Fun
and educat
Places
to go
With Kids and adults
in Southern California

"I have bought this book at least 20 times - it is by far my favorite baby present, grandparent present, parent of kids present, etc. How great to get something that does not add clutter but rather fun to a kids life. The indexes are EXCELLENT as are the directions and website references. Susan Peterson is very funny in person - she spoke to our MOPS group and was just excellent."
Louise Valente
Speech Pathologist
Co-owner of Pacific Coast Speech Services

"This is a wonderful resource that has all sorts of gems and suggestions. The book is well organized by county/region/type of place and the index gives you the option to search by price, area or specific place. Each entry has a detailed description of the place and gives suggestions about what to do, what is at the site, and even sometimes suggests what to do to prepare before you go (like books to buy about art so that the kids enjoy it more). Each entry also has a recommended age level which I think is really realistic. This woman really knows kids and obviously has gone to most of these sites (pretty amazing actually because there are so many!). I have a 4 year old and a 2 year old and have been using this book for the past year. It made my summer with the kids so much fun and I pull it out whenever we want to find some interesting place to go as a family . . . I HIGHLY recommend this book for families with children living or visiting SoCal. It's been amazing for me since I didn't grow up in SoCal and all the usual travel guides like LonelyPlanet and RoughGuides don't have most of these places listed and aren't written for families . . . I'm in awe at the amount of work put into this book. Thank you Susan Peterson."
Tiffany F. Jones, PhD.
Department Chair & Associate Professor of African History
California State University, San Bernardino

"It's 10:30 and I've already had five telephone calls from leaders thanking me for inviting you to the meeting last night, praising your fun-filled presentation, pleasant personality, great ideas, . . . Believe me, Susan, I have never looked so good. It's just not that easy to impress *or* entertain the "been there, done that" woman in Irvine. . . You may be sure that you have substantially improved the quality of Girl Scout field trips in Irvine so I feel confident that I can offer you the appreciation of the 1600 girls affected."
Mary Pearlman
Membership Development Director for Girl Scouts, Orange County

"Over 20 copies of *Fun and Educational Places to go With Kids* are continually checked out in the Orange County Public Library System; we can't keep them on the shelves! Children's librarians feel confident referring parents to this title. It's perfect for planning local inexpensive family outings."
Elke Faraci
Senior Administrative Librarian
Orange County Public Library System

"As a travel industry professional, I find Susan Peterson's book to be my #1 reference when designing group tours & outings for families in Southern California. Her easy-to-use guide, with its complete listing of activities by location, cost and age range, allows me to tailor every outing to meet each client's particular needs. Because she's an experienced mother of three I know I can trust her judgment, and that's why Pack the Kids will always pack her guide!"
Daniel McCollum
Director of Operations Pack the Kids Family Tour Adventures

Fun
and educational
to go
Places
With Kids
and adults
in Southern California

Susan Peterson

A comprehensive guide to Los Angeles, Orange, Riverside, San Bernardino, San Diego, Santa Barbara, and Ventura counties

Fun Places Publishing, California
www.funplaces.com

Cover art by the talented Andie Beahn!

Published by Fun Places Publishing
6124 Capetown Street
Lakewood, California 90713
susan@funplaces.com
www.funplaces.com

ISBN 978-0-9833832-3-9

Printed in the United States of America

Eleventh edition - August, 2018
Tenth+ edition - July, 2016
Tenth edition - April, 2014
Ninth edition - April, 2011
Eighth edition - April, 2009
Seventh edition - April, 2006
Sixth edition - June, 2003
Fifth edition - March, 2001
Fourth edition - October, 1998
Third edition - May, 1997
Second edition - May, 1996
First edition - May, 1995

ACKNOWLEDGMENTS

Thank you to you who are reading this guidebook for the first time; my hope is that it will give you a wealth of ideas of where to go with your kids and that you spend precious family time together (because kids actually *do* grow up fast). Thank you to those of you who have been faithful readers. I've had the pleasure of meeting and talking with many of you. May this edition continue to bless you in creating memories together and - there are GREAT new places to explore!
A special thanks is needed for the following people:

Lance - 34 years of being married to you continues to be one of the greatest privileges and blessings of my life. I love partnering with you in all facets of life and appreciate that we partner so well in working together on this book, too. (And laugh a lot.) I know I still get the fun part of exploring the places, writing and speaking, and you do the computer work, so thank you for your diligence because without you, there would be no book. Thank you, my love.

My three boys, whom I had the privilege (plus tears, trials and triumphs) to homeschool and now be great friends with - Kellan, Bryce, and T.J. They have literally come along for the ride (mostly willingly) to all the fun places. We continue to be richly blessed by enjoying whatever time we get to spend together.
Kellan, my oldest son, who is married to Carolyn, one of my favorite daughters-in-law: You are a gifted writer and speaker, and you do both with conviction, passion, depth, humor and an extensive vocabulary. Yea for you for becoming a pastor ! (So not the path you were on when you were younger!) I love seeing your life and faith grow in maturity and strength as you purposely choose God on a daily basis. You are my favorite.

Bryce, my middle son and married to Channelle, my other favorite daughter-in-law: The career you have is wonderful. More than that, you keep your priorities right by being a godly and devoted husband, and a wonderful father. You are a man of integrity and faithfulness. You are personable and genuinely care for people, and it shows. And you've given me two grandsons - you are my favorite.

T.J., my youngest: Your dedication to bring to light sexual abuse prevention via teaching self defense classes and your other jobs have given you an intense focus. I don't know how this will continue to unfold, but I know God has a purpose and plan for it all. Your devotion and love for God shines as you seek hard after Him via mission's trips and life, and how intentional you are with relationships. You are my favorite.

A very special shout out (or write out) to **Diana Clay -** you were my absolute rock!!! You worked tirelessly in making phone calls and checking websites to verify every big and little detail of information in these pages. I know it's not the fun part of the job, but it's so important! All the inaccuracies are mine. (Sorry for them!) Thank you, Diana. And thank you some more.

Thank you to all of the people associated with places mentioned in this book that were so willing to talk with me, send me information, and enable my family to come and visit - thank you, THANK YOU, **THANK YOU!!**

I want to dedicate this edition to my mom, who died in October, 2017. This incredible woman taught me how to choose joy, love one another, and make the most of every minute of life. I miss her, yet I'm so very thankful for her.

I also want to dedicate this edition to Jax and baby boy Peterson #2 (not his real name) whose on his way. I so enjoy taking you places, Jax, and seeing such the fresh excitement of discovery on your face. I can't wait for more and to take your brother, too. I'm loving this whole grandma thing!

ABOUT THE AUTHOR:

I love my family, traveling (almost anywhere and everywhere), reading, walking, talking with friends, working out, doing projects, speaking to groups, and so much more. I've also been honored to be able go to the jungles of Ecuador for the last 12 years on short-term mission's trips to continue relationships there with incredible people, to support our national and local missionaries, and to serve and love by faith and action.

I really like to explore fun places and new things, yet I have the same thing for lunch every day - go figure.

I would appreciate your ideas about and for this book. Do you have a wonderful place to go with kids that wasn't included in this edition? Please let me know and I'll share it in the next one. You can contact me at:

FUN PLACES TO GO WITH KIDS
email: susan@funplaces.com
www.funplaces.com

Share your experience with others by commenting on my Facebook page - photos, things you liked (or didn't like) about the attraction. My goal is for readers and adventurers to be prepared, experience new things, grow, enjoy family time and maybe even discover some new interests for your kids (and yourself).

www.facebook.com/funplacestogo

TABLE OF CONTENTS

INTRODUCTION and LEGEND EXPLANATION

In this world there are specifically fun places to go with kids, and there are places we go and bring our kids, anyhow. I think going shopping is great, but when my boys were younger, while I was looking at clothes, they thought it was fun to climb in the clothing racks and maybe even pull off a ticket or two to bring home as "prizes." That did not make for a fun family outing. I've tried to do the weeding for you so that anywhere you choose to go in this guidebook, whether it's an all-day outing or just for an hour, would be an enjoyable time for you and your child. Some places are obvious choices; some are places you might have simply forgotten about; some are hidden treasures; and some are new attractions.

The book is set up by county. Under each county, categories are listed alphabetically; and under each category, attractions are listed alphabetically. Note: The names of places in all capital letters used in a description (e.g., DISNEYLAND) are attractions listed separately elsewhere in the book and usually referenced by a page number. An explanation of what each category means is on the following pages simply titled, "What Do the Categories Mean?" If you still have a hard time figuring out in which category I have placed an attraction (and that is a strong possibility), look up the place in one of the four indexes in the back of the book: Name, City, Price, or Theme.

Next to most of the places described are symbols, meant to be at-a-glance guidelines. The **sun** indicates the average amount of time needed to see this attraction. You might decide you need more or less time - this is just a guideline. The **dollar signs and exclamation mark** are price guidelines. They incorporate *the entrance cost for one adult, a 10-year-old child, and the parking fee* (if there is one). If you have more than one child, or one who gets in for free, your cost will vary. **Ages** stands for recommended ages. It is meant to be an aid to help you decide if an attraction is appropriate and/or meaningful for your child. Some of the age restrictions, however, are designated by the place you visit. The **birthday cake** symbol represents an attraction that is a good place to 1) have a birthday party (the place may or may not have a separate party room), or 2) incorporate with a birthday party.

☀ =	15 minutes to 1 hour	
☀ =	1½ hours to half a day	
☀ =	all day	
🎂 =	good for birthday parties	

!	=	Free!
!/$	=	Free, but bring spending money.
$	=	1¢ - $5
$$	=	$5.01 - $10
$$$	=	$10.01 - $20
$$$$	=	$20.01 - $40
$$$$$	=	$40.01 - $100
6/$	=	Over $100

GO Los Angeles Card and **GO San Diego Card** provide great deals in these and surrounding counties. See www.smartdestinatons.com for more info.

Discounts: Always check the attraction's website for online discounts. If you belong to AAA (i.e., Auto Club), ask if there is a discount for members.

Check www.CITYPASS.com for another way to save at some major attractions.

WHAT DO THE CATEGORIES MEAN?
(and other helpful information)
Each attraction in every county is listed under one, or more, of the following categories.

AMUSEMENT PARKS
Webster's definition of amusement is: "To cause to laugh or smile; entertainment; a pleasant diversion." So, from roller coasters to water slides - have fun!

ARTS AND CRAFTS
Children have creative urges and need a place to express themselves. Since art classes are offered in a dizzying array and with fluctuating times and prices, many of the places listed in these sections are paint-it-yourself ceramic studios to assist your young artists in developing their talents - move over Monet! There are other unique places listed, too, that aid in artistic endeavors. Note: Museums are also great resources for arts and crafts workshops.

BEACHES
Beaches are a *shore* bet for a day of fun in the sun. Along with sand and water play, some beaches have playgrounds, picnic tables, and waveless waters that make them particularly younger-kid friendly. Some also have paved pathways for biking, strolling, or rollerblading. These sections includes *just a few* suggestions of where to go beaching. Check the following website for more beaches and more beach information: www.beachcalifornia.com.

On a sad note, some beaches' waters get polluted, either temporarily or longer term. Before your visit, please contact Heal the Bay at (800) HEAL BAY (432-5229) / www.healthebay.org and see the rating/report card for that particular beach.

EDIBLE ADVENTURES
I am not a food critic. The places I mention have an "eatertainment" atmosphere and serve at least decent, if not delicious, food. From themed restaurants to high tea, from farmer's markets to a fun place to get an ice cream cone, the Edible Adventures sections cover some of the best. For a fairly comprehensive listing of tea rooms and customer reviews for Southern California (and beyond), look up www.teamap.com.

FAMILY PAY AND PLAY
The family that plays together, stays together. Indoor play areas, miniature golf courses, rock climbing centers, laser tag arenas, paint ball fields, indoor skateparks, and more, are great places to go to spend some special bonding time.

GREAT OUTDOORS
Contrary to popular belief, Southern California consists not only of concrete buildings, but also of the great outdoors. Explore the region's natural beauty by visiting open-space preserves, botanic gardens, nature centers, and a plethora of designed parks. Go take a hike - with your kids! For a complete listing of state-run parks, contact (916) 653-6995 / parks.ca.gov. Hiking is a favorite way to really see the fantastic outdoors of Southern California. Here are two websites to check for hiking trails to get you started: www.alltrails.com and www.socalhiker.net.

Parks in Orange County have a fantastic resource with Michele Whiteaker's Nature Play Trips. Check out her website at www.funorangecountyparks.com. She describes each park in detail and has great photographs.

Enjoy almost 300 gardens nationwide for one membership price with a reciprocal membership program offered by American Horticultural Society. The program includes fifteen gardens just in Southern California! Members also receive the magazine, *The American Gardener*, discounted or free admission to flower and garden shows, the annual Seed Exchange, and special discounts on gardening products. See ahs.org for more info.

Also listed under the Great Outdoors sections are outdoor skateparks. Check www.socalskateparks.com or call your city hall to keep up on newly-opened skateboard parks.

MALLS
These sections are not necessarily to tell you where to go shopping, but rather to inform you of free kids' clubs, programs, and "shoppertainment" features that your local mall has to offer. We included just a few of our favorite unique malls, also. Be entertained, enjoy, and create - and maybe get in a little shopping, too!

MUSEUMS

There is a whole world of learning in the huge variety of museums in Southern California. Captivate kids' imaginations, hearts, and even their hands by treating them to a visit. Here are a few tips about museums:

*Exhibits rotate, so be flexible in your expectations.

*If you really like the museum, become a member. Besides supporting the foundation, you'll reap benefits such as visiting the museum year round at no additional fee, being invited to members-only events, receiving newsletters, getting discounts on store merchandise, and lots more.

*Join NARM - North American Reciprocal Museum Association, which has 1,013 member institutions. See narmassociation.org for details.

*The California Science Center in Los Angeles, Children's Museum at La Habra, Columbia Memorial Space Center, Discovery Science Center in Santa Ana, Kidspace Children's Museum, Natural History Museum of Los Angeles, Reuben H. Fleet Science Center of San Diego, San Diego Natural History Museum, and Santa Barbara Museum of Natural History have reciprocal memberships, but exclude museums within 90 miles of the museum where membership was purchased. These memberships are also reciprocal - usually for the permanent exhibits only - with more than 300 other museums nation and worldwide. Check www.astc.org for more information.

*If you're a Bank of America cardholder know that you can get into 200 museums nationwide for free the first full weekend of every month, including fourteen great museums in Southern California. Check museums.bankofamerica.com for more details.

*Blue Star Museums offers free admission to active-duty military personnel and their families from Memorial Day weekend through Labor Day. See www.arts.gov for more details.

*If you're looking for a special present, most museum gift shops carry unique merchandise that is geared toward their specialty.

*Museums offer a fantastic array of special calendar events. Check their websites or get on a mailing list.

*Contact www.museumsusa.org for a wealth of info.

*Take a guided tour! You and your kids will learn a lot about the exhibits this way.

*Call first and ask if they are hosting a school field trip and if so, what time. Don't visit the museum then. Go whenever field trips aren't as it will be less crowded then.

PIERS AND SEAPORTS

It ap*piers* that walking around seaport villages, looking at boats, fishing off piers, and taking a cruise are delightful ways to spend a few hours with your child.

POTPOURRI

The dictionary defines potpourri as: "A miscellaneous mixture; a confused collection." This accurately describes these sections! Unique stores, cemeteries, libraries, Catalina Island, Tijuana, and more fill these pages. Whatever you do, there are a potpourri of ideas to explore.

SHOWS AND THEATERS

How about a day (or evening) at the theater? The listings here include theaters that have performances specifically for children, planetarium shows, dinner and show productions, and musical extravaganzas.

TOURS

These groupings are all about insight into ordinary and unique places. Many tours are also offered under the museums sections and a few other sections. Note: See the Ideas and Resources section toward the back of the book for general tour ideas regarding a particular profession or topic.

Tip: Many restaurants, especially chain restaurants, offer tours of their facility. I've listed only some restaurants in the main sections of the book. The tours usually require a minimum number of participants (usually school-aged children), and could include a tour of the kitchen, and a partial or full meal. Tours are usually free. I suggest that if you see a place you're interested in taking a tour of, call the place and ask. They might not be set up to do it for the general public, but they might be willing to take your group around.

TRANSPORTATION

For a truly "moving" experience, take a journey with your child by bike, plane, train, automobile, ship, carriage, or another mode of transportation. Note: There are numerous boating companies up and down the coastline. I've mentioned only a few, giving just some pertinent facts. Anchors away! Many beaches and parks have bike paths, so look under the Beaches sections and Great Outdoors sections for additional suggestions.

ZOOS AND ANIMALS

Kids and animals seem to go hand-in-hoof - both are adorable and neither is easy. Zoos, aquariums, farms, animal rescue facilities, and more are listed here. Animal lovers - these sections are for you!

MISCELLANEOUS TIDBITS

CAPTURE YOUR MEMORIES:
1. Camera / Smart phone - Capture these precious moments in a snap. Make movies involving the whole family. This is also a great way to document trips (remember to state the date and/or video the location) and interview kids, as well as get genuine reactions and impromptu stories, songs, and arguments.

SAFETY PRECAUTIONS (just a few to get you started):
1. Dress your kids in the same shirt (no, I don't mean one big shirt), or at least shirts of the same color (orange, yellow, and red are bright choices) when you go on an outing. I thought this would look silly, but while we did get stares and comments, I could find my kids at just a glance. If kids balk at wearing the same-colored shirt, invest in solid colored baseball caps. Not only can you spot your children quickly, but hats help shade their faces from the sun.
2. Dress kids in brightly colored or easily identifiable shoes. If someone should try to snatch your child, shoes are the hardest thing for a kidnapper to change.
3. Have a current picture of your child on your cell phone. In fact, take one on the day of your outing, in their outfits, for easy identification purposes.
4. Instruct your child where to meet and who to talk to (and not to talk to) in case you get separated from each other.

EXPECTATIONS:
1. Be Aware - Simply because you have a fun outing planned, whether it's going to the "happiest place on earth" or just an hour of play, please don't expect your child to necessarily enjoy every moment of it. Know and expect that your child will probably fuss about something, or seemingly nothing. Beware of the fun-stealers - tiredness and hunger. With younger children, visit places before or after nap time, and always bring food, even if you just ate.
2. Be Prepared - Call ahead and make sure the place you want to visit is open, especially if there is something that you particularly want to see. Also, check off your list of essentials from the next page; set realistic expectations for all participants; be flexible; and go for it!
3. Family Mottos - We didn't promise our kids that we'd take them on an outing. A promise, as any parent knows, cannot be broken; it is an absolute. A plan, however, can be altered depending on weather, circumstance, finances, and/or attitude! One of our family mottos is, "It's a plan, not a promise." Another one is, "Oh well." Feel free to use either or both as the situation warrants.

NEVER LEAVE HOME WITHOUT THESE ESSENTIALS

1) **SNACKS**: Always carry snacks and a water bottle with you and/or in the car. Listening to a child whine because he is hungry or thirsty can drive any sane parent over the edge. (And kids will not stop this endearing behavior until they actually get their food or drink!)

2) **TISSUES AND/OR WIPES**: For obvious reasons.

3) **QUARTERS**: A few quarters tucked away in a container in the car can come in handy for metered parking, arcade games, or purchasing those snacks I told you to pack but you forgot.

4) **TOYS/BOOKS/GAMES**: Keeping little fingers busy helps keep little hands out of trouble. Add your own ideas to this short list - stickers books, pipe cleaners, threading/weaving of some sort (preferably things that are all attached together), finger puppets (attached to something). . .

5) **IPOD, SMART PHONE or audio source**: Get kids singing instead of fussing. (And if kids cry really loud, just turn up the volume even louder!) We've also found good storytelling, in particular, to be a wonderful way to learn listening skills, use imaginations, and become educated. (See the IDEAS and RESOURCES section, on page 767, for some suggestions and resources.)

6) **FIRST AID KIT**: Fill it with the essentials, including band aids, ointment, adhesive tape, scissors, an ice pack, Benedryl, disposable gloves, a sewing kit, and Tylenol (both children's and adults').

7) **ROADSIDE EMERGENCY KIT**: This kit should contain jumper cables (know how to use them!), flares, a flashlight, batteries, extra drinking water, tools, matches, screwdrivers, wrenches, etc.

8) **JACKET**: Pack a light jacket or sweater for an unexpected change in weather, or change of plans. Throw in a change of clothes, too, for little ones who spit up, for youngsters who don't always make it to the bathroom in time, and for those who have the gift of finding water wherever you go or for getting really dirty. (This tip could save your outing from being cut short.)

9) **BLANKET**: We use ours mainly for picnics, but it doubles as an "I'm cold" helper, and is handy for other emergencies.

10) **BACK PACK**: Even if your kids are still in the diaper/stroller stage, a back pack is great for storing snacks and water bottles, and keeping your hands free to either help your children or grab them before they dart away. Get the kids their own backpack, too, so they can carry their own snacks and souvenirs.

11) **SUNSCREEN**: Always!

12) **CAMERA / CELL PHONE:** A picture is still worth a thousand words and brings to mind just as many memories.

13) **PORTABLE POTTY**: Caught somewhere without a potty around? Been there; done that; really not that fun. Adults might be able to hold it, but not so for little kids. My Carry Potty is just one brand available. (I will say from experience that boys just sometimes need a funnel and a bottle.)

14) **GROCERY BAG**: It holds trash, excuse me, I mean treasures, that kids collect such as rocks, sticks, and creepy crawly things. The bag helps keep your car clean and makes it easier to throw things away once you get home!

15) **CONTAINER**: A good thing to have if your kids are prone to motion sickness.

16) **A SENSE OF HUMOR!**: Some things (not everything!) will be funny later on. They will - I promise.

SOME IDEAS TO EXTEND THE MEMORIES OF YOUR OUTING

1. **PHOTO SHARING** - Don't just post photos on social network, with a caption, but also have your kids write a blog of some sort so family and friends can share the experiences (and your kids practice their writing and photography skills).

2. **JOURNALING** - Have your child write about the fun you have together. See my website, www.funplaces.com, for information on ordering the *Fun Places to go Journal*. Keep ticket stubs and brochures to attach them to journal pages. Use stickers for decorations.

3. **COLLECTIONS** - Collect key chains, refrigerator magnets, mugs, pencils, decks of cards, smashed pennies, or something else inexpensive from each place you go. Display them.
   A. Patches - I have collected patches and sewn them on a quilt, so each of my boys has his own quilt or "travel blankets".
   B. Postcards - Ask your younger children, "What's the most fun thing you remember about this place?" and jot down the answers on the back of this inexpensive memory-keeper. Make older kids write out the answers themselves. Be sure you date the postcard. Keep all the postcards in a small, three-ring binder. Another option: If you're going away on a trip, bring stamps and mail the postcards home. Kids love to receive mail.

4. **EDUCATION** - Spend some time doing a little (or a lot of) research about a particular place, person, or time period before your visit. It will make your outing more meaningful and make a lasting impression upon your child. Think of your field trip as curriculum supplement! Call the attraction to get a brochure on it and/or do some online research. Other educational activities to enhance your outing include:
   A. Read stories - If you're going apple picking, for instance, read stories, or read about characters, that have something to do with apples, such as Johnny Appleseed, William Tell, Snow White, Adam and Eve, Sir Isaac Newton, and specifically, *The Giving Tree* by Shel Silverstein or *Ten Apples on Top* by Theo LeSieg.
   B. Theme books - There are thematic study books for almost every subject written. Teacher Created Materials, Inc. at (888) 434-4335 / www.teachercreated.com, for instance, has over fifty, thematic unit study books available. Each book includes lessons and projects that incorporate math, arts and crafts, history, science, language arts, and cooking, into a study about one particular subject (i.e., weather, birds, the human body, holidays, and more).
   C. Spelling words - Give your child a spelling list pertaining to the attraction you're visiting.
   D. Maps - Have older children use a map to track your way to and from your outing - this is an invaluable skill, especially if they learn to do it correctly!
   E. Flash cards - Take photographs of the places you go. Put the photos on a piece of cardstock paper and write the facts about the attraction on the back. "Laminate" it with contact paper or clear packing tape. Use the cards as flash cards. Tip: If you're not a picture-taker, buy postcards instead.
   F. Use my *Fun Places to go Journal*. (See the back of the book for ordering information.)

These are just a few ideas - I'm sure you have many of your own!

5. **YOUR IDEAS -**

ROAD GAMES

"Are we almost there yet?" and "I'm bored!" (along with "I have to go to the bathroom!") are common cries from children (and adults) who are traveling. CDs, books, toys, electronic entertainment, and snacks all help to keep kids amused, as do car games. Here are just a few of our favorite games with brief explanations on how to play:

FOR THE YOUNGER SET:

MISSING LETTER ABC SONG - Sing the ABC song, leaving out a letter. See if your child can figure out what letter is missing. Now let your child sing (or say) the alphabet, leaving out a letter. Suggest correct (and incorrect) letters and see if your child agrees with you on what letter is missing. (Tip: Know your alphabet!)

MISSING NUMBER GAME - Count up to a certain number and stop. See if your child can figure out what number comes next. Now let your child do the counting. See if he/she agrees with what you say the next number should be.

COLOR CAR GAME - Look out the window for just red cars (or just blue or just green, etc.). Each time your child sees a red car, he/she can shout "red!" (or "blue!" or "green!", etc.) Count together the number of cars of a particular color you see on your trip. Your child can eagerly share at night, "Daddy, we had a fifteen-red-car day!" A variation of this game is to count a particular type of car; VW Bugs is the popular choice for our family.

ABC WORD GAME - A is for apple; B is for bear; etc. Encourage your child to figure out words that start with each letter of the alphabet.

FOR OLDER CHILDREN:

ALPHABET SIGN GAME - Each person, or team, looks for a word outside the car (i.e., on billboards, freeway signs, bumper stickers, etc.) that begins with each letter of the alphabet. When the words are found, the person, or team, shouts it out. The words must be found in alphabetical order, starting with the letter A. Since words beginning with a Q, X, or Z are hard to find (unless you're near a Quality Inn, X-Ray machine, or a Zoo), players may find these particular letters used <u>in</u> any word. A word on a sign, billboard, etc., can only be used once, by one player or team member. Other players must find their word in another sign, billboard, etc. The first one to get through the alphabet wins! Warning #1: Try to verify that the word has been seen by more than just the player who shouted it out, or learn to trust each other. Warning #2: From personal experience: If the driver is competitive and wants to play, make sure he/she keeps his/her eyes on the road!

ALPHABET WORD GAME - This is a variation on the above game. Instead of finding words that begin with each letter of the alphabet, each player must look outside the car and describe his surroundings using letters of the alphabet, in sequential order. This game can be played fast and gets creative, depending on the quick-thinking skills of the people playing. Example: Someone who is on the letter "D" might look at the land and see dirt; a person looking for an "S" might say soil; someone else who is on the letter "G" might say ground. All are correct. Players may use the same point of reference as long as the exact same word is not used. Whoever gets through the alphabet first wins.

GHOST - (Or whatever title you choose.) The object of this game is to add one letter per turn and be in the process of spelling a word, without actually spelling out a word. Players take turns adding letters until someone either spells a word, or can't think of another letter to add without spelling a word. A player may try to bluff and add a letter that doesn't seem like it spells a word. If he gets challenged by someone asking what he is spelling, he must come up with a legitimate word. If he doesn't, he loses the round. (If he does have a word, however, than the challenger loses that round.) Whoever spells a word or can't think of a letter to add, gets a G. The second time he loses a round, he gets an H, etc. Whoever earns G-H-O-S-T (i.e., loses 5 rounds) is eliminated from the game. Example: Player 1 says the letter "B." Player 2 adds the letter "E." (Words must be at least 3 letters long to count as a word.) Player 3 says "T." Player 3 gets a G, or whatever letter-round he is on. He loses the round even if his intent was to spell the word "better" because "bet" is a word.

WORD SCRAMBLE - Make sure players have a piece of paper and a writing implement. Using a word on a sign or billboard, or using the name of the place you are visiting, see how many other words players can make out of it. To spice up the game, and add stress, set a time limit. Whoever has the most words wins. A variation is that letters are worth points: 2 letter words are worth 2 points, 3 letter words are worth 5 points, etc. The player with the most points wins. (Although a player may have fewer words, he/she could win the game by being long-worded.) Note: This game can be played for only a brief period of time by players who are prone to motion sickness.

FOR ALL AGES:

BINGO - This is the only game that you have to prepare for ahead of time. Make up bingo-type cards for each child. Cards for younger children can have pictures of things kids would typically see on their drive (although this depends on where you are traveling, of course): a blue car, McDonalds, a cow, a pine tree, etc. Cards for older children can have pictures, signs, license plates, and/or words that they would typically see on their drive: exit, stop, a traffic light, curvy road ahead, etc. Use magazines, newspapers, etc., and glue the pictures and words onto posterboard, one card per child. Tip: Have your kids help you prepare the cards as it's a fun project. Use raisins or M&M's as markers and when your child has bingo (or has seen a certain number of objects on his card), he can eat his reward. For those parents who intend to use the bingo boards more than once, "laminate" them with contact paper or clear packing tape. Put small pieces of velcro on a part of each picture or sign on the card and make (non-edible) markers that have the other part of velcro on them. (This will keep markers from sliding off the cards during sudden turns!) Keep the cards and markers together in a plastic baggy in the car.

20 QUESTIONS - This time-honored game has many variations. (Our version is usually called 40 Questions.) The basic rules are for one player to think of a well-known person, or at least someone well-known to your children, and for other players to ask questions about the person to try to find out his/her identity. Only yes or no answers can be given. Whoever figures out the mystery person, in 20 questions or less, wins. Tip: Encourage players to ask general questions first to narrow down the field. (Inevitably, my youngest one's first question was, "Is it George Washington?") Teach them to ask, for instance: "Is it a man?"; "Is he alive?"; "Is he real?"; "Is he a cartoon?"; "Is he on T.V.?"; "Is he an historical figure?"; "Is it someone I know personally?" You get the picture. For a variation of the game, think of an object instead of a person. (Tip: Tell the others players first, though, about the switch in subject matter.)

3 THINGS IN COMMON - This is a great thinking game that is easily adaptable for kids of all ages. One person names 3 words (or things) that have something in common. Everyone else takes turns guessing what that something is. Examples for younger children: #1) sky, ocean, grandpa's eyes (or whomever). Answer: Things that are blue. #2) stop sign, fire truck, Santa's suit. Answer: Things that are red. Examples for older kids and adults: #1) house, butter, horse. Answer: Things that have the word fly at the end of them. #2) chain, missing, sausage. Answer: Things that can end with the word "link." #3) tiger, nurse, sand. Answer: Kinds of sharks.

I'M GOING ON A PICNIC . . . . - This game tests a player's abilities to remember things and remember them in order. Player 1 starts with the words, "I'm going on a picnic" and then adds a one-word item that he will bring. The next player starts with the same phrase, repeats player 1's item, and then adds another item, and so on. Play continues until one of the players can't remember the list of things, in order, to bring on a picnic. Example: Player 1 says, "I'm going on a picnic and I am going to bring a ball." Player 2 says, "I'm going on a picnic and I'm going to bring a ball and a kite." Variations of the game include adding items in alphabetical order or adding items beginning with the same letter.

THE PERSON NEXT TO US - Driving on the road, you glance at someone in the car next to you. Who is he? What kind of job does she have? Is he married? What are her hobbies? Where is he going, and why? Kids (and adults) can give a made-up answer to these, and an almost endless array of other questions. Include reasons in your response, such as "That man is a golfer because he has a good tan." I like playing this game at airports, too, albeit more quietly, while watching people disembark, especially those who are greeted by someone.

PLEASE be aware that although the facts recorded in this book are accurate and current as of July, 2018:

• HOURS CHANGE!
• EXHIBITS ROTATE!
• ADMISSION COSTS ARE RAISED WITHOUT FANFARE!
• PLACES CLOSE, EITHER TEMPORARILY OR PERMANENTLY!

To avoid any unexpected (and unpleasant) surprises:

Always, ALWAYS, *ALWAYS*
CALL BEFORE YOU VISIT AN ATTRACTION!!!

LOS ANGELES COUNTY

Ciudad de Los Angeles; City of Los Angeles; "City of Angels": This international city of Mexican heritage is one of extremes with its concrete jungles, acres of parkland, pockets of poverty, and renown cultural meccas. Almost 10 million people live in this county, which is a sprawling metropolis that encompasses the glitz of Hollywood, the incredible wealth of Beverly Hills, the quirkiness of Venice, the beach-city attitudes of Manhattan Beach and Malibu, the charm of Pasadena, the deserts of Lancaster, and the daily living of families in every community.

Brave the freeways to reach mainstream attractions such as Universal Studios Hollywood, California Science Center, Aquarium of the Pacific, Huntington Library, Magic Mountain, and the Music Center, as well as the numerous "smaller" jewels that make L.A. a gem of a place to visit.

—AMUSEMENT PARKS—

BUCCANEER BAY - SPLASH! LA MIRADA AQUATICS CENTER

(562) 902-3191 / www.splashlamirada.com

13806 La Mirada Boulevard, La Mirada

$$$$$

Arrgh - calling all scallywags (and non-scallywags) to come play and get wet at the family-friendly Buccaneer Bay. Piratey-themed, this clean and lovely small water park has three body slides (no raft slides) for which riders must be 48". One is enclosed, short, straight, and very fast; another is longer and mostly enclosed; and the third is open, twisty, and meanders downward at a slower speed. Catch the gentle current at the circular river and grab an inner tube to float around in it if you want. This river also has fountains on the side to get you extra wet and buckets overhead that fill up and pour over on floaters (that's you!) at random times.

A good-sized and colorful kiddie water playground makes up a third of the water park. Here, in zero depth waters, young ones (47" and under) can zip down several short slides, climb on the cargo nets, and squirt and play on the play equipment. And watch out below - the huge pirate's head on top of the play structure fills up with water and tips over, gushing down tons of water. Free life vests are available. An adjacent sprayground has water shooting up from the ground and raining down from above, as well as large tubs of water on short stands for kids to play with toy boats.

Splash! has two adjacent, swimming pools which are part of the La Mirada Aquatics Center. Open year round, one pool is for team competitions (swimming and water polo) and the other is for recreational swim (and lap swim, at times) so it is open to Buccaneer Bay attendees to also splash around and even shoot some hoops at the water basketball net. Adults, only, are invited to unwind in the adjoining, fenced-in hot tub.

Attractively landscaped, the water park is surrounded by rolling grassy hills and lawn dotted with palm trees. Ahoy mateys! Kids definitely enjoy playing in and on the landlocked, cutaway, large, wooden pirate ship and on the boulders that are designed to look like a skull. The skull has caves carved inside it, which are actually the eyeballs of the skull.

No outside food/drinks (except bottled water) are allowed in, but the on-site snack bar offers an array of tasty food such as a cheeseburger ($5), chicken Caesar salad ($8.45), and personal cheese pizza ($6.50), plus funnel cake and shaved ice. There are plenty of tables and chairs, lounge chairs, umbrellas, and nice, private cabanas for pool side relaxing. Music plays in the background. There is a small store here if you forget a bathing suit, sunscreen, or other sundries. Note that nearby amenities include LA MIRADA REGIONAL PARK (pg. 69), a gymnasium, and a library.

Hours: Buccaneer Bay is open the end of May - mid-June, and mid-August to the beginning of October, Sat. - Sun., 10:30am - 5:30pm. Open daily, mid-June - mid-August, 10:30am - 5:30pm. Family Fri. Nights is 3pm - 8pm. Recreational swim is open most of the year, Sat. - Sun. from noon - 5pm. Rec swim is open mid-June - Labor Day, Mon. - Fri., 1pm - 4pm; Sat. - Sun., noon - 4pm.

Price: Buccaneer Bay is $21.95 for 48" and taller; $16.95 for 47" and under; children 2 and under are free. Family Fri. Nights is $16.95 per person. Recreational swim is around $4 for adults; $3 for ages 3 - 12. Parking is free.

Ages: 2 years and up.

DRY TOWN WATER PARK AND MINING CO. and PALMDALE OASIS PARK AND RECREATION CENTER

(661) 267-6161 - water park; (661) 267-5100 - parks and rec / www.cityofpalmdale.org

3850-B East Avenue S, Palmdale

$$$$$

Is that a mirage? No, it really is a water park out here in the desert, surrounded by mountains! Mosey on beyond the weathered buildings grouped together to look like an Old West town (but with prettier landscaping) into the mid-sized water park. Note that a real, modern-day sheriff is always on duty here. Grab a tube and go down the three tube slides that jut out of a thirty-five-foot-high slide tower; some enclosed, some open air. Spin around (and around) on a vortex-like slide, called the Devil's Punch Bowl, until you drop into the splash pool. Shoot down Dusty's Mineshaft Racer, a four-lane slide with mats. Take a ride in the circular, lazy river. Little Miners Camp is a children's water playground, ideal for youngsters to splash and play on the slides and colorful apparatus. Umbrella sprays, cargo nets, water hoses, and large water rings that shoot out water to walk through, plus a huge bucket that fills up with water and then tips over drenching those below, await here, too. Life jackets and tubes are available free of charge. Drier choices include a few arcade games, lounging areas, or indulging in a food break utilizing the concession stands. Locker rentals are $5. As always at water parks, wear water shoes of some kind as the pavement can get really hot.

The adjacent Oasis Park has a regulation competition swimming pool that is open year round. It also has a grassy area to let kids run (relatively) wild and a basin that is ideal for soccer and football. The recreation center has a gym with open play and a youth room with a large screen TV, foosball, ping pong, air hockey, basketball court, and other games.

Hours: The water park is open Memorial weekend - mid-August daily, 11am - 6pm. It is open mid-August - mid-September, weekends only, 11am - 6pm. It is open most Fri. nights, too, from 7pm - 10pm. Oasis Park is open daily. Call for pool hours.

Price: The water park, for Palmdale residents, is $22 for 48" and taller; $17 for seniors and kids 47" and under; children 2 and under are free. Admission for nonresidents is $25 for 48" and taller; $20 for seniors and kids. In and out privileges are allowed. Discounts are offered for active military. Twilight rates are offered every day after 3pm and all day (ironically) on Tues. - $17 for resident adults, $14 for resident seniors and kids; $20 for non-resident adults; $17 for non-resident seniors and kid. Parking is free. The Oasis Park is free. The swimming pool at Oasis cost about $2 per person.

Ages: 18 months and up.

PACIFIC PARK

(310) 260-8744 / www.pacpark.com; www.smgov.net $$$$

380 Santa Monica Pier, Santa Monica

The major kid-attraction on the Santa Monica pier is Pacific Park with its twelve family-oriented amusement rides, including six kiddie rides, that are all clustered tightly together. The rides include a huge Ferris wheel (130 feet high!), which gives a great view at the top for miles around; a roller coaster; spinning shark cars; bumper cars; a pirate ship and a sea dragon that both swing back and forth like giant pendulums; Pacific Plunge, which launches riders forty-five-feet into the air over the ocean (at least a portion of it) before it drops; a scrambler; and, specifically for little ones, are scale patrol trucks, a mini hot air balloon-looking ride, and little sea planes for young pilots. A mini bungee ride and Gyro Loops (a 360-degree rotating ride/attraction) are also available. Lots of carnival-style and midway games are here, as are plenty of arcade games. An historic carousel (with horses, camels, and lions) is not park of the park, but still on the pier.

If your belly starts rumbling, grab a bite at oceanfront restaurants, snack bars, or ice cream shops. See SANTA MONICA PIER / SANTA MONICA BEACH (pg. 161) for details about the pier and its other attractions.

Hours: Hours here fluctuate a lot!!! Most of the year a few rides, plus the Ferris wheel and some games, are operational Sun. - Thurs., 11am - 8pm, with all rides and games available Fri. and Sat., 11am - midnight. May - September all rides and games are up and running Sun. - Thurs., 11am - 11pm (usually); Fri. - Sat., 11am - 12:30am, though they sometimes open at 10am on Sat. and Sun. Definitely call or check the website before you visit.

Price: Individual rides cost $5 for the kiddie rides, up to $10 for the bigger kids' rides, each. An all-day rides wristband is $32.95 for 8 years and up; $17.95 for 7 years and under. Online prices are discounted. AAA members and active military personnel receive discounts. Parking on the pier (open 24/7) is about $3 an hour. Parking in Lot 1, just north of the pier at 1550 Pacific Coast Highway (and open daily, 6am - midnight) is $6 a day, Mon. - Fri. from November to March; $8, Sat. - Sun. Parking there April - October can be $15 a day. There is very limited metered street parking nearby.

Ages: 2 years and up.

RAGING WATERS

(909) 802-2200 / www.ragingwaters.com $$$$$

111 Raging Waters Drive, San Dimas

What a cool place to be on a hot day! Raging Waters is out*rage*ous with its fifty acres and almost fifty attractions of chutes, quarter-mile-long white-water rapids, slides, drops, enclosed tubes (which make these slides dark and scary), a wave pool, lagoons, and sandy beaches. The rides run the gamut from a peaceful, quarter-mile river raft ride in only three feet of water to the ultimate for daredevils, such as descending into Dr. Von Dark's Tunnel of Terror with its forty-foot drop, vertical banks, and 360° spins, all in total darkness. Or, plunge headfirst on a mat on High Extreme, a 600-foot ride off a 100-foot tower. Drop Out is an extreme body slide where the feeling that you are free falling (a seven-story drop) is terrifyingly fun. (I guess.) The Bermuda Triangle has three, enclosed, twisting body slides snaking out of its tower. Jump in your tube and drop down Dragon's Den, a ten-story-high, twisting, enclosed flume that spins you around a gigantic bowl. Race against seven others in the huge slide (with bumps) of Raging Racer. The five-person raft ride of Thunder Rapids is wild and wonderful, like riding a wild bronco. Aqua Rocket is unique in that it is a four-person raft water coaster - going up inclines and zipping down several drops. Ride high and try your boogie boarding best at the waves from the Flow Rider wave machine and at the Wave Cove, where water surges and swells into waves every ten minutes, or so. There is even a small beach here.

The younger set reigns at the huge Kids Kingdom as they splash around in this water area designed just for them.

It has a big water play structure to climb on that shoots out water, plus tyke-size water slides, a maze of tubes and tunnels, showers under waterfalls, and a tire swing. The Little Dipper lagoon is also for youngsters, 48" and under, with its wading pools, shooting fountains, and waterfalls. Elementary-school-aged kids have their own, separate, fantastic, activity pool with slides, a ropes course, and Splash Island Adventure. The tropical-themed Island is a five-story treehouse with slides, water cannons, cargo nets, swinging bridges, and a huge bucket on top that spills over gallons of water. Holy smoke! The Volcano Fantasea is a smoking volcano with several enclosed slides oozing down its sides into hip-deep water and more water activities. For a challenge, use an overhead rope for balance while trying to cross the length of the pool on hard foam pads.

Life vests are available at no extra charge. Locker rentals are available starting at $12. A picnic area is located just outside the main entrance gate. Outside food is not allowed inside, but there are several food outlets throughout the park. Hot tip: Wear water shoes, or sandals, because the walkways get very hot.

Hours: Open mid-May - May, and the end of August - September on weekends and holidays, Mon., 10am - 6pm, or 11am - 5pm. Open June - end of August, daily, 10am - 6pm or 7pm. Call first as hours fluctuate.

Price: $45.99 for 48" and taller; $35.99 for seniors and 36" - 47"; children 35" and under are free. Purchase season passes by May or purchase tickets online to save $. Parking is $15.

Ages: 1½ years and up.

SIX FLAGS HURRICANE HARBOR   ☼

(661) 255-4111 / www.sixflags.com $$$$$
26101 Magic Mountain Parkway, Valencia

This twenty-five-acre and twenty-three-slide water park is awash with amphibious fun set in a jungle and lagoons of a forgotten world. Older kids enjoy the thrill of the vertical drops, speed slides, body slides, open tube rides, and two of the tallest enclosed speed slides this side of the Mississippi. Stand in one of six upright launching tubes in Bonzai Pipelines. Then, as the bottoms drop out, you'll experience a fifty-foot free fall in clear tubing, and then an additional 200 feet (!) in enclosed tubes (i.e. darkness), including twists and turns and a 360 degree loop. Taboo Tower, with its multiple slides, is 65 feet high!! Writhe down the four ultra-fast water slides at Black Snake Summit, two of which are 75 feet high, fully-enclosed (i.e. pitch black), body slides. The other two slides are similar, but you use a raft. Reptile Ridge is another tower complex with five scary slides slithering from it. Tornado might just feel like the real deal with a 75 foot drop through a huge opening of a 132-foot tunnel/funnel. Bamboo Racer pits six contestants against each other as they race down the slides into the water. The wave pool, with two-foot waves, is a hit for those practicing surfing techniques. A five-person raft ride is fun without being too scary, and the lazy, looping river ride in only three feet of water is great for everyone in the family. If you want to avoid some waiting in line, purchase The Flash Pass which saves your place, virtually, in line so you can play elsewhere and be line when the pass indicates its your time.

Relax in lounge chairs while your younger children play in Castaway Cove, a shallow pool with mini-slides, cement aquatic creatures, and a wonderful, fortress-like water play structure with waterfalls, swings, water-spurting gadgets, and more. Kids not only get a cove to call their own, but they get their own island at Splash Island. With rain curtains, slides, squirting fountains and water play platforms, they can happily play here all day. An activity pool, Lizard Lagoon, is great for swimming, plus it has a net for water volleyball and, of course, it also has several slides. Forgotten Sea Wave Pool has gentle waves to ride or just bob along. Check out the website for times that dive-in movies are shown.

Food is available to purchase inside the Harbor as outside food is not allowed in. Hot tip: Wear water shoes, or sandals, as the walkways get very hot. Note: The Harbor shares the same parking lot as Magic Mountain.

Hours: Open Memorial Day to mid-June and in September on weekends only (plus Fridays in June), 10:30am - 6pm. Open mid-June - Labor Day daily, usually 10am - 6pm or 7pm. Hours vary so check the calendar website or call first.

Price: $43.99 for 48" and taller; $35.99 for kids 47" and under; children 2 and under are free. Online tickets are discounted, as are tickets bought with AAA cards. Season passes are a great deal. The Flash Pass is an additional $25. Parking is $25. Combo tickets for Hurricane Harbor and Magic Mountain are available.

Ages: 1½ years and up.

SIX FLAGS MAGIC MOUNTAIN   ☼

(661) 255-4111 or (661) 255-4103 / www.sixflags.com $$$$$
26101 Magic Mountain Parkway, Valencia

Thrill seekers and/or roller-coaster aficionados consider action-packed Magic Mountain the most daring place to go with its more than forty-five rides and attractions geared mostly for kids 8 years and older. Nineteen roller coasters here range from the updated, but still iconic, wooden and steel (i.e. hybrid) Twisted Colossus (with stalls, lifts, impressive drops and zero G rolls) to some of the world's tallest and fastest rides, including Goliath, which is a 255-foot drop and Superman, which zips you 100 mph in seven seconds and then reverses the direction so mere humans zoom backwards! I was yelling for Superman at this point - the hero, not the ride. Lex Luthor Drop of Doom is currently the world's tallest vertical drop with a 400-foot tower. Full Throttle is the world's tallest and fastest looping coaster. Scream is a floorless coaster that has a 150-foot initial drop, seven loops, and a top speed of 65 mph where riders, yes - scream. Ride the ultimate - Tatsu, with four inversions, zero gravity rolls, sharp dives, and more - all in one ride. Become completely immersed in another world while riding the revisited New Revolution - now a VR coaster. Strap on your headset and become a virtual jet fighter pilot firing upon the alien mother ship, extraterrestrial drones and more and as you virtually fly up and down, and bank around and through city buildings while you are literally going up and down and around loops on the physical coaster. Whew!

This extreme theme park also boasts X2, yet another ripping coaster ride, that spins its vehicles (360 degrees forward, backwards, and head-over-heels) independently of one another with sound and fire effects while going along the tracks. Green Lantern is the first vertical spinning coaster (with three 360-degree turns) in the U.S. And then there is Batman, one of the most popular rides as it combines more thrills and turns and loops than any Gotham City citizen can withstand. On the flip side, try Riddler's Revenge, a stand-up coaster that goes upside down (and fast). This area, Metropolis, is also where Justice League hero/characters are on hand for meet and greet and photo ops. CraZanity is a pendulum that swings seventeen stories high and then swings down (and back up) at up to 75mph. My stomach and I prefer to just watch some of these rides and not actually participate. If you don't want to wait in line for the more popular rides consider purchasing The Flash Pass, which is an electronic device that reserves your place in line while you enjoy other attractions. You'll get an alert when it's your turn.

Other highlights here include the Log Ride, Jet Stream, and Tidal Wave (all very wet rides); bumper cars; Buccaneer, a swinging (like a pendulum) pirate ship for mateys to ride; scrambler; and the exciting Justice League: Battle for Metropolis, a 3-D ride/game experience of battling with DC super heros against super villains by shooting lasers and scoring points through wind, fire, fog and special effects while riding through the streets of Metropolis as your vehicle moves with the on-screen motion. A few thrill rides with an extra fee include go-cart racing around an Indy 500-like track ($8 - $10); Slingshot ($30); and getting harnessed into Dive Devil - a leap off a 152-foot tower into the air to free fall down and then a guided, swinging, sky dive back down to earth ($35 for a single, $50 for a double).

A visit to Bugs Bunny World is ideal for the younger crowd, ages 2 to 8 years. Looney Tunes characters are often here for hugs and pictures. The rides include a pint-size free fall, train ride, truck ride, balloon ride, pirate ship, carousels, four roller coasters (of course), and Tweety's Escape, which is a ride in an oversized bird cage. Another high-ranking attraction in this section is the Looney Tunes Lodge, a two-story funhouse. Visitors in here use cannons and other creative gadgets to shoot, drop, or hurl hundreds of foam balls through the air at one another. To complete this world is a fountain area where Looney Tunes statues spew out water.

Cyclone Bay is toward the back of the park, where specialty shops are the specialty. Cartoon Candy Company is an especially sweet stop as kids can watch fudge, caramel apples, and all sorts of mouth-watering delights being made before their very eyes. If it's real food that you're hankering for there are plenty of selections throughout the park representing several countries - buon appetito!

Although there are lots of grassy, shady areas to rest, Magic Mountain is spacious and hilly, so wear walking shoes. Believe it or not, educational field trips are offered here, such as Math & Science Day that focuses quite a bit on physics. Tip: Visit this Mountain on a Monday or Tuesday, if possible, as it is normally less crowded then. Note: If you want wet, summertime fun, check out SIX FLAGS HURRICANE HARBOR (pg. 4), which is right next door.

Hours: Open daily, usually at 10:30am. The park closes anywhere from 6pm - 1am, depending on the date. Definitely check the website calendar as hours fluctuate a lot!

Price: $84.99 for 48" and taller; $59.99 for kids 47" and under; children 2 and under are free. Discounts are available online (pre-purchase and save up to $25 per ticket!) and through AAA. Season passes can be a great deal, especially if purchased before summer. A Flash Pass, for priority boarding, costs $45 - $120, depending on the day and level of your pass, plus the price of an admission ticket. Parking is $25. Combo tickets for Magic Mountain and Hurricane Harbor are available.

Ages: 1½ years and up.

UNIVERSAL STUDIOS HOLLYWOOD   ☼

(800) UNIVERSAL (864-8377) or (818) 622-3750 / www.universalstudioshollywood.com $$$$$

100 Universal City Plaza, Universal City

This huge, unique, Hollywood-themed amusement park is really one of the world's biggest and busiest motion picture and television studios. My personal advice is to either go on the 50-minute, guided studio tram tour first or visit the Wizarding World of Harry Potter, as lines for each of these most popular attractions get longer later on. Each tram on the studio tour is outfitted with monitors that show numerous film clips, as well as how various sets and sound stages have been used in productions over the years. The tram takes you behind the scenes and through several of Hollywood's original and most famous backlots including Courthouse Square, Western facades, little Europe, and the set for *Desperate Housewives*. You'll also learn about the shows currently being filmed at Universal, plus see sound stages and lots of props, including parts of the town from *The Grinch* and the real (completely wrecked) airplane and detailed scene of devastation caused by the plane crash in *War of the World*s. Some of the elaborate special effects that you'll encounter along the way are enraged dinosaurs attacking King Kong in enormous 3-D; the shark from *Jaws*; an earthquake in a subway station, where buildings collapse and a run-away big-rig crashes within inches of you, followed by fire and a flood coming toward you; a flash flood; and, by entering a tube, you'll feel like you are in a high-speed race with loud, adrenaline-pumping, immersive motion simulator and hologram action, riding along with the cast from *Fast and Furious:* Supercharged. It's just like being in the movie(s). Some of it can get a bit overwhelming for younger kids.

Leave the muggle world behind when you enter the 6-acre Wizarding World of Harry Potter. Walk through the archway to snow-capped, pitched roofs and crooked-looking shops of Hogsmeade Village and Diagon Alley, recreated with great attention to detail to the books and movies. Notice the Hogwarts Express train and platform that includes worn luggage, a leather trunk, and an empty bird cage.

Shop at Zonko's novelty items and joke shop; Honeydukes candy store (filled with exploding bonbons, chocolate frogs with wizard trading cards, and more); Filch's Emporium of Confiscated Goods gift shop; Dervish and Banges (with brooms, school robes and Quaffles to buy); Owl Post stationery shop (where you can send postcards and letters home with a genuine Hogsmeade postmark); and more, as well as the most beloved - dusty, Ollivander's wand shop filled with boxes and boxes of wands. An interactive mini "show" here includes seeing which wand chooses a wizard (customer)! Purchase your own wand from Ollivander's, choosing from a selection of character wand replicas. There are 11 medallions on the streets of Diagon Alley that work with special, interactive wands that are available for purchase - imagine that! Wave the wand, recite the spell, and watch the animatronic window displays come to life, like magic! Original props, music from the films, sounds, and fun extras (like Moaning Myrtle echoes in the bathrooms) lend authenticity to this unique world.

Hungry? Eat at the Three Broomsticks tavern with its genuine-looking decor like the gigantic beam ceiling and a broomstick rack. This buffeteria-style restaurant serves fish and chips, shepherds pie, bangers and mash, huge smoked turkey legs, and kid's meals of mac and cheese, fish and chips and chicken nuggets. Try a frosty mug of non-alcoholic, very sweet-tasting (and delicious) Butterbeer ($10 a pop with a souvenir mug), or the Butterbeer Potted Cream for dessert.

It's a short walk to a star attraction - the massive (200 foot tall!) replica of Hogwarts Castle with magical creatures guarding it, moss growing on the castle's stone walls and the Weasley's flying car crashed outside, its engine still running. Inside, the queue for the Forbidden Journey ride is an attraction in and of itself as you meander through the castle and encounter a Hogwarts classroom; a portrait gallery where the paintings come to life and talk to you and each other; Professor Dumbledore's office (and his hologram); the Room of Requirement; a secret staircase; the dungeon; and the Gryffindor common room, plus interactive "conversations" with Harry, Ron, and Hermoine. Enter the story as you enter the 3D-HD, motion-based, simulator Forbidden Journey ride which takes you along for non-stop action with the main characters as you fly high over the castle, play a Quidditch match, battle with Dementors, narrowly escape a dragon attack (and literally feel it's hot breath) and arrive safely back at the Great Hall. Back outside the castle, walk past Hagrid's hut to ride the family-friendly Flight of the Hippogriff roller coaster. Then, back through the archway to the "real" world.

On an eight-passenger *Simpsons* ride the characters join you (kind of, as they are on screen) to experience an almost out-of-control roller-coasterish ride through Krustyland and, just like the TV show (characters voices and all), you'll encounter wacky happenings, plus 4-D effects and the sensation of being immersed in the surroundings. The eateries and shops in this section of Universal reflect Bart's world and you can taste your own (nonalcoholic) Flaming Moe or Phineas O Butterfat's d'oh-nut sundae (exactly as it sounds).

Enjoy the building facades of the neighborhood of *Despicable Me*. Tip: Ring the doorbells and see what happens. Then, put your goggles on and go on the 3-D motion simulator ride, *Despicable Me: Minion Mayhem*, complete with super-villain, Gru, and his girls. Riders, or minions as they are now known, cruise and swerve through Gru's laboratory and then go through a minion training mission. Afterward (or before), play at the adjacent Super Silly Fun Land, a water play area with squirting fountains, splash pools, and huge buckets of water that overturn on unsuspecting guests. You will get wet. Tip: Bring a change of clothing. There is also a good-sized dry play area here where youngsters can climb on cargo nets, slide, and jump around, plus a themed ride with vehicles that spin and transport riders in the sky for a bird's eye view of Fun Land.

You can (or not) walk zombie-like through the *Walking Dead* labyrinth featuring real people in costumes that jump out to scare you, plus animatronic figures, props, and lots of blood and gore. This attraction is not for the faint-hearted.

Take the Starway (i.e., a really long escalator) to the lower lot where, if you are at least 46" tall, you can enter through the gates of Jurassic World Ride to river raft through the primordial forest. It starts off as a peaceful ride, but it ends up as a very wet, terrifying, face-to-face encounter with bellowing dinosaurs and realistic scenes that immerse you in the movie's storyline! You will get drenched. Ponchos are available for purchase at a nearby vending machine. Note that this ride has a single rider line which is usually faster than the regular line. Also note that there is an adjacent, small, dino-themed play area for younger ones. The very short *Revenge of the Mummy* ride hurtles thrill-seeking passengers through dark (and cold!) Egyptian chambers and passageways as a ceiling of flame, skeleton warriors, and other ghoulish robotic figures, a few pyrotechnics, and laser images seek to terrify. The roller coaster ride also goes backwards for a brief duration. Be on the lookout for the Egyptian-dressed guys and females on stilts that walk around this ride area and scare unsuspecting people - fun to watch. Fight alongside Optimus on the 3-D *Transformers* ride, based on the movies. Your car jerks forward and back and up and down, as the mega sensory and special effects battle with gigantic animatronic robots that fight loudly play out all around you: It could be a transforming experience. Note: A parent who waits with a younger child while the other adult goes on the ride can then go to the front of the line instead of waiting in the line again. The nearby NBC Universal Experience room holds rotating exhibits of authentic props and wardrobe from past and present movies, including the DeLorean used in *Back to the Future*.

As the name Universal Studios is synonymous with quality productions, the live shows here are wonderfully entertaining and highlighted with special effects. Animal Actors employ a lot of laugh-out-loud humor with a variety of well-trained animals including dogs, birds, cats, guinea pigs, ducks, and more. *Waterworld*, the "coolest" production here, and truly a favorite, has explosive stunts and special effects that blow you out of the water. The Special Effects Stage show reveals how sleight-of-sight effects were created and used in various Universal movies. See behind-the-camera work here with computer graphics and green screen technology, as well as the art of sound effects, and be a part of the half-hour show through audience participation. Kung Fu Panda like you've never experienced it is in the DreamWorks Theatre. This fifteen-minute, multi-sensory, visual immersion, animated show starring Master Po and the rest of the cast incorporates quite a few special effects to keep participants really feeling a part of the adventure, right down to the shaking and rocking theater seats.

Notes: Beat the crowds and get an early start for your adventure at Universal Studios. Look for the many costumed characters around the park. Get a free birthday button (if it's your birthday) from Guest Relations. Parents can participate in Child Switch where parents and kids wait in line together and then take turns riding rides without children without re-waiting in line. If time is of the essence, or you don't like waiting, purchase an Express Pass that allows you to go to the front of line one time for each ride/attraction, plus priority and reserved seating at the shows. Lines that can take an hour, or more on busy days, can take only five minutes with this pass. Another speciality is the VIP Experience, which includes breakfast and lunch; exclusive back lot access, such as actually walking around sound stages and sets closed to the public; unlimited front of the line access to all rides and attractions; a personal tour guide; and more. Educational workshops are offered for students to get behind-the-scenes look into all the aspects of filmmaking and special effects. Check out the adjacent UNIVERSAL CITYWALK (pg. 176) for unusual shopping and dining experiences. The show *EXTRA* films in front of a live audience, often in front of the Universal Globe, just outside the entrance gate to Universal Studios. Check the website to see which celebrity is being interviewed when.

Hours: Open every day of the year. Open the majority of the year daily, 10am - 6pm. Summer and some holiday hours are usually Mon. - Fri., 9am - 9pm; Sat. - Sun., 9am - 10pm. Check the web calendar for the day of your visit as hours fluctuate a lot. Tours are available at times in Spanish and Mandarin.

Price: $129 at the gate for ages 10 and up, or $109 - $119 for pre-purchased tickets, depending on the day/month; $123 for ages 3 - 9, or $103 - $113 pre-purchased; children 2 and under are free. CA residents get a discount. Two-day admission is $129 - $169. Always check online as many specials are offered. Express passes range from $179 - $259. Annual passes are usually a good deal. Parking is $25 until 6pm; $10 after 6pm. Or, park near the Universal Station (www.metro.net) at 3913 Lankershim Blvd. (note that there are 773 free parking spaces there), cross the street, then take a free shuttle up to Universal Studios, saving driving time and a parking fee.

Ages: 3 years and up.

—ARTS AND CRAFTS—

AS YOU WISH (Los Angeles County)

Palmdale - (661) 224-2000; Valencia - (661) 255-1177 / www.asyouwishpottery.com

Palmdale - 1233 Rancho Vista Blvd., in the Antelope Valley Mall; Valencia - 24201 Valencia Blvd., suite 3412, in the Westfield Valencia Town Center

$$$$

Pick it, plan it, paint it - perfect! Choose from an array of ceramics such as mugs, bowls, figurines, holiday items, sports items, plates, picture frames, Disney items, and much more. Create a design or just randomly paint your keepsake. Or, choose a canvas - a blank one to create your own design or pick from a plethora of stock designs to trace onto the canvas and then paint it. Kids love participating in making something they will keep and maybe even use, or give away as a special gift. Paints, supplies, and firing are all included in the studio fee. Your ceramic masterpiece will be ready for pick up in about five days. An ideal location for field trips, scout groups, parties or celebrations of any kind, so in the words of Westley from *The Princess Bride*, make something "As You Wish." Check the website for many special classes and events. Tip: As both of these studios are in malls, see the mall's websites for other things to do at them.

Hours: Palmdale - Open Mon. - Wed., 10am - 8pm; Thurs. - Fri., 10am - 9pm; Sat., 10am - 8pm; Sun., 11am - 6pm.
Valencia - Open Mon. - Thurs., 10m - 9pm; Fri. - Sat., 10am - 10pm; Sun., 11am - 6pm.

Price: $7.50 studio fee, plus the cost of your item.

Ages: 4 years and up.

AUNTIE'S CERAMICS

(626) 339-8916 / www.facebook.com/AuntiesCeramics

116 E. Badillo Street, suite B, Covina

$$$$

Create a unique gift at this ceramic art painting studio that stocks frames, holiday decorations, sports items, figurines, plates, refrigerator magnets, and more. Paints, brushes, stencils, and even design guidance, are included in the cost of your bisque piece. Auntie's also offers classes on cleaning and painting greenware, and on painting porcelain dolls.

Hours: Open Mon. - Thurs., 10am - 5pm; Sat., 10am - 2pm. Closed Sun. and Fri.

Price: $5 per person to paint, plus the price of your piece and a firing fee.

Ages: 4 years and up.

BITTER ROOT POTTERY

Los Angeles - (323) 938-5511; Valencia - coming soon; Woodland Hills - (818) 703-7008 / www.bitter-root-pottery.myshopify.com

Los Angeles - 7451 Beverly Blvd.; Valencia - 24201 Valencia Blvd., #150 at Westfield Valencia Town Center; Woodland Hills - 6230 Topanga Canyon Blvd at The Village

$$$$$

Throwing a pot is different than throwing a fit - just sayin'. This funky pottery studio, and I mean in the best possible way, has shelves showing a collection of finished products for purchase, including potted plants, bowls, and more, and an area for sitting at the pottery wheels which is sectioned off with a wall of tree trunks. Take a two-hour class that includes step-by-step instruction (and help!) with all the tools that you need - stamps, slump molds, cookie cutters, rolling pins, and more - to create your one-of-a-kind masterpiece from clay. Check the website for class listings, plus seasonal kids camps, birthday party and other party ideas. After you're done creating, pick the color you want for glaze and pick up your piece at a later date. See WESTFIELD TOPANGA and THE VILLAGE (pg. 96) for other things to do at that mall.

Hours: Check the website for dates and times.

Price: Usually $50 for a two-hour class.

Ages: 6 years and up.

COLOR ME MINE (Los Angeles County)

www.colormemine.com

Beverly Hills; Burbank; Calabasas; Encino; Glendale; Long Beach; Los Angeles; Pasadena; Porter Ranch; Redondo Beach; Santa Monica; Studio City; Torrance; Valencia; Whittier

$$$$

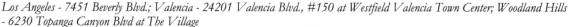

Do your kids have an artistic flair? Or think they do? Color Me Mine is a delightful, cozy, paint-your-own ceramic store. Kids can express themselves by first choosing their own ceramic piece and then their own palette. White dinosaurs, dolphins, mugs, plates, and much more will be transformed into vibrant works of art that will be treasured forever, or at least a while. My boys were so intent on their artistry that the hours just flew by. Warning: This recreational activity can become quite addicting! Pieces are glazed and fired, then ready to be picked up in a few days. Each store has a computer that has 25,000 drawings that can be printed out and traced. Photos and logos can be added to your items, too.

If you won't come to the party, the party will come to you. Some stores offer Party in a Box or To Go Party packages that include a ceramic or bisque item per person, plus paints and brushes. Glazed pieces can be picked up at the studio about a week after the party.

Note: The Encino and San Diego stores offer glass works and mosaics. Ask about other Color Me Mine's specialty classes, such as holiday classes, kids night out and the array of educational classes. We thoroughly enjoyed the Paint Like the Masters class and Art Around the World class where students learn about the subject matter or person, and then do a painting reflecting that style. Some stores offer preschool classes, as well as opportunities for boy and girl scouts to earn badges. There are a multitude of Color Me Mine's Los Angeles County. For info about a particular store, that website is that city's name.colormemine.com (i.e. longbeach.colormemine.com).

Hours: Most stores are open Sun. - Thurs., 11am - 9pm; Fri. - Sat., 11am - 10pm. Call your store first as hours vary.
Price: Studio painting rates fluctuate depending on the store - most charge $10 for the day for ages 11 and up; $7 - $8 for ages 10 and under. Prices for mugs and vases start at $10.
Ages: 4 years and up.

THE LONG BEACH DEPOT FOR CREATIVE REUSE ☼

(562) 437-9999 / www.thelongbeachdepot.org $
320 Elm Avenue, Long Beach

If you can think of it, you can create it by using items from this shop. Well, almost! (And if you can't think of it, look up Pintrest ideas.) This store has bins and jars and shelves filled with corks, baby food jars, egg cartons, buttons, bottlecaps, yarn, paper, cardboard, milk jugs, string, fabric, beads, and much more to create works of art, or at least to do art projects. There is also an exchange area where you can take items if you leave some in return.

Hours: The store is open Mon. - Sat., 11am - 6pm. Close Sun. and holidays.
Price: Technically free, but it is hard to leave without buying something.
Ages: 7 years and up.

PAINT N' GLAZE ☼

(562) 421-8000 / paintnglaze.wixsite.com/paintnglaze $$$$
3690 Studebaker Road, Long Beach

Do your kids have that glazed look in their eye? Then bring them to Paint 'N Glaze. This paint-it-yourself ceramic store is well supplied with an array of pieces to paint, so let your creative juices flow! Choose from mugs, vases, bowls, figurines, and more. My kids sometimes choose very interesting color combinations, but that is part of what makes their pieces (and them) so special. Designing your keepsake can take time, so be prepared to spend a few hours here. The studio price includes all of your paints, brushes, and stencils. Ask about the after school Kids Club, summer classes and other special events, as well as select times for painting on canvas.

Hours: Open Tues. - Thurs., 11am - 8pm; Fri. - Sat., 10am - 10pm; Sun., noon - 6pm. Closed Mon. and holidays. Closed on the 3rd Sat. at 5pm for adult canvas painting.
Price: $8 per person studio fee, plus the cost of your product. Check website for special pricing on different days.
Ages: 4 years and up.

PAINT 'N' PLAY ART STUDIO ☼

(626) 256-4848 / www.paintnplayartstudio.com $$$$
418 S. Myrtle Avenue, Monrovia

This funky, contemporary art studio offers something for every artistic bent. It is also very kid-friendly. Shelves of boring, white ceramics are waiting to become vibrant, colorful masterpieces at the touch of a paintbrush (and some paint). The room goes back surprisingly far with tables that are set with paint-splattered cloths. A separate party area is toward the back. Choose from a large variety of pieces such as mugs, plates, vases, statues, coin banks, cookie jars, and novelty items. Paint, smocks, and help from the friendly staff are included in your price. Stencils, rubber stamps, and a design center are available to assist the artistically challenged.

Paint N' Play also offers classes for learning oil painting, working a potter's wheel, and sculpting with clay. Inquire about Mommy and Me workshops, school field trips, Girl Scout badge-earning programs, and other specialty programs.

The studio also offers To-Go kits and/or will come to your venue with all the supplies needed for a painting party. Note that the studio is located in Old Towne, so there are numerous fun shops to investigate. The Krikorian Theater is just four doors down, as well.

Hours: Open Wed. - Thurs., noon - 7pm; Fri., noon - 9pm; Sat., noon - 7pm; Sun., noon - 5pm. Closed Mon., Tues., and holidays.

Price: There isn't a studio fee. The cost is the price of the piece, which start at about $16, plus about $6 for glaze. Acrylic-painted items may be taken home that day.

Ages: 4 years and up.

REDISCOVER

(310) 393-3636 / www.rediscovercenter.org
12958 W. Washington Boulevard, Los Angeles

Part warehouse, part studio, part lab - reDiscover supplies the raw materials and kids supply the creativity. Bins and bins and shelves and shelves and walls are filled with recycled and reusable goods - cardboard, rubber bands, tubes, ribbon, pipe cleaners, tile pieces, beads, spools, tote bags, electronic components, jars, fabric, cork stoppers, buttons, doohickeys, thingamajigs and so much more! Besides a place to purchase materials, support staff help direct in making some pretty cool projects such as making rope sandals, kites, ball runs, puzzles, games and contraptions of all sorts. At the Crafting Corner, younger kids can make small crafts using things like beads, paper, feathers, felt, pipe cleaners, dowels, stickers, jewels, crates, markers and tons more. For kids aged 7 to 12, the Tinkering Club allows them to use real tools and materials, under supervision of the staff, to make bigger projects such as picture frames and even go karts.

Other programs include private parties, educational programs and camps. Educational programs can be adapted to any curriculum. Samples topics include Simple Machines, Life Cycles, Home and Habitat, and Music. Adults can get in on the action, too, with educators' workshops.

Hours: Open Mon. - Fri., 3pm - 6pm; Sat. - Sun., 11am - 5pm.

Price: Materials are available for purchase. About $5 per person, per project. The Tinkering Club is $20 for the first 2 hours and then $10 an hour after that. Other programs range from $10 to $100 per student.

Ages: 4 years and up.

TWO BIT CIRCUS FOUNDATION

(310) 527-7080 / twobitcircus.org
12815 S. Western Avenue, Gardena

This big, green building is where the saying, "One man's trash is another man's treasure" comes into play. The "trash" in this warehouse is huge bins and bins, and more bins, filled with all sorts of upcyclable materials and items and manufactured overruns or defects from over 200 companies that you get to recreate into art, or a project of some kind. Check out what their walls and partitions are made of - they practice what they preach. I love their mottos: "minimizing waster; maximizing education" and "filling minds instead of landfills". Not only does the company promote STEAM (Science, Technology, Engineering, Art and Math) and thus work with schools, but they offer any group or individual help in learning technology, physics, and to have fun by repurposing. They also host field trips, teacher training courses, corporate events and birthday parties. It's a free-for-all creating time.

Hours: The warehouse is open Wed., 9am - 4pm; Sat., 9am - noon.

Price: $100 allows you to choose 100 units of material, to be used within a year's time. (Comes out to about $2 a pound.)

Ages: 3 years and up.

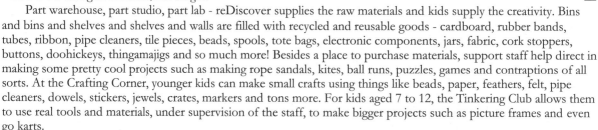

—*BEACHES*—

BELMONT SHORE BEACH, LONG BEACH CITY BEACH and BAYSHORE BEACH & PLAYGROUND

(562) 570-3100 or (562) 570-3170 - beach; (562) 570-1715 - Bayshore Playground / www.longbeach.gov; www.beachcalifornia.com

!

39th Place, along Ocean Boulevard (off Livingston Dr.), Long Beach

This very long and fairly wide expanse of beach hugs the shoreline of the Pacific Ocean, with plenty of places to play, swim, and ride bikes along the paved pathway. See BIKE TRAIL: LONG BEACH SHORELINE (pg. 209) for info on the bike trail. Along with the sand, there are lots of volleyball nets, a few palm trees, a specific dog zone (watch where you step), and Belmont Veterans Memorial Pier, featuring a place for fishing (no license required), a bait and tackle shop, a snack shop and an Aqua-link stop. (For just a few dollars, take the aqua-link, a.k.a. water taxi, around the waters, up to the Queen Mary and Shoreline Village.) Parking at the pier is $1 an hour; $10 max. Adjacent to the pier is an indoor, Olympic-size pool with stadium seating. There is also an outdoor pool at Belmont Plaza, a few beach-side restaurants next door, and tons of places to shop and eat just up the street.

South of the pier, starting around 5415 East Ocean Blvd. and Bay Shore Avenue, is Bayshore Playground and Bayshore Beach. The small, enclosed playground at 14 54th Place has a few swings, slides, and talking tubes, plus an adjacent basketball court, roller hockey rink, racquetball court, and cement picnic tables under shade trees. The small and very popular Bayshore Beach strip / Alamitos Bay is near the yacht club. It has waveless waters, but check out the water quality before swimming. Bring your rafts or kayaks (or rent kayaks at KAYAKS ON THE WATER - STAND UP PADDLEBOARDS (pg. 212)) to paddle this area and beyond, through the narrow water channels of Naples Island canals (Long Beach's version of Venice, Italy), under bridges and past lovely (and expensive) waterfront home. Note: This is where GONDOLA GETAWAY (pg. 211) is also located.

Hours: Open daily, 5am - 10pm.
Price: Free
Ages: All

CABRILLO BEACH

(310) 548-2645 or (310) 548-7554 / www.sanpedro.com
3720 Stephen M White Drive, San Pedro

This sometimes windy beach has a gated entrance, wonderfully wide sandy expanses, picnic tables, grass areas, barbecue pits, volleyball nets, and fire rings. It has a playground, too, with slides, climbing apparatus, swings, and a rock-like climbing structure. Beyond the breakwater is ocean surf; inside the breakwater is a gentle harbor. Check the water quality first at (800) 432-5229 or www.healthebay.org, as this beach has had a history of problems.

A paved, wheelchair-accessible trail runs from the parking lot across the beach to the water's edge at the tidepools. On wheels or by feet, take the sidewalk along the water to go out onto the rather long cement fishing pier. (Bring your own pole.) Although daring visitors walk the almost two miles on the rock jetty to the little lighthouse at the end, this is not advised. On the west beach, which is like a private little beach, you may hike the Cabrillo Coastal Park Trail that hugs the coastline. The trail, which is paved for a bit and then turns into a dirt pathway, dead ends at a gate barring entrance into Point Fermin Park.

See CABRILLO MARINE AQUARIUM (pg. 219), as this great, mid-size aquarium is adjacent to the beach. Ask about the seasonal grunion runs.

Hours: Open daily, 5:30am - 10:30pm.
Price: Parking is $1 an hour; $9 max, cash only. If you get here early enough (before crowds), you can park for free on the street.
Ages: All

COLORADO LAGOON

(562) 570-3215 or (562) 570-1888 / www.longbeach.gov; www.coloradolagoon.org
5119 E. Colorado Street & E. Appian Way, Long Beach

This half-mile stretch of lagoon water is fed through a large pipe from the ocean. The water quality is tested daily and usually deemed good, except after rain. Kids can swim the length of the lagoon, or a much shorter distance across it, from shore to shore. They can also jump off a wooden dock that spans across the water. Just beyond the sandy beach area is a grassy area. A playground, featuring a large plastic boat with slides and climbing apparatus, is shaded by a canopy. A few scattered picnic tables, shade trees, and barbecue pits make this an ideal location for a picnic.

Although the lagoon borders residential quarters with a fairly busy street on one side of it and a golf course on the other, we found it to be a relatively quiet place to spend the day. Lifeguards are on duty daily, mid-June through mid-September. See the Calendar entry, COLORADO LAGOON (pg. 717), for information on the Colorado Lagoon Model Boat Shop for a first-rate, boat-building opportunity that's available only in the summer.

Hours: Open daily, 8am - dusk.
Price: Free
Ages: All

EL MATADOR STATE BEACH

(818) 880-0363 / www.parks.ca.gov

$$

32350 32215 Pacific Coast Highway, Malibu

   Under the umbrella of Robert H. Meyer Memorial State Beach, El Matador is one of a series of small, cliff and cove beaches, and it is one of the best of the series. Topside are a few picnic tables with an incredible view. Take the dirt trail and steep steps way down to the beach below. There is sand there, but the standout features and main draws, besides the tidepools, are the rock formations on the beach and the sea caves contained within them. (Check out the "secret" passage at the northern end of the beach, but only during low tide!) This beach is great to explore and great for photo ops; no bull!

Hours: Open daily, 8am - sunset.
Price: $8 - $10 per vehicle at the drop box. Note that no change is given.
Ages: 4 years and up

LEO CARRILLO STATE PARK AND STATE BEACH

(310) 457-8143 or (818) 880-0363 - beach; (800) 444-7275 - camping reservations / www.parks.ca.gov

$$$

35000 Pacific Coast Highway, Malibu

   Leo Carrillo combines the best of everything that's enjoyable about the beach - 1.5 miles of beautiful, sandy beach; good swimming and surfing; a few sea caves to carefully explore; lots of rocky points and rocks littering the beach; rich and fairly large tidepools; and lifeguards, seasonally. Camping near the beach (campsites are a five-minute walk from the beach, under the freeway) makes this one of our favorite campgrounds. Each campsite has a fire pit and picnic table, and usually an oak tree and some bushes at the perimeter. Some sites are creek side. Pack a sweater, even in the summer!

Hours: Open daily, 7am - 10pm.
Price: $12 per vehicle for day use. Tent camping is $45 a night, plus an $8 camping reservation fee; $60 with hook-up.
Ages: All

MANHATTAN COUNTY BEACH

(310) 802-5000 / www.californiabeaches.com; www.citymb.info

!/$

Manhattan Beach Boulevard, at the end of Manhattan Beach Pier, Manhattan Beach

   This is definitely an iconic Southern California beach - great sand and wide stretches of it; waves for surfing; tons of volleyball courts for amateurs to play and where professional tournaments are held, including the Manhattan Beach Open; palm trees saluting the shore; a bike trail (see BIKE TRAIL: SOUTH BAY (pg. 210)); and a pier for fishing. See ROUNDHOUSE AQUARIUM TEACHING CENTER (pg. 225) for information about the small aquarium at the end of the pier. There are numerous shops and restaurants within walking distance.

Hours: Open daily, sunrise - sunset.
Price: Free. Metered parking is $1.25 an hour.
Ages: All

MARINA BEACH or MOTHER'S BEACH

(310) 305-9545 or (310) 305-9503 / beaches.lacounty.gov; www.visitmarinadelrey.com

$$

4135 Admiralty Way, Marina Del Rey

   This tiny patch of waveless water lagoon, where younger children can swim, is adjacent to a large marina. A half circle of sand has play equipment, such as a big pirate play boat, several swings, a tire swing, and slides. Lifeguards are on duty here in the summer. There are numerous picnic tables set up under a covered area right on the beach, near volleyball nets. It's pleasant scenery. Tip: A visit to the adjoining Cheesecake Factory makes it an extra fun (and tasty) excursion as does visiting the Farmer's Market that's here every Thursday morning. See MARINA DEL REY WATERBUS (pg. 213) for an inexpensive and fun water excursion, WATERSIDE MARINA DEL REY KIDS CLUB (pg. 96) at Waterside Marina Del Rey for free entertainment on Tuesday mornings, and FISHERMAN'S VILLAGE and surrounding area (pg. 159) for other activities in the immediate area.

Hours: Open daily, sunrise - 10pm.
Price: Free. Parking is usually 25¢ every 15 min. in the lots. Beach lots - Memorial Day - Labor Day, Mon. - Fri. are $8 for all day; Sat. - Sun., $10. Parking the rest of the year, Mon. - Fri. is $6; Sat. - Sun., $8.
Ages: Toddler to 8 years old.

MARINE PARK or MOTHER'S BEACH

(562) 570-3100 / www.longbeach.gov/park
5839 Appian Way, Long Beach

    This beach is aptly nicknamed because it is a mother/child hang out. There are waveless waters in this lagoon-type setting, plus lifeguards, barbecues, a volleyball court and a good playground surrounded by a small, grassy park. If you get hungry and forgot your picnic breakfast or lunch, grab a bite to eat at the quaint Mom's Beach House Cafe, located next to the playground. Mom's is open weekends, only, most of the year and daily during the summer. Call (562) 477-6820 for more info.

Hours: Open daily, sunrise - 10:30pm.
Price: Bring either lots of quarters for parking, or get here early to park on the street for free.
Ages: All

POINT DUME STATE BEACH

(310) 457-8143; (805) 488-1827; (818) 597-9192 / www.parks.ca.gov
Westward Beach Road, just off PCH, Malibu

    There are two parts, kind of, to this beach area. The free, northern one is a very long and fairly wide stretch of beach, with fine sand and several volleyball courts and nets, plus lifeguard stations. Be on the lookout for the dolphins that frequent these waters. A section of this beach parallels the road, then leads south to a paid area that is almost cove-like as it follows along part of the cliffs. A huge rocky point (hence the name, *Point* Dume) towers over this southern section of beach. We saw people repelling off this rock and there are, apparently, several climbing routes marked on it. Just a short drive down the road is POINT DUME NATURAL PRESERVE (pg. 79).

Hours: Open daily, sunrise - sunset
Price: Parking at the southern end of the state beach is $3 from 6am - 9am and 4pm - closing; $6 from 9am - 4pm. There is free street parking for the northern part of the beach.
Ages: All

SANTA MONICA BEACH

    Look up SANTA MONICA PIER / SANTA MONICA BEACH (pg. 161), under PIERS AND SEAPORTS, for details.

Hours: Open daily, sunrise - sunset.
Ages: All

SEASIDE LAGOON

(310) 318-0681 / www.redondo.org/seasidelagoon
200 Portofino Way, Redondo Beach

    Have a swimmingly good time at the gated Seaside Lagoon. This large saltwater lagoon, next to an ocean inlet and rock jetties, is heated by a nearby steam generating plant, so the average water temperature is seventy-five degrees. Warm, waveless waters, plus a lifeguard, make it an ideal swimming spot for little ones. A large water fountain statue sprays out water in the shallow end of the lagoon and there are a few, tallish, enclosed slides in the deeper end. There is also a sandy beach area that semi-surrounds the swim area; grass areas that ring some of the sand; playgrounds with a big, plastic pirate ship plus swings; barbecues; picnic tables; and a volleyball court. (Bring your own ball.) Tips: Bring your own beach chair and pack a picnic lunch. An easily-accessible snack bar is sponsored by RUBY'S (Los Angeles County) (pg. 26). Several other restaurants are in the immediate vicinity. Note that this is a prime spot for watching fireworks on the 4th of July; gates open at 2pm for that event. Tickets for this day/night are $20 for adults; $12 for kids.

Hours: Open Memorial Day - Labor Day daily, 10am - 5:45pm.
Price: $7 for adults; $6 for ages 2 - 17; children under 2 are free. Season passes are available. Parking is $2 per hour, $6 max with validation - cash only.
Ages: All

VENICE BEACH

(310) 396-6794 / www.laparks.org; www.venicechamber.net
1800 Ocean Front Walk, between Washington Boulevard and Rose Avenue, Venice

    I think Southern California's reputation of being offbeat, quirky, funky, etc., comes directly from Venice Beach. This area actually has a three-mile stretch of beach, but visitors also come to gawk at, and mingle with, the eclectic Venice population of street performers. These include jugglers (one juggler specializes in chain saws), musicians, artists, magicians, mimes, and fortune tellers, as well as people sporting unusual and colorful haircuts, and numerous tattoos, plus bikini-clad women (and men), skaters, and more. Self expression reigns. A hot spot here is Muscle Beach, where weight lifters of all levels pump iron. Venice Beach also has a bike path, playground, basketball courts, pagodas, volleyball courts, handball courts, shuffleboard, souvenir shops, a boardwalk, and restaurants. A cement skate park is here, too, complete with bowl, ramps, rails, and other street elements. A helmet and pads are required in the skate park.

Hours: Open daily, sunrise - sunset.
Price: Free, although parking may cost.
Ages: All

WHITE POINT / ROYAL PALMS STATE BEACH

(424) 526-7878 / beaches.lacounty.gov; www.sanpedro.com
1799 Paseo Del Mar, San Pedro

Park on the top of the bluff or drive down to the "beach." I put this word in quotes because there is precious little sand here, as the shoreline is composed of tons of rocks. Numerous tidepools are just beyond the parking lot, so you'll have a great day of exploring and searching for small marine organisms. My boys, of course, also loved climbing out on the rocks and the jetty. Note: A lifeguard is on duty here, too, in season. Tip: Come during low tide. We've also come during high tide, though, and watched the waves slam into the rocks and shoot high into the sky. Bring your camera!

One side of the beach has a cement patio with picnic tables (and restrooms) under the palm trees (hence the name of the park) that are snug up against the cliffs - very picturesque. A small playground is here, too.

Hours: Open daily, 6am - sunset.
Price: Parking is $3 from 6am - 9am; $6 - $10 at other times, depending on the season.
Ages: 4 years and up.

WILL ROGERS STATE BEACH

(310) 457-9701 - beach; (310) 821-1081 - parking / www.beaches.lacounty.gov
17000 E Pacific Coast Hwy, Pacific Palisades

At about three miles long, this lovely, clean stretch of beach offers wide sandy expanses, as well as lots and lots of volleyball courts, a playground, some fitness equipment, showers, a snack bar, and a bike trail/walkway that cuts through it. Note that the shoreline can sometimes be rocky. This beach is usually much quieter than its neighbor, Santa Monica Beach.

Hours: Open daily, sunrise - sunset.
Price: Parking is $5 - $15 during the summer (peak season); $4 - $9 during the winter.
Ages: All

ZUMA BEACH

(310) 457-2009 - beach; (818) 597-7361 - beach bus / beaches.lacounty.gov; www.ci.agoura-hills.ca.us - beach bus
30000 Pacific Coast Highway, Malibu

This is one of the biggest, busiest, and cleanest beaches in Southern California. Besides the miles of sand, good swimming, body surfing, lifeguard stations, volleyball courts, a swing set, snack bar, and ample parking (8 lots and 2,000 spaces), these ocean waters are often home to schools of dolphins that ride the waves. *This* is what Southern California beaches are all about! Tip: Locals can catch the Beach Bus mid- June through mid-August, weekdays starting at 9:15am to Zuma Beach, #6. Pick up and drop off points are Lindero Canyon Middle School, Agoura High School and the corner of Liberty Canyon and Agoura Rd. Tickets are $2 each way for all ages.

Hours: Open daily, sunrise - sunset.
Price: Parking in the lots can range from $6 - $15, depending on the time of day and season. There is some free parking on PCH if you arrive early.
Ages: All

—EDIBLE ADVENTURES—

94th AERO SQUADRON (Los Angeles County)

(818) 994 - 7437 / www.94thvannuys.com
16320 Raymer Street, Van Nuys

See 94th AERO SQUADRON (San Diego County) (pg. 469) for a description of this aviation-themed restaurant.

At this location, the restaurant overlooks the Van Nuys airport.

Here the lunch menu includes crab stuffed mushrooms ($14), 94th gourmet burger ($17), chicken lettuce wraps ($13), roasted turkey and avocado croissant club ($15), prime rib French dip ($17), and beer battered fish and chips ($18). The dinner menu includes filet mignon ($37), roasted lamb shank ($30), chicken pot pie ($23), and more. Their Early Flight dinner, served from 4pm to 5:30m, is $25.95 and includes the roast prime rib, chicken scallopini or fresh salmon as a main entree, plus starters and dessert. The Sunday buffet brunch has an incredible assortment of delectable foods - made-to-order pasta, omelets, fresh seafood, carving stations, desserts, and much more. Catch the next flight to the 94th Aero Squadron!

Hours: Open Mon. - Thurs., 11am - 9pm; Fri. - Sat., 11am - 10pm; Sun., 9am - 3pm for brunch, 4pm - 9pm for dinner.

Ages: 4 years and up.

AMERICAN GIRL PLACE

See AMERICAN GIRL PLACE (pg. 162), under POTPOURRI, for details about this outing.

$$$$$

BELLADONNA GIFT BOUTIQUE AND TEA ROOM

(661) 942-0106 / www.belladonnatea.com

$$$$

44054 10th Street West, Lancaster

Step in the door at Belladonna's (which translates as "beautiful lady") and relax - you are now on a mini-vacation. A small, renovated, purple, Victorian-style home has seven rectangular tables with a mixture of high-back chairs that seat a maximum of twenty-two total; walls that are decorated with hats (you may choose one to wear, if you wish); an eclectic arrangement of pictures; and whimsical decor. Enjoy the friendly service and settle down for a good cup of tea (choose from eighty-five flavors of loose leaf, or several tisanes [herbal tea]), freshly-made scones, and time to chat with your tea companion(s). This is how a tea experience should be!

Menu selections include (bottomless) tea and scone, $12.95; tea, sandwich, and scone, $17.95; and a full tea lunch, $26.95. The latter is served with tea; soup or a petite salad; tea sandwiches, such as turkey curry and black olives, chicken with walnut and cranberries, and cucumber with garden cream cheese; and a few desserts. The Princess Tea, for children, comes with a teacup full of fruit, a peanut butter and jam tea sandwich in a heart shape, a crown-shaped cheese sandwich (it is the details that count!), sweetened tea (or another beverage), chocolate chip scone, petite dessert, plus a goody bag of princess items for $17.95. Scones are freshly made and the variety can include cranberry, apricot, and butterscotch with coconut.

The gift boutique is packed with tea sets, jewelry, decorative hand towels, gloves, tea accessories, and several other gift items.

Hours: Open Tues. - Fri., 11am - 5pm; Sat., 11am - 4pm, with the last seating at 2pm. Note that only full lunch is served on Sat. and the seatings are at 11am and 2pm. Closed Sun. and Mon. Reservations are highly suggested.

Price: Menu prices are listed above.

Ages: 5 years and up.

BENIHANA OF TOKYO (Los Angeles County)

Arcadia - (626) 340-2276; City of Industry - (626) 912-8784; Downey - (562) 372-9210; Encino - (818) 788-7121; Santa Monica - (310) 260-1423; Torrance - (310) 316-7777 / www.benihana.com

$$$$

Arcadia - 400 South Baldwin Ave.; City of Industry - 17877 Gale Avenue; Downy - 8801 Apollo Way; Encino - 16226 Ventura Blvd.; Santa Monica - 1447 Fourth St.; Torrance - 21327 Hawthorne Blvd.

Enjoy the "show" and the food at Benihana. With their choreographed cooking, the chefs prepare the food on a sizzling grill right in front of you, hibachi-style. Knives flash as the food is chopped up seemingly in midair, as well as on the frying table, with lightning speed - this is the show part. (Don't try this at home.) Although my kids are not normally prone to trying new foods, they readily taste new entrees here because the food is fixed in such an intriguing way. The onion ring volcano is especially cool!

Just some of the food choices include chicken - picante or hibachi with lemon; seafood - scallops, lobster tail, and tuna steak; steak - filet mignon or teriyaki steak; and fresh vegetables. Sushi is also available, but there's not much of a show with that entree. The communal tables seat up to ten people. Lunch prices for adults range from $12 to $16.80; for dinner, $20 to $47. Kids' meals range from $9 to $13.25 for a choice of chicken, hibachi steak, or shrimp. Their meals also come with salad, shrimp appetizer, rice, and ice cream.

Ever want to "Be the Chef"? Try this package with its one-on-one training session to learn the art of teppanyaki which includes some of Benihana's signature tricks and preparing their special fried rice. Wear your commemorative apron and hat when you put on a special performance (i.e. making a meal) for three of your friends. All for $200.

Note that several Benihana locations have a koi pond and a traditional Japanese arched bridge as part of their outside decor.

Hours: Most locations are open daily for lunch, 11:30am - 3pm; for dinner, 5:30pm - 10pm. Call first as hours vary.
Price: Menu prices are listed above.
Ages: 5 years and up.

BUCA DI BEPPO (Los Angeles County)

(866) EAT BUCA (328-2822) for all locations; Claremont - (909) 399-3287; Encino - (818) 995-3288; Los $$$$
Angeles - (323) 370-6560; Pasadena - (626) 792-7272; Redondo Beach - (310) 540-3246; Santa Clarita - (661)
253-1900; Universal City - (818) 509-9463 / www.bucadibeppo.com
Claremont - 505 West Foothill Blvd.; Encino - 17500 Ventura Blvd.; Los Angeles - 6333 W. 3rd St. at the Farmer's Market;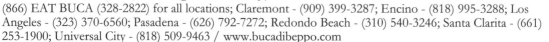
Pasadena - 80 West Green St.; Redondo Beach - 1670 South Pacific Coast Highway; Santa Clarita - 26940 Theater Dr.;
Universal City - 1000 Universal Studios Blvd., G101 (on Universal CityWalk)

O Solo Mio! Eating at Buca Di Beppo (the name translated means, "Joe's Basement") is the epitome of Italian-style, family dining - good food, comfortable atmosphere for sitting and talking (boisterously so at times), and meals meant to be shared. In fact, many meals here come in two portion sizes - small, which feeds two or more, and large, which feeds four or more. (Single portions are also available.) The restaurant has other outstanding features that pay homage to Italian heritage. The walls are crammed with photographs and pictures of Italian people - actors and actresses, and a lot of just ordinary folk. (The Santa Monica location has 1,500 pictures!) Some pictures are like family portraits and other pictures feature people of all ages who don't have many clothes on. Paintings, art, statuary (some of it PG-13) also fill up the alcove walls, semiprivate room, and large rooms. Every spare inch is taken up with something that is purposefully kitschy and over-the-top, in a fun and colorful way. Italian music plays in the background.

The circular Pope's Room seats up to twenty people. The ceiling is painted, a la Sistine Chapel, and all of the pictures, art objects, and memorabilia are papal-oriented, including a bust of the present Pontiff. A favorite room, and you'll need to make a reservation, is the kitchen. Yes, the kitchen. Up to six people can eat at the one table in the kitchen while watching food being prepared and servers scurry back and forth. Note that some of the locations offer outside dining as well.

Menu prices can change according to location. Most menu choices, of the large size (which serves up to 5), include a pepperoni pizza ($29.99); spaghetti with meatballs ($36.99); stuffed shells with sausage, spinach, and ricotta cheese and Parmesan ($33.99); shrimp Florentine or salmon Sorrento ($40.99); and much more. Single, lunch options can include soup or salad ($9.99); baked rigatoni or lasagna ($12.99); and chicken limone or chicken parmigiana ($14.99).

Hours: Most locations are generally open Mon. - Thurs., 11am - 10pm; Fri. - Sat., 11am - 11pm; Sun., 11am - 9pm.
            Redondo Beach and Encino location aren't open for lunch. Call the specific restaurant for its hours.
Price: Menu prices listed above.
Ages: 4 years and up.

CAFE 50'S

(310) 479-1955 / www.cafe50s.com $$$
11623 Santa Monica Blvd., Los Angeles

Well, shake it up, baby! This small hamburger joint is jumping with 50's memorabilia and atmosphere. The front room consists primarily of a soda counter (thirty-two types of shakes are offered) and a wall taken over by signed pictures of celebrities. Each red or green vinyl booth has a personal jukebox. For 25¢ you get two songs from the good old days. The walls and ceilings are crammed with nostalgic movie star posters, magazine covers, license plates, old-fashioned advertisement tin signs, serving trays, and pictures. Playing cards are another ceiling decoration. The rooms also boast bubble-gum machines, a case of signed sports paraphernalia, and glass displays of old TV collectibles such as Mickey Mouse ears, lunch boxes, box cartons, and more. On top of the lockers in the back room are board games that you can play - just ask. Besides the eye-catching decor, other entertaining features of this cafe include table top magic shows (usually on Sunday afternoons), and the "Food For Thought" newsletter packed with trivia, stories, jokes, and such.

Breakfast specialities include blueberry pancakes ($9.95), cheese blintzes with blueberry sauce and sour cream ($11.95), breakfast burritos ($12.95), and a variety of omelettes ($13.95 average). Lunch and dinner selections include appetizers of sweet potato fries ($8.95) and chili cheese fries ($8.95); salads such as Cobb ($14.95) and grilled chicken ($14.95); cheeseburgers ($8.69); and sandwiches such as a Monte Cristo ($12.95), BLT ($10.49), and patty melt ($11.49). Desserts, besides the shakes, include fruit pie ($6.49), hot fudge chocolate cake ($7.69) and cheesecake ($6.49). Shake flavors include rocky road, orange dreamsicle freeze, apple pie, Butterfinger, and strawberry cheesecake for $5.95 each. Join the free Frequent Dining Club for great, free rewards. The Big Bopper never had it so good!

Hours: Open Mon. - Thurs., 7am - midnight; Fri., 7am - 1am; Sat., 8am - 1am; Sun., 8am - midnight.
Price: See menu prices above.
Ages: All

CANDLELIGHT PAVILION DINNER THEATER

See the entry for CANDLELIGHT PAVILION DINNER THEATER (pg. 179), under SHOWS AND THEATERS, for details.

$$$$$

THE CANDY FACTORY

(818) 766-8220 / www.thecandyfactoryla.com
1819 West Verdugo Blvd., Burbank

$$$$

How sweet it is! The Candy Factory is one of the largest and oldest candy-making suppliers on the West Coast. The store does not actually have a lot of the finished product to purchase, but it has an abundance of the supplies needed, such as a wide variety of molds, flavorings, chocolates in every color (to melt), and lollipop sticks. Birthday parties are offered for ages 7 years and up for groups of ten to twenty-five. The $30 per person fee includes ninety minutes of making candy (and eating it) - swirling and pouring three chocolates and four molds (guitars, race cars, stars, and other fun shapes) and, while they're freezing, eating cake and drinking punch. Participants get deliciously messy and leave on a sugar high and with at least a pound of chocolate. And if that's not enough sugar, this "factory" also sells homemade ice cream, including redneck root beer floats that come in a mason jar you get to keep. My children offered (begged) to live at the Factory for a while - imagine that!

Hours: The store is open Tues. - Fri., 10am - 5pm; Sat., 10am - 4pm. Birthday parties are usually offered on Sun. from 1pm - 3pm or 2pm - 4pm.
Price: Some prices are listed above.
Ages: 6 years and up.

CANDY WAREHOUSE

(310) 343-4099 / candywarehouse.com
2520 Mira Mar Avenue, Long Beach

$$

I've always been a sucker for a candy store. ☺ This place, with hard-to-miss M&M statues outside, has one room filled with warehouse shelves packed with all kinds of candy - top brands and generic - to purchase mostly in bulk, although there are $1, $5 and $10 shelves. The aisles are sorted by colors of candies. I can't decide if I like the red aisle better or the blue aisle. Since you'll need somewhere to put all the candy, purchase a giant pinata!

There are other fun things, too. (But is there anything more fun than candy, tho? Seriously.) In the small front room, sit on a bench that looks like it's made out of dot candy. One of the coolest things is the steampunk desk made with giant gears that are visible under glass. Sit behind the desk on a purple, throne-like chair, wear the Willa Wonkesk hat, and with an enormous lollipop and a large bubblegum machine framing you, it's a great photo op. There are also other smaller, plush purple chairs to sit in, plus t-shirts, individual candies, and a huge jelly belly dispenser with a wide variety of flavors to buy. And yes, you can have a really sweet birthday party here, too, in the separate party room.

Hours: Open Mon. - Fri., 8am - 6pm; Sat., 9am - 5pm. Closed Sun. and major holidays.
Price: Free, but you'll spend money.
Ages: 3 years and up.

CARNEY'S

Studio City - (818) 761-8300; West Hollywood - (323) 654-8300 / www.carneytrain.com
Studio City - 12601 Ventura Blvd.; West Hollywood - 8351 Sunset Blvd

$$$

Railroad the kids and take them to Carney's for a bite to eat on board passenger train cars. The West Hollywood location has a 1920's Union Pacific dining car. The Studio City location has two 1940's train cars and a caboose. Grab a burger - no chili ($4.45), hot dog with chili ($4.59), spicy Polish dog ($4.40), small chili fries ($3.25), chicken breast filet sandwich ($6.50), beef or chicken soft tacos ($4.25 each), Thai chicken wrap ($7.25), tuna salad ($8.90), or tuna melt ($6.50).

Hours: Studio City - open Sun. - Thurs., 11am - 10pm; Fri. - Sat., 11am - midnight. West Hollywood - open Sun. - Thurs., 11am - midnight; Fri. - Sat., 11am - 3am.
Price: Menu prices listed above.
Ages: All

CHARLIE BROWN FARMS

(661) 944-2606 / www.charliebrownfarms.com $$$

8317 Pearblossom Highway, Littlerock

This innocuous-looking store appears to be a kind of old-fashioned general store. Walk through its doors, however, and you will be utterly amazed at the massive size of the store and the astonishing variety of goods offered here.

The immediate section has an impressive selection of more than 1,000 food items including nuts; dried fruits; pretzels and chips; locally-grown fruits and vegetables; a plethora of honey, molasses, and jams and jellies; sixty kinds of jerky; homemade cookies; ostrich eggs; soda flavors and brands that are no longer readily available; and so much more. The candy selection includes over 1,000 kinds - a multitude (over fifty) of flavors of saltwater taffy, plus brittle, horehound candies, chocolate, and hard-to-find speciality and novelty candies. Walk through several rooms filled with vast assortments of everything under one major roof. One room is devoted to collectible, porcelain, and vinyl dolls - more than 1,000 of them. Another room is packed with games and toys, including reproductions of classics, collectibles, and newer ones, and too many choices of marbles. Another is devoted to hundreds of teapots, plus dishes, cookie jars, collectibles, and home products. Christmas ornaments and holiday decorations are available year round in a room toward the back. Another room features larger-than-life-size statues of pirates, penguin butlers, Betty Boop, cavemen, an old English phone booth, and more. Dinosaurs from miniature to life-size are ensconced in another room. There are also rooms filled with all things military; one for just gnomes; another for gift items; and much more! To sum up Charlie Brown Farms in two words - fabulously kitschy.

Outside there are large statues of knights, lions, dinosaurs, elephants, etc. Order your food at the counter and then sit indoors, with its Western ambiance, or outside, where you are surrounded by more large statues and creations. The decor is both odd and fun. The food is delicious with a choice of Texas barbecue tri-tip (this was my favorite), barbecued chicken, pulled pork, or brisket, plus a choice of two sides for about $9.95. A half rack of ribs is $12.95. Or, order burgers of venison, buffalo, or ground steak for an average of $6.95 per ($9.95 for an ostrich burger). Frog legs, alligator, wild boar, kangaroo, and rattlesnake meats are available at times, too. And that's just the beginning! There are also breakfast and sandwich wraps (average $7.95), bread bowls (about $6.95), a slew of salads to choose from (average $6.95), deli sandwiches (about $6.75), side orders (sweet potato fries, cowboy beans, garlic cheese fries, pepper bellies), plus the good stuff like shakes (choose from the fifty kinds offered), frozen custard, homemade fudge, funnel cakes, kettle korn, pie shakes (i.e. cherry pie shake, banana cream pie shake, etc.), deep-fried Oreos, Hawaiian shaved ice, and lots more. Kid's meals are about $5 for a meal, with sides, ice cream and drink! The coffee menu is also fairly extensive, of course.

Note that peach and other U-pic fruit orchards are just down the road.

Hours: Open daily, 8am - 8pm.
Price: Technically free, but bring money!!
Ages: 1½ years and up

CHUCK E. CHEESE'S (Los Angeles County)

www.chuckecheese.com $$$

These popular indoor eateries and play lands for young kids offer token-taking kiddie rides and video and arcade games, as well as the all-important prize redemption centers. Many facilities also have play areas with tubes, slides, and ball pits. Chuck E. Cheese's, the costumed rat mascot, is usually walking around giving hugs and high fives. An electronic version of Chuck E. performs several stage shows throughout the day.

Every child's favorite food is served here - pizza! An extra large cheese pizza (16 slices) is $17.49 and all-you-can-eat salad bar is $8.99. Other menu choices are personal gluten-free pizza ($7.49), Italian sub ciabatta ($8.99), buffalo wings ($10.99), club wraps ($8.99), and sandwiches, plus dessert options of churros and cinnamon dessert pizza. All purchases come with a few tokens, but kids always want more. Bring in their report cards (especially if they have good grades!) to redeem for extra tokens. Check out the website for online coupons, too. Note: This place is often noisy at peak lunch and dinner times, especially on weekends when crowds descend.

Hours: Call for a particular location's hours.
Price: Free admission, but count on spending money on pizza and tokens.
Ages: 2 - 11 years.

CLIFTON'S REPUBLIC

(213) 627-1673 / www.cliftonsla.com $$$

648 S Broadway, Los Angeles

Originally founded in 1932, Clifton's is a wonderful mixture of eclecticness and entertainment. With its cafeteria (i.e. The Marketplace) and several bars, each area of Clifton's four floors have different and novel surroundings and themes. The best is the atrium eating area which boasts a massive mural of woods (Yosemite Valley and Muir Woods) along with real tree bark on some trees popping out from the mural, making it 3-D. There is also a huge stone mantle and fireplace with plants on the top and giant stones and grottos around the rest of the room, complete with mini caves. The faux redwood tree in the center of the room, standing a few stories high, has a fireplace in its split open trunk base. A taxidermied grizzly bear (one of several such stuffed animals in Clifton's) overlooks it all from his raised perch. A waterfall is adjacent to the stairs on the second floor. The old-school cafeteria here serves a plethora of cafeteria food - soups, salads, pizza, sandwiches, pastas, veggies, breads in animal shapes, and a full selection of dessert options. There is seating in this area, too. The Exposition Marketplace here offers fun and collectable retail options and artisanal foods from around the world to bring home.

Kids can only take a look at the other floors, as they are mostly bars, but they should because of the quirkiness of the decor such as antique furniture and lamps, a chair made of horns, a nine-foot-tall buffalo behind glass (impressive!), and wooden bar stools made from beautiful slats of wood with mushroom stools (not real ones) for foot stools. The Monarch bar sports a 1935 Art Deco-era soda fountain. The Brookdale room is an upscale restaurant atmosphere and ballroom on the third floor that also features a stuffed lion posed in a "natural" diorama setting, as well as a deer being chased by a coyote. The Gothic Bar is from another era with a brick wall mural of a forest, old-time furnishings, and golden highlights everywhere. Pacific Seas bar is my favorite: It has a huge Art Deco Map Room (from travels of yesteryear); brick walls that are muralized with a South Seas theme; a wooden boat as a centerpiece; a sea diving helmet; and carved tikis and other artifacts paying homage to this locale. Live entertainment with bands /concerts, for ages 21 and over, are invited at nighttime.

Hours: The bars are opened at various times - see the calendar. The atrium eating area and cafe/marketplace is open Thurs., 11am - 9pm; Fri., 11am - 10pm; Sat., 10am - 10pm; Sun., 10am - 9pm. It's closed Mon. - Wed.

Price: Free to walk around. Restaurant prices - average $17+ per person.

Ages: 3 years and up.

DALE'S DINER

(562) 425-7285 / www.dalesdiner.com
4339 E. Carson Street, Long Beach

Hey Daddy-O! This small 50's diner is a really happenin' place. It's decorated with black and white checkered tile floor, turquoise vinyl seats, and a few special booths that look like they were made from the back section of cars from this era. Each table has its own small jukebox. At 25¢ for two songs, your kids can now be introduced to such classics as *Chantilly Lace* and *Purple People Eater.*

For breakfast, tasty morning choices, which range from $9 to $12, include omelettes, with side dishes; a waffle, two eggs, bacon or sausage patty; or blueberry flapjacks. Kids' meals, for ages 9 and younger, include two oreo pancakes (about $7), or one egg and one pancake and a piece of bacon (about $6). The lunch menu, ranging from $10 to $13, and dinner menu, ranging from $13 - $15, offer a Cobb salad, pork chops, sirloin tip steak kabob, deli sandwiches, hamburgers, and more. Top off your meal with a chocolate, vanilla, or cherry soda. Kids can choose a burger and fries, grilled cheese with fries, chili, or a pepperoni pizza for about $6 per. Beverages are extra. Come in sometime just for dessert and try a slice of freshly baked pie ($4); a malt, sundae, or float (average $5); or a scrumptious Brownie Saturday, which is alternating layers of brownies with vanilla ice cream, topped with hot fudge and whipped cream ($6).

Hours: Open Mon. - Thurs., 6am - 9pm; Fri. - Sat., 7am - 10pm; Sun., 7am - 9pm. Closed Christmas.

Price: Menu prices are listed above.

Ages: All

ELISE'S TEA ROOM

(562) 424-2134; after hours - (562) 715-6281 / www.elisestearoom.com
3924 Atlantic Avenue, Long Beach

This refined, yet welcoming and feminine tea room, off a main street in Long Beach, offers a pleasant respite and time to relax while enjoying a cup of tea. The decor is artfully arranged pictures on the walls and hutches filled with dolls and china plates and tea cups, plus lovely murals on the wall and ceiling. Tables are set with white linen tablecloths accompanied by matching padded chairs. A small shop selling tea paraphernalia and collectibles is located toward the back.

There are several types of teas to choose from - I've only listed a few of them. A scone with jam and a pot of tea is $8.99. Child's Tea with a heart-shaped (and kids notice these things!) peanut butter and jelly sandwich or chicken nuggets, a cookie, and tea or lemonade is $12.99. Full Tea consists of two scones with jam, six tea sandwiches, one petite dessert, and a pot of tea for $25.99. High Tea is the Full Tea, plus quiche and a house salad for $38.99. A sampling of the a la carte items include one scone ($2.99), one tea sandwich ($2.99), a small pot of tea ($3.99), and a bagel with cream cheese ($5.99). Chicken salad is available for $15.99, and soup and salad for $12.99. There seems to be something at Elise's to fit everyone's budget and palate.

Hours: Open Tues. - Fri., 11am - 5pm; Sat., 10am - 5pm; Sun., noon - 4pm. Open the first Fri., 7pm - 9pm for a dance party (no cover charge) in conjunction with First Fridays Art Walk in Long Beach. Closed Mon., except for private parties. Reservations are suggested at all times and necessary on the weekends.

Price: Menu prices are listed above.

Ages: 5 years and up.

THE ENCHANTED ROSE TEA PARLOUR AND GIFT BOUTIQUE

(909) 394-4588 / www.enchantedrosetea.com $$$$

120 W. Bonita Avenue, suite G, San Dimas

Surrounded by the ambiance of bygone days in Old Town, the Enchanted Rose blooms among a garden of antique shops. The vintage parlor setting is enhanced by hutches and shelves that hold tea sets, dolls, china plates, hats, bird houses, candles, frames, floral arrangements, and all sorts of tea embellishments. The various chandeliers add a charming touch, as does a faux fireplace with a lace mantel covering. If you want to play dress up (because we are never too old for that), you may choose from an assortment of hats and/or feather boas.

Not only is the atmosphere inviting, but the food is good as well. The namesake Enchanted Tea, $17.75, includes a raspberry vinaigrette salad or cup of soup; a fresh-baked scone with Devonshire cream, jam and lemon curd; tea sandwiches; chocolate-dipped seasonal fruit; dessert; a pot of tea; and a signature pink chocolate rose. The Lady Sheila Tea, $14.75, offers a scone or dessert; chocolate-dipped seasonal fruit; tea sandwiches; a pot of tea; and chocolate rose. Little Prince or Princess Teas, for ages 5 to 11, $12.75, include a mini scone, petite children's sandwiches, fresh fruit, dessert, pot of tea, punch, or lemonade, and a chocolate rose. Ask about the special-occasion tea parties for adults and for children ages 5 and up.

Nice gift items and teas in tins available to purchase are interspersed throughout the tearoom. Take the time to stroll around and browse through the numerous shops of Old Town San Dimas. Of special interest to kids is a train store toward the west end of town. There are real trains that run by the town as well. A small park and a small historical museum are also in the immediate vicinity.

Hours: Open for tea Wed. - Sat., 11am - 3pm. The shop is open 10am - 5pm. Reservations are suggested. Open Sun. - Tues. by special reservation, only.

Price: Menu prices are listed above.

Ages: 5 years and up.

FAIR OAKS PHARMACY AND SODA FOUNTAIN

(626) 799-1414 / www.fairoakspharmacy.net $$$

1526 Mission Street, South Pasadena

Fair Oaks is a small "store" with a quaint ambiance, located a few miles from Old Town Pasadena, which has lots of shops and restaurants. It is part pharmacy, that also sells retro collectibles, jewelry, and home accents; and part 1900's restaurant and soda fountain, complete with a marble counter top and antique fixtures. Both sides of the store are decorated with memorabilia, unique toys, and fun stuff to look at.

Lunch items include a grilled chicken sandwich ($10.95), chili cheese dog ($8.95), burger ($8.95), and chicken Caesar salad or Cobb salad ($12.95). The kid's menu, $5 - $6, includes grilled cheese sandwich, hot dog, hamburger and chicken fingers - add fries and a soda for an additional $3. Now for the good stuff - dessert. Ask the soda jerk (who is actually quite nice) to fix you an old-fashioned phosphate ($3.50); an ice cream soda or float ($6.95); a hot fudge brownie topped with ice cream and whipped cream ($7.95); or a specialty drink. There is a small eating area inside, as well as a few tables and chairs outside.

Hours: The soda fountain counter, for desserts and beverages, is open Mon. - Thurs., 9am - 9pm; Fri. - Sat., 9am - 10pm; Sun., 10am - 8pm. The kitchen, for meals, is open daily, Mon. - Thurs., 10am - 6pm; Fri., 10am - 7pm; Sat., 9am - 7pm; Sun., 10am - 6pm. Closed Easter, Thanksgiving, and Christmas.

Price: Menu prices are mentioned above.

Ages: All

FARMERS MARKET

(323) 933-9211 / www.farmersmarketla.com

!/$$

6333 W. 3rd Street, Los Angeles

This unique outdoor market, originally founded in 1934 and almost unchanging in its "small-town" ambiance, is an eclectic mixture of more than sixty fresh food and produce vendors, and over twenty kitchens that make and sell all sorts of homemade domestic and international favorites. The market can be crowded, but it is a fun place to shop or enjoy lunch. Patrons can order their favorite ethnic food and eat at an outdoor table. Kids love stopping by Littlejohn's English Toffee House stall to watch (and sample) mouth-watering candy being made. At Magee's House of Nuts, they can see peanuts steadily pouring into a large machine behind glass, being churned around to make very fresh-tasting peanut butter. Across the way from the main marketplace, more than sixty-five retail stores offer unique clothing items and specialty gifts. I will say a standout is Dylan's Candy Bar, (323) 930-1600 / www.dylanscandybar.com, with its huge array and kinds of candy in a store with candy wallpaper and cool lollipop lights. It also features homemade ice cream, and they do parties.

Check the Farmers Market website for special events and celebrations held at the market. See the entry for THE GROVE - KIDS' THURSDAYS (pg. 95) for details about the uptown mall just across the road, plus the LOS ANGELES MUSEUM OF THE HOLOCAUST (pg. 132) and PAN PACIFIC PARK / RENEE'S PLACE (pg. 77) which are just around the corner.

Hours: Open Mon. - Fri., 9am - 9pm; Sat., 9am - 8pm; Sun., 10am - 7pm. Closed major holidays.
Price: Free, but bring spending money. Parking is free for the first ninety minutes with validation; $1 for each additional 15 minutes. Parking is $2 for each 15 minutes without validation.
Ages: 2½ years and up.

FARMER'S MARKETS (Los Angeles County)

www.goodveg.org; www.ocagcomm.com/services/markets; www.ocfoodies.com; lbfresh.org; orangehomegrown.org

Many cities host a weekly farmer's market. These markets usually consist of open-air (outside) booths set up for customers to purchase fresh produce, bakery goods, meats, and more - taste the difference! Freshly cut flowers are often available, too, as is entertainment of some sort, whether it's rides or activities. Indulge yourself and let your kids pick out "new" foods to try. The food and ambiance of a market is much more enticing than a grocery store. Search the web to see if there is a farmer's market near you. Here are just a few of the cities that I know of that host a market: Bellflower, Beverly Hills, Burbank, Calabasas, Cerritos, Coronado, Costa Mesa, Culver City, Encino, Gardena, Long Beach, Los Angeles, Malibu, Mission Valley, Monrovia, Montrose, Northridge, Ocean Beach, Oceanside (with llama rides!), Ojai, Oxnard, Pacific Beach, Pasadena, Pomona, Redondo Beach, Riverside, Santa Barbara, Santa Maria, Santa Monica, Studio City, Temecula, Torrance, Tustin, Ventura, Vista, and Westwood.

Hours: Vary
Price: Free
Ages: 5 years and up.

FOUR SEASONS TEA ROOM

(626) 355-0045 / www.thefourseasonstearoom.com

$$$$

75 North Baldwin Avenue, Sierra Madre

You are invited to take tea in one of two very sweetly decorated tea rooms, or on the outside patio. The rooms have just the right touch with a few old-fashioned pictures, and some greenery and lace outlining the windows. Antique furniture, beautiful china settings, soft music, and friendly service bespeak of a more genteel time. The covered outdoor patio has a trellis with vines and a gently bubbling fountain.

Afternoon Teas, $22, consist of scones that come fresh from the oven accompanied by cream and raspberry jam; five finger sandwiches, such as egg salad, cucumber with dill butter, and chicken salad with cranberries; tea breads; a selection of dessert bites; and tea. Add a good-sized salad to the previous and now it's a Royal Tea, $28.50. Sandwich Tea, $17.50, includes five sandwiches and tea. Salad Tea, $17.50, comes with a house salad and tea. Cream Tea, $17.50, is served with a scone and cream and jam, and a selection of petite desserts. The menu items change seasonally. (Hence the name of the tea room.) Note that Four Seasons offers only a few types of tea. Although the presentation is grown-up, children will rise to the occasion and enjoy it as well. Check the website for seasonal enter*tea*ment like Faerie Tale Teas, Murder Mysteries, and more.

Hours: Open Tues. - Fri., 11am - 4pm; Sat. seatings are at 11am and 2:30pm. Reservations are recommended, especially for Fri. and Sat. Closed Sun., Mon., and holidays.
Price: Menu prices are listed above. Tues. - Fri. there is a $17.50 minimum per person; $22. on Sat.
Ages: 6 years and up.

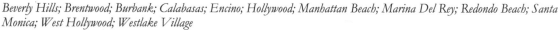

FRESH BROTHERS (Los Angeles County)

www.freshbrothers.com

$$$

Beverly Hills; Brentwood; Burbank; Calabasas; Encino; Hollywood; Manhattan Beach; Marina Del Rey; Redondo Beach; Santa Monica; West Hollywood; Westlake Village

Ciao means "hello" or "goodbye" in Italian. It's pronounced chow, which means "food". So, ciao - say hello to some good, Italian food at Fresh Brothers. This pizza place offers a variety of build your own pizza options with various toppings and crusts, including skinny (half everything and on thin crust), deep dish and gluten free, (average $19), plus personal pizzas ($7.49), as well as meatball sliders ($8.99), buffalo wings ($11.99), vegan tenders ($10.99) and create-your-own salad (starting at $8.99).

The reason I'm including this entry in the book, though, is that they offer kid's parties where kids can make their own pizzas. First, the kids get a personal pizza box that they decorate with stickers and markers. Then, they get to play with dough and make their own 7" pizza - with whatever toppings they want. The pizzas get baked, presented to each child in their box, and eaten! Drinks are included in the party and so is a Fresh Brothers t-shirt for each participant. Now, that's amore!

Hours: Call to schedule a party. Restaurants are open Sun. - Thurs., 11am - 9pm; Fri. - Sat., 11am - 10pm.

Price: The basic party package for twelve kids is $275. There are several add-ons available.

Ages: 4 years and up.

FRISCO'S CARHOP DINER

(626) 913-FOOD (3663) / www.friscos.com

$$$

18065 Gale Avenue, City of Industry

Pop quiz: What are skatetresses? Answer: Waitresses on skates! Frisco's has them, and more throwbacks to the 50's. The restaurant's prominent colors are hot pink and cool turquoise, along with white-and-black-checkered flooring. The walls and ceilings are painted blue with clouds that feature artists from the 50's (e.g., Jimmy Dean, Elvis, Marilyn Monroe, and others) with wings, as in heavenly angels. There are also some neon thunderbolts and a few 3-D images popping out. Other decor includes parking meters, traffic signals, dice, drive-in movie speakers, a juke box, and an old gas pump. Many of the booths have the front or back end of a car incorporated in them. The restaurants offer cruise nights, special events, and even live entertainment.

The food is a combination of American and Greek, served in a fifties-themed restaurant - and somehow it works! Breakfast selections include eggs and bacon, $7.99; steak and eggs, $12.49; breakfast burrito, $8.99; and waffles, $6.99. Kids 10 years and under can choose from two pancakes or French toast, eggs, and bacon or sausage for $5.75. Lunch options include a variety of burgers starting at $9.49; Greek salad, $10.99; lots of sandwich choices, such as turkey avocado melt on sourdough, $11.49; chicken souvlaki, $10.99; gyro, $11.49; charbroiled chicken tacos, $9.49; and more. Kid's meals are $6.49 for a choice of burger, hot dog or corn dog, chicken strips, pizza, or grilled cheese, plus fries and a soft drink. Desserts include hot fudge sundaes or shakes, $5.99 - $6.99; and chocolate brownie a la mode, $6.99. Keep on cruisin'!

Hours: Mon. - Thurs., 10am - 9pm. Fri. - Sat., 9am - 10pm; Sun., 9am - 9pm.

Price: Menu prices are listed above.

Ages: All

GRAND CENTRAL MARKET

(213) 624-2378 / www.grandcentralmarket.com

$$$

317 S. Broadway Street, Los Angeles

This is a fun, aromatic, cultural experience for kids who are used to shopping at a traditional grocery store. There are more than forty stalls inside this covered structure that spans a city block. Everything from exotic fruits and vegetables to octopus, chicken feet, honeycomb tripe, chiles, fresh tortillas (made on-site), birch bark, shrimp powder, and lambs' heads are sold here. There are also meat stalls, restaurants, and bakeries. Stop here to shop and/or eat on your way to visit other fun and educational places listed in this book! See DOWNTOWN LOS ANGELES / GRAND PARK (pg. 167) for information on Grand Park and all the other places to go within this fairly immediate area.

Hours: Open daily, 8am - 10pm. Closed New Year's Day, Thanksgiving, and Christmas.

Price: Parking is $3 for the first 90 minutes; $2 for every 15 min. after that.

Ages: 3 years and up.

GYU-KAKU (Los Angeles County)

Beverly Hills - (310) 659-5760; Burbank - (818) 846-0779; Canoga Park - (818) 888-4030; Cerritos - (562) 809-3800; Los Angeles - (310) 234-8641; Pasadena - (626) 405-4842; Sherman Oaks - (818) 501-5400; Torrance - (310) 325-1437; Valencia - (661) 254-2355 / www.gyu-kaku.com

Beverly Hills - 163 N. La Cienega Blvd.; Burbank - 116 S. San Fernando Blvd.; Canoga Park - 6600 Topanga Canyon Blvd., suite 1010B (inside Westfield Topanga Center); Cerritos - 11324 South St.; Los Angeles - 10925 W. Pico Blvd.; Pasadena - 70 W. Green St.; Sherman Oaks - 14457 Ventura Blvd.; Torrance - 24631 Crenshaw Blvd.; Valencia - 27025 McBean Parkway

$$$$

Be your own chef at this restaurant that integrates Korean barbeque and Japanese-style grilling. Each table has its own grill in the center that uses hot coals which are replaced for you when necessary during your dinner. Place portions of specially marinated beef, chicken, pork, and seafood items, as well as vegetables, to barbecue them just the way you like 'em. If cooking isn't one of your gifts, or you're not sure of how to do the pieces you selected, ask your server for tips and instructions.

The wide selection of individual menu choices (from the Cerritos menu) include skirt steak, $9.75; short ribs, $10.50; filet mignon, $8.25; spicy pork, $5; duck breast, $8.50; four pieces of butterfly shrimp with garlic, $7.25; salmon, $6.25; scallops, $7.50, and much more. Grill vegetables directly, or in tin foil, such as assorted veggies, $7; corn, $3.75; and broccoli, $4. Rice (and bibimbap), noodles (fried or ramen), soups and salads are also available. The food is tasty, especially with marinades and dipping sauces, and there is a communal feel to sharing a meal like this, kind of like sitting around a campfire. Kids, 12 and under, select a meat to grill and also receive a small salad, rice, dumplings, juice and s'more for $7. Try big kid desserts such as chocolate lava cake, $6.50; s'mores, $3; and mango, strawberry, vanilla, coffee or green tea ice cream sandwiches, $4.50. Note that menu choices do vary from location to location.

Hours: Most of the restaurants are open Mon. - Thurs., 11:30am - 10:30pm; Fri. - Sat., 11:30am - 11:30pm; Sun., 11:30am - 9:30pm.

Price: Menu prices are listed above. There are good discounts during their happy hours. Most of the restaurants are open Mon. - Thurs., 11:30am - 10:30pm; Fri. - Sat., 11:30am - 11:30pm; Sun., 11:30am - 9:30pm.

Ages: 5 years and up.

HARD ROCK CAFE

Hollywood - (323) 464-7625; Universal City - (818) 853-0600 / www.hardrock.com

Hollywood - 6801 Hollywood Blvd. suite 105 at Hollywood & Highland Center; Universal City - 100 Universal City Plaza at Universal CityWalk

$$$$

This is an "in" place to eat and hang out if you are a rock 'n roll fan, or even if you're not. Each Cafe has its own unique music-related memorabilia displayed in the open and in glass cases covering the walls, but the essence of all the cafes is the same - to pay tribute to music industry legends and the hot artists of today, and to promote the environmental motto, "Save the Planet." Hard Rock Cafe is part restaurant and part museum, so before or after your meal take a walk around to see your favorite musician's guitar, record album, or stage costume on exhibit. And, oh yes, rock music is played constantly. Souvenir t-shirts and glasses bearing the Cafe's logo and location (as there are restaurants throughout the world) have become collectible items among Hard Rock Cafe enthusiasts.

The Cafe at UNIVERSAL CITYWALK (pg. 176), for instance, features a gigantic (seventy-eight foot) electric guitar out front. Inside are numerous guitars (one is covered with snake skin), a few saxophones (including a chandelier made of thirty-two of them), a cool-looking '57 Cadillac convertible spinning on a pedestal, a gleaming Harley Davidson motorcycle, gold records, autographed items, and an outfit worn by Elton John. This location also has outside, patio seating.

Menu items include Caesar salad (about $12.50), burgers (average $17), grilled chicken ($14.95), fajitas for two (about $22), New York strip steaks (about $30), and sandwiches (average $13). Personal dessert favorites include Oreo® cheesecake (about $6) and chocolate molten cake (about $8). Kids' meals (10 and under) are $8.50. Choices include burger, hotdog, pasta, fish sticks, chicken tenders (shaped like guitars), or chicken salad. Most of their meals also come with fries and a beverage in a souvenir cup.

Hours: Hollywood is open Sun. - Thurs., 11am - 11pm; Fri. - Sat., 11am - midnight. Universal is open Sun. - Thurs., 11am - 9pm; Fri. - Sat., 11am - 11pm. Note that parking at Universal is $25 until 6pm; $10 after 6pm, but it's $15 for up to 3.5 hours with restaurant validation.

Price: Menu prices are listed above. Certain discounts are available through AAA.

Ages: 5 years and up.

JOE'S CRAB SHACK (Los Angeles County)

(310) 406-1999 / www.joescrabshack.com $$$$
230 Portofino Way, Redondo Beach

    If you're in a *crab*by mood, this is the restaurant for you! Most of the shacks, as there are multiple locations, really do resemble tacky-looking shacks - it's part of the charm. The servers must have fun because they sometimes dance on the tables and break out into song.

    Outside the Newport Beach restaurant, for instance, is a collage of large, marine-related items such as a life-size carved wooden captain, a whale's tail, a surfboard, fishing nets, and a wooden alligator. Inside, a lot of stuff fills the walls and ceiling. From the corrugated tin roof hangs plastic seagulls, netting, crab and lobster decorations, animals made out of shells, surfer clothing, and small boats - you get the picture. The wall is completely covered with photographs of everyday people, some holding fish, some not. At almost any of the wooden tables, the waterfront view of the harbor is terrific.

    Most of the meals are large enough to be shared; even the kid's meals are more than adequate. Crab is the featured specialty, but other foods are available. My oldest son fell in love with the crab cake sandwiches ($12.29). Other entrees include top sirloin ($16.49); hamburger ($10.59); crab nachos - my favorite ($10.99); fish and chips ($13.49); shrimp platter - fried, coconut, and crispy with delicious sides ($17.29); Dungeness crab ($33.99); twin lobster tails ($20.49); fried chicken ($15.29); crab cake chipotle Caesar salad ($11.99); and an appetizer of fried calamari with marinara ($8.69). One of the lunch specials is fish and chips ($8.49); another is bottomless soup and salad ($8.29). Kids' meals come with fries and are about $6 for a choice of chicken fingers, corn dog, mini burgers, popcorn shrimp, pizza, or mac and cheese. They can even get snow crab for $10. Drinks are extra. Save room for desserts - Crabby Apple Crumble ($8.89) or campfire s'mores ($8.29).

  Hours: Open daily, 11am - midnight.
    Price: Menu prices are listed above.
    Ages: All

JOHNNY REBS' SOUTHERN ROADHOUSE (Los Angeles County)

Bellflower - (562) 866-6455; Long Beach - (562) 423-7327 / www.johnnyrebs.com $$$$
Bellflower - 16639 Bellflower Blvd.; Long Beach - 4663 Long Beach Blvd.

    This roadhouse restaurant serves up southern hospitality, as well as good ol' southern cookin'. Walk past the bales of hay and cow bells into the main room with its wood-beam ceilings, wooden tables and benches, and rustic ambiance. Large U.S. (and a few other) flags hang from the ceiling. The walls and counter tops are decorated with straw hats, old wash basins, musical instruments, license plates, old-fashioned kitchen gadgets and tools, and pictures of farms framed by shutters. Bluegrass music plays in the background.

    The immediate attraction for kids (and adults) is the bowl of peanuts on each table because the peanut shells are to be thrown on the floor! (My floor at home looks like this too, sometimes. The only difference is that kids are allowed to do it here.) I have to mention that even the bathrooms fit into the Ma and Pa Kettle theme because they look like (nice) outhouses, and barnyard noises are piped in.

    Our waiter, who wore a "long johns" shirt, served our beverages in canning jars. Going along with the southern attitude toward food - anything tastes better when fried - dinner choices include fried green tomatoes ($7), okra ($9.50), fried pickles ($8), Jalapeño hushpuppies (i.e. fried cornbread)($7.50), catfish ($20), jambalaya ($20), Creole shrimp over cheddar grits ($21), beef ribs ($31.50) and chicken fried steak ($19.25). Also, y'all may select ribs, hamburger, smoked tri-tip, pulled pork, blackened T-bone steak, stuffed Cajun sausage sandwich, chicken salad, and more. Meals come with all the fixin's. The homemade desserts are delicious, especially the peach cobbler, key lime pie, and fried apple pie. The lunch menu is the same as the previous dinner menu, only the portions are smaller, so prices are lower. Kid's menus are $6.50 for breakfast and $7.50 for lunch/dinner. An extensive breakfast menu include grits, omelettes (average $13), flapjacks ($10), catfish and eggs ($15.95), beignets ($7.25), chicken and waffles ($15.50), and a side order of biscuits and gravy and sausage. Personal advice - don't even think about dieting, at least for the meal you eat here. Beverages are extra and include peach or cherry lemonade, mint julep, buttermilk, sodas, etc. "Put some south in your mouth" and grab some grub at Johnny Rebs'!

  Hours: Open Sun. - Thurs., 7am - 9pm; Fri. - Sat., 7am - 10pm.
    Price: Menu prices are listed above.
    Ages: 2 years and up.

LAKESIDE DINING at THE LANDING

(818) 865-0095 - Zin Bistro Americana; (818) 889-8300 - Boccaccio's / zinwestlake.com; boccacciosrestaurant.com

32123 / 32131 Lindero Canyon, Westlake Village

$$$$

The above entry name is not a formal title - I'm simply using it to explain these dining experiences. There are several upscale restaurants along the scenic lake in Westlake Village. Each one offers a small, outside dining section overlooking a patch of grass and a pretty view of the lake, with its bordering homes and private boats. The ducks and geese seem more than a little eager for a hand out. (Signs ask that you don't feed them.) A sidewalk hugs the lake around a few of its curves, so you can go for a short stroll.

The restaurant at the south end of the shopping center is Boccaccio's, which has lunch offerings of lobster bisque ($7.50); Cobb salad ($17.95); linguini and clams ($20.95); chicken parmigiana ($18.95); and more. The Landing Grill and Sushi Bar is a few shops in, as is one of my favorites, Zin Bistro Americana. Lunch prices at Zin include bbq chicken wrap ($12); lobster Cobb ($19); build-your-own omelet ($15); fish and chips ($15); filet mignon ($36); and more. Bon appetit!

Hours: The restaurants are usually open from 11am - 9pm, or 10pm.
Price: See menu prices above.
Ages: 4 years and up.

MONROVIA STREET FAIR & MARKET

(626) 932-5550 / www.cityofmonrovia.org

708, 700 S Myrtle Ave, Monrovia

!/$$

Enjoy Friday night date night in Old Town Monrovia amid street vendors selling crafts, art, flowers, fresh fruit, decor, clothing, and other unique items. Food trucks and vendors, a petting zoo, face painting, bounce houses, and live music complete the ambiance and make for a fun family outing.

Hours: Every Fri., 5pm - 10pm, with an emphasis on kid-friendly activities on the first Fri. of every month.
Price: Free, but bring spending money.
Ages: 3 years and up.

THE OLD SPAGHETTI FACTORY (Los Angeles County)

(626) 358-2115 / www.osf.com

1431 Buena Vista, Duarte

$$$

These elegant "factories" have posh, velvet seats in a variety of colors. The overhead fabric lamps are from a more genteel era. The old world antiques and the dark, rich furniture exudes a quiet, classy atmosphere. Yet, the restaurants are also very kid friendly. Old Spaghetti factories usually have a train or trolley car to eat in - this is a highlight. The franchised restaurants differ only in regional decor. For instance, the one in Riverside, being in a citrus city, has orange crate labels on the walls.

The food selection, which include gluten-free options, is focused on spaghetti (what a surprise!), with a large selection of sauces to choose from. Lasagna, tortellini, and ravioli are served here, as well. Lunches average $9 and three-course dinners (soup or salad, bread and dessert) range in price from $16.75 (for jumbo crab ravioli) to lasagna ($15.25) to chicken marsala ($14.95). Kids' meals are $6.25 for a choice of mac and cheese, grilled cheese sandwich, and six 'sghetti and ravioli meals with different sauces. Their meal comes with a salad, beverage, and dessert.

Hours: Most locations open Sun. - Thurs., 11:30am - 9:30pm; Fri. - Sat., 11:30am - 10pm. Hours may vary according to location - call first.
Price: Menu prices are listed above.
Ages: 4 years and up.

OLIVIA'S DOLL HOUSE TEA ROOM (Los Angeles County)

(310) 257-1199 / olivias4tea.com

2051 Palos Verdes Dr. North, Lomita

$$$$$

Walk through the door into princess fantasyland. Each room in this small house is tastefully decorated with classy flowery carpets, feminine wallpaper, lacy curtains, tea party furniture, frills, roses hanging from the ceiling, animated stuffed animals and dolls, and shelves and curios filled with collectable dolls and tea paraphernalia. Not a kitschy, cheap, glittery facade, Olivia's is the real deal - a little girl's (and big girl's!) dream come true for a private, dress-up tea party or any kind of celebration. (The website offers great visuals.)

The first part of the two-hour party is dress up, where young ladies get gussied up in Disney princess gowns and other fancy dresses - and there are soooo many to choose from - and accessorize with feather boas, hats, gloves, parasols, and all kinds of jewelry, plus "diamond" tiaras. Each guest gets her hair in a up-do with glitter, befitting her new princess look, plus her make-up and nails done at the salon room with a long mirror and comfy stools. (Forget about little girls - this sounds like a mom's dream come true!) Each partygoer participates in a fashion show and gets her picture taken. Then, story time with the in-character presiding princess. At the heart-shaped table lemonade is served along dessert. (You may bring in your own food.) Party favors are doled out, too. The birthday girl gets very special treatment - a princess made to feel like a queen. The cost for a birthday party is $385, that includes most of the above, for up to 9 kids. Mini tea parties that include all of the above, plus some extra surprises, are $450 for up to 6 children. Storytime is where your child can come dressed as their favorite princess or dress-up in one of the costumes here, and a costumed princess reads and sings her story. Pictures, autographs and a gift from the treasure box are included for $15 per child. Note that this is a great place for bridal and baby showers, too.

Hours: Open only for private parties and by reservation.
Price: Prices are listed above.
Ages: 4 years and up.

QUEEN MARY

See the entry for QUEEN MARY (pg. 147), under MUSEUMS, for details.

$$$$$

ROCKET FIZZ SODA POPS AND CANDY SHOP (Los Angeles County)

Burbank - (818) 846-SODA (7632); Lancaster - (661) 948-FIZZ (3499); Long Beach - (562) 433-8880; Valencia - (661) 253-FIZZ (3499); Westwood - (310) 208-4509 / www.rocketfizz.com
Burbank - 3524 Magnolia Blvd.; Lancaster - 43530 10th Street W. suite 105; Long Beach - 5282 E. 2nd St.; Valencia - 24300 Town Center Dr., suite 103; Westwood - 1067 Broxton Ave.

$

Looking for a uniquely flavored soda to perk up your taste buds? How about S'Mores, Cotton Candy, Mud Pie, Green Apple Jalapeno, Shirley Temple, Peanut Butter, Sweet Corn, Ranch Dressing, or Australian Style Hot Ginger Ale? There are literally hundreds more funky flavors well as a slew of traditional sodas to choose from. But that's not the only thing that brings customers in - it's also the collectible gifts, gag gifts, retro toys, tin signs and colorful posters from yesteryear, as well as the huge array of novelty, nostalgic and more current candies. Try salt water taffies, Gold Nugget gum, Toblerone, black licorice buttons, Charleston Chew, Necco wafers, bacon-flavored suckers, candy cigarettes, band aid bubble gum, and so many more. The walk down Memory Lane isn't very far, after all.

Hours: Hours vary by store but all are open daily, usually around 10am until 9pm - 11pm, depending on the night and location of the store.
Price: Technically, free
Ages: 3 years and up.

RUBY'S (Los Angeles County)

(800) HEY RUBY (439-7829) - for all locations. / www.rubys.com

$$$$

See the entry for RUBY'S (Orange County) (pg. 252) for details. LA County has Ruby's in the following cities: Downey, Long Beach, Los Angeles, Redondo Beach, Rolling Hills Estates, and Whittier.

SHOGUN (Los Angeles County)

La Verne - (909) 596-9393; Pasadena - (626) 351-8945 / www.restaurantshogun.com
La Verne - 2123 Foothill Blvd.; Pasadena - 470 N. Halstead St.

$$$$

This Japanese-style restaurant has built-in tabletop grills where chefs prepare the food with rapid slicing and dicing movements (and cool tricks) in front of your eyes. See BENIHANA OF TOKYO (Los Angeles County) (pg. 15), as it is a similar type of restaurant. The "entertainment" is great and the food is delicious. Kids get a real kick out of the presentation, and are more likely to try "new" foods now that they've seen the unique way it has been prepared. Chicken, seafood, and steak are some of the menu selections. Lunch ranges from $11.49 to $24.99; dinners from $21 to $45. Kids' meals average $10.99. (Kids are served the same meals as adults, just smaller portions.)

Hours: Open Mon. - Thurs., 11:30am - 10pm; Fri., 11:30am - 10:30pm; Sat., noon - 10:30pm; Sun., noon - 9:30pm.
Price: Menu prices listed above.
Ages: 4 years and up.

SPEEDZONE

See the entry for SPEEDZONE (pg. 41), under FAMILY PAY AND PLAY, for details.

$$$

—FAMILY PAY AND PLAY—

ADVENTURE PLEX

(310) 546-7708 / www.adventureplex.org
1701 Marine Avenue, Manhattan Beach

Let's get physical! The large, four-story, indoor play structure, known as the Adventure Room, is a big draw and just plain fun for you and your child; mainly your child. Crawl through tunnels, go down slides, climb up ladders, play in the ball pit, bounce on the air bounces, bop through the soft foam obstacle course, and just get good and tired. Socks are mandatory. Toddler Town is a cutely done, separate play room for ages 5 and under, only. The farm mural is adorable and kids can ride kid-size tractors, play in a ball pit, and rake and even harvest plastic oranges, apples, strawberries and tomatoes straight off the walls. They can shop for healthy food in an adjacent little market with carts, play food, and a check-out stand. Then, kids can complete the food cycle in the just-their-size kitchen complete with a dining table, refrigerator, microwave, cabinets and sink, plus play fireplace and ocean "view". An arts and crafts room; a classroom with internet access; a reading nook (no library card needed) with books and comfy bean bags; and an outdoor gardening area are here, too.

Adventure Plex also offers numerous classes for kids of all ages, including sports psychology, rock climbing, karate, pop star dance, coaching skills for teens, arts and crafts, homework tutoring, Mad Science programs, and more. Drop-ins are also welcome. Come with your child to the Sports Court, for instance, so he or she can pick up a game of basketball or volleyball. Two, twenty-eight-foot-tall rock walls, located outside, are other appealing options for sports play. Kids, who must be at least 5 years old, learn skills, confidence, and even strategy planning by literally climbing the walls. A staff belayer is provided and so is safety equipment. An adjacent ropes course is equally fun and challenging for kids at least 8 years old.

If you (and your kids) work up an appetite, you can order food - pizza (including gluten-free), salad, and wings - delivered to Adventure Plex from Fresh Brothers. Note that MARINE AVENUE PARK and SKATE PARK (pg. 73) is located just across the way.

Hours: Drop-in sessions for the Adventure Room, Toddler Town, and reading corner are for two-hour increments. It is all open Sun. - Thurs., 10am - 6pm; Fri. - Sat., 10am - 7pm. Rock climbing is available Mon. - Fri., 10am - dusk. The ropes course is available by reservation, only.

Price: Each two-hour session is $12 for one adult and one child. Add-on admission for the rock climbing wall is $8, or it's $10 by itself. The ropes course is an additional $10 with purchase of general admission, or $15 by itself. The Sports Court is $5 for one child and one adult for an hour. Note that one hour before closing all admission is half off. Check the website for class and membership prices.

Ages: 2 years and up, depending on the class or activity.

AGOURA HILLS / CALABASAS COMMUNITY CENTER ROCKWALL

(818) 880-2993 / www.ahccc.org
27040 Malibu Hills Road, Calabasas

Thirty-five-feet off the ground is pretty high up, and that's the top height of this rock climbing wall which has various other different heights and slants. Just keep putting one hand and foot a little higher than the last placement, gripping the simulated rock outcroppings to reach your goal. If your child, or you, has never rock climbed before, take a class together to learn how to wear a harness, tie in, and belay: $30 will teach you all the rock climbing basics that you need to know, and you must be able to pass a test before you can climb unsupervised. Come for a thirty-minute Try-A-Climb (with a belayer supplied), an after school program, and/or for a birthday party. Waivers are required for all climbers. Have a galactically good time here at a Cosmic Climb party where the rocks, the holds, and even the ropes glow neon colors under black lighting. Note that this is not a rock gym, but a few walls, in a separate area than the rest of the community center facility, with a very small amount of floor space. I like the price, though.

Hours: The Try-A-Climb is offered Tues. - Wed., 5:30pm - 7:30pm; Sat. and Sun., 11am - 1pm. Open climb is Mon. - Fri., 6am - 10pm; Sat., 7am - 7pm; Sun., 7am - 6pm. Closed most major holidays.

Price: Try-A-Climb is $10 for a half-hour. Open climb (for 15 year olds and up for tested climbers, or younger kids accompanied by a tested adult) is $7 for adults; $3 for ages 11 and under. Class fees vary. Climbing equipment is included in the admission price.

Ages: 5 years old and up.

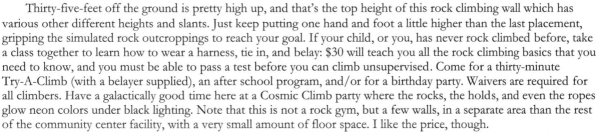

AMY'S PLAYGROUND

(626) 799-0304 / www.amysindoorplayground.com

1115 Mission Street, Pasadena

$$$

With its brick walls and with white fluffy clouds painted on the sky-blue ceiling, the atmosphere in this mid-sized, clean room is inviting. Amy's is a young child's haven that has four main play components - a structure with an enclosed, maze-like (think Habitrail) tube system that is great to climb up, crawl through (parents can, too, if you can), and slide back down; a large bounce house with a giant bounce slide; a playhouse with a kitchen; and a toddler section with foam shapes and blocks. There are a few other toys to play with and ride, also.

Bring your own food or purchase fruit cups, chips, or other snacks and a beverage at the register to enjoy at the indoor picnic tables. Remember to wear socks, or you can purchase them here for $2. A gift shop is also on the premises.

Hours: Open Mon. - Thurs., 10am - 6pm; Fri., 10am - 5pm. Open on weekends for private parties.

Price: $12 for ages 6 - 11; $10 for ages 2 - 5; $8 for children under 2. Adults are free.

Ages: 1 - 7 years

ARROYO MINIATURE GOLF

(323) 255-1506

1055 Lohman Lane, South Pasadena

$$$

This older-style, nine-hole miniature golf course, adjacent to a real golf course, is a "hole" lot of fun. It has classic buildings such as a (small) castle, red barn, windmill, church and more, and just the right amount of difficulty. It's a good little course for practicing your short stroke game, so for the inexpensive price, practice, and fun of it, why not bring the kids and come play a couple of rounds?! There is a cafe on site, too, with burgers, etc.

Hours: Open daily, 7am - 10pm.

Price: $6 per person.

Ages: 4 years and up.

AUTO CLUB RACEWAY AT POMONA / POMONA RACEWAY

(800) 884-NHRA (6472) or (909) 593-7010 / www.nhra.com

2780 Fairplex Drive at the Pomona Fairgrounds, Pomona

$$$$

Start your engines! Host to several National Hot Rod Associations, with events beginning in February and ending in November, the quick track offers exciting races and 40,000 grandstand seats to accommodate fans. Pit passes are included with the purchase price of tickets, depending on the race.

Hours: Call or check the website for a schedule.

Price: Tickets range from $15 and up for adults for general (not reserved) seating, depending on the day and event. General seating can be as low as $15 for ages 6 - 12, and free for ages children 5 and under, depending on all the above factors. Parking is about $12.

Ages: 5 years and up.

BILLY BEEZ (Los Angeles County)

(661) 460-5558 / billybeezus.com; www.westfield.com/valencia

24201 Valencia Boulevard in Valencia Town Center, Valencia

$$$

See BILLY BEEZ (Orange County) (pg. 256) for details. This location does not have a Honeycomb Village, but it does have the Mini Beez play area. Check out the Valencia Town Center web site above for more things to do at this mall.

The cafe here sells food / snacks such as a grilled cheese sandwich ($3.99); wraps ($5.99); personal pizza ($7.95); soft pretzel ($2.49); and ice cream bars ($2.49).

Hours: Open Mon. - Sat., 10am - 9pm; Sun., 10am - 8pm.

Price: $3.95 for the first adult; $6.95 for the second adult (but only on the weekends); seniors are free with a paid child; $15.95 for ages 5 - 17; $12.95 for ages 1 - 4; infants are free with a paid family member or $9.95 for one infant and one adult. The price is good for all-day access, with re-entry.

Ages: 1 - 14 years.

BOULDERDASH INDOOR ROCK CLIMBING (Los Angeles County)

(818) 700-1300 / www.boulderdashclimbing.com

19801 Nordhoff Place, Unit 110, Chatsworth

$$$$

See BOULDERDASH INDOOR ROCK CLIMBING (Ventura County) (pg. 658) for details. This location is larger than the one in Thousand Oaks.

Hours: Open Mon. - Fri., 11am - 10pm; Sat., 10am - 8pm; Sun., 10am - 6pm.
Price: Daily climb fees are $17 for adults; $15 for ages 17 and under. Rental gear - harness, shoes, and chalk - is $6, inclusive. Off the Deck is $25 per child. Climb Time is $20 per person.
Ages: 6 years and up.

CHUCK E. CHEESE'S (Los Angeles County)

See the entry for CHUCK E. CHEESE'S (Los Angeles County) (pg. 18), under EDIBLE ADVENTURES, for details.

DAVE & BUSTER'S (Los Angeles County)

Arcadia - (626) 802-6115; Hollywood - (323) 603-2400; Los Angeles - (310) 846-9950; Torrance - (888) 300-1515 / www.daveandbusters.com $$$

Arcadia - 400 S. Baldwin Ave. at Westfield Santa Anita Mall; Hollywood - 6801 Hollywood Blvd. at Hollywood & Highland; Los Angeles - 6081 Center Dr. at the Promenade at Howard Hughes; Torrance - 21880 Hawthorne Blvd. at Del Amo Fashion Mall

See DAVE & BUSTER'S (Orange County) (pg. 259) for details. See the malls that these are located in for other attractions.

Hours: Open Sun. - Wed., 11am - midnight; Thurs. - Sat., 11am - 1am.
Ages: 7 years and up.

GET AIR TRAMPOLINE PARK (Los Angles County)

(626) 225-8665 / www.getairpomona.com $$$

2735 South Towne Avenue, Pomona

See GET AIR TRAMPOLINE PARK (Riverside County) (pg. 347) for details.

Hours: Open Mon., 10am - 10pm; Tues., 10am - noon for Toddler Time, noon - 10pm all ages; Wed., 10am - 10pm; Thurs., 10am - noon for Toddler Time, noon - 10pm all ages; Fri. - Sat., 10am - 9pm, and 9pm - midnight for Club Air; Sun., 10am - 8pm.
Price: $15 per hour for 46" and taller; $10 for 45" and under. Toddler Time is $10 per child, one adult is admitted for free. Club Air is $15 for 2 hours or $20 for all 3. Always check the website for special offers.
Ages: 2 years and up.

GIGGLES N' HUGS

Canoga Park - (818) 610 - HUGS (4847); Glendale - (818) 956 - HUGS (4847) / www.gigglesnhugs.com $$$

Canoga Park - 6600 Topanga Canyon Blvd., suite 2008 in the Westfield Topanga Plaza; Glendale - 3222 Glendale Galleria Way in the Glendale Galleria

You can play. You can eat. Or, you can play and eat (though not play with your food) all at the same place at Giggles N' Hugs. The play half of the really spacious room has several, good-sized, castle-like turrets to climb up into. The turrets are all connected to each other by crawl bridges, enclosed with cargo nets, on the second "story" of the castle. There is also a long, high-off-the-ground crawl bridge that connects to the Pirate boat. Play in the boat's large ball pit (parents, too!), and go down some short slides. The few other free-standing structures are also fun - one is platform that is lollipop themed and another has a longer, twisty slide. A small, enclosed toddler area has a tunnel and some soft blocks. There are also Little Tyke cars, big balls to play with, and other toys. Socks are required at all times. Music is playing in the background. Kids are loud and loving it all.

A stand-out feature are the activities that all Giggles N' Hugs encourages by having various princesses and other characters and staff lead the children in singing, crafts, dancing, storytelling, magic shows, concerts, puppet shows, face painting, parachute games, or something else that kids like to join in on. This happens periodically on the stage or simply throughout the restaurant.

The restaurant half, divided by a clear, short fence, is truly a restaurant with tables and chairs along wonderful, fairytalish murals, and a few TV's. Menu choices include mostly high-end, organic foods, like a breakfast burrito ($11.95); French toast ($9.95); two eggs, plus potatoes, bacon and toast ($9.95); freshly made BBQ chicken pizza ($13.95); veggie wrap ($11.95); Ahi poke ($16.95); wild Alaskan salmon ($17.95); citrus kale salad ($12.95); hummus platter ($7.95); hamburger (gluten free buns available) ($11.95); shrimp tacos ($14.95); and more. Kid's menu selections include chicken littles ($8.95); grilled cheese ($7.95); cheeseburger ($8.95); fruit plate ($8.95); make your own pizza, at the table, and it gets baked for you to eat ($10.95); and more. Smoothies, ice blended drinks and espresso drinks are also available. This is not just a kid-friendly restaurant; this is a restaurant for kids and adults to <u>really</u> enjoy together.

At the Topanga Plaza location, just below Giggles N' Hugs, is a two-story(!) carousel and a play place for kids. Look up both the associated malls for what else they have to offer.

Hours: Open Mon. - Thurs., 10:30am - 8pm; Fri., 10:30am - 9pm; Sat., 10am - 9pm; Sun., 10am - 7pm. Call first on weekends at all locations as they shut down for private parties.

Price: Entrance to Giggles N' Hugs is $13 for kids who are walking; $10 for siblings; $7 for crawlers; babies and adults are free. Restaurant prices are listed above.

Ages: 9 months - 8 years

GLOWZONE LA

(818) 918-3964 / wdh.glowzoneca.com
$$$$

6051 De Soto Avenue, Woodland Hills

You have a glow about you! Or, maybe it's just the neon colors under the black lights on of all the attractions. LA Underground Laser Tag is 2,400 square feet of a cleaned up downtown LA vibe with painted trash containers, alleyways, and more to run and spy behind, then zap your opponent. Skyscraper Ropes Course is a glow-in-the-dark obstacle course that's almost ten feet off the ground so it's safe, as participants are harnessed in, but still a thrill. Walk on tightropes up here as well as planks, bridges, and more. Hot pink, orange and green "rocks" are your hand and foot holds to scale the ten individual walls that are twenty feet high. You can race against friends on the time climbing walls, too. Just like the real freeway, the 405 Bumper Cars move riders forward, backward or spinning in circles as they bump into each other. Play 18 holes of mini golf indoors with a city scape theme around obstacles of scale tall city buildings, a small version of the Golden Gate bridge, and other fun elements. Don't trip the laser maze as you crawl under, step over and move around the beams to get to the other side. Atomic Rush is a hitting-the-colorful-large-buttons-on-the-wall-race game that you play against up to three other people. These latter two games aren't long at all, but they are fun. Bazooka Ball - shooting foam balls at each other in a free for all is another fun and active thing to do here. And yes, it is dark and noisy in the Zone. Note that there are nights here just for adults, so kids aren't the only ones who have all the fun. There is also an arcade area here.

Little ones, ages 7 and under, have their own city to play in - Soft City, where socks are required for all participants. One room has little go cars that kids can pedal around on the floor that is designed to look like a road, with tires in the middle and walks with a cartoon-like city scene. Another room has a good-sized, multi-story play structure with ball pit, slides, a climbing tower, hard foam obstacles and shapes, and obstacle courses. On the ground are a few kiddie rides and a crawl tunnel. There is also a separate area for ages 3 and under to play on and with hard foam shapes and blocks on a padded floor.

Hours: GlowZone is open Mon. - Thurs., 2pm - 10pm; Fri. - Sat., 11am - midnight; Sun., 11am - 10pm. Soft City is generally open daily, 11am - 9pm, although it is closed sometimes for private parties, so call first.

Price: Laser tag is $8 a game. Skyscraper and the rockwall are $7 each. $6 for bumper cars. Laser maze is $4. Atomic Rush is $3. Bazooka Ball is $8. You can also purchase package deals. Soft City is $10, Mon. - Thurs. for all day play; $10, Fri. - Sun. for two hours of play.

Ages: 18 months - 10 years old.

GO KART WORLD

(310) 834-3700 or (310) 834-3800 / www.gokartworld.com
$$$

21830 Recreation Road, Carson

Get supercharged here by racing around on the six race tracks. The Kiddie Track has battery-operated cars that go about 3 mph on an L-shaped track. This ride is for children at least 3 years old and under 75 pounds. Mini Indy is for drivers at least 45" tall and goes about 9 mph on a B-shaped track. A double-seater car can hold a driver who is at least 16 years old with a passenger who is at least 32" tall. The Bumper Car track is for drivers at least 43" tall. These cars can be individually manipulated to go forwards, backwards, and even spin all the way around. For a slick ride, drivers at least 56" tall can race on the Slick Track. We vote the Turbo Track the most-like-a-real-race-track ride. Race over and under passes and around banked, hairpin turns. Drivers must be at least 58" tall. The one-third-mile Super Trak is really super. It is two stories tall, strobe lit, and twenty-five feet wide with track space for up to twenty riders, with bank turns. All rides last four minutes. An electronic scoreboard keeps track of your time. If you have a group of ten or more, you may rent the track for a private party. Minors must have release waivers for Turbo Track or Super Track. A large (3,000 square feet) video and arcade game area, with redemption-playing games, is inside. Racers (and observers) can refuel at the Pit Stop Cafe, which offers pizza, chips, sodas, and more.

Hours: Open Sun. - Thurs., 10am - 10pm; Fri. - Sat., 10am - midnight.
Price: Each of the rides listed cost $6 per ride, or purchase 5 rides for $25. You may also purchase a wristband for
$30 which allows sixty minutes of unlimited rides, with a minimum of 8 rides.
Ages: 3 years and up.

GOLF N' STUFF (Los Angeles County)

(562) 868-9956 / www.golfnstuff.com
10555 E. Firestone Boulevard, Norwalk

What course of action will you take? This big family fun center offers several different ways to have fun with four
themed **miniature golf** courses designed with whimsical buildings like castles, Big Ben, a lighthouse, a tree house, a
haunted mansion, a Western scene, and more, plus challenging obstacles - $11 for adults; $10 for seniors; one free
child 3 years and under with each paying adult. Other attractions include **Disc'O Thrill** (a huge flying disc ride that
goes forward and back up a short roller coaster ramp while spinning around) - $6.50 a ride; **kiddie train** - $3 per ride;
go-karts - $8 for drivers, $4 for passengers; and **bumper boats** - $8 for drivers, $4 for passengers. Height restrictions
apply for drivers and passengers. Look in the website for discount coupons and wristband specials, like two hours of
unlimited attractions (not the arcade games) for $30.

Yes, there are also lots of arcade games to be played here along with a prize redemption area. I actually enjoy
some of the interactive virtual reality games. This can keep you and the kids busy for hours - just bring quarters! A
snack bar is on the premises, too, offering nachos, pizza, and hot dogs.
Hours: The golf course and arcades are open September - mid-June, Mon - Thurs., 10am - 10pm (rides open 4pm -
9:30pm); Fri., 10am - midnight (rides open 4pm - 11:30pm); Sat., 10am - midnight (everything is open); Sun.,
10am - 10pm (everything). Golf and arcade are open in the summer and school holidays Mon. - Thurs., 10am
- 11pm (rides open noon - 10:30pm); Fri., 10am - midnight (rides open noon - 11:30pm); Sat., 10am -
midnight (everything); Sun., 10am - 10pm (everything). Golf and rides sometimes begin to shut down about
an hour before closing time.
Price: Attractions are individually priced above. Parking is free.
Ages: 4 years and up.

HANGAR 18 (Los Angeles County)

Hawthorne - (310) 973-3388; Long Beach - (562) 981-3200 / www.climbhangar18.com
Hawthorne - 4926 W. Rosecrans Ave.; Long Beach - 2599 E. Willow St.

See HANGAR 18 (San Bernardino County) (pg. 408) for details about these 12,000 square foot indoor rock
climbing gyms.
Hours: Both are open Mon. - Fri., 10am - 10pm; Sat. - Sun., 10am - 8pm.
Price: $18 for adults for a day pass; $13 for ages 13 and under. Shoe rentals are $3.
Ages: 5 years and up.

HOLLYWOOD SPORTS COMPLEX

(562) 867-9600 or (877) GIANT97 (442-6897); (562) 716-0487 - BMX / www.hollywoodsports.com;
www.bellflowerbmx.com
9030 Somerset Boulevard, Bellflower

The huge, twenty-eight acre paintball area, carved out in the midst of the city of Bellflower, has different fields
sporting a variety of scenarios and props from actual movie sets with stone walls, buses, beat up automobiles, cargo
nets, buildings, piles of tires, and so much more. One looks like something out of a *Terminator* movie (without even
entering the fields!) with its futuristic/techno look. Another is Forbidden City, with gigantic Egyptian statues, pillars,
and wall ruins. Mad Max and Apocalypse both have rusted vehicles and lots of themed scenery to engage with.
Another paintball arena features inflatable obstacles. Warriors, I mean players, run, hide, and generally try to ambush
and shoot the enemy with paintballs while rock music plays in the background. (Getting hit can hurt.) There is also a
speedball stadium, an airsoft field, and a separate area for beginners and kid's paintball games. Spectators can watch
some of the action from a second-story observation deck. A target range for practice is here as well and the fields have
lighting for nighttime play. A pro shop is on the premises for purchasing supplies. Note that paintballs for play here
can only be purchased here. Wear old pants, a long sleeve sweatshirt, high-top boots or old tennis shoes, and
protective clothing and mask.

Airsoft is a tactical game played with plastic bb's being shot from realistic-looking guns. A little softer, perhaps,
than paintball and not as messy, players usually wear much the same gear as paintballers, and the military. Paintball Soft
is where participants use a .50 caliber paintball so the impact isn't painful, it costs less, and is friendly to newcomers

and players as young as 7 years old. This is my kind of game!! Call or check the website for details, and to make reservations. Groups can also use the beach volleyball, the banquet room, and the fifty-foot rock climbing wall, which looks more like a mountain. It features several routes, ranging from easy (kind of) to difficult, including various angles of the rock face to climb.

The adjacent BMX track is well kept up and ready for action with all of its curves and hills. Riders must be active ABA members to race.

Hours: Open most of the year, Mon. and Thurs., 4:30pm - 9pm; Fri., 4:30pm - 10pm; Sat., 9am - 10pm; Sun., 9am - 8pm. Open Tues. and Wed. for private groups only. Open extended hours in summer and on holidays. Call for BMX hours.

Price: Paintball field admission is $37 with all day air, if you bring your own equipment; $59 for entrance and all the rentals needed, plus 200 paintballs. Paintball soft is $42 for admission and rentals, plus paintballs. Airsoft entry is $28 - not including any rental equipment. BMX is usually $12 to race; call for clinic prices.

Ages: Must be at least 10 years old to play paintball or airsoft; 7 for paintball soft.

IRWINDALE EVENTS CENTER

(626) 358-1100 / www.irwindalespeedway.com
500 Speedway Drive, Irwindale

If your family likes fast cars, speed on over to a NASCAR, Speed Truck, Winston West, or USAC Midget and Sprint Cars event held at the speedway. This banked, one-half-mile super speedway track packs in thrills-a-minute for the racing enthusiast.

Hours: The season runs April through November. Races are held on Saturdays.

Price: Admission fees for regular events are usually $15 for adults; $7 for ages 6 - 12; children 5 and under free. Special event nights are $20 - $35 for adults; $10 for ages 6 - 12; children 5 and under are free.

Ages: 5 years and up.

THE JUMP AROUND

(818) 993-JUMP (5867) / www.thejumparound.com
21515 Parthenia Street, Canoga Park

This place is made for kids (and adults) who love to jump around, which is every child I've ever met! Good, healthy physical activity is a great alternative to video games, and the weather isn't ever a factor. There are four, colorful, giant inflatables in this indoor playground that have slides, jumps, obstacle courses, a wall-climbing bounce, and a boxing ring where contenders wear oversized, blown-up gloves. There is also a two-story, padded castle to play in. Free foosball, air hockey, dual basketball, computer usage, satellite TV, and coffee (for adults) offer something fun for everyone. A toddler room has a little playhouse and toys geared for youngsters. All the action takes place in one big room. Socks must be worn at all times. There is a separate room for parties, and special nights with Cosmic Lighting using black lights, disco lights and strobe lights. Note that this facility allows "big" kids to have a party here, too - yea!

Hours: Open Mon. - Fri., 10am - 6pm, but call first to make sure a private party is not going on. Weekends are usually reserved for private parties.

Price: $7 for ages 3 - 13 for a two-hour session; $5 for 1 - 3 years; infants and adults are free.

Ages: 3 years and up.

JUMPING JACKS (Los Angeles County)

(909) 599-4199 / www.jumpingjacksparty.com
186 Village Court, San Dimas

See JUMPING JACKS (San Bernardino County) (pg. 408) for details. This facility is 7,000 square feet larger (more jumping fun!) and it offers a glow-in-the-dark room with planet murals, plus a basketball court.

Hours: Open play, family fun times are Tues., 10:30am - 1pm; Wed., 2pm - 5pm; Wed. - Thurs., 6pm - 9pm.

Price: $10 per child for ages 2 and up; children under 2 with a paid sibling, and adults, are free.

JUMP 'N JAMMIN (Los Angeles County)

Arcadia - (626) 821-9120; West Covina - (626) 337-2232 / www.jumpnjammin.com
Arcadia - 400 South Baldwin Ave. in Westfield Santa Anita Mall; West Covina - 112 Plaza Dr. at Plaza West Covina

See JUMP 'N JAMMIN (Orange County) (pg. 261) for details about this big and fun indoor play place. Also see WESTFIELD SANTA ANITA (pg. 96) and the Plaza West Covina website, www.shoppingplazawestcovina.com, for other fun things to do and places to shop and eat at these malls.

Hours: Open Mon. - Thurs., 10am - 8pm; Fri. - Sat., 10am - 9pm; Sun., 10am - 7pm. Closed Easter, Thanksgiving, and Christmas.

Price: $14.95 for ages 2 and up, which includes one free adult admission; $6.49 for children 23 months or younger, which includes one free adult admission. Additional adults are $3.95.

Ages: 2- 12 years

K1 SPEED (Los Angeles County)

(310) 532-2478 / www.k1speed.com

$$$$

19038 S. Vermont Avenue, Gardena

See K1 SPEED (San Diego County) (pg. 482) for details. This location has an etched concrete racing surface, which is different from the asphalt on the other locations.

KID CONCEPTS U.S.A.

(310) 465-0075 / www.kidconceptsusa.com

$$

22844 Hawthorne Boulevard, Torrance

What a concept! The main feature within this 9,000 square-foot room is a good-sized, terrific, multi-level play structure. It has several tubes (large enough for adults to crawl through), slides, ball pits, a bounce room, obstacle courses, and lots of nooks and crannies to discover. Note: The black slide is <u>really</u> fast. Kids can also sit in a child-sized rocket ship or helicopter and "fly" away to parts unknown. (Doesn't that sound appealing sometimes?!) Although this area is well-ventilated, my kids got sweaty having such a good time. Wearing socks is a must!

A separate, upstairs section has a small game center to be played on Xbox Kinect. The games get kids moving and are hands free as the game detects body heat and movement. It may be puzzling, but your kids can figure out how to make puzzles on the puzzle wall, with pieces that have velcro backing, stick to the wall. Dress up at the small costume section. Be an engineer using the train table. Play air hockey at $2 for fifteen minutes. A small, separate area has a good array of soft foam blocks for building. The arts and crafts room is for your creative genius to create. A room just for toddlers, painted in primary colors, has mats, little slides, tunnels and age-appropriate toys to play with and on. The party rooms are cutely-decorated. The toy store has a great selection of educational and fun toys. Check out the numerous classes and special events hosted here.

There is a sitting area, with tables and chairs, where you can just sit and relax, or use to eat at when ordering food from the cafe. The cafe serves up delicious selections including regular pizzas ($5.49 for an individual pan cheese); specialty pizzas, such as barbecue chicken ($15.99 for a twelve-inch); chicken veggie pasta ($9.49); cream of broccoli soup ($3.99); a variety of salads ($8.99); hamburgers or turkey burgers with fries (about $7); angel hair pasta (about $9); fruit bowl ($5.99); zucchini sticks ($4.99); and brownies (about $1.99). Kid's meals are about $5 for a choice of pizza, chicken strips, a burger, grilled cheese, or a hot dog, plus fries and a drink.

Hours: Open Mon. - Thurs., 10am - 8pm; Fri. - Sat., 10am - 9pm; Sun., 10am - 6pm. Closed New Year's Day, Easter, 4th of July, Thanksgiving, and Christmas.

Price: Two-hour sessions are $10 for ages 3 and up, with one free adult per child (additional adults are $4); $7 for ages 1 - 2; children under 1 are free with a paid child. Admission Mon. - Thurs. after 5pm is $7. Ask about prices for gym classes.

Ages: 9 months - 10 years.

KID-CO PLAY & LEARN CENTER

(661) 253-2277 / www.kid-co.com

$$$

26529 Carl Boyer Drive, Santa Clarita

Where can you visit a post office, grocery story, school, house, library, workshop and kidzerria (restaurant) all under one roof? At Kid-Co indoor play place, where everything is kid-sized for kid fun. Each small "building"/room has a different theme and is stocked with toys and items for make believe play. For instance, the kidzerria has a little wooden stove (with pots and pans), sink, frig, shelves, etc.; the grocery store has a cash register, shopping carts, and shelves with boxes, plastic fruit and veggies, and other containers of play food; the house has a kitchen and even a small living room; and the post office has small postal office boxes for mail and it has a map on the wall. The small, open play area has short tunnels, padded foam shapes, and little vehicles to ride on. You may bring outside food to eat at their picnic tables. Wearing socks is a must! Come for open play, or to take a class.

Hours: Open play is Mon., Wed., and Fri., 2pm - 5pm.

Price: $12 for the first child; $10 for siblings; parents and caregivers are free as are children under 1 with a paid sibling.

Ages: Geared for 6 month to 5 years old

LA BOULDERS

(323) 406-9119 / www.touchstoneclimbing.com/la-boulders
1375 E. 6th Street, suite 8, Los Angeles

$$$$

Bouldering is a form of indoor rock climbing without ropes or harnesses or incredibly tall walls, though they are 17 feet high. Move sideways, upside down, onto overhangs and archways, in a cave, and just up - bouldering is definitely a physically and mentally challenging sport as climbers solve 200 "problems", which is what the routes are called. Come to learn the ropes of bouldering (so to speak), or advance your skills by signing up for a class on technique at this nicely-laid out bouldering gym with contemporary-looking walls. The staff is helpful and wants to see people succeed in their climbing endeavors. See DOWNTOWN LOS ANGELES / GRAND PARK (pg. 167) for information on Grand Park and all the other places to go within this fairly immediate area.

Hours: Open Mon. - Thurs., 7am - 11pm; Fri., 7am - 10pm; Sat - Sun., 10am - 6pm.

Price: A day pass for adults is $20 on weekdays (except on holidays) before 3pm; $25 after 3pm; $20 for ages 12 and under (at any time). Shoes rentals are $4.

Ages: 5 years and up.

LASER STORM

(310) 373-8470 or (310) 378-2265 / www.gablehousebowl.com
22501 Hawthorne Boulevard, Torrance

$$$

Laser tag is taking kids (and adults) by storm! Power up your laser gun as two teams of up to thirty people compete against each other and "shoot" it out in a darkened room. Take cover behind neon-colored partitions, decorated with gak splats, as an opponent aims at you. Or, use the partitions as cover to stealthily sneak up on someone. The fifteen-minute games are action-packed, and all the running around can literally take your breath away! Note that there are two arenas here and that they are located right next to Gable House Bowl, which offers Rock and Glow bowling in addition to regular bowling. A full-service snack bar and arcade games are here, too.

Hours: Open during the school year, Mon. and Thurs., 3pm - 9pm; Fri. - 3pm - 11pm; Sat., 10am - 11pm; Sun., 10am - 8pm. Closed Tues. and Wed. Open in the summer and school holidays, Mon. - Thurs., 11am - 10pm; Fri., 11am - 11pm; Sat. - Sun., 10am - 9pm.

Price: There are a lot of specials offered throughout the week, so check the website or call. Games Mon. - Fri. are generally $6 per person; Sat. - Sun., $7.

Ages: 6 years and up.

LE FUNLAND (Los Angeles County)

(626) 810-1450 / www.puentehills-mall.com
1600 S. Azusa Ave. in Puente Hills Mall, City of Industry

$$$

This location is a little more spacious than some other Le Funlands, all of which are located inside malls. The indoor play place has padded floors and play equipment of mostly pastel blue, pink, green, and yellow, accompanied by mostly white walls. There are a few mini buildings designed to look like a library; a market and fire department for some pretend play; four, very short, side-by-side slides that end in a ball pit; a soft block building area; some easy obstacle courses; another ball pit; a carousel with what looks like upside lollipops to sit on that all hang from a palm tree while spinning gently around; peanut-looking seats on a tiny carousel; a train on a wall that contains several puzzles, gears, and toys; a horizontal spiral climbing apparatus; and some other fun things to play on and with, plus party rooms. All participants, kids and adults, must wear socks. Parents, the equipment is too small for you to play on. Note: There is no bathroom or changing area inside Funland, but there one fairly close by in the mall, and there is re-entry. As this location is in a mall, extend your time here by shopping and eating, and checking out ROUND1 BOWLING AND AMUSEMENT (Los Angeles County) (pg. 38), at this location.

Hours: Open Mon. - Fri., 10am - 9pm; Sat., 10am - 8pm; Sun., 11am - 6pm.

Price: $15 for a child; adults are free.

Ages: 52" and under, only

LEGO STORE - MINI MODEL BUILD (Los Angeles County)

Canoga Park - (818) 884-8597; Glendale - (818) 549-0733 /
www.lego.com/en-us/stores/events/mini-model-builds

!

Canoga Park - 6600 Topanga Canyon Blvd. at Westfield Topanga mall; Glendale - 2148 Galleria Way at Glendale Galleria

See LEGO STORE - MINI MODEL BUILD (San Diego County) (pg. 485) for info on this great, free LEGO

mini model build. Check out the malls listed above for other activities to do there.
Hours: The first Tues. and Wed. of each month, between 3pm - 7pm.
  Price: Free
  Ages: 6 - 14 years old, only.

MB2 RACEWAY (Los Angeles County)

(866) 986-RACE (7223) / www.mb2raceway.com
13943 Balboa Boulevard, Sylmar

  Go cart yourself to this indoor go kart facility where the quarter-mile long racetrack has eleven turns. Keep control of the car and zoom around the turns, trying to beat other drivers' times. Kids must be at least 48" to drive.
Hours: Open Mon. - Thurs., noon - 9pm; Fri. - Sat., 11am - 11pm; Sun., 11am - 8pm.
  Price: Licensed drivers are $23 for a fourteen-lap race; juniors are $20 for a nine-lap race.
  Ages: At least 48" tall.

MONARX PARKOUR

(818) 889-6326 / monarx.monarchsgym.com
5331 Derry Avenue, Suite I, Agoura Hills

  If your child has a style all his/her own, then parkour might just be the right activity for him/her! Free flow the time at open gym, or take classes that include running up and down walls; swinging on bars; leaping on and over padded and wooden shapes; climbing cargo nets and rope ladders; jumping off platforms; and more all in an atmosphere conducive to promoting and teaching physical fitness and agility. With MonarX, X marks the spot for challenging oneself while trained coaches support and teach every step of the way. And parents, check out the weekly Parents Night Out - 3 hours of activities, games, free play and pizza for the kids = 3 hours of time together out for parents.
Hours: Open gym, for ages 8 and up, is Wed., 8pm - 9pm. Parents Night Out is every Fri., 7pm - 10pm for ages 8 -
      15 years old.
  Price: Open gym is $12 an hour. Parents Night Out is $22 for the first child; $37 for two siblings.
  Ages: 8 years and up. (6 years and up for the classes.)

MOUNTASIA FUN CENTER

(661) 253-4FUN (4386) / www.mountasiafuncenter.com
21516 Golden Triangle Road, Santa Clarita

  Mountasia offers a mountain of fun for your family! Play either one of two **miniature golf** courses that feature a cascading waterfall. Note that the zebra course has a hole that goes under the waterfall and inside a cave, and that the elephant course has nine wheelchair-friendly holes. Zip around the race track in **go karts**. Drivers must be at least 58" tall and passengers must be 42". Try to avoid getting wet (or go for it) in the **bumper boats**, which have a short waterfall and squirt guns that are activated in warmer weather. All attractions are $9 each. Seniors play mini golf for $8 and children 3 years and under are free; early birds (tickets purchased in the first 30 minutes of opening) are $7. Kids at least 48" tall and 6 years old can improve their batting average at the **batting cages**.

  Inside Mountasia are family-oriented video and arcade games and a redemption center; a **rock climbing wall** ($9 for two climbs); and a spacious, L.A. future-city themed **lazer tag arena** where players put on vests and use their laser guns to "tag" opponents and score points ($10 per game). For eats, order food at the counter at Boardwalk Grille and then find a seat. The streamlined menu offers hamburgers, chicken sandwiches, pizza and salad, plus a good selection of ice cream dessert, including shakes and malts.
Hours: Open most of the year, Mon. - Thurs., 2:30pm - 8:30pm; Fri., 2:30pm - 10pm; Sat., 10am - 10pm; Sun., 11am
      - 9pm. Usually open in the summer, most holidays and school breaks, Mon. - Thurs., 10am - 9pm; Fri. - Sat.,
      10am - 11pm; Sun., 11am - 9pm - but call first!
  Price: Attractions are individually priced. Ask about unlimited play and Family Fun specials.
  Ages: 4 years and up.

MULLIGAN FAMILY FUN CENTER - Palmdale

(661) 273-1407 / palmdale.mulliganfun.com
525 West Avenue P-4, Palmdale

  Do you have a Tiger in your house? A Tiger Woods, I mean. Practice a modified golf swing at the three themed, nine-hole **miniature golf** courses here - $10 for ages 10 and up for all twenty-seven holes; $7 for ages 9 and under. A five-minute ride on a two-seater **go-kart** is $7.50 for drivers, who must be at least 56" tall, and $3.50 for passengers, who must be at least 40" tall. **Rookie go-kart**, where the driver must be a minimum 40", is $7.50. Get wet on **blaster boats** (i.e., bumper cars in the water that are open seasonally) at $7.50 for drivers, who must be at least 44" tall, and $3.50 for passengers, who must be at least 44" tall. I always enjoy a round of **lazer tag** and this arena seems futuristic with neon colors and lights. The cost is $7.50. The **rock climbing wall** is $7.50 for three attempts. Instead of hanging on by a thread, try a rope, or at least the **ropes course**. This multi-level attraction looks like a play structure, but you are harnessed in while walking a ropes bridge, over a tightrope, and on an adventure trail of more challenges. It costs $10 for one time use. Other attractions at Mulligan include batting cages, a large game arcade area, and a cafe. The cafe serves pizza - $14.99 for a large cheese; buffalo wings - $8.99 for eight pieces; grilled chicken sandwich - $6.49; and kids meals - $6.49 for a choice of chicken strips, cheese quesadilla, or mini corn dogs.

Hours: Open most of the year, Mon. - Thurs., 3pm - 8pm; Fri., 2pm - 10pm; Sat., 11am - 10pm; Sun., 11am - 8pm. Open in the summer and on holidays longer hours, so call first.

Price: Individual attractions are listed above. Ask about special package pricing, such as all-day, unlimited play for $30.99.

Ages: 4 years and up.

MULLIGAN FAMILY FUN CENTER - Torrance

(310) 325-3950 / torrance.mulliganfun.com $$$$

1351 W. Sepulveda Boulevard, Torrance

    Fore a fun time of golfing come play at the two wonderful **miniature golf** courses that feature great add-ons such as a mining cave to go through, a haunted mansion obstacle, huge boulders to go under, a castle, an old West "town", a train and a fire house - $11 per person, per game. This center also has **batting cages** - $2 for ten pitches; **go-kart** racing - $9.50 for drivers for a five-minute ride (drivers must be 56" and passengers 40") and $4.50 for passengers; **rookie go-karts** for ages 5 minimum, $7.50; **paddle boats** for ages 3 to 80lbs. - $5; a glacier-looking **rock climbing** wall - $7.50 for two attempts; **laser tag** - a hi-tech battle game in a 2,200-square-foot arena - $8.50; and the ever-present arcade games. A small, free, **kids play area** for young kids of a maximum 54" tall, is available to climb (think gerbil habitat on steroids for the enclosed tubes), slide, jump, and play. A driving range is also here, as is a full-service snack bar serving nachos, pizza, hot dogs, and more.

Hours: Open most of the year usually, Mon. - Thurs., 1pm - 8pm; Fri., 1pm - 10pm; Sat., 10am - 10pm; Sun., 11am - 8pm. Open in the summer and school holidays usually, Mon. - Thurs., 10am - 9pm; Fri. - Sat., 10am - 10pm; Sun., 11am - 9pm.

Price: Attractions are individually priced above. Ask about special package pricing, such as all-day, unlimited passes for $39.99.

Ages: 2 years through 54" tall for the play area; 4 years and up for miniature golf.

PAINTBALL U.S.A. CLOSE ENCOUNTERS

(800) 919-9237 / www.paintballusa.org $$$$$

15114 Sierra Highway, Santa Clarita

    Play this version of Capture the Flag while armed with markers (i.e., guns) filled with paint. This makes the game a bit more colorful! You'll be placed on one of two teams. The object of the game is to get the flag from your opponent's base, while dodging paintballs by hiding behind objects such as bunkers and trees. There are fourteen fields here that incorporate bales of hay; huge wooden wheels; trenches; dunes; and a maze. Two fields resemble real battlefields in the middle-East; others have more natural obstacles, such as trees and ravine; and some feature man-made buildings and inflatables. A referee is on the playing fields to insure fair play and to help out. Each game lasts about twenty minutes. After you're rested, go for another round. Tip: Wear pants and other clothing you don't care about, and shoes with good traction. Getting hit stings, so wear a padded shirt, or multiply layers to help absorb the hits. Players 17 and under must have a waiver.

    Participants can also play airsoft and infrared games (similar to laser tag, but played outside) here. In between games, enjoy shaded picnic facilities with BBQs - just bring your own food. Or order pizza from the onsite cashier, as it can be delivered.

Hours: Open Sat. - Sun., 9am - 4pm. Groups of 25 or more can reserve play time during the week.

Price: If you have your own equipment, admission is $30, which includes all-day air. For rentals, prices are $45 for ages 10 - 17, which includes 200 paintballs; $50 for ages 18 and older.

Ages: 10 years and up, only.

PEEKABOO PLAYLAND

Bel Air - (424) 341-2321; Eagle Rock - (323) 255-1400 / www.peekabooplayland.com

Bel Air - 2321 Roscomare Road; Eagle Rock - 2030 Colorado Boulevard

    This two-story, high-ceiling, airy home with lots of natural light has been converted to a sweet and casually elegant kid's play place. Stairs, with gates and fencing all around, lead up to a big white bird to climb into, an entrance to a slide, and a large upper play area with a puppet theater, book nook, and plenty of toys and puzzles. Downstairs is a small ball pit, raised train tables, mini bounce, Little Tykes cars, mini slides, and a little kitchen room with a play oven, sink, and table. Kids can do Peekasso art projects once a week, here, too. There are couches for parents to relax and watch. All kids and adults must wear socks. Note: The Bel Air location has a small, lovely outdoor patio, too, with a beautiful view, and a big hallway set up like a road, complete with street signs and cars to race around on it.

Hours: Open Mon. - Thurs., 10am - 6pm; Fri., 10am - 5pm. Open Sat. - Sun. for private parties only. Closed Thanksgiving and Christmas.

Price: $10 per child; $8 for siblings and children 1 and under; adults are free.

Ages: 1 - 8 years

PINT SIZE KIDS

(310) 339-7452 / www.pintsizekids.com

13323 Ventura Boulevard, Sherman Oaks

    The mid-sized room with cement flooring is painted to look like streets; a few Little Tyke cars and street signs add to the setting. Along the perimeter of the wide road are a few different little rooms, such as a workshop with Duplos and other toys; a medical center with doctor's coats, stethoscopes, an examining table, and toy body parts; a little kitchen with a play stove and frig, plus a table and chairs and painted fireplace; and a grocery store with a cash register, shelves with fake food, and bins of plastic fruits and veggies. A gated infant/toddler area has stuffed animals and toys for tots. A carpeted book nook in the front has plenty of books to peruse, a train table, and large stuffed animals to use as pillows.

    This facility also offers a myriad of art, music, dance, sport and other classes geared for your pint-sized darlings. Wear socks as they are required.

Hours: Open Mon. - Fri., 9am - 6pm; Sat., 9am - noon. Closed Sun.

Price: $12 for the first child, ages 9 months and up; $10 for siblings. Parents are free.

Ages: 1 - 7

PUMP IT UP (Los Angeles County)

Torrance - (310) 533-9377; Van Nuys - (818) 994-1100 / www.pumpitupparty.com

Torrance - 1780 Oak Street; Van Nuys - 6862 Hayvenhurst Avenue, Unit B

    See PUMP IT UP (San Diego County) (pg. 487) for details. The Torrance location also offers Pre-K only Open Jump times, Family Nights and Drop Off Play Dates, where children, ages 4 years and up, can be dropped off to play, have snacks and do a craft for 3 hours for $25. Torrance attractions include huge, variously-shaped foam blocks and a jousting inflatable. Van Nuys calls Open Jump, Pop N Play Time.

Hours: Check the location's website calendar for details on Open Jump and other specialty jump times as the times vary even within a particular month.

Price: $11 per child at Torrance; $10 per child at Van Nuys. Adults are free.

Ages: 2 years and up.

ROCKIN' JUMP (Los Angeles County)

Palmdale - (661) 233-9907; San Dimas - (909) 660-4930 / palmdale.rockinjump.com; sandimas.rockinjump.com

Palmdale - 1301 W Rancho Vista Blvd. at the Antelope Valley Mall; San Dimas - 533 West Arrow Hwy.

    Lots of fun and lots of exercise - all at one time! This friendly, indoor trampoline park has a lot of rockin' features - an large, open jump arena; a dodgeball room (yes, to play while trampolining!); a stunt area to practice flips and jumps safely into a foam pit or onto stunt bags; a slam dunk zone to practice your (literal) jump shots; X-Beam, where two players use padded lances to "joust" knock their opponents off the beam into a foam pit; a hurricane simulator, which is an upright tube to enter while winds of hurricane force swirl around you; and a vertical ops rock climbing wall, where climbers race up the wall to beat their opponents, all while harnessed in. Note: The Palmdale location doesn't have a hurricane simulator and the San Dimas location doesn't have a rock wall.

    There is a cafe, party rooms, and places for parents to watch their kids (or they can join in and jump with them), too. There are also times just for tots (ages up to 6 years old), on select mornings; times just for older kids (ages 11 to 17), on Rockin' Fri. and Sat. nights with black lights, music, and a D.J.; and some locations have a special needs jump time and a home schoolers time. All jumpers at all times must use the Rockin' Jump socks ($3), and must have signed waivers.

Hours: Palmdale: Open Mon., Tues., Thurs. for open jump, 3pm - 8pm; plus Tues., tots only, 9am - 11am. Open Wed., tots only, 9am - 11am, then open jump, 1pm - 8pm; Fri., open jump, 3pm - 9pm; Rockin' Fri., 9pm - 11pm; Sat., tots only, 8am - 10am then open jump, 10am - 9pm, Rockin' Sat., 9pm - 11pm; Sun., open jump, 11am - 8pm. San Dimas: Open Mon. - Fri. for open jump, 3:30pm - 8pm; Fri., Rockin' Fri., 8pm - 10pm. Open Sat., tots only, 8am - 10am, then open jump, 10am - 8pm, Rockin' Sat., 8pm - 10pm; Sun., open jump, 11am - 7pm.

Price: Palmdale: $12 for 60 min. of jump time; $16 for 90 min., etc. $15 for tots only time - for one parent and child ($3 each additional child); $15 per person for Rockin' Fri. and Sat. San Dimas: $16 for 60 min. of jump time; $25 all-day pass. $15 for tots (same as Palmdale). $20 per person for Rockin' Fri. and Sat.

Ages: 18 months and older, depending on the time and day.

ROCKREATION (Los Angeles County)

(310) 207-7199 / www.rockreation.com
11866 La Grange Avenue, Los Angeles

$$$$

See the entry for ROCKREATION (Orange County) (pg. 265) for details. This location is a little smaller at 9,000 square feet.

Hours: The gym is open Mon. and Wed., noon - 11pm; Tues. and Thurs., 6am - 11pm; Fri., 6am - 10pm; Sat. - Sun., 10am - 6pm. Closed major holidays. Climb Time is offered Sat. - Sun., 1pm - 3pm. Kids' Climb, for ages 6 - 12, is offered Mon. - Fri., 4pm - 6pm; Sat. and Sun., 3pm - 5pm.

Price: $20 for adults for a day pass; $15 for ages 11 and under, but they must have a belayer. Rental equipment - shoes and harness - is an additional $8. Climb Time is $25 per hour. Kids Climb is $35 for the two-hour session - both include the necessary equipment. Reservations are needed.

Ages: Must be 6 years old and up.

ROUND1 BOWLING AND AMUSEMENT (Los Angeles County)

City of Industry - (626) 964-5356; Lakewood - (562) 408-2937 / www.round1usa.com
City of Industry - 1600 S. Azusa Ave. suite 285, in the Puente Hills Mall; Lakewood - 401 Lakewood Center Mall in Lakewood Center Mall

$$$

Lights! Action! Noise! And lots of it all! Talk about a place where kids (and adults) can be entertained for hours. On one side of the escalators (in the Lakewood Mall) are the twenty, trendy bowling lanes, each with their own screen to watch sporting events or music videos, while bowling. Distracting to me, but others love it. Bumper lanes are available for kids. Come at nighttime to play cosmic bowling, where the lanes are lit by neon lights. Five billiard tables are next to the alleys, as are two private rooms for karaoke (with songs available in English, Spanish, Chinese, Japanese and Korean); two ping pong tables (with netting over the doorway to help catch stray balls); dartboards; and a bar and cafe. The cafe serves 8" pizzas ($6.99), hamburgers ($4.49), nachos ($4.99), sweet potato fries ($3.49), buffalo chicken wings ($7.99), raviolis ($2.50) and more.

The other side of the escalator is taken over by over 200 of the newest and most popular arcade and video games in a rather large space. Redeem your tickets for some good prizes. Along with the games there is an entire section(!) of photo booths here in which to take pictures and then add cool extras to them. There are also a plethora of crane games with some big ticket items to win.

As Round1s are in malls, there are numerous eating options and even other fun things to do and shop for in the immediate area.

Hours: Round1 is open daily, 10am - 2am; ages 18 and over only after 10pm.

Price: All prices depend on the day and time. Bowling, for instance, for 90 minutes, ranges from $9.99 -$17.99. Shoe rentals are $3.50. Karaoke ranges from $9 - $24 an hour for up to three people. Billiards, darts, and ping pong range from $8 - $14 an hour.

Ages: 5 years and up.

SCOOTER'S JUNGLE (Los Angeles County)

El Segundo - (310)848-1380; Valencia - (661) 877-4400 / www.scootersjungle.com
El Segundo - 606 Hawaii Street; Valencia - 28230 Constellation

$$

See SCOOTER'S JUNGLE (Orange County) (pg. 266) for details. The Valencia location has three arenas, each geared for a different age group.

Hours: Most locations have really varied calendars, so check the websites. A few have regular times: El Segundo - Toddler Times are usually Tues. - Thurs., 10:30am - noon. Family Fun and All Ages are usually every other Wed. from 5:30pm - 8:30pm. Valencia - Toddler Times are usually Wed. - Thurs., 10:30am - noon.

Price: All Ages is $10 per child. Toddler Time is $9 per child. Family Fun is $11 per child. All playtimes include one adult; additional adults are an additional $4.

Ages: 2 years and up.

SENDER ONE LAX (Los Angeles County)

(714) 881-3456 - rock climbing; (714) 881-3FUN (3386) - Sender City / www.senderoneclimbing.com $$$$
11220 Hindry Avenue, Los Angeles

Bigger and taller than its sister site, SENDER ONE (Orange County) (pg. 267), this location has an amazing (and eye-appealing) 31,000 square feet of climbing space including sixty-foot-high walls with over eighty foot routes; a World Cup standard speed climbing wall; two stories of bouldering upstairs and downstairs with seventy-five-feet-wide walls; viewing areas; a training mezzanine; yoga classes; a fully-equipped, fitness center with free weights, weight machines and cardio equipment; a training wall and area to learn belaying using GriGri belay devices; and a myriad of classes ($39 for an intro to climbing class) including clinics, youth camps, parents night out, climbing teams, and other opportunities. The one-hour Kids Climb in the main gym is a time for kids, ages 6 - 13, to actually learn the ropes of rock climbing - $29. Waivers are required for all climbers. Truly, it has it all in a great environment for all levels to practice, train and enjoy.

Another stand-out feature is Sender City, a huge room designed just for kids. The fantastic, padded, and colorful climbing room has imaginative and challenging (but doable) configurations that will get kids active and excited. Some of the creative walls to climb up include a (very long) giraffe's neck; several short ladders spaced at adjacent angles to reach the next level, and then the next one, etc.; ropes that look like a spider's web; two "ladders" made out of tires; and, using apples as hand and footholds on a tree to then branch out onto the leaves on the treetop, moving around colorful owls perched there. Also, kids can climb up a colorful island, in and over the faux water and sand and mountains to reach the treasure chest at the top. (I think the treasure is just making it to the top!) Go King Kong and leap from the top of one free-standing (scale) city skyscraper to the next, while harnessed in. And try to Jump Catch - where all is takes is a leap of faith to grab the trapeze bar. All this is just to whet your appetite for all there is to do here. Each session at Sender City is an hour long, reservations are required, kids must weigh at least 35 pounds to "play", and kids 13 and under must have an adult with them. The entire floor is thickly padded. Party rooms are right off this main room.

Sender One is legitimately one of my favorite places to climb, and a favorite for kids to climb, too.

Hours: Open Mon. - Fri., 6am - 11pm; Sat., 8am - 10pm; Sun., 8am - 8pm. Sender City is open Mon. - Fri., 9:30am - 8:30pm; Sat. - Sun., 9:30am - 6:30pm. Closed New Year's Day, 4th of July, Thanksgiving and Christmas. Closed early on some other days.

Price: A day pass, which includes climbing, yoga classes and use of the fitness room, is $24 for ages 14 and up, with your own gear; $19 for ages 13 and under. A package rental of shoes, harness and chalk is $7. An hour-long session in Sender City is $25 per person most weekdays; $29 on weekends, holidays and summer/school breaks.

Ages: 4 years and up.

SHERMAN OAKS CASTLE PARK

(818) 756-9459 / www.laparks.org/castlepark $$$
4989 Sepulveda Blvd., Sherman Oaks

This Castle Park offers royal fun for the whole family. Adjacent to the parking lot is a small, outdoor eating area with picnic tables. Go through the castle onto grounds that are beautifully landscaped (palm and pine trees and plants) so puttin' around on the three majestic **miniature golf** courses is a real pleasure. All the fun elements are here - obstacles, hairpin turns, miniature buildings, themed holes, bridges, waterways, a gingerbread house, a lighthouse, and more. There are also nine **batting cages** (kids must be 8 years old, or at least 54" tall), over 100 arcade games surrounded by wall murals of a king and his subjects, a redemption center, and a full-service snack bar.

Hours: Open Mon. - Thurs., 10am - 11pm; Fri., 10am - midnight; Sat., 9am - midnight; Sun., 9am - 11pm. Open during the summer and school breaks, Mon. - Fri., 10am - midnight; Sat. - Sun., 9am - midnight.

Price: Miniature golf is $6.50 for the first round for adults; $5.50 for seniors and for children 5 - 12; ages 4 and under are free with a paying adult; $3 for replays for all ages. Pay only $3 a round for early bird specials on Sat. and Sun. morning, 9am - 10:30am.

Ages: 4 years and up.

SKY HIGH SPORTS (Los Angeles County)

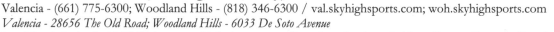

Valencia - (661) 775-6300; Woodland Hills - (818) 346-6300 / val.skyhighsports.com; woh.skyhighsports.com $$$
Valencia - 28656 The Old Road; Woodland Hills - 6033 De Soto Avenue

The sky's the limit! Well, almost at this indoor trampoline place that is veritably wall-to-wall trampolines because, yes, they are on the walls, too. The main jumping arena, for freestyling, has a huge network of trampolines that line the floor like a grid - you can't fall off. Parents, note that all pads and springs are covered by two inch thick safety pads and that there are staff supervisors. Just jumping around proves that cardio can be fun.

Other fun features include a dodgeball trampoline court; a really large foam pit for extreme sports to either bounce into when trying out tricks and flips, or swing over with a rope (think Tarzan) and then letting go; and Sky High Dunk - a place to shoot hoops while trampolining. Everyone wants to be a ninja, so practice your moves on the Ninja Course where you'll try to master floating boards, rings, poles, monkey bars and more and then finish by running up a warped wall to hit the buzzer and beat the clock. Ninjas must be at least 52", wear closed-toed shoes and pay an additional $8. The Valencia location also has Kids Court, a special trampolining section just for little ones, plus a lane in the foam pits just for them.

Lockers, a few video games, free Wi-Fi, a couch, a big screen TV, and a cafe that offers pizza ($15 for cheese), spicy chicken wings ($10.99), mini corn dogs ($7.50) and family-sized salads and sandwich platters make this an up-lifting destination. Ages 17 and under must have a parent-signed waiver. All jumpers must wear grip socks ($2 a pair here). A separate party room of trampolines and an eating area is also available to reserve for any age group and any celebration. Check the website for special and deals plus Special Needs Days, AIRobics classes, Munchkin Mondays, Home School Days, Family Night, Wild Wednesdays, and Cosmic Jumping which is hours of jumping on Fri. and Sat. nights with music on and lights off (except for black lights). Knowing how much my kids love this place, so I'm confident yours will literally flip for Sky High!

Hours: Valencia - Open Sun. - Mon., 11am - 9pm; Tues. - Thurs., 2pm - 9pm; Fri. - Sat., 11am - midnight. Woodland Hills - Mon., 11am - 9pm; Tues. - Thurs., 2pm - 9pm; Fri., 11am - midnight; Sat., 10am - midnight; Sun., 10am - 9pm. Both locations are open extended hours for holidays and open in the summer daily at 11am.

Price: $15 for the first hour; $20 for ninety minutes; $25 for two hours. Children under 2 are free with paying adult. Always check the website for specials.

Ages: 4 years and up.

SKY ZONE (Los Angeles County)

Covina - (626) 331-3208; Gardena - (310) 323-4500; Van Nuys - (818) 946-0082 / www.skyzone.com $$$
Covina - 1314 North Azusa Ave.; Gardena - 1625 West 190th St.; Van Nuys - 7741 Hayvenhurst Ave.

How high can you jump? How long can you jump? (I can only last ten minutes.) With its wall-to-wall trampolines, Sky Zone can test your limits, and take you beyond. The main room has over forty individual trampoline rectangles that form one big patchwork grid. And that doesn't include the angled trampolines on the walls which then have you literally bouncing off the walls. At some facilities toddlers have their own room to bounce in so they can join in on the fun.

The Foam Zone is an area to practice flips and tricks at your own risk, or just to jump into the soft foam block pit for the fun of it. Play dodgeball like never before - on a trampoline! There are several courts just for this game. Other sports offered here while trampolining include volleyball, and sky slam (i.e. mini basketball) on a few free-throw courts. Most locations offer a few extras like jousting with padded lances (over a foam pit); slack lining; going up a trick ladder (called a fidgety ladder); and running up the Warped Wall - a curved incline wall, just for the fun of it. For more of a work-out take a Skyfit *air*obics class! You can also rest and watch others be active at tables and chairs both downstairs and up. A few arcade games are available to play.

You can't bring in outside food, but there are some snacks (and lots of candy) available for purchase. Sky Socks (with tread) are mandatory and available to purchase for $2. (Some locations include this sock fee in their admission price; some don't.) Waivers must be signed by a parent or legal guardian before jumping can commence. Always check the website for specials, events, and classes including Toddler Time, Glow, College Night, Hoppy Hour, special needs time, SkyJam, Family Fitness, and more. Tip: Sometimes sessions sell out, so you might want to prepurchase your ticket.

Hours: Most locations are generally open Mon. - Thurs., 3pm - 9pm; Fri., 3pm - 11pm; Sat., 10am - 11pm; Sun., 10am - 9pm. Hours fluctuate by location, so call first.

Price: Covina and Van Nuys: $17 for 60 min., $22 for 90 min. Toddler Time is $7 an hour or $10 per session. Gardena: $13 for 30 min.; $18 for 60 min.; $23 for 90 min.

Ages: 2 years and up.

SPEEDZONE

(626) 913-9663 / www.speedzone.com

$$$$

17871 Castleton Street, City of Industry

Ahhhh, the smell of gasoline and the sound of engines being revved! Although SpeedZone is advertised as a racing park for adults, kids can go full throttle here, too. The huge mural of formula race cars on the outside of the massive black-and-white-checkered building reinforce the park's intentions of being dedicated to speed, racing, and competition. Three of the tracks, along with their minimum height requirements, are: Top Eliminator Dragsters, with 300-horsepower cars (4'8"); Turbo Track, a two-seater sidewinder racer which allows wheel-to-wheel racing with up to nineteen other drivers (5'); and Slick Trax, for a spin around a concrete track (5'). SpeedZone is the closest thing to professional racing available to the public. Kids between 42" and 54" are not left out - they have their own track called Lil' Thunder.

Two, eighteen-hole miniature golf courses are done in the racing theme motif and include paraphernalia such as gas pumps, tires, and guard rails, plus waterways and bridges. Inside, SpeedZone decor consists of racing flags, murals, photos, a few cars (on the floor and suspended from the ceiling), and signed memorabilia such as helmets and jumpsuits.

Enjoy American classic food in the Johnny Rockets restaurant. Meal choices include hamburgers ($7.99), grilled chicken breast sandwich ($8.99), chicken salad ($9.99), Philly cheesesteak ($9.99), chili cheese dog ($7.99), and a full selection of shakes and floats ($5.49). Kid's meals are $5.99 to $6.99 for a choice of two mini burgers, chicken tenders, or grilled cheese sandwich.

Keep the adrenaline pumping with more than 100 video, virtual reality, and arcade games in the Electric Alley, plus a prize redemption area. Play basketball or skee ball, or try virtual jetskiing, motocross, or downhill skiing. Strike it rich at the Strike Zone where it's not "real" bowling (no special shoes or ball size needed), but it is mini bowling and fun, and the lanes look like streets (of course!). At the Daytona simulators up to eight drivers can race against each other on the same track. A day at SpeedZone is not just another day at the races!

Hours: Open Mon. - Thurs., 11am - 10pm, racing opens at noon; Fri., 11am - midnight, racing opens at noon; Sat., 11am - midnight, racing opens at 11am; Sun., 10am - 10pm, racing opens at 11am. Open one hour earlier in the summer. All visitors at SpeedZone after 10pm must have a valid California driver's license.

Price: Free entrance. Top Eliminator - $20 for 3 races; Turbo Track ($2 for a passenger) and Slick Trax are $10 each for 5 minutes; Lil' Thunder is $8 per race. Speedway miniature golf is $10 for adults; $5 for seniors; ages 5 and under are free with a paying adult. Strike Zone is $5 per 5 frames.

Ages: 4 years and up for the restaurant and miniature golf; see above restrictions for driving cars.

STRONGHOLD CLIMBING GYM

(323) 505-7000 / www.strongholdclimb.com

$$$$$

650 S. Avenue 21, Los Angeles

Like a good cliff hanger? Come climb the walls at this indoor rock climbing gym where the wall are up to 46 feet high with hundreds of routes, plus top-roping, lead climbing terrain, and three cracks (which is a good thing to practice on in terms of climbing). An auto-belay system is available. The huge bouldering area, with the numerous angles, overhangs, arches and "caves", offers a great and enjoyable workout. Stronghold is a cool ambiance with a mixture of warehouse-style facility with brick walls and it's very kid friendly, too - they even offer summer camps, classes and Open Climb / Kids' Climb. The latter is offered every Saturday and Sunday from 2pm to 4pm and includes everything that climbers need, plus a belayer and a day pass.

The 2,000 square foot work-out mezzanine features weights, cardio machines, pull-up bars, rings and more. There is also a specific training area for climbing with hang-boards, campus boards, a systems wall and a super Moon board. Top this all off with yoga and fitness classes to know that Stronghold offers a complete workout and training.

Hours: Open Mon. - Fri., 6am - 11pm; Sat. - Sun., 8am - 9pm. Closed Thanksgiving and Christmas.

Price: $25 for the day for adults; $20 for ages 18 and under. $20 a day for adults, Mon. - Fri. before 3pm (except holidays); $15 for youth. Open Climb / Kids' Climb is $40 preregistration; $50 walk in.

Ages: 4 years and up.

TEMPEST FREERUNNING ACADEMY - Hawthorne

(310) 644-7686 / www.tempestacademy.com
3337 Jack Northrop Avenue, Hawthorne

See the Tempest Freerunning entry below for a full explanation about the academy. With all of the same ideas and physical challenges as the Northridge location, but almost twice the size, this facility is set up with different scenarios. A few colorful and crazy sections look like mazes - one is called Minecraft. The Antfarm space is unique in that one must crawl in and through some spots. One section looks like a cement, cubed building; another like a castle with stone-like walls and partitions with a fire escape; and another is all poles attached to each other for swinging on and around. These sections look so different under colored lights! A Santorini space has a beautiful mural of this city on a hill, which becomes 3-D with stairs jutting out of it, plus a balcony and poles. A trampoline area with a foam pit is here, as is a central, gymnastics spring floor. Read the below entry regarding classes and open gym.

Hours: Open Gym for adults (17 years and up) is Mon. - Thurs., 8pm - 11pm; Sat., 3pm - 5pm. Monitored Open Gym, for ages 9 - 16 years only, is Fri., 6pm - 9pm and Sat., noon - 2pm. Open Gym for mixed ages (9 years and up) is Mon. and Thurs., 6pm - 7pm. Closed Sun. and certain holidays. Call or check online for a schedule of classes.

Price: $15 for ages 17 and up for Open Gym, and per child (ages 9 - 16) for Open Gym mixed ages; $20 per child for Monitored Open Gym. Classes start at $100 a month for a one-hour class once a week; $30 to drop in a class (must call in advance).

Ages: 4 years and up for classes; 9 and up for open gym.

TEMPEST FREERUNNING ACADEMY - Northridge

(818) 717-0525 / www.tempestacademy.com
19821 Nordhoff Place, suite 115, Northridge

"Developed by the founders of Team Tempest and X-Games course designer Nate Wessel, our facility offers a real-world environment where you can learn everything from the basics of parkour to the advanced maneuvers and tricks of freerunning." (Quoted from the company's website.) Even if you don't know what the terms "freerunning" or "parkour" mean, if you have kids who enjoy X-treme sports (and/or you just want to physically wear your kids out), this innovative and even artsy training facility is the place to take them. Both practices involved running; running up or scaling walls; wall spins; flips; vaulting over street elements; and other acrobatics and street stunts. Parkour is more regimented and directed than freerunning which is a more free form and aesthetically-pleasing way of moving your body in motion.

Take all of the above and this is what you get with Tempest - a huge indoor warehouse-like facility (7,000 square feet) with different sections created to look and feel very unique from one another. With columns, ledges, ramps, steps, benches, doorways, poles, and more, to run and jump on and over, one area has a fourteen-foot, warped wall (like a half pipe) designed and built for these sports; another is like a wildly colorful urban street scene; another has a blackboard along a long wall; yet another looks like a brick house. With a trampoline at one end and an eight-foot edge at the other, the huge foam pit (30 ft. long by 10 ft. wide by 6 ft. deep) is ideal for practicing flips. Another trampoline helps practitioners gauge just the right amount of bounce needed for certain tricks. A gymnastics spring floor is integrated into the center of the hardcore Parkour Park, giving some cushion to landings.

Is it safe? The sports lend themselves to physical extremes, but the qualified staff and coaches here do parkour and freerunning professionally (in competitions and for movies), so they train on the how to's and don't allow participants to go beyond what they've proven they can handle. At least seven classes are offered for different age brackets and abilities, from beginners to the advanced athlete. There is even a Kinderkour class offered, for ages 4 and 5 years old. Tempest also offers open gym hours for participants to just run, practice, and experience parkour. The open gym times are separated by sessions for adults, 17 years and over, who have access to the entire gym; sessions just for kids, 16 years and under, which is a staff-monitored time where participants are allowed in certain areas of the gym and must be accompanied by a parent or legal guardian; and mixed ages sessions for ages 9 and up. Waivers must be signed. Come dressed in clothes that are comfortable to move in (not too tight and not really baggy), and wear gym shoes.

Hours: Open Gym for adults, ages 17 and up is Mon. - Thurs., 8pm - 11pm; Sat., 3pm - 5pm. Monitored Open Gym for ages 9 - 16 is Fri., 6pm - 9pm; Sat., noon - 2pm. Open Gym for mixed ages is Mon. and Thurs., 6pm - 7pm. Closed Sun. and certain holidays. Call or check online for a schedule of classes.

Price: $10 for adults for Open Gym; $20 for kids for Monitored Open Gym. Classes start at $90 a month for a one-hour class, once a week; $30 to drop in a class (must call in advance).

Ages: 4 years and up, depending on the class.

THE PLAYROOM

(818) 784-PLAY (7529) / www.theplayroomvalley.com
14329 Ventura Boulevard, on the second floor of Oak Ridge Plaza, Sherman Oaks

$$

This mid-size, clean, open, airy indoor play area and enrichment center, geared for younger children, has lots of colorful toys and equipment. It has a small bounce; short rock climbing wall; little ball pit; playhouse; little play gym; plenty of sturdy plastic cars to ride on; rockers; stand-alone slides; a wall of chalkboard; air hockey; small desks with puzzles and manipulatives; and a few mini roller coasters to roll down a little track. A nook with table and chairs offers a place for hungry visitors to chow down on food they bring in. Remember to wear socks!

Hours: Open Mon. - Fri., 10am - 6pm. Sat. - Sun. are usually reserved for private parties.
Price: $10 per child; adults are free; $8 additional children.
Ages: 10 months - 5 years.

TOP OUT CLIMBING

(661) 288-1813 / www.topoutclimbing.com
26332 Ferry Court, Santa Clarita

$$$$

Help your kids reach new heights in this beautiful, state-of-the-art, indoor rock climbing gym. Topping out at almost 12,000 square feet, Top Out offers two types of climbing - auto belay, which is an automated braking system so you can scale the walls without a partner, and bouldering. The bouldering area is the main emphasis of the gym, featuring a 100-foot long steep wall that wraps around, a twenty-foot high top out wall, and a fifteen-foot high freestanding boulder. Climb away! I'm a fan of this sport for all that does for participants, both in building up physical strength and agility, and in building up mental acuity. A signed waiver must be filled out.

In the center of the gym is a lounge area with couches, benches, a pool table and free WiFi. This is the area for parties, too. A viewing deck with seating overlooks one of the bouldering areas. Yoga classes are offered on the second floor. Ask about rock climbing classes (the Intro to Rock Climbing is $40), recreational and competitive youth climbing teams, and special events.

Hours: Open Mon. - Fri., 10am - 11pm; Sat., 10am - 9pm; Sun., 10am - 7pm.
Price: A day pass is $17 for adults; $15 for military and students; $12 for ages 10 and under. Come Mon. - Fri. before 2pm for $12 for all ages. Rentals are $4 for shoes and $2 for a harness.
Ages: 5 years and up.

ULTRAZONE (Los Angeles County)

Alhambra - (626) 282-6178; Sherman Oaks - (818) 789-6620 / www.lalasertag.com; www.zonehead.com
Alhambra - 231 E. Main St.; Sherman Oaks - 14622 Ventura Blvd., suite 208

$$$

It's almost pitch black, tho some walls are painted to appear other-worldly in neon colors. You're going through mazes and tunnels trying to find your way to the enemy's base before your enemy finds you. Suddenly, ZAP - you get hit! You realize you've lost your power and now you have to recharge. Where *is* the recharging site? After getting lost several times you find it, and now your infrared sighting helps spy one of "them"! You fire, hit, and score one for your team!

Ultrazone, with over 5,000 square feet of high tech excitement, is the ultimate in laser tag. Wearing a vest and laser gun, you play with up to forty-five people, or three teams. After a five-minute briefing, you'll play for twenty intense minutes in this futuristic-looking arena. The first game will wear you out, but it's just practice. Now that you've got a handle on how the game is played, go for a second round. Laser tag - there is fun to be had with a game this rad!

Notes: The Alhambra facility is a two-story arena. Both facilities have separate party rooms and a few arcade games in the lobby plus a snack bar.

Hours: Alhambra - open most of the year, Wed. - Thurs., 3pm - 8pm; Fri., 3pm - midnight; Sat., 11am - 1am; Sun., 11am - 8pm. Closed Mon. and Tues. for private events and closed most major holidays. Sherman Oaks - open Tues. - Thurs., 3pm - 10pm; Fri., 3pm - midnight; Sat., 10am - midnight; Sun., 10am - 10pm. Closed Mon. and certain holidays. Both locations are open extended hours during summer and on school breaks.
Price: Alhambra - $9 a game. Sherman Oaks - $11 a game. There are a lot of weekly specials.
Ages: 6 years and up, or not afraid of the dark.

UNDER THE SEA

(310) 915-1133 / www.undertheseaindoorplayground.com
3871 Grand View Blvd., Culver City

$$$

Murals of mermaids, octopuses, and even pirates submerge your children in a world of play at Under the Sea. This aquatically-themed indoor play area has bounce houses; multi-level structures with tubes and tunnels to crawl through;

slides; a ball pit; soft play mats; Little Tykes™ cars; playhouses; free standing slides; soft play shapes; huge balls; air hockey; and a Baby Corner with a toddler swing, slide, and carousel. Socks are required in the play area. Ask about classes, including modern dance and Mommy & Me. You are welcome to bring your own food in and enjoy a meal at the picnic tables toward the entrance.

Hours: Open Mon. - Fri., 10am - 6pm; open Tues. until 8pm. Open Sat. and Sun. for private parties only.

Price: $11 for ages 9 months - 14 years. Adults are free.

Ages: 9 months to 8 years.

VALENCIA LASER BLAST

(661) 255-1600 / www.valencialaserblast.com

23460 Cinema Drive, Valencia

For some out-of-this-world fun, play laser tag in this 5,000 square foot, multi-level arena with spacey decor and shapes painted on the walls and on the maze-like partitions. There are also mirrors (to add confusion and fun), two platforms, three bases and a few mines to activate during this adrenaline-pumping game of tag.

The lobby has some arcade and video games, plus air hockey, basketball, skee ball, and more, along with tickets and a prize redemption area. The snack bar serves good-tasting pizza ($18.95 for large with pepperoni), Greek salads and yummy cupcakes. There are separate party rooms available.

Hours: Open most of the year, Tues. - Thurs., 3pm - 9pm; Fri., 3pm - 11pm; Sat., 11am - 11pm; Sun., 11am - 10pm. Open in the summer and holiday hours, Mon. - Thurs., noon - 10pm; Fri., noon - 11pm; Sat., 11am - 11pm; Sun., 11am - 10pm.

Price: $9.50 per game; $29 for 3 hours of unlimited play. Check the website for specials.

Ages: 6 years and up.

VAULT PK

(310) 977-4478 / www.vaultpk.com

1275 Sartori Avenue, Torrance

If I was creative and had the space, money and man-power, I'd like to have something like Vault PK in my house for my kids (and me). In a cool setting these parkour elements make moving incredibly fun - a trampoline; cargo nets; hard-padded shapes; movable and variously-sized wooden shapes; a spring floor; a 16 foot and a 10 foot wave wall; rings; steps; rails; a foam pit; a large boat structure; and movable wall modules. Flipping, running, jumping, leaping, rolling, climbing, and more are offered via classes and open gym time. Also check out Kids Night Out, Preschool Play, Homeschool classes, and other special events.

Hours: Open gym for all ages, Mon., 2pm - 3:10pm. Open gym for ages 13 and up, Fri., 8:30pm - 10:30pm. Open Thurs. and Sun. for private events only.

Price: Open gym is $10 for ages 13 and up; $15 for ages 12 and under.

Ages: 4 years and up.

WARPED PAINTBALL PARK / WARPED OPS AIRSOFT FIELD

(661) 450-9400 or (661) 450-9401 / www.warpedpaintballpark.com

34481 Ridge Route Road, Castaic

See AMBUSH PAINTBALL & AIRSOFT PARK (pg. 657) for information on this park as they are owned and operated by the same company. Spread over forty acres, Warped has eight scenario fields and two tournament grade fields that include the Spool field, Graveyard field, Castle, the Hyperball field, and the town of Baghdad, plus lots of natural obstacles such as hills and trees, as well as man-made ones such as a life-size tank and buildings.

Hours: Open Sat. - Sun., 9am - 4pm.

Price: $25 for full day of paintball or airsoft with your own equipment; $40 for all day admission plus rental equipment for both games.

Ages: 8 - 11 years for Splatmaster; 10 years and up for airsoft and paintball.

WE ROCK THE SPECTRUM KIDS GYM (Los Angeles County)

www.werockthespectrumkidsgym.com

Agoura Hills; Glendale; Lawndale; Long Beach; Northridge; Pasadena; Santa Clarita; Santa Monica; Studio City; Tarzana; Whittier ; Woodland Hills

These places rock! More than "just" an indoor play place in that these gyms for kids, bursting in primary colors, encourage lots of movement and sensory experience with equipment to help facilitate just that. There is a rope ladder for climbing; wooden monkey bars; trampolines (with safety nets); mini exercise equipment; hula hoops; big balls; little slides; play tunnels; mini zip lines; balance beams; and fun swings for all sizes, including a tire swing, sack swing, and plastic vehicle swings, hanging from the ceiling. All of this is on a padded floor. In the large central room there could also be a small puppet theater, a train table, toys, dress up clothes, soft foam blocks, arts and crafts area, and puzzles at tables, depending on the location. There are adult-size tables, too. Ask about classes, including those offered for kids with special needs. And give yourself a break by taking advantage of the Break Time program where you can leave your kids in care of the staff and go run errands, or just go. Note that there are several more locations slotted to be opening up soon.

Hours: Open daily - hours vary by location, but most are open at 9am and close between 6pm - 8pm. Sometimes private parties are held on weekends, so call first (of course!).

Price: All gyms, except Santa Monica, are $12 per child; $10 for siblings. Adults are free. An all-day pass, offered at some locations, is $20, which allows you in and out privileges of the facility. The Break Time program is $12 an hour with 1 hour minimum, 3 hours max for ages 2 and up, as well as those in special ed. Santa Monica's prices are $16 per child, $14 for siblings, $25 all day pass and $15 per hour for Break Time.

Ages: 6 months - 10 years. Different locations are geared for various ages - call first.

WONDER OF DINOSAURS

(951) 543-6011 / www.wonderofdinosaurs.com

1815 Hawthorne Blvd. in the South Bay Galleria, Redondo Beach

Dinosaur-lovers aren't extinct, as evidenced by how kids react to playing at Wonder of Dinosaurs. There are two floors of dinosaur-themed activities and exhibits. The second floor, the "museum", has over 100 static and robotic dinosaurs, accompanied by information about them, interspersed among rides and activities, which cost extra. All kinds of colorful, life-size dinosaur statues (some of them are scary looking), with an occasional dino skeleton, are in settings of rocks, grasses (astroturf), and small trees, and some have dino eggs to look at or get inside to hatch from. A few robotic ones even come "alive". Remembering that everything here is dinosaur themed, so play the prehistoric 18-hole miniature golf course ($4 per person) with rocks, dinosaurs (of course!), palm trees and more as obstacles and decor; ride a mini Triassic train ($2 per person, up 165 pounds); go around on the tiny dino egg carousel ($2 per person, up to 220 pounds); ride a robotic T-Rex like a dino cowboy ($2 per person, up to 120 pounds, tho an upstairs one is included with admission); work your way through a maze; color dino pages for free; and more.

On the third floor is more action and more dinosaurs, with a room filled with lots of dino-related bounces, including an obstacle course with slides and "rocks" to climb, and a mini mini, inflatable golf course. Note that ages 13 and up are not allowed on the inflatables. There is even a set of bouncers specifically for younger kids, ages 2 to 4 years. All children must wear socks. Besides bounces there is a dino dig pit to uncover bones using brushes - a paleontologist in the making; and a sluice so you can pan for a special dino rock to take home. Or, pan for real fossils and gemstones by purchasing a preloaded bag at the gift shop. Same day re-entry is handy since this dino-mite place is located inside a mall.

Hours: Open Mon. - Fri., 10am - 8pm; Sat., 10am - 7:30pm; Sun., 11am - 6:30pm. Closed Thanksgiving and Christmas.

Price: General admission Mon. - Fri. is $8 for ages 13 and up, $7 for seniors, $16 for ages 2 - 12; Sat. - Sun., $10 for ages 13 and up, $7 for seniors, $18 for ages 2 - 12. Children under 2 are free. Extra activity prices are listed above. Happy Hour is Mon. - Thurs., 6pm - 8pm, with admission being $3 for adults with a paying child; $10 per child. Tot-o-saurus, for ages 5 and under only is Mon. - Thurs., 10am - noon, with admission being $3 for adults with a paying child; $10 for ages 2 - 5. All Tot-o-saurus guests must exit by noon. Happy Hour and Tot-o-saurus discounts are not valid on holidays or spring break, etc.

Ages: 3 years and up.

—GREAT OUTDOORS—

ABALONE COVE SHORELINE PARK

310-544-5366 or (310) 377-1222 / www.palosverdes.com/rpv/recreationparks

5970 Palos Verdes Drive South, Rancho Palos Verdes

This beautiful, cliff-side park on the Palos Verdes Peninsula has a grassy park area at the top and plenty of picnic tables. The ocean view (and sighting of Catalina on a clear day) is spectacular. This park is the only way down to Abalone Cove and the great tidepools at Portuguese Point, which you are welcome to explore. Check the tide schedule before you come and ask for a tidepool map at the entrance when you do. A paved pathway follows along the street for a short while before veering downward. The quarter-mile dirt path is a bit more direct, as well as a bit steeper. Be prepared to carry your gear (chairs, towels, food, etc.). Lifeguards are on duty at the cove during the summer months. Fishing is allowed. Note: The WAYFARERS CHAPEL (pg. 178) is directly across the street.

Hours: Gates are open daily, 9am - dusk. Closed New Year's Day, Thanksgiving, Christmas Eve, and Christmas Day.
Price: Parking is free for the first 30 min.; $6 for up to two hours; $12 for three hours and up. No charge for seniors and handicapped.
Ages: 4 years and up.

AIDAN'S PLACE - WESTWOOD PARK

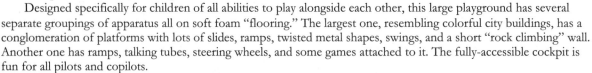

(310) 473-3610 / www.laparks.org
1350 S. Sepulveda Boulevard, Los Angeles

Designed specifically for children of all abilities to play alongside each other, this large playground has several separate groupings of apparatus all on soft foam "flooring." The largest one, resembling colorful city buildings, has a conglomeration of platforms with lots of slides, ramps, twisted metal shapes, swings, and a short "rock climbing" wall. Another one has ramps, talking tubes, steering wheels, and some games attached to it. The fully-accessible cockpit is fun for all pilots and copilots.

The construction zone has three structures that look like trucks. The attached misters come on with the touch of a button. A covered sand pit has three diggers and an elevated sand area that is wheelchair accessible. There are lots of "extras" around the playground, too - a teeter-totter, a square springboard, and short, tube tunnels.

Aidan's Place, which is part of Westwood Park, has a large grassy area, a basketball court, traditional playgrounds, picnic tables, wonderful shade trees, an indoor pool, huge sculptures toward the "back" of the park, workout stations with great equipment, and eight lighted tennis courts. Call (310) 477-5550 for information on playing at the Westwood Tennis Center - courts are usually $8 an hour. The pool is open year round (closed Mondays) for lap and recreation swim - call (310) 478-7019 for hours as they vary. Swimming is $3 for adults; $1 for seniors and ages 17 and under.

Hours: Open Mon. - Fri., 8:30am - 10pm; Sat., 9am - 6pm; Sun., 10am - 5pm.
Price: Free
Ages: All

ANNENBERG COMMUNITY BEACH HOUSE / BACK ON THE BEACH CAFE

(310) 458-4904 - beach house; (310) 393-8282 - Back on the Beach Cafe / www.annenbergbeachhouse.com; $$/$$$$
www.backonthebeachcafe.com
415 Pacific Coast Highway, Santa Monica

Though it has a private, somewhat exclusive feel, this beach and grounds are open to the public. A boardwalk-style walkway on the beach separates the beach from the pool and buildings. The wide and very clean beach sports fine sand; a lifeguard stand (and a lifeguard in the summer); six beach volleyball or beach tennis (a combo of volleyball, tennis and badminton) courts that are free to use or can be reserved for $10 an hour; part of the twenty-six mile bike path that runs from just north of here all the way south to Torrance; and two beach soccer fields. There is also paddle board rentals available ($25 an hour) and a small playground with some odd shapes to play on/with, a half sphere "rock" climbing wall, and swings. Note that volleyballs, soccer balls, and beach tennis equipment can be borrowed from guest services.

On the other side of the walkway is a lovely, heated pool with plenty of lounge chairs under umbrellas and even some couches under the contiguous Pool House building awning. The Pool House has lockers, changing rooms, and a Rec Room that is open daily, mid-June through Labor Day (11am to 5pm) for playing a board game or ping pong, or relaxing with an ocean view. Next to the pool, one level up and separated by a fence, is a splash pad as well as a deck area with round tables and chairs under umbrellas and palm trees - a place to relax, read and watch the sand, surf and people.

A half-hour tour through the adjacent Marion Davies Guest House, originally built in the 1920's, is great for older kids and adults who are interested in the unique architecture and the stories of movie stars and other celebrities from that era.

The on-site, casual and beach-classy Back on the Beach Cafe has some indoor and lots of outdoor seating, and is right on the beach. A walkway allows easier access for strollers and wheelchairs. Menu options include: Breakfast - blueberry pancakes ($11); bananutella French toast with Nutella, bananas, crushed almonds, and whipped cream ($14); granola sundae ($10); and a variety of omelettes with grilled potatoes ($13). Lunch - chicken, apple, and goat cheese salad ($17); salmon, Angus or quinoa burger ($17); and fried shrimp tacos entree ($17). Starters - fried calamari ($14); seafood bisque ($8.75); and sweet potato fries ($4.75). Dinner - short ribs ($15); salmon mousse ($12); crab raviolis ($11); eggplant ($10); and skirt steak ($21). Desserts - cinnamon roll bread pudding; s'more preserve with house-made graham cracker, dark chocolate fudge, and marshmallow brulee; and summer berry cobbler with vanilla ice cream for $9 each. Kid's menu - pasta ($7); kosher hot dog with fries ($7); cheeseburger ($9); and chicken tenders ($8.75).

In the summer, reservations are available for the pool, parking, beach volleyball and "tennis" courts, beach soccer fields, and canopies.

Hours: The parking lot is open daily, 7am - 7pm (or 9pm, depending on the season). The beach and playground are open 24/7. The Beach House grounds - the courtyard, splash pad, and view deck - are open daily, 8:30am - about 8pm - depending on the season. The pool is open Memorial Day weekend, 10am - 6pm, and the first few weekends in June and weekends in September, 11am - 5pm. It's open mid-June - Labor Day, Sat. - Mon., 10am - 8pm; Tues. - Fri., 10am - 6pm. Pool passes go on sale starting at 9am each day. The pool is also open Tues. from 6:30pm - 9:30pm for 17 years and older. The Cafe is open daily, April - September, 8am - 8pm. It's open the rest of the year, Mon. - Fri., 8am - 3pm; Sat. - Sun., 8am - 4pm. Hours do fluctuate, so call first. The splash pad is open most of the year, Mon. - Fri., 10am - 1pm; Sat. - Sun. and holidays, 9am - 3pm. It's open in the summer daily, 9am - 6pm. Marion Davies Guest House tours are offered mid- June - Labor Day on the hour, Mon., Wed., Fri., Sat. - Sun., 11am - 2pm. It's open the rest of the year, usually, Fri. - Mon. for tours between 11am - 2pm.

Price: The Beach House grounds - the beach areas, playground, courtyard, splash pad, view deck, and Marion Davies House - are free. The pool is $10 for adults; $5 for seniors; $4 for ages 1 - 17. Dollar Splash Day Mondays are only $1. Parking: April - October, $3 an hour, $12 a day; November - March, $3 an hour, $8 a day.

Ages: All

ANTHONY C. BEILENSON PARK / LAKE BALBOA / PEDLOW FIELD SKATE PARK / SEPULVEDA DAM RECREATION AREA

(818) 756-8187 - park /Lake Balboa; (818) 756-9642 - sports center; (818) 995-6570 - tennis; (818) 654-5296 - skate park; (818) 756-9710 - Sepulveda Basin Wildlife Reserve; (818) 212- 4263 - Wheel Fun bike rentals / www.laparks.org; www.laparks.org/horticulture; www.sepulvedabasinwildlife.org; www.wheelfunrentals.com
6300 Balboa Boulevard, Encino

Is there anything you can't do at the massive Sepulveda Dam area?! It's very spread out: On the east side of the street are three golf courses; on the west side is an enormous field with sixteen soccer fields, four lighted baseball diamonds, sixteen lighted tennis courts (and a backboard), lighted basketball courts, and lots of open space and gently sloping hills. The Encino Velodrome is also in this vicinity. A paved, relatively easy, ten-mile round-trip bike trail goes through and encompasses the east and west side of the park.

The favorite place to play is a little further north, just south of Victory Boulevard, near Lake Balboa at Anthony C. Beilenson Park. This massive, shaded, boundless, nautical-themed playground with rubberized and sand flooring is fantastic for all abilities! Wide ramps for wheelchairs have interactive play stations along the way with Braille boards, tic-tac-toe, sensory panels, talking tubes, and places to create music (or make noise) by playing bells and piano keys. The sprawling playground features play boats; a lighthouse-shaped play structure; a tactile sea wall with fish and mosaics imbedded; slides of all heights - both open and enclosed; swings; raised sand play areas; sand diggers; rocks to climb on; and metal shapes to spin and twirl on.

The adjacent twenty-seven-acre, man-made Lake Balboa, is made from reclaimed water and patrolled by lifeguards. Bring some old bread for the always-hungry ducks swimming around here. Wait - are those giant swans on the lake? Yes, and no - they are pedal boats (cleverly disguised as swans). Hourly rentals are $11 per adult, $6 per child, per swan. Swan boats seat 2 to 5 people. Numerous walkers take advantage of the 1.3-mile cement pathway that loops around the scenic lake - no bikes, blades, or skateboards are allowed. Bikes are allowed at the several other bike paths that wind throughout the park. Contact Wheel Fun Rentals if you'd like to rent a surrey ($25 an hour), chopper ($12), kids bike ($6), or another type of bike. Fishing is allowed at the lake. A license is required for those 16 years and older. Also, enjoy watching or racing electric, remote-controlled boats through the boating cove.

At Pedlow Field Skate Park, at 17334 Victory Boulevard, an enclosed, supervised, huge, cement skate park is a highlight. It includes handrails, steps, a funbox, plenty of ramps, a pyramid, and a waterfall (which is just the name of a ramp - there is no actual water). Wearing safety gear - a helmet and knee and elbow pads - is mandatory.

Drive east through the park, past a golf course, and you'll reach the adjacent Woodley Park. One of its outstanding features is model aircraft flying at the Apollo Field. Members of the San Fernando Valley Flyers club are often seen here, using (and fixing) their remote-controlled aircraft on a scale runway, and then flying them. See if you can tell the difference in the air between the models and the real planes coming to and from the nearby Van Nuys airport. Other park features include an archery range (short and long range); four cricket fields (come watch a game on the weekends, April through October); and work-out stations with great exercise equipment. 225-acres of a seemingly hidden Sepulveda Basin Wildlife Reserve is a refuge where an abundance of trees and other plants and animals (more than 200 species of birds!) dwell in a place so removed from yet smack in the middle of city life. At the Reserve, located at 6350 Woodley Avenue, stroll the nature trails, walk to the eleven-acre lake created from reclaimed water, cross over bridges, try to shut out the noise of the streets that filter in, and enjoy. Call to join in on the monthly bird walks. Look up the THE JAPANESE GARDEN (pg. 66) as it is located in this area, as well.

Hours: The park and wildlife reserve are open daily, sunrise - sunset. The skate park is open Tues. - Fri., noon - sunset; Sat. - Sun., 10:30am - sunset. Closed Mon. and holidays. The sports center is open Mon. - Fri., 9am - 10pm; Sat. - Sun., 9am - 5pm. Wheel Fun Rentals is open daily, 9am - sunset.

Price: Free to the park, lake, skatepark, and reserve.

Ages: All

APOLLO COMMUNITY REGIONAL PARK

(661) 940-7701 / parks.lacounty.gov

4555 W. Ave. G, Lancaster

This *space*ious park has three man-made lakes that are named after the astronauts from Apollo XI: Lake Aldrin, Lake Armstrong, and Lake Collins. The lakes are stocked seasonally with trout (November through April) and catfish (the rest of the year), and while there is not a fee for fishing, a California state fishing license is needed for those over 16 years of age. There is a floating dock, here, too. Popular spring and fall fishing derbies are held for both adults and children. Tip: Bring duck food to feed the relentlessly friendly ducks and geese. This ritual alone took us over half an hour!

The park, though surrounded by the desert, is picturesque with its shade trees, bridges over portions of water, walking path, and plenty of run-around room. There is also a great abstract playground here, the kind that looks like abstract art, where creative play on the poles, colorful knobs, ropes, and more ensues. My kids were also intrigued by the glass-enclosed, well-built mock-up of a command module. The placard describes the dedication of the park to the Apollo program. (Don't you love sneaking in a history lesson?)

Hours: Open daily, dawn - dusk.

Price: Free

Ages: All

ARATANI JAPANESE GARDEN

(909) 869-7659 / www.cpp.edu

3801 W. Temple Avenue, on the campus of California State Polytechnic University, Pomona

Japanese gardens are steeped in tradition and symbolism. This 1.3-acre garden features plants of East Asia; a reflection pond with koi; a short waterfall; a little, bubbling stream; bridges; a sculptured rock garden; a small amphitheater; a patch of lawn with trees; and a paved pathway that winds throughout it all. Meant to be enjoyed and imbue visitors with a sense of peace, the garden succeeds in being a mini-retreat. Check out the Index by City in the back of this book to see what other attractions Cal Poly holds.

Hours: Open daily, sunrise - sunset when the campus is open.

Price: Free. Parking on campus is $2 an hour, $8 for the day Mon. - Fri., $5 on Sat. - Sun. There is some metered parking.

Ages: All

AVERILL PARK

(310) 548-7675 / www.laparks.org; www.sanpedro.com

1300 South Dodson Avenue, San Pedro

This verdant, tranquil park has a series of linear, rock-lined streams and ponds that gently cascade into each other. A stone bridge and botanic-like garden add beauty to this area. The paved pathways on both sides of the stream have chain-link safety "ropes" and numerous trees - palm, bamboo, oak, banyan, and other shade trees. Picnic tables, small barbeques, and benches are tucked into nooks along the waterway. While ducks and turtles inhabit the waters, squirrels have free reign of the trees that cover one side of the hill. Grass covers the other side and the top. A picnic lunch here is a way of refreshing the soul.

Hours: Open daily, sunrise - sunset.

Price: Free

Ages: All

BALDWIN HILLS SCENIC OVERLOOK

(310) 558-5547 - visitor center; (310) 558-1444 - park / www.parks.ca.gov

6300 Hetzler Road, Culver City

 Climbing the seemingly unending stone stairs that go straight up the hill - that's the tough part. Reaching the overlook and looking out over Los Angeles and, on a clear day, to the mountains beyond - that's the beauty of this park. Not for the faint of heart, but heart smart, the almost 300 steps up the 511-foot peak are not evenly or easily spaced as some are wider apart and some are taller to step up onto, but it sure is a popular place to come, even at sunrise (I can attest). Walk up a little farther (you've already come this far) and along a dirt trail to the attractive visitor's center (which has a bathroom - bonus!). If don't want to go back down the same way, there is a one-mile trail at the east end of the center that winds back down via switchbacks that are still steep, but not as directly steep as the staircase. You can also walk down the paved road that cars take to get to the top. Parking is at the bottom of the hill, for walkers, and at the top, near the visitors center, for those who just want to soak in the view. Note that CULVER CITY PARK (pg. 54) is nearby.

Hours: Open daily, 8am - sunset. The visitor center is open Fri. - Mon., 9am - 4pm.

Price: Free. Parking in the lot at the top of the hill is $2 an hour; $6 for the day. There is some free street parking down below.

Ages: 8 years and up.

BELLFLOWER SKATE PARK and CARUTHERS PARK

(562) 866-5684 or (562) 804-1424 / www.bellflower.org

10500 Flora Vista Street at Caruthers Park, Bellflower

 This 8,000 square-foot, supervision-free park features benches, ramps, rails, a curb, pyramid, snake run, hips, and bowls. A helmet and pads are encouraged. The adjacent, 20-acre, frequently-used Caruthers Park offers access to the bike path that runs along the riverbed (see BIKE TRAIL: LOS ANGELES RIVER TRAIL (pg. 210)); large grassy areas; picnic tables; barbecue pits; swing sets and other playground equipment (I like the four interconnected ponies that you can ride and bounce on); a grouping of exercise/fitness equipment; lighted tennis, basketball, volleyball and handball courts; lighted ballfields; and a wading pool for kiddies that's open the summer.

Hours: Open daily, sunrise - sunset.

Price: Free

Ages: All

BIXBY MARSHLAND

(562) 908-4288 / www.lacsd.org

24501 S. Figueroa Street, Carson

 Unexpected, so close to the freeway, this restored 17-acre marshland is a unique habitat and lovely spot for numerous species of plants, as well as birds, lizards, frogs, turtles and other critters as well as humans to enjoy. As you walk the trails and over the bridges near the ponds and through the trees and brush, you'll learn about its inhabitants via a naturalist-led guided tour. It's a breath of fresh air in the city of Carson.

Hours: Open for tours, the only way to experience the marshland, the first Sat. of every month, 8am - noon. Schedule group tours by appointment.

Price: Free

Ages: 4 years and up.

BRAND PARK

(818) 548-3782 / www.glendaleca.gov

1601 W. Mountain Street, Glendale

 The front part of this thirty-acre park is composed of green lawns, playgrounds, a few basketball courts, volleyball courts, a seasonal wading pool for kids, and picnic tables. The back part, behind the museum and library, is a huge hilly area with miles of dirt and asphalt hiking trails (and for mountain bikers who like a real workout) that lead through a chaparral into the Verdugo Mountains and around a reservoir. An almost three-mile fire road "trail" starts on the asphalt road up the hill and to the left of the fire road fork. There is a great view from the top. The park sees a lot of action on the weekends. Look up THE DOCTORS HOUSE MUSEUM (pg. 106) as it, and the beautiful adjacent Glendale Library, are located in the park.

Hours: The park is open daily, 7am - 10pm.

Price: Free

Ages: All

BROOKSIDE PARK - REESE'S RETREAT

(626) 744-7500 / ww5.cityofpasadena.net

360 N. Arroyo Boulevard, Pasadena

This large - 62 acre - park is located in the middle of the Arroyo Seco, an eight-mile natural area with a river, wildlife, woods, meadows, trails, and much, much more. It is also just south of KIDSPACE CHILDREN'S MUSEUM (pg. 125). Its amenities include a fitness trail, five tennis courts, three baseball fields with stadium seating and lights, a basketball court, soccer and football fields, horseshoe pits, a swimming pool, and a wonderful, piratey playground.

Although there are two other playgrounds, the universally accessible, pirate-themed playground, called Reese's Retreat, is kind of hidden, making it a more special find: It is near the Aquatics Center. It features a large pirate boat that is anchored in blue padding with sea creatures emblazoned on them, including sharks at the end of the low planks. Play in, on, and under the boat with its periscopes, cannons, ropes and chains to climb, plus ramps, slides, swings, pirate maps, and sea creatures to ride. Just off this main area is a stack of cannon balls; a ride that sways back and forth, and one that spins; and a shipwrecked water play area with a treasure chest that shoots water into an adjacent large sandbox. Bring buckets and shovels. Expect the kids to get wet because of the little shallow pool area and small fountains.

Enjoy the walking, running and bike trails; trees; lots of grassy areas; picnic tables; and bbq areas and mountain scenery. Note that the twenty-three-hole Oak Grove Disc Course (the first permanent disc golf course in the world!) is located in the upper Arroyo Seco, in Hahamongna Watershed Park which is north of the 210 freeway, at 4550 Oak Grove Drive. The course is played through mature oak trees, over rocks and throughout the Arroyo's natural elements.

Hours: Open daily, 6am - 10pm.

Price: Free

Ages: All

CASTAIC LAKE RECREATION AREA

(661) 257-4050 - lake information; (661) 775-6232 - boat rentals / parks.lacounty.gov; www.castaiclake.com; www.rockymountainrec.com

32132 Ridgeroute Road and Lake Hughes, Castaic

There are so many ways to play in the great outdoors at the massive (8,000 acres) Castaic Lake Recreation Area! The gigantic, upper lake is mostly for motorized watercraft (jet skis, etc.) and fishing - both the lake and lagoon are stocked with rainbow trout and bass. A California state fishing license is needed for those who are over 16 years old. Boating activities are available in the Lower Lake (i.e. the lagoon), too, as is aluminum boats rentals. Life-guarded swimming at the lagoon (i.e. swim beaches), with its small sandy beaches (which can get very crowded), is a great and refreshing summertime activity.

The "typical" park part is wonderfully huge and fun. There are acres and acres of rolling, grassy hills spotted with all kinds of shade, pine and other trees, plus paved pathways meandering and crisscrossing all over the park. Just beyond the dam are fire roads and dirt hiking/biking trails - up to seven miles of trails, with three access points. The trails range from an easy stroll to rugged hikes. Maps are available. There is also a horseshoe pit here.

There are plenty of picnic tables and some great playgrounds which all differ from one another. At the northern end of the lagoon, one playground is kind of an abstract metal configuration with some ropes and hoops to climb on and through; another has the metal frame of a ship with a two-story cabin in middle with slides and steps and poles to play in and under; and another is comprised of big, flatish rocks to climb up that also have double ropes connecting them to tightrope walk on. The latter also has some fake logs and other scattered "rocks" - imaginative play! Another great playground is located at the southern end of the park - it is a big, multi-story structure with all the newest and best amenities.

Come spend the night around the corner and up the road at one of sixty standard campsites that features both tent and RV camping; no hook up. Several sites overlook the lagoon. However long you choose to visit, an escape to Castaic Lake fits all your recreational desires!

Hours: Open daily, sunrise - sunset. Closed Christmas. The swim lagoon is open Memorial Day - Labor Day, Thurs. - Sun., 10am - 5pm.

Price: $11 per vehicle; $5 for seniors on weekdays - cash only! November - February the entry fee is waived Mon. - Fri. Camping is $20 a night. A fourteen-foot aluminum, nine-horse-power boat rents for $35 for two hours and $55 for the day during the week; $35 for two hours and $78 for the day on the weekends. Seniors get a discount.

Ages: All

CASTRO CREST

(818) 880-0367 / www.nps.gov; www.lamountains.com; www.localhikes.com

Corral Canyon Road, Malibu

My kids jumped out of the almost-stopped car and made a bee-line for the rock formations directly in front of us, the tallest of which they dubbed Pride Rock. A variety of moderately difficult trails lead hikers past just a few more formations. The trails roller-coaster either along the ridgeline offering panoramic views, on fire roads, or on roads that cut through a gorge. Although the green, velvety-looking hills were covered with trees when we visited, we found relatively little shade along the trails we walked. Note that Backbone Trail, a trail that extends nearly seventy miles across and through the Santa Monica Mountains, is part of the Castro Crest trail system. For more information on Backbone, call the Santa Monica Mountains National Recreation Area at (805) 370-2301 or www.nps.gov/samo. Also note that there are no restroom facilities here. Tip: Bring your own water.

Hours: Open daily, 8am - sunset.

Price: Free

Ages: 6 years and up.

CERRITOS REGIONAL COUNTY PARK / CERRITOS SPORTS COMPLEX / DON KNABE COMMUNITY REGIONAL PARK

(562) 924-5144 - regional park; (562) 407-2611 - Cerritos Park East; (562) 916-8590 - sports complex; (562) 809-8079 - tennis center; (562) 403-7498 - pool; (562) 916-1254 - skate park / www.cerritos.us

19900 & 19700 Bloomfield Avenue, Cerritos

I've combined three different parks into one entry (as you can see by the entry title) as they are adjacent to one another and seemingly indistinct from each other. Fourteen lighted tennis courts (free, or $5 an hour for a reserved court); several baseball diamonds with stadium seating and lights; six soccer fields; basketball courts; a few playgrounds with mostly traditional equipment; an area with almost gym-worthy exercise equipment; a walking/running track; a good-sized lake (fishing is permitted); a swimming pool (open seasonally, to Cerritos residents and their guests, only); several, immense, open grassy areas; picnic tables and shelters; cement pathways that crisscross throughout; and a large, outdoor skate park make these parks a delight for the whole family.

The gated, 10,000-square-foot concrete skate park has a grinding pole, pools, ramps, bowls, and a small fish bowl. The posted rules (enforced by patrolling policemen who <u>do</u> give out citations) state that skaters (no bikes allowed) must wear a helmet and elbow and knee pads. Aluminum benches are available for visitors and tired skaters. My kids love to skate and rollerblade here - I just don't like the foul language that is often prevalent.

Hours: The park is open daily, dawn - dusk. The skate park is open Mon., 11am - dusk; Tues. - Sun., 8am - dusk. It's closed on some holidays. The pool is open toward the end of June through August.

Price: Free. The pool is $2 and for residents only.

Ages: All

CHANTRY FLAT - STURTEVANT FALLS

(818) 899-1900 - park; (626) 447-7356 - pack station / www.bigsantaanitacanyon.com; www.adamspackstation.com; www.fs.fed.us

Santa Anita Avenue, Los Angeles

Take the Gabrielino Trail about a mile-and-a-half into the tree-lined Big Santa Anita Canyon. Cross the Winter Creek Bridge up the trail and go straight through the three-way junction. Ford the creek, then re-cross it where it takes a sharp bend to the left, and scramble over boulders to reach the foot of Sturtevant Falls, a fifty-five-foot cascading waterfall. Note that climbing up the waterfall can be dangerous. The small rocky pool at the top of Hermit Falls, about 2 miles from Chantry, is just right for wading or just a dip. Depending which trail you take, it will be 6 to 7 miles to loop back. The canyon is beautiful - oak trees line the stream bed, along with maples and spruce trees. There are numerous other hiking trails to take in the immediate area (over forty miles), depending on how far you want to go.

The Adams' Pack Station at Chantry Flat offers a general store and a great historic place as this might be the last pack station of its kind in the U.S. The people at the station deliver supplies by donkey year-round to a community up the hill accessible only by footpath. If you, or a group of your friends, really want to get away from it all (and I mean no cell phone service, too), consider renting a cabin at Sturtevant Camp, which includes a hike in twice as far as the falls (about 3 hours). Pack in your stuff or have the Pack Station do it for you. See their website for full details.

Hours: Open daily, 6am - 8pm. The pack station/general store is open Fri. - Sun., 7am - 5pm.

Price: Hiking is $5 per vehicle to park for an Adventure Pass, available at the general store when they're open, and elsewhere.

Ages: 7 years and up.

CHARLES WILSON PARK

(310) 328-5310 or (310) 328-4964 / www.torranceca.gov; www.southerncalifornialivesteamers.org
2200 Crenshaw Boulevard, Torrance

This large, elongated park has a delightful, sand-based playground for younger children with its twisty slides, swings, and animals on giant springs to ride back and forth on. The park also has a roller hockey rink that is available by reservation; four baseball diamonds; grassy "fields"; gently rolling hills lined with shade trees; stroller-friendly pathways that crisscross throughout; a horseshoe court in the northeast corner; several tennis courts; paddle tennis courts; basketball courts; sand volleyball courts; a fitness course; a fountain in the middle of the wading pond that ducks are very fond of; and a huge treehouse. The elevated treehouse is wheelchair accessible with wooden ramps going in every direction - what fun!

On select weekends of each month, the Southern California Live Steamers Club offers free rides on their electric, steam, or diesel-powered scale trains. The train goes through a little wooded section which make is seem like more of an adventure. Every Tuesday and Saturday a Farmer's Market is held in the main parking lot from 8am to 1pm.

Hours: The park is open daily, 6am - 10pm. Train rides are offered the first Sun., 11am - 3pm and the third Sat., noon - 3pm.
Price: Free
Ages: All

CHARMLEE WILDERNESS PARK

(323) 221-9944 or (310) 457-7247 / www.lamountains.com; www.malibucity.org
2577 Encinal Canyon Road, Malibu

Explore the wilds of Malibu (and Malibu can be wild!) via Charmlee Park. The park is 532 acres with eight miles of dirt and fire road hiking trails that meander through the Santa Monica Mountains. Visitors enjoy magnificent views of the coastline, as well as experience oak woodland areas, meadows, chaparral, some interesting rock formations, and seasonal wildflowers. Most of the trails are fairly easy. Download a map route from the website before you head out. There are numerous picnic tables amongst the grove of trees toward the entrance, plus ones that overlook the ocean. A small nature center is the headquarters for several educational programs. Note that docents lead hikes with school children in grades K - 12 on Thursday mornings.

Hours: The park is open daily, 8am - sunset. The nature center is open Sat. - Sun., 9am - 5pm.
Price: $4 per vehicle, bring dollar bills.
Ages: 4 years and up.

CHATSWORTH PARK

(818) 341-6595 - both; (818) 756-8189 - north; (818) 341-6596 - south / www.lamountains.com; www.laparks.org
22360 Devonshire (South) or 22300 Chatsworth (North), Chatsworth

There are two Chatsworth parks; a north and a south. The north park has gigantic, sprawling, and climbable old oak trees; a lot of picnic tables under the trees; a rundown baseball diamond; a play area with some equipment (I like the play cannon); a basketball court; a volleyball court; some pathways to explore; and a small hill with a group of boulders to climb around on. Note: Don't go up on the rocks on the northern hills of rocks - it's not safe.

Chatsworth Park South offers two tennis courts; a basketball court; a more up-to-date playground (with climbing apparatus, slides, swings, and some interactive, creative elements); open grassy areas; a community center building that offers lots of activities (including a wheelchair hockey league); a small natural stream running throughout; and picnic tables. There are a few trails around the perimeter of the park, some of which lead into to the surrounding rocks.

Hours: The parks are open daily, sunrise - sunset.
Price: Free
Ages: All

CHEESEBORO CANYON

(818) 597-9192 or (805) 370-2301 / www.nps.gov/samo; www.localhikes.com
5792 Chesebro Road, Agoura Hills

Hike or bike on the numerous dirt trails here that go through canyons, grasslands, and riparian areas. The road most traveled is the one immediately accessible; the Cheeseboro Canyon Trail. The hike starts off moderately easy along a streambed and through a valley of oak trees. A picnic area is about a mile-and-a-half from the parking lot. Stop here, or continue on to more strenuous hiking. Bring your own water! You'll reach Sulphur Springs (almost another two miles), where the smell of rotten eggs lets you know you've arrived. This particular trail goes on for another mile through a variety of terrain. Several trails branch off and connect to the Cheeseboro Trail. Note that on weekends mountain bikers tend to take over the trails. Pick up a trail map at the SANTA MONICA MOUNTAINS NATIONAL PARK HEADQUARTERS - VISITORS CENTER (Anthony C. Beilenson Interagency Visitor Center) (pg. 85), which is down the road a bit.

Hours: Open daily, 8am - sunset.
Price: Free
Ages: 6 years (for shorter hikes) and up.

CHEVIOT HILLS RECREATION AREA

(310) 837-5186 - park; (310) 202-2844 - pool; (310) 836-8879 - tennis / www.laparks.org
2551 Motor Avenue, Los Angeles

This large park really fits the bill of a recreation area with its basketball courts (indoor and outdoor), volleyball courts (indoor), baseball diamonds, tennis courts, and gated, somewhat shaded playground. It has twisty slides, bridges, tubes, rings, leaf stepping pads, and multi-level structures, plus a separate little playhouse, a sandbox and more. During the hot summer months, when kids have played hard and need to cool off, they can take a dip in the outdoor, municipal swimming pool.

Hours: The park is open Mon. - Fri., 9am - 10:30pm; Sat. - Sun., 9am - 7pm. Summer sessions for the pool are Mon. - Fri., 10am - 1pm and 2pm - 5pm; Sat. - Sun., 1pm - 5pm.
Price: The park is free. Each swim session costs $2 for adults; ages 17 and under are free.
Ages: All

CLAREMONT SKATE PARK and CAHUILLA PARK

(909) 399-5460 / www.ci.claremont.ca.us; www.socalskateparks.com
1717 N. Indian Hill Boulevard, Claremont

This medium-sized, concrete skate park has a bowl, grinding poles, grinding boxes, and some flat area to skate and gain momentum. Lights make it one of the few skate parks available at nighttime (although they don't always work). Wearing a helmet and knee and elbow pads is required. The rest of the park offers shade trees, lots of grassy space, picnic areas, and eight tennis courts, baseball fields, a basketball court, and a playground.

Hours: Open daily, 6am - 10pm.
Price: Free
Ages: 7 years and up.

COLDWATER CANYON PARK / TREEPEOPLE

(818) 753-4600 or (818) 623-4845 / www.treepeople.org; www.lamountains.com
12601 Mulholland Drive, Los Angeles

The 45-acre Coldwater Canyon Park is beautiful, with large oak and California bay laurel trees that shade the meandering trails, making this a sanctuary for nature. Some of the five miles of hiking trails are covered with sawdust and small broken twigs - great for walking, though bumpy for strollers - and some are hard-packed dirt. Most of the trails, including two that immediately branch off in opposite directions, eventually lead up along hillsides, affording hikers great vistas of the valley and mountains beyond. A very short hike from the main building leads up to a shaded overlook that has picnic tables.

If you and your kids are concerned about environmental issues, come visit the TreePeople, whose headquarters are in the park. This organization is dedicated to replenishing the diminishing number of trees and to encouraging recycling. Visit the greenhouse and walk through a part of a drainage tube to a watershed garden with a small scale river that flows and shows how modifications to it can help rain have a healthy impact our immediate environment. School groups and individuals can check out the educational resource center and sign up for a guided eco-tour and hike, such as the monthly Moonlight Hikes, to learn about conservation and sustainable living, as well as the importance of planting trees in areas damaged by pollution. Interactive games are sometimes offered to children, especially for the Family Hikes, as they explore and hike the trails.

Hours: The park is open daily, 6:30am - sunset. Call to make a reservation for a TreePeople tour.
Price: The park and parking is free. Tours are usually $5 per person for nonmembers; some activities are free.
Ages: 6 years and up.

CULVER CITY PARK

(310) 253-6650 or (310) 253-6470 / www.culvercity.org

9700 Jefferson Boulevard, Culver City

This is one fine city park! The playground is the newer style with free-thinking play apparatus and several independent units. It has polygon spheres with rock-climbing holds; poles that spin; cargo netting and metal bars in assorted shapes to climb; a few slides; rides on huge springs; elevated sand containers (that are wheelchair friendly) attached to a water pipe; and a few swings. Adjacent to the playground are two spots of green lawn with big shade trees, picnic tables, barbeque pits, two half-court basketball courts, and a great skate park.

The enclosed 1,300-square foot skate park features a Trog Bowl, Waterfall, Hubba Ledge, Ramp, Pier 7 Block, Wall Ride, 90 degree banked hip (all terminology that will mean something to your pro-skater wanna-be), and more street features making this place a hit for skaters. Although unsupervised, we saw all the skaters wearing helmets and pads - yea! - as the posted sign states is required.

Across Duquesne Avenue the park continues with a long, raised, wood-slat trail and wood fencing that is ADA accessible (and looks really cool). The interpretative trail/boardwalk zig zags through trees and hillside up to the next level, to baseball diamonds and a soccer field, and a great view. Note that back at ground level is The Boneyard, a good-sized dog park with all the accouterments a canine could want. Really close by is BALDWIN HILLS SCENIC OVERLOOK (pg. 49) and STAR ECO STATION (pg. 229).

Hours: The park is open daily, sunrise - sunset. The skate park is open Mon. - Fri., noon - 7pm or sunset, whichever comes first; Sat. - Sun., 9:30am - 4:30pm.

Price: Free

Ages: All

DEL VALLE PARK

(562) 866-9771 / www.lakewoodcity.org

5939 Henrilee Street, Lakewood

Known as "Airplane Park" because of the Douglas F3D "Skynight" jet fighter perched on a pedestal, this park celebrates community life via special events offered here, a seasonal wading pool, horseshoe pits, a Vietnam War Memorial, grassy areas and picnic tables, and a terrific airplane-themed playground. It features the frame of a grounded airplane on a runway that's fun to play in - it even has a captain and co-pilots seats (with a pseudo instrument board) and a climbing wall on its tail. There are smaller airplanes to sit on and ride, too. A large and long elevated "airport" structure has ramps, slides, rock climbing, bars, games (with wheels and gears and moveable parts), play space underneath, a cave, and even a control tower. The playground also has a rope climbing contraption, other climbing walls, zipline, swings, stools with poles, and some other free-standing, fun units.

The park features another, smaller playground that has a good-sized play fire truck with slides, a ladder, and wheels to crawl thru, and some other more traditional equipment such as swings, a play house, and objects to ride on for little kids. There are grassy areas to run around, baseball fields, basketball courts and bbqs. You'll be glad you came in for a landing at Airplane Park.

Hours: Open daily, sunrise - sunset.

Price: Free

Ages: 18 months - 12 years.

DESCANSO GARDENS

(818) 949-4200 - garden; (818) 949-0120 - tour info; (818) 790-3663 - cafe / www.descansogardens.org $$$

1418 Descanso Drive, La Canada

Descanso Gardens is over 150-acres of incredible beauty. It's not just a bed of roses here though, as there are acres of lilacs, camellias, tulips, dogwood, California poppies, and other flowers also bloom. Although flowers do bloom here year round, you can call for a specific bloom schedule. A network of stroller-friendly trails wind through the grounds and around the pond, which is an enchanting destination. One trail that is particularly delightful goes through a forest of mature California oaks. The edible garden looks good enough to eat, but don't. The fruit trees (such as apples, orange, and pomegranates) and seasonal vegetables (including pumpkins, corn, and squash), along with herbs and edible flowers, are enclosed by vines trellises, arches, bushes, and other greenery. There are also open grassy areas to run around, chaparrals to explore, and a bird observatory station overlooking a lake. Hop aboard a five-minute model train ride - the Enchanted Railroad - for a kid-oriented trip.

The tranquil Japanese garden is intriguing because of its unique, maze-like layout. It also has ponds and a stream. Be on the lookout for squirrels and for more than 150 species of land and water birds, as this is their haven. (You don't have to find all 150.)

Ask about summer camps for kids and the numerous educational programs offered throughout the year - there is even one for toddlers. Hour-and-a-half guided tours are offered for school groups and other groups with advance registration. On a hilltop above the Gardens is the historic and elegant Boddy House - a museum and interpretive center for the history of this area.

Sandwiches, wraps, salads, fruit and other lunch options, including homemade desserts and ice cream, are available at the cafe daily, 9am to 4:30pm, with lovely outside seating. The Japanese Tea Garden in the Full Moon Teahouse is open in the summer only. Call (818) 790-3663 for more info. Or, bring your own food and use the picnic grounds outside the garden, adjacent to the parking lot.

Hours: The gardens are open daily, 9am - 5pm. Closed Christmas. Train rides are available Tues. and Fri., 10am - noon; Sat. - Sun., 10am - 4pm.

Price: $9 for adults; $6 for seniors and students; $4 for ages 5 - 12; children 4 and under are free. Admission is free on the third Tuesday of each month. The train ride is $3 per person. See American Horticultural Society (pg. x) for info on reciprocal memberships.

Ages: 2½ years and up.

DEVIL'S PUNCHBOWL

(661) 944-2743 / parks.lacounty.gov; www.localhikes.com

28000 Devil's Punchbowl Road, Pearblossom

The "punchbowl" is a spectacular geological formation that looks like a huge, jagged bowl created from rocks. The 1,310-acre park consists of rugged wilderness rock formations along the San Andreas Fault, plus a seasonal stream. The hiking trails vary in degree of difficulty. We hiked down into the punchbowl and back up along the one-mile Loop Trail in about half an hour. The eight mile, or so, (round-trip) hike to Devil's Chair and back is obviously tougher. The terrain is diverse, ranging from desert plants to pine trees, as the elevation changes from 4,200 feet to 6,500 feet. Rock climbing is a popular sport here, whether you prefer climbing on boulders or scaling sheer rock walls.

The nature center museum contains a small number of taxidermied animals and displays that pertain to this region, as well as a few live rattlesnakes, boas, scorpions, ant colonies, bees, and some insects. Outside, the center houses a few live birds, such as barn and great-horned owls. The park also offers picnic areas and equestrian trails, and is host to many special events throughout the year. School field trips are welcome.

Hours: The park is open daily, sunrise - sunset. The nature center is open Tues. - Sun., 9am - 5pm. Closed Mon. and Christmas.

Price: Free

Ages: 5 years and up.

DEY REY LAGOON PARK

(310) 836-1040 / www.laparks.org

6660 Esplanade Street, Playa Del Rey

Come play in Playa Del Rey at this little hidden gem of a park. It has a ball field and basketball court, plus palm trees, run-around space of grass and sand that borders a long lagoon which is home to lots of birds and ducks, and a playground. The playground has swings, a free-standing rock climbing rock "wall", slides, fun play structures with climbing elements, platforms, rings, a play ship and more. It's the setting, as well as the amenities, that make this park a winner. Also see FISHERMAN'S VILLAGE and surrounding area (pg. 159) for others things to do and see in the immediate vicinity. Note that Dockweiler Beach is just down the road.

Hours: Open daily, sunrise - sunset.

Price: Free

Ages: All

DOUGLAS PARK

(310) 458-8310 or (310) 458-8300 / www.smgov.net

2439 Wilshire Boulevard and 25th Street, Santa Monica

This pleasant respite is just off a busy street. At the northern end is a wonderful playground for young children with a tennis court on either side. In the center of the park is a little nature area with a pond (and ducks, of course) and a cluster of trees. An expanse of lawn, a smaller pond, shaded concrete pathways throughout, and bridges add to the specialness of this park. One wooden picnic table is built around a mature, shade tree and another is built around, and almost into, a large boulder. Another unique feature is a very shallow concrete "pool" used for trikes and skaters, although not at the same time. In the summer, a few fountains shoot water up here at unexpected intervals, providing a refreshing way to cool off and eliciting giggles.

Hours: Open daily, sunrise - sunset.
Price: Free
Ages: 1 - 10 years old.

DRY TOWN WATER PARK AND MINING CO. and PALMDALE OASIS PARK AND RECREATION CENTER

See DRY TOWN WATER PARK AND MINING CO. and PALMDALE OASIS PARK AND RECREATION CENTER (pg. 2), under AMUSEMENT PARKS, for details about the park.

!/$$$

EARL BURNS MILLER JAPANESE GARDENS

(562) 985-8885 / www.csulb.edu/~jgarden

$$

1250 Bellflower Boulevard at Earl Warren Drive on the campus of California State University Long Beach, Long Beach

This beautiful, one-acre Japanese garden has two waterfalls, a meditation rock garden, a quaint teahouse (to look in), and a koi pond. Kids can help feed the koi, so bring a quarter for the food dispenser. As you cross over the zigzag bridge into the gardens, share with your kids that it was built in this shape to sidestep spirits because, according to Japanese tradition, spirits can only travel in straight lines! $1 per person guided tours are provided for school and educational groups. The garden is ADA accessible.

Hours: Open Tues - Fri., 9am - 4pm; Sun., noon - 4pm. Closed Mon., Sat., spring break, Thanksgiving, winter break, and state furlough days (check the website calendar).
Price: $5 for adults; $4 for seniors; $2 for ages 4 - 18; children under 4, SCULB students and faculty are free. Park on the street or use metered parking (to your right) in Student Lot 16.
Ages: 3 years and up.

EAST AND RICE CANYONS

(310) 589-3200 or (310) 858-7272 / www.lamountains.com; www.localhikes.com

!

24255 The Old Road, Newhall

A year-round stream and a wide variety of plants and trees line trails that lead hikers away from city life and straight into nature. The Rice Canyon Loop Trail is a round trip of a little over two miles. It is a moderate walk that gets harder toward the end as it goes uphill. The trail follows along the stream and crosses over it a few times. If you smell petroleum, it's not coming from cars, but from natural oil seeping near the creek. This area was once part of an oil boom town. The East Canyon trail is almost four miles round trip. As you go steadily up in elevation, you'll pant harder, but you'll also see big-cone Douglas-fir trees and vistas of the Santa Clarita Valley. Be on the lookout for wildlife such as deer, foxes, skunks, and an abundance of birds. This trail doesn't loop, so I hope you like the way you came, because you get the opportunity to see it all again! Or, continue further up and further in as there are many more miles of trails to explore. Also look up ED DAVIS PARK IN TOWSLEY CANYON (pg. 57).

Hours: Open daily, sunrise - sunset.
Price: Free
Ages: 3 years and up.

EATON CANYON COUNTY PARK

(626) 398-5420 / www.ecnca.org; www.lamountains.com

!

1750 N. Altadena Drive, Pasadena

Located in the foothills of the mountains, this 190-acre wilderness park has several rugged dirt trails leading up into the mountains. One of the most popular hikes starts at the nature center and continues a little over a mile on an easy trail through oak and sycamore trees to the Mt. Wilson toll bridge. If you feel like pushing it a bit, take the ½-mile stretch past the bridge with some creek crossings and climbing over boulders up to Eaton Falls, where a 50-foot waterfall and large shallow pool could greet you (depending on the prior rainfall). Hardy hikers can take a trail up to Mt. Wilson, a "mere" ten-mile hike. Approximately two-thirds of this park was burned in a 1993 brush fire. As the slopes and flats continue (still!) to recover from the fire, new plant growth continues to restore the park's beauty and this is marked along the Fire Ecology Trail. There are shorter trails in the immediate vicinity of the nature center. One such trail is only a quarter of a mile and has a self-guiding pamphlet (pick it up from the nature center) that helps identify the plants. The first (and most important) plant to recognize is poison oak.

The Eaton Canyon Wash (river bed) is filled with rocks and is fun to explore - when it's dry, of course. Eaton Creek usually flows through the canyon, except during the summer months. Pretty, shaded, and almost hidden picnic areas are found just off the parking lot. Remember to B.Y.O.W. - Bring Your Own Water.

The nicely laid-out nature center contains display cases that hold rocks and animal skulls, mounted insects, and several stuffed birds such as a great horned owl, quail, and a hummingbird. A diorama of the area is complete with a (stuffed) crouching mountain lion peering down. There are also several cases of live critters - snakes, including a rattlesnake, plus lizards, tree frogs, scorpions, and more. A few cubicles contain books, animal puppets, and some games. A 3-D map of the park shows the area's trails. Outside, a 150-seat amphitheater is the setting for environmental programs. The park offers many special events, such as free family nature walks which are given every Saturday from 9am to 11am, and tours for school children.

Hours: The park and trails are open daily, 7:30am - 5pm. The nature center is open Tues. - Sun., 9am - 5pm. It's closed Mon. (except Mon. holidays), New Year's Day, Thanksgiving, and Christmas.

Price: Free

Ages: 3 years and up.

ECHO PARK

(213) 250-3578; (213) 847-0095 / www.laparks.org; www.wheelfunrentals.com   !/$$$$

1632 Bellevue Avenue, Los Angeles

This iconic lake/park is right between the freeway and an older, lower income Los Angeles neighborhood, with city skyscrapers in the background. The long, man-made lake, which is occasionally stocked with trout (you can fish here), has a cement pathway looping all around it (about a mile, or so), as well as some shade trees and palm trees, park benches and picnic tables, and some grassy, run-around space. The north end also has a bridge on it that reaches over to a small island and an enclosed playground. There is a little cafe along the lakeside, too.

If you want to get closer to the three fountains in the lake that shoot water up (really high!), or if you just want to toodle around and get some exercise, rent a swan pedal boat for $11 an hour for adults; $6 an hour for ages 2 to 17 years. The lake is home to turtles, visiting ducks and other waterfowl and birds, and to lotus plants/pads that burst into beautiful flower in the late spring thru summer time. They are especially celebrated every July in the Lotus Festival.

Across the street and right next to the freeway is the Echo Park Recreation Center and a park. The park boasts a standard, but fun playground with lots of swings, too - all in sand; some picnic tables with shade trees; and six lighted tennis courts. Note: Just down the street at 1419 Colton Street is an indoor swimming pool that is open year round for lap and recreational swim. The cost is $2.50 for adults per session; seniors and ages 17 and under are free. Call (213) 481-2640 for more info.

Hours: The park is open daily, sunrise - sunset. Call for hours for specific activities. Swan pedal boat rentals are available daily, 9am - sunset, weather permitting.

Price: Free

Ages: All

ED DAVIS PARK IN TOWSLEY CANYON

(661) 255-2974 / www.lamountains.com   !

24335 The Old Road, Newhall

This beautiful mountain wilderness park contains some special geological structures. First, visit the nature center, located near Canyon View Loop Trail / Wiley Canyon trailhead, which contains displays on the history of the park. These include old photographs, taxidermied animals, and artifacts from the days when this area was an oil boom town. A picnic area and restrooms are here, too. Hiking trails range from easy to difficult. The two-mile Canyon View loop trail is a mostly moderate hike with a few short, steep grades. The five+ mile Towsley View Loop Trail definitely has more strenuous grades, plus varying scenery. This trail parallels the creek as it goes past grassy areas, up to the Narrows (where there are unique, nearly vertical rock formations), and old oil drilling grounds. The view from the top can be spectacular on a clear day. Be on the lookout for seasonal wildflowers, plus valley and coastal live oak trees, and animals that share this habitat. Also see EAST AND RICE CANYONS (pg. 56), as that park is just down the road.

Hours: Open daily, sunrise - sunset.

Price: Free

Ages: 3 years and up.

EL DORADO EAST REGIONAL PARK

(562) 570-1771 / www.longbeach.gov/park $$

7550 E. Spring Street, Long Beach

El Dorado has hundreds of acres of lush green park with lots for kids to do! There are two stocked fishing lakes that also have ducks clamoring for handouts. The park has a model glider field, several playgrounds, and four-and-a-half miles of paved biking/running/stroller trails, including access to the San Gabriel River cement embankment. The park has a nature feel, but is adjacent to the freeway so you hear and see the cars. The archery range provides targets, but you must bring your own equipment. Note that free archery instruction, for all levels, is available on Saturday mornings. A small, enclosed dog park is also here. Pedal boats, which can hold up to four people per, rent here for $8 per half hour. Rentals are available on weekends, 11am to 5pm, most of the year (closed November through January). Call (562) 824-7717 for more info. If you want to rent a bike contact Wheel Fun at (562) 400-8923. They are open weekends and holidays year round, 10am to sunset. Cruiser bikes are $12 an hour; surreys, $25 an hour; etc. A one-mile, gasoline-powered, scale train ride, the El Dorado Express, runs Saturdays and Sundays, March through October from 10:30am to 4pm. The cost is $3 per person. Call (562) 824-7725 / www.caboosecorners.com for more information. Organized youth groups (which is an oxymoron) are invited to camp at the park overnight. You can be as active or relaxed as you want (or as the kids let you!) at El Dorado Park. Also see the following entries for EL DORADO NATURE CENTER and EL DORADO PARK WEST.

Hours: Open March - October, daily, 7am - 8pm; November - February, daily, 7am - 5pm. Closed Christmas.
Price: $5 per vehicle Mon. - Thurs.; $6 on Fri.; $7 on Sat. - Sun.; $8 on holidays. Entrance fee is good for a same-day visit to the Nature Center located across the street. Annual passes are $60; if you are 50+ years old or have a disabled placard, the pass is only $35.
Ages: All

EL DORADO NATURE CENTER

(562) 570-1745 / www.longbeach.gov/park
7550 E. Spring Street, Long Beach

The 105-acre El Dorado Nature Center is part of the El Dorado East Regional Park. When crossing over the wooden bridge leading to the museum and trail-heads, look down to see the many ducks and turtles swimming and sunbathing in the water below.

The Nature Center has skulls, antlers, and other artifacts to touch; bugs to look at under a magnifier; a few cases of live insects and reptiles; a display of feathers and wings; and a huge book depicting various animal habitats. Contact the center for information on their many terrific special programs such as educational field trips for schools, the Turtle and Reptile Show, and summer camps.

Walk over another bridge (lots more turtles in the water!) and onto a short, quarter-mile paved trail that good for strollers and wheelchairs. Or, walk the one or two-mile, mostly stroller-friendly, dirt trails that immerses you in nature as they go under and through pine, oak and other trees; wildflowers; over bridges; and wind around two ponds and alongside a stream. Be on the lookout for egrets and herons. These trails are very popular with walkers (no jogging allowed), and parents with kids. I know the freeway is close by, but I don't hear it here: I love being in God's beautiful creation! Picnicking is not allowed inside the Nature Center, but picnic tables and shade trees can be found outside the gates at the end of the parking lot. The Nature Center is truly "an oasis of greenery and woodland in the middle of Long Beach", and my local go-to place of refreshment. Also see EL DORADO EAST REGIONAL PARK and EL DORADO PARK WEST.

Hours: The trails and park are open Tues. - Sun., 8am - 5pm. The nature center is open Tues. - Sun., 8:30am - 4pm. The trails and center are closed Mon., New Year's Day, 4th of July, Thanksgiving and Christmas.
Price: $5 per vehicle Mon. - Thurs.; $6 on Fri.; $7 on Sat. - Sun.; $8 on holidays. Walk ins or bicyclists are free. Entrance fee is good for a same-day visit to El Dorado East Regional Park located across the street. Annual passes are $60; if you are 50+ years old or have a disabled placard, the pass is only $35.
Ages: All

EL DORADO PARK WEST

(562) 570-3225 - park; (562) 425-0553 - tennis courts / www.longbeach.gov/park; www.longbeachtennis.com
2800 Studebaker Road, Long Beach

This city park is just around the corner from its neighbors, EL DORADO EAST REGIONAL PARK and EL DORADO NATURE CENTER. (See above entries.) Sprawling across both sides of Willow Street, this huge park features lots of grassy areas; picnic tables under shade trees; a popular disc golf course; a couple of ponds with ducks; baseball diamonds; playgrounds (some old-school ones with metal vehicle frames); a large library; fifteen tennis courts; and an outdoor skate park. The concrete skate park offers street-type skating with ramps, bowls, grinding boxes, and more. Wearing safety equipment - a helmet and elbow and knee pads - is enforced.

Hours: Open daily, sunrise - sunset. The tennis courts are open Mon. - Fri., 7am - 9:30pm; Sat. - Sun., 7am - 8pm.
Price: Free to the park and skate park. Tennis courts are $8 per hour most daylight hours; $13 per hour after 4pm during the week, on weekends and on holidays.
Ages: All

ERNEST E. DEBS REGIONAL PARK / AUDUBON CENTER

Park - (213) 485-5054; Audubon Center - (323) 221-2255 / www.lamountains.com; debspark.audubon.org

Park - 4235 Monterey Road, Highland Park; Audubon Center - 4700 North Griffin Avenue, Los Angeles

Nearly 300 acres of nature - with California black walnut and oak woodland, hilly grassland, and coastal sage scrub - comprise this park in the otherwise asphalt-covered Los Angeles. The inner-city park features a fairly well-manicured area near the main entrance off Monterey Road. This section has a playground, baseball fields, 100 picnic tables, and twenty barbecue pits. The majority of the park, however, is untamed open space, with some hiking trails, and an abundance of wildlife, such as snakes, lizards, rabbit, raccoons, and coyotes. Families can participate in docent-led hikes or walk the almost nine miles of hilly dirt paths and fire roads at their leisure. Atop the hill is a pond/lake where locals often fish. (Look for dragonflies around here, too.)

The Audubon Center, located in the western side of the park, is a "green" center that hosts workshops, children's bird counts (there are about 138 species of birds within the park - can you find them all?), nighttime astronomy hikes, and a myriad of other educational programs. Inside are interactive displays such as listening to bird calls via the touch of a button and touching a hummingbird's nest. The center also loans out backpacks that contain activities for the great outdoors. Outside is a ¼-acre Woodland Play Area with a courtyard, a small pond, a children's garden, a native American hut, climbing trees, and picnic tables under shade. School tours are welcome.

Hours: The park is open daily, dawn - dusk. The Audubon Center is open April - October, Wed. - Sat., 9am - 5pm;
November - March, 8am - 4pm.

Price: Free

Ages: All

EXPOSITION PARK

(213) 744-7458 or (213) 763-0114 / www.laparks.org

701 State Street, Los Angeles

$$$

The expansive Exposition Park encompasses the CALIFORNIA AFRICAN AMERICAN MUSEUM (pg. 101), CALIFORNIA SCIENCE CENTER (pg. 102), IMAX THEATER (pg. 185), NATURAL HISTORY MUSEUM OF LOS ANGELES COUNTY (pg. 140), and Los Angeles Memorial Coliseum. Most of the park is simply grassy areas and trees, surrounding these attractions. More developed landscaping is just outside of the Natural History museum.

Enjoy the sunken Rose Garden, adjacent to the California Science Center, which has always been a *scent*ral part of the park. Its seven acres of beauty cultivates 16,000 specimens of 190 varieties of roses. (I bet your kids didn't know there are so many different varieties.) The gardens are wonderful for walking, smelling the perfumed air, and picture taking, plus it's stroller accessible. There is also a huge fountain in the middle of this park. Often on weekends, people of various nationalities have their wedding ceremonies in the garden. (We like looking at the different types of wedding attire.)

Hours: The rose garden is open daily, 9am - sunset. Closed January through mid-March for maintenance.

Price: Free. Parking in the lots is $12.

Ages: 3 years and up.

FORT TEJON STATE HISTORIC PARK

(661) 248-6692 / www.forttejon.org

4201 Fort Tejon Road, Lebec

$

A long time ago, when battles were fought here, the U.S. Dragoons were garrisoned at this fort. Near the entrance is a very small museum with several informational panels and a few military uniforms. Come and explore the long barracks building, walk through the officers' quarters that display war-time memorabilia, and pretend to shoot the cannons at unseen enemies. Portions of the fort are still intact, such as a few foundational remains of buildings and a small cemetery. There are plenty of picnic tables and wide-open grass areas, plus a few trails for hiking. Note: Primitive overnight camping is permitted here.

I highly recommend coming here when Frontier Army Days/Dragoon Living History Days are presented, or during Civil War Reenactments. Dragoon program activities, with a different focus every month, could include adobe brick making, playing old-fashioned games, participating in chores from days of yore, and more. Visitors could also see a blacksmith in action, open hearth cooking, military drills, and the everyday life of a soldier. During Civil War Reenactment days troops of the Union and Confederate armies are authentically uniformed and equipped. Meet soldiers and civilians, and tour their camps. See demonstrations of weapons and watch half-hour battle skirmishes at 10:30am, noon and at 1:30pm. Guided tours of the fort are given in between battles. Come see history in action.

Come <u>live</u> history in action by participating in a day and/or overnight program called Students Living History program. Kids will live life as it was in the 1800's and participate in activities at different stations. The price includes two meals and most program materials. Note: Teachers must attend a teacher training session first.

Hours: The grounds are open daily, sunrise - sunset. The buildings are open daily, 9am - 4pm. Closed New Year's Day, Thanksgiving, and Christmas. Dragoon Era Programs are the first Sat. of most months, 10am - 3pm. Civil War Reenactments are held a few times a year - check the website calendar. The student overnight program is usually offered March - June.

Price: Regular day use is $3 for adults; $1 for ages 7 - 17; children 6 and under are free. Frontier/Dragoon Days are $5 for adults; $2 for ages 7 - 17 and scouts in uniform; $14 for family (parents and all kids 17 and under). Civil War Reenactments, other battle enactment, and special events are $7 for adults; $3 for ages 7 - 17 and scouts in uniform. Tours are $7 for adults; $5 for students. The student overnight program is $25 for students; $15 for adults. Camping is usually $15 a vehicle.

Ages: 3 years and up.

FOX HILLS PARK

(310) 253-6650 or (310) 253-6470 / www.culvercity.org
6161 Buckingham Parkway, Culver City

    This attractive little park, surrounded on the street level by office buildings and condos, is tucked away on a hill and offers a pleasant respite from city life. The hillside is landscaped with flowers, bushes, and trees and has a packed-dirt jogging/walking trail winding all around it. Like a gym at a park, the isometric and resistance exercise equipment here allows visitors to get a real workout (if they actually use the machines!).

    For kids, and for those who work nearby and have extended lunchtime, the top of the hill has a sand volleyball court, a basketball court, several tennis courts, a large flat grassy area (baseball field!), climbing trees, picnic tables and a playground. Replacing more traditional equipment, this playground sports poles, bars, slides, great climbing structures, and other objects to encourage more creative play.

Hours: Open daily, 9am - 6pm.
Price: Free
Ages: All

FRANK G. BONELLI REGIONAL COUNTY PARK - PUDDINGSTONE LAKE

(909) 599-8411 / www.bonellipark.org; www.lacountyparks.org; www.sandimas.net
120 E. Via Verde Park Road, San Dimas

    This sprawling park (almost 2,000 acres!) is centered around the huge, man-made Puddingstone Lake Reservoir, which is an ideal water hole for all your fishing and boating desires. A fishing license is required for those over 16 years old. If the fish are biting, catch bass, catfish, crappie, carp, and trout. There are two fishing piers that go out a bit over the water. Feed the plentiful ducks and observe the wildlife at the lake area. We saw a heron and a crane, which my kids thought was pretty cool, plus lots of other birds and ducks. You can also launch your own boat here, but it must pass an inspection first. Jet skiing, fast boating, and water skiing are allowed on alternate days with personal water craft.

    A portion of the lake is sectioned off in the summer months for swimming. Lifeguards are on duty. There is a sandy beach here, as well, that gets very popular.

    The park boasts a vast amount of open, grassy space with trees and lots of picnic tables and BBQs. There are some great playgrounds here, too. One has a three-level play structure with tall slides, platforms to play on and under, "rock" climbing walls, metal spiral structures to climb, and toys on big springs to move back and forth on. Another is circular and has fake logs and lots of boulders with holes to climb through and over, plus sturdy ropes that connect the boulders - wonderful for cowboy or explorer play. One more play area worth mentioning looks like abstract art. It's made of rope structures, twisted shapes, poles (confused yet?), and more, all excellent for imaginations to soar.

    There are over fourteen miles of hiking and biking trails here. The scenery along the trails changes and ranges from cacti to pine trees - only in California!

Hours: Open March through September daily, sunrise - 9pm. Open October through February daily, sunrise - 7pm. Closed Christmas. The swim beach is open Memorial Day weekend through mid-June on weekends only; open mid-June through September, Thurs. - Sun., 10am - 6pm.

Price: March through October, $10 per vehicle daily. November through March, it is $10 on weekends and holidays, only, and $5 for seniors. Thus, it's free during the week.

Ages: All

FRANKLIN CANYON

(310) 858-7272 / www.lamountains.com

2600 Franklin Canyon Drive, Beverly Hills

Franklin Canyon, almost 600 acres in size, proves that there is more to Los Angeles than just skyscrapers. The lower canyon is the site of an old ranch house, which is now an office. A big, green lawn and a few picnic tables are the only things down here. Follow the creek along the mile-and-a-half trail leading to the Upper Canyon and the Nature Center. The canyon has a variety of trees such as California live oaks, black walnuts, and sycamores. Wildlife here includes deer, bobcats, coyotes, rabbits, and lizards. A moderate 2.3-mile trail, the Hastain Trail, leads to an overlook of the reservoir and summit of west Los Angeles and the coast. You'll pass an active apiary (i.e., bee houses) along the way. The Upper Reservoir has reverted to a natural lake and is a wetland area for herons and other waterfowl, as well as frogs. There are a few other, easier trails to hike, as well. Check out the "Heavenly Pond," a smaller nature section and pond accessible for persons with disabilities.

Inside the Sooky Goldman Nature Center are mounted displays of the type of animals that live in the canyon, such as mountain lions; a scale model of the Santa Monica Mountains; an interactive exhibit and dioramas on Native Americans; and an exhibit on the importance of water conservation. For your tactile child, there are fossils, antlers, furs, bones, and even a few bird's nests to touch.

This Center is also the headquarters of the William O. Douglas Outdoor Classroom, which is really the name for numerous, on-going, free nature programs. Docent-led tours are open for the general public daily. Tours are available for school groups, Wednesdays and Thursdays by reservation. There are several programs for all ages that range from a stroller-friendly walk on a paved trail and nature crafts, to Nearly Full Moon Hikes (geared for older kids to have a howling good time), to Family Campfires (in the summer) with singing, stories, and s'mores. Whatever you do, enjoy your day in the wilds of L.A.

Hours: The canyon entrance is open daily, sunrise - sunset. The Nature Center is open Wed. - Sun., 10am - 4pm. The center is closed on major holidays.

Price: Free

Ages: All

FRED HESSE JR. COMMUNITY PARK

(310) 544-5350 / www.rpvca.gov

29301 Hawthorne Boulevard, Rancho Palos Verdes

Behind the very nice community center, just down the steps, are a few playground areas cut into the slope of the hill with huge shade trees "covering" them. One play area has cement creatures to ride - a tortoise and dolphin. Another, larger playground has twisty slides, metal spiral elements to climb, wind chimes and pipes to play, and a short rock climbing wall, all in a sand base. Picnic tables and BBQ grills are clustered under a tightly bunched grouping of trees. The view from up here of the coastline just beyond the houses is stunning. This pretty park is popular on weekends.

An S-shaped, ¼-mile-dirt trail leads down the hill (that is brown and kind of ugly in the winter and a lovely green in the spring) - it's good for hiking or bike riding. At the level, base part of the trail and hill is a soccer field, baseball diamond, climbing trees, sand volleyball court, and more picnic tables.

Hours: Open Mon. - Fri., 9am - dusk; Sat. - Sun., 10am - dusk. Closed New Year's Day, Thanksgiving, and December 24 and 25.

Price: Free

Ages: All

GATES CANYON PARK / BRANDON'S VILLAGE

(818) 880-6461 / www.cityofcalabasas.com

25801 Thousand Oaks Boulevard, Calabasas

Gates Canyon Park is a seven-acre park with open grassy areas and mature trees surrounding and interspersed with a basketball court, tennis courts, fitness course, cement pathways, picnic tables, and BBQ pits. The featured attraction for youngsters is Brandon's Village, an expansive, boundless playground designed by the Shane's Inspiration organization. There are two main separate play areas created for both younger kids (in a sand base), bigger kids (in a rubber base) and kids with all abilities. Each play pavilion is shaded. There are long ramps, tubes, tunnels, slides, swings (some that accommodate wheelchairs), objects to ride on, short rock climbing walls, metal ladders (both horizontal and vertical) and poles, raised sand tables, sand digger tools, a big play ship that rocks back and forth, and a pretend horse stable that looks like it has forts on either side of it. I love the fact that kids can play on the equipment as well as under it in little houses and such - so creative, so safe, so fun! A misting pole gently refreshes visitors during hot summer months.

Hours: Open daily, sunrise - 10pm.
Price: Free
Ages: All

GEORGE F CANYON NATURE CENTER

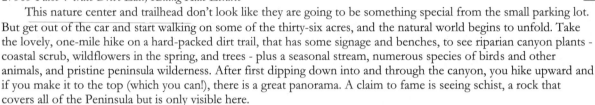

(310) 547-0862 or (310) 541-7613 / www.pvplc.org
27305 Palos Verdes Drive East, Rolling Hills Estates

 This nature center and trailhead don't look like they are going to be something special from the small parking lot. But get out of the car and start walking on some of the thirty-six acres, and the natural world begins to unfold. Take the lovely, one-mile hike on a hard-packed dirt trail, that has some signage and benches, to see riparian canyon plants - coastal scrub, wildflowers in the spring, and trees - plus a seasonal stream, numerous species of birds and other animals, and pristine peninsula wilderness. After first dipping down into and through the canyon, you hike upward and if you make it to the top (which you can!), there is a great panorama. A claim to fame is seeing schist, a rock that covers all of the Peninsula but is only visible here.

 The nature center has a viewing deck and a small demonstration garden outside. Inside there are maps; books; taxidermied animals - foxes, possum, hawks and more; microscopes with slides; an exhibit of pinned insects; and small live critters (in glass displays) that inhabit these lands - snakes, lizards, turtles and frogs. They do great eco-friendly birthday parties here with nature crafts, learning about the live animals, a short hike, and more. Look on the calendar for night hikes, guided family nature hikes, and more.

Hours: The trail is open daily, dawn - dusk. The nature center is open Fri., 1pm - 4pm; Sat. - Sun., 10am - 4pm.
Price: Free
Ages: 3 years and up.

GRAND PARK

(213) 972-8080 / www.grandparkla.org
200 North Grand Avenue, Los Angeles

 See DOWNTOWN LOS ANGELES / GRAND PARK (pg. 167) for information on Grand Park and all the other places to go within this fairly immediate area.

GREYSTONE MANSION AND PARK

(310) 285-6835 or (310) 285-6830 / www.beverlyhills.org
905 Loma Vista, Beverly Hills

 Edward Doheny made an oil discovery that enabled him to become one of the world's largest oil producers. In 1927 he put a great deal of his wealth into constructing the fifty-five room Greystone mansion, designed in Gothic and neo-classical styles. It was built using mainly gray stones (hence the name), plus limestone facing, a slate roof, and seven magnificent brick chimneys. Opened, iron gates at the end of a stone driveway lead to an outside porch that's made of marble. The basement used to house a bowling alley and billiards room. This multi-story, castle-like mansion is the epitome of opulence and, although you may not go into it on your own, you are welcome to peer through the windows. We looked and saw an elegant entry way with black-and-white-checkered tiles, a gorgeous chandelier, elaborately carved wooden banisters, and several archways that are followed by incredibly long hallways. There isn't any furniture inside. Quite a few shows have been filmed here, including episodes of *Murder She Wrote* and the movie, *Ghostbusters II*. Walk around to the front sundeck for a gorgeous view of Beverly Hills and the Los Angeles area.

 Behind the mansion is a dungeon (according to my boys) built into the hillside. The adjacent, closed, control room has levers and a high voltage sign, which clinched the dungeon notion. Imagination definitely reigns here!

 Tiered, lush gardens and extensive grounds lavishly landscaped into and around the hillside are immaculately maintained. Go up the stone steps or walk the pathways to see the acres of grassy areas, courtyards surrounded by trimmed hedges, shade trees, some koi and turtles in the ponds, several reflecting pools, fountains, and a few park benches. This is a great place for taking photographs! A highlight for my kids was simply running down the long, sloping stone driveway - then panting their way back up. Two-hour park ranger tours of the mansion and gardens are held the first Saturday of the month December through April where you can go inside the mansion and learn more, too. The tour costs $15 per person for ages 12 and over.

Hours: Open March through October, 10am - 6pm. Open November through February, 10am - 5pm. Closed New Year's Day and Christmas.

Price: Free
Ages: All

GRIFFITH PARK

(323) 913-4688 or (323) 644-6661 / www.laparks.org; www.ci.la.ca.us
4730 Crystal Springs Drive, Los Angeles

The vast 4,200 acres of the eastern Santa Monica Mountains, known as Griffith Park, is really several parks in one. One part consists of enormous stretches of grassy lawns with several picnic areas and children's attractions, such as the merry-go-round and playground equipment near Park Center. A particularly interesting picnic area is the Old Zoo Picnic area on Griffith Park Drive, kind of just west of Shane's Playground. It has tables near obsolete caves and cages that were once part of the original zoo. The caves, or concrete and stone outcroppings, were very small "natural" settings for lions and tigers and bears. Kids can prowl and roar in front of them. At the back of the shallow caves are locked, steep, stony steps leading up to other cages. There are several barred cages, too, along the same row of enclosures as the caves. More cages, a large empty building, and hiking trails are just steps away on a pathway that hairpins back over the caves. Explore away, but be safe!

Another part of the park incorporates the zoo, observatory, museums, and scale model train rides. Look up LOS ANGELES ZOO (pg. 222), GRIFFITH OBSERVATORY AND PLANETARIUM (pg. 115), THE AUTRY MUSEUM (pg. 153), LOS ANGELES LIVE STEAMERS RAILROAD MUSEUM / WALT DISNEY BARN (pg. 131) and TRAVEL TOWN (pg. 154) for more information. Note: The Greek Theater, a nationally renowned venue for concerts and other events, is just down the road.

The largest part of the park, two-thirds of it, is the wilderness area with fifty-three miles of trails for hiking and horseback riding. Be on the lookout for deer, red-tailed hawks, opossums, coyotes, and other critters. One of the most popular hikes is three miles round trip, beginning at the observatory and extending up to one of the highest points in the park - Mt. Hollywood. On a clear day the view is unbeatable. The famous Hollywood sign is easily seen from the observatory, too. At the southwest side of the park, at 3200 (or 2960) Canyon Drive, is Bronson Canyon or Bronson Caves. A quarter-mile walk up the drive leads to a cave, which looks more like a tunnel, that was used as the Bat Cave from the *Batman* TV series. Rugged wilderness trails, as well as easy walking trails, network throughout this gigantic park located in the middle of L.A. Call or visit the ranger station in the park for all trail information. Also check out the Los Angeles Orienteering Club which offers nature walks for all skill levels. They incorporate learning survival skills, such as map and compass reading, with their hikes.

Ride on the bike trail that runs along a portion of the LA. River which passes by Griffith Park (see BIKE TRAIL: LOS ANGELES RIVER TRAIL (pg. 210)), or just ride along the fairly level roads inside the park. Rentals are available at Spokes 'N Stuff at 4730 Crystal Spring Drive, in the park, for about $10 an hour. Bikes are available year round, Saturday and Sunday from 10am to sunset. From Memorial Day to Labor Day they are also available Monday through Friday from 2pm to 6pm. Call (323) 662-6573 for more information.

Other noteworthy attractions, from the northern end of the park to the southern end, include: 1) The two **train places** (mentioned above) - located west of the Victory Boulevard entrance to the park. 2) **Merry-go-round** - located off Griffith Park Drive, south of the Zoo. The antique carousel, with its sixty-eight carved horses, offers rides daily in the summer, and on weekends and holidays only, the rest of the year from 11am to 5pm. Rides are $2 for all riders over 11 months old. A snack stand is here, too. Call (323) 665-3051 for more information. Free **tennis courts** are nearby. 3) **Shane's Inspiration Playground**, a large boundless playground. It is also located in this same section. It was constructed for physically challenged children and has several age-appropriate play areas with paved pathways, lowered monkey bars, high-backed swings, rocket ship and airplane apparatus, signs in Braille, ramps to interconnect the play areas, raised sand tables to accommodate wheelchairs, courts with lowered basketball hoops, and stainless steel slides for hearing-impaired kids. At Shane's Inspiration able-bodied and disabled children can play together side-by-side as it's just a great playground. 4) **Pony rides** - located at the Los Feliz entrance to the park. Each ride is $5 for kids 1 year old to 100 pounds. The rides are available March thru October, Tuesday through Friday, 10am to 4pm; Saturday through Sunday, 10am to 5pm; open November thru February, Tuesday through Sunday, 10am to 4pm. Call (323) 664-3266 / www.griffithparkponyride.com for more information. 5) **Train rides** and **simulator** - located at the Los Feliz entrance to the park. The eight-minute, mini-train ride chugs past weathered Western town facades and costs $2.75 for ages 19 months and older; $2.25 for seniors; children 18 months and under are free. (During the Christmas season, the train makes a stop in the "North Pole" and kids can visit with Santa all for $4 per passenger.) The simulator, which simulates bobsledding, riding a roller coaster, or being in an airplane, costs $3 per person. Both attractions are open daily from 10am to 4:15pm, or 5pm (daylight savings). Call (323) 664-6903 / www.griffithparktrainrides.com for more information on either attraction. 6) **Tennis courts**, **soccer fields**, **rugby fields**, a **swimming pool**, and **golf course** - located at the Los Feliz entrance to the park. (The cross street is

Riverside.) The twelve tennis courts, at 3401 Riverside Drive, are open during the week, 5pm to 9pm, and weekends and holidays, 7am to 7pm. The cost is free during the week from November through March; $8 an hour to play on all weekends, holidays, and daily during spring/summer months. Call (323) 661-5318 / www.laparks.org for more information. The pool is open mid-June to September, Monday through Friday, 11am - 2pm and 3pm - 6pm; Saturday and Sunday, 1pm - 5pm. Adults are $2.50 per session; seniors and kids 17 years and under are free. Call (323) 644-6878 seasonally, for pool information. This area also has the well-used, Los Feliz par-three, nine-hole course, which is great for beginners. It's only $5.50 per round; $4 for seniors. Call (323) 663-7758 / www.golf.lacity.org for more information. 7) **Bird Sanctuary** - located on Vermont Canyon Road, northeast of the Observatory. This verdant area has a short, stroller-friendly nature trail that crosses over a creek and loops around. A wide variety of birds flock here and make it their home. It's open daily from 10am to 5pm. 8) **Ferndell** - located near the Western Avenue entrance. This is a pretty spot to rest and picnic. Ferns and flowers growing along the brook make it an attractive, cool haven on hot days, and nature trails take you into the heart of the park. Check out FAERY HUNT (Los Angeles County) (pg. 183) for information about an interactive "production" where kids are invited to go on fairy hunts and learn about nature, too. The Trails Cafe snack stand, open Tuesday through Sunday, 8am to 5pm, is also available at this area. Contact the cafe at (323) 871-2102. There are other refreshment stands located throughout the park, as well as restaurants at golf courses and at THE AUTRY MUSEUM (pg. 153).

The following are some of the equestrian centers around the park: **LA Horse Rentals,** (818) 242-8443 - located at 1850 Riverside Drive in Glendale. It's open daily, 8am to 5pm, 6pm in the summer. Riding, available on a first come- first served basis, costs $30 per hour per person. Cash only. The minimum age is 8. Special sunset rides usually begin at 5pm (4pm in the winter) and include ninety minutes of riding, followed by a dinner break at a restaurant, and then riding "home." reservations are required. Sunset rides without dinner are also available. **Circle K Horse Rentals**, (818) 843-9890 / www.circlekhorserentals.com - located at 914 Mariposa Street in Burbank. It's open daily, 7:30am to 5pm, 6pm in the summer. Riding costs $30 for one hour; $55 for two hours. Cash only. The minimum age is 7 years old. **Griffith Park Horse Rentals**, (818) 840-8401 / www.griffithparkhorserental.com or www.la-equestriancenter.com - located at 1820 Riverside Drive in Glendale. It's open daily, 10am to 4pm (last ride). Riding costs $30 per hour (more if you weigh over 200 pounds) and the minimum age is 7 years old (and four feet tall). Cash only. Younger kids, and even adults, can take a twenty-minute lead ride on a trail for $25. Take a private ride, minimum two people - one hour, $95 per rider, and up. **Sunset Ranch Hollywood Stables**, (323) 464-9612 / www.sunsetranchhollywood.com - located at 3400 N. Beachwood Drive in Los Angeles. It's open daily, 9am - 5pm. Riding is $50 an hour; $75 for two hours, with a minimum age limit of 8 years. The much-acclaimed sunset rides, for ages 16 and up, begin around 4:30pm and are $95 per rider. For something extra special, every Saturday is the Best View and BBQ option where you ride over the hills for about two hours, then come back to the ranch for a dinner of barbecue chicken, beans, potato salad, and rolls, and music - $135 per person. Other options are lunch rides, kids parties, Girl Scout programs, horse and carriage rides, and more. This people-friendly place invites families to just come and visit and pet the horses - no charge.

Hours: The park is open daily, 5:30am - 10:30pm.
Price: Free
Ages: All

HANSEN DAM RECREATION AREA

(818) 899-8087 or (818) 756-8189 - recreation; (818) 899-3779 - aquatics center; (818) 756-8189 - skate park / www.laparks.org
11770 Foothill Boulevard, Lake View Terrace

This large park offers a few hiking trails (some of which hook up to equestrian trails), a picnic area, ball fields, soccer fields, trees and shaded areas, and a few scattered playgrounds. The huge, boundless playground is terrific(!) and it features equipment for all abilities. Slides, ramps, swings for wheelchairs, and lots of activities at the connecting platforms and in between them offers hours of fun. The almost 13,000 square foot concrete skatepark has ledges, banks, a huge "flow bowl" and several freestyle features for grinders.

Two of the park's other best features are the smallish, nine-acre, man-made lake and an adjacent, year-round swimming pool. The man-made recreation lake, with cement sides, offers kayaking and SUP classes, and usage of remote controlled boats. Catfish and trout fishing are also available and stocked in their proper season. A fishing license is needed for ages 16 years and up.

The non-heated, gated pool, which is referred to as the swimming lake, is four-feet deep all around, very large, and extremely long. It also has two twisty water slides (one is enclosed) for those 48" tall and 8 years and up. Lifeguards are on duty when it's open. Coarse sand all around the pool, a sand volleyball court, and no shade offers a quasi-beach-like atmosphere. A snack stand is open in the summertime and showers are here, too. Make sure you also check out the adjacent, great DISCOVERY CUBE (Los Angeles County) (pg. 105)!

Hours: The park is open daily, 7am - sunset. The pool is open Memorial Day - mid-June, and the month of September on weekends only, 11am - 6pm. It's open mid-June - Labor Day daily, 11am - 6pm. Closed 4th of July.

Price: Park entrance is free. Pool admission is $3.50 for adults; $1 for seniors and ages 17 and under. Youths 7 and under must be accompanied by an adult.

Ages: 3 years and up.

HAZARD PARK

(213) 485-6839 / www.laparks.org
2230 Norfolk Street, Los Angeles

Hazard Park features another great playground built by Shane's Inspiration! Created for able-body and disable-body children to play together, this playground features a large area with interconnecting ramps and learning activities along the way and at the covered mini platform areas; tunnels; slides; swings; a few rock-climbing structures; rope climbing; sand diggers toys; and much more. The surrounding park has mature trees, lighted tennis courts, indoor and outdoor basketball courts, handball courts, lighted baseball diamond, utility fields, BBQ pits, picnic tables, and lots of grassy, run-around space with a jogging trail crisscrossing throughout.

Hours: Open daily, sunrise - sunset.
Price: Free
Ages: All

HERITAGE PARK - Cerritos

(562) 916-8570 / www.cerritos.us
18600 Bloomfield Avenue, Cerritos

One if by land, two if by sea . . . . The most unique feature of this noteworthy park is an island with a kid-size version of Boston, circa 1770. Cross the covered bridge and be transported back in time. (Not literally; it's just the atmosphere of the island.) This multi-level, stone-wall-built "town" has a replica of Paul Revere's house and a North Church Tower, which has two slides and climbing chains. (Creative parents can reinforce a Paul Revere history lesson here. Check out the Paul statue and plaques to do with the *Midnight Ride of Paul Revere*.) The town is also composed of a series of little buildings - apothecary, saddler, printer, etc. - with play space, sliding poles, and more slides in them, as well as outside (one enclosed slide comes out from the second story of a small building!) and inside bridges that connect them. There are also small cannons to sit on or "fire", and small replicas of British ships harbored in the water, which are designed for pint-sized sailors to climb aboard. The island has a rock-lined brook running through it with small waterfalls and plenty of shade trees, so it is refreshingly cool even on hot days.

The ducks swimming in the "moat" surrounding the island are always looking for a handout, and watch for the sun-bathing turtles. Across the water is a wonderful, expansive, play area with swings, slides, and climbing apparatus. The park also has picnic tables, a few barbecues, basketball courts, large grass areas, climbing trees, and a baseball diamond with stadium-type benches.

Hours: The main part of the park is open daily, sunrise - sunset. The island is open Mon., Wed - Sun., 10am - dusk; Tues., 2pm - dusk.
Price: Free
Ages: All

HIGGINBOTHAM PARK / THOMPSON CREEK TRAIL

(909) 399-5490 / www.ci.claremont.ca.us
625 Mt. Carmel Drive, Claremont

A small, train-car playground makes this park worth mentioning and stopping by to play if you are in the vicinity. The main car looks like a steam engine so kids can climb aboard. They can also climb on top and through the windows and down the short slide. Dream about riding the (real) rails, bring a picnic lunch and hike about as the rest of the park is in a natural setting. In fact, the 2.8 mile, dirt, single-track Thompson Creek Trail goes right past this park. Walk to the end of the trail and connect to Sycamore Canyon, a 144-acre natural area. All this from an unassuming park!

Hours: Open daily, sunrise - 10pm.
Price: Free
Ages: 3 - 8 years.

HOPKINS WILDERNESS PARK

(310) 318-0668 - park; (310) 318-0670 - reservations / www.redondo.org
1102 Camino Real, Redondo Beach

Escape to the wilderness of Redondo Beach. This gated, eleven-acre hilltop park has two streams running through it, two ponds (home to turtles, fish and ducks) surrounded by large flat rocks, and a wonderful view of the city. Hike along the nature trail that takes you through California Redwood and pine trees; through a meadow - be on the lookout for butterflies and lizards; and to the small waterfall and pond where turtles, crayfish, and bullfrogs have made their homes. Wilderness Park also has several campgrounds and is a popular spot for local, overnight camping for groups. Reservations are required. Picnic tables and barbecue pits are available for campers.

Hours: Open Thurs. - Tues., 10am - 4:30pm. Closed Wed., New Year's Day, Thanksgiving, Christmas, and in bad weather.
Price: The park is free to walk through. Day camping/reserving the park is available for $30 per 3 hour session. Fri. and Sat. overnight tent camping (no stakes allowed) is $5 a night for adults; $3 a night for ages 17 and under, plus a staffing fee of $240.
Ages: 3 years and up.

HUNTINGTON LIBRARY, ART COLLECTIONS AND BOTANICAL GARDENS

$$$$

See the entry for HUNTINGTON LIBRARY, ART COLLECTIONS AND BOTANICAL GARDENS (pg. 121), under MUSEUMS, for details.

JAMES IRVINE GARDEN

(213) 628-2725 / www.jaccc.org
244 South San Pedro Street, Los Angeles

!/$

Go through the doors of this community center, down the elevator, to the "basement", and then outside for a brief bit of serenity in the midst of bustling L.A. This small, hidden, lush oasis is filled with plants, boulders, wooden footbridges, short waterfalls, a small pond, and a rock-lined pathway and stream that meander throughout the flowers, bamboo, and willow, pine, and other trees. Visit Little Tokyo and the JAPANESE AMERICAN NATIONAL MUSEUM (pg. 124), which are both just down the street. Also checkout DOWNTOWN LOS ANGELES / GRAND PARK (pg. 167) for information on Grand Park and other places to go within this fairly immediate area.

Hours: Open Tues. - Fri., 10am - 5pm; Sat. - Sun., 10am - 4pm. Call for weekend availability as it is sometimes closed for special events. Closed Mon. and holidays.
Price: Free. Metered parking on the street.
Ages: 3 years and up.

THE JAPANESE GARDEN

(818) 756-8166 / www.thejapanesegarden.com
6100 Woodley Avenue, Van Nuys

$$

Sharing the same address (and waters) as the Donald C. Tillman Reclamation Plant, but worlds apart, is this hidden and tranquil Oriental gem. The 6.5-acre garden is based on designs of 18th- and 19th-century gardens that were created for Japanese feudal lords who used them for contemplation.

While you'll like the dry, Zen meditation garden that makes up a small portion of the grounds, you'll really enjoy a stroll on the paved pathway through the startlingly lovely main garden that gracefully curves in and around a lake and waterway. Interspersed throughout are numerous trees, plus small bamboo groves; manicured shrubbery; several bridges, including a zigzag one; a Shoin-zukuri building, which was a traditional type of dwelling used by samurais and aristocrats; a weeping willow tree; a variety of stone lanterns; Ginko trees; and a three-tiered waterfall. A narrow pond with water lilies runs along an entire wall of the garden. Be on the lookout for herons, egrets, grebes, and cliff swallows here. Peek into a formal tea house and tea garden also on the premises. Read the information on the website to gain a greater appreciation of all the symbolism used in the layout and elements in the garden, or listen to your docent on a one-hour-and-fifteen-minute guided tour. Note: You will smell an unpleasant odor at times - this is the downside of using reclaimed water.

From a viewing platform, you can see the adjacent reclamation plant. In fact, free tours of plant are available (see LA SANITATION (pg. 200)) where you can learn how solids and waters are processed and learn how the plant water brought about the existence of the garden. Note that the garden is adjacent to the ANTHONY C. BEILENSON PARK / LAKE BALBOA / PEDLOW FIELD SKATE PARK / SEPULVEDA DAM RECREATION AREA (pg. 47) parks and recreation area.

Hours: Open Mon. - Thurs., 11am - 3:15pm (last admission, the garden closes at 4pm); Sun., 10am - 3:15pm (garden closes at 4pm). Closed Fri. and Sat. Always call the day of your visit as many special events are held here and the gardens may be closed then. Guided tours are offered Mon. - Thurs. with advanced reservations.

Price: $3 for adults; $3 for seniors and children 12 and under. Guided tours are free with admission. See American Horticultural Society (pg. x) for info on reciprocal memberships.

Ages: 7 years and up.

JOHNNY CARSON PARK

(818) 238-5300 / www.burbankca.gov

400 Bob Hope Drive, Burbank

Despite the proximity of the freeway, this pleasant park offers a refuge, of sorts, in downtown Burbank. Kids enjoy the large grassy areas, small woods, climbing and shade trees, and stroller-friendly dirt pathways that run throughout the park. The Tonight Show Playground, for today's kids, inspires creativity with its variety of climbing apparatus, including twisty tubes, poles and ropes, plus it has slides, swings, bridges, wheels, and all sorts of shaped objects all under shade awnings. Picturesque bridges go over what I first thought was a seasonal stream, but it is only a drainage "creek." Come enjoy a picnic here before or after you take the WARNER BROS. STUDIO TOUR HOLLYWOOD (pg. 206) studio tours.

Hours: Open daily, sunrise - 10pm.

Price: Free

Ages: All

KENNETH HAHN STATE RECREATION AREA

(323) 298-3660 / www.lacountyparks.org

4100 S. La Cienega Boulevard, Los Angeles

This spacious, 336-acre natural parkland in the heart of Baldwin Hills has hilly grasslands, forest areas (including the Olympic section, which has a tree representing each participant country from the 1984 Olympics), and several dirt hiking trails that extend up to seven miles. A favorite is the one-mile hike to the waterfall. The park also features a large lake that is stocked with trout in the winter, and catfish, bluegill, and bass in the summer. The fishing is free, but ages 16 and up need a license. Swimming in the water is not allowed. You may, however, feed the ducks who are always looking for a handout. Make sure to check out the Japanese garden with its koi and little bridges. There are seven picnic areas complete with barbecue grills for families to enjoy, as well as a few scattered playgrounds, plus basketball and volleyball courts, soccer fields, and workout stations with equipment. And the view can be lovely and all-encompassing.

Hours: Open daily, sunrise - sunset. Closed Christmas.

Price: Free during the week; $6 per vehicle on weekends and county holidays.

Ages: All

KING GILLETTE RANCH

(805) 370-2301 / www.nps.gov/samo

26800 Mulholland Highway, Calabasas

At 588 acres, maybe this ranch is king! On the grounds are a twenty-five room mansion, a single-family resident's home, a few other buildings that you can see, but not go into, and one that you are welcome to go into - the current home of the SANTA MONICA MOUNTAINS NATIONAL PARK HEADQUARTERS - VISITORS CENTER (Anthony C. Beilenson Interagency Visitor Center) (pg. 85). Stop off to get some information here first. Bring a picnic lunch to enjoy at the picnic tables outside.

The ranch also has a walking path leading to a California native plant nursery; a pond to walk around where great blue herons, mallards, cormorants, and other birds visit; and a one-mile trail to Inspiration Point which is a steep climb, but worth it for the rewarding view. The chaparral and mature trees are naturally beautiful. If you are so inclined, walk another 1.5 miles along the ridge. There are numerous educational programs offered here for kids of all ages. Note that PETER STRAUSS RANCH (pg. 78) and PARAMOUNT RANCH (pg. 78) are just around the corner.

Hours: Open daily, sunrise - sunset.

Price: Free for the first 2 hours; $7 per vehicle for the day.

Ages: 5 years and up.

LACY PARK

(626) 300-0790 or (626) 300-0700 / www.cityofsanmarino.org

!/$$

1485 Virginia Road, San Marino

This is one of the prettiest parks we've visited - it's so well maintained and beautifully landscaped. In the center is a large expanse of immaculately kept grass. Encircling it are several varieties of trees, including oak, pine, and lots of palm. A paved pathway, about a mile "round trip", loops around the center and is perfect for walkers, joggers, strollers, etc. There are also several scattered benches and picnic tables, and pockets of tree-shaded respite areas.

The playground is "enclosed" by low bushes and by a fence, as well as park benches. The woods-themed play structures inspire kids' free-thinking play and physical activity. One has an almost cartoonish treehouse at the top of a (fake) tree, with a slide coming out from it, plus a short tunnel, some bridges, monkey bars, and more. Another shaded, multi-level structure has more tunnels and slides, climbing apparatus, and rock climbing wall, plus swings and under-the-structure play space. A good-sized, free-standing, rope climbing structure that kind of looks like a spider web is also here.

Six tennis courts, operated by the San Marino Tennis Foundation, are on the grounds, open 7:30am to sunset, with lighted courts. The cost is $10 for non-members. Call (626) 793-1622 for more info.

Hours: Open year-round, Mon. - Fri., 6:30am - sunset. Open May through October on weekends, 8am - 8pm; November through April, 8am - 6pm. Closed New Year's Eve, New Year's Day, Thanksgiving, Christmas Eve, and Christmas Day.

Price: Free Mon. - Fri. for everyone. Entrance is $4 for ages 5 and up on Sat. - Sun. for nonresidents; free for residents.

Ages: All

LADERA LINDA COMMUNITY CENTER

(310) 544-5370 - community center; (310) 541-7073 - park; (310) 544-5264 - hikes / www.rpvca.gov

!/$

32201 Forrestal Drive, Rancho Palos Verdes

This park features a wilderness area (with a gorgeous view of the ocean, and beyond, from the top), a basketball court, a small playground, and, closer to where the additional parking lot is located, two paddle tennis courts and (up the wooden stairs) soccer and baseball fields. There are picnic tables and a few shade trees, too. The community center building is a former elementary school which now hosts educational programs and a Discovery Room. Besides history information about the area, the small Discovery Room has a few live animals; displays of rocks, fossils, and animals skins to gently touch; skulls of a racoon, coyote, fox and skunk; an ostrich egg and hummingbird egg; and stuffed racoons and great horned owl. Another little playground is here as are two basketball courts.

Two-hour, docent-led hikes offered by the center enable groups of kids to explore the coastal habitat of the Palos Verdes Peninsula. Look out for and learn about coastal sage scrub, native trees, and wildflowers, as well as important critters such as lizards, butterflies, and birds. Hikes are moderately difficult, so bring a water bottle and wear sunscreen. The hike/tours can focus on a topic of your choice, such as plants, animals, fossils, or the geology of the area, including a visit to a rock quarry. A visit to the Discovery Room, with explanations about the exhibits, is included in your time here.

Hours: The park is open daily, sunrise - sunset. The Discovery Room is open Mon. - Fri., noon - 5pm; Sat. - Sun., 10am - 5pm. Closed major holidays. Tours are set up by reservation.

Price: Free to the park and Discovery Room. Tours are $2 for adults; $1 for children 13 and under.

Ages: All for the park; 7 years and up for the tours.

LA LAGUNA DE SAN GABRIEL / VINCENT LUGO PARK

(626) 308-2875 / www.sangabrielcity.com

!

300 W. Wells Street, San Gabriel

The front portion of this park is a tree-lined expanse of green lawn, bordered by a lovely, short paved nature trail and a dry, rocky creek with several bridges. Walk back just a bit, to La Laguna, or Dinosaur Park, to discover a nautical park that's a treasure of a modern-day find. Originally created in the 1960's, children can play on the 14 oversized concrete sea creatures that have surfaced here, such as an octopus, snail, sea serpent, seals, and a whale, all based in sand (of course). Shouts of "This is the best!" came from my kids as they slid down the sea serpent that is wrapped around a lighthouse. Another giant sea serpent is curled around a short, rocky hill which has a huge shade tree growing from it and a slide to go down. The large treasure chest and sunken piece of pirate ship add to the ambiance and kid's imaginative play here. There are also pockets of trees and grassy spots, plus picnic tables and even some work-out equipment here.

Hours: Open daily, 7:30am - 10pm.
 Price: Free
 Ages: 2 - 11 years old.

LA MIRADA REGIONAL PARK

(800) 404-5888 or (562) 902-5645 / www.cityoflamirada.org; www.lmdgc.org
13701 Adelfa Drive, La Mirada

Green rolling hills and other grassy expanses; a plethora of mature trees (for shade and for climbing); picnic tables; two pretty and hilly 18-hole acclaimed disc golf courses (some of our favorite ones to play for the seasoned and beginner player); twelve lighted tennis courts; a lighted baseball field; a cement pathway that meanders throughout; playgrounds; exercise stations and equipment; and a lake with a tiny island in it constitute this 100-acre, lovely park. Benches and trees line the lakeside, while the resident (and requisite) ducks look for handouts. Bring your fishing pole because the lake is stocked with rainbow trout in the winter and spring, and catfish in the summer and fall. Bass and carp can also be caught here.

Entrenched in a wood-chip base the covered play structure is elevated so not only can kids run around on its swinging bridges and fort-like outlooks, and slide down the short slides and crawl through tubes, but they can also engage their imaginations as they play under it. Toddler swings; a truck and plane on giant springs to rock back and forth on; a small rock climbing wall; and a little clubhouse nestled in the sand (bring bucket and shovel) round out this playground. Another playground boasts web-like cargo nets attached to a sphere to climb on and around, plus abstract shapes to play on and other creative equipment.

The fully-stocked pro shop sells discs for the golf course (they hold tournaments here) and snack items, and offers sign-ups for the twelve tennis courts. Call Lifetime Sports / La Mirada Tennis Center at (562) 902-6371 for more information. Note - they also have a tennis wall here so you can practice without a partner. Just around the corner is a water park and swimming pools - see BUCCANEER BAY - SPLASH! LA MIRADA AQUATICS CENTER (pg. 2) for details.

Hours: Open sunrise - sunset. The tennis courts are open from sunrise - 9pm (when the lights go off).
 Price: Free. Tennis courts are free for unreserved courts; $5 for reserved courts, which must be made 2 hours before play time.
 Ages: All

LA PINTORESCA PARK

(626) 744-4724 / ww5.cityofpasadena.net
45 E. Washington Boulevard, Pasadena

This mid-size, neighborhood park is located just behind the La Pintoresca Branch Library. The park offers huge, shady oak trees to climb and relax under; a few barbeque pits and picnic tables; a paved pathway for biking or strolling; a basketball court; and a lighted, portable skate park with wooden ramps, a funbox, a small, quarter-pipe, and a pyramid. Parental consent for minors, and helmets and pads are required for skaters. A playground with wood-chip ground cover has several slides and a variety of climbing apparatus, plus a swing-set and a merry-go-round. In the summertime, kids enjoy water play on a cemented section of the park that has colorful loops and poles which act as fountains as water squirts out through them.

Hours: The park and skate park are open daily, 6am - 10pm.
 Price: Free
 Ages: All

LAS FLORES CREEK PARK

(310) 456-2489 / www.malibucity.org
3805 Las Flores Canyon Drive, Malibu

What a creativity-inspiring little park located right off the highway! It has a wooden raft (with sides and handles) on huge springs to create movement of the sea; giant frog and fish statues; a small merry-go-round with a rope tepee structure on it; a wooden teeter-totter; wood blocks and large fake rocks with ropes attaching them to climb on and through; and a wooden boat to climb in. Very fun - very different. There are also sycamore trees with low-hanging branches that beckon climbers, other plants and shade trees, and a seasonal creek on one side of the park. Note: There are picnic tables here, but no restrooms.

Hours: Open daily, 8am - sunset
 Price: Free
 Ages: 2 - 12 years

LIBERTY PARK - Cerritos

(562) 916-8565 / www.cerritos.us

19211 Studebaker Road, Cerritos

Experience the freedom at Liberty Park to do almost anything. The park offers long grassy areas to run around. There are two good playground areas - one has a rocking "boat", plus enclosed slides, swings, platforms, play areas, etc., and the other small one has some innovative elements, like vertical bars to climb, and other climbing and balancing apparatus, plus rings, twisty poles, a few slides and some swings. Picnic tables; barbeque pits; picnic shelters; three sand volleyball courts; a 330-yard walking/jogging track; a softball field; a small disc golf course; outside exercise clusters equipped with pull up bars and more; two pickle ball courts; and six lighted tennis courts make up the rest of the park. Tennis is free for Cerritos residents (show a driver's license or utility bill for proof of residency) and $7 per hour for nonresidents, starting at 10am daily. A bike path runs along the Los Angeles River just outside the park gates. See BIKE TRAIL: SAN GABRIEL RIVER TRAIL (pg. 210) for more information.

Inside the community building are racquetball courts ($7 per hour for residents, $11 for nonresidents) and a weight room.

Summertime offers the refreshing pleasures of a small water park with sprayers and other fun features. This area is open daily, 1pm to 4pm. You can ask in the office to turn the water on, if it's not already. During the summer, too, is Monday night family time at the movies ('G' rated) and Wednesday night family entertainment consisting of puppets, magicians, or storytellers.

Hours: The park is open daily, sunrise - sunset. The community center is open Mon. - Fri., 10am - 9:30pm, plus Sat. - Sun., 10 - 8pm in the summer; 10am - 6pm in the winter. Call for times for special programs.

Price: Free to the park. Fees for activities are listed above.

Ages: All

LINCOLN PARK

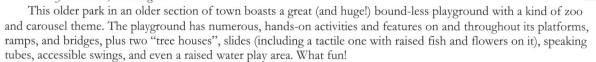

(213) 847-1726 or (213) 485-5572 / www.laparks.org

3501 Valley Boulevard, Los Angeles

This older park in an older section of town boasts a great (and huge!) bound-less playground with a kind of zoo and carousel theme. The playground has numerous, hands-on activities and features on and throughout its platforms, ramps, and bridges, plus two "tree houses", slides (including a tactile one with raised fish and flowers on it), speaking tubes, accessible swings, and even a raised water play area. What fun!

The park also has rows of picnic tables under huge pine and oak trees; paved pathways that crisscross throughout; four tennis courts; another playground with a sand base for younger children; grassy expanses; artwork/murals on wooden walls; a community building; and sometimes quite a few homeless people. A big lake (with a large fountain in it) is stocked with fish and home to numerous ducks. A fishing license is needed for ages 15 and over. We also enjoyed the large, grass-covered hill - walking up it and running back down Kamikaze-style! For those who like even more action, try the plaza-style, big skate park which has ramps, quarter- and half-pipes, and other skateboarding elements.

Hours: The park and skate park are open daily, 6am - 10pm. The community center is open Mon. - Fri., 10am - 9pm; Sat., 8am - 5pm; closed Sun.

Price: Free

Ages: All

LINDBERG PARK

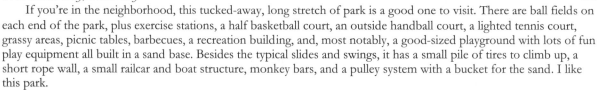

(310) 839-0127 / www.culvercity.org

5401 Rhoda Way, Culver City

If you're in the neighborhood, this tucked-away, long stretch of park is a good one to visit. There are ball fields on each end of the park, plus exercise stations, a half basketball court, an outside handball court, a lighted tennis court, grassy areas, picnic tables, barbecues, a recreation building, and, most notably, a good-sized playground with lots of fun play equipment all built in a sand base. Besides the typical slides and swings, it has a small pile of tires to climb up, a short rope wall, a small railcar and boat structure, monkey bars, and a pulley system with a bucket for the sand. I like this park.

Hours: Open daily, sunrise - sunset.

Price: Free

Ages: All

LIVE OAK PARK

(310) 545-5621 or (310) 802-5000 / www.citymb.info

1601 N. Valley Drive, Manhattan Beach

This park is formed around a bend in the road and is divided into various park pockets with grassy sections. The northern section has baseball diamonds, picnic tables, and some short, bent, gnarled trees - so great for climbing. Other pockets have playground equipment (one has little play trains), a lighted basketball court, soccer fields, places just to run and play, and tennis courts. The six courts are open weekdays and holidays from 7am to 10pm ($8 per hour until 5pm; $10 per hour after 5pm - for lights), and on weekends from 7am to 8pm. Call (310) 545-0888 for more info.

Hours: Open daily, dawn - dusk.

Price: Free

Ages: All

LOS ANGELES COUNTY ARBORETUM & BOTANIC GARDEN

(626) 821-3222 / www.arboretum.org; www.pasadenasymphony-pops.org

301 N. Baldwin Avenue, Arcadia

Do you have a budding horticulturalist in your family? Come visit this awesome arboretum and explore the more than 127 acres of plants and trees from around the world grouped mainly by geography. The blooming flowers and the variety of gardens are astounding. We walked along the southern (and most interesting) route first. There are numerous paved pathways as well as several dirt pathways leading through trees, bushes, and jungle-like landscape which makes the walk an adventure for kids. Ducks and geese loudly ask for handouts at Baldwin Lake. Look for the turtles in the lake's water. Learn about drought-tolerant landscape here and more about California native plants.

For your history lesson for the day, peek into the spacious Hugo Reid Adobe House, where each room is furnished with period furniture. The adobe grounds are beautiful and reflective of the mid-1800's. Peer into the gracious Queen Anne "Cottage" for another glimpse of the past. You'll see mannequins dressed in old-fashioned clothes, elegantly furnished rooms, and a harp in the music room. The nearby immaculate Coach Barn has stalls ornately decorated with wood paneling and iron grillwork. Instead of horses, they now hold farm tools, blacksmith tools, and a coach. Also, via tours offered at certain times throughout the week, go inside the Santa Anita Depot that houses a train master's office and railroad paraphernalia. A little farther away are the Tongva kis (huts).

The lush greenery around the fifty-foot waterfall makes it one of the most enchanting spots in the arboretum. Walk up the wooden stairs for a panoramic view and "discover" a lily pond. Back down on Waterfall Walk you'll see a serene woodland area and rock-lined stream. I was utterly content to sit while the kids let their imaginations kick into gear and play. Colorful koi are just around the "corner" at the Tule Pond.

The northern section has a few greenhouses with exotic flowers and plants. An African and Australian section at this end has an abundance of trees. Peacocks are everywhere - strutting their stuff and calling out in plaintive-sounding wails. Note that peacock feathers are available at the gift shop for about $2 each, although I don't think these two facts are related. Picnicking is not allowed on the grounds, but there is a shaded, grassy area between the parking lots. Or, eat at the Peacock Cafe, which has reasonably-priced food, though note that it is closed on Mondays.

Tip one: Take a half-hour tram ride around and through the extensive arboretum, or get off at any one of the seven stops along the way and reboard at a later time. Trams run on Saturdays only, noon to 3pm, on the hour. Tickets are $5 per person. Tip two: It gets hot here during the summer, so bring water bottles (and look for the sprinklers to run through).

Involve the kids even more in their surroundings by picking up a scavenger hunt guide at the Rotunda for them to look for and check off plants, animals, and other items as they walk around. Wonderful, family geared events are held here several times throughout the year. Science Adventure Day Camps, which include classes on space and rocketry, magic, and more, are offered in the summer. The Pasadena Symphony POPS offers five Summer Concerts during the summer. The Saturday concerts start at 7:30pm and the arboretum closes at 3:30pm on these days. See the June Calendar section for more details.

Hours: Open daily, 9am - 5pm. Closed Christmas.

Price: $9 for adults; $6 for seniors and students with ID; $4 for ages 5 - 12; children 4 and under are free. The third Tues. of every month is free. Free parking. See American Horticultural Society (pg. x) for info on reciprocal memberships.

Ages: 2 years and up.

LOS ARBOLES PARK

(310) 328-5310 or (310) 618-2930 / www.torranceca.gov

5101 Calle de Ricardo, Torrance

What a blast! One of the few parks left that has a classic, metal rocket ship play structure for kids, this is a launching place for imaginations. The four-story rocket ship is the main feature with a ladder going all the way up, and a tall slide with which to come back down to earth. Nearby, fittingly, is a metal lunar module model (say that five times fast!) based in sand, perfect to spy out alien life forms, like siblings. It has a short ladder, a fireman's pole and controls. This smallish playground has a few other elements such as grassy areas and trees, plus an incredible, almost astronaut's view of the world. Well, the Los Angeles basin world. Note that the playground is unfenced and there are no restrooms.

Hours: Open daily, 6am - 10pm.
Price: Free
Ages: 4 - 12 years

MADRONA MARSH

(310) 32 MARSH (326-2774) or (310) 782-3989 / www.friendsofmadronamarsh.com   !/$$
3201 Plaza Del Amo, Torrance

Tucked away in a business and suburban area is the ten-acre Madrona Marsh. It's a vernal marsh, meaning that it's a depression flooded by runoff water from surrounding upland slopes. It has a seasonal pond and four different plant habitats that are home to small mammals (namely squirrels); insects, such as dragonflies and butterflies; and numerous bird species. Educational nature walks for kids (and adults) of all ages are given throughout the year. During the hour, or so, guided tour you'll see and learn mostly about birds, plus ground animals, like tree frogs, and varieties of plant life. Ask about the numerous other programs offered, such as junior naturalist, astronomy, art classes, and habitat restoration. (It does my heart good to see kids pulling weeds.) Bring snacks and a water bottle.

Across the street from the marsh, the handicapped-accessible, mid-sized Nature Center contains a room with large information and picture panels that explain the plants and animals of the marsh and about the marsh; glass display cases with several stuffed birds and other animals depicted in their natural habitats; and some interactive exhibits. The hallways offers a book nook; a place to color and display kid's artwork; live animals, such as turtles and snakes; furs to touch; and a microscope with prepared slides to look at. A classroom, a project lab and a little gift shop are also on-site. As the Nature Center and marsh are somewhat hidden, even if they aren't big enough to make you feel like you've gotten away from all of city life, they are at least big enough to make you feel like you've gotten away from some of it.

Hours: Marsh and Nature Center are open Tues. - Sun., 10am - 5pm. Closed on Mon. and holidays. Guided walks of the marsh are given at various times throughout the week, as are field study tours. Call for details or to schedule a field trip.
Price: Free; donations gladly accepted. Field trips are $5 per person.
Ages: 6 years and up.

MALIBU BLUFFS PARK

(310) 317-1364 / www.malibucity.org   !
24250 Pacific Coast Highway, Malibu

As the name suggests, this park is on a bluff top, right across the street from Pepperdine University. The view is fantastic, especially on a clear day, and there are playgrounds here, too. One small, enclosed play area, adjacent to the community center, has one structure with three different slides coming out from it, plus metal twisty things to climb on. Other play elements scattered throughout the park include a mini zip line; a sand area with diggers; a large turtle statue to climb on; and a funky, curved horizontal rock climbing wall with a tube and metal and spherical balls to play on. You can also sit on a whale's fluke bench to whale watch (or use the telescopes). Hike the dirt pathway down and around the surrounding preserve, or all the way down to the beach below.

An ample plot of grass is dotted with a few picnic tables, boulders, and trees, plus a soccer field, two baseball fields (with concession stands that are open on game days), and a cement walkway around the perimeter.

Hours: Open daily, sunrise - sunset.
Price: Free
Ages: All

MALIBU CREEK STATE PARK

(818) 880-0367 - park; (800) 444-7275 - camping reservations / www.parks.ca.gov; www.localhikes.com $$$
1925 Las Virgenes Road, Calabasas

Of the many hiking, mountain bike, and horseback riding trails to choose from in the Santa Monica Mountains, one of our favorites is the Malibu Creek Trail. Starting at the broad fire road, veer to the right as the trail forks onto

Cragg Road. The scenery keeps getting better the further in you hike. Oak trees shade part of the trail as you follow the high road along the creek. Man-made Century Lake is a great place to stop for a picnic, take in the beauty of your surroundings, fish, or even use the rope to swing over and in the water. This spot marks a four-mile round trip. Continue on an additional two miles (round trip) to the former M*A*S*H set, which contains just a few of the shows artifacts, such as the ambulance and other vehicles. Being here might not have any meaning for your kids, but they'll at least think the rock formation, named Goat Buttes and used in the opening scene of the show, is worth a "wow."

A mile in from the parking lot is the Visitor's Center, which also has a small museum. One room contains taxidermied animals, rocks, shells, and other displays. There is also M*A*S*H memorabilia and a room for school groups to work on craft projects.

Feel like taking a dip in cool, refreshing water? About a half mile beyond the Visitor's Center, over the bridge to the left and over a short trail of rocks, is Rock Pool, a rock-lined swimming hole. (*Swiss Family Robinson* and some *Tarzan* movies were filmed here.) It's a drag to have to hike food and such in, but it's like a hidden oasis (though it's crowded on the weekends), so it's worth it. My boys thought jumping off the boulders into the "pool" formed by the creek was the ultimate.

Take advantage of all that the park offers by spending a night, or two, here. Each of the seasonally-open, sixty-two campsites, some of which are shaded, has a picnic table and charcoal-use fire pit. Eight people per campsite are allowed. No RV hook-ups.

Hours: The park is open daily, 8am - 10pm. The Visitor's Center is open Sat. - Sun., noon - 4pm.
Price: $12 per vehicle all day; $9 for 3 hours. Camping prices are $45, plus a reservation fee of $8.
Ages: 3 years and up.

MARIE KERR PARK - MARIE KERR SKATE PARK

(661) 267-5611 - park and skate park; (661) 267-6145 - pool / www.cityofpalmdale.org
39700 30th Street West, Palmdale

Airborne! At least my kids keep hoping for this state when they skate at this skate park. I just hope they land unharmed. This sometimes supervised, 8,500-square-foot skate park has all the necessary ramps, grinding boxes, and other street elements to make it fun. A helmet and knee and elbow pads are required. A parent or guardian must sign a waiver if the participant is under 18 years old. Also, kids must show a city-issued photo I.D. card (available at the parks and recreation office - 38260 10th St. East - during regular business hours) each time they enter the park.

The surrounding park has tennis courts, basketball courts, a playground, soccer field, a seven-field softball complex and sports play field, baseball diamonds, gymnasium (at the recreation center), and picnic areas. A well-used walking/jogging/biking trail (.9 miles long) circles the perimeter of the park. Enjoy a refreshing dip in the pool which is open for lap swim year round and open in the summer for recreational swim. B.Y.O.B. (Bring Your Own Blanket, or lawn chair) for the free, summer Starlight concert series, and bring a picnic dinner, or purchase something from the food vendors.

Hours: The park and skate park are open daily, 6am - 10pm.
Price: Free. The pool is $3 for residents; $4 for non-residents; $1.50 for seniors.
Ages: 7 years and up.

MARINE AVENUE PARK and SKATE PARK

(310) 802-5410 or (310) 802-5000 / www.citymb.info
1625 Marine Avenue, Manhattan Beach

The park has a turf soccer field, baseball diamond, basketball courts, cement picnic tables, exercise stations, and two playgrounds - a newer-style abstract playground with domes, metal hoops, and ropes to climb in various configurations, and another with swings and a short rocket ship to climb up into and blast off to parts unknown, and then to slide down. A small (6,000 square foot) skate park is here with a street section in the center with stairs, rails and ledges. Restrooms, an activity center, and indoor racquetball courts are available here, too. Note that ADVENTURE PLEX (pg. 27) is located just across the way.

Hours: The park is open daily, sunrise - sunset. The skate park is open daily, 8am - dusk.
Price: Free
Ages: All

MASSARI PARK - CHRIS O'LEARY SKATE PARK

(661) 267-5593 or (661) 267-5611 / www.cityofpalmdale.org
37716 55th Street East, Palmdale

This large park boasts a huge, sprawling, multi-level playground with several, separate elements. There are numerous slides (some enclosed), tunnels, ramps, bridges, peek holes, bars, climbing apparatus and more, from and connected to kid-sized towers. There are also some huge dragonfly statues to sit in and on their wings; a giant, metal caterpillar with a tunnel for a belly; rainbow arched poles and other free-form play elements; and boulders. Other park amenities include soccer fields, baseball diamonds, basketball courts, tennis courts, a sand volleyball court, picnic areas, and a walking/jogging trail.

The 12,000-foot, lighted, cement skate park has all the "tight" street features that challenge kids - ramps, bowls, steps, and more. A helmet and knee and elbow pads are required.

Hours: The park and skate park are open daily, sunrise - sunset.
Price: Free
Ages: All

MATHIAS BOTANICAL GARDEN AT UCLA

(310) 825-1260 / www.botgard.ucla.edu
777 Tiverton Dr, Los Angeles

See the entry for UNIVERSITY OF CALIFORNIA, LOS ANGELES / UCLA (pg. 177) for details.

MAYFAIR PARK

(562) 866-9771 or (562) 866-4776 - park; (562) 804-4256 - pool (in season) / www.lakewoodcity.org
5720 Clark Street, Lakewood

Mayfair Park is a very fair park indeed! The sand-based boundless playground, accessible for all abilities, has ramps; metal monkey bars and other metal climbing apparatus; a tire swing; interactive panels; rock climbing walls and fake rocks to climb on with hand and foot holds; swings; slides; and other really fun elements and shapes to spark imaginations. Open grassy fields are plentiful here, plus there are basketball courts, tennis courts (free), baseball diamonds with lights and stadium seating, barbecue pits, a wading pool, and a (very popular) swimming pool.

Hours: The park is open daily, sunrise - sunset. The pools are open mid-May through mid-June, weekends only; open daily in the summer. Swim sessions are 1pm - 2:30pm and 2:45pm - 4:15pm. Call for extended nighttime hours.
Price: Free to the park. For Lakewood residents each pool session costs $1.50 for adults, $1 for children 17 and under; non-residents are $3 for adults; $2 for kids. The wading pool is free.
Ages: All

MEMORIAL PARK - Claremont

(909) 399-5460 / www.ci.claremont.ca.us
840 N. Indian Hill Boulevard, Claremont

The site for many community events, this stately old park has delightful, huge, gnarled oak trees all around with plenty of grassy, run-around space. It also has a picnic grove, BBQ pits, a tennis court, a basketball court, a wading pool that's open in the summer, two sand volleyball courts, a bandshell for outdoor concerts, and a small playground. The play area has toddler and bigger kid's swings, plastic tunnels, slides, and chain ladders to climb.

Hours: Open daily, sunrise - sunset.
Price: Free
Ages: All

MEMORIAL PARK - Santa Monica / THE COVE SKATEPARK

(310) 458-2201 - park; (310) 458-8237 - skatepark / www.smgov.net
1401 Olympic Boulevard, Santa Monica

Several baseball fields, soccer fields, four lighted tennis courts, and a gated children's playground with slides, swings, animals on large springs, and other equipment, plus a gym with indoor volleyball and basketball make this a memorable park.

In-line skaters and BMX bikers should check out the terrific, gated, lighted, 20,000 square feet skate park, complete with ramps, bowls, stairs, a pool, an over vert bowl, and rails. Park skaters (and bikers) must register annually, in person at the park office, and youths 17 and under must have a waiver signed. Helmets and knee and elbow pads are required and are not available for rent here.

Hours: The general park is open daily, 6am - 11pm. The skate park is open during the school year daily, noon - 10pm, with designated times for bikes only and for adult skaters (18 years and over). Call or check the website for those specific days and times. The park is open extended hours in the summer and on holidays.

Price: Free to the general park. The registration fee for the skatepark is $10 for ages 6 - 17 years; $15 for resident adults; $16.50 for non-resident adults, which includes one daily pass, too. Daily passes are $3 for youth; $5.50 for adults.

Ages: All for the park; 7 years and up for the skatepark.

MENTRYVILLE / PICO CANYON

(310) 589-3200 or (661) 222-9536 / www.lacountyparks.org; www.santa-clarita.com; www.scvhistory.com; www.lamountains.com

27201 Pico Canyon Road, Newhall

Mentryville was once an oil boom town. Of the few old buildings that remain, the Felton schoolhouse, built in 1885, is the only one open to the public. Inside are wooden school desks, a potbellied stove, blackboards, and a very small library room that no longer contains books. A dual-seat outhouse is just outside. Other structures on the grounds include Mr. Mentry's house, a barn and chicken coop, and a jail that was built for a movie. Short, guided tours of the town, where visitors learn the history of it and the area, are given by appointment.

Picnic tables are set up under shade trees. A seasonal creek runs through this area. Take a short hike on a service road that is stroller/wheelchair accessible. The road, a little over half a mile, leads to Johnson Park, a picnic spot featuring a replica of a wood oil derrick. Hike a bit further through the surrounding hills of Pico Canyon, past foundation remains and up to some overlooks. Head south for about three miles on the service road which has a gentle grade. After that, the trail changes and only experienced hikers should continue as there are several very steep and strenuous sections. Tip: Bring your own water.

Hours: The park is open daily, sunrise - sunset.

Price: $5 per vehicle.

Ages: All

MILLARD CANYON FALLS

(818) 899-1900 / www.fs.usda.gov

W. Loma Alta Drive and Chaney Trail, Los Angeles

Past the picnic tables and camping area is a fire road. Follow it for about a half mile - the walk is fairly easy and short. There are some boulders to climb over, but that's part of the fun. The sixty-foot falls are beautiful, and really flowing after a rain. The pool at the bottom is not very deep, but it is refreshing in the summer.

Want s'more time here? Bring your own everything and camp in one of the five primitive sites along the creek. There are fire rings, a pit toilet, and a campground host, but little else except for canopies of oak trees, being away from the city, stars, and the calls of nature - crickets, owls, and more.

Hours: Open daily, 6am - 8pm.

Price: Parking is $5 for an Adventure Pass (prepurchase at sporting goods stores or close by at Webster's Pharmacy - 2450 N. Lake Ave. in Altadena.) The cost of camping is just the $5 Adventure Pass.

Ages: 5 years and up.

MONROVIA CANYON PARK

(626) 256-8282 / www.cityofmonrovia.org

1200 N. Canyon Boulevard, Monrovia

This canyon park, bordering on the Angeles National Forest, backs into the wildlife corridor. The twenty developed acres contain a lovely nature center and several grassy and wooded picnic areas. Note that there is a cabin to rent near the nature center that sleeps up to twenty-eight people in sleeping bags - no beds. It comes with a fireplace, kitchenette, and other amenities.

The nature center contains taxidermied animals such as foxes, coyotes, two small black bears, raccoons, a mule deer, and more. There are live lizards and walking sticks here, as well as gopher snakes, rosy boas, and king snakes. A mural depicts animals in their natural habitat. A historical display features the story of the original settlers to this area, a reproduction of some of their tombstones, and remnants from Deer Park lodge, which was a supply cabin just up the road.

The sixty other acres are woodland nature at its best, supporting wildlife like deer, mountain lions, and bears, as well as small mammals and lizards and such. One of the most popular and beautiful trails, which is only one-and-a-half miles round trip from the nature center, leads to a year-round, thirty-foot-high waterfall that's fed by springs. For a longer hike, take the trail from the entrance station of the park, or go another route completely and hike the Ben Overturff Trail. Take the fire road a portion of the way on this trail or go all the way on the footpath. The trail is a moderate grade of seven miles that leads through virtually undisturbed wilderness, including an overlook, through trees, brush, a creek and more, and ends at the Deer Park lodge site.

Hours: The park is open daily, sunrise - 9pm for pedestrians. For vehicles, it's open Mon., Wed. - Fri., 8am - 5pm; Sat. - Sun., 7am - 5pm. Closed Tues. The nature center is usually open (if staffing is available) Wed. - Sat., 11am - 1pm; Sun., 9am - 5pm.

Price: $5 per vehicle during the week; $6 on weekends and holidays.

Ages: 4 years and up.

MOUNT WATERMAN SCENIC RIDES and DISC GOLF

(818) 790-2002; (619) 708-6595 / www.mtwaterman.org $$$$

Angeles Crest Hwy/CA 2, Mount Waterman

Mount Waterman does have ski lifts, but in the summer time, it's also a great place to go mountain biking on groomed trails. The trails range from fairly easy fire road trails at the base of the mountain and up to perhaps-a-bit-of-insanity-but-I-gotta-try-it trails. There are no bike rentals on the hill. If biking isn't your thing, go hiking, as there are miles and miles of it. And if that isn't either, just enjoy a fourteen-minute lift ride to the top to take in some fabulous scenery (and fresh air).

The Warming Hut at the top serves food and drinks, and has picnic tables outside among the trees. Bring your own disc and play on the 18-hole disc golf course up here amid the natural "obstacles" of trees, boulders, and walking up and down a mountainside. Great exercise and fun way to spend time together (unless you lose a disc).

Hours: Open late spring - early fall, Sat - Sun., 9am - 4pm (the Warming Hut is open these hours, too).

Price: Scenic lift, no bikes - $20 for adults; $15 for teens; $10 for seniors and ages 7 - 12 years; children 6 and under are free. Mt. bike lift tickets are $30 for all day usage. Disc golf is free with purchase of scenic lift ride - $20.

Ages: 2 years and up for just the scenic lift ride.

NORWALK PARK

(562) 929-5702 or (562) 929-5566 - park; (562) 929-5754 - museum and house; (562) 929-5622 - pool /   !/$
www.ci.norwalk.ca.us

13000 Clarkdale Avenue, Norwalk

The park has a spacious grassy area, plus a playground for younger kids, picnic tables, a basketball court, a pool, and skate park. The enclosed skate park has several ramps, a pyramid, and a few other street elements. Skaters and bikers (as there are set times for each) must wear a helmet and pads. The lovely, adjacent pool is open in the summer for recreation swim.

The Sproul Museum and Hargitt House are also on the park grounds. They contain artifacts from early Norwalk, including pictures, a few articles of clothing, and some furniture. They are usually open to tour on the third weekend of the month from 1pm - 4pm - call for more specifics.

Hours: The park and skate park are open daily, sunrise - dusk.

Price: Free. Swim sessions are $4 for adults; $3 for seniors and ages 17 and under.

Ages: All

ORANGEWOOD PARK - SKATE PARK

(626) 939-8430 / www.westcovina.org

1615 W. Merced Avenue, West Covina

Orangewood Park is soccer-oriented with two soccer fields and a soccer-themed playground. The playground follows the trend of creative features with twisty poles, lots of rope climbing elements and climbing walls, bridges, rings, seats to stand on the base of long poles, and more. There is more to do here, too, as there is a walking trail, picnic areas, basketball courts and two covered roller rinks for open play most days, but used by leagues in the evenings. The unsupervised 12,000-square-foot skate park welcomes in-line bladers and skaters to get some big air. Participants must wear safety gear.

Hours: Open daily, dawn - dusk.

Price: Free

Ages: All

ORCUTT RANCH HORTICULTURE CENTER

(818) 346-7449 / www.laparks.org   !

23600 Roscoe Boulevard, West Hills

This horticultural center was originally created in the early 1900's. A stroll through these nostalgic gardens is a delightful way to pass a half an hour, or so. A short, wide, stroller-friendly, dirt trail leads into a grove of shady oak trees and through grounds that are lush with greenery and wildflowers, and quite a few statues. The adjacent pathway along Dayton Creek, which borders one side of the ranch's perimeter, is not for strollers. The path does have stone benches for resting and leads to a few bridges that extend over the water. On the other side of the creek is a cozy picnic area. Look for ancient live oaks throughout the ranch; one is over 700 years old (and still growing)! Also on the grounds are a picnic table in the small bamboo grove, and more formal gardens consisting of maze-like hedges around the rose gardens. Note: Visitors may not walk through the adjacent acres of citrus trees.

The adobe building, once the Orcutt's home, is now used for park offices and group rental functions. A quick walk around and through the mostly unfurnished building allows you to see the Mexican-influence architecture and hand-painted, South-of-the-Border tiles.

Hours: The grounds are open daily, sunrise - sunset. Many private functions are held here, however, so call first. (But you would do that anyhow, right?)
Price: Free
Ages: All

OSCAR GARCIA SKATEPARK / RECREATION PARK

(626) 256-8246 - park / www.cityofmonrovia.org
843 East Olive Avenue and 620 S. Shamrock Avenue, Monrovia

The nice-sized Recreation Park features an enclosed playground with traditional and fun features, picnic areas with shade trees, ball fields, tennis courts, basketball courts, sand volleyball court, a roller hockey rink, a youth center, and lots of grassy run-around space under mature shade trees. A skate park here offers over 10,000 square feet of skating fun. The concrete skate park has two sections; a street side, with rails, stairs, ramps, kickers, and ledges; and a bowl side, with a kidney-shaped pool with roll-overs. Areas to watch the skaters are available. All participants are required to wear safety protection. The MONROVIA HISTORICAL MUSEUM (pg. 136) is also located inside Recreation Park.

Hours: The park is open daily, sunrise - sunset. The skate park is open daily, sunrise - 10pm.
Price: Free
Ages: All for the park; 7 years and up for the skate park.

PALOS VERDES PENINSULA LAND CONSERVANCY

(310) 541-7613 / www.pvplc.org
Various locations throughout the Palos Verdes and San Pedro areas

Once-a-month guided Nature Walks, most of them family oriented and suitable for children, are given by naturalists, historians, and geologists. Tour guides share information about the history of the area, wildlife, plants, and more. It's a great time and way to learn, enjoy fresh air, and spend time together. The walks range from one- to three-hours, and from easy to more difficult. All are on dirt paths. Starting points include Abalone Cove/Portuguese Bend, Madrona Marsh, and George F. Canyon Preserve, which are each listed separately in this section. Call or check the website for a calendar of events as there are also night hikes, special events, volunteer workdays on the trails, and more.

Hours: Public nature walks are usually given on the second Sat. of each month.
Price: Free, but donations are often requested.
Ages: 4 years and up.

PAN PACIFIC PARK / RENEE'S PLACE

(323) 939-8874 / www.laparks.org
7600 Beverly Boulevard, Los Angeles

The train-themed, all-abilities playground has train cars (about the size of small cars) in a semi circle around one of the playgrounds. Kids can climb aboard, use the steering wheels, actually listen to sounds of the whistle blowing and trains chugging along the tracks, and poke their heads out the windows to go full steam ahead. An elevated play structure has slides, a short rock-climbing wall, bridges, tactile learning panels, space to play underneath, swings (some that are wheelchair accessible), monkey bars, climbing apparatus, and more fun and imaginative elements all on rubberized flooring. Another play structure, lower to the ground for the younger set, has a textured slide, ramps, tunnel, slides, and speaking tubes. The park also boasts a little sprayground for wet, summertime fun; two basketball courts; yet another playground on the lower level the tiered grassy lawn with a castle, a ship, and play houses; an exercise area with some legitimate workout equipment; a lighted baseball diamond; a soccer field; an amphitheater; plenty of picnic tables and BBQs under shade trees; a pavement for jogging, strolling, etc., that crisscrosses throughout the park; and a massive amount of grass to play on.

This multi-ethnic park is a good park in and of itself and it's surrounded by more fun and educational places - the original FARMERS MARKET (pg. 21); THE GROVE - KIDS' THURSDAYS (pg. 95), an uptown, outdoor mall; and, sharing immediate park space, the LOS ANGELES MUSEUM OF THE HOLOCAUST (pg. 132). The park also shares space with a gym.

Hours: Open daily, 6am - 10pm.
 Price: Free
 Ages: All

PARAMOUNT RANCH

(805) 370-2301 / www.nps.gov/samo; www.lamountains.com
2903 Cornell Road, Agoura Hills

Howdy partners! Western Town, in Paramount Ranch, was once owned by Paramount Studios. The town was and still is used as a Western movie and TV set. Walk the dusty roads and inspect the weathered buildings from the outside. These buildings, which change slightly depending on the production being filmed though they always remain a Western motif, have included V. Shank Undertaker; a two-story, Hotel; a General Store (peer into the windows because it is usually stocked with clothing, canned good, supplies and more); a Saloon; a store "selling" mining equipment; a Blacksmith; Farmer's Exchange; a jail (again, peer into the windows to see the jail cell and sheriff's desk); and even a train depot, with actual tracks and a train. It all looks so real! Dress up your cowboy or cowgirl and bring your camera. Better yet bring props and a "script" and video them in their own Western mini-movie. Free, guided walking tours that describe the set and history of the area are usually given on the first and third Saturdays of each month at 9:30am.

Meanwhile, back at the ranch. . . over the bridge, next to the main part of town, is a huge meadow with a few picnic tables and some gigantic, old trees. At the end of the meadow is a wonderful, wooded trail that follows along a creek. It's only one-eighth of a mile round trip. If the kids are in the mood for hiking into the mountains, go up Coyote Canyon Trail, just behind Western Town. This uphill, half-mile, round-trip trail goes through green chaparral-covered canyons overlooking the valley. The picnic spot up here has a view that is worth the effort. Ask about ranger-led naturalist programs and special and seasonal events that the ranch hosts. Note that PETER STRAUSS RANCH (pg. 78) and KING GILLETTE RANCH (pg. 67), with the SANTA MONICA MOUNTAINS NATIONAL PARK HEADQUARTERS - VISITORS CENTER (Anthony C. Beilenson Interagency Visitor Center) (pg. 85), are just around the corner.

Hours: The park is open daily, 8am - sunset. Closed New Year's Day, Christmas, and some other federal holidays.
 Price: Free
 Ages: All

PETER STRAUSS RANCH

(805) 370-2301 / www.nps.gov/samo; www.lamountains.com
30000 Mulholland Highway, Agoura Hills

This rarely-frequented, sprawling park, once owned by actor Peter Strauss, has an easy, about a mile, mostly shaded, hiking trail that weaves amongst the chaparral and oak trees. More ambitious walkers can take the Malibu Lake Connector Trail. Inspect the ranch house; the huge grassy front lawn (good for picnicking); the waterless, fenced in swimming pool (once the biggest one in California); the remnants of the dam, aviary and some buildings; and other parts of this park, too. Off the ranch grounds, but in the immediate vicinity, are some funky stores and restaurants. Note that KING GILLETTE RANCH (pg. 67), with the SANTA MONICA MOUNTAINS NATIONAL PARK HEADQUARTERS - VISITORS CENTER (Anthony C. Beilenson Interagency Visitor Center) (pg. 85), is just around the corner.

Hours: Open daily, 8am - sunset.
 Price: Free
 Ages: 4 years and up.

PIONEER PARK

(909) 394-6200 or (909) 394-6230 / www.cityofsandimas.com
225 S. Cataract Avenue, San Dimas

This park offers a playground in a sand base, two basketball courts, two tennis courts, fitness equipment, picnic tables, and, most importantly for my boys, an 8,000 square-foot concrete skate park. It has all the elements of a good

skate park - ramps, a grinding box, and more. A helmet and knee and elbow pads are required.
Hours: Open daily, dawn - dusk.
Price: Free
Ages: All

PIRATE PARK

(562) 804-1424 / www.bellflower.org
16559 Bellflower Boulevard, Bellflower

Shiver me timbers! This very small, gated, pirate-themed park has young mateys running, climbing, playing, swabbing the deck, and searching for pieces of eight. Go under the Spanish fort entrance and then cross the short suspension bridge to the fort's top, look out through its windows, and descend the ladder on the other side. Besides a large treasure chest, pint-sized slide (painted blue to look like water) cutting through rocks, small boat, and tiny island of boulders and palm trees, the main attraction is the pirate ship decorated with skulls on its side and two tall masts with netting for sails. Kids clamber aboard and play in and on the deck, sides, inset cannons, and gangplank. Another great feature of the park is the little cave where kids can crawl into and look up and out through barred rock windows. Parents appreciate the many flat-topped boulders that line the inside perimeter creating ample places to sit and watch their buccaneers, and the rubbery flooring of the park.

Just outside the gates is a courtyard with a fountain, eateries, and a wall mural of a pirate and his ship at dock, with the ocean behind him - great as a backdrop for pictures.
Hours: Open daily, usually about 9am - 5pm (hours vary a little monthly).
Price: Free
Ages: 2 - 12 years.

PLACERITA CANYON NATURE CENTER AND PARK

(661) 259-7721 / www.placerita.org; www.lacountyparks.org
19152 Placerita Canyon Road, Newhall

Placerita Canyon was the site of one of the first gold discoveries, small though it was, in California. In fact, the famed oak tree where gold was first discovered, Oak of the Golden Dream, is just a short walk from the parking lot. There is a wealth of history and wilderness to be found at this Nature Center and park.

The Center has rescued live owls, hawks and other birds in cages outside. Inside are display cases with animal skulls, skins, and rocks; several taxidermied animals in dioramas such as mountain lions and a bear; some equipment that monitors weather conditions; and a few live spiders, snakes, and lizards.

An immediate large picnic area on the hillside of the park is nestled in a huge grove of oak trees. Play equipment is here, although the main attractions are the beauty of the area (I love this park!) and a few short hiking trails. Call to find out more about the Saturday nature hikes, the animal presentations from 1pm to 2pm, twilight hikes, nature tots walk, summer camps, and other special programs.

Extended hiking is great here, especially for slightly more experienced hikers. Canyon Trail, for instance, is a two-mile gradual climb, following along a stream and crossing over it several times, leading up to Walker Ranch, a cabin that has been refurnished and restored for a glimpse of yesteryear. The left fork leads to a Scout campground. The right fork leads to the Waterfall Trail, where, yes, about two-thirds of a mile back is a waterfall. Canyon Trail also hooks up to Los Pinetos Trail, which is a hardy, eight-mile hike.
Hours: The park is open daily, sunrise - sunset. The nature center is open Tues. - Sun. and holiday Mon., 9am - 5pm. Closed other Mon. and Christmas.
Price: Free
Ages: 2 years and up.

POINT DUME NATURAL PRESERVE

(310) 457-8143; (818) 597-9192 / www.lamountains.com; www.parks.ca.gov
Cliffside Drive, between Birdview Ave. and Dume Dr., Malibu

This overlook of the beach offers great shoreline views, but be careful as not all the cliffs have secure fencing. A dirt trail leads along the topside of the cliffs, while another trail, lined with chain link fence, meanders down to wooden steps that lead to the mostly rocky beach below. The somewhat narrow beach is great for walking and for tidepooling, as well as seeing and hearing seals. See POINT DUME STATE BEACH (pg. 13) for a nearby swim beach.
Hours: Open daily, sunrise - sunset.
Price: Free
Ages: 4 years and up.

POLLIWOG PARK and BEGG POOL

(310) 545-5621 - park; (310) 374-7575 - museum; (310) 802-5428 or (310) 802-5448 - Begg pool /
www.citymb.info

1601 Manhattan Beach Boulevard, Manhattan Beach

This expansive park is wonderfully deceptive. The part seen from the street is beautiful, with lots of grass and trees, a nine-hole disc golf course, and even a two-third-acre botanical garden with different, themed areas at the southwest corner of the park. There is also an exercise area with several pieces of equipment that offer a legit workout via lifting, running (gliding), pushing and pulling. The large, red and blue, all-abilities playground has long ramps, bridges, curvy tube slides, speaking tubes, mini zip line, climbing equipment, and towers to play on and under, plus traditional swings along with swings that are wheelchair accessible. A huge portion of the lawn is graded for free summer concerts. (Check the city's website calendar.) Some of the trees have low branches that beckon to climbers. An enclosed dog run is also here. The original, red, beach cottage in the park is a small historic museum. The rooms feature photos, old-fashioned bathing suits and other clothing, accessories, furniture and other artifacts of the olden days. Nearby is a rose garden.

As you take the stroller-friendly pathway leading down toward the interior of the park (there are pathways all around the park), you'll discover some "hidden" delights, such as a good-sized pond where marshy reeds and ducks abound. (Signs ask that you don't feed the ducks.) Tip: Watch your children around the water as there are no guard rails. Two other playgrounds are here - one is large and boat-themed with portholes, spiral tube slides coming out of the tall, multi-level structure, and lots of fun components, plus a good-sized cement lighthouse with misters, and a little cement play ship. Younger kids have another separate play area especially for them with swinging bridges, slides, and swings. This area also has grassy lawns, shade trees, cement picnic benches, and a small amphitheater.

Across the street from the main park are a baseball diamond and four lighted tennis courts. On the campus of Manhattan Beach Transition School, adjacent to the park, is Begg Pool. The pool is open during the summer for recreation swim, and at other times during the year for lap swim and lessons.

Hours: The park is open daily, dawn - dusk. The museum is open weekends, noon - 3pm; closed on major holidays. The pool is open for recreational swim mid-April through May, Sat., 1pm - 2:45pm, and June through September, daily. Call for specific session times.

Price: Free to the park and museum. The pool is $4 per person.

Ages: All

PRIME DESERT WOODLAND PRESERVE

(661) 723-6000 - city/preserve; (661) 723-6234 - nature center; (661) 723-6257- tours /
www.cityoflancasterca.org

43201 35th Street West, Lancaster

This stretch of desert preserve is carved out of the surrounding suburbia, which is within eyesight. Easy-walking, rope-lined, hard-packed dirt/sand trails meander through desert topography while interpretative signs allow visitors to learn about the plant and animal life they see. The longest trail is one mile, round trip.

The small nature center building displays a few taxidermied animals, pictures of old Lancaster, and a touch table with lots of great objects - fossils, feathers, an ostrich egg, and several replicas of dinosaur parts such as skin, claws, and a tooth. Check out the fairly extensive list of upcoming events on the website as well as information on guided tours and educational presentations for all ages.

Hours: The trails are open daily, 6am - dusk. The building is open Wed., Sat., and Sun., 10am - 4pm.

Price: Free

Ages: All

PYRAMID LAKE

(661) 295-7155 - lake; (661) 294-9403 - shop; boat rental; campground / www.rockymountainrec.com

Smokey Bear Road off Interstate 5, 20 miles N. of Santa Clarita Valley, Gorman

This huge sparkling reservoir lake, surrounded by hills, offers a myriad of activities for families. Year-round boating, including waterskiing, canoeing, rowboating, and rubber rafting, is allowed. B.Y.O.B. (Bring Your Own Boat) or rent one here. 12' to 14' aluminum fishing boats, which seat up four adults, are $35 for two hours, $5 for additional hours; pontoon boats are $90 for up to ten people for two hours. Rentals are available daily, year-round. Shaded picnic shelters and barbeques are near the docks. Some of the beach and picnic sites across and at the lake are reachable only by boat. Fish for seasonal bass, trout, catfish, crappie, and bluegill. A bait and tackle and snack shop is on the grounds.

A California state fishing license is required for those 16 years old or older. There are two waveless swim beaches open during the summer season at Emigrant Landing and Vaquero Day Use Area. They are patrolled by lifeguards on the weekends.

Meander on trails along the lake, enjoy a picnic meal, visit the nearby VISTA DEL LAGO VISITORS CENTER (pg. 156), and/or camp near the lake at Los Alamos Campground, which is two miles up the road and has room for ninety-three family units and three group units. No hook-ups or showers.

Hours: The lake and shop is open early September through April daily, 7am - 5pm; May through early September daily, 6am - 7pm. The swim beach is open the same hours in the summer. The park is closed New Year's Day, Thanksgiving, and Christmas.

Price: $11 per vehicle, which includes the swim beach. Camping is $20 per night.

Ages: All

RANCHO SANTA ANA BOTANIC GARDEN

(909) 625-8767 / www.rsabg.org

$$$

1500 N. College Avenue, Claremont

This lovely, eighty-six-acre botanic garden is beautiful in scope and sequence, and abundant with plants native only to California. Thousands of different kinds of plants grow in our state, so this garden covers a lot of ground with its giant sequoias, fan palms, California live oak, manzanitas, cacti, wildflowers, and more. There is also a replica Tongva Village on site that visitors can walk through and even go into some of the buildings.

The numerous trails, many of which are stroller friendly, afford good walking opportunities. Since the diverse vegetation attracts a wide variety of birds, bird lovers can pick up a bird check list at the gift shop, or join an organized bird walk on the first Sunday and third Saturday of each month at 8am. Butterfly lovers can enjoy these beautiful insects May through July at the California Butterfly Pavilion here for an additional $3 per person. I don't know how much horticulture my kids take in when we visit botanic gardens, but it's a good introduction to the variety and importance of plant life, plus a beautiful walk is always enjoyable.

Hours: Open daily, 8am - 5pm. Closed New Year's Day, July 4th, Thanksgiving, and Christmas.

Price: $9 for adults; $6 for seniors and students, $4 for ages 3 -12; children 2 and under are free. See American Horticultural Society (pg. x) for info on reciprocal memberships. Free on National Public Garden Day.

Ages: 3 years and up.

ROBERT E. RYAN PARK

(310) 544-5362 or (310) 544-5200 / www.rpvca.gov

30359 Hawthorne Boulevard, Rancho Palos Verdes

From the parking lot of this nine-acre park, you get a glimpse of the California coastline and, on a clear day, Catalina Island. Steps lead down into the park itself. Note: Strollers and wheelchairs can take a ramp that leads all the way down to the playground. The play equipment is ADA approved and wheelchair accessible. Set sail on a large ship-like structure with slides, rope climbing, bridges, and portholes, or on a smaller ship with similar apparatus. Play in the tot area on a climbing structure, swing on swings, and ride on springy whales. Stroll under shade trees on cement pathways that go through a good portion of the park. Bring a sack lunch to enjoy at the picnic tables, or grill food at the barbecues. This is one of my favorite parks for the play equipment, view, and openness of it.

The community center has some play equipment to check out, as long as you leave your driver's license in exchange. Play a game of basketball or baseball, or just romp around on the large, open, grassy areas.

Hours: Open daily, 9am - dusk.

Price: Free

Ages: All

ROXBURY PARK

(310) 285-2537 - park; (310) 285-6840 - community center; (310) 550-4979 - tennis / www.beverlyhills.org

471 S. Roxbury Drive, Beverly Hills

This beautiful 11-acre park fits right in with its surroundings of well-manicured lawns and stately homes. Although it is off a main street, it still seems somewhat removed from city life. The park offers a wealth of activities to choose from, such as tennis (four lighted courts, plus backboards), sand volleyball, and basketball. Along with a few picnic tables, barbecue pits, and some large shaded grassy areas with lots of mature trees, there is a good-sized playground with some innovative equipment to climb on, spin around, slide down, and swing from.

Hours: The park is open daily, 6am - 10pm.
Price: Free. Tennis courts before 5pm are $8 an hour for residents; $11 an hour for nonresidents; after 5pm and on weekends, prices are $9 for residents; $12 for nonresidents.
Ages: All

RUNYON CANYON PARK

(818) 243-1145 or (213) 485-5572 / www.laparks.org
2000 Fuller Street, Hollywood

Hike the hills of Hollywood in the popular Runyon Canyon. The dirt trail starts off at an upward slant, leading past ruins where house foundations and a few chunks of wall still remain. We walked the scenic, mostly woodland, main trail all the way up the mountain, as it affords a spectacular view of the famed city and of the Hollywood sign. We chose the looping hike, which we walked counter-clockwise, which is strenuous as it goes up steeply, then along the rim of the hills. The trail eventually levels off, then loops back down at a more gentle grade. The two-mile round-trip hike is not stroller/wheelchair accessible, nor is the slightly longer hike out to Mulholland. Bring water! Note: Look where you walk as this is a popular park for walking dogs. Also note the street signage when parking your car.
Hours: Open daily, dawn - dusk.
Price: Free
Ages: 5 years and up.

RUSTIC CANYON RECREATION CENTER

(310) 454-5734 - park; (323) 906-7953 - aquatics info; (310) 230-0137 - pool / www.laparks.org
601 Latimer Road, Pacific Palisades

This pretty park is nestled in a somewhat secluded area of Pacific Palisades, but it's worth making the effort to visit here. Shade trees line the perimeter of a paved pathway that leads down into the park. A baseball field, basketball court, playground, grassy area, climbing trees (always a hit with my family), a wooden pyramid structure (to climb on and around), two picnic areas, and barbeque pits, make up the central part of the park. Several tennis courts are located in one corner. Up near the parking lot is an older-style recreation center which offers a variety of classes. An adjacent, medium-sized community swimming pool is open seasonally.
Hours: The park is open daily, sunrise - sunset. The pool is open mid-June through Labor Day. Swim sessions are usually Mon. - Fri., 11am - 4pm; Sat. - Sun., 1pm - 5pm.
Price: Free to the park. Swim sessions are $3.50 for adults; $1 for seniors and ages 17 and under.
Ages: All

SADDLEBACK BUTTE STATE PARK

(661) 727-9899 or (661) 946-3055 / www.parks.ca.gov
17102 Avenue 'J' East, Lancaster

This state park is 3,000 acres of desert landscape, with Joshua trees scattered throughout and a huge granite mountain top, Saddleback Butte, jutting up almost a 1,000 feet above the valley. Be on the lookout for wildlife such as desert tortoises, rabbits, coyotes, kit foxes, kangaroo rats, and lots of reptiles and birds. Several hiking trails are available here, including a two-and-a-half-mile trail that leads to the top of the Butte with a view that makes the hike worthwhile. Springtime is particularly beautiful at the park because the wildflowers are in bloom. Near the entrance and visitor center/park headquarters are several covered picnic areas, complete with barbecues. The visitor center features displays and some hands-on exhibits about the geology, history, plants, and animal life of the area. You can also pick up a trail map here. Please remember that desert weather is hot in the summer and cold in the winter, so dress accordingly. Overnight camping is available. Saddleback is located just a few miles down the road from the ANTELOPE VALLEY INDIAN MUSEUM (pg. 99).
Hours: Open daily, sunrise - sunset.
Price: Day use is $6 per vehicle; $5 for seniors; $3 for disabled. Camping is $20 per night and on a first come, first served basis.
Ages: 5 years and up.

SALT LAKE PARK / HUNTINGTON PARK SKATE PARK

(323) 584-6218 / www.hpca.gov
3401 Florence Avenue, Huntington Park

This twenty-three-acre park comes fully equipped for a day of sports fun. It has four fenced-in baseball diamonds, plus basketball courts, a soccer field, tennis courts, a gym, picnic area with grills, and a good-sized playground. The latter has a few really tall structures to climb up with slides going down, plus ramps, climbing elements and swings. An adjacent colorful sprayground has a huge animated pole spider and a frog and other shapes that spurt water. A 12,000-square-foot, gated skate park is near the park's center. The lighted skate park has rails, pyramids, ledges, ramps, and a few smooth "open" sections for skating. Safety gear - a helmet and pads - is required.

Hours: The park is open daily, sunrise - sunset. The skate park is open Mon. - Fri., noon - 9pm; Sat. - Sun., 10am - 6pm. It is open longer in the summer and during school holidays.

Price: Free

Ages: All

SAND DUNE PARK

(310) 545-5621 or (310) 802-5448 / www.citymb.info

At the corner of 33rd Street and Bell Avenue, Manhattan Beach

This little park has a big surprise. While there is a tiny playground for younger children, the park is "beachy" and really popular because of its steep wall of sand (100 feet high) that is perfect for running, jumping, or rolling down. Take the 200 steps on the switchback that lead to the top of the hill, or just climb up the hill. Bring your own bucket and shovel to play with at the bottom. Here is a local's favorite tip: After it rains, take a snow sled down the hill! Look below for sand dune reservation information as it's the only way to access it, and only twenty people are allowed on the hill per hour.

Behind the playground is a green grassy stretch. Picnic tables and a few barbecue pits under a shelter are also available. Parking is limited.

Hours: Use of the dune is by reservation only, one hour only, per day. Must submit printed online reservation to hand to dune attendant. $1 is due with your reservation form - no change is available. The dune is open at certain time slots, daily, 8am - 4:30pm (last reservation time) most of the year, and 3pm (last reservation time) in the winter time. The playground is open daily, 8am - 7pm and is free; no reservations needed.

Price: $1 for the sand dunes for ages 13 and up; kids 12 and under are free and no reservations are needed. Monthly memberships are available, too.

Ages: All

SAN DIMAS CANYON COMMUNITY REGIONAL PARK

(888) 239-6700 or (909) 599-7512 / parks.lacounty.gov

1628 N. Sycamore Canyon Road, San Dimas

Nestled in the foothills of the San Gabriel Mountains, adjacent to Angeles National Forest, is a wonderful county park/museum/wildlife sanctuary. The small nature museum contains a few live snakes, such as the California king and gopher snakes; taxidermied animals such as a mountain lion, fox, and birds; and several small collections including rocks, arrowheads, insects, and butterflies.

The outside wildlife sanctuary offers a caged home to several injured or non-releasable native animals. Red-tailed hawks, heart-faced barn owls, and great-horned owls are part of the bird rehabilitation area - not part of the bird "rebellion" area as my son misread the sign. (Hmm - could be something to do with his childhood. . . .) Other live animals here include a few deer, tortoises, and snakes, plus many squirrels running around freely. The type of animal rotate according to need.   An almost one-mile, self-guiding nature trail begins in the oak woodland just behind the nature center building and loops around. There are plenty of picnic tables under the cover of shady oak trees. Some of the picnic areas have barbeques. The area below the museum has a baseball diamond, a half basketball court, horseshoe pits, large grassy areas and a few really good, multi-story play structures that feature slides, tubes, rock climbing rocks, play space underneath and more. A portion of a long bike route goes through part of the park. Come visit the park on your own, take a guided tour, or come via a Jr. Ranger Program which is offered through the park system. A visit to the San Dimas Canyon Park is great for temporarily escaping city life.

Hours: The park is open daily, sunrise - sunset. The nature center and animal sanctuary are open Tues. - Sun., 9am - 4:15pm. Closed Mon. and Christmas.

Price: Free

Ages: All

N MARTIN PARK

(562) 866-9771 / www.lakewoodcity.org
5231 Ocana Avenue, Lakewood

How do you get to a ball, if you're Cinderella? In a pumpkin coach, of course. This park, also known as Pumpkin Park, has fairy tale elements with a huge pumpkin coach to get into and "ride" (and benches on the front and back of it), and two life-size horse statues pulling it. The rest of the large playground resembles a castle with rock-climbing turrets (some tall ones) that have slides coming out of them, ramps, and play spaces underneath. It also has a good-sized zip line; bars; swings; orange stools to sit on or play on; an orange and a green climbing structure; a rope structure; and spheres with big holes to sit in and large circles to climb through, plus other creative elements to live happily ever after.

There is a wading pool that's open seasonally sandwiched between the pumpkin playground and an adjacent playground which has a castle-style top over the picnic tables. It features more traditional play pieces geared for younger kids, all in a sand base.

Hours: Open daily, sunrise - sunset.
Price: Free
Ages: 18 months - 12 years.

SANTA CLARITA SPORTS COMPLEX - AQUATIC CENTER - SKATE PARK

(661) 250-3700 - sports complex; (661) 250-3740 - skatepark; (661) 250-3766 or (661) 250-3761 - aquatics / www.santa-clarita.com; www.scskatepark.com
20850 Centre Pointe Parkway, Santa Clarita

Indoor, outdoor, year-round fun for the family is available at the nicely-landscaped Sports Complex. Those who got game can use the two, inside, full-sized basketball courts, badminton courts, and four racquetball/handball courts. Outside, on the upper level of the park, are two basketball courts, a sand volleyball court and an area with green, plastic, fun-looking, but serious exercise equipment that appeals to kids and adults alike for training.

Take the cement pathway to the lower level (or park down here) to the unsupervised, massive (40,000 square feet!), lighted cement skate park for skaters and bmx riders - beginners to pros. It features large bowls, a street plaza, half-pipe tunnel, a bridge, snake runs, skate-able planters, rails, stairs, a perimeter path, and more. Riders must wear a helmet and pads.

The adjacent Aquatic Center has three pools - a fifty-meter competition pool, a dive pool, and an activity pool. The good-sized activity pool is comprised of a 160-foot, twisty slide (must be 48" or taller to slide); a shallow splash pool; and a colorful, water play structure for young kids that has a small slide, several water pipes with steering wheels and nozzles that squirt out water, and an inverted umbrella that overflows with water. Proper swimwear must be worn. Lounge chairs are welcome. Picnic tables are here.

Hours: The skate park is open daily, 8am - 8pm. Skaters 12 and under, only, skate from 8am - 10am on weekend mornings. Lap swim is open year round. Rec swim is open Memorial Day weekend - mid-June on weekends only, then mid-June - Labor Day, daily, 10am - 2pm. The rest of the park is open daily, sunrise - sunset.
Price: The gym is $3 for adults; $2 for seniors and 17 years and under. The skate park is free. Recreational swim is $6 for adults; $4 for seniors and ages 3 - 17; children 2 and under are free. It's $5 for lap swim.
Ages: 3 years and up, depending on the activity.

SANTA FE DAM RECREATIONAL AREA

(626) 334-1065 - park; (626) 334-6555 - boat, bike, bait and fishing poles rentals / parks.lacounty.gov; www.sgmrc.org; www.wheelfunrentals.com
15501 E. Arrow Highway, Irwindale

Though located in the middle of an industrial section, city sounds fade away while at this enormous recreational area that sports a mountainous backdrop. Our first stop was at the nature center trail, at the northern end of the park, which has info on the area and a few live snakes in cages. The rock-lined, three-quarter-mile looping trail here is paved, level, and a delight to walk. Desert is the predominant theme. We observed an abundance of cacti and other plant life, and animals such as jackrabbits, lizards, roadrunners, and hummingbirds. You can also take a longer trail, such as the Santa Fe Dam Loop Trail, which is 4 miles.

The huge lake toward the entrance offers a nice-sized beach with a life guarded swimming area. A water play area for children 52" and under is located by the picnic area. It has a good-sized structure with a few slides, ramps, pipes, wheels that turn, and some colorful climbing and water squirting apparatus all in shallow water. This lakeside area, with its shade trees and acres of green grass, is vastly different from the northern desert area. Other attractions in the park include picnic facilities; a snack bar (usually open in the summer); unpaved walking trails; fishing - a California state license is required for those 16 years of age and older; and quiet boating activities (no gasoline powered boats allowed), with boat rentals of kayaks and pedal boats available on weekends and holidays year round. Note that model rockets and model airplanes can fly from here, too. The playgrounds are great for adventurers who like to climb as they have huge rope climbing configurations and other climbing apparatus, plus more standard and fun equipment.

Ready for a bike ride? Choose your route and go the distance all the way north to San Gabriel Canyon, or south to Long Beach and Seal Beach, using various trails that go through this park. Parts of the thirty-seven-mile bike trail are paved, while other parts are not. Bike rentals, for within the park, start at $20 for a surrey which can seat three adults and two kids.

Hours: The park is open May - October daily, 6:30am - 8pm; November - April daily, 6:30am - 6pm. Closed Christmas. The nature center is usually open daily, 10am - 1pm, but it's staffed by volunteers so hours can vary. The swim beach is open Memorial Day - Father's Day on weekends only, then Father's Day - Labor Day, Thurs. - Sun., 10am - 6pm. The water play area is open Memorial Day - Labor Day, Sat. - Sun., 10:30am - 6pm. Boat and bike rentals are usually available on weekends most of the year, and daily during the summer, 11am - 4:30pm.

Price: $10 per vehicle March - October; $10 on weekends and holidays, but free on weekdays, November - February. There is no extra charge to use the swim beach. The water play area is $2 per person for each hour-and-a-half session. Rowboats are $30 an hour. SUPs are $12 an hour. Pedal boats start at $20 an hour for one person; $30 for a double. Kayaks are $12 an hour for one person; $20 for two.

Ages: All

SANTA MONICA MOUNTAINS NATIONAL PARK HEADQUARTERS - VISITORS CENTER (Anthony C. Beilenson Interagency Visitor Center)

(805) 370-2301; (805) 370-2300 / www.nps.gov/samo; www.lamountains.com; www.localhikes.com   !
26876 Mulholland Highway at King Gillette Ranch, Calabasas

From the thousands of acres of mountains, to the coastline beaches, to the inland grounds, the enormous Santa Monica Mountain National Park covers a major part of the wilderness and parkland in Southern California. This includes hiking, biking, and equestrian trails, plus camping, swimming, scenic drives, ranger-led programs, and more. One reason I'm writing about this place is because maps, for purchase and for free, and a calendar schedule of events for the numerous parks within the Santa Monica Mountains Park system can be found here. The parks, most of which can be found listed individually under the Great Outdoors Section, include Circle X Ranch, Coldwater Canyon Park, Franklin Canyon Ranch, Leo Carrillo State Park, Malibu Creek State Park, Malibu Lagoon State Beach, Paramount Ranch, Peter Strauss Ranch, Rancho Sierra Vista, Temescal Gateway Park, Topanga State Park, Will Rogers State Historical Park, and the UCLA Stunt Ranch. If you are a hiker extraordinare, or want to just hike a fantastic trail, ask for information on the Backbone Trail, a trail that extends nearly seventy miles across and through the Santa Monica Mountains.

The center has a few interpretative displays; a gift shop containing hiking and nature books and other items; a twenty-minute movie in the small theater about the history of the Santa Monica mountains; and a place to crawl into a cement short tunnel to see what it's like being a coyote in suburbia. Outside are a few picnic tables, a CA native plant section and two hiking trails that begin from here, as it is located at the KING GILLETTE RANCH (pg. 67). See the Ranch to find out what else there is to see on the premises. You could spend some time just at the visitors center! Note that PETER STRAUSS RANCH (pg. 78) and PARAMOUNT RANCH (pg. 78) are just around the corner.

Hours: Open daily, 9am - 5pm. Closed on some federal holidays.
Price: Free. Parking is free for the first 2 hours.
Ages: 5 years and up.

SCHABARUM REGIONAL COUNTY PARK

(626) 854-5560 / parks.lacounty.gov   !/$$
17250 E. Colima Road, Rowland Heights

Looks can be deceiving. This park doesn't look like much from just driving by, but it goes deep. At 640 acres huge, this country has lots of green rolling hillsides and is seemingly removed from city life as ninety percent of it is left in its natural state. Toward the entrance are scattered picnic tables, barbeque pits, an exercise area with machines to use, a fun playground featuring a pirate ship, shade trees, and open space to run around. Take a quick stroll through the hummingbird and butterfly garden - you might see some! About a mile of paved trail follows along a creek as it winds through part of the park. There are twenty miles of mostly unshaded dirt hiking and equestrian trails (get a map!) that weave through the rest of the sprawling countryside, leading past shrub, a few groves of trees, wild flowers (in the spring), and cherry trees, which are beautiful in bloom. Come in the summertime and enjoy free Tuesday nights concerts in the park.

Hours: Open October - March, 7am - 6pm; April - September, 7am - 8pm. Closed on Christmas Day.
Price: The park is free during the week; $6 per vehicle on weekends and holidays.
Ages: All

SMITH PARK

(626) 308-2875 / www.sangabrielcity.com
232 W. Broadway, San Gabriel

A beautiful and intricate tile wall encompasses basketball courts, lighted tennis courts, handball courts, and youth and toddler playgrounds which are shaped like a ship (and has a dinosaur on springs - hmmm). A swimming pool, a wading pool, picnic areas, grassy run-around space, and more, are yours for coming to Smith Park. Another play area, based on Native American Tongva peoples, incorporates a picnic area, rolling green lawns, and a few concrete animals, such as dolphins and seals. Take a look at the large concrete compass at this spot, too. Walkways crisscross throughout the park.

Hours: Open daily, 7:30am - 10pm. The swim pool is open mid-June through Labor Day for recreation swim.
Price: Free to the park. Swim sessions are $2 for adults; $1.50 for ages 17 and under. The wading pool is free.
Ages: All

SOLSTICE CANYON

(805) 370-2301 or (310) 457-8494 / www.nps.gov/samo
Corral Canyon Road, Malibu

This canyon offers a variety of trail lengths and terrain, from huge shady oak woodlands to shrubs to an intermittent stream. Short, easy trails include the 1.2-mile round trip on Dry Canyon Trail, that has some stone steps, which ends near a seasonal waterfall and the stone and brick ruins of a ranch house. The slightly longer Solstice Canyon Trail is a 2.1-mile-round-trip paved road for bikers as well as hikers. Longer trails include the 3.9-mile Sostomo Trail/Deer Valley Loop. We found the canyon to be a peaceful and beautiful place to explore nature. A few picnic tables in a lovely grove are located near the parking lot. Note: There are restroom facilities. Tip: Bring your own water.

Hours: Open daily, 7am - sunset. Closed federal holidays.
Price: Free
Ages: 4 years and up.

SOUTH COAST BOTANICAL GARDENS

(310) 544-6815 or (310) 544-1948 / www.southcoastbotanicgarden.org
26300 Crenshaw Boulevard, Rolling Hills Estates

This attractive, eighty-seven-acre garden is a breath of fresh air for Southern Californians. Plants from around the world include exotic trees (redwoods, palms, and others), shrubs, and flowers from Africa and New Zealand. There are several different specialty areas here including a cactus garden, a rose garden (we love taking pictures of roses here - such color and variety), a woodland walk (one of my favorites!), and a Garden for the Senses. In the latter, vegetation with unique fragrances, textures, and color schemes flourish. Follow the yellow brick road to and through the Discovery Garden, a fanciful children's garden that features old-fashioned storybook figures and structures, as well as plants. Can your child spot Humpty Dumpty, or the three little kittens who lost their mittens?

Stroll along the cement and dirt pathways through the gardens, under shade trees, and up and down the gently rolling hills and grassy areas. It feels good to be surrounded by such beauty! Feed ducks at the man-made lake and look for koi, turtles, and heron and other waterfowl who make their home here. Outside food can't be brought in, but a picnic area is just outside the gates in a little grove.

Hours: Open daily, 9am - 5pm. Closed on Christmas.
Price: $9 for adults; $6 for seniors and students; $4 for ages 5 - 12; children 4 and under are free - cash only. Admission is free the third Tues. of every month. See American Horticultural Society (pg. x) for info on reciprocal memberships.
Ages: 3 years and up.

STONER PARK

(310) 479-7200 / www.laparks.org

!/$

1835 Stoner Avenue, Los Angeles

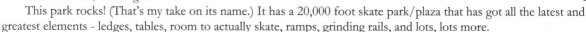

This park rocks! (That's my take on its name.) It has a 20,000 foot skate park/plaza that has got all the latest and greatest elements - ledges, tables, room to actually skate, ramps, grinding rails, and lots, lots more.

Other facilities here include a basketball court; baseball diamonds; tennis courts; volleyball courts; picnic area with BBQs; a rec center; grassy, run-around space with lots of mature shade trees; and a long, narrow, all-abilities playground. The rubberized and sand-based playground has swings, raised sand basins, ramps, slides, misters (and a few missus), and places to play both on and under the play structures.

A tiny, shady, Japanese nature garden, complete with a few cherry trees and a wonderful, gnarly tree that's great for sitting in, is located in front of the gated pool area. The pool has a graduated slope from the slightly deep waters (4.5 feet) into the more shallow end that sports a sprayground. This aquatics area has a tall "mushroom" that water flows off, plus colorful pipes and tubes that squirt, spurt and rain down water. Note that the ratio is 1 adult to 1 child. A lifeguard is on duty. An adjacent, small, separate pool features a long and twisty waterslide. Proper swimwear must be worn in the pools by everyone coming inside the gates, even non-swimmers.

Hours: The park and skate park are open daily, sunrise - sunset. The pool and water play area are open mid-June - mid-September, usually for four-hour increments during the day, although they are open daily, 11am - 6pm the end of June through mid-August. Call or check the website for specific times.

Price: The park and skate park are free. The pool and water play area are $2.50 for adults; free for seniors, persons with disabilities, and ages 17 and under.

Ages: All

STONEY POINT

(818) 756-8189 / www.laparks.org; www.lamountains.com

!

11000 Topanga Canyon Boulevard, Chatsworth

Do you have a rock-climber wannabe in your household? Stoney Point, so named for the large boulder perched at the top of the sandstone hill, is a famous (at least locally) rock climbers' delight. Practice repelling on this small mountain of stone, or just hike the trail up to the top. Either way, it can be an exhilarating way to spend part of the day. Be on the lookout for the numerous alcoves and caves to crawl into, but use caution, too. There is a dirt path toward the "back" of the hill that visitors can hike for a bit.

Hours: Open daily, sunrise - sunset.

Price: Free

Ages: 6 years and up to hike; your discretion about rock climbing.

STOUGH CANYON NATURE CENTER - WILDWOOD CANYON PARK

(818) 238-5440 / www.burbankca.gov; www.lamountains.com

!

2300 Walnut Avenue, Burbank

Snuggled right into the mountains, this nature center offers a variety of displays around the perimeter and some in the center, as well as in a few classrooms. The exhibits include taxidermied animals, such as bobcat, raccoons, deer, quail, and an owl; a few live tarantulas and snakes (which visitors can touch), and a few nonliving ones; a touch table with animal skins and bones; a beekeeping display; and several colorful information panels. Ask about the numerous educational programs and recreational opportunities, ranging from organized nature hikes to astronomy workshops. Tip: Pick up a trail map here.

The fire road behind the nature center winds its way up the mountain and leads to a main trail, the Verdugo Mountainway Trail, which traverses the Verdugo Mountains. Taken in the other direction, where the road branches, the path eventually leads to Brand fire road and BRAND PARK (pg. 49).

Just down the street from the nature center is Wildwood Canyon Park, at 1701 Wildwood Canyon Drive. A two-mile trail system here snakes around on the Burbank side of the Verdugo Mountains and a steep, three-plus-mile Vital Link Trail hooks up with the Verdugo Mountainway. There are a few places at Wildwood to park, picnic, and play, with some grassy areas to run around.

Hours: The nature center is open September - May, Mon., 1pm - 5pm; Tues. - Sat., 9m - 5pm; Sun., 11am - 5pm. It is open June - August, Mon. - Sat., 9am - 5pm; Sun., 11am - 5pm. Closed most holidays. The trails are open daily, dawn - dusk.

Price: Free

Ages: 3 years and up.

SWITZER FALLS

(626) 574-5200 or (626) 574-1613 / www.hikespeak.com

Angeles Crest Highway, Los Angeles

Ah - the rewards of a hike! Follow the moderately graded Gabrielino Trail on the west end of the picnic area about a mile to the remnants of Switzer's Camp, which is a backpacker's campground, to reach the top of the falls, a fifty-foot chute. To reach the bottom, and your destination of a refreshing (i.e., cold!), rock-lined swimming hole surrounded by rock walls, continue hiking on the Gabrielino Trail, along the right-hand side (or west) of the canyon wall and over some boulders. Note: Please use caution around any waterfall - wet rocks are slippery rocks, and watch out for poison oak. If you don't like heights, this is not the hike for you. The hike is about 4.5 miles roundtrip.

Another alternative is to take the three-mile-or-so hike to Bear Canyon. Once you've hiked down the initial trail and reached Switzer's Camp, go up the canyon to Bear Canyon trail. A primitive campsite, a seasonal stream, and careful boulder hopping await. Bring a water bottle.

The small parking lot fills up early on the weekends. Many families stay near the entrance to picnic and wade in the Arroyo Seco Creek.

Hours: Open daily, 8am - dusk.
Price: $5 per vehicle for an Adventure Pass.
Ages: 7 years and up.

TEMESCAL GATEWAY PARK

(310) 454-1395 or (310) 589-3200 / www.lamountains.com

15601 W. Sunset Boulevard, Pacific Palisades

This 140-acre, comely wilderness park is particularly pretty in the spring when the wildflowers are blooming profusely, though anytime is a good time to visit. Dirt trails meander throughout that are often shaded by large oak, sycamore and other trees. Follow the one-and-a-half-mile trail that winds uphill, back through the canyon along the seasonal creek to a bridge and waterfall. Other trails allow access to Topanga State Park and Will Rogers State Historic Park.

Picnic tables are scattered throughout the park, so bring a sack lunch. Ask about the Outdoor Education Program - a hands-on outdoor experience for urban youth.

Hours: Open daily, sunrise - sunset.
Price: $10 per vehicle. There is some free parking on the street, with lots of extra walking involved to get to the park, though.
Ages: All

TIERRA BONITA PARK

(800) 735-2922 / www.cityoflancasterca.org

44910 North 27ᵗʰ St. East, Lancaster

Located next to an elementary school, Tierra Bonita, which means "beautiful land", fits its namesake with 27-acres of loveliness and fun. Park amenities include lighted softball fields, exercise stations, picnic tables, and lots and lots of open space and lots and lots of trees, with paved pathways gently meandering thruout.

The playgrounds are very different from one another - one boasts a really high, multi-story tower/building to climb up and in, and has long, enclosed slides emerging from it; another has a shorter structure, plus swings. An adjacent area has small buildings/houses for kids to use for pretend, that include fences, doors and windows. It also has a train, fire truck and a few other play vehicles. A plain, but refreshing, splash pad has water spurting up from the ground and fountains seasonally.

Hours: Open daily, sunrise - sunset. The splash pad is open spring - early fall.
Price: Free
Ages: 18 months - 12 years.

TONGVA PARK

(310) 458-8310 / tongvapark.squarespace.com

1685 Main Street, suite 200, Santa Monica

This architecturally unusual, 6.2-acre park in the midst of Santa Monica offers a place of respite as plants flow around fountains and as a spiral pathway leads up to a viewpoint of the ocean that's encased in an oval grid (lovelier than it sounds). Other features include nice landscaping, tiered cement and grass seating, a lawn, alcoves, some palms and shade trees, and forty-nine stainless steel poles in a grid that alternate in height and have a weather vane, or anemometer, on the ends - collectively, it's a sculpture. A stone stairs cascading waterfall spills into a small, zero depth splash walkway.

Discovery Hill is a section just for kids. One play structure is kind of in the shape of the frame of a hut that kids can climb on. They can also climb the rope ladders inside it. One area has slides that go down a covered surface hill. A rock climbing element is adjacent to it and to a boulder-enclosed water play area (i.e. fountains shooting up). Check out the music wall, sculpturers that double as play equipment, and more in this aesthetically-pleasing and fun park. It is located across from Ken Genser Square, a one-acre park.

Hours: Open daily, 6am - 11pm. The splash pad is open daily, 10am - 6pm.
Price: Free
Ages: 3 years and up.

TOPANGA STATE PARK

(310) 455-2465 / www.lamountains.com; www.parks.ca.gov $$
20828 Entrada Road, Topanga

Believe it or not, this massive state park, actually a huge natural preserve, is all contained within the Los Angeles city limits. Thirty-six miles of hiking, biking, and equestrian trails go through canyons, hills, and cliffs of the Santa Monica Mountains. One of the main access for the trails is Trippet Ranch. Which trail you choose depends on how long you want to hike. A two-mile hike to Eagle Junction leads to the looping Eagle Springs trail. We like this one because of the boulders. Or, choose the broad Topanga Fire Road, or various other routes. Another popular trailhead is at WILL ROGERS STATE HISTORIC PARK (pg. 158). A small museum/visitor's center has a few exhibits and maps for the area, plus it hosts education programs. It's open January through July on Sundays from 10am - 3pm. Regardless of where you start (or finish), bring your own water and wear sunscreen. Note: No dogs allowed on the trails.

Hours: Open daily, 8am - sunset.
Price: $10 per vehicle. (Parking at Will Rogers is $12.)
Ages: 5 years and up.

TRANCAS CANYON PARK

(310) 317-1364 / www.malibucity.org
6050 Trancas Canyon Road, Malibu

Move 'em on, head 'em out, rawhide! This great, Western-themed playground feels like the Old West for young uns. On a plateau, surrounded by mountains with a view of the beach, the playtown has boulders and trees around it, and even some in it. The little town is comprised of a few, two-story buildings on wooden poles, named Rindge Hotel, General Store, Malibu Post Office, and Tile Store. The buildings have slides coming out from them; rock-climbing walls (one has a boot, horseshoe, and sheriff's star as the "rocks"); a series of wagon wheels to climb up; doorways; platforms; and lots of space under the raised buildings with benches and short tunnels for more creative play. Ride the range on play horses and a buffalo on huge springs. Logs, cargo nets, tunnels to crawl through, bridges to cross (one crosses over a blue, recycled rubber area designed to look like water); a configuration of blocks; and swings (including toddler swings) complete this truly out-West little town.

There is a huge expanse of grass (i.e. an athletic field) adjacent to the playground, plus shaded picnic benches. There is a really large, dirt, enclosed dog park (with bridges and other play elements for canines) on an upper level from the playground.

Hours: Open Mon. - Fri., 8am - dusk (or 7pm, whichever is earlier); Sat. - Sun., 9am - dusk (or 7pm)
Price: Free
Ages: 2 - 11 years

VALLEY PARK and SKATE PARK

(818) 238-5300 - park; (818) 238-5390 - skate park / www.burbankca.gov $
1625 N. Valley Street, Burbank

Skate one, skate all! This enclosed, good-size (over 10,000 square feet), concrete skatepark with a small bowl, pool, a street course, a small pyramid, rails and skating area is supervised and good, I understand, mostly for beginners to intermediate skaters. (It all looks hard to me.) There are separate sessions for skaters and for BMX riders, and lights for nighttime use. All participants must have a signed waiver and must wear a helmet and pads (yea!).

The rest of the park has a good, sand-based playground, plus picnic tables, grassy areas, shade trees, paved pathways, and a ball field.

Hours: Open during the school year, Mon. - Thurs., 4pm - 8pm; Fri., 4pm - 9pm; Sat., 10am - 9pm; Sun., noon - 7pm. Open during the summer and on holidays, Mon. - Fri., 11am - 9pm; Sat., noon - 9pm; Sun., noon - 8pm.
Price: There is an annual pass fee of $50 for Burbank residents, $60 for non-residents; then daily rates of $3 for residents; $5 for non.
Ages: 4 years and up.

VASQUEZ ROCKS

(661) 268-0840 / parks.lacounty.gov

10700 W. Escondido Canyon Road, Agua Dulce

This park became an instant favorite with my boys with its 932 acres of eye-catching, spectacular and unusual rock formations, many of which are sandstone and almost triangular in shape, jutting practically straight up from the ground. They have ridges along their sides making them moderately easy to climb, although my kids also climbed much higher (to the tops!) than my heart could take. For those who don't like heights, there are several smaller rocks to conquer, and plenty of walking trails offering stunning views, plus Tataviam Indian sites and a seasonal stream.

If you experience "deja vu" while here, it's probably because this park has been used in numerous commercials and films, such as *The Flintstones* (the stones do look prehistoric), as well as several westerns and science fiction thrillers. Tip: Call before you come because sections of the park are closed when filming is taking place.

The Ranger Station / interpretative center, housed in a barn with corralled horses outside, enhances the mood for this all-natural, rustic park. Be forewarned - drinking water is not available in the park. Camping for organized youth groups is allowed.

Hours: Open daily, sunrise - sunset. The Ranger Station is open Tues. - Sun., 8am - 4pm.
Price: Free
Ages: 3 years and up.

VERDUGO PARK AND SKATE PARK

(818) 548-2786 or (818) 548-6420 / www.glendaleparksfoundation.org

1621 Canada Boulevard, Glendale

This lighted, 15,000-square-foot skate park has two bowls, a kidney-shaped pool, ramps, slide rails, and more, all on a concrete surface. The park is fenced-in and staff is on hand at all times. Skaters under 17 years must have a parent or legal guardian sign a waiver. Wearing a helmet and knee and elbow pads is a requirement. No rentals are available.

The surrounding, forty-acre park has mature oak trees providing lots of shade and places to climb, picnic tables, a good-sized playground, baseball diamond, basketball court, horseshoe court, and more.

Hours: Open during the school year, Mon. - Fri., 4pm - 10pm; Sat., 10am - noon (for ages 14 and under) and noon - 10pm (all ages); Sun., 10am - 10pm. Open school holidays and summer Mon. - Fri., noon - 10pm; weekends same as above.
Price: The park is free. The skate park is $4 a day for adults; $3 for ages 17 and under.
Ages: 7 years and up.

VIRGINIA ROBINSON GARDENS

(310) 550-2065 / www.robinsongardens.org $$$
1008 Elden Way, Beverly Hills

Once the estate of the department store magnate, Robinsons (of Robinsons-May), this house has the distinction of being one of the first homes built in Beverly Hills. A ninety-minute- guided tour of the grounds includes a brief guided tour through the house, showing off the furnishings and other collections gathered from around the world. Visitors walk through the living rooms, bedroom, kitchen, and other rooms.

Probably of more interest to older kids is the bulk of the tour through the six acres of botanic gardens. The hilly gardens, which are not stroller or wheelchair friendly as there are numerous stairs, feature lush tropical and subtropical plants, roses, and more. Brick pathways connect the diverse areas of foliage that are also landscaped with ponds, fountains, and an Olympic-size pool. The grounds are a gardener's delight!

Hours: Open by reservation only, made 4 - 6 weeks in advance, Tues. - Sat. Closed during the month of May.
Price: $11 for adults; $6 for seniors and students; $4 for ages 5 - 12; children 4 years and under are free.
Ages: 9 years and up.

WHIT CARTER PARK

(800) 735-2922 / www.cityoflancasterca.org
45635 Sierra Hwy, Lancaster

This is a funky playground with so many imaginative and separate elements, it's hard to describe. There are several free-standing rock climbing rocks. There are also curved "walls", some that are really high and long, with climbing foot holds as well as holes in them; huge balls with holes to sit in and climb thru; cargo ropes; colorful poles in all shapes and sizes; swings; slides; play areas; and more. The park also features acres of walking trails, picnic tables and lots of run-around space.

Hours: Open daily, sunrise - sunset.
Price: Free
Ages: 18 months - 12 years.

WILDERNESS PARK

(626) 355-5309 or (626) 574-5113 / www.arcadiaca.gov
2240 Highland Oaks Drive, Arcadia

This huge wilderness park/preserve in the foothills of the mountains and on the same street as residential housing, offers a little for visitors to do. A short dirt trail through the shade trees loops around a large grassy area. The nature center contains quite a few glass-encased, taxidermied animals. We looked at barn owls, ravens, a gold eagle, black bear, mountain lion, coyote, raccoon, and lots more. The building also has a mounted insect collection, a few live snakes, and small waterfall and "pond." Ask about the many classes that the park offers, including merit badge classes.

Plenty of picnic tables are scattered among the woods. As this is primarily used as a group camping spot a picnic shelter with enough picnic tables for a busload, or two, is on the grounds, next to the kitchen facility that has two sinks, a freezer, a refrigerator, and an oven. This shelter area is available for group/overnight rental and also has a fire ring with amphitheater-type seating.

Hours: Open October through April, Mon. - Fri., 8:30am - 4:30pm. Open May through September, Mon. - Fri., 8:30am - 7pm. Weekend admission is by advanced reservation only, year round.
Price: Free to daytime visitors.
Ages: All

WILLIAM S. HART MUSEUM AND PARK

See the entry for WILLIAM S. HART MUSEUM AND PARK (pg. 158), under MUSEUMS, for details.

—MALLS—

THE AMERICANA AT BRAND - KIDS CLUB

(818) 637-8900 or (818) 637-8982 / www.americanaatbrand.com
889 Americana Way, Glendale

Glitz and glamour don't just belong to Hollywood anymore. This fifteen-acre, upscale shopping (over seventy-five shops); dining (from Sprinkles Cupcakes, Pinkberry, CrepeMaker, Pie Hole, and Granville Cafe); entertainment (including Pacific Theatres, with its 3D movies and Monday Morning Mommy Movies, too); and residential center offers a luxurious experience. Moms with kids in strollers or carriers are invited to participate in the hour-long Stroller Strides classes for moms of all fitness levels. Come and make new friends, while getting in shape. Classes are offered every Wednesday and Friday from 9am to 10am. The mall also includes rolling green lawns (not usually associated with a mall experience); awesome fountains that shoot water really high (eighty-feet!) in the air and "dance" to music (the lights at nighttime are especially pretty!); live music on the quad on weekends; trolley rides along the mini streets; uniformed elevator men; and concierge personnel who offer an incredible range of services, for a fee.

Kids have their own entertainment event every Tuesday on the green, or in the Community Room on rainy days. Singers, comedians, magic, storytime, cultural performances, crafts, or animal presentations - every week is something different. There is even free food for kids on Tuesdays at many of the restaurants; either a free item or a free meal with purchase of another meal. Check the website for more info and print out the flyer because some places require it.

Hours: The Kids Club is every Tues., 11am - 1pm.
Price: Free. Parking is free the first hour, $3 the second hour, on up with a max of $18, although it can be less with merchant validation.
Ages: Geared for ages 2 - 7

ANTELOPE VALLEY MALL - ANTELOPE ADVENTURES KID'S CLUB

(661) 266-9150 / www.av-mall.com

1233 Rancho Vista Boulevard, Palmdale

Kids, 3 to 11 years, can galvanize their artistic side monthly near the food court by participating in a seasonal craft. Paint an umbrella. Have fun with shamrocks. Ring in the holidays with a Christmas craft. Whatever the craft, it is fun (and free!). This mall also has AS YOU WISH (Los Angeles County) (pg. 8); BUILD-A-BEAR WORKSHOP (Los Angeles County) (pg. 162); ROCKIN' JUMP (Los Angeles County) (pg. 37); special events; a soft play area for younger ones; and of course, numerous shops and restaurants.

Hours: Kid's Club is the second Wed. of every month, 4pm - 7pm.

Price: Free

Ages: 3 - 11 years

DEL AMO FASHION CENTER / KIDGITS CLUB

(310) 542-8525 / www.simon.com/mall/del-amo-fashion-center

3 Del Amo Fashion Center at Carson Street and Hawthorne Boulevard, Torrance

Join in the fun and frivolity on select Saturday mornings near Joann's. The activities vary so it could be kids' entertainers encouraging your children to laugh, sing, and dance along with them as they tell stories, sing songs, and more, or an art and craft project to make and take. There are free drawings after every show. Membership to Kidgits is free (sign up on the website), which includes free goodies at the club events and spinning the wheel for a prize any time you visit the mall.

The Fashion Center also hosts seasonal events and programs. This mall, by the way, is the largest one in the western U.S. - one mile of shopping! There are over 200 stores, including DISNEY STORE (Los Angeles County) (pg. 167) and BUILD-A-BEAR WORKSHOP (Los Angeles County) (pg. 162); three food courts - talk about choices! and lots of restaurant, including DAVE & BUSTER'S (Los Angeles County) (pg. 29); an AMC theater that also has IMAX and 3-D movies; and two kid's play places. One is a large, free, semi-enclosed play space with a woodland theme in its murals and padded flooring, as well as its hard foam animals to climb on, fake log to crawl through, and other shapes. It also features several interactive elements on the wall partitions, such a firefly wall, a pixel light wall, and ball machine with levers to pull as balls go thru tubes and drop down. The other is Le Funland. See LE FUNLAND (Los Angeles County) (pg. 34) for more a description. Note that this Le Funland is $15 per child. Call (310) 370-8838 for more info.

Hours: Kidgits is on selected Saturdays, usually at noon.

Price: Free

Ages: 1½ - 8 years.

FIGAT7ᵗʰ KIDS CLUB

(213) 955-7170 / www.figat7ᵗʰ.com

735 S. Figueroa Street at the Figat7ᵗʰ shopping center, Los Angeles

All sorts of wonderful crafts are created at these free, arts and crafts workshops for kids which meets at the lower level food court. They'll make and treasure a mini fairy garden, a tube space rocket, animal murals, flower bouquets out of colorful tissue paper, paper kites, Mardi Gras masks, wands, weathervanes, cornucopias, and seasonal projects. Besides the Kids Club, enjoy the shops and dining here, plus art walks, movie nights, music, arts and crafts for adults, and other special events. If you're around on Thursdays from 10am to 2pm, buy something fresh at the Farmer's Market.

Hours: Kids Club is every second and fourth Sat., 2pm - 4pm.

Price: Free. Parking, with validation, is $1 for the first hour, $2.50 for the second, etc.

Ages: 3 - 11 years

GLENDALE GALLERIA

(818) 246-6737 / www.glendalegalleria.com

100 West Broadway, Glendale

Besides great shopping, a centerpiece for children is the carpeted Tot Lot, near JCPenney. Climbable, soft-sculptured letters and numbers in this enclosed area add up to fun, as do other alphabet activities. Musical accompaniment is triggered as kids go down the slide and crawl under the arches and other shapes. There is also a little, kid's clubhouse, and a small area for them to sit and watch kids TV, plus soft benches for parental units.

Check out the interactive and magical DISNEY STORE (Los Angeles County) (pg. 167), as well as the LEGO

STORE - MINI MODEL BUILD (Los Angeles County) (pg. 34). Visit GIGGLES N' HUGS (pg. 29) - a great kid restaurant and indoor play place. Look up the website for special events such as the Lego Americana Roadshow and others.

Hours: The mall is open Mon. - Sat., 10am - 9pm; Sun., 11am - 7pm.
Price: Free
Ages: 42" and under for the Tot Lot.

KID'S CLUB AT THE COMMONS

(818) 637-8922 / www.shopcommons.com
4799 Commons Way, Calabasas

Weekly kids' entertainment at The Commons, usually about an hour, can include magic shows, mime, puppetry, storytelling, science demonstrations, animal presentations, or music. The Kid's Club meets at the community stage, which is between Mi Piace and Marmalade Cafe. Prizes are raffled off every week and some stores offer Kid's Club members discounts.

The Commons occasionally offers other events such as cooking classes, live music, pet adoption, Stroller Strides classes, holiday special events, and more. This lovely, upscale, outdoor mall also has several shops and restaurants to entice you, plus an Edwards cinema. Or, just come for the somewhat peaceful ambiance with rock-lined, small, connecting ponds with real turtles, koi and ducks (and really neat, playful statues) at one end, and a waterfall and more nice landscaping at the other.

Hours: The Kid's Club meets every Tues., 6pm - 7pm.
Price: Free
Ages: 3 - 10 years.

LAKEWOOD CENTER KIDS CLUB

(562) 531-6707 / www.shoplakewoodcenter.com/kidsclub
200 Lakewood Center Mall, Lakewood

Teaming up with National Geographic Kids, the Kids Club features one hour of thematic activities, games, crafts, and performances once a month for young ones by Center Court. Themes have included castles, dinosaurs, under the sea, winter fun, big cats, and more. The mall other special events throughout the year, too, so check the events section on the website.

Near Target is a small, semi-enclosed, soft-play area designed for younger ones. Against a colorful background mural, they can play on giant, padded, foam pieces representing picnic food, including a spilled soda, hot dog, and fruit. A mini train runs on a small oval track at the other end of the mall, near JCPenney. Rides are about $2. Also see ROUND1 BOWLING AND AMUSEMENT (Los Angeles County) (pg. 38) for more fun and games. Some favorite stores might include the DISNEY STORE (Los Angeles County) (pg. 167) and Book-off, an inexpensive bookstore. Note that there is a Farmer's Market across from El Torito Restaurant on Saturdays from 8am - 1pm, May through mid-November. Enjoy current-release movies with your baby with Monday Morning Mommy Movies at Pacific Theatres here, too.

Hours: Kids Club is the fourth Fri. at 11am.
Price: Free
Ages: 1 - 9 years.

MANHATTAN VILLAGE KIDS CLUB

(310) 546-5555 / www.shopmanhattanvillage.com
3200 Sepulveda Avenue, Manhattan Beach

This Village plays host to a fun kid event every second Thursday from 10am to 11am. The morning includes music to get kids clapping, singing, and moving to rhythms; interactive storytime; dress up; arts or crafts; and a magical cloak.

The indoor/outdoor mall of Manhattan Village also does family-friendly special events throughout the year, as well as Stroller Strides, which is a free fitness class for moms to work out with babies in strollers. A slew of shops and restaurants are also available here.

Hours: The mall is open Mon. - Fri., 10am - 9pm; Sat., 10am - 8pm; Sun., 11am - 6pm. Kids Club day and hours are mentioned above.
Price: Free
Ages: 1½ - 10 years.

MOMMY & ME KID'S CLUB AT THE POINT

(310) 414-5280 / www.thepointsb.com

850 South Sepulveda Boulevard at The Point, El Segundo

The full name is Mommy & Me and Daddies too Free Kids Club - so it's not just for mommies. Come join the fun of arts and crafts, live entertainment (sing-a-longs, puppet shows, dancing and more), balloon animals, face painting and more, depending on the weekly theme. The club meets outside on the lawn in the Plaza.

Hours: The third Thursday of every month, May - Dec., 10am - noon.

  Price: Free

  Ages: 18 months - 5 years old.

NORTHRIDGE FASHION CENTER

(818)701-7051; (818) 885-9700 / www.northridgefashioncenter.com

9301 Tampa Avenue, Northridge

Located on the lower level, near Macy's, this mall features a large, free, soft-play area with a hard-padded giant starfish, surfboards, and dolphins, plus play sports cars and a backdrop scene of the Hollywood Hills. There is also a train ride ($4) that choo choos around the lower level, and not on tracks. A *beary* fun store for kids here is BUILD-A-BEAR WORKSHOP (Los Angeles County) (pg. 162) and a magical one is DISNEY STORE (Los Angeles County) (pg. 167). Enjoy current-release movies with your baby with Monday Morning Mommy Movies at Pacific Theatres here, too. Note that on Wednesdays, from 5pm to 9pm, April through October, the mall parking lot hosts a Farmer's Market with fresh fruit and vegetables, as well as a bounce house, pony rides, crafts to make, and a petting zoo for kids.

Hours: Mon. - Sat., 10am - 9pm; Sun., 11am - 7pm.

  Price: Free

  Ages: 18 months - 6 years old.

NORWALK TOWN SQUARE - KIDS FUN ZONE

(562) 868-2291 / www.norwalk-townsquare.com

11633 The Plaza, at the corner of Pioneer Boulevard and Rosecrans Avenue, Norwalk

Have you got crafty kids? They are invited to make free, seasonal crafts once a month at this outdoor mall. Tables are set up with supplies and staffed with volunteers who help out with the chosen craft - decorating aprons, creating gift boxes, making a Christmas ornament, etc. The Town Square also hosts special events throughout the year, such as an Easter Eggstravaganza, Trick or Treating, Santa Claus, and a snow play area.

Hours: Kids Fun Zone is held the last Sat. of every month, noon - 3pm.

  Price: Free

  Ages: 2 - 12 years.

PASEO COLORADO KIDS CORNER

(626) 795-9100 or (626) 795-8891 / www.thepaseopasadena.com

300 East Colorado Boulevard at The Paseo, Pasadena

What to do, what to do with the kids? Take them to Kids Corner in Garfield Promenade at the stage where are entertained and become a part of the performance as they sing and dance along with the performers. They'll also play musical instruments, watch a show with marionettes, or perhaps do a craft - it all depends on what is featured that week.

Hours: Tues., 10am - noon.

  Price: Free

  Ages: 18 months - 5 years

SANTA MONICA PLACE - KIDS CLUB

(310) 499-2928 or (310) 260-8333 / www.santamonicaplace.com

395 Santa Monica Place, Santa Monica

This huge, upscale, mostly outdoor mall, located at the end of THIRD STREET PROMENADE (pg. 95), which is lined with shops and restaurants, offers more shops and restaurants! The DISNEY STORE (Los Angeles County) (pg. 167); the incredible ZIMMER CHILDREN'S MUSEUM (pg. 159); pop-up "museums"; Johnny Rockets, a 50's dining experience; ArcLight Cinemas; rooftop dining, where you can see the ocean and (maybe) beyond; and Crepe Maker and are just a very few favorites here.

Kids Club takes place on Wednesdays in the Food Court (level 3). Bring the kids to enjoy puppet shows (which includes puppets for the kids to use, too); music with interactive songs; story time; sometimes true production extravaganzas (depending on who/what is going on and performing); and more. Adjacent to the food court is Samo's Clubhouse, a large play area for kids. They'll have a whale of a time climbing in and through the frame of a full-size humpback whale made of steel, netting and wood. Play panels, stairs, a slide, a balance beam, a short tight-rope, talking tubes, a periscope and other creative elements complete the nautical fun at the Clubhouse.

Just some of the other events at the mall include free Zumba classes on Saturday mornings at 9am in Center Plaza, live music, and more.

Hours: Kids Club is every Wed., 11am - noon.
Price: Parking is available in 8 public parking structures, including Structure 7 and 8, immediately adjacent to Santa Monica Place. The first 90 min. are free; $1.25 the next hour; then $1.85 for each 30 min.; $17.50 max. Library parking at 601 Santa Monica Blvd. is $1 an hour, $5 max on weekends.
Ages: 2 - 6 for the Kids Club

SOUTH BAY GALLERIA - KIDS CLUB

(310) 371-7546 / www.southbaygalleria.com
1815 Hawthorne Boulevard, Redondo Beach

Once a month kids can come to the Galleria and enjoy an hour of free entertainment such as stories, puppets, animal presentations, magic shows, sing-alongs, or seasonally-oriented arts and crafts activities presented on the third level near the food court. After each show, raffles or drawings are held for mall certificates. Make new friends as you and your child become regulars! Make sure you sign up to become a Kids Club member (membership is free) because a postcard is mailed out once a month listing a schedule of events and giveaways from retailers. There are a lot of retailers and eateries here, so enjoy an extended visit to the mall.

Hours: Usually the first Tues. of each month at 6pm.
Price: Free
Ages: 2 - 10 years.

THE GROVE - KIDS' THURSDAYS

(888) 315-8883 or (323) 900-8080 / www.thegrovela.com
189 The Grove Drive, Los Angeles

What a contrast in malls! The definitely upscale Grove is located just across the way from the down-to-earth, original FARMERS MARKET (pg. 21). The Grove is an outdoor complex with pedestrian streets that boasts of beautiful landscaping, including a large pond (or small lake); a choreographed "dancing" fountain that moves every half hour to a variety of musical selections; a free ride on the double-decker trolley with a bell-ringing conductor who conveys patrons from one end to the other; lots of shops; a variety of eateries and restaurants (including the hands-down winner for young girls, AMERICAN GIRL PLACE (pg. 162)); and special activities offered throughout the year, such as book signings by famous authors, plus concerts, and more. Pacific Theaters has fourteen screens here and, in keeping with the posh atmosphere, the theater has an elegant lobby, stadium seating (with some reclining seats!), and loge seating for private parties. Enjoy current-release movies on Monday Morning Mommy Movies from 11am to 1pm where infants (even crying ones) and younger children are welcome. Check www.pacifictheatres.com for more info.

On Thursdays (hence the title of the club, Kids' Thursdays), kids are invited to listen to storytellers, make crafts, hear and join in on songs, watch a marionette show, or enjoy something else equally entertaining. Story time is shared every Tuesday at 11am at Pottery Barn Kids with rewards given along the way.

Note that PAN PACIFIC PARK / RENEE'S PLACE (pg. 77) with great playgrounds and picnic areas and more, and the LOS ANGELES MUSEUM OF THE HOLOCAUST (pg. 132) are just around the corner.

Hours: Kid's Thursdays are Thurs., 11am - 1pm, with other family activities often throughout the week. Call or check the website for a schedule. The stores are open Mon. - Thurs., 10am - 9pm; Fri. - Sat., 10am - 10pm; Sun., 11am - 7pm. Restaurants and the movie theater are open later.
Price: Free, but bring spending money. Kids' Thursdays are free. Parking in the structure is free for the first hour, $4 for the second hour, etc.
Ages: 2 years and up.

THIRD STREET PROMENADE

(310) 393-8355 / www.downtownsm.com
3rd Street Promenade, Santa Monica

This three-block pedestrian walkway is a fascinating, outdoor mall experience. It rates an A+ for people-watching as the international mix of people, converging here from the nearby Los Angeles International Airport, make it a cultural adventure. Nighttime and weekends bring out performers who want to show off their talents, however glorious or dubious they might be. We've seen and heard African drum playing, tap dancing, folk songs, acrobatics, men acting like robots, clowns making balloon animals, and an organ grinder monkey begging - all within the span of an hour. Benches are plentiful, so if you really enjoy some of the entertainment, sit down and watch. A plethora of artsy and unique stores and boutiques, plus movie theaters, line the "street." Vendor carts are along the sidewalks. Choose from a multitude of restaurants of numerous ethnicities that range from upscale to grab-a-bite, or snack at a bakery or ice cream shop. A few fountains, featuring dinosaurs spouting water, complete the eclectic ambiance at the promenade. Farmer's Market is nearby on Arizona Avenue between Second and Fourth streets on Wednesdays and Saturdays from 8:30am to 1pm. Check the November Calendar section in the book for information about the ice-skating rink that's just down the street here during winter months. Note that SANTA MONICA PLACE - KIDS CLUB (pg. 94) is at the end of this Street.

Note: The Big Blue Bus, (310) 451-5444 / www.bigbluebus.com, runs a loop from Main Street to Third Street Promenade every fifteen minutes, from 6am to midnight at a cost of $1.25 per person; 50¢ for seniors; children 4 and under are free.

Hours: Most stores and restaurants are open daily, 10am - 9pm.
Price: Free, but bring spending money.
Ages: All

WATERSIDE MARINA DEL REY KIDS CLUB

(818) 637- 8921 / www.shopwaterside.com
4700 Admiralty Way at the Waterside Marina Del Rey shopping center, Marina Del Rey

Conveniently located in front of Starbucks (so adults can indulge and get some energy first!), usually once a week entertainment for the kids at the outside Waterside Marina Del Rey shopping center can include magic shows; animals to pet and learn about; puppet and marionette shows; storytelling; songs and games; and more. And of course there are plenty of shops and restaurants to peruse, plus MARINA BEACH or MOTHER'S BEACH (pg. 12), MARINA DEL REY WATERBUS (pg. 213) and FISHERMAN'S VILLAGE and surrounding area (pg. 159) just around the corner.

Hours: Every Tuesday, March - October, 11:15am - 12:15pm.
Price: Free
Ages: 2 - 8 years

WESTFIELD SANTA ANITA

(626) 445-3116 or (626) 462-8528 / www.westfield.com
400 S. Baldwin Avenue, Arcadia

Inside, the mall features a semi-enclosed PlaySpace for kids with soft play objects to climb, slide, and ride on (like critters and cars) to keep them occupied, plus comfortable seating for adults. A Family Lounge is a place to sit and relax, with a few games and kid-friendly TV programs playing. Check out the great indoor play area here called JUMP 'N JAMMIN (Los Angeles County) (pg. 32), plus the DISNEY STORE (Los Angeles County) (pg. 167) and DAVE & BUSTER'S (Los Angeles County) (pg. 29). Outside the mall, on the promenade, is a small play area where a friendly dragon is partly hidden in the ground, but his wide face, eyes, and body bumps are on the surface to play on. A rope climbing structure, and spiral objects to twirl around on, plus benches complete this playground. Check the website or call about special events throughout the year such as making a candle, for free, for Mother's Day; watching dance competitions; and more.

Hours: Mon. - Sat., 10am - 9pm; Sun., 11am - 7pm.
Ages: 2 - 7 years for the play areas.

WESTFIELD TOPANGA and THE VILLAGE

(818) 594-8740 or (818) 227-5514 / www.westfield.com
6600 Topanga Canyon Boulevard, Canoga Park

Shopping at the huge Westfield Topanga mall and at The Village mall (just across street) can have benefits for both parents and kids. At Topanga - parents can rest their weary bodies at the Family Lounge with a few games and kid-friendly TV shows, or on the padded benches (or on chairs at the outer counter tops) that encircle the enclosed, free Playtown area called The Canyon, located near Target. At The Canyon younger kids enjoy climbing on, around and in the hard foam play figures of fake rocks, a huge snake, mountain lions and other critters. The Canyon plays host to storytelling one Tuesday a month at 11am where a book is read followed by an applicable art and craft, sing-a-long, or another form of entertainment. The free storytelling is put on by the mall's partnership with GIGGLES N' HUGS (pg. 29), a fantastic restaurant with an imaginative play area for kids that is located just above this play spot, on the second floor.

Adjacent to the Canyon is a unique, two-story (!) carousel with a dinosaur, bunny, tigers, hummingbird, zebras and other wondrous animals to ride. The cost is $3 for a child; free for an adult to stand with the child. My Gym Express is another play section that looks like a small train but has tunnels, cargo nets, and foam obstacle course for little kids to run around. The cost is about $4 a child. One more noteworthy place here especially for kids is the LEGO STORE - MINI MODEL BUILD (Los Angeles County) (pg. 34) where kids can make a free mini model. For fresh food, come to the farmer's market, open every Sunday from 9am to 1pm, December through June.

The Village, a lot trendier, also has a Family Lounge; splash fountains to run thru at both end; lots of places to sit and chill, especially the koi pond with lots of Adirondack chairs at the northern end; book exchange stations (leave one and borrow another); and the Kids Climber, near 24 Hour Fitness, which is an enclosed, netted climbing structure that houses huge, staggered, fake "plant" pads to climb on. If you're feeling creative, be sure to check out BITTER ROOT POTTERY (pg. 8).

To get from one mall to the next, or just for a fun ride, ride the Westfield Topanga Trolley. The free Trolley usually runs every 20 minutes or so, between Westfield Topanga and The Village, Mon. - Sat., 11am - 10pm; Sun., 11am - 8pm. Check the website for the full schedule.

Note that both malls offer a variety of special events seasonally, including Circus Vargus, concerts, and being completely decorated for Christmas.

Hours: Storytelling is the first Tues. of each month at 11am. The mall is open Mon. - Sat., 10am - 9pm; Sun., 11am - 7pm.

Price: Free. Parking is free at Topanga. Parking (which can be hard to find!) is free for the first hour at the Village, then $1 after up to 5 hours, etc.

Ages: 1 - 8

—MUSEUMS—

ACADEMY MUSEUM

(310) 247- 3000 / www.academymuseum.org

6067 Wilshire Boulevard, Los Angeles

And the Oscar goes to.... this museum, opening in 2019, that "will be simultaneously immersive, experimental, educational, and entertaining. More than a museum, this dynamic film center will offer unparalleled experiences and insights into movies and movie making." I've been watching the construction of the building and it will be six stories! It will have more than 50,000 square feet of exhibition galleries, an education studio, an almost 300-seat theater (of course), a restaurant and cafe, and a store. I can't wait to see the props, plus photos, screenplays, posters, costumes, design drawings, artwork and more representing all facets of movie-making and production. The Academy Museum has actively been acquiring three-dimensional motion picture objects since 2008. Its holdings now number approximately 2,500 items representing motion picture technology, costume design, production design, makeup, and hairstyling. The north end will have a massive, open-ended glass dome terrace offering fantastic views of L.A. and the mountains, including the Hollywood sign. Inside the sphere-shaped addition will be a 1,000 seat state-of-the-art theater for premieres, productions, performances, and more. I think it will all be a winner!

Hours: TBA

Price: TBA

ADAMSON HOUSE AND MALIBU LAGOON MUSEUM

(310) 456-8432 - museum; (310) 456-1770 - docent, during museum hours / www.adamsonhouse.org; www.parks.ca.gov $$$

23200 Pacific Coast Highway, Malibu

The Adamson House and its adjacent museum are on beautifully landscaped grounds just a few feet away from the Malibu Surfrider Beach and lifeguard station, and the Malibu Lagoon - definitely beach-front property. The outside of the house and the fountains integrate the colorful Malibu tiles in their design. We wandered around the grounds on flagstone walkways that wove through grassy lawns, beneath shade trees, along several small gardens (including a rose garden), past a pool that was once filled with salt water from the ocean, and to the chain-link fence which marks the house boundaries. Here, just a short distance from the pier, we watched surfers do their thing.

The small museum features exhibits pertaining to the history of Malibu, including cattle brands, arrowheads, maps, fossilized shells, and numerous photographs. I liked the Malibu Colony of Stars' pictures of Robert Redford, Bing Crosby, Clara Bow, Joan Crawford, and others.

The two-story house was built in 1929. The rooms and grounds can only be seen on a ninety-minute, guided tour.

Adults and older children will appreciate the bottle-glass windows, hand-painted murals, additional tile work (especially in the kitchen), furnishings, and unique decor throughout the house. You'll hear explanations regarding the history of the railroad, the dam, and the movie colony and more on your tour.

There isn't any direct access to the lagoon (i.e., the parcel of water and land that is a haven for various bird species) from the house. You can get to this area by walking or driving over the bridge and down Cross Creek Road. We observed pelicans, herons, sandpipers, and other birds coming in for a landing before taking to the skies once again.

School tours are a combination of cultural and natural history as a tour of the house is accompanied by learning about the lagoon/park's biological diversity. Using binoculars and magnifying glasses, a day at the beach becomes more educational with topics such as Chumash Indian culture; ecology; plant, fish and animal life; and environmental pollution.

Note: Although the beach is accessible by going through the museum parking lot, the waters are for surfers only. If your kids want to go swimming, head toward Malibu Pier, just east up the street.

Hours: The house and museum are open Thurs. - Sat., 11am - 3pm. The last house tour begins at 2pm. A tour of the garden is included every Fri. at 10am. Closed New Year's Day, July 4th, Thanksgiving, and Christmas Day, plus rainy days. Call for information on lagoon tours and programs.

Price: The house and museum tour is $7 for adults; $2 for ages 6 - 16; children 5 and under are free. Cash only. Parking in the county lot adjacent to the museum costs about $10 per vehicle. Some free street parking is available.

Ages: 7 years and up.

ADOBE DE PALOMARES (aka Ygnacio Palomares Adobe)

(909) 620-0264 or (909) 623-2198 / www.pomonahistorical.org $

491 E. Arrow Highway, Pomona

This thirteen-room restored adobe was originally built in 1854, during the California Gold Rush. A guided tour of the house includes seeing the courtyard, with its horno (i.e. outdoor oven); the simple, but lovely, authentic period furniture; cooking utensils (how did they live without so many technical doohickeys?!); tools; antique clothing; canopy beds; and children's toys. The rooms look quite livable, even by today's standards. The landscaped grounds are very pleasant. A blacksmith shop is also on site and features saddles, ranching tools, branding irons, and a horse-drawn carriage, circa 1880's.

Adjacent to the adobe is Palomare Park, so bring a picnic lunch and enjoy some running around space.

Hours: Open Sun., 2pm - 5pm. Closed Easter, Memorial Day weekend, Labor Day weekend, and Thanksgiving weekend. Special tours are given by appointment.

Price: Donations of $2 for adults; $1 for ages 18 and under are suggested.

Ages: 6 years and up.

AFRICAN AMERICAN FIREFIGHTER MUSEUM

(213) 744-1730 / www.aaffmuseum.org   !

1401 S. Central Avenue, Los Angeles

This small, beautiful, two-story museum in a Los Angeles neighborhood was actually Fire Station #30, one of two segregated firehouses in Los Angeles between 1924 and 1955. It chronicles the history of black firefighters by honoring them as well as their white colleagues who pushed for integration. The walls and reference books contain photographs and stories. For instance, although black and white men battled fires and fought side-by-side to save lives, they couldn't cook or eat together. African Americans even slept in beds designated "black beds." Exhibits include a fire engine, vintage fire apparatus, uniforms, boots, fire extinguishers, badges, helmets, and other mementos.

Hours: Open Tues. and Thurs., 10am - 2pm; Sun., 1pm - 4pm. Special tours can be arranged by appointment. Closed Mon., Wed., Fri., Sat., and major holidays.

Price: Free, donations are suggested. Groups over 10 people pay a tour fee of $50.

Ages: 5 years and up.

AMERICAN MILITARY MUSEUM

(626) 442-1776 / www.tankland.com $$

1918 N. Rosemead Boulevard, South El Monte

Attention! Over 170 pieces of equipment, representing all branches of the United States military, can be found at this outside museum. The collection contains vehicles and weapons from World War I through Desert Storm. It includes Jeeps, amphibious trucks, ambulances, helicopters, cannons, gun turrets, and thirty-ton Sherman tanks. The vehicles can be looked at, but not sat in or touched.

To the untrained eye it looks like a random compilation of old military equipment. And it is. However, some pieces are in the process of being restored, and some have been used in movies and T.V. shows. The volunteers are knowledgeable and know many of the "inside" stories about the vehicles. Pick up a booklet to learn more about the pieces of equipment here. Tip: This is an ideal setting if your kids are studying any of the wars and want to make a video, or to have a birthday party here and play Army (or Navy, or Marine, etc.). Picnic tables are here, too.

Hours: Open Fri. - Sun., 10am - 4:30pm. Open at other times for group tours by appointment only. Closed on rainy days.
Price: $5 for adults; $4 for seniors and military; $3 for ages 10 - 16; $1 for ages 5 - 9; children 4 and under are free. Fridays are free to educational non-profit organizations by advanced reservation.
Ages: 4 years and up.

ANTELOPE VALLEY INDIAN MUSEUM

(661) 946-3055 / www.avim.parks.ca.gov
15701 Avenue 'M', Lancaster

Built into and around rock formations of the Mojave Desert, the outside of this Indian museum looks incongruously like a Swiss chalet. The inside is just as unique. Once the home of artist Howard Edward, portions of the interior (i.e., walls, ceilings, and flooring) are composed of boulders. My kids' reaction was simply "WOW!"

The first small rooms contain stone and mortar pestles, old photos, and info about the Native Americans that once lived in this area. A hallway room contains beautiful rugs; several glass-cased displays of pottery shards that were once used for money and jewelry; cradle-boards; baskets; and various items made from plants, such as yucca fiber sandals. The large main, Swiss Chalet and boulder room is lined with Kachina dolls on the upper shelves and colorfully-painted panels of the dolls on the ceiling. (The Hopi people believed that Kachina dolls brought rain.) The unusual furniture and the support beams are made from Joshua trees. Rugs, woven plates and baskets, paintings, and more pottery are also in here.

Kids love climbing up the narrow stony steps into another exhibit room, which is also carved out of rock. There are numerous glass displays cases in the walls, and several items not in cases. These collections include arrowheads, whale bone tools, shells, whale ribs, necklaces, more cradleboards, harpoons, pottery, and weapons. Read the descriptions because although most items are authentic, the designer of the exhibits made up some stories to go along with some of the artifacts - creative license! Go back down a few of the steps. Stop. Look up. You'll see Indian dioramas and recreated cave paintings.

Outside, you'll pass by a series of small cottages that were once used as guest houses. On guided tours, or at special events, there are hands-on activities for kids such as grinding corn with stone mortars and pestles, trying their hand at using a pump drill to drill holes, "sawing" with a bow drill to create smoke, and learning how to make a pine needle whisk broom. (The brooms may not have much practical use nowadays, but it's a fun and educational project.) Docents gladly explain the use of various seeds and other plant parts. Note that every October the museum hosts an American Indian Celebration with native dancing, crafts, demonstrations and more. December is the Holidays on the Homestead event.

The museum is part of the California Department of Parks and Recreation. Enjoy an easy, yet unshaded, quarter-mile loop trail just behind the Indian Museum. You'll walk through some desert, surrounded by mountains, and get a fantastic view of the valley below. A guidebook ($1) explains the fourteen Native American symbols on the posts along the trail.

Hours: Open Sat. - Sun., 11am - 4pm.
Price: $3 for adults; ages 12 and under are free. (Cash or checks only.)
Ages: 5 years and up.

AUTOMOBILE DRIVING MUSEUM

(310) 909-0950 / www.automobiledrivingmuseum.org
610 Lairport Street, El Segundo

The cars are the stars at this unique automobile museum. Some of the over 130 restored, rotating classic and vintage automobiles on display include Eleanor Roosevelt's limo; Joseph Stalin's Packard; the convertible Howard Hughes gave his wife (valued at 1.2 million dollars!); muscle cars; 1886 Benz Motowagon; 1999 350Z concept car; 1931 Ford Model A Roadster; 1929 Durant; 1909 Model T; 1936 red and roaring Packard Roadster; 1948 DeSoto; 1982 DeLorean DMC 12; lots of Packards; and many more. Is it *driving* you crazy to just look at cars? Here, you can see the cars up close, touch some of them, and even get inside one of them. Take a guided tour offered on the weekends if you'd like to hear their history. The docents are friendly, knowledgeable and enthusiastic.

What really makes this museum an *auto*matic favorite is that guests 10 years and older (minimum height of 56") can actually take a two-mile joyride back through time in select museum's cars - what a classic (and classy) way to see L.A.! Check the website to see which three will be going out for a spin on any given Sunday, weather permitting. As you ride, you'll hear the back story of the cars - about the owners, how to start the car, its horsepower and what makes it so special. Kids will also enjoy the small kid's corner set up like a garage with dress up clothes, car-related toys, a mechanic tent, scavenger hunt and two cars they can "play" in - photo op! See their website calendar for special events like Ladies Car Care, Hot Wheels garage of life-size cars, Summer STEAM days for kids, camps for kids, etc.

There's a small, 1950's themed ice cream parlor on-site, too, so enjoy an ice cream dessert - maybe even have a birthday party here! Sometimes there are craft activities after your car tour in the parlor, too. Tip: The Toyota Training Center for the Kings is on Nash Street, just two blocks away, where the Kings can often be found practicing during weekday mornings.

Hours: Open Tues. - Sun., 10am - 4pm. Close Mon. and holidays. Automobile rides are offered on Sun., only, starting at 10am, with the last ride given at 3:30pm.

Price: $10 for adults; $8 for seniors; $5 for ages 10 - 17; children 9 and under are free. A family of 4 (2 adults and 2 kids) is $25. Admission includes museum entrance and rides on Sundays.

Ages: 5 years and up; 10 years for Sunday automobile ride.

BANNING MUSEUM   ☀

(310) 548-7777 / www.banningmuseum.org $$
401 E. M Street, Wilmington

This huge Victorian museum, where the founder of Wilmington once lived, is reflective of the Banning family lifestyle in the 1800's. The one-hour guided tours are best suited for older children as there is much to see, but not to touch. First, walk through the photo gallery, past a display of brilliant cut glass, and into the house where each of the seventeen rooms are beautifully decorated with period furniture and eclectic art work. (Note: The house is completely decked out at Christmas time and looks particularly splendid.) Check out the hoof inkwell in the General's office. Get the kids involved with the tour by asking them questions like, "What's missing from this office that modern offices have?" (Answer - a computer, a fax machine, etc. Surprisingly, a copy machine *is* here.) The parlor doubled as a music room and contains a piano, violin, and small organ as well as an unusual-looking chair made out of buffalo hide and horns. Other rooms of interest are the children's nursery; the bedrooms - one has a unique hat rack made of antlers, while another has a stepping stool that is actually a commode; and the kitchen with its potbellied stove and all of its gadgets. (Obviously some things never change.) Make sure to see the Stagecoach Barn, a fully outfitted, nineteenth-century working barn with real stagecoaches. Ask your children if they can figure out how some of the tools were used.

School groups are given two-plus-hour tours, one geared for third graders and one for fourth, that include attending class in the one-room schoolhouse which has old-fashioned desks, slates, and McGuffy primers. Kids don an apron or ascot, get a math or English lesson from that time period, learn about family living from this era, and go out for recess to play games of yesteryear. Ask about Heritage Week in April and October, when the house is closed to the public for special school programs that encourage visitors to partake in activities from the 1880's. Also see the Calendar section in the back of this book for the variety of seasonal events hosted here throughout the year.

The museum is situated in the middle of a pretty, twenty-acre park that has a small playground, a few picnic tables, a rose garden, eucalyptus trees, giant bamboo trees, and grassy areas.

Hours: Tours are given Tues. - Thurs. at 12:30pm, 1:30pm, and 2:30pm; Sat. - Sun. at 12:30pm, 1:30pm, 2:30pm, and 3:30pm. Closed during Heritage Week on weekdays and on national holidays.

Price: $5 per adult; $1 for children 11 and under.

Ages: 7 years and up.

BORAX VISITOR CENTER   ☀

(760) 762-7588 / www.borax.com   !
Borax Road, Boron

Borax isn't something that my family normally spends a lot of time thinking about. However, visiting this center made us realize how widely this mineral is used. As you drive past the active mine (and past the sign that states the speed limit is 37½ mph, which is a little tricky to actually do), you'll see what appears to be a little city, complete with buildings, trucks, and Goliath-type machines used to extract and process the borax. This area supplies nearly half the global need for the mineral!

Up the hill is a state-of-the-art visitors center. Outside are original twenty mule team wagons, with harnessed fiberglass mule statues, that were once used to haul the ore over 165 miles through desert and rocky terrain (the wagons, not the statues). Inside is a large sample of kernite, a type of borate ore, plus a pictorial time line of the Borax Company, and an exhibit that shows the process of ore being transformed (crushed, actually) into fine dust. The Borax at Home display shows the mining and geology processing of raw ore into everyday finished products such as glass, ceramic glazes, detergent, shaving creams, and plant fertilizer. For products closer to a child's heart, the display features footballs, Play Doh™, and nail polish. Borax is also added to commodities to make them sparkle, including toothpaste and fireworks.

An adjacent room shows continuously running videos of Borax commercials starring Ronald Reagan, Dale Robertson, Clint Eastwood, Star Trek stars, and others. A ten-minute video titled *The World of Borax* gives a history of the mining process. An all-glass wall shows an unobstructed panorama of the entire open pit mine. High-powered microscopes are available for closer inspection of borax and other in-house crystals. Free, organized school tours of the center are given, and fun supplemental materials are available to aid learning, including a mineral collection area where students may do their own "rockhounding" to collect and take home their own borate samples. Don't forget to stop off at the TWENTY MULE TEAM MUSEUM (pg. 155) and the adjacent SAXON AEROSPACE MUSEUM (pg. 151), which are just down the road.

Hours: Open daily, 9am - 5pm, excluding major holidays and during inclement weather.
Price: Free
Ages: 4 years and up.

BURBANK POLICE AND FIRE MUSEUM

(818) 238-3235 or (818) 238-3000 / www.burbankpd.org
200 North Third Street, Burbank

In a partnership between the police and fire departments, this museum is a peek into the history and current status of both departments via different equipment on display including a variety of older (and newer) fire trucks engines, and police motorcycles and cars, plus mannequins in uniforms, weapons, badges, photographs, tools of the trade, information panels and tributes to those who gave up their lives.

Hours: Open one Sat. a month from 10am - 2pm.
Price: Free
Ages: 5 years and up.

CALIFORNIA AFRICAN AMERICAN MUSEUM

(213) 744-7432 / www.caamuseum.org
600 State Drive, at Exposition Park, Los Angeles

$$$

This museum portrays the works of African-American artists documenting the African-American experience in this country. There are two large, permanent galleries containing an array of wood-carved masks and headdresses (one looks like a baby crocodile), plus statues, a room showcasing famous African Americans, and more works of art. Traveling exhibits in the rotating galleries could be painting, sculptures, huge pieces/objects of art and/or history, often coming from other major galleries. See the nearby CALIFORNIA SCIENCE CENTER (pg. 102), EXPOSITION PARK (pg. 59), IMAX THEATER (pg. 185), and NATURAL HISTORY MUSEUM OF LOS ANGELES COUNTY (pg. 140).

Hours: Open Tues., - Sat., 10am - 5pm; Sun., 11am - 5pm. Closed Mon., New Year's Day, Memorial Day, Thanksgiving, and Christmas.
Price: Free. Parking costs $12; $15 after 5pm.
Ages: 5 years and up.

CALIFORNIA HERITAGE MUSEUM

(310) 392-8537 / www.californiaheritagemuseum.org
2612 Main Street, Santa Monica

$$

Inside this two-story house/museum, originally built in 1894, the downstairs living room is cozy and rustic-looking. The dining room atmosphere fluctuates, depending on the current exhibit, so it could be set with fine china, or pottery, etc. The restored kitchen is the one Merle Norman originally used to cook-up her cosmetic recipes. (From such humble beginnings . . .) Both the downstairs and upstairs are redecorated each time a new exhibit is installed. Often the exhibitions are aimed at appealing to the younger generation. Past themes have focused on cowboys; guitars from all over the world; children's books and illustrations; and model trains. Call for information on the current display. The guided tour illuminates the heritage and nuances in the exhibit pieces.

Outside, a grassy lawn welcomes picnickers. Note that several gourmet food trucks gather here on Tuesday from 5:30pm to 9:30pm (the museum is not open then) for outdoor family dinner time and that a Farmer's Market is held on the grounds on Sundays from 8:30am - 1:30pm.

Hours: Open Wed. - Sun., 11am - 4pm. Closed Mon., Tues., and major holidays.
 Price: $5 for adults; $3 for seniors and students; military and children 11 and under are free.
 Ages: 5 years and up.

CALIFORNIA SCIENCE CENTER

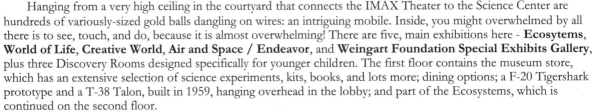

(323) SCIENCE (724-3623) or (213) 744-7400 / www.californiasciencecenter.org
700 State Drive, Exposition Park, Los Angeles

Hanging from a very high ceiling in the courtyard that connects the IMAX Theater to the Science Center are hundreds of variously-sized gold balls dangling on wires: an intriguing mobile. Inside, you might overwhelmed by all there is to see, touch, and do, because it is almost overwhelming! There are five, main exhibitions here - **Ecosytems**, **World of Life**, **Creative World**, **Air and Space / Endeavor**, and **Weingart Foundation Special Exhibits Gallery**, plus three Discovery Rooms designed specifically for younger children. The first floor contains the museum store, which has an extensive selection of science experiments, kits, books, and lots more; dining options; a F-20 Tigershark prototype and a T-38 Talon, built in 1959, hanging overhead in the lobby; and part of the Ecosystems, which is continued on the second floor.

The massive **Ecosystems** is comprised of eleven different, recreated environments or zones, each one containing several hands-on experiments that pertain to that particular zone. The following are some highlights: Walk through a long room with a video screen on the walls that immerse you in different environments - under the sea, in a city, etc. In the Island Zone room shoot a ping pong ball toward the small center "island" to show how birds, insects, and the wind carry plant and animal life to populate islands. The room also contains live fish native only to Hawaii; a display case with skulls, insects, and more items native to islands; and an interactive exhibit to see how different kinds of beaks enable birds to eat various foods. In Extreme Zone go outside to Rocky Shore where a machine creates coastal waves, a touch tank has sea stars and anemones, and you can behave like a barnacle by reaching your gloved hand into a large glass box and trying to grab food. Extreme Zone also features Poles with a wall of real ice, polar bear fur, and a time line for visitors to create using wood's growth rings. The actually hot Desert room has dioramas with rocks and cactus, an infrared camera to find endothermic animals, mini flash floods, and bats in the small caves. Test an ROV at Deep Sea Vents and learn about the animals that survive here. The Global Zone stars a giant globe with various projections on it that show how climate and temperature affect conditions all over the world. I know decay is a part of life (and death), but the Rot Room is gross with its live maggots, a wheel to spin to see decomposition (of strawberries, a rabbit, and more), and log with live bugs (in display cases). The cartoonishly-decorated Family Discovery Room off of this room is ideal for ages 7 and under (and I think its apropos that kids have their own zone!) with its living room, kitchen, and bedroom (geared for toddlers) filled with furniture, toys, books, and games that are educationally oriented (and fun). There is also an outdoor area here with picnic tables and a gardening plot for kids to work. The adjacent River Zone has interactive water/river elements, real river fish, and a whole wall made of silver discs that flow and ripple like water when air from the fan you turn on hits them. My favorite room is the Kelp Forest with several tanks of live sea animals, a walk-through tunnel of fish (that swim overhead), and a capacious kelp forest tank with a school of fish, leopard sharks, Garibaldi, and bat rays. I also like watching the moon jellies.

The west wing of the second floor stars **World of Life**, packed with exhibits that pertain to human and animal lives. Look closely at cells via a microscope and a video. Crank a knob to watch how a model's digestive system unravels to stretch over eighteen feet and listen to the sounds we make when digesting food. Watch a movie of an actual heart transplant as it is laser-beamed onto a statue patient. Drive a simulator car to experience the difference in driving sober and driving drunk. See preserved fetuses in jars ranging from a few weeks old to nine months. View a movie on conception (suitable for older children). Sit on a clear, no-butts-about-it chair filled with over 200 cigarettes and watch a film clip on lung cancer. Press buttons to match recorded heartbeats to real hearts that are on display, from the huge elephant's to the medium-sized cow's to the tiny mouse's. Look at the real brains of a human, monkey, and a rat. Learn about the basic needs of plants and animals through other interactive displays. Look at the chick hatchery and maybe you'll get to see chicks break out of their eggs. Tess, the reclining, fifty-foot human figure, comes to "life" in a well-done, fifteen-minute presentation in the BodyWorks room. A large movie screen above her head stars a cartoon character who helps Tess explain how her body parts work together to keep her system in balance (i.e., homeostasis). Periodically, her muscles, organs, and circulatory system are illuminated by fiber optics. An adjacent Discovery Room allows younger children to put on puppet shows and look at small live animals such as frogs, spiders, lizard, and a boa constrictor. Use the Discovery Boxes that are filled with creative and educational toys, games, musical instruments, and more.

A star of the **Air and Space / Endeavour** exhibit is the historic and absolutely colossal space shuttle, *Endeavour*. Enter the separate pavilion to see it (wow!!! it is so impressive!!) and learn *Endeavour*'s story with photos and info panels regarding its twenty-five completed missions, including the first service mission to the Hubble Space Telescope and a trip to the International Space Station. You can touch the *Endeavour*'s tires, and only the tires, that show wear from landing on the runway. You'll also see a Spacehab module, a kind of astronauts' workshop/extra *space* (haha!) area. Just outside, you can't miss the gargantuan, orange, External Tank (or ET), a "gas tank" for the space shuttle orbiter. A "sister" to Columbia's, this fifteen-story-building-high (though it's horizontal), ET-94 (which never flew) is the last flight-qualified external tank in existence, thus making this science center only place in the world to see a complete shuttle stack of orbiter, external tank, and solid rocket boosters, which will eventually displayed in launch configuration.

Back inside the main building, other air and space exhibits include a SSME rocket engine; actual space capsules, including the Gemini 11 and Mercury-Redstone 2; a J47 turbo engine; a full-scale model of the Sputnik 1; a real Apollo spacesuit; pieces of meteorites; a Velie Monocoupe; a full-scale flying replica of the 1902 Wright Glider; several scale model space telescopes; a few interactive space exhibits; and more. Make sure you also check out the A-12 Blackbird, which looks like the spy plane that it was, located out front and the F/A-18A Hornet on a pedestal in the back, near the Rose Garden.

The major portion of the east wing, **Creative World**, features temporary exhibits. We recently saw Goose Bumps! The Science of Fear where visitors actually faced their fears of animals (by seeing and interacting with a few, smaller critters), falling (laying down on an upright bed and it falling backward) and (receiving a mild!) electric shock, plus seeing a huge body outline on a wall that demonstrated, via videos for the body parts, how the brain and body work together to respond to fear and danger. There was also information on how to cope with various fears and a fear theater, which showed how fears are dealt with in movies and in real life.

Visitors in this section can also experience the shake, rattle and roll of an earthquake by standing on a platform as a simulated earthquake hits; constructing buildings using scale model parts and watching what happens when an earthquake strikes via a shake table; and building archways using foam blocks to learn about the strength of compression. Another section of this area focuses on transportation. Direct fans to blow wind to move model sailboats, and to race solar-paneled cars in the exhibits here. A space devoted to motion and fuel features prototype cars and how to design more fuel and energy efficient ones; use hand- cranks to turn light into electricity; a display of solar panels; and crash dummies that demonstrate how to be safer. The Discovery Room here has a play house that resembles a city street with several rooms such as the Hardware Store, so kids can "purchase" supplies and build structures using tools and gadgets, and - "Quiet on the set!" - a TV Studio with costumes, puppets and a camera. The Discovery Boxes have more games and toys to use. Computers for younger kids incorporate more learning in the Tech Lab.

Also on the third floor is the **Weingart Gallery**, featuring wonderful, usually hands-on, special rotating exhibits. One exhibit focused on geography, so kids learned about people, customs, plants, and unique geological formations from all over the world, via interactive displays. Another was simply *Marvel*ous - it was the Marvel Super Heroes exhibit with artwork, hands-on attempts at super hero powers (such as testing the strength of spider webs against a strong, man-made material), and lots to do with heroes and villains. More geared for adults was Pompeii: The Exhibition which featured over 150 excavated artifacts from this ancient Roman city, including marble statues, Gladiator helmets and shin guards, coins, and more, and a shaking reenactment of the volcano that covered the city and its inhabitants. The incredible King Tut exhibit was worth its weight in gold!

Ever want to join the circus and try the high-wire act? Here's your chance. At the Science Center you can pedal a weighted bike across a cable wire that is forty feet above the ground. Although you're strapped in and safety netting is in place, it is still a slightly scary venture, especially when the staff person tilts the bike before pushing it across the cable wire! ($3) Other interactive exhibits include a motion simulator ride with themes from the Air and Space Exhibits ($5), and "Cliff Climb," a twenty-three-feet high rock climbing wall ($4). Height requirements apply. Do all three activities for $9.

Live, audience-participatory shows, including Science Spectacular!, are presented for various age groups throughout the day. Make sure to check out the numerous special classes, programs, camps, and events offered for children and adults.

In a separate building, but sharing the same campus, is Big Lab (also titled Wallis Annenberg Building for Science Learning and Innovation), an enormous building and parcel of land for school group field trips, plus homeschool and Scout days, to learn via multi-sensory experiences in this fun and educational environment. Programs include roller coaster engineering, cow eye dissection, slime lab, ladybugs and life cycles, and much more. The cost is usually $200 for up to fifteen students; $10 for each additional student. Call (213) 744-2019 or (213) 744-7444 for more info.

Tips on visiting the Science Center: 1) School kids come in busloads on weekday mornings, so several exhibits require waiting in line to view or use during these peak hours. Therefore, consider either arriving early to watch an IMAX movie and explore the grounds and other nearby museums first, or come here in the early afternoon. 2) On-site food options include a grill with burgers, hot dogs, specialty sandwiches, salads, and soup; a market with pre-made sandwiches, fruit, bottled water, and snacks; and a coffee bar with beverages and ice cream. 3) Avoid food lines by packing a lunch. There are several shaded grassy areas for picnicking. 4) Locker rentals are available on the first floor. 5) Plan on coming back - there is too much to see and do all in one day! Note: The center is stroller/wheelchair accessible. Check out the nearby CALIFORNIA AFRICAN AMERICAN MUSEUM (pg. 101), IMAX THEATER (pg. 185), and NATURAL HISTORY MUSEUM OF LOS ANGELES COUNTY (pg. 140).

Hours: Open daily, 10am - 5pm. Closed New Year's Day, Thanksgiving, and Christmas.

Price: Free. Note that some special exhibits have a fee. For instance, King Tut was $29.95 for adults; $19.50 for ages 4 - 12. There is a $2 reservation fee per person for the Endeavour and reservations are required Mon. - Fri. before 1pm, and weekends and holidays all day. (Free after 1 during the week!) Parking is $12 per vehicle. Membership here is a great deal for $65 as it includes four IMAX tickets, two parking vouchers, four high-wire bike rides or cliff climbs, discounts to on-site activities and shopping, and free admission to more than 300 other science centers and museums nationwide. See info on the Association of Science - Technology Centers (pg. xi) for reciprocal museum memberships.

Ages: 3 years and up.

CHEN ART GALLERY

(310) 781-3808 when open; (310) 222-9192 after hours / www.chenartgallery.org

1625 Abalone Avenue in the Sunrider International headquarter building, Torrance

Enter through cool looking red doors, protected by guard dog/lions, for your ninety-minute guided tour, the only way you can explore the gallery. Encompassing 5,000 years of Chinese history you'll see a Qing dynasty imperial throne room, a Ming dynasty bedroom, porcelains, jade carvings (a favorite being the 5,000 year old dragon), silk textiles, scroll paintings, snuff bottles, cloisonne, clothing, Buddhist statues, vases, bowls, ancient pottery, and artifacts owned by former Chinese emperors, as well as Picasso and Matisse paintings. There are also special exhibits, so call before you come as they are sometimes closed in between exhibitions. This museum is much more than you would first expect, as rooms and galleries unfold to reveal more of this incredible collection. As the tour guide explains the various items, you'll learn so much about China - its history and its people. Note that there is nowhere to sit during the tour, so you'll be walking and standing. Just outside are botanic gardens, a pagoda, manicured lawns and a rock-lined koi pond.

Hours: Open Tues. - Fri., 10am - 4pm, with tours usually given around 10am and 2pm. Reservations for tours are mandatory. Closed all major holidays.

Price: Free

Ages: Children 10 years and under are not allowed.

COLUMBIA MEMORIAL SPACE CENTER

(562) 231-1200 / www.columbiaspacescience.org

12400 Clark Avenue, Downey

Ignite a desire within your child to reach for the stars by visiting this medium-sized, unique space center. Rich in aerospace history, including the site of the development of the first cruise missile in the 50's and the engineering and building of the Apollo space capsules, this former Boeing/NASA development site is now, fittingly, the home of an official national memorial to the Space Shuttle *Columbia* with an emphasis on engaging kid's hands and minds in the present and future of space exploration.

Outside is the Apollo Boiler Plate 12, an unmanned test vehicle. In the lobby, an 18' by 18' photo mosaic of the crew and shuttle of the *Columbia* moves visitors to learn about their lives, the mission, and the tragedy. Another wall shows a visual and informational time line of the history of Downey and the city's relationship with the aerospace industry. Launch a pneumatic model rocket inside a tube at the touch of a button - the noise is surprising! A rotating display case contains photos and artifacts regarding astronauts and other people in the field, as well as space-related technology, instruments, and perhaps a model rocket. A huge video wall shows the latest launch, or a visit to the space station. The few hands-on experiments here include the orbital velocity exhibit, a fancy name for kids gently throwing marbles, which represent planets and space debris, and watch as they spin around a vortex (demonstrating orbit) and drop into the center hole; a paper airplane make and launch station; a model plane in a cage that visitors can fly and steer using the wheel and the throttle; a space-themed claw machine; and a long, vertical pole to attach a miniature capsule with a parachute which you crank up to the top, release and watch it float down to the landing zone. (Mine missed.)

Sign up to use the robotics lab where fourteen computers interface with fourteen, nine inch high, or so, robots in the Lego Mindstorm "game". Participants program their robot to walk on a tabletop that represents the surface of Mars and to rescue items, research a project, or whatever else they program it to do - both challenging and fun.

The upstairs gallery wall murals depict the space station, views from the Hubble telescope, our solar system, people involved in the space program, and more. A small area for ages 6 and under has a nice play area with a crawl tunnel, large foam blocks and toys and books. Astronaut wanna bes can sit at the at the controls of the scale model flight simulator and blast away to parts unknown. An earth exhibit is a spherical video projector with touch screen panels that shows the view of the earth from the moon, planets, or other points in space. Try on a spacesuit - major photo op. Use a touch screen to illuminate and animate planets and moons. At another exhibit match and piece together large photo cubes to form a from-space view of the earth - or is it Mars? Similar to the hand and footprint cement signature squares of movie stars in Hollywood, one wall is dedicated to signature blocks, where astronauts signed their names in concrete after their mission was completed. The blocks with signatures, that are accompanied by photos and explanations of the missions, include Alan Shepard from Apollo XIV, Richard O. Covery with *Discovery*, and many more.

The apogee of the center is the Challenger Learning Center with three mission simulations, set up for field trips and school classes for 5th graders and up, for $3 per person with a minimum of fifteen students. Enter the Mission Control room, which looks like the real deal, and become immediately immersed in space travel, made more real with interactive screens. The situation room has medical, research, and scientific elements. Participants in both rooms interact with each other via camera and computer collaboration, working together to solve problems and deal with situations that arise on the space station and during space travel. In this two-hour program students, who switch rooms midway through their session so all have the opportunity to be mission controllers and spacecraft astronauts, learn teamwork and practical math and science applications in an unforgettable, interactive way.

Columbia Memorial Space Center also offers a stellar array of day camps to learn about engineering, astronaut training, robotics, and 3D printing. There are programs for all ages regarding potential careers in aerospace, geographic information systems, principles of flight, understanding our solar system, and so much more.

Hours: Open Tues. - Sat., 10am - 5pm. Closed Sun., Mon. and all major holidays.

Price: $5 per person; children 3 and under are free. See info on the Association of Science - Technology Centers (pg. xi) for reciprocal museum memberships.

Ages: 4 years and up.

DISCOVERY CUBE (Los Angeles County)

(818) 686-CUBE (2823) / la.discoverycube.org

11800 Foothill Blvd, Los Angeles

$$$$

Like its sibling DISCOVERY CUBE (Orange County) (pg. 304), this multi-story Discovery Cube is an great, interactive gem for kids (and adults) to hands-on explore. Environmental stewardship is a cornerstone principle here and is experienced in numerous interactive exhibits. Sit in kayaks (just because) located just outside the Aquavator - a special "elevator" that, once inside, makes you feel like you're descending deep into the earth's crust as you see the various geological layers - ground level, sand, rock, fossil bed, etc. - via large screens as you journey to the center of the earth, learning about underground water aquifers. Watch out for the mythical Megalodon! In the darkened Planetary Research room look at the huge suspended, animated earth that shows historic weather patterns and storms, as well as real-time weather around the world. Climb aboard a helicopter facade into a room with passenger seats (and insides more spacious than any helicopter I've been in) and consol boards with huge screens that simulate the skies above Los Angeles - the skyscrapers and buildings to the snow-covered mountains - then dive beneath into an aqueduct to view the vast water system. Inspector Training is like a scavenger hunt: In a setting that looks like a backyard and the rooms of a house, kids strap on an touch screen tablet and become a home inspector to see if the house is earthquake proof, energy efficient and more.

One reason kids stick to it at the fabulous and very hands-on Science of Hockey exhibit, created in association the LA Kings, is they can "drive" the almost life-size model of a Zamboni machine stationed on the ice-like flooring of the room. Wannabe sportscasters can try out their chosen career in the broadcast booth. Compare surfaces as you see whose puck goes the fastest at the ice and friction table. Gear up as a goalie as virtual versions of real players shoot the hockey puck that then actually comes out of holes in the wall toward you, the goalie. Or, be a hockey player by taking a real stick and shoot a puck at a simulated goalie. Your kids will actually want a time out in the Penalty Box as it has hockey-oriented ways to learn math equations, statistics, physics, and more sports applications. Learn about training and nutrition, uniforms, equipment in action, force and power exchange dynamics, the locker rooms, safety tips, and more via interactive games and interactive videos.

Set up like a real grocery store, the Discovery Market is a game of shopping. Grab a cart, go down the aisles and using touch screens and scanners, learn to make wise, healthy food choices. At Race to Zero Waste, stand at an conveyor belt as trash comes out of a truck and race against others to quickly and correctly sort recyclables and other waste to divert trash from our landfills. What fun! And learning! Take a virtual trek through the real, neighboring Hansen Dame Recreation Area while rock climbing on a low, short wall with "rocks" that light up and standing in a wind tunnel to feel the Santa Anas. Sit down on a pulley seat and pull your own weight up to the top (or not). Turn wheels, looks through lenses, push buttons, interact with various scenarios at galleries that promote and educate about the environment. Play areas just for younger kids are terrific for them to build using extra large blocks and connectors; enjoy a life-size Thomas the Tank; play at a huge train table; and more. Watch and be a part of live demonstrations at the stage area. See a show in the 4D theater. Don't miss the wonderful rotating exhibits here, too, such as Dora the Explorer, Curious George, and Storyland, where you could read books in the recreated book settings.

When you get hungry, enjoy the relatively healthy food options at the on-side cafe. Inquire about field trips, sleep overs, summer camps and so much more. Take some time to explore the immediate area of HANSEN DAM RECREATION AREA (pg. 64), too.

Hours: Open daily, 10am - 5pm. Closed Thanksgiving and Christmas.
Price: $17.95 for adults; $14.95 for seniors; $12.95 for seniors and ages 3 - 14; children 2 and under are free. Purchase tickets online for a discount. Shows at the 4-D Theater are an additional $3 per person. See info on the Association of Science - Technology Centers (pg. xi) for reciprocal museum memberships. See info on the Bank of America Museums on Us (pg. xi).
Ages: 2 years and up.

THE DOCTORS HOUSE MUSEUM

(818) 242-7447 or (818) 548-3782 / www.glendalehistorical.org $
1601 W. Mountain Street, Glendale

Tour through this delightfully restored, Queen Anne Eastlake-style home that was once owned by four doctors, in succession. (Hence the name.) Docents point out and discuss the doctors' office with its instruments and vials, period furniture from the early 1900's, clothing, and other artifacts from the Victorian time period. One-hour, free, school tours, for third graders and above, are given during the week. In addition to the house tour, students also play outdoor Victorian games. Ask about special functions throughout the year, such as the candlelight tour in December.

Just outside the house is an expansive green lawn and a gazebo. A Japanese tea garden, complete with a waterfall, koi, and a Japanese tea house, Whispering Pine, to peek into is also on the grounds. The Doctors House Museum and the adjacent beautiful Glendale Library are located in BRAND PARK (pg. 49).

Hours: Open Sun., 2pm - 4pm, except major holidays, inclement weather, and the month of July. Tours are also given the second and third Sat. in December from 6:30pm - 8:30pm.
Price: The museum is $5 for adults; ages 16 and under are free.
Ages: 6 years and up.

DOMINGUEZ RANCHO ADOBE MUSEUM

(310) 603-0088 / www.dominguezrancho.org   !
18127 S. Alameda Street, Compton

Site of the First Spanish land grant in California by King Carlos III in 1784, of a skirmish in the Mexican-American War, and of an oil discovery in 1921, this site and rancho have a rich history. Walk through the sprawling and beautifully-restored adobe to see the family dining room, with the table set for a meal; the simply furnished yet stylish bedrooms - make sure to look at the wood bed frame that uses rawhide to hold the straw mattress and Manuel Dominguez's more elegant bed with a canopy; the parlour with a piano and phonograph; the living room with its elegant furniture; the display room exhibiting photographs in glass and wood cabinets; the room containing intricately-carved wood furniture; and the outside kitchen with big vats. Other artifacts around the Rancho include hides, saddles, branding irons, a spinning wheel, and a replica of an ox-driven carreta used during the rancho period.

The spacious grounds are lovely with rose gardens and pathways in the front and lots of grass areas with mature trees and picnic tables. On the guided tour you'll learn, among other interesting facts, about the cattle once raised here for hide, beef, and tallow, as well as how tallow was processed. School tours incorporate many hands-on activities to allow students to really experience history, and what students experience, they remember. Call or look online for the numerous the special events and programs such as Battle Reenactments; Living History Night, Adobe Brick Making, Nature Craft Classes, and garden tours.

Hours: Guided tours are offered Wed., Sat., and Sun. and the first Thurs. and Fri. at 1pm, 2pm, and 3pm. Tours are available in Spanish the 2nd Sun. of each month. Call to arrange a school or group tour for at least ten people or more. Closed New Year's Day and Christmas.
Price: Free
Ages: 6 years and up.

THE DRUM BARRACKS CIVIL WAR MUSEUM

(310) 548-7509 / www.drumbarracks.org

1052 Banning Boulevard, Wilmington

The year is 1861 and the Civil War has broken out. Although most of the fighting was done in the east, troops from Camp Drum, California, fought on the Union side. Your forty-five-minute tour of the medium-sized barracks/house/museum starts in the library research room. (This is the last remaining original Civil War era military facility in the L.A. area.) A six-minute video tells the history of Camp Drum through reenactments, with a costumed character narrating. Apparently, a few good ghosts from the Civil War still hang out here. Needless to say, my kids heard "ghostly" noises throughout the rest of our visit.

The parlor room is where the officers entertained. Besides period furniture and a few pianos, it also has a stereoscope, which is an early Viewmaster™, to look through. Q: Why didn't people smile for photographs back then? A: Many people had bad teeth, plus it took a long time to actually take a picture.

The hallway shows a picture of the Camel Corps. which was a regiment that actually rode camels. It also has a flag from an 1863 battlefield - have your kids count the stars (states). Upstairs, the armory room has a few original weapons, like a musket and some swords. Look into a barracks room where soldiers once slept, and the Model Rooms with scale models of the original camp with all of its buildings. The officer's bedroom has furniture, a pump organ, personal effects, and old-fashioned clothing. Q: Why did women usually wear brown wedding dresses? A: You'll have to take the tour to find out! Check the website Calendar for special events such as a Civil War Technology Fair, Civil War Christmas with free carriage rides, and more.

Hours: Tours are given Tues. - Thurs. at 10am and 11:30am; Sat. - Sun, 11:30am and 1pm.

Price: $5 for adults; students and children 11 and under are free.

Ages: 5 years and up.

EL MONTE HISTORICAL MUSEUM

(626) 444-3813 - museums; (626) 580-2001 - city hall / www.ci.el-monte.ca.us

3150 N. Tyler Avenue, El Monte

A visit to this adobe-style museum offers fascinating glimpses into the history of the United States, as well as the history of the pioneers of El Monte. There is plenty to see and learn to keep young people's interest peaked, even though no touching is allowed. Items in the numerous glass displays are labeled, making it easy to self-tour. However, I highly recommend taking a guided tour, given for groups of ten or more people, so your family, or school group, doesn't miss out on the many details and explanations of the exhibits.

My kids were captivated by the hallway showcasing Gay's Lion Farm, which was a local training ground in the 1920's for lions used in motion pictures. The photos depict the large cats interacting with people in various circus-type acts. There are also several adorable shots of lion cubs. A lion's tail and teeth are on display, too. The Heritage Room, toward the back, looks like an old-fashioned living room with antique furniture and a piano, plus cases of glassware, ladies' boots, and clothing. The walls are lined with pictures of walnut growers and other first-residents of El Monte.

The Pioneer Room has wonderful collections of typewriters, lamps/lanterns, dolls, toys, books, bells, quilts, army medals, and Bibles. It also contains ornate swords, a flag (with two bullet holes in it) from the battlefield at Gettysburg, a piece of the Berlin wall, George Washington's lantern, and an actual letter written by the Father of our Country who, by the way, had nice handwriting! The Frontier Room is equally interesting with early-day policeman and fireman hats, police badges and guns, a 1911 Model T, a wall of old tools, early Native American artifacts, and a recreated old-time law enforcement office.

The huge Lexington Room is subdivided into smaller, themed "rooms" such as a turn-of-the-century schoolroom with desks, maps, and schoolwork; an old-time general store filled with shelves of merchandise; a barber shop with a chair; a music shop with ukuleles, violins, a Victrola, and more; and a dressmaker's shop with beautiful dresses, sewing machines, elegant hair combs, and beaded handbags. Most of the rooms also have period-dressed mannequins. This section of the museum also contains rooms that would have been found in a house of the early 1900's - a parlor, bedroom, kitchen, and library. Each room is fully furnished and complete to the smallest detail. The El Monte Historic Museum, with a plaque that commemorates it as "the end of the Santa Fe Trail," offers a window to the world!

For further study, or just for the joy of reading, the El Monte Public Library is only a few buildings down. Directly across the street from the museum is a park. This pleasant corner park offers plenty of picnic tables and shady oak trees, plus a few slides and some metal transportation vehicles to climb on.

Hours: Open Tues. - Fri., 10am - 4pm. Open on Sat. by appointment and during the week for school tours. Closed Sun., Mon., Sat., and holidays.

Price: Free

Ages: 5 years and up.

EL PUEBLO DE LOS ANGELES HISTORICAL MONUMENT / OLVERA STREET / CHINESE AMERICAN MUSEUM / ITALIAN AMERICAN MUSEUM OF LOS ANGELES

$$$

See EL PUEBLO DE LOS ANGELES HISTORICAL MONUMENT / OLVERA STREET / CHINESE AMERICAN MUSEUM / ITALIAN AMERICAN MUSEUM OF LOS ANGELES (pg. 168), under POTPOURRI, for details about the museums here.

FASHION INSTITUTE OF DESIGN & MERCHANDISING MUSEUM & GALLERIES

$$

(213) 624-1200 or (213) 623-5821 / fidmmuseum.org
919 S. Grand Avenue, Los Angeles

Project Runway and other shows have helped promote the world of fashion and design to the average person. The small museum is located at the Fashion Institute school and you will definitely notice a difference in the very trendy way the students on this campus dress versus other downtowners! The museum showcases two major (and popular) exhibits a year that are particularly interesting to kids - The Art of Motion Picture Costume Design (usually mid-February through mid-April) and The Outstanding Art of Television Costume Design. These exhibits feature over 120 costumes (headdresses and all) from current Academy Award-nominated films (about twenty-five films are represented) and Emmy Award-nominated television shows, respectively. Do you recognize the costumes? Which ones do you think are winners? The galleries also include traveling exhibits (a past one was a tribute to Barbie), FIDM's student's work, and select costumes from the thousands of pieces from the permanent collection from international couture, theater, and film. The galleries are closed in between exhibits. Upstairs is a tiny exhibit gallery with rotating exhibits - perfume bottles, period shoes and accessories, etc.

Look into the museum gift store that offers unique accessories and gifts for sale, and especially check out the adjacent Scholarship Store. The latter store sells a great array (and often only one-of-a-kind) of new clothing (from evening dresses and wedding dresses to t-shirts and jeans), jewelry, fabric and accessories all donated by top fashion companies and by students for sale at a fraction of the "real" cost - really. For more shopping opportunities, note that the Los Angeles Fashion District (www.fashiondistrict.org) is just a few blocks away.

In front of the campus is Grand Hope Park, a lovely sprawl of green grass and trees, benches, statues, a pavilion, and a playground with slides, bridges, swing, poles and extra large animals to sit and rock back and forth on. See DOWNTOWN LOS ANGELES / GRAND PARK (pg. 167) for information on Grand Park (a different Grand Park) and all the other places to go within this fairly immediate area.

Hours: Open Tues. - Sat., 10am - 5pm. Closed Sun., Mon., and holidays.
Price: Free. Parking costs about $6.
Ages: 7 years and up.

FLIGHT PATH MUSEUM AND LEARNING CENTER

!

(424) 646-7284 / www.flightpathmuseum.com
6661 West Imperial Highway, Los Angeles

Located right next to LAX, this commodious and unique museum displays the history (and future) Los Angeles Airport has played regarding flight, airlines, and even movies. The ample rooms hold pictures, murals, information panels and memorabilia regarding flying, pilots, and airplanes.

Outside is a burnt motorcasing, or part of a third stage of a rocket, that survived re-entry to earth. Walk into the museum past a display of old luggage and the front end of a plane. Windows take up most of the central room which looks out onto the terminals and airspace so visitors can watch planes take off. You can even sit in airplane seats to do so. You can also listen to the radio control tower being transmitted in here. Exhibits in this room include the bright blue, eight-foot Stinson Model U used in the movie *Indiana Jones*; hanging model airplanes; goggles and a leather flying cap worn during WWI; flight schedules; navigational aids; and a glass display of cups, plates, and other items used on board a plane.

One room is devoted to the changing styles of flight attendant uniforms and has lots of them on display, from the short skirts of the sixties to polyester to Hawaiian-themed ones - how styles have changed! In the hallways and in the corner of rooms, several airlines, such as Pan Am and TWA, are represented with a grouping of uniforms, model planes, and commemorative items. Be sure to check out the Flying Tigers gallery. A section devoted to space travel has pictures of the planets, videos of space exploration, model rocket ships and even a few space suits. The large conference room has several flight simulators - computers, foot pedals, and cockpit wheels - used for teaching and education. There is a research library available, too. Out back, visitors can board a 1935 DC-3 Spirit of Seventy Six plane and go up (walking at a tilt) to the cockpit area and take control, so to speak.

Ask about the numerous special programs offered here. Groups are offered guided tours of the facility often given by retired pilots. Sometimes included in the school tours is a police dog demonstration (the kennel is right next door) where the dogs show how they sniff for drugs and bombs, and a fire truck demonstration where the highlight is having the kids come outside and watch the water cannon blast into the air.

Hours: Open Tues. - Sat., 10am - 3pm. Closed Mon., Sun., and major holidays.
Price: Free
Ages: 6 years and up.

FOLK MUSIC CENTER AND MUSEUM

(909) 624-2928 / www.folkmusiccenter.com
220 Yale Avenue, Claremont

"We pluck dulcimers, not chickens" is the true, but quirky motto for the Folk Music Center. The shop, here since the 1950's, has an incredible variety of instruments - hundreds of them - from around the world for sale and in its small museum. Browse the store for banjos, guitars (there's a wall full of them), chimes, drums, gongs, sitars, percussion instruments, musical toys, and an assortment of ethnic instruments. The adjacent museum room has shelves and shelves of rare and antique musical instruments and artifacts from various cultures across the globe.

Informal, but informative, hour-long tours/field trips are tailored for whatever age group visits - kids or adults. The folk music educator shares the history of specific instruments and the culture of the people playing them, and then demonstrates their sounds. Listen to the call of the Tibetan Temple Horn (which is a very long instrument!). Hear the call of the sea via a conch shell. And check out the size of the giant harmonica. Then, a mini jam session takes place and visitors are encouraged to clap and sing along. So, take *note:* This museum and tour can help fine *tune* your kids' musical appreciation. The minimum number of people for a tour is ten; the maximum is about seventy.

Hours: The store and museum are open Tues. - Sat., 10am - 6pm; Sun., noon - 4pm. Closed Mon. and major holidays. Tours are offered, by reservation only, on Wed. at 10:15am.
Price: Free. Tours are free, as well.
Ages: 5 years and up.

FORT MACARTHUR MUSEUM - ANGEL'S GATE PARK

(310) 548-2631- museum; (310) 548-7705 - Angels Gate Park / www.ftmac.org
3601 S. Gaffey Street, San Pedro

This concrete World War II coastal defense battery building really fires up kids' imaginations as they walk the grounds and tour the few open concrete rooms that contain mines, gun casings, uniforms, pictures, newspaper clippings, a gun tube, a twenty-two-foot-long rammer, a missile, GM-12 generator set, and other war memorabilia. You can even walk through some underground hallways! Another set of rooms includes one filled with World War II information, a mess hall, and a communication display room that holds numerous restored radio equipment including WWII radio sets used on B-17 and B-24 Bombers, squad radios, transmitters, a Lane Victory radio room, and more. A sixteen-minute video shows recoil guns shooting, as well as the history of this museum. Go into the soldier's barracks displaying typical army articles of cots and some uniforms.

Talking through the speaking tube system can keep kids busy for a time, as one person speaks through one end while someone else tries to find the receiving end. Don't forget to take the steps up to the top of the defense building once used by lookouts with guns to watch for incoming, attacking ships. Note: Check the Calendar entry for OLD FORT MACARTHUR DAYS (pg. 725) and ask about other events, such as "living history" days. Ask to take a guided tour if you're interested in learning more about this site and about WWII, and /or take a school group here on a fascinating trip through time.

Just east of the museum, on a hill in Angels Gate Park, sits the seventeen-ton Korean Friendship Bell set in a traditional, Korean-style pagoda. Let the kids run loose to enjoy the grassy knolls. There is a small playground here and a basketball court, and since it's a fairly treeless area, it's also ideal for kite flying. On a clear day the coastal view is gorgeous, and you can see Catalina Island. Note that the MARINE MAMMAL CARE CENTER AT FORT MACARTHUR (pg. 223) is just around the corner. Also note that entrance to the museum is via 32nd Street gate.

Hours: Open Tues., Thurs., Sat. - Sun., and holidays, noon - 5pm. Docent tours are offered by appointment. The park is open daily, sunrise - 6pm.
Price: Free. Suggested donations are $3 for adults; $1 for ages 12 and under.
Ages: 3 years and up.

THE GAMBLE HOUSE

(626) 793-3334 / www.gamblehouse.org $$$
4 Westmoreland Place, Pasadena

    Wood, and the way various types are crafted and blended, is the primary focus of the Gamble House. Teak, maple, cedar, redwood, and oak were used in the furniture, cabinetry, paneling, carvings, and exterior walls in a way that represents the best of the Arts and Crafts movement from the turn-of-the-century. Not that kids care about these details, but they are impressed by the natural beauty of the rooms, original furnishings, and terraces. A one-hour guided tour explains the history of the house, the era in which it was built, and the architecture's harmonious use of wood and natural light in the home in accord with its environmental surroundings. Highlights, besides the use of wood, include the appealing open porches (used as sleeping porches), and the Tiffany glass throughout. Note: Only the first floor of the house is stroller/wheelchair accessible. If you don't feel like you've seen it all, you haven't, but you can on a more leisurely, two-hour+ tour called Behind the Velvet Ropes - $45. There are other special focus tours available, as well.

    The outside grounds are classy looking, with beautiful landscaping, rolling green lawns, and a brick walkway and driveway. It's so nice here that mini-tours, called Brown-Bag, are offered on Tuesdays. This consists of a twenty-minute tour and the opportunity to just enjoy the grounds while enjoying a picnic lunch (that you supply) for a few hours.

Hours: Open Tues. for Brown-Bag from 11:30am - 1:30pm; mini-tours given at 12:15pm and 12:45pm. Advanced reservations are necessary. Open for regular tours, which leave every 15 min., Thurs. - Fri., 11:30am - 3pm; Sat. - Sun., noon - 3pm (last tour), although ticket sales begin at 10am Thurs. - Sat. and at 11:30am on Sun. Closed Mon., Wed. and national holidays.

Price: Brown-Bag tours are $8 per person. Regular tours are $15 for adults; $12.50 for seniors and students with ID; children 12 and under are free.

Ages: 6 years and up.

THE GETTY CENTER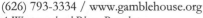

(310) 440-7300 / www.getty.edu $$$
1200 Getty Center Drive, Los Angeles

    Everything wonderful you've heard about the Getty Center is true! Your adventure begins with a four-and-a-half-minute tram ride up a winding track that seemingly hugs the edge of the road. You may also hike up the 1.9-mile road, but you'll get enough exercise walking around the Getty.

    The architecture of the museum is stunning - it elicited several exclamations of admiration from my kids. The all-white travertine (i.e., marble-like) structures can also be blinding, so bring sunglasses. Once inside the lobby, make your first stop at one of two theaters that show a ten-minute orientation movie regarding the center. Next, use an app or borrow a free ipod touch GettyGuide that offers several types of tours in several languages, such as suggestions of special stops for families; descriptions, commentary, and interviews of more than 300 works in a total of nine hours (which is longer than you'll be here, I know); animals speaking about the artwork they star in; how food and wine connect to works of art in An Art Tasting tour; a tour - Demons, Angels, and Monsters - where listeners hear those aforementioned voice their perspectives; and more. Specific guided tours are available almost each day that cover an exhibition, the Getty architecture, the gardens, and 17th and 18th century art as is a Collection Highlights tour. Tours and classes for school and other groups are available by reservation.

    Stroll down the courtyard toward the boulder fountain as you aim for your next destination, the Family Room. This room is subdivided into five discovery "coves," each one highlighting a different form of art - photography, painting, sculpture, decorative arts, and manuscript and drawings. Each cove also contains a hands-on activity, such as making a mask, experimenting with mirrors and photographic lenses, reading books on an 18th century-style bed, designing and coloring a portion of an illuminated manuscript, and, most fun of all, rearranging foam tubes into a grid of holes on the wall to recreate a metal tubular sculpture. A treasure hunt wall containing about seventy peepholes at various heights allows guests to peer in and see detailed portions of art on display throughout the museum. (Can you match the portion with the whole piece of art?) You can get Art Detective Cards at the entrance or the Family Room that enables your kids to go from mere observers to interactive participants in the galleries as they look for certain pieces of art. Make up your own activities, too, such as having your children imitate portrait poses, or encourage them to be on the lookout for paintings with bridges or dogs or the color red. Note: The museum offers several kid-oriented tours and family workshops that include looking at kid-intriguing artwork and perhaps doing a related art activity. One more room/activity - for all ages - is the drawing room with easels, paper, colored pencils, and still life objects for aspiring artists to use for drawing their own masterpiece.

    Now it's time to actually see the world-renown art. Forgive me for not going into detail here about the works -

they are too numerous and grand. Suffice to say that the five magnificent, multi-level galleries feature paintings, sculptures, drawings, photography, and decorative arts (e.g., elegant, gold-gilded furniture, tapestries, vases, and more) in natural-light conditions, which enhance the beauty of the work. My boys were fascinated with the overhead sun panels that automatically adjust to let in the right amount of light. Many of the works have stories about the pieces printed alongside them, making them more interesting than just another pretty picture. A separate, darkened room features medieval, illuminated (i.e., hand-painted) manuscripts with still-vivid colors painted on vellum (i.e., sheep skin). From Van Gogh to Rembrandt to Renoir, the spectacular Getty it a "must see" and it has something to please every *palette*.

Hardwood floors and elevators make the Center stroller/wheelchair accessible, although the doors that connect the galleries are heavy to push and pull open. As the Getty is on a hill, the several terraces offer magnificent vistas from Mt. Baldy to Catalina to the surrounding Beverly Hills area. We particularly liked the cactus garden on top of a building outside the South Pavilion. Another outside attraction is the tiered, maze-like, central garden which you may walk in and around. In fact, garden tours, specifically, are offered because they are so remarkable

Hungry visitors have several options. Two cafeterias have both indoor and outdoor seating, and serve a sandwiches, burgers, salads, tacos, pizza, and more for an average of $10.50. The on-site restaurant is an elegant, sit-down dining experience, and entrees range from $24 to $38. You may also bring a lunch to enjoy at the large picnic area by the base of the tram ride. It has grassy green lawns and numerous covered picnic tables. This last choice entails taking the electric tram down to the parking lot and then back up to the museum.

Here are a few tips to make your day more memorable: 1) Consider pre-purchasing (through the Getty bookstore or elsewhere) *A is for Artist*, a Getty museum pictorial alphabet book that inspires children to be on the lookout for certain works of art. (Familiarity, in this case, breeds pleasurable recognition.) Or, buy *Going to the Getty* by J. Otto Seibold and Vivian Walsh, a book that gives a solid and fun overview of the museum, as well as a look at a few pieces in particular. 2) Look for fossils embedded in the Getty walls, particularly at the plaza where the tram arrives. 3) Pre-warn your children to stand 6" to 12" away from the art. There are no ropes in front of the pieces, and while the security guards are friendly, they are also insistent. 4) A free coat/bag check is available in the entrance hall. 5) Going outside, just to another building, is almost unavoidable, so if it's raining bring an umbrella. 6) Wear comfortable walking shoes! Our eyes were glazed over when we left the Getty, but our minds and hearts were filled with wondrous works of art.

Hours: Open Tues. - Fri. and Sun., 10am - 5:30pm; Sat., 10am - 9pm. Closed Mon., New Year's Day, Thanksgiving and Christmas.

Price: The museum is free. Parking is $15 per vehicle; $10 after 3pm. Visit the Getty Villa on the same day and pay just one parking fee.

Ages: 4 years and up.

THE GETTY VILLA   ☀

(310) 440-7300 / www.getty.edu $$$
17985 Pacific Coast Highway, Pacific Palisades

In a setting that would please the ancient gods, this utterly magnificent "villa," integrated into a terraced hillside, showcases antiquated works of art from Greece, Rome, and Etruria (i.e., part of Italy). The architecture blends elements inspired from first-century Rome and from the modern world, with columns, skylights, marble staircases, and a 450-seat outdoor, classical, coliseum-style-seating theater. The theater is host to year-round, classical dramas, concerts, and presentations. The four gardens are an intrinsic part of the villa experience, comprised of over 300 varieties of plants known to have grown in the bygone Mediterranean world, plus statues, fountains, and decorative columns. The large, formal, Outer Peristyle garden is most impressive with its 225-foot-long reflecting pool. And do take a look at the astounding beauty of the surrounding vistas.

Begin your visit by viewing a twelve-minute film that gives an overview of J. Paul Getty's vast collection, the architecture of the villa, and how antiquities are preserved. "Rent" a free GettyGuide audio guide which features commentary on over 150 works of art. Book/pamphlet guides are available as are various free tours throughout the day that spotlight different segments of the Villa. Forty-five minute Art Odyssey tours, geared for kids, are offered on weekends year round and during the week, additionally, in the summer. When kids are involved with art their visit has more of an impact.

Dating from 6,500 B.C. to 400 A.D., select objects d'art are elegantly exhibited in twenty-three permanent galleries and five rotating galleries that flow from one into another. Depictions of gods and goddesses, and renderings of the Trojan War, plus vases, glass, pottery, mosaics, gems, coins, jewelry, and sculptures are presented in galleries organized by theme and context, making your visit a walk through history. Kids are especially intrigued by the sculptures. (Note that there are many nude statues here.) Make sure to look where you walk as the floors are made of bronze, marble, and terrazzo pieces designed and inlaid in intricate, geometric patterns.

Just a few exhibit highlights: On the first floor, the Temple of Herakles room, featuring a stunning statue of Herakles; the resplendent Basilica with statues of divinities (don't *myth* this one); Dionysus, near the inside theater; and two interactive rooms - the TimeScape Room and Family Forum. The TimeScape Room features a colorful, visual time line incorporating audio commentary, sculptures, and rock strata for archeology buffs. In the hands-on Family Forum draw on urn replicas, use props and a shadow screen to imitate poses of famous works of art (or whatever) for an audience, and peek inside a simulated kiln to see how ceramics are fired. Upstairs, are bronzed animals of old; a real mummy; statues of athletes in various poses, including the bronze Statue of a Victorious Youth (i.e., an Olympian); funerary sculpture; and renderings of women and children in one room, men in another. The GettyGuide Room is here, as well, where you can view videos of art-making techniques and interact with a time line of the collection.

The Villa is host to numerous special events and cultural functions. Educators may obtain curriculum aids. A cafe on the grounds serves, fittingly enough, Mediterranean fare, and beyond, such as salads, soups, pizza, Greek chicken wrap, and beef brisket. Bambini (i.e. children's) menu offers pastas or grilled chicken with French fries. Sit at the cafe or order a boxed lunch to go to enjoy on the grounds. A full-on tea is also served with scones, grilled vegetable panini, roast beef, shrimp toast, chocolate toffee crunch and more on Thursdays and Saturdays at 1pm for $39 per person. One thing is certain - this Getty isn't resting on its laurels.

Hours: Open Wed. - Mon, 10am - 5pm. Closed Tues., Jan. 1, July 4, Thanksgiving, and Dec. 25. A timed ticket, obtained in advance, is required.
Price: Free. Parking is $15; $10 after 3pm. Visit the Getty Center on the same day and pay just one parking fee.
Ages: 7 years and up.

GLIB MUSEUM OF ARCADIA HERITAGE

(626) 574-5440 / www.arcadiaca.gov; www.visitarcadiacalifornia.com
380 West Huntington Drive, Arcadia

This small museum is well laid out, chronicling the history of Arcadia in a timeline format with newspaper articles, photographs, documents, and plenty of memorabilia from various time periods. The artifacts include an old fire hose cart, coppering tools, military uniforms from several wars, a man's fur coat and mittens, pianos, a school desk, old cameras, tiaras from past Rose Queens, and even an alcove set up like a dining room with table, chairs, china, and a cupboard of kitchen implements. A hands-on table holds military helmets, phones, a typewriter, and cameras. The Museum offers a plethora of school and other guided tour groups, as well as speakers, family days, and workshops for adults.

Hours: Open Tues. - Sat., 10am - noon and 1pm - 4pm. Closed Sun., Mon. and most holidays.
Price: Free
Ages: 7 years and up.

GO FOR BROKE NATIONAL EDUCATION CENTER

(310) 328-0907 / goforbroke.org $$$
355 E. 1ˢᵗ Street, Suite 200, Los Angeles

This small, unique Education Center is really more of a focused exhibit and powerful experience, than museum, per se. The current exhibit (at the time of this writing), Defining Courage Experience, has maps, photos, personal belongings (i.e. furniture, clothing, etc.), portraits, videos, and computer screens that encourage visitors to not just look at pictures and read the info, but also, really, to engage with the programs and concepts offered. After explaining the atrocity of Japanese Americans being rounded up and sent to concentration camps, Defining Courage explores the idea of what it means to be courageous as depicted thru the lives of young Japanese Americans - soldiers and civilians - during WWII. You walk through a few rooms to view the exhibits and displays, and then into the main exhibit room to answer experienced-based surveys and questions that ultimately invite guests to see relevance in similar circumstances of their own lives today. This room also has exhibits on propaganda and a station to make your own two-minute movie based on certain choices. Check the museum website for group and educational tours offered.

Go For Broke is just down the street and associated with JAPANESE AMERICAN NATIONAL MUSEUM (pg. 124), so make sure you visit both while in the area, as well as the monument around the corner.

Hours: Open Tues. - Wed., Fri., and Sun., 11am - 6pm; Thurs., noon - 8pm; Sat., 10am - 6pm. Closed Mon., New Year's Day, 4th of July, Thanksgiving and Christmas.
Price: $9 for adults; $5 for seniors, teachers with ID, students, and ages 6 - 17; ages 5 and under are free. Admission is free every Thurs. from 5pm - 8pm, and all day on the third Thurs. of every month. Check the website for other free days. Combo admission to this museum and to Japanese American is $15 for adults; $8 for seniors and youth.
Ages: 7 years and up.

GORDON R. HOWARD MUSEUM - MENTZER HOUSE

(818) 841-6333 / www.burbankhistoricalsoc.org
115 Lomita Street in the George Izay Park, Burbank

!

Make sure to save a weekend afternoon to come and explore the Gordon Howard Museum and other immediate buildings. The hallway has old toys and dishes on display, plus a drawing room and a music room. The salon contains wedding dresses, old dresses (that are now back in style), including a stunning 1898 dress with beads and lace, plus ladies boots, jeweled hat pins, and dolls.

The Historical Room is large and filled with interesting slices from Burbank's past. Along one wall are glass-enclosed rooms, each one complete with furniture and period-dressed mannequins. As you look into the rooms, pick up an old-fashioned telephone receiver, press a button that corresponds to the room, and listen to stories about Dr. Burbank (does that name ring a bell?), a family-owned winery, a 1920's hotel lobby (when $1 paid for a room!), a country store, and the *Jazz Singer*, Al Jolson. Other exhibits in this room include military uniforms, flags, and other war memorabilia; an ornate desk used by Spanish noblemen; a mannequin of world heavyweight champ James J. Jeffries in a ring and his old boxing gloves; and a display devoted to Lockheed, composed of numerous pictures and model airplanes. A tribute to Walt Disney features animation techniques and cells, audio animatronics, photographs, posters, and a wall collage of every Disney movie made (up to a certain date). Use the zoetrope to see how early animation worked. A Warner Brothers Studio exhibit displays costumes from a *Batman* movie and from an old Errol Flynn movie. You can watch continuously running oldie cartoons.

Another room is packed with lots of antique "stuff," such as an old switchboard, tools, parking meters, a huge Gramophone, a hotel telephone booth, and fire hats. It also showcases classic cars in mint condition, and several vintage vehicles including a 1922 Moreland Bus, a 1909 Ford horseless carriage with a crank, a spring wagon, and a 1949 fire engine with a huge target net that my kids thought was a trampoline. The small upstairs gallery has pictures and paintings, as well as a complete collection of old cameras. A video on the history of Lockheed is shown at 1:10pm and again at 2:30pm.

Follow the walkway from the museum courtyard to the reconstructed Mentzer House, which was originally built in 1887. On your walk-through tour you'll see two bedrooms, a dining room, and a living room containing period furniture, plus old-fashioned items such as a phonograph, an old telephone, and a vacuum cleaner. The kitchen has a beautiful coal-burning stove, plus china dishes, and cooking gadgets. Adult and children tours are given during the week for groups of ten or more by reservation.

A farm house holds a fully-equipped spring wagon and other farm equipment. Note that right next door is the Olive Recreation Center, easily identified by the model F-104 Starfighter in the front. The park has picnic tables and a playground, plus tennis and basketball courts.

Hours: Open Sat. - Sun., 1pm - 4pm.
Price: Free; donations gladly accepted.
Ages: 5 years and up.

GRAMMY MUSEUM

(213) 765-6800 / www.grammymuseum.org
800 W. Olympic Boulevard, Los Angeles

$$$$

And the Grammy goes to . . . the Grammy Museum for most relevant music museum in L.A. There are a considerable amount of artifacts here, but really, it's all about the music. Ride the elevator to the fourth floor of this state-of-the-art, contemporary museum to start your time here at the top. The wall videos in the hallway are popping with images and sounds of Grammy winners singing. You become immediately engaged with the music, which is one of the purposes of the museum. The others include learning the history, the creative process, the art and technology, and the celebration of music from song writing to recording. This is accomplished mostly through multimedia displays that encourage interaction with the music and those who create it.

The next huge room features Crossroads, which is a long touch screen table with headphones at different stations for numerous users. Touch a photo, song, or story on the tabletop and listen to learn about the almost 160 genres of music, their history and how they are interconnected - pop, blues, jazz, hip hop, barbershop, folk, ambient, opera, disco, Southern gospel, and so much more. Explore the roots of key traditional music inside four pods that contain videos, interviews, and music regarding sacred, folk, pop, classical, and jazz genres. The outside of the pods contain personal memorabilia such as hand-written lyrics from artists, signed album covers, personal photographs, hand-written letters (e.g. from Elvis to a fan), and instruments. What is your musical heritage? At Music Epicenters a wall-size map of the U.S. connects with touch screens so visitors can see and hear who and/or what type of music states, cities, and time periods have contributed. Music generates passion. Culture Shock is an audio/video time line that features singers whose songs and/or styles have created controversy, including Elvis Presley, Bob Dylan, Kurt

Cobain, and 50 Cent. The Grammy Archives and Hall of Fame showcases the history of the awards and nominations, as well as clothing donated from some of the winners. Sit and listen to any of the Grammy shows and songs. The display case of Influential Instruments contains, on a rotating basis, incredibly rare instruments from legendary musicians. It Starts With a Song is the kiosk area where significant songwriters describe their creative process and share the stories behind their songs.

Revolutions of Recorded Sound, on the third floor, focuses on the behind the scenes processes; the technology behind the recorded song. In this, the Roland Live exhibit contains electronic instruments for you to play and participate in the music-making process. It's fascinating to see and hear the impact the technological leaps have made on songs - from records to tapes to CDs and digital. Eight glass-enclosed, self-contained pods, like real recording rooms, offer more individual interaction with the touch screen and footage of top professionals in their specific area of expertise in the recording industry - engineering, producing with Eddie Kramer, mastering with Bob Ludwig, rapping with Jermaine Dupri, and more. You have input to how the sound, track, and song turns out with your creative and technical choices. Can you make great music? There is also personal memorabilia displayed here, on a rotating basis. We saw eight of Michael Jackson's beaded and bejeweled jackets (one was worn on his Victory tour), and two of his gloves, and a huge selection of Kate Perry's outrageous stage outfits/costumes. Another rotating display area shows dresses, suits, and outfits worn on the red carpet for the Grammys, including Jennifer Lopez's almost dress from the 2000 Grammys. Behind the glamour, literally behind the showcase of outfits, is a small gallery that shows and describes how the nomination and award's process works and how it all comes together looking so polished (most times). Current winners are honored here and the Latin Grammys are highlighted here, too. Then, sit, relax and watch some of Grammys most memorable moments on the big screen.

The second, and last floor of exhibits, is set aside primarily for premiere, traveling exhibits. We saw Songs of Conscience, Sounds of Freedom which featured multimedia kiosks, footage, music, photographs, and personal items from private collections that aided in exploring the impact and connection between music and politics; music as a political force. Very powerful. It covered and displayed everything from an abolitionist songbook, J. Edgar Hoover's FBI summary of the MC5, Civil War memorabilia, Woody Guthrie's guitar, to the Dixie Chicks. This floor also has a 200-seat theater that shows the twenty-minute film *Making of a Grammy Moment* two times each hour. The theater is used for concerts, chat time with famous artists and producers, career panels, Civil War Reenactments, and much more.

Music is an effective tool to capture the attention of youth and bring history, sociology, and technology to life. The Grammy Museum has an assemblage (over fifty annually!) of public, family, and school educational programs. Guest speakers from all walks of the music industry and world renown performing artists offer the public uncommon opportunities to hear and see them. The school educational programs, geared for K through high school students, are equally all-encompassing with just some of the selections including Analyzing Lyrics; Careers in Music: The Grammy Museum; the Music of War; and Behind the Scenes: Building Exhibits. Monthly workshops change and have included Learning the History of Music; Connecting Music, Politics and Social Change; Celebrating Hispanic Heritage Month through Music; and more. Each field trip, which meets California state standards, includes a self guided tour of the museum and/or a workshop or performance - $8 per student for tour only or tour plus a workshop. Tour only visits require a minimum of ten students; workshops are for a minimum group of twenty-five up to 200. Note that the museum is in the middle of the L.A. LIVE complex, which also has Staples Center, Microsoft Theater, a Regal L.A. Live Stadium 14, Lucky Strike Lanes, and plenty of restaurants. See DOWNTOWN LOS ANGELES / GRAND PARK (pg. 167) for information on Grand Park and all the other places to go within this fairly immediate area.

Hours: Open Mon. - Fri., 10:30am - 6:30pm; Sat. - Sun., 10am - 6:30pm.

Price: $12.95 for adults; $11.95 for seniors and students; $10.95 for ages 6 - 17; children 5 and under are free. Parking in the lots start at about $10 for two hours.

Ages: 9 years and up.

GRIER MUSSER MUSEUM

(213) 413-1814 / www.griermussermuseum.org $$$

403 S. Bonnie Brae Street, Los Angeles

This thirteen-room, two-story, green and rust-colored Queen Anne-style house/museum was built in 1898. It was the Grier Musser family home. Since many of the tour guides are family relatives, they know and share the history and interesting stories of the memorabilia. The house is literally packed with personal ~~stuff~~ treasures accumulated over the years. The front parlor contains an original chandelier, Delph plates, a grandfather's clock, and other antiques. The family room has a 1950's television set, a piano, and a fainting couch for women who did just that. The dining room's fireplace is decorated with ornate tiles and beautifully carved wood work. The kitchen has a wood-burning stove, a gas stove, a beaded chandelier from the 1915 Exposition Fair, dishes from the Depression era, a collection of cookie jars, kitchen gadgets, and china cabinets filled with original boxes of Ivory Soap, Morton's Salt, and more. At the foot of the stairs is a red velvet chaperone's seat. While a gentleman courted his lady love, a chaperone would sit out of the way, but within eyesight.

An upstairs study contains a desk, grandma's diploma from high school, and a pictorial history of the Red Cross, plus a closet full of nursing uniforms from WWII. The master bedroom and adjoining bedroom have maple furniture, and closets full of hats, dresses, and boots. The children's bedroom is filled with toys, stuffed animals, dolls, and dollhouses. The dresser displays old bottles and hairbrushes as well as a more unique sign of the past - a container of leg makeup from WWII. Women would put this makeup on their legs to make it look like they were wearing nylons - seams and all. The sundeck is a favorite room for kids because of the numerous games and toys, and extensive Disney collection. Open the printer drawers to see even more treasures, such as jewelry.

Using the maid's stairway, go down to the basement to see pictures of the family and the Los Angeles area, and an extensive postcard collection from around the world. A visit here makes you wonder if maybe you should have kept that bottle cap collection, or at least your great grandfather's fishing pole as a potential museum piece. Tip: Check the Calendar website for fun annual and special events.

Hours: Open Wed. - Sat., noon - 4pm. Reservations are necessary for all visitors.
Price: $12 for adults; $7 for seniors and students; $6 for ages 5 - 12; children 4 and under are free. Cash only.
Ages: 5 years and up.

GRIFFITH OBSERVATORY AND PLANETARIUM ☼

(213) 473-0890 / www.griffithobservatory.org   !/$$
2800 E. Observatory Road, in Griffith Park, Los Angeles

The landmark copper domes and architecture of this world-famous observatory beckon star trackers. On a cloudless day the terraces around the building allow it be one of the best places to view the sprawling city of Los Angeles, and beyond, including a fairly close-up view of the iconic Hollywood sign. On a clear night, a magnificent view of the city lights and the stars await. Zeiss, the largest public telescope in California, is available to use (for free) every clear evening in the summer from dusk to 9:45pm, as are other "lesser" telescopes. It is available the rest of the year Tuesday to Sunday from 7pm to 9:45pm. Call the Sky Report, (213) 473-0880, for twenty-four-hour recorded information.

On the front lawn of the observatory is an almost forty-foot-tall statue featuring Copernicus, Hipparchus, Galileo, Kepler, Newton, and Herschel. Inside the lobby is the large Foucault pendulum which knocks over pegs, illustrating the rotation of the earth. Look up at the rotunda ceiling to see heavenly murals. The two exhibit hallways contain niches with displays of models, orbiting planets (always look overhead at museums!), photographs, pictures, videos, and buttons to press for cause and effect. The Hall of the Sky features displays of the moon phases; day and night; sun and stars pathway; tides - rising and falling; seasons; and eclipses. At the end of this corridor is a small, semi-circular room that offers real time images of the sun viewed via a filter on a solar telescope, as well as videos of eruptions on the sun, pictures of sun spots, and super nova explosions. The periodic table is shown in small, individual cases with its elements in their mineral forms. Press buttons to see which elements light up, accordingly, that comprise super novas, stars, humans, gases, and more.

The Hall of the Eye holds a model of the Hale telescope; observatory instruments; a replica of Galileo's telescope; information on astronomy and the history of it in California; a Tesla coil (watch the sparks jump as lightening is created!); and a camera obscura.

35,000-square-feet of underground space focuses on the exploration of space. The mezzanine showcases real meteorites, including a 395-pound fragment, and information on their origins and impact (literally). One video allows visitors to design their own velocity and density of a meteorite, and its destination. At another interactive display you answer questions either meteorite or meteorwrong! A corner exhibit has a huge, spinning model of the moon, information panels regarding where Apollo missions have landed, and a moon rock. The steeply graded, 200-seat Leonard Nimoy (yes, the Vulcan) Event Horizon Theater is used for special programs, lectures and free presentations, such as the twenty-four minute film about the observatory's history. A gift shop and cafeteria-style cafe are in this area, too.

The walls of the lower level are decorated like the night sky, full of constellations and our Milky Way. Each planet is represented along one wall in its own kiosk that promotes a rotating model of the planet, plus pictures, videos and facts about it - temperature, days per year, and more. Watch out - each one also has a scale that, when stepped on, allows all the other visitors to see how much you weigh on Earth, Venus, Mars, Saturn, etc. (Pluto rules!) Behind the Earth kiosk is an old planetarium projector; an enormous model of the earth, rotating and showing the changing surface; and a seismograph - jump on the floor to simulate an earthquake and see what it registers.

For a truly stellar experience, don't miss the planetarium shows as the seamless, seventy-seven feet across projection dome and the fiber optics make the stars appear incredibly realistic and vibrant. (Enjoy the plush seats that recline!) There are four live shows (i.e. with a narrator) with eight half-hour+ presentations (there are a variety of show titles to choose from) offered each weekday, and ten shows each weekend day. Children 4 and under are admitted ONLY to the first show each day - 12:45pm on weekdays; 10:45am on weekends.

Check the website for information on school tours, which are usually geared for fifth graders. For other close-by attractions look up GRIFFITH PARK (pg. 63). Note: The Greek Theater, a nationally renown venue for concerts and other events, is just down the road.

Hours: Open Tues. - Fri., noon - 10pm; Sat. - Sun., 10am - 10pm. Closed Mon., and most major holidays.

Price: Admission to the observatory is free. The planetarium shows are $7 for adults; $5 for seniors; $3 for ages 5 - 12; children 4 and under are free and they must sit on parent's lap.

Ages: 4 years and up.

GUINNESS WORLD OF RECORDS MUSEUM

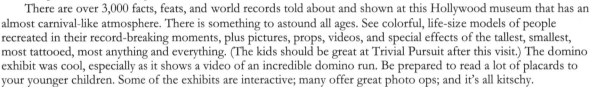

(323) 463-6433 / www.guinnessmuseumhollywood.com

$$$$

6764 Hollywood Boulevard, Hollywood

There are over 3,000 facts, feats, and world records told about and shown at this Hollywood museum that has an almost carnival-like atmosphere. There is something to astound all ages. See colorful, life-size models of people recreated in their record-breaking moments, plus pictures, props, videos, and special effects of the tallest, smallest, most tattooed, most anything and everything. (The kids should be great at Trivial Pursuit after this visit.) The domino exhibit was cool, especially as it shows a video of an incredible domino run. Be prepared to read a lot of placards to your younger children. Some of the exhibits are interactive; many offer great photo ops; and it's all kitschy.

Prep your children before their visit: Q: Do you know who holds a record for the most fan mail in one day? A: Mickey Mouse. He received 800,000 letters one day in 1933. Q: What animal had the smallest brain in proportion to his body? A: Stegosaurus. Q: What was the longest length a human neck was stretched using copper coils? And why? A: Fifteen and three-quarter inches. I don't know why, though. Watch some fascinating footage of intriguing and bizarre facts about our world and the people and animals in it: *The Human World*, *The Animal World*, *Planet Earth*, *Structures and Machines*, *Sports World*, and a salute to *The World of Hollywood*. Look up HOLLYWOOD - the downtown tourist mecca (pg. 171) for details on other close-by Hollywood museums and attractions.

Hours: Open Sun. - Thurs., 9am - midnight ; Fri. - Sat., 9am - 1am.

Price: $20.99 for adults; $10.99 for ages 4 - 11; children 3 and under are free. Combo tickets for this museum, plus HOLLYWOOD WAX MUSEUM (pg. 120) and RIPLEY'S BELIEVE IT OR NOT! ODDITORIUM (pg. 150) are $35.99 for adults; $19.99 for kids.

Ages: 4½ years and up.

HACIENDA HEIGHTS YOUTH SCIENCE LEARNING CENTER

(626) 854-9825 / www.youthsciencecenter.org

!

16446 Wedgeworth Drive in room 17 at Bixby Elementary School, Hacienda Heights

The Youth Science Center has a lot of science packed into a classroom at Bixby Elementary School. YSC uses the BB-8 robot (as in *Star Wars*) and several of the Sphero SPRK robots, controlled by hand-held iOS and Android devices, to help teach kids math and science. Kids can mold and sculpt shapes, such as mountains, lakes and rivers, with the Kinetic Sand on the table-top Reality Watershed Sand Box. Via a Kinect 3D camera and computer, projected images then show topographical lines and simulated water ways. A Virtual Reality exhibit teaches students about astronomy, anatomy, dissection and more. An augmented Reality exhibit is for entomology, chemistry and more. There are some fossils, insects, and a few live critters here, too.

A terrific array (almost 100!) of science-related classes are available after school and especially during the summer for kids in grades K - 8 that range from 90-minute classes to week-long to six week long classes. Just some of the classes offered include model rocket-building, plant dissection, Minecraft, GoPro filmmaking, Quadcopter filmmaking, 3D Printing, water filtration, kitchen chemistry, slimy science, woodworking, designing and flying paper airplanes, and much more. Wow!!! See the website for a complete schedule. The Center also offers a digital Starlab, an inflatable planetarium, for up to thirty-five students, that comes to your site. The program includes hand-outs regarding constellations.

Hours: Open year round, by appointment, Mon. - Fri., 8am - 4:30pm. Note that summer science camps are held in June and July, daily, 8:30am - 6pm.

Price: Free

Ages: 4 years and up.

HAMMER MUSEUM
(310) 443-7000 / www.hammer.ucla.edu $$
10899 Wilshire Boulevard, Westwood

The fairly large Hammer art museum features an interesting array of paintings, sculpture, photographs, lithography, and graphic arts in both its permanent and rotating exhibits. Impressionist and Post-Impressionist works include paintings by Monet, Pissarro, Cassatt, and Van Gogh. Samples from European old masters to more modern American artists are creatively displayed on the walls and sometimes, on the floors. Modern art is definitely intriguing, if somewhat baffling, to kids. Ask about the weekly guided tours, as well as lectures, classes, readings, screenings, and variety of educational programs.

Hours: Open Tues. - Fri., 11am - 8pm; Sat. - Sun., 11am - 5pm. Closed Mon., New Year's Day, 4th of July, Thanksgiving and Christmas.

Price: Free. Parking is $6 for the first three hours.

Ages: 8 years and up.

HERITAGE JUNCTION HISTORIC PARK
(661) 254-1275 / www.scvhs.org   !
24101 Newhall Avenue, Santa Clarita

A steam locomotive is on the tracks out in front of this restored, late 1800's train station/museum. Inside is a large room, used also as a classroom, that displays photographs, information, and artifacts that show and tell the history of this valley, including the Spanish era, the petroleum and mining areas, and its rich film history. Another small room here, attached to a great gift shop, is re-decorated to look like what it was back in the day - a ticket master's office, complete with a period-dressed mannequin, old-fashioned communication equipment and more.

Go into the furnished adobe abode that is part house and part school room. An outhouse is here, too (not to use), plus picnic tables (to use). Walk up the road to a cluster of buildings that have been restored and comprise the rest of the junction that include the Edison house, the Kingsbury house that contains nineteenth-century furniture, a very little red schoolhouse, and a tiny and picturesque chapel. We weren't here long, but it was an interesting, historical, and photogenic stop. The historical society offers fantastic school field trips here. Note: The junction park is right next to WILLIAM S. HART MUSEUM AND PARK (pg. 158).

Hours: Open daily, 9am - 5pm, just to walk the grounds. The train museum and buildings are open Sat. - Sun., 1pm - 4pm. Open for school tours during the week by appointment.

Price: Free

Ages: 6 years and up.

HERITAGE PARK - Santa Fe Springs
(562) 946-6476 - park; (562) 944-1027 - cafe / www.santafesprings.org   !
12100 Mora Drive, Santa Fe Springs

Heritage Park is like a breath of fresh air among the historical parks. Its six acres of beautifully landscaped grounds make any length visit here a pleasure. The high-ceiling, two-story, wood Carriage Barn, which holds turn-of-the-century exhibits, is a must-see. Two carriages from horse and buggy days take the center floor. Behind glass is a large display of period clothing, including a wedding dress, plus dolls, toys, and books. The small touch and play area has clothing to try on, an old telephone to dial (it's not a touch tone or cell phone), and a few other articles to play with. Inventing a Better Life display features old phonographs, typewriters, bikes, roller skates (not in-line skates), plus cameras and other equipment. It's interesting to see how the inventions of yesteryear benefit us today.

Walk down a short pathway to a thirty-two-foot dome-shaped dwelling that is the centerpiece of a recreated Native American village of the Tongva tribe. You can go into it. A small creek, a granary, a sweatlodge, and a canoe (that you can sit in) are also featured. This area often showcases storytellers, a craft time, demonstrations, and Journeys to the Past presentations.

Grab a bite to eat at Lolita's Cafe located in the park. It's open Monday through Friday from 8am to 3pm; weekends, 9am to 2pm. The cafe serves Mexican food such breakfast burritos ($5.99), chicken nachos ($6.99), and cheese quesadillas ($2.99), as well as pancakes, sandwiches, salads, and hamburgers (average $6.99). Or, bring your own lunch, and enjoy the garden setting with beautiful old shade trees and plenty of tables and chairs.

Outside, walk around the outside of an aviary that houses parakeets, canaries, and a few other birds. A small window to an archeological pit shows excavated trash such as cattle bones and pottery. There are remain sites marking original fireplace and basement foundations, but kids cannot go in them to explore. A hedge around the beautiful formal gardens gives way to an old fig tree with huge roots that are almost irresistible for kids to climb on. Walk through the small greenhouse. An immaculate, wood-paneled tank house, once used to store water, is at the far end of the park. On a school tour, kids can go inside the windmill building and walk up the crisscross stairs to the top, then go outside, and take in the view.

I can't emphasize the beauty of this park enough. It's clean, green, and the walkways throughout make every area accessible. Ask about the park's special programs throughout the year.

Just outside the park gates are three restored railroad cars on a piece of track. Climb into the cab of the classic-looking locomotive and ring the bell, then look to see where coal was stored. Look at the caboose, the colorful refrigerated boxcar and go inside the depot. There is a small picnic area, here, too.

Exceptional, two-hour, school tours of Heritage Park include lots of historical information, presented in a kid-friendly way, plus hands-on activities. These are offered on Wednesdays and Thursdays for ages 8 and up. The tours are free. Just a short walk away, near the pedestrian bridge on Norwalk and Telegraph, is an outdoor sculpture garden with artwork, fountains, and grassy areas - a nice reprieve.

Hours: The park is open November - April, Mon. - Fri., 7am - 5pm; Sat. - Sun., 9am - 5pm. It's open May - October, Mon. - Fri., 7am - 8pm; Sat. - Sun., 9am - 8pm. The Railroad cars area is open daily, noon - 4pm. The Carriage Barn hours are Tues. - Sat., noon - 4pm. Everything is closed on major holidays.

Price: Free

Ages: All

HERITAGE SQUARE MUSEUM

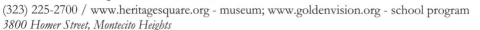

(323) 225-2700 / www.heritagesquare.org - museum; www.goldenvision.org - school program $$$
3800 Homer Street, Montecito Heights

This little "town" behind a gate at the end of a residential street has eight historic structures, including five houses, plus a carriage barn (used for storage), a church building, and a train depot. The elegant Victorian homes, originally built between 1865 and 1914, have been relocated here and are in various stages of restoration. Each one has a different architectural style and coloring. One is white with columns, almost colonial-looking, while another is green and pink, gingerbreadish in style, and has brick chimneys. The octagon-shaped house is the most unique-looking house here. Its unusual configuration makes it interesting to look at as well as walk through. Only on the one-hour guided tours can you go through some of the homes. The Queen Anne house on the tour is the only one completely furnished and restored. The grassy grounds are ideal for picnicking.

Hour-long group and school tours are offered Monday through Thursday, starting at 10am for $2 for K through 6, and $3 for 7 through 12 graders. These living history school programs fit with California state standards. A several-day program, called Golden Vision, involves having a costumed docent come to the classroom to teach a lesson, followed by students doing assignments and activities, and culminates with coming to the museum and participating in real life living of 100 years ago. There are also many functions open to the general public throughout the year such as the Vintage Fashion Show and Tea; living history days; the Holiday Lamplight Celebration, where lamp lights give a warm glow to the houses and area; and Museums of the Arroyo Day in May, where this and some of the other local museums, including the Gamble House, Pasadena Museum of History, and Los Angeles Police Museum, are free admission.

Hours: Open Fri. - Sun. and most federal holiday Mon., 11:30am - 4:30pm. Guided tours are available from noon - 3pm (last tour), on the hour. Closed New Year's Day, Easter, 4th of July, Thanksgiving, and Christmas and after heavy rains.

Price: Admission is $10 for adults; $8 for seniors; $5 for ages 6 - 12; children 5 and under are free. Discounts are available through AAA. Group tours are $10 a person for 10 - 40 people.

Ages: 6 years and up.

HOLLYWOOD BOWL MUSEUM

(323) 850-2058 / www.hollywoodbowl.org   !
2301 N. Highland, Hollywood

While at the Hollywood Bowl for a concert, or if you're in the area, stop by the Hollywood Bowl Museum. This 3,000 square-foot museum displays musical instruments, memorabilia, photographs of performers (from opera to rock to Native American dancers) and conductors. Re-created rooms in a house represent various eras: They are the settings that surround music from that time period. For instance, the 1930's parlor features a radio playing Fred Astaire singing in a live broadcast from the Bowl. A 1970's/1980's teenage bedroom shows TV clips from *The Brady Bunch*, and a boom box that gently blasts Pink Floyd's music. A commercial recording (the first ever made) of a symphony orchestra outdoors plays on a Victrola in a 1920s ladies dressing room. Touch screens show concerts featured at the Bowl and other film footage (even cartoons).

Check out the Hollywood Bowl: Music For Everyone exhibit, on the main floor of the museum. It's organized into sections on dance; pop, rock, jazz and world music; symphonic music and opera; architecture and history of the Bowl; and the Hollywood Bowl Hall of Fame, featuring videos of the honorees.

The second story has rotating exhibits; the history of the Bowl displayed via photographs and audio and video kiosks; and some past museum exhibits.

Picnic areas are available so pack a lunch. Attend rehearsals of the Los Angeles Philharmonic and Hollywood Bowl Orchestra during the summer when available. Call Audience Services at (323) 850-2000 for a rehearsal schedule.

Hours: Open mid-June through mid-September, Tues. - Sat., 10am - showtime; Sun., 4pm - showtime. Open mid-September - mid-June, Tues. - Fri., 10am - 5pm; open Sat. by appt. Closed New Year's Day, Thanksgiving and Christmas.

Price: Free. Parking is free until 4 hours before a performance.

Ages: 7 years and up.

THE HOLLYWOOD MUSEUM

(323) 464-7776 / www.thehollywoodmuseum.com $$$$
1660 N. Highland Avenue, Hollywood

Do you know who coined the phrase "makeup"? The cosmetic king, Max Factor. Located inside this landmark Max Factor building, originally constructed in 1914, is a tribute to Hollywood, old and new. Most of the first floor retains the essence of "old" Hollywood, with architectural elegance and several small rooms dedicated and denoted by the color of one's hair. The "redheads" room has pale green walls, photographs of red-headed stars, and a case of makeup and accessories that harmonize with a redhead's hair and skin tones. Blondes, brunettes, and brownettes each have different, colored rooms with similar, specialized exhibits. Several hundred of Joe Ackerman's 6,000-piece autograph collection, often accompanied by pictures, are on view throughout the hallways. The photo library room displays 1,000 black-and-white photos of the changing Hollywood community, as well as head shots and "casual" pictures of stars and their homes. An eclectic mix of props are also on display on this floor, including gigantic bunny legs from the movie *Along Came Polly*, the space capsule and costumes in a re-created setting from *Planet of the Apes*, and a Rolls Royce that belonged to Cary Grant. A small screening room shows classics throughout the day.

Take a ride in the freight (or fright!) elevator that was once used to transport stars' cars to storage below. The elevator is decorated with movie posters and a continuously playing silent movie. It takes you down to the basement, to the Chamber of Horrors, which is comprised mainly of the original set of Hannibal Lector's jail. The brick walls, pipes, and four cells are realistically creepy looking. Enter into the padded cell and look into the one that holds Hannibal's mask, reading materials, and other props. Other exhibits down here include blood-splattered costumes from *Sweeny Todd*; Jason's mask; costumes and props worn by Elvira; a guillotine with a severed head; an Iron Maiden; torture beds; mummies; and more gory memorabilia.

The ample second and third floors are packed, containing a multitude of well-labeled, both permanent and rotating exhibits, many of which are behind floor-to-ceiling glass displays. A majority of the displays contain costumes, such as gowns worn by Mae West, Lucille Ball, and Joan Crawford. Other costumes that we saw were used on the set of *Moulin Rouge, Master and Commander, Star Trek, Flintstones,* and *Gladiator*. Often props from the corresponding movie are exhibited alongside the costumes, such as cannons from *Master and Commander* and the bed from *Gladiator*. We also saw signed boxing gloves from *Rocky*; the Batmobile and Batcycle and original costumes worn not just by Adam West and Burt Ward (i.e. Batman and Robin in the iconic TV series), but also costumes by guest villains, plus life size sculptures of the three women who portrayed Catwoman; Roddy McDowall's powder room (moved from his house); masks and molds; Pee Wee Herman's bike; torture equipment from *Quills*; large, stuffed creatures from *Monster's Inc.*; vintage lighting and camera equipment; lots of movie posters; a tribute to Bob Hope composed of letters, photos, and personal artifacts; a section devoted to silent movies; Elvis Presley's bathrobe; and more. *Harry Potter* fans will love seeing Harry's ultimate broom, his robe, and his quill and ink bottle, plus blueprints of Hogwarts, a collection of wands and their boxes, the actors' shoes, photos, and posters. The museum also has an extensive collection of the ultimate movie icon - Marilyn Monroe. Memorabilia such as gowns, documents regarding her death, personal accessories, dolls in her image, and a wall display of photographs of her in the nude are on the second floor.

Take a guided tour to learn more about the displays and the people and props behind the scenes of movie- and television-making. "Fame is fickle, and I know it. It has its compensations, but it also has its drawbacks, and I have experienced both." - Marilyn Monroe. Note that the museum also houses Mels Drive-In, which is a 50's hamburger diner that is no longer a drive-in. Serving all three main meals, it features sliders, a wide selection of salads and of burgers, sandwiches (including meat loaf, turkey melts, and club), chicken pot pie, fish and chips and New York steak.

Look up HOLLYWOOD - the downtown tourist mecca (pg. 171) for details on other close-by Hollywood museums and attractions.

Hours: Open Wed. - Sun., 10am - 5pm. Close Mon., Tues. and certain holidays.
Price: $15 for adults; $12 for seniors and students; $5 for children 5 and under.
Ages: 10 years and up.

HOLLYWOOD WAX MUSEUM

(323) 462-5991 / www.hollywoodwax.com

6767 Hollywood Boulevard, Hollywood

Hundreds of celebrities from the world of television and movies are presented in waxy, kind of lifelikeness, immersed in settings appropriate to a favorite character that they've played, or just being themselves (which might be a character they're playing). You can be a part of the movie-making magic as you interact with them (and take lots of photographs!) - practice a karate kick with the cast from Charlie's Angels; grab a mic and sing in front of renown singers like Celine Dion and Madonna; follow the yellow brick road with Judy Garland as Dorothy from *The Wizard of Oz*; have a chocolate (bring your own) with Tom Hanks as Forest Gump; walk the red carpet with other A-list stars; and try on clothes and props while getting up close and personal with Johnny Dep, Julia Roberts, Elvis, Robin Williams, Sylvester Stallone (dressed as Rambo), Clint Eastwood in his "make my day" attire, and so many more. We enjoyed debating how realistic each statue depiction was. New icons are being added on a regular basis. A word of caution: There are also recreated sets and characters from horror flicks which might frighten younger children.

Learn facts about your favorite stars by taking multiple choice quizzes on your self-guided tour in the museum. Look up HOLLYWOOD - the downtown tourist mecca (pg. 171) for details on other close-by Hollywood museums and attractions.

Hours: Open Sun. - Thurs., 9am - midnight; Fri. - Sat., 9am - 1am.
Price: $22.99 for adults; $12.99 for ages 4 - 11; children 3 and under are free. Combo tickets for this museum plus GUINNESS WORLD OF RECORDS MUSEUM (pg. 116) and RIPLEY'S BELIEVE IT OR NOT! ODDITORIUM (pg. 150) are $35.99 for adults; $19.99 for kids.
Ages: 4 years and up.

HOLYLAND EXHIBITION

(323) 664-3162 $

2215 Lake View Avenue, Los Angeles

I could take this tour at least three more times and still not see and learn everything this museum has to offer! The Holyland Exhibition is an inconspicuous two-story corner house that was built in the late 1920's. It contains an incredible collection of priceless Egyptian and biblical items. Most of the two-hour tour is not hands on. It does involve a lot of listening and learning. An incredibly well-informed costumed docent will take you first to the tapestry-rich Bethlehem/Egyptian room which, like all the rooms, is not large, but <u>packed</u> with artifacts. You'll feel transported to a different time and country. Some of the items explained in depth are the 2,600-year-old mummy case; the hand-made brass art pieces and plates; papyrus; shoes made of camel hide and ram skin; headdresses; and a lunch bag made of goat skin. Each item is presented with its history and its biblical connection. You'll also see jewelry, engraved leather goods, a 2,000-year-old lamp, and much more.

The Bible Art and Archaeology Room has stones, shells, pottery, spices, and more from Nazareth, Bethlehem, the Jordan River, and surrounding areas. You'll view the type of large thorns used in Christ's crown of thorns; a big chunk of salt called Madame Lot; a very comprehensive family tree detailing lineage from Adam to Jesus; the kind of stones crushed and used for pitch on Noah's ark; a picture of Mt. Ararat where *ark*eologists believe the ark landed; and a recreated Ark of the Covenant. Make sure your tour guide explains how Mr. Futterer, the museum founder, went on an expedition to find the ark and how this was the basis for the movie *Raiders of the Lost Ark*. (This will definitely spark your children's interest.) Again, amazing amounts of Bible references are given with the presentation of each article.

The Damascus Room has an intricate game table inlaid with mother-of-pearl that took fifty man-years to make - kids may not play games on it! The room also contains beaded lamps, musical instruments, a camel saddle, animal skin (to write on), and many unique pieces of furniture. In another room, enjoy a taste of Israel while sitting on oriental rugs around low tables, as you're served small samples of Holy Land refreshments. The Jerusalem Bazaar is a gift shop with souvenirs (and great teaching aids) made of olive wood, mother-of-pearl, and other materials, at bargain prices. Come, take a trip to the middle east, via the Holyland Exhibition, and learn about its peoples and customs. The interdenominational museum is frequented by Christians, Jews, Muslims, and people of various other faiths.

Hours: The museum is open to tour seven days a week, including holidays and evenings, 7am - 7pm. Call ahead of time to choose the most convenient time for your or your group.

Price: $2.50 for adults; $2 for ages 3 - 15; children 2 and under are free.

Ages: 6 years and up.

THE HOMESTEAD MUSEUM

(626) 968-8492 or (626) 968-8493 / www.homesteadmuseum.org

15415 E. Don Julian Road, City of Industry

The Homestead Museum resides on six acres of land. A major portion of the property is an open, grassy area between the main group of buildings and the old mausoleum. A shady picnic area is here, too, plus a fish pond, gazebo, and some pretty landscaping. A forty-five-minute guided tour, starting at the water tower, will take you behind the gates. Kids will see and learn about the history of the United States, and about California in particular. They'll learn, for instance, that our state was once Mexican territory, and how that influence has factored in the development of our culture. They will also learn about the art and architecture of the 1830's through the 1930's.

The tour goes into the two residences on the premises. The Workman adobe home has exhibit space and one period room inside, but outside are a few artifacts that kids can touch. La Casa Nueva house is spacious with twenty-six rooms, mostly furnished in 1920's decor. Kids will also get information about the on-site pump house, tepee, mausoleum, and cemetery, where Pio Pico, the last Mexican governor of California, is buried. Ask about tours specifically for students and for programs for younger kids and the many events that go on year round.

Hours: The historic houses and grounds are open for guided tours, only, Wed. - Sun., 1pm - 4pm, on the hour. Open for tour groups, minimum ten people, at other times throughout the week. Call for a reservation. Closed major holidays and special tour weekends.

Price: Free

Ages: 6 years and up.

HUNTINGTON LIBRARY, ART COLLECTIONS AND BOTANICAL GARDENS

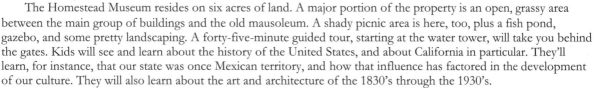

(626) 405-2141; (626) 405-2100 / www.huntington.org $$$$

1151 Oxford Road, San Marino

The Library houses one of the world's greatest collections of rare books, manuscripts, and documents including a Gutenberg Bible; Ellesmere Chaucer's *The Canterbury Tales*; Shakespeare's First Folio; Benjamin Franklin's autobiography, in his own handwriting; original works by Whitman and Dickens; and letters written by George Washington, Thomas Jefferson, and Abraham Lincoln. In the west wing of the library is the permanent, five-gallery exhibit titled, Beautiful Science: Ideas That Change the World. One gallery is a reading room with reference copies. Each of the other four focus on a specific area: astronomy, natural history, medicine, and light. Original books are the core of the exhibit including *Origins of Species* (in several languages), Louis Pasteur's personal diaries, and Isaac Newton's own copy of *Opticks*, plus Robert Hooke's 1665 incredibly detailed drawings of insects viewed under a microscope and more. Listen to an audio excerpt from written works at fourteen stations. The mural in the astronomy room portrays a supernova explosion in 1605. There are interactive components in each gallery such as computer terminals, a prism experiment, a camera obscura, and a replica of a 17th century microscope and of Galileo's telescope to look through.

The Huntington Art Gallery is the epitome of opulence. This mansion contains the collection's European art of sculptures (including the life-size bronze of the Roman goddess of the hunt, *Diana the Huntress*), rare tapestries, miniatures, period furniture, and famous paintings, including Gainsborough's *The Blue Boy*. Get kids involved with observing the paintings by pointing out the ones with children in them and ones with different styles of dress than theirs. Read to them the accompanying information (stories) about the subjects. For instance, sweet-faced *Pinkie*, which hangs opposite *The Blue Boy* by Sir Thomas Lawrence, died soon after her portrait was finished, and the boy in *Lavina, Countess Spencer and her son Viscount Althorp* was one of Princess Diana's great great (great, etc.,) grandparents. This is a gentle way to introduce children to some truly great works of art. Pick up a free Family Guide at the entrance that encourages kids to participate in certain artworks by striking similar poses, drawing a particular element, or listing objects in a painting. The Huntington has a world class collection of art so I'm thankful the atmosphere is not off-putting for kids.

The breathtaking Virginia Steele Scott Gallery of American Art and the Erburu Gallery display over 500 pieces of American art (all of which I won't all list here!); paintings (by John Singleton Copley, Mary Cassatt, and Sam Francis, to name just a few); and other media such as glass, ceramic, silver (by Paul Revere and others), sculpture, and furniture (some designed by Frank Lloyd Wright). The Boone Gallery building showcases stunning, changing exhibits; some from the Library's collection and others from around the world.

The Botanical Gardens are composed of twelve, separate, themed, massive, amazing gardens that cover 120 acres of the 200-acre estate. As Lisa Blackburn, a museum associate says, "The gardens . . . have wide-open spaces and vast rolling lawns; great for running, somersaulting, cartwheeling, shrieking, and releasing all that boundless energy that is sometimes stifled in traditional museum settings." There are waterfalls, lily ponds, koi, ducks, turtles, and frogs to capture kids' attention - almost more than can be seen in one day. The Desert Garden has, again to quote Lisa, "twelve acres of some of the most bizarre, colorful, creepy-crawly plants that a child could imagine." The Shakespeare Garden features plants mentioned in the bards' plays, accompanied by placards of pertinent poetry phrases. My Tarzans said one of the best part of coming to the Huntington, though, is hiding in the bamboo groves in the Jungle Garden. Another favorite garden is the nine-acre Japanese garden, which is a quarter-mile west of the main entrance. This has a traditionally-furnished Japanese teahouse (that overlooks so much of the Huntington below from its high vantage point); stone ornaments; an old temple bell; a much-photographed, arching bridge; and a bonsai court. The tranquility and beauty of this garden is aided by the waterfall and stream, as well as the lawns and picturesque trees and plants. The three-acre Rose Garden, with its incredible varieties of roses, by any other name would smell as sweet (a paraphrase). The Camellia Garden boasts a comprehensive collection (and flowering) of camellias.

Think Ming Dynasty and you'll get a picture of the five-acre (in the process of expanding to twelve acres), authentic Chinese Garden, also called Garden of Flowing Fragrance. With a glimpse into the Chinese culture, it classically displays a 1.5-acre man-made lake with seasonally blooming lotus plants and rocks imported from China that line its edge. It invokes a sense of serenity with lush landscaping of pine, bamboo, lotus, plum, and mature California oak trees; five stone bridges; a rockery; a boat pavilion; several other pavilions (most in Pagoda-style); a tea house and tea shop; pebble-embedded-in-cement pathways; and streams, waterfalls, and other waterways.

A one-acre Children's Garden, aimed toward younger children, is an absolute delight. Each of the four ancient elements - air, earth, fire, and water - has a section. In Air, a grotto surrounded by plants fills with fog every few minutes, then dissipates. Kids run around, temporarily "lost" in the mist. At Earth, create shapes with magnetic sand and, near the globe, drop pebbles through a maze of metal posts to compose a cacophony of sound. Crawl through a prism tunnel with rainbow arches in the front. See a topiary volcano. Watch for rainbows as you walk through the mist surrounding the rainbow room in Fire. In Water, this liquid reacts to sound vibrations and dances in response, so you can "feel" the sound waves. Jets make water jump from one pot of water to another, and just a touch changes the shape of small, dome-shaped waterfalls at the vortex and water bells exhibit. Interspersed throughout this magical garden are fragrant and colorful plants, tunnels, bridges, stepping stones, and a little playhouse formed mostly by vines and other plants. An adjacent Teaching Greenhouse offers youngsters an opportunity to get their hands dirty at the potting benches and provides a place for horticultural and botany programs for young people and adults.

The Conservancy, which looks like a huge greenhouse, is also located in this area. It has four different environments (most are somewhat hot and humid), each incorporating fascinating hands-on experiments and learning stations of some sort that appeal equally to kids and adults. The Tropical Forest, in the central rotunda, showcases giant palm fronds and huge water lilies. The Cloud Forest is lush with orchids, bromeliads, and pitcher plants. The Bog has carnivorous plants, such as the Venus flytraps. The large Plant Lab holds the widest variety of plant exhibits. Look through microscopes, use a refractometer to measure the amount of sugar in nectar samples, and smell fragrances to match them with a photo of their pollinator.

Choose from a wide selection of tours including free garden tours, audio and podcast tours, and tours geared for specifically for adults, for kids or for the family. Take advantage of Kid's Crafts, which is offered the first Saturday of every month and the interactive, bi-monthly Family Workshops. Ask about the numerous educational classes and programs. Just one of the great programs involves the Ranch, a fifteen-acre fruit tree and vegetable garden where participants get their hands dirty as they learn about agriculture.

Picnicking is not allowed on the grounds at the Huntington. However, a special treat for you and your daughter, as it's not really a boy's cup of tea, is to dress up and sip English tea in the Rose Garden Tea Room, which overlooks three acres of roses. The menu includes a variety of finger sandwiches (egg salad, chicken, English cucumber, and avocado mushroom); smoked salmon and caviar; quiche; tea; scones served with clotted cream and jam; and delightful petit desserts of chocolate raspberry ganache tart, mango cupcake, strawberry cheesecake and more. The cost is $35 per person. Children 9 and under have their own tea menu of nutella, grilled ham and Swiss, and pb and j sandwiches; egg salad; ants on a log; fruit; scones; and desserts - all for $20 per. Reservations are recommended; walk ins are accepted by availability. Call (626) 405-2236 for more info. Beside the Rose Garden Patio offering grab-and-go sandwiches and snacks, there is also a cafe, by the entrance; a coffee shop; and a restaurant in the Chinese Garden that specializes in authentic dumplings and noodle dishes.

The Huntington is absolutely one of the top five "don't miss" destinations in Southern California - it's that fantastic.

Hours: Open Sun. - Mon., 10am - 5pm. (the last entrance is 4pm); the library and art galleries close at 4:30pm. Closed Tues., New Year's Day, 4th of July, Thanksgiving, Christmas Eve, and Christmas Day. On the free Thurs., you can reserve a morning entry at 10am, or afternoon entry at 1pm.

Price: Mon. - Fri., $25 for adults; $21 for seniors and ages 12 - 18; $13 for ages 4 - 11; children 3 years and under are free. Sat. - Sun., holidays and holiday Mon., $29 for adults; $24 for seniors and ages 12 - 18; $13 for ages 4 - 11. Admission is free the first Thurs. of every month with advanced ticket reservations online - you may reserve up to 5 tickets. Tickets are available the first day of the month prior to your visit at 9am, and they go fast (i.e. July 1 for an August visit). You may not purchase regular admission tickets on the free day.

Ages: 4 years and up.

INTERNATIONAL PRINTING MUSEUM

(310) 515-7166 or (714) 529-1832 / www.printmuseum.org

$$$

315 Torrance Boulevard, Carson

With the smell of ink in the air and the ambiance of an old-fashioned printing press office (albeit a really large one), the printed page comes to life with a visit to this museum. The one-hour, general, guided tour is informative, interactive, and presented in a fun, even spellbinding, manner. You'll walk around the museum and see and learn about several rare and working antique presses, including a wooden one from 1750, the ornate Columbian hand press from 1838, and a replica of Gutenberg's first press, plus numerous printing artifacts. General tours are offered for the public and specific tours are offered for groups of up to seventy people. A separate room, across the parking lot, contains an incredible array of typeset letters (drawers and drawers of them), more presses, and storage equipment. This museum is always a work in progress.

The two-hour Book Arts Tour includes components of the Ben Franklin Gallery Tour (see below) in learning, seeing, and understanding the history and importance of paper and the printed word. After printing their own pages of the Gutenberg Bible, students help set metal type and print pages for a book. Then, they sew and bind this book. They will also make paper (from "scratch"), learn about color and design, and gain knowledge regarding lithography and typography. Check out the day-long Book Arts Institute classes, and other specialty classes, to learn papermaking, fine printmaking, and more - print is truly a work of art. The library here houses almost 8,000 books on all the facets of printing history.

There are two other outstanding, two-hour tours for students, which include a general museum tour. The first one is the Ben Franklin Gallery Tour, geared for 3rd graders and up, where the fascinating journey of the printed word began thousands of years ago when the Chinese first invented paper and "wrote" on it using carved blocks of wood. Children continue traveling to the period when Egyptian scrolls were written on papyrus, then on to the time of Gutenberg's invaluable contribution. Students learn about the tools of the trade while listening to anecdotes and information on writing, printing, and bookbinding. They also learn how long it took to make a hand-written book (three to five years); the price of a book; the increase in availability of books to the common people because of the press; and a lot more. The next stop on the tour is the Heritage Theater where a costumed appearance by Benjamin Franklin - not the real one, but a marvelous reenactor who looks and speaks just like him - then follows. Utilizing slides and equipment, Ben explains his numerous inventions and discoveries, such as electricity, an unsteady chair (i.e., rocking chair), markers called milestones, bifocals, swim fins, and more. Eager audience members participate in experiments that demonstrate static electricity and electricity generated through a replica 1750 electro static generator. He regales listeners about his life in Colonial America and encourages children to get educated by reading. The second tour is the Constitutional Convention Tour, geared for 5th graders and above. It is a reenactment of the Constitutional Convention. Divided into thirteen groups (colonies), students use pre-written cards to debate foundational issues, such as representation taxation, election of the president, and slavery. Ben Franklin presides over the meeting which ends with the colony deputies signing the Constitution. This is an exceptional, experiential history lesson/tour!

Other options include an hour-long school assembly titled The Inventive Benjamin Franklin, where Ben takes students from inception to finished product of several of his scientific inventions, or an outstanding, almost two-hour, Museum on Wheels tour where a component of the museum, similar to the Ben Franklin Gallery Tour, comes to your site. Geared for 3rd graders and up, the show consists of a traveling van carrying a working Colonial printing press and many other visuals. Kids are enthralled as they learn and experience the history of print and books, and "help" Ben Franklin with his experiments and discoveries as they hear about his life from a master storyteller

There are several family days where touring the museum and making a print craft of some sort is offered as well as classes for older students and adults, such as making mini books, screen printing, and letterpress printing. Also note that the museum hosts Boy Scout Merit Badge Days and annual standouts such as the Kids Krazy Krafts Day in April, Los Angeles Printer's Fair in October, and the Dickens Holiday Celebration in December. (See the Calendar section for more details.) I can't recommend this museum and its tours highly enough.

Hours: Open Sat., 10am - 4pm. Open for groups and other individuals by appointment, Tues. - Fri. Closed Sun., Mon., and certain holidays and special event days.

Price: $10 for adults; $8 for seniors and ages 5 - 18; children 4 and under are free. The Book Arts Tour is $250 for up to 25 people, then $10 per person up to 50. In-house group educational tours are $200 for up to 25 people, then $8 per person, up to 70. The school assembly is $450 for the first show; $200 for an additional show for the same day, for up to 120 students. Museum on Wheels is $650 for up to 150 students.

Ages: 6 years and up for the tours; 3rd graders and up for the school assemblies or Museum on Wheels tours.

JAPANESE AMERICAN NATIONAL MUSEUM

(213) 625-0414 / www.janm.org $$$

100 North Central Avenue, Los Angeles

During World War II more than 120,000 people of Japanese ancestry, most of whom were American citizens, were incarcerated in American relocation/concentration camps from 1941 to 1946. This museum is dedicated to preserving the memory of that time period, and learning from it. The glass building is nicely laid out and has seven gallery rooms, plus a research library, classrooms, and a theater room. The exhibit rooms holds rotating displays, varying from art exhibits, to the history of Japanese Americans, to athletes of Japanese ancestry. Permanent displays include authentic wooden barracks from an internment camp in Wyoming, plus videos of people's personal stories, and a gallery reminiscent of an Ellis Island tribute with suitcases and immigrants' belongings, such as clothing (e.g., wedding dresses, uniforms, and everyday clothing), personal articles, board games, and numerous photographs. Articles on discrimination in the 1920's and on the loss of citizens' rights during WWII offer both shameful and fascinating information. Videos in several galleries complete the museums' offerings.

Numerous tours are offered here with various educational emphasis, such as Taiko Drumming, Storytime, Origami Art, Object Analysis (showcasing some artifacts), and more for $5 per student. Many times throughout the year the second Saturday of the month is Free Family Day where admission is free, and crafts, workshops, and performances throughout the whole day are included.

The adjacent building, National Center for the Preservation of Democracy, is another part of the museum and is essentially an auditorium and center for presentations and classes.

The museum also anchors the east end of Little Tokyo Historic District which is composed of ethnic shops and restaurants. Try mochi, a Japanese rice cake made of short-grain glutinous rice that is pounded into paste - it's better than it sounds. Small balls of ice cream wrapped in mochi come in unusual flavors, such as green tea, red bean, and mango. Check out Fugetso-Do or a concoction at Mikawaya Mochi. Also check out the nearby GO FOR BROKE NATIONAL EDUCATION CENTER (pg. 112), which is a sister museum of this museum, and JAMES IRVINE GARDEN (pg. 66). See DOWNTOWN LOS ANGELES / GRAND PARK (pg. 167) for information on Grand Park and all the other places to go within this fairly immediate area.

Hours: Open Tues., Wed., Fri. - Sun., 11am - 5pm; Thurs., noon - 8pm. Closed Mon., New Year's Day, 4th of July, Thanksgiving, and Christmas.

Price: $12 for adults; $6 for seniors and ages 6 - 17; children 5 and under are free. Admission is free every Thurs. from 5pm - 8pm, and all day on the third Thurs. of every month. Check the website for the free Sat. Combo admission to this museum and to GO FOR BROKE is $15 for adults; $8 for seniors and youth. Parking is about $10.

Ages: 7 years and up.

JOE DAVIES HERITAGE AIRPARK AT PALMDALE PLANT 42 / BLACKBIRD AIRPARK   !

(661) 267-5100 - City of Palmdale; (661) 267-5611 - airpark; (661) 267-5345 - Joe Davies - tours; (661) 274-0884 - Blackbird Airpark / www.cityofpalmdale.org/airpark; www.afftcmuseum.org

2001 Avenue P at the Flight Test Installation at Plant 42, Palmdale

Plant 42 took the aeronautics industry soaring to new heights and now features two collections of vintage aircraft. The Joe Davies airpark pays tribute to those contributions and its heritage of aircraft flown, tested, designed, and produced here by displaying twenty-one retired restored, military, important planes, with room (and plans) for more. The collection currently includes an F-104 Starfighter, F-86 Sabre, C-140 Jetstar, F-4 Phantom II, and F-105 Thunderchief, plus a scale model of the B-2 Spirit and a AGM-28 Hound Dog Missile. Walk around the planes to read the placards to understand their importance. Call to schedule a guided tour, offered Mondays through Saturdays.

Beside the planes, aviation buffs (and others) see salvaged aircraft parts used creatively as "decoration" elements. Plans for this acreage include buildings to house aerospace memorabilia and a visitors center.

Blackbird Airpark, at 2503 E. Avenue P, is just a building over from Joe Davies. Three historic, sleek-looking planes are on display here - the Lockheed SR-71A, the A-12, the spy plane U-2D, and the once-top-secret, D-21 drone. The A-12 is perhaps the best known because it is the first Blackbird ever built and flown. The inscribed, inlaid tiles recognize record setters and program participants. A gift shop is on the premises, as well. This park is not connected with Joe Davies, but they are too close to not see both in one day. Blackbird is an annex of, and maintained by, the Air Force Flight Test Center Museum at Edwards Air Force Base.

Hours: Both are open Fri. - Sun., 11am - 4pm. Closed federal holidays.
Price: Free
Ages: 7 years and up.

JOHN FERRARO BUILDING - LOS ANGELES DEPARTMENT OF WATER AND POWER - HEADQUARTERS

(800) 821-5278 / www.ladwp.com
111 North Hope Street, Los Angeles

This sixteen-story building is completely surrounded by a moat! Well, technically it's a water fountain that circumscribes the building, but it looks as cool as a moat. Part of the fountain is on top of a parking garage, too. Walk around the building because it all looks neat, especially as the fountains shoot upward.

Inside the light and airy lobby are surprisingly interesting displays regarding the history of the department of water and power. They consist of huge murals, an old switchboard, models, a replica of part of an aqueduct, pipes, tools and equipment used, historic artifacts, and some informational panels. As this building is near so many other attractions (see DOWNTOWN LOS ANGELES / GRAND PARK (pg. 167) for details), it's definitely worth a stop, look, and visit. Note that tours to LADWP operating facilities are available for grades five and up.

Hours: Open Mon. - Fri., 9am - 5pm. Closed weekends and holidays.
Price: Free, except for parking.
Ages: 7 years and up, as there are no guard rails around the water.

JUSTICE BROTHERS RACING CAR MUSEUM

(626) 359-9174 / www.justicebrothers.com
2734 E. Huntington Drive, Duarte

Justice Brothers is an established name in car care products. In the main lobby of their headquarters office building is a slick exhibit of their collection containing thirteen-plus cars and a few motorcycles. Featured models include gleaming and colorful vintage Kurtis midget and sprint cars dating back to the 1930's, a 1968 Ford GT-40 LeMans, a Ford Model T, and a classic Corvette and Thunderbird. Other memorabilia includes numerous gasoline pumps, a great display of lights from the top of old gasoline pumps, models, photographs, engines, and even a biplane "flying" overhead. The winner for most unique motorcycle goes to an ice motorcycle, or "icycle," with its steel spikes on the tires to grip ice in Russia and a few other cold countries. There are two other, smaller display areas in adjacent buildings that showcase a few more race cars and a Chevy truck.

Hours: Open Mon. - Fri., 8am - 5pm. Closed Sat. and Sun.
Price: Free
Ages: 6 years and up. Visitors under 18 must be accompanied by an adult.

KIDSPACE CHILDREN'S MUSEUM

(626) 449-9144 / www.kidspacemuseum.org
480 N. Arroyo Boulevard at Brookside Park, Pasadena

Welcome to Kidspace - one of the best children's museum around! Go through the park and walk through a short tunnel that looks like the inside of a kaleidoscope with colorful pieces of odd-shaped tile and mirrors on the walls and ceiling. The large courtyard has picnic tables (purchase food at the cafe or bring your own), huge rubber balls, and splash dance - sections of ground fountains that spurt up water at irregular intervals. (Tip: Bring a change of clothing.) The early childhood learning center, geared for ages 4 and under, has padded floors. It contains soft foam blocks and shapes, short climbing apparatus, and entertainment such as story time and music, plus seats for parents to relax and watch.

Enter the main pavilion building and into other fun worlds. Some of it is furnished with everyday objects that are disproportionately large so that things are seen from a bug's eye perspective, such as a wall made of pencils and tables made of bottle caps. An adjacent room has several live, caged insects, scorpions, and millipedes, as well as a live bee house. Gently move the table-top maze and see if you can roll the ball through the town, waterways, and around the nature trails without it falling into a trap. In the nature art center, paint an oversized leaf (using water colors) and play with push pins that make up the large flower heads.

The climbing towers are highlights for agile kids, and for parents who think they can keep up. Big, bluish-clear circles (that represent gigantic raindrops) spiral around and up forty feet to the top. Very cool. (Parents, duck your heads.) The second structure is shaped like a wisteria vine. Climb the large leaves, surrounded by netting, to the top for a view of the museum and surroundings. I let my kids do this one on their own as the zigzag leaf pathway is more narrow than the raindrop tower.

A central section of the pavilion features a paleontologist dig where kids can hop in the Land Cruiser to "drive" to the fairly large size dig site. Here kids can don gloves and use brushes and their hands to uncover plant and animal fossils (like a T-Rex!) imbedded into the fake rock walls and recycled "dirt" trenches. Learn about earthquakes and earthquake preparedness by viewing survival kits, interacting with retrofitted wooden model houses, and pushing large tectonic plates against each other to cause quakes. Get a bug's perspective and try the Ant Climber, a small climbing structure of curved leaves surrounded by netting. Go down the staircase to a trench to experience a dig site where trash is embedded in the walls as are insect burrows. Visitors can climb back via a short tunnel (or use the stairs).

The Nature Exchange is an information center housing books, shells, and numerous containers of rocks and minerals, such as quartz, amethyst, sodalite, coal, and garnet. Bring your rocks, plant life, and other natural finds to show to and discuss with the staff. In exchange, you'll earn points used to trade for the collections in the containers in order to build your personal collection.

The Imagination Workshop is a really cool place for kids to repurpose old radios, gears, electronics, toys, craft items and more into whatever they design. Staff is on hand to help design and create projects, too. Everyone has a story to tell and Storyteller Studio, also in the pavilion, allows kids to do that and express themselves via dressing up and acting out on a small stage with props and all; putting on puppet shows; and drawing and coloring.

If you can't see the forest for the trees, look at a different forest, such as the Galvin Physics Forest, located just outside. Instead of trees there are thirteen oversized exhibits outdoors for kids to interact with as they learn about launching bottle rockets; a cool fan that transforms energy into wind power; centripetal force and momentum by constructing a roller coaster; a giant lever; and so much more. Another great element to this area are the huge and numerous soft play blocks in all sorts of shaped and sizes. Kids create marvelous buildings, animals, robots - wherever their imaginations can think of. Adjacent to this section is a greenhouse for kids to hands-on learn about plants.

All this and there is still the "backyard" acres with crisscrossing paved trails, to explore! The back patio is paved like a road, complete with street signs, and kids can use Kidspace's sturdy trikes to ride the course. An outdoor amphitheater, with tiered seating, is put to good use for presentations and shows. Walk underneath an arbor to reach a sand pit and climb on a spider's "web" made from rope. (I'd rather be the spider than the fly.) Other exhibits here include the bee and butterfly garden, an interactive garden (learn about, make, and take home garden-related projects); a wildlife pond (with frogs, turtles, and fish); and a redwood bridge over a stream. Kids will get wet playing in and around this stream. A main attraction is the short, but wide, rock climbing wall designed with strata formations. Kids must place their feet and hands in strategic crevasses and footholds to get across. Younger children will also enjoy climbing a huge inverted tree root.

Kirby's Kids Corner is an outdoor section just for little ones with padded flooring and several colorful play structures to stimulate imaginative play including a playhouse, tables, slides, and raised water basins for H2O fun water element. (Remember that change of clothing?)

Arroyo Adventure has even more fun things for kids to do - play instruments (like a xylophone) made out of natural materials; climb out to a way oversized hawk's nest that overlooks part of garden and beyond; learn about by doing with gardening, composting, and harvesting crops; and just be a kid in some of favorite, "old-school" areas where kids can build forts and other structures out of natural materials; play in the mud by making bricks; create new worlds in the rock-lined shallow water area with sand, small stones, and sticks; and dig in a sandy area just for little ones to explore and enjoy.

Ask about the thirty- to forty-five-minute educational programs and field trip options aimed at kids pre-K to fourth grade. Participants learn about the rocks, water, bugs, gardening, and more, via an array of arts, sciences, games, and activities. Tip/ be aware: Many school groups come here for field trips on weekdays mornings, so you might want to visit in the afternoons!

The on-site Cafe offers food selections such as a hamburger ($5.95); turkey or tuna sandwich ($7.25); Chinese salad ($7.75); veggie and humus wrap ($7.50); cheese cubes and grapes ($3.50); grilled cheese sandwich ($4.95); mac and cheese ($5); sunbutter and jelly sandwich ($3.50); yogurt with fruit and granola ($4.50); bagel with cream cheese ($2.50); and six piece chicken nuggets ($4); plus cookies and beverages.

Just outside the museum grounds is BROOKSIDE PARK - REESE'S RETREAT (pg. 50), another place for kids to run around and play. The park has a baseball diamond, lots of open, grassy areas, and playground equipment and Reese's Retreat, an all-accessible, pirate-ship themed playground.

Hours: Open September through mid-March, Tues. - Fri., 9:30am - 5pm; Sat. - Sun., 10am - 5pm. Closed Mon., except for holiday Mon. Open mid-March - Labor Day, Mon. - Fri., 9:30am - 5pm; Sat. - Sun., 10am - 5pm. Closed New Year's Day, 4th of July, Thanksgiving and Christmas, plus certain Saturdays because of football games at the Rosebowl.

Price: $14 per person; children under 1 year are free. Admission is free on the first Tues. of every month from 4pm - 8pm. Educational programs are about $9 per person. See info on the Association of Science - Technology Centers (pg. xi) for reciprocal museum memberships.

Ages: 1½ - 12 years old.

LA BREA TAR PITS & MUSEUM

(323) 857-6300; (323) 934-PAGE (7243) / www.tarpits.org $$$$
5801 Wilshire Boulevard, Los Angeles

Kids boning up on becoming paleontologists will really dig this place. Forewarn your kids, though, that dinosaurs had been extinct for many years before the tar pit entrapments occurred, so there isn't anything here regarding dinosaurs, but what they will see and experience is terrific.

The La Brea Tar Pits Museum has over thirty different exhibits including several skeletons of sabertooths in life-like poses (what fangs!), a giant ground sloth, mastodons, extinct birds, and a Columbian mammoth (these animals were absolutely gigantic!). What has been excavated outside has been brought inside to the museum. Besides murals and dioramas, the walls are filled with fossils behind glass - skulls, jaws, femurs, claws, and more - of bison, deer, condors and other birds, etc. One wall contains over 400 dire wolf skulls found on the grounds. An animated model of a young mammoth startled me. Visitors can pit their strength against the force of asphalt by pulling on glass enclosed cylinders stuck in the sticky stuff. The futility of this effort makes it easier to understand why animals, of any size, couldn't escape the tar pits. And check out the sabertooth hologram, which changes from skeleton to "fleshed out" creature, and back.

Observe through the huge, semicircle of windows a working paleontologist's laboratory, fittingly referred to as the Fishbowl Lab, and the on-going process of cleaning, studying, and cataloging newly excavated fossils. When Kellan, my oldest son, was younger, he wanted to become a *bone*afide paleontologist until he saw how tedious the work can be. Toward the exit is a room with a pectoral and informational time line regarding the theory of evolution for animals. Walk through the lovely atrium in the center of the museum filled with plants and a pond with koi.

Pick up a pencil scavenger hunt at the front desk to get the kids more involved with the exhibits and/or check online before your visit for information and a scavenger hunt. Take a guided tour offered throughout the day, especially the forty-five-minute Excavator Tour to visit and learn about active excavation spots outside at the Observation Pit and Project 23, where live excavations are on-going, and inside at the Fossil Lab, watching and talking with a paleontologist.

Ice Age Encounter is a fifteen-minute live and film presentation that also incorporates a life-size (and life-like) saber-tooth cat puppet that "comes to life" as it roars and stalk the museum floor, and visitors. (Younger children might get scared.) The Encounter is usually offered only Fridays through Sundays. The theater is currently showing the twenty-five-minute, *Titans of the Ice Age: The La Brea Story in 3D*, which intersperses excellent animation of the icy world of wooly mammoths and other animals with re-enactments and current discoveries - definite worthwhile to view. The cost for either of the above attractions is an additional $5 per person; children 2 and under are free.

Outside, enjoy a walk around the twenty-three acres of beautifully landscaped Hancock Park, otherwise known as the La Brea Tar Pits. The pits are composed of asphalt that has seeped to the surface to form sticky pools in which the animals got trapped and died. There are several active tar pits in the park, with hundreds more having been dug out and filled in. One gated pit out front has several, "stuck" mastodons statues. Look into the Pit 91 excavation site, open 10am to 4pm, to see undisturbed fossils. Project 23, open 6am to 10pm, is a live excavation site with people working there. The park, with its outdoor amphitheater and picnic facilities, is also a backyard, and has connecting walkways, to the LOS ANGELES COUNTY MUSEUM OF ART (pg. 130). Note: If all else fails, kids will have a great time rolling down the hills outside the museum and climbing on the statues!

Hours: Open daily, 9:30am - 5pm. Closed New Year's Day, July 4th, Thanksgiving, and Christmas.

Price: $15 for adults; $12 for seniors and students with ID; $7 for ages 3 - 12; children 2 and under are free. General admission is free on the first Tues. of the month, except July and August, and free every Tues. in September. L.A. County residents get free admission Mon. - Fri., 3pm - 5pm - bring valid ID. Parking in the lot behind the museum is $15. There is some free and metered parking on 6th St. Read parking signage carefully.

Ages: 3½ years and up.

LANCASTER MUSEUM OF ART AND HISTORY

(661) 723-6250 / www.lancastermoah.org   !/$

665 W. Lancaster Boulevard, Lancaster

This small, multi-story, modern museum has rotating exhibits featuring art interests that include paintings, sculptures, drawings, and photography. It doesn't take long to go thru the exhibits so check out the calendar to see which ones might appeal to you. School tours, art classes, and Discover traveling trunk programs (where trunks are filled with hands-on educational and historical items) are offered here.

There are lots of restaurants and eateries nearby including the small, 50's style Katz N' Jammers on 44801 Beech Ave. Open for breakfast and lunch it has black and white checkered flooring, red vinyl booths, 50's memorabilia on the walls - records, posters, murals, and Coca Cola items, plus that-decade music playing in the background, all of which equals a fun extension of your outing.

Hours: Open Tues. - Sun., 11am - 6pm; open until 8pm on Thurs. Closed Mon. and some holidays.

Price: Free; suggested donation is $2 per person.

Ages: 5 years and up, depending on the current exhibit.

THE LEONIS ADOBE, and area

(818) 222-6511 / www.leonisadobemuseum.org $

23537 Calabasas Road, Calabasas

Step back over 100 years in time when you visit the Leonis Adobe. The restored buildings help kids to picture the wealthy ranchero as it once was. The rustic grounds, complete with grape arbors, old farm equipment, windmills, and a corral containing longhorn cattle, horses, turkeys, sheep, and goats, enhance the yesteryear atmosphere. Officially Los Angeles' Historic Cultural Monument No. 1, the adobe was once owned by Miguel Leonis, a Basque who led a very colorful life, and Espiritu, his Native American wife. Both the museum and its owners have a rich and fascinating history that kids will enjoy hearing.

The visitor's center is actually the relocated Victorian-style Plummer House, the oldest house "in" Hollywood. It contains a few glass-cased displays of mannequins dressed in period clothing and a gift shop. Outside, a huge, 600-year-old oak tree dominates the grounds. You are welcome to explore the barn, complete with wagons and buggies; a blacksmith's shop that is outfitted with saddles and tools; and the adobe. The bottom story of the adobe has a kitchen with a wood-burning stove and other old-fashioned kitchen implements; a pantry for preserving and drying food (kids like the hanging cow with fake blood); and a dining room with adobe floors. Upstairs is the Leonis' elegant bedroom that has a red velvet bedspread over the canopy bed, plus ladies' boots, and leather trunks. You'll notice that the hallway floor tilts at a downward angle, slanting away from the house. It was built like that to ensure that rains would run away from the walls, not seep into them. The Juan Menendez (bed) Room has a ghost story associated with it. (Every good historical home has at least one such story!) Also up here is an office, complete with desk, ledger, and guitar.

Elsewhere on the ranch grounds are penned sheep, goats, turkeys, ducks, chickens, horses, and a few longhorns; a covered beehive oven which was used for baking bread; and steps leading up to the tank house, or worker's bedroom. The Leonis Adobe is a classy reminder of the relatively brief, but pivotal Mexican/California era. Ask about the terrific year-round school programs offered here where kids immerse themselves in this time period. They might get to grind corn, make tortillas, churn butter, learn about branding and the role of a blacksmith, rope with a lasso and feed the livestock. Docents dress in period costumes.

Just a short walk eastward, past the Sagebrush Cantina restaurant, is the small, but beautiful Calabasas Creek Park. It offers a pleasant picnic area and respite with a rose garden out front, wrought-iron benches throughout, massive shade trees, re-created Chumash village, and bridges over the duck pond. The only drawback to this serene scene is the ever-present freeway noise. Notes: There is a Farmer's Market here every Saturday morning, 8am to 1pm. Add a trolley ride to your adventure, for free! Catch a free ride on the Calabasas Trolley that makes an hourly loop with twenty-four stops, including near the Adobe. The Trolley runs Saturday 10am to 10pm (all 24 stops) and Sunday, noon to 4pm (5 stops only). Contact (818) 224-1673 / www.cityofcalabasas.com for more details.

Hours: The Leonis Adobe is open to the public Fri., 1pm - 4pm; Sat., 10am - 4pm; Sun., 1pm - 4pm. Half-hour guided tours are given on the weekends at 1:15pm, 2:15, and 3:15pm. Closed Mon. - Thurs. to the public, but open then for school groups. Closed main holidays.

Price: $4 for adults; $3 for seniors and students; $1 for children 11 and under.

Ages: 4 years and up.

LOMITA RAILROAD MUSEUM

(310) 326-6255 / www.lomita-rr.org

2137 W. 250th Street, Lomita

Stop, look, and listen! This small, recreated, turn-of-the century train depot is as charming to look at - with its decorative wrought iron, gingerbread molding, and brick patio - as it is to tour. Inside the depot museum/souvenir shop, visitors will see various train memorabilia, such as an old-time station agent ticket office, scale model train cars, telegraph equipment, locomotive whistles, marker lights, an exhibit of railroad ties, and glass cases filled with photographs, and more artifacts. Hanging from the ceiling and the walls is a collection of hand-lanterns.

Outside, on real train tracks, are several railcars including an all-wood, 1910 Union Pacific "bobber" (i.e., caboose) to explore, a 1949 Santa Fe Caboose and a 1902 Southern Pacific Steam locomotive with a cab that the kids can climb in and let their imaginations go full steam ahead. Note that the valves and handles are labeled with explanations for their use, but they are not for touching. You look at, but not go into, the 1923 Union Oil Tank Car and 1913 Union Pacific Boxcar. And it's hard to miss the adjacent, 35-foot tall water tower - an important part of that era.

Half-hour tours, for all ages are offered that incorporate the history of the museum and trains, and the importance of train transportation.

Extend your visit by picnicking at the adjoining small grassy area, or the museum annex just across the street. The annex is a pretty little grassy spot, with a picnic table under shade trees, that boasts a real wood box car and a 1923 Union Oil tank car; both are for display purposes only.

Hours: Open Thurs. - Sun., 10am - 5pm. Closed all major holidays.

Price: $4 for adults; $2 for 3 - 12; children 2 and under are free.

Ages: 1½ years and up.

LONG BEACH FIREFIGHTERS MUSEUM

(562) 599-3985 or (562) 570-8628 / www.lbfdmuseum.org

1445 Peterson Avenue, Long Beach

This historic museum, housed in a fire station, holds a wonderful conglomeration of old equipment and numerous old engines. Throughout the main hallway and large rooms and into the crew room and captain's room are displays of breathing apparatus, nozzles, hats, alarm bells, hoses, ladders, a life net, basket stretcher, helmets, uniforms, medals, and even a horse hitching post. The vehicle collection includes an 1890 Rumsey ladder wagon, 1907 Amoskeg steam fire engine, 1897 hand pumper, 1901 hose cart, 1935 squad wagon, 1965 Mack fire truck and several Ahrens Fox pumpers. Visitors are allowed to climb into some of the vehicles. The docents are knowledgeable and love to share information and stories, so ask away and listen.

Hours: Open Wed., 8am - noon; the second Sat., 10am - 3pm.

Price: Free

Ages: 4 years and up.

LONG BEACH MUSEUM OF ART

(562) 439-2119 / www.lbma.org

2300 E. Ocean Boulevard, Long Beach

This small, two-story art venue by the beach contains a permanent collection of paintings, drawings, sculptures, decorative furnishings, ceramics, and more. The rotating exhibits vary in medium and content, so call to see what's currently showing to see if it has kid-appeal. Note that on the third Sunday of every month (and every Sunday in the summer), from 11am to 3pm, a family art-making workshop is hosted for ages 5 and up. The museum also offers Summer Art Adventures (i.e., day camps) for kids to learn how to draw and paint, as well as education programs, music programs, and other special events.

Grab a bite to eat next door at Claire's at the Museum Restaurant. The food is good - soups, salads, sandwiches, pastas, and more. Eat outside on the patio, by the cool-looking water sculpture, for an incredible view of the beach and Catalina!

Hours: Open Thurs, 11am - 8pm; Fri. - Sun., 11am - 5pm. Closed Mon. - Wed., New Year's Day, July 4, Thanksgiving, and Christmas.

Price: $7 for adults; $6 for seniors and students; children 11 and under are free. Free admission Thurs., 3pm - 8pm and all day Fri.

Ages: 7 years and up.

LOS ANGELES COUNTY MUSEUM OF ART

(323) 857-6000 or (323) 857-6010 / www.lacma.org $$$$
5905 Wilshire Boulevard, Los Angeles

Art, according to Webster, is: "The use of the imagination to make things of aesthetic significance; the technique involved; the theory involved." This leaves the interpretation of what constitutes art wide open! The world-class, massive Los Angeles County Museum of Art campus is composed of a grouping of several, multi-story buildings each featuring a different style and/or country of origin of art, plus the Bing Center of theater and movies for older audiences. The following just touches on some of the buildings and art.

The Art of the Americas building showcases art from the United States, as well as art from Latin America. Ancient and contemporary furniture, clothing, paintings, sculptures, and various other mediums are presented here on a rotating basis.

The Ahmanson Building contains both modern and contemporary art and more traditional works from Medieval European, the Romantic, and the Renaissance periods. Classic paintings and portraits by Picasso, Giovanni Bellini, Desportes, Koninck, and so many more hang in various galleries throughout the stately, three-story building. Gilbert gold and silver pieces, such as elaborate bowls and candelabras, are on display here, as are incredibly detailed, inlaid stone pictures. Other works of art on view include Islamic, African, and Oceanic art. Contemporary art appeals to kids in that they are attracted and puzzled by the larger-than-life sculptures, abstract paintings on gigantic canvases (that sometimes, to my untrained eye, just look like blotches of color), and common objects that express artistic creativity, like a kitchen sink, or an arrangement of cereal boxes.

The Hammer building features Chinese and Korean Art. The permanent and temporary exhibits here portray other mediums of artistic endeavor as they also specialize in photography, impressionism, drawings, textiles, and prints. This building also houses the Boone Children's Gallery, the most interesting places for kids as it's really a place for them to create art, supervised themes and just draw time, with everything they need supplied. Storytelling in Boone's is every Monday and Friday at 2 pm.

The adjacent Pavilion for Japanese Art is architecturally unique, inside and out. It houses mostly paintings and a few sculptures in a serene, natural-light setting. The Samurai warrior statue, dressed in eighteenth-century black chain mail armor, gets our vote for the most interesting piece here. The ramp spirals downward, toward the small waterfall and pond on the lowest level.

Under a covered walkway, go outside to the neighboring Broad Contemporary with 60,000 square feet of exhibition space. Take the long ride up the open-air escalator and check out the view of the surrounding city and mountains from the top. This building has three galleries focusing on always the interesting, rotating, contemporary art, which translates as "anything goes", with some extraordinarily large pieces, such as *Band*. For kids, don't miss *Metropolis II* . This amazing exhibit is like a Hot Wheels racetrack on steroids. It looks like a mini futuristic city and freeway system, during rush hour. The massive little city, which takes up the space of a small room, is comprised of small skyscrapers, single family homes, and other buildings all surrounded by a miniature commuter rail line, several roads, and a freeway that kind of resembles a roller coaster. Watch, and listen - then feel stressed out - as 1,100 mini cars and other vehicles race along these roads Fridays every hour on the half hour, starting at 11:30am until 6:30pm, and on Saturdays and Sundays, 10:30am until 5:30pm. View this electrically-run metropolis from the ground or, better yet, from the balcony.

Between the Broad Contemporary and the Ahmanson, in the front plaza, is Urban Light - a variety of over 200 antique lampposts, which are great for picture taking, day or night. By the Resnick, on the north lawn, is Levitated Mass, 340-ton granite megalith (kind of cool!) perched on top a slanted cement walkway that runs underneath it. These exhibits are free and open to the public: Urban Light is available 24/7 and Levitated Mass is open 7am - sundown (but not when it's raining).

Behind the Broad Contemporary, the glass and stone, single story, spacious Resnick Exhibition Pavilion houses special exhibitions showcased in natural lighting. These have included massive sculptures, such as stone heads of ancient Mexican warriors (weighing up to 24 tons); a collection of over seventy European and royal court clothing items from the 1700's, and accessories; paintings; art deco furniture; and more.

Although many docents are on hand to insure that nothing is touched in the LACMA buildings, the atmosphere is not stifling. Andell Family Sundays are held for the general public almost every Sunday from 12:30pm to 3:30pm with different themes each month. These free days include a family gallery tour (which is also given in Spanish) and learning about a particular exhibit followed by art workshops and sometimes live performances. Contact the museum about their numerous and wonderful art classes, school tours, and family programs offered throughout the year. For instance, our school group took the free sculpture tour where we went on a guided tour of the sculptures and then went to the on-site classroom to make sculptures out of the provided clay. A cafe serving reasonably priced food and an eating area, plus a more formal sit-down restaurant are part of the outdoor, central courtyard.

Enjoy walking around the museum's spacious backyard, Hancock Park. The parks hosts concerts and presentations at the amphitheater; has picnic tables, grassy areas, and trees; is home to the La Brea Tar Pits; and is near LA BREA TAR PITS & MUSEUM (pg. 127) and PETERSEN AUTOMOTIVE MUSEUM (pg. 144). Tip: Sign up (in person or on-line) for the free NexGen Arts program that gives free museum membership (which translates to free museum admission year round!) to youths 17 and under and to one accompanying adult. Note: Just across the street are several, colorfully painted chunks of the Berlin wall!

Hours: Open Mon. - Tues., and Thurs., 11am - 5pm; Fri., 11am - 8pm; Sat. - Sun., 10am - 7pm. Select galleries are open Fridays in July and August until 11pm. Note that the Boone Children's Gallery closes at 5pm. School tours are often given in the morning hours. LACMA is closed Wed., Thanksgiving, and Christmas.

Price: $25 for non-Los Angeles resident adults, $20 for LA residents; $21 for non-resident seniors and students; $16 for residents; ages 17 and under are free. Admission is free Mon., Tues., and Thurs., 3pm - 5pm, and Fri., 3pm - 8pm for residents. General admission is free for everyone on the second Tues. of each month and certain holiday Mon. NexGen members have free general and special exhibit admission. Parking is $16 onsite. There is some free and metered parking on 6th St. (and metered parking is free on Sundays). Read the street signage carefully. See info on the Bank of America Museums on Us (pg. xi) free museum days.

Ages: 6 years and up.

LOS ANGELES FIRE DEPARTMENT HOLLYWOOD MUSEUM

(323) 464-2727 / lafdmuseum.org

1355 N. Cahuenga Blvd. Hollywood

You can have a hot time at this Fire House museum, housed in Old Fire Station 27. This restored, two-story facility, originally built in the 1930's, looks like it's back in action! The three bays are filled with a great collection and lots of fire-fighting vehicles and equipment from various decades (as far back as the 1880's), including old hook and ladder trucks, engines, pumpers, and rescue cars. There are displays of nozzles, masks, model toy fire trucks, an area set up with a bed and boots, uniforms, an enormous exhibit of helmets from around the world, and more. Upstairs has an area for kids to play with toy fire trucks and try on fireman jackets and boots, plus a place to look down the fire pole. Exhibits up here highlight the various methods to be saved in the event of a fire or disaster, and honors just some of the firefighters that have done so. A video plays that shows families how to prepare for a fire, earthquake, etc. The docents are mostly former LA firefighters so the stories and information they share often come first-hand. The gift shop is great and the memorial statues out front are powerful.

Old Station 27 also includes a Fire Service Research Library and a learning center where fire and life safety lessons are shared with both children and adults.

Hours: Open Sat., 10am - 4pm.

Price: Free

Ages: 3 years and up.

LOS ANGELES HARBOR FIRE MUSEUM - OLD FIRE STATION 36

(323) 464 - 2727 / www.lafdmuseum.org

638 Beacon Street, San Pedro

This small museum is housed in the original fire station 36 - on the ground floor of city hall, built in 1928. Come inside to see four fire engines/apparatus, some old and some slightly more modern, plus a fireboat and diver display, hoses, fire extinguishers, photos, and a variety of tools related to the field of fire fighting and rescue.

Hours: Open Sat., 10am - 3pm.

Price: Free. Metered parking (.50¢ an hour) is available.

Ages: 4 years and up.

LOS ANGELES LIVE STEAMERS RAILROAD MUSEUM / WALT DISNEY BARN

(323) 662-8030 or (323) 661-8958 - Live Steamers; (818) 934-0173 - Disney barn / www.lals.org; www.carolwood.com

5202 Zoo Drive, Los Angeles

Right next to TRAVEL TOWN (pg. 154) this park-like museum features a stationary steam plant (which is fired up on the third Sunday). The park/museum has seven working steam engines, three cabooses, a Union Pacific baggage dorm car and sleeper car. Most of the cars now serve as museum offices, *training* rooms (really!), and workshop rooms.

Walt Disney was a railroad aficionado and his actual backyard barn/workshop where he built and ran railcars and layouts, is here at this museum. Some say that inside this small barn was the genesis of Disneyland. Open to tour through on the third Sunday of the month, see several scale locomotives, photographs, an antique phone, Walt's control board, tools, some of his hats, drawings of the Main Street Station, toys, books, railroad paraphernalia, and Disney memorabilia. (And unlike anything else Disney, this is free!) Enjoy a lunch at the picnic tables here and maybe become inspired.

One of the best features of this museum is the large-scale train ride visitors can take over 1.5 miles (about twelve-minutes) through this part of Griffith Park. You'll pass by three miniature towns, plus water towers, bridges, train stations, and other buildings and scenery. See GRIFFITH PARK (pg. 63) for more things to do in this immediate area. Check the October Calendar section for info on their annual Ghost Train Ride.

Hours: Open most Sun. (weather permitting), except the Sun. before Memorial Day and the first Sun. in October, 11am - 3pm. Walt Disney's barn is open the third Sun., 11am - 3pm.

Price: $3 per person, per train ride.

Ages: 1 ½ years and up; at least 34" for the train ride.

LOS ANGELES MARITIME MUSEUM

(310) 548-7618 / www.lamaritimemuseum.org; www.portoflosangeles.org $$
600 Sampson Way, Berth 84, San Pedro

If you have older children who dream of sailing the oceans blue, they will enjoy walking through the two-story, nicely-laid-out galleries of changing exhibits in this maritime museum, which is housed in an old ferry terminal. Arranged in the rooms and up and down the hallways, there are hundreds of ship models to look at, many of which are glass-enclosed, ranging from several real boats to scale sized to ones inside a bottle. (How do they do that?) An impressive twenty-one-foot scale model of the *Queen Mary* (made for and renamed *Poseidon* for the same-name movie) and two cut-away models of the *Titanic* and *Lusitania*, give your kids the inside scoop on ocean liners. Other exhibits put the spotlight on the fishing industry in San Pedro and commercial diving. Check out the ship figureheads and maritime crafts. A highlight is the Amateur Radio Station where your child might be able to talk to someone on the other side of the world. It's *knot* impossible to practice tying any of the sixty-four types of seaman's knots on display. On the second floor younger kids also enjoy the children's area with toy cranes, cars, containers and cargo; binoculars to look out the window; some nautical-themed dress up costumes and uniforms; and a small row boat to get into and pretend sail on the wave murals and story time. Free, guided tours for all ages are also offered. Classes for the public include scrimshaw, celestial navigation, and ship model building. Check out the gift shop for nautical finds.

A ship's anchor (which is gigantic!), a propeller, torpedo, mast, bow peak, and bell are out in front of the museum. There is a cannon on the small back deck where you can also watch the ships in the harbor. Nearby is Fire Station #112, which shelters a classic behind glass - fireboat #2. The boat, commissioned in 1925, sports pumps and just looks really neat. A history of Los Angeles fireboats, and this one in particular, are on panels in front of the boat. There is no charge for viewing the fireboat.

Hours: Open Tues. - Sun., 10am - 5pm. (Last admission is at 4:30pm) Closed Mon., New Year's Day, Thanksgiving, and Christmas.

Price: $5 for adults; $3 for seniors; ages 12 and under are free.

Ages: 5 years and up.

LOS ANGELES MUSEUM OF THE HOLOCAUST

(323) 651-3704 / www.lamoth.org   !
100 S. The Grove Drive, adjacent to Pan Pacific Park, Los Angeles

Enter through a long, narrow tunnel/hallway that goes at a slant, kind of underground. Get a free printed and/or audio tour which describes the exhibits and behind-the-scenes in more detail, making the personal stories around the museum hit the heart and mind. A video featuring a U.S. soldier who helped with the liberation of a concentration camp is the first stop. Several rooms then flow into the next, each containing necessarily graphic (i.e., piles of naked bodies) photos and informational panels, plus numerous artifacts. In the first room is a large and long, touch-screen table with images and videos that reveal the lives of Jewish people - education, family, culture, sports, etc. - before the Holocaust. In another room video terminals show actual footage from and of, and locations of, eighteen concentration camps, plus newsreels from WWII Germany that depict life in the camps. A seventy-screen video testimonial wall, called the Tree of Testimony, features powerful interviews with Holocaust survivors that interconnects each one just as leaves and branches from a single tree are connected. Other displays throughout the museum include a model layout of the Sobibor death camp; family belongings; religious antiques (including an old Torah once stolen by the Nazis);

music of that era; artwork by Jewish artisans; and a walk through a recreated (human) cargo train car.

One-hour+ guided tours for school or other groups, tailored to meet the need of the given age group for fifteen to fifty people, are also offered. Allow another hour, or so, if you will, to incorporate into your tour the opportunity to meet and hear the powerful, first-hand testimony of a Holocaust survivor, when offered. On Sundays, docent-led tours for the public are offered at 2pm, followed by a Holocaust Survivor talk at 3pm.

At the north end of the adjacent PAN PACIFIC PARK / RENEE'S PLACE (pg. 77) is a martyr's memorial monument with its six black granite, triangular columns - please read the website for all of its symbolism. Note that the museum is also close to THE GROVE - KIDS' THURSDAYS (pg. 95) and FARMERS MARKET (pg. 21).

Hours: Open Mon. - Thurs., 10m - 5pm; Fri., 10am - 2pm; Sat. - Sun., 10am - 5pm. Closed some major holidays.
Price: Free. A $100 donation is suggested for group tours.
Ages: 4th graders and up.

LOS ANGELES POLICE MUSEUM

(323) 344-9445 or (877) 714-LAPD (5273) / www.laphs.org
6045 York Boulevard, Los Angeles

$$

Here's an APB - this police museum offers arresting pieces of history while capturing the impact of the LAPD from its inception in 1869 through modern day. Take an audio tour, which is great, or take a one-hour, or so, guided tour, often given by an ex-law enforcement officer, through the building which was a police station from 1925 to 1984. It looks like a classic police station from a Hollywood set. Actually, Clint Eastwood did much to restore and renovate it when he filmed *Blood Work* here.

The first floor contains a pictorial history of the city's changing styles and people, plus crime scene pictures. A display case contains blackjacks, batons, and handcuffs from various eras. Down the passageway, enter a cell block of five jail cells, once used to hold those who committed misdemeanor crimes. You may go in the cells (and leave them) of your own free will. Take pictures as you emphasize to your kids that this will be the only time they will ever be inside a jail cell. You can also take mug shots with your camera, here. The three display cases in this section hold foreign and American handcuffs and thumbcuffs, leg irons, and old jail locks. You can even stand in a line-up and hope no one chooses you!

The backyard has a helicopter you can climb into, a military armored personnel carrier (that looks like a small tank), and a few bullet-ridden and some vintage police cars and emergency vehicles. A suspects' car, from a robbery, is also here - check out its shattered windshield. Put on a helmet and sit on a police motorcycle.

Back inside, another room contains old communications equipment - radios, radars, car computers, and bull horns, plus light bars and helmets. Pass by the felony jail cells to see various hand-held radios and an exhibit of items that came from the New York 911 site, including a piece of the towers, some helmets, and newspaper clippings.

Upstairs, visitors can try on body armor (which is really heavy), helmets, an equipment belt, and a gas mask. Other displays are of the SLA (i.e., posters and a pipe bomb); part of a bomb shield on wheels; mannequins wearing uniforms from different time periods; a Jack Webb display case; and cases of various weapons, mostly firearms. Watch the almost twenty-five minute, riveting video of mostly real footage (and some reenactment) from a 1997 bank robbery involving two suspects and over thirty officers. There are some graphic scenes of people getting shot, and even killed. Then, walk into the next room which contains mannequins of these robbers dressed in gear and toting their AK-47s, plus other real weapons and bullet casings used in the shootout. Note that the suspects' getaway car you saw outside earlier belonged to these robbers.

A visit here increases knowledge about the police force and elevates understanding and respect for them. If you want to bring home something more tangible, stop off at the gift store - it would be almost criminal not to.

Hours: Open Tues. - Fri., 10am - 4pm; and on the third weekend, 9am - 3pm. Closed Mon., most weekends, and holidays.
Price: $9 for adults; $8 for seniors; children 12 and under are free.
Ages: 5 years and up.

LOS ENCINOS STATE HISTORIC PARK

(818) 784-4849 / www.historicparks.org; www.parks.ca.gov
16756 Moorpark Street, Encino

!

Just off the very busy Ventura Boulevard is a little oasis. With a good-sized gated pond and plenty of ducks (purchase duck food for 25¢), expanses of grassy lawn under mature shade trees, and picnic tables, this park is delightful to visit in and of itself. Other reasons to visit include taking a tour of the De La Ossa Adobe, originally built in 1849. Walk through the rooms to see a writing desk, an antique wedding dress and shoes, pictures of families that once owned the adobe, and the simply-furnished rancho office and kitchen. Guests can also peer into the working blacksmith's shop, made of stone, to see the furnace and all the tools of the trade. The small visitors center holds displays of photographs, branding irons, and other artifacts.

Guided tours are offered to the public and to school groups. A docent dressed in historical costume usually tours the school groups who play 19th-century games, use the water pump outside, and do a few other old-fashioned chores while learning about the time period.

Hours: The park and visitor's center is open Wed. - Sun., 10am - 5pm. Closed Mon., Tues. and most national holidays. Free tours of the adobe are offered by appointment only.

Price: Free

Ages: 2 years and up for the park; 7 years and up for the adobe.

MADAME TUSSAUD'S HOLLYWOOD

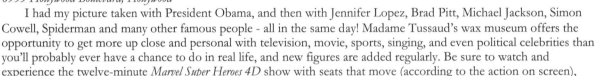

(323) 798-1670 / www.madametussauds.com/hollywood $$$$$

6933 Hollywood Boulevard, Hollywood

I had my picture taken with President Obama, and then with Jennifer Lopez, Brad Pitt, Michael Jackson, Simon Cowell, Spiderman and many other famous people - all in the same day! Madame Tussaud's wax museum offers the opportunity to get more up close and personal with television, movie, sports, singing, and even political celebrities than you'll probably ever have a chance to do in real life, and new figures are added regularly. Be sure to watch and experience the twelve-minute *Marvel Super Heroes 4D* show with seats that move (according to the action on screen), smells and other sensory components.

This multi-level wax museum is unique from others of this genre in two ways in particular: One is that the over 125 wax figures, for the most part, look amazingly lifelike and truly like the person they are modeled after. (My top pick for realistic lookalike is the Steven Spielberg figure.) You can see this for yourself because of the second distinction - you can get close enough to touch the figures and to interact with them because there aren't any barriers.

There are several genres, or sections, of the museum - A-list Party, Crime, Action Heroes, Sports, Modern Classics and more. Many of the wax statues are set in famous scenes, backdrops and all, along with props that you can use so you can pose with them or even imitate them. Make sure to bring your camera! It was fun, for instance, to put on a robe and boxing gloves, get into the ring, and pretend to box next to Sylvester Stallone; sit on a camel next to Peter O'Toole in a setting from *Lawrence of Arabia;* pull up a chair at the table and join Audrey Hepburn in a replicated scene from *Breakfast at Tiffany's;* hop on a motorcycle and join Hugh Jackman as Wolverine; yell "hi ya" while chopping a wooden block in two near Jackie Chan; put on a jacket and twirl a cane around while standing alongside Charlie Chaplin; set a cowboy hat on your head and hang out with John Wayne, or with Robert Redford and Paul Newman from *Butch Cassidy and the Sundance Kid;* sit in the captain's chair onboard the deck of the *Star Trek Enterprise* alongside Captain Kirk and the rest of the waxy crew; and in an office room setting with Spiderman, pretend to be hanging upside down on the furniture and then reverse the picture on your computer at home - perfect! Many of the settings have sound effects to go along with them, such as the sound of swords clashing. Kiosks are interspersed throughout the attractions, too, where you can test your knowledge of the stars, movie terminology, trivia, and more.

From David Beckham to Clark Gable to Quentin Tarantino to Beyonce to Lady Gaga and Madame Tussaud herself (kind of) - there is someone here for everyone to get excited about seeing and posing with.

On the last floor you mingle with a bevy of stars (who are wearing clothing worn by the actual celebrities) at the Oscars as paparazzi camera lights flash. The final room in the museum allows visitors to see the intricate details of how a wax model is made (over 800 hours of work per statue) and the painstaking details and measurements (of everything!) taken on a person being immortalized (unless there is a heat wave). You'll see the diagrams, models in various stages of being created, colorful locks of hair (which are inserted in the figure's head one strand at a time) and color and sizes of eyeballs to choose from. For an additional $12 you can dip your hand in a vat of wax to make a mold of your hand to give to someone special.

Day campers and students have additional options in viewing the wax museum. They can participate a forty-five minute, educational scavenger hunt and/or a field trip that incorporates subjects such as Hollywood History, where students follow script notes throughout the museum to learn about Hollywood's influence on people and communities; World History, where historical figures that shaped our world are studied; Modern-Day Superheroes which looks at real superheroes and fictional ones; and Special Effects where students study visual and technical special effects. There are also specialty themes such as Black History and Hispanic Heritage. The field trips also offer pre- and post-lesson plans and are for groups of fifteen or more students. Another option is a briefer, educational and interactive workshop/presentation to see some wax pieces up close for an additional $5 per person.

Check out the HOLLYWOOD - the downtown tourist mecca (pg. 171) entry for an abundance of other things to see and do in the immediate area, including the Hollywood Walk of Fame and much more.

Hours: The hours fluctuate a lot! It is open every day, except Oscar day, and usually at 10am (9am in the summer). Closing times vary from 7pm on weekdays and 8pm on weekends most of the year, to 10pm daily in the summer.

Price: $30.95 for ages 13 and up; $18.99 for ages 3 - 12; children 3 and under are free. Purchase tickets online to save up to 30%! Entry is even more steeply discounted after 5pm. Parking is available at Madame Tussaud's garage, accessible off Orange Dr., at $15/$20 max. At this center you can also park for $2 for first two hours with validation from a business or Visitor Information Center. Madame Tussaud's does not validate parking.

Ages: 5 years and up

MARTIAL ARTS HISTORY MUSEUM

(818) 478-1722 / www.martialartsmuseum.com
2319 W. Magnolia Boulevard, Burbank

Small, but mighty, this unique museum artistically and creatively visually portrays the history of martial arts while also dispensing a wealth of readable information. It was designed with the aid of Disney and other artists and animators. Enter under the long, paper dragon through the faux stone castle archway (and guard) and begin your journey. In chronological order, each country with a history of martial arts is represented in separate sections showcased by colorful picture panels, stories, memorabilia, and three-minute videos with tie-ins of the arts (opera, dance, and more.). Note that overhead is a pictorial timeline of important events and people in martial arts history. Many martial arts pioneers, including Funakoshi, Kano, and Ueshiba, are honored in photos. Kids - ask for a paper scavenger hunt.

The Chinese section tells of how Kung Fu began and features a wonderful, huge lion "puppet" used for lion dancing, plus a wall of weapons and uniforms. The Art of the Samurai in the Japanese section shows and tells that story with three pieces of incredible armor from the style of the late 1500's (poised to look like three scary men) and over fifteen swords against a mural of Japanese warriors. Big pictures display the art of Sumo. Kabuki features more uniforms, weapons, and photos of masters, plus explanatory information such as sickles were originally farming tools, then modified. Ninjas are next with a life-sized torso of a hidden-faced Ninja, plus climbing claws weapons and a video that includes the introduction of Judo in the Olympics. After Korea, and its uniforms, is the tiki-hut-themed Hawaiian arts with a large tiki figure and shark teeth on the edges of several of its weapons. This is followed by Kali, and then the U.S. with its intro of mixed martial arts and UFC. Huge photos of champions line the walls here.

The last section is devoted to the influence of martial arts on comic books, film, televison, print, and other media. Cartoon-style panels and some movie memorabilia are in the last room, which is a theater that shows a three-part documentary called *Martial Arts in Film, TV and Print*. It also shows other films. Some of the movie props are the shield used in *Mortal Combat*, Billy Jack's hat from *Billy Jack*, the headband worn by Ralph Macchio in *The Karate Kid*, and Kato's mask from the *Green Hornet*.

The museum hosts a variety of events and seminars including special screenings, Samurai history, language workshops, sushi seminars, animation drawings, craft displays, martial art demonstrations (sometimes featuring celebrities), sword cutting performances, the annual Dragonfest Expo, and more. Adult and kid groups can take educational tours; just call to make a reservation. Is it wrong that I still have these song lyrics running through my brain? - "Everybody was Kung Fu Fighting, those kicks were fast as lightning. . ."

Hours: Open Thurs. - Sun., 11am - 6pm.

Price: $10 for adults; $8 for seniors; $5 for ages 6 - 15; children 5 and under are free. Admission is free on the first Thur. from 3pm - 6pm. Take a tour with 20 people, or more, for $3 a person.

Ages: 5 years and up.

MISSION SAN FERNANDO REY DE ESPAÑA

(818) 361-0186 / www.missionscalifornia.com
15151 San Fernando Mission Boulevard, Mission Hills

What was life like in the early days of California? Take a self-guided tour of one of my family's favorite missions to find out. Mission San Fernando Rey, founded in 1797, was the seventeenth mission in the chain of outposts along the coast of California. It has a beautiful, large courtyard, with a small sundial at the north entrance, and west gardens that are surrounded by numerous rooms. These rooms lead to small, alcove rooms - what delightful exploration! The Museum Room is a good place to begin as it's filled with old photos (including one of a bathroom that looks like a small indoor pool), statues, bows and arrows, peace pipes, a bell collection, and several more artifacts. The Madonna Room is fascinating as it contains over 100 representations of the Madonna, each depicted by different nationalities and cultures. From simplistic versions to ornate ones, there are Chinese, African, and Native American Madonnas, plus one that looks like a prairie woman, another like an Eskimo, and more.

Other rooms and items of interest we saw include a hospice that held beds made with rope supports (before box springs); simply furnished bedrooms; plain wooden tables and chairs; the Convent, where meat was hung to dry; mission vestments; a library containing shelves of very old books including a colorful, hand-illuminated liturgical book with large Gothic lettering; brick ovens; and pipe organs. The workshop and weaving rooms are interesting because they hold, respectively, blacksmith tools, saddles, and scythes, and a large wooden loom with cowhide chairs. The church, which still holds regular worship services, has adobe walls and an ornately decorated altar with gold-leaf overlay. A small cemetery behind the church opens into a huge, neighboring cemetery. In the midst of all this history, my boys loved seeing the many peacocks that wandered the grounds. They even "discovered" a few roosters that were tame enough to pet.

Brand Park, once a part of the mission, is just across the street. This grassy park has a lot of shade trees, plenty of picnic tables and running around space, but no playground. It also has vats where mission wines were once produced.

Hours: Open daily, 9am - 4:30pm. Closed Thanksgiving and Christmas.
Price: $5 for adults; $4 for seniors; $3 for ages 7 - 15; children 6 and under are free. Admission to Brand Park is free.
Ages: 5 years and up.

MISSION SAN GABRIEL ARCANGEL

(626) 457-3035 or (626) 457-3048 / www.sangabrielmissionchurch.org $$
428 S. Mission Drive, San Gabriel

Located in the Mission District, California's fourth mission is aptly nicknamed "Queen of the Missions." The graceful buildings and pleasant grounds transport you back to 1771, when the mission was founded. They also offer a wonderfully visual way to learn about California's Spanish/Mexican heritage.

In the midst of the cactus garden are tanning vats, with a placard describing the tanning process. Walk up a few stone steps to see four large holes in the ground, which were once the soap and tallow vats. The San Gabriel Mission supplied soap and candles to most of the other missions. There is one fountain and several statues distributed throughout the mission gardens. In the cemetery, for instance, is a life-size crucifix - a memorial to the 6,000 Indians buried on the grounds.

The Mission Church is still in use. The wall behind the altar is eye-catching as it is ornately decorated. The small baptismal room is equally impressive. Next to the church, the small and somewhat dark museum contains only a few articles that were of interest to my kids - big, old books covered in sheepskin dating from 1489 and 1588, and a Spanish bedroom set. Knowing that the museum was once a series of rooms, such as sleeping quarters, weaving rooms, and carpenter shops, made it a bit more interesting.

Located in the center of the mission is the Court of the Missions. Models of each of California's twenty-one missions, varying in size and layout, but similar in style, are on display here. Vaya con Dios! (Go with God!)

Hours: Open Tues. - Sat., 9am - 4:30pm; Sun., 10am - 4pm. Closed Mon., New Year's Day, Easter, July 4th, Thanksgiving, and Christmas.
Price: $6 for adults; $5 for seniors; $3 for ages 6 - 17; children 5 and under are free.
Ages: 5 years and up.

MONROVIA HISTORICAL MUSEUM

(626) 357-9537 / www.monroviahistoricalmuseum.org   !
742 E. Lemon Avenue, Monrovia

One room of this small, local museum features artifacts and photos of the early city, including a police motorcycle and uniforms, along with other displays. Another features memorabilia of early Native Americans, such as pottery and arrowheads. The 1907 classroom has desks, blackboard, and even a teacher (i.e. a mannequin dressed in clothing from that time period). I love the display of telephones from the ages - some of those styles are making a comeback. The turn-of-the-century parlour holds a piano, furniture, and other items from this era. There is a courtyard and garden area out back. Call to book a tour for a school group, scouts, etc. Check out the gift shop that sells vintage military uniforms, postcards, etc. See OSCAR GARCIA SKATEPARK / RECREATION PARK (pg. 77) for details about the surrounding park.

Hours: Open Thurs. and Sun., 1pm - 4pm.
Price: Free
Ages: 8 years old and up.

MONTEREY PARK HISTORICAL MUSEUM and GARVEY RANCH PARK

(626) 307-1267 / www.ci.monterey-park.ca.us; www.laas.org

781 S. Orange Avenue, Monterey Park

    This small museum's claim to fame is its twenty-one scale models of the California missions. The adobe-like museum has three reconstructed rooms that also house Indian artifacts, household items (such as toys and a phonograph), tools, period clothing, photographs, and a corner dedicated to Laura Scudder (who lived in Monterey Park) - of the potato chip fame.

    Adjacent to the museum is a small observatory, operated by the L.A. Astronomical Society, that is open for public viewing on Wednesdays from about 7:45pm - 10pm. The next-door Garvey Ranch Park is a nice park with grassy areas, trees, a few covered picnic areas, paved pathways, two lighted baseball diamonds with stadium seating, basketball courts, nice playgrounds, and two tennis courts, just up the hill.

Hours: The museum is open Sat. - Sun., 2pm - 4pm and open weekdays by appointment only for tours. Closed the 5th Sat. and Sun. of the month, holidays and bad weather. The park is open daily, sunrise - sunset.

Price: Free

Ages: 5 years and up.

MUSEUM OF CONTEMPORARY ART / GEFFEN CONTEMPORARY / PACIFIC DESIGN CENTER

$$$$

(213) 626-6222 - Grand; (213) 621-1741 - Geffen; (310) 289-5223 - Pacific Design Center / www.moca.org

250 S. Grand Avenue, Los Angeles

    The elegant Museum of Contemporary Art (MOCA), located on top of a plaza, presents rotating exhibits of eclectic art work - paintings, sculptures, photos, and more. This type of museum is a fun one to bring kids to as an introduction to art because the pieces are unusual, imaginative, and sometimes puzzling. Idea: After visiting the museum, have the kids come home and create their own contemporary or abstract piece of art. As we looked at the huge paintings on canvas, my boys and I took the liberty of renaming several pieces. (I think some of their title choices were more apropos than the ones the artists chose.) This involved the kids in studying the art and therefore enhanced our visit here. Downstairs in the museum is a reading room with several books, many geared for children, that pertain to the art and artists currently featured at the MOCA.

    Free, family friendly tours are given on the first Sunday of every month that include art/crafts, music, a Toddler Town for young children and even food trucks. The plaza just outside has tables and chairs, a few trees and reflection pools.

    One satellite building of MOCA, the Geffen Contemporary, is located one mile away at 152 N. Central Avenue in Little Tokyo, across the plaza from the JAPANESE AMERICAN NATIONAL MUSEUM (pg. 124). Another satellite is the Pacific Design Center (PDC) at 8687 Melrose Avenue in West Hollywood. The Center features rotating exhibits of architecture, design, and selections from MOCA's permanent collection. The Museum of Contemporary Art, then, is actually one museum in three buildings! See DOWNTOWN LOS ANGELES / GRAND PARK (pg. 167) for information on Grand Park and all the other places to go within this fairly immediate area.

Hours: Open Mon., Wed., and Fri., 11am - 6pm; Thurs., 11am - 8pm; Sat. - Sun., 11am - 5pm. Closed Tues., New Year's Day, July 4th, Thanksgiving, and Christmas.

Price: $15 for adults; $10 for seniors; $8 for students with ID; ages 11 and under are free. Admission is free every Thurs., 5pm - 8pm. Admission to 1 of the MOCA museums is valid for all 3 if visited on the same day: the Pacific Design Center is always free. Parking starts at $8 in the various areas for the museums.

Ages: 6 years and up.

MUSEUM OF FLYING and AIRPORT PARK

$$$

(310) 398-2500 / www.museumofflying.com

3100 Airport Avenue, Santa Monica

    Consider this entry your boarding call to make a direct flight to the Museum of Flying. A Douglas DC-3 aircraft outside the museum hanger lets you know you've arrived. There are several other aircraft outside, too, including a Douglas A-4 Skyhawk, Blue Angels Naval plane, and the nose of a Fed Ex. plane.

    Enter the mid-sized museum to gawk at planes suspended overhead such as a BD-5 Microjet, Cassutt III Formula One Air Racer, and Monerai Sailplane, and some that are grounded such as a replica of the Wright Flyer, a hot air balloon, a replica of a Lockheed Vega, a Douglas World Cruiser, and more - there are almost two dozen planes of all sizes. Some are undergoing restoration. Airplane seats, video kiosks, aviation artwork, model planes, airplane parts (engines, flight computer, etc.), mannequins in airline uniforms, rescue vehicles and artifacts from aviators are also important components of the museum.

Play pilot and adjust the instruments in the cockpit of a Convair CV-240; sit inside a T-33 Jet Trainer; and go inside the cockpit of the Fed Ex. Boeing 727 (the one belonging to the nose you see outside) to listen to the live feed from the Santa Monica air traffic control tower. To experience flight, go on Maxflight, a full-motion simulator ride that allows 360 degree pitches and rolls, stunt flying and can even go upside down, though hopefully you won't experience that on a real flight! Participants, who must be at least 4 feet tall, can choose from a variety of aircraft such as air combat in a P-38 or cruising in a CD-3 over L.A. Non-participants can view what is showing on the screen, as well.

The Mezzanine features a replica of the Douglas Aircraft Company executive boardroom and office of its founder, Donald Douglas. The theater on this level features various aviation films.

The museum offers guided tours for all ages, as well as birthday parties for kids that include use of a party space, a guided tour, viewing of a Charlie Brown aviation movie in the theater and exploring the museum after the party.

Note that just down the street from the museum is Airport Park. This park has a small, gated tot lot in the sand with swings; toys on huge springs to sit and ride on; and a fun, artsy-shaped object to climb on and play. There are also picnic tables, a few bbq pits, a block of grass with huge trees, an enclosed dog run area, and best of all, perhaps, is that it is close to the airport so you can watch planes land and take off.

Hours: Open most of the year, Fri. - Sun., 10am - 5pm. Open in the summer, Wed. - Sun., 10am - 5pm. Simulator rides are available Fri. - Sun. The park is open daily, 6am - 11pm.

Price: The museum is $10 for adults; $8 for seniors and students; $6 for ages 3 - 12; children 2 years and younger are free. The Maxflight Simulator is $8. Airport Park is free.

Ages: 4 years and up.

MUSEUM OF LATIN AMERICAN ART

(562) 437-1689 / www.molaa.com

628 Alamitos Avenue, Long Beach

$$

A nicely laid out main gallery and surrounding gallery rooms create a welcoming ambiance for exploring Latin American culture and heritage while experiencing its art. Rotating exhibits feature sculpture, paintings, and mixed media art by Latin American artists. Take a stroll through the outdoor sculpture garden to look at unique pieces set amongst cacti, palm trees, and other plants. The museum regularly hosts hands-on art workshops and even live performances on select Sundays for children, usually geared for ages 6 and up, that tie-in with the present exhibit. Note: The gift shop is filled with wonderful selection of cultural items to purchase.

Hours: Open Wed., Fri. - Sun., 11am - 5pm; Thurs., 11am - 9pm. Closed Mon., Tues., New Year's Day, 4th of July, Thanksgiving, Christmas Eve and Christmas.

Price: $10 for adults; $7 for seniors and students; children 11 and under are free. Admission is free every Thurs., after 5pm and all day Sun. A $5 parking fee is charged on Sunday free admission days and other special event days. See info on the Bank of America Museums on Us (pg. xi) free museum days.

Ages: 6 years and up.

MUSEUM OF NEON ART

(818) 696-2149 / www.neonmona.org

216 S. Brand Boulevard, Glendale

$$

MONA, not as in Mona Lisa, but as in the Museum of Neon Art, preserves neon, electric and kinetic art, so a visit here is enlightening. Yes, I went there. I speak of the rotating exhibits - which consist of signs, shapes, designs and other art forms - in glowing terms. Besides coming to the museum for a visit you can also take a class in creating your own neon art sign or sculpture, or go for a nighttime Neon Cruise. This Saturday night bus tour cruise goes past neon signage and such, like movie marquees and advertising, in downtown L.A., Chinatown and Hollywood while your tour guide explains more about the "urban electric jungle".

Hours: $10 for adults; $8 for seniors; $5 for Glendale residents; ages 12 and under are free. Parking at 120 S. Maryland Ave. is free for the first 90-min. The Neon Cruise is $55.

Price: Thurs. - Sat., noon - 7pm; Sun., noon - 5pm.

Ages: 6 years and up.

MUSEUM OF TOLERANCE / SIMON WIESENTHAL CENTER

(310) 772-2505 or (800) 900-9036 / www.museumoftolerance.com

9786 W. Pico Boulevard, Los Angeles

$$$$

Simon Wiesenthal, the museum's namesake, was a Holocaust survivor who became a famed Nazi hunter that unearthed over 1,100 war criminals. The Museum of Tolerance, an educational component of the center, is unique in its format of numerous technologically advanced and interactive major exhibits, and in its focus on personal prejudice, group intolerance, the struggle for civil rights in America, and the Holocaust. Begin your journey on the lower level as you enter through the door marked Prejudiced. A video wall exhibit (which changes), currently called the Power of Words, shows famous politicians speaking - Joseph Stalin, President Kennedy, and several others; history has told us the effect of their words. In a mock 50's diner, called Point of View, visitors use jukebox monitors to watch various scenarios and answer a menu of questions about personal responsibility regarding drinking, drugs, hate speeches, and other issues. Enter the Millennium Machine where participants add their input by answering questions about global crimes, human rights abuse, and the threat of terrorism. You'll be riveted and affected by the sixteen-screen video Civil Rights Wall; an interactive U.S. map that discloses 250 hate groups in America called GlobalHate.com; and *We The People*, a timeline on a very long wall with photos and information from 1565 to the present day regarding the diversity of Americans and the struggles and intolerance that the people and country has and continues to overcome. An intense film called *In Our Time* focuses on Bosnia, Darfur, Rwanda, genocides, and contemporary hate groups that have violated human rights throughout the world.

The Holocaust section starts as you take a passport photo card of a real person who was sent to the concentration camps, making the experience more personal. On a semi self-guided tour you then walk along a series of chronological stylized vignettes, starting in the late 1920's, that light up when you stand in front of them, while listening to narration that explains the events leading up to the Holocaust. This factual and emotional one-hour tour is one of the most informative and visual ways to witness what happened. You then walk through a replica of the gates of Auschwitz into a recreated gas chamber to watch more detailed film clips regarding what happened to people at the camps; their stories and testimonies. Powerful. Your time here culminates when you receive a printout of the fate of the person whose passport you hold. The next area contains Simon Wiesenthal's actual office from Vienna with all of his papers, SS directories, books, videos, and more. You'll also see genuine artifacts from Auschwitz, including clothing, medical instruments, and more; and the floor to ceiling wall exhibit called Appeasement with videos of leaders taking the appeasing route instead of calling Hitler out.

The second floor of the museum contains rotating exhibits and a multimedia learning center with work stations. Numerous films - on Anne Frank, Harriet Tubman, Helen Keller, and others - are available for viewing. Also housed here are copies of letters from Anne Frank. One of the most compelling experiences at the museum is hearing Holocaust survivors share their testimonies. They usually speak here for an hour every day; call to confirm.

Don't miss the one-hour Anne Frank exhibit/experience. Walk down a corridor with panels decorated to look like a Frankfort streetscape, then turn around to see Anne's profound words printed on the other side. Enter a hidden room, her Secret Annex, to immerse yourself in her story in so many different ways. Playing on the expanse of walls is a riveting film that re-creates what it felt like to live as Anne Frank, from being locked up in the attic to exploring her feelings and hopes and dreams to the nightly attacks of war just outside. Real footage is also shown throughout the rest of the exhibit, including a shot of Anne, as well as displays of prison uniforms, yellow felt Stars of David, copies of handwritten letters, photographs, and many more artifacts. The displays are interspersed on and with a wall of tightly folded shirts that wraps around and progress in color from pinkish pastels and colors to dingy grays and blacks as Anne's life progresses from childhood towards her untimely death. Kiosks in the Interactive Action Lab encourage visitors to become more involved with Anne's world and the Holocaust by responding to issues she brings up, ones that still need thought and action today. The words from her world-famous and poignant diary are printed around walls and pillars, as well as heard from a continually-playing audio narration hauntingly read by actress Hailee Steinfeld. An evocative exhibit/experience.

The third floor main exhibit is titled Finding Our Families, Finding Ourselves that aims at encouraging visitors to seek their own history and recognize commonalities between all peoples. The first display is a collection of personal belongings - all stuff actually left behind at Ellis Island. Bon voyage as you walk the gangplank onto a realistic-looking part of a boat, bypassing luggage and other artifacts. Walk past the ships's exam rooms while listening to Billy Crystal narrating what immigrants experienced. Through a hall of celebrities, such as Michelle Kwan and Kareem Abdul-Jabbar, who share how their heritage has affected them, you then enter a series of four rooms. Each room was decorated and chosen as a pivotal place to four famous Americans who also tell their story and influence of their family via videos: Dr. Maya Angelou and her grandmother's general store in Arkansas; Joe Torre and his family's Italian-influenced family room; Billy Crystal and his cartoonish-styled kitchen and living room; and Carlos Santana and his recording studio. There is a nook of computer monitors to assist visitors on how to research their own genealogy.

The fourth floor has a cafeteria that serves light snacks and refreshments. Notes: Each of the three main exhibit places take at least an hour. Going through the Anne Frank exhibit takes another hour. Cameras are not allowed in the museum. The educational programs offered are wonderful - for school groups, and for adults and professionals. The programs include Tools For Tolerance, From Hate to Hope, where a former White Supremacist and one of his victims share their story; hearing survivors of human trafficking; and much more.

Hours: The museum hours, except for the Anne exhibit, are Sun. - Thurs., 10am - 5pm, with the last ticket sold at 3:30pm. Fri. hours are 10am - 5pm, April - October; 10am - 3:30pm, November - March, with the last ticket sold at 1pm on Fri. when the museum closes at 3:30pm. The Anne exhibit is open Sun. - Thurs., 10am - 6:30pm, with the last entrance at 5:30pm. Fri. hours are 10am - 5pm, April - October; 10am - 3:30pm, November - March. Everything is closed Sat. and national holidays, and either closed or closed early on Jewish holidays. School tours for twenty or more students are offered as early as 8:30am.

Price: Admission to all the exhibits, except Anne, is $15.50 for adults; $12.50 for seniors; $11.50 for students with I.D., active military, and ages 5 - 18; children 4 and under are free. Admission to Anne is an additional $15.50 for adults; $13.50 for seniors; $12.50 for students, active military, and ages 5 - 18. Advanced reservations are highly suggested for your visit to the museum. Free parking is available underground, under the museum, on Pico Blvd.

Ages: 10 years and up - it's too intense for most younger children.

NATURAL HISTORY MUSEUM OF LOS ANGELES COUNTY   ☼

(213) 763-3466 / nhm.org $$$$

900 Exposition Boulevard, Los Angeles

Your natural history experience begins (for free) before you enter the museum, while outside in the extensive North Campus, in urban nature. This Nature Garden features a pond with plant and animal pond inhabitants, like turtles and dragonflies, plus a variety of garden zones and microclimates. Small groves of native trees, fruit trees, and plants beautify the park while butterflies, lizards, birds, and people enjoy it. I especially like the pollinator garden planted to attract hummingbirds, bees (not my favorite), and butterflies (my favorite). See what is living in and on the Living Wall. A cafe is outside here, too, as are benches, picnic tables under shade trees, and walkways all around.

This extensive museum has a lot of a little bit of just about everything. In the foyer complete skeletons of a Tyrannosaurus rex and triceratops engage in battle with each other. A few enormous, long halls showcase numerous North American, African, and exotic mammals mounted in a backdrop of their natural habitat (i.e., huge dioramas). The gigantic walrus, buffalo, and elephant are the most impressive. Take a walk through time in the American history room (1st level) and California history room (basement). They contain early vehicles, such as tractors, stagecoaches, and a streetcar; mannequins dressed in period clothing; early weapons; and numerous other pioneer artifacts. The lower level also features the Nature Lab, a place to learn about the plants and animals that dwell in L.A. It also houses live rats, snakes, frogs, turtles, ants, geckos, tarantulas, spiders and more.

Back on the first floor is the Gem and Mineral Hall, with over 2,000 outstanding rocks and minerals, including fluorescent minerals (which shine neon colors under black light); spectacular rock pieces from all over the world that are so brilliant in color, or so oddly shaped that they look unreal; a touch area with a meteorite, a giant slab of jadeite, and more; 300 pounds of natural gold, plus mining artifacts; and a vault to walk through which contains cut rubies, emeralds, sapphires, and topaz. (I'm not coveting here; just admiring.) Other exhibits on this floor include a real mummy; a preserved, unusually long, and flat-looking fish - the oarfish; and the rare Megamouth shark. Walk around and be amazed at the colossal skeleton of a fin whale in this long gallery leading to some of the most popular exhibits - dinosaurs and mammals.

The two-story, two room Dinosaur Hall, guarded by a triceratops, contains dinosaurs in life-like poses. Visitors can walk around and even view them up close; some even face-to-face. One of the massive animals is the thirty-foot skeletal form of Thomas the T. rex, who shares the limelight with two other, smaller rexes near the remains of a duckbill dinosaur. An allosaurus is locked in mortal combat with a stegosaurus. Some of the other twenty full-body, ancient creatures and 300 fossils include the head of a horned dinosaur, and a Mosasaur and a 68-foot-long-necked Mamenchisaurus (dinosaur speak is like learning a foreign language) - giant sea reptiles. There are also videos, illustrations, and interactive components speculating how dinosaurs may have looked and acted with the acknowledgment that science is always evolving and learning.

Under the beautiful stained glass sky light rotunda are rotating exhibits from the museum's vast collection - one currently features a platypus egg and an ancient Peruvian gold feather, among other objects; another exhibit has incredible paintings of extinct animals (and places).

In stage-like settings, under natural lighting, the two-story Age of Mammals room showcases skeletons of animals - a mastodon, ancient horse, saber-tooth cat, thunder beast (great name!), giant jaguar, walking whale, and others. It also features fleshed-out animals - a zebra, tiger, polar bear, alpaca, and more, in action poses. The flow of the room represents the evolution of animals, especially in regards to climate change. Marine mammals skeletons - a sperm whale, sea lion, and more - are suspended overhead. Interact here by using multimedia technology to learn how movement of land masses affected temperature and weather changes. Be a paleontologist and use the bones here to rebuild a Paleoparadoxiid skeleton.

The city of Los Angeles might not seem "natural", but four galleries are devoted to its history - how nature and culture and habitation have grown and changed it. A scale model of downtown L.A., circa 1940, a 1902 wooden automobile (the first manufactured in L.A.), a sword from the Mexican War of Independence, an animation stand used by Walt Disney for the first Mickey Mouse cartoon, a costume donated by Charlie Chaplin, Native American artifacts, cattle displays, WWII exhibits and much more comprise this eclectic collection that celebrates our city.

Upstairs more wonders await. An entire wing is devoted to our fine feathered friends. There are taxidermied penguins, vultures, ostriches, ducks, turquoise cotingas (guess what color they are?), and more. Pull out the drawers of the cabinets in the hallway to see a variety of feathers and bird eggs. A large part of the ornithology (study of birds) exhibit is interactive. Turn a disk to get a magnified view of wings, feathers, and bones. Step on a scale to see how much just your bones weigh - they make up 17% of your body weight. (Although I'm sure my bones weigh more than that.) Walk over the bridge of recreated marshlands to reach a dark, two-story rainforest habitat that resounds with bird noises and has a waterfall. Another room here presents an in-depth look at marine life via murals, mounted animals, and information.

Look into the Dino Lab through huge windows to watch real paleontologists unearthing and working meticulously on fossilized dinosaur bones and casts. Touch a real T. rex toe bone and dinosaur footprint here.

"Hands-on" is the motto at the wonderful Discovery Center where visitors are greeted by a nine-foot tall, stuffed polar bear. Mounted animal heads, including moose, warthogs, a variety of deer, and more, plus models of large fish, decorate the walls and ceiling. Smaller taxidermied animals, as well as skulls and bones, are in display cases that guests are encouraged to rearrange; to play museum curator. Kids can touch (or wrap themselves in) skins of deer, fox, skunk, opossum, sheep, and other animals. Touch tables have rocks, minerals, horns, and shells to sort, and a saber-toothed cat to assemble. There are also stuffed animals, microscopes with slides, and more hands-on items and activities in this room.

The adjacent Insect Zoo room is a buzz with activity, too, because of the cases swarming with live insects! Show no fear (or disgust) in front of your kids - some of the little buggers are quite interesting. You'll see scorpions, millipedes, tarantulas, beetles, and more (than you've ever wanted!). Gorgeous photos of insects grace the walls. A small room, next door, in a vault, is devoted to pre-Columbian archaeology. Just some of the extensive Native American artifacts on display include baskets, beadwork, pottery, statues, and jewelry.

Inquire regarding the usually daily live animal presentations and the don't-miss Dinosaur Encounters. The latter, twenty-minute presentation uses juvenile, life-size (and life-like) puppets of a fourteen-foot T. rex and nine-foot Triceratops that "come to life" as they roar and stalk the museum floor, and visitors. Cool and just a little scary for younger ones (and some older ones). Check the schedule for show times. Ask about the museum's numerous, in-depth field trips for various age groups, as well as their special events held on site - there is always something good going on. One such event is the once-a-month, Family Fun Days where thematic activities, science experiments, and/or crafts are included in museum admission. You can also have a "night at the museum" experience (kind of) by having an overnight adventure here. From mid-March through the beginning of September, for an extra fee, walk into the Butterfly Pavilion, which is an enclosed, outdoor butterfly garden, and be enthralled as butterflies of every color of the rainbow alight on the plants and on you. If you visit here late September through mid-November go into, look at, learn about and interact with all kinds of spiders at the Spider Pavilion. Look at the May Calendar entry, too, for details about the BUG FAIR (pg. 711).

Picnic tables and lots of grassy areas surround the museum. Also see the nearby CALIFORNIA AFRICAN AMERICAN MUSEUM (pg. 101), CALIFORNIA SCIENCE CENTER (pg. 102), EXPOSITION PARK (pg. 59), and IMAX THEATER (pg. 185).

Hours: Open daily, 9:30am - 5pm. Closed New Year's Day, 4th of July, Thanksgiving, and Christmas.

Price: $15 for adults; $12 for seniors and students; $7 for ages 3 - 12; children 2 and under are free. Buy tickets online and save $2 for adults. L.A. County residents, with valid ID, receive this same discount at the door during the week. Special exhibits may raise the admission price a few dollars. Entrance to each the seasonal butterfly pavilion and spider pavilion is the entrance fee plus an additional $5 per person; children 2 and under are free. General admission is free the first Tues. of the month, except July and August, and free every Tue. in September. Admission is free for L.A. County residents Mon. - Fri., 3pm - 5pm, and for CA teachers and military, daily. Parking in the lot costs $12. See info on the Association of Science - Technology Centers (pg. xi) for reciprocal museum memberships.

Ages: 2½ years and up.

NETHERCUTT COLLECTION and NETHERCUTT MUSEUM ☼

(818) 364-6464 / www.nethercuttcollection.org   !
15200 Bledsoe Street, Sylmar

There are two buildings that hold an impressive array of vintage automobiles - over 250 - as well as hood ornaments, mechanical musical instruments, and time pieces collected by J. B. Nethercutt, the cofounder of Merle Norman Cosmetics. The Nethercutt Collection, housed in a five-story box-like building, offers two-hour guided tours. The inside is opulently decorated with marble floors and columns in the Grand Salon room, plus chandeliers, elegant wood paneling, and spiral staircases elsewhere. The Lower Salon features more than two dozen classic American and European luxury cars in pristine condition, including a 1934 Packard Dietrich Convertible Sedan, a one-of-a-kind 1933 Dusenberg Arlington Torpedo Sedan, and a few Rolls Royces and Cadillacs. There are also numerous dolls, coins, nickelodeons, and music boxes on display. The third floor mezzanine showcases over 1,000 "mascots" (i.e., hood ornaments), including some made out of crystal, and ornate, eighteenth-century French furniture (both originals and reproductions). The spacious fourth floor, known as the Music Room, displays rare and elegant mechanical musical instruments such as music boxes, reproducing (i.e., player) pianos, nickelodeons, and the crown jewel - the Mighty Wurlitzer Theater Pipe Organ. The tour guide describes the mechanical system of each instrument and also plays a few of them. Check the website for the calendar of free organ concerts and silent movie showings. The Louis XV-style dining room has a chandelier similar to the one in Versailles, a stunning grandfather clock, and a collection of musical pocket watches

The Nethercutt Museum is another huge building, across the street, that displays over 130 more antique and immaculate automobiles, described as "rolling works of art." Let me whet your appetite for this stunning collection by mentioning just a few makes and models on display here from antiques to post-war: a 1913 Mercedes Dusenberg, Packard, Pierce Arrow, Rolls Royce, an 1898 Eisenach Runabout, a 1967 Ferrari 365, and a classic 1913 steam pumper fire truck. Again, the cars are displayed in beautiful surroundings. A fully-staffed automotive restoration facility, where classic cars are striped to the bare "bone" and then painstakingly rebuilt according to original specifications, is also on the premises. Outside are an immaculately restored 1937 Royal Hudson steam locomotive and a 1912 Pullman private rail car on tracks. Fifteen-minute tours of the railcars are available Tuesday through Saturday at 12:30pm and 3:45pm, but not on rainy days.

Hours: The Collection is open for guided tours only, Thurs. and Fri. at 10am or 1:30pm; Sat. at 10am and 1:30pm. Reservations are required, and usually well in advance. The Museum is open Tues. - Sat., 9am - 4:30pm - peruse at will. Both are closed Sun., Mon., and most major holidays.

Price: Free

Ages: Must be at least 10 years old for a tour of the Collection; ages 8 years and up will enjoy the Museum.

NHRA MOTORSPORTS MUSEUM ☾

(909) 622-2575 or (909) 622-2133 / nhramuseum.org $$$
1101 W. McKinley Avenue, suite 3A, Pomona

To see some really hot wheels, visit this stylish hot rod museum that showcases very cool cars in mint condition, both up on the walls and on the floor. The cars chronicle the colorful history of drag racing, from its days as an illegal street activity to its current status as a major spectator event. Some of the legendary cars on display include Kenny Bernstein's 1992 Budweiser King Top Fuel Dragster, the first car to break the 300 mph barrier in NHRA competition; Warren Johnson's 1997 GM Goodwrench Pontiac Firebird, the first Pro Stock machine to break the 200 mph barrier; and John Athans '29 Highboy, once driven by Elvis Presley; plus Indy roadsters, midgets, and much more. Glass cases that run almost the length of the museum contain trophies, photographs, helmets, driving uniforms, and more. Murals and paintings decorate the other walls.

The Chrisman, Brinker Gallery of Speed showcases some of the vehicles that were pivotal to the early days of racing such as a 1932 Ford Deluxe 3-window coupe, a McMullen '32 Ford highboy roadster, the Chrisman #25 dragster, and the Beast III Bonneville streamliner. The gallery also contains life-sized sculptures, hands-on activities, and interactive touch screens that allows visitors to customize their own hot rod.

With all of this inspiration, what kid (or man) wouldn't dream of being behind the wheel of any one of these cars and racing toward the finish line?! School tours, group tours, and participating in the L.A. Fairkids program are just a few of the way the museum reaches out to educate the community.

Want to do some cruising of your own? The first Wednesday of each month, April through December (but not September), from 3pm to 7pm, join in on the Twilight Cruise. Over 300 of the finest early rods, customs, muscle cars, and classics fill the parking lot outside the museum. Cruise around on your own two legs to check out the autos and/or purchase some food and drink. Admission is free to this event and the museum is free after 3pm, too. So, don't be a drag; race to this museum.

Hours: Open Wed. - Sun., 10am - 5pm. Closed Mon., Tues., and most major holidays. During the L.A. County Fair in September, the museum observes Fair admission prices and hours of operation. See www.lacountyfair.com for more info.

Price: $10 for adults; $8 for seniors and ages 6 - 15; children 5 and under are free. AAA discounts given.

Ages: 3 years and up.

NORTON SIMON MUSEUM

(626) 449-6840 / www.nortonsimon.org $$$

411 W. Colorado Boulevard, Pasadena

The museum brochure describes some of the masterpieces as "highly important works" and "glorious compositions," which lets astute readers know that this is not a hands-on museum for younger children. A visit to the museum and observing the numerous museum employees/security guards confirm this impression.

The Norton Simon is, however, a treasure for art connoisseurs as the pieces are truly outstanding and tastefully displayed in an atmosphere of quiet elegance. The permanent collection of this thirty-eight gallery, two-story, fine arts museum consists of seven centuries of European art, from the Renaissance to the twentieth century. A sampling of the featured artists includes Raphael, Botticelli, Rembrandt, Renoir, Rodin, Monet, van Gogh, Goya, Picasso, and Matisse. Western art and South and Southeast Asian art and sculpture are also well represented. A special exhibits section presents more of the permanent collection on a rotating basis.

Beginning at 12:30pm and running alternately throughout the day, the museum theater presents a thirty-minute orientation documentary movie on the life and collections of Norton Simon called *Art of Norton Simon*. The theater room is also a venue for other film, plus concerts and lectures.

Tip: Ask for a free family guide to get the kids more involved with the paintings and sculptures. Another way to get children (and other family members) interested in the pieces is to rent one of two, self-guided audio tours. One is geared for adults, covering eighty works; the other, for children and families, covers thirty-six works. The audio guides are $3 each

Check out the lovely garden, styled after Monet's Giverny. Stroll the lush pathways that meander around groves of stately trees, garden flowers, and a pond with water lilies. And appreciate the numerous sculptures that are placed throughout.

Educational tours, and accompanying study guides with activity sheets, are available by reservation for students. Personally, I benefit greatly from the "insider" information and explanations. Note that there is a cafe on the grounds. Check out the Saturday family day projects, story time, and kids' workshops in the summer.

Hours: Open Mon., Wed., Thurs., noon - 5pm; Fri. - Sat., 11am - 8pm; Sun., 11am - 5pm. Closed Tues., New Year's Day, Thanksgiving, and Christmas.

Price: $15 for adults; $12 for seniors; free for students and ages 18 and under. Admission is free on the first Fri. from 5pm - 8pm.

Ages: 10 years and up.

THE PALEY CENTER FOR MEDIA

(310) 786-1000 or (310) 786-1091 / www.paleycenter.org   !/$$$

465 N. Beverly Drive, Beverly Hills

Tune into The Paley Center for Media, which houses the ultimate collection of broadcasting programs - almost 160,000 of them covering almost 100 years. Inside the upscale, contemporary-looking building are various rooms to watch and listen to shows, with just the touch of a button. The lobby has rotating exhibits of costumes, set pieces, props (photo ops!), scripts, artwork, mementos, video clips, storyboards, and more from your favorite TV shows. I saw Warner Brothers feature items from *The Bugs Bunny Show, Big Bang Theory, Kung Fu, The Closer, Murphy Brown, Fringe, The Mentalist, Friends, Seinfeld, Smallville*, and many more shows.

The Radio Listening Room is just what its name implies. The room is quiet as visitors use headphones to choose from five preset radio channels. A sampling of the rotating selections can include comedy, rock 'n roll, history of radio, witness to history (e.g., historic speeches), etc. There is also a fully-equipped radio station in here to do live broadcasts. Next door, watch a preselected show in the fifty-seat Screening Room, or watch a film or program in the 150-seat Theater Room. Call or check the website to see what or who is playing as there are numerous special events such as appearances, interviews, and panel discussions with cast members of television shows, movie celebrities, and creative teams from the news and entertainment fields.

Use the upstairs computer library to select your choice of radio or television shows. For example, key your television selection into the computer, then view it in the adjacent Console Room. This room has individual monitors as well as family consoles, which accommodate up to four people. Your child is in couch potato heaven here, able to choose his own television programs from literally thousands of titles available.

Some of the other benefits of this center include viewing (and listening to) historic shows both for school-aged children and for researchers. Ready access to programs is also great if you just want to choose a favorite show. Call for information on special children's events. Check the website for the wonderful and current live shows, discussion panels with today's media stars, and great programs.

Hours: Open Wed. - Sun., noon - 5pm. Closed Mon., Tues., New Year's Day, July 4th, Thanksgiving, and Christmas.
Price: Admission is free as it's a non-profit. Suggested donations are $10 for adults; $8 for seniors and students; $5 for children 13 and under. Parking is free.
Ages: 6 years and up.

PASADENA MUSEUM OF HISTORY

(626) 577-1660 / www.pasadenahistory.org $$$
470 W. Walnut Street, Pasadena

Pasadena's stately heritage landmark Fenyes mansion showcases turn-of-the-century gracious living. A one-hour+ guided tour through the house allows visitors to see original (now antique) furnishings which came from all over the world. The stories about the artifacts are intriguing, especially the legend of flying carpets, which is thought to come from prayer rugs supposedly endowed with magical powers. A prayer rug is located in the studio. Some of the highlights include the wood-paneled study; the elegant living room with its exquisite furniture and period-dressed mannequins; a grandfather clock in the foyer that has rotating, colored-glass slides of early Pasadena; old-fashioned utensils in the kitchen (my boys needed an explanation about the rug beater); china in the butler's pantry; numerous volumes of books in the hallway and office; the solarium; fine wooden tables and chairs; and chests in the living room and studio ornately finished with tortoise shell, ivory, and mother-of-pearl. The elegantly decorated master bedroom and a child's bedroom are upstairs. A few small rooms downstairs hold old tools, a piano, a collection of old cameras, and several military uniforms.

Another component of the Pasadena Museum of History is the two galleries that display changing exhibits. A past exhibit was of children's toys, quilts, and clothing from 1850 to 1950. It showed how life was before video games (was there life before video games?) and how things change over time, at least in design, with displays of dolls, trucks, stuffed animals, books, games, clothing, and more. Educational tours are offered for groups of all ages, as are special programs.

The well-stocked gift shop carries some unique items. The grounds are beautifully landscaped with plants, trees, a pond, and a rose garden. The Finnish Folk Art Museum, just next door, is a homey, three-room replica of a Finnish farmhouse that contains handmade furniture, plus utensils and folk costumes. Pasadena is a city steeped in rich cultural history that is well represented by this mansion and museum.

Hours: Mansion tours, which includes entrance to the Finnish Folk Art Museum, are offered Fri. - Sun. at 12:15. The galleries are open Wed. - Sun., noon - 5pm. The gardens are open daily, 9am - 5pm. Everything is closed all major holidays and big Rose Bowl events.
Price: Mansion tours are $17 for adults, which includes admission to the galleries, too. Gallery admission, only, is $9 for adults; $8 for seniors and students. Admission is free for children 11 and under in all of the buildings.
Ages: 6 years and up.

PETERSEN AUTOMOTIVE MUSEUM

(323) 930-CARS (2277) / www.petersen.org $$$$
6060 Wilshire Boulevard, Los Angeles

For car aficionados, the driving force behind this state-of-the-art museum is dedication to the art, culture, and history of the automobile. The exterior is comprised of stainless steel ribbons, flowing and highlighted by the red of brake lights behind it. Inside are hundred of automobiles and twenty-five motorcycles in three, distinctive floors all accompanied by a modern-looking, grey-toned interior with touch screens, huge wall projections (for an immersive experience) and a multitude of 3D displays of engines and scale models. Rev up your engines and get into gear to cruise through this museum. Start at the 3rd floor to work your way down, somewhat chronologically.

History of cars is the theme of the third floor. A glitzy Hollywood Gallery stars cars that were featured in movies and television shows, and/or that were owned by celebrities. Some of the cars even show the movies/TV shows behind them. Check out the changing exhibits here that can include the 1963 Volkswagen Beetle used in *Herbie the Love Bug;* John Travolta's car Greased Lightning; the black, pop-up car used in *The Great Race;* Bond cars; the Batmobile and Bat motorcycle; Heisenberg's Aztec from *Breaking Bad;* Elvis Presley's 1971 Pantera, complete with bullet holes (he shot it when it wouldn't start); and a 1966 Mongrel T, a custom roadster built for the movie *Easy Come, Easy Go,* starring Elvis Presley, and also driven by the Joker in the television series *Batman*. The car incorporates parts from numerous different vehicles - thus the "mongrel" moniker. What a concept! Concept cars are also shown on this floor, along with numerous vintage cars - classics in prime condition. Cameras out - you can actually sit in a 1910 Ford Model T.

The second floor, **Industry**, is another favorite. Hot rods and customs - cars modified for speed and cool-looking - are lined up, like parked in a (very nice) garage, making it easy to see and ooh and ahh over them. A few are stationed high overhead so visitors can walk and see under them. The art and design center give perspective to new ideas of cars of the future. Biking enthusiasts will enjoy seeing the motorcycles, displayed in a linear fashion, that include everything from modified bicycles with single-cylinder engines to fully-outfitted motorcycles of today.

Cars Mechanical Institute here will spark a child's imagination. In partnership with Disney/Pixar, stars from *Cars* engage visitors in interactive stations. Animated drawings on the wall, displays of car parts and a life-size model of Lightning McQueen inspire visitors to paint and personalize virtual cars, trace and color their own *Cars* character to take home, race toy cars around a racetrack, and compete in an Ipad game against other *Cars* drivers. Note that at peak times the Institute is open by hourly, timed entry only, so reserve a time slot at the front desk. Another popular attraction here is the Forza Motosports Racing Experience. Sit in one of ten racing car simulators to pit your driving skills against a professional, or against one another. The stand alone kiosks also engage guests with another element of hands-on fun.

The first floor is dedicated to **Artistry**. It features "rolling sculptures" and how the automobile has been interpreted as the subject of fine art. Befittingly, gleaming, one-of-a-kind cars are classily presented on short pedestals, with drapes in the background. See such treasures as a 1925/34 "Round Door" Rolls-Royce Phantom I Aerodynamic Coupe, a 1939 Bugatti given to the Shah of Iran as a wedding present, and 1947 Cisitalia 202 Coupe. The Precious Metals exhibition has incredibly rare cars - such as a 1936 Duesenberg and 1937 Horch - all in silver, that are like 3D works of art cast in a silver setting. A few BMW's are canvases (very expensive ones!) showcasing artwork by Alexander Calder and David Hockney.

Just some of the cars that you'll see along your travels include a 1934 La Salle Series 350 Convertible Coupe; 1993 Jaguar XJ220; 1954 Plymouth Explorer; 1933 Deusenberg Model SJ; 1964 Porsche 901; 1932 Ford-Foose 0032 Roadster; 1979 Volkswagon Transporter; 1953 Dodge Storm Z-250; 1931 Ford Model A Station Wagon; 1900 Smith Runabout; and 1982 Ferrari 308GTSi.

For an extra treat, visit underground - The Vault. This is where 120 rotating premium, prize cars are on view including the Ferrari given to Henry Ford II by Enzo Ferrari; a presidential limo used by President Nixon; a Jaguar XKSS once owned by Steve McQueen; and a Mercedes used by Sadam Hussein; plus hot rods, muscle cars, Hollywood vehicles, vehicles used by heads of state, motorcycles, and even a Popemobile. Choose either a 75-minute or a two-hour guided tour of The Vault where the difference is the number of cars you'll see and learn about. Photography is not permitted here and guests must be at least 10 years old.

An Italian inspired restaurant, Drago Ristorante, is on the first floor, as is a gift shop. Field trips, guided tours, and so much more will definitely accelerate your interest in cars. Note that right across the street is the LOS ANGELES COUNTY MUSEUM OF ART (pg. 130) and the LA BREA TAR PITS & MUSEUM (pg. 127).

Hours: Open daily, 10am - 6pm. Both of The Vault tours are offered daily. Petersen is closed Christmas.
Price: $16 for adults; $13 for seniors and students with I.D.; $8 ages 3 - 12; children 2 and under are free. The Vault is an additional $20 per person for the 75-min. tour; $30 for the two-hour tour. Enter the museum parking structure from Fairfax - $15 for all-day parking, or use metered parking along the side streets.
Ages: 6 years and up.

PETTERSON MUSEUM   ☀

(909) 399-5544 / www.pilgrimplace.org/petterson_museum.php   !
730 Plymouth Road, Claremont

This small, intra-cultural museum is housed on the grounds where a community of retired pastors, missionaries, and other church professionals live. Those who shared the gospel in far corners of the globe often return with significant mementos of their host culture and crafts, covering many centuries of human history. The museum consists of three galleries filled with these mementos. Some of the exotic artifacts in display cases include costumes, textiles, masks, statues, dolls, shells, and pottery. Exhibits do rotate, bringing in unusual displays from all over. The docent-guided tours give insight into the exhibits. Note: Check the Calendar entry for the annual PILGRIM PLACE FESTIVAL (pg. 750) in November.

Hours: Open to the public, Fri. - Sun., 2pm - 4pm. Call to make a reservation to take a tour at another time.
Price: Free
Ages: 6 years and up.

PIO PICO STATE HISTORIC PARK

(562) 695-1217 / www.piopico.org

6003 Pioneer Boulevard, Whittier

Pio Pico was the last governor of Mexican California. His once-sprawling ranch is now a three-acre state park and house/museum. The restored adobe home, made from large, sun-dried bricks, is sparsely furnished, yet interesting to tour. You walk into and past bedrooms, a living room, dining room, and kitchen. Photos of Pio Pico, clothing that belonged to his wife and him, ranch tools, wine barrels, and personal items are on exhibit throughout. Some parts of the wall were purposely left unpatched and exposed, so that visitors can view the adobe underneath.

The garden and beehive oven outside are worth learning about and seeing. After your tour, enjoy a lunch at the picnic tables surrounded by the expansive green lawn. School and other groups are welcome to take a guided tour by making a reservation. Check out the summer programs for kids, such as the Jr. Rangers program.

Hours: The park is open Fri. 9:30am - 3:30pm; Sat. - Sun., 9:30am - 4pm. The adobe is open Fri., 10am - 3pm; Sat. - Sun., 10am - 3:30pm. Call to make a reservation for a guided tour. Closed major holidays.

Price: Free

Ages: 8 years and up.

POINT FERMIN PARK AND LIGHTHOUSE

(310) 548-7756 - park; (310) 241-0684 - lighthouse / www.sanpedro.com; www.pointferminlighthouse.org

807 W. Paseo del Mar, San Pedro

This good-sized corner park has lots of green grassy areas, shade trees and huge climbing trees, and a few, good play structures. I love the cliff-side picnic tables tucked in several nooks that overlook the coastline and the ocean - what a great view!!

One of the park's best features is the charming, Stick Style (i.e., early Victorian) lighthouse, built in 1874. The white picket fence and variety of flowers and other plants in the garden surrounding it make it very picturesque. There is even a small vegetable garden. Best of all, the lighthouse is open for one-hour guided tours for individuals or groups of no more than ten. (Lighthouses aren't large buildings.) Use your imagination as you tour the unfurnished rooms and learn the history of this lighthouse, its inhabitants, and the area. The lighthouse keeper's office is a small room where kids they can try on lighthouse keeper uniforms and hats. Children under 40" may not climb the winding tower steps to the top which lead to an incredible 360-degree view. The lantern up here has been removed from here to display on the first floor. All in all, though, it is an enlightening experience.

Hours: The park is open daily, sunrise - sunset. Lighthouse tours are offered Tues. - Sun. at 1pm, 2pm, and 3pm. The grounds are open until 4pm. Closed Mon., major holidays, and some holiday weekends.

Price: Free; donations requested.

Ages: All

POINT VICENTE INTERPRETIVE CENTER, PARK and LIGHTHOUSE

(310) 377-5370 - interpretive center; (310) 541-0334 - lighthouse / www.sanpedro.com; www.rpvca.gov; www.vicentelight.org

31501 Palos Verdes Drive West, Rancho Palos Verdes

Just inside this 10,000 square feet interpretative center/museum is a large corner exhibit of underwater rocks and tidepools, with animals underneath, that begin to immerse you in the sights and sounds of being under the sea. A life-size baby gray whale "swims" overhead. The 3-D kelp forest, the mural in bright ocean blue, and the walk through underwater cave with tunnels that have ocean sounds, like waves crashing overhead, add to the effect.

The hallway is filled with exhibits including a natural and cultural time line of the peninsula. This includes a shark mural; fossils, starring a large shark fossil; and viewing holes to peer into to see a saber tooth cat and a ground sloth. Press the corresponding button to view the animal's habitat. A full-size diorama showcases a recreated tule hut of the Tongva, plus related artifacts such as arrowheads and soapstone bowls. Whale baleen is in the next display case. An adjoining room contains shells, pictorial history of the ranchos and models and an ode to Marineland, Bubbles (the pilot whale), and Shamu. This area has feeding buckets from Marineland, pictures, uniforms, and gift shop items.

Next, lift the flaps on the model whale to see pictures of a whale's insides. See how different whales measure up when compared side to side. The adjacent room contains models of dolphins and porpoises, part of a gray whale's cranium, and a huge try pot for rendering blubber. Objects made from whales include a piece of Eskimo armor (made of baleen), an umbrella with a baleen handle, a bracelet, Eskimo goggles, wolf whirlers, candles from sperm whale blubber, whale oil soap, and a whale's eye (made out of a whale's eye).

Enjoy a walk on the beautiful grounds. This gorgeous viewpoint of the ocean, the sailboats, and beyond is also a premier whale watching site during the annual migration of the Pacific gray whale from late December through mid-April. Enjoy a picnic lunch in the grassy grove surrounded by palm, pine, and other trees. Kids will like the waist-high rock wall encircling the south end of the park. Walk a paved pathway to the lighthouse. And yes, you'll hear the foghorn blow about every thirty seconds. (I timed it.)

To shed a little light on the subject of what the inside of a lighthouse looks like, take a tour of the adjoining landmark Point Vicente Lighthouse. There isn't a lot to actually see in it, as it is sparsely furnished, but walk up the somewhat steep steps for a view atop the cliffs overlooking the ocean. On a clear day, this is spectacular. The light still sends out its beacon, albeit automatically, and the foghorn still blows. At the base of the sixty-seven-foot tower is a very small museum that displays signal flags, photos, lights, and other lighthouse memorabilia.

Hours: The interpretive center is open daily, 10am - 5pm. Closed Jan. 1, Thanksgiving, Dec. 24 - 25. Adjacent park grounds are open daily, dawn - dusk. The lighthouse is open the second Sat., 10am - 3pm.

Price: All are free.

Ages: 3 years and up for the center; 7 years old and up only for tours of the lighthouse.

QUEEN MARY   ☼

(877) 342-0738 or (562) 435-3511 / www.queenmary.com $$$$$

1126 Queens Highway, Pier J, Long Beach

Cruise over to Long Beach Harbor to see the Queen, *Queen Mary* I mean - one of the largest luxury passenger liners ever built. We thoroughly enjoyed walking through the enormous ship on our own self-guided tour, using the audio headsets and listening to history and stories that added a lot to our experience. The step-by-step audio guide, available in several different languages, covers everything in and about the ship, from bow to stern. On the lower deck, watch a video called *The Queen Mary Story* about its construction, maiden voyage, and service during WWII. The Hall of Maritime Heritage, a small museum, displays navigating instruments, and pictures and stories of famous doomed ships, including the *Titanic*. The Model Gallery hosts a collection of thirty-seven model passenger ships that span 130 years of shipbuilding. The craftsmanship and attention to detail are marvelous! Inspect another type of model - the *Queen Mary* made out of Legos (250,000 of them). This brick model is twenty-six feet long. When the kids (and adults) are done oohing and aahing over it, they can creative their own model whatever at the Lego building stations.

Everything in the engine room is clearly marked, making it easy to explain the machinery's function to youngsters. The last remaining propeller on the ship is in an open-top, propellor box in water. It looks like a shark fin at first. Tell your kids that the life-size diver in the water is just a model. We toured the bridge, the wheel house where officers were quartered, and the state room exhibits. A highlight for my boys was playing on the gun turrets on the bow of the ship, as they fought off invisible enemies. The view from the top deck of the shoreline and beyond is fairly amazing. The long, wooden upper decks are great for strolling around. Note: As an older ship, there are many narrow staircases, but not many ramps on board. Elevators enable those using strollers or wheelchairs to get from deck to deck.

Enjoy the Queen Mary 4-D Theater where seats move and whatever is on-screen is felt, smelt or dealt to the audience, too, such as the feel of wind, the smell of roses, or getting tickled. These about ten-minute movies are varied such as a documentary on whales and other sea creatures, to Spongebob Squarepants.

Take a one-hour, guided tour, called The Glory Days, which is a behind-the-scenes tour with fact and stories explaining the ship's fascinating history, her time serving as a troopship during WWII, and her glory days as once the world's most extravagant ocean liner. Only on this tour can you see the dining room/ballroom, an original first class suite, and much of the elegant interior decor materials and artwork. Younger children might get antsy.

Capitalizing on the numerous ghost reports, the Haunted Encounters tour is a one-hour walking tour that shows where reported apparitions and the paranormal have been sighted and tells stories about the ship's purported hauntings. Visitors through very dark hallways and rooms (with occasional apparition sightings and things hanging down from the ceilings) to the lower decks of the forward work areas, into the six-story boiler room (which I would like to see in the light), and the swimming pool filled with fog. Other special effects designed to make the paranormal experiences come alive, so to speak, include changes in temperature in certain rooms and the finale - a shudder like two ships colliding and a deluge of water that seemingly bursts through the hull of the *Queen Mary*. This is way too scary for younger kids. Nighttime tours with an emphasis on the paranormal are also offered. Note that these specialty tours are only offered at certain times, so if you are interested in taking one, check the website for a current schedule.

The *Queen Mary* also hosts temporary (two to five years), outstanding exhibits such as *Titanic*, which featured numerous artifacts, facts and stories about the ship and people on board. Another one was Diana: Legacy of a Princess, where visitors got the inside scoop on royalty an exhibit that elegantly showcased nine of her evening gowns and dresses, plus personal accessories, photographs, writings, letters and more intimate memorabilia.

There are several fine shops and restaurants on the ship that run the gamut from the very fine and expensive at Sir Winston's (entrees average $45); to Chelsea Chowder House & Bar (entrees average $26; salads, $11 - $18; spaghetti and meatballs - $18); to a more family-style and family-priced eatery, Promenade Cafe (French toast - $12, build your own omelet - $15; hamburger, club sandwich or bbq chicken salad - about $16; desserts, $9 - $10).

For understanding beyond school books and even good history movies, several one-hour educational tours are available, with a minimum of fifteen students (or scouts or senior citizens), and are a great deal - kids are impressed by the size and history of this ship as they focus mostly on the WWII aspects. Tours start at $5 per student, which includes general admission onto the ship after the tour.

Tips: 1) For a ~~cheap~~ inexpensive family date, come on board after 6pm when there isn't an admission charge, just a parking fee. Although some stores and many parts of the ship are not open then, it's fun for kids to walk around, and the sunsets are beautiful. Most of the restaurants are open, so you can indulge in dinner, or just a dessert. Don't miss the ship on this one! 2) Remember, that you can sleep on board the *Queen Mary*, as it functions as a floating hotel, too, with 314 rooms. 3) Look up SHORELINE VILLAGE (pg. 161) and AQUARIUM OF THE PACIFIC (pg. 217) for information on these nearby attractions. Also, catch the AQUALINK / AQUABUS (pg. 209) for a cruise around the harbor. 4) Check the Calendar section of this book or the Queen Mary website for fantastic annual attractions such as Scottish Festival in February and Chill in November and December.

Hours: Queen Mary is open most of the year daily, 10am - 6pm. Sir Winston's is open Sun., Tues. - Thurs., 5pm - 9pm; Fri. - Sat., 5pm - 10pm. Closed Mon. Smart casual attire is required. Chelsea is open Sun. - Thurs., 4pm - 10pm; Fri. - Sat., 4pm - 11pm. The Cafe is open daily, 6:30am to 4pm.

Price: There are several admission options and I've included just some: General admission is the Queen Mary Passport, which includes the self-guided audio tour, most permanent exhibits, the 4-D movie, and one choice of either Glory or Haunted tours for $32 for adults; $25 for ages 4 - 11. The First Class Passport incorporates the Queen Mary Passport, plus both tours for a total of $37 for adults; $27 for kids. These are the discounted online prices. Ask about AAA discounts. Parking for up to 1 hour is $3; $18 per vehicle all day. If you eat at a restaurant on board, parking is $8 for 3 hours, with validation, though Sir Winston's offers free parking. Beat parking prices by catching the free Passport shuttle that runs from downtown Long Beach - check out www.lbtransit.com for more info.

Ages: 3 years and up.

RANCHO LOS ALAMITOS

(562) 431-3541 / www.rancholosalamitos.com
6400 E. Bixby Hill Road, Long Beach

This beautiful, historic ranch appeals to kids of all ages. The barn has several horse stalls, a few of which have been converted into small rooms, or self-contained history lessons. They display photographs, animal pelts, branding irons, and a suspended horse harness (which is a favorite because it looks like a horse just escaped and left that behind), showing how a horse was hooked up to help plow. Other buildings of particular interest, in this area, contain a blacksmith shop filled with old tools, and a room with lots of saddles and branding irons. A ranch is not complete without animals, so goats, sheep, chickens, ducks, and Shire horses are in outside pens.

A ninety-minute, guided tour includes going inside the adobe ranch house. It's always fun to try to guess the name and use of gadgets in old kitchens. The bedroom, library, music, and billiards rooms are interesting to older children and hold period furniture, clothing, photographs, and other objects. An Artifacts Room is open at certain times so kids can touch - that's right - artifacts! Most of the site is wheelchair/stroller accessible. Ask about the rancho's terrific school tours and their slew of seasonal events. Check the Calendar section at the back of the book.

The front (and side) of the house has five acres of truly lovely botanic gardens with dirt pathways that meander through them including two, 150-year-old Moreton Bay fig trees with huge roots; a bamboo section (listen to them when the wind blows); and picnic tables under weeping willow trees.

Hours: Open Wed. - Sun., 1pm - 5pm. Tours are offered on the half hour. School tours are given at various times throughout the week. Call to make reservations. The rancho is closed on holidays.

Price: Free; donations appreciated.

Ages: 3 years and up for the outside grounds; 6 years and up for a tour of the house.

RANCHO LOS CERRITOS

(562) 206-2040 or (562) 570-1755 / www.rancholoscerritos.org
4600 Virginia Road, Long Beach

This picturesque historic adobe rancho, originally built in 1844, is situated almost at the end of Virginia Road. The perimeter gardens are beautifully landscaped around a grassy center area. There is also a huge old Moreton Bay fig tree with tremendous roots. A one-hour tour takes you through the house which is furnished as it was in the late 1870's. You'll walk through the study, dining room, parlor, simply furnished bedroom, and other rooms to see furniture, clothing, hair wreaths (yes, wreaths made from hair), oil portraits, and a velocipede (an early bicycle). This is a terrific way to see and learn about our Mexican-California heritage. Outside is a blacksmith shop.

Kids can more easily relate to the bigger picture of state history when they explore a small part of it. Ask for a Kids' Activity Treasure Hunt, where young visitors use pencil and paper as they look for particular items throughout the museum - it makes a visit here that much more interesting. Bring a sack lunch as there are picnic tables on the grounds. Ask for a schedule of the Rancho's special family events - they are great. See the Calendar entry for MUD MANIA (pg. 724).

School group tours include hands-on fun, such as candle-dipping and playing old-fashioned games. Students also have the opportunity to do chores, such as butter churning and washing clothes, the way they were done years ago.

Hours: Open Wed. - Sun., 1pm - 5pm. Guided tours are usually given on the hour. School tours are given on Wed. and Thurs., 9:30am - noon. The Rancho is closed Mon., Tues. and most holidays.
Price: Free; donations appreciated.
Ages: 7 years and up.

RAY CHARLES MEMORIAL LIBRARY

(323) 737-8000 / www.theraycharlesmemoriallibrary.org; www.theraycharlesfoundation.org
2107 West Washington Boulevard, Los Angeles

This historic RPM building, originally built in 1964, is where Ray Charles had his office and his recording studio, and were also used in the movie, *Ray*. Open for groups only, the one-hour guided tour includes B.B. King, Quincy Jones, and other luminaries welcoming visitors via video to each of the seven galleries of this library/museum, all located on the first floor. Huge photos of Ray Charles, fellow musicians, and celebrities don the walls. You'll see flashy and classy suits, and stage costumes worn by Ray, in display cases; a selection of his dark glasses; gold records; seventeen Grammy awards; his contracts; one of his customized chess boards; his personal piano and saxophone; his collection of microphones; letters he received from Bill Clinton, George W. Bush, Johnny Cash, and others; film footage of Ray; and more. Touch screens allow visitors to listen to his recordings and learn the background of why he wrote certain songs.

Feeling inspired? The library also includes a mixing station, where creative guests can compose their own mixes incorporating Charles' music; his rhythms and melodies. In a karaoke room, sing along with Charles and the Raelettes.

The second floor holds his wardrobe and current administrative offices of the foundation. The foundation was created to give underprivileged children, and especially those with hearing difficulties, an opportunity to experience music and gain confidence in their abilities. *Let the Good Times Roll.*

Hours: Tours are offered Mon. - Thurs. from 9am - 4pm by appointment only, for groups between 10 - 25 people.
Price: Free
Ages: 7 years and up.

RAYMOND M. ALF MUSEUM

(909) 624-2798 / www.alfmuseum.org; www.dinosaurjoe.com
1175 W. Baseline Road on the campus of the Webb Schools, Claremont
$$$

Make no bones about it, this unique, circular museum displays dinosaur skeletons, trackways, fossils, and archaeological finds from all over the world often displayed in front of wall murals. See the complete (and very large) skeletal cast of the Allosaurus fragilis (how do you measure up?), the skull of a Tyrannosaurus rex, a giant fossil alligator skull, dinosaur eggs, saber toothed cats, three-toed horses, and more. A kid's area has computer games, books, dinosaur puzzles, and a small sandpit for archaeologists-in-training to "dig" for fossils (and they are guaranteed to find them - not quite like being out in the field). The touch table has mastodon tusks, vertebrae, rocks, and a fossilized turtle shell, which is surprisingly heavy.

The downstairs room, Hall of Footprints, consists mainly of trackways, which are rock slabs with castings of dinosaur, camel, the only known trackway of a "bear-dog" carnivore, and horse, plus extinct spiders and scorpions. The trackways are displayed on the walls, around the room, and under glass-encased coffee tables (albeit, priceless ones). Footprints in the Sands of Time is an unusually large rock slab containing numerous reptile footprints that is reportedly 250 million years old. Video and exhibits describe how trackways are formed and studied, including field research and curation. Visitors can also view behind-the-scenes via windows cut into the fossil preparation lab and through to the center storage area where students work on specimens.

Good-sized rock and mineral specimens, like geodes and petrified wood, abound, as do fossils such as mammoth molars and fern imbedded in rock. Have your kids look at the rocks and ask them if they know the difference between a fossil and a mineral.

This museum is great for older kids who are interested in paleontology, or for younger ones to just see the sheer size of some of the animals from long ago. Two-hour school/group tours are offered at 9:30am, with reservations, for second through fourth graders. Ask about research expeditions, which combine fossil collecting and camping, are available for high school students during summertime, and how highschoolers can work in the lab to get hands-on experience.

Hours: The museum is open Mon. - Fri., 8am - 4pm; Sat., 1pm - 4pm. Closed Sun., during school breaks, July 4th, Thanksgiving weekend, and between Christmas Eve and New Year's day.

Price: $9 for adults: $7 for seniors, students and ages 5 - 18; children 4 and under are free. Cash or checks, only. Tours are $75 for up to 30 students.

Ages: 4 years and up.

RIPLEY'S BELIEVE IT OR NOT! ODDITORIUM

(323) 466-6335 / www.ripleys.com $$$$

6780 Hollywood Boulevard, Hollywood

As a reporter, Robert Ripley traveled all over the globe visiting over 200 countries and meeting with kings and queens, cannibal chieftains, and tribesmen to collect interesting, humorous, and bizarre items and facts. This two-story museum displays nearly 300 unusual and amazing items and facts collected from around the world - pictures, life-size models, special effects, statues, and assorted odd artifacts, in fifteen themed galleries. Just to mention a few of them, you'll see a portrait of Michael Jackson made out of candy; bowls made from skulls; a two-trunk elephant; a Bigfoot (perhaps) footprint; a twelve-foot tall Transformer sculpture made of scrap car parts; an authentic vampire killing kit; Marilyn Monroe made from a quarter million shredded dollars (and other Marilyn items, such as a portrait made of nail polish and one of her sweaters); Duct tape "art"; a two-headed goat; a 1950's prop Ray Gun from a sci-fi movie; a genuine shrunken head; and the world's largest tire (nearly 12 feet tall). Whew! My son, Bryce, summed up the exhibits best by saying, "They're kind of cool and kind of gross."

There are also videos throughout the museum that show amazing feats such as unusual body contortions, swallowing razor blades, and more. (Don't try these activities at home.) There is a small optical illusion room that also contains old-time, coin-operated machines featuring fortune tellers, bars to squeeze to test your strength, and more. At the Smash and Dash room, it's you vs. time when you test your reflexes as buttons light up and buzz, and you dash around the room to hit them in the right order before you are buzzed out - $2. Warning - If you take an inquisitive child who can't read the explanations to this museum, be prepared to read a lot of information and answer a lot of questions! Note: Look up HOLLYWOOD - the downtown tourist mecca (pg. 171) for details on other close-by Hollywood museums and attractions.

Hours: Open daily, 10am - midnight.

Price: $22.99 for adults; $11.99 for ages 3 - 11; children 2 and under are free. Combo tickets for Ripley's, HOLLYWOOD WAX MUSEUM (pg. 120) and GUINNESS WORLD OF RECORDS MUSEUM (pg. 116) are $35.99 for adults; $19.99 for kids.

Ages: 5 years and up.

SANTA MONICA HISTORY MUSEUM

(310) 395-2290 / www.santamonicahistory.org $$

1350 7th Street next to the Santa Monica Public Library, Santa Monica

This museum is small, but interesting to explore. The first room features rotating exhibits. The main room has a few sides rooms that, along with several information panels, contain old dolls and vintage dresses; an old movie camera and some props; bathing suits from yesterday in front of photographs from that time period; the Pacific Ocean Park wheel; very old barbells used on the original Muscle Beach; a player piano; a huge fiberglass seahorse (from the Park, too); a replicated section of a Douglas C-47 aircraft to walk into; skateboards from Z-Boys; "stylish" Hotdog on a Stick outfits; and a room dedicated to the local Outlook Newspaper (1875 to 1998), detailing the history of the area and beyond. In this room, you can use a green screen and camera to take a picture of yourself in a scene from Santa Monica's past. With the "Then & Now" exhibit use a touchscreen to bring up various locations to see the landscape change from then to now. This room also has an old school desk and typewriter. The last small room is a Research Library.

Docent-led school tours are free. Adult group tours are available for $5 per person. Free Craft and Story workshops for kids are held on the second Saturday of each month from 10:30am to 11:30am. Note that this museum is adjacent to the Santa Monica Public Library. The complex also has a small, but lovely courtyard and a cafe.

Hours: Open Tues. and Thurs., 12pm – 8pm; Wed., Fri., Sat., 10am – 5pm. Closed Sun., Mon. and holidays.
Price: $10 for adults; $15 for two adults; $5 for seniors; children 11 and under and veterans with ID are free. Metered parking on the street, or park underground near the Santa Monica Public Library for $1 for the first hour.
Ages: 7 years and up.

SAXON AEROSPACE MUSEUM

www.saxonaerospacemuseum.com
26922 Twenty Mule Team Road, Boron

The F-4 fighter, Saab 35 Draken, and a few other planes outside lets you know you've reached the right destination. The museum was built to look like a hangar and the artifacts kind of packed inside all reflect aviation interests. There are several models, some experimental aircraft, a replica of the Voyager, a few computers with aeronautic programs, uniforms, lots of pictures, a rocket engine, missiles, and other interesting exhibits to look at and learn about. Come for a tour or explore it on your own. Just across the street is a small park with a roadside display that includes an antique fire engine. Make sure to visit the adjacent TWENTY MULE TEAM MUSEUM (pg. 155) and the nearby BORAX VISITOR CENTER (pg. 100).

Hours: Open Wed., 10am - 4pm. It might be open other days, depending on volunteer staff; call first.
Price: Free; donations appreciated.
Ages: 4 years and up.

SKIRBALL CULTURAL CENTER

(310) 440-4500 / www.skirball.org
2701 N. Sepulveda Boulevard, Los Angeles

$$$

This architectural gem of a cultural center tells the story of the Jewish people, from post-biblical days and journeys, to present day life in America. The core exhibit, Visions and Values, features objects from the museum's permanent collection and traces the history, accomplishments, and values of the Jewish people over 4,000 years. Exhibits include ancient and modern artifacts, photographs, art, film, a recreation of an immigrant's kitchen, and video screenings all housed in a building beautifully designed with archways and high-ceilings. The variety of the unique Torah mantles and Hanukkah lamps on display is outstanding. One of our favorite menorahs has each of its eight branches fashioned like the Statute of Liberty.

The Liberty Gallery features a reproduction of the hand and torch of the Statue of Liberty at seventy percent of full scale. It's huge! This room also contains documents from past United States Presidents that supported nondiscrimination, including a display paying homage to President Lincoln. This section contains cases filled with personal belongings of Jewish immigrants, too - clothing, shoes, mugs, toiletries, and more.

Rotating exhibits have featured Jewish holidays and the memorabilia that aids the rich traditions; Einstein - the Man and His Science; Jewish Life in Ancient Egypt; a room set for the Sabbath; and the altar and front portion of a beautiful temple. The third floor of Winnick Hall is also a venue for major traveling exhibitions.

The stairway heading down to the Archaeology Discovery Center is lined with ancient, palm-sized oil lamps. The centerpiece of this small room is a tomb in a rock with ledges that contain pottery. Surrounding the rock tomb are displays that show what objects remain intact over centuries; a table to see the Hebrew alphabet and do some rubbings; and a computer game called Dig It! Check out a free gallery kit, geared for ages 4 to 8, which contains games, books, related objects, and activity cards that motivate children to investigate the items in the galleries.

The much acclaimed (and rightly so!) main destination for kids (and adults) is the area adjacent to the archaeology room - Noah's Ark. WOW! FANTASTIC! I can try to describe it to you, but this truly is a must-see. A metal-framed Asian elephant, also comprised of Thai rain drums and vegetable steamers, stands just inside this gallery alongside zebras that have piano keyboards for manes and black and white wind turbines for bodies. The whimsical, hand-crafted, life-size animals in this incredible menagerie were created from recycled and found materials and put together in the most innovative manner. Before you enter the wooden ark, made of almost Biblical proportions, interact with some of the animals outside by tugging on the pulley to make the coyote throw back his head and howl; manipulating bars to make the gigantic giraffe's neck move; sitting on the wooden camels; and loading small foam animals on a conveyor belt and turning a wheel so they go up to the ark, two by two. Also, help recreate (kind of) the epic storm and flood by pushing a button to watch torrential rain fall upon a mini ark in a glass display and spinning a wheel to watch leaves in a tube swirl around from the wind. Note the striking animal and plant life silhouettes on the walls and how several animals are peering and hanging out of the ark openings.

Inside the ark are numerous more animals to see and things to do. See kiwi birds made of oil cans; a chicken with a red cowboy boot body; a turtle with basketball skins for his shell; plus crocodiles (accompanied by rubber poop), aardvarks, owls, penguins, walruses, sheep, lions, and just about every other animal God created - 350 in all, although

God may have created more than that. Guests are invited to look at, touch, sit on, and play with the animals, including all the stuffed animals and puppets. They can also climb up and down cargo ladders, crawl in and through rope tunnels in the ark rafters, and explore nooks and crannies, while hopefully gaining a sense of taking care of the animals while playing house (or playing ark, as the case may be). Don't forget to peer into the small room with corn on its walls and slide open the ceiling - it reveals tiers of fake food for storage.

Once through the ark, the adjacent large room has a real rainbow prism on the wall and a (fake) dove with an olive branch hanging from the ceiling. Storytelling, puppetry, and making crafts are offered here. There is also a small play area on the carpet for younger kids.

Outside, in the arroyo garden over a wooden bridge, is a short pathway leading to and around an arched metal sculpture that is reminiscent of a rainbow (that's horizontal, not vertical) which emits mist on hot days - look for the rainbows formed from the water (and get just a little wet).

There are numerous educational opportunities available at the Skirball, such as Immigration Journeys, performing arts programs, teen open mic night, speciality tours/programs, concerts, family musical matinees, and an archaeology study where students go outside and excavate roads, walls, an altar, and more, at a small mock dig site. Make sure you ask if a film is playing on the day of your visit as many classics are shown. Weekends during the summer, check out the family programs at the amphitheater - storytelling, magic acts, live animals, and more.

Zeidler's Cafe is a full-service restaurant within the center that offers reasonable prices for lunch or for afternoon coffee. Menu choices include pizza, pasta, sandwiches, omelettes, salads, fish, house-baked breads, and chocolate desserts. The lovely courtyard just outside the cafe is a pleasant place to take a break and to gaze at the reflecting pool.

As you enter and exit the Skirball Center you'll see, etched in stone, words fit for everyone - "Go forth . . . and be a blessing to the world." (Genesis 12: 1 - 3)

Hours: Open Tues. - Fri., noon - 5pm; Sat. - Sun., 10am -5pm. Closed Mon., 4th of July, Yom Kippur, Thanksgiving and Christmas. Noah's Ark has ticketed, timed entry, for up to two hours. While walk-up tickets might be available, getting advance tickets is highly recommended on weekends, school holidays, and Thursdays. Same-day advance tickets are not available.

Price: $12 for adults; $9 for seniors and students; $7 for ages 2 - 12; ages under 2 are free. Admission is free on Thurs. (Note that advance Noah's Ark tickets are not available on free days, only walk up.) See info on the Bank of America Museums on Us (pg. xi) free museum days.

Ages: 2 years and up.

SOUTHERN CALIFORNIA MEDICAL MUSEUM

(909) 273-6000 / www.socalmedicalmuseum.org $$

350 S. Garey Avenue at the Western University of Health Sciences' (WUHS) Nursing Science Center, Pomona

You'll never complain about our health care again after a visit to this museum whose collection showcases the history and evolution of medicine, medical equipment and healthcare from ancient times to current day. Not for the squeamish, the room is filled with display cases that do a clear job of explaining the time period of the artifacts and how they were used - fascinating! Displays include wartime surgery kits from the Civil War to WWII, including an amputation kit and a bullet extractor from 1870; bottles holding salves and elixirs; bleeding bowls; a variety of dentistry drills and real teeth; birthing helps (and hurts); syringes; a collection of invalid feeders designed to provide liquids to patients unable to sit up in bed; lobotomy tools; an oxygenator; photographs; a medical library; and so many more instruments and devices. A fully-outfitted doctor's office and dentist's office, circa 1930's, has mannequins in period dress, a doctor's table, typewriter, and an old-fashioned telephone, plus all the instruments they used at that time. Oddities of medicine include quack products such as snake oil; a Violet Ray Generator (for healing baldness, cramps and paralysis!); artifacts used in blood letting; and a head with an ice pick near his eye because that was used in that way at one time. (Remember what I said that this isn't necessarily for the squeamish?!) Tours offer more insight and learning regarding our civilization, cultures and history via medical advances.

Hours: The museum only open by advanced reservations.

Price: $5 for ages 18 and over; $3 for students and ages 6 - 17; children 5 and under are free (but don't bring them).

Ages: 8 years and up.

S. S. LANE VICTORY

(310) 519-9545 / www.lanevictory.org $$

3600 Miner St. (the end) at Berth 49, San Pedro

This seventy-year-old ship served as a cargo ship during World War II, the Korean War, and the Vietnam War. The large Victory ship is a seaworthy museum that some parts of it you may explore unaccompanied. You and your kids will get shipshape by climbing up and down ladders and walking the hallways through the crew's quarters, past the radio room and kitchen, and on deck where there are guns and superstructures to investigate. (Tell your kids that they are on a poop deck - it will make your outing a big hit!) One-hour guided tours are given by retired merchant marines (advanced notice is usually needed) and this is the only way to see the bridge and the huge, multi-level engine room with its noises and bulk machinery.

Below deck, there are two museum rooms. One features memorabilia such as flags, whistles, photographs, newspaper clippings, lanterns, numerous model ships, uniforms, and navigational tools. The Gift Shoppe here sells wonderful nautical items from clothing to medals to model ship kits. The museum room, on the other "side" of the ship, contains an anti-ship mine, riveting gun, rivets, three jeeps from the Vietnam War (one with a bullet hole in the windshield), a torpedo, a degaussing control unit, and a wall display of knots. Visitors can lift block and tackles (i.e., a pulley system) to see which ones are easier and why, and push buttons on a board that has a hand-held (non-working) radio. Batten down the hatches and be sure to wear tennis shoes for your ship-to-shore adventure. Note that the ship is not stroller/wheelchair friendly.

Hours: Open daily, 9am - 4pm. Closed most holidays.
Price: $7 for adults; $3 for ages 5 - 15; children 4 and under are free.
Ages: 5 years and up.

THE AUTRY MUSEUM

(323) 667-2000 / www.theautry.org
4700 Western Heritage Way, in Griffith Park, Los Angeles

The cowboy lifestyle lassos our imagination. Bryce, my middle son, wanted to become a cowboy missionary (yes, he is special) and this museum really *spurred* on his interest, at least regarding the cowboy part of his career choice. It will also delight fans of the Old West with its complete array of paintings; clothing, both Native American and cowboy; tools; and weapons (one of Annie Oakley's gold-plated guns with pearl grips!), especially the collection of Colt revolvers and of Winchester rifles and other guns used in hunting and trapping, and displayed to better understand the role they played in the history of the settling the frontier. Movie clips, videos, movie posters, and lots of authentic film and television props (including the original *The Lone Ranger* costume and numerous other costumes) used in Westerns are throughout the museum, highlighting specific areas of this romanticized period. One interactive exhibit includes sitting on a saddle and making riding motions to become part of an old western movie showing on a screen behind the rider - this is a big hit. Others include trying out the hands-on sound effects station; sitting on a huge horse statue for a photo op; exploring a full-size chuck wagon and using the tools of the cowboy trade; and discovering the museum via themed scavenger hunts (ask at the front desk or pre-print the hunt from online). The entire museum is interesting, yet keep your kids somewhat corralled as most of the exhibits are not touchable ones.

Don't be a fool - try your hand at gold panning at the outdoor, recreated miner's panning area. It's available every weekend, weather permitting, from 11am to 3pm and is free with museum admission. It's available daily (except Mondays) mid-June through July. Weekend guided tours, plus craft programs, Western music showcases, tours geared specifically for families that are interactive with storytelling, games, and even sing alongs, are also offered. Ask about the museum's Drop-In Summer Family Fun, summer camps for kids and more. The Autry also offers numerous outstanding programs throughout the year, even sleepovers. A plethora of age-appropriate, guided tours for school groups (and scout groups) are a bargain for the insider information dispensed and the price - $2 per person! Tour topics include role playing of Plains Indians, cowboys, and cowgirls; the CA Gold Rush with gold panning; Animals of the West; exploring Western lands and cultures; and more.

At the on-site Crossroads West cafe try frybread tacos, buffalo burgers, or red corn chicken tortilla soup, or a variety of salads and sandwiches. A children's menu is available. Note that there is also a wonderful, large, grassy area for picnicking, here too. See GRIFFITH PARK (pg. 63) for more things to do and see in the immediate area.

Hours: Open Tues. - Fri., 10am - 4pm; Sat. - Sun., 10am - 5pm. Closed most Mon. and government holidays.
Price: $14 for adults; $10 for seniors and ages 13 - 18; $6 for ages 3 - 12; children 2 and under are free. Prices may vary for special events and theatrical programs. Admission is free for active military, veterans, peace officers, and park rangers with ID. Certain discounts available through AAA. Admission is free on the second Tues. of each month, as well as New Year's Day. See info on the Bank of America Museums on Us (pg. xi) free museum days.
Ages: 4 years and up.

THE BROAD

(213) 232-6200 213-232-6250 / www.thebroad.org
221 S. Grand Avenue, Los Angeles

This incredible contemporary art museum houses the vastly *broad* collection of more than 2,000 works and 200 artists; about a tenth of which are on exhibit at any one time. The lobby is very white and very stark and almost cave-like, funneling the focus on the escalator. The long escalator ride up is like going through a tunnel as it takes you to where most of the museum is located, on the gigantic third floor - an acre of art. Art is also showcased on the massive second floor, and much more of it resides in the storage vault/archives. The escalator ride down goes through a staircase designed to allow visitors a glimpse into sections of this vault.

The Broad is all about experiencing art. From 1950's until current day, including Andy Warhol and Roy Lichtenstein, prominent artists' works are on display in classy and artistic arrangements with purposed lighting. Some of the pieces are absolutely enormous - such as a giant's wooden table and chairs (you can easily walk under them); Jeff Koon's blue balloon dog sculpture and colorful balloonish tulips; and several canvas paintings. Art is exciting here and kids of all ages will enjoy what they see, including the cool pop art, like that featured in the Murakami room. There are numerous tours and special events offered, so check their calendar website.

Located next to the uniquely-designed Walt Disney Concert Hall, the Broad building has stand-out architecture, as well, with its honeycomb-like diamond shapes forming the outside structure that allows filtered natural light in. See DOWNTOWN LOS ANGELES / GRAND PARK (pg. 167) for information on Grand Park and all the other places to go within this fairly immediate area.

Hours: Open Tues. and Wed., 11am - 5pm; Thurs. and Fri., 11am - 8pm; Sat., 10am - 8pm; Sun., 10am - 6pm. Closed Mon., Thanksgiving and Christmas.

Price: General admission is free, but tickets are still needed. All tickets have entry times. All tickets should be ordered online in advance as tickets are available on the first of each month for the following month and they go fast. Standby lines on the day of your visit can be long, up to 3 hours on weekends. A fee (around $25 for adults; free for ages 17 and under) is charged for temporary, special exhibitions, though the third floor exhibits are still accessible for free. Parking at The Broad garage is $15 for three hours on weekdays and all day on weekends.

Ages: 7 years and up.

TOURNAMENT HOUSE and THE WRIGLEY GARDENS

(626) 449-4100 / www.tournamentofroses.com

391 S. Orange Grove Boulevard, Pasadena

The Tournament House, more aptly referred to as a mansion, is used throughout the year as the meeting headquarters for committees, float sponsors, and practically everything else associated with the annual Tournament of Roses Parade. Once owned by Wrigley, of the chewing gum fame, each room is elegantly furnished. The downstairs contains a spacious living room, a library, meeting rooms, and the Eisenhower bathroom - so named because when the president was Grand Marshall, he got stuck in here and no one knew where he was, not even the Secret Service agents.

The second floor is interesting to kids who have some knowledge and interest in the Rose parade and Rose Bowl games. Each former bedroom is dedicated to various elements of Tournament of Roses' traditions. The Rose Bowl Room showcases pennants and football helmets from Rose Bowl teams, plus photographs, trophies, and other memorabilia dating back to the first game in 1902. The Queen and Court Room is femininely decorated to allow the reigning Queen and her Court, who attend over 100 events a year, a place to recuperate. A display case in here features past winners' crowns, tiaras, and jewelry. The Grand Marshall's Room shows photographs of past Grand Marshals like Bob Hope, Shirley Temple Black (do your kids know who she was?), Hank Aaron, Walt Disney, Charles Schultz, and others. Out in the hallway is an impressive 240-pound sterling silver saddle - heigh ho, Silver, away! The President's Room has pictures and other mementos of past presidents of the Rose Parade, plus models of the current year's winning floats. You are also invited to watch an interesting fifteen-minute behind-the-scenes film on how the floats and parade are put together.

The beautifully-landscaped grounds, with over four acres of flowers (over 1,500 varieties of roses!) have a fountain surrounded by one of the rose gardens.

Hours: Tours of the house are given February through August on Thurs. at 2pm and 3pm.

Price: Free

Ages: 7 years and up.

TRAVEL TOWN

(323) 662-5874 - Travel Town; (323) 662- 9678 or (800) 438-1297 - train rides / www.traveltown.org; www.griffithparktrainrides.com; www.laparks.org

5200 W. Zoo Drive, Los Angeles

"All aboarrrrrd!" This wonderful outdoor "town" has a "trainriffic" atmosphere. There are real boxcars, a few cabooses, and some steam locomotives to climb into (but not on top of). A few of the trains, still on tracks, are located in an open pavilion for preservation purposes. Grassy areas invite you to rest (one can always hope), play, and/or picnic. A scaled model train takes you for a ride around the small town - $2.75 for adults; $2.25 for seniors; free for ages 18 months and under.

Inside the buildings are old-fashioned carriages, wagons, and some period automobiles. It's tempting to touch the vehicles, but don't give in to temptation. For a listing of other things to do in this area see a neighbor train museum, the LOS ANGELES LIVE STEAMERS RAILROAD MUSEUM / WALT DISNEY BARN (pg. 131) and GRIFFITH PARK (pg. 63).

Hours: Open most of the year, Mon. - Fri., 10am - 4pm; Sat. - Sun. and holidays, 10am - 5pm. Train rides close a half hour to an hour before the rest of Travel Town, and they close during the week from 12:15pm - 1pm. The town is closed Christmas.

Price: Free; donations appreciated. Train prices listed above.

Ages: 2 years and up.

TWENTY MULE TEAM MUSEUM

(760) 762-5810 / www.borax.com

26962 Twenty Mule Team Road, Boron

This small-town museum is built around its claim to fame - the Twenty Mule Team wagons. Beginning in 1883, these wagons were used for five years to haul borate ore 165 miles through the desert and rocky outcroppings, from Death Valley to the Mojave railhead. The museum displays the history of the surrounding area from the late nineteenth century up to the present day via enlarged photographs, a continuously running video, and four small rooms that contain artifacts. Some of the items on exhibit include samples of kernite and borate ore (components of Borax); mining equipment, such as replica scale mine cars, and caps that held candlesticks and lamps; models of planes tested at Edwards Air Force Base; clothing worn during the turn-of-the-century; a man-pulled fire wagon, and handcuffs and prison garb from the nearby federal prison. A small kitchen displays household items, and a beauty shop, circa 1930, which has tools of the trade and period-dressed mannequins. A big hit is the animated mule team.

Stroll around outside to see more exhibits, such as rusty agricultural and mining equipment, a large granite boulder with holes (it was used for drilling contests), water pumps, an ore bucket, a surrey, and a miner's shack. There is also a shade area with a few picnic tables. Just across the street is a small park with a roadside display that includes an antique fire engine. Make sure to visit the adjacent SAXON AEROSPACE MUSEUM (pg. 151) and the nearby BORAX VISITOR CENTER (pg. 100).

Hours: Open daily, 10am - 4pm. Closed most major holidays.

Price: Free; donations appreciated.

Ages: 4 years and up.

USS IOWA

(877) 446-9261 or (310) 971-4462 / www.pacificbattleship.com $$$$

250 S. Harbor Boulevard, San Pedro

Built in 1940, this Goliath battleship, once home to over 2,700 military personnel, served in WWII, the Korean War and Cold War. Her nickname was the "World's Greatest Naval Ship" because of her heavy armor, fast speed, longevity, and because of her big guns: Nine, 16 in (in diameter) Mark 7 guns/turrets; twelve, 5 in. Mark 12 guns; thirty-two Tomahawk cruise missile launchers; sixteen harpoon anti-ship missile launchers; and four, 20 mm/76 cruise missile defense phalanx guns. With its more than fifty years of service, including hosting three U.S. Presidents, when you tour the ship, you tour history.

Board the gangway to the wooden decks of the ship to begin your adventure where you'll see the guns and all other parts of the five-levels of ship up close. Although you explore the ship on a self-guided tour, there are explanatory placards everywhere and former shipmates stationed throughout to answer questions and dispense intriguing, behind-the-scenes information. The kids can get more involved, too, with a scavenger hunt around the ship and looking for picture of Victory, the mascot dog, posted in various places.

Much of the ship is outdoor exploration, so dress accordingly, and enjoy views of the harbor. You will climb up and down several narrow and steep ladders (the ship is in process of becoming more stroller and ADA accessible); step up and go through hatch doors; stroll past (unarmed) missiles and launchers; walk through the Captain's room (where FDR once stayed) which boasts the only bathtub at sea; walk through the enlisted men's very tight quarters (may your kids never again bemoan the size of their bedrooms!); go onto the bridge (armored with 18" of steel - very safe for the captain and others to be stationed); meander down hallways; go through the crew's gallery and mess deck; and enter the ship's museum area. This latter area contains information and photographic panels about the *USS Iowa*; a tribute to

Pearl Harbor including a naval uniform, newspaper headlines, and other artifacts from that era; and a theater showing Iowa's history and its tows into L.A.

Check out the great gift shop on board! Also, check out the website calendar as there are sooooo many fun offerings and special events throughout the year such as a sleepover with a behind-the-scenes tour that includes dinner and breakfast, offered for groups of 25 or more; curator tours focusing on engineering; STEAM programs; and special holiday happenings, especially at Christmas. And look up San Pedro in the Index by City in the back of the book to see other close-by attractions.

Hours: Open daily, 10am - 5pm (last entry at 4pm). Closed Thanksgiving and Christmas Day.
Price: $19.95 for adults; $16.95 for active military and seniors; $11.95 for ages 6 - 11 years; children 5 and under are free. Order online tickets at a discount. Parking is free for the first hour; $2 each additional hour, max of $18.
Ages: 5 years and up.

VISTA DEL LAGO VISITORS CENTER

(661) 294-0219 / www.water.ca.gov/recreation   !
Vista Del Lago Road, Gorman

Overlooking Pyramid Lake via a view from the balcony, is a hexagon-shaped building showcasing California's liquid gold - water. This surprisingly interesting museum features many educational and interactive exhibits that show the State Water Project's water supply and delivery systems throughout California. Audio tours are available at no cost. Step on special scales in the first room and find out how much of your body is composed of water (60%), and how much you actually weigh. (Or, skip this exhibit.) Video presentations, projected on a giant map of California, and information panels point out that although water is abundant in the north, most of the population is in the south, so we need ways to transport it down. Learn how water is treated before it is delivered to homes and how it is tested for quality. The ancient waters diorama shows how water systems used to be and work. The Nasa-created, interactive globe shows water cycles all over the world. Thirsty yet? Streamline your interest by playing the computer games and using the touch screens in each of the three display rooms.

The theater room shows several short films, ranging from five to seventeen minutes, that present various aspects of water, such as *Wings Over Water*. Educators take note: Not only can the videos be rented, but there is a lot of information given here on a field trip. Pamphlets, comic book-style booklets, teacher's guides, and lots more add to a guided tour of the facility.

The Visitors Center is a great place to quench your child's desire to learn about irrigation, flood control, and water conservation. Tip: After your visit here, enjoy the rest of the day at PYRAMID LAKE (pg. 80), where you can boat, fish, swim, picnic, hike, and even camp.

Hours: Open daily, 9am - 5pm. Closed New Year's Day, Thanksgiving, and Christmas.
Price: Free
Ages: 4 years and up.

WELLS FARGO HISTORY MUSEUM

(213) 253-7166 / www.wellsfargohistory.com $$
333 S. Grand Avenue at the Wells Fargo Center, Los Angeles

Discover the Old West in the middle of downtown Los Angeles. The history and development of the West (and of Wells Fargo) are laid out like booty in this small and interesting museum that shares space with a bank. Highlights include a 110-year-old stagecoach, which kids may not climb on; a replica stagecoach, that they are welcome to climb in; a replica of an 1850's agent's office; a mining display with yes, real gold; a gold miner's rocker; a telegraph machine to try out; photographs; murals; and a fifteen-minute film that depicts the hardships of a journey taken in 1852 from Omaha to San Francisco. Buy a pan (and some gold) here so kids can try their hand at working a claim in their own backyard! "Rent" a free audio guide for the exhibits. On free field trips here students will learn about the Gold Rush, and touch gold nuggets and coins; imagine travel conditions while riding on a stagecoach; see and hear about life and work in the 19th century; understand the importance of the invention of the telegraph, plus try using one; and more golden opportunities. Curriculum support materials are provided to teachers.

Note that there is a picnic spot with tables and chairs and eateries just outside the museum. See DOWNTOWN LOS ANGELES / GRAND PARK (pg. 167) for information on Grand Park and all the other places to go within this fairly immediate area.

Hours: Open Mon. - Fri., 9am - 5pm. Open one Sat. a quarter, noon - 5pm. Closed bank holidays. Tours are available with advanced reservations and a minimum of fifteen people.
Price: Free. Parking in nearby lots is between $6 - $11.
Ages: 4 years and up.

THE WESTERN HOTEL MUSEUM

(661) 723-6250 / www.lancastermoah.org

!

557 W. Lancaster Boulevard, Lancaster

This small, quaint Western Hotel/Museum has been restored to look like it did when it was originally built in the late 1800's, when room rentals were only $1 a day. The downstairs has a few bedrooms and a parlor that contain old furniture, a wheelchair, and a phonograph that belonged to the last owner, Myrtie Webber. Kids are interested in hearing some of the stories about her, and are impressed that she lived until she was 110 years old! (She doesn't look a day over 70 in her photographs.)

Upstairs is a room with antique clothing; one that is a recreated, turn-of-the-century schoolroom; another featuring Native American artifacts; and one that was Myrtie's bedroom, which displays some of her clothing and hats, along with her bedroom furniture. The highlight for my boys was seeing the vivid black-and-white pictures of jack rabbit hunts. The rabbits were hunted, corralled, and then clubbed to death. Although it is not a pretty sight, it is an interesting slice of Lancaster history.

Hours: Open the second and fourth Fri. and Sat., 11am - 4pm.
Price: Free
Ages: 4 years and up.

WESTERN MUSEUM OF FLIGHT

(310) 326-9544 / www.wmof.com

$

3315 Airport Drive, Red Baron #3, at the Torrance Airport, Torrance

A rendition of "Off we go, into the wild blue yonder, flying high into the sky . . ." goes through one's mind when visiting this museum. The Western Museum of Flight "houses" plenty of model planes and about sixteen rare planes, like the YF23A Black Widow II, YF17 Cobra, a F-5A Freedom Fighter, and JB-1Bat glider prototype from 1942, plus target drones from WWII and an exact replica of the first controlled aircraft, an 1883 glider. Some planes inside the hangar are in the process of being restored, so kids have the opportunity to see this process. Also in the hangar, which overall somewhat resembles a workshop, are displays of engines, an extensive model plane collection, medals, leather helmets and jackets, and other memorabilia from WWI and WWII, as well as a nook that is dedicated to space flight. This museum is ideal for school fields trips, too. For those interested in doing aeronautical research, a library is available. Call for more details.

Hours: Open Tues. - Sun., 10am - 3pm. Closed Mon. and most major holidays.
Price: $5 for adults; children 11 and under are free.
Ages: 6 years and up.

THE WHITTIER MUSEUM

(562) 945-3871 / www.whittiermuseum.org

!

6755 Newlin Avenue, Whittier

Journey back in time to the early days of Whittier, circa 1900. Stroll along a wonderfully recreated, full-size Main Street. The Victorian style is predominate in both the store and home fronts, and in the fully furnished, walk-through rooms. A stereoscope and an old-fashioned stove and bathtub are some of our favorite items. Authentically dressed mannequins all around make the visitors feel a part of this era.

The next few rooms feature an outhouse; a water pump that kids can actually try; photos; murals depicting early Whittier as a farming community; a tractor; old farm tools; and a model of an oil derrick. Sitting on old church pews, kids can watch a video that shows the history of Whittier. The transportation room has photos and an encased display of old medical instruments and medicine vials, plus a doctor's buggy, a racing plane, and a replicated front end of the historic Red Car. Walk up through the Red Car into the children's room filled with hands-on delights, such as old typewriters, adding machines, telephones, and a switchboard. There are also old-fashioned toys to play with and clothes for dressing up. The Library Room is an archival room housing documents on the history of Whittier. Upstairs is a large gallery room with changing exhibits. Call to see what's currently showing. Kids enjoy walking through history at this museum.

Hours: Open Fri. - Sat., 1pm - 4pm. Group tours are also given by appointment.
Price: Free
Ages: 4 years and up.

WILLIAM S. HART MUSEUM AND PARK

(661) 254-4584 - museum; (661) 259-0855 - park and camping / www.hartmuseum.org;
www.friendsofhartpark.org; www.lacounty.gov
24151 Newhall Avenue, Newhall

William S. Hart was a famous western star of the silent films - a bit before my time. (Just a bit.) His Spanish, colonial-style home is now a museum. It is a relatively short, but uphill hike to reach the house/museum on the hill. Note: Seniors and physically disabled people can get a pass from the park ranger to drive up the side street to the house. The half-hour guided tour of his home is quite interesting, as the house is filled with Western and Native American art and furnishings. Kids can look at, but not touch, the saddles, guns and other weapons, forty-pound buffalo coat, bear skin rug, stuffed buffalo head, paintings, and Western movie memorabilia.

The park covers over 265 acres, with almost 110 acres set aside for wilderness area. A herd of American bison roam the grounds (which definitely adds to the Old West ambiance), within an enormous fenced-in enclosure. Their feeding area is just down the road from the house museum. Many deer consider this area home, too. Hiking and nature trails through a chaparral and woodland start behind the museum, and loop back around. Camping is available for organized youth groups here, too.

Back at the bottom of the hill, a large picnic area, with tables and lots of grassy lawn, is located next to a grouping of bunk houses which contain period artifacts. A smaller picnic area is behind the on-site Barnyard Zoo where sheep, ducks, horses, llamas, bunnies, chickens, pigs, burros, and a few deer are kept in pens. Purchase some animal feed to entice them to come within petting distance.

The park offers many special events throughout the year, such as free, family friendly movies on Friday nights during the summer; craft boutiques; Pow Wows; and more. Note: See the adjacent HERITAGE JUNCTION HISTORIC PARK (pg. 117). Also note that just down the street on Main Street in old town Newhall is the Western Walk of Stars. Kind of like the Hollywood Walk of Fame with its stars on the sidewalk, Western stars - cowboys and cowgirls - are commemorated with their name and a brass saddle embedded in the sidewalk here. Look for the stars of William S. Hart, John Wayne, Melissa Gilbert and more.

Hours: Hart park is open daily, 7am - 5pm; open in the summer until 7:30pm. The gate to the animals opens at 10am. The museum is open mid-June - Labor Day, Wed. - Sun., 11am - 4pm. It's open the rest of the year, Wed. - Fri., noon - 3pm; Sat. - Sun., 11am - 4pm. The last tour is a half hour before closing. Docent-led tours are given every half hour on weekdays and every hour on the weekends. The museum is closed Mon., Tues., New Year's Day, July 4th, Thanksgiving, and Christmas.

Price: Free
Ages: All

WILL ROGERS STATE HISTORIC PARK

(310) 454-8212 / www.parks.ca.gov; www.willrogerspolo.org $$$
1501 Will Rogers State Park Road, Pacific Palisades

"I never met a man I didn't like." These famous words were spoken by the "cowboy philosopher," actor, columnist, humorist, and philanthropist - Will Rogers. His ranch house was deeded to the state, and is now a museum. It has been left virtually unchanged (except for maintenance) from when he lived here in the late 1920's. The rustic, wood-beamed living room features many Indian blankets and rugs, saddles, animal skins, a longhorn steer head over the fireplace, a wagon wheel "chandelier," Western statues, Will's boots, and furniture. On the guided tour you'll also see his library/drawing room, upstairs bedrooms, and an office, which are all simply and comfortably furnished, and decorated with a western flair, of course. The Visitors Center shows a free, continuously playing twelve-minute film on Will Rogers, featuring some of his rope tricks. An audio tour of the grounds is also available.

Picnic tables are plentiful at the park. The huge grassy area is actually a polo field. Games are held on Saturdays from 2pm to 5pm and Sundays from 10am to 1pm, mid-April through September, but not on Memorial Day, 4th of July and Labor Day weekends. So come, have fun, learn a little history about a fascinating man, and if you feel like horsing around, watch a polo match. There is also a roping and training area for horses so you can watch them being put through their paces. You can even take riding lessons or take a guided trail ride. Fifty-minute horse rides through the park are available Tuesday through Sunday and holiday Mondays in the summer, 9am to 5pm; fall and spring, 10am to 4pm; and winter, 10am to 3pm. The cost is $75; kids must be at least 8 years old. Contact (310) 662-3707 / www.willrogerstrailrides.com for more information.

There are several trails leading from the park that connect with its "backyard" neighbor, the massive TOPANGA STATE PARK (pg. 89). One of the most popular hikes is the almost three-mile loop trail to Inspiration Point which, on a clear day, gives an inspirational, breathtaking view. Note that Backbone Trail, a trail that extends nearly seventy miles across and through the Santa Monica Mountains to Point Mugu, has a trailhead here. For more information on Backbone, contact the Santa Monica Mountains National Recreation Area at (805) 370-2301/www.nps.gov/samo.

Hours: The park is open daily, 8am - sunset. Guided tours of the house are offered Thurs. - Fri., 11am - 3pm (last tour), on the hour; and Sat. - Sun., 10am - 4pm. School and special group tours are offered Thurs. and Fri., 10am. The visitor center / gift shop is open weekends, 11am - 4pm. Tours are closed New Year's Day, Thanksgiving and Christmas.

Price: $12 per vehicle; $11 for seniors. House tours and polo matches are included in the price of admission. (There is very limited, free street parking before Villa View Rd., just before you enter the park.)

Ages: 5 years and up.

ZIMMER CHILDREN'S MUSEUM

(323) 761-8984 / zimmer.sharewell.org; www.santamonicaplace.com

395 Santa Monica Place at Santa Monica Place, Santa Monica

This fantastic children's museum has a new location as of the end of 2018 - on the 3rd floor of the huge, outdoor, Santa Monica Place mall, next to ArcLight Cinemas. 20,000 square feet of immersive play and learning to cultivate social and environmental awareness and action is excellently offered through the hands-on activities and scenarios, and the wide variety of programs such as arts, music, cross-cultural exchange and YouThink, which reaches students in middle and high school providing leadership, classes, and community opportunities. Whew! All this inside a colorful, creative and fun place for kids to play.

Exhibits at the previous, much smaller, location have included the front end of a real airplane, with cockpit controls, flight simulation, and headsets where passengers could watch a video of a flight to and around Israel and other countries; a theater that encouraged imaginations to reign with its dressing area, a great array of costumes, makeup tables, and props; a blue screen backdrop that allowed a video camera to superimpose children over a variety of locales, while showing the action on the monitor; a giant, neon-lit Tzedakah pinball game where kids inserted disks to symbolize giving money, time, or of oneself (the latter disk is mirrored); a play cafe which had a bar and stools, plastic food, kitchen, and clocks set in time zones all over the world; a market; a ball pit; a mini emergency room complete with medical uniforms, a wheelchair, and X-ray machines, plus a full-size ambulance parked "outside" that was stocked with crutches and bandage wrappings; a place to experience life down on the farm with a wall farm mural, a patch of fake grass, toy farm animals to ride and kid-size tools to use; a space to build a dam at the water table, or just splash around a bit; virtual technology exhibits where kids could compose their own music, play drums, and engage in a musical matching game; and so much more. This location will offer so much more, and better.

Hours: Call or check the website for hours.

Price: Call or check the website for prices. Parking is available in 8 public parking structures, including Structure 7 and 8, immediately adjacent to Santa Monica Place. The first 90 min. are free; $1.25 the next hour; $1.85 for each 30 min.; $17.50 max. Library parking at 601 Santa Monica Blvd. is $1 an hour, $5 max on weekends.

Ages: 18 months - 12 years.

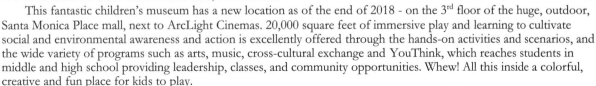

—PIERS AND SEAPORTS—

FISHERMAN'S VILLAGE and surrounding area

(310) 822-6866 or (424) 526-7900 / www.visitmarinadelrey.com

13755 Fiji Way, Marina Del Rey

This small, turn-of-the-centuryish restaurant and boating complex is located on the main channel of the Marina Del Rey harbor. It offers pier fishing (with a fishing license) and boat rentals. See the Los Angeles County Transportation section in this book for the kayak rentals, harbor cruises, gondola rides, and more.

Some of the best things in life are free, or at least relatively inexpensive. It's fun just walking along the waterfront, looking at the boats, maybe grabbing a snack, checking out the souvenir shop, and feeling the ocean breeze. If you want more activity, then walk, bike, or skate along the twenty-six-mile BIKE TRAIL: SOUTH BAY (pg. 210) that runs through the Marina along the coast. (It runs from Malibu to Palos Verdes.) Bring your own bikes or skates or rent them at Daniel's Bicycle Rental and Sales, located in Fisherman's Village. Call (310) 980-4045 / www.danielsbikerentals.com for more information.

There is a lot else to do in the immediate area: Catch the Farmer's Market just down the road at Waterside, Marina Del Rey - 14101 Panay Way. It's here every Saturday morning from 9am to 2pm. See MARINA DEL REY WATERBUS (pg. 213) for an inexpensive and fun summertime water excursion. Visit MARINA BEACH or MOTHER'S BEACH (pg. 12) for a place for little ones to swim in a lagoon. Drive a short distance to DEY REY LAGOON PARK (pg. 55) and/or Venice Beach.

Hours: The Village is open Sun. - Thurs., 9am - 9pm; Fri. - Sat., 9am - 10pm.

Price: Free. Two-hours of free parking with validation, $15 max.

Ages: All

MALIBU PIER

(888) 310-PIER (7437); (310) 456-8031 - The Ranch; (310) 456-8850 - Malibu Farm Rest.; (310) 456-1112 - Cafe / www.malibupier.com; www.parks.ca.gov

23000 Pacific Coast Highway, Malibu

Malibu Pier is famous first of all because it's in Malibu. And it's the pier. Walk out on the long wooden pier to enjoy the view, to fish and to peruse The Ranch, a gift shop that sells sundries, surf and skate clothing, and souvenirs, plus it has bait and fishing rentals. Grab a bite to eat at the Cafe at the end of the Pier. They serve fried egg sandwiches with bacon and arugula, $18; Swedish mini pancakes with whipped cream and berries, $10; yogurt and granola, $9; chicken ricotta and bacon burger, $15; grilled cheese panini, $9; crab cakes, $18; skirt steak sandwich, $21; cauliflower pizza, $11; and more. Or, eat at the upscale Malibu Farm Restaurant, located at the base of the pier, where prices range from Greek Salad for $14 to salmon for $29.

Walk under the pier during low tide and enjoy tidepools at the rocky area on the adjacent beach. This stretch of beach and surf, called Surfrider Beach, is actually quite famous for surfing because of its three-point break.

Hours: The beach and pier are open daily, 6:30am - sunset. Malibu Cafe is open Mon. - Thurs., 8am - 4pm; Fri. - Sun., 8am - 9pm. Malibu Farm Restaurant is open Mon. - Fri., 11am - 9pm; Sat., 9am - 10pm; Sun., 9am - 9pm.

Price: Free. There is some free parking north of the pier. Parking at the pier is $10, Mon. - Fri.; $14 on the weekends.

Ages: All

REDONDO BEACH INTERNATIONAL BOARDWALK, REDONDO BEACH PIER and KING HARBOR MARINA

(310) 374-3481 - marina; (310) 376-6911 - visitor's center / www.rbmarina.com; www.redondopier.com

100 W. Torrance Boulevard, where Torrance Boulevard meets the sea, Redondo Beach

This is no ordinary pier, but a fascinating place to explore with your family! Starting at the north end of the harbor, come hungry because enticing food smells waft through the air. Choose from egg rolls, gyros, hamburgers, or pizza as the international restaurants run the gamut from grab-a-bite to elegant. We munched as we watched the ducks and boats in the water, and soaked up the ambiance. Stop off at Quality Seafood - it's like a mini sea-zoo with tanks of live crabs, lobsters, shrimp, and shellfish, as is the Fun Fish Market next to the Fun Factory.

You cannot entirely avoid the Fun Factory, which is a huge, under-the-boardwalk, amusement center. It is open daily and has over 200 video, arcade, and carnival-style games, plus kiddie rides, tilt-a-whirl, and other rides for all ages. All this adds up to a lot of noisy stimulus. Call (310) 379-8510 for more information. Come up for a breather and take a boat ride.

Back on the cement, horseshoe-shaped pier, have your kids look down at the various sea etchings, including blue whales and sting rays. Try your luck at fishing off the pier - no license needed. The gift shops on the older, wooden part of the boardwalk offer a variety of merchandise for sale.

This boardwalk and harbor area really extends outside of this immediate area. For instance, there are numerous restaurants to choose from, both in the marina confines and next "door" or within walking distance. Check out RUBY'S (Orange County) (pg. 252), a 40's diner; Polly's On the Pier; "Old Tony's" On the Pier; or Captain Kidd's, a fresh seafood waterfront restaurant with a "kidd's menu" and more. Look at this book's transportation section and/or the city index for information on cruises and watercraft rentals, including a semi-submersible sub with a viewing window, and for more attractions in the immediate vicinity, such as THE SEA LAB (pg. 227).

Last, but not least, there are rock jetties here. Deeming them fairly safe for the kids to walk on, my husband and I won the coveted, "You guys are the greatest!" award from our children. Ah, the simple pleasures. A two-mile stretch of beach, with fine sand, is adjacent to the pier and harbor.

Veteran's Park, located just south of the pier on Catalina Avenue and Torrance Boulevard is a large, grassy park with plenty of trees, some picnic tables, and a great view of the ocean. Look for the nearby Whaling Wall. This incredible mural of the California gray whale, painted by marine artist, Wyland, decorates the massive wall of the Redondo Generating Station building located on Harbor Drive at Herondo Street. It's worth a drive by, or a stop and stare.

Hours: Most restaurants are open daily for breakfast, lunch, dinner, and after dinner. Most of the stores and attractions are open daily, 10am - 6pm; open later in the summer. The Fun Factory is open Fri., 6pm - midnight; Sat. - Sun. (and some holidays), noon - 10pm.

Price: Parking is about $2 an hour.

Ages: All

SANTA MONICA PIER / SANTA MONICA BEACH

(310) 458-8900 / www.santamonicapier.org; www.smgov.net

at the foot of Colorado Avenue, Santa Monica

This renowned wooden pier offers a lot to do, including just soaking up the beach atmosphere. There are food stands, restaurants (including Bubba Gump Shrimp Company, and Soda Jerks with its numerous specialty sundaes, shakes, phosphates, and other drinks), and great shops that carry a little bit of everything. Peek in the fresh fish store as it has tanks of live lobsters, crabs, and other shellfish. Or, go fishing off the pier to catch your own fresh meal; no license needed. Rent a pole for about $4 an hour at the bait and tackle shop at the end of the pier.

A major kid-attraction on the pier is PACIFIC PARK (pg. 3). A food court is near the amusement park to service your tummy. A beautiful, vintage carousel is usually open Monday, Wednesday through Friday, 2pm to 7pm; Saturday and Sunday, 11am to 7pm. Open extended hours in the summer. Rides are $2 for adults; $1 for children. Call (310) 394-8042 for more info. The Playland Arcade draws kids like a magnet with its video and arcade games. It's open most of the year, Monday through Thursday, 10am to 10pm; Friday through Sunday, 10am to midnight, with extended hours in the summer. A friendly warning: Weekends in the summer can be almost overwhelmingly crowded here. Note that free concerts are given on certain nights at 7pm during the summer.

Do you believe you can fly? The Trapeze School New York on the pier gives you a chance to practice doing just that with two-hour flying trapeze classes at a cost of $55 to $65, plus a one-time $10 registration fee. Other classes include silks, trampoline, static trapeze (i.e. a bar hung from ropes), lyra/aerial hoop, and more. Contact (310) 394-5800 / www.trapezeschool.com for more information.

An attraction found under the boardwalk, down by the sea, is the wonderful SANTA MONICA PIER AQUARIUM (pg. 226), a place to discover teeming, touchable tidepool life.

The popular Santa Monica Beach offers plenty of long stretches of beach (three-and-a-half miles), great surf, and several playgrounds. On the south side of the pier is the original location of Muscle Beach. (The more famous one is in Venice Beach.) The beach gym is great for athletes (future Olympians?) to train with parallel bars of various heights, uneven metal bars, and ten, high-hanging single rings and several double rings. It's also great for kids who simply want to work out or just have some fun. Across from this workout park, you and your mate should check out Chess Park, at 1652 Ocean Front Walk. Here you'll discover 14 large tables with four chess boards per table and 10 smaller tables with individual chess boards. Watch players of all levels play the traditional game or speed chess. Bring your own pieces and try your skills. Rookie, or not - if you're feeling bold, make a gambit and play on the gigantic chess set with two-foot tall (or so) plastic chess pieces. The pieces are kept locked up so just ask for the keys to the locker at the Police Substation on the pier. Call (310) 458-845 if you have any questions.

Feel like going for a ride? A twenty-six-mile bike path goes through Santa Monica; from the north at Wills Rogers State Beach to the south at Torrance Beach. If you forget your wheels, a little snack shop in front of Muscle Beach doubles as a bike and skate rental agency. Or, call Blazing Saddles at (310) 393-9778 as they have in-line skates, bicycles, and boogie boards for rent.

Hours: The pier is open 24 hours a day. The stores are usually open year round, 10am - 6pm and open extended hours in the summer.

Price: Free to the pier. Parking on the pier (open 24/7) is about $3 an hour. Parking at beach lots (open sunrise - sunset) ranges from $7 - $14 during the week; $8 - $10 on weekends. Parking in Lot 1, just north of the pier at 1550 Pacific Coast Highway (open daily, 6am - midnight) November through March is $6 a day, Mon. - Fri.; $8 Sat. - Sun. Parking there April - October is $12 a day. There is very limited metered street parking nearby.

Ages: 2 years and up.

SHORELINE VILLAGE

(562) 435-2668 / www.shorelinevillage.com; www.visitlongbeach.com

419 Shoreline Village Drive, Long Beach

Shoreline Village is a turn-of-the-century coastal "village" with specialty shops, like Pirates Cove for all your piratey needs, and places to eat such as Parkers' Lighthouse Restaurant, a multi-story landmark lighthouse building on the water's edge with a great harbor view. Check out the all-important candy store, funnel cake, and ice cream shops. The Pelican Pier Pavilion offers an old-fashioned style carousel with horse, lights and music ($2 per person, per ride), as well as seventy video games and skee-ball, air hockey and more. Collect tickets and redeem them for prizes here. Call (562) 980-1415 / www.funfactorygames.com for more info.

Weekday mornings are a great time to enjoy serenity here. Stroll along the walkways and/or amble the cement pathway that winds along the waterfront with its various attractions. Catch a narrated harbor cruise via SPIRIT CRUISES (pg. 215). Take a water taxi or AQUALINK / AQUABUS (pg. 209) to the Aquarium or the QUEEN MARY (pg. 147). Rent your own type of boat at LONG BEACH BOAT RENTALS (pg. 212). Rent a surrey, beach cruiser, or skates at Wheel Fun Rentals. Call (562) 951-3857 / www.wheelfunrentals.com for more information.

Walk along the shoreline to the other end of the pathway, to the AQUARIUM OF THE PACIFIC (pg. 217). Continue on around to a grassy park with a small lighthouse and a view of the *Queen Mary*. Toward the aquarium, near the Bubba Gump's restaurant, is a pedestrian bridge with sides that looks like a roller coaster ride. Take this bridge over the street to The Pike Outlets which has outlet stores and restaurants.

Hours: The stores and restaurants are open daily, usually, 10am - 9pm. The Pelican Pier Pavilion is open Mon. - Thurs., noon - 10pm; Fri. - Sat., 10am - midnight; Sun., noon - 10pm. Most places are open extended hours in the summer.

Price: Free for the Village. Parking is $2 for the first 2 hours with validation/$10 purchase at any store or restaurant; $16 max.

Ages: 2 years and up.

—POTPOURRI—

AMERICAN GIRL PLACE

(877) AG PLACE (247-5223) / www.americangirlplace.com
189 The Grove Drive at The Grove, Los Angeles

$$$$

Playing with dolls has been a favorite past time of girls since time began. The American Girl phenomenon has a place of its own in L.A. It is a combination of retail boutique, Cafe, and meeting place for American Girl enthusiasts. Come visit whether you are a fan, or are unfamiliar with this line of books; of eighteen-inch dolls and accessories based on nine-year old fictional heroines from America's past, as well as contemporary culturally diverse models; and of other products that foster celebrating girlhood.

The main floor is a bookstore and boutique that sells everything related to past and present American Girl dolls, including outfits and furniture, and Bitty Baby dolls for preschool children as well. Several unique features add to the experience: One is a Doll Hair Salon, where your doll can get a new 'do for $10 to $25. Ask about classes to learn how to braid or create fancy hairstyles, too. Doll piercings and earrings run $16. Another, located upstairs, is a Peek into the Past which is a series of nooks decorated as scenes or rooms from the homes of American Girl characters from the past. See how they lived. There is more boutique merchandise upstairs, too. If your doll needs fixing, take her to the Doll Hospital. Ask about special events such as cooking classes, author book signings, and more.

The adjacent Cafe is the ideal location to treat your daughter to lunch, afternoon tea, or dinner. The decor lends a casual, but upscale ambiance with linen table cloths, fresh flowers, and nice table settings. All meals come with warm cinnamon buns. A charming dessert standard is the chocolate mousse flowerpot with a piece of cake and a cookie. Lunch is served with appetizers of artichoke spinach dip, hummus, and veggies. Your choice of several entrees includes a burger; grilled vegetable sandwich; pastas; salmon; pizza; or chicken tenders. Dessert and a beverage accompany your meal. The cost is $24 per person. Afternoon Tea, at $20 per person, comes with appetizers of a fresh fruit kabob, rainbow of jello, and petite fruit muffin; a variety of finger sandwiches, such as soy nut butter and jelly, turkey and cheese, mini hot dog, and cucumber and cream cheese; and desserts and beverage. Dinner options are similar to lunch, with a cost of $24 per person. Note that menu items are subject to change. And yes, dolls are welcome to dine - in fact, the cafe even has special chairs just for the dolls. Outdoor dining is available on the terraces.

See THE GROVE - KIDS' THURSDAYS (pg. 95) or more information about the mall.

Hours: The boutique is open Mon. - Thurs., 10am - 7pm; Fri. - Sat., 10am - 9pm; Sun., 10am - 6pm. The Cafe is open Mon. - Thurs., 11am - 2:30pm; Fri. - Sat., 11am - 6:30pm; Sun., 11am - 4pm.

Price: The boutique is free to walk through the doors. Prices are listed above for the special attractions, including Cafe costs.

Ages: 3 years and up for the boutique; 5 years and up for the Cafe.

BUILD-A-BEAR WORKSHOP (Los Angeles County)

Headquarters - (877) 789-BEAR (2327); Cerritos - (562) 263-2390; Culver City - (310) 754-2619; Glendale - (818) 254-3113; Montebello - (323) 720-9424; Northridge - (818) 772-5587; Palmdale - (661) 538-1096; Torrance - (310) 921-2327; West Covina - (626) 646-2833 / www.buildabear.com

$$$

Cerritos - 239 Los Cerritos Center in Los Cerritos Center; Culver City - 6000 Sepulveda Blvd in Westfield Mall; Glendale - 100 W Broadway in Glendale Galleria; Montebello - 2134 Montebello Town Center in Shops at Montebello; Northridge - 9301 Tampa Ave. in the Northridge Fashion Center; Palmdale - 1233 Rancho Vista Blvd. in Antelope Valley Mall; Torrance - 3525 Carson St. in the Del Amo Fashion Center; West Covina - 112 Plaza Drive in Plaza West Covina

See the entry for BUILD-A-BEAR WORKSHOP (Orange County) (pg. 315) for details.

Hours: Most of the stores are open Mon. - Sat., 10am - 9pm; Sun., 11am - 7pm.

CAMERA OBSCURA

(310) 458-2239 / www.smgov.net

1450 Ocean Avenue at Palisades Park inside the senior center, Santa Monica

A visit to the Camera Obscura takes just a little longer than it takes to snap a picture, but not much. The Camera's building design involves a revolving metal turret that pokes through the roof of the building with a mirror inside the turret angled at forty-five degrees. The outside surrounding city street and beach scene is reflected through a convex lens down onto a large circular table screen. Artists and drafts people have used this type of camera in years past to sketch landscapes. The bottom line is that kids can see a 360-degree view of the outside world and learn how a camera operates by (kind of) being inside one. Tips: 1) Come on a sunny day as the Camera Obscura depends on sunlight to work effectively, and 2) turn off the light in the small viewing room!

Palisades Park is a long, grassy park above the beach, with a paved pathway that parallels the beach. The park is popular with both joggers and transients.

Hours: Open Mon. - Fri., 9am - 3pm; Sat., 9am - 4pm. Closed Sun.

Price: Free

Ages: 6 years and up.

CATALINA ISLAND

(310) 510-1520 - Visitors Bureau; (310) 510-7410 - Descanso Beach; (877) 778-8322 or (800) 626-1496 - $$$$$
Catalina Island Company / www.catalinachamber.com; ww.visitcatalinaisland.com

Across the water!

Catalina Island is a resort in the truest sense of the word. It's twenty-one miles long, eight miles wide, 85% natural (meaning development is only allowed on 15% of the land), only twenty-two miles from the mainland, and packed with all sorts of things to see and do, or not - just relax. The city of Avalon has an abundance of shops and restaurants along the beach and harbor, and all within walking distance of each other. (It's only one-square mile and there is no traffic light.) Come to Catalina to fish in the deep blue sea; take a glass bottom boat ride; go horse-back riding, hiking, or camping on the untamed side of the island; take an Island safari, where kids thrill at seeing real buffalo; or just enjoy the beach and all the water activities, such as swimming, snorkeling, and canoeing in its crystal clear blue waters. Catalina has a quaint ambiance and is a wonderful family day trip, weekend, or even week excursion. The following information covers most of the main attractions and a few of the minor ones.

Walk parts of the island, bike it (pedal or electric), rent a golf cart around Avalon, or take the electric bus, the Garibaldi, around town, which is like a mini tour, plus it stops at several different places. It runs daily Monday through Thursday from 7:20am to 6pm; Friday, 7:20am to 7pm; Saturday, 8:10am to 7pm; and Sunday, 8:10am to 6pm. The cost is $2 for adults; up to two children, 5 and under, are free with a paying adult. Exact change, only. Call (310) 510-0081 for more information or check out www.catalinatransportationservices.com for this and other means of getting around the island.

There are two main, waveless beaches in Avalon - the very long, very narrow, very popular strip in front of the main harbor, and the more secluded Descanso Beach, which is a short walk away around the harbor on the other side of the Casino. Descanso is a beach cove, abutting at the rocky hillside, which costs $2 per person for admission. It is open year round. It has a resort feel, with cabana rentals (starting at $250, with some complimentary services) and chaise lounge rentals ($80), plus palm trees, and a restaurant/bar on the beach ($10 - $14 for salad; $13 for carne asada tacos; $12 for a cheeseburger; shakes and more). Kayak and snorkel rentals are also available here. (See below paragraphs.)

How much time you have in Catalina will dictate what you should do. I highly recommend ordering or downloading the Visitors Guide (at the above website) as it has all the information you need. Consider taking a tour or two as you'll see more of the island. Catalina Island Company, (800) 626-1496 / www.visitcatalinaisland.com offer numerous and diverse tours. Note: Children's admission prices are for ages 2 to 11, unless otherwise stated. Get acquainted with Catalina by taking a fifty-minute, narrated **Avalon Scenic Drive tour** to see the Wrigley estate, the city streets, and an unparalleled view of the picturesque harbor while hearing about Catalina's history - $20 for adults; $17 for seniors and children. During the narrated, two-hour+, kind of bumpy (but fun!) bus ride on the **Skyline Drive tour** with the Island Company tour, you'll go ten miles into the surrounding wilderness area and see breathtaking views of the ocean and coastlines from mountain ridge tops and canyons, plus maybe wild bison, turkeys and foxes. The information about the history of the island and its inhabitants from the tour guide/bus driver is really interesting. A stop at Airport-in-the-Sky is good for stretching your legs, watching small planes land and takeoff and trying a buffalo burger at the on-site cafe. This tour costs $51 for adults; $47 for seniors and children. A similar tour, but in a open-air Hummer H1, so half the fun is in the ride, is the two-hour **East End Adventure** - $85 for adults; $82 for seniors and children. One of my favorite Island Company options is the almost four-hour **Expedition tour**, which includes all of the above two-hour tour listings, but going thirty-one miles into the inner island, plus a stop at the Pacific side of Catalina (a rugged beach overlook), then through Middle Ranch for more plant and animal nature. It also follows the 1800's stagecoach route - $90 for adults; $87 for seniors and children. For more of an adventure, take the **Cape Canyon Expedition** tour, a four+-hour, off-road excursion in an open-air Hummer where the ride is as wild as the scenery, really. You can purchase lunch (a buffalo burger and other options) at Airport in the Sky - $129 for adults; $119 for seniors and children (ages 4 and under are not allowed). Or, take an open **jeep tour** of the rugged inland with Jeep Eco-Tours, (310) 510-2595 ext. 108 / www.catalinaconservancy.org, starting at $70 per person for a two-hour tour, with a minimum of two people.

There are several cruise and water taxi options, at about $5 per person, (available during the summer only), if you want to see Catalina from the water. A forty-minute, narrated **glass-bottom boat rides**, which is *clearly* one of the best ways to see the many varieties of fish and underwater gardens, is just around the "corner" at Lover's Cove, a protected undersea area. Prices are $18 for adults; $14 for seniors; $12 for ages 3 to 11. A forty-five-minute **semi-submersible sub** ride, on board the Sea Wolf, is where visitors use specially designed tubes to feed the fish food, so you get to watch the feeding frenzy. (It's just like the dinner table at home!) A ride is $37 for adults; $31 for seniors and children. Take an hour boat ride out (and back) out to Seal Rock, on **Seal Rock Safari**, where seals sunbathe, bark, and are just plain fun to watch. Tickets are $16 for adults; $12 for seniors and children. That safari is available Memorial Day through Labor Day. The hour-long **Ocean Runner** is a thrilling ride on a twelve-seater, high-speed, RIB (rigid inflatable boat) that heads straight into waves so riders are airborne at times, then land with a thud, and then airborne again; a little hard on the body, but what a thrill - I loved it! Dolphin sightings can be a fun part of the ride and if they are spotted, the captain stops and drifts alongside them. Great info about them and about the island is dispensed. This excursion is $55 for adults; $51 for seniors and ages 5 - 11. You will also see sea lions up close at their buoy hang out. In the summer, don't miss the amazing the Island Company tour's **nighttime Flying Fish Boat Trip**, where yes, the fish really do "fly" across the water, as far as a couple hundred feet. This movement is brought about by a bright searchlight from the boats that hits and excites (i.e., scares) the fish. Hour-long excursions cost $35 for adults; $29 for seniors and children.

There are a myriad of other water activities to choose from, too, besides the obvious choice of **swimming**. Rent a SUP (Stand Up Paddle board) or Jet Ski. Take a **guided kayak excursion** with Ocean Sports, (310) 510-1226 / www.kayakcatalinaisland.com. Two-hour guided tours, for instance, are really natural history field trips because of the all the knowledge imparted. These include two miles of kayaking for about $54 for adults; $40 for children 11 years and under. A four-hour **kayaking and snorkeling trip**, which includes all the gear and wetsuits, lunch, snacks, bottled water, and dolphin-watching on the way back, is $109 for adults; $72 for children 11 years and under. There is an abundance of other options, including classes for kids; just **kayaking**, starting at $15 an hour for single and $22 an hour for a double; and **snorkeling** - rentals are about $10 an hour for mask, snorkel and fins. Or, bring your own snorkeling gear! Tip: Great snorkeling is found at Lover's Cove, too - a protected marine sanctuary just a few minutes walk south of town. The clear waters, with visibility ranging from 40 to 100 feet, is home to undersea kelp gardens and hundreds of fish. Contact Wet Spot rentals, (310) 510-2229 / www.catalinakayaks.com for snorkeling equipment ($10); kayaks ($15 for a single for one hour, $22 for a double); and glass bottom kayaks ($25 for a single, tho a child under 50 lbs can join in on this ride, too, for free). Walking on land is good, but walking underwater is way cool! **Sea Trek tours** allows even non-swimmers to walk under the water, wearing a special helmet attached to air hoses, plus a wetsuit and booties. Walk among the kelp forest, as schools of fish surround you. See the bright orange garibaldi, perhaps a bat ray, and observe sea lions in their element. The actual underwater time with this unique, ninety-minute aquatic adventure is about half an hour. The trek is $79 per person. Contact (310) 510-0330 / www.catalinadiverssupply.com for more info about this and **SNUBA** (a cross between scuba and snorkeling) tours.

Parasailing: Via California Parasail, (310) 510-1777 / www.parasailcatalina.com, offers the thrill of flying - about ten minutes air time - for $65 to $75 per person, depending on the height of the flight, with options of singles, tandems, and triples. The flying and boat ride take about an hour total. You fly off and land on the boat, with a toe dip in the water, if you want. Additional, non-flying passengers are $25, if there is room in the boat. Ask about discounts for reserving online and free flight for the birthday person (on their actual birthday) with one paid 800ft. flight; must fly tandem. Tubing (being pulled on inner tubes behind a boat), snorkeling, and other fun rentals are also available.

Dryer, land activities are fun, too. One of the most exciting tours in Catalina is the **Catalina Zip Line Eco Tour**. This two-hour walking and zipping journey consists of five consecutive zip lines up to 300 feet above the canyon floor. All of the lines are more than 500 feet long and one of the lines is over a 1000 feet long. At nighttime, the heights and lengths sure seem amplified! Ziplines during are $129 per person in the spring and summer; $119 in the fall and winter. Climb a 32-foot **rock climbing wall/tower,** with eight routes, located near Descanso Beach. The cost is $10 for three climbs. It is open seasonally on weekends and holidays. Be a part of an ancient art today by doing the **Falconry** experience. Hold the trained bird of prey on your gloved hand, give signals and watch as he zips through the sky at amazing speed to chase his lure/prey, and then come back. You'll also "meet" an owl and learn about it and hold, it, too. Offered June through mid-September at 9:45am and 11:45am for $89 per person, ages 7 and up. Call (800) 626-1496 for more details. Visit the lovely, thirty-eight acre **Wrigley Memorial & Botanic Garden** on your own (a twenty+ minute walk, uphill, from town, or take a bus up here for $2) and walk the flowers and plants native to California. One of the many island trails, the four-mile looping **Garden to Sky Hike**, begins here. (There is also an entrance to the hike just below the Botanic Garden, at the campground, where an admission fee then doesn't apply.) The garden is open daily 8am to 5pm (closed major holidays). The cost is $8 for adults; $6 for seniors and Vets; $4 for students and children 6 to 12; free for active military (with ID) and children 5 and under. See American Horticultural Society (pg. x) for info on reciprocal memberships. Call (310) 510-2897 / www.catalinaconservancy.org for more information. Get it in gear and rent a **bike** at Brown's Bikes, (310) 510-0986 / www.catalinabiking.com, to explore the island - $8 an hour for a beach cruiser; $20 an hour for an electric bike. In the center of town, play a beautifully-landscaped **miniature golf** course with some really challenging holes at Golf Gardens, (800) 626-1496 - $15 for adults; $12 for seniors and children. Just down the street is **Three Palms Avalon Arcade,** (310) 510-0967 / www.threepalmsavalonarcade.com, with four lanes of mini or duckpin bowling (no special shoes needed), plus a small Pirate-themed laser shooting gallery, and some video and arcade games. Another noteworthy short stop is the small **Nature Center at Avalon Canyon**, (310) 510-0954 / www.catalinaconservancy.org, which has mostly pictorial and informational displays, plus rocks that were found on the island. Push to listen to whale sounds. There are a few video exhibits, a topographical map of the island from the early days of its first inhabitants, and history of the island. Open seven days a week during peak season, 10am to 4pm. Admission is free. Take a tour of the famous **Casino** building, which isn't a Vegas casino, but as in a "social gathering place", which is what the word means in Italian. There are also movies shows here nightly. Call (310) 510-0179 for more info. The **Catalina Island Museum**, at 217 Metropole Avenue, (310) 510-2414 / www.catalinamuseum.org, has a wall with some trophy fish such as Marlin; a few models of ships; old switchboards; lots of ceramic pieces and tile; a digital theater; and informational and photographic displays, plus lots of archaeological material of the island's history as well as one of the largest collections of Tongva and Gabrielino artifacts in the world. There are rotating exhibits such as Houdini: Terror on the Magic Isle, and Jaws: The Art of Fear in Filmmaking. The museum is open daily, 10am - 5pm. It's closed on major holidays. Admission is $17 for adults; $15 for seniors and students; children 15 and under are free with a paid adult. Catalina is famous for its colorful clay tiles so come make two at **Silver Canyon Pottery** studio, just a mile outside of Avalon, for $58 for adults; $52 for seniors and ages 5 to 16. Put on an apron and get to work pounding, molding and creating - the finished products will be shipped to you. Call (310) 499-8799 / www.silvercanyonpottery.com for more info.

To really get away from it all, explore Catalina by **camping** and/or **hiking**. Reservations are always recommended, and are necessary in July and August. For more information regarding campgrounds, for reservations, to inquire about equipment rental (e.g., tents and such), and for bus/transportation information, call (310) 510-8368 / www.visitcatalinaisland.com. **Hermit Gulch**, the only camping site in Avalon, has forty campsites and seven tent cabins, all surrounded by trees. This is getting-away-from-it-all camping, but not too far away. Camp in your tent or rent a tent cabin that sleeps up to six people for $70 a night; fabric cots, a two-burner stove, and lantern are provided. Camping at Hermit Gulch and Two Harbors is $27 for adults; $18 for children per night; sometimes more on holidays. A two- to three-night stay is required on certain weekends and holidays. **Two Harbors Campground**, which is on the other side of the island, has forty-two sites and twelve tent cabins. Four-man tents, sleeping bags, firewood, and other equipment rentals are available here. This campground is a quarter-mile from the small town of Two Harbors; at an isthmus. The seaside camping feels like being in another part of the world. The site is also popular because of its accessibility and water activities, such as kayaking and snorkeling. Two Harbors also has a snack bar, general store, and restaurant, as well as a twelve-room B&B (Banning House Lodge) in an historic building. Call (800) 626-1496 for more info. The **USC Wrigley Marine Science Center**, (310) 510-0811 / www.dornsife.usc.edu/wrigley, is an easy two mile hike away. The center is a marine lab and a teaching facility and laboratory for researchers, but it is open to the public Memorial Day through Labor Day on Saturdays from 10am to noon. Admission is free. Touch tanks, demonstrations of the staff feeding moray eels, a science lecture and a tour of a hyperbaric chamber (unless it's in use) are offered to visitors. Ask about their other education outreach programs or book a private tour with a minimum of ten people at about $5 per. FYI - a two-hour bus drive from Avalon to Two Harbors is $57 one way for adults; $42 for children. **Parson's Landing Campground** is remote, located at the complete opposite end of the island from Avalon. A mandatory $14 additional fee is charged for firewood and water. It is beautiful, and suitable for older kids who like to backpack. **Little Harbor Campground** is on the east side of the island from Avalon. The campground is near two sandy beaches under small, but somewhat shady, palm trees, so it is great for kayaking, snorkeling and lazing about in the water. It is accessible by taking a shuttle bus or an intense hike (16 miles from Avalon). **Blackjack Campground** is situated among a grove of pine trees, away from the water, toward the interior of the island. It's for hardy campers. The surrounding area is great for hiking. The latter three campgrounds cost $23 for adults; $14 for children in the summer; $18 for adults and $8 for children other seasons. Various length hiking trails intersect mainly through the campgrounds, or experienced hikers can do the Trans-Catalina Trail - 37.2 miles, one way. A hiking permit is required.

Note: Catalina's busiest season is the summer. September and October, however, provide balmy weather and travel discounts.

Channel crossing time takes about an hour. Prices quoted are round trip. Some numbers to call for cruise information, with various points of departure, are: *Catalina Express*, (800) 481-3470 / www.catalinaexpress.com - departs from Dana Point for an hour-and-a-half cruise for the price of $76.50 for adults; $70 for seniors; $61 for ages 2 to 11; $5 for infants under 2. Departing from Long Beach or San Pedro Harbor for an hour cruise, prices are $74.50 for adults; $68 for seniors; $59 for ages 2 to 11; $5 for infants under 2. (Tip: Sit on the right-hand side of the boat, or starboard, to get better views of the *Queen Mary* and of Catalina island, especially of the iconic casino.) This company also leaves from San Pedro and cruises to Two Harbors (same prices as above from San Pedro). Bikes and surfboards are an additional $7 on any voyage. All-day parking is $14 at Dana Point; $18 at San Pedro; and $17 at Long Beach. *Catalina Flyer*, (800) 830-7744 / www.catalinainfo.com, departs from Balboa in Newport Beach at 9am and returns at 5:45pm daily. The hour-and-fifteen-minute cruise costs $70 for adults; $65 for seniors; $53 for ages 3 to 12; $6 for children 2 years and under. All-day parking is $21.75. If time is of the essence, take a fifteen-minute helicopter ride with *Island Express Helicopter Service*, (800) 2-AVALON (228-2566) / www.iexhelicopters.com, which departs from Long Beach (or San Pedro or Santa Ana, for more money) - $135, plus tax, one way for all ages; children under 2 ride free on a parent's lap. Once on the island, you'll need to walk fifteen minutes to get to town, or take a taxi which costs about $12 for two people.

Price: Prices given above. Note: See if *Catalina Express* is still offering free travel to Catalina on your birthday.
Ages: All

CERRITOS LIBRARY

(562) 916-1350 / www.menu.ci.cerritos.ca.us; www.cerritos.us
18025 Bloomfield Avenue, Cerritos

This is one of the coolest libraries in Southern California. From the titanium exterior to the fanciful fountains outside - enhanced by oversized fake flowers and a dolphin that looks ready to swim away - to the "extras" inside, this is the place to read, learn, and let imaginations soar.

Inside the library is a large, wall aquarium - ten feet high by twenty-one feet wide - filled with colorful tropical saltwater fish, and sharks! Ask about educational aquarium programs.

Enter into the amazing children's library through enormous model books placed over the archway. There are over 80,000 kids' books and rows of computer cubicles. Special reading nooks are decorated with large fake rocks and plants. One nook has a lighthouse and a little wooden pier. Other intriguing elements in this huge room include constellations on a dome-shaped ceiling; a life-sized Tyrannosaurus rex skeleton on a rock, watching over a puzzle table (ever feel like someone is looking over your shoulder?); a scale model of a NASA space shuttle; and a large (fake) Banyan tree that's accompanied by piped in rain-forest sounds. Toward the back is an art area that has ready-to-do art projects and a geology wall with 3-D layers of rock formations. A corner theater has walls that contain three portholes showing fish videos. Learning should always be this entertaining! Stand in front of the green screen and act out what is showing on the screen in front of you. Pick up a brochure or ask about the numerous programs that the library offers including reading programs, performances, storytelling, puppet shows, magic workshops, arts and crafts classes, and tours.

The rest of the multi-story library is almost equally exciting. There is a multimedia presentation room; a circulation desk built to resemble a time machine; a small, elegant/vintage reading room across from the children's library with a holographic fire; a very small, local and multi-cultural history museum; and a gift shop - and that's just the first floor.

Upstairs are computer stations, reading rooms, and more books.
Hours: Open Mon. - Fri., 10am - 9pm; Sat., 9am - 5pm; Sun., 1pm - 5pm. Closed most major holidays.
Price: Free. Residents can check out books for free; nonresidents must pay $100 for a library card.
Ages: 3 years and up.

CHINATOWN

(213) 680-0243 / www.chinatownla.com

N. Broadway Street, Los Angeles

!/$

Instead of digging a hole to China, hop in the car and drive to Chinatown. Walk along North Broadway to meander through the red and gold decorated stores - I love the faux palace architecture. A few of our favorite shopping areas include the plaza around 737 Broadway. The two-story market is amazing (to me) with its grocery goods downstairs of shark fin, snail, reindeer antlers, and a variety of fish products, as well as the upstairs household items. I judge it to be authentic as Chinese is spoken here and by the number of Chinese people shopping here. Across the street, next to Bank of America, is a shopping mecca. It looks small from the sidewalk, but walk back and you'll discover a plethora of stores, with more that branch off from the main pathway.

You can also immerse yourself in this Far East experience by entering the pedestrian plaza through the large Chinese-style gate, West Gate, with a sign that announces "Chinatown." (This entrance is just past College Street.) Take along a few coins to toss at the wishing well inside that has signs directing you to throw your money at appropriate desires: love, health, wealth, etc. (And may all your wishes come true!) Among the open air booths here small stores tucked away, and stores with neon signs, your kids will see touristy stuff as well as authentic Chinese items. You'll find Chinese-style silk dresses, fortune cookies (which did not originate in China), whole barbecued ducks hanging in windows, robes with beautiful embroidery, chopsticks, jewelry, dragon statues, toys, weapons, and lots, lots more. The herb shops are fascinating, and many people swear by the concoctions. The bakeries are tantalizing. Hungry for something more substantial? Give your taste buds (and stomach) a surprise by trying ostrich, fried large intestines, or other unusual fare.

Another cultural adventure here is CHINATOWN TOURS (pg. 196).

Hours: Most stores are open daily, 10am - 6pm, or so.
Price: Free, but bring spending money. Metered parking is available on the street or in lots.
Ages: 4 years and up.

DISNEY STORE (Los Angeles County)

www.disneystore.com

!/$$

Arcadia; Cerritos; Culver City; Glendale; Lakewood; Montebello; Northridge; Santa Monica; Sherman Oaks; Torrance; Valencia; West Covina;

See DISNEY STORE (Orange County) (pg. 316) for details about this interactive, Disney store - it's a whole new world! Check out all the above malls, some of which have separate listings in this book, for the other activities, kids clubs, and specialty stores that they have to offer.

Hours: Call for individual store hours. Most are open Mon. - Sat., 10am - 9pm; Sun., 11am - 7pm. Closed Thanksgiving and Christmas.
Price: Free
Ages: 1 - 10 years.

DOWNTOWN LOS ANGELES / GRAND PARK

(213) 972-8080 / www.grandparkla.org

$$

200 North Grand Avenue, Los Angeles

The above address is just one of the many for the twelve-acre long, no-playground, Grand Park. I chose the park because it's fun (see the last paragraph) and as a point of reference. This Downtown Los Angeles entry is mostly a listing of a conglomeration of fairly immediate places to go in downtown Los Angeles, either within walking distance from one another, or very short drives. The attractions are listed alphabetically and most are found under that name elsewhere in the book, so look in the Alphabetical Index or Index by City in the back.

Here goes: Angels Flight, Cathedral of Our Lady of Angels, China Town, Chinese American Museum, Dodger Stadium, El Pueblo De Los Angeles Historic Monument, Fashion Institute of Design and Merchandising, Federal Reserve Bank, Grammy Museum, Grand Central Market, James Irvine Garden, Japanese American National Museum, John Ferraro Building, Kyoto Gardens, LA Boulders, L.A. Live, Little Tokyo, Los Angeles Central Library, Los Angeles Times, Music Center, Museum of Contemporary Art, Microsoft Theater, Olvera Street, Staples Center, The

Broad, Union Station, and Wells Fargo History Museum. Whew!

A word about GRAND PARK; well, a few of them. This park stretches from City Hall, where there is a Farmer's Market and food vendors on Tuesdays, all the way to the Music Center, crossing over several streets. Entrances are at the 200s of N. Grand Ave., N. Hill St., N. Broadway and N. Spring St. It is mostly lawn and a few shades trees, dotted with startling pink tables, chairs, and benches. I love the Little Libraries concept - freestanding, pink (of course) bookcases where people are encouraged to leave a book and/or take a book. The Flags of the U.S. Court flies the different flags flown by our nation, along with explanations. One of the park's best features, besides creating lovely respites, are the fountains. The one on the lowest level, called California Plaza, is enormous and, here's the best part - it is allowable for kids (and adults) to splash around in its ankle-deep waters with jets that shoot up. Other notable features - the perimeter, or edge, of the fountain disappears by your feet; there are more tables and chairs here, some food stands, a Starbucks, and a restroom; and the fountains look beautiful at nighttime, when they light up and change colors. Check the website for special events held at the park such as concerts, free yoga classes, community celebrations, food truck days, and more.

Hours: Grand Park is open daily, 5:30am - 10pm.
Price: Free, except for parking. Parking can be $3.50 per 15 min. or $20 for the day. A flat fee of $10 after 4:30pm is on weekends and for special events.
Ages: All

EL PUEBLO DE LOS ANGELES HISTORICAL MONUMENT / OLVERA STREET / CHINESE AMERICAN MUSEUM / ITALIAN AMERICAN MUSEUM OF LOS ANGELES

(213) 485-6855 or (213) 628-1274 or (213) 625-3800 / www.elpueblo.lacity.org; www.lamountains.com $$$
125 Paseo de la Plaza, suite 400, Los Angeles

This attraction is not a single monument, but the oldest part of the city of Los Angeles. It contains twenty-seven historic buildings, eleven of which are open to the public, and four of those are restored as museums. A traditional Mexican-style plaza and Olvera Street are also here. Tip: Read up a little on the history of this area, as it will make your visit here more meaningful.

One of the museums is the **Chinese American Museum**, located at 425 North Los Angeles Street, across from Union Station. Follow the hanging red lanterns to the restored building to see art, history, and other exhibits on both ancient and contemporary Chinese culture. The museum is open Tuesday through Sunday from 10am to 3pm. Admission is free, though suggested donations are $3 for adults; $2 for seniors and students; children 12 and under free. Contact (213) 485-8567 / www.camla.org for more information.

Bravissimo for the small **Italian American Museum of Los Angeles**, located at 644 North Main Street, in the historic Italian Hall originally built in 1908. The building was once a speakeasy during prohibition - you can even see the original door and its sliding cover and peep hole. The tiling and entrance chandelier are pretty cool. Well set up displays celebrate and document Italian history and Italian influences in entertainment, politics, businessmen, arts, vintners, and other fields via photographs, clothing, touchscreen info and videos. Paraphernalia such as Tommy Lasorda's baseball jersey, Valentino's typewriter, a cape worn by Lady Gaga while on tour, Flintstones original artwork and other cartoons from Hanna Barbera, and more are also here. Capisci? Seats are in the middle of the large room to take a moment and to soak it all in. The museum is open Tuesday through Sunday, 10am to 3pm. Admission is free. Contact (213) 485-8432 /italianhall.org for more info.

The circular plaza is the central hub of El Pueblo and has some interesting statues to look at. Usually a docent is on hand giving out maps and other information. Across the way is the **Firehouse Museum**. Inside is a restored, old fire engine that was once hooked up to a horse and a few other pieces of fire-fighting paraphernalia. The walls are decorated with different fire hats.

Olvera Street is one of the oldest streets in Los Angeles. In 1930 it was closed to through traffic and reborn as a Mexican marketplace. It is very commercial and a definite tourist attraction for shopping, but it still conveys the flavor of old Mexico and bonus - you don't need a passport. Enjoy a walk down the brick-paved/cobblestone "street" to look at the eye-catching displays, watch a glassblower at work, see candles being dipped, hear strolling mariachi bands, and munch on bakery goods. There are inexpensive and expensive Mexican handicrafts to purchase both inside the stores and at the center stalls, such as little guitars, leather purses, ceramic banks, colorful clothing, Mexican pottery, toys, and so much more. Note: Kids love the variety of candy that is conveniently placed at their grabbing level. Olvera Street offers several full-service restaurants. A favorite one is La Luz del Dia, located toward the entrance, because the food is good and kids can climb the ornately tiled steps and peer into the kitchen to see tortillas being made by hand.

The Sepulveda House is a few doors down from the entrance on the west side of Olvera Street. You can also enter it from Main Street. It has an encased display of Mrs. Sepulveda's bedroom, and her kitchen as it appeared in the late 1800's. It contains books, a small gallery around the corner with some interesting artifacts from the area, and a mural by a renown Latino artist.

The Avila Adobe is located almost directly across from the Sepulveda House. This is the city's oldest building, constructed in 1818. It has rooms to walk through that reflect the style of a wealthy ranch owner in the 1840's. Some of the more interesting items include a child's bed that used rope and cowhide instead of box springs, a wooden bathtub, and a Chinese shawl that was used as a bedspread. The Courtyard, which is really a packed-dirt patio, was used as a kitchen because most of the cooking was done outside. We enjoyed the side trip here, and learned a little along the way. It also houses a **visitor's center** with maps and gift items. Inside, watch an eighteen-minute film, *Pueblo of Promise* about the early history of Los Angeles. (My kids actually watched and enjoyed the movie.) The Visitors Center offers a free, one-hour guided walking tour of the highlights of El Pueblo Monument. Best suited for ages 10 years and up, it is offered Tuesday through Saturday at 10am, 11am, and noon. Reservations are required for groups, but not for individuals. There is even a curriculum guide available online.

A few other buildings/attractions worth mentioning and visiting briefly are **LA Plaza De Culturas y Artes**, a center to promote Mexican American culture; **América Tropical Interpretative Center**, dedicated to the life and legacy of David Alfaro Siqueiros and his influential mural, América Tropical; and **The Gateway to Nature Center**, with its goals of connecting kids (and adults) to national parks and nature. It does this mostly by educating visitors of their importance via visuals, such as a huge wall map highlighting forest info, plus information, free pamphlets, and nature-oriented books and other items to purchase.

As you walk around this historic area, either with a guide or on your own, enjoy soaking up the atmosphere of a different country while so close to home! Tip: Consider taking the train from your area to Union Station, which isn't too far away from Olvera Street. See DOWNTOWN LOS ANGELES / GRAND PARK (pg. 167) for information on Grand Park and all the other places to go within this fairly immediate area.

Hours: Olvera Street is open daily in the summer, 10am - 10pm. Open the rest of the year, 10am - 7pm. The Sepulveda House and Firehouse Museum are open Tues. - Sun., 10am - 3pm. The Avila Adobe is open daily, 9am - 4pm.

Price: The entrance to everything is free. Parking is available at lots that charge about $15 max during the week, $9 on weekends. Lot #4 on 426 N. Los Angeles St. is $7 - $9 flat rate.

Ages: 3 years and up.

FAIRPLEX GARDEN RAILROAD   ☀

(909) 623-3111 / www.fgrr.org

1101 W. McKinley Avenue at the Pomona Fairgrounds, Pomona

"I've been workin' on the railroad, All the live long day. I've been workin' on the railroad, Just to pass the time away. Don't you hear the whistle blowing?. . ." You don't have to work on this railroad; just come and enjoy one of the oldest (since 1927) and perhaps the largest miniature (which is ironic phrasing) railroads in the U.S. This outdoor, 100 x 300 foot model town has numerous ponds and rivers, mountains, deserts, residential buildings, bridges, tunnels, mining, a circus, a section of the Old West, missions, oil fields, farms, and everything else that a town (or state) might have, and then some. And because it's a garden railroad, the landscaping is exquisite. In fact, school groups are welcome to take a tour as they can learn about California history by seeing the varied terrain and the role the railroads have played. Over thirty G gauge trains can run at one time on the over 9,800 feet of track - that's a lot of train!

Hours: Open November - July, the second Sun. of the month from 11am - 4pm. It's open the end of August - September daily (during the L.A. County Fair), noon - 8pm. Call as hours fluctuate.

Price: Free

Ages: All

FANFARE FOUNTAINS AT GATEWAY PLAZA   ☀

(310) 732-3508 / www.portoflosangeles.org

Harbor Boulevard and Swinford Street, San Pedro

If you are in the area, the fountain, encircled by tall palm trees with the iconic Vincent Thomas Bridge in the background, is worth seeing, especially when the "show" is on. Covering a total of ¾ of an acre, the two main fountains, 250 by 100 feet, are accompanied by programed jets shooting as high as 100 feet, choreographed with music for three-minute presentations that go on periodically throughout the day. In the evening, lights add a little color and flare to the show. Kiosks usually abound in the summer time.

Even without the music and jets shooting, it's worth a visit. Feel like you're walking through water on the walkway that divides the twin fountains because the black granite infinity edge spills over the rim, over the basin ledge. (You can get all wet here, too, when the fountains dance, or just your feet by the continuous water flowing.) Just north of the fountains is a reflection pool and south of the fountains, on Harbor Boulevard at 2nd Street, is a small, interactive fountain where waters jet up from the pavement at random intervals and kids can play and get wet (if mom and dad say it's OK). The pools are all connected by a nice, tree-lined, wide walking pathway.

Hours: "Shows" are daily 10am to 9pm (winter hours) to 10pm (summer hours) - one song plays every 30 min. From noon to 1pm, and 7pm to 8pm (winter hours) or 8pm to 9pm (summer hours) one song plays every 10 minutes.

Price: Free. Some free parking on Swinford or in the lot for $1 an hour.

Ages: All

FOREST LAWN MEMORIAL PARK

(323) 340-4742 or (800) 204-3131 or (888) 204-3131 / www.forestlawn.com

Glendale - 1712 S. Glendale Ave.; Los Angeles - 6300 Forest Lawn Dr. in Hollywood Hills

A cemetery might seem like an odd addition to this book, but most of the Forest Lawn Memorial parks have outstanding works of art, including beautiful works of stained glass. Tip: Pick up a map at the entrance. In reference to the Glendale location: The Great Mausoleum at this park contains Leonardo da Vinci's Last Supper recreated in gorgeous stained glass, as well as replicas of Michelangelo's La Pieta and Moses. Note that many of the statues are naked. A larger-than-life replica of David is on the grounds, as are several other statues and a huge mosaic titled Signing of the Declaration of Independence. You can also walk the labyrinth here.

Make sure to visit the Hall of Crucifixion/Resurrection. A twenty-two-minute "show" features an audio presentation of Christ's last days on earth, complete with various voices, sound effects, and a narrator. As the dramatic story is told, a spot light shines on parts of one of the largest religious oil paintings ever created, a 45-foot by 190-foot painting titled *Crucifixion*. At the end, the picture is seen in its entirety. The *Resurrection* painting, a close runner up in size and impact at 51-foot by 70-foot, is also highlighted in the same manner during the retelling. Did you ever think there could be so much history and art at a mortuary?

Next door, the on-site museum contains stained glass pictures, coins mentioned in the Bible, statues, medieval armor, and an art gallery with exhibits that rotate every three months. Take an audio tour using your cell phone by calling (323) 209-4143. A variety of educational and artistic, hands-on activities are offered here throughout the year, particularly for each of the holidays. Past activities included making a chocolate rose for Valentine's Day, creating a work of "stained glass", making a Father's Day bookmark, enjoying a pumpkin patch, and lots more.

The Hollywood Hills Forest Lawn in Los Angeles has several impressive art pieces and tributes to American history. There is a huge memorial and statue of George Washington, as well as larger-than-life commemorations of Abraham Lincoln and Thomas Jefferson. A 30-foot by 165-foot tiled mosaic graces the outside of the Hall of Liberty building. The colorful, chronological, mosaic scenes of freedom depict the surrender of General Cornwallis, the crossing of the Delaware, Betsy Ross making the flag, and the signing of the Declaration of Independence. Inside the hall is a replica of the Liberty Bell.

Note: See the Calendar entry for a VISIT WITH MICHELANGELO AND LEONARDO DA VINCI (pg. 705)- Forest Lawn's terrific, free, History Comes Alive program.

Hours: The museum is open Tues. - Sun., 10am - 5pm; closed Mon. The Crucifixion/Resurrection paintings and "show" can be seen Tues. - Sun., on the hour, 10am - noon and 2pm - 4pm. The Last Supper can be seen daily, 9:30am - 4pm.

Price: Free

Ages: 7 years and up.

FRY'S ELECTRONICS (Los Angeles County)

Burbank - (818) 526-8100; City of Industry - (562) 463-2400; Manhattan Beach - (310) 364-3797; Woodland Hills - (818) 227-1000 / www.frys.com

Burbank - 2311 North Hollywood Way; City of Industry - 13401 Crossroads Parkway North; Manhattan Beach - 3600 Sepulveda Blvd.; Woodland Hills - 6100 Canoga Ave.

I know this is an odd addition (another one!) to the book, but some of these stores are so fancifully themed in their decor that I had to at least mention them. My husband and boys love to look around in here, and as much as I love to shop, electronics (over 50,000 per store!) doesn't do it for me. I do, however, like looking at the imaginative "decorations." The store in **Woodland Hills**, for instance, is themed after Lewis Carroll's *Alice in Wonderland*. Rose bushes, with white and red roses, and other huge topiaries, as well as gigantic cards "flying" overhead comprise an eye-catching entryway. Other objects throughout the store include a flying dragon, a large "thatched" roof house, and oversized (ten- to fifteen-foot high) figures representing characters from the book. Very fun.

The other stores are equally well done: **Anaheim**: This one features a replica of the NASA flight deck for the Endeavor Space Shuttle, complete with launches on big screen TV's, and other space ships in flight. It also has a cafe that's open the same as store hours. **Burbank**: An alien space ship apparently crash landed into the entrance over this store. Inside, travel back in time to the 1950's with a retro space theme from Hollywood, complete with a Martian-style robot, army figures fighting aliens, spaceships overhead, and a giant octopus holding up a computer display. A cafe here, serving sandwiches, salads, and beverages, is designed to look like a drive-in movie, complete with three booths made from convertibles so you can eat and watch black and white movies on a big screen. **City of Industry**: This location has a factory setting that is a salute to the Industrial Revolution, complete with oversized gears and cogs. **Fountain Valley**: It hails the ruins of ancient Rome, complete with a flowing aqueduct. **Manhattan Beach**: Tahiti is recreated with sculpted lava Tiki heads and its own rainforest. **Oxnard**: Wood decor and wall murals depicting the coastal community, such as Hollywood Beach, and agriculture of this area pay tribute to this town. **San Marcos**: This store is one of my favorites! It is reminiscent of the lost city of Atlantis, with its huge aquarium and exotic fish, statues of gigantic seahorses, marine-oriented murals, and submarine windows (complete with rising bubbles in them) in the customer service section. This store has a sit-down cafe in its center that offers sandwiches, salads, pizzas, shakes, coffee, and smoothies. The cafe's corners are composed of more fish tanks. Any of the stores are worth a stop and peek if you're in the neighborhood.

Hours: Call for store hours.
  Price: Technically, free.
   Ages: 5 years and up.

HOLLYWOOD - the downtown tourist mecca

(323) 467-6412 - Hollywood & Highland Center; (323) 469-8311 - Hollywood Chamber of Commerce and   !/$
visitors center / www.hollywoodandhighland.com; www.hollywoodchamber.net; www.discoverlosangeles.com
Hollywood and Highland, Hollywood

Lights! Camera! Action! Get ready for your closeup of the heart of Hollywood (at least the family-friendly part) that is glorified on screen and in the media, and embedded in the minds of moviegoers. Glamorous? No. Not at all. In fact parts of this area are equally overly touristy and kind of sketchy. But, it's an interesting tourist mecca to see in real life. Look down and walk (and walk) to see **Hollywood's Walk of Fame**, which is actually hundreds of stars' names, each adorning a star on the sidewalk. Bring a pink strip of paper (to blend in with the pink terrazzo of the star) with your child's name on it and place it on a blank star. Take a picture of your child next to that star - he or she is now famous! (It's just that easy!) Find out when the next celebrity will be honored with a ceremony dedicating his/her star along this famous "walk" by contacting the chamber. All kinds of shops line Hollywood Boulevard - many of them offering kitschy and touristy souvenirs. This is a great place to people watch, including all the people dressed up as super heroes and movie and TV characters; some are better costumed than others. They all want to take a photo with you - to charge you for it.

Take the palatial-like steps up to the **entertainment complex of Hollywood & Highland**. Hmm - notice how the facade looks like an old-time movie set? It, and the center's Babylon Court, which incorporates giant, rearing elephants atop columns, were inspired by D.W. Griffith's silent film, *Intolerance*. Look through the archway to see the famed Hollywood sign on the hill. The tiered complex has sixty, mostly brand-name, retail shops; numerous eateries and restaurants, including HARD ROCK CAFE (pg. 23) and DAVE & BUSTER'S (Los Angeles County) (pg. 29), plus crepes, pizza, poke and more; and an upscale bowling lounge, called Lucky Strike, which has twelve lanes, video screens, retro decor, American bistro food fare, and a bar. The DOLBY THEATRE (pg. 182) is located here, as well. Little ones will enjoying running through the water fountain at this complex, where water spurts up seemingly randomly - bring a change of clothing. For nostalgia and a good laugh, walk through the small museum called Museum of Failure that showcases about 100 products that failed along with funny placards as to why it failed. Contact (323) 672-8075 / www.failuremuseum.com for more info. If you want to see stars' homes or go sightseeing in the city on a double decker bus, contact Starline Tours, (800) 959-3131 / www.starlinetours.com, or another such company.

Look up these nearby attractions, most of which are within walking distance: TCL CHINESE THEATRE (pg. 192), EGYPTIAN THEATRE / AMERICAN CINEMATHEQUE (pg. 198), EL CAPITAN THEATER (pg. 183), GUINNESS WORLD OF RECORDS MUSEUM (pg. 116), THE HOLLYWOOD MUSEUM (pg. 119), HOLLYWOOD WAX MUSEUM (pg. 120), MADAME TUSSAUD'S HOLLYWOOD (pg. 134), PANTAGES THEATER (pg. 190), and RIPLEY'S BELIEVE IT OR NOT! ODDITORIUM (pg. 150). For about $3 per person for an all-day pass, have more of an adventure by catching the Metro Red Line subway for a twenty-minute ride from Union Station in Los Angeles to Hollywood Boulevard and

Highland Avenue.

Hours: The mall is open Mon. - Sat., 10am - 10pm; Sun., 10am - 7pm. Some restaurants are open later.

Price: Free, technically. Park in the lot is $2 for 2 hours with validation from participating shops or restaurants; 4 hours with validation from the movie theater.

Ages: 8 years and up.

HOLLYWOOD FOREVER CEMETERY

(323) 469-1181; (818) 517-5988 – walking tour / www.hollywoodforever.com; cemeterytour.com

6000 Santa Monica Boulevard, Hollywood

"That's all folks". This saying is engraved on Mel Blanc's tombstone, the "man of 1000 voices", who spoke Bugs Bunny, Porky Pig, Tweety Bird and 997 other voices into existence. Hollywood Forever doesn't quite give the legendary actors, producers, musicians, and others buried here immortality, but it does give the public a place to see their tombstones and other memorials, and remember them. Other celebrities buried here include Charlie Chaplin, Jr., Don Adams, Vampira, Fay Wray, Rudolph Valentino, Cecil B. De Mille, John Huston, and many more. If you want to take a 2.5 hour guided walking tour and learn more about who is here (and their lives) call to make a reservation.

This cemetery has also become a popular gathering place to watch movies, shown on the side of a mausoleum, and even attend concerts and other special events. Who knew?! Note: Another resting place for the famous (i.e. Marilyn Monroe, Natalie Wood, Ray Bradbury, etc.) is down the road a bit at PIERCE BROTHERS WESTWOOD VILLAGE MEMORIAL PARK AND MORTUARY (pg. 175).

Hours: Open daily, 8:30am - 5pm. Walking tours are given most Sat. at 10am.

Price: Free. Walking tours are $20 per person.

Ages: 8 years and up.

IFLY (Los Angeles County)

(818) 985-4359 / www.iflyworld.com/hollywood $$$$$

100 Universal City Plaza at Universal Studios CityWalk, Universal City

Have you ever dreamt you could fly? Me, too. Skydiving is one way to get as close as you can to actually flying. This indoor skydiving/vertical wind tunnel allows you to fly safely and relatively inexpensively (for flying, that is). A single flight lasts only a minute, so I recommend the double flight (two minutes). First-time flyers will participate in training to get important information and practice correct body position - back arched, arms and legs slightly bent upward, and chin up. (So natural - not!) Put on a jumpsuit, earplugs, elbow and knee pads, and helmet, and get ready. Participants enter the doorway of a small, glass-enclosed room at the base of a 40+-foot-tall, vertical wind tunnel that is a skydiving simulator (i.e., flight chamber). Here wind speeds of up to 250 mph blast through the grids on the floor and air gets sucked up from overhead fans. (Note that the tunnel operator controls the windspeed based on the flyer's weight and skill level.) At first, the wind makes it difficult to breath, but then - lift off. As you go horizontal, for a few minutes you experience the sensation of free falling. An instructor is standing by your side, aiding you at all times. First-time flyers generally don't fly higher than about five feet above the ground, but oh - what a feeling!!

This facility has its glass-encased tower right on the main strip of the entertainment mecca, UNIVERSAL CITYWALK (pg. 176), so family and friends (and strangers) can watch you flying around inside it, and you can watch them. Look into other flying options, too, such as parties, flight school and their iFLY STEM education program for K through 12 graders. At the latter, students learn grade-appropriate interactive presentations with real-world application of STEM with wind tunnels, experiments, flight training and then the best part - experiencing it all by flying! Participants under 17 must have a signed parental waiver. Visit the rest of CityWalk and enjoy shopping and eating before or after your flight.

Hours: Open Mon. - Thurs., 11am - 9pm; Fri, 11am - 11pm; Sat., 10:30am - 11pm; Sun., 10:30am - 9pm.

Price: A double flight for first time flyers is $69.95. Parking is free for the first 2.5 hours for first time flyers; or $25 for the day until 6pm; $10 after 6pm.

Ages: 4 years and up.

LONG BEACH MARINE INSTITUTE

(562) 431-7156 / www.longbeachmarine.org $$$$

6475 East Pacific Coast Highway, suite 281, Long Beach

"The Long Beach Marine Institute is an association of researchers and educators dedicated to bringing marine field research into the classroom and the classroom into the field." (A quote from the institute's brochure.) L.B.M.I. offers over twenty different programs to encourage hands-on learning about marine life and habitats. Most programs are offered for groups of twenty-five or more, for K - through college.

Being on board the *RV Challenger* is a main attraction. This 118-foot, shipshape vessel is the host and means of transportation for several field trips. The ninety-minute Sea Creature Safari, $25 per student, is a popular expedition. After a boat orientation, set sail for adventure on this floating laboratory. Organisms from the sea are gathered in two ways, at two stops: One is mud from the harbor floor that is gathered on board to be inspected and sorted through. Kids love being able to put their hands in this fascinating pile of gunk to find "treasures." The second is a trawl where a net is thrown into the waters and dragged for about ten minutes to see what is collected, then sifted through as well. Kids also examine their findings under a microscope. The Oceanographer for a Day, $35 per student, is the above Safari with the add-on of an entrance tickets and self-guided tour through the Aquarium of the Pacific to enhance your time and learning. Another field trip is a guided tidepool tour of the Cabrillo tidepools. You can also use the wonderful collection of information given on the Institute's website for a self-guided tour of that tidepool, or any other one. Summer day camps are held here, as well as overnight camps and excursions to the Catalina Island Marine Science Camp, which are offered in the fall and spring. One camp session is worth at least a semester of school (in my opinion!) with all that you get to see, do, explore and study. L.B.M.I. will also come to your school or group for a presentation.

Hours: Call for times for various excursions.

Price: Some prices are listed above. Prices are $10 per person for a tidepool tour.

Ages: 7 years and up, depending on the activity.

LOS ANGELES PUBLIC LIBRARY

(213) 228-7000 - library; (213) 228-7250 - children's literary info; (213) 228-7025 - cultural and educational activities; (213) 228-7168 - tours / www.lapl.org

630 W. 5th Street, Los Angeles

This 125-year-old library is an absolute classic. From the unique architecture to the millions of books to the areas and exhibitions that focus on special interests (such as Forty Years of Sesame Street Illustrations), it is an oasis to researchers and readers of all ages who can easily spend hours here. The Language Learning Center offers audio aid and instruction manuals in twenty-eight languages. What a unique adventure for your children's ears! Over 250 newspapers and periodicals are offered in numerous languages. The children's section is a haven for young book lovers with its Old World library atmosphere, comfy furniture and shelves of books that open their imagination to new worlds.

One-hour free tours are given of the library that allow visitors to see, know and appreciate its rich history. Walk-ins are welcome. If you don't take the tour, at least walk around to see the beautiful rotunda, old library card boxes, the eight-story atrium with its funky chandeliers, murals (especially the murals of CA history in the Children's Literature Department), and much more. Just outside are some small, park-like areas with grassy spots, trees, a walkway and a fountain. One-hour school tours are given Thursdays and Fridays for kindergarten to fifth graders at 10am and 11am. Tours consist of a half-hour tour of the library and a half hour of story time, making a craft, or book reading.

Besides weekly story times (for different ages and abilities - check the website for times), the Children's Literacy Department and the KLOS Story Theater offers puppet shows, crafts and other programs throughout the week. Various past shows have featured magic tricks, instructions on how to make a book (followed by actually making one), creating a Lego model, and storytelling with puppets. At least once a month, on the first floor of the library, at the Mark Taper Auditorium ALOUD presentations are given for teens and up. These are free, dramatic readings of a favorite story by the author, or a discussion by an artist or scientist, or whomever, usually followed by a Q & A. Also note that the Mark Taper offers numerous other performances and it contains galleries of rotating exhibits. (The one on pop-up books was wonderful!) Look at the library calendar events for more details. See DOWNTOWN LOS ANGELES / GRAND PARK (pg. 167) for information on Grand Park and all the other places to go within this fairly immediate area.

Hours: The library is open Mon. - Thurs., 10am -8pm; Fri. - Sat., 9:30am - 5:30pm; Sun., 1pm - 5pm. Closed most major holidays. Library tours are offered Mon. - Fri. at 12:30pm; Sat. at 11am, 12:30pm and 2pm; Sun. at 2pm.

Price: Free. Enter the parking structure under the library on 524 S. Flower St. - $1 for the first hour, $4 for the second hour - with validation for library card holders at the times the library is open. For cars entering after 3pm, until the library closing, and on Sat., 9:30am - 5:30pm - $1 flat rate.

Ages: 3 years and up.

MOUNT WILSON OBSERVATORY and SKYLINE PARK

(626) 793-3100 or (626) 793-3065 - observatory; (818) 899-1900 - ranger station; (800) 427-7623 - Caltrans $
road closures / www.mtwilson.edu

Angeles Crest Highway, Los Angeles

Observant kids will enjoy the incredible view from atop the world, above the clouds, and also seeing the observatory, which was founded in 1904. Hike around the grounds on your own on the aptly named Skyline Park, see the towers that house some massive telescopes, and then come into the visitors gallery and museum and gawk at the 100-inch Hooker telescope through a big window. Inside the small museum are numerous photographs taken of the skies and planets and stars, accompanied by information about the photographed objects, plus a scale model of the observatory, and a few star-searching tools.

Or, sign-up for a two-hour, guided tour. Besides walking the area quite a bit, the tour takes visitors into the visitor's gallery and the astronomical museum. Tours also go into the telescope domes to see the 60-inch Hale telescope and 100-inch Hooker telescope up close, once the world's largest telescopes and which played a part in discovering our place in the Milky Way and more. The only time, though, that you may view through the famous Hale and/or Hooker is by either booking a group tour, or by joining in on a public tour, offered a few times a year. The public tour is limited to 20 people, open from 8pm to 1am and costs $95 per person for viewing through the 60-inch, $225 for the 100-inch. "Seeing" up at Mt. Wilson is extraordinary and this research facility, the CHARA (Center for High Angular Resolution Astronomy), makes the most of this opportunity with optical interferometric array of six telescopes, and more.

Via the website, pre-print a self guided tour brochure before you come up. The Cosmic Cafe, offering sandwiches, hot dogs, snack, beverages, and even souvenirs, is open on weekends from 10am to 5pm, April through November. Note the elevation of Mt. Wilson is 5,800 feet and it is often cold, or at least cool, up here. There is frequently snow on the ground in the winter.

Hours: The grounds, park gate, and museum are usually open April through November, weather permitting, Mon. - Fri., 10am - 5pm; Sat. - Sun., 8:30am - 5pm. Closed December through March. Guided tours are offered April through November, Sat. and Sun. at 1pm, and also at 9am during the summer months, weather permitting. Call to make special arrangements during the winter, or for private tours.

Price: Admission is free. Tours are $15 for adult; $12 for seniors and ages 6 - 16; children 5 and under are not permitted. To park you must first purchase a $5 Adventure Pass, which is available at the Clear Creek Ranger Station halfway up the road to Mt. Wilson, or at a sporting goods store. Carpool as space is limited.

Ages: 6 years and up.

NATURALIZATION CEREMONY

www.cacd.uscourts.gov $$$

Naturalized citizens must meet three requirements: be lawful, permanent residents of the United States; have lived here for at least five years; and pass a written citizenship test. Many applicants study our history so intensely that they know it better than those of us who have lived here all our lives.

The naturalization ceremony takes place a few times a month at different locations - courthouses as well as convention centers - and as 600 up to 5,000(!) people are inducted at one time, it can take a few hours. Almost-new citizens renounce any foreign allegiance and promise to uphold the U.S. Constitution. A judge pounds the gavel and administers the Oath of Allegiance and ta da - new American citizens have been born! A guest speaker talks about the role and value of citizenship. Usually, depending on the place of the ceremony, the US citizens and are usually given kits for "new citizens" that contain info, a small U.S. flag, a copy of the U.S. Constitution, and a registration form for voting. Sometimes ceremonies include a reception after the ceremony itself or music, or something celebratory.

I mention this ceremony as an outing because I think older kids who are studying the Constitution or immigration might be interested in seeing this process and perhaps even catch a little national fever. Note that the public is welcome, but they must sit or stand near the back of the huge hall.

Hours: Call for dates.

Price: Admission is free. $12 - $15 for parking.

Ages: 10 years and up.

OLVERA STREET

See EL PUEBLO DE LOS ANGELES HISTORICAL MONUMENT / OLVERA STREET / CHINESE AMERICAN MUSEUM / ITALIAN AMERICAN MUSEUM OF LOS ANGELES (pg. 168) for details about this historic, Mexican street full of restaurant and shopping opportunities.

OUE SKYSPACE LOS ANGELES

(213) 894-9000 / www.oue-skyspace.com

$$$$$

633 West Fifth Street in the U.S. Bank Tower, Los Angeles

Not only is the view amazing from waaay up on the open-air observation deck (nearly 1,000 feet above the city), but so is the rest of the experience. When you get off the elevator at the 54th floor, your first stop is to step onto the glass covered, lit up, elevator shaft and look down, into infinity. Well, not really into infinity, but it looks cool and is a great photo op. Next, pose and dance as an interactive shadow wall moves to form your silhouette. A few other interactive exhibits are here plus several walls that display the development and history of Hollywood and Los Angeles via photos, videos and time lines. Look down as you walk to read interesting facts imbedded on the Hollywood stars the floor.

Take another elevator up to the 69th floor to arrive at the almost top of the building. Outside, protected by glass walls, is Los Angeles, in all of its 360-degree panoramic view glory. ♪On a clear day rise and look around you .... you'll feel part of every mountain, sea, and shore♫... Visit on a clear day to see Catalina Island, Glendale, Los Angeles, the Hollywood sign, mountains and more. Walk around or sit down and enjoy the view; look through the telescopes; make the most of the photo ops, especially the one with the angel wings painted on one of the glass walls and another one at a green screen area; and perhaps eat at the cafe, too. The skyslide is an all-glass enclosed slide on the outside of the building that you zip down on a mat. It is a unique, but incredibly short ride (maybe 5 seconds). Tips: Visit OUE Skyspace on an uncloudy day. Parking right near the building is more expensive than parking and walking a bit. OUE Skyspace entrance is not the same as the bank building, so go up the steps on the side to the actual entrance.

Hours: Open daily, 10am - 10pm (last ride up is 9pm). Timed tickets are available every half an hour.

Price: $25 for ages 13 and up; $22 for seniors; $19 for ages 3 - 12; children 2 and under are free. A slide ride is $8. The Sun and Stars admission fee, which is for two entries within 24 hours, is $35 for adults; $30 for seniors; $25 for youth. Look for deals on the internet and thru AAA.

Ages: 6 years and up.

OXMAN'S SURPLUS, INC.

(562) 921-1106 / www.oxmans-surplus.com

!

14128 East Rosecrans Avenue, Santa Fe Springs

Outside is a replica nose of the Columbia space craft, as well as an array of military flags. Inside, at the front section of this unique army surplus store is a very small museum filled with an eclectic mix of items, mostly from WWII. These include ejection seats, uniforms, a gun collection, a whale harpoon, a periscope, a B-17 cockpit (which visitors may sit in), a 15th century suit of armor, a few surface-to-air missiles, a WWII oxygen breathing tank, Hitler's bayonet, helmets, patches, a Devil fish skeleton, a corner set up with sandbags, gas masks, a display of rations, a B-29 engine, a Dog Tag machine, grenades, field equipment, a Choctaw helicopter tails section (from the Korean War), and more. Many of the articles are labeled so a self-guided "tour" works. Hint - Boy Scouts love this sort of place! The surplus store part carries everything camouflage, plus camping gear, knives, boots, tarps, tools, swords, clothing, and lots more.

Hours: The store and museum are open Mon. - Sat., 9am - 6pm. Closed Sun. Short tours are given by appointment.

Price: Free

Ages: 6 years and up.

PIERCE BROTHERS WESTWOOD VILLAGE MEMORIAL PARK AND MORTUARY

(310) 474-1579 / www.dignitymemorial.com

!

1218 Glendon Avenue, Los Angeles

This hard-to-find, and very small, cemetery is worth a visit if you are interested in where some big name stars are laid to rest. Some of the celebrities here include Marilyn Monroe (who's grave is very simply marked), Natalie Wood, Rodney Dangerfield ("There Goes the Neighborhood" is on his tombstone), Farrah Fawcett, Ray Bradbury, Don Knotts, Truman Capote, Donna Reed, Frank Zappa, Dean Martin, and many more. There are names you might recognize here, too - not just from the entertainment industry. A few of the graves are from the early 1900's. Another well-known cemetery is HOLLYWOOD FOREVER CEMETERY (pg. 172) where you can pay respects to Mel Blanc, Charlie Chaplin, Cecil B. De Mille, and many others.

Hours: Open daily, 8am - 5pm.

Price: Free

Ages: 7 years and up.

SKELETONS IN THE CLOSET

(323) 343-0760 / www.lacoroner.com   !/$

1104 N. Mission Road, Los Angeles

Maybe it's morbid, but my kids thought coming to this tiny gift shop located inside the Los Angeles County Department of Coroners building was cool, in a weird sort of way. (Maybe it's a guy thing?) Park next to a coroner's car, walk into the building, ride up the elevator, and walk down the hallway past offices into the gift shop where an unusual selection of items are for sale. You may purchase, for instance, a welcome mat with a body outline (about $30), a crime scene beach towel ($35), toe tag key chains (and other ones) ($5 each), t-shirts ($20 and up), plastic skulls ($18), crime scene party tape ($6.50), BBQ aprons that read "spare hands, spare ribs" ($18), water bottles ($12), mugs (starting at $12), and mouse pads with a body outline and a phrase proclaiming "We're dying for your business." The proceeds from the gift shop support the Youthful Drunk Driving Visitation Program.

Hours: Open Mon. - Fri., 8:30am - 4:30pm. Closed weekends and holidays.

Price: Free

Ages: 8 years and up.

THE VOID (Los Angeles County)

(818) 246-6737 / www.thevoid.com $$$$$

1164 Glendale in the Glendale Galleria, Glendale

See THE VOID (Orange County) (pg. 320) for a description on this hyper-reality experience.

Hours: Open Mon. - Wed., 10am - 9pm; Thurs., 10am - 10pm; Fri. - Sat., 10am - 11pm; Sun., 10am - 8pm.

Price: $29.95 per person

Ages: Must be at least 10 years old.

UNIVERSAL CITYWALK

(818) 622-4455 / www.citywalkhollywood.com $$$

100 Universal City Plaza by Universal Studios, Universal City

CityWalk is an outdoor, multi-level mall built in theme-park style with stores, unique restaurants, and unusual entertainment. Everything here, from the larger-than-life neon signs (including a giant, neon gorilla - think King-Kong) to the oversized, Disneylandish-decorated storefronts is done with spectacular Hollywood flair, and that's just the outside of the buildings! On weekend nights, outdoor concerts and other live entertainment, such as jugglers, magicians, and musicians can add to the carnival-like atmosphere. The crowds, activities, music piped in everywhere, and rock videos playing on a large screen outside the movie theaters, however, might be a bit too stimulating for younger children (and sometimes adults!). Look at the Calendar for concerts and other special events offered.

Here are just a few of the major attractions along the walkway: Socks featuring everything and anything are popular at The Los Angeles Sock Market. The Universal Studios Store has all the Universal-oriented merchandise you could possibly want to purchase including a huge selection of Harry Potter items. The water fountain in the center circle of CityWalk spouts up to the rhythm of flashing colors and music, and kids (and adults) love walking/running through it when the weather is hot. On the storefront of Things From Another World the back half of a spaceship, which is still emitting smoke, is all that remains from a crash landing. IFLY (Los Angeles County) (pg. 172), an indoor skydiving venue, will literally blow you away. Movie entertainment is available at AMC's nineteen-screen movie theater, (818) 508-0711 / www.fandango.com, and a 3-D IMAX theater that shows both 3-D and 2-D movies on a screen six stories high. 3-D tickets, on average, are $17 for adults; $14.50 ages 2 to 12.

Restaurants and eateries on the walk, including a food court with all the usual fast food places, aim to please any tastebud and wallet, as the wide-ranging food selections indicate. Eat Chinese, Mexican, Italian (BUCA DI BEPPO (Los Angeles County) (pg. 16)), seafood (featuring Bubba Gump Shrimp Co.), sushi, hamburgers, steaks, crepes, deli, and ice cream (at Ben and Jerry's). Outside the HARD ROCK CAFE (pg. 23) is a huge, neon guitar. Inside this restaurant, dedicated to the preservation of rock 'n roll, personal items from famed musicians decorate the walls as do their guitars, costumes, and posters.

UNIVERSAL STUDIOS HOLLYWOOD (pg. 5) is at one end this pedestrian thoroughfare. (Read that entry for parking tips.) The show EXTRA films in front of a live audience, often in front of the Universal Globe, just outside the entrance gate to Universal Studios. Check the CityWalk website to see which celebrity is being interviewed when.

You can experience practically all of Hollywood at CityWalk - all at one time!

Hours: Most stores and restaurants are open Sun. - Thurs., 11am - 9pm or 10 (until 11pm in the summer); Fri. - Sat., 11am - 11pm (until midnight in the summer). Check for hours for individual places as they vary.

Price: Free. Parking is $25 until 6pm; $10 after 6pm. End up paying only $5, with validation, if you see a movie here. Valet parking is $15 for the first 2.5 hours and $35 after that. Valet parking, with validation from a participating restaurant, is $7 for the first 2.5 hours, $15 for the next hour, $35 after that.
Ages: 2 years and up.

UNIVERSITY OF CALIFORNIA, LOS ANGELES / UCLA

(310) 825-4321 / www.ucla.edu/visit

$$$

off Westwood Blvd. at UCLA Campus, Westwood

University of California at Los Angeles is a classic campus with huge old brick buildings and stately trees. I know our visit here planted some dreams in my children's mind of going to college. If, in fact, you have a college-bound high schooler, take the free, two-hour walking tour of the campus which highlights housing, academics, financial aid, and, most importantly, social activities. There are also guided tours for K- 8th graders and other groups. The following are some of our "discoveries" as we simply walked the campus on our own. Tip: There are several places on campus to eat lunch or grab a snack, and since you've paid for parking, you might as well make a day of it!

Mathias Botanical Garden, located on the lower part of the campus, gave us the feeling of being in a secret garden, with its stony pathways through a lush "forest" and a hidden dirt path along a small creek. Trails crisscross through cactus and various other plant sections, all of which are as interesting to study as they are beautiful. The gardens are open Monday through Friday, 8am to 5pm; Saturday and Sundays, 9am to 5pm; closed school holidays. Admission is free. Call (310) 825-1260 / www.botgard.ucla.edu for more information.

We took a free shuttle to the north end of the campus to the Murphy Sculpture Garden, which has over seventy sculptures by masters of the nineteenth and twentieth centuries scattered around an open grassy area. My middle one summed it up best from a kid's perspective; "I thought this was supposed to be great art. How come it's just a bunch of naked people?"

The **UCLA Fowler Museum of Cultural History,** (310) 825-4361 / www.fowler.ucla.edu is also on the north end of campus. The majority of the exhibits are sophisticated, with a focus on anthropology. Older kids might enjoy them. Call for a current schedule of exhibits showing in the gallery rooms. Inquire about their children's programs and family workshops. The museum is open Wednesday, noon to 8pm; Thursday through Sunday, noon to 5pm. Admission is free.

The **Athletic Hall of Fame,** (310) 206-6662/ www.uclabruins.com, is a showplace for UCLA athletes. It houses numerous displays of photos, trophies, memorabilia, Olympic mementos (including an Olympic torch), and equipment used by Bruin athletes who have excelled at tennis, basketball, football, volleyball, and other sports. Walk through Coach John Wooden's den where he wrote, entertained guests, and watched TV. Sit in a stadium seat in the small theater to watch highlight clips of Bruin athletes in action. The hall is open Monday through Friday from 8am to 5pm and every 1st Saturday of the month from 10am to 4pm. Admission is free.

Visit a 357-pound chunk of a meteorite in the center of the **Meteorite Gallery** in the small Room 3697 of the Geology Building, along with 999 other space rock specimens in glass display cases lining the walls. Posters and other explanatory signs aid visitors in learning the composition of meteors, where these were found and more. It's open weekdays from 9am to 4pm and Sundays from 1pm to 4pm. Admission is free. Check www.meteorites/ucla.edu for more info. For information on the **planetarium** and its free shows, look up UCLA PLANETARIUM (pg. 194).

UCLA abounds with other forms of entertainment, too. Check out the CENTER FOR THE ART OF PERFORMANCE AT UCLA (pg. 180) for first-rate theater productions.

Hours: The campus is usually open daily, 8am - 5pm. Attractions are usually closed on university holidays.
Price: Parking is $6 for two hours; $12 for the day.
Ages: 7 years and up.

VENICE CANALS

In a grid between Washington Blvd. and Venice Blvd., and Pacific Ave. and Ocean Ave., Venice

!

Not quite Venice, Italy, but this town, originally founded after its namesake in 1900 with a network of twenty miles of canals, has a remnant of canals that still afford a lovely and unusual neighborhood to stroll around. Waterfront homes, most with huge glass windows, border the narrow, cement walkways that hug the shallow canals. Set in an enclosed, square grid the canals sport rowboats moored to the homeowner's parcels; numerous and variously designed bridges that arch over the water; lots of ducks; and a multitude of plants, making the area very picturesque. One-way streets and no parking make this a walk-around attraction. Note that some houses <u>really</u> decorate for Halloween and Christmas! A very small, gated park is located on Linnie Canal that has play equipment - slides, twisty apparatus to climb, and swings - in a sand base, plus a tiny patch of grass. Remember, the beach is just down the street!

Hours: Open daily, sunrise - sunset.
Price: Free
Ages: All

WAYFARERS CHAPEL

(310) 377-1650 / www.wayfarerschapel.org

5755 Palos Verdes Drive South, Palos Verdes

This unique, small church, is nicknamed the Glass Church because it's built almost entirely of glass (and some stone). It's nestled in a few overgrown trees so it looks to be almost a part of them - very picturesque. You can go inside of it when it's not being used. It was designed by Lloyd Wright, son of Frank Lloyd Wright. The church is built on a bluff overlooking the Pacific Ocean, surrounded by redwoods and gardens. The chapel is unique and charming, and the landscaping is beautiful. The Visitors Center is worth a quick go-into. This is a short stop off, so look up ABALONE COVE SHORELINE PARK (pg. 45), REDONDO BEACH INTERNATIONAL BOARDWALK, REDONDO BEACH PIER and KING HARBOR MARINA (pg. 160), or SOUTH COAST BOTANICAL GARDENS (pg. 86) for other things to do in this area.

Hours: The church and grounds are open daily, 9am - 5pm. The visitor's center is open daily, 10am - 5pm. Church functions take precedence over public accessibility.

Price: Free

Ages: 5 years and up.

WORLD WAR II STORE

(310) 533-4992 / www.wwiistore.com

1422 Marcelina Avenue, Torrance

Known as The Greatest Generation, a phrase coined by onetime NBC Nightly News anchor, Tom Brokaw, in his book by the same name, are those who came of age during the Great Depression and World War II. This store pays homage to the soldiers who fought, especially during WWII. More like a museum than a store (but you can buy things here!!), peruse and purchase genuine WWII artifacts, uniforms, military medals, books, flags, gas masks, helmets, hats, radio equipment, canteens, instruments, ammo belts, and more. Mannequins in period attire and music from the 40's playing in the background complete the ambiance. Bonus - the staff is knowledgeable and helpful regarding war items and history. They do buy items, as well.

Hours: Open Mon. - Sat., 10am - 5pm; Sun., 10am - 4pm.

Price: Free, but bring spending $.

Ages: 7 years and up.

—SHOWS AND THEATERS—

AHMANSON THEATER

(213) 628-2772 or (213) 972-7211 / www.musiccenter.org

135 N. Grand Avenue at the Music Center of Los Angeles, Los Angeles

See the MUSIC CENTER OF LOS ANGELES (pg. 189) for details.

ALEX THEATRE

(818) 243-ALEX (2539) - box office; (818) 243-2611 - tours / www.alextheatre.org

216 N. Brand Boulevard, Glendale

The gorgeous Alex Theatre seats 1,450 and offers a wide variety of performances and programs, for both professional and community performing arts groups. These include Peking Acrobats; dance ensembles; holiday shows; musical theater, with shows such as *The Music Man* and *Ain't Misbehavin'*; concerts starring the L.A. Chamber Orchestra and Glendale Youth Orchestra (both are resident companies); Shakespearean school performances; and family-oriented and classic feature films and cartoons. (Look up www.alexfilmsociety.org for more information on the films.) Special kid's presentations that are given occasionally on Sunday afternoons at 2pm and 5pm have featured Parachute Express, Beakman's World, Gizmo Guys, and more. Ask about educational outreach programs for students including special school presentations, matinees, open rehearsals, and pre-performance lectures.

Free, two-hour "backstage" public tours are given so visitors can learn the history of the ninety-old theater, especially regarding its architecture and artwork. Seeing the dressing rooms, green room, lobby, and backstage are all part of the tour, too. This walking tour includes climbing many stairs. Call to make a reservation. Check their website calendar for information on the free Open Arts and Music Festival usually held in September.

Hours: Call or check the website for a complete schedule. Tours are offered on select Sat. at 10am.

Price: Prices vary depending on the show. Sun. afternoon kid's shows are $10 - $16 per person. Parking is $1 for 4 hours with validation.

Ages: 4 years and up, depending on the show.

BOB BAKER MARIONETTE THEATER

(213) 250-9995 / www.bobbakermarionettetheater.com

$$$$

1345 W. 1st Street, Los Angeles

The Bob Baker Marionette Theater has been around since 1961, proving its staying power in this ever-changing world. Interactive marionette performances are given while children sit on a horseshoe-shaped carpet around the stage, and parents sit in chairs behind them.

The musical revues feature marionettes, and some stuffed animals, that range in size from very small to the size of a two-year-old. They "sing" and "dance" their way right into your child's heart. The puppeteers, dressed in black, become invisible to the audience as the kids get swept away in the magic of the show. The performance is done within touching distance of the kids, and sometimes the marionettes even sit in their laps! This is a great way to keep short attention spans riveted. If the story line seems a little thin to you and your attention drifts, watch the puppeteers manipulate the strings - it's a good show in itself. After the hour-long show, chat with the puppeteers and enjoy a sack lunch (that you supply) at the picnic tables in the lobby - no strings attached. If you're here for your child's birthday he/she will get special recognition with a crown, a little present and maybe a song just for him/her. Note that there are puppets and marionettes for sale here, too. Field trippers are welcome! Reservations are required for all shows.

Hours: Performances are given most Wed. - Fri. at 10:30am; Sat. - Sun. at 2:30pm. There are additional shows given during the month of December.

Price: $15 for ages 2 and up; children under 2 (lap sitters) are free. $20 for the holiday show. Free parking next to the theater.

Ages: 2½ - 11 years.

CALTECH PRESENTS - SCIENCE SATURDAYS

(626) 395-4652; (626) 395-6059 / www.events.caltech.edu

$$$

332 S. Michigan Avenue at Beckman Auditorium at California Institute of Technology, Pasadena

Science Saturdays are just one of the numerous series and special events, including performing arts, held at Caltech. Check their website for the full listing, and I mean full!. On selected Saturdays, come watch a screening of a variety of science movies. Titles have included *Weird Nature - Marvelous Motion, Planet Earth - Seasonal Forests, The Roachmobile*, and more. After the film a Caltech scientist leads a discussion on the science behind nature and space. School groups are invited to come on select Fridays at 10am for Reel Science - a movie and time of discussion with a scientist, too, or for a performing arts event such as *Sounds of Korea, Lakota Sioux Dance Theatre, The Dancing Scientist* or *The Iliad*.

Hours: Science Saturdays are at 4pm. School group science or performing arts presentations are Fri. at 10am.

Price: $10 per person for Science Saturdays. Parking is free.

Ages: 8 years and up.

CANDLELIGHT PAVILION DINNER THEATER

(909) 626-1254 / www.candlelightpavilion.com

$$$$$

455 W. Foothill Boulevard, Claremont

This family-owned, elegant dinner theater serves gourmet cuisine along with its ninety-minute, professional musical productions. Families dress up in their Sunday best and sit down in padded booths with linen tablecloths. Larger groups may sit at equally nice, long tables. Tiered seating is available on the main floor, or choose terrace seats. Candlelight wall chandeliers and candles on the table add to the ambiance. (My sons liked the draped stage curtains, too.)

Dinner is served for almost two hours before the show begins. (If kids get antsy, wander outside on the cement pathways, near the fish pond.) Entrees differ with each show but usually include variations of tri tip, chicken, fish (we had grilled salmon with shrimp mousse strudel), or a vegetarian dish. Meals come with vegetables or another side dish. The children's menu changes, offering macaroni and cheese, spaghetti and meatballs, chicken strips with french fries, or something equally tasty. Full waiter service makes dining here a real treat. The dessert selection varies and can include cheesecake, lemon raspberry martini trifle, and (my personal favorite) chocolate strawberry euphoria - brownies topped with ice cream, fresh strawberries, chocolate mousse, and chocolate. Champagne brunches are served Saturday and Sundays at the matinee seating. A performance is included with the brunch. Note: The show and dinner/brunch are included in the admission price, but appetizers, beverages, and desserts are extra.

The eight yearly musical productions are first-rate, and most of them are suitable for children. Past shows have included *My Fair Lady, Joseph and the Amazing Technicolor Dreamcoat, Big River, Shrek: The Musical*, and the annual *A Candlelight Christmas*. Reservations are required for all shows. Dress up attire is requested. The theater also hosts other events, such as concerts (band tributes and more).

Hours: Dinner seatings are Thurs. - Sat. at 6pm; Sun. at 5pm. Brunch is on Sat. and Sun. at 11am. Shows begin at 8pm, 7pm, and 12:45pm, respectively.

Price: Prices range from $63 for a weekend matinee to $78 for an evening terrace seat. Children's rates for Fri. evenings and Sat. matinees (excluding the holiday performance) are $30 in section A and on the main floor; $35 in the terrace. Children must be 12 or under to order a children's entree. (If a child's entree is desired at another show time, you must call ahead of time.)

Ages: 6 years and up.

CANYON THEATRE GUILD

(661) 799-2702 / www.canyontheatre.org
24242 Main Street, Newhall

Come see live performances in this 280-seat theater with mostly family-friendly shows that have included *Willy Wonka, Damn Yankees, Little Women*, and *A Christmas Carol*, plus concerts. Kids and school groups should check out the youth workshops and school field trips that feature productions such as *The Lion, The Witch and the Wardrobe* and *Once Upon a Leprechaun*. Be in a play, not just the audience - check out the website for information about auditions.

Hours: Call for evening and matinee show times.

Price: $15 - $35 per person, depending on the show, date, and time.

Ages: 5 and up, depending on the show.

CARPENTER PERFORMING ARTS CENTER

(562) 985-7000 - box office; (562) 985-4274 - tours / www.carpenterarts.org
6200 Atherton Street, on the campus of California State University Long Beach, Long Beach

Lovers of musical theater, dance, dramatic theater, juggling, concerts, and children's performances will enjoy the professional performances given at this center ranging from circus acts, Garrison Keller, Shakespeare Aloud, comedians, *Pirates of Penzance* and more. Note that there is a program called Classroom Connections where professional performers visit local elementary classrooms to talk about and demonstrate their art with a follow up of the students coming to see a full performance at the theater. Also see MUSICAL THEATRE WEST (pg. 189) for Broadway musicals performed at the Carpenter center. Come join the fun!

Hours: Call for show dates and times.

Price: Prices range in price depending on your seat location, the date, and show. Parking is $8.

Ages: Some shows are for ages 5 and up; some shows are recommended for older kids.

CENTER FOR THE ART OF PERFORMANCE AT UCLA

(310) 825-2101 / www.cap.ucla.edu; www.roycehall.org; www.tickets.ucla.edu
340 Royce Drive, in the North Campus of UCLA, Los Angeles

Name it, and it plays at UCLA. There are several different concert and theater venues here - the huge, 1,800-seat Royce Hall, the 580-seat Freud Playhouse, the 500-seat Schoenberg Hall, and a smaller theater that seats 200. Over 200 performances, combined in all the theaters, are featured here annually including a wide variety of musicals, classical music, chamber music, ballet, dance, circus-type performances, Broadway's best, theater, concerts, and for-the-family shows, including family film festivals. If UCLA doesn't have it - does it exist? One of our favorite shows was *Stomp,* a high-energy show where performers created rhythm and music using brooms, trash can lids, and other unusual "instruments".

Hours: Call or check the website for a schedule of current shows.

Price: Prices vary depending on the show, date, and time. Parking is $12 - cash only.

Ages: It depends on the show.

CENTER FOR THE ARTS, PEPPERDINE UNIVERSITY

(310) 506-4522 - box office; (310) 506-4766 - ARTS reach coordinator / www.arts.pepperdine.edu
24255 Pacific Coast Highway at Pepperdine University, Malibu

Pepperdine offers a wide variety of programs including orchestral, choral concerts, guitar competitions, musicals, comedies, and plays. Family shows at the theater, sometimes under the title of Family Performances and Art Days, include magic, acrobatics, puppetry, song, dance and other entertaining shows for kids. Show titles have included

Mermaid, The Very Hungry Caterpillar and Other Eric Carle Favorites, The Flying Karamazov Brothers, Recycled Percussion, Story Pirates, Golden Dragon Acrobats, and *Rhythmic Circus.* Some of the performances allow talk-back sessions, a chance to meet the performers, or a hands-on art activity. Educators - check out the free performances specifically for students!

The Weisman Museum of Art, adjacent to the theater, is open one hour prior to most performances and through intermission, besides its regular operating hours of Tuesday through Sunday, 11am to 5pm. The museum features rotating temporary exhibits of historic and contemporary art. Call (310) 506-4851 for more details.

Hours: Call or check the website for other show dates and times.

Price: Show prices are $20 - $40 for adults; $10 - $17 for ages 17 and under. Call or check the website regarding prices for other shows. Parking in the lot is about $5, cash only, and a free shuttle is available at the Theme Tower parking lot.

Ages: 3 years and up.

CERRITOS CENTER FOR THE PERFORMING ARTS

(800) 300-4345 or (562) 916-8500; (562) 467-8844 - shows for students; (714) 589-2770 - 3-D Theatricals / www.cerritoscenter.com; www.3dtheatricals.org

12700 Center Court Drive, Cerritos

$$$$$

Every season this absolutely beautiful Center (with grounds that are equally lovely) features four or five top-rate performances specifically for families, such as puppetry, dance, circus acts, or dramatic theater. The packed calendar at Cerritos also features classical music, Broadway musicals, the Moscow Circus, star-studded headliners, and numerous others. Educators, ask about the free or minimal cost, professional performances given especially for students throughout the year - fantastic shows at a fantastic price.

3-D Theatricals is a resident theater company that offers terrific productions, many geared especially for kids. See shows such as *Joseph and the Amazing Technicolor Dreamcoat, Once on this Island, Young Frankenstein* and *Oklahoma!.* Check the website, or call, to see what's playing. This company also performs at REDONDO BEACH PERFORMING ARTS CENTER (pg. 191).

Hours: Call or check the website for a schedule.

Price: Show prices vary.

Ages: 5 years and up.

CINEMARK 18 + XD

(310) 568-9950 or (310) 568-3394 / www.cinemark.com

6081 Center Drive, suite 201, in the Promenade at Howard Hughes Center, Los Angeles

$$$$

Cinemark is a classy movie theater located in an upscale, outdoor mall. It features a cafe and bar, and more importantly, a crazy soda machine with an incredible number of choices that you select via a touch screen. The cushy theater seats can be classified as a cut above as they recline and you reserve your seat when you purchase a ticket. A fun option is watching a movie in the XD theater here with a massive, over-sized screen. (XD means the movie format/projector is capable of up to 35 trillion colors. That seems like a lot.) Shows are available in 2-D, 3-D, XD and D-Box (in which you control motion of your own seat to parallel the action going on in the movie). 3-D movies are a visual and sensory experience as the images seem to come out of the screen and right into the theater. The show titles change so there is always something new to see.

Inquire about school field trips. A summer bonus is the Summer Movie series where flicks are only $1 per. Note that this theater is in the Promenade at Howard Hughes Center, so there are numerous restaurants and shops.

Hours: Check the website for show times.

Price: Admission prices change depending on the movies being shown. Matinee XD tickets are usually $13 for adults, $8.25 for seniors and children; $15 for adults and $9.75 for seniors and kids on weekend evenings. Regular movies usually cost $10 for adults; $5.25 for seniors and kids. Tues. prices are discounted. Parking is $2.80 with a movie validation; $3 for up to 4 hours, otherwise.

Ages: 4 years and up.

COMEDYSPORTZLA at the NATIONAL COMEDY THEATRE

(323) 871-1193 / www.cszla.com

5269 Lankershim Boulevard at the El Portal Theatre, Hollywood

$$$$

This theater is the home of the nationally acclaimed ComedySportz, a ninety-minute, audience-participatory, improvisational comedy "show." Played like a sport in the sense that there are team competitions with a referee, uniforms, fans (i.e., the spectators), and even a rendition of the National Anthem, the audience yells suggestions (when asked) to the six players on stage, and the games begin.

Each scene in a series has a time limit, so the quips are fast and the musical bits snappy and clever, usually. Of course no two shows are alike because the players, the audience, the input, and the witticism of the lines blurted out are different on any given evening. Fouls are given for poor taste (being unclean), being boring, and bad jokes. Not only is ComedySportz interactive and funny, it is also clean, musical, and all-round entertaining. When we went, we laughed throughout the entire evening.

Special shows and performances include college night, where the players are trained and talented college "kids"; Airwaves, the Golden Age of radio entertainment as a variety show; and more. Celebrate a birthday party here using the back patio to serve pizza, cake, and party bags. The birthday person gets a starring segment in a show. Note that the theatre also provides workshops, sleepover camps, and high-school improv leagues.

Hours: ComedySportz shows are Fri., 8pm and 10pm (this is the college team performance); Sat., 8pm; Sun., 7pm. Check the website for other performances and events.

Price: College team shows are $10 per person. ComedySportz on Fri. and Sat. is $18 for adults, $10 for ages 14 and under; Sun., $15 for adults, $10 for 14 and under. Prices are for tickets purchased in advance; tickets at the door can be more.

Ages: 7 years and up.

CREATING ARTS COMPANY

$$$$

(310) 804-0223 or (310) 204-4440 / www.creatingcentral.com; www.thepico.com
10508 W. Pico Boulevard, Los Angeles

This musical theater company was formed to perform for kids (40 shows a year!) - to engage them in classic Broadway shows at a level that they understand and enjoy. They offer four different "styles" of shows: Twinkle Theater - thirty-minute, upbeat (i.e. no scary villains) musical shows for ages 5 and under; Mini Musicals - one-hour musical theater for ages 3 and up that is interactive as the audience is encouraged to sing and dance with the characters, cheer, boo (the villain), clap, and then play the musical instrument they are given when entering the theater; Pint Size Plays - a play version of the Mini Musicals; and Jr. Broadway - ninety-minute versions of Broadway plays and musicals for ages 9 and up. After many of the performances, the kids get to meet the actors and take pictures with them. Past shows include *School House Rock, Cinderella, Babes in Toyland, The Wizard of Oz, Thumbelina,* and *Peter Pan.*

I remember taking my oldest son to a live Broadway-style show when he was 4 years old - he was mesmerized! Check the website for the educational outreaches and numerous classes that the Company offers to get your child really involved in loving theater.

Hours: Most of the shows are on weekends. Check the website for specific dates and times.

Price: General seating (not reserved): $15 a show; ages 2 and under (lap sitters) - are free. VIP (reserved seating): $30 for one show; $40 for two.

Ages: 3 - 16 years, depending on the show.

DOLBY THEATRE

$$$$

(323) 308-6300 / www.dolbytheatre.com
6801 Hollywood Boulevard, suite 180, in the Hollywood & Highland Center, Hollywood

"I'd like to thank the Academy . . ." The elegant 3,332-seat Dolby Theatre, which is host to the Academy Awards telecast. Although the theater was built for the awards, it is also used throughout the year for numerous Broadway plays and musicals, headlining concerts, opera, ballet, comedy acts, classic music events, motivational speakers, *American Idol,* and family events. The marvelous theater offers tiered levels, opera boxes, and a special media pit.

You are invited to take a thirty-minute guided tour of the theater - it might be the only time you'll stand behind the velvet rope. Touch and discover how the "silver screen" got that name; see an actual Oscar statuette; find out how Oscar got its name; visit the Dolby Lounge with its intriguing glass windows that alternate between foggy and clear; look at photographs of stars accepting their awards; learn where nominees sit and why; get a feel for what goes on behind the curtains; and walk where winners do after their Oscar acceptance speech. Depending on what's currently playing at the theater, you might also get to step onto the stage. Although this walking tour includes several flights of stairs, disabled guests are accommodated as well. (No strollers, however.) Check the plaques outside, honoring the Best Picture winners from past years. Look up HOLLYWOOD - the downtown tourist mecca (pg. 171) for details on other close-by Hollywood museums and attractions.

Hours: Check the website for a schedule of shows. Tours are offered every half hour, daily, from 10:30am - 4pm, when a show is not in progress. Call for tour schedule updates as tours are also not given on holidays, special event days, or mid-February through mid-March to prepare for the Academy Awards.

Price: Call or check the website for show prices as they vary greatly. Tours are $23 for adults; $18 for seniors, students with I.D., and ages 3 - 17; children 2 and under are free. Parking is $2 for 2 hours; $15 max.

Ages: 6 years and up for shows, depending on what's playing; 7 years and up for the tour.

DONALD E. BIANCHI PLANETARIUM

(818) 677-2488 - office or 818 677-5601 - info / www.csun.edu/science-mathematics/physics-astronomy $$$
18111 Nordhoff Street at California State University Northridge, Northridge

It's written in the stars, or so it seems when you visit this 100-seat planetarium. The show titles might change, but all explore different aspects of our universe. Show titles have included *Winter Sky Show* and *Spring Sky Show*, which highlight planets inside and outside our solar system, plus the Voyager encounters, the light years from Andromeda, Mars Quest and more; *Magellan: Report from Venus*, a narrated program about the Magellan Mission to Venus; and *Total Solar Eclipse at the Navel of the World*, which combines travel, science and history as a 2017 solar eclipse at Douglas, Wyoming is showcased. Two shows are given each night with a price discount for viewing both of them. Be on time as latecomers will not be admitted. Weather permitting, come look through the telescopes after the shows.

Hours: Shows are usually given every other Fri. at 7:30pm and 8:30pm, February - mid-March; and select Thurs. and Fri., the end of March - mid-May. Check the website for the schedule during the traditional school year.

Price: $6 for one show for adults, $10 for two shows; $4 students for one show, $7 for two. Parking is $6 per car.

Ages: 8 years and up.

DOROTHY CHANDLER PAVILION / LOS ANGELES OPERA

(213) 972-7211 / www.musiccenter.org $$$$
135 N. Grand Avenue at the Music Center of Los Angeles, Los Angeles

See the MUSIC CENTER OF LOS ANGELES (pg. 189) for details.

EL CAPITAN THEATER

(323) 467-7674; (800) 347-6396 / www.elcapitan.go.com $$$$
6838 Hollywood Boulevard, Hollywood

This Disney-owned, tiered theater is lavishly decorated, reminiscent of the late 1920's, with ornate edifices and a sense of grandeur. Besides regular Disney movies and those shown in 3-D, this theater also holds premiers of new Disney movies which are often accompanied by special exhibits, or a live show of some sort. For instance, *Avengers: Infinity Wars* had sixteen of the costumes worn in the movie on display. *Solo: A Star Wars Story* had reserved seating, a beverage, a souvenir popcorn tub and poster, plus a live DJ for its opening. Regular showings of the movie included displays of props and costumes from the movie. *The Incredibles* showing was accompanied by a fashion show, a character show and special, in-theater effects, and more. Note that Tiny Tot Tuesday, specifically for little ones, is at 10am during the run of most movies.

If you need more Disney in your day, check out the mini Disney store/Ghiradelli shop next door. Also, look up HOLLYWOOD - the downtown tourist mecca (pg. 171) for details on other close-by Hollywood museums and attractions.

Hours: Call for show dates.

Price: Ticket prices sometime vary according to opening night, or what is playing. Regular movies are $16 - $18 for adults; $13 for seniors and ages 3 - 11. Ask about VIP admission. Parking is $2 for 4 hours with validation; $15 max at the Hollywood and Highland Center across the street.

Ages: 4 years and up.

FAERY HUNT (Los Angeles County)

(818) 324-6802 / www.afaeryhunt.com $$$$

With or without pixie dust, you can join *A Faery Hunt* as cast members of this interactive theater production, dressed as fairies, hide amongst the trees and bushes of various parks (and props of indoor places) mostly throughout Los Angeles County on select weekends. Locations include Corriganville Park, Crestwood Hills Park, Fern Dell at Griffith Park, Los Angeles Arboretum and Botanic Garden, and South Coast Botanic Garden, plus indoor venues such as Sunset Theatre Company, libraries, and Tarzana Community and Cultural Center. Visitors are invited to sing, dance, play games, and go on a fairy hunt, romping into and through the forest, looking for fairies (and squealing as they find them) and other fantastic creatures, while learning fairy lore. Strollers are welcome on the gentle outdoor hikes, as participants also learn about respect for nature and kindness. What imaginative and delightful fun!

Hours: Usually at 10:30am. Arrive at 10am, though, for the pre-show.

Price: The cost is usually $12.50 - $15 per person. Ages 23 months and under are free. Library shows are free.
Check the website for specific locations, calendar information, special programs and to make reservations.

Ages: 2 - 9 years.

GLENDALE CENTRE THEATRE

(818) 244-8481 / www.glendalecentretheatre.com

324 N. Orange Street, Glendale

Many block-buster musicals and comedies suitable for the family are performed here throughout the year. This theater puts on at least two terrific, one-and-a-half-hour shows for children. Past productions have included *The Little Mermaid, Sleeping Beauty, Hansel and Gretel,* and *Jack and the Beanstalk.*

Check out the theater's Shakespearience summer camp programs for junior and senior high. It includes select interactive performances from the Bard, workshops, and study materials.

Hours: Children's shows are usually performed Sat. at 11am. Call for other show times.

Price: Children's show prices are usually $12.50 per person. Other show prices are $34 for adults; $28 for seniors; $20 for ages 4 - 16; children 3 and under are not allowed. Note that the Christmas show sells out quickly.

Ages: Depends on the show.

HARRIET AND CHARLES LUCKMAN FINE ARTS COMPLEX

(323) 343-6600 / www.luckmanarts.org

5151 State University Drive, on the California State Los Angeles campus, Los Angeles

The modern-looking buildings of the Luckman Fine Arts Complex consist of a 1,152-seat theater, which is the main presentation arena for modern dance, ballet, opera, and other musical performances; a modular 250-seat theater, which is a more intimate setting for solo artists; a contemporary art exhibits gallery; and a small amphitheater for concerts and Street of the Arts presentations. Check out their website for annual events such as the Global Arts Fest and the World Arts Day which offer a variety of activities, performances, arts and crafts and workshops all pertaining to that year's theme or country.

Hours: Call or check the website for show dates and times.

Price: Tickets range from $40 - $80 for adults; $20 - $25 for students, depending on the show. Parking is $2 per hour; $4 for 4 hours. The art gallery is free.

Ages: Depends on the show.

HAUGH PERFORMING ARTS CENTER

(626) 963-9411 / www.haughpac.com

1000 W. Foothill Boulevard at Citrus College, Glendora

Family-friendly shows are a great way to introduce live theater to children. The variety of past performances have included *The Broadway Princess Party, Baskerville: A Sherlock Holmes Mystery, Magic Shadows, Beauty and the Beast, Christmas Is, Curious George,* and more. The center also hosts numerous headliner artists, dancers, comedians, acrobats, Christmas performers, and musicians - jazz, big band, pop, and more. School performance matinees are offered at 10am on select days for a cost of $4 to $8 per student, depending on the performance.

Hours: Family friendly shows are presented mostly on Sun. at 2pm. Check the website for a schedule of other performances.

Price: Family friendly shows are $30 for adults; $25 for seniors and students; $15 for ages 16 and under - if ordered online. Call for prices for other shows.

Ages: 4 - 13 years, depending on the show.

HOLLYWOOD BOWL

(323) 850-2000 / www.hollywoodbowl.com

2301 N. Highland, Hollywood

Jazz, world music, classical, and every genre you can think of - that's what the historic Hollywood Bowl has to offer. With a seating capacity of just under 18,000, this outdoor amphitheater offers over seventy-five programs in the summer alone! Check the schedule because there is something here (almost) year-round to entertain everyone in your family. A few past programs that kids can relate to in particular included *Video Games Live,* featuring orchestra and choir music from some of the most popular video games, and *Sing-A-Long Sound of Music*.

The hills surrounding the bowl are alive with music and offer the perfect spot for picnicking. So, pull up a piece of lawn, bring your own chairs, or snag a picnic table if you get here early enough. You are welcome to bring your cooler to your seat to enjoy, as well, while watching the concert. Some areas open four hours before the show begins. If you forgot to pack a meal, or just didn't want to, enjoy tasty options from the Rooftop Grill, Marketplace, a gourmet boxed dinner, or the refreshment stands. Coming to the Bowl is not just coming to a concert, but experiencing an event.

Make sure you check out HOLLYWOOD BOWL MUSEUM (pg. 118). Note about parking: It's painful. On-site parking is very limited and you can wait for hours (literally) to get in and especially out. Take the Metro Red Line and walk, or take the Bowl Shuttle bus (free with Metro Red Line ticket), or park at one of three lots close by and take the Bowl Shuttle for $5 - cash only. Parking is free at two of the lots. My favorite? Taking a Park & Ride bus. The cost is $6 (prepaid online) or $10, cash only at the lot, round trip per person, and is offered from several venues (up to fourteen for philharmonic performances) around L.A. Bonus - you don't have to drive in the traffic. Check the website for specifics.

Hours: Call or check the website for a schedule.

Price: Prices vary according to the show, date, and time.

Ages: 7 years and up, depending on the show.

IMAX THEATER

(213) 744-7400 or (213) 744-2019 / www.californiasciencecenter.org $$$$

700 State Drive, Exposition Park, Los Angeles

Moviegoers can enjoy 3-D film format at this large screen IMAX Theater. In the 3-D format, the use of polarized glasses, a surround sound system, and the seven-story high, ninety-foot-wide screen takes you and your child on wonderful adventures. You might explore the depths of the ocean and swim with fish (watch out for the sharks!); river raft through the Grand Canyon; enter the world of outer space; and more. In other words, you'll feel like you actually experience whatever is on the screen, without ever leaving your seat. "Edutainment" is what this theater is all about! Tip: Pre-purchase your tickets to make sure you'll get in and note that there is a $3 service charge per ticket on all phone orders. Bonus: Timed reservation tickets to see the Endeavour at the adjacent Science Center are not needed with any purchase of an IMAX ticket. Look up the following attractions as they are all in the same complex: CALIFORNIA AFRICAN AMERICAN MUSEUM (pg. 101), CALIFORNIA SCIENCE CENTER (pg. 102), EXPOSITION PARK (pg. 59), and NATURAL HISTORY MUSEUM OF LOS ANGELES COUNTY (pg. 140).

Hours: Call for show titles and show times. Shows run most of the year every hour, Mon. - Fri., 10:30am - 5:30pm; Sat. - Sun., 9:30am - 5:30pm. In the summer, shows start daily at 9:30am.

Price: Most movies are $8.95 for adults; $7.95 for seniors and students; $6.75 for ages 4 - 12; children 3 years and under are free. Prices might fluctuate depending on the film. Parking is $12.

Ages: 3 years and up.

INTERNATIONAL CITY THEATRE

(562) 436-4610; (562) 495-4595 / www.ictlongbeach.org   !/$$$$$

300 E. Ocean Boulevard at the Long Beach Performing Arts Center, Long Beach

The five-play season offers some Broadway-type musicals, a little cabaret, dramatic and comedic plays, and other good theater for older kids. Past shows have included *The Glass Menagerie*, *Is He Dead* (by Mark Twain), and *Songs for a New World*. The theater also offers six community and education outreach programs. One of the best deals in town is the Free Saturday Family Theatre Series with two to three performances a year. Some shows are funny and some are thought provoking. Although these shows are free, online reservations are required. The Staged Play Reading series is also free. Be sure to check out the summer youth conservatory performance.

Hours: Most shows start at 8, but Sun. shows are at 2pm. The Free Saturday performances start at 11am.

Price: Preview night is $35. Opening night is $55. Regular tickets are $47 on Thurs. - Fri.; $49 on Sat. and Sun. Parking at the garage is $15.

Ages: 4 and up for the Free Saturdays; 10 and up for the plays.

JOHN DRESCHER PLANETARIUM

(310) 434-3005 - ticket office; (310) 434-4767 - school tours / $$$
www.smc.edu/AcademicPrograms/Planetarium

1900 Pico Boulevard on the campus of Santa Monica City College in room 223 of Drescher Hall, Santa Monica

Do your kids have stars in their eyes? Bring them to the planetarium, then lean back, look up at the nighttime sky, and watch some of the mysteries of the heavens unfold. The first presentation, titled *Night Sky Show,* is a fifty-minute, weekly interactive update on the night sky, highlighting the latest news in space exploration and astronomy. There is a time to ask questions at this show. The second show, a lecture and changing fifty-minute presentation, has titles such as *Neutron Stars; Colliding Black Holes and Gravitational Waves; Tilt: Equinoxes and Solstices Explained;* and *Mars INSIGHT Mission Preview.* These shows focus on different aspects of astronomy. The December show, *A Winter's Solstice,* discusses the various observances of the Winter Solstice and looks at a scientific explanation of the Star of Bethlehem as the astronomer/lecturer incorporates Bible passages and the research known to astronomers from that time period.

The planetarium is available for special showings for school, or other groups, on Tuesdays and Thursdays at 10am and 11:30am. The cost is $100 for up to twenty people, and $5 per person after the minimum is met, with a maximum of fifty.

Hours: Shows for the general public are on select Fri. nights at 7pm and 8pm. (The latter time is the feature presentation.) There are no shows on holidays.

Price: $6 for adults for a single show, $11 for both shows; $5 for seniors and ages 12 and under for a single show, $9 for the double feature. Cash only.

Ages: 7 years and up, only.

JOY COMEDY THEATRE

(818) 505-9355 / www.joytheatre.com

14366 Ventura Boulevard, Sherman Oaks

Giggle along with kid performers (ages 4 to 11 years) in the Giggle Gaggle troop who, after attending classes and doing auditions, perform standup comedy, improv out of scenarios suggested to them by the audience, character bits, and more. Your kids will laugh and after watching them, may aspire to the stage, themselves. Also for kids are classes in fencing, Shakespeare for Fun, Jedi training, stunts, and even puppet/mask making. This playhouse is also home to several adult comedy classes whose participants then perform standup, improv, and sketch comedy for audiences.

Hours: Giggle Gaggle - Sun., 2pm. Check the website for all other shows and dates.

Price: $5 per person for Giggle Gaggle; $10 for some of the adult performances. Cash only.

Ages: 5 years and up.

L. A. CONNECTION COMEDY THEATER

(818) 710-1320 / www.laconnectioncomedy.com

3435 W. Magnolia Boulevard, Burbank

The Comedy Theater produces numerous shows appropriate for adults, however, you can also tickle your children's funnybones by bringing them here for special comedy improv performances by kids, for kids. The almost hour-long improvisational show is given in a small room (sixty seats) with tiered, theater-type seating. There are two casts for the kids improv shows - one consisting of teenagers and another of one adult and usually six kids that are 5 to 13 years old. The kids are members of the Comedy Improv for Teens/Kids and are trained in the L.A. Connection's Improv Workshops.

Audience participation is mandatory as the actors ask for help in creating characters, or supplying ideas to use in a skit. Your children love to see their suggestions acted out. Remember, the performers are kids, so there is a lot of kid-type humor. As with any improv show, the success of a skit depends on the improvisationalists and the audience. The L.A. Connection really connected with my kids! If your child thinks the whole world is a stage, then maybe he should be on it. Sign him up for comedy improv classes and the next performance you see could be his.

Hours: Kids performances are Sun. at 3:30pm; teens are Sat. at 5:30pm.

Price: $7 per person for kids performances; other performance tickets are $10.

Ages: 5 years and up - younger ones won't get the humor.

LA MIRADA THEATER FOR THE PERFORMING ARTS

(562) 944-9801 - theater; (714) 690-2900 - Phantom Projects / www.lamiradatheater.com

14900 La Mirada Boulevard, La Mirada

Symphony concerts, Broadway productions, youth presentations, and education programs are some of the offerings that this 1,250 seat theater hosts. Enjoy comedies, musical, dramas, and concerts. Just a few of the productions have included Moscow's Ballet *Great Russian Nutcracker, Vicki Lawrence and Mama, Newsies, Donny and Marie, Happy Days,* and *The Simon and Garfunkel Story.*

Under the name of Phantom Projects (www.phantomprojects.com), teens have their own plays dealing with issues for their age, as well as plays that they study in school, such as *The Diary of Anne Frank, The Outsiders,* and *The Crucible.*

Ages 5 and up are enthralled with one-hour Programs for Young Audiences which have included *James and the Giant Peach*, *Sid the Science Kid Live*, *Pippi Longstocking*, and *Seussical the Musical*.

Hours: Programs for Young Audiences are offered about eight times a year on Sundays at 1pm and 3:30pm. Call or check the website for a schedule of other shows.

Price: Tickets for Phantom Projects are usually $10- $15 for all ages for field trip performances; 7pm shows are $15 - $55 for adults, depending on the show and seat location. Tickets for Programs for Young Audiences are $15 - $30 for adults; $13.50 for children, depending on the show. Tickets for Broadway and other shows range from $20 - $70; prices are higher for special shows and concerts.

Ages: 5 years and up.

LANCASTER PERFORMING ARTS CENTER

(661) 723-5950 / www.lpac.org

$$$$

750 W. Lancaster Boulevard, Lancaster

The theater productions here run the gamut of Broadway musicals; classical ballet and other dance; jazz or big band music; comedies; and dramas. Past performers and shows include Earth, Wind and Fire; B.B. King; *The Music Man*; Cirque Eloize; Howie Mandel, The Lettermen, Chinese acrobats, and *Jack and the Beanstalk*. The Arts for Youth program is geared for schools to bring kids to see live theater, so performances are held weekdays, usually at 9:15am, 10am, and 11am, with a minimum of ten students. Past productions have included *Rumpelstiltskin*, *Math Magic*, *Story Pirates*, *Sleeping Beauty*, and *Revenge of the Space Pandas*. If you're interested in taking a behind-the-scenes tour of the theater, call (661) 723-5876 for information.

Hours: Call or check the website for show dates and times.

Price: The Arts for Youth program is usually $5 per person. Other performances range from $18 - $79 for adults; $8 - $15 for youth tickets, depending on the show, date, seat and time.

Ages: 3 years and up, depending on the production.

LONG BEACH SHAKESPEARE COMPANY

(562) 997-1494 / www.lbshakespeare.org

$$$

4250 Atlantic Avenue at the Richard Goad Theatre, Long Beach

Who wrote - "This above all; to thine own self be true." and "What's in a name? That which we call a rose by any other name would smell as sweet."? Maybe the title of the company gave it away, but yes, Shakespeare. This classical theatre company presents several Shakespeare plays throughout the year with traditional performances in period costumes, accompanied by music, dancing, and fencing. It also presents Shakespeare farces, plus guest speakers, specials programs, and reading performances of old-time radio shows aided by Foley-type sound effects. With great prices and even several free events (at the park, not at the theatre), the theatre troupe is advancing its mission of promoting literacy to all ages in engaging and creative ways.

Hours: Most shows are Fri. - Sat. at 8pm; Sun. at 2pm, but check the website for specific show dates and times.

Price: Tickets for Shakespeare plays are usually $22.50 for adults; $12.50 for students. A Flex Pass card is $100 for 10 show tickets per season. Check the website for other show prices.

Ages: 9 years and up.

LOS ANGELES PUBLIC LIBRARY

See the entry for LOS ANGELES PUBLIC LIBRARY (pg. 173), under POTPOURRI, for details.

$

MAGICOPOLIS

(310) 451-2241 / www.magicopolis.com

$$$$$

1418 4ᵗʰ Street, Santa Monica

Abracadabra - make a place of magic appear! Magicopolis, meaning "City of Magic," was created by veteran magician, Steve Spill, to make magic shows available to the public. The building is older and a bit worn, and so are some of the magic acts, but there were still many times that I sat with my mouth wide open, thinking, "How did he do that?"

While waiting for the main show to begin, watch what a resident magician might have up his sleeve. Being close-up to the performers, however, does not insure that audience members will "get" the sleight of hand tricks, at least it didn't in my case. The main show with Steve Spill, and sometimes other magicians, incorporates some audience participation (so beware), some off-color jokes/humor/innuendoes (not appropriate for kids, and sometimes for me!), and some wonderful, larger-scale illusions, like levitation and Houdini-like escapes. The performances can entertain and mystify visitors. For those who want to try a little magic of their own, check out the in-house retail shop.

Hours: Shows are given Fri. at 8pm; Sat. at 2pm and 8pm; Sun. at 2pm.

Price: $36 per person for an evening performance; $26 for a matinee. Parking in the lots is usually free for first 90 minutes and $1.25 for hour after that.

Ages: 15 years and up.

MARK TAPER FORUM

$$$$

(213) 628-2772 or (213) 972-7211 / www.musiccenter.org

135 N. Grand Avenue at the Music Center of Los Angeles, Los Angeles

See the MUSIC CENTER OF LOS ANGELES (pg. 189) for details.

MICROSOFT THEATER

$$$$$

(213) 763-6020 or (213) 763-6030 / www.microsofttheater.com

777 Chick Hearn Court and Figueroa Street, Los Angeles

Hosting an amazing array of over 120 premiere events a year, this 7,100-seat venue offers some of the hottest tickets in town. Awards shows, headlining concerts, dance performances, boxing matches, family shows - Neil Young, Mary J. Blige, So You Think You Can Dance? tour, Sesame Street, Power Rangers Live, and American Music Awards - just to name a few. Note that the theater is in the middle of the L.A. LIVE complex, which also has Staples Center, a Regal L.A. Live Stadium 14, GRAMMY MUSEUM (pg. 113), Lucky Strike Lanes, and plenty of restaurants. See DOWNTOWN LOS ANGELES / GRAND PARK (pg. 167) for information on Grand Park and all the other places to go within this fairly immediate area.

Hours: Call for show times or check the website.

Price: Call for show prices or check the website. Parking adjacent to the theater and in lots on Olympic Blvd. and around the (big) block range from $10 for 2 hours to $30 for all day.

Ages: 4 years and up, depending on the show.

MORGAN-WIXSON THEATRE

$$$$

(310) 828-7519 / www.morgan-wixson.org

2627 Pico Boulevard, Santa Monica

Home of the Santa Monica Theatre Guild, this community theater produces several productions a year and also has Y.E.S. (i.e., Youth Education/Entertainment Series) which helps develop talent in children 7 through 17 as they audition and perform five productions every year. Past shows have included *Frog Prince*, *A Wrinkle in Time*, *Midsummer Night's Dream*, *Velveteen Rabbit*, and *Curious George*.

Hours: Y.E.S. shows are performed Sat. and Sun., usually at 11am. Other performances are usually on Fri. and Sat. at 8pm; Sun. at 2pm.

Price: Y.E.S. show tickets are $12 for adults; $10 for ages 12 and under. Y.E.S. musicals are $20 for adults; $15 for ages 12 and under. Other prices fluctuate according to show, date, and time.

Ages: Depends on the show.

MOUNT SAN ANTIONIO COLLEGE PLANETARIUM

$$$

(909) 468-4050 or (909) 274-5795 - box office; (909) 594-5611, ext. 4774 - show info / www.mtsac.edu/planetarium

1100 N. Grand Avenue at Mount San Antonio College, Walnut

Star gazers can take an almost one-hour journey through the solar system to learn about our sun and about our constellations in the night sky - the moon, comets, and meteors - via a state-of-the-art, Zeiss Skymaster projector. Check the website calendar for shows that are particularly for kids such as *One World, One Sky: Big Birds Adventure* and *Secrets of the Cardboard Rocket*, plus "tonight's sky" talk, and more. The 75-seat planetarium holds shows for the general public, as well as shows for specific groups such as students, first graders through twelfth graders, and boy scouts, girl scouts, etc. Rocket building and launching can be add-ons to the field trips.

Hours: Shows to the general public are offered on Fri. and Sat. at 4:30pm, 6pm and 7:30pm. They are offered for school groups Tues. - Fri. at 9:30am and 12:15pm; for other groups, including birthday parties, Sat. at noon. Reservations are necessary and can be made up to 6 months in advance.

Price: Shows for the general public in the evening are $6 for adults; $4 for seniors, students, and ages 6 - 13; $1 for ages 5 and under. Matinee shows are $5 for ages 6 and up; $1 for ages 5 and under. School and group tours are $4.50 per person. Parking is $4 per vehicle.

Ages: 1st graders and up.

MUSICAL THEATRE WEST

(562) 856-1999 / www.musical.org
$$$$$

6200 E. Atherton Street at the Carpenter Performing Arts Center on the campus of California State University Long Beach, Long Beach

Broadway's top musicals are performed locally, incorporating lavish sets and costumes, a live orchestra, and professional casts. Each production runs for three weeks and includes special performances for schools. Past shows include *Annie, Nice Work If You Can Get It, Oliver, The King and I, Young Frankenstein, The Music Man, West Side Story*, and many more. Teachers, the outstanding special matinee programs for classrooms are $5 per student with shows on Thursday at 10am.

Hours: Call or check the website for show schedules.
Price: Regular show prices range from $20 to $92 per person. Parking at the Carpenter Center is $10 a vehicle.
Ages: 7 years and up, depending on the show.

MUSIC CENTER OF LOS ANGELES

(213) 972-7211 or (213) 628-2772; (213) 972-8030 - shows for students / www.musiccenter.org
$$$$$

135 N. Grand Avenue, Los Angeles

The Music Center is one of the crown jewels of the Los Angeles cultural scene. This sprawling, two-city block Los Angeles complex features four powerhouse entertainment venues, each with a resident company. The **Ahmanson Theater** seats about 1,700 and puts on world-class, big-name, mainstream and Tony-award winning musical productions, many of which are terrific for the whole family. Past productions have included *Phantom of the Opera* and *Les Miserables*. It is home to the Center Theatre Group. The **Dorothy Chandler Pavilion**, which seats almost 3,200, is home to the Los Angeles Opera. Kids who can read can now be drawn into the story as supertitles, the English translation of the words being sung, are projected above the stage at the performances. This Pavilion is also home to numerous kid-friendly programs. School programs offer low-cost to free, professional shows! The fabulous **Walt Disney Concert Hall** is home to the Los Angeles Philharmonic and the Los Angeles Master Chorale. There are several other performance and education facilities associated with the Disney Hall, too. Wow! The 2,265-seat, acoustically sophisticated, state-of-the-art, wheel-chair friendly concert hall is gorgeous. The fantastic-looking pipe organ in the back is particularly eye-catching. The hall also has two outdoor amphitheaters; the 350-seat W.M. Keck Foundation Children's Amphitheatre, located on the rooftop of the Disney Concert Hall, and a 120-seat venue for preconcert events. The 750-seat **Mark Taper Forum**, also a base for the Center Theatre Group, produces spectacular theater such as *Big River* and *Bring in 'Da Noise, Bring in Da' Funk*. See MUSIC CENTER (tours) (pg. 202) for information on tours of the Music Center.

Call, or check the website, for the numerous family and educational events, some of which are free. Join in the Active Arts program which incorporates dance, drumming outdoors, sing-alongs, joining in playing music at different venues, and more throughout the year.

Notes: 1) Just down the road at 2nd and Hope streets performances are given at the Roy and Edna Disney/CalArts Theater (REDCAT) that seats up to 266 patrons. 2) Walk around the various buildings at the Music Center as there are hidden pleasures such walkways, views of L.A., and the pocket Blue Ribbon Garden on the rooftop of the Disney Concert Hall which is a delight of trees, tables and chairs, and a huge rose statue fountain made of Delft porcelain mosaic pieces. 3) The twelve-acre Grand Park, kind of broken into variously landscaped chunks, begins here and extends to City Hall. The fountains, a performance lawn, hot pink benches and tables, and grassy areas make it a pleasant place to gather and relax in the outdoors and enjoy some special events such as concerts, dance performances, movie nights, farmer's markets, and more. See DOWNTOWN LOS ANGELES / GRAND PARK (pg. 167) for information on Grand Park and all the other places to go within this fairly immediate area.

Hours: Call or check the website for show dates and times.
Price: Varies, depending on the show. Parking in the Music Center and Disney Concert Hall garages is $9 on event weekdays (cash only), starting at 4:30pm, and all day Sat. and Sun. Parking is $20 max on non-event weekdays.
Ages: 5 years and up, depending on the show.

OLD TOWN MUSIC HALL, INC.

(310) 322-2592 / www.oldtownmusichall.org
$$$

140 Richmond Street, El Segundo

Step back in time, to the golden era of film where silent movies and "talkies" dominated the screens. The rich red drapes, chandeliers, intimate seating, and the sound of the mighty Wurlitzer pipe organ, which is like a one-man band, create an atmosphere of yesteryear. The proprietors are two older gentlemen who have been in business together here for over thirty years, sharing organ duty and running the movies. The audience gets warmed up with four or five sing-alongs while on-screen slides provide lyrics and hokey cartoons. The Wurlitzer is played at every showing and accompanies silent epic and comedy films. Past films have included *The General*, *Wings*, *Phantom of the Opera*, and the original *Ben Hur*. Talkies have included *The Firefly* with Jeanette MacDonald; *Donkey Serenade*; *Roaring Twenties* starring James Cagney and Humphrey Bogart; and *The Little Princess* with Shirley Temple. Grand pianos are on hand for ragtime and jazz concerts that are also given here. What a great this-is-the-way-it-was experience for kids (and adults!).

Hours: Show times are Fri., 8:15pm; Sat., 2:30pm and 8:15pm; Sun., 2:30pm. Most concerts are Sun. at 2:30pm, or at 7:30pm at night at other times. Check the website.

Price: $10 per person; $8 for seniors. Concerts are $20 per person. Cash or check only.

Ages: 5 years and up.

PALMDALE PLAYHOUSE

(661) 267-5684 - playhouse; (661) 267-ARTS (2787) - recorded info; (661) 267-5685 - box office / www.palmdaleplayhouse.com

38334 10th Street East at the Antelope Valley Community Arts Center, Palmdale

Comedy, drama, country music, jazz, magic, improv, ballet, community theater, and more is yours to experience throughout the year at the 350-seat Playhouse. Past performances have included a smorgasbord of shows from *A Victorian Holiday*, Sing Along With Santa, *Annie Get Your Gun*, *1776*, *Shrek*, and *The Lion, the Witch, and the Wardrobe*. Annual festivals include the Children's Spring Fest which is a day of arts, crafts, pony rides, and fun zone. There are several workshops offered in the summer.

Hours: Call for show hours.

Price: Tickets range from $15 - $18 for adults; $7 - $12 for seniors, active military, and children.

Ages: It depends on the show.

PALOS VERDES PERFORMING ARTS CENTER

(310) 544-0403 / www.palosverdesperformingarts.com

27570 Norris Center Drive, Rolling Hills Estates

Ballet, big band, off-Broadway shows, Chinese acrobats, storytelling, puppetry, and comedy are just a few examples of the assortment of programs and shows put on at this Palos Verdes theater. Past kid-friendly productions have included *Carnival of the Animals*, *Much Ado About Nothing*, *Dora the Explorer*, *Flat Stanley*, *Ugly Duckling*, and the *Nutcracker*.

Hours: Call or check the website for show dates and times.

Price: The kid-friendly productions are usually $20 - 25 for adults; $17 - $20 for ages 17 and under. Other shows range from $30 - $80 per ticket, per person.

Ages: 3 years and up, depending on the show.

PANTAGES THEATER

(800) 982-2787; (323) 468-1770 / www.hollywoodpantages.com

6233 Hollywood Boulevard, Hollywood

This classic venue showcases the absolute finest in Broadway musicals, as well as dramas and hot-ticket comedies. Theater doesn't get much better than this. A few of the past productions include *Peter Pan*, which starred Cathy Rigby, *Beauty and the Beast*, *School of Rock*, *Frozen - the musical*, *Charlie and the Chocolate Factory*, and the Magic of Adam Trent. Check the website for a current schedule. Look up HOLLYWOOD - the downtown tourist mecca (pg. 171) for details on other close-by Hollywood museums and attractions.

Hours: Call for show dates and times.

Price: Prices vary, depending on the show, but range from $35 - $275. Parking is $10 - $20, depending on the lot.

Ages: Children 5 years and under are not admitted.

PASADENA PLAYHOUSE

(626) 356-7529 - box office; (626) 689-2319 - tours / www.pasadenaplayhouse.org

39 S. El Molino Avenue, Pasadena

The 100-year old Playhouse offers two arenas of interest for kids. The first is the plays themselves. The Playhouse does not have a family series, but often the plays are appropriate for middle-school-aged children and older. The second area of interest is a one-hour tour. See PASADENA PLAYHOUSE (tour) (pg. 202) for details.

Hours: Check the website for dates and times of shows.
Price: Show prices vary according to show, date, and time.
Ages: 4th graders and up.

REDONDO BEACH PERFORMING ARTS CENTER

(310) 937-6607 / www.redondo.org; www.3dtheatricals.org
1935 Manhattan Beach Boulevard, Redondo Beach

This lovely theater, which seats about 1,450 patrons, puts on outstanding musicals that are often enthralling for the whole family. Past productions, via the 3-D Theatricals troupe, have included *Joseph and the Amazing Technicolor Dreamcoat, Young Frankenstein, Once on this Island*, and *Oklahoma!*. The troupe also performs at CERRITOS CENTER FOR THE PERFORMING ARTS (pg. 181).

The center is also host to numerous other prestigious productions including ballets; dance troupes; folk ensembles, such as Aman; magicians; jazz musicians, such as David Benoit; country and rock and roll musicians; comedians; national athletic championships, such as California Bodybuilding Championship; and much more. The Distinguished Speakers Series, www.speakersla.com, has featured David McCullough, Ron Howard, Margaret Thatcher, Joe Biden, Kareem Abdul Jabar, and many others.

Hours: Call for a schedule of events.
Price: Prices range depending on the show, date, and seating.
Ages: 5 years and up, depending on the show.

SANTA CLARITA PERFORMING ARTS CENTER

(661) 362-5304 / www3.canyons.edu/Offices/PIO/CanyonsPAC
26455 Rockwell Canyon Road on the campus of College of the Canyons, Santa Clarita

This community college has a professional-style theater that seats over 880 guests and a state-of-the-art sound system that all work together to showcase community and professional performances of dance, theater, music, comedy, and more, as well as instructional programs. Past shows have included the Olate Dogs (winning participants from America's Got Talent); *Oliver!*; Santa Clarita ballet ([661] 251-0366 / santaclaritaballet.net); master chorale; Air Force band; a dance and light show; and more.

Hours: Check the website for the show schedule.
Price: Free to $50, depending on the show.
Ages: 4 years and up, depending on the show.

SANTA MONICA COLLEGE PERFORMING ARTS CENTER

(310) 434-3412; (310) 434-3005 - box office; (310) 434-3560 - education / www.thebroadstage.org
1310 11th Street, Santa Monica

The acoustics are grand, yet the performing arts center theater is still intimate with 499 seats, each offering a clear view of the stage. See and hear first rate performances at the Broad Stage, which offers a broad range of categories. These include operas, symphonies, dance companies, musicals, plays, and films. For a really intimate experience see a show at the adjacent 99-seat theater, The Edye, which is just right for smaller audience shows, readings, and experimental theater. Note that there is an art gallery on the premises, as well. Check the website or call the above phone number for more information on the select, free, matinee shows for students to see and/or the workshops to participate in.

Hours: Check the website for a schedule of shows.
Price: Prices depend on the show.
Ages: 9 years and up.

SANTA MONICA PLAYHOUSE

(310) 394-9779 / www.santamonicaplayhouse.com
1211 4th Street, Santa Monica

For over fifty years this ninety-two-seat Playhouse has offered original, one-hour, family-style musicals every weekend. Most of the productions are based on well-known characters and have titles like *Alice and the Wonderful Tea Party, Captain Jack and the Beanstalk*, and *Barnyard Madness with the Three Little Pigs*. There is a intermission with cookies and punch. Young and old will enjoy this theater experience. Ask about their much-acclaimed Theatre Field Trips for all age students. Younger kids come to the theater so see the play, then participate in a question and answer with the cast, take a backstage tour, and attend a workshop which encourages them to use and stretch their imaginations and critical thinking skills. Each participant also receives free tickets for a future production and an activity booklet. Sixth through twelfth graders have a similar program with the focus on Shakespeare, learning to understand and appreciate the language and seeing the modern relevance in his plays. Inquire about their special classes and workshops for acting, too, and come see international touring shows, concerts, and more.

Hours: Every Sat. at 2pm; Sun. at 12:30pm.
Price: $15 for adults; $12.50 for ages 12 and under. The school field trips are $695 for one show, $975 for two shows on the same day. Call for prices for other shows.
Ages: 3 years and up.

STORYBOOK THEATER AT THEATRE WEST

(818) 761-2203 / www.theatrewest.org
3333 Cahuenga Boulevard West, Los Angeles

$$$$

Every Saturday, October through June, Storybook Theater presents a fun, musical, audience-participatory play geared for 3 to 9 year olds. Classics are redone to appeal even more to children (with all the violence eliminated), like *Little Red Riding Hood*, *Ugly Duckling* and *Jack In The Beanstalk*. There is a cookie and apple juice intermission in this hour-long show. Afterward, the cast stays around to talk with the kids. What a wonderful "first theater" experience! Call or check the website to find out what's playing. Ask, too, about on-site school field trips for a minimum of 80 students.

Hours: The shows are Sat. at 1pm.
Price: $15 for adults; $12 for ages 3 - 12; children 2 and under are free. Cash or check only.
Ages: 3 - 9 years.

TCL CHINESE THEATRE

(323) 461-3331 or (323) 463-9576 / www.tclchinesetheatres.com
6925 Hollywood Boulevard, Hollywood

!/$$$$

The classic theater, built in 1927, used to be called Grauman's. It looks like a giant Chinese pagoda, with a huge dragon snaking across the front and two stone lion-dogs guarding the entrance. However, the big tourist draw is not just the architecture, but the *concrete* evidence of stars' shoe and hand sizes, and how well they write their name. Over 200 past and present stars have left their imprints - shoe prints, hand prints, and autographs - in the cement front courtyard. Step into and see if you can fill the shoe prints of John Wayne, Marilyn Monroe, Harrison Ford, Tom Cruise, Jimmy Stewart, Jack Nicholson, Shirley Temple, Julie Andrews, Tom Hanks, Arnold Schwarzenegger and Darth Vader to name a few of the immortalized stars. Celebrity lookalikes (some more so than others) and costumed cartoon characters (again, some more so than others!) are always outside the theater trying to entertain, take pictures with tourists (and charge money for doing so), and just to be odd.

Inside the exotic theater, the lobby is rich with Asian motif murals. The actual theater continues along the same theme with more, although subtle, murals and friezes. The huge auditorium, under a Hollywood-esque, star-burst chandelier, faces the screen that plays first-run movies, as well as IMAX movies (on an extra large IMAX screen) and MX4D movies, which is where seats move and emit fog, air blasts, smells, etc., that correlate with the action on the screen.

Thirty-minute, walking tours (called VIP) are offered where visitors see beyond the red carpet - it is essentially a guided tour of the lobby and exhibits inside. (A short tour for the money.) You'll learn the history of the theater (inside and out) and of the costumes and props on display, plus stories of the stars who left their imprints. Look up HOLLYWOOD - the downtown tourist mecca (pg. 171) for details on other close-by Hollywood museums and attractions.

Hours: VIP Tours are given daily, every 20 min. or so, usually starting at 10:15am, with the last tour at 6:45pm.
Price: Free to the front courtyard. VIP tours are $18 for adults; $14 for seniors; $8 for ages 12 and under. Call or check the website for movie ticket information. IMAX movies are $21.75 for adults; $20 for srs., $19 for children. MX4D movies are $25 per ticket. Parking in the lots cost between $5 - $9; with validation, the price is $4 for up to 4 hours.
Ages: 6 years and up.

TERRACE THEATER

(800) 776-7469; (562) 436-3661 - box office / www.longbeachcc.com
300 E. Ocean Boulevard at the Long Beach Convention and Entertainment Center, Long Beach

$$$$

This beautiful and modern 3,051-seat theater is situated by the ocean and has a ocean view from the eastside of the facility. It plays host to a variety of performances such as Broadway musicals (like *Grease* and *Cats*), celebrity headliners, Long Beach Symphony, *Sesame Street Live*, the Long Beach Ballet, and local performing arts groups.

Hours: Call or check the website for show times.
Price: Call or check the website for ticket prices. Parking is $15.
Ages: 5 and up, depending on the show.

THE BROAD STAGE ☼

(310) 434-3200 - college; (310) 434-3005 - box office / www.thebroadstage.com $$$$
1310 11th Street at the Santa Monica College Performing Arts Center, Santa Monica

Come and see world-class performances of every kind - Broadway musical theater; dramatic theater; concerts from the world of opera, pop, jazz and every other venue; dance, including ballet; family performances; and so much more. Other offerings include free or low cost education and outreach activities; free, student matinees; student workshops; family events; master classes; and more.
Hours: Check the website for show dates and times.
Price: Prices vary depending on the show, date and time.
Ages: 5 years and up, depending on the show.

THE YOUNES & SORAYA NAZARIAN CENTER FOR THE PERFORMING ☼
ARTS

(818) 677-3000 - box office; (818) 677-8800 - tours / www.soraya.org $$$$$
18111 Nordhoff Street on the campus of California State University Northridge, Northridge

The curtain rises on big-name talent at this 1,700-seat, very classy, glass-paneled, performing arts center. Performances have included Tyne Daly, the China Philharmonic Orchestra, Joel Grey and Marvin Hamlisch, Soweto Gospel Choir, Los Angeles Chamber Orchestra, Patti LuPone, Mandy Patinkin, the Russian National Ballet, Sergio Mendes, Arianna Huffinton, and many more. The Arts Education program offers a Student Matinee Series for school groups with shows such as *The Stinky Cheeseman and Other Fairly Stupid Tales*, *A Midsummer's Night Dream*, *Drums of India*, *Beakman on the Brain*, and *Step Afrika! Jabber*. An art gallery is located on the loge level of the Center and is open one hour prior to performances and during intermission for ticket holders.

The Bistro on the Terrace, (818) 677-2076, offers prix-fixe dinners prior to the Friday, Saturday and Sunday evening performances. Reserve them in advance. Concession stands are open during intermission, too.

Tours are offered of the Center on the last Tuesday of each month for a behind-the-scenes look into the world of performing.
Hours: Call or check the website for a schedule.
Price: Tickets range from $37 - $109, depending on the show. Parking is $8 per vehicle, though it might be free with pre-purchased tickets.
Ages: 7 years and up.

TORRANCE CULTURAL ARTS CENTER ☼

(310) 781-7171 / www.torrancearts.org $$$$
3330 Civic Center Drive, Torrance

The center is composed of several buildings that serve the community in various capacities. The Armstrong Theatre has a 500-plus-seat theater with plush seats. It's host to a variety of professional and community productions, as well as film screenings and family friendly shows. The George Nakano Theatre is an intimate setting with only 180 seats for its productions. Past family productions have included *Petra and the Wolf* and *Doktor Kaboom - It's Just Rocket Science*, plus *Peter Pan*, *Amadeus*, *Twelfth Night*, and more.

The Torrance Art Museum has three galleries usually showcasing local artists' work. It is open Tuesday through Saturday, 11am and 5pm. A music room; performing arts studios, utilized mainly for classes and as dance and exercise studios; a jewelry-making studio; a radio studio; and two outdoor plazas complete the complex. A small, traditional Japanese garden in the plaza area is a lovely way to connect all the buildings. It has a waterfall, koi pond, stone pathways, and something not so traditional - a redwood amphitheater. Check the website for the annual South Bay Festival of the Arts held here.
Hours: Call or check the website for show times and dates.
Price: Prices vary for each show, starting at $10.
Ages: 3 years and up.

TOYOTA SYMPHONIES FOR YOUTH SERIES

(323) 850-2000; (323) 850- 2050; (213) 972-0704 / www.laphil.com/tsfy

$$$$$

135 N. Grand Avenue at the Walt Disney Concert Hall, Los Angeles

At least four times a year the Los Angeles Philharmonic offers one-hour concerts under the collective title of Toyota Symphonies for Youth. They are designed to excite kids, particularly between the ages of 5 to 11, about the wonderful world of orchestral music. First, enjoy a variety of preconcert activities. Different stations can include arts and crafts, storytellers, dance, and/or meeting with musicians who will demonstrate their instruments. All the activities help to introduce (and reinforce) the morning's concert theme. Then, onto the concert. Past concerts include *Magical Melodies, Fun with Bach,* and *Peter and the Wolf.* See MUSIC CENTER (tours) (pg. 202) for details about taking a tour of this gorgeous facility and MUSIC CENTER OF LOS ANGELES (pg. 189) for more about the facility and surroundings. See also DOWNTOWN LOS ANGELES / GRAND PARK (pg. 167) for information on Grand Park and all the other places to go within this fairly immediate area.

Hours: Preconcert workshop activities begin at 10am. Concerts begin at 11am on selected Sat., usually in the months of November - April.

Price: $25 per person. Parking in the Disney Concert Hall garage is $9 - cash only.

Ages: 5 to 12 years.

TWO MILK MINIMUM

(818) 845-9721 / www.flapperscomedy.com

$$$

Burbank - 102 East Magnolia at Flappers Comedy Club; Claremont - 532 W First Street at Flappers Comedy Club

I love to laugh. And I love to laugh with my kids, but I wouldn't bring them to most comedy clubs. Two Milk Minimum is geared for family and kids to laugh out loud at the funny, crazy and interactive one-hour comedy acts, comedy magic acts, juggling, improv artists, musical acts and more. This will be a new favorite place to take the kids! The energetic host and performers are professionals who have appeared on Nickelodeon TV, Disney Channel and Cartoon Network. Enjoy a meal out here, too, with choices of burgers, mac and cheese, and pizza for only $7 per entree, plus a menu for adults, too. So, eat, drink (milk!), and be merry at Two Milk.

Hours: Shows are every Sat. at 4:30pm at Burbank; 4:30pm on Sun. at Claremont.

Price: $10 per person; children 1 and under are free.

Ages: 3 years and up.

UCLA PLANETARIUM

(310) 825-4434 / www.astro.ucla.edu/planetarium

$

405 Hilgard Ave. on the 8th floor of the UCLA Mathematical Sciences Building on the campus of UCLA, Los Angeles

The planetarium offers a free, three-part presentation every Wednesday night during the traditional school year. The first part consists of a thirty - forty-minute talk and show about the current night sky in both hemispheres, and the configuration of the galaxies in the night sky - covering stars, constellations, and other astronomical phenomena. A twenty-minute special-topic slide or video presentation follows. These shows are used as a teaching tool for astronomy students, but open to the public. Each program varies with the presenters. Afterward, is part three - viewing the real sky, weather permitting, through three department, rooftop telescopes.

Free private shows are given to educational and school groups for a maximum of thirty-five students. Advanced reservations are required. See UNIVERSITY OF CALIFORNIA, LOS ANGELES / UCLA (pg. 177) for more things to do here.

Hours: Public shows are Wed. at 7pm (8pm during daylight savings time). Late arrivals will not be seated.

Price: Free - donations appreciated. Parking is $3 an hour.

Ages: 8 years and up.

WALLIS ANNENBERG CENTER FOR THE PERFORMING ARTS

(310) 746-4000 - box office; (310) 246-3800 / www.thewallis.org

$$$

9390 N. Santa Monica Boulevard, Beverly Hills

The broad-reaching performing arts center has two theaters - one is the smaller, historic 1933 Italianate-style, 150-seat Lovelace Studio that once was the Beverly Hills Post Office, and the other, connected by a grand staircase, is the contemporary, 500-seat Bram Goldsmith Theater. Both offer a variety of top-notch programs of theater, musicals, dance, music - classical, pop, opera, etc. - as well as children's theater and programs geared for the whole family. Classes for youth are also offered. On Sunday nights in the summer, 5pm to 7pm, join in on free dance lessons - salsa, hip hop, African, Vogue, and more - with Dance Sundays by Debbie Allen. A cafe, small sculpture garden and artwork are part of the Wallis experience, too.

Hours: Call for show dates and times.

Price: Prices vary depending on the show, date and time. Student matinee performances are $7 a ticket. Parking for matinee performances is $6; $8 for nighttime ones.

Ages: 5 years and up, depending on the show.

WALT DISNEY CONCERT HALL, LOS ANGELES PHILHARMONIC and LOS ANGELES MASTER CHORALE

(213) 972-7211 / www.musiccenter.org

135 N. Grand Avenue at the Music Center, Los Angeles

$$$$

See the MUSIC CENTER OF LOS ANGELES (pg. 189) for details. For information on tours of the hall, check out MUSIC CENTER (tours) (pg. 202).

WILL GEER THEATRICUM BOTANICUM

(310) 455-3723 - box office; (310) 455-2322 - more info / www.theatricum.com

1419 N. Topanga Canyon Boulevard, Topanga

$$$$$

Set in rural Topanga, a professional resident acting company uses repertory to perform mostly classical plays, with an emphasis on Shakespeare, along with some contemporary plays, at this 300-seat outdoor amphitheater. Past productions have included *Taming of the Shrew, Our Town, A Midsummer Night's Dream,* and *Harold and Maude.* June through October, Family Fundays Kid's Shows are also presented. (Check out Creative Playground, a company that performs literature-based theater here and at other venues - www.creativeplayground.org). They feature stories and plays such as the *Velveteen Rabbit, Ferdinand the Bull* and *Legend of King Arthur.* Dress warmly for evening shows, bring a blanket, and a seat cushion. If you arrive early enough before your production you can hike at the nearby Topanga State Park, enjoy some of the unique shops that line the Boulevard, and/or pack a picnic lunch or dinner to eat under the trees.

Besides the above performances, the Botanicum presents several other theater options for children including classes (for both kids and adults); a summer youth drama camp; The Americana Series; in-school Shakespeare Assemblies or excerpts from great plays or novels (i.e., Mark Twain, Victor Hugo, or F. Scott Fitzgerald); and School Days educational programs. In the latter, students receive a resource packet and an in-class visit by an actor/teacher who explains the language and the story. This is followed by a visit to the theater. Once here, students meet costumed actors such as Queen Elizabeth I and William Shakespeare, J. R. R. Tolkien, or President and Mrs. Lincoln, depending on the time period being studied. Some students rehearse for the play while others participate in workshops which include Stage Illusion, Mime, and Elizabethan Dance. After lunch, students watch the play.

Hours: Call or check the website for a schedule. The Fundays are usually performed every Sunday and on the third Saturdays, June - October at 11am.

Price: Prices for the plays range from $25 - $38.50 for adults, depending on the seat; $15 - $25 for seniors and students; $10 for ages 5 - 15; children 4 and under are free. The Fundays are $9 per person; children under 2 are free. Parking in the lot is $7; some free parking on the street is available. The School Days program is $14 per student for the full day and all the preliminaries; $9 per student for just the play. Call about other program offerings, such as kid's concerts and comedy improv.

Ages: Plays - 8 years and up. Programs can be adapted for K - 12 graders.

—TOURS—

ALEX THEATRE (tour)

(818) 243-7700 / www.alextheatre.org

216 N. Brand Boulevard, Glendale

!

See ALEX THEATRE (pg. 178) for details about taking a tour.

Hours: Tours are offered on select Sat. at 10am.

Price: Free

Ages: 8 years and up, depending on the show.

BRAILLE INSTITUTE (Los Angeles County)

(323) 663-1111 / www.brailleinstitute.org

741 North Vermont Avenue, Los Angeles

!

See BRAILLE INSTITUTE (Santa Barbara County) (pg. 641) for details. Each campus has a slightly different feel, equipment and buildings to explore for their tours. Ask about speakers coming to your group, too.

Hours: Tours are available weekdays with appointments.

Price: Free

Ages: 8 years and up.

CALIFORNIA INSTITUTE OF TECHNOLOGY - SEISMOLOGY TOUR

(626) 395-3298, (626) 395-6327, or (626) 395-6811 / www.seismolab.caltech.edu

1200 E. California Boulevard on the Caltech campus in the South Mudd Building, Pasadena

Too often in Southern California there is a whole lot of shakin' going on. What causes this? Find out by taking a seismology tour. Much of the information is technical, but older children can appreciate it. The one-hour tour starts in the lobby, which has a timeline that shows how information comes into the lab. The lobby also has interactive displays and a computer that shows recent earthquake activity around the world and a computer with a touch screen that shows (with sound and animation) information on the Northridge quake and others. From here you go through the seismology lab, where researchers and scientists are at work, to see giant drums where seismic data are recorded, and learn how to read the seismographs. You also go through the media center, where press conferences are held after a quake. Note: This is not a hands-on tour and tours must be reserved one week in advance.

Tours must comprise of at least ten people, maximum twenty-five. If your group has less than ten, or you are a general public individual, you will be assimilated in with another group, if possible. Students must be at least 12 years old or in the sixth grade. All school tours must book the date at least two months in advance so participants have time to receive and review the provided educational materials before coming. Note: It is a requirement that all tour participants be familiar with the materials prior to taking a tour as this outing is meant to supplement, not introduce, knowledge of seismology.

Hours: Just the lobby is open to the public Mon. - Fri., 8am - 5pm. School tours are offered on the first Tues. and
          first Thurs. of the month at 10am and 11am, October - December and February - June.

Price: Free

Ages: At least 12 years old or 6th grade and up.

CALIFORNIA PIZZA KITCHEN (Los Angeles County)

(800) 91-WE CARE (919-3227) / www.cpk.com

For curious kids who wonder what actually happens from the time they order something in a restaurant to the time it arrives on their table, take them on a tour of California Pizza Kitchen. They get to walk around the restaurant before it opens to the public, see behind-the-scenes, learn about the various positions that workers hold, and to top it all off, they get to make their own pizza! Each child also receives a free activity book and a coupon to come back for a free kid's meal. Such a deal! The tour is usually geared for children 6 to 10 years old. Call your local restaurant for more details, such as minimum number (which is usually twelve children) and maximum number of students, and to set up a tour.

CPK is also a fun place for a kids birthday party as all the party-goers can be pizza chefs for a day and make their own. The party also includes all of the above-listed tour features, plus a CPK chef coat for the birthday child.

Hours: Tours are usually offered, by appointment, at 9am or 10am - before the restaurant opens for lunch.

Price: Tours are free for schools and non-profit organizations. Birthday parties start at $10 per child.

Ages: 6 - 10 years.

CHINATOWN TOURS

(213) 680-0243 / www.chinatownla.com

947 N. Broadway, Los Angeles, CA

One option is to simply take a walking tour around Chinatown by yourself. (See the website for route ideas.) We opted for a two-and-a-half hour guided walking tour, "The Undiscovered Chinatown Tour". As we walked, our guide pointed out buildings of interest, so we learned the hows and whys of the colorful architecture throughout Chinatown, as well as a history of the Chinese people, particularly the ones in this vicinity, and a history of this area. It does depend on the tour guide as to exactly what you will see and learn about. We visited a local school, a bank, a temple, herb stores, and a few other places, plus we went shopping and found great bargains as we went through the maze of Chinatown through alleyways and shopping stalls. Shopping is definitely an emphasis on this excursion.

Hours: The walking tour is given the first Sat. of every month, 10:30am - 1pm.

Price: The two+ hour walking tour is $20 per person.

Ages: 8 years and up.

DODGER STADIUM

866-DODGERS (363-4377) / www.mlb.com/dodgers/ballpark/tours

1000 Vin Scully Avenue, Los Angeles

$$$$

Let's go Dodgers, let's go! For a "fan"tastic tour of one of the best baseball teams in the National League (at least the best one based in Los Angeles!) take this 90 minute, behind-the-scenes tour to see some of the normally restricted and non-public areas. This third oldest baseball stadium has quite a storied history, with a long roster of famous players. Note that this is a walking tour, which includes climbing stairs and ramps. Some of the places you'll see and learn about include the press box, the Dodger dugout, the actual playing field (a highlight!), and the exclusive Lexus Dugout Club, which is the VIP restaurant and lounge located behind home plate. This is also home to the World Series trophies, Most Valuable Player (MVP), Cy Young awards and Rookie of the Year awards. Go Dodger Blue!!!

If you want more, two hour Clubhouse Tours include all of the above, plus a visit to the Dodger bullpen, weight room, batting cages, Dodger Clubhouse and the interview room. It's like being a team player! 45 minute pregame tours offer a briefer version, and not visiting all the places of a standard tour, but you will see Club Level Memorabilia Hall highlighting the story of Dodger baseball, the Lexus Dugout Club, et. all, and the interview room. Note: All tours meet just outside the Top of the Park Store on the Top Deck level, adjacent to Lot P.

Hours: Regular tours are given almost daily at 10am, 11:30am and 1pm. Arrive 15 min. early. Pregram tours, only, are given on daytime home games when games start at 12:10pm or 1:10pm. Clubhouse Tours are offered on select Sat. and Sun. at 2:30pm and 4:30pm. No tours are given on select national holidays.

Price: $20 for adults; $15 for seniors, military and ages 4 - 14; children 3 and under are free.

Ages: 5 years and up.

DOLBY THEATRE

See DOLBY THEATRE (pg. 182), under SHOWS AND THEATERS, for details on the Academy Awards theatre tour.

$$$$

EDWARDS AIR FORCE FLIGHT TEST CENTER MUSEUM

(661) 277-3824 or (661) 277-3510 / www.edwards.af.mil; www.afftcmuseum.org

Edwards Air Force Base

!

Your tour starts off at the parking lot where you'll board a bus that goes to the Air Force Flight Test Center Museum. You'll spend ninety-minutes listening to a talk about the history of the Air Force and Edwards, explanations of the items in the museum, and have time to look around. The museum has over twenty aircraft on display outside such as a B-52D, T-33, F-104A, YA-10B, SH-34G helicopter, UC-45, SR-71A Blackbird, and F-86. Inside are several grounded airplanes while others are suspended in air. You'll see an F-16, F-22, NA-37, AQM-34 Firebee drone, the X-25B concept demonstrator, and a full-scale replica of the Bell X-1 and Orange X-1. The museum is packed with memorabilia fitting for the birthplace of supersonic flight. One section is dedicated to Mach Busters, the men who broke sound barriers, including, of course, Chuck Yeager. It shows and tells how planes (and men) were tested for this significant breakthrough. The First Flights Wall is a model display of the more than 100 aircraft that completed their first flight at Edwards AFB. Other items on exhibit include aircraft propulsion systems, rocket engines, life support equipment, photographs, fine art, flight jackets, personal memorabilia, and the geology, or history, of the formation of the lakebeds.

The second part of the tour consists of a ninety-minute windshield tour which includes a bus ride along the flightline to see test planes taking off, looking at several unmanned vehicles and more test planes, and seeing whatever else is going on the base that particular day as well as a drive through the community of Edwards to see how life there is lived. You'll continue to learn about the missions and the history of this center, too. Some of the information on the tour is technical, so I was a little surprised how much my boys (as they range in ages) enjoyed it. Any and all questions (and my kids had a lot) are fully answered, and the knowledge that does sink in helps make this a memorable tour.

There are two types of tours offered. One is a General Public Tour, for individuals or small groups like families. These are offered once a month and fill up months in advance. The other is Large Group Tours, for groups of at least 15 people with more flexibility in booking time and date. Reservations for all tours are necessary. All visitors must provide place of birth, state I.D. or driver's license number (for those of age), last six digits of social security number, and other pertinent information. Drivers must show current registration and proof of vehicle insurance.

Hours: The museum is open only for tours to the general public, or those who already have base access. General Public Tours are offered one Friday a month, except December, from 9:30am - 1pm. Large Group Tours can be given Tues., Wed. and Thurs,. and on non-General Tour Fridays. No tours are given on federal holidays, special engagements, or shuttle landing days. All tours are by reservation only.

Price: Free

Ages: Must be 5 years or older.

EGYPTIAN THEATRE / AMERICAN CINEMATHEQUE

(323) 461-2020 or (323) 466-FILM (3456) / $$$
www.americancinemathequecalendar.com/egyptian_theatre_events
6712 Hollywood Boulevard, Hollywood

Walk like an Egyptian or just come see a movie on a giant screen at the Egyptian Theatre. This restored, 616-seat theater, built in 1922 and originally managed by Sid Grauman, shows a variety of films offered by American Cinematheque, a film and cultural arts organization. Your children might be more interested in taking a one-hour walking tour of the building. You'll go behind the scenes and learn about the history and renovation of the theater, plus see the old dressing rooms, the projection room (and talk with the projectionist about the evolution of film technology), and more. See the one-hour movie, *Forever Hollywood*, which shows at select times throughout the year. Made exclusively to show at this theater, the movie shows some of today's biggest stars narrating the history of movies and Hollywood by using numerous film clips and by being interviewed, themselves, in casual settings. Also note that this theatre shows many classic films - look at the theatre website for a listing. Look up HOLLYWOOD - the downtown tourist mecca (pg. 171) for details on other close-by Hollywood museums and attractions.

Hours: Tours are given one Sat. a month at 10:30am. Check the website for a schedule. Groups of 10 or more can schedule a tour on other dates as well. Check the website for show times.

Price: Tours are $9 for adults, $7 for seniors and students. Movies are $12 per person. Parking is $10 - $12, depending on the lot.

Ages: 8 years and up.

FEDERAL RESERVE BANK OF SAN FRANCISCO

(213) 683-2900 / www.frbsf.org $$
950 S. Grand Avenue, Los Angeles

What actually happens to our money once it's deposited in a bank? Find out by taking a tour of the Los Angeles branch of the Federal Reserve Bank. The ninety-minute tour starts with a fifteen-minute video that describes the bank and the role of the Federal Reserve System in the U.S. economy. The rest of the tour focuses on the cash and check processing operations. You'll see how coin, currency, and checks are processed by high speed machines. You may also peruse the World of Economics exhibit in the lobby of the bank. The exhibit attempts to simplify the complex ideas of American economics by using a timeline, computer games, videotapes, colorful murals, and some samples of rare and historic bills. The best is the pachinko-like game where students rate the safety and soundness of a financial institution and the money wheel to identify counterfeit notes. Over 100 free publications are available to render further aid. High school students are invited to stay after the tour for a forty-five minute finance training session where they will learn the importance of saving and investing, how to develop a budget, and the relationship between risk and rate of return. (I need this.)

Rules are enforced at the bank as a matter of security. Visitors must wear badges at all times, pass through a metal detector, and stay with the tour. No cameras are allowed. Tours need a minimum of fifteen participants, a maximum of thirty, and must be arranged in advance, online. There are three type of tours: one for high-schoolers, one for Girl Scouts who must be in 5th grade or older, and one for college students. See DOWNTOWN LOS ANGELES / GRAND PARK (pg. 167) for information on Grand Park and all the other places to go within this fairly immediate area.

Hours: Group tours are by appointment only, Mon. - Thurs. at 10am and 1pm, excluding national holidays.

Price: Free. Parking costs about $10 for 2 hours.

Ages: 9th graders and up only.

GOODWILL INDUSTRIES (Los Angeles County)

Long Beach - (562) 435-3411; (323) 223-1211 - Los Angeles / www.goodwillsocal.org; www.thinkgood.org   !
Long Beach - 800 W. Pacific Coast Highway; Los Angeles - 342 North San Fernando Road

See the entry for GOODWILL INDUSTRIES (San Bernardino County) (pg. 437) for details. There are three campuses in the Los Angeles area and two are recommended to take tours of. The facility on San Fernando Road is the biggest facility in the L.A. area and the main one for tours. The best tour time is usually between 10am and 11am, otherwise you might not see a lot of action going on. Purchase a lunch in the cafeteria for about $5, or bring a sack lunch and enjoy it on the patio. There is a donation center there and retail store, too.

Hours: Long Beach - Tours are offered by reservation only. Los Angeles - Tours are offered Mon. - Fri. at 10am by reservation only.

Price: Free

Ages: Preferably 5th graders and up.

GUIDE DOGS OF AMERICA

(818) 833-6437 - tours; (818) 362-5834 - general info / www.guidedogsofamerica.org   !
13445 Glenoaks Boulevard, Sylmar

Guide Dogs of America is a center that breeds, raises, and trains Labrador retrievers, golden retrievers, and German shepherds for the blind. It is also a school that teaches blind men and women how to use guide dogs. These services are offered free of charge. Free tours, which last about an hour and a half, are given of the facility.

First, you watch a twenty-minute video that shows puppies frolicking, students getting to know their dogs and testimonies on their lives being changed by being mobile. The film tugs at your heart. You'll walk past the administrative offices and hallways lined with photos of graduates and tour the dormitories where students stay for a month while receiving training. Note: If students are in residence, this part of the tour is bypassed. The best part, according to kids, is seeing the kennels and whelping bays of future guide dogs. Tip: Call first to see if there is a puppy litter because seeing them makes the field trips extra special. Tours are offered for groups of fifteen to fifty people (if you have less than fifteen you can be added onto another group) with an advance registration of thirty days. Walk-in tours, or individuals, may join in on an on-going tour if one is scheduled.

Have you ever thought about being a foster parent - for a dog? Guide puppies, or future guide dogs, need temporary homes for the first eighteen months of their life. If you are willing to teach them basic obedience, love them, and encourage them to be well socialized (sort of like raising children), call for more information. The heartbreak of separation from your pup can be offset in the knowledge that your family enabled a blind person to be mobile and independent. You're invited to attend the graduation ceremony of your dog and the student you've helped.

Hours: Group tours are given Tues. - Thurs. at 10am and 1:30pm, by reservation only. Groups must be a minimum of 15 and max of 50.

Price: Free

Ages: Kids must be at least 9 years old or in fourth grade.

JET PROPULSION LABORATORIES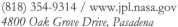

(818) 354-9314 / www.jpl.nasa.gov   !
4800 Oak Grove Drive, Pasadena

"Space, the final frontier." JPL is a leading research and development center for NASA, with 160 buildings on 177 acres of land. Its mission is to observe earth, explore new worlds (via unmanned, robotic spacecraft), send back pictures, and ultimately, find the answer to the question, "Are we alone?" A twenty-minute film, *Journey to the Planets,* starts at the sun and then takes viewers through the solar system, to its outer limits. It made my family aware of the incomprehensible vastness of our universe. My boys were awed by this realization - I just felt very small and insignificant. (Did you know that one light year translates as six trillion miles?) The tour guide then dispenses information about JPL - its history and accomplishments.

The next stop is the museum, or visitors center. It contains vivid photographs of star fields and pillars of gas; replica models of the Voyagers; and a Voyager gold record made for other intelligent life forms to listen to and learn about planet earth. Press the display button and listen to a sampling of the recording. The actual recording contains greetings in fifty-five languages as well as photographs of our culture, and sounds of music, the rainforest, a heartbeat, and much more. We watched a short "animated" movie about the Mars Rover, too. There are also replicas of early and modern space craft including the 1958 Explorer, the Mars Pathfinder, a full-scale model of the Galileo, and the Cassini. Our tour guide talked extensively about the models and their actual missions. Although some of it was a bit too technical for my kids (and me - I guess I'm no rocket scientist), we learned a lot.

Trekking over to another building, we watched Mission Control in action. The viewing room allows visitors to see the Operations Chief and others tracking and (maybe) communicating with spacecraft - it depends on what's going on. While here the docent explains all about the current space programs, hopeful future ones, and how transmission is accomplished. The last stop is the huge Spacecraft Assembly Facility (i.e. the assembly area, or clean area), where, again, depending on what is in process, you might see actual spacecraft being assembled. Maybe you'll see a piece of history in the making!

JPL facilities can be seen on a two-plus-hour walking tour, which involves covering a bit of ground and going up and down several flights of stairs. You are welcome to take pictures. Note that special events could preclude the regular tour route. Reservations for tours are required at least five months in advance and a final roster of names must be submitted online. Guests 18 and up must provide a photo I.D. Check out the annual Explore JPL open house, which happens in June. Bring your space cadets here and have a blast!

Hours: Tours are offered for ten individuals or family members, on alternating Mon. or Wed., usually at 1pm. Tours are offered to groups comprising 20 - 80 people, Mon. - Fri. at 9:30am and at 1pm.

Price: Free

Ages: Must be 3rd grade or above.

LA SANITATION

(800) 773-2489 - main #; Los Angeles, Los Angeles-Glendale Water Reclamation Plant - (818) 778-4226; Playa Del Rey, Hyperion Water Reclamation Plant - (310) 648-5363; San Pedro, Terminal Island Water Reclamation Plant - (310) 548-7520; Van Nuys, Donald C. Tillman Water Reclamation Plant - (818) 778-4226 / www.lacitysan.org

Los Angeles - 4600 Colorado Blvd.; Playa Del Rey - 12000 Vista Del Mar; San Pedro - 445 Ferry St.; Van Nuys - 6100 Woodley Ave.

How can you refuse to learn about refuse, especially if it's offered in such a "clean" manner? Although "all drains lead to the ocean", according to *Finding Nemo*, find out what actually happens when something goes down the drain by taking a part-tram, part- walking tour of one of L.A.'s four water reclamation facilities.

You'll see and learn about the steps of some of the various treatment processes at the plants - 1) preliminary treatment where solids (as large as tree branches and as small as sand) are screened, pumped out and removed from wastewater; 2) primary treatment which allows settling of leftover solids then removal; and 3) secondary treatment which incorporates helpful bacteria for final processing. So, solids are separated from water for the wastewater to be treated then ultimately recycled, and solids are processed into energy resources, soil amendments, and more. Don't waste this knowledge!

At the 144-acre Hyperion Plant, for instance, there are two tours, each a little over an hour long. The first is an interesting and informative tour of the plant, including a tram ride around the plant, seeing and following raw waste (kind of yucky!) to enclosed tanks and to its final processing - just go with the flow. The second tour includes the environmental learning center with three floors of exhibits, some that are interactive. These include "working" in a lab, turning gears to enable bacteria to help settle the solids, learning about disposing of hazardous waste and playing recycle games, like which items go in which trash/recycle bins. Tip: You can take both tours in one visit. Check the website for information on LA Sanitation Sewer Science Program which teaches and aids environmental awareness and stewardship for high school students.

Note that the Donald C. Tillman Water Reclamation Plant in Van Nuys is adjacent to the lovely Japanese Garden (THE JAPANESE GARDEN (pg. 66)) which is fed by the plant's reclaimed water. Also note that LA Sanitation hosts six Discover Recycling Open Houses throughout the year, April thru June, at their watershed district yards (not the above facilities). The free Open House features trash trucks and equipment demonstrations in addition to facility tours, information booths, recycling games, and refreshments. See DISCOVER RECYCLING OPEN HOUSE (pg. 706) in the Calendar section for more info.

Hours: Tours are by appointment only. Call the number for the corresponding plant.

Price: Free

Ages: 9 years and up, only.

LONG BEACH AIRPORT TOUR

(562) 570-2678 - tours; (562) 570-2600 / www.lgb.org

4100 Donald Douglas Drive at the Long Beach Airport, Long Beach

Take a pretend trip and a real visit to this great little historic airport for a sixty to ninety-minute, behind-the-scenes tour, tailored to your group's interests and age level. Depending on airport activity, kids and adults walk through the terminal and see model airplanes, photographs, and artifacts from early aviator, Earl Daugherty, while learning about aviation history and exactly what goes on at an airport. The facilities art, such as mosaic murals, and architecture (the terminal was built in 1940) is also viewed and discussed.

If the schedule permits, groups will be treated to a demonstration of the huge rescue vehicles, with all of its lights and sirens, by members of the airport's Fire and Rescue team. The tour concludes with a visit to the Observation Deck which is great for, well, observing planes landing and taking off. Flexibility is a key for this high-flying tour. Seventy-five is the maximum number of people for the tour and kids must be at least 8 years old.

Hours: Tours are available by appointment only. Book your tour at least a month ahead of time. Extreme weather cancels all tours.

Price: Free

Ages: At least 8 years old.

LOS ANGELES TIMES

(213) 237-5757 or (800) LATIMES (528-4637) ext. 75757 /
www.latimes.com/about/mediagroup/latimes/tour
202 W. 1ˢᵗ Street, Los Angeles

$$

Children who are at least 10 years old with journalistic tendencies will enjoy seeing how a newspaper is put together. (So will adults.) The beautiful, historic building with marble flooring has a lobby that contains old printing artifacts, murals, a gorgeous globe, and an informational and visual timeline which chronicles the inception of the Times through present day. The one-hour Editorial Tour goes through the editorial offices, where news from all over the world is gathered, written, and edited; the composing room, where news stories, advertisements, and graphics are incorporated; the entertainment and features office; the sports area; and where TV spots are made incorporating newsworthy people. There are numerous empty desks and it might not look busy, but staff members are off getting, reporting and writing the news, nonetheless. Walk through the archives office where every article and every photograph is still kept on file! Look into the test kitchen, where recipes are tested and photographed for the Food Section. Along the way visitors learn the history of the company, how times have changed (pun intended!), and some of the how-to's of journalism and photojournalism.

One-hour Plant Tours are also given down the street, at 2000 E. 8ᵗʰ Street, through the aptly named Olympic plant - the enormous warehouse facility where over half a million copies of the newspaper are made each evening and temporarily stored. Pass through a pressroom, which is twice the size of a football field; the newsprint storage area, where robot-like automated vehicles carry rolls of newsprint weighing 2,500 pounds; the plate-making area, where newspaper pages go from photographic negatives to aluminum printing plates; and the mail room, where an automated distribution system takes newspapers from presses to the delivery trucks. Depending on the day of your visit, you might view the presses actually running, from the lobby. And yes, it can be loud.

Kids (and adults) rarely realize what it takes, on a daily basis, to put together the internationally acclaimed newspaper that gets read with a cup of coffee every morning. Individuals and groups (maximum of thirty for the Editorial Tour and forty-five for the Plant Tour) are welcome; just need to make reservations for either tour in advance. Tours are disabled accessible. Tip: Our group took both tours and found plenty to see and do in between tour times. See DOWNTOWN LOS ANGELES / GRAND PARK (pg. 167) for information on Grand Park and all the other places to go within this fairly immediate area.

Hours: Call for tour times of the Times offered on weekdays by reservations only.
Price: Free. Parking is $11 max.
Ages: Children must be at least in 4ᵗʰ grade/10 years or older.

MELODY RANCH MOTION PICTURE STUDIO VIP TOURS

(661) 286-1188 - tours; (661) 259-9669 - studios / www.melodyranchstudio.com $$$$$
24715 Oak Creek Avenue, Newhall

Well, Pilgrim, if you're an Old West fan, you'll love taking a tour of this working studio built in 1915 specifically as a Western town for shooting films. Walk along the dusty main street and you'll be walking in the boot steps of John Wayne, Tom Mix, Gene Autry, Hopalong Cassidy, The Lone Ranger, and many others. You walk past and into the furnished buildings along here - the jailhouse, saloon, church, bank, hotel lobby, town hall, and more.

There are props galore around town and in the Prop Shop. Barrels, brooms, bottles, blankets, and other items that don't begin with the letter b. The museum, originally a house, contains over twenty-five mostly-military vehicles used in movies and television, plus a lot of photos from past and present shows filmed here - over 2,000 productions to date! Film fanatics favorite flicks are featured here, including *Django* and *The Last Stand*.

If you're interested in the film industry - acting, directing, camera work, etc. - you'll appreciate the behind-the-scenes and insider's knowledge dispensed throughout your two-hour walking tour. You'll also learn about the history of film-making and the history of the ranch. The information and tone of this casual tour adapts to the age group and interest level of the visitors.

Because filming is frequently being done here and studios might have it under contract for up to nine months at a time if a series is being shot and the ranch isn't open then, tour times are extremely limited. Groups can comprise as few as two and only up to ten people. It is imperative that you call before visiting.

Hours: Call to schedule a tour.
Price: $75 for adults; ages 17 and under are free with a paying adult.
Ages: 8 years and up.

MUSIC CENTER (tours)

(213) 972-4399 or (213) 972-7211 or (213) 972-3688 / www.musiccenter.org $$
135 N. Grand Avenue at the Music Center of Los Angeles, Los Angeles

    This two-city block Los Angeles complex features powerhouse entertainment venues - the Ahmanson Theater, Dorothy Chandler Pavilion, Walt Disney Concert Hall, and Mark Taper Forum. For show information and knowing what else there is there check out MUSIC CENTER OF LOS ANGELES (pg. 189). The free, ninety-minute, guided Symphonian Tour, meeting in the lobby of the Disney Concert Hall, goes into a portion of all four of the buildings, concentrating on their history, architecture, and resident companies. For more insight and knowledge specifically about the Disney Concert Hall take a free, hour-long guided tour that highlights the garden and architecture while going through parts of the interior as well. Another option is the free, sixty-minute self-guided audio tour, narrated by John Lithgow, for individuals or groups of fourteen or less. This tour focuses on the history and conception of the concert hall, as well as the final implementation. Note that tours include only the lobby of the Disney hall without going into the auditorium as it is almost constantly in use for rehearsals and productions. See DOWNTOWN LOS ANGELES / GRAND PARK (pg. 167) for information on Grand Park and all the other places to go within this fairly immediate area.

Hours: The Symphonian tours are usually given Tues. - Sat. at 10:30am and 12:30pm. Disney Concert Tours are usually offered on select days at noon and 1:15. Check the schedule first as these days and times do fluctuate. Audio tours are usually available most days, 10am - 2pm.

Price: Note that tours are free for individuals and families of 14 or fewer - first come, first served. Tours for 15 or more people must have advanced reservations and are charged $10 per for the audio tour; $15 for Symphonian and Disney. Parking in the Music Center and Disney Concert Hall garages is $9 for 3 hours with validation. Parking is $20 max on non-event weekdays.

Ages: 3rd graders and up.

PARAMOUNT PICTURES

(323) 956-1777 / www.paramountstudiotour.com   6/$
5555 Melrose Avenue, Hollywood

    Insider knowledge in Hollywood is of *paramount* importance, so take a two-hour, behind-the-scenes guided tour of this working movie and television studio. You will walk around this historic, Oscar-producing studio visiting several finished and furnished sets and seeing some still in the process of being built, depending on the current need. You'll see the daily operations of a studio; learn information about the shows, past and present, filmed here; and maybe see someone famous - it's all in a day's work!

    For even more behind-the-scenes tour, take the 4.5 hour VIP cart tour of the studios and backlot where you have access to some of the more private areas - special effect, prop warehouse, sign shop and other sound stages, as well as the opportunity to perhaps meet and chat with some people who make the magic happen. Lunch is included.

    Free, reserved tickets are also available here to see a television show being filmed. This is a very fun, very Hollywood thing to experience. Call for a schedule of shows and show dates and times. You may also contact Audiences Unlimited, Inc. at (818) 260-0041 / www.tvtickets.com for more information about television shows as they are listed thirty days prior to show taping.

Hours: Tours are available daily, by advance reservations only, every half hour from 9:30am - 3:30pm. The VIP Tour is given Mon. - Fri., 9:30am and 1pm. Closed Easter, 4th of July, Thanksgiving and Christmas.

Price: $58 per person for the regular tour; $178 for the VIP tour. Parking is $15 for the regular tour.

Ages: 10 years and up only.

PASADENA PLAYHOUSE (tour)

(626) 792-8672 / www.pasadenaplayhouse.org; www.friendsofthepasadenaplayhouse.org $
39 S. El Molino Avenue, Pasadena

    The renowned and historic Playhouse offers tours that last a little over an hour that involved some walking and walking up and down steps. Visitors see first hand what the audience normally doesn't see - behind-the-scenes. The tour usually include seeing the green room, where the actors await their time on stage; dressing rooms; the shop where the scenes are designed and built; and other rooms and areas of interest, while hearing the history of the theater as well as this particular region. A minimum of five people is necessary. See PASADENA PLAYHOUSE (pg. 190) for details about the shows presented here.

Hours: Tours are conducted Mon. - Fri., 10am - 3pm.

Price: Free, but donations are customary and appreciated. Parking is $5.

Ages: 4th graders and up.

PORT OF LOS ANGELES SCHOOL BOAT TOUR PROGRAM

(310) 732-3508 or (310) 732-3960 / www.portoflosangeles.org/education/sbtp.asp !
600 Sampson Way, Berth 84 adjacent to the Los Angeles Maritime Museum, San Pedro

The Port of Los Angeles is America's busiest container port in the nation. It is incredibly impressive to see these massive container ships - that contain furniture, electronics, and anything and everything consumers use - up close. The facility itself, situated on the nearby manmade island, is almost 500 acres huge!

Free, one-hour educational boat tours are offered to school groups (fourth grade through college) so that as they visually experience what the port does, they also learn how it actually operates. They are also educated about the operations of world trade, environmental issues and initiatives, and security measures. Teachers, resource materials and information is provided for you on any area of focus - local history, international trade, or environmental awareness. Combine a tour here with a visit to the LOS ANGELES MARITIME MUSEUM (pg. 132). Other programs offered by the port include scout programs; speakers for schools; the *Los Angeles Times* in Education series; and the TransPORTer, a mobile exhibit truck with interactive exhibits, displays, computer simulation games, "Sounds of the Port" listening center, and more. (The latter is for a minimum 400 students.) Note that one Saturday a year, in May, free, educational boat tours of the port are open to the public.

Hours: Go on the website to schedule a tour.
Price: Free
Ages: 4th grade - college

RAIN BIRD BIOTREK

(909) 869-4072 / (909) 869-7659 - BioTrek; (909) 869-6701 - campus / www.cpp.edu/~biotrek/ $$
3801 W. Temple Avenue at California State Polytechnic University, Pomona

"It sure is hot in here!" is a comment from kids as they enter the humid jungle atmosphere of the rainforest. Rain Bird BioTrek is a three-building learning facility that features the rainforest, an ethnobotany area, and an aquatic biology center, all designed for visitors to learn about environmental preservation.

Enter the huge greenhouse - the rainforest environment, replete with 100 species of tropical plants. Via a self-guided (or guided) tour learn about the global impact and importance of the rainforest, especially the different plants of the rainforest and their use - some are used to make spices, some for food, and some for other functions. The animals here representing this section of the world include dwarf caimans, which is related to the crocodile; the odd-looking matamata "snorkeling" turtles; stick insects, which visitors can hold; blue tongue skinks; and Madagascar hissing cockroaches. The building also houses a museum of sorts, showcasing the five biomes of Southern California in a diorama style; the impact man has had on the rainforest via mining and logging; and artifacts and exhibits that pertain to the Tongva and Gabrielino Indian tribes.

Outside, adjacent to the rainforest green house, is the ethnobotany learning center garden. (Ethnobotany means the study of how different cultures use plants.) Native plants of indigenous people and other "wild" vegetation are landscaped around a pathway, running brook, and a pond. Visitors learn fascinating facts about the relationship between the Tongva and plants. They also can try their hand at grinding acorns with stones and a few other activities. There is also a Mesozoic (or age of reptiles/dinosaurs) garden - a small garden with plants for that time period and a seating area of large boulders. And look for the Monarch and other butterfly species in the nearby butterfly garden.

The aquatic biology component of this trek is in another adjacent building that holds a few large aquarium tanks, as well as several smaller ones. Set up by habitat, the facility includes a flood zone, representing when the Amazon River floods the rainforest and fish feed off treetops. One of the fish here is a lungfish, which adapts to search for food in muddy water. The mangrove habitat holds scat and puffer fish. Colorful, tropical fish can be seen in the coral reef tank, such as the clownfish, foxface, and even an eel. The kelp forest contains bass, sting rays, a horned shark, and sculpin fish. Other intriguing creatures include fish that make loud sounds and ones that generate electricity. A table sink allows visitors to see tidal animals up close.

Guided group tours of BioTrek last about ninety minutes and require a minimum of sixteen people and not more than ninety. At certain times the facility is open to the public and although the tours are not guided then, per se, staff members are available to answer questions. Note: There is a grassy area to enjoy a picnic lunch or go to the on-campus eateries. Another food choice is to visit the Farm Store just around the corner at 4102 S. University Drive. They have farm-fresh produce, incredible chocolate milk, health foods and other products. Contact the store at (909) 869-4906.

Hours: Open September through mid-June. Group tours are given Tues. and Thurs. from 10am - 11:50am. Call to schedule. It is usually open to the public the third Sat. of the month from 11am - 3pm, but you can take a self-guided tour whenever the doors are open. Call first to confirm.

Price: Free to visit and walk around on your own. School field trips for K - 12th grade are $6 per person, with a minimum of $180. Parking is $8 a day, Mon. - Fri.; $5 on Sat. - Sun.

Ages: 5 years and up.

SANITATION DISTRICTS OF LOS ANGELES COUNTY TOURS

(562) 699-7411or (562) 908-4288 / www.lacsd.org

1955 Workman Mill Road, Whittier

Do your kids run after trash trucks? Mine did when they were little. Now it's a struggle to get them to take out the trash. The sanitation department offers two different tours regarding trash and sewage treatment. The ninety-minute landfill tour takes visitors into and kind of through one of the largest landfills in the country. (Don't breathe in too deeply.) There are several stops along the way including the station where trucks are weighed; the disposal yard where trash is sorted and separated by category such as recyclables, appliances, yard waste, etc.; and an area where biogases, namely methane, are converted to electricity and clean-burning automobile fuel. Visitors learn about ecology and what happens when a landfill closes. Note that for this tour for students, only one vehicle (i.e., a bus) is allowed on the premises.

The one-hour walking tour of a water treatment plant can be taken in conjunction with the landfill tour, or separately. Students walk through the control room of the plant and see tanks of water where solids have settled. They'll learn how water is cycled, recycled for use like landscape irrigation, about water quality, conservation, and see pictures and samples of treated water. The minimum number of participants on each tour is ten; the maximum is thirtyish. If you can't come to the plant, staff members will come to your facility to talk about wastewater treatment, solid waste management, and even environmental careers. Various resources are available for teachers, such as a down loadable teacher's guide. Note that the facilities are open to the public a few Saturdays, too, and at these tours ages 7 and up are invited.

There are numerous water reclamation facilities in L.A. County - Carson, Cerritos, City of Industry, El Monte, La Canada Flintridge, Lancaster, Long Beach, Palmdale, Pomona, Saugus, Valencia, Whittier - and several Solid Waste facilities - Calabasas, Commerce, Long Beach, Los Angeles, Palos Verdes, Puente Hills, Walnut, and Whittier. Most of the facilities offer tours to schools and groups living within these communities, with the most popular sites being the San Jose Water Reclamation Plant and Puente Hills Materials Recovery Facility both in Whittier.

Hours: Groups need to call to schedule a tour at least a month in advance. Tours are offered Mon. - Fri. from 8am - 3pm. Tours for the general public are offered at least once a quarter, on select Sat., 9am, 11am or 1pm for a water reclamation plant; 10:30am - 12:30pm for a landfill.

Price: Free

Ages: Must be 10 years old and up.

SONY PICTURE STUDIOS TOUR

(310) 244-TOUR (8687) / www.sonypicturesstudios.com $$$$$

10202 W. Washington Boulevard, Culver City

Catch a glimpse of great moments in movie and television history that have been made on this forty-four-acre lot. After seeing the hard-to-miss, 94-foot tall Rainbow sculpture arching over the studio, your two-hour-plus walking tour begins in the lobby of the architecturally gorgeous Sony Plaza building. Some of the costumes we saw on display behind glass here included Captain Hook's pirate outfit, Tinkerbell's dress, and dresses (as well as furniture and a stagecoach) from the 1994 version of *Little Women*. Exhibits do rotate.

First watch a twenty-minute movie on the history of Columbia/Tristar/Sony, including some classic film footage. Then, walk across the street to the main cluster of buildings. In a park-like setting, visit the Thalberg building which houses two original Oscars, as well as several others made for the studios, for Best Picture awards. The tour continues past numerous buildings that were once dressing rooms to stars and are now less-glamorous editing or business offices. You'll hear a little bit about Louis B. Mayer, Judy Garland, Joan Crawford, and other famous alumni.

Because this is a real working studio, what you see next differs from tour to tour, depending on the day, the time of day, and what shows are being filmed. We saw the scoring stage, with chairs and microphones ready for musicians to record; the wardrobe department, where seamstresses were busy at work and where the clothes "closet" was almost as big as my house; and we walked through many of the sound stages, including the one housing the Jeopardy set. The huge sound stages, which have padded walls that block out 98% of sound, are in a constant state of flux - either under construction, being torn down, or containing sets of shows currently on the air. Not to take away from the magic of

Hollywood, but we saw a lot of equipment, free-standing doorways, stairs that led nowhere, props of all kinds, and lots of stuff (e.g., nails, trash, and boards) just left around. Watch your step! You'll see the RV used in *Breaking Bad* and other famous vehicles. Our tour guide pointed out the sound stage where the yellow brick road once wound through Munchkinland, the one where agents from *Men in Black* battled outlaw aliens from outer space, and another one that holds a pool (i.e., tank) where Ethel Merman swam. You also might be able to visit the sets of *Jeopardy* or *Wheel of Fortune*. If you want to see a taping of either of these shows on the day of your tour, call (800) 482-9840 for more info. Tip: Call ahead to get a schedule of other shows being filmed to combine a tour with the possibility of being part of their studio audience.

Finish your time here by shopping on Main Street, which is the only place picture-taking is allowed. The "street" is composed of a row of stores, including an emporium stocked with Sony products, and a few places to grab a bite to eat such as the Commissary; The Museum Marketplace; Gower Cafe, with Wolfgang Puck's pizza and more (this restaurant interior features costumes and props direct from movies and shows); and cafes.

Want to feel more like a movie star? Take another tour option - the three-hour VIP Lunch Tour which gives you a personal cart ride around the studio; more and personal behind-the-scenes; some time at the Sony Museum which has actual props and artifacts from some of the most iconic films, plus a Virtual Reality experience there; a three-course lunch at the Commissary; and a souvenir photo. All yours for $150 per person.

Hours: Tours depart Mon. - Fri., at 9:30am, 10:30am, 1:30pm, and 2:30pm. Purchase tickets online. Additional tour times are available at peak seasons. VIP tours are offered during the week at 11am. Reservations are highly recommended for all tours. Government-issued photo IDs are required for all adults. Closed weekends and all holidays. Groups may schedule tours at other times.
Price: $45 per person.
Ages: 12 years and up only.

TOPSAIL   ☀

(310) 833-6055 / www.lamitopsail.org $$$$$
Berth 78 at Ports O'Call Village, San Pedro

Get ready to sail the ocean. The traditionally-rigged, official tall ships of Los Angeles, the 110-foot twin tall ships / brigantines *Exy Johnson* and *Irving Johnson,* are wonderful to behold, but a cruise, or tour, on them is even better. Experience the wind in your hair, the sun on your face, and sea lions and dolphins (hopefully!) in the water. Participants will enjoy the high (well, medium) seas adventure while literally learning the ropes of sailing as the sea teaches about life.

Topsail, which partners with the Los Angeles Maritime Institute, offers choices of Topsail use or Topsail STEM educational programs. They are geared for youth primarily between 6th to 12th grades, but flexible enough to accommodate almost any age and ability with school and organized youth groups. The ships don't feel like a classroom (which is good!), yet students learn seamanship, navigation (geometry and algebra), history, charts, piloting, marine biology, geology, sail training, team-building, problem-solving, planning, leadership and so much more, all in an adventuresome and participatory way on day sails and overnight voyages.

And sailing isn't just for youth as there are monthly Community Sails offered where individuals and families can purchase a ticket and sail the LA Waterfront aboard one of the tall ships, experiencing a hands-on program, firsthand, for 2.5 hours! Each month is a different theme. Check the website calendar for these special days, as well as others such as Explore the Coast / Explora la Costa, a bi-lingual sail and program. Note that Topsail offers a myriad of volunteer opportunities, for youth and adults, at sea and on land such as boat restoration, woodshop, boat building, training sails and more. Youth can also check out the Sea Scouts organization.

Hours: Call or check the website for program dates.
Price: Community Days start at $60 for adults; $30 for ages 12 and under. Topsail starts at $1700 per day for a five-hour day sail for up to 40 participants, which is $42.50 per person. Title 1 pricing is available for those schools who qualify.
Ages: 70 lbs and up.

VAN NUYS AIRPORT TOUR   ☀

(818) 442-6526 / www.lawa.org   !
Roscoe Boulevard at Van Nuys Airport, Van Nuys

Here's a way to stay grounded while touring an airport - take the ninety-minute bus tour of the Van Nuys airport. Groups can provide their own bus, or, with a minimum of twenty people, ask if the airport has one available for the tour. There are several stops along the way, depending on what's available on the day of your visit. You cruise along the service road and runway, and look inside hangars. Stops could include seeing the fire station and the radar facilities.

You will definitely learn the history of the airport and importance of it in aviation and even in its use of Hollywood and TV shows. Visit Vinny, the airport's kid-friendly, hands-on, educational airplane. As the children watch planes land and take off, they'll learn the history of the airport and gain some high-flying knowledge. Bring a sack lunch and eat at the observation site while watching the planes in flight.

Hours: Call and schedule a tour date; times are 9:30am and 11am. Reservations are required.
Price: Free
Ages: Must be at least in the 1st grade.

WARNER BROS. STUDIO TOUR HOLLYWOOD

(818) 972-TOUR (8687) / www.wbstudiotour.com   6/$
3400 Riverside Drive, Burbank

"What's up, doc?" An almost three-hour, behind-the-scenes tour of the world-renown Warner Bros. studio - that's what's up! First, watch a ten-minute film that shows a montage of highlights of shows created by Warner Bros., just to get you in the mood. Hop on board the twelve-passenger tram (such a small number allows the tour to be intimate) for a part-driving and part-walking tour around some of the 110-acre studio that incorporates thirty sound stages, a gas station, a multitude of outside sets, the four-story prop building, and much more.

The first stop is a few streets that look familiar as they have been, and continue to be, used in a multitude of movies, including the *Spiderman* films. You'll learn that doorknobs denote a time period; that the trees are potted in the ground and removable or ready to show foliage with fake leaves tied on; that many of the realistic looking buildings are merely facades; and so much more insider information and facts you never knew about movie-making. The tour will either take some of the romance out of picture-making, or make your child want to be involved in the process!

You'll see numerous backlots and exterior sets from classic to current movies and television shows, lots of equipment, and the inside of some sound stages (but not all thirty). See what you recognize from your favorite flicks. You might see a celebrity. The interior sets rotate, depending on what is currently being filmed here. We went onto the set of *Chuck* and saw where *Gilmore Girls, The Mentalist, Big Bang Theory, Ellen DeGeneres Show, La La Land* and so many more shows and movies were filmed. The set from *Two and a Half Men* is here, as is the authentic Russian Soyuz capsule from *Gravity*. We saw sets being constructed at the craft/production shop and learned that Stage 16 is one of the tallest in the world and was used in the *Batman* trilogy and *Perfect Storm*. We drove past *ER*'s emergency room entrance and learned how movie "snow" is made. (They use instant mashed potato flakes - we can do this at home!) We walked into the immense prop building and saw rooms and rooms packed with eclectic stuff - rooms of just lamps, antique furniture, contemporary furniture, bunny heads, statues, globes, cameras, trunks, signs, dinosaurs, costumes used in *Last Samurai*, and everything else you could imagine (and some you can't), all rentable for a huge price tag.

Enter the Batcave, a very cool room full of just the incredible Batmobiles used in the films and series. Bathammer, Batblade, Tumbler and other bat vehicles are the stars, surrounded by city-scape wall hangings, a huge Batman statue in the center and flashlight bat signs shining.

You can enter into the recreated, real set of *Friend's* Central Perk coffee shop here that has authentic props, like the actual couch that you can sit on for a photo op. Get behind the camera and act out some of your favorite lines from the show. Note that in another area a full, working replica of the Cafe allows you to purchase Central Perk coffee to share with some of your friends and/or purchase breakfast or lunch here during the week.

Besides Central Perk, Stage 48 - Script to Screen, is also a huge interactive sound stage that you can explore for 45-minutes on your own. Costumes, hot off the actors from current movies, and props abound, plus there are screens to move in front of that mimic movements of animated screen stars; a computer design station to create your own costumes and see how professionals go from rough sketches to final scenes; a touch screen to view head shots and audition reels from your favorite actors; a screen to build your own Batmobile; and more - everything to give you real insight from script development to post production. While here stand in front of a green screen and ride a Nimbus 2000 from *Harry Potter*, or ride a Bat-pod through the streets of Gotham, while learning about 'motion capture' used also in *The Matrix* and other films. Again, great photo ops. The fully equipped, state-of-the-art recording studio shows how speech, sound effects and music are all added to film.

DC Universe: The Exhibit is a great 20-minute stop. The large room features super heros and super villains with mannequins and statues wearing authentic costumes in their proper settings - Superman, Wonder Woman, and more. Plus there are original comic books - all seven Super Heroes of the Justice League, and super hero-themed games to play.

Another exciting stop is Wizarding World with props, costumes, and parts of sets from some of the Harry Potter movies, including Fantastic Beasts - it's like living in parts of the movies. See the bedroom and trunk from Newt's case of creatures; costume designs from inception to finished products, including all of Lord Voldemort's transition; and get sorted into your right house by the sorting hat, too. Fans love this place!

If you are hungry before or after your tour, enjoy a bite to eat at the adjacent Studio Plaza Cafe (open weekdays only). A small gift shop is stocked with movie and TV merchandise. No matter what you see and do, this tour affords visitors a great opportunity to see what actually goes go on behind the scenes. No video or tape recording is allowed, but cameras are allowed at many of the stops. The tour is partly outside, so dress warmly for the tram ride. Other tour options include the Classics Made Here - a tour with the emphasis on Warner Bros. golden age of classic films and TV shows ($75 for adults; $65 for ages 8 - 12), or if you really want to experience all that the studio has to offer, the five-hour Deluxe Tour which includes a lot more behind-the-scenes, a visit to the costume department, post production, the private screening room, and breakfast and lunch ($295 per person). FYI - JOHNNY CARSON PARK (pg. 67) is just down the street if you're looking for a place for kids to run around or have a picnic before or after your tour.

Hours: Tours, for no more than 12 people at a time, leave every twenty minutes, daily, most of the year, 9am - 3:15pm; in the summer, 8:15am - 4pm. Closed Christmas. Tours in Spanish are available Mon. - Fri. at 12:15am and 3:15pm. Reservations for all tours can be made for the first three tour times of the day - all other times are first come, first served basis. You must arrive at least 20 minutes before your allotted tour time. Adults must have a valid form of government ID.

Price: $68 for ages 13 and up; $58 for ages 8 - 12. (Tickets are discounted online.) Parking is $12 at gate 6.

Ages: Children must be at least 8 years old.

WILDLIFE SANCTUARY TOUR   ☼

(909) 274-4794 - tours; (909) 594-5611, ext. 4794 / www.mtsac.edu/about/getting-around/tours.html   !
1100 N. Grand Avenue at Mount San Antonio College, Walnut

A forty-five-minute guided tour of this ten-acre wildlife environment includes walking the dirt footpath, which is not stroller-friendly, to see and learn about the plants and animals and their eco systems. Look for the turtles in the pond and the variety of birds that visit. The sanctuary also has a lake, a swamp, a pond, and a stream. There aren't any caged animals here, but free-roaming lizards, squirrels, raccoons, insects, and a few other critters. A guide from the college explains why the plants and animals need protection and what visitors can do to help - check out the website for curriculum supplements. The minimum number of students is ten; the maximum, thirty.

Hours: Tours are offered Tues. and Thurs. on the hour from 9am - 4pm (last tour). Reservations are required.

Price: Free, but donations are appreciated.

Ages: Elementary-school age kids.

—TRANSPORTATION—

AIR COMBAT USA, INC.   ☼

(714) 525-7590 / www.aircombat.com   6/$
3280 AirFlite Way, Suite #C103, Long Beach

If being a Top Gun is your top dream, here's the opportunity to make it a reality. You, perhaps being an unlicensed pilot and leading an otherwise normal life, will actually fly and fight air-to-air combat. "The SIAI Marchetti SF260 is a current production, Italian-built, fighter aircraft. It has 260 horsepower, can fly at 270 MPH, FAA certified to +6 to -3 G's and can perform unlimited aerobatics. It was originally designed to transition student pilots to jet fighters. It is maneuvered by the stick grip complete with gun trigger, identical to the F4 Phantom. The pilot and guest pilot sit side-by-side with dual controls." (Excerpted from Air Combat's brochure.) If all this has your adrenaline pumping, go for it!

You'll be prepped for your flight in a one-hour ground school which covers the basics, with emphasis on tactical maneuvers. After being fitted with a flight suit, helmet, and parachute, you'll soar for one hour with the birds over L.A. and Catalina waters, which in itself is exciting. You're actually in control of the aircraft 90% of the time, while receiving constant instruction on how to get the "enemy." More excitement! After practicing maneuvers, you'll engage in three or more (depending on your package) "g-pulling" (i.e., gut wrenching) dogfights and combat encounters against a real opponent (e.g., friend, spouse, etc.). A direct hit registers through an electronic tracking system, complete with sound effects and smoke trailing from the other aircraft. What a sensational experience! It's as close to the real thing as you can possibly get without being in the military. I will confess that after a few high/low yo-yos and roll overs, I used that special white bag and became part of the 10% that share in this ritual. Too much excitement for me.

After you've landed, come down from your high, and gone home, you can view and relive your flight and your "hits" again and again via the SD card which recorded your flight from three cockpit cameras. Air Combat is an unforgettable experience! Combat and Advanced Aerobatics, which is a more intense flight with more maneuvers, are two different ways to experience flight here. Note that SKYTHRILLS (pg. 214), offering thrilling aerobatic airplane rides, shares the same location.

Hours: Several classes/flights that accommodate two people each are offered almost every day. Check the website for flight schedules.

Price: Advanced Aerobatics is $695 per person. The Intro combat package, 3 engagements, is $895 per person. Super Phase 1, 8 engagements, is $1,695.00. Ask about specials, such as discounts for two people.

Ages: Pre-teenager and up.

ALFREDO'S BEACH CLUB

(562) 314-8778 / www.alfredosbeachclub.com

Alfredo's has six concessions within Los Angeles County; along the beach and in many parks. They rent kayaks - $15 an hour for single, $25 an hour for double; pedal boats - $35 an hour; as well as bikes ($10 an hour), three-person surreys ($25 an hour), stand-up boards, boogie boards and skim boards. Depending on the location, they also rent beach chairs, umbrellas, fishing poles, and more. Check the website for their locations and specific details.

AMERICAN PRIDE - CHILDREN'S MARITIME INSTITUTE

(562) 758-7525 / www.americanpride.org

Rainbow Harbor, off Shoreline Drive, Long Beach

$$$$

Isn't she a beauty? *American Pride*, a three-mast tallship originally built in 1941, now serves as a historic nautical educational tool for students and adults. Several programs, both at dockside and at sea, are offered throughout the year - what a *sea*sational time of student teamwork and learning about geology and environmental systems, with an emphasis on marine biology. Other programs include overnight programs on the ship, sailing to Catalina, and multi-day programs / journeys. Teachers note that there is a minimum of twenty-six students per program and that classroom prep resources arrive about a month before your excursion.

Adults, do not despair! Whale-watching tours are given in season - December through April - with a marine biologist on board. Participants look for whales as well as help raise the sails, dissect fish, and learn elementary navigation skills. Bring binoculars, a jacket, and sunscreen.

Hours: Call for a schedule of events or to book a tour.

Price: Check the website for current pricing.

Ages: Most programs are geared for 4th graders and up.

AMTRAK (Los Angeles County)

(800) USA RAIL (872-7245) / www.amtrakcalifornia.com

$$$$$

Trains are a great alternative to driving. By incorporating a train trip into your day's excursion, it makes the journey almost as much fun as the destination, whether you're visiting a park, a special restaurant, or a major attraction.

The Amtrak phone number and website gives fares and other pertinent information. For example, from Union Station in Los Angeles to San Juan Capistrano, the round-trip fare is $42 for adults; $36.80 for seniors; $22 for children ages 2 through 15. (One child rides for half price with each paid adult fare.) Ask about AAA discounts.

Check out the website for information on the Kids 'N Trains Program. This program is offered mid-September through June, Monday through Thursday (except some blackout dates). It allows teachers, designated leaders, chaperones, and kids - students, scouts, church groups, and other community groups (minimum of twenty, ages 5 to 18) - to ride the rails from Los Angeles to Santa Barbara (and up to San Luis Obispo) for $11 per person one-way or round trip (on the same day), and from Los Angeles to San Diego (or somewhere in between), for $13. Reservations must be made online at least a month in advance of departure date.

Note that Union Station, at 800 N. Alameda Street in Los Angeles, is not only a hub for Amtrak and Metrolink, but a gorgeous, historic building. Starring in numerous movies, the station, which is open from 4am to 1am, is just across the street from EL PUEBLO DE LOS ANGELES HISTORICAL MONUMENT / OLVERA STREET / CHINESE AMERICAN MUSEUM / ITALIAN AMERICAN MUSEUM OF LOS ANGELES (pg. 168).

ANGELS FLIGHT RAILWAY

(213) 626-1901 / angelsflight.org

$

The top station is at 350 South Grand Avenue at California Plaza, Los Angeles; the lower station at 351 South Hill Street, across from Grand Central Market.

The definition of a funicular is - of a railroad, especially one on a mountainside, operating by cable with ascending and descending cars counterbalanced. "The Shortest Railway in the World" may only be 298-feet long, but the quick ride up (or down) the steep slope of Bunker Hill is a memorable side trip aboard the 117-year-old funicular. The railway connects the residential streets with the California Plaza and the Grand Central Market and other cultural

attractions, plus they offer a great view.
   Hours: Open daily, 6:45am - 10pm.
   Price: One-way fare is $1 per person.
   Ages: All

AQUALINK / AQUABUS

(562) 591-2301 / www.lbtransit.com $$
Shoreline Drive, Long Beach

    "Taxi!" The AquaLink, or water taxi, is a fun and inexpensive way to see a part of the Long Beach Harbor. The seventy-five-seat catamaran cruises by the *Queen Mary*, past charter fishing boats, and past the working port in the fifth largest city in California. A snack shop is available on board. One-way fare covers departing from the QUEEN MARY (pg. 147), which is a wheelchair-accessible boarding area, to AQUARIUM OF THE PACIFIC (pg. 217), which is also wheelchair accessible, and arriving at Alamitos Bay Landing (toward Seal Beach), or vice versa. The *Queen Mary* leg to the Aquarium takes twenty minutes; to Alamitos Bay takes about an hour. If you de-board at the *Queen Mary*, you'll have to pay another fare if you want to resume your cruise.
    The Aquabus is an open-air water shuttle, too, but its route is much shorter as it's within the Queensway Bay; basically from the Aquarium to Shoreline Village to the Queen Mary and back.
   Hours: The Aquabus is open mid-April - Memorial Day weekend, and the months of September and October, Fri. - Sun., 11am - 6pmish. It is open daily May - August, 11am - 6pmish. It is closed November - mid-April. The Aqualink is open the same dates and days, but 11am - 10:30pm. Check the website for specific times and points of departure.
   Price: The Aqualink is $5 per person each way. The Aquabus is $1 per person. Kids under 2 are free with a paying adult.
   Ages: All

BEVERLY HILLS TROLLEY TOUR

(310) 285-2500 or (310) 285-1128 / www.beverlyhills.org/exploring/trolleytours   !
Departs from the southwest corner of Rodeo Drive and Dayton Way, Beverly Hills

    This is the best bargain in Beverly Hills! If you're in the area and want to give your kids a taste of the posh lifestyle, for free, hop on board an old-fashioned looking trolley (which is a fun mode of transportation) for a forty-minute ride by some of the most famous sights in Beverly Hills (but no celebrity homes), including Rodeo Drive, film locations, some of the high-priced boutiques, and the elegant hotels. You'll also see some of the most significant art and architectural locations around town, including City Hall, galleries, Creative Artists Agency, The Paley Center for Media, and more. Note: Parking in the structure is free for the first two hours so you've got time to window shop on Rodeo Drive. Note, also, that there is a lovely and nicely-landscaped, outdoor courtyard /park with tables and chairs between buildings by the parking structure on Beverly Dr., so bring a picnic and enjoy.
   Hours: Rides are offered most of the year on weekends only on the hour, 11am - 5pm. They are offered July - Labor Day weekend, Tues. - Sun., 11am - 5pm, on the hour. Closed on major holidays and a chunk of December.
   Price: Free. Tickets are available from the trolley driver on a first come, first serve basis.
   Ages: 5 years and up.

BIKE MAPS (Los Angeles County)
    See BIKE MAPS (Orange County) (pg. 328) for information.

BIKE TRAIL: LONG BEACH SHORELINE

(562) 570-3100   !/$
Bay Shore Avenue to Shoreline Village, Long Beach

    This 3.1-mile (one-way) easy, paved riding path follows along the Pacific Ocean. An ocean breeze and a practically flat trail makes it a delightful ride for the family. Stop and shop at SHORELINE VILLAGE (pg. 161) with its nice array of quaint-looking restaurants and stores. Also, check out other places nearby - AQUARIUM OF THE PACIFIC (pg. 217) and QUEEN MARY (pg. 147). At the other end, check out BELMONT SHORE BEACH, LONG BEACH CITY BEACH and BAYSHORE BEACH & PLAYGROUND (pg. 10).
   Hours: Open daily, dawn - dusk.
   Price: Free, although parking at Shoreline Village is $2 for the first 2 hours with validation/$10 purchase at any store or restaurant; $16 max.
   Ages: 5 years and up.

BIKE TRAIL: LOS ANGELES RIVER TRAIL   ☼

(323) 223-0585 - Friends of the L.A. River; (323) 913-7390 - Griffith Park / www.labikepaths.com;   !
www.folar.org; www.thelariver.com

Griffith Park, Los Angeles

The first five miles of this urban bikeway are not always quiet, as some of it parallels the Golden State Freeway. The paved bike trail is, however, entirely off-road. Although the riverbed is up against concrete slopes, there are also trees, flocks of birds, and even a few ponds along the way with ducks and some fish, plus portions of it are lit at night. The next forty-seven miles are still in the planning and making-it-work stage, although the next three-mile stretch, which heads past the huge Elysian Park and through the neighboring, small Egret Park toward downtown L.A., has already begun. Eventually, the pathway will stretch from the mountains all the way to sea along the Los Angeles River. A good place to park is inside Griffith Park, near the bike trail entrance where Zoo Drive meets Riverside Dr./Victory Blvd. The longest contiguous bike path along the LA River is 17 miles from Atlantic Blvd. in Vernon to the Shoreline Bikeway in Long Beach.

Just across the river from Egret Park, which is also an entrance/exit point for the bike trail, on Riverside Drive, is the Los Angeles River Center located at 570 W. Ave. 26. You can also start down the road at Frogspot, at 2825 Benedict Street, Los Angeles, which is a headquarters for Friends of the LA River. The bike path, for now, goes along GRIFFITH PARK (pg. 63), so enjoy a side trip into the park. (See that entry for more details about the park, its zoo, and its museums.)

Hours: Open daily, sunrise - sunset.
Price: Free
Ages: 6 years and up.

BIKE TRAIL: SAN GABRIEL RIVER TRAIL   ☼

bike.lacity.org; www.labikepaths.com   !

Lakewood, Long Beach, Seal Beach

This two-way, concrete river trail, a right-of-way for bicyclers and skaters, actually travels almost the whole length of the San Gabriel River (i.e., flood control waterway) - 38 miles. It begins (or ends, depending on how you look at it) in Seal Beach at Marina Drive, just west of 1st Street, and ends (or begins) in Azusa at San Gabriel Canyon Road, north of Sierra Madre. The pathway has several access points along the way. The route sometimes follows along main streets, although it just as often veers completely away from them. Depending on where you catch the trail, it passes under bridges; goes through some scenic areas that are a delight to behold; past parks; past people's backyards; and even through sections that don't feel as safe as I'd like.

One of our favorite stretches starts at LIBERTY PARK - Cerritos (pg. 70) and goes all the way to SEAL BEACH (pg. 247). Along the way, we sometimes stop off at Rynerson Park, which has playgrounds and paved pathways throughout; the Long Beach Town Center, which has restaurants, fast food places, a movie theater, Barnes & Noble, Sam's Club, and lots more stores; and EL DORADO NATURE CENTER (pg. 58) and EL DORADO PARK WEST (pg. 58). The latter park is beautiful and there is no admission fee from the bike path. Sometimes we actually make it to Seal Beach! We then ride to the ocean's edge and go along Main Street into the quaint town of Seal Beach, where there are plenty of shops and restaurants. (We also cheat sometimes and invite my husband to meet us for lunch or dinner, and then have him drive us, and our bikes, all home in the van!) Nonstop from Liberty Park to Seal Beach takes my older children and me about an hour. This section of the riverbank route is also great for birdwatching. We've seen numerous herons, egrets, and pelicans.

Hours: Open daily, dawn - dusk.
Price: Free
Ages: 4 years and up.

BIKE TRAIL: SOUTH BAY   ☼

bike.lacity.org; www.labikepaths.com; www.traillink.com   !

Torrance County Beach to Pacific Palisades

Life's a beach and this twenty-six-mile, two-lane, relatively flat concrete bike trail emphasizes that by cruising mostly right along the sandy shores of California's beaches. From Malibu/Pacific Palisades to Torrance/Palos Verdes, it passes through Venice beach, the Santa Monica Pier, and other state treasures. There are many stores and eateries (and restrooms!) to stop off at along the strand. Of course weekends, especially in the summer, are very crowded. Don't forget your sunscreen. From Torrance, find an entrance near Esplanade Ave. From Pacific Palisades, you can start at Will Rogers State Beach, by the intersection of PCH and Sunset Blvd.

Hours: Open daily, sunrise - sunset.
Price: Free
Ages: 4 years and up.

GONDOLA AMORE

(310) 376-6977 / www.gondolaamore.com 6/$
208 Yacht Club Way, King Harbor Marina, Redondo Beach

Now this is amore! This one-hour gondola cruise is a unique way to see the Redondo harbor and shoreline. During the day you'll also see Catalina Island (on a clear day), sailboats, waterfowl, and maybe a few seals. Nighttime rides bring about their own magic (and romance). The two gondolas, operated by the owner and by lifeguards, seat up to four people, have canopies for privacy, and small twinkling lights around the boat and canopies. Amore provides blankets, as the ocean air can get chilly even on a summer night, and cups for the drinks that you provide. Your other list of things to bring includes jackets, a music CD, and your camera. Champagne (or sparkling cider) rides, where your beverage, glasses, fresh fruit, chocolate, and bread and cheese are provided, are also offered. Tips: Before or after your cruise, take some time to walk around the pier. Look up REDONDO BEACH INTERNATIONAL BOARDWALK, REDONDO BEACH PIER and KING HARBOR MARINA (pg. 160) for details.

Hours: Open daily. Reservations are required. Note: Holiday seasons book quickly.
Price: $109 for two people; $20 for each additional person. Champagne rides are $135 for two people. Parking is validated.
Ages: 4 years and up.

GONDOLA GETAWAY

(562) 433-9595 / www.gondolagetawayinc.com 6/$
5437 E. Ocean Boulevard, Long Beach

Long Beach, California is transformed into Venice, Italy when you go on this gondola ride. I know this attraction is thought of as a romantic excursion, and it is. It is also a wonderful treat for your child. Step into a Venetian gondola and for one hour, gently slip in and out through the waterways and canals of Naples. Your gondolier will serenade you with Italian music, regale you with interesting tales, or quietly leave you alone. After our kids plied my husband and me with questions about the possibility of sharks and whales in the canal, they settled down to enjoy the ride and look at the incredible homes along the waterfront. Christmas time is particularly spectacular, as many of the houses are decked out with lights, animated figures, etc. Make reservations for this time period far in advance.

A bucket of ice is provided, as is a blanket for the colder nights. Bring your own liquid refreshment. Your child will now be dreaming of visiting a tiny little town far away in a boot-shaped country. Ciao!

Hours: Open daily for cruises, 11am - 10pm. Suggested reservations are two weeks in advance.
Price: Gondolas carry two to six people - $100 for the first two passengers; $30 for each additional person. Gratuity not included. The Carolina carries seven to fourteen people - $354 for up to ten, $35 for each additional person. Fleet cruises carries twenty-one to sixty people - $30 per person. Check the website for special holiday and dinner cruises.
Ages: 4 years and up.

GONDOLAS D'AMORE

(310) 736-7301 / www.gondolasdamore.com 6/$
14045 Panay Way, Marina Del Rey

Glide through the becalming waters of Marina Del Rey, enjoying the scenery of yachts, houses, and even the sea life of seals and birds, and most of all, enjoying this peaceful ride with someone you care about in an Italian-style gondola with a small canopy on the top. Soft Italian music can be playing in the background and while your gondolier gently oars you through the waters, you can enjoy a picnic lunch or dinner (that you supply) at the small table on board while snuggled under a warm blanket that's provided for you. Also provided are an appetizer plate, candles, music, and an ice bucket. Nighttimes are especially pretty with the lights on the houses and in the sky. Doesn't this make you want to go, right now?!

Hours: Make reservations online.
Price: Rates start at $145 for an hour for two people.
Ages: 12 years and up, only.

HARBOR BREEZE CRUISES

(562) 432-4900 / www.2seewhales.com; www.harbor-cruises.com; www.californiadolphincruises.com　　$$$$

100 Aquarium Way, dock #2, Long Beach

　　Enjoy a forty-five-minute cruise of the inner and outer harbor, past supertankers, cruise ships, a Coast Guard station, Terminal Island, a Federal Prison, and Angels Gate Lighthouse. Three-hour blue whale-watching cruises are available May or June through September. Two-and-a-half-hour gray whale-watching and dolphin /sea lion cruises are available November through May.

Hours: Forty-five-minute cruises depart from the Village Boat House daily at 11:30am, 12:30pm, 1:45pm, 3:15pm, 4:45pm and 6:15pm. Call for summer and school break hours. Gray whale-watching and dolphin cruises depart daily at noon and 3pm, with an additional time on weekends, at 9am. Check for hours for blue whale cruises during the summer.

Price: Prices for the forty-five-minute cruises are $15 for adults; $10 for seniors; $6 for ages 5 - 11; children 4 and under are free. Gray whale-watching and dolphin cruises are $40 for adults on weekdays and $45 on weekends; $40 for seniors; $30 for kids. Blue whale-watching cruises are $45 for adults on weekdays and $50 on weekends; $40 for seniors; $30 for kids. Check online for specials and discounts.

Ages: 4 years and up.

KAYAKS ON THE WATER - STAND UP PADDLEBOARDS

(562) 434-0999 / www.kayakrentals.net; www.standuprentals.net　　$$$

5411 East Ocean Boulevard, Long Beach

　　Sometimes it's nice to lay on the beach. Sometimes we need to be more active. Kayaks launched here allow newbies at kayaking, and those more experienced, to get their feet wet, so to speak, around the harbor; the Naples Island canals (which is a lovely and calm-water route in front of gorgeous, waterfront homes); to a restaurant or snack place; or to a cove where you'll see floating moon-jellies, in season. At high tide you can kayak to see birds at a small wildlife refuge. All kayakers <u>must</u> know how to swim. After kayaking, go back and enjoy, again, the stretch of beach at Los Alamitos Bay.

　　Stand ups are at first challenging to stand up on! If you qualify to use a stand up paddle board (and you can take lessons here and/or join lifetime membership for $10), then rentals are $16 for the first hour, for members. If you are trying it out, it is $25 for an hour with an instructor. Also check out the SUP dolphin adventures which entails taking a boat ride out to find a pod of dolphins, then paddling and interacting with them as they swim around and under your stand up board. This adventure is about $150; prices may vary.

Hours: Rentals are available April through September, daily, 9am - 5pm. Open October through March, Sat. - Sun., 9am - 4pm.

Price: $10 an hour per person for single or double kayaks; $25 an hour per person for SUPs.

Ages: 5 years and up - all kayakers and paddle boarders must know how to swim.

LONG BEACH BOAT RENTALS

(562) 491-7400 / www.boats4rent.com　　$$$$$

401 Shoreline Village Drive, Long Beach

　　Boat rentals include jet skis - $125 for the first hour; electric boats (that seat eight) - $80 for the first hour; pontoon boats - $105; and six-passenger power boats - starting at $80 for the first hour. Before, or after, your boating excursion, stroll along SHORELINE VILLAGE (pg. 161) and its environments for a myriad of great places to shop, eat and sightsee.

Hours: Open daily most of the year, daily 10am - 5pm. Closed during inclement weather.

Price: Prices listed above, plus a surcharge of $5 - $9 depending on the rental.

Ages: 5 years and up.

LONG BEACH WATER BIKES

(562) 546-2493 / www.lbwaterbikes.com　　$$$$$

110 North Marina Drive, Long Beach

　　Not quite like walking on the water, but maybe its the next best thing. Biking on water you won't/shouldn't get wet, unless you want to, as the bikes are very stable. There is so much to see along the way, besides the coastline and water, such as the homes along Naples Canal, shops, restaurants, a jellyfish cove, and more. If your kids legs can't reach the pedals, they can ride on the center platform of one of the side-by-side bikes, sandwiched between two riders. Single and tandem bikes are available. Bring a water bottle and a hat - enjoy!

One favorite excursion is to rent a bike a little before sunset. Another is to rent a decorated bike during the ninety-minute Holiday Lights (group) Tour between the day after Thanksgiving through the end of December to be a part of the celebration and to see the spectacular lights up close. These nights include a few extra surprises, too.

Hours: Bike rentals are available daily advanced reservation and for walk-ins, Wed. - Sun., noon - 4pm. Call first to insure you'll get a bike.

Price: $25 an hour per person. The Holiday Lights Tour is $40 per hour, per rider. Glow lights (lights on the bikes) are $30 an hour and available Fri. and Sat. evenings.

Ages: 4 years and up.

LOOKING GLASS TOURS

$$$$

(310) 909-3179 or (310) 755-8359 / www.fastkayak.com; www.rbmarina.com

233 N. Harbor Drive, Redondo Beach Pier at the marina, Redondo Beach

Hourly rates for single kayaks are $15, double kayaks are $25; pedal boats are $10 for adults, $5 for ages 16 and under, but at least 25 pounds; stand up paddle boards are $15 an hour (tours are available if booked in advance). For a different point of view, try a ride on the *Looking Glass*, a bright yellow, semi-submersible underwater viewing boat with two, seven-foot long windows to see the fish, rays, and other harbor sea life, including sea lions. The forty-minute sub ride is $15 for adults; $10 for kids and is only open Friday through Monday. See REDONDO BEACH INTERNATIONAL BOARDWALK, REDONDO BEACH PIER and KING HARBOR MARINA (pg. 160) for adjacent activities.

Hours: Open October - mid-May, Fri. - Mon., 11am - 4pm or 5pm, for the *Looking Glass*. All rentals and rides are available mid-May - September, Mon. - Fri., 11am - 6pm; Sat. - Sun., 10am - sunset.

Price: Prices are listed above. Park in the lot (not the parking structure) for two free hours of parking with validation.

Ages: 4 years and up.

MARINA DEL REY BOAT RENTALS

$$$$

(310) 306-4444; (310) 306-2222 - parasailing / www.marinadelreyboatrentals.com

13717 Fiji Way, Marina Del Rey

Located in FISHERMAN'S VILLAGE and surrounding area (pg. 159), Marina Boat Rentals rents kayaks - $15 per hour for a single, $25 an hour for a double; power boats - beginning at $80 an hour for a four-passenger boat; $120 for waverunners; $25 an hour for a stand up paddle board; and electric boats (which hold twelve people and are much quieter than motor boats) starting at $120 an hour. For an uplifting experience, go parasailing - go 500 feet up for $85 per person, or 800 feet for $90. Observers, with a reservation, are $50.

Hours: Open year-round, daily - the hours vary greatly, but they are almost always open until sunset; weather permitting. Parasailing is closed November - early Feb.

Price: Prices listed above.

Ages: 4 years and up.

MARINA DEL REY WATERBUS

$

(310) 628-3219 / www.marinawaterbus.com

13755 Fiji Way, Marina Del Rey

The waterbus (i.e. boat) is one of the best deals in town! From eight different locations, including Fisherman's Village, plus Burton Chace Park and Marina Beach / Mother's Beach, hop on board with the kids and take in the sights of the marina and coastline. You can hop off at any stop and then reboard, though you'll have to pay another fare for the ride.

Hours: Open the end of June through Labor Day, Thurs. - Sat. (and 4th of July), 11am - midnight; Sun., 11am - 9pm.

Price: $1 per person, one way. Cash only.

Ages: All

METROLINK (Los Angeles County)

$$$

(800) 371-LINK (5465) / www.metrolinktrains.com

See the entry for METROLINK (Orange County) (pg. 331) for details.

Hours: Trains run daily and offer limited service on most major holidays.

Ages: All

METRO RAIL

(323) GO METRO (466-3876) / www.metro.net $

    This rail mode of transportation is terrific and also a work-in-progress as there are more miles to the tracks being added. That said, the rail lines that are complete make going to a destination an adventure. The advantages of riding the rails are numerous, such as it's inexpensive, you don't have to fight traffic, you don't have to try to find a parking spot, and kids consider it a treat. Pick up a map of the routes at Union Station or check online for maps, as well as park and ride lots, of which there are over 100 in the county. Most of the lots offer free parking. Trains run every ten minutes.

    With numerous stops along the way (and the website makes the lines and where to pick up the buses very easy to understand), here are the basic lines: The Blue Line runs north/south, between 498 Pacific Avenue in Long Beach through Compton and San Pedro, just south of Pershing Square at 7th Street/Metro Center at 660 S. Figueroa St. in downtown Los Angeles. The Silver Line runs parallel to the Blue Line for a bit, starting from Artesia Transit Center in Long Beach (the next stop is Rosecrans Ave.) to 3501 Santa Anita Ave. in El Monte. The Green Line runs east and west, connecting at 12901 Hoxie Ave. in Norwalk to 2406 Marine Ave. in Redondo Beach. Trains run alongside, but separate from, the 105 freeway. The Red Line runs from 801 N. Vignes St. at Union Station in downtown Los Angeles through Hollywood and Highland and Universal City to Lankershim Blvd. in North Hollywood. The Orange Line picks up where the Red Line stops - North Hollywood to west through Van Nuys and Reseda to 6101 ½ Owensmouth at Warner Center. The Purple Line parallels the Red Line for a bit - going from Union Station through Pershing Square to 3775 Wilshire Blvd. near Western. The Gold Line runs from 149 N. Halstead at Sierra Madre Village in Pasadena through Chinatown in downtown L.A., Union Station, and Little Tokyo to end (or begin) at 5150 E. Pomona Blvd. in E. Los Angeles. Note that Union Station, at 800 N. Alameda Street in Los Angeles, is not only a hub for Amtrak and Metrolink, but a gorgeous, historic building. Starring in numerous movies, the station, which is open from 4am - 1am, is just across the street from EL PUEBLO DE LOS ANGELES HISTORICAL MONUMENT / OLVERA STREET / CHINESE AMERICAN MUSEUM / ITALIAN AMERICAN MUSEUM OF LOS ANGELES (pg. 168).

Hours: Trains usually run daily, 6am - 11pm; some lines run 24 hours.
Price: About $1.75 for adults, plus 50¢ for a transfer; 75¢ for seniors, 25¢ for transfers; $1 for kids K - 12; two children 4 and under are free with each paid adult ticket. The Silver Line has a different fare structure, so check online for prices. A day pass is $7 for adults; $2.50 for seniors.
Ages: All

REDONDO BEACH WHALE WATCH   ☼

(310) 372-2111 / www.rbwhales.com $$$$
140 International Boardwalk at the marina, Redondo Beach

    View the ocean and some of its inhabitants at a somewhat leisurely pace. Be on the lookout for the colony of sea lions that usually hangs around. Two-and-a-half whale-watching cruises are offered the day after Christmas through mid-April to look for migrating whales as well as common and bottlenose dolphins, plus maybe a shark and some sea lions. Another option is to cruise around the harbor, and just beyond, on forty-five minute, guided nature rides offered May through October - a great time of learning while experiencing.

Hours: Whale watching tours are offered daily at 10am with a minimum of 10 paying passengers - call first. Boat rides are offered Sat. - Sun., 1pm - 6pm, on the hour.
Price: Whale watching is $35 for adults; $30 for seniors; $25 for ages 4 - 12; $5 for ages 3 and under. Nature cruises are $20 for adults; $15 for ages 4 -12; $5 for ages 3 and under.
Ages: 4 years and up.

SKYTHRILLS   ☼

(714) 402-4888 / www.skythrills.com   6/$
3280 AirFlite Way, Suite #C103, Long Beach

    Be a stunt pilot for a day! The son of the owner of AIR COMBAT USA, INC. (pg. 207), and who shares the same building space, also shares a passion for something equally thrilling at SkyThrills of encouraging people to experience the joy of high-performance flying.

    There are several different styles of rides to choose from. A mild ride of sightseeing over Los Angeles and Orange County - of Catalina Island and the stunning California coastlines, and even over some landmarks like Knott's Berry Farm - can be done in an historic open cockpit 1935 WACO biplane, a 1957 Beech Super 18, or other aircraft. There is a more extreme wild ride of performing aerobatics in a Pitts S-2C, Extra 300L, Marchetti SF-260, or a Waco YMF-5. And G-forces? Oh yes. Up to 250 mph and 6 Gs. Pure power. What a rush! (Think of a dog in a car on the freeway, with the window rolled down, only much more so. This visual is for the feel of the force, as well as the dog's/your look of pure enjoyment.) You can also choose an in-between option because your ride is customized as to how you, the passenger and co-pilot, want to fly. And you are a co-pilot because you can fly as much as 90% of the time - a real hands-on (please be hands-on!) experience with no prior flying experience necessary.

The first part of your time is spent in a fairly comprehensive ground school briefing that covers what you need to know immediately about flying and performing aerobatics in an aircraft - the loop, the roll, the hammerhead, the spin and the intricacies of more advanced maneuvers, if that's your choice. Gear up by changing into your flight suit, putting on your parachute, and away you go! Experience of a lifetime? Yes. Rides are recorded, so take your video home to, ironically, relive the experience of a lifetime more than once. Note that aerobatic and formation flight training are also available here.

Hours: Flight times are usually on the weekends, but can be arranged to fit your schedule. All flights are by reservation only and depend on weather conditions. Closed on some holidays.

Price: 45 min. sightseeing tours start at $545 per person. A 25 min. flight with 10 min. of aerobatics starts at $595. There are numerous options to choose from with full explanations - check the website.

Ages: 8 years and up.

SPIRIT CRUISES

(562) 548-8080 / www.spiritmarine.com $$$$
429 Shoreline Village Drive, suite 100, Long Beach

Spirit Cruises offers one-hour cruises, year-round, often weekends only. Ninety-minute and two-hour cruises are offered on select days and times throughout the year. Each cruise is narrated as it goes through Queen's Way Bay, past the QUEEN MARY (pg. 147) and AQUARIUM OF THE PACIFIC (pg. 217). The longer the tour, the more you'll see and learn. During the two-hour cruise you'll navigate past cargo ships and tankers, cross under four bridges, and much more. Adults can enjoy the two-hour plus dinner cruise, with prime rib and chicken on the menu, plus dancing, and more. Reservations are required for all cruises.

Hours: See their website for cruise availability.

Price: The one-hour harbor cruise is $15 for adults; $7 for ages 5 - 12. The ninety-minute cruise is $18 for adults; $10 for kids. The two-hour cruise is $25 for adults; $15 for kids. Dinner cruises start at $49.50 per person. Prices fluctuate so call first.

Ages: 5 years and up.

WILLOW SPRINGS INTERNATIONAL MOTORSPORTS PARK

(661) 256-6666 / www.willowspringsraceway.com $$$
3500 75th Street West, Rosamond

This sprawling 600-acre complex has enough vrooooom for six very different race tracks, ranging from clay oval, paved oval, a kart track, a lighted speedway, a road course, and the original 2.5 mile, nine-turn raceway built in 1953. Call or check the website for the complete schedule to make sure you're seeing the cars, karts, and motorcycle races that you want. General admission also allows you access to the pit area as long as kids are supervised by parents or other adults. A diner and gift shop are on the premises.

Hours: Fri. are testing and tune up days, but you are welcome to come and observe. Races are usually held on Sat. and Sun. See the website for a schedule.

Price: Usually $10 for adults; children 8 and under are free with a paying adult. Free parking and overnight camping; $40 with RV hookup.

Ages: 5 years and up.

WINDSPORTS

(800) 644-8988 / www.windsports.com   6/$
Sylmar - 12623 Gridley Street at Sylmar Flight Park; Los Angeles - 12501 Vista Del Mar at Dockweiler State Beach

Fly with the birds and planes! Kind of. The Los Angeles location is just south of LAX, at Dockweiler State Beach. During the pre-flight briefing and flight demonstration you'll pay close attention, knowing that you are actually going to be doing this same thing in just a minute. Starting atop the 30-foot bluffs (i.e. training hills), you run and glide above the beach (about 10 feet) to land on the sand about 100 yards from your starting point. As baby birds learn to fly in increments, so will you with these lessons, and if you're getting the *hang* of it, your instructor may allow you to go higher on subsequent flights. Four solo flights, with the mini beach lessons, take about two hours total. Seven flights take three hours, with the hope that you fully learn how to control the glider. This is a fun activity to just come and watch, too. (But, I'd rather fly!)

Really fly high at the Sylmar location where you fly tandem, with an instructor, off the top of a 3,500 foot mountain!! You'll first drive 45 minutes up Kagel Mountain, help set up the hang glider, have a time of pre-flight ground instruction, then hang on to your instructor, run and - you're off! During your fifteen minute, or so, flight you'll experience the silence, the exhilaration, and the view, plus you get to even steer the glider while gently soaring through the air to eventually land on a grass strip about two miles from your original starting point. Wow! Wow!! Wow!!!

Hours: Beach lessons are offered Wed. - Sun. Mountain tandem lessons are offered daily.
Price: 4 flights, mini beach lessons are $99; 7 flights are $160. Parking at the lot near the beach is $8 - $10 per day. Mountain tandem flying is $249.
Ages: Must be at least 15 years old, 90 lbs, and 4'11".

YOUNG EAGLES PROGRAM (Los Angeles County)

National number - (877) 806-8902; Compton, Hawthorne and Torrance, Chapter #96 - (310) 374-4812 - Glen; Long Beach, chapter #7 - (562) 500-0173; Pacoima, chapter #40 - (818) 725-4AIR (4247); Santa Monica, chapter #11 - (610) 628-9008 - airport / www.youngeagles.org; #96 - www.96.eaachapter.org; #7 - www.7.eaachapter.org; #40 - www.eaa40.org; #11 - www.11.eaachapter.org

Compton - 901 West Alondra Blvd.; Hawthorne - 12101 South Crenshaw Blvd.; Long Beach - 4100 Donald Douglas Dr.; Pacoima - 12653 Osborne St.; Santa Monica - 3233 Donald Douglas Loop South; Torrance - 3301 Airport Dr.

"They will soar on wings like eagles." (Isaiah 40:31) I think all kids (and adults) dream of flying, and the Young Eagles Program helps those dreams become a reality. Young Eagles is a national program sponsored by the EAA (Experimental Aircraft Association) to introduce children to the joy of aviation. There are a multitude of Young Eagle chapters throughout Southern California that offer kids, between the ages of 8 and 17 years, the opportunity to actually fly, one time only, for free!, in a two- or four-seater airplane. Please remember that everyone here is volunteering their time, including pilots, so be patient with a process that will take at least two to three hours. Although the following information is fairly standard, call the particular program you're interested in for specific dates, times, and other details. Reservations are necessary at most of the airports. A signed consent form by a parent or legal guardian is required for each child.

At the airport, after your child registers, he/she will participate in a preflight inspection training, which means looking over an airplane to make sure it's mechanically sound while learning some technical aspects of how to fly a plane. Then, he/she will fly! The flight is usually twenty minutes round trip. What a thrill! If it becomes too thrilling for your child, airsick bags are provided. Two more wonderful freebies are a certificate upon completion of the flight, and a magazine called *Sport Aviation for Kids* that comes later in the mail. Plan on bringing something to munch on as many airports have picnic tables available. Kids who are grounded will enjoy watching the planes take off and land. Blue skies and tail winds to you!

Some locations offer a tour of the control tower, if available. Kids will need to keep their voices low so they don't disturb the tower operators. Most chapters have an education program of some sort. Notes: Compton, Hawthorne, Torrance - Most pilots at this program try to let the kids have a turn at the controls, for just a short period of time. Pacoima - Kids fly over Magic Mountain, which makes their flight extra special. Santa Monica - Check the website for a phone number to call for this chapter.

Hours: Compton, Hawthorne, Torrance - Jan. - November, the 3rd Sat. at 10am. Long Beach - call the national number for more info. Pacoima - The fourth Sat. of every month, usually, starting at 10am. Santa Monica - Three or four select Sat. a year, starting at noon.
Price: Free
Ages: 8 - 17 years old.

—ZOOS AND ANIMALS—

ANIMAL TRACKS

(661) 268-1314 / www.animaltracksinc.org
10234 Escondido Canyon Road, Agua Dulce

Pet a baby alligator? Sit at a picnic table and have "lunch" with a baboon? Stroke the soft fur of a kangaroo? Allow a monkey to inspect me close up and jump on my head? Rub the belly of a wolf hybrid? Feel the scales and the strength of an albino Burmese python? Hear a cockatoo "sing" (more like yelling)? Touch an armadillo, skunk, serval, fennec fox and more???!!! YES! Make tracks to Animal Tracks, one of the best animal encounters I've ever had.

Our tour started off with seeing (not touching) scorpions and a huge, ugly African bull frog (think Jabba the Hutt - no, really), then touching the 14 foot python. Then, onto mammals including possums, ferrets, a skunk, porcupines, raccoons, cavies, a Bengal cat, a pig and the critters I previously mentioned. Note that the animals you actually encounter are up to staff discretion. Most of the animals you can touch (but not all) and as you do, or even as you just look at them, the staff is doing an incredibly wonderful job of explaining all about the animals, as well as why they are here since they are all rescues and can't be returned to their natural habitats. Many were kept illegally (and foolishly) as exotic pets. I learned so much, was overjoyed with being able to actually handle such animals and I appreciated the cleanliness of the cages. Each animal is lovingly trained to be social so that visitors have a unique experience and are educated about them. All tours are by reservation only. Tip: Look at the grocery wish on their website before you come and bring some food for the animals when you do.

A public tour is one where anyone may come; a private tour is just you and your party. Here are just a few of the tours offered (check the website for others): The Ranch Tour, for ages 13 and up, is a two-hour tour of the facility where you might have a hands on experience with reptiles, ferrets, an armadillo, opossums, a fennec fox, wolf hybrids, cavies, a pig, a serval, kangaroos, and Chrissy, the baboon. The tour is $45 per person for the public tour; $100 per person for a private tour. The Monkey Experience, for ages 16 and up for the public tour, ages 10 and up for a private one, is a one-hour time of monkeying around by possibly interacting with capuchin monkeys, a squirrel monkey and the baboon. This tour is $85 per person for a public tour; $125 for a private. Children's tours, which can be for all ages though geared for ages 8 and under, is a one-hour experience to meet some of the most popular animals (but not monkeys). It is $25 for ages 13 and up; $20 for ages 2 - 12; children under 2 are free. Note that VASQUEZ ROCKS (pg. 90) is just down the street.

Hours: All tours are by reservation only.

Price: Prices for some of the tours are listed above.

Ages: 2 years and up, depending on the tour.

AQUARIUM OF THE PACIFIC

(562) 590-3100 / ww.aquariumofpacific.org

$$$$$

100 Aquarium Way, Long Beach

Something fishy's going on at one of the largest aquariums in the United States. The first stop in this multi-level, incredible aquarium is the spacious entryway where your attention is immediately riveted by a life-size, eighty-eight-foot blue whale (no way can a creature be so large!) hanging overhead with her calf "swimming" beside her. This hall also contains preview tanks of the main exhibit regions. Watch a sea-related film in the theater or even a 4-D special presentation movie for an additional $3. Information and breath-taking footage on the audio/video screens throughout the aquarium answer many of the questions visitors have about the animals here. Note that almost everything in the tanks, besides the fish, is man-made, although it is incredibly realistic looking. Note, too, that small Discovery Labs are located in each area of the main exhibits and are staffed with docents to answer questions, give demonstrations, and allow you to touch selected sea creatures. All exhibits are handicapped accessible. There are five main exhibit areas to view: California/Baja, Northern Pacific, Tropical Pacific, Explorer's Cove, and Pacific Visions.

The natural flow of the aquarium leads visitors toward the back of the building, to the **Southern California/Baja** area. Watch the mesmerizing moon jellies' milky white bodies and other exotic drifters float gracefully around in their tanks. Peek at the Swell Shark egg cases where baby sharks are getting ready to be born. A kelp display shows those of us who aren't marine biologists that kelp is used as an ingredient in lipstick, Jell-O, toothpaste, and other household items. Catch an underwater look at the seals and sea lions splashing around. (Ask about feeding times, when divers often interact with the animals.) Walk up the stairs and outside to see these mammals sun themselves on the surface of the rocky "shoreline." Tiered cement seating allows good viewing for everyone. This outdoor plaza also features sea turtles, shore birds (that are unable to fly away), and a touch tank that holds stingrays and batrays, which feel like rubber. It's a weird sensation and worth it. The Discovery Lab here contains sea urchins, anemones, sea stars, and crabs to gently touch. A favorite is the penguin habitat that holds about twenty Magellanic penguins, which are native to South America. You can see them swimming around from above and below, and even at eye level at a crawl-in space. Back inside, on the second floor of the gallery, you'll see aptly named garden eels and a rocky reef that holds unusual looking fish, particularly the Lookdowns, which are a vertically-flattened fish.

For a change in venue and temperature, enter the **Northern Pacific** gallery. The most popular attractions here are the playful sea otters in a tank with underwater and above-water viewing. Ample information is given about their fur (for which they've been voraciously hunted), their food, their habitats, and more. Other draws include the tank of anchovies (no pizza!), diving puffins (seabirds), monstrous-looking Giant Japanese Spider Crabs, and a Giant Pacific Octopus, which is not menacing, but so shy that you might not even see him.

Ocean on the Edge Gallery explores the top ten ocean issues. This hallway, with small nooks, showcases great visuals of wall-sized photos, maps, videos, 3-D models of the earth and parts of the ocean, wheels to turn to uncover facts, and animal exhibits on rays, coral reefs, and jellies. The information presented deals with global warming, destructive fishing, ocean pollution, and more. The Ocean Science Center here offers a unique and visual way to view and understand the effects of climate change and rising sea levels, and maritime trade and ports via "science on a sphere". Both stories are told through the medium of satellite images and videos projected onto a rotating, six-foot diameter globe.

The **Tropical Pacific** is one of the most colorful sections. It's set up so you'll "travel" through the reef and into deeper waters as you venture deeper into this gallery. The coral lagoon showcases brilliantly colored fish - electric blue, canary yellow, jade green, and vivid purple. The largest tank, containing a tropical reef and its 1,000 inhabitants, offers various levels of viewing which is interesting because of the diversity of life shown in here. You'll see clown fish, zebra sharks, giant groupers, puffer fish, Picasso Triggerfish, and more. At feeding time the divers are equipped with aquaphones to answer any questions. A partial water tunnel allows visitors to see sharks, and every parent knows that an aquarium visit is not complete without seeing sharks. Other outstanding exhibits in this gallery include deadly sea snakes; sea horses; the strange-looking leafy sea dragons and weedy sea dragons; upside-down jellies, who were created to live like this; orange-spined unicorn fish; sex reversal fish (mainly wrasses) who change from females to males as they mature or undergo stress - go figure; and beautiful, but venomous or poisonous fish, such as the lionfish. The lower level has an array of colorful jellies including the Leidy's comb jelly with iridescent pink and green flashing lights, and sea nettles with their long, stringy tentacles. Also on display here are Flashlight fishes, which live in the dark depths of the sea. These truly odd, but practical, creatures have headlights located under their eyes that they can switch on and off.

Outside is a favorite area - the shark lagoon. It contains 150 sharks, many of which swim right up to the glass partition so you can clearly see and count all three rows of their teeth. A favorite of ours is the sawshark with a nose that looks like a saw. Try to come by at feeding time, usually at 11am and 2pm, to see a frenzy of activity. At a nearby shallow "petting" tank, roll up your sleeves and touch a variety of sharks (which feel like sandpaper) and rays. Come on Shark Lagoon Nights, offered almost every Friday, when the public is invited for free to see these predators up close and to touch some. Behind the shark exhibit is Molina Animal Care Center which provides onsite healthcare for animals. Visitors can come in and see veterinarians at work.

Also out this way is a walk-through lorikeet aviary, open daily from 10:30am to 4:30pm. Purchase a small cup of nectar to feed these colorful birds. Take pictures of your astonished kids as the birds land on their head and arms. The canopied-covered Marine Life Theater has fifteen-minute presentations of an animal or storytelling time. Beyond the lorikeet aviary is Harbor Terrace, a small outdoor space to relax for a minute that also feature mudskippers and the Moon Jelly Touch Lab.

The outdoors, and covered, classroom - Our Water Future - is strongly educational in teaching what happens to water once it rains or flows down from the mountains; water conservation; and drought-resistant plants. It has an interactive, 3-D watershed model where visitors can manipulate a map, "make" it rain, learn about conserving water, and more.

Pacific Visions (opening in spring, 2019) is located just inside the entrance and is comprised of four main components. The first is a museum-like Art Gallery, with a focus on various aspects of marine life art in photos, sculpture and more. The second is the Orientation Gallery, a room made up of numerous multi-media screen panels showcasing fact and discoveries about sea creatures and marine habitats to prep visitors for going into the next room, the theater. The two-story, 300-seat theater features a 30' high by 130' long screen that is both interactive and immersive, with 4-D elements of seeing, hearing, and smelling what's on the screen, along with a 30'-diameter floor projection disc all allowing visitors to experience a virtual ocean environment more fully. Ocean stories play out on the massive screen. This room also hosts live performances of music and dance, scientists talks and other educational programs. The Changing Exhibit Gallery is just that - a gallery of various tanks of live animals and more touch screen walls that invite visitors to make choices about marine environments and see how they are played out.

Cafe Scuba has good food and indoor tables, plus outdoor tables that overlook the seal and sea lion exhibit and Rainbow Harbor. And yes, fish is on the menu.

There are "shows" every day for visitors, such as the feeding times for the animals, learning how certain animals are cared for, and more. Ask about the multitude of special events and programs offered to families and school groups including sleep-overs, which are so fun to do with your child ($90 per person); one-hour animal encounters with sharks, otters, penguins, or seals and sea lions ($109 each person - aquarium admission included); one-hour, behind-the-scenes tours, which incorporate feeding the fish at Tropical Reef ($19 per person + aquarium admission);

whale watching tours; and studies of a particular animal or species. Check their calendar online for annual events. Two classrooms in the educational wing are fully stocked with lab equipment, live systems (touch-tank animals), terrestrial aquariums, craft projects, and other good stuff. An educator's room, available for teachers, contains computers, books, arts and crafts resources, and more.

Note: Weekend and holidays are peak attendance times, which translates as lots of people and waiting in line to get in. Prepurchase tickets at a discount online and avoiding waiting in line.

The aquarium is adjacent to Rainbow Harbor. In between the aquarium and harbor are an esplanade and a large green lawn. Feel free to bring a blanket and a picnic lunch. Head out on the esplanade (i.e., cement walkway) to the colorful-looking buildings of SHORELINE VILLAGE (pg. 161), a shopping and eating complex. Head the other way around the harbor toward a quasi park (i.e., an expanse of green lawn with a few picnic tables) where you can view the QUEEN MARY (pg. 147) just across the waters. Take an aquabus around - see AQUALINK / AQUABUS (pg. 209) for details. Catch a free ride to the aquarium on a bright red Long Beach Passport shuttle bus that cruises Pine Ave., Shoreline Dr., and Ocean Blvd. in the downtown area, and connects to the Metro Blue Line at the Transit Mall on First Street. Passport buses will also deliver you to the *Queen Mary*.

Hours: Open daily, 9am - 6pm. It's open on select nights throughout the year and on Sunday nights in the summer, 5pm - 8pm. Shark Lagoon Nights (when only the shark area is open) are almost every Fri., 6pm - 9pm throughout the year and they are free! Closed Christmas and sometimes during the Grand Prix in April.

Price: $29.95 for adults; $26.95 for seniors; $17.95 for ages 3 - 11; children 2 and under are free. AAA members receive a discount. The 5pm - 8pm nighttime only tickets are only $14.95. Combo tickets are offered for the aquarium plus other local attractions. Parking is $8 for the day, with aquarium validation. With validation from an area business it's free for the first 90 min.; $3 for up to 3 hours, etc.

Ages: All

CABRILLO MARINE AQUARIUM

(310) 548-7562 / www.cabrillomarineaquarium.org
3720 Stephen M White Drive, San Pedro

!/$$

Explore the underwater treasures of Los Angeles Harbor without ever getting wet! The mid-size Cabrillo Marine Aquarium specializes in the marine life of Southern California. Originally built in 1935, it doesn't have the polished look or feel of more modern aquariums, but that is absolutely part of its charm. It features quite a few smallish tanks, mostly at kids' eye-level, filled with a wide variety of sea life.

The front courtyard has full-size killer whale, shark, and dolphin models, plus a full-grown gray whale outlined on the cement. Kids are welcome to touch the whale bones in the adjacent Whale Graveyard.

The exhibit halls and rooms have tanks filled with several kinds of live jellies (usually referred to as jellyfish), crustaceans, octopuses, fish, leopard sharks, seahorses, moray eels, the kelp forest and inhabitants, and other sea animals. Some of the animals - the sea stars, some of the fish, and a lobster - are huge, having lived here for a long time. There are numerous displays of preserved animals, such as seals and sea lions; bones, skeletons, jaws, and teeth of sharks and a full whales skeleton; shells; pictures; and other models of sea life. My boys liked pushing the button to hear the recording of a whale singing, although their renditions of it were more grating than musical. We also watched a shark blend into the sandy ocean floor; touched a sample of shark skin and compared it to a sample of sandpaper; and saw a video presentation at the auditorium. Call to see what's currently showing.

As most kids have this inherent need to explore the world with their hands and not just their eyes, a definite favorite is the tidepool touch tank. At timed sessions throughout the day, kids can gently touch sea anemones, sea stars, and sea slugs.

The adjacent buildings feature an Exploration Center and an Aquatic Nursery. The educational-oriented Center has a tank that allows kids to crawl up into the middle so it looks like they are surrounded by fish. (And they are!) It also contains touch screens; a puppet theater with puppet sea creatures, and costumes for kids and adults, along with a monitor so actors can watch themselves; a craft station; microscopes with lots of slides; a no-touch tank of sea slugs and fish; a short tunnel of a recreated mud flat with hinged informational panels on the outside; and a touch table of fossils, shells, and jarred specimens. The Nursery looks like a scientist's lab with large, bubbling tubes that contain sea monkeys (i.e., brine shrimp) and phytoplankton, along with other equipment. See the breeding area for baby seahorses and other sea animals, and look at live abalone. Lift the panels for more information, learn about salmon farming and abalone, and listen as staffers explain about the inhabitants and the function of the nursery.

The Cabrillo Aquarium offers seasonal events such as whale watching (January through April) and grunion hunting (March through July), plus various workshops and programs, such as Sleep With the Fishes. At low tide - call for particular times and seasons - tidepool tours are given at the beach in an area called Point Fermin Marine Life Refuge. A paved, wheelchair-accessible trail runs from the parking lot to the aquarium, across the beach, and to the water's edge at the tidepools. You are welcome to explore this area on your own, too.

Don't forget to pack your swimsuits and beach towels as CABRILLO BEACH (pg. 11) is right outside the aquarium. Wonderful sandy stretches and a playground await your children. There are also some rock jetties to explore and a fishing pier. Enjoy your day playing by the ocean, and learning more about it.

Hours: The Aquarium is open Tues. - Fri., noon - 5pm; Sat. - Sun., 10am - 5pm. Closed Mon., Thanksgiving, and Christmas. The touch tank doors open for twenty minutes at a time Tues. - Fri. at 1:30pm, 2:30pm, and 3:30pm; Sat. - Sun. at 11:30am, 1:30pm, 2:30pm, and 3:30pm. Slide shows are presented Tues. - Sun. at 11am and 2pm. The beach is open daily, 6am - 10pm.

Price: $5 (suggested donation) for adults, $1 for seniors and ages 12 and under. Parking is $1 an hour, $9 max. If you get here early enough, you can park on the street and just walk through the beach/aquarium entrance gate.

Ages: All

CAL POLY POMONA PETTING FARM

(909) 869-2217 - petting farm; (909) 869-4906 - Farm Store / www.cpp.edu/~agriscapes/petting-farm.html
4102 S. University Drive at California State Polytechnic University, Pomona

Farm fresh animals in this case means a petting farm, located in the AG area of Cal Poly Pomona. Enter the pens to gently stroke and even feed miniature horses, goats, sheep, calves, rabbits and small breed pigs. Bring your camera! Picnic tables are available here, too. If you didn't bring food, grab a snack (and something to take home for dinner) at the adjacent Farm Store which offers farm-fresh produce, pork, and beef; incredible chocolate milk; health foods; plants; and other products.

Hours: Open March - October, on most Sat., 10am - 2pm, weather permitting. Open in the month of October, along with the adjacent, huge pumpkin patch, Sat. - Sun., 10am - 4pm.

Price: $4 per person. Food cups are $1.

Ages: 1 - 12 years.

EFBC'S FELINE CONSERVATION CENTER / THE CAT HOUSE

(661) 256-3332 - recorded info; (661) 256-3793 - live person / www.cathouse-fcc.org
3718 60th Street West, Rosamond

This place is the cat's meow! In the middle of desert and dirt, this nicely-landscaped, mid-sized compound has seventy exotic wild cats living here, representing over nineteen different species. Since it is a breeding compound, you're almost guaranteed to see a few kittens, too. Unlike traditional zoos, the safety fences keep you only a few feet (not yards) away from the caged animals. This allows for plenty of up-close viewing and photo opportunities.

Stroll along the cement pathways to see jaguars, panthers, pumas, lynxes, ocelots, fluffy Amur leopards, regal-looking servals, weasel-like jaguarundi, snow leopards, sand cats and lots of Chinese leopards. Read the information plaques at the enclosures or ask for a guided tour to learn about the animals - what they eat, how much they weigh, their life span, and more - and about the importance of this breeding compound.

In the center of the grounds is nice, green and shady spot and some tables. You can enjoy a picnic lunch here; just don't feed the animals. The gift shop has a few displays showing some of the reasons these cats are facing extinction - one fur coat was made from fifteen bobcats, and another was made from over fifty leopards. Tip: Late afternoon and cooler months are the best times to visit the center as this is when the felines are more active. Special Twilight Tours are offered three times a year for ages 18 and older. At those times you'll see areas not open to the daytime public, like the Siberian tigers, and have your picture taken with a cat (if one is cooperating). Call if you want to schedule a tour for ten or more people. Educational outreach programs are also available. Check out the special Kid's Day, too, in October.

Hours: Open Thurs. - Tues., 10am - 4pm. Closed Wed., Thanksgiving, and Christmas.

Price: $10 for adults; $8 for seniors; $5 ages 3 - 12; children 2 and under are free. Twilight tours are $20 per person.

Ages: 4 years and up.

FARM SANCTUARY'S SOUTHERN CALIFORNIA SHELTER

(661) 269-5404 / www.farmsanctuary.org					$$$
5200 Escondido Canyon Road, Acton

This lovely, twenty-six acre ranch is sanctuary to over 100 barn animals - horses, cows, pigs (some weigh up to 1100 pounds!), goats, turkeys, chicken, ducks, and sheep - that have been rescued from slaughter houses and animal cruelty. A four-minute video at the beginning of the guided tour emphasizes the sanctuary's stand on not eating animals and caring for all creatures equally. The casual, one-hour tour allows visitors to ask lots of questions, hear the animal's rescue stories, and walk around interacting with the mostly free-roaming animals by petting them, feeding them, and giving them love, thus educating and maybe changing minds and diets when people "meet what they eat."

Hours: Open Fri., Sat. and Sun. for one-hour guided tours at 11am, 1pm and 3pm. School and other groups may call to make an appointment at other times. Always call first as sometimes there are special events so the Sanctuary is closed to the public.

Price: $10 for adults; $5 for ages 4 - 12; children 3 and under are free.

Ages: 2 years and up.

GENTLE BARN

(661) 252-2440 / www.gentlebarn.org					$$$$
15825 Sierra Highway, Santa Clarita

The over 120 animals at the farm-like Gentle Barn sanctuary have been rescued from abusive situations and have found a new home here where people lovingly connect with them. Watch and stroke horses playing in the grassy field and go to their stalls to feed them carrots ($5 a bag). Brush the cows and give them a hug. Go into the pen to pet llamas, sheep, goats, an emu, chickens, and turkeys, and give the big pigs a belly rub. Hands on, your own leisure timing, education about where the animals (and each one has a name) came from and why, and many volunteers to assist you and answer your questions make Gentle Barn a warm, welcoming, and therapeutic animal encounter. There is a picnic area here, too, plus snacks and a little gift shop for purchases. Special needs groups, at-risk kids, school field trips, and other groups are invited during the week.

Hours: Open to the public Sun., 10am - 2pm, with groups allowed into the upper barnyard at 11am, noon and 1pm. Sometimes tickets get sold out ahead of time.

Price: $20 for adults; $10 for ages 12 and under.

Ages: All

GIBBON CONSERVATION CENTER

(661) 296-2737 / www.gibboncenter.org					$$$
19100 Esquerra Road, Santa Clarita

What's the difference between a monkey and an ape? If you answered, "Monkeys have tails," you are correct. Next question: Are gibbons monkeys or apes? Hint - they have no tails. A one-hour, or so, guided tour of this outdoor facility takes you past sixteen enclosures that hold over forty gibbons in their natural family groupings. The enclosures are sizable chain-link cages, scattered over the hard-packed dirt grounds and under shade trees. The tours are informative, entertaining, and vary according to the interests and ages of the participants in the group, from elementary-age kids to anthropology professors. Note: To ensure the safety of the gibbons, visitors must be in good health, not have had any recent contact with a person or animal with an infectious disease, and stay a minimum of five feet away from all enclosures.

Gibbons are arboreal apes - they swing from tree to tree - and are found in the rainforests of Southeast Asia. This research facility, which has five out of the nineteen existing species, studies their behavior and helps to increase their endangered gene pool, which means you could see babies on your visit here. Gibbons are the only nonhuman primates to walk upright and they have earned the name of loudest land mammal. Every species has a different way of singing (that's the technical name - I call it screaming) to each other, usually in the morning hours. They can project their voices a distance of up to two miles. We heard them. I believe it. The kids loved it. Siamangs have vocal sacs that inflate to the size of a large grapefruit (reminiscent of a bullfrog) when they sing. This is fascinating to listen to and watch. Males and females in certain species are born one color and change colors as they mature. (Is this the same thing as humans "going gray"?) We also learned about gibbons' nutrition, why they are dying off, preventative medical care, and more. My boys went ape over this center!

Hours: Open to the public, Sat. - Sun., 9:30am - noon, except for rainy days and holidays. Guided tours are at 10am. Open by appointment at other times for groups of twenty or more people, or a minimum of $120 for 8 people. These tours preferably start between 8:30am and 10:30am, when gibbons are most active. Individuals may call to see if they can join an already scheduled tour. Closed New Year's Day and Christmas.

Price: $15 for adults; $10 for seniors; $12 for teens and students; $5 for ages 6 - 12; children 5 and under are free.

Ages: 4 years and up.

KELLOGG ARABIAN HORSE CENTER

(909) 869-4988; (909) 869-2224 / www.wkkelloggarabianhorsecenter.com

3801 W. Temple Avenue at California State Polytechnic University, Pomona

The Kellogg Arabian Horse Center at Cal Poly houses over 130 purebred Arabian horses. The center's thirty-eight scenic acres are set in the hills and encompass a huge pasture, three barns, foaling stalls, a breeding area, a veterinary clinic, a farrier shop, an arena, and a covered grandstand that seats 900.

Staff members, and students of horse husbandry and equine sciences, present hour-long shows that put the horses through their various paces. Guests see demonstrations of English and western riding, with riders in appropriate costumes, as well as drill team and precision maneuvers, and horses jumping over small fences. Riders in silver and gold flowing Arabian dress are crowd pleasers as their horses, decorated in jewel-toned brocade and tassels, prance around the ring. Our favorite act was the horse that performed several tricks, including walking a baby carriage and rocking a cradle.

After the show children can ride a horse on a lead around a path for $4, walk around the stables where families can watch the beautiful horses being bathed and groomed, and simply enjoy the ambiance. Springtime is the best time to visit as there are newborn foals to see - ten to fifteen are born here each year. Note that visitors are welcome to visit the horse center, just to walk around and through the stables as it's usually open daily, 8am to 4pm. Guided tours are offered during the academic year Tuesdays at 11am and Wednesdays at 1:30pm. Call (909) 869-4988 to arrange a tour.

Be sure to visit the Farm Store just around the corner at 4102 S. University Drive for farm-fresh produce, pork, and beef; incredible chocolate milk; health foods; plants; and other products. It's open daily from 10am to 6pm. For more info contact the store at (909) 869-4906 / www.csupomona.edu/~farmstore.

Hours: Shows are offered October through May on the first Sun. of each month at 2pm.

Price: $4 for adults; $3 for seniors and ages 6 - 17; children 5 and under are free. Parking on Sun. is $4.

Ages: 3 years and up.

LOS ANGELES ZOO

(323) 644-4200 / www.lazoo.org

5333 Zoo Drive, Los Angeles

All the big-name animals star at the Los Angeles Zoo - Asian elephants (in six acres of their own exhibit - see the training demonstrations daily at 11am), tigers, African lions, bears, okapi, kangaroos, alligators, jaguars, wolves, and rhinoceros. With 1,100 animals living here, there are also lots of little name stars here, too. Many of the animals live in the context of their natural environment with plants, rocks, etc., and yet plenty of viewing areas, too. Our favorites are the gorillas, apes, orangutans, chimps, and other primates - they provide entertainment that tops television any day - all in their own habitats that also immerses visitors because of the plants and other authentic setting "props". An aquatic area features otters and seals splashing in the water, or posing or sleeping on rocks. You'll want to catch the sea lion training in the aquatics section and the keeper talk. Actually, catch several keeper talks, which take place at select animal enclosures as great information and insight is dispensed regarding that animal. The hippos have an underwater pool with glass walls so visitors can view their below the waterline activities. Tip: You can learn about and see hippos more up close on weekends and holidays for an additional $20. The darkened Koala House has koalas in their nighttime environment, since they are supposed to be more active at that time. Don't forget to sssssstop by the two-building LAIR (Living Amphibians, Invertebrates and Reptiles) to see snakes and lizards from all over the world, and my favorites, the Komodo dragons and the Chinese alligators. Don't just see the giraffes, but feed them from 11am to 1pm and 2pm to 4pm daily for an additional $5.

If your kids get tired of walking around this huge and hilly zoo (and it is hilly), or you get tired of pushing a stroller, purchase an all-day shuttle pass for about $4 for adults, $1.50 for seniors and disabled, $2 for ages 2 to 12. The shuttle goes around the perimeter of the zoo, and will drop you off or pick you up at various stops along the way.

Enter the children's zoo (which closes daily at 4pm) to pet and even brush goats and sheep, and see miniature horses, rabbits, and potbellied pigs. Don't miss the fifteen-minute "Animals and You" presentations here to see, maybe touch, and definitely learn about an assortment of critters in an intimate setting on weekdays at 10:45am and 11:45am, with an additional show on weekends at 12:45pm. Spelunkers can explore a man-made cave, which offers tunnels to crawl through, exhibits on cave creature dwellers to look at, and (pretend) stalactites and stalagmites to see. One cave features Desert Trail, a tunnel exhibit showcasing tortoises, bearded lizards, scorpions, and tarantulas. At the prairie dog exhibit kids can pop their heads up from underneath the ground into a plexiglass dome while real prairie dogs are looking at them! This is a fun photo opportunity. The Animal Care Center (i.e., nursery) houses small mammals, birds, and newborns that need special care.

An animal-themed, boundless playground has climbing sculptures; slides, including a textured slide; a bridge; a toddler area; and larger play structure that are suitable for kids with and without disabilities. It also has water misters and a picnic area. Take a spin on the huge carousel ($3) featuring sixty-four animals including giraffes, bears, tigers, a poison dart frog, and a dung beetle.

Look - it's a bird, it's a plane, it's Superman! No, it's a bird! The World of Birds show features about twenty, mostly free-flying birds that perform Wednesday through Monday at noon and 2:30pm - a ~~flight~~, sight not to miss.

On select dates during warmer months, join in a Creature Camp Out ($85 per person) where your family (kids must be at least 5) can join numerous others and sleep in tents on the zoo grounds. Enjoy a campfire snack and continental breakfast, plus enjoy special nighttime and early morning behind-the-scenes tours of the animals and an animal encounter, plus a souvenir t-shirt. What a great experience! Ask about their numerous other special programs and events, such as Safari Days ($75) for K through 6th graders, with activities and animal encounters; Zoopendous Nights for groups and scout troops ($60 per person), which is an overnight adventure that includes working on badge-related activities; daytime patch programs for scouts; free guided tours given to mid and upper elementary school-aged kids; and annual events, such as the wonderful L.A. Zoo Lights in November and December. Stroller and wheelchair rentals are available. A free audio tour regarding some of the weirdest animals is available by using on your cell phone at the zoo. Look under GRIFFITH PARK (pg. 63) for other attractions in this immediate area.

Hours: Open daily, 10am - 5pm. Closed Christmas.

Price: $21 for adults; $18 for seniors; $16 for ages 2 - 12. Discounts can be available through AAA. Parking is free.

Ages: All

MARINE MAMMAL CARE CENTER AT FORT MACARTHUR

(310) 548-5677 / www.marinemammalcare.org

3601 S. Gaffey Street, San Pedro

Can you hear them barking? Injured or sick marine mammals, mostly sea lions and seals, are brought here, doctored, and taken care of until they can be released back into the wild. Rehabilitation can take one to three months, depending on the case. We saw one seal that was severely underweight and another that had numerous shark bites. This small facility houses from five to ninety marine mammals outside in chain-link fence pens, depending on the season. Stormy weather and pupping season (February through July) bring in more injured or abandoned animals. However, the staff has more time to spend with visitors during non-busy times. Your children have an opportunity to learn more about these animals as knowledgeable volunteers are on hand to answer any questions kids might ask. And they do ask! Try to visit at feeding time (for the seals and sea lions, not the kids), which are usually at noon and 4pm, because this is when the animals are most active. Call first to make sure of the times. You can only see the seals through chain link fences so you won't be here long, but it's interesting stop off.

A variety of educational tours and classes are offered for K - 12th grade that incorporate a visit with the animals, a video, reinforcement activities, and pre- and post-visit materials. Fourth graders and up may also utilize the laboratory inside the adjacent building, operating the microscopes and computers and looking at the aquarium. Tours are an hour for preschoolers through kindergartners, and ninety minutes for older children, with an emphasis on the academics. Inquire about the MMCC Seal Day event in May.

Look up FORT MACARTHUR MUSEUM - ANGEL'S GATE PARK (pg. 109) as it is located just across the street. Check out the nearby Angels' Gate Park for picnicking, kite flying, basketball, and running around.

Hours: Open daily, 10am - 4pm.

Price: Free. Tour groups of less than 10 are $30; groups of 11 - 30 people are $3 per person.

Ages: All - younger ones will just enjoy seeing the animals, while older ones can learn about them and appreciate what the Center does.

MONTEBELLO BARNYARD ZOO and GRANT REA PARK

(213) 718-5442; (323) 887-4595 / www.montebellobarnyardzoo.com

!/$

600 Rea Drive, Montebello

A very small Barnyard Zoo is at one corner of the Grant Rea Park. It has a small pond for ducks, an aviary with a few doves and peacocks, and pens holding goats, pigs, a cow, llamas, bunnies, horses, chickens and sheep that kids can pet through the fences. A quick visit to this "zoo" makes a stop at the park a little more special. The entrance fee to the zoo is $5 per person. Other activities include a short "train" ride around - $5 per person; a merry-go-round with small horses - $4 per person; pony rides for younger children, twice around the walking track - $6; and mining for "gems" at a sluice - $3. Animal feed is $1. A snack bar is open here on the weekends with hot dogs, churros, beverages, and more. School groups, with a minimum of twenty kids, pay $7 per child ($4 for adults, teachers are free) for one ride on each attraction and admission to the petting zoo.

The surrounding, nice-sized park is pretty. It has baseball diamonds, batting cages (open at certain times), picnic tables under shade trees, barbeques, a playground, and bike trails along the river bed.

Hours: The park is open daily, 7am - dusk. The zoo is open most of the year, Wed. - Fri., 10am - 4pm; Sat. - Sun., 10am - 5pm or 6pm. It is open in the summer daily, 10am - 5pm. The rides are usually available during zoo hours.

Price: Free to the park. Prices for the zoo and rides are listed above.

Ages: 1 - 10 years.

NEWHALL AQUARIUM

(661) 220-5512 or (310) 795-2851 / www.facebook.com/newhallaquarium/

$$

24631 Arch Street, Newhall

This small aquarium holds several tanks filled with angelfish, anthias, clown fish, grouper, jellyfish, moon jellies, crabs, octopus, leopard sharks, seahorses, Moray eels, and more. Come at feeding time when the animals are more active. Touch-tubs contain a variety of seastars and sea hares that visitors can carefully hold, as well as bat rays to gently stroke. Overhead hangs a stuffed hammerhead shark. The room is surrounded by shelves filled with opportunities to touch sea shells and much more. There are some long tables set up like a classroom with microscopes and other equipment for hands-on learning. Contact them to book school field trips, outreach programs, birthdays and other special events during the week.

Hours: Open to public Sat. - Sun., 3pm - 5pm.

Price: $5 donation per person.

Ages: 3 years and up

PASADENA HUMANE SOCIETY

(626) 792-7151 / pasadenahumane.org

!

361 S. Raymond Avenue, Pasadena

This atypical animal shelter is quite lovely with open-air kennels and plants all around. Besides the numerous dogs and cats, there are rabbits in penned play yards, guinea pigs, birds, iguanas, turtles, peacocks, and other kinds of animals that need a home. (Sometimes even wildlife, such as deer, show up.) The permanent residents here include an alligator, some parakeets and cockatiels in the aviary, and a few snakes.

Free, forty-five-minute tours are offered for school children, scouts, and other groups. Note that the program will come to your facility as well. Kids learn about why the animals are here (i.e., homelessness or abuse), facts about pet care, animal safety, how animals communicate, careers with animals, and more. After a presentation with various animals such as reptiles, birds, a chinchilla, and others, the group takes a guided walk around the shelter. Smaller groups may go into the veterinary hospital, depending on the happenings there. Your kids come away with a better understanding of animals and of the humane society's resources. Ask about summer workshops, camps, internships and other programs.

Hours: Open to visit Tues. - Fri., 9am - 5pm; Sat., 9am - 4pm; Sun., 11am - 4pm. Closed Mon. Open for tours Tues. - Fri., 9:30am - 4:30pm. Call to schedule a tour. Closed holidays.

Price: Free

Ages: 4 years and up.

POLO MATCH - WILL ROGERS STATE HISTORIC PARK

(310) 454-8212; (818) 509-9965 / www.willrogerspolo.org; www.parks.ca.gov

$$$

1501 Will Rogers State Park Road, Pacific Palisades

   If you feel like horsing around, come watch a polo match on the beautiful grassy field at Will Rogers State Historic Park. To learn more about what a game entails, look up SANTA BARBARA POLO (pg. 648). Picnic tables are plentiful at the park. And if you want to incorporate a tour of Will's house and/or a hike through the adjacent Topanga State Park, look up WILL ROGERS STATE HISTORIC PARK (pg. 158).

Hours: Games are held mid-April through September, Sat., 2pm - 5pm; Sun., 10am - 1pm. The park is open daily, 8am - sunset.

Price: $12 per vehicle; $11 for seniors. House tours and polo matches are included in the price of admission.

Ages: 5 years and up.

PONY TIME

(562) 916-7669; (951) 201-3928 / ponytimeatlakewood.weebly.com

$$

11369 E. Carson Street at the Lakewood Equestrian, Lakewood

   In the midst of the Lakewood Equestrian Center is this short adventure for young children. They can ride a pony that's on a walking lead around a small, center ring, and/or go for a short walk and a trot on a pony in a more open walking area. Come inside the little farm to pet and feed several goats, rabbits, sheep, and chickens. An alpaca, llama and a cow are in their own enclosures to see up close. Ask about the hour-long Mommy (Daddy) and Me classes where kids can brush, saddle and ride ponies, too. Picnic tables under shade trees are reservable for parties.

Hours: Open Wed. - Sun., 10am - 4pm., until 5pm at spring daylights savings time. Trot ponies are available on Sat. and Sun., only.

Price: $6 per ride/walking; $9 per ride/trot ponies (weekends only). $2 for the petting zoo. $2 for food for the animals.

Ages: 1 ½ years - 100 pounds for the walking ring; 3 years - 100 pounds for a pony trot.

ROUNDHOUSE AQUARIUM TEACHING CENTER

(310) 379-8117 / www.roundhouseaquarium.org

!/$

Manhattan Beach Boulevard at the end of Manhattan Beach Pier, Manhattan Beach

   Come see the stars of Manhattan; sea stars that is. The Roundhouse Aquarium is a small, two story marine learning center that offers a wonderful variety of tanks (some are floor to ceiling) along with lots of information via media kiosks and more, plus exhibits all set in a background of ocean and sky blue. (Look down at the marine-themed flooring!) The shark tank (always a favorite!) contains three species of sharks common to this area, plus moray eels, and some fish. Watch the sharks be fed - a feeding frenzy. A lobster and crab tank hold a California spiny lobster, giant spider crabs, and more. The nursery tank shows off just-hatched babies of the sea. A petting pool contains several types of rays to gently stroke. Rainbow stars, sunflower stars, and the sheephead are in the deep ocean habitat tank. You'll also see clownfish, Garibaldi (our state fish), an octopus, hermit crabs, and more. A tidepool touch tank containing mostly sea stars, a surge tank, and a few other aquariums with tropical fish and local invertebrates round out the collection at Roundhouse Aquarium. Upstairs is a play and study center that is complete with sea animal puppets, books, whale bones and shark's teeth to examine, more aquarium tanks, and videos.

   The aquarium offers several marine science programs, field trips for students, and fun family activities such as Sunday story times (with a craft and teaching time), sleeping with the sharks, summer camps, and more. A popular option for students is a three-hour class, given for kindergartners through twelfth graders, includes a lot of fa*sea*nating information, pollution awareness, beach exploration, animal anatomy, and hands-on fun such as touching sea stars and even petting a shark.

   On your way out to the aquarium, which is located at the end of a concrete pier, check out all the beach activity - lots of sand volleyball, surfing, swimming, and of course, sun bathing. You can also, ironically, fish from the pier. Sidewalk shops are just down the street.

Hours: Open Labor Day - Memorial Day, Mon. - Fri., 2pm - 5pm; Sat. - Sun., 10am - sunset. Open Memorial Day - Labor Day, Mon. - Fri., 2pm - 8pm; Sat. - Sun., 9am - 8pm.

Price: Free entrance to the aquarium; donations of $2 per person or $5 per family are encouraged. Metered parking ($1.25 an hour) is available on Manhattan Beach Blvd. by the stores, or wherever you can find it.

Ages: 2 years and up.

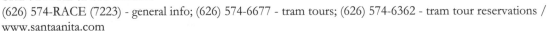

SANTA ANITA PARK

(626) 574-RACE (7223) - general info; (626) 574-6677 - tram tours; (626) 574-6362 - tram tour reservations / $$
www.santaanita.com

285 W. Huntington Drive, Arcadia

Hold your horses! One of the most famous thoroughbred horse racing parks in the United States is surprisingly family-friendly. Watch the horses being put through their paces during their morning workouts from 5am (this is a little too early for me!) to 9:30am, and while you're at it, grab a bite to eat at Clocker's Corner Cafe breakfast counter (open everyday, 7am to 10am). The Cafe offers inexpensive items that can be eaten at the outside patio area overlooking the track, or bring your own food to enjoy here.

On most Saturdays and Sundays during the season, and weather permitting, at 8:30am or 9:45am, take a free, fifteen-minute, behind-the-scenes, narrated Seabiscuit Tram Tour. Arrive fifteen minutes early. Reservations are highly suggested. You'll ride along dirt "roads," through a hub of horse activity, and past rows of stables where walkers, trainers, and jockeys are exercising, bathing, and grooming horses. The guides point out Barn 38 where Seabiscuit was stabled from 1937 to 1940, and the locations where the movie *Seabiscuit* was filmed, plus you'll see the equine who actually starred in the movie. A forty-five-minute walking tour follows the tram tour where you can peek into a jockey's room and saddling paddock, see behind-the-scenes action, and much more. Tip: Call first as the tram ride is not offered on days of major races. Catch the tram near Clocker's Corner Cafe in the parking lot near the west side of the grandstands.

Walk in the beautifully landscaped Paddock Gardens, located just inside the admission gate, to look at the flowers, statues, and equine-themed topiary plants. In the gardens, twenty minutes prior to post time, there is a brief "show" as jockeys, in their colorful silks, walk and ride their mounts around the walking ring before going on to the race track. Note: The first race on Monday usually begins at 1pm while races Wednesday through Sunday begin at 12:30pm. Weekends bring special events such as mariachi bands and dancers, costumed park mascots strolling about, and more. Look at the website for a schedule of their family-oriented events for both on and off season.

Go through a paved tunnel from the gardens to the infield (i.e., interior of the racetrack) to reach a playground. Kids can horse around on the large play structure with slides, monkey bars, a merry-go-round, and swings. One end of the playground is best suited for toddlers and the other for slightly older kids. The infield, which is only open on weekends and holidays, also features large grassy areas for running around and picnicking, so pack a lunch. Family Fun Zones are here most weekends that include huge inflatables, face-painting, rock climbing walls, pony rides, some rides and other fun things to do with attractions priced individually or buy an all-day wristband. Note: You may stay in the infield during races.

From the time the starting gates (which are portable) and jockeys are in position, to the finish line, enthusiasm runs rampant through the crowd. The actual races, although over quickly, are thrilling, even for nonbetters. (The numerous manned windows and wagering machines receive a lot of frantic activity.) My boys "scientifically" deduced who to root for - according to the horse's name and/or the color of the jockey's silks. Tip: Sitting in grandstand seats is the best way to see the action as the slanted cement standing area in front of the seats fills up quickly with people who are always taller than you. Note: It is almost a half an hour between races.

Lunchtime food can be purchased at concession stands; at the casual, but nice Turf Terrace; or the posh FrontRunner. Prices vary according to venue. I wager your kids will have a good time watching the Sport of Kings.

Hours: The season runs the end of December through June. Racing is usually Thurs. - Sun. and holiday Mon. (sometimes on a Wed.), with the first post time usually 12:30pm.

Price: There is often free admission before the gates open at 10:30am so watch the horse workouts and, on weekends, go on the tram ride. General admission and parking is free on Thurs. and Fri. If you arrive after gates open on weekends and holiday Mon., general admission is $5 for adults; free for kids 17 and under when accompanied by an adult. Clubhouse admission on weekends is $10. Parking is $4 after 9:30am.

Ages: 4 years and up.

SANTA MONICA PIER AQUARIUM

(310) 393-6149 / www.healthebay.org/smpa; parking.smgov.net $$$

1600 Ocean Front Walk, at the foot of Santa Monica Pier, Santa Monica

Discover what really lives in the Santa Monica Bay at the aquarium, located under the Santa Monica Pier. This small, but fascinating center, part of the Heal the Bay community program, has several tanks of live sea creatures to look at and touch. One large aquarium holds crabs, sea stars, California sheepshead, halibut, and other fish. Other tanks contain octopus, seahorses, and sea jellies plus a kelp forest and a rocky reef tank, which holds a moray eel and other sea life. Use the provided flashlight to see tiny swell sharks (which aren't necessarily wonderful sharks, it's just the name of that shark species) developing inside their hanging egg cases. Mature swell sharks, sand crabs, sand dollars, leopard sharks, and bat rays are too fragile for fingers to touch, but they are easily seen in shallow tanks placed at a child's eye level. In three touch tanks, however, kids can gently touch tidepool life such as sea stars, sea anemones, and sea slugs, and even sharks! (Albeit horn and swell sharks). A touch table displays a shark's jaw and individual teeth. It also has a microscope for a closeup look at scales, shells, etc.

A fantastic, interactive (with panels to open and more), 3-D and kid-friendly wall mural allows visitors to visually dive into the path water takes from ocean to mountain.

A kid's corner is filled with age-appropriate activities, games, and/or books. A small puppet theater stars sea creatures that kid's make come to life. The microscope lab, with its array of microscopes, computers, and viewing screens offers a closer perspective of sea organisms. On select days a short, ocean-related film (usually about sharks) is shown, plus you can participate in a shark craft and watch the feeding of the horn and swell sharks. Help feed the sea stars at 2:30pm on Fridays.

Informative, wonderful, and interactive one and two-hour programs are offered year round for students of all ages, and adults, and often include a "field trip" to the adjacent Santa Monica Beach. The programs also give great info on what Heal the Bay, "Southern California's water watchdog", does. Inquire about other classes and special events. Make a day of your visit to the aquarium by taking a walk on the SANTA MONICA PIER / SANTA MONICA BEACH (pg. 161), enjoying some rides at PACIFIC PARK (pg. 3), or just playing at the beach!

Hours: Open most of the year, Thurs. - Fri., 2pm - 5pm; Sat. - Sun., 12:30pm - 5pm. Open in the summer until 6pm. Call first as hours sometimes fluctuate. Closed Mon. - Wed., except for school programs. Closed most major holidays, including the week before Christmas.

Price: $5 for adults; children 12 and under are free. $3 per person for groups of 10 or more. Parking on or right next to the pier is $8 during the week; $12 on weekends. There is very limited metered parking nearby.

Ages: 3 years and up.

THE SEA LAB

(310) 318-7438 / www.lacorps.org/programs/the-sea-lab
1021 N. Harbor Drive, Redondo Beach

Inside the very small building of the SEA Lab are tanks containing a variety of sea creatures such as octopus, eels, Garibaldi, seahorses, coral, horn and swell sharks, moonjellies, and skates (not roller, but ones that look like rays), yet with funny looking faces. A small display on a storm drain vs. sewage, and the subsequent effects that trash has on the oceans and sea animals is here as is the ocean supermarket exhibit showcasing products on a shelf, like at a supermarket. When visitors use a scanner on a product, it reveals how much of what ocean element is used in that particular everyday item, such as seaweed in ice cream.

Outside is a good-sized tidepool touch tank with sea stars, sea anemones, and more. Beyond the gate, and open to the public on a guided "tour" given at the top of the hour only, are several large tanks, that look like small pools, containing an assortment of sea life. There are lobsters, large halibuts (sorry, no fishing allowed) that are part of the halibut hatchery, giant sea bass, bat rays, sea stars, and more. Most of these creatures arrive at this destination via saltwater intake systems from generating stations that suck in, and sometimes trap and even injure, the animals. Many of them are here only briefly before being released back to the ocean. Big "selling points" for a visit to the lab are that kids can ask as many questions as they want, and they can see and touch almost all of the animals here. The staff will even take the lobsters and sea stars out of the tanks for a closer look and touch. Saturdays at noon you can either watch the feeding of the fish or participate by purchasing a tray of food for $2 and then feeding it to them. A native plant nursery at the facility is also a butterfly habitat.

Coming here is a fun family outing, especially on the first Saturdays when there are "fishtivities" of crafts, music, games, and more. There are oceans of opportunity for school field trips, too. Three-hour, age-appropriate classes cover a gamut of topics that not only meet the state science standard, but are engaging. Time is spent at the lab, learning about the animals, and seeing and touching them. A portion of the time is also spent at the big lab, the beach. One project that the kids do is look at the water from a different perspective, through a microscope, and test for water quality. After expending some energy and gaining more knowledge about aquatic life, it's back to the building for a related craft or hands-on activity. Can't come to the SEA Lab? Then they'll come to you. Note: If you have a teen who is 14 years or older inquire about the volunteer program.

Hours: Open September - June, Tues. - Fri., 9am - 3:30pm; Sat., 10am - 4pm. Open July and August, the same hours plus Sun., 10am - 4pm. Tours of the touch tank are at the top of each hour. The first Sat. of each month includes special fishtivities. Closed Mon., most Sun., and holidays.

Price: $5 for adults; children 14 and under are free. Free admission on the first Tues. Fishtivity Sat. are $5 per person; children 3 and under are free. School field trips are about $5 per student.

Ages: 4 years and up.

SHADOWLAND FOUNDATION

(661) 724-0291; (818) 766-1825 / www.shadowlandfoundation.org

$$$$$

18832 Pine Canyon Road, Lake Hughes

Like *Dances With Wolves* without the dancing, this 11-acre ranch sanctuary, called Shadowland, is home to a pack of ten Alaskan Timber wolf hybrids whose original line was rescued out of Denali National Park. The owners of Shadowland have hand-raised and socialized this pack purposely so the public can learn about them, touch them and get to know them as "educate, not eradicate" is their main motto. On the two hour tour you first watch a video about wolves and are invited to learn the rules such as don't come at them and don't run (you don't want to be thought of as prey!) and be slowly introduced to them. The wolf hybrids are put through their paces in that you see how they are trained to do certain actions or tricks. All the while you learn about wolves, their habits and habitats, and the importance of them existing in the world. And then comes the best part - you get to pet them and even play with pack. And they are beautiful! You also get to feed them and receive wolf kisses (especially when they gently grab their snack from your mouth or face)! They like to howl, which is incredible to hear this up close. This rare opportunity is offered via tours and through educational programs for all ages and organizations, and by reservation only.

Hours: Public tours are offered on Sat. from 10am - noon. Private tours can be booked Tues. - Thurs. Reservations are mandatory for all tours.

Price: Public tours are $50 dollars for adults; $30 for kids. Private tours are $300 for up to 5 people.

Ages: 8 years and up.

SHAMBALA PRESERVE

(661) 268-0380 / www.shambala.org

$$$$$

6867 Soledad Canyon Road, Acton

The word Shambala means "a meeting place of peace and harmony for all beings, animal and human". This is a preserve for over forty exotic big cats - African lions, Bengal and Siberian tigers, bobcats, servals, a lynx, a liger (a hybrid of tiger and lion), cougars, and black, spotted, and Asian leopards - all who have been rescued from people and/or agencies that owned them and often abused them. The three-hour Safari tour, for those 18 years and older only, includes a one-hour guided walking tour that is sometimes hosted by Tippi Hedren, actress and founder of The Roar Foundation, the supporting foundation of the preserve. While learning about the history of the preserve and stopping at most cages, visitors see the magnificent cats and learn their stories - some good and some horrible. Visitors are also educated about legislation regarding illegally owning exotic felines and the unfortunate need for sanctuaries, while hopefully spurred on to become active in caring for these animals and others like them. The animal enclosures are natural and lovely with some run-around room, trees, plants, toys, and more creature comforts. You'll hear the animals communicating, like tigers chuffing and lions roaring. All this makes a power impact. The walking tour is mostly on hard-packed dirt trails, with some steps, on the beautiful, park-like grounds. There is even a lake with a picnic area and a wooden walkway, so bring a lunch to enjoy at the conclusion of your guided tour. If you enjoy the nighttime, come to a Sunset Safari during the summer and know that animals are often more active then, too. A gift shop is also on the premises. Note that there are other opportunities, besides the Safari, to support the preserve, as well. Bottom line - a lion is not a pet!

Hours: Open one weekend a month (usually the second one), noon - 3pm (gates open at 11:30am), for a Safari by advance reservation only.

Price: The safari tours are $50 per person.

Ages: 18 years and up only.

STAR ECO STATION

(310) 842-8060 / www.ecostation.org

10101 W. Jefferson Boulevard, Culver City

The inside of the Eco Station is done in the style of a lost Mayan temple, complete with archways, wall friezes, floor tiles with "fossils," (fake) greenery all around, and murals so the ECO Station's message of teaching kids the importance of preserving the environment and protecting wildlife comes across in an inviting manner. This place is, in fact, a designated wildlife sanctuary and works with the Department of Fish and Game, as well as other organizations. Illegal articles and animals, seized from people trying to smuggle them into the country via airports, seaports, and over the border, are displayed here for show and tell.

One hour-plus guided tours, the only way to see the station, are given to see the rooms and their inhabitants. The tour guides continually share interesting stories of how and why the animals are here and emphasize why wild animals should not be kept as pets. Note: The critters at the Station vary at any given time because of newcomers.

Two aquarium rooms contain tanks with colorful angelfish, blue tangs, Picasso fish, coral that's been harvested, lionfish, seahorses, pufferfish, red-ear slider turtles, and other aquatic creatures taken from people attempting to bring them into the U.S. Walk through a room painted like a kelp forest that simulates scuba diving, while learning about the food chain and how to keep the ocean healthy and free from litter that comes through storm drains.

The reptile room houses chameleons, numerous iguanas, geckos, bearded dragons, Burmese and ball pythons, boas, several caimans, and some tortoises. There are also quite a few tarantulas here and other arachnids. Guests are invited to touch some of the chameleons and iguanas and/or wrap the pythons around themselves, or for the more squeamish, to merely stroke them (or not). You'll be greeted with loud "caw"s inside the large bird room, filled with green-cheeked Amazons, toucans, cockatoos, African gray parrots, Macaws, and others. Some of them are practically bald as they pick at their feathers, habits they had previously that can't be undone.

An adjacent Environmental Village room contains information about saving the environment and wildlife and it features Chumash and Hope artifacts, such as drums, tools, and headdresses. The mammal rescue center room provides temporary homes for various animals, depending on which creatures are in need of the Eco Station facilities. We also saw bobcats and servals.

Two-hour school or group tours are offered during the week for $6 per person, $120 minimum. There is a park nearby for picnic lunches. If you can't come to the station, the station will come to you with mobile exhibits and workshops. Check the website for information about camps and special events, including the popular Dinofaire and Earth Day. Note that CULVER CITY PARK (pg. 54) is just down the street.

Hours: Open to the public Sat. - Sun., 10am - 4pm (last tour is at 3om). Tours leave every hour on the hour. Open for school/group Mon. - Fri. from 10am - noon or noon - 2pm.

Price: $8 for adults; $7 for seniors; $6 for ages 2 - 12; children under 2 are free.

Ages: 2 years and up.

WHALE WATCHING

See the TRANSPORTATION section.

WILDLIFE LEARNING CENTER

(818) 362-8711 / www.wildlifelearningcenter.org

16027 Yarnell Street, Sylmar

This mid-size center, with rows of cages that hold over fifty species of animals, is prettified with lots of plants in, around, and on the enclosures, as well as huge shade trees all over, so it's an attractive place to visit. Of course the reason to come is to see and learn about the unusual animals here - bobcats, lynxes, and servals; Arctic, red, gray, and fennec foxes; porcupines; sloths; owls; coatimundis; squirrel monkeys; armadillos; alligators; woodchucks; tortoises; macaws; and kinkajous (which you might not have seen before). There is also a small reptile and amphibian room starring the blue poison dart frog, red-eyed tree frog, anaconda, tarantula, scorpion, lizard, and others. Catch a Trainer Talk every hour on the hour starting at noon to see, learn about and maybe even touch an animal. Stroll the pathways to view the animals.

If you'd like to really learn about particular critters and even have the opportunity to interact with some of them, sign up to take one or more of the Individual Animal Experiences, which take about ten minutes each. For instance, gently stroke a fennec fox (so soft!); hold an owl (with a gloved hand); go into the porcupine habitat and feed them (this was one of our favorites!); meet a prairie dog; touch an alligator; meet a giraffe; hold a huge python; and more.

Bring your camera for great photo ops! A ninety-minute Zoofari Tour combines several of the above interactions, which is what we did and it really added to our experience. The center also does school and scout programs, birthday parties, and assemblies, summer camps, and much more.

Hours: Open daily, 10am - 5pm. Closed New Year's Day, Thanksgiving, and Christmas.

Price: $10 for adults; $8 for seniors, students, and ages 3 - 15; children 2 and under are free. The Individual Animal Experiences range from $25 - $40 per animal for most of the animals, for 1 to 4 people (additional people are extra), up to $100 for up to 4 people for a sloth encounter. The Zoofari Tour is $250 for up to 4 people, $50 each additional person.

Ages: All

ORANGE COUNTY

Upwardly mobile urbanites live in this county designed to meet the needs of growing families. It boasts a great number of parks and playgrounds, including the most famous one of all - Disneyland. The intimate San Juan Capistrano, the upscale Laguna Beach, the natural preserves of Coto de Caza, the bustling Anaheim, the hills of Mission Viejo, and every city in between comprise a county that offers numerous places to sightsee. From Knott's Berry Farm to Huntington Beach to Medieval Times to Rainforest Café to Richard Nixon Library to Dana Harbor to Fullerton Arboretum - "orange" you glad you came to visit?

—AMUSEMENT PARKS—

ADVENTURE CITY

(714) 236-9300 / www.adventurecity.com

$$$$

1238 S. Beach Boulevard, Anaheim

My family travels a lot and one of our favorite cities to visit when the kids were younger was Adventure City. This clean, two-acre little, amusement park is perfect for younger children. The colorful city scene facades throughout resemble storybook illustrations. The seventeen rides and attractions, many designed to accommodate parents, too, include a wonderful train ride around the "city," a few mild roller coasters (including one that goes forward and backward!), a carousel, an airplane ride, a hot-air balloon ride, a bus with wheels that go 'round and 'round, and Crank n' Roll, a kid-powered little car ride. Kids can have a really hot time dressing up in full fireman apparel before (or after) they "drive" around on the Rescue Ride 9-1-1 ambulance, police, and firemen vehicles.

The Thomas the Tank Engine play area has several huge layouts and wooden train sets that encourages toddlers' imaginations to go full steam ahead. A small petting zoo has goats, sheep, a pig, and bunnies. At twenty-four-feet high the rock climbing tower is just the right size for kids (and adults) to scale and cost about $3 extra per person to climb. Adventure City also offers a few video and arcade games, plus interactive puppet, magic, and other shows at the theater.

The food onsite is good and reasonably priced. Note: You may not bring your own food inside, but there is a small picnic area just outside the gates, and with a hand stamp you have free re-entry throughout the day of your visit. Up a tree for a different place to have a birthday party? Have one on-site, or have one in the building adjacent to Adventure City which was created to look like a big trunk of a tree, both inside and out.

Hours: Open most of the year sometimes on Fri., 10am - 5pm; and usually Sat., 11am - 8pm; Sun., 11am - 7pm. Open in the summer and during school breaks, Mon. - Thurs., 10am - 5pm; Fri., 10am - 7pm; Sat. - Sun., 11am - 8pm. Call for holiday hours and check the schedule before you come as hours fluctuate.

Price: $19.95 for ages 1 and up; $15.95 for seniors; children 12 months and under are free. Certain discounts are sometimes available through AAA.

Ages: 1 - 10 years.

BUCCANEER COVE WATERPARK (Boomers)

949) 559-8341 / www.boomersparks.com

$$$$

3405 Michelson Drive adjacent to Boomers!, Irvine

See BOOMERS! - Irvine and BUCCANEER COVE WATERPARK (pg. 257) for more information on this small waterpark.

Hours: Open Memorial Day - mid-June, and mid-September - September, Sat. - Sun., 11am - 7pm; open Memorial Day - Labor Day, Mon. - Fri., 11am - 6pm; Sat. - Sun., 11am - 7pm.

Price: $19.99 per person; $5 for dry, non-participants; children 2 and under are free.

Ages: 2 years and up.

CALIFORNIA ADVENTURE

(714) 781-4565 - recorded information; (714) 781-4636 - operator / www.disneyland.disney.go.com

6/$

1313 Harbor Boulevard, Anaheim

This is a Disney version of vintage California and much more, so it's sometimes realistic, and always entertaining. Take a Red Car trolley from the entrance through and around the main street, and beyond.

To the left of the entrance is **Hollywood Pictures Backlot** area, which describes exactly what it looks like. The main road looks like a real street with a huge backdrop of blue sky and a few white clouds at the end. Famous Hollywood movie facades line the streets. Take a ride through scenes from the show, *Monsters Inc.*, as Mike and Sulley help Boo escape Monstropolis. Inside the Disney Animation building are several activities: Interact, via questions and answers, with a computer-animated Crush (the turtle from *Finding Nemo*) - this is so cool. Or, learn how to draw a Disney character in fifteen minutes at the Animation Academy - an instructor and paper and pencils are provided. A small adjacent "museum" shows the creative process of animation - inception to the final product - via sketches and sculpture of several famous Disney characters. In the Sorcerer's Workshop, which is decorated in a dark, dungeon-style tone, draw your own Zoetrope (i.e., an early animation strip) and then enter the Beast's Library, which looks like a set from *Beauty and the Beast*, to match up your personality traits with a Disney character by having your picture taken and pressing buttons on a "magic" book.

Just next door is Disney Junior Dance Party, where you can dance to Disney tunes with your favorite Disney characters. At the end of the street is the Hyperion Theater, which seats 2,000, that features a forty-five-minute, professional, theatrical and musical show (think Broadway!), *Frozen* - a true musical spectacular. The sets, music, acting, special effects, costumes, humor, and more make this a fantastic production not to be missed. In the adjacent Guardians of the Galaxy - Mission: BREAKOUT! ride, walk through the Collector's fortress, filled with an assortment of encased extraterrestrial artifacts and creatures from all over the universe (i.e. some are actual props from the movies), to join Rocket (and impressive special effects) in rescuing fellow Guardians held captive. After you take the elevator ride to the top floor to help them, you are hurtled down -then bounced back up, and then back down a few stories, again - in a free-fall-style, while viewing scenes from the movies. Mission accomplished.

"a bug's land" is themed around the animated film, *A Bug's Life*. Walk back to Flik's Fun Fair where several kiddie rides, and the scenery, are oversized, supposedly reducing visitors to a bug's size. The rides include Heimlich's Chew Chew train, very slow bumper cars; spinning ladybugs (similar to the teacups ride); and pretend hot-air balloons. There is also a water play area with a few water fountains that spurt up at unexpected times. (Bring a change of clothing.) Bug's land also features *It's Tough to be a Bug* 3-D animation show - not for those with arachnophobia. The show features bugs of all kinds, such as termites, huge tarantulas that seemingly come out of the screen, stink bugs (with an olfactory emission), an angry hoard of hornets that buzz loudly in a blackened room as a "stinger" pokes through the back of your chair. Not my favorite attraction. Next door is a cluster of restaurants with outside seating only. This area also features a ten-minute walk through tour (looking at videos and the kitchen) of a sourdough bread "factory", along with bread samples. The adjacent restaurant offers salad or soup in a very freshly-made bread bowl. And make sure you pick up your free Ghiradelli chocolate square (the flavor of the sample changes with the seasons) at the next door Ghiradelli Soda Fountain and Chocolate Shop. Just across the way watch a seven-minute film on the making of wine at Wine Terrace where wine and wine sampling is available for adults.

Carthay Circle Restaurant is an upscale restaurant and bar in the center of "town" with dining inside and dining outside on the terrace overlooking Buena Vista Street. Elegantly and beautifully furnished with numerous, tasteful tributes to Walt Disney via photographs, this is the place to go for a fine dining experience while at the park, with prices that reflect that.

To the right of the main entrance is **Condor Flats** and **Grizzly Peak**, which includes the highly touted, and rightly so, Soarin' Around the World ride. Walk through its hangar (with great photos and stories of real California aviators), then sit in a chair, with your feet dangling over the edge, in front of a giant screen that will immerse you in an amazing, virtual hang gliding adventure over, through and around landmarks and some of the most scenic parts of the world: "Fly" over the snowy Swiss Matterhorn; seemingly dip your feet into the waters of Iguazu waterfalls; swoop over Sydney Harbour (and literally feel the mist); travel with a herd of elephants; glide past the Taj Mahal (and smell the roses); and see and experience the Pyramids, Paris and more. You will get wet on the next ride, Grizzly River Run, which is an eight-passenger raft ride that goes down mountain sides, through caverns, under waterfalls, and down a river onto a spouting geyser. At the extra large, outdoor play area, Redwood Creek Challenge Trail, kids expend energy by running around, scaling a short rock climbing wall, going up fire towers, down slides, and across cargo nets, zip lines, and swaying bridges.

Walk to the back of the theme park to a star attraction, the incredibly well-themed **Car's Land**. Besides Mater's Junkyard Jamboree where trailers are pulled by a tractors in a figure 8 configuration, and the anthropomorphic, dancing, Luigi's Rollickin' Roadsters ride, it is home to one of the most popular rides at the park - Radiator Spring Racers. The massive and eye-catching mountain scenery (look for the disguised tail fins of Cadillacs that create the mountain range) is reminiscent of the Grand Canyon, with colorful rock formations and a waterfall. Cars ride through parts of the movie, basically, and conclude with a very fast and fun race to the finish line, high-banked turns and all. Eat at either the Crazy Cone Motel area, where ice cream and everything else is served in orange safety cones, or at Flo's V8 Cafe, refueling while eating comfort food by the kitschy gas tanks outside or inside with completely-themed 1950's and *Cars* decor. Ordering a kid's meal here allows little crew members to take home a sporty car-shaped container.

Enjoy a meal at the Pixar-themed restaurant. Drop in or call (714) 781-DINE (3463) to make a reservation. Just across the way is The Little Mermaid; Ariel's Undersea Adventure which wondrously steeps guests in an under-the-sea-like experience as passengers ride clam shells through scenes from the movie, aided by music, special effects, animation, and favorite, colorful characters.

On the bridge and located across the water is **Pixar Pier** where favorite Pixar characters from *The Incredibles*, *Inside Out* and *Toy Story* come to life. This Disneyfied boardwalk carnival is also filled with old-fashioned-style rides, such as a carousel, and some carnival-type games featuring Pixar characters. The best of the classic midway games here is Toy Story Midway Mania! where guests wear 3-D glasses and take a ride as they compete by shooting lasers at targets for points and interacting with other video-enhanced games while the movie's characters coach vocally from the sidelines. The "E-ticket" ride here is the well-themed Incredicoaster, a colossus roller coaster with steep hills, high speed drops, enclosed tubes and a loop-de-loop around the emblem. The giant Ferris wheel, sporting a colorful Mickey's face in the middle, is another heart-stopper. Each gondola, featuring a different Pixar character, swings independently of each other, so passengers go around and around, _and_ around and around! Rides in the adjacent area, called Paradise Park, include Silly Symphonies swing ride; Goofy's Sky School, a really goofy coaster ride; the Jumpin' Jellyfish parachute ride; and old-fashioned-looking rocket ships. Good Mediterranean and Italian food are available, as well as some of the best corn dogs ever at Corn Dog Castle.

Live shows, including another rendition of _Frozen_, are performed throughout the day and evening. See the colorful and animated Paint the Night and Pixar Play Parade with floats starring characters from favorite films, plus dancing and acrobatics; periodic, interactive entertainment; and even dance parties for tweens and teens, with live bands (think - safe concert!).

My favorite nighttime attraction is the twenty-five-minute World of Color at the Pier lagoon where over 1,200 water fountains reach as high as 200 feet (!). Colors pulsate through the fountains as the waters dance and sway to the music, enhanced by other lighting and effects, and fire, to create a truly memorable and magical show. Scenes from _Finding Nemo_, _The Lion King_, _Pocahontas_, _Toy Story_, and other classics are projected during the show on the water screen that is 380 feet wide by 50 feet tall. Make sure you get a fast pass for the show/time of your choice to reserve a spot in the viewing area and then get to the show early to get a good place to stand and watch. It is standing room only, no sitting, and on a first-come, first-served basis. Two dining options that reserve you a spot in the preferred viewing section for this water extravaganza include full-service, three-course (starter, entrée and dessert) meals from prix-fixe menus: Wine Country Trattoria - lunch ($34.55 for adults; $22.66 for ages 3 to 9) or dinner ($48.58 for adults; $26.98 for kids); or Carthay Circle Restaurant - lunch ($44.29 for adults; $23.76 for kids) or dinner ($66.96 for adults; $27.01 for kids). One more option is the World of Color Dessert Party - $79 for a sweet and savory dessert selection and sparkling beverage, plus reserved _seating_ at Paradise Park. Be sure to make reservations for any option!

Note: Everyone loves a hero, especially the _Marvel_ous ones! Spider-Man, the Avengers and other heros are making their presence known now and preparing for an immersive Super Hero universe at the park with characters visits, attractions and rides in years to come.

Tips: 1) Make use of the Fastpass system, which means that timed passes are dispensed from ticket machines (or use your phone), one ride at a time, to reserve a designated time for each ticket holder to be in line to board the ride - you bypass others in the "regular" line. Fastpasses are available for Incredicoaster, Guardians of the Galaxy, Goofy's Sky School, Grizzly River Run, Radiator Springs Racers, Soarin' Around the World, Toy Story Midway Mania and World of Color. 2) Single rider seats are for those willing to not ride with others in their party, but to fill in when a single rider is needed. You usually radically reduce your ride wait time and are only a departure or two away from others in your party. Single rider is available on Incredicoaster, Goofy's Sky School, Grizzly River Run, and Radiator Springs Racers. 3) Parent swap system - Everyone waits in line. Then, show and tell the line attendant that one parent is going to wait and that waiting parent/person will receive a pass to then go to the front of the line, once the first parent is done. Almost every ride honors this. 4) For guests with disabilities and/or in wheelchairs, download the Guide for Guests With Disabilities to know which rides offer special, and usually faster, entrances. 5) Note that there are traditionally fewer crowds here on Mondays and Tuesdays. 6) My family often packs a meal to save money by renting a locker for the day (about $15), which fits a cooler and some jackets. 7) Download a free Disney app to check wait times for rides, where which Disney characters currently are, and more. See DISNEYLAND (pg. 235) which is just across the walkway from California Adventure, and DOWNTOWN DISNEY (pg. 316) a huge pedestrian "street" adjacent to both amusement parks that offers unique shopping and dining experiences.

Hours: Usually open daily in the summer, 8am - 1am. Open the rest of the year usually, Mon. - Thurs., 10am - 8pm; Fri. - Sun., 10am - 10pm. Hours fluctuate a lot, so check before you visit.

Price: Tickets range from $97 - $135 for adults, depending on the day and season; $91 - $127 for ages 3 - 9; children 2 and under are free. Parking is $20. A park-hopper pass (good for entrance and re-entrance to both Disneyland and California Adventure on the same day) is $147 - $185 for adults; $141 - $177 for kids (though you can't do both entirely in one day). Check out 2 to 5 day passes. Several times throughout the year Southern California residents are offered a discount on admission.

Ages: 2 years and up.

DISNEYLAND

(714) 781-4565 - recorded information; (714) 781-4636 - operator / www.disneyland.disney.go.com
1313 Harbor Boulevard, Anaheim

6/$

The world-famous "happiest place on earth" amusement park has so many things to do, see, and ride on, that entire books are written about it. The following description is a brief overview along with some tips.

Orient yourself by taking a train ride, Disneyland Railroad, located just inside the Disneyland entrance at **Main Street, U.S.A.**, that goes around the perimeter of the park. You'll see the whole park and go through some fun, old, and "hidden" attractions, like the dinosaur diorama and the mining cave. It stops at each main section of Disney. Main Street is perfect for all your mini (and Mickey) shopping needs. It also features restaurants and ice cream eateries. One of our favorite stops is the Candy Palace, where you can watch delicious confections being made before your eyes. (No free samples, though - sigh.) At Christmas, the candy makers create candy canes - a fascinating process. Also inside this palace are a few penny arcades to see short, old-time "movies." This street also has a cinema house that shows Disney cartoons, including the 1928 *Steamboat Willie,* and an opera house showcasing Disney history culture and a model of the White House. A very patriotic, almost documentary-style presentation of Great Moments With Mr. Lincoln in here has stirring film and music and gives and shows a condensed history of the Civil War. An animatronic President Lincoln appears and speaks towards the end.

The park is "divided" into different sections and each section favors a particular theme. The following attractions are just *some* of the highlights in these various areas. **Fantasyland** is located mostly in the courtyard of the park's centerpiece - Sleeping Beauty's castle. Actually walk inside the castle walls (up and down several staircases) to see this classic story retold in film vignettes. The Bibbidi Bobbidi Boutique is to bring out the princess in young girls. Prices start at about $60 for the Crown Package which includes a choice of hairstyle (plus a tiara or hairpiece), sparkly makeup, nail polish, a Princess sash, face gems and more, and go up to $200 for the Castle Package which includes all of the above, plus a Disney Princess costume, some accessories and photos. Your child can also meet a "real" Disney princess just outside the castle walls at Royal Hall (bring your camera and autograph books) and even see a condensed show of *Rapunzel* and/or *Beauty and the Beast* at performances at the Royal Theatre in this same area. The rides in Fantasyland include Mr. Toad's Wild Ride (which has things popping out at riders, loud noises, and even a dark and fiery section of hell, complete with demons); Alice in Wonderland (where the ride vehicle is shaped liked a caterpillar); Mad Tea Party (a spinning tea cups ride); Casey Jr. Circus Train; King Arthur Carousel; Peter Pan's Flight - to Never Land and back (I like this gentle and flying-high ride); and more. Although this area is definitely geared for the younger set, some of the images on the rides may be scary for them. Storybook Land is a boat ride through canals lined with miniature buildings that are from Disney's classic tales. Fantasyland also features the jolting Matterhorn Bobsled roller coaster with a few roaring abominable snowmen, and the iconic "it's a small world," where a slow-moving boat takes you past animated children figures from all over the world dressed in their culture's attire and singing the theme song in their native language. (If you didn't know the song at the beginning of the ride, you will never forget it afterward.) Look for characters from Disney and Pixar movies, too, situated in their country of origin. Just down the road is Pixie Hollow where visitors go down enchanted walkways to meet Tinker Bell and other fairies.

Mickey's Toontown has buildings put together at colorful, crazy, cartoonish angles. Walk through and meet Mickey and Minnie in "person" at each of their houses and get your picture taken with him/her. Kids enjoy playing in Goofy's Playhouse; riding on the scaled-down roller coaster; climbing all around the tree house and cargo nets at Chip n' Dale Treehouse; simply sitting in cars that look like they are straight out of a cartoon; and just running all around this toddler-friendly "town." Roger Rabbit is the most popular ride here as riders sit in a car that they can actually spin around. Catch the twenty-minute, great musical and dance production of Mickey's Magical Map just outside Toontown.

Frontierland features Big Thunder Mountain Railroad (a roller coaster); Mark Twain River boat (which looks authentic); Sailing Ship Columbia (an intriguing fifteen-minute ride around Pirate's Lair on a replica, three-masted ship from the 18th century); and Pirate's Lair on Tom Sawyer's Island. Visitors are rafted to the island where they can climb up, on and under (fake) rocks; go through secret passages in caverns; go up in a treehouse; enter a spherical cage made of bones and skulls; cross a suspension bridge; and just run around. Back on the mainland, make a reservation (on busy days) to eat at the Golden Horseshoe revue where a fun, hillbilly-type musical/comedy show accompanies your meal. You can also just come in to watch a show. Practice shooting skills at the shooting gallery with 100 interactive targets set up like the Tombstone, Arizona in the Old West.

The adjacent **New Orleans Square** continues the pirate theme in the classic ride, Pirates of the Caribbean. Yo ho, yo ho - with its catchy music, cannons blasting, and piratey scenes all under a realistic-seeming nighttime setting, it's a pirate's life for me. Captain Jack Sparrow makes multiple appearances. A different place to eat here is at the Blue Bayou Restaurant, where a nighttime sky is always in effect and the seating overlooks a section of the Pirate's ride. The Haunted Mansion is a ride through, well, a haunted mansion, that showcases various ghosts.

Critter Country features everyone's favorite bear, Winnie the Pooh. Take a "hunny" of a ride through the

Hundred Acre Wood, a very popular attraction with the younger set, and enjoy the rest of the similarly themed area, including a photo op with Pooh and Tigger. This country also has Splash Mountain, a wet roller coaster ride, with entertaining characters on the sidelines. For an early American experience, pick up a paddle and go on Davy Crockett's Explorer Canoes. These real, twenty-passenger canoes (no motors or tracks) go around Tom Sawyer's Island. They operate seasonally and close at dusk.

Adventureland has the thrilling (and bumpy) Indiana Jones roller coaster ride. You'll encounter snakes, skeletons, a huge boulder rolling toward your jeep, and other "dangers". Height restrictions apply as younger children will most likely be frightened by the content. Be sure to take the slow-moving Jungle Cruise where the hysterical one-liners tossed off by the boat captains about the jungle animals and activities are the highlight. (Your kids will repeat these same lines for a long time to come.) Walk the narrow stairs up and through Tarzan's (giant) Treehouse to see how the ape man (and his family) lived. And who doesn't love the old-school and wonderful Enchanted Tiki Room where the birds sing words and the flowers croon? And you must try the tasty Dole Whip, here!

Tomorrowland, with its sixty-four-foot mobile of gold spinning planets at the entrance and Astro Orbitor ride, ushers in a new era. Zoom through the darkness of outer space, with *Star Wars* overtones, in Space Mountain, one of the fastest (and darkest) roller coaster rides at Disneyland. Bump along through Star Tours, an exciting 3-D motion simulator ride that has riders battle with the Empire in over fifty possible scenarios portrayed on screen. Fun fact: The retail store here sells make-your-own light sabers! Turn 360 degrees in your Star Cruiser pod as you blast DayGlo intergalactic enemy targets with hand-held laser guns in Buzz Lightyear Astro Blasters. (It's like a shooting gallery ride.) Check your score at the end. Look for Nemo and other friends in the Finding Nemo Submarine Voyage which plunges you into the ocean's depths, kind of. At the Autopia course, drivers 52" and taller can rev up the engines and drive. Bring a bathing suit (or change of clothing) in the summertime if you want to get wet running through the huge fountain in Tomorrowland. The water shoots up in some sort of pattern, but my kids usually just got wet, pretty much on purpose, I think. The two-story building here features rotating exhibits. With everything being *Star Wars*, it is currently home to Star Wars Launch Bay with some Star Wars-themed video games, authentic movie props and settings, and costumed characters to meet and greet. Outside, next door, the interactive Jedi training academy stage is a fun place for knight wanna-bes. And yes, the monorail is still here to offer a (low flying) bird's eye view of the park as it meanders throughout.

Star Wars: Galaxy's Edge, a remote and rocky outpost on the galaxy's edge, is an epic, completely immersive experience for space and time travelers. At 14-acres huge(!), entering this land feels like entering the movies, or another world from a long time ago in a galaxy far, far away.... Here can board a re-creation of the Millennium Falcon, docked in front of massive buildings that are built into sheer cliffs, and pilot your way through outer space while firing laser cannons and earning galactic credits (or not!), all in the midst of the battle between the First Order and the Resistance. The other major ride has the feel of being in a Star Destroyer hangar bay. *Star Wars* characters, engaging live action and screen shows, and even captivating queues that add to the adventure are enhanced by shops and restaurants that are totally themed in atmosphere and food choices (even blue milk). Such incredible attention to detail! Live *Star Wars*.

For a breakfast buffet with Disney characters, join Minnie and Friends Breakfast in the Park at the Plaza Inn on Main Street. A delicious array of food - made-to-order omelets, Mickey-shaped waffles, fresh fruit, biscuits and gravy and more - is served in old-fashioned, spacious rooms decorated in pink and white. Best of all, Minnie, and sometimes Daisy, Max, Hook, Tigger, Eeyore and other costumed friends come around to dispense hugs and take pictures with your children. Bring your camera! The cost is about $32 for adults and $18 for ages 3 to 9. Reservations are usually necessary - call (714) 781-DINE (3463). Open until 11am. Note that Plaza Inn does serve lunch and dinner, but Disney characters aren't visiting then.

The daily, nightly, and seasonally-themed parades and shows are memorable. They are often based on Disney's latest animated films. *Fantasmic* is usually shown daily in the summer, and on weekends only the rest of the year. This somewhat dark, twenty-five-minute show, presented near Tom Sawyer's Island, centers around Mickey Mouse's imagination battling forces of evil. Fountains of water create a misty "screen" for laser-projected images from *The Sorcerer's Apprentice*, *Dumbo*, and other films. Lighted boats cruise by with costumed characters on board acting out scenes from Disney movies. Fire flashes on the water, fireworks explode, and the finale is played with a thunderous symphony of music. Get a reserved viewing area for this incredible show via a dinner-and-entertainment package that includes a three-course prix fixe meal at the Blue Bayou Restaurant ($65 per adult; $25 for ages 3 to 9) or River Belle Terrace ($45 per adult; $25 per child). Sit-down, restaurant viewing is an additional $15 per. An On-The-Go Dining option is $29.99 per adult and $19.99 per child, which includes picking up a meal at Hungry Bear Restaurant and a voucher for reserved viewing. Reservations must be made in advance.

Weekend evenings throughout most of the year and every night during the summer showcases an utterly fantastic, choreographed fireworks extravaganza accompanied by music and narration. Sleeping Beauty's castle magically changes color and even projects patterns according to the music. Call for a complete list of show information and times, and arrive early to get a good viewing spot for each show.

If you want to have more knowledge than the average tourist, take a guided tour of the park, such as "A Walk in Walt's Footsteps". This tour provides a deeper understanding of Walt's life and dreams, a peek into many places unaccessible to the average visitor, two rides, and lunch (or dinner) for $109 per person, plus park admission. The Youth Education Series is offered to students of all ages to incorporate a field trip to the park with learning about the world of physics, animation, history of California, or leadership strategies, and more. Contact (877) WD-YOUTH (939-6884) / www.disneyyouth.com for more information.

Disney goes all out and is completely redecorated for Halloween. Some of the rides are even switched up to include ghosts and monsters. Another Halloween addition is Mickey's Halloween Party on select nights and usually extended hours, open only to special event ticket holders. For five hours (plus an optional, additional three hours before the event), visitors dress up in costume, go trick or treating at various stations, encounter Disney villains, go on rides, watch a special parade, join in a dance party, create a creepy craft, and more, for the whole family. The cost is $95 - $120 per person, with the greater cost being closer to Halloween.

Christmas brings many exceptional elements such as the park, and some rides, being thoroughly decorated (especially the outstanding "it's a small world"), plus two other special offerings - the Candlelight Processional and the holiday tour. The Candlelight Processional is a one hour, riveting presentation of traditional Christmas carols and music rousingly and beautifully sung by hundreds of choir members who enter Main Street carrying candles, and some of whom configure into the shape of a Christmas tree. The choir is joined by an orchestra. The music is interspersed with the Christmas story read from the Bible by various celebrity narrators. Held twice a night, for only a few nights, it is presented on Main Street. Seating for the show is available usually to VIPs and sometimes to annual pass holders by lottery, but there is lots of standing room to at least hear it, if not see it. Tip: Get a spot early! The Holiday Time at Disneyland tour is a winner, providing the holiday history of Disneyland, as well as holiday legends and cultures throughout the world. It also allows express boarding for "its a small world" and the Haunted Mansion; a commemorative pin; reserved, front row seating for the Christmas Fantasy Parade; and some hot chocolate in a keepsake mug ($85, plus park admission). Note that World of Color, at California Adventure, presents a special Christmas-themed light and water show that is spectacular.

Tips: 1) Your child's favorite Disney characters are strolling all around the park, so keep your eyes open and your camera ready. Quite a few of the characters are gathered at Town Square when Disneyland opens in the morning. The lines to see them are shorter then. 2) Make use of the Fastpass system, which means that timed passes are dispensed from ticket machines (or use your phone), one ride at a time, to reserve a designated time for each ticket holder to be in line to board the ride - you bypass others in the "regular" line. Fastpasses are available for Autopia, Big Thunder Mountain Railroad, Indiana Jones Adventure, Matterhorn Bobsleds, Roger Rabbit's Car Toon Spin, Space Mountain, Splash Mountain, Haunted Mansion, Buzz Lightyear, and Star Tours. A fast pass for Fantasmic gets you a reserved, preferred viewing spot. 3) Single rider seats are for those willing to not ride with others in their party, but to fill in when a single rider is needed. You usually radically reduce your ride wait time and are only a departure or two away from others in your party. Single rider is available on Indiana Jones Adventure, Splash Mountain, and Matterhorn Bobsleds. 4) Parent swap system - Everyone waits in line. Then, show and tell the line attendant that one parent is going to wait and that waiting parent/person will receive a pass to then go to the front of the line, once the first parent is done. Almost every ride honors this. 5) For guests with disabilities and/or in wheelchairs, download the Guide for Guests With Disabilities to know which rides offer special, and usually faster, entrances. 6) Note that there are traditionally fewer crowds here on Mondays and Tuesdays. 7) My family often packs a meal to save money by renting a locker for the day (about $15), which fits a cooler and some jackets. 8) Download a free Disney app to check wait times for rides, where which Disney characters currently are, and more. 9) For a free Disney souvenir, go to City Hall and get a free button commemorating a first visit, birthday, wedding, just celebrating, and more. 10) For the fun of it: Check the website www.findingmickey.squarespace.com for fun facts and to find hidden mickeys throughout Disneyland. See CALIFORNIA ADVENTURE (pg. 232), which is the other Disney theme park adjacent to Disneyland, and DOWNTOWN DISNEY (pg. 316), a huge pedestrian "street" adjacent to both amusement parks that offers unique shopping and dining experiences.

Hours: Open daily in the summer, 8am - 1am. Open the rest of the year, Mon. - Thurs., 10am - 8pm; Fri. - Sun., 9am - 11pm or 8am - midnight, depending. Hours fluctuate a lot, so check before you visit.

Price: Tickets range from $97 - $135 for adults, depending on the day and season; $91 - $127 for ages 3 - 9; children 2 and under are free. Parking is $20. A park-hopper pass (good for entrance and re-entrance to both Disneyland and California Adventure on the same day) is $147 - $185 for adults; $141 - $177 for kids (though you can't do both entirely in one day). Check out 2 to 5 day passes. Several times throughout the year Southern California residents are offered a discount on admission.

Ages: All

KNOTT'S BERRY FARM

(714) 220-5200 / www.knotts.com

8039 Beach Boulevard, Buena Park

The atmosphere of the Old West is recreated throughout a good portion of California's original theme park via authentic and vintage-looking period buildings - almost a town's worth of them. Almost all of the stores in the section of the park called **Ghost Town** have a Western motif, including a real working blacksmith shop, a wool spinning shop, and numerous arts and crafts stores. There is a surprisingly big rock store which has such a variety of rocks, gems, and fossils for sale, including mammoth fossils for $2,500, dinosaur poop for $12, and geodes that you purchase whole to be cut right there and see what's on the inside - some with amazing crystals. The Western Trails Museum here is an interesting and wonderful dusty museum - filled with items from that time period such as brands, saddles, a gun collection, buttons, toys, dolls, a wagon, knick knacks, and much more. There is small, fake cemetery here, too, with humourous headstones. Go inside the genuine Old School House and sit at a desk and chat with the docent schoolmarm, but you don't have to do homework. Find the small jail and go back to visit the criminal behind bars because this mannequin "talks" to visitors. (I won't tell the secret.) And don't be a fool - you can even pan for real gold here. A lot can actually be learned about the Old West and Native American life styles by talking to some of the costumed employees and using some of the stores and places as mini-museums in the Ghost Town and Indian Trails areas.

Enough about stores and onto the real reason kids visit - rides and attractions. Ghost Town has a twenty-minute, slap-stick, western-themed stunt show with cowboys, gunfights, and stunts; a ride in an old-fashioned Butterfield Stagecoach around the park (with real horses) - a favorite; a very short ride in steam engine trains from the early 1900's; Calico Mine Ride - a fairly mild roller coaster ride through a mine; the log ride (on which you will get splashed, if not soaked); and one of the quickest rides, time-wise, I've ever been on - a modern-day Pony Express where you straddle your "horse coaster" and bank around tight turns and Old West features. The mail (and rider) must go through! One of the longest and tallest wooden-trestle roller coasters in the world, Ghost Rider, is a fast, high-*spirited* thrill ride. (Part of the time I was lifted out of my seat - the first drop is 108 feet!) Reputed to be the longest, tallest suspended (i.e., inverted) roller coaster in the West is the Silver Bullet: It climbs up to 146 feet, drops fast and furious, turns riders upside down several times and includes a vertical loop. This ride endears Knott's to thrill seekers. I think, however, that the bumper cars are more my kind of style. Beware - the Bigfoot Rapids raft ride <u>will</u> get you completely drenched. The Mystery Lodge is a "show" that hosts a mystical Native American storyteller narrating his tales around a fire that produces images to his stories.

The adjacent **Indian Trails** section has tepees to go into, Native American crafts to see, and terrific outdoor small-stage shows featuring live Native American storytellers and dancers. The energetic hoop dance is our favorite. We learn something new about the featured tribe every time.

Fiesta Village's rides and shops have a Mexican theme, for the most part. Enter Jaguar, a roller coaster, through a Mayan-styled pyramid temple and experience ancient wonders (and a fun ride!). Sol Spin is like a pinwheel with six spinning arms, that each rotate 360 degrees independently of each other, on a stand that is over 6 stories high. A dragon, pendulum-type swing ride; a merry-go-round; the hat dance (similar to a spinning teacup ride, only with hats); and Montezuma's Revenge roller coaster are all here, as is La Revolucion with inward-facing passenger seats that rotate and spin, simultaneously.

The **Boardwalk** section has some of the most exciting rides. HangTime towers 150 feet over the Boardwalk area, with gravity-defying inversions, a vertical lift hill that incorporates a 96-degree drop (yikes!) and a mid-air suspension, plus a twisting dive track. Go straight up about 250 feet and take a free fall, dropping at faster than 50 mph in the appropriately named Supreme Scream. And this is fun? My boys responded to that question with a resounding, "YES!" Your heart rate will accelerate on the Xcelerator, a 50's-themed roller coaster that both rocks and rolls. Coast Rider has plenty of tracks that zig zag on the top before plunging downward, then up again. Be a hero on the 4-D interactive ride of Iron Reef. Once onboard a submarine, dive the animated depths and blast your laser guns at an iron octopus, metal sharks, and deadly fish to save the submerged and almost destroyed Knott's Berry Farm. The 3-D effects are pretty cool. Old West meets new West in the immersive VR Showdown in Ghost Town where participants don virtual reality headsets and move about, blasting robotic enemies, dodging attacks and more in this futuristic Ghost Town setting. Play is $6 per person. The Boardwalk also has an arcade and quite a few mid-way games. A favorite venue here is the Charles M. Schulz Theatre, where major entertainers, including Snoopy, perform in extravaganzas. (My favorite are the ice skating shows.)

Kids 2 to 8 years old can spend the whole day in **Camp Snoopy** with its numerous rides and attractions. Many of Snoopy's friends, such as Peppermint Patty, Lucy, and Charlie Brown, are on hand dispensing hugs, along with Snoopy himself. This "camp" has a kiddie roller coaster; a Huff and Puff (kid-powered); Flying Ace airplane ride; Charlie

Brown's kite flyer (a swing-type ride) with kites caught in trees, of course ; little trucks to ride; a mini-scrambler; Pig Pen's mud buggies (mini ATV's that give a bouncy fun ride); Linus' "blanket" that launches riders ten feet in the air, then around and around; a scaled-down steam train ride; hot-air balloon ride; a rocking tug boat ride; Ferris wheel; a camp bus (with wheels that go round and round); and several other attractions geared just for young Peanut's fans. The Camp Snoopy Theater features the Peanuts Gang in musical performances throughout the day. Just outside of Camp Snoopy is Sidewinder, a spinning cars coaster with dips and turns and speed and rotation - yea!

Knott's goes all-out for major holidays in decor and special events, and offers a variety of shows, concerts, and dancing during the summer. In addition to Knott's Berry Farm's rides, attractions, shops, and eateries, there are several shops and delicious restaurants, including the famous Mrs. Knott's Chicken Dinner Restaurant, directly adjacent to the amusement park. For dining in the park, purchase an all-day dining pass, which is valid at six participating restaurants for $31.99, and a souvenir cup with discounts on refills. There are also many truly terrific educational tours (for students and scouts) available through KNOTT'S ADVENTURES IN EDUCATION (pg. 326). Across the street is a full-size reproduction of INDEPENDENCE HALL (pg. 318) and a water park, KNOTT'S SOAK CITY U.S.A. (See the next entry.) Note: Mondays and Tuesdays are the best days to come here as it's usually less crowded.

Hours: It almost always opens at 10am (occasionally at 9am). Closing times fluctuate between 5pm - 11pm, so call or check the website calendar before you go. Closed Christmas.

Price: $79 for adults; $49 for seniors and ages 3 - 11; children 2 and under are free. Knott's usually offers substantial discount tickets online, including some for Southern California residents only, and sometimes admission is discounted after 4pm. Certain discounts available through AAA. Fast Lane passes start at an additional $60 - they allow purchasers to bypass the lines to the most popular rides, repeatedly, throughout the day. Parking is $19. The first 3 hours of parking are free, with $18 of purchases validation, if you're eating at one of the restaurants, doing some shopping, or visiting Independence Hall.

Ages: All

KNOTT'S SOAK CITY

(714) 220-5200 / www.soakcityoc.com; www.knotts.com

8039 Beach Boulevard, across from Knott's Berry Farm, Buena Park

$$$$$

Located just next to Knott's Berry Farm come hang ten at this fifteen-acre water park with a 1950's and early 1960's Southern California beach cities theme. Long boards and surf woodies dot the landscape and surf music plays in the background.

At over 60 feet tall, Shore Break towers offers six different water slides; four that start off with the floor suddenly dropping out from underneath your feet, plunging you into a high-speed, almost vertical free fall! Some of the other twenty-two rides and attractions include several other high-speed slides - lie on your back and let 'er rip; seven tube rides (both open flumes and dark enclosed fumes) that range from a little thrilling to hair raising; a long (one-third mile!) relaxing tube ride that circles around a portion of the park in two-and-a-half feet of water; a six person, side-by-side, racing slide that utilizes mats; the Wedge, which is an open-air family raft ride with fun turns and twists; and Tidal Wave Bay, where a series of waves roll out into a good-sized "bay" every few minutes for body surfing or boogie boarding. Two activity areas for kids include the Beach "House", a three-story structure of hands-on water fun with big, stationary, squirt guns, slides, and a huge bucket that periodically unloads hundreds of gallons of water to deluge everyone below. For younger children, the colorful Gremmie (surfer lingo for "young surfer wannabe") Lagoon is a pint-sized playground with gadgets to squirt, sprinkle, and soak fellow playmates. Climb aboard a submarine in the middle of the lagoon which is covered by an octopus with slides for tentacles. Sit and play on sea turtles and crabs that spurt out water, too.

A few grassy areas and plenty of lounge chairs round out this way cool water park. Hot tip: Wear water shoes or sandals as the walkways get very hot. Note that swimsuits or boardshorts may not have plastic or metal rivets. Rent your own tube for about $5. Locker rentals are available for about $5. Full-service food and snack stations abound, of course. Tip: Bring a picnic lunch to enjoy on the grounds of INDEPENDENCE HALL (pg. 318), located just outside the gates.

Hours: Open mid-May to mid-June, Mon. - Fri., 10am - 5pm, or 6pm. Open mid-June to mid-August daily, 10am - 7pm. Open mid-August to Labor Day and on weekends through mid-September, 10am - 5pm or 6pm. Call or check the website first as hours fluctuate.

Price: $50 for adults; $40 for seniors and ages 3 - 11; children 2 and under are free. Save money by pre-ordering tickets online. With proof of residency, Southern Californians sometimes receive a discount. Parking is $19.

Ages: 1½ years and up.

—ARTS AND CRAFTS—

COLOR ME MINE (Orange County)

Brea - (714) 671-2808; Costa Mesa - (714) 241-8072; Mission Viejo - (949) 367-9757; Tustin - (714) 505-3975
/ www.colormemine.com

Brea - 260 W. Birch St., suite 5; Costa Mesa - 949 South Coast Dr., suite 103 at Metro Pointe; Mission Viejo - 27741 Crown Valley Pkwy., suite 323 in the Kaleidoscope mall; Tustin - 2875 El Camino Real, at the Tustin Marketplace

$$$$

See the entry for COLOR ME MINE (Los Angeles County) (pg. 8) for details.

Hours: Hours vary at each location. Most open daily at 10am or 11am and close at 9pm - call first.

DRAGONFLY SHOPS AND GARDENS

(714) 289-4689 / www.dragonflyshopsandgardens.com

260 N. Glassell Street, Orange

$$$

Amidst the charming shops of Old Towne Orange is a stand out - Dragonfly Shops and Gardens. The shop is in an old Victorian home where each room showcases a different artisans' merchandise, including distinctive gifts for the home, clothing, accessories, gourmet food, jewelry, paintings, collectibles, and more. Outside is a garden bursting with colorful flowers and plants for sale, surrounded by charming and funky statuary, mosaics, and garden art.

Shopping here is gratifying, but for more satisfaction, take one of the many classes offered. For instance, have you ever needed (or wanted) a bracelet, necklace, earrings, or anklet to match an outfit, or just for the fun of it? Make it yourself at the Dragonfly. Need some help in design? The Bead Lady (aka Beth Davidson) holds jewelry workshops and classes for all ages including girl scouts, birthday parties, a get together with friends, etc. She has a plethora of beads to choose from - glass, vintage, seed, crystals, and so much more. From the simple to the elegant, you can make a memorable piece of wearable art and have a delightful time doing it. If you don't mind getting down and dirty, take a potting class with the on-site gardener who helps fashion attractive arrangements in a unique pot or container. A truly enchanting, one-hour class geared for ages 5 to 10 years, is the Fairy Garden Workshop. Kids paint a pot and then create a fairy garden complete with plants, mini critters, and fairy dust. The Miniature Garden workshop is similar, just geared for adults. Decorate a pot, incorporate the plants you want and then add in miniature furniture, accessories, statues and more. I love mine!

The Dragonfly also offers classes in making boxes, wire wrapping, mosaic tiling, watercolors, cooking, soap-making, scrapbooking, candles, stamping, designing and making cards (go home with a set of six to eight custom cards!), succulent container planting, and so much more. There are even make-it-and-take-it projects (starting at $5) available to create any time, for any age, whenever you visit the shop. Kids, especially, take note of the Arts & Crafts camps offered in the summer and on school breaks.

Hours: The store is open Mon. - Fri., 11am - 6pm(ish); Sat., 9am - 5pm; Sun., 11am - 4pm(ish). Call or check the website for a schedule and description of classes and workshops.

Price: Fairy Gardens and Miniature Garden workshops are $25 per person. Call or check online for the several types of beading classes and other workshops offered.

Ages: 4 years and up.

FIRED UP

(949) 498-3929 / www.firedupsanclemente.com

143 Avenida Granada, San Clemente

$$$$

Get fired up to paint a unique ceramic piece to give as a gift or make for yourself. This inviting studio, with several round tables and chairs, also has a small outside area with picnic tables. It has a wide selection of items to choose from including boxes, mugs, plates, (mini) surf boards, animals, and seasonal figurines. If you're not sure how to paint your hand-picked item there are books, stamps, stencils, and staff personnel to help ignite your creativity. Finished, glazed, and fired masterpieces may be picked up after a few days. Food and beverages may be brought in. Scouts can earn their ceramics badge here. Check out the website for other class and fun offerings such as Create Your Own Macrame Plant Holder, pottery making (using a wheel), and Parents Night Out for Kids Only.

Hours: Open Mon. - Thurs., noon - 6pm; Fri., noon - 9pm; Sat. - Sun., noon - 6pm.

Price: There is no studio fee. Prices for your item start at about $15, which includes your time, paint, and glaze.

Ages: 4 years and up.

HIDDEN TALENTS CERAMIC STUDIO

(714) 840-6833 / www.hiddentalentsceramicstudio.com
16917 Algonquin Street, suite E, Huntington Beach

Do you have a hidden talent? This small, but airy paint-it-yourself ceramic place could be just the venue to showcase that artistic flair. Walls are lined with shelves holding mugs, vases, figurines, plates, and more, that await your masterful brush strokes and clever designs, or at least some paint. Bring a child or bring a friend and share some time creating memories and a keepsake. Paints, firing, and glazing are included in your price.

One wall is covered with a mural of a mountain, a wizard, and a fairy. This area also has a tiny play area for young children with a dollhouse, toys, and books. Child-size tables are here, too. Ask about clay hand and foot prints, tile wall fundraisers, classes and summer camps.

Hours: Open most of the year, Tues. - Fri., 11am - 6pm; Sat. - Sun., 11am - 5pm. Closed most Mon., except school holidays and during the summer. Closed on major holidays.
Price: The price of a piece plus a flat studio fee of $8 for ages 13 and up; $6 for ages 12 and under.
Ages: 4 years and up.

—BEACHES—

1,000 STEPS BEACH

(949) 661-7013 / www.ocbeachinfo.com
Pacific Coast Highway and 9th Avenue, Laguna Beach

Not sure if you're in or out of shape? Come find out! Although there is actually only 227 steep, cement steps down to the beach, it can feel like 1,000 coming up! The beach itself is scenic (and romantic), so you could just enjoy a day of water and sand and staring at the beauty. There is also a volleyball court here. Look up to see magnificent mansions on the bluffs - I love the ones with private elevators built into the hillside.

If you head to the left from the stairs, past the abandoned building, you'll reach rocks and tidepools, and the best thing - a good-sized sea cave. Exploring this, in low tide, is a fun and memorable adventure. We stayed for sunset and got awesome photos. Note that coastal access sign is easy to miss.

Hours: Open daily, 6am - 10pm.
Price: Free
Ages: 5 years and up - the stairs are tough.

ALISO BEACH PARK

(949) 923-2280 or (949) 923-2283 / www.ocparks.com; www.lagunabeachinfo.com
31131 Pacific Coast Highway, Laguna Beach

You can smell the ocean here! Surrounded by million dollar homes (some are perched on the cliffs overlooking the beach) this beautiful beach in a cove has a wide section of sand dotted with palm trees, tidepools among the rocky promontories that are just around the "corner", and a few fire pits. Part of Aliso Creek empties into a section of this beach, too. The nice, mid-size playground has swings; an elevated sand play area (accessible for wheelchairs); and a structure with two towers that has slides, a chain ladder and a short, rock climbing wall. Another component, a play ship dubbed Adventure Ship, has portholes, talking tubes, climbing apparatus and more. A food concession stand is open here seasonally, usually on weekends only. Note that Aliso Beach Park is one in a series of cove beaches in Laguna Beach, and it connects with the northern TREASURE ISLAND PARK - BEACH (pg. 247), which is a walk around the bend over some difficult and rocky terrain.

Hours: Open daily, 6am - 10pm.
Price: $1 an hour for parking, or catch a (free) ride - see LAGUNA FREE TROLLEY (pg. 331).
Ages: All

BALBOA BEACH

(949) 644-3309 / www.visitnewportbeach.com; www.newportbeachca.gov
Main Street, Newport Beach

See BALBOA PIER (pg. 315) for details.

Hours: Open daily.
Price: Balboa Pier Parking Lot is $1.90 per hour, May - Sept.; $1.30, Oct. - April; $19+ max.
Ages: All

BOLSA CHICA STATE BEACH

(714) 846-3460 - beach recording; (714) 377-5691 - beach live person; (800) 444-7275 - camping reservations / www.parks.ca.gov; www.beachcalifornia.com; www.stockteam.com

Pacific Coast Highway, between Golden West and Warner Ave., Huntington Beach

$$$

There are miles and miles of beach here that are ideal for families because of the picnic areas, outdoor showers, four cafe/snack bars (open in the summer), beach rentals, and the lovely 8.5 miles of paved beachside trail that runs between Bolsa Chica and Huntington State Beaches. A beach wheelchair is available for loan. The waves can be great (or not). This beach is popular year round because of the 200 fire rings - bring your own wood and even your own barbecue. Tip: Arrive early to save one for a weekend or holiday evening. There is also a small interpretative center at the front entrance of the beach parking.

A *shore* way to learn more about the beach and its environment is by taking one of four, one-hour, educational programs offered for K-12 school groups: Marine Debris & Recycling, which incorporates some beach clean-up; Marine Mammal Life; Beach Animals; and Aquatic Safety & State Park Careers, which includes a tour of the Lifeguard Headquarters. Note that several 45-minute Outreach Programs are also offered where the programs comes to you.

Camping in self-contained vehicles at the 50 parking lot sites is allowed, but there are no hook ups. No tent camping is permitted. Check out the adjacent SUNSET BEACH (pg. 247), as well and note that the Bolsa Chica Ecological Reserve is just across the highway.

Hours: Open daily, 6am - 9pm.
Price: $15 per vehicle. Camping is $65 for a beach-front site, $50 for one in the "back" row. The educational programs are $1 per person with free parking, and school groups may stay at the beach after the tour without an additional fee.
Ages: All

CORONA DEL MAR STATE BEACH / PIRATES COVE / INSPIRATION POINT

(949) 644-3309/(949) 644-3151 - beach; (949) 723-0502 - Tackle Box / www.parks.ca.gov; www.newportbeachca.gov; www.tackleboxoc.com

Marguerite Avenue and Ocean Boulevard, Corona Del Mar

$$$

Beside a large, wide parcel of sand and water, the popular "Big Corona" (as it is known) provides fire rings, picnic tables, and volleyball courts. A rock jetty forms around one part of the beach and has a cement walkway that reaches out to it. Beach equipment rentals are available seasonally, but Tackle Box cafe is open year round. Tackle Box (at 3029 E. Shore Ave.) offers upscale and really good food, especially for a beach cafe. Menu choices include breakfast sandwiches ($8.50), French toast ($9.75), cheesesteak ($12.75), fried catfish sandwich $12, buffalo cauliflower ($9), burger ($13), baby kale salad ($10), chicken club sandwiches ($11) and more.

Avast! Just below Lookout Point Park is **Pirates Cove**, or Rocky Point Beach - found at the north end of Corona beach and accessible via stairs, or over and around some sandstone caves and rocky hill (all part of the adventure!). It yields the treasure of waveless waters and some cave alcoves for mateys to explore and pretend. Walk around the rocks during low tide, or carefully climb over more of the stony hill, to reach another, very little cove. A small square lawn and picnic area, with BBQs, is almost hidden among the trees in front of Pirate's Cove.

Inspiration Point, located at the south end of the beach, has two worthwhile viewpoints - one along the bluff-top pathway, dotted with benches, that offers a stunning overview of the beach and ocean, and one at beach level where you can see for miles. For free beach access from this point, head down to the beach by climbing down a short nature trail or take the steep, cement, ramp.

Check out the tidepools at LITTLE CORONA DEL MAR BEACH and TIDEPOOL TOURS (pg. 244) at the very southern end of Big Corona. Know that grunion runs are held a few times in the spring and summer at Big Corona.

Hours: Open daily, 6am - 10pm. Tackle Box is open Tues., 11am - 4pm; Wed. - Sun., 9am - 3pm, then 3:30pm - 6pm (open until 7pm on weekends). Closed Mon.
Price: Some free parking can be found on Ocean Blvd.; just beware that you must hike down a bit (and then back up) on steep ramps to access the beach. The main parking lot is $4 an hour, 9am - 6pm ($2.50 before and after that), May - Sept.; $1.50 an hour, 6am - 10pm on weekdays, $4 on weekends, Oct. - April. $15 max a day; $20 on peak holidays.
Ages: All

CRYSTAL COVE STATE PARK

See the entry for CRYSTAL COVE STATE PARK (pg. 277), under GREAT OUTDOORS, for details.

$$$

DANA COVE PARK, "BABY BEACH" and TIDEPOOLS

(949) 248-3500 or (949) 923-2280 / www.danapointharbor.com

24256 Dana Point Harbor Drive, Dana Point

The protected harbor of "Baby Beach" (called so because of its waveless waters) offers picnic tables on the bluffs, plus barbecues, free parking, showers, and lifeguards. Check for water quality first, however, at (800) 432-5229 or www.healthebay.org or www.ocbeachinfo.com as this beach has had a history of problems. A good tidepool area is just around the "corner." See DANA POINT HARBOR (pg. 315, 755), DOHENY STATE BEACH PARK (pg. 243), and the OCEAN INSTITUTE (pg. 311) for more details about the surrounding area.

Hours: Open daily, sunrise - sunset.

Price: Free

Ages: All

DOHENY STATE BEACH PARK

(949) 496-6171 - beach; (800) 444-7275 - camping reservations / www.dohenystatebeach.org; www.parks.ca.gov

25300 Dana Point Harbor Drive, Dana Point

Doheny State Beach Park is big and absolutely gorgeous. It is divided into three parts: The northern area, also accessible by metered parking off Puerto Place, is for day use. It is five acres of grassy, landscaped picnic area, with barbecue grills and fire rings along the beach. The adjacent butterfly garden is a delight. Walk through the wooden entrance frame with huge butterflies (additionally marked with a large sign) on a gravel trail. Each fall the Monarch butterflies roost and hibernate here, ultimately on their way to migrating south. A small picnic area is inside. The rocky area is ideal for tidepool exploration during low tide. Since DANA POINT HARBOR (pg. 315, 755) is right next door, this is also a perfect spot to watch the boats sail in and out. The central section, south of the San Juan Creek, is a campground with 118 sites. Farther south is another day use area with fire rings, beach volleyball, and showers. Throughout the entire stretch of the park there are sandy beaches and beckoning ocean waves. Word of caution: Check for water quality first, at (800) 432-5229 / (310) 451-1500 or www.healthebay.org, as this beach has had a history of problems. While you're here, check out the nearby OCEAN INSTITUTE (pg. 311).

Towards the entrance of the beach park is a nice little Interpretive Center (and gift store) with a small aquarium of five tanks holding a variety of fish, lobster, and eels in a rocky grotto; a tidepool; and display cases containing rocks, shells, skulls, and various taxidermied birds and mammals. Look for the life-sized paintings of whales on the front walkway of the park - can you name the type of whale you see? Note: This state beach offers a wide choice of year-round educational programs for school groups, scouts, jr. rangers, and more.

Hours: The park is open daily, 6am - 10pm. The Interpretive Center is open Wed. - Sun., 10am - 4pm.

Price: Parking is $2 per hour; $15 all day; $14 for seniors. Admission to the Interpretive Center is free. Camping prices are $40 - $60, depending on campsite location. The camping reservation fee is $8.

Ages: All

HUNTINGTON CITY BEACH

(714) 536-9303 - recorded beach info; (714) 536-5281; (714) 733-3167 - Surf City Nights / www.ci.huntington-beach.ca.us; www.surfcityusa.com; www.surfcitynights.com; www.huntingtonbeachevents.com; www.hbartafaire.com; www.sunsetvistacamping.huntingtonbeachca.gov

Pacific Coast Highway at the end of Main St., Huntington Beach

The combined beaches of Huntington Beach (both the city and connecting state beach), known as Surf City USA, have waves; about eight miles total of long and wide sandy beach; thirty public volleyball nets (as competition games are played here, too) - bring your own ball or rent one; fire pits; and one of the longest concrete piers in California, with a RUBY'S (Orange County) (pg. 252) at its end. The Kite Connection is a well-known kite shop located on the pier. You can also make use of the bait and tackle shop on the pier and fish off the pier's sides.

The Strand is a very popular, almost nine miles of paved biking, jogging, and blading pathway that hugs this same span of coastline, as it expands north from Warner Boulevard at Sunset Beach to south on Brookhurst Boulevard almost into Newport Beach. Several of the parking lot entrances have Beach Cafes that offer food, snacks, and beach rental equipment, including bikes, seasonally. Tip: Always check for the water quality before you visit. Top-rated surfing, skateboard, volleyball, and BMX competitions are held here in the summer. A plethora of funky and fun shops and restaurants await you just across the street on Main Street. Surf City Nights, a truly great weekly street fair and art fair (90 vendors!), and Farmers Market, is held on Main Street every Tuesday night from 5pm to 9pm. A Farmer's

Market and Art Afaire is held here on Fridays - noon to 5pm for the market; open until 7pm for the Art Afaire.

This is one of our preferred beaches, year round, for beach bonfires. (Bring your own wood and lighter.) Arrive early to claim a pit on weekends and holidays, especially during the summer. RV camping is available in the parking lot south of the pier, October thru May.

Hours: Usually open daily, 5am - 10pm. Winter hours can fluctuate.

Price: The lots near the pier are $1.50 per hour; $15 all day. Parking on peak holidays is $20; on 4th of July it's $27. RV camping is $70 ($60 for seniors), plus a $10 reservation fee.

Ages: All

HUNTINGTON STATE BEACH

(714) 536-1454 / www.parks.ca.gov; www.beachcalifornia.com; www.surfcityusa.com $$$

Pacific Coast Highway, Huntington Beach

See the above entry for detailed information on this renown beach which is just south of the city beach. See BOLSA CHICA STATE BEACH (pg. 242) for information on the educational programs offered. Note: We have found the Magnolia Street entrance to be one of the few open during "off" season.

Hours: Open daily, 6am - 9pm.

Price: Parking is $1.50 per hour; $15 for all day; $14 for seniors. There are parking lots are off Brookhurst, Magnolia, Newland, and other streets.

Ages: All

LAGUNA BEACH BEACHES

(949) 497-3311 / www.lagunabeachcity.net; www.visitlagunabeach.com; www.californiabeaches.com

Laguna Beach is replete with individual as well as interconnected small coves and stretches of beach. Most of them are kid-friendly, but not all because of the difficulty of access and riptide conditions. Victoria Beach, for instance, located next to the address 2713 Victoria Drive, has a long stairway to reach the beach. It's cool, tho, because a hike out on the rocks and around the point allows a great photo op of Victorian La Tour Tower, a cement stair tower built in the 1920's. See the above websites for specific information and locations of all the coves and beaches, as well as my write-ups in this section about some we like, in particular.

Hours: Usually open sunrise to sunset.

Price: Free

Ages: All

LITTLE CORONA DEL MAR BEACH and TIDEPOOL TOURS

(949) 644-3151/3309 - beach info; (949) 644-3038 - tidepool reservations / www.parks.ca.gov; $$$
www.city.newport-beach.ca.us

On Poppy Avenue and Ocean Avenue, Corona Del Mar

Tidepools are a rich natural resource and a fascinating way to learn about marine life, so come for a few hours to explore some of the best tidepools in Southern California, then spend the rest of the day playing at the adjacent beach. It's a great kids' hangout! See CORONA DEL MAR STATE BEACH / PIRATES COVE / INSPIRATION POINT (pg. 242) for more info on the big beach just a short drive away.

Hours: Open daily, 6am - 10pm. Guided tidepool tours are given by reservations only.

Price: There is some free street parking, and some that is $2 for 2 hours. $15 per vehicle for the day at the adjacent Corona Del Mar State Beach.

Ages: 3 years and up.

MAIN BEACH / HEISLER PARK

(949) 497-0706 / www.lagunabeachcity.net; www.visitlagunabeach.com $

Cliff Drive and Myrtle Street at Pacific Coast Highway, Laguna Beach

I mention this park and beach together because they are on either side of Highway 133/Broadway Street. Both are incredibly popular (i.e., crowded) and noted for their unparalleled views of the ocean. The water is clear, and the horizon seems to go on forever.

Heisler Park offers a paved, picturesque (palm trees, flowers, etc.) walkway along the cliff top, plus benches, picnic tables, and a small grassy area with a few fun climbing trees all overlooking the beach and horizon. The cove beaches below, namely Diver's Beach, Picnic Beach, and Rockpile Beach, have stairs access at several points, as well as a ramp access. A few spots are more rock than beach, so there is some great tidepooling here, too.

The large and wide Main Beach, adjoining Sleep Hollow Beach, offers (besides the beach) a few, decent-sized grass expanses along with two, half basketball courts; several sand volleyball courts with nets; a few barbecues pits and picnic tables; and a short boardwalk that parallels the shoreline. A small playground on the beach has a play lifeguard station in its center with slides jutting out from the top story and several swinging bridges connected to the bottom story, with dolphin statues leaping out of the blue flooring, encircled by wooden posts. Rock jetties and tidepools add to a day of fun and exploration.

This nice stretch of sand is lined with houses and condos on one side, and is just across the street from the heart of the city of Laguna Beach with its variety of restaurants and shops, including Main Beach Toy store that offers beach rentals. All in all, these are good places for beaching it and for swimming. Park can be tight!

Hours: Both are open daily, sunrise - sunset.
Price: Free. Metered parking is available or park in lots, which vary from free, to $3 for 3 hours, and up, and/or catch a free shuttle ride - see LAGUNA FREE TROLLEY (pg. 331).
Ages: All

NEWPORT DUNES WATERFRONT RESORT MARINA

(800) 765-7661 or (949) 729-3863 / www.newportdunes.com
1131 Backbay Drive, Newport Beach

Toddlers to teens enjoy the enclosed acres of clean beach here, along with a waveless lagoon and a myriad of boating activities. There is a large fiberglass, stationary whale, nicknamed Moe B. Dunes, in the water for kids to swim out to, and another one on the beach. The playground equipment includes swings, slides, short tunnels and a colorful ship, that's split into two parts, to climb aboard - ahoy mateys! Picnic tables under shade trees and outdoor showers are also available.

Remember the joys of collecting seashells? Newport Dunes is one of the rare beaches around that still has shells. Note: Shellmaker Island and UPPER NEWPORT BAY NATURE PRESERVE / PETER AND MARY MUTH INTERPRETIVE CENTER (pg. 298) are adjacent to the resort marina.

Make sure you check out MOE B'S WATERSPORTS (pg. 331), located across the water in the park, for your kayaking, pedalboat, electric boat, Stand Up paddleboards and windsurfing needs, and for info on the Water Playground.

If you forget to bring food, have no fear of a growling tummy as a grocery store and the Back Bay Bistro, (949) 729-1144, are inside the gates, just around the corner from the beach. The Bistro offers California-style cuisine for breakfast, lunch, and dinner, with indoor or outdoor seating that overlooks the water.

Overnight camping is available and there are plenty of RV hookups; some on the waterfront. There are a few spaces for free-standing (i.e., no stakes) tent camping, too. Various cottages, with kitchens, are available as well. Not only are the surroundings pretty, but activities for campers are offered, such as crafts, ice cream socials, and free, family-friendly movie showings on a large inflatable screen (May through September on weekend nights for both campers and the public). The Dunes also has a swimming pool, indoor showers, and laundry facilities. What more could you want out of life? This local resort is my kind of "roughing it" vacation!

Hours: Open daily, 8am - 10pm.
Price: Day parking is $10 for 30 min. - 2 hours; $15 for 2 - 5 hours; $20 for all day. Camping prices/small RV sites start at $64 - $123 a night during the winter, and $79 - $150 a night during the summer, depending on location and camping equipment. Studio "camping" cottages start at $90 - $163 in the winter, and $155 - $237 in the summer.
Ages: All

NEWPORT MUNICIPAL BEACH

(800) 94-COAST (942-6278); (949) 644-3309 / www.visitnewportbeach.com; www.beachcalifornia.com
Balboa Boulevard at Oceanfront and 21st, Newport Beach

This fine, five-mile stretch of clean sandy beach offers plenty of summer fun for swimmers, surfers (near the jetty), and sunbathers. Walk out onto the pier and/or bring your fishing pole to catch a meal. If you don't have success, catch something fresh Wed. - Sun., 6:30am - noon, at Dory Fleet Market, located at the base of the pier. Fresh fish and crab are hauled in and sold by local fishermen at this open air market. Contact (949) 632-5939 / www.doryfleet.com for more details.

Tired of lying around? Walk or ride the bike path, which goes around most of the peninsula. Bike, skate, and board shop rentals are available, too, plus there quite a few retail shops and restaurants close by.

Hours: Open daily, 6am - 10pm.
Price: Parking in the lot is $1.50 per hour; $15 max; $25 on Memorial Day, 4th of July and Labor Day.
Ages: All

NORTH BEACH

(949) 361-8200 - beach / www.san-clemente.org; www.traillink.com/trail/san-clemente-beach-trail-/
Pacific Coast Highway and Avenida Pico, San Clemente

Cross over the train tracks to reach this wide, not too large and sometimes pebbly stretch of beach, which is north (of course) of the city beach and pier. Amenities, besides the main attraction of sand and water, are a playground, a fire ring, a railroad, and the ending/beginning point of the 2.5 mile, one-way, flat, hard-packed dirt and sand San Clemente Beach Trail that parallels the coastline (and rail tracks) down to the State Beach and Calafia State Beach Park (see those separate entries).

Hours: Open daily, 4am - midnight
 Price: Free. Metered parking in the lot is $1.50 an hour from 9am - 6pm.
  Ages: All

SALT CREEK BEACH

(949) 923-2280 / (855) 886-5400 / www.ocparks.com; www.beachcalifornia.com
33333 S. Pacific Coast Highway, Dana Point

Way cool beach! Walk along the street (good for strollers and wheelchairs) through the underpass to reach the park/beach. The grassy, seven acre hillside, called Bluff Park, is spotted with some shade trees and picnic tables with an amazing view from the top of the Pacific Ocean and beyond. This park area also boasts a half basketball court and fire pits. The seasonal snack stand sells cheeseburgers, chili, quesadillas, and Hawaiian shaved ice, and Boogie board, chair/umbrellas rentals are also available then.

The wide and long expanse of beach is clean, has rocky promontories, a lifeguard in the summer, tidepools to the south, and a bike path to the north that runs parallel to the ocean. Surfing is good here (so I'm told).

Hours: The parking lot is open 5am - midnight.
 Price: Parking is $1 an hour.
  Ages: All

SAN CLEMENTE PIER CITY BEACH and MUNICIPAL PIER

(949) 361-8200 or (949) 276-8866 / www.san-clemente.org; www.beachcalifornia.com
Avenida Del Mar and Avenida Victoria, San Clemente

This beach (a compilation of beaches, really) is a two-mile long, narrow strip of sand on either side of the pier, dotted with palm trees and a few, scattered picnic tables. It is bordered by the sea on one side and train tracks that run parallel to the water on the other. (An Amtrak station is here, too.) Amenities include a few pieces of play equipment, a restroom, fire pits, volleyball courts, and the Fisherman's Restaurant and Bar, in case you don't catch any of your own lunch or dinner off the pier. This beach is also the center point for the 2.5 mile (one-way), hard-packed dirt and sand, San Clemente Beach Trail - go south to the State Beach and Calafia State Park Beach, or head north to North Beach (see those separate entries). The scenic, flat trail follows the coastline. I have to admit I'm partial to the antique and other fun stores and restaurants that line Avenida Del Mar, too.

Hours: Open daily, 4am - midnight.
 Price: Free. Parking is $1.50 an hour at metered spots.
  Ages: All

SAN CLEMENTE STATE BEACH / CALAFIA STATE BEACH PARK

(949) 492-3156 / www.parks.ca.gov; www.beachcalifornia.com;
www.traillink.com/trail/san-clemente-beach-trail-/
225 and 250 Avenida Califia, San Clemente

These adjacent beaches, located mostly under steep cliffs, offer swimming and sand, in addition to the 2.5 mile (one-way), hard-packed dirt and sand, San Clemente Beach Trail (the entrance is marked by the Calafia Park Trail head placard) that heads north to City Pier Beach and North Beach (see those separate entries) while hugging the coast line. It's a lovely trek. Each tent and RV camp site here, open year round, has a fire ring and picnic table. Railroad tracks parallel the beach. Carefully explore some of the water-carved caves and pathways along the beach, too. Ask about the educational programs offered - school field trips, junior ranger programs and more - and/or guided hikes, and check out the small visitor's center in the cottage.

A cafe is opened seasonally offering grilled food and beach rentals.

Hours: Open daily, 6am - 10pm.
 Price: $15 per vehicle. Camping is $40 for tent; $65 for hook-ups.
  Ages: All

SEAL BEACH

(562) 431-2527 - city; (562) 430-2613 - lifeguard station / www.sealbeachca.gov; www.beachcalifornia.com
the end of Main Street, W. of PCH, Seal Beach

This beach is one of my local favorites. It has lifeguards, the second longest wooden pier in California, great swimming, a good beach and a playground with swings and slides. My kids love to gather the crabs crawling along the pier wall and put them in buckets. (We let them go before we go home.) Take a walk on the pier as the coastline view is terrific. No license is required for fishing off the pier and bait is available to purchase.

Directly across the street from the beach is Main Street, which is lined with unique shops and restaurants from casual to upscale, plus a few ice cream stores.

Hours: Open daily, sunrise - sunset.
Price: Park along the street, or in a nearby lot for $3 for two hours; or pay a $6 entrance fee for the day at the parking lot at the beach.
Ages: All

SUNSET BEACH

(714) 969-3492 or (949) 923-2295 / www.surfcityusa.com; www.beachcalifornia.com
Pacific Coast Highway at the intersection of Warner Avenue, Huntington Beach

Sandwiched between BOLSA CHICA STATE BEACH (pg. 242) and SEAL BEACH (pg. 247), is a great stretch of sand. We frequent this beach often as it offers (limited) free parking and it has lifeguard stations, restrooms, outdoor showers, generally decent waves for boogie boarding and surfing, plus it's a short walk to the fire pits at Bolsa Chica. Although I'm usually good about bringing food to the beach, the Jack-in-the-Box here is very convenient.

Hours: Open daily, 5am - 10pm
Price: Free
Ages: All

TREASURE ISLAND PARK - BEACH

(949) 497-3311 - city hall; (866) 271-6953 - Montage Resort / www.lagunabeachinfo.com
30801 South Coast Highway, Laguna Beach

Not buried, but a little hidden, the scenic and beautiful Treasure Beach is accessed and viewed from the utterly lovely landscaped cement pathway that gently winds around the cliff top in front of the gorgeous Montage Resort. Enjoy the stroll, or sit on one of the numerous benches up top to gaze at unforgettable panoramas. Flowers, palm trees, cactus, and other plants cover the hillside and line the several stair access points leading down to the beach. A ramp is available, too. Go down to one of several coves and enjoy sweet stretches of beach, dotted with juts of rocks, where swimming and snorkeling are popular in the blue/green waters. A few tidepool areas are here, too. Note that this a marine reserve so look, but don't touch.

This beach is also accessed (although it's a difficult passage through water and over rocks) by the southern, adjoining ALISO BEACH PARK (pg. 241) for details.)

Hours: Open daily, 8am - 7pm.
Price: Parking at the Montage Resort off Wesley into very small underground lot is $1.50 an hour with a 3 hour limit. There is also metered street parking. Or, catch a (free) ride - see LAGUNA FREE TROLLEY (pg. 331).
Ages: All

—EDIBLE ADVENTURES—

ANGELO'S AND VINCI'S RISTORANTE

(714) 879-4022 / www.angelosandvincis.com
550 N. Harbor Boulevard, Fullerton

Attenzione - this ristorante and full bar not only bears the names of two of Italy's finest artists, but the cuisine and atmosphere are sure to please any *palette*. The dimly lit restaurant creates a cozy and kitschy ambiance by its eclectic decor packed around a main square room and upstairs mezzanine. Look up to see recreated Italian marketplace stalls along the walls. The fruit store, meat market, wine shop, etc., display realistic-looking fruit, hanging sausages, jars of pasta, hanging grapes and grapevines, and more, all with toddler-sized dolls dressed as merchants. There are also small knights in shining armor, framed art work, angel mannequins, signs, posters of the Mona Lisa, banners, a doll-sized stage, and bottles of wine all around, as well as trapeze figures and white Christmas lights suspended from the ceiling -

always something to keep one's attention. A chapel wall holds statues, including a replica of the David, and old family photographs. There are a few uniquely decorated banquet rooms at the restaurant, too. Take a quick peek, if you want, at the small basement/dungeon with its display of movie props and monsters, such as Dracula and Frankenstein.

Luncheon menu specialties include Old World-tasting pizza with a huge variety of toppings ($18 to $22.95 for a medium); extra large calzone, that feed 2 or 3 ($19.95); spaghetti (average $10); ciccaglione ($11.95); and linguini and clams ($15.95), plus chicken, shrimp, salads, and more. There isn't a children's menu, but young ones can easily share a meal. The all-you-can-eat buffet lunch is $10.95 for adults and $5.95 for ages 9 and under during the week from 11am to 2pm for chicken wings, pasta Alfredo, spaghetti, lasagna, salad, soup, breads, and more. The champagne brunch buffet on Sunday, from 11am to 3pm, is $21.95. It includes all the aforementioned food choices, plus an omelet bar, Belgian waffle bar, chocolate fondue station and, of course, champagne.

Hours: Open Sun. - Thurs., 11am - 9pm; Fri. - Sat., 11am - 10pm. Closed Thanksgiving and Christmas.
Price: See menu prices above.
Ages: All

BENIHANA OF TOKYO (Orange County)

Anaheim - (714) 774-4940; Newport Beach - (949) 955-0822 / www.benihana.com
Anaheim - 2100 E. Ball Road; Newport Beach - 4250 Birch Street
See the entry for BENIHANA OF TOKYO (Los Angeles County) (pg. 15) for details.

BUCA DI BEPPO (Orange County)

(866) EAT BUCA (328-2822) for all locations; Brea - (714) 529-6262; Garden Grove - (714) 740-2822;
Huntington Beach - (714) 891-4666 / www.bucadibeppo.com
Brea - 1609 East Imperial Hwy.; Garden Grove - 11757 Harbor Blvd.; Huntington Beach - 7979 Center Ave. at Bella Terra shopping center.
See BUCA DI BEPPO (Los Angeles County) (pg. 16) for details.

CHIP 'N DALE CRITTER BREAKFAST and BRUNCH AT STORYTELLERS CAFE

(714) 956-6755 or (714) 781-DINE (3463) / www.disneyland.disney.go.com
1600 Disneyland Drive at Storytellers Cafe in the Grand Californian Hotel, Anaheim

Which one is Chip and which one is Dale? Only kids know for sure. The two chipmunks, often accompanied by Pluto or another Disney character, walk around to greet each guest at breakfast and brunch, sign autographs, lead in sing-alongs, and hug (or high five) little guests. The breakfast buffet offers a wide variety of tasty dishes like made-to-order omelets, sausages, French toast, fresh bakery items, Mickey-shaped waffles, fruit, juices, and more. The weekend brunch includes all of the delicious breakfast choices, plus chicken nuggets, pastas, salads, salmon, potatoes and assorted desserts. In addition to weekends, this brunch is available select Mondays and holidays, too. Lunch and dinner a la cart menu choices are also available, but the Disney characters do not make an appearance at those times.

The restaurant is done in turn-of-the-century style and decorated with storytelling murals. Ask your server to tell you a few of the stories. Visit the adjacent DOWNTOWN DISNEY (pg. 316) for more fun things to do and see. DISNEYLAND (pg. 235) and CALIFORNIA ADVENTURE (pg. 232) are just next door.

Hours: Open for the breakfast buffet daily, 7am - 11:30am (characters appear off and on from 8:30am - 11:30am). The weekend brunch, with character appearances, is 11:30am - 2pm. Reservations are highly recommended for both. The cafe is also open daily for lunch, 11:30am - 2pm and for dinner, 5pm - 10pm, but the characters don't make an appearance at these times.
Price: The breakfast buffet is $36 for adults; $21 for kids ages 3 - 9; children 2 and under eat for free. The brunch buffet is $39 for adults; $23 for kids, etc. Parking is free at Downtown Disney with restaurant validation.
Ages: All

CHUCK E. CHEESE'S (Orange County)

See the entry for CHUCK E. CHEESE'S (Los Angeles County) (pg. 18) for details.

FARMER'S MARKETS (Orange County)

See the entry for FARMER'S MARKETS (Los Angeles County) (pg. 21) for details. I will have to mention three markets here because they are especially good, fun, and good and fun for kids. Admission is free to all of them. The **Fullerton Market** (www.cityoffullerton.com) offers farm-fresh produce, flowers, fresh-baked breads, and live entertainment, plus arts and crafts and other activities for children. The market is open on Thursdays, 4pm to 8:30pm, April thru October. It's located on Wilshire Ave., between Harbor Blvd. and Pomona Ave., right next to the Fullerton

Museum Center, which offers $2 off admission during market hours on the first Thurs. of the month. **Farmer's Market at Orange County Great Park** (#www.cityofirvine.org) is held every Sunday, 10am to 2pm with artisans bringing fresh bread, fruit, veggies and other goodies. To uninterruptedly enjoy everything else that the ORANGE COUNTY GREAT PARK (pg. 288) has to offer, purchase breakfast and/or lunch here. The Groves Antique Market is also held here on the first Sunday of every month, so the Farmers Market opens early then, at 8am. **Surf City Nights Street Fair and Farmers Market in Huntington Beach** (www.hbdowntown.com) on Main St., between Orange and Pacific Coast Highway, is held every Tuesday night, 5pm to 9pm. Just down the street from the beach and pier are booths with fresh produce plus all kinds of street vendors with food, jewelry, art, clothing, and live music, plus bounce houses, and kiddie train.

FRESH BROTHERS (Orange County)

$$$

Irvine (Harvard Place) - (949)797-9044; Irvine (Market Place) - (714) 598-2828; Laguna Niguel - (657) 999-0800; Newport Beach - (949) 759-1212; Newport Beach (Newport Mesa) -(657) 845-2345 / www.freshbrothers.com

Irvine (Harvard Place) - 17655 Harvard Ave.; Irvine (Market Place) - 13258 Jamboree Rd.; Laguna Niguel - 24002 Aliso Creek Rd #16; Newport Beach - 1616 San Miguel Dr.; Newport Beach (Newport Mesa) - 1124 Irvine Ave.

See FRESH BROTHERS (Los Angeles County) (pg. 22) for details.

GOOFY'S KITCHEN

$$$$$

(714) 781-DINE (3463) or (714) 956-6755 / www.disneyland.disney.go.com
1150 Magic Way at the Disneyland Hotel, Anaheim

Gawrsh! This all-you-can-eat breakfast/brunch and dinner buffet is described as "character dining." I'm still not sure if the "character" reference refers to Disney characters or to my children! Your kid's favorites put on a little fun show along with some music, and they come by the tables for a hug. We were visited by Pluto, Mickey Mouse, Chip (or was it Dale?), Aladdin, Miko and, of course, Goofy. Kids even eat a bite or two in between hopping up to touch the costumed characters. Remember to bring your camera for photos with the characters, especially in front of the cartoony kitchen backdrop, and bring your autograph book!

The breakfast/brunch buffet includes an array of delicious foods such as omelets made any way you like 'em (my boys considered watching the cook make omelets part of the entertainment), salads, fruit, vegetables, pastas, chicken, Mickey-shaped waffles or pancakes, cheese blintzes, home fries, cereal, oatmeal, yogurt with toppings, omelets, and peanut butter and jelly pizza. We stuffed ourselves at the dinner buffet with prime rib, ham, chicken, seafood, fruit, salad, and scrumptious desserts. (The way my family suffers just to be able to share with you!) The kids have their own food bar that offers familiar favorites like macaroni and cheese, mini-hotdogs, spaghetti, breaded shrimp, and chicken strips.

Goofy's Kitchen offers good food in a fun, family atmosphere. Make your outing even more of a treat by coming early, or staying after mealtime, to walk around and enjoy the hotel grounds and the adjacent DOWNTOWN DISNEY (pg. 316). DISNEYLAND (pg. 235) and CALIFORNIA ADVENTURE (pg. 232) are just next door.

Hours: Open for breakfast/brunch, Mon. - Fri., 7am - 11:30am; Sat. - Sun., 7am - 1:30pm. Open for dinner, Mon. - Fri., 5pm - 9pm; Sat. - Sun., 4pm - 9pm.

Price: Breakfast/brunch buffet is $39 for adults; $23 for ages 3 - 9; children 2 and under eat for free. The dinner buffet is $45 for adults; $25 for kids. Parking is free with restaurant validation.

Ages: 1½ years and up.

GYU-KAKU (Orange County)

$$$$

Brea - (714) 671-9378; Huntington Beach - (714) 842-8333; Tustin - (714) 731-1719 / www.gyu-kaku.com
Brea - 120 S. Brea Blvd., suite 1; Huntington Beach - 7862 Warner Ave., suite 109; Tustin - 14181 Newport Ave.

See the entry for GYU-KAKU (Los Angeles County) (pg. 23) for information on this grill-it-yourself restaurant.

Hours: Open Mon. - Thurs., 11:30am - 10:30pm; Fri. - Sat., 11:30am - 11:30pm; Sun., 11:30am - 10pm.

HOUSE OF BLUES GOSPEL BRUNCH (Orange County)

$$$$$

(714) 778-BLUE (2583) / www.houseofblues.com
400 W. Disney Way, Suite 337, Anaheim

Got the blues? Gospel Brunch at the renowned House of Blues is the cure. Inside the multi-story House's sound and lighting system gently screams state-of-the art while interspersed throughout are chandeliers juxtaposed with an impressive amount of artwork, consisting of eclectic original folk (and other) art done in various mediums, wall murals, a large Buddha statue and more. (And do look up at the ceilings.) This House boasts an 1,800 seat main concert hall, a 400-seat room designed for more intimate performances, a VIP Foundation Room, and special event spaces. The large restaurant spills out to include an open-air patio with live music - the better to enjoy the Southern California weather.

Concerts include world-famous headliners, as well as up-and-comers, however, my reason for including this venue in this book is the two-hour gospel brunch - a feast for the body, mind, and spirit. Indulge in eating some of the finest Mississippi Delta cuisine this side of, well, the Mississippi. Some of the southern-style, all-you-can-eat buffet items includes croissants; banana bread; corn muffins; omelets fixed any way you like 'em; bacon; sausage; shrimp; Greek salad; seasonal fresh fruit; breakfast potatoes; waffles with berries and whipped cream (and with or without fried chicken); fried chicken salad; Caesar salad; biscuits and gravy; grits; carved meats; maple glazed ham; brisket; smoke bbq chicken; Creole Chicken Jambalaya; and desserts, such as sticky buns, fresh cookies, or white chocolate banana bread pudding. Menu items are subject to change, but it's all finger-licking good!

The food is a precursor to the uplifting, high-energy, praise-the-Lord, hour-long concert that follows. Many people don't remain seated throughout the concert as they stand up, dance around, clap their hands, sing along, and at times, even join the musicians on stage. Every week features different artists or groups from traditional ensembles and choirs to contemporary gospel that include nationally known singers to locally famous ones. It's a delicious and upbeat way for a family to spend a Sunday afternoon.

Before or after your gospel brunch, walk around the adjoining Anaheim GardenWalk, an outdoor mall with a plethora of other dining and shopping, or go around the "corner" to DOWNTOWN DISNEY (pg. 316)) and DISNEYLAND (pg. 235).

Hours: Gospel Brunch is every other Sunday (usually the second and fourth Sunday), usually at 10:30am - check the web calendar. Get here earlier than the scheduled time. Ask about holiday Sun., such as Easter and Mother's Day.

Price: $45 for ages 10 and up; $21 for ages 3 - 9; children 2 and under are free.

Ages: 5 years and up.

JOE'S CRAB SHACK (Orange County)   ☀

Garden Grove - (714) 703-0505; Newport Beach - (949) 650-1818 / www.joescrabshack.com $$$

Garden Grove - 12011 Harbor Blvd.; Newport Beach - 2607 W. Coast Hwy.

See the entry for JOE'S CRAB SHACK (Los Angeles County) (pg. 24) for details.

JOHNNY REBS' SOUTHERN ROADHOUSE (Orange County)   ☀

(714) 633-3369 / www.johnnyrebs.com $$$

2940 E. Chapman Avenue, Orange

See the entry for JOHNNY REBS' SOUTHERN ROADHOUSE (Los Angeles County) (pg. 24) for details. This location's building looks like an authentic ramshackle shack, complete with a corrugated tin roof. The enclosed patio's lampshades are tin buckets with holes, which just add to the down and out old Southern atmosphere.

Hours: Open Sun. - Thurs., 7am - 9pm; Fri. - Sat, 7am - 10pm.

JOHN'S INCREDIBLE PIZZA CO. (Orange County)   ☼

Buena Park - (714) 236-0000; Westminster - (657) 242-1111 / www.johnspizza.com $$$$

Buena Park - 8601 On the Mall (at Buena Park Mall); Westminster - 1025 Westminster Mall (at Westminster Mall)

Incredible is a good way to describe this pizza play place. The broad selection of all-you-can-eat buffet food offers pizza with toppings that include, besides the traditional standards, BBQ chicken, cheeseburger, spicy peanut butter, margherita, Hawaiian, design-your-own, and other specialities. Gluten free personal pizza is an additional 99¢. Other choices are the salad station, with lots of options, and bread sticks; the pasta bar with mac and cheese, marinara sauce, chipotle, etc.; fried chicken; soup; baked potato with various toppings; and desserts of soft serve ice cream, cinnamon rolls, fudge cake, donuts fresh from the donut machine, and more. Yum!

Enjoy your meal in any one of several themed rooms such as Fusion, which has optical illusion framed images on the walls and magic tricks showing on the screen; Hall of Fame, showcasing baseball and other sports; Toon Time Theater that shows cartoon films and poster art; Cabin Fever with stone and timber decor, plus a fireplace and antler chandelier; and Vertical, the surfer and skateboard themed room with thatched roofs and beach umbrellas. Room types vary depending on location.

John's is more than just fun food. The game center, laid out on colorful star carpet, has rides for big and little kids, and games to play, including arcade and redemption games. (Tickets and prizes are always fun.) Rides, which are different at different locations, can include bumper cars, twister, little rockets, frog hopper, little roller coaster, and others. Play skee ball, UFO stomper, feel-like-you're-really-the-driver car games, Deal or No Deal, jumping jackpot, Guitar Hero, basketball, six-lane mini bowling, air hockey, and more. A toddler play room has Little Tyke slides, a playhouse, and small rocking rides.

One hit here is Dance Heads Recording where for $5 per CD you (and a friend or two) enter a small photo booth, choose a song to sing along with while your head is superimposed on an animated dancing body. Song choices include Barbie Girl, Jailhouse Rock, Car Wash, Wild Thing, Achy Breaky Heart, and more.

An almost two-hour, behind-the-scenes tour, for twelve or more students who are 12 and under (plus chaperones), also includes participating in creating pizza - from making dough to eating their own finished product; buffet lunch and beverages; 20 game credits; and a ride of their choice. This tour, offered Monday through Friday from 8am to 3pm, is $10.99 per person.

Check out John's other group and party options, as well as their kid's reward cards, VIP awards cards ($10 to join and you get a free buffet during the month of your birthday plus other great deals!), and exchanging credits for good grades. Note that different locations may differ on what they offer. The Buena Park location offers child match, where a child is given a wristband linked to the adult who is supervising that child. If the child attempts to leave John's without being verified upon exiting, an alarm will sound. Cost is $1 for up to 4 children.

Hours: Open Mon. - Thurs., 11am -10pm; Fri., 11am - 11pm; Sat., 10am - 11pm; Sun., 10am - 10pm. Both locations are usually open an hour earlier Mon. - Fri. during school breaks.

Price: Everyone entering John's must pay for the buffet: $11.99 for adults; $10.99 for seniors; $7.49 for ages 7 - 12; $5.49 for ages 3 - 6; children 2 and under are free with a paying adult. Prices Mon. - Fri. from 11am - 3pm, only, are $8.49 for adults; $7.49 for seniors; kids' prices are the same. Unlimited fountain or coffee beverages are an additional $1.99 per person. Video and redemption games and rides operate on a credit system: one credit is .25¢, or purchase a FunCard Special where $20 = 90 credits and 1 ride. Games range from 1 - 6 credits while rides and attractions cost up to 10 credits.

Ages: 2 years and up.

MCKENNA'S TEA COTTAGE

(562) 431-0200 / www.mckennasteacottage.com
237 Main Street, Seal Beach

This cute, quaint and comfortable, dressed-up cottage tea room has lace tablecloths under glass; chandeliers with beads hanging from them; and wood and glass curios and wood dressers filled with plates, teapots, bric-a-brac, candles, teas, tea paraphernalia, and gift items for sale. There is also an attached gift shop.

Just a sampling from the liberal menu includes: Queen Mums Tea of tea, a scone with Devonshire cream and jam, soup of the day or salad, assorted finger sandwiches, seasonal fruit, and dessert for $27. Lady Hamilton Tea is tea, scone with cream and jam, and five finger sandwiches for $20.50. Little Duchess Tea is a pot of tea and two scones with cream and jam for $11.50. Prince and Princess Tea, for 10 years and under, is a pot of lemonade (or decaf tea); miniature scone with cream and jam; a choice of peanut butter and jelly, turkey or cheese sandwich; and petite dessert for $16. Meal choices include a variety of quiches served with salad or soup for $14.50; tuna, chicken, roast beef or turkey sandwich served with soup or salad for $14; and a selection of salads that start at $10.50. Sides and desserts are also available. Both adult and themed children's parties (Snow White, Little Mermaid or other characters can even come and visit) can be enjoyed inside, or out in the small private garden surrounded with plants and lattice work. Parties of twenty or more can make reservations for evening parties.

Hours: Open Mon. - Fri., 11am - 2pm; Sat., 11am - 4pm; Sun., noon - 3pm. Closed most major holidays.

Price: Tea and menu prices are listed above.

Ages: 4 years and up.

MEDIEVAL TIMES

See the entry for MEDIEVAL TIMES (pg. 321), under SHOWS AND THEATERS, for details.

THE OLD SPAGHETTI FACTORY (Orange County)

Fullerton - (714) 526-6801; Newport Beach - (949) 675-8654 / www.osf.com
Fullerton - 110 E. Santa Fe Ave.; Newport Beach - 2110 Newport Blvd.

See the entry for THE OLD SPAGHETTI FACTORY (Los Angeles County) (pg. 25) for details.

PARIS IN A CUP

(714) 538-9411 / www.parisinacup.com
119 South Glassell Street, Orange

$$$$

If you can't meet at the Eiffel Tower, the next best thing might be to meet for tea at Paris in a Cup. (It does have a photo mural featuring the Eiffel tower.) Located in the heart of Old Town Orange (which you need to walk around before or after your visit!), this intimate tea room, with its black, white and gold decor, padded wrought iron chairs, mirrors, and chandeliers oozes chic, French charm and elegance.

A sample from le menu, served with tea or coffee, includes Claudette - baked potato soupe in croc and breads for $17; Maurice - soupe du jour in croc and chicken salad on croissant for $18; Louis - French dip sandwich and soup or salad for $19. The teas include Marie Antoinette - scones with creme and jam, soup, four assorted tea sandwiches, petite salad, and petit fours for $37; Madame de Pompadour - three assorted tea sandwiches and soup or salad, plus tea for $18; and Scones and Tea - two scones with Marion-berry jam and creme, plus tea for $13. Other desserts a la carte to tantalize your tastebuds include chocolate filled croissants, with cream and chocolate sauce for dipping for $7; creme brulee for $9; and chocolate ganache cake with raspberries, cream and chocolate-raspberry sauce for $9. A pot of tea is $6. Paris in a Cup also hosts special*tea* teas and special events.

The front part of the restaurant has shelves stocked with French gourmet chocolates, teas, jellies, other food gift items, plus teapots, books, music, Paris-themed items and a selection of fragrances.

Hours: Open Wed. - Sun., 11am - 3pm. Closed Mon., Tues. and major holidays.
Price: Prices are listed above.
Ages: 5 years and up.

PIRATE'S DINNER ADVENTURE

See PIRATE'S DINNER ADVENTURE (pg. 322), SHOWS AND THEATERS, for all the swashbuckling details.

$$$$$

ROCKET FIZZ SODA POPS AND CANDY SHOP (Orange County)

Irvine - (949) 453-0992; San Clemente - (949) 492-0099 / www.rocketfizz.com
Irvine - 823 Spectrum Center Drive at Irvine Spectrum Center; San Clemente - 107 Avenida Del Mar

$

See ROCKET FIZZ SODA POPS AND CANDY SHOP (Los Angeles County) (pg. 26) for details on this shop with an incredible array of unusual sodas, candy and more.

Price: Technically, free.
Ages: 3 years and up.

RUBY'S (Orange County)

www.rubys.com
Anaheim; Balboa; Corona Del Mar; Costa Mesa; Huntington Beach; Irvine; Laguna Beach; Laguna Hills; Mission Viejo; Orange; San Clemente; San Juan Capistrano; Santa Ana; Tustin; Yorba Linda

$$$

These 1940's-style diners offer good food and have a terrific atmosphere for kids. They've readily become one of our favorite places to eat. Old-fashioned-looking jukeboxes that play favorite oldies; red vinyl booths and bar stools; decorations that match the time period ambiance; and the kind of attentive service that all but disappeared years ago, are some of Ruby's trademarks. Since the restaurants are franchised, each one is slightly different in decor (some have trains going around on tracks overhead), and in their choice of menu items. Most breakfast choices include omelettes (about $10 to $11), waffles (about $10), etc. Lunch and dinner foods include a wide selection of burgers (beef, turkey, veggie, or chicken), or a sandwich for an average cost of $11. Salads and soups are available, too. The delicious concoctions from the soda fountain, including flavored sodas and old-fashioned ice cream desserts, keep us coming back for more. Kids' meals are about $6 for a choice of a grilled cheese sandwich, corn dog, hamburger, or chicken fingers. Their meals come with fries, a beverage, and a toy. Note: You'll often find Ruby's at the end of several Southern California piers, kind of like a pot of gold at the end of a rainbow. Orange County cities that have a Ruby's are: Anaheim, Balboa, Corona Del Mar, Costa Mesa, Huntington Beach, Irvine, Laguna Beach, Laguna Hills, Mission Viejo, Orange, San Clemente, San Juan Capistrano, Santa Ana, Tustin and Yorba Linda.

Hours: Most locations are open Sun. - Thurs., 7am - 9pm; Fri. - Sat., 7am - 10pm. Call for hours to the specific restaurant you're going to.
Price: Menu prices are listed above. Kids 12 and under eat free Tues., 4pm - close, with the purchase of an adult meal.
Ages: All

SURF'S UP CAFE

(714) 842-1111 / www.boomersparks.com
16800 Magnolia Street, Fountain Valley

$$$

Adjacent to the BOOMERS! - Fountain Valley (pg. 256), this separate cafe is colorfully Surf City-themed with surfboards, beach scenes, wooden planks, surf photos and signs, and fake palm trees on the walls, plus real boards hanging overhead, netting with sea stars, and a small boat to sit in with a surfboard as a table and part of the mast. This tri-level room doesn't have games, but the smallish adjoining room does. Themed with a city-scape mural, there are token-taking video and arcade games here and a prize redemption center at the cafe entrance. Menu choices include nachos, $4.99; chicken Caesar salad, $7.99; personal cheese pizza, $7.49; cheeseburger with fries, $8.99; corn dog with fries, $5.99; and more.

Hours: Open Mon. - Thurs., noon - 8pm; Fri. noon- 11pm; Sat., 10am - 11pm; Sun., 10am - 8pm.
Price: Prices are listed above.
Ages: All

SURF'S UP! BREAKFAST WITH MICKEY AND FRIENDS

(714) 781-DINE (781-3463) / www.disneyland.disney.go.com
1717 S. Disney Drive at PCH Grill, Paradise Pier Hotel, Anaheim

$$$$$

Hang ten with Mickey and four or five of his friends that come by to give guests high fives! Mickey leads the way in fun, too, as he invites kids to be a part of singing, dancing, hula hooping, or other activities intermittently throughout the morning. Decor and music from the California beach scene, hugs, photo ops, and signing autographs enhance the aloha ambiance.

In between dances and laughs, enjoy a variety of food selections. The all-you-can-eat buffet includes fresh fruits, Mickey Mouse-shaped waffles; French toast topped with berries and maple syrup; build-your-own-parfait stations; omelettes and eggs fixed any way you like 'em; breakfast burritos; smoked salmon; bakery goods; bacon; sausage; fruit; and more. Make sure to check out the adjacent DOWNTOWN DISNEY (pg. 316) and, of course, DISNEYLAND (pg. 235) for more places to go and things to do.

Hours: Open daily, 7am - 11:30am.
Price: $39 for adults; $23 for ages 3 - 9; children 2 and under are free. Parking is free with restaurant validation.
Ages: 2 years and up.

SWEET PETES CANDY / FARRELL'S ICE CREAM PARLOUR RESTAURANTS

Sweet Pete's and Farrell's, Buena Park - (714) 484-2674; Farrell's, Brea - (714) 990-4FUN (4386) / Buena
Park - www.farrellsusa.com; Brea - www.farrellsbrea.com
Buena Park - 8650 Beach Blvd.; Brea - 215 S. Brea Blvd.

$$$$

Located inside Farrell's Restaurant in the Buena Park location, your visit gets sweeter with a visit to Sweet Pete's Candy store with a plethora of candy to choose from - handmade chocolates and caramels, retro and premium candies, plus toys and lunch boxes and games and stuff. The favorite thing to do, though, is to take one of several candy-making "classes" offered here. We took the forty-five-minute Hand-Pulled Lollipop Class where we sat on bar stools and, after choosing colors and flavors, we watched our candy maker add and boil ingredients, then knead it together to create our sweet concoction, all the while learning about its chemistry and cooking elements. Then we got to participate and craft our lollipops into fun shapes and eat them (and take some home)! The cost is $15 per person and includes a scoop of delicious ice cream, too. Other classes include Hand-Pulled Taffy Class - for ages 5 and up (which includes a scoop of ice cream) for $15; Chocolate Bar Your Way, where you create three custom chocolate bars ($18), or Chocolate Pizza Class ($18). Field trips for all grades, costing $8.50 per student, include science and history curriculum, plus a hands-on candy-making session, restaurant tour, and more. And of course, it's a sweet place for a birthday party! Call to make a reservation.

Updated, but designed to pay homage to the "old" Farrell's from the 70's and 80's, the adjacent restaurant has red patterned wall paper, Tiffanyesk hanging lamps, street lamps, and a menu printed on newspaper type add to the atmosphere of yesteryear. The Brea location still makes a loud deal out of a birthday or celebration with singing, drums and a player piano.

The smallish menu includes Southwest steak salad, $14.50; three parlour street tacos, $9.50; pretzel dog, $10.25; NYC pastrami, $11.95; and build-your-own. The latter offers options of beef patty, chicken breast, turkey or veggie patty for $11.25, then choice of "bun" (brioche, French roll, pretzel frank bun, sourdough bread), cheeses, sauces and toppers that include the usual (lettuce, tomatoes, bacon, etc.) plus avocado, egg, tri tip, chili, and more. The kid's menu offers a burger, pizza, grilled cheese or chicken nuggets for $6. The best is yet to come - dessert. Farrell's has the classic fare of shakes and malts, plus a Trough ($16), which is two banana splits piled high with goodies, eaten from a trough and awarded a blue ribbon if you eat it yourself; Parlour's Tin Roof ($9.50); and the Zoo ($65), a huge sundae which feeds up to ten people, featuring 30 scoops of chocolate, strawberry, and vanilla ice cream, with strawberry, chocolate, and marshmallow topping, then topped with bananas, sprinkles, whipped cream, a cherry! The build-your-own sundae allows you to pick your flavor ice cream (the standards, plus chocolate malted crunch, coffee, animal cookie, incredible-tasting berry sorbet and more) at $3.95 for a single scoop, then, from a cart, add toppings ($1 per) of a variety of sauces, marshmallow fluff, salted caramel whipped cream, candies, cookies, brownies, apples, and more.

Hours: Brea - Open Mon. - Thurs., noon - 10pm; Fri. - Sat., 11am - 11pm; Sun., 11am - 9pm. Buena Park - Open Mon. - Thurs., noon - 8:30pm; Fri., noon - 10pm; Sat., 11am - 10pm; Sun., 11am - 8:30pm.
Price: Prices are listed above.
Ages: All

TEA HOUSE ON LOS RIOS

(949) 443-3914 / www.theteahouseonlosrios.com
31731 Los Rios Street, San Juan Capistrano

Take a sip of tea and just relax. The ambiance of this historic district flows with Old World charm, as does this tea house which is in a restored, 1911 cottage. The rustic garden has a profusion of flowering plants growing every which way. The white picket fence, trellis, and covered veranda, with plenty of outdoor seating on an enclosed patio that wraps around the house, and some stained glass windows, add to the atmosphere. Inside are three intimate rooms decorated with flowered wall paper, plates, tea cups, other tea time paraphernalia, and fresh flowers. Fine china and linens are used at the tables.

A wide variety of teas are offered here, ranging from Cottage Tea, with scones, cream, preserves, and fruit, plus a selection of tea for $18.95 to the ultimate of Victorian Tea, with scones et. al, and tea, plus soup and salad, assorted finger sandwiches, fresh fruit with heavy cream, dessert, and champagne for $42.95. Children 9 years and under will especially enjoy the Tree House Tea which consists of a peanut butter and jam or grilled cheese sandwich, fruit, a scone with cream and jam, and a soft drink or tea for $15.95. A la carte lunch entrees include a cup of soup, ($5.95), petite salad ($8.95), Mediterranean salad ($15.95), Shepherd's Pie ($17.95), island-style rice with chicken breast ($18.95), and prime rib ($33.95). Dessert options include English trifles with fresh strawberries, or warm bread pudding with brandy sauce and raisins, or an ice cream parfait with hot fudge sauce for $7.95 each.

Weekend brunch, served from 9:30am to noon, includes salmon benedict with a poached egg and a crumpet, home fries and seasonal fruit for $16.95; classic quiche with potatoes, fruit and crumpet for $15.95; and prime rib and eggs with a crumpet and preserves for $19.95; as well as other items.

Before or after your tea time, take a stroll around the Los Rios district and the streets of San Juan Capistrano to enjoy the rest of what this quaint city has to offer. Watch out for younger children around the nearby train tracks. Look up ZOOMARS PETTING ZOO / LOS RIOS PARK (pg. 337) and MISSION SAN JUAN CAPISTRANO (pg. 309) for more to do in this immediate area.

Hours: Open Tues. - Fri., 11am - 5pm; Sat. - Sun., 9:30am - 5pm. Closed Mon., Easter, Thanksgiving and Christmas.
Price: Prices are listed above. Note: There is a $10 per person minimum.
Ages: 4 years and up.

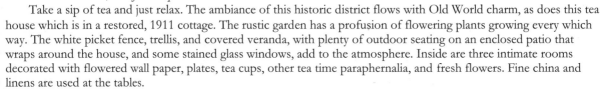

—FAMILY PAY AND PLAY—

AESTHETIC CLIMBING GYM

(949) 716-7116 / www.aestheticclimbinggym.com
26794 Vista Terrace, Lake Forest

This indoor rock climbing gym was designed by climbers for climbers and for those who want to give the sport a try. It's huge! About half of the gym is bouldering and the other half is lead climbing and numerous top rope stations. The ambiance is a little hipper than some other indoor climbing places as there is artistic graffiti painted on the walls and some of the top rope walls (and some seemingly unattached walls) are red and not the more typical granite-like textured walls. The bouldering area includes all competition grade angles along with a cave, overhang roof climbing, and a top out slab.

Scale the rocks using various hand and foot holds that incorporate different routes; some with sharper angles and some just vertical. Climbing is a great alternative to more traditional physical activities! A variety of both indoor and outdoor classes are available, as well as deals and special events. There is also a weight and cardio room, plus ping pong and foosball tables.

Hours: Open Mon - Fri., noon - 11pm; Sat., 10am - 10pm; Sun., 10am - 6pm.
Price: $18 for a day pass for adults; $15 for students, which includes all the equipment needed.
Ages: 5 years and up.

ALISO VIEJO AQUATIC CENTER

(949) 425-2559 / www.swimoc.com; www.cityofalisoviejo.com
$$$
29 Santa Barbara Drive, Aliso Viejo

This gated, nice aquatic center is set on a hilltop, next to a golf course, with a breathtaking view of the surrounding mountains. It has a junior Olympic five-lane lap pool, a recreational swimming pool, an adult whirl pool, a children's wading pool, a small sprayground on recycled rubber ground in between the pools, and a shower area. There is also a picnic area inside the gates with an outdoor fireplace, a full-service snack bar called the Oasis Cafe, and locker facilities. No outside food is allowed in. Just outside the center is a small playground with slides, a little rock climbing wall, and some climbing apparatus.

Hours: Lap swim is open daily, year round. Open May and September, Mon. and Wed., 10am - 6pm; Tues. and Thurs., 6:30am - 6pm; Sat. - Sun., 9am - 5pm. Open Memorial Day - Labor Day, daily, 10am - 6pm. The Cafe is open May and September, weekends only, 11am - 4pm; open in the summer daily, 11am - 4pm.
Price: $7 for non-resident adults; $5 for residents; $5 for non-resident seniors and ages 2 - 13; $3 for residents.
Ages: Toddler and up.

BALBOA FUN ZONE

(949) 675-8915 - fun zone; (949) 438-6273 - Ferris Wheel / www.ocfunzone.com;
$$
www.balboaferriswheel.com; www.balboaislandferry.com
600 E. Bay Avenue, Newport Beach

This strip, called the Fun Zone, is across the road from the BALBOA PIER (pg. 315) and is fun in a casual sort of way. The Ferris wheel is $4 a ride. Other attractions, at $5 per, include a multi-person, swing; a (fake) coconut tree climb to the top; and a short Tower Drop. The bungee "ride" that goes up 20 feet is $10. There are several classic arcade games at Bay Arcade and a small nautical museum, OCEAN QUEST (pg. 312), to explore.

Kids also enjoy walking the short pedestrian street, shopping, or eating a famous Balboa Bar, which is an ice-cream bar topped with chocolate, sprinkles, and nuts. If you're looking for physical activity, bike rentals ($10 for two hours), and even surreys, kid's bikes, and child trailers are available in the immediate area at Seaside Bike Rentals at (949) 270-6911 / wwwseasidebikes.com. See the Transportation section for information on the numerous boat rentals and harbor cruises launched from the Fun Zone.

Take the historic Balboa ferry which runs Sunday through Thursday from 6:30am to midnight, and Friday and Saturday from 6:30am to 2am (starts at 6am everyday in the summer), across the water to Balboa Island. At only $1 for adults, 50¢ for ages 5 - 11, and free for children 4 years and under, or $2 for car and driver - the ferry is a fun, affordable way to get to the island and kids love this mini-adventure. (You can even bring your bike for $1.25 for adults; .75¢ for kids.) Once on the man-made island, there is not a lot for kids to do. Enjoy a walk or ride on the paved pathway along the beach, or perhaps head east toward the main shopping street. Note: The Island can also be reached by exiting Pacific Coast Highway [1] S. on Jamboree Road, where it turns into Marine Ave.

Hours: Stores, restaurants, and most attractions along the Balboa Fun Zone are open Mon. - Thurs., 11am - 6pm (until 8pm in the summer); Fri., 11am - 9pm; Sat., 11am - 9pm (open at 10am in the summer); Sun., 11am - 7pm (open 10am - 9pm in the summer). Most parking along the street is metered, or park at the lot at Balboa Blvd. and Palm St.
Ages: All

BIG AIR TRAMPOLINE PARK

Buena Park - (714) 831-1092; Laguna Hills - (949) 305-9788 / www.bigairusa.com
$$$
Buena Park - 8320 On The Mall; Laguna Hills - 23251 Avenida De La Carlota

The term "big air" means "a high jump in an extreme sport" - and that's exactly what this place is! The huge, main room with a floor of trampolines (and some up on the walls, too) is perfect for working off all the excess energy, and then some. Other rooms, divided by netting, include two dodgeball courts; two basketball courts; a foam pit area for jumping and spinning and trying tricks; and a room, called Lil' Air, just for younger jumpers who are ages 8 and under. And a resting room - different than a restroom! - with couches and TV.

This facility also offers some unusual and fun features such as good-sized rock climbing areas for bouldering, with overhangs, that have foam pits under the climbers for them to fall into; a bull pen (riding a mechanical bull); and a Battlebeam®. The latter is a padded beam over a foam pit that contestants joust on using large, hard-foam "lances". The Laguna location also features Lazer Maze - dodging and bouncing your way across, up and over a series of laser beams that crisscross in a large room. Cosmic Nights (with lights down and music up, plus lasers and strobes); Toddler Time (for ages 6 years and under); Special Needs Days; Homeschool Days; cardio workouts; and more give Big Air a leg up on similar parks. Purchase pizza, corn dogs, and other snacks and beverages at the snack bar inside, or bring your own food to enjoy on the picnic tables outside. Notes: All jumpers must wear non-skid socks (sold here for $2). Signed waivers are required.

Hours: Buena Park - Usually open Mon. - Thurs., 3pm - 9pm; Fri., 3pm - 11pm; Sat., 10am - 11pm; Sun., 11am - 8pm. Cosmic Nights are Fri. - Sat., 8pm - 11pm. Toddler Time is Tues., 9am - noon; Sun., 9am - 11am. Laguna Hills - Open Mon. - Tues., 3pm - 9pm; Wed. - Thurs., 1pm - 9pm; Fri., 3pm - 11pm; Sat., 10am - 11pm; Sun., 10am - 8pm. Cosmic Nights are Fri. - Sat., 8:30pm - 11pm. Toddler Time is Wed. - Thurs., 10am - 1pm. Both locations are usually open during school holidays and summer, Mon. - Fri. at 11am.

Price: Buena Park - $15 an hour. Subsequent hours are $7. $20 for Cosmic Nights. $8 per jumper for Toddler Time. Laguna Hills - $15 an hour. Subsequent hours are $8. $19 for Cosmic Nights. $8 per jumper for Toddler Time. Spectators are always free. Check on-line for specials and deals.

Ages: 3 years and up.

BILLY BEEZ (Orange County)

(657) 207-4841 / billybeezus.com
$$$
400 West Disney Way, Suite 189 at Anaheim GardenWalk, Anaheim

Your kids will swarm to this wonderful indoor play place like bees to honey! The multi-level play structure has got everything kids need to *bee* busy, active and entertained. With lots of padding along the way, there are hard-foam obstacles to conquer, cargo nets to climb, slides, tubes, tunnels, knotted ropes, padded steps, and more. Enter the ball arena, if you dare! On the lower level the foam balls spew out of the machine in the center and kids try to catch them. The kids (and adults) on the top level are using their cannon/guns to target the kids down below, each other (as its in a circular enclosure), and at actual bull's-eye targets just below each other's guns. This is just one of the places here that they can play all day! The six, tall, curvy, side-by-side, rainbow-colored slides are fun to zip down. And of course there's other slides, too - some wide enough for the family to go down together, some enclosed in a tube, and some short ones. Shoot some hoops or kick in a goal at the sports courts.

Honeycomb Village is a mini-city, complete with flooring that looks like streets (plus tyke-size cars to drive around) that lead to different rooms for younger kids to use their imagination and play as hard as worker bees. The hospital room has small beds and doll patients, plus play doctor equipment. The house has a living room / kitchen with tot-size furniture and frig, sink and stove, and other homey touches. The schoolroom has desks and chairs, colorful learning posters, and some games and puzzles. (Maybe kids can do a spelling bee in here!) The pizzeria has all the ingredients need for a meal and little chef outfits to wear, plus a mural of a wood burning oven. The grocery store is fully stocked with lots of plastic food, and mini grocery carts. Kids can become tellers at the bank. They can also board a "fire truck" that has a steering wheel, gear puzzles on its walls, and a game where the hood should be. Every city needs a playground, so a Mini Beez central play structure here keeps young visitors all abuzz as it has similar components to the older kids play structure, but on a smaller scale, plus huge soft blocks and hard foams rockers.

Socks must be worn by all participants. An on-side cafe sells food / snacks such as a slice of cheese pizza ($2.99); hot dog ($2.99); 4pc chicken wings ($5.99); and ice cream bar ($2.49). This location is at Anaheim Gardenwalk where just outside this busy hive are more fun places to explore and eateries to indulge.

Hours: Open Sun. - Thurs., 10am - 8pm; Fri. - Sat., 10am - 9:30pm.

Price: $3.95 for the first adult; $6.95 for the second adult (but only on the weekends); seniors are free with a paid child; $15.95 for ages 4 - 17; $12.95 for ages 1 - 3; infant is free with paid toddler or child, or $9.95 for one infant and one adult. The price is good for all-day access, with re-entry.

Ages: 1 - 14 years.

BOOMERS! - Fountain Valley

(714) 842-1111 / www.boomersparks.com
$$$$
16800 Magnolia Street, Fountain Valley

Boomers is fun for the whole family. The attractions here include **two miniature golf courses** with hazards of a schoolhouse, pagoda, mini Eiffel Tower, windmill, fountain, and pond, plus lots of (real) palm trees for landscaping attractiveness - $10 for ages 5 and up; children 4 and under are free with a paid adult; **bumper boats** - $9 for a six-minute ride, and drivers must be at least 44" tall to ride by themselves (passengers under 40" can ride with an adult for $2); **batting cages** - twenty-five pitches for $3; **go karts** - $9 for a five-minute ride, and drivers must be at least 54" tall to drive by themselves, $2 for additional passengers who must be at least 40" tall; a **rock wall** - $9 for two climbs up the thirty-two-foot wall; and a game room with ticket redemption center. The **kiddie rides**, geared for ages 7 and under, include a Ferris wheel, a roller coaster, train ride, whirly bird, and balloon ride -$5 per. Picnic tables are here, as well. A full-service SURF'S UP CAFE (pg. 253) is on-site, too.

Hours: Open Mon. - Thurs., noon - 8pm; Fri. noon- 11pm; Sat., 10am - 11pm; Sun., 10am - 8pm. Open extended hours during holidays and in the summer.

Price: Attractions are individually priced above, or purchase an all day play pass starting at $44.99.

Ages: 2 years and up.

BOOMERS! - Irvine and BUCCANEER COVE WATERPARK

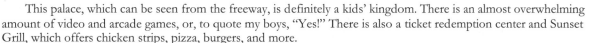

(949) 559-8341 / www.boomersparks.com

$$$$

3405 Michelson Drive, Irvine

This palace, which can be seen from the freeway, is definitely a kids' kingdom. There is an almost overwhelming amount of video and arcade games, or, to quote my boys, "Yes!" There is also a ticket redemption center and Sunset Grill, which offers chicken strips, pizza, burgers, and more.

Outside, are two terrific, themed **miniature golf** courses with windmills, castles, houses, and other mini buildings - $12 for ages 5 and up; children 4 years and under are free. **Rock climbing** is $9 for two climbs up the wall. Splash Island **bumper boats** are $9 a ride and drivers must be 44" tall; $2 for additional riders who must be over 40" tall. I allowed my youngest to steer the boat and he did so gleefully - right under the fountain's waters. Oh, the joy of spending time together! **Go-carts,** where drivers must be a minimum of 58" tall, are $10 per ride; $2 for additional riders who must be at least 40" tall. Younger speedsters, at least 42" tall, can drive their own cars at **Kiddie Go-karts** for $8 a ride. **Flame Thrower**, which goes up and over and spins around, is $8 ride; riders must be 52" tall (but not over 76" tall). **Sidewinder** - a swinging pendulum that rotates around, too - is $8. **Batting cages** are here, too. In **Laser Tag**, you and your at least 5-year-old child (personal recommendation) enter a darkened, maze-like room with walls that are three-feet high and lit by fluorescent markings. For about five minutes you'll engage in laser tag, which entails alternately safeguarding your base while shooting at the players on the opposing team. It's a blast. The cost is $9 per game. King Arthur's Carnival has **five kiddie rides** - an open-air little train, a mini-boat ride, teacups, a jumping ride, and a carousel. Each ride is $5.

Get splash happy at the small **Buccaneer Cove Waterpark**. The pirate and nautically themed, one main play structure is five stories high with six enclosed and open twisty slides (the blue one is in the shape of a figure 8). It also has tunnels; bridges; burst pipes that squirt water every which way; steps; water cannons to shoot at people (and be shot at); an aqua dome; buckets that fill up and splash down; short, kiddie slides; and lots more wet fun. The adjacent cement sprayground has a partial, stationary boat to get into and shoot water; pipes in all configurations that spray out water; and good clean fun. If wet isn't for you, watch those playing from a lounge chair on the perimeter.

If the urge strikes, go next door to the nicely appointed Irvine Lanes. It has plenty of bowling lanes (40!) and Galaxy Bowling (like Cosmic Bowling), featuring music, lights and lasers, is offered at certain times.

Hours: Open Mon. - Thurs., 11am - 9pm; Fri., 11am - 11pm; Sat., 10am - 11pm; Sun., 10am - 9pm. Hours may fluctuate. Buccaneer Cove is open Memorial Day - mid-June, and mid-September - end of September, Sat. - Sun., 11am - 7pm. It's open Memorial Day - Labor Day, Mon. - Fri., 11am - 6pm; Sat. - Sun., 11am - 7pm.

Price: Prices are listed individually above or get an all day, all play pass starting at $44.99. Entrance to the waterpark is $19.99 per person; $5 for dry, non-participants; children 2 and under are free.

Ages: 2 years and up.

BOUNCEU

Huntington Beach - (714) 892-4842; Orange - (714) 744-JUMP (5867) / www.bounceu.com

$$

Huntington Beach - 5445 Oceanus Dr., suite 115; Orange - 428A W. Katella Ave.

Jumping, hopping, sliding, bouncing, laughing, running, playing - this is what happens at BounceU. Kids can knock themselves out (not really!) in the inflatable boxing ring where participants wear oversized, inflatable boxing gloves and protective helmets. The huge interactive inflatables include obstacle courses, basketball, and bounce houses. One really cool element in one of the bounces is a tiered, web-like rope climbing structure that kids love. The red, white, and blue theme lends itself a fun place for younger kids and older kids, too, as it's not too cutesy for them. Remember that all participants must wear socks and that reservations, even for open play, are recommended and necessary for certain programs.

Celebrate birthday parties, team parties, fundraisers, field trips, or anything you can think of here. Family Bounce is for everyone to get in on the action. Be the light of the party by having a Cosmic Bounce party where the black lights, disco lights, and glow-in-the-dark accessories are especially a hit with teens. Parent's Night Out is a popular drop-off program as kids get to play and eat dinner for over three hours while parents go out somewhere else to play and eat dinner. Check out the variety of camps offered for kids, especially during the summer, as one incorporates art and another engineering with Legos.

Hours: For both locations - Check the calendar for open play dates, cosmic bounce, parent's night, camps, Preschool Playdates, and all other events as they frequently change.

Price: Orange - $10 per session for open play. Preschool Playdates are $12 per child. Huntington Beach - $10 (1.25 hours) - $12 (2 hours) per session for open play and for family nights. Parents and children under 2 are free. Cosmic Bounce is $10 per child. Parent's Night out is $20 (at Orange), $25 (at Huntington Beach) for the first child; $15 for siblings.

Ages: 3 years and up.

BUENA PARK RACEWAY

(714) 827-9979 / www.bpraceway.com
6161 Lincoln Avenue, Buena Park

$$$

Slot cars are four to eight inches long, look like real cars (i.e. race cars, hot rods or muscle cars), run on a slot in a track, and are powered electrically with speeds manipulated by a hand-held controller operated mostly by the male gender! This store not only has all the supplies one needs to build, own and run slot cars, but several tracks to race competitively, and even rental cars for those who want to test drive the sport first. Race you to the finish line!

Hours: Open Wed. - Fri., 3pm - 9:30pm; Sat., 8am - 10pm; Sun., 11am - 7pm. Racing is usually held on Thursday nights and on the weekends.

Price: Free to watch. Track time is $7.50 per 30 minutes with your own car and controller. Or, $3.75 for a rental car, $3.75 for a controller, $7.50 for 30 min. of track time = $15 total.

Ages: 6 years and up.

CAMELOT GOLFLAND

(714) 630-3340 / www.golfland.com/anaheim
3200 E. Carpenter Avenue, Anaheim

$$$

In short, there's simply not a more congenial spot for happy ever aftering than here in Camelot! This huge castle has dragons, knights in shining armor, and anything else your prince or princess might consider fun decor. Choose from four, exciting **Miniature Golf** courses with obstacles and "decorations" to putt through - $10.49 for adults; $9.49 for seniors and ages 4 - 11; free for ages 3 and under with paid adult admission. One additional replay is $5.49. **Lazer Knights** is an exciting game of tag using laser guns - $7.49 for the first game, with a replay game for $6.49. Get your engines running as you race around the **Fast Car Raceway** - $7.49 for the six-minute ride; drivers must be at least 58". A little less fast, and definitely more bumpy, are **Bumper Cars** - $4.99. For bumping around in the water, go on **Bumper Boats** - $5.49. The five-story **Water Slides** are $15 for an all-day rides pass, or $8 after 3pm. There are over 200 video and arcade games (ask about arcade-mania pricing - if you want) and a full-service snack bar serving fresh pizza, sandwiches, and Dryer's ice cream.

Hours: Most of Camelot is open Mon. - Thurs., 11am - 10pm; Fri., 10am - midnight; Sat., 9am - midnight; Sun., noon - 10pm. Note that the race track and bumper boats open at 5pm during the week, most of the year. Call first as hours fluctuate a lot! The water slide is open Memorial Day - mid-June on weekends only from noon - 5pm; open mid-June - Labor Day, Mon. - Sat., noon - 5pm. Closed Sun.

Price: Attractions are individually priced above. Check the discounted online specials before you go!

Ages: 2½ years and up.

CHUCK E. CHEESE'S (Orange County)

See the entry for CHUCK E. CHEESE'S (Los Angeles County) (pg. 18) for details.

CIRCUSTRIX

(949) 445-1340 / www.circustrixoc.com
25222 El Paseo, Mission Viejo

$$$

A huge grid of over 60 trampolines include angled walls to springboard off of, launching decks, and one high area that you drop off, vertically, onto the trampoline below and climb the walls (or just air). The Ninja course is really fun, and hard!, with running up and down obstacles, catching bars, and more. Basketball "courts", extreme dodgeball courts, slacklining over a foam pit, and foam pits that feature a "waterfall trampoline" (series of trampolines) add to the fun here. For circus-like elements, fly thru the air with the greatest of ease and be a daring person on the flying trapeze when you use the trapeze bar and even the aerial silks - both over foam pits, of course. Check the calendar for special weekly events such as trampoline fitness where you can burn 1,000 calories per hour (so at 16.66 calories a minute - I could burn almost 84 calories!); Club Nights with black lights, lasers, music and more for ages 15 and up; theme nights; college jump; KidJump; and more. CircusTrix grip socks are mandatory and cost $3 per pair.

Hours: Open Mon. - Thurs., 9am - 10am for KidJump only, 10am - 9pm for the general public; Fri. - Sat., 9am - 10am for KidJump only, 10am - 9pm for the general public, 9pm - midnight for Club Night; Sun., 9am - 9pm.

Price: Mon. - Fri., $17 for the first hour for ages 7 and up, $27 for 2 hours; $13 for the first hour for ages 6 and under, $23 for 2 hours. Sat., Sun. and school holidays, $17 for the first hour for ages 7 and up, $34 for 2 hours; $13 for the first hour for ages 6 and up, $26 for 2 hours. Discounts are given for KidJump and other special events. Observers are free.

Ages: 2 years and up.

DAVE & BUSTER'S (Orange County)

Irvine - (949) 727-0555; Orange - (714) 769-1515 / www.daveandbusters.com

Irvine - 661 Spectrum Center Drive at Irvine Spectrum; Orange - 20 City Boulevard West at The Outlets at Orange

Sometimes, adults just want to play. Dave & Buster's is mainly geared for adults as it has a full bar in the restaurant area and another centrally located in the massive arcade room, plus there are some more mature/intense video games, but kids are welcome here, too. Loud and often packed, as any video arcade, there are over 200 games to play, both classics and the newest of motion simulator rides, plus arcade, video and virtual reality games such as Star Wars Battle Pod, Speed of Light, Candy Crush Saga, Angry Birds, Mario Kart Arcade Grand Prix Deluxe, Monopoly, Simpson's Soccer, Snow Down, Typhoon, Temple Run, Dizzy Chicken, Time Crisis 5, Harpoon Lagoon, and Dark Escape 4-D.

On top of a ticket redemption area with prizes, plus table shuffleboard, billiards, sports games, several big screen HDTV's (up to 180"), and more attractions, is the restaurant feature. Menu choices include many delicious selections such as, for appetizers - four mini-cheeseburgers, buffalo wings and fries ($13.99), potato skins, and calamari; main meals (between $10 to $30) - bacon-wrapped sirloin medallions and grilled shrimp, Black Jack bbq chicken, sweet apple pecan salad, chicken and waffles, peppercorn New York strip steak, burgers, pastas, sandwiches, and more; and decadent desserts like Belgian chocolate fondue. The kid's menu, ranging from $6 to $9, offers kids surf and turf, cheeseburger, grilled cheese sandwich, pretzel dog, or salad. For a non-alcoholic beverage try the grape candy chill which is grape juice and sprite over snow-cone ice, gummy worms and a color-changing straw.

Guests under the age of 18 or 21 (it varies by location) must be accompanied by a parent or guardian 25 or 30 years of age, or older. One parent or guardian can accompany up to a maximum of six underage guests who, in turn, must remain with their authority. Check the website for specials. See IRVINE SPECTRUM CENTER (pg. 300) and VANS SKATE PARK (pg. 269) for more details about the respective mall attractions.

Hours: Open Sun. - Wed., 11am - midnight; Thurs. - Sat., 11am - 1am.

Price: Some prices are listed above. Always check the website first as there are always specials offered.

Ages: 7 years and up.

FIRESTORM FREERUNNING & ACROBATICS

(714) 458-3733 / www.firestormfreerunning.com

2533 South Main Street, Santa Ana

Remember *The Office* segment where Michael, Dwight and Andy did parkour? They could really have used coming here to practice! Firestorm offers colorful and creative ways and equipment to jump on walls, over obstacles, off foam blocks, on a trampoline, into a foam pit, swing over bars on scaffolding, tumble on the spring floor, and so much more. Several different areas, devoted to different facets and configurations of these physical arts, make up this unique playground! Test your abilities and learn the how-tos of parkour, acrobatics, and body agility with classes and training in aerial silks, freerunning, ninja warriors, and more, or come for the open gym hours to practice and play. At the kids open gym coaches offer participation-optional games, obstacle courses, and other activities, or the kids can just run around. Check out the Parents Night Out, camps, and other happenings, here. Ages 17 and under must have a parent, or legal guardian, 25 or older, sign a waiver.

Hours: Open gym for adults, ages 18 and older, is Mon. - Thurs., 8:30pm - 11pm; Sun., 6pm - 8:30pm. (Closed Fri. and Sat.). Open gym for kids, ages 4 - 17 years, is Mon., Wed. and Fri., 1pm - 2pm and 4:30pm - 5:30pm; Tues. and Thurs., 1pm - 2pm and 5:30pm - 6:30pm; Sat., noon - 1pm; Sun., noon - 1, 2pm - 3pm, and 4pm - 5pm.

Price: $10 per session, per person.

Ages: 4 years and up.

FLIGHTDECK AIR COMBAT CENTER

(714) 937-1511 / www.flightdeck1.com

1650 South Sinclair Street, Anaheim

$$$$$

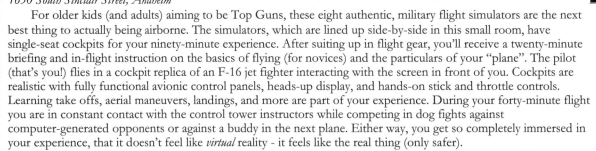

For older kids (and adults) aiming to be Top Guns, these eight authentic, military flight simulators are the next best thing to actually being airborne. The simulators, which are lined up side-by-side in this small room, have single-seat cockpits for your ninety-minute experience. After suiting up in flight gear, you'll receive a twenty-minute briefing and in-flight instruction on the basics of flying (for novices) and the particulars of your "plane". The pilot (that's you!) flies in a cockpit replica of an F-16 jet fighter interacting with the screen in front of you. Cockpits are realistic with fully functional avionic control panels, heads-up display, and hands-on stick and throttle controls. Learning take offs, aerial maneuvers, landings, and more are part of your experience. During your forty-minute flight you are in constant contact with the control tower instructors while competing in dog fights against computer-generated opponents or against a buddy in the next plane. Either way, you get so completely immersed in your experience, that it doesn't feel like *virtual* reality - it feels like the real thing (only safer).

Fly with the big birds by piloting the Boeing 737 commercial jetliner simulator for thirty minutes ($98), where you'll take-off, fly a short itinerary and land at your destination airport; or fly for an hour ($189) with a more complex flight plan. Be a part of a military combat squadron where squadron members also learn advance piloting skills such as air combat maneuvering, precision bombing, and navigation. Ask about the education programs that are offered here, too, as well as Top Gun kids birthday parties for ages 7 and up.

For those who remain grounded, go upstairs to the small room called the Officer's Club, or watch the action on monitors from the observation deck that show exactly what each pilot is experiencing.

Hours: Usually open Wed. - Fri., 11am - 8pm; Sat. - Sun., 10am - 9pm. Open 24/7 for private events. Make a reservation as walk-ins are only accommodated if there is an available flight.

Price: Forty-minute missions on the F-16 are $59. Special programs have different fees.

Ages: Must be at least 11 years old with a minimum height of 4'11". Top Gun kids birthday parties are for ages 7 and up.

FROGG'S BOUNCE HOUSE

(714) 418-0442 / www.froggsbouncehouse.com

16121 Brookhurst Street, Fountain Valley

$$$

With a welcoming and almost a jungly feel, this 9,000 square foot, big, long room, decorated with primary colors on the walls, is filled with six inflatables on each side of a center isle. The isle, with its clustering of comfy couches and tables and chairs, and even large-screen TV in one area, is a great place for parents to chat, relax, and watch their kids bounce around. The inflatables include a giant double slide; an island-themed jumper combo with slide and bounce; a mega obstacle course with "hills" and slides and tunnels; a bounce for ages 10 and under only; and a round, birthday cake bounce.

Frogg's also has a train table, bean bag chairs, Little Tykes cars, air hockey, karaoke and a play treehouse There is an eating area too, so bring a lunch so you can stay and play longer. The party room in the back has murals featuring sunshine, mountains, trees, and happy frogs. Love those kids, but drop them off here so you and yours can go out for date night - offered every Friday. It includes pizza for the kids. Note that socks are required for everyone and liability waivers must be signed for all ages. The fun is here, just waiting for you, so hop to it!

Hours: Open Sun. - Thurs., 10am - 7pm; Fri. - Sat., 10am - 8pm. Closed all major holidays. Date night every Fri., 5pm - 8pm.

Price: $4 for adults; $12 for ages 4 - 17; $8 for ages 3 and under; $10 per person for a group of 10 or more kids. The last two hours of every day admission is $10 for ages 4 and up. Check the website or call for specials.

Ages: 2 years and up.

GET AIR TRAMPOLINE PARK (Orange County)

(714) 916-5815 / www.getairsurfcity.com

5142 Argosy Avenue, Huntington Beach

$$$

See GET AIR TRAMPOLINE PARK (Riverside County) (pg. 347) for details. This facility is 10,000 square feet. It does not have a slack line, Ninja course, or fidget ladder, but it has everything else great!

Hours: Open Mon., 10am - 10pm; Tues., 10am - noon for Toddler Time and noon - 10pm all ages; Wed., 10am - 10pm; Thurs., 10am - noon for Toddler Time and noon - 10pm all ages; Fri. - Sat., 10am - 9pm, and 9pm - midnight for Club Air; Sun., 10am - 8pm.

Price: $14 per hour for 46" and taller; $10 for 45" and under. Toddler Time is $10 per child; one adult is admitted for free. Club Air is $15 for 2 hours, or $20 for 3. Always check the website for special offers.

Ages: 2 years and up.

GREAT WOLF LODGE

See GREAT WOLF LODGE (pg. 317) for all the details.

HANGAR 18 (Orange County)

Mission Viejo - (949) 454-8043; San Clemente - (949) 388-0480 / www.climbhangar18.com
Mission Viejo - 23812 Via Fabricante, suite A4; San Clemente - 1031 Calle Trepadora, unit A

These Hangar 18 facilities are different from the other Hangar 18s in that they are bouldering-only gyms. That said, with 4,200 square feet, it is a bouldering paradise with walls jutting out at various angles that prove a fitting challenge for your young athletes, and for those who are not so athletically inclined. Both seasoned climbers and those new to the sport will experience a sense of accomplishment as they conquer the rocky obstacles and terrain. The routes are changed to continually stimulate your mind and body. So, if you're feeling caught between a rock and a hard place, come to Hangar 18 for safe, challenging, fun exercise for the whole family! Note that the San Clemente location also has a yoga studio.

Hours: Open Mon. - Thurs., 10am - 10pm; Fri., 10am - 9pm; Sat. - Sun., 10am - 8pm.

Price: $18 for adults for a day pass; $13 for ages 13 and under. Shoe rentals are $3.

Ages: 5 years and up.

JOHN'S INCREDIBLE PIZZA CO. (Orange County)

See JOHN'S INCREDIBLE PIZZA CO. (Orange County) (pg. 250), under EDIBLE ADVENTURES, for details.

JUMP 'N JAMMIN (Orange County)

(949)582-5890 / www.jumpnjammin.com
27741 Crown Valley Parkway in the Kaleidoscope mall, Mission Viejo

Truly, this children's entertainment center is jumpin' and jammin! The gigantic, multi-story play structure is the main draw and it can keep kids (and adults) busy for hours. It has large plastic tubes to crawl through on all levels, slides to zip down, bridges to cross, nets to climb up, inflatable and foam obstacle courses to power through, zip lines, large balls to roll around on, barrels to roll around and through, and a totally fun feature - guns to shoot out foam balls at other guests. A fountain in the center, on the floor, gushes out more colorful foam balls. This is an ideal play place to let off some steam and have a blast doing it. Adults are invited to join in the fun, too, and they do.

Other activities include a bounce house, a short rock climbing wall, and virtual jump rope - all so fun! Toddlers have a separate, enclosed space just for them with soft foam objects to play on. Each child has a wristband that corresponds to the adult that brought them. Socks must be worn at all times by kids and adults.

No outside food may be brought in, but since you're in a mall, there are plenty of places to grab lunch or just a snack before or after your visit, plus you are welcome to leave and reenter Jump 'N Jammin all day. Try Islands for burgers, El Torito Grill, or the pizzeria, and top it off with a visit to Yogurtland. The mall also features COLOR ME MINE (Orange County) (pg. 240) and LASER QUEST (Orange County) (pg. 262).

Hours: Open Sun. - Thurs., 10am - 6pm; Fri. - Sat., 10am - 8pm. Closed Easter, Thanksgiving, and Christmas. Jump closes at 4pm on several other holidays.

Price: $14.95 for ages 2 and up, which includes one free adult admission; $6.49 for children 23 months or younger, which includes one free adult admission. Additional adults are $3.95.

Ages: 2 - 12 years.

K1 SPEED (Orange County)

Anaheim - (714) 632-6999; Irvine - (949) 250-0242 / www.K1speed.com

$$$$

Anaheim - 1000 East Edward Court; Irvine - 17221 Von Karman Ave.

See K1 SPEED (San Diego County) (pg. 482) for details. The Irvine location is huge at 100,000 square feet and three tracks.

Price: The first race in Anaheim is $22; the first in Irvine is $19.99.

LASER ISLAND (Orange County)

(714) 985-9966 / www.laserisland.com

$$$$

1840 N. Placentia Avenue, Placentia

See LASER ISLAND (San Bernardino County) (pg. 409) for details.

Hours: Open Mon. - Thurs., 3pm - 9pm; Fri., 3pm - midnight; Sat., 10am - midnight; Sun., noon - 9pm. Open in the summer and on holidays at noon with same closure times.

Price: Laser tag is $9. Mini golf is $6. CoCo Climb is $6. Check out the numerous specials offered like after school specials of unlimited laser tag or, my favorite - Family Dinner Adventure for 4 people. This includes pizza, a pitcher of soda, garlic bread and 2 laser games per person for only $50.

Ages: 6 years and up.

LASER QUEST (Orange County)

Fullerton - (714) 449-0555; Mission Viejo - (949) 367-1421 / www.laserquest.com

$$$

Fullerton - 229 E. Orangethorpe Ave.; Mission Viejo - 27741 Crown Valley Pkwy., Suite #315A Kaleidoscope Courtyards

This large arena, with fantasy decor, sets the stage for an exciting game of laser tag. Armed with laser guns, and vests with target lights, enter the multi-level maze with mirrors on the walls, lots of corners, columns, and obstacles to hide behind. Amid the strobe lights, black lights, ramps, catwalks, partitions, fog, and pulse-pounding music (which covered up my heavy breathing from being out of shape), race against the clock to "tag" the opposing team members with laser shots, and score. The fifteen-minute games are fast-paced, and leave you either tired or fired up to play another round! The lounge has video games and three separate party rooms.

For a new adventure "play" Key Quest, variously themed, live action escape room where 3 to 6 participants must work together using observation and critical thinking skills to discover clues, solve puzzles, and ultimately, find the "key" (whatever it might be) to escape the room within the 45-minute time limit. You will find out who works well under pressure!

Ask about their laser tag special events, such as themed overnight events from 11:45pm to 6am, and field trips for third through tenth graders. There are even school field trips where students learn about optics and refection or how lasers work, lasers as a form of light, and the history of mazes and how they are a part of everyday life. These programs include watching a short video, activities, learning and actually playing two games of laser tag, with an educational perspective, of course. That two-hour program is $10 per students with a minimum of twenty students.

The Mission Viejo location is in the Kaleidoscope Mall which also boasts COLOR ME MINE (Orange County) (pg. 240), a ceramic place, JUMP 'N JAMMIN (Orange County) (pg. 261), an indoor play center, plus shops and restaurants.

Hours: Fullerton - Laser Tag is open Tues. - Thurs., 6pm - 9pm; Fri., 4pm - 11pm; Sat., noon - 11pm; Sun., noon - 8pm. It's closed most Mon. except holiday Mon. Key Quest is available on the hour. Mission Viejo - Laser Tag is open Mon. - Thurs., 4pm - 9pm; Fri., 4pm - 11pm; Sat., 11am - 11pm; Sun., 11am - 7pm. Key Quest is available on the hour. Both locations are open extended hours in the summer and on holidays.

Price: $10 per game of laser tag. Key Quest is $15 a person, with a minimum of 3 people.

Ages: 6 years and up.

LEGO STORE - MINI MODEL BUILD (Orange County)

Anaheim - (714) 991-6512; Costa Mesa - (714) 668-9017; Mission Viejo - (949) 347-6867 /

!

www.lego.com/en-us/stores/events/mini-model-builds

Anaheim - 1585 Disneyland Dr. at Downtown Disney; Costa Mesa - 3333 Bristol St. at South Coast Plaza; Mission Viejo - 555 The Shops at Mission Viejo

See LEGO STORE - MINI MODEL BUILD (San Diego County) (pg. 485) for info on this great, free LEGO mini model build. Check out the malls listed above for other activities to do there.

Hours: The first Tues. and Wed. of each month, between 3pm - 7pm.

Price: Free

Ages: 6 - 14 years old, only.

LUV 2 PLAY (Orange County)

Lake Forest - (949) 916-0877; Irvine - (855) PLAY-002 (752-9002) / www.luv2play.com

Lake Forest - 26741 Rancho Pkwy; Irvine - 13722 Jamboree Road

See LUV 2 PLAY (Riverside County) (pg. 349) for details on this great indoor playground. The Lake Forest location has a relax room with comfy chairs and WiFi. One kinetic sand play table here is surrounded by cute, strawberry-themed chairs and the other has octopus stools. A separate, padded area is just for crawlers and has with foam shapes and hard foam colorful objects to create with.

Hours: Open Mon. - Thurs., 9am - 8pm; Fri. - Sat., 9am - 9pm; Sun., 10am - 6pm.

Price: Parents, kids 0 - 5 months old, and siblings 13 and older are free, as are ages 11 months and under with a paid sibling. Special needs kids are $5.95. Mon. - Thurs., ages 6 months - 4 years are $11.95; 5 - 12 years are $13.95; siblings are $10.95. Fri. - Sun. and holidays, ages 6 months - 4 years are $13.95; 5 - 12 years are $15.95; siblings are $12.95.

Ages: 12 months - 12 years

OC_RC RACEWAY AND HOBBIES

(714) 892-6699 / www.ocrcraceway.com

15282 Jason Circle, Huntington Beach

Remote-controlled, off-road racing is a fun sport to watch, and a funner one to participate in. Come race your car or truck at this indoor high-bite clay track with plenty of turns and bumps to maneuver around. Spectators are welcome, as are racers. The adjacent hobby shop is fully stocked with everything you need to get started, or for repairs.

Hours: Open for practice Mon. - Fri., noon - 11pm, with racing at 7pm on Wed. and Fri.; Sat., 11am - 9pm; Sun., noon - 2:30, with racing at 3pm.

Price: The practice fee is $15 for members; $20 for non-members. The racing fee is $20 for members; $25 for non-members. Membership is $40 a year. Rentals are $20 an hour for the Short Course Trucks which run on the small track, or $30 an hour for the 2WD Buggies that can run on the big track.

Ages: 7 years and up.

PRETEND CITY CHILDREN'S MUSEUM

(949) 428-3900 / www.pretendcity.org

29 Hubble, Irvine

Kids (and parents) will have real fun at this Pretend City. Much more than just an indoor play place this large "city" has fifteen different, interconnected stores, offices, and areas that motivate kids to interact and to expand their understanding of how a healthy community can work together.

Citizens walk down main "street," complete with streetlights and a park centerpiece, and go into the buildings around its perimeter and linking roads. Here are some of the city components: Trader Joe's grocery market is a spacious mini mart fully stocked with groceries, plus shopping baskets and cash registers. The farm has a wonderful mural with fake apples to pick from trees imbedded in the walls, as well as carrots and cabbage and other produce to harvest, plus an elevated gardening box. It also has fertilized eggs and live baby chicks in the incubator. Kids can use wood pieces and PVC pipes at the construction site to create (small) buildings. Acting out is encouraged on the amphitheater stage which is complete with lighting and music and costumes. Storytellers ply their trade here often, too. A complete little house has all of its rooms redecorated every few months with furniture and accessories pertaining to various ethnicities and the family room TV shows films starring a family explaining their culture. The beach section has ocean and whale murals, and a boat to get into, as well as beach chairs and a play area with buckets, shovels, and real sand. Adjacent to the beach is the marina with raised tables of water to create waterways using wind and water machines. Put together a sailboat here, too. Learn about the environment by looking down at the transparent street drain to see pollution travel from trash to the sea. The STEM lab is a room to play with building blocks, like Legos, on raised tables. Dress the part with uniforms and get into the appropriate child-size vehicles at the tiny fire, police, and gas stations. There is even a small jail here. The dispatch desk has buttons and a real siren. Is your child a chef? She can try her hand at the restaurant (which changes the ethnicity of its food and ambiance every few months) by working in the real-size kitchen. Customers are welcome at the tables. The health center is has a fully equipped dental office and doctor's office with X-rays, charts, models of body parts, a doctor's table and dentist chair (and check out the teeth chairs!), sinks, uniforms, and even crutches, all designed to ease kids' fears in going to visit a real doctor's office. A good-sized room toward the back of the city features special traveling exhibits. And these are just some of the city's structures and elements!

Other important areas include the Real Cafe, where outside food can be eaten (note that food, such as packaged sandwiches, snacks, and beverages, can be purchased here, too); the Art Studio where lots of supplies (and some instruction) for arts and crafts masterpieces are provided; and a mesh-enclosed, infant play area with toys and padded shapes just for them. An educational ingredient is the time cards which can be stamped at certain offices and stores here to be turned in for play cash from the ATM or bank, to be used at other stores. And be sure to call (or answer) the phones located at several stations throughout the city. One more feature worth mentioning - the bathrooms. Behind each toilet is a glass panel, revealing pipes, titled "Where does the poop go?"

Parents are helped in leaving with joyful (not tearful) kids at closing time as the staff head a parade involving all the kids that leads them around and out of the city to the front door. Hmm, wonder if I can get keys to this city? Ask about the numerous events, camps and programs, including those for kids specifically with autism.

Hours: Open Mon., 10am - 1pm; Tues. - Sat., 10am - 5pm; Sun., 11am - 5pm. Closed all major holidays.
Price: $12.50 per person; children 12 months and under are free. Admission after 4pm is half off.
Ages: Infants - 9 years

PUMP IT UP (Orange County)

Anaheim Hills - (714) 408-2585; Huntington Beach - (714) 847-9663; Irvine - (949) 261-7867; Lake Forest - 951-9663 / www.pumpitupparty.com

Anaheim Hills - 5397 E. Hunter Ave.; Huntington Beach - 16351 Gothard St.; Irvine - 16871 Noyes Ave.; Lake Forest - 26242 Dimension Dr., suite 100

See PUMP IT UP (San Diego County) (pg. 487) for details. The Anaheim location has a Cannonball foam ball blaster and inflatable rock wall only available for parties. The Lake Forest location has a Ninja Adrenaline Combo (a really cool obstacle course), Cannonball foam ball blaster, and Motion Mania, which are interactive games projected on the floor. It also offers a variety of Open Jump options including PreK only, Open Jump Glow, and more.

Hours: Check the location's website calendar for details on Open Jump and other speciality jump times as the times vary even within a particular month.
Price: Open Jump is $10 per child; adults are free. Lake Forest PreK Open Jump is $7 per child.
Ages: 2 years and up.

ROCK CITY CLIMBING CENTER

(714) 777-4884 / www.rockcityclimbing.com

5100 E. La Palma, suite 108, Anaheim Hills

I'm gonna rock 'n roll all night! Well, I'll at least rock for a good portion of the day at one of my favorite indoor rock climbing facilities. This large gym is very family oriented and particularly kid-friendly, including a wall specifically for younger climbers. Rock City has thirteen top ropes, numerous lead routes on variously angled walls, a bouldering wall, a bouldering cave, and a tunnel to crawl through. Take glow stick through the latter (because it is pitch black!) and crawl through the tunnel which is angled, has ladders, a short fire pole, and other elements to make it an extra-ordinary venture.

Each climb here is a unique experience because of the different colored-coded routes. Rock climbing is not just a physical challenge, but a mental one as well. Done on a regular basis, it builds confidence and discipline. Perfect for first time climbers and still very challenging for experts, Rock City offers the best of both worlds. Parents, learn to belay your kids (which is so easy to do!) so it's something you can do with them.

A huge variety of classes are available for all skill levels. Inquire about climbing programs for kids including camps, joining the climbing team, and more. Note that Boy Scouts can earn merit badges here. A separate party room is available, too. I've had numerous parties and team-building gatherings here. A two-hour party/team building for any age, for 7+ climbers, includes two hours of rock climbing, use of the party room, and the staff teaching how to belay other climbers, all for $17 a person; $100 minimum. You can also use a staffer as the belayer for an additional $35. A signed waiver and liability form, available online, is required for all rock climbers.

Hours: Open Mon. - Fri., noon - 10pm; Sat., 10am - 8pm; Sun., 10am - 6pm.
Price: Day passes are $15 for top rope and boulder for adults; $10 for ages 8 and under for either. Rent both harness and shoes for an additional $7.
Ages: 5 years and up.

ROCKIN' JUMP (Orange County)

(714) 249-7676 / orangecounty.rockinjump.com

1411 S. Village Way, Santa Ana

See ROCKIN' JUMP (San Diego County) (pg. 488) for details and for the attractions. Note that this location does not have a mini golf course, but it has two dodgeball areas, not just one, plus it has a wall hurricane simulator, and a trip wire laser maze. The latter is just like it sounds - a maze thru a web of laser beams that you can roll under, jump over, whatever - as long as you don't touch them - to make it to the other side.

Check the website for info on homeschool hours, special needs jump time, fitness classes, and more. Note that all jumping participants must wear the Rockin' Jump socks - $3.

Hours: Open Mon. - Thurs. - open jump, 3pm - 8pm. Tues. - tots, 9am - 11am, and Neon Jump, 5pm - 8pm. Thurs. - Neon Jump, 5pm - 8pm. Open Fri. - open jump, 3pm - 11pm with Neon Jump, 8pm - 11pm; Sat. - tots 8am - 10am then open jump, 10am - 11 with Neon Jump, 8pm - 11pm; Sun. - open jump, 11am - 8pm with Neon Jump, 5pm - 8pm. Homeschoolers, in particular, are invited to jump Mon. - Thurs., 1pm - 3pm.

Price: $16 for 60 min. of jump time; $25 for 120 min., etc. Tot time is $15 for one parent and child; $3 each additional child, $5 each additional parent. $10 for homeschool jump time. $15 for Neon Jump on Tues., Thurs., and Sun.; $18 on Fri. and Sat.

Ages: 18 months and older, depending on the time and day.

ROCKREATION (Orange County)

(714) 556-ROCK (7625) / www.rockreation.com

1300 Logan Avenue, Costa Mesa

Get the kids geared up - it's time to *rock* out at Rockreation! This huge (12,000 square feet) indoor warehouse/rock climbing gym is devoted mostly to Top Roping, where belayers (i.e. those who hold the rope so if you slip you don't fall) are needed. It's a great place for beginners to learn climbing techniques in a safe and controlled environment and it provides lots of rocky terrain for serious climbers to train. The multi-colored rocks of various shapes and sizes jut out from the twenty-seven-foot geometrical walls for handholds and footholds, offering over 250 different climbing routes. Some of the walls are straight up and down, others have slight inclines, while still others have very challenging angles and overhangs. Even if you were to hit rock bottom (which you won't), it's "carpeted" with black foam padding. A bouldering cave here offers another type of challenge for using climbing technique and strength without ropes.

Belayers are provided when you reserve an hour, or two, of Climb Time. The Time is for those who want to try climbing, but might be unsure, or who need a belayer. Bouldering is for ages 16 and up. Kids Climb is specifically for kids, ages 6 and up. Kids warm up using a short practice wall and then go for it. Although when my boys were younger they were a bit intimidated at first, by the end of our time here, they were really climbing the walls - all the way to the top.

Enroll your child in a summer camp, a climbing league, or one of the year-round classes offered for various levels and ages. A separate party room is available. Waivers are needed for all climbers. Hang out with your kids here, or better yet, tell them to go climb a rock!

Hours: The gym is open Mon., noon - 10pm; Tues. - Thurs., 6am - 10pm; Fri., noon - 10pm; Sat. - Sun., 10am - 6pm. Closed major holidays. Call to reserve Climb Time which is usually offered Sat. - Sun., 1pm - 2pm and 2pm - 3pm. Kids Climb is usually offered Wed. and Fri., 4pm - 6pm.

Price: Day passes, for adult climbers who must pass a test, are $20 for adults; $15 for 11 and under. Seniors, and students with ID, receive a discount. Equipment rental - shoes and harness - is an additional $9. Climb Time is $15 per hour; Kids Climb is $30 for two hours - all equipment is provided for both. Reservations are needed.

Ages: 6 years and up.

ROUND1 BOWLING AND AMUSEMENT (Orange County)

(714) 619-6840 / www.round1usa.com

2800 N. Main Street at Main Place Mall, Santa Ana

See ROUND1 BOWLING AND AMUSEMENT (Los Angeles County) (pg. 38) for details. This location doesn't have darts or ping pong.

Hours: Open Mon. - Sun., 10am - 2am.

Ages: 5 years and up.

SAN CLEMENTE AQUATICS CENTER

(949) 429-8797 / www.san-clemente.org

987 Avenida Vista Hermosa, San Clemente

Located right next to COURTNEY'S SANDCASTLE (pg. 275), this aquatic center sports a competition and recreation pool, as well as a very small, but fun water play structure for little ones in almost zero depth. The colorful structure has a few slides, steps, pipes, and buckets that squirt out water. Lounge chairs on the ample deck are available.

Hours: The rec pool and playground pool are open year round, Mon. - Fri., 1pm - 3pm; Sat. - Sun., noon - 4pm. Check the web calendar for lap swim times.

Price: $4 a day for resident adults, $8 for non-residents; $2 for resident seniors and ages 17 and under, $6 for non-residents.

Ages: 2 years and up.

SCOOTER'S JUNGLE (Orange County)

Aliso Viejo - (949) 349-9090; Placentia - (714) 223-5730 / www.scootersjungle.com

Aliso Viejo - 25 Journey; Placentia - 921 S. Via Rodeo

Grab a vine and swing on over to Scooter's Jungle. The small lobby has a few toys and some fun-house mirrors to keep kids occupied before they enter the main play room. Palm tree murals in the large play room add to the tropical theme ambiance. Your little monkeys will go bananas! There is a huge inflatable bounce structure that is a twenty-foot-high slide; a sport's inflatable for playing basketball, soccer, and volleyball, as well as boxing (with oversized, inflatable gloves) and jousting - very fun!; and a third bounce with a zip-line and place to just play. Each of these bounces rate off the charts with kids. There is also a multi-story play structure with a slide, cargo nets, tunnels and more - for all ages to play. Free air hockey, foosball, and ping pong just make a fun outing funner. Socks are always required.

An adjacent party room has long tables and chairs and a throne for the birthday child. Although Scooter's is mostly open for private parties, there are three ways for the public to come play: 1) ninety-minute, open play for young kids, called Toddler Time, as it's for ages 6 and under, is offered several times during the week; 2) three-hour Family Fun Events, where everyone plays and pizza by the slice may be purchased for an additional $2.50 per slice; 3) All Ages Open Play (exactly what it says) which gives two hours of fun for everyone. Call or check the website for day camp information. Catch jungle fever and visit Scooter's Jungle!

Hours: Most locations have such varied calendars, so check the websites.

Price: All Ages is $10 per child and one adult at Aliso Viejo, $8 at Placentia; extra adults are $5 per at Aliso Viejo, $3 at Placentia. Toddler Playtime is $9 per child and one adult at Aliso Viejo, $7 at Placentia; extra adults are an extra $4 at Aliso Viejo, $2 at Placentia. Family Fun nights are $10 per child.

Ages: 2 years and up, depending on the activity.

SEASCAPE KIDS FUN

(714) 970-7100 / www.seascapekidsfun.com

4771 E. Hunter Avenue, Anaheim

Escape to Seascape, an indoor play area for younger children. With cutely animated sea creature murals in the lobby and actually throughout, the underwater theme carries into the different rooms. The Aquarium Room has fish, shark, and sea turtles swimming on the walls (mostly in various shades of soothing and fun blues) and a super large bounce with obstacle courses, inflatable palm trees, inflatable logs to roll on and over, and areas to bounce. The Beach Ball room is the bomb. Enter the play space, enclosed with netting, and get bombarded by soft foam balls erupting from a fountain in the middle and by being shot at from kids manning the ball guns up above. There is a fun game with balls to play in here, too. Kids can also go up and down this multi-level jungle gym to shoot at someone below, go down the wavy slides, run around, blitz through an obstacle course, cross over a bridge, and more. Foosball and air hockey are free table games offered here. Seascape also has a place for parents to sit in a room that has a playhouse and other toys for younger children. Socks are required for everyone. *Sea* you here!

Hours: Open Play is usually Mon. - Fri., 10am - 6pm; sometimes on Sat. Call, or check the calender on the website as open play hours sometimes fluctuate.

Price: $10 for ages 1 and up; children under 1 are free with one paid admission; adults are free.

Ages: 1 - 14 years

SENDER ONE (Orange County)

(714) 881- 3456 - rock climbing; (714) 881-3386 - Sender City / www.senderoneclimbing.com $$$$
1441 S. Village Way, Santa Ana

Scale new heights, literally, at one of the best, biggest and most innovative climbing gyms I've had the pleasure to "play" at. Sender One, meaning "one who ascends" plus the number one, is creative, clean, colorful and wonderfully designed to encourage the beginner and challenge the more experienced climber. The massive rock climbing room is 25,000 square feet with 108 top ropes and walls that are up to fifty feet high! The central wall sports a huge vertical wave in it while other cavernous walls are built at various angles in and around pillars, arches, cracks, and other inclines. There is a lounge area in the pit, the center of the room, with couches and chairs, etc, and a very relaxed vibe. Walk up the stairs for an overlook of the gym, or to use the exercise bikes up here.

An archway and tunnel connect the top roping side of the gym to the other side, an extensive bouldering element which boasts eighteen-foot high walls and a topout boulder. There is a lot of space and problems to move around and to clamber the walls both vertically and horizontally. The central lounge area works here well, too.

A fantastic and unique feature at Sender One is a separate Sender City room, geared specifically for kids, but so much fun for all ages. Using the hydraulic OnBelay auto device system there are at least ten distinct walls that present different challenges. For instance, one wall has hand and foot holds that are gears so they turn as you climb and another is a fire escape wall has a backdrop that looks like windows and ladders so as you touch particular holds (ladder rungs), the background fire lights up. Another wall has a brick facade with jutting bricks that are the climbing holds, incorporating the Spiderman effect. One very easy route/wall just has smiley cut outs and another is inside a tower with black light holds. Two walls, positioned side-by-side, have rocks on the end of flat levers that pop out. These walls offer three challenges. One is called Chase, where the levers with rocks slap back into the wall behind you as you go up the wall - the knowledge that the holds are disappearing faster and faster and the loud clacking sound they make puts a little motivation in the climb. Another is called Random, where the levers disappear randomly, maybe even while you're stepping or pulling up on them. The last takes teamwork as each person, climbing side-by-side, at each level must push a button for the other person's levers to pop out.

Just a few more great activities to do in Sender City include attaching yourself to a velcro wall (and peeling yourself off); climbing a tower and taking a leap of faith off (while in a harness) to a rope bar or to a padded pole; and holding onto a bar to be lifted up, then let go to go down a long, curved slide. One more that was scary and fun was stepping onto the tops of a series of padded pillars (while harnessed) that gradually get higher and higher, and then jumping off! The entire floor is thickly padded. There are also big padded blocks to play and learn with, as well as bean bags chairs to just hang and relax in. Party rooms are right off this main room. All sessions in Sender City are one hour long, starting on the hour. All participants must weigh at least 35 pounds and those under 14 years old must be accompanied by an adult. Call to make a reservation, although drop ins are welcome if there is space.

Start them young! Kids must be under 35lbs to play in the Toddler Park which has short walls to climb that are decorated with the alphabet and rocks, and plenty of fun foam building blocks to play with.

Sender One also has a separate room for strength training and working out with free weights, weight machines and cardio equipment; a training wall and area to learn belaying using GriGri belay devices; several specific training walls for serious climbers; yoga classes; and a myriad of classes ($39 for an intro to climbing class) including clinics, youth camps, parents night out, climbing teams, and other opportunities. The one-hour Kids Climb in the main gym is a time for kids, ages 5 - 13, to actually learn the ropes of rock climbing - $25. Waivers are required for all climbers. Come to this gym and begin to reach your summit.

Hours: Open Mon. - Fri., 6am - 11pm; Sat., 8am - 10pm; Sun., 8am - 8pm. Sender City is open Mon. - Fri., 10:30am - 8pm; Sat., 9am - 8pm; Sun., 9am - 7pm. Toddler Park is open normal gym hours. Call first to guarantee your spot here. Closed New Year's Day, 4th of July, Thanksgiving and Christmas. Closed early on some other days.

Price: A day pass, which includes climbing, yoga classes and use of the fitness room, is $24 for ages 14 and up, with your own gear; $19 for ages 13 and under. A package rental of shoes, harness and chalk is $7. An hour-long session in Sender City is $24 per person most weekdays (but not in the summer) and $27 on weekends, holidays and summer/school breaks. The Toddler Park is $10.

Ages: 4 years and up.

SKY ZONE (Orange County)

Anaheim - (714) 693-0250; Westminster - (714) 415-5867 / www.skyzone.com $$$$
Anaheim - 1301 N. Kellogg Drive; Westminster - 1025 Westminster Mall at Westminster Mall

See SKY ZONE (Los Angeles County) (pg. 40) for details. The Anaheim location also has a rock wall and a

Warrior Course where you race against a balance beam, ropes, rings, obstacles, and an opponent!

Hours: Anaheim - Open Mon. - Thurs., 2pm - 9pm; Fri., noon - midnight; Sat., 9am - midnight; Sun., 10am - 10pm. Westminster - Open Mon. - Thurs., 2pm - 9pm; Fri., 2pm - 11:30pm; Sat., 10am - 11:30pm; Sun., 10am - 9pm. Open extended hours in the summer and on holidays.

Price: Anaheim - $19 for 60 min.; $22 for 90 min. Westminster - $17 for 60 min., $21 for 90 min. Check the website for specials.

Ages: 2 years and up.

TAC CITY AIRSOFT

(657) 888-6111 / www.taccityairsoft.com
2430 Artesia Avenue, Fullerton

Tac City is in a 30,000 square foot large warehouse. It's nothing fancy or pretty, but who cares? This indoor airsoft battle field is part obstacle course and part maze, with ladders and window cutouts in particle-board walls and buildings which are in various configurations - clumped together and standing separate - to hide behind and tactically maneuver around in order to shoot members of the opposing team. There is also a ladder leading to an overhead walkway. Does it hurt to get hit? I think so, but wearing protective clothing helps and facial protective gear is mandatory, plus the thrill is in the hunting. Join in open games, or get a team together to come play. Waivers must be signed for players 17 years and under. There is an upstairs parent's lounge with chairs and free WiFi.

Hours: Open Mon. - Fri., 5pm - 11pm; Sat. - Sun., 1pm - 10pm. Closed New Year's Eve, New Year's Day, Christmas Eve and Christmas Day.

Price: $15 on weekdays for 1 player, or $20 for 2; $25 on weekends, but $15 on weekends after 7pm. There are lots of specials offered. Bring your own gear or rent it here: full auto M9, $15; full face mask, $5; body armor vest, $5.

Ages: Minimum 10 years old.

THE FACTORY BOULDERING

(714) 639-ROCK (7625) / www.thefactorybouldering.com
1547 W. Struck Avenue, Suite A, Orange

The phrase "you rock" takes on a whole different meaning here with over 11,000 square feet of just bouldering terrain for beginning to advanced climbers with 325 boulder challenges and angles from 85 degree slab to steep cave climbing. Don't be deceived just because the walls aren't as tall as other rock climbing gyms: it's all in the angles, overhangs, and color-coded routes. There are no ropes or belaying - it's navigation, problem solving, technique, and strength. The three walls, with thick padding underneath, are descriptive - the Wave Wall, Slab Wall and Steep Wall, which practically runs the length of the gym, is just that - steep. It also has a small cave. The staff is not only helpful, but they make everyone feel invited, like being part of a community.

A lounge area is centrally placed with couches, benches, free Wi-Fi and a pool table for non-climbers or those needing a break. The Factory also has a fitness area with a treadmill, rower, and weights, plus a campus board and system wall for dedicated climbers seeking to advance in technique. Inquire regarding classes, specials, and events. Ages 17 and under must have a waiver signed by a parent or guardian.

Hours: Open Mon. - Fri., 9am - 11pm; Sat. - Sun., 10am - 9pm.

Price: $18 for adults for a day pass; $16 for college students and ages 18 and under. Mon. - Thurs. before 1pm is only $12 per person. 10 visits (on a prepaid punch card) are $135. Shoe rentals are $4.

Ages: 8 years and up

THRILL IT FUN CENTER

(714) 937-1600 / www.thrillit.com
20 City Boulevard W. at The Outlets at Orange, Orange

In the midst of this outdoor shopping mall, this medium-sized center for kids has a little bit of everything for a thrill, including a mechanical bull ride. Apparently I thought more highly of my hanging-on skills than I ought and of course people are watching! P.S. No skirts or dresses as you will be thrown off the bull at one point or another. The ride is $7 for three minutes. A twenty-one-foot rock climbing wall with auto belay and three levels of difficulty is $7 for five minutes. Look up! Several short, safe yet adventurous, high ropes challenges are right above patrons' heads. Participants wear harnesses as they start from platforms then walk on and across multiple ropes courses - $9 for ten minutes. The Area 51-themed, two-story, laser tag arena has black lights, numerous partitions to hide behind, and murals of planets on the walls - $9 for ten minutes. Ballocity is a decent-sized, colorful, three-level, interactive play area. Its centerpiece is a plethora of foam balls that kids shoot out of several cannons and ball blasters, located on all the levels, at other kids. Ballocity also has padded obstacle courses, cargo nets, tunnels, huge balls, fast slides, and lots of other fun elements - $12 for all day play. Thrill It also has a few arcade games, tables and chairs in the center of all the activity stations for easy viewing (and to relax), and private party rooms.

The mall has lots of other fun things to do, see, shop and eat. See VANS SKATE PARK (pg. 269) for another fun outing and more details regarding The Outlets.

Hours: Open Mon. - Thurs., 1pm - 9pm (Ballocity and arcades open at 10am); Fri., 1pm - 10pm (Ballocity and arcades open at 10am); Sat., 10am - 11pm; Sun., 10am - 8pm. Open longer on school holidays and summer. Closed Christmas.

Price: Prices listed above. Package deals are a good deal cheaper.

Ages: 4 years and up, depending on the activity.

VANS SKATE PARK

(714) 769-3800 / www.vans.com/skateparks-orange.html
20 City Boulevard West, Orange

Wow! Awesome! Incredible! And these were just the first few words out of my boys' mouths. This part-indoor, part-outdoor skate park at this outdoor mall has 46,000 square feet of wooden ramps, concrete bowls, a Combi pool, half-pipes, pro and outdoor street courses, mini and vert ramps, and more, all at a mega mall. Rollerbladers and skateboarders, and cyclists can all use the park at various times. It is a training "camp" for competitors as well as a practice place for enthusiasts of all levels. Beginners and Pee Wee skaters have certain areas that have scaled-down elements just for them. Observers can sit anywhere on the multi-level stadium seats that semi-surround the main skate area. Our first few times here we just watched before my older boys actually ventured out on the ramps, and then they were off! Participants under 18 must have a waiver signed by a parent or legal guardian. Waivers are available online. An attached pro-shop hawks Vans brand merchandise and everything that a skateboarder needs and wants. It also provides rentals of helmets, knee pads, and elbow pads, all of which are mandatory. There is also a small arcade inside.

The over 120 stores and fun restaurants at The Outlets include THRILL IT FUN CENTER (pg. 268); DAVE & BUSTER'S (Orange County) (pg. 259); BUILD-A-BEAR WORKSHOP (Orange County) (pg. 315); Cafe Tu Tu Tango (an art-themed restaurant, often with artists painting here); Johnny Rockets (a 50's themed diner); Lucky Strike, an upscale bowling alley with billiard tables and more; and an AMC Theaters, with an IMAX and 3-D theater.

Hours: Open for skateboarding Mon., Wed. and Fri., 10am - 10pm; Tues. and Thurs., 10am - 6pm; Sat., 10am - 10pm; Sun., 10am - 5pm. It is open for BMX only, Tues. and Thurs., 6pm - 10pm; Sun., 5pm - 9pm. Closed Christmas.

Price: Free

Ages: 3 years and up to watch; 7 years and up to participate.

WE PLAY LOUD

Huntington Beach - (949) 328-9616; Lake Forest - (949) 328-9616 / www.weplayloud.com
Huntington Beach - 7470 Edinger Avenue; Lake Forest - 24350 Swartz Drive

Playing loud is one of the things that kids do best, isn't it?! This wonderful, 12,000 square foot indoor playground has padded floors and is bright and colorful (lots of pinks, blues and greens) and encourages fun. A two-story play structure has an obstacle course; a ball machine in the middle of one area that gently shoots out foam balls; an enclosed twisty slide; side-by-side slide racers; webbed netting bridges; and play panels, plus a small separate area with big balls to throw, catch and bounce on top of, and a bounce house. There is floor space here and wonderful and unique stand-alone play objects to play on (some of them move!), like a mini airplane to board and pilot; a small boat; a friendly octopus; a coconut tree with balls hanging down to sit and swing on, that spins around; and an inflatable, spaceship-looking piece. A gated, spacious area, for toddlers only, has animal-shaped toys and short things to climb on and over; a little ball pit; big foam blocks; a train with some fabric tunnels; slides; rocking creatures; and lots more. No outside food is allowed in. There is a cafe with beverages and pre-packaged snacks available. Socks are required for all guests.

Hours: Open daily, 10am - 6pm.

Price: $15 for the first adult and child for 2 hours of play; each additional child, or adult, is $7.

Ages: 51" and under.

WE ROCK THE SPECTRUM KIDS GYM (Orange County)

(949) 337-1049 / www.werockthespectrumkidsgym.com
23572 Moulton Parkway Unit 102-104, Laguna Hills

See WE ROCK THE SPECTRUM KIDS GYM (Los Angeles County) (pg. 44) for details.

Hours: Open Mon. - Sat., 9am - 7pm; Sun., 9am - 6pm
Price: $12 per child; $10 for siblings; adults are free. An all-day pass is $20, which allows you in and out privileges of the facility.
Ages: 6 months - 10 years.

—GREAT OUTDOORS—

ADVENTURE PLAYGROUND / UNIVERSITY COMMUNITY PARK

(949) 724-6818 / www.cityofirvine.org
1 Beech Tree Lane, Irvine

Let the adventures begin! Located within University Community Park is the completely gated Adventure Playground, which is staffed. The playground space is multi-level and has engaging elements to encourage kids to creatively play in an unstructured environment all in various grounding of recycled rubber, dirt, and mulch/bark. An open portion just has some wooden poles sticking out of the ground. Just because. There are giant Lego blocks available to build here, plus oddly-shaped pieces (some with flexible hoses and holes), and big dump trucks and diggers for the adjacent sand area. In another favorite area pump water out onto the ground and into the small dirt creek creating, yes, mud. Let the kids get down and dirty in this little mud hole and mud creek lined with tall grasses and a few huge rocks. There is a station to wash off, so bring a towel and change of clothing. There are also a few water play tables.

The generously-sized, wooden, fort playground has several structures with some high towers; enclosed and open slides; bridges; cargo nets; climbing ropes, climbing poles, and climbing walls; and much more. Concrete slides; a sensory garden (which looks like a meditation maze in design); a huge art wall (paint and paint brushes provided); shaded picnic tables; other games like a ping pong table, fusbol, giant checkers and chess; and gravel and concrete pathways throughout add to making this a kids' happy place.

University Community Park is a spacious grassy park with a non-muddy playground that has free-standing climbing rocks, ropes, slides, abstract ladders, standing/spinning discs and more, plus lighted sports areas of a basketball court, handball court, sand volleyball courts, tennis courts, a baseball diamond, and open areas for field sports. The library is right next door.

Hours: Adventure Playground is open March - Oct., daily, 10am - 6pm; Nov. - Feb., daily, 10am - dusk. Closed New Year's Day, Easter, Thanksgiving, and Christmas. University Park is open daily, 6am - 10pm.
Price: Free
Ages: 2 years and up.

ALISO AND WOOD CANYONS WILDERNESS PARK

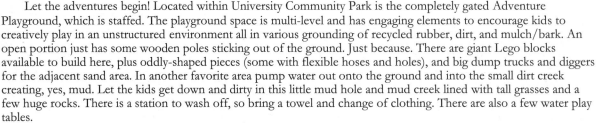

(949) 923-2200; (949) 923-2201 / www.ocparks.com
28373 Alicia Parkway, Laguna Niguel

This regional park has about 4,000 acres of wilderness sanctuary and thirty miles of trails to explore by hiking or biking. You and your child will see everything that patience allows - coastal sage, chaparral, oak woodlands, open grassland meadows, canyons, and creeks, plus possibly wildlife such as deer, possums, coyotes and lizards.

Start at the visitor center, pick up a map and look at the interpretive exhibits area before you hit the trails. This huge park is like life, offering many paths to choose from. Take a trail from here into the adjacent Laguna Niguel Regional Park; ride the twelve-mile Aliso Creek Bikeway, which basically follows along Alicia Parkway; or choose from several other hiking trails inside the park. We walked the Aliso Trail. Note that there is also a small picnic area at the trailhead. The first part is wide, paved and rather bland, scenically speaking. As we reached the dirt pathway and went into the hills, the terrain and scenery became much more interesting. (Strollers and bikes can go here, but it does get a bit bumpy. Cyclists under 18 must wear helmets.) Note that this trail can be very busy on weekends.

There are numerous caves, or overhangs, throughout the park. A few are open to the public. Past the Nature Center, or Gate 2, is Cave Rock. Kids enjoy climbing up into Cave Rock, and sliding back down. Further back on the trail, is Dripping Cave, also called - and this has much more kid-appeal - Robbers Cave. Legend has it that bandits used this cave as a hideout after a robbery! At one time the holes inside supposedly had wooden pegs to hold their saddle bags, and bags of booty. Tell this to your kids and let their imaginations take over. Now, it's a resting place. If you have the time and energy, keep on going to Coyote Run, deeper into the heart of the park, with more hills to climb, or go all the way to the 13.9 loop trail to and thru ALTA LAGUNA PARK (pg. 271). Tip: Bring water!

Hours: The park is open daily, 7am - sunset.
Price: $3 per vehicle, or park across the street for free.
Ages: 2 years and up.

ALTA LAGUNA PARK

(949) 497-0711 / www.lagunabeachcity.net

3299 Alta Laguna Blvd, Laguna Beach

  The park on a hilltop makes it almost feel like you're at the top of the world, almost. The park has a baseball field, six tennis courts, a half basketball court, picnic tables and a playground with twisty slides, bridges, a rock climbing wall, cargo net and more all in a sand base. All this and an ocean view to boot. The park also gives access to, and is a trail head for, a 13.9 loop trail that goes to and thru ALISO AND WOOD CANYONS WILDERNESS PARK (pg. 270).

Hours: Open 5am - 1pm. The trail closes at sunset.

Price: Free

Ages: All

AROVISTA PARK / BREA SKATE PARK

(714) 990-7103 / www.ci.brea.ca.us

500 West Imperial Highway at Berry Street, Brea

  The park has baseball diamonds, two lighted basketball courts, sand volleyball courts, an amphitheater, a playground, soccer and football fields, and open grassy areas with picnic tables and barbecues. The 10,000-square-foot cement skate park has a kidney pool, pyramid, table top, quarter-pipes, rails, and street section. Skateboarders and rollerbladers only - no bikes allowed. Spectators are welcome to gather 'round and watch the show. Wearing a helmet and knee and elbow pads is strictly enforced.

Hours: The skate park is open daily, 7am - dusk. The park is open daily, 7am - 10pm.

Price: Free

Ages: All

ATLANTIS PLAY CENTER

(714) 892-6015 / www.ci.garden-grove.ca.us; www.ggparksandrec.com

13630 Atlantis Way, Garden Grove

  This "lost island" park is quite a find. Atlantis Play Center is a wonderful, large, enclosed play area for kids of all ages that has been around for over 50 years! Several, different, aquatic-themed playgrounds are scattered around the park that feature slides, tubes, swings, sand pits, grassy expanses, and big, concrete aquatic creatures to play on, like whales and sharks. The sea serpent slide is a favorite. The green rolling hills are perfect for picnicking. Numerous shade trees make the park surprisingly cool, even in the heat of the summer. One of my boys' favorite things to do when they were younger was to play in and amongst the bushes that go around the perimeter of the park. The bushes become hideouts, forts, a pirate's landing, or whatever - a little imagination goes a long way!

  To keep even cooler, run around in the wonderful water-play area with colorful marine sea creatures that squirt out water and fountains that shoot up at random times encased by a sitting area that gets wet. The surrounding walkway has other fun water elements, like an extremely long pelican head and shorter sea dragons that spew out water, plus more ground fountains and artsy-looking bars with water coming out.

  Check the city website calendar for the several events held here throughout the year. Note that a full-service snack bar is open here daily during the summer, only. Also note that just outside Atlantis is Garden Grove Park, with more play equipment and wide open grassy areas.

Hours: Open most of the year, Tues. - Fri., 10am - 2pm; Sat., 10am - 4pm; Sun., noon - 4pm. Open in the summer, Tues. - Sat., 10am - 4pm; Sun., noon - 4pm. Closed Mon. and most major holidays. The water park element is open June - August, only.

Price: $2 for ages 3 and older (cash only); children 2 and under are free. Adults are not admitted without a child.

Ages: 1½ - 12 years.

BEEBE PARK / MISSION VIEJO SKATE PARK

(949) 470-3061 / www.cityofmissionviejo.org

24190 Olympiad Road, Mission Viejo

  This 9.8-acre sports park also sports the "latest" in sports - a skateboard (and in-line skates') park. The 9,000-square-foot unsupervised concrete park has bowls, a vert wall, bauer box, rails, spine, pyramid, hips, steps, and ramps. Helmet and elbow and knee pads are required. Other park amenities include a lighted soccer/football field, lighted baseball diamond, a sand volleyball court, playgrounds, short walking trails, and picnic tables.

Hours: Open daily, 8am - dusk.

Price: Free

Ages: All

BLUEBIRD PARK

(949) 497-0716 / www.lagunabeachcity.net; www.funorangecountyparks.com

798 Bluebird Canyon Blvd. / (730ish) Cress Street, Laguna Beach

   Walk through the decorated gates to see for yourself that the bluebird of (park) happiness has landed on this nicely-landscaped park with imaginative play equipment. One structure is comprised of ropes, knobs, poles, rock-climbing walls and artistic-looking structures - they can be whatever you want them to be. Blast off in an adjacent, really tall, multi-story, rocket ship with an enclosed metal slide. Climb over, under, and on a good-sized, metal, half-spherical object.

   Another sand-based, younger-kids-oriented playground is just up the steps that has slides, swings (and toddler swings), and more colorful, fun apparatus. Two short tunnels (through rocks) and a little wooden bridge are located in this area, too.

   A spacious grassy lawn has trees and benches around its perimeter, plus an older, half basketball court. The southern end features a large, brilliantly-colored mosaic turtle to ride, plus picnic tables and BBQ grills. One side of the lawn also has steps up it that connect kids to several slides that whoosh down the short hillside.

   The bathroom, which looks like a stone cottage, has a Boys and Girls Club perched above it. Every element of this park adds up to a welcoming atmosphere and fun play times.

Hours: Open daily, sunrise - sunset.

Price: Free

Ages: All

BOLSA CHICA ECOLOGICAL RESERVE

(714) 846-1114 - interpretative center; (714) 840-1575 - tour info / www.bolsachica.org

17851 Pacific Coast Highway, Huntington Beach

   This 300-acre, saltwater wetland reserve is home to a variety of plant and waterfowl such as avocets, egrets, plovers, sand pipers, ducks, and terns. We also saw herons, and a few brown pelicans that swooped down to scoop up fish. Bird lovers should bring binoculars. The nesting and breeding islands are protected by a chain-link fence. You may, however, cross over the wooden bridge to walk along an easy and stroller-friendly, mile-and-a-half trail that loops through the reserve, and partially along the highway. No bikes or dogs are allowed. My little explorers especially liked walking down to inspect the water and its inhabitants, a little closer than I felt comfortable with. Free, guided tours are given the second Saturday of every month from 10am - noon.

   A small Interpretative Center is housed in a trailer on the corner of the reserve, at 3842 Warner Avenue and Pacific Coast Highway. Inside are local ecology displays such as pictures of birds in the area, a rattlesnake skin, taxidermy animals (opossums, and birds), a touch table, a salt water aquarium with native species (stars, sea cucumbers, fish, etc.), and live snakes, lizards and spiders, plus information panels on the value of wetlands. Come see the animals being fed and learn about them and their habitats every Saturday from noon - 1pm. There are also numerous science and marine-based education programs, some with labs, offered here for students/people of all ages, for $5 per. Interested in helping take care of this area? Clean-ups are held the second Sunday and last Saturday of each month, where volunteers, as young as 6 years old, pick up trash and remove nonnative plants from 9am - noon. Note: For more fun in the sun, BOLSA CHICA STATE BEACH (pg. 242) is directly across the street from the reserve.

Hours: The Reserve is open daily, 6am - 8pm. The Center is open daily, 9am - 4pm.

Price: Free

Ages: All

BOMMER CANYON / QUAIL TRAIL

(949) 724-6835 / www.cityofirvine.org; www.letsgooutside.org

Community Park - 11 Bommer Canyon Rd.; Trailhead - 6400 Shady Canyon Dr.; Quail Hill Trailhead - 34 Shady Canyon Dr.

   Bommer Canyon was once part of the Irvine Ranch Cattle Camp and the cattle camp area, with some of its original structures, like the water tower, is available to rent.

   Some of the adjacent trails, lined with oak and sycamore groves (but there really isn't a lot of shade), rock outcroppings, and even a few bridges, are open for hiking, mountain biking and horse-back riding, while several more are open only for docent-led "tours" due to sensitive habitat. Open trails include the paved 2.8 mile Shady Canyon bike trail, which leads up to the 1.8 mile Quail Hill Loop and down to the 1.3 mile Quail Trail. (There is a Quail Hill Community Park, too, with some basketball courts, baseball diamonds, picnic tables, and playground.) Or, go another direction and take the 2 mile Turtle Ridge Trail, then the Community trail for another .8 miles to reach a vista point. The more immediate Bommer Nature Loop (which doesn't loop) is only .7 miles. Also look up COASTAL PEAK

PARK (pg. 274), LAGUNA COAST WILDERNESS PARK / LITTLE SYCAMORE CANYON STAGING AREA / NIX NATURE CENTER (pg. 285), and TURTLE ROCK PARK and NATURE CENTER (pg. 297) since these areas and trails interconnect and intersect.

Hours: Open daily 7am - sunset.
Price: Free
Ages: 3 years and up.

BOYSEN PARK and ANAHEIM TENNIS CENTER

(714) 765-5155 - park; (714) 991-9090 - tennis center / www.anaheim.net; www.anaheimtenniscenter.com
971 S. State College Boulevard, Anaheim

Take off to this park with a main attraction at the small playground being a large red, white, and blue cement airplane. The wings are tipped just enough so kids can climb up on them (wingwalkers!) and into the instrumentless cockpit. The other featured play structures are a real blast - one is a really tall space ship (the other is a shorter one) to climb up into with slides coming out from them, and ramps and a rock walls - the sky's the limit. There is also an independent rock wall rock, a dome climbing structure, swings and little plane vehicles to sit in and rock back and forth.

Other park amenities include picnic tables, baseball fields, and sand volleyball courts. The adjacent schoolyard, available to use when school is not in session, has basketball courts, a few scattered playgrounds, and more baseball diamonds. The park wraps around the Anaheim Tennis Center. Get in the swing of things by playing on one of the Center's twelve lighted courts and/or the ball-machine court.

Hours: The park is open daily, sunrise - sunset. The Tennis Center is open Mon. - Fri., 7am - 10pm; Sat. - Sun., 7am - 6pm.
Price: The park is free. Call for hourly tennis court fees.
Ages: All for the park.

BROOKHURST COMMUNITY PARK / ANAHEIM WEST SKATEPARK

(714) 765-5263 or (714) 765-3373 or (714) 765-5155 / www.anaheim.net; www.socalskateparks.com
2271 W. Crescent Avenue, Anaheim

Baseball diamonds, a basketball court, a few picnic tables, mature shade trees, and barbecue pits are here, but more importantly, your kids can come to this park and walk on the moon. Crater Park, our nickname for it, resembles the surface of the moon with crater-shaped areas that contain play equipment such as swings, a small rock climbing wall, and several older-style metal climbing structures. Wood chips cover the play area ground. Alien-looking white shapes are plopped in clusters, while a few long, curvy, white, raised cement walkways (which look like open-top tunnels) - complete with arches and holes - interconnect the play areas. This is a great area for tag and hide-and-go-seek. Being here almost eclipses playing at other parks, but I will also say it is a bit run down.

The enclosed, 10,000 square-foot skatepark that is in the park has a six-foot deep concrete pool, steps, grinding rails, planters, and other street elements. Although it is not supervised, wearing protective gear - helmet, knee pads, and elbow pads - is required in the skate park and is often enforced (and ticketed if riders aren't doing so) by local police and security.

Hours: The park is open daily, sunrise - sunset. The skate park is open daily, 10am - dusk.
Price: Free
Ages: 2 years and up

CARBON CANYON REGIONAL PARK

(714) 973-3160 or (714) 973-3162 / www.ocparks.com
4442 Carbon Canyon Road, Brea

Talk about recreational opportunities! Carbon Canyon is 124 acres big and offers everything for the sports-minded and fun-loving family. There are eight lighted tennis courts, three sand volleyball courts, horseshoe pits, softball fields, a huge open field for whatever other sport you feel like playing, plenty of picnic areas scattered throughout the park, tons of run-around space with huge shade trees in abundance, and five great playgrounds that are kind of grouped together. The playgrounds alone are worth visiting the park. Based in sand, a few of them are huge and offer lot of slides, covered platforms, animals on large springs, intricate climbing apparatus, swings, learning stations, bridges, and a series of metal and chain ladders.

A good-sized butterfly garden with lots and lots of birdhouses (have the kids count them) among a shady grove of trees, is located just by the trail head. Hikers and cyclists can take this hard-packed dirt nature trail (very wilderness-like), which is not good for strollers, 1.1 miles to the ten-acre Redwood Grove. Equestrians can ride here or even take a trail that accesses the adjoining Chino Hills State Park. The beautiful four-acre lake in the middle of the park has two, short fishing piers. A license is required for ages 16 and up. Bring sunscreen and food, and have a great day.

Hours: Open November through March daily, 7am - 6pm. Open April through October, 7am - 9pm.
Price: $3 per vehicle Mon. - Fri.; $5 on Sat. - Sun.; $7 on some holidays.
Ages: All

CARL THORNTON PARK

(714) 571-4200 or (714) 647-5400 / www.ci.santa-ana.ca.us
1801 W. Segerstrom Avenue, Santa Ana

The front part of this park is a huge open area, with some trees interspersed, as well as a small playground. A small creek runs through this area, ending in a big pond that attracts a lot of ducks, geese, and sea gulls. (Don't get goosed by the geese!) For your sporting pleasure, there are also three baseball diamonds.

At the northeast corner of the park, accessible by pathways and beyond the basketball court, is a large playground that has stone turrets, giving it a castle-like setting. Some of the fun elements include playful dino statues; enclosed tube slides coming from the castle walls; a free-standing climbing rock; and a rock climbing tower attached to a huge play structure with slides and bridges and a DNA-looking climbing ladder. There are also two little ship-like structures with short slides and more for little kids.

Hours: Open daily, 10am - 10pm.
Price: Free
Ages: All

CEDAR GROVE PARK

(714) 573-3326 / www.tustinca.org
11385 Pioneer Road, Tustin

This park has play equipment for all ages, including two half-basketball courts (which don't equal a whole) and two grassy, volleyball courts. Starting at the parking lot, follow the winding pathway to the nature-themed play area with a large cement frog and a huge snake that wraps around rocks for kids to climb on, in and over. The rest of the playground has some shaded, elevated platforms that interconnect via short tunnels and bridges, all with slides, interactive play boards, short rock climbing walls, and talking tubes. Plenty of picnic tables line the playground's pathway. Towards the back is a fitness area with man-powered machines that can offer a genuine workout.

The huge, adjacent grassy area has numerous cedar trees around its perimeter, and a pathway all the way around. Next to this is a grove of shady pine trees with picnic tables nestled underneath. The park also has a trail that connects to PETERS CANYON REGIONAL PARK (pg. 291).

Hours: Open daily, sunrise - sunset.
Price: Free
Ages: All

CENTENNIAL REGIONAL PARK

(714) 571-4200 or (714) 571-4254 / www.ci.santa-ana.ca.us
3000 W. Edinger Avenue, Santa Ana

Good-sized lakes stocked with carp and other fish, plus ducks, scattered large rocks, shade trees, barbeques, picnic tables, gently rolling green hills, and two play structures - one in ship-shape (or the shape of a ship) and the other with slides, bridges, swings, metal climbing structures, and talking tubes - make this park a fun family destination. At more than seventy acres, Centennial also boasts a skatepark with all the street elements, baseball diamonds, basketball court, fields for soccer or football, and paved hiking/biking trails within the park's boundaries.

Hours: Open daily, 8am - 10pm.
Price: Free
Ages: All

COASTAL PEAK PARK

(949) 644-3151 - Coastal Peak Park; (714) 508-4757 - Irvine Ranch Conservancy / www.newportbeachca.gov; www.letsgooutside.org; www.ocparks.com
20403 East Coastal Peak, Newport Beach

The Coastal Peak Park is a winner on so many levels. One is the playground. And one of the playground's best feature is the big, Spiderman-like rope web/climbing structure - way fun. Other elements include fairly tall slides on a raised platform that leaves play space underneath; two huge fake rocks for climbing and imaginative play; poles with disc to sit and spin; other climbing components; seats (or whatever) that lend themselves to creative play on the sea-blue recycled rubber flooring; swings; little vehicles; diggers in the sand; and attached short walls with interactive dials and games. The park also features a basketball court, baseball fields, cement picnic tables and benches, shade trees, and plenty of grassy areas for running around and to use as soccer fields.

This is also a major access point for the almost 7,000 acres and forty miles of Laguna Coast Wilderness Park via the Pacific Ridge Trailhead. (See LAGUNA COAST WILDERNESS PARK / LITTLE SYCAMORE CANYON STAGING AREA / NIX NATURE CENTER (pg. 285) for more info.) Take in the incredible on-top-of-the-world scenery - on a clear day you can see forever. The several trails lead off in different directions - some go opposite ways on ridges up and along the mountaintop (i.e. the Bommer Ridge Trail); another, Boomer Canyon trail, leads up the mountain (and under the freeway to go further up); others leads directly down the mountain surrounded by oak, sycamore, coast scrub, flowers, and other vegetation and mountain vistas, with wooden railings along one side; and others, one which is fairly direct, go down to the beach and hiking area at Crystal Cove State Beach. See CRYSTAL COVE STATE PARK (pg. 277) for more information. Some of the trails/fire roads are hard-packed dirt so they are popular for hikers, bikers, and parents with strollers, while the more mountainous routes tend to have ruts, rocks, and lots of hills. See the websites for detailed trail maps.

Hours: Open daily, 7am - sunset.
Price: Free
Ages: All

COLONEL BILL BARBER MARINE CORPS MEMORIAL PARK

(949) 724-6714 / www.cityofirvine.org; www.funorangecountyparks.com
4 Civic Center Plaza, Irvine

I salute the outstanding, patriotic-themed, huge playground at this forty-two acre park. Ramps connect most of the three separate play areas with their numerous platforms and play structures, make them accessible for everyone. Equipment includes slides, metal climbing apparatus, tunnels, raised sand (or water) basins, little play houses, and swings, plus places to play on, through and under the playgrounds. Nearby are walkways and a garden area that surrounds a fountain where city celebrations are held.

Besides the playgrounds, other huge draws to the park include a main baseball stadium, three lighted softball diamonds (and three soccer overlay fields), two concession stands, batting cages, six lighted tennis courts, open run-around areas, and lots of picnic tables and barbecue pits.

Hours: Open daily, sunrise - 9pm.
Price: Free
Ages: All

COURTNEY'S SANDCASTLE

(949) 361-8264 / www.courtneyssandcastle.com
987 Avenida Vista Hermosa, San Clemente

The central, multi-story, universally-accessible, castle-themed play structure is huge!! I love it. It features so many fun and unique components: ramps; bridges; towers and turrets; multiple slides; several rock climbing-type walls; poles; gears; play space under the castle; educational activity boards (one with music keys so you can actually play songs); rope ladders; and more. A smaller play area here is ship themed with masts, low portholes, speaking tubes, slides, ramps and activity panels. The playground also features several swing sets, with swings for all abilities; a sand play area with raised sand basins, digger toys, and a dragon to sit on; free-standing tall and wide rocks to climb on and climb through its holes; run-around space; a xylophone; a lovely sensory garden with plants and a floating granite water sphere; boulders just plunked around; and shaded picnic tables in the center of it all. There is a also a raised, interactive, rock-lined, simulated touch tank (with real water). All of it is enclosed.

A ¼ mile trail loops around an adjacent park. Just next door is the SAN CLEMENTE AQUATICS CENTER (pg. 266) with a water playground for kids.

Hours: Open daily, 6am - 10pm.
Price: Free
Ages: 1 - 12

CRAIG REGIONAL PARK

(714) 973-3180 / www.ocparks.com

3300 N. State College Boulevard, Fullerton

    Much of these 124 acres are hilly and woodsy, blessed with lots of mature pine, oak, alder, and sycamore trees, lending it a peaceful ambiance. Holidays, however, can be extremely busy here, so it's not so peaceful. The playground in the upper area, near one parking area, has slides and animals on oversized springs to ride on. A cement pathway - great for walking and biking - meanders all throughout the park, leading down and through much of the park's rolling hills and alongside the year-round creeks (water play time - whether or not you want your kids to!). Besides other playgrounds, including one for older kids with steeper slides, there are picnic gazebos, baseball diamonds, volleyball courts, horseshoe pits, basketball courts, racquetball courts, and a lake. Fishing is allowed in the 3-acre lake, but it isn't stocked so bring your wiggliest worms. Ages 16 and up must have a fishing license.

Hours: Open April through October daily, 7am - 9pm. Open November through March daily, 7am - 6pm.

Price: $3 per vehicle Mon. - Fri.; $5 on Sat. - Sun.; $7 on some holidays.

Ages: All

CREEKSIDE PARK

(949) 248-3530 or (949) 248-3500 / www.danapoint.org

25743 Stonehill Drive, Dana Point

    A favorite! This attractive park has several reasons that make it so great. A large wooden (so, rustic-looking) playground has separate, spread out, components all based in wood chips. These include monkey "bars" (that are rings); a small, shaded wooden seat that glides horizontally across a pole; a chain bridge (on the ground) with curvy metal hand railings; a tire swing; other swings; a balance beam; and a legit, really good-sized curved, bouldering wall with hand and foot holds and a little cave, plus a sign that explains exactly how to climb effectively. A multi-story play structure has slides, steps, twisty poles, a rope ladder, a small tunnel and three short, side-by-side racing slides. There are a few other, smaller, play structures, too, with vehicles to ride on; assorted shapes to simply play on; mini play houses in sand and a digger toy; a seesaw; a train-shaped play structure for littler ones; a wooden fort; and more. All around are benches, a few picnic tables, mature shade trees, landscaping, and grassy areas.

    Walk further into the park as it narrows to reach the half basketball court, then along the paved trail that leads pretty far back to the end, over bridges, through several more grassy spots, and picnic tables. A paved walking/bike trail - the San Juan Creek Trail - parallels the San Juan "creek" and passes by the park.

Hours: Open daily, 6am - 10pm

Price: Free

Ages: 1 - 12 years.

CROWN VALLEY COMMUNITY PARK

(949) 425-5100 / www.cityoflagunaniguel.org

29751 Crown Valley Parkway, Laguna Niguel

    This prince of a park is worthy of a crown as it has something that will appeal to each member of your family. A network of trails wind through the eighteen-acre hillside Niguel Botanical Preserve. Some of the trails are cement, and therefore stroller-friendly (although uphill), and some are dirt paths with wooden steps. Enjoy beautiful landscaping, shade trees, evergreen forest, children's garden with a small maze and a fort, and benches along the hike up to the picturesque viewpoint where, at the top, a labyrinth awaits as does a small butterfly garden and cactus garden.

    At the base of the hill, two playgrounds have woodsy themes - one is smaller and geared for young children, another is larger, for older kids. Both have fake trees on poles, fort platforms that interconnect with short bridges, plus fake rocks to climb on, climbing apparatus, twisty slides (one really tall one!), play space beneath the structures, and a large animal statues to play on. Next to the playgrounds is a gated sprayground with wildly colored poles of all sizes and shapes spurting and pouring out water, as well as some in-ground fountains randomly shooting up gentle water jets, and some other fun elements. Numerous picnic tables are scattered throughout the park. Summer concerts are given on an outdoor stage with tiered seating on a grassy hill. At the top of another hill is a soccer field and baseball field.

    Between the park office and the adjacent Y.M.C.A. is a regulation-size swimming pool that is open year round to the public and for swim meets. Diving competitions also take place on the two low diving boards, two high dives, and a (really high) diving platform. Cement stadium seats are on one side of the pool. The canopy-covered wading pool is great for your little tadpoles. Finally, a three-quarter-mile bike path here connects to Laguna Niguel Regional Park. This park is a crown jewel in Laguna Niguel.

Hours: The park is open daily, dawn to dusk. The pool is open for public swim sessions year round, Mon. - Fri., 9am - noon and 1pm - 4pm; Sat. - Sun., noon - 4pm. It's open in the summer Mon. - Fri., 1pm - 4pm; Sat. - Sun., noon - 5pm. The sprayground is open Memorial Day - Labor Day daily, 10am - 5pm. It's open on weekends in September and October (weather permitting), and sometimes on spring break, 10am - 4pm. The park is closed on city holidays.

Price: Free to the park and the sprayground. Swim sessions are $4 for adults; $3 for seniors and children 2 - 13.

Ages: All

CRYSTAL COVE STATE PARK

(949) 494-3539 - beach; (949) 497-7647 - guided field trips; (800) 444-7275 - camping reservations / $$$
www.crystalcovestatepark.com; www.parks.ca.gov; www.reserveamerica.com; www.crystalcovecottages.com
8471 N. Coast Highway, Laguna Beach

This expansive state park is a combination of 2,400-acres of largely undeveloped park land that encompasses everything from coastal and canyon areas on one side of the freeway, and three-and-a-half miles of beach on the other side.

The 3.5 miles of rocky and sandy shoreline has seven small coves, surf, sand, numerous tidepools and an underwater park in the offshore waters that is popular with scuba and skin divers. A paved, moderate hiking/biking trail goes along the eighty-foot bluff top and through the coastal sage scrub and dunes. There are restrooms and playgrounds along the way. Activity and relaxation - both are opportunities to commune with nature. Day use at Moro Canyon offers beach access and picnic tables, too. Camping with a beach view is available at Moro Campground for tent and RV's.

Want to explore and learn more? Take a guided field trip. Choose from programs that include tidepool exploration, whale migration, endangered species, and marine debris, plus ecology of Crystal Cove which incorporates a moderate backcountry 3-mile loop trail hike. The fee is $2.50 per student for up to 60 classroom students and 40 homeschool students. Programs incorporate curriculum, hands-on exploration, games, music and fun.

The backcountry, mountain side of the park, has numerous, and fairly strenuous, hilly, multi-use trails - hiking, mountain biking, and equestrian. One such trail is the Moro Canyon Trail, with various offshoots making it anywhere from five to almost twenty miles, which is especially pretty in the spring time when the wildflowers are blooming. Reference COASTAL PEAK PARK (pg. 274) for more trail info and free parking. Bring water!! Environmental camping - meaning whatever you backpack in, you take out - is a rugged three-mile hiking adventure to reach the three campgrounds - Lower Moro (in a canyon) and Upper Moro and Deer Canyon at higher elevations. No open fires are allowed. There are also sixty campsites at the southern end of the park. Parking is at Moro Canyon behind El Morro School at 8681 N. Coast Highway. Maps are available at the ranger station here.

From the Los Trancos parking lot there is a pedestrian tunnel under the highway that leads to the Beachcomber restaurant and to the beach. The twenty-one cottages down here, originally built in the 1920's to 1930's, are available for rent. If interested, go to the cottages website at 8am on the first of each month for seven months in advance - they fill up quickly.

Hungry? The oceanfront Beachcomber, open daily from 7am to 9:30pm, serves upscale meals - breakfast, lunch, and dinner. The indoor/outdoor restaurant, with a train set and station displayed in the dining room, can be reached at (949) 376-6900 / www.thebeachcombercafe.com. Three-hour parking validation, thus entry to the beach, with a purchase of $15 or more, is included. Walk from Los Trancos parking lot or pay $1.50 for a one-way shuttle ride. (Kids 12 and under are free.) You can also grab a bite at Ruby's Crystal Cove Shake Shack which serves eggs, oatmeal and pancakes for breakfast and sandwiches, hamburgers, hot dogs, soups and fries for lunch, across the way at 7703 E. Coast Highway, (949) 464-0100. This little "shack" also offers up a tasty selection of almost 30 shake choices including chocolate chip cookie dough, mocha, oreo, date, orangesicle, and peanut butter cup. There are a few benches and tables here, too, overlooking the ocean for a vista of the shoreline and beyond. It's open daily, 7am to 7pm; sometimes later in the summer.

Hours: The park is open daily, 6am - sunset. Closed Thanksgiving and Christmas.

Price: $15 per vehicle for day use. Primitive camp sites are $25 a night; other camping is $50; and RV's are $75 - all require an $8 reservation fee.

Ages: All

DEERFIELD COMMUNITY PARK

(949) 724-6725 / www.cityofirvine.org
55 Deerwood West, Irvine

A good-sized park with lots of fun things to do is what works for parents with kids. The smaller playground, designed for younger kids, has climbing chains, slides, and swings in a sand base. The slightly bigger playground has a rock climbing wall, twisty slides, and fun metal shapes to climb and play on. The park also has open grassy areas, two sand volleyball courts, a nine-hole disc golf course, four lighted tennis courts, two racquetball courts, a fitness course, bicycle trails, picnic tables, and BBQ pits.

Hours: Open daily, dawn to dusk.
Price: Free
Ages: All

EDISON COMMUNITY CENTER

(714) 960-8870 or (714) 536-5486 / www.huntingtonbeachca.gov; www.stockteam.com
21377 Magnolia Street, Huntington Beach

Although the park is not outstandingly pretty to look at, it is packed with fun things to do. Within its forty acres it has four lighted tennis courts, open to play on a first-come, first-*served* basis; six racquetball courts; four full basketball courts and several half courts, with lights; two baseball diamonds; lots of open space; a paved trail throughout; a covered picnic area with barbeque pits; a community center building; sand and grass volleyball courts; horseshoes pits (bring your own horseshoes); and a large, sand-based play area complete with slides, swings, tot swings, climbing apparatus, and a section boasting a ship motif.

Hours: The park is open daily, 5am - 10pm. The community center is open Mon. - Thurs., 9am - 9pm; Fri., 9am - 8pm; Sat., 9am - 12:30pm. It is closed Sun. and on holidays.
Price: Free. Tennis costs only if you make a reservation.
Ages: All

EISENHOWER PARK

(714) 744-7272 / www.cityoforange.org/depts/commserv/parks_and_facilities
2864 N. Tustin Avenue, Orange

Driving down Lincoln Boulevard, it's easy to miss Eisenhower Park, but it's worth finding. At the south end of the park is a good-sized lake with a paved pathway all the way around it. Fishing is allowed, although it is only stocked annually. Ages 16 and up need a license. No license needed to watch the ducks, though!

This big park has a stream running through a good portion of it, with almost irresistible stepping stones. There are two small play areas for slightly older kids. Plenty of green rolling hills and a wide variety of mature shade trees (oak, willow, and pine), plus a few scattered picnic tables and barbecue pits make your day picnic perfect. Cement pathways make the entire park stroller accessible.

Hours: Open daily, sunrise - 11pm.
Price: Free
Ages: All

ENVIRONMENTAL NATURE CENTER

(949) 645-8489 / www.encenter.org
1601 16th Street, Newport Beach

This small, three-and-a-half acre nature center is an almost hidden gem that has been here for more than forty years! Walking back to the trailhead, notice the rocks along the path containing imbedded fossilized shells. Although buildings are around the perimeter of this wooded area, you'll still feel like you're in the midst of nature while walking along the various crisscrossing trails. You'll see a cactus garden, pine trees, woodland trees, and a small rock-lined stream.

The attractive, eco-friendly green learning center has shelves and tables that contain rocks, shells, animals' skins, turtle shells, taxidermied animals, skulls, feathers, and bird's nests, plus many nature-inspired craft ideas and interactive exhibits. My boys also liked seeing the live snakes, crickets, and lizards in here. The center hosts numerous programs for all ages - school groups, scouts, summer camps, and more. Note that the ENC Nature Preschool, a nature preschool and nature play area, borders the Nature Center's redwood forest.

During warmer weather, make sure you walk through the small butterfly house - a greenhouse that is home at various times to chrysalises and Painted Ladies, Red Admirals, Mourning Cloaks, and several other species. Someone once said that butterflies are like flying flowers; what a lovely description!

Hours: Open Mon. - Fri., 8am - 5pm; Sat. - Sun., 8am - 4pm. The butterfly house is open May through September, daily, 10am - 3pm, weather permitting. Call first as sometimes it is booked for educational programs. Both are closed on major holidays.
Price: Free
Ages: 2½ years and up.

ETNIES SKATE PARK OF LAKE FOREST

(949) 916-5870 / www.etniesskatepark.com

20028 Lake Forest Drive, Lake Forest

At 62,000 square feet, this lighted cement park designed by several pro skaters is a skater's paradise! The park is composed of a plaza that features open space with ledges and rails; a street course with a street run that features fun boxes, more ledges, a vert wall, and rollers; and bowls, a pool, pyramids, and other exciting elements. Safety gear for skaters - a helmet and pads - is required and enforced. A signed waiver is necessary for all skaters 17 years and under. Children 8 years old and under must have a parent or guardian stay with them. This is a great place for birthday parties. Skating camps are also offered here.

Hours: Open the school year, Mon. - Thurs., 11am - 9pm; Fri., 11am - 10pm; Sat. - 10am - 10pm; Sun., 10am - 9pm. Open daily in the summer, 10am - 10pm.

Price: Free for residents. An annual fee of $15 is charged for non-residents.

Ages: 7 years and up.

FAIRVIEW PARK

(949) 54TRAIN (548-7246) - engineers; (714) 754-5009 or (714) 754-5300 - park / www.ci.costa-mesa.ca.us; www.ocmetrains.org

2501 Placentia Avenue, Costa Mesa

Fairview Park has two main attractions - dirt trails and model train rides. There are miles and miles of dirt trails, which are great for jogging, but kid-wise, they are ideal for riding dirt bikes. Up and down, over hill and dale, and to the outer edge of the natural park, which is lined with coastal shrubs, the trails are just plain fun. There is also a wetlands area. The large size of the park, slight wind factor, and layout also lends itself to flying kites and model glider airplanes.

Just across the road is a station that hosts one of the largest scale model layouts of its kind in Southern California. The Orange County Model Engineers run five miles of track and offer rides, about fifteen minutes long, for free, to park-goers. Bring a picnic, a bike, a kite, and make a day of it.

Hours: The park is open daily, dawn - dusk. The train is here on the third weekend of each month, 10am - 3:30pm, weather permitting.

Price: Free

Ages: Minimum height is 31" and kids must be able to walk in order to ride the train.

FLORENCE JOYNER OLYMPIAD PARK

(949) 470-3061; (949) 470-3095 / www.cityofmissionviejo.org; www.funorangecountyparks.com

22760 Olympiad Road, Mission Viejo

Named for the Olympiad athlete, this popular, pretty, and colorful park has tons of fun elements. The big pirate ship, with its slides, poles, talking tubes, and portholes, encourages little ones to yo ho ho. Based in both recycled rubber and sand, there are two other covered major play structures that have several twisty and straight slides, metal bars and poles to climb, monkey bars with steps to go across, tunnels, bridges, a climbing configuration, rocks, and much more. There are also swings; smiley face free-standing walls; and several separate, kid-sized buildings with cut outs in the walls, plus windows, steering wheels, tables, and hands-on imaginative elements. A covered area with picnic tables and BBQ grills, expansive grassy lawn, plenty of mature trees, a landscaped perimeter, and an adjacent sports field round out this winning park.

Hours: Open daily, 7am - 11pm.

Price: Free

Ages: All

FORSTER RANCH COMMUNITY PARK

(949) 429-8797 or (949) 361-8264 / www.san-clemente.org; www.funorangecountyparks.com

3207 Camino Vera Cruz & 1291 Sarmentoso, San Clemente

Land ho! Play areas shaped like ships (making them shipshape!) with portholes, treasure maps, slides, and more; big alligators "swimming" through the sand; fake palm trees; and a large playground in a sand surface make this island-themed park the perfect getaway for kids. The large, central play structure has steps, plus wooden and chain bridges; tunnels; several slides; monkey bars; climbing apparatuses made of ropes, chains, metal and plastic; a zip line; a short tunnel through an open lion's mouth; and climbing ropes. Two stationary jeeps to "drive" around in, a low and fairly wide balance beam, and swings, including toddler and wheelchair accessible swings, make the enclosed island park seem not so deserted. Ball parks and grassy areas are adjacent.

Hours: Open daily, 6am - 10pm
Price: Free
Ages: All

FOUNDERS PARK

(714) 990-7103 / www.ci.brea.ca.us
777 Skyler Way, Brea

We found a great playground at Founders! It has a dynamite rock climbing wall - wider and taller than most other parks, like part of one that you'd find at a rock climbing gym, but not too high. The playground has lots of fun elements within its two play structures including slides, overhead wheels to hang on (like monkey bars), and a favorite - a raised sand play area that's kind of inset into fake rocks. Bring sand toys. The park also has a basketball court, two tennis courts, grassy areas, and picnic tables.
Hours: Open daily, sunrise - sunset.
Price: Free
Ages: All

FRONTIER PARK

(714) 573-3325 or (714) 573-3000 / www.tustinca.org
1400 Mitchell Avenue, Tustin

This nice corner park features a plastic playground in sand with a fort-like/Western theme. It has many slides, some bridges, and a rope wall to climb. There is a small water feature play area with just a few poles that spurt out water and some fountains that shoot up from the ground. Other components are a short frisbee golf course with chain baskets, fitness stations with exercise equipment, plus picnic tables, barbecue pits, shade trees, and a grassy area to run around.
Hours: Open daily, dawn - dusk.
Price: Free
Ages: All

FULLERTON ARBORETUM

(657) 278-3407 / www.fullertonarboretum.org
1900 Associated Road, Fullerton

This comely, twenty-six-acre botanical garden, with more than 4,000 plants, is a delight to wander around. Divided into four main sections, the Cultivated Garden section is a favorite because it is a verdant refuge, with flower-lined pathways, a pond (look for turtles and koi), a stream, and a few bridges. It's also big enough to let the kids run loose, a little. Take a whiff - the air is perfumed with the scent of roses, mint, and citrus, from the rose garden, herb garden, fruit grove, and deciduous orchard, respectively. Garden benches here (and everywhere, actually) offer a picturesque resting spot, underneath shade trees in the midst of the plants and flowers. Bring your camera for some potentially great shots in a garden setting.

The Woodland section features redwoods, pines, bamboo grove, rainforest plants, a meadow, and a colorful subtropical garden with a small pool. The Mediterranean area showcases chaparral and shrubs, while the Desert section grows a variety of cactus. The small, delightful Children's Garden is created particularly for kids to enjoy. There are fanciful super-sized garden tools; a very small house made out of sand bags; a section where visitors can touch plants (some are fuzzy; one is cotton), and see unusual ones; and another spot called sniff n' seek so kids can make *scents* of gardening!

An 1894 Victorian Heritage House, once the home and office of the first physician in Orange County, is also on the grounds. Older kids will appreciate a tour through the house that has turn-of-the-century furnishings. The visitor's center/museum contains rotating displays.

There are many special events going on at the Fullerton Arboretum throughout the year, including Science Adventure programs, volunteering opportunities, Victorian teas, planting how-to's for all ages, educational presentations and workshops, and much much more. Call or check the website for details. Note that picnicking is not allowed on the grounds.
Hours: The Arboretum is open daily, 8am - 4:30pm. Closed New Year's Day, Thanksgiving, and Christmas. The house is open for tours Sat. and Sun., 2pm - 4pm. Call to make an appointment for other days and hours. The house is closed for tours in January and August.

Price: The Arboretum has a donation box by the entrance gate - $5 suggested. The house tour is a $3 for adults; $1 per child. See American Horticultural Society (pg. x) for info on reciprocal memberships.

Ages: All

GREEN PARK

(714) 536-5486 / www.ci.huntington-beach.ca.us

18751 Seagate Drive, Huntington Beach

Up a gently sloping hill covered with grass and sprinkled with shade trees is a great playground for young 'uns on recycled rubber flooring. A large, multi-level play structure, with plenty of room for imaginative play underneath, has several slides sprouting from it, including two twisty enclosed ones, and circular and twisty metal climbing shapes. The tall platforms and ramps are lined with protective bars. A shorter play structure has more slides, including side-by-side slides, plus a bridge, steps, talking tubes, and climby things. Kids can also climb in and on a play fire truck and dump truck, ride on large cement turtles, play giant tic-tac-toe, swing, and climb a free-standing rock wall. (Seems like the word "climb" comes up a lot for this park.) The park also features a tennis court, sand volleyball court, basketball court, and picnic tables in and out of the shade. Alas, there are no restrooms here.

Hours: Open daily, 5am - 10pm.

Price: Free

Ages: All

HARRIETT M. WIEDER REGIONAL PARK

(949) 923-2250 / www.ocparks.com

19251 Seapoint Avenue, Huntington Beach

What a crazy fun park this is! The play equipment looks like abstract art, albeit sturdy and colorful, and lets unrestrained imaginations invent ways to play on the circular, cylindrical, straight up, and twisted shapes. Kids can climb, swing, spin, slide, and even zip on the good-sized playground that offers a view of the Bolsa Chica Wetlands. One area is designed for ages 6 to twelve years; the other for toddlers. Both have rubberized surfaces and play components comprised of recycled materials. Several picnic tables are here, as well. The few short walking trails will be maintained and expanded in the future.

Hours: Open daily, 7am - sunset.

Price: Free

Ages: 2 - 14 years

HARRY M. DOTSON PARK

(714) 379-9222 / www.ci.stanton.ca.us

10350 Fern Street, Stanton

This 1.3 acre park is packed with kid-friendly amenities that include a half basketball court, cement pathways, open grassy areas, climbing area, pirate ship for mateys to climb aboard and say "aarrrgh" a lot, and a water play area. The pirate ship is large, has three masts, porthole windows, ramps, and has play equipment attached to it, like climbing apparatus and a few slides. Several big boulders, with hand holds, are placed around the ship to increase the fun of "let's pretend", and there is a partially buried treasure chest next to an X, which marks the spot. The small, covered, Western-themed Wet Saloon water play area has fountains that erupt water from the ground, water cannons, poles disguised as cactus, and a play structure that looks like the frame of a pioneer wagon. Picnic tables are in this immediate area, under shade trees, so parents can dryly watch their wet little darlings.

Hours: Open daily, sunrise - sunset. The water "park" is open Memorial Day - Labor Day, daily, noon - 5pm.

Price: Free

Ages: 1 ½ years and up.

HART PARK

(714) 744-2225 or (714) 744-7274 - park; (714) 744-7266 - pool / www.cityoforange.org/depts/commserv/parks_and_facilities

701 S. Glassell Street, Orange

Stone walls add to the beauty of this spacious park. The northern section has lots of picnic tables (57!) and barbecue pits, a playground, trees to climb, a few tennis courts (although kids were roller skating on them when we visited), horseshoe pits, a sand volleyball court (or, for younger kids, a sandbox with a net), and a swimming pool. Come for a concert at the amphitheater on Wednesday nights in the summer.

The southern section has a large open grassy area lined with trees, plus soccer fields and a few baseball diamonds. One of the diamonds has stadium seating and lights. Note that there is a bike/creek trail that goes from Hart Park to SANTIAGO PARK / NATURE RESERVE (pg. 294), near the DISCOVERY CUBE (Orange County) (pg. 304). And kids will discover the rocky creek bed that begins at the parking lot and goes under the freeway and along the bike/creek trail. Just sayin.

Hours: The park is open daily, 5am - 11pm. The pool is open mid-June - Labor Day daily, with one-hour-and-fifteen-minute swim sessions, Mon. - Tues., and Thurs. - Fri., 1:30pm - 4:15pm; Wed., 1:30pm - 4:15pm and 7:15pm - 8:30pm; Sat. - Sun., 1pm - 5:15pm.
Price: The park is free. Each swim session costs $2.50 per person.
Ages: All

HARVARD COMMUNITY PARK

(949) 724-6821 - park; (949) 337-6577 or (949) 724-6830 - skate park / www.cityofirvine.org
14701 Harvard Avenue, Irvine

This expansive park has four soccer fields, seven lighted baseball/softball fields, picnic tables, barbecue grills, and open play areas. The big attraction for skateboarders is the 10,000 square foot concrete corner skate park which has a pool, ramps, verts, grind boxes, grinding poles, and other standard skate street equipment. Safety equipment - helmet and knee and elbow pads - is required.

Hours: The park is open daily, dawn - dusk. The skate park is open during school hours, Mon. - Fri., 2pm - 8pm; Sat., 10am - 9pm; Sun., noon - 8pm. During the summer and on school breaks, it is open Mon. - Sat., 10am - 9pm; Sun., noon - 8pm. Closed major holidays.
Price: Free
Ages: All

HAWES PARK

(714) 536-5486 / www.huntingtonbeachca.gov; www.stockteam.com
9731 Verdant Drive and Everglades Drive, Huntington Beach

The large and colorful play structure has some great features such as two, short rock climbing walls; twisty slides; swaying bridges; a domed, metal climbing apparatus with cross bars; monkey bars; and more. A separate play area has swings, enclosed slides, and a long curvy slide stationed in a sand pit. Other amenities include picnic tables, basketball courts, shade trees, expanse of lawn, and ball fields. Note that since this park is adjacent to an elementary school the playground is often in use during school hours.

Hours: Open daily, 5am - sunset.
Price: Free
Ages: All

HERITAGE PARK - Irvine

(949) 724-6750 - youth services center; (949) 724-6717 - Aquatics Complex; (949) 724-6824 - athletic field / www.cityofirvine.org
14301 Yale Avenue, Irvine

Heritage Park is an extensive community park with the emphasis on community. The park has a terrific and large, low-to-the-ground playground with several, interconnected play areas in ship and castle configurations and motif. They incorporate lots of slides; talking tubes; ramps; rope and metal climbing structures; a rock climbing wall; play panels; a boat-shaped teeter-totter with plastic mini couches on each side; other teeter totters; several sand pits with fine sand; wheels to spin around on; raised sand tables; swings; animals on large springs; and more - all to stimulate creative play, and all surrounded by small, grassy hills, shade trees, and benches. A small water play area is here, too, with a few fountains that shoot water up from the ground.

The centerpiece of the park is a beautiful small lake with numerous ducks and a fountain in the middle. Skate or stroller around the paved pathway, play on the boulders that also ring it, and run around on more of the grassy, gently rolling hills. There are also basketball courts, twelve lighted tennis courts, three soccer fields, volleyball courts, racquetball courts, and four fields for organized sports play at the park.

Several buildings line the perimeter of the park, such as the community services center, which has a few billiard tables and other games; the library; and the Irvine Fine Art Center, which has a small art gallery and offers art classes. The William Woollett Junior Aquatics Complex is just around the corner at 4601 Walnut Avenue. Two of their pools are open for recreational swim in the summer.

Hours: The park is open daily. The pools are open daily in the summer, Mon. - Fri., 1:15pm - 3:15pm; Sat. - Sun., 1pm - 2:30pm.

Price: The park is free. Swimming costs $4 for adults; $2 for seniors and ages 17 and under.

Ages: All

HILLCREST PARK

(714) 738 - 6575 / www.cityoffullerton.com

1200 N. Harbor Boulevard, Fullerton

For some Fullerton fun, try Hillcrest Park. This huge, hilly park has a winding road throughout, with parking lots in several different spots and levels along the way. Originally opened in 1922, some of that older ambiance shows in a classic way with graded, grassy areas, dotted with numerous mature trees, and stone steps leading to various levels. We saw some creative kids using cardboard to slide down a hill, which probably isn't great for the grass, but it looked like fun.

Hillcrest has a few woodland areas with dirt paths for hiking. There are also picnic tables, grassy expanses and barbecue pits. One main play area, located at the base of the hill, at N. Lemon St., has a playground with fort-like structure on stilts with curvy slides attached and climbing ropes, plus monkey bars and a semi-circles climbing "steps", all in bark ground cover. Just around the corner is a recreation center.

Lion's Field, at 1440 N. Brea Blvd., has four baseball/softball fields with bleacher seating; a soccer/football sports field; tables and chairs on cement under trees; and another way to get fit, Pine Forest Stairs. This series of 467 wooden steps, ramps and dirt trails zig zag and go up and down and over the hill, interconnecting to Hillcrest Park. The hillside stairs are lit, have three decks to stop and breathe and take a look, and offer a great view from the top.

Hours: Open daily, sunrise - sunset.

Price: Free

Ages: All

HUNTINGTON CENTRAL PARK / SHIPLEY NATURE CENTER

(714) 536-5486 - park; (714) 842-4772 - Shipley / www.huntingtonbeachca.gov; www.shipleynature.org; www.stockteam.com

18000 Goldenwest Street, Huntington Beach

This gigantic park offers many options for all kinds of fun. Fish at the stocked lake, which is tucked in the corner. Let the kids go wild on the four different playgrounds. Ride bikes along the six miles of cement pathways that crisscross all over. Walk on the several other miles of dirt trails. Romp on the expansive green lawns. Retreat under shade trees. Enjoy lunch using the picnic tables or barbeque grills. Work it out on the exercise stations located throughout. The equipment, such as pull up bars and rings, is provided as are how-to instructions. Score on the disc golf course located on the west side of Goldenwest Street, which offers instructions, maps, and an opportunity to purchase your own disc. It's much more fun than golf (personal opinion!) as the discs are thrown into above ground metal baskets (if you're good). If you can throw a frisbee, or disc, you can play. Call (714) 931-4559 for more information.

Check out books from the huge HUNTINGTON BEACH CENTRAL LIBRARY and CULTURAL CENTER (pg. 318) off Talbert Street. Get dirty at ADVENTURE PLAYGROUND (pg. 715) for summertime fun. Play at the adjoining Huntington Beach Central Sports Complex with its eight baseball and soccer fields, batting cages, concession stand, and imaginative children's play area. The latter has a short rock climbing wall, lots of slides, monkey bars, and metal climbing structures.

If all this exercise gets you hungry, Kathy May's Lakeview Cafe, located at 6622 Lakeview Dr. in the park and on the lake bank, has an extensive menu serving omelettes ($10.99), breakfast burritos ($9.29), French toast ($8.29), chicken wraps ($10.49), Cobb salads ($12.29), sweet potato fries ($6.49), meatball sandwiches or roast beef dips ($11.49), N.Y. steaks ($15.49), salmon ($17.49), and much more. There is seating inside, but why do that on such a gorgeous day? There is outside patio seating and seating even more outside with an unencumbered view of the lake, too. Contact (714) 842-7700 /www.kathymayslakeviewcafe.com for more info. The tiny Park Bench Cafe, located at 17732 Goldenwest Street, serves up breakfast and lunch with some tables inside and most outdoors. They also have a Doggie Diner section where you can eat with (and order for) your pooch. Contact (714) 842-0775 / www.parkbenchcafe.com for more info.

Shipley Nature Center is a fenced-in, eighteen-acre preserve with a very family friendly walking trail, a pond, and an interpretive building with animal skins, rocks, and other exhibits on wildlife and ecology. Come on your own, or join in on one of several presentations and programs offered for all ages, and/or a volunteer opportunity for maintenance, etc.

Hours: The park is open daily, 5am - 10pm. The disc course is open Mon. - Fri., 9am - 5pm; Sat. - Sun., 8am - 5pm. Shipley is open Mon. - Sat., 9am to 1pm. Closed Sun. and major holidays.

Price: Free to the park and Shipley. The disc course is $2 for adults to play on weekdays; $3 on weekends; ages 15 and under are free. Disc rentals are $2.

Ages: All

INDEPENDENCE SKATE PARK

(714) 738-5369 / www.cityoffullerton.com

801 W. Valencia Drive, Fullerton

12,000 square feet of cement bowls, rails, ledges, and mini ramps are great for practicing. Although self-supervised, helmet and pads are required. The adjacent recreation building houses a basketball court, racquetball courts, and the Janet Evans Swim Complex for recreation swim. There is also a Farmer's Market on Wed., 8am - 1pm.

Hours: The skate park is open daily, 9am - dusk.

Price: Free

Ages: 7 years and up.

IRVINE REGIONAL PARK

(714) 973-6835 or (714) 973-3173 / www.ocparks.com

1 Irvine Park Road, Orange

Spend entire days exploring all there is to see and do at this 477-acre regional park, which is one of my favorites. A multitude of huge, old oak (and other) trees spread their large branches and roots, so enjoy some back-to-nature time. The middle area is "carved out," with lots of grass for picnic areas, several great playgrounds, and baseball diamonds.

Toddlers through about 8 years old can ride ponies around a track that is open Tues. - Fri., 11am to 4pm; Sat. - Sun. and holidays, 10am to 4pm. Rides are $5 each, cash only. Call (714) 559-9147 for more details. Kids 8 years and older can take a guided horseback ride inside the park past coastal live oaks, sycamore trees, and chaparral. Rides are available Tuesday through Sunday for $55 an hour by reservation only. Call Country Trails at (714) 538-5860 / www.ctriding.com for further horseback riding rental information. More fun can be had with pedal boat rentals - $20 per half hour, and bike rentals - $12 an hour for a BMX bike, $30 an hour for a small surrey. Both pedal boat and bike rentals are available daily, 10am to 4pm; open until 6pm on spring and summer weekends. Irvine Park Railroad offers ten-minute, one-third-scale model train rides around the park daily (closed major holidays), 10am to 4pm (open until 6pm on spring and summer weekends) at $5 per person; children 12 months and younger ride free. This is a fun little trip! Call (714) 997-3968 or (714) 997-3636 / www.irvineparkrailroad.com for more information. The railroad also offers 2.5 hour-long school field trips for 4th graders, incorporating panning for gold, miner's camp, and more, that corresponds with the California history curriculum for $15 a student. The train's website is good for all the above-listed attractions.

The Interpretive Center, (714) 973-3187, has taxidermied animals to look at; skulls, furs, and animal pelts to touch; a grinding rock to try out; plus displays and information about the wilderness part of the park. Biking, paved and unpaved hiking, and equestrian trails are plentiful in Irvine Regional Park with creeks, sagebrush, and animals throughout. Rangers are available for school and scout tours for park trails. Note that the twenty-two-mile Mountains to Sea Trail, accessed from this park, begins at Weir Canyon in Anaheim Hills and reaches to the Bay in Newport Beach. Hikers and mountain bikers follow the trail system that encompasses all of Irvine Ranch and passes through some of the most scenic topography of parkland and open spaces that Orange County has to offer. Check www.IrvineRanchLandReserve.com for more information. Also, look up ORANGE COUNTY ZOO (pg. 335), as the zoo is located inside the park.

Hours: Irvine Park is open April through October daily, 6am - 9pm. It's open the rest of the year daily, 6am - 6pm. The Nature Center is usually open Sat. - Sun., 11:30am - 3:30pm, providing a volunteer is available.

Price: $3 per vehicle Mon. - Fri.; $5 on Sat. - Sun.; $7 on some holidays.

Ages: All

IRVINE TERRACE PARK

(949) 644-3151 or (714) 605-6085 / www.newportbeachca.gov

721 Evita Drive, Newport Beach

Up a hill, via grass or the cement pathway, is a delightful playground with a two-story play structure that has enclosed slides shooting out, metal climbing apparatus, steps, platforms with steering wheels and games, monkey "bar" rings, and metal wheels to hang from. Underneath is a plenty of space for pretending. A shorter play structure, partly in the sand, is just as much fun with slides, tunnels, wide plastic climbing "rocks", and raised sand basins, plus a little house underneath. A four-sided, free-standing rock climbing wall; a play ship on large springs; talking tube; diggers; four-person teeter-totter; and swings complete this section.

The park also sports a basketball court, two tennis courts, wide open grassy areas, pine and other mature trees, and a view of the bay via a very small Zen garden with plants and statues.

Hours: Open daily, sunrise - sunset.
Price: Free
Ages: 1 - 10

LAGUNA COAST WILDERNESS PARK / LITTLE SYCAMORE CANYON STAGING AREA / NIX NATURE CENTER

(949) 923-2235 or (949) 923-3702 / www.lagunacanyon.org; www.ocparks.com
18751 Laguna Canyon Road, Laguna Beach

The headquarters for the massive Laguna Coast Wilderness Park is this small nature center which has a wall mural, corn and stone pestle, and informational panels about the Native Americans, as well as a phone to pick up and hear a recording about spirit animals. Pick up trail maps here (42 miles of trails!) and enjoy the use of the picnic tables. An easy, half-mile loop trail just outside the nature center is a fun starting point. We opted to take another, about five-mile, dirt trail that looped around after it went up and up (and up) a hill, got steep and rocky at times, rewarded us with a fantastic view of the entire area as we walked along the perimeter amongst a few trees, sage, etc., and left us with a feeling of accomplishment and joy at seeing such beautiful creation as we headed back down to the center. Bring water and know there is not a lot of shade at the top!

Just down the road are other parts of this 7,000-acre park, which is part of the 17,000-acre South Coast Wilderness Park system. This includes Willow Canyon Staging Area, on 20101 Laguna Canyon Road, which is just south of the El Toro Road intersection and James Dilley Preserve, and just north of the 73 Toll Road. Also see COASTAL PEAK PARK (pg. 274) for more trail information.

Hours: Parking is open daily, 8am - 5pm. The trails open at 7am. The nature center is open daily, 9am - 4pm (ish).
Price: Parking is $3.
Ages: All

LAGUNA HILLS SKATE PARK

(949) 707-2608 / www.ci.laguna-hills.ca.us
25555 Alicia Parkway, Laguna Hills

The skate park is part of a community park and sports center. Skateboarders and bladers can skate at the lighted, 10,000-square-foot cement park that features a pyramid, cones, steps, grinding rails, volcano, and ramps. All participants must wear a helmet and knee and elbow pads.

Hours: Open Mon. - Sat., 8am - 10pm; Sun., 8am - 6pm.
Price: Free
Ages: 7 years and up.

LAGUNA LAKE PARK

(714) 738-6575 / www.cityoffullerton.com; www.wildlife.ca.gov
3120 Lakeview Drive, Fullerton

In contrast to my earlier thinking, I now know that parks don't require a playground to make them "good." They simply must have kid-appeal, and this one does. The dirt path around the long lake, seasonally stocked with trout, is bike and stroller friendly. The marshy reeds are a great place for dragonfly hunting. Bring duck food for the ducks, bait for your fishing pole (over 16 needs a fishing license), and enjoy this unusual park. Barbecue pits and picnic tables are here, too. There is a longer Fullerton loop to hike or bike on, too.

Hours: Open daily, sunrise - sunset.
Price: Free
Ages: All

LAGUNA NIGUEL REGIONAL PARK

(949) 923-2240 - park; (949) 362-9227 - fishing / www.ocparks.com; www.lagunaniguellake.com
28241 La Paz Road, Laguna Niguel

This park is 236 acres of adventures waiting to be had. It offers volleyball courts, horseshoe pits, tennis courts, bike trails, an area for flying remote-controlled airplanes, several toddler-friendly playgrounds, open grass areas, barbecue pits, and picnic shelters, plus a forty-four-acre lake for fishing. The lake is seasonally stocked with catfish and bluegill, with a limit of five fish per person. Bass are strictly catch and release. Fish from the floating docks or along the lake shoreline. A fishing license is required for ages 16 and up. The park tends to get crowded on weekends and holidays, so get an early start!

Hours: Open daily, 6am - 6pm. Fishing closes at 5pm.
Price: $3 per vehicle Mon. - Fri.; $5 on Sat. - Sun.; $7 on some holidays.
Ages: All

LAGUNA NIGUEL SKATE & SOCCER PARK

(949) 916-7766 or (949) 916-7755 / www.cityoflagunaniguel.org
27745 Alicia Parkway, Laguna Niguel

The 22,000 square-foot concrete lighted skate park has all the features both intermediate and advanced skaters look for; bowls, rails, funbox, a street course, and more. It is a supervised park and requires a parental waiver on file for ages 17 and under. Skaters must wear a helmet and pads. The adjacent soccer park's playing field is synthetic grass. The field has lights for night play.

Hours: The skate park is open during the school year, Mon. - Fri., noon - 9:30pm; Sat. - Sun., 9am - 9:30pm. Holidays, school breaks, and summer time hours are daily, 9am - 9:30pm. BMX bikers can utilize the park Tues., 7pm - 9:30pm, Fri., noon - 4:30pm and Sun., 4:30pm - 9:30pm.
Price: $10 per person for the skate park per day, or purchase an annual pass for $40 for residents; $80 for nonresidents.
Ages: 7 years and up.

LANTERN BAY COUNTY PARK

(949) 248-3530 / www.danapoint.org
25111 Park Lantern Road, Dana Point

This bluff top park offers spectacular vistas of the ocean and features a large, grassy, run-around area; barbecues; picnic tables under pine trees; a full basketball court; a bocce ball court; physical fitness clusters; a playground with short slides and other play equipment; and a paved pathway that winds throughout and around the park.

Hours: Open daily, 6am - 10pm.
Price: Free
Ages: All

LEMON PARK

(714) 738-3161 / www.cityoffullerton.com
701 S. Lemon Street, Fullerton

The two small playgrounds here have climbing apparatus, including twisty metal climbing structures, plus slides, short walkways, swings and some other fun elements. Added features are basketball courts; a rec center; picnic tables in full and partial shade; grassy areas; a series of workout stations with equipment; and a rejuvenating feature on a hot day - a gated splashpad that gushes water up and out from the ground and the pipes. Wear swimwear!

Hours: The park is open daily, sunrise - sunset. The spray park is open June - mid-August, daily, 1pm - 5pm; mid-August - September, weekends only, 1pm - 5pm.
Price: Free
Ages: All

LIBERTY PARK & SKATE PARK - Westminster

(714) 895-2860 or (714) 898-3311 / www.westminster-ca.gov
13900 Monroe Street, Westminster

The park is a typical, medium-sized park with open grassy areas, a few trees, a few picnic tables, a basketball court, and a sand-based playground. The major draw, I think, is for skateboarders and bladers. Their play area is a mid-size cement skate park which has a mini-pool, kidney pool, stair-rail plaza, funbox, and a street course. Wearing safety gear - a helmet and knee and elbow pads - is enforced.

Hours: The park and skate park are open daily, 8am - dusk.
Price: Free
Ages: 7 years and up for the skate park.

MILE SQUARE REGIONAL PARK

(714) 973-6600 or (714) 973-3197 - park; (805) 895-8480 - Wheel Fun Rentals / www.ocparks.com; www.wheelfunrentals.com

16801 Euclid Avenue, Fountain Valley

Have a full day of family fun at Mile Square Park; be there or be *square*. Enjoy picnic areas with lots and lots of tables and barbecue grills; cement bike/stroller pathways that crisscross throughout and that go around the park perimeter; an archery range (bring your own equipment); two playgrounds (with several short, curvy and enclosed slides, swings, and a short climbing wall); a nature area; two soccer fields; baseball fields; a good-size, boulder-lined lake (with a bridge and small island of palm trees) toward the north end and another (smaller) one in the south; a stream; and sand volleyball courts. You may fish in the two man-made lakes - a license is needed for ages 16 and up. Ask about the fishing derby. There are plenty of lovely shade trees interspersed throughout the park with some open grass areas. One-Night Stay Overnight Camping for organized youth groups, for ages of 6 to 12 years old, only, is also available here.

The Fountain Valley Recreation Center is on Brookhurst Avenue, sandwiched between golf courses. This center has several basketball courts, twelve tennis courts, outdoor racquetball courts, two sand volleyball courts, numerous baseball diamonds, and a playground.

Get physical on the weekends with various pleasure rentals by the hour - a small surrey bike (seating two adults and two small children) is $25; quad sport (similar to a go-cart) or cruisers are $10; and single pedal boats are $20 for half an hour. All rentals are available on weekends only, February - November, 11am - dusk.

Hours: Open March - October daily, 7am - 9pm. Open November - February daily, 7am - 6:30pm.

Price: $3 per vehicle Mon. - Fri; $5 on Sat. - Sun.; $7 on holidays. Some free street parking is available on Euclid and Edinger Ave.

Ages: All

MOULTON MEADOWS PARK

(949) 497-0716 / www.lagunabeachcity.net; www.funorangecountyparks.com

Balboa Avenue at the intersection of Capistrano Avenue, Laguna Beach

For kids who like to climb, this great little park's main attraction is the section dedicated to thick, crisscrossing ropes in different configurations to climb up and on. What fun! More climbing apparatus includes a short rock climbing wall and several tall, big, fake boulders. The sand-floor playground also offers shade-covered platforms with several slides, monkey bars, twisting metal structures, toy animals to rock back and forth on, swings (including toddler swings), and flat, inverted triangle seats (some with poles through them) to incorporate with creative play.

The park also has two, half basketball courts; two tennis courts (with parking meters to keep track of court time); a soccer field in the upper area; a fitness course along the pathway to the field; and small portions of grassy green lawn with trees and a few picnic tables and BBQ grills. There is a short, dirt, nature trail leading through some of the landscaping and around parts of the park, too.

One of the most inviting elements of Moulton Meadows is the breathtaking view driving up (and up!) to this hilltop park - wow! Laguna Beach and the ocean is laid out before you and on a clear day you can see Catalina.

Hours: Open daily, sunrise - sunset.

Price: Free

Ages: All

NORTHWOOD COMMUNITY PARK (aka Castle Park)

(949) 724-6728 - park; (949) 724-6620 - community center / www.cityofirvine.org

4531 Bryan Avenue, Irvine

The focal point of this park is the big, fortress-like structure which is great for climbing on and around. It has slides, steps, a fireman's pole, and castle-like walls built into the rocky side, completing the fortress image. The large, sprawling, wonderful, all-abilities playground also has tire swings, ramps, a balance beam, more slides, bridges, short tunnels, animals on large springs to ride, a wooden and cement pirate ship, and raised sand boxes.

The surrounding park has soccer fields, large grass areas, two tennis courts, fitness course, two basketball courts, two racquetball courts, and baseball diamonds, plus a paved pathway all around the fields. You can check out play equipment, free of charge, at the community center building, which also has an exercise room and classroom space.

Hours: The park is open daily 8am - 9pm. The community center building is open Mon - Fri., 9am - 9pm; Sat. 9am - 10pm; Sun noon - 6pm.

Price: Free

Ages: All

OAK CANYON NATURE CENTER

(714) 998-8380 / www.anaheim.net
6700 Walnut Canyon Road, Anaheim

This rustic Nature Center is a fifty-eight-acre natural park nestled in Anaheim Hills. Surrounded by such beauty, it doesn't seem possible that there is a city nearby. Take a delightful, easy hike along the wide pathways along the creek and through the woods that boast of huge oak and other shade trees. Or, opt for more strenuous hiking on the six miles of trails offered here. No bikes or picnicking is allowed, so that the animals and plants that consider this canyon their home can continue to live here unharmed.

The good-sized, interpretative center building houses live critters, plus several trays of mounted butterflies and other insects. The small stage area is great for putting on shows using the animal puppets. The Nature Center offers many different programs, including a Discover Nature Family Program held every weekend from 10:30am to 11:30am. The program is free, but a $5 per family is suggested. On Wednesday evenings throughout the summer, Nature Nights for families begin at 7pm with a twilight walk through the canyon followed up by a presentation at 7:30pm at the outdoor amphitheater ($5 per family donation). Ask about their summer day camps and school programs.

Hours: The park is open daily, sunrise - sunset. The interpretive center is open Sat. - Sun., 10am - 4pm.
Price: Free to the park. The nature center asks for a $2 donation per family.
Ages: All

OLINDA RANCH PARK

(714) 990-7603 / www.ci.brea.ca.us
4055 Carbon Canyon Road, Brea

This beautifully landscaped and maintained park has a long paved pathway that runs along Lambert. It also has stretches of green grass, a baseball field, picnic tables, lighted basketball courts, a mini skate park, and a small, but good playground with swings, slides, some play panels (a favorite is one that is like a mini piano where you can strike the keys to play songs) and climbing apparatus all in a sand base. The park is across the street from CARBON CANYON REGIONAL PARK (pg. 273).

Hours: Open daily, sunrise to sunset.
Price: Free
Ages: All

O'NEILL REGIONAL PARK / ARROYO TRABUCO

(949) 923-2260 or (949) 923-2256 / www.ocparks.com
30892 Trabuco Canyon Road, Trabuco Canyon

As we explored parts of this over 2,000 acre park, I kept thinking of how absolutely gorgeous it is. O'Neill Park is a canyon bottom and so filled with trees, it's like being in a forest. A creek runs throughout, creating lush greenery. The abundant nature trails (about 23 miles!) are mostly hilly dirt trails, though a few are paved "roads".

The play structure has a short bridge, poles, rings, mini-zip line, climbing wall, and a few slides. Inside the small Nature Center are taxidermied animals around the perimeter of the room. A few tables in the middle display skulls, furs, and rocks to touch. Join in a morning, ranger-led hike to learn how to identify animal tracks and find out other facts about the park's inhabitants.

Arroyo Trabuco is a more than 900-acre parcel of pristine wilderness preserve adjacent to O'Neill park area. Hiking, mountain biking, and equestrian trails and wildlife observation are the main recreational activities available here. The park also has beautiful campgrounds for tents, RVs and equestrians. This entire park is nature at its finest.

Hours: The park is open daily, 7am - sunset. The Nature Center is usually open Sat. - Sun., 8am - 4pm.
Price: $3 per vehicle on Mon. - Fri.; $5 on Sat. - Sun; $7 on holidays. Camping starts at $20 per night.
Ages: All

ORANGE COUNTY GREAT PARK

(949) 724-6247 - Visitor's Center; (949) 724-6599 - hot air balloon; (714) 733-3167 - Farmer's Market / www.cityofirvine.org
Trabuco Road, Irvine

Still in the process of being built (for years and years to come) on the former Marine Corps Air Station at El Toro this absolutely gigantic park (1,347 acres) has and will have a lot to offer.

Here are the current attractions, which are all grouped together on site, surrounded by a whole lot of space: The runway has a **walkable historical time line** painted on it that commemorates 162 significant historical events from around the globe - a kind of interactive educational tool. The big, orange, tethered, **hot air balloon** is hard to miss, especially as it rises up, up, and away - 400 feet up in the air, overlooking the park and surrounding neighborhoods. The gondola (i.e. passenger basket) can hold up to twenty-five adults, depending on wind conditions. All ages are invited to go airborne, as there are safety nets in place surrounding the basket area. "Flyers" can walk around the basket for different panoramic viewpoints during the seven-minute ride. Note that a waiver must be signed for all riders and children 12 and under must be accompanied by an adult. Visitors can also ride the thirty+-animal **carousel** which was moved here from Fashion Island. A small, but fun **Kids Rock Playground** features a few fake boulders to climb on and through, with a kid-size cave thrown in, all on cushy, recycled rubber. Misters operate during the hotter months. There are plenty of picnic tables and chairs scattered throughout, so bring a lunch. A terraced-lawn serves as an outdoor performance venue. **Palm Courts Arts Complex** is a huge courtyard, lined by extra large palm trees, that hosts two buildings - the Great Park Artists Studios, an interactive space (mini concerts, etc.) with offerings on weekends from 10am - 4pm, and the Great Park Gallery with rotating art exhibits. It is open Thurs. - Fri., noon - 4pm; Sat. - Sun., 10am - 4pm. Both are free. The adjacent **Heritage and Aviation Exhibition** is located in historic Hangar 244. It features displays and artifacts that show and tell the story of the Great Park from its agricultural roots to its role in the military. It also has WWII airplanes - a N3N-3 Canary and SNJ-5 Texan, and an Air Force Memorial. It is free and open Thurs. - Fri., noon - 4pm; Sat. - Sun., 10am - 4pm. Call (866) 829-3829 for more info.

The massive South Lawn, near Ridge Valley and Phantom, features two reflecting ponds/fountains; a long, redwood viewing pier near the Marine Way entrance; and a **mile long walking/jogging path**. These connect to the walkable time line and the recreation field and **Sports Complex**. The recreation field is an open play area with grassy spots for picnics and to run, run, run around, plus soccer fields and four **basketball courts**. You can even check out soccer balls, footballs, jump ropes, Bocce ball sets, giant chess sets, and frisbees for free at the Visitors Center. The Sports Complex, mostly in the North Lawn and located off Great Park Blvd., boasts several components including a championship **soccer field** and stadium with seating for 2,500 spectators, plus locker rooms, training facilities and concession areas. And because you can't get too much soccer, there area six lighted grass soccer fields with spectator viewing areas for anyone to play if not occupied by teams. Five lighted **sand volleyball courts** include one championship court with seating for 178 spectators. The Tennis Center offers 25 **tennis courts** for drop-in and league play. It's open daily, 6am - 10pm. Call (949) 724-6400 for more information. Near this section, too, is a **children's playground** that's pretty spread out. There is a short hill to run up and down that also has slides flowing down it. A stack of large, pentagon-shaped crates for kids to climb up and in and on is unique. A short log tunnel; a pop-up shape covered with ropes to climb; a bee statue; toddler swings; a really fun zip line; and a few geometric shapes and spheres for imaginative play engage kids here. A baseball stadium, ten baseball diamonds, and more multi-use fields are opening soon.

For a hands-on gardening experience, take a class at the adjacent **Farm & Food Lab** which has a conglomeration of garden beds and a variety of plants and flowers with activities and information. The public is welcome to view all this. We saw strawberries, oranges, and lemons growing; and a butterfly garden. Some plaques show and tell visitors ingredients and toppings that go into meals, such as the Pizza and Spaghetti Garden, which grows ingredients for sauces. There is information to learn about and do composting, planting, fertilizing and more. The **Farmer's Market** offers fresh seasonal fruits and produce (some produced from the 105-acre Great Park Farm), plus flowers and bread every Sunday from 10am to 2pm. Breakfast and lunch are available to purchase here then, too. The 4.5 acre Incredible Edible Farm grows vegetables that are harvested by Second Harvest Food Bank volunteers (that could be you!) who pick the food to help feed the hungry in Orange County. See www.FeedOC.org for more info. A lot of special events are held at the Great Park throughout the year, so check the website calendar, and/or just come to hang out, play and relax any time.

Hours: The park is open Mon. - Wed., 10am - dusk; Thurs. - Fri., 10am - 10pm; Sat. - Sun., 9am - 10pm. The hot air balloon ride is open Thurs. - Fri., 10am - 3pm and 7pm- 10pm; Sat. - Sun., 9am - 3pm and 7pm - 10pm. Note that registration for this ride begins thirty minutes before morning operating hours and an hour before nighttime operating hours. Always call first as wind conditions effect flights. The carousel and Visitors Center are open Thurs. - Fri., 10am - 3pm and 7pm - 10pm; Sat. - Sun., 9am - 3pm and 7pm - 10pm. Closed Mon. - Wed. The Farmer's Market is open Sun., 10am - 2pm. Farm and Food Lab is open daily, 10am - 3pm. The balloon and carousel are open on certain Monday holidays. The whole park is closed on New Year's Day, Veteran's Day, Thanksgiving, Christmas Eve, and Christmas Day.

Price: The carousel is $2 per person a ride or $3 for all day. Balloon flights are $10 for ages 19 and up; $5 for ages 12 - 18 without a paid, accompanying adult; free for ages 18 and under with a paid adult. Parking is usually free, except for special events, such as the Great Park Pumpkin Harvest, and Flights and Sounds Summer Festival, when the fee is $10 per car.

Ages: All

ORANGE COUNTY ROPES COURSE

(714) 616-1026 - ropes course; (714) 637-0210 - Canyon RV Park / www.ocropescourse.com; www.canyonrvpark.com

24001 Santa Ana Canyon Road at the Canyon RV Park in Featherly Regional Park, Anaheim

$$$$$

Are you up for a challenge? Up at least sixty feet off the ground, that is? Constructed with telephone poles, steel cables, and ropes, there are several elements (over 30 different challenges) to mentally and physically test participants in this ropes course. The emphasis here is not on speed, but on attempting and doing. (Just don't look down!)

The course consists of a rock climbing wall, Burma bridge, cargo net traverse, cat walk, rope bridges, other aerial obstacles, and two zip lines extending up to 277 feet each in length. On some of the elements you stand and walk the ropes, while on others you might move from one swing (made from two ropes with a bar between them) to another in the series. (Did I mention to not look down?) Every phase is supervised and each person wears a safety harness. The 2.5-hour ropes course challenge is designed for groups of at least two people as it's great for team building, birthday parties, scout outings, youth group gatherings, etc. A signed waiver and liability form, available online, is required by all participants.

The surrounding park also offers lots of picnic tables and hundreds of shade trees, a playground, grassy areas, horseshoe pits, a pickle ball court, and the beginning (or end) of the Santa Ana River Bike Trail, plus youth group camping, cabin rentals ($90 a night), and 140 RV hookup sites ($75 a night). The park does not offer day use. Campers have use of the pool (open seasonally) and other amenities. Located within a wildlife preserve, the long and somewhat narrow Featherly Park is bordered by the Santa Ana River. The river adds another scenic element to the park, as well as another place to explore, which when done safely, is fun for kids.

Hours: Call to schedule an outing.
  Price: 2 participants is $70; 4 is $128; 10 is $280. $2 per Spectator. Parking is $5.
  Ages: 7 and up, 50 - 250 pounds. Children 6 and under must climb with an adult.

OSO VIEJO PARK / OSO CREEK TRAIL

(949) 470-3095 / www.cityofmissionviejo.org; www.funorangecountyparks.com

the park - 24931 Veterans Way, Mission Viejo; the southern trailhead - 25552 Marguerite Parkway

Oso (which means "bear" in Spanish) Viejo Park features a playground, sports park, nature hiking trail, and community center. The center has a lovely outside patio to sit at and enjoy the nature of the park and/or have a picnic. Behind the center is a sand-based playground that boasts a three-story-high play tower with two, very long, enclosed slides jutting from the top, plus a few shorter slides, rock-climbing walls, metal climbing apparatus, and platforms. The playground also includes another, less-imposing play structure, plus a rope climbing wall, talking tubes, a swing set surrounded by a large rainbow imbedded in the ground, a teeter-totter, and more.

The park is almost at the center point of the 5.5 mile Oso Creek Trail. To catch the trail from the park, head south of the community center, down past the playground and baseball diamonds, or head north to PAVION PARK (pg. 290) which boasts a good-sized playground with a huge funnel and play equipment. The southern trailhead is located at 25552 Marguerite Parkway and the northern at 24051 Pavion. The fairly wide, pretty Oso Creek Trail is stroller-friendly and often shaded with huge trees. It parallels a rock-lined creek, green beltways, and an upper walking trail. Be on the lookout for ducks, turtle, bunnies, lizards, birds and other wildlife. Along the way there are short wooden bridges, a butterfly garden, a plant maze created from bushes, mosaic wall murals, garden spots, animal statues, picnic tables, and benches to rest.

Hours: Open daily, 7am - 11pm.
  Price: Free
  Ages: All

PAVION PARK

(949) 470-3061 or (949) 470-3093 / www.cityofmissionviejo.org; www.orangecounty.net

24051 Pavion, Mission Viejo

The five-acre Pavion Park is a playground in the best sense of the word - it has huge play structure that is wheelchair accessible with lots of zig zaggety ramps, plus bridges, several short slides, climbing structures, and slides coming out of a treehouse. There is a huge, open, colorful, creative play space (one area has flowers and animal tracks decorating its flooring) with objects and equipment for the kids to use however their imagination dictates that includes bent poles with a standing space at the base, poles with pods, raised big bowls to sit in, 3 different types of swings, and more. Vibrant Adirondack chairs in groupings are all around. There is also a large free-standing rock climbing rock, picnic tables, barbecues, and a soccer/football field.

The park can be the starting or ending point for your walk along the 5.5 mile paved walking/biking pathway, Oso Creek Trail. See OSO VIEJO PARK / OSO CREEK TRAIL (pg. 290) for details about the trail and another park along the way.

Hours: Open daily, sunrise - sunset.
Price: Free
Ages: All

PEARSON PARK

(714) 765-5274 - amphitheater; (714) 765-5155 - park; (714) 635-9622 - pool / www.anaheim.net
400 N. Harbor Boulevard, Anaheim

At the north end of this attractive, nineteen-acre park is a series of small, interconnecting, rock-edged ponds with a few bubbly fountains and lots of friendly ducks. Besides an abundance of palm trees and a variety of mature shade trees (which make good climbing trees!), there is plenty of green lawn, some scattered picnic tables and barbecue pits, and cement pathways throughout which allow the whole park to be accessible. The sports oriented will enjoy the six tennis courts, sand volleyball courts, baseball diamond with stadium seating and the swimming pool (which is run by Anaheim YMCA) with a small, adjacent, two-and-a-half-feet pool.

The playground, with wood chip flooring, has a swing set, slides, a short "rock" climbing wall attached to a good-size play structure with steering wheels in place of monkey bars, and a giant plastic climbing thing that it looks like an oversized leaf.

A large, enclosed amphitheater, located on the east side of the park, is the hot spot for terrific family entertainment during the summer months, such as Friday night Family Series ($3 for ages 8 and up; children 7 and under are free) and movie nights. This venue, with flower-lined walkways, has a box office and a refreshment stand in the courtyard.

Hours: The park is open daily. The pool is open mid-June - Labor Day, Sat. - Sun., 1pm - 5pm.
Price: The park is free. Swimming is free, too.
Ages: All

PETERS CANYON REGIONAL PARK

(714) 973-6611 or (714) 973-6612 / www.ocparks.com
8548 E. Canyon View Avenue, Orange

My boys and I have decided that this huge, 354-acre undeveloped park, bordered by occasional housing developments, is best geared for at least somewhat hardy hikers and bikers. The seven miles of narrow dirt trails are sometimes barren and sometimes lined with sage scrub, grassland areas, and willow and sycamore trees, as they traverse up and down and through the hills and canyon. (Bring drinking water and know that it is hot during the summer!) The 2.5 mile upper Lake View Trail loops around the reservoir, while the lower East Ridge Trail and Peters Canyon Trail provide a panoramic view of the canyon and the surrounding area. Be on the lookout for lots of wildlife.

The reservoir by the parking lot offers one of the most scenic spots, as it overlooks the water often teeming with diverse waterfowl - bird watchers flock here. Picnic tables under a few shade trees are also here. Another scenic area is along the Creek Trail as it goes along a creek.

Hours: Open daily, 7am - sunset.
Price: Parking is $3 per vehicle.
Ages: 5 years and up.

PIONEER ROAD PARK

(714) 573-3000 / www.tustinca.org
10250 Pioneer Road, Tustin

Round up your young 'uns and bring 'em to this Western-themed park. Its most unique feature are the several, hardy, wooden-sided, wire-meshed and open-topped stagecoaches with wagon wheels and short ladders to climb aboard. The wagons are arranged in a semi-circle, just like the old days. The park also has wonderful, covered, multi-story play structures that have enclosed tube slides, open slides, ropes and chains to climb, twisty metal apparatus to climb, lots of swings, a zip line, a clear tunnel connector, bridges, and nooks and crannies to play in and on. There is even room underneath one of the towers with a little table and chairs. Other amenities include a basketball half court, grass volleyball court, walking trail encircling the park, grassy areas, and a seasonal water spray area. In this area, water spurts up from the ground and feels good on our hot summer days. An open-sided log cabin eating area has numerous picnic tables under its roof, as well as barbecue pits. The facilities here are nice, not rustic.

Hours: Open daily, sunrise - sunset. The water play area is open Memorial Day - Labor Day daily, 10am - 4pm.
Price: Free
Ages: All

PREHISTORIC PLAYGROUND

(949) 707-2680 / www.ci.laguna-hills.ca.us
25555 Alicia Parkway, Laguna Hills

See LAGUNA HILLS COMMUNITY CENTER AND SPORTS COMPLEX (pg. 308) for details about this great, primordial playground. The sports complex also has ball fields, a roller hockey rink, and a huge skate park. The Community Center features a museum, of sorts, showcasing locally found fossils.

RALPH B. CLARK REGIONAL PARK

(714) 973-3170 / www.ocparks.com
8800 Rosecrans Avenue, Buena Park

This 100-acre park is one of the most aesthetically pleasing parks we've seen. It has all the things that make a park great - a lake to fish in, short waterfalls, ducks to feed, tennis courts, horseshoe pits, three softball fields, a baseball diamond, volleyball courts, and a few small playgrounds. Take a short hike around Camel Hill, or let the kids climb on the small, therefore ironically named, Elephant Hill. A paved bicycle trail goes all around the perimeter of the park. The playgrounds are wonderfully rustic-looking. One has duel slides, swings, climbing structures, and shaped, fake rocks plopped around to climb on and pretend with, all in a big area of sand.

The Interpretative Center has a working paleontology lab where kids can look through a big window and observe the detailed work being done. The Center also houses a twenty-six-foot Baleen whale fossil; a skeletal sabertooth "attacking" a skeletal horse; fossils of a ground sloth and a mammoth; shells; and more.

Kids really dig the marine fossil site across the street where a *bone*afide paleontologist conducts Family Fossil Day four times a year, usually in February, May, September, and December. This three-hour class is geared for youngsters 6 years and up. They can practice their fossil-finding skills by looking for fossilized shells at the marine site, then study and classify them back at the lab at the Interpretive Center. They may also make a craft, play a game, or enjoy another activity related to that day's theme. The price for the field trip is simply the price of admission to the park.

Hours: The park is open November through March daily, 7am - 6pm; April through October daily, 7am - 9pm. The Interpretative Center is usually open Tues. - Fri., 12:30pm - 5pm. Call first to make sure it's staffed, thus open.
Price: $3 per vehicle Mon. - Fri.; $5 on Sat. - Sun.; $7 on some holidays.
Ages: All

RANCHO MISSION VIEJO LAND CONSERVANCY

(949) 489-9778 / www.rmvreserve.org
Off Ortega Highway, San Juan Capistrano

The Land Conservancy manages a 1,200 acre wilderness reserve in the coastal foothills. They offer an incredible array of special programs to the general public and to school groups that give intimate glimpses into the wilderness of Orange County. Programs include guided nature walks, bird watching (and finding), wildlife workshops, astronomy nights, owl outings, bat walks, butterfly classes, butterfly counting (for research purposes), trail maintenance, and much more. The programs are given by trained docents, or professionals in that field of study. What a wonderful opportunity for kids to become aware of wildlife, and what they can do to help protect it. Also see RONALD W. CASPERS WILDERNESS PARK (pg. 293) which is just down the road.

Hours: Check the website for program hours and to look at the calendar of events. Visitors are not allowed on property without a conservancy staff member.
Price: Depending on the program, the fees range from free to $10 for adults; $5 for ages 16 and under.
Ages: Varies, depending on the program.

RICHARD T. STEED MEMORIAL PARK / RALPH'S SKATE PARK

(949) 361-8264 / www.san-clemente.org
247 Avenida La Pata, San Clemente

The memorial park has several ball fields and is home to many tournaments - it even has a concession stand. There are also batting cages, a playground (with twisty slides and cargo nets), picnic areas, volleyball courts, and a skate park. This great, unsupervised 14,000-square-foot, concrete skate park features bowls, ramps, stairs, rails, and pyramids. It has lights, too. A helmet and knee and elbows pads must be worn for safety's sake and because the patrolling police will cite offenders.

Hours: The park is open daily, 6am - 10pm. The skate park is open daily, dawn - dusk. Note that the skate park is closed Fri., 8am - 10am, for maintenance.
Price: Free
Ages: All

RONALD W. CASPERS WILDERNESS PARK

(949) 923-2210 or (949) 923-2207 - park; (800) 600-1600 - camping reservations / www.ocparks.com
33401 Ortega Highway, San Juan Capistrano

Orange County's largest park is massive, and consists mostly of canyon wilderness such as seasonally verdant valleys, groves of live oak and sycamore trees, meadows, and running streams. We saw mule deer and jackrabbits scampering through the woods and quail walking/running alongside the dirt road. The over thirty miles of hiking trails range from easy walks to strenuous, mountain-man hikes. The moderate, four-mile Bell Canyon loop is a nice jaunt. Start on the nature trail loop, go through oak trees, left on the Oak Trail cutoff that heads north along a streambed then onto a fire road. Your best bet is to pick up a trail map at the front entrance. Give kids the freedom to hike, but beware that mountain lions sometimes roam this area, too. Mountain bike usage is permitted on designated roads only. Visitors can also enjoy a barbecue under shade trees and playing on the large wooden playground with swings and slides, surrounded by trees. Check out the Nature Center that has a few taxidermied animals and hands-on activities.

The numerous camp sites are picturesque, wonderful for enjoying nature. Campsites have picnic tables, charcoal-burning stoves, fire rings, and a nearby water source. Also see RANCHO MISSION VIEJO LAND CONSERVANCY (pg. 292) which is just down the road.

Hours: Open daily, 7am - sunset. The nature center is open Sat. - Sun, 9am - 3pm.
Price: $3 per vehicle Mon. - Fri.; $5 on Sat. - Sun.; $7 on some holidays. Camping is $20 a night; $15 for seniors.
Ages: All

SAN JOAQUIN WILDLIFE SANCTUARY / SEA & SAGE AUDUBON

(949) 261-7963 / www.seaandsageaudubon.org
5 Riparian View, Irvine

Who would have imagined that there would be this beautiful, peaceful bird sanctuary smack in the midst of the Irvine business district? Park at the grouping of buildings, one of which is the Audubon center. The center contains a collection of taxidermy birds and is a great place to pick up information and maps, and perhaps even purchase something from the small gift shop. Binoculars and birding guides are available for loan here, too. The nicely landscaped grounds have an open green lawn, a few picnic tables, and restroom facilities. Note: Across the road from the center is the San Diego Creek, which offers more diverse wildlife (and a walking trail alongside).

There are twelve miles of fairly level, dirt, walking trails through the almost 300 acres of the sanctuary, as well as five large ponds (and several smaller ones), nesting islands, and riparian habitat. What a delight! This area is home to 223 species of birds, as well as rabbits (we saw several), raccoons, coyotes, lizards, dragonflies (by the marshy areas), and bats. Come to look for Canada geese, snowy egrets, peregrine falcons, great blue herons, black-necked stilts, and more birds, or just come to enjoy being in nature.

Explore the sanctuary on your own or join in any number of programs, such as the free monthly wildlife walks offered on the first Saturday of the month at 9am; workshops for teachers and students, including classroom kits on owls, songbirds, butterflies, and more; nature camps; and two-hour hands-on field trips for schools on wetland birds and pond life. If you're *pond*ering what to do, come here and let your imagination take flight!

Hours: Trails are open daily, dawn - dusk. The center is open daily, 8am - 4pm. Closed major holidays.
Price: Free
Ages: All

SANTA ANA RIVER LAKES

(714) 632-7830 / www.fishinglakes.com
4060 E. La Palma Avenue, Anaheim

Not incredibly scenic and just off the main road, the reason to come here is for the fishing. Stocked twice a week in the winter with rainbow trout and lightning trout (you gotta be quick as a flash to catch these!) and catfish in the summer, plus bass and crappie, the lakes are great for fishermen of all ages. The lakes are also known for the large size fish that are often caught. A fishing license is not required. There is a five fish limit for adults and a three fish limit for children. The area is handicap accessible as you can drive right up to the lake's edge to fish. Motor boat rentals ($50 a day), rowboats ($20 a day), and pontoons for up to eight people ($100 a day) are available.

The park also offers picnic tables, a grassy area, and some large shade trees. Kids are almost guaranteed to catch a fish, or two, at the enclosed, small, rock-lined Huckleberry Pond, which is a nice-looking spot. There are chairs, a big shade tree, ducks, and picnic tables. Rod rentals are available for $3. Via the Huckleberry Mining Company, visitors can also purchase mining rough planted with minerals, gemstones and fossils. Pour it onto screens, shake and rinse it out to catch some rocks!

Other amenities include an on-site tackle shop that carries bait, as well as snacks and sandwiches to satisfy humans. There are lots of birds - I saw storks, kingfisher, herons, and ducks. Camping here is free and pretty much on the dirt, but for those who like to get an early start in the morning, it's ideal.

Hours: Open daily, 6am - 4pm for the day session; 12:30pm - 11pm for midday; and 5pm - 11pm for the evening session. There are also 24-hour sessions. Mining is open Wed. - Fri., 9am - 1pm; Sat. - Sun., 9am - 4pm.

Price: Day and night sessions are $28 for ages 13 and up; $15 for ages 4 - 12; children 3 and under are free. Midday session are $5 more with a fish limit of seven for adults; four for kids. Ask or check the website for specials. Huckleberry Pond costs $3 (per rod) and fish from there costs $8 a pound.

Ages: 3 years and up.

SANTIAGO OAKS REGIONAL PARK

(714) 973-6620 or (714) 973-6622 / www.ocparks.com
2145 N. Windes Drive, Orange

Get back to nature at this 1,269-acre park that has beautiful hiking and equestrian trails that connect to the Anaheim Hills trail system. Take a short path along the creek leading to a waterfall at the dam, or travel more rugged terrain into the heart of the park. Be on the lookout for animals such as lizards, squirrels, deer, and birds. Mountain lions have been seen on rare occasion, too.

A favorite activity here is cooking breakfast over the charcoal barbecues early in the morning, while it's still quiet and cool. A small playground and a few horseshoe pits round out the facilities under a canopy of oak trees. The small Nature Center has taxidermied animals, pictures, and a few hands-on activities. Free, ranger-led tours are given on the first Sunday of the month at 10am, by reservation only.

Hours: The park is open daily, 7am - sunset. The nature center is open the first Sun., 10am - 2pm, more hours if staffed.

Price: $3 per vehicle Mon. - Fri., $5 on Sat. - Sun.; $7 on some holidays.

Ages: All

SANTIAGO PARK / NATURE RESERVE

(714) 571-4200 - park; (714) 571-4230 - nature reserve / www.ci.santa-ana.ca.us
600 E. Memory Lane, Santa Ana

You can literally stroll along Memory Lane here, simply because that's the name of the street adjacent to the park. This long park, located directly across the street from the DISCOVERY CUBE (Orange County) (pg. 304), has several areas with play equipment, plus scattered picnic tables, shade trees, grassy patches, and barbecue pits. We usually spend most of our time at the first play area, with its slides, swings, sand area, wooden bridges, tunnels, and a green, wooden fort-like structure. A little further east is a slightly sunken grassy area (perfect for a group party), a lawn bowling center, a baseball diamond, an archery range, tennis courts, and more play equipment.

There is a small nature center building toward the east part of the park - the Santiago Creek Wildlife and Watershed Center. It has two rooms with nature wall murals, and information on the Santa Ana River and wildlife around, plus taxidermied animals, skulls, animal scat, bird eggs and nests, a few live animals (snakes and lizards), and other display. Find out info about nature walks and storytime for kids.

A rocky riverbed path follows along one side of the park. There is a bike/creek pathway that leads all the way to HART PARK (pg. 281), that follows along a rocky creek bed.

Hours: The park and nature center are open daily, sunrise - sunset, though the nature center hours can depend on staffing.

Price: Free

Ages: All

SIGLER PARK and SPLASH PAD

(714) 895-2860 / www.westminster-ca.gov
7200 Plaza Street, Westminster

This long park has various components including three and a half basketball courts, two racquetball/handball courts, a tennis courts with lights, BBQ pits, a multipurpose field at one end, and a small playground at the other. The colorful playground has twisty slides, a slide shaped like a fish, swings (including toddler swings), a short rock-climbing wall, some rope climbing walls, play areas under platforms, and metal configurations to climb.

What really makes this park stand out, though, is the gated water playground with lots of fun elements. Palm trees dot the area. Poles with pelican heads squirt out water, as do sea dragons, and kids can run under arches and whales tales that shoot out water. H2O also shoots up from the ground at certain points. There are cement benches for parents to sit and watch. The splash pad may be rented out for private parties.

Hours: The park is open daily, sunrise to sunset. The water park/splash pad is open Memorial Day - mid-June, weekends, noon - 5pm; open daily mid-June through Labor Day, noon - 5pm.

Price: Free

Ages: All for the park; toddler - 8 year old for the water park.

STANTON CENTRAL PARK

(714) 890-4268 / www.ci.stanton.ca.us

10660 Western Avenue, Stanton

Like any good central park, this one is a central gathering place for fun and community. It consists of an exercise loop trail dotted with several pieces of legitimate workout equipment; two half-basketball courts; four tennis courts; sports fields and huge, grassy areas to run around; picnic tables; a bandstand and plaza; a butterfly garden (easy to find because of the butterfly statue); and a gated, good-sized, cement skate park with rails, ramps, pipes and steps. There are also two playgrounds - one has a very small structure and a few swings, and the other is quite big. It has a large, multi-story, round water tower structure (paying homage to the city's past) to climb into and up connected by a tunnel to a raised, tiered, train-like structure with an enclosed slide and other twisty slides attached to it, plus climbing apparatus, short tunnels, mini zip line, and more interactive elements. Several free-standing fake rocks of various heights to climb on, over and thru, and spider like rope courses almost complete this park. There is also a seasonal water playground with some unique features like a huge can on a tower with a spout where water pours out; a fake stone archway; small, animal statues; and a train engine that water squirts and sprays out of. Bring your own chess pieces (or check them out from the park office) to play on chess boards embedded into some of the concrete picnic tabletops.

Hours: The park is open Mon. - Fri., 6am - 8pm; Sat. - Sun., 6am - 7pm. The skate park is open during the school year, Mon. - Fri., 2pm - 8pm; Sat. - Sun., 9am - 5pm. It's open during summer and other school breaks, Mon. - Fri., 10am - 8pm; Sat. - Sun., 8am - 6pm. The water play area is open Memorial Day - Labor Day, daily, noon - 5pm.

Price: Free

Ages: All

TEWINKLE MEMORIAL PARK / VOLCOM SKATE PARK

(714) 754-5300 / www.costamesaca.gov

970 Arlington Drive, Costa Mesa

The fifty-acre Tewinkle Memorial Park is another one of my favorite parks. The huge, colorful and shaded Angel's Playground is a barrier-free playground, meaning it's accessible for those in wheelchairs, as well as those who aren't. Several ramps adjoin the various play elements like the many slides, tunnels, and platforms, plus tic-tac-toe, chimes, metal spiral climby things, short climbing walls, spinning wheels, and monkey bars and monkey bars with handles. There is also lots of play space and components underneath the platforms with little houses, portholes, and more.

Other parts of the play area are sand based (so bring your bucket and shovel) and incorporate diggers, along with raised sand basins, and swings. There are also pedals on poles, green stools (or seats), and a large plastic vehicle to sit in and move back and forth propelled by kid motion. Picnic tables and barbecue pits are interspersed along the cement pathways that flow throughout and there are plenty of wide open grassy areas and big shade trees. The trees help make the park cool, even on a hot day.

Nature-loving kids will also enjoy this park (just ignore the planes flying overhead from the nearby airport) as at least half of the park is dedicated to three separate lakes connected by streams and short waterfalls, with wooden bridges and a walking path around them. There are numerous (!) ducks of all varieties here having a swimmingly good time. A large hill, with hefty rocks imbedded in and around it, divides the playground from the lakes. A short hike up the hill, dotted with pine trees, yields the treasure of a pond in a small, forest-like setting at the top.

For the sports-minded, there is also a basketball court and baseball fields, and across the street are tennis courts at the Costa Mesa Tennis Center plus a skate park. The popular and nicely-laid out Volcom Skate Park is 15,000 square feet of free skate fun with all the necessary street elements of ramps, rails, bowls, and steps. Helmet, knee and elbow pads are required.

Hours: The park is open daily, dawn - dusk. The skate park is open Mon., Wed. - Sun., 9am - 9pm; Tues., 3pm - 9pm.

Price: Free

Ages: All

THOMAS F. RILEY WILDERNESS PARK

(949) 923-2265 / www.ocparks.com

30952 Oso Parkway, Coto de Caza

This hilly, 544-acre wilderness preserve is a sanctuary for native wildlife - coyotes, mountain lions, raccoons, mule deer, a multitude of birds, and lots more. It's composed of hills with protected sagebrush, oak trees, and other plant life, plus a pond and two seasonal creeks. Five miles of rugged dirt trails (stroller occupants would have a bumpy ride) loop throughout the park and visitors are asked not to stray from them. Although housing developments border part of the park, miles of undeveloped canyons, tree groves, and Santa Ana Mountain peaks can still be seen from the viewpoints.

Take a self-guiding nature hike, or sign up for a guided walk or program. The park makes a wonderful outdoor "classroom" and offers students of all ages firsthand knowledge about the environment. Some of the programs offered include merit badge classes, which could include a topical game and craft; Critter Talk, which emphasizes learning about animal life styles and their habits and habitats, and includes animal presentations; Star Watch, designed for viewing and learning about the stars and moon; Jr. Rangers, which is a six-week, springtime class; special classes for toddlers; and more. Most of the programs have a minimal fee.

The small nature center contains a few taxidermy animals and a game that kids can take on the trail to help them identify objects they find along the way. A few picnic tables are under shade trees in front of the nature center. A butterfly garden is here, too. Note: The rangers are very friendly and dedicated to enabling children to learn more about the wilds of Orange County.

Hours: Open daily, 7am - sunset. Call for seasonal hours.

Price: $3 parking fee.

Ages: 4 years and up.

TIERRA GRANDE PARK

(949) 361-8264 / www.san-clemente.org; www.funorangecountyparks.com

399 Camino Tierra Grande, San Clemente

Old McDonald might have had a farm, but kids can invite all their barnyard friends to Tierra Grande Park (also known as Red Barn Park) - a farm-theme park without the smell and mess of a real farm! The main, multi-level, interconnected, large structures are comprised of platforms and red poles and bars that sport barn facades, along with short bridges, mesh-like roofs, several slides, a large tic tac toe game, wheels, speaking tubes, metal spiral elements, tubes to crawl through, fireman poles, and more fun. Based in sand and recycled rubber, kids can play on, in, through and under the "barn."

Other components of the playground include a corral with animals on large springs to ride on; a hay and milk tractor cut outs with play equipment behind them; a big circle to sit on and spin around and around; swings, including toddler swings and a wheelchair-accessible swing; and sandy areas for digging and building. The park also features a large expanse of open grass with trees and a paved pathway around the perimeter; softball/multipurpose fields; two lighted basketball courts; horseshoe pits; and a large area with picnic tables, sinks, and barbecue pits. Come cock-a-doodle-do and more at this playground.

Hours: Open daily, 6am - 10pm

Price: Free

Ages: All

TRI-CITY PARK

(714) 973-3180 / www.ocparks.com

2301 N. Kraemer Boulevard, Placentia

Named for being in close proximity to Brea, Fullerton, and Placentia, the centerpiece of this established park is a large lake for fishing, feeding ducks, and gazing at. Benches are placed around the lake's perimeter. Picnic benches overlook the park giving it an air of restfulness. There are a multitude of old trees, a considerable amount of grassy areas, paved pathways that meander throughout, a sand volleyball court, bicycle trails, and a playground toward the south end of Tri-City.

Hours: Open April through October daily, 7am - 9pm. Open November through March daily, 7am - 6pm.

Price: Free

Ages: All

TUCKER WILDLIFE SANCTUARY

(714) 649-2760 / www.tuckerwildlife.org

29322 Modjeska Canyon Road, Silverado

At the end of a windy, tree-lined country road is this twelve-acre wilderness destination that's adjacent to the Cleveland National Forest. It's owned by Cal State Fullerton and used for research purposes. The small, welcoming, natural history/interpretative center contains taxidermied wildlife such as a cougar, bobcat, eagle, squirrel, owl, grizzly bear, and lots of local birds. Live animals include some snakes, frogs, lizards, and a millipede. Look under microscopes at insects, butterfly wings, cat hair, vacuum cleaner lint, and more. One wall mural has the food web; others are equally informative and colorful. Play with animal puppets; look at X-rays of animals; dissect owl pellets; and study and touch animal skins and bones, fossils, and rocks, that are on display and in drawers to pull out. A small gift shop and snack shop is here, too.

Just outside is a patio with a picnic area under the canopy of large oak trees. A little, children's garden has interesting plants to look at, touch, and smell. Seasonally, you'll see butterflies fluttering around, attracted to the garden's plants.

Across the road are several easy walking trails that take visitors in and amongst the trees and chaparral. A looping trail, partially paved, is 1.5 miles around the sanctuary. Along the scenic and well-maintained trail you'll encounter a creek that runs through the property; two ponds that contain mosquito fish, turtles, and water lilies; desert tortoises in an open air enclosure; lots of benches; trees, sage plants, cactus, and more; squirrels and lizards; and a bird observation porch. Sit quietly inside the porch area and watch hummingbirds and other species fly in and fill up at the feeders hanging just outside. Identify the birds by using the pictures and info on the porch wall. I think this tranquil place is a human sanctuary as much as a bird sanctuary.

Other popular trails include the Harding Truck Trail, which is a fire road from the sanctuary that goes uphill (at least one way!) and extends twenty-five miles into the forest (although you can stop and turn around whenever you want), and the Laurel Springs Trail, which is about a 5.5 miles round-trip and leads up to natural streams and even little waterfalls that appear after a rain.

Guided tours are offered for grades K through 12, Tuesdays through Fridays, that include hiking part of a trail, and insight and education regarding native plants and animals.

Note that the ARDEN - THE HELENA MODJESKA HISTORIC HOUSE AND GARDENS (pg. 301) is nearby.

Hours: Open Tues. - Sun., 9am - 4pm. Closed Mon. and major holidays.

Price: Free. $3 donation per person is recommended. Guided tours are $6 per participant, or a minimum of $80 and must be scheduled in advance.

Ages: 4 years and up.

TURTLE ROCK PARK and NATURE CENTER

(949) 724-6734 or (949) 854-8144 - park; (949) 724-6738 - nature center / trail / www.cityofirvine.org; www.letsgooutside.org

1 Sunnyhill Drive, Irvine

The lovely Turtle Rock Park has lighted tennis courts, a basketball court, baseball diamond, sand volleyball courts, a community center, and a decent-sized playground with slides, rings, fort-like towers, and climbing structures, all amidst shade trees. There is also a nature trail that goes over a seasonal creek.

The nature center building is also the entrance way to a small, five-acre nature preserve. The preserve has both a desert habitat and pine trees, so that the short, stroller-friendly trail is partially in the sun and partially in the shade. A ranger here said that going around a little pond, over a few bridges, and looping back around takes "ten minutes if you don't see anything, thirty minutes if you follow the trail guide. The longer you're here, the more you'll learn." For a small fee, guided tours of the trail are offered by reservation, as are tours for scouts earning badges, with a minimum of ten people. Also check out the nearby BOMMER CANYON / QUAIL TRAIL (pg. 272), for more of a hike.

Hours: The park is open Mon. - Fri., 9am - 9pm; Sat., 9am - 10pm; Sun., noon - 6pm. The nature center is open Mon. - Fri., 9am - 5pm; Sat., 9am - 4pm; closed on Sun.

Price: Free

Ages: 2 - 13 years.

UPPER NEWPORT BAY NATURE PRESERVE / PETER AND MARY MUTH ☼
INTERPRETIVE CENTER

(949) 923-2290 or (714) 973-6820 - interpretive center; (949) 640-9958 - Back Bay Science Center; (949)   !/$$
923-2269 - Back Bay tour / www.newportbay.org; www.ocparks.com

2301 University Drive, Newport Beach

The impressive-looking Peter and Mary Muth Interpretive Center, which is not visible from above as it's tucked under the observation bluff overlooking the northern portion of the reserve, offers several hands-on activities for kids. Lift panels to find answers to questions such as "Why does mud stink?". Walk through a short tunnel of (fake) mud to see what lives there. The center also has numerous information panels and displays around the inside perimeter; an exhibit on what comprises an estuary, accompanied by a real fish tank; taxidermied animals; a cut away to show life above and below the waterline; a theater room with several TV screens to view films; and a kids room filled with some live critters (i.e. snakes, turtles and lizards), a fake tree with a hollowed out trunk, fun and educational equipment and games, and kid-size tables. Look for butterflies in the butterfly garden planted just outside the building.

A short, somewhat stroller-friendly dirt hiking trail in this immediate area takes visitors to vistas overlooking the bay and reserve. A three-and-a-half-mile paved biking/walking trail goes around the reserve, mostly along the one-way street, Backbay Drive, where cars can only go fifteen miles an hour. This is a great way to explore the estuary. Note: You will frequently hear planes flying overhead from the nearby John Wayne Airport.

This ecological reserve, a remnant of a once-extensive wetland, is part of an endeavor to conserve wildlife in the Upper Bay. Although surrounded by urban development and ringed by roads, the bay and small islands are home to sea critters, a variety of plants, and hundreds of waterfowl as it's a stopover for migrating birds on the Pacific Flyway.

Introduce your children to the valuable natural resources that God originally put on the earth by involving kids in the wide variety of interactive and interpretive programs offered at the interpretive center, at the Back Bay Science Center, at 600 Shellmaker Drive, (www.backbaysciencecenter.org), and at the California Department of Fish and Game. Curriculum aids are available. Join in on a free walking tour, or participate in youth fishing programs, clean-up day, or shark study - mere samplings of what is offered here. Special tours are offered for students, scouts, and interested adults. The Science Center is open to the public every Sunday from 10am to 2pm to take a tour of facility, touch animals at the tidepool touch tank, walk the short loop trail, and do some hands-on activities.

A knowledgeable naturalist from the Newport Bay Conservancy is the guide for a two-hour kayak tour of the Back Bay, the wildlife estuary reserve, every Saturday and Sunday at 10am. In the estuary, you can see crabs, blue herons, snowy egrets, and other birds and animals in their natural habitat. We took this tour and learned why this reserve is becoming endangered, as well as some of the clean up projects that we can get involved with. What a workout of paddling for those of us not physically fit! But it is also a fun and educational way to spend some family time together. The cost is $25 for ages 8 and up, which is the minimum age. Call (949) 923-2269 / www.newportbay.org for more info.

For swimming, camping, and more water-sport fun, look under the NEWPORT DUNES WATERFRONT RESORT MARINA (pg. 245) and MOE B'S WATERSPORTS (pg. 331), which are at the southern end of the bay.

Hours: The interpretative center is open Tues. - Sun., 10am - 4pm. Closed Mon. and major holidays. The reserve is open daily, sunrise - sunset.

Price: Free to the interpretative center. Program prices vary.

Ages: 5 years and up.

WHITING RANCH WILDERNESS PARK ☼

(949) 923-2245 / www.whitingranch.com; www.ocparks.com $

27901 Glenn Ranch Rd, Trabuco Canyon or 26701 Portola Parkway, Foothill Ranch

"Real" hikers can explore the hills of Trabuco Canyon via the 2,500 acres and 17 miles of trails of Whiting Ranch Wilderness Park. Follow the trails through forested canyons with huge oak trees, along streams, and past huge boulders. A moderate hike starts at the Borrego Trail and leads to the Red Rock Canyon trail, which is about five miles round trip and loops back around. Note: This trail is more easily reached from the Market Street entrance. The scenery is outstanding. The size and beauty of this park offers the opportunity to enjoy some good, back-to-nature time with your kids. I'm not trying to give contrary information, but also remember that this is a wilderness area and wild animals, including mountain lions and rattlesnakes, inhabit this place. The on-site ranger station has some taxidermied animals and historical info about the region.

Hours: Open daily, 7am - sunset.

Price: $3 per vehicle.

Ages: 5 years and up.

WILDCATTERS PARK

(714) 990-7100 / www.ci.brea.ca.us
3301 E. Santa Fe Road, Brea

The two playgrounds here, built on recycled rubber, are really fun as they feature some usual elements - slides and swings and places to climb, plus some unusual ones such as a little log tunnel; a tree trunk with "cut" branches and steps; a good-size fake boulder to climb on; a quirky-shape that has drums and a piano-like panel to create music (or just noise); and play horses on big springs to ride.

The rest of the nicely-landscaped park is part of a sports complex with a baseball field; a football/soccer field; concession stand; and basketball court, plus picnic tables (and lots of benches), bbq, and a .6 mile paved, looping walking trail.

Hours: Open daily, sunrise - sunset.
  Price: Free
  Ages: 2 ½ years and up.

WILLIAM R. MASON REGIONAL PARK

(949) 923-2223 or (949) 923-2220 / www.ocparks.com
18712 University Drive, Irvine

This 345-acre park is serene (even with kids!) and beautiful. The picturesque lake is a central feature. You can bring your model boat for sailing on it. Fishing, with a license, is allowed, but be forewarned - the lake isn't stocked. Honking gaggles of geese will vie for your attention (and food). There are three different playgrounds with modular plastic equipment such as tunnels, slides, swings, forts, etc. The park also boasts of two sand volleyball courts, a ball field, a fitness course, horseshoe pits, picnic shelters, open grassy expanses, large shade trees, a butterfly habitat and two miles of lovely paved walking/biking trails that crisscross throughout.

Hours: Open November through March daily, 7am - 6pm. Open April through October daily, 7am - 9pm.
  Price: $3 per vehicle Mon. - Fri.; $5 on Sat. - Sun.; $7 on some holidays.
  Ages: All

YORBA REGIONAL PARK

(714) 973-6615 or (714)973-6838 - park; (714) 461-1652 - Wheel Fun rentals / www.ocparks.com; www.wheelfunrentals.com
7600 E. La Palma Avenue, Anaheim

This pleasant, 140-acre elongated park follows along the Santa Ana River. It offers a myriad of activities such as nice, flat, paved and unpaved trails for healthy distances for family hiking, horseback riding biking, and biking, including going the distance on the twenty-mile Santa Ana River Trail which leads all the way to the ocean! (See BIKE TRAIL: SANTA ANA RIVER (Riverside County) (pg. 372) for bike route information.) Other amenities include four softball fields and a lighted baseball diamond; an exercise course; horseshoe pits; several volleyball courts; and a few noteworthy playgrounds. The playgrounds are colorful and have fun, twisty tunnels to go through, plus some good, metal, climbing apparatus. One of the playgrounds has a whimsical fish ladder, poles with seats to move and spin on, swings, and more.

A wonderful urban get away to nature (though the freeway is right there), this park is flush with a variety of trees including wooded areas, shade trees, and great climbing trees, plus lots and lots of grassy run-around space, barbecue pits and numerous (over 400!) picnic tables. Water is always a draw. (I think of this from Psalm 23 - "He leads me beside quiet waters, He refreshes my soul.") The lakes here are really scenic, with bridges to connect them and some short piers for fishing. Note that a valid fishing license is necessary for fishermen over 16 years. One of the lakes allows operating model boats and another is great for kayaking and paddle boating. Streams also weave their way throughout the park. Note that bikes and boats are available to rent here: Hourly rentals include $25 for a small surrey; $10 for a cruiser bike; $6 for a kid's bike; $15 a half hour for a pedal boat; $10 a half hour for a single kayak; $15 for a double.

Hours: The park is open April through October daily, 7am - 9pm; November through March daily, 7am - 6pm. Rentals are available September - mid-June, Sat., Sun. and holidays, 10am - sunset; mid-June - August, Wed. - Fri., noon - 7pm; Sat., Sun., and holidays, 10am - sunset.
  Price: $3 per vehicle during the week; $5 on Sat. - Sun.; $7 on some holidays.
  Ages: All

—MALLS—

ANAHEIM TOWN SQUARE - KIDS FUN ZONE

(714) 956-3411 / www.anaheimtownsquare.com

2100 East Lincoln Avenue, Anaheim

You can shop at the store and eat at the restaurants here any day, but only on the last Saturday of each month can kids gather together at the long tables set up then to make a free, seasonal craft such as heart art for Valentine's Day or painting a tote bag (for the fun of it). Kids are offered merchant discounts on those days, too. The Square also hosts events throughout the year, so check the online calender.

Hours: The last Sat. of the month, 11am - 3pm.

Price: Free

Ages: 3 - 12 years

BELLA TERRA - KIDS CLUB

(714) 897-2534 / www.bellaterra-hb.com

7777 Edinger Avenue, Huntington Beach

This lovely, outdoor mall features a Kid's Club at the amphitheater outside the Century Theaters that can include magicians, jugglers, puppet shows, storytellers, and/or musicians. The performances are often interactive, so kids become part of the show. Wholesome entertainment in the California sunshine surrounded by shops and restaurants, including BUCA DI BEPPO (Los Angeles County) (pg. 16) - this is the place to be. During the summer, sign up for the Summer Movie Clubhouse where children's movies are shown for $1 a movie on select days at 10am.

Bella Terra also offers live music on most weekend evenings ranging from alternative rock to Latin contemporary to jazz, as well as family crafts and special events throughout the year. Check the website for more info.

Hours: Kids Club is usually the last Mon. of the month from 10:30am - 11:30am.

Price: Free

Ages: 2 - 10 years

IRVINE SPECTRUM CENTER

(949) 789-9180 or (949) 753-5180 / www.shopirvinespectrumcenter.com

71 Fortune Drive, Irvine

How can I choose favorites from a choice of over 120 shops, restaurants, and entertainment venues? I vote for the Edwards with an IMAX and 3-D theater (with king-size recliners in certain theaters!), ROCKET FIZZ SODA POPS AND CANDY SHOP (Los Angeles County) (pg. 26), Barnes & Noble Bookstore, and STORYMAKERY (pg. 319). Kid favorites include playing (and getting wet) on the turtle statues in the fountain outside the food court, or in the small, shaded playground towards the Target. They also enjoy riding the carousel ($3) with its three rows of animals to ride on such as bears, deer, a rabbit, tigers and more; the kiddie train ride ($3); the 108-foot Giant Wheel ($5), found at one end of the spectrum (which is lit up beautifully at night); and The Ride 7D, located next door to the Wheel. The Ride 7D (yes, 7D) is an eight-passenger, seven-minute, immersive, interactive motion ride experience as you feel the elements you experience on the screen, coupled with the joy of using laser guns, too. There are three adventures to choose from that could include zombies, robot cowboys, monsters, racing and more. Rides are $10 per. Call (949)769-6772 / www.theride7d.com for more information.

Hungry? This outside mall includes a gigantic a DAVE & BUSTER'S (Orange County) (pg. 259); a food court; and restaurants such as California Pizza Kitchen, Cheesecake Factory, RUBY'S (Orange County) (pg. 252), Johnny Rockets, and more. The Cold Stone Creamery can help you (or hurt you) in the dessert area.

For entertainment, there is almost always something special going on, including live music/concerts on the weekends by the Giant Wheel. Sometimes the center features Toddler Tuesdays for a time of free arts and crafts, as well as music, dancing, storytelling and more. Check out the website for the complete calendar of events. Sign up for the free Kid's Birthday Club where your children get a free ride on the kiddie train, Giant Wheel and carousel on their birthday.

Note that there is an Improv Comedy Theater here, too - for adults. Call (949) 854-5455 / www.improv.com for dinner and show information. Check the November Calendar, under HOLIDAY ON ICE (pg. 748), for details about the seasonal ice-skating rink.

Hours: Most shops are open Mon. - Thurs., 10am - 9pm; Fri. - Sat., 10am - 10pm; Sun., 10am - 8pm; restaurants and the movie theater are open later.

Price: Technically, free.

Ages: All

MAINPLACE MALL

(714) 547-7000 / www.shopmainplacemall.com
2800 N. Main Street, Santa Ana

The mall features Picture Show (pg. 774), ROUND1 BOWLING AND AMUSEMENT (Orange County) (pg. 265), DISNEY STORE (Orange County) (pg. 316) and a younger child's indoor playplace with hard-foam, fanciful, large critters to climb on and in, and padded benches surrounding it.
Hours: The mall is open Mon. - Fri., 10am - 9pm; Sat., 10am - 8pm; Sun., 11am - 7pm.
  Price: Free
  Ages: All

PLAYCLUB AT THE SOURCE

(714) 521-8858 / www.thesourceoc.com
6940 Beach Boulevard, Buena Park

When all else fails go to The Source! This Source has a free, weekly kid's program at the outdoor, Main Plaza, or the first floor Step Plaza (with tiered seating), featuring different activities and/or themes. Along with interactive science shows/experiments, magic acts, singing, dancing, arts and crafts, face painting, festivals, hero sightings, photo ops, and more, there are also special events going on for the entire family. Check their calendar and come be a part of it all.
Hours: PlayClub is every Sat., 2pm - 3pm. Check the website for special events.
  Price: Free
  Ages: 2 - 11

SOUTH COAST PLAZA

(714) 435-2034 or (800) 782-8888 / www.southcoastplaza.com
3333 Bristol Street, Costa Mesa

With 250 stores restaurants, this upscale mall is REALLY big! Of particular kid interest are Pottery Barn for Kids, (714) 427-0813 / www.potterybarnkids.com, because it hosts storytelling every Tuesday at 11am; the interactive and magical DISNEY STORE (Orange County) (pg. 316); LEGO STORE - MINI MODEL BUILD (Orange County) (pg. 262); RUBY'S (Orange County) (pg. 252); Puzzle Zoo toy store; a glass elevator (just to ride in); and smallish carousel. The mall also hosts seasonal and special events.
Hours: The mall is open Mon. - Fri., 10am - 9pm; Sat., 10am - 8pm; Sun., 11am - 6:30pm.
  Price: Free. Carousel rides are $1.
  Ages: All

—MUSEUMS—

ARDEN - THE HELENA MODJESKA HISTORIC HOUSE AND GARDENS

(949) 923-2230 / www.helenamodjeska.net; www.ocparks.com
29042 Modjeska Canyon Road, Silverado

Waaaaay off the beaten path is the fourteen-acre, wooded parklands and picturesque old cottage plus surrounding gardens that have withstood the test of time in a gracious manner. Once owned by a renowned Shakespearean actress, Madame Modjeska who died in 1909, the public is invited to tour through the residence to admire the furnishings and the architecture. The porches and gables are reminiscent of a more romantic era. Besides the main attraction of the white cottage home, there is a cabin, guest cottages, a hexagonal building (once a music room), reflection ponds, lily ponds, a well, and two stages extending into the gardens. The wooded area around the house is alive with oak trees, a grove of redwoods, palms, and other plants. Walk along the rock-lined pathway through the Forest of Arden, so named from Shakespeare's play *As You Like It*. On the guided tour, which is the only way to see Modjeska, the docent explains the history of the home and the theatrical lifestyle of the original owners. Note that the TUCKER WILDLIFE SANCTUARY (pg. 297) is close by.
Hours: Guided tours are offered every Wed. and Sat., 10am by advanced reservations only - no walk-ins allowed.
  Price: $5 per person.
  Ages: 10 years and up.

BEALL CENTER FOR ART AND TECHNOLOGY

(949) 824-6206 / beallcenter.uci.edu $

712 Arts Plaza at Claire Trevor School of the Arts at University of California, Irvine

"The mission of the Beall Center is to support research and exhibitions that explore new relationships between the arts, sciences, and engineering, and thus, promote new forms of creation and expression using digital technologies." So, the rotating, technologically-based exhibitions are really intriguing. For instance, "Sight and Sound" was a varied group of artists who presented beautiful footage along with a cacophony of sounds and music. Virtual reality images, along with sound sculptures, were featured in the accompanying exhibit "Wall of Sound". Other past exhibit titles have included "Information as Art" and "Morphonano", which were interactive works through space and time created by an artist and nanoscientist. Intriguing, right? Call if you'd like a tour. Definitely check out their events and STEAM programs, with hands-on art and science activities, and demonstrations. Note that robotics camps are offered during the summer.

Hours: Open Mon. - Sat., noon - 6pm. Closed Sun. and major holidays.
Price: Free. Parking at 4000 Mesa Rd. structure is $2 an hour.
Ages: 8 years and up.

BLAKEY HISTORICAL PARK AND MUSEUM

(714) 891-2597 or (714) 893-0134 / www.westminsterhistorical.wordpress.com; www.westminster-ca.gov   !

8612 Westminster Boulevard, Westminster

Like many other cities that want to preserve their roots for future generations, the city of Westminster has a historical museum. It houses displays from its founding in 1870 to the present day. The museum building, which looks like a converted auditorium, has exhibits, mostly in glass cases, set up in chronological groups. Each grouping has a number that corresponds to an information sheet which explains the memorabilia, thus making for an easy self-guided tour. If you prefer, a docent will explain articles more fully and allow children to touch just a few items - this is a mostly "eyes-on" (as opposed to hands-on) museum. Some of the more interesting items to see include a very small 1897 child's bed; an old stove, washboard, butter churn and other kitchen implements; an antique, wind-up phonograph that still works; old-fashioned ladies' hats and clothing; a collection of dolls from around the world; war posters; and the head of a water buffalo.

Four other small buildings are on the park's grounds. A California Crazy, or Shutter Shack, is a little, picture-perfect "store" that looks like a camera. (It was once used for dropping off and picking up film.) A docent will take you through the other buildings: The small, restored McCoy-Hare House was the community's first drugstore, as well as a home. The front room contains a pump organ, plus shelves filled with jars of medicine, bolts of fabric, and sundries. The adjacent living room has some period furniture and clothing. Next, walk through the Warne Family Farmhouse to see the parlor, which holds a 1749 grandfather's clock and a piano; a dining room, with its table set with china; the bedroom that contains a bed (people were much shorter back then!) and a ceramic pot (i.e., port-a-potty); and the kitchen with its stove and old-time telephone. A sink wasn't necessary as water and garbage were simply thrown out the back door to feed the plants and the chickens, respectively. The adjacent large barn contains antique saddles, large farm equipment, a wooden sugar beet wagon, tools, and a blacksmith shop. Everything is well-labeled. Walk into the barn and discover two fire engines and an antique paramedic "van." Kids may climb into the cab of the 1959 white fire engine and "drive" around. A few grassy areas and a picnic table on the premise complete this park.

Hours: Open to the public the first Sun. of each month, 1pm - 4pm. School groups may call to book a tour during the week.
Price: Free
Ages: 5 years and up.

BOWERS MUSEUM

(714) 567-3600 / www.bowers.org $$$

2002 N. Main Street, Santa Ana

This culturally-rich museum contains permanent exhibits showcasing art from pre-Columbian, Art of the Pacific, Art of Africa, Art of Asia, First Californians (Native Americans), and early California history, with a focus on ranchos and missions in the Segerstrom gallery. This collection includes baskets, statues, body adornment pieces, clothing, spurs, a huge copper brandy still from early 1800's, murals, and paintings. Another permanent gallery is the Ancient Arts of China: A 5,000 Year Legacy. Bronze vessels, ivory carvings, robes, sculptures, porcelains paintings, and more are on display here. All the art in the galleries and in the hallway are classically displayed.

The first-class, temporary exhibits have included treasures from Tibet; portions of the Dead Sea Scrolls;

gemstones; and Beethoven: The Late Great with drafts of scores, a personal letter, locks of his hair and more. Just a few of the blockbuster exhibits have included Egyptian mummies and funerary objects on loan from the British Museum, and the Terra Cota Warriors. Don't miss these special exhibits - these have been absolutely incredible!!

Download an audio guide which aids in interpreting the various artifacts and exhibits. One-hour guided tours are available for all ages, as are one-hour cultural art classes. School groups also receive a curriculum guide for select galleries. Enjoy the outdoor courtyard before or after your visit. For fine dining on the museum grounds, indulge in Tangata, a restaurant that serves salmon Cobb salad ($19), short rib pasta ($20), tuna melt panini ($16), and burgers ($16), or just go straight for the creme brulee ($8).

KIDSEUM (pg. 307), located just down the street, is geared specifically for kids (obviously), and is associated with Bowers. Tip: Adults are admitted free into Kidseum with a same day ticket stub from the Bowers Museum; you just have to pay for kids.

Hours: Open Tues. - Sun., 10am - 4pm. Closed Mon., New Year's Day, 4th of July, Thanksgiving, and Christmas Day.

Price: $13 for adults Tues. - Fri., $15 on Sat. - Sun.; $10 for seniors and students, Tues. - Fri., $12 on Sat. - Sun.; children 11 and under are free with a paying adult. Note that special exhibits, which include general admission, cost extra. For instance, Mummies of the World was $25 during the week; $27 on weekends. Admission is free to the permanent exhibits every Sun. for Santa Ana residents, only. Parking at the lot is $6. There is some free parking on the streets and 2 blocks down the street at Kidseum, as well as some metered parking.

Ages: 8 years and up.

CHILDREN'S MUSEUM AT LA HABRA

(562) 905-9793 or (562) 383-4236 / www.lahabracity.com

301 S. Euclid Street, La Habra

This great museum, housed in a renovated Union Pacific Railroad Depot, has a child's interest at heart. Out front are (fake) dinosaur print trackways of a Tyrannosaurus rex, sauropod, and theropod, and a replica nest containing unhatched "dino" eggs, plus a wonderful wooden train engine with a bench attached.

Inside, a Science Station room encourages hands-on exploration with a Dino Dig (i.e., digging in sand for "fossils") and a huge T. rex skull that hangs from the ceiling, watching you. The room also features a cut-away of a bathroom and kitchen that partners with an exhibit (with fake rocks and clouds) on evaporation; a shadow wall that takes a temporary picture; and a gas pump to fill 'er up. The STEAM area offers physics-based fun with a flight lab tower, magnetic tube play wall and kinetic play space. The adjoining room has a carousel to ride, a mini-market for kids to shop like grownups (without the grownup bills), and the front end of an Orange County Transit bus to get in and practice driving skills. The next room has wonderful, interactive, changing exhibits. Past themes have included Cowboys and the Wild West, which featured western gear to try on, a wooden horse with a saddle, and a guitar to strum on the range; and Would You Look At That?, which featured fun with lenses, light, and optical equipment. This room is always enlightening! Just outside this room is a train caboose, filled with train memorabilia, that is open to walk through at certain times. See how tiny the bathroom is and look at the seats perched up high for good viewing.

Do you hear trains chugging, clanging, and whistling as they come around the mountain? A connecting room contains a large model train layout. The train room then leads to Nannies Travels, a living room-like setting that features a collection of cultural artifacts - masks, costumes, games, artwork, furniture, and more - from all over the world. The next connecting room is the nature room. Listen to the sounds of nature (e.g., birds chirping) as you go through a little cave and look at the taxidermied wildlife, such as bears, mountain lions, a raccoon, a wart hog, and birds "flying" overhead. Real critters are here, too - snakes, lizards and other reptiles. Hanging on the wall are stuffed animal heads of deer, moose, and buffalo. A touch table holds furs, bird's nests, and skulls.

Quiet on the set! The large dress-up area, with a stage, piano, numerous and varied costumes (including several fireman uniforms), and even prepared scripts, inspires future actors and actresses. The lighting booth, with all of its working buttons, is perfect for aspiring directors. The adjoining playroom, for children 5 years and under only, has a fake tree to climb, a little puppet theater, toys, building blocks, books, a stuffed cow that kids can milk, and a play castle.

The museum often hosts special programs such as craft projects in the Family Art room, storytelling, or shows for kids to enjoy and participate in. Call or check the website for a schedule of events.

Portola Park, the museum's backyard, is open daily and features a playground (with a fun play bus), baseball fields, tennis courts, picnic tables, and barbecue grills.

Hours: Open Tues. - Fri., 10am - 4pm; Sat., 10am - 5pm; Sun., 1pm - 5pm. Closed Mon., Mother's Day, Father's Day, and major holidays.

Price: $10 for ages 2 and up; children under 2 are free. $9 for La Habra residents. Usually the first Sun. of the month is free admission with themed workshops and performances, too. See info on the Association of Science - Technology Centers (pg. xi) for reciprocal museum memberships.

Ages: 1½ - 10 years.

DISCOVERY CUBE (Orange County)

(714) 542-CUBE (2823) / www.discoverycube.org

2500 N. Main Street., Santa Ana

This two-story, high-caliber science center, with full-size mock up of the space shuttle outside, has over 100 hands-on exhibits, plus live science demonstrations, 4-D movies (with wind and fog effects that you can feel!) in the theater, and special programs. Press your flesh against a wall of pinheads to create a 3-D impression (and some mighty odd poses). See yourself in a "new light" inside a room with a camera that takes real time pictures of your movements. Watch your image reflected on a screen in vivid colors and lights. If you can't get enough of the real California quakes, enter the Shake Shack, a room with a platform that simulates major and minor quakes. Or, use a seismograph and construct a model building to see if it's up to earthquake code. Walk through an eight-foot-tall artificially-generated tornado and even redirect its pattern. Speak through a tube that changes your voice from normal to sound like you're underwater, in an opera, inhabiting an alien, and more. Use wind to blow sand into dunes or other formations. Form dams or create erosion, or just get your hands dirty, at the stream and silt table. Create a cloudy day (inside!) by pushing on large rings around a cloud machine which then form various-sized clouds. Fly a model airplane into the wind using a throttle. Experience what you would weigh on the moon or on Mars by hoisting yourself up on a properly weighted pulley system. See what speed you get clocked at when you pitch a ball. Balance yourself on a board resembling a seesaw. (This is much harder than it looks!) Duck underneath to go into a giant kaleidoscope. Play virtual volleyball and learn about green screen technology used in movies. Participate in live science shows. Climb a rock wall. Play a laser beam harp. Log on to computers to play educational games and/or take a computer class at the Digital Lab.

Environmental stewardship is a responsibility that the Cube enables kids to learn about via several exhibits: In Water Gallery and Lab look through magnifying glasses and see what's really in drops of water; discover water content in salt water, ice, and vapor; and test water's reactions to various movements and temperatures. At the Planetary Research Station stare at the ginormous globe in the center of a room and see a hurricane swirling around, rain pouring down, and all other kinds of weather all around the world, in real time from satellites. Learn about the planets from the interactive stations. Set up like a real grocery store, try your skills at a game of shopping. Grab a cart, go down the aisles and using touch screens and scanners, learn to make wise, healthy food choices. At Eco Challenge, stand at an conveyor belt as trash comes out of a truck and race against others to quickly and correctly sort recyclables and other waste to divert trash from our landfills. What fun! And learning! Board a helicopter to watch a movie - a virtual helicopter tour over the parks and wildlands (and animals and plants) of Orange County that many earthbound citizens don't realize exist. In an area set up like a backyard and by using a touch screen tablet, become an Inspector Trainer to learn about and find invading vectors (i.e. mosquitoes, rodents, and flies), the diseases that they carry and how to eliminate them. Yuk, but a good thing to learn about! Complete this scavenger-hunt-style game and earn a badge.

One reason kids stick to it at the fabulous and very hands-on Science of Hockey exhibit is they can "drive" the almost life-size model of a Zamboni machine stationed on the ice-like flooring of the room. Wannabe sportscasters can try out their chosen career in the broadcast booth. Players can try their skating skills with an interactive video game. Compare surfaces as you see whose puck goes the fastest at the ice and friction table. Be the goalie, or at least hear the game from his perspective in the goalie sound room. Your kids will actually want a time out in the Penalty Box as it has hockey-oriented ways to learn math equations, statistics, physics, and more sports applications.

In the underwater-themed KidStation, designed for children five years and younger, kids dress up and act out a scene in front of a background screen that can change from a shark, to a school of fish, to other nautical images. Youngsters can climb in a submarine and slide down it, fingerpaint electronically (a lot less messy than the real thing), play with puzzles, and read books.

The eighty-five-foot tall Delta III rocket and gigantic cube aren't the only outside museum attractions you see from the freeway; you can't miss the 120-foot long, almost friendly-looking Argentinosaurus and the skeletal, life-size T. rex. Walk inside the partly-fleshed and partly-exposed Argentinosaurus to see its innards. Young kids can slide down its tail, put together dino bone puzzles, and ride on small dinosaurs at the playground.

3... 2...1... blast off! You can go up inside the cube and experience a rocket blasting off, kind of. Enter a real Delta Rocket RS-68 booster engine, press the launch button, and with sound effects, smoke (i.e. fog), and video screens that simulate a rocket taking off. Three interactive stations enable visitors to work the buttons and screen while seeing the real life enactment of fueling a rocket, launching one (and if you don't get the right ratio of water to air, you might get wet), and the gasses a rocket leaves behind as it thrusts and takes off.

Enter Mission Control, a replica of the Jet Propulsion Lab's control room, where young space engineers can land a rover on Mars, dock at the International Space Station or complete other missions via computers and huge wall screens - an immersive experience that kind of feels like the real thing.

Uniting education with entertainment in an appealing format for all generations, the Discovery Cube also hosts terrific traveling exhibits, such as *Sesame Street Presents: The Body*, plus workshops, science camps, scout programs, and a packed calendar of events including a favorite - the BubbleFest, held in April. Note that the on-site fairly healthy eatery, BeanSprouts, has an indoor and outdoor eating area. It also serves up imaginative sandwiches - sunflower butter and jam in the shape of piano keys, grilled cheese in the shape of a butterfly, and crocamole (guess the ingredients and shape). Also, see SANTIAGO PARK / NATURE RESERVE (pg. 294), which is across the road, but accessible by an underpass. Parking at the park is free. Note that there is a DISCOVERY CUBE (Los Angeles County) (pg. 105) in Los Angeles.

Hours: Open daily, 10am - 5pm. Closed Thanksgiving and Christmas.

Price: $17.95 for adults; $14.95 for seniors; $12.95 for ages 3 - 14; children 2 and under are free. Up to 4 free admissions for Santa Ana residents (bring a valid photo ID with your Santa Ana address) is offered on the first Tues. of every month. Shows at the 4-D Theater are an additional $3 per person. Parking is $5 per vehicle, cash only. See info on the Association of Science - Technology Centers (pg. xi) for reciprocal museum memberships. See info on the Bank of America Museums on Us (pg. xi), but note that this museum offers it only on that Sunday.

Ages: 2 years and up.

FULLERTON MUSEUM CENTER   ☀

(714) 738-6545 - museum; (714) 738-3136 - tour info / www.cityoffullerton.com $$
301 N. Pomona Avenue, Fullerton

This small cultural museum has two galleries with rotating exhibits that often have kid-appeal, plus a video that explains more about what is currently showing. Past exhibits have included The Nature of Collecting, which featured different collections ranging from *I Love Lucy* paraphernalia to pencil sharpeners and old radios; Touchable Sculptures, with over seventy touchable, lifecast sculptures of contemporary and historic figures such as George Bush, Clint Eastwood, and Dizzy Gillespie; Anne Frank, a recreation of the life and times of Anne Frank through photographs and facsimiles of her diary, plus commentary; and Prehistory of North Orange County with hands-on arts and crafts for the whole family, a simulated fossil dig, a guided tours of the exhibit and more.

A gallery honoring Leo Fender, the man who revolutionized guitars with Telecaster, Stratocaster, and Precision Bass Fender guitars, is towards the back. It exhibits several of his classic guitars such as a 1962 fiesta red custom color Telecast guitar, a (wild looking) paisley Telecast from 1968, and a 1990 Celtic guitar inlaid with rich, Celtic symbols. A continuously running film shows Fender being interviewed, as well as celebrities and more of the history of his guitars. A visual time line with more guitars and old amps are also on display.

Ninety-minute school tours are given that include an in-depth tour of the museum and a hands-on activity that correlates to the current exhibit. Also inquire about Family Days; Wednesday Art Studios; after-school programs; summer art camps; Stroller Brigade for docent-led stories, crafts and games - for free; and other special programs and events.

Just across the street is the fun Plaza Park. It has fountains that squirt to life at random intervals (great for cooling off), benches under shade trees, grassy spots, a few picnic tables, and a funky playground. The playground has a wall for rock climbing and metal objects (think modern art) to motivate the imagination - saucer shapes to swing, play and climb on; bars that spin; and more.

Hours: The museum is open Tues. - Sun., noon - 4pm; open Thurs. until 8pm. Closed Mon., 4th of July, Thanksgiving and Christmas. The park is open daily.

Price: $5 for adults; $4 for seniors and students; $3 for ages 6 - 12; children 5 and under are free. Admission is free on the first Fri. every month from 6pm - 10pm.

Ages: 5 years and up.

HERITAGE HILL HISTORICAL PARK

(949) 923-2230/2232 / www.ocparks.com; www.lakeforestca.gov

!

25151 Serrano Road, Lake Forest

Heritage Hill consists of several lovely, restored historical buildings in a beautiful gated setting. Four buildings that reflect part of Orange County's heritage are open to tour. The Serrano Adobe dates from 1863 and has furniture from the late nineteenth century. The Bennet Ranch House, built in 1908, reflects a ranching family's lifestyle from the early twentieth century. St. George's Episcopal Mission, built in 1891, has many of its original interior furnishings. El Toro Grammar School was built in 1890. The school is a favorite with kids because it has school books from that era, as well as desks and other school-related items. The Historical Park has a few picnic tables on the grounds.

Three school tours are offered. The third grade tour is called "Hands On". It is ninety-minutes long, costs $2 per person, and is designed for ten to sixty students. Groups go through the houses and do an activity in each one, such as grinding corn in the adobe and participating in a mini school session in the school house. The fourth grade tour is called "Living History". It is two hours long and cost $2 per person. Seventeen to thirty-five students participate in hands-on lessons in the school house. The Native American Tour incorporates knowledge of native inhabitants with activities. Learning was never so interesting! Reservations for tours are required.

If your kids need more running around space, visit Serrano Creek Park, just behind Heritage Hill. Serrano is a long, narrow, wooded park with a paved walkway and a creek running through it. There are a few different play structures with bridges, short slides, tunnels, big wheels to turn, and metal climbing apparatus, plus fake rock walls and rope nets to climb, too.

Hours: Heritage Hill is open Tues. - Sat., 9am - 5pm. Guided tours are the only way to see the interior of the buildings and they are offered for walk-ins Tues. - Fri. at 2pm; Sat., 11am and 2pm. Groups of 8 or more and school groups must make reservations for tours at other times throughout the week. Closed major holidays.

Price: Free to the public. Groups of 8 or more are $2 per person.

Ages: 6 years and up.

HERITAGE MUSEUM OF ORANGE COUNTY

(714) 540-0404 / www.heritagemuseumoc.org

$$$

3101 W. Harvard Street, Santa Ana

Travel back to Victorian times as you visit the Kellogg House (i.e., the Heritage Museum), built in 1898. Take a few moments to walk around the truly lovely grounds. Tours begin in the parlor where kids can play a pump organ, crank an old telephone, listen to music played on an Edison talking machine, and look through a stereoscope - an early version of the modern-day View Master™. The kitchen has wonderful gadgets that kids can learn about as well as touch. The wood dining room is oval-shaped with cabinets specially made to bend with the curves, like the inside of a ship. The spiral, wooden staircase got "cool" raves from all the kids, as did the wooden pole going thru the center, from floor to ceiling, because it is actually a ship's mast. Upstairs, children play a game that teaches them the parts of a Victorian house. The master bedroom is now a room to dress up in Victorian-style clothing, with beautiful dresses for the girls and dapper coats and vests for the boys. The children's room has old-fashioned toys to play with.

Outside, on the back porch, children can practice *real* chores like "washing" clothes on a scrub board and drying them with the clothes wringer. Sometimes visitors are invited to make their own butter or learn how to play Victorian-era games. Make sure you take a look into the working blacksmith's shop. After the official tour, kids are welcome to go back and explore their favorite rooms, with parental supervision, of course.

Enjoy a picnic lunch in the gazebo area. Throughout the year the museum offers special events, such as themed teas where kids are invited to make crafts and participate in topical projects, and family activities, such as storytelling, a craft, blacksmith demonstrations, or a nature hike through some of the adjacent natural area and wetlands. Call for a schedule and for pricing. School groups, with a minimum of ten students, should inquire about their wide array of programs, such as Journey in Time, Mind Your Manners, Great Grandpa's House, several agriculture education opportunities (organic farming methods and more), and Gold Rush. The latter has a gold mine set with a small mine shaft, a mine car on tracks, and a head frame that feeds water to a small stream where students pan "gold". Two-hour classes start at $10 per student. Add the blacksmith option for $3 more per person.

Of all the historical homes we've toured, and we've been through quite a few, this one has earned one of the highest ratings from my boys. Most houses, while beautiful and worthy of a tour, are understandably hands off. The Heritage Museum has hands-on activities, plus the docents gear the tour toward whatever age group is taking the tour, both in the tour length and the way the information is presented. Come here and let your kids touch history!

Hours: Open to the public Fri., 1pm - 5pm; Sat., 10am - 2pm; Sun., 11am - 3pm, but always call first as they host many special events that affect their public hours. Open to tour groups of ten or more by appt. only, Mon. - Thurs., 1pm - 5pm. Closed most holidays.

Price: $7 for adults; $5 for seniors and ages 3 - 12; children 2 and under are free. Santa Ana residents are free on the first Sun. of the month.

Ages: 3 years and up.

INTERNATIONAL SURFING MUSEUM

(714) 465-4350 / www.surfingmuseum.org

411 Olive Avenue, Huntington Beach

Surf's up at this small museum that celebrates surfing and surf culture, from its roots in Hawaii to the present day. Feel like catching a wave? Check out some of the famous and unique surfboards here. Look at early examples of slalom and vertical to current long boards and motorized boards. The most famous and eye-catching board is a <u>huge</u> star - it is the world's largest surfboard at a whopping 42 feet long! This is a fun selfie! It is also part of a Guinness World Record because it held 66 people riding it unassisted for 12 seconds.

The museum also has trophies, clothing, and photographs. Past rotating exhibits have included Surf 2 Skate, with a lifeguard stand, numerous surfboards, and walls completely covered with skateboards, old-school metal rollerskates, and more, plus clothing, posters and movies featuring skateboards completing the display. Another included a skin-diving exhibit featuring early face masks, fins, spear guns, and other diving gear, as well as photos and information panels. Surfing movies play continuously, and there is a gift shop. Note that the Surfing Walk of Fame, honoring thirty-six people, is just down the street. Summertime brings free surf-music concerts in the parking lot on Sunday afternoons.

Hours: Open Tues. - Sun., noon - 5pm. Closed Mon. and holidays.

Price: $2 per person.

Ages: 6 years and up.

KIDSEUM

(714) 480-1520 - museum; (714) 567-3680 - tours / www.bowers.org

1802 N. Main Street, Santa Ana

Kidseum is a smallish, hands-on, cultural museum designed to assist kids, preschoolers to 12 years old, develop an appreciation of art and the ways of life in cultures from around the world. Cross over the short (symbolic) rainbow bridge (from a Chumash legend) from the lobby into the main gallery.

The main room has wonderful, changing, interactive exhibits always geared towards the above-stated, central goals. Check the website to see what is currently "showing" here. For instance, Once Upon a Time... Exploring the World of Fairy Tales focused on the significance of fairy tales throughout history and around the world. Kids played a harpsichord in the *Beauty and the Beast* scene; hammered and worked on shoes in *The Elves and the Shoemaker*; and climbed a beanstalk in *Jack and the Beanstalk*.

Your kids will love the small, colorful music and story room. It has mostly drums, but they can also play unique musical instruments, like deer hoof shakers and some string instruments. Stories are told on the TV screen to the kids (and sometimes live). Kids can take a ride through history on the Wells Fargo stagecoach. They can watch themselves as they dress up and "travel" to Machu Picchu, Stonehenge, the Great Wall of China, Coliseum, and Giza Pyramids using green screen technology. Enter the Glow Cave that has paintings on the walls and ceiling that glow in the dark (and so do white clothes!), as well as florescent crayons for kids to color and draw on the white paper.

The side Archaeology Room is done in wall-to-wall in Egyptian motif with vivid paintings of gods and animals and a huge screen of the pyramids. It holds a small (fake) sarcophagus; an Egyptian vessel; rubbings (of world symbols, the Aztec calendar, and more); a large Languages of the World map to press buttons and hear phrases in languages from all over the globe (my Swahili is rusty!); touch screens; and puzzles. Elsewhere in the museum, play games from foreign lands; learn through discovery box projects; dress up in a variety of ethnic costumes; climb into kid-size tepees; work in the computer lab that is in the original bank's safe; put on a show at the puppet theater; participate in an archaeological dig; and do other engaging activities.

Stop by the Art Lab, where kids can paint, color, experiment with sand art, and more at different times throughout the year. Most activities are included in the price of admission. School tours here are my favorite combination of hands-on fun and learning and ask about their after-school programs. The museum also has kits available to classrooms for rent; cultural and arts Scouts' badge requirements with special art projects and presentations; summer art camp adventures; and more. Kidseum proves that learning about other cultures can be exciting!

Note: The BOWERS MUSEUM (pg. 302), located just down the street at 2002 N. Main Street, is the parent museum of Kidseum. It contains carvings, pictures, and other art work from African, Asian, and Native American cultures, as well as top-notch traveling exhibits. Older kids might appreciate a walk through the galleries. Admission to Kidseum is free for adults with a same day ticket stub from Bowers Museum - so why not visit both?!

Hours: Open most of the year, Sat. - Sun., 10am - 4pm; open in the summer, Tues. - Sun., 10am - 4pm; open on other school breaks and holiday Mon., 10am - 4pm, too. Closed Mon, New Year's Day, 4th of July, Thanksgiving and Christmas. Call to make a reservation to take a group tour during the week.

Price: $10 for ages 2 and up. Admission to Kidseum is free for adults with a same day ticket stub from the Bowers Museum. Admission is free every Sun. for Santa Ana residents, only. Note that there are usually fun events/crafts going on then, too.

Ages: 3 - 8 years.

LAGUNA HILLS COMMUNITY CENTER AND SPORTS COMPLEX

(949) 707-2680 - center; (949) 707-2692 - school tours / www.ci.laguna-hills.ca.us
25555 Alicia Parkway, Laguna Hills

This huge community center is more than just a beautiful building filled with great activities for families to enjoy. Built on a rich fossil site, it's a museum, of sorts, that showcases prehistoric fossils and bones unearthed during its construction. Various display cases, highlighted by murals that illustrate the paleo-environments and changing landscape of this site, are situated in the lobby and throughout the building. You'll see teeth from Great White sharks, seashell fossils, whale vertebrae, Mammoth tusks, bison and mastodon bones, and skulls of a bottlenose dolphin, extinct sea lion, and sabertooth. The displays have descriptive placards, or you can rent (for free) headphones and CD, available in English and Spanish, that auditorily explains each item, along with scientist's recordings. To enhance the educational value of your self-guided tour, ask for a paleopack, which is a folder that contains age-appropriate worksheets. School tours for elementary-aged kids are also available, Tuesdays through Thursdays. There is a wagon with dirt and fossils to find and match to a chart, too.

The adjoining sports complex features baseball fields, a soccer field, a roller hockey rink, and, behind the center and next to the high school, a really big (20,000 square feet!) cement skate park with a bowl, rails, stairs, pyramid, and other street elements. Pads and helmet are mandatory when using the skate park.

For more primordial-style fun, walk up the stone-line pathway past the ball fields and covered picnic areas, to the adjacent, extra large, two-level, dinosaur-related, Prehistoric Playground (or Fossil Reef Park) with its several nooks and crannies. A jeep is parked toward the entrance to get visitors in the exploring mode. A shallow cave here is embedded with numerous real marine fossils! Under a bridge is a short tunnel with more shell fossils and a fossil of a duck-billed dinosaur. At the several, multi-level play structures, kids can climb up a chain ladder; slide down a long, enclosed slide and other slides; swing on swings, including a tire swing; and engage in play using apparatus on the good-sized playground. The flooring is alternately padded recycled rubber and sand-based. The latter has two diggers that kids can sit on and operate the hand levers. Children can also play on and under the whale skeleton and on cement turtles, which are actually water features, plus splash in a stone-tiered fountain. There is a small parcel just for toddlers. Shade awnings cover certain portions of the play area. Modern-day kids of all ages will delight in this excellent "primitive" playground.

Hours: The Community Center is open Mon. - Sat., 8am - 10pm; Sun., noon - 6pm. The playground is open daily, sunrise -sunset. The skate park is open Mon. - Sat., 8am - 10pm; Sun., 8am - 6pm.

Price: Free

Ages: All

LOCK MUSEUM OF ORANGE COUNTY

(714) 630-0800 / www.keedex.com/Main_Pages/about_us/about_us.html
1051 Grove Street, Anaheim

I just can't keep this unique little museum under lock and key! The locksmith owner, who began avidly accumulating keys and locks when he was a kid, has an amazing and varied collection that now shares space with a consumer-products warehouse. He has the keys to many cities from all over the U.S. and the world, including ones made from steel, glass, and ivory. He also has amassed ten locks and keys that belonged to Houdini; ensembles that have been used in movies; manacles dating back to days of slavery; time locks used to thwart bank robbers; leg irons and neck cuffs with spikes; over 175 handcuffs (and some thumbcuffs); and keys and locks to jails and to a castle. Feeling all keyed up? Half-hour, interactive tours are offered to school groups, adults, Boy Scouts (who can earn a patch), or any group.

Hours: Open Mon. - Wed., 7am - 5:30pm. It's good to call first. Closed Thurs. - Sun.
Price: Free
Ages: 6 years and up.

LYON AIR MUSEUM

(714) 210-4585 / www.lyonairmuseum.org
19300 Ike Jones Road, Santa Ana

With a view through huge glass windows of the John Wayne Airport runway, this clean and well laid out aviation museum specializes in beautifully restored and operational WWII aircraft and vehicles. A centerpiece is the gleaming American Airlines DC-3. Kids are most intrigued by the Douglas A-26 Invader - perhaps because it has a face with sharp teeth painted on the front. One highlight is the B-17 Flying Fortress, complete with machine guns, that you can actually look into. It once transported generals Dwight Eisenhower and Douglas MacArthur. Other planes include a Cessna O-1E Birddog, Douglas C-47 Skytrain, B-25 Mitchell, WWII trainer plane - AT+6F/SNJ6, and more.

The vehicles include a 1935 Packard Model 1208 Convertible Sedan; 1940s Helms Bakery Truck; a shining, like-new 1929 Duesenberg Model J Murphy Dual Cowl Phaeton; military jeeps; and a 1941 Dodge half ton command & reconnaissance truck; plus motorcycles, such as a crazy-looking 1943 German NSU Kettenkrad HK 101 Tracked Motorcycle, a 1945 Indian Chief, and a 1943 Japanese Rikuo. The most intriguing automobile is the Mercedes Benz G4 touring wagon, which has bullet-proof glass - it was once used by Adolph Hitler. The history of each vehicle and plane is told with signage, and also by the knowledgeable docents, many of whom are WWII veterans.

A few display cases exhibit helmets, documents, and other memorabilia. Large maps on the walls show USAF deployments. Enter through the realistic-looking theater (because it is one) to watch continuously running aviation-themed movies. Individuals, tour groups, and school groups are welcome to walk around, and even under, some vehicles to get close up. Some of the planes might not be here at all times are they are flown for special events.
Hours: Open daily, 10am - 4pm. Closed Thanksgiving and Christmas.
Price: $12 for adults; $9 for seniors and vets; $6 for ages 5 - 17; children 4 and under are free. School groups are free.
Ages: 7 years and up.

MARCONI AUTOMOTIVE MUSEUM

(714) 258-3001 / www.marconimuseum.org
1302 Industrial Drive, Tustin

The museum's main purpose is to raise money for children's charities by showcasing automobiles from Dick Marconi's private collection, and renting out the facility. That said, the public, too, can come and look. The front hallway of this classy museum is lined with gleaming motorcycles. Inside are over seventy-five cars (specific ones sometimes rotate) that are housed here and kept in mint condition. They vary in style, shape, and color. His collection includes a 1929 Ford Model 'A' Cabriolet; 1937 Ahrens-Fox Fire Engine; 1954 green Chevrolet; 1973 canary-yellow convertible Ferrari Daytona Spider (once owned by Cher); restored 1964 Corvette Sting Ray; and a jet-black 1989 Lamborghini Countach, plus seventeen racing Ferraris, an assortment of motorcycles, and a few kid-size cars. Marconi's prized possession is the last car Mario Andretti drove to victory at the 1993 Phoenix International Raceway. It is signed by Andretti. My boys' favorite was the rather colorful car completely decoupaged with magazine covers featuring boxing champions. Racing flags, trophies, drivers' jumpsuits and helmets, and a huge, shining silver horse constructed out of old car bumpers complete this museum.
Hours: Open Mon. - Fri., 9am - 4:30pm, but always call first as it is often closed for special events. Closed on most major holidays.
Price: $5 for adults; children 12 and under are free.
Ages: 8 years and up.

MISSION SAN JUAN CAPISTRANO

(949) 234-1300 - mission; (949) 234-132 - program coordinator / www.missionsjc.com
26801 Ortega Highway, San Juan Capistrano

The Mission, founded in 1776, is the oldest building in California. It is ten acres of historic stone buildings and beautifully landscaped gardens, courtyards, and walkways. It's easy to see why the San Juan Mission was considered the "Jewel of the Missions." There are many parts to the Mission, so there is something to interest almost any age child. It's a history treat for the public and for school kids as they visit and "experience" the early Native American, Spanish, and Mexican lifestyles, depicted in separate rooms. Walk through rooms that contain murals such as Indians hunting, and artifacts such as bone weapons. The Soldiers' Barracks room looks lived in, just as it did many years ago. It contains life-size models of soldiers and their (few) possessions. Note: Outside, behind the barracks, are some picnic tables. Kids will especially enjoy the brick Mission Clubhouse room with colorful informational posters all over and the activities offered. They can practice weaving a basket in the traditional way, using an extra large model basket; be a mission architect and build a Roman archway with blocks; and spin a wheel to find out their chore/ job could have been back then.

The extensive grounds are a maze of pathways. The Central Courtyard, the cemetery, the areas of archaeological excavation, and the industrial center are all interesting. For instance, tanning vats in the industrial center were used to turn animal skin into sellable leather, while the ovens were used to turn animal fat into candles, soap, and ointments.

The Mission has two churches. One is the Serra Chapel, the oldest building in California, where mass is still regularly performed. The glittery baroque altar, made of gold leaf overlay, is eye-catching. The other church, the Great Stone Church, was once a magnificent cathedral. Some of it was destroyed by an earthquake in 1812. Today, the ruins have been handsomely preserved and stabilized.

Mission San Juan Capistrano offers many special, educational activities such craft days, storytelling, playing games, making old-fashioned toys, panning for gold, adobe brick making, and more. Guided school and group tours are also available that offer historic insight into the mission and this area.

If you're looking for somewhere fun to eat, RUBY'S (Orange County) (pg. 252) is across the street and up the stairs at the shopping district. This 1940's diner has a train going around overhead, red vinyl seats, and kids' meals that are served in a forties-style, cardboard car. Or, have tea at TEA HOUSE ON LOS RIOS (pg. 254). Afterwards, take a walk around Camino Capistrano, which is a street with many interesting stores with truly unique merchandise. Idea: Take a train into town and really make a day of your visit here! The train depot is only two blocks away from the Mission. Definitely look up ZOOMARS PETTING ZOO / LOS RIOS PARK (pg. 337) for a fun, close-by, petting zoo adventure and other ideas of what else to do in the immediate area. Check the Calendar entry for the FIESTA DE LAS GOLONDRINAS (Festival of the Swallows) (pg. 702) held at the mission.

Hours: Open daily, 9am - 5pm. Closed Thanksgiving and Christmas. Closed at noon on Good Friday and Christmas Eve. Sometimes closed due to rainy days; call first.

Price: $10 for adults; $9 for seniors; $7 for ages 4 - 11; children 3 and under are free. All admission includes a free audio tour. Discount coupons are available online.

Ages: 5 years and up.

MUZEO

(714) 95-MUZEO (956-8936) / www.muzeo.org
$$$
241 S. Anaheim Boulevard, Anaheim

This urban cultural museum showcases several traveling exhibits each year. Vastly diverse in theme, past titles have included Chicano Art and Soul; The Color of Rock (about rock legends); Bizarre Beasts Past and Present; Imperial Rome: Discovering the Ancient Civilization; How to Make a Monster (the process of designing and molding life-size finished monsters for major films); and Treasures of Napoleon. The high quality, integrity, and feeling of immersion is consistent in all the exhibits.

In the exhibit Under African Skies, for instance, the rooms were transformed into an African veldt, a village, and even a slice of America. African maps depicting various peoples and languages lined the entryway. Videos of jelis (i.e. singing historians), cultural dances, a sheep herder, and more people and places played against the backdrop of pictures, costumes, weapons, and even jewelry. Piped-in African music and chants filled the air adding to the "you are there" experience. Plaster-cast faces of gorillas were available to touch and feel their patterned wrinkles and I listened to the sounds of gorillas. Doors on a camel opened to see and learn about what the hump consists of (fat). I also learned that fine camels are a sign of wealth to the Tuarey, as sports car are to Americans. One room contained a tribal dwelling. I also walked down a hallway that was like the inside of a slave-carrying ship, with silhouettes on the wall and a voice speaking about the hardships of sailing. It opened to a platform and when I stood on the small balcony portion inside designated footprints, a slave auctioneer's voice was selling me. Timelines, pictures, a recreated cabin, and artifacts told the story of the cost of slavery in America.

A second, smaller building - the Carnegie Gallery - just across the way, continues with the main exhibit. This building also holds a one-room, permanent exhibit regarding the history of Anaheim. Displays include clothing, fine jewelry, boots, irons, a hair wreath, a rabbit skin cape, shell and bone necklaces, a (replica) saber tooth cat skull, items from the grape/wine industry and the citrus industry, an homage to Disneyland, and uniforms and news headlines from WWI and WWII.

Educational field trips at the museum meet the California State standards and lesson plans are available. Ask about numerous special programs, free workshops with fun activities, lectures, and events. Note that the museum gift store sells rotating merchandise that is pertinent to the current exhibit. Surrounding the museum are courtyards and a few retail stores and eateries. Catch a (small) farmer's market here on Thursdays.

Hours: Open Wed. - Sun., 10am - 4pm. Closed Mon., Tues., Thanksgiving and Christmas Day.

Price: Admission is free to the Carnegie Gallery. Admission fees vary for the main gallery exhibits. For instance, The Art of Woodcarving was $7 for adults; $6 for seniors/students/military; $5 for ages 4 - 12; ages 3 and under were free. Educators, check the website and download a form for a free pass. The first Thurs. of every month is free for Anaheim residents and city of Anaheim employees.

Ages: 5 years and up, depending on the exhibit.

NEWLAND HOUSE MUSEUM

(714) 962-5777 / www.hbnews.us/nwhouse.html $

19820 Beach Boulevard, Huntington Beach

Once the only building on acres of land, the restored, two-story Queen Anne Victorian house, originally built in 1898, is now next door to a shopping complex. It does, however, retain its elegance with its upkeep and well-manicured lawn, and it makes an interesting slice of history to learn about and explore.

A half-hour tour includes walking through the various rooms of the house that are furnished not only from that time period, but with many items that belonged to the original owners. See an old-fashioned kitchen with a stove, wall telephone, and cupboard of glass containers; a sunroom with wicker and Mission oak furniture; a dining room with a table all set for a meal; a patterned-wallpapered parlour with a grand piano and 1924 Victrola, and; several bedrooms with mannequins wearing clothing from that era (check out the wool bathing suits!), wash basins, and ¾ size beds; a nursery with a rack of children's clothing and rocking chair; a playroom that contains christening gowns, a few toys, and a cabinet of old dolls; a sleeping porch with brass beds; and a boy's room where three young boys slept on the one bed (until they got too big).

Hours: Open the first and third Sat. - Sun., noon - 4pm. The museum is closed on major holidays and rainy days.

Price: $2 for adults; $1 for ages 12 and under.

Ages: 8 years and up.

OCEAN INSTITUTE

(949) 496-2274 / www.ocean-institute.org $$$

24200 Dana Point Harbor Drive, Dana Point

The Ocean Institute's series of buildings consist of a research center; classrooms designed to teach maritime history and facts about the marine environment to kindergartners through highschoolers; exhibits; touch tanks; a place for hands-on discovery; and more. Note: Peek into the lecture hall to see the whale skeleton hanging from the ceiling.

Walk inside the lobby and immediately feel immersed undersea as kelp hangs from the very tall ceiling with (fake) sea life interspersed. The main exhibit hall here contains Headlands and Beyond, featuring (real) sea creatures that can be found locally in the Rocky Reef tank such as octopus, crabs, squid, flatfish, and perch. It also features hands-on science and sea activities, such as an interactive globe that allows visitors to interact with weather and water patterns over all the earth, and ROV touch screens.

The courtyard has a fun play area for younger kids, themed with extra large sea stars, octopus, a crab and sea anemones on fake rocks (that kids can climb on) and a sea cave. A 100-foot-long pier and 300-foot-long dock, part of The Maddie James Seaside Learning Center that floats on the harbor, is home port to several vessels and nautical learning stations. These include an aquapen for raising White Sea Bass; ROV's used to listen to the sounds of the ocean and its underwater inhabitants; and a flourishing biodiversity aquarium and other tanks of sea life; plus other opportunities to learn by "playing" with exhibits, such as learning to tie a nautical knot. Because students and teachers visit the Institute in force during the week, the public may explore just these parts - Headlands and Beyond, courtyard play area, and Seaside Learning Center - on weekdays.

On the weekends, however, all of the above, plus the rest of the campus and the Tallship *Pilgrim* (on Sundays only), is open. Come into the Ocean Education Building that has several learning stations complete with wet tables, hydrophones, microscopes, and magnification cameras for up-close viewing. You can even do a squid dissection if you want. Some of the tanks in here have large bubbles where kids can stick their heads up "inside" and get a fish-eye view. See moon jellies, and small sharks and rays. Gently touch and even hold some of the sea creatures in the touch-tank. Help out with animal feedings at certain times. The adjoining theater is used for virtual underwater experiences, interactive shows, puppet shows, or other presentations.

A 130-square-foot replica of the historic Tallship *Pilgrim,* rigging and all, is moored in front of the building and open to walk through most Sundays - it's like walking through history. Dressed in period costume docents lead you in singing sea chanteys, sharing sea-faring lore, and help you raise a sail or, you can just enjoy the nautical ambiance. *Pilgrim* offers one- to eighteen-hour on-board programs which recreate the austere life of a sailor in the early nineteenth century. Students learn sea chanteys, how to raise the sails, load cargo, and other period-related activities. See the Calendar entry, TALL SHIPS FESTIVAL (pg. 734) for details on the terrific annual Toshiba Tallships Festival.

Just one of the many cruises the Institute offers is Living Systems program, for older students, aboard the R/V Sea Explorer. The lab includes a fish dissection, water chemistry, invertebrate classification, and Jelly biology. Check out the living-history program aboard the tallship *Spirit of Dana Point,* a replica clipper schooner. Head out to sea and learn sail handling and helmsmanship, plus experience a firing of the ship's cannon. This is an extension of a dockside program or overnight experience with specific curriculum. Of course, you'll get the bigger picture by looking at the waters, too, for dolphins and whales, in season. Want to swab the decks, matey? You can with a three-hour, It's a Sailors Life. This engaging and educational program is an introduction to early California history and the world of a merchant sailor. As you can see, The Institute offers an incredibly full range of outstanding classes for school kids of all ages, from one hour to five days! Check out the extensive field trip list that incorporates literature, social sciences, and history with a maritime theme. Ask about guided tidepool hikes, too.

Behind the Institute is a small park overlooking the harbor, with rock jetties, a few picnic tables, and tidepools. See DANA POINT HARBOR (pg. 315, 755) for details.

Hours: The Institute is open Mon. - Fri., 10am - 4pm; Sat. - Sun., 10am - 3pm. The *Pilgrim* is open most Sun., 10am - 2:30pm. Call for school group tours. Everything is closed on major holidays.

Price: Mon. - Fri., $5; Sat. - Sun., $10 for adults, $7.50 for seniors and ages 2 - 12, children under 2 are free.

Ages: 3 years and up.

OCEAN QUEST

(714) 542-2823 / www.oceanquestoc.org $$

600 E. Bay Avenue, Newport Beach

This satellite museum of Discovery Cube is a small waterfront destination within a destination of going to Balboa Fun Zone and the surrounding area. It currently has just a few rooms with exhibits that include a great white shark hanging on the wall, at a touchable level (good for photo ops); a sailing exhibit showing model ships from early explorers; a play submarine to climb aboard with a short slide; a knot-tying station; a ships' wheel to spin; two short, table-top water lanes to sail the sail boat you helped make; a place to practice Morse code; a weather green screen; a costume area with a few costumes like a kid's captain's uniform and shark outfit; and a few table-top tidepool touch tanks (what a tongue twister!) containing sea stars, sea slugs, limpets, and more. The museum also offers educational programs for students and whale watching cruises. For more to do in this immediate area see BALBOA FUN ZONE (pg. 255) and BALBOA PIER (pg. 315).

Hours: Open most of the year, Sat. - Sun., noon - 5pm; open daily in the summer and on some school holidays, 11am - 6pm.

Price: $5 for ages 3 and up; children 2 and under are free.

Ages: 4 years and up.

OLD COURTHOUSE MUSEUM

(714) 973-6605 - courthouse; (714) 973-6607 - tours / www.ocparks.com   !

211 W. Santa Ana Boulevard, Santa Ana

Order in the court! Older kids interested in the history of our legal system, or in seeing what an actual courtroom looks like, will enjoy visiting the oldest courtroom in Southern California. Built in 1901, this huge, red sandstone building contains three floors of Orange County history. The bottom floor has a few glass cases of archaeological artifacts, such as fossils and bones. The second floor, which is the entrance, has two displays containing information about the museum, the history of the courthouse, and the court of law.

The third floor is the most interesting destination. It features a turn-of-the century courtroom, jury room, and judge's chambers, plus a court reporter's room that has original transcribing machines, a candlestick telephone, and an old roll-top desk. My boys and I role-played a bit here so they could get a feel for how the court system is set up. The museum, which is a room of changing exhibits, is across the way from the Superior Courtroom. Past exhibits have included displays of sheriff's badges, war posters, a mock-up of a 1940's living room, and World War II artifacts from Orange County. A visit to the Old Courthouse Museum is a good beginning for future lawyers. I rest my case.

Hours: Open Mon. - Fri., 9am - 4:30pm. Closed on holidays. Forty-five-minute guided tours are available by appointment.

Price: Free

Ages: 6 years and up.

OLINDA OIL MUSEUM AND TRAIL

(714) 671-4447 or (714) 671-4452 / www.ci.brea.ca.us   !
4025 Santa Fe Road, Brea

Still pumping out about two barrels a day, Olinda's first oil well (dug in 1897) keeps on giving. Located in a residential area this twelve-acre historical site is wonderfully maintained. The building holds artifacts regarding oil, photos, and even small warehouse, yet I think the outside holds a kid's interest more. On the grounds is a pump, the original oil well #1, a records vault, a steam boiler (from 1910), and a rusted 1924 Model T. There are also a few picnic tables on the grass under shade trees. School and group tours are welcome.

Just behind the office building is a moderate, two-mile, looping hiking dirt trail which actually retraces the footsteps of oil pioneers. Going to the top rewards hikers with panoramic views of Orange County.

Hours: The museum is open Wed., 10am - 2pm; Sun., noon - 4pm. The park is open daily, 9am - 4pm. The hiking
       trails are open daily, sunrise - sunset.
Price: Free
Ages: 7 years and up.

ORANGE COUNTY DENTAL SOCIETY MUSEUM

(714) 634-8944 / www.ocds.org   !
295 S. Flower Street, Orange

This small museum doesn't floss over America's early dental period. It contains several old dental chairs, including an 1855 wooden chair with a straight back and a spittoon - no running water on this device; an 1876 velvet, rose-colored chair with fringe and a spittoon; and a modern-day chair with all the amenities. The glass-enclosed display shelves are lined with old dental tools that made me wince just to look at them, such as extraction forceps, clamps for separating teeth, and small saws. My youngest son commented, "I'm going to brush my teeth ten times a day from now on!" We also saw a lot of false teeth, porcelain shade guides (used to match teeth for bridge work or capping), metal swagging sets (for making gold crowns), a buffalo horn mallet (used before plastic), and numerous steel instruments - some made with ivory and some with mother-of-pearl handles. The crowning jewel here is in a silver trinket box - a partial denture of four of George Washington's ivory teeth! You are welcome to explore the museum on your own, as everything is labeled, or ask for further explanations across the hall at the Dental Society. This museum is something you can really sink your teeth into!

Hours: Open Mon. - Thurs., 7am - 4:30pm - please call at least one hour in advance of your visit.
Price: Free
Ages: 9 years and up.

RICHARD NIXON PRESIDENTIAL LIBRARY AND BIRTHPLACE

(714) 983-9120 / www.nixonlibrary.gov; www.nixonfoundation.org $$$$
18001 Yorba Linda Boulevard, Yorba Linda

This museum/library/grave site/rose garden features nine acres of galleries and gardens, plus the restored birthplace of - here's a quiz - what number president? (The answer is at the end of this description.).

The theater presents a half-hour film, documenting Richard Nixon's political career with vintage news footage, campaign clips and more. It's a great introduction to who he was, both personally and presidentially. There are numerous videos, touch screens, and immersive media experiences throughout the museum presented in somewhat of a timeline, that showcase various aspects of his life, from childhood to president, and beyond. These include the Kennedy/Nixon debates, footage from his speeches, a tribute to Pat Nixon, and a presidential forum with over 300 questions to choose from. I was pleasantly surprised at how interested kids were in all of this. The Road to Presidency starts from Nixon's beginnings and takes visitors through his growing up years, on the campaign trails, and into the White House.

The exhibit of ten, life-size statues of world leaders (some of whom were very short) is impressive. Touch screens offer comments and biographical summaries on the leaders. Gifts of State - jewelry, carved ivory, statues, and more - and gifts from the people are unique treasures to view. My oldest son thought the pistol from Elvis Presley was the coolest present. The Structure of Peace gallery features presentations about Nixon's strategy for peace regarding Peoples Republic of China, the Soviet Union, and Vietnam which includes a replica of a South Vietnamese house and uniforms belonging to former POWs. A twelve-foot high chunk of the Berlin Wall is also in this gallery, as is a Soviet missile replica, providing a tangible backdrop for information about the global issues of communism and the Cold War. Other pieces of history include the presidential limo that at various times held Johnson, Ford, Carter, and Nixon; a fully furnished recreation of the White House's Lincoln Sitting Room (which is quite small); numerous photographs; Nixon's daughters' wedding dresses and some of Pat's dresses; the Woody Station Wagon Nixon used for campaigning; memorabilia from Pat Nixon's world travels; and Nixon's private study from his New Jersey home, complete with hand-written letters and speech notes. Enter the Oval Office, a full-size replica and decorated as when Nixon was President, and sit behind the president's desk to take a selfie. Enter a room in the White House that you can digitally explore some of the events and entertaining that occurred therein, plus information on the Nixon family. Step inside Army One (circa 1974) where President and Mrs. Nixon are sitting aboard, having given his farewell speech. Look thru the windows at an audioscape and experience the Nixon's departure from the White House, too.

A small room dedicated to the space program contains an astronaut suit, a piece of moon rock, photographs, and the recording between the president and Apollo 11 astronauts when they landed on the moon. The Domestic Affairs Gallery contains info and touch screens regarding Nixon's achievements in many reforms - space, health, environment, crime, etc. Listen to the "smoking gun" tape in the Watergate exhibit, as well as hundreds of other Watergate tapes and interviews. Use the interactive screens, watch videos, and read the section called "Dirty Tricks and Political Espionage". The comprehensive, really well-done, bipartisan pictorial and descriptive timeline of this historic scandal takes up an entire room. Tip: At the very least, know how to explain the term "impeach" to your kids. Docents are available in most rooms to give some brief, interesting, and helpful background on the exhibits and to answer questions.

Step thru a moon gate portal into the colorful China exhibit which commemorates the historic 1972 trip that Nixon made to China (first U.S. president to do so) and the lasting significance of it. On display are a rendering of part of Air Force One and bronze-plated statues of Nixon shaking hands with Chinese Premier Chou En-lai, as well as huge video screens and photos that give details and visuals as to the planning that went into this trip, and touring China. You can even pose for a photo on the Great Wall of China with President and Mrs. Nixon.

On the other side of the U-shaped building is a room with rotating exhibits and a full-size replica of the White House East Room. This large room has beautiful crystal chandeliers, an ornate ceiling and wall carvings, and some information panels. It is often used for private functions or museum events. Kids usually make just a brief visit here.

Walk outside, through the First Lady's beautiful rose gardens (which look pretty when they're in bloom), past the large reflecting pool, to the home where Nixon was born. A tour of the small house only takes fifteen minutes. A million dollar, restored Sea King helicopter, also known as Marine One, used by this elected official, as well as Kennedy, Johnson, and Ford, is stationed near the house. Walk through it and get a feel for being presidential. Richard Nixon was, by the way, our thirty-seventh President.

Ask about the numerous special programs offered here including Sunday Family Concerts, war reenactments, a myriad of political speakers, and much more. Two-hour, free, guided tours are given Monday through Friday for fifth through twelfth graders, with advanced reservations.

Hours: Open Mon. - Sat., 10am - 5pm; Sun., 11am - 5pm. Closed New Year's Day, Thanksgiving, and Christmas.
Price: $16 for adults; $12 for seniors; $10 for students; $6 for ages 5 - 11; children 4 and under are free. Certain discounts are available through AAA.
Ages: 6 years and up.

SANTA ANA FIRE MUSEUM

(714) 547-9645 / www.santaanafiremuseum.com $$
120 W. Walnut Street, Santa Ana

Don't be alarmed - this museum, housed in a working fire station, is open for you to see both vintage fire-fighting engines, equipment and memorabilia along with contemporary fire trucks and such. Climb into the fully restored 1921 Seagrave fire engine, with all of its bells and whistles, plus other original apparatus. Display cases contain old speaking trumpets, fire lanterns, badges, uniforms, boots, dispatch equipment, and more. Maybe a desire will be sparked to learn more about fires, safety and becoming a fireman by talking with some of the knowledgeable and friendly firemen at the open houses!

Hours: Open 6, or more, Sat. a year. Check the website for the dates and times.
Price: $5 for adults; $4 for seniors; $3 for K - 12 graders; preschoolers and under are free.
Ages: 3 years and up.

SUSANNA BIXBY BRYANT MUSEUM AND BOTANIC GARDEN

(714) 694-0235 / www.santaanahistory.com $
5700 Susanna Bryant Drive, Yorba Linda

Pockets of history are revealed via a tour of this house built in 1911. Walk the grounds and then through this lovely home to see and hear about the history of Yorba Linda, and beyond. The parlour has a piano, stone fireplace and a vintage rug and other furnishings, as well as mannequins dressed in period clothing. There are several other rooms, including a kitchen, with displaying lots of old photographs, road signs, maps, farm implements, household furniture, lanterns, medical equipment, a mastodon jaw, cast iron stove, and other equipment and artifacts. They are open for school and group tours during the week.

Hours: Open Sun., 1pm - 4pm. Closed on holidays.
Price: $2 for adults; $1 for ages 5 - 12; children 4 and under are free.
Ages: 6 years and up.

—PIERS AND SEAPORTS—

BALBOA PIER

(949) 644-3309 or (800) 94-COAST (942-6278) / www.newportbeachca.gov; www.visitnewportbeach.com $
Main Street by E. Oceanfront, Newport Beach

Enjoy the miles of sandy beach for sunning and surfing; fish from the pier just for the fun of it; or grab a bite to eat at the small RUBY'S (Orange County) (pg. 252) at the end of the pier. Peninsula Park is on the east side of the pier. This decent-size, grassy park (that's good for flying kites!), shaded only by palm trees, has barbecues, picnic tables, and even a small playground with a fun, triangular, rope-climbing structure. Note that there are many trendy cafes and equipment rental places in the area. Combine BALBOA FUN ZONE (pg. 255) and OCEAN QUEST (pg. 312) attractions, located just across the road, for a full day of fun.

Hours: Open daily, 6am - 10pm.
Price: Free. Balboa Pier Parking Lot is $1.90 per hour, May - Sept.; $1.30, Oct. - April; $19+ max.
Ages: All

DANA POINT HARBOR

(949) 923-2255 / www.danapointharbor.com   !/$
34675 Street of the Golden Lantern, Dana Point

Dana Point Harbor has beaches, tidepools, a seaside shopping village, boat rentals, picnic areas, and more. The shopping village offers many specialty stores, from Indian jewelry to seafaring items. Food choices range from the elegant to the quick bite, plus ice cream and candy shops, of course. Your young sailor can watch boats of all sizes, shapes, and colors sail in and out of the harbor and up and down the coast. See the Transportation section for details about cruises, whale watching, and ocean fun craft rentals.

At the western end of the harbor, next to the Ocean Institute, is Dana Cove Park, or "Baby Beach." There are a few picnic tables here overlooking the bluffs, a long rock jetty to climb out on, a waveless beach, and a youth group facility which holds classes for water sports. On the other side of the Institute is a rocky patch of beach and the tidepools of the marine preserve, which you can explore on your own or call for a guided tour. Tip: Wear shoes with good tread.

Enjoy the day with your family at Dana Point, whatever you choose to do! See DOHENY STATE BEACH PARK (pg. 243) and OCEAN INSTITUTE (pg. 311) for other things to do here.

Hours: Most shops are open daily, 10am - 8 or 9pm.
Price: Parking is free.
Ages: All

—POTPOURRI—

BUILD-A-BEAR WORKSHOP (Orange County)

Mission Viejo - (949) 347-6992; Orange - (714) 922-2763 / www.buildabear.com $$$
Mission Viejo - 555 The Shops Blvd. at The Shops at Mission Viejo; Orange - 20 City Boulevard West at The Outlets at Orange.

Make your own new best friend at Build-A-Bear stores. First, choose a furry bear, frog, dinosaur, monkey, kitty, unicorn or dog body. Add a sound or record your own message to put inside the critter. Then, help stuff it by pressing on a pedal that (gently!) shoots stuffing into your animal, fluffing him/her until he/she is just right. After putting a little heart inside your new buddy, have the last few stitches sewn up, and choose a name to put on a personalized birth certificate or inside of a storybook. The stores also offer over 200 outfits and accessories (including Star Wars, Marvel, holiday, and so many other fun themes) to dress up your furry friend. What a fun excursion or *bear*thday party idea! Note that there are several workshops throughout Southern California and most of them located inside malls.

Hours: Mission Viejo is open Mon. - Fri., 10am - 9pm; Sat., 10am - 8pm; Sun., 11am - 6pm. Orange is open Mon. - Thurs., 10am - 9pm; Fri. - Sat., 10am - 10pm; Sun., 10am - 8pm.
Price: The "bear" minimum prices are $12 - $35, depending on the size of the bear. Clothing, accessories, and storybooks are all extra.
Ages: 2 years and up.

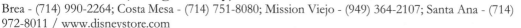

DISNEY STORE (Orange County)

Brea - (714) 990-2264; Costa Mesa - (714) 751-8080; Mission Viejo - (949) 364-2107; Santa Ana - (714)   !/$$
972-8011 / www.disneystore.com

Brea - 1065 Brea Mall; Costa Mesa - 3333 Bristol St. at South Coast Plaza; Mission Viejo - 555 The Shops at Mission Viejo Blvd.; Santa Ana - 2800 North Main St. at Main Place Santa Ana

These Disney stores have several extra, magical and immersive components, besides the world of Disney merchandise. One child is chosen every morning to participate in an opening ceremony of officially "unlocking" the store with an oversized lock and key. Inside, the glittery walkway (sprinkled with pixie dust, I presume) leads to a kid-sized bejeweled castle door. Walk through and come face-to-face with a set of mirrors. Wave special wands in front of the main one (employees will show your kids which wands) and it becomes animated, showing scenes starring Disney princesses. Look up at the enchanted trees - they periodically come to life with changing colors and seasons, and Disney images and footage.

Another special feature is a small theater that continuously shows favorite Disney trailers, music videos, cartoons, and movie clips - you can sometimes even select which ones you want to view. This area is where free teas and mini parades (both events encourage kids to come dressed as their favorite Disney character), storytelling, how-to-draw, and other celebrations/events are held throughout the day. There are also crayons and coloring pages here, too, to use any time. Parents shop leisurely (or rest a bit), kids are mesmerized and happy - a fairy tale ending.

Hours: Most stores are open Mon. - Fri., 10am - 9pm; Sat., 10am - 8pm; Sun., 11am - 6pm. Call for the hours of your specific store.

Price: Free, but bring spending money.

Ages: 1 - 10 years.

DOWNTOWN DISNEY

(714) 300-7800; (714) 635-2300 - Grand California Hotel / disneyparks.disney.go.com   !/$$$

1580 Disneyland Drive, Anaheim

Downtown Disney has an uptown feel. It is a wide, non-gated, beautifully-landscaped pedestrian walkway, lined with unique restaurants, shops, and nightclubs. Nighttime can bring a (clean) party atmosphere, especially when it has street entertainers, live music, and fun kiosks. Favorite stores in this eclectic mixture, include the massive World of Disney, which is one of the world's largest collections of exclusive Disney merchandise. If you can't find it here, they don't make it! Lego Imagination Center carries a huge variety of Lego products. Try your luck at Splitsville Luxury Lanes, a 2-story, upscale bowling alley with 20 lanes, 25-plus flat-screen TV's, live music and a restaurant that features indoor/outdoor dining. Groups of 4 people at a time live Star Wars, or another virtual reality scenario, for about 15 minutes in THE VOID (Orange County) (pg. 320).

Downtown Disney is located in between DISNEYLAND (pg. 235) and CALIFORNIA ADVENTURE (pg. 232), and connects with the Disneyland Hotel and Disney's Grand Californian Hotel and Spa. The latter gigantic (and expensive) hotel is done in the Arts and Crafts design with a woodsy yet understated elegant theme. Take a walk through and gawk at the high, high beam ceiling, at the lobby fireplace that dominates the room because of its size, and at the timber trusses that look like a castle gate door. The lobby actually feels like an inviting living room/family room. You can just relax in the plush chairs here for a bit. The hotel does offer free, hour-long tours a few times a week, by reservation. For a usually quiet nook or picnic area, go through the hotel onto its grounds' walkway where you'll be surrounded by trees. There you'll find a few cafe-style tables and chairs. This hotel also has two, on-site restaurants; the comfortable, Storyteller's Cafe with CHIP 'N DALE CRITTER BREAKFAST and BRUNCH AT STORYTELLERS CAFE (pg. 248), and the more refined Napa Rose, with incredible food, views of the chef's in the kitchen fixing the meals and an entire children's food and dessert menu. Other fun places to eat that are just around the corner are SURF'S UP! BREAKFAST WITH MICKEY AND FRIENDS (pg. 253) and GOOFY'S KITCHEN (pg. 249).

Hours: The "street" is open daily, 7am - 2am. The Void is open daily, 9am - 11:45pm. Most of the stores and restaurants open at 9am. Closing times vary.

Price: Free. The first 3 hours of parking are "free" when you make a $20 minimum purchase and receive validation from any Downtown Disney location; up to 5 hours of parking with validation from any Downtown Disney table-service restaurants. There is a 15-minute grace period to allow those dropping visitors off.

Ages: All

FRY'S ELECTRONICS (Orange County)

Anaheim - (714) 688-3000; Fountain Valley - (714) 378-4400 / www.frys.com

Anaheim - 3370 East La Palma Ave.; Fountain Valley - 10800 Kalama River Ave.

See the entry for FRY'S ELECTRONICS (Los Angeles County) (pg. 170) for details.

GREAT WOLF LODGE

(714) 530-9653 / www.greatwolf.com

12681 Harbor Blvd, Garden Grove

$$$

Who's afraid of the big bad wolf? No one who comes to this fantastic, massive, wolf-themed lodge to play! The lobby is huge and has a relaxing side room with fireplace, antler chandeliers and statues of bears and wolves.

You don't have to be a guest at the hotel to enjoy some of its kid-friendly amenities, located mostly on the lower level. For instance, play laser frenzy ($4) - a game where you try to leap over or crawl under the web of laser beams that crisscross all over the room to get to the other side without the lights touching you, therefore wining the game. Go "miniature" bowling with smaller, five-pound balls on lanes that are half the regular size, but all the regular fun ($6 a game). Play nine holes of miniature golf ($7) on an inside, blacklit course. The detailed, fanciful creatures that glow-in-the-dark and the murals are nature-themed. Watch/be immersed in a four-minute, interactive 4D show at the Howly Wood XD Theater when your chair moves with the action on screen and special glasses make objects pop out ($8). Similar to Build-A-Bear, Creation Station has plush animals that you create (stuff) for about $34.99, plus more for accessories and outfits. Your new animal friend also has a chip that interacts with about nine stations throughout the hotel for a game for younger kids to play. A colorful arcade is filled with kid-friendly games of skill (and luck) such as air hockey tables, skee ball, basketball, motorcycle and car racing, Stinky Feet (involving a character in a bubble bath and a toilet), and more. Earn Paw Points to redeem for prizes. Kind of Harry Potterish, go on a MagiQuest by purchasing and using a special wand that reacts to magical spots throughout the hotel, played like a scavenger hunt game. These thirty-four interactive stations, set up like decorated vignettes with videos screens, are located throughout the hotel, even on the upper floor hallways. They give clues to solve a mystery, part of a game that kids can play over and over again, or they can purchase a new adventure. Quests can take a half hour or three hours, depending on the quest. Wands double as a fun souvenir. The cost is a $14.99 wand activation fee, plus $17.99 to $23.99 for the wand. And there are a lot of wands to choose from, plus wand toppers (fairies to dragons); costumes, so kids can dress up in character for their quests; stuffed animals; and more in the on-site store.

Here's the scoop at Scooops Kid Spa: They offer dessert-themed pampering such as fizzy soaks with an ice cream motif, sherbet scrubs and a rainbow of nail colors for pedicures or manicures, each given while resting on a banana split throne and wearing a take-home tiara. A quick, sweet treat is Sprinkled Scoops which is a sampling and application of ice cream-flavored lotion, hair scent and lip gloss, and a take-home tiara and sash, for $9.99 a child. Call (714) 530-9653 to make an appointment.

There are several restaurants and eateries throughout the lodge and I can attest that the food is really good. Burgers, sandwiches and salads are about $13. Definitely try the Bear Paw Sweet & Eats shop (lower level) with its ice cream flavors and freshly-made fudge. Enjoy character dining at the woodsy-decorated Loose Moose Family Kitchen. A costumed and friendly wolf, bear, raccoon, and chipmunk (the lodge cartoon mascots) greet your kids and are available for photo ops. The all-you-can-eat breakfast buffet includes eggs, any way you want them, bacon, waffles, Danish, and more goodies. Breakfast, served daily from 7am to 11am, is $19.99 for adults; $9.99 for ages 4 to 11; children 3 and under are free with a paying adult.

If you stay at the Lodge, a super fun element, open only to hotel guests, is the mostly inside and a little bit outside water park. The relatively big waterpark has all the elements that make a water park great (plus you don't need to wear sunscreen) - a side-by-side racing slide; a short lazy river; a Flowrider pool to practice boogie boarding; a swimming area (up to five-feet deep); long, enclosed, twisty tubes; a pool with basketball hoops and play area; a gigantic, enclosed, funnel-shaped slide to spin around and around before you drop down; and a large, colorful and themed, central, multi-story play structure for older kids with several slides, tubes, steps, bridges, water going up and under and over everywhere, a big bucket that pours over soaking visitors, and more. A fanciful water play area designed for little ones in zero depth has colorful fake flowers on long stems/poles (that pour down water), animals and short slides, plus water spurting up gently from the shallow pool area. The outside, shallow pool has more of the same elements with animated objects dropping water from tall poles, a few basket ball hoops, things to play on and around, and just fun! There is a full-service snack bar inside and out, lots of lounge chairs, and room to relax. There is also a fully-stocked shop that sells a wide variety of swimsuits, towels, and everything else you might have forgotten. There are standard rooms, that start at about $299, as well as themed rooms, which include a "separate" room for the kids that looks like a cabin with bunkbeds. However you come to play or stay, you'll have a howling good time.

Hours: The attractions are open daily, usually 9am - 11pmish. The arcade is open 24 hours.
Price: Prices are listed above.
Ages: 4 years and up

HUNTINGTON BEACH CENTRAL LIBRARY and CULTURAL CENTER

(714) 842-4481 / www.hbpl.org
7111 Talbert Avenue, Huntington Beach

When is a library more than just a place to peruse books (as if that weren't enough)? When it is the Huntington Beach Public Library! This multi-level facility is a delight to visit. Kids are captivated by the huge center fountain inside and the spiraling paved walkway that encircles it. The fountain is loud, especially on the lower level, in contrast to the normal quiet tones associated with a library. On the bottom floor is a cafe stand that sells sandwiches, salads, corn dogs, muffins, and a range of coffees. Use the adjacent tables and chairs for enjoying a snack, reading, and/or studying. Look up and see returned books being transferred to be re-shelved via a metal conveyor belt. (Only kids notice this sort of thing.)

The Huntington Beach Playhouse is located on the lower level. Several, mostly adult-oriented performances, are given throughout the year. Children's productions are occasionally offered here, although usually given in the upstairs theater room. These can include marionette and puppet shows, musicals, and so on.

One side of the main floor has an incredible number of books organized on several levels within the library. A map is available to help you find your topic of interest. There are even a few small art galleries in this wing. Adjacent to this room is a large section with used books and videos for sale. The library also has a small gift shop.

Just outside the Children's Room is a circular aquarium - look for the eel. The Children's Room has a large selection of books. It also contains a reading area, a toddlers' section, and a wooden frame of a boat for tots to play in. The adjacent Tabby Storytime Theater, which is used throughout the week for various storytimes, and crafts, plus a media/computer room make this library complete. Check the website for a calendar listing of children's events, including the Lego Club, school reading programs, homework help, and more.

HUNTINGTON CENTRAL PARK / SHIPLEY NATURE CENTER (pg. 283) surrounds the library. Directly behind the library is a trail leading down to a pond. Acres of trails, rolling green hills, shade trees, and picnic areas are all here to enhance your visit. For summertime fun, check out ADVENTURE PLAYGROUND (pg. 715), just up the hill from the library.

Hours: The library is open Mon., 1pm - 9pm; Tues. - Thurs., 9am - 9pm; Fri - Sat., 9am - 5pm; Sun., 1pm - 5pm.
          Closed on certain holidays. Call for hours for special events, and for the shows.
Price: Free to the library.
Ages: All

INDEPENDENCE HALL

(714) 220-5244 or (714) 220-5080 / www.knotts.com
8039 Beach Boulevard, Buena Park

Right across the street from KNOTT'S BERRY FARM (pg. 238), this full-size, brick-by-brick, reproduction of Independence Hall houses, among other things, a replica of the Liberty Bell. Press a button to hear a prerecorded history message about the bell. See the recreated room where the Declaration of Independence was signed. Every half hour, a twenty-minute "show," called *Storm in Philadelphia*, is presented. It consists of sitting in the darkened room while candle lights flicker and a "storm" rages outside, and listening to voices debate the ratification of the Declaration of Independence. It is very well done and stirs up patriotism in an American's heart. The gift shop here has patriotic memorabilia to purchase at good prices. Tip: Bring a dime to put in the machine to watch the miniaturized Spirit of '76 army march around. It also has period-dressed mannequins and artifacts, such as a cannon. Tip: Pick up a copy of the self-guided tour brochure before you bring a group here, just to acquaint yourself with all the hall has to offer. Before you visit Independence Hall, you might want to call first and see if a school tour will be in progress. See KNOTT'S ADVENTURES IN EDUCATION (pg. 326) for a list and details on the outstanding educational programs offered.

The surrounding, lush park area has a pond with ducks, shade trees, and grass - perfect for picnicking.

Hours: Open daily, 10am - 4pm. Closed Christmas.
Price: Free. The first hour of parking is complimentary; an additional 2 hours of parking (so 3, total) are free with
          proof of at least $18 of purchases if you're eating at one of the restaurants or doing some shopping. Or, pay
          $18 for parking for the day in the Knott's Berry Farm lot (not the Marketplace where all-day parking is $30).
Ages: 5 years and up.

IRVINE RANCH OUTDOOR EDUCATION CENTER ☼

(714) 923-3191 / www.iroec.webs.com $$$
2 Irvine Park Road, Orange

Being a big advocate of "the world is our classroom" learning makes me appreciate all the programs that Irvine Ranch has to offer groups for half-day, full day, and overnight school field trips, scouting excursions, team building and more. Programs can include really cool science experiments (like firing rockets) and astronomy; going into a mine to dig and learn about rocks, earthquakes, panning for gold, geology and mining; experiencing a day at the rancho at the citrus grove, seasonal vegetable garden, windmill, and solar-powered well to learn about compost, plants, the water cycle and more; archery; shooting BB guns; zip lining; obstacle courses; high ropes courses; hiking; swimming; and much more. Tent and cabin camping, plus nighttime activities are also available.

Hours: Call for a schedule or to create a schedule for your own group.
Price: Depends on the activities and time.
Ages: Depends on the activity.

ROGER'S GARDENS ☽

(949) 640-5800 / www.rogersgardens.com   !
2301 San Joaquin Hills Road, Corona Del Mar

Enter the world of gardening fantasy; a fantasy for me as I have a black thumb. Roger's Gardens sells an enormous variety of plants and shrubs in a beautifully landscaped, garden-like setting. Walk the two-tiered paved trails and fill your eyes with an explosion of color. My kids loved the unusual plants as well as seeing ones that could supposedly bloom in our garden, too. There are a few good-sized gift shop rooms that sell gardening tools, books, dried flower arrangements, specialty soaps, cards, and other paraphernalia.

The kid-draw happens from the end of October through the middle of January when a large patch of elevated grass on the grounds has an extensive model train layout set up and completely decked out. The train, smoke and whistles and all, runs over hill and dale, around miniature cities and scenery. There is also a section at the gardens adorned with decorated Christmas trees.

Hours: Open January - February, 9am - 5pm; March - October, 9am - 6pm; November - December, 9am - 8pm. Closed New Year's Day, Easter, Thanksgiving, and Christmas.
Price: Free
Ages: All

STORYMAKERY ☽

(949) 431-5061 / www.storymakery.com $$$$$
825 Spectrum Center Drive #825, at Irvine Spectrum Center, Irvine

Everybody has a story to tell, and now your child (and you!) can write a personalized story and get it published, all at the same place and day. Storymakery™ is a self-publishing experience designed for children. Who will star in the story? Your child? A character they created? Family and friends and pets? Will it be a mystery story? Adventure? Superhero? Real life? Kids can type in their own stories or use standardized stories with Story Maker which prompts kids with simple questions to enable them to personalize their story. (Adults, you can create a story here, too.)

Characters can be designed by using a base person or thing on the computer, and then customizing it with coloring, features, clothing, accessories, etc., then adding magical powers, or favorite foods and activities, etc. So much imagination to build on! And it's not overwhelming because not only does this studio have tables and chairs, with short, white, stand-alone trees, and kid-friendly workstations with computers to blend creativity with technology for an inspired and unique story, but it has staff members ready to render one-on-one help every step (or page) along the way. The book makes a great gift idea! Maybe a sequel is waiting to be told, too.

And because your child is already on their way to becoming famous, you can also purchase their character design on mugs, t-shirts, tote-bags and more. Read all about it (or write all about it!) and join in on an author summer camp, scouting event, birthday party, or other previously unscripted event.

Hours: Open Sun. - Thurs., 10am - 9pm; Fri. - Sat., 10am - 10pm.
Price: Prices start at $34.99 for preschoolers (using more ready-made story formats) to $54.99 for 5 years and up (inputting more original content), although there are some less expensive options for ages 9 and up, starting at $19.99.
Ages: 3 years and up.

THE VOID (Orange County)

(385) 323-0090 / www.thevoid.com

$$$$$

1580 S. Disneyland Drive at Downtown Disney, Anaheim

    Live the adventure in hyper-reality, a fully immersive, whole body experience where you touch, smell, hear, see and become a part of the reality that now surrounds you. Groups of 4 people at a time suit up, with VR goggles, a vest and usually a proton blaster of some sort, and enter another world for about 15 minutes. It's like a holodeck - it's crazy! Different scenes, stories or worlds are offered such as Star Wars where participants become stormtroopers who try to capture Imperial intelligence vital to the rebellion's survival. Touch a "real" wall, feel the heat and other sensations, and walk around freely, interacting with other Star War's characters and talking to each other! Check the website to see what is currently "showing". Liability waivers are mandatory. Reserve your ticket/time slot beforehand.

Hours: Open daily, 9am - 11:45pm.

  Price: Mon. - Thurs., $32.95 per person; Fri. - Sun. and holidays, $34.95. 3 hours of validated parking.

   Ages: Must be at least 10 years old.

—SHOWS AND THEATERS—

COSTA MESA CIVIC PLAYHOUSE

(949) 650-5269 / www.costamesaplayhouse.org

$$$$

661 Hamilton Street, Costa Mesa

    School House Rock Live!, *The Diary of Anne Frank*, and *Seussical - the Musical* are just three of the shows that have been produced at this seventy-three-seat community theater. Of the four productions put on each year, at least one of them is geared specifically for family and kids.

Hours: Show times are generally Fri. and Sat. at 8pm; Sun. at 2pm. Call for a schedule.

  Price: Tickets are generally $20 for adults; $18 for seniors and students.

   Ages: 7 years and up, depending on what's playing.

CURTIS THEATER - CITY OF BREA GALLERY

(714) 990-7722 - theater; (714) 990-7731 or (714) 990-7730 - gallery / www.ci.brea.ca.us;

$$$$

www.breagallery.com

1 Civic Center Circle, Brea

    The 199-seat Curtis Theater and Brea's Youth Theater boast a variety of plays and productions, musicals and comedies, that are family friendly. The theater's regular season has put on shows such as *West Side Story*, *Peter and the Wolf*, *The Alley Cats* (singing group), and *4 Stand Up Dads* (comedians). The Youth Theater is made up of a talented cast of young actors and actresses (i.e., kids) who put on two musical extravaganzas a year; one in the summer and one in the winter. Past productions include *Peter Pan*, *Aladdin*, and *Bye-Bye Birdie*. Call for information about signing your kids up to be in a future production.

    Across from the theater, the Civic Center has a small gallery, called City of Brea Gallery, where rotating exhibits from around the world of painting, photography, sculpture and more are shown. The gallery hosts workshops for adults and also a Children's Art Workshop where young visitors, ages 5 to 13, may create their own masterpiece related to the current exhibits on select Sundays from 1pm to 3:30pm. The cost is tiered, from $25 - $75, so call and see what works for you. The Brea Gallery is usually open on performance nights and allows kids to peruse art while waiting for the theater doors to open.

Hours: Call for a schedule of performances. Youth Theater productions are usually in July and January. The gallery is open Wed. - Sun., noon - 5pm. Closed holidays.

  Price: Ticket prices vary greatly depending on the show. Tickets for the Youth Theater usually run $12 per person. The gallery is $3 for adults; free to youth 12 and under and Brea residents.

   Ages: 5 years and up.

IRVINE BARCLAY THEATER

(949) 854-4646 / www.thebarclay.org

$$$$$

4242 Campus Drive, Irvine

    This theater offers four to five family-oriented shows a year, plus several touring shows geared for kids, and for adults. The various types of shows include circus acts, folk singers, Indian dancers, ballet, chorus music, modern dance, ensembles, youth orchestras, acrobats, and specifically, the *Nutcracker Suite*. Applause, applause - not a seat in the house is more than sixty feet away from the stage.

Hours: Call for show dates and times. Even children sitting on your lap must have a ticket.
Price: Ticket prices vary greatly from free - $150. Parking is $10 at the UCI parking structure.
Ages: 5 years and up.

THE LAGUNA PLAYHOUSE

(800) 946-5556 or (949) 497-9244; (949) 497-2787 - box office / www.lagunaplayhouse.com
606 Laguna Canyon Road, Laguna Beach

"Orange County's Award-Winning Theater for Young People and the Young at Heart!" The playhouse offers a main stage season, a youth theater showcase where youth acting companies perform, and Theatrereach - an ensemble that comes to schools for on-site performances. Four great-for-the-kids plays are presented here each year. Past productions include *Charlotte's Web*, *Treasure Island*, *Wizard of Oz*, and *The Best Christmas Pageant Ever.*

Hours: Call for show dates and times.
Price: Tickets by the youth companies are usually $10 - $25, depending on the show. Other tickets usually run from $30 - $70, depending on the show. Parking is $10.
Ages: 5 years and up.

MEDIEVAL TIMES

(800) 899-6600 or (714) 521-4740; (714) 521-2342 - student field trips / www.medievaltimes.com; educators.medievaltimes.com
7662 Beach Boulevard, Buena Park

Joust the sight of this eleventh-century-style castle sets the mood for a *knight* to remember. Upon entering the castle hall, wear the crowns given ye, good Lords and Ladies, as the color designates which one of the six knights you'll cheer for. The Lord of the castle and his daughter-in-law, the princess, have invited you and hundreds of your closest friends, neighbors, and foes to a two-hour royal tournament. Bring your camera to take pictures with the knights in shining armor all around the castle. Note: The Museum of Torture is open before the show. This unusual museum displays over thirty reproductions of instruments of torture and ridicule used during the Middle Ages, like the Rack, and the Stock and Pillories. Each instrument is explicitly labeled as to its use. Personally, I wouldn't go through the museum again. Admission is $2 per person.

Tiered spectator seating encircles the dirt floor arena where fog starts to rise up and the music swells - the story and show begin. Hear and become part of the tale where the king, the princess, a master of arms, and six knights and their squires first celebrate a victory, and then discover a treachery.

As dinner commences, the invited guests (that's you and your family) are first entertained by silky-maned horses that prance, high-step, and even jump. These elegant displays of horsemanship delight horse fans young and old. The royal falconer then commands his trained birds of prey as they swoop around the arena. As the story continues to unfold (and you continue to eat) the main event is held - an authentic jousting tournament over which the castle Lord presides. Six knights on horseback compete against one another as they perform feats of real skill in several medieval games before the king and his daughter, and a wildly cheering crowd. (Yelling is encouraged!) After every game, the winning knight throws flowers out to his rooting section. As the show progresses, the knights engage in choreographed battle by pairs, with their swords actually sparking as they strike each other. The knights fight on horseback and on foot until there is just one victor. The traitor is subsequently revealed, beaten in battle, and vanquished to the dungeon.

Throughout the evening serfs and wenches serve a four-course feast, eaten without utensils, of course. The finger-licking delicious meal consists of half a roasted chicken, bread, spare ribs, potatoes, vegetable soup, a pastry, and beverage. We enjoyed the food and were riveted by the action. After the show, the gift shop selling medieval memorabilia is open. Sometimes there is dancing at the in-house Knight Club. Note: If you have a birthday or anniversary or some sort of celebration to celebrate, let your server know immediately so that person(s) can be given a shout out by the king in front of everyone.

Student Field trips/matinees are offered several times a month, year round, during the week, on selected dates from 11:30am to 1pm for kindergartners through twelfth graders. In place of some of the pageantry of the nighttime show, a medieval history lesson is presented in an engaging, storytelling style, delivered while on horseback, by a Master of Ceremonies. The topics covered include knighthood, feudalism, weaponry and combat, and even geography. Kids still see, though, the knights engaging in period games, sword fights, and all the good stuff. This excellent educational outing includes a lunch of chicken, potato, corn cobette, garlic bread, a cookie, and soda. Teachers take note: The matinee also includes an educational resource packet which meets the California state standards. The packet emphasizes reading, writing, and social studies in a story that revolves around the famous Spanish knight, El Cid.

Hours: Knightly performances are usually Mon. - Thurs., 7pm (6pm during July and August); Fri., 6:30pm and 8:45pm; Sat., 3:30pm, 6pm and 8:15pm; Sun., 3:30pm and 6pm (or Sun., 2:30pm and 5pm). Call first as the times fluctuate greatly.

Price: The price, for the dinner and show, is $61.95 for adults; $36.95 for ages 12 and under. Note that children 2 and under are free if they sit on your lap and share your food. Upgrade your package to include preferred "royalty" seating, commemorative program, a knights cheering banner, and a behind-the-scenes" DVD (one per party) for $12 more per person. Reservations are required. Certain discounts available through AAA, and there is usually a discount of some sort offered online. Note: A person gets in free during the month of his/her birthday, with proof that it really is his/her birthday, as long as there is another adult in the party paying the full amount. Advance registration is required. Student matinees are $27 per person.

Ages: 3 years and up.

MERLIN'S MAGIC DINNER SHOW

$$$$$

(714) 744-9288 / www.merlinshow.com; www.ribtrader.com
2710 E. Chapman Avenue at the Rib Trader (restaurant), Orange

It's no illusion, Merlin's Magic Dinner Show is very entertaining. Located in a room that seats about 100 people, guests are invited to sit at long tables for two-hours of down-home magic, comedy, and food. Medieval music plays in the background. Homemade soup is served as Merlin opens with jokes and sleight of hand tricks. Then, comes more delicious food, served by wenches. The adults are given baby back ribs, barbecued chicken, honey-baked corn bread, beans, and coleslaw. Kids receive chicken strips, fries, and fresh fruit. Appetizers, beverages, and desserts are extra. Merlin periodically appears on stage for interludes of more magic and comedy.

After dinner, he performs the bulk of his show, which includes a lot of audience participation. He confounds guests with his cards, ropes, and rings tricks, as well as numerous other magical feats. There were several times after he finished a trick that no one clapped immediately, only because we were trying to figure out how he did it. (In fact, we're *still* trying to figure out how he did it!) Most of the comedy is kid appropriate. Reservations are required.

Hours: Shows are performed Fri., 7:30pm; Sat., 5pm and 8pm; Sun., 5pm. Seating is half-hour before the show.

Price: Admission includes the show and dinner, but not tax and tip: $29.99 for adults; $18.99 for ages 12 and under.

Ages: 4 years and up.

MUSCO CENTER FOR THE ARTS

$$$$

844-OC-MUSCO (844) 626-8726 / www.muscocenter.org
One University Drive at Chapman College, Orange

Stars are born, or realized, at this incredible performing arts venue that seats 1,044 on three levels. Students, faculty, and renown featured entertainers from all walks of the industry are showcased here in song, dance, theater, music, stage productions, ensembles, festivals, and much more. Note that Old Town Orange, with a plethora of restaurants and fun shops, especially DRAGONFLY SHOPS AND GARDENS (pg. 240), is just down the street.

Hours: Call or check the website for show titles and times.

Price: Prices depend on the show. Parking for four hours is $3.

Ages: 5 years and up, depending on the production.

PIRATE'S DINNER ADVENTURE

6/$

(866) 439-2469 or (714) 690-1497 / www.piratesdinneradventure.com
7600 Beach Boulevard, Buena Park

Pillaging, plundering, rifling, and looting aside, pirate's have an un*arrrr*guable appeal. Arrive before show time to enjoy some appetizers of meatballs, cheese and crackers, and chips (buy your own drinks); purchase souvenirs at the gift shop; and witness a preshow. The slapstick preshow involves audience participation and introduces some of the main characters in the featured production.

The audience, up to 750 people, then enters the main room and, on tiered seats, surrounds a replicated 18th-century Spanish galleon with a flying skull and crossbones flag and forty-foot masts anchored in an actual indoor lagoon. Guests are separated into six different groups and assigned a color. That color represents the pirate that you cheer for throughout the ninety-minute dinner and over-the-top show and musical performance. The storyline is classic - a princess is kidnaped and her life is saved when the pirate Captain's son falls in love with her. The dastardly Captain's crew consists of his shrewish wife and the pirates who are sometimes funny, sometimes silly, and often loud as they taunt each other, interact with the audience, encourage the audience to drink beer and rum (and drink and drink), and engage in stunts. The pirates sing, fist fight (accompanied by cheesy sound effects), perform acrobatics, fire cannons, duel with swords, and fight a sea dragon who rises out of the water. The sea dragon has been guarding treasure. They also use audience members to aid them in competitive games. Guests throw balls to their team's pirates, help raise flags, toss around money bags, and more. A captured gypsy woman (the princess' friend) entertains the crew (and audience) by performing acts of balance and gymnastics on a pole using ropes and silks, and on a trapeze-like swing. A battle to save the princess breaks out and there is more fist fighting, swordplay, and choreographed stunts.

Food is served along with the swashbuckling action. The fare consists of soup or salad; roasted chicken or BBQ beef; rice or mashed potatoes; and vegetables. Vegetarian and Captain Kid's meals are available upon request. Brownie a la mode is your just dessert. After the dinner and show, you're invited to meet the pirates and take pictures with them and, on Friday and Saturday evenings after the last show, get your booty together and join the dancing.

Hours: Shows are Mon. - Thurs., 7pm; Fri., 7pm; Sat., 5pm and 8pm; Sun., 3:30pm and 6:30pm. Call first, especially as show times can fluctuate. The doors open ninety minutes before showtime for appetizers and the preshow.

Price: $67.11 for adults; $42.11 for ages 3 - 11; children 2 and under are free. Tax and gratuity are not included. Discounts available online.

Ages: 3 years and up.

ROSE CENTER THEATER

(714) 793-1150 / www.rosecentertheater.com
14140 All American Way, Westminster

$$$$$

Four Broadway-style musicals are produced here every season. Past features have included *A Chorus Line*, *Phantom*, *Music Man*, *Gypsy*, *Nutcracker* and *1776*. Youth and cultural presentations are also offered here.

Hours: Check the website for show times.

Price: Tickets usually run between $15 - $25 for adults; $10 - $20 for seniors and students, depending on the show.

Ages: 6 years and up, depending on the show.

SADDLEBACK COLLEGE PERFORMING & VISUAL ARTS

(949) 582-4656 / www.saddleback.edu/arts
28000 Marguerite Parkway, Mission Viejo

$$$$$

Saddleback College attracts local and featured guest talent from all over and the shows here - music, dance, theater, concerts, art galleries, and more - represent that. Past performances, from all genres, include The New Shanghai Circus (acrobats of China), An Evening of Comedy and Magic, jazz concerts, Beatles music, Dance Collective, Big Band music, *Seussical Jr. The Musical*, orchestra music, and much more.

Hours: Call for performance hours.

Price: Call for performance admissions. Parking is $5.

Ages: 7 years and up.

SEGERSTROM CENTER FOR THE ARTS / FAMILY MUSICAL MORNINGS

(714) 556-2787 - performing arts center; (714) 755-5799 - Pacific Symphony / www.scfta.org; www.pacificsymphony.org

$$$$$

600 Town Center Drive, Costa Mesa

This world-class Center offers top-rate performances that include Broadway plays and musicals, cabaret, jazz, ballet, concerts, opera, symphony performances, dance, and much much more. Past productions have included National Acrobats of China, *Oklahoma*, *Lord of the Dance*, Cirque Du Solei, *Blues Clues! Live*, *Forever Plaid*, a sing-a-long of *Sound of Music*, headlining entertainers, etc. The complex is comprised of Segerstrom Center Hall, 3,000 seats; Segerstrom Concert Hall, 1,700 seats; Samueli Theater, 500 seats; and the Julianne and George Argyros Plaza and Center for Dance and Innovation, an outdoors stage and pavilion. Note: One hour prior to most performances in the Dance, Jazz, and Chamber Music Series, a noted expert gives a free, informative talk, open to all ticket holders, to share insights about the performance. Call to verify there will be a lecture if you are interested in this. Also, for select Broadway performances, stay afterward on Thursdays for post-show Talkbacks with the cast to ask questions and learn details about the life of a performer. Teachers, the Center offers student performances/field trips at incredible prices - what a fantastic, affordable opportunity for students to engage in the arts! See SEGERSTROM CENTER FOR THE ARTS (tour) (pg. 327) for information on taking a tour of this center.

Five Saturdays a year the Pacific Symphony presents Family Musical Mornings. Designed especially for kids ages 5 to 11, they are more than just concerts. Fun for kids, as well as interactive, the forty-five-minute performances vary in content, but aim to be pieces and stories that children are familiar with, such as music from *Nutcracker Suite* or *Peter and the Wolf*, from cartoons, or a famous fairytale. Come at 9am (for a 10am program) and stay afterward for the latter show as kids are then invited to a Musical Carnival where they can try out a variety of instruments, talk with performers, and do a craft pertaining to the featured show.

Hours: Call for a show schedule. Family Musical Mornings are on select Sat. at 10am and 11:30am.

Price: Performance prices vary according to show, date, and time. Family Musical Mornings, depending on your seat, range from $16 - $35. Parking is $10 - cash only.

Ages: 4 years and up, depending on the show.

SOKA PERFORMING ARTS CENTER

(949) 480-4ART (4278) / www.soka.edu/pac

$$$$

1 University Drive at Soka University, Aliso Viejo

This 1,000 seat concert hall is big enough to attract some big names, but small enough to still be somewhat intimate, with front row seats actually on the stage floor. Concerts feature classical music, jazz, chamber orchestras, piano concertos, the pop classic series and, my favorite, the World Music Series with multi-cultural music and dance performances. The adjacent Maathai Hall features a black box theater with 180 seats and a dance studio.

Hours: Check the website for show dates and times.

Price: Ticket prices can be $10 for children; $15 for adults; and up.

Ages: 9 years and up.

SOUTH COAST REPERTORY

(714) 708-5555 or (714) 708-5577 / www.scr.org

$$$$$

655 Town Center Drive, Costa Mesa

Come to this acclaimed theater for year-round professional productions. Note that most plays are geared for older children and adults. There is a series of three family productions a year, titled Theatre for Young Audiences, that run for about three weeks. Productions have included *The Emperor's New Clothes*, *James and the Giant Peach*, *The Stinky Cheese Man*, and *Wind in the Willows*. These shows range average $27. Kids, ages 4 to 15, can also sign up to be in a production that, after months of rehearsals, culminate in performances given for the public, such as *Jack and the Giant Bean Stalk*.

Or, invite the theater to come to your child's school as the repertory has fantastic educational outreach programs. Musicals and dramatic presentations correlate with school curriculum on a variety of subjects, including multi-cultural themes, dealing with relationships, and even Shakespeare. Call for a schedule and pricing information.

Hours: Call for show dates and times.

Price: Varies, depending on the show. Parking is $10.

Ages: 10 years and up, depending on the show.

TESSMANN PLANETARIUM AT SANTA ANA COLLEGE

(714) 564-6356 or (714) 564-6680 / www.sac.edu

$$$

1530 W. 17th Street, Santa Ana

Twinkle, twinkle little star, how I wonder what you are? Your kids can begin to find the answers to this question, and many more, at shows in the 100-seat planetarium. Several hour-long programs, such as *How Rare is Earth?*, *What Color is Your Planet?*, *Mysteries of the Cosmos,* and *A Tour of Our Solar System* (this is followed by going outside for Night Sky Live on Saturday evenings) are wonderful trips around the galaxy, as you see and learn about planets, constellations, our solar system, comets, and more. There is also a shorter show, written by a former preschool teacher, geared for kindergartners and first graders called, *Can You See in the Dark?* This show is only $3. All the shows have live narrations given by an astronomer. Various programs appeal to guests 5 to 95 years old. There is time after the presentation for questions and answers. If you have a group of thirty-five or more, ask about reserving the auditorium for your group. Dates depend on availability and reservations are required. See the Calendar entry for more information on the wonderful Christmas show, PLANETARIUM SHOWS - CHRISTMAS SHOW / STAR OF BETHLEHEM (pg. 750).

Hours: Shows are presented on selected dates year round, Mon. - Fri. at 9:30am and 11:15am, and sometimes at 3pm; Sat. at 7pm. Reservations are needed. School, or other groups, are welcome to make reservations, too, and large groups, of 35 or more, can book the planetarium at other times.

Price: $6 per person weekdays; $7 on Sat. Parking is $2.

Ages: Must be at least 5 years old, except for the shorter show mentioned above.

THE PLANETARIUM AT ORANGE COAST COLLEGE

(714) 432-5072 / www.orangecoastcollege.edu

2701 Fairview Road at Orange Coast College, Costa Mesa

The galaxy might seem light years away, but it's actually available in Orange County. This state-of-the-art planetarium offers a 125-seat theater with a fifty-foot dome, showing wonderful media and presentations to learn about and view the earth, heavens, and beyond. The rest of the building, and grounds, boast a Foucault Pendulum, which is huge device that visually demonstrates the rotation of the earth; interactive science hall exhibits; a sphere NOAA display globe; telescopes outside; and more. Student field trips for all ages, as well as public programs are part of the way the planetarium is helping us chart our way to the stars.

Hours: Check the website for the schedule.
Price: Check the website.
Ages: 5 years and up.

—TOURS—

ANGEL STADIUM

(714) 940-2045 or (714) 940-2230 / www.mlb.com/angels
2000 Gene Autry Way, Anaheim

"Let me root, root, root for the home team . . ." . Take this behind-the-scenes, seventy-five-minute tour to see areas that you don't normally see during a ball game. You'll visit the press box, press conference room, stadium clubhouse, dugout (not onto the playing field) and more. The walking tours, which can have parts that are wheelchair accessible, are a must-do for fans! Tours are not offered on dates when the Angels have a home game. Reservations are highly suggested. Note that the team store is open for groups after the tour.

Private tours, for groups of 20 or more, are available, too - for birthday parties, class field trips, baseball teams, just because, and more.

Hours: Tours are offered April - September, usually Tues., Wed., and Fri. at 10:30am, 12:30am, and 2:30pm, when the team is out of town. Tours are not offered when the Angels have a home game. No tours are given on major holidays, or when there is a special event at the stadium.
Price: $8 for adults; $6 for seniors, active military, and ages 4 - 17. Parking is free.
Ages: 5 years and up.

CALIFORNIA PIZZA KITCHEN (Orange County)

See the entry for CALIFORNIA PIZZA KITCHEN (Los Angeles County) (pg. 196) for more information.

FULLERTON AIRPORT

(714) 879-0161 or (714) 612-5317 - general public tours; (714) 738-3136 - Museum Dept. of Ed. / www.cityoffullerton.com
4011 W. Commonwealth, Fullerton

If your child, or you, has lofty ambitions, take a one-hour tour of the airport led by a docent who is a member of the Fullerton's Pilot Association. The walking tour includes going onto the airfield (and usually looking inside or sitting in a small plane), while learning about how an airport operates, airport businesses, the types of airplanes that use this airport, how planes fly, some history of the area and more. The tour usually ends on a high note as souvenirs, like plastic wings for future pilots, are given out. Tours are offered for a minimum of five people up to fifteen. Note that Wings Cafe is located just inside the airport terminal and is open daily, to the public, from 7am - 2pm.

Educators - Sign up your kindergartners, or older students, for the Wings Over Fullerton half-day field trip which covers most of the above same material, as well as curriculum standards of earth's weather patterns, local and regional history, and more. The docents are knowledgeable as they are FMC staff and sometimes pilots or instructors.

Fullerton hosts the Antique Aircraft Display Days every second Sunday of the month from 9am to 2pm. Join the owners and admirers to look at warbirds and homebuilts, and perhaps a few antique cars, and more. Free admission.

Hours: Public tours are available Mon. - Fri., usually at 11am, by advanced reservation only. Wings Over Fullerton tours are given for school groups, only, on the second Tues., by appointment. Call in August to book for the upcoming school year.
Price: Public tours are free. School tours are free to Fullerton School District schools - all other groups are $3 per child; chaperones are free.
Ages: 5 years and up.

GOODWILL INDUSTRIES (Orange County)

(714) 480-3355; (714) 547-6308 - ask for public relations / www.ocgoodwill.org   !

410 North Fairview Street, Santa Ana

See the entry for GOODWILL INDUSTRIES (San Bernardino County) (pg. 437) for details.

Hours: Tours are usually given twice a month - call for specific information.

Price: Free

Ages: At least 8 years old

JOHN WAYNE AIRPORT THOMAS F. RILEY TERMINAL TOUR

(949) 252-5296 or (949) 252-5168 / www.ocair.com $

3151 Airway Avenue, Costa Mesa

This terrific, ninety-minute tour is tailored toward the participants' ages and interests, showing all aspects of the airport. Guests see the public access places while learning about the history of the airport and some basic information on aviation, such as the answer to what makes a plane fly. The tour starts at the statue of John Wayne and goes all around the terminal to see and learn about the various activities, such as terminal architecture, airline ticket counter areas, security checkpoints, historical photo displays, the Wright Brothers flight, the baggage carousels, skycap activity and more. There are huge windows all along the field, and a V-shape one jutting into it that offers a wonderful view of the planes taxiing, landing and taking off, being serviced, and baggage being loaded and unloaded. A fun remembrance, such as an airplane activity guide, is given out at the end of the tour. Happy landings! The docents are knowledgeable and some are even retired pilots. A minimum of seven people and maximum of twenty-five are needed for a tour. Note that high school and college tours may be arranged with aviation career speakers provided.

Hours: Tours are available Mon. - Fri. at 10:30am and 2:30; call for other times. Sat. tours can be accommodated. Reservations are required at least 2 weeks in advance.

Price: Free. Parking is $2 per hour.

Ages: Must be at least 5 years old and/or in first grade.

KNOTT'S ADVENTURES IN EDUCATION

(714) 220-5244 or (714) 220-5166 / www.knotts.com $$$

8039 Beach Boulevard, Buena Park

The education department with KNOTT'S BERRY FARM (pg. 238) provides over twenty, outstanding, guided tours for all grade levels and for scouts, as well. The tours incorporate aspects of the amusement park, and sometimes a few rides, such as Ghost Town - a very real, Western part of Knott's Berry Farm; a visit with a re-enactor, like Benjamin Franklin; and/or a visit to INDEPENDENCE HALL (pg. 318). Park admission can be added onto all tours.

The programs are offered year round and range from ninety-minutes to five hours. Some of the programs are: Geologist - Panning for Gold (gold panning can actually be added to any tour for an additional $10 per person); Native American Cultures; Transportation Past and Present (which includes a ride on the Knott's stagecoach); Early American Heritage; Early California (this incorporates a 1830's trapper re-enactor, blacksmith demonstration, and candlemaking demonstration); Energy in Motion - Physics (one physics program taught by a physics teacher is for jr. and sr. highers, and another is geared for younger kids); and Classic Christmas.

Adults (40 years and older) and with a minimum group of fifteen - you are not left out! Choose either two-hour tour: 1) Early American Heritage tour, which highlights significant moments in Early American history including a tour of Independence Hall; meeting Benjamin Franklin or Abigail Adams or Patrick Henry; and more, or 2) Pathways to the Past, which focuses on the Old West throughout Ghost Town, including the blacksmith shop, the school house, a ride on restored train cars from the 1880's, and more. The latter tour has a lot of walking involved. Stay for lunch, at your own cost. Admission to the park for the day is also extra.

Hours: All tours are offered by reservation only.

Price: Tours start at $13 per student, and go up from there. Tours for adults are $14. Parking is $19 for the day. There is some validated parking at the California MarketPlace.

Ages: K - 12th grade; or adults.

ORANGE COUNTY SANITATION DISTRICT

(714) 962-2411 / www.ocsd.com   !

10844 Ellis Avenue, Fountain Valley

The ninety-minute education program is geared for students at least 11 years old and up (really for teenagers) - adults are welcome to take tours, too. A fifteen-minute video explains how water is treated. The rest of the program, including a bus tour of the facility, is spent hearing about and seeing the different levels of water treatment and how the public health is protected. Students learning about microbiology, for example, will look at various water particles under a microscope and identify what they see. Visitors also learn why it's important to conserve. The minimum number for a tour is ten, the maximum, twenty-five, although there are tours for groups under ten people offered five times a year - usually on Tuesdays from 9am - 10:30am. Check the website for more details.

Hours: Tours can be scheduled Mon. - Fri. between 9am - 3pm.
Price: Free
Ages: Must be at least 11 years old.

SEGERSTROM CENTER FOR THE ARTS (tour)

(714) 556-2122 / www.scfta.org   !
600 Town Center Drive, Costa Mesa

All the world's a stage! Get a behind-the-scenes look at both halls, usually, that comprise the Center - the Renée and Henry Segerstrom Concert Hall and the 3,000-seat Segerstrom Hall. This, latter, grand facility is where major symphony concerts, operas, ballets, and Broadway musicals are presented.

Tour one building (one hour) or both (ninety minutes), beginning at the ticket box office, then through the theaters, to the star's dressing rooms and wardrobe area, finishing up backstage, and seeing and learning insider information about the current productions. Tour routes may vary due to rehearsal and performance schedules, and backstage set construction. Visitors will also see and learn about the architecture, sculptures, and other art objects that grace the interior and exterior of the Center. For show information, please see SEGERSTROM CENTER FOR THE ARTS / FAMILY MUSICAL MORNINGS (pg. 323, 778).

Hours: Guided tours are offered few times a month on Mon. and Wed. or Sat. at 10:30am. Reservations are required. Private tours for a group of 10 or more people can be also be made. Closed on some holidays.
Price: Free. There is limited street parking and several parking garages that cost about $10.
Ages: 10 years and up.

TANAKA FARMS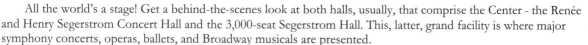

(949) 653-2100 / www.tanakafarms.com $$$$
5380 ¾ University Drive, Irvine

Tanaka Farms incorporates three of my favorite things all in one tour: food, being outside, and learning. The specific type of tour depends on the season as that determines what's growing, but most of the tours are similar in content. Each one is about one-hour long; includes a tractor-drawn wagon ride around the thirty-acre farm and seeing the various fruits and vegetables; and learning about farming methods, and the history of farming and the area. Participants get to sample the crops in season, too. The last stop is usually picking and eating the featured crop and taking home a one-pound basket. You can pick more and pay for it. Tours are offered on the weekends, in season, every half hour from 9:30am - 2:30pm for the general public. Reservations aren't needed for less than ten people. School or group tours are offered during the week and reservations are required. Tours are $18 per person; children 2 and under are free.

Strawberry Tours are offered February to June. Watermelon Tours are offered July through August. U-Pick Pumpkin Patch Tours are in October. Christmas Tree Tours are in December. Weekend tours are often accompanied by games, crafts, samples, cooking demos, ATV rides, face-painting, petting zoos and more, for an additional cost.

There are a few other options, as well. U Pick Tours, available March through August, offer free wagon rides around the farm so you can more readily get to the various crops and pick your own fruits (usually not strawberries, tho) and vegetables, directly. They are only offered when there is an abundance of crops and could include carrots, kale, tomatoes, lettuce, and more. Pick and then simply pay the market stand price, by pound or by bunch. If you want to pick strawberries without a tour, that is sometimes available to do directly behind the market stand for $5 a pound. Lastly, for a really fresh farm to table experience, sign up for one of the special luncheon events offered at various times throughout the year. Seasonal crops are prepared, along with a BBQ main dish and other delicious food, to enjoy at the picnic tables.

Tour tips: The fields are on uneven ground, so remember to wear closed toe shoes that you don't mind getting dirty. There isn't any public drinking water here, so bring your own. Tours are great experiences for kids and adults! The produce stand sells whatever is ripe, plus other goodies, including fresh squeezed strawberry lemonade on the weekends, in season. The market stand hours are daily in season, 9am - 5pm.

Hours: Mentioned in the entry.
Price: Tour prices are given in the entry.
Ages: 3 years and up.

—TRANSPORTATION—

AMTRAK (Orange County)

(800) USA RAIL (872-7245) / www.amtrakcalifornia.com
Ride the rails! See AMTRAK (Los Angeles County) (pg. 208) for more information.

BALBOA BOAT RENTALS

(949) 673-7200 / www.boats4rent.com

$$$$

510 E. Edgewater, Balboa

Rentals include kayaks - $18 per hour for a single, $30 an hour for a double; stand up paddle boards - $25 an hour; powerboats - $75 for the first hour for a six-passenger boat that doesn't leave the harbor, and starting at $120 for the first hour for a six-passenger boat that does; pontoon boats (in harbor) that seat up to twelve - $105 for the first hour; and electric boats (which are much quieter than motor boats, hold eight to twelve people, and some are enclosed - start at $85 an hour. See BALBOA FUN ZONE (pg. 255) for more things to do in this immediate area.

Something to keep in mind when Christmas lights are turned on: Tour the harbor to see all the houses and boats that are decorated magnificently - before, during or after the wonderful parade of lights - by either renting a Duffy electric boat or a pontoon, or take a narrated tour of the waterfront homes in a "private" boat that seats twelve. Make your reservation early.

Hours: Open daily in the summer, 10am - 8pm. Open the rest of the year daily, 10am - 6pm. Call first. Reservations are highly recommended for all rentals.

Price: Prices listed above. Parking validation is $5 for the first two hours; $12 for the day. There is some metered street parking available.

Ages: 6 years and up.

BIKE MAPS (Orange County)

These websites - .bike.lacity.org, www.labikepaths.com and www.traillink.com - are fantastic resources. They actually cover all of Southern California, not just L.A., with links to specific counties for maps, bikeways, and other cycling information. They can be your three-stop shopping sites for maps and info. Another great website is www.trails.com for mountain bike trails. Caltrans Office of Bicycle Facilities: (916) 653-0036 / www.dot.ca.gov/hq/tpp/offices/bike gives you tons of options all over.

Also contact the Orange County Transportation Authority at (800) 636-RIDE (7433) or (714) 560-OCTA (6282) / www.octa.net for (paved and unpaved) maps and more information. For the city of Irvine, check out www.cityofirvine.org/bikeways. Many Orange County buses are equipped with bike racks. To inquire about trail closures and detours on county-operated off-road trails (i.e., mountain biking), call the EMA - Harbors, Beaches, and Parks Operation at (714) 834-2400 or County of Orange RDMD/Harbors Beaches & Parks at (866)-OCPARKS (627-2757) or (714) 973-6865 / www.ocparks.com.

BIKE TRAIL: HUNTINGTON BEACH

www.huntingtonbeachca.gov; www.bike.lacity.org; www.labikepaths.com

!

Pacific Coast Hwy between Warner Ave. and Brookhurst St.

Huntington Beach is known not only for its great roads but also for the well-maintained, 8.5 mile cement bike path that runs parallel to Pacific Coast Highway. Located on the ocean side of the highway, this path can see hundreds of bicyclists, joggers and walkers on a daily basis. The scenic paved path (which some prefer to call a promenade, boardwalk or road) stretches from Sunset Beach (1 mile in length), through Huntington Beach (8.5 miles) and through Newport Peninsula (nearly 3 miles). It is possible to get a twelve-mile workout one direction or twenty-four miles total. For the distance workouts, you can take the underpass that connects to the Santa Ana River Trail near the bridge beyond Brookhurst Street. That trail goes all the way through Orange County, via Yorba Linda and Featherly Park, for an estimated additional thirty-two miles one direction.

Bicyclists and roller bladers share the paved Huntington Beach path with pedestrian traffic. Be aware and ride defensively as you will find people and pets crossing the path. State law requires children riding bicycles in public to wear helmets for protection. Bicycle lanes are often provided on city streets; cyclists must travel the same direction as traffic, obeying vehicle rules and regulations. Speed limits along beachfront paths in Huntington Beach are enforced.

Orange County Transportation Authority (OCTA) buses are public buses connecting this section of Huntington Beach with all of Orange County, and even Long Beach to the north and San Diego to the south. There are several bus stops along the paved path route in Huntington Beach with buses that have bicycle racks. For OCTA routes and times, there are posted signs at bus locations that include the Warner Avenue and Pacific Coast Highway turn around area near Jack in the Box restaurant. You can also call OCTA at (714) 636-RIDE (7433).

BIKE TRAIL: SANTA ANA RIVER (Orange County)

(714) 973-6615 / www.ocparks.com; www.bike.lacity.org; www.labikepaths.com

7600 E. La Palma Avenue in Yorba Regional Park, Anaheim

See BIKE TRAIL: SANTA ANA RIVER (Riverside County) (pg. 372) for information.

Hours: The trail is open daily. The park is open April through October daily, 7am - 9pm; November through March daily, 7am - 6pm.

Price: $3 per vehicle during the week; $5 on weekends; $7 - $10 on holidays.

Ages: 5 years and up.

CALIFORNIA PARASAIL

(949) 485-4665 / www.balboaparasail.com

600 East Bay, Newport Beach

Come sail away, high in the air (800 feet!) above the sea, while safely tethered to a boat. Parasailing is an exhilarating experience and this venue allows for one, two, or three people to ride at a time (side-by-side). The ninety-minute boat trip includes eight to ten minutes of airtime for each passenger that's flying. Flyers can dip their feet in the water toward the end, or remain completely dry - their choice. Bring your camera only if it's waterproof! Reservations are highly recommended. Note that it's usually better to fly in the morning as winds might pick up later on.

Hours: Open daily, 9am - 6pm. Boats depart every ninety minutes.

Price: $80 for each flyer. Non-flying passengers may go on the boat only IF there is room - $25 per person. Discounts are often offered for online reservations. Ask about flying for free on your actual birthday when you can fly tandem with someone paying full price.

Ages: 5 years old to parasail. Guests younger than 18 must have an adult sign them in. You must weigh at least 125 lbs to fly alone.

CAPTAIN DAVE'S DOLPHIN AND WHALE SAFARI

(949) 488-2828 / www.dolphinsafari.com

24440 Dana Point Harbor Drive, Dana Point

Captain Dave is a marine naturalist who is passionate about dolphins and whales. He has four vessels for sea exploring, with his fifty-foot catamaran, the *Manute'a*, a most popular option since it is the only one with an underwater viewing compartment and camera, speakers, and a hydrophone for listening to the mammals and playing music to them. The two-and-a-half hour safaris are a time of learning about and observing the dolphins, whales (in season), sea lions, and other sea life in the wild aquarium (i.e., the ocean). Note: Dana Point is one of the best locales in Southern California for actually seeing whales on whale-watching tours. Models of dolphins and whales, plus whale vertebrae and baleen are also on the vessel for teaching aids. Bring some munchies and a jacket or windbreaker, and set sail.

For a trip with more zip, go out on the twelve-person zodiac for whale and dolphin watching for ninety-minutes of fun at $65 per person, ages 8 and up.

Hours: Open year round - check the website calendar or call for cruise departure times.

Price: $65 for adults; starting at $45 for ages 1 - 12; children 1 and under starts at $5.

Ages: 6 years and up.

DANA WHARF SPORTFISHING, CHARTERS, AND WHALE WATCHING

(888) 224-0603 / www.danawharf.com

34675 Golden Lantern, Dana Point

Cruise the coastal waters in the lovely ninety-five-foot vessel, *Dana Pride*. Two-hour whale-watching cruises are offered November through April for the gray whale and May through October for the blue whale. Sunset cruises and sport fishing are available as well.

Hours: Whale watching cruises usually depart daily in season at 10am, noon, and 2pm; sometimes 4pm, also, on weekends. Check the website for other cruise hours and options.
Price: Whale watching cruises are $45 for adults; $35 for seniors; $29 for ages 3 - 12; children 2 years and under are free. Half-price off the adult fare is offered on Tuesdays! See the website for info about parking.
Ages: 6 years and up.

DAVEY'S LOCKER

(949) 673-1435 - whale watching; (949) 673-1434 - fishing / www.daveyslocker.com $$$$$
400 Main Street, Newport Beach

Skiff rentals, fishing, and two-and-a-half-hour whale-watching cruises are offered here. See BALBOA FUN ZONE (pg. 255) for more things to do in this immediate area.
Hours: Cruises are offered November - April, Mon. - Fri. at 10am and 2pm; Sat. - Sun. at 10am, 1pm and 3:30pm. May - October, daily at 10am, 1pm, 3:30pm and 6pm.
Price: $32 for adults for whale-watching on weekdays, $36 on weekends; $26 for seniors and ages 3 - 12 on weekdays, $30 on weekends; ages 2 and under are $2.50. $105 for a half day for skiffs.
Ages: 7 years and up.

DUFFY ELECTRIC BOAT COMPANY

(949) 645-6812 / www.duffyofnewportbeach.com   6/$
2001 W. Coast Highway, Newport Beach

Be your own captain as you pilot the canopy-topped electric boat around the harbor and through the channels of Newport Beach. The boat, which seats up to twelve people (ten comfortably), is an ideal way to see the multimillion-dollar homes on the waterfront and enjoy a relaxed time on the water with family and friends. Note that several restaurants offer dock side service, or bring your own food on board. For more things to do, check out the nearby BALBOA FUN ZONE (pg. 255).
Hours: Open daily, 10am - 8pm. Reservations are highly recommended, especially during weekends and holidays.
Price: Rentals $199 for a two-hour minimum. Closed New Year's Day, Thanksgiving and Christmas, and in inclement weather.
Ages: 3 years and up.

FUN ZONE BOAT COMPANY

(949) 673-0240 / www.funzoneboats.com $$$$
600 E. Edgewater Place, Balboa

Board the *Pavilion Queen* for a forty-five-minute narrated cruise that is perfect for kids as they'll go around Balboa Island and, hopefully, see some sea lions. On the other forty-five-minute cruise see several stars' homes and hear the history of Balboa Island Peninsula. The ninety-minute cruise is a combination of both cruises - the best of both worlds. Ninety-minute sunset cruises are also available mid-May through September. You are welcome to bring your own food on board. Special sightseeing tours are available in December during the Parade of Lights - what a view! See BALBOA FUN ZONE (pg. 255) for more things to do in this immediate area.
Hours: Summer tours depart daily every half hour from 11am - 6pm. Sunset cruises leave at 6pm or 7pm, depending on the time of sunset. The rest of the year, tours depart every hour from 11am - 4pm.
Price: $14 for adults for a forty-five-minute cruise; $11 for seniors; $7 for ages 5 - 11; children 4 and under are free. $19 for adults for the ninety-minute cruise; $14 for seniors; $7 for ages 5 - 11; children 4 and under are free. Closed Thanksgiving and December 25.
Ages: 4 years and up.

GONDOLA ADVENTURES, INC.

(855) GONDOLA (466-3652) or (949) 200-8037; (888) 480-9472 - educational tours / www.gondola.com   6/$
3101 W. Coast Highway, suite 110, Newport Beach

O sole mio! These authentic Italian gondolas are made out of mahogany, have leather seats and a canopy, and are operated by gondoliers either dressed in the traditional Venetian outfit, or a tuxedo, depending on the occasion. Yes, of course it's romantic to take this peaceful cruise along the waterways of Newport Beach Harbor and Newport isle, viewing the boats and waterfront homes, and kissing under bridges (mandatory). But a gondola ride can also be a family-friendly excursion. It's a time to relax and enjoy down time together, soaking in the sights and ambiance. We enjoyed learning a little about the area, seeing the variety of birds, and gliding through the waterways as a gentle breeze over the harbor.

The gondoliers begin your cruise from the harbor office, or pick you up at one of several harbor-side restaurants. Gondola Adventures provides a chilled bottle of Martinellis and Godiva chocolates, or it can provide a completely catered dinner served on china - definitely an upscale adventure! If interested, ask about taking an educational tour.
Hours: Open daily, call for reservations.
Price: Prices begin at $135 for two people, $25 each additional person, for a one-hour classic cruise.
Ages: 4 years and up.

LAGUNA FREE TROLLEY

(949) 715-4405; (949) 497-9229; (949) 497-3311 / www.lagunabeachcity.net/cityhall/transit_and_trolleys
The transfer point between the North, South and Canyon routes is at the Transit Center/Bus Depot on Broadway (where Laguna Canyon/the 133 ends), Laguna Beach

Consider taking a trolley around Laguna Beach, where parking is usually at a premium, especially in the summer months. The route includes twenty-one stops along Pacific Coast Highway, south of Broadway/133, plus nine stops north of Broadway/133 - so all of the major beaches are covered. It also includes a few stops actually on Broadway/133. It runs every twenty minutes. Check the website's map to see where you can park your car for the day.
Hours: The trolley runs mid-June - Labor Day, daily 9:30am - 11:30pm (July 4th from 9:30am - 7pm). It runs the rest of the year Fri., 4pm - 11pm; Sat., 11am - 11pm; Sun., 11am - 8pm.
Price: Free
Ages: All

METROLINK (Orange County)

(800) 371-LINK (5465) / www.metrolinktrains.com $$$

Metrolink offers a fairly hassle-free mode of transportation that links the counties of Ventura, Los Angeles (mostly in the Antelope Valley), San Bernardino, Riverside, and Orange. Teachers, ask about traveling with students at great discount rates, such as $3 per student, round-trip, for groups of fifteen or more students, ages 5 - 18 years. Reservations are mandatory six weeks prior to travel date. Ask about taking a rail safety program for school, organization, or community groups.

Forget the hassle of driving in traffic and parking fees on weekends, and take the MetroLink Weekends, where unlimited rides to the beach, amusement parks and beyond, and hundreds of free connections, are only $10 per person, per day! Other prices include weekday ride prices for a round trip from Rialto to Oceanside, for instance, at $32.50 for adults; $16.25 for seniors; $25 for ages 6 - 18; up to three children 5 and under ride free with a paid adult.
Hours: Trains run daily and offer limited service on most major holidays.
Price: One-way tickets start at about $3.50; round trip, $7 and go up to about $30/$60 - depending on the origin and destination. Senior rate is 50% discounted off regular rate. The discount for students with I.D. and youth, ages 6 to 18, is 25%. Kids 5 and under ride for free with a paying adult. Weekend price for unlimited riding is $10 per day.
Ages: All

MOE B'S WATERSPORTS

(949) 279-4507 - summer #; (949) 999-3181 or (949) 999-3180 - marina/market the rest of the year. / $$$$$
www.newportdunes.com
1131 Backbay Drive, Newport Dunes Resort, Newport Beach

Located in NEWPORT DUNES WATERFRONT RESORT MARINA (pg. 245) (see that entry for all that this resort has to offer to day visitors and campers), this rental facility has everything you need to make your day at the beach even more exciting. Hourly rates are: $24 for a two-person pedal boat, $29 for a four-person; $180 for an electric-powered boat; $20 for stand up paddle boards; $25 for a hydro bike; $35 for 14' catamarans; $22 for single kayaks; and $29 for double kayaks. Prices are discounted at least $4 an hour during off-summer hours. Rentals for land play include two-rider surreys for $25 an hour, four-rider for $35, six-rider for $45; and bikes at $15 an hour.

The Water Playground is a beach with a huge, sectioned-off water play area. It also has several, giant inflatables to climb up and on, such as a climbing "iceberg" with hand and foot holds and a slide on one side; a water version of a teeter-totter that can help launch participants into the water; a climbing dome; a water trampoline; twelve-foot slides connected to obstacle inflatables; and more. The Water Playground is $25 for up to two hours in the summer; $18 at other times.

Hours: Rentals are available October - February., Sat. - Sun., 10am - 4pm; March - mid-May, Thurs. - Sun., 10am - 5pm; mid-May - August daily, 10am - 6pm; September daily, 10am - 5pm. The Water Playground is open Memorial weekend, 10am - 6pm; mid-May - mid-June, Sat. - Sun., 11am - 5pm; mid-June - Labor Day, Mon. - Sun., 10am - 7pm; September, Sat. - Sun., 11am - 5pm.

Price: Prices are stated above, plus day-use vehicle entrance fee ($20 for all day).

Ages: 5 years and up.

NEWPORT AQUATIC CENTER

$$$$

(949) 646-7725 / www.newportaquaticcenter.com

1 Whitecliffs Drive, Newport Beach

Enjoy a serene kayak ride in the calm harbor waters. Single kayak rentals are $15 an hour; doubles and stand up paddle boards are $20. Two-hour naturalist tours of the Upper Newport Bay Ecological Reserve are given so as you paddle, you'll learn about the herons, egrets, and numerous other birds and animals, as well as the geology of the area, and the history of the bay and native plants you see along the way. These tours are offered every weekend at 10am for $25 per person. The minimum age is 8. A day of learning and fresh air - an unbeatable combination.

Hours: Rental hours are Mon. - Fri., 7am - 4pm; Sat. - Sun., 7am - 3pm. The center closes early on holidays.

Price: Prices are listed above.

Ages: 7 years and up for kayaks; 14 and up for paddle board.

NEWPORT BEACH BOAT RENTALS

$$$$$

(714) 263-3911 / www.newportbeachboatrentals.com

600 E. Edgewater Place, Balboa

What kind of boat would you like to captain in Newport Bay? Newport Beach Boat Rentals can make much of that happen with their fleet of rental boats. For instance, 16 foot runabouts (seats four) are $69 an hour; deck boats for six passengers are $79 an hour; eight passenger electric bay cruisers (a Duffy) are $85 an hour; single kayaks are $20 an hour; and tandem kayaks are $30 an hour. Stand up paddle boards are $20 an hour.

What can you do while on the water? Take a self-guided tour past the homes along the waterfront; zip amongst the seven islands; get a good workout on the kayak; bring your own lunch or dinner to enjoy on a pontoon; or stop off at one of the several restaurants on the way. See BALBOA FUN ZONE (pg. 255) for more things to do in this immediate area.

Hours: Open most of the year, daily, 10am - 5pm. Open in the summer and school breaks, Mon. - Thurs., 10am - 6pm; Fri. - Sun., 10am - 7pm.

Price: Prices are listed above.

Ages: 5 years and up.

NEWPORT LANDING SPORTFISHING

$$$$$

(949) 675-0550 or (949) 647-0551 / www.newportwhales.com

309 Palm, suite A, Newport Beach

Two-and-a-half hour whale-watching cruises are available here November through April to see the California gray whale, and May through October for giant blue whales and finback whales. Full-service snack bars are on all vessels. See BALBOA FUN ZONE (pg. 255) for more things to do in this immediate area.

Hours: The boats depart November - February, Mon. - Fri. at 10am and 1pm; Sat. - Sun. at 9:30am, noon, and 2:30pm. They depart March - October, daily at 10am, 1pm, and 3:30pm; sometimes at 6pm, too.

Price: Weekday prices are $32 for adults; $26 for seniors and children 12 and under. Weekend prices are $36 for adults; $30 for seniors and kids.

Ages: 7 years and up.

OCEAN INSTITUTE

$$$

See the entry for OCEAN INSTITUTE (pg. 311), under MUSEUMS, for details about boat outings.

PURE WATERSPORTS

(949) 661-4947 / www.purewatersports.com
34671 Puerto Place, Dana Point

$$$$

Tour the harbor and beyond! Jet ski rentals, for up to three people, range from $95 an hour to $125, depending on the day and time. Single kayaks are $15 for one hour and double kayaks are $20. SUP boards are $15 for one hour. Surfboards are $10 for one hour.

Hours: Usually open Mon. - Fri., 10am - 5pm, or 6pm; Sat. - Sun., 9am - 5pm, or 6pm.
  Price: See above for prices.
  Ages: 3 years and up, depending.

SOUTHWIND KAYAK CENTER

(949) 261-0200 / www.southwindkayaks.com
100 N. Bayside Drive, Newport Beach

$$$

This company knows kayaks. Around since 1987 with a retail store in Irvine, rentals are available on the waterfront - $14 an hour for single sit-on-top kayaks; $20 for tandems kayaks, stand up paddle boards, single Hobie Mirage kayak, or pedal boats; $25 for a double Hobie Mirage kayak.

Hours: Open most of the year, Fri. - Sun., 9am - 4pm. Open in the summer daily, 9am - 5pm.
  Price: Prices are listed above.
  Ages: 3 years and up, depending on where you go.

SUNSET GONDOLA

(562) 592-3295 - gondola; (800) 979-3370 - reservations / www.sunsetgondola.com
16370 Pacific Coast Highway, Huntington Beach

$$$$$

That's amore! Steeped in the tradition associated with an authentic gondola ride, such as the gondolier wearing a nautical-looking outfit and singing an Italian song, and kissing under bridges (for the passengers, not the gondolier!), riders enjoy a serene cruise around islands, gliding in and out of channels and inlets, past estates and mansions of Huntington Harbor. Time of day and year help create a variety of moods - a daytime jaunt; a romantic, moonlit evening out; a sunset reverie; or a Christmas-time ride to see all the decorated houses and brightly lit boats. Bring your own beverage and/or snack. Note that there are several restaurants in the immediate area.

Hours: Open daily, 11am - 11pm. Reservations are required.
  Price: Prices range from $60 for a forty-minute ride for two people; $80 for one hour ride for two people; etc., plus a $3 handling fee. (Holiday prices can be higher.)
  Ages: 4 years and up.

YOUNG EAGLES PROGRAM (Orange County)

National number - (877) 806-8902 / www.eaa92.org; www.youngeagles.org
4011 W. Commonwealth Avenue at Fullerton Airport, Fullerton

$$$

See both the entry for YOUNG EAGLES PROGRAM (Los Angeles County) (pg. 216) for details.

Hours: The program is offered once a year through this airport, usually in June, but the chapter also flies out of the Chino airport.
  Price: A $20 donation is asked per youth that is flying - it covers lunch, fuel costs, materials, and more.
  Ages: 8 - 17 years old.

—ZOOS AND ANIMALS—

CENTENNIAL FARM

(714) 708-1619 / www.ocfair.com/farm
88 Fair Drive, Costa Mesa

This outdoor working farm has pigs, chickens, sheep, bunnies, llamas, and cows. During the springtime, in particular, be on the lookout for the many animal babies that are born here, like squealing piglets that are so ugly they're cute. Walk around the grounds to learn about other aspects of farming. Younger kids will probably be amazed to see vegetables such as carrots, zucchini, lettuce, and corn being grown, not already picked and packaged, as in the grocery stores. (Please do not pick the vegetables or feed the animals.) The Millennium Barn has animal stalls, a tack room, a small museum area, and a milking parlor. A few picnic tables are here at the farm too, so pack a sack lunch. The huge parking lot is usually empty at this time, so bring skates or bikes. Note that on Thursdays there is a Farmer's Market just next door from 9am to 1pm.

A ninety-minute guided tour of the farm is for kindergarten through third graders for groups of ten or more students. The tour includes walking all around the farm; milking a cow (this is fun to watch); going into the main building and petting or holding baby chicks; planting a seed (and then taking it home); and learning about the food groups. Reservations are required. All age groups, with a minimum of six students, are invited to take a self-guided tour which encompasses much of the same elements of a guided tour, during the week between 9am and noon (arrive by 11am).

Hours: The farm is open to the public August - June, Mon. - Fri., 1pm - 4pm; Sat. - Sun., 9am - 4pm, and extended hours in the summer. It's closed for special events, so call or check the web calendar first. Tours for kindergartners and up are given October - May, Mon. - Fri. at 9am and 11am. The farm is open in July only with paid admission to the ORANGE COUNTY FAIR (pg. 725). Closed on state holidays.

Price: Free. All tours are also free.

Ages: 2 years and up during public hours.

LAGUNA KOI PONDS

(949) 494-5107 / www.lagunakoi.com
20452 Laguna Canyon Road, Laguna Beach

This fun little stop off has several cement tanks filled with koi and a store carrying fish supplies. We enjoy just looking at these colorful fish with their beautiful patterns. Who knows, you may want to purchase a few to raise at home. You may also feed them at certain times with a handful of pellets. It's fun to watch their large mouths open quickly and bite at the food. Combine a trip here with a visit to the PACIFIC MARINE MAMMAL CENTER (pg. 335), which is located just south of the ponds.

Hours: Open Mon. - Sat., 9am - 5pm; Sun., 10am - 5pm

Price: Free

Ages: All

LOS ALAMITOS RACE COURSE

(714) 820-2800; (714) 995-1234 / www.losalamitos.com
4961 E. Katella Avenue, Los Alamitos

Thoroughbreds and quarter horses are the attractions here. Have your child cheer for his favorites! Call for schedule information.

Hours: Races are usually held in April, May, September, and December. Call or check the website for specific races and hours.

Price: $3 for adults for grandstand seats, $5 for the clubhouse, $10 for Vessels Club; ages 17 and under are free. Parking is free for general; $5 for preferred.

Ages: 4 years and up.

MAGNOLIA BIRD FARM (Orange County)

(714) 527-3387 / www.magnoliabirdfarms.com
8990 Cerritos, Anaheim

Take your flock of kids to visit their fine feathered friends at the Magnolia Bird Farm pet shop. Birds here range from common doves and canaries to more exotic cockatoos and macaws. A small-bird aviary is located just outside the main building.

The Bird Farm has bird accessories, including a wide assortment of bird cages. Here's a craft idea: Buy a simple wooden cage for your kids to paint and decorate, then fill it with bird seed, and hang it up in your backyard. While you're here, have your kids take the bird challenge - see if they can get one of the talking birds to actually speak to them! Short, free tours are offered for groups of ten to fifteen people during the week. Also see MAGNOLIA BIRD FARM (Riverside County) (pg. 374).

Hours: Open Tues. - Sat., 9am - 5pm. Closed Mon., Sun. and holidays, and for two weeks during the summer.

Price: Free

Ages: All

ORANGE COUNTY POLO CLUB

(714) 791-8369 / www.ocpolo.com
27271 Silverado Canyon Rd., Silverado

To find out the "how-tos" of a polo game, see SANTA BARBARA POLO (pg. 648). The public is welcome to watch year-round practices/games and tournaments at the two polo arenas at this O.C. club. If you're interested in picking up the sport, lessons are offered here. Come watch! Come play!

Hours: Practices/games are usually held Thurs. at 6pm; Sat. and Sun. at 11am, but not usually in December. Check the website for tournaments.

Price: Free to all the events.

Ages: 3 years and up.

ORANGE COUNTY ZOO

(714) 973-6840 or (714) 973-6847 - zoo; (714) 973-6846 - tours / www.ocparks.com/oczoo
1 Irvine Park Road, Orange

Take a trip to the zoo while you're in the park! Tucked away in the massive IRVINE REGIONAL PARK (pg. 284) is the eight-acre Orange County Zoo. The zoo has barnyard animals such as sheep, goats, and potbellied pigs to pet through fence pens. Food dispensers are here, too. The main section of the small zoo features primarily animals native to the southwestern United States, such as mountain lions, bobcats, deer, beaver, coyotes, a coati, an Island fox, a black bear, burro, porcupines, and a variety of birds, including a bald eagle, golden eagle, and several types of owls. Look for Discovery Carts scattered around in the zoo with hands-on artifacts.

Toddler programs ($5 per person) and scout programs ($3 per person) are offered, as are one-hour school tours for any grade level for $3 per person. These all include a zoo guide and animal presentation. Topics covered may include habitats, adaptations, feeding habits, and general information about animals native to the southwestern United States. A train ride at Irvine Park Railroad may be added to any tour for an additional fee of $3 per student. Check the website or call about special events.

Hours: Open Mon. - Fri., 10am - 3:30pm; Sat. - Sun., 10am - 4:30pm. Closed New Year's Day and Christmas.

Price: $2 for ages 3 and up; children 2 and under are free. This admission is in addition to the vehicle entrance fee to the park which is $3 per vehicle, Mon. - Fri., $5 on Sat. - Sun; $7 - 10 on holidays.

Ages: All

PACIFIC MARINE MAMMAL CENTER

(949) 494-3050 / www.pacificmmc.org
20612 Laguna Canyon Road, Laguna Beach

This Center is a small, safe haven and rehabilitation hospital for pinnipeds - more commonly known as sea lions, elephant seals, and harbor seals. When these animals are abandoned, injured, or in need of medical attention they are temporarily housed in the facility's small outdoor pools until they are ready to be released back into the wild. This is a good opportunity for kids to see these animals up-close, tho thru the fences, while learning more about them and the effects that we have on our ocean environment. The volunteers are great at answering the numerous (and sometimes off-the-wall) questions kids ask.

Feeding time, usually around 10:30am and 3pm, is lively as the sea lions go wild, barking in anticipation of a meal. (It sounds like mealtime at our house.) There are anywhere from ten to 100 mammals here, as many of them arrive when pups are weaned from their mothers - January through July. One-hour educational programs that feature a slide presentation and a guided tour are $25 plus $10 per person; with a minimum of eight people. Ask about summer day camp, after-school programs, Kids Club, and Girl Scout troop workshops. Note that there are a multitude of plants, including butterfly gardens, purposely cultivated along the fence here with small info plaques that allows visitors to learn about pollination and being water-wise. Also see LAGUNA KOI PONDS (pg. 334) located just north of the center.

Hours: Open daily, 10am - 4pm. Closed New Year's Day, Thanksgiving, Christmas Eve, and Christmas Day.

Price: Free; donations gladly accepted.

Ages: 2 years and up.

PREHISTORIC PETS / THE REPTILE ZOO

(714) 964-3525 / www.thereptilezoo.com; www.jurassicparties.com   !/$$$

18822 Brookhurst Street, Fountain Valley

The word "prehistoric" evokes imagery of a reptilian world where creatures roam and forage under canopies of trees. This huge, 10,000-square-foot pet store and zoo does a good job of fleshing out this concept.

A rock-rimmed pond with lots of greenery is near the entrance of the retail store. It is filled with a multitude of turtles, giant tortoises, and giant catfish, while a large monitor lizard, or two, usually basks on a rock in the middle. You may purchase food to feed the always hungry critters for $5. Jungle-theme music through the speakers and tiki-style decor add to the atmosphere.

The glass cages lining the store are filled with exotic animals such as skinks (not skunks), chameleons, frogs, scorpions, tarantulas, iguanas, lots of monitor lizards, rattlesnakes, other snakes and more to purchase (and stare at).

There is an entrance fee to go into the adjoining area, The Reptile Zoo. This zoo contains reptiles that you will gawk at such American alligators (which eat raw chicken); an albino iguana; anacondas; several different types of pythons; a cobra; water monitors (one weighs about 60 pounds!); bearded lizards; skinks; and the star - Twinkie (an albino reticulated python), reputed to be one of the world's largest snake at over twenty-feet long and weighing in at 300 pounds!

Brave visitors are invited to pet and even hold a rotating variety of ball pythons (grab a hug from one of these and don't forget your camera), bearded dragons, leopard and crested geckos, and others at the Hands-On Learning Zone in the Zoo. Another section houses the husbandry facility, egg incubators, life cycle learning zone, and more. There are usually at least three fifteen-minute, educational presentations throughout each day, always with one at 11:30am - check the website to see the rest of the schedule. A frog, tarantula, tortoise and/or other critters are presented, talked about and available to touch.

Schedule a hands-on, educational tour, or a unique birthday party in a Jurassic party room. A two-hour party allows up to thirty guests (adults and children) an hour in a private party room and an hour presentation with twelve to fifteen animals - snakes, frogs, lizards, bugs, etc., that guests get to touch, hold and learn about. Visitors of all ages will enjoy the animals as they come out to play, crawl, coil, and slither. The cost starts at $200. A thirty-minute Reptile Zoo Tour includes admission to the Reptile Zoo and a private, thirty-minute presentation of six to twelve animals, such as snakes, frogs, lizards, bugs, etc. That cost starts at $150 for up to fifteen people. Other options are available. Prehistoric Pets will also bring the critters to you for a party or function of some sort.

What makes this pet store/zoo so spectacular is not just the variety, rareness, and number of reptiles and such, although those elements are worthy in and of themselves, but the greatness of size of so many of them. I would not want to meet some of them outside their cages!

Hours: Open Mon. - Sat., 11am - 7:30pm; Sun., 11am - 5:30pm. Closed Thanksgiving and Christmas, and early on other holidays.

Price: Free for Prehistoric Pets, the retail store. The Reptile Zoo admission on weekdays is $10 for adults; $8 for ages 4 - 12; children 3 and under are free; admission on weekends is $12 for adults; $10 for ages 4 - 12.

Ages: 3 years and up.

SANTA ANA ZOO

(714) 836-4000 or (714) 953-8555 - zoo; (714) 647-6568 - education coordinator; (714) 569-0779 - cafe / $$$
www.santaanazoo.org

1801 E. Chestnut Avenue at Prentice Park, Santa Ana

Lions and tigers and bears - not here! This small zoo, however, is perfect for young children. They can easily walk around it, see all the animals, and still have of time to play on the playground, all within just a few hours. The zoo houses llamas; wallabies; a dromedary camel; hedgehogs; cavies; emus; anteaters; rheas; porcupines; a sloth; ocelots; birds, including a bald eagle, toucans, macaws (who squawk loudly!), and scarlet ibises; and a wide variety of monkeys, our personal favorites. In fact, the zoo is mandated to have at least fifty monkeys living on its premises at all times so you'll see golden-headed lion tamarins, emperor tamarins, capuchins, black howlers, spider monkeys, gibbons (which are technically apes), and others, most living on Monkey Row. The cages and animals are not far off in the distance, but right along the pathways so you can see (and hear) all the antics. Walk through the wonderful aviary where you can observe beautiful and exotic birds close up. The Santa Ana Zoo abounds in all kinds of green plants, too.

The Crean Family Farm area has several small, farm-looking buildings each home to a particular barnyard animal such as pigs, bunnies, goats (no *kid*ding!), cows, and sheep which you can pet through pens. A few owls are here, as well. A hatchery holds newborn chicks at certain times. Catch a six-minute ride on a scale model electric locomotive that circles around this enclosure and northern part of the zoo for $4.50 per person. Ride on the thirty-three animal conservation carousel for $3. Ages 2 and under are free for both. Note that these attractions close at 2pm or 3pm during the week. Not quite like flying monkeys, but the 64-foot high Fifty Monkey Ferris Wheel is still fun. Each of the 15 gondolas features a description of a unique monkey species, and a great view of the zoo from the top for $6 per person. Read the signs along the walkway that tell the story of founder, Joseph Prentice, and his fifty monkeys.

Come for a presentation near the stage to see and learn about Macaws, snakes, and other inhabitants. Stop by the jungle-like, large room called Jaguar Exploration Outpost, modeled after a real outpost, to learn research techniques regarding the Amazon rainforest animals, plus weather patterns and conservation efforts via hands-on experiments. And look at the insects here, including a bird-eating tarantula - the Amazon grows them all bigger! Open at certain times, go through the not-scary Rainforest Adventure maze with four interactive learning stations. If you answer questions correctly regarding the rainforest, you venture deeper into the maze; if you don't, the info panels shows cliffs and dangerous animals and you're at a dead end.

The on-site playground has two play structures with a rope tower, slides, rings, and other fun elements. The Knollwoods Cafe, with an adjacent covered eating area, offers hot dogs (average $3.15), hamburger (average $5), chicken sandwich ($5), tacos ($3), Chinese chicken salad ($7.95) and kids meals ($4.50). Or, enjoy a sack lunch right outside the zoo gates at the adjoining Prentice Park which offers picnic tables, grassy areas, and shade trees.

A wonderful variety of educational and interactive programs are offered throughout the year. Note that membership at Santa Ana Zoo is reciprocal for free or discounted admission at 150 other zoos throughout the United States.

Hours: Open daily, 10am - 4pm. (The grounds close at 5pm.) Closed rainy days, New Year's Day, Thanksgiving, and Christmas Day. Train and carousel rides open at 11am and close at 3pm in the summer, and 2pm the rest of the year.

Price: Weekday admission is $10 for adults; $7 for seniors and ages 3 - 12; children 2 and under are free. Weekend admission is $12 for adults; $9 for seniors and ages 3 - 12. Admission after 2pm is $2 off. Admission is free the third Sun. of each month for Santa Ana residents. AAA discounts are available.

Ages: All

WHALE WATCHING

See the TRANSPORTATION section.

ZOOMARS PETTING ZOO / LOS RIOS PARK

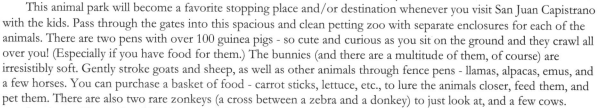

(949) 831-6550 / www.zoomars.com

31791 Los Rios Street, San Juan Capistrano

This animal park will become a favorite stopping place and/or destination whenever you visit San Juan Capistrano with the kids. Pass through the gates into this spacious and clean petting zoo with separate enclosures for each of the animals. There are two pens with over 100 guinea pigs - so cute and curious as you sit on the ground and they crawl all over you! (Especially if you have food for them.) The bunnies (and there are a multitude of them, of course) are irresistibly soft. Gently stroke goats and sheep, as well as other animals through fence pens - llamas, alpacas, emus, and a few horses. You can purchase a basket of food - carrot sticks, lettuce, etc., to lure the animals closer, feed them, and pet them. There are also two rare zonkeys (a cross between a zebra and a donkey) to just look at, and a few cows.

Starting at 12 months old, kids up to eighty pounds can take a hand-led pony ride around a dirt track. Scale model train rides around a short track are also available (and fun). An a*maize*ingly interesting place for kids to play is the covered corn box (i.e. like a sand box) filled with un-popped kernels of corn. Buckets and toys are provided. Kids are happy and not sandy. Parents are happy and not sandy, too! A little playground here has a slide and raised, wooden forts to play in. Parents can rest on some of the picnic tables and stone benches scattered around. Against a nicely-done backdrop of Old West building facades, miners-in-training can pan for rocks, minerals, and other treasures at Miner's Gulch. As water comes down the sluice young prospectors take their chosen bag, which is filled with sand and minerals, and sift it over a screened pan. We got some great rocks, an arrowhead, and even a shark's tooth - felt like we struck gold. Field trippers and birthday party goers are welcome as Zoomars has several separate areas to accommodate each group.

Behind Zoomars is a lovely area with a butterfly garden, stone and wood picnic tables under shade trees, and a paved path leading to **Los Rios Park**. The well-landscaped, good-sized park has some great features - raised, fort-like, wooden play structures with steps, plus a swinging connecting bridge, slides, a fireman's pole, and swings; a separate section with boulders to climb on, under and through; a wading pool filled in with sand; plenty of trees; and lots and lots of benches all over, plus a grouping of picnic tables under a trellis of grape vines.

In the same immediate area is the 100-year-old Olivares Home. Next door is the O'Neill Historic Museum. A short stroll down the quaint street is the TEA HOUSE ON LOS RIOS (pg. 254). Fun and funky places to eat include the Hummingbird House Cafe with Mediterranean appetizers and desserts; sandwiches, wraps, gyros and salads at $8.50 each; and a kids' menu - average $3.50. The Cafe is located directly next to the railroad tracks, so you have front row seats to the rumbling trains! The vintage, beautiful, bricked old depot of Sarducci's Capistrano Depot (restaurant) has window seats and outside seating next to the tracks, too (and elsewhere). Note that MISSION SAN JUAN CAPISTRANO (pg. 309) is only a block, or so, away. If you don't live near here, consider traveling to San Juan by train as that adds a whole other adventure element to your outing. (The train station is located right next to the parking garage.)

Hours: Open, weather permitting, Mon. - Fri., 10am - 4pm; Sat. - Sun., 9am - 5pm. Closed Thanksgiving and Christmas, and sometimes other holidays.

Price: $10 for ages 14 and up; $9 for seniors; $8 for children 12 months - 13 years; infants are free. Pony rides are $5 for one lap around the track. Train rides are $3 per person. A basket of food for the animals is $4. Miner's Gulch bags are $8 - $10 per.

Ages: 2 - 10 years.

RIVERSIDE COUNTY

Once a grove of orange trees that spawned a thriving citrus industry, the southern Inland Empire is now very diverse. It claims the city of Temecula, a fast-growing community that still maintains its small-town feel; historic downtown Riverside with its famous Mission Inn; and Palm Springs (and the surrounding desert cities) - an oasis that's no mirage. With all of the county's attractions and small cities, Riverside still has plenty of open spaces left to explore.

Note: Since the Palm Springs area is often a multi-day destination, its attractions are listed in a separate section in the back of this county.

—AMUSEMENT PARKS—

CASTLE PARK / BUCCANEER COVE

(951) 785-3000 / www.castlepark.com
3500 Polk Street, Riverside

The family-fun amusement park, **Castle Park**, has a lot of action packed into its twenty-five acres. The compactness of the park makes it easy to walk all around. It has four scenically-landscaped and challenging eighteen-hole, miniature golf courses complete with waterfalls, bridges, a miniature Big Ben, Dutch windmill, Chinese pagoda, castle, and western fort. The huge, multi-level arcade has over 200 video games and games of skill including virtual boxing, Dance Dance Revolution, bass fishing, and Daytona race car simulations, plus a prize redemption center. Check out the fun and kind of hokey Ghost Blaster ride, within the arcade, where riders go into a haunted house and shoot moving ghosts with their laser "Boo Blaster" to receive redemption points.

The rest of the park contains over thirty-five rides and attractions. There are many classic Midway rides and other rides, including the short log ride (which *will* get you wet); a huge carousel with all sorts of interesting animals; roller coasters; swing rides; a scrambler; bumper cars; an airplane ride; a free fall; a sea dragon ride; a Ferris wheel; two train rides; and lots more. Besides the "big kids" rides, there are plenty of kiddie rides - tea cups that spin, small coasters, antique car rides, train rides, mini motorcycles, and more.

The atmosphere at Castle Park reminds me of Coney Island in that the flashy rides are interspersed with carnival-type games. There are also kind of unusual features for an amusement park, such as the reproduction of the Liberty Bell, proclaiming liberty throughout the park, and an authentic gypsy wagon.

Summer is funner (and wetter) at **Buccaneer Cove**. This small, piratey-themed water park, next to the castle building, has a main, colorful, multi-level play structure in zero depth water. Attached to it are five water slides; water tunnels; interactive aqua domes; spray cannons; colorful loops and cylinders with spray fountains shooting everywhere; a huge bucket that fills up with water and pours out intermittently; and several other interactive water elements, including water spurting up from the cement ground. Lounge chairs and some shade are around the perimeters for those who need a break. Bring a change of clothing to enjoy the drier rides and attractions.

For big time fun, come eat at Big Top Restaurant. The good-sized restaurant resembles a circus big top, complete with a lifelike statue of a circus elephant outside. The inside feels like a circus, too. (Then again, meal times at our house always felt like a circus what with balancing plates of food, kids acting clownish, etc.) The food is good, with pizza being the featured item - $7.99 for a personal one. Burgers ($8.99, which includes fries and a drink); corn dogs ($3.49); chicken tenders ($8.99); and sandwiches are also available. Children's meals are $5.99. The Big Top bear mascot occasionally appears on stage for a short show on Sat. There are a few kiddie rides, a small arcade room with G-rated games, and a redemption center inside here, too. Other places to eat at the Park offer fried oreos, fried pb and j sandwiches, wings, pasta, funnel cakes, chili dogs and more.

The restaurant and Castle Park are good places for a birthday party. Special events and package deals are on-going at the park, including scout programs, so call for a schedule and more information. Motivate your kids because good grades and school attendance are rewarded here with free tokens!

Hours: Most of the year, miniature golf and the arcade area are open Mon. - Thurs., 1pm - 9pm; Fri., 1pm - 10pm; Sat., 11am - 10pm; Sun., 11am - 9pm. Rides are open Fri., 5pm - 9pm; Sat., noon - 9pm; Sun., noon - 8pm. During the summer and on holidays, golf and arcades are open Mon. - Thurs., 11am -8pm; Fri. - Sat., 11am - 11pm.; Sun., 11am - 10pm. Rides are usually closed on Mon. Call first as the hours fluctuate a lot. Buccaneer Cove is usually open from Memorial Day - Labor Day, Mon. - Fri., noon - 6pm; Sat. - Sun., noon - 7pm. It is sometimes open on weekends in May and September, too. Big Top Restaurant is open Sat., noon - 5pm, and usually Sun., noon - 3pm. Check the website for other hours.

Price: Just entering the park costs $9.99. The following deals include admission: Duke's Deal - Choose either unlimited rides or entrance to Buccaneer Cove for $12.99; Duke's Duo - Choose two unlimited attractions - mini golf, rides or Buccaneer cove for $15.99; Dukes's Deluxe - Includes unlimited rides, mini golf, and Buccaneer Cove for $17.99. Everything includes admission to Castle Park video games. Check online for discounts and promotions. AAA members receive a discount. Unlimited mini golf is $9.99. Parking is $10.

Ages: All

DROPZONE WATERPARK

(951) 210-1600 / www.dropzonewaterpark.com
2165 Trumble Road, Perris

Fitting with the theme that prevails throughout the city of Perris, of being a premier location for sky diving and thus, drop zones, this delightful, mid-size (12-acre) waterpark is an ideal place to drop in.

Terminal Velocity Slides and Mat Racers are three slides that spill out from a high tower - one is enclosed and twisty; one is open with curves; and "one" is actually a side-by-side racer for participants to zoom down on mats. The Jet Stream Continuous River allows single or double tube riders to float leisurely around a small island (which has a fun, little play seaplane to board), under a bridge, and just relax for a minute. The small, Meridian Springs pool, at four-feet deep, offers a place for even young swimmers to stay afloat and splash. Lil' Jumper's Landing is for little jumpers to land a good time. The colorful, main structure is uniquely themed like an air control tower. An airplane's huge wings, with propellers, are on both sides of the tall stand that holds a giant bucket which tips over when filled with water. This structure also has three short slides, stairs, water cannons, pipes that burst with water, and other stand-alone equipment to squirt at frienemies, all in just enough water to get wet. Kids gleefully run through the Launch Pad, a concrete area with a huge target painted on it that has geysers that shoot up water at random intervals. Practice surfing skills at Hydroplane FlowRider® - a wave simulator that allows riders to body board or stand-up surf on the custom Flow Boards. The FlowRider is actually open at certain times throughout the year, also. A competition pool, with diving boards and grandstand seating, is open for lap swim. For some dry fun, play volleyball (balls are for rent) on the sand volleyball courts, or just have the kids build sand castles here.

Outside food is allowed in if you pay a cooler fee - $20 for a small; $50 for a large, but the on-site cafe can satisfy your fliers' taste buds: A hamburger is $4.50; individual pizza, $7.95; chicken wrap, $6.95; and chicken tenders meal, $7.95, plus funnel cake fries, soft pretzels and dippin dots. Locker rentals are $2. Cabanas are available to rent for $50 during the week; $55 on weekends. Free usage of lounge chairs abound. A small shop for sundries that you might have forgotten to bring is also on the grounds.

Hours: Open mid-May - mid-June, and mid-August - September, Sat. - Sun., 11am - 6pm. Open during the summer daily, 11am - 6pm. There are also night swims on some evenings from 6pm - 9pm.

Price: $18 for 48" and taller; $14 for seniors, military, and 37" - 47"; $9 for 30" - 36"; children 29" and under are free. The lap and rec pool is $3 for non-residents ages 13 and up; $2 for residents and non-residents 12 and under.

Ages: 2 years and up.

LAKE PERRIS WATERPARK

(951) 287-4990 / www.lakeperrisrecreation.com
17801 Lake Perris Drive, Perris

$$$$

Yes, you can swim in water, but why just do that? This water playground has several inflatables to jump and climb on, through and over. A 14-foot climbing structure (that looks like an iceberg), huge slides, a giant trampoline (flip into the water), teeter totter, blob, balance beam, obstacle course, and a Giant Action Tower with several physical challenges to attempt all add to your day of fun. Then, you can swim, just float on a raft, or enjoy the beach. Know that a lifeguard is on duty, everyone must wear a life jacket, proper bathing attire is required, and guests must be 48" and 7 years old to play on most of the inflatables, though there is a small area for younger kids. Also note that there are other areas designated for just swimming and other water (and land) activities at Lake Perris - see LAKE PERRIS STATE RECREATION AREA (pg. 357) for more info.

Hours: Open Memorial Day weekend - September (and maybe beyond), Sat. - Sun., 11am - 7pm.

Price: $15 for adults; $10 for ages 8 - 17; $5 for ages 7 and under. Access to the beach area with waterpark play is $5. Parking is $10. Rent 2 chairs and an umbrella for the day for $20.

Ages: 4 years and up.

THE COVE WATERPARK - JURUPA AQUATIC CENTER

(951) 360-1974 / www.covewaterpark.org
4310 Camino Real, Riverside

$$$$

'ey mon! This smallish, Caribbean-themed water park has huge (fake) parrots, plus overturned ships, cargo netting, treasure chests, and tiki "umbrellas" with lounge chairs underneath, decorating the deck. The suitably-named Crow's Nest is a tower with three twisty slides (one is totally enclosed) that plummet, plunge and plop. Catch a gnarlatious wave while surfing at the double-sized Flowrider at Riptide Reef. Take it easy in an inner tube and float along the Ne'er Endin' River that encircles part of the park as it goes under bridges and waterfalls. A colorful activity pool for younger kid is the pirate-themed, Lil' Mates' Lagoon. It has several slides, even enclosed curvy ones; huge barrels of water that tip over periodically; squirting water elements; and plenty of room for splashing around, all in very shallow waters. An adjacent pool for older kids (and adults) is fun to just play around in. Landlubbers can play on a ship that is torn apart enough to let mateys board it and pretend they are adventuring on the high seas. Locker rentals are $1.

Traditional swimwear is required. Ask about the summer camps here for kids.

The snack bar serves made-to-order grilled food - hotdogs ($3.50), cheeseburgers ($4.50), chicken wrap ($6.95), chicken salad ($7.95), and snacks of soft pretzels ($3.75) and funnel cakes fries ($4.95). Kids meals, like a grilled cheese combo, are $5.75. Outside food is allowed in if you pay a cooler fee - $20 for a small; $50 for a large.

The adjacent competition pool, 25-yard by 35-meter, has a diving board and spectator seating. It is open for lap swim during park hours.

Hours: The water park is open daily, Memorial Day weekend - mid-August, 11am - 6pm. Open mid-August - September on weekends only (and Labor Day Monday), 11am - 6pm. Check the website for night swims offered from 6pm - 9pm.

Price: The water park is $18 for 48" and taller; $14 for seniors, Riverside county employees and 36" - 47"; $9 for tots 30" - 35"; children 29" and under are free. Entrance to the waterpark includes use of the pool. Parking is free.

Ages: 2 years and up.

—ARTS AND CRAFTS—

CERAMIC & ART STUDIO OF NORCO

(951) 737-3521 / www.ceramicandartstudio.com
$$$$
1660 Hamner Avenue, suite 10, Norco

This is a full-service, more-than-a-ceramic art studio! There is, of course, a wide selection of ready-to-paint objects to make the perfect gift for someone special. All the paints you want and need, stencils, and instruction, plus firing, are included in your studio price. Other ways to play here include clay-works, mosaics, glass painting, pottery wheel workshops and rentals, and drawing and painting classes where even non-artists can feel like they've created a masterpiece, or at least an apprenticepiece. Another bonus feature is that the studio store carries the supplies and mechanisms for finishing particular projects, such as clock workings, music boxes, trivets, and more. Ask about kids' club and classes, as there are a variety of them available.

Hours: Open Mon. - Sat., 11am - 6pm; open Sun. for private events only.

Price: $6 per person per day for painting ceramics, plus the price of your item. Check the website for other class prices.

Ages: 4 years and up.

COLOR ME MINE (Riverside County)

(951) 687-1630 / www.riverside.colormemine.com
$$$$
1299 Galleria at Tyler in the Galleria at Tyler mall

See the entry for COLOR ME MINE (Los Angeles County) (pg. 8) for details.

Hours: Open Mon. - Sat., 10am - 9pm; Sun., 11am - 7pm.

Price: The studio fee is $8 per person.

Ages: 4 years and up.

CRAFTY U TOO!

(951) 684-2645 / www.craftyutoo.com
$$$$
5225 Canyon Crest Drive, suite 16, Riverside

Feeling crafty (and not in a devious way)? Come in a pick out a mug, dish, figurine, bank, or any of the other numerous objects that you then paint into a one-of-a-kind keepsake. All the materials - paint, brushes, ideas, and space to work on your design - are provided. Check out the calendar for all of the special events offered, such as kid's night out; storybook and painting (listen to a story and do a related painting or craft); two can paint for the price of one days; and more.

Hours: Open Mon. - Thurs., 10am - 8pm; Fri. - Sat., 10am - 9pm; Sun., noon - 6pm.

Price: The studio fee is $10 for adults; $6 for ages 12 and under; plus the price of your piece.

Ages: 4 years and up.

PAINTED EARTH

Menifee - (951) 679-6800; Temecula - (951) 676-2447 / www.paintedearthpottery.com
$$$$
Menifee - 30010 Haun Road; Temecula - 27507 Ynez Road at Tower Plaza

Paint your own ceramic masterpiece at Painted Earth. Choose from decorative figurines to microwavable plates and mugs. All the paints, brushes, and glazes are included in the studio fee, so feel free to express yourself and enjoy a lasting, hand-crafted treasure. The web calendar lists special events such as kid's night, two for one nights of painting and even plant your own terrarium classes.

Hours: Open Mon. - Thurs., 10am - 9pm; Fri. - Sat., 10am - 10pm; Sun., 11am - 7pm. Closed Christmas.
Price: $6 per person, all-day studio fee, which includes the price of glazing and firing. The price of the item is an additional fee ranging from $10 to $70.
Ages: 4 years and up.

—EDIBLE ADVENTURES—

AFTERNOON TEA AT MISSION INN

(800) 843-7755 - tea; (951) 784-0300 - Inn / www.missioninn.com
3696 Mission Inn Avenue, Riverside

$$$$$

This elegant, old Inn is an ideal setting for the tradition of afternoon tea, served on the Spanish Patio, weather permitting. See MISSION INN and MISSION INN MUSEUM (pg. 366) for details about the Inn, and even taking a tour.

Your delectable offerings for Grand Afternoon Tea could include a selection of savory sandwiches on a variety of breads, such as smoked salmon with egg; cucumber; ham; chicken salad; and citrus shrimp. The sweetest part, of course, is dessert with scones and lemon curd and cream; tea breads; custard eclairs; brownies; and other tasty options. The cost is $34 for adults; $18 for ages 5 to 11 years. Refreshments of strawberry milk, an ice cream float or a Shirley Temple for younger ones is extra. Royal Afternoon Tea, at $44, is the same as Grand, but includes alcoholic beverages (for adults!). To really feel like royalty, indulge in Tea and Tiaras, offered one Saturday a month for $34 for adults; $20 per child. This includes sparkling apple cider, orange floats, the Grand Tea, and a tiara, of course.

Hours: Tea is served daily with seatings at 2pm to 4pm - call to make a reservation.
Price: Prices are listed above. Parking at the Inn is $11 for 3 hours.
Ages: 4 years and up.

BOMBSHELTER RESTAURANT & BAR

(951) 943-4863 / www.skydiveperris.com
2091 Goetz Road, Perris

$$$

Drop in for a bite to eat at Bombshelter, a restaurant adjacent to one of the best drop zones for sky divers in the United States. The two rooms in here are decorated wall-to-wall with photos and posters of skydivers. Flags, jumpsuits, and even two painted, real bombs hang from the ceiling. A large-screen TV shows the flyers from the neighboring, indoor wind tunnel on live-feed camera. See PERRIS SKYVENTURE (pg. 350) for more information on this thrilling adventure.

Look out the huge picture windows to view the mountains, and watch skydivers floating down. A pool table is also here.

Breakfast items include two eggs with bacon or sausage ($8.99); breakfast burrito ($7.49); four pancakes ($6.49); or two biscuits and gravy ($3.99). For lunch, order cheeseburger and fries ($9.79); chicken strips and fries ($8.49); Philly cheese steak ($10.99); Cobb salad ($9.99); hot dog with fries ($5.49); or a deli sandwich (from $5.99 to $11.49). Dinner selections consist of appetizers - mozzarella sticks ($8.99) and buffalo chicken wings ($9.99); and real meals of NY steak with baked potato ($19.99); lemon rosemary chicken ($16.99); grilled steak and shrimp ($23.99); and more.

And by the way, the outside pool and lounge chair area is free to use for skydiving customers.

Hours: Open daily, 8am - sunset.
Price: Menu prices are listed above.
Ages: All

CHINESE BISTRO

(951) 928-3837
28490 Highway 74, Romoland

$$$

Located just before the city border of Hemet, this isn't a slow train to China; it is a parked train restaurant serving Chinese cuisine. Inside the railcars, which are actually on a track, each small table has flowers, padded chairs, and a window seat. Hanging lanterns overheard and plenty of red and gold decor add to the Chinese ambiance.

A large selection of food includes crispy spicy shrimp ($12.95); pineapple shrimp ($12.95); Kung Pao beef ($11.95); orange peel beef ($11.95); sweet and sour pork ($11.95); and vegetable egg fu yong ($9.95); plus black pepper filet mignon, cream cheese won tons, and a wide variety of soups, appetizers, and lunch and dinner combinations.

You're guaranteed to find something (or some things!) to please your palate.
Hours: Open Mon. - Sat., 11am - 9pm; Sun., 11am - 8pm.
Price: Menu prices are listed above.
Ages: 4 years and up.

CHUCK E. CHEESE'S (Riverside County)

See the entry for CHUCK E. CHEESE'S (Los Angeles County) (pg. 18) for details.

FARMER'S MARKETS (Riverside County)

See the entry for FARMER'S MARKETS (Los Angeles County) (pg. 21) for details.

JOHN'S INCREDIBLE PIZZA CO. (Riverside County)

(951) 656-5555 / www.johnspizza.com
6187 Valley Springs Parkway, Riverside
See JOHN'S INCREDIBLE PIZZA CO. (Orange County) (pg. 250) for details.
Hours: Open Mon. - Thurs., 11am - 9:30pm; Fri., 11am - 11pm; Sat., 10am - 11pm; Sun., 10am - 9:30pm. Usually open an hour earlier Mon. - Fri. during school breaks.

THE OLD SPAGHETTI FACTORY (Riverside County)

(951) 784-4417 / www.osf.com
3191 Mission Inn Avenue, Riverside
See the entry for THE OLD SPAGHETTI FACTORY (Los Angeles County) (pg. 25) for details.
Hours: Open Sun. - Thurs., 11:30am - 9:30pm; Fri. - Sat., 11:30am - 10pm.

SHOGUN (Riverside County)

Corona - (951) 737-3888; Temecula - (951) 296-9133 / www.restaurantshogun.com
Corona - 275 Teller Street, suite 130; Temecula - 41501 Margarita Road
See the entry for SHOGUN (Los Angeles County) (pg. 26) for details.
Hours: Corona - Open Mon. - Thurs., 11:30am - 9:30pm; Fri., 11:30am - 10pm; Sat., noon - 10pm; Sun., noon - 9pm; Temecula - Open Sun. - Thurs., 11:30am - 9pm; Fri. - Sat., 11:30am - 10pm.

TIOS TACOS #1 MARISCOS

(951) 788-0230 / www.tiostacos1.com
3948 Mission Inn Avenue, Riverside
Eclectic. Odd. Unusual. Cool! These are the first words I can think of to describe this restaurant's fairly extensive (one acre) ground and decor. Not really stroller friendly, but you can walk around outside to see folk art at its finest, or is it at its weirdest?! There are several groupings of outdoor eating areas with patio chairs, and multicolor tiled tables and benches. But you'll first notice the odd statues and unusual things all around, all made from recycled products. And some of the statues are gigantic! One long walkway is imbedded with beer bottles, shells, and rocks as wells as a bike, dolls, dishes, computer components, fishing rod, curling iron, and just about anything else you can possibly think of. Some of the colorful plaster statues here have masks; some don't. One is holding a sword while astride a horse statue. Many of the creations are shaped using chicken wire and stuffed with a variety of objects - Barbie dolls, little plastic toys, coconuts, junk, etc. A few, shaped like humans, have plants growing out of them with plaster heads wearing wigs. One section has a stone slab with a cascading fountain. Water shoots over (and onto) the cobblestone circular pathway under trees, while busts, a waterfall made out of shovels, a tree with circular saws sticking out, lamps, ant statues, and other bizarre, non-related items surround it. On the rooftop of the old house are little kid figures riding trikes and scooters, and one riding a bike E.T. style, with its front wheel suspended in air. There is a small chapel made out of white, green, and brown beer bottles, forming various designs, plus mosaics, all held together by cement. Angel statuary and even windows complete the chapel. Inside, with its vividly-painted ceiling of a Bible scene, are benches, an altar, Jesus and Mary statues, and the lip of the bottles. You have to see this whole outside place to believe it. The art on display, changes, too, so come back to view new creations.

The inside of the adjoining small restaurant is decorated with sea-themed mosaic floors, a ceiling painted like blue sky with clouds, and a large wall collage of sea stars, shells, sea anemones, coral, and more creating a 3-D effect. Fanciful. Unique. Cool. The authentic Mexican food, all served with complementary fresh chips and salsa, is absolutely delicious and reasonably-priced. Bring your appetite because the restaurant has a huge variety of foods, juices, and smoothies. Try a steak taco, $2.50; huevos rancheros, $6.99; breakfast burrito with ham and eggs, $5.99; BBQ pork burrito, $5.99; tongue burrito, $5.99; beef tostada, $4.99; nachos (the works), $9.99; taco salad, $8.99; twenty shrimp, $12.99; whole, deep fried catfish, $12.99; half a dozen oysters, $9.99; and a fish filet meal, $12.99, plus tortas, garlic cheese fries, enchiladas, salads and lots of combo plates and other a la carte items. Desserts include flan, $2.75; frozen bananas; and a delicious Hawaiian-Bionic which is an apple, strawberry, banana, papaya, and mango fruit salad topped with yogurt and condensed milk, $3.99.

Hours: Open Sun. - Thurs., 8am - 10pm; Fri. - Sat., 8am - midnight.
Price: Prices are listed above.
Ages: 2 years and up.

TOM'S FARMS

(951) 277- 4422 - Farm; (951) 277-1002 - Senor Toms / www.tomsfarms.com
23900 Temescal Canyon Road, Corona

Tom's Farms consists of several separate buildings, each one selling different products. The front building has a terrific selection of farm fresh produce, dried fruit, nuts, and candies. This is a delicious stop, as is the Fresh Fudge & Gourmet Popcorn Shop. If you want real food, though, eat at Señor Tom's Mexican Restaurant (open Monday through Friday, 11am to 8pm; Saturday through Sunday, 10am to 8pm), which offers breakfast, lunch, and dinner - the whole enchilada. Menu items include burritos ($6.99 to $7.99), tacos ($2.99 a la carte), salads, nachos ($9.99), BBQ trip tip sandwich ($8.99), shredded chicken sandwich ($7.99), half rack of ribs ($14.99), and more, either in a combo plate or a la carte. Kid's meals are $4.99 - $5.99 for a choice of burrito, quesadilla, enchilada, or taquitos. If you prefer American-style food, the small restaurant, Tom's Hamburgers (notice a reoccurring theme?), offers large portions of food. Tasty hamburgers start at $3.99 or order a pastrami sandwich ($7.29), bacon and egg sandwich ($5.59), Chinese chicken salad ($7.39), or jumbo chili cheese fries ($5.29). Kids have their choice of a grilled cheese sandwich, chicken strips, or a burger, plus fries and a drink, for $4.99. Shakes and malts are $4.99. This restaurant is open at 7am for breakfast, too. A wine and cheese store also offers baked goods and a gourmet deli, as well as pizza ($10.99 for a 14" cheese), sub sandwiches and more. A lovely outside eating area is set up around a series of small ponds and bridges.

Just beyond the pond, open on weekends only, the farm takes on the feel of a small "old tyme" country fair with craft booths, face painting, and shaved ice, as well as a carousel ride ($3 per person); tractor ride around a small dirt track ($3); pony ride around a small ring ($5); tiny petting zoo, which opens at 11am ($2); shooting gallery ($1); a chance to play with the mini-tractor digger in the dirt ($1); and a train ride ($3) through a portion of the ten acres of countryside and under a bridge. The train is a reproduction of an 1800's steamer. Enter Tom's Mining Company to pan for gold, or work a sluice and unearth fossils and gems ($4 to $8, depending on your bag of rock treasures). Live music and a magic show are free, added attractions. There is also a koi pond in this back area and a large spread of lawn with picnic tables. Ask about the seasonal activities, such as the Pumpkin Patch in October and Festival of Lights at nighttime in November and December. Come grab a snack, or eat a meal at this "farm" with a folksy ambiance.

Hours: The main part of Tom's Farms is open daily, 8am - 8pm. The craft fair is every weekend, 8am - 5pm, and the country fair, with its rides and attractions, is every weekend, 10am - 6pm in the summer, 10am - 5pm all other seasons, weather permitting.
Price: Free entrance.
Ages: All

—FAMILY PAY AND PLAY—

ACTION STAR GAMES

(909) 793-6743 / actionstargames.com
681 East Ellis Avenue, Perris

Gear up and get ready for some serious (and seriously fun) paintball action at seven different Action Star Games field scenarios that include Concrete Jungle, Civil War, The Graveyard, Crate Fields, The Mall and more. Many things make this particularly good with one being the friendliness of the staff and another that there are continuous games, so no waiting in between - jump in and keep the action going.

Hours: Sat. - Sun., 9am - 3:30pm. Open during the week for private parties.
Price: $30 per person includes entry and all-day air fills. Rental packages are $50 for entry, air fills, semi-auto paintball marker and a mask. Other rental equipment is available.
Ages: 8 years and up.

ADAMS MOTORSPORTS PARK

(800) 350-3826 or (951) 686-3826 / www.adamsmotorsportspark.com $$$$$
5292 24ᵗʰ Street, Riverside

Kart racing, drifting, time attack, pocket bikes/mini-moto, motorcycles, or supermoto racing can all be had at Adams Motorsports Park. The main track, which is six-tenths of a mile long with fourteen turns and twists and a long straight-away, is a great introduction to real racing. Junior karts and "full-size" karts are available. This race track school offers classes for kart racing, available for kids 5 to 7 years, and 8 years and up. Call for a class schedule.

Hours: The track is open Mon. - Fri., 10am - 5pm and Sat. - Sun., 8am - 5pm for practices, classes, and events. Kart racing is Fri. - Mon., 11am - 5pm. Call or check online for the nighttime events. Closed New Year's Day, Thanksgiving, and Christmas.

Price: Standard race track is $25 per 10 min. race, which includes the kart, racing suit, helmet, etc. Bring your own kart for the main track - $45 a day for nonmembers; $30 for members; $10 for pit person/spectator. Classes start at $179 for two hours of instruction and racing.

Ages: 5 years and up for a class; at least 8 years old, 56" and able to reach the gas and brake pedals can race in "Arrive & Drive" racing format; 18 years and up (or 56" and with a legal guardian) to race.

AEROSPORTS

Corona - (951) 278-9769; Murrieta - (951) 696-5867 / www.corona.aerosportsparks.com; $$$
www.murrieta.aerosportsparks.com
Corona - 280 Teller Street, Ste 120; Murrieta - 39729 Avenida Acacias

A huge main arena with so many trampolines and other fun "extras" has kids flipping over this place. Come play on slanted wall trampolines to launch from; foam-padded landing pit to practice tricks; a few long trampoline runways; basketball and dodgeball courts; and a nice-sized area for younger jumpers (48" and under only) to practice their best moves (or just to move!) along with a mini foam pit. Hado is a non-trampoline activity. Hado is like VR, but called AR (Augmented Reality), which combines wearing goggles with wrist motion censors to play a very active futuristic-type of game of team techno sports via shooting laser balls and using shields against opponents. A snack bar area, small arcade room, a sitting area with couches plus tables and chairs complete this sporty place. Note that there are special events offered like dodgeball tournaments, black lighting and music on certain Friday nights, and Aerofit work-out classes, too.

Hours: Open Sat. - Thurs., 10am - 10pm; Fri., 10am - midnight.

Price: $12 for the first hour for ages 6 and up, $8 for the second hour; $6 for the first hour for ages 3 - 5, $4 for the second; ages 2 and under are free with a paying adult. Hado is an additional $10 for 5, 80 second games.

Ages: 2 years and up.

CHILD'S PLAY

(951) 699-7696 / www.childsplaytemecula.com $$
28860 Old Town Front Street, suite A2, Temecula

One big room, brightly decorated in primary colors, filled with toys and activities in a clean and safe environment make this an ideal destination for younger children. Child's Play has a small ball pit; a treehouse with two slides; little go karts; Little Tyke cars; a caterpillar tube to crawl through; mini-trampolines; soft play blocks; dress-up areas; short slides; an infant area; and more. Note that every participant must wear socks. You are welcome to enjoy outside food and drinks in the lobby/eating area.

Hours: Open play is Mon. - Fri., 10am - 6pm; Sun., 2pm - 6pm. Open Sat. for private parties only. Closed major holidays.

Price: $9 for the first child; $7 for a sibling; $5 for 10 months - 1 year. Parents are free.

Ages: 6 months - 6 years. (Older children are invited to be in the lobby/eating area only.)

CHUCK E. CHEESE'S (Riverside County)

See the entry for CHUCK E. CHEESE'S (Los Angeles County) (pg. 18) for details.

DEFCON 1

(951) 262-8123 / www.defcon1games.com $$$$
26201 Ynez Road, Suite 101, Temecula

Somewhere in between laser tag and paint ball is Defcon 1. Its name and term means the first stage of readiness, or alert, for the U.S. Military - so get ready! In a warehouse-like arena, with cool wall murals and black light,

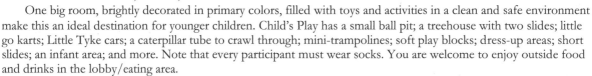

participants play tactical combat games using dart blaster guns with foam bullets as they run around props of boxes, tires, cans, and other objects, plus cubicle rooms and walls with window openings. It's a fun twist on hide and seek! Lock and load, and soldier on. Vests, safety glasses and a basic gun is included in the admission price. Note that Defcon 1 is in the same building as GET AIR TRAMPOLINE PARK (Riverside County) (pg. 347).

Hours: Open Mon. - Thurs., 10am - 10pm; Fri. - Sat., 10am - midnight; Sun., 10am - 8pm.
Price: $12 for one hour; $20 for two hours. Gun upgrades and magazine clips are an additional fee.
Ages: 46" and taller only.

FREEDOM IN MOTION GYM

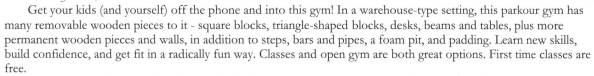

(951) 397-2070 / www.freedominmotiongym.com $$$
41513 Cherry Street, Murrieta

Get your kids (and yourself) off the phone and into this gym! In a warehouse-type setting, this parkour gym has many removable wooden pieces to it - square blocks, triangle-shaped blocks, desks, beams and tables, plus more permanent wooden pieces and walls, in addition to steps, bars and pipes, a foam pit, and padding. Learn new skills, build confidence, and get fit in a radically fun way. Classes and open gym are both great options. First time classes are free.

Hours: Open gym for ages 13 and up, only, is Fri., 7:50pm - 10pm. Open gym for ages 12 and under, only, is Tues., 3:30pm - 4:25pm. Open gym for all ages is Wed., 3:30pm - 4:25pm; Thurs., 12:10pm - 1:15pm and 3:30pm - 4:25; Fri., 3:30pm - 4:25pm; Sat. - Sun., 3pm - 4:45pm. Close Mon.
Price: $10 - $15 per person, per open gym session.
Ages: 4 years and up.

GET AIR TRAMPOLINE PARK (Riverside County)

Hemet - (801) 917-1935; Temecula - (951) 268-3850 / www.getairhemet.com; www.getairtemecula.com $$$
Hemet - 869 W. Florida; Temecula - 26201 Ynez Road, Ste 101

Put a bounce in your step (a big one!) by coming to play at this 20,000 square foot indoor trampoline park. The open jumping area is fun by itself, with its checker-board style of small trampolines making up one big room, and with trampolines curved up on the walls and even some platforms to leap from (reminiscent of a skate park or parkour). For more of a challenge try the dodgeball court, or Slam Ball (i.e. air basketball), and practice new tricks by landing in the foam pit, which also has flat screen monitors with delayed playback to see how good, or not, you really are. Try your hand, or feet, on the competition style slack line - a flat, narrow, strap - over padded cushions. Test your coordination on the fidget ladder (or trick climbing ladder) that flips over readily if you misstep. Ever want to be a ninja? Maybe Ninja Course can help prepare you for just that! Race against time in this short obstacle course by running up a ramp, on a cargo net, up and over a "fence", moving from ring to ring and bar to bar (over a foam pit) and bounce on some trampolines - all to reach the buzzer on the other end. Good luck! Kiddie Court, a small, separate room just for younger jumpers, 46" and under, contains trampoline slides and their own foam pit (and a couch for parents to simply watch). If all of this is too much, relax in the massage chairs here. Ahh - there we go.

Note that there are several special classes and events offered. Toddler Time, for instance, is only for kids 46" and under and their parents. Club Air, for jumpers 46" and taller and at least 9 years old, is way more fun than any other night club with high energy trampolining to music and lights. Get Air also has private rooms for parties and other gatherings. Signed waivers and non-skid socks are always required for all participants. Also note that the Temecula facility shares the same building with DEFCON 1 (pg. 346).

Hours: Open Mon., 10am - 10pm; Tues., 10am - noon for Toddler Time, and noon - 10pm all ages; Wed., 10am - 10pm; Thurs., 10am - noon for Toddler Time, and noon - 10pm all ages; Fri., 10am - 9pm all ages, and 9pm - midnight for Club Air; Sat., 8am - 10am for special needs jumpers and their families only; 10am - 9pm all ages, and 9pm - midnight for Club Air; Sun., 10am - 8pm.
Price: $12 per hour for 46" and taller; $6 for 45" and under. Toddler Time is $6 per child; one adult is admitted for free. Club Air is $15 for 2 hours, or $20 for all 3. Always check the websites for special offers.
Ages: 2 years and up.

GLO MINI GOLF

(888) 896-8419 / www.glominigolf.com $$$
1299 Galleria at Tyler in the Galleria mall, Riverside

Ready, aim, and putt! In *glo*uncertain terms, this glow-in-the-dark, 27-hole, indoor, mini golf course is a great way to have fun while golfing. Under black lights and electric neon colors, wonders of the world are lit up as the featured decorations at the holes. See the Great Pyramids, Niagra Falls, the running of the bulls, Eiffel Tower, Great Wall of China, Amazon Jungle, and more - how many do you recognize? (Teachers - tie in playing golf with learning about these travel destinations!) Eight-foot tall, colorful wall murals accompany these landmarks. Add another dimension to your experience by wearing 3D glasses that are provided.

The XBox gaming room has ten stations equipped with gamer chairs and 48" wall-mounted screen, with all of the big-ticket games to choose from. The arcade room boasts thirty-plus arcades from the newest to retro ones. Put on the equipment and immerse yourself in the Virtual Reality Arcade where you can walk on a moon, battle aliens and zombies, dive with whales, or paint a masterpiece (kind of). There are even multi-player games where teams can work together to diffuse a bomb and partake in other missions. Virtual games, but real fun. I have to say that watching someone do Virtual Reality can be entertaining, too.

Party rooms; food (like an ice cream shop with 11 different flavors and 165 different combinations, and delicious shakes, including coffee and pineapple); drinks; and glow in the dark accessories are available here, too. Relax here while choosing from thousands of music videos to watch.

Hours: Open Mon. - Thurs., 10am - 10pm; Fri. - Sat., 10am - 11pm; Sun., 11am - 9pm.

Price: $12 for 27 holes of golf; $10 for military and seniors; children 2 and under are free. 3D glasses are an additional $2 per. $7 an hour for XBOX rental, or $15 for the day. Virtual Reality is $9 for 15 min., $15 for 25 min., etc.

Ages: 3 years and up.

HANGAR 18 (Riverside County)

Riverside, Arlington Ave. - (951) 359-5040; Riverside, Iowa Ave. - (951) 742-8479 / www.climbhangar18.com	$$$$
Riverside - 6935 Arlington Avenue; Riverside - 2111 Iowa Ave, Unit A

Stick it. That's rock climbing terminology for having a sure grip in a climbing move. The Arlington Ave. location has one of the largest freestanding bouldering walls in the U.S., plus 12,000 square feet of textured climbing terrain, a huge top-rope area, with lead area and autobelays.

The Iowa Ave. location has almost 9,000 square feet of climbing terrain with lots of bouldering, plus top roping and lead routes (over thirty feet high) using an auto belay system, for both the beginner and expert to conquer and utilize to improve their skills. This facility also has an upper level observation deck and a WiFi lounge with couches. Members are invited to also use the yoga studio and the full work-out gym with weights, treadmills, ropes, and more. For more info, see HANGAR 18 (San Bernardino County) (pg. 408).

Hours: Open Mon. - Thurs., 10am - 10pm; Fri., 10am - 9pm; Sat. - Sun., 10am - 8pm.

Price: $18 for adults for a day pass; $13 for ages 13 and under. Shoe rentals are $3.

HANGAR TRAMPOLINE PARK

(951) 682-JUMP (5867) / www.hangartrampolineparks.com	$$$
12125 Day Street, Riverside

For some off the wall fun, experience Hangar Trampoline Park with a huge room of trampolines that has some low platforms to jump off, trampolines curved against the wall, and a really long tumbling/jumping run; dodgeball courts; foam pits for safely trying tricks, as well as a huge air bag to land on top of; a kid's area with trampolines and a foam pit; and bubble soccer which is wearing bubble balls and running around (not on a trampoline!) - fun to play and funnier to watch! Check out the special deal like College Night; DJ Night on Fridays with black lights, music, and trampolining; and Toddler Times. All participants must wear Hangar socks - $3 per pair.

Hours: Open Mon., Tues., and Thurs., 4pm - 8pm; Wed., 2pm - 8pm; Sat. - 11am - 10pm; Sun., 11am - 7pm; Fri., 10am - noon (Toddler Time only); 4pm - 7pm (general public) and 8pm - 10pm - DJ Night. Open more in the summer and on school breaks.

Price: $15 for the first hour for ages 6 and up, $20 for 2 hours; $8 for the first hour for ages 5 and under, $12 for 2 hours. Toddler Time is $10 for 2 hours and one parent per child is free.

Ages: 2 years and up.

JOHN'S INCREDIBLE PIZZA CO. (Riverside County)

See JOHN'S INCREDIBLE PIZZA CO. (Riverside County) (pg. 344), under EDIBLE	$$$$
ADVENTURES, for details.

JUMP 'N JAMMIN (Riverside County) ☼

(951) 867-9513 / www.jumpnjammin.com $$$

22500 Town Cir. at Moreno Valley Mall, Moreno Valley

    See JUMP 'N JAMMIN (Orange County) (pg. 261) for details about this big and fun indoor play place. Look up MORENO VALLEY MALL - KIDS CLUB (pg. 361) for other fun activities to do, plus shopping and places to eat.

Hours: Open Sun. - Thurs., 10am - 7pm; Fri. - Sat., 10am - 8pm. Closed Easter, Thanksgiving, and Christmas.

Price: $14.95 for ages 2 and up, which includes one free adult admission; $6.49 for children 23 months or younger, which includes one free adult admission. Additional adults are $3.95.

Ages: 2- 12 years

JUNGLE ISLAND PAINTBALL PARK ☼

(951) 775-9316 / www.jungle-island.com $$$$$

14881 Temescal Canyon Road, Lake Elsinore

    It's a jungle out there! Actually, there are thirteen themed, paintball-playing fields on fifty-six acres and the Jungle, called the Kong field, is only one of them. The Castle field has cement fortresses, archways, and steps galore to hide and seek. The Guns of Normandy field has a mock battle field with a camouflage truck, ambulance, defensive hill, foxholes, and more. Pipes field has countless cylindrical cement pipes. Volcano field looks like there were several eruptions. City field looks like an inner city with vehicles and eighteen buildings. There is also Congo (with monster tire truck bunkers), and more. Games last about twenty minutes. 6 to 12 year olds have their own arena called Little Warriors where they play a version of Paintball called Splatmaster. The markers (i.e., paintballs) have a softer hit and lighter equipment is used. Adults are welcome to play here, too, with a private group. Other game alternatives include paintball lite and nerf wars games for group parties. Airball is available here, too. There are also five fields here exclusively for airsoft. See WILDLANDS AIRSOFT PARK (pg. 353) for more information on them.

    A snack bar serving pizza and beverages is on the premises. A picnic table is out front. Wear appropriate attire - old, long sleeve shirts, jeans, and running boots. A parental waiver, available online, is necessary for ages 17 and under.

Hours: Open Sat. - Sun., 8am - 4pm. Open most school holidays; closed Thanksgiving and Christmas. Little Warriors Arena is open Sat. - Sun., 9am - noon and 1pm - 4pm.

Price: $25 for walk ons with their own equipment. Package deals, which include all the necessary gear, start at $55. Little Warriors arena is $20 with their own equipment; $30 for admission and rental gear.

Ages: Must be 10 years or older for paintball.

LUV 2 PLAY (Riverside County) ☼

Riverside - (855) PLAY-002; (752-9002); Temecula - (951) 404-7126 / www.luv2play.com $$$

Riverside - 4790 La Sierra Avenue; Temecula - 26469 Ynez Road

    Who doesn't Luv 2 Play at this great indoor play place? It's massive, three-level, multi-colored play structure is filled with things kids love to play on, with and around: tunnels to crawl through; ball pits; a ball blower pit with some compression air guns; twisty slides; climbing ropes; obstacle courses; a climbing wall for slightly older kids; a mini zip line; stairs to climb up; and much more. Bar stools line a good portion of the structure so it's easy for parents to sit and keep an eye on their kids.

    Other unique elements include a floor-size map of the U.S.; an enclosed, nice-sized toddler play area with a mini ball pit, big foam shapes, and mini carousel; giant balls to bounce; and a separate area with a large racing car table with cool cars to race, a space to build with Duplo-like blocks, and kinetic sand play tables with a global theme for clean, creative fun. Inexpensive, mostly kid-friendly arcade redemption games are interspersed with throughout.

    Parents are welcome to get in and play with their kids. Or, they can relax at the centrally located dining area with WiFi. The cafe serves pizza, hot dogs, fruit, cookies, and other snacks, as well as beverages.

Hours: Open Mon. - Thurs., 9am - 8pm; Fri. - Sat., 9am - 9pm; Sun., 10am - 6pm.

Price: Parents, kids 0 - 5 months old, and siblings over 13 are free, as are ages 11 months and under with a paid sibling. Mon. - Thurs., ages 6 months - 4 years are $10.95; 5 - 13 years are $12.95; siblings are $10.95. Fri. - Sun. and holidays, ages 6 months - 4 years are $12.95; 5 - 13 years are $14.95; siblings are $12.95.

Ages: 12 months - 12 years.

MULLIGAN FAMILY FUN CENTER - Murrieta ☼

(951) 696-9696 / www.mulliganmurrieta.com $$$$

24950 Madison Avenue, Murrieta

    Calling all ranch hands: Git 'long to Mulligan Family Fun Center for some family fun! Take a look at all the fun props outside, like cowboy mannequins literally hanging around. This western-themed miniature golf center has two impressive **miniature golf** courses, with water hazards and sand traps. (Note: You can see the red rock boulders, small western buildings, and stagecoaches from the freeway when you're heading southbound on the I-15.) A round of golf costs $10 for ages 13 and up; $7 for seniors and children 12 and under; replays are $3. Other attractions include **batting cages**; **go-karts** - $7.50 for drivers, $3 for passengers (height restrictions apply); **rookie go-karts** in a police and fire engine cart for guests 40" to 58" and at least 5 years old, $5; **lazer tag** in a 3,500 square-foot arena, which is a lot of running around and shooting space, that's decorated with neon bright colors lighting up some obstacles - $7.50; a twenty-one-foot-high **rock climbing wall** - $6 for two climbs; **extreme air** where you are literally strapped in to fly/bounce twenty-five high, and back again - $7.50 for one session; and Kiddie Korral there are three **kiddie rides** - tea cups, train ride, and frog hopper - $4 per ride. The hot summers have met their match with **Waterworks**, a water play structure with several slides; pipes bursting with water; a huge bucket that dumps over water by the, well, bucket loads; stairs; and places to play under the structure where water pours out everywhere, and almost all in zero water depth - $15.99.

Complete your day (or night) on the town by coming inside into the spacious "town hall," which is done up right fine with a jail and kids' saloon (cafe). There are plenty of modern-day, shoot-out games (i.e., arcade and video games), including two mini bowling lanes with bumper rails and smaller-than-usual balls. A prize redemption station is here, too.

The cafe serves grilled chicken salad ($6.99); pizza ($13.99 for a large cheese); hot dogs ($2.79); chicken strips ($14.99 for an eight-piece); grilled chicken sandwich ($6.99); and other food essentials. Kids' meals are $4.99 for a choice of chicken nuggets, hot dog, or grilled cheese.

Hours: Open Mon. - Thurs., 1pm - 8pm; Fri., 1pm - 10pm; Sat., 10am - 10pm; Sun., 11am - 8pm. Open in the summer, Mon. - Thurs., 10am - 9pm; Fri. - Sat., 10am - 10pm; Sun., 11am - 9pm. Closed Thanksgiving and Christmas. The water play area is open mid-May - May and mid-August - September (plus Memorial Day and Labor Day), Sat. - Sun., 11am - 6pm. It is open June - mid-August, Mon. - Fri., 11am - 5pm, Sat. - Sun., 11am - 6pm.

Price: Attractions are individually priced above. Unlimited all-day passes are available Fri. - Sun. and holidays most of the year, as well as daily during the summer for $39.99, which includes a $10 arcade fun card. Kiddie Korral and rookie go-kart all-day passes are $14.99. Ask about or check their website for other specials.

Ages: 3 years and up.

PERRIS SKYVENTURE

(800) 832-8818 or (951) 940-4290 / www.skydiveperris.com

2093 Goetz Road, Perris

Have you ever dreamt you could fly? Me, too. Skydiving is one way to get as close as you can to actually flying. This indoor skydiving facility offers both a safe and utterly exhilarating experience. The 96-foot-tall tower houses a wind tunnel that is a skydiving simulator. Walk up stairs to a small classroom to watch a video, learn the hand signals of a flyer, and practice correct body position - back arched, arms and legs slightly bent upward, and chin up. (So natural - not!) Put on a jumpsuit, earplugs, elbow and knee pads, and helmet, and get ready. Participants enter the doorway of a small, glass-enclosed room (i.e., flight chamber) where wind speeds of up to 120 mph blast through the grids on the floor and air gets sucked up from overhead fans. At first, the wind makes it difficult to breath, but then - lift off. As you go horizontal, for a few minutes you experience the sensation of free falling. An instructor is standing by your side, aiding you at all times. First-time flyers generally don't fly higher than about five feet above the ground, but oh - what a feeling!!

Family and friends can watch through the flight chamber windows, or at home via the live-feed web cam. Just tell them your flight time. Souvenir t-shirts ($10 - $20) and hats and a flashdrive of your flight ($45) are available for purchase. Ask about the other flying options, such as group flying, camps, aerobatic shows, and yes, school field trips. At the latter, students learn about velocity, force, Newton's Law of Motion, and acceleration. They also learn how to pack a parachute, do experiments inside the chamber, see aircraft - and then get to experience it all by flying for 2 minutes! Adults, 18 years and up, can go one step further and actually sky dive onto the huge field adjacent to the tower. Classes, instructors, gear, and encouragement are all part of the package. If you opt out of skydiving, sit on the lawn under shade trees and watch the colorful show as the divers jump from the planes and float down onto the landing field. Some of the formations are thrilling. Listen to the parachutes open - they sound like firecrackers. This is a premiere facility to see skydivers from all over the world.

If all of this sounds like more than you want, or can afford to do for now, grab a meal at the onsite BOMBSHELTER RESTAURANT & BAR (pg. 343) and just watch the action. The restaurant offers good food and the opportunity to watch skydiving via the huge picture windows. A small, outdoor, gated pool with lounge chairs is available for skydiving customers and families to use free of charge. How cool is that! Children under 18 years must be supervised by an adult and have a signed waiver to use the pool.

Hours: Indoor and outdoor skydiving is available Mon. - Thurs., 8am - 5pm; Fri. - Sun., 8am - 6pm. Reservations are highly recommended. Closed Thanksgiving and Christmas.

Price: Indoor Skydiving: For first time flyers - about thirty minutes in the staging area and two minutes of flight time is $59 per person. Each extra minute of flight time is an additional $20 (and worth it!). Ask about specials, like Sundays being $39 for two minutes. Block rates are available, starting at $200 for ten minutes of flight time for returnees. This can be split among multiple flyers. Ask about skydiving rates.

Ages: 3 and up for the indoor skydiving; 18 and up for real skydiving.

POLE POSITION RACEWAY

Corona - (951) 817-5032; Murrieta - (951) 461-1600 / www.polepositionraceway.com $$$$
Corona - 1594 E. Bentley Drive; Murrieta - 41810 McAlby Court

Not quite ready for the Grand Prix? This clean, spacious, indoor kart racing facility is the place to race. You will zoom around the state-of-the-art track for about ten minutes, wearing provided helmets, in fast electric karts that look like the real thing. Junior karts are also available. The intensity, adrenaline rush, and competition (against opponents or the clock) are all part of the experience. Check the event calendar for tournaments. Before or after your race, take a look at the collection of racing memorabilia, watch major sporting events on big screen TVs, play some video games or air hockey or pool, or grab a bite to eat at the snack bar. Kids must be at least 48" tall and able to safely operate the kart in order to drive. Minors must have a signed waiver.

Hours: Corona - Open Mon. - Thurs., 11am - 9pm; Fri. 11am - 11pm; Sat., 10am - 11pm; Sun., 10am - 8pm. Murrieta weekend hours are different - Sat., 11am - 11pm; Sun., 11am - 7pm. Both are closed Christmas. Call for holidays hours.

Price: For non-members, the price is $19.95 for adults, 56" and taller, for a 14-lap race; $16.95 for kids, 48" - 55", for a 10-lap race. Everyone must purchase a race license, good for one year, for $5.95.

Ages: 48" and taller.

PUMP IT UP (Riverside County)

(951) 677-1933 / www.pumpitupparty.com $$
41785 Elm Street, suite 203, Murrieta

See PUMP IT UP (San Diego County) (pg. 487) for details. This location encourages Open Jump for ages 2 - 17 years. It also has a rock wall and Cannonball foam ball blaster.

Hours: Check the website calendar for details on Open Jump and other speciality jump times as the times vary even within a particular month.

Price: Open Jump is $9 per child; adults and ages 2 and under are free.

Ages: 2 years and up.

ROMP-O-RAMA

(951) 432-7707 / www.romporama.com $$
4300 Green River Road, Corona

Romping, jumping, crawling, sliding, playing and squealing with delight are all part of a child's experience here. There are a few adjoining rooms featuring different facets. The largest play structure is multi-storied and kind of decorated to look like a castle. It, and the smaller structure, has colorful tunnels and tubes, obstacles courses, climbing areas, several mini trampolines (one with a foam pit for jumping into), ball pits, slides (even short, side-by-side racing slides), and an enclosed area to shoot plastic balls. An adjacent, two-story wooden fort has a ladder inside, plus windows, a slide, climbing wall, and more.

A little play town is a complete area with kid-size rooms that have a few pieces of equipment and dress up clothes for the police station, fire department, market, hair salon, restaurant (with an outdoor bistro-like eating area), doctor's office, movie theater and more. So cute! Romp-O-Rama also has a separate, soft play toddler area and a parent's lounge with Wi-Fi and TV. Note - you must wear socks and a parent or legal guardian must sign a waiver for the child(ren) entering the facility.

Hours: Open daily, 10am - 8pm.

Price: 2 hours of play time is $10 for ages 13 months - 17 years; unlimited play is $17 per. Children 12 months and under are free; adults are $1.

Ages: 1 - 10 years.

ROUND1 BOWLING AND AMUSEMENT (Riverside County)

(951) 697-0260 / www.round1usa.com

$$$

Moreno Valley - 22500 Town Circle at Moreno Valley Mall; Temecula - 40820 Winchester Road at Promenade Mall
Moreno Valley - (951) 296-0975; Temecula - (951) 296-0975 (general mall number)

See ROUND1 BOWLING AND AMUSEMENT (Los Angeles County) (pg. 38) for details. Also see MORENO VALLEY MALL - KIDS CLUB (pg. 361) for details about what else this mall offers.

Hours: Round1 is open daily, 10am - 2am; ages 18 and over only after 10pm.

Price: All prices depend on the day and time. Bowling, for instance, for 90 minutes, ranges from $9.99 - $17.99. Shoe rentals are $3.50. Karaoke ranges from $9 - $24 an hour for up to three people. Billiards, darts, and ping pong range from $8 - $14 an hour.

Ages: 5 years and up.

S.C. VILLAGE PAINTBALL PARK

(949) 489-9000 or (562) 867-9600 / www.scvillage.com

$$$$$

8900 McCarty Road, Corona

Rambos, Terminators, Xenas, and people from all other walks of life are invited to play paintball on this massive, sixty-acre premiere playing field with seventeen different settings for paintball and three for airsoft. Battle it out in desert terrain, jungle tracts, or even in the city of Beirut. Each field has special props which may include a downed helicopter, ambulance, tents, tanks, radar towers, huts, bridges, tunnels, swamp, camouflage netting, and acres of woods or brush. In this updated version of Capture the Flag, paintball guns and nontoxic gelatin capsules (i.e., paintballs) are used. Two teams compete against each other using the props to run around and hide behind. The object of the game is to somehow capture your opponent's flag and return it to your team's flag station. However, if you are hit with a paintball (which can sting), you are out of the game. Games last twenty to thirty minutes. All games have referees to insure safe and fair play. There are two levels of play - beginner and advanced. Come by yourself or with a group of friends. All amenities, including a food concession, equipment rentals, and supplies are on-site. Participants under 18 must have a waiver signed by a parent or guardian. Airsoft is similar, just a gentler sting of the pellets and no paint.

Hours: Open Sat., 9am - 7pm; Sun., 9am - 4:30pm. Weekday games are by appointment only for groups of twenty or more.

Price: General admission is $27 for all day paintball - $28 for airsoft - if you come with your own equipment, plus $11 for air. Rental equipment varies in price according to what you want. Goggles/face masks (mandatory) are $7; jumpsuits are $10; guns are about $14; and paintballs start at $19 for 200 rounds. Package deals are available. For instance, a $59 starter package includes all-day admission, full mask, pump rifle, 200 rounds of paintball, and initial tank of CO_2 air. For an additional $5, play all day.

Ages: At least 10 years old.

SKY HIGH SPORTS (Riverside County)

(951) 681-5867 (JUMP) / ont.skyhighsports.com

$$$

3230 Cornerstone Drive, Mira Loma

See SKY HIGH SPORTS (Los Angeles County) (pg. 40) for details about this fantastic, indoor trampoline place. This location has extra features of Ninja Course and Lazer Maze.

Hours: Open most of the year Mon., Wed. and Thurs., 2pm - 9pm; Fri. and Sat., 2pm - 11pm; Sun., 2pm - 8pm. Closed on Tues. Hours change during school breaks and holidays. Note that you can call ahead of time and book your time as there are a limited number of participants allowed.

Price: $14 for the first hour, daily; Mon. - Thurs., $6 each additional hour; Wed., $3 each additional hour; Fri. - Sun., $10 each additional hour. Check for specials. The Ninja Course is an additional $3 per hour. The Lazer Maze is an additional $3 for 1 trip or $5 for 2 trips. The 3-hour Fri. and Sat. Cosmic Nights are $15.

Ages: 4 years and up.

SKY ZONE (Riverside County)

(951) 643-0099 / www.skyzone.com

$$$$

4031 Flat Rock Dr., Riverside

See SKY ZONE (Los Angeles County) (pg. 40) for details.

Hours: Open Mon. - Thurs., 3pm - 9pm; Fri., 3pm - 11:30pm; Sat., 10am - 11:30pm; Sun., 10am - 9pm. Open during the summer and holidays extended hours.
Price: $16 for 60 min., $21 for 90 min.
Ages: 2 years and up.

VITAL CLIMBING GYM (Riverside County)

(951) 251-4814 / www.vitalclimbinggym.com
29990 Technology Drive, suite 22, Murrieta
See VITAL CLIMBING GYM (San Diego County) (pg. 492) for details.
Hours: Open daily, 11am - 9pm. Holiday hours fluctuate. (Open 24-hours for members.)
Price: $12 per person for a day pass.
Ages: At least 5 years, and up.

WILDLANDS AIRSOFT PARK

(951) 775-9316 / www.wildlandsairsoft.com
14881 Temescal Canyon Road at Jungle Island Paintball Park, Lake Elsinore
Sharing the acreage with JUNGLE ISLAND PAINTBALL PARK (pg. 349) the airsoft games are played like military simulation and players are treated kind of like soldiers. Players are encouraged to dress in military attire - at least a military-style jacket. There are five combat-themed fields for players to crawl through trenches and high grass; hide in or behind walls, boulders or vehicles; run through buildings and up and down stairs; and other incredibly realistic props and settings. Waivers must be signed.
Hours: Open Sat. - Sun., 8am - 4pm. Groups of 20 or more can book games during the week.
Price: $25 for self-equipped walk ons. $55 for all-day admission which includes a rifle, BBs, and a mask.
Ages: 8 years and up.

—GREAT OUTDOORS—

ARLINGTON PARK

(951) 826-2000 / www.riversideca.gov/park_rec
3860 Van Buren Boulevard, Riverside
This nice corner park has a playground and well-used shuffleboard courts. It also has basketball courts, tennis courts, barbecue pits, and a swimming pool.
Hours: The park is open daily. The pool is open mid-June - August, Mon. - Thurs. and Sat., 1pm - 4pm, and Tues. and Thurs., 7pm - 8:30pm. Closed Fri. and Sun.
Price: Free to the park. Swim sessions for residents are $2.50 for adults; $1.75 for seniors; $1 for ages 17 and under. Non-residents are $3.25 for adults; $2.25 for seniors; $1.25 for ages 17 and under.
Ages: All

CALIFORNIA CITRUS STATE HISTORIC PARK

(951) 780-6222 - park; (951) 637-8045 - visitors center / www.parks.ca.gov
Van Buren Boulevard and Dufferin Avenue, Riverside
Take a whiff - the park, with its acres of citrus groves, captures the spirit of Riverside's slogan, "The land of citrus and sunshine." The main section is attractively landscaped with plenty of shade trees and has a big, grassy area for running around and for picnicking. Around the corner is a small visitor's center/gift shop/museum in a restored home. The center, which resembles a citrus packinghouse, features mostly historical photographs with narrative regarding the citrus industry. Two-hour school tours, for third and fourth graders, include a guided tour of the museum, the grove, and citrus tasting. Yum! Adults, you are not left out - free tours are offered Fri. - Sun. at 11am and 2pm to learn the history and sample fresh fruit from the tree.
A good short (1.25 miles round trip) nature hike starts at the gazebo (where interpretative pamphlets are usually available), goes through the groves and to the canal. Don't forget to stop and smell the oranges along the way!
Hours: The park is open daily, 8am - 5pm. It's open April - September on Sat. and Sun until 7pm. The visitor center is open Fri - Sun., 10am - 4pm.
Price: $5 per vehicle. If you just want to visit the visitor center, you can get a pass for free.
Ages: 2 years and up.

CEDAR CREEK

(951) 727-3524 or (951) 685-7434 / www.jcsd.us
6709 Cedar Creek Road, Eastvale

This little park is great for the little ones. It has a tot lot and play area, grassy lawn, a cement pathway, picnic tables, BBQs, and a small water play area that is self activating. Turn the green cone on to start the water running. The water play area/splash pad just has fountains that shoot up, but sometimes that's all you need to cool off.

Hours: The park is open daily, sunrise - 10pm. The water feature is available April - September daily, sunrise - sunset.
Price: Free
Ages: 1 year - 10 years old.

CITRUS PARK

(951) 736-2241 / www.coronadwp.com or www.incorona.com/parks.asp
1250 Santana Way, Corona

The twenty-acre Citrus Park is like a park within a park. The park itself has two great playgrounds side-by-side, with slides, speaking tubes, several small towers, ramps, swings, and more. There are also softball fields, picnic tables, and lots and lots of grassy areas to run around.

The park within is a waterpark/splash pad, the base of which looks like an orange slice, with leaves on poles sprouting up (3-D) out from the center. It has several interactive features, such as fountains spurting up from the ground, large rings to walk through that spray, and water cannons to shoot. It's all a slice of refreshment on hot summer days.

Hours: The park is open daily, 5:30am - 10pm. The waterpark is open May - September daily, 10am - 7pm. (Hours may fluctuate.)
Price: Free
Ages: 1 year and up.

DAIRYLAND PARK

(951) 685-7434 / www.jcsd.us
14520 San Remo, Eastvale

Some of the best features of this park are the water features on the splash pad. It is self-activating in that when you pass your hand over the yellow rod, the water features turn on. Fountains jet water up from the ground rather randomly, boulders dot the area, and fake palm trees not only decorate the circular wet area, but water rains down from them, too. Benches, with shade, are around the perimeter so parents can dryly watch their kids run, play, and get wet. The rest of this neighborhood park has picnic tables, a nice and enclosed dog park, and plenty of wide open space.

Hours: Open daily, sunrise - sunset. The water park is open April - September, daily, sunrise - sunset.
Price: Free
Ages: 1 year - 10 years old.

DIAMOND VALLEY LAKE

(951) 926-7201 - marina / www.dvmarina.com; www.dvlake.com
Domenigoni Parkway, Hemet

This enormous, man-made lake (i.e., reservoir) holds 260 billion gallons of water - enough to secure a six-month supply in case of an earthquake emergency. (I knew you wanted to know that!) With its twenty-six miles of shoreline, you can fish from designated areas at the water's edge, seasonally, for perch, catfish, bass, and trout, or try your luck from a boat. Sailing and other boating opportunities are available - check the website for boating regulations. There are also two large dams (and one smaller one) to contain the water - one on the west end of the lake, and one on the east.

West of the marina entrance, from Winchester Road, turn onto Newport Road and Viewpoint Road to reach the Clayton A Record Jr. Viewpoint, which offers a panoramic vista of the lake, surrounding mountains, the dam, and the open space /wild animal corridor. You won't be here long, but it's an interesting stop and see for free. The viewpoint is open 8:30am - 4pm Thursday to Sunday. Feeling in good physical shape? Hike the six-mile pedestrian/equestrian trail that starts near the viewpoint (parking, picnic tables, and water for horses is available here), and stretches to just north of the visitor's center, on Searl Parkway. Or, start at the visitor center.) Bring water. Feeling in great shape? Hike or bike the 21.8-mile pedestrian/bicycle trail (or a portion of it) that circumnavigates the lake. Restrooms, and some shade, are found along the hilly Lakeview Trail. You'll also get great views of the lake, the dams, and the quarry where rocks were mined for the dams.

Just up the road is the WESTERN SCIENCE CENTER (pg. 369)and DIAMOND VALLEY LAKE

COMMUNITY PARK AND AQUATIC CENTER (pg. 355).

Hours: The lake is open Wed. - Sun., sunrise - 1 hour before sunset; closed Mon. - Tues.

Price: The lake is $9 for parking; $7 for adults for a fishing access permit; $5 for ages 11 and under. All fishermen/fisherwomen must have a valid fishing license, which they sell here. Boat rentals are $30 an hour; $75 a half day for a basic fishing boat; $205 for a half day for an eight-person pontoon. Hiking is $2 for adults (trail fee); free for ages 12 and under.

Ages: 4 years and up.

DIAMOND VALLEY LAKE COMMUNITY PARK AND AQUATIC CENTER

(951) 929-0047 - aquatic center; (951) 926-5917 or (951) 654-1505 - park / www.gorecreation.org

1801 Angler Avenue, Hemet

This park's best summertime feature is the heated 25-meter pool that has a long, twisty water slide. Riders must be at least 48" tall. Younger ones can splash around in the connected, but kind of separate, colorful, water playground which has a few short slides, an enclosed slide, tunnels to crawl through, a cargo net bridge, and water equipment that sprays, squirts, drips, and waterfalls, all in an ankle-deep wading area. Lots of lounge chairs make it a nice place for mom and dad to hang out, too. No coolers or outside food are allowed in. Dive in movie night and ice cream socials are offered on special nights, with extended hours, during the summer.

The park also features eight lighted baseball diamonds, four basketball courts, three soccer fields, two pickleball courts, six tennis courts, seven volleyball courts, picnic areas, a fitness trail, and play areas. What a fun place to spend the day! Just up the road is the WESTERN SCIENCE CENTER (pg. 369) and DIAMOND VALLEY LAKE (pg. 354).

Hours: The park is open daily, sunrise - sunset. The pool is open weekends only, May through mid-June, noon - 4pm. Open in the summer, Mon. - Sat., noon - 5pm; Sun., noon - 4pm.

Price: The park is free. The pool is $8 for ages 3 and up; $7 for seniors; $4 for ages 2 and under.

Ages: 1 and up.

FAIRMOUNT PARK

(951) 826-2000 - park / www.riversideca.gov/park_rec

2601 Fairmount Boulevard, Riverside

This lush park has a lot to offer. The huge, all-access and very fun circus and carousel-themed playground has swings, slides, bridges, metal climbing apparatus, interactive panels, places underneath the raised platforms to imagine and play, a mini Ferris wheel, and an entire section that is covered by the big top. A zero-depth splash pad offer a fun and welcome reprieve during the summer months. The surrounding grassy area is large, with plenty of shade trees and picnic tables. With all this, plus tennis courts, basketball courts, and horseshoe pits, kids can play here all day. Pedal boats are available to rent from Memorial Day to Labor Day. The park's rose garden is located at the corner of Redwood and Dexter drives.

Take a winding drive around the lakes, and watch out for the ducks - they're everywhere. Don't forget your fishing poles as you can stop almost anywhere to fish, including from a small, horseshoe-shaped pier. A fishing license for ages 16 and up is required. You'll have a better than fair day at Fairmount Park!

Hours: The park is open daily, sunrise - 7pm. Pedal boat rentals are available Sat. - Sun., 10am - dusk. Splash pad hours are 11am - 5pm.

Price: Free. Pedal boat rentals are $10.50 for half an hour.

Ages: All

HARVESTON LAKE PARK

(951) 694-6411 - park; (951) 662-3141 - boats / temeculaca.gov

29005 Lakehouse Road, Temecula

This long, large and lovely lake allows lingering and lollygagging, as well as liveliness. Ringed with houses, a cement pathway loops around the lake with lots of green grassy areas along the way, and interspersed with trees. Ducks flock to the lake, as do turtles, but don't feed them human food, please. Fishing is allowed. A good-sized nautical-themed playground is here with slides, climbing elements, twisty shapes, swings, poles and more fun. There are gazebos, here, too that look especially pretty lit up at nighttime. For extra fun rent an electric pedal boat that holds up to four people, $15 for a half hour; $25 an hour.

Hours: The park is open daily 6am - 11:30pm. Pedal boats rentals are usually open Thurs. - Sun., noon - sunset.

Price: Free

Ages: 2 years and up.

HIDDEN VALLEY WILDLIFE AREA

(951) 785-7452 / www.rivcoparks.org $

11401 Arlington Avenue, Riverside

Aptly named, this 1,500-acre wildlife area is indeed off the beaten path. There are several options to see at least parts of this "park": Drive along the ridge to see vast expanses of treeless stretches that are close to the road, and wooded areas that are further back into the park; hike along the numerous trails (twenty-five miles!) and view the wildlife closer up; or horseback ride, which is obviously a popular option judging from the number of horse trailers we observed.

As Hidden Valley is located along the Santa Ana River, much of the wildlife encouraged and seen here are migratory birds. There are many ponds, too, as you'll discover if you hike into this sprawling park. A small Nature Center is up the road a bit. Several educational programs are offered here, by reservation and for $5 per student, that include information regarding the wetlands, Native Americans, geology and more. Programs could include a hike, craft, game and even live animal presentations.

Hours: Open most of the year daily, 7am - 4:30pm; open Memorial Day - Labor Day daily, 7am - 7pm. The Nature
Center is open Sat., 10am - 4pm; other days by appointment.

Price: $5 per vehicle. $2 per dog.

Ages: 4 years and up.

HUNTER PARK

(951) 826-2000 - park; (951) 779-9024 - Live Steamers train rides / www.riversideca.gov/park_rec;   !
www.steamonly.org

1400 Iowa Avenue, Riverside

Hunter Park is composed mostly of grassy playing fields. Its best feature occurs on the second and fourth Sunday of each month when scale model train rides are offered. Kids love taking a ride on the track that encircles the park.

Hours: Steam train rides are on the second and fourth Sun., 10am - 3pm.

Price: Free

Ages: All

HUNT PARK

(951) 826-2000 or (951) 351-6132 / www.riversideca.gov   !

4015 Jackson Street, Riverside

This park has several family-fun amenities such as a softball field (with lights); basketball court (with lights); volleyball court; playground; run around space; picnic facilities; soccer field; swimming pool; a community center; and a 17,000 square-foot, lighted, cement skate park that has street course elements such as ledges, stairs and rails, as well as a cement bowl and other features. A helmet and pads are required for skateboarding.

Hours: The park is open daily, sunrise - sunset. The skate park is open daily, 10am - dusk. The pool is open mid-
June - August, Mon. - Thurs., 1pm - 4pm; Tues. and Thurs., additionally, 7pm - 8:30pm; Sat., 1pm - 4pm.
Closed Sun.

Price: The park and skate park are free. Admission to the pool is cash only - $2.50 for adults; $1 for ages 17 and
under for residents; non-residents are .75¢ more.

Ages: All

JEAN'S CHANNEL CATS

(951) 679-6562 $$$$

28393 Somers Road, Murrieta

Ironically, Jean's Channel <u>Cats</u> is a fishing spot! Just off a dirt road, this enclosed, quite lovely, old-fashioned, nice-sized, stocked, fishing pond is a relaxing place to take in the scenery of the distant mountains while fishing for catfish during the warmer months, and rainbow trout during the cooler months. Picnic tables, some shade trees, a bait and tackle/snack shop, fish-cleaning area, and outhouse complete the amenities here. Fishing poles are available to purchase for $20 per, or bring your own. Hopefully, you'll bring some dinner home.

Hours: Open Fri. - Sun. and holiday Mon., 8am - 5pm.

Price: $5 per person. The fish (no throwbacks allowed) cost $8 per pound. Cash only.

Ages: 3 years and up.

LAKE PERRIS STATE RECREATION AREA

(951) 940-5600 or (951) 940-5603 - general info; (951) 657-2179 - marina; (951) 657-0676 - Indian Museum; (800) 444-7275 - camping reservations; (951) 940-5657 - school tours. / www.parks.ca.gov

17801 Lake Perris Drive, Perris

Come for at least a day of play at the popular Lake Perris. This gigantic (8,800 acres!), man-made lake supports a multitude of water activities. (It's hot out here in the summer, so you'll need them.) There are two swim beaches with placid waters along sandy shores, plus adjacent grassy areas, a small playground, and barbecue pits. Check out LAKE PERRIS WATERPARK (pg. 341), too. For your boating pleasure choose a four passenger boat for $35 for the first two hours (two hour minimum), and $10 an hour after that, or a pontoon boat for $85 for the first three hours. Waterskiing is available, if you bring your own boat. A cove is here for non-motorized boats, such as sail boats and kayaks. Fish at the lake and catch a big one, or at least try to. A license and day permit is required for those 16 years and over. Licenses and bait are available at the Lake Perris Store.

Drier activities include geocaching; picnicking; rock climbing (just around on the boulders or, specifically at Big Rock, which has 110 bolts, so you must bring your own equipment); and biking or hiking on the fairly-level, nine-mile, mostly-paved trail that goes around the lake. What more could nature-loving kids want?! Camping! There is so much to do at Lake Perris that you'll want to spend a night, or two, here. Ask about their summer programs, such as campfire times held on Saturday evenings and the Jr. Ranger program for ages 7 to 12. Also check out the Ya' Heki' Regional Indian Museum, which is free with paid park admission. The museum highlights this area's Native Americans via photos, dioramas, and artifacts.

Hours: Mid-November - mid-March, the lake is open daily, 6am - 6:30pm; the rest of the park is open daily, 6am - 8pm. Mid-March - mid-November the lake is open daily. 6am - 8:30pm; the rest of the park, daily, 6am - 10pm. The Ya' Heki' Indian Museum is open Fri., 10am - 2pm; Sat. - Sun., 10am - 4pm. School tours can call to make an appointment for other times.

Price: $10 per vehicle; $9 for seniors; $8 per vessel/watercraft. Tent camping is $30 a night March - November; $25 during off season. Seniors are $2 less. RV camping is $45. Prices include vehicle admission, but not the $8 camping reservation fee.

Ages: All

LAKE SKINNER COUNTY PARK

(951) 926-1505 - store; (951) 926-1541 - park; (800) 234-7275 -camping reservations. / www.rivcoparks.org

37701 Warren Road, Winchester

Here's the skinny on Lake Skinner. The main attraction is fishing, either from a boat (a four-passenger motorboat is $35 for the first two hours, which is the minimum, $10 for each additional hour), or from the shore. A California state license is required for ages 16 and up and sold here. Day permits for fishing are $10 for adults; $8 for children 12 years and under. Ten passenger pontoon boats are $85 for two hours, which is the minimum, and $20 each additional hour. It's a $100 deposit for motorboats and $250 deposit for pontoon boats. The well-equipped marina offers all sorts of fishing supplies as well as a cafe/restaurant for those who didn't have much luck catching their own meal.

Other activities include overnight camping, hiking, picnicking, and playing on the two, modern, two-story playgrounds with their twisty slides, chain climbing "walls", and other fun elements. Cool off at the good-size garden - a splash pad that has oversized "flowers", leaves and plant stalks that spout water along with water that shoots up from the ground. Boulders are inter-sprinkled. A smaller, separate, water play area has a giant faucet - that pours out water - and handles, and more water shooting up from the padded ground.

Hours: The park and fishing are open daily, 6am - dusk. The splash pad is open April - Labor Day weekend, Mon., noon - 6pm; Tues. - Sun., 10am - 4pm.

Price: $6 per adult; $3 per child under 12 years, except holidays and special events when higher prices are charged. Dogs and horses are $2 per. Tent camping is $25 a night. RV camping is $40 with full hook ups. The camping reservation fee is $8.

Ages: All

MOUNT RUBIDOUX

(951) 826-2000 / www.riversideca.gov/park_rec

Mount Rubidoux Drive and 9th Street, Riverside

For kids who enjoy a somewhat rugged hike, climbing Mount Rubidoux is a great adventure. The steep, three-mile+ (roundtrip) trail winds around the hill that is barren except for boulders and cacti. "The trail is two miles up and one mile down." Just below the summit is a stone tower and bridge. There is another railroad track bridge up this way, too. Reaching the top is a climax. At the top is a cross and a flag. There are also rocks to climb. On a clear day, the panoramic view of the San Gabriel and San Bernardino Mountains is beautiful. On the western slope of the hill, watch vintage planes take off and land at Rubidoux's Flabob Airport. Hiking here in the summer gets hot, so bring a water bottle. Plan on about an hour-and-a-half round trip. Next door, along the river, is the Mount Rubidoux Park. The bike trail at the base of the mountain goes a few miles back to Martha McClean/Anza Narrow Park and beyond.

Hours: Open daily, sunrise - sunset.
Price: Free
Ages: It depends how far up you want to hike!

RANCHO JURUPA PARK

(951) 684-7032 - park; (800) 234-PARK (7275) - camping and cabin reservations / www.rivcoparks.org
4800 Crestmore Road, Riverside

This huge (200-acre) mountain-wilderness park, which is part of the even bigger Santa Ana River Regional Park system, provides a delightful escape from the city. Where to start? The three-acre lake is stocked with trout in the cooler months and catfish in the summertime. Fishermen (and women) 16 years and older must have a state fishing license, which are sold here. Near the lake is a big play structure with slides, swings, monkey bars, towers, twisty-metal climbing apparatus, and more. Horseshoe pits are located over here, too.

Enjoy a day (or two or three) here by camping in one of the 140 camp sites that are slotted in a big open space near one end of the lake. Coin-operated showers (be quick!), a general store, and laundry facility are available. If camping isn't your thing, rent a cabin. The six cabins sleep up to four people and have bunk beds, a room with a queen-size bed, a bathroom, and a room with full kitchen facilities, an eating area with table and chairs, a couch, and central air and heat. Each cabin has a front porch, too, and a picnic table in the small front yard.

On the other side of the main lake are a few smaller lakes; big, grassy open spaces for baseball or whatever; plenty of picnic tables; and barbecue pits. The boulder play area is great for kids to use their unlimited imaginations to hide, play cowboy, or whatever else they pretend. The good-size splash pad for kids (or anyone who wants to get wet) is open usually April through Labor Day. It features poles that hold buckets of water that spill over onto waiting kids below, pipes bursting with water from their seams, water cannons, and a water play structure with steps, ropes, poles, and other fun elements. A pretty, rustically-landscaped with lots of boulders, eighteen-hole miniature golf course, surrounded by waterfalls, adds to the fun here. The cost to play is $5 per person. Flip your wrist with just the right amount of twist to make the disc fly and land in the holes at the disc golf course, which is free to play with entrance into the park. Bike rentals are available, starting at $10, and help you enjoy your time here that much more.

Hiking trails throughout the wooded landscape and meadows, and an easy hike along the river trail, plus rocks to climb on await your kids.

Hours: Open Sun. - Thurs., 6am - sunset; Fri. - Sat. and holidays, 7am - 10pm.
Price: Day use is $6 for adults; $3 for ages 11 and under. Dogs and horses are $2 each. Fishing is $10 for ages 16 and older; $8 for ages 6 - 15; children 5 and under fish for free with a paid adult. A campsite is $35; with full hook-ups, it's $45. Group rates are available. Camping entry is $6 per vehicle. Cabins are $100 a night, Sun. - Thurs.; $120 a night, Fri. - Sat. with a two-night minimum. Holidays are extra.
Ages: All

ROCK VISTA PARK

(951) 736-2241 / www.incorona.com
2481 Steven Drive, Corona

Climbing on rocks makes kids happy - it just does. And that's pretty much what this park has to offer. An enormous grassy area has a looping dirt trail, interspersed with groupings of trees and boulders, that leads up to the surrounding hills. Some of the hills have houses on top, but one in particular just has a cluster of rocks and boulders that are high enough, but not too high. This might not sound like fun, but imaginations are given reign here. I also like the "stream" of rocks that wind down a portion of the park.

Hours: Open daily, 6am - 6pm.
Price: Free
Ages: 2 years and up.

RONALD REAGAN SPORTS PARK AND COMMUNITY RECREATION CENTER / TEMECULA SKATE PARK

(951) 694-6410 - park; (951) 695-1409 - skate park / www.cityoftemecula.org
30875 Rancho Vista, Temecula

Have a ball at this terrific sports park! It has twelve ball fields, seven soccer fields, lots of open grassy areas for running around, two great playgrounds, shade trees, picnic shelters, and barbecue grills. The roller hockey rink has some open time, although it is used mostly by leagues. Bring your Tony Hawk wannabes to practice at the gated, one-acre, staffed, outdoor cement skate park which is equipped with all the "necessary" features. The sixty-foot-diameter bowl has ramp entry which also leads to an upper bowl with a street plaza that consists of a pyramid, fun box, curbs, ramps, stairs, and a hand rail. All participants must have a signed waiver form prior to park entry. Proper safety equipment is mandatory - helmet, elbow pads, and knee pads.

The indoor gym offers basketball, but it can be set up for volleyball, too. Keep your cool in the twenty-five-meter outdoor swimming pool that has a diving board and a water slide. There is also a shallow pool just for tots. The Teen Center is a great place for 12 to 18 year olds to hang out. It offers pool, air hockey, ping pong, foosball table, X Box and more. This park offers everything active kids need - my boys would be very happy living there!

Hours: The park is open daily, sunrise - 10pm. The skate park is open Mon. - Fri., 4:15pm - 8pm (plus 1:30pm - 3:30pm on Wed.); Sat., 3:15pm - 8pm; Sun., 1:15pm - 6pm. The sessions vary for scooters or skateboards - check the website calendar. The skate park is open in the summer Mon., Wed., Fri., Sat., 2pm - 8pm; Tues., Thurs., 9am - 3pm; Sun., 1pm - 6pm. The roller hockey rink is usually available for open play Mon. - Fri. before 3:30pm and all day Sun. After 4pm and on most Sat. it's booked for league play. Call for pool hours, as they fluctuate.

Price: The park is free. Skateboard sessions are free for residents ($1 for a year's membership); $5 for nonresidents. Pool sessions are $2.50 for adults; $1 for seniors and ages 12 and under for residents; $5 for nonresidents of any age. The Teen Center asks that a resident card be purchased - $1 for a year's membership.

Ages: All ages for the park. Skateboarders under 7 years must be accompanied by an adult. Kids must be from 12 to 18 years to hang out inside the Teen Center.

SANTANA REGIONAL PARK

(951) 736-2241 / www.coronadwp.com; www.incorona.com
598 Santana Way, Corona

One of the park's best features is the nice cement skate park with a pool, fun boxes, steps, grinding rails, and pyramids. Lighted ball fields, soccer fields, cement pathways, grassy areas, a playground (with a mini zip line), and more round out this twenty-one-acre park.

Hours: Open daily, 5:30am - 10pm.
Price: Free
Ages: 6 years and up.

SANTA ROSA PLATEAU ECOLOGICAL RESERVE

(951) 677-6951 / www.santarosaplateau.org
39400 Clinton Keith Road, Murrieta

From riparian stream sides to basalt-capped mesas, this gigantic 9,000-acre reserve covers the gamut of topography. The thirty-plus trails range from easy, one-mile hikes to hardier five-mile round-trip hikes. Depending on which trail you choose, you'll hike through oak woodlands, acres of grasslands, chaparral, up the Santa Ana mountains, and down to creek beds. Look for tree frogs and turtles in the water, and ground squirrels, woodpeckers, hawks, and horned lizards along the wooded pathways. There is a picnic spot at the vernal pools, which is a four-mile round-trip hike. Pick up a trail map from the visitors center where there are also a few displays to look at. Guided hikes are offered - call for dates and times, and other interpretive programs are offered at various times by reservation. A plethora of school, scouting, and other programs and tours are offered.

Hours: Open daily, sunrise - sunset. The visitor's center is open Tues. - Sun., 9am - 5pm. Closed Mon.
Price: $4 for adults; $3 for children 12 and under.
Ages: 3 years and up.

SKULL CANYON ZIPLINE

(951) 471-0999 / www.skullcanyon.com
13540 Temescal Canyon Boulevard, Corona

Skull Canyon is a great local place to go for a combination of good hiking and ziplining. Get geared up in this shaded outdoor facility nestled into the 160 acres of canyons and hillsides. One choice is the Original Course, which incorporates a ten-minute hike uphill and has six different ziplines varying between 200 and 660 feet long. The weight limits are 60 lbs up to 250 lbs and the cost is $85 per person. The other choice is for those who are a little more daring - the Extreme Course. The thirty-minute hike is followed by five ziplines with a total length of more than double that of the Original Course. It is higher, longer and faster, and not for those with a fear of heights. The weight limits are

100 lbs up to 250 lbs and the cost is $115 per person. No more than ten people go on either of the two-hour excursions, so the attention from the guide is personal. Ziplining is a thrilling adventure! The guides here not only make it a fun and educational excursion, as you learn about the eco-systems, but a memorable one as well. This is a great group bonding activity.

For those who are impatient, or want a quick adrenaline fix, do the Speed Run. It's actually the last run of the Extreme Course, a 1,700 foot, side-by-side, racing zipline. The Speed Run is yours for $40, or an additional $20 if added to the original course run. Spectators, for any of the outings, can hang in the shade and enjoy a picnic here.

Hours: Open daily, by reservation only.
Price: Prices are listed above.
Ages: 60 lbs to 250 lbs.

STAGECOACH PARK

(951) 736-2241 / www.coronaca.gov
2125 Stagecoach Road, Corona

Seems like this town is big enough for the both of us, or even more than that! This little playground is set up like an Old Western town, with smaller buildings and funner things to play on. The two-story Post Office and connected General Store have stairs, slides, balconies, short rock climbing walls, wagon wheel climbing walls, ladders, and poles. There are a few other free-standing play apparatus with bridges, climbing structures, and slides, including one that is a stagecoach. Climb aboard to ride it, looking out the little side windows, and whoosh down the attached slide. There are also speaking tubes, swings, a decent-sized rock climbing rock, monkey bars (rings), chin up bars, and black ponies on huge springs to ride back and forth on, plus benches with wagon wheels on the sides of them, a covered picnic area with bbqs, grassy spaces, and a .4 miles paved pathway.

Hours: Open daily, sunrise - sunset.
Price: Free
Ages: 2 - 9 years.

STONEY MOUNTAIN PARK

(951) 658-3211 / www.sanjacintovalley.info/parks.html
Inglestone Drive and Cinnabar Avenue, Hemet

This small playground has colorful equipment with a short tower, slides, and other equipment. There are also two half basketball courts here and, best of all, a short trail dotted with trees and surrounded by grass, that leads to a good-sized hill of boulders and rocks. I love climbing and scrambling around on rocks and my kids share this passion, so we think this park is "boulderdacious."

Hours: Open daily, 6am - sunset
Price: Free
Ages: 2 - 12 years old.

UNIVERSITY OF CALIFORNIA AT RIVERSIDE BOTANIC GARDENS

(951) 784-6962 or (951) 827- 4650 / www.gardens.ucr.edu
Campus Drive, at the University of California, Riverside

Riverside's climate ranges from subtropical to desert to mountains, all within forty acres and four miles of hilly trails. A gently-sloping walkway provides access to the gardens' main areas for wheelchairs and strollers. Explore the botanic gardens to see rose gardens, fruit orchards, an herb garden, saguaros, barrel cacti, pine trees, giant sequoias, and more.

Besides the diverse plant life, numerous animals share this habitat. Be on the lookout for bunnies, lizards, squirrels, snakes, coyotes, and numerous bird species. A main trail loops around and is walkable in forty-five minutes. At the far end of the trail is a pond supporting more wildlife such as frogs, turtles, dragonflies, and koi. A dome-shaped building made of cedar that houses a "living fossils" collection and a greenhouse are more discoveries you'll make along the way. Come with your kids to enjoy the beauty of the gardens, and/or come for an educational field trip. Check the web calendar for great events such as Birdwalk and Breakfast, Children's Adventure Series, Art in the Gardens, etc.

Hours: Open daily, 8am - 5pm. Closed New Year's Day, Primavera Day (sometime in mid-May), July 4th, Thanksgiving, Christmas and all academic and administrative holidays.
Price: Free; $5 donation is suggested. Parking is $2 an hour. See American Horticultural Society (pg. x) for info on reciprocal memberships.
Ages: All

—MALLS—

GALLERIA AT TYLER

(951) 351-3110 / www.galleriatyler.com
1299 Galleria at Tyler, Riverside

The Galleria offers a plethora of fun things to do, so check outDISNEY STORE (Riverside County) (pg. 370) BUILD-A-BEAR WORKSHOP (Riverside County) (pg. 370); COLOR ME MINE (Riverside County) (pg. 342); GLO MINI GOLF (pg. 347) and the adjacent CASTLE PARK / BUCCANEER COVE (pg. 340). It also features a Farmers Market every Sunday, 8:30am to 12:30pm outside, and inside, a carousel and a free, semi-enclosed, carpeted, kids play area with colorful, hard-padded foam letters to climb on and around, and even mini slide. I always appreciate the benches inside here for parents to watch and hang.

Hours: The mall is open Mon. - Sat., 10am - 9pm; Sun., 11am - 7pm.
Price: Free
Ages: All

KIDS OUTLET at LAKE ELSINORE OUTLETS

(951) 245-0087 / www.lakeelsinoreoutlet.com
17600 Collier Avenue, suite 106 at Lake Elsinore Outlets, Lake Elsinore

Every week kids have a special time of entertainment, learning, and creating at the Outlet. The one-hour event has featured a drum circle workshop where kids (and adults) were taught how to play the drums; a puppet show; storytelling; making and decorating a picture frame; making a flip book; decorating an umbrella (♪ella, ella); doing science experiments; a presentation of tidepool animals to learn about and then gently touch; and more. Call or check the website to see what's coming next.

The Outlet has about fifty name-brand stores and a few eateries for your shopping and dining pleasure.

Hours: Kids Outlet meets every Fri., 11am - noon.
Price: Free
Ages: 3 years and up.

MORENO VALLEY MALL - KIDS CLUB

(951) 653-1177 / www.morenovalleymall.com
22500 Town Cir., Moreno Valley

The Kids Club is held once a month in the food court and features a specific craft, usually seasonal, for kids to make and take home. Come play and then have lunch and go shopping. A few favorite fun stores/restaurants and things to do include Dollar Book Fair; Kelly's Coffee and Fudge; a free, Raceway Nissan Play Area with themed, hard-foam play objects; JUMP 'N JAMMIN (Riverside County) (pg. 349), a great indoor play area; ROUND1 BOWLING AND AMUSEMENT (Riverside County) (pg. 352); and Harkins Multiplex theatre with its indoor PlayCenter for you to drop off the kids, on-site, as you go and watch a movie.

Hours: The Kids Club is third Sat. of each month from 11am -noon.
Price: Free
Ages: 2 - 9

PROMENADE SUMMER KIDS CLUB and PROMENADE MALL

(951) 296-0975 / www.promenadetemecula.com
40820 Winchester Road at Promenade Mall, Temecula

Malls just wanta have fun, and this one has more fun than some others. Check the website for the many special events held here throughout the year, such as Circus Vargus, Teen Expos, a Farmer's Market every Wednesday from 9am - 1pm, and more. Two kid-favorite stores are here, too - DISNEY STORE (Riverside County) (pg. 370) and BUILD-A-BEAR WORKSHOP (Riverside County) (pg. 370), as well as ROUND1 BOWLING AND AMUSEMENT (Riverside County) (pg. 352), plus numerous other stores and restaurants to choose from.

In the summer, keep your kids occupied and entertained by signing them up for the Promenade Summer Kids Club, for ages 3 - 10. Every week there is a different theme with a different show, craft or educational activity offered, as well as some discounts and other benefits. Kids Club is usually held on Wednesdays from 11am - 1pm. Check the Edwards Cinemas here, too, as they sometimes offer discounted kids' movies in the summer.

Hours: The mall is open Mon. - Sat., 10am - 9pm; Sun., 11am - 7pm.
Price: The Kids Club is free.
Ages: 3 - 10 years old for the Kids Club.

—MUSEUMS—

CALIFORNIA MUSEUM OF PHOTOGRAPHY

(951) 784-FOTO (3686) or (951) 827-4787 / www.artsblock.ucr.edu

3824 Main Street, Riverside

Expose your kids to the photographic arts at the unique, three-story California Museum of Photography. The main level has rotating photo exhibits, with an emphasis on various photography styles or photographers, such as Ansel Adams. The back area houses a part of the museum's vast collection of vintage cameras, including working miniature cameras (my boys refer to them as "spy" cameras), old-fashioned cameras with the drape cloth, a Spiderman camera, and one that is part of a radio-controlled car!

Take the spiral stairs up to the mezzanine terrace, which is a catwalk-like hallway gallery. The top floor often focuses on kids with its small, interactive gallery with rotating exhibits. When we visited, children used the Zoetropes to draw pictures and spin them around in a drum, creating moving images - early animation! We also learned that not all shadows are black as the images shadowed here produced a rainbow of colors. The next display visually explained how the aperture of a camera is similar to the pupils in eyes. We looked into a light and watched in the mirror as our pupils enlarged or contracted, according to the amount of light entering in. The Shadows Room temporarily imprinted body outlines on the photosensitive wall when a light flashed. Use computers in the Digital Studio to see some of the wonders that can be performed with digital photography.

Camera Obscura is a small, dark room with a tiny hole of light that projects an upside-down image of the outside scene on its wall. This is a visual demonstration of how a camera lens works. Kids will get a wide angle view of photography at this Museum! Note: Guided school tours are available for 7th through 12th graders. This museum, and several others in the area plus galleries, are open for free, October through May for community events: the first Sunday of each month for First Sundays, with crafts and activities for families, 11am to 4pm, and on the first Thursday, 5pm to 9pm, for Riverside Artswalk. Adjacent to the museum, and part of the Artblock, is the Sweeney Art Gallery, a cafe, a seventy-five seat film screening room, and a natural light atrium gallery and performance space.

Hours: The museum is open Tues. - Thurs., 11am - 5pm; Fri. - Sat., 11am - 7pm; Sun., 11am - 4pm. It's also open the first Thurs. from 5pm - 9pm. Closed Mon., New Year's Eve, New Year's Day, 4th of July, Veteran's Day, Thanksgiving, Christmas Eve and Christmas.

Price: $6 for adults; $3 for seniors; college students and children 11 and under are free. Entrance is free on the first Thurs., 5pm - 9pm and the first Sun., 11am - 4pm, October - May. There is a small fee for parking during the week, but it's free after 5pm weekdays and free on the weekends.

Ages: 3 years and up just to look at things; ages 5 and up will begin to really appreciate it.

EDWARD-DEAN MUSEUM AND GARDENS

(951) 845-2626 / www.edward-deanmuseum.org

9401 Oak Glen Road, Cherry Valley

This elegant, medium-sized fine arts museum seems almost out of place in the rural town of Cherry Valley. It is situated on beautifully-landscaped grounds with formal gardens, accompanied by grassy lawns, small garden maze and a small koi pond. Just outside the museum is a fountain surrounded by a rose garden.

The two-story museum has seven galleries that specialize in interior decorative art from the late 16th to early 18th centuries. The North wing gallery has rotating exhibits. We saw "Art in Miniature," which showcased buildings, artwork, and scenes in miniature. The permanent upstairs galleries are situated in a home-like atmosphere. They feature European and Oriental art which includes furniture; china; a Buddha exhibit in a room with ornate wood wall carvings; silk tapestries; portraits; a beautiful oriental robe; statues; and a music room with a piano and a harp. Downstairs is a small reference library, plus a wing displaying a pope's wooden traveling desk and few other items. The docents we encountered were friendly and readily explained many of the exhibit pieces. There are several group tours and free school programs offered. Note that the museum is just down the road from all the fun at OAK GLEN / APPLE PICKING (pg. 403).

Hours: Open Thurs. - Sat., 10am - 5pm. Call to make a reservation for a school tour.

Price: $5 for adults; children 12 and under are free.

Ages: 7 years and up.

FINGERPRINTS YOUTH MUSEUM

(951) 765-1223 / www.fingerprintsmuseum.com

123 S. Carmalita Street, Hemet

This place has kids' fingerprints all over it! The huge, rectangular room is divided into sections with various hands-on exhibits and activities. Each one emphasizes a particular educational aspect that visitors can touch, learn about, and test. Note: Some exhibits do rotate.

The first section allows open play with building supplies, puzzles, and bins of arts and crafts materials, plus colorful tables and chairs. The adjacent party room has a great undersea mural. Kids can uncover bones at a paleontology pit that uses recycled rubber instead of sand. To the right is a book nook to sit and read. Great animal and habitat murals are the backdrop against the enclosed Little Critters Kingdom (for your little critters) that has a wooden play boat; petite army jeeps; really big blocks; short play structures; and a play kitchen with all the appliances.

Be green: A Waste Management truck is parked in a section on composting and recycling information. Storm the castle, or at least climb the wall designed to look like a castle as rocks jut out from it, providing hand and foot holds. Become a temporary member of law enforcement by wearing a helmet and hopping on one of the two real police motorcycles, complete with a radio and working lights, or climbing into a real police car. Practice rescuing techniques in a fully-equipped ambulance with gurney, lights, and a two-way radio that is connected to the police motorcycles. Respond to an emergency by dressing up in firemen outfits and boots, and using the hoses on board the mock fire engine.

Along the back and side walls are several city-themed, mini rooms. These include a post office with boxes and a desk; a bank with a teller's desk; and a Walmart with mini shopping carts, shelves stocked with fake food, and a check out stand, scanner, and cash register. The kid-size humane society has a fire hydrant out front, and inside, an examination table, stethoscope, lab coat and stuffed animals. The doctors office is equipped with white lab coats for visiting "doctors", as well as stethoscopes, crutches, an examination table, scales, and more. Work out in the small fitness center with some exercise machines, hula hoops and pretend weights. Helmets and a police desk await next door at the police station. Future anchormen and women can first get glamed up with some costumes before going on air in the next room, Kids TV Station. Sit behind a desk here with lights and buttons - action!

Ninety-minute school tours are offered that focus on a particular theme and include plenty of just play time. Special workshops and events are offered for families throughout the year. Tip: Just around the corner from the museum, at 4080/4090 Park Avenue, pull over to stop and stare at some domestic and exotic animals that belong to a private residence. You'll see horses and goats, as well as zebras, camels, gazelles, a buffalo, and peacocks.

Hours: Open October - May, Wed. - Fri., 11am - 4:45pm; Sat., 10am - 4:45pm. Open June - September , Tues. - Fri., 11am - 4:45pm; Sat. - Sun., 10am - 4:45pm. No admittance after 4:15pm. Closed most holidays.

Price: $5 per person; $4 for seniors; children under 2 are free.

Ages: 1 - 12 years.

GILMAN HISTORIC RANCH AND WAGON MUSEUM   ☀

(951) 922-9200 / www.rivcoparks.org $$

1901 West Wilson Street, Banning

Wagons, ho! Take the dirt road back to the Gilman Historic Ranch and Wagon Museum and explore life as it was over 150 years ago. The exhibits are set up in a chronological order. Over fifteen wagons from yesteryear are inside the museum including chuck wagons, stagecoaches, and prairie schooners. Some of the wagons are hitched to large wooden horses. Learn how our pioneer ancestors traveled across the country, and hear about the hardships that they endured. Also on exhibit are photographs, saddles, a bedroom set with a ladies' riding habit and surrey, a blacksmith's shop, and Indian artifacts. I really enjoy all this museum and ranch have to offer.

The adjacent section of the ranch has a few historic buildings, including the beautifully-restored, furnished Ranch House, which looks like it did in the 1890's (but with a fresher coat of paint). It is open to tour. Walk around and enjoy the grounds as there are old wagons and other equipment scattered around, shaded picnic tables and some hiking trails. Some of the trails go across the creek and to the upper reservoir, while others go deeper into the canyons. Be on the lookout for rabbits, deer, and other wildlife.

School groups, geared for third and fourth graders, with a minimum of ten students and maximum of sixty, can take outstanding and informative two-hour tours which include a tour of the museum, grounds, and adobe ruins, plus a craft to make and take home. For instance, for $8 per person in the California Gold Rush program, students will also go on a nature hike, including walking on the wagon trail originally blazed here; pan for real gold flakes in sluices set in the woods (you may keep whatever you pan); use hand-powered drills and tools to drill holes in logs; and learn about ranch life by making rope, branding a piece of wood, and more. The Native Americans program, also $8 per person, incorporates the above tour, plus seeing and learning about indigenous plants for medicine and other purposes, grinding seeds with a mano and metate, demonstrations of primitive skills, and making a relevant craft. Scout groups may use the campfire sites and fire rings, and choose badge-earning activities. Whatever you choose to do here, enjoy your day reliving the past!

Hours: The museum and grounds are open to the public Fri., noon - 4pm and the second and fourth Sat., 10am - 4pm. Crafts for kids are offered on the second Sat. from 11am - 3pm, for an additional fee. Tours for school and other groups are offered throughout the week by reservation.
Price: Admission/self-guided tours are $5 for adults; $3 for ages 12 and under; $1 for dogs. Guided tours are $5 per person.
Ages: 5 years and up.

HERITAGE HOUSE

(951) 689-1333 or (951) 826-5273 / www.riversideca.gov/museum/heritagehouse $$
8193 Magnolia Street, Riverside

Heritage House is a beautiful Victorian house built in 1892. It is fully restored and filled with elaborate, turn-of-the-century furniture. Adding to its charm is the wrought-iron fence in front, the well-kept grounds, the backyard windmill, and the barn complete with clucking chickens.

Given by a docent in period dress, your older children will appreciate the forty-minute guided tour as they see and learn about a different era and style of living. Downstairs is the formal dining room, elegant parlor, kitchen with a brick oven, and music room. Kids are invited to look through the stereo-optic, which is an early version of today's View Master™ and view a unique, old music box. Explaining the Edison phonograph is a lot harder now that record players are also a thing of the past! The formal oak stairway leads upstairs to bedrooms, the library with trophy animal heads and a bearskin rug, and the servant's quarters. Heritage House graciously displays the life of an affluent citrus grower.

Forty-five-minute group tours, for a minimum of twenty people, are offered by appointment. Check out the free ice-cream social given in May, with Victorian games and musical entertainment, and the December event of Victorian Christmas Open House.
Hours: Open Fri. - Sun., noon - 3:15pm. Closed July and August.
Price: $5 per person, cash only.
Ages: 7 years old and up.

JENSEN-ALVARADO RANCH HISTORIC PARK

(951) 369-6055 / www.rivcoparks.org $$
4307 Briggs Street, Riverside

This historic site brings the history of the 1880's to life. The front part of the park is a large area with picnic tables. Rusty old farm equipment lines the main pathway. The corral and animal pens, with a few horses, sheep, potbellied pig, chicken, and other ranch animals, are located next to the Jensen-Alvarado Ranch House. Behind the house was a winery; it's now a small museum. Inside is period furniture, plus wine-making presses, barrels, and other equipment.

A three-hour school tour, for minimum of forty students, includes seeing all of the above, plus hearing a living history presentation from a costumed docent; participating in hands-on demonstrations such as making ice cream, butter, or tortillas; and, maybe, feeding the animals. Reservations for the upcoming school year start in May. Ask about special events.
Hours: Open to the public Tues. - Fri., 2pm - 4pm, by reservation only. Open the first Sat. from 11am - 3pm for tour and a craft and the third Sat. for tours, only, from 10:30am - 4pm. Closed other Sat., plus Sun., Mon. and holidays. Open Tues. - Fri. in the morning for school and large groups only, by reservation.
Price: Public admission is $4 for adults; $3 for ages 12 and under. Cash only. School tours are $7 per person.
Ages: 6 years and up.

JURUPA MOUNTAINS DISCOVERY CENTER / EARTH SCIENCE MUSEUM

(951) 685-5818 / www.jmdc.org   !/$$$
7621 Granite Hill Drive, Riverside

This center is a rock hound's paradise where kids can either start or add to their rock collection. The main building is a gigantic warehouse/gift shop with an incredible array of rocks, minerals, dinosaur skeletons, and fossils of all sizes and quality, for display and purchase, at good prices. (My best purchase - fossilized dinosaur dung!) The store also sells jewelry and toys. Just outside the gift shop is a tortoise barn and paddock housing huge desert tortoises.

The adjacent Earth Science Museum has outstanding rocks, minerals, fossils, and Native American artifacts displayed according to classification. The large crystals, geodes, carbons, etc., are worthy of a few "oohs" and "aahs." A major hit with kids is the *egg*straordinary dinosaur egg collection. A camptosaurus, a plant-eating, bird-hipped dinosaur, awaits here, too. The assemblage of ancient and modern Native American artifacts includes tools, weapons, a wonderful arrowhead exhibit, an 1100-year-old corn cob, and costumes - in particular, a beautiful fringed and beaded wedding dress. Products, like Borax, are shown in their commercial form next to their original mineral form. Other unique exhibits are the florescent exhibit, which literally highlights rocks with luminescent characteristics; the space exhibit, which includes moon rocks; a mining display; and the ivory exhibit, which has examples of intricately carved scrimshaw. Watch the video, hosted by a talking mammoth, that discusses how the Jurupa Mountains were formed. Note: The outside of the building is made with petrified wood and fossils.

If your kids want to take home their own hand-picked treasures, go on a Dino Walk on Saturdays. This drop-in, ninety-minute family field trip starts at the magnetic rock, proceeds to the small, petrified wood "forest," and has several other stops along the way, with kid-appropriate explanations about the fascinating plants and rocks you see. (I finally understand that fossil simply means, "something that was once living.") You'll go past botanic gardens (that you can explore later on), boasting lots of cactus and succulents; a nursery; and some dino statues hanging out in the gardens. You can't miss the seventy-foot brachiosaurus sculpture near the entrance to your destination, Dinosaur Mesa. This hilly area has numerous dinosaur statues including a pachyrhinosaurus, styrachosaurus, velociraptors, T. rex, and more. The highlight of the excursion is sorting through the huge spread of rocks and rock chips strewn at the dinos' feet, and picking out twelve to take home! Crystals, jasper, malachite, petrified wood, amethyst, chrysocolla, and sulphur are some examples of what can be found here. Egg cartons are provided to carry your rocks. Back at the warehouse/store, you can label each of your treasures, with a geologist's help, if needed. Bring a picnic lunch to enjoy at the outside tables, as well. If you'd like to add on a short hike to an outing hike up the back hill to "meet" Eddie, a Columbian Mammoth and get a great view of the Jurupa Valley.

Several onsite gardens are the Iris Garden (beautiful in full bloom); the Enabling Garden, where people in wheelchairs can work the raised garden beds; Cactus and Succulent Gardens; and the Biblical Garden, where once you've walked past a cedar of Lebanon and through a Middle-Eastern style arch, you enter grounds where all the plants are mentioned in the Bible. Each one has a placard with a biblical reference. Also here is Granite Hills Nursery with a variety of plants for sale. Look for all the red ear slider turtles in the turtle pond in this area, as well as some gold fish.

The Jurupa Cultural Center offers a wide variety of terrific school group programs (with a minimum of twenty-five students) and a slew of scout programs, such as gold panning at sluices, adobe brick-making, lapidary workshops, creating an Indian pictograph, forestry, textile, first aid, insect study, environmental science, archaeology, nuclear science, weather, and lots more. A visit to the Earth Science Museum is usually included in the programs. The Center also comes to schools for on-site classes. Toddler Time is Fridays from 1pm - 3pm, for $10, for story time and activities relating to arts, math, science, etc. Call for information on their week-long camps of Nature School in the summer that range from hiking and survival to Indian lore to dinosaurs and fossils.

Hours: The gift shop and Earth Science Museum are open Tues. - Sat., 8am - 5pm; Sun., noon - 5pm. Both are closed on Mon. and national holidays. Dino Walk is held Sat., 9am, 11am and 2pm, weather permitting.

Price: Entrance to the warehouse/gift store, the botanical gardens, and the museum is free. Dino Walk is $9 per person; children under 2 are free. School programs range from $9 - $15 per person, depending on the activity and materials. Scout programs are $20. Call for specific information and a class schedule or check the site's website.

Ages: 3 years and up.

MARCH FIELD AIR MUSEUM

(951) 902-5949 / www.marchfield.org

$$$

22550 Van Buren Boulevard, March Air Reserve Base

March Field Museum is the proud home to one of the most extensive collections of military aircraft and aviation artifacts in the United States. The walkway is lined with airplane engines, plus a jeep that kids can get into and "drive" around. Outside, over eighty historic airplanes are on display, from the smaller F-84 to the massive B-52 to the sleek Blackbird SR-71. Forty-five minute narrated tram tour rides are offered that go around the perimeter of the airfield every hour on the hour (except noon) - weather permitting. The cost is $3 per person. Kids are welcome to look at the planes, but they may only climb aboard them on open-cockpit days, on Saturdays. At these times three, or so, airplanes are opened up to climb aboard and there are pilots and mechanics to speak with. Sometimes there are extra things to do and see, too.

Inside, the two huge hangars display a replica of the Wright Brothers flyer, as well as everything possible pertaining to the Air Force, starting from 1918 to present day. Airplanes, such as a biplane trainer, have landed in here, plus there are exhibits of flight uniforms, a "war dog" memorial, photographs, model planes, engines, medals, weapons, control panels, aerial cameras, and equipment from both World Wars, Korea, Viet Nam, the Cold War, and Desert Storm. Other highlights include a PT-13D Kaydet with bombs below, a rare P-59 fighter, and a Firebolt missile. (Exhibits do rotate.) In the simulated barracks from WWI a replica Nieuport 11 (7/8 scale) flies overhead while a documentary of the conflict appears through trench periscopes mounted on the trench wall. Space exploration is paid tribute in a room devoted to NASA with space artifacts and articles, and mission control. Three computers offer mission control programs of jet simulators. Hanger 2 houses the library, several more planes and memorabilia and is used for educational programs and special events. Your pilots-in-training will also enjoy the interactive area in here with ejection seats, a little mock plane to board, and clothing, including flight suits, to get dressed up in with a biplane on a mural in the background. You can tour the restoration hangar on Saturdays at 1:30pm. This museum defines the word "comprehensive"!

Fire Base Romeo Charlie is a half-acre adjacent to the museum's education hanger. It replicates a Vietnam-era fire base complete with helicopters of the period including an AH-1 Cobra gunship, two UH-1 Iroquois, H-21 Shawnee, and others. Sandbags and other defensive walls; bunkers; a flight control tower; and vehicles add to the immersion experience and authenticity of the tough living conditions.

School and other group tours are offered for a minimum of twelve people. Call or check the website for air show dates. By the way, the museum has a great gift shop.

Hours: Open Tues. - Sun., 10am - 5pm. Closed Mon., New Year's Day, Thanksgiving, and Christmas.
  Price: $10 for adults; $5 for ages 5 - 11; children 4 and under and active duty are free.
  Ages: 3 years and up.

MISSION INN and MISSION INN MUSEUM

(951) 784-0300 - Inn; (951) 788-9556 - museum; (951) 781-8241 - school tours / $$$
www.missioninnmuseum.com; www.missioninn.com

3696 Mission Inn Avenue, Riverside

Is it a European castle? Not quite, but this elegant, old, sprawling Inn is beautiful to look at and tour. The hour-plus tour shows much of its eclectic architecture and furnishings. Mediterranean style, emphasized in the colorful tiles, spiral columns, and bells, is fused with an Oriental influence. This combo is reflected in a hotel kitchen chimney which is in the shape of a pagoda, plus other unique touches. Only through the tour can you see all four wings of the hotel with highlights including the gilded eighteenth-century altar in the wedding chapel; the music room; the Court of Birds (there are no actual birds still here, but the stories about them give wings to the imagination); the Taft Chair, that seats up to five kids at one time; and the open-air, five-story spiral staircase in the rotunda, which is quite grand looking. If your kids are interested in architecture or hearing about the Inn's history, they will enjoy the tour. If not, at least take a quick walk through the grounds. Note that one-hour school tours are given that are aimed toward certain age groups. Combine your time here with Afternoon Tea! See AFTERNOON TEA AT MISSION INN (pg. 343) for details. See the Inn's calendar of events for the Festival of Lights spectacular at Christmas time.

A small museum is located on the pedestrian walkway, next to the Inn's gift shop. Frank Miller, the Inn's builder, had an international collection that reflected his tastes. Housed in the museum are encased figurines, artifacts, and photos. Exhibits rotate and some are hits with kids, some aren't.

Hours: The Inn is a functioning Inn so it is open daily. Tours are given Mon. - Fri. at 10am, 11:30am, 2pm, and 4pm; Sat. - Sun. at 10am, 11:30am, 1:30pm, 2:30pm, and 4pm. Reservations are recommended. The museum is open daily, 9:30am - 4:30pm. It is also open until 5pm, Mon. - Wed. and until 8pm, Thurs. - Sun. during the Festival of Lights.
  Price: You can walk around the hotel at no charge. The tour costs $13 for adults; children 12 and under are free, except during the Festival of Lights when the cost is $17 per person. The museum is $2 per person donation. Both are closed during all major holidays.
  Ages: 8 years and up.

MOTTE HISTORICAL MUSEUM

(951) 928-3210 / wwww.mottemuseum.com   !

28380 Highway 74, Menifee

Housed in a huge old barn are about two dozen beautifully and lovingly restored, gleaming vintage automobiles that are from the personal collection of the Motte family. From the horseless carriage through the 50's some of the cars here include an old Ford Tractor, an early fire truck, a 1924 Model T School Bus, 1926 Chevrolet Touring Car, 1951 Studebaker, and more. The cars all have info about them and that time period on placards. Some of the cars are in vignettes that describe the car era, such as the 50's car with a mini soda fountain in the background, or one car surrounded by a garage setting (albeit a clean one!) with tools. On the walls are giant photos and murals of old Menifee and more history. Upstairs are display boards that show and tell the local history of the valley. School and other groups are welcome to take a guided tour that include a movie in the old time cinema, too.

Hours: Open Wed. - Sun., 10am - 4pm.

Price: Free
Ages: 4 years and up.

PENNYPICKLE'S WORKSHOP - TEMECULA CHILDREN'S MUSEUM

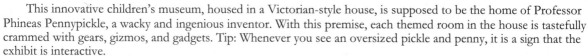

(951) 308-6370 - workshop; (951) 308-6376 - gift shop / www.pennypickles.org
42081 Main Street, Old Town Temecula

This innovative children's museum, housed in a Victorian-style house, is supposed to be the home of Professor Phineas Pennypickle, a wacky and ingenious inventor. With this premise, each themed room in the house is tastefully crammed with gears, gizmos, and gadgets. Tip: Whenever you see an oversized pickle and penny, it is a sign that the exhibit is interactive.

The small center room in the hall (i.e., the flight and aviation room) has a hot air balloon basket to climb into where kids can ring a bell, tug on a rope to activate pretend flames, pull on knobs, and peer through a periscope and telescope. Experiment with the Bernoulli effect using a vacuum and ball, and "use" an old-fashioned switchboard, telephone, and adding machine. Peer into a doorway window in the hall to see an adjoining looooong hallway - an optical illusion.

The library contains a time-travel chair (not really) that uses centrifugal force via modified bike wheels. This room is packed with books, maps, and clocks that tell the time all over the world. There are also clothes, hats, and costumes to dress up in. The best part of this room is the secret passageway. Walk through the fireplace into a maze with black lights that leads to the bedroom, or perception and illusion room. Try grabbing the springs in a broken clock (you can't); duck under a triangular-shaped fence to look at yourself through a kaleidoscope of mirrors; and walk into a wardrobe closet to look through a one-way mirror that hangs over a sink in an adjacent bathroom (not a real bathroom). The people on the bathroom side tend to make very funny faces in the mirror at what they think is just themselves.

The music room contains a grand piano that is hooked up to numerous other instruments that hang on the wall - drums, banjo, flute, trumpet, and more - that play when corresponding piano keys are pressed. Speak into an old-fashioned mike, which is really a voice modulator that delays speech and changes voices with a turn of a dial. A jukebox and records decorate this room. The kitchen, or chemistry and physics room, has a sink filled with very small magnet pieces that can be sculpted into various shapes. Open the frig, stove, microwave, and other appliances. Check out the fake cake hovering in a plastic container - it demonstrates how maglev (short for magnetic levitation) trains operate. I like the peanut butter and jelly maker invention on the wall with the ingredients going through all the coils and jars. The small room off the kitchen, the pantry, demonstrates earthquake safety via a seismograph, shake table (press the button), and proper food storage.

The dining room features an electrolight-o-later chandelier that uses disco lights, a bug zapper, and other unique items. Flip switches on and off to see the power usage of incandescent, fluorescent, and other wattage and redirect lines of current. Harness power by touching a static wall and see how your body acts as a conduit. Run a magnet across a TV screen to see all the colors change as beams of electrons move. (Don't do this at home.) Best of all, go through a secret passageway crawl space which leads to a recycling basement room. The recycling room shows how bottles can be transformed into t-shirts and how cans are crushed, recycled, repackaged, and reused. In the back of the house, a small toddler room has great murals plus stuffed animals, soft foam shapes to build with and crawl into and through, and a play cash register to purchase toys and food. One more bright feature to this museum is Everbright, a large, hanging panel with hundreds of colorful, rotating LED lights with which to create patterns and designs.

The gift shop offers one of the best selections of scientifically-oriented toys and games that I've encountered. There are also tables available in a room off the gift shop to eat snacks and food. This is definitely a field trip and school outing destination. Ask about or peruse the website for information on the numerous special programs that explore topics from the science of jellybeans to knights to hot air balloons to slime factory dinosaurs. Since the museum is located in Old Town, take some time to shop around.

Hours: Open Tues. - Sat., 10am - noon, 12:30 - 2:30pm, 3pm - 5pm; (Fri. night, 5:30pm - 7:30pm for science adventures); Sun., 12:30 - 2:30pm and 3pm - 5pm. (The museum is closed for a half hour in between sessions for clean up.) Closed Mon. (but open some holiday Mon.) and major holidays.
Price: $5 per session for ages 3 and up; children 2 and under are free.
Ages: 1½ - 12 years.

PERRIS VALLEY HISTORICAL MUSEUM

(951) 657-0274 / www.perrismuseum.com
Fourth Street and D Street at the Santa Fe Depot, Perris

This 1892 renovated, Victorian red brick building, once the home of the historic Santa Fe Depot, now displays a restored survey wagon originally used by city founder, Fred. T. Perris. The museum also exhibits farming equipment, mining tools, vintage clothing, and artifacts regarding Native Americans, and from families from the surrounding area. Note that the SOUTHERN CALIFORNIA RAILWAY MUSEUM (pg. 373) is just down the street.

Hours: Open Thurs. - Sun., noon - 3:45pm.
Price: Free, donations appreciated.
Ages: 6 years and up.

RIVERSIDE ART MUSEUM

(951) 684-7111 / www.riversideartmuseum.org $

3425 Mission Inn Avenue, Riverside

This beautiful and historic two-story art museum, originally built in 1929, contains a printmaking center, classroom and youth gallery, library, atrium restaurant, rooftop courtyard, and over twenty rotating exhibits a year in four of the galleries. The galleries display traditional and contemporary paintings, photographs, and sculptures with a focus on American, Californian, and specifically, Inland Empire artists. Just outside the museum is an expanse of green lawn to walk or run around. Down the street is the RIVERSIDE METROPOLITAN MUSEUM (pg. 368) and TIOS TACOS #1 MARISCOS (pg. 344), which is a folk art experience and great place to eat. This museum, and several others in the area plus galleries, are open for free, October through May for community events: the first Sunday of each month for First Sundays, with crafts and activities for families, 1pm to 4pm; and on the first Thursday, 6pm to 9pm, for Riverside Arts Walk.

Hours: Open Tues. - Sat., 10am - 4pm; Sun., noon - 4pm. It is also open the first Thurs. of every month during Riverside Artswalk from 6pm - 9pm. Closed Mon., and most holidays, plus the week of Christmas until the day after New Year's.
Price: $5 for adults; $3 for seniors, students with I.D. and educators; ages 11 and under and military are free. Entrance is free on the first Thurs., 6pm - 9pm and the first Sun. (October - May), 1pm - 4pm. See info on the Bank of America Museums on Us (pg. xi) free museum days.
Ages: 7 years and up.

RIVERSIDE METROPOLITAN MUSEUM

(951) 826-5273 / www.riversideca.gov/museum

3580 Mission Inn Avenue, Riverside

This museum contains numerous collections and a wealth of information and fun for both kids and adults. At the time of this writing, it was undergoing a major renovation. So, please check the website for the re-opening and details on exhibits, prices, hours, etc. as it has been a great museum that they are making even better!

Ages: 2 years and up.

SOUTHERN CALIFORNIA RAILWAY MUSEUM

See the entry for SOUTHERN CALIFORNIA RAILWAY MUSEUM (pg. 373), under   !/$$$
TRANSPORTATION, for details.

TEMECULA VALLEY MUSEUM / TEMECULA - OLD TOWN

(951) 694-6450 / www.temeculavalleymuseum.org   !/$

28314 Mercedes Street, Temecula

Mosey on over to Old Town Temecula and enjoy an hour or so shopping along Main Street. This western strip of town looks and feels authentic, right down to its wooden sidewalks. The over 100 antique and specialty shops offer many unique gift items for sale, making it an alluring place to shop, even with children.

The museum is located by a corner park - Sam Hicks Park, which has a small playground, and a large rock inscribed with the names of pioneers. The small museum is an interesting glimpse into Temecula's past. On the first floor a few tools, household goods, guns, saddles, and army equipment portray life on the local ranches and frontier towns. There are also some Native American artifacts, plus memorabilia from Erle Stanley Gardner, the author of the Perry Mason stories and a one-time resident of Temecula. At the more interactive second-floor room, there are rotating exhibits. When we visited, my boys became a part of the Old West mostly by dressing up in vintage clothing and sitting on a pretend horse (I brought my camera!), plus looking at facades that depicted a frontier town. Kids also sold or bought pretend items at the well-stocked mercantile store; put on a puppet show; cooked over a play 1880's stove; made imaginary s'mores over the pretend fire at the Mormon Battalion campsite; and more. Don't miss PENNYPICKLE'S WORKSHOP - TEMECULA CHILDREN'S MUSEUM (pg. 367) which is a great children's museum located just down the street.

Hours: Open Tues. - Sun., 10am - 4pm. Closed Mon. and holidays. Main Street shopping is usually open daily, 10am - 6pm.

Price: Suggested donation of $5 per person; $10 per family.

Ages: 5 years and up.

WESTERN SCIENCE CENTER

(951) 791-0033 / www.westerncentermuseum.org

2345 Searl Parkway, Hemet

Kind of in the middle of nowhere (no insults intended) this small, yet terrific, state-of-the-art museum complex holds a fascinating array of history, such as ice age beast fossils unearthed while preparing for construction on the adjacent Diamond Valley Lake. The huge room to the right of the entrance holds three particularly eye-catching exhibits: Max, a colossal (i.e. ten-feet high) mastodon whose remains were discovered on the grounds; Xena, a behemoth mammoth; and an almost seven-foot tall composite of a giant ground sloth. Another mastodon has been somewhat reburied beneath the room's floor; it is visible via tempered glass. Visitors can actually walk on the glass and look down into the re-created dig site. Also on display are skulls of dire wolves and an extinct bison; the skull and leg bone of a sabertooth; the teeth and jawbone of mammoths and mastodons; and mammoth tusks.

This room, set up to look like a study lab, is very hands on. Supplies are given to do rubbings of a short-faced bear, sloth, saber-toothed cat, and more. Look through large magnifying glasses to view fossils of gophers, owls, kangaroo rats, and snakes. Rotate a knob that triggers a brush and blower (under glass) to sweep away sand and dirt from imbedded fossils. Become a critter-scene investigator and study case files to determine how victims die. Follow the tracks on the ground. And best of all, cast your own fossil mold to take home by using the provided lump of clay and pushing it into molds of a saber-toothed cat tooth, a golden eagle talon, or mastodon tooth. Let it air dry while you explore the rest of the museum. This room also hosts rotating exhibits, such as Brain Teasers with twenty-one mind boggling puzzles, and Art meets Science where guests design bridges, towers, and more using planks.

And don't miss the Harley Garbani - Dinosaur Hunter exhibit which features some unusual treasures - a replica skull of a giant dinosaur Tyrannosaurus rex and one of a baby Triceratops, plus part of an extinct camel and other original and replica fossils that this local namesake found on his digs.

The central hallway is set up like a geological time line, with alcoves containing displays. The Big Dam Hole (you might want to rephrase that one when you mention it to the kids) answers the question - Where are the dinosaurs? It also visually and textually explains about the inhabitants (people and animals) that once lived in this area. Press a button to hear about hydrology, climate, native peoples, water, and the dam. See a cut-away adobe-style home in another section. Other alcoves host rotating exhibits such as heirlooms from families of this area and Remains of the Day, which has Native American baskets and scenes from years ago accompanied by sound effects.

Make sure to see a show in the 270-degree immersion theater which is set up like a cave, with boulders for seats, albeit comfortable ones with flat tops. Watch the seven-minute animated *Echoes of the Past* about how this valley looked thousands of years ago, and the ten-minute *Discovery and Recovery* documentary regarding the excavation here. Both are excellent and kid and adult friendly. The very cool thing is that when the heavy-footed mammoths and mastodons thunder on the screen, you feel it - literally! The theater floor and seats vibrate and rumble along with the movies.

If fact-finding is your passion, incorporate the audio tour for an additional $2. Visitors, school groups, scouts, day campers, and others are invited to participate in a multitude of down-to-earth programs such as working a simulated dig site; workshops; summer camps and labs; and the monthly Science Saturdays, offered the first Saturday of every month for a time of learning, talking with scientists, and doing a craft. More than just a sandbox, the dig site excavations take place on site with elements such as heat, wind, and dust aiding in recreating an actual dig. Replicas of artifacts and fossils are buried to be exhumed through real-life scientific methods. Perhaps your child's future career of archaeology or paleontology will be discovered in the past!

Note that the on-site curation unit, research labs, and education and learning center with several classrooms take up almost half of the Center's buildings. These facilities provide space and resources for research and advanced educational training, as well as acting a repository for paleontological and archaeological materials and finds.

See details on the neighboring DIAMOND VALLEY LAKE COMMUNITY PARK AND AQUATIC CENTER (pg. 355) and DIAMOND VALLEY LAKE (pg. 354).

Hours: Open Tues. - Sun., 10am - 5pm. Closed Mon., New Year's Day, Easter, Thanksgiving, Christmas Eve, Christmas Day, and New Year's Eve.

Price: $8 for ages 13 and up; $6.50 for seniors and students (13 - 22); $6 for ages 5 - 12; free for children 4 and under and military with current ID.

Ages: 4 years and up.

WORLD MUSEUM OF NATURAL HISTORY

(951) 785-2209 or (951) 785-2500 / www.lasierra.edu

4700 Pierce Street in Cossentine Hall on the campus of La Sierra University, Riverside

This quality museum is tremendous in its comprehensive scope of minerals and unique (and several endangered), taxidermied animals. Full-grown and young animals are displayed according to species. The old and new world primates - or monkeys, gorillas, and chimps - all look so life like! The size and variety of the Crocodiles of the World is impressive. We had not heard of at least half the ones featured here. The Indian Gavial is especially unique with a snout that resembles a long, thin saw blade. The numerous types of turtles are similarly astounding. They range from the very small to the gigantic alligator snapping turtle. Snakes of the World boasts another record-breaking variety, ranging from boas, pythons, and common garters, to venomous snakes and even a two-headed snake. Other reptiles, including the world's largest Komodo dragon (365 pounds at time of death!), are also on display. Birds from all over the world are represented here, such as pelicans, flamingoes, penguins, an eagle blue-face, and a blue-hued hunting green magpie. Some of the more unusual animals on display are the flat-headed cat, bats (one is just the size of a pin), armadillos (one is rolled up into a ball), a bush dog, pangolin, linsang, Columbian little spotted cat, a kangaroo, and an Indian rhino.

An outstanding collection of rocks and minerals are grouped, in one section, according to color. (I loved the blue agate.) These include large specimens of amethyst, malachite, etc. Other groupings include meteorites, fluorescent minerals (look at them under black light), geodes, opals, and huge slabs of petrified wood. There is also a large display of sphere balls or, in kidspeak, "cool-looking bowling balls." Part of this display shows the progression of a chunk of raw rock to a cube and then to the finished, sphere product. A fine display of Indian artifacts, such as arrowheads and headdresses, is also noteworthy. Pick up a copy of the paper scavenger hunt to help kids partake in what they see. The World Museum of Natural History is a gem of a place!

Hours: Open Sat., 2pm - 5pm, or weekdays by appointment.

Price: Free; donations gladly accepted.

Ages: 2 years and up.

—POTPOURRI—

BUILD-A-BEAR WORKSHOP (Riverside County)

Riverside - (951) 688-8690; Temecula - (951) 719-1389 / www.buildabear.com

Riverside - 1299 Galleria at Tyler; Temecula - 40820 Winchester Rd. at the Promenade Mall

See the entry for BUILD-A-BEAR WORKSHOP (Orange County) (pg. 315) for details.

Hours: The stores are open Mon. - Sat., 10am - 9pm; Sun., 11am - 7pm.

DISNEY STORE (Riverside County)

Riverside - (951) 687-1581; Temecula - (951) 296-0557 / www.disneystore.com

Riverside - 1149 Galleria at Tyler; Temecula - 40820 Winchester Road in The Promenade

See DISNEY STORE (Orange County) (pg. 316) for details about this interactive and magical store! See PROMENADE SUMMER KIDS CLUB and PROMENADE MALL (pg. 361) for details on other things offered at the Temecula location.

Hours: Open Mon. - Fri., 10am - 9pm; Sat., 10am - 7pm; Sun., 11am - 6pm.

Price: Free

Ages: 1 - 10 years old.

—SHOWS AND THEATERS—

LANDIS PERFORMING ARTS CENTER - PERFORMANCE RIVERSIDE

(951) 222-8100 / www.performanceriverside.org; www.inlandarts.com; www.landispac.com

4800 Magnolia Avenue at Riverside City College, Riverside

Performance Riverside is the resident troupe that performs Broadway-style musical theater at the Landis Performing Arts Center. Most of their productions are suitable for the family and all are professionally produced and presented. Past shows include *The Music Man*, *Ragtime the Musical*, and *Evita*. The Children's Series is the perfect introduction to theater for youngsters. Past shows have included *The Elves and the Shoemaker*, *Tom Sawyer*, *The Little Mermaid* and *Schoolhouse Rock Live!* Teachers note that school field trip performances, called Discovery Theatre, are usually given on a Friday morning at 10am and cost about $8 per student ($16 for teachers and parents), but field trip

reservations must be made by the May prior to the next performance season. Check the website for more information.
Hours: Call for a schedule.
 Price: Prices can range from $29 - $50, depending on the seating and the type of show.
 Ages: 5 years and up, as children 4 and under are not admitted to shows other than Sat. matinees.

OLD TOWN TEMECULA COMMUNITY THEATER

(866) OLD TOWN (653-8696) / www.temeculatheater.org
42051 Main Street, Temecula

$$$$

In the heart of Old Town is a contemporary theater. With over 350 seats, an orchestra pit, balcony, and box seats (even a courtyard outside), the theater accommodates all manner of shows - musicals, dramas, community presentations, concerts, plays, dances, and more. The theater, and the quality and variety of its productions, is another jewel for the city of Temecula.

Make sure to spend some time, probably before your show, walking and shopping Old Town. Also see PENNYPICKLE'S WORKSHOP - TEMECULA CHILDREN'S MUSEUM (pg. 367) which is a great children's museum in the immediate vicinity.
Hours: Call for a schedule of shows.
 Price: Prices vary, ranging from $15 - $50, depending on the show.
 Ages: 4 years and up, depending on the show.

RIVERSIDE COMMUNITY COLLEGE PLANETARIUM (ROBERT T. DIXON PLANETARIUM)

(951) 222-8090 / www.rccshows.weebly.com
4800 Magnolia Avenue at Riverside Community College, Riverside

$$

Come see a truly star-studded show at the college planetarium! The theater seats fifty-five people and each presentation has a live narrator. Different shows study various aspects of astronomy such as constellations, revolutions (the earth's, not a country's), galaxies and measuring distances between them, lunar eclipses, and what makes the sun shine.

School groups, or other groups, of up to fifty-five people can schedule a time to rent out the theater for $75 to see fifty-minute shows such as *Sun's Family*, or *Finding Your Way in the Sky*, or others. These shows are geared specifically for elementary-aged kids. There are several shows and programs geared for secondary grade levels, too. *Christmas Star* is offered only in the month of December, to the public and for groups. It explores the possible origins of the Star of Bethlehem, utilizing biblical passages and astronomer's technology and understanding of the heavens.
Hours: Public shows are offered March - May and December, once or twice a month on Fri. nights at 7pm. Groups
             can call to make reservations at other times.
 Price: Public shows are $5 for adults; $4 for students; $2.50 for children 12 and under. Cash or checks, only.
 Ages: 7 years and up.

STARLIGHT DOS LAGOS 15 THEATRES

(877) 795-4410 - show times; (951) 603-0654 - other inquiries / www.starlightcinemas.com
2710 Lakeshore Drive, The Shops at Dos Lagos, Corona

$$$

Movie showings include: 3-D movies; EPEX; one "new" classic on the big screen that shows for a week for only $7 per person; special presentations; first-run films; and a summer series for kids for $1 per kid-friendly movie (and popcorn and soda for another $1 each) on select weekdays.
Hours: Call for show schedules.
 Price: Check the website for show prices. The first shows of the day are $5. Shows all day and evening on Tues. and
             Thurs. are also only $5 (an additional $2 for 3-D movies and $1 for EPEX), and on Sun. before 6pm.
 Ages: 3 years and up, depending on the film.

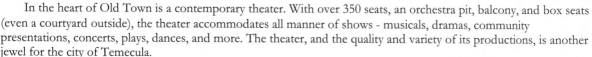

—TOURS—

CALIFORNIA PIZZA KITCHEN (Riverside County)

See the entry for CALIFORNIA PIZZA KITCHEN (Los Angeles County) (pg. 196) for more information.

DEJONG'S DAIRY

(951) 674-2910 / www.dejongsdairy.com

31910 Corydon Road, Wildomar

$$

    This thirty-two-acre, family-owned-and-operated dairy invites you to come and buy really fresh eggs and milk, as well as pre-packaged snacks, beverages, souvenirs, and animal feed from its little convenience store. You might come here just to pet and feed the enclosed animals including goats, ducks, geese, a pig, rabbits, sheep, peacocks, and a variety of birds.

    With a minimum of fifteen people, take a one-hour+ tour and learn all about the daily dairy operations, from cow to bottled milk. (Note: If you have less than fifteen people for a tour, you might be able to be added onto another group.) See the over 100 cows, perhaps watch a baby calf get bottle-fed, walk through the barn where the cows are milked and then through the processing plant where milk is put into containers. Included in the tour are fun "extras" such as feed for the farm animals, and chocolate milk and cookies. (I brought a cooler to purchase and bring home even more chocolate milk - it is so rich and creamy!)

Hours: The dairy is open daily, 8am - 8pm. Tours are offered Tues., Wed., and Fri. between 9am and 11am, by reservation.

Price: Tours are $5 per person; ages 1 and under are free. Groups of over 30 are $3 per person.

Ages: 4 years and up.

FENDER VISITOR CENTER

(800) 856-9801 / tours@fender.com / www.guitarfactorytours.com

$$$

301 Cessna Circle, Corona

    Tune in and take the hour-long Fender Factory Tour to see the step-by-step transformation from raw wood and other materials to the glossy finished product of an acclaimed Fender guitar. As the guided walking tour goes through each section of the factory - the wood mills, metal shop and final assembly - you see and hear about the process that goes into creating a guitar and amp, and you see and even meet many of the workers. The rows and rows of necks hanging are amazing as is the quantity (thousands) of wooden bodies which are sanded, painted (look overhead at one point and see hundreds of them drying), buffed, and polished and finally, assembled. It's a very up close, personal, informative and fun tour and it's interesting to see how much is truly hand crafted. For the "wow" factor, the last area of the tour is the "Dream Factory". This is the custom shop where you will see, and salivate over, some of the most unique and high-end custom guitars. And this is as close as I will ever get to owning one. Know that you must wear closed-toed shoes for the tour, there is a maximum of six people, and that reservations are made through email: tours@fender.com. Note: The Visitor's Center isn't open at the time of this writing. Rock on.

Hours: Tours are given on Thurs. at 10am by advance reservation only.

Price: $10 per person.

Ages: Must be 10 years and up.

—TRANSPORTATION—

AMTRAK (Riverside County)

(800) USA RAIL (872-7245) / www.amtrakcalifornia.com

    Ride the rails! See AMTRAK (Los Angeles County) (pg. 208) for more information.

BIKE MAPS (Riverside County)

    See BIKE MAPS (Orange County) (pg. 328) for information.

BIKE TRAIL: SANTA ANA RIVER (Riverside County)

(714) 973-6615 - Yorba Regional Park / www.santa-ana-river-trail.com; www.bike.lacity.org

Beginning point: 5215 Green River Road, Corona. Great entry point: 7600 E. La Palma Avenue in Yorba Regional Park, Anaheim. Ending points: Pacific Coast Highway, Sunset County Beach, Huntington Beach

    This bike path is planned to eventually be 110 miles long - from the mountains to the sea. In the meantime, the continuous, almost thirty mile, mostly easy-riding trail extends from Green River golf course in Riverside County through beautiful Yorba Linda Regional Park to a premiere beach, Huntington Beach. Some parts of the bike path are paved; some are packed dirt. Some sections go along a street, while others encounter more nature. Another chunk of trail ranges from Waterman Avenue in San Bernardino to the beginning of the National Forest line, just after the City of Mentone. The first website is wonderfully detailed about entry points, amenities, etc.

The first five miles from the Green River golf course have moderate hills, while the rest of the trail is fairly flat. Starting from or continuing through Yorba Linda park, these few miles are park-scenic, then meander through an adjacent wilderness area with shade trees and flocks of birds, mostly waterfowl such as ducks and egrets. A good stopping point (and maybe turning around area?) is about the fifteen-mile mark, just before the Honda Center at 2695 E. Katella Avenue, where a pocket park has the necessary amenities. (Bring your own snacks, though.) Hearty bikers - bike on!

Hours: The regional park is open daily, 7am - 8:45pm.
Price: The regional park charges $3 per vehicle Mon. - Fri.; $5 on Sat. - Sun.
Ages: 5 years and up.

METROLINK (Riverside County)

(800) 371-LINK (5465) or (951) 222-7000 / www.metrolinktrains.com

$$$

See the entry for METROLINK (Orange County) (pg. 331) for details.

Ages: All

PERRIS AUTO SPEEDWAY

(951) 940-0134 / www.perrisautospeedway.com

$$$$

18700 Lake Perris Drive at the Lake Perris Fairgrounds, Perris

Get up to speed and race to this premier half-mile oval dirt race track. Competitions include super stocks, street stocks, champ trucks, dwarfs, sprint cars, cruisers, night of destruction and more. Join in on the dance contest (or not) that happens before the race begins. A sound system in the 8,000-seat grandstand is hooked up to speakers so the audience can hear, even over the roar of the engines. Huge tip: There is adamantly no reentry once you go in!

Hours: Call for a schedule of events - often times Sat. at 5pm.
Price: Tickets start at $15 for adults; $5 for ages 12 and under.
Ages: 6 years and up.

SOUTHERN CALIFORNIA RAILWAY MUSEUM

(951) 657-2605 or (951) 943-3020 / www.oerm.org

!/$$$

2201 S. 'A' Street, Perris

If you are a train aficionado, make tracks to the Southern California Railway Museum where you can really go full steam ahead! This sixty-five-acre, unique, outdoor museum is best described as a continuous work in progress. Numerous railcars from all over the country, in various states of disrepair, find their way here. Some are being restored while others are just stationed at the yard and inside buildings. Walk around the massive property to see which railcars the volunteers are working on, take pictures, soak in ambiance from yesteryear, and/or learn more by taking a guided tour.

Walk through the several car houses (i.e., buildings that house railcars) to see historic Yellow Cars (which my kids thought looked like school buses), a San Francisco cable car, electric railway streetcars and locomotives dating from 1900, steam engines, and wood passenger cars. The car houses are open during the week whenever volunteer staff is available; they are almost always open on the weekends.

Check out the Middleton Collection that includes old toy and scale model railroad cars, and others. There is an ongoing video that shows how tracks are laid. We got derailed at the gift shop, which offers videos, books, and all sorts of train paraphernalia.

The museum is open daily, but weekends are the prime time to visit as this is the only time when train and trolley rides are available. Purchase an all-day ride ticket which is good for rides on a locomotive, electric trolley, streetcar, freight car, and/or passenger car. (Three types of cars are usually running.) Note: Steam locomotives operate on the third weekend of the month between September and May, and during certain special events and major holidays. Each ride lasts about fifteen minutes and a conductor explains the history of the vehicles and the museum, and the impact of train transportation in Southern California. The train's whistle, the clickety-clack of its wheels, and the clanging of streetcar bells add excitement to your adventure.

A real treat for an engineer wanna-be is to actually be one, for an hour, with a program called Run One. Up to four people can share the rental hour to ride with an engineer and actually operate the locomotive on the museum railway. You must be 18 years old to actually "drive," but ages 5 and up can ride along with an adult. This activity is available on Mondays, Wednesdays, and Fridays, and ranges between $250 to $350, depending on the type of train; $750 for a real steam locomotive. They all include a true fashion statement - an engineer's cap. Reservations are required. Another option is to simply ride with an engineer in the cab on regular operating day (when a train is available) - ages 5 and up can do this for an additional $10 per person for a diesel-powered train and $20 per on a steam engine train. Cab riders must wear long pants and closed-toed shoes.

A few picnic tables and grassy areas are also on site. Ask about the special events throughout the year, such as the bunny train, Rail Festival, Civil War reenactment, pumpkin train (and pumpkin patch), Thomas the Tank Engine appearance and rides, Santa Christmas train, and Railroadiana Swap Meet. The museum also conducts school, scout, and several other acclaimed program and group tours throughout the week; you can even charter a trolley and train ride for your group for $5 to $7 per person. Note that just up the street, at the corner of Ellis and A Street, is Rotary Park - you passed it on the way to the museum. The small, sand-based playground has swings, slides, a twisty metal climbing structure, picnic tables, and a few trees.

Hours: The grounds are open daily, 9am - 5pm. Train and trolley rides are available only on weekends and major holidays, 11am - 5pm. Closed Thanksgiving and Christmas.

Price: The museum is free. Weekend, all-day ride passes are $12 for adults; $8 for ages 5 - 11; children 4 and under ride free. A $40 family pass is good for 2 adults and all the kids in the family.

Ages: All

YOUNG EAGLES PROGRAM (Riverside County)

(877) 806-8902 - national number; (951) 847-5474 - chapter #1 / www.flabob.org; www.eaach1.org; www.youngeagles.org

4130 Mennes Street at Flabob Airport, Riverside

See the entry for YOUNG EAGLES PROGRAM (Los Angeles County) (pg. 216) for details. This particular airport also features a half-hour ground school and preflight instructions, plus a snack bar and small souvenir store, and perhaps a chance at the controls while in the air. Reservations are required.

Hours: Usually the second Sat. of the month, except December, starting at 7:15am.

Price: Free

Ages: 8 - 17 years old.

—ZOOS AND ANIMALS—

MAGNOLIA BIRD FARM (Riverside County)

(951) 278-0878 / www.magnoliabirdfarms.com

12200 Magnolia Avenue, Riverside

See the entry for MAGNOLIA BIRD FARM (Orange County) (pg. 334) for details. The main difference between the two is size, with this location being almost three times as large. The aviary here includes parakeets, love birds, finches, and quail, as well as doves and pigeons.

As springtime brings the birth of new baby birds, kids can sometimes see them being hand fed through the glass walls. Tour groups, for ten to fifteen people, will learn about seed, such as which kind is best for what species; see and study a (live) white dove; and more.

Hours: Open Tues. - Sat., 9am - 5pm. Closed Sun., Mon., the first two weeks of August, and some holidays. Reservations are needed for the free, half-hour tour.

Price: Free

Ages: All

MR. JOE'S FARM

(951) 657-8408 / www.mrjoesfarm.org

20850 Old Elsinore Road, Perris

Of the twenty, or so, animals, that consider this farm home, there are typical farm animals - chickens, goats, a few sheep, donkeys, cows, miniature horses, and some pigs, plus dogs and cats -and there are non-traditional farm animals - ducks, geese, tortoises, alpacas, llama, peacocks, and a two-hump camel. It's a rural, low-key atmosphere for kids to interact with the animals as most of them (the animals, not the kids) like to be pet. Many of the animals aren't in enclosures, but just like to hang out with humans and their other animal friends. The owners can take you on a tour where you learn each animal's name and preferences. One of the owners' visions is to enable special needs kids to connect with the animals. Looking for a place to have a birthday party and/or to donate your time to help in upkeep? Contact Mr. Joe.

Hours: Tours/entrance is available by appointment only, Mon. - Sat., 10am - 4pm; Sun., 1pm - 4pm.

Price: By donation.

Ages: All

—PALM SPRINGS—

PALM SPRINGS (and the surrounding desert cities)

I know that Palm Springs, and the surrounding desert communities, are officially part of both Riverside and San Bernardino Counties. I've grouped them all together under "Palm Springs" because I think most people refer to this area as a destination in and of itself. Creative liberties? (Or just thinking like a tourist!)

A collage of words and images used to come to mind when I thought about Palm Springs and the other areas - desert, hot, resort, homes of the rich and famous, golf, and shopping mecca. Now that my family has thoroughly explored them, I can add to this list - kid-friendly, fun, beautiful, great hiking opportunities, and educational treasures. Note that the Palm Springs Bureau of Tourism publishes free guides that have up-to-the-moment happenings. Call (800) 347-7746 or (760) 778-8418, or check their website at www.visitpalmsprings.com. for information. To get around downtown and uptown Palm Springs easier, catch the BUZZ, a free trolley service with thirty stops and four trolleys operating Thursday through Sunday from 11am to 1am.

ADVENTURE HUMMER TOURS

(877) WE-HUMMER (934-8663); (760) 285-0876 / www.adventurehummer.com   6/$

74880 Country Club Drive, Palm Desert

The great outdoors is awesome, and sometimes it is wonderful to see it from inside a really cool car like an open-air Hummer H1 or more luxury, air-conditioned H2. (A little pampering doesn't hurt.) The all-terrain vehicles do quite a bit of climbing - up and down mountain sides, taking you into some incredible places.

One of the most popular tours is the Joshua Tree Adventure, an excursion that goes into Joshua Tree National Park, a place that boasts the highest bio diversity in the U.S. And the 360-degree view is spectacular! The open-air hummer (my preference for the Indiana Jones-style ride) is mostly back roads in and through parts of Joshua Tree not seen by regular tourists - along the Big Game Corridor and to and around incredible rock formations with opportunities to get out and walk around to explore. You'll see and learn about geology, Native American plants, earth's history and more as each of the tours are hosted by a learned and versatile naturalist who makes your time an outstanding and educational experience. This tours also goes through the canyons of the San Andreas Fault, which is marvelous to see and encounter first-hand. Take this daytime tour or see your surroundings in a new light and book this as a sunset tour.

Several other tours are offered, as well - one with a focus along the San Andreas Fault, one to the Salton Sea near bubbling mud holes, and another throughout the city of Palm Springs. Depending on your adventure, your tour will last between one to ten hours.

Hours: Open daily - call to schedule a tour.

Price: The four-hour Joshua Tree open-air tour is $169 for adults, $139 for ages 16 and under; the Joshua Tree luxury H2 tour is $229. The three-hour, open-air San Andreas Fault tour is $149. Check the website for substantial discounts.

Ages: 7 years and up.

AGUA CALIENTE CULTURAL MUSEUM

(760) 323-0151 or (760) 778-1079 / www.accmuseum.org   !

219 S. Palm Canyon Drive, Palm Springs

This small, tribal museum relates the history and culture of the Agua Caliente Band of Cahuilla Indians via changing exhibits. Baskets and the meaning behind the street names in Palm Springs are included. School tours feature an explanation of the exhibits, demonstrations, and a video presentation. The museum also offers classroom visits and field trips.

Hours: Open September - May, Wed. - Sun., 10am - 5pm; June - August, Fri. - Sun., 10am - 5pm. Closed New Year's Day, Easter, Thanksgiving, and Christmas.

Price: Free

Ages: 7 years and up.

BAGDOUMA PARK

(760) 347-3484 or (760) 347-4263 / www.coachella.org; www.myrecreationdistrict.com
84620 Bagdad Avenue, Coachella, CA

This sprawling, forty-six acre park has several baseball/softball fields (with stadium seating) and soccer/football fields, tennis courts, several basketball courts, three play areas, and a swimming pool. The gated swim center has a pool with two enclosed slides, a small grassy area with a picnic table, and a covered wading pool for younger ones. One playground has twisty and straight slides; colorful, metal climbing apparatus; a raised tube to crawl through; monkey rings (instead of monkey bars); and a play car. The other two play areas have similar equipment, although one is much smaller and one has a really big - tall, wide, and double-sided - rock climbing wall. A seasonal water spray ground is here, too, with water fountains shooting up from the ground on a somewhat covered, cement pad.

Hours: The park is open daily, sunrise - sunset. The pool is open mid-June - Labor Day, daily, 12:30pm - 3:30pm, plus Mon. - Thurs., 7pm - 9pm and Fri. - Sun., 6pm - 9pm.

Price: The park is free. The swim center is $3 for adults; $2 for ages 17 and under.

Ages: All

BIG MORONGO CANYON PRESERVE

(760) 251-4800; (760) 363-7190 / www.bigmorongo.org; www.blm.gov
11055 East Drive, Morongo Valley

This massive preserve is a favorite and a visual treat as it can be unexpectedly lush with a variety of trees and plants, and fresh water marshes and springs in contrast to the more traditional dry desert landscape. The quietness of this peaceful preserve was broken by shouts from my kids whenever they spotted a lizard, bunny, roadrunner, or other animals. Other wildlife here includes bighorn sheep, raccoons, coyotes, and so many species of birds that people come just to observe them. Bring binoculars!

The trails are relatively easy to walk, and many of them go in and through the canyon and trees, along the willow-lined seasonal creek. There are several short, looping trails on the boardwalk, making them stroller and wheelchair friendly, as well as a longer hike of almost ten miles (round trip) along the Canyon Trail, extending the length of the canyon. Note that the preserve's terrific website offers a great trail map and detailed description of the trails.

Several educational programs and tools, such as microscopes and field guides, are available to school groups.

Hours: Open daily, 7:30am - sunset. No dogs or pets allowed.

Price: Free

Ages: 3 years and up.

BOOMERS! - Cathedral City

(760) 770-7522 / www.boomerspalmsprings.com
67-700 E. Palm Canyon Drive [111], Cathedral City

This huge, family-fun center (the first castle off Highway 111), offers a variety of entertainment for everyone. Choose from two funtastically-themed **miniature golf** courses; **go carts**; **bumper boats** (avoid the shooting fountain waters or get refreshed); and two climbs at a thirty-two-foot tall **rock climbing wall**. Each of the above attractions are $9 apiece (ages 4 and under are free for mini golf), $2 for passengers, if that's applicable. Boomers also has **batting cages**, over 200 video and sport games, a prize redemption center, and a snack bar serving pizza, corn dogs, nachos, and more. Kids should do well in school for a lot of reasons, but also because they earn free tokens for good grades.

Hours: Open most of the year, Mon. - Thurs., noon - 8pm, with go karts, bumper boats, and rock wall opening at 4pm; Fri., noon - 11pm, with go karts, bumper boats, and rock wall opening at 4pm; Sat., noon -11pm; Sun., 11am - 8pm. Open later hours in the summer and on school holidays.

Price: Attractions are individually priced above, or purchase one of packages, such as all day, unlimited play starting at $22.99. Purchase tickets online for discounts.

Ages: 4 years and up.

BRAILLE INSTITUTE (Rancho Mirage)

(760) 321-1111 or (800) 272-4553 / www.brailleinstitute.org
70251 Ramon Road, Rancho Mirage

Kids, as well as adults, often have preconceived ideas on what visually impaired people can and cannot do. A forty-five-minute tour through this institute enables visitors to see, firsthand, how well blind people can function. A tour guide, who is legally blind, takes your family or group (up to thirty people) around the campus and classrooms to look at the computers, art room, cooking facility, garden, and any other area that teaches life skills. Visitors are encouraged to ask questions - it's the best way to learn! You can also arrange to watch a film on being visually impaired and/or to have a special speaker, and you may be able to stand on a talking scale, something I personally opted out of doing. Visitors receive a card with the Braille alphabet - try it and see if you can discern the difference in letters.

Hours: Tours can be arranged any day with a minimum of 10 participants.

Price: Free

Ages: 8 years old and up only.

CABAZON DINOSAURS

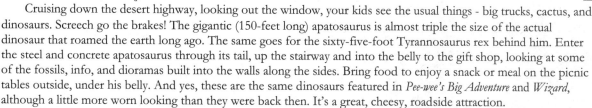

(951) 922-8700 or (951) 922-0076 / www.cabazondinosaurs.com   !/$$$$
50800 Seminole Drive, Cabazon

    Cruising down the desert highway, looking out the window, your kids see the usual things - big trucks, cactus, and dinosaurs. Screech go the brakes! The gigantic (150-feet long) apatosaurus is almost triple the size of the actual dinosaur that roamed the earth long ago. The same goes for the sixty-five-foot Tyrannosaurus rex behind him. Enter the steel and concrete apatosaurus through its tail, up the stairway and into the belly to the gift shop, looking at some of the fossils, info, and dioramas built into the walls along the sides. Bring food to enjoy a snack or meal on the picnic tables outside, under his belly. And yes, these are the same dinosaurs featured in *Pee-wee's Big Adventure* and *Wizard*, although a little more worn looking than they were back then. It's a great, cheesy, roadside attraction.

    More fun starts when you head toward the back, to Mr. Rex's Dinosaur Adventure. Go through a cave-like entrance, with an inset of baby dinos in the cave wall, into a huge gift shop filled with everything dinosaur (and then some) - books, models, t-shirts, stuffed animals, stones, etc. There are two robotic dinosaurs in here that move and roar; two large dinos to actually ride ($2 a ride); and a big dino skeleton. Colorful posters and info panels abound sharing facts and fiction regarding the origins of dinosaurs and of man from a creationist perspective. In a separate video room the best seats are the dino eggs chairs where visitors can watch films and documentaries given from a creationist's view point.

    Stroll through the outdoor dino garden (my term for it) on a gravel and hard-packed pathway lined with over fifty dinosaurs of all sizes and species amidst palm trees and other plants with a backdrop of desert hills. There are stegosauruses, scary-looking velociraptors, T. rexes, brachiosauruses, and dimetrodons, as well as dinosaur families and a statue of a lion and lamb. Photo ops abound! This garden also boasts a good-sized, covered, hands-on dino dig (basically a place to play in the sand), plus a sluice where you can pan for gemstones for free, trying your luck with leftovers, or purchase a bag of dirt with gems planted in it - $5 to $10 per bag, depending on size and quality of gems.

    A highlight (pun intended) is climbing the steps (that get narrow and steep towards the top), which are lined with greenery, logs, info posters, and models of dinosaurs, to the top of the extra large T. rex you saw from the parking lot (i.e. this is the T-Rex Museum). You are now in his mouth, behind his rows of sharp teeth! Tip: Look up and see why his eyes glow red at nighttime.

    School field trips, play groups, or any type of or age group are welcome, as are individuals and families. Note that there are some fast-food restaurants in the immediate vicinity as well as a sit-down restaurant. All in all, this is a *dino*-mite stop!

Hours: Open daily, 10am - 4:30pm. Closed Thanksgiving and Christmas. The apatosaurus store is open on select weekdays and on weekends, 10am - 4:30pm.

Price: Free to look and just walk around the two dinosaurs out front. Entrance to the museum/dino garden is $12 for adults; $8 for seniors and military; $10 for ages 3 - 12; ages 2 and under are free.

Ages: All

CABOTS PUEBLO MUSEUM

(760) 329-7610 / www.cabotsmuseum.org $$$$
67616 E. Desert View Avenue, Desert Hot Springs

    This four-story, thirty-five-room, Hopi-style pueblo with sixty-five doors and 150 windows, was built out of the side of a mountain. Cabot, the owner and builder, believed in mysticism and an Indian belief that symmetry retains an evil spirit, so he constructed the abode with slanted doorways and floors, uneven walls, windows with odd shapes, and small, narrow doorframes and staircases. (It looks like our house before we remodeled.) The almost one-hour tour includes the fascinating history of Cabot and his pueblo.

On the first floor is a cave-like bedroom (raised off the floor to avoid rattlesnakes), a living room with a dirt floor, a Kiva (i.e., prayer room), a small art gallery, a smaller Alaskan room, and a kitchen. Some of the artifacts in these rooms include ceremonial Indian costumes, headdresses, drums, carvings, pottery, baskets, and a rock collection. The upstairs belonged to Cabot's second wife and contains a series of rooms - a tiny bathroom, bedroom, kitchen, and more - displaying "finds" from Cabot's travels. It also has a short and small (one to two people at a time can go up) meditation tower that oversees some of the grounds.

The outside grounds are almost as eclectic as the inside house, with an enormous (forty-three-foot tall) Indian statue carved from a giant Sequoia, old signs, and some rusted tools and equipment. There is also a small picnic facility, a multi-room gift shop and visitor's center. School tours and other group tours offer a wide range of topics - call to schedule one.

Hours: Open October - May, Tues. - Sun., 9am - 4pm. Tours are offered at 9:30am, 10:30am, 11:30am, 1:30pm, and 2:30pm (last tour), and limited to 12 people at a time. Open June - September, Wed. - Sat., 9am - 1pm. Tours are offered at 9:30am, 10:30am and 11:30am. Closed Mon., Tues., (in the summer), and on major holidays.

Price: $13 for adults; $11 for seniors and ages 6 - 12; children 5 and under are free. The grounds and gift shop are free.

Ages: 7 years and up.

CAP HOMME / RALPH ADAMS PARK

(760) 346-0611 / www.cityofpalmdesert.org
72500 Thrush Road, Palm Desert

The park offers twenty-seven acres of natural desert - hills and cactus - to hike through, plus a picnic table under a thatched roof near a few palm trees by the trailhead. The Homestead Trail winds up into the mountains (take a moment to soak in the sights of the sprawling desert and the valley below) and just before it connects with the much longer Hopalong Cassidy Trail, there is a shaded rest stop. Continue along the narrow dirt trail, up and down some steep grades, and keep right to the Gabby Hayes Loop. Follow the trail along the road for the final bit, making your hike about 2.5 miles in length. Cap Homme is just part of the Cahuilla Hills Trails System. Bring water and sunscreen.

Hours: Open daily, dawn - dusk.

Price: Free

Ages: 6 years and up.

CHILDREN'S DISCOVERY MUSEUM OF THE DESERT

(760) 321-0602 / www.cdmod.org
71701 Gerald Ford Drive, Rancho Mirage

The desert, well known for golf and retirement living, boasts of a terrific museum for children. The building is deceptive. Its architectural style befits an art museum, and its high ceilings are complemented by numerous windows and tall, pastel, modular room dividers. Upon entering the lobby, my middle son whispered, "Are you sure this is a hands-on place for kids?" Most definitely!

The exhibits flow easily from one to another, and they do change, so the ones written about here might not be here when you visit, but they give you an idea of how wonderful this kids' museum is. Note that no strollers are permitted inside.

Some of the scientific exhibits in the front include a music machine of sorts, where a touch on a metal sculpture produces a jazz or percussion musical sound, and a stroboscope, which is a display where kids can draw their own design, attach it to the fan, and watch it "dance" in the strobe light. Follow any one of three colored ropes through a kid-size, spider-web-looking rope maze. Get properly suited up with a safari hat, goggles, and gloves and use the tools provided to find faux artifacts in a simulated dig. Climb a rock wall, complete with hand and foot holds. Pull! Or at least pull yourself up on the pulley system and see how much weight you can pull. Try to follow light and sound patterns by tapping different icons. Design and implement a sort of tunnel/roller coaster using tubes and platforms that balls go through. Build with Keva planks and blocks. Turn the gears to see a chain reaction at the gear wall. The relatively large MakerSpace work area is a real treat for kids who like to take apart radios, computer components, and other household gadgets and repurpose them. They can even use the screwdrivers, glue, pieces of wood, and recycled materials to make a new creation to take home. (Parents will be thrilled!) The magnetic wall promotes ingenuity by creating a sculpture from magnetized household objects. Young weavers can add a few layers on the giant loom. The

Art Corner has paper, markers, and a computer with art programs. Animation is harder than it seems as kids try to make their own short movie at this station. The Braille station and wheel chair racer enable kids to experience how those physically challenged have to maneuver differently to get around in the world. Toward the back of the museum is a well-stocked, pretend grocery store with mini-carts and a checkout counter. Pizza, every child's favorite food, can be made to order just next door. This pizzeria has all the ingredients (made from cloth) to make pizzas, as well as aprons, hats, and a pretend brick oven, plus tables and chairs for "customers." An enclosed toddlers' play area and a real CHP motorcycle are also located in this wing.

Walk up the snake-like, winding ramp to the second story to Grandma's Attic Room. This area is decorated with old trunks, hat boxes, fishing poles, pictures, and adding machines and telephones. One of the best features is the quality costumes in which to play dress up. They range from princess dresses with sequins to military uniforms to suits and everything in between. Lots of hats, an assortment of shoes and boots, plus boas and ties are some of the accessories.

The above merely lists the highlights of the museum! Parental supervision is required at all times but, as each activity was so much fun, I was delighted to participate, too. Both the adjacent Dinah Shore theater and the outdoor amphitheater put on a variety of performances year round. Note that there is a grassy play area between the buildings, along with a sand table, balls and other toys, plus a garden and small maze. Ask about plethora of special programs and classes offered for children, such as art classes, ballet lessons, manners classes, educational tours for students (of course!) and lots, lots more.

Hours: Open Labor Day - November, Tues. - Sat., 10am - 5pm; Sun., 1pm - 5pm. Also open on school holidays, Mon., 10am - 5pm. Open December through Labor Day, Mon. - Sat., 10am - 5pm; Sun., 1pm - 5pm. Open every third Wed., 5pm - 8pm. Closed New Year's Day, Thanksgiving, and Christmas.

Price: $9.95 per person; $7.95 for active military; children under 1 are free. Admission on the third Wed. from 5pm - 8pm is $5 per person.

Ages: 2 - 11 years.

CHUCK E. CHEESE'S (Palm Springs area)

See the entry for CHUCK E. CHEESE'S (Los Angeles County) (pg. 18) for details.

CIVIC CENTER PARK AND AQUATIC CENTER

(760) 568-9697 or (760) 346-0611; (760) 565-7467 - aquatic center / www.cityofpalmdesert.org; www.palmdesertart.com; www.desertymca.org; www.pdpool.com

73510 Fred Waring Drive (and San Pablo Avenue), Palm Desert

The beautiful seventy-acre park, bordered by the civic center and the sheriff's station, encompasses a good portion of land and offers a wide variety of things to do and see. There are four baseball fields; six tennis courts; pickleball courts; a dog park; four volleyball courts; three basketball courts; a YMCA building; a tot lot; a playground for older kids with great play equipment and imagination-inspiring apparatus; an amphitheater for concerts and special events; jogging paths; a beautiful lake with bridges and fountains; a rose garden; acres of wildflowers; artwork; and a skate park. There are about twenty-five works of art, mostly bronze sculptures and some memorials, scattered throughout the park land. Favorite pieces include the large abstract baseball catcher titled "Today"; "The Dreamer," a two-piece work of art depicting a young man reposed on the grass with his stomach being part of the lawn; and the figures of children. The Holocaust Memorial is powerful with the faces of the statues etched in pain, an eternal flame, and a place to repose and ponder.

15,000 square feet of the skate park are designed for the advanced skater. It has two connected bowls, one four feet in diameter and one six feet, plus boxes, pyramids, rails, drop ins, and stairs. The other 5,000 square feet are geared for beginners with a shorter pyramid, box, drop in, and rails. The skate park is lighted, fenced, and monitored. Skaters must wear a helmet and pads, have a signed parental waiver for ages 17 and under, and have a registration card, which costs $5 a year. Note that there are special days/times for bikes only to use this park, too.

Located at 73751 Magnesia Falls Drive, at the northeast corner of the park, the aquatic center has an Olympic-size pool, with competition diving platforms, and a recreation pool and a zero depth area, all of which are open year round. The splash pool, open seasonally, is ideal for kids to enjoy its wavy slides, fun fountains, and colorful water play structures. There are a few slides in this section, too. The center also features changing rooms, a multipurpose room, and a concession stand open to all pool and park users. Consider it your civic duty (and a lot of fun!) to visit the Civic Center Park.

Hours: The park is open daily, sunrise - 11pm. The skate park is open during the school year, Mon. - Fri., 2pm - 9pm; Sat. - Sun., 8am - 9pm. It is open during the summer and on holidays daily, 8am - 9pm. The lap and rec pool in the aquatic center are open year round, Mon., Wed., Fri., 11am - 3:45pm; Tues. and Thurs., 11am - 7pm; Sat. - Sun., 11am - 5pm. The splash pool is open in warmer weather, daily, usually mid-March - September. Call for specific hours as they might vary.

Price: Free. The skate park is $5 per year. The aquatic center is $4 for adult Palm Desert residents, $6 for adult non-residents; $3 for senior and ages 6 - 12 residents, $4.50 for non-residents; $2.50 for ages 2 - 5 residents, $3.75 for non-residents.

Ages: All

COACHELLA VALLEY HISTORY MUSEUM ☀

(760) 342-6651 / www.cvhm.org $$$

82616 Miles Avenue, Indio

Each city desires to preserve its history and make it available for future generations. The Coachella Valley Museum does so through various collections inside the three buildings on the park-like grounds and gardens. Each room inside the Smiley-Tyler House is dedicated to a different aspect of the valley. The first room, fittingly, contain baskets, pottery, stone mortar and pestles and other artifacts from the first settlers, the Cahuilla Indians, as well as photos (not of the Cahuilla!) and diagrams. Visitors are encouraged to touch sandals made of plants, shell necklaces, baskets, and plants. Other rooms focus on water and agriculture, with an interactive exhibit where you can touch a button corresponding to a photo and hear about supply and demand; plus a railroad room with a desk, signs, lanterns and other railroad memorabilia; a fully-arrayed 1926 kitchen with cans, jars, pots and pans, a butter churner, very old toasters, icebox, stove and other appliances; and an homage to farming set up like a feed store with some old farm tools, a telephone, crates of food, and old-time photographs. Another room is a fully-equipped doctor's office with all the instruments and devices a physician would need.

85% of the nation's dates are exported from the Coachella Valley, so go inside the nicely-laid out Date Museum to see displays, videos and explanations of date farming and learn the date's non-romantic history. Go under the huge fake date palm leaf to see a video, then enjoy a pictorial timeline and glass displays containing equipment used to farm dates, colorful Middle Eastern costumes, packaging, and related date items.

If you ever wondered what school was like in the early 1900's, visit the handsomely-restored, 1909 Indio Schoolhouse to answer that question. The one-room schoolhouse is set up with desks, blackboards, old books, crayons, and other implements - let the lessons begin! School groups, especially, enjoy hands-on learning in the schoolhouse - so different from modern-day ones.

Outside, on the beautiful grounds, are lots of old agricultural tools, machinery, and farm equipment, plus fire and railroad equipment, and even an outhouse. Peek inside the blacksmith shop to see forges, anvils, tongs, and other tools and look at the saw mill and adobe replica. Check out the desert submarine (a "hut" for RR workers to keep warm) and water tower. Stroll among the garden sections in the "back" of the museum which include a Japanese garden, rose garden, and a lovely desert garden growing native plants that the Cahuilla Indians used, interspersed with boulders. The working date garden is spacious and help connect the learning gained from the museum into real life. Take a guided tour of the entire museum to learn background information on the articles here and to get a rich, visual sampling of history.

Hours: Open October - May, Mon. and Thurs. - Sat., 10am - 4pm; Sun., 1pm- 4pm. Open June - September, Fri. - Sat., 10am - 4pm. Open at other times for school and private tours. Closed New Year's Day, Thanksgiving and Christmas.

Price: $8 for adults; $6 for seniors; free for ages 18 and under and active duty military. Admission is free on the first Sun.

Ages: 5 years and up.

COACHELLA VALLEY PRESERVE ☼

(760) 343-2733 - visitor's center; (760) 343-1234 - park / www.coachellavalleypreserve.org; www.cnlm.org

29200 Thousand Palms Canyon Road, Thousand Palms

This 18,000-acre preserve, with its twenty-eight miles of hiking trails, is not only immense, but diverse in topography and wildlife. The preserve straddles Indio Hills and the infamous San Andreas Fault. Thousand Palms Oasis (I'm not sure it contains quite this many palm trees) is at the heart of the Coachella Valley Preserve. The oasis is supported by water constantly seeping along the fault line.

Start at the rustic visitor center that has a few natural history exhibits behind glass. The displays include arrowheads, mounted insects, birds' nests, and eggs. Just outside the center is a small oasis with very large palm trees, including "shaggy" ones, that have several picnic tables nestled among them. From here, first walk on planks that cover the swamp-like surrounding ground and then hike the one-mile trek to the most popular destination, the pond. Most parts of the path are not very stroller/wheelchair friendly.

Kids begin to appreciate the many faces of the desert as they hike through the preserve. It's sandy, dry, and rocky, and these elements create sand dunes, bluffs, and mesas. It is also mountainous and interspersed with dense palm trees, cacti, and various other vegetation. Some of the trails are as short as one-quarter mile, while others are longer at one-and-a-half miles, and more. If the visitor's center is closed, a downloadable hiking trails map is available on the website.

Bring a water bottle and/or a picnic lunch and have a delightful time exploring desert wilderness at its finest.

Hours: The preserve is open October - April, daily, 7am - 5pm; open May - September, daily, 6am - 8pm. The visitor's center is usually open daily, 8am - 4pm, but closed June - August and all major holidays.

Price: Free

Ages: 4 years and up.

COACHELLA VALLEY WILD BIRD CENTER

(760) 347-2647
!

46500 Van Buren Street, Indio

This center offers a wonderful opportunity to learn about native wild birds in a variety of ways. The small inside exhibit room has taxidermied animals, literature, and a few other displays, as well as several iguanas and live snakes such as rosy boas, racers, and king snakes. Outside are enclosures that hold birds that have been injured, imprinted, or abused. Some are releasable; some are not. The enclosures hold several owls, including great horned owls, plus hawks, geese, quail, and others. Knowledgeable volunteers are on hand to answer questions about the birds - why they are here, what they eat, why they are not good to have as pets, and lots more good information. Beyond this area are fenced-in wetlands with reeds, a few ponds, and more life-sustaining elements. Sandpipers, mallards, pelicans, and other waterfowl nest here, or at least drop in for a visit. Bring binoculars and/or take a look from the viewing towers. Bring a sack lunch to take advantage of the on-site picnic area. School and other tours are available.

Hours: The center and wetlands are open daily, 8am - noon. A guided bird walk tour is offered the first Sat. of each month, October - May at 8am.

Price: Free; donations are appreciated.

Ages: 4 years and up.

COVERED WAGON TOURS

(800) 367-2161 or (760) 347-2161 / www.coveredwagontours.com
$$$$$

Washington Street, Thousand Palms

Travel in a mule-drawn, covered wagon for a two-hour narrated tour of the Coachella Valley Preserve. You travel along the San Andreas fault and see three oases and perhaps some wildlife as the naturalist shares information about the geology, plants (which ones were used for food and which ones for medicinal purposes), animals, and way of desert life, both past and present. Occasionally, you get out and walk a bit along the way. The wagons are not the primitive ones that pioneer ancestors used, as these have padded seats, springs, tires, and other amenities, although part of the fun is the bumpiness of the ride. This is a great family outing as the Old West appeals cross generationally. School groups guides will tailor the tour to include facts about Western expansion, and an emphasis on geology and earthquakes.

Take just the tour, or add on a chuck wagon cookout lunch or dinner and cowboy entertainment for the full western experience. The tasty barbeque lunch/dinner consists of chicken, tri-tip, beans, coleslaw, garlic bread, and pie with topping, plus beverages. The entertainment usually consists of a singer with a guitar, although sometimes it's cowboy poetry or Native American dancing. After your meal and the show, you are invited to grab a skewer and roast some marshmallows over the campfire. The whole experience takes about three-and-a-half hours.

Hours: Open end of October - end of April. Call for tour and dinner times. A minimum of 12 adults are needed for any outing. If you are a family group, ask to add on to another group. Reservations are required.

Price: Tours only are $40 for adults; $20 for ages 7 - 16; children 6 and under are free. Tour and lunch, or dinner, costs $76 for adults; $38 for ages 7 - 16; children 6 and under are free. Ask about group rates.

Ages: 5 years and up.

DATELAND PARK

(760) 398-3502 / www.coachella.org
51805 Shady Lane, Coachella

This terrific park equals fun. The spacious skate park (about 12,000 square feet) has the necessary street elements - ramps, rails, pyramids, boxes, and plenty of skating area and spectator seating enclosed in perimeter fencing. The small, seasonal water-play spray area has water that spurts up from the ground and down from fake palm trees. There are also grassy fields for open play; a covered picnic area; lots of pavement, and a kind of dirt trail for bikes, scooters, and strollers where one loop around the park equals one-quarter of a mile; and sizable, wonderful, covered playgrounds with wood chip flooring. One of the play areas has a giant, geo-shaped climbing structure with heavy duty ropes crisscrossing all over its inside and bars on the outside. A slide tower, with several curvy and straight slides emanating from it, also has a rock climbing wall attached. There are numerous slides, swings, bridges, large metal climbing coils, platforms, talking tubes, and plenty of places to play on and under the structures. Make a play date with your kids to come to Dateland Park.

Hours: The park is open daily, sunrise - 10pm. The skatepark is open daily, 6am- 10pm.
Price: Free
Ages: All

DEMUTH

(760) 323-8272 - city; (760) 320-6430 - community center / www.palmsprings-ca.gov
3601 E. Mesquite Avenue, Palm Springs

This long and large park has several amenities for families - a grass volleyball court; four tennis courts; lots of picnic tables with shade trees; plenty of run-around, grassy areas; two soccer fields; six baseball diamonds; walkways throughout the park; and several climbable, colorful, sculptured metal shapes. The two good-sized playgrounds have a few twisty slides and even enclosed slides, plus swings, and a rock climbing wall on what looks like a large sandwich board. A community center is open Mon. - Sat.

Hours: Open daily, sunrise - 10pm.
Price: Free
Ages: All

DESERT ADVENTURES

(888) 440-JEEP (5337) or (760) 324-5337 / www.red-jeep.com   6/$
67555 E. Palm Canyon Drive, Cathedral City

Explore the natural wonders of the desert by choosing from several different excursions via a two- to five-hour, seven-passenger jeep ride. I almost feel like these adventures should be required for school kids and anyone else who has a desire to learn, as all the guides are wonderfully knowledgeable about history, geology, plants, animals, Native American heritage, and more.

The three-hour San Andreas Fault tour is a great combination of learning Native American culture and heritage, and seeing geography (hopefully not too much in action!). Guests go through archaeology sites; an authentically recreated Cahuilla Indian village; a hidden, lush oasis; and a stream, all the while learning about the history of the Palm Springs area and the Cahuilla Indians, plus how they used the local plants. Also on this tour, through no *fault* of their own, visitors may also straddle the San Andreas Fault line, as well as inspect a fossil bed and look at the great geography. Going at sunset and adding stargazing was a personal favorite. Besides seeing God's masterpiece sunsets on His original canvas, you also walk into the San Andreas Fault as the area is transformed by shadows and, eventually, the dark of night. Millions of stars appear in the sky (at least out here in the desert!) and you study them using telescopes and even laser light pointers.

Besides the Adventures privately-owned 800 acre Metate Ranch, other tours can involve hiking around different areas, such as the Indian Canyons Jeep & Hiking tour and the Mecca Hills/Painted Canyon Jeep tour. Bighorn sheep, coyotes, and other wildlife are abundant along these back roads, so keep your eyes open. Bring your camera! Dress appropriately with closed-toed shoes and a hat, and bring sun block, sunglasses, and a water bottle. Be informed that restrooms are nonexistent, except for the bushes beyond the bend in the road. Check out the Desert Adventure website for year round and seasonal adventures, as well as additional excursions, such as the tour with the wind turbines and Whitewater Preserve.

Hours: Open year round, weather permitting. Call first to make a reservation.

Price: Three-hour tours are $139 for adults; $124 for seniors; $114 for ages 12 and under. Call for other tours and prices and check the website for specials.

Ages: 6 years and up.

EL DORADO POLO CLUB

(760) 342-2223 - games info; (760) 831-POLO (7656) - Clubhouse reservations / www.eldoradopoloclub.com
50950 Madison Street, Indio

This club features ten polo fields (and just one is really big as it's the size of nine football fields!), a stick and ball field, an exercise track, and stabling for 400 horses. Visitors are invited to come and watch an exciting game of polo where the thundering hooves and "whack" of the mallet keep eyes riveted on horses and riders. Practice matches are generally held during the week. View matches from the Cantina restaurant and field side patio on Saturday at noon and Sundays at 10am. Arrive early as seating is first-come, first- served. For $10 per person, view Sunday afternoon games from the Clubhouse, which offers a full-service menu and bar as well, or bring a picnic lunch to enjoy on the grass or have a tailgate party (Sundays only) in areas north and south of the Clubhouse, for free. Make reservations at the restaurants or arrive early to grab a picnic/tailgate spot.

Hours: Practices are Wed. - Fri. and spectators are welcome. Games are played some Sat. at 10am and noon, and sometimes 2pm; Sun. at 10am, noon and 2pm. The season runs (or gallops!) January - mid-April. Call or check the website for a schedule for other specific practice and game times.

Price: Watching the practices and games is free (as is tailgating), unless it's a special event, when parking could be $10. Parking on Sun. is $10

Ages: 3 years and up.

FELLOW EARTHLINGS WILDLIFE CENTER

(760) 363-1344 / www.fellowearthlings.org
11427 West Drive, Morongo Valley

"Awwww - so cute!" That's the first thing we exclaimed when we entered the enclosure with the small mob (i.e. group) of about seven meerkats at this unique center. We spent our allotted two hours sitting on the ground as the meerkats ran around (constantly!), dug holes (constantly!), climbed up the fence, climbed on us, fed out of our hands (we wore gloves), and entertained us by their constant antics. As we took pictures and played with them using paper bags, balls, stuffed animals, and other items, Pam, the proprietor, taught us so much about the cute little critters. We learned about their habits, their personalities, how to care for them, that they do not make good pets, and much more. Note that this center partnered with Animal Planet for *Meerkat Manor* and that Pam consulted for Disney for Timon's character in *Lion King*.

The encompassing rustic grounds are beautiful with numerous huge old oak and pine trees, a quaint-looking cottage, and a rock-lined pond with a large paddlewheel and short waterfall. Don't *meer*ly read about Fellow Earthlings, come by for a visit! Each visit is considered an adoption and you are sent a portfolio for the meerkats and information on them. Each visit is for two hours, costs $100, and is for up to four people - no more. It is a private visit - your group is the only one on the grounds. Visitors must be in good health and be able to sit relatively quietly for two hours, on the ground. The facility and enclosure are not handicapped accessible.

Hours: Visits are available May - September on select Fri., Sat., and Sun. You must call or email beforehand to schedule a visit.

Price: $100 for up to 4 people.

Ages: Must be at least 8 years old.

FORTYNINE PALMS OASIS

(760) 367-5500; (760) 367-5502 / www.nps.gov; www.hikespeak.com
Fortynine Palms Canyon Road, Twentynine Palms

Part of Joshua Tree National Park, this moderate, delightful, three-mile (round trip) trail cuts through desert hillside and sparse vegetation and around red boulders leading to a cool, green oasis in the canyon. Depending on the season, the water trickles or streams into a smallish pool that provides a drinking hole for the wildlife and waters the numerous fan palm trees here. (The palm trees look like they're wearing shaggy coats.)

The view from the hilltops is great - you can see all around the valley and Twentynine Palms area. You can also clearly see some of the surrounding fault lines. It's too hot to hike here in the summer, but its a great hike through rugged scenery at other seasons. Regardless of when you come, bring plenty of water!!!

Hours: Open daily, sunrise - sunset.
  Price: Free
  Ages: 7 years old and up.

FREEDOM PARK

(760) 346-0611 / www.cityofpalmdesert.org
77400 Country Club Drive, Palm Desert

Feel free to find something wonderful to do at the twenty-six acre Freedom Park. It has three baseball fields, with stadium seating and a concession stand; three basketball courts; two tennis courts; two sand volleyball courts; two huge fields for soccer or football; plenty of open, grassy areas; a small, narrow skating area with a few ramps and rails; a small and a large dog park; plenty of covered picnic tables; hard packed dirt/sand walking paths throughout; gardens (it's a usable and scenic park!); and three playgrounds. One play structure looks ready to set sail as it is designed like a ship with portholes, plus slides and ladders. Another area has swings, animals on big springs to ride and rock on back and forth, slides, and cargo rope to climb. The last playground captures the imagination as the apparatus looks like abstract art. There is a curved rock climbing wall; shapes to sit on and climb; cables with discs to climb up and on; a tilted trampoline ring (with no trampoline); a twisted metal pole with a small platform to twirl around on; and other unique elements.

Hours: Open daily, dawn - 10pm.
  Price: Free
  Ages: All

GENERAL PATTON MEMORIAL MUSEUM

(760) 227-3483 / www.generalpattonmuseum.com
62510 Chiriaco Road, Chiriaco Summit

Any study of World War II includes at least one lesson on war hero, General George Patton. Even if kids don't know who he is yet, they will like all the "war stuff" at the museum. Outside the memorial building are over a dozen tanks from WWII to Vietnam. Kids can't climb on them, but they can run around and play army. There are several Walls of Remembrance on the grounds with names engraved of honorees from all branches of the service and from all wars. There is a picnic area located by tanks and other vehicles.

Inside, the front room is dominated by a five-ton relief map depicting the Colorado River Aqueduct route and surrounding area. The large back room is filled with General Patton's personal effects, and lots of WWII memorabilia such as uniforms, weapons, flags, artillery, helmets, and more. Our favorite exhibits include a jeep, a lifelike statue of General Patton (who looks amazingly like George C. Scott), and rounds of machine gun bullets. Special displays showcase Nazi items taken from fallen Nazi soldiers; a small, but powerful pictorial Holocaust display; and items found on the battlefield of Gettysburg. There are also exhibits and items from WWI, the Afghanistan, Iraq and other wars, plus photographs, flags, guns, and more.

Over one million servicemen and women were trained at this huge Desert Training Center site during WWII. If your child is especially interested in this period of military history, take him to the remnants of the training camps, accessible by four-wheel vehicles. Call the museum for directions and more details. Note that the gift shop features a good selection of military-themed toys, clothing, and souvenirs.

Hours: Open daily, 9:30am - 4:30pm. Closed Thanksgiving and Christmas.
  Price: $8 for adults; $7 for seniors; $4.50 for ages 7 - 12; children 6 and under and active military are free.
  Ages: 3 years and up.

GET AIR TRAMPOLINE PARK (Palm Springs area)

(760) 206-7211 / www.getairpalmdesert.com
34450 Gateway Drive, Palm Desert

See GET AIR TRAMPOLINE PARK (Riverside County) (pg. 347) for details.

Hours: Open Mon., 10am - 10pm; Tues., 10am - noon for Toddler Time, noon - 10pm all ages; Wed., 10am - 10pm;
    Thurs., 10am - noon for Toddler Time, noon - 10pm all ages; Fri. - Sat., 10am - 9pm, and 9pm - midnight for
    Club Air; Sun., 10am - 8pm.

Price: $15 per hour for 46" and taller; $10 for 45" and under. Toddler Time is $10 per child, one adult is admitted for free. Club Air is $15 for 2 hours or $20 for all 3. Always check the website for special offers.

Ages: 2 years and up.

GUIDE DOGS OF THE DESERT

(760) 329-6257 / www.guidedogsofthedesert.com

60740 Dillon Road, Whitewater

Thirty, or so, dogs consider this place their temporary home as they are trained to become guide dogs for their blind owners. Visitors learn about the program which takes pups, places them in loving homes for eighteen months or so, then brings them back for serious training as guide dogs, and matches them with a new master or mistress. Explore the kennels where the puppies are raised (call first to see if any puppies are currently here); tour the dormitories (if they are unoccupied) where owners stay for their orientation; watch dogs being trained; learn how to treat guide dogs (i.e., when it's acceptable to touch them and when it's not); and learn how to put a harness on the dogs. Tours can last a half hour up to an hour and a half, depending on the interest of the visitors.

Hours: Tours are given by reservation, Mon. - Fri.

Price: Free; donations appreciated.

Ages: 3 years and up.

HI-DESERT NATURE MUSEUM / YUCCA VALLEY COMMUNITY CENTER

(760) 369-7212 / www.hidesertnaturemuseum.org; www.yucca-valley.org

57116 Twentynine Palms Highway, Yucca Valley

I *highly* recommend the Hi-Desert Nature Museum. It offers lots of activities and has fascinating exhibits on wildlife, geology, culture, and science. Just some of the rotating exhibits in the front room have included Wild on Wildflowers; Shake, Rattle & Roll - Living With Earthquakes; and Holiday Traditions from around the world. We saw one called Black Widow. Arachnophobia aside, the fantastic photographs, video, and information combined with live and dead specimens made learning about this feared insect interesting. The far wall in this room contains several encased displays of Indian baskets, arrowheads, pottery, and Kachina dolls.

Another good-sized room has taxidermied waterfowl, plus animals that are unique to the desert such as mule deer, quail, roadrunners, jack rabbits, and coyotes. A touch corner in here has skulls and soft fur to match to the stuffed animals.

Fossils, a sabertooth cat skull, and a wonderful rock and mineral collection comprise the earth science room. The petrified logs are unusual, as are the sphere balls. Rocks such as amethyst and malachite are shown in their rough, natural state, and also in a polished version. Raw minerals are shown next to their commercial counterparts such as fluorspar next to toothpaste and talc next to baby powder. This helps kids to make connections and understand that man-made products were first God-created resources.

A mini-zoo has live lizards, Madagascar hissing cockroaches, snakes, a tarantula, and some furry little creatures, too. A docent is often on hand to assist your child in holding one of the animals. I'm proud to write that, after recovering from my cold sweat, I held the (large!) tarantula.

The Kids' Corner is action packed. There is a small sand pit (I mean archaeological dig); animal puppets; a butterfly and insect collection; stone mortar and pestles with corn kernels to grind; animal tracks to match with animals; a touch table with whale bones, rocks, and shells; books; and containers of construction toys. The Hi-Desert Nature Museum also offers special events, kids craft programs, educational tours, and themed traveling classroom programs on insects, wildflowers, a particular animal, and more.

The community center/park just behind the museum is equally fine. It has four basketball courts; a baseball field; a skateboard park with cement ramps and steps; a sand volleyball court; a covered picnic area; grassy areas; and three playgrounds complete with slides, climbing apparatus, and swings. All this and a few shade trees are against the backdrop of Joshua trees and the desert mountains.

Opening an oyster and finding a pearl created by a grain of sand is comparable to opening the doors to this museum and finding a part of the sandy desert that has been transformed to a treasure of great worth.

Hours: Open Thurs. - Sat., 10am - 5pm. Closed Sun. - Wed. and major holidays.

Price: Free

Ages: 1 year and up.

HISTORICAL SOCIETY PALM DESERT

(760) 346-6588 / www.hspd.org
72861 El Paseo Drive, Palm Desert

This historical museum has four small rooms. The lobby holds numerous styles and models of cameras throughout the ages; a display case of marionettes used in TV shows, including the "mother" of Howdy Doody; an homage to Hopalong Cassidy; and photographs of Palm Desert as it was in the olden days. There are also photographs and some memorabilia from the famous people who have called Palm Springs home and some of the famous places in Palm Springs.

The second room holds firefighting memorabilia as this museum is located in the old firehouse. (A fire truck out front advertises this fact.) There are helmets, axes on one wall, hose nozzles, copper and brass fire extinguishers, a leather fire bucket, little plastic fire coats for kids to try on, a Darth Vaderish smoke helmet from the 1900's, and an 1820 Molly Stark fire engine pump. The next room has a 3-D wall map tracking the Cahuilla Trail (Road) and exhibits regarding water - a precious commodity especially for the desert. The tiny room off here contains a collection near and dear to my heart - chamber pots. Some of the porcelain ones are quite decorative, like the one fit for royalty made in England in 1891, as well as some basic bed pans. Hmmm. An outhouse door is attached to the wood paneled wall in here - you can open it if you want. A Nolan organ is also in this room and a few other household items. Guided tours are offered as are several annual events, such as fire safety training to school children.

Hours: Open October - May, Fri. - Mon., 10am - 3pm. Closed Tues. - Thurs., and June through September.
Price: Free
Ages: 6 years and up.

HOVLEY SOCCER PARK

(760) 346-0611 / www.cityofpalmdesert.org
74735 Hovley Lane, Palm Desert

This elongated park is mostly comprised of five full-size soccer fields. Around the perimeter of the fields is a disc golf course which is very technical because of the straight drives. Along the side of the fields, near the concession stand, are two small, covered playgrounds - one is ship-themed - with metal climbing apparatus, a short chain ladder, swings, and slides. Past the playgrounds are three horseshoe pits, which can see a lot of action, plus three shuffleboard courts, and a basketball court.

Hours: Open daily, dawn - 11pm.
Price: Free
Ages: All

INDIAN CANYONS

(760) 323-6018 - canyons; (800) 790-3398 - office / www.indian-canyons.com
38529 S. Palm Canyon Drive, Palm Springs

Vast, spectacular, and awesome are three words that come to mind when exploring Indian Canyons. Long ago, ancestors of the Agua Caliente Cahuilla Indians made their homes in these canyons and the surrounding area. Today, a large number of Indians still reside on the reservation here. The Tribal Council has opened the canyons for the public to explore.

A mile, or so, past the entrance gate is the trading post. Kids enjoy looking at the trinkets, jewelry, and Indian art work. Beyond the store are picnic grounds and hiking and horse trails.

Palm Canyon is fifteen miles long and abundant with palm trees - a stark contrast to the surrounding rocky hills. The moderately graded, paved walkway into this valley leads you along a stream and to a picnic oasis. The scenery almost makes you forget that you're hiking! Andreas Canyon is unexpectedly lush with fan palms and more than 150 species of plants, all within a half-mile radius. Walk along a stream and see unusual rock formations. Challenge your kids to look for shapes or people in the rocks. There are also Indian caves back in the canyon and old grinding stones. Learn more by joining in on a ninety-minute, one-mile, ranger-led tour offered on Friday, Saturday, and Sunday at 8am, 10am, noon and 2pm.

Hike to Murray Canyon from Andreas Canyon. Murray is smaller and less accessible, but no less beautiful. There are caves here also, which always sparks a child's imagination. Hiking in Indian Canyons is a wonderful opportunity to explore the desert wilderness surrounded by the stunning backdrop of the rocky mountains and there are several trails for all levels of difficulty. See TAHQUITZ CANYON (pg. 397) for information on another nearby canyon.

Hours: Open October - June, daily, 7:30am - 5pm (last entrance at 3:30pm). Open July - September, Fri. - Sun., 7:30am - 5pm (last entrance at 3:30pm).
Price: $12.50 for adults; $5 for ages 6 - 12; children 5 and under and military are free.
Ages: All, but older kids for real hiking.

JOE MANN PARK

(760) 346-0611 / www.cityofpalmdesert.org
77810 California Drive, Palm Desert

    This nice neighborhood park has a sand volleyball court; a basketball court; one large, gated, covered playground with plenty of space to play under the raised elements and lots of activity to play on them; an open grassy area; covered picnic tables; some BBQs; and a small waterplay area used seasonally. The waterplay is just one twisty piece of metal that shoots out water from its various holes, but sometimes that's all you need to cool off and have fun. The playground has slides, bridges, tic-tac-toe, swing, curvy metal pieces of equipment to climb on and up, ladders, and a stepping structure that looks like a small hillside.

    Adjacent to the park is a gated Rose Garden, promoted as a quiet area. It contains old shade trees, picnic tables, grass areas, and a rose garden.
Hours: Open daily, 7am - 10pm.
Price: Free
Ages: All

JOSHUA TREE AND SOUTHERN RAILROAD MUSEUM

(760) 366-8503 or (760) 366-8879 / www.jtsrr.org
8901 Willow Lane, Joshua Tree

    Nestled into the rocky, desert hillside, this site is great for those who are *loco* about trains! The trains range from two-and-a-half-inch scale models to full-size rail cars. If it's running, you're invited to ride on model trains - fully operational 15" gauge, 7 ½" gauge, and G-scale trackage - which covers about a mile of track, some of which is elevated over the ground and supported by trestles, and some goes on bridges and through desert terrain. Take a tour of the full-size cars including a diner, with its old-fashioned stove and icebox; a mail car, with small pigeonholes that are labeled with city names; a Pullman sleeping car, which always makes sleeping on a train seem romantic; and the grand finale - a caboose. Both the Live Steam Club and the railroad museum are located here. Model railroad enthusiast members cannot only work on their hobby, but engineered it so that they and guests can camp here, too.

    Inside the museum, a replicated railroad station, are model steam engines and lots of railroad memorabilia from Francis Moseley's collection. Ask to watch the video which shows how a model train operates.
Hours: Check the calendar to visit at an open event, or call to make an appointment for a ride and tour.
Price: Free; donations of $5 per adult are asked for group visits. On-site tent camping is $15; RV is $25.
Ages: 3 years and up.

JOSHUA TREE NATIONAL PARK

(760) 367-5500 - park; (760) 367-5522 - Keys Ranch tour / www.nps.gov/jotr $$$$
South entrance - on Pinto Basin Rd. at the Cottonwood Springs Visitor Center; North entrance - at 74485 National Park Dr. for the Oasis Visitor Center in Twentynine Palms; West entrance - at 6554 Park Blvd. for Joshua Tree Visitor Center. This is the best way to reach Keys View and Hidden Valley. In Yucca Valley, Black Rock Nature Center is located at 9800 Black Rock Canyon Rd., Joshua Tree

    This over 900,000-acre park gets its name from the unique Joshua trees that Mormon visitors likened to the biblical Joshua reaching up to God. Explore the riches of this national treasure by car, by foot, and/or by camping.

    Entire books are written on Joshua Tree National Park, so consider the following information a very condensed version. Just a few phrases attributed to this enormous park are "wind-sculpted boulders"; "massive granite monoliths"; "five fan palm oases dotting the park"; "wildflowers and wildlife"; "mountainous"; and "rugged." Start your visit at the main headquarters/visitors center in Oasis of Mara, located off the north entrance. You can get a map here, look at the botanical displays, and watch a slide show that gives a good overview of the park. You can also sign your youngsters up here to be Junior Rangers. Like many other national parks, when your ranger, usually between the ages of 5 to 13 years old, completes special activities and shares their answers with a park ranger, they receive a Junior Ranger badge. Who knows where this interest might take them?

One destination worth mentioning, in particular, is Keys Ranch. Explore and learn about the ranch and its colorful owners and see the numerous vestiges of the people that once lived here, including the schoolhouse and workshop. Against a backdrop of boulders, the ranch grounds are strewn with old rusty equipment and half-buried cars, and vestiges of a Desert Queen Ranch, a gold mine turned into a ranch. Ninety-minute guided tours, the only way to see the ranch, are offered Thursday through Sunday at 2pm. The cost, plus vehicle fee, is $10 for ages 12 and over; $5 for ages 6 to 11; children 5 and under are free.

If you are automobile adventurers, which is a good way to get a lay of the land, there are many roads to travel. Keys View is the most popular destination because of its breathtaking view of the valley, mountains, and deserts. (Take a panoramic shot on your camera.) If you don't mind a few bumps along the way, and kids usually don't, there are many dirt roads accessible only by four-wheel drive. Particularly outstanding is the eighteen-mile Geology Tour Road, which showcases some of the most incredible landscape the park offers.

Hiking runs the gamut from easy, one-tenth-of-a-mile trails, to strenuous, over thirteen-mile long trails. Three of the trails that offer fascinating terrain also lead to special destinations. The first one is the one-mile loop, Hidden Valley, with trails winding through massive boulders. It leads to and through legendary cattle rustlers' hideouts and past petroglyphs. The second is Barker Dam, which was built almost 100 years ago and is now a reservoir that many desert animals frequent. Approach it in whispers, if possible, so as not to scare away any critters. Encourage your children to look for some of the "hidden" wildlife in the water. The third is Lost Horse Mine, which is a rugged four-mile round-trip hike. This mine was used for prospecting and gold mining. Maybe there still is gold in them thar hills! **Bring water** no matter which trail you take because it is not supplied in the park.

Rock climbing is a very popular sport here. Even if your kids are too young to participate, they'll get a vicarious thrill at watching more experienced climbers. Boulder hopping is also fun, and that can be done by kids of all ages. There are many groups and classes that come here to climb, including a locally-based school called Joshua Tree Rock Climbing School. Call (800) 890-4745 / www.joshuatreerockclimbing.com for more information.

Camping is primitive at most of the 500 sites of the nine campgrounds in Joshua Tree. Many campsites are located in the shelter of rocks, while others, at higher elevations, offer spots of shade. It is hot during the day, much cooler at night (even cold), and at times quite windy, but kids revel in it all. Water is only provided at Cottonwood and Black Rock Canyon campgrounds, so other sites are really back to basics.

National parks are sometimes referred to as "universities of the outdoors." Joshua Tree National Park is an outstanding university to attend. Everyone will go home with a special memory, and a different reason for wanting to come back.

Hours: Open daily, 24/7. Joshua Tree visitors center is open daily, 8am - 5pm; Oasis is open daily, 8:30am - 5pm; Cottonwood is open daily, 8:30am - 4pm; Black Rock is open October - May daily, 8am - 4pm (8am - 8pm on Fri.)

Price: $30 per vehicle, which is good for 7 days admittance. (An annual pass is only $55) $15 per person if by foot, bike, horse, etc. Free for residents with permanent disabilities. Admission is sometimes free, as with all national parks, on Martin Luther King, Jr. Day; National Park Day in April; National Public Lands Day in September; and Veterans Day in November. Family campgrounds are $15 - $20 a night, depending on location.

Ages: All

KOBE JAPANESE STEAKHOUSE

(760) 324-1717 / www.koberanchomirage.com
69838 Hwy. 111, Rancho Mirage

$$$$

Knives, flames, and food - it doesn't get any better than this for my boys. Go past the waterfall over the footbridge and the koi pond to enter the somewhat dark restaurant. Quality food - seafood, Angus (not Kobe) steak, chicken, and even Oriental vegetables - with sauces and such are sliced, diced, and prepared at communal Teppanyaki grill tables, so it's kind of like having your own personal chef. Some of the menu items are teriyaki chicken, $22.00; file mignon, $37.50; scallop and tiger prawns, $32.90; Halibut steak, $36.90; teppan shrimp, $29.90; Kobe poke, $14.50. Dinners include shrimp appetizer, white rice, miso soup, vegetable blend, and hot green tea. Sherbet or green tea ice cream is dessert. Sashimi choices include maguro tuna, $13.25 and shake salmon, $12, while sushi choices include rainbow roll of snowcrab meat, cucumber and avocado topped with five kinds of sashimi, $14.90; California roll, $7.50 and several other selections. (The onion volcano is a fun thing to watch the chef cook.) Kids meals include the same appetizer, soup, veggie, and dessert as an adult. Choose from teriyaki chicken, $13.90; sirloin steak, $14.90; steak and chicken, $17.90 each; or steak and shrimp, $19.90.

Hours: Open Sun. - Thurs., 5pm - 8:30pm; Fri. - Sat., 5pm - 9pm. Reservations are highly recommended.

Price: Prices are listed above. Check out the Early Bird specials.

Ages: 5 years and up.

LAKE CAHUILLA

(760) 564-4712 - lake; (800) 234-PARK (7275) - camping reservations / www.rivcoparks.org

58075 Jefferson, La Quinta

Escape from the heat at Lake Cahuilla recreation park. The gigantic, stocked lake is a prime spot for fisherboys and girls to reel in the catch of the day. Kids 16 years and up need a state fishing license, which are not sold at the lake. Night fishing is open Friday and Saturday until 9pm April through October. Although swimming in the lake is prohibited, there is a pool available for your aquatic pleasure. (The pool is open for anyone to use, not just overnight campers.) A playground is located behind the pool - youngsters always have energy to play, no matter what temperature it is!

The park is not abundantly blessed with shade trees, but there are large grassy areas and palm trees to enhance its beauty. Hiking trails traverse the park, so make sure you've got plenty of sunscreen and water. Almost 100 campsites are available here, complete with barbecues and other amenities. Come escape the city life, if just for a day or night.

Hours: The park is open October - April daily, 6am - 10pm. It is open May - September, Fri. - Mon., 6am - sunset. The campground is open October - April, daily, but May - September Fri. - Sun., only. The pool is open April - October on weekends only, for two hour sessions starting at 11am, 1:30pm, and 4pm.

Price: Park entrance is $6 for adults; $3 for ages 2 - 12. The swimming pool is an extra $4 per person, per session. Primitive camping (space and a table - no shade trees) is $20 a site (reservations are not necessarily needed); a site with full hookups is $35 a night. The camping reservation fee is $7. Fishing permits are $8 for ages 12 and up; $5 for ages 6 - 11; children 5 and under are free. Fishing licenses are an additional fee and not available here.

Ages: All

THE LIVING DESERT ZOO and GARDENS

(760) 346-5694 / www.livingdesert.org

47900 Portola Avenue, Palm Desert

Kids can experience a lot of living in the 1,200-acre Living Desert! Choose one of three areas of interest - botanical gardens, wildlife, or hiking - or partake in some of each.

Start your visit at the good-sized children's Discovery Room with great murals and an eight-foot giant ground sloth skeleton. Replica bones and skulls are on the fossil wall. Children can get a real "feel" for desert life as they touch live snakes, turtles, and a big hairy tarantula, plus feathers, bones, rocks, and fur. They can also put together puzzles, do rubbings, look at a seismograph, and watch ants (10,000 of them) run here and there inside the ant lab. Stand in a darkened room here with a nighttime sky lit up by constellations, listening to sounds of the desert, seeing animal projections and glow in the dark animal tracks. Watch sand dunes reform as the sand blows around in an encased display.

The northern section of this "like a zoo, only better" park is mostly botanical. The pathways weave in and out amongst an incredible variety of desert floral including saguaros, yuccas, and towering palm trees. Caged bird life is abundant along the walkways, too. We took the time to really watch our feathered friends' activities and learned quite a bit.

Eagle Canyon houses twenty desert animal species living in their natural element. Powerful mountain lions, Mexican wolves, and the small fennec foxes dwell in their own craggy retreats that are easily viewed through glass. Don't miss the tree-climbing coyote! The three-acre African Village, WaTuTu has hyenas, camels, leopards, a petting zoo (but not with the aforementioned animals!), and a time for story telling. This section also houses the hospital where examinations and medical procedures occur. You can go in and see a part of this facility on your own, or take a docent-led tour.

A trail system lies to the east, traversing through some of the 1,000-acre wilderness section of the park. Three loops offer something for every level hiker: An easy three-quarter-mile hike; a moderate one-and-a-half-mile hike; and a strenuous five-mile, round-trip hike to the base of Eisenhower Mountain, all of which is open in cooler months, closed in the summer. Don't get me wrong, however, even the walk around "inside" the park is a hike in itself. If you get tired, take a shuttle ($6 for adults; $3 for ages 3 - 12) which you can hop on and off throughout the park at eleven stops throughout the day.

Animals in the Living Desert dwell in outdoor enclosures that resemble their natural habitat. A rocky mountain is home to the Bighorn sheep. Look for them leaping among the boulders. Other exotic animals include Arabian oryx, aardwolves, zebras, cheetahs, small African mammals, giraffes, and birds. We saw several other animals in the wild, too, such as a snake slithering across our path and the ever-speedy roadrunner darting out of the bushes. Seeing them authenticated the unique setting of this park. Want to see more animals, more up close? Animal Encounters is an intimate stage "show" at the outdoor theater featuring smaller residents that you see, touch, and learn about, such as hedgehogs, foxes, snakes, owls, birds of prey and others. Also check the schedule for Keeper Chats, where the animal keepers visit and talk about five different critters each day at their enclosures, such as cheetahs, hyenas, big horn sheep, and more. Help feed the giraffes at the Giraffe Feeding, between 9:30am - 2:30pm, for $6. Go on a safari ride without going to Africa by taking a camel ride here for only $6 per person for a three-minute ride. (Every day is hump day!) Go inside the aviary and hand feed small lorikeets; $3 for a cup of nectar. Every few years the aviary exhibit changes and there are butterflies housed here, so walk gently through Butterflies! Winged Wonders where 300 butterflies, from more than thirty species, fly in the enclosure. Aviary exhibits are open October through April, only. Admission is an additional $3 per person. Become a Gecko explorer - a member of a naturalist club to see more than meets the eye, for kids 6 to 12 years old, held on most Saturday mornings.

Kids will especially enjoy Gecko Gulch, a one-acre play area for youngsters. There are oversized reptile sculptures to climb on, a saguaro cactus slide (not a real saguaro), a tortoise shell to crawl into and hide, underground animal burrow tunnels, sand dune play area, a "gold" panning trough, and shade area for parents (thank goodness!). Ride the endangered species carousel for $2.

Train afficionados of all ages enjoy the acre-large, G-scale, model train exhibit with three loops and five distinct layouts. Trains make tracks past the Grand Canyon, Mount Rushmore, a California mining town, the Swiss Alps, and much more. The exhibit is usually shut down June through October for maintenance and construction.

Inquire about the numerous programs offered during the year, such as family evening adventures; almost three-hour behind-the-scene safaris; summer zoo camp; and (a favorite) Starry Safaris (i.e., sleepovers), which include a wildlife presentation, dinner, walking through the park at dark, s'mores, breakfast, and a pass to stay at the zoo for the day. Visit here during the spring when the desert flowers and trees explode in a profusion of colors, or come in the winter to see WILDLIGHTS (pg. 752). Anytime you choose to visit the Living Desert will be a time of wonder, relaxation, and education.

Hours: Open October - May, daily, 9am - 5pm; open June - September, daily, 8am - 1:30pm. Closed Christmas.

Price: $19.95 for adults; $17.95 for seniors; $9.95 for ages 3 - 12; children 2 and under are free. School groups, with reservations and a minimum of 10 students, are $6 per student for admission, $9 for parents and teachers, or $20 per person for admission plus a two-hour guided tour. See info on the Bank of America Museums on Us (pg. xi) free museum days.

Ages: All

LUCKIE PARK

(760) 367-7562 - park; (760) 367-5777 - pool / www.ci.twentynine-palms.ca.us
Two Mile Road and Utah Trail, Twentynine Palms

The best park in town, Luckie features a great playground with a twisty slide; swings; funky-shaped, metal climbing apparatus; a short rock climbing wall; and more, all on chipped wood flooring. Green grassy lawns (a rarity in the desert), three lighted basketball courts, baseball fields, a soccer field, indoor racquetball courts, horseshoe pits, a pool that's open seasonally, and a nice skate park complete this park. The mid-size skate park, which is just across the street from the park on Joe Davis Road, has a bowl, ramps, and other street elements. Helmet and pads are mandatory

Hours: The park and skate park is open daily, sunrise - sunset. The pool is open Memorial Day - mid-June, Sat. - Sun and mid-June - August daily, 1pm - 5pm.

Price: The park is free. The pool cost $3 per person; $1.50 for seniors.

Ages: All

MCCALLUM THEATRE

(760) 340-ARTS (2787) / www.mccallumtheatre.org
73000 Fred Waring Drive, Palm Desert

This beautiful theater seats over a thousand people and has three levels of seating, including box seats. First class productions include *Sound of Music, Riverdance, Cats,* and *The Nutcracker Suite,* as well as famous individual acts and artists

There are also several productions that are enjoyable for the entire family, such as the Peking Acrobats. Ask about the Field Trip Series in which slightly abbreviated dance and theater performances are given for free for students and educators - fantastic! Art is important! Tours often focus on the stage and technical aspects of the facility. Contact the McCallum for more information.

Hours: Call for a program schedule.
Price: Tickets range from $50 - $127, depending on the show.
Ages: 4 years and up.

MOORTEN BOTANICAL GARDEN

(760) 327-6555 / www.moortenbotanicalgarden.com $$
1701 S. Palm Canyon Drive, Palm Springs

This place has plenty of prickly plants along pleasurable pathways. In other words, this compact botanical garden, specializing in cacti, is a delightful stroll and an interesting way to study desert plant life. There are over 3,000 varieties of cacti, trees, succulents, and flowers, plus lots of birds! You'll see giant saguaros, ocotillos, and grizzly bear cactus, and you may walk through a greenhouse (or cactarium). Toward the entrance are petrified logs, and a few, small desert animals in cages. Enjoy this spot of greenery in the midst of the sandy, brown desert.

Hours: Open most of the year, Mon. - Tues., Thurs. - Sun., 10am - 4pm. Open in the summer, Mon. - Tues., Thurs. - Sun., 9am - 1pm. Closed Wed., Thanksgiving, and Christmas.
Price: $5 for adults; $2 for ages 5 - 15; children 4 and under are free.
Ages: All

OASIS DATE GARDEN

(800) 827-8017 / www.oasisdategardens.com   !
59111 Hwy. 111/Grapefruit Boulevard, Thermal

Is your date worth the drive? I think so. Take a twenty-minute tour first which includes watching an eight-minute movie about date growing. The video room also has date artifacts - palms, cultivating and harvesting tools, hats worn by harvesters, and the fruit. Although you can't walk through the date grove, you can go outside and hear more about date pollination and see male and female trees. Tour groups of all ages are welcome. The outside has lovely picnic grounds with a grassy area and plenty of picnic tables surrounded by towering date trees from the 175-acre ranch. Bring your own lunch, or purchase a meal in the small Oasis Date Gardens cafe inside. Meals average about $7.50 to $9.95 and include salads (try the spinach date salad), hamburger, deli sandwiches, and more, plus a wide variety of shakes from date to butterscotch to cactus and pineapple.

Back inside, choose from a variety of dates to sample and purchase, other souvenir merchandise, and a date shake. (Tip - the Palm Desert Visitor Center often has brochures regarding Oasis that include a coupon for a free, small date shake.)

Hours: Open daily, 9am - 5pm. Close Thanksgiving and Christmas.
Price: Free
Ages: 6 years and up.

OFFROAD RENTALS

(760) 325-0376 / www.offroadrentals.com $$$$$
59511 Hwy. 111, Palm Springs

Come ride the sand dunes in Palm Springs! After watching a ten-minute video on safety in a cave-like setting, put on a helmet and goggles (provided by Offroad), hop on your single-seater, four-wheel ATV, and go for an exhilarating ride. An expansive, flat area immediately in front of the rental facility is great for beginners, and it is the only place children may ride. The "course" has tire obstacles, too. More experienced riders (i.e., older) can venture out on the large sand hills beyond this area. Machines are suited to the age and size of the rider, and speed limits are built into the vehicles. (Yea!) For instance, children 6 to 10 years, or so, are assigned vehicles that can't exceed four mph. The ride here was a highlight for all of us. A beverage is included in your admission price, but bring your own sun block. Riders must wear long pants and closed-toed shoes. Ask about their two-hour, educational dune buggy tours.

Hours: Open daily, 10am - sunset. Hours might vary during the summer.
Price: Thirty and forty-five-minute rides start at $40 per person (those who obey the rules get a little longer).
Ages: 6 years and up.

THE OLD SCHOOLHOUSE MUSEUM

(760) 367-2366 / www.29palmshistorical.com   !
6760 National Park Drive, Twentynine Palms

Originally built in 1927, the old schoolhouse museum looks like an old schoolhouse room, complete with wooden desks, a flag, phonograph, books, and a blackboard. The books on display are on Native Americans, gold miners, cowboys, and homesteaders. It also houses a small research library and historical exhibits of the early settlers, mostly via pictures and written information. The small gift shop carries pamphlets on the history of this area, as well as cards and gift items. Call if you would like information on a school field trip.

Hours: Open September - May, Wed. - Sun., 1pm - 4pm; open June - August, Sat. - Sun., 1pm - 4pm.
Price: Free
Ages: 7 years and up.

THE OLD SPAGHETTI FACTORY (Rancho Mirage)

(760) 341-5600 / www.osf.com $$$
71743 California 111, Rancho Mirage

See the entry for THE OLD SPAGHETTI FACTORY (Los Angeles County) (pg. 25) for details.
Hours: Open Sun. - Thurs., 11:30am - 9pm; Fri. - Sat., 11:30am - 9:30pm

PALM CANYON THEATRE

(760) 323-5123 / www.palmcanyontheatre.org $$$$$
538 N. Palm Canyon Drive, Palm Springs

Palm Canyon Theatre specializes in light, musical theater so you'll enjoy such productions as *Oklahoma*, *The King and I*, *Noises Off*, and *Little Shop of Horrors*. Other productions include dramatic plays and Shakespeare.

Hours: Performances are usually given September - May and in July, Thurs., 7pm; Fri. - Sat., 8pm; Sun., 2pm. Kid's camps are held in June and July.
Price: Tickets usually range from $29.50 - $36.
Ages: 6 years and up.

PALM SPRINGS AERIAL TRAMWAY

(888) 515-TRAM (8726) - tram info; (760) 325-4537 - Peaks Restaurant / www.pstramway.com $$$$$
1 Tramway Road, Palm Springs

In only ten minutes, an eighty-passenger, rotating, enclosed car, carries you seemingly straight up the side of Mount San Jacinto. The scenery change in this short amount of time is almost unbelievable - from cactus and desert sand below, to evergreen trees and cool air up above. Call ahead to see if there is snow at the top because Mount San Jacinto State Park is at an altitude of 8,516 feet.

The Mountain Station at the top has a game room, a gift shop, restaurants, a snack bar, and observation areas where you can see a panoramic view of the entire valley, including the Salton Sea which is forty-five miles away. The bottom floor of the Station also has a few taxidermied animals and an interesting, twenty-minute film on the history of the tramway.

Outside, behind and down the Mountain Station building, is Mount San Jacinto Wilderness State Park, with fifty-four miles of great hiking trails, campgrounds, and a ranger station. Download a map from the website. The Desert View Trail is a delightful beginner trail at 1.5 miles, or, for younger kids the ¾ mile loop. The San Jacinto Peak is 5.5 miles, one way and leads you to the second highest point in Southern California for a spectacular view. Call (951) 659-2607 / www.parks.ca.gov for (primitive) camping information; permits are $5 and must be reserved at least 10 days in advance. Though we just walked along the easier trails, the mountain scenery anywhere up here is unbeatable! Just remember that the trail you go down from the peak Mountain Station, you must also go back up to catch the tram. During the summer on the weekends, free, forty-minute, guided nature walks are offered. In the winter you can rent cross-country skis ($21 for adults for the day) and snow shoes ($18 per person for the day) at the Adventure Center. These are available November 15 through April 15 (weather permitting), Thursday through Monday, and holidays, from 10am to 4pm. There are also plenty of areas to go sledding, snow-tubing, and, most importantly, snowman-making and snowball-throwing. Tip: Always bring a jacket and wear closed-toed shoes - it **really** does get cold up here, no matter the temperature down the mountain!

If you're hungry, inside the Mountain Station is the Pines Cafe, a cafeteria-style restaurant open from 11am to

8pm, serving pizza, $3.95; French dip sandwich, $8.95; chili, $3.95 and nachos, $4.95. Entrees for Ride 'n' Dine include vegetarian lasagna, chicken, ½ rack of pork ribs, beef burgundy, roasted potatoes, and a house salad. Fine dining is available at Peaks Restaurant for lunch - Arugula salad, $11; Avocado BLT, $15; steak and fries, $22; burger, $15; chicken club, $15; and dinner - filet of beef, $42; grilled salmon, $30; or brick chicken, $26. Children's meals are $12 for a choice of grilled shrimp, grilled cheese sandwich, pizza or grilled chicken. If you venture up the tramway after 4pm (and only after 4pm), you can purchase a Ride 'n' Dine ticket which includes a round trip tram ride plus dinner at Pines Cafe, which is served starting at 4:30pm.

Hours: Cars go up every half hour, Mon. - Fri., starting at 10am; Sat., Sun., and holidays starting at 8am. The last car goes up at 8pm, and the last car comes down at 9:45pm.

Price: $25.95 for adults; $23.95 for seniors; $16.95 for ages 3 - 10; children 2 and under are free. Ride 'n' Dine tickets are $36 for adults; $23.50 for ages 3 - 10. Parking is $5 a vehicle. Parking is free for residents of the Coachella Valley.

Ages: 3 years and up.

PALM SPRINGS AIR MUSEUM

(760) 778-6262 / www.palmspringsairmuseum.org
745 N. Gene Autry Trail, Palm Springs

Enjoy happy landings at this classy air museum, conveniently located next to the Palm Springs Airport. Inside the three hangars and outside on the grounds are usually thirty vintage WWII and Korea/Vietnam era aircraft; some come and go on a rotating basis. Most of the planes are in flight-ready condition and some are being restored. The collection can include a Grumman F4F Wildcat, Grumman 56F Hellcat, Grumman F7F Tigercat, Grumman A6 Intruder, P-40 Warhawk, P-51 Mustang "Bunny", B-17, and many more. The planes are not cordoned off, making it easier to look at them close up, although touching is not allowed. Walk under and look up into the belly of an A-26 Invader attack bomber. My kids were thrilled to see the places where it actually held real bombs!

The hangars are designated European (Army), Pacific (Navy), and B17. The planes are fascinating for the part they've played in history, and they are visually exciting for kids because most have decorative emblems painted on their sides. In the Pacific (Navy) hangar, the Pearl Harbor diorama is narrated by Tom Brokaw. Visitors can climb aboard a Grumman Goose and/or Nomad N22 cockpit and pretend to pilot it. Bunkers and displays around the perimeter of the airy hangars honor different eras of flight by featuring various uniforms, flight jackets, combat photographs, patches, model planes, combat cameras, murals, and more. Other exhibits include maps of missions, touch screens, documentaries showing on five TV screens throughout, and five, ten-foot-long replicated warships. Highlights of the European (Army) hangar include the B-25 Mitchell Bomber, P-47 Thunderbolt, P-63 King Cobra, the PT-17 Stearman, the Spitfire and the C-47 (when it's not flying).

Tour the inside of a B-17 for a donation of $5 per person; or just admire it from the outside. The children's area in this hangar has modified airplanes for them to pretend pilot (or be a passenger!), a fire truck to climb into, a mock-up tower control, a radio transmitter, airplane simulators, a spiral wishing well, where you drop a coin and watch as it spins around (and around and around), and other interactive exhibits.

Starting at 11am, the Buddy Rogers Theater continuously shows military documentaries, combat videos, or interviews with war heroes - all with an emphasis on WWII. Kids always enjoy watching small planes land and take off at the adjacent runway. For more entertainment with an *altitude*, every other Saturday hear a special guest speaker in a program that can conclude with a flyover or flight demonstration. Or, take a twenty-minute flight on a C-47 Skytrain for $195 per person, with five passengers necessary per flight. Call (844) 377-4151 to book a flight. Contact the museum to ask about their almost two-hour school and group tours (minimum age is 8) offered on weekdays. If you'd like to hear the complete history of all the planes at the museum, ask a docent as they gladly answer any and all questions. This museum also offers a plethora of other programs and events and all of them are exceptionally well done. And if all this travel has made you hungry, grab a bit to eat at the on-site cafe.

Hours: Open daily, 10am - 5pm. Closed Thanksgiving and Christmas.

Price: $17 for adults; $15 for seniors and ages 13 - 17; $10 for ages 6 - 12; children 5 and under are free. The family deal is $37 for 2 adults and 3 kids, ages 12 and under.

Ages: 4 years and up.

PALM SPRINGS ART MUSEUM

(760) 325-7186 or (760) 322-4800 / www.psmuseum.org $$$
101 N. Museum Drive, Palm Springs

There are many facets of this mid-size, museum jewel that showcases modern and contemporary American works. Different components include paintings, some specifically California-oriented and some very modern; photography; classic western art (i.e., cowboy art); Native American pottery, basketry, and blankets; and sculptures - from abstract designs to Old Couple on the Beach, which looks exactly like an old couple just sitting on a bench (although the older I get, the more I think they look middle age).

The fine arts galleries are thematically grouped and some have rotating exhibits. The George Montgomery Collection features the western star's movie posters, plus furniture, paintings, and bronze sculptures of cowboys and Indians that Montgomery designed. The William Holden Collection offers some of Holden's prized art pieces. A small gallery contains art from ancient Latin American civilizations.

The upper level room and mezzanine level have over 100 rotating exhibits of twentieth century art, which means expect the unexpected. I love seeing what's new up here. Some favorite pieces from the glass studio include Virtual Waterfall, which is a bronze, blown-glass depiction of a waterfall, and End of Day, which is an explosion of colorful and funky glass pieces shooting in different directions. My middle son has an artistic temperament, so I'm hoping art exposure will develop his talents, too! Actually, there are ample opportunities to do that at the museum as they often offer hands-on activities on the second Sunday of the month (when admission is free) with activities themed around a featured artist include, as well as KidStudio projects, camps, classes, and school tours.

The downstairs, 433-seat Annenberg Theater presents shows geared mostly for adult audiences, such as plays, ballets, operas, and concerts. Call (760) 325-4490 for more info. Even if you don't eat at the gallery cafe, which sells fresh salads, sandwiches, soups, desserts and specialty coffees, at least take a stroll through it to check out its colorful mobiles and art deco decor. Outside, all-age visitors will enjoy the small, twentieth-century sculpture garden. Inquire about the variety of guided tours offered for the public, and for school or other groups.

Hours: Open most of the year, Fri. - Tues., 10am - 5pm. Closed Wed. and major holidays.

Price: $12 for adults; $10 for seniors; ages 18 and under and active military are free. Admission is free on Thurs. from noon - 8pm during the street fair VillageFest and on the second Sun. of every month. See info on the Bank of America Museums on Us (pg. xi) free museum days.

Ages: 8 years and up.

PALM SPRINGS ART MUSEUM IN PALM DESERT

(760) 346-5600 / www.psmuseum.org/palm-desert   !
72-567 Highway 111, Palm Desert

This small branch of the Palm Spring Art Museum features four galleries that hold rotating exhibits of various media - sculpture, painting, photography, and more. Call first and see what is showing to see if it will appeal to your kids (and you). The Baroque to Bling! was a fun one with funky jewelry, a fringed neckpiece made out of rubber inner tubes, theater lights, and mirrors and glass created into works of art, or as the word baroque implies - lavishly ornate design. There is also an education wing for programs that accompany each exhibition to draw visitors in more and learn about them. Ask about classes, summer camps, etc.

The four-acre, outside, sculpture garden displays ten sculptures - Acrobats and Ball Suspended are favorites - surrounded by beautifully landscaped gardens with pathways meandering through native plants and rock benches placed throughout. Note: There is a Farmer's Market every Wednesday in the parking lot from 8am - 12:30pm.

Hours: The museum is open June - Labor Day, Fri. - Sun., 10am - 5pm. Closed Mon. - Thurs. It's open Labor Day - May, Tues. - Sun., 10am - 5pm, and open until 9pm the first Fri. of each month from November - May. Closed Mon. and major holidays. The Sculpture Garden is always open.

Price: Free

Ages: 8 years and up.

PALM SPRINGS VILLAGEFEST

(760) 320-3781 or (760) 325-1577 / www.villagefest.org; www.pschamber.org   !/$
Palm Canyon Drive between Baristo and Amado, Palm Springs

It's Thursday night and you're in Palm Springs with the kids, wondering what to do. Then, you pick up this terrific book called *Fun and Educational Places to go With Kids and Adults* and read about VillageFest - problem solved! The

VillageFest, or international old-time street fair, is held along several blocks on Palm Canyon Drive in the heart of Palm Springs where businesses stay open late and admission is free to the PALM SPRINGS ART MUSEUM (pg. 394). There is food, arts and crafts vendors, boutiques, cafes, and entertainment, such as live music. For kids, various attractions could include pony rides, magic shows, a bounce house, a gyroscope, school band competitions, or a stage for children's productions.

Hours: Thurs. nights, October - May, 6pm - 10pm; June - September, 7pm - 10pm. Closed Thanksgiving.
Price: Free entrance.
Ages: 4 years and up.

PIONEERTOWN

(760) 365-7001 / www.pioneertown-motel.com
53626 Mane Street, Pioneertown

I enjoy the drive to Pioneertown, up a windy mountain road through hillsides dotted with desert boulders and funky-looking Joshua trees. Most of our "knowledge" of the Wild West comes from TV shows or movie screens. This very small town, about a half-hour drive north of Palm Springs, was used for numerous western films and looks like time has stood still. Although there are actual homes and businesses here, the Old West permeates the atmosphere and physical structures. Check out the real hitching posts and bullet holes on some of the signs.

Most Saturdays, from April through October, the Mane Street Stampede, all dressed in period attire, performs mock gunfights and Old West Re-enactments. Shows commence about 2:30pm, staged along Mane Street.

Since you're in the area, eat at the honky tonk Pappy and Harriet's Pioneertown Palace, (760) 365-5956 / www.pappyandharriets.com, a restaurant and bar for locals and tourists where bands play almost every night. The menu includes a cheeseburger ($14); Santa Maria steak sandwich ($15); chop salad ($13); chicken quesadilla ($13); and chili dog ($11); plus, with mesquite barbeque, rib eye steak ($32); half-rack of baby back pork ribs ($21); and one-half of a smoked chicken ($19). Kid's meals are $3.95 - $5.50 for a cheeseburger, chicken fingers, grilled cheese, hot dog, or cheese quesadilla. The restaurant is open Monday, 5pm to midnight, and Thursday through Sunday, 11am to 2am, although the kitchen closes at 9:30pm. It is closed Tuesday and Wednesday.

If you like it so much you want to stay, the ranch-style, rustic and basic Pioneertown Motel has eighteen rooms furnished in very simple, Old West decor, starting at $180 a night. This place is great for star-gazing and just relaxing. Or, look into tent, RV, or car camping next door at Pioneertown Corrals for $10 per person and $10 per horse, per night. Cash only. Bring your own everything. Contact (760) 365-7580 / www.pioneertowncorrals.biz for more info.

Price: Free, for the most part.
Ages: 4 years and up.

ROCKET FIZZ SODA POPS AND CANDY SHOP (Palm Springs area)

(760) 424-8018 / www.rocketfizz.com
155 South Palm Canyon Drive, Suite A-2

See ROCKET FIZZ SODA POPS AND CANDY SHOP (Los Angeles County) (pg. 26) for details on this shop with an incredible array of unusual sodas, candy and more.

Price: Technically, free
Ages: 3 years and up.

RUBY'S (Palm Springs area)

(800) HEY RUBY (439-7829) - for all locations. Cabazon - (951) 849-3850; Palm Springs - (760) 406-RUBY (7829) / www.rubys.com
Cabazon - 49000 Seminole Drive by the Morongo casinos; Palm Springs - 155 S. Palm Canyon Drive on the main shopping drag.

See the entry for RUBY'S (Orange County) (pg. 252) for details.

SHIELDS DATE GARDEN / BIBLICAL GARDENS

(760) 347-7768 - date store; (760) 775-0902 - cafe / www.shieldsdategarden.com
80225 Highway 111, Indio

Wanna date? Since 1925, this date garden has been a staple in the desert area, growing a variety of dates, some of which are exclusively sold here. And you can't miss the sign - a gigantic knight, pointing to the store holding a shield that says "Shields". The old theater, with 108 seats, shows the old, fifteen-minute movie with a catchy title, *The Romance & Sex Life of the Date*. The film is informative and tells the history of the date and how fruit is produced. (Forty-nine females to one male within one acre of land - that's not dating, that's a harem.)

You can look at the huge trees outside. Better yet, and even walk the pathway that meanders through a Biblical Garden that goes through parts of the seventeen-acre date farm. The Garden is lovely, good-sized and has a small lake, plus overlooks and bridges. There are fourteen different scenes scattered throughout that chronologically depict Christ's life, from birth to resurrection, and in between. Twenty-three life-like statues, props and Bible texts at each of the fairly lush scenes, help the Bible become real - from manger to John the Baptist to healings to the cross to the cave-tomb and resurrection. It takes a minimal of half an hour to walk around. Listen to an audio narrative using your smart phone describing the scenarios. It's a destination for me, not just a side trip.

The on-site, classy Cafe, with indoor and outdoor seating, offers breakfast - the works omelet ($12.50); French toast ($11); pancakes with dates ($13); a fruit plate with cottage cheese ($11); and lunch - Shields signature salad ($13); N.Y. steak sandwich ($14); chicken tacos ($12.25); date burger (bacon, cheese, and sauteed dates, $15); and chicken club ($11.50). Kid's meals are about $8.75. Get a date shake, purchase some dates or date crystals from the large gift shop, definitely sample the dates and other treats at the sampling counter, and enjoy this little, but not really romantic, excursion.

Hours: Open daily, 9am - 5pm. The Cafe is open daily, 7:30am - 3:30pm. The Garden walk is open daily, 7:30am - 4pm; closed for 2+ weeks in August for maintenance. Everything is closed Thanksgiving and Christmas.

Price: Free. The Garden is $5 for adults; free for ages 12 and under, though if you have a meal at the Cafe, admission is free, as it is (for 2 people) if you spend $25 or more at the store.

Ages: 7 years and up.

SHOGUN (Palm Springs area)

(760) 346-1223 / www.restaurantshogun.com

$$$$

74225 HWY 111, Palm Desert

See the entry for SHOGUN (Los Angeles County) (pg. 26) for details.

Hours: Open for lunch Mon. - Fri., 11:30am - 2pm; Sat., Sun., and holidays, noon - 2:30pm. Open for dinner Mon. - Thurs., 5pm - 9:30pm; Fri. - Sat., 5pm - 10pm; Sun. and holidays, 4:30pm - 9:30pm.

SUNNYLANDS CENTER AND GARDENS

(760) 202-2222 / www.sunnylands.org

!

37977 Bob Hope Dr, Rancho Mirage

What lovely grounds!!! The nine acres of gardens are aesthetically pleasing with similar types of cactus grouped together, some even some in rows, amidst shade-giving desert trees. The easy walking paths that meander through the land and fifty species of plants are also home to lizards, jackrabbits, birds, butterflies and other insects. A short labyrinth, twin reflecting pools, and an expanse of lawn, along with scattered benches, enhances the relaxing ambiance felt here. Sit for a spell, too, on the backyard patio and enjoy light refreshment from the cafe.

Inside the center/museum is a grand living room with an open view to the outdoors. A twenty-minute film on the history of Sunnylands plays continuously. Sunnylands, an architectural gem built by the Annenbergs as one of their homes, has hosted seven U.S. presidents, Queen Elizabeth and other members of the Royal family, Hollywood icons (like Bob Hope, Frank Sinatra, Jimmy Stewart, and Ginger Rogers), and numerous other world-famous people.

There are some interactive displays throughout; sculptures, paintings, cloisonne, glass, furniture, and other works of art from the Sunnylands Collection; and gifts from their famed visitors on display.

Hours: Open Thurs. - Sun., 8:30am - 4pm.

Price: Free

Ages: 3 years and up for a walk outside; 8 years and up for the museum.

SUNRISE PARK / PALM SPRINGS SWIM CENTER AND SKATE PARK

(760) 323-8278 - swim center; (760) 323-8272 - park/skate park / www.palmsprings-ca.gov

!/$$

401 South Pavilion Way, Palm Springs

This park has activities that will keep your family busy and refreshed from sunrise to sunset. Besides the wonderful grassy areas and big playground with bridges, slides, and swings, there is an extra large (30,000 square feet!!) skate park. It has three bowls, ranging from features for entry-level skaters to an area in one of the bowls that is nine-and-a-half feet deep with three feet of vert wall. Street elements include rails, hips, pyramids, stairs, ramps, and quarter-pipes. Touted as one of the best skate parks in Southern California, participants relish skating here at night, too because of the unique, no-shadow, lighting. A helmet and pads are mandatory. There is an adjacent, lighted baseball stadium.

Another important attraction of the park is the Olympic-size swimming pool that has a shallow end for younger kids to cool off. Bring your own lawn chairs.

Hours: The park is open daily, sunrise - sunset. The skate park is open Mon. - Fri., noon - 10pm; Sat. - Sun., 9am - 10pm. The pool is open year-round for recreational swim - Mon. - Fri., 11am - 5pm; Sat. - Sun., 9am - 3pm. Night swimming is available in the summer.

Price: The park and skate park are free. Swim sessions are $5 for non-resident adults; $4 for resident adults; $3 for ages 4 - 12; children 3 and under are free with a paid adult.

Ages: All

TAHQUITZ CANYON

(760) 416-7044 or (760) 323-6018 / www.tahquitzcanyon.com
500 W. Mesquite, Palm Springs

☀
$$$

At the visitors center, watch the short video called *Legend of the Tahquitz Canyon* to get a feel for the history of this region. There are also a few indigenous displays here, as well. This gorgeous canyon doesn't have palm trees, so during the day it just gets hot without shade. It does, however, have other trees and plants along with the major reason to visit - a sixty-foot waterfall. The one looping, hiking trail goes to the base of the waterfall and is almost two miles long. It's rated easy to moderate, with some rock steps that vary in height, along the Tahquitz Creek. (The trail is not stroller friendly.) Be on the lookout for wildlife, caves, rock art, and impressive landscape.

A free, two-and-a-half-hour ranger-led interpretative hike goes along the same path that gives insight as to the topography, history, Cahuilla Indians, animal life, and plant life along the way. Such knowledge gives participants a deeper appreciation for what they see. Check out INDIAN CANYONS (pg. 386) for details about nearby canyons.

Hours: Open October - July 4, daily, 7:30am - 5pm; open July 5 - September, Fri. - Sun., 7:30am - 5pm. Visitors must be inside the gate by 3:30pm as the canyon closes at 5pm. Free ranger hikes are offered when the canyon is open at 8am, 10am, noon, and 2pm.

Price: $12.50 for adults; $6 for ages 12 and under. Free to active military.

Ages: 6 years and up.

THE BEST OF THE BEST TOURS

(760) 320-1365 / www.thebestofthebesttours.com
490 S. Indian Canyon Drive, Palm Springs

☀
$$$$$

This tour company offers several types of tours, most of them in an open-air jeep. We took the Windmill Tour and if you like learning about alternative energy sources and are fascinated by the power that wind can generate, you'll be (literally) blown away by this tour. To state the obvious, it is usually very windy out here. Why? Because cool coastal air comes inland and pushes the hot air through the narrow mountainous San Gorgonio Pass. Driving around on the grounds of one of several wind farms in the world, you'll hear the thumping noise created by the huge pinwheels in motion. Blades, by the way, can span more than half the length of a football field. You'll see the older-style wind turbines and new, sleeker, more efficient ones. You'll get to stop and get out of the 21-passenger van twice during your tour. And, yes, you'll finally find out if these wind mills are simply tax shelters or actually producing usable, affordable energy and other related environmental and economic issues. A lot of technical information is given during this two-hour tour, and though some of it might be long winded for kids, even I understand a bit more now about electricity, sources of clean energy, and what makes a kilowatt hour. The tour is $40 for adults; $35 for seniors; $10 for ages 12 and under. Other tours include the two-hour+Indian Canyon tour ($50 for adults; $45 for seniors and ages 12 and under); ninety-minute Rich and Famous tour ($40; $35); and the almost four-hour Bonanza tour - a combo of Windmill, Indian Canyon, and Rich and Famous ($99; $94).

Hours: Tours are offered daily. Reservations are suggested.

Price: Prices are listed above.

Ages: 9 years and up.

ULTRASTAR CINEMAS DESERT IMAX-1

(760) 324-7333 / www.ultrastarmovies.com; www.desertimax.org $$$$

68510 East Palm Canyon Drive, Cathedral City

Larger than life! That's the images shown on the huge IMAX screen, which features several films on any given day. Some of the films are entertaining and some are educational. I am personally partial to the 3-D format, also available here, as viewers get more involved with the on-screen action as things and people seemingly pop out. Nature films are especially fun viewed this way. Ask about double feature specials and school group discounts. Just across the street is the UltraStar Mary Pickford Cinemas for more movie selections.

Hours: Call or check the website for movie time.

Price: 2-D (IMAX large screen) and 3-D movie tickets vary - from $7.50 for matinees and Tues. and Thurs. discount days to $13.25 for evening shows for adults.

Ages: 4 years and up

WET 'N' WILD

(760) 327-0499 / www.wetnwildpalmsprings.com $$$$$

1500 Gene Autry Trail, Palm Springs

This twenty-two-acre waterpark is truly an oasis in the desert. Six water slides for big kids range from mild uncovered slides, to enclosed forty-mph slides, to a seventy-foot, free-fall slide. Cowabunga - the four-story interactive water playground is really rad with water squirting everyone, squirt guns, so visitors can tag other visitors, slides, a bucket that dumps 1,000 gallons of water at regular intervals, several more slides and everything fun. Get carried away in the gentle, three-foot-deep, circular, Sunset River inner tube ride. Catch a wave, dude, in the large wave pool where kids can body or board surf. Almost really catch a wave by surfing in the desert at the FlowRider, a simulated surfing machine. Hang ten on Surf Rider, a multi-person, open raft ride. Literally go for a spin as a two-to-four person ride spins rafters around and around and then through a funnel-shaped hole. Younger children can take the plunge in their own small water play area that has two slides and a large mushroom that showers water.

Wet 'n' Wild offers locker rentals (about $11 for a small), private cabana rentals, a few full-service snack bars, and an indoor restaurant for all your creature comforts. There is a video arcade here, too. Bring water shoes or flip flops because the cement gets really hot. Note: You cannot bring a cooler or your own food inside the park. Proper swimwear must be worn, meaning that anything with rivets is not allowed. Family-friendly dive-in movies are some Friday nights in July, when the park is open, on a limited basis, until 10pm.

Hours: Open mid-March - mid-May, usually Fri. - Sun. (on some weekdays as well), 10am - 5pm, or 6pm. Open Memorial Day - Labor Day daily, usually 10am - 7pm, or 8pm. Open September until the second weekend in October on weekends only, usually 11am - 5pm. Call or check the website first as hours fluctuate a lot!

Price: $39.99 for adults; $29.99 for seniors and ages 3 - 11; children 2 and under are free. Buy in advance online and save. Admission prices after 3pm are $19.99. Parking is $12.

Ages: All

SAN BERNARDINO COUNTY

Originally settled by the Serrano Indians, the land has changed hands many times over the years and today incorporates a flavor from all of its past inhabitants. Tour through a restored rancho in Rancho Cucamonga. See a once-working silver mine in the revitalized ghost town of Calico. Take a walk in the deserts of Barstow (but not in the summertime). Enjoy the mountainous woodlands of Big Bear Lake. Pick apples in Oak Glen. Shop at Ontario Mills Mall. Visit airplane museums in Chino. This Inland Empire has something to cater to every interest.

Note: Since Big Bear is often considered a resort destination, you'll find its attractions listed in a separate section in the back of this county.

—ARTS AND CRAFTS—

COLOR ME MINE (San Bernardino County)

Chino Hills - (909) 628-7744; Redlands - (909) 792-2622 / www.chinohills.colormemine.com;
www.redlands.colormemine.com

Chino Hills - 13865 City Center Drive, suite 3065 at the Promenade; Redlands - 9900 Alabama Street, suite A in the Redland Town Center

See the entry for COLOR ME MINE (Los Angeles County) (pg. 8) for details.

THE SAWDUST FACTORY

(909) 946-0866 / www.thesawdustfactory.com

1525 Howard Access Road, Upland

*Wood*n't your kids enjoy making a craft to take home? The aptly-named Sawdust Factory allows kids (and adults) to do just that. Gather inspiration from the many country crafts, toll-painted items, and practical products in the retail part of the store. Then, choose a project to paint and/or assemble to take home to do, or complete a project on-site and make it yours, through and through. Even if you are craft deficient, like me, you'll leave with a finished project that pleases you.

The good-size workshop room towards the back of the store is set up with long tables. Choose from hundreds of precut items including picture frames, signs, notepad holders, treat boxes, bug boxes, bird feeders, toolboxes, holiday items, and much more. Customize your project by adding wood figures for a 3-D effect, or by painting and adding embellishments such as buttons, wire, raffia, bows, and wiggle eyes. If you can't decide what to do, sign up to take a special workshop with a predetermined craft which usually revolves around a particular theme. Come here on a walk-in basis, or come for a scheduled workshop. Birthday parties, scout outings, and school field trips are welcome. On field trips, kids won't *leaf* without learning about trees, the milling process, and wood tools on their twenty-minute guided presentation, plus they see a demonstration of how a drill press and scroll saw work, and make a pre-selected woodcraft project. Once a month Storytime for pre-schoolers include a story (hence the name of the event) and craft pertaining to the story.

Hours: Open Mon. - Fri., 9am - 4pm; Sat., 10am - 4pm. Open Sunday for special events and parties. Closed major holidays. Call or check the website for scheduled workshop dates and times.

Price: Walk in workshop fees are $5 per person, plus the cost of the project, which range from $10 to $40. Call first to check on availability of accommodating walk-ins. Check the calendar for the no-workshop-fee days. Scheduled workshops are an all-inclusive fee, starting at $10, depending on the project.

Ages: 3 years and up.

—EDIBLE ADVENTURES—

BARSTOW STATION

(760) 256-0366 / www.barstowstation.net

1611 E. Main Street, Barstow

Several retired railroad cars are grouped together to form a unique, albeit brief, shopping and eating experience. Eating McDonald's food in an old train car might taste the same as eating it elsewhere, but the atmosphere here makes it fun. Other rail cars offer Subway, Panda Express, ice cream, candy, souvenirs, and knickknacks. The Station fulfills its goal of being an interesting, edible adventure.

Hours: Open Mon. - Thurs., and Sat., 7am - 8pm; Fri. and Sun., 7am - 9pm. McDonald's is open daily, 5am - 11pm.

Price: Free to enter; bring spending money.

Ages: All

BENIHANA OF TOKYO (San Bernardino County)

(909) 483-0937 / www.benihana.com

3760 E. Inland Empire Boulevard, Ontario

See the entry for BENIHANA OF TOKYO (Los Angeles County) (pg. 15) for details.

CENTER STAGE THEATER

See the entry for CENTER STAGE THEATER (pg. 436), under SHOWS AND THEATERS, for details on terrific dinner and stage shows.

CHUCK E. CHEESE'S (San Bernardino County)

See the entry for CHUCK E. CHEESE'S (Los Angeles County) (pg. 18) for details.

FARMER'S MARKETS (San Bernardino County)

See the entry for FARMER'S MARKETS (Los Angeles County) (pg. 21) for details.

GRANLUND'S SWEET TEMPTATIONS

(909) 790-6266 $$$$

12164 California Street, Yucaipa

The inside of this restaurant reminds me of a floral store (not a florists). First, you walk through the oak and glass door through an archway full with fake greens twisted with vines of bright red berries into a room filled with greenery which is dripping from the ceiling, and deftly placed along the walls, on oak shelves, and on round tables topped with topiary wrapped with white lights. The greenery is also interspersed among other plants, statues, lamps, and picture frames, plus pitchers and vases in classic white, all artfully arranged and for sale. Wooden floors and wooden tables and chairs, touches of red, wood ceiling fans, and ornate gold ceiling (tin-plated) tiles that look like they've been hand tooled, plus Big Band music, all work together to create a classy, yet relaxing dining experience. There are seven tables, well spaced to give room to the diners, along with a semi-circular counter top imbedded with small red tiles with red vinyl stools to eat at. The room is kind of divided by wood and glass display cases. In the back area is a long display case holding tantalizing desserts. How hard is it to eat a meal back here while being tempted with dessert!

Food selections, with approximate prices, include soup in a sourdough bread bowl (a personal favorite), $8.25; chicken Caesar salad, $10.25; summer fruit salad with sherbet, surrounded by fruit served with cinnamon swirl bread, $10.75; brioche - sweet, egg bread stuffed with spinach or mushroom or tomato/basil, and topped with cheese, then toasted, $9.50; smoked turkey breast sandwich, $10.75; French dip, $9.95; cheese enchilada, $9.75; and lasagna, $11.50. Try some hand-churned ice cream, fresh pastries, or hand-made chocolates, truffles, and other sweet temptations from the dessert case. Note that there is some outdoor seating, as well.

Hours: Open Tues. - Fri., 11am - 4pm; Sat. - Sun., 9am - 4pm. Closed some major holidays.

Price: Prices are listed above.

Ages: 5 years and up.

GYU-KAKU (San Bernardino County)

(909) 899-4748 / www.gyu-kaku.com $$$$

7893 Monet Ave. in the Victorian Gardens Shopping Center, Rancho Cucamonga

See the entry for GYU-KAKU (Los Angeles County) (pg. 23) for information on this grill-it-yourself restaurant.

Hours: Open Mon. - Thurs., noon - 10pm; Fri., noon - 11pm; Sat., 11am - 11pm; Sun., 11am - 10pm.

ISLAMORADA FISH COMPANY

(909) 922-5400 / www.restaurants.basspro.com $$$$

7777 Victoria Gardens Lane, in the Bass Pro Shops Outdoor World, Rancho Cucamonga

Located inside the fantastic, sportsman's dream, BASS PRO SHOPS OUTDOOR WORLD (pg. 432) and adjacent to VICTORIA GARDENS REGIONAL TOWN CENTER - VG KIDZ CLUB - CULTURAL CENTER (pg. 422), this small, wood-paneled, nautically-themed restaurant offers the taste of the outdoors inside. With sword fish and other fish mounted on the wall and on the ceilings (check out the huge ray), and a large (13,000 gallon!) salt water fish tank, the mood is set for eating fresh fish. There is also a large fireplace in the center.

Served with most meals, the mini loaf of bread topped with sugar is delicious. Appetizers include breaded American alligator, which doesn't taste like chicken ($13.50); fried crawfish tails ($10.50); and venison-stuffed mushrooms ($10). Meal choices include tropical salad with greens, red pepper, mango, toasted coconut and cashews ($8); fish tacos ($13); a bowl of clam chowder ($6); fish and chips ($13.50); pulled BBQ pork sandwich ($10); burger ($11); wild boar burger ($15); salmon ($20); and top sirloin ($15). Kid's meals range between $5.99 to $6.99 for a choice of popcorn shrimp, pizza, mini corn dogs, and more. Drinks are included.

Hours: Open Mon. - Thurs., 11am - 9pm; Fri. - Sat., 11am - 10pm; Sun., 11am - 8pm.

Price: Menu prices listed above.

Ages: 2 years and up.

JOHN'S INCREDIBLE PIZZA CO. (San Bernardino County)

Montclair - (909) 447-7777; Victorville - (760) 951-1111 / www.johnspizza.com

Montclair - 5280 Arrow Highway; Victorville - 14766 Bear Valley Road

$$$$

See JOHN'S INCREDIBLE PIZZA CO. (Orange County) (pg. 250) for details.

Hours: Montclair - open Mon. - Thurs., 11am - 10pm; Fri., 11am - 11pm; Sat., 10am - 11pm; Sun., 10am - 10pm. Victorville - open Sun. - Thurs., 11am - 9pm; Fri. - Sat., 11am - 10pm. Both locations are usually open an hour earlier Mon. - Fri. during school breaks.

LEGENDS BURGERS

Rancho Cucamonga - (909) 941-9555; Upland - (909) 949-6363; Upland (College Park) - (909) 445-9400 / www.legends-burgers.com

Rancho Cucamonga - 8775 Baseline Rd.; Upland - 1645 N. Mountain Ave.; Upland (College Park) - 2420 W. Arrow Rte.

$$$

A fun homage to the 50s, this restaurant's walls are completely filled with memorabilia from that era, such as old movie posters, street signs, license plates, and record albums - even the blinds are decorated with movie star's portraits. Vintage-type cars run on a track overhead, 50's music plays in the background, and the floor tiles are black and white checkered.

The food is good and prices decent. For instance, a cheeseburger is $3.99 (or try a buffalo burger or ostrich burger!); steak sandwich, $9.49; chicken breast club, $8.99; hotdog, $3.69; Greek salad, $7.99; chicken burrito, $7.99; and zucchini fries, $3.99. Most kid's meals are $6.49.

Hours: Open daily, 7am - 11pm. Closed Easter, Thanksgiving and Christmas.

Price: Menu prices are listed above.

Ages: All

MANIAC-MIKES CAFE AT CABLE AIRPORT

(909) 982-9886 / www.maniac-mikes.com; www.cableairport.com

1749 West 13th Street at the Cable Airport, Upland

$$$

The planes might be up in the air, but the food here is down-to-earth. The small cafe is located just off the airport runway, so you can readily observe the small planes landing and taking off, whether you're eating inside or out on the patio. The airport is snuggled next to the mountains, so the view is tremendous. Note that the YOUNG EAGLES PROGRAM (San Bernardino County) (pg. 441) flies from this airport.

The retro cafe (vintage 1940's) has a few model airplanes on the ceiling and leather aviation jackets on hangers, plus a speaker to listen to the radio control tower. Typical American breakfast menu choices include eggs (a three-egg, cheese omelet served with hash browns or fries starts at $8.10); pancakes - short stack ($4); country-fried steak and two eggs ($9.45); and French toast ($5.90). Lunch items are burgers ($7.55); BLT ($8.05); chef salad ($8.45); bowl of chili ($6.15); or turkey or ham sandwich ($8.55). Kid's meals are $4.50 each and served with chips or fries, and a cookie. Choices include French toast with bacon, grilled cheese, hot dog, or peanut butter and jelly sandwich.

Hours: The cafe is open daily, 7am - 3pm. Closed New Year's Day, Easter, Thanksgiving and Christmas.

Price: See menu prices above.

Ages: 3 years and up.

MILL CREEK CATTLE CO. & DIAMOND JIM'S SALOON

(909) 389-0706 / www.millcreekcattlecompany.com

1874 Mentone Boulevard, Mentone

$$$

From the outside, this very unique restaurant looks like building fronts along Main Street in an Old West town. Wooden facades are labeled saloon, hotel (complete with balconies), barbershop, and U.S. Marshall's office, with a painted silhouette of a cowboy marshal. Bales of hay, cactus, antlers, and travel trunks complete the ambiance.

Enter through the restaurant doors for inside and inside/outside seating. The lobby continues the Old West theme with saddles hanging on the walls, old lanterns, old-time photographs, steer skulls, and an old-fashioned furnace. Eat inside the bar area, decorated with bits, bridles, a fireplace, a bear head over the piano, swords, and a flag that is half Confederate and half Union, plus pictures of Robert E. Lee and Ulysses S. Grant.

The other dining area is really quirky. It is inside the restaurant walls, but the roof is only camouflage netting. (Tip: Find an alternative place to eat on a rainy day. Just kidding - the restaurant is big enough.) Two real, tall, palm trees shoot up through the "ceiling," surrounded at their base by an odd combination of fake flowers and real cactus. The decor is an eclectic mix of more Old West building fronts, highlighted with neon signs, plus a corner waterfall enhanced by fake rocks and colorful fake flowers. The room also has heat lamps, old posters, and mounted deer and wild boar's heads.

Amid the unusual atmosphere of the Cattle Co., enjoy great food. Appetizers include jalapeno peppers stuffed with cream cheese ($8.95); spicy buffalo wings ($8.95); and quesadillas ($9.25). Meal menu items include chili ($5.95); Cobb salad ($12.95); liver and onions ($13.95); burgers (start at $8.25); smoked tri-tip sandwiches ($9.95); pork spareribs ($17.95); spicy sausage links ($10.95); smoke house chicken ($12.95); rib eye steak ($24.95); jumbo gulf shrimp ($17.95); and catfish ($15.95), plus a choice of pastas. Check out the website for the weekly specials. Kids' meals are $5.75 for either chicken tenders, grilled cheese, hamburger, barbecue ribs, barbecue chicken, or spaghetti. Drinks are extra. Breakfast, with cowboy beans, biscuits and gravy, and apple coffee cake, is also available.

While here, visit the adjacent MB's Gift Shop and General Store. It stocks all sorts of country store goodies, collectibles, antiques, dolls, and more.

Hours: Open Mon. - Thurs., 11am - 9pm; Fri., 11am - 1am; Sat. - Sun., 8am - 9pm.
Price: Menu prices are listed above.
Ages: 3 years and up.

MOUNT BALDY SCENIC LIFT RIDE

See the entry for MOUNT BALDY SCENIC LIFT RIDE (pg. 417), under GREAT OUTDOORS, for more information.

$$$$

MY ENCHANTED COTTAGE & TEA ROOM

(760) 264-4141 / www.myenchantedcottage.com
214 W. Ridgecrest Boulevard, Ridgecrest

$$$$

High tea out in the desert? Is it proper? I don't know, but it is a delightful treat. This very small, old cottage has been freshened up and radiates charm. The first few rooms contain gift items and collectables such as jams, tea accessories, pillows, and hand-painted keepsakes. Tea is served in the last room, as well as outside near the garden.

All of the food is made on the premises, based on traditional recipes that have been tweaked and enhanced with fun flourishes. Enchanted Tea, $15.95, consists of freshly-made scones with cream and preserves; three tea sandwiches with unusual combinations; a petite salad; dessert; and choice of tea. (There are over 100 teas to choose from!) For ages 10 and under, Princes Ali Tea, $12.95, includes four tea sandwiches, fruit, sweet treat, and mini-scones, and tea. A la carte items are also available such as a pot of tea, $6; scone with cream and preserves or another dessert, $3.50; tea sandwiches, $4 to $6; and a small salad, $3.

Hours: Open Tues. - Sat., 11am - 3pm(ish) for tea; the tea room is open extended hours. Hours change so call first.
Reservations are required for formal teas, but walk-ins are usually accommodated by the la carte selections.
Price: Menu prices are listed above.
Ages: 4 years and up.

OAK GLEN / APPLE PICKING

(909) 797-6833 / www.oakglen.net
Oak Glen Road, Oak Glen

$$

Your *delicious* journey into Oak Glen takes you on a five-mile loop through a town that is *ripe* with fun things to do. Several orchards offer U-pic, which means you pick your own apples, raspberries, blackberries, pears, and pumpkins, all in season, of course. Apple varieties range from the exotic, such as Ida Red, Pearmain, Winesap, Cameo, and Cinnamon Spice, to the more familiar ones of Jonagold, Granny Smith, Pippin, Braeburn, Rome, and Red Delicious. Most orchards also have wonderful country stores with all sorts of apple concoctions and apple-related items for sale. Even though berry-picking season starts in late July and apple season runs from September through the middle of November, there are many year-round reasons to visit Oak Glen. Tips: Although weekends in the fall (especially mid-September through mid-October) can be crowded, some orchards will only let you pick apples then, so get an early start on your day's adventure. Call the orchards to find out when your favorite type of apple will be ripe. Buy an apple-recipe book, as kids get a little carried away with the joy of picking apples! Here are a few of our favorites stops:

Parrish Pioneer Ranch, 38561 Oak Glen Road, (909) 797-1753 / www.parrishranch.com: The Ranch has a picnic area, pre-picked apples for sale, a few gift shops, a toy store, a small artists gallery and a restaurant. Goats, alpacas, a miniature donkey, miniature horse, peacocks, turkeys and a dwarf cow are in pens by the parking lot - to be looked at, not petted. August through November, harvest season, entertainment includes a country singer and, on Sundays, an over-the-top pirates stunt show is performed in melodrama-style in a professional-looking set at the outside theater at noon and 2pm, weather permitting. Call first. Admission is free; donations are appreciated. The barn and restaurant are open during apple season, Mon. - Fri., 9am to 5pm; Sat. - Sun., 9am - 6pm. The store opens at 10am. Out of season, the barn and restaurant are open Thurs. - Mon., 9am - 5pm; the store opens at 10am.

Oak Tree Village, 38480 Oak Glen Rd., (909) 797-4420 / www.oaktreevillage.info: Located in the center of Oak Glen is the Village - a wonderful place to shop, play, and eat. See OAK TREE VILLAGE (pg. 434) to find out all of the fun things to do in this village including the Animal Park, pony rides, fishing, and so much more. Open Mon. - Fri., 10am - 5pm; Sat. - Sun., 8am - 5pm. Closed Christmas.

Mountain Town, 38480 Oak Glen Rd., (909) 797-4420 / www.oaktreevillage.info: Just up the walkway from the Oak Tree Village is MOUNTAIN TOWN REPTILE MUSEUM (pg. 443), an unusual, animal/reptile museum that has some live reptiles and some taxidermied animals inside in a recreated cave/mountain setting.

Snow-Line Orchard, 39400 Oak Glen Road, (909) 797-3415 / www.snowlineorchard.com: This short drive up the road offers rows and rows of U-pic raspberries in season. (We pick basketfuls and freeze them.) In the store, purchase fresh apples and tasty blends of raspberry/apple cider and cherry/apple cider. Tip: Watch the doughnut machine at work providing sweet concoctions seven days a week - there is always a line with people waiting to purchase these. Also, taste samples of their thirty-eight kinds of apples (depending on what's available at the time) before you decide which ones you want to purchase. The orchard/store is open September through November, daily from 9am - 5pm; open the rest of the year on weekends only, 10am - 4pm.

One-hour tours are offered for a minimum of twenty-five students (or adults) and a maximum of 125 at $6 per person; call first to verify prices. The tours include learning about this orchard, which has been here for more than a century, and seeing how it operates, plus making cider and packing and grading fruit. For school tours, teachers receive a bag of apples and the children get an apple and a cup of cider (and a lot of knowledge). Tours are offered Monday through Friday mornings (except October); call first to make a reservation. If you are interested in the history of Snow-Line orchard, or Oak Glen or apple farming, specifically, you'll enjoy the Orchard Walk tour. Call to make a reservation.

Riley's at Los Rios Rancho, 39611 Oak Glen Road, (909) 790-2364 / www.losriosrancho.com: This working apple ranch has acres of orchards that are ready to be picked, baked, sauced, and pressed in the fall; a large store selling everything apple, including up to twenty varieties of apples (depending upon the season), plus apple cider, apple butter, and gift items; a delicious deli and bakery (really fresh apple pie!); a BBQ open daily, only in season, serving up tri-tip sandwiches, chili, Polish or chicken apple sausages, and more; wonderful nature walking trails (see Wildlands Conservancy below); and two picnic areas. One picnic area is the large, grassy front lawn that has picnic tables. The other is a pretty, wooded area with picnic tables, located behind the store. Also, a free packing house tour is offered to the general public on weekends at 1pm, during apple season, Labor Day - Thanksgiving.

Los Rios offers wonderful school/group tours in the spring and fall. See RILEY'S FRONTIER EVENTS (pg. 440) for full details. Call or check the Los Rios website regarding the numerous special events here. Enjoy once-a-month, year-round, special entertainment such as hometown jamborees with dinner and gospel nights. Mark your calendar for the Apple Butter Festival in November, Currier & Ives Christmas in December, and Old West Days in August. U-pic raspberries are available mid-August through September, or so, and U-pic pumpkins are ready in October. The country store and cafe are open daily, 10am to 5pm.

Southern California Montane Botanic Garden / Wildlands Conservancy, 39611 Oak Glen Road, (909) 797-8507 or (909) 790-3698 / www.wildlandsconservancy.org: The conservancy shares and operates the land with the above-mentioned Los Rios Rancho. The botanic garden is hundreds of acres and five miles of trail in and amongst some of nature's finest. See SOUTHERN CALIFORNIA MONTANE BOTANIC GARDEN / OAK GLEN PRESERVE (pg. 421) for more info on this lovely and free nature excursion.

Oak Glen School House Museum - see OAK GLEN SCHOOL HOUSE MUSEUM (pg. 428) for details.

Willowbrook Apple Farm, 12099 S. Oak Glen Road, (909) 797-9484 / www.willowbrookapplefarm.com: Stop here briefly as this farm sells candied apples, preserves, blackberries and raspberries (in September) and Winesap apples, exclusively. You can pick your own Winesaps (one of my favorite apples) and press your own cider. A tour is available for groups of twenty-five or more which includes cider pressing, a tractor ride in the orchard, interacting with the farm animals, learning about farming and apples, and eating a fresh-dipped caramel apple - $8 for adults; $12.1 for children. The farm is open August through mid-November, weekends only to the public, 10am to 4pm. Call for tour times.

Riley's Apple Farm, 12201 S. Oak Glen Road, (866) 585-6407 or (909) 797-4061 / www.rileysapplefarm.com: In the tradition of various Riley's farms up on the mountain, this original farm offers exceptional Colonial-era tours, activities (including archery, corn husk doll-making, and rope-making), and sweet treats. See RILEY'S APPLE FARM (pg. 438) for more details.

Riley's Farm, 12261 S. Oak Glen Road, (909) 797-7534 / www.rileysfarm.com: These members of the Riley's dynasty offer a variety of attractions, including outstanding school and group tours with an emphasis on early America, U-pic fruits, and a re-created Colonial restaurant which is open for breakfast and lunch. See RILEY'S FARM (pg. 439) for more information.

Ages: All ages for most activities; 5 years and up for the educational tours.

THE OLD SPAGHETTI FACTORY (San Bernardino County)

Rancho Cucamonga - (909) 980-3585; Redlands - (909) 798-7774 / www.osf.com
Rancho Cucamonga - 11896 Foothill Blvd.; Redlands - 1635 Industrial Park Ave.

See the entry for THE OLD SPAGHETTI FACTORY (Los Angeles County) (pg. 25) for details.

OLIVIA'S DOLL HOUSE TEA ROOM (San Bernardino County)

(909) 982-6060 or (626) 708-1223 / www.oliviastearoomupland.com
569 N. Central Avenue, Upland

See the entry for OLIVIA'S DOLL HOUSE TEA ROOM (Los Angeles County) (pg. 25) for details, but also check this website for specific prices and teas exclusive to this location.

PEGGY SUE'S 50's DINER

(760) 254-3370 / www.peggysuesdiner.com
35654 Yermo Road, Yermo

If your cruisin' for food served in a really happening place, head over to Peggy Sue's. (This is the "Peggy Sue" that Buddy Holly crooned about.) This original roadside diner has a few rooms, including several small ones packed with booths, and a larger room with chairs and tables. The walls are filled with an impressive and eclectic array of movie and television personality memorabilia, including Lucille Ball, Ricky Ricardo, Cary Grant, Marilyn Monroe, Elvis, James Dean, Buddy Holly, Laurel and Hardy, and the gang from the *Wizard of Oz*, all portrayed in pictures, posters, masks, dolls, and paintings. Gaudy decor (i.e., paintings on black velvet and cheesy trinkets) is interspersed with nicer mementos (i.e., fine portraits of celebrities and expensive-looking paraphernalia). An occasional mannequin dressed in period clothing adds to the wonderful kitschyness. The jukebox plays 50's music every night except Friday nights, when live music is performed.

The diner also features a full pizza parlor toward the back and a small arcade. Outside is a small park with picnic tables, a pond for ducks, fountains, grass, a koi pond, a few shade trees, and some quirky statues on small dirt hill - dinosaurs, King Kong, and other creatures. Toward the front of the restaurant is a soda fountain for old-fashioned drinks and desserts, and an attached Five and Dime Store that sells touristy television and movie souvenirs, older-style toys from a simpler time, and collectors items. Look at the thirteen-foot Marlin here and life-size model of Betty Boop. Note that CALICO GHOST TOWN (pg. 433) is just down the road.

Breakfast options include three eggs any style with ham ($9.39) or pancakes ($7.49). Lunch fare includes a burger ($9.29); club sandwich ($10.79); or meatloaf ($9.29). For dinner, try a New York steak ($14.39); Southern fried chicken ($13.89); or chef salad ($10.59). Dessert beverages include Green River or cherry phosphates ($2.89); malts or shakes ($4.89); Chuck Berry pie ($3.89); or pineapple cheesecake ($4.69). Kid's menu choices for breakfast include an egg with toast ($3.19); one egg, two strips of bacon or sausage and hash browns ($5.49); French toast and two strips of bacon or sausage ($5.19); and a hot cake with bacon or sausage ($5.19). Lunch and dinner selections, which all include french fries, range from grilled cheese sandwich or chicken nuggets to a hot dog or a hamburger. Each kid's meal is $4.69 - $5.29 and drinks are an additional $1.49. Note: The food is O.K., but the atmosphere gets top ratings.

Hours: Open daily, 6am - 10pm (open in the winter until 9pm). Closed Christmas.
Price: Prices are listed above.
Ages: All

RAINFOREST CAFE

(909) 941-7979 / www.rainforestcafe.com
4810 Mills Circle in Ontario Mills Mall, Ontario

A (pretend) life-size crocodile in the front of the store resides in a small swamp. He moves around and roars every few minutes. Then, enter the Cafe under a huge fish tank archway that holds a colorful array of saltwater fish. Two more aquariums are inside the cafe and one contains beautiful, but poisonous, lionfish. Deep in the heart of the Rainforest Cafe, realistic-looking animatronic beasts come to life - gorillas beat their chests, elephants trumpet, and parrots squawk. Periodic thunder and lightning "storms" explode through the restaurant. This is not a quiet place to eat. Cascading waterfalls, fake dense foliage, and "rock" walls add to the atmosphere, as do the jaguars and cheetahs that are partially hidden in the banyan trees. Rain drizzles down from the ceiling around the perimeter of the cafe, ending in troughs of misty waters. There is always something to grab your attention here!

Savor your meal at a table, or on a bar stool that is painted to look like a giraffe, zebra, frog, or another animal. The delectable menu offers everything from salmon, flatbread pizza, coconut shrimp, rotisserie chicken, Oriental chicken salad, and hamburgers. Prices start at about $14.49 for hamburgers and go up to $30.49 for steak and fish. Portions are large. Children's meals average $6.99 for a choice of a grilled cheese sandwich, hot dog, Jurassic chicken nuggets, popcorn shrimp, mac and cheese, or pizza and a beverage. Desserts are deliciously unique, especially the sparkling volcano overflowing with chocolate. Tip: Join the Select Club. For $25, in which you receive $25 towards the purchase of food or retail items, you also save money whenever you eat here (or at 500 other Landry-owned restaurants), are given a $25 credit to be redeemed in your birthday month, and you get priority seating.

The adjacent Rainforest Cafe Retail Village (i.e., store) is themed with equal attention to detail. Ask about educational programs that take students on a half-hour safari through the restaurant to learn about endangered species, conservation, and the environment. Tours include an early lunch and a lesson plan. Catch jungle fever and experience the Rainforest Cafe! See ONTARIO MILLS MALL (pg. 422) for other things to do at the mall.

Hours: Open Mon. - Sat., 11am - 9:30pm; Sun., 11am - 8:30pm.
Hours: Menu prices are listed above.
Ages: All

—FAMILY PAY AND PLAY—

BOOMERS! - Upland

(909) 946-9555 / www.boomersparks.com
1500 W. 7th Street, Upland

Upland Boomers fun center offers fun for everyone in your family! This giant fun center has two, themed outdoor **miniature golf** courses with all the whimsical decorations such as waterfalls, windmills, and more obstacles that make each hole fun. Two other courses, the Old West and Storybook Land, are indoors so rainy days won't put a damper on your swing. The Old West is seen in a different light with **cosmic golf**, where holes glow neon colors in the dark under black lights. All golf prices are $10 a round per person; children 4 and under are free. Unleash your inner warrior with **lazer tag** - $9 for a 5 minute game. Over 150 arcade and video games are also inside the building. Little ones, under 58" tall, can ride on **rookie go karts** for $8. Take a spin on a non-rookie **go kart** at $10 a ride (no sandals allowed) - drivers must be over 58" tall. An additional passenger under this height is $2. Or really spin around (and around) on Spin Zone **bumper cars** with a disco twist for $8 a ride. **Bumperboats**, a seasonal attraction, are always fun - $9 for kids over 44" tall, $2 for riders under this height. There are a few **kiddie rides** here including a Ferris wheel, mini jets, and tubs of fun. Each ride is $5. The **rock climbing wall** is $9 for two climbs, for participants who weigh at least forty pounds. Kids can also practice for the big league at the **batting cages.** And of course there are virtual reality games. If you've worked up an appetite, Be-Bop Cafe is right next door. Your choice of hamburgers, pizza, or chicken, plus Icees to slurp on, all served in a fun atmosphere, where there are more arcade games to play. (There is no escape from them.)

Hours: Open most of the year, Mon. - Thurs., 3pm - 9pm; Fri. 1pm - 11pm; Sat., 10am - 11pm; Sun., 11am - 9pm. Open longer hours in the summer and during school breaks.
Price: Attractions are individually priced above, or purchase an all day, all fun pass starting at $44.99. Definitely check the website regarding specials.
Ages: 3 years and up.

CHINO SKATE PARK - AYALA PARK

(909) 334-3257 or (909) 591-9834 / www.cityofchino.org
14225 Central Avenue, Chino

At almost 28,000 square feet, this huge, free-flowing, gated, cement skate park has received many well-deserved kudos. Street, vert, and pool riders rate this park as one of the best in the area - worth driving for, especially because of its stairs, funboxes, rails, three-leaf clover bowl, nine-foot bowl, and several other bowls and banks. The adjacent park has some open grass areas, ball fields, and a playground.

Hours: Open April - September, 7am - 10pm; open October - March, 8am - 10pm.
Price: Free
Ages: 7 years and up.

CHUCK E. CHEESE'S (San Bernardino County)

See the entry for CHUCK E. CHEESE'S (Los Angeles County) (pg. 18) for details.

DAVE & BUSTER'S (San Bernardino County)

(909) 987-1557 / www.daveandbusters.com
4821 Mills Circle at Ontario Mills Mall, Ontario
     See DAVE & BUSTER'S (Orange County) (pg. 259) for details. See ONTARIO MILLS MALL (pg. 422) for other things to do at the mall.
Hours: Open daily, 11am - midnight.
  Ages: 7 years and up.

FIESTA VILLAGE

(909) 824-1111 / www.fiestavillage.com
1405 E. Washington Street, Colton
     Just off the freeway, come party at Fiesta Village! The two, Western-motif **miniature golf** courses, are well kept up and have some crazy, fun holes complete with fountains, palm trees, and small structures such as a lighthouse, castle, windmill, mini Western town facade, and more. Unlimited use of the two courses is $13.95 for players 53" and taller, $11.95 for seniors and children 37" to 52", kids 36" and under are free (with a paying partner). The **go karts** in the raceway are a blast to zip around the track - drivers must be at least 53" tall and the cost is $11.95 for a five-minute ride. Six amusement **rides** include a Gear Jammer (i.e., swinging arm); Bizzy Bear (like a teacup ride); Tilt a Whirl - 3 tickets; Dragon roller coaster - 3 tickets; plus a bounce house - 2 tickets, and a giant, super slide - 1 ticket. The maze-like, **lazer tag** arena is really a fun one with numerous nooks and crannies to hide behind and shoot your opponents. The eight-minute games can have up to fifteen players and costs $11.95 for a single mission; $14.95 for two. The outdoor **roller blade and skate rink** is a great way to burn off some extra energy or try some fancy moves - $11.95 for unlimited skating, with rentals an additional $4.95. **Batting cages** are also on the grounds. During the summer enjoy wet refreshment at **Pyrite Rapids Waterpark** which consists of three water slides - a double tube, a body slide, and a high-speed plunge, with a lounging area for spectators - $17.95 for an all-day pass for 48" and taller; $13.95 for juniors - those under 48". Note: No swimming around in the landing pool.
     Video arcades are in the main lobby with ticket redemption center. Picnic tables are located outside and a few are inside, as well. Eating places include Dairy Queen, with a full snack bar, and Nickelodeon Pizza restaurant, which has more video and arcade games like Jumpin' Jackpot and Deal or No Deal.
Hours: Usually open Mon. - Thurs., 11am - 9pm - arcade, go karts, mini-golf, roller skating, and lazer tag - no other rides. Fri., 11am - 11pm - arcade, go karts, mini-golf, roller skating, and lazer tag; 4pm - 10pm - everything, plus carnival rides. Sat., 10am - 10pm - all attractions; Sun., 11am - 9pm - all attractions. Check the calendar or call for summer hours. The water park is open mid-May - mid-June, and August - mid-September on Sat., 11am - 6pm; Sun., noon - 5pm. It is open mid-June - July daily, noon - 5pm.
  Price: Attractions priced above. Amusement rides are by tickets - 6 tickets cost $10.95 and 24 tickets cost $26.95. Ask about package deals, such as unlimited go karts, rides, mini golf, rollerskating (plus skate rentals) and 1 game of laser tag for $29.95.
  Ages: 4 years and up.

FONTANA PARK - SKATE PARK - AQUATIC CENTER

(909) 349-6900 - park; (909) 899-5320 - skate park; (909) 854-5111 - pool / www.fontana.org
15556 Summit Avenue (park) - 15610 Summit Avenue (aquatic center), Fontana
     Wahoo - this 25,000 square-foot mega skate park is fantastic for both beginners and advanced skaters. It has four cement bowls - from one- to three-feet, up to seven- to nine-feet, and one is a full capsule (skaters can go 360° around it inside); street elements with fun boxes, rails, and stairs; one sidewalk that meanders around the perimeter of the skate park and another that encircles an island of grass and shade trees; and a small pro shop and concession stand. Safety equipment - a helmet and pads - must be worn as police officers will cite offenders. Lights are here for nighttime fun. Lessons, summer camps, friendly competitions, and birthday parties are all available here.
     The surrounding park has plenty of amenities including picnic tables, BBQ pits, a hockey rink, walking and biking pathways, health and fitness community center, dog park, sports pavilion, palm trees, and a playground. The huge playground inspires lots of creative play. It features a sunken ship play area with a whale and dolphin "swimming" alongside; big fake boulders to climb on and under; four tall, kinetic sculptures that have elements that twirl in the wind, adding to the cool factor of the park; and colorful sculptures of frogs, caterpillars, a snail, and ladybugs to climb on as they reside underneath wildly-oversized (metal) flowers and butterflies - all on recycled rubber flooring.
     This large aquatics center has two heated pools open year-round; one for rec swim and the other for lap and competitive swim. Along with two diving boards, the center has three slides that swoosh down from a tower - one

enclosed slide and two open ones that end in a catch pool. These are for guests 48" and taller only. The good-sized splash pad (zero depth water play area) for younger kids has large buckets on the end of tall poles that look like trees that fill up with water and tip over; fountains that squirt up from the ground; a rainbow arch to run under with misters that spray; and some other play elements - all fun and refreshing, especially on hot summer days. There are also lounge chairs and picnic tables.

Hours: The park is open daily, sunrise - sunset. The skate park is open most of the year, Mon. - Thurs., 2pm - 9pm; Fri., noon - 9pm; Sat. - Sun., 9am - 9pm. It is open during school breaks and the summer starting at noon during the week. BMX riding is available Sun., 6pm- 9pm. The pools are open year round, Sat. - Sun., noon - 5pm. They, and the splash pad, are open Memorial Day - Labor Day, or so, daily, noon - 4pm.

Price: The park is free. The skate park is $5 a month for residents; $7 for non-residents. Yearly passes are available. Rec swim is $5 for adults for just the pool, $7 for the pool and slides; $1.50 for seniors; $3 for ages 3 - 17 for just the pool, $5 for the pool and slides; children 2 and under are free.

Ages: 1½ years and up.

GET AIR TRAMPOLINE PARK (San Bernardino County)

(760) 205-0578 / www.getairvictorville.com

12410 Amargosa Road, Suite A , Victorville

See GET AIR TRAMPOLINE PARK (Riverside County) (pg. 347) for a description.

Hours: Open Mon., 10am - 10pm; Tues., 10am - noon for Toddler Time, and noon - 10pm all ages; Wed., 10am - 10pm; Thurs., 10am - noon for Toddler Time, and noon - 10pm all ages; Fri., 10am - 9pm all ages, and 9pm - midnight for Club Air; Sat., 8am - 10am for special needs jumpers and their families only; 10am - 9pm all ages, and 9pm - midnight for Club Air; Sun., 10am - 8pm.

Price: $14 for one hour for 46" and taller, $23 for two hours; $8 for one hour for 45" and under, $14 for two. Toddler Time is $8 per child; one adult is admitted for free. Club Air is $15 for 2 hours or $20 for all 3. Always check the website for special offers.

Ages: 2 years and up.

HANGAR 18 (San Bernardino County)

Rancho Cucamonga - (909) 476-1438; Upland - (909) 931-5991 / www.climbhangar18.com

Rancho Cucamonga - 9004 Hyssop Dr.; Upland - 256 Stowell Street, suite A

Love a good cliffhanger? The Upland location of Hangar 18 boasts 12,000 square feet of overhangs; a forty-foot-long roof climb across the ceiling; two huge top rope areas; textured climbing walls dotted with numerous multi-colored stones that represent different routes; and a gigantic bouldering wall with a large lead cave. The Rancho Cucamonga facility has 4,200 square feet of bouldering terrain with all styles and levels of difficulty. Both lead climbing and the bouldering areas give seasoned climbers, as well as beginners, the opportunity to practice their bouldering technique. Rock climbing is a fun and safe activity that teaches balance and thinking while building confidence and stamina. (Have you ever noticed how most rock climbers don't have an ounce of fat on their bodies? After attempting the sport - I know why!) There is also a viewing platform and rails at the top for non-climbers to look down at the climbers.

The Adults Intro package and the Kid's Intro package (for ages 13 and under), which is mandatory for first-time climbers, includes a belay lesson, for the attending adults, or learning bouldering techniques; gear - shoes, harness and chalk; and a day pass. Notes: A party room is available. Waivers must be signed for all climbers. Hangar 18 also has youth climbing teams which compete all over the U.S.

Hours: Open Mon. - Thurs., 10am - 10pm; Fri., 10am - 9pm; Sat. - Sun., 10am - 8pm.

Price: Day passes are $18 for ages 14 and up; $13 for ages 13 and under. Rental equipment - shoes and a harness - is $5. Adults Intro package is $33; Kids Intro package is $28.

Ages: 5 years and up.

JOHN'S INCREDIBLE PIZZA CO. (San Bernardino County)

See JOHN'S INCREDIBLE PIZZA CO. (San Bernardino County) (pg. 402), under EDIBLE ADVENTURES, for details.

JUMPING JACKS (San Bernardino County)

(909) 989-6820 / www.jumpingjacksparty.com

7945 Cartilla Avenue, Rancho Cucamonga

Jumping Jacks makes me want to hop to it and play, slide, and bounce on these crazy fun and massive inflatables. Working up a good sweat never hurt anyone! There are numerous "jumps" in this 19,500-square-foot, carpeted, play place and some run-around space in the three rooms. One room is Jungle themed, one is Carnival themed and the other Jurassic Park - murals help with the themes. One of the rooms can glow in the dark and another has a light up game to play on the floor. One enormous slide looks like a pinball machine where you can throw balls or be the ball; another is a conglomeration of bounce, slide, and obstacle course; and another is underwater themed. The jousting arena is great with it's inflatable pugil sticks as is the boxing ring where contestants use oversize, inflatable boxing gloves.

Free game tables like air hockey are also part of the deal. If parents want a time out they can retreat to a place with a couch and wireless internet. Jumping Jacks is also carpeted, air conditioned, and has a sound system. Socks are mandatory.

Hours: Open play, family fun times are Tues. - Wed., 11am - 2pm; Wed. - Thurs., 5pm - 8pm. The rest of the time is for private parties.

Price: $10 per child for ages 2 and up; children under 2 with a paid sibling, and adults, are free.

Ages: 4 years and up.

K1 SPEED (San Bernardino County)

(909) 980-0286 / www.k1speed.com

5350 East Ontario Mills Parkway, Ontario

See K1 SPEED (San Diego County) (pg. 482) for details. See ONTARIO MILLS MALL (pg. 422) for other things to do at the mall.

Price: The first race is $19.99.

LASER ISLAND (San Bernardino County)

(909) 982-0044 / www.laserisland.com

207 E. Foothill Boulevard, Upland

Playing tag on a deserted island. Can it get any better than this? Yes, when it's laser tag - running around black-lit erupting volcanos and ducking behind an island temple into a jungle hut, or alongside and in the scattered parts of a plane wreck that "crashed" here. Even the walls and partitions are painted and decorated with the theme - bamboo-looking forests, jungle plants, rocks, etc. Up to thirty-six players are divided into two teams that "tag" each other with lasers and try to score the most points, while strategically hiding to avoid getting "hit" for about twenty minutes per game.

This island offers even more fun with a nine-hole, Tiki-themed miniature golf course, arcade games with tickets and redemption prizes, and Coco Climb where climbers strap in and shimmy up a twenty-foot fake coconut tree. All this adventuring can build up an appetite so grab a pizza ($15 for a 16") in the tiki cafe/lobby, or a salad ($4 for a small), toasted sandwich (about $8), nachos ($3.50), buffalo wings ($8), or a root beer float with freshly-made ice cream ($3.50).

Hours: Open most of the year Mon. - Thurs., 3pm - 9pm; Fri., 3pm - midnight; Sat., 10am - midnight; Sun., noon - 9pm. Open in the summer and on holidays at noon with the same day closure times.

Price: Laser tag is $9. Mini golf is $6. CoCo Climb is $6. Check out the numerous specials offered like after school specials of unlimited laser tag or, my favorite - Family Dinner Adventure for 4 people. This includes pizza, a pitcher of soda, garlic bread and 2 laser games per person for only $50.

Ages: 6 years and up.

LEGO STORE - MINI MODEL BUILD (San Bernardino County)

(909) 758-9303 / www.lego.com/en-us/stores/events/mini-model-builds

One Mills Circle, Space 631, at Ontario Mills mall, Ontario

See LEGO STORE - MINI MODEL BUILD (San Diego County) (pg. 485) for info on this great, free LEGO mini model build.

Hours: The first Tues. and Wed. of each month, between 3pm - 7pm. Check out the malls listed above for other activities to do there.

Price: Free

Ages: 6 - 14 years old, only.

LOL KIDS CLUB

(909)948-8588 / www.lolkidsclub.com

735 N. Milliken Avenue, Ontario

Come inside, play and laugh out loud! A favorite place to come, LOL has a huge, multi-level play structure, all enclosed by safety nets, with several ball pits (one has a piratey ship in its midst), a compressed air gun for shooting balls, plus slides, obstacle courses, tubes and tunnels, climbing ropes, a trampoline, steps, ramps, rollers and so much more. Sensory overload, or maybe just fun overload! There are also several party rooms, a toddler play section and a good-size ball pit, plus hard-foam animals to climb on. Socks are mandatory. Check out the field trip packages.

The seating area and cafe make it easy to keep an eye on the kids and grab a bite to eat. Food prices are decent: BBQ chicken nachos, $5.75; a slice of pizza, $2.25; and a choice of salads for $6.25 and sandwiches, like panini steak and cheese, for $5. Kid's meals are $5.25 for a choice of quesadilla, grilled ham and cheese, chicken nuggets or spaghetti and meat balls. They come with a veggie or fruit, cookie and a beverage.

Hours: Open Sun. - Thurs., 10am - 9pm; Fri. and Sat., 10am - 11pm.

Price: The first adult is free; additional adults are $5 per. The first child, age 3 - 17 years, is $16.95; additional children, and toddlers (10 months - 2 years) are $9.95 each. Infants, 9 months and under, are free. Ask about specials. Mon. - Fri. you can leave LOL and come back for free on the same day - note that ONTARIO MILLS MALL (pg. 422) is just across the road.

Ages: 2 - 14 years

PARTY KINGDOM

(909) 628-9900 / www.partykingdomchino.com

3937 Schaefer Avenue, Chino

Party Kingdom rules as an indoor play place because it has so many of the best elements under one roof. The three-story play structure has a side-by-side, 35-foot, wave slide; a roller slide; a slide that ends into a ball pit; air blasters (shooting foam balls at each other); an area with really thick, crisscrossing webbing (like a spider's web) to crawl over and around; a rings obstacle course; other obstacle courses; tubes; swings; and so much more - love it! The giant inflatables are slides, obstacle courses, physical challenges, mazes, mini ziplines, sports themed (one has a basketball hoop for jump shots and the other is to throw a football), and a joust with inflatable lances. Some are even geared just for younger children. The trampoline room is fun to just bounce around, and also to play dodge ball. And for parties - nerf wars while trampolining! There is colorful, enclosed area just for toddlers with huge, soft blocks, mini slides, and several big toys to play with and on.

There is open space so moms and dads can sit and chat while keeping an eye on their little darlings. Grip socks must be worn by all participants and are available here for $2. Private, themed party rooms are available.

Hours: Open playtimes are Mon. - Fri., 10am - 1pm and 5:30pm - 8:30pm.

Price: $10.95 per child; free for children 11 months and under with a paying child, and for adults.

Ages: 18 months - 10 years for open playtimes.

PUMP IT UP (San Bernardino County)

Chino Hills - (909) 597-2828; Rancho Cucamonga - (909) 466-0806 / www.pumpitupparty.com

Chino Hills - 4510 Eucalyptus Avenue; Rancho Cucamonga - 11966 Jack Benny Drive

See PUMP IT UP (San Diego County) (pg. 487) for details. The age limit at the Rancho Cucamonga facility is 2 - 10 years old.

Hours: Check the location's website calendar for details on Open Jump and other speciality jump times as the times vary even within a particular month.

Price: Open Jump time is $10 per child; adults are free.

Ages: 2 years and up.

REVELATION RACEWAY

(909) 628-9909 / www.revrace.com

4871 E. State Street, Ontario

Race your smaller, remote-controlled version of a real race car around the street track and/or off-road dirt racetracks, over big bumps and around tight corners. 1/10 and 1/8 scale, electric and gas-powered - all are welcome. If you don't want to participate, just watch the cars, trucks, and buggies fly around the track (we saw some going 45mph), jumping, turning, and even tumbling. Spectators are welcome to sit at the bleachers, or to stand. Rows of tables are available for drivers to work on their cars, like a pit area.

The track is attached to the incredibly well-stocked Revelation Shop, which can take care of any car parts needs you might have.

Hours: Both the track and store are open Mon., Wed., Fri., 10:30am - 6:30pm; Tues. and Thurs., 10:30am - 10pm; Sat. - Sun., 8am - 6pm. Racing on the street track is the 1st Sat. of the month; racing on the dirt track, the 3rd Sat.
Price: Free for spectators. Practice fees are $10 on Mon., Wed., and Fri., $15 the other days. The last hour is only $5.
Ages: 5 years and up.

SAN BERNARDINO RACEWAY

(909) 824-7804 / www.sbraceway.com
217 E. Club Center Drive, San Bernardino

Gas-powered, indoor go karts zoom around the track at 35+ mph, with a maximum of twelve to fifteen cars on the track at any one time. Each race lasts ten minutes, which is about twelve to seventeen laps around. Participants without a valid driver's license or permit, can race, too, as at least once an hour unlicensed drivers start at half speed for two laps to demonstrate their ability to handle the karts. If they are good to go, they can compete full throttle and can then join in on other, regular races. Get more amped up on weekends nights with Cosmic Karting as you race surrounded by laser, strobe and black lights.

Hours: Open Mon. - Thurs., 11am - 10pm; Fri., 11am - midnight; Sat., 10am - midnight; Sun., 10am - 8pm. Cosmic Karting is available Fri. - Sat., 5pm - 8pm for all ages; 8 - midnight for 16 years and older, only.
Price: $18.99 for a race + $6 racing license. Two-seater karts are $27 for one race. Cosmic karting is $20.99 + $6 license. Check the website for specials and membership prices.
Ages: All drivers must be at least 52 " and 8 years old.

SCANDIA AMUSEMENT PARK

(909) 390-3092 / www.scandiafun.com
1155 S. Wanamaker Avenue, Ontario

Vikings might have come to this country just to play at this amusement park! Well, maybe not, but it is a lot of fun and very well kept up. Attractions include two Scandinavian-themed **miniature golf** courses with unlimited play at $11.75 for 48" and taller; $8.95 for 47" and under. The sixteen **amusement rides** include some for big kids, such as a roller coaster, bumper boats, Tilt-A-Whirl, go-karts, Swedish Swing, Viking boat (pendulum motion), free fall, and scrambler; and some for little kids, such as a small semi-truck ride around a track, a carousel, a mini coaster, train ride, a fire truck ride, and a slide. The rides have various height requirements. Tickets cost $1.25 each or $28.75 for twenty-five of them. Children's rides require one to two tickets; big kids' (or adult) rides usually require five tickets. There are also **batting cages**, 150 arcade and video games with a prize redemption center, and a full-service snack bar here, too. Incorporate fun and education with a field trip to Scandia. Learn about gas and electric motors, hydroelectric energy, centrifugal force, gravity and friction, and more, and then experience it via rides. Call for times, prices and more info.

Hours: Open most of the year daily, noon - 10pm for almost everything, however rides are only open Thurs. - Fri., 3:30pm - 9pm; Sat. - Sun., 12:30 - 9pm. Everything is open during holidays and school breaks daily, 12:30pm - 9pm.
Price: Attractions are individually-priced above, or purchase an unlimited pass (excluding arcade games) - $28.25 for 48" and taller; $20.25 for 47" and under. Inquire about weekday specials.
Ages: 3 years and up.

SCANDIA FAMILY FUN CENTER

(760) 241-4007 / www.scandiafun.com
12627 Mariposa Road, Victorville

Enjoy some high desert fun at this Scandia location. There are two Scandinavian-themed **miniature golf** courses, with castles, bridges, and other small buildings that add interest - $8.95 for unlimited play for 48" and taller; $6.50 for 47" and under. **Go-karts, bumper boats, Sky Screamer**, which earns its name by spinning riders in complete circles at 55mph at sixteen stories off the ground, and three other rides (just one for younger kids) are purchased via tickets that are $1 per, and 24 tickets for $19.95, with rides taking at least a few tickets each. **Batting cages**, a full-service snack bar, arcade and video games, and prize redemption center are also here for your enjoyment. Incorporate fun and education with a field trip to Scandia. Learn about gas and electric motors, hydroelectric energy, centrifugal force, gravity and friction, and more, and then experience it via rides. Call for times, prices and more info.

Hours: Open most of the year, Mon. - Thurs., 3pm - 10pm (note that the rides are not open at all on these days); everything is open - Fri., 3pm - 11pm; Sat., noon - 11pm; Sun., noon - 10pm. Everything is open during the summer and school breaks, Sun. - Thurs., noon - 10pm; Fri. - Sat., noon - 11pm. Hours can fluctuate, so call first.

Price: Attractions are individually-priced above, or buy an unlimited pass for $19.95 for 48" and over; $9.95 for 47" and under, which includes some tokens, and is available on weekends, holidays and in the summer.

Ages: 4 years and up.

SKY HIGH SPORTS (San Bernardino County)

(951) 681-5867 / ont.skyhighsports.com

$$$

3230 Cornerstone Drive, Mira Loma

See SKY HIGH SPORTS (Los Angeles County) (pg. 40) for details about this fantastic, indoor trampoline place. This facility has Ninja Course and Laser Maze. Laser Maze challenges players to attempt to reach the other side of the room by going over and under the crisscrossing beams, without breaking them. There is also a Sky Tykes area for kids 8 years old and under, only, to jump around and play on inflatables. The Sky High Cafe serves up pizza ($16 for a whole cheese); sub and wraps ($6.25 for an Italian sub); hot dog combo ($4.25); nachos ($3); dippin dots ($4); and more.

Hours: Open most of the year Mon., Wed., and Thurs., 2pm - 9pm; Fri., 2pm - 11pm; Sat., 11am - 11pm; Sun., 11am - 8pm. Closed Tues. It is open more hours during the summer and other school breaks. Hours can vary, so call first!

Price: Jump time Mon. - Thurs. is $14 for the first hour, $6 each additional hour; Fri. - Sun., $14 for the first hour, $10 each additional hour. Laser Maze is $3 a play. Ninja Court is an additional $3 an hour.

Ages: 4 years and up.

ZIPLINES AT PACIFIC CREST

(760) 705-1003 / www.ziplinespc.com

$$$$$

6014 Park Drive, Wrightwood

Exhilarating! Ziplining through the treetops and over mountain terrain is literally quite breathtaking and simply exhilarating!!! One of several zipline adventures offered is called the Canopy Tour. For about three and half hours you trek into and through the forest; cross three sky bridges (i.e. suspended bridges that swing) that are high up in the air; cross sky stairs; rappel down trees (from as high as ninety feet); and whoosh across and down eight ziplines, some of which are up to 300 feet high and as long as 1,500 feet. There is even a side-by-side zipline so you can race someone to the finish line.

The two-and-a-half hour Mountain View Zipline Tour includes six ziplines up to 135 feet high and 1,100 feet long; leaping off tree platforms (free fall rappels) that can be sixty feet off the ground (while in a safety harness and gear and auto-belay); and hiking, because ground to air perspective is impactful. (No bridges on this tour.) Quest Tour is ninety-minutes of zipping on four ziplines. There is an adventure for everyone. There is also an Ultimate All Day Adventure, which, not surprisingly, is all day.

With no more than eight people per tour, you get a lot of personal attention from the two guides and a lot of information about conservation, geography, history, and safety, plus - what an adventure!

Come prepared by wearing layers (note that tours operate, rain or shine); wearing pants or long shorts (these are more comfortable in the harness); and close-toed shoes (a must). Requirements include being in good health, weighing at least 90 pounds and no more than 250 (participants will be weighed), and being at least 10 years old. Waivers must be signed and kids under 14 must be accompanied by a parent or adult designated as his chaperone. Come and see and experience the mountains from the treetops!

Hours: Open year-round, depending on weather/snow: Canopy Tours are available Thurs. - Mon.; closed Tues. and Wed. Open the two weeks after Christmas daily. Mountainview Tours and Quest Tours are available weekends only. Always call to make a reservation. The first tour starts around 9am and the last leaves about 2pm.

Price: The Canopy Tour during the week is $119; on weekends it's $129. Mountain View Tours are $109. Quest Tours are $65.

Ages: At least 10 years old, and up.

—GREAT OUTDOORS—

AFTON CANYON

(760) 252-6000 / www.blm.gov

Afton Road off I-15, between the Afton Rd. and Basin Rd. exits, Baker

Referred to as the "Grand Canyon of the Mojave," the canyon is at the site where the river surfaces after being underground for more than fifty miles. Since this is one of the few places in the desert where water is available, several wildlife species consider the canyon home, including bighorn sheep, migratory birds, and birds of prey. There are a few established roads through the multi-colored canyon, as well as hiking and equestrian trails. Washes and dry stream beds make for good hiking trails, too, although not during a flash flood. Hobby rock collecting is permitted. Primitive camp sites are available with a picnic table and single tap. Bring your own firewood and water. Note that hunting is permitted here in season.

Hours: Open daily, sunrise - sunset.
Price: Free to the park. $6 to camp.
Ages: 6 years and up.

AMBOY CRATER

(760) 326-7000 - crater; (760) 733-1066 - Roy's / www.blm.gov

National Trails Highway (Old Route 66), off Kelbaker Rd., Amboy

What do volcanoes look like? Well, instead of seeing one erupt (which would be thrilling, but potentially deadly), you can see the aftermath by hiking to and around this cinder cone. The surrounding lava flows surface is black with specks of green-colored, olivine crystals. The surface texture is alternately rough like jutting rocks or smooth like glass. There are twelve, bowl-shaped depressions that add even more variety to the volcanic features.

The Bureau of Land Management suggests a minimum of three hours hiking time to hike around the entire crater rim. The cone is about one mile from the parking lot and it is one mile in circumference. If you follow the trail to the right of the cinder cone, you'll head up to its wide opening where an eruption breached the crater wall. From here, the climb to the top is only an eighty-foot incline. There are a few, scattered picnic tables, some informational kiosks, and even restrooms. A favorite time to visit is from March to May when the desert flowers are blooming, and the sunrises and sunsets are often pink and purple hued.

Tips: Download this app for trails - Owlsheadgps.com. Carry water! Wear tough boots or tennis shoes as the lava rock can cut bottoms of shoes. Winters can be really cold here, and summer is blazing hot. If you drive east a few miles on National Trails Highway past the crater turn off, the "town" of Amboy, and Amboy Gas / Roy's you'll see the shoe tree, which has fallen over. This large shade tree is "decorated" with shoes of all sizes and styles that are still being tossed into its branches. But this is just a *foot*note for your trip.

Hours: Open daily, 7:30am - 4pm. (In the summer it is waaaaay too hot!)
Price: Free
Ages: 7 years and up.

BLAIR PARK

(909) 384-5233 / www.ci.san-bernardino.ca.us

1466 West Marshall Boulevard, San Bernardino

The area isn't the best, but it's OK and this park has a lot to offer: 34 acres include some hiking trails - some are steep ones, but the reward is a panoramic view from the top, plus a walking track with exercise and fitness equipment along the way. There are also two baseball diamonds; a basketball court; outdoor racquetball court; horseshoe pits; three lighted tennis courts; two fairly standard playgrounds; picnic tables with open grassy space; and a gated, cement skateboard park complete with several bowls and pools, ramps, step and rails.

Hours: Open daily, sunrise to sunset.
Price: Free
Ages: All

CUCAMONGA-GUASTI REGIONAL PARK

(909) 481-4205 or (909) 38 PARKS (387-2757) / cms.sbcounty.gov

800 N. Archibald Avenue, Ontario

Guasti Regional Park offers seasonal catfish and trout fishing at its nice-sized lakes. Note that ages 16 and up must have a fishing license (not sold here) and a fishing permit (sold here). The playground has a tire swing, monkey bars, and cement tubes with holes to climb through, plus open grassy areas for running around.

During the summer have some wet fun by going down the two water slides (must be 48" or taller), swimming in the half-acre lagoon, and playing in the zero-depth water play splash pad with colorful nozzles that squirt out water, tube arches to run under and fountains spurting up water from the cement. You can also just beach it on the sandy area around the lagoon and grassy area beyond that. Lifeguards are on duty.

Hours: The park is open most of the year daily, 7:30am - 5pm; open on summer weekends, 7:30am - 7pm. Fishing is usually closed on Thurs. for restocking. Water fun is available Memorial Day - Labor Day, Fri. - Sun.

Price: $8 per vehicle Mon. - Fri.; $10 on Sat. - Sun. and holidays. Pedestrians are $3; dogs are $1. Fishing permits are $10 per person during the week; $12 on weekends. Swimming Fri. - Sun. is $7 for ages 4 and up, plus the entrance fee. Swimming and all day water slides is $12 per person during the week; $17 on weekends, holidays and special events, plus entrance fee.

Ages: All

DANA PARK COMMUNITY CENTER / BARSTOW SKATE PARK

(760) 256-5617 / www.barstowca.org

850 Barstow Road, Barstow

Dana Park has a community center, picnic shelters, some grassy hills to roll down, a playground, and a 12,000-square-foot cement skate park with elements for beginning and advanced skaters, including a bowl, pyramid, and grind rails. Note that the park is just across the street from the MOJAVE RIVER VALLEY MUSEUM (pg. 427) and down the street from the DESERT DISCOVERY CENTER (pg. 424).

Hours: Open daily, 7am - dusk.

Price: Free

Ages: All

ENGLISH SPRINGS PARK

(909) 364-2700 / www.chinohills.org

2201 Grand Avenue, Chino Hills

This picturesque park, located on the corner of Grand Avenue and Chino Hills Parkway, has a small playground, a few picnic tables, and grassy area with plenty of mature trees surrounding the centerpiece pond that has a short waterfall. The other end of the park has a volleyball court and two basketball half courts, and more run-around space.

Hours: Open daily, dawn - dusk.

Price: Free

Ages: All

ETIWANDA FALLS

www.inlandempire.com; www.alltrails.com

near 4890 Etiwanda Avenue, Rancho Cucamonga

Depending on the rain fall, this popular, very rocky, 3.5 mile round trip hike leads to a lovely waterfall. The trail is mostly uphill, but only on the way up! The vista of Rancho Cucamonga from the top is wonderful as is the stream and water rushing over the rocks and the actual fall. Bring drinking water.

Because the Falls is accessed through the North Etiwanda Preserve, park at the trailhead, at the parking lot (if you park just outside the lot you could get towed), and look at the map there for this particular hike.

Hours: Open daily, sunrise - sunset.

Price: Free

Ages: 5 years and up.

FERGUSSON PARK

(909) 421-4949 / www.yourrialto.com

2395 W. 2345 Sunrise Drive, Rialto

This popular community park offers a baseball field, basketball court, horseshoe pits, a walking track, open grassy areas, picnic tables, tennis courts, and two nice playgrounds - one for tots and one for older kids, plus a cement skate park with all the necessary components to make it a really good one.

Hours: Open

Price: Free

Ages: All

GLEN HELEN REGIONAL PARK

(909) 887-7540 / cms.sbcounty.gov/parks

2555 Glen Helen Parkway, San Bernardino

$$$

This scenic 1,340-acre park, nestled in the mountains, is worth the drive. It offers an assortment of year-round fun, such as catfish, bass and trout fishing in the stocked and sizeable lakes (a license is needed for those over 16 years old) - note that there is a bait shop, here, too; volleyball courts; a baseball diamond; eighteen holes of disc golf; horseshoe pits; wide open grassy areas; lots of trails for hiking up and down the mountain; and playgrounds. These atypical playgrounds, partly based in the sand, spark the imagination with metal configurations to climb on, under, and through; slides; talking tubes; hanging monkey bar rings; netting to climb on; gyro twister; and more.

Favorite summer activities include sunbathing on the surrounding beach; swimming in the pool; playing in the a zero-depth water play area that has a huge "umbrella" with water pouring over it and more; and slip-sliding down the two water slides (minimum 48" tall) that end in a small pool. Replenish your energy at the nearby snack bar. Many special events occur at the massive outdoor pavilion including concerts and other programs, as well as at the Glen Helen Raceway. Camping, no hookups, is available here, too.

Hours: Open daily in the summer, 7:30am - 8pm; open the rest of the year daily, 7:30am - 5pm. Fishing is usually closed on Thurs. for restocking. Water activities are open Memorial Day - Labor Day, Wed. - Fri., 10am - 4pm; Sat. - Sun., 10am - 5pm.

Price: $8 per vehicle Mon. - Fri.; $10 per vehicle Sat. - Sun. and holidays. $3 for pedestrians. Fishing permits are $10 per person during the week; $12 on weekends. Swimming and water slides are $9 per person, Wed. - Fri.; $11 on Sat. - Sun.; $17 on holidays. Campsites are $25 a night during the week; $35 a night on weekends and holidays.

Ages: All

HESPERIA LAKE PARK

(760) 244-5951 / www.hesperiaparks.com

7500 Arrowhead Lake Road, Hesperia

!/$

This good-sized, enclosed lake park, surrounded by mountains, is mainly great for fishing and camping, although it's fun for day use, too. A rock-lined, seasonal creek runs throughout the park which is rich with large shade trees and picnic tables. Other facilities include barbeque pits, a soccer field, volleyball court, and sizable playground with a wood-chip base. The latter has swings, including toddler swings, a talking tube, and twisty slides.

The picturesque lake, which has small marshy islands in the middle, is apparently home to numerous ducks and birds, all eager for a hand-out! We saw pelicans, herons, swans, wood ducks, and other ducks and birds I can't identify. The lake is stocked every week, October through March, with trout, while catfish are stocked April through September. No state fishing license is required. If you are so inclined, you can even walk around the lake - about a mile round trip.

Tent, RV, and equestrian campers can stay here and get away from it all for a weekend, or week. All sites have a picnic table and fire ring. The on-site store offers camping supplies, food, drinks, bait, and tackle.

Hours: The park is open daily, 6am - 7pm. Fishing is open daily, 6am - sunset.

Price: Day use is free. Fishing sessions are $18 for adults for a 5 fish limit; $6 for ages 10 and under with a 2 fish limit (or pay the adult rate for a 5 fish limit). Camping starts at $35 per site, with a two-night minimum; dogs are $2 per dog, per night. Camping fees do not include fishing fees.

Ages: All

JACK BULIK PARK AND SKATE PARK

(909) 823-8751 - skate park; (909) 349-6900 - park / www.fontana.org

16581 Filbert, Fontana

!/$

The park offers plenty to do to keep everyone in the family happily busy. There are several ball fields, picnic facilities with BBQ pits, soccer fields, snack bar, covered basketball courts, tennis courts, a covered roller-hockey rink, a playground, teen center, and a skate park.

The massive and well-laid-out skate park (27,000 square feet) has rails, ledges, a three-bowl clover, a eight- to nine-foot round vert bowl, banks, steps, and more street elements. Again (and always) - skaters must wear safety equipment and those 17 and under need signed waivers. The park is supervised. Lessons, summer camps, friendly competitions, and birthday parties are all available here.

Hours: The park is open daily, 9am - 9:30pm. The skate park is open Mon. - Fri., noon - 9pm; Sat. - Sun., 9am - 9pm.

Price: The park is free. The skate park is $5 a month for residents; $7 for non-residents. Yearly passes are available.

Ages: All

JESS RANCH LAKES

(760) 240-1107 / www.jessranchlakesnews.com

11495 Apple Valley Road, Apple Valley

$$$

Serious, and not so serious, fishermen and women will have a great time angling for their fish limit at the two large lakes here. The area around the lakes has dirt pathways, as well as trees and other plants, plus a view of the mountains beyond. The fishing limit is five - trout or catfish and an additional three bluegill - for adults, for $20; and three trout or catfish for ages 12 and under, plus two bluegill, for $10. No fishing license is needed. Each angler must have his/her own string or basket, and children 12 and under must be accompanied by and supervised by adults.

If lake fishing didn't pan out at all for you, you may catch one trout, instead, at the nice-sized angling pond. The pond, surrounded by shade trees, grass, a short protective wall around some of it, and benches, is also available for those who just want to fish from there. The entrance fee for the angling pond is $3 for adults; ages 12 and under are free with a paying adult. The trout cost $4.50 per. Poles are available to rent for $5. The cleaning fee is $1 per fish. The fish hatchery on the grounds supplies trout for the weekly stocking. Lake One is for float tubers only, with a minimum of two tubers. The lake entrance fee is $25 for a half day, and bass are catch and release only.

There is a picnic area with BBQs for those who can't wait until they get home to eat their fish. You are also welcome to bring in a picnic meal and/or purchase something from the snack and bait shop. (Snack food for you; bait for the fish - just to be clear.) Be on the lookout for an amazing array of birds around here, too, such as woodpeckers, herons, road runners, quail, and egrets, plus ducks and geese, of course. Enjoy your day of fishing and fun in the great outdoors!

Hours: Open Fri. - Sun., 7am - 4pm.

Price: Day parking is free. Overnight RV parking is $10 a night. Other prices are listed above.

Ages: 3 years and up.

MARTIN TUDOR JURUPA HILLS REGIONAL PARK and SPLASH PARK

(909) 349-6900 - park; (909) 428-8822 - splash park, in season / www.fontana.org

11925 Sierra Avenue, Fontana

!/$$

This is another good park nestled into a rocky mountainside. It has a great wooden playground for slightly older kids, with wavy slides, a big spiral slide, swaying bridges, and swings. The lower level of the park has a grassy picnic area, along with a baseball diamond, horseshoe pits, volleyball courts, and a few swings.

Summertime fun got just a bit cooler - literally. The good-sized splash park has a rainbow arch that sprays water to run through; several, free-standing and colorful poles that shoot out water and some taller ones with buckets and flowers on top that spill over; plus water jets that stream up randomly from the cement ground. Some of this area is shaded, too, and there are a few picnic tables scattered about, adjacent to a grassy space. Two curvy water slides add a little extra zip to your time here.

Look at the MARY VAGLE MUSEUM AND NATURE CENTER (listed below) because it is just around the corner. In fact, a hiking/biking trail at the south end of the park goes around the base of the hill to the nature center. Another trail goes up and over the hill.

Hours: The park is open daily, 9am - sunset. The Splash Park is open Memorial Day - Labor Day daily, 11am - 5pm.

Price: Free to the park. The Splash Park is $5 for adults; $1.50 for seniors; $3 for ages 2 - 17; children under 2 are free.

Ages: All

MARY VAGLE NATURE CENTER

(909) 349-6994 / www.fontana.org

11501 Cypress Avenue, Fontana

This delightful nature center is at the foothills of a rock-covered hill, which is great for climbing and hiking on trails. One such trail leads up to petroglyphs. A winding bike trail goes around the base of the hill to connect to the MARTIN TUDOR JURUPA HILLS REGIONAL PARK (look at the above entry) on the other side.

The front of the nature center has a pond and acres of land for wildlife. Inside the building are live animals such as snakes, tarantulas, a chinchilla, lizards, and a tortoise. A small touch tidepool tank has sea stars and sea anemones. Other touch tables with bones, furs, rocks and more are also available here. Join the staff of the center in an array of family programs and classes on Saturday afternoons, guided nature walks, camps, and seasonal events. Teachers, inquire about the three-hour school field trips which incorporate a nature craft, tour of the center, and hands-on live animal experience. Field trips are $5 per student for grades K through 12th.

Hours: The center is open Wed. - Sun., noon - 5pm. Closed Mon., Tues., and major holidays. The grounds are open daily, sunrise - sunset.
Price: Free
Ages: All

MOJAVE NARROWS REGIONAL PARK

(760) 245-2226 / cms.sbcounty.gov/parks
18000 Yates Road, Victorville

This delightful, 840-acre park features two lakes. The larger one, Horseshoe Lake, is great for fishin' (no license needed for ages 15 years and under), has a bait shop near the entrance, and an island in the middle of it. The pond is seasonally stocked with trout and catfish. A stream runs through part of the park which boasts of wide open grassy spaces; lots of trees, including willow thickets and patches of cottonwoods; some hiking and riding trails; and pasture land for the numerous horses boarded at the on-site stables. Decent tent and full hookup RV camp sites (with showers) are here, but be aware that trains run by this park frequently; day and night. An equestrian campground is also onsite.

Picnic shelters, a disc golf course, a water play park for younger children with zero depth water, and a few dry-land playgrounds complete the park. Part of one good-sized playground is for all abilities with a ramp leading up to platforms and the slides. There is also twisty metal and plastic apparatus to climb, a tire swing, and other fun elements. The water play park has fountains and poles in colorful configurations that squirt water to drench kids running around the splash pad.

Hours: Open Thurs. - Mon., 7:30am - 4pm. Closed Tues. and Wed.
Price: $8 per vehicle Mon. - Fri.; $10 on Sat. - Sun. and holidays. Pedestrians are $3. Tent camping (which includes park entry) is $30 a night ($40 during holidays); $40 with hookup ($50 during holidays). Fishing permits are $10 per person Mon. - Fri., $12 on Sat. - Sun.
Ages: All

MOUNT BALDY SCENIC LIFT RIDE

(909) 982-0800 - chair lift; (909) 981-8238 - Top of the Notch / www.mtbaldyskilifts.com
8401 Mount Baldy Road, Mount Baldy

Mt. Baldy is a year-round destination, with numerous, adventuresome options. Those with intrepid spirits (and physical stamina) can walk up (and I mean almost straight up) the direct, steep route, under the chair lift, over one mile, to reach a summit. Slaloming on the fire road takes longer, 2.4 miles, but it's easier, and still gets up there. Or, take the almost twenty-minute scenic lift ride up for a gorgeous panoramic view - almost 8,000 feet high. Now that you've worked up an appetite (by hiking or riding), enjoy a good meal at Top of the Notch Restaurant and Bar. This large, cabin-style restaurant has been here for a while and its comfortable ambiance shows. Eat inside or outside, and know that sunsets up here are breathtaking. Breakfast options include a short stake of pancakes, $7 to an Awesome Burrito stuffed with scrumptious items, $10. The lunch and dinner menu, served with fries or salad, includes nachos, $10; hummus wrap, $10.95; burger, $12; chili bowl, $8; tri tip sandwich, $12; teriyaki stir fry, $12; and more.

Just a few of the various hiking trails from Top of the Notch include Thunder Mountain, a few miles from the Notch; and Devil's Backbone Trail. Head left from the Notch to take the Devil's trail, also known as Old Baldy, which climbs 3.5 miles (one way) to San Gabriel's tallest peak, Mt San Antonio, at 10,064 feet! Hiking this trail during non-winter months is recommended, and even then it is recommended for advanced hikers as the altitude can cause altitude sickness and the trail hugs the backbone ridge of the mountain (so it's narrow with some drops on either side). Bring water - lots of it!! Mountain biking is suggested only for very experienced riders as the terrain is rough. Check the website for weekend Moonlight Hikes in which you can hike (or ride) up to the restaurant and enjoy a bbq dinner and/or a lift ride up and down.

Zip it - ride one of four, side-by-side ziplines from Desert View back down to the Top of the Notch restaurant. The 600-yard is short, but fun - what a view! What a sensation! Feeling a little teed off? Start from the Notch and disc golf your way on the extreme 18-hole course to the bottom of Thunder Mountain, and back up to the Notch. The course, only open in the summer, is challenging and fun as your throw your disc through (and into) trees, mountain sides, and other natural obstacles as you walk up and down steep slopes and over loose rocks - yahoo! Discs are available for sale or for rent ($3) at the Notch.

So much to do up here and so little time? Spend the night in one of twenty tent cabins - canvas "cabins" on a platform - furnished with just a basic queen or twin bed, night stand, locking door and window, and electric lantern, plus a picnic table outside. Some are closer to the Notch, and some are a little more secluded. A tent cabin booking includes a round trip lift ticket, dinner on arrival night and breakfast in the morning for each guest. Actual tent camping (not in a cabin) is available for large groups, only.

Skiing, tubing and snow boarding at Mt. Baldy, with rentals available, are great winter sports. With four chair lifts and twenty-six runs, plus tubing at the base of the mountain, there is something for every level. See SKIING, SNOWBOARDING, SNOWSHOEING, SNOW PLAY (pg. 455) for more info.

Hours: Hiking is available any time, year round. The chair lifts are open during snow season and from Memorial Day - Labor Day, daily, 7am - 7pm(ish). They are usually open Fri. - Sun., only the rest of the year. The Notch is usually open the same days as chair lifts, usually 8am - 6pm. However, in the winter, it is only open 11am - 5pm. Skiing, snowboarding and tubing are offered daily, seasonally, 8am - 5pm. The disc course is only open in the summer time the same time as the chair lifts. Check the calendar for special events.

Price: Scenic lift tickets are $25 roundtrip for adults, $15 going up only (so hike down), $12 going down (so hike up); $20 roundtrip for ages 13 - 18, $13 for going up only, $9 going down; $15 roundtrip for seniors and ages 12 and under, $10 for going up only, $6 for going down; free for children 35" and under with a paying adult. Check out combo and discount tickets on the web, such as one round-trip chairlift ticket and a $10 voucher for the restaurant for $35 (regularly $50) for adults. Technically, disc golf is free if you hike up to the first tee at the Notch; or take a chair lift. Ziplining is $50 for adults, which includes the lift ticket; $40 for seniors and ages 12 and under; $45 for ages 13 - 17. Canvas cabin rentals are $200 per person for one night for a double. Parking is $5.

Ages: 40" and up to ride the lift chair; 8 years old to zipline; 6 years and up (recommended) for the hike.

MOUNT BALDY TROUT POOLS

(909) 982-4246
6945 Mount Baldy Road, Mount Baldy Village

No waders (or fishing license) are needed to catch fish at this delightful fishing spot up in the mountains. The clear, spring water ponds are surrounded by shady oak trees. The first pond stocks fish 13" through 18"; the second holds smaller fish, 9" through 13". The fish are abundant here, so chances are your young fisherboy/girl will make at least one catch of the day! All fish caught must be kept and paid for. After you've caught your fill, or the kids need more action, take a hike through the woods on the surrounding trails.

During the summertime, enjoy a refreshing dip in the nearby stream. There are places to hike and bike here year-round, plus the MOUNT BALDY SCENIC LIFT RIDE (see the entry above) for rides up and down the mountain to biking and hiking trails (and skiing during the winter), or for a meal at the top, Top of the Notch restaurant, that is. And while you're in the area, check out Mount Baldy Village, which has a few shops and places to eat, and the MOUNT BALDY VISITOR CENTER (the entry below), where you can pick up a map of the area hiking trails and a wilderness permit.

Hours: The ponds are open Sat., Sun., and holidays (including week-long school holiday breaks), 9am - 4pm. Additionally, they are open July through August, Fri. - Mon., 9am - 4pm. Note: You must be here at least a half hour before closing time. Closed Thanksgiving and Christmas.

Price: $1 if you bring your own pole; $2 to rent a pole. You may share poles. Fish prices range from $9 for 12" to $20.75 for 18". Price includes bait, cleaning, and packing fish in ice.

Ages: 3 years and up.

MOUNT BALDY VISITOR CENTER

(909) 982-2829 - visitor center; (909) 982-2879 - education/field trips / www.sgmha.org; www.fs.fed.usda.gov
1113 Mount Baldy Road, Mount Baldy Village

This place is worth a stop off on your way up or down the mountain. Inside the pleasant center's building, which was originally a schoolhouse built in 1921, are taxidermied animals - great horned owl, eagle, gray fox, bighorn sheep, mountain lion, and more. Display panels and photographs show the history of the area and its inhabitants. You can also pick up hiking trail maps, your Adventure Pass ($5), and other information here for your day of fun at Mt. Baldy. (Also see the previous two entries regarding other things to do in the immediate vicinity, plus skiing and snowboarding in the winter.)

Explore the wooded grounds, and sneak in a history lesson, as you see and go into a small, re-created village of the Gabrielino/Tongva native inhabitants. Here you'll find a replica ceremonial enclosure, a mountain lodge made of poles, and a traditional, dome-shaped house made of tules. The gold mining camp here has a canvas, miner's wedge tent; a general store (not like our current-day ones); a gravesite; and sluice boxes. One of the oldest buildings in the Mt. Baldy area, built in 1912, is here and made out of river stones and mortar. Bring a picnic lunch to enjoy at the tables under the trees. Scouting programs and other educational programs are offered through the ranger's station - $8 per student.

Hours: Open to the public Fri., 8am - 3pm; Sat. - Sun., 7am - 3pm. Open Tues. - Thurs. for educational programs/tours only.

Price: Free. An Adventure Pass is $5, which is needed for hiking around.

Ages: 3 years and up.

PACIFIC ELECTRIC INLAND EMPIRE TRAIL

(909) 477-2700 / www.cityofrc.us; www.traillink.com

These 18 mile parallel trails of asphalt and concrete and crushed stone, follow the old Pacific Electric Railway (hence the trail name) and now interconnect parks and community centers linking cities starting (or ending) in Montclair thru Upland, Rancho Cucamonga, Fontana and ending (or starting) in Rialto for the joggers, walkers, cyclists and horseback riders who use them. The trails sometimes go thru parks, alongside and across streets, past houses, and into more rural places. Portions of trail have night lighting, like the seven miles in Rancho Cucamonga. Users can choose from several trailheads. Some of the more easily accessible entry points include 4681 Huntington Dr., Montclair (an endpoint); 8500 Foothill Blvd.; Central Park at 11200 Base Line Rd.; Ellena Park at 7139 Kenyon Way; Red Hill Park at 7484 Vineyard Ave.; and 144 N Cactus Ave., Rialto, the other endpoint.

Hours: Open daily.

Price: Free

Ages: 3 years and up.

PERRIS HILL PARK and WATER PARK

(909) 384- 5233 - park; (909) 384-5419 - swim center/water park / www.ci.san-bernardino.ca.us

1135 E. Highland Avenue in Perris Hill Park, San Bernardino

Perris Hill Park has numerous amenities - a small playground with slides, swings, and a speaking tube; a large shady area packed with cement picnic tables; a few dirt trails up and around the hillside; an outdoor amphitheater with stadium-style seating built into the hillside; a tennis center with seven courts; horseshoe pits; a baseball diamond at one end; and a swim center with a splash playground. The enclosed, Jerry Lewis Swim Center / Water Park, is open seasonally, has a pool with a diving board and a good-sized water playground on cement. The latter has several rainbow-colored shapes that squirt out water; a large frog statue slide that ends in a wading pool; a long twisty water slide; an area where water fountains spurt up randomly; and umbrellas that drip water showers.

Hours: The park is open April - September daily, 6am - 8pm; open October - March daily, 6am - 6pm. The swim center/water park is open Memorial Day - beginning of June, and mid-August - September, weekends only, noon - 2:30pm and 3pm - 5:30pm. It is open the beginning of June - mid-August, daily, noon - 2:30pm and 3pm - 5:30pm.

Price: Free to the park. The swim center is $3 per 2½ hour session for adults; $1.50 for seniors and ages 8 - 17; $1 for ages 2 - 7.

Ages: All

PRADO REGIONAL PARK

(909) 597-4260 - park information; (909) 597-5757 - horse rentals / www.sbcounty.gov

16700 S. Euclid Avenue, Chino

This is another, has-it-all regional park! Besides the three softball diamonds; two soccer fields for tournament games or family fun; a nice, eighteen-hole disc course; and several playground areas, there is year-round fishing at the massive, stocked lake for trout and catfish - over 16 years old needs a license. Bait and tackle are available to purchase on weekends. There is a special area for radio-controlled boats on the lake, too.

On top of a large slab of cement is a small water play park, open seasonally, that has a few shapes that squirt out water to run through and under. The extra large "Fun for All" playground (a Shane's Inspiration one) is divided into several sections, with one being shaped like a ship. The playground is absolutely wonderful and accessible for all children, regardless of physical ability or disability. There are several ramps; bridges; many slides; monkey bars; climbing steps; a rock climbing wall; and activities to play and learn (i.e. Braille alphabet, a musical section - press a key to play a note and then play a song, and tic-tac-toe); plus swings, stepping stones, talking tubes, and much more, with places to play on the apparatus, as well as under it. Note that when you touch the sea creatures imbedded in the water wall, they will splash, squirt, and/or make their animal noise.

For those of you with delicate noses, you have correctly detected the nearby presence of horses, cattle, and sheep, as this is farm country. There are herds and ranches all up and down Euclid Street. The Prado Equestrian Center is located at the northern end of the park. Children 7 years old and up can take a one-hour guided trail ride through the park and to the basin. Rides are $30 an hour; $10 for an additional hour. Kids 2 to 7 years can be led inside the arena for $20 for a half hour; a helmet, that is provided, is required.

The paved street that winds all around the park will have to suffice for most skating or hiking desires, although there is a dirt trail along the lake and Chino Creek about a mile and a half long. Just down the street is a radio-controlled model plane airport and flying facility. Across Euclid Street, the park also has trap and skeet fields, an Olympic shooting range and an archery range.

If you like it here so much that you don't want to go home, stay and camp. The campgrounds are at the far end of the park and are O.K. looking. A few of the seventy-five sites have shade trees and a majority of the campsites are near barren, gently sloping hills. This area does have laundry and shower facilities.

Hours: The park is open most of the year daily, 7:30am - 5pm; open Memorial Day - Labor Day daily, 7:30am - 7pm. Horseback riding is available Sat. - Sun., 9am - 5pm (last ride leaves at 3:30pm), or Wed. - Fri., with advanced reservations.

Price: $8 per vehicle, Mon. - Fri.; $10 on Sat. - Sun. and holidays. $3 for pedestrians; $1 for dogs. Fishing permits are $10 per person Mon. - Fri., $12 on Sat. - Sun. Camping begins at about $40 a night; reservations are $7.

Ages: All

RAINBOW BASIN

(760) 252-6000 / www.blm.gov

Fossil Canyon Loop Road, 8 miles N. of Barstow

ROY G BIV (red, orange, yellow, green, blue, indigo, and violet) and all the in between, somewhat muted, colors of the rainbow are represented at the aptly-named Rainbow Basin. Note: Although the dirt roads are a bit bumpy, the destination is worth the jolting. (Four-wheel drive vehicles are highly recommended, but our mini van made it without too many problems.) Tip: Bring water! The colorful sedimentary rock formations are eye catching. We stopped the car several times to get out and look more closely at the variety of rocks, and to hike and climb the peaks, valleys, and cave formations, although there are no developed trails. We didn't find any, but we read that this area is rich with mammal fossil remains as mastodons, pronghorns, "dog-bears," and horses have been found here. Collecting fossils, however, is forbidden.

The adjacent Owl Canyon Campground has twenty-two fairly primitive sites. Facilities include fire rings, grills, and vault toilets. Bring your own firewood and water. Remember that, as with any desert area, extreme temperatures occur.

Hours: Open daily, dawn - dusk.

Price: Free. Camping is $6 a night.

Ages: 4 years and up.

SILVERWOOD LAKE STATE RECREATIONAL AREA

(760) 389-2281or (760) 389-2303 - park office; (760) 389-2299 - marina boat rentals and beach store; (760) 389-2288 - boat rentals / www.parks.ca.gov

14651 Cedar Circle, Hesperia

As we traveled north on Interstate 15, almost at the Highway 138 turnoff, we noticed trains on several different tracks, so we pulled off to watch them intersect and chug by below us.

The upper area of the huge lake, by Highway 173, is for waterskiing and boating activities. The overlook of the lower section reveals surprisingly blue waters that reach into the several nooks and inlets all around the lake. Three miles of maintained hiking trails branch off in various directions and two swim beaches are complete with sections of sand. Note that a portion of the colossal Pacific Crest Trail, the 2,650 mile trail which spans from Mexico to Canada, passes through Silverwood Lake. Fish from the shore for striped bass, crappie, catfish, largemouth bass, and trout (which are stocked during the cooler are months), or from fishing boats and float tubes. Fourteen-foot aluminum fishing boats ($35 for two hours) are available to rent year round, weather dependent, and pontoon boats are $85. Summer rentals include kayaks ($18 an hour), two-seater paddle boats ($23 an hour) and jet skis ($99 an hour). Note that there are a few picnic areas that can only be reached via boat. Bait, tackle, fishing licenses (a must for ages 16 and up), snacks, drinks and sundries are available past the main entrance at the marina/beach store.

Down near the waterside, the Cleghorn area has a big grassy spot, picnic tables, and barbecues under shade trees, plus a rock-lined brook, one of the swim beaches, and the stunning beauty of the surrounding mountains. A short drive down the road is Sawpit Beach, just in front of the store, the most popular spot (i.e., crowded) for swimming, sunbathing, and picnicking. The close-by Black Oak picnic area is just a short walk to Sawpit, but it boasts of fewer people, lots of grass, large oak trees, and picnic tables. Miller Canyon picnic area is a few miles past the main entrance east on Highway 138 and is more secluded. It's ideal for fishing, kayaking, hiking, and relaxing. Note: Cleghorn area is closed November through April.

If you like it so much that you want to stay here, do. Bring your camping gear. The 136 developed campsites for tents and RVs are decent and there are plenty of outdoor activities, including all the above-mentioned, plus eleven miles of biking trails. Ride around the relatively easy paved trails which loop around a part of the lake.

Hours: Open April - September daily, 6am - 9pm; open October - March daily, 7am - 7pm.
Price: $10 per vehicle; $9 for seniors. $5 for pedestrians and bikers. $3 per person to fish off the docks. Camping starts at $45 with no hookups; $50 with hookups.
Ages: All

SKY HIGH DISC GOLF

(760) 249-5808; (888) 754-7878 / www.mthigh.com/discgolf
24510 Hwy. 2, Wrightwood

It's a bird, it's a plane - no, it's - a disc? Maybe your disc won't be flying that high, but the course is almost 8,000 feet above sea level, on the north side of the Mountain High Ski resort. Talk about a view! To complete the three nine-hole courses is a 2.5 mile hike up and down and along the mountainside, which is part of the Angeles National forest. Players throw the discs around trees and wildlife - perhaps hawks and even deer - and then players must walk wherever they threw the disc and try to find it.

If you don't have a disc, don't worry because you can purchase one (or more) from the full line of accessories at the onsite, woodsy lodge/pro shop, which also sells food. A combo meal of a freshly grilled hamburger, plus chips and a soda is about $8.50. You can also purchase a hot dog or pizza, or even bring your own food. There are picnic tables inside and outside for your dining pleasure. Special events and tournaments are hosted here, too, as Sky High is rated high on the list of the top courses to play in the country. I'm not good at throwing a disc, but this was a blast, if just for the hiking. Extreme disc golf; extremely fun.

Hours: Usually open mid-April - the beginning of October, Sat. - Sun., 8am - 5pm. Open holiday Mon., 9am - 5pm. Hours fluctuate depending on if the there is snow for skiing, so call first.
Price: $9 per person for 27 holes.
Ages: 7 years and up - or able to throw a disc, and walk a lot.

SOUTHERN CALIFORNIA MONTANE BOTANIC GARDEN / OAK GLEN PRESERVE

(909) 797-8507 or (909) 790-3698 / www.wildlandsconservancy.org
39611 Oak Glen Road at Los Rios Rancho, Oak Glen

The botanic garden is nature, pure nature. Period. In all of its naturalness and loveliness. The botanic garden, located within the 908-acre preserve, has coniferous forests, chaparral, meadows, woodlands, a pond (with a short floating bridge and pier), streams, small pools, giant sequoias, a champion-sized oak tree (almost 500" around and 97 feet tall!), a man-made waterfall and waterfall plants, plus plants and lots of wildlife all nestled in mountain foothills and overlooking apple orchards. Seasonally you will also see hummingbirds and tons of other birds, as well as CA poppies and five other acres of wildflowers. Come walk some (or all) of the five miles of trails, especially the two mile loop trail, and breathe it all in. You are welcome to explore on your own, or sign up for a guided hike and/or other special events offered by the conservancy like Night Walks, Little Pines (for little kids), Fun Unplugged summer program, Volunteer Day and more. The amazing school tours, for all age students, could incorporate lessons and experiments with erosion, plants, weather, animals, micro habitats, pond life, the food chain, seed dispersal and more. Note that the conservancy shares the land with Los Rios Rancho, so enjoying seasonal apple products and picking, the country store, and the picnic tables on the front lawn. See OAK GLEN / APPLE PICKING (pg. 403) for more details.

Hours: The trails are open daily, 8am - 4:30pm, open til 5:30 with d.s.t.
Price: Free
Ages: All

YUCAIPA REGIONAL PARK

(909) 790-3127 / cms.sbcounty.gov/parks
33900 Oak Glen Road, Yucaipa

Nestled in the rocky San Bernardino Mountains is this huge, beautiful oasis of a park offering year-round fun. Fish in any one of the three very large, picturesque, stocked lakes to catch seasonal bass, trout, or catfish. A fishing license is required. Try your hand at the eighteen-hole disc golf course and at horseshoes.

During the summer months, get in the swim of things in the one-acre swim lagoon, and/or go for the two long water slides. White sandy beaches frame the water's edge, with grassy areas just beyond them. A few steps away is a full-service snack bar, which also carries bait / worms for your fishing needs. A wonderful playground is right outside the swim area. Another playground, designed specifically for disabled children, is across the way.

RV and tent camping is available for those who really want to get away from it all for a weekend or so. The grassy areas, trees, and mountains are a scenic setting for the camp sites. There are plenty of picnic tables and shelters, as well as barbecue pits. Hiking is encouraged on either paved trails or along the few dirt pathways. See OAK GLEN / APPLE PICKING (pg. 403) for nearby places to go.

Hours: The park is open most of the year daily, 7:30am - 5pm; open in the summer daily, 7:30am - 6pm. Swimming is available Memorial Day - mid-June, and mid-August - Labor Day, weekends only, 10am - 5pm; mid-June - mid-August, Tues. - Sun., 10am - 5pm.

Price: $8 per vehicle Mon. - Fri.; $10 on weekends and holidays. Pedestrians are $3; dogs are $1. Fishing permits are $10 per person Mon. - Thurs., $12, Fri. - Sun. Entrance to the swim lagoon is park admission, plus $7 per person for ages 4 and up. An all-day water slide and swim pass is $12 per person, plus park admission. Camping prices range from $39 (no hook-ups) to $40 (hook-ups) per night; holidays are an additional $10. Hot showers, grills, and fire rings are available.

Ages: All

—MALLS—

ONTARIO MILLS MALL

(909) 484-8300 / www.simon.com/mall/ontario-mills

One Mills Circle, Ontario

Ontario Mills is one of California's largest outlet malls with over 200 outlet, speciality, and name brand retail stores. Kids favorites include LEGO STORE - MINI MODEL BUILD (San Bernardino County) (pg. 409), The Disney Store Outlet, and Sweet Factory. The mall also offers various forms of "shoppertainment." Other entertainment offered at the mega mall includes DAVE & BUSTER'S (San Bernardino County) (pg. 407), a combination restaurant/bar and game/arcade center geared for adults;IFLY (San Bernardino County) (pg. 434); an AMC 30 Theatre; and Improv Comedy Theater and Dinner Theatre for adults - (909) 484-5411 / www.improv.com. Kids will love making their own teddy bears here at BUILD-A-BEAR WORKSHOP (San Bernardino County) (pg. 432). Note that Circus Vargas is usually here the end of March. Get tickets and more information at (877) 468-3861 / www.circusvargas.com.

The food court is fancifully-decorated with large, colorful, inflatable foods. Other tantalizing eating experiences in unique surroundings include RAINFOREST CAFE (pg. 405).

Hours: The mall and most attractions are open Mon. - Sat., 10am - 9pm; Sun., 11am - 8pm.

Price: Technically, free.

Ages: All

VICTORIA GARDENS REGIONAL TOWN CENTER - VG KIDZ CLUB - CULTURAL CENTER

(909) 463-2830 - guest services; (909) 477-2720 - library; (909) 820-4600 - carriage rides / www.victoriagardensie.com; www.vgculturalcenter.com

10500 Civic Center Drive, Rancho Cucamonga

The "mall", for lack of a better word, is a shopping complex of over 170 shops and restaurants (and places to indulge in dessert). Part of it is a typical mall, but the other part is a cohesive, classy, outdoor venue stretching several city blocks with pedestrian streets and a park-like ambiance of grassy areas and fountains interwoven between groupings of stores. Some of the draws for kids are the free rides up and down the streets on a vintage-style trolley; the AMC movie theater; a ride on the trackless scale model train ($3 for ages 3 and up); the fountains that spurt up at random intervals for them to play in and run through; horse-drawn carriage rides ($5 per person for about a fifteen-minute ride); all the lights at Christmas time; and the special events, especially those held at Chaffey Town Square. The latter includes family-oriented entertainment such as free spring and summertime movies (bring your own blanket or lawn chair), and concerts. The free, VG Kidz club meets one Saturday a month from 11am to 1pm at Chaffey Town Square. Past activities have included a flower pot craft, summer luau, back to school event, tree craft, and other seasonal happenings. Buy something special at the Farmer's Market and Craft Fair that meets here every Friday from 10am to 2pm.

Check out BASS PRO SHOPS OUTDOOR WORLD (pg. 432), for all (and I mean all) of your outdoors needs, and for the ambiance. You'll see what I mean. Other favorites include It's Sugar, GYU-KAKU (Los Angeles County) (pg. 23) Japanese BBQ, Richie's Real American Diner, and lots more.

The Victoria Gardens Cultural Center is one of the anchors for the town center. One component is the stylish LEWIS FAMILY PLAYHOUSE PERFORMING ARTS CENTER (pg. 437), which hosts a multitude of terrific shows and performances. Adjacent to the Playhouse is a state-of-the-art public library with a themed children's section, storytelling theater, and, of course, lots and lots of books. Enjoy the outdoor landscaped courtyards, interactive learning stations, wishing fountain, and the glass elevator. (Take a ride!) Just outside the center is a small playground and a food hall with several, express-food options.

Hours: Call or check this center's website for a schedule of events. The VG Kidz meets one Saturday a month from 11am - 1pm. The shops, restaurants, and entertainment times vary. Little train rides are offered Mon. - Thurs., 11am - 8pm; Fri. - Sat., 11am - 9pm; Sun., 11am - 7pm. Trolley rides are usually offered Fri. - Sat., noon - 9pm; Sun., noon - 6pm. (Open extended hours during holidays.) Horse-drawn carriage rides are usually offered Fri., 7pm - 10pm; Sat., 8pm - 10pm; Sun., 5pm - 7pm. (Open extended hours during holidays.)
Price: Free; bring spending money.
Ages: All

—MUSEUMS—

BARSTOW ROUTE 66 "MOTHER ROAD" MUSEUM

(760) 255-1890 / www.route66museum.org
681 N. First Avenue, Barstow

The small Mother Road museum has a few mother lode exhibits. Some of the vehicles on exhibit here from the Route 66 heyday are a 1947 Police Servi-Car, a 1964 red Mustang convertible, a 1915 Model T, and an old, wooden, one-horse carriage, sans horse. Other memorabilia includes gas station pumps; lots of roadway signs; old toys (anyone else remember trolls?); a camera collection; display of products and the minerals from whence they came; license plates; WWII paraphernalia (ration books, hair curlers, and more); toy cars; photographs of the local area from around the turn of the century; and lots of information on Route 66. The gift shop sells postcards, t-shirts, and other souvenirs. Note that the WESTERN AMERICA RAILROAD MUSEUM (pg. 430) shares this same brick building, which is located in a working railroad depot, first reached by going over a trestle bridge.
Hours: Open Fri. - Sat., 10am - 4pm; Sun., 11am - 4pm.
Price: Free
Ages: 7 years and up.

CALIFORNIA ROUTE 66 MUSEUM

(760) 951-0436 / www.califrt66museum.org
16825 D Street, Victorville

You can still get your kicks on Route 66! The more you know about the history and the culture of Route 66, the more you'll appreciate this terrific museum. Actually, the museum was once a Route 66 road house. The rooms are now packed with memorabilia and artifacts that encapsulate this era, such as Hula Ville art, roadway signs, gas pumps, neon signs, lots of photographs and information on local history, a Model-T, toy cars, and some decorative roadside art saved for posterity. (Exhibits do rotate.) The attached gift shop is filled with nostalgic-type items.
Hours: Open Mon., Thurs. - Sat., 10am - 4pm; Sun., 11am - 3pm. Closed Tues., Wed. and major holidays.
Price: Free
Ages: 7 years and up.

CHINO YOUTH MUSEUM

(909) 334-3270 / www.chinoyouthmuseum.com
13191 6th Street, Chino

This compact children's museum has a main room with several smaller rooms that branch off from it. Each room is themed around a particular function, or career, found within a city. The themes are enhanced with a colorful mural or building facade, and a prop or two. For instance, kids can become a fireman for a day by putting on firemen uniforms, sliding down a short pole, and sitting on a wooden fire engine. They can "shop" in a market with play food; work at a bank behind the teller's window with cash registers; and be a newscaster behind the desk with the camera pointed on them. Ah, to be young again and just have to pretend at working a job! The museum also has a room just for arts and crafts, and an area to play with puzzles, Legos and other hands-on fun. Ask about monthly shows and activities, such as First Friday when the museum is open between 3pm and 5pm, for free, and offers a free craft project, entertainment, and snack; and Kid's Night Out, a one Saturday a month night, when ages 4 to 10 can be dropped off from 6pm to 9pm for hours of play, games, storytelling, and a light dinner.

Just outside the museum is a plaza with a fountain, cement picnic tables, and a grassy area with trees.

Hours: Open most of the year, Wed. - Sun., 10am - 4pm. Open in the summer Mon. - Fri., 10am - 5pm; Sat. - Sun., 10am - 4pm. The museum closes at 2pm on the days of First Friday events to reopen at 3pm. Closed Mon., Tues. and most major holidays.

Price: $4 for ages 1 and up. The first Fri. of each month is free admission from 3pm - 5pm. Kid's Night Out is $15 per child.

Ages: 2 - 8 years.

DESERT DISCOVERY CENTER

(760) 252-6060 / desertdc.com

831 Barstow Road, Barstow

This center, in partnership with several other organizations, is the nucleus of a wide range of educational programs exploring the resources in association with the vast Mojave Desert. It is also a museum. The building houses the renown Old Woman Meteorite, weighing in at 5,000+ pounds. It is the second largest meteorite found in the U.S. Other displays include native plants and taxidermied animals indigenous to the area, such as big horn sheep, foxes, birds, snakes, and more. Animal tracks dating from prehistoric times include those of camels, other mammals, and even some dinosaurs. Fossils, skulls, rocks, replicas of petroglyphs, tools from the Calico mine site, and exhibits on the water cycle are also found here.

The garden outside consists of native plant species and a short hiking trail with a bridge. The small pond out back hosts numerous turtles and quite a few dragonflies. And look for the several desert tortoises that consider the center home. (They hibernate, though, November through February.)

Area school kids benefit greatly from all the free programs offered, including plant and animal adaptation, recycling, geology, and the all-inclusive Jr. Naturalist certification program. The latter has requirements in nine categories including biology, botany, history, paleontology, archeology, and learning environmental stewardship. The hands-on approach makes it fascinating and fun for primarily elementary-school-aged kids. Check the website or call to ask about day camps and their annual events.

Hours: Open Tues. - Sat., 11am - 4pm. Closed Sun., Mon., and holidays. Call for program information.

Price: Free

Ages: All

GRABER OLIVE HOUSE

(800) 996-5483 or (909) 983-1761 / www.graberolives.com

315 E. Fourth Street, Ontario

This is an unusual pit stop for kids. On the lovely grounds are picnic tables, a grassy area with shade trees in the front, and old machinery, plus a small museum, an olive processing plant, a gift shop, and the owner's house. The one-room museum shows a pictorial history of olive processing. It also has an eclectic mix of antiques such as a big wooden olive grader, a Singer sewing machine, a sausage stuffer, and more.

Take a twenty-minute tour around the working olive plant. Harvesting, the "on-season", is mid-October through December, when the machinery and workers are in full production. This, then, is the best time to take a tour. Walk into the grading room, where olives are sorted by size and quality, and peer into the enormous olive vats. The boiler room, where olives are sterilized, the canning machine, and the labeling machine are all interesting to look at. A ten-minute video, that shows the history of the packing plant, is also available to watch.

One of the gift shops carries unique kitchen and cooking utensils. The other is very classy with etiquette videos, stationery, delicious jams, and elegant candies. (The chocolate-covered cherries are to die for!) Kids can sample Graber olives, and this brand might mean more to them after a tour.

Hours: Open most of the year Fri. - Sun., 10am - 5pm. Open mid-October - December daily, 10am - 5:30pm. Closed major holidays.

Price: Free

Ages: 5 years and up.

HISTORICAL GLASS MUSEUM

(909) 798-0868 / www.historicalglassmuseum.com

!/$$

1157 N. Orange Street, Redlands

Housed in a 1903 Victorian-style home this small museum, which boasts the largest collection of American-made glass in the West, contains a plethora of glassware, displayed mostly on glass shelves in curio cabinets. Plates, vases, cups, bottles, pitchers, cruets, candlesticks and other beautiful and colorful pieces are grouped together in various rooms, showcasing glass from factories that are becoming extinct as well as "current" producers. I wouldn't want to be the one in charge of dusting! Learn more of the history of glass, and the United States, by taking a guided tour. Note that there is also a gift shop here.

Hours: Open Sat. - Sun., noon - 4pm. Closed on some holidays.
Price: Free - $5 suggested donation.
Ages: 12 years and up.

INLAND EMPIRE MILITARY MUSEUM

(909) 885-6324 or (909) 888-0477 / www.juanpollo.com

!

1394 N. E Street, San Bernardino

Operated by a veteran, this relatively small museum holds a lot of great memorabilia from WWI, WWII, Korea, Vietnam, Gulf, Afghan, and Iraq wars. Divided into sections according to each branch of the military, on display are military dress uniforms, hats, helmets, medals, flags, a 1953 restored Willis Jeep, a model of an aircraft carrier, photographs, and more. Take a guided tour and/or take the time to read the information accompanying the artifacts and learn the stories and history behind the items. Note that this museum is right next door to the MCDONALD'S MUSEUM (unofficial) (pg. 426).

Hours: Open Sat. - Sun., 11am - 5pm. Open during the week by appointment only.
Price: Free
Ages: 7 years and up.

JOHN RAINS HOUSE - CASA DE RANCHO CUCAMONGA

(909) 989-4970; (909)798-8608 / www.sbcounty.gov/museum

$$

8810 Hemlock Street, Rancho Cucamonga

Built with bricks in 1860, this restored rancho residence is a lovely example of a house from this era. Tours are given through the historical home to see period furniture in the bedrooms, living rooms, and other rooms, and around the beautiful grounds, complete with green lawns, trees, picnic tables in the backyard, and the central courtyard. Docents recount stories about the people who once lived here. Their lives were like soap operas, complete with affairs, murders, buried treasure, and more sordid happenings - kids love this! (And they are learning history.) Ask about school and group tours and the special events that the Rancho hosts, such as Rancho Day, where each year the house is decorated according to a different theme, accompanied by costumed docents and activities for kids. Note: The house is exquisitely decked out at Christmas time.

Hours: Open Tues. - Sat., 10am - 3pm for tours by advanced reservation. Closed Sun., Mon., New Year's Day, Thanksgiving, and Christmas.
Price: $5 for adults; $4 for seniors; $2.50 for students and ages 6 and up; children 5 and under are free.
Ages: 6 years and up.

KIMBERLY CREST HOUSE AND GARDENS

(909) 792-2111 / www.kimberlycrest.org

$$$

1325 Prospect Drive, Redlands

This exquisite-looking, three-story, rather large (7,000 square-foot!), light lime green and gray French chateau, with yellow trim, was originally built in 1897. The turrets add to its eye-catching appeal, as do the formal Italian-style gardens and grounds, complete with lotus blossoms and koi in the lily ponds under the stone steps and bridge, a series of cascading pools, and mature cypress, magnolia, palm, and orange trees.

See the period (replicated) furniture and decor, which is as grand as the outside, with gilt furniture, glass mosaics, and silk damask wall coverings on the forty-five-minute guided tour. Explore the French parlor, library, living room, dining rooms (set with crystal), bedrooms, and other beautifully-accessorized rooms - the first two floors of the house and the Carriage House Museum. The tour requires walking up and down stairs.

The gift shop is located in a one-hundred-year-old carriage house, as is a small picture gallery/museum with some memorabilia. Specialized tours include a two-hour Behind the Scenes Tour geared for older kids and for adults that includes seeing the house, including the third floor, the basement and Carriage House, with an emphasis on the architecture and preservation of it all. See the web calendar for other events like the Second Sunday program with activities geared for kids; the specialty teas, including some specifically for younger children, such as the Wonderland Tea Party; and the very popular Princess at the Castle event for children. See the April Calendar section for details.

The Crest House is nestled in one end of the lush, Prospect Park. After your tour, enjoy a walk on the dirt trails through the park.

Hours: Tours are given Thurs., Fri. and Sun., 1pm - 3:30pm, every 30 minutes, with the last tour at 3:30pm. Closed holidays and the month of August. The surrounding park is open daily, 9am - 5pm.

Price: $10 for adults; $8 for seniors; $5 for ages 6 - 12; children 5 and under are free.

Ages: 6 years and up.

LINCOLN MEMORIAL SHRINE

(909) 798-7636 - Shrine; (909) 798-7632 - Heritage Room at the Smiley Public Library / www.lincolnshrine.org

125 W. Vine Street, Redlands

"Fourscore and seven years ago . . ." begins the Gettysburg Address. If your older children are studying our revered sixteenth president, but can't make it to Washington D.C., bring them to the Lincoln Memorial Shrine in Redlands. The central, octagon-shaped building has a main room and two wings, all devoted to Abraham Lincoln and Civil War memorabilia. The building contains research books; surgical instruments; letters and documents written from and about Abraham Lincoln, Robert E. Lee, and Stonewall Jackson; Civil War photographs; bullets found on battlefields; officers' uniforms; medals; and a lifemask (i.e., an exact likeness of a person via a mold) and handcast of Abraham Lincoln. Mementos from his assassination include his cuff links, a strand of his hair, mourning bands, and the wreath that laid on his casket. The shrine also displays other Civil War artifacts such as swords, an 1863 Springfield rifle, hardtack, documents, models, and pictures of Abraham Lincoln, Robert E. Lee, and Ulysses S. Grant.

Come view the materials here on your own. Better yet, take a guided tour and benefit from knowledgeable docents who explain the exhibits in more detail. Exhibits at the memorial rotate because the small shrine cannot contain the 3,000-plus manuscripts and other items in the archives. The outside of the building is inscribed with excerpts from Lincoln's inaugural addresses and various other speeches. Look at the Calendar entry LINCOLN SHRINE OPEN HOUSE (pg. 699) for information on the annual Open House.

The shrine is located behind the Smiley Public Library which has a lovely expanse of green lawn, old shade trees, and benches in between. The multi-level library, established in 1894, is an architectural and book-lovers delight.

Hours: Open Wed. - Sat., 10am - noon and 1pm - 5pm. Closed holidays, except for Lincoln's birthday. Small group tours can be arranged for morning hours.

Price: Free

Ages: 7 years and up.

MCDONALD'S MUSEUM (unofficial)

(909) 885-6324 / www.juanpollo.com

1398 North 'E' Street, San Bernardino

"We love to see you smile!" is just one McSlogan touted at this museum. The building is on the site of the first McDonald's Restaurant, which was established in 1948. Inside, half of the space is used for the administration offices of Juan Pollo Restaurants, the company that now owns the building. The other half is a tribute to McDonald's and a refuge for all of its merchandising paraphernalia throughout the years - that's a lot of Happy Meal toys! (Kind of makes you wish you hadn't thrown out all of those toys; kind of.) Besides the toys, games, and array of promotional products, display cases hold old menus; to-go bags; a 1940's milk shake machine; a 1950's potato press for making French fries (check out the old, moldy fry that is a eleven feet long); and lots of photographs and articles on McDonald's, including the ones detailing the feud between the McDonald's brothers and Ray Kroc. There are also a few pieces of Playland equipment and character costumes - lots of McMemories!

In the back of the museum are some artifacts, such as road signs, souvenir mugs, and posters, plus information panels from and about historic Route 66. Note that just next door to this museum is the INLAND EMPIRE MILITARY MUSEUM (pg. 425).

Hours: Open Mon. - Fri., 9am - 5pm; Sat. - Sun., 10am - 5pm.

Price: Free

Ages: 5 years and up.

MOJAVE RIVER VALLEY MUSEUM

(760) 256-5452 / www.mojaverivervalleymuseum.org

270 E. Virginia Way, Barstow

This little, and sometimes dusty, museum is full of interesting artifacts and displays. The rock and minerals on display include nice specimens of arrowheads, quartz, calate, and black and gold forms of chalocopyrite, plus fluorescent minerals that glow neon colors under black light. Other glass-encased exhibits are an eclectic mixture, such as lanterns, irons, rug beaters, pottery, clothing, a collection of glass insulators used by telegraph companies, and more. Kids can try their hand at grinding corn with stone mortar and pestle. They can also touch various animal skins, a turtle shell, bones, pinecones, rocks, and cotton. Short nature films are available to watch upon request. Call to arrange a field trip for students.

Outside of the museum is some large mining equipment - ore carts, picks, and other tools, as well as a jail cell and one of only two Drover cars left in the world. Across the street is the small Centennial Park, which is actually an extension of the museum. It has a caboose, an army tank, and a mining display, which are representative of the three industries that helped formed Barstow. Note that DANA PARK COMMUNITY CENTER / BARSTOW SKATE PARK (pg. 414) is just across the street and the DESERT DISCOVERY CENTER (pg. 424) is just down the road.

Hours: The museum is open daily, 11am - 4pm. Closed Christmas.

Price: Free to the museum, though donations are appreciated.

Ages: 3 years and up.

MUSEUM OF HISTORY AND ART, ONTARIO

(909) 395-2510 / www.ontarioca.gov

225 S. Euclid Avenue, Ontario

The Museum of History and Art captures the flavor of historic Ontario. The small museum's galleries feature artifacts regarding early inhabitants from Native Americans and California Rancheros to early twentieth century settlers and, in particular, the founder of Ontario. Displays represent home and community life, and exhibits from the agricultural heritage, citrus groves, and industry and social life. The artifacts consist of saddles, bikes, toys, irons, clothes, military uniforms, pictures, and a replicated assay office from the 1900's. Another section focuses on locally famous roads, such as Euclid Avenue and Route 66. I like the big neon eagle sign that lights up when you walk into that section. The north wing presents changing exhibits every two months or so. Ask about docent guided gallery tours and family workshops that include a hands-on, theme-related projects, or the classroom outreach programs. Set in a Mediterranean-style building with a big fountain out front, huge shade trees, and a grassy area, the museum is a pleasant way to learn more about local roots.

Hours: The museum is open Thurs. - Sun., noon - 4pm. Closed Mon. - Wed., and holidays.

Price: Free

Ages: 6 years and up.

NASA GOLDSTONE VISITOR CENTER

(760) 255-8688 / www.gdscc.nasa.gov

681 North First Avenue, Barstow

Who knew that you can't really learn all about deep space from *Star Trek* and *Star Wars*?! Goldstone, working alongside NASA and JPL, is only one of three facilities in the world where a network of antennas receive ALL the information transmitted from ALL the interplanetary spacecraft missions, as well as radio and radar astronomy observations, for processing. Wow! This includes signals and pictures from the over thirty-year-old Voyager I to the more current Mars Exploration Rover and Earth-orbiting missions. While you can't visit the Goldstone facility, located on Fort Irwin, you can come visit the Visitor Center and still gain a world of knowledge.

The Goldstone visitor center / museum, located on the second floor of the historic Harvey House (Casa Del Desierto), is set up partly like a (visually stimulating) classroom, with numerous colorful posters, models, photos from space telescopes of exploding supernovas, and more. Explore it on your own, yet a guided tour adds such great information. We learned that the 10th planet Eris, was discovered years ago; Pluto has three moons, not one; signals from our moon come back in 2 ½ seconds, while they return from Voyager 1 in over twenty-nine hours; and there is definite proof that liquid once flowed on Mars. This stellar tour, given for school students and adults, makes exploring our vast solar system and universe relevant, important, and down to earth, so to speak.

The two rooms here also contain history timelines via information panels and pictures; a dichroic plate with holes that allow frequencies to pass through; tools; an astronaut's uniform; a huge gear box for antennas; an orb to spin that shows the turbulence in flowing water; an astronaut photo op; computer programs; and more. Free NASA stickers and posters are given out, too - yea! See the other museums in this immediate vicinity: BARSTOW ROUTE 66 "MOTHER ROAD" MUSEUM (pg. 423) and WESTERN AMERICA RAILROAD MUSEUM (pg. 430).

Hours: Open Mon. - Fri., 9am - 4pm; Sat. - Sun., 10am - 2pm. Closed on federal holidays.
Price: Free
Ages: 7 years and up.

OAK GLEN SCHOOL HOUSE MUSEUM

(909) 797-1691 / www.oakglenschoolmuseum.com; www.oakglen.net
11911 S. Oak Glen Road, Yucaipa

The small, one-room school house museum was originally built in 1927. The stone exterior encompasses a room containing old-fashioned desks facing a black board, a potbelly stove, a phonograph, a stereoscope, newspaper clippings, apple crate labels from ranches, and old pictures. Tours are offered to the public upon request. School groups can take the basic fifteen-minute tour and then add on additional activities, such as making a candle by rolling up a sheet of beeswax, dipping pen in an ink bottle and writing, and taking a short nature walk. Teachers are welcome to bring their own curriculum to teach, too.

The adjacent, picturesque small park has grassy lawns, shade trees, picnic tables, and a multi-story play structure with slides (even an enclosed one) and climbing rock. See OAK GLEN / APPLE PICKING (pg. 403) for more attractions in this area.

Hours: Open most of the year, Sat. - Sun., noon - 4pm, weather permitting. Open in the fall (apple-picking season), Wed. - Sun., noon - 4pm. Closed the month of December. Call to make a reservation for a school tour.
Price: Free. Suggested donations are $1 for adults; 50¢ for children. School tours cost 50¢ per student, per activity.
Ages: 4 years old and up.

PLANES OF FAME AIR MUSEUM

(909) 597-3722 / www.planesoffame.org
7000 Merrill Avenue, Chino

For some *plane* old fun, come see over 150 rare and vintage aircraft (about thirty of which are flyable) that have landed here, including the only original and air-worthy Japanese Zero in the world. Many of the planes are touchable without any formal barriers to keep visitors away, making it a comfortable place to take children. The model aircraft collection, displayed in numerous cases throughout the several hangers, is one of the largest we've seen in one place.

The two south hangars hold numerous colorful and historic airplanes. The adjacent USS Enterprise hangar, which currently has ten planes on display, is dedicated specifically to Navy and military planes that were on the carrier. Take the catwalk around the interior part of that building and look into the built-in exhibit windows that hold uniforms, artifacts, and the carrier's timeline, Just a few of the planes on display in these hangers (with the understanding that some aircraft are out flying or on loan) include the Cessna 0-1Bird Dog, Douglas A-4B Skyhawk, Formula One Racer "Mr. D", Lockheed P-38J Lightning, Grumman J2F-6 Duck, P-51D Mustang, Piper L-4, and Stearman PT-17 Kaydet. There is also an "office" display with posters and information about the B-17 Fortress (which is actually located out front), as well as some upper gun turrets, a replica of the Wright Brothers plane, and a mock up of an Apollo space capsule here.

Across the way is the restoration hangar, where planes in various stages of repair and restoration are being worked on. Planes, parts of planes, jet aircraft, and tanks and other military vehicles are stationed outside the north hangar. Read the history of the aircraft on the placards or ask a docent for their fascinating stories.

Inside another hangar are foreign planes; Japanese and German aircraft from WWII, some of which are "flying" around overhead, while others are grounded. My boys were drawn to the "Wild Grinning Face of the Green Dragon Unit" - a nose of a plane that has machine guns and is decorated with a fire-breathing dragon painted on its side. A G4MI Hamaki (code named "Betty") bomber on display looks like it has crashed landed in a jungle, complete with an overgrowth of plants and camouflage covering, plus dirt and a background mural. Hitler's very rusted and bullet-holed jet fighter, the Heinkel HE-162A1 Volks Jager, is here, too. Watch a video interspersed with real footage that tells the story of what happened. This building also displays airplane engines and small models of Japanese army aircraft, plus news clippings regarding Pearl Harbor.

One smaller hanger contains the P-38 Lightning and 475th FG displays; another is devoted to a variety of colorful jets and air racers.

Kids who are aeronautically inclined will be in their element at the Aviation Discovery Center with interactive displays such as flight simulators, wind tunnels (don't get blown away!), a control tower simulator, an aviation movie theater, and educational programs such careers in aviation, historic and scientific significance of planes and more.

A B-17 Bomber is available on weekends, only, to walk through or sit down in and "fly." The first Saturday of every month, Living History Flying Days, features a particular plane, or type of planes, plus a seminar at 10am with panelists or veteran pilots who were directly associated with that plane. Whenever possible, this event concludes with a flight demonstration.

Planes of Fame is on the grounds of the Chino airport, so kids can experience the thrill of seeing planes take off and land. Don't miss the annual Air Show in May, PLANES OF FAME AIR SHOW (pg. 713). If you get hungry, pilot your way to Flo's Cafe, which is also on airport grounds. It's open Sunday through Thursday, 5:30am - 7pm; Friday and Saturday, 5:30am - 8pm. Note that just three blocks west of this museum is another one - YANKS AIR MUSEUM (pg. 431) for details.

Hours: Open Sun. - Fri., 10am - 5pm; Sat., 9am - 5pm. Closed Thanksgiving and Christmas. The Aviation Discovery Center for kids is open Sat. only, 10am - 2pm, but also during the week for groups with reservations.

Price: $11 for adults; $10 for seniors; $4 for ages 5 - 11; children 4 and under are free. AAA discounts are available.

Ages: 3 years and up.

SAN BERNARDINO COUNTY MUSEUM
(909) 798-8608; (909) 307-2669 / www.sbcounty.gov/museum
2024 Orange Tree Lane, Redlands

The distinctive half-dome attached to the main building of the San Bernardino County Museum is the Fisk Gallery of Fine Arts, which features changing exhibits. The Hall of History room is down the ramp from the main level. Here you'll find a covered wagon, 1888 buggy, 1901 fire wagon, a Wells Fargo stage coach, a beautiful convertible from the 50's, along with cut outs and mannequins dressed in period clothing. The anthropology section has Indian artifacts, such as arrowheads, dolls, pottery, an Eagle feather dance kilt, and painted rock art. An Edison exhibit displays hydro-electric generators, guns used by mountain men, and more bring history to life.

Enter the huge room at the lower level, the Hall of Earth Sciences, where a life-size mastodon and her calf reside in a naturalistic diorama setting of rocks and some plants. The rest of the rocky wall, as well as the glass display cases all around, contain fossilized animal bones, horns, and teeth, the skull of a sabertooth, some dinosaurs and a triceratops skull, the Old Woman meteorite, and lots more. Bug collectors will be bug-eyed at the comprehensive collection of mounted insects of all sizes, shapes, and colors. Visitors can also learn about plate tectonics and earthquakes and find out why there's a whole lotta shakin' goin' on.

Stairs lead up to the second story of Earth Sciences which overlooks the first floor. One room up here continues with the theme and features taxidermied animals that have lived in the surrounding mountains, deserts and other Western climates and geography such as big horned sheep, mountain lions, a bison, an Alaskan brown bear, a California Condor, a polar bear (it's so amazingly tall!) and more. Along the walls are dioramas of smaller taxidermied animals and reptiles, such as spotted skunks, possums, raccoons, beavers, and turtles. Another portion of the Hall of Earth Sciences features the exhibit, Sculpted by Time: Our Mountains, Faults, Lakes, and Caves. Walk through the geology of our county by exploring a cave, inspecting the rocks that make up our mountains, seeing the skeleton of a giant ground sloth, and more.

If your kids show any interest in ornithology, which is the study of birds (and calling each other bird brain doesn't count), they will be enjoy another area up here, the Hall of Biodiversity. Many birds and types of taxidermied birds are often flocked together including penguins, woodpeckers, swans, ostriches, hawks, geese, and many more. The substantial collection of bird eggs varies in size from extra large elephant bird eggs to very small hummingbird eggs. The water and land birds here takes you on flights of fancy, although with taxidermied birds you won't get very far. Press a button at one exhibit to match the call of the bird to its picture on the wall.

Outside, between the main building and the Exploration Station, is a patio area. One diorama has a mining car carrying "explosives" on track toward a tunnel. A find-a-fossil sand pit has "hidden" fossils and brushes with which to uncover the finds. Look for the dinosaur statues in the garden. There is also a full-size caboose and steam engine on tracks. Picnic tables are here for snack attacks - bring your own food. (Other picnic tables are located just outside the museum entrance.)

The Exploration Station is a learning center that has small, live critters such as bunnies, bearded dragon, python, king snake, an alligator lizard, frogs, turtles, scorpions, tarantulas, giant hissing cockroaches, tortoise, gecko, cockatiel, and walking sticks. Kids can touch fossils, animal furs, antlers, snake skin, and casts of bones and dinosaur fossils, as well as look at a variety of animals skulls from kitty cat to an American (yes, American) lion. Taxidermied animals scattered around the room include birds, raccoon, and a cougar, plus a rhino head and hippo head. Often times there are free, nature-oriented crafts to do, too.

Check the calendar for special programs and know that the museum's field trips are wonderful.

Hours: Open Tues. - Sun., 9am - 5pm. The Exploration Station is open Tues. - Fri., 9:30am - 12:30pm; Sat. - Sun., 1pm - 4pm. The museum is closed Mon., New Year's Day, Thanksgiving, and Christmas.

Price: $10 for adults; $8 for seniors and active military; $7 for students with ID; $5 for ages 5 - 12; children 4 and under are free. See info on the Bank of America Museums on Us (pg. xi).

Ages: 2 years and up.

SAN BERNARDINO HISTORY AND RAILROAD MUSEUM

(909) 888-3634 / www.sbdepotmuseum.com

!

1170 W. Third Street at the Santa Fe Depot, San Bernardino

Located at the restored Santa Fe Depot, originally built in 1918, the small museum is in the former baggage room and has brick flooring. It displays a collection of lanterns, railroad signs, horse-drawn fire wagon and hose reel, block signals, dining car memorabilia, china dishes, baggage-handling equipment, uniforms, and other artifacts, plus lots of historical photographs and a six-foot long model of a steam engine. The museum is adjacent to a working Metrolink station. The lobby is open for morning and evening Amtrak stops.

Hours: Open Sat., 10am - 3pm.
 Price: Free
 Ages: 5 years and up.

SAN BERNARDINO RANCHO ASISTENCIA

(909) 793-5402; (909)798-8608 / www.sbcounty.gov/museum

$$

26930 Barton Road, Redlands

This lovely restored set of buildings was once an outpost as part of Mission San Gabriel's Rancho. A grassy courtyard, surrounded by a few small adobe buildings, a bell tower, a fountain, and a grist mill complete this picturesque asistencia. Explore a part of the ranchero history as you walk through the main structure. The tour guide helps bring the past to life, explaining the people that once lived here and their way of life. School groups are welcome; just call to make a reservation.

Hours: Open Tues. - Sat., 10am - 3pm. Closed Sun., Mon., and all county-observed holidays.
 Price: $5 for adults; $4 for seniors; $2.50 for students and kids; children 4 and under are free.
 Ages: 6 years and up.

VICTOR VALLEY MUSEUM

(760) 240-2111; (909) 798-8608 / www.sbcounty.gov/museum/

$$

11873 Apple Valley Road, Apple Valley

This small, but classy, off-the-beaten-track museum is like an oasis in the desert that stays true to its motto of "Discover Your Own Backyard". You can't miss it - it has the giant tortoise statue out front.

Inside, it has displays, with lots of information plaques, that cover desert living, specifically of the Mojave desert and Death Valley with dioramas with sand and taxidermied animals, including a desert fox; skulls; and wall plaques and murals depicting animals and wildlife. The geology room, or Mine Room, has rocks and fossils, such as giant mammoth tusks and remains of extinct large camels; plus a beautiful and large amethyst, and a short, mock-up mine. The archaeology section, or Sacred Earth Room, features Native American groups from the local area and their craft, such as baskets and jewelry, and even clothing. Another item of interest is a stagecoach (with John Wayne posed beside it). Kids enjoy the touch stations with interactive things for them to do.

School tours are offered that include learning about heros, such as Native Americans - how they made and did so much with seemingly so little - and Earl Bascom, a local rodeo star. As we inspected Native American baskets we learned that the weaving was so tightly done that the baskets could hold water. And we gained more knowledge about the rocks, minerals, and numerous other artifacts on display. Check the website for special events as many are kid-oriented, including the Annual Train Day in April.

Hours: Open Wed. - Sun., 10am - 4 pm. Closed all county-observed holidays.
 Price: $5 for adults; $4 for seniors; $2.50 for students; children 5 and under are free.
 Ages: 6 years and up.

WESTERN AMERICA RAILROAD MUSEUM

(760) 256-WARM (9276) / www.barstowrailmuseum.org

!

685 N. First Street, Barstow

Train enthusiasts are invited to get on track by visiting W.A.R.M. The museum is dedicated to preserving railroad history and to getting the public involved with train "culture." Outside the building are several railcars, locomotives, and rolling stock - specifically, the Santa Fe 95; cars used to ship horses and their trainers; a CE-8 and a CA-8 caboose; a flat car used for freight service, now carrying an old neon sign; and a General Electric 44 tonner.

Inside the nice-sized museum are a few rooms that hold an assortment of train-related paraphernalia: two small, track inspection cars - one hand pump and one gas engine; photographs; a huge collection of date and pole nails (i.e., nails with the date stamped on the head driven into railroad ties for record keeping purposes); uniforms; scale model steam engine; recording equipment; tools; china used on old train cars; locks and keys; timetables; artwork; switch lights; Harvey girl displays; and old signs. Visitors also enjoy the thirteen-foot model train layout with all its bells and whistles. Ask about their special events.

This beautiful brick building, reached by first going over a trestle bridge, is an authentic train depot, currently home to an Amtrak station and a welcome center, as well as the BARSTOW ROUTE 66 "MOTHER ROAD" MUSEUM (pg. 423).

Hours: Open Fri., 11am - 3pm; Sat. - Sun., 11am - 4pm. Closed all major holidays.
Price: Free
Ages: 4 years and up.

YANKS AIR MUSEUM

(909) 597-1734 / www.yanksair.com $$$$
7000 Merrill Avenue, Chino

"The Yanks are coming!" That phrase was uttered in celebration as the Yanks brought liberation for the people throughout Europe and the Pacific during WWII. This museum, which encompasses four clean hangars, as well as some outside space, is dedicated to American aircraft and aviation with one of the largest collection of single-engine, WWII aircraft on display, with a focus on fighters and dive bombers. Many of the over 200 planes have been restored, maintained, and are air-worthy, while other planes are in process of, or awaiting, this same fate/hope. The signage in front of each plane lets visitors know why that plane, in particular, is special - whether it is vintage, one-of-a-kind, or it has a unique history. A very short list of some of their planes includes a Bell P-36C King Cobra; Grumman F-14 Tomcat; Curtiss JN-4DJenny biplane (with exposed frame, no skin); Bell 47B1 medical evacuation helicopter; P-40E Warhawk (with a shark's mouth painted on it); a 1950's F-106B Delta Dart (a trainer and interceptor plane with supersonic and nuclear capabilities); Blue Angels; and Republic P-47M Thunderbolt. The museum also contains a replica Wright Brother's 1903 Wright Flyer and other history-making aircraft.

One of the hangers is a restoration warehouse where you'll see frames of helicopters and planes, siding, wings, engines, propellers, lots of shelves with dusty parts, and mechanics working on their projects. (Get a whiff of the lacquer!)

Just beyond the workroom is a room containing flight suits from Viet Nam, survival kits, gas masks, photos, newspaper articles, NASA space suits, military dress, hats, and an array of helmets and goggles. Other paraphernalia in the hangers include instruments, medals, and a large collection of scale models planes. Take a self-guided tour, or schedule a guided one to get all the information.

The third Saturday is Open Cockpit Day, from 10am to 3pm, which could include cockpit access into a Blue Angels F-18 Hornet, WWII Bomber, E-2C Hawkeye, P-51 Mustang, or other historic aircraft; touring the Super Constellation; or joining WWII reenactors and jumping from a (grounded) C-47 Skytrain. Food, posters and, for little ones, a ride in the small planes amusement ride, are all included in admission.

Note that just down the road is the PLANES OF FAME AIR MUSEUM (pg. 428) and Flo's Cafe which is open Sun. - Thurs., 5:30am - 7pm; Fri. - Sat., 5:30am - 8pm.

Hours: Open Tues. - Sun., 9am - 4pm; closed Mon. and holidays.
Price: $16 for adults; $15 for seniors; $5 for ages 5 - 11; children 4 and under are free. Ask about AAA discounts.
Ages: 3 years and up.

YORBA & SLAUGHTER FAMILIES ADOBE

(909 597-8332 / www.sbcounty.gov/museum/ $$
17127 Pomona Rincon Road, Chino

Just for the record, the name "Slaughter" refers to a family that once lived here - not the slaughtering of animals. The adobe was built in 1852 and therefore receives the distinction of being the oldest standing residence in San Bernardino. A tour through the adobe, which is fairly well kept up, allows visitors to see its low beam ceilings; a dining room, with a table set for company; a living room and music room with period furniture and artifacts that include a piano, sewing machine, and dolls; a kitchen; a potbellied stove; a bedroom; and a few, simply-furnished rooms upstairs.

There are a few other buildings on the grounds that are also original, and very weathered in appearance. Step inside the post office/general store which contains advertising from the 1890's, artifacts, and even exhibits of agricultural animal husbandry. A shed with a stone chimney, a winery building, a one-ton solid copper pot (used for tallow), a grist mill, and a few pieces of old farming equipment complete the homestead. Note: Group and school tours are given by appointment.

Hours: Open to the public Tues. - Sat., 10am - 3pm. Closed Sun., Mon., New Year's Day, Thanksgiving, and Christmas.
Price: $5 for adults; $4 for seniors; $2.50 for student and kids; children 4 and under are free.
Ages: 7 years and up.

—POTPOURRI—

BASS PRO SHOPS OUTDOOR WORLD

(909) 922-5500 / www.basspro.com

7777 Victoria Gardens Lane, Rancho Cucamonga

"Welcome fishermen, hunters, and other liars" reads the sign over the doorway. Saying that this wholly outdoor-themed store is massive is almost an understatement. Wood, boulders, antlers (more of those than I've ever seen anywhere, collectively); taxidermied animals (such as bears, deer, moose, wild boar, buffalo, elk, rams, birds, and more) - more than 400 wildlife and trophy fish mounts; and murals of Joshua Tree National Monument, Big Bear Lake, and Silverwood Lake fills the walls and ceilings. *Any*thing pertaining to the great outdoors dominates every inch of the building. I've never seen so much outdoors underneath one roof.

Downstairs, besides the large boat showroom section, is a marine and fishing area with schools (and schools) of fish hanging overhead and every piece of equipment I can imagine (and some I can't) that you'd need/want for fishing. Clothing, a kid's toy and games area, home decor, and a fudge shop selling homemade fudge and coffee are also downstairs. There is a forty-foot-high rock climbing wall just for looks.

Last, but not least downstairs, near the lodge fireplace, is a cascading waterfall creating a mini retreat with benches and a boulder-lined stream at its base, replete with posed stuffed animals, model fishermen, and real fish - bass, catfish, stripper, and blue gill - in the indoor trout stream. View and help with the fish feeding every Saturday at noon. Free classes are offered to learn or improve an outdoor skill - fishing, first aid, hunting, camping, amateur radio, predator seminar, intro to archery, and a lot more. Scouting merit badges can also be earned here during summer months.

Upstairs, you'll find everything camouflage, plus camping gear, bows and arrows, guns, and a fine gun room (i.e. expensive guns) with even more stuffed animal heads. There is a gun range here, too - $10 an hour. Use the indoor archery range (i.e. an enclosed long hallway) if you purchase a bow here, or bring in your own and use it for a half hour for $7, if the department isn't busy. If you've got your sights on using the laser shooting gallery, the cost is only $1 to play.

If you're hungry and don't have time to hunt or fish immediately, eat at the small, nautically-decorated ISLAMORADA FISH COMPANY (pg. 401) which is inside the store. Theoretically, Pro Bass is a store, but it's so much more. Note that Pro Bass is adjacent to VICTORIA GARDENS REGIONAL TOWN CENTER - VG KIDZ CLUB - CULTURAL CENTER (pg. 422).

Hours: Open Mon. - Sat., 10am - 9pm; Sun., 10am - 8pm.

Price: Free, technically.

Ages: All

BOTTLE TREE RANCH

www.roadsideamerica.com

24266 National Trails Hwy, Oro Grande

Quirky art is the best way I can describe this two-acre bottle tree farm along Rte. 66 where hundreds of "trees" are made of metal poles with branches (think hat rack) that have colorful vintage bottles (mostly blues, green, amber and clear) attached to the ends. Atop these trees are random items such as a radiator, street signs, wagon wheel, saxophone, typewriter, gun, waterpump, hubcaps, birdhouse - you get the picture. Interspersed throughout the "forest" are other found and collected eclectic, rusted things such as a gas pump, a few cars, antlers, tools, a railroad crossing sign, other road signs, a fire hydrant, cow skull, lanterns, park benches, and more. There are also several wind chimes that make a pleasant noise as the breeze sweeps gently through. If you get a chance to speak with Elmer, the resident, owner, and artist he'll intrigue you with his stories. You won't be here long, but it's a funky fun little stop off (and great for photographs).

Hours: Open daily, around 10amish. The gates are just usually open.

Price: Free

Ages: 5 years and up.

BUILD-A-BEAR WORKSHOP (San Bernardino County)

(909) 980-0520 / www.buildabear.com

One Mills Circle in Ontario Mills Mall, Ontario

See the entry for BUILD-A-BEAR WORKSHOP (Orange County) (pg. 315) for details. See ONTARIO MILLS MALL (pg. 422) for more information on the mall.

Hours: Open Mon. - Sat., 10am - 9pm; Sun., 11am - 8pm.

CAL-EARTH

(760) 956-7533 / www.calearth.org

10177 Baldy Lane, Hesperia

!/$

Nestled among Joshua trees, the California Institute of Earth Art and Architecture (aka Cal-Earth) has an educational facility that emphasizes building structures utilizing the four basic elements - earth, water, air, and fire. Domed, igloo-like structures made out of superadobe bricks, which look like sand bags, are on the grounds; prototypes for future buildings. The structure uses archways instead of the typical, box-like corners and doorframes. Both the United Nations and NASA have expressed interest in the designs and environment-friendly building materials.

The general public is invited to come, learn, and tour around the first Saturday of every month. Bring a potluck dish, enough to feed four to five people, on this day, too, or contribute $5 if you want to share the meal. At other times, a minimum group of fifteen students is offered three-hour or full-day workshops. In the "class," they learn how (by hearing about and by physically working) to build homes with arches and vaults using the earth (i.e., dirt); how to build emergency housing that is flood and fire-proof; teamwork; and how to live in harmony with the environment, using solar energy for glazing buildings and for cooling them. Deforestation is examined as alternative choices are shown and worked with. Prepare the kids for some hard labor and for out-of-the-box thinking here. Note: Located a short drive away at the end of Main Street is HESPERIA LAKE PARK (pg. 415). This lake offers picnic tables, fishing, a children's play area, and camping.

Hours: Open the first Sat. (but closed in August), 10am - about 3pm. Call first. Tours are given by appointment or for school groups during the week at 1pm.

Price: Free on the first Sat. School tours are a minimum of $100 - $350, depending on the length of the program and activities.

Ages: 8 years and up.

CALICO GHOST TOWN

(800) TO CALICO (862-2542) or (760) 254-2122 / www.visitcalicoghosttown.com; cms.sbcounty.gov/parks; www.calicoattractions.com

36600 Ghost Town Road, Yermo

$$$

Once upon a time a rich vein of silver was found in a mine underneath some multi-colored mountains. Word about the strike spread like wildfire, and pretty soon there were 5,000 people, of twenty different nationalities, living in and around this mining town. The town was called Calico because the varied minerals that created the different colors of the mountains were "as purty as a gal's Calico skirt." Between 1882 and 1907, the 500 mine claims produced eighty-six million dollars worth of silver and forty-five million dollars worth of borax. Then, the price of silver dropped. And the boom town went bust. Thankfully, the story doesn't end here.

Nowadays, this small, authentic western town has over twenty unique shops and eateries on both sides of the wide, dirt, main road that snakes up the mountainside - put your walking shoes on. Some of the current shops are even housed in original buildings. Topping our list of favorite shops are the rock and fossil shop, the print shop, the leather works, and an 1890's general store.

There are several other attractions here. Gun fights break out every Saturday, every hour on the half hour starting at 10:30am. Visit the recreated schoolhouse at the end of the road where an authentically-dressed schoolmarm will gladly teach your kids what going to school was like in the olden days. There is a sturdy wooden teeter-totter and swing outside the schoolhouse. Don't be a fool when you pan for gold 'cause it's only fool's gold. The Mystery Shack is a small house of optical illusions where water rolls uphill, a broom stands up at an angle without falling over, and more. Before you walk through Maggie Mine, a real silver mine, look at the mining tools on display, such as a stamp mill, ore cart, recreated assay office, and more. Just inside the mine is a display of a few rocks and minerals mined from these parts, including fluorescent ones that glow in neon colors when the lights are turned off. Take the short walk through the mine, which has mannequin miners in action and audio explanations of the mining process. The Odessa Railroad is simply an eight-minute train ride on a narrow-gauge railcar. It takes you around part of a mountain where you'll see small cave-like openings that were front doors to miners' homes. On your ride you'll learn that the huge pile of "tailing" from the Silver King Mine still contains six million dollars worth of silver ore, but it would cost nine million dollars to process. Oh well! Sharpshooters can test their skill at the shooting gallery. Look at and into the house made of bottles - it's the ultimate in recycling.

Ask about school tours offered to educate students on the history of the town and this era. Any "group" of at least 3 can take an extreme 3+-hour Silver King Mine Tour into parts of the actual mine to learn firsthand what the conditions and lives were like of miners in the 1880's. This tour also offers behind-the-scenes sights and info of the town - $50 per person; minimum $150. The Off Road Tour follows along the same trail as the 20 Mule Team Borax

Wagon Train, but in a jeep. This 3+-hour tour is off the property, exploring the surrounding landmarks and mining districts along the wagon train road, up to Borax, and back. Call for a schedule of special events or check the Calendar section for information on a CALICO CIVIL WAR DAYS (pg. 698) on President's Day Weekend, CALICO DAYS (pg. 731) the last weekend in September, and HOLIDAY FEST (pg. 747) on Thanksgiving weekend. Oh, and do explain to your kids that the term, "ghost town" doesn't mean that there are ghosts here, but just that the town went from being inhabited to being deserted.

Tent, RV, or cabin "camping" is available just below the town, as are bunkhouses, which sleep from twelve to twenty people. The basic, dirt sites are small, but the surrounding area can make it attractive for kids because there are (small) caves all over. In fact, seeing and even going into a few caves, was one of the things my children liked best about Calico. If you have a four-wheel drive vehicle (trust me, a mini-van doesn't cut it), turn left after leaving Calico and head for the hills on Mule Canyon to explore some of the hiking trails and go rock hunting in this area.

Hours: Open daily, 9am - 5pm. The town is closed on Christmas.

Price: Entrance is $8 for adults; $5 for ages 4 - 11; children 3 and under are free. On special event days/weekends, prices are usually $10 - $20 for adults; $5 - $10 for ages 4 - 11, depending on the event. Train rides are $4.50 for ages 11 and up; $2.50 for ages 5 - 10; free for ages 4 and under. Maggie's Mine or the Mystery Shack is $3 for ages 11 and up; $2 for ages 5 - 10. Gold Panning is $3 for ages 11 and up; $2 for ages 5 - 10. Packages for the mine, shack and gold panning is $6.50 for ages 11 and up; $5 for ages 5 - 10. School or youth groups, with a minimum of 20 students, is $5 per person. Tent camping is $30 a night; hookup sites are $40; the cabin is $65; the bunkhouse is $160 a night for up to 20 people, 2 night minimum.

Ages: All

DISNEY STORE (San Bernardino County)

!/$$

Montclair - (909) 624-4548; Ontario - (909) 980-9070; San Bernardino - (909) 386-7347 / www.disneystore.com

Montclair - 5060 East Montclair Plaza Lane; Ontario - 1 Mills Circle
Ontario at Ontario Mills; San Bernardino - 428 Inland Center

See DISNEY STORE (Orange County) (pg. 316) for details about this fabulous hands-on store.

Hours: Open Mon. - Sat., 10am -9pm; Sun., 11am - 7pm. Closed Thanksgiving and Christmas.

Price: Free

Ages: 1 - 10 years

IFLY (San Bernardino County)

$$$$$

(909) 531-4359 / www.iflyworld.com/ontario

4510 Ontario Mills Parkway, Ontario

See IFLY (Los Angeles County) (pg. 172) for more information about this high-flying experience.

Hours: Open Mon. - Thurs., noon - 9pm (last flight at 8pm); Fri. - Sun., 9am - 9pm (last flight at 8).

Price: Double flight, first time flyers is $69.95.

Ages: 4 years and up.

OAK TREE VILLAGE

!/$$

(909) 797-4420 - museum; (909) 797-2311 - Apple Annies; (909) 797-1517 - tour info / www.oaktreevillage.info; www.oakglen.net

38480 Oak Glen Road, Oak Glen

Oak Tree Village is fittingly located in the heart of Oak Glen. See OAK GLEN / APPLE PICKING (pg. 403) for information on the surrounding apple orchards and places to enjoy along Oak Glen Road. This fourteen-acre village, with a Western motif, is a funky and wonderful conglomeration of family activities, animals, shopping, and eating. The row of shops and restaurants, with plenty of outdoor picnic tables under huge oak trees, beckons travelers to buy, eat, and visit. Craft booths are located throughout the village on weekends. Definitely indulge in a slice of apple pie or a caramel-dipped apple!

Walk up the road where, on the weekends during apple season (which is September through November), kids enjoy pony rides that are led around in a circle attached to a wheel ($4); scale model train rides ($3); and several large bounces and slides ($3 to $5) in front of a Western town facade. Other special activities include piglet races, fishing contests, and live entertainment.

Kids really enjoy walking on the hilly dirt trail through the good-sized **Animal Park**, which is open daily. Over 100 animals reside here including penned deer, zebra, alpacas, llamas, steer, Angora goats, ostriches, emus, kangaroos, wallabies, zebu, singing dogs, and birds, ducks, and swans, plus a lot of squirrels and peacocks that freely roaming the grounds. The petting zoo in the Animal Park contains long-haired (and long horned) goats, pot-bellied pigs, and big woolly sheep. Admission to the Animal Park is $6 per person; children 1 year and under are free.

Inside the Animal Park are three picturesque, stocked rainbow trout ponds (with a short waterfall and stream). They are usually open weekends only, year round. Fishing fees are the $6 entrance fee to the Animal Park, plus $2 per fisherman to rent a pole (no license needed), plus a $1 per-inch fee for each fish. No catch and release. Fish can be cleaned and packed in ice, also.

Just up the walkway is MOUNTAIN TOWN REPTILE MUSEUM (pg. 443), an unusual, animal/reptile museum that has some live reptiles and some taxidermied animals inside in a recreated cave/mountain setting.

Numerous group tours/field trips are offered year round such as: Fishing Tour - Learn about fish and the importance of the ecosystem, plus you actually get to fish and keep what you catch in this two hours - $20 per person. (Fish will be packed in ice to take home.) Pioneer Farm Life - Learn what life was like on the farm as participants milk a goat, collect eggs, make butter, and learn the chores of an 1800's homesteader - $10 per person. California Gold Rush - A two-hour tour at $15 per person with the main activity of gold panning in an actual stream for real gold (which is a lot harder and not as much fun as it seems). Learn about the importance of the Gold Rush and keep whatever you find. Harvest Tours (this is great one for older folk, too) are offered in season. They include lunch, an entire apple pie (per person) to take home, and an informative talk on the history of Oak Glen and all about apples - $40 per person. All tours/field trips include entrance to the Animal Park, feed for the animals, admission to Mountain Town, a twenty-five-minute animal presentation (i.e. learning about them and touching them), and fun. The docent is very flexible, gearing tours around particular interests or studies. A minimum of twenty is needed per tour/field trip. Check the website for other tours. Note that picnic facilities are available here.

Hours: Open daily for shopping and food, depending on the weather.
Price: General admission is free. Other prices are listed above.
Ages: All

WIGWAM MOTEL

(909) 875-3005 / www.wigwammotel.com $$$$$
2728 W. Foothill Boulevard, Rialto

Originally built in 1949 along the famous Route 66, this classic and kitschy motel consists of nineteen, wood-framed, cement and stucco tepees that are thirty-feet tall arranged in a kind of semi-circle around a grassy area and gated, kidney-shaped pool. The pool is open seasonally and has a few lounge chairs around it. There are a few picnic tables and benches on the grounds near the pool. Bring your camera and take some fun pictures of the Wigwams. The surrounding area is run down, but the motel itself feels safe and offers clean rooms; comfy beds with decorative, half-wagon-wheel headboards; a mini fridge; and free internet, cable and TV (just the Old West days). The bathrooms are very small and ours didn't have an electric outlet, but we didn't care - we were sleeping in a wigwam and that's a cool adventure! And for being on a major street, we were pleasantly surprised not to hear traffic noises inside our room. This motel is also pet friendly.

Outside the office are great retro signs and inside are Route 66 souvenirs to purchase. I have no reservations about sleeping at the Wigwam Motel again. Note: Check the San Bernardino area in the back of this book for close-by places to explore.

Price: Rooms run from about $80 - $229 for a queen-size bed, depending on day and season.
Ages: All

—SHOWS AND THEATERS—

AT THE GROVE

(909) 920-4343 / www.grovetheatre.com $$$$
276 E. 9th Street, Upland

Fine, professional, dramatic live theater is performed at the grove, along with comedies, concerts, six musicals per season, and children's workshops. Past shows have included *My Fair Lady*, *Fiddler on the Roof*, and *Barnum*.

Hours: Call for show dates and times.
Price: Varies, depending on the show.
Ages: Varies, depending on the show.

CALIFORNIA THEATER OF PERFORMING ARTS

(909) 885-5152 / www.theatricalarts.com

562 West 4th Street, San Bernardino

It's show time! This beautiful old theater, which originally opened in 1928, seats 1,700 patrons inside its classical Spanish colonial design with ornate moldings, elegant chandeliers, tapestries, inlays, and wide, sweeping staircases. Will Rogers is featured on the exterior in two huge murals. Home to musicals, Broadway shows, plays, the San Bernardino Symphony, the Inland Dance Theater, ballet, concerts, and even naturalization ceremonies, this historical building hosts some kind of entertainment for everyone. Past shows have included The Righteous Brothers, Blue Man Group, *Hunchback of Notre Dame, Cats, Chronicles of Narnia, Madagascar: A Musical Adventure,* and *Les Miserables.*

Hours: Performances are usually given on Fri., 8pm; Sat., 2pm and 8pm; Sun., 2pm.

Price: Tickets for plays and musicals range from $38.50 for the rear balcony to $77.50 for orchestra. Contact the theater for ticket prices as they vary depending on date, time, and performance.

Ages: 6 years and up, depending on the show.

CENTER STAGE THEATER

(909) 429-SHOW (7469) / www.centerstagefontana.com

8463 Sierra Avenue at Center Stage Theater, Fontana

Center Stage is both an historic and contemporary, gorgeously renovated "theater" that showcases and hosts several performance series - Tibbies Center Stage Dinner Theater; Broadway; Cabaret; Celebrity; and special events.

Tibbies, which runs from April to June, offers more than just dinner, and more than just a show - it is a wonderful, two-hour dinner and musical song and dance revue in an upscale, classy atmosphere that is not off-putting for kids. The eight waiters and waitresses also serve up the entertainment as the shows's performers. They start the show by singing as they bring in the salad, and they entertain all the way through dessert. They perform on the stage, as well as all around you. Their high energy, beautiful voices, numerous costumes changes, and well-choreographed dance moves make any show here a delight. Past show titles have included *From Stage to Screen* (favorite Broadway show tunes and movie music), *Forever Fifties* (songs from the 50's), and *Singin' in the Rain.* Audience participation and other surprises throughout the evening add to your family's enjoyment.

The delicious dinner selections, which change for each show, can include salmon, a chicken entree, chef's pasta special, or prime rib roast for adults. Meals usually come with oven roasted potatoes or rice, fresh bread, veggies, and an ice cream or cheesecake dessert. Children are offered creamy mac and cheese or chicken strips, with a salad, bread, garlic mashed potatoes, and veggies, plus a beverage and the special dessert. If your child or another member of your party is celebrating a birthday, graduation, or other special occasion, be sure you tell Tibbies beforehand so they will mention it sometime during the show. Call for particular show titles.

Center Stage is also home to excellent Broadway productions, such as *Five Guys Named Moe, Dream Girls, 25th Annual Putnam County Spelling Bee,* and *You're a Good Man, Charlie Brown,* with a menu similar to Tibbies, although the adult main selections are top sirloin, almond crusted mahi, roasted garlic chicken, or vegetable pasta. The Cabaret and Celebrity series, such as *Barbara and Frank The Concert That Never Was, The Platters Live!,* and *Ticket to Ride* offer similar menus and equally choice talent. Special events can include murder/mystery shows, dazzling magic performances, Latin music and dancing, and a variety of other shows or community involvement.

Enjoy your night out on the town at either Tibbies, Broadway or another Center Stage production, where the food is good and the entertainment is clean and fun. One to two week reservations are suggested.

Hours: Tibbie and Broadway dinner shows are usually Fri. at 7:30pm; Sat. at 7pm (tho sometimes there is a matinee show at 2pm and then nighttime show at 7:30pm); Sun. at 2pm. Arrival time for Tibbies and Broadway shows only (no dinner) are Fri., 8:15pm; Sat., 7:45pm (or Sat., 2:45pm and 8:15pm); Sun., 2:45pm. Ask about their expanded holiday hours.

Price: Tibbies and Broadway shows, dinner, and dessert are usually $46.95 - $56.95, depending on the meal; $34.95 for children 12 and under. Prices for the show only (no dinner) are $21 per person. Cabaret and Celebrity series dinner and show tickets, or show only, are usually more expensive. Prices can change according to the show in any of the series, so call or check the website first.

Ages: 6 years and up.

GEORGE F. BEATTIE PLANETARIUM

(909) 384-8539 / www.valleycollege.edu

701 S. Mount Vernon Avenue at San Bernardino City College, San Bernardino

Join in a gathering of the stars, the celestial stars that is. The sixty-seat planetarium shows the night sky and a live narrator discusses what the heavens are up to. Shows titles have included *Star Tales*, *The Little Star That Could*, and *The Amateur Astronomer's Universe*. Hour-long show topics change frequently so you can come back more than once. *The Christmas Star* shows in December with a presentation regarding the star of Bethlehem.

Hours: Shows are presented September through April, twice a month on Fri. at 7pm; doors open at 6:30pm. No late seating.

Price: $3 for adults; $2 for seniors and students; $1 for ages 10 and under. Cash only.

Ages: 6 years and up.

LEWIS FAMILY PLAYHOUSE PERFORMING ARTS CENTER

$$$$

(909) 477-2752 / www.lewisfamilyplayhouse.com

12505 Cultural Center Drive at the Victoria Gardens Cultural Center, Rancho Cucamonga

The 540-seat Lewis Family Playhouse Performing Arts Center brings a plethora of top-notch talent and productions such as popular children's literary pieces (that come to life via stage productions), Broadway musicals, marionette shows, world renown guest artists, opera, dance, concerts, and authors. Past shows include *Aesop's Fables*, *Willy Wonka*, *Sid the Science Kid - Live*, *Ferdinand the Bull*, *Noises Off*, Riders in the Sky, Diavolo, Art Garfunkel, Clint Black, Rockapella Holiday, and more. Ask about school field trips, workshops, and educational programs because they offer an amazing array for students and teachers. See VICTORIA GARDENS REGIONAL TOWN CENTER - VG KIDZ CLUB - CULTURAL CENTER (pg. 422) for details about the upscale mega mall surrounding the Playhouse.

Hours: Call for performance times.

Price: Prices vary depending on the show.

Ages: 3 years and up - depending on the performance and activity.

—TOURS—

CALIFORNIA PIZZA KITCHEN (San Bernardino County)

!

See the entry for CALIFORNIA PIZZA KITCHEN (Los Angeles County) (pg. 196) for more information.

GOODWILL INDUSTRIES (San Bernardino County)

!

(909) 885-3831 / www.goodwillsocal.org

8120 Palm Lane, San Bernardino

Learn how to spread goodwill as you accompany your kids on a one-hour tour of this facility. This location is a main donation center, where goods get consolidated and processed. It also has manual production lines and a work activity area. You'll get an overview of what Goodwill Industries does by observing people, including many disabled people, being trained to work in several different areas. Watching assembly lines are interesting, as things are put together and packages are shrink wrapped. Kids will also see recycling in action, as old stuffed animals and toys get fixed up for someone else to play with and love. Check out the receiving dock where the donations are piled. Idea: Clean out your closets and have your kids bring their old toys and clothes to Goodwill on your tour date. Tip: Next door to this facility is a thrift store. (I think we bought as much as we brought!) There is no minimum number of people required for a tour, but a maximum of 12 and a week's notice is requested. There are other GOODWILL INDUSTRIES in Los Angeles County.

Hours: Tours are offered Mon. - Fri., 10am - 4pm, by reservation.

Price: Free

Ages: 7 years and up.

NTC BOX TOURS

!/$$

ntcboxtour@yahoo.com; (760) 380-3078 / www.irwin.army.mil

Fort Irwin Road, past Barstow - you'll be on that road for about 30 min., Fort Irwin

Ever wonder how our soldiers get the on-site training they need to fight insurgents on their turf during war? Come see for yourself at Fort Irwin, home to the National Training Center (NTC). The NTC is renowned by all branches of the military for its tough and realistic training - a place to train for war just before overseas deployment.

This unique outing begins at 9am at Painted Rocks, a huge monument/hill of - yes, painted rocks. The boulders are colorfully painted with military insignias from various squadrons of the armed services. Quite a sight to behold!

The approximately forty-seater van/bus then takes visitors onto and through a portion of the absolutely massive base, while a military tour guide dispenses information about the base, the area, our armed forces, and more. The entire tour is somewhat informal so questions are welcomed.

You are given an MRE - a soldier's lunch, then, on to the "Box", or training area, for the most intriguing part of the tour, where you are first briefed as to your time here. You are driven, even more out into the desert, to a re-created village - complete with buildings of homes, cafes, and shops, plus mosques, statues, live goats, and roads - to look and feel like a village in Iraq or Afghanistan, depending on what is needed at the time of training. The scene is complete with actors dressed in appropriate cultural attire who speak the language and stay in character, mannerisms and all, as you walk down the main road, past street vendors who call out to you, wanting to sell you bread or other items. You are escorted to a roofless second story room of a building to safely stand not only to watch the action below, but you are given a gun (with blanks!) to become part of the action.

For about an hour a real time battle unfolds. Tension builds as soldiers in full gear search the streets for the enemy. Tanks roll into the village. Shots are fired, from and at snipers and soldiers, and the citizen bystanders. People are "wounded". Body parts are blown off, portrayed by hired amputees whose limbs squirt "blood". "Bombs" explode, in cars or buildings. Sometime, it is intense and loud, with gunfire and bombs. Sometimes, it is very quiet and there is seemingly no action taking place. The Box is not a show, or for entertainment purposes. It is to prepare units for combat; to ultimately learn how to save lives. Soldiers are learning how to interact with and respond to Afghan-speaking role players, terrorist cells, insurgents, civilian authorities and military forces.

After the battle, you might gather in an old hotel and recap with some military personnel. The last stop before arriving back to the Painted Rocks at about 3:30pm is the 11th Armored Calvary Regiment Museum. Inside are displays of weapons, mannequins in uniforms (including one with a model camel), re-created war times scenarios, a helicopter, photographs, and more, plus a gift shop. Outside are several tanks to look at and touch, and even a playground.

Important notes: All participants must have a valid government ID, or drivers license. Closed toe shoes and eye protection (i.e. sunglasses or goggles) are required. No tank tops. Sunscreen and hats are recommended, especially in the summer when temperatures soar, because you are outside, without shade. Participants must be able to walk short distances and stand for approximately one hour, or more. To sign up for the tour email your name, date of tour, and driver license/ID number and expiration date to the above email address.

Hours: Tours are usually conducted once a month, from 9am - 3:30pm, weather permitting. There are no tours given in December. Check the website for dates.

Price: Free

Ages: Must be at least 12 years old for the tour.

OAK GLEN / APPLE PICKING

See the entry for OAK GLEN / APPLE PICKING (pg. 403), under EDIBLE ADVENTURES, for details.

RILEY'S APPLE FARM

(866) 585-6407 or (909) 797-4061 / www.rileysapplefarm.com
12201 S. Oak Glen Road, Oak Glen

This orchard looks like it is set in the same time period as *Little House on the Prairie*. It has a delightful store that offers colonial-times toys and games, books, hand-made soaps, candles, and more modern purchases. On weekends in July and August come pick berries, some apples, and a few other types of fruit. In the fall, thirteen different varieties of apples, plus pumpkins, are ripe for visitors to harvest.

A bountiful crop of fall tours are yours to participate in. One includes learning frontier skills such as chopping wood, washing clothes on a washboard, writing with a quill pen, starting a fire with flint and steel, pumping water, and gardening and harvesting crops; building a log cabin; chopping and grinding corn and baking Johnny cakes; learning about the 1800 Land Act; archery; tomahawk throwing, rope-making, corn husk doll making; gold panning; hayride; and pressing apple cider. That tour requires a minimum of 60 people. Other tour options range from two hours (25 people minimum) to four hours (40 people minimum) and cost from $14 to $17 per person. If your group is smaller than that, come to a Home School Days. Tours begin Labor Day weekend until the end of November and are offered Tuesday through Thursday, usually starting at 10am. Rope making, kazoo making, a nature walk, crafting a corn husk doll, and creating a water carrier are the other activities offered. You can order lunch for $5.95 to $9.95, or bring a sack lunch to enjoy by the pond picnic area. Two-hour weekend tours, that include some of the above activities, are offered to groups, families, scouts, etc., of at least 20 people for $14 per person in August and September. Advanced reservations are needed for all tours.

Riley's is also open on weekends during the fall, from 10am to 4pm, for individuals and families to stop by. Visitors are welcome to pick their own apples and/or partake in some activities such as pressing cider at $22 a gallon -

soooo good! (this shuts down at 3pm); archery, tomahawk and knife throws ($2 each); and eating hot-dipped caramel apples for $4. (Winner!) Lunch is available here, too, as is fresh-baked apple pie. Sometimes entertainment on Saturday includes fiddle and banjo playing. The farm also hosts occasional musical programs and hoedowns at Los Rios Rancho, just down the road.

Spring tours are given in March through June that are similar to the fall tours, with the added bonus of apple tree planting.

Hours: See tour info above.

Price: Prices are listed above. Parking mid-September through October is $5 on weekends, or park on Oak Glen Rd.

Ages: 5 years and up, depending on the tour.

RILEY'S FARM

(909) 797-7534 or (909) 790-TIME (8463) / www.rileysfarm.com $$$
12261 S. Oak Glen Road, Oak Glen

Enjoy a meal at Hawk's Head Public House, a re-creation of an 18th-century Colonial restaurant with simple wood floor and tables and chairs, brick fireplace, pewter mugs, etc., and where servers are dressed in period clothing. Breakfast choices fit for a country squire include homemade bread for French toast with apples ($11); scrambled egg with bacon or sausage; or biscuits and gravy at an average cost of $10. Lunch and dinner fare includes roast beef, ham, or turkey sandwich, $9; chicken pot pie, $14; and apple walnut salad, $12. Kid's meals are $5 for chicken drumstick, pb & j, hot dog or grilled cheese (plus applesauce and chips). The restaurant is open Monday through Friday, 10am to 4pm; Saturday, 8am to 4pm. It's closed Sundays. Special Living History dinner events are offered throughout the year on select Saturdays and they might incorporate a barn dance, an evening in the colonies with Patrick Henry, Sleepy Hollow, and more.

Dinner theater combines family-friendly theater production (with fun extras and interactive activities), maybe some music, usually based on classic literature, plus farm-fresh food in a rustic setting. Each one has a different theme and menu. Past shows have included Sherlock Holmes, Riding Hood Goes West (which included a hay ride and dancing), Dracula, Ragtime Melody, and Christmas in the Colonies. Prices are $38 - $110 for adults; $33 - $80 for ages 3 to 12, depending on the show.

Pluck, pick, press, squeeze, and savor a myriad of fruit here from the end of May through November. Crops include strawberries, watermelon, raspberries, pears, peaches, and apples. Call to find out when the fruit is ripe. You can pick twenty different varieties of pumpkins here in the fall, too. Some picking is done by appointment only. U-pic hours, in season, are Sat., 9am to 4pm.

The year is 1775. The Revolutionary War is imminent. Students can learn first hand how it felt to be involved with this radical war by participating in a four-hour reenactment. Upon arrival, students are broken into "townships" and each group then visits various stations to experience life in this era. Some of the activities they participate in include visiting a blacksmith; witnessing Colonel Fenton's attempt to bribe Sam Adams; encountering British soldiers; learning about the Stamp Act; going through a court trial; grinding wheat; churning butter; learning etiquette of the times; and in a grand finale - marching across the orchard lands with arms (i.e., sticks and fake gun stocks) in a battle recreation. Kids become a part of the history - living it and learning it. A typical fare of a lunch ration is handed out: cornbread, slice of cheese, piece of fruit, and beef jerky. Tip: Bring some of your own food for lunch. This tour was a favorite for my troops! The tour begins at 10am at cost of $18 per person, for a group of fifteen or more. Important note: All tours listed, which are offered year-round, must have minimum of at least fifty participants to have the event; smaller groups can be joined together to make up one big group! Once the minimum is met, individuals/families are welcome to join in the group tour paying $5 to $9 more per person, per event. The Revolutionary War Overnight combines the above reenactment with more of the same - sentry duty against the redcoats, period dancing, skirmishes, sleeping on rope bunk beds, and eating.

If kids are studying the Civil War, Riley's also has a reenactment for this pivotal time period that is almost as engrossing (no shooting, though) and just as authentic. The Civil War requires prep work as students have drama assignments, costume guides, vocabulary helps, etiquette information, and more for this recreation. A similar, learn-it-by-living-it, two-hour Colonial Farm Life tour offers a choice of activities including playing 18th-century games, making cheese and butter, pressing cider, weaving, baking bread, learning etiquette, making candles, stamping, and eating a hot-dipped caramel apple. This tour is $12 per person (for fifteen or more). The four-hour Gold Rush field trip, 10am to 2pm, offers gold panning in a sluice box, panning for gold, dry mining, digging in a mine shaft, looking inside a miner's cabin, etiquette and manners "class," a rope climbing challenge, and tomahawk throwing, as well as a lesson in California economics and a drama involving a gold theft. The price is $19 per person (minimum of fifteen guests); $27 per person for individuals, or per family member, that want to join a tour. A period lunch, a ration, is served. Again, bring lunch! (Food is important!) Ask or check the website for other tours.

Each Saturday is a "new" experience from the 18th century, incorporating a different demonstration or performance each month, and opportunity to try your hand at it, be it spinning wool, throwing tomahawks, dipping a candle, playing games, writing with quill and ink, etc. These activities usually cost $3 per.

Riley's Farm, set in the hills of Oak Glen, has a naturally rural ambiance with running streams, apple orchards, and dirt trails. See OAK GLEN / APPLE PICKING (pg. 403) for more on fruit picking at this farm and for other things to do in this immediate area.

Hours: Tours are offered by reservation.
Price: See above for prices.
Ages: 3rd graders through high schoolers, depending on the tour.

RILEY'S FRONTIER EVENTS   ☼

(909) 790-2364 / www.losriosrancho.com $$$
12211 S. Oak Glen Road, Oak Glen

The Riley's name is big up here in apple country. In fact, these Riley's also operate Riley's at Los Rios Rancho (see entry OAK GLEN / APPLE PICKING (pg. 403)) where wonderful school/group tours are offered in the spring and fall.

The Frontier Life Tour incorporates choices of taking a horse-drawn hayride through the woods; visiting an authentic log cabin (set up for a pioneer family), pressing your own cider, eating a hot-dipped caramel apple, toy making, tin-smithing, leather-making, candle-dipping, cabin chores, a walk in the orchard walk and visit with the barnyard animals. The tour require a minimum of twenty-five students and cost $10 per person.

The Apple Farm Tour, available in the fall, invites kids and adults to learn about apple farming - the industry and history - as they explore the 1906 barn; pack apples on the packing line and take a box home; visit the large, 1932 cider press; press your own cider and drink it with lunch; and take a walk with Johnny Appleseed through the orchards. The cost is $7 per person and a minimum of twenty-five people are needed. Extra options include a caramel apple ($3), and pumpkin picking (in October), with the price for the pumpkin depending on the size of it.

Take a Little Seedling Tour where youngsters, ages 2 to 5, can taste apples with Johnny Appleseed; visit, pet, and feed barnyard animals; and go through a hay bale fort for $7 per person. You can also add on a lunch of hot dogs, chips, and drink for $7 per and/or caramel apple for another $3 per person. Reservations are required for all tours.

Price: Prices are listed above.
Ages: 6 years and up.

—TRANSPORTATION—

AMTRAK (San Bernardino County)

(800) USA RAIL (872-7245) / www.amtrakcalifornia.com
Ride the rails! See AMTRAK (Los Angeles County) (pg. 208) for more information.

BIKE MAPS (San Bernardino County)

See BIKE MAPS (Orange County) (pg. 328) for information.

CALIFORNIA SPEEDWAY   ☼

(800) 944-RACE (7223) / www.autoclubspeedway.com $$$$$
9300 N. Cherry Avenue, Fontana

The best in NASCAR racing roars to life in Southern California! Located on over 525 acres, this state-of-the-art speedway features a two-mile, D-shaped oval super speedway with a 1.3-mile infield road course. The track can accommodate three to four cars side-by-side. (Racers clock average speeds of up to 200mph!) The stadium seats allow great views of the races. Gigantic screens and hundreds of smaller monitors show the action to spectators, too. Thirteen huge message boards, an incredible speaker system, a car-themed children's play area, sometimes live entertainment, and "real" food (including lobster), as well as standby's of hot dogs and hamburgers, all aid in making this a very fan-friendly speedway. Check out the website for information on the Lefty's Kids Club for more offerings, including going to select races for free. The street festival atmosphere is enhanced by a concert stage, town center, retail store, and cuisine by Wolfgang Puck. RV camping (no hookups) is available at certain times. Note there are many special happenings, including motorcycle racing, driving a NASCAR race car yourself, exotics racing, racing schools, and more.

Hours: Call or check the website for a race schedule.
Price: Prices vary greatly according to the race. Fri. practices are $30 for adults; ages 12 and under are free; Sat. assigned seating is usually $55 for adults while general seating is $35 for adults; ages 12 and under free. Sun. assigned seating ranges from $45 - $155. Pay an additional $60, in addition to a grandstand pass, for a pit pass.
Ages: 5 years and up.

METROLINK (San Bernardino County)

(800) 371-LINK (5465) / www.metrolinktrains.com

See the entry for METROLINK (Orange County) (pg. 331) for details.
Ages: All

YOUNG EAGLES PROGRAM (San Bernardino County)

National number - (877) 806-8902; Upland - (626) 705-5773; Redlands - (909) 771-3279 /
www.youngeagles.org; Upland - www.448.eaachapter.org; Chino - www.eaa92.org; Upland / Riverside -
www.eaach1.org
Chino - 7000 Merrill Avenue at Chino Airport; Redlands - 1755 Sessums Drive; Upland - 1749 W. 13th Street, Cable Airport

See the entry for YOUNG EAGLES PROGRAM (Los Angeles County) (pg. 216) for details. The Upland chapter, #488, partners with chapter #1 from Riverside at the Flabob airport.

The Chino program is run by the Orange County chapter, #92, and has an educational emphasis and a lot of excitement about the program. The ground school first covers what makes an airplane fly, special instruments in the plane, how pilots navigate using charts and maps, careers, pre-flight checks, and making and testing a model glider. Then, they fly! Afterward, they get a lunch, a certificate and a bag that contains a few treasures for them. The whole program takes about 3.5 hours. Young Eagles aids Boy Scouts in getting their aviation merit badge. Since you are here, check out the adjacent PLANES OF FAME AIR MUSEUM (pg. 428) and YANKS AIR MUSEUM (pg. 431). Pre-register your child early!

Hours: On select Sat. throughout the year. Upland / Riverside fly the 2nd Sat. of the month. Chino / Orange County flies almost once a month.
Price: Free for Young Eagles. At the Chino location a $20 donation is asked per youth that is flying - it covers lunch, fuel costs, materials, and more.
Ages: 8 - 17 years old.

—ZOOS AND ANIMALS—

AMY'S FARM TOURS

(844) 426–9732 / www.amysfarm.com
7698 Eucalyptus Avenue, Chino

Breathe in the country smell (i.e. cows); breath out the city. For a really mooooving tour, visit Amy's Farm, which is really a family-run, working ten-acre cow ranch and crop farm. Other animals that consider the farm home, besides the over 100 cows, include penned ducks, bunnies, sheep, goats, pigs, and horses, plus chickens that are roaming all over the place. Note that you are welcome to come and visit, walk around, and shop at the produce stand any time the farm is open, but school tours abound and take over on weekday mornings. A tour, with a minimum of ten paying guests and maximum of sixty, is the best way to visit the farm and reservations are required. If you have a smaller group, you can be added on to another, larger one. Tours are age-appropriate. For $8 per person, tours for elementary-aged children last about an hour and include learning all about the animals; the story of milk - from cow to grocery store; petting goats and sheep; grooming mini horses; feeding the pigs; perhaps harvesting crops from the vegetable garden; perhaps petting newborns (depending on the season); and milking a cow - this is a highlight! In October, the pumpkin tour includes taking home a pumpkin for an additional $2 per person. One hour plus tours for middle school through high schoolers ($10 per person) and college students ($15 per) have more of an emphasis on ecological and sustainable farming incorporating composting, crop rotation, seasonal planting and more. A visit here is an awesome way to gain first-hand introductory knowledge and experience with and on a farm.

Although the tours involves walking around, it is also set up for special needs groups. A picnic area, with attached grassy area, is on the grounds, as is a farm stand with fresh produce for sale. Check the website regarding other seasonal events, such as summer camps, and for information about specialty classes such as Fun on the Farm and the Science of Farming. See the Calendar entry, AMY'S FARM PUMPKIN TOUR (pg. 735), for information about the pumpkin tours. Note that PLANES OF FAME AIR MUSEUM (pg. 428) and YANKS AIR MUSEUM (pg. 431) are just down the street at the airport.

Hours: The farm is open Mon. - Sat., 9am - 5pm. Tours are offered in the morning, Mon. - Sat. starting at 9am, with the last tour at 11:15am. Closed Sun. and major holidays. Book tours online.

Price: Prices listed above.

Ages: 2 years and up.

FOREVER WILD

(760) 686-2775 / www.foreverwildsanctuary.org

8545 Buttemere Road, Phelan

$$$

This small place is packed with animals to see and learn about, as it is a rescue and rehabilitation sanctuary for captive-bred animals. Start in the lobby/gift shop, which is free to visit. It has a separate room with a lot of poisonous snakes - King cobras, black mambas, rattlesnakes, vipers, puff adders and more. In the larger lobby area is a sloth, a few birds, a hedgehog, a monkey, large mouth bass, geckos, Gila monsters, and other reptiles.

Outside, you'll see rows of cages with several tigers, black leopards, bobcats, a lion, and servals. Another section features raccoons, capuchin monkeys, falcons, alligators, foxes, hawks, and tortoises. A more domesticated section has llamas, horses, and zonkey-zebra mix. There are also two small playgrounds here and a picnic area.

An add-on that is so worth it is Extreme Feed - for $5 for ages 17 and under, $10 for adults, you can feed a big cat by giving it meat on a long, long fork. Take a behind-the-scenes guided tour to learn more - schools and scout groups can do this for only $5 per person. Look at the website for the wild, special annual events.

Hours: Open Mon. - Fri., noon - 5pm; Sat. - Sun., 10am - 5pm. It is closed Tues. and Wed. in the fall. The facility is located 1.3 miles up a dirt road, so it could be closed due to inclement weather.

Price: $10 for adults; $8 for seniors; $6 for ages 3 - 12; children 2 and under are free.

Ages: 3 years and up.

HESPERIA ZOO

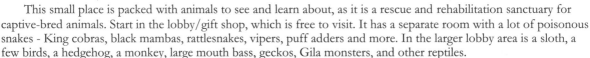

(760) 948-9430 / www.thehesperiazoo.com

19038 Willow Street, Hesperia

$$$

The animals at this very small, ten-acre zoo (which is surrounded by a housing development), who have either been rescued or purchased, spent time in the spotlight as they have been featured in movies, TV commercials, and print ads. Do you recognize any of them? See the animals close up in their small, hard-packed-dirt floor pens and learn more about them because the guided tour (which is the only way allowed to experience the zoo) is given by an animal trainer. You hear stories about the animals - where they came from, their traits, habitats, and some of their personality quirks. You see a black bear, ostriches, llama, tiger, lion, camel, baboon, prairie dogs, monkeys, birds, hoofed animals, porcupine, alligator, reindeer, and other exotic animals. Some domestic animals are here, as well.

Your tour usually finishes with a presentation of some sort, like watching certain animals be led through paces to show how they use their instincts in the wild. Kids, especially, enjoy the petting zoo, also, which has llamas; Australian sheep (who have hair, not wool); goats; pigs; and more. There are also boas, scorpions, tarantulas, and other such critters at this zoo.

Visitors can also take the one-hour guided Feeding Frenzy Tour where they can help feed spider monkeys, lemurs, reindeer, tigers and more animals. Private guided tours, educational programs, and kids summer camps are offered during the week by reservation. Check the website for special events such as Boo at the Zoo Halloween flashlight tours.

Hours: Open Sat. and Sun. at 4pm, only, for regular tours or Feeding Frenzy tours. All tours must be reserved in advance. Closed New Year's Day, Easter, 4th of July, Thanksgiving, Christmas, and rainy days.

Price: The one-hour guided tour is $7 for adults; $5 for seniors and ages 3 - 12; children under 2 are free. The Feeding Frenzy Tour is $20 per person. Cash only.

Ages: 2 years and up.

MOJAVE STATE FISH HATCHERY

(760) 245-9981 or (909) 484-0167 / www.wildlife.ca.com

!

12550 Jacaranda Avenue, Victorville

This facility is the largest trout-producing hatchery in California. Six raceways (i.e., holding tanks for the fish) at 1,000 feet long each, hold six strains of rainbow trout that supplies seven counties. You won't be here long, but come see them at feeding time, if possible, as the fish practically leap in the air to snatch their food. And note that tempting though it may be, you may not bring your fishing pole. Tours are offered upon request. There is a picnic table under a shade tree on a small patch of grass here, too.

Hours: Open daily, 7:30am - 3:30pm.
Price: Free
Ages: 2 years and up.

MOUNTAIN TOWN REPTILE MUSEUM

(909) 797-4420 / www.oaktreevillage.info

38480 Oak Glen Road, Oak Glen

Inside, just beyond the gift shop/lobby is a huge, long, funky room with a "mountain" built in its middle, complete with a number of fake trees (which add ambiance) and mannequins; niches inset into its sides; and dioramas along the perimeter walls. Taxidermied animals are perched on the mountain, in the mountainside and in dioramas including bear, big horn sheep, ostriches, deer, raccoons, a mountain lion, birds in flight, ducks, and a wolverine, all in life-like poses. One collection, in a cave-like setting, has a polar bear, a family of Emperor penguins, seals, and an Arctic fox. Another diorama is a one-room log cabin with a period-dressed mannequin, a stove, and animal furs. The niches inset into the mountain hold small, live animals such as a variety of snakes, frogs, lizards, and insects. Another room along the wall contains several live snakes (in glass enclosures) including boas, pythons, corn snakes, and milk snakes, plus a skink, a legless lizard (which is somehow not a snake), and tortoises. Other live animals in Mountain Town include Nile monitors, Flemish giant rabbits (about 20 lbs. each) and other rabbits, plus Madagascar hissing cockroaches, African grey parrots, macaws, and more. In the fall, animal and reptile presentations are given at 1:30pm and 3:30pm.

In the Mountain Town lobby is a souvenir shop and a few more taxidermied animals, such as a bear and deer heads. Just outside the shop are fallow deer in enclosures. You can purchase food for the animals at $1 a cup. In the fall, gold pan here at the sluice on weekends for $17 per person (with a minimum of 20 people) and keep what you pan. See the entry for OAK GLEN / APPLE PICKING (pg. 403) and OAK TREE VILLAGE (pg. 434) for more things to do in this immediate area and for information on great school and group tours that explore the area and allows participants to interact with the animals in the adjacent Animal Park.

Hours: Open daily, 10am to 5pm, weather permitting.
Price: $3 per person.
Ages: 3 years and up.

OAK TREE VILLAGE

See OAK TREE VILLAGE (pg. 434), under POTPOURRI, for information on the Animal Park and other fun things to do here.

—*BIG BEAR*—

BIG BEAR LAKE / LAKE ARROWHEAD (and the surrounding area)

Instead of categorizing Big Bear Lake and Lake Arrowhead attractions in my usual way throughout San Bernardino county pages, I've grouped them together in their own section because I think most people think of these areas as destinations in and of themselves.

These four-season mountain resorts are close enough to escape to for a day or a weekend, although they offer enough activities for at least a week's vacation. The pine trees and fresh air that beckon city-weary folks, plus all the things to do, make them ideal family get-aways. November through March (or so) the mountains become a winter wonderland with lot of opportunities for snow play and skiing. This section, however, also covers a broader base of activities because Big Bear Lake and Lake Arrowhead are great any time of year!

For specific information on events held during the time you plan to visit Big Bear Lake, call (909) 866-4607 / www.bigbearchamber.com - chamber of commerce, or www.BigBeartodaymag.com. I appreciate www.bigbearlake.net for general information, as well, plus www.openairbigbear.com. as the best resource for <u>all</u> outdoor activities, gear rentals and events in Big Bear Valley! For lodging information and visitor's guide, call (800) 4BIG BEAR (424-4232) / www.bigbearinfo.com. For similar information about Lake Arrowhead, call (909) 337-3715 / www.lakearrowheadchamber.com or www.lakearrowhead.com. Camping information can be found by contacting the Forest Service at (877) 444-6777 / www.recreation.gov. Note: Fishing in Big Bear Lake is available to the public; those 16 years and older must have a valid license. Fishing in the lake in Lake Arrowhead is open only for Arrowhead Lake Association members and their guests. Check road conditions first in the winter time before heading up - (800) 427-ROAD (7623).

ACTION TOURS CALIFORNIA

(909) 866-0390 / www.actiontourscalifornia.com   6/$
40957 Big Bear Boulevard, Big Bear Lake

    With Action at its core (and name), this company offers a variety of thrilling adventures. **Zipline**: Take your leap of faith as literally zipping through forest tree tops is an incredible adrenaline rush! And you get to do this nine times! The three-hour zipline tour even starts off exciting, in a Pinzgauer (safari-type jeep) that rides and climbs the mountainous terrain, incorporating several stops along the way. Hiking is part of the trip as is walking across a suspension bridge (the bouncing always gets to me!) all the while learning the history of the area. There are nine zip lines to zoom across, ranging from the baby step one at 140 feet all the way to 860 feet. Zip lines are cables suspended really high up (85' at one!). Riders wear a harness with a carabineer attached to a pulley to let 'er rip from one side of the cable to the other. Coming back from this adventure, you might just be ready to do it again as the experience is different in the cold and snow, than in the warmth of spring or summer. Participants must be at least 8 years old and weigh between 65 and 250 pounds.

    Tree rope climbing: Branching out to try a new skill? This three-hour adventure, for ages 12 and up, starts by taking the company van a little deeper into the forest to the climbing site, which is a high-point of the National Forest; really. Harnessed and helmeted, learn the ropes (literally) by tying the magic knot (which slides up and down, allowing movement, but still holds you in place) and safety knot; foot stirrups to pull you up the trees; and leaning back and taking small jumps to rappel down. The trees look tall to just look up at them - they are so much taller to actually climb as you go about forty-five-feet up. This is a great physical activity because you are doing it - it's not a guide pulling you along, plus you'll be learning about trees, the history of the area, etc. along the way. Wear close-toed shoes; bring water bottles; go for it!

    Add to any of your adventures by going off-roading, through the forest and through town on a **Segway**! Take this two-hour tour and learn and see the area while zipping along in another fashion. One more fun offering is the seasonal, three-hour **snowshoe** tour for ages 10 and up. "Walk" amongst the Jeffrey and Ponderosa pine trees along trails not always accessible any other way. Enjoy the pristine beauty here and get a great work out at the same time. All equipment is provided, but dress for cold weather and bring hydration, energy bars, camera, and an attitude of being up for a wonderful time.

Hours: Open daily, weather permitting. Call for specific tour times.
Price: Zipline tours are $129 per person. Tree rope climbing is $99. Segway tours are $85. Showshoeing is $87.
Ages: 8 years and up - depending on the adventure.

ALPINE SLIDE at MAGIC MOUNTAIN

(909) 866-4626 or (909) 866-4627 / www.alpineslidebigbear.com $$$
800 Wildrose Lane, Big Bear Lake

    Alpine Slide lifts family fun to new heights! Take the chairlift up the mountain. Then, you and your child sit on heavy-duty plastic toboggans and rip down the quarter-mile, cement, contoured slide that resembles a bobsled track. Control your speed by pushing or pulling on the lever. We were cautious only on our first ride. Your child can go down by himself if he's at least 7 years old.

    The compact, eighteen-hole miniature golf course, Putt 'N Around, has just a few frills, but kids still enjoy puttin' around on it. Single and double go karts are available for drivers at least 57" tall. Inside the main building are a few video games, of course, and a snack bar. That delicious food you smell is a burger (about $4) or hot dog (about $2) being barbecued right outside, or it may be a bowl of soup or chili (but not being barbecued).

    Summer play is enhanced by two zippy water slides. You'll end with a splash in the three-and-a-half-feet deep pool, but it's not for swimming in. Winter allows you and the kids a chance to inner tube down the snowplay hill on four side-by-side runs that resemble a snake's trail. Instead of trudging back up the hill with tube in hand (which you're not allowed to do), ride the covered Magic Carpet which is similar to a moving conveyor belt covered in plexiglass. Nighttime runs add an extra touch of magic. You'll have mountains of fun any season you come to Alpine Slide at Magic Mountain.

Hours: The Alpine Slide, miniature golf, and go karts are open mid-June - mid-September, Sun. - Thurs., 10am - 6pm; Fri. - Sat., 10am - 9pm. Open weekends only in the spring and fall, 10am - 5pm, or 6pm; open in the winter, daily (weather permitting), Mon. - Fri., 10am - 4pm; Sat. - Sun., 10am - dusk. (Mini golf and go karts are also open in the winter on Fri. and Sat. until 9pm.) The water slide is open Memorial Day weekend - Labor Day weekend, 10am - 4pm. The snow play area is usually open November - Easter (they make their own snow here) daily, 10am - 4pm. Night sessions are Fri., Sat., and holidays, 5pm - 9pm.

Price: Alpine ride - $6 for one ride; $25 for a five-ride book. Miniature golf - $5 a round for adults; $4 for ages 12 and under. Go karts - $6 a single car; $8 a double car. Water slide - $2 for one ride; $10 for a ten-ride book; $15 for an unlimited day pass. Snow play - $35 for an unlimited day-pass which includes a tube as you may not bring your own. Nighttime tubing sessions are $30 per person. Children 2 to 6 are free on the Alpine slide, water slide, and snow play area, as long as they are accompanied by a paying adult.

Ages: 3 years and up.

BALDWIN LAKE STABLES AND PETTING ZOO

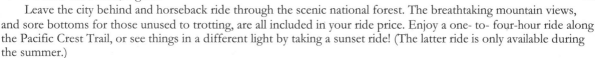

(909) 585-6482 / www.baldwinlakestables.com

$$$$$

46475 Pioneer Town Road, Big Bear

Leave the city behind and horseback ride through the scenic national forest. The breathtaking mountain views, and sore bottoms for those unused to trotting, are all included in your ride price. Enjoy a one- to- four-hour ride along the Pacific Crest Trail, or see things in a different light by taking a sunset ride! (The latter ride is only available during the summer.)

Hand-led pony rides for young bronchos are $10 per child that last about fifteen minutes - a few laps around the track. A petting zoo here has bales of hay all around and a barn-like small building. For $3 per person enter the pen to pet the llamas, bunnies, goats, sheep, potbellied pigs, a chinchilla, guinea pigs, and ducks.

Hours: The stables are open daily most of the year, weather permitting, 10am - 5pm, although hours fluctuate. Call before you come as rides are by reservation only. Pony rides and the petting zoo are open most of the year on weekends only, 11am - 3pm; open daily in the summer the same hours.

Price: Horseback riding is $55 an hour per person.

Ages: At least 7 years old and 4' tall for horseback riding.

BIG BEAR DISCOVERY CENTER

(909) 866-3437 or (909) 382-2790 / www.mountainsfoundation.org

!

40971 N. Shore Drive, Highway 38, Fawnskin

This classy-looking ranger station is the best place to visit (or call) for hiking and biking trail maps, and camp sites. Exhibits at the center include informational and pictorial panels, animal pelts, and stuffed animals such as a black bear, bobcat, gold eagle, barn owl, and raven. A seventeen-minute film about the history of Big Bear Lake runs continuously. An hands-on exhibit hall includes an explanation and visual of the formation of mountains, plus touchable rocks. Activities in here include mining limestone, building dams, climbing through a hollow log, and building a log cabin. You may buy a bite to eat at the snack bar to enjoy at the outside patio tables and chairs. Outside, too, is a huge, 370-year old pine slab displaying a time line, of sorts, via its rings that indicate the year Mickey Mouse was created; the year the Dodo bird became extinct; the War of 1812 (guess which year?); and more.

A special place for kids, ages 2 to 7, is the Nature Discovery Zone, an outdoor space for them to have outdoor exploration with areas for unstructured play in a safe environment, for free. The areas include a gathering area; nature art; messy materials (using sticks and logs and more nature materials to create or play); building (using wooden blocks); cargo ropes and webs for climbing and crawling; music and movement (a wooden boardwalk/stage, and wood xylophone and other instruments); walking on stone steps to various areas of plants, etc.; dirt and sand digging boxes (yea!); a quiet area (a bench under a tree - time to breathe!); and just an area to hang out in nature.

The center, which boasts a 300-seat, outside amphitheater, is also host for a variety of special programs, held mostly in the summer, such as weekend campfires. Another program focuses on Native American lifestyles and includes arts, crafts, and demonstrations such as drum making, working with clay, and gourd painting. Hour-long Nature Nights presentations, held every Thursday night during the summer and every other Friday in other seasons, cover various topics. Half-hour guided nature walks are offered every weekend, twice a day. Ask about Jr. Forest Ranger programs for kids and the educational programs for school groups. One of the winter jaunts is a three-hour, guided snowshoe excursion (based on snow availability). The trip is ideal for both beginners an experienced snowshoers of all ages.

Pick up an Adventure Pass at the center. This Pass is required for all vehicles parking on national forest property for recreational purposes.

Hours: Open Thurs. - Mon., 9am - 4pm. Closed Tues., Wed., New Year's Day, Thanksgiving, and Christmas. Snowshoe trips are offered December thru mid-March on the weekends, IF there is enough snow.

Price: The Adventure pass is $5 per day, or $30 for an annual pass. The snowshoe excursion is $30 for adults; $20 for ages 8 - 12.

Ages: All

BIG BEAR VALLEY HISTORICAL MUSEUM

(909) 585-8100 / www.bigbearhistory.org   !
800-B Greenway Drive, Big Bear City

The past is definitely present at the Big Bear Valley Historical Museum. The buildings that comprise the museum are very old (and old looking). The small main building contains a good assortment of taxidermied animals such as a golden eagle, skunk, red fox, badger, and others, displayed mostly behind glass in "natural" settings. Other exhibits include birds' nests, eggs, arrowheads, rocks, fossils, unique leather carvings, old photographs of old Big Bear, Native American artifacts, and old-fashioned toys. Outside on the porch are turn-of-the-century post office boxes, plus mining equipment and mining artifacts.

An on-site, furnished, 1875 one-room log cabin offers a real look into the pioneer lifestyle. The docents in here are wonderful at explaining to kids how pioneer families lived, and the uses of some of the household items. My boys couldn't believe that chamber pots were really used as portable potties. It finally dawned on them that entire families lived together in this one room; sleeping, cooking, eating, and playing together. I hope they'll be more thankful about their own living arrangements!

One log structure here is actually a mule barn used to house mules. A stamp mill used to crush gold bearing ore and hard rock to recover gold, and lots of old, rusted agriculture equipment are also on the grounds. Note that the adjacent Big Bear City Park is good mostly for visitors to just run around in its fields; no shade.

Hours: Open Memorial Day to the second Sun. in September on Wed., Sat., and Sun. (and holiday Mon.), 10am - 4pm.
Price: Free; donations gladly accepted.
Ages: 3 years and up.

BIG BEAR MARINA BOAT RENTALS / BIG BEAR QUEEN CRUISE

(909) 866-3218 - marina; (909) 744-4948 - Big Bear Queen / www.bigbearmarina.com; www. $$$$
bigbearqueen.com
500 Paine Road, Big Bear Lake

The Marina offers a boatload of fun for the family. Four-passenger motorized fishing boats start at $55 for two hours. Kayaks and stand up paddle boards rent for $25 an hour per. Two-seater wave runners are $130 an hour (early bird special is $100). Peddle boats are $40 an hour. Rent a small pontoon, a flat-bottomed boat that is almost seasick proof, for $80 an hour, plus $20 fuel, so $100 an hour. It seats up to six people. A larger pontoon, which seats up to twelve people, is $115 an hour, plus $20 for fuel, so $135 an hour.

Take an hour-and-a-half, narrated tour around Big Bear Lake on the paddlewheel boat, *Big Bear Queen*. You'll learn the history of the marina and the town of Big Bear, plus the happenings of the area. Tours are given daily, May through October, always at 2pm, and sometimes at noon and 4pm, if at least fifteen people are signed up. Prices are $22 for adults; $20 for seniors; $15 for ages 3 to 12; children 2 years and under are free. There are sunset cruises available, too - mostly for adults.

Hours: Open daily, seasonally, usually spring through October, 7am - 7pm.
Price: Prices are listed above.
Ages: 3 years and up.

BIG BEAR OFF-ROAD TOUR

(310) 508-7687 / www.offroadadventure.com $$$$$

Up to twelve passengers can ride in this six-wheel drive Pinzgauer on this 2.5 hour, fun and educational adventure/tour. The trip isn't just about riding in a cool-looking vehicle (although that counts) or gaping at the spectacular mountain scenery of forest, lakes, streams, canyons, and more (although that really counts); it is also about incorporating learning about the history of the land and the people. Your tour guide shares info about the lake, the mining town of Belleville in the Holcomb Valley, Native Americans, old pioneers, and miners. In fact, there are usually miners working their claim, so a stop and chat with them is often part of your experience. Note that a minimum of four adults (or the price for four adults) are needed for a tour. You will be picked up at your place of lodging or agreed on meeting place. Bring your own snacks and water.

Hours: Open year round, weather permitting. Call to schedule a tour.
Price: $50 for adults; $25 for ages 12 and under.
Ages: 5 years and up.

BIG BEAR PIRATE SHIP

(909) 878-4040 or (909) 866-5706 / www.bigbearhollowaysmarina.com
398 Edgemoor Road at Holloway's Marina, Big Bear Lake

$$$$

        If it's adventure you're seekin' matey, then climb aboard and hoist the sails! This jet black, three-masted galleon, with white and red trim, is a one-third-scale replica of a 16th century pirate ship and it comes complete with its own crew of pirates, well, at least a captain. The completely restored ship, *Time Bandit*, is named after the 1981 movie in which it was featured. Sail across Big Bear Lake (which is kind of like sailing the seven seas, just a shorter trip) on a ninety-minute narrated cruise. Stops include the BIG BEAR DISCOVERY CENTER (pg. 445) and Whaler's Pointe restaurant. Night sails often offer live entertainment on board.

Hours: Usually open mid-May - October, weather permitting, with tours are guaranteed to leave Sat. - Sun. at 2pm. It can also depart Mon. - Fri. at noon and 2pm, if enough people are signed up (the ship holds 25), and on weekends, additionally, at 10am, 4pm and 6pm.
Price: $22 for adults; $20 for seniors; $14 for ages 12 and under. Infants or lap-sitting toddlers are free.
Ages: All

BIG BEAR SOLAR OBSERVATORY

(909) 866-5791 / www.bbso.njit.edu
40386 North Shore Lane, Big Bear Lake

!

        The world's largest solar telescope, 1.6 meters, is housed in the dome-shaped observatory located on a strip of land that juts into Big Bear Lake. The observatory offers a unique way to study the often sunny skies (300 days on average) in Big Bear. Opening the shutter allows sunlight in, at almost any angle, to strike the central mirror of the telescope. Other observatory instruments also monitor and record often dramatic images of the sun, which are then displayed on video monitors. Cameras can show sharper details than the unaided eye can see. Take a forty-five-minute tour to get the hot facts about the sun. School groups may call to schedule an appointment.

Hours: Tours are offered at a limited capacity - April - Labor Day, on the second Thurs. from 1pm - 2pm.
Price: Free
Ages: 8 years and up.

Biking

www.mountainbikebigbear.com; www.mybikesite.com; www.bigbearhostel.com

        There are several places to rent mountain bikes and helmets; most include a free bike map of the area. Pedal your way across town, down a mountain, or along forest trails. Some of the rental shops also offer guided tours. This list is not exhaustive by any means, but includes several favorite trails.

Bike Trails
BIG BEAR LAKE:
Alpine Pedal Path
        A five-mile (round trip), very easy, asphalt path that meanders along the north shore of Big Bear Lake. (You'll share this path with joggers, skaters, and strollers.) It starts (or stops) at Stanfield Cutoff and ends (or begins) near the solar observatory, connecting with the BIG BEAR DISCOVERY CENTER (pg. 445), as well.
John Bull Loop Bike Trail
        This almost fifteen-mile intermediate loop starts at the base of Van Dusen Canyon, climbs up for several miles to Holcomb Valley, becomes level for a stretch, and then ends with the road being steep and rutted.
Snow Summit Adventure Park
        Catch a ride up the mountain and cruise across and down over forty miles of trails. The terrain varies, meaning that trails range from easy, wide, forest service roads to arduous, single-track, dirt trails so there are routes for the novice, intermediate, and advanced riders. The Grand View Pointe Loop, one of the most popular routes, is nine miles long and great for intermediate riders. Seven miles of serious downhill trails await experienced mountain bikers. Those who prefer flatter trails may skip the sky chair entirely and bike beginner-friendly trails running through and from the base area of the resort, including Bristlecone Trail and Towne Trail. See more under SNOW SUMMIT ADVENTURE PARK / SCENIC SKY CHAIR (pg. 456) and check www.bigbearmountainresorts.com for more details.

Bike Rentals
BIG BEAR LAKE:
Bear Valley Bikes - (909) 866-8000 / www.bvbikes.com
        40298 Big Bear Boulevard, across from Alpine Slide and Magic Mountain Recreation Area

Bear Valley has mountain bikes, BMX bikes, trailers for children, toddler bikes, and helmets.

Open daily most of the year, 10am - 5pm. Closed in the winter on Mon. Call for hours, just to be on the safe side.

Mountain bikes, kids bikes and trailers start at $10 an hour; $30 for 4 hours.

Chains Required Bike Shop - (909) 878-3280 / www.chainsrequiredbikeshop.com

    41869 Big Bear Boulevard

Bicycle repairs, as well as rentals of full suspension, $16 an hour; K2 comfort bike, $9 an hour; Tandem, $16 an hour; and children's K2, $9 an hour.

Open Mon. - Fri., 9am - 6pm; Sat., 8am - 6pm (7pm in the spring/summer); Sun., 8am - 5pm (6pm in the spring/summer), weather permitting. Open earlier in the summer, about 7:30am.

Snow Summit Rental Shop - (888)-SUMMIT-1 (786-6481) or (909) 866-5766 /844.GO2.BEAR for 3 hour rentals

    www.bigbearmountainresorts.com /

    880 Summit Boulevard, at the base of Snow Summit; the Adventure Academy

For those serious about mountain biking, the shop has a full line of bikes and protective equipment to rent. Freeride or cross country full suspension bikes, for instance, begin at $56 for 3 hours; $110 for a downhill bike. Purchase a lift ticket to access the bike trail at the top of the mountain.

Open mid-June - Labor Day, daily; open weekends mid- May - mid-June, and in the fall. Closed in the winter and beginning of spring.

CHILDREN'S FOREST

(909) 382-2773 or (909) 867-5996- children's forest; (909) 382-2600 - national forest service /

www.mountainsfoundation.org

32573 California 18, Running Springs

    The small, Children's Forest Visitor Information Center is located at the gateway to the Children's Forest, which is a spread of 3,400 acres within the San Bernardino National Forest. The center, staffed primarily by youths, offers information on recreation opportunities in the forest, education programs, the opportunity to purchase the Adventure Pass, themed workshops, and more. There are a few displays of local flora and fauna, and a hands-on nature table.

    Drive four very winding miles on the narrow Keller Peak Road (or hike or bike it if you're brave) to reach the Children's Forest Interpretive Trail. Note: Drive another mile on the road to reach KELLER PEAK FIRE LOOKOUT TOWER (pg. 451). At the trailhead there are a few picnic tables and restrooms and a drinking fountain. Use a self-guided brochure as you walk the mildly hilly, three-quarter-miles of looping paved trails that are also readily stroller and wheel-chair accessible; ideal for younger children. Among the scrubs and, further in, the pine trees and by a pretty lake and boulder formations, be on the lookout for wildlife such as birds, deer, squirrels, unusual insects, etc. Interpretive trail signs designed by children help mark the paths and tell stories of the plants and animals. A longer hiking option is the 4.5-mile Exploration Trail that winds through backcountry. More mileage, but still family friendly. Don't forget to pack lunch, water, sunscreen, and binoculars. With all that it offers and set in such beautiful surroundings, I'm glad the Children's Forest is open to adults, too!

    The main purpose of the information center is to encourage children to develop a passion for the environment by training youth naturalists and offering opportunities for kids to take a hike. There are several outstanding educational programs offered through this center, both to the public and to school groups. A sampling includes Forest Ecology - learning how plants and animals depend on each other for survival; Finding the Wild Things - learning how animals adapt to the environments, where they live, what they eat, and how to read the signs of their presence; Soil Erosion - physically working to prevent soil erosion; and Charting Your Course - learning map and compass reading techniques. Seasonal snowshoe field trips are available to aid in learning about winter ecology. Get a workout while following animal tracks! School exploration programs are offered Monday through Friday, year round. Each program is four hours long. The majority of the time is spent in the forest, plus there are games and hands-on activities.

Hours: The visitor's center is only open May - September, Sat. - Sun., 9am - 5pm. Keller Peak Road, the paved trail, and this part of the forest are open in the spring, summer, and fall daily, sunrise - sunset. It's closed in winter. Call for a schedule of programs.

Price: $5 per vehicle per day to stop anywhere in the forest. Call for various program prices.

Ages: All for the hiking trails, depending on which one you choose. Age requirements vary for the programs.

GOLD RUSH MINING ADVENTURE

(800) 363-8303 / (909) 866-5678 / www.goldrushminingadventures.com $$$$

40016 Big Bear Boulevard, Big Bear Lake

    Modern-day mining, rock treasure hunting and gold panning at this part gift shop, part experience store makes it a lot easier to find the mother lode than in days of yore. Expect to pay modern-day prices, tho, too. The touristy advertising out front of the cabin-like shop (including a fake hanging shark, an outhouse, and a life-size donkey statue) is indicative of the type of things to do inside. Knowing this, enter the fun.

Purchase a bag of mining ore, that come in a variety of sizes with pre-planted "finds", then pan for gold and other rocks and mineral gems in your ore bag using a grated tray in the water trough just outside. For drier mining, go inside and dig at the dino discovery station, or in a sand box for fossils. Wet and dry finds can include polished gemstones, whale or dinosaur bones, amethyst, quartz, garnet, arrowheads, rubies, shark teeth, and much more - over 70 varieties from all over the world. Other activities include choosing a geode and breaking it open using a machine to see what it reveals; opening up a "dinosaur" egg to find a fossil; and harvesting a pearl, yourself, from an real oyster. It really is fun to take part in the discoveries and take home your treasures, plus it can be a genuine learning experience, too.

The gift shop is packed with stuff, from kitschy to authentic, and divided into different themes such as a faux dino cave with dinosaur items such as fossils and artifacts, plus sections featuring pirates, mermaids, *Frozen*, etc, offering jewelry, rocks, shells, toys, and kits, as well as fudge and soda, and more. You can also take a bag of minerals in mining rough to unearth at home. Your prospects will pan out at Gold Rush! Note that just across the way is a very small, Old West "town" made of wooden buildings - good for photo ops.

Hours: Open daily, 9am - 5pm; open until 6pm or 7pm in the summer. Closed Christmas day.
Price: General admission is free. Prices start at $2 for a geode, $18 to open an oyster, and $15 for a small mineral bag and go up to $95 for a large sea chest. Plan on at least $30 for your adventure.
Ages: 4 years and up.

GREEN VALLEY LAKE

(909) 867-2009 or (909) 867-2165 - camping and lake info.; (714) 920-1689 - cabins; (877) 444-6777 - camping reservations / www.green-valley-lake.com; www.mountaininfo.com; www.recreation.gov - camping
Green Valley Lake Road, Green Valley Lake

Can you keep a secret? This somewhat secluded, small, pristine, ten-acre, private lake is an ideal and idyllic spot, especially for younger children. Surrounded by pine and oaks trees, families can swim at the little beach that has a lifeguard, and rent boats by the hour - kayaks ($10 for a single, $12 for a double), rowboats ($10), swan-shaped pedal boats ($52), and SUP ($15). Note that no motorized or personal boats are allowed. You can also fish for trout (the lake is stocked); enjoy a picnic and/or barbecue meal; and hike or bike on the mile-long, looping, dirt path that goes through the forest and around the lake. At the Sports Court play volleyball, basketball, tennis, and badminton. A convenience store and bait shop are here. A fishing license is required for fishermen 16 years and over and can be purchased here.

About a half mile from the lake is a campground. The almost forty campsites are snuggled amongst tall pine trees, with a meadow closeby. Reservations are recommended. Cabin rentals are available here, too. Also, since you're in the area check out the free, small Lilleberg Museum at 33659 Green Valley Lake Road. It displays the history of the mountain area in pictorials and dioramas, as well as a few pieces of equipment such as an old telephone system and train apparatus. The museum is open on Saturdays from 2pm to 4pm. Note that the town of Green Valley has only 400 permanent residents.

Hours: The lake is open year round for fishing, daily, 5:30am - 8pm, though it isn't stocked year round. Water activities and camping are available late April - October, daily. The swim beach is open Memorial Day Weekend - Labor Day, daily, 8am - 7pm (tho it might be closed one day a week for maintenance - call first).
Price: Day use is free. The swim beach is $5 for adults; $3 for ages 10 and under. Fishing costs $15 for adults (plus a license); $10 for ages 15 and under. Tent camping is $25 - $27 a night, plus a $10 reservation fee. Cabin rentals start at $125 for a one bedroom, two night minimum.
Ages: All

HIKING

(909) 866-3437 - Big Bear Discovery Center; (909) 382-2709 - Arrowhead Ranger Station; (909) 382-4802 - $ national forest / www.mountainsfoundation.org; www.bigbearinfo.com; www.fs.usda.gov

There are many, *many* places to go hiking in the Big Bear Lake and Lake Arrowhead areas. In Big Bear Lake, visit the BIG BEAR DISCOVERY CENTER (pg. 445), a ranger station where you can obtain trail maps. In Lake Arrowhead, visit the Arrowhead Ranger District at 28104 Highway 18 in Skyforest for maps and other information. Several hiking trails are associated with or begin (or end) with some of the campgrounds in Lake Arrowhead and the surrounding areas, as well. Note: Anywhere you park in the national forest for recreational reasons, you must pay $5 a car for an Adventure Pass. Take necessary precautions while hiking and always bring water. I've listed just a few of the trails my family has enjoyed trekking.

Hiking Trails
BIG BEAR LAKE:
(Also see BIKING (pg. 447) as biking trails can usually be hiked as well, especially the very easy and accessible Alpine Pedal Path.)
Castle Rock:
(FROM HIGHWAY 18, THE TRAILHEAD IS ABOUT ONE MILE EAST PAST THE DAM. PARKING IS VERY LIMITED ON THE HIGHWAY.)

The trail is only eight-tenths of a mile, but it is an uphill walk over some rocky terrain. The destination is Castle Rock, a large rock that kids love to climb on. Its name gives lead to a lot of imaginative play time here. All of my kids wanted to be king - what a surprise! If everyone still has the energy, keep hiking back to the waterfalls, and/or to Devil's Woodpile. The scenery along the way is spectacular.

Cougar Crest Trail:
(THE TRAIL STARTS JUST WEST OF THE BIG BEAR DISCOVERY CENTER)

This four-and-a-half-mile (about three hour) moderate to difficult hike goes up a gentle hill, but it does get you out of breath at this altitude. Note that there is very little shade along this route. It ends at the juncture of the Pacific Crest Trail. (See the next few entries below for more information on this trail.) If you can, however, hike another half mile to reach the summit of Bertha Peak (where the transmitting equipment interferes slightly with the wilderness perspective) for an almost 360-degree view of Bear Valley and Holcomb Valley, and even the Mojave Desert on a clear day.

Pineknot Trail:
(FROM HIGHWAY 18, EXIT SOUTH ON MILL CREEK ROAD AND LOOK FOR THE TRAILHEAD.)

For a panoramic view of Big Bear Lake and the surrounding San Bernardino Mountains, hike this moderate to difficult, six-mile round-trip trail. It begins at the Aspen Glen Picnic Area, winding from the valley amongst white fir and Jeffrey pines up to the ridgeline at Grand View Point, where you deserve to rest and eat snacks that you've packed in.

Snow Summit Adventure Park:

Look up SNOW SUMMIT ADVENTURE PARK / SCENIC SKY CHAIR (pg. 456) for details about the over forty miles of trails around the Snow Summit mountain.

Woodland Trail:
(ON HIGHWAY 38, PARKING IS ALMOST DIRECTLY ACROSS THE STREET FROM M.D. BOAT RAMP, JUST WEST OF THE STANFIELD CUTOFF ROAD.)

This one-and-a-half-mile loop is an easy walk, as the dirt trail follows more along the side of the mountain, rather than into the mountain. Although you can hear the traffic from certain sections of the trail, the changing landscape, from pine trees to coastal shrub to cactus, still offers the sense of being immersed in nature. An interpretative trail guide is available through the Ranger Station. Make it an educational field trip as well as a nice walk!

LAKE ARROWHEAD:

Some of the trails that I've not mentioned below, such as Crab Creek Trail and Seeley Creek Trail, are beautiful, but know that the trail passes crosses through a creek, which can be fun, but can be dangerous for kids when the water runs high.

Children's Forest: See the entry for CHILDREN'S FOREST (pg. 448) for details.
Heap's Peak Arboretum:
(JUST OFF HIGHWAY 18, ABOUT A MILE-AND-A-HALF EAST OF SKYFOREST.)

This almost-a-mile, relatively easy loop begins on pavement and continues on hard-packed dirt the rest of the way. The trail winds through tall Sequoias and pine trees, past wildflowers (depending on the season), over a creek, and alongside numerous native plants. It is never quite completely quiet as the highway noise filters through the forest, but it is still beautiful and serene. Pick up a brochure that highlights the botanical points of interest to make the walk a learning experience as well as a nature excursion.

Indian Rock Trail
(ON HWY. 173, EAST OF ROCK CAMP STATION.)

This very, easy half-mile walk is educational in that it leads to the bedrock mortars used by the Serrano Indians to grind acorns. A stone monument here depicts the encampment of the Serrano Indians.

North Shore Recreational Trail:
(TRAVELING NORTH ON HWY. 18, TURN L. ON HWY. 173 FOR 1.6 MILES, R. AT THE STOP SIGN, STILL ON HWY. 173, R.

ON HOSPITAL RD. AND ENTER THE NORTH SHORE CAMPGROUND. OR GO EAST ON TORREY RD., OPPOSITE THE LAKE ARROWHEAD MARINA AND FOLLOW THE DIRT ROAD ½ A MILE UNTIL YOU REACH THE TRAILHEAD.)

Not quite two miles long, this scenic trail is moderately difficult as it takes you over hills, down into the forest, past boulders, and along Little Bear Creek. There you'll catch up to a forest service road.

Pacific Crest National Scenic Trail:

This 2,600-mile long (yes, you read that correctly) trail, reaches from Canada to Mexico - not quite a day hike. About forty miles traverse the Big Bear/Arrowhead Ranger District. If that's still too much of a hike (which it is for me), there are several portions of it to enter and exit and still get in some decent, but not exhausting, hiking time. How fun to be a part of something so huge! Contact the ranger station using the phone numbers or websites listed above for details and maps.

Hours: Open daily, sunrise - sunset.
Price: $5 a day per car for an Adventure Pass. (The pass allows you to park on and hike in national forest land.)
Ages: 4 years and up.

HOLLOWAY'S MARINA AND RV PARK AND BOAT RENTALS

(909) 866-5706 - Marina and RV; (909) 878-4FUN (4386) - kayaks, canoes, wave runners rentals - North Shore Landing / www.bigbearhollowaysmarina.com

398 Edgemoor Road, Big Bear Lake

Holloway rents flat-bottomed pontoons for up to eight people for $80 for one hour, plus $15 for gas. Aluminum motorized fishing boats start at $70 an hour for two hours. Kayaks are $20 for a single for an hour; $30 for a double. SUPs are $25 an hour. The sister company is NORTH SHORE LANDING (pg. 454), which rents jet skis. Look up BIG BEAR PIRATE SHIP (pg. 447) for information on taking a tour on board a cool-looking pirate ship that departs from this marina.

The adjacent RV park has all the amenities including a playground, horseshoe pits, basketball court, small convenience store, showers, and place to do laundry.

Hours: Open April - October, 6am - sunset, weather permitting. Kayaks and SUPs are usually available starting Memorial Day.
Price: Prices are mentioned above, but they vary quite a bit, so call first. RV camping is about $50 a night.
Ages: 2 years and up, depending.

KELLER PEAK FIRE LOOKOUT TOWER

(909) 225-1025 or (909) 382-2600 / www.mountainsfoundation.org/fire-lookouts/keller-peak

Keller Peak Road, Running Springs

This is a hot ticket: You can see the world, or a good portion of it, from lookout towers, which were originally designed in the 1920's and 1930's to aid rangers in spotting forest fires. The towers were strategically built on the highest points of the mountains. This also means that they are located off the beaten track and incorporate a drive on a winding road. Keller Peak is about five miles off Highway 18; five miles of narrow, winding mountain roads with no guards rails, but breath-taking views. (Or maybe it's the drive that takes your breath away!)

Visitors are now encouraged to visit the towers, climb up the steep ladder (which may be scary for younger kids and older adults), go into the small observation room (only five visitors are allowed in the tower at a time), see the equipment, perhaps even try the Osborne Fire Finder, and enjoy the vista. On a clear day, of which morning times are best, you can see incredibly far. Bring binoculars or borrow ones at the towers. Volunteer staff are on hand to explain the equipment, history of fire lookouts, and the process and procedures for putting them out. Kids might receive Smokey Bear fire prevention materials to take home. While you're here, make sure to hike the CHILDREN'S FOREST (pg. 448) trail, which is one mile back on Keller Peak Road, and stop by the Visitor Center there, too. Note - you won't be here long, but it is an interesting stop.

Hours: Open during fire season - Memorial Day through October daily, 9am - 5pm.
Price: $5 for an Adventure Pass - the Pass is not needed for fire lookout, but it is for any other part of this area that you stop and explore.
Ages: 6 years and up.

LAKE ARROWHEAD QUEEN

(909) 336-6992 / www.lakearrowheadqueen.com

28200 Hwy. 189, Lake Arrowhead

Cruise around beautiful Lake Arrowhead during a fifty-minute narrated tour on board a restored paddle boat.

Guides share the history of the 100-year-old lake and the city, and tidbits about some of the old-time celebrities that used to live here. You'll see the many gorgeous homes/mansions that dot the shoreline. Kids are invited to help steer the boat. See the next entry for details about Lake Arrowhead Village.

Hours: Winter/fall hours are Mon. - Fri., 11am - 3:30 (last tour); Sat. - Sun., 11am - 5pm. Tours leave every ninety minutes. Spring/summer hours are Mon. - Fri., 11am - 5pm; Sat. - Sun., 11am - 6pm. Tours leave every hour.
Price: $17 for adults; $15.50 for seniors; $13 for ages 3 - 11; children 2 and under are free.
Ages: 7 years and up.

LAKE ARROWHEAD VILLAGE / LOLLIPOP PARK

(909) 337-2533 - village info; (909) 337-3715 - visitors's center; (909) 337-2999 - Lollipop Park /   !/$$
www.lakearrowhead.com; www.thelakearrowheadvillage.com; www.lakearrowhead.net; www.lollipoppark.com
28200 Hwy. 189, Lake Arrowhead

Built on the lake's peninsula, this two-level, open-air Village has over fifty shops (including outlet stores) and eateries, plus some fun activities for the family, making it a worthy destination. Some of the kid-friendly shops include Mr. G's for Toys and Rocky Mountain Chocolate Factory, which is an adult-friendly shop as well. From May through Labor Day free concerts are given on the center lawn every Friday and Saturday night, and occasionally on Sundays and Mondays, starting at 6:30pm.

The north section of the Village holds a small, fenced-in park with a grass area and free playground, and Lollipop Park, which is a small-scale kiddie amusement park. Fun attractions at Lollipop Park include a nine-hole miniature golf course, $4 per person; village train ride, $4; bumper cars; go-carts, $7 for the driver and $3 for a passenger; plus, for little ones only, a small, horse carousel; swing ride; mini train ride; and a pirate ship that swings up and down. The cost is $3 per child per ride, or four rides for $10.

For food, try the family-owned Lake Arrowhead Pizza, Deli and Arcade on the second story. Menu choices include a hand-tossed, medium cheese pizza for about $16, plus pastas, salads, sandwiches, and appetizers. There is an arcade room and eleven TV screens inside, including one huge screen, but a much better picture is found by sitting at an outside table: The view of the lake is stunning. Call (909) 337-0723 for more information.

McKenzies Water-Ski School and LAKE ARROWHEAD QUEEN tour boat (see above entry) are also located and launched here. With all there is to see and do at the Village, you could easier spend a day or two learning, playing, eating, and shopping.

Hours: Most stores are open daily, 10am - 6pm. Closed Christmas. Lollipop Park is open September - May, Thurs. - Sun., 10am - 5pm, weather permitting. Open Memorial Day - Labor Day, Sun. - Thurs., 10am - 6pm; Fri. - Sat., 10am - 8pm. It is also open on school holidays - call for hours.
Price: Free, but bring spending money. Prices are listed above for the amusement park.
Ages: All

LAKE GREGORY

(909) 338-2233 - Lake Gregory / www.lakegregoryrecreation.com; www.sbcounty.gov; $$$
www.crestlinechamber.net
24171 Lake Drive, Crestline

Crestline is a little mountain town that people usually just pass through on their way to Lake Arrowhead or Big Bear Lake. But, stop here! The mid-size Lake Gregory is located near the edge of town, nestled in the foothills of the San Bernardino mountains. During the summer months, a four-acre section of the waveless water is roped off for swimming, water play, and paddle boarding, all patrolled by lifeguards. The two smallish swim beaches (across the lake from each other) also offer sand volleyball courts, a basketball court, and horseshoe pits, plus barbecue pits and picnic tables. Bring your own food or grab a burger and fries, sandwich, and other grub at the full-service cafe.

Swim at the lake and/or enjoy the Water Park with its numerous, huge inflatables of slides; climbing structures (i.e. pull yourself up by ropes on one and by inflatable steps on another); obstacle courses; a trampoline; ones to jump off of; and ones to just play on. So fun! (And tiring in a good way.) Other aquatic options are long twisty slides that zoom guests down a small hill at the edge of the lake into the water. These areas are for ages 7 and up and at least 48" tall. Little ones can enjoy the Zero-depth Water Play Park which has nozzles to point and shoot, tall tubes that look like flowers squirting water, and fountains spurting up from the ground, all in cement.

The rest of the lake is open year round for boating and fishing for trout, bass, catfish, crappie, carp and bluegill. Note that there is free Youth Fishing Derby every May for kids 15 years and under with cash prizes. The on-site bait and tackle shop rents poles. Rowboat rentals are available for $45 for a half day; motor boats are $85. Pedal boats, which seat four people, and Aqua Cycles (i.e., big-wheel-type water cycles that seat two people) both use pedal power and rent for $15 a half hour, per. Kayaks and SUPS are also $15 a half hour. The long, thin paddle boards (i.e. belly boards) boards rent for $10 a half hour and must be handled with some finesse if you want to stay topside. The above are available daily in the summer and on weekends through October.

There are also over two miles of hiking trails that stretch around a good portion of the lake with ten fitness stations along the way.

Hours: The lake is open year round, daily, sunup to sundown, for fishing and boating activity. The swim beach and water park activities are open Memorial Day - mid-June on weekends only, 10am - 6pm; open mid-June - Labor Day, daily, 10am - 6pm.

Price: $10 for ages 5 and up for the swim cove and beach area (not Water Park); $6 for seniors; children 4 and under are free. An unlimited day pass is $25 which includes the swim beach, Water Park, and park entrance fee. A fishing access pass is $8 for the day. A California state license is necessary for ages 16 and up. Parking is $10 per vehicle in the gated lots.

Ages: All

MOONRIDGE ANIMAL PARK and ZOO

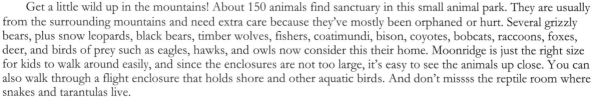

(909) 584-1299 or (909) 866-9700 / www.bigbearzoo.com

43285 Goldmine Drive, Big Bear Lake

Get a little wild up in the mountains! About 150 animals find sanctuary in this small animal park. They are usually from the surrounding mountains and need extra care because they've mostly been orphaned or hurt. Several grizzly bears, plus snow leopards, black bears, timber wolves, fishers, coatimundi, bison, coyotes, bobcats, raccoons, foxes, deer, and birds of prey such as eagles, hawks, and owls now consider this their home. Moonridge is just the right size for kids to walk around easily, and since the enclosures are not too large, it's easy to see the animals up close. You can also walk through a flight enclosure that holds shore and other aquatic birds. And don't misss the reptile room where snakes and tarantulas live.

Daily events include hour-long Animal Presentations at noon which take place at several enclosures. They include an animal being talked about, feeding it, learning why it's here, its habits and more. We've always found the docents and trainers willing, even eager, to answer our kids' questions, so it makes our visit here more memorable. The animal park also offers some seasonal special programs, too, such as Flashlight Safaris. Traveling exhibits are offered to school groups.

A small, grassy picnic area inside the zoo has a few picnic tables. The lobby doubles as an educational center with a few nature exhibits such as bird eggs and nests, fossils, animal jawbones, and live bunnies and snakes (but not in the same enclosure).

Hours: Open May - Labor Day weekend daily, 10am - 5pm. Open the rest of the year daily, 10am - 4pm, weather permitting.

Price: $12 for adults; $9 for seniors and ages 3 - 10; children 2 and under are free.

Ages: All

MOUNTAIN SKIES ASTRONOMICAL SOCIETY ASTRONOMY VILLAGE

(909) 336-1699 / www.mountain-skies.org

2001 Observatory Way, Lake Arrowhead

Observe the universe, or parts of it, from the astronomy village which consists of two main buildings - a combination gift shop/library/research facility, and a 500-square-foot observatory that houses a 16", F/10 Schmidt-Cassegrain with a top mount of a 4" refractor. Purchase a piece of space at the gift shop such as asteroid pieces, blue smoke, and rare, space shuttle memorabilia. The small library/museum has several shelves of books and videos regarding astronomy, as well as a few displays of meteors, Mars rocks, Apollo display models, and signed astronaut photographs. There are picnic tables outside, too.

The best time to visit is on a Saturday night for the Sky Quest Program. This two-and-a-half hour program starts off with a lecture, discussion, and question and answer time. A half-hour slide show follows. A powerful laser pointer is used to point out constellations, specific stars, and other cosmic happenings outside. Finally, guests have the opportunity to look through the telescope. Topic titles include Exploring the Known Universe, Meteorites, Basic Astronomy, and How to Use a Telescope. Ask about school education programs and workshops, other special events, and teacher resource equipment.

Hours: Open Fri., 11am - 2pm. Sky Quest Programs for the public are offered on selected Sat. evenings, usually once a month: Winter/fall shows are 7pm - 9pm; spring/summer, 8pm - 10pm.

Price: Free to walk around and visit. Sky Quest Programs are $7 for adults; $5 for ages 16 and under. Prepurchase tickets or pay $2 more at the door.

Ages: 6 years and up.

NORTH SHORE LANDING

(909) 866-4386 / www.bigbearhollowaysmarina.com $$$$$
North Shore Drive, about 2 miles off Hwy 38, Fawnskin

Rent one to two person jet ski/ waverunners for $85 an hour; kayaks are $20 for a single, $30 for a double; and SUPs are $25. Wakeboarding, waterskis, and tubing are also available here to do and rent.

North Shore Landing is associated with HOLLOWAY'S MARINA AND RV PARK AND BOAT RENTALS (pg. 451), who has other boat and water fun rentals. Look up BIG BEAR PIRATE SHIP (pg. 447) for information on taking a tour on board a cool-looking pirate ship that departs from Holloways.

Hours: Open around Memorial Day - October, 7am - 9am, depending on the time of year, until sunset, weather permitting.

Ages: 4 years and up, depending on the boat choice.

PINE KNOT LANDING BOAT RENTALS / MISS LIBERTY CRUISE

(909) 866-6463 or (909) 866-7766 or (909) 866-BOAT (2628); (909) 866-IFLY (4359) - parasailing / $$$$
www.pineknotmarina.com
400 Pine Knot Boulevard, Big Bear Lake

Boat rentals here are "knot" a problem! Cruise around on your own via a ten-passenger pontoon boats at $114 an hour, or a twelve-passenger pontoon for about $125 an hour. Motorized fishing boats start at about $49 an hour. Wave runners are $125 an hour; kayaks are $35 for two hours for a single; $45 for a double; and paddle boards are $35 for two hours.

Come on board the double decker *Miss Liberty* paddlewheel boat for a ninety-minute, narrated excursion. Sit inside or out on the deck - the lower deck is enclosed and wheelchair accessible, while the upper deck is out in the open. Learn the history of the lake, famous people who have or still live here, and general information about Big Bear Lake Valley. You'll see million-dollar estates (which are something to gawk at), the Solar Observatory, brown (in the summer) ski slopes, other boaters, and fishermen. The *Miss Liberty* has a snack bar stocked with beverages, chips, cookies, and such. Another special way to tour the lake and enjoy a front row view of the surrounding purple mountains majesty is to go on a sunset cruise, which starts at 6pm.

Ever had dreams where you can fly? Parasailing is the next best thing. Start off (and end) on the boat's landing platform, attached by a harness to the parasail and by a tow rope to the boat. As the boat pulls away, you are lifted into the air for ten minutes of flight. You can stay dry if you want, and if all goes well, or take a quick dip (more like a toe touch) in the lake before being airborne again. This is a thrill-seeking experience for kids and adults. If you just want to ride along as an observer, you may, if there is room.

Hours: The rentals are open seasonally, usually May - October, although hours fluctuate: Mon. - Fri., 6am - 7pm; Sat., Sun., and holidays, 6am - 8pm. Always call first as hours are weather dependent! The *Miss Liberty* cruise is available June - September daily, at noon, 2pm, 4pm, and sometimes 6pm, with a minimum of 15 passengers per tour. The cruise is offered throughout the year on weekends only, if the minimum quota is met. Reservations are necessary for all outings. Parasailing is open seasonally, Memorial Day - early fall, Mon. - Fri., 9am - 5pm; Sat. - Sun., 8am - 6pm.

Price: The narrated, *Miss Liberty* cruise is $22 for adults; $20 for seniors; $14 for ages 3 - 12; children 2 and under are free. Parasailing is $80 for single; $160 for tandem (go with your child, though the minimum age is 6); $20 for an observer just riding on the boat. Other prices are listed above.

Ages: 4 years and up.

PLEASURE POINT MARINA

(909) 866-2455 - marina; (909) 556-3345 - wakeboarding, etc. / www.pleasurepointmarina.net; $$$$
www.designatedwakesports.com
603 Landlock Landing Road, Big Bear Lake

What a pleasure to rent a boat from Pleasure Point Marina and tootle around Big Bear Lake. The starting rental price for pontoon boats (i.e., flat-bottomed) that hold up to eight people is $100 an hour; a twelve passenger, $130. Pedal boats are $30 an hour. SUPs and single kayaks are $20 an hour per. Double kayaks are $30. Fishing boats are $85 for two hours. Retail services here include purchasing fishing licenses, lake permits, bait and tackle, and snacks and drinks. The more adventuresome can go wakeboarding, water-skiing and/or tubing at a cost of $150 an hour for up to 6 people. This includes all equipment, the boat, and driver. Not quite sure if you're ready for all of that, or you just want to practice? The Cable Park gives you the above adventures, without a boat. You are attached to a controlled cable and towed 500 feet one way on the water course, and then back. Experienced riders can hit big air and small ramps. The Cable Park is $15 an hour. Helmet, life jacket and wakeboard or wakeskate rentals are an additional $15 for the package.

Hours: Open seasonally daily, 7am - 7pm, weather dependent.
Price: See above for prices.
Ages: 4 years and up, depending on the activity.

SKIING, SNOWBOARDING, SNOWSHOEING, SNOW PLAY ☼

$$$$$

The following is a list and quick bites of information on ski slopes and snow play areas in and around the Big Bear/Lake Arrowhead area because there's no business like snow business! The website: www.onthesnow.com/CS/skireport.html, is helpful for up-to-the-minute ski conditions. Also check www.mountaininfo.com. Ask each resort about beginner specials, other special promos, half-day tickets, and even a free lift ticket on your birthday.

SKIING / SNOWBOARDING:

Bear Mountain: 43101 Goldmine Drive, Big Bear Lake - (909) 585-2519 or (909) 866-5766 / www.bearmountain.com. Bear Mountain has 12 lifts and 24 runs on 200 acres, with the longest run being 2 miles. Top elevation is 8,800 feet. The Park boasts a Superpipe for airdogs with 195 acres of freestyle terrain that incorporates jumps, step-ups, step-downs, spines, rollers, a half-pipe, rails, and boxes. Non-holiday rates for all-day skiing are $69 for adults; $57 for ages 13 - 21; $28 for ages 5 - 12; children 6 and under are free, with a paying adult. Holiday rates and peak weekends are $84 for adults; $69 for ages seniors and ages 13 - 19; $34 for ages 5 - 12. (Ski free on your birthday.) Night skiing is available on Friday, Saturday, and holidays, 3pm - 9:30pm. On Friday it is $35 for adults; $30 for ages 13 - 21; $15 for ages 7 - 12. On Saturdays and holidays the prices are $45 for adults; $35 for ages 13 - 21; $25 for ages 7 - 12. Lift tickets are interchangeable with Snow Summit, and a free shuttle runs in between both mountains.
Mountain High: 24510 Hwy. 2, Wrightwood - (888) 754-7878 or (760) 249-5808 / www.mthigh.com. Wrightwood has mountain conditions without the winding, mountain drive. (It's 20 minutes west off the I-15). It has 13 chairs and 47 runs on 220 acres. The elevation is 8,200 feet. Mt. High has three separate resorts - East, West, and North, offering a variety of skiing and snowboarding. Note: North is mostly beginner and intermediate terrain. Ski the mountains with free shuttles going in between the three resorts. Lift tickets (which are interchangeable among the resorts) are offered in 4 hour and 8 hour blocks; Mon. - Thurs., 4 hours of skiing is $74 for adults; $40 for ages 7 -12; ages 6 and under are free with a paying adult. 8 hours is $79 for adults. Fri. - Sun. is by a point system - Purchase 500 points (can be shared by 2 people) for $169 with each lift costing 20 points per. Night skiing, 5pm - 10pm, is available at $45 per person.
Mount Baldy: 8401 Mt. Baldy Road - (909) 981-3344 or (909) 982-0800 / www.mtbaldyskilifts.com. Mt. Baldy has 4 lifts and 26 runs. The elevation is 8,600 ft. Lift tickets are $69 for adults; $29 for seniors and ages 12 and under; $49 for ages 13 - 21. (Ski free on your birthday.) Rides in the sky chairs are also available for non-skiers. Parking is $5. See MOUNT BALDY SCENIC LIFT RIDE (pg. 417) for more info.
Mount Waterman: on Angeles Crest Hwy, (Hwy. 2), 7 Miles past Newcombs Ranch, E. of Wrightwood - (818) 790-2002 or (619) 708-6595 / www.mtwaterman.org. Mt. Waterman has 3 lifts and 25 runs on over 115 acres. It does not have a snow-making machine, so it isn't always open. The top elevation is a little more than 8,000 feet. Skiers can also go "tree skiing", meaning they can venture off the marked runs and go through the forest. Ski rentals are not available here, but they are just down the hill. Lift tickets are $50 (½ day) - $60 (full day) for adults; $25 for seniors; $40 (½ day) and $50 (full day) for ages 13 - 17; $25 for ages 7 - 12. The resort is usually open on weekends only, 9am - 4pm. See MOUNT WATERMAN SCENIC RIDES and DISC GOLF (pg. 76) for info on the summertime fun.
Snow Summit: 880 Summit Road, Big Bear Lake - (909) 866-5766 / www.bigbearmountainresort.com. Summit has 14 chairs and 31 runs on 240 acres. The elevation is 8,000 feet. Family Park is great for beginner snowboarders, while intermediate and advanced terrains are also here. See the Bear Mountain entry, above, as the prices are identical. Lift tickets are interchangeable with Bear Mountain and a free shuttle runs in between both mountains.
Snow Valley: on Hwy. 18, 5 miles E. of Running Springs - (909) 867-2751 / www.snow-valley.com. Snow Valley has 13 lifts and 27 runs on 240 acres. The elevation is 7,440 feet. The snowboarding parks have spines, rails, boxes, tabletops, and banks. Lift tickets are $64 on regular days, $79 on holidays, for adults; $54 - $69 for seniors and ages 13 - 19; $27 - $35 for ages 7 - 12; children 6 and under are free with a paying adult. Night skiing is also available at $12 more per person on select Fridays and Saturdays. Ski free on your birthday.

SNOWSHOEING:

Rim Nordic Ski Areas: on Hwy. 18, E. of Running Springs, across from Snow Valley Mt. Sports Park - (909) 867-2600 / www.rimnordic.com. They offer cross country skiing and snowshoeing, plus rentals, and have 10 miles of trails. Trail passes are $20 for adults; $13 for ages 11 - 16 years; children 10 and under are free. Cross country ski rentals (skis, boots and poles) or snowshoe rentals, are $18 for ages 11 and up; $10 for children 10 and under. All snowshoers must purchase a trail pass. Open daily, 9am - 4pm. In the summer, the area offers mountain biking. Also see BIG BEAR DISCOVERY CENTER (pg. 445) for more information about trails.

SNOW PLAY:
Note: A National Forest Adventure Pass ($5) is required in the national forest while playing in the snow if you just park along the side of the road.
Alpine Slide at Magic Mountain - See ALPINE SLIDE at MAGIC MOUNTAIN (pg. 444) for details.
Big Bear Snow Play: 42825 Big Bear Blvd., Big Bear Lake - (909) 585-0075 / www.bigbearsnowplay.com. Two magic carpet lifts (i.e. like riding an uphill escalator), one covered with plexiglass, take tubers and tobogganers up the hill where natural snow is helped by snow-making machines. This area has some of the longest tubing runs in Southern California. A heated base lodge is here, too. Open daily, November through Easter(ish), 10am - 4pm. The cost is $35 per person, which includes inner tubes. Children 2 to 6 are free with a paying adult, but must ride on their lap (or purchase a separate ticket). $30 per nighttime glow tubing session, Fri., Sat., and holidays, 5pm - 9pm.
Mount Baldy: See Mount Baldy in the above section for location. (909) 981-3344 or (909) 982-0800 / www.mtbaldyskilifts.com You must purchase a scenic chair ride ticket to access the tubing park. 90 minute, weekday ride/tubing tickets are $29 for adults; $25.75 for ages 13 - 17; $22.50 for ages 12 and under. These are the discounted, online prices. Children must be at minimum of 40". Session times are 8:30am, 10:30am, 12:30pm and 2:30pm. Weekend prices are $6 more per session. All tickets are more expensive when buying in person. Parking is $5.
North Pole Tubing Park: See Mountain High in the above section for location. (888) 754-7878 or (760) 249-5808 / www.mthigh.com. This 20-acre tubing facility has 6 lanes and handle tows. It's open Sat. - Sun. and holidays, 8:30am - 4:30 through mid-March. Two-hour tube sessions (including the use of a tube) are $30 for adults; $25 for children 36" - 42", who must ride in their own tube. Children under 36" are not allowed.
Snowdrift Winter Playground: Hwy. 18, 4 miles E. of Running Springs - (909) 867-2640 / www.snowdrift.net; www.mountaininfo.com/sledding.html. Tube down the 6 hills on your belly, Mon. - Fri., 10am - 4pm; Sat. - Sun., 9am - 5pm. Admission is $17 per person per hour. Children 36" and under are free with a paid adult. Cash only. Tubes are included - no private equipment allowed. No snowman making. Limited parking is available and is $6. A $5 Adventure Pass is also required.
Snow Valley - See Snow Valley in the above section for location. (909) 867-2751 / www.snow-valley.com. At the base of the mountain, Snow Play is open daily (in season), 10am - 4pm. On Fri., Sat., and Sun. the cost, which includes sleds (and a lift ride), is $34 for ages 7 and up; $19 for ages 6 and under. Holidays are $37 for 7 and up; $27 for 6 and under. On weekdays (no lift available), the cost is $19 for ages 7 and up; $15 for ages 6 and under.

SNOW SUMMIT ADVENTURE PARK / SCENIC SKY CHAIR

(909) 866-5766 / www.bigbearmountainresorts.com
880 Summit Boulevard, at Snow Summit ski area, Big Bear Lake

$$$$

Do your kids appreciate the awesome scenery of mountains, trees, and Big Bear Lake, plus breathing clean air? If not, they'll still enjoy the mile-long, almost fifteen-minute (each way) life chair ride up the mountaintop. At the top, there is a picnic and barbecue area, as well as other food/beverage options, so bring your own food, or purchase a cheeseburger, chicken sandwich, bratwurst, or smoked turkey wrap for about $10 each from the Skyline Taphouse snack bar. What better way to spend a day than up here in a place readily described as "God's country".
As there are over forty miles of trails through the forest and wilderness areas, hikers and biking enthusiasts are in their element up here. The terrain varies, so hiking trails range from easy, wide, forest service roads to arduous, single-track, dirt trails. The most direct route is a service road that is one mile long. The Bike Park has great trails with elements for the intermediate and advanced (black diamond) biker with banked turns, switchbacks, drops, steps ups and bridges. Besides the three top-to-bottom trails for adventuresome bikers (and more on the way), there are also beginner trails at the top and around the bottom of the hill. In fact, if you want to hone your mountain-bike riding skills with scaled down versions of the terrain and features at the more advanced levels, ride at Skill Builder Park (SBP). Features include Small Wonder, a half-mile beginner trail features a 6% grade, two paver turns, small wood feature, dirt berm, and baby rock garde; Worm's World Pump Track, the place to warm up or perfect track technique; a Party Wave Trail; and Turtle Trail. Note that mountain bikes may be transported only up the sky chair; not down. Bike rentals, including those specifically designed for downhill riding, plus helmets (which are required for all riders), elbow and shin guards, chest protectors, etc., are available at the rental shop at the base of mountain, and elsewhere in town.

Hours: The Scenic Sky Chair operates beginning of June - mid-June, and in the fall, Fri. and Sun., 9am - 4pm; Sat., 9am - 5pm. It's open mid-June - Labor Day, Sun. - Fri., 9am - 4pm; Sat., 8am - 5pm, weather permitting. Closed in the winter and most of spring, but open then for skiing!

Price: Scenic Sky Chair is, round trip (no bike) - $20 for adults; $15 for seniors and ages 13 - 17; up to 2 kids, ages 5 - 12, ride for free with 1 paying adult; additional children are $10. Lift and Lunch Packages that include a round trip sky chair ride and lunch at Skyline Taphouse are $30 for adults; $25 for seniors and youth. Lift and Lunch Packages include a one-way sky chair ride, access to the bike park and lunch at Skyline Taphouse - $46 for ages 13 and up; $33 for ages 5 - 12. A one-day park pass (with bike) that includes unlimited day access to the downhill and cross-country trails is $45 for adults during the week; $35 for youth. There are other options available such as a single use bike pass (one way chair lift and once going down and on the course), half-day, and more. Save $ by pre-purchasing tickets online. Tip: You receive a free lift ticket on your actual birthday! Parking in the upper lot is $20 - cash.

Ages: 3 years and up.

STRAWBERRY PEAK FIRE LOOKOUT TOWER

(909) 382-2600 / www.mountainsfoundation.org

$

Bear Springs Road, Twin Peaks

See KELLER PEAK FIRE LOOKOUT TOWER (pg. 451) for detailed information on fire towers. I think the view and bragging rights of being able to say you were in a fire tower make the drive worth it, although you won't be here long. From the top of this tower you can see three lakes - Arrowhead, Gregory, and Silverwood.

Hours: Open a few weeks before Memorial Day through a few weeks after Labor Day on weekends and most weekdays (call first as it is staffed by volunteers), 9am - 5pm.

Price: $5 for an Adventure Pass

Ages: 6 years and up.

SUGARLOAF CORDWOOD CO.

(909) 866-2220

!/$

42193 Big Bear Boulevard, Big Bear Lake

The gigantic, wooden, chain-saw carvings of bears, Indians, and other figures, will attract your attention as you drive along Big Bear Boulevard. This unique store is worth a stop. Take a walk through the lot and inside the rooms to see smaller carvings and other unusual, artistic, gift items. Note that there is a similar store if you head west for a few blocks on Big Bear Boulevard.

Hours: Open most of the year, daily, 10am - 4pm.

Price: Free

Ages: 3 years and up.

SUGARLOAF PARK

(909) 866-9700 / www.bigbearparks.com

!

44828 Baldwin Lane and Maple Lane, Big Bear Lake

It is a beautiful drive to this well-worn park, but where up here isn't the scenery beautiful? Sugarloaf Park has a softball field, a few tennis courts, a sand volleyball court, a basketball court, and playground equipment with slides, swings, a short rock climbing wall, spirals to climb on and twirl around. A picnic shelters, barbecue pits, and some exercise stations with some solid workout machines let you work off what you just ate. It also features a skate park with ramps, rails, quarter pipes, stairs, boxes, and plenty of skate around room.

Hours: Open daily, sunrise - sunset.

Price: Free

Ages: All

TOWN SKATE/BMX PARK

(909) 866-9700 / www.bigbearparks.com

!

40946 Big Bear Boulevard, Big Bear Lake

Skaters can hit the ramps and rails at this very small, gated park, while bikers have just a few jumps available at the adjacent "park". Both are located on the church parking lot, so they are small, but it gives the kids something to do!

Hours: Open daily, sunrise - sunset.

Price: Free

Ages: 5 years and up.

VICTORIA PARK CARRIAGES, LTD. / BEAR VALLEY STAGE LINES

(909) 584-2277 / www.buggies.com

$$$$

on the corner of Pine Knot and Village Drive, Big Bear Lake

There is no more elegant, storybook way to explore Big Bear than by horse and carriage. Take a ride through the village, and down to the lake. Carriages seat from four to seven people. Go for a quick, fifteen minute ride or enjoy a more leisurely one.

Hours: Shorter rides are available most weekends and holidays from 11amish until no one else wants a ride. Call to make a reservation for longer carriage and stagecoach rides.

Price: Shorter rides are $18 for adults; $8 for ages 13 and under, with a $40 minimum. Hour-long rides are $250. Prices might fluctuate depending on date and time of day.

Ages: 2 years and up.

WILDHAVEN RANCH

(909) 337-7389 or (909) 337-1391 / www.wildhaven.org

$$$$

29450 Pineridge Drive, Cedar Glen

Wildhaven Ranch is a wildlife sanctuary for over twenty indigenous wild animals. The mission statement proclaims to "serve as stewards of God's creation through rescue, protection, and preservation of the earth's wild creatures." Most of the animals were brought here because they've been orphaned or injured and cannot be rehabilitated and released back to the wild. Others have imprinted with humans, so this is now their home. Species native to the San Bernardino mountains that can be seen include eagles, mule deer, raccoon, coyote, bobcat, black bear, and birds of prey such as owls, hawks, and falcons. Little Bear (who is a bear) is a favorite as this personable creature goes through paces of climbing up on a platform and plays with a ball for a food reward. We learned about California grizzly bears and their extinction; bear habitats and their habits in general; and the American Black bears that have "replaced" them in this ecosystem.

On a guided tour, the only way to see the sanctuary, you'll see the animals in their enclosures and learn about their habits and value. Programs are generally a combination of a thirty-minute, or less, raptor or other animal presentation held in the barn and then a half hour walking tour of the facility. The Wings & Things and Paws 'n' Claws presentations allows visitors to observe and learn about falcons, hawks, owls, eagles, and other birds of prey as handlers walk around with them, and/or indigenous mammals of the sanctuary - bears, bobcats, deer, coyotes and raccoons. Bear Watch is a program that teaches visitors about California black bear, their habits and habitats - and how they live in the surrounding area of the forest and mountain community. A special time is watching a trainer interact with the bears, up close and personal. Adults can also participate in feeding a bear. Call about school and scout group tours, or having a presentation come to your school/location. Volunteer opportunities abound, from helping with small tasks to completing internships.

Hours: Open year-round, weather permitting for Wings & Things Sat. at 11am and Paws and Claws at 1pm. Bear Watch is offered on Wed. and Fri. at 1pm. Reservations are necessary for all visits and tours, as are signed waivers.

Price: $15 per person. $25 for Feed A Bear (adults only). Private tours for 2 guests are $200.

Ages: 5 years and up.

YOUNG EAGLES PROGRAM - Big Bear

(909) 547-0832 / www.bigbearcityairport.com; www.youngeagles.org

501 W. Valley Boulevard. Big Bear City

See the entry for YOUNG EAGLES PROGRAM (Los Angeles County) (pg. 216) for details. No reservations needed.

Hours: Offered the second Sat. of each month, May - September, 9am - 11am.

Price: Free

Ages: 8- 17 years old.

SAN DIEGO COUNTY

San Diego is the site of the first permanent European settlement on the California coast - the West Coast equivalent of Jamestown. From coastal cities to beaches that are the epitome of California dreaming, the county is also home to Legoland; the extensive military base of Camp Pendleton and other San Diego bases; the enchanting town of Julian; Old Town San Diego, which is steeped in early California heritage; several missions founded by Father Junipero Serra; the resort town of La Jolla; and vast acres of trails to hike. A visit to this county probably wouldn't be complete without seeing the world-class San Diego Zoo, San Diego Zoo Safari Park, and/or SeaWorld, as well as some of the first-class museums located in the massive Balboa Park. Drive just to the south and go over the border to Mexico - into a whole other world.

Tip: Contact the San Diego Convention and Visitors Bureau at (619) 236-1212 / www.sandiego.org. because it offers discount coupons on attractions, tours, harbor cruises, trolley rides, restaurants, hotels, and more.

—AMUSEMENT PARKS—

AQUATICA SEAWORLD'S WATER PARK

(800) 257-4268 / www.aquaticabyseaworld.com

2052 Entertainment Circle, Chula Vista

6/$

G'day mates! Put on your togs (Australian slang for "swimsuit") and enjoy a bit of Australia in Southern California. San Diego's liquid gold attraction is very colorful, beautifully-landscaped, fun, and, most important, very wet. The park is spread over acres and acres of land with several groupings of waterslides. Guests can plunge down the sixteen twisty, water slides; both body and inner-tube raft rides. Some of the tubes are open, some are completely enclosed, and a few are long, straight, speed drops. Daredevils can zip down Taumata, a 375-foot long, high-speed racing water slide, in and out of tunnels and around a 180-degree hairpin turn. Tassie's Twister is a two to four person enclosed raft ride that spits out riders into a massive funnel to be spun around and around, and eventually down into an exit pool. Another family-size raft ride, Walhalla Wave, is open-air and more gentle.

Ankle biters (Australian slang for "kids") thrill at the four-story, interactive, water play structure that has water hoses and jets, decent-sized slides, cargo nets to crawl and climb on, and bridges, all in shallow water. And watch out below! A huge bucket fills up and then turns over, dumping hundreds of gallons of water on unsuspecting (and suspecting) visitors. Another section for younger ones, Slippity Dippity, has a few short, wide slides all jutting out from one central rock formation, plus some waterfalls and a splash and swim area. There is also a very small pool just for relaxing. Or, really relax on a tube in Loggerhead Lane - a circular, slow-moving river that has a waterfall, plus palm trees and bushes that line the river banks.

Ride the waves at the enormous Big Surf Shores wave pool, where periodic swells can reach up to five feet high. Don't wipe out! Just outside the Shores area look for the display of live, fresh-water turtles, swimming in their own pool pond.

One of my favorite Sea World elements at Aquatica is the flurry (or flock) of flamingos that greet visitors as soon as they enter. Their (artificial) grassy enclosure also has a mini lagoon and the flamingos are just simply fascinating to watch.

The water park has plenty of lounge chairs and other seats mostly placed in sand, giving it an overall beachy feel. Aquatica also has lockers (fees start at $14, which includes a $5 merchandise voucher upon return of the key), private cabanas for rent, free usage of life vests for all ages, and showers. If you get hungry, choose from several full-service eateries, or snack from one of the "stands" scattered throughout the park. No outside food is allowed inside. Have a ripper (i.e. fantastic) time!

Hours: Open Memorial Day - Labor Day daily from 10am - 5pm at the beginning of the season, then usually 10am - 6pm (open 10am - 7pm on certain weekends). Open in September - mid-October, Sat. - Sun., 10am - 5pm. Call or check the website first as hours fluctuate, especially due to concerts at the adjacent Mattress Firm Amphitheater.

Price: $47.99 for ages 10 years and older; $42.99 for ages 3 - 9; children 2 and under are free. Parking is $15. Check out combo membership to SeaWorld and Aquatica

Ages: 2 years and up.

LEGOLAND

(760) 918-LEGO (5346) / www.legoland.com

One Legoland Drive, Carlsbad

6/$

Lego mania reaches an all-time high at the 128-acre Legoland California which features over sixty family rides, shows, and interactive attractions, as well as areas to build and play with Legos™, and restaurants. (There are three other Legolands in the world.) Over thirty-five *million* Legos create the models used in and around this unique amusement park (and you will get tired of reading the word "Lego" by the end of this entry). The Lego builders really are incredible! Note that some of the rides have height restrictions. The following are some highlights of the main attraction areas:

Explorer Island features Coastersaurus, which curves around animated and life-size Lego brick dinosaurs. Kids can try out paleontology skills digging for "skeletal" remains in sand pits. Take a boat ride through an enchanted forest, past animated classic fairy tale characters and settings. A short ride in a Lego jeep treks you through a "jungle" that has ninety animated animals made of Legos. Choo choo around the railroad track on the Legoland Express. At the waterworks area turn a handle and aim water spray at objects and at pretend animals to bring them to "life." Kids can get wet here, too, as they play in and amongst the fountains that spurt up at unexpected intervals. (Bring a change of clothing.) Younger children can happily while away the day creating and playing at the Duplo playground. It has a maze to crawl through, a train ride, an ambulance, and police motorcycle to "drive," and lots more. At the theater see the live, comedy performances that uses people from the audience as well as behind-the-scenes from the *Lego Movie* including the sound stage, movie footage and some incredible models.

Heartlake City has a 62-horse carousel, and area to build and play (and not just horsin' around!), and an interactive, live, singing and dancing stage show featuring Heartlake City friends.

Fun Town offers two driving schools, one for young kids, one for younger kids - no adults allowed. Drive Lego-looking electric cars (not on a track!), complete with stop signs, traffic lights, turns, and traffic jams. (And you'll see the reason kids this young do not have licenses!) At the Power Tower, sit in outward-facing seats and pull yourself up a thirty-foot tower, then experience a controlled "free fall" down. For another perspective, pedal the Sky Cycle around an elevated circular track. Other attractions and activities in this area include piloting a kid-size helicopter up and down via a joystick; maneuvering a bumper boat around buoys (and other boats); taking a walk through Adventures' Club building to see ancient lands, the Arctic, and more, all depicted in Legos; touring a small-scale Lego factory to see how the bricks are made and packaged; and playing at the Club House with online games for multiplayers and/or shopping at the bins (and bins) to purchase bulk bricks. Kids can pick out the color and shape of the Lego bricks to create their own specialty masterpiece. The bricks are sold by weight. Get a picture perfect present at the Lego Clubhouse: After a digital photo is taken, you receive all the bricks needed to make the portrait in 3-D. At the funny, live Big Test show kids (and adults) belly-laugh when acrobatic/clownish firefighters try to teach safety tips. Get a workout by using a handcart fire truck or police car in a race to a "burning" building to then pump out water fast and furious through a hose and put out the fire. Tip: The Marketplace in this area offers fresh cooked, good, non-fast food.

Pirate Shores has a great seasonal water zone play area - Swabbie's Deck - where water jets pop up at random times, fountains are fun to frolic in and through, squirt cannons are a blast, and the large Soak-N-Sail play structure is pure water play pleasure with sixty interactive gadgets to spray, pump, and get wet. This shores also has a water log ride; Splash Battle, where mates ride piratey ships on a track and shoot water at bystanders (and each other); Pirate Reef, where two larger boats battle via water cannons with each other; and a huge boat that swings you back and forth and back and forth in the air. So much water and an unarrrrrguably good time! Bring a swimsuit and towel for this area and note that swim diapers are required for children 4 and under.

Past the rocks that sing "we will rock you" is the medieval-themed **Castle Hill.** Ride the roller coaster that takes all-age riders through a castle and into a cave past a fire-breathing dragon. Kids (only) can also mount a "horse" and take part in a simulated joust ride. A real quest is Knights' Tournament where robotic arms swing seated passengers up and down and upside down. This robo-coaster allows riders to choose their own maneuvers and intensity level, so each ride is unique. (I saved my stomach and just observed this one.) Everyone can have adventures at a huge, multi-level playground that has rope ladders, cargo nets, obstacles courses, wooden bridges, and slides. Visitors can also pan for "gold" to be exchanged for a Lego medallion, and take a nature walk past models of native animals. Immerse yourself in the Deep Sea Adventure submarine ride where eight real submarines, that hold twelve passengers each, navigate around more than 2,000 real sea animals such as tropical fish, stingrays, and sharks, amid Lego critters and scuba divers. The subs don't actually submerge, but it feels like it and they stay in the water as visitors use the touch screens at the portholes to look and help the Lego diveteam find the lost treasure from a sunken Lego shipwreck.

Miniland recreates several areas of the U.S., constructed in 1:20 scale. Each area has fourteen to thirty-three animations and some interactivity such as volcanos erupting in Las Vegas and a man covering himself with a manhole when a vehicle comes around. *New England Harbor* has farmlands, a traditional harbor and a shipyard, and underwater divers exploring a sunken ship. *Washington, D.C.* is impressive with its Lincoln Memorial, Washington Monument, White House, a presidential motorcade, baseball games, and more capital activities. *New York City* showcases the Manhattan and Brooklyn bridges, Central Park (e.g., joggers, the zoo, etc.); Times Square complete with police cars with lights and sirens; and the Statue of Liberty. *Southern California* combines beaches and mansions in Beverly Hills with Hollywood, Griffith Observatory, TCL Chinese Theatre (used to be called Grauman's), and sights in San Diego. *San Francisco* boasts cable cars, Pier 39, Ghiradelli Square, Lombard Street, and more. *New Orleans* offers paddle steamers on the river front, plantation houses, Mardi Gras, and the sound of jazz. *Florida* highlights Cape Canaveral and the Daytona International Speedway, where you can race remote Lego cars. Daytona Speedway racers complete with boaters and jet skiers at Lake Lloyd and speed around the course to cheering fans. *Las Vegas* has all the casinos and glitz, in miniature scale. Not in the U.S. but from a long time ago in a galaxy far, far away, come many *Star Wars* scenes from all of the movies, including "The Force Awakens" and the T.V. show that all feature sounds, lights and special effects! Pose with life-size, Lego versions of Darth Vader, Darth Maul and Chewbacca, and see three-foot models of Han Solo, Luke Skywalker, Princess Leia, Yoda and other characters, plus a 16-foot long model of the Star Destroyer Finalizer. Below the model of the incredible Lego Death Star, you can construct your own starships at building stations. All the *Star Wars* weapons and spacecraft look awesome in Legos, too.

Another picturesque part of Legoland is a large lake where families take a cruise and see - what else - more Lego animals and characters!! The Block of Fame is like a 3-D art gallery with likenesses of George Washington, Abe

Lincoln, and several more.

The ancient land of Egypt is the theme for **Land of Adventure**. Inside the tented area of Pharaoh's Revenge shoot hundreds of foam balls, out of mounted guns, at each other. At the interactive Lost Kingdom Adventure take a jeep ride through the dark temple ruins where guests shoot laser guns at targets and make animated scenes come to "life". There are also a few kiddie rides and slides here.

The mostly hands-on **Imagination Zone** offers both free-play opportunities (with both Legos and Duplos) and structured workshops and contests for all ages. Visual inspiration is all around, such as a Technic T. rex, and a fifteen-foot Einstein. A learning center here allows kids at least 9 years old to build and operate Mindstorms robots. Tip: Sign up first thing on the day of your visit for a class as space fills up. Xbox Family Game Space is gaming fun for everyone. The Hero Factory is for creating and building new heros, and using the ones that Lego built. The Imagination Zone theater shows twelve-minute, 4-D films based on the *Lego Movie* on a giant screen, a favorite for kids as music and other sounds pulsate and viewers are immersed in the sensations - actually feeling the wind and water, and smelling smoke - whatever the onscreen show is depicting. Ride the Technic Coaster for a fun and fairly fast (for Legoland standards) trip on the switchback tracks. Take a spin around (and around and around!) on the Bionicle Blaster - individual cars that spin around as much as you want them to. Imposing giant Bionicles stand guard here. Aquazone participants circle around in power ski-like water vehicles as spectators press buttons that control blasts of water directed toward the riders.

Just behind the Imagination Zone is a practice center just for ninjas. OK - others can play, too, at **Ninjago World.** Using certain hand motions guests blast fireballs, lightning, shockwaves, and ice (while feeling the heat and wind) to train and then defeat the Great Devourer and earn ninja status - all on one ride! Other ninja-themed attractions are helping to build an impressive model of the old Ninjago Monastery with Zane, the Ninja of Ice; honing your balance while spinning; practicing rock climbing skills; and testing your lightning fast (or not) reflexes.

Do try the decadent Granny's Apple Fries - Granny Smith apples covered with batter and fried, then topped with cinnamon sugar and a creamy vanilla sauce. The on-site Legoland store is the largest one in the U.S. It carries everything Lego, including hard-to-find pieces and kits. The store gets mobbed toward the end of the day, so shop early and have them hold your package.

Other notes/tips: Moms (or caregivers) who are looking for get-togethers at Legoland should visit on the first and third Thursday of the month when other moms with children 4 years and under meet here and interact via playgroups and stroller strides fitness walks. Look online into the Model Mom Club for details. Check out the variety of educational programs and field trips, plus homeschool days offered here, too - fun learning and great prices. For info on parent swap, miniature figure trading with park employees, Reserve 'N' Ride (to reserve your spot at 12 of the most popular rides) and other good-to-know facts, check the website. There are photo ops with character meet and greets. Download the park's mobile app. SEA LIFE AQUARIUM (pg. 593) and LEGOLAND WATER PARK (pg. 462) share the same property. If you have a real Lego fanatic, definitely check out the adjacent LEGOLAND HOTEL (pg. 564) and LEGOLAND CASTLE HOTEL (pg. 563).

Hours: Open most of the year, Mon., Thurs. - Sun., 10am - 5pm. (Closed on select Tues. and Wed., September - February, except for holiday periods.) Open daily in the summertime, 10am - 8pm. Check the hours before your visit as they fluctuate a lot!

Price: $95 for adults; $89 for ages 3 - 12; children 2 and under are free. Discounts are available online through AAA and through some local stores and restaurants. An annual pass is $159 per person. Parking is $20. Reserve 'N' Ride starts at $25. Check out the website for specials and for combo passes that include Sealife Aquarium and the Water Park.

Ages: Most of the rides and shows are geared for ages 2 - 11, but you are never too old to play with Legos.

LEGOLAND WATER PARK
(760) 918-LEGO (5346) / california.legoland.com   6/$
One Legoland Drive, Carlsbad

Not really made out of just Legos, which is good, this water park is definitely Lego-themed and is colorful, creative, and totally fun with an entrance only accessible through Legoland. The centerpiece of the water park is a forty-five-foot tall tower that sports lots of traditional Lego characters and elements. The tower has four slides for those 42" or taller - two enclosed; one open-body, twisting slide; and a slide for up to four riders on a raft. There are actually 50 fun features here in Cragger's Swamp (but whose counting?). For younger ones, ages 6 and under, who can't ride the big slides, Duplo Splash Safari is the place to be. The large pool (only twenty-four inches deep) has a gradual entrance with the elephant, polar bear and alligator Duplo figures to ride on that also squirt out water; several shorter slides; a lazy river called Kid Creek for little ones; an area to shoot water cannons and listen to a Lego Joker tell jokes and then dump gallons of water; and plenty of pool space to just splash around in. The Splash Zoo is ideal for toddlers: A giant Duplo lion, giraffe, and zebra make their home on a big splash pad that also has fountains, a teeter-totter, and more water-fun toys.

Catch a wave at Surfer's Bay where racers slide down a mat to compete on six side-by-side water slides. A "spray ground" is here, too, with Lego models and elements shooting water jets everywhere and on everyone.

A wild world of adventure awaits at the Legends of Chima area (based on that same-name Lego hit where animal tribes compete in a mystical land). Go through the lion temple archway to a gentle wave pool for young children; slide down through the head of a massive crocodile, then shoot water cannons and play in the jets; spend hours doing an almost dry activity - making boats from a raft of Legos pieces then testing their seaworthiness; and more. Fire water cannons on battling pirate ships and/or board a "ship" to race down a flume between the battling boats.

Build-a-raft river adds a unique element to riding a tube around the 800-foot-long lazy river - you get to add on large, soft foam Lego bricks to your raft sides, thereby customizing your raft. Over twenty Lego models are around the edges of the river, some squirting water on you as you drift by. Use Duplos at Imagination Station to build boats, bridges, and more all in a raised, long narrow "table" filled with flowing water. Cover various fountain holes at AquaTune to create different notes of music.

Lounge chairs are available on cement and on the beach which has finer sand than you normally find at the beach. You may bring your own umbrella. Private cabanas are also available for rent. Note that proper swimwear must be worn here and wearing just bathing suits is not allowed in the Legoland Park.

Hours: Open mid-March - mid-April sporadically, noon - 5pm; open on the weekends in May; open the bulk of the summer, daily, 10am - 7pm; open weekends only after Labor Day (in September) through October, noon - 5pm. Check for hours first because they fluctuate a lot. If you have a real Lego fanatic, definitely check out the adjacent LEGOLAND HOTEL (pg. 564) and LEGOLAND CASTLE HOTEL (pg. 563). Also see SEA LIFE AQUARIUM (pg. 593) and LEGOLAND (pg. 460) for info on the park.

Price: The entrance to the Water Park is only through Legoland and therefore includes entrance to Legoland - $125 for adults; $119 for ages 3- 12; $5 for ages 2 and under. Parking is $20. Call or check the website first as sometimes specials and discounts are available.

Ages: 2 - 12

THE WAVE WATERPARK

(760) 940-WAVE (9283) / www.thewavewaterpark.com
101 Wave Drive, Vista

Catch a wave at The Wave on the Flow Rider wave machine. Then, swoosh on down the four water slides here - two are enclosed, and two are convertible-style (no tops). Some height restrictions apply. Slip 'n slide down the fifth slide, which is short, slopes gently, and ends into Crazy River, is a large ring of water that encircles the slide and lounge area. Those 48" and under especially enjoy the multi-story children's water play area with a maze, climbing apparatus that has water spouting out, and slides. The large rectangular pool, usually used for lessons and the swim team, is open to the public during Wave hours.

There are a limited number of picnic tables here, as well as a few grassy areas for picnicking or sunbathing. You may bring in your own lounge chairs. Lockers ($4), double inner tubes ($8), and cabanas ($55) are available. Use of single inner tubes and body boards are included in your admission price. Outside food is not allowed in, but there is a full-service snack bar here that sells food at very reasonable prices. Have big time fun at this small water park!

Hours: Open the end of May - mid-August, Mon. - Fri., 10am - 4pm; Sat., 11am - 5:30pm; Sun., noon - 5:30pm. Open mid-August - end of August, weekends only, (see previous weekend hours) and in September, weekends only from noon - 5pm. Check out the select Fri. splash nights from 4pm - 8pm.

Price: $19.95 for 42" and taller; $13.95 for seniors; $15.95 for 41" and under and spectators; children 2 and under are free. The last two hours entry is just $9.95 per person as is Fri. splash nights.

Ages: 1½ years and up.

—ARTS AND CRAFTS—

CERAMICAFE ART LOUNGE

Del Mar - (858) 259-9958; La Mesa - (619) 466-4800 / www.ceramicafe.com
Del Mar - 3435 Del Mar Heights Road; La Mesa - 5500 Grossmont Center

These well-lit, paint-your-own ceramics stores have a great array of objects to choose from. We painted dragon figurines, deep mugs, a vase, and a heart-shaped tile. (We were busy!) I used the stencils and stamps, while my boys free-formed it. All the artistic aids, paints, and brushes are included in the price. Finished masterpieces are ready for pick up in about five days. Ceramicafe also offers scout programs, fundraisers and after-school activities where kids can learn painting techniques, clay prints, mosaics, and more.

Hours: Del Mar - Open Mon. - Sat., 10am - 9pm; Sun., 10am - 6pm. La Mesa - Open Mon. - Thurs., 10am - 8pm; Fri. - Sat., 10am - 9pm; Sun., 10am - 6pm. Closed Thanksgiving and Christmas.

Price: There is no per-hour studio fee. All-inclusive prices range from $6 - $65. Mugs, for instance, are $16 - $24; bud vases, $15 - $24; and 4 x 4 tiles are four for $20.

Ages: 4 years and up.

CLAY 'N LATTE

$$$$

(760) 726-9293 / www.claynlatte.net
20 Main Street, suite H-110, Vista

A ceramic piece, some paint, and a little latte goes a long way in making a ceramic masterpiece to take home. Choose from a wide selection of items (over 1,000!), such as plates, bowls, flower pots, goblets, salt and pepper shakers, animal figurines, and more. Kids will have a field day picking out colors (over 100 to choose from) and thinking of ways to design their chosen piece. Warning: This recreational activity can become habit forming! Paints, paintbrushes, and stencils are all provided - you simply provide the artistic creativity (and the money). Look into their summer art camps. Also ask about creating with mosaics, glass fusing, and clay imprints, as well. Scouts can earn badges here!

Hours: Open Mon. - Thurs., 11am - 9pm; Fri., 11am - 10pm; Sat., 10am - 10pm; Sun., noon - 6pm.

Price: $8 studio fee for adults, $6 for children 12 and under, plus the price of item (average price is $10- $35). Ask about specials.

Ages: 4 years and up

CLAYTIME CERAMICS MULTI-MEDIUM ART STUDIO

$$$$

(619) 223-6050 / www.claytime-ceramics.com
1863 Bacon Street, Ocean Beach

A vase with little handprints; a kitty-cat bank; a plate bordered with flowers; or a picture frame in art deco style - these are just a few of the multitude of ideas and items you can paint at this ceramic store. Choose from a variety of objects, get creative, and paint. All the paints, brushes, and aid you need are included in your price.

Don't like what you see or want to create your own design? Sign up for a molding session and sculpt your own. As a multi-media art studio classes include potters wheel, making ceramic masks, mosaics, clay imprints, painting on canvas, henna tattoos, and pregnant belly bowls. You can also book a party that comes to you! And ask about their painting classes and summer camps where a walk on the beach and maybe tidepool exploration is followed by incorporating found objects into a craft.

Hours: Open Mon. - Thurs., 10am - 7pm; Fri. - Sat., 10m - 9pm; Sun., noon - 5pm.

Price: The price of the object - there is no studio fee.

Ages: 4 years and up.

COLOR ME MINE (San Diego County)

$$$$

(858) 312-5500 / www.ranchobernardo.colormemine.com
10550 Craftsman Way at 4S Commons Town Center, suite 183, San Diego

See the entry for COLOR ME MINE (Los Angeles County) (pg. 8) for details. This location also offers Color Me Mine To Go, where the party comes to you.

Hours: Open Sun. - Mon., 11am - 7pm; Tues. - Thurs., 11am - 8pm; Fri. - Sat., 11am - 9pm.

Price: The studio fee is $10 for ages 13 and up; $6 for ages 12 and under.

MISSUS POTTS

$$$$

(760) 517-6319 / www.missuspotts.com
4225 Oceanside Boulevard, suite D, Oceanside

Missus Potts pottery painting place presents pottery pieces to be procured, personalized and painted! The mid-size, airy room has tables of various heights in the center and walls filled with useful and decorative items to artistically bedeck such as vases, plates, figurines, mugs, picture frames and more. All the materials of paint, brushes, inspiration, staff help, and firing and glazing are included. Clay impressions, canvas paintings, Mommy and Me, after-school classes, parties, and field trips for kids are all offered here, too. The studio (parts of it!) will even come to you for a minimum of ten people.

Hours: Open Tues. - Thurs., 11am - 8pm; Fri. - Sat., 11am - 9pm; Sun., 11am - 6pm. Closed on Mon. and some holidays.

Price: $8 studio fee for adults, plus the cost of the pottery; $6 for ages 12 and under. Ask about AAA and military discounts.
Ages: 4 years and up.

THE HOT SPOT

(619) 223-1339 / www.thehotspotstudio.com
2770 Historic Decatur Road at Liberty Station Barracks 14, San Diego

$$$$

Located next to CORVETTE DINER (pg. 471), this place IS the Hot Spot for candle-making, pottery painting, and making a fairy/gnome succulent garden! The large room has wood tables and chairs, plenty of windows, and music playing that all make for an inviting atmosphere to create and do so together with friends. You can even bring your own food and beverages. There are hundreds of pottery pieces to choose from on the wooden shelves - pet dishes, jewelry boxes, mugs, vases, plates, and more. I love watching artistic people design and paint their masterpieces freehand. I, on the other hand, rely on other's ideas and using stamps and stencils. Either way, it's a great activity and the finished product is always a special keepsake. Leave your item overnight to be fired (which makes it food and microwave safe), or pick a non-fired decorative item to paint and take home that same day.

Let your light shine bright by making a very personalized candle. Choose from a variety of shape molds, or a container. Fill that with colorful cubes of wax. Add a fragrance of cotton candy, ocean, chai tea, Plumeria, bubble gum, etc. Finish it off with a few other special touches of gems or sea shells or glitter. Now, you have a *scent*sational gift! Candle- making can also come to your event site.

Plant it and they will come. Pick a planter, some decorative succulents, add soil, and choose a fairy or gnome figure and/or mini garden accessories and voila - a sweet garden to enjoy.
Hours: Open daily, 10am - 9pm. Closed most holidays.
Price: There are no studio fees. Prices range from $15 - $60, with the average being about $20.
Ages: 4 years and up.

—BEACHES—

BUCCANEER BEACH PARK

(760) 435-5041 / www.ci.oceanside.ca.us
1500 S. Pacific Street, Oceanside

Avast ye! This very small, very family-friendly beach park has a beach area designated for swimmers (and water splashers) on the west side of the highway. Surfing is only allowed, then, on either side of this parcel of shoreline. (Go further north for more beach - Tyson Street Beach and Oceanside City Beach.) On the east side of the highway is a grassy park adjacent to railroad tracks. It has restrooms, a basketball court, and a playground that inspires creativity with several free-standing cargo nets to climb; rock climbing walls; a giant, free-standing tilted "wheel"; ladders; slides; swings; and several, tiered play structures. A snack bar here is open during the summer that sells hamburgers, quesadillas, hot dogs, and drinks at reasonable prices. There is even a kid's menu! There are also picnic tables with BBQ grills and outdoor showers here.
Hours: Open daily, sunrise - sunset; open in the summer 6am - 9pm.
Price: Free
Ages: All

CARDIFF STATE BEACH

(800) 777-0369 or (760) 753-5091 / www.parks.ca.gov
S. Coast Hwy. 101, Cardiff-by-the Sea

$$

We promptly nicknamed one section of this beach "Rocky Beach." There isn't a lot of uncovered sand on that narrow strip (know your tides table!), but there are literally tons of multi-colored, round, smooth rocks here. Wear sandals. Walk a little further north to reach a huge stretch of sand. So, go into the ocean here as the water is just fine. Bathrooms are available and lifeguards are on duty here, too. The tidepools can be pretty amazing to explore during low tide. Note that this beach is adjacent to SAN ELIJO STATE BEACH (pg. 467) on the north end and TIDE BEACH PARK (pg. 469) on the south end. Free usage of beach wheelchairs is available at the San Elijo State Beach Campground entrance on a first come, first served basis.
Hours: Open daily, sunrise - sunset.
Price: Limited street parking, or pay about $15 for parking in the lot.
Ages: 3 years and up.

CARLSBAD STATE BEACH (and SOUTH CARLSBAD STATE BEACH)

(760) 438-3143 / www.parks.ca.gov

7201 Carlsbad Boulevard, Carlsbad

This long, somewhat narrow strip of beach has several different parts to it. In the "center" of the beach, south of Tamarack Blvd. is a surf beach and in just this area no swimming is allowed. There is a free parking lot here (or park along the streets) and restroom facilities. A cement walkway stretches along a good portion of Carlsbad Beach, with most of the sand accessible via stairs placed every few hundred feet.

There are 110 bluff-top camping sites (220 total sites) available at South Carlsbad Beach, near Poinsettia Ln. The small sites, which remind me of parking lot camping, are bound by the main street on one side and a chain-link fence protecting them from the cliffs on the other. Showers are available with tokens.

Hours: Open daily, sunrise - sunset.

Price: Camping is $35 for an inland site; $50 for beachfront.

Ages: All

CORONADO BEACH

(619) 522-7346 / www.coronadovisitorcenter.com

920 Ocean Boulevard, Coronado

This beach offers a lovely, long stretch of sand, plus a lifeguard station, volleyball courts, a few sand dunes, restroom facilities, stairs to the beach, a view of Navy vessels who use this waterway, and usually Navy personnel working out. If you park or walk southward, toward Flora Avenue, you can climb over a few boulders that line the street and head to the wide expanse of clean, fine sand in front of the famous Hotel Del Coronado. Rocks in front of the hotel beach act as a breakwater. This is a favorite beach for all ages.

Hours: Open daily, sunrise - sunset.

Price: Free

Ages: All

FLETCHER COVE BEACH PARK

(858) 755-1569 or (858) 720-2400 / www.ci.solana-beach.ca.us

111 S. Sierra Avenue, Solana Beach

A local favorite, this little bluff side beach is reached by a wide, sloping ramp. Its cozy size invites a more personal time, and hopefully one of relaxation as well as play. Lifeguards are here year round for swimmers and surfers.

Topside is a little park with grassy lawns, picnic tables, bbqs, a half basketball court, showers, restrooms, and a small, nice playground with swings, slides, and such, and an impressive view of the ocean and beyond - particularly great for watching sunsets. There are several restaurants within walking distance.

Hours: Open daily, 6am - 10pm.

Price: Free, with free parking.

Ages: All

HARBOR BEACH - BREAKWATER WAY

(760) 435-4500 or (760) 435-4030 - harbor; (760) 435-3065 - city of Oceanside / www.ci.oceanside.ca.us; www.oceansidechamber.com

Pacific Street, near Harbor Dr., Oceanside

Adjacent to Oceanside Harbor, this spread of beach (one of the widest in San Diego County) offers amenities such as swimming; kayak rentals and other boat rentals (see OCEANSIDE BOAT RENTALS (pg. 581)); barbeque grills and fire rings; picnic tables; a snack bar (open seasonally); volleyball courts (bring your own net and ball); as well as a few shops and eateries. You can also fish from the jetties. Overnight camping is allowed in parking lot 12 for $20 a day (which is the overnight parking fee) mid-September - mid-May, only. No tents allowed.

Breakwater, just south of Harbor Beach, also provides the above "extras", plus the frequent appearance of a sand bar, which is a good surf break. See OCEANSIDE PIER and HARBOR AREA (pg. 560) for more information about the pier, its beaches, and the surrounding area.

Hours: Open daily, sunrise - sunset.

Price: Metered parking and/or paid lots -$10 mid-September - mid-May; $15 mid-May - mid-September.

Ages: All

LA JOLLA SHORES BEACH

(619) 236-5555 or (619) 221-8899 / www.sandiego.gov/lifeguards/beaches
8200 Camino del Oro, La Jolla

This beach comes fully loaded for a full day of fun! The one-mile-plus fairly wide stretch of beach that ends near the Scripps pier and is adjacent to the Underwater Ecological Reserve has a separate area for surfers and for swimmers. Note that the very small, but incredibly picturesque La Jolla Cove is also right here. Year-round lifeguard service, rest rooms, showers (a parent's essential), cement barbecue pits, and a few playgrounds for the kids, complete with swing sets and climbing apparatus, add up to make the Shores Beach a fun place to go with kids. A temporary rubber walkway allows limited access to the beach for wheelchairs and strollers. A beach wheelchair is available, on a first-come, first-served basis, near the main lifeguard station. Kellogg Park, the adjacent grassy area behind the main lifeguard station, offers another way to enjoy this length of coastline. A cement boardwalk parallels a portion of the beach between the park and the sand.

Look up SNORKEL SAN DIEGO (pg. 584) for a kayaking adventure that's just around the "corner." To incorporate a visit to the beach with a drive around picturesque La Jolla, see SCRIPPS PARK / LA JOLLA COVE and COASTLINE (pg. 516) for several other places to visit in the nearby area.

Hours: Open daily, sunrise - sunset.
Price: Free - good luck with parking!
Ages: All

LEUCADIA STATE BEACH or BEACON'S BEACH

(760) 633-2740 / www.parks.ca.gov; www.ci.encinitas.ca.us; www.beachcalifornia.com
948 Neptune Avenue, Encinitas

This hidden, non-populated beach is locally known as Beacon's. It is accessible only by walking down a series of steps where a lifeguard stand is stationed here during the summer. The size (or width) of the beach varies with the tide. At low tide, there is plenty of beach under the cliffs. At high tide, the beach is rather skimpy. The beach is a good getaway for swimming and surfing. Note that there are no restrooms here.

Hours: Open daily, 4am - 2am.
Price: Free
Ages: 4 years and up (because of the steps)

MISSION BAY PARK

See the entry for MISSION BAY PARK (pg. 508), under GREAT OUTDOORS, for details.

MOONLIGHT BEACH

(760) 633-2740 / www.ci.encinitas.ca.us; www.parks.ca.gov; www.beachcalifornia.com
400 B Street, Encinitas

Moonlight can be romantic, but Moonlight Beach is great for the whole family. A short, wide expanse of beach offers clean sand (at least when we visited), three volleyball courts with nets, a great playground for the younger set, cement picnic tables, fire rings, a lifeguard station, restrooms, outdoor showers, and a seasonal snack shop offering hot dogs, hamburgers, chips, and drinks. Forgot your boogie board? No problem - there is a small beach rental shack, also open seasonally, that can equip you with boards, surfboards, wet suits, chairs, and even umbrellas. Note that this beach has a polyethylene walkway that extends toward the ocean for wheelchairs and strollers.

Hours: Open daily, 4am - 2am.
Price: Free
Ages: All

SAN ELIJO STATE BEACH

(760) 753-5091 - beach; (800) 444-7275 - camping reservations / www.parks.ca.gov
S. Coast Hwy. 101, south of Encinitas Blvd., Cardiff-by-the-Sea

This beach entrance is a little challenging to find, is accessible via many wooden steps, and is only good at low tide. Having said that, it offers several places for tidepooling, swimming, and snorkeling. Lifeguard stations are manned daily in the summer and mostly on weekends in the spring and fall.

The bluff-side camping spots each have a patch of dirt, separated by a row of trees and bushes, a fire ring and picnic table. (My youngest thinks that it's worth spending the extra money for camping on the beach side, with direct views of the ocean, versus the "inland" sites right by the side of the road. Of course, it wasn't his money.) A camp store, snack bar, laundry room, and showers are available here.

The San Elijo Lagoon inlet separates this beach from the next door CARDIFF STATE BEACH (pg. 465).

Hours: Open daily, dawn - dusk.
Price: $15 per vehicle. Campsites on the bluff are $50; with hook-ups $75. Campsites more inland are $35; with hook-ups $60.
Ages: 3 years and up.

SHELTER ISLAND - SHORELINE PARK

(619) 686-6200 / www.sandiego.org
Shelter Island Drive, San Diego

A stunning view of the skyline and San Diego Harbor awaits visitors at Shelter Island. A marina is on one side of the island while the other side boasts a nice stretch of beach across the water from the boat launch. This area also has a playground, fire pits, restrooms, rocks on the shore to climb, a T-shaped fishing pier with a bait and tackle shop, and shade spots with benches along the paved pathway that hugs the shoreline. At one end is the Yokohama Friendship Bell, a large bronze bell housed in a pagoda structure. April through October, the island also boasts Humphreys Concerts by the Bay (via Humphreys Half Moon Inn & Suites) headlining some of the biggest names in music and comedy. See www.halfmooninn.com for more info on the concerts.

Hours: Open daily, 6am - 10:30pm
Price: Free
Ages: All

SUNSET CLIFFS NATURAL PARK

(619) 224-4591 or (858) 581-9978 / www.famosaslough.org; www.sandiego.gov
1253 Sunset Cliffs Boulevard, San Diego

This natural park runs over a mile, north and south, along Sunset Cliff Boulevard, from Adair to Ladera Streets. It then reaches inland for another sixty+ acres which are grouped together from the beach to a hillside bordering the 650-acre Point Loma Ecological Reserve, Navy property and Point Loma Nazarene University.

The linear stretch has numerous places to pull over and park (for free!) that parallel Sunset Cliff Boulevard. Visitors can get a front row to admire the incredible (and very popular) view, especially the sunsets - hence the name - and walk along the cliffs - hence the other part of the name. Use caution! A dirt walking/running path follows along the street and shoreline. There are several places to access the beach, such as just north of Hill Street, a lovely section of beach, and at the "corner" of Sunset and Ladera down a steep flight of stairs. Overlooks are by Adair, Osprey, and Froude streets. Note that each patch of sandy beach is surrounded by rocks, making them good places for tide pool exploration. There are also several beach caves, too, but be mindful of high tides. There is a sinkhole (and non-accessible sea caves) across from Monaco St. Head north on the beach, a narrow, but nice tract of sand, for some good , accessible sea caves. There are some to the south as well.

The hillside section of the park has several crisscrossing trails where a biodiversity of native plants, reptiles, small mammals, and birds thrive. Some of the trails lead down to the beach. May your sunset at Sunset Cliffs be a beautiful end of, hopefully, a wonderful day.

Hours: Open daily, sunrise to sunset.
Price: Free
Ages: 4 years and up.

SWAMI'S BEACH

(760) 633-2740 / www.ci.encinitas.ca.us
1298 S. Coast Highway 101, Encinitas

Swami's Beach is not just for mystics! It is worth going down the steep, over 100 wooden stairs to reach the smallish beach, which changes size according to the tide. During low tide the tidepools appear so you can check out the sea anemones, crabs, sea stars, and other critters. Indulge in swimming, or watch the surfers, since this is a popular surfing spot. The kelp beds offshore are supposed to be great for divers, too.

Up top, at Seacliff Roadside Park, is a patch of grass, some shade trees, a few benches to take in the majestic view, a few bbq grills, restrooms, and a small parking lot. You can watch (and hear) the trains roll past behind you, too.

Hours: Open daily, 4am - 2am.
Price: Free
Ages: All

TIDE BEACH PARK

(858) 755-1569; (858) 720-2400 / www.ci.solana-beach.ca.us
302 Solana Vista Drive, Solana Beach

This is a beach for tidepool explorers and rock collectors. The beach, accessible by stairs at Solana Vista Drive and Pacific Avenue, is under part of a cliff that overhangs and creates small caves, or nooks and crannies, along the shoreline. Don't hang out here during high tide! The tidepools are not the best I've seen for observing marine life, but they are fun nonetheless. We did see lots and lots of limpets, plus muscles, sea anemones, and some small crabs. Just north of the tidepools is CARDIFF STATE BEACH (pg. 465). Tide Beach is life-guarded during the summer and good for swimming and snorkeling.

Hours: Open daily, 6am - 10pm.
Price: Free
Ages: 2 years and up.

TYSON STREET BEACH and PARK

(760) 435-4500; (760) 435-3065 / www.ci.oceanside.ca.us; visitoceanside.org
Pacific Street and Tyson Street, Oceanside

Accessible by stairs, this pleasant, long stretch of beach is located just south of Oceanside Pier. Amenities include lifeguard stations, bathrooms, patches of grass and some picnic tables, and even a few small playgrounds. The Strand is a driveable strip of pavement between the grass side and beach, so use caution when crossing it. Note that there are beaches, just with different names, north and south of Tyson.

Hours: Open daily, sunrise - sunset.
Price: Parking in the lot is about $5 for the day, or there is metered parking on the street.
Ages: All

—EDIBLE ADVENTURES—

94th AERO SQUADRON (San Diego County)

(858) 560-6771 / www.94thsandiego.com
8885 Balboa Avenue, San Diego

The ivy-covered brick restaurant is a replica of a French WWI-era farmhouse. Outside, cannons are in a semicircle around sandbags. Bales of hay are suspended over wooden carts that look like they're falling apart. A bi-plane, trees, and a wooden fence are also out front. Listen to swing and other older-style music being piped outside.

Inside, the ambiance is just as rustic and charming. Dark wood beam ceilings; huge brick fireplaces with large kettles; and walls and ceiling tastefully lined with helmets, war posters, photos, medals, plane parts, vests, farm implements, and even sandbags add to the somewhat romantic atmosphere. There are even a few pocket booths that contain headphones so diners can listen to the FAA control tower on the adjacent Montgomery Field Airport. Out back, tables on a grassy embankment overlook the airfield, bunkers with camouflage netting, more grounded airplanes, an army jeep, and a duck pond.

The lunch menu includes escargot in mushroom caps ($9.95), fried calamari ($8.95), Cobb salad ($14.95), hamburger ($10.95), prime rib French dip sandwich ($17.95), blacked chicken breast sandwich ($11.95), grilled salmon ($17.95), and pastas. The dinner menu includes some of the aforementioned foods plus filet mignon ($32.95), lobster tail ($34.95), rack of lamb ($44.95), and more. The Sunday Champagne Brunch ($32.95 for adults, $15.95 for ages 4 to 10) has an incredible assortment of delectable foods - blintzes, carved roast beef, crab legs, an omelette bar, fish, a fajita bar, a waffles station, barbecue ribs, muffins, crepes, cheesecake, eclairs, and more. Catch the next flight to the 94th Aero Squadron.

Hours: Open Mon. - Thurs., 11am - 9pm; Fri., 11am - 11pm; Sat., 4pm - 10pm; Sun., 9am - 2:30pm - brunch; 4pm - 9pm - dinner.
Price: Some menu prices are listed above.
Ages: 4 years and up.

ANTHONY'S FISH GROTTO

(619) 463-0368 / www.anthonysfishgrotto.com
9530 Murray Drive, La Mesa

Shell I tell you about this restaurant that resembles an underwater sea cave? It's a pearl of a place. Enter through a giant clam shell. Fish are "swimming" around on the ceiling. Octopus-covered lamps are at the front desk and a fish mosaic covers the wall here. The booths are upholstered with fish designs. Waist-high coral barriers separate the restaurant into sections. (Look for eel and other creatures peeking out from the coral rocks.) The bar is in a cave-like setting. Even the restrooms maintain the theme!

Dining is available inside, or outside under shade trees on patio tables and chairs. Both seating arrangements allow guests to overlook the grotto's small lake. Duck feed is available from the restaurant. A dry-docked boat on the lawn houses a small video arcade.

The Fish Grotto specializes in a wide variety of fresh fish and shellfish, of course, although it offers chicken and steak, as well. Here's a sampling of the menu: Crab stuffed mushrooms ($12.95); clam chowder in a sourdough bread bowl ($7.95); shrimp, scallop and fish kabobs ($17.25); tuna melt ($10.95); grilled squid steak Milanese ($17.95); coconut fried shrimp ($21.50); chicken picatta ($16.95); top sirloin steak ($17.95); and fresh mussels ($16.95). The kid's menu offers fish dippers ($6.65), grilled cheese ($5.65), pasta ($5.65), and chicken ($6). Drinks are extra. Note: Take some of Anthony's fish home as this location also has a retail market, along with the fresh catch of the day.

Hours: Open Sun. - Thurs., 11am - 8:30pm; Fri. - Sat., 11am - 9pm. Closed all major holidays.
Price: See menu prices above.
Ages: All

AUBREY ROSE TEA ROOM

(619) 461-4TEA (4832) / www.theaubreyrosetearoom.com
8362 La Mesa Boulevard, La Mesa

I just fell in love with this place. It's the epitome of a tea room. Covered with pretty wallpaper and without feeling cramped or crowded, almost every imaginable space of the Aubrey Rose Tea Room is decorated with tea accouterments and cupboards that hold tea pots, tea cups and saucers, books, napkins, quaint placards, hats, dolls, jewelry, and collectibles. Almost all of the merchandise is for sale. Each of the table and chair settings are nestled in their own nook, giving a sense of privacy and intimacy. If you forgot to wear a hat or feather boa, you are welcome to borrow one.

The Lady Anne Tea consists of assorted tea sandwiches (served in a style befitting a queen, or lady), along with seasonal fresh fruit, freshly-baked scones with lemon curd and Devonshire-type cream, pastries, and, of course, tea for $26.95 per person. The Queen Victoria Tea is similar, but also offers an additional course of soup du Jour and savories, such as sherry-mushroom turnovers, artichoke heart fondue, and/or something equally scrumptious for $29.95 per person. The Princess Sophia's Tea, for ages 5 through 10 years, includes tea sandwiches (with peanut butter and jelly as a standard), fruit, sconettes, pastries, and a beverage for $26.95 per person. For just a spot of tea, walk-ins can indulge in the Cream Tea of a scone, fruit garnish, and tea for $13.95 per person. Inquire about theme teas, birthdays, or any occasion to celebrate. Note that there are gluten-free menu choices, here, too.

Bonus - Aubrey Rose is located in the midst of La Mesa Village surrounded by its numerous antique and collectibles shops!

Hours: Open Wed. - Sat., 10:30am - 4pm, with seatings Wed. - Fri. at 11am, 11:30am, 1:30pm and 2pm, and seatings Sat. at 11am and 1:30pm. Open Sun., 1pm - 4pm, with seatings at 1:30pm. Closed Mon. - Tues. and most holidays. Reservations are always highly recommended.
Price: Menu choices are listed above.
Ages: 5 years and up.

BENIHANA OF TOKYO (San Diego County)

Carlsbad - (760) 929-8311; San Diego - (619) 298-4666 / www.benihana.com
Carlsbad - 755 Raintree Drive, suite 100; San Diego - 477 Camino Del Rio S.

See the entry for BENIHANA OF TOKYO (Los Angeles County) (pg. 15) for details.

BUCA DI BEPPO (San Diego County)

(866) EAT BUCA (328-2822) for all locations; Carlsbad - (760) 479-2533; Mira Mesa - (858) 536-2822; San
Diego - (619) 233-7272 / www.bucadibeppo.com
Carlsbad - 1921 Calle Barcelona; Mira Mesa - 10749 Westview Parkway; San Diego - 705 6th Avenue

See BUCA DI BEPPO (Los Angeles County) (pg. 16) for details.

BUGA KOREAN B.B.Q. AND SUSHI BAR

(858) 560-1010 / www.bugabbq.com
5580 Clairemont Mesa Boulevard, San Diego

Authentic Korean cuisine (and sushi) is served at this restaurant, but the real reason that I include it in the book is that you can cook your own food (not the sushi) on your own grill in the middle of your own table. A waiter comes by to give instruction. So, yes, you still have to cook dinner, but it's different, it's a fun atmosphere, and the kids enjoy participating.

Menu selections include marinated beef, spicy pork, grilled salmon, prime short ribs, and lots more. If you don't understand what to order, because the food names are hard to decipher, just pick something and be surprised. Try, for example, bulgogi for $22.99; daiji samgyubsal (i.e., pork, fresh bacon-style) for about $18; BibimBap for $10.99; Maeun Daeji Galbi Jim (spicy pork short ribs) for $17.95; and saewoo gui (i.e., grilled king prawn shrimp) for $23.95. Buga has a full sushi bar and serves sashimi. Kid's meals are available for $9.95 for beef or chicken teriyaki.

Hours: Open daily, 11am - 10pm.
Price: Some menu prices are listed above.
Ages: 5 years and up.

CHUCK E. CHEESE'S (San Diego County)

See the entry for CHUCK E. CHEESE'S (Los Angeles County) (pg. 18) for details.

COBBLESTONE COTTAGE TEA SHOPPE

(619) 445-6064 / www.cobblestonecottageteashoppe.com $$$$
1945 Alpine Boulevard, Alpine

With a lovely decor blend of country chic and elegance, Cobblestone Cottage is in a picture-perfect setting with its antique glass windows and miniature gables. It is a delightful place to relax and enjoy life for a bit with friends and family. Each of the tables is set with different color and floral schemes, fine china, and with patio-style chairs. If it's a nice day, have your tea outside amidst a country garden/woods setting underneath a pine tree, with a bubbling fountain and old wooden buildings.

Perk up your attire with a feathery boa, hat, and/or gloves from the Cottage's selection. Feel pampered with the service and the homemade food. Cottage High Tea is $27.95 per person and is like a lunch. It includes tea (over forty choices); scones (with Devonshire cream, preserves, and lemon curd); several savories; fresh fruit; soup; tea sandwiches (cucumber and cream cheese, ham, and chicken curry) cut into fancy shapes served with fresh flowers on a tiered tray - presentation does count; and delectable, dainty desserts. The tea is kept hot, and I've learned to appreciate trying new flavors. Cottage Afternoon Tea is $23.95, does not include soup and is less one savory. If you want tea in the more English tradition of just tea and two scones with embellishments, plus fruit, walk-ins may order this for $12.95 per person.

The attached retail shop has teacups and saucers for sale, as well as plates, jewelry, tea cozies, books, napkin rings, and other gift items. Make time to meander in and around the antique and collectibles shops that are next door to the tea room.

Hours: Open Wed. - Sat., 11am - 4pm (tho they may close on days with no reservations). Reservations are highly
suggested. Always call first. Closed Sun. - Tues.
Price: Menu prices are listed above.
Ages: 4 years and up.

CORVETTE DINER

(619) 542-1476 / www.cohnrestaurants.com/corvettediner $$$$
2965 Historic Decatur Road, San Diego

This ultimate 50's-style diner is the best bebopping place to eat! The central dining room is decorated with posters of musicians and stars from the 50's, old license plates and signs, neon signs, hub cabs on the walls, old gas pumps, Bazooka bubble gum displays, and a gleaming vintage car, all while 50's music plays in the background. Some of the padded vinyl booths are sparkly silver and hot pink, and some that particular color of turquoise. Checkered tiles cover the floors and part of the walls. A back room has vintage-shaped TV screens on the walls that play black and white TV shows from that era. Another room is dedicated to the 60's with black-lit flower power and peace signs on the walls and ceiling, and booths with a streamlined look, from that time period. Most evenings after 6pm a live DJ plays 50's and 60's music and takes requests. Down the hallway that's lined with more celebrity posters from the 50's, is an arcade room, still decorated with the theme of the restaurant, but filled with modern-day video and arcade games, plus air hockey. There is also a prize redemption area.

The food here is great and the menu extensive! Try a Hawaii 5-O chicken sandwich with pineapple ($11.99), Greek salad ($10.50), Rory hamburger with peanut butter ($11.99), Reuben ($11.50), Philly steak sandwich ($12.99), shrimp platter ($14.50), meatloaf ($14.50), or spaghetti and meatballs ($12.50). Other food choices include grilled ribs, blackened chicken pasta, and more. Kids' meals are $8.49 for their choice of spaghetti, burger sliders, corn dog, grilled cheese sandwich, mac and cheese, or chicken fingers, plus fries or veggies, and a soft drink. Desserts are delectable, such as brownie hot fudge sundae, apple pie a la mode and cotton candy. Specialty sodas and shakes range from Kahlua Mocha Chocolate Shake and Green River to egg cream and nutella & banana (or twenty other flavors). Was life really this good in the fifties?!

Hours: Open Mon. - Thurs., 11:30am - 9pm; Fri., 11:30am - 11pm; Sat., 11am - 11pm; Sun., 11am - 9pm.
Price: Menu prices are listed above.
Ages: All

FARMER'S MARKETS (San Diego County)

See the entry for FARMER'S MARKETS (Los Angeles County) (pg. 21) for details.

FRESH BROTHERS (San Diego County)

(858) 252-7000 / www.freshbrothers.com
5950 Village Way #103, San Diego

See FRESH BROTHERS (Los Angeles County) (pg. 22) for details.

GILLESPE FIELD CAFE

(619) 448-0415 / www.gillespiecafe.com
2015 N Marshall Avenue, El Cajon, CA 92020

The Cafe, located just off the airfield near the air traffic control tower, is a great place to eat while watching small planes land and take off. Inside is plane paraphernalia on the walls and a display case with model airplanes, plus views of the airstrip. The outside patio is delightful and has even better views.

The food is good! Breakfast options, which are served all day, include omelettes, pancakes with all the fixings, blueberry muffins and more while lunch options include patty melts ($9.95), Philly steak ($9.75), fish and chips ($11.50), plus soups and salads. Happy landings! Visit the nearby museum AIR GROUP ONE COMMEMORATIVE AIR FORCE WORLD WAR II FLYING MUSEUM (pg. 523).

Hours: Open daily, 7am - 3pm.
Price: Prices are listed above.
Ages: 1 year and up.

GYU-KAKU (San Diego County)

(858) 693-3790 / www.gyu-kaku.com
9844 Hibert St., G-1, San Diego (Scripps Ranch)

See the entry for GYU-KAKU (Los Angeles County) (pg. 23) for information on this grill-it-yourself restaurant.

Hours: Open Mon. - Sat., 11am - 10:30pm; Sun., 11am - 9:30pm.

HOUSE OF BLUES GOSPEL BRUNCH (San Diego County)

(619) 299-BLUE (2583) / www.houseofblues.com
1055 Fifth Avenue, San Diego

See HOUSE OF BLUES GOSPEL BRUNCH (Orange County) (pg. 249) for details on this southern sensation. This location's building has different decor, but it follows the theme of eclectic folk art with a hip appeal.

Hours: Gospel Brunch is offered on select Sun., usually once a month, at 11am. Get here earlier. Ask about holiday Sun., such as Easter and Mother's Day. All seating is reserved. Reservations are highly recommended.
Price: $44 for ages 13 and up; $22 for ages 6 - 12; children 5 and under are free. Prices include tax and gratuity. Parking costs about $10 in a lot across the street.
Ages: 5 years and up.

JANET'S MONTANA CAFE

(619) 659-3874
2506 Alpine Boulevard, Alpine

Janet's is a good-sized, authentic, rustic-themed restaurant with ceilings of timber-hewed logs, wooden floors, antler chandeliers, chairs made of tree branches (strong ones!), and decor of stuffed moose and deer heads and Western art. Outside seating gives an equally country feel while on a covered back porch overlooking lots of shade trees, rocks, a waterfall, old stagecoach, and a little brook with wooden bridges. A few very small shops are also on the premises.

The generously-proportioned, American-style breakfast - usually served with hash browns, home fries, or fresh fruit and a choice of toast, biscuit, muffin or pancakes - consists of: biscuits and gravy ($8.75), ham and cheese omelet ($11.95), waffles with strawberries ($10.25), two pancakes ($7.45), granola French toast ($10.95), and country fried steak. And this is just a sampling of the breakfast menu! For $5.95 kids can order two pancakes, an egg and bacon; French toast; or a ham and cheese omelet with bacon. Hearty lunches and dinners include a buffalo burger ($11.25), turkey melt ($10.95), Reuben ($10.95), chicken quesadilla ($11.95), taco and enchilada ($10.95), roasted turkey breast ($15.45), grilled halibut ($21.95) and baby back ribs ($16.95 - half rack). Kid's meal choices include hamburger, grilled cheese, pizza, popcorn shrimp, or chicken fingers, plus a dessert for $5.95 each.

If it's a nice day, and most are in Southern California, wander over to the adjacent nursery to look at the lovely and unique selection of plants and pottery.

Hours: Open Mon., 6am - 2:30pm; Tues. - Thurs., 6am - 8:30pm; Fri. - Sat., 6am - 9pm; Sun., 6am - 8:30pm. Closed Thanksgiving and Christmas.

Price: Menu prices are listed above.

Ages: All

JOE'S CRAB SHACK (San Diego County)

Oceanside - (760) 722-1345; San Diego (Harbor Dr.) - (619) 233-7391 / www.joescrabshack.com

Oceanside - 314 Harbor Dr.; San Diego - 525 E. Harbor Dr.

See the entry for JOE'S CRAB SHACK (Los Angeles County) (pg. 24) for details.

JOHN'S INCREDIBLE PIZZA CO. (San Diego County)

(619) 472-5555 / www.johnspizza.com

3010 Plaza Bonita Road in Westfield Plaza Bonita (mall), National City

See JOHN'S INCREDIBLE PIZZA CO. (Orange County) (pg. 250) for details.

Hours: Open Mon. - Thurs., 11am - 9pm; Fri., 11am - 10:30pm; Sat., 10am - 10:30pm; Sun., 11am - 9pm. Usually open one hour earlier Mon. - Fri. during school breaks.

JULIAN TEA & COTTAGE ARTS

(866) 765-0832 or (760) 765-OTEA (0832) / www.juliantea.com

2124 Third Street, Julian

This quaint (what in Julian isn't quaint?), 100-year-old house is a *tea*lightful place to take your daughter for an afternoon of one-on-one time, or to go with a group of friends. Tea is served in the tea room (and the front porch) and the white room looks like you would picture a tea place to be with white wood walls and cute stencils; small round tables with flowery tablecloths and doilies; and tea cups and saucers, china plates and cute artwork on the walls. The retail shop has several other rooms packed with items for sale - china, tea pots, a really huge selection of teas, baby gifts, bridal gifts, books on teas, cards, aprons, cooking utensils, food products (i.e. sauces, jams, candies), lace, and cottage arts, such as weaving. Such an assemblage!

The Cottage Classic Tea ($26.96) is a four-course meal starting with the house pumpkin soup and mini cheese scone; then five finger sandwiches and savories; fruit; a scone with whipped cream, lemon curd and jam; all topped off with dessert, and, of course, a bottomless pot of tea. Afternoon Tea ($21.95) is a three-course tea with most of the same as the Cottage Classic, minus the soup. An example of a lunch/tea is the Drew Bailey Lunch ($21.95). It comes with a full sandwich - a choice of house curried chicken salad; turkey or ham with cheese; egg salad; or hummus; on either a croissant or whole grain bread. It also includes a cup of soup or a salad, dessert, and tea. Cream Tea ($9.95) is two scones with traditional toppings, and tea. Fruit n' Cheese Tea ($10.95) offers fruit, cheeses, a cookie and tea. And these are just a few of the options! Add-ons include a cup of soup or a salad, $3.95; a scone with toppings, $4; and a cheese scone with ham and cheese, $5.95. Children's Tea ($9.95), for ages 12 and under, includes a peanut butter and jelly sandwich or turkey sandwich; a scone with "toppings"; a cookie; and a beverage choice of children's tea, apple juice or hot chocolate. Note that there are some tea foods you can purchase to take home, like the pumpkin soup and scones. Holiday teas, such as ones offered for Valentines' Day, Mother's Day, and the Victorian Tea at Christmas, are always extra special.

Hours: The shop is open Thurs. - Sun., 10am - 4pm. Seatings are at 11:30am, 1pm, and 2:30pm. Reservations are recommended and required on weekends. Closed Tues., Wed. (but open daily during holiday seasons), New Year's Day, Thanksgiving, and Christmas.

Price: Prices are listed above.

Ages: 5 years and up.

KILLER PIZZA FROM MARS

Escondido - (760) 741-MARS (6277); Oceanside - (760) 722-6060 / www.killerpizzafrommars.com
Escondido - 1040 W. El Norte Parkway; Oceanside - 3772 Mission Avenue, suite 127

With a name like this, you have to expect something far out of this world! Both of the pizzerias are similar in theme, but have slightly different, quirky decor. At the larger and more decorated Oceanside location, first look through the window to be greeted by life-size figures of ET, Darth Mal, Jar Jar Binks, and a few other creatures. Inside, the science fiction/outer space theme is continued throughout this large pizza joint. The black ceilings feature constellations, inflatable aliens and astronauts, and small model space ships from *Stars Wars*, *Star Trek*, and more hanging from the ceiling. Some of the hanging objects glow in the dark.

The walls are covered with an eclectic assortment of anything remotely related to space, such as alien-themed movie posters, magazine covers featuring NASA happenings, and pictures of the cosmos. Bookcases and a large shelf on the wall are packed with more of this type of paraphernalia including games, collectibles, action figures, Jetson figurines, Conehead models, Buzz Lightyear dolls, toys, stuffed animals, more aliens, lunch boxes, glasses, masks, and more. Yoda, a Chewy head, and a few other such items are also featured. T.V. monitors and a couple of arcade-style games complete the kitschy ambiance.

The food is good and ranges from an assortment of pizzas (about $21 for a large with one "space partikul") to chicken salads ($8.29) to "spagatte with meetballz" ($8.99). Men might be from Mars, but I daresay that female folk enjoy the offerings from here, too.

Hours: Usually open Sun. - Thurs., 11am - 9pm; Fri. - Sat., 11am - 10pm. Call individual stores for specific hours.
Price: Prices are listed above. Discount coupons are available on the website.
Ages: All

THE OLD SPAGHETTI FACTORY (San Diego County)

San Diego - (619) 233-4323; San Marcos - (760) 471-0155 / www.osf.com
San Diego - 275 Fifth Ave.; San Marcos - 111 N. Twin Oaks Valley Rd.

See the entry for THE OLD SPAGHETTI FACTORY (Los Angeles County) (pg. 25) for details.

PARK HYATT AVIARA RESORT

(760) 448-1234 / www.parkaviara.hyatt.com
aviara.park.hyatt.com
7100 Aviara Resort Drive at Four Seasons Point, Carlsbad

All dressed up and nowhere to go? Then go to Park Hyatt and indulge in an elegant repast of tea time at this fine resort hotel. Tables in the lobby/lounge are covered with white linen, sprinkled with rose petals, and set with fine china. A three-tiered silver cake plate bears scrumptious edibles of finger sandwiches; scones with rose petal jelly, lemon curd, and Devonshire cream; and petit fours and delicate pastries. Sip your choice of teas, including herbal and fruit infusions. A pianist plays, adding ambiance.

Hours: Tea is served Sat. - Sun. from 12:30 - 2:30pm.
Price: $45 per person for adults, add $5 for a glass of port or wine; $25 for ages 12 and under (no alcohol!). Valet parking is complementary, with the tea.
Ages: 4 years and up.

PETER PIPER PIZZA

(619) 477-1788 / www.peterpiperpizza.com
3007 Highland Avenue, National City

This huge, fun-filled pizza place is very similar to Chuck E. Cheese's. Obviously the main food offered here is pizza (a large cheese pizza is about $14.49), but chicken wings ($9.49 for 10-piece) and a salad bar are also available. All-you-can-eat lunch buffets, offered Monday through Friday from 11am to 2pm, are only $6.99 for adults, $4.99 for kids.

For entertainment, there is a play area with a few short slides, plus plenty of arcade games with prize redemption, and video games, and a merry-go-round that is free (yea!). You will have to purchase tokens for the games - twenty tokens for $5. Bring in a good report card and you've earned tokens on the house. The kids love coming here - just cover your ears to block out the din. Note that for a minimum of ten kids, one-hour tours are offered where youngsters see the kitchens, learn about dough and oven temperature, and, most importantly, top off their own 7" pizza and eat it. A drink and ten tokens are included in the $5.99 per child price. Adults, you're on your own!

Hours: Open Sun. - Thurs., 11am - 9pm; Fri.; 11am - 10pm; Sat., 10am - 10pm. Tours start at 9:30am - call to
schedule a date.
Price: Admission is free, but bring money for food and tokens.
Ages: 1½ years and up.

RUBY'S (San Diego County)

(800) HEY RUBY (439-7829) - for all locations. / www.rubys.com
Carlsbad; Oceanside; San Diego (this one has a recreation of the 1939 World's Fair pavilion)
See the entry for RUBY'S (Orange County) (pg. 252) for details. Ruby's can be found in Carlsbad, Jamul,
Oceanside, and two locations in San Diego.

SHAKESPEARE'S CORNER SHOPPE & AFTERNOON TEA

(619) 683-BRIT (2748) / www.ukcornershoppe.com; www.sandiegoafternoontea.com
3719 India Street, San Diego
"I count myself in nothing else so happy as in a soul rememb'ring my good friends." This Shakespearian quote is
appropriate in sharing time with a friend over a spot of tea. Inside Shakespeare's Corner (which is small enough to be
about corner size), the shoppe sells a lovely selection of British goods - food, gift items, flags, tea accessories, clothing
items, and more.
Seating, for up to fifteen people, is on the outside patio at wrought-iron tables and chairs. Authentic British
Afternoon Tea includes finger sandwiches, sausage roll, a home-baked scone with Devon cream and jam, biscuit
selection, cake medley, and choice of tea for $28.95. A Child's Afternoon Tea, for ages 12 and under, offers similar
fare for $19.95. If you don't want a full tea, order a pot of tea and a scone with cream and jam for $12.95, an
assortment of finger sandwiches for $6.95, or something from the bakery. Beverages, besides tea, include British sodas,
hot chocolate, and juice. Reservations are required. Check the website for specially themed teas such as Alice in
Wonderland, Mary Poppins, Dr. Who, Harry Potter, Princess (the latter two include a magician's wand or fairy wand,
respectively, for each child) and more.
Hours: The shoppe is open Mon. - Fri., 10am - 8pm; Sat. - Sun., 9am - 8pm. Tea is served Mon. - Fri. starting at
11am, with the last sitting at 4pm; every ninety minutes. Seatings on Sat. and Sun. are at 11am, 1:30pm and
4pm. Closed Thanksgiving and Christmas.
Price: Prices are listed above.
Ages: 4 years and up.

SHOGUN (San Diego County)

San Diego - (858) 560-7399; San Marcos - (760) 744-6600 / www.restaurantshogun.com
San Diego - 5451 Kearny Villa Road; San Marcos - 695 S. Rancho Santa Fe Road
See the entry for SHOGUN (Los Angeles County) (pg. 26) for details.
Hours: San Diego - Mon. - Thurs., 11:30am - 9:30pm; Fri., 11:30am - 10pm; Sat., noon - 10pm; Sun., noon - 9:30pm.
San Marcos - Mon. - Thurs., 11:30am - 2pm and 5pm - 9pm; Fri., 11:30am - 2pm and 5pm - 9:30pm; Sat.,
12:30pm - 9:30pm; Sun., 12:30pm - 9pm.

SUMMER SUNSET LUAU ON MISSION BAY

(858) 488-1081 or (800) 422-8386 / www.catamaranresort.com
3999 Mission Boulevard, Mission Bay
See SUNSET LUAU ON MISSION BAY (pg. 721) in the Calendar section for more information on this
Polynesian experience.
Hours: Open mid-June to beginning of September, every Fri., 6pm - 9pm, plus mid-July to mid-August, every Tues.,
6pm - 9pm.
Price: Non-hotel guests prices are $72 for adults; $32 for ages 5 - 12; children 4 and under are free.
Ages: 5 years and up.

THE GRAND TEA ROOM

(760) 233-9500 / www.thegrandtearoom.com
145 W. Grand Avenue, Escondido
Tea time, not tee time! Not overdone cutesy, but more like charming, this full service tea room has long tables
(and several smaller round ones) covered with lace tablecloths; a mixture of wooden chairs and padded side chairs; a

countryside garden wall mural; chandeliers; teapots and china in cabinets; and lamps, photos and hats tastefully arranged, hanging on the walls. There is also a few tables on the small, out front patio. There are several teas to choose from, as well as a la carte menu items such as three tea sandwiches, $6.50; a grilled chicken garden salad, $14; and a cup of soup and baguette, $5. The Grand Tea comes with soup and a savory; assorted tea sandwiches; fresh seasonal fruit; a scone with cream, lemon curd and jam; petite desserts; and a choice of over forty teas - $29.95. The Children's Tea, for ages 10 and under, includes two tea sandwiches and a savory; fresh seasonal fruit; a scone with all the good stuff; two petite desserts; and tea or milk - $19.95.

The gift shop is brimming with feminine treasures of tea hats, tea pots, teas, collectables and more.

Hours: Open Tues. - Sat., 11am - 5pm; closed Sun., except for private parties, and Mon.
Price: Some prices are listed above.
Ages: 5 years and up.

—FAMILY PAY AND PLAY—

ALTITUDE TRAMPOLINE PARK

(760) 842-5142 / www.altitudevista.com
1928 Hacienda Drive, Vista

Altitude is everything. Wait - maybe that's attitude, but here it is altitude that counts. This park has a large room of trampoline grids; foam pit; rock climbing wall; dodgeball court; performance trampolines with jumping walls of 4 and 6 feet; two basketball dunking lanes; a battlebeam (padded jousting over a foam pit!); a stunt jump; a trapeze; a gymnastics tumble area; and an area just for younger kids. Trampoline fitness classes are available, as are toddler times, teen nights and other special events and dates. Note: You must wear their socks - purchase them here for $2.

Hours: Open Sun. - Thurs., 10am - 9pm; Fri., 10am - 11pm; Sat., 9am - 11pm. Toddler Time is usually Mon. - Fri., 10am - 1pm.
Price: 30 min. is $8.95; 60 min. is $14.95, etc. Toddler Time is $8.95 for toddlers, $2.95 for parent/guardian.
Ages: 2 years and up.

ATLANTIS LASER TAG

(619) 420-3824 / www.atlantislasertag.com
510 Broadway, suites 1-3, Chula Vista

This fantastic, family-friendly, huge (6,000 square feet), multi-level, state-of-the-art laser tag arena is underwater themed. There are cool fish murals (I like the shark ones) that incorporate sea turtles and coral, plus underwater-looking statues on top of the walls in the arena and hanging from the ceiling. The maze-like setting has walls to shoot around, over, and under, as well as ramps, windows, doorways, pillars, and other hiding spots. Fog, music, blue neon lighting, and never knowing where your enemy will pop out keeps the adrenaline rushing and keeps you coming back for more. Up to forty-four people can play at one time.

Another element that sets this laser tag arena apart from others is that it offers over twenty different games or strategies, for both individual players and team play. Some of the game options include tag, fugitive, gladiator, time warp, capture the flag, deadaim, and masters. The lightweight, flashing phasers have a variety of settings which can also add to the challenge.

For another type of challenge try Lazer Maze where laser beams crisscross inside a smallish room and players must avoid them (i.e. dive under, jump over, etc.) to reach the targets - race against teammates!

The lobby has video arcade games, with a prize redemption area, plus air hockey and a full-service snack bar that serves pizza, popcorn, Icees, and soft drinks. Enjoy use of the themed, private room for parties.

Hours: Usually open Tues. - Thurs., 4pm - 9pm; Fri., 3pm - midnight; Sat., noon - midnight; Sun., noon - 9pm. Open Mon. by reservation. It is open during the summer and school breaks Mon. - Thurs. at 2pm - the rest is the same.
Price: $7 for one game of laser tag; $18 for 3 games. Lazer Maze is $2 a game. Always call or check the website for specials.
Ages: Must be 7 years old or 48" tall.

BELMONT PARK

(858) 228-WAVE (9283) or (858) 488-1549 - park and amusement rides; (858) 488-1971 - arcade, mini golf, lazer blast, and other attractions; (858) 228-9300 - the Wave House; (858) 412 - 5914 - Escapology / www.belmontpark.com; www.lazerblastarcade.com
3146 Mission Boulevard, San Diego

This relatively small area is packed with a few shops; restaurants, including the fine dining of Cannonball with seating on the beachfront rooftop; eateries, including an ice cream store and a candy shop; and an arcade and games center that encircle the ten, or so, **amusement rides** and other attractions at Belmont Park. In the center is the Giant Dipper Roller Coaster ($6) which doesn't have any loops, but has plenty of ups and downs! A replica of the Looff Liberty wooden carousel ($3) has horses as well as an ostrich, giraffe, and tiger to ride on. Other amusement rides include traditional Bumper Cars ($4); Krazy Kars, which are bumper cars that bump and spin all around ($4); Tilt-A-Whirl ($4); Beach Blaster, which swings riders standing up sixty feet in the air at randomly occurring G-forces ($5); Control Freak, a vertical ride where riders control the forward, backward and flip motions of the car ($5), which is similar to the Octotron roller coaster ride in which riders control the motion, as well as the speed ($5); Vertical Plunge, a three-story drop ($4); and the kiddie rides of Crazy Submarine ($3) and Speedway ($3). Certain height restrictions apply to the rides. Play some **Midway games** that are interspersed among the rides.

Face your fear of heights on **Sky Ropes**, an outdoor, suspended, obstacle ropes course where you are harnessed in and move over rope bridges and along beams among real and fake tree tops ($8). Scale the thirty-foot rock wall of **Sky Climb** that offers a few different routes ($8), as well as two, side-by-side, more modern-looking walls to race up. A short, but zippy **zipline** above it all is $15. Sink your shots at the eighteen-hole Tiki Town Adventure Golf, a **mini golf** course that is tropically themed. The course is extra fun with some holes that are inside and some that are out. Check out the erupting volcano - one of the best attractions on the course! $9 a game. Don't just watch a movie, experience it with **Xanadu 7D**, motion sensor ride. 3D glasses and seats that move you to the motion on screen (sometimes wildly, like a roller coaster!) enable you to be a part of the action, whether you're laser blasting pirates, zombies, or aliens. The **Laser Maze** challenge looks like something from a spy movie as players try to go over and dive/roll under the lasers, in a vault setting, without breaking them so an alarm won't be tripped. This game can be over quickly as it stops as soon as you "break" a lazer. The reverse option is Beam Buster, to break as many as you can in a time period. $4 a game/try, or $10 unlimited. Is there fun to be had in a Tron-themed world? According to this **Laser Tag** game - yes! The three levels and 3,000 square-foot arena lets all the action be unleashed for $8 a game, or $20 for unlimited games. Classics and the latest in **video** and **arcade** games are also here. Earn tickets and redeem them for prizes at the redemption center.

Escape. That's what it's all about. There are three differently themed escape rooms at **Escapology**, where for 60 minutes you work with your team of 2 to 6 players (or detectives!) in a completely decorated room to unlock codes by thinking strategically and using mental muscle to solve the puzzles and the "crimes". It's an intense, challenging, and fun experience.

Besides these other activities, you can continuously surf or body board the perfect five-foot wave via the **FlowRider** machine at the Wave House Athletic Club. Take lessons or just let it rip. Hourly fees are $20, plus a one-time registration fee of $10 for non-club members. Feeling adventurous? Try ten-foot waves on the advanced FlowRider called FlowBarrel, or Bruticus Maximus (which is definitely tougher sounding). Hourly fees are $40, plus a one-time registration fee of $20. While at Belmont Park, take a plunge at **The Plunge**. This large, indoor swimming pool boasts a beautiful underwater/whale mural, painted by renown marine artist, Wyland. The enclosed pool, kept at 84 degrees, is surrounded by huge windows looking out on palm trees, suggesting a tropical atmosphere. Swim sessions are $7 for adults; $6 for seniors and children 6 months to 17 years.

Too nice a day to go swimming inside? Go for a dip outside, as the ocean is just a few steps away. The surf, sand, and bike trail on the beach are "shore" to help make your day at the park a good one!

Hours: The stores and restaurants are open daily, usually 10am - 7pm. Most of the rest year, most rides and attractions are usually open only Fri. - Sat., 11am - 10pm; Sun., 11am - 8pm. Call first as hours fluctuate a lot! In summer, the rides are open Sun. - Wed., 11am - 11pm; Thurs. - Sat., 11am - midnight. Flow Riders are open to ride Mon. - Fri. starting at noon; Sat. - Sun. starting at 11am. The Plunge is open Mon. - Fri., noon - 4pm and 8pm - 10pm; Sat. - Sun., noon - 8pm.

Price: Attractions are priced above. An unlimited rides pass is $30 for 48" and taller; $20 for 47" and under. Always check the website or call for special deals.

Ages: All, although most of the rides are geared for ages 7 and up.

BOARDWALK

619) 449-7805 / www.boardwalk-parkway.com

1286 Fletcher Parkway, El Cajon

This Boardwalk is not made of boards, nor is it by the seaside; it is, however, a large indoor amusement center for kids. It's clean with brightly-colored games and rides that elicited several, "This is FUN!" comments from young kids. The main attractions are the **carousel** ($1), **castle bounce** ($1.25), **frog hopper** ($2.25), **Himalaya** coaster ($2.25),

kart wheel ($2.25); **krazy kars** ($3.75) and **soft play gym** ($2.25). The two-story soft play gym area, for kids 60" and under, has ball pits, a mini zip line, slides, and obstacle courses, plus tubes to crawl through. The best bet is buying an unlimited play wrist band (which doesn't include Krazy Kars) for $9.95, Monday through Thursday, and $10.95, Fridays - Sundays, and holidays. A decent-sized, glow-in-the-dark **Laser tag** arena is another exciting element at the Boardwalk. Almost eight minutes of running around and "zapping" people costs $4 for the first game, $3 for each game thereafter, or special deals at times of $7.95 per person for unlimited play. Numerous arcade and video games are also here with a prize redemption center.

The full-service snack bar offers salads ($5.39 for chicken Caesar), pizza ($14.79 for a large cheese), pasta, sandwiches ($5.19 for a turkey breast or meatball), chicken tenders ($5.09), and more, plus weekly family deals. Kids meals are regularly $3.39 for a choice of corn dog, chicken nuggets, burger, or pizza, plus fries and a drink. If you feel like scoring more fun, strike out to Parkway Bowl, a connecting bowling alley, with sixty lanes of regular or cosmic bowl. Parkway also has a room of video games and a billiards table.

Hours: Open Mon. - Thurs., 3pm - 9pm (noon - 9pm on school breaks and holidays); Fri., 3pm - 11:30pm, tho rides close at 10pm (open noon - 11:30pm on school breaks and holidays); Sat., 11am - 11:30pm, tho rides close at 10pm; Sun., 11am - 9pm. Laser tag is open Mon. - Thurs., 5pm - 9pm; Fri., 5pm - 11pm; Sat., noon - 11pm; Sun., noon - 9pm. Open longer hours during the summer and school breaks.

Price: Attractions are individually priced above. Laser tag prices are listed above.

Ages: 1½ years - 12.

BOOMERS! - El Cajon

(619) 593-1155 / www.boomersparks.com
1155 Graves Avenue, El Cajon

Come to this family fun center to play for just an hour, or have fun all day. Green fees pay for two rounds at any of the three, nine-hole themed **miniature golf** courses. Choose Memory Lane (fairy tale motif), Iron Horse (western), and/or Lost Crusade (Egyptian) - $10 for adults, children 4 and under are free with a paying adult. Other attractions include **bumper boats** - $9 for adults, $2 for passengers (height restrictions apply); **go-karts** - $10 for drivers who must be at least 58" tall, $2 for passengers who must be at least 40" tall; **batting cages**; and the **Kid's County Fair**. The latter consists of four rides for young children, 36" to 48" tall: a roller coaster, train ride, Ferris wheel, and mini-planes. Each ride costs $5. A 32-foot high **rock wall** costs $9 for two climbs - make the most of them. The two-story arcade and video game building is attractively set up. A full snack bar is also at this fun center, including pizza, corn dogs, chicken tenders and more. Food and fun - what more could you want?!

Hours: Open Mon. - Thurs., noon - 8pm; Fri., noon - 11pm; Sat., 11am - 10pm; Sun., 11am - 8pm, or 9pm. Hours fluctuate, especially as they are open longer hours over holidays and school breaks, so call before you come. Kids' County Fair is generally open the same hours, but usually closes earlier.

Price: Attractions are individually priced above, or purchase an all day, unlimited play pass starting at $44.99. Check online for specials.

Ages: 2½ years and up.

BOOMERS! - San Diego

(858) 560-4211 / www.boomersparks.com
6999 Clairemont Mesa Boulevard, San Diego

So much fun can be had at just one place! Choose from two themed **miniature golf** courses: Storybook Land, which has a castle, Cinderella's pumpkin, the shoe from the old woman who lived in one, and more; or Western Town with a bank, jail, storefront facades, a livery stable, and wagons - $10 per person, ages 4 and under are free. Other attractions include **go karts** - $10 for a five-minute ride (drivers must be at least 58" tall), $2 for a passenger; **bumper boats** - $9 per driver, who must be at least 44" tall, $2 per passenger; **Flame Thrower**, a two-person thrill ride that goes up and over a tall, rotating "arm" and upside down - $8; a 32-foot high **rock climbing wall** - $9 for two tries; and **batting cages.** The **Kid's County Fair** has six rides, including teacups, a Ferris wheel, a train ride, a swing, and a fire engine that goes in the air and around and around. Rides cost $5 each. Of course there is a video and arcade game area, and a prize redemption center. There is also a separate section for less violent kiddie video games. A Boomer's cafe serving pizza, nachos, chicken tenders and other necessary foods is on-site here.

Hours: Open Mon. - Thurs., noon - 8pm; Fri., noon - 11pm; Sat., 10am - 11pm; Sun., 10am - 8pm. Open extended hours in the summer. The Kids County Fair is open generally the same hours, but it sometimes closes earlier.

Price: Attractions are individually priced above or buy an all-day, play pass starting at $44.99.

Ages: 2 years and up.

BOOMERS! - Vista

(760) 945-9474 / www.boomersvista.com
1525 W. Vista Way, Vista

This family fun center really has it all! If you're in a mutinous mood, play the pirate-themed **miniature golf** course with its piratey ship and fountains. If you're feeling rather noble, play King Arthur's course with its huge (relatively speaking) castles and dungeons, and a bridge over water. Golf prices are $8 per person; ages 4 and under are free. **Laser Tag** is an every man/woman/child-for-himself laser tag game played inside an inflatable battleship bounce. There are soft obstacles to hide behind (or jump on), and even small rooms to run around in. The game is action-packed, sweaty, and fun. The cost is $8 for a five-minute game, and children must be 5 years old to play. **Kidopolis** is a huge, four-story, soft-play area with slides, obstacle courses, ball pits, tubes and tunnels. This major gerbil run was a major hit with my boys. Participants must be under 48" and wear socks. Kids can also take a spin on a **mini-helicopter** or **spinning tea cups** - any of these two attractions for $8 per. Other attractions here include **batting cages**; **go karts** - $8 for drivers, who must be at least 58" tall, $2 for passengers, who must be at least 40" tall; and **bumper boats** - $8 a driver, who must be at least 44" tall, $2 for passengers.

The noisy, but attractive, main two-story building houses numerous video and arcade games. Note that good grades translate into free tokens here! A nickel arcade section is upstairs. Johnny Rockets is a full-service restaurant where freshly-cooked hamburgers, hot dogs, Philly cheese steak, BLT, and other tasty family fare, along with a kid's only menu, is served along with a fun atmosphere.

Hours: Open Mon. - Thurs., noon - 8pm; Fri., noon - 11pm; Sat., 10am - 11pm; Sun., 10am - 8pm. Open extended hours in the summer and on school breaks.

Price: Attractions are individually priced above, or purchase an unlimited pass starting at $19.99. Check the website for discounts and coupons.

Ages: 2 years and up.

CARMEL VALLEY SKATEBOARD PARK / CARMEL VALLEY COMMUNITY PARK and POOL

(858) 552-1616 - park; (858) 552-1623 - pool / www.sandiego.gov/park-and-recreation
12600 El Camino Real - skate park / 3777 Townsgate Drive - park and pool, San Diego

Is your child a ripper? This means a really good and consistent skater in skate-speak. At 13,500 square feet, this night-lighted park has what it takes to give your kids the edge. It has a challenge course, a concrete bowl, and urban elements of railings, stairs, banks, and ledges. Amenities include a restroom, shade structure, and observations area. Helmet and knee and elbow pads are required. A parent or legal guardian must accompany kids 12 years and under.

The surrounding park amenities include picnic areas; grassy open areas; several tennis courts; a multi-purpose athletic field; horseshoe pits; basketball courts; fitness stations; a recreational center with a game room and gym; and a great, multi-level playground with short slides, low bridges, climbing apparatus, interactive games attached to the main play structure, and lots of fun elements under the structure like play houses, kid-size benches, and tunnels. A cement pathway winds around the perimeter of the park. Check out all the rec opportunities offered for kids!

The adjacent aquatic facility has a main swimming pool, plus two large water slides that end in a catch pool. There is also a children's wading pool and a small water play structure with a short slide and tunnel, steps, and water spurting out from tubes and pipes.

Hours: The park and skate park are open daily, 10am - 8pm. The pool is open most of the year for recreational swim Mon., Wed., Fri., 12:30 - 4pm; Sat., noon - 4pm. The slides and water play structure are open Memorial Day - Labor Day.

Price: Free to the park and skate park. The pool is $4 for adults; $2 for seniors and ages 15 and under.

Ages: 7 years and up.

CHUCK E. CHEESE'S (San Diego County)

See the entry for CHUCK E. CHEESE'S (Los Angeles County) (pg. 18) for details.

CHULA VISTA SKATEPARK / LEN MOORE SKATEPARK

(619) 409-5979 / www.chulavistaca.gov
1301 Oleander Avenue, Chula Vista

This unsupervised skate park is huge at 55,000 square feet of concrete and 10,000 square feet of wood. It also has a courtyard with a park-like ambiance, including picnic tables. (It feels safe - as safe as one can be doing ollies, flips, and other stunts!) The wood section has a mini half-pipe and a series of ramps. The concrete skate area has separate components of bowls, rails, steps, reservoirs, three- to nine-foot banks, a pyramid, ledges, fun boxes, and lots of just-skating space.

Hours: Open daily, 8am - dusk, weather permitting.

Price: Free

Ages: 7 years and up.

CITY OF SANTEE AQUATIC CENTER at CAMERON FAMILY YMCA

(619) 449-9622 / www.cityofsanteeca.gov

10123 Riverwalk Drive, Santee

Beat the heat at this very fun aquatic center which is part of the YMCA. There are three recreation pools: one is a lap pool, one has a twisty slide for bigger kids (48" and taller), and one is an interactive pool. A separate water play area for younger children is in one-and-a-half-feet of water. The water play area has mini slides, swings (over the water), climbing apparatus, and a structure that squirts out water in all different directions. Bring a picnic to enjoy on the large lawn just outside the gated aquatic center. (There is not much shade around, though.) Note that children 6 years and under must be accompanied by an adult in the water; there is a maximum of two children per adult; and waivers for kids 17 and under must be signed.

Hours: The lap pool is open daily, year round. The interactive pool/slide, etc. is open April - mid-June, and September - October, usually on Sat. - Sun., noon - 2pm and 2:30pm - 4:30pm. Open in the summer daily, extended hours, and sessions are often 3 hours long, not 2.

Price: $3 per person per two-hour water play session for Santee residents; $8 per person for non-residents. Lap swim is $3 for Santee resident; $8 for non-residents.

Ages: 2 years and up.

DAVE & BUSTER'S (San Diego County)

Carlsbad - (760) 576-3800; San Diego - (619) 280-7115 / www.daveandbusters.com

Carlsbad - 2501 El Camino Real, Ste. 140 at The Shoppes at Carlsbad; San Diego - 2931 Camino del Rio North, San Diego

See DAVE & BUSTER'S (Orange County) (pg. 259) for details.

Hours: Open Sun. - Wed., 11am - midnight; Thurs. - Sat., 11am - 1am.

FUNBELIEVABLE

(619) 456-2474 / www.funbelievableplay.com

11655 Riverside Drive, suite 155-157, Lakeside

Tropically-themed, this huge indoor play place, is almost as good as an island get-away; almost. The main, tri-level, mega play structure, decorated with surfboards and fake palm trees, sports tiki-faced foam obstacles; side-by-side racing slides; cargo ropes to climb; tubes and tunnels to crawl through; a ball pit; a ball suction dispenser; hop on bounces to swing on; a rock-climbing wall; large balls; a mini zip line; and oversized Lego-like bricks to build things. Socks are required.

An enclosed, Hawaiian-looking area just for toddlers has play surfboards; a tiny ball pit; a short play structure with foam stairs; mini slides; and soft play toys to play on and with.

There is also a basketball and (mini) soccer area, with netting all around, and a lounge and cafe right in front of the play structures for easy viewing. The cafe serves coffee drinks and smoothies, as well as sandwiches, salads, paninis and more. Funbelievable offers fun for parents, too, with Date Night drop offs ($18 per child) and Family Fun Nights every Friday from 5pm to 8pm. There are also camps and special events - check the website for specific information.

Hours: Open Mon. - Thurs., 9am - 6pm; Fri., 9am - 8pm; Sat. - Sun., 10am- 6pm. Call first as sometimes they are closed for a private event. Closed all major holidays.

Price: $12 for the first child; $10 for a sibling; non-walkers are free with a paid sibling, or $6 without one; adults are free with paid child.

Ages: 1 - 12 years

GET AIR TRAMPOLINE PARK (San Diego County)

Poway - (858) 848-1AIR (1247); Vista - (760) 478-5867 / www.getairpoway.com; www.getairvistaca.com

Poway - 12160 Community Road; Vista - 2755 Dos Aarons Way

See GET AIR TRAMPOLINE PARK (Riverside County) (pg. 347) for a description.

Hours: Open Mon., 10am - 10pm; Tues., 10am - noon for Toddler Time and noon - 10pm all ages; Wed., 10am - 10pm; Thurs., 10am - noon for Toddler Time and noon - 10pm all ages; Fri. - Sat., 10am - 9pm, and 9pm - midnight for Club Air; Sun., 10am - 8pm.

Price: Jumpers 46" and taller are $16 an hour; jumpers 45" and under are $10 an hour at Poway, $9 an hour at Vista. Toddler Time is $10 for one child and one adult at Poway, $9 at Vista. Club Air is $15 for 2 hours, or $20 for all 3. Always check the website for special offers.

Ages: 2 years and up.

GIANT SAN DIEGO

(562) 867-9600 / www.giantpaintball.com

$$$$$

1800 Wildcat Canyon Road, Lakeside

You look like (and probably feel like) a weekend warrior in this game of paintball. Suited up with a full, wrap-around face shield and a paint ball gun (and maybe even some camouflage clothing), you are ready to run and play an incredibly intense game of "tag" and "capture the flag" at one of the outdoor "battlefield" options. Nestled in the hills, this massive arena offers several, separate, fully-themed fields include Western, which is not the Old West, but more like urban west with junky, metal vehicles and other things to hide behind; Concrete, that looks like a bombed out city with its numerous concrete tubes and half buildings; Castle, which is a huge "castle" and its grounds; and Death Valley and Bunker Hill, both of which are heavy on natural terrain meaning lots of brush, some trees, and some hills, as well as props. Moving stealthily through the scenarios, using cover, you spy an opponent, then pull the trigger, and splat - he/she has been tagged (ouch!) with a paint ball (or airsoft pellet) and is out of the game. (Realize that this can happen to you, also.) Each game lasts about fifteen minutes. Strategizing and staying focused are key elements. Oh yea, and having fun, too.

Your admission fee includes all-day play, which is about fifteen games, and one tank of CO_2. Wear dark clothing that you don't care much about, and expect it to get very dirty. Ask about kids-only events. Participants under 18 must have a waiver signed by a parent or guardian.

If you don't like the pain of a paintball, play Paintball Soft - a lower impact paintball game (.50 caliber paintballs vs. .68 in regular paintball) and lighter equipment. Airsoft players get their shot of fun here, too, on the same fields (but not at the same time as paintballers), just without all the color of paintballs! Tip: All these games are great ways to burn calories!

Hours: Open Sat. - Sun., 9am - 4pm.

Price: Field entrance is $37 for paintball players with your own equipment, plus air. A Bravo package is $55 for entry, gun, mask, all-day air and 200 paintballs. Other rentals include masks, caliber assault rifle, paintballs, etc. Airsoft is $28 per person, with your own equipment, and includes air.

Ages: Paintball Soft is great for ages 7 and up; paintball for ages 10 years old with a parent; 12 years and up on their own.

HOUSE OF AIR

(760) 201-1313 / www.houseofair.com

$$$

6133 Innovation Way, Carlsbad

What does a kangaroo, a rope, a frog and House of Air have in common? They all have to do with jumping! House of Air, described as in "indoor adrenaline park", is a huge facility with different sections that offers literally wall-to-wall trampolines - a matrix of connected, square trampolines; jousting with padded lances on a padded beam over an airbag pit; a launch pad area to safely practice new (or old) tricks; a drop zone where you can drop or leap off a 21-foot tower onto airbags, just like a stuntman; basketball dunk and dodgeball courts on trampolines; and a free-standing climbing tower with several walls (not on trampolines) using autobelay. Decorated with minimal color lends House of Air a clean look. There are also some indoor metal picnic tables and a few couches here, too.

I like that there are three small areas just for kids 3 to 6 years old - a trampoline court, a short climbing wall and a bounce house. Other special features include Air Conditioning classes (great name!) which is a full body workout class; training camps; and a three-hour parent's night out every Saturday night. All jumpers must wear special jumping socks - $2. I think House of Air lives up to its lofty name.

Hours: For ages 7 and up, Sun. - Mon., 10am - 8pm; Tues. - Thurs., 10pm - 9pm; Fri., - Sat., 10am - 10pm. For ages 3 - 6, daily, 10am - 6pm. Air Conditioning is Wed. and Sat. at 9am.

Price: 1 hour is $16 and 2 hours is $26 for ages 7 and up; $10 an hour for ages 3 - 6. Air Conditioning is $20 per 50 min. class. Parent's night out is $35 a child, ages 7 and up.

Ages: 3 years and up.

INFLATABLE WORLD

(619) 216-0199 / www.inflatableworldsd.com

$$$$

1640 Camino Del Rio North, at Westfield Mission Valley mall, San Diego

Inflatable World is just what it says it is - a world of just inflatables. There are over fifteen, giant inflatables with lots of eye appeal such as a massive tiger, menacing dinosaur, chomping shark, and a ferocious King Kong, plus super heros, monster trucks, tropical island themes, and more. Some of the inflatables are huge slides; some are obstacle courses and mazes; and some are combo bounce houses. There are a few for younger children, but they are mostly geared for kids 5 years and up. Running and playing on them will wear your kids out and they will get sweaty = fun!

During the hot summer months, slip and slide into more fun in the wet zone part of Inflatable World with a few water slides and a water balloon station. Bring your bathing suit and towel, and enjoy.

Located in the parking lot of the mall, this world offers very little shade. Know that. There are a few tables and chairs, and some have umbrellas. The floor between the inflatables is "carpeted" with artificial turf. Be prepared for your time here, too, by bringing water bottles; lots of them, as kids get thirsty while working up a sweat having fun. No outside food is allowed in, but as your wristband allows all day re-entry you can leave to grab a bite to eat at the adjacent mall. There is also an on-site concession stand that sells pre-packaged snacks and beverages, and shaved ice. It's recommended to wear long shirts and long pants, even in the summer, so participants won't get burned or rashes from the inflatables when they are hot. Socks are mandatory.

Hours: Open the end of March - August, Wed. - Fri., noon - 6pm; Sat. - Sun., 10am - 6pm. The water slides open in June.

Price: $23 for ages 13 and up (non-jumping adults are free); $20 for ages 8 - 12; $17 for ages 2 - 7; under 2 is free with a paying adult. Admission includes in and out privileges throughout the day.

Ages: 4 years and up.

INVASION LASER TAG

(760) 571-9191 / www.invasionlasertag.com

$$$

1290 W. San Marcos Boulevard, suite 101, San Marcos

Enter the future. Well, just this 5,000 square foot, multi-level laser tag arena that is futuristically and space themed. The black and gray walls and partitions (designed to look like broken stone) have occasional shots of color, mostly from exploding planets, and the props (like robots) and even the ramps are really cool looking. Fog, lights, music, and the adrenaline rush of shooting your opponents with a laser gun while trying to evade getting tagged yourself are all part of the excitement. Call or check the website for specials and info about Midnight Madness games on the weekends.

Ever see spy movies where the spies must step or jump over, and roll or crawl under lasers to get through and reach the goal on the other side of the room? Laser Maze offers you the opportunity to try your skills at dodging laser beams while incorporating mirrors, haze, and neon images into the maze-like challenge. See how high you score (i.e. how fast you complete the course without touching lasers) - mission accomplished.

Hours: Usually open Wed. - Thurs., 3pm - 8pm; Fri., 3pm - midnight; Sat., noon - midnight; Sun., noon - 8pm. Open longer hours, usually opening at 1pm, on school breaks. Closed Mon. (but open some holiday Mon.), Tues., New Year's Day, Thanksgiving, and Christmas.

Price: Laser tag is $8 for one game; $19 for 3. Lazer Frenzy is $1 for one game.

Ages: 7 years and up.

JOHN'S INCREDIBLE PIZZA CO. (San Diego County)

See JOHN'S INCREDIBLE PIZZA CO. (San Diego County) (pg. 473), under EDIBLE ADVENTURES, for details.

$$$$

K1 SPEED (San Diego County)

Carlsbad - (760) 929-2225; San Diego - (619) 241-4740 / www.k1speed.com

$$$$

Carlsbad - 6212 Carte Del Abeto; San Diego - 1709 Main Street

Kids don't have to wait until their sixteenth birthday to drive anymore (that's a scary thought!) as they can put the pedal to the metal at this large (i.e., 60,000-square-foot) indoor kart track. Accompanied by an adult, kids between the ages of 5 and 13, and between 48" to 58" tall, can drive junior karts. In separate races, adults, who are at least 58" tall, accelerate around the corners in the real race cars and go for their best time in fully-computerized, electric-powered karts - no gas fumes! Head-sock, helmet and a driver's briefing are standard. Leagues, for all ages, are also available where participants learn about cars and racing - throttle, braking, brake point, and on-track etiquette - as well as do some racing.

A public viewing area allows nonparticipants to watch the action, or play some games in the lobby, such as air hockey and video simulations. Stop off at the Pit Cafe and refuel your body. Drivers over 18 must have a valid driver's license. Younger drivers must have a waiver signed by a parent or legal guardian.

Hours: Mon. - Thurs., noon - 10pm; Fri., 11am - midnight; Sat., 10am - midnight; Sun., 10am - 10pm. There are no jr. races after 8pm on Fri. and Sat. Closed on some major holidays.

Price: $22 for one race, which is about 14 laps for adults (12 laps for juniors), or 10 minutes, plus an $8 annual membership that's required for all drivers.

Ages: Jr. racers must be at least 48"; adult racers must be at least 4' 10"

KIDSVILLE PLAYGYM

(760) 730-9022 / www.kidsvilleplaygym.com
2375 Marron Road, Carlsbad

Part gym, part indoor play place, and all exploratory, Kidsville is a clean, bright and fun destination just for little ones. Much of the flooring of the large room is padded so children using the colorful padded shapes for gymnastics, the tumbling mats, uneven bars, low balance beam, ladder attached to the wall, cargo nets, rings, and the three small trampolines won't get hurt.

Towards the back of the room is a large castle wall with a room behind it for kids to play in. It contains a very short rock climbing wall and a ladder that takes climbers up to an enclosed slide. Across the way, a little red schoolhouse has a chalkboard and some toys. A niche room has couches, a round climbing structure, and lots of toys on tot-size tables that sport various scenes. A few small, themed rooms hold an array of costumes for dress-up play, and while the construction junction also has lots of toy trucks and tools, the kitchen is fully supplied. A cute, carpeted room just for little, little ones contains a bitty ball pit, Little Tyke slides and cars, and lots of toys and stuffed animals. A fake rock hill has a slide coming out of it - great for imaginative play.

A lounge section in the front has couches for parents, plus tables and chairs. Ask about calendar events, story times, classes, membership opportunities, and Parents' Night Out.

Hours: Open play is usually Mon. - Fri., 9:30am - 6pm; Sat., 11:30am - 6pm; Sun., 11am - 6pm. Call first, especially on the weekends, as there is no open play when a birthday party is booked.

Price: 9:30 am - 2:30 pm (peak hours), $13 per child, $9 for each sibling; 2:30pm - close (non-peak hours), $8 per child. Non-walking children are $5 each, or free with full price paid sibling. The first adult is free, $5 for each additional adult.

Ages: 7 years and under, only.

KID VENTURES (4S RANCH)

(858) 207-6088 / www.kidventuresplay.com
10760 Thornmint Road, San Diego

Sometimes it does take a village - a village to entertain and encourage creative thinking and play for kids to grow and learn. This play village has life-sized buildings and stores lined up in long rows on both sides of a pathway designed to look like a street, interspersed with patches of green and even stone-looking sidewalks. Kids can immerse themselves in roles as they pretend real life.

In the little ranch market, they shop for groceries and use the cash register. Or, they can don an apron in the fully-equipped diner and make meals on the little kitchen appliances and serve them, or be waited on. They can work on Little Tyke cars at the garage. The nursery allows little ones to be big brothers or sisters as they take care of baby dolls and use strollers. Time to get dolled up, literally, in the beauty salon and spa with its vanity mirrors, brushes, dolls and more. Dress up in proper fire attire and then climb aboard the old-fashioned fire truck at the Fire Station to turn its wheel, push pedals and use the hose to rescue someone. Paints, stamps, glue, playdough and other art mediums allow every child to be an artist at the Art Studio. In front of the inviting, beach-themed mural that showcases water, a city line and a pier are some tables and chairs for adults to sit, watch, read, chat, etc. A small sand box for infants is here, too.

In another section, Kid Ventures has added fantasy and exploration elements with its good-sized pirate ship and a castle to play in, on, under and through, as well as to slide down. Dress up in princess and knight attire, and ride a rocking horse. Young adventurers can also negotiate a rock wall that is designed on a wall painted to look like a grassy hill. Toys throughout the facility include Little Tyke cars, tunnels, balls, and more

I appreciate the attention to detail at Kid Ventures - the openness of all the areas - all within easy viewing; the colorful, but not cutesy wall murals; the size of the room and kinds of furnishings and toys; and how kids can have a blast while parents can equally enjoy their time here relaxing at the table and chairs. The cafe offers sandwiches, salads, muffins, smoothies, a variety of coffee drinks and other snacks.

Enrichment activities are offered about every hour, such as games, arts and crafts projects, story time, sing-a-longs, and more. Check out camps, classes (such as Super Hero training), parties, and other events. Note: Socks must be worn by kids and adults. No outside food is allowed in. Note that this location is bigger than the Eastlake location and has more play places.

Hours: Open Mon. - Fri., 9:30am - 5:30pm; Sat., 9am - noon. Closed Sat. afternoon and Sun. for private parties. Closed major holidays.

Price: $18 a child - walking and older; $9 for sibling; $5 for ages under 1 if not accompanied by a paid child.

Ages: 1 ½ - 7 years.

KID VENTURES (EASTLAKE)

(619) 651-8622 / www.indoorplaysandiego.com
851 Showroom Place, Chula Vista

See above entry for details about this fantastic, indoor play place for kids. This location is set up like a village in one, large room with several stores and buildings all around it. As 4S Ranch, it features a pretend market, nursery, and fire station; castle and pirate ship playgrounds; and cafe with a sit down area for adults. This location also has a toddler room for little ones with art supplies and books and toys; a theater that offers a place to see a show, one that your kids put on; and a place to saddle up on a stick horse or rocking horse, dress up in cowboy duds, and mosey on over to the Western Saloon with its hitching post, horse mural and corral. There are also two outside areas - a small one in front with a few tables and chairs, and a much larger one in the back that has some covering, wooden fencing all around, a few benches and artificial grass covering the ground - good for hanging out, or a party.

Hours: Open Mon. - Thurs., 10am - 6pm; Fri., 10am - 8pm; Sat., 9am - noon. Closed Sat. afternoon and Sun. for private parties.

Price: $18 a child - walking and older; $9 for sibling; $5 for ages under 1 if not accompanied by a paid child.

Ages: 1 ½ - 7 years.

KID VENTURES (LIBERTY STATION)

(619) 573-9625 / www.indoorplaysandiego.com
2865 Sims Road, San Diego

See KID VENTURES (4S RANCH) (pg. 483) for details about this wonderful indoor play place for kids. This location is much, much smaller. It does have a fire truck/station area, market store, play cafe, nursery, and cafe, plus castle and pirate ship play area. There is an outside lawn area, too, and the whole Liberty Station complex with restaurants, shops and open play space to enjoy.

Hours: Open Mon., 9:30am - 4pm; Tues. - Thurs., 9:30am - 5:30pm; Fri., 9:30am - 8pm; Sat., 9am - noon. Closed Sat. afternoon and Sun. for private parties.

Price: $18 a child - walking and older; $9 for sibling; $5 for ages under 1 if not accompanied by a paid child.

Ages: 1 ½ - 7 years.

KRAUSE FAMILY SKATE AND BIKE PARK

(858) 246-6731 - skate park; (619) 298-3576 - Y.M.C.A. / www.ymca.org
3401 Clairemont Drive, San Diego

Skateboarders, scooter-riders, BMXers, and roller bladers flip (sometimes literally) for this huge (55,000 square feet!), gated, outdoor skate park that's associated with the Mission Valley Y.M.C.A. It has numerous and variously-sized, mostly wooden ramps and half-pipes, plus grinding boxes, rails, and other street skate elements, as well as areas to simply skate. A large, in-ground, concrete bowl has a maximum ten-foot depth - a favorite feature. There is also a good-sized beginner area. Sessions are about three hours long. The park is supervised and all participants must wear elbow and knee pads and a helmet. There are no rentals available. Bikes are allowed on certain days/times. Skaters and bikers 17 and under must have a waiver signed by a parent in person, or notarized, for their first session. Ask about skate camps and/or lessons. Note that SOUTH CLAIREMONT RECREATION CENTER and POOL (pg. 516) is right next door.

Hours: Open most of the year (traditional school year) Mon. - Fri., 2pm - 5:30pm; Sat. - Sun., 11am - 5:30pm. Open in the summer daily, 11am - 8pm. Check on holidays hours.

Price: $10 per session; or $40 for a membership, then $5 per session.

Ages: 7 years and up.

LE FUNLAND (San Diego County)

(619) 209-7368 / www.shoppingparkwayplaza.com

415 Parkway Plaza inside Parkway Plaza mall, El Cajon

See LE FUNLAND (Los Angeles County) (pg. 34) for details on this small indoor play place.

Hours: Open Mon. - Sat., 10am - 9pm; Sun., 11am - 7pm.

Price: $15 per child; adults are free.

Ages: 52" and under, only.

LEGO STORE - MINI MODEL BUILD (San Diego County)

San Diego, Fashion Valley - (619) 294-9437; San Diego, Westfield UTC - (858) 824-9170 / www.lego.com/en-us/stores/events/mini-model-builds

San Diego - 7007 Friars Road, suite 965A in Fashion Valley mall; San Diego - 4545 La Jolla Village Dr. in Westfield UTC

A free LEGO mini model? I'm in! Bring your child, ages 6 to 14 years old (strict age restrictions), to your favorite LEGO store on the first Tuesday or Wednesday of every month and they get to build (and take home) a really cool and unique mini model for free. Unique because the model kits are not available to purchase, per se, and are themed. Quantities are limited. Note that kids must be a registered LEGO VIP member to participate, but it's free to sign up. Registration begins online at 10am EST on the 15th of the month prior to the next month's event (i.e. sign up in April for May, etc.). Check out the malls listed above for other activities to do there.

Hours: The first Tues. and Wed. of each month, between 3pm - 7pm.

Price: Free

Ages: 6 - 14 years old, only.

LUV 2 PLAY (San Diego County)

(855) PLAY-002 (752-9002) / www.luv2play.com

1962-1964 Hacienda West Drive, Vista

See LUV 2 PLAY (Riverside County) (pg. 349) for details on this great indoor playground.

Hours: Open Mon. - Thurs., 9am - 8pm; Fri. - Sat., 9am - 9pm; Sun., 10am - 6pm.

Price: Parents, kids 0 - 5 months old, and siblings 13 and older are free, as are ages 11 months and under with a paid sibling. Mon. - Thurs., ages 6 months - 4 years are $11.95; 5 - 12 years are $13.95; siblings are $10.95. Fri. - Sun. and holidays, ages 6 months - 4 years are $13.95; 5 - 12 years are $15.95; siblings are $12.95.

Ages: 12 months - 12 years

MESA RIM CLIMBING AND FITNESS CENTER

Mira Mesa, San Diego - (858) 201-4411; Mission Valley, San Diego - (619) 908-1611 / www.mesarim.com

Mira Mesa, San Diego - 10110 Mesa Rim Rd.; Mission Valley, San Diego - 405 Camino Del Rio. S.

Step by step, rock by rock - a journey up the rock climbing walls is exciting, physically challenging, and self-confidence building. These facilities are more than 30,000 square feet huge! They sport numerous rock climbing walls - some of which are short, and some are really, really tall at fifty-two feet - at interesting angles. Some are relatively easy and some are just crazy hard. All of it is good for bouldering, top roping, and lead climbing opportunities. Everyone from novices to experts will find routes that fit their level and even take them to the next. These are premier facilities dedicated to the sport of rock climbing. A separate room upstairs has the latest gym equipment, a yoga room with classes, and a party room (I mean for birthday parties, and such). The second floor also has a nice overlook room with some comfy chairs and couches, and WiFi.

A day pass includes the climbing gym, yoga classes, and usage of the fitness equipment. Don't know how to belay? Take a lesson, offered for ages 14 and up, for only $10, and know that climbers must pass the belay certification test prior to top rope climbing. Street shoes are not allowed on the walls, so you can rent them here. Signed waivers are required for all participants. Mesa Rim offers numerous classes, competitions, camps, and expeditions for adults and kids, including the two-hour Mini Monsters (for ages 4 - 6), the two-hour Rock Monsters (for ages 7 to 12), and Merit Badge Programs. And if you are really serious about climbing technique and improving yourself on a whole new level check out The Academy, located next door to the Mira Mesa facility, for individual and team training.

Hours: Open Mon. - Fri., 6am - 11pm; Sat. - Sun., 8am - 9pm. Call for the holiday schedule.

Price: $22 for a day pass for adults; $18 for military, student, and ages 11 - 17; $14 for children 10 and under. Gear package rental, which includes shoes, harness, chalk bag, and belay device, is $8. The Monsters classes are $30 per lesson, which includes gear rental and day pass.

Ages: 4 years and up.

MR. PAINTBALL FIELD U.S.A.

(760) 737-8870 / www.mrpaintballusa.com

25320 Lake Wohlford Road, Escondido

$$$$$

Armed with semiautomatic paint guns and dressed in goggles, mask, and layers of clothing (to reduce the somewhat painful impact of the paintballs), you are now ready to play the wildly exhilarating and intense game of paintball. Twelve different fields on 90 acres of land are the playing area where hills, valleys, trees, props, man-made huts, huge spools, villages, natural obstacles, and trenches are used for both offensive and defensive tactical maneuvers. Try to zap your opponents with paintballs, without getting hit yourself. Games last fifteen to thirty minutes. Bring running shoes, a water bottle, and, most of all, stamina. Note: Participants 17 and under must have a signed parental waiver. With all the sport and intensity and just as much fun, though a little less colorful, is the game of airsoft, also played here. Note that there is a pro shop and a snack bar on the premises.

Hours: Open for paintball and airsoft, Wed. - Fri., 9am - 3pm; Sat. - Sun. and most holidays, 8:30am - 3:30pm. Closed Christmas. Open during the week over holidays and for groups of 20 or more, with reservations.

Price: $25 per player (airsoft or paintball) if you come self-equipped. Prices start at $50 per person for the basic rentals which includes all-day play, face mask, a marker, air, and paintballs.

Ages: 10 years and up.

NED BAUMER AQUATIC CENTER

(858) 538-8083 / www.sandiego.gov

10440 Black Mountain Road, Mira Mesa

$$

Perfect for a hot summer day! The aquatic center has a large main pool for both lap and recreational swim, and a short, twisty slide, as well as two shallow pools for kids. The water play structure has hoses with water squirting out from the sides, a short enclosed slide, and other fun apparatus.

Hours: Open most of the year, usually Mon., Wed., Fri., 12:30pm - 3pm; Sat., noon - 3pm. Closed Sun., tournaments, and major holidays. Open extended hours in the summer.

Price: $4 for adults; $2 for seniors and ages 15 and under.

Ages: 3 years and up.

PELLY'S MINI GOLF

(858) 481-0363 / www.delmargolfcenter.com

15555 Jimmy Durante Boulevard, Del Mar

$$$

Though many of the obstacles on these two rock-lined, mini golf courses are simply twists and turns or bumps on the blue course ways (i.e. not super challenging), the surrounding themed embellishments are creative and fun. The Ocean Adventure, for instance, sports sculptures of dolphins, seals, an octopus, and a gray whale, including one that spouts water; an almost life-size shark cage on hole #11 (enter through the bars); huge whales tails in a water feature; and a good-sized ship. The Surfing Safari features a wave sculpture with water spurting, surfboards, and more. Other adornments include a large pond and more water elements, bridges, palm trees (for the Southern California feel), and ambiance music.

The courses are eco-friendly in that facts about recycling, water conservation and protecting the environment are posted at holes. There is even developed educational programs on these topics geared for scouts to earn badges and for school groups. A snack bar is on the premises. Note: Older kids might want to try out a bigger back swing at the adjacent driving range with sixty-five teeing stations.

Hours: Open Sun. - Thurs., 9am - 9pm; Fri. - Sat., 9am - 10pm. Closed Christmas.

Price: $9.50 for adults; $7.50 for seniors, military and ages 12 and under for the first round; $4.50 for round two for adults; $3.50 for kids.

Ages: 4 years and up.

PLAYTOWN INDOOR PLAYGROUND

(619) 447-PLAY (7529) / www.goplaytown.com

858 Jackman Street, El Cajon

$$$

Imagine your young children playing in a safe, clean, indoor environment, and having a blast, while meeting new friends, as you keep an eye on them and enjoy socializing with friends, as well. Welcome to Play Town! Geared with young ones in mind the small bounces, toy cars to drive, tubes to crawl through, play treehouse, play houses, mini ride-on coaster, soft play area, castle, and other fun elements keep them busy for hours in one large, brightly-colored room. (Note that everyone must wear socks.) You are welcome to bring in your own food, or purchase beverages here. Check out the website for info about weekly special programs for crafts, messy activities, music, and more.

Hours: Open Mon. - Sat., 9am - 6pm; Sun., 9am - noon. Note that weekend hours fluctuate, depending if there is a private party. Closed New Year's day, Easter, Mother's Day, 4th of July, Thanksgiving, Christmas Eve, and Christmas.

Price: $11 for the first child 1 year and older; $9 for a sibling; $5 for an infant under 1 if he comes with just an adult, otherwise under 1 is free with paid sibling. The first two adults are free.

Ages: Infant - 6 years.

PLAYWERX

(760) 804-1600 / www.playwerx.com

6060 Avenida Encinas, suite B, Carlsbad

PlayWerx is not work at all - it's just fun. The clean, large room has a main, enclosed (with netting), multi-story, play structure with foam obstacles, a ball pit, lots of climbing up and down levels, crawling space, rope swings, slides, and some foam blocks. Socks are required. The room is airy as a big portion is open, though gated, to the outdoors via a warehouse-style, rolled up door. Along with shelves of books, this room also has comfy couches and lounge chairs in groupings, making it so easy to keep an eyes on (and ears alert to) your kids. A smaller, offshoot, simple room is for toddlers that contains stuffed animals and other toys. There is a cafe here, too, with an array of coffee beverages, smoothies, pizza, sandwiches, snacks and gluten-free snacks. PlayWerx is "next door" to VITAL CLIMBING GYM (San Diego County) (pg. 492).

Hours: Open Tues. - Fri., 10am - 6pm; Sat., 9am - 7pm; Sun., 10am - 6pm. Closed Mon. and some holidays. Check the website for early closings due to private parties.

Price: $12 for ages 4 and up; $9 for ages 3 and under; parents are free.

Ages: 1 - 10 years old.

PUMP IT UP (San Diego County)

Chula Vista - (619) 216-9812; Poway - (858) 679-5867; San Marcos - (760) 510-8000 / www.pumpitupparty.com

Chula Vista - 751 Design Court, suite A; Poway - 12760 Danielson Court, suite J; San Marcos - 445 Ryan Drive, suite 103

The term "pump it up" used to mean getting buff by working out, but now it means "Have a fantastic time playing in this inflatable indoor playground!". Two rooms that are filled with huge, primary-color inflatables such as giant slides, creative obstacle courses, bounce houses, a jousting pit (using foam-type lances), sports bounces (for shooting hoops, or soft play soccer or softball) and a rock-'em-sock-'em ring, plus gigantic hard-foam blocks, shapes and gears make this place an absolute blast for kids (and adults). This place has rightly won "best party ever" awards among guests. And, actually, all that bouncing around makes it quite a workout, too.

Open Jump times are offered on select dates and times and, as each location varies, call or check the website of the one you want to visit. Note that in San Marcos, Open Jump is for ages 10 and under, only. The rest of the days and times the facilities are available only for parties for all ages (up to 150 pounds per), plus field trips, boy scout/girl scout badge programs, special times for kids on the autism spectrum, or other outings. Socks and a signed waiver are required for each person at each facility. Check out the Glow Parties which add another element of fun when the regular lights are turned off and the black lights and special effect lighting are turned on. Kids are given glow necklaces as well.

Hours: Check the location's website calendar for details on Open Jump and other speciality jump times as the times vary even within a particular month.

Price: Open Jump is $10 per child. In San Marcos, siblings 22 months and under are free with a paid sibling. Adults are free at all locations.

Ages: 2 years old or 34" and taller, depending on the location.

RANCHO PENASQUITOS SKATE PARK

(858) 538-8131 / www.sandiego.gov/park-and-recreation/centers/skateparks

10111 Carmel Mountain Road, Rancho Penasquitos

A good mixture of wood and cement, this 22,000-square-foot, unsupervised skate park - labeled an Advanced Street Park - is pretty amazing. It features four stair handrails; grind boxes; multi-height grind ledges; hipped bank ramps; flat rails; half-pipes; quarter-pipes; a spine; a multi-height pyramid with ledges and rails; straight and curved bench style ledges; and more. There are also shade sails to help keep off the heat. A helmet and knee and elbow pads are required by city mandate. A parent or legal guardian must accompany children 12 and under. Rollerbladers and skateboarders are welcome.

Hours: Open daily, 10am - dusk. Closed holidays.

Price: Free

Ages: 7 years and up.

RICOCHET

(760) 919-9800 / imperial.aerosportsparks.com
450 W. Aten Road, Imperial

Like its parent company, Aerosports, this indoor trampoline play space has a large main arena with so many trampolines and other fun "extras" that it has kids flipping over coming here. Play on slanted wall trampolines used to launch yourself; foam-padded landing pit to practice tricks; a few long trampoline runways; and basketball and dodgeball courts. There is also a nice-sized area for younger jumpers (48" and under only) to practice their best moves (or just to move!) along with a mini foam pit and a bounce house. A snack bar area, a small arcade and video room, and a sitting area with couches plus tables and chairs complete your time here. Note that there are special events offered like dodgeball tournaments and black lighting and music on certain Friday nights.

Hours: Open Sun. - Thurs., 10am - 9pm; Fri. - Sat., 10am - 11pm.
Price: $12 for the first hour for ages 9 and up, $8 for the second; $8 for the first hour for ages 3 - 8, $4 for the second; ages 2 and under are free with a paying adult. A basketball pass (no trampoline time) is $5 for the day.
Ages: 2 years and up.

ROCKIN' JUMP (San Diego County)

(858) 693-5867 / sandiego.rockinjump.com
8190 Miralani Drive, San Diego

This places is really jumping! It has a huge open jump arena with a patchwork of a multitude of trampolines; a dodgeball area (so fun to play this on a trampoline!); the X-Beam which is using a padded lance to bop your opponent off the fairly wide, padded beam into a foam-padded pit; a Stunt Bag area for safely practicing flips, or just jumping onto the massive, air-filled stunt bag; and a slam dunk zone (mini-basketball) and yes, this is on a trampoline! Non-trampolining activities include climbing up the rock climbing wall (because visitors don't have enough physical activity here as it is!); playing 18 holes at the outdoor, miniature golf course (which doesn't have any special features, but is lovely); playing arcade games; snacking on pizza, hot dogs, salads, sandwich wraps and more; and even a place to rest and hang for a bit. Note that all jumping participants must use the Rockin' Jump socks - $3.

Hours: Open Mon., Tues., Thurs., Fri., open jump, 3pm - 8pm; plus Tues. for tots, 9am - 11am. Open Wed. for tots, 9am - 11am then open jump from noon - 8pm; Fri., Rockin' Fri./Neon, 8pm - 10pm; Sat., tots, 8am - 10am, then open jump from 10am - 8pm, followed by Rockin Sat./Neon, 8pm - 10pm; Sun., open jump, 11am - 6pm.
Price: $16 for 60 min. of jump time; $21 for 90 min., etc. $7 for tots only time - for one parent and child ($3 each additional child). $18 for Rockin' Fri. or Sat. Add mini golf to any open jump time for $5 per person. Mini golf by itself is $8.50 for adults; $7 for ages 17 and under.
Ages: 18 months and older, depending on the time and day.

SALVATION ARMY RAY AND JOAN KROC CORPS COMMUNITY CENTER

(619) 287- KROC (5762) / www.sd.kroccenter.org
6845 University Avenue, San Diego

Oh my gosh - this facility is amazing! This long series of buildings contains so many wonderful activities and programs that if it's not offered here, it must not be fun. (That might be a slight exaggeration, but only a slight one.)

Join in and play a game of basketball, volleyball, and badminton in the gym. Ages 16 years and up are welcome to use the fitness area for aerobics, weight training, kickboxing, and other exercise equipment and classes. Just hang out in the adjoining recreation room, or pick up a game of air hockey, billiards, table tennis, foosball, and/or play a board game. Swim a couple of laps in the twenty-five meter competition pool or just splash around on a hot summer's day in the rec pool. Check out the recreation field for soccer, flag football, and lacrosse. The field also has a walking track. Open to group, or individuals, is a thirty-foot tall rock climbing tower that allows participants to actually go climb a rock! A parental waiver must be signed for kids 17 years and under. The indoor ice arena is open for general skating sessions, skating lessons, and for hockey leagues. Nonparticipants can watch from ringside seats. (Brrrring a jacket!)

The performing arts center boasts a 600-seat theater where family-appropriate shows are presented, often by youth theater. This is also where Kroc Community Church meets on Sunday mornings at 10:30am - all are welcome. The center also has a dance studio, band and orchestra room, large multi-purpose room, art workshop rooms, and vocal practice room. The adjacent education center is comprised of the Cox Technology Center, Kroc Center Library, visual arts studio, study hall, and tutoring rooms. The Cox Technology Center has twenty-four computer terminals for guests to access the internet and get school or work done. An abundance of programs (e.g., day camps, after-school programs, etc.) for all ages and interests complete this center. Also note that this is the Salvation Army's food and toy distribution center during the holidays. Whew! And if all this activity makes you hungry, there is a snack and coffee shop on site.

Each activity has its own hours, prices, skill levels, and age requirements, so please call first. Check the website for the many special events held here throughout the year. Note that there is a Play Care Center (child care) onsite.

Hours: Public ice skating sessions are usually available Mon., 3:30pm - 5:30pm; Wed., 10:30am - 12:15pm and 3:30pm - 5:30pm; Fri., 10:30am - 12:15pm and 3:30pm - 5:30pm; Sat.1pm - 3pm; Sun., 1:30pm - 3pm. Rock climbing is open Thurs., 4pm - 6pm; Fri., 6:30pm - 8:30pm; Sat., 10am - 1pm; Sun., 1pm - 4:30pm. Recreation swim is open Mon. - Fri., 1pm - 4:30pm, plus Fri., 7pm - 8:30pm; Sat. - Sun., 1pm - 5:30pm. The recreation center is open daily. The Cox Tech Center and library are open Mon. - Sat., 10am - 6pm. Closed Sun. The facility is closed on most holidays.

Price: Day passes are a fantastic deal at $10 for adults; $8 for ages 3 - 17. Day passes include recreational swimming, access to the field, the rec room, the game room, computer lab, the fitness center (age restrictions apply), and the gym (basketball courts, etc., when open), plus a single session of rock climbing. Ice skating, $10 per session, includes skate rentals; after-school specials and some Sunday sessions are $8. Ask about membership here or about multi-use passes.

Ages: 6 years and up.

SAN DIEGO RC RACEWAY

(858) 831-0477 / www.sdrcraceway.com
8725 Production Avenue, Miramar

$$$

Racing your remote control car or truck on this indoor track can be a fun activity for the family, and it's easy to get hooked on this hobby. The relatively huge, hard-packed dirt track (that gets changed up frequently) always has lots of bumps (i.e. jumps), turns, and banks, making it a great course to race. Beginners and kids, particularly, have a class on Saturday mornings (beats watching cartoons!) to learn the how-tos. The class is from 9am to 10am. If you need any automotive parts, the store is fully stocked and the large pit room has plenty of long tables to repair whatever parts need fixin', as well as staff and other people around to help out. Even if you don't race a car (and this facility doesn't have rentals), it's a fun sport to watch.

Hours: Open Mon. - Fri., 2pm - 10pm; Sat., 10am - 10pm, Sun., 10am - 8pm. Race days are usually Wed. and Fri. at 7pm, and Sat. at 4.

Price: Free to watch. $20 for non-members to race for the day/night.

Ages: 5 years and up.

SKY ZONE (San Diego County)

Chula Vista - (619) 754-9782; San Marcos - (619) 609-0960 / www.skyzone.com
Chula Vista - 851 Showroom Place, suite 100; San Marcos - 860 Los Vallecitos Blvd.

$$$$

See SKY ZONE (Los Angeles County) (pg. 40) for details. Ask about Toddler Times, special needs times, discounts, and more.

Hours: Chula Vista - Open Mon. - Thurs., 2pm - 9pm; Fri., 2pm - 11pm (ask about Glow restrictions); Sat., 10am - 11pm; Sun., 11am - 9pm. San Marcos - Open Mon. - Thurs., 2pm - 8pm; Fri., 2pm - 10:30pm; Sat., 10am - 10:30pm; Sun., 10am - 8pm. Open during the summer and holidays extended hours.

Price: Chula Vista: $15 for 60 min. during the week, $17 on weekends; $20 for 90 min. during the week, $22 on weekends. San Marcos: $16 for 60 min., $19 for 90.

Ages: 2 years and up.

SPEED CIRCUIT and LASER TAG

(858) 586-7500 / www.miramarspeedcircuit.com
8123 Miralani Drive

$$$$

It's all about speed. Well, maybe control and speed. This facility boasts an indoor, quarter-mile, asphalt track that allows drivers to race around corners and on the straightaway. Get all geared up with a helmet, racing suit (if you want), and neck guard for your experience. Regular go karts are for drivers 60" and taller, while junior karts are for drivers 48" to 59" tall. Kids 12 years or under and at least 48" tall can sign up for a Saturday or Sunday morning beginning driving class where safety is the focus. Plenty of drive time is included in that $40 fee. Reservations are required.

The thrill of the chase is also on in the 5,000 square-foot, multi-story, futuristic-themed, Laser Tag arena. Music, flashing lights, neon colors, really cool atmosphere and fog all add to the intensity of the game as you run, hide, seek and zap your opponents while defending the base.

There are tables to sit at in the lobby, as well as some arcade games, plus air hockey or billiards to play. Food is available on site at the cafe which offers a small, but good, selection of food of sandwiches, salads, snacks and beverages.

Hours: Open Mon. - Thurs., 11am - 11pm; Fri., 11am - midnight; Sat., 10am - midnight; Sun., 10am - 11pm.
Price: $19.95 per person per race (10 min. of track time), plus an annual race license for $7. Laser tag is $9 per game/course. Closed-toed shoes are required.
Ages: 48" height requirement.

TEMPEST FREERUNNING ACADEMY - Vista

(760) 305-8926 / www.tempestacademy.com
2620 Progress Street, Vista

$$$$

See TEMPEST FREERUNNING ACADEMY - Northridge (pg. 42) for details about this fantastically-themed and charged up place to parkour and do advanced maneuvers and tricks of freerunning. This location is set up much like the one in Hawthorne, but with black and white "bricks" that are set up like a combo of Minecraft and Legos, and even half an airplane to jump on/off. So creative and challenging!

Hours: Open Gym for ages 17 and up is Mon. - Thurs., 8pm - 11pm; Sat., 3pm - 5pm. Open Gym for mixed ages (9 years and up) is Mon. and Thurs., 6pm - 8pm. Monitored Gym for ages 9 - 16 is Fri., 6pm - 9pm; Sat., noon - 2pm. Closed Sun. and certain holidays. Check on line for a schedule of classes.
Price: $15 for ages 17 and up for Open Gym; $20 per person per Monitored and Open Gym for mixed ages.
Ages: 4 years and up, depending on the class.

THE PAINTBALL PARK

Alpine - (866) 985-4932; San Diego - (866) 985-4932 / www.thepaintballpark.com
Alpine - 25 Browns Road; San Diego - 2522T Maxam Avenue

$$$$$

See THE PAINTBALL PARK - Camp Pendleton (pg. 490) below for a description. At the Alpine location there are 3 fields up in the mountains. The terrain is more hilly and tho props are definitely added, there is a lot of nature to hide in and behind, and to ambush from. At the San Diego location there over 30 acres and 3 main fields to play paintball, including Base Camp and Western Town with small, dilapidated, one-room buildings, and rusted vehicles and other props, plus palm trees and brush to run around. It is open for civilian access via the military shuttle.

Hours: Both are open Sat. - Sun., 8:30am - 5pm. Open during the week for private parties.

THE PAINTBALL PARK - Camp Pendleton

(866) 985-4932 / www.thepaintballpark.com
1700 Vandegrift Boulevard (near Rodeo Grounds), Camp Pendleton, Oceanside

$$$$$

Although the paintball park is on in the marine base, anyone can play. The park is thirty acres huge with four turf tournament-size fields that boast of bunkers, buildings, trenches, big trees, sandbag fortifications, and real tanks and other military vehicles to keep play interesting and challenging. There are also ten rec fields, including a 6,000 square foot Castle Field. Capture the Flag is the most common game played, although alternatives include Center Flag, where two teams go for just one flag, and Elimination, where the winning team must annihilate (figuratively speaking) all members of the opposing team. Wear a long-sleeve shirt and long pants, even on summer days. Protective gear is necessary. A few alternatives to paintball are no-bruises Paintball Lite (low-impact paintball for kids and beginners [and wimpy people like me!]) and playing airsoft at the military-like Airsoft Park with two close-combat killhouses, a village marketplace, and tanks and vehicles.

For parties, try Splatmaster, ideal for ages 6 to 9, where kids are engaged in paintball-type games, running around inflatable bunkers and shooting at targets, but with smaller paintballs and lightweight guns that shoot about half as fast.

A snack bar has, yes, snacks, and soda, plus there are fast food restaurants just down the road. You are welcome to bring in your own food. Participants under 18 must have a waiver signed by a parent or guardian.

Note: As the paintball park is on base at Camp Pendleton, all participants are required to show photo ID at the entrance gate. Plus, there is a short form on the website to fill out that must be received a minimum of 7 days prior to your first visit. Drivers must have proof of insurance and registration for the vehicle. Entrance is off Highway 76 and left on College Blvd.

Hours: Open most of the year, Fri. - Sun., 8:30am - 5pm. The fields are open for night games by reservation only. Open in the summer, Wed. - Sun., 8:30am - 5pm. Always call ahead to check on rental gear availability. Open during the week for groups of 15, or more.

Price: Paintball is $20 per person if you have your own equipment; $54 per person with rental equipment - (goggles, semiautomatic paint gun [upgrades available], CO2 refills, and 500 paintballs). Paintball Lite is $45, which includes everything. Airsoft is $25 for self-equipped walk-ons; $54 for full rental equipment with a pistol; $10 more for a rifle. A three-hour Splatmaster party is $44 per child, with a minimum of 10 kids, that includes all the equipment.

Ages: 6 - 9 years for Splatmaster; 8 years and up for Airsoft; 10 years and up for paintball.

ULTRAZONE (San Diego County)

(619) 221-0100 / www.ultrazonesandiego.com
3146 Sports Arena Boulevard, suite 21, San Diego

Come play laser tag - the tag of the future! Put on your vest, pick up your laser gun, and for fifteen minutes you'll play hard and fast. Laser tag is action packed, and the thrill of the chase really gets your adrenaline pumping! This Ultrazone, with its dark, cave-like setting, is themed "Underground City." The multi-level city, or playing arena, is maze-like and huge. Run up and down ramps; seek cover behind floor-to-ceiling walls; duck into partly hidden doorways; find your way in and around the myriad of partitions and obstacles; and zap your opponents. For more interaction and acceleration of the game there are robotic enemies and targets that allow players to acquire more points. Tip: The best times for younger kids to play is weekday afternoons and early evenings, or during the day on weekends. Older kids come out here in hordes at nighttime.

Hours: Open Mon. - Thurs., 4pm - 10pm; Fri., 2pm - 1am; Sat., 10am - 1am; Sun., 10am - 10m. Open in the summer at 2pm Mon. - Thurs. - the rest of the hours are the same.

Price: $9 a game. Although game play is not exclusive for kids at this time, ages 7 - 10 pay only $7.50 per game Sat. and Sun. from 10am - 2pm. Games must be completed by 2pm. Games are only $7.50 per, too, Fri. - Sat., 11pm - 1am.

Ages: Must be at least 7 years old.

URBAN JUNGLE

(619) 334-6107 / www.urbanjunglefunpark.com
8711 Magnolia Ave #300, Santee

Urban Jungle, decorated like a city scape, has a little bit of everything to keep kids active and happy. The huge, multi-story play structure (definitely not just for little kids!) has tubes, tunnels, steps, slides, obstacles, cargo nets, and lots more. A free-standing tower to climb is designed to look like a sky scraper on one side (though it's really not quite as tall as one at 24') with window sills and stories to go up, and a rock-climbing wall on the other side. Climbers are hooked into a harness and top-rope.

A 50' long inflatable obstacle course on the top level, with tons of fun elements, has the kids racing up and over and under and through - it will wear them out in healthy ways! Then, they can whoosh down the four tall, curvy, side-by-side slides. Life-size video games encourage more movement and some dance moves. A small, separate toddler room has fire poles, big foam blocks, little slides, and toys. Bounce away in the trampoline room that's divided for younger kids and older kids to bounce, try tricks and even play dodgeball. Parents, you have your own spaces to relax and chill, all within sight of most of the action. A small snack bar is in the lobby. All participants must wear grip socks and have signed waivers.

Hours: Open most of the year Mon. - Thurs., 1pm - 8pm (open Wed. for ages 5 and under, only, from 10am - 1pm); Fri., 1pm - 9pm; Sat., 10am - 9pm; Sun., 10am - 8pm. Open longer on school breaks and holidays.

Price: Mon. - Fri., $10 for one hour, $14 for two hours; Sat. - Sun., $12 for one hour, $18 for two hours. Observers are free.

Ages: 3 years and up.

VERTICAL HOLD

Poway - (858) 748-9011; San Diego - (619) 299-1124; San Marcos - (760) 480-1429 / www.verticalhold.com
Poway - 13026 Stowe Dr.; San Diego - 2074 Hancock St.; San Marcos - 992 Rancheros Dr.

Experience the thrill and physical challenge (i.e., you'll get sweaty) of rock climbing in a safe, indoor, controlled atmosphere. Novice climbers can learn the basic skills and importance of a well-placed foot and/or hand, while experienced climbers will enjoy the opportunity to continue training by sharpening their skills. This is a great sport to introduce kids to because it builds confidence, physical fitness, and strategic thinking. (All this just by rock climbing - and we thought school was important!) Staff members are experienced climbers and are always around to instruct and encourage, and if you don't have a friend to belay with, use the auto belay system - no partner needed. Children must be 13 to use auto belay without supervision.

Multi-colored stones mark various routes on the walls, overhangs, and arches for top roping and lead climbing, as well as on the bouldering cave. Although a child may be tentative at the beginning, by the end of the first time, he/she is usually literally climbing the walls, and having a great time doing it. So, if you're looking for a creative way to channel your child's excess energy, turn off the cartoons, then come *rock* and roll! Note: A party room is on the premises. Programs are available at all location for scouts, teen climbing camps, and more. Lessons and membership are available. Signed waivers are required for all climbers.

Hours: Poway - Open Mon. - Fri., 9am - 10pm; Sat. - Sun., 9am - 9pm. San Diego - Open Mon. - Fri., 9am - 11pm; Sat. - Sun., 9am - 9pm. San Marcos - Open Mon. - Fri., noon - 9pm; Sat. - Sun., 9am - 9pm. Close some national holidays.

Price: An all-day pass, $17 per person. Harness and shoe rentals are an additional $7. Beginner class is $30, which includes an all-day pass and rental gear.

Ages: 5 years and up.

VITAL CLIMBING GYM (San Diego County)

Carlsbad - (760) 689-2651; Oceanside - (760) 385 - 8209 / www.vitalclimbinggym.com

Carlsbad - 6102 Avenida Encinas, suite L; Oceanside - 525 S Coast Hwy.

$$$$

All that energy and nowhere to go to expend it? Then, it might be Vital to come to these bouldering gyms! Bouldering is a little different from straight up rock climbing in that ropes and harnesses aren't necessary - it's a matter of you clinging to (at least I cling to) and climbing the "rocks" that have the thick safety crash pads underneath. This type of dynamic exercise is great for the body and mind. Follow any one of the color-coded duct tape routes up the walls and up and over the angles. The walls are about sixteen feet tall, and the longest one is about sixty feet.

There is a little snack area with beverages, plus a loft/chill area overseeing some of the routes that has a couch and some chairs. The Oceanside location has a sweet little wood-paneled room with some couches to relax in, as well as a weight room/work out room with weights, rings and more equipment, and another small area with more equipment. Lockers are available. Ages 15 and under must have a parent present while they climb. Waivers for all ages must be signed. Members perk - these facilities are open 24 hours to its members. The staff leaves at 9pm so members then own the gym - the type of music played, using the equipment, working out, or just hanging out. Note that the gym in Carlsbad is around the corner from PLAYWERX (pg. 487).

Hours: Open daily, 11am - 9pm. Holiday hours fluctuate. (Open 24 hours for members).

Price: Carlsbad - $14 per person for a day pass. Oceanside - $17 per. Optional shoe rentals are $2. Climb for free on your birthday!

Ages: At least 5 years, and up.

—GREAT OUTDOORS—

AGUA CALIENTE COUNTY PARK

(760) 765-1188- park; (877) 565-3600 - reservation / www.sdparks.org

39555 County Route S2, Julian

$$

For a more therapeutic take on life, come visit Agua Caliente Springs County Park. It features a big, glass-enclosed pool with water temperature maintained at 102 degrees as it is fed by underground hot mineral springs. Ahhhh - feels so good! However, only ages 14 years and up may use the indoor pool. The two outdoor pools are available for all ages, and the fifteen-foot by thirty-foot shallow one is especially fun for children.

The park also has a general store, shuffleboard courts, horseshoe pits, play areas, hiking trails, over 140 campsites, and seven camping cabins that are outfitted with a table, two queen size bed frames (no mattresses or bedding!) and a bathroom, plus a fire ring and picnic table outside. There are several trails to choose from, including a half-mile loop called Ocotillo Ridge Nature Trail and a more arduous 1.7-mile loop trail called Moonlight Canyon Trail. The park is pretty, and parts of it are lush with lots of plants and trees fed by the natural springs that run throughout. Look for the many species of birds and other wildlife that call it home. Note that this park is adjacent to ANZA BORREGO STATE PARK (pg. 494).

Hours: The park is open Labor Day weekend - Memorial Day for camping and for day use, daily, 9:30am - sunset. The indoor pool is open daily for ages 14 and up, 10:30am - 5pm and for adult campers only, Fri. - Sat., 6pm - 9pm. The outdoor pool is open daily, 9:30am - 5pm and for all-age campers only, Fri. - Sat., 6pm - 9pm. The park is closed June - August.

Price: $3 per vehicle for day use. Pool entry (for non-campers) is $3 per person. Camping costs from $29 (tents) - $38 (full hook-ups) a night - $75 for a cabin.

Ages: 3 years and up.

ALGA NORTE COMMUNITY PARK

(760) 268-4777 or (760) 434-2826 / www.carlsbadca.gov

!/$$$

6565 Alicante Road, Carlsbad

This wonderful and expansive park features numerous great elements. Dive into the aquatic center that consists of two outdoor pools (a 25-yard instructional one and a 50-meter competition pool), plus a warm water spa for adults, a snack bar, and a small splash pad area for kids. The splash pad has gigantic flowers and pipes that spray water, and fountains that spurt up at random times offering refreshment and squeals of delight. There are also sessions when a pool has huge inflatables in it - slides, climbing and obstacle courses. The whole aquatic area is nicely laid out, with palm trees, some huge umbrellas for shade, plenty of space for moving around, and even lights for nighttime swims.

The skate park is one of the largest in San Diego, at 22,200 square feet. Part of it is designated more towards beginners while the majority is for those with higher skills. I describe it as epic as the lighted, unsupervised park boasts a long, straight street course with variously-sized ramps, steps, rails, ledges, a bell tower, and two adjacent, wide and deep, big bowls.

The extra extra large, tri-level, ADA playground, based partly in a hard foam base and partly in sand, has several separate play sections with ramps, slides, climbing poles, slopes, boulders, swings, bridges, walkways, ropes, and all the fun things for kids to expend their considerable energy.

Alga Norte also offers three ball fields; lighted basketball courts (one full and one half); picnic areas; lots of green open space to run, play and throw a frisbee or football; and two sizable dog parks. This community park truly services the entire community.

Hours: The park and skate park are open daily, 8am - 10pm. Recreational swim is open year round, Mon. - Fri., 5:45am- 7pm; Sat. and holidays, 8am - 4pm; Sun., 9:30am - 4pm. The pool is open weekends in the summer until 5pm. The splash pad is open year round when the air temp is warm. The inflatable zone days are offered in the summer on Tues., Thurs. and Fri., usually 1pm - 3pm. Tickets do sell out.

Price: The park and skate park are free. Recreational swim is $5 for adults; $3 for ages 17 and under; $2 for spectators. The inflatable zone day session fee is $10 per person.

Ages: All

ALTA VISTA GARDENS / BRENGLE TERRACE PARK

(760) 945-3954 - Alta Vista gardens; (760) 726-1340 - Brengle / www.altavistagardens.org; www.ci.vista.ca.us

!/$

1270 Vale Terrace Drive (the gardens are on Jim Porter Pkwy.), Vista

This is a two-for-one entry as these side-by-side attractions, each with a different emphasis, are both great places to visit. The fourteen-acre Alta Vista botanic gardens are an absolute delight to walk around with their blending of distinct plant sections; colorful and funky artwork interspersed; easy trails that crisscross throughout; places to sit and contemplate; areas designed for kids; and a wonderful view from the hilltop. Children will enjoy running all around, as well as going through short cement drainage tubes; pretend playing at the stone piano and playing real music created from natural elements, like the pebbles chime; incorporating big stone animals based in sand in their imaginative play; and the variety of the unusual plants and flowers. The types of gardens include Desert, Prehistoric, South American, Pan Asian, Jungle, Herb, Rose, and more. A Children's Garden is in the works, as is a water play area and so many other wonderful projects. The art includes sculptures, mosaics, chimes, statues, and more. Enjoy seeing butterflies, as it's a certified butterfly habitat; sacred lotus; rare pine trees; a pond and its inhabitants; numerous fruit trees; and walking through a small labyrinth, plus sitting at a patio table and chairs that overlook the view of the valley below and beyond. Educational field trips, and classes on farming, the environment and botany are just some of the offerings - check the website for a full listing and for special events held here, such as Earth Day celebration.

Adjacent to the gardens is a really tough disc golf course - up and down hills; one hole is in the midst of a cluster of trees! Brengle Terrace Park offers lighted ball fields, multi-purpose fields, basketball courts, tennis courts, volleyball courts, picnic tables, a tot lot play area, horseshoe pits, and an amphitheater. Come play! See MOONLIGHT STAGE PRODUCTIONS (pg. 719) for information on the programs at Moonlight Amphitheater here.

Hours: The gardens are open Mon. - Fri., 7am - 5pm; Sat. - Sun., 10am - 5pm. Closed most major holidays. The park is open daily, 8am - sunset.

Price: $5 is asked for entrance to the gardens - put it in the donation box. The park is free.

Ages: All

ANZA BORREGO STATE PARK

(760) 767-5311 - state park; (760) 767-4205 - visitor center; (760) 767-4684 - wildflower hotline; (800) 444-7275 - camping reservations. / www.parks.ca.gov; www.theabf.org; www.galletameadows.com

200 Palm Canyon Drive, Borrego Springs

This massive state park is over 600,000 acres of living desert - palm trees, flowers, oases, bighorn sheep, and lizards, plus sand, rocks, mountains, and much more. The following description merely touches on a few of the activities and places that this park has to offer. Remember that this is a desert and the temperatures can reach over 125 degrees during the summer - always bring water!!! Nighttime temperatures can drop drastically, no matter what time of year, so be prepared for anything!

As with any major park, your best bet is to start at the Visitor's Center - this one is located in the small town of Borrego Springs, which is north of Highway 78. Get familiar with the park by watching the slide show that is presented upon request, and looking at the exhibits such as taxidermied animals and photographs. Be sure to pick up trail guides and a map.

Dinosaurs! Camels! Battling horses! A sea serpent! Sloths! Giant tortoises! All of these, and much more (140 in all) can be found in Borrego Springs, fantastically recreated in gigantic metal sculptures. Drive along Borrego Springs Road (and other branch roads) to see the magnificent sculptures scattered about and rising out of the desert floor. They are easily accessible to see up close, too, so bring your camera. One of my favorites is the 350-long sea serpent whose head and mouth looks like its breathing fire and whose body ripples above and below the ground, and on both sides of the main road. Get a map of the sculptures online or pick one up at the visitors center. It's all free to view!

Anza Borrego has some of the most incredible scenery in Southern California and although much of it can be seen by driving through the park, the really awe-inspiring vistas and landscape can only be seen by hiking. Within the park, take your choice of hiking trails which range from easy loops to arduous "mountain man" trails. One of the most popular hikes is the three-mile round-trip nature trail from the Borrego Palm Canyon campground up through the canyon. The end of the trail is a sight for sore eyes (and hot bodies) - a refreshing waterfall with a pool (when there is water)!

There are two developed campsites available in this gigantic park, and one, Whittier Horse Camp, for camping with horses. There are places you can also open camp - pull over wherever you choose. Tip: Try to choose a site that has some shelter from the desert winds that blow in seemingly at random times. For more information call the park office at the number above. Note that Borrego Springs is a Dark Sky Community, meaning that there aren't any street or many other artificial lights at night so you can really see a multitude of stars.

See AGUA CALIENTE COUNTY PARK (pg. 492), as it is located at the southern part of Anza Borrego park, as well as OCOTILLO WELLS STATE VEHICULAR RECREATION AREA (pg. 581).

Hours: The park is open for day use daily, dawn - dusk. The Visitor's Center is open October - May, daily, 9am - 5pm. It's open June - September on weekends and holidays only, 9am - 5pm.

Price: Free for the sculptures and driving through Borrego Springs. Entrance into Anza-Borrego Desert State Park is $10 per vehicle on Fri. - Sun., and holidays. Overnight camping prices for developed campgrounds range from $25 - $35 a night, depending on location and facility. Camping reservations are an additional $8.

Ages: 3 years and up.

BALBOA PARK

See the entry for BALBOA PARK (pg. 524), under MUSEUMS, for details.

BATIQUITOS LAGOON ECOLOGICAL RESERVE and NATURE CENTER

(760) 931-0800 / www.batiquitosfoundation.org

7380 Gabbiano Lane, Carlsbad

A nature center, housed in a trailer at this end of the trail, has birds, rocks, a few other exhibits and some reference materials. Stop by here if you get a chance. You can also get a free trail guide either inside the center or at the outside bird boxes. Enjoy the view from the deck and/or use one of the picnic tables here, too.

This pretty walking trail (no bikes allowed) is a fairly level hard dirt pathway, for the most part. The trail is sandwiched between a golf course at one end (that boasts a beautiful waterfall) and the lagoon. There is even a branch of the trail that goes closer to the water for short distances. Bring binoculars for a more up-close look at the wide variety of birds that flock here. Along the almost two-mile, non-looping trail are trees, benches, and interpretive signs that describe the critters that call this salt marsh their home. Fishing is allowed at one point, with a permit. School field trips and guided walks of the lagoon are available.

Hours: The lagoon is open daily, dawn - dusk. The nature center is usually open daily, 9am - 3pm, but call first as they sometimes close earlier during the week.

Price: Free

Ages: All; strollers/wheelchairs are O.K. for a good part of the path.

BLUE SKY ECOLOGICAL RESERVE

(858) 668-4781 / www.blueskyreserve.org

16275 Espola Road, Poway

Head for the hills! From the parking lot, that is your only option. The large, mostly hard-packed dirt fire road follows along a seasonal creek into the hills. The main trail, leading to 700 acres of nature, is surrounded by tall, leafy oak and sycamore trees, and shrubs. One trail branches off to hook up at the neighboring LAKE POWAY RECREATION AREA (pg. 505), where trail maps are available. Bring your own water. No bikes allowed. Guided groups hikes, such as Owl Prowl and Star Party, are offered several times throughout the year. Wildlife/plant walks are offered every Saturday and Sunday at 9am.

Hours: Open daily, sunrise - sunset.

Price: Free

Ages: 4 years and up.

BORDER FIELD STATE PARK

(619) 575-3613 / www.trnerr.org; www.parks.ca.gov

1500 Monument Road, San Diego

The best thing, and really the only thing exciting, about the hilltop Border State Park is that its boundaries go up to the border of Mexico. Only a chain-link fence separates the two countries! There is a small monument that is exactly half on U.S. soil and half on Mexican soil. This small, immediate area, a half-circle in front of the monument, is called Friendship Park. This Park is actually only accessible on weekends from 10am to 2pm, and visitors must have any document verifying legal residence in the U.S.

A tall, rusted fence goes down the hillside/cliffside onto the beach and actually out into the water for about fifty feet to divide the lands as well as the peoples. We saw families swimming on the Mexico side, but swimmers are not allowed in the water on the U.S. side, purportedly because of riptides and foul water from the Tijuana River. There are always border patrol officers here, in trucks and in helicopters, encircling the park. This is, also, a great place to go whale watching during their migration season.

The park does have a grassy area for running around, picnic tables, restroom facilities, and pathways to hike into the adjacent Tijuana Estuary. See TIJUANA ESTUARY - VISITORS CENTER (pg. 518) for more information about the estuary and visitor's center.

Hours: Open most of the year daily, 9:30am - 5pm. It is open in the summer until 7pm. It is only accessible and open for pedestrians and equestrians - no vehicles, Mon. - Fri. It is open to vehicles, Sat., Sun., and holidays (and Fri. in the summer). The park is closed during and after rain.

Price: $5 per vehicle.

Ages: All

CABRILLO NATIONAL MONUMENT

(619) 557-5450 / www.nps.gov/cabr

1800 Cabrillo Memorial Drive, at the southern end of Point Loma, San Diego

In 1542 Juan Rodriguez Cabrillo sailed into San Diego Bay and claimed it for Spain. A huge statue of Cabrillo, commemorating his epic voyage along the western coast of the U.S., resides on the tip of the peninsula at this national park. Press the button near the monument to hear the history of Cabrillo and the bay area.

Older kids will appreciate the exhibit hall in the building behind the monument. Displays include maps and drawings of the areas Cabrillo and other explorers "discovered"; lots of written information; examples of food eaten on board ship, like dried fish and hardtack; and models of ships. The adjacent Visitors' Center offers pamphlets, film programs, and guided walks of this area, plus a book shop and an incredible view. There are a number of ranger-led education tours and programs (for students of all ages) offered here with emphasis on either history or science. This is also where your young ones can earn a Junior Ranger badge, as they can at any national park. Ask for a free "Just For Kids" newspaper and check out various places around the park to learn more about 16th century exploration, ships and aircraft, whales, natural and military history. Then, come back, and when your kids share their answers with a Park Ranger, they will be awarded a Junior Ranger badge.

Before walking out to Point Loma Lighthouse, which was used from 1855 to 1891, listen to its history by pressing an outside storyboard button. We listened to it in Japanese and German (as well as English) - just for the fun of it. Kids think it's great to actually climb up the spiral staircase inside the refurbished lighthouse. The odd-shaped bedrooms are fully furnished with period furniture and knickknacks, as is the small living room, kitchen, and dining room. The entrance to the top floor/tower is closed by a grate (and only open 3 days a year), but you can look through it and see the huge light that was a beacon to so many sailors.

Your only opportunities to tour the bunkers on Point Loma - to learn about and see where soldiers were stationed here during WWII and see the weapons and instruments - are on select Saturdays from 10am to 3pm, with a tour guide.

Take the Bayside Trail, about 2.5 miles round trip, to walk further out to the point. Along the way look for remnants of a coastal artillery system used during both world wars. The trail goes down through a coastal sage scrub "forest." Topside of the trail, behind plexiglass, is a whale overlook. From late December through March, catch a glimpse of the gray whales during their annual migration. Audio information is, again, available at the touch of a button. (This time we listened to explanations in French and English.) Even if you don't see a whale, the view is spectacular.

From this viewpoint, look down to see the rocky marine environment of the tidepools. A driveable road from the monument leads down to them. (You must pay the parking fee to enter this area.) Exploring tidepools is always a wondrous adventure for my kids. See and touch (but don't bring home) sea stars, anemones, and limpets, and be on the lookout for crabs and even octopus. Tip: Be sure to bring your camera, wear rubber-soled shoes (the rocks get slippery), and keep a close eye on your little ones! Ask about free, ranger-guided school tours for third to fifth graders for the tidepools, monument, and surrounding parkland.

Hours: Open daily, 9am - 5pm. Sometimes open an hour later in the summer.
Price: $15 per vehicle, which is valid for up to 7 days (an annual pass is only $30!); $5 for walk-ins; free for military and residents with permanent disabilities. See MUSEUM MONTH, SAN DIEGO (pg. 700), in the calendar section, for details about half-price admission in February. Admission is often free, as with all national parks, on Martin Luther King, Jr. Day; National Park Week in April; National Park Service Birthday in August; National Public Lands Day in September; and Veterans Day in November.
Ages: 3 years and up.

CARLSBAD SKATE PARK

(760) 434-2826 or (760) 602-4684 / www.socalskateparks.com
2560 Orion Way, Carlsbad

This good-sized, non-supervised, lighted skate park features cement bowls and other fun street elements, plus a beginner's area. The park is located between the police and fire departments. Wearing safety gear is enforced by the policemen that drive by. A small circle of grass is across the way and a baseball diamond is just down the hillside.

Hours: Open daily, 8am - 10pm.
Price: Free
Ages: 8 years and up.

CHOLLAS LAKE

(619) 527-7683 / www.sandiego.gov
6350 College Grove Drive, San Diego

This sixteen-acre reservoir lake, surrounded by trees, is a designated fishing lake just for youth, ages 15 and under only. How great to be a kid! A looping, dirt path (not quite a mile) that goes around the lake is popular with bicyclists, joggers, and kids. There are picnic tables with barbecue grills, a play area, and a small basketball court. Ask about the fishing clinics and ranger-guided nature walks.

Hours: Open daily, 6:30am - a half hour before sunset. Closed New Year's Day, Thanksgiving, and Christmas. Closes early on state holidays.
Price: Free
Ages: All

COTTONWOOD CREEK PARK

(760) 633-2740 / www.ci.encinitas.ca.us
95 N. Vulcan Avenue, Encinitas

This delightful park has several appealing facets. The good-sized playground, with sand and foam padded flooring, has several slides; swings; toddler swings; an "M" shaped climbing structure; wiggly stepping stones attached to poles; a tiny house with a sand table; a tiered rock fountain for splashing water; and other creative play equipment. Another fun element is a ten-foot-high large rock designed for kids to climb up and on.

The park also boasts grassy lawns, including one gently sloping hill to roll down; picnic tables and benches scattered throughout; two tennis courts; and two half basketball courts. A creek flows through the south side of the park with several semicircular turnouts that have wooden foot bridges and information panels regarding creek life.

There is also a war memorial here.
Hours: Open daily, 5am - 10pm.
  Price: Free
  Ages: All

COTTONWOOD PARK

(619) 397-6197 / www.chulavistaca.gov
1778 E. Palomar Street, Chula Vista

    This large, traditional park has several noteworthy amenities. The playground, that has a sand and rubber base, has enclosed, twisty slides and other slides; curved, metal climbing ladders; swings (and toddlers' swings); and a large camel and elephant statue to climb. Covered picnic tables, a cement bike/stroller trail that winds throughout, a basketball court, a ball field with stands (for seating, ironically), and restrooms complete this facility.
Hours: Open daily, sunrise - sunset.
  Price: Free
  Ages: All

CUYAMACA RANCHO STATE PARK / LAKE CUYAMACA

(760) 765-3020 or (760) 765-0755 - park; (800) 444-7275 - camping reservations / www.parks.ca.gov; $$
www.crspia.org
12551 Hwy 79, Descanso and 13652 Hwy 79, Julian

    Retreat from the buildings, noise, and general busyness of city life to this outstanding state park with its 25,000 acres of pristine wilderness - a balm to the mind and soul. Take in the trees, grassy meadows, streams, peaks, and valleys that this park has to offer. There are over 120 miles of hiking trails and forty miles of biking trails along the fire roads and access roads. As the terrain varies, hiking trails vary in their degree of difficulty. Be on the lookout for birds, mule deer, lizards, coyotes, and other critters.

    Pick up a trail map ($2) at the park headquarters, or check online. While at the headquarters, go through its interactive museum which features a taxidermied bobcat, mountain lion, fox, racoon, and rattlesnake. Touch (or wear!) the pelts of some of these animals, too. The museum also has informational panels to lift and learn; a section of a mine with an ore cart; Native American artifacts; a fireman suit and map of the wildfire from 2003; and a video room. Ask about the jr. ranger program. Outside are picnic tables under a shady tree grove.

    Seasonal changes at this altitude of 4,000 feet are often drastic and beautiful: Autumn bursts on the scene with its rich colors of gold, red, and orange; winter brings a white blanket of snow; spring explodes with a profusion of brilliant wildflowers; and summer offers refreshment, by sitting near a stream, under a canopy of trees.

    Campgrounds in the park, and some near rivers, are available for families at either Paso Picacho or Green Valley. You can hike to waterfalls from the latter campground. The campsites have picnic tables, fire rings, and heated showers (bring lots of quarters!). Paso Picacho also has a few one-room cabins available (you must bring your own bedding, etc.). You can camp with your horse at specific campgrounds. Note that there are some great trails heading out directly from the campgrounds. We hiked up to the peak, which was arduous, but worth it.

    Fishing or boating at Lake Cuyamaca, (760) 765-0515 / www.lakecuyamaca.org, is another way to enjoy this area. Motorboat rentals are $50 a day, *oar* rent a row boat at $50 a day. Pontoons are $125 for the day during the week. Pedalboats are $15 an hour. Kayaks are $14 per hour for a single; $20 for a double. Fishing permits are $8 for adults; $4 for kids 8 to 15 years; children 7 years and under are free with a licensed adult. A California license is also required for ages 16 and up for $15.12 for a day. Depending on the season (and your luck), you can catch trout, catfish, bass, bluegill, and crappie. The lake is at the northern end of the park and a bait-and-tackle shop are located here. Rod and reel rental is $10. There is also a full-service restaurant at the lake - in case you don't catch your own meal! Camping at the lake is $25 for tent camping and $35 for RV.
Hours: The park is open daily, sunrise - sunset. The gift shop and museum are open Sat. - Sun., 10am - 4pm. Fishing and boat rentals are open daily, 6am - sunset. Call for extended summer hours.
  Price: There are several designated scenic turn-outs along Hwy. 79 that offer picnic tables and hiking trails; parking here is free. Parking for day use of a campground is $10 per vehicle. Camping is $30 a night per person for primitive camping; $35 per vehicle for developed camping. The camping reservation fee is $8. 12 x 12 cabins are $75 a night.
  Ages: 2 years and up.

DALEY RANCH

(760) 839-4680 or (760) 839-4880 / www.escondido.org; www.daleyranch.org; www.fodr.org
3024 La Honda Drive, Escondido

This 3,058-acre ranch is a hiking/mountain biking wilderness habitat preserve that offers a variety of terrain, from meadows to open grasslands to hills with rugged boulders. Twenty-five miles of main trails and offshoots traverse the property and range from wide, easy, paved fire roads to narrow, up and down, dirt trails. We hiked the somewhat steep East Ridge route (1.6 miles) and reached two decent-sized ponds. Boulder Loop Trail (2.5 miles) offers a great view and rock "gardens." The wide Ranch House Loop Trail (2.5 miles) passes the site of Daley's original (unrestored) log cabin. Bring your own water. Note: DIXON LAKE, see the next entry, is just "next door."

Hours: Open daily, dawn - dusk.

Price: Free

Ages: 5 years and up.

DIXON LAKE

(760) 839-4680 - ranger station; (760) 741-3328 or (760) 839-4045 - camping / www.escondido.org
1700 N. La Honda Drive, Escondido

This beautiful getaway offers year-round fishing with promising areas of the reservoir titled Trout Cove, Catfish Cove, and Bass Point. Fish off the shoreline, off the piers, or rent a motorboat or row boat to try your luck. No license is needed. Paddle boat rentals are also available. The lake is cradled in pines, poplars and other vegetation along the surrounding hillsides. There are a few short walking trails along the lake, and the rocks make it a fun destination for rock climbing. (For longer hikes, go "next door" to DALEY RANCH; see the previous entry.) One picnic area, with a small playground and a patch of grass, is at the entrance of the park. Another larger one, with some picnic shelters and more play equipment, is farther in. A concession stand is open year round.

Camping spots are up on the mountain ridge and overlook the valley on one side, the lake on the other. Some of the sites are a very short hike down from the parking area and therefore a bit more private than other sites. There is an accessible cabin here, too, for $40 a night - bring your own bedding. All in all - Dixon Lake is scenic and peaceful. Note: No swimming or biking is allowed.

Hours: Open daily, 6am - dusk.

Price: $5 per vehicle on the weekends and on holidays; free during the week. Fishing is $7 for ages 16 and up; $5 for seniors and ages 8 - 15; children 7 and under are free. A fishing license is not required. Night fishing is available during summer months. Row boat rentals are $14 for half a day; $17 a full day. Motorboats are $30 for half a day; $35 a full day. Pedal boats are $12 a half hour for up to 4 people. Camping is $25 a night, $35 with RV hook-up, plus an advance registration fee of $5.

Ages: All

DOS PICOS REGIONAL PARK

(858) 694-3049 or (760) 789-2220 / www.sdparks.org
17953 Dos Picos Park Road, Ramona

This is my kind of "secluded" wilderness - close to a small town, yet seventy-eight acres that are mostly au natural. Huge boulders dot the hillsides and a trail leads up amongst them. The valley of the park is filled with numerous oak trees that provide wonderful shade, but there are also open grasslands and chaparral. The park provides a pond (those over 16 years old need a fishing license), play area, horseshoe pit, picnic area, exercise course, open play areas, and tent and RV camping, plus 2 cabins with bed frames (no mattresses) and bathrooms. Ask about the programs offered here, such as the junior ranger program and the campfires that incorporate some old-fashioned family fun. The town of Ramona is just around the bend.

Hours: Open daily, 9:30am - sunset. Closed Christmas.

Price: $3 per vehicle per day. Tent camping is $24 a night; RV, $29, plus a $5 registration fee, and cabins are $67.

Ages: All

DOYLE COMMUNITY PARK

(858) 581-7170 or (858) 552-1612 / www.sandiego.gov
8175 Regents Road, La Jolla

This has-it-all park goes back much deeper than it first appears. The "bottom level" of the park is composed of a huge playground with different features appealing to various ages. The kiddie playground, geared for ages 2 to 5 years, has a wooden ship, a spiderweb made of nets, and ropes to climb, plus baby and bigger kid swings. The larger, two-story play structure has ramps, bridges, twisty slides, a mini zip line, and tire swings, among other features. The entire playground has a sand base and there are benches all around it along with cement picnic tables and barbecue pits. A basketball court and recreation center offering a myriad of activities are also on this level.

On the upper level there are more basketball courts, a sand volleyball court, a grass area, three ball fields, a small playground, cement picnic tables, a horseshoe pit, and two dog parks; one for smaller dogs and one for larger ones. A cement pathway goes all around the park. There is also an easy hiking trail, the Rose Canyon Trail, which is about 9 miles but goes amidst roads and houses, sometimes, too.

Hours: Open daily, sunrise - sunset. The rec center is open Mon. - Sat. usually at about 11am.
Price: Free
Ages: All

ELFIN FOREST RECREATION RESERVE

(760) 632-4212 - ranger station; (760) 753-6466 - water district / www.elfinforest.olivenhain.com
8833 Harmony Grove Road, Encinitas

San Diego always surprises me with all of its city attractions and yet its wealth of natural habitat. Elfin Forest encompasses over 750 acres of open space with oak trees, coastal sage, chaparral, wildlife (such as mule deer, lizards, squirrels, snakes, and such), and scenic hilltop/mountaintop vistas - such a variety of topography! Eleven miles of hiking, biking, and equestrian dirt trails and about six miles of the boulder-lined Escondido Creek meander throughout the reserve.

A main hike from the trailhead is a little over three miles round trip and moderately difficult, which means there are some steep climbs and some level walking areas. There are several switchbacks, many of them in the shade. Bring a fanny pack or backpack for water, and snacks for the kids. The Way Up Trail is tough, but the top-of-the-world scenery makes it worthwhile. An easier, fun, family trail is the self-guided botanical loop trail (about one mile), marked with over twenty-five stops for plant identification. For a more strenuous hike, follow the trail to Lake Hodges. An Interpretive Center is also on the grounds and offers ranger-led hikes and special activities.

Hours: Open daily, 8am to 30 minutes before sunset. The Interpretive Center is open Sat. - Sun., 9am - 3pm; and sometimes during the week. Hours fluctuate, depending if they have staff or not. Closed Christmas and on rainy days.
Price: Free
Ages: 5 years and up.

EUCALYPTUS PARK

(619) 397-6197 or (619) 425-9844 / www.chulavistaca.gov
4th Ave. and C Street, Chula Vista

The best thing this twenty-one-acre corner park has going for it is the fantastic, very purple and yellow playground. Besides the brightly colored twisty slides, tunnels, platforms, ladders, talking tubes, swings, activity panels, curvy metal structures, monkey bars, and little vehicles on giant springs, there is a yellow mini truck and bulldozer to play on, a good-size rock climbing wall, and lots of area to play on and under.

The rest of the park is not so exciting. The baseball diamond, basketball courts, and even the grassy areas and picnic areas are a bit run down, plus it's located on a very busy corner (but the tennis courts are nicely resurfaced). Maybe the cool playground will be an inspiration to maintain/upgrade the rest of the park?

Hours: Open daily, sunrise - sunset.
Price: Free
Ages: All

FELICITA PARK

(760) 745-4379 / www.sdparks.org
742 Clarence Lane, Escondido

This spacious, truly-lovely woodland park beckons guests to play, hike, picnic, and climb on boulders. A large grassy area for running around and several, elevated play structures - with tubes, bridges, slides, creative climbing apparatus, and swings, etc. - help make the park younger-child friendly. Older kids will enjoy the ball fields, horseshoe pits, volleyball courts, and the small museum. Walk on trails through huge shady oak groves or near the rock-lined seasonal creek. Join in on the many ranger programs offered here that specialize in local and Native American history. For instance, take a tour to the Indian grinding holes and learn about the village life of the local Indian tribes, learn the brutal history of "treeing" a thief, or learn about backcountry safety. This park is also home to the ESCONDIDO RENAISSANCE FAIRE (pg. 707). Get the kids more involved with nature by, ironically, using an app called Track Trails - they can even earn prizes.

Hours: Open daily, 9:30am - sunset. Closed Christmas.
Price: $3 per vehicle.
Ages: All

FLINN SPRINGS COUNTY PARK

(858) 565-3600 or (619) 390-1973 / www.sdparks.org
14787 Olde Highway 80, El Cajon

Although the park is just off a main street, it feels more like it's somewhere in the countryside. Lots of old oak trees give the rural park plenty of shade in the picnic areas and along the hiking trails. The dirt paths lead up and around the grassy and rocky hillsides. Be on the lookout for wildlife. A rock-lined, seasonal stream meanders through the park, allowing kids hours of outdoor, imaginative play. Both upper and lower lots have small playgrounds (one is enclosed), picnic tables, and barbecue pits. There is even a grass section, too.

If you're hungry, bring along a picnic lunch or eat next door at the very small Mary Ettas Cafe. Breakfast (eggs, French toast, and other staples) and lunch (hamburgers and such) are served daily from 6am to 1:30pm.

Hours: Open daily, 9:30am - sunset. Closed Thanksgiving and Christmas.
Price: $3 per car.
Ages: All

GLEN PARK

(760) 633-2740 / www.ci.encinitas.ca.us
2149 Orinda Drive, Cardiff-by-the-Sea

This nicely landscaped and maintained park, situated just across the highway from the beach, is a pleasant choice if you're in the neighborhood. The playground, with typical equipment and lots of sand surrounding it, is at the base of the park, along with a basketball court and horseshoe pit. Grassy lawns, palm trees, and large eucalyptus trees follow the gentle slope up toward the back. A few barbecue pits, scattered picnic tables, a cement pathway throughout, a volleyball court, a tennis court, and restrooms complete Glen Park.

Hours: Open daily, 5am - 10pm.
Price: Free
Ages: All

GUAJOME REGIONAL - COUNTY PARK

(760) 724-4489 or (858) 694-3049; (877) 565-3600 - camping reservations / www.sdparks.org
3000 Guajome Lake Road, Oceanside

This over 550 acre, mostly nature park has it all! Active visitors can partake in basketball, hiking the 4.5 miles of trails, fishing in the lake, kicking or throwing a ball on the acres of green lawn, and playing at either, or both, of the playgrounds. The mostly flat hiking trails meander through wooded sections, plus some chaparral, marshlands, and grass areas. The playgrounds are great - with swings, slides, metal shapes to climb on, and some rock climbing walls. More relaxed-minded visitors can enjoy the beautiful scenery, soak up some nature in the midst of suburbia and read a book under a shade tree. Get the kids more involved with nature by, ironically, using an app called Track Trails - they can even earn prizes.

There are thirty-five campsites with partial hookups for $29 a night (plus a $5 reservation fee). Each of the sites has a picnic table, fire ring, and some large trees for shade and some semblance of privacy. There is also a cabin for rent, $100 a night, on the premises. The cabin sleeps up to six people (with 2 bed frames - no mattresses, and 4 cots) and has a full kitchen, outside patio and fire pit.

Note that the RANCHO GUAJOME ADOBE (pg. 547) is at the far, far end of the park and that the ANTIQUE GAS & STEAM ENGINE MUSEUM, INC. (pg. 523) is just down the street.

Hours: Open daily, 9:30am - sunset.
Price: $3 a car for day use.
Ages: All

HERITAGE PARK and COMMUNITY CENTER - Chula Vista

(619) 421-7032 / www.chulavistaca.gov
1381 E. Palomar Street, Chula Vista

This fairly large park has cement pathways that crisscross throughout (great for bikes and strollers); play equipment with swings, slides, and a good-size sand base, so bring bucket and shovel; lighted basketball courts; open, grassy areas; barbeque pits and picnic tables; and - a big draw - a pond with lots of friendly/hungry ducks. There is also a very small skate park here with the basic elements. The community center is open for all sorts of activities.

Hours: Open daily, sunrise to sunset.
Price: Free
Ages: All

HILTON HEAD COUNTY PARK

(858) 694-3030 or (858) 565-3600 / www.sdparks.org
16005 Hilton Head Road, El Cajon

    This ten-acre park offers acres of fun. (Ten acres of it, actually.) A basketball court, sports field, exercise stations, picnic area, BBQs, grassy areas, some paved pathways throughout, a boulder-lined dry creek bed, a playground, and an aquatic playground make it ideal for the family. The sand-based playground has a fairly tall tower with enclosed slides, steps, and places to play underneath, plus swings and a tire swing. The big and wide, pulled-apart ship on rubber flooring is a centerpiece play structure to climb in, on, and around. It has slides, port holes, a chain climbing ladder, and a large, purple sea creature that looks likes it's coming up out of the ground. The adjacent water play area has fountains that squirt up from a circular pad and several straight and curved poles that spurt out H2O. Note that there isn't a lot of shade at this park.

Hours: The park is open daily, 7:30am - dusk. The waterplay area is open May - October daily, 11am - 4pm.
  Price: Free for the park. $3 per child for the waterplay area - purchase a wristband at the vending machine there.
  Ages: All

HOSP GROVE PARK

(760) 434-2826 / www.carlsbadca.gov
Jefferson Street and Marron Road, Carlsbad

    I know the cars are right there, but this 5.5 acre park feels like a little nature refuge. Dirt trails zig zag up (sometimes steeply) and go around the wooded hillside, for a total of about three miles, offering a nice overlook of the adjacent Buena Vista Lagoon. The trails even continue to the other side of Monroe Street, at the East Grove park.

    The base of the park is in eucalyptus groves with a stone-lined seasonal stream and a playground. The sand flooring of the playground supports the swings, slide, play equipment and boulders. Make your mini retreat complete by enjoying a picnic under the shade trees.

Hours: Open daily, 8am - 10pm.
  Price: Free
  Ages: All

IMPERIAL SAND DUNES / ALGODONES DUNES

(760) 337-4400 / www.blm.gov/visit/imperial-sand-dunes
On Highway 78, Glamis

    The expansive Imperial Sand Dunes, also referred to as the Algodones Dunes, extend for over forty miles - almost as far as the eye can see. They change in appearance from smooth surfaces to rippling waves, depending on the prevailing winds. They conjure up images of science-fiction flicks, or of a lone, sunburnt person clothed in rags crawling across the dunes crying out desperately, "Water, water!" Tip: Bring your own water.

    Stop off first at the Osborne Overlook, located two miles east of Gecko Road along SR78. Here you'll see a great view of the dunes and the surrounding Imperial Valley. The appropriately named "wilderness" area is north of the 78, between Ted Kipf Road and the Coachella lands. A viewing area is two miles north of Glamis along Ted Kipf Road. Awe-inspiring dunes are toward the west side, while the east side has mostly smaller dunes and washes. The region is open for you to walk, run, jump, and roll down the dunes. Horseback riding is also allowed. Note that summer temperatures can rise to 110 degrees, so the most favorable months to visit are October through May. Bring your sunglasses, camera, and a bucket and shovel.

    The area south of the highway is open for tent and RV camping (inclusive of the vehicle pass you purchase), off-highway vehicles (OHVs), and all-terrain vehicles (ATVs). Dune buggies are not readily available for rent, so you must bring your own vehicle. Camping is primitive, and trash must be packed out. For more information and an area map, call the BLM (i.e., Bureau of Land Management) at the above number.

Hours: Open daily, sunrise - sunset.
  Price: A permit is required Oct. 1 through April 15. Purchased in advance the fee is $35 for a week pass. On-site the pass is $50.
  Ages: It depends on how far you want to hike, or if you are content with just playing in the sand.

JACK'S POND

(760) 591-0827 or (760) 744-9000 / www.san-marcos.net
986 La Moree Road, San Marcos

    This clean, small park with two barn-like structures offers a large, fenced in grassy area/corral for kids, not horses;

a good playground with slides, tallish towers, a bridge and more; and a Nature Center. The good-sized nature center is comprised of several small, themed rooms on each side of the large, main room. Each room contain some hands-on exhibits, or activities, such as live bugs and other critters; microscopes; animals felts; and information on the area's natural history. Outstanding educational programs for students of all ages are offered that usually incorporate doing a craft, or two, as well. Take the quarter-mile, partly-dirt, partly gravel lovely nature trail which leads back to a pond. The a non-looping trail goes about a half-mile around the perimeter of the pond, and back. Fishing in this pond is allowed and kids under 16 years do not need a fishing license. Be on the look out for lizards, bunnies, bugs and birds. You can also enjoy a longer walk as you go past the pond on a nice, wide, gravel trail that meanders through the hillside, past adjacent homes, etc.

Hours: The park is open daily, sunrise - sunset. The nature center is open to the public Sat., 9am - noon. It is open for school groups during the week.

Price: Free

Ages: 10 years and under.

KEARNY MESA RECREATION CENTER

(858) 573-1387 - park; (858) 573-1389 - pool; (619) 561-3824 - BMX   !/$$
/ www.sandiego.gov; www.kearnybmx.com

3170 Armstrong Street, San Diego

This park has a decent playground (with a tube slide), basketball courts, tennis courts, a recreation building, six ball fields, soccer fields, a BMX course (behind the park), an enclosed dog park, and a swimming pool.

Hours: The park is open daily, sunrise - sunset. The pool is open January - September; call for specific hours of operation. The BMX course usually hosts practices and races Wed. and Fri., starting at 5:30pm; Sun. starting at 11am.

Price: Free to the park. The pool is $4 for adults; $2 for seniors and ages 15 and under.

Ages: All

KIT CARSON PARK / ESCONDIDO SPORTS CENTER

(760) 839-4691 - park; (760) 839-5425 or (855) 372-4255- sports center / www.sportscenter.escondido.org;   !/$$
www.escondido.org

3315 Bear Valley Parkway, Escondido

Come to where the action is! A state-of-the-art, outdoor sports center is located in the heart of Kit Carson Park. Besides an eighteen-hole disc course (discs are available in the skate shop, in the sports complex), it has an arena soccer field with bleachers, two roller hockey arenas, a 22,000-square-foot skate park, and a pro shop and concession stand. The lighted skate park, open to riders of BMX bikes and scooters, too, is complete with variously sized ramps, a full street course with rails, spine, pyramids, quarter-pipes, a bowl, hips, ledges, and much more - impressive! At times the skate park is open for bikers as well as skaters. Bring your own safety equipment because it is mandatory. A parental waiver is required for participants 17 and under. Sign up for leagues, camps, and/or skate sessions, or just come to watch the action. A pond is located across the way from the Sports Center.

Just north of the center is the rest of Kit Carson Park with its 185 undeveloped acres and 100 developed acres. It's very family friendly with pretty landscaping, bridges over a seasonal creek, plenty of picnic tables, barbecue pits, green grassy areas for running around, nine ball fields (some with stadium seating), lighted tennis courts, soccer fields, an amphitheater, a fitness course, a fitness trail with markers, hiking trails, and a few playgrounds (plus one just for tots). Whew! The playgrounds feature a gigantic multi-arched cement snake, a Paul Bunyan-sized wagon tilted to slide down, a few climbing trees, and some paved pathways.

Back behind the playground, on the Iris Sankey Magical Garden Trail, or Queen Califa's Magical Circle, is a unique artistic sculpture garden. Several enormous snakes made of both polished and rough stones and colorful tiles encircle this section of the park. Walk through a maze-like section of black and white tile pieces, interspersed with pieces of mirror to a circular courtyard. This area features several gigantic and brilliantly colorful fantastical sculptures that are, again, created with tile and rock. Queen Califa, perched on a royal blue bird figure is in the center, with other mosaic statues scattered around. There are a few benches in here, but very little shade.

Kit Carson Park handily accommodates all of your family's different activities.

Hours: The park is open daily, dawn - dusk. Call for hours on the various sporting center activities. Queen Califa's Magical Circle is open Tues. and Thurs., 9am - noon, and the second Sat., 9am - 2pm. The skate park is open for two-hour sessions, November - March, Mon. - Fri., 3pm - 9pm; Sat., 1pm - 9pm. The skate park is closed New Year's Eve, New Year's Day, Christmas Eve and Christmas Day.

Price: The park and Queen Califa's are free. Skate/bike sessions are $10 per two-hour session. Year memberships are available at $25 per person, which brings the cost of each session down to $5.

Ages: All; 6 years and up for the skate park.

LAGUNA MOUNTAIN RECREATION AREA

(858) 673-6180 or (619) 473-8547 - visitors center; (619) 445-6235 - Laguna Mountain Volunteer Association
/ www.fs.usda.gov/recmain/cleveland/recreation; www.lagunamountain.com;
www.tourguidetim.com/cleveland-national-forest.com

10678 Sunrise Highway, Mount Laguna (this is the address for the centrally-located lodge and general store - the visitors center is just north, next door, at Los Huecos Rd.)

Beautiful! Stunning! So glad we did this! A breath of fresh air (literally). The absolutely lovely drive into the mountains, reaching an elevation of 6,000 feet, entices visitors to pull over and take in the vistas where row after row of mountains are vividly seen on clear days as are majestic panoramas and the valleys below. And come up in the fall when the leaves change their colors.

The mountain, part of the massive Cleveland National Forest, offers fantastic hiking, mountain biking, sledding and playing in the snow in the winter, wildflowers in the spring, and camping.

I advise going to the visitor's center first to purchase a hiking map of the area - I like to know where I'm going. The small visitor's center has some nice displays, too - a number of taxidermied animals, animals pelts to touch, rocks, photos of the area, books, and more. It also has restrooms. Adjacent to the visitor's center is the Laguna Mountain Lodge and Store. The general store, open daily from 9am to 5pm, is pretty much that as it is carries a little bit of everything, including food and various sundries. Stay at the lodge a night, or two, in a motel-like room, or in one of 17 cabins. Call (619) 473-8533 for more info. Another way to spend the night is to stay at either of the two campgrounds, each with over 100 campsites. Burnt Rancheria Campground, open Memorial Day to mid-October, is open for tent and RV camping, and it's close to the general store and visitor's center. Laguna Campground, open year round, has 104 sites and is closer to the Julian entrance Pine Valley. It isn't too far away from Little Laguna Lake. Both campgrounds are $22 a night; $7 for day use.

There are two day use picnic areas here, surrounded by pine and oaks trees. One is just down the road from the visitor's center called Desert View Picnic Area with several picnic tables and bbq pits nestled into the mountainside. Walk the moderately easy trail here and you can peer into the adjacent desert; Anza Borrego Desert State Park. What a difference in topography as you follow along the rim of the mountain! The second day use picnic area is Pioneer Mail, which is much further north, closer to Julian.

There are miles and miles (and miles and miles) of hiking/mountain biking trails on the mountain. The mighty 2,650-mile Pacific Crest Trail, which stretches from the border of Mexico through California and Washington and into Canada, even intersects on some of them. The 1.5 mile Wooded Hill Nature Trail reaches the highest peak on the mountain. About two miles south of the visitor's center is an information kiosk for the trails. Park here and start on the not-too-difficult-but-still-challenging Sunset Trail (then onto the 6.7 mile Big Laguna Trail, if you want) to reach sections of the 900-acre Laguna Meadow. Several lakes are found in the meadow lands, as well as a wide variety of plants and animals. All this just to whet your appetite, or get your hiking boots dirty.

Tips: Bring water - always. Bring bug spray in the non-winter months. The climate is almost always cooler up here than down the mountain, so layer up. Bring tire chains in the winter time. In the summer, take advantage of the campfire programs, guided nature walks and other special events offered here. Laguna Mountains is not that long of a drive from the city of San Diego, but it is seemingly another world away.

Hours: The visitor's center is open Fri., 1 pm - 5pm; Sat., 9am - 5pm; Sun., 9am - 3pm.

Price: $5 Adventure Pass is required if you stop anywhere along the mountain, which you will.

Ages: 6 years and up.

LAKE HODGES

(619) 668-2050 - park; (760) 432-2023 - concession/boat rentals; (619) 465-3474 - recorded fishing info /   !/$$
www.sdrp.org; www.sandiego.gov

20175 Lake Drive, near Del Dio Community Park, or on Lake Hodges Way, Escondido

This massive and winding lake, and its surrounding green hills (at least in the spring), are stunning; we also visited on a gorgeous day. We followed a part of the shoreline to the boat launch area and saw kayaks, sailboats, and row boats being used. We found a grassy picnic area with tables and were greeted by ducks eagerly awaiting a handout. The island in the lake was most intriguing. You may fish from the lake shoreline or rent a boat to try your luck elsewhere. A fishing license, which is not sold at the lake, is needed for ages 16 and up. A fishing permit is $8 for ages 16 and older;

$2.50 for ages 8 to 15; children 7 years and under are free with a paid adult. Row boat rentals are $30 for the day. Motor boats are $35 for two hours. Single kayaks are $10 an hour; double kayaks are $12. Fishing pole rentals and bait and lures are available here, too.

It was a delight for us to simply walk around the area, as well. In fact, Lake Hodges has numerous, long hiking trails. The Piedras Pintadas Trail is 3.8 miles long. Mule Hill, located on the north side of the lake, is an historic site as it's the site of an 1846 Mexican-American battle. There are two interpretive stations along the multi-use trail that tell the story of battle and other interesting facts for history buffs. The trail connects with Sikes Adobe; the trailhead is at Sunset Drive. Kids will especially appreciate the Ruth Merill Children's Interpretive Walk, which is actually the first mile of the Highland Trail, south of the lake. There are numerous markers along the Walk that show and tell about the native plants, animals, and importance of the river systems. Pamphlets with the trail map and more info can be obtained at the River Park office. Cool fact and mini adventure: The David Kreitzer Lake Hodges Bicycle Pedestrian Bridge, the world's longest stress ribbon bridge, goes over and connects the north and south end of the lake. It's located just west of the I-15 freeway bridge off West Bernardo Dr. and connects Coast to Crest Trail and San Dieguito River Trail on the north with the Piedras Pintadas and Bernardo Bay Trails in the Bernardo Bay Natural Area on the south. Whew!

Hours: The lake is open for fishing, boat rentals and concession, February - October, Wed., Sat., and Sun., 30 minutes before sunrise - sunset. Open for walk-ins/hiking daily. Closed New Year's Day, Thanksgiving and Christmas.

Price: Free to the lake.

Ages: 3 years and up.

LAKE JENNINGS COUNTY PARK

(619) 390-1623 - camping/day use or (619) 443-2510 (lake and bait shop) / www.lakejennings.org
9535 Harritt Road, Lakeside

Fishing is the main attraction at this beautiful lake with trout, catfish, bass, and bluegill yours for the catching, depending on the time of year (and your luck). Fish from the shore seven days a week at the various coves, or venture out on the sprawling lake via boat Fridays through Sundays. Row boat rentals are $19 a day; $40 a day for a motorized boat. A daily permit and a California fishing license for those 16 years old and over, which is not sold here, are required. Permits are $9 for adults; $4 for ages 8 to 15; children 7 and under are free with a paying adult. Free classes on how to fish are held on Sundays at 1pm. The Lake Jennings Bait & Tackle Shop sells permits, bait, tackle, snacks, and beverages. Picnic tables overlook the lake.

Miles of hiking across the chaparral-covered hills, with the lake view on one side and the city scape on the other, is another reason to visit Lake Jennings. There is also a large playground on at the park. And don't forget about tent and RV camping where the campsites have shrubs and trees, plus picnic tables. There are some walk-back tent sites which offer a bit more seclusion. If you want to camp like a native, there are five large tipi sites (complete with tipis) for rent, too. Ask about the Saturday programs offered on the grounds. They can include making bird feeders, taking a nature walk, seeing and learning about snakes, and more.

Hours: The park and fishing from the campsite area of the lake is open daily, 7:30am - 5pm. The park and fishing from any shoreline and from a boat is open Fri. - Sun. and some holidays, sunrise - sunset.

Price: Day use entrance is $2 per adult; ages 15 and under are free. Camping fees range from $30 a night for tent - $44 a night for full hook-ups, plus an $8 processing fee. Tipis are $65 - $75 a night.

Ages: All

LAKE MORENA

(619) 579-4101 - general info; (858) 565-3600 - reservations; (619) 478-5473 - fishing info / www.sdparks.org; www.lakemorena.com
2550 Lake Morena Drive, Campo

This large, remote reservoir/lake is surrounded by over 3,000 acres of wilderness. The landscape includes chaparral, oak woodlands, marshy grass areas, and more. The land really belongs to the wildlife - bald eagles, mountain lions, mule deer, migratory waterfowl, and others that roam (or fly over) the backcountry. Fishermen are lured to the lake in hopes of catching the big one or, at least, one. Fish from the boulder-lined shore, or rent a boat. Hook trout in the winter and bass starting in the spring. Sometimes the fish are tagged so the anglers who catch them win a prize. A fishing license is required, but not sold here.

Hikers have a field day here. Explore the well-known Pacific Crest Trail, but don't try to reach the end of it as the trail terminates in Canada. Get the kids more involved with nature by, ironically, using an app called Track Trails - they can even earn prizes. Overnight tent and RV camping are available. The eighty-five sites are largely located under huge oak trees. Ten primitive cabins (i.e., no electricity, no water, beds, but no mattress and cooking that must be done outside at the fire ring) sleep four to six people. The lakeside view from the cabins is my kind of roughing it.

Hours: Open daily, sunrise - ½ hour before sunset. Fishing hours are 30 min. before sunrise to 30 min. after sunset.
Price: $3 per vehicle for day use. Tent camping is $27 a night; RV with hook-up, $34; cabins are $55, plus a $5 reservation fee. Rowboat rentals are $15 a day during the week, $25 on weekends. Motor boats are $30 during the week, $50 on weekends. Fishing for adults is $5 Mon. - Fri., $7 on Sat. - Sun and holidays; $3 Mon. - Fri. and $5 on Sat. - Sun. for seniors; $2 Mon. - Fri. and $3 Sat. - Sun. for ages 10 - 15; ages 9 and under are free.
Ages: 5 years and up.

LAKE MURRAY

(619) 465-3474 or (619) 668-2050 - lake; (619) 466-4847 - boat rentals / www.mtrp.org; www.sandiego.gov
5540 Kiowa Drive, La Mesa

At the southern part of MISSION TRAILS REGIONAL PARK (pg. 509) is a beautiful, stocked reservoir allowing fishing and boating activities, with some boats and kayaks for rent, as well. A fishing license is required for ages 16 and up, which is not sold here, plus daily permits which are $8 for ages 16 and up; $4 for seniors; $2.50 for ages 8 to 15; children 7 and under are free with a paid adult. There is a concession stand here which sells bait and tackle and some refreshments. It's open by 6am in the fall/winter, Wednesday through Sunday; in the spring/summer, daily. A paved trail, 3.2 miles long, goes partly around the lake and is popular for biking, hiking, and walking. Plenty of picnic tables and barbecue pits are also available here.

Hours: The park grounds and shoreline fishing are open daily, sunrise - sunset. Closed New Year's Day, Thanksgiving, and Christmas.
Price: Entrance is free. Rowboats are $15 for half a day. Kayaks are $10 for a single per hour, $20 for a double per hour. Pedal boats are $15 an hour.
Ages: All

LAKE POWAY RECREATION AREA

(858) 668-4770 or (858) 668-4772- general info; (858) 668-4778 - concession stand / www.poway.org
14644 Lake Poway Road, Poway

Nestled between mountains, this pretty park features green grassy rolling hills, two playground areas, thirteen exercise stations, ball fields (one that is lighted), a sand volleyball court, picnic tables overlooking the lake, horseshoe pits, an archery range, and miles of dirt pathways and hiking trails. One trail, great for hardy hikers and mountain bikers, is a scenic, three-mile rocky trail that goes a good distance around the lake. Much more rugged trails include the 8-mile round trip hike up to Mt. Woodson, and back, and trails leading into the adjacent BLUE SKY ECOLOGICAL RESERVE (pg. 495). Be on the lookout for wildlife such as red-tail hawks, raccoons, and even deer.

The large Lake Poway is seasonally stocked with trout or catfish. Bait and fishing permits (a fishing license isn't needed) and refreshments can be purchased at the concession stand. Looking for something fun to tackle on summer nights? Sometimes night fishing is offered on Friday and/or Saturday nights from 4pm to 11pm early July through mid-September. Boat rentals are available year round: Rowboats - $20 a day; motorboats - $30 a day; pedal boats - $15 an hour. Half-day rentals are also available. Ask about the summertime Family Campout programs hosted by Lake Poway.

Hours: Open daily, 6am - dusk. Closed Thanksgiving and Christmas. The lake is open for fishing and boating, Wed. - Sun., 6am - sunset. The concession stand is open the same schedule as the park.
Price: Free for Poway residents; $10 per car for nonresidents is charged on weekends and holidays, only. Fishing permits are $7 for adults; $3 for seniors and ages 8 - 15; free for ages 7 and under with a paying adult.
Ages: All

LAKEVIEW PARK and DISCOVERY LAKE

(760) 744-9000 / www.san-marcos.net
650 Foxhall Drive, San Marcos

This attractive park has a main, wood-themed play structure with several slides emanating from it, steps, a rock climbing wall, bars, and a few play areas under it, too. It also has a grassy area, a covered picnic pavilion, and steps leading down to a wading fountain to splash around in on hot days. The fountain turns on for fifteen minutes at 11am, 12:30pm, 2pm, 3:30pm and 5pm - plan your time accordingly. An eight-acre lake is ringed by a ¾-mile smooth trail, half of which is paved in asphalt, the other half is hard-packed dirt. The pathway makes for a nice stroll or bike ride. A two-and-a-half-mile trail branches off and leads up to the ridgeline (1,000 foot gain of elevation) for a wonderful view. Another trail, one mile long, follows along Discovery Creek.

Fishing is allowed in the lake, although one has to be fairly optimistic or incredibly lucky to catch anything as the lake is not stocked. You do need a permit.

Hours: Open daily, dawn - dusk.
Price: Free
Ages: All

LAKE WOHLFORD

(760) 839-4346 - lake; (760) 749-6585 - cafe / www.escondido.org; www.lakewohlfordcafe.com
25453 Lake Wohlford Road, Escondido

    This beautiful, large, stocked lake offers boating and fishing - catfish, rainbow trout, crappie, bass, and bluegill - but no swimming. Rocks and boulders line the lake. Picnic tables are on the grounds. If you don't catch anything for lunch or dinner, catch something at the Smokey's Lake Wohlford Cafe, just across from the lake. This is also the place to purchase bait and boat rentals.
Hours: Open most of the year daily, 6am - dusk. Open September - mid-December weekends only, 6am - dusk.
Price: Fishing permits are $7 for adults; $5 for seniors and ages 8 - 15; children 7 years and under are free with a paying adult. Fishing licenses are also required. Row boats are $17 for the day; $14 after 1pm. Motor boats are $35 for the day; $30 after 1pm.
Ages: 5 years and up.

LA MESITA PARK / SKATE MESA

(619) 667-1300 / www.cityoflamesa.com
8855 Dallas Street, La Mesa

    This nicely kept-up little park has four lighted tennis courts, a playground with a sand base, grassy lawns for run-around play, horseshoes, picnic tables, and a skate park. This unsupervised skate park is especially good for beginners to intermediate skaters as there aren't any bowls, but plenty of ramps and other challenging features. Helmet, elbow, and knee pads are required and must be brought by the skater as there are no rentals available.
Hours: The park and skate park are open daily, 6am - 10pm.
Price: Free
Ages: All for the park; 7 years and up for the skate park.

LAS POSAS AQUATIC CENTER

(760) 744-9000 or (760) 599-9783 / www.san-marcos.net
1387 W. Borden Road, San Marcos

    The park has two tennis courts, a huge treeless field, a soccer field, and a baseball diamond. The main attractions here are the heated pool that has a shallow water area for children and a small, water play "sprayground" on the deck adjacent to the pool. The sprayground has water troughs of various heights at little kids waist level, as well as a water umbrella and pipes that spurt out water, helping everyone to have a "cool" time. Restrooms and showers are here, too.
Hours: The park is open daily, dawn - dusk. The pool (and sprayground) are open Feb. - June and holidays, and in the fall months on Sat. and Sun., 12:30pm - 4:30pm. They are open mid-June - mid-August daily, 12:30pm - 4:30pm.
Price: The park is free. Admission to the pool and sprayground is $4 for ages 3 and up.
Ages: All

LIVE OAK COUNTY PARK

(760) 728-2303 - ranger station; (760) 728-1671 - community center / www.sdparks.org
2746 Reche Road, Fallbrook

    Ah - the pause that refreshes. As its name implies, this inviting rustic park has a bounty of huge, old, shady oak trees. Scattered picnic tables, a few play areas, softball fields, sand volleyball courts, horseshoe pits and a few hiking trails also make this park a worthwhile place to visit. There is also a small botanic garden to meander through, plus a seasonal creek with bridges over it, stroller-friendly pathways, and exercise areas.
Hours: Open daily, 8am - sunset. Closed Christmas.
Price: $3 per vehicle
Ages: All

LOS PENASQUITOS CANYON PRESERVE / CANYONSIDE RECREATION CENTER COMMUNITY PARK

(619) 525-8213 or (858) 538-8066 - preserve; (858) 484-7504 - ranch house; (858) 484-3219 - friends of the preserve/hike schedule; (858) 538-8131 - recreation center / www.sandiego.gov; www.penasquitos.org; www.sdparks.org

12020 Black Mountain Road / 12350 Black Mountain Road, San Diego

This is a great "combo" destination, meaning it has a combination of elements that appeal to various ages and interests. One part is the Canyonside Recreation Center which has a small playground, ten lighted tennis courts, picnic tables, grassy areas, seven baseball fields, and a community building.

Another aspect of the park/preserve grounds is the 1824 adobe Rancho Santa Maria de los Penasquitos on Canyonside Drive. Forty-five-minute guided tours are offered on weekends of this second-oldest, standing residence in San Diego. Check out the three-foot-thick walls of the adobe, and the Mexican and Indian artifacts as you tour through the kitchen, bedrooms, office, and mock schoolroom. A natural year-round spring is on this site, too.

The largest portion of this attraction is the thousands of acres and six miles of Canyon Preserve. Hike through chaparral, wildflowers, sage, and riparian woodlands with oaks, sycamores, willows, and cottonwoods. Walk along a year-round creek, among dense canyon vegetation, and past several ponds populated by fish, crayfish, and frogs (and tadpoles in season) to reach the year-round waterfall. The boulder-lined waterfall carves through bedrock. It is reached by hiking inland about three miles, or approximately half the length of the preserve. Coming from the western route, it is also reached by going through a few creek crossings. Bring drinking water. The wildlife at the preserve is as rich and diverse as the plant life. Be on the lookout for mule deer, small mammals, lizards, birds, and, specifically, waterfowl. The crisscrossing trails are frequented by hikers, mountain bikers, and horseback riders. Ask about the numerous naturalist programs such as the geology hike, tracker walks (learn how to track animals), and ecology scavenger hunts.

Hours: The reserve is open daily, 8am - dusk. The ranch is open for guided tours Sat. at 11am and Sun. at 1pm. Call to reserve a school group tour during the week. The community park is open daily, 7am - 10pm.

Price: The preserve is free or $1 per vehicle, depending on where you park. Tours of the ranch free. The community park is free.

Ages: All

LOUIS A. STELZER PARK

(619) 561-0580 - park; (619) 390-7998 - Discovery Kit Program / www.sdparks.org

11470 Wildcat Canyon Road, Lakeside, CA

What a delightful respite! The 310-acre, back-country park has a horseshoe pit, two playgrounds, a seasonally dry creek bed, and several clusters of picnic tables with barbecues under sprawling oak and sycamore trees. (My boys also found a few good climbing trees, of course.) Some of the pathways are wheelchair/stroller accessible. A series of short hiking trails almost form a full loop. The .7-mile Riparian Trail begins near the ranger/visitor center and goes over a series of bridges as it follows along the seasonal creek. It connects to the Wooten Loop and then you have a choice: Go left onto the .6-mile Stelzer Ridge Trail, which meanders through oak groves, or go straight, which is a relatively quick climb up to the summit and promontory point. Get the kids more involved with nature by, ironically, using an app called Track Trails - they can even earn prizes.

The small visitor center has a few taxidermied animals and a Discovery Kit program. Each kit features pre- and post-visit materials for teachers and involves hands-on, interactive learning for elementary-aged children to learn about Native Americans, geology, birding, or general ecology.

Hours: Open daily, 7am - sunset. Closed Christmas.

Price: $3 per car; bring quarters.

Ages: All

MAGDALENA ECKE FAMILY YMCA SKATE PARK

(760) 942-9622 / ecke.ymca.org

200 Saxony Road, Encinitas

This YMCA really knows how to reach active kids. A great, outdoor, lighted, 37,000-square-foot skate park at the Y features a thirteen-foot-high vert bowl ramp, and six-foot-high double-bowled and double-hipped ramp, a clover bowl, and an eleven-foot kidney bowl, plus a full street course (with some interchangeable features) with a handrail station, quarter-pipes, bank ramps, pyramids, roll-in's, and slider station. Street course ramps are layered in Masonite, and half-pipes are layered in steel. The course is challenging for experienced skaters, yet allows less-experienced ones the opportunity to try some more difficult maneuvers. Younger (or beginning) skaters have a separate, gated area with lower ramps so they can build confidence as they attempt trickier moves.

All skaters are required to wear helmets and those 17 years and under must also wear knee pads and elbow pads. A parent waiver consent form must be signed, on-site, for participants 17 years and under.

Hours: Usually open during the school year, Mon. - Fri., 3pm - 6pm; Sat. - Sun., 9am - 11:30am and 2:30pm - 6pm. Open longer hours in the summer, and on some school holidays.
Price: Sessions are $6 for members, $8 for nonmembers. Membership is $50 a year and comes with a t-shirt and photo ID card.
Ages: 7 years and up.

MAST PARK

(619) 258-4100 / www.cityofsanteeca.gov
9125 Carlton Hills Boulevard, Santee

    This attractive park, that's located along a bank of the San Diego River, can get very populated. The front of the park has a play area with a basketball court, an exercise course, and a small, well-loved playground in a sand foundation. The large, plastic boat-like shape is fun for climbing into. Shade trees, picnic tables, and barbecues add to the family-friendly ambiance. And bring along your disc to play on the disc golf course!

    There are two looping, paved trails that go around the wooded back side of the park: a shorter trail, and a slightly more extensive one that weaves in and out and amongst the dirt and grassy open areas. We came in autumn as the trees were losing their leaves, crunching them underfoot as we walked the pathway.
Hours: Open daily, sunrise - sunset.
Price: Free
Ages: All

MIRAMAR RESERVOIR

(619) 668-2050 - reservoir / www.sandiego.gov
10710 Scripps Lake Drive, Scripps Ranch

    Take a gander at all the geese and ducks waiting for a hand out at the reservoir. This lovely lake offers fishing, lakeside picnic tables and barbecue areas. Fishermen 16 years and older need a fishing license and a permit. A paved, almost 5-mile looping service road extends around the lake and, judging by the number of people we saw, it's ideal for walking, biking, rollerblading, and skateboarding.
Hours: Open daily, sunrise - sunset. Closed New Year's Day, Thanksgiving, and Christmas.
Price: Free. Fishing permits are $8 for adults; $2.50 for ages 8 - 15; children 7 and under are free with a paying adult.
Ages: All

MISSION BAY PARK

(619) 525-8213 - park office; (858) 581-7602 - ranger station; (619) 235-1169 - reservations / www.sandiego.gov; www.infosandiego.com
2688 E. Mission Bay Drive, San Diego

    Mission Bay Park is not a singular bay or park like the name implies - it is thousands of acres of incredibly beautiful vistas, and of beaches, water, pathways, playgrounds, grassy areas, and various attractions. Generic things to do include jogging; cycling; in-line skating (especially the three-mile path along Mission Beach Boardwalk which runs along Mission and Pacific Beaches); swimming (there are nineteen miles of beaches here!); picnicking; fishing; kayaking; sailing; paddle boating; and camping. Park at any one of the scenic spots you see along Mission Bay Drive, or Ingraham Street, and enjoy. Hot spots include: **Pacific Beach**, just north of Mission Beach on Mission Boulevard - a favorite hang out for surfers, swimmers, joggers, and others; **Fiesta Island**, just northeast of SeaWorld, and **Vacation Isle**, on Ingraham Street north of Sea World Drive - both have numerous biking trails, delightful picnic areas, and a few playgrounds; **South Mission Beach** and **North Mission Beach**, both along Mission Boulevard - popular beaches for swimming and lying out; and **De Anza Cove**, on E. Mission Bay Drive - a nice area for swimming.

    A helpful name and phone numbers in the Mission Bay area is Campland on the Bay, (858) 581-4260 / www.campland.com, for camping, with over 650 sites. Campland also has a marina, (858) 581-4224, that has pedal boats, kayaks, catamarans, wave runners, aqua cycles, paddle boards, ski boats, power boats, and pontoon boats rentals, plus surries, beach cruisers, and recumbent trikes for rent.

    Attractions listed separately in Mission Bay Park are: BELMONT PARK (pg. 476), SEAWORLD (pg. 594), and TECOLOTE SHORES NORTH PLAY AREA (pg. 518). Check the website for a lot more information on this park.
Hours: Open daily, sunrise - sunset.
Price: Free
Ages: All

MISSION TRAILS REGIONAL PARK

(619) 668-3281 / www.mtrp.org; www.sdparks.org

One Father Junipero Serra Trail, San Diego

This massive, over 7,000-acre recreational area is composed of several major areas and points of interest, and sixty miles of trails. **The Visitor and Interpretive Center** - This architecturally-beautiful building blends in with the natural rock setting of the park, and it is a great starting place for an adventure. Every thirty minutes the small theater presents a film on the park. Pick up trail guides, program information, and/or enjoy some interactive exhibits inside. Kids gravitate to the Indian faces carved from "rocks." Several touch screens offer information about the park - where to go and all about the plants and animals. Walk to the upper story of the center amid bird and animal sounds. See ancient volcanic rock and a great view of your surroundings. Outside the center is a small stage and rocks that are almost irresistible for kids to climb. The kids sweated (I glowed) as we hiked on the moderate looping trail around the Visitors Center, which took us a good hour. Our mission, should we decide to accept it, is to come back to Mission Trails and experience more of what it has to offer!

Cowles Mountain - Hiking is the main sport here. For an outstanding 360-degree view of the city, take the one-and-a-half-mile trail (about two hours) to the top of the mountain. The trail begins at Golfcrest and Navajo. **Old Mission Dam Historic Area** - This is a starting point for several hikes. Picnic tables are here, too. People of all abilities can go on a self-guided, paved pathway from the parking lot to the footbridge across the San Diego River, lush with foliage. Further along is the gorge with rock cliffs. Press buttons along the trail to listen to explanations of the area. Take a longer hike, too. So many trails - so little time! **East Fortuna Mountain** - This area offers some of the most diverse environments of the park. Check out some of the canyons. **Kumeyaay Lake** - This small lake, accessible from Father Junipero Serra Trail, is fun for shoreline fishing, and it has 46 non-shady campsites for overnight camping on Friday and Saturday nights at $24 a night. The campground is also open daily for day-use, only. A relatively flat one-and-a-half-mile trail goes around the lake. **West Fortuna Mountain** - You can hike or mountain bike up plateaus and series of canyons. Climb the 100+ steps up to the south portion of the mountain for a breath-taking (literally) view of the area. Also see LAKE MURRAY (pg. 505) for another part of this massive regional park.

Hours: The trails and park are open daily, sunrise - sunset, although the car entry gates are open 9am - 5pm. The Center is open daily, 9am - 5pm. Closed on New Year's Day, Thanksgiving, and Christmas.

Price: Free

Ages: 3 years and up.

MONTEVALLE PARK

(619) 691-5269 / www.chulavistaca.gov

840 Duncan Ranch Road, Chula Vista

Adjacent to Salt Creek Open Space, you'll find plenty to do for the day at this expansive, twenty-nine-acre park, in somewhat of a natural setting. The amenities include three multi-purpose fields; a softball field; tennis courts; basketball courts; off-leash areas - one for large dogs and one for smaller ones; picnic tables and shelters; paved and gravel walking trails lined with a wooden fence that meander through some marshy areas, amongst trees, and over bridges; a community center; a terrific playground; and a skate area. The small skate park has rails and ramps, but no bowls.

It's worth coming here just for the huge playground with its foundation in wood chips and rubber. One section is designed especially for disabled children with long ramps that have lots of interactive gadgets and activities along the ramp walls, plus speaking tubes and a learning Braille section. This area also has a small playhouse with a raised table and several basins on stands filled with sand for wheelchairs to readily fit under. A sand pit is on ground level, too. Toddler swings and swings to accommodate wheelchairs; animals on large springs to ride on; numerous slides; a cargo net to climb; twisted metal pieces to play on; benches; peek-a-boo play spaces under the play platforms; a seasonal water sprayer (that looks like a shower); and two jumbo-size xylophones (one metal and one wood) to make (beautiful?) music complete this playground.

Hours: Open daily, sunrise - sunset.

Price: Free

Ages: All

MORLEY FIELD

(619) 525-8262 - park; (619) 692-3607 - disc golf; (619) 692-4920 - pool; (619) 295-9278 - Balboa Tennis Club / www.sandiego.gov; www.morleyfield.com; www.balboatennis.com

2221 Morely Field Drive, San Diego

The massive, multi-use park and sports complex is located at in the northeastern section of BALBOA

PARK (pg. 524). It has soooo much to see and do! It has a fitness course with 18 stations encircling a good portion - 2.5 miles - of the park; boccie ball, which is an Italian sport similar to lawn bowling and Petanque, a French game that's also similar to lawn bowling; a velodrome, that hosts races and offers classes; an archery range; baseball diamonds; playgrounds - one near Upas St. and Pershing Dr., and one behind the swimming pool complex; picnic areas; a dog park; a remote control race car track (at the southern end); lots and lots and lots of grassy areas and trees; some walking and hiking trails; and a disc golf course. The disc golf course is off Pershing Dr. and is open daily sunrise to sunset. It cost $4 to play all day during the week; $5 on the weekends. The pro shop has rental discs for $1.50 per. The Bud Kearns Memorial swimming pool here is open seasonally - call for hours. Swim sessions cost $4 for adults, $2 for seniors and children. The 25 public, lighted, tennis courts are available for $10 per person for adults (for all day use); $8 for seniors; $6 for ages 17 and under. Call the Tennis Club for reservations. Courts are open Mon. - Fri., 8am - 9pm; Sat. - Sun., 8am - 8pm.

Just south of the tennis courts is a Nature Exploration Area - an area set aside and furnished by the city with fort-building and other natural building materials such as branches, reeds, pine cones and tree cookies (1" thick log rounds), along with numerous large logs and huge boulders to climb on. Imagination and nature - still a winning combination. For more of nature, hike the 2 mile loop Florida Canyon Trail, which crosses Florida Drive and Zoo Drive, and the offshoot trails, which don't. The trail is hilly, with some erosion, seasonal wildflowers and a creek bed, and near civilization. The offshoot trails on the west side of Florida Dr. are in Morely Field (park off Pershing and Jacaranda Dr near the disc golf course), and the ones on the west side are a hidden pocket of Balboa Park (park near 2581 - 2699 Park Blvd.) Whew! And then, go play some more at Balboa Park and all of its museums and gardens.

Hours: The park is open daily, sunrise - sunset.
Price: Free, for most of the activities.
Ages: All

MOUNTAIN HAWK PARK

(619) 397-6042 / www.chulavistaca.gov
1475 Lake Crest Drive, Chula Vista

This 12-acre, scenic park has a basketball court, an amphitheater, a gazebo that overlooks Otay Lake, a lovely walking trail along the lake and park, open grassy fields, and two play areas: One has a free-standing rock climbing wall, a large ring and another creative play structure that has a large metal arc and climbing elements at both ends; the other is a more traditional structure with short slides, a little bridge connecting two short towers and play space beneath it. The cement splash pad, open daily April through November, is basic - it just has water spurting up from fountains on the ground - but it is effective in the hot summer months.

Hours: Open daily, sunrise - sunset.
Price: Free
Ages: All

OCEAN BEACH ATHLETIC AREA / ROBB FIELD SKATEBOARD PARK

(619) 531-1563 / www.sandiego.gov/park-and-recreation/centers
2525 Bacon Street, Ocean Beach

This huge park has something for every athlete in the family. It boasts several baseball diamonds, racquetball courts, twelve tennis courts (available through Peninsula Tennis Club), basketball courts, and a massive grass area for North American football or "futebol" (i.e. soccer). There are also smaller grassy areas, picnic tables, a bike path that follows along the adjacent San Diego River, and a terrific skate park at the east end.

In front of the massive skate park (40,000 square feet!) are a few very shallow cement pools (more like a toe-dip area than pool) and cement area - a good place for young skaters to practice. The outdoor, smooth concrete-surface skate park has numerous pools of varying depths along with ramps, steps, a split fun box, ledges, blocks, an octagon volcano, and pump bump, plus a few flat areas and a pathway around the perimeter. Robb Field was the first skatepark in San Diego and is still one of the best. Benches are just outside for ~~anxious~~, I mean, observing parents. Vending machines carry beverages; bring your own lunch. Helmet, elbow and knee pads are required by the signs via the signage.

Across the street, Dusty Rhodes Park offers more picnic and run-around area, plus a playground. To the west is Dog Beach, where furry visitors from all over come to romp and play frisbee on this stretch of beach. Tip: Watch where you walk.

Hours: The park is open daily, sunrise - sunset. The skate park is open daily, 10am - dusk.
Price: The park and skate park are free.

Ages: All

OLD POWAY PARK

See the entry for OLD POWAY PARK (pg. 566), under POTPOURRI, for details.

OTAY LAKE COUNTY PARK

(619) 482-7361 - park; (619) 668-2050 - boat rentals / www.sdparks.org
2270 Wueste Road, Chula Vista

The view from atop this small park is beautiful as it overlooks lower Otay Lake. The playground has slides, swings, and climbing equipment, plus talking tubes and a mini zip line. A grassy area, picnic tables, horseshoe pits, a demonstration garden, and three short hiking trails up the hillside complete this scenic park. Enjoy kayaking or motor boating, and fishing in the lake that is stocked once a year with catfish.

Hours: The park is open Mon. - Fri., 9:30am - 5pm; Sat. - Sun. and holidays, 9:30am - sunset, tho pedestrians can walk in daily, sunrise - sunset. Closed Christmas. Fishing and boating are available at Lower Otay February - October, Wed., Sat., and Sun., sunrise - sunset. No fishing or boating is allowed November - January. (It's duck season.) Shore fishing - catch and release only - is allowed at Upper Otay the same schedule as Lower Otay.

Price: Free for walk ins. $3 per vehicle to the park. Fishing is $8 for adults, plus a fishing license, which isn't sold at the park; $2.50 for ages 8 - 15 (no license necessary); children 7 and under are free with a paying adult. Motorboats are $35 for two hours. Single kayaks are $10 per hour; tandems are $12.

Ages: All

PALOMAR MOUNTAIN STATE PARK / PALOMAR OBSERVATORY

(760) 742-2119 - observatory; (760) 742-3462 - state park; (800) 444-7275 - camping reservations. / www.parks.ca.gov; www.astro.caltech.edu/palomar; www.friendsofpalomarsp.org
35899 Canfield Road - observatory / 19952 State Park Drive - state park, Palomar Mountain

Up in the Palomar Mountains, at the end of a long and winding road, is the Palomar Observatory. A short hike up to the observatory allows you to see the famed 200" Hale telescope. But forewarn your children - you can only look at the telescope which is housed behind glass panes; you cannot look through it, even on a guided tour. The telescope is magnificent in size and scope and seeing it is almost worth the drive here! The small one-room museum displays outstanding photos of star clusters, galaxies, and clouds of glowing gas. It also shows a continuously running video about the workings of the telescope and about our universe. Hour-long, guided tours are offered to the public on the weekends, April through October, at 11am and 1:30pm.

Just a few miles down the road is Palomar Mountain State Park. If you're planning on coming to the observatory, I suggest making the park a destination, too, as just walking around the observatory and museum took us only half an hour. Palomar Mountain General Store, (760) 742-3496, is at the junction of S7 and S6 at 33120 Canfield Road, making it a natural stopping place before going on to the park. The store has a bit of everything, including fossils, gems, Indian jewelry, and artifacts. And if you're hungry, Mother's Kitchen is just next door, serving breakfast and lunch.

Continue about three miles on S7 to reach the park. The 2,000 acres and eleven miles of trails throughout this Sierra Nevada-like park are incredibly beautiful. It also can get snow in the winter. The Boucher Hill Lookout trail, for instance, is a looping four-mile hike with marvelous vistas. Note that the Boucher Fire Tower is usually open Mid-May through October, 9:30am - 5pm, if it is staffed. The Doane Valley Trail is fairly easy at only one mile, but it includes two stream crossings and a few steep areas. Fishing is available at Doane Pond, which is stocked with trout regularly. There is a five-fish limit per day, and those 16 years old and older need a California state license. The park also provides areas for picnicking and overnight camping. Each of the thirty-one family campsites has fire rings and picnic tables, plus community, coin-operated hot showers. Call the ranger station (park office) for more information.

Hours: The museum and the observatory are usually open daily, 9am - 3pm. Always call first as weather affects closures. The museum gift shop is open Fri. - Wed. (closed Thurs.), 9:15am - 2:45pm. All are closed Christmas Eve and Christmas Day. The state park is open daily, sunrise - sunset.

Price: Free to the observatory and museum. Guided tours of the observatory are $5 for adults; $3 for ages 5 - 12 (children under 5 aren't permitted). A $10 vehicle entrance fee is charged for day use of the park. Overnight camping is available at Doane Valley Campground at about $35 a night, plus a $8 camping reservation fee, or camp at the forty-two site Observatory Campground which is open May - November.

Ages: 8 years and up for the observatory and the museum; ages 3 and up for the park.

POTRERO COUNTY PARK

(619) 478-5212 or (858) 694-3030 / www.sdparks.org

24800 Potrero Park Drive, Potrero

Waaay out here is an expansive park (115 acres) that is reminiscent of the olden days in California. Hundreds of enormous oak trees, plus grassy meadows, rocky hillsides, nature trails (look for rocks with holes where the Indians ground acorns into meal), lots of picnic tables, ball fields, playgrounds, exercise stations and machines, and camping and RV sites, plus two cabins with a bathroom and bed frames (no mattresses) are here. Be on the lookout for all kinds of wildlife.

Hours: Open daily, 9:30am - sunset. Closed Christmas.

Price: Free for day use. Camping fees range from $27 - $34 a night, plus a $5 reservation fee. The cabins are about $65.

Ages: All

POWAY COMMUNITY PARK

(858) 679-4366 or (858) 668-4671 or (858) 668-4687 - park, skate park and tennis; (858) 668-4680 - swim center / www.poway.org

13094 Civic Center Drive, Poway

This park offers something for almost everyone in the community. An unsupervised cement skate park with bowls, ramps, and stairs is on the corner, just behind the public library. Riders of scooter, skates and bikes are also allowed in the skate park. Children 12 and under must be accompanied by parent or legal guardian. A helmet and pads are necessary. Note that officers of the neighboring Sheriff's office often drop by for a visit. Drive further in to play on the two lighted tennis courts (call for reservations), or walk over the grassy embankments to the good-sized Adventure Playground. The playground has swings, a swaying bridge, several slides, circular monkey bars, and a big wheel to spin around, all on top of a rubberized surface. There are plenty of picnic tables here, as well.

Other park amenities are a dog park (watch where you step), a tot lot, a few ball fields, a soccer field, a basketball court, bocce ball courts, and a compact exercise "course" with bars for pull ups and sit ups, and pieces of wooden equipment. The swim center has a fifty-meter pool that is open year round and a wading pool for kiddies that is closed in the winter. Children 7 years and under must be accompanied by an adult.

Hours: The park is open daily, 8am - sunset. The skate park is open daily, 8am - 8pm. The swim center hours fluctuate greatly - check the website or call first.

Price: The park and skate park are free. The swim center for nonresidents is $5 for adults; $4 for seniors and ages 17 and under. For residents, $2.50 for adults; $2 for seniors and ages 17 and under.

Ages: All

RANCHO BERNARDO-GLASSMAN RECREATION CENTER

(858) 538-8129 - park; (858) 487-5002 - tennis club / www.rbcommunitypark.com; www.sandiego.gov/park-and-recreation/centers

18448 W. Bernardo Drive, San Diego

This community park has a playground, eight baseball diamonds, basketballs courts, the Rancho Bernardo Swim and Tennis Club (with a woodworking shop, too), two lawn bowling areas, picnic tables, barbecue pits, and lots of grassy areas and paved pathways throughout for all kinds of wheels. All of this is nice, but what helps make this park a stand out is the adjoining open area with some fairly easy dirt hiking trails. The area has hard-to-resist-climbing-on large rocks scattered throughout, gentle hills, and a trail that leads to Lake Hodges, a lake within visual range from the park. A portion of the park is also a leash-free dog park.

Hours: The park is open daily, sunrise - sunset. The recreation building is open Mon. - Sat.; closed Sun. and holidays. Play tennis daily, 7am - 10pm. (Of course you'd be tired if you played that long.)

Price: Free. There is a fee for tennis and swimming.

Ages: All

SALTON SEA STATE RECREATION AREA

(760) 393-3052 or (760) 393-3059 - park and camping; (760) 393-3810 - visitor center / www.parks.ca.gov

100-225 State Park Road (for the North Shore), Mecca

Firstly, I know this isn't really in San Diego county, so with that said. . . . Salton Sea is California's largest lake and is one of the world's lowest spots on earth at 236 feet below sea level. It is also incredibly salty, so while fishing is big here, a limited type of fish can be caught. And yes, it does smell like rotting fish, especially during hot days, because fish skeletons/dead fish litter the shores. The "sand" is made up mostly of crushed bones and shells - wear shoes. The sunsets are camera-worthy.

Salton Sea is a strange and fascinating place to visit, as there is beauty in the midst of decay. We weren't here long, but it was intriguing. Most of the action takes places at the North End, near Varner's Harbor and the visitor center. Inside the center is a very small nature center and a video regarding the Salton Sea, plus photographs of the area and information as to how it was formed, its salinity, preservation efforts, and more. There is also a playground located here and a fishing jetty.

Boating is a preferred recreational sport and there are numerous launching points. Twitching is also immensely popular. Not as in a body part twitching or jerking around, but as in bird-watching lingo, "the pursuit of a previously located rare bird." The Salton Sea is located along the Pacific Flyway and about 400 species of birds have been counted here including grebes, brown pelicans, great blue herons, ospreys, gulls, owls, tern and many more. Bring your binoculars and make it 401!

Spend the night at one of the over 1,600 campsites, ranging from primitive to full amenities. Note which ones are closed in the summer, though that wouldn't be the best of times to come here, anyway. Make sure to visit SALVATION MOUNTAIN (pg. 566) and the INTERNATIONAL BANANA MUSEUM (pg. 533) because they are just down the road a bit.

Hours: Open daily 24/7. The visitor center is open October - May, Wed. - Sun., 10am - 4pm; June - September, Fri. - Sun., 10am - 4pm.

Price: $7 per vehicle for day use; $5 for seniors. Camping is $20 - $30.

Ages: 5 years and up.

SAN DIEGO BOTANIC GARDEN

(760) 436-3036 / www.sdbgarden.org

230 Quail Gardens Drive, Encinitas

$$$$

Desert, exotic tropical, tropical rainforest, palm, bamboo, native California, Mexican, Mediterranean, African, New Zealand, and other garden sections (twenty seven in all!) makes it feel as if you are walking all over parts of the world as you meander the trails throughout these thirty-seven beautifully-landscaped acres.

The bamboo forest, which grows a variety from very thick to quite thin bamboo, contains a pond with lily pads and koi. An array of tropical fruit trees, such as papaya and bananas, grow their fruit upside down, while figs and jujube (not the candy!) are also ripening here. The desert gardens have twisted-looking cactus and other succulents. The Mexican garden features life-size figures made from plants and sculpture parts. The lush foliage of the rainforest showcases the amazing size of some leaves and beyond Crayola colors of green. Throughout the gardens the incredible array of flowers, the wandering trails (some dirt, some paved), the beautiful waterfall, the ponds, the benches under shade trees, and even the fanciful sculptures (for sale) that unexpectedly crop up all invoke the sensation of visiting a secret garden. Add to that the sounds and sights of woodpeckers and a variety of other birds such as wrens, finches, scrub jays, and hermit thrushes, and the outdoors come alive. Take a short hike up to the Overlook Pavilion for a 360-degree view of the gardens, mountains, ocean, and surrounding community.

Kids can spend almost all day in the one-acre Hamilton Children's Garden with its fifteen activities. The colorful sculptures throughout this area add a touch of whimsy. Bloom with learning at the Spell and Smell Garden where a plant for each letter of the alphabet and the plant's function, is labeled, such as C is for chocolate mint (smell) and L is for lamb's ear (soft, velvety texture). Check out the Seussian elephant foot tree. Play in dirt and sand at the good-sized Earth Builders portion with small logs to build forts, plus toys and toy trucks. Go through a little maze to the center where you become the sundial's shadow to tell time. Make music (or noise) with natural elements at Garden Rhythms with a stone xylophone, a drum, bamboo wind chimes, stone pianos, and more. Splash a bit in the small, shallow, rock-lined stream. Birds and butterflies are attracted to certain plants and in this area you see them as they land and flutter about. Practice chalkboard skills and other artistic endeavors in the Art's Garden, complete with oversized chairs and other objects. The Hamilton Children's Garden also contains an awesome Tree House - a twenty-foot high, multi-platform, banyan tree (part real, part man made) with steps up to the separate areas. What kid doesn't dream of living at a place like this? Climb over and through the tree roots and up the rope ladder, too. I'm sure they also become rooted in a love and knowledge of plants here.

The Seeds of Wonder is south of the parking lot and is a small section specifically for preschoolers. It has a few fanciful topiary figures; a hand water pump; animal sculptures to climb on (including some small dinosaurs and some eggs); a small, sandy dig site with buried "bones"; short, hidden pathways for young children to explore; a shed with plants growing on the roof; a miniature train on tracks through a garden area; and a sweet, little playhouse with kitchen utensils and books inside. Adjacent to this section is a short hiking trail through a representative canyon of sorts - the Native Plants/Native People region. It is reminiscent of the landscape hundreds of years ago with its coastal sage, a pond, and a Native American (Kumeyaay) dwelling.

Plan to be at the Botanic Garden on a Thursday night in the summer when the garden stays open until 8pm and activities and live music are included with the price of admission. Ask about guided tours; plant sales; family programs, such as art in the garden, Fairy Festival, or the annual Insect Festival; summer science camps; the beautiful Garden of Lights in December; and other listings in the packed calendar of events. Just to let you know that all this write-up doesn't do this amazing garden justice - it is a "must see".

Hours: Open daily, 9am - 5pm. Closed Christmas.
Price: $14 for adults; $10 for seniors, military, and students; $8 for ages 3 -12; children 2 and under are free. Admission is free on the first Tues. for San Diego residents. Parking is $2. See MUSEUM MONTH, SAN DIEGO (pg. 700), in the calendar section, for details about half-price admission in February. See American Horticultural Society (pg. x) for info on reciprocal memberships.
Ages: 2 years and up.

SAN DIEGUITO COUNTY PARK

(858) 755-2386 / www.sdparks.org
1628 Lomas Santa Fe Drive, Del Mar

San Dieguito's 125 acres of nature park offer a variety of trails to hike that crisscross all over the park; lots of grassy, open and wooded spaces to play and picnic; bbq pits; a swinging suspension bridge; two small ponds at one end with ever-present ducks and some turtles; a lookout tower with great views; a basketball court; a seasonal creek; two great playgrounds; exercise stations; and a baseball field that is fully accessible for players with special needs. This park feels, to me, like a great and close by nature retreat. Trees actually change color here in the fall! Get the kids more involved with nature by, ironically, using an app called Track Trails - they can even earn prizes.

Hours: Open daily, 9:30am - 5pm.
Price: Parking is $3.
Ages: All

SAN DIEGUITO RIVER PARK

(858) 674-2270 / www.sdrp.org
18372 Sycamore Creek Road, Escondido

Beautiful and startling scenery await at this enormous natural habitat within San Diego County with 65 miles of trails for every level. Most trails are open to hikers, bikers, and equestrians. The backbone trail - the Coast to Crest Trail - extends a great distance in chunks (i.e. not all connected), from the ocean at Del Mar almost to the San Dieguito River's source on Volcan Mountain near Julian - with lots of places from which to access it in-between, plus 20 miles of auxiliary trails. A favorite section for me goes around LAKE HODGES (pg. 503). Check the website for detailed trail maps. The above address is the headquarters for the River Park, not a trailhead.

Hours: Open daily, sunrise - sunset.
Price: Free
Ages: 5 years and up.

SAN ELIJO LAGOON ECOLOGICAL RESERVE AND NATURE CENTER

(760) 634-3026 - nature center; (760) 436-3944 - lagoon conservancy / www.sanelijo.org; www.sdparks.org
2710 Manchester Avenue, Cardiff-by-the-Sea

One of San Diego's largest coastal wetlands protects nearly 1,000 acres and hundreds of plants, birds, and other animals in the water and on land, even as a highway divides a portion of it. Walk any part, or all, of the seven miles of the eight mostly flat trails that wind through the reserve, past estuaries and salt marshes, and through sagebrush and chaparral, many with interpretive signage. The ADA accessible, half-mile loop trail by the nature center is on paved and boardwalk surfaces. The 3.5 mile La Orilla Trail really traverses through distinct areas, including some woodland. Get the kids more involved with nature by, ironically, using an app called Track Trails - they can even earn prizes.

Join in on a free, one-hour, naturalist-led walk on the first and last Saturdays at 10am and learn about what you are seeing; help out with the monthly habitation restoration (i.e. clean up!); and/or attend free Family Fun Days on the first Sundays from 11:30am - 1:30pm with crafts, hands-on exhibits, an opportunity to earn a Junior Ranger Badge and other activities. School, and other, groups are welcome to set up a time for guided tours.

The green, lovely and airy nature center allows visitors to see a whole new world - well, at least it offers a good view of the lagoon and surroundings from the second-floor Observation Deck. The inside features informational and photographic panels; interactive displays to learn about the surrounding plant and rock and animal life; taxidermied animals such as a bobcat, coyotes, and hawks; and a few live animals such as snakes, lizards, tree frogs, and crabs.

Hours: Trails are open daily, dawn to dusk. The nature center is open daily, 9am - 5pm. Closed Christmas.

Price: Free

Ages: All

SAN PASQUAL BATTLEFIELD STATE HISTORIC PARK

(760) 737-2201 / www.parks.ca.gov

15808 San Pasqual Valley Road (SR78), San Pasqual

This is the site of the worst (i.e., bloodiest) battles in California during the Mexican-American War. Kids need to know this fact for its historical significance, and because it will make their visit here more exciting. The grounds have picnic tables and a quarter-mile, looping trail. The visitors center overlooks the battlefield, which is actually across the highway, on private land. The small center has interpretive panels, a few uniforms, weapons, and a ten-minute video entitled *Mr. Polk's War.* Living History Days are held the first Sunday of each month from 10am to 4pm, October through June. Docents are dressed in period costumes and visitors get to participate in old-fashioned chores, crafts, and other activities. Periodically, you can also see a cannon being fired. Guided school tours are given during the week, by appointment. Note: The battle is reenacted in December. See the Calendar entry SAN PASQUAL BATTLE REENACTMENT (pg. 763) for details. Note that the park is located right next to SAN DIEGO ARCHAEOLOGICAL CENTER (pg. 550).

Hours: The park is open Sat. - Sun., 10am - 4pm, October - March; 10am - 5pm, April - September. Closed New Year's Day, Thanksgiving and Christmas.

Price: Free

Ages: 6 years and up.

SANTA CORA PARK

(619) 397-6197 / www.chulavistaca.gov

1365 Santa Cora Avenue, Chula Vista

This Chula Vista park has some unique elements such as a hopscotch court, funky playground, a rock climbing wall, and a big, wide, grassy hill to roll down, with plenty of run-around space at its bottom. The playground has geometric shapes to climb up and on; poles with seats to twirl around and up; cargo ropes; platforms; ladders; a spinning chair that looks like an upside down plunger; and other fun structures. A separate apparatus looks like a frameless helicopter with a steering wheel.

The sizeable, free-standing, ten-foot-high (or so), curved, rock climbing wall has colorful hand and foot holds (just like an indoor rock climbing gym), an archway with an overhang, and an accompanying panel with instructions on how to practice bouldering skills. The park also has a tennis court, lighted basketball court, barbecue pits, and several cement picnic tables. Note that there aren't any restroom facilities here. See COTTONWOOD PARK (pg. 497), which is just down the street, for facilities and a different type of park.

Hours: Open daily, sunrise - sunset.

Price: Free

Ages: All

SANTEE LAKES REGIONAL PARK AND CAMPGROUND

(619) 596-3141 / www.santeelakes.com

9310 Fanita Parkway, Santee

Nestled in the hills, this lovely, narrow, 2.5 mile long regional park is made up primarily of a series of seven lakes. Paved trails for walking and biking loop around the lakes, and all around the park. There are several playgrounds: One specifically designed for children with disabilities; one with a bouldering adventure course with "rocks" to climb; and one, towards the entrance, has a very small sprayground with fountains that spurt up and a misting ring to run through.

Bring your fishing pole as the lakes are seasonally stocked with trout, catfish, bluegill, and bass. There are a few short fishing piers here. A permit is required and available for purchase at the park entrance. No state fishing license is required. No swimming is allowed, but there a myriad of other fun water options with kayak, canoe and rowboat rentals at $17 an hour per, and four-seat pedal boats at $16. Bike rentals, including surreys, are also available.

Three hundred campsites (only nine for tent camping), a swimming pool (for campers only), a general store, laundry facilities, horseshoe pits, volleyball courts, and a recreation center are on the grounds, too. The camp playground, open to day user, too, is very fun with a pirate-ship-looking structure to climb up and thru and slide down, and a short rock climbing wall. Full hook-up campgrounds are $45 to $61 a night, depending on the day and site. Each campsite has a picnic table. Seven fully-furnished and equipped lakeside cabins with kitchenettes, that sleep six, range from $99 to $170 a night, depending on the day and date. For the ultimate waterbed, rent one of three side-by-side cabins that float on the water(!) near a dock. They sleep four and range from $99 to $190 a night.

Hours: The park and fishing are open Mon. - Thurs., 8am - one hour before dusk; Fri. - Sun., 6am - 6:30pm. Closed Thanksgiving and Christmas day. The pool is open seasonally.

Price: $4 per vehicle during the week; $6 per vehicle on the weekends and holidays ($1 discount if paying by cash). Note that you can park for free at the adjacent Padre Dam Municipal Water District parking lot and walk in for free. It's near the first lake and has a patch of grass and cement picnic tables. The sprayground, open seasonally, is $2 for ages 13 and under during the week; $3 on weekends and holidays. Fishing permits are $9 for adults; $6 for seniors and ages 15 and under.

Ages: 2 years and up.

SCRIPPS PARK / LA JOLLA COVE and COASTLINE

(619) 221-8899 or (858) 581-9976 / www.sandiego.gov
1180 Coast Boulevard, La Jolla

This delightful grassy park overlooks a gorgeous stretch of the California coastline and the Pacific Ocean. The park itself has few amenities - picnic tables, a few palm and cypress trees, and a covered overlook. It's an ideal place for flying a kite and to catch a concert on Sunday afternoons in the summer from 2pm to 4pm (when concerts are given). Take a walk on the cement sidewalk that follows up and down a good distance along the coast and revel in the breathtaking scenery and in the variety of landscape.

Just to the north of the park is tiny Shell Beach (good for collecting seashells) and La Jolla Cove, a tiny patch of beach with palm trees swaying in the wind on top of the adjoining sandstone cliffs. There are a few rocks here to climb on and through, like short caves. You may go swimming here. The cove's water visibility can sometimes exceed thirty feet, making this a favorite spot for snorkelers and scuba divers. (Think Hawaiian waters, kind of.) The cove is part of the San Diego La Jolla Underwater Park Ecological Reserve which safeguards marine life in the area, so bring your own snorkel gear and head out to sea.

Further north is the LA JOLLA SHORES BEACH (pg. 467). Heading just south of the park, within easy walking distance, is the SEAL ROCK MARINE MAMMAL RESERVE / CHILDREN'S POOL (pg. 594). Continue on to small South Casa Beach and Wipeout Beach (hard to tell where one stops and the other begins), which has a semicircular portion of sand (embraced by rocks), sea caves, and rocks - large, flat rocks to climb on and jump off (at least the shorter ones). My boys loved this aspect of the beach. Tide pooling is a great activity to do at certain nooks along the coastline.

Note that parking anywhere around this area in the summer time can be ridiculously difficult, but worth it. Go "off-season" and enjoy all the same benefits. Look up LA JOLLA CAVE and THE CAVE STORE (pg. 563) and SNORKEL SAN DIEGO (pg. 584) for information on other nearby attractions.

Hours: Open daily, sunrise - sunset.

Price: Free

Ages: All

SHADOW HILL PARK

(619) 258-4100 / www.cityofsanteeca.gov
9161 Shadow Hill Road, Santee

If you are in this area, this is a nice little park to release some energy. The sand and rubber-based playground has fun apparatus, plus there is a basketball court, a small lawn, a few picnic tables, a little garden with a picnic nook, short paved pathways for cycling or skating, and a short hiking trail up the hill and around the two tennis courts.

Hours: Open daily, dawn - dusk.

Price: Free

Ages: All

SOUTH CLAIREMONT RECREATION CENTER and POOL

(858) 581-9924 - recreation center; (858) 581-9923 - pool / www.sandiego.gov
3605 Clairemont Drive, Clairemont

This large community park offers various activities for families to enjoy. Green grassy areas and scattered picnic tables provide a picnic atmosphere, while the older-style playground, complete with hopscotch, slides, swings, and climbing apparatus, provides the fun. Check at the community center building for special classes, programs, and events. There is also one tennis court, a basketball court, and a good-sized, outdoor swimming pool, plus a wading pool that is open year round. During the week, only half of the pool is open for public use because the swim team uses the other half. On weekends, the whole pool is open for the public to use. Note that KRAUSE FAMILY SKATE AND BIKE PARK (pg. 484) is next door to the pool.

Hours: The park is open daily, sunrise - sunset. The pool is open daily, noon - 3pm. Call for hours as they do fluctuate.

Price: The park is free. Swimming sessions cost $4 for adults; $2 for seniors and ages 15 and under.

Ages: All

STAGECOACH COMMUNITY PARK

(760) 434-2826 or (760) 602-4690 / www.carlsbadca.gov

3420 Camino de los Coches, Carlsbad

Although stagecoaches no longer use this park as they once did, there are some preserved adobe ruins from those bygone days. The ruins are housed in a building residing beneath a large, wide expanse of stones (set in a spiral, with benches, for visitors to sit and rest, or play on). The ruins are worth a look. The adjacent community center has a gym.

The park has three multi-use, athletic fields; four lighted tennis courts; a lighted basketball court and some half-courts; paved pathways that traverse throughout the open grassy play areas and trees; picnic tables scattered throughout; and a delightful, stone-lined brook with a wooden bridge - like a mini woodlands area. There is also a short trail towards the back. A good-sized, sand-based playground has several, separate, elevated play structures, including one designed to represent a stagecoach. The main playground has lots of slides, including two that are enclosed, plus climbing apparatus, swings, and more.

Hours: Open daily, 8am - 10pm.

Price: Free

Ages: All

SUNSET PARK

(760) 744-9000 / www.san-marcos.net

909 Puesta del Sol, San Marcos

Good playgrounds are important at a park and this one has two; a smaller one for younger kids and a larger taller one for older kids. Imagination inspired, the structures have the prerequisite slides and swings, but they also have several innovative climbing elements such as curved walls with holes and shapes, twisted bars and play space underneath, a teeter totter and mini zip line, all in wood chips and under shade awnings. Adjacent to that is a really large, flattish snake head to climb on (just because) and a splash pad with nothing fancy (but cool water always feels good on a hot day) - it's a sun design with water spurting up and a small rock fountain in the middle.

The park also features a volleyball court; half-basketball court; disc golf course; multi-purpose sports field; a lighted indoor soccer arena; picnic tables; lots of grassy run-around space; a dog park; a bridge over a usually dried creek bed; and some walking trails.

Hours: Open daily sunrise to sunset.

Price: Free

Ages: All

SWEETWATER REGIONAL PARK / ROHR PARK

(619) 472-7572 - campground; (619) 397-6197 - park; (877) 565-3600 - camping / www.sdparks.org; www.chulavistalivesteamers.org

3218 Summit Meadow Road / 4548 Sweetwater Road, Chula Vista

Sweetwater Regional Park is a long stretch of land that runs between Sweetwater Road and Bonita Road. Fred Rohr Park is a nice oblong park, within Sweetwater Park, that parallels a golf course, and has a 3.3 mile walking trail. The lake here is home to numerous ducks. Picnic tables are scattered throughout the park along with a few barbecue pits. Entertainment is provided by using swing sets, jungle gyms, volleyball courts, softball fields, basketball courts, grassy areas, shade trees, fitness stations with legit equipment, and cement bike and rollerblade paths. A monthly highlight is a ride on a scale-model steam locomotive around the park. The Live Steamers, who run the locomotive, also operate ⅛-scale diesel and electric trains.

Sweetwater offers a sweet escape from city life. It has over 100 campsites that can accommodate RVs (with full hook-ups) or tents, each with a picnic table and fire ring, and panoramic view of the surrounding mountains. There is even equestrian camping at the summit site of the park that overlooks the reservoir. There are fifteen miles of hiking trails in the area. Sweetwater also has a lakeside (well, reservoir-side) community recreation building with fireplaces, an outdoor deck and amphitheater, and a simple, but imaginative, playground. One section has boulders to climb on and a rock-climbing wall with an archway. Another area has a tower with slides, monkey bar rings, and more climbing apparatus. Down the hill in the day-use area is another playground and a gated, colorful water playground which sports a rainbow with misters; fountains that spurt up water intermittently and a good-size area to run around and squeal; water cannons; and a tall pole with buckets attached that dump out water on people standing below them. An exercise circuit, expanses of grass, and a sense of getting away for a bit add to your day (or weekend) of enjoyment.

Hours: Sweetwater is open daily, 9:30am - sunset. The trains run on the second full weekend of each month (but on Labor Day weekend in September) from noon - 2:30pm. The water playground is open daily, May - October, same hours as the park.

Price: $3 per vehicle for Sweetwater Park. Rohr Park is free. Train rides are $1 per person. The water playground is $3 per child. Camping is $29 - $36 a night, plus a $5 reservation fee.

Ages: All

TECOLOTE SHORES NORTH PLAY AREA

(619) 236-5555 or (619) 235-1169 / www.sandiego.gov

1590 E. Mission Bay Drive, San Diego

　　Head for some big time fun at the large Tecolote Shores Play Area. This wonderful playground has a great combination of old and new equipment. In the main area, with its sand-covered grounds, there are slides, swings, and cement turtles to climb on (and under). Other sections include aquatic cement creatures, a good-sized pirate ship, mini-obstacle ropes course, bridges, and various other climbing apparatus. There are plenty of picnic tables and grassy areas here, too. As the playground is right on the bay, the view is beautiful. Tip: There aren't many tall trees here, at least right now, so this is a great place to fly a kite.

Hours: Open daily, sunrise - sunset.

Price: Free

Ages: 1- 10 years old.

THE PARK AT THE PARK

(619) 795-5000 / www.petcoparkevents.com; www.sandiegopadres.com

100 Park Boulevard, San Diego

　　See PETCO PARK - THE PARK AT THE PARK (pg. 576) for details.

TIDELANDS PARK / CORONADO SKATE PARK

(619) 686-6200 or (619) 522-7300 - park; (619) 708-8341 - skatepark / www.portofsandiego.org - park; www.coronado.ca.us - skatepark

2000 Mullinex Drive, Coronado

　　This delightful, large, corner park offers a spectacular view of San Diego across the bay, plus pathways, a bike path (that stretches from Silver Strand to the Old Ferry Landing), playgrounds (with a sand flooring and palm trees sprinkled in the midst), a fitness course, picnic tables, ball fields, grassy areas, and a sandy beach for swimming (no lifeguards).

　　A good-sized (16,000 square feet), supervised and gated skate park near the beach has several concrete pools along with steps, rails, ramps, and grinding boxes. A parent or legal guardian must sign a waiver, that is kept on file, for skaters 17 years and under. Helmets are required for all ages skaters; knee and elbow pads required for ages 17 and under. (There is some equipment here to borrow.) A small snack shop is on the premises.

Hours: The park is open daily, 6:30am - 10:30pm. The skate park is open most of the year, Mon. - Fri., 1pm - sunset; Sat. - Sun., 10am - sunset. It's open daily in the summer, 10am - sunset. Closed New Year's Day morning, Easter morning, Thanksgiving, and Christmas.

Price: The park is free. The skate park has an annual fee of $10 (which includes your first session), then $5 per day after that.

Ages: All

TIJUANA ESTUARY - VISITORS CENTER

(619) 575-3613 / www.trnerr.org

301 Caspian Way, Imperial Beach

　　First things first - an estuary is: "The wide part of a river where it flows near the sea; where fresh water and salt water mix." (That's why this book is called *Fun and Educational* . . .) The Visitor's Center has several wonderful interactive exhibits. One of our favorite displays is the ordinary-looking, black-and-white sketched pictures of habitats that magically reveal brightly colored birds, insects, fish, and other animals when viewed through a polarized filter. The touch table contains snake skin, nests, skulls, and a dead sea turtle. The food chain is portrayed through pictures and graphs. The Beneath the Sand exhibit entails pressing the bills of bird puppet heads into holes in various levels of "sand." A light on the side panel displays what birds with shorter beaks eat (insects and plant seed) compared to what birds with longer beaks eat (crabs and worms). Upon request, a small theater shows films such as *Coastal Wetlands of San Diego* and *Tijuana River Watershed*.

Eight miles of walking trails are interspersed throughout the reserve. Ask for a map at the center, as there are different entrance points. You can borrow binoculars here, too. Some of the trails follow along the streets, while others go deeper into the coastal dunes and near the Tijuana River. Be on the lookout for terns, egrets, herons, curlews, and other birds and wildlife. On a very short loop around the center, my boys and I saw interesting plants and birds, plus thirteen bunnies! Take a guided walking tour to learn more about the flora and fauna at the estuary, or sign the kids up for one of the numerous programs available. The Jr. Ranger Program, for students 7 to 12 years old, is offered every Thursday from 3:30pm to 4:30pm. During the program kids will enjoy a walk, earn patches or buttons, and/or make a craft - all free of charge! Ask about other educational programs, including one specifically for Scouts, as well as special events.

Just south of the estuary is a park which borders Mexico. See BORDER FIELD STATE PARK (pg. 495) for more details.

Hours: The Visitors Center is open Wed. - Sun., 10am - 5pm. Closed Mon., Tues., New Year's Day, Thanksgiving and Christmas.

Price: Free

Ages: 3 years and up.

TORREY PINES STATE RESERVE

(858) 755-2063 / www.torreypine.org
12500 N. Torrey Pines Park Road, La Jolla

$$$

The Torrey pine tree grows only in this and one other reserve (that's also in Southern California) in the whole world! My kids were impressed with this fact and by the beauty of the park. Our favorite trail was the Guy Fleming Trail. It's an easy loop, only two-thirds of a mile, and incredibly scenic through the trees and out to a cliff overlooking the ocean. Tip: Hold on to younger children! Other trails include the half-mile Parry Grove looping trail; the two-thirds-of-a-mile Razor Point Trail with dramatic views of gorges; the steep, three-quarters-of-a-mile (one way) Beach Trail which ends at the San Diego - La Jolla Underwater Park; and the two demanding Broken Hill Trails. There are also a few miles of short trails in the reserve extension, closer to North Beach, that offer views of the lagoon, marsh and main reserve.

The Visitor's Center /Museum / Ranger Station shows a short film that gives an overview of the reserve - just ask to see it. The exhibits here offer good visual information regarding the plants and animal wildlife of the reserve. On display are taxidermied raccoons, skunks, and birds; a pine cone display; a pine needle display; and more. We appreciated Torrey Pines Reserve for its glorious nature trails and its breath of fresh air!

There is no eating allowed at the reserve, but you can at the lifeguarded Torrey Pines City Beach right below the reserve, plus you'll enjoy the sand and surf there. Note that the north side of the beach, the state beach also known as Black's Beach, is a clothing-optional beach.

Hours: The reserve is open daily, 7:15am - sunset. It is closed during and immediately after rain. The visitors center is open daily during summer daylight savings time 9am - 6pm; during winter standard time, 9am - 4pm.

Price: The South Beach lot is $10 - $15 per vehicle Mon. - Thurs.; $12 - $20, Fri. - Sun. and holidays, depending on the day of the week, and low or high season. Fees paid at South Beach kiosk are valid for the parking lot in the reserve at the top, too. Parking at just the reserve is $10 a vehicle. The North Beach lot is $3 for all day, Mon. - Thurs. in the winter. The rest of the year it is $4 - $6 for the first hour; $6 - $8 for two hours; $12 - $15 for the day, depending on day of the week and the season. Walk-ins are free. There is some free parking down the hill along Hwy. 101.

Ages: 3 years and up.

TUBING ON SAN LUIS REY RIVER / LA JOLLA INDIAN RESERVATION CAMPGROUND / LA JOLLA ZIP ZOOM

(760) 742-1297 or (760) 742-3771 - campground; (760) 742-3776 - zipline / www.lajollaindians.com;
www.lajollazipzoom.com

$$$

22000 Highway 76, on the La Jolla Indian Reservation, Pauma Valley

The La Jolla Band of Luiseño Indians, one of five California Luiseño tribes, have lived in North San Diego County for thousands of years. Come to the campground owned and operated by the Band for a day, or spend a night or two here in the lush, semi-wilderness of the foothills of the beautiful Palomar Mountains. Hike amongst the beautiful foliage along the San Luis Rey River; climb the rocks on the river banks; try your luck at fishing; or wade in the river waters.

For more wet thrills, depending on the water level, you can go inner tubing down the river along a two-mile stretch, which takes about an hour. Hike back up to go again, or better yet, come here with a friend who drives and leave one car at each end. Parts of the river are idyllic, while other parts are a bit more exciting (and bumpy) - and the flow depends on the water level. Be prepared for this adventure by wearing a hat, tee shirt, sunscreen, and sneakers (for painlessly stepping on the rocks on the river bottom). B.Y.O.T. (Bring Your Own Tube) or rent an inner tube here for $10. Tip: Tie your inner tube to your child's so you can stay together!

Dry thrills include zooming along the four zipline courses ranging from 300 feet to over 2500 feet in length with speeds up to 55mph! Side-by-side lines allow you to share (or race!) in your adventure with fellow adventurers. Trek to and climb up the platforms during this two-hour guided "tour" which also showcases panoramic views of the surrounding area - mountains, Pauma Valley, and beyond. Zippers must be at least 48" tall and weigh between 65 - 275 pounds.

Most of the camping sites are located right by the river. (The water can be soothing or loud, depending on how you interpret its sound.) If you are coming for the day, you are advised to bring your own table, chairs, and barbecues as those items are limited in number in the camp. Chemical toilets are scattered throughout the camp, and hot showers are available at designated places. Campfires are allowed. Firewood, tackle, supplies, and food are available at the small Trading Post on the grounds, but better yet, bring your own. Note that weekends in the summer get really packed.

Hours: Open mid-March - November, 6am - 6pm for day use. Camping is available mid-March to mid-April, Fri. - Sun., then open daily for the season. Tubing is usually available daily the end of April - September, 8am - 6pm. Call first. The zip line is open daily year-round. Times vary on the season, but usually the first tour is at 10am.

Price: $20 per vehicle for day use. River tubing is included in this price. Tube rentals are $10. Camping is $35 per vehicle for tent campers for up to four people - more than 4 people is charged $2/person/per night; $44 for RVs with hook-up. No pets allowed. Zip lining is $99 per person; $75 for campers. Parking for zipliners is an additional $15 and includes day use of the campground.

Ages: 4 years and up.

VOLCAN MOUNTAIN NATURE PRESERVE

(760)765-4098 or (760) 814-0208 - ranger; (760) 765-2300 / www.volcanmt.org; www.sandiegocounty.gov

1209 Farmer Rd., Julian

This preserve has God's fingerprints all over it with its spectacular wilderness scenery. Hikers can start at this trailhead and go halfway up the mountain, about a mile-and-a-half one way, to the gate, passing through meadows, high chaparral, and forests of oak and pine. Or, since you're here, hike the almost six-mile round trip to the summit for a 360-degree panoramic view of the surrounding area, including the Salton Sea. Note - bring water!!!!!!

Hours: Open daily, sunrise to sunset.

Price: Free

Ages: 3 years and up.

WALKER PRESERVE TRAIL

(619) 258-4100 / www.cityofsanteeca.gov

9500 Magnolia Avenue, Santee

Wooden fencing lines this 1.3 mile walking and biking trail, made from compressed decomposed granite, which parallels the San Diego River. Along the way, and at the trailhead, are a few picnic tables, historical artifacts, and interpretive signs. There is not a lot of shade on the trail, itself, but there are trees and shrubs on the sides. This segment of the trail ends at Lakeside Baseball Fields (where there is a restroom). You can keep going another mile on the trail that goes across a street, along a golf course, in some nature and through various other parts of Lakeside, ending at Lakeside River Park.

Hours: Open daily, sunrise - sunset.

Price: Free

Ages: 2 years and up.

WATER CONSERVATION GARDEN

(619) 660-0614 / www.thegarden.org

12122 Cuyamaca College Drive West on the campus of Cuyamaca College, El Cajon

Take a leisurely stroll on the stroller/wheelchair-friendly pathways through this eye-appealing, five-acre garden. The garden is designed to be an Xeriscape™ demonstration learning center to educate the public on how to create lovely, yet water-wise, landscapes. The front courtyard has a few picnic tables and a cement tube with steam pouring out into a very small pond with plants. Sit on a rock here and meditate.

Sprinkled throughout the garden are a few topiary animals, shade trees, a gazebo, fountains, irrigation options with mini water towers and sluices, and larger-than-life art objects, such as pencils that frame the entrance, huge gardening shears, and a purple sprinkler head (that I thought looked like a lighthouse). The plants are well marked and conservation ideas abound on both placards and by implementation. En route, you'll see an edible garden; fragrance garden (for the visually impaired); practical garden (to aid in soil erosion); wildlife garden (to attract butterflies); a Native American section; cactus and succulent areas; a gazebo and lawn area; a variety of grasses alongside the number of gallons of water they cost to maintain; irrigation systems; and the how-to's of planting on a slope. Enter the butterfly pavilion year-round, but if you are visiting mid-April through May, that's when you'll usually see a host of live native butterflies fluttering around. A few more components of this unique garden experience include mulch displays; concrete bins with a variety of soil aids - manure, fir shavings, compost, and more; an intriguing display of pipes and fittings on raised tables; a tower compass; and a mini weather station. A short children's discovery trail leads to a potting shed, a sand box, and hidden animals to discover. No doubt you'll "leaf" here with more ideas on what to do in your own yard.

A small gift shop and bathrooms are also on the premises. Ask about tours, workshops, and special events, especially (for kids) those involving Miss Smartyplants. Note that the garden is adjacent to the HERITAGE OF THE AMERICAS MUSEUM (pg. 532) and the Cuyamaca College Nature Preserve.

Hours: Open daily, 9am - 4pm. Closed on major holidays.

Price: Free. See American Horticultural Society (pg. x) for info on reciprocal memberships.

Ages: All

WATERFRONT PARK

(619) 232-PARK (7275) / www.sdparks.org

1600 Pacific Highway, San Diego

Located in the waterfront heart of San Diego, this twelve-acre park offers a series of huge, rectangular, shallow fountains with arcs of water that visitors are welcome to splash around in (bring bathing suits and a towel), built with steps all around them so parents can sit and watch kids easily. It also has a massive expanse of lawn (for festivals, playing games, and hanging out); a wide pedestrian (and bike) walkway; lovely and diverse garden sections; and an intriguing playground in cushy padding. The latter has separate areas. One area that has large play sculptures that with metal spheres with ladders and poles and netting to climb up and on; swings; a metal saucer; slides; discs with poles to stand on and twirl around; and rock climbing on a wide, twisty metal band. Another has a plateau at the top of short hill, slides, and hoops and balls dotting the "hill"side to use in creative play, like running up and down the sides, etc.

There are pockets of things to see and do in and amongst the park, such has statue of a cat sitting upright, made of mosaic tiles and stones, which is open at the paws so people can go inside. The view of the waterfront is beautiful, especially at sunset. Note that the MARITIME MUSEUM OF SAN DIEGO (pg. 536) is also located here.

Hours: Open daily, 6am - 10pm.

Price: Free

Ages: 1 year and up.

WEST SYCAMORE - MISSION TRAILS REGIONAL PARK

(619) 668-3281 / www.mtrp.org

17160 Stonebridge Parkway, San Diego, or where Sycamore Canyon Road dead ends at the Goodan Ranch.

This 1,128 acres and seven miles of miles of hiking, mountain biking and equestrian trails is part of the much larger Mission Trails Regional Park system, tho located on the other side of the Marine Corps Air Station (MCAS) in Miramar. Several trails of various lengths go up, down, and through the hillsides. Pick up a trail guide as there are only a few looping trails.

Hours: Gates are open daily, 8am - 5pm, November - mid-March; 8am - 7pm, mid-March - October.

Price: Free

Ages: 5 years and up.

WILLIAM HEISE COUNTY PARK

(760) 765-0650 - park; (877) 565-3600 - reservations / www.sdparks.org

4945 Heise Park Road, Julian

Consider this forest-like park a family destination. With eight miles of hiking and equestrian trails to choose from in the 1,000-acre park, there is bound to be a trail or two suitable for each member of the family. Select an easy pathway that leads through a mountain meadow and a cedar forest; a moderate, three-mile, round-trip trail that goes through canyon live oak; or choose a rugged trail for more experienced hikers, such as the 5.75-mile Kelly Ditch Trail which leads to Lake Cuyamaca. Two shaded picnic areas, a horseshoe pit, a playground, and a pond are all available here, too. And the quaint town of Julian is just a short drive away.

Over forty tent sites, sixty RV sites, and fourteen cabins with electricity and a few furnishings, provide overnight camping in this beautiful area. The campgrounds have piped-in water, showers, barbecues, and fire rings. Bring your own firewood. The small, one-room cabins each have a fireplace and sleep up to six people. Bring your own bedding and know that reservations usually need to be made at least three months ahead of your arrival date.

Hours: Open daily, 9:30am - sunset.

Price: $3 per vehicle. Camping is $29 for tents; $34 for RV's and partial hook-ups, plus $5 reservation fee. The cabins are $67 a night.

Ages: All

WILSON MEMORIAL SKATE PARK / MEMORIAL COMMUNITY PARK and POOL

(619) 235-1125 or (619) 525-8213 - park; (619) 235-1139 - pool / www.sandiego.gov

702 South 30th Street, San Diego

The unsupervised skate park has 22,000 square feet of cement surface. Railings, stairs, beginner's bowl, 90-foot long "snake run" and a 10-foot key-hole are some of the park's more fun elements. Helmets and pads are required. Note that police do monitor this area.

Adjacent to the skate park is the Memorial Recreation Center and Community Park with a playground, open fields, basketball court, and baseball field. The swimming pool is great for lap and recreational swim. It boasts a sprayground at one end with rainbow arched pipes to run through, poles that squirt out water, and fountains in the cement the spurt up water at random times.

Hours: The park is open daily, sunrise - sunset. The skate park is open daily, 10am - dusk. Recreational swim and the sprayground are open year round Mon., Wed., and Fri., 11am - 4pm. They are also open the end of March - October, Sat. - Sun., noon - 3pm.

Price: Free. The pool/sprayground is $4 for adults; $2 for seniors and ages 15 and under.

Ages: 6 years and up.

WOODGLEN VISTA PARK AND SKATE PARK

(619) 258-4100 / www.cityofsanteeca.gov

10250 Woodglen Vista Drive, Santee

Woodglen has a little something for everyone. The two nice-sized playgrounds, with wood chip "flooring", have swings, slides, and several big plastic animals to ride. There are lots of trees and open grassy play areas, plus a rocky, seasonally dry creek bed to explore, and a few bridges. A ball field, tennis court, basketball court, and small skate park motivate the sports enthusiast to get moving. The gated cement skate park, aptly nicknamed a "pocket," has a half pyramid, grinding wall, rails, spine, steps, and four-foot-high half bowl. Skaters must wear safety equipment and have a signed waiver. There are times just for BMX riders, as well.

Hours: The park is open daily, dawn - dusk. The skate park is open during the traditional school year, Wed. - Fri., 2pm - sunset; Sat. - Sun., 10am - sunset, with alternating hours for skaters and bikers. It is open Mon. and Tues. during school holidays and in the summer from 10am or 11am - sunset.

Price: Free

Ages: All

WOODLAND PARK AND AQUATIC CENTER

(760) 744-9000 - community services; (760) 746-2828 - pool complex / www.san-marcos.net

671 Woodland Parkway, San Marcos

A large, picturesque fountain and a small, man-made, rock-lined pond decorate the corner section of this park. A short, paved walkway winds around the pond and up through the park inviting strollers to use it. Several tennis courts, a children's play area, and a long grassy area, plus picnic tables and barbecue pits, make the park a fun outing. Try your hand (and foot) at the free-standing, decently-high, rock climbing wall.

Up the small hill from the park is an aquatic center with three pools, one of which is a wading pool. The swimming pool has a fifty-foot, curvy water slide and the diving has a high dive and low diving board - fun features. Showers are available here, too.

Hours: The park is open daily, dawn - dusk. The pool is open Memorial Day - Labor Day. Call for weekday hours; open Sat., Sun., and holidays, 12:30 - 4:30pm.

Price: Free for park facilities. $4 per person for pool usage; children under 2 are free.

Ages: All

—MALLS—

WESTFIELD UTC

(858) 546-8858 / www.westfield.com/utc
4545 La Jolla Village Dr., San Diego

As with the other Westfield malls, this huge outdoor one offers a few special things for kids. Storytime is on two Tuesdays a month from 10:30am - 11am, usually at the PlaySpace in front of Macy's. The PlaySpace is a semi-enclosed area with large puzzles and brightly-colored, hard-foam objects for kids to climb on and over. A small kids play area outside has a slide, rope climbing structure, and a few other elements. Inside, a Family Lounge is a nice place for a respite with a sitting area and a tiny area with books and kid-friendly videos. The mall also has LEGO STORE - MINI MODEL BUILD (San Diego County) (pg. 485), lovely outdoor seating areas and landscaping, an indoor ice skating rink, a fountain pool with statues of dolphins leaping around, and more.

Price: Free

Ages: 18 months - 8 years old.

—MUSEUMS—

AIR GROUP ONE COMMEMORATIVE AIR FORCE WORLD WAR II FLYING MUSEUM

(619) 259-5541 / www.ag1caf.org
1921 N. Marshall Ave. Hangar #13, El Cajon

This very small aviation museum is operated by WWII aviation buffs who are a wealth of information. There are numerous prints and photos of WWII and other aircraft, with accompanying binders, to learn about the planes and their roles in various wars. The other displays include some model planes; goggles; equipment; a Norden bombsight, which was once top secret; front pages of newspapers highlighting events from the war; uniforms; and other paraphernalia.

Visitors will also enjoy watching small planes land and take off here and at GILLESPE FIELD CAFE (pg. 472). Would you, or someone you know (who is 12 years or older), enjoy flying in a WWII warbird? The SNJ-5 is available and ready to fly - tailwinds to you. A twenty-five-minute flight, for $350, gives you an incredible view of San Diego in a memorable manner. Or, experience some combat maneuvers and more flight time for $525. Make sure to check the Calendar entry for a yearly event, the AIRSHOW SAN DIEGO (pg. 715), and for other special events such as the WarBird Expo.

Hours: Open Tues., Thurs., Sat., 10am - 2pm.

Price: Free

Ages: 6 years and up.

ANTIQUE GAS & STEAM ENGINE MUSEUM, INC.

(800) 5-TRACTOR (587-2286) or (760) 941-1791 / www.agsem.com; www.sdparks.org
2040 N. Santa Fe Avenue, Vista

California has a museum for almost any interest. This one answers the age-old question, "Where do engines go when they run out of gas (or steam)?" The fifty-five acre, mostly outdoor museum, has hundreds of tractors, combines, gas and steam engines (that's a given from the name of the museum), horse-drawn carriages, and equipment used in mining, oil drilling, construction, agriculture, and more. The machines have been (or are in the process of being) restored to working condition. In fact, some of the equipment is used to help farm the adjacent lands. Walk around on your own to just look, or make a reservation for a tour, which is offered for preschoolers through college-internship students. Kids will see many of the machines in action and learn a lot about the history of agriculture via harvesting. Another option is to visit on the third and fourth weekends of June and of October during the ANTIQUE ENGINE AND TRACTOR SHOW (pg. 716) when they also host tractor shows/parades and a lot of the engines here come to "life". Watch or take part in planting, harvesting, household chores, early American crafts, blacksmithing, log sawing, parades, square dancing, scale model railroads, wagon rides, train rides, and shopping. We went and it's definitely worth it!

Some of the museum's collection is housed in structures that collectively resemble a small town. Featured buildings include a huge (and complete) blacksmith shop (with demonstrations on Sat. from 9am to 3pm) and wheelwright shop, a farm house with parlor, a sawmill, a one-third-scale train with a telegrapher's office (open Saturdays from 9am to 1pm only), a handweaver's building (open Thurs. and Sat., 10m to 2pm) and a barn. A (non-working) gas station is also on the premises. If you have the time, check out the West Coast Clock and Watch Museum displays that feature hundreds of unique and beautiful clocks and watches from the 1680s through the 1920s. See a clock from the 1893 Chicago World's Fair with a Ferris wheel on top; an organ clock that plays music; ornate pocket watches; and much more.

There are also picnic tables on the premises and even a small playground with two small, stationary tractors to climb on. The museum is interesting to visit any time, but it's especially exciting to visit on special event days.

Hours: Open daily, 10am - 4pm. Closed New Year's Day, Christmas, and rainy/muddy days.

Price: $5 for adults; $4 for seniors; $3 for ages 6 - 12; children 5 and under are free. Special event admission is usually $10 for adults; $9 for seniors; $7 for ages 6 -12; $5 for parking.

Ages: 4 years and up.

BALBOA PARK

(619) 239-0512 - Visitors Center; (619) 232 - 2282 - Friends of Balboa Park / www.balboapark.org; friendsofbalboapark.org

1549 El Prado Balboa Park, San Diego

This immense, 1,158-acre park is the cultural and recreational heart of San Diego. An incredible number of programs and seasonal events are held here, so see the Calendar section in the back of the book, call or check their website for a schedule of events, or pick up a copy of their bi-monthly events guide. Scattered throughout the plethora of museums and buildings, the park has shade trees, grassy areas, numerous gardens (of all kinds!), picnic areas, and a multitude of walking trails that crisscross all over the land. Playgrounds are located at Pepper Grove Picnic Area on Park Boulevard, south of the San Diego Zoo (this park is ADA accessible), and at the north end of Balboa Drive. Also see MORLEY FIELD (pg. 509) for more things to do in this immediate area.

Balboa Park is home to a majority of the city's best museums, as well as the world famous SAN DIEGO ZOO (pg. 591). Individual museum entries are found elsewhere under the Museums section, listed by their official titles: MINGEI INTERNATIONAL MUSEUM (pg. 537), MUSEUM OF PHOTOGRAPHIC ARTS (pg. 540), MUSEUM OF PHOTOGRAPHIC ARTS (pg. 540), REUBEN H. FLEET SCIENCE CENTER (pg. 547), SAN DIEGO AIR AND SPACE MUSEUM (pg. 549), SAN DIEGO ART INSTITUTE (pg. 550), SAN DIEGO AUTOMOTIVE MUSEUM (pg. 551), SAN DIEGO MODEL RAILROAD MUSEUM (pg. 552), SAN DIEGO MUSEUM OF ART (pg. 553), SAN DIEGO MUSEUM OF MAN (pg. 553), SAN DIEGO NATURAL HISTORY MUSEUM (pg. 554) and the VETERANS MUSEUM AND MEMORIAL CENTER (pg. 558), which is across the street. Multi-day passes, which are good for one week from the date of purchase, can be bought to visit sixteen participating museums (including the Japanese Garden) for $57 for adults; $30 for ages 3 to 12. (Note that many museums are free for younger children.) There are also day passes good for visiting any five of the participating museums in one day for $46 for adults; $27 for children. Annual passes for all seventeen institutions are $129 for 18 years and up; $99 for seniors and children. Below is a list of museums that are free on particular Tuesdays for San Diego County residents and active military and their dependents: First Tuesday: S.D. Natural History (permanent exhibits only), Reuben H. Fleet Science Center, Centro Cultural de la Raza, and S.D. Model Railroad; Second Tuesday: Museum of Photographic Arts, Veterans Museum and Memorial Center, and S.D. History Museum; Third Tuesday: Japanese Friendship Garden, Mingei International Museum, S.D. Art Institute, S.D. Museum of Art (permanent exhibits only), and S.D. Museum of Man; Fourth Tuesday: S.D. Air and Space Museum (permanent exhibits only), S.D. Automotive Museum, and select cottages of House of Pacific Relations International Cottages whose Hall of Nations films, such as *Children Around the World,* show at 11am to 3pm. Check out www.balboapark.org/residents-free for the complete list.

The park also offers many other attractions that are worthy of mention. The beautiful, latticed **Botanical Building** is located at the north end of the lily pond next to the San Diego Museum of Art. It has (labeled) tropical and subtropical plants on display. It is open Friday through Wednesday, 10am to 4pm. (Closed Thursdays and holidays.) Admission is free. Ranger-led tours of the gardens are available on Tuesdays and Sundays at 11am. The small **Timken Museum of Art** is located next to the Visitors Center. Housed here are collections of works by European Old Masters, eighteenth- and nineteenth-century American paintings, and Russian icons. It is open Tuesday through Saturday, 10am to 4:30pm; Sunday, noon to 4:30pm. Admission is free. The **Japanese Friendship Garden**, (619) 232-2721 / www.niwa.org, is a small, but beautiful, and serene garden replete with symbols of the Japanese culture. It contains a tea pavilion and Japanese-style exhibit house with a main room that has a traditional table set with (fake) Japanese food. Other elements include a bridge, deck, and a short path leading to the garden, koi pond, stream, and short waterfall, plus a cherry tree grove and places to sit and relax. Admission is $10 for adults; $8 for seniors; ages 6 and under are free. There is an extra cost for special exhibitions. Admission is free on the third Tuesday of every month for San Diego residents. See American Horticultural Society (pg. x) for info on reciprocal memberships. The exhibits are open daily, 10:45am - 4:45pm; the gardens, 10am - 7pm. It's closed New Year's Day, Thanksgiving and Christmas, and closed early on some holidays. The **Centro Cultural de la Raza** is hard to miss with it colorful murals on the outside (and inside) of an old water tower building. It exists to maintain and promote Chicano, Mexican, Indigenous and Latino art and culture via rotating exhibits and performances with dance, music, and film. It's open Tuesday through Sunday, noon to 4pm. A $5 donation is suggested. Free outdoor concerts are given on the famous **Spreckels Pipe Organ**, (619) 702-8138 / www.spreckelsorgan.org, year-round on Sundays from 2pm to 3pm, plus on Mondays from 7:30pm to 9:30pm, for the Summer Organ Festival, June through August. The organ is located at an architecturally beautiful building set in a huge half circle. My kids think the steps here are a great place for picnicking. The **House of Pacific Relations**, (619) 234-0739 / www.sdhpr.org, is located behind the United Nations Building, across from the Spreckels Organ. The "House" encompasses seventeen small cottages that are home to thirty-three different nationalities. Exhibits, such as traditional dress, musical instruments, flags, and furnishings, in each small cottage pertain to specific ethnic groups. Special lawn programs of music, dance, crafts, and ethnic food are held on Sundays from 2pm to 3pm, March through October. Nations are represented on a rotating basis. The cottages are open every Sat. and Sun. from 12pm to 5pm, tho closed some holidays. Admission is free. The **Spanish Village Art Center**, (619) 233-9050 / www.spanishvillageart.com, is just north of the San Diego Natural History Museum. The "village" has retained its old-world charm with its Spanish architecture and colorful courtyard tiles and flowers. The thirty-seven art studios and galleries include woodcarvings, sculptures, glass blowing, and gems and minerals for show and sale. Oftentimes, the artisans demonstrate their craft, which makes the Spanish Village Center an intriguing stop for slightly older kids. The small **San Diego Mineral & Gem Society Museum** here has rocks, minerals and gems on display. It is free to enter, offers lapidary and jewelry arts classes, and is fun to peruse for hobby and serious collectors. For more information, contact (619) 239 - 8812 or www.sdmg.org. The Village is open daily, 11am to 4pm; closed New Year's Day, Thanksgiving and Christmas. Two other kid-friendly attractions are the **miniature train ride** and **carousel**. Located just outside the San Diego Zoo exit and north of the Spanish Village Center is a three-minute train ride, operated by the zoo. It is open Fridays through Sundays, 11am to 4:30pm (longer during the summer) and costs $3 for ages 1 and older (under 1 is free). Call (619) 239-4748 or www.zoo.sandiegozoo.org for more info. The old-fashioned carousel has horses, giraffes, dragons, camels, ostriches, and other animals to ride on, and still offers a chance to grab at the brass ring - $3 per person. The carousel is open most of the year Saturdays, Sundays and school holidays, 11am to 5pm, and open daily in the summer, 11am to 5:30pm. There are several restaurants and cafes scattered throughout Balboa Park and located inside several of the museums, although we usually bring a picnic lunch. There are also a few theaters, such as MARIE HITCHCOCK PUPPET THEATER (pg. 571) and OLD GLOBE THEATRE (pg. 571).

At any time during your visit to the park, you are welcome to hop aboard the Balboa Park Tram. This free, intrapark transportation system can take you from Presidents Way and Park Boulevard, up to the carousel, through where the museums are, to the Visitors Center and House of Hospitality, and up north to 6th Street. It makes several stops along the way, so you can catch it coming or going. It operates November through May, daily, 9am to 6pm; June through October, daily, 9am to 8pm. Plan to visit Balboa Park many times, as you obviously cannot see it all in one, two, or even three days! Photographer's tip: At night the lighting and beauty of the buildings is wonderful, especially of the Museum of Man edifice, the fountain in front of the science museum, and the series of archways of the Spreckels pavilion.

Hours: The park is open daily. The Visitor's Center is open daily, 9:30am - 4:30pm (extended hours in the summer); closed New Year's Day, Thanksgiving, and Christmas. Individual attractions are listed in separate entries.

Price: Entrance to the park itself is free. Parking is free. Individual attractions are listed in separate entries.

Ages: All ages for the park.

BANCROFT RANCH HOUSE MUSEUM !

(619) 469-1480 / www.svhistoricalsociety.org

9050 Memory Lane, Spring Valley

I love visiting old house-museums because I always learn some history about the original owners and the time period that they lived there. With every new tidbit learned, it's like fitting in another piece of a huge, historical puzzle. For instance, in the early 1900's Howe Bancroft, one-time owner of this adobe ranch house, was a renowned historian who wrote and compiled thirty-nine books describing the civilization of the Old West.

A truth window, where visitors can see the layers of original adobe - mostly mud and hay - is one of the first things the guide points out. One small room contains a few display cases of Native American artifacts such as grinding stones, arrowheads, and baskets. Another room contains a straw bed, Bancroft's history books, and few period household goods. A connecting room has an old school desk and a map. The last room holds display cases of boots, clothing, tools, kitchen implements, and, most exciting of all because kids can hold them - ship-to-shore cannon balls, and tumbler balls used to crush rocks. School groups are encouraged to visit.

There are a few picnic tables under shade trees in front of the house and an indigenous garden. Although the surrounding area is a bit rundown and the museum grounds are a work in progress, seeing and hearing a portion of history makes the Bancroft Museum a worthwhile visit.

Hours: Open Fri. - Sun., 1pm - 4pm. Closed Easter and Christmas.

Price: Free, but donations are appreciated.

Ages: 8 years and up.

BARONA CULTURAL CENTER AND TRIBAL MUSEUM ☀

(619) 443-7003 / www.baronamuseum.org !

1095 Barona Road, Lakeside

Haawka, or hello, and welcome to this classy little museum! A large rock in the lobby features numerous recreated Indian pictographs and the logo of the tribe. The large, glass wall display case usually contains items such as pottery, baskets, photographs, tools, and personal items. The displays do change. Press the buttons located near several of the displays to hear the history and other information about the artifacts, as well as audios of the indigenous language. We especially liked hearing the voices of the Bird Singers who sang ceremonial songs, accompanied by gourd rattles. Other exhibits in this front area include a small roundish house made of willows, and metates and manos (i.e., grind stones) that visitors can actually try out.

An adjacent small room celebrates Native American athletes, especially Matt LaChappa, who played for the San Diego Padres, with personal memorabilia and photographs. Just around the corner is a little room featuring rotating exhibits with tools from a homestead and bricks.

School tours are offered during the week with a minimum of just five kids. The tour encompasses the museum with more insight into the Barona/Kumeyaay people's heritage, and can incorporate a craft or learning a native game. Outreach programs come to other facilities, too. Note that there are picnic facilities south of the museum at Louis Stelzer County Park.

Hours: The museum is open Tues. - Fri., noon - 5pm; Sat., 10am - 4pm. Closed Sun., Mon. and major holidays. Other tours are offered by appointment.

Price: Free

Ages: 7 years and up.

BUENA VISTA AUDUBON NATURE CENTER ☀

(760) 439-BIRD (2473) / www.bvaudubon.org !

2202 S. Coast Highway, Oceanside

This nature center is not just for the birds! The exhibits inside this small, 3, 500 square foot building consist mainly of taxidermied, local birds (some in flight) such as a pelican, a great blue heron, a red-tailed hawk, a colorful yellow western tanager, and more. A stuffed owl has a mouse in its beak and a pellet at its feet that contains partially digested animal parts. Other mounted animals on display include a bobcat, red fox, possum, and more. The touch table has a raccoon skin, petrified wood, and whale bones, among other things. Look through a kid-level porthole on the central display to see fish "swimming" underneath. Spread your arms against a wall to measure your "wing span" up to a variety of birds' span. A book corner for children has a nice selection of nature books to read. Other items of interest are a small rock and mineral display, and a live tarantula. Go upstairs to the viewing deck to see more of a bird's eye view.

Outside, take a walk on the ¼ mile nature trail through the marshy reeds to the lagoon. This area is home to a wide variety of birds. Migrate over to the picnic tables which are available to make your day just ducky!

Guided field trips, always, are one of the best ways to really learn about the abundant wildlife at Buena Vista. Call for reservations. Free, ninety minute tours are offered for kindergartners through 5th graders that cover a variety of topics such as what makes a bird a bird, birds of prey, local history and migration. Other special programs offered include natural history classes (for adults, too!); Preschool Nature Storytimes (not for adults) with a craft and songs; field trips; annual events; and more.

Hours: Open Tues. - Sat., 10am - 4pm; Sun., 1pm - 4pm. Closed Mon., Thanksgiving, and Christmas.
 Price: Free; donations accepted.
 Ages: 3 years and up.

CABRILLO NATIONAL MONUMENT

See the entry for CABRILLO NATIONAL MONUMENT (pg. 495), under GREAT OUTDOORS, for details.

CALIFORNIA SURF MUSEUM

(760) 721-6876 / www.surfmuseum.org
312 Pier View Way, Oceanside

Surfing is the heart of the Southern California beach culture. This small museum aims to preserve the history and lifestyle of surfing so it won't be wiped out. It displays a diverse selection and variety, and a timeline of and with surfboards. To the inexperienced eye, some might look simply like thick boards, but I'm learning that there is more to the board than meets the eye. A Hawaiian hut made of palm leaves pays homage to surfing's roots, as do the many photographs, art, and information regarding surfing, plus body surfing gear, hand planes, and fins on display. Long term exhibits include World Surfing Champion Kelly Slater's surfboard and Bethany Hamilton's surfboard she was riding on that day, plus the bathing suit she was wearing, the documentary *Heart of a Soul Surfer*, and photographs. Exhibits rotate yearly and have included a tabletop wave and California surfriders from 1900 to 1940. Check the website for special events.

Hours: Open daily, 10am - 4pm; open Thurs. until 8pm. Closed New Year's Day, Memorial Day, 4th of July, Labor Day, and Christmas.
 Price: $5 for adults; $3 for seniors, military and students; ages 11 and under are free. Admission is $1 on the first Tues.
 Ages: Surfer dudes 8 years and up.

CAMP PENDLETON

(760) 725-5758 or (760) 725-5727 - tours and museum; (760) 763-6081 - weekdays for Amphibious School Battalion, (760) 763-6082 on weekends; (760) 725-5799 - community relations / www.themech.org; www.pendleton.marines.mil/About/HistoryandMuseums.aspx
Camp Pendleton, Oceanside

Driving on I-5 between Orange County and Oceanside, it's hard to miss the sprawling Camp Pendleton, the major West Coast base of the United States Marine Corps. There are several aspects of Camp Pendleton open to the public.

As it is on an historical site where early Spanish explorers traveled, take an almost two-hour tour to explore this earlier time period via the on-site ranch house complex - Santa Margarita Ranch House - comprised of the huge ranch house (once home to Pio Pico, the last governor of Mexican California), the chapel, and the Bunkhouse Museum. (The Las Flores adobe is 14 miles away and needs restoration.) Photos, including one of President Roosevelt's visit, antiques, and other artifacts are visual aids as the buildings retain the essence of yesteryear in both landscaping and interior furnishings.

Make time to see the Marine Corps Mechanized Museum, located in building 2612 on Vandegrift Blvd. at the base of Rattlesnake Canyon. This museum contains a good number of transport and battle vehicles from Vietnam and Desert Storm era, plus a Vietnamese road marker from the road to Hue City.

The one-room World War II and Korea LVT Exhibit is located in Building 21561 in the base's boat basin and maintained by the Assault Amphibious School Battalion. It contains L.V.T.'s (Land Vehicle Tracks) - amphibious vehicles used in combat. These large relics are accompanied by war mementos such as uniforms, weapons, and personal artifacts. You may ask to watch the video on the history of the L.V.T.'s. You must make reservations to see the museums.

Note: THE PAINTBALL PARK - Camp Pendleton (pg. 490) is located on base, and don't miss the wonderful MARINE CORPS RECRUIT DEPOT COMMAND MUSEUM (pg. 535).

At the entrance gate all visitors must present government photo ID, and drivers must show proof of car insurance and registration, along with a letter of tour confirmation.

Hours: Note: Call first to see if the base is currently open to the public. Tours and visits must be made in advance. Historic Ranch tours are offered 10am - noon, between the last week in September to the end of May. The Mechanized Museum is open Mon. - Thurs., 8am - 4pm; Fri., 8am - 1pm.

Price: Free

Ages: 6 years and up.

CLASSIC ROTORS - THE RARE AND VINTAGE ROTORCRAFT MUSEUM

(760) 650-9257 / www.rotors.org

2690 Montecito Road at Airport Hangar #G at the Ramona Airport, Ramona

Home to forty-five, or so, rotorcraft this large hangar holds a collection of some of the most unique helicopters I've ever seen, all kind of packed together, including many Hillers. Come look at a Vertol H-21B Shawnee "Flying Banana" that looks like a Dr. Doolittle PushMe-PullYou; a Monte Copter model 15 Triphibian; a Brantly 305; a Sikorsky S-55/H-19; a gyrocopter; a collapsible copter; and several others. Most of the rotors are flight ready, while others are in the process of being restored, so you'll probably see some being worked on. The star attraction is the unusual-looking Roton Rocket ATV (Atmospheric Test Vehicle) experimental aircraft. It was once used to test and validate a unique spacecraft atmospheric reentry system using helicopter rotors.

As a volunteer takes you on a tour of the aircraft, you learn the history of the machines - where they flew and why - and technical information. Many times, too, visitors are welcome to climb into the helicopters and take it out for a spin; at least an imaginary spin. The museum not only houses the rotors, but it is also a tribute to the pioneers of vertical flight technology.

Hours: Open Tues. - Fri., 10am - 4pm; Sat., 10am - 6pm. Open Sun. by appointment. Closed Mon. and most holidays. Sometimes the museum isn't open as everyone's at air shows. Call to arrange private tours.

Price: Free; donations gladly accepted.

Ages: 6 years and up.

COMIC-CON CENTER

www.comic-con.org

2131 Pan American Plaza in Balboa Park, San Diego

Comic-Con, the largest purveyor of promoting appreciation for and contributions of comics to art and culture, is in the process of creating a permanent center. While still facilitating their wildly-popular conventions, the center will celebrate comics, movies, television and other popular arts via rotating exhibits, panels, film screenings, virtual reality interactions, and Comic-Con's history and legacy, along with comics, movie props and more from pop culture. The Center will be as unique as Comic-Con is with fans still driving what is featured and educational programs that will excite students to learn with graphics and heroic (and not) storylines. Keep checking the website and/or goggling Comic-Con, San Diego for details.

Hours: TBA

Price: TBA

CREATION AND EARTH HISTORY MUSEUM

(619) 599-1104 / www.creationsd.org

10946 Woodside Avenue North, Santee

The enormous T-Rex out front lets you know you've arrived. Inside, the fairly extensive bookstore/gift shop, with a massive, fossil-imbedded rock in the lobby, is the entry point.

Genesis 1:1: "In the beginning, God created the heavens and the earth." This walk-through creation museum is a richly visual way of seeing the biblical account of how the earth and its inhabitants have developed. Each phase of the earth's history is graphically represented by murals, photographs, models, or audio sounds, plus biblical references, questions to ponder, and lots of technical information. Start at the beginning, of course, and proceed through to modern day. Day four (when the sun, moon, stars, and planets were created) is the first dramatic depiction of the unfolding wonders of our universe. This small room is basically dark, with spotlights on stunning photos of the planets, constellations, and our sun. Each photograph is accompanied by factual explanations. Enter the small room for days five and six where greenery abounds alongside a few cages of small live animals such as birds, fish, and snakes. One wall shows models of man, his inner workings, diagrams, and pictures of families.

Continue on and see the fall of man, illustrated by a tiny display of bones, decay, and the sound of crying; onto a wood-paneled room with a mural depicting Noah's ark, complete with storm sounds and lightning flashing. The next room has 3-D, touchable walls that are layers of the earth, explaining the flood, enhanced by Grand Canyon murals, and mineral and animals fossils (a whale jaw, a sabertooth cat, etc.) in display cases imbedded into the walls. There is also a replicated Mt. St. Helens' erupted volcano that you can walk through with a life-size dinosaur (behemoth?) outside of it. Walk into The Age of the Earth Mineral Cave, a recreated cave complete with stalactites and stalagmites, and an ore cart and tracks. Videos, minerals, and data are inset into cave walls. The cave's purpose is to support the young earth view. Next, is a short, blue hallway representing the Ice Age with icicles hanging overhead and models of woolly mammoths. A scale model of the (originally) enormous Tower of Babel takes center stage in the Egyptian room, which also contains several Egyptian artifacts. The Stone Age room comes next; followed by the room of civilization immortalizing (so to speak) Greek and Roman cultures; and the hallway of modern man, including pictures and philosophies of evolutionists and creationists. Most of the rooms offer various free pamphlets that discuss the scientific and biblical ideas and facts presented throughout the museum.

The next large wing has several long hallways, and a few rooms, packed with detailed and intricate displays on the human body. Wall murals, photo panels and models, many of which are touchable and 3-D, are really thorough renditions of each part of the human body - the eye, ear, cells, body systems, stages of a baby's development in the womb, bones, muscles, and so much more. There are also videos to watch. It's like taking visual anatomy classes! Psalm 139: 14 - ". . . I am fearfully and wonderfully made; your works are wonderful. . ." The displays also detail more recent scientific advances in the biologic and geologic fields regarding DNA, RNA, cloning, and even plate tectonics. The Creation Museum is a great, interactive timeline.

The Dinosaurs & the Bible Exhibit has pieces of the actual horn from the triceratops where soft tissue was discovered. This exhibit also has information panels, pictures, and other visuals.

The Tabernacle Theatre (which is the actual size of the biblical tabernacle) is a long room with seats on one side and a "stage" divided into three sections one the other. Each section has just a few (not Disney quality!) representations of a different component of the tabernacle - a replica of the Ark of the Covenant and a life-size model of a High Priest in period clothing, plus an Altar of Incense and Golden Lampstand. The props here are a bit hokey, but the half-hour video highlighting and explaining the objects and their meanings from Old Testament times through modern day, incorporating scripture in the references, is really good and informative. The video is shown at 10am, noon, 2pm, and 4pm (or at other times if requested).

Two-hour guided tours are available by appointment for any age group. Kid's Creation Club workshops are given the first Saturday of every month that involve a topical science or history presentation, a craft, and maybe a movie. Afterward, participants can explore the museum on their own.

Hours: Open Mon. - Sat., 10am - 5pm; Sun., 1pm - 5pm. Closed New Year's Day, Thanksgiving, Christmas Eve and Christmas Day. Much of the museum is geared for at least slightly older children as a lot of the information is very technical; however, the visuals make quite an impact on any age.

Price: $8 for adults; $6 for seniors; $3 for ages 5 - 12; children 4 and under are free. Admission is free on the first Tues. Kid's Creation Club workshops are $5 per person.

Ages: 5 years and up.

ESCONDIDO HISTORY CENTER / GRAPE DAY PARK

(760) 743-8207 - history center; (760) 839-4691 - park and pool / www.escondido.org
321 N. Broadway, Escondido

Grape Day Park has a charming ambiance created by a rose garden, large grassy areas, shade trees, picnic tables, a military tribute in statues and a remembrance wall, Victorian buildings, a restored train depot, and a unique playground. Note: There has been an upsurgence in recent years of the homeless population hanging around this park. The small playground has a colorful climbing structure that looks like giant grape vines, along with grape leaf seats and a purple slide coming out of the middle of a bunch of grapes. (No sour grapes at this play area.) There is another, larger and taller fort-like play structure with slides, a rock wall, a variety of climbing apparatus, and poles in sawdust. The park has rocks around the perimeter of it and five horseshoe pits. Play equipment can be checked out Tuesday through Saturday between 10am and 4pm, including bocce ball, a giant chess board with toddler-size chess pieces, giant checkers, giant dominos and giant pick up sticks. (Parental supervision is required.)

There are five buildings that comprise the museum complex that were relocated here in 1976. The ones open to the public are: 1) Escondido's first library; 2) A quaint, completely furnished, two-story 1890's house with a living room, parlor, and kitchen, plus four small bedrooms upstairs; 3) A blacksmith's shop (that's open on Saturdays - fascinating to watch them at work and they offer classes!); and 4) An 1888 Santa Fe Depot. The two-story depot building is nice looking and interesting to explore. Some highlights include a train master's office, a working telegraph station (send a message to someone!), and a Q & A board of Escondido history. The depot also has a real train car that can be toured. It contains a model train set with an historic layout that makes tracks around realistic-looking landscape.

A tank house and a small herb garden can also be seen on the short walk around the history center. The park is a fun place for kids to play, yet bring them sometime to see the museum part of it, also. Call for tour information. Note that the SAN DIEGO CHILDREN'S DISCOVERY MUSEUM (pg. 551) is located right across the street. If you're looking for a place to cool off June through August, the James Stone Municipal pool is just next door. It has a small tube slide and a kiddie wading pool, too. Call for hours and prices, though it's usually $3 for adults.

Hours: The park is open daily, sunrise - sunset. The museum complex is open Tues., Wed., Thurs. and Sat., 1pm - 4pm. It's closed Mon., Fri., Sun., Thanksgiving weekend, all major holidays, and during rainy weather.

Price: Free. Donations of $3 for adults and $1 per child for the History Center are requested. School tours are $3 per student for Escondido residents; $5 per for non-residents.

Ages: All for the park; ages 5 and up for the museum.

FALLBROOK GEM AND MINERAL SOCIETY MUSEUM

(760) 728-1130 / www.fgms.org
123 W. Alvardo, suite B, Fallbrook

This very small museum has display cases of quartz, feldspar, garnet, topaz, pink rhodochrosite, azurite, beryl, aquamarine, tourmaline, and other very fine specimens. Check out the fluorescent mineral gallery where flecks of bright red, green, orange, blue, and purple show-up on rocks under black lights. A touch table holds a mastodon head, petrified wood, and other objects. There are several types of stones, fossils, and minerals to purchase at decent prices from the small gift shop.

Free, hour-long school field trips, usually geared for elementary-aged kids, are given on Fridays that could include gold panning and arrowhead making, and definitely learning all about about minerals.

Hours: The museum and gift shop are open Thurs. - Sat., 11am - 3pm, but call first. Call to make a tour reservation.

Price: Free

Ages: 5 years and up.

FALLBROOK HISTORICAL SOCIETY

(760) 723-4125 / fallbrookhistoricalsociety.com
1730 Hill Avenue, Fallbrook

Marcus Garvy said, "A people without the knowledge of their past history, origin and culture is like a tree without roots." This museum helps rectify this by promoting Fallbrook's past throughout this small and well done museum and other buildings on-site. The central building contains sections with displays from yesteryear such as books, quilts, clothing, pottery, military uniforms, kitchen tools, scouts, and an organ and pew from First Baptist Church. The center display is a large table with a train chugging around, going past dollhouse-size recreations of old Fallbook buildings. On the lower level is a converted garage that holds a few vintage automobiles and photos, and the small Rock and Mineral Museum. The museum is a private collection of mostly found locally geodes, petrified wood, thunder eggs, quartz, and fossils in glass display cases.

Tour through the Pittenger House, built in 1895, with its parlor, holding an authentic Civil War Uniform, a pump organ and a phonograph; and the bedroom with an original rope bed, a child's trundle bed and a cradle, and a framed hair picture (i.e. framed "art" made from hair). The dining room has a sewing machine, a cabinet with books and games for the children, and more typical dining room furniture and decor. The kitchen features a wood burning stove, an ice box and an authentic Hoosier Cabinet. Also on the grounds is a picnic area under shady oak trees; lots of rusted farm implements (combines, scapers, and more); and the barn/interpretive center. The latter features exhibits and collections on the agricultural and dairy heritage of the Fallbrook area, including barb-wire. A highlight is the restored 1860's "Brougham Ladies Afternoon Carriage". Come on your own to explore it all or take a guided tour.

Hours: Open Thurs. and Sun., 1pm - 4pm.

Price: Free

Ages: 6 years and up.

FLYING LEATHERNECK AVIATION MUSEUM

(858) 693-1723 / www.flyingleathernecks.org
4203 Anderson Avenue, Miramar Road at U. S. Marine Corps Air Station, Miramar

This aviation museum is the only one dedicated to United States Marine Corps (USMC) aviation, preserving and promoting its history with this collection of vintage aircraft flown by Marine pilots. There are over thirty aircraft on display (and army trucks and tanks, and missiles) both inside and outside the museum, including a Sikorsky 53A/D cargo helicopter, HOK, Iraqi Bell 2145, MiG-15, Intruder, McDonnell F2H-2 "Banshee," WWII-era Douglass Dauntless SBD bomber and North American FJ-3 "Fury." The planes and copters date from World War II up to modern day. Several aircraft are undergoing restoration, a process that ranges from a complete overhaul to simply a new coat of paint, so displays do rotate. Visitors are invited to see the planes, learn their histories, and ask questions of the docents.

The display cases, hallways, and rooms inside the barrack building contain military and aviation artifacts such as uniforms (including a POW uniform), engines, a captured Japanese flag, memorabilia from WWII battlefields, equipment, historic documents, model aircraft, photographs, a collection of patches (2,400!), and more. A favorite item is the F4 flight-simulation cockpit where kids (and adults) can climb into the cockpit to check out all the instruments, gauges, and the joystick. Don't forget to take a look through the great gift shop. Guided tours of the museum are given by appointment. For the more technically oriented, there are numerous videos and documents in the museum's library. Bring your little pilot wanna-bes here, especially, on Open Cockpit Days, usually held on certain weekends from May to September, where cockpits of selected aircraft are open to climb in and "fly". Note that there is a playground on the base just down the street from the museum.

Hours: Open Tues. - Sun., 9am - 3:30pm. Closed Mon., for the annual air show, Veteran's Day, and Thanksgiving Thursday and Friday. It closes at noon on Christmas Eve and New Year's Eve.
Price: Free
Ages: 5 years and up.

GASKILL BROTHERS STONE STORE MUSEUM

(619) 663-1885- museum, weekends only; (619) 478-5566 / www.cssmus.org; www.sdparks.org
31330 Highway 94, Campo

This small museum is exactly as its name implies - a museum created from an old store built out of stones, by brothers, from 1885 to 1887. The exhibits in the main room consist of a stocked, old-fashioned general store with jars, bottles (filled with tonics) and tins on the shelves; plus dolls, Native American pottery, scales, adding machines, etc.; a small, turn-of-the-century kitchen; tools; appliances; a furnace; a school desk; odds and ends from that time period; and lots of photographs and documents. The back room is a tiny man-made cave blasted from rock, once used for storing food (i.e., a really old-fashioned refrigerator) and other items. Upstairs is a military room, mostly representing the American Legion, with several mannequins in uniforms, including the Buffalo Soldiers Cavalry, plus saddles, some equipment, and photographs and information about this area's military region.

A stream runs in front of the museum and a woods surrounds it. Out back, up a very short hill, is a picnic table under a shade tree. Just around the corner is the PACIFIC SOUTHWEST RAILWAY MUSEUM (pg. 582) and MOTOR TRANSPORT MUSEUM (pg. 539).

Hours: Open Sat. - Sun., 11am - 4pm(ish). Closed during inclement weather.
Price: $2 per person.
Ages: 7 years and up.

GUY B. WOODWARD MUSEUM OF HISTORY

(760) 789-7644 / www.woodwardmuseum.net
645 Main Street, Ramona

A complex of buildings makes up this small, early western museum "town." The outside courtyard has a stage wagon - no springs made for a bumpy ride! A red barn houses an old medicine wagon (an RV prototype). The long garage contains a 1920's tractor, old buggies, an antique fire engine, fire fighting equipment, and lots of old tools, such as saws and wheat scythes, in neat rows on the walls. Just around the corner is a Honey House which contains beekeeping equipment. A narrow Millinery Shoppe features real mink stoles, outrageous feather hats, and a few beaded dresses. Other buildings here include a real jail; an outhouse; a recreated post office; a blacksmith shop complete with all the tools of the trade; a bunkhouse where cowboys used to live; a tack room with dusty, rusty saddles; a one-room schoolhouse; and a hobby room, which is really a catch-all room filled with old typewriters, bottles, and one of the first T.V. sets. Farm machinery is displayed all around the cluster of buildings. See if your kids can recognize washing machines, butter churns, the large incubator, a cream separator, and a machine for bottling milk.

The museum contains the heritage (and furnishings) of the older citizens of Ramona. The 1886 main house has roped-off rooms to look into including a turn-of-the-century doctor's office with a mannequin nurse and a collection of early medical instruments and vials; a beautifully decorated parlor, which is a combination of living room and music room, with mannequins dressed in period clothing; a library; a bedroom; and a kitchen that is packed with irons, dishes, butter churns, and other implements. The screened in back porch is set up like a bedroom - my kids were ready to move in!

The downstairs used to be a wine cellar, and the temperature is still cool here. The conglomeration of "stuff" now stored and displayed here includes Civil War artifacts, such as uniforms and cannon balls; a collection of cameras; a turkey-feather cape; a six-foot long Red Diamond Rattlesnake skin; Native American artifacts, such as stone mortar and pestle, and pottery; a hair perming machine that looks like something out of a science fiction film; a Casey Tibbs memorial exhibit dedicated to this World Champion rodeo rider; mining equipment; and more.

This unique museum is more than a glimpse into the past - it is a good, long, and interesting look into our ancestors' way of life. Note that school group tours are given by appointment. While you're here, enjoy a stroll around historic Old Town Ramona, located on both sides and across the street from the museum.

Hours: Open Thurs. - Fri., 1pm - 3pm; Sat. - Sun., 1pm - 4pm. Call first and they can open at other times, too. Closed the month of September and for major holidays.

Price: $5 for adults; $1 for children 12 and under.

Ages: 5 years and up.

HERITAGE OF THE AMERICAS MUSEUM

(619) 670-5194 / www.heritageoftheamericasmuseum.com

12110 Cuyamaca College Drive West at Cuyamaca College, El Cajon

This museum makes learning about our heritage much more exciting than simply reading about it in a history book. Four different exhibit halls branch off diagonally from the reception desk and four different pamphlets are available that give details about exhibits in each of the halls. The **Natural History Wing** contains rocks and minerals, including a lodestone (i.e., a hunk of rock with a magnetic "personality") with nails sticking out from it. The meteorite display is out of this world. Other favorite items in this wing include a fossilized turtle shell, a Tyrannosaurus rex tooth, Duckbill dinosaur eggs, an Allosaurus claw, trilobites, a rattlesnake skin, a prehistoric bee trapped in amber, shells, coral, and seahorses. The many taxidermied animals include a leopard, deer, coyote, and the head of a cape buffalo.

The **Archaeology Wing** contains an incredible arrowhead collection, gathered from all over the world, and from different periods of time. Some of them are practical, while others are more ornamental. Other displays in the glass cases include stone artifacts, such as hoes and ax heads; Mayan treasures of stone and clay; necklaces (more than 500 are in the collection) made of jade, quartz, and amethyst; and various forms of money, such as shells and copper. Weapons, of course, are always a hit with my boys.

The **Anthropology Wing** showcases impressive Native American artifacts such as eagle feather headdresses, ceremonial costumes, and exquisitely beaded moccasins, gloves, and vests. More intriguing, however, are the elk tooth and eagle claw necklaces; beaded mountain lion paw bag; knife made from a blackfoot bear jaw; shark tooth sword that looks like a small chain saw; and rattles (used for dances) made out of turtle shells and trap door spiders' nests. This section also displays tomahawks, guns from the Old West, and a buffalo robe.

The **Art Wing** features Western art with cowboys and Indians portrayed in drawings, paintings, photographs, and sculptures. It also contains Chinese artifacts dating back over 2,500 years, including a jade burial suit. Two more stunning exhibits are the fifteen-foot long scroll from the Song Dynasty and just above the scroll, a five-foot long carved Jade Dragon Ship from the Qing Dynasty with detailed work of dragons and phoenixes.

Call to schedule a school field trip here for 2nd through 6th graders. The museum gift shop has fossil, beaded items, rocks, and shells at affordable prices. This hilltop museum also has two smallish gardens; one with an emphasis on tropical plants, the other, desert. There are also picnic tables here, plus a stunning 360-degree view. See WATER CONSERVATION GARDEN (pg. 521) for another great place on the campus.

Hours: Open Tues. - Fri., 10am - 4pm; Sat., noon - 4pm. Closed Sun., Mon., and major holidays.

Price: $3 for adults; $2 for seniors; children 17 and under are free. See MUSEUM MONTH, SAN DIEGO (pg. 700), in the calendar section, for details about half-price admission in February.

Ages: 5 years and up.

HERITAGE PARK VILLAGE AND MUSEUM

(760) 435-5041 - city; (760) 435-5540 or (760) 801-0645 / www.visitoceanside.org; www.oceansidechamber.com; www.ncmrs.org

220 Peyri Drive, Oceanside

This re-creation of an Old West main street came into existence when several original buildings (circa 1893) were relocated to this spot, giving birth to Heritage Park Village and Museum. The park/short main street includes a schoolhouse, newspaper building, a hotel and saloon, general store, blacksmith shop, livery stable, doctor's office, jail, and museum, plus an area for picnicking and a much-photographed gazebo and surrounding grassy area. Amble along the tree-lined street to soak in the ambiance, which won't take long, as, currently, you can only see the outside of the historic buildings, not the insides. Maybe video a fun Old West-type of movie here as the backdrops are already in place!

Note that the North County Model RR Society is located at the park as well. Toot toot! It's open every Saturday for the Trains for Kids program, where kids are invited to run and operate the model trains on the huge layout.

Hours: The grounds are open Wed. - Sun., 9am - 4pm. The trains are open Sat., 10am - 3pm.

Price: Free

Ages: 5 years and up.

HISTORICAL MAGEE PARK

(760) 434-9189 or (760) 602-7513 / www.carlsbadhistoricalsociety.com; www.carlsbadca.gov
258 Beech Avenue, Carlsbad

This quaint, historic park qualifies as a park with its grassy lawns, picnic tables, barbecues, lovely rose garden, and shuffleboard courts all overlooking the Pacific Ocean. The "historic" part enters the equation because of the 1926 town meeting hall on the grounds and the vintage, 1887 one-story Magee House, a small home open to tour through on the weekends. See the living room with its piano and old-fashioned camera; vintage clothing (some of which is now back in style); the tiny kitchen with its ice box and stove; and bedrooms. The house is decked out in Victorian finery during the month of December. Inside the barn is a buggy, farm tools, and a few more displays. Come enjoy a slice of history.

Hours: The park is open daily, 10am - 8pm. The house is open for tours Fri. - Sun., 11am - 3pm.
Price: The park is free. Donations are requested for the Magee House.
Ages: 8 years and up.

INTERNATIONAL BANANA MUSEUM

(619) 840-1429 / www.internationalbananamuseum.com
98775 State Hwy 111, Mecca

Come, Mister Tally Man, tally me banana, daylight come and me wan' go home. This very small, but fascinating, International Banana Museum is in the middle of nowhere; in the tiny town of Mecca. It makes for an interesting and quick stop off as you journey further out into the desert. Stop to gape at the myriad of banana items packed inside here for show and tell, and to purchase - from keychains to mugs, furniture, salt n pepper shakers, slippers, book, dishes, and so much more. Definitely try an edible banana creations at the snack bar, such as a chocolate-covered frozen banana, or a truly delicious and thick banana shake - just ripe for your taste buds. Drive a little further to see SALTON SEA STATE RECREATION AREA (pg. 512), SALVATION MOUNTAIN (pg. 566), and ANZA BORREGO STATE PARK (pg. 494).

Hours: Usually open on weekends. Call first. It's run by the owner and his daughter.
Price: The Museum costs $1 to look around, unless you buy $1 worth of something. (Another excuse to eat a banana shake.)
Ages: 4 years and up.

J. A. COOLEY MUSEUM

(619) 295-1611 or (619) 296-3112
4233 Park Boulevard, San Diego

As a book shouldn't be judged by its cover, a museum shouldn't be judged by the way it looks from the outside, at least this one shouldn't. J. A. Cooley's is a treasure trove of collections, with a rotating array of items gathered and garnered by owner and history buff, Jim Cooley. The museum contains over twenty-four rare, vintage, and beautifully restored cars including an 1886 Benz (one of the first cars ever built), 1906 Cadillac, 1936 Ford, 1895 buggy, and a HP 2000 Buick Concept Car. The cars are packed in here on a wooden floor. A plethora of other collections are unassumingly displayed. War posters and other types of posters line the walls.

Over fifty phonographs are here, including a duplex model (like an early stereo!), a 1901 Victor, and an Edison prototype, one of two in the world. (The other is in the Smithsonian.) Most of the phonographs are in working condition, so ask to listen to one. If you have the time, take a look at the numerous clocks. Actually, you can't help but hear them ding dong and tic toc. The eclectic collections also consist of irons, cameras, antique iron toys, train cars, baby carriages, beaded handbags, telephones, wood planes, bells (including a camel bell), bottles, ink "bottles," typewriters, and more. Note that not every item is labeled, so ask Mr. Cooley to show you around - he is a wealth of fascinating information.

Ever-stylish, the working nickelodeons and player pianos are a joy to listen to and fun to watch as the keys move unassisted. Our favorite instrument here is the 1900's Wurlitzer Band Organ. It plays the drums, cymbals, organ, xylophone, and more, all within one glorious machine. The sound makes you want to march or dance, or at least twirl around.

The museum shares its entrance with Mr. Cooley's store, Frank the Trainman. The retail store sells everything train-oriented, especially the Lionel line of cars, tracks, and accessories.

Hours: Open Mon. - Sat., 10am - 4pm; Sun., noon - 4pm. Closed major holidays.
Price: $5 for adults; $2 for ages 12 and under.
Ages: 7 years and up.

JULIAN PIONEER MUSEUM

(760) 765-0227 / www.julianpioneermuseum.org; www.julianca.com; www.sdparks.org

2811 Washington Street, Julian

If I were to clean out my grandparents' and great-grandparents' attics, closets, and garages, I would probably find many articles similar to what is inside this multi-room, pioneer museum made of rock-hewn walls and high, wood-beam ceilings, and a few murals. The wide assortment of items packed in here in display cases and all around include carriages; mannequins dressed in period clothing; guns; saddles; eyeglasses; mining equipment; rocks; bottles; clothing; arrowheads; a ceremonial Indian costume; kitchen implements; a metal bathtub; a potbellied stove; an American flag (with forty-five stars); taxidermied animals; a safe; cannon balls; horseshoes, branding irons and ranching tools; lanterns; old photographs; fireplaces; rattlesnake skins; Native American baskets; dishes; furniture; lots of old, handmade lace; pianos; a doll collection; and a small touch area with furs, feathers, and animal skulls. One of my favorite exhibits is a perm machine from a 1930's beauty shop. With the wires and rods sticking out all over the mannequin's head, it looks more like something from a science fiction film! Tips: Ask for a pencil scavenger hunt for the kids. Bring a lunch and enjoy a picnic on the tables outside this rustic and interesting museum.

Julian is a charming town with unique shops along Main Street. Your kids will enjoy a stop-off at the Julian Drug Store and Candy Mine for a trip downstairs to the "candy" mine. Go next door to Miner's Diner for an ice cream at its old-fashioned, marble-topped soda counter or enjoy a full breakfast, lunch, or dinner meal. The drug store and diner are located at the corner of Main Street and Washington Street. Note that on Sundays at 1pm and 2pm, weather permitting, Julian Doves & Desperados (a Western-themed reenactment group) performs free, comedic gunfights and skits near the Julian Market & Deli on the main street. Also see EAGLE MINING COMPANY (pg. 574) to take a tour of a real gold mine.

Hours: Open Thurs. - Sun., 10am - 4pm. Closed most major holidays.

Price: Free, but a donation of $3 for adults; $1 for ages 8 - 18 is requested.

Ages: 5 years and up.

JUNIPERO SERRA MUSEUM

(619) 297-3258 or (619) 232-6203 / www.sandiegohistory.org

2727 Presidio Drive, San Diego

Located just above OLD TOWN SAN DIEGO and STATE HISTORIC PARK (pg. 544), picturesque Presidio Park has green rolling hills and lots of old shade trees. Follow the signs and walk along the Old Presidio Historic Trail and you'll be walking in the footsteps of settlers from centuries ago.

On a hilltop in the park sits the mission-style Junipero Serra Museum. It was built in 1929 to commemorate the site where Father Junipero Serra and Captain Gaspar de Portola established California's very first mission and fortified settlement. Outside the museum is an old wine press. Inside of this somewhat stark museum, (because the building itself is a main part of the museum), the first and second floors contain some 400-year-old Spanish furniture, some of which is quite elegant, plus some exhibits of clothing, weapons (such as a cannon and cannon balls), art, artifacts from the outside dig site, and house wares that belonged to Native American and early Spanish/Mexican residents. There is also a room dedicated to the founder, Father Serra, that contains personal belongings and items given to him. A seven-minute video is shown throughout the day that describes San Diego's beginnings. Information panels throughout help, too. Upstairs, in a bell-like tower, look through the windows for an unparalleled view of San Diego. Tours are given for all ages, with a minimum of 10 participants.

Hours: The park is open daily, sunrise - sunset. The museum is open to the public September - May, Sat. - Sun., 10am - 4pm (closed 1pm - 1:30); open June - August, Fri. - Mon., 10am - 5pm (closed 1pm - 1:30). Closed Thanksgiving and Christmas.

Price: The park is free. The museum is free; donations gladly accepted. Tours are $4 per person.

Ages: The museum is best suited for ages 7 and up.

LA MESA DEPOT

(619) 465-7776 / www.sdrm.org/la-mesa

4650 Nebo Drive, La Mesa

This restored train station, circa 1894, boasts of a few cars still on the tracks - an engine, and caboose. The small depot building contains several railroad artifacts, including an antique baggage scale.

Hours: Usually open Sat., 1pm - 4pm.

Price: Free

Ages: All

LEO CARRILLO RANCH HISTORIC PARK ☼

(760) 476-1042 / www.carrillo-ranch.org; www.carlsbadca.gov   !
6200 Flying Leo Carrillo Lane, Carlsbad

Once a working rancho and once home to actor Leo Carrillo, this sprawling parcel of land currently contains restored ranch structures that pay tribute to Old California culture and architecture. The dirt pathways are uneven and the grounds are fairly extensive and a little hilly so just a walk around is fun and interesting. Take the winding, paved pathway down through the extensive landscaped grounds to the visitor's building, which houses a few of Carrillo's personal effects. As an intro to the ranch, watch a thirteen-minute film on the history of the ranch and life of Leo Carrillo in the adjacent Barn Theater that is lined with old movies posters.

The rest of the delightful grounds are composed of a ¾-mile trail that loops up and around several buildings. These include a wash house; cabana and pool area; U-shaped hacienda and adobe house with several sparsely furnished rooms such as a dining room, kitchen, and bedrooms; stable; barn; and a carriage house with lots of old farm equipment and old vehicles. The interior of the buildings can only be peeked into whenever the park grounds are open, but going inside them is limited to guided tours. The one-hour-or-so tours are the best way, of course, to really learn the history of the ranch and the era it represents.

My kids enjoyed seeing the buildings and courtyard, but they also really enjoyed seeing the numerous peacocks on the grounds (and yes, giving chase occasionally despite my warnings), as well as the lizards, squirrels, and rabbits. Keep your younger kids involved in your visit by having them count the number of times they see the Leo Carrillo brand throughout the park. There are picnic tables here so bring a lunch to enjoy.

Hours: The grounds are open Tues. - Sat., 9am - 5pm; Sun., 11am - 5pm. Closed Mon. Free, guided tours of the grounds and interiors are offered Sat., 11am and 1pm; Sun., noon and 2pm, or on other days by advanced reservation.

Price: Free

Ages: 3 years and up for the grounds; 8 years and up for the tour.

MARINE CORPS RECRUIT DEPOT COMMAND MUSEUM ☼

(619) 524-6719; (619) 524-6038; (619) 524-4200 / www.corpshistory.org;   !
www.mcrdmuseumhistoricalsociety.org
Marine Corps Recruit Depot on Pacific Highway and Washington Street, San Diego

The first thing my kids noticed were the Japanese 70mm Howitzers outside the museum. Inside, the downstairs California Room displays numerous paintings of war, including battles involving Native Americans, blue coats verses gray coats, and more. The hallway has photos of movies and television shows that have featured Marines. An on-going, twenty-minute narrated film is presented in the small theater. It shows all the different phases of Marine training, from boot camp to graduation. Naturally, the "coolest" parts of it, according to my boys, were the maneuvers where rounds and rounds of ammunition were shot, and the nighttime target practice where spots of light were seen when the guns were fired. After the movie my youngest son, with his eyes shining, declared, "I want to be a Marine!" The visitor's lounge looks like a large living room with couches and chairs. Around the perimeter of the room are exhibits such as helicopter and ship models, various military hats, and small models of physical fitness courses that make me tired just looking at them.

The upstairs rooms are filled with military memorabilia. The extensive exhibits include uniforms, swords, medals, grenades, posters, pictures, flags, mannequins dressed in camouflage, rocket launchers, jeeps, police motorcycles, a collection of knives (including machetes and bayonets), weapons used by Marines or captured from their enemies, and a room devoted to guns and ammunition. The Vietnam gallery and Iraqi Freedom gallery contain photographs, video and audio information, and artifacts from those time periods. Other galleries chronicle the history of the Marine Corps in San Diego; their collective history in wars, including a Ford Ambulance from WWI; a model of barracks for recruits; and displays and descriptions of what recruits go through.

The museum encompasses the history of the Marines from its inception 243 years ago, through WWI and WWII, and up to the present day. Always looking for "a few good men and women," the Marine Corps maintains a museum that is historically important, and that will enlist your child's attention. Free educational programs that incorporate world history, geography, current events, the history of the Marine Corps, and the values of honor and courage and commitment are available, as well as guided tours. Scout programs are also available. Tip: Groups may make reservations to eat in the mess hall. Note: All visitors must show valid government issued identification. Drivers must have a valid driver's license, proof of vehicle insurance, and proof of vehicle registration.

Forty-four Fridays out of the year the Marine Corps holds a brief "morning colors ceremony," where the flag is raised and the *National Anthem* is played. It begins at 8am sharp. During the year, there is also a "pass and review" parade, mini band concert, and a graduation ceremony. The graduation might be long for young kids, but it does stir up patriotism. The public is welcome to attend one or both ceremonies. Call for specific dates.

Hours: Open Mon. - (most) Sat., 0830 - 1600 (8:30am - 4pm) - open Thurs. until 5pm. Closed Sun. and most federal holidays.

Price: Free

Ages: 5 years and up.

MARITIME MUSEUM OF SAN DIEGO ☼

(619) 234-9153 / www.sdmaritime.org $$$$

1492 N. Harbor Drive, San Diego (Can I just say how fitting this address is for a maritime museum?)

"I saw a ship a-sailing, a-sailing on the sea; and, oh! it was all laden with pretty things for thee!" (An old rhyme.) The eight historic ships and two submarines that comprise the Maritime Museum - the *Star of India*, *H.M.S. Surprise*, the *Berkeley*, the *Medea*, the *Pilot*, the *Californian*, a *Swift Boat*, the *San Salvador* and the *Dolphin* sub and "Project 641" B-39 Foxtrot sub - are laden with wonderful, nautical artifacts. The 1863 *Star of India*, the flagship of the fleet, is beautiful to behold with its intricate-looking rigging, interesting figurehead, and polished wooden exterior. Inside, kids can look out the portholes; check out the very narrow bunks that once held emigrants; look at the old tools and displays of knots; and marvel at the variations of ships in bottles. Not only are the ships in the bottles unique, but the shapes of the bottles vary, too. Our favorite is the ship in a lightbulb. A video onboard *Star* depicts action at sea. A play boat, below deck, is for youngsters to climb aboard and dress up in the costumes. Top board is the small captain's cabin, a few passengers' cabins (which passengers had to furnish themselves), a dining room, and the chart room.

Be your own *Master and Commander* (from) *The Far Side of the World* when you board the *H.M.S. Surprise*, the actual boat used in the above-mentioned movie. Tour this fully-rigged, 18th-century replica Royal Way frigate and you'll see the costumes, artifacts, weapons (including cannons), props, and furnishings used during the filming, as well as movie clips, the Captain's private quarters, and the gun deck.

Now home in former enemy territory, the B-39 Soviet Attack Submarine, classified as "Foxtrot," was once used to track U.S. and NATO warships. It carried twenty-four torpedoes (you can see into the tubes as the hatch doors are open), including some with nuclear warhead capability. The sub is intriguing to explore as you walk past the sonar room, officer's accommodations, galley, and engine room with all the gauges, wheels, and knobs. Be forewarned, though, that the cramped spaces and narrow doorways that must be climbed up and through can make one feel claustrophobic. A fellow sub, the *U.S.S. Dolphin*, is the last diesel-electric sub in the U.S. Navy, used in undersea naval research because of its extreme diving capacity. Once on board, make sure to look through the periscope.

The 1898 steam ferryboat, *Berkeley*, contains a number of fascinating model ships and yachts. A model ship construction and repair shop is on board, and we watched a builder at work. He told us a model takes an average of five years to complete! Such detailed work! One section of the Berkeley has a whaling gun on exhibit and displays of fish (mostly tuna) and fisheries. Downstairs is the engine room which you can explore on your own. The room is alluring with its huge machinery and gears, narrow walkways, and slightly spooky ambiance. Also below deck is another room that showcases memorabilia from pleasure boating. The triple expansion steam engine is put to work and demonstrated at various times throughout the day. Cross over the bridge from the *Berkeley* to the 1904 steam yacht, *Medea*, which is a very small vessel. Peek into the elegant, Edwardian-decorated smoking room and into the galley that contains a coal-burning stove, big copper pots, and a wooden ice box.

The *Pilot*, a restored harbor pilot boat, is now used as a teaching vessel. It also sails out around and beyond the bay with students to study marine animals. The public is also invited to take a forty-five-minute tour of the harbor on most days, too, for an additional $7 per person. The majestic tallship *Californian* (the official tall ship of California - hence its name) has nine sails that unfurl to catch the wind just as its model did, an 1847 Revenue Cutter. It also has gun ports for fake battles. Seasonally, the *Californian* sails out of port and offers terrific on-board educational living history programs where costumed crew members teach participants about maritime history, about the art of sailing tallships, how shipmates must work together as a team (including swabbing the deck), and how to sing sea chanteys. What a unique way to study the maritime lifestyle! These three-hour sails are $62 for adults; $57 for seniors; and $48 for ages 3 - 12. Reserve your spot online or come early to ensure your spot and explore the other ships. Light snacks and soft drinks are available to purchase on board as coolers are not permitted. Tours and cruises are offered on the restored, fifty-foot-long *Swift Boat*, an important training vessel for sailors going off to war, especially to Vietnam and serving in Malta. Narrated tours - seventy-five minute cruises that describe this boat's role in those pivotal places and times - are offered on weekends at 10am and 1pm. The cost is $28 for adults and $10 per child. The 100-foot-long *San Salvador* with a 100-foot-tall mast (and two other masts) is an historically accurate galleon replica of the first ship to land in San Diego, circa 1542. It has taken years to build at Spanish Landing Park (fittingly!) to take mateys sailing around the San Diego Bay and up the coast. Limited, four-hour sailing trips are available for $99 for adults; $49 for kids.

The museum offers a full array of classes and programs for kids and adults from the science of seafaring to living history to elementary physics to docent-guided ship tours via dock side, plus overnight programs, even dockside family sleepovers, and Pirate Buccaneer Birthday Bashes. Note that school programs can book up to a year in advance. Check the calendar for special events such as the Sea Chantey Festival, Festival of Sail on Labor Day weekend, Tall Ship Adventure Sail, Pirate Days, annual day-time excursions, and so much more. One of the daytime sailing trips even ends with a cannon salute. Ask about Family Fundays where, on certain Sundays, two kids under 12 are admitted free with a paying adult and there are special activities on board such as sing-a-longs and crafts. Know that WATERFRONT PARK (pg. 521) is adjacent and the USS MIDWAY MUSEUM (pg. 557) is just down the road. Chart your course to have a merry time at the Maritime Museum.

Hours: Open daily, 9am - 8pm. Open one hour later Memorial Day - Labor Day. Four-hour sails board at noon.

Price: $18 for adults; $15 for seniors, students (13 - 17 years), and active military; $8 for ages 3 - 12; children 2 and under are free. Ask about AAA discounts. The Family Packages is $47 for 2 adults and 2 kids. See the internet for other offers. School programs vary in price. Sometimes general admission is free on Earth Day. During the month of October, 2 kids are free with a paying adult. See MUSEUM MONTH, SAN DIEGO (pg. 700), in the calendar section, for details about half-price admission in February. Parking in the lots start at $10 for the day; some metered parking is available.

Ages: 5 years and up.

MARSTON HOUSE MUSEUM AND GARDENS ☀

(619) 297-9327 or (619) 298-3142 / www.marstonhouse.org; www.sohosandiego.org $$$$

3525 7th Avenue, San Diego

This 1905 mansion was built to provide "function, simplicity and good design." The sixteen various rooms, covering four floors, plus a basement, are decorated in American Arts and Crafts, Oriental, and Native American styles. What a fun and different way to learn the many facets of American history! The forty-five-minute tours are better for older kids who can appreciate the lifestyle changes that occurred during the early twentieth century. Also enjoy touring through the carriage house and the five acres of landscaped grounds that include formal gardens and rustic canyon gardens, a teahouse, and fountain. School and other groups, $5 per person, are invited to come, see and learn.

Hours: The mansion is open only for guided tours, Fri. - Mon., 10am - 5pm. Tours are given every half hour. Garden tours are self-guided. Closed Thanksgiving and Christmas.

Price: $15 for adults; $12 for seniors and students with ID; $7 for ages 6 - 12; children 5 and under are free.

Ages: 9 years and up.

MINGEI INTERNATIONAL MUSEUM ☀

(619) 239-0003 / www.mingei.org $$$

Plaza de Panama, Balboa Park, San Diego

"Min" is the Japanese word for "all people"; "gei" means "art", so mingei translates as "art of all people", or folk art. Outside are colorful, fanciful statues made of stone and tile. Fun photo op. A child's enjoyment of this folk art museum depends on the current exhibits. We saw many tapestries, handcrafted furniture, ceremonial masks, currency, Chinese woodblock prints, statues from the Ming Dynasty, and beautiful pieces of jewelry. Past exhibits have included toys and dolls from around the world, Mexican folk art, ceremonial objects, and the horse in folk art. Check out the video rooms that offer in-depth glimpses into the countries and their art. Call first, or go on the third Tuesday of the month when admission is free for residents. The museum's gift shop offers colorful and unique items. Note that tours are free for all K-12 and college groups when booked in advance. Add on a hands-on craft workshop for $5 per student. See BALBOA PARK (pg. 524) for a listing of all the museums and attractions within walking distance, as well as information and prices on multi-day museum passes.

Hours: Open Tues. - Sun., 10am - 5pm. Closed Mon. and national holidays.

Price: $10 for adults; $7 for seniors, students (with ID) and ages 6 - 17; children 5 and under are free. Admission on the third Tuesday of every month is free to San Diego County residents. See MUSEUM MONTH, SAN DIEGO (pg. 700), in the calendar section, for details about half-price admission in February.

Ages: 8 years and up.

MINIATURE ENGINEERING CRAFTSMANSHIP MUSEUM ☀

(760) 727-9492 / www.craftsmanshipmuseum.com   !

3190 Lionshead Avenue, Carlsbad

This unique museum houses an eclectic collection of hundreds of (mostly) miniature models and projects of metalwork built by experts, many of them working models, displayed in rows and rows of glass cases all in one big room. Some of the items include an aluminum Corsair and P-51; plane engines; three miniature V-8 engines; iconic buildings made out of toothpicks, like the Eiffel Tower and Big Ben; a Ferrari V-12; ships; several cases of miniature guns and knives, like a 1854 Smith & Wesson "Volcanic" lever action pistol in ⅓ scale; delicate brass sculptures by Szymon Klimek; a fancy Napoleonic coach; a Curtiss P-40 Warhawk; a motorcycle made from watch parts; steam engines (with sounds and steam); an Epicyclic Train Clock; an electric typewriter; a working 1/14 scale Bridgeport mill model; and a ¼ scale Marmon Coupe built by the factory craftsmen in 1921 - almost every "little" thing you can imagine! Groups tours are welcome - call to make a reservation.

A small, back room is dedicated to an extensive collection of small machine tools, including everything from simple, hand-cranked, watchmaker lathes to the electronically-speed-controlled laser engraved machines made today. There are exposed machine tools in the working shop, where a machinist is often at work, so children under 12 must be supervised at all times. There are miniature engine demos at 10am, noon and 2pm each day. If your kids enjoy building things and working with tools, bringing them here would be a constructive use of time.

Hours: Open Tues. - Sat., 9am - 4pm. Closed Sun., Mon. and holidays.
Price: Free
Ages: 9 years and up.

MISSION BASILICA SAN DIEGO DE ALCALA

(619) 283-7319 or (619) 281-8449 / www.missionsandiego.com $$
10818 San Diego Mission Road, San Diego

Father Junipero Serra came to California on a mission - to start missions. The Mission San Diego de Alcala was the first church in California, founded by the Padre in 1769. As with a visit to any of the twenty-one missions, coming here brings the past vividly back to life. The church is long and narrow and, of course, housed in an adobe structure. The gardens here are very small, but pretty. The Padre Luis Jayme Museum, named after the missionary who was killed here by an Indian attack, contains some interesting excavated artifacts such as flintlock pistols, swords, buttons, and pottery. Other exhibits here include vestments, old photos, and small dioramas of all the missions. The monastery ruins have partial walls and the outlines of where the padres living quarters, the library, and other rooms once stood. Tips: Read the pamphlet about the mission as you explore it because knowing its history makes it much more interesting.

Hours: Open daily, 9am - 4:30pm. Closed Thanksgiving and Christmas.
Price: $5 for adults; $3 for seniors and students over 12; $2 for ages 11 and under.
Ages: 7 years and up.

MISSION SAN ANTONIO DE PALA

(760) 742-3317 / www.missionsanantonio.org $
3015 Pala Mission Road, Pala

This mission, founded in 1816, is the only remaining Spanish California Mission to continue in its original purpose of proselytizing and serving Native Americans. The adjacent school is for Native American children and the gift shop is run by Native Americans. The small mission is located on an Indian Reservation, a fact that greatly enhanced its value in my children's eyes.

The museum part of the mission consists of two small wings. One contains arrowheads, pottery, clothing with intricate beadwork, the Padre's small quarters, and an altar. Hand-carved religious figures and the Southwestern-style painted ceilings are eye-catching. The other wing is the Mineral Room, showcasing nice specimens of jasper, petrified wood slabs, and amethyst. The room also has a marine display that includes a stuffed puffer fish, corral, huge shells, and a giant clam shell.

The small back courtyard has a nicely landscaped garden, an altar, and a fountain with koi. The old bell tower is around the side of the mission, next to the cemetery.

Hours: Open Wed., 9am - 4pm; Thurs., noon - 4pm; Fri., 9am - 4pm; Sat., 9am - 5pm; Sun., 9am - 2pm. Closed Mon., Tues. and the week between Christmas and New Years.
Price: $2 donation for adults; $1 for children 12 and under.
Ages: 6 years and up.

MISSION SAN LUIS REY DE FRANCIA

(760) 757-3651 / www.sanluisrey.org $$
4050 Mission Avenue, Oceanside

Founded in 1798, this mission has been nicknamed "King of the Missions" because it is the largest of the twenty-one missions. It is also one of the most interesting. The extensive grounds cover nearly six and a half acres, though not all of it is open to the public. The first series of rooms contain several glass-encased displays that document the history of the mission. Next, is a Friar's small bedroom with a knotted rope bed, and monks' robes. (Several Franciscan friars still live here in a separate section of the mission.) The weavery and work rooms have a loom, spinning wheel, and implements for leather tooling, respectively. The kitchen contains pots, pans, a brick oven, and glassware typical of the Mission period. The next few rooms display embroidered vestments, statues of angels and the Madonna, and other religious art work. The big Mission Church is gorgeous. Exit the church through the Madonna Chapel into the cemetery which contains a large wooden cross to commemorate the 3,000 Indians buried here.

The grounds are equally interesting to explore. Large grassy areas, with plenty of picnic tables, are outside the mission's front doors. Just past this area are ruins of soldiers' barracks. Further down, toward the street, is an ornate stone arch and a tiled stairway that lead to an old mission laundry area and large sunken garden, where Indians bathed. The garden looks like it was left over from Babylonian times; once elegantly landscaped, but now overgrown. Mission San Luis Rey de Francia is a great one to cover for those fourth grade mission reports! Of course, guided tours are available, by reservation. A seventy-five-minute, Behind-the-Scenes Tour is offered most Saturdays and Sundays at 1pm for $12 for adults; $10 for seniors. Visitors can see areas not normally open to the public, such as the private rose gardens, and docents share interesting historical facts and stories about the church, the cemetery and the site in general. Check out taking a day or overnight individual or group retreat here, even a personal quiet day.

Hours: Open Mon. - Fri., 9:30am - 5pm; Sat. - Sun., 10am - 5pm. Closed New Year's Day, Easter, Thanksgiving and Christmas Day.
Price: $7 for adults; $5 for seniors; $3 for ages 6 - 18; children 5 and under are free, as are active military.
Ages: 5 years and up.

MOTOR TRANSPORT MUSEUM

(619) 478-2492 / www.motortransportmuseum.org
31949 Highway 94, Campo

It might seem like a glorified junkyard, but this outdoor "museum" will make a car enthusiast's heart rev. Located in the building and mostly on the grounds of the old mill, over 200 vehicles from the early days of automobiles to current day, reside here; some waiting to be restored, but in real life, most have found their resting place. Old and rusted vehicles in no particular order are lined up, side by side; cars, buses, trailers, tractors, moving vans, military vehicles, and all kinds of trucks - cargo, fire, fuel, lumber, milk, dump, and more. Manufacturers include Mack, Ford, Nash, Fageol, Garford and many more. Walk the grounds to see the cars close up, but don't get inside them; take photos - great for photo ops!; hold onto little ones as you watch out for tires and other parts lying around; and enjoy this quirky and fascinating display of history.

Inside the massive building are a few prized, restored vehicles and some in process of, such as a Mack truck, WWII jeep and 1917 Nash Quad, plus old gas pumps and lots of tools as this is, basically, a workshop. Tours, clubs and school groups are welcome during the week. Note that just down the road are the GASKILL BROTHERS STONE STORE MUSEUM (pg. 531) and the PACIFIC SOUTHWEST RAILWAY MUSEUM (pg. 582).

Hours: Open Sat., 9am - 5pm, or, if you're in the area and the gate is open and someone is working, you are usually welcome, then, too.
Price: Free
Ages: 6 years and up.

MUSEUM OF CONTEMPORARY ART - La Jolla

(858) 454-3541 / www.mcasd.org
700 Prospect Street, La Jolla

I admit two things about contemporary art museums: 1) I enjoy visiting them, and 2) I don't always "get" the art on exhibit. I've learned not to step on things lying on the floor or to touch anything, even things as seemingly innocuous as a pole in the center of the room - it could be an exhibit. Displays here rotate about every three months, so there are new eclectic paintings, sculptures, photos, and other pieces to figure out every few months.

Our favorite past exhibits include a room-size metal spider carrying a nest of eggs; toddler-size figures made out of wax in various stages of melting because of the heat lamps directed on them; the "Reason for the Neutron Bomb," which had 50,000 match tips glued onto nickels on the floor, each one representing a Russian tank; and a darkened room with a large church bell which, when my kids pulled on the rope, triggered a hologram of the Virgin Mary and baby Jesus to appear.

You can enjoy a light meal at the cafe, or a cappuccino. By the way, the view of the coastline from the museum is spectacular. NOTE: At the time of this writing, this museum was closed for a major renovation, increasing its gallery space from 10,000 square feet to 40,000! So, check the website or call to see the progress, and when it will reopen. Also see the following entry, MUSEUM OF CONTEMPORARY ART - San Diego.

Hours: TBA
Price: TBA
Ages: 6 years and up.

MUSEUM OF CONTEMPORARY ART - San Diego

(858) 454-3541 / www.mcasd.org $$
1001 and 1100 Kettner Boulevard, San Diego

Comprised of two artsy-style buildings, across the street from each other, the mood is set for your visit to San Diego's contemporary art museum. What kinds of materials are used in the art that you're looking at? Traditional materials, like paint? Or nuts, bolts, wires, or other improbable materials? These are a few of the questions listed in the (free) children's guide on discovering contemporary art, which is found at the reception desk. The guide helps your child become more involved with the art, and enables him/her to understand the artist's vision in creating their work. Free, guided tours are also available Saturdays at 2pm and the third Thursdays at 5:30pm. Contemporary art is fun because it is eclectic. Some art pieces might be as unusual as a box of cereal, while other paintings, sculptures, and/or photos are a more daring combination of design, light and texture. The museum, which has quarterly rotating exhibits, is a branch of the M.C.A. in La Jolla. (See the previous entry.)

One of the art buildings is three stories, allowing more light-filled gallery space and innovative showings, including large-scale sculptures. There are also multiple-channel video capabilities to gain knowledge and insight as to the works. Free tours are given on Sat. at 2pm.

Hours: The 1100 Kettner Blvd. location (Jacobs Building) is open Mon. - Tues. and Thurs. - Sun, 11am - 5pm; open the third Thurs. until 8pm. Closed Wed. The 1001 Kettner Blvd. location is open Thurs. - Sun., 11am - 5pm; open the third Thurs. until 8pm. Closed Mon. - Wed. Both are closed on major holidays.

Price: $10 for adults; $5 for seniors and older students; ages 25 and under are free. Admission is valid for 7 days at both MCASD locations. Admission is free on the third Thurs. from 5pm - 8pm. See MUSEUM MONTH, SAN DIEGO (pg. 700), in the calendar section, for details about half-price admission in February.

Ages: 6 years and up.

MUSEUM OF MAKING MUSIC

(760) 438-5996 / www.museumofmakingmusic.com $$$
5790 Armada Drive, Carlsbad

"It makes no difference if it's sweet or hot, just give that rhythm everything you got." (From *It Don't Mean A Thing* by Irving Mills and Duke Ellington.) This would be a fitting motto for this *note*-worthy museum. The museum is nicely laid out and chronologically traces the history of music from the late 1800's through present day in an audibly and visually stimulating way. Paintings and wall-sized historic photographs of musicians add to the museum's ambiance.

Each section showcases, behind glass, instruments (over 450 total!) typical for that particular era which could include trumpets, banjos, mandolins, harmonicas, guitars, electric guitars (one signed by Stevie Ray Vaughan), keyboards, pianos (one signed by Henry Mancini), horns, and drums. The sections also have listening stations where visitors can, at the press of a button, hear samplings of popular music, sounds of specific instruments, and even some of the key innovations and inventions that changed the style of music being produced. Expose kids to the sound of ragtime, big bands, jazz, blues, hillbilly, country, and more. Rooms toward the end emphasize music probably more familiar to them - rock and roll, heavy metal, new wave, jazz infusion, and the Latin scene. Videos, instead of just audios, accompany the latter years of music.

End your visit on an upbeat tune by letting the kids play the instruments in the interactive, Innovations Studio area. Children are encouraged to try out the drum pad set, keyboard, African strum stick, theremin (an instrument played by hand movement, without ever touching it!), a banjo, and electric guitars all of whose sounds, thankfully, can only be heard through headsets. Although the gift shop doesn't sell instruments, it does have a wide variety of them on display and it does sell some unique, music-related gifts. Forty-five-minute to ninety-minute (depending on the size of the group and age level) guided tours for the general public and for school groups are available by advanced reservation.

Hours: Open Tues. - Sun., 10am - 5pm. Closed Mon., New Year's Day, July 4th, Thanksgiving, and Christmas.

Price: $10 for adults; $7 for seniors, students, and ages 4 - 18; children 3 and under are free. See MUSEUM MONTH, SAN DIEGO (pg. 700), in the calendar section, for details about half-price admission in February.

Ages: 7 years and up.

MUSEUM OF PHOTOGRAPHIC ARTS

(619) 238-7559 / www.mopa.org   !/$$
1649 El Prado, Balboa Park, San Diego

Your shutterbugs will appreciate this large showroom, with five galleries, that features changing exhibits of photographic works. Some exhibits zoom in on portraiture work or the history of American photography, while others focus more on pictures taken from all over the world. We enjoy the artistry in the pictures as well as comparing styles and choice of subjects. Ask about the variety of guided tours for adults and students, along with curriculum supplements, plus workshops, photo classes and more.

A 200-seat theater shows a variety of movies such as *Matilda*, *Princess Bride*, and *Casablanca*, as well as documentaries and special events. See BALBOA PARK (pg. 524) for a listing of all the museums and attractions within walking distance, and for information and prices on multi-day museum passes.

Hours: The museum is open Tues. - Sun., 10am - 5pm; open on Thurs. in the summer until 8pm. Closed Mon., New Year's Day, Martin Luther King Day, Thanksgiving, and Christmas Day. Open some holiday Mon. and other holidays, 10am - 3pm. Call for specific hours for the theater shows.

Price: Admission is pay what you wish. It is also free on the second Tues. of every month for San Diego County residents. Theater admission for children's movies is usually free with admission; call for prices for other shows.

Ages: 7 years and up.

MUSEUM OF SAN DIEGO HISTORY

(619) 232-6203 / www.sandiegohistory.org

1649 El Prado, Balboa Park, San Diego

!/$$

This museum presents the history of San Diego, from the 1850's to the present, via numerous photographs, plus maps, works of art, costumes, household goods, furniture, a 1910 railcar, 1901 buggy, and other artifacts. An authentic stagecoach is the first item you'll see, plus the giant floor map, and it sets the mood for your visit here. We always enjoy seeing history and understanding more about our past generation's lifestyles. See BALBOA PARK (pg. 524) for a listing of all the museums and attractions within walking distance, and for information and prices on multi-day museum passes.

Hours: Open daily, 10am - 5pm. Closed Thanksgiving and Christmas.

Price: $10 suggested donation for adults, but pay as you wish. Admission the second Tues. of every month is free for San Diego County residents. See MUSEUM MONTH, SAN DIEGO (pg. 700), in the calendar section, for details about half-price admission in February.

Ages: 5 years and up.

NATIONAL CITY DEPOT MUSEUM

(619) 474-4400 / www.sdera.org

922 W. 23rd Street, National City

!

Once a working train depot, the building now houses a few historic railroad artifacts and some merchandise to purchase, and it has a picnic table outside. The museum also has several rail cars in the process of being restored. The main kid-draw, if you're in the neighborhood, is the huge, multi-track, O-scale model train layout. The trains run through valleys, hills, and towns. All of the "add-ons" that make model trains fun to watch are here. Across the street is a glass-enclosed gazebo that protects a restored 1887 passenger coach and a cover that protects an unusual streetcar, Car 54. Group tours are given with advanced reservations.

Hours: Open Sat. - Sun., 10am - 4pm. Closed Thanksgiving and Christmas.

Price: Free

Ages: 3 years and up.

THE NEW CHILDREN'S MUSEUM

(619) 233-8792 / www.thinkplaycreate.org

200 W. Island Avenue, San Diego

$$$$

This 50,000 square feet, tri-level, modern, environmentally-friendly building is a unique blend of contemporary art museum and interactive children's museum. The spacious rooms have high ceilings that are infused with natural light (even rooms without walls that open directly to the outside), and contain outside-the-box exhibits along with, always, space and inviting nooks to just hang out, a much needed factor. Note that exhibits change because "new" is part of their name! What doesn't change is the quality and excitement that kids express by coming here. Hungry for both a fun and educational place to take your kids? Below is what we experienced at the exhibit "Feast, the art of playing with your food".

The entrance bridge, which is redecorated with every new exhibit, was ap*peel*ingly covered in a banana mural. The lobby/main room had grove of oranges at the ends of ropes which were dangling from the ceiling, plus some curved, metal monkey bars. As kids (and absolutely adults, too) climbed on the bars, and sat and swung on the roped oranges, or even just walked by, their movements produced a cacophony of sounds, amplified by the speakers. The sounds changed according to how fast people moved and what kind of movement was being produced. You can't see wind, only the effects of it. We experientially learned more about wind - movement, interaction and manipulation - in the Wind Vessel section.

The next areas are permanent: A creative arts and craft room with low tables for kids and supplies, and a wall-sized blackboard. Outside, a large balcony features a vehicle of some sort (I've seen VW bugs and a small tractor) and other items that await visitors to paint and repaint and repaint them. Aprons and paint are supplied. Tables and chairs are set up outside here, too, for making clay creations or other art projects. Museums staff post a schedule of their daily art workshops, but also check out the special events and programs, too.

Make/Shift takes an outside play concept and brings it inside. Custom-made plywood shapes and furniture on wheels, plus fabric, cardboard boxes, ropes and other parts are pulled and shifted around to continually recreate and redesign. Other learning play areas include a costume, dress-up nook; a cool tree-house/fort-like structure for climbing up, in and around; a make-it and take-it innovators lab; and more.

Back inside another room for the special exhibit was set up like a mini road/warehouse with play food delivery trucks to drive around a grouping of tires in the center. The next room was like a musical house with kitchen counters made of marimbas; a drum set made of huge pots and cymbals out of lids (ideas for a real homemade band!); cans strung in a row to strike like a xylophones; and recording devices. In another room were building blocks made of dried and compressed mushrooms for both *fungi*s and fun girls.

Across from the lobby is an eating area and Bean Sprouts Cafe that serves fairly healthy food and cute food - like a pb&j cut to look like piano keys ($5); butterfly-shaped grilled cheese; and crocamole ($5.50) with carrots for teeth and cucumbers for eyes served in a half of an avocado. Pizza ($7.50), soups, sandwiches (average $9.50) and salads are also on the menu, as in an espresso bar (so you can keep up with your kids). You've gotta love (and contribute to) the wall contraption to put in donation money and watch it go up and down and through a clear tubing system to the end basket. (I have some wall space in my house. . . .)

On the third floor, a huge fruit and vegetable bounce made kids jump for joy regarding eating their veggies. Inside a big, wooden playhouse (which is redecorated according to the museum theme), was a place for kids to play with huge foam puzzles, and relax. A fun, indoor soft play spot had a watermelon boat; a huge piece that looked like Swiss cheese to crawl in and out and through and on; an orange slice to get into; soft foam melon slices to rock on; an enormous water spigot with padded water; and more. More permanent stations of a paper-making studio; a small area with some tables and chairs; and a few more interactive (and clever) toys and exhibits; plus a big bubble station outside with large trays of bubble solution on raised tables make up the rest of this floor.

Downstairs, via stairs or the glass elevator, is a space with bean bags in two big pits to read or watch something on the screen. Look out the window to see a chicken coop. Visitors can pet and feed the chickens via daily workshops. At the food exhibit we crawled under a gigantic dining room table to play on the carpet and see footage (showing on the tablecloth) of kids eating vegetables and other good-for-you foods. An adjacent room, the Arts Education Center, is for educators as it is stocked with resources. Note: Check the website for great crafts ideas and what else to do at home to extend the learning and creating inspired from these exhibits.

Across the street from the museum is a one-acre park. A triangle-shaped grassy lawn proceeds a small stage area, plus a small playground with twisty sculptures to twirl around on and a few swings on cement. A garden project is on one side and an adjoining, enclosed play area, with an abstract climbing structure with fun and imaginative elements, plus a sand pit inside, is on the other. A bike path, train tracks, and across the road, another park with circles of grass, pine trees, and small grassy mounds add to the uniqueness and enjoyment of your outing.

Hours: Open Mon., Wed. - Sat., 9:30am - 4pm; Sun., 11am - 4pm. Closed Tues., New Year's Day, 4th of July, Thanksgiving, and Christmas. Hours fluctuate so call first.

Price: $14 for ages 1 and up; $10 for seniors and military; children under 1 are free. The second Sun. of the month is $3 per person. Parking in the structure behind the museum is $10 during the week, $15 on weekends. Or, park at the lot on 450 2nd Ave. for a discount for museum attendees. There is limited street parking for free and some metered parking.

Ages: 1 ½ years and up.

NORTH COUNTY MODEL RAILROAD SOCIETY   ☾

(760) 801-0645 / www.ncmrs.org   !

220 Peyri Dr at Heritage Park, Oceanside

Come watch museum quality HO gauge model trains go around the seventy-five-foot by forty-foot track. Get a handle on what's like to be an engineer by operating up to four trains, though not at the same time, at another display area. The volunteers here gladly answer your kid's questions.

Hours: Open Sat., 10am - 3pm.
Price: Free
Ages: 3 years and up.

OCEANSIDE MUSEUM OF ART

(760) 435-3720 / www.oma-online.org $$
704 Pier View Way, Oceanside

    This pleasing, two-story art museum is located in the heart of the attractive city buildings in "downtown". It contains five galleries with rotating exhibits. Some of the modern and contemporary exhibits will appeal more to kids than others, so check to see what is showing. Some of the exhibits are more traditional in the presentation (i.e., art hanging on walls) and some exhibits are more unusual, such as the pop culture one that was called Icons of Desire with shiny, tiled, gum-ball machines, ice cream cones, candy and toys. The museum offers several ways for kids (and adults) to get involved with the art via classes and program - take advantage of them! (please)

Hours: Open Tues., Wed., and Sat., 11am - 5pm; Thurs. and Fri., 11am - 8pm; Sun., noon - 5pm. Closed Mon., New Year's Day, Easter, July 4, Thanksgiving, and Christmas.
Price: $8 for adults; $5 for seniors; students 17 and under and military are free. Admission is free the first Sun. of each month.
Ages: 8 years and up.

OLAF WIEGHORST MUSEUM AND WESTERN HERITAGE CENTER

(619) 590-3431 / www.wieghorstmuseum.org $
131 Rea Avenue, El Cajon

    These lovely grounds, landscaped with a wide variety of cactus and even a small pond, were once the home of Western painter, Olaf Wieghorst. The museum building has two rooms - one features his landscape paintings and the other features his cowboy paintings, plus other objects such as saddles, Native American baskets, photographs, jewelry, Kachina dolls, dream catchers, and a beautiful beaded Indian dress and bag.

    Walk outside to his home - a weathered, wooden building from 1947. You can see his period furniture in some of the rooms including the living room couch and old TV set, and several Native American rugs and baskets. A huge mural (twenty feet high) of his is painted on one side of yet another building.

Hours: Open Tues. - Fri., 10am - 3pm; last Sat. of the month, 11am - 2pm. Closed Mon., Sun., and holidays.
Price: $2 suggested donation for adults.
Ages: 8 years and up.

OLD TOWN MODEL RAILROAD DEPOT

(619) 299-9015 !
2415 San Diego Avenue, Old Town San Diego

    Being at this very small museum is like being at a train station - you're not there long, but you enjoy the ambiance while you are. In one room it's daytime and the scenery is more of a typical train layout (tho fantastic!) with miniature mountains, tunnels, trees, countryside, a farmhouse, lake, and lots more. The adjoining room depicts nighttime so it's dark and this is a total city scene with a multitude of small buildings all lit up, plus a plethora of scale vehicles, people, scenery enhancements and other embellishments in the vignettes. The attention to detail is amazing, so look closely at it all (there are stepping stools for little ones to see the trains better) to take it in, and look for the subtle humor. Visitors are welcome to push buttons to activate sound effects - whistles, bells, etc. - and make things and people move in the scenarios. O-scale model trains go around the tracks - one freight (diesel) and one passenger (steam). McDonald's, an airplane cloud scene, diners, Elvis, a mock fire, fireworks, a baseball game, a truck depot and so much more are some favorites. Look at OLD TOWN SAN DIEGO and STATE HISTORIC PARK (pg. 544) for a myriad of other attractions in the immediate vicinity.

Hours: Open Wed. - Mon., 11am - 6pm. Closed Tues. and major holidays.
Price: Free
Ages: 18 months and up.

OLD TOWN SAN DIEGO and STATE HISTORIC PARK   ☼

(619) 220-5422 - Robinson-Rose House and park ranger / www.parks.ca.gov;   !/$
www.oldtownmarketsandiego.com; www.oldtownsandiegoguide.com; www.historictours.com

Taylor, Juan, Twiggs, and Congress Sts., Old Town, San Diego

Old Town is a six-block area, which is closed to automotive traffic and bound by Taylor, Juan, Twiggs, and Congress streets. The places mentioned below encompass this area, plus a little bit more of the immediate, walkable vicinity.

This wonderful conglomeration of unique shops, scrumptious places to eat, vintage houses, museums, and Mexican bazaars are all located along dirt "roads" and on paved sidewalks inside the "town." Old Town contains many original and restored buildings from San Diego's Mexican period before 1846, and the early California period. A day here is a combination of history lessons and fun shopping! Just a quick note about some of our favorite stores here: Through the window at the Cousin's Candy Shop come watch salt water taffy being pulled; then go inside and buy yourself a treat of taffy or homemade fudge. At Miner's Gems & Minerals you can find some items at rock bottom prices, as well as more expensive ones, plus fossils and meteorite pieces. Become a miner 49er here for $5. You wash a mineral pan that's filled with "tailings" from the Stewart Tourmaline Mine and "salted" with pyrite, quartz crystals, agate, jasper, shark's teeth, and more - all yours to keep. For about $10, you can make your own candle at Toby's Candle Company - choose a mold, dip it in the colors that you like and build up the wax.

The route for the museums/attractions listed below starts at the Robinson-Rose House - the park headquarters at the opposite end than Old Town Market - then proceeds east, south, and north before looping back around. Admission is free, unless otherwise noted. All historic buildings are closed on New Year's Day, Thanksgiving, and Christmas. Free maps of the area are available at the park headquarters, in many of the stores in Old Town, and in local hotel lobbies. Free walking tours that cover all of the old buildings, not just the more kid-friendly ones I've listed here, are offered at 11:30am Monday through Thursday, and at 11:30am and 2pm Friday through Sunday, beginning at Robinson-Rose House. Various Living History activities go on throughout the month including soap making, mountain men, blacksmithing, carpentry, games, card-printing, and more. Check the calendar for a full list and days.

ROBINSON-ROSE HOUSE is located at 4002 Wallace Street, on the other side of the parking lot from Taylor Street. This 1853 adobe structure houses the park headquarters/visitors center and has walking tour maps available for purchase. It also has a few exhibits, such as photo murals and a scale model of Old Town as it appeared in the mid 1870's.

OLD TOWN PLAZA is located directly in front of the Robinson-Rose House. This area is essentially a large grassy area for kids to run around, with olive, fig, cork, and eucalyptus trees providing beauty and shade. A large fountain is in the middle of this park and there are plenty of benches for weary travelers (or shoppers). The row of stores across from the Plaza are in reconstructed buildings dating from around 1830.

COLORADO HOUSE / WELLS FARGO MUSEUM is located on San Diego Street in the heart of Old Town. This museum has the appeal of the Old West, with an 1868 stagecoach prominently displayed in the center. Other exhibits include a colorful wall display of Wells Fargo featured in comic books, trading cards, and even a board game; rocks with gold, bags of gold found in treasure boxes, and gold coins; mining tools; Old West posters; and more. Try sending a Morse code message, using the provided "how to" sheet, to someone across the room. A video shows and describes this time period and the history of Wells Fargo. A more modern feature is the ATM machine.

CASA DE MACHADO Y STEWART is located almost directly behind the Colorado House/Wells Fargo Museum. This plain-looking adobe is an exact replica of the original house, complete with a dirt walkway leading to it. The brick-floored house contains few furnishings, including a dining table, shelves with dishes and pottery, a sparsely furnished bedroom, and some tools. Just beyond the front porch is a beehive oven and open fire stoves, evidence of the outdoor cooking that pioneers once employed.

MASON STREET SCHOOL is located on Mason Street, diagonal to the Casa de Machado y Stewart. This 1865 red schoolhouse is a child's favorite historical stop in Old Town. It was the first public schoolhouse in San Diego and retains its old-fashioned ambiance with twenty school desks, a school bell, flags, a chalkboard, a wood-burning stove, the dunce's corner (and cap), and old pictures and books. It's open daily, 10am to 4pm.

SAN DIEGO UNION BUILDING is located on San Diego Avenue. The first edition of the San Diego Union came off the presses here way back when. Now, kids can see an old Washington handpress (printing press), typeset letters and tools, and the adjacent small newspaper office.

OLD TOWN MARKET, (619) 278 -0955 / www.oldtownmarketsandiego.com is at the other end of the park complex at 4010 Twiggs Street. It has a very small museum with historical displays of old San Diego, text panels, a video on this area, and artifacts found while excavating this site. The majority of the market is for shoppers because it has forty outdoor booths that offer unique gifts, plus artisans who sometimes demonstrate their craft as they work, such as a silversmith, a painter, and a bonsai sculptor. The adjacent stage is used for free shows such as storytelling, concerts, magic shows, and other presentations appealing to families.

OLD TOWN TROLLEY TOURS - See OLD TOWN TROLLEY TOURS (pg. 581) for details.

WHALEY HOUSE - See WHALEY HOUSE (pg. 559) for details. This haunted, historical house is just outside the park grid. Take a quick peek into the Old Town Drug Store Museum, located behind this house/museum. Kids can see an old-time pharmacy containing bottles, patented medicines, and a mortar and pestle.

OLD TOWN MODEL RAILROAD DEPOT - See OLD TOWN MODEL RAILROAD DEPOT (pg. 543) for details. This is further south outside the park grid.

SHERIFF'S MUSEUM - See SHERIFF'S MUSEUM AND EDUCATIONAL CENTER (pg. 556) for details. The southern most of my stops in Old Town San Diego.

HERITAGE PARK VICTORIAN VILLAGE, (858) 565-3600 / www.sdparks.org is located west of the Whaley House, on Harvey and Juan streets. This group of seven buildings is enchanting to simply look at.

THE MORMON BATTALION VISITOR CENTER, (619) 298-3317 / www.lds.org/locations/san-diego-mormon-battalion-historic-site, is located on 2510 Juan Street, and part of the park. For over half an hour, an informative and costumed tour guide (the only way to see the center) will show your family around this Old West center with a covered wagon in the front. The talking pictures in frames are pretty fun, especially as they leave the frames in each room to continue on with the visitors.

The museum has a few themed rooms that are filled with interesting artifacts from the Old West including canons and a big box camera in an adobe-style room, plus several interactive exhibits. One room is set up to look like a campsite in the mountains with logs and tents and trees. Another room, with its wooden floors, walls, and cross beam ceiling, is a general store with barrels, bedrolls, lanterns, and shelves packed with clothing and equipment for "sale". We were led into another room and shown huge paintings of Jesus during various times of his ministry.

Although the 500 men of the Mormon Battalion never fought a battle, the 1846 volunteer unit marched 2,000 miles across country to San Diego to help fight in the Mexican/American war. Their arduous trail blazing efforts and accomplishments are reenacted in an interesting fifteen-minute film shown in a room with rocky outcroppings along the perimeters of the walls, plus real plants, and a mural that pulls you into the mountain scenery of the Old West. The staff interact with the videos (and photos in frames), making it a 4-D experience. In the backyard there are activities for visitors including using a water pump, making a brick, dressing up in period clothing and panning for fools gold (that can be kept) in a sluice. You can also get a free souvenir here - an old time photo of yourself. As our tour concluded, we were offered a Book of Mormon and asked if we could have someone call on us regarding the Mormon religion. The visitor center is open Mon. - Sat., 9am to 9pm; Sun., 1pm - 9pm. Admission is free.

SEELEY STABLES is located on Calhoun Street. This huge, reconstructed barn contains several exhibit stalls. The saddles, bells, and harnesses, plus at least ten stagecoaches, surreys, and carriages, are great visual aids for picturing the past. Free slide shows are presented in the downstairs theater at 11am and 1:30pm so come and rest, and learn a little history. The upstairs loft has more exhibits of the wild, wild west, such as branding irons, spurs, more saddles, a Mexican cowboy hat, and furniture including an unusual chair made out of steers' horns. A native American display features Kachina dolls, a feather headdress, and baskets. Other exhibits up here include an old-fashioned slot machine, a roller organ, an antique telephone, a case of model horses, and a child's room with toys. Open daily, 10am to 5pm.

The backyard of the stables is an open courtyard with early farm equipment around its perimeter, plus several more carriages and stagecoaches in glass-cased enclosures. Also back here, or accessible from Mason Street, is THE BLACK HAWK LIVERY STABLE AND BLACKSMITH. This large blacksmith workshop usually holds demonstrations on Wednesday and Saturdays throughout the day. Kids might see the hot fires help bend pieces of metal into horseshoes or heavy chains, or they might hear a hammer clank against the anvil to create a sword or branding iron. The stable room is filled with finished pieces and tools.

LA CASA DE ESTUDILLO has a good-sized, outer courtyard and garden that leads the way to a large, U-shaped, adobe home. Notice the reconstructed beehive oven off to the side. As you tour the furnished house of this once-prominent family, you'll see the kitchen, dining room, several bedrooms, living room, priest's room, chapel, workroom, and study. The house/museum is open daily, 10am - 5pm. Admission is free.

GEORGE JOHNSON HOUSE is located on Calhoun Street, near Mason Street. This small building has a room to walk through - it took us five minutes, maybe. It displays archaeological findings of the area such as bottles and pottery, plus tools of the trade and pictures showing the painstaking work of excavation and cleaning.

FIESTA DE REYES has nineteen shops and restaurants with strolling mariachis, folklorico dancing, outdoor dining with authentic Mexican food - a taste of across the border. Try Old Town Jerky and Root Beer for 50 brands of root beer (and other sodas), a root beer float (buy one, get one free), and elk, alligator, turkey, bacon, and numerous other kinds of jerky. Also check out Geppetto's (toy and games store), del Cobre for copper smithing products, and Treasures of Mexico (for treasures from Mexico). For more info about Fiesta De Reyes, contact (619) 297-3100 / www.fiestadereyes.com

BAZAAR DEL MUNDO, (619) 296-3161 / www.bazaardelmundo.com, is a little bit of a walk, just north from the main park - catty-corner to it, located at 4133 Taylor Street on the corner of Juan and Taylor streets, behind Casa Guadalajara Restaurant. This gaily decorated, traditional, Mexican courtyard/shopping/eating area is festive in appearance and atmosphere. Occasionally, Mariachi bands play, costumed dancers entertain, and all the colorful storefronts and wares beckon shoppers of all ages to come in and buy. If your tummy is saying, "Tengo hambre" (that's Spanish for "I'm hungry"), sample and savor some of the culinary delights here. Shops are open Tues. - Sat., 10am to 9pm; Sun - Mon.,10am - 5:30pm.

Look up the JUNIPERO SERRA MUSEUM (pg. 534), which is located just north of Old Town.
Hours: The visitor center and most of the museums/attractions are open October - April, Mon. - Thurs., 10am - 4pm; Fri. - Sun., 10am - 5pm. Open May - September daily, 10am - 5pm. Shops are usually open until 9pm in the spring and summer.
Price: Free, but bring spending money. See individual listings.
Ages: 4 years and up.

PACIFIC SOUTHWEST RAILWAY MUSEUM
See the entry for PACIFIC SOUTHWEST RAILWAY MUSEUM (pg. 582), under TRANSPORTATION, for details.

$$$

RANCHO BUENA VISTA ADOBE
(760) 639-6164 / www.ranchobuenavistaadobe.com; www.cityofvista.com
640 Alta Vista Drive, Vista

$

    Follow the signs through the park and over the footbridge to the adobe. Guided tours, the only way to see the inside of the rancho, begin just outside the gift shop in front of an eye-catching, hand-painted map of the surrounding cities. The brick-paved patio and pathways leading to the eleven-room adobe add to the old-time ambiance. The immaculately kept grounds and adobe are often used for weddings, meetings, and other functions.
    The first stop is simply to check out the thickness of adobe walls. Walk into each room, all of which are furnished with items donated by area residents. The kitchen is constantly in use and it contains numerous old-fashioned implements. In one bedroom touch cowhide (which is hard) and calf hide (which is supple) draped on a bed. The bathroom has ornate tiles from the 1930's and a cool-looking bathtub. Another room contains a loom and other workman's tools of trade. A living room contains an old piano with candle holders (used before electricity was invented), a phonograph with cylinder "records," pictures, and paintings. My boys especially liked the light fixtures with wood-carved knight figures on them. Outside are a few neatly arranged washing machines and farm tools.
    Listen to the fascinating history and stories of this home, from rancho to Hollywood hangout. A few samples to

pique your interest: One room supposedly still contains a skeleton in the wall because when it was discovered years and years ago, it was just covered back up again. Once a bandit came to steal a horse and instead, wound up ordering his gang to protect the owner who had befriended him. A few of the rooms were originally not enclosed and used as a thoroughfare for horses. One owner slept with his prize stallion in his room. And so on.

Two-hour California history programs, offered for groups comprising of ten to thirty-three students, include a forty-minute guided tour and two activities. Choose from candle dipping, cooking, branding, roping, weaving, Native American games, and/or Native American crafts. Activities take place in the adobe or in the backyard. Teachers may request a curriculum notebook with lesson plans and worksheets. Three-hour Scout programs are also available.

The small park adjacent to the rancho has a grassy area, picnic tables, and a stage.

Hours: The rancho is open Thurs. - Fri., 10am - 2:15pm (last tour); Sat. at 10am - 12:15 (last tour). School programs are offered Mon. - Fri., 9:30am - 11:30am and 11:30pm - 1:30pm, with advanced reservations. The park is open daily, dawn - dusk.

Price: The rancho is $4 for nonresident adults; $3 for seniors and Vista residents; $1 for students; 50¢ for ages 12 and under. School programs are $12 per student; $10 for the Scout programs. The park is free.

Ages: 7 years and up.

RANCHO GUAJOME ADOBE

(760) 724-4082 or (858) 694-3030 / www.sdparks.org

2210 N. Santa Fe Avenue, Vista

This "Cadillac of adobes," built in 1853, contains twenty-two rooms and is one of the finest examples of early California hacienda architecture. (Count all the archways!) It was built for some of the same reason missions were built; to protect residents from intruders and maintain a small community of family and servants on the grounds.

Encircling a large inner courtyard, the rancho consists of a schoolroom, spacious family living quarters, dining room, a separate chapel, servants' quarters, the kitchen, sheds, stables, and a Victorian-style garden. It has all been beautifully restored. The furnishings, plus the buggy in the carriage courtyard and the docent's information, make the past seem vividly present. You can walk the Santa Fe Trail that goes behind the museum, too.

School groups are offered guided tours that correspond with California state curriculum for third and fourth graders. One of the highlights for students is making adobe bricks. (Dress accordingly!) Note that the ANTIQUE GAS & STEAM ENGINE MUSEUM, INC. (pg. 523) is next door, and GUAJOME REGIONAL - COUNTY PARK (pg. 500), for picnic and playtime, is just down the street. The park's grounds and trails are open daily and admission is free.

Hours: Open Wed. - Sun., 9:30am - 4pm for self-guided tours, with scheduled guided tours given Wed. - Fri. at noon and Sat. - Sun. at noon and 2pm, except in rainy weather. Closed Thanksgiving and Christmas.

Price: $3 for adults; $1 for ages 4 - 12 years; children 3 and under are free. School tours are $1 per student.

Ages: 7 years and up.

REUBEN H. FLEET SCIENCE CENTER

(619) 238-1233 / www.rhfleet.org $$$$

1875 El Prado, Balboa Park, San Diego

This huge Science Center is a fascinating place for hands-on exploration, experimentation, and discovery with over eighty permanent exhibits covering perception, astronomy, technology, and science. One permanent exhibit geared specifically for younger kids is the good-size Kid City with a floor that looks like a street. Shop at the grocery store with lots of play food, shopping carts, an interactive food pyramid, and all the accouterments. Climb in and around the factory, which has four levels of climbing and play. Sit in the little fire engine and turn levers and knobs. On the ball wall, push buttons and pull levers and watch balls go down through the see-through chutes, track, and big gears to show cause and effect. Kid City also has soft blocks, computers with educational games, a book nook, funhouse mirrors, magnetic letters, and a craft area. Infants have a separate play area just for them.

Just a few of the several other permanent exhibits and gallery rooms throughout include a periscope that literally goes through the roof to view the outside world; So WATT!, which is an illuminating look at how solar panels generate electricity, visual comparisons of energy resources, and energy conservation; Exploration Bar where interactive demonstrations and scientific experiments take place; and Gallery of Illusions and Perceptions which plays games with your brain. Dream! Design! Build! is all about being an architect or engineer, a wonderful place to invent, create and build using blocks - LEGO bricks and LEGO DUPLO pieces; pipes - PVC pipes in all different configurations; and wood pieces - thousands of uniform KEVA wood pieces to design and make towers, structures, bridges, and more without glue or connectors. At Nano learn about nanoscale science, technology and engineering. If that seems overwhelming for your kids (or you), this exhibit makes it more accessible by building a giant carbon nanotube and making connections while learning about atoms; using magnetite sand and seeing how small can be mighty; playing with a table top neighborhood to try to not tip it, but balance our nano future; and more. In a long hallway on the mezzanine is Power Play San Diego, an interactive exhibit where the entire power grid for San Diego is in your hands. Sections, panels and routes light up (or not) as you decide how much and what kind of power to deliver to homes, schools, offices, etc. and try to avoid a blackout! (No pressure!) Studio X (formerly known as Tinkering Studio) is a place to invent, design, and build using cardboard, plastic, origami, re-purposed materials and supplies, as well digitally designing projects. Making it extra special are Make-It Workshops, where participants learn to build something and get to take it home, and 3D printing workshops. So much to do, learn and become!

There are also numerous outstanding temporary exhibits here that rotate every year, or so, such the ExploraZone, courtesy of the Exploratorium in San Francisco. A favorite display there was called Memory, featuring thirty-eight interactive exhibits about making memories, retrieving memories, and . . . I forget what else. Another favorite was Animal Grossology, which featured 3-D and hands-on exploration of a cow's insides, blood-sucking and slime-making creatures, and other disgusting (but intriguing) animal functions. MythBusters: The Explosive Exhibition was like the TV show come to life, aided by a lot of props, gadgets, and sets from the show. Visitors could recreate some of the same scenarios and see for themselves if they worked or not, plus there were live demonstrations. Check the website to see what's currently at the museum. I guarantee that whatever is here is well worth at least one visit, if not several.

The second floor hosts many changing displays as well such as TechnoVation, the corporate name for numerous, technology-based exhibits. You could watch, for instance, a film showing laser eye surgery being performed; learn the history of computers from punch card to P.C.; have a video conference with someone across the room; see technological breakthroughs; and find out where water comes from and how it gets clean - from rain water to tap water. Live science demonstrations are also given on this floor.

The geodesic dome-shaped IMAX theater shows one-hour films on a screen several times the size of screens in regular movie theaters, therefore drawing you into the on-screen action. The shows, including a show once a month in Spanish, are usually educational and are always interesting. Another stellar production is the one-hour planetarium shows given on the first Wednesday of every month at 7pm and 8:15pm.

There is an abundance of education programs and workshops for all ages - youth to senior citizens, plus camps, outreach programs and clubs. Tip or warning: The gift shop appeals to all ages who are even slightly scientific or hands-on oriented. See BALBOA PARK (pg. 524) for a listing of all the museums and attractions within walking distance, and information and prices on multi-day museum passes.

Hours: The exhibit gallery is open Mon. - Thurs., 10am - 5pm; Fri. - Sun., 10am - 6pm. It is also open until 8pm on Fri. in June, July and August. IMAX films are shown throughout the day.

Price: Exhibit gallery admission is $16.95 for adults; $15.95 for seniors; $14.95 for ages 3 - 12; children 2 and under are free. IMAX tickets are an additional $3. Admission to the exhibit gallery, only, is free on the first Tues. of every month for San Diego County residents. See MUSEUM MONTH, SAN DIEGO (pg. 700), in the calendar section, for details about half-price admission in February. See info on the Association of Science - Technology Centers (pg. xi) for reciprocal museum memberships.

Ages: 4 years and up.

ROYNON MUSEUM OF EARTH SCIENCE & PALEONTOLOGY

(442) 999-4449 / roynonmuseum.org $$$

457 East Grand Avenue, Escondido

So many skulls, with the hadrosaur, saber tooth tiger, triceratops and T-Rex being some of the best, as well as a large variety and number of fossils, real dinosaur eggs, and life-size dino reproductions (such as the 25' Tarbosaurusa and the skeletal "fighting dinosaurs"), plus rocks and minerals. this place isn't huge, but it's good sized and amazing in breadth and depth!! Species I had never heard are here in the flesh, so to speak, in well done displays accompanied by great information. See a T-Rex tooth; a wall filled with imbedded fish fossils; petrified (not as in "scared") dung; a fluorescent room with rocks that light up when the overhead lights go out; geodes; bones; shark jaws; and so much more. What an incredible private collection that's now open to the public.

A group tour, or scout program, really makes the time here rock. This is where you dig into learning about the items here, from the Precambrian to the Pleistocene and "newer" eras, with stories about how the specimens were acquired, the science in what you are seeing and touching, earth's history, and climate changes, plus students get to make a specimen box and put in nine really cool rock and mineral specimens to take home. This is a fantastic tour/field trip!

Hours: Open the traditional school year Mon. - Fri., 1pm - 5pm; Sat., 10am - 4pm. Open for school programs and guided tours Mon. - Fri., 8am - 12:30pm. Open mid-July - August, Mon. - Sat., 10am - 4pm. Closed Sun. (except by appointment), New Year's Day, Memorial Day, Independence Day, Labor Day, Thanksgiving, Christmas Eve and Day, and New Year's Eve.

Price: $12 for adults; $10 for seniors and military; $8 for ages 5 - 17; $5 for ages 2 - 4; children under 2 are free.

Ages: 4 years and up.

SAN DIEGO AIR AND SPACE MUSEUM

(619) 234-8291 / www.sandiegoairandspace.org

$$$$

2001 Pan American Plaza, Balboa Park, San Diego

Take to the skies in this marvelous museum that visually chronicles the history of aviation from the dawn of flight through the age of space travel with over sixty real, replica, and mock-up aircraft, as well as hundreds of other exhibits. Outside are a Navy Convair Sea Dart and A-12 Blackbird on pedestals. In the lobby is the only flying replica of a NYP-3, as well as the real Apollo 9 command module, plus models hanging overhead, and an XJ-5 simulator ride and two-seater, full-motion, flight simulator called the FS2000. Simulator rides are is $8 per person. The following is information on the permanent exhibits - just know that the museum also hosts fabulous temporary exhibits such as Ripley's Believe It or Not!, the Centennial of Naval Aviation, and much more.

The rooms circle around the center pavilion, which contains a PBY-5A Catalina, an F-4S Phantom II, and a Ford 5-AT-B Trimotor, among others. The first few rooms, formally titled the International Aerospace Hall of Fame, give homage to the aero-engineers, pilots, and aviation founders that didn't fly off course in their vision for creating aircrafts and the aerospace industry. The hall contains a hot air balloon, as well as photos, plaques, and medals of aviation heroes. Portraits of Armstrong, Aldrich, and other astronauts, especially, caught my children's eyes. An Apollo XI display features a replica of the plaque left on the moon, the box used to collect lunar samples, and more.

The next rooms are packed with exhibits of early flying machines and models of inventions such as gliders, "birdmen" who used bicycle tires, bi-planes, and the Wright Brother's flyer, plus narrated videos that show pictures of early flying attempts. Consecutive eras are also well defined and enhanced with colorful wall murals, period-dressed mannequins, and other fine details. Wood-paneled rooms, complete with sandbags and army netting, house WWI and WWII planes and other memorabilia such as helmets, goggles, and uniforms. The flying aces and the fighter planes that served them, including the SPAD, the Nieuport, Spitfires, Hellcats, and Zeros, are well represented. In between wars, the U.S. Mail service was introduced. Displays here include a Curtiss JN-4 Jenny, wall posters of stamps blown up in size that commemorate aviation, and a replicated 1918 mail office. Kids love the next exhibits of barnstormers and pictures of daredevils using planes to entertain. These showmen of the air are doing headstands on wings, transferring from a plane to a speeding car, and other feats.

The next series of rooms honor women aviators; house engines, cylinders, and propellers; and display lots of model airplanes. Enter a pilot's ready room to watch the film *Sea Legs*. The armed forces are saluted with their contributions and a scale model of the *U.S.S. Yorktown*, and the *U.S.S. Langley* - the Navy's first carrier.

Enter the Jet Age with the F-4 Phantom, and the spy plane, the Blackbird. This exciting time period is followed by the Space Age. This last set of rooms feature bulky astronaut uniforms, capsules, modules, a moon rock, and more. An adjacent theater room showcases the history of model making.

At the Kid Aviation Action Hangar, tailored for pre-schoolers through elementary age, kids can get blown away at the wind tunnel U-Fly-it ride, which is a flight simulator in a real wind tunnel. There are also two other flight simulators in here, plus pedal planes to pilot around the play airport; a simulated moon surface to walk around in a space suit; mini parachutes to make and launch; a F-104 Starfighter cockpit mock-up to climb into and captain; toys; games; and more.

Hold on to your seats as they actually bump and jolt you as you engage in an immersive experience at the 3-D/4-D Zable Theater. The various shows are entertaining (and usually flight-oriented) and you are a part of the special effects that take place on screen - with objects flying out at you and feeling the visual sensation of flying - and off screen with the seats moving, misters, and more. The shows are given continuously throughout the day and are included in your price of museum admission.

Soar to new heights as you and your children explore this aerospace museum! Guided tours, summer camp programs, field trips, educational events, paper airplane festivals, book signings, and much more are offered throughout the year. The museum also has Flight Path Grill, an outdoor restaurant serving hamburgers, pizza hot dogs, salad, and more for about $7 per. Sometimes it's open only on weekends. See BALBOA PARK (pg. 524) for a listing of all the museums and attractions within walking distance, and information and pricing on multi-day museum passes.

Hours: Open most of the year daily, 10am - 4:30pm. Open in the summer daily until 5:30pm. Closed Thanksgiving and Christmas.
Price: $19.75 for adults; $16.75 for seniors; $10.75 for ages 3 - 11; active duty military and children 2 and under are free. Special exhibits usually have an extra charge. General admission is free on the fourth Tues. of every month (except December) for San Diego County residents. See MUSEUM MONTH, SAN DIEGO (pg. 700), in the calendar section, for details about half-price admission in February.
Ages: 4 years and up.

SAN DIEGO AIR AND SPACE MUSEUM GILLESPIE FIELD ANNEX

(619) 258-1221- direct line; (619) 234-8291 - Air and Space Museum in Balboa Park / www.sandiegoairandspace.org
335 Kenney Street, El Cajon

Even I couldn't miss this museum - it has an Atlas missile on the front lawn! This museum consists of two hangars and lots of outside space that is a depository for "work-in-progress" planes from the SAN DIEGO AIR AND SPACE MUSEUM (pg. 549) in Balboa Park as numerous planes here are in the process of being restored or rebuilt. They have completed restoration of a Convair F-102A Delta Dagger and are currently working on a Wright Flyer. What a great "eyes-on" experience young aviators and engineers can gain by visiting this unique museum! There are also several other planes on display inside the hangars, plus a few engines and aeronautical artifacts, and a glass display case of model planes.

Outside, besides the missile, are an F-14A Tomcat, F-86F Sabre, and A-4C Skyhawk, plus an army helicopter and other jet fighters. Exhibits do rotate.
Hours: Open Mon., Wed. - Fri., and Sat., 8am - 3pm.
Price: Free, but donations gladly accepted.
Ages: 5 years and up.

SAN DIEGO ARCHAEOLOGICAL CENTER

(760) 291-0370 / sandiegoarchaeology.org
16666 San Pasqual Valley Road, Escondido

Dedicated to preserving San Diego's past for the future generations, this small museum and education and research facility will interest those who appreciate a more traditional approach.

Glass display cases containing pottery and pottery pieces, glass bottles, donut hole rocks, grinding rocks, shells, a drum, and items uncovered from Fort Guijarros, including some swords and other weapons, whale bones and more. The display cases also hold pictural and information panels on the objects. A small section of the museum also holds a place for younger kids to dress up in archaeologist's clothing (which look like a construction worker's) and there is a blue sand box where they can excavate "treasures" from a shipwreck. There is also a small botanic garden outside, and some picnic tables. Note that SAN PASQUAL BATTLEFIELD STATE HISTORIC PARK (pg. 515) is right next door.

The Center offers an impressive array of adult workshops and lectures, K-12 classroom outreach and field trips, scouting programs, and more. The programs are interactive and intriguing as attendees are challenged to become jr. archaeologists, themselves. Some of the programs involve not just learning about a specific artifact, but making one, such as pottery and rock art, to take home. Programs can be as low as $7 per student.
Hours: Open Mon. - Fri., 9am - 4pm; Sat., 10am - 2pm. Closed Sun., New Year's Day, Memorial Day, 4th of July, Labor Day, Thanksgiving and Christmas.
Price: $2 per person; $5 per family (for 3+ visitors)
Ages: 5 years and up.

SAN DIEGO ART INSTITUTE

(619) 236-0011 / www.sandiego-art.org
1439 El Prado, Balboa Park, San Diego

New exhibits showcasing regional artists open every four to six weeks. This small gallery features works in various mediums, depending on the selected artist, including photography, sculpture, oil, watercolor, and more. A small side gallery debuts work from local schoolchildren. See BALBOA PARK (pg. 524) for a listing of all the museums and attractions within walking distance, and information and prices for multi-day museum passes.
Hours: Open Tues. - Sat., 10am - 5pm; Sun., noon - 5pm. Closed Mon., New Year's Day, Thanksgiving and Christmas.

Price: $5 for adults; $3 for seniors and students; children 12 and under are free. Admission to the museum is free on the fourth Tues. of every month for San Diego County residents.

Ages: 6 years and up.

SAN DIEGO AUTOMOTIVE MUSEUM

(619) 231- AUTO (2886) / sdautomuseum.org $$$

2080 Pan American Plaza, Balboa Park, San Diego

Jump start your child's interest in automobiles at this museum that has more than eighty vehicles on display. Most of the gleaming cars are in a line and readily viewable. Some of the vintage automobiles are on display in appropriate settings, such as a fifties car in front of a backdrop of a drive-through. Understand that the vehicles on display are here on a rotating basis. Classics here range from old-fashioned Model A's to futuristic-looking DeLoreans. Other favorites (that were on display when we visited) include a 1948 Tucker "Torpedo" (only fifty-one were ever built); a 1934 convertible Coupe Roadster; a 1955 Mercedes Benz (300SL Gullwing); a 1957 Chevrolet; and Packards from 1929 to 1936. Prototypes and concept cars, model cars, a race car, a recreated mechanics shop complete with tools, and an engine room for those who want the inside scoop on cars, are also found at this museum. "Gentlemen, start your engines" applied to my boys as they raced over to see the over sixty motorcycles on display. They were particularly elated by the Harley Davidsons, the Indian Chief, and an army cycle.

A kid's corner features a motorcycle to sit on; a frame of a race car for kids to sit in and shift gears; a floor mat designed with city streets for youngsters to race around play cars; and car pictures to color. Tip: Ask for a paper and pencil scavenger for the kids and turn in it to the admission counter before you leave for a prize. See BALBOA PARK (pg. 524) for a listing of all the museums and attractions within walking distance, and information and prices for multi-day museum passes.

Hours: Open daily, 10am - 5pm. Closed New Year's Day, Thanksgiving, and Christmas.

Price: $10 for adults; $6 for seniors and students; $4 for ages 6 - 15; children 5 and under are free. Admission on the fourth Tues. of every month is free for San Diego County residents. See MUSEUM MONTH, SAN DIEGO (pg. 700), in the calendar section, for details about half-price admission in February.

Ages: 6 years and up.

SAN DIEGO CHILDREN'S DISCOVERY MUSEUM

(760) 233-7755 / www.sdcdm.org $$$

320 North Broadway, Escondido

Come play! Our kids always urged my husband and I to share in playing with them because it's important to them and they like to be with us. (I'm thankful!) This small children's museum is a delightful place to do just that.

The good-sized room is divided into various sections to explore and *plearn* (play/learn) about international cultures, communication, and imagination. A wooden, boat-like play structure has sails, a slide, a tunnel, wheels to spin, and more for sailors to imaginatively travel the oceans. The enclosed (and dry) tiny Toddler Tidepool is an area specifically for ages 3 and under with soft block climbing structures and more. Building is also encouraged with more traditional blocks, wooden Keva planks, and using colorful plastic pieces at the light table. Construct different routes for a ball to race down at the magnetic ball wall. See real science at Aquaponics where water and plants interact to make life possible. Order an exotic something at the Global Village marketplace/cafe counter using pretend money, a cash register and fake food. Dress up in animal costumes or ethnic costumes or in uniforms, like a firefighter, and other career choices. Use props and hats to complete the outfit and enact a story. Or, use the puppet theater to put on a mini play. There are other activities here, too, such as using an air tunnel, beating some drums, looking through large microscopes, and more. I also like the fact that there is some created space to be low-key, to just sit and read books.

The outdoor patio is green with gardens growing seasonal crops, plants that attract butterflies, and plants to touch and smell - all "fertilized" by composting and by worms. And there are chickens, here, too! Other things to do outside include painting a huge canvas fabric; manipulating and designing with gigantic large foam blocks, mats, and noodles (I wish I had room for these at my house!); blowing bubbles; climbing the short rock mound; playing with Legos at a water play table; jumping on hay; climbing on and in some of the play equipment; and digging in a sand pit (i.e. base camp) to brush up on archeological and paleontological skills. Ask about the programs the museum offers such as camps, school field trips, and workshops. Bring a lunch to enjoy at the inside cafe, the picnic tables outback, or even across the street at the ESCONDIDO HISTORY CENTER / GRAPE DAY PARK (pg. 529).

Hours: Open daily, 9:30am - 4:30pm. Closed major holidays.

Price: $8 for ages 1 and up; $5 for military.

Ages: 6 months to 7 years.

SAN DIEGO CHINESE HISTORICAL MUSEUM

(619) 338-9888 / www.sdchm.org $

404 3rd Avenue, San Diego

    This very small museum, originally a Chinese mission, contains dishes and bottles dug up from the original Chinatown; replicas of the Terra Cota soldiers; the bed of Feng Yu-hsiang, a warlord of the early Republic of China; some traditional clothing; ancient Chinese coins; a sixteen-panel pictorial history; and more. Changing exhibits have included Chinese opera costumes, calligraphy, paintings, and children's hats. A stone path, outside, leads to a memorial gate and tiny Asian garden with a short waterfall and a fish pond. One-hour guided tours are offered that include this building and the sister building across the street that contains a few more exhibits. Classroom presentations are available that focus on the art of Chinese writing, dragons, or Chinese paper cutting. Girl Scouts are invited here to earn badges. Extend your time immersed in Chinese culture by going out to a nearby Chinese restaurant.

Hours: Open Tues. - Sat., 10:30am - 4pm; Sun., noon - 4pm. Closed Mon. and holidays.

Price: $5 for adults; children 11 and under are free. Metered parking is available in front of the museum.

Ages: 8 years and up.

SAN DIEGO FIREHOUSE MUSEUM

(619) 232-3473 / www.sandiegofirehousemuseum.com $

1572 Columbia Street, San Diego

    Have a hot time in downtown San Diego by visiting the Firehouse Museum! Housed inside an old fire station, the museum features ten antique fire engines from different time periods and other displays in several rooms. Note that sometimes exhibits rotate. Some antique pieces of fire-fighting equipment in the Steamer Hall include a 1905 hand-drawn fire engine and 1841 hand pumper, and tools of the trade like fire helmets, lanterns, and claim buckets (and a cool-looking spiral staircase). A small room off the back features elements to teach children about fire safety, such as a stove and sink to show and tell young visitors how not to grab a pot or pan. A fireman mannequin in full gear is in here, as are escape ladders, to illustrate what to do in case of fire in a multi-story home. School groups are welcome to tour.

    The Main Room has several engines, plus collections of helmets, badges, fire nozzles, fire alarms, photos, and speaking trumpets through which chiefs would shout their orders. Another room has old hook-and-ladder trucks, which are really long trucks! A September 11th memorial display includes pictures and World Trade Center artifacts. Most of the staffers are firemen, so they are knowledgeable about the equipment, history, and fire fighting tactics. Note that there is a small gift shop that sells fire fighting apparel here, too.

Hours: Open Thurs. - Fri., 10am - 2pm; Sat. - Sun., 10am - 4pm.

Price: $3 for adults; $2 for seniors and children. Admission is free on the first Thurs. of every month.

Ages: 4 years and up.

SAN DIEGO MODEL RAILROAD MUSEUM

(619) 696-0199 / www.sdmrm.org $$$

1649 El Prado, Balboa Park, San Diego

    You won't have to railroad your children into coming to this museum. Just one of the things I learned here was the difference between model trains and toy trains. (Hint: The way they operate and the way they look are very different.) The museum houses the largest operating model railroad exhibits in America. Kids (and short adults) can step up onto platforms to get a closer look at the several huge layouts. Watch scale model trains make tracks through and around authentically landscaped hillsides and miniature towns that are complete with scale cars, trees, and people. One of the exhibits depicting the development of railroading in Southern California includes the Tehachapi Pass, and others incorporate the Cabrillo and Southwestern, and a Civil War era live steam locomotive. One of our favorites is the Pacific Desert Line, which has a model train going through a town, citrus groves, and a gorge, all of which can be seen by looking through real train car windows! A huge relief map of San Diego County is accompanied by a touch screen to aid visitors in taking a virtual tour of the area.

    Kids will have the most fun in the toy train gallery, which features Lionel type 3-rail trains and more. Turn knobs, push buttons, and pull back on throttles to operate trains, make signal crossers flash, windmills turn, and toy trucks haul "rocks" to a loading dock. One model train even features sounds and smoke. A wooden Brio train set for younger children completes this interactive and at*track*tive room. (Next door is a club room/party room.) The kid's corner, upstairs, hosts storytime, crafts, and games at certain times during the week. As the railroad museum is always in the process of re*model*ing, it is fun and different every time you visit. See BALBOA PARK (pg. 524) for a listing of all the museums and attractions within walking distance, and information and pricing on multi-day museum passes.

Hours: Open Tues. - Fri., 10am - 4pm; Sat. - Sun., 11am - 5pm. Closed Mon., Thanksgiving, and Christmas. Call for holiday hours.

Price: $11 for adults; $9 for seniors; $6 for students; $5 for ages 6 - 14; children 5 and under are free. Admission on the first Tues. of every month is free for San Diego County residents. See MUSEUM MONTH, SAN DIEGO (pg. 700), in the calendar section, for details about half-price admission in February.

Ages: 2 years and up.

SAN DIEGO MUSEUM OF ART

(619) 232-7931 / www.sdmart.org
1450 El Prado, Balboa Park, San Diego

$$$

This ornately edificed building primarily features European, American, Asian, and twentieth-century art. As with any art museum, my children's interest was sparked by having them look for differences in artistic styles or color, and looking at various choices of subject. Kids need to somehow participate with the art in order to enjoy it. My boys were intrigued most by the statues, especially the fighting Minotaur. The small Image Gallery room has touch screens that introduce and teach children (and adults) more about the paintings and sculptures throughout the museum.

Although the museum has more appeal for older children, the Family Drop-In Days, held on select Sundays from 1pm to 3pm, are geared for all ages. Hands-on activities that relate to a current exhibit and other activities make this an outing to look forward to. Other great draws for families include Search & Find activity sheets (kids can complete and get a prize!); incorporating the Gallery Game, a set of five cards that each feature a work of art to find and learn about; and ARTie, a free activity book with games, puzzle and coloring activities. Check out summer camps and free guided tours. Note that a cafe is on the premises, too. See BALBOA PARK (pg. 524) for a listing of all the museums and attractions within walking distance, and information and prices on multi-day museum passes.

Hours: Open Mon., Tues., Thurs., Sat., 10am - 5pm; Fri., 10am - 8pm; Sun., noon - 5pm. Open Thurs. in the summer until 9pm. Closed Wed., New Year's Day, Thanksgiving, and Christmas.

Price: $15 for adults; $10 for seniors and military; $8 for students with I.D.; free for ages 17 and under. An additional admission fee is sometimes charged for some special exhibitions. Admission on the third Tues. of each month is free to view the permanent collection, for San Diego County residents. See MUSEUM MONTH, SAN DIEGO (pg. 700), in the calendar section, for details about half-price admission in February. See info on the Bank of America Museums on Us (pg. xi) free museum days.

Ages: 8 years and up.

SAN DIEGO MUSEUM OF MAN

(619) 239-2001 / www.museumofman.org
1350 El Prado, Balboa Park, San Diego

 $$$

Both permanent an rotating exhibits here are to be vivid and thought provoking regarding man's past, present and future and the reasons, results and relationships with other humans. One section of the first floor permanent exhibits are in a jungle-like setting and contain plaster casts of tall, engraved, stone monuments (called stelae) recounting Mayan stories and histories of gods and rulers, in hieroglyphics. And check out the terrific graffiti art murals that surround and expound upon the Mayans! Enter the imaginative world of Monsters - magical, mythical and real. Where did some of them come from and why? There are artifacts to touch and look at, and interactive fun to be had with making a monster of your own to take home (and put under your bed! jk), discovering monster habitats, discerning which stone age creature's skull was thought to belong to a monster, putting on a monster puppet show and more. Beerology is a study not offered in public schools, but it is here. With wooden barrels, information panels to lift and read, and even beer tastings at certain times, it is the study of the ancient craft of brewing to modern day micro breweries with interesting facts, stories, and displays.

Upstairs is a permanent exhibit called Race: Are We So Different? It explores physical and cultural differences, including the impact racism has had on history; how and why there is racism today and the origins of race and racism; looking at skin under a microscope (no difference in races); and asking what you believe and why. Tip - look really closely at the picture there.

PostSecret was originally started by Frank Warren. It is a part of a massive collection of people anonymously writing their secrets on hand-created postcards and sending them to him. That's this exhibit - thousands of unique postcards from all over the world where people share their innermost thoughts and/or deeds. Some messages are heart-breaking; some are encouraging; some are awkward. Entertainment? Healing? Disgusting? Emotional? Connection? Would you share your secrets with a stranger?? A portion of the exhibit is comprised of postcards from San Diego residents sharing local city secrets.

Peoples of the Southwest are represented by displays of pottery, Kachina dolls, and jewelry. A full-size, traditional, thatched Kumeyaay "house" is in this section, too. Hunters are represented by displays of weapons, tools, and foods. Our favorite exhibits, pertaining to this latter category, are the rabbit skin blanket, eagle feather skirt, shoes from fibers, and a quiver made out of a raccoon.

Ancient Egypt is *tut*tilating with over 400 objects including real mummies, dating from around 330 B.C., plus wooden coffins, coffin masks covered with symbols of Isis, X-rays of mummies, mummified animals, and exotic jewelry. You can even print your name in hieroglyphics. More graffiti art murals make the walls explode with color and explanation. Experience Ancient Egypt, too, in the well-done, hands-on Children's Discovery Center by dressing up in appropriate clothing and headwear, building pyramids with blocks, trying your hand at hieroglyphics, shopping at a grocery store (with plastic food), and playing ancient games - all in a replicated noble's home.

Some intriguing temporary exhibits include Cannibals: Myth and Reality which included, but went way beyond, the Donner Party; Counter Culture, the Secret Lives of Games, which was a huge hit with its 1,400 games, from classic to board to computer, from all over the world and many able to be played; and Strange Bones: Curiosities of the Human Skeleton which had bones displaying results of dwarfism, scurvy, neck rings, fused bones, and more.

Ever wonder what it would be like to go up into the tower on top of the museum? Quench your curiosity and go up a staircase (recently opened to the public after 80 years of not), climb seven floors (125 steps) up and up, looking out the narrow windows along the way, up the last metal spiral stairway and finally you are outside, looking over the surrounding San Diego area. Good things to know about going up California Tower: 12 people can go up at a time per timed ticket; children must be at least 6 years old and able to climb by themselves; the guided tours last 40 minutes, including 10 to 15 minutes on the viewing deck; and you don't go to the tippy top of the tower, for safety reasons, but to the first deck which offers wonderful views (and a physical challenge!). There are lockers at the base of the stairs to stow your stuff.

See BALBOA PARK (pg. 524) for a listing of all the museums and attractions within walking distance, and information and prices on multi-day museum passes.

Hours: Open daily, 10am - 5pm. Closed Thanksgiving and Christmas.

Price: Basic admission is $13 for adults; $10 for seniors, military, and ages 6 - 17; children 5 and under are free. Admission to California Tower is an additional $10 per person. Special exhibits may have an additional charge. Basic admission on the third Tues. of every month is free for San Diego County residents. See MUSEUM MONTH, SAN DIEGO (pg. 700), in the calendar section, for details about half-price admission in February.

Ages: 5 years and up.

SAN DIEGO NATURAL HISTORY MUSEUM

(619) 232-3821 / www.sdnhm.org

$$$$

1788 El Prado, Balboa Park, San Diego

Naturally, this multi-story museum is a favorite for kids to visit! The south entrance features a giant Foucault pendulum that provides visual proof of the earth's rotation. (Visitors usually stay here for a while, waiting to see if the pendulum will knock down a peg.) This hallway and adjoining rooms feature a child's favorite - dinosaurs, and more. Hanging overhead and standing on display are a thirty-foot model of the extinct megalodon shark; a whale calf; a T. rex; a fossil of an Ankylosaur; "fleshed" out models of dinosaurs; mastodons, saber-toothed cats, and wooly mammoth skeletons; a model of an extinct giant sea cow and baby; a pterosaur (your child will know what this is); a compost cast of a lambeosaur; and numerous animal fossils to look at and some to touch, such as skulls and other bones, and a number of shells. You can even sit in the shell of a dinosaur egg. Murals painted by a paleoartist enhance the exhibits.

Take a walk on the wild side through a series of rooms which are recreated rainforests complete with animals, sounds, and hands-on exhibits such as swinging like a gibbon by grabbing the knobs on the wall. Put together a puzzle of dinosaur bones in the fossil lab or dig for bones in the sandy dino pit. Touch really large rocks, minerals and more on display such as obsidian, petrified wood, amethyst, jade, magma, marine fossils imbedded in marble, and a meteor.

Camping isn't allowed inside the museum - so the Airstream trailer, surrounded by a starry night, is here is help depict the desert at night, along with boulders that hold a taxidermied ram and cougar in motion. The San Diego canyon, Torrey Pines State Park, forests and oceans are all here, too, in striking scale, to showcase the area's incredible biodiversity.

In the downstairs main exhibit room is Water, A California Story. The room contains some taxidermied animals such as a mountain lion, sea otter, owl, and several waterfowl, as well as some insects that live in water plus live rattlesnakes, scorpions, lizards, and tarantulas - all behind glass. There are also photographs, fossils, the massive jaw of a finback whale, the cut-away of a dolphin, and some interactive exhibits that deal specifically with water. The 300-seat, giant-screen theater, also on the lower level, shows twenty-five-minute and forty-minute movies throughout the day. Past titles have included *Ocean Oasis, Dinosaurs Alive! 3-D,* and *Titans of the Ice Age 3-D.* The Flying Squirrel Cafe offers food for foragers of all ages.

The third floor has rotating photography and sculpture exhibits that are stylishly displayed, as you'd see in an art museum. We also saw a display devoted to animal skulls. Call or check the website to see what is currently being showcased. This museum also features standout, major, national traveling exhibits such as the Dead Sea Scrolls, Real Pirates, and artifacts from the ancient city of Pompeii.

The museum offers many classes for all ages students (including field trips for minimum ten people for $10 per student), tours, guided nature walks, family programs, monthly events, camp outs, and even camp-ins. Several lab classrooms are also available. See BALBOA PARK (pg. 524) for a listing of all the museums and attractions within walking distance, and information and prices on multi-day museum passes.

Hours: Open daily, 10am - 5pm. Closed Thanksgiving, and Christmas. During special exhibits, daily museum hours are sometimes extended - 9am - 6pm.

Price: $19 for adults; $17 for seniors, students and military; $12 for ages 3 - 17; children 2 and under are free. Giant 3-D screen theater shows are included with admission, except on free Tues. when the cost is $5 a show. Special exhibits can cause prices and hours to fluctuate, so always call first. Admission is free on the first Tues. of every month to the permanent exhibits, for San Diego County residents. See MUSEUM MONTH, SAN DIEGO (pg. 700), in the calendar section, for details about half-price admission in February. See info on the Association of Science - Technology Centers (pg. xi) for reciprocal museum memberships.

Ages: 3 years and up.

SAN DIEGO POLICE MUSEUM

(619) 726-6151 / www.sdpolicemuseum.com   !
4710 College Avenue, San Diego

You have the right to remain silent, but not about this museum! Each of the several rooms is filled with police artifacts and memorabilia almost from its inception in San Diego to modern day, along with a multitude of mannequins dressed in uniforms from throughout the decades.

The first room has a wooden police desk with lamps, a typewriter, photographs and badges. Lining the upper shelf that goes around the room are police hats from all over the world. There is also a public telephone booth in here. For show, not for use. An open conference room is across the way with a huge display of badges, more photos and posters. The jail cell, a replica of one used until the 1970s, holds two prisoners, a sink, a toilet and a shelf of personal items, plus a bell used in 1913. Outside of the cell is a motorcycle police officer, standing next to his motorcycle. There is also a parking meter, street sign, mural, more photographs and badges.

The large, main room holds a life-size statue of a saddled horse, saddlebags and all, to represent the mounted police. There are also street signs in here; another motorcycle; saddles; the first polygraph machine; manuals from 1889; old photographs; a police switchboard; a jackpot (which are legal if over 25 years old and not used for commercial purposes); helicopter models and uniforms; a tribute to WWII; and several display cases containing police helmets, handcuffs, batons, billy clubs, and lots of bullets and guns and other weapons. One section showcases narcotics and all kinds of drug paraphernalia, evidence kits, and a skull as a reminder of what drugs do. A mini crime lab features all the equipment used in solving a case, including fingerprinting identification and composite sketches.

A hallway is lined with plaques honoring policemen killed in the line of duty. The small back room pays homage to S.W.A.T. team members with mannequins wearing gas masks, a sniper on an overhead shelf, shields, weapons, and gas canisters. Don't forget to pull over and check out the on-site gift shop.

Hours: Open Wed. - Fri., noon - 4pm; Sat., 10am - 2pm. Closed Sun. - Tues., and major holidays.

Price: Free

Ages: 5 years and up.

SAN DIEGUITO HERITAGE MUSEUM

(760) 632-9711 / www.sdheritage.org   !/$
450 Quail Gardens Drive, Encinitas

With a gas station and a cluster of other buildings on this mostly dirt parcel of land, guests can fill 'er up with history at this ranch house museum. Besides the buildings, a wickiup, some picnic tables and a random collection of vehicles, including a fire truck and stagecoach, the museum consists of a home that houses displays of cases of tools, a variety of barbed wire, household items, dolls, toys, maps, old photos, Mexican Ranchero costumes, a few surfboards, period-dressed mannequins, and a bed. The vintage toys were fun to look at. I appreciate the docent's willingness to explain the items, and the paper and pencil treasure hunt that got the kids involved with the exhibits.

Educational tours are offered to students (and other groups) to learn pioneer and Native American history by a guided tour of the museum and then hands-on learning as participants barter, make butter, make shanties, do a sand painting, and play Native American games. Check the website or call to find out about free family activities often offered on weekends such as soap making, cattle roping, seed planting, adobe brick making and more.

Hours: Open Thurs. - Sun., noon - 4pm.

Price: Free; suggested donations are $4 for adults; $3 for seniors. Special tours are $4 a person.

Ages: 5 years and up.

SHERIFF'S MUSEUM AND EDUCATIONAL CENTER

(619) 260-1850 / sheriffsmuseum.org

$

2384 San Diego Avenue, San Diego

Get deputized at this two-story, innocuous-looking adobe building. A helicopter (with realistic copter sounds) is outside in the courtyard as are two Sheriff's cars (one you can sit in and use the radio). The museum houses two jails, lots of weapons (all made inoperable), and a wealth of displays and information. The two jails are from different eras: one is a replicated 1850's jail with saddles, guns, an old desk, and a safe all adding ambiance; the other is a more modern-day facility. Come on in! Just a few minutes behind these bars will hopefully make an impact upon kids so that they won't want to do any time anywhere else. The weapons include Winchester rifles, colt revolvers, a submachine gun, numerous pistols, a pen gun, and a cane gun, among others.

One room contains a booking area with fingerprint and picture-taking stations. Some of the displays in here include inmate art and items that inmates have created to try to escape (e.g., "rope" made from sheets). Other exhibits include billies and cuffs; a roped-off crime scene and information panels on forensics; and a crime laboratory showing target papers revealing various gunshot angles, plus pipe bombs, mortars, and more. Listen to real police scanners. Sit on the police motorcycle that has working sirens and lights. Visitors can also pick up a bullet proof vest and "play" with handcuffs.   Upstairs walk through a working metal detector and into a recreated courtroom - you be the judge. A display on gangs, narcotics paraphernalia, and confiscated toy weapons is also here, plus a mannequin in full S.W.A.T. regalia. A corner honoring Search and Rescue teams has a wounded mannequin on a stretcher and a sheriff rendering aid. One display case shows what a washed check is and how to detect counterfeit money. A recreation and display about Heaven's Gate (cult) is up here, too. A gallery here is dedicated to the memory of fallen officers and another area salutes the K-9 units.

Check out the gift shop before you check out - it's got some unique and fun items for sale. A deputy sticker badge, a McGruff coloring book, and other information about the history of San Diego sheriffs and about prevention of crime are available here at no cost. School tours are given that fit in with California fourth-grade curriculum. (Younger and older kids, too, will glean a lot of helpful insight and information with a tour.) Don't forget to patrol the rest of Old Town while you're here - look up OLD TOWN SAN DIEGO and STATE HISTORIC PARK (pg. 544).

Hours: Open October - March, Wed. - Sun., 11am - 5pm; open April - September, Wed. - Sun., 11am - 6pm. Closed Mon., Tues. and major holidays.

Price: $5 for adults; ages 12 and under are free.

Ages: 5 years and up.

SOLANA BEACH HERITAGE MUSEUM

(858) 259-7657 / www.solanabeachcivicandhistoricalsociety.org

!

715 Valley Avenue, Solana Beach

The house looks like just a regular home from the outside, but it was first built in 1887. Step inside to experience a bit of history with furnishings from that time period. The rooms hold antique treasures such as a wood-burning stove that looks ready to use; an ice box; hand water pump; old fashioned clothes washer and wringer (so NOT fun looking to have to use); treadle sewing machine; phonograph; and more. It's enlightening to compare these implements with those of a 1930's kitchen and living room that are also here. These rooms contain a washing machine with a spin dryer, wall phone (still old-fashioned), player piano, a huge radio, and much more. A photo and informational time line shows the progression of the inhabitants of early California. Note that docents dress in period costumes for school, scout, and seniors tours.

Hours: Open to the public the first and third Sat. from 1pm - 4pm. Group tours can call to arrange a visit at other times.

Price: Free

Ages: 8 years and up.

STEIN FAMILY FARM ☼

(619) 477-4113 / www.thesteinfamilyfarm.org   !

1808 F. Avenue, National City

    Smack in the middle of urban life, this "as-is" farm "museum" is a work-in-progress with its gardening plots and wild grass covering the grounds; a small farmhouse; a weather-beaten stable; and some rusting, dilapidated farm equipment. Informal tours allow visitors a present glimpse into the past.

    The farm house has original furnishings, such as a potbellied stove, clothing from the 1800's in the bedroom, and a stereo optic view finder. The barnyard animals include a few pigs, ducks, a donkey, chickens, emus, goats, and bunnies. The animals, the information dispensed about yesteryear, and the casual tone of the tour makes the family farm interesting for kids. School and other groups are encouraged to come visit and learn, as well.

Hours: Open to the public on Sat., 10am - 2pm. Call for other days and times.
  Price: Free
   Ages: 5 years and up.

USS MIDWAY MUSEUM ☼

(619) 544-9600 / www.midway.org $$$$

910 North Harbor Drive, alongside the Navy Pier, San Diego

    At 1,001 feet in length, this floating city is utterly gigantic and fascinating for all ages to see and explore! The USS Midway, launched in 1945, is the longest-serving carrier in naval history with participation in WWII, the Korean, Vietnam, and Persian Gulf wars. It has supported up to seventy-two aircraft and had a crew of 4,500. Currently, there are over sixty aircraft on display with twenty-nine in the process of being restored. Pick up a free audio guide narrated by various people, many whom have lived and served on board the Midway. They dispense valuable facts and captivating stories involving the carrier's history and personnel. There are more than thirty labeled stops along the way. Note that by following instructions on an audio tour designed specifically for them and going to the locations specified throughout the aircraft carrier and completing tasks (and learning so much via interaction!), your kids can receive jr. pilot wings. Live docents are located throughout the museum and they are always eager and willing to share stories and information - wonderful and wonderfully helpful!

    Walk up the stairs to the hangar deck to start your tour. Note that the Midway has only been somewhat spruced up as a museum, so it still feels like a genuine aircraft carrier. Climb aboard authentic Navy cockpits and aircraft throughout the museum. First up is a multi-media theater experience to get a better understanding and sensation of the actual Battle of Midway. This hangar deck contains aviation weapons, photo displays, an A-4C Skyhawk, an F-14 Tomcat, Bird Dog light plane, F4U Corsair, TBM Avenger, and SNJ Texan utility plane. Behind the information counter are berths - confining, triple-layered bunk beds with small, attached metal lockers to store belongings. May your children never quibble about their rooms being too small again. This gallery deck contains the fo'c'sle of the ship (i.e. the forward part of a ship with the sailors' living quarters) where you can see the humongous anchor chains of the ship. You can also learn how to tie a variety of knots here. Walk through the darkened Command Information Center (CIC), the tactical center of the ship, with its screens and lights - it's like entering a giant video game. Enter a F/18 twelve-person simulator and experience the sensation of being yanked to a stop from 150 mph and engaged in a catapult launch toward the heavens, for $6 per person. The two-seater Air Combat 360 simulator lets you control the rolls, spins, and loops into the wild blue yonder for $8 per person for double occupancy.

    Below, on the second deck, are recreated areas, along with mannequins, such as the galley and mess hall (low ceilings, so watch your head) complete with tables and a chow line with fake cafeteria food ready to be served. Since space was at a premium on warships, sailors had to be careful what they ate because mess decks also served as areas to assemble bombs and missile components before they were taken topside. The sick bay and dental exhibit has mannequin doctors and a patient on an operating table, plus all the real equipment. There is also a machine and metal shop, and post office. Several decks below is the restored engine room and main engine control to walk thru.

    The top "floor," or flight deck, offers a breathtaking view of the San Diego Harbor. On this four-acre deck (equivalent to eight football fields) are 26 restored military jets and helicopters, including a Huey Gunship assault helicopter, some F-4s Phantom II, an A-6 Intruder, an A-7 Corsair, and an E-2C Hawkeye. Again, there are some planes to actually board (tho not fly!). Line up for two tours, as each destination can hold only about twenty people at a time: With access by metal ladder stairs, one tour goes to the top of the carrier, and the other goes moderately high. Up in the tiny Pri-fly office, you'll learn about the air boss's job as told by ex-navy docents. You may even sit at the control panels and visualize how jets are catapulted into flight and "trapped" when coming back, with a wire. The captain's at-sea cabin, the chart room, and the open-air bridge are also in the immediate vicinity.

    One-hour, behind-the-scenes, guided tours are available throughout the day for $32 per person for groups of ten or more. This fee includes entrance to the museum so participants can continue to explore the ship on their own.

Youth have numerous other options available to them such as two-hour educational programs that includes visits to the decks and detailed information about and interactions with the aircraft on display, plus learning labs with an emphasis on science, math, and or social studies for $7 to $10 per student. Experience life as a Navy seaman (or woman) by joining an Overnight Program for $100 per person. This can incorporate the previously-mentioned student programs, plus sleeping in the berths, eating in the mess hall, using the simulators, taking behind-the-scenes tours, and more. Your pilot wanna-be (no matter the age) can also enjoy a birthday party on board the ship.

The two cafes - one open year round and one on the flight deck open in the summer only - serve snacks, salads, sandwiches ($7 to $12), pizza, burgers, hot dogs, kids' meals, and beverages. A gift shop that's really ship shape is also on board the carrier. Approximately 60% of Midway's exhibits are wheelchair accessible. Loaner wheelchairs are available on a first come, first served basis. See MARITIME MUSEUM OF SAN DIEGO (pg. 536) for information on another close-by, waterfront attraction. You can't miss the giant statues closeby, along the waterfront. One is the famous scene of a WWII sailor kissing a nurse. *A National Salute to Bob Hope and the Military* has fifteen life-size, bronze statues, representing servicemen and women from different wars, "listening" and cheering on a likeness of Bob Hope as he holds a microphone to entertain the troops.

Hours: Open daily, 10am - 5pm. (The last ticket is issued at 4pm.) Closed Thanksgiving and Christmas.

Price: $23 for adults; $21 for seniors; $18 college students and ages 13 - 17; $11 for retired military and ages 6 - 12; free for children 5 and under and active military personnel. Tickets are discounted if purchased online. Parking in the lot is $10 - $20 for up to 12 hours. Some metered parking is available along N. Harbor Blvd. See MUSEUM MONTH, SAN DIEGO (pg. 700), in the calendar section, for details about half-price admission in February.

Ages: 5 years and up.

VALLEY CENTER HISTORICAL MUSEUM

!

(760) 749-2993 / www.vchistory.org
29200 Cole Grade Road, Valley Center

This small museum's centerpiece is a 100-year-old stuffed grizzly bear. (Grizzly bears have been extinct in California since 1924.) Other exhibits and pieces of history include a 19th-century reed pump organ, a saddle, typewriters, a school desk, and photos of stars who've passed this way. Check out the fully furnished settler's cabin from 1862 that contains a potbelly stove, clothing, furniture, and old kitchen implements and tools. It seems that the famous cook, Betty Crocker, was really Agnes White, a local resident; some of her cook books are featured here as well. A corner niche displays a Native American habitation site with pestle, acorns, baskets, and reed plants. Note that the five-by-eight-foot building outside, crafted in 1898, is listed in the Guinness World Book of Records as the world's smallest post office. A stagecoach and a few other vintage coaches are also on the grounds.

Friendly docents offer tours to the general public and to school-age children during morning hours, by appointment. The museum is located next to the county library.

Hours: Open Tues. - Sat., noon - 4pm. Closed Sun., Mon., and most holidays.

Price: Free

Ages: 7 years and up.

VETERANS MUSEUM AND MEMORIAL CENTER

$

(619) 239-2300 / www.veteranmuseum.org
2115 Park Boulevard, San Diego

"The nation which forgets its defenders will be itself forgotten." (Calvin Coolidge) The Veterans center is a memorial dedicated to honor all the men and women who served in all branches of the U.S. Armed Services, including the Merchant Marines.

The small museum is located in the former chapel of the Naval Hospital, which was built in the early 1940's and still retains the original stained glass windows. Display cases contain plaques, medals, gas masks, uniforms, and more memorabilia from WWI, WWII, the Korean War, Vietnam War, and Desert Storm. The Navy Seal's exhibit describes the skills and expertise required in underwater demolition. Several mannequins are dressed in military attire. Multitudes of military flags hang from the ceiling, with several versions of the American flag prominently displayed. A display table has a few uniforms and hats for kids to try on, as well as some war time field phones to use. Docents who have served in the military now serve as tour guides, so the information comes from those who have been there, done that. Memorial plaques are on the back lawn of the museum. See BALBOA PARK (pg. 524) for a listing of all the museums and attractions within walking distance, and information and prices on multi-day museum passes.

Hours: Open Tues. - Sun., 10am - 4pm. Closed Mon. and most major holidays.

Price: $5 for adults; $4 for seniors and veterans; $2 for students; free for military and children 11 and under. Admission is free on the second Tues. of every month for San Diego County residents. See MUSEUM MONTH, SAN DIEGO (pg. 700), in the calendar section, for details about half-price admission in February.

Ages: 7 years and up.

VISTA HISTORICAL MUSEUM

(760) 630-0444 / www.vistahistoricalsociety.com

2317 Old Foothill Drive, Vista

The Vista Historical Museum contains one large hall and four smaller halls with a little bit of everything such as old clothing, gloves, hats, a collection of typewriters, rock specimens, arrows, tools, a hair curler machine that looks like it's out of a science fiction story, and more. Take a self-guided tour around the museum or ask for a docent to explain the items. School groups are welcome.

Hours: Open Wed. - Fri., 10am - 2:30pm; the 1st and 2nd Sat., 10am - 2:30pm. Closed most holidays.

Price: Free

Ages: 7 years and up.

WHALEY HOUSE

(619) 297-7511 / www.whaleyhouse.org; www.sdparks.org $$

2476 San Diego Avenue, San Diego

Built in 1847, this two-story brick house/museum is definitely worth touring. It has served in the community as a residence, store, theater, and courthouse, and is filled with numerous early California artifacts. It is also one of two authenticated haunted houses in California. The first room you're ushered into, the courthouse room, is fascinating. As you listen to the ten-minute tape explaining the history of the house and this time period, look around. Behind the railing is an old wooden judge's desk, and chairs for the jury. Along one wall is a bookshelf given to Ulysses S. Grant on his inauguration, and an 1860 lifemask (only one of six in existence) of Abraham Lincoln. Display cases in this room feature documents, spurs, pistols, Spanish helmets and swords, clothing, and ornate hair combs and fans. An early copy machine, a letter press, a handmade U.S. flag from 1864 (how many stars does it have?), plus pictures and portraits of George Washington, Abraham Lincoln, Ulysses S. Grant, and Robert E. Lee are also here.

The kitchen, with all of its gadgets, is downstairs, as is the beautifully decorated parlor and a small music room that contains a spinet piano used in the movie, *Gone With the Wind*. There are several bedrooms upstairs that can be viewed through the protective glass in the doorframes. The bedroom behind the staircase has a decorative wreath, framed on the far wall. It is made from the Whaley girls' hair gathered from hairbrushes and then braided - something to keep the family busy on pre-television nights. The children's bedroom has dolls and toys, while the other bedrooms contain a soldier's dress uniform, mannequins clothed in elegant, ladies' dresses, a lacy quilt covering a canopy bed, and period furniture.

Exit through the backdoor into a small, picturesque, tree-shaded courtyard. A quick peek into the Old Town Drug Store Museum allows kids to see an old-time pharmacy containing bottles, patented medicines, and a mortar and pestle. Push a button to hear more of the building's history.

I highly recommend taking a guided tour so you don't miss out on any of the background information. Note that nighttime admission includes a half-hour guided tours that talks about the history, as well as the mystery - the alleged hauntings. Private tours for a minimum of 2 people are given after hours, starting at 10pm, that include paranormal investigation information - $75 per person for the first hour. See OLD TOWN SAN DIEGO and STATE HISTORIC PARK (pg. 544) for details about other attractions in this immediate area.

Hours: Open day after Labor Day - day before Memorial Day, Sun. - Tues., 10am - 4:30pm; Thurs. - Sat., 10am - 9:30pm (last tour begins at 9:30pm). Closed Wed. Open summer and school breaks daily, 10am - 9:30pm. Closed Thanksgiving and Christmas. Call to check the hours for Christmas week.

Price: Daytime admission is: $8 for adults; $6 for seniors and ages 6 - 12; children 5 and under are free. Evening admission Thurs. - Fri., 6pm - 9:30pm and Sat., 5pm - 9:30pm is $13 for adults; $8 for seniors and ages 6 - 12; children 5 and under not recommended.

Ages: 7 years and up.

—PIERS AND SEAPORTS—

OCEAN BEACH MUNICIPAL PIER

(619) 224-4906 / www.oceanbeachsandiego.com

5099 Niagara Avenue, Ocean Beach

At 1,971 feet into the ocean, the pier is purportedly the longest, T-shaped concrete pier in the world. Drop a fishing line and see what's biting - no license needed. If the fish aren't biting, grab a bite to eat at the Ocean Beach Pier Cafe on the pier, (619) 226-3474, which also has a bait and tackle shop attached to it. Ironically, you can order fish and chips, plus tacos, burgers, and more - and what an ocean view! Just the right ambiance for a cafe on a pier - a little weathered, and views of and over the ocean.

Underneath and just south of the pier, and by the rock jetty, are tidepools - great for exploring during low tide. North of the pier, bordering the sandy beach, is Ocean Beach Park, which is a patch of grass and some palm tress. The beach itself is a long stretch of sand and fairly wide as it kind of goes around a "corner" - popular for swimmers, surfers, and sunbathers.

Ride the Ocean Beach bike path, a separate pathway paralleling the street and part of the 8 freeway. It starts (or ends) at Voltaire Street, where there is a parking lot, and extends to Hotel Circle/Hotel Circle Place.

Hours: The pier is open 24/7.
Price: Free
Ages: All

OCEANSIDE PIER and HARBOR AREA

(760) 435-4030 - harbor; (760) 435-3065 - city of Oceanside / www.ci.oceanside.ca.us; www.oceansidechamber.com

At the end of Pier View Way at The Strand, Oceanside

The Oceanside Pier is one of the longest piers in San Diego County, and the majority of it is made from wood planks. It stretches out over the ocean almost 2,000 feet, or twenty minutes of walking, depending on the age of your youngest child. The spacious RUBY'S (San Diego County) (pg. 475) at the end of the pier is a 40's diner, serving great all-American food at good prices in a very kid-friendly atmosphere. Another pier-related activity is fishing. It doesn't require a license, so reel 'em in! A bait and tackle shop on the pier has pole rentals available. During low tide, look waaay down, over the edge of the pier to see the pylons covered with hundreds of barnacles and sea stars. The other end of the pier (the land end) offers an outdoor amphitheater (used for in-line skating when concerts aren't in session), and a community center.

On the beach is a playground with wooden climbing structures, sand volleyball courts, fire rings, picnic tables, bbqs, and, of course, miles of surf and sand. The beach north of the pier (Pier View North) has more sand than its southern counterpart, so there is more room. Pier View South draws more of a crowd because of the amphitheater and activities here. (Look under "Oceanside" in the city index for adjacent beaches, or just walk south for a little ways.) Wear shoes with tread to carefully walk along the tidepools and go out on the rock jetties.

Breeze on over to the Oceanside Harbor, just a few streets north of the pier. The Harbor offers a choice of boat rentals at OCEANSIDE BOAT RENTALS (pg. 581). A few eateries, including JOE'S CRAB SHACK (San Diego County) (pg. 473) and some shops make up a small "village" here. This area also has HARBOR BEACH - BREAKWATER WAY (pg. 466), offering more fire rings and picnic areas with barbecues, plus covered cabanas and RV camping.

Hours: Most restaurants are open daily, 10am - 6pm. Open extended hours in the summer.
Price: Parking costs about $8 at the beach from 4am - 8pm. There is some metered parking along Pacific St.
Ages: All

SEAPORT VILLAGE

(619) 235-4014 / www.seaportvillage.com

849 W. Harbor Drive at Kettner Boulevard, San Diego

This delightful harbor-side shopping area is in an expansive, beautiful, park-like setting. There are three themed plazas here representing early California, a New England fishing village, and the Victorian era. Along its boardwalk and cobblestone "streets" the Village offers almost fifty unique shops, including Seaport Village Shell Co. and a Magic Shop. There are several wonderful waterfront restaurants to choose from as well as numerous places for snackers to munch. Kids will enjoy riding a menagerie of fifty-four animals on the 100-year-old Looff Carousel located in the West Plaza. The carousel is open daily, 10am to 9pm. Rides cost $3 per person. Check the online calendar to see what special events are going on at Seaport.

Hours: Open daily, 10am - 9pm. Open in the summer and on holidays until 10pm.
Price: Technically, free. Parking is $5 for the first three hours with validation - a minimum of $10 purchase. Non-validated parking is $8 per hour. Or, take a trolley or bus here - look at the Transportation section for details.
Ages: All

—POTPOURRI—

BATES NUT FARM

(760) 749-3333 or (800) 642-0348 / www.batesnutfarm.biz

15954 Woods Valley Road, Valley Center

Is your family a little nutty? Then join nuts from all over the world at Bates Nut Farm. This 100-acre ranch features acres of open green grassy areas with shade trees and picnic tables. It is a welcoming and charming place to stop and relax. Nice-sized pens hold a variety of animals to feed (bring your own or purchase a bag here for 50¢) and pet through the fences - sheep, goats, llamas, an emu, ducks, mini donkeys, chickens, peacocks and geese.

The one-hour, Nuts For You tour, with a minimum of fifteen people, is offered year round, except October when pumpkin tours are in season. The tour includes learning how nuts are grown and harvested and their nutritional value; taking a walk through the roasting and packaging rooms; going through where fudge is made; walking around the facilities; feed for the animals; and taking a tractor-drawn hayride. Bring a picnic lunch to enjoy on the grounds. You are invited to seasonally pick your own pumpkins at the eight-acre pumpkin patch, BATES NUT FARM PUMPKIN PATCH (pg. 735), and weave your way through a maze. In fact, groups of fifteen or more can take the Life of a Pumpkin a tour at that time that includes a walk through the maze, a hayride around the farm, learning all about pumpkins, and taking a pumpkin home. Check the farm's website for their other great calendar events and tours.

The larger store here has rows and rows of nuts (pecans, cashews, walnuts, and more), dried fruits, and candies, plus antiques, baskets, country crafts, and more. The smaller, adjacent Farmer's Daughter gift boutique sells books, dolls, collectibles, jewelry cards, and more country crafts. Remember, you've got *nutin'* to lose by coming here for a visit!

Hours: Open daily, 9am - 5pm.
Price: Admission is free. Nuts For You tours are $6.50 per person.
Ages: All

BUILD-A-BEAR WORKSHOP (San Diego County)

Chula Visa - (619) 482-9622; San Diego - (619) 542-1565 / www.buildabear.com

Chula Vista - 2015 Birch Road at Otay Ranch Town Center; San Diego - 7007 Friars Road in Fashion Valley

See the entry for BUILD-A-BEAR WORKSHOP (Orange County) (pg. 315) for details. The San Diego location is part of a mall that features a DISNEY STORE (San Diego County) (pg. 562) and LEGO STORE - MINI MODEL BUILD (San Diego County) (pg. 485), plus other fun stores.

Hours: Stores are open Mon. - Sat., 10am - 9pm; Sun., 11am - 6pm (7pm at San Diego store).

CHULA VISTA ELITE ATHLETE TRAINING CENTER

(619) 656-1500 or (619) 482-6220 / www.easchulavista.com; www.chulavistaca.gov

2800 Olympic Parkway, Chula Vista

This beautiful facility is nestled in a mountain range by the blue waters of Otay Lakes. The 155-acre campus is the training grounds for future Olympians and Para-Olympians, as well as other athletes - international, college, or youth teams for tournaments or camps - as they prepare for the thrill of victory (hopefully not the agony of defeat). Throughout the day, the visitors' center shows a free ten-minute video that arouses the Olympic spirit in all of us.

You can walk the nine-tenths of a mile (each way) paved path that slices and winds through a center portion of the facility. It is elevated so you get a bird's eye view of the fields and sports that are played on both sides of it, including soccer, field hockey, tennis, track and field, cycling, baseball, beach volleyball, and archery. Water sports, such as rowing, canoeing, and kayaking can also be observed from this vantage point, if there is anyone using the facility. The walk only takes 15 minutes or so.

If you want to know more of what goes on here, the history of the Training Center and about the athletes that train here, take a guided tour. The twenty-minute basic Bronze Tour goes along the paved path - $5 per person. The Silver Tour includes a behind-the-scenes walkthrough of the strength and conditioning center and the dining hall, for $15 per person. The Gold Tour, $35 per person, includes all of the above plus "Eat Like An Athlete" - lunch in the dining hall. Check the website for VIP and other tours, and school tours, as well. The facility also has athlete housing, a medical facility, and more.

Hours: Tours are offered Mon. - Fri., 9am - 3:30pm. The best times to come are between 10am and 11:30am when a majority of the athletes are training (and seeing them makes the center come alive). Tours are also offered June - September, on Sat., 9:30am - 3:30pm (last tour).
Price: Basic admission is free.
Ages: 6 years and up.

DISNEY STORE (San Diego County)

Carlsbad - (760) 517-0073; El Cajon - (619) 441-0536; National City - (619) 470-3391; San Diego - (619) 299-0652 / www.disneystore.com

Carlsbad - 5610 Paseo Del Norte at Carlsbad Premium Outlets; El Cajon - 621 Parkway Plaza at Parkway Plaza; National City - 3030 Plaza Bonita Road at Westfield Plaza Bonita; San Diego - 7007 Friar Road at Fashion Valley Mall

See DISNEY STORE (Orange County) (pg. 316) for details about this interactive, Disney store - it's a whole new world!
Hours: Open Mon. - Sat., 10am -9pm; Sun., 11am - 7pm. Closed Thanksgiving and Christmas.
Price: Free
Ages: 1 - 10 years

FORT CROSS OLD TIMEY ADVENTURES

(951) 847-1904 / www.fortcross.com
4425 Hwy 78, Santa Ysabel

I think part of this name describes this place best, "Old Timey". Like a throw-back to the olden days when kids learned by doing farm and other household chores, visitors today can partake in some of those same activities. Incorporating historical education and outdoor family fun, all in beautiful Julian area, you can do archery; tomahawk throwing; slingshot paintball (at targets in front of a very colorful, small, wooden house structure); candle dipping (takes longer than you'd think!); petting zoo (goats, rabbits, guinea pigs, bearded lizard, chickens, ball python, and more); hayrides; pressing apples for apple cider (in season); musical sessions; gold panning; rope making; fairy/dino garden making; hoedowns; and more.

There are certain times when Fort Cross is open on the weekends for the public and there are more times available for a broad series of tours for school kids of all ages. The two-to-four hour school/group tours usually need a minimum of 25 students and include some of the above listed activities as well as making a craft, or playing old fashioned games, or something else that pertains to that specific tour focus, plus learning about that era or historical figure. The field trip can also come to your location!
Hours: Usually open to the public Sat. - Sun., noon - 4pm. Call or check the website for festivals and other special events.
Price: $5 per most activities; $10 for archery; $10 is the starting price for making a garden. Tour prices start at about $20 per student.
Ages: 3 years and up.

FRY'S ELECTRONICS (San Diego County)

(760) 566-1300 / www.frys.com
150 Bent Avenue, San Marcos

See the entry for FRY'S ELECTRONICS (Los Angeles County) (pg. 170) for details.

GEMS OF PALA

(760) 742-1356 / gemsofpala.com
35940 Magee Rd., Pala

Located on the Pala Indian Reservation, the rustic, small Gems of Pala store offers a flawless selection of rocks and minerals. Both raw and polished emeralds, amethyst, opals, tourmaline, and more are available here. Outside, large bins hold chunks of rocks for sale.

Although the nearby Stewart Mine is no longer open to the public, it is still worked regularly and buckets of mine run, or tailings, are sold at this store. Purchase a bucket of the rocks and dirt, and dump the contents onto a screen on top of the tables outside located on a parcel of dirt. A worker will get you started, telling you what to do and what to look for. To look for "treasure," shake the screens and pour water over the rocks, and start sifting. This can be a bit arduous. Kids will be delighted with almost anything they find, although the jackpot is finding tourmaline. This precious stone comes in a rainbow of colors, with pink being the rarest and most highly prized color. The mine also produces kunzite, morganite, lepidolite, and more, but there are no guarantees as to what you'll find because it's straight from the mines. If, however, you purchase a pre-dug gem bag for $50, you are guaranteed to find some gems, pun intended. Call first to make sure mine run is available and to reserve a bucket, if this is your goal for coming, although reservations aren't necessary. If you don't want to take the time and screen the bags here, take one to go.

Hours: Open Sat. - Sun., 10am - 3pm, with buckets ready at 10:30am and 1:30pm, but arrive 15 min. before that time. Closed holidays that fall on a weekend and sometimes in the winter - call first.

Price: $30 for a bucket of mine run, cash only!

Ages: 3 years and up.

IFLY (San Diego County)

Oceanside - (760) 606-4359; San Diego - (619) 432-4359 / Oceanside - www.iflyworld.com/oceanside; San Diego - www.iflyworld.com/san-diego

$$$$$

Oceanside - 3178 Vista Way; San Diego - 2385 Camino Del Rio North

See IFLY (Los Angeles County) (pg. 172) for more information about this high-flying experience.

Hours: Oceanside - Open Mon. - Thurs., 10am - 10pm; Fri., 10am - 11pm; Sat., 9am - 11pm; Sun., 9am - 10pm. San Diego - Sun. - Thurs., 8am - 9pm; Fri. - Sat., 8am - 10pm.

Price: Double flight, first time flyers is $79.95.

Ages: 4 years and up.

LA JOLLA CAVE and THE CAVE STORE

(858) 459-0746 / www.cavestore.com

$$

1325 Cave Street, La Jolla

This small building houses a few antiques and artwork. The real draw, literally located in the center of the store, is a natural sea cave locally known as Sunny Jim Cave. It's accessible via a 145-step downward "tunnel" dug in 1902. Once down in the small cave, the only things to see are a view of the ocean through the cave openings, and crabs crawling around on the rocks below. The trip down the steps, which get slippery toward the bottom, was the primary adventure. My boys were excited to tell everyone that they had been inside a real sea cave, though, so it was worth it. The store also sells jewelry and some clothing.

Just outside the cave store are steps leading down close to the water's edge, enclosed by a fence. Look for the numerous pelicans on the rocks, the sea lions that frolic in the bay waters below, and the multitude of caves carved out of the cliff side. Facing the ocean and to the right is a quarter mile, or so, dirt trail leading along the hillside overlooking the ocean. Facing the ocean and to the left, just down the street, is the entrance to the sea caves. A fence blocks anyone tempted to go down, but you can see the opening to the caves. Continue walking along the sidewalk just a short distance to SCRIPPS PARK / LA JOLLA COVE and COASTLINE (pg. 516) and further on to reach SEAL ROCK MARINE MAMMAL RESERVE / CHILDREN'S POOL (pg. 594). Look up LA JOLLA SHORES BEACH (pg. 467) and SNORKEL SAN DIEGO (pg. 584) for information on other nearby attractions.

Hours: Open daily, 10am - 5:30pm (last cave "tour" is at 5pm).

Price: Going down to the cave cost $5 for adults; $3 for ages 16 and under. Walking around to the other nearby sites is free.

Ages: 3 years and up.

LEGOLAND CASTLE HOTEL

(888) 690-5346; (877) 534-6526 / www.legoland.com

$$$$$

One Legoland Drive, Carlsbad

There isn't a lot of castles in the United States. And only one made using Legos. And this is it. This three-story, 250 room hotel/castle is definitely fit for a king who appreciates Legos. Outside is a royal statue made of 250,000 Lego bricks. Inside, surrounding by castle archways and other castle architectural elements, a giant Lego wizard greets visitors in the lobby, as do other figures either made out of Legos or portraits of them. The wizard is standing on a pile of Lego books all in a huge tub of Legos that kids can climb in and build something magical. Take a slide ride that connects the lobby to the first floor and your adventure has already begun.

The hallways to the rooms have colorful and castle-themed carpet and wall artworks. Each room - from floor to wall mural, is completely true to its theme, including Lego models throughout and such attention to detail on the bedspreads, decor, bathrooms and more. The kids' bunk-beds are in a somewhat separate, fully-decorated area with a space (and Legos) to build their own Lego whatever. They can also do a scavenger hunt. Choose from three room themes - 1) Knights and Dragons, decorated with boy and girl knights, dragons (including a 3-foot-tall Lego dragon), play swords, treasure and adventure in gold and blue and "stone" castle walls; 2) Magic Wizard, decorated with wizards, Lego owls, Fiberglass potion bottles, crystal balls, moons and stars all in purple and gold; and 3) Royal Princess, decorated with princesses, flowers, outdoor scenes of sunshine, hills, cute animals, archery(!), and fairy tales, all in pinks, purples, greens and gold.

Dine at the Dragon's Den, a 425 seat, full-service restaurant open for all three meals and decorated mainly with red and blue booths and yellow walls, and Legos. Breakfast, which is included in every guest's stay, includes made-to-order items along with a buffet. There is also an open kitchen here for little ones (and big ones) to watch chefs prepare food.

Outside, the royal courtyard awaits honored guests. There is outdoor seating for the restaurant; for watching live shows on the outdoor stage starring fairies, princesses, elves, dragons and of course dragon trainers; and for watching movies on a giant screen. The series of playgrounds here include a Duplo play area for tots; a knights training play area with a rock climbing wall, monkey bars and other themed and innovative equipment, and where you can be knighted at the end of your time; and an outstanding knights /fortress play area.

The pool has some interactive features, like a water umbrella and large foam bricks to float on and build with, plus a zero entry point, plenty of lounge chairs, cabanas to rent, and a hot tub.

There are so many other fun and funny surprises here, like a knock knock door, talking portraits, musical seats, nightly entertainment for kids and more - I don't want to spoil it all. Treat your princess and prince to a royal night (or two) at this unique castle. Check out SEA LIFE AQUARIUM (pg. 593), LEGOLAND WATER PARK (pg. 462), LEGOLAND (pg. 460) and LEGOLAND HOTEL (pg. 564) for more details about these attractions as they share the same property.

Price: Breakfast is included with hotel reservations. Hotel rates for a deluxe room (king bed, bunk beds and pull out trundle) is about $500, plus a $28 per day resort fee.

Ages: 1 year and up.

LEGOLAND HOTEL

(888) 690-5346; (877) 534-6526 / www.legolandhotel.com $$$$$

One Legoland Drive, Carlsbad

Just driving up to the three-story, 250 room hotel and you'll know you have arrived at Lego heaven - even the hotel looks like it was constructed out of Legos. It's not - it's sturdier. Enter the lobby, where your kids could play for hours. Beyond the large Lego dragon that is spewing out Lego bricks and an enclosed play area with more bricks, is a room that beckons. Follow the Lego-brick road up to it with its pirate ship, and the house-size castle with a moat filled with Legos. Cross over the drawbridge, under the Lego ogre (pull the lever), and behind castle walls to a carpeted play area with a wall-size chalkboard where there are more Lego-building areas (surprise!). Climb aboard the pirate ship (that looks like it's made from several gigantic Lego blocks) and steer the wheel on a course for adventure. I love the blue sky and cloud murals on the walls and ceilings, and the hot air balloonist hanging from the ceiling. The adjacent sitting area is Mini's Lounge serving drinks and snacks - cereal, fruit cups, muffins, kids and grown-ups sandwiches, beverages and desserts.

Behind the registration desk in the lobby is a humongous wall of hundreds of Lego figures and an oversized Lego person who moves back and forth along the wall on a bike with wheels that act as magnifying lenses to more clearly (and largely) show all those tiny figures.

Walk past life-sized Lego figures to the buffet-style Bricks Family Restaurant. It features more intricately-made and fanciful characters, and Lego touches and adornments, plus you can interact with Lego heroes as you dine and sing and dance with them every hour during operating hours. The paper tablecloths have designs of Lego shapes and people to color. Crayons are supplied. Food choices include a wide array of breakfast or dinner items - eggs, cereal, yogurt, bacon, potatoes, salad, chicken, Mexican food, pizza, mac and cheese, Chinese food, and more. In primary-colored chairs, outside patio dining is available, too, that is directly in front of the Legoland amusement park entrance. (The Lego dragon in the soap bubble bath out here gently passes gas.) You can also eat at the Skyline Cafe that has an entire glass-enclosed wall containing a 3-D city skyline - impressive. Note: Even the bathrooms downstairs are bedecked in Lego images. Even if you don't stay at the hotel, you are welcome to come and eat at the restaurants, as long as it is not maximized with hotel guests dining, and your kids can play in the lobby rooms. If you are here for dinner, you can even join in on the kid entertainment that usually starts at 6pm in the lobby. Tip: For dinner and play here, you can park in the hotel parking lot - just tell the attendant you are here for a meal.

Each of the three floors of the hotel is themed differently and completely - even the hotel hallways are Lego-themed, from the carpeting to the wall decor to the doorframes! The first floor is shared with Ninjas - Kai, Jay, Cole, and Master Wu to name a few, and dragon's caves; and with Heartlake City Friends, complete with "stables" and a tree house room. The second floor is all about pirates, and the third is Adventure, meaning mostly Egyptian-style digs. Each room of each theme has a separate, fully-decorated kid's area with two bunk beds and a trundle bed. In these just-for-kids "rooms" is a kid's treasure chest safe with toys inside - only to be opened after they complete a treasure hunt; a kid's TV; and their own, embellished bathroom. The attached adult sleeping quarters have a queen sized bed, (a king size in the suites) with their own TV, plus a mini fridge and other amenities. Lego models prevail in each room - at least seven of them. The wall murals and hangings, pillows, bathrooms, shower curtains, and style of furniture immerse guests in one of the four themes (and even more thoroughly in the premium rooms and suites) - it's like living out a childhood fantasy.

Ride the elevator (spoiler alert) because when the doors close, disco lights pulsate against the mirrored ball and music blares while kids break out and boogie (and some younger ones get scared). Each floor is given different sound effects, too. What goes on outside the elevator? Umm - electronic whoopee cushions and other kid-giggle surprises.

Hotel guests enjoy nightly kid's entertainment with character visits, games, and brick building contests, plus early access to Legoland. The lovely outdoor pool offers lots of seating and lounge chairs (and more Lego figures - go figure). Build it and they will come. Build it with Lego bricks and they will come with their kids. Check out SEA LIFE AQUARIUM (pg. 593), LEGOLAND WATER PARK (pg. 462), LEGOLAND (pg. 460) and LEGOLAND CASTLE HOTEL (pg. 563) for more details about these attractions as they share the same property.

Hours: Brick Family Restaurant is open for breakfast, 7am – 10:30am and dinner, 5pm – 9pm. Minis Lounge is open 7am - noon and 2pm - 9pm. Skyline Cafe is open 11am – 10pm.

Price: Breakfast is included with hotel reservations or, for non-guests around $18 for adults; $9 for ages 3 to 12. Dinner is around $25 for adults and $13 for ages 3 to 12. If you are staying at the hotel you can pre-purchase a dinner package for four people, at time of booking, for about $65. Children 2 and under eat free. Hotel rates start at about $400, but average more in the $500+ range, plus a $28 per day resort fee.

Ages: 1 year and up.

MOUNT SOLEDAD VETERANS MEMORIAL   ☀

(877) 204-7661 or (858) 459-2314 / www.soledadmemorial.com   !
6905 La Jolla Scenic Drive South/Soledad Road, La Jolla

The twofold goal of this jaunt off the main road is to visit a Veteran's memorial and to get a fantastic, 360-degree view of San Diego county, encompassing the mountains to the ocean (on a clear day). Names and photos are engraved on black granite plaques that honor veterans from all wars. These plaques decorate the walls surrounding steps that lead up to a huge cross at the pinnacle of the mountaintop. We read many of the plaques and then enjoyed the magnificent view. There is a small grass area up here, a few benches, and some walkways that descend into the surrounding chaparral. At annual military-oriented events, bands and political and military speakers are part of the program.

Hours: Open daily, 7am - 10pm.
Price: Free
Ages: 8 years and up

OBSERVER'S INN   ☀

(760) 765-0088 / www.observersinn.com $$$$
3535 Highway 79, Julian

Star light, star bright, first star I see tonight; I wish I may, I wish I might, have this wish I wish tonight. Fulfill a wish by visiting this unique Inn located in the mountains of Julian. Observant guests will see and appreciate the *star* attraction - the night sky displaying all its heavenly beauty. Us city folk rarely get the full picture of the vast array of celestial bodies, but in the mountains the people-manufactured lights fade away and God's lights take over in a dazzling display. A nineteen-foot by twenty-four-foot observatory with a retractable roof, houses several research grade telescopes, although visitors are invited to bring their own, as well. Take a one-hour "sky tour," as the Inn's owner (who used to work for NASA) acts as a guide around the visible universe, using a laser pointer to outline constellations and telescopes to focus on a star cluster, ring nebula or other heavenly bodies. The homey observatory is carpeted, has heat, a sound system, and couches, and is decorated with lots of astronomical photos. Beverages and cookies are offered, too.

This is an Inn, also, which means you may spend the night here. A detached guesthouse has two nice, private, star-themed rooms (although the rooms can be adjoining) with queen-size beds and full baths decorated with celestial photographs. A living room-like lobby with TV, library, and CDs are also here. Single night booking is allowed

Monday through Wednesday; at other times guests must stay for a two-night minimum, unless the weekend isn't booked by the Thursday prior. If you spend the night you are welcome to spend hours on the concrete observing pads just outside the observatory using your own telescope. Bring your camera to attach to a telescope for great moon pictures. Dress warmly, even during summer months, as nighttime temperatures can drop rapidly. Other activities include hiking on nearby trails, picnicking, resting in a hammock under shady oak trees (although technically, this isn't an activity), and seasonally sledding down hills. (B.Y.O.S. - Bring Your Own Sled.) An on-site gift shop is an authorized Meade dealership.

Hours: Call for hours.

Price: $30 per person for just the sky tour - advanced reservations are required. Guests of the Observer's Inn pay $20 per person for the sky tour. Overnight rates start at $160 for single or double occupancy, which includes a Continental breakfast each morning of your stay. (No credit cards.)

Ages: 7 years and up.

OLD POWAY PARK

(858) 668-4576 - park; (858) 486-4063 - Poway-Midland R.R.; (858) 486-4575 - Hamburger Factory /
www.poway.org; www.powaymidlandrr.org; www.hamburgerfactory.com
14134 Midland Road, Poway

This charming park is set up like a small historic western village, complete with its own train depot. The two-acre grassy park boasts of shade trees, a gazebo, picnic tables, barbecues, crisscrossing pathways, and bridges over the creek. Come during the week to simply enjoy the park. Come on a weekend, however, for some action, because that's when the "town" is open and everything comes to life! Regular weekend activities include a farmer's market with 65 vendors on Saturday mornings from 8am to 1pm; tours through the museum and house; and train rides. There are also arts and crafts booths from 8am to 2pm on the first Saturday of the month from February through May, then most Saturdays the rest of the year. The small Heritage Museum has glass-encased displays containing items from olden times in Poway such as pictures, clothing, a guitar, glassware, and a piano. The small Nelson House contains a turn-of-the-century, fully furnished kitchen, living room, music room, and bedrooms. The blacksmith's shop puts on demonstrations of its craft, occasionally. Last, but not least, take a short ride around town on a vintage, genuine steam engine train, trolley, or speeder car on a full-size, narrow-gauge railroad. Check the website calendar for a schedule of which trains are operating on which weekends. Take a look into the train barn which houses the steam engine, a 1938 Fairmont Speeder, ore cars, and a 1894 Los Angeles Yellow Trolley. Don't forget to check out the many special events that go on here throughout the year, like summer concerts in the park and the RENDEZVOUS IN POWAY (pg. 734). Two-hour guided tours to learn the heritage of the park for organized groups of twenty or more are offered for $4 per person, March - June, Tuesday - Thursday, between 10am - 3pm.

Bring a picnic lunch, or enjoy good old American food at the on-site Hamburger Factory. The Factory has wood-paneled walls that are decorated with buffalo heads, steer skulls, and more, giving it a rustic ambiance. The restaurant is open daily for breakfast, lunch, and dinner, with a full selection for every meal. Burgers average $11, and there are turkey and buffalo burgers available, too. Other options includes breakfast burrito ($10.99); blueberry pancakes ($5.99); two-egg combo ($9.39); sandwiches (tri tip melt - $12.29, chicken mushroom - $10.29); salads (Chef's - $10.49); shrimp ($10.40); baby back ribs ($19.99 for a half rack); salmon $17.49; and lots more. Kids' meal choices include hamburger, chicken nuggets, a hot dog, or a grilled cheese sandwich. Meals come with fries and a drink for an average of $5.79.

Hours: The park is open daily. Rail cars operate on weekends Sat., 10am - 3:45pm; Sun., 11am - 1:45pm - no railcars operate on the second Sunday. The museum and Nelson house are open Sat., 10am - 2pm; Sun., 11am - 2pm. All of the proceeding attractions are closed on Easter and the last few weeks in December. The restaurant is open daily, 7am - 9pm.

Price: The park is free. The following pricing for train rides is for adults (as children 12 and under are $1) - $3.50 each for the locomotive and cable car; $2.50 each for the trolley and speeder. Donations are requested for the museum and Nelson House.

Ages: All

SALVATION MOUNTAIN

(760) 624-8754 / www.salvationmountaininc.org
601 East Beal Road, Niland (It's actually in Imperial County, east of San Diego County.)

You might not find salvation on this mountain, though the words "God is LOVE" is predominant, but you will find a divinely interesting place to explore. An incredibly eclectic and colorful collage of mostly Bible sayings and pictures painted and built on the mountainside by incorporating adobe clay, straw, found materials, and half a million gallons of latex paint, grabs visitors visually and then fills their minds and hearts with a little bit of wonder. You'll see lots of flowers; a painted waterfall going down the mountainside; trees supporting some domed roofs; pictures of some recognizable things; the Lord's Prayer; the nine fruits of the spirit (from the New Testament book of Galatians); and lots and lots of color.

Follow the yellow brick road (i.e. yellow steps) up and around the mountain, which is about 100 feet high and 150 feet across, to the top where a cross reigns. The view from there is terrific. Walk underneath the mountain, too, which has a few tunnels and cave-like rooms - all wildly decorated. Call it folk art; call it whimsical; the creator (as well as the Creator) of this Mountain desired to spread the message of God's unconditional love to the world, and this mountain has been his canvas.

If you continue northeast on Beal Rd. for a few minutes and turn left at the end and onto where there is literally a huge fork in the road, you'll discover that art is not just in the eye of the beholder - it is also in the "town" of East Jesus. Definitely an add on visit, not a destination, the eclectic artists that live out here express themselves in various mediums such as cars completely covered in stuff (i.e. hubcaps, signs, random junk); a statue made of recycled tires; bottle trees; and so much many more interesting pieces. Entrance is free! Note: Other attractions back on the main road, several miles away are the SALTON SEA STATE RECREATION AREA (pg. 512) and INTERNATIONAL BANANA MUSEUM (pg. 533).

Hours: Open daily, sunrise - sunset.
Price: Free
Ages: 3 years and up.

SUMMERS PAST FARMS

(619) 390-1523 / www.summerspastfarms.com
15602 Olde Highway 80, Flinn Springs

Experience a genteel way of life (yes, even with kids) at Summers Past Farms. Although the Farm is not large, it's beautifully landscaped gardens, blooming with a variety of flowers and herbs, almost ensure a delightful (and fragrant) *thyme* here. The plants are both for show and sale. One of the small gardens has a little creek with a bridge over it. There is a grassy area with trees, trellises, and white wrought-iron benches. The lavender field has a Provence-style facade. No farm is complete without its resident animals, such as cats, dogs, a few birds, and rabbits.

One of the retail shops, housed in a big red barn, offers potpourri, wreaths, baskets, teas, essential oils, lotions, dried and fresh flowers, and more. Craft classes are available. The other shop is Ye Old Soap Shoppe offering a wide variety of *scent*sational herbal soaps. Pick up a free sample (I chose Lavender/French Vanilla), and maybe you'll even get to see (and smell) the owner mixing essences for his soaps. You may purchase soap-making supplies, or a complete soap-making kit that includes <u>everything</u> you need to make eight pounds of herbal soap for about $74.

Enjoy coffee, ice tea, and pastries on weekends here. Be sure to check out the Farms website for calendar events like a pumpkin patch and fairy festival.

Hours: Open January - September, Thurs. - Sat., 9am - 5pm; Sun., 10am - 5pm. Closed Mon. - Wed. Open October - December on Wed., too, 9am - 5pm.
Price: Free
Ages: 5 years and up.

TIJUANA, MEXICO

(888) 775-2417 - Tijuana Tourism Board; (800) 44MEXICO (446-3942) / www.tijuana.com; www.tijuana.com $$$

Hola! Come spend the day in a foreign country without the European price tag (or luxuries, majestic sights, etc.). YOU MUST HAVE A PASSPORT - not to enter the country; only if you want to get out! There are several ways you can arrive at and enter into Mexico: 1) Drive into Mexico; 2) Take a tram from downtown San Diego to the border, and then take a taxi or walk across; or 3) Drive your own car almost to the border, park on the U.S. side, and then walk or take a shuttle across. Following are more details about the above options: **Option 1** - If you drive into Mexico you must buy Mexican automobile insurance because American insurance doesn't mean anything over there. The border town of San Ysidro has several places to purchase Mexican insurance. The cost depends on the coverage you are buying and the value of your car but about $30 for the day. A few other things to take into account if you drive into Mexico: You will experience lines getting into and especially getting out of Mexico in the afternoon as it's rush hour traffic (actually this occurs no matter what mode of transportation you use); parking can be a problem (I mean challenge); and if you think that Los Angeles drivers are scary - you ain't seen nothing yet! For those who like to live life on the edge - drive into Tijuana. **Option 2** - Take the blue line trolley/bus to Mexico from Santa Fe's station in downtown San Diego, which costs $2.50 one-way for ages 6 and older; $1.50 for seniors. Trolleys run every few minutes, from 5am to 1am. Check the website for all the stations, from American Plaza and downtown at the northern end to San Ysidro. Check (619) 595-4949/(619) 557-4555; www.sdmts.com for locations, maps, and information. There are several stations that offer free parking, like Bayfront and E St. - check the website. The trolley takes you to the border where you can walk across the bridge or take a taxi into Mexico. It's about a mile from the border to the main shopping area in Tijuana. Even if you walk into Tijuana, you might consider taking a cab or shuttle out because you'll be carrying shopping bags, and your children will be tired (and so will you!). Taxis are plentiful, but determine exactly where you are going first, and decide on a price before you get into the cab. The fare is usually $8 to Avenida Revolucion. **Option 3** - This was our personal choice, and it was fairly hassle-free. We parked on this side of the border at Border Station Parking - signs off the freeway direct you to the huge parking lots at 4570 Camino de La Plaza in San Ysidro. The cost is $7 during the week; $20 on weekends for all-day parking, and attendants are on duty twenty-four hours. (Note: Just behind Border Parking are factory outlet stores. More shopping!) Call (619) 428-9477 / www.borderparking.com for more info. Then, we took a Tourismo Express shuttle, located at 3060 E Beyer Boulevard in San Ysidro, ($10 per person, round trip), which runs every half hour or so from 8am to 9pm, from the parking lot into the heart of the oldest Tijuana shopping district - Avenida Revolucion, which is seven blocks of tourist-shopping heaven. You may buy up to $400 of duty free goods in Tijuana. You then can take the bus back, walk over the border to show your passport, and board the bus again to the parking lot. Call (619) 428-0011 for more information.

Shopping along Avenida Revolucion is an experience. The numerous small shops, most of which are open daily, 10am to 9pm, have goods almost overflowing onto the sidewalks that practically scream at your children to buy them. Vendors are constantly hawking their wares, enticing you, begging you, to come into their store. Be tough. Tips to keep in mind when shopping: 1) Don't feel obligated to buy just because you asked the price. 2) I can almost guarantee that you will see that exact same item at least ten more times. 3) Never pay the original asking price. Bargaining is expected. As a rule of thumb, pay around half (or a little more) of the asking price. Be willing to go higher if it's something you really want or can't live without. (Decide beforehand how much the item is worth to you.) Haggle if you want it, but be prepared to walk away in order to get a better price, or if it isn't the price you want. 4) Prepare your children beforehand that they won't always get the item being bargained for, if the price is still too high, etc. 5) Lastly, and most importantly, teach your children to not say, "I love it - I must have it!" in front of the merchants.

Merchandise that appeals most to kids includes leather vests, hats, boots, purses, gold and silver jewelry, kids' guitars, gaudy ceramic figurines, watches, blankets, ponchos, and knickknacks. The more mature shopper will enjoy leather goods and jewelry, too, as well as perfumes, pharmaceutical supplies, clothing, and more. On every street corner you'll find the touristy-looking carts hooked up to donkeys (painted to look like zebras) along with gaudy sombreros available for you to wear while having your picture taken - $5 for a Polaroid, $1 with your own camera. (Our pictures turned out nice!)

There are other places to shop in Tijuana besides Avenida Revolucion. Try Avenida Constitucion, which is the next street over, and Plaza Rio Tijuana Shopping Center - near the Cultural Center - which has a few major department stores and specialty shops. The latter is a long walk, or a short drive, from Avenida Revolucion. Mercado Hidalgo is only five minutes from the border and often overlooked. It is a true Mexican marketplace where locals shop for produce and specialty items, such as spices and cookware.

We walked around downtown Tijuana, just beyond the shopping district. Tijuana has been cleaned up and renovated in certain areas, but we also saw a lot of poverty, broken sidewalks, and people setting up shop in much less healthy environments than would be allowed in the States. It was an eye-opener for my kids. And, since they couldn't read any of the signs, it gave them an understanding of how difficult it is for foreigners in America to get around. Tip: Bring your own water, still.

There are several nearby attractions in Tijuana. Note: The 01152-664 number designates making an international phone call and the area code; the other digits are the actual phone number. **Bullfights** at Plaza Monumental de Playas, near the border, and on Agua Caliente Blvd. at the Tijuana Bullring: Fourteen fights are held May through September on Sunday afternoons. Tickets range from $16 to $50. Call (01152-664) 680-1808, (01152-664) 686-1510 for more info. **Centro Cultural Tijuana** at Paseo de los Heroes y Mina: The Museum of the Californias is good, although the art gallery wasn't that exciting to my kids. The Centro also has a planetarium/Omnimax theater. (The shows, of course, are in Spanish.) Contact (01152-664) 687-9600 / www.cecut.gob.mx for more info. **Hipodromo Caliente** at Blvd. Agua Caliente y Tapachula: Greyhound races takes place here. There is a small zoo on the grounds, too. Check (01152-664) 682-3110 / bet.caliente.com.mx for more info. **Mexitlan** at Calle 2 and Avenida Ocampo: This city-block-long attraction houses about 200 scale models of Mexico's most important monuments, buildings, churches, plazas, archaeological sites, and more. This is a great way to get an overview of the country. Call (01152-664) 638-4101 for more info. **Mundo Divertido** (Family Entertainment Center) at 2578 Paseo de los Heroes y Jose Ma: This Family

Fun Center offers the same fun, and at comparable prices, as the Boomers! fun centers in the States - miniature golf, batting cages, bumper boats, go karts, video and arcade games, and amusement rides such as a roller coaster and a kiddie train. Call (01152-664) 634-3213 for more info. Another **Mundo Divertido** is located at Mundo Divertido Plaza in La Mesa. This facility offers bowling, too. **Rodeos** at Lienzo Charro and Avenida Bravlio Maldonado: Call (01152-664) 680-4185 for dates, times, and prices. **Parque Estatal Morelos** at Blvd. Insurgentes 16000: This state park and ecological reserve has large open spaces, grassy lawns for picnicking, and a Creative Center for children that offers a lake, an open-air theater, botanical gardens, children's rides, and games. Call (01152-664) 625-2469 for more info. **Wax Museum of Tijuana** at First Street 8281 near Avenida Revolucion: This museum is home to over eighty waxy, lifelike historical figures and movie stars such as Mikhail Gorbachev, Emiliano Zapata, Elvis Presley, Marilyn Monroe, and Christopher Columbus. It's open daily from 10am - 6pm. Admission is about $2; children 5 years and under are free. Call (01152-664) 688-2478 for more information.

Hours: Most shops are open daily, 10am - 9pm.

Ages: 5 years and up.

WALTER ANDERSON NURSERY

(858) 513-4900 / www.walterandersen.com

12755 Danielson Court, Poway

Nurseries aren't a normal entry for a children's guidebook, but if you are in the Poway vicinity and your child is a train buff, this is a great little stop off. Walk through the building and then through the abundance of plants (I wish my yard, or any portion of my yard, looked like this) to reach the massive train layout with 1,400 feet of track. Watch the train make tracks around and through an almost magical area of waterfalls, bridges (fifteen of them), a trestle (118 feet), tunnels, a variety of plants, a lake with real pond plants, rocks, and a "populated" city. Delightful!

Hours: The nursery is open Mon. - Fri., 9am - 5pm; Sat. - Sun., 9am - 5pm. The train runs daily, usually 10am - 4pm. Closed New Year's Day, Easter, 4th of July, Thanksgiving, and Christmas.

Price: Free

Ages: All

—SHOWS AND THEATERS—

BALBOA THEATRE

(619) 570-1100 - box office; (619) 615-4000 - administration / www.sandiegotheatres.org $$$$$

868 Fourth Avenue at E Street, in the Gaslamp District, San Diego

Originally built in 1924, this renovated and incredibly beautiful and ornate, 1,335-seat theater gives kids (and adults) the opportunity to experience real theater in a formal setting. Come see a top-notch show, concert, comedian, play, or other performance.

Hours: Call, or go online, for a show schedule.

Price: Tickets start at $25. Price depends on the performance, time, and date. Parking in the Gaslamp district (which can be reserved in advance online) can be a little interesting, so allow yourself time before the start of the performance to find a spot.

Ages: 6 years and up, depending on the show.

CALIFORNIA BALLET COMPANY

(858) 560-6741 or (858) 560-5676 / www.californiaballet.org $$$$

This professional ballet company tours throughout San Diego giving performances at the San Diego Civic Center and other places, plus in-school performances and out-reach performances. They perform three to four, ninety-minute ballets a year. Past family-oriented shows, usually put on in the spring, have included *Alice in Wonderland* and *Snow White*. The associated junior ballet company, with performers between the ages of 12 and 17 years, put on a yearly show. The company also offers dance classes of ballet and jazz for children 3 years and up.

Hours: Call for a schedule.

Price: Prices depend on the theater venue.

Ages: 6 years and up.

CALIFORNIA CENTER FOR THE ARTS, ESCONDIDO AND FAMILY PERFORMANCES

(800) 98-TICKETS (988-4253) or (760) 839-4138; (760) 839-4140 - tours; (760) 839-4174 - museum / www.artcenter.org

340 N. Escondido Boulevard, Escondido

All the world's a stage and kids are invited to come watch the world, or at least a part of it. Broadway musicals, comedies, dramas, dance troupes, classical concerts, operas, and other of the finest, top-name entertainment around is performed at the center. Many productions are perfect for the entire family. Some of those past productions have included *The Sound of Music, Joseph and the Amazing Technicolor Dreamcoat*, a barbershop quartet, *Late Nite Catechism, The Magic Schoolbus, Lazer Vaudeville*, and *The Hobbit* (which was performed with large puppets). Special matinee student performances are offered throughout the year, too. Children's performances can also include art projects, meeting the artists, and museum admission. And check out First Wednesdays when performances are free for the public. They are given September through June on the first Wednesdays (of course!) at 4pm and 7pm, but get here earlier because show seating can fill up fast. Reserved seats for these performances are $12.

The small museum at the center focuses on contemporary and twentieth-century art. Hour-long, docent-guided tours of the museum are offered for kindergartners to adults. Through the education program, tours are followed by another hour, or so, of making exhibit-related projects. The projects are geared for a maximum of thirty-five kids, for $4 per student. Take advantage of this terrific way to *really* learn about art - what kids participate in, they will remember better. The second Saturdays are pay what you can with free art lessons at 10am and 11am (with advanced reservations).

Hours: Check the website for a performance schedule. Family Performances are usually on the weekends. The museum is open Thurs. - Sat., 10am - 5pm; Sun., 1pm - 5pm; closed Mon. and major holidays. Museum tours are offered by reservation. See the company's website for classes and special events.

Price: Prices vary depending on the show. Family-oriented performances can start as low as $12 per person. The museum is $8 for adults; $5 for seniors and students with ID; children 12 and under are free. The museum is free on the first Wed. of every month and often free to ticket holders on the day of performance. See MUSEUM MONTH, SAN DIEGO (pg. 700), in the calendar section, for details about half-price admission in February.

Ages: 5 years and up.

CLASSICS FOR KIDS

(619) 231-2311 / www.classics4kids.com

all around San Diego County, with a primary venue of Balboa Theater.

Committed to introducing elementary-school aged kids to, and getting them involved with, a life-long love for theater arts, Classics for Kids produces professional musical performances at various venues throughout San Diego. *The Magic Flute*, for instance, incorporated the symphony music of the Philharmonics and City Ballet of San Diego dancers. Concerts for families and for schools, even school assemblies with curriculum supplements, are scheduled throughout the year.

Hours: Check the website for the schedule.

Price: Family show tickets are usually $15 for adults; $12 for ages 2 - 17. School show tickets are $7 per person for groups of ten or more.

Ages: 6 - 12 years

IMAX DOME THEATER

(619) 238-1233 / www.rhfleet.org

1875 El Prado, Balboa Park, San Diego

See the entry for REUBEN H. FLEET SCIENCE CENTER (pg. 547) for details as the museum houses the IMAX Theater.

LAMB'S PLAYERS THEATRE

(619) 437-6000 / www.lambsplayers.org

1142 Orange Ave, Coronado

This theatre troupe offers five great, usually musical, productions a year and most of them are very kid-friendly. Past shows include *Joseph and the Amazing Technicolor Dreamcoat, You're a Good Man, Charlie Brown, Noises Off, Dracula*, and *American Rhythm*, a journey across America through music. Inquire about immersion programs the theater offers for school groups and about summer camps for children aspiring to the stage and screen. Note that there is an on-site cafe open two hours before performances, serving quiche, sandwiches, soups, salads, and more.

Hours: Check the website for show dates and times, though usually there is a show every day/night, except Monday.

Price: Tickets usually range from $24 - $82 for adults, depending on the date and time; $5 off for seniors and ages 5 - 17. Tickets are half-price for active military. Children 4 and under are not admitted. Rush tickets are sometimes available.

Ages: 5 years and up.

MARIE HITCHCOCK PUPPET THEATER

(619) 544-9203 / www.balboaparkpuppets.com

2130 Pan American Place, Balboa Park, San Diego

$$

This 200+ seat, intimate theater, located behind the San Diego Automotive Museum, presents kid-approved, half-hour, puppet shows. The type of puppets vary from show to show, and can include hand puppets, marionettes, dummies (for ventriloquists), life-size puppets, and puppets made from anything and everything found around the house. The shows themselves are similar in that they never fail to capture a child's imagination. From *Cinderella* to *The Ugly Duckling* to *The Frog Prince* and *Peter Rabbit*, stories are told as only puppets can tell them (with a little bit of human help)! Shows change weekly so watch out - bringing the kids here can become habit forming. Note that the theater also hosts birthday parties, and sometimes puppet-making workshops for ages 3 and up - $7 for each child with a minimum of $49 total. See BALBOA PARK (pg. 524) for a listing of all the museums and attractions within walking distance.

Hours: Labor Day - Memorial Day performances are Wed. - Fri., at 10am and 11:30am; Sat. - Sun., 11am, 1pm, and 2:30pm. Memorial Day - Labor Day performances are Wed. - Sun., 11am, 1pm and 2:30pm.

Price: $5 general admission; $4 for seniors; children under 2 are free.

Ages: 1½ - 10 years.

NATIONAL COMEDY THEATRE

(619) 295-4999 or (818) 953-4933 / www.nationalcomedy.com

3717 India Street, San Diego

$$$$

Your belly will be bustin' from laughing so hard at this troupe who perform fast-paced, quick-witted, improvisational comedy. Two teams, usually composed of three comedians each, compete in a series of scenes (i.e., games) which can involve singing, mime, and always fast repartee. The general guidelines of each game is explained then the audience suggests situations, activities, names and more. The audience also judges and picks the winning team. The referee keeps everything in check, including the suggestions and actions. A stand-out feature of the ninety-minute long shows is that material is clean, so they are appropriate for kids (and adults). So, enjoy a hilarious outing with the family. Alternative shows include MashUp, a mish mash and variety of the normal performances and Cage Match where two competing teams (of current and former students from the workshops) present a half-hour show, with audience voting on the winner. The troupe also offers improv comedy training, high school improv leagues, and summer camps, plus a connection program for autistic teens.

Hours: Thurs. at 7:30pm; Fri. and Sat. at 7:30pm and 9:45pm; Sun. at 7:30pm, and the College Team at 9pm.

Price: College Team performances are $12 per person; Thurs. and Sun. (7:30pm show), $14 per person; other shows are Fri. and Sat., $18 for adults; $14 for seniors and students.

Ages: 7 years and up.

OLD GLOBE THEATRE

(619) 23GLOBE (234-5623) or (619) 239-2255 / www.oldglobe.org

1363 Old Globe Way, Balboa Park, San Diego

$$$$$

Originally modeled after Shakespeare's Globe Theatre in London, this 580-seat classic theater is accompanied by two other theaters; the Conrad Prebys Theatre Center and the 612-seat, outdoor Lowell Davies Festival Theatre. Combined, the theater complex puts on about fifteen productions and 600 performances, usually plays, a year. Of course, Shakespeare's plays are a draw, especially during the Shakespeare Festival in summer. Many of the other productions appeal mostly to adults, but the Globe's holiday musical program, *How the Grinch Stole Christmas*, is definitely family fare. It runs November through December.

Call regarding programs, such as Shakespeare Intensive for students, acting workshops, tours, and educational opportunities, as well as free student matinees. See OLD GLOBE THEATRE (tour) (pg. 576) for details about the tour.

Hours: Call for a schedule.

Price: Prices vary depending on show, date, and time.

Ages: Depends on the show.

PALOMAR COLLEGE PLANETARIUM

(760) 744-1150 / www.palomar.edu/planetarium

$$

1140 West Mission Road at Palomar Community College, San Marcos

This planetarium seats 138 people under a fifty-foot dome for an immersive experience under the nighttime sky. The first show, *The Sky Tonight*, is a live, narrated show highlighting heavenly objects visible from San Diego. The moon, planets, and several constellations and their mythology are discussed. The second feature presentation varies with some being more of a movie and others perhaps more documentary-style. Telescopes are out on the patio for viewing stars in real life after every show. Purchasing tickets in advance is recommended.

Ninety-minute field trips are offered for schools, 3rd graders and up, year round on Tuesdays and Thursdays, from 10am to 11:30am. A presentation is followed by a time for Q and A. Afterwards, enjoy lunch on campus in a parkish setting - a taste of college at a young age!

Hours: Doors open every Fri. night at 6:30pm. The first show is 7pm - 8pm; the second show is 8:15pm - 9pm. There is no late seating.

Price: Each presentation on Fri. is $6 for adults; $4 for seniors, students and military with ID, and ages 5 - 12. School groups are $120 for groups with less than 30 people; $4 per person for groups of 30 or more. Park in lot 5 for free parking; otherwise it's $5.

Ages: 5 years and up only.

POWAY CENTER FOR THE PERFORMING ARTS

(858) 668-4693 or 858-668-4798 - info; (858) 748-0505 - box office / www.powayarts.org; www.powaycenter.com

$$$$

15498 Espola Road, Poway

This 800-seat capacity theater offers a variety of family entertainment throughout the year, as well as a few outstanding children's programs. Past productions have included Jim Gamble puppets; a troop that performed juggling, acrobatics, and comedy combined with a laser light show; the Boys Choir of Harlem; *The King and I*; and *Cinderella*. Other performances include Broadway musicals, big band productions, comedy routines, and more.

Hours: Call for performance times.

Price: Ticket prices vary depending on show, date, and time.

Ages: 4 years and up.

SAN DIEGO CIVIC THEATRE

(619) 570-1100 - box office; (619) 615-4000 - administration / www.sandiegotheatres.org

$$$$$

1100 3rd Avenue at B Street, San Diego

The elegant, almost 3,000-seat theater gives kids (and adults) the opportunity to experience real theater in a formal setting. One of the central companies that consider the Civic Theatre home is Broadway San Diego. Broadway-billed shows and top-name stars perform with this West Coast Broadway company. Past shows include *Phantom of the Opera*, *Stomp*, *Beauty and the Beast*, *Doctor Doolittle*, *Paw Patrol Live*, *School of Rock* and *Wicked*. Indulge in a show - it is a memorable treat.

Other companies at the Civic, who deserve as much recognition and write-up, include the California Ballet and La Jolla Music Society.

Hours: Call or go online for a show schedule.

Price: Tickets start at $22.50. Price depends on the performance, time, and date. Parking at the Concourse Mon. - Fri., is $12 for 2 hours. After 5:30pm daily and all day Sat. it's $10.

Ages: 6 years and up, depending on the show.

SAN DIEGO MUSICAL THEATRE

(877) 778-1258 / www.sdmt.org

$$$$$

444 Fourth Avenue at the Horton Grand Theatre, San Diego

I appreciate their slogan - "Your local way to see Broadway." So, come see and enjoy shows like *South Pacific*, *Young Frankenstein*, *Hairspray*, *Bring It On*, *Annie Get Your Gun*, *White Christmas* and much more. Note that shows are currently at the Horton Grand Theatre; the location could change.

Hours: Check the website for performance dates and times.

Price: Usually $30 - $70, depending on the show and date.

Ages: 8 years and up, depending on the show.

SAN DIEGO SYMPHONY / JACOBS MUSIC CENTER / COPLEY SYMPHONY HALL

(619) 235-0804 - concert box office; (619) 615-3955 - tour / www.sandiegosymphony.org $$$$
750 B Street, San Diego

Jacobs Music Center is home to the San Diego Symphony and the performance hall known as Copley Symphony Hall. Performing at the beautiful, classic, and historic 2,231-seat theater and at the outdoors amphitheater during the summer for the Bayside Summer Nights, the renown symphony plays over 100 concerts a season. Offering a huge range of musical experiences and opportunities, there is a production that will intrigue almost any age. One-hour family performances on select Sunday afternoons are a terrific way to introduce your children to classical music. Free, preconcert activities can include "What's the Score" conversations, face painting and a musical "petting zoo," which is touching or even playing an instrument to get familiar with it. The center is host to other venues of entertainment such as comedy shows, film screenings, and other type of concerts.

School groups, geared for second graders through 8th, are especially welcome at matinee performances (given at 10am and 11:30am) of Young People's Concerts, when tickets are usually $5 per. Reservations are required. Open rehearsals are on select mornings that include over an hour of rehearsal combined with a Q & A time with the musicians, and even a tour for ages 12 and up. Make reservations. Free, one-hour tours are offered once-a-month on Wednesdays starting at noon, the end of October through May, when visitors see and learn about the magnificent building. Check the website for a complete listing of the offerings here.

Hours: Call or go online for concert times.

Price: Prices begin at $25 for ages 13 and up; $10 for ages 3 - 12 (lap-sitting kids 2 and under are free) for family performances, and go up according to performance and date. Check online for Family Pack discounted tickets. Discounts are also available for students and seniors for all performances. The closest lot is the Symphony Tower Garage - $20 for 9 hours; or walk from B Street where parking is $8.

Ages: 5 years and up, depending on the show; 8 years and up for the tour.

ULTRASTAR CINEMAS MISSION VALLEY - HAZARD CENTER

(619) 685-2841 / www.ultrastarmovies.com $$$
7510 Hazard Center Drive, San Diego

This theater shows films in regular format, 3-D and DBox (where seats move and vibrate, synchronizing with the on-screen action). The cafe inside the theater has a coffee bar and serves sandwiches and specialty popcorn, as well as some other slightly upscale options.

This theater also caters to parents when it's not a crying shame to bring a baby to the movies. Parent Movie Morning, with changing facilities in the auditorium and movies that adults want to see, are Wednesdays at 10am. Baby's Night Out is on select nights at 7pm. And more for kids (and parents): Check out the Kids Summer Series when a different, kid-appropriate film is shown every week during the summer, Monday - Thursday, at 9:30 am. Summer movies are $1 each, or $5 for a 10-pack deal.

Hours: Check the website for show times and ticket info.

Price: Prices range from $7 for early bird matinees; $9 all day Tues.; up to $19 for DBox. Check online for deals and other specials.

Ages: Infants and up, depending on the movie!

WELK RESORT THEATRE

(855) 455-9355 or (760) 749-3000 / www.welkresorts.com/san-diego/theatre/ $$$$$
8860 Lawrence Welk Drive, Escondido

This "wannaful" (i.e., that's the way Lawrence Welk used to say "wonderful") theater offers several different, full-production Broadway musicals a year, as well as concerts, magical acts and other specialty performances. Audiences in the intimate 330-seat theater have seen the likes of *My Fair Lady, The King and I, Seven Brides for Seven Brothers, Forever Plaid,* and its annual, *Welk Musical Christmas Show.* As you can tell by the titles, many of the musicals are family oriented. Note that some of the shows, usually the musicals, can include a meal of pot roast, chicken, fish or vegetarian, plus side dishes. Or, grab a bite to eat at one of the restaurants, like the pizzeria, in the nearby Welk Village shopping area. Personally, I was glad we arrived early enough to also shop in the village.

Before or during intermission, take a short "tour" around the lobby/museum that showcases a few pictures, props, and instruments from the Lawrence Welk Show.

Hours: Check the website for matinee and nighttime performances.

Price: Pricing starts at $35 for adults, depending on the show time and date.

Ages: 6 years and up. (Children 2 and under are not allowed.)

—TOURS—

BRAILLE INSTITUTE (San Diego County)

(858) 404-5009 or (858) 452-1111 / www.brailleinstitute.org

!

4555 Executive Drive, San Diego

What would it be like to have limited vision, or not be able to see at all? Take a 45-minute tour of the Braille Institute campus to learn how the visually impaired can get around, and learn about the tools that help them be independent. Depending on the availability and the day, visitors might also have the opportunity to talk with a librarian who reads Braille and/or hear a talking book; see the school's classrooms and computer labs; see a cooking demonstration; or partake in other interests your group might have.

Hours: Tours are available Mon. at 1pm and Fri. at 10am, with advanced reservations, only.

Price: Free

Ages: 8 years and up.

CALIFORNIA PIZZA KITCHEN (San Diego County)

See the entry for CALIFORNIA PIZZA KITCHEN (Los Angeles County) (pg. 196) for more information.

!

DEERING - THE GREAT AMERICAN BANJO COMPANY

(800) 845-7791 / www.deeringbanjos.com

!

3733 Kenora Drive, Spring Valley

Banjos just have that happy and bright sound to them, don't they? Come and see and learn how that sound is made by taking a one-hour, intimate and casual tour through the factory. The tour begins in the showroom with a brief history of the family-owned company and an explanation about the parts of a banjo. (You get to see the finished product first and then how each component is made.) You'll walk through the various departments along narrow aisles, stopping at each one to look at the skilled craftsmen who use both machines, as well as their hands to fine tune each part. From the various types of wood in choosing the neck and rim, to the metal bands around the banjo head, the hardware, gluing, sanding, polishing, fretting, spray painting, intricate detail work (especially the inlays), strings, and the tuning - there is so much attention to each step of the process! It takes anywhere from three to twenty man hours to craft a banjo, depending on the elaborateness of it.

The tour ends back at the showroom where you can take your pick of banjos to play, or purchase, as well as other items to buy. You'll have a Goodtime at this factory tour! Note that there is a maximum of fifteen people per tour, so call to make a reservation. The minimum age is 6.

Hours: Tours are given Tues. and Thurs. at 1pm. Call first!

Price: Free

Ages: At least 6 years old and up.

EAGLE MINING COMPANY

(760) 765-0036; (760) 440-6352 / www.theeaglemining.com

$$$

2320 C Street, Julian

Eureka! There's gold in them thar hills! Original mining equipment and a few old buildings make it look like time has stood still here. One of the rustic and dusty buildings is a small museum/store with rock specimens, mining tools, and a glass-cased display of memorabilia from the early 1900's.

Trek through time on your one-hour, guided walking tour through two genuine gold mines that were founded in 1870: the Eagle Mine and the connecting, High Peak Mine. My kids studied about the forty-niners, but to actually go through a gold mine, walk on ore-cart tracks, see stone tunnels hand carved by picks, and learn the hardships of mining, really made a lasting impact on them. We saw the vein that the miners worked and realized, along with hundreds of other people both past and present, that gold wasn't easily obtainable. It took one ton of rock to yield a sugar-cube-size amount of gold! We went up two of the eleven levels in the mines, saw the hoist room where ore buckets were used as olden-day elevators, and experienced darkness so black that we couldn't see our hands in front of our faces. I admire the fortitude of our early engineers. It's interesting to note the difference between the earlier smooth rock tunnels that were hand drilled and the later jagged edges left from blasting with charges. Don't forget to look up at the amazing shaft tunnels (and duck your head)!

Outside, we saw the milling equipment used to crush rocks, and learned the tedious process of extracting gold.

ry your hand at panning for gold (it's harder than it looks) in a "stocked" water trough on the premises. This activity s included in the tour price. And just remember: All that glitters isn't gold.

Julian is a quaint town with unique shops along Main Street. Your kids will enjoy a stop-off at the Julian Drug tore and Candy Mine for a trip downstairs to the "candy" mine. Go next door to Miner's Diner for an ice cream at its ld-fashioned, marble-topped soda counter or enjoy a full breakfast, lunch, or dinner meal. The drug store and diner re located on the corner of Main and Washington Sts. Note that every Sunday at 1pm and 2pm, Julian Doves & Desperados (a Western-themed reenactment group) performs free, comedic gunfights and skits near the Julian Market Deli on the main street. Look up Julian under the city index for other, close-by attractions.

Hours: Open Mon. - Fri., 10am - 4pm; Sat. - Sun., 10am - 5pm; weather permitting and depending on if people are here. Closed Thanksgiving and Christmas.

Price: $10 for adults; $5 for ages 5 - 13; $1 for children 4 and under.

Ages: 4 years and up.

GEMOLOGICAL INSTITUTE OF AMERICA

800) 421-7250 or (760) 603-4116

345 Armada Drive, Carlsbad

Diamonds are a girl's best friend, but both sexes will enjoy learning more about these and other gemstones. The nstitute is a school for those interested in learning and applying knowledge about gemology and the jewelry manufacturing arts. Quiz: What are the 4Cs of diamond value? Answer: color, clarity, cut, and carat weight. A ne-hour tour begins to familiarize the public with gem analysis and grading, and tools of the trade. The best parts, owever, are looking at the numerous stones in raw form and at the finished products of world-class gems. (Sorry, no ree samples.)

Many items, such as pearl necklaces, diamond rings, antique tools, and sculptures, are behind glass in the small otunda. Look, too, at the incredibly, intricately carved piece of ivory. Peek through classroom windows to glimpse tudents of all ages work at computer-aided designs, wax techniques, grading a stone, or other projects. You'll be nthralled by the over sixty labeled window boxes (i.e., glass display cases) lining the hallways that contain rubies, meralds, aquamarines, garnets (including red, orange, and green ones), zircons, tourmaline, opals, and peridots, plus culptures made of gems and stunning jewelry pieces.

The guide explains, among other things, the difference between synthetic and real gem stones, and how faux ones re produced. You'll also hear interesting stories about royalty and their jewelry. One small picture gallery shows the ntire diamond process, from mining to the sale of the stone to its cutting to its becoming a piece of glittering jewelry. small museum showcases rotating exhibits that come from the Smithsonian and from all over the world.

The two-hour GemKids program, for fourth through twelfth graders, is a different tour in that it is geared pecifically for children, is hands on, and it meets state standards. Groups, composed of fifteen to forty students, see amples of diamonds in rough and polished forms, as well as other minerals. They use jewelers' loupes and microscopes to examine stones up close. Aided by other visuals, the class includes elements of mineralogy, geology, rystal structure, and an introduction to identifying inclusions. Note that there are ninety-minute programs for boy couts and girls scouts, too. Have kids bring a sack lunch to enjoy at the picnic tables on site. A gift shop is also on the remises. What a gem of a place!

Note that advanced reservations are required for both the general tour and GemKids program, and that openings ll up quickly. A photo I.D. is required for everyone.

Hours: The museum and tours are offered Mon. - Fri. and are only available with advanced reservations.

Price: Free

Ages: 11 years and up for the general tour; fourth through twelfth graders for the GemKids program.

ULIAN MINING COMPANY

951) 313-0166 or (951) 312-9940 / www.julianminingcompany.com

444 Highway 78, Julian

Rural America is alive and well at the Julian Mining Company. Open year round for individuals, families, and field ips this outdoor country space offers a variety of "living history" experiences such as panning for gold - which is arder than it looks - at a good-sized "stocked" sluice where you can keep whatever you pan ($9 for adults; $7 for kids 2 and under); petting animals at the small petting zoo; pressing cider (in season); riding on a tractor-drawn hayride; cking seasonal fruit (such as apples and raspberries); throwing a tomahawk; and gem mining ($11.50 a bag up, to $70 bucket) which contains ore rough that is shaken over a screen to find an assortment of tiger eye, pyrite, quartz, gates, shark teeth, and more.

One of the several, hands-on, school field trips is the two-hour Farm Life Tour which includes cider pressing, visiting the petting zoo, candle dipping, hayride, pioneer chores, wool carding, and pie or butter making. A minimum of twenty-five people is needed and the cost is $11.75 per person. At the four-hour Native American Tour participants make jewelry, shoot a bow and arrow, watch a tanning demonstration, visit a Sioux tipi, and more, for a cost of $14.75 per person. Via lecture and hands-on demonstrations and experiments regarding carbon dating, laws of thermodynamics, micro and macro evolution, archaeological dig, worldwide flood, the creation account, and more the Creation Science tour helps to answer the question - What is the origin of life? This tour is $15 per person with a minimum of fifteen people. Participate in an almost four-hour Civil or Revolutionary War reenactment (which are excellent) with battles that you soldier in, on one side or the other. Live that life while you also learn colonial etiquette, garden, practice militia drill and march, make soap or candles, and more. Each tour is $14.75 per person. Note that if you have a smaller group, or just a family, that would like to take a tour, you might be able to add on to a group tour.

Enjoy lunch at the picnic tables and/or purchase additional refreshments at the on-site store. The store also sells old-time toys, animal pelts, unique gifts, books, and other fun stuff. Note that you can also spend the night here in a fully-furnished, small and homey, one-bedroom cabin for $100 per night for a minimum two nights, or $130 for one night.

Hours: Generally open to the public on Sat., 10am - 4pm; Sun., noon - 4pm. Open longer during summer, and at other times for field trips and private events.

Price: A few hours of activities can cost $10 - $15 per person. See some prices listed above.

Ages: 4 years and up.

KUMEYAAY-IPAI INTERPRETIVE CENTER

(858) 668-4781 or (858) 668-1292 / www.poway.org

13104 Ipai Waaypuk Trail (formerly Silver Lake Drive), Poway

Rich in Kumeyaay-Ipai history, a paved trail weaves around and through this six-acre village site. Recreated parts of the village include round houses made of reeds, ramadas that provide shade, milling stations where acorns were ground, native plants, and interpretative signs. The docent-led tours, for the general public and for school groups, are wonderfully informative and make the past seem present. A modern building contains exhibits regarding the Kumeyaay such as baskets, photos of rock art, and artifacts from the site. Two-hour school tours, geared for third graders, include a docent-led tour and hands-on activities like creating their own rock art, playing a stick game and grinding acorns.

Hours: Open to the general public for docent-led tours on the second and fourth Sat., 10am - noon; for school tours Thurs. - Fri. 9am - 11:30am.

Price: Public tours are free. School tours are $4 per student.

Ages: 7 years and up.

OLD GLOBE THEATRE (tour)

(619) 23GLOBE (234-5623) or (619) 239-2255; (619) 231-1941- reservations / www.oldglobe.org

1363 Old Globe Way, Balboa Park, San Diego

Take a ninety-minute tour of the Old Globe Theatre, which was originally modeled after Shakespeare's Globe Theatre in London. You'll see behind-the-scenes of this theater and the two other ones in the complex while learning their histories; architecture; how sets are built to look like stone castles; costumes and their designs; the miniature bug orchestra; and about the current plays. Look up OLD GLOBE THEATRE (pg. 571) for show information.

Hours: Tours are given on selected days throughout the week, and almost every weekend at 10:30am. Check the website for specific dates.

Price: $5 for adults; $3 for seniors and students.

Ages: 3td graders and up, only.

PETCO PARK - THE PARK AT THE PARK

(619) 795-5000 or (619) 795-5011; (619) 231-6664 - Omni Hotel / www.mlb.com/padres

100 Park Boulevard, San Diego

Take me out to the ball game, or at least take me out on a tour of a ballpark. Home to the world-famous San Diego Padres, this stadium offers behind-the-scenes tours that last not quite ninety minutes. Fans can see the press box, dugouts, bullpen (maybe warm up your arm with a pitch or two?), a luxury suite, warning track, the Park at the Park, the Padres Hall of Fame and Museum, and the team store. All this while learning the history of the team and players, and of the historic Western Metal Supply Co. building, which was constructed in 1909. Although the tour includes climbing stairs and getting a workout by walking about a mile and a half, it is also wheelchair accessible. Families and individuals are welcome to take the tour on a walk-in basis. There is a limit of twenty-five people per tour so groups need to call to make a reservation. Educational tours are also offered with advanced reservations. Note that the Omni Hotel, located next to Petco Park at 675 L Street and actually connected to the ballpark via a skybridge, has awards, autographed baseballs, bats, vintage uniforms, and documents such as contracts and correspondence on display on various floors.

The Park at the Park is a 2.8-acre park just beyond the outfield fence. It boasts a small infield used for supervised wiffle ball games, a grassy hill, a playground for tots with some fun apparatus, and a few picnic tables.

Come see a game via the park as a variety of seating is available. Spots on Picnic Hill are the least expensive, as are seats on the side of the giant scoreboard, which actually obstructs the view from the higher-numbered seats. Enjoy a picnic lunch, or dinner, with seats on the picnic terrace, where mesh fences are absent (so the view is clear), and at smaller picnic tables, with advanced reservations. On game days the park closes about five hours before the game, except for visitors with tickets. Tip: You can even enjoy a tailgate party at Tailgate Park on 12th and Imperial sts., with advance reservation.

Hours: Off-season, usually October through March, tours are daily at 10:30am; 12:30pm and 3pm. When the Padres are playing and at home, tours are still given, but times are effected - check the website or call first. The park is usually open daily sunrise to sunset, and is free.

Price: The tour is $17 for adults; $12 for seniors, military and children 12 and under. Parking in lots ranges from $10 - $35, depending on the proximity. There is some metered street parking available for the tour. Note that tours begin at the Western Metal Building ticket windows on 7th Ave./Tony Gwynn Blvd. and K St.

Ages: 6 years and up.

SAN DIEGO CITY LIGHTS NIGHT TOUR

(866) 754-0966 / www.trolleytours.com

$$$$$

470 Kettner Boulevard at Harbor Drive at Seaport Village, San Diego

Lights, camera, awesome! From the Gaslamp Quarter to Balboa Park to the top of Coronado Bridge - with a 20-minute stop at Coronado's Ferry Landing where the skyline is beautifully lit up (photo op!) and you can stroll along the beach - all this can be yours with this tour. Then, back to the bay and the ships all along it. The nighttime route is very similar to the one offered during the day with this company, but during this ninety-minute narrated tour you see the city in a different light, literally. The commentary about the history of the city and the buildings as you drive past them help make the tour even more memorable and meaningful.

Hours: Call or check the calendar for dates and times.

Price: $29.95 per person; children 3 and under are free.

Ages: 7 years and up.

SAN DIEGO INTERNATIONAL AIRPORT - TERMINAL TO TARMAC TOUR

(619) 400-2404 or (619) 400-2880 / www.san.org

!

Harbor Drive at Lindbergh Field, San Diego

Pilot your way to the airport for a well-organized, two-hour tour of the San Diego International Airport. Tours include a walk through a majority of the facility while learning about architecture, travel, communications, career opportunities, and the history of aviation. Hear about Charles Lindbergh while looking at a replica of the Spirit of St. Louis. See some of the works of art on display, view the endangered-species Least Tern area, and see planes land and take off while safely driving around the runway. Go through the baggage claim area, find out about courtesy phones, and how to use the maps on the walls. Kids only tours might get to see a demonstration of what the on-site fire station does and the harbor police K-9 unit. The tour enables children and adults to find out all about travel without experiencing jet lag, or the cost of a trip! Groups are limited to a maximum of twenty-two people.

Hours: General public tours are offered on select Thurs. and Fri. from 10am - noon. Student tours are offered one Wed. and Fri. a month from 10am - noon.

Price: Free. Parking is validated.

Ages: Kids must be at least 7 years and up. Student tours are for second - eighth graders.

SAN DIEGO SYMPHONY HALL

!

See SAN DIEGO SYMPHONY / JACOBS MUSIC CENTER / COPLEY SYMPHONY HALL (pg. 573), under SHOWS AND THEATERS, for tour information.

TAYLOR GUITARS

(619) 258-6957 or (619) 258-1207 / www.taylorguitars.com
1980 Gillespie Way, El Cajon

What do Aerosmith, Pearl Jam, President Clinton, and Garth Brooks have in common? They each own Taylor guitars. This over-an-hour-long tour is "Taylor"-made for guitar fans. Starting in the lobby, which features an informational and pictorial timeline of the guitar company, visitors then walk outside to a storage area and through the buildings, into each room and the warehouses to see and learn how a guitar is put together, from start to glossy (or satin) finish. The tour is intimate and casual, and you'll see every aspect of guitar-making up close and get to ask the questions (and get answers) from the workers and tour guide. Cherry, Sapele mahogany, Sitka spruce, Big Leaf maple, cedar, Indian rosewood, Hawaiian koa, and walnut are just a few of the common and exotic woods used in Taylor guitars. Once the wood is cut to precise specifications, it is kept in climate controlled rooms and containers, then carved, sanded, and assembled. Specially designed (loud!) machines, such as the ones that slice grooves in the neck of the guitar, are fascinating to watch as are the workers who are involved in each step of the process. Note: It takes at least a week to ten days to complete just one guitar.

The tour is geared for guitar aficionados (we had some people on ours who asked lots of "technical" questions), but kids will appreciate the different shapes, woods, colors, and sounds of the guitars. I, who am not musically inclined at all, thought it was fascinating and enjoyed seeing every component and the hand crafting still employed. After the tour, guests are invited to purchase a wide selection of merchandise (guitar picks, jackets, etc.) imprinted with the Taylor logo. Guitars are not sold on the premises. The tour is geared for small groups, is not wheelchair friendly, and visitors must stay within specified lines and resist the temptation to touch anything in the factory warehouses. School and other groups are welcome to book a special tour at least two weeks in advance. Photography is permitted.

Hours: Tours are offered Mon. - Thurs. at 1pm., excluding holidays. Reservations are not required, but suggested as only 60 people per tour are allowed. Tours are not given for a week toward the end of June, at the beginning of July, and for a week before Christmas through New Year's Day.

Price: Free

Ages: 7 years and up.

—TRANSPORTATION—

AMTRAK (San Diego County)

(800) USA RAIL (872-7245) / www.amtrakcalifornia.com

Ride the rails! See AMTRAK (Los Angeles County) (pg. 208) for more information.

BIKE AND KAYAK TOURS $$$$$

(858) 454-1010 / www.sandiegobikeandkayaktours.com
Coronado - 1201 1st Street, suite 215; La Jolla - 2158 Avenida De La Playa

There is almost no better way to see the sea than from a kayak: So close to the water, sea creatures and even geological formations - it's a thrill! In La Jolla, kayak the seven caves on a guided tour where the naturalist glides you there and points out the sights along the way. Going through the La Jolla Ecological Reserve you should see sea lions, garibaldi, leopard sharks, and other critters. Two-hour tours start at $39 per person. Other tours offered are combo kayak and snorkel tours, and sunset tours, and, for those who want to be on dry land, bike tours.

Rentals are also available for those who want to do it on their own. Single kayak rentals are $29 for ninety-minutes; doubles are $49; triples are $69. Note that prices are less expensive for the first departures in the morning and the last one in the afternoon. Snorkel gear rentals - mask, fins, wetsuit and snorkel - are $29 for the day. Bike rentals are $9 an hour, or $29 for the day.

Hours: Tours and rentals are usually available daily, 9am - sunset.

Price: Prices are listed above.

Ages: 6 years and up and can swim.

BIKE MAPS (San Diego County)

See BIKE MAPS (Orange County) (pg. 328) for information. Note that bike racks are available on many buses and on Coaster commuter trains.

CALIFORNIA WATER SPORTS - CARLSBAD LAGOON

(888) 5- LAGOON (552-4666); (760) 434-3089 / www.carlsbadlagoon.com

$$$$

4215 Harrison Street, Carlsbad

    This very popular place is located right off the 5 freeway. Three marina/lagoon areas are located here for separate water activities on calm waters. Wave rentals are $99 for an hour. Single kayaks are $20 an hour. Double kayaks, canoes, pedalboats, aqua cycles and stand up paddle board rentals are $30 each, per hour. Power boat rentals are $135 for an hour. Liability waivers must be signed for everything. You may not take the equipment out of this marina, but the area is plenty big enough. In between boating activities, lie out on the private beach or play volleyball, eat lunch at the picnic tables, or shop at the pro shop. Enjoy!

Hours: Open the end of March - September, daily, 9am - 6pm. Open the rest of the year, Wed. - Fri., 10am - 3pm; Sat. - Sun., 9am - 4pm.

Price: Prices are listed above.

Ages: 6 years and up.

COASTER

(619) 685-4900 - automated system for the coaster, bus, and trolley; (619) 233-3004 - transit office / www.gonctd.com/coaster/coaster.html; www.sdmts.com

$$$

San Diego County

    Coast stress-free from Oceanside to Old Town to further south in San Diego, with stops at Carlsbad, Encinitas, Solana Beach, and Sorrento Valley via the sleek transit express rail line. Pick out a destination in the above-mentioned cities, or let the ride be the adventure as you travel along the shoreline. Note that bike racks are available on the Coaster commuter trains. Automated fare machines at the Coaster stations make obtaining a ticket a breeze, although calling to find out the schedule on the automated number can drive one a little nuts.

Hours: It operates Mon. - Fri. starting at about 5am and ending at about 6:30pm - depending on destination; Sat., 8:30amish - 78:15pmish. Check the website for the holiday schedules.

Price: $4 for adults one-way; $2 for seniors; children 5 and under are free.

Ages: All

FLAGSHIP CRUISES AND EVENTS

(800) 44CRUISE (442-7847) or (619) 234-4111 / www.flagshipsd.com

$$$$$

990 N. Harbor Drive, Broadway Pier, San Diego

    Enjoy a one- or two-hour-narrated harbor cruise along San Diego's coast in a nice excursion ship. A snack bar is on board. During a one-hour cruise, you'll explore either the north part of the bay, or the south part. Depending on which cruise you choose, you'll see the *Star of India*, the Naval Air Station, Coronado Bridge, U.S. Navy Seal base, Point Loma Lighthouse, and the San Diego shipyards that hold merchants' vessels, fishing boats, and more. The two-hour cruise encompasses both the north and south parts of the bay. Three-and-a-half-hour whale-watching trips are given early December through mid-April. The trips are narrated by a naturalist from the Birch Aquarium. A sighting is guaranteed or you ride again for free. Tip: Bring a jacket or sweater (and camera) on any journey by sea. Note that for fine dining, this cruise line also offers dinner cruises and sometimes a brunch buffet cruise.

Hours: Harbor cruises depart daily, 10am to about 5pm. Seasonal three-and-a-half-hour whale-watching cruises depart daily at 9:45am and 1:30pm.

Price: One-hour cruises are $25 for adults; $22 for seniors and active-duty military; $12.50 for ages 4 -12; children 3 and under are free. Two-hour cruises are $30 for adults; $27 for seniors and military; $15 for ages 4 - 12. Whale watching, Mon. - Fri., is $42 for adults, $37 for seniors, $21 for ages 4 - 12; on Sat. - Sun. it's $47 for adults, $42 for seniors, $24 for ages 4 - 12. Dinner cruises are $96.27 for adults, $64.57 for ages 4 - 12. The brunch buffet cruise is $83.70 for adults; $56.20 for kids. Parking at the Broadway pier is $18 all day.

Ages: 3 years and up.

GONDOLA COMPANY

(619) 429-6317 / www.gondolacompany.com

6/$

503 Grand Caribe Causeway, Coronado

    This part of Coronado becomes a part of Italy via an authentic gondola cruise through the exclusive waterway of the Coronado Cays. Romantic? Yes, but it can also be a peaceful, almost hour-long adventure with children. The gondolier dresses in the traditional costume of striped shirt and black pants. Italian music plays in the background. An ice bucket and glasses are provided, and you supply your own choice of beverage. Most of the gondolas can take up to six people; a few can up to fourteen passengers.

Hours: Open Mon. - Fri., 3pm - 10pm; Sat. - Sun., noon - 11pm.
Price: $115 for two people (sunset cruise is $130); $20 per additional person. The Carolina Cruise - for 7 to 14 people - is $32 per person + 18% gratuity). Children under 3 are free. Reservations are required for all rides.
Ages: 4 years and up.

H & M LANDING

(619) 222-1144 / www.hmlanding.com
2803 Emerson, San Diego

$$$$$

San Diego's oldest whale-watching expedition company offers three-hour cruises during whale-watching season, which is late-December through March. Besides whales, be on the lookout for sea lions, dolphins, and elephant seals.
Hours: Cruises depart daily at 10am and 1:30pm.
Price: $50 for adults on weekends; $30 on weekdays; $26 for seniors, military, and ages 15 and under, every day. All-day parking is $8.
Ages: 6 years and up.

HORNBLOWER

(888) 467-6256 or (619) 686-8715 / www.hornblower.com
970 N. Harbor Drive, San Diego

$$$$

Hornblower offers one- and two-hour narrated harbor cruises. You'll see numerous ships including air craft carriers and other military vessels, the *Star of India*, the Navy Seals Training base, Hotel Del Coronado, the Coronado Bay Bridge, and (hopefully) lots of marine animals. The company also offers three-and-a-half-hour whale-watching cruises in the winter and four-hour ones in the summer that include narration by the Captain; watching a documentary on whales; viewing sea lions, birds, and whales; indoor/outdoor seating; and a snack bar with hot food and drinks available. Whale sighting is guaranteed or you receive a whale check, good for another cruise. This yacht company also offers other specialty cruises, including brunch and dinner cruises, throughout the year.
Hours: One- and two-hour harbor cruises depart year round, 10am - 4:15pm. During the summer, both tours depart from 8:45am - 4:15pm. Whale-watching cruises, mid-December through mid-April, are offered daily at 9:30am and 1:30pm. Summer whale-watching cruises are given late June - early September, Fri. - Mon. at 9am. Reservations aren't necessary, but call first (of course!). All cruises are weather dependent.
Price: One-hour harbor tours are $25 for adults; $23 for seniors and active military; $12.50 for ages 4 - 12; children 3 and under are free. Two-hour cruises are $30 for adults; $28 for seniors and military; $15 for ages 4 - 12. Winter whale watching is $47 for adults, $45 for seniors and military, $23.50 for ages 4 - 12. Summer whale watching is $65 for adults; $63 for seniors and military; $32.50 for kids.
Ages: 5 years and up, depending on the tour.

JULIAN CARRIAGE COMPANY

(760) 705-7085 or (520) 686-0935 / www.julianca.com
2202 Main Street, Julian

$$$$

Clip clop, clip clop - a horse-drawn carriage ride through Julian fits in perfectly with the ambiance of this quaint town. On the narrated ride you'll see and hear about the history of Julian, including mining and apple picking, while enjoying the sights and sounds of the countryside. And any special event - birthday, moonlight rides, and whatever else you think of - can be made more special with a carriage ride. Note that most of the tours begin in front of the Julian Market and Deli.
Hours: Look for a carriage Sat. - Sun., 1pm - 5pm, or call first as reservations are always recommended.
Price: A 15 min. ride for up to 6 people is $10 per adults; $5 per for ages 12 and under. A 30 min. ride is $75 for everyone. Gratuities are always appreciated.
Ages: All

LA JOLLA KAYAK

(858) 459-1114 / www.lajollakayak.com
2199 Avenida De La Playa, La Jolla Shores

$$$$$

Come kayak the waters of gorgeous La Jolla on your own, or with a guide, during the day or at sunset. You'll paddle past sea cliffs, as well as past and through caves. An underwater reserve, featuring reefs and diverse marine life, is in this area, too, so bring or rent snorkel gear. And don't be surprised by the sea lions and harbor seals that swim by your kayak or stop for a friendly visit. Stunning scenery, good exercise, and a fun family excursion - life doesn't get any better than this! You can also experience whale watching from a kayak for a more up-close visit with these sea mammals. The company offers land excursions, too, of bike tours.

Tours include a lesson, life vest, and guide. Wear your swim suit. Kids must be at least 6 years old to kayak with an adult and 15 to kayak by themselves. Note that you can combine your kayak adventure with snorkeling so you see the best of both worlds - above and below the water. The company also offers surfboard, boogie boards and stand-up paddle board rentals.

Hours: Tours and rentals are available daily, 8am - sunset, weather permitting. Call for specific tour times.
Price: Kayak rentals are $30 for ninety-minutes for a single; $40 for a double. Snorkel gear is $12 for mask and snorkel; $10 for fins; $20 for wetsuit for two hours, or all of it for $30 for 4 hours. Two-hour kayak tours (which are actually just one hour on the water) start at $45 per person; $75 for two people. Two-hour kayak and snorkel tours start at $60 per person; $95 for two people, depending on the date and time. Whale watching is $59 for a single; $89 for a double.
Ages: 7 years and up.

OCEANSIDE BOAT RENTALS

(760) 722-0028 / www.boats4rent.com

256 Harbor Drive South, Oceanside Harbor, Oceanside

$$$$

Rentals includes kayaks - $20 per hour for a single, $33 an hour for a double; pedal boats - $23 an hour for up to two people; sailboats - $45 the first hour for a fourteen footer; motorboats - $75 for the first hour for a six-passenger boat that doesn't leave the harbor, and starting at $110 for a six-passenger boat that does (plus a fuel charge); electric boats (which are much quieter than motor boats and seat eight) start at $80 for the first hour; stand up paddle boards - $27 an hour; and wave runners -$125 for the first hour (plus a fuel charge). Make some time to shop around in the Harbor Village before or after your excursion.

Hours: Open daily, 10am - an hour before sunset, weather permitting.
Price: Prices listed above. The first two hours of parking in the village area are free.
Ages: 4 years and up.

OCOTILLO WELLS STATE VEHICULAR RECREATION AREA

(760) 767-5391- ranger; (760) 767-5393 - district office / ohv.parks.ca.gov

5172 Highway 78, Borrego Springs

!

For a little off-roading fun, try Ocotillo Wells Recreation Area where you can go up hills, over sand dunes, and through dry washes. You must provide your own vehicles (and have them registered), but the entrance is free and so are primitive camping sites. A visitor center is open daily, October thru Memorial Day weekend, from 8am - 4:30pm; closed the rest of the year. It has shaded areas for bbqs and even has pay showers. It hosts campfires, junior ranger programs and events such as star gazing, geo caching, interpretive lectures, and more.

Hours: Open daily.
Price: Free
Ages: 6 years and up.

OLD TOWN TROLLEY TOURS

(619) 298-8687 or (866) 754-0966 / www.trolleytours.com

4010 Twiggs Street, San Diego

$$$$$

Ding, ding, ding goes the bell of the trolley! Really get to know the city of San Diego by taking a narrated tour on board an old-fashioned looking trolley. The tour guide will tell you the history of San Diego, plus lots of fun stories. One of the best features about this tour is that you can take a continuous two-hour tour, a 25-mile loop, or jump off (so to speak) and rejoin the tour at any time throughout the day. There are ten stops covered on the loop, including Old Town, Seaport Village, Horton Plaza, Hotel Del Coronado, San Diego Zoo, and Balboa Park. Appropriately nicknamed "transportainment," we enjoyed the commentary, the freedom of stopping at attractions, staying for a bit, and getting back on board when we were ready. Hassle-free parking to all these attractions is another plus. Note that this Old Town San Diego address is just one of the stops.

Hours: Trolleys run daily most of the year, 9am - 5pm; open in the summer, daily, 9am - 6pm, or 7pm. No tours are given on Thanksgiving or Christmas.
Price: The trolley tour is $39.95 for adults; $24.95 for ages 4 - 12; children 3 and under are free. Prices are discounted if booked through the internet and kids are free with a paying adult in October.
Ages: 5 years and up.

PACIFIC SOUTHWEST RAILWAY MUSEUM

(619) 465-7776 - recording; (619) 478-9937 - weekends / www.psrm.org

750 Depot Street, Campo

$$$$

The sound of a train whistle blowing has always been a signal for adventure! Start your adventure at the old Campo Depot where there are a few stationary push carts, a gift shop, several picnic tables, and even a small playground with swings, old tires, and a sandbox with toys. Then, come aboooooard the *Golden State Limited* train for an hour-and-a-half ride (twelve-miles) your children will never forget. You'll depart from the depot/ticket office and ride in restored 1930s passenger coaches. My boys loved the freedom of moving about while traveling. They walked from car to car (parents are asked to accompany minors), watched the scenic mountains and meadows roll past, saw a few cows, and played cards. Tip: We brought a picnic lunch, as only snack food is available to purchase on the train. At the halfway point, kids can view (from the windows) the engine being switched around to pull you back the way you came. The conductors were friendly and shared a lot of information about railroads and the history of the area.

If you conduct yourself really well and would like to pay $40 per person for the privilege, two people per excursion can ride in the locomotive cab. Share this experience in that one person rides in the cab and another on the train, and then switch positions for the return trip. Only two riders are allowed in the cab at one time. Go a step further and be an engineer for an hour for $175. You'll sit in the engineer's seat and operate the locomotive after a quick instructional session from one of our engineers; sound the horn and ring the bell; and be at the controls. Up to 3 people can split this exciting hour.

The train stops for all passengers to depart at the museum on the way back. Inside the display building, or museum, are some terrific train treasures - a Southern Pacific Engine, pull carts, photos, tools, a wooden train car desperately awaiting lots of help, and a beautifully restored, oak, segregated passenger and baggage car (look at the signs above certain seats that say "for colored") built in 1886. Walk through this car and to the attached mailroom car with its cubicles and bags. Outside, on the tracks, are numerous more old and restored rail cars such as passenger, steam and diesel locomotives, cabooses, Pullman, and freight cars. #104, even rusted and sporting some holes, is a classic as it is the last surviving steam locomotive of the SD & A railway. The docents willingly share their knowledge about the history of the cars, people or freight that rode on them and anything else railroad related. Don't hesitate to ask them any questions!

On the walk back to the Depot is more of the outdoors museum, as the grounds are strewn with old and weathered rail cars, some being restored, some not, plus plaques describing the history of this railway. Check out the sign that has hobo codes carved into it.

Ninety-minute school train tours/rides on the 1930's vintage cars are offered on the third Tuesday of every month at 10am, by reservation. (A minimum of thirty students is required.) A train ride is a great "living" classroom. Then, there is time to explore the museum. The general public is welcome to come along if there's room.

Check the train website for special excursions such as dinner rides, the Bunny Train (at Easter), Pumpkin Trains, the North Pole Limited, and more. Note that MOTOR TRANSPORT MUSEUM (pg. 539) is around the corner.

Another fun ride is aboard the Valley Flyer caboose. A half-hour round-trip shuttle service goes around some of the museum grounds and then connects the depot with the GASKILL BROTHERS STONE STORE MUSEUM (pg. 531). Visit the museum and then ride the caboose back as tickets are good for the day. This train ride is $14 for adults; $7 for ages 3 to 12; children 2 and under are free. A cab ride here is $25. See the website for times.

Hours: The museum is open most of the year, Sat. - Sun., 9am - 5pm. It's open between Father's Day and mid-October, Sat., noon - 7pm; Sun., 10am - 3pm. Trains depart on select Tues. (call for times), and most of the year on Sat. and Sun. at 11am, 1pm and 3pm. Father's Day and mid-October a train departs on Sat. at 5pm and 7pm, as well. You must have a reservation for all train rides. Closed Christmas and the two weekends following it.

Price: Train rides, which include the museum, are $18 for adults; $15 for seniors; $9 for ages 3 - 12; children 2 and under are free. Special event rides might cost more. The student train rides are $5 per person; the general public pays the regular price. Entry to just the museum and grounds is $10 for adults; $8 for seniors; $5 for ages 3 - 12.

Ages: 3 years and up.

SAN DIEGO BAY FERRY and OLD FERRY LANDING

(800) 44CRUISE (442-7847) or (619) 234-4111 / www.flagshipsd.com

990 N. Harbor Drive at the Broadway Pier in downtown San Diego, and the Ferry Landing Marketplace in Coronado

$$$$

Take a fifteen-minute ride over to Coronado (and back) on the San Diego Bay Ferry. Enjoy the Ferry Landing Marketplace on the Coronado side, with its Victorian-style shopping and eating complex. Bike, blade, or walk along the waterfront paved pathways. You can also romp in the grassy lawns along the pathways, or sunbathe on the beach. A farmer's market is held on the island on Tuesdays from 2:30pm to 6pm. TIDELANDS PARK / CORONADO SKATE PARK (pg. 518) is next to the Marketplace. If you want to go to Hotel Del Coronado, take the bus (#904) from the landing. It runs approximately every hour from 10am to 6pm, with a few stops along the way. The shuttle is about $2.25 for adults; $1.10 for seniors; and up to 2 children, ages 5 and under, ride for free with a paying adult. Or, enjoy a scenic walk to the hotel (one-and-a-third miles), though it might get a little long for younger children. See FLAGSHIP CRUISES AND EVENTS for information on longer and more scenic boat rides offered from this company.

Hours: The ferry departs from the pier every hour on the hour, Sun. - Thurs., 9am - 9pm; Fri. - Sat., 9am - 10pm. It leaves Coronado every hour on the half hour.

Price: $4.75 for adults (one-way); children 3 and under are free; bikes are included in the price. Parking at Five Star parking at the Broadway pier is $18 - $24 for the day. Parking at the USS Midway lot starts at $10.

Ages: All

SAN DIEGO PARASAIL ADVENTURES

(619) 223-4(FUN) (4386) / www.goparasailing.com
1548 Quivira Way / 844 W. Mission Bay Drive, San Diego

$$$$$

Experience the thrill of soaring up in the air, "flying" over San Diego waters, and getting a bird's eye view of this lovely city. Rides last about seven minutes, although participants are in the boat for about ninety minutes, to ensure that everyone gets their turn. Take off and land directly on the boat. Single or tandem flights are available.

Hours: Open March - Memorial Day and Labor Day - December, weekends only, 10am - 4pm. Open daily during spring break, and Memorial Day - Labor Day, 9am - 6pm. Closed Jan and Feb.

Price: $99.95 for going up 600 ft.; $129.95 for going up 800 ft., plus a fuel charge and taxes per person. Observers can ride in the boat for $29 a person, if there is room.

Ages: At least 95 lbs.; minimum age 6 years old.

SAN DIEGO SEAL TOURS

(619) 298-8687 or (866) 754-0966 / www.sealtours.com; www.trolleytours.com
470 Kettner Boulevard at Harbor Dr., Seaport Village, San Diego and 1004 North Harbor Dr. at Embarcadero Marina Park, San Diego

$$$$$

Is it a bus or a boat? Yes! The amphibious vehicle on this SEAL (which stands for SEa And Land) tour takes passengers on a ninety-minute, narrated ride on the streets through the heart of San Diego, explaining the history of the city and highlighting points of interest. Then, splash! Drive into the waters of Mission Bay (this is an odd sensation at first). You'll spend some more time back up on land before another plunge, this time into the San Diego Bay waters where you'll cruise past (and learn about) the maritime and military history of the area. "Sail" past the sky line, Navy ships, fishing vessels (don't forget to wave), and tugboats. Be on the lookout for sea-lions and other aquatic creatures. The tour is an unforgettable way to learn about San Diego in an exciting manner. And yes, people in cars and all along the land and sea route do stare as the bus/boat is unusual looking. (Or is it the people inside who are unusual looking?!)

Hours: Tours depart daily, with more tours offered in the spring/summer. Tours leave from both addresses listed above, starting at 10am and then every hour, or so, until 3pm, 4pm or 5pm, depending. Check the website or call for an exact schedule.

Price: $42 for adults; $25 for ages 4 - 12; $10 for ages 3 and under (but it's not recommended for younger kids.) Book tickets online for a discount.

Ages: 4 years and up.

SAN DIEGO TROLLEY

(619) 685-4900 - 24-hour information line; (619) 233-3004 - trip planning; (619) 234-5005 - for persons with hearing impairments. / www.sdmts.com/trolley/trolley.asp
San Diego

$$

The San Diego Trolley (and bus) line is a great way to get around San Diego. The Blue line extends from Mission San Diego all the way down to San Ysidro. From this last stop at the border, you can either walk into Mexico, or take a cab. Park for free at the Old Town Transit Center, or all day at the MTS tower garage at 12th and Imperial for about $1.50 an hour, or $6 max. They are closed on weekends. Park at Tailgate parking, then, on K St. for $8. The Orange line goes from El Cajon to Santa Fe Depot and downtown. There are several places to catch the trolley line along the routes, with many of the stops being at major attractions. Part of the fun for a child is just the ride. Check out the website for specials, such as family weekend deals and friends ride free. Also see OLD TOWN TROLLEY TOURS (pg. 581), for another, and more expensive, way to get around San Diego.

Hours: It runs daily, 5am - 1am, with service every fifteen minutes most of the day.

Price: Travel between any two stations is $2.50 for adults; $1.25 for seniors. A day pass is $5, which is also good for most bus routes for one operating day. Up to two children, 5 and under, ride for free. Family days are every weekend where up to 2 kids, 12 years and under, ride for free with a paying adult. Tickets are usually dispensed from machines.

Ages: All

SAN DIEGO VINTAGE TROLLEY

(619) 557-4555 / www.sdmts.com $

12th and Imperial Transit Center, San Diego

Take a "ride back in time" when you board a restored, vintage trolley, circa 1946. Ride the Silver Line trolley past, or stop at, downtown San Diego's most popular destinations including the Gaslamp Quarter, Seaport Village, Petco Park, and along the waterfront. The trolley also has other stops along the way - check the full, 2.7 mile round trip route online. The ride is about twenty-five minutes if you stay on it the whole way. Note that if you disembark and reboard, you pay the fare, again.

Hours: Tues. and Thurs., 9:54am - 1:54pm; Sat. - Sun., 10:54am - 3:24pm - every 30 minutes, from 12th and Imperial Transit Center, and along the way. Closed on most holidays and during special events.

Price: $2.50 for adults, round trip; $1.25 for seniors; free for two children, 5 years and under, with one paying adult. Exact change only.

Ages: All

SNORKEL SAN DIEGO

(619) 260-1880 / www.snorkelsandiego.com   6/$

1166 Coast Blvd. at La Jolla Cove, La Jolla

Daytime snorkeling at the La Jolla Cove Underwater Park is an exciting excursion. A guide aids you in exploring the near-to-shore, underwater ecosystem and points out some of the most colorful fish off the coast, including the brilliant orange Garibaldi, the California state fish. You'll also encounter sea lions at the sea lion rookery and explore a sea cave. All gear is provided with the tour. Snorkelers must be able to swim, be at least 13 years old, and weigh at least 100 pounds. You'll be in the water about an hour and a half.

Scuba Adventures, for non-divers, include 45 minutes of instructions, plus 45 minutes of dive time, down to about twenty-five feet. It includes all the equipment you need and a guide.

See LA JOLLA SHORES BEACH (pg. 467) for information on the immediate beach area and SCRIPPS PARK / LA JOLLA COVE and COASTLINE (pg. 516) for more information on the close-by La Jolla area.

Hours: Snorkel tours are usually offered daily at 10am and 1pm.

Price: Snorkel tours are $70 per person. Scuba Adventures are $195 per person.

Ages: 13 years and up for snorkeling.

TORREY PINES GLIDER PORT

(858) 452-9858 / www.flytorrey.com   !/$$$$$

2800 Torrey Pines Scenic Drive, La Jolla

Man has had dreams and aspirations to fly since the beginning of time. Hang gliding and paragliding are the closest things we'll get to it in this lifetime (and they are much better than Icarus' attempt!) Kids may participate in this uplifting sport, or come to just watch. We brought a picnic lunch, as there are tables at the cliff tops, although a full-service snack bar, the Cliff Hanger Cafe, is here, too, selling breakfast items, plus deli sandwiches, salads, and soups. Besides the exhilarating sight of gliders soaring and dipping along the coastline, there is a breathtaking view of the ocean and beach. The small planes you see flying overhead are really remote control planes that have a take-off/landing site right next "door."

Hours: Open daily for flights, 9am - 5pm, although if you're coming to watch, you might want to call first to see if anyone is actually flying that day. Closed Christmas.

Price: Free, unless you're flying! Paragliding tandem flights start at $175, usually take about a half hour, which includes ground school instruction and about 20 minutes of flight time. Hang gliding tandems start at $225. Air conditions determine flight capability.

Ages: All to come and watch; 5 years and up for tandem; at least 100 pounds for solo flights.

YOUNG EAGLES PROGRAM (San Diego County)

☀

!

National number - (877) 806-8902; San Diego - EAAChapter14@gmail.com, or (619) 920-8069 - airport; Chapter 286 - (760) 598-5784; Chapter 1279 - (951) 775-8909; Chapter 14 - (858) 273-4051 / Fallbrook - www.eaa1279.org; San Diego - www.eaa14.org; Oceanside - www.286eaachapter.org; National - www.youngeagles.org

Fallbrook - 2155 S. Mission Road at the Fallbrook Airport; Oceanside - 480 Airport Road; San Diego - 1409 Continental Avenue Hangar 1, Brown Field

See the entry for YOUNG EAGLES PROGRAM (Los Angeles County) (pg. 216) for details. Fallbrook, chapter #1279 - This chapter usually flies twice a year. Preregister as the 35 to 40 spaces available fill up quickly. Their website is very up-to-date. San Diego, chapter 14 - The flight is over the city of San Diego and over the ocean. Younger children who are grounded can ride in a simulator that has a radio, earphones, and all the instruments that are in a cockpit. The ride moves and turns as the wheel is turned. Ask about this chapter's other Young Eagle programs.

Hours: Fallbrook - One Sat. in April and one in October, with registration beginning around 8:30am. Oceanside - Usually once a quarter from 10am to 1pm, or so. San Diego - Usually the second Sat. of each month from 9am - noon, but no flights in December.

Price: Free

Ages: 8 - 17 years old.

—ZOOS AND ANIMALS—

BIRCH AQUARIUM

☼

$$$$

(858) 534-FISH (3474) / www.aquarium.ucsd.edu

2300 Expedition Way, La Jolla

Visually exciting statues of leaping, large whales grace the fountain outside the entrance of the Birch Aquarium. There are also picnic tables and a snack stand out here. This outstanding, sizable, aquarium-museum has three main exhibit areas. The aquarium section contains over thirty-three large tanks filled with an incredible variety of creatures found in the Earth's oceans - from monkey face eels to sharks to flashlight fish that glow (or blink on and off) in the dark. Just some of our favorite sea animals showcased here include the almost mesmerizing moon jellies; sunflower starfish; bat rays; very large grouper fish; nurse sharks; odd-looking, longhorn cowfish; the leafy sea dragons; garden eels that look like hoses "standing" upright in the sand; the amazing giant octopus; and the beautiful, but venomous, striped lionfish. I also like some of the other colorful fish at the coral reef displays. This exhibit also posts information, coupled with interactive displays, about the harvesting of coral - the harm that's been done and the help that coral can be medically. The largest tank at Birch has a huge (two-story) kelp forest which makes it easy to view animals that are normally hidden on ocean floors. See divers feed the fish in the forest Tuesdays and Thursdays at 12:30pm, Saturdays at 2pm, and Sundays at 10:30am. (These times may change.) In fact, check the website for all the feeding times at the different exhibit areas.

Outside, the small rocky Tidepool Plaza connects the aquarium and the museum. A wave machine gently creates natural water motion in a simulated tidepool. Kids will see up close (and can gently touch) sea stars, sea urchins, sea cucumbers, and more. Also, take in the magnificent panoramic view of the La Jolla coastline (and the world famous Scripps Institute).

The museum has several fine components. Find out everything you ever wanted to know about seahorses in the incredibly interesting and thoroughly researched Seahorse Exhibit. Did you know that seahorses adapt by changing color to blend in with their environment? See the same type of seahorse in various background settings, and therefore, various colors. Learn about threats to these creatures and how they are dried and ground up to use as medicinal aids. Watch short videos on (seahorse) dating, mating, and giving birth. Note that males give birth - this could make for some very interesting conversation. Look for the tiny baby seahorses in the nursery. And check out the utterly bizarre-looking, weedy and leafy sea dragons - cousins to the seahorse. One rotating exhibit we saw was Whales - Voices in the Sea, where visitors listen to seven types of whales, including humpback, sperm, beaked, gray, and blue whales, and then try to mimic them. (We call this whale karaoke.) Videos showed the elegance of whales in their natural habitat while spotlighting their struggles of survival in an increasingly threatened environment.

Another component of the museum is the rotating oceanographic exhibit with numerous interactive display areas that incorporate touch screens and activities that demonstrate and explain the integral part that oceans play in relation to how the Earth functions. Kids participate in exhibit experiments to learn about various aspects of ocean sciences such as currents, tides, and waves; and how solar heat falls on the ocean unevenly via a long wave tank. The experiments are actually quite fun! My kids also really enjoyed a past exhibit called the Ocean Supermarket, where they used scanners on common household products to see which ingredients came from the ocean. (Did you know that ice cream uses carrageenan [i.e., red seaweed] to make it smooth and creamy?!) Another exhibit is Feeling the Heat: the Climate Challenge which encourages participants to test their knowledge of if everyday items contribute to climate change and other aspects of global warming. Step into the 8-foot Infinity Cube where projections of images of bioluminescence in various stages, plus sounds, surround you. It's kind of cool.

Kids can expend energy at Boundless Energy, an outdoor, educational playground. Power a mechanical fish here with solar energy. Contrast and compare the wind turbine innovations. Ride a teeter-totter. Generate your own electricity to harness solar, wind, and water power.

The back courtyard features a fascinating destination - the shark tank. The large tank is clear so you can easily see all the angles of the many species of shark swimming around. Feeding times are usually at 10:30am on Tuesdays, Thursdays, and Saturdays. There is also a feeding area for humans at the aquarium at the Splash Cafe. The Birch Aquarium has a lot to offer - come "sea" it for yourself! Call about the many special activities, programs, and camps offered through the aquarium including tidepool tours, whale-watching cruises, grunion hunting, snorkeling, sleep overs, and the popular Shark Discovery Days.

Hours: Open daily, 9am - 5pm. Closed New Year's Day, Thanksgiving, and Christmas.

Price: $18.50 for adults; $15.50 for seniors; $15 for college student with ID; $14 for ages 3 - 17; children 2 and under are free. Parking is free for three hours. See MUSEUM MONTH, SAN DIEGO (pg. 700), in the calendar section, for details about half-price admission in February. See info on the Bank of America Museums on Us (pg. xi) free museum days.

Ages: 3 years and up.

BUTTERFLY FARM

(760) 613-5867 / www.butterflyfarms.org $$

3012 Oleander Ave, Vista

This place is small and you won't be here long, but it has butterflies and that's all I need to know. Enter the enclosed Vivarium, or butterfly house, which isn't always lush with vegetation, but has enough to sustain caterpillars/chrysalises that transform into a variety of butterflies such as Cloudless Sulfur, Cabbage Whites, Painted Ladies, Gulf Fritillaries, Anise Swallowtails, and Monarchs. One-hour educational workshops, with a minimum of fifteen people, are offered here, too, that discuss conservation, research and the importance of restoring pollinator habitats. It includes a visit to the vivarium, of course.

Enjoy a picnic lunch and/or purchase some butterfly-attracting plants from the on-site nursery.

Hours: Open daily, 10am - 4pm, but the best months to visit are "one-season" - March - November. Closed on holidays.

Price: The general public is $5 per person; children 2 and under are free. School tours are $8 a person.

Ages: 3 years and up.

CALIFORNIA WOLF CENTER

(619) 234-WOLF (9653) or (760) 765-0030 / www.californiawolfcenter.org $$$$

KQ Ranch Road (off Highway 79), Julian

Who's afraid of the big bad wolf? And why? Clear up many misconceptions about Mexican gray wolves and Alaskan gray wolves at the education and conservation wolf center during a two-hour presentation/tour. First, gather in a room filled with wolf paraphernalia for a twenty-minute video presentation. See and learn about what wolves eat; how they communicate (yes they howl, but not at the moon); the pack's pecking order, starting with an alpha (i.e., dominant) male and female; and their predators (man). Learn the difference between a fox, a coyote, and a wolf (this being the largest of the three) via a touch table with skins, skulls, teeth, and plaster footprints. Also hold and learn about tracking collars that researchers use on wolves.

A highlight is going out to the enclosures to actually see these majestic creatures. There are currently about twenty-one wolves here, but you won't get to see them all as most are kept off the main path. The ones seen on the tours and in the education programs are usually more curious and often come close up to the fence where visitors line up - all the better to see you, my dear. There are no guarantees that the wolves will approach, though, as they are wild animals. Bring your camera. Take a short hike up a hill to see the other wolves who may, or may not, come over to check out the group. Two tours are offered and both include the education presentation and seeing two packs of wolves. The Wolf Pack Tour is a smaller group, a maximum of 15 people, lending a more intimate time with the guide and more time observing the wolves.

The center also offers private tours, school field trips, off-site presentations (wolves "attend" via Skype), and photography tours for ages 18 and up, August through December. Photography tours, for up to two people at a time, are the only way visitors are allowed into an enclosure, animal behavior permitting, although no physical contact is ever allowed. Have a howling good time here!

Hours: Wolf Recovery Today tour is offered Sat. and Sun. at 10am and 2pm. Wolf Pack Tours are offered Mon. at 10am and Fri. at 2pm. Arrive 30 minutes prior to any tour. Latecomers will not be admitted because a truck picks you up from the bottom area of a hill (near the sign that says Kenis/ Christiansen Private Road) for a bumpy ride on a dirt road up and through a gate. Reservations are required. Call to set up a time for group programs during the week.

Price: Wolf Recovery Today tours are $20 for adults; $15 for seniors, military, students, and ages 12 and under. Wolf Pack Tours are $30 for adults; $20 for everyone else.

Ages: 7 years and up.

DEL MAR FAIRGROUNDS - RACETRACK

(858) 755-1141 or (858) 793-5533 / www.dmtc.com $$$
2260 Jimmy Durante Boulevard, at Del Mar Fairgrounds, Del Mar

For unbridled fun, check out horse racing season at the famous Del Mar Fairgrounds. Kids have good horse sense - they aren't here to bet, but to enjoy the races. View the races from the stands or go through a tunnel to the infield area. Most weekends bring a special event such as the One and Only Truly Fabulous Hats Contest on opening day, and family day when the infield is transformed to a fun zone for children with pony rides, face painting, an inflatable jump, obstacle course, and more. Admission is free for children, when accompanied by a parent.

Check out the summertime Camp Del Mar, where adults watch the races while kids, ages 5 to 12, are supervised by counselors to enjoy activities on the grounds such as an inflatable jump, crafts, mini golf, fun tournaments, air hockey, and/or other games and events, plus lunch and snacks. Camp usually runs from noon to 30 min. after the last race. Also inquire about horse shows, rodeos, and polo games, and know that the fairgrounds are host to the county fair, holiday light shows, and other special events.

Hours: The season runs mid-July - early September, with some dates in November and maybe December, Wed. - Sun., 9am - 5pm and some Mon., 9am - 1pm. Post time is usually 2pm, although it's at 4pm on Fri.; and 1pm on Pacific Classic Day. Gates usually open 2 hours before the first post. The track is closed Mon. (except Labor Day Mon.) and Tues.

Price: General admission for adults in the summer is $6 for Stretch Run (west of the finish line); $10 for clubhouse (both east and west areas of the finish line). Admission is free for children 17 and under. Reserved seats for all ages are an additional $5 on Wed. and Thurs., $8 on Fri., $10 on Sat. and Sun. (Seats are less in the fall.). Prices are more expensive on Opening Day and Pacific Classic Day. Camp is $24 per day, per child. Parking is $10.

Ages: 5 years and up.

ECO VIVARIUM

(760) 975-9690 / www.ecovivarium.org $$$
136 S. Juniper Street, Escondido

Who does not want to hold a huge boa constrictor or false water cobra (named Taco)???! Or hug a tegu? Or a bearded dragon, iguana, geckos or other reptiles and some insects? Several, large, glass displays contain those animals, plus tortoises and some really cool bugs from the jungle, in this very small exhibit facility. While a primary function of the Eco Vivarium is education via outreach programs, especially with special needs and at-risk students, as well as birthday parties and other presentations, the hands-on approach with these animal ambassadors (98% of whom are rescues) allows every visitor the opportunity for personal interaction with them. So, when you come to visit you'll not only get to touch and hold many of the friendly critters (what a unique and wonderful opportunity!), but you'll learn their stories and more about their natural environment and habitats from the knowledgeable and dedicated staff who work hard to socialize them. One bearded dragon even helps kids to read - come visit and learn how. Note that there are numerous reptiles housed here, yet there are only about thirty in the displays at any given time; they do rotate.

Classroom programs cover ecology, environmental impacts, threatened and endangered species, exotics in the pet trade/pet responsibility, the food web, humans' role in species survival, and more. A variety of live animals are presented to be handled, too, of course. Classroom programs are up to an hour long and begin at $195.

Hours: Open to the public Wed. - Fri., noon - 5pm; Sat., 10am - 5pm; Sun., 10am - 3:30pm. Closed Mon., Tues. and major holidays.

Price: $10 for adults; $9 for seniors and military; $8 for ages 3 - 17; children 2 and under are free.

Ages: 3 years and up.

FREE FLIGHT

(858) 481-3148 or (858) 755-9351 / www.freeflightbirds.org
2132 Jimmy Durante Boulevard, Del Mar

This permanent little outdoor boarding house is for the birds, literally, and specifically for parrots - about forty-five of them. Some of them are here for behavioral issues and some are rescues for various reasons. There are also birds up for adoption. There are more than thirty perches along the short pathway in this tree-lined and jungle-like "backyard". Look at and even gently touch some of the brilliantly-colored cockatoos, macaws, and other exotic parrots and birds. It's a good place to get some great pictures! Note: Loud squawking of the birds is set off by loud kids who are set off by the loud squawking, etc. Young children might be startled. Also, many of the birds have strong talons which could scare or hurt visitors, so young ones are better off simply looking at, and not handling, the birds. Children under 13 years must be accompanied by a parent. Bring some change to purchase food to feed the birds and fish, as there is also a koi pond here.

Freeflight offers guided tours that explain the different types of birds, their habitats, and educates visitors as to the care of exotic birds, and more. Call to make a reservation. Tip: Visit on sunny days, if possible, as there are more birds brought out then. Note: There is no public restroom here!

Hours: Open Thurs. - Tues., 10am - 4pm; Wed., 10am - 2pm. Closed on rainy days and some holidays.

Price: $7 for adults; $3 for ages 12 and under.

Ages: 3 years and up.

LEELIN LLAMA TREKS

(800) 6WIKIUP (694-5487) or (760) 765-1890 / www.wikiupbnb.com
1645 Whispering Pines Drive, Julian

Looking for an unusual outing? Sign up for a llama trek! Choose from a variety of destinations - to the lake, through the mountains, or through the town of Julian. Each member of your group leads his/her own llama that carries trekkers' lunches and other necessities. Most kids, and adults, aren't used to being around llamas so the intrigue, as well as the scenery, makes the five-mile, four-to-five-hour expeditions unique experiences. The animals are gentle, enjoy being petted, and by the end of the trek, your children will want to take theirs home. They can't. A deli sandwich or salad, chips, cookie, and cold drink are included in your outing. Bring sunscreen and a water bottle. One of the best excursions for kids is the Eagle Mine Trek, which takes about five hours round trip, and includes an almost sixty-minute tour of the gold mine. See EAGLE MINING COMPANY (pg. 574) for details on the mine.

LeeLin Wikiup is a bed and absolutely scrumptious breakfast(!), geared for couples, owned by LeeLin Llama Treks. (The llamas actually live on the grounds here.) Each of the five rooms of the Wikiup, although adjacent to each other, has its own unique, themed decor - Native American, Victorian, Stargazer, or garden, and some have private hot tubs. There is a nice-sized common lounging area with TV, games, and books. An outdoor hot tub, outdoor deck, horseshoe pits, the llamas, and the lovely surroundings complete this inn's offerings.

Hours: Open year round except during inclement weather. Reservations are required. At least two people must sign up for any of the day treks that begin about 9:30am or 10am.

Price: Prices start at $95. The Eagle Mine trek is $95 for adults; $75 for ages 10 and under. Wikiup rates start at two nights for $330 - $430 per couple.

Ages: 7 years and up.

LIONS, TIGERS & BEARS

(619) 659-8078 - rescue facility; (800) 979-3370 - reservations; (619) 445-0997 - White Oak overnight Wild Nights / www.lionstigersandbears.org
24402 Martin Way, Alpine

Oh my! This accredited rescue facility is located on a sprawling, ninety-three-acre ranch, only a portion of which currently is being used. There is room for more animals, but funding is needed. Salvation for the animals and education for the public regarding exotic animal trade and care are the main goals. A ten minute intro movie talks about this and states that there are thousands of more tigers in captivity than in the wild. I didn't know that.

About sixty animals, many which have come from abusive residences, find permanent sanctuary here, including (at least at the moment of this writing) eleven big cats (and they are BIG!) - six majestic African lions (one weighs 500 pounds!), two Bengal tigers, a leopard, a serval, a mountain lion and four bobcats.

The big cat, double-fence enclosures are nicely landscaped with natural rock, trees, water (i.e. pools), grass, and even a hammock or two for catnaps. There is also a larger exercise area for the cats with a run around area and rock pool with a waterfall. The facility is also home to ten black bears, including the famous Meatball, and several ranch animals.

Ninety-minute (or so) tours are offered for visitors to walk around (on uneven ground) to each enclosure with a knowledgeable and passionate keeper who discusses each animal - their history, their personal habits, and more, in an informal manner, which is great for Q and A. Tip: Feed A Wild One experience is offered to visitors 18 years and older. For a few minutes, these guests go in between the first and second fence enclosures, stab a piece of meat, or chicken, with a very long fork and then poke it through the fence holes to feed the cat or bear of their choice. For participants the thrill of being so close to such a powerful animal, and perhaps being roared at, is worth it! After all this, walk the grounds on your own and/or even bring a picnic lunch to enjoy here at tables in the shade in front of the cat enclosures.

Hour-long group tours, for up to thirty students (or other age groups), are encouraged to come for even more of an educational outing. They'll see the big cats and learn facts and rescue stories about each of them, while similarities and differences between domestic and wild animals are pointed out and discussed. There is plenty of time for questions and answers. Book a tour in the morning, if possible, as that's when the cats are most active. Waivers must first be filled out by parents of minors.

Tips: Read over the wish list on the website before a visit and bring one or more of the items needed. Check the website for special events, such as overnight stays at the on-site, elegant, White Oak cottage with all of the amenities; brunches; activities just for kids; photography workshops; Keeper for a Day; and more. Since you're in the area, about ten minutes eastward in Pine Valley are two notable outings: 1) Pine Valley County Park at 28810 Old Hwy 80 - a 17-acre park with oak and pine trees, a seasonal creek, ball fields, tennis courts, shuffleboard, horseshoe pits, and a playground; and 2) Major's Diner at 28870 Old Hwy 80 / (619) 473-9969 - a cute, 50's decor diner, with indoor and patio outdoor seating, offering good food at reasonable prices. It's open Mon. - Fri., 6am to 2pm; Sat. - Sun., 6am - 4pm.

Hours: Open Wed. - Thurs. for a tour at 10:30am; Fri. and Sat. for tours at 10:30am and 1:30pm. You must call first to make a reservation before you visit.

Price: Member-for-a-day (i.e. a tour) is $33 for adults, Wed. - Fri., $38 on Sat.; $16 for ages 12 and under. Annual membership starts at $85 for adults, which includes unlimited visits for the year. Feed A Wild One is $130 and includes general admission. Educational visits for school groups (of 20 or more) or scouts are $13 for students/scouts; $28 for adult chaperons.

Ages: 5 years and up.

LIVING COAST DISCOVERY CENTER

(619) 409-5900 / www.thelivingcoast.org $$$$
1000 Gunpowder Point Drive, Chula Vista

Putting their hands in a pool of sharks is only one of the special things that kids (and adults) are invited to do at the Living Coast Discovery Center, which is located in the Sweetwater Marsh National Wildlife Refuge. You'll start your visit by taking the free trolley into the refuge, as cars are not allowed.

Flanking the entrance are deep-water aquariums with green sea turtles. The medium-sized center is full of interactive exhibits, and plants and animals that correspond to certain environmental zones - the bay, the marsh, and the upland. There are several tanks in the main room containing seahorses, lion fish, piranhas, eels, clown fish, sheephead, crabs, octopus, garibaldi, steelhead trout, and the almost ethereal moon jellies who reside in a glowing blue aquarium. Other live critters that dwell here include snakes, poison frogs, and alligator snapping turtles.

My boys proudly boast that they've touched a shark, and lived! as an adjacent building houses an aquarium with a shallow-water touch tank. It contains leopard and horn sharks, as well as batrays, stingrays, and the odd-looking, shovel-nose guitarfish. Some of these creatures actually come within petting distance. Feeding time is 11am and 1:30pm. There is also a deep water tank for larger sharks and rays that is just for looking at, not touching.

An outside overlook affords an opportunity to observe migrating shore birds such as terns, killdeer, plovers, and more wetlands wildlife. A walk-through bird aviary features snowy egrets, sandpipers, herons, black-necked stilts, and other water birds, as well as some interactive exhibits such as rubbing tables and an oversized clapper rail nest for kids to crawl inside. Other bird enclosures contain non-releasable birds of prey, such as owls, hawks, and some eagles, including a bald eagle, whose feeding time is 2:30pm. A hummingbird and a butterfly garden are also on the grounds.

Short, stroller-friendly trails in front of the Center branch off in several directions leading towards the water, allowing visitors to get closer to the bay to see geese and egrets, or smaller water inhabitants. Look for other wildlife along the trail such as bunnies and lizards.

Feel like a Very Important Person? Take one of the five, twenty-minute, VIP Animal Encounters - $50 each for up to 6 people. We did the one with the sea turtles where we saw and touched sea stars and other tidepool animals, saw rescued animals in holding tanks, and then went into the sea turtle area and got to feed them. It was wonderful to see them up close and learn so much about them! We also did another intriguing VIP experience - feeding the sharks and rays, which felt like they had slimy lips as they took the food from our fingers. I'm looking forward to doing the owl one next. Note: If a particular VIP encounter is not booked on a weekend, walk-in guests, only, can sign up at that time for $10 per person. The Living Coast offers a variety of other on-site special activities, such as guided tours given Wednesday, Saturday and Sunday; make-it take-it crafts ($1) on most weekend afternoons; day camps; family overnights; and educational programs.

Hours: Open daily, 10am - 5pm. Closed Thanksgiving, and Christmas. Trolleys run approximately every fifteen minutes.

Price: $16 for adults; $11 for ages 3 - 12; children 2 and under are free.

Ages: 3 years and up.

OASIS CAMEL DAIRY

(760) 787-0983 / www.cameldairy.com $$$

26757 Old Julian Hwy, Ramona

Do camels spit? Are they mean? Where do they live and why? What do they really store in their humps? Find the answers to these questions and more as you learn about these intriguing animals on Open Farm day. This first part of this time, a "show", consists of sitting outside on bleacher seats listening to Nancy, one of the owners, who is both funny and passionate, as she talk about camels, camel care, etc. She also brings out several camels for show and tell. And there are a few other animals make an appearance, too, like a talking parrot, plus turkeys and farm dogs. After her talk, go visit the eighteen, or so, camels that roam the acreage and you'll get to see them up close and gently stroke them. You might see a baby camel and even watch one being bottle fed. Thought about riding a camel in the Sahara Desert? Closer, less expensive, and not nearly as lengthy, but still a unique opportunity, visitors can take a very short, hand-led camel ride around a ring. The dairy has a few other animals as well, including a donkey, cows, sheep, a bull, a potbellied pig, turtles, and several birds, such as macaws, parrots, kookaburras, turkeys, and an African crowned crane. Don't forget your camera!

Camel milk products are sold here, too, such as lip balm, camel milk chocolate (not made here), and camel milk soap made from the camels milked here. The luxurious soaps come in a variety of scents, including Gold, Frankincense, and Myrrh.

Private group tours are offered whenever you want to make a reservation with a minimum fee of $100 (for up to ten people); $200 for other options and larger groups. Camel rides are available on private group tours for an additional fee. Photo safaris and even hands-on camel clinics are also offered. All of these require reservations.

Hours: Open Farm days are usually held one weekend a month starting at 1pm; gates open at 12:30pm. Call or check the website for specific dates. The dairy is only open during this time.

Price: Open Farm day admission is $12 for adults; $10 for seniors; $8 for ages 4 - 14 and under; children 3 and under are free. Camel rides (must be at least 3 years old) are an additional $12 for ages 15 and up; $7 for ages 3 - 14.

Ages: 3 years and up.

SAN DIEGO HUMANE SOCIETY

(619) 299-7012 - society; (619) 279 - 5939 - camps; (619) 243-3432 - education dept. / www.sdhumane.org $$

5500 Gaines Street, San Diego

Animals and kids have an almost intuitive connection. Via birthday parties, outreach programs, scout tours, and Animal Adventure Camps, this Humane Society offers ways to foster and deepen that relationship. Pet Pals, offered one Friday a month, is a one-hour interactive time of learning and is just doggone fun - $10. Week-long Adventure Camps are generally held over school breaks and in the summertime. At other times, one-hour guided tours are offered for a minimum of five people that are geared for the age group that's visiting. The tour provides information about guidelines in choosing a pet, being responsible, and pet care. Depending on the animals available, sometimes visitors are allowed to pet or hug a cat or dog. Note that there is an on-site cafe offering sandwiches, snacks, and beverages. There are Humane Society facilities in Oceanside and Escondido that hold some of the above-listed programs, too. If you're *feline* like it's a dog-eat-dog world and you want to help animals out in some way, unleash your potential and call the society.

Hours: The center is open daily, 9am - 6pm. Call to schedule a tour or sign up for a program or camp.
Price: Prices vary depending on the program.
Ages: 5 years and up, depending on the program.

SAN DIEGO ZOO

(619) 231-1515 / www.sandiegozoo.org

$$$$$

2920 Zoo Drive, San Diego

The world-famous San Diego Zoo is home to some of the rarest animals in captivity and almost every animal imaginable, at least that's what it seems like. Put your walking shoes on because this huge and fantastic zoo covers a lot of ground! In fact, you'd be hard pressed to try to see all 4,000 animals in one day, at least with young children in tow. The flamingos, just inside the entrance, are a colorful way to start your day. Personal favorites are the orangutans and siamangs in a naturalistic setting behind a huge glass observation window. I could watch these guys for hours and apparently, vice-versa. The monkey trail has an elevated walkway that allows visitors to walk through a tree canopy (just like in the jungle) and about three acres of exotic habitat. Although the monkeys, especially the mandrills with their colorful faces (and red behinds), and gorillas are some of the most fascinating creatures here, there are several other species sharing this section including tigers, hippos (be amazed at how enormous they really are), otters, tapir, several other species of mammals, and lots of birds. Enjoy a walk through aviaries to see brilliantly-colored jungle birds amidst tropical foliage; watch the antics of the bears, especially the sun bears; see koalas in their trees; and take the opportunity to observe kangaroos, buffalo, zebra, exotic okapis, camels, giraffes, African lions and other big cats, meerkats, and other animals in enclosures that simulate their natural habitat.

Experience panda-monium and see the giant pandas amidst the bamboo - what unique-looking animals! See the immense polar bears and enjoy other parts of their exhibit area where visitors can read a huge book about polar bears, pop their heads up through fake ice, and learn about real Arctic ice. Elephant Odyssey features an extensive area for the really big stars - elephants. This 2.5-acre habitat for Asian elephants showcases them like never before with an open-sided food area, plus educational panels on their history and culture, and a place to speak with and see their keepers at work. Don't misssssss the Reptile House which contains enormous snakes - anacondas, pythons, boas, and cobras - plus Gila monsters, Komodo dragons, poison frogs, snake-necked turtles, and many more uncommon-looking creatures.

The Discovery Outpost is a children's area, but adults can visit, too. It is always a highlight with its petting zoo; 4-D theater (additional $6); playground; and insect house with terrariums housing tarantulas, praying mantises, stick insects, scorpions, beetles, and more. This section also features naked mole-rats, spider monkeys, hedgehogs, and alligators. Interactive animal encounters and keeper talks go on throughout the zoo at various times, daily.

The forty-minute, double-decker, narrated bus tour is not only fun and informative, but it's a great way to get a good overview of most of the animals here. You can also use the Kangaroo Express bus, a vehicle that travels around the zoo enabling riders to hop on and off at five locations, as often as desired throughout the day. The Skyfari Aerial Tram ride, which is pretty cool, is another way to view a portion of the zoo as it takes you from one end to another.

There are numerous educational programs/experiences available to the public and for school groups. Programs for the public include the two-hour, Inside Look Tour ($89 + zoo admission) where visitors see behind-the-scenes and learn interesting info about how the animals are taken care of, and Crazy About Cats ($109 + zoo admission), a two-hour tour just about felines. Sleepovers are a great way to see animals at night and during early morning hours when they tend to be more active (the animals, not the kids). During sleepovers, you'll take a bus tour, see live animal presentations, do a craft, sing and have s'mores around a campfire, and, for additional fees, enjoy a buffet dinner and breakfast. Prices start at $90 per camper. Individuals and small groups can sometimes be added on to a larger group. Call (619) 718-3000 for tour dates, reservations, and more information for all the above programs, and more.

Hours: Open daily - most of the year, 9am - 5pm; open in the spring and summer, 9am - 6pm, or 7pm - check the website calendar or call first.
Price: $54 for adults; $44 for ages 3 - 11; children 2 and under are free, which includes unlimited use of the guided bus tour, Kangaroo Express Bus, and skyfari aerial tram. Certain discounts are available through AAA. Parking is free. Admission to the zoo is free during the month of October for ages 3 - 11.
Ages: All

SAN DIEGO ZOO SAFARI PARK

(760) 747-8702 or (619) 231-1515 / www.sdzsafaripark.org   6/$

15500 San Pasqual Valley Road, Escondido

Go on an incredible safari and see the exotic animals that live in the African veldt and Asian plains, without ever leaving Southern California. The 2,000-acre Safari Park (which equals a lot of walking for you!) has tigers, rhinos, lions, elephants, giraffes, lots of birds, a variety of antelope and gazelle, and many more, in atypical zoo enclosures. The animals roam the grasslands freely, in settings that resemble their natural habitats which is why you don't always see them up close. The best way to see quite a few of these animals is via the Africa Tram which is a two-mile, thirty-minute, narrated journey. You ride around the perimeter of (although it seems like through) the African section, stopping for better vantage points and photo ops. I suggest doing the tram tour early in your visit as the lines get longer later in the day.

The ride ends/begins near the Park's pride - the pride of lions, that is, at Lion Camp, which is a terrific place to see lions close up. If it's a hot day, kids can cool off at the small water play area next to the camp. Also in this area is more of Africa, a great starting point for the rest of your wild animal adventure. A paved, circuitous, path winds through some of the thirty acres that comprise this section. The trail leads you past plains that are home to wildebeest and cheetahs, and even a station, open at designated times, where visitors can hand-feed giraffes for an additional fee. Their long, black tongues always elicit a few "eeews" from kids. Cross over a bridge to a small island that has a mock research station and see dart guns and lab equipment. Stop off at Jameson Research Island for stories about animals and some more water play. Walk past and look at warthogs, rhinos, flamingos, and foxes, and into the forestry area to see antelope, the unusual-looking okapi, and a favorite for me - the secretary bird.

I have to admit that I always spend at least a half hour in front of the gorilla enclosure, just watching their interactions and the expressions on their faces. Walk thru a lemur enclosure. Go into the petting zoo. Observe the numerous elephants as they lumber gracefully through their savanna. If you can't fly to Australia, don't worry mate - Walkabout, the walk-through kangaroo exhibit, lets you see these animals up close and personal, as well as wallabies, wombats, echidnas, and more! Further up into the park, look for the tigers often hidden (or sleeping) in their habitat. And at this northernmost end of the park take the trail up (and up!) to look through telescopes on the observation deck of Condor Ridge to see the habitats of dozens of endangered species, including, obviously, California condors. This area also has prairie dogs, roadrunners, ferrets, and big horned sheep, as well as botanical gardens. Actually, the whole park is like a botanical garden, with brilliant and unusual plants and flowers throughout.

There are numerous other attractions at the Safari Park. Watch the interactions and antics of the monkeys, the glares of the gorillas, and the curiosity of the meerkats. Go batty at the bat exhibit where these odd creatures are kept in their home surroundings - a dark cave. The Petting Kraal has small deer and sheep to pet and feed. Check the time for the animal shows presented here. One of our favorites is the funny and fantastic, Frequent Flyers Bird Show - daily at noon and 2pm. Animals Encounters and Keeper Talks are great ways to visually and auditorily learn about select animals. Hand-feeding rainbow-colored lorikeets, who look like small parrots, is a thrill. Bring your camera to capture your child's expression as the birds land on his arms or even his head. Check for feeding times and bring $4 for a cup of food. I was enchanted by the Hidden Jungle offered in spring because the "room" in here is filled with lush green plants and colorful butterflies fluttering all around. Enjoy some down time at the Discovery Station where children can read books, do puzzles, and work on craft projects. Younger visitors can play on the safari-themed jungle gym for free, and/or take a twirl on the sixty-one creature carousel for $6 for unlimited rides. Guests 10 years and older can soar on Flightline, a ⅔ mile long zipline over wild parts of the park. The entire experience, orientation and practice, takes an hour and costs $79 per person, in addition to regular park admission. Walk among the treetops for ninety minutes during the Jungle Ropes Safari with rope bridges, aerial tightropes, platforms to negotiate and more in this high ropes challenge course. The cost is $54 per person (ages 7 and up, only), plus park admission. Get a ringside seat to watching a cheetah accelerate, and then see this powerful animal close-up, no bars between you - $59 per person. Take a hot air balloon ride 400 feet up in the air and overlook the park for an additional fee, as well. Enjoy all your travels through the animal kingdom.

Want to make your day picture perfect? A variety of Caravan Safaris (ages 6 and up) offer several photo opportunities as you feed some of the animals, learn all about them, and go into some of the animal enclosures on an open, flat-bed truck. The cost is $125 for a two-hour caravan specifically for kids and $175 (for ages 8 and up) for 3.5 hours, plus admission cost to the park. Numerous other family, scout, and other group programs are offered including a favorite - Roar and Snore overnight tent-camping safaris. These are for kids as young as 6 years old and include nature hikes, a campfire, food, photo opportunities, close-up encounters with wild (and more mild) beasts, and more! The cost ranges from $140 per person ($30 for ages 2 and younger,) plus park admission, depending on tent size and placement within the park. There is a two person, per tent minimum. Check the website or call (619) 718-3000 for information and a complete schedule of special programs.

Hours: Open daily most of the year, 9am - 5pm; open in the spring and summer, 9am - 6pm, or 7pm - check the website calendar or call first.

Price: Admission, which includes park entrance, the Journey into Africa tour, and a ride on the carousel, is $54 for adults; $44 for ages 3 - 11; children 2 and under are free. Certain discounts are available through AAA. Parking is $15. Admission to the zoo is free during the month of October for ages 3 - 11.

Ages: All

SEA LIFE AQUARIUM

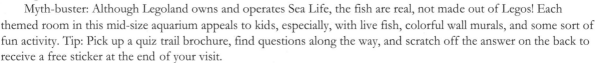

(760) 918-LEGO (5346) / www.visitsealife.com/california

$$$$$

One Legoland Drive, Carlsbad

Myth-buster: Although Legoland owns and operates Sea Life, the fish are real, not made out of Legos! Each themed room in this mid-size aquarium appeals to kids, especially, with live fish, colorful wall murals, and some sort of fun activity. Tip: Pick up a quiz trail brochure, find questions along the way, and scratch off the answer on the back to receive a free sticker at the end of your visit.

Start in the Lake Tahoe room where trout and other fish swim in small brooks and kids can cross a bridge and slide down a short tree trunk slide. In the next rooms are shovelnose guitar fish, rays, octopus, leopard sharks, and bright orange Garibaldi (the California state fish) all in eye-level tanks and enclosures that resemble their native habitats. Note that many of the "kelp" and "coral" in the tanks are not real. Listen to sounds of nature piped in, such as sea gulls and waves breaking, and stop to read the fin facts. Did you know that octopus have three hearts and blue blood? Get sucked into the interactive octopus gardens to really understand how their camouflage and jet propulsion works. Kids can crawl through tunnels, pop their heads up (via a protective bubble) in a fish tank, look for the Lego figures everywhere, learn, and play.

The centerpiece of the aquarium is the Lost City of Atlantis where sharks swim in the thirty-five foot tunnel overhead and in the gigantic viewing tank, along with rays and a large variety of other tropical fish. Seeing a huge statue of King Neptune, the Lego submarine, and Lego divers in the tank is pretty cool, too. Other highlights include the Mayan-themed seahorse room (such variety even within the species!); the realistic-looking Shipwreck room with eels slinking in and out of the undersea vessel; the tank of rays; the discovery touch pool and tide pool where visitors are encouraged to gently stroke sea stars and sea anemones; and the kelp forest. Besides marine life, household products made from kelp are on display here, such as toothpaste, ice cream, and paint. For an other-worldly feel, stand in the center of the Shoaling Ring room as thousands of silvery fish encircle you, swimming around in the almost 360 degree tank.

Take time to watch a short film on marine animals in the theater; jam over to the jellyfish area where over 100 jellyfish are on display; let the crab exhibit grab your attention with its Japanese spider crabs and lobsters; build a coral reef out of Lego bricks in the cafe area; and definitely check out the schedule of feedings (octopus, seahorse, sharks, rays, and sea stars) and activities (divers cleaning tanks while interacting with visitors, and a really funny, interactive puppet show). Look into guided and self-guided educational programs, fields trips, homeschool discount days, youth camps, and scout patch programs, too, at very reasonable prices. There is much to *sea* and do here! Note: This aquarium is towards the entrance of LEGOLAND (pg. 460) and LEGOLAND WATER PARK (pg. 462). Also, if you have a real Lego fanatic, definitely check out the adjacent LEGOLAND HOTEL (pg. 564) and LEGOLAND CASTLE HOTEL (pg. 563).

Hours: Usually open daily, 10am - 5pm; open longer hours on holidays, certain weekends. Summer hours are usually daily, 10am - 8pm.

Price: $22 per person; children 2 and under are free. Save $ and order tickets online. Re-entry during the same day is free. A combo ticket to Sealife and Legoland is $115 for adults; $109 for ages 3 - 12. Parking is $20.

Ages: 1½ - 13 years

SEAL ROCK MARINE MAMMAL RESERVE / CHILDREN'S POOL

850 Coast Boulevard, La Jolla

From a distance, we saw what looked like lots of lumpy rocks on the beach. As we got closer, however, we could see that they were really seals sprawling on the sand and on the nearby rocks. The seals have taken over what used to be known as Children's Pool Beach, so named because the rocks form a breakwater. My boys and I were thrilled that we were almost close enough to touch the seals, although doing so and getting too close is forbidden. (Even seals are protected by harassment laws!) Walk out on the rock jetty for more of a view. A normal family might be here for just a few minutes; we were here for an hour because we were enthralled. Warning: Seals are not sunbathing here constantly, so seeing them is a hit or miss deal, although they are usually on the beach during cooler months, such as November through June; in the water more frequently the warmer months; and often lay on the rocks for the late afternoon sun. Pupping season is usually February through April.

On either side of the reserve, you'll see beaches, large rocks to climb on, and even grassy park areas. A paved sidewalk trail runs along the coastline. See SCRIPPS PARK / LA JOLLA COVE and COASTLINE (pg. 516) for lots more information about this immediate area.

Hours: Open daily, sunrise - sunset.
Price: Free
Ages: All

SEAWORLD

(619) 222-4SEA (4732) / www.seaworld.com

500 Sea World Drive, San Diego

6/$

Submerse yourself into Sea World via a giant wave sculpture that ushers you into the underwater world of animals and activities, starting with Explorer's Reef. This immediate, themed area consists of four touch tanks filled with bamboo sharks and literally thousands of fish.

SeaWorld entertains and educates people of all ages with its wide variety of sea animal exhibits and shows. *Porpoise*ly catch the shows here, such as the dazzling, high-jumping dolphin show. It gets top ratings as they are part of a huge, twenty-five minute aquatic production along with human acrobatic performers who are dressed in fanciful costumes. And don't miss the silly sea lion show, where the animals hilariously interact with trainers - arrive early or you will miss out on some of the pre-show antics. The Pets Rule show is just so darn cute with all the different and funny animal acts. The Mission Bay Theater showcases a variety of special acts such as Madagascar Live! where the costumed characters sing and dance with more human-looking performers inside the theater. The theater can also star Chinese acrobats, magicians, and more.

Orcas, or killer-whales, have always been a staple at SeaWorld so make sure you these magnificent animals at Orca Encounter. This is where a 140-foot long Infinity Screen, that's almost three stories tall, acts as a backdrop with documentary videos of Orcas in the wild showing on it as real orcas jump out of the water, spin around, and splash around showcasing natural behaviors for hunting, playing and living together. The adjacent Ocean Explorer land features four rides, including a Tentacle Twirl swing and kiddie drop tower, plus an educational Submarine Quest track ride where riders play games and score points as they spot ocean critters. For a more electrifying ride, wait in a line that goes thru a massive tank of moray eels to board the Electric Eel roller coaster, a ride with twists and loops and a 154-foot-tall barrel roll. Nearby aquariums feature giant octopus, moray eels and enormous Japanese spider crabs.

At Rocky Point Preserve visitors can actually touch and feed bottlenose dolphins; check for feeding times first so you don't miss out. (The food costs about $4.) These mammals feel rubbery. If you stretch your arms far enough, you can touch bat rays and other marine animals at Forbidden Reef and the California Tide Pool. The penguin exhibit features penguins and the penguins' cousins, the funny-looking puffins who fly through the air and sea. A simulated helicopter ride at Wild Arctic lands you at a remote research station. (Actually, you're still at SeaWorld.) Blasts of Arctic air greet you as you view beluga whales, harbor seals, walruses, and polar bears. A unique attraction is Shark Encounter which culminates in a fifty-seven-foot-long, glass-enclosed, people-mover tube that takes you "through" shark-infested waters(!) Learn about and watch more than sixty endangered sea turtles gracefully glide by the immense underwater viewing windows at Turtle Reef, as well as thousands of tropical fish in this exhibit area.

Journey to Atlantis is a combination roller coaster and water ride that zooms passengers past dolphins as they ride through mist, up the hills, and then plunges them down into mythical waters (that get you actually wet). Another wet activity is the Shipwreck Rapids ride where a nine-passenger raft swirls past several realistic-looking shipwrecks, real sea turtles, through "rapids," and partially (or completely, depending on the season) under a roaring waterfall. Ride a manta, well a Manta roller coaster, a ride that incorporates projection screen images of swimming manta rays to give riders the feeling of being immersed in the water with the mantas, all the while getting gently sprayed with real water. Ride Riptide Rescue, an airboat-like ride that goes around (and around) in a big circle. DeepSEE VR: Orca 360 is a seven-minute virtual reality film/experience like feels like you're in the ocean with Orcas (additional $10). Ride up, up, up and away in the Skytower for a panoramic view. Swing on the Bayside Skyride, a gondola ride over Mission Bay. And don't miss walking around to see the numerous unique fish and other sea creatures in various other aquariums throughout Sea World.

The Sesame Street Bay of Play is two-acres of pure kid delight. It has three rides modeled after Sesame Street characters - Elmo's Flying Fish, Abby's Sea Star Spin (don't get too dizzy!), and Oscar's Rocking Eel mini roller coaster. It also has tubes, slides, ropes, balls, a sandy beach, a moon bounce, an outdoor theater for kid-oriented entertainment, and a large fun water ship for mates to climb aboard and get wet. For those who want (or are allowed) to get wet (more wet?), there are even water fountains to splash in and water tubes to go through. Tip: Bring a towel or change of clothing. Be on the lookout for Sesame Street characters here, too - they love hugs.

If you are planning to be here all day, check out the all-day dining deal for $35.99 for adults and $18.99 for children, at participating restaurants in Sea World. Or, start your visit here having Breakfast with Orcas. The buffet is delicious - bacon, sausage, eggs, oatmeal, toast, muffins, fresh fruit, and more. The best thing, of course, is seeing the killer whales up close by the pool side and watching as a trainer puts them thru some behaviors. The cost, plus park admission, is $26 for ages 10 and up; $16 for ages 3-9; free for ages 2 and under.

SeaWorld also offers a lot and a variety of outstanding educational tours, such as a sleep over "with" sharks or other animals, summer camps, marine science investigation, Shamu Adventurers, and much, much more. What fun! One-hour Dolphin Interaction Program allows visitors, who must be at least 10 years old and 49" tall, to put on a wet suit, wade into waist-high water for about twenty minutes with the dolphins, then touch, feed, and interact with them while learning about their anatomy and personalities. The cost is $215 per person. Interact with penguins and go where guests aren't normally invited on a one-hour tour - $50 for ages 10 and up; $44 for ages 6 - 9. Call or check the website for information on the times, hours, and admission for all the other unique family and field trips. Ask about the monthly school days specials where admission is greatly reduced for students. Special summertime highlights at SeaWorld include fireworks; Sesame Street Parade (weekends only); a laser and light spectacular called Electric Ocean; and an annual favorite - Cirque de la Mer, a sister act to the mesmerizing Cirque Du Soleil, with dazzling costumes, humor, and seemingly impossible feats of strength and acrobatics.

Although no outside food is allowed inside the park, a picnic area is set up just outside. Spending a day (or night) here is a great way for the whole family to "sea" the world!

Hours: The hours really fluctuate. Open daily most of the year, 10am - 5pm, but sometimes until 7:30pm. Open daily in the summer, 9am - 11pm. Check for seasonality.

Price: $89.99 for per person; children 2 and under are free. Prepurchase tickets for a big discount. Definitely check the website before you visit for other specials, such as the Fun Card, where for the price of a single day admission, you get the rest of the calendar year free. Parking is $20 per day.

Ages: All

WHALE WATCHING
See the TRANSPORTATION section.

WILD WONDERS & ZOOFARI FOUNDATION
(760) 630-9230 / www.wildwonders.org $$$$$
5712 Via Montellano, Bonsall

This place is a favorite! About 150 animals consider this almost six-acre animal rescue and wildlife education conservation center home. The mission is to educate the public, especially kids, and rescue injured and non-releasable animals. The one-hour guided tours, given by professional biologists and animal trainers, are informative regarding the animals' stories as to why they are here, descriptions of their personalities, and facts about their species. The numerous different kinds of exotic creatures here aren't readily seen elsewhere, especially this close up and interactive!

The keepers enter most of the enclosures and bring out whatever animals they can to hold and play with so that you are able to touch, feed, and definitely take great photos of or with some of them. You will see binturongs; foxes; alligators (no feeding!); precious-looking kinkajous (what? - look them up); a massive albino Burmese python; a leopard; porcupines (that are really cute!); owls; Arctic foxes; turtles; wallabies; macaws; a serval; tamarins; lynx;

coatimundi; wide-eyed bush babies; hedgehogs; and a myriad of insects and reptiles. I had never seen armadillos run around before coming here, or been able to pet one! The tours are personal, relaxed, and wonderful.

Most of the enclosures aren't large so it's an easy walk to see them all, though sometimes on uneven, slightly hilly ground and up stairs. The enclosures are nicely kept up with shade, mini pools, trees, and whatever else is needed for care for the animals.

Educational programs abound (even those that bring animal ambassadors to your school or location), as do zoology day camps for ages 8 to 13 ($80 per half day, per child); a zookeeper mentor program; a variety of scouting programs; special experiences, like meet and greet a cheetah for $250 for 2 people; and other calendar events.

Hours: Reservations are required to visit the facility.

Price: General tours are $30 for adults; $15 for ages 17 and under, with a minimum of $130 for all tours. (Sign up with friends or check the online calendar to see if you can join another, prescheduled tour!)

Ages: 4 years and up.

SANTA BARBARA COUNTY

Although Chumash Indians were this county's original inhabitants, its name came from a Spanish explorer's party. Seeking shelter in the channel from a severe storm, the fleet was saved on Saint Barbara's feast day. The hub of this multi-faceted county is the compact city of Santa Barbara. The city offers a culturally-rich assortment of things to do and see in a setting that is both elegant and friendly. Visitors are minutes away from the beach or the mountains. The Los Padres National Forest makes up almost half of this county! The hub's spokes, or other cities that complete the county, each have their own distinct "personality." The town of Goleta is home to Santa Barbara's University, as well as miles of coastline. The small town of Lompoc is known for its murals. Solvang is the "Danish Capitol of America." Los Olivos, originally a stagecoach stop, is now a fine arts destination. Santa Ynez boasts of pioneer history. The far flung Santa Maria, with its farming roots, has both a quaint and lively town center, as well as the unique sand dunes.

—AMUSEMENT PARKS—

MUSTANG WATERPARK

(805) 489-8898 / www.mustangwaterpark.com

$$$$$

6800 Lopez Drive, Arroyo Grande

See LOPEZ LAKE RECREATION AREA / MUSTANG WATERPARK (pg. 613) for details on this waterpark and lake recreation area.

—ARTS AND CRAFTS—

ART FROM SCRAP CREATIVE RESUSE STORE and EXPLORE ECOLOGY

(805) 884-0459 / www.exploreecology.org

$$

302 East Cota Street, Santa Barbara

Crafters (and teachers) are absolutely in their element at this store with odds and ends and all sorts of stuff ready to be used for art projects, costumes, school endeavors, etc., and all at great prices. Shop for paper, thread, ribbons, tiles, picture frames, beads, sacks, fabric, mirrors, wire, baby food jars, paint, buttons, and so much more - individually or by bulk. Stock continually changes so you never know exactly what you'll find, but you will find treasures and inspiration.

Art workshops are held here throughout the week, for adults and for kids, plus every Saturday from 10am to 2pm for ages 7 and up. Some have different themes each week and with titles such as Shadow Puppets, Make Music, Miniature Universes, Creative Containers, Exquisite Bugs, and more. Ages 6 and under must be accompanied by an adult.

More than just a store, Art From Scrap leads the way with environmental educational programs, teaching the "new" three R's - reduce, reuse, and recycle. The store is under the umbrella of Explore Ecology, a nonprofit environmental education organization that works with over 30,000 children a year combining art and ecology to "foster creative thinking and connection between people and the environment." They are also associated with the WATERSHED RESOURCE CENTER / EXPLORE ECOLOGY (pg. 635) and hold many classes there, too.

Check the website calendar for the many other environmental programs that Art From Scrap hosts and co-sponsors including worm composting workshops, beach cleanup days, creek testing kits, teacher's workshops, summer camps, and educational field trips with titles such as Natural Resources, Water Quality, School Gardens, etc.

Hours: The store is open Thurs. - Fri., 11am - 6pm; Sat. - Sun., 10am - 4pm. Closed Mon. - Wed., and many holidays.

Price: Free, bring spending money. Sat. workshops are $8 per artist.

Ages: 3 years and up.

—BEACHES—

ARROYO BURRO "HENDRY'S" BEACH PARK

(805) 687-3714 or (805) 681-5650 / www.countyofsb.org

Cliff Drive from Las Positas Rd., Santa Barbara

This lovely stretch of beach has plenty of sand, plus a lagoon that extends into it and bluffs that hang over a portion of it. Highlights include surfing, tidepooling, swimming, fishing, and whale watching, in season. (Bring your binoculars.) Day-use showers, a small park for picnicking, and bbq grills complete the scene.

Hours: Open daily, 8am - sunset.

Price: Free

Ages: All

CARPINTERIA STATE BEACH

(805) 684-2811 or (805) 968-1033 - beach; (800) 444-7275 - camping reservations / www.parks.ca.gov;

$$

www.reserveamerica.com; www.californiasbestbeaches.com

at the south end of Palm Avenue near Carpinteria Ave., Carpinteria

I know that it depends on the season and even the day, and that most kids don't care much about the scenery around a beach, but Carpinteria has a wonderful shoreline as well as a magnificent view from the beach of inland palm trees and the mountains beyond.

Dubbed as the "world's safest beach" because a reef helps protect the shoreline from heavy ocean swells, this beach features very fine sand, sand dunes with vegetation, some volleyball courts, lifeguards during the summer, outdoor showers, reservable covered picnic areas, and large rafts at swimmable distances to climb aboard. The reef to the right of the beach, that circles off from the mouth of Franklin Creek, is great for kayaking or snorkeling. Tip: Kayak and SUP rentals are available at the Boathouse building on Ash Avenue during the summer for $15 an hour for adults; $10 for children 12 and under with a paying adult. Also check Carpinteria Beach Store for rentals or to purchase beach umbrellas, toys, sunscreen etc. Call (805) 566-9482 for more info.

Across from the beach's main parking lot is a small, adjacent Visitor's Center offering an indoor tidepool exhibit, interpretative panels, and programs, such as the Jr. Ranger's Program. One of our favorite parts of the long and wide expanse of Carpinteria State Beach, besides playing in the sand and the water, are the tidepools toward the southern end of the state beach, below San Miguel Campground at Tar Pits Park. A short walk down the stairs and over some tar-covered rocks leads to some wonderful tidepool exploration at low tide. We have found some wonderful shells and some unusual rocks here, too. Guided tidepool walks are offered October through May. Call for more information. At the southernmost end, with very limited parking, is Jellybowl scenic vista, which is a decent place to fish. A fishing license is required. If you feel like a hike or bike ride, keep heading south on the adjacent dirt trail of the CARPINTERIA BLUFFS NATURE PRESERVE AND TRAIL (pg. 608) until you reach the HARBOR SEAL PRESERVE (pg. 647), and then to the end, about five miles round trip.

About 65 of the 216ish family campsites, for up to eight people per site, allow tent camping, no hook-ups; the others are for RVs with full hook-ups. There are also seven group campsites. Some of the sites are definitely better than others. A majority of the RV sites are literally like setting up camp in a parking lot, although each one still has a fire ring and a picnic table. Choice sites are nestled up to the beach and most of the tent camping spots include a grassy area and a sprawling oak tree or greenery of some kind. The camp offers coin-operated showers. Reservations, which are site-specific, are suggested throughout the year and required in the summer and on weekends and holidays. Note: Railroad tracks parallel the campground and though the trains run about 5 times during the day, starting at 7am and ending at 11pm, they don't run during the night.

Freebies adjacent to and outside of the State Beach boundaries include Linden Field, a decent-size open grassy area that also has chin-up and sit-up bars and a few other pieces of exercise equipment; TOMOL INTERPRETATIVE PLAY AREA (pg. 620), a great little park next to Linden Field; and, at the end of Linden Avenue, a beach area with limited free parking in a lot and on the street. There are several cement picnic tables here along with palm trees, volleyball courts, and a good stretch of beach. Since you're in the Carpinteria area, you might want to stop off at the small Robitailles Fine Candies on 900 Linden Avenue. They carry homemade fudge, candies from the 50's (although their stock is fresh), and other goodies. Look up Carpinteria in the Index by City in the back of this book for other area attractions.

Hours: Open daily, 7am - sunset. The Visitor's Center is open Fri. - Sun., 10am - 4pm.

Price: $10 for day-use parking. December - February, camping is $45 - $70 a night, depending if it's tent or full-hook RV, and inland or more toward the beach; March - November, camping is $45 - $80. There is a $8 camping reservation fee.

Ages: All

EAST BEACH   ☼

(805) 564-5433 / www.californiasbestbeaches.com $

E. Cabrillo Boulevard off Castillo, Santa Barbara

Easily one of Santa Barbara's most popular beaches, East Beach stretches from the east, at ANDREE CLARK BIRD REFUGE (pg. 606), to the west, at Stearns Wharf. On the other side of the wharf is the adjacent WEST BEACH (pg. 601).

Miles of white sand; fourteen volleyball courts (come watch a tournament!); a playground; a grassy area; and the Pacific Ocean - what more could a body want?! At low tide, hike along the beach eastward all the way to Butterfly Beach, which is opposite the Four Seasons Hotel. Look up SANTA BARBARA HARBOR / STEARNS WHARF (pg. 635) for more details as to what else is in the immediate vicinity.

Hours: Open daily, sunrise - 10pm.

Price: Free. Parking in beach lots is $2 an hour; $12 max. There is some free street parking.

Ages: All

EL CAPITAN STATE BEACH

(805) 968-1033 - beach; (800) 444-7275 - camping reservations / www.parks.ca.gov $$
El Capitan State Beach Road, off the 101, Goleta

    The stone-lined stretch of beach offers swimming, a few tidepools toward the southern end, dune trails, and camping. The almost private campsites off the road in El Capitan are an interesting combination of camping near the beach, yet surrounded by sycamore and oak trees, giving them a woodsy atmosphere. Note that while the upper campgrounds are nice, they are closer to the freeway and railroad tracks. Showers are available at a nominal additional cost. Other amenities include open fire pits, a seasonal snack bar, and a camp store. A cycling trail connects El Capitan to REFUGIO STATE BEACH (pg. 601), which is three miles further west. Look for the Monarch butterflies that gather here November through January.

Hours: Open daily, 8am to sunset.
 Price: $10 per vehicle for daily use; $9 for seniors. Camping is $45 a night. There is a $8 camping reservation fee.
  Ages: All

GAVIOTA STATE PARK

(805) 968-1033 - park; (800) 444-7275 - camping reservations / www.parks.ca.gov $$
Refugio Beach Road off the 101, Goleta

    Just when you think Santa Barbara beaches and vistas can't get any better, visit Gaviota. This beach, though, is better described as a cove that's fenced in by natural rock walls. A creek from the mountains empties into the ocean, making it ideal for wading and fishing. Spend the night in this lovely countryside at any of the forty-one campsites which come complete with fire pits and picnic tables. No RV hook-ups. The park also has a playground, grocery store, and snack bar.

    Hike inland, on the other side of the road, through the huge park. One trail, across the highway, is called Trespass Road. It's about two-and-a-half miles long and leads to the hot springs in the Los Padres National Forest. Continue on up the trail (and I mean up!), about six miles, round trip, to reach Gaviota Peak.

Hours: Open daily, 7am - sunset.
 Price: $10 per vehicle for day use; $9 for seniors; or $10 to hike and bike. Camping is $45, plus a $8 camping reservation fee. Camping is first come, first served, although reservations are required Memorial Day - Labor Day.
  Ages: All

GOLETA BEACH PARK

(805) 967-1300 - beach; (805) 964-7881 - Beachside Cafe / www.countyofsb.org; www.beachside-barcafe.com
5968 Sandspit Road, Goleta

    Sand, gentle surf, lifeguards, a long pier (bring your own fishing pole), a playground, a horseshoe pit, volleyball courts, picnic tables on the adjacent lawn, barbecue grills, a paved bike trail - this twenty-nine-acre beach park, complete with palm trees, has it all! Bring food for a picnic lunch, or eat at the Beachside Bar and cafe where you can sit and eat at a table while digging your toes into the sand.

Hours: Open daily, 8am - sunset. The cafe is open Sun. - Thurs., 11:30am to 9:30pm; Fri. - Sat., 11:30am to 10pm.
 Price: Free
  Ages: All

JALAMA BEACH

(805) 736-6316 - recorded info; (805) 736-3504 - beach; (805) 736 - 5027 - store & grill / $$
www.countyofsb.org; www.jalamabeachstore.net
9999 Jalama Road, Lompoc

    The word "windy" means full of wind, which is something that Jalama boasts of quite frequently. After the winding, scenic drive, enjoy the view from a cliff-top vantage point, overlooking the crystal clear ocean waters. You'll see kelp beds, kayakers, surfers, windsurfers, a long stretch of classic California shoreline, and campsites. This isolated beach, with its fine sand and a few small sand dunes, offers all of the above, as well as fishing from the surf or rock outcropping; playing horseshoes,,volleyball and basketball; and flying a kite. Bring your own equipment for any activity. Also bring your fishing license, as they are not sold here, but you can purchase bait and tackle onsite.

    Swimming is allowed at the beach, but with waves breaking on the shore and riptides, the surf can be dangerous. There is a small lagoon, and lifeguards are on duty during summer months. Rock hounds will enjoy the rocks that can be found in this area, such as agate and travertine. Also, look for gray whales as they migrate seasonally - January through March, and September through November.

About one hundred campsites, some with RV hookup, are available for reservation and some on a first-come, first-served basis. The few sites directly on the beach are separated by hedges on both sides. Tip: Bring tent pegs because of the wind. The other sites' boundaries aren't as clearly delineated. If you want to camp, but not, rent one of the cabins which can sleep up to six people. Each one has a kitchen and other amenities. Hot showers, a general store, and grill (collectively, the Jalama Beach Store & Grill), are also located here. Known for its Jalama burgers (which cost about $7.50), the beach grill also serves up, for lunch - chicken breast sandwiches ($7.50), bread bowl with chowder ($9.50), and a kid's menu of nuggets, grilled cheese, corn dogs and more for about $5 per. The breakfast menu includes bacon and eggs ($9.95), breakfast burritos ($7.95), and sandwiches ($7.50), pancakes ($5.95) and fruit. Yum!

Hours: The beach is open daily, 6am - sunset. Jalama Beach Store & Grill is open daily, 8am - 4:30pm.

Price: $10 per vehicle for day use; $3 for dogs. Tent camping fees October - March are $30 a night, or $50 for sites on the beach; April - September, $35, $50 for the beach. A $7 reservation fee is also charged. Partial hook-ups are $45 -$50. Cabin rentals are Mon. - Thurs., $190 a night; Fri. - Sun and holidays, $240 a night, plus a $20 reservation fee. Pets are an extra $20 a night.

Ages: 5 years and up.

LEADBETTER BEACH

(805) 564-5433; (805) 568-0064 - cafe / www.californiasbestbeaches.com

Shoreline and Loma Alta drives, Santa Barbara

Located between WEST BEACH (pg. 601) and the adjacent harbor, and under the cliff-top Shoreline Park, this popular beach is noted for swimming because of moderate waves, tidepooling during low tide, beach volleyball courts, a playground, a grassy run-around area, and a picnic area underneath palm trees. A stairway leads from the park down to the beach. When the tide is low, you can walk to the connecting beaches. Note that at the nearby Shoreline Beach cafe you can feast on a battered shrimp taco, grilled seafood burrito or a variety of salads and sandwiches, all while sitting at a table in the sand.

Hours: Open daily, sunrise - 10pm. The cafe is open fall / winter, Mon. - Thurs., 9am - 6:30pm; Fri. - Sun., 8am - 6:30pm. Open daylight savings time, Mon. - Thurs., 9am - 8pm; Fri. - Sun., 8am - 9pm.

Price: Free. Parking in beach lot is $2 an hour; $12 max. There is some free street parking.

Ages: All

REFUGIO STATE BEACH

(805) 968-1033 - beach; (800) 444-7275 - camping reservations / www.parks.ca.gov; www.californiasbestbeaches.com

10 Refugio Beach Road, Goleta

The beach offers swimming under the watchful eyes of lifeguards during the summer (watch out for rocks on the shore), some tidepools, a basketball court, a playground, picnic tables, barbecue pits on the beach, a grocery store, a grassy area, a lagoon/marsh inlet, a few palm trees for ambiance, and a beach wheelchair. There are over sixty camp sites nearly on the beach (no RV hook-ups), so be lulled to sleep by the sound of waves. However, you might be startled awake by the sound of the not-too-distant freeway traffic or the very nearby trains as they thunder by. If you're in the mood for pedaling, head east for about three miles on the bike trail that leads to EL CAPITAN STATE BEACH (pg. 600). Take a guided kayak tour, led by a lifeguard, offered from Memorial Day weekend through August and paddle along the coast, seeing and learning.

Hours: Open daily, 8am - sunset.

Price: $10 for day use fee. Camping is $35 - $55 a night. Camping reservations are required. There is an $8 camping reservation fee.

Ages: All

WEST BEACH

(805) 564-5418 or (805) 564-5523 / www.santabarbaraca.gov; www.californiasbestbeaches.com

W. Cabrillo Boulevard by Castillo Street, Santa Barbara

EAST BEACH, STEARNS WHARF, WEST BEACH, and LEADBETTER BEACH are all along one strip of land. (Each of these beaches has their own entry.) They are broken up by different names and by different attractions in between beaches. Eleven acres of sandy beach includes some volleyball courts; swimming in the relatively gentle waves; palm trees waving in the wind; the BIKE TRAIL: CABRILLO BEACHWAY (BIKEWAY) (pg. 642) on the beach's perimeter; watercraft, both large and small, sailing in and out of the harbor; launching your own kayak; and a playground. Look up SANTA BARBARA HARBOR / STEARNS WHARF (pg. 635) for details as to what else to do in this immediate area.

Hours: Open daily, sunrise - 10pm.
Price: Free. Parking in beach lot is $2 an hour; $12 max. There is some free street parking.
Ages: All

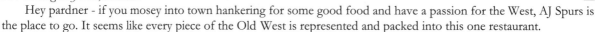

—EDIBLE ADVENTURES—

AJ SPURS

(805) 686-1655 / www.ajspurs.com $$$$$
350 E. Highway 246, Buellton

Hey pardner - if you mosey into town hankering for some good food and have a passion for the West, AJ Spurs is the place to go. It seems like every piece of the Old West is represented and packed into this one restaurant.

Outside, on top of the wooden building, are a few parked stagecoaches. One is also in front, on ground level. Cactus, life-size cowboy cutouts, a small waterfall, a mill wheel, jar lanterns, wooden porch swings with ends made from wagon wheels, antlers, and scenic western murals decorate the outside of this log cabin-style eatery.

Inside, the theme continues. Past the small coin fountain in the lobby, the wood walls and ceilings showcase more murals, mounted animals heads (both deer and buffalo), saddles, stirrups, cowboy hats, dangling horse bits, canteens, branding irons, bearskins, steer skulls, and stuffed ducks - you get the picture. There are also a few taxidermied grizzly bears lurking around corners in ferocious poses.

A smattering of options from the bill of fare includes eight-ounce top sirloin ($25.95); a full rack of ribs ($31.99); bbq chicken ($24.99); burger ($17.99); shrimp scampi ($31.50); lobster tail (market price, about $51); Cajun chicken tortellini ($29.50); and filet mignon ($30.50). All meals come with vaquero soup, tequila beans, salad, spuds, garlic bread, and a root beer float. Little pardners, ages 10 and under, can order a meal for $10.99, when an adult meal is ordered. Their choices include popcorn shrimp, chicken tenders, chicken Alfredo, BBQ chicken, hamburger, or ribs. A clean plate earns a trip to the treasure chest. (This applies just to the kids - not the adults.)

Hours: Open Sun. - Thurs., 5pm - 9pm; Fri. - Sat., 4pm - 9:30pm.
Price: Menu prices are listed above.
Ages: 3 years and up.

COLD SPRING TAVERN

(805) 967-0066 / www.coldspringtavern.com $$$$
5995 Stagecoach Road, Santa Barbara

Imagine dusty, hungry, and parched travelers arriving over 130 years ago at this stagecoach stop. Not much has changed since then.

Seemingly in the middle of nowhere, and surrounded only by woods and a seasonal stream, is a cluster of buildings with an enchantingly rustic tavern as the centerpiece. The log cabin eatery has several small dining rooms, each with wood-beam ceilings, animals' heads mounted on the walls, and other decor that consists of old tools, jugs, and other artifacts from bygone days. The small main room has a fireplace and a bar. Outside are a few tables under shady oak trees, as well as some rough-hewn log benches.

Modern-day folk enjoy this rest stop, too, for the ambiance as well as the food. Breakfast (served on the weekends only) - omelettes ($10.75); N.Y. steak with eggs ($12.95); homemade whole wheat French toast ($9.50); blueberry pancakes ($9.25); and more. Lunch - wild game chili ($8.50); buffalo burger ($12.50); venison sandwich ($13.50); French dip ($10.75); Cobb salad ($10.75); baby back ribs ($13); etc. Dinner (which all include an array of fresh breads; soup or salad or chili; vegetables; and potato or rice) - sauteed duck breast ($27.50); New Zealand rack of lamb ($33); sauteed medallions of rabbit ($25); New York steak ($26); and center cut pork chop ($26). Don't miss out on the homemade desserts such as Granny Smith apple cobbler and cheesecake - just like grandma used to make. Note that there is usually live music on the weekends and that weekends, in general, are very crowded. Reservations are highly recommended. Tip: Drive just around the bend to get a good view of the arch bridge.

Hours: Open for breakfast, Sat. and Sun., 8am - 11am. Open for lunch daily, 11am - 3pm. Open for dinner nightly, 5pm - 9pm, or 10pm. Closed Christmas.
Price: See above for menu prices.
Ages: 5 years and up.

FARMER'S MARKETS (Santa Barbara County)

See the entry for FARMER'S MARKETS (Los Angeles County) (pg. 21) for details.

KLONDIKE PIZZA

(805) 348-3667 / www.klondikepizza.com

2059 S. Broadway Street, Santa Maria

Alaskan pizza? It seems to work at Klondike. The family pizzeria is decorated with memorabilia from our 49th state on the walls and on the ceiling. The adornments include a grizzly bear, elk head, Alaskan crabs, a red fox, small totem poles, advertisements about Alaska, skis, sleds, baleen from whales, and more. The sawdust on the floor and the fact that peanuts are given to hungry diners with the understanding that peanut shells are to be tossed on the ground, add to the fun atmosphere. Kids will love ordering (and eating) Road Kill pizza (i.e., all meat), or perhaps trying a pizza topped with reindeer sausage. There are numerous "normal" pizza selections ($19.99 for an extra large pizza with cheese, $27.99 for chicken cordon bleu), as well as cheeseburgers ($5.99), chicken entrees ($7.99 for an Hawaiian chicken salad) and sandwiches ($7.29 for a sub sandwich; $6.29 for Alaskan reindeer sandwich). Tuesday night is usually all-you-can-eat. Of course, what good would a place be without arcade games?! There are numerous here.

Hours: Open Sun. - Thurs., 11am - 9pm; Fri. - Sat., 11am - 10pm.

Price: Menu prices are listed above.

Ages: All

PADARO BEACH GRILL

(805) 566-9800 / www.padarobeachgrill.com

3765 Santa Claus Lane, Carpinteria

There is very little seating inside this restaurant because why would you want to sit inside? The enclosed outside area is one, big, delightful, mostly unshaded, grassy space spotted with plenty of wooden picnic tables (some have umbrellas) and some palm trees. While there isn't direct access to the beach, the beach is brought to you via a large sandy zone with buckets, shovels, and other toys. Just like a picnic (but better because you don't have to prepare and lug all the food), you'll be outdoors enjoying a meal while the kids run around on the grass and play in the sand. There is also a pretty little pond here.

Food choices include appetizers of calamari ($9.95) or the Trio of French fries, sweet potato fries and onion rings with bbq sauce and ranch - so healthy! ($6.50); sandwiches or burgers (about $7.50), fish and chips ($11.25), Cobb salad ($9.75) and more. Kid's choices include a burger, chicken tenders or quesadilla for $5.95 each. Top off your meal with a chocolate fudge or caramel latte shake ($4.75 each). Enjoy the food; enjoy the scenery. Tip: Before or after your meal, pull over on the side of Santa Claus lane and watch the trains go by.

Hours: Open Sun. - Thurs., 10:30am - 7:30pm; Fri., 10:30am - 8pm; Sat., 11am - 8pm.

Price: Menu prices listed above.

Ages: All

ROCK AND ROLL DINER

(805) 473-2040 / www.rockandrolldiner.com

1300 Railroad Street, Oceano

Come on, baby - let's rock & roll! Two, long, renovated railcars serve as the dining areas for this authentic 50's-themed restaurant serving American and Greek food. Twist and shout (albeit quietly) to the music on the table jukeboxes. Munch on appetizers such as fried zucchini ($6.95); jalapeno poppers ($8.50); or bacon cheese fries ($8.50). Choose from a variety of "real" foods such as a chicken fajita salad ($10.75); cheeseburger ($9.29); French dip ($9.50); meatloaf ($12.95); beef ribs ($16.95); shrimp scampi ($18.95); spaghetti ($10.95); tacos asada ($11.75); or Greek entries, like gyros ($10.95); falafel ($10.95) and moussaka ($15.95). Save room for a shake. There's a whole other menu for breakfast, which is served until 2pm.

Kid's meals range from $5.50 to $10.50 and include choices of burger, spaghetti, chicken fingers, or corn dogs. Most meals come with fries. Drinks are extra. Note: I do know this diner isn't really in Santa Barbara county, but if you are visiting the RANCHO GUADALUPE-NIPOMO DUNES PRESERVE / OSO FLACO LAKE NATURAL AREA / OCEANO DUNES STATE VEHICULAR RECREATION AREA / DUNES CENTER (pg. 616) or going out to THE GREAT AMERICAN MELODRAMA & VAUDEVILLE (pg. 639), this is a fun place to grab a bite to eat.

Hours: Open daily, 8am - 8:30pm.

Price: Menu prices are listed above.

Ages: All

ROCKET FIZZ SODA POPS AND CANDY SHOP (Santa Barbara County)

(805) 568-0099 / www.rocketfizz.com $

1021 State St., Santa Barbara

    See ROCKET FIZZ SODA POPS AND CANDY SHOP (Los Angeles County) (pg. 26) for details on this shop with an incredible array of unusual sodas, candy and more.

  Price: Technically, free.

  Ages: 3 years and up.

WOODY'S BODACIOUS BARBECUE

(805) 967-3775 / www.woodysbbq.com $$$$

5112 Hollister Avenue, Goleta

    Wowser! Woody's is a quirky, rustic mix of the Old West and everything else, plus the kitchen sink. The lobby, for lack of a better word, contains an outhouse (just for atmosphere) and an old washtub to wash your hands. Place your order at the counter and go sit at any one of the old wooden benches and tables, covered in red-and-white checkered tablecloths, located in several small rooms where shutters and wood-paneled walls are "decorated" with pots, pans, skis, a toilet, stuffed fish, a lantern, surfboards, and lots of antlers, plus numerous license plates, traffic signs, neon signs, and more stuff. (Look at the ceiling, too.) Most of the rooms also contain a T.V., usually showing rodeos or other sporting events. A few arcade games are scattered throughout. Outdoor seating is available, too.

    Bodacious is an appropriate word to describe the savory ribs (pork, beef, and bison) and homemade barbecue sauce that has made Woody's famous. Menu options include burgers ($9.95 to $12.45); all-you-can eat salad bar ($8.95); grilled chicken breast sandwich ($11.95); tri tip dinner ($17.95); Southern style pork ribs ($14.95); or prime rib ($19.95 for a roadhouse cut). Portions are large, tasty, and usually come with their special, seasoned fries. Also try the nuclear waste buffalo wings if you *really* like hot food ($9.45). The kid's menu offers a hot dog or burger for $5.95, ribs for $10.95, or chicken strips for $7.95. These meals come with fries, a drink, and a toy. Woody's became an instant favorite with my family.

  Hours: Open daily, 11am - 9pm. Closed 4th of July, Thanksgiving, Christmas Eve and Christmas Day.

  Price: See above menu prices.

  Ages: All

—FAMILY PAY AND PLAY—

ADVENTURE CLIMBING CENTER at UNIVERSITY OF CALIFORNIA, SANTA BARBARA

(805) 893-3737 or (805) 893-3738 / www.ucsb.edu $$$$

Ocean Road, Recreation Building #516, University of California Santa Barbara, Isla Vista

    This recreation building on the university campus is open to the public mostly during the summer; call for other times. At certain times, kids may use the two pools, one of the basketball courts, and the rock climbing facility.

    The glass-enclosed, indoor rock climbing area has three main sections with walls up to thirty feet tall, over twenty top ropes, a belay edge, six auto-belay stations, three crack features, and a dedicated bouldering section, where a harness is not needed. To climb the walls, so to speak, bring your own belayer, become one by taking a lesson, use the auto belay, or use their staff at certain times offered on Belay Days. Ages 17 and under must have a parent-signed waiver for all activities. If you are interested in doing some team building (or birthday parties), ask about their Adventure Programs Ropes Course, available for groups (usually of 15 or more), that includes games, the course (most of which is almost twenty feet in the air), a rope bridge, and a short zipline. The cost is $375 for up to 15 people. If you are wondering what to do with your active little darlings during the summer, sign them up for rock climbing summer camp.

  Hours: The Rec Center, which contains the rock gym, is open during the academic year for adults, Mon. - Thurs., 11:30am - 10:30pm; Fri. - Sat., 11:30am - 8:30pm; Sun., 11:30am - 9:30pm. It is open mid-June - Labor Day, Mon. - Thurs., 11:30am - 9:30pm; Fri. - Sun., 11:30am - 8:30pm. Closed July 4th and 5th. Note that kids are invited to climb on weekends, only, during school months from 10am - 6pm, but daily in the summer.

  Price: $15 for an adult day pass; $10 for ages 13 - 17; $8 for ages 12 and under. Rentals are shoes, $5; harness, $5; $8 for both. Parking is about $3 an hour; $5 for two hours.

  Ages: 5 years and up.

BOOMERS! - Santa Maria

(805) 928-4942 / www.boomersparks.com
2250 N. Preisker Lane, Santa Maria

At this family playland try for a hole-in-one at either one of two **miniature golf** courses ($10 for adults; ages 5 and under are free). Both feature fun obstacles and scale buildings, such as a colorful gingerbread house, a windmill, and a castle. Bump and splash each other in **bumper boats** ($9; passengers are $2 - drivers must be at least 44" tall. Big kids, who must be at least 58" tall, can race in go-karts ($10; passengers are $2), while younger kids, 40" to 58", can zoom around in their own **lil' thunder road** ($8). Climb the thirty-two-foot **rock wall** ($9 for two climbs). Take a swing at the **batting cages**. Play over 125 video and sport games at the arcade. A snack bar here offers nachos, pizza, and drinks. Note that Boomers is across the way from PREISKER PARK (pg. 616).

Hours: Open most of the year, Mon.- Thurs., 11am - 8pm; Fri., 11am - 11pm; Sat., 10am - 11pm; Sun., 10am - 8pm. Open longer summer and school holidays. Call first as hours fluctuate. Some attractions close during inclement weather.

Price: Prices listed above or buy an all day, all play pass starting at $44.99.

Ages: 4 years and up.

ROCKIN' JUMP (Santa Barbara County)

(805) 266-7080 / santamaria.rockinjump.com
142 Town Center East, Suite G-58 in the Santa Maria Town Center, Santa Maria

This location has most of the attractions listed in the ROCKIN' JUMP (Los Angeles County) (pg. 37) entry except the hurricane simulator and rock wall. It does, however, have a Vertigo Climbing Tower which is like a rock wall, but climbing ropes, instead, and a Junior Jump Zone for smaller kids to experience the same sort of trampolining fun as the bigger kids with a main jump arena, foam pit, climbing wall and more.

Hours: Open Mon. - Fri., 10am - 2pm for Junior Jumpers, only; open 3pm - 8pm for open jump. Also open Fri., 8pm - 10pm for Neon Jump. Open Sat., 10am - 8pm for open jump; 8pm - 10pm for Rockin Sat.; Sun., 11am - 7pm for open jump.

Price: $12 for 60 min. of jump time; $16 for 90 min., etc. $7 per hour for Junior Jumpers. $18 per person for Neon and Rockin' Sat.

Ages: 18 months and older, depending on the time and day.

SANTA BARBARA ROCK GYM

(805) 770-3225 / www.sbrockgym.com
322 State Street, Santa Barbara

This place really rocks! The mid-size (8,500 square foot), airy room offers top roping, and bouldering in a cave, and beyond. Gaining in popularity, rock climbing and bouldering give participants a workout physically and mentally as it sharpens one's decision-making processes while literally stretching one physically to reach and be flexible. What's great, too, is that rock climbing is something that can be relished both by those who've never done it before and by skilled climbers. Enjoy climb time on your own or sign up for one of the many classes offered, such as Family Introduction to Climbing, after-school programs for almost all ages, kids climbing club, camps, and more. A signed wavier must be filled out. The Rock Gym location is really nice, on a level just above the main street, and the facility is equally pleasant - it even has a small lounge area inside and patio area outside. Tip: Parks down the street at REI.

Hours: Open Mon. - Fri., noon - 10pm; Sat. - Sun., 10am - 8pm.

Price: $17 for an adult day pass; $15 for students and ages 14 and under. $35 for 4 climbs with an instructor, which includes rental harness and auto belay orientation. Rentals are $6 for shoes, $6 for harness, $2 belay device, $3 for chalk bag, or $12 for everything.

Ages: 5 years and up.

—GREAT OUTDOORS—

ALICE KECK PARK MEMORIAL GARDENS

(805) 564-5418 or (805) 963-0611 / www.santabarbaraca.gov
1500 Santa Barbara Street, Santa Barbara

This small, 4.6-acre, botanical garden park located in a residential neighborhood, is astoundingly beautiful. Lush grassy expanses are interspersed and bordered by a rich variety of trees, plants, and flowers. The mix includes palm trees, Chinese flame trees, coastal live oaks, Ficus, pink clover blossoms, wisteria, trumpet vines, bougainvillea, camellias, morning glories, roses, Spanish bluebells, and so much more.

A hard-packed dirt path meanders throughout the park and winds around the centerpiece pond. The pond teems with life - blooming lily pads, koi, turtles, ducks, and dragonflies. A few speakers are located around this area that, with the press of a button, quietly tell the history of the park and describe some of the plant life. A rock-lined stream gurgles its way around a portion of the park. Look for and test the sensory garden; plants with particular smells and feels. Check out the butterfly garden that attracts a variety of the beautiful winged insect. Note that KID'S WORLD / ALAMEDA PARK (pg. 611) is just across the street.

Hours: Open daily, sunrise - 10pm.
Price: Free
Ages: All

ANDREE CLARK BIRD REFUGE

(805) 564-5418 / www.santabarbaraca.gov/gov/depts/parksrec/parks/features
1400 E. Cabrillo Boulevard, Santa Barbara

This forty-acre, artificial, fresh-water lake and marsh pond attracts native and migratory birds that come here to rest and nest. Bring binoculars and utilize the observation platforms located on the north side of the lake. Don't forget to read the educational panels along the way. A paved pathway encircles the lagoon and is very popular with parents with kids in strollers as well as bicyclists, joggers, and skaters. Take the flat pathway from here, which is part of the BIKE TRAIL: CABRILLO BEACHWAY (BIKEWAY) (pg. 642), the whole three miles to EAST BEACH (pg. 599). Combine an outing here with a visit to the adjacent SANTA BARBARA ZOO (pg. 649), where you can see more exotic birds, and other animals.

Hours: Open daily, sunrise - 10pm.
Price: Free
Ages: All

ARROYO HONDO PRESERVE

(805) 567-1115 or (805) 966-4520 / www.sblandtrust.org
4 miles W. of Refugio State Beach off Hwy. 101, Gaviota

782 acres of wide open spaces are kept in their natural condition, with the exception of a few added hiking trails. This canyon, surrounded by mountains, sage, shaded streams, oak trees, sycamore trees, yuccas, views of the coastline, and meadows is breathtakingly beautiful. Bring your own water bottles. Picnic tables and portable restrooms are on site.

Hours: Open to the public the first and third full weekends of the month; free, guided nature hikes are held on these days too, at 10am. It is also open every Mon. and Wed., for free, for school and community groups. Advance reservations are required for everyone.
Price: Free for individuals and school groups.
Ages: 4 years and up.

BEATTIE PARK

(805) 875-8100 or (805) 736-1261 / www.cityoflompoc.com
East Olive Avenue and Fifth Street, Lompoc

Located at the southeast corner of town, this fifty-acre park, which is a little tired looking, offers not only a great view of the city, but kid-interesting amenities, as well. Enjoy the basketball courts, sunken soccer/football field, a playground, horseshoe pits, a walking trails, a disc golf course and a picnic pavilion with grills. A small "urban forest" also offers a popular winding dirt fitness trail.

Hours: Open daily, sunrise - sunset.
Price: Free
Ages: All

CACHUMA LAKE RECREATION AREA

(805) 686-5054 or 5055 - general recreation area; (805) 693-0691 - Nature Center; (805) 568-2460 - all camping reservations; (805) 686-5050 (Mon. - Fri.), (805) 686-5055 (Sat. - Sun.) - nature cruise; (805) 688-4040 - boat rentals / www.countyofsb.org; www.clnaturecenter.org; www.rockymountainrec.com
225 Chumash Highway (154), Santa Barbara

Situated in the mountain footholds and only twenty minutes from both Solvang and Santa Barbara city, this fully-equipped recreation area offers a smorgasbord of activities including boating, fishing (including bow fishing), hiking, camping, and relaxation. The park also has a nature center, two swimming pools that are open in the summer, and nice playgrounds with twisty slides, rock climbing walls, and metal apparatus to climb on. A relatively large (for a campground) general store carries all the necessary accouterments and plenty of just-for-the-fun-of-it items. Other lake amenities include a coin laundry, showers, and a gas station.

Man-made Lake Cachuma is seven miles long with forty-two miles of shoreline. Its marina is open year-round and offers boat rentals such as outboards, rowboats, kayaks, and patio deck boats, as well as launch facilities, a bait and tackle shop. Drop a line off a pier, shoreline, or boat to catch bass, bluegill, perch, catfish, and trout. Ask about the annual fishing derbies. No swimming in the lake allowed.

Other outstanding lake features are the two-hour narrated nature cruises onboard a pontoon. On the Eagle Cruise tour, given November through February, be on the lookout for migratory bald eagles, Canada geese, teals, and loons. On the Wildlife Cruise, given March through October, the on-board naturalist points out the water fowl such as osprey, great blue herons, plovers, hawks, and mallards, and even the hovering turkey vultures. Tip: Bring binoculars! You'll learn to identify the various birds by their wingspan, nests, and their habits. (We learned that turkey vultures projectile vomit as a defense mechanism.) As the boat maneuvers close to shore look for mule deer, wild turkeys, and the elusive bobcats. The naturalist guide informs listeners of the surrounding, diverse plant life along the shoreline, and in the inaccessible interior land. Both tours are casual in the sense that questions are welcome. The tours are interesting and educational. Tip: Arrive at least a half hour early or you may miss the boat, literally.

The mostly hands-on, surprisingly good-sized Neal Taylor Nature Center has several small rooms branching off from its central room. That room contains a please-touch table and shelves of labeled rocks, fossils, feathers, furs, and a few stuffed animals, including a black bear. Other exhibits include a display of arrowheads, Chumash grind stones, and discovery drawers filled with games and activities. Another room features mounted birds - a great horned owl, an eagle, a snow goose, and more. Compare your wing to other birds against a labeled bird outline on the wall. A display case holds nests and eggs. Look out the two-way mirror and (without scaring them away) observe the numerous species of birds snacking at the outside bird feeders. A plant room showcases indigenous plants and cones, and a tree slab. (Count its rings.) The adjacent room has taxidermied animals such as coyote, mule deer, gray fox, raccoon, and mountain lion. Touch an animal fur and guess what kind of animal it is. (Lift the panel for the answer.) Other exhibits in the center include a light up board to match true statements with pictures of animals; skulls and jawbones of various animals; rocks with geological fact sheets; and stone mortar and pestle to try. The center hosts fishing workshops and educational school field trips throughout the year, including the Junior Ranger program; free, guided nature walks every Saturday; a trout derby in April; and a live animal program in May.

There are five short hiking trails within the park. The Sweetwater Trail, an extended 2.5-mile one-way hike, starts here and winds its way between campgrounds to the Bradbury Dam Overlook. Tequepis Trail, directly across the road from the lake, is an eight-mile hike to the Santa Ynez Mountains ridge line. There is no direct access to this trail from the recreation area and a parking permit is required.

Campers can choose from over 520 sites, many with RV hook-ups available. Some sites have trees, most have grass, and numerous have a lake view. Several yurts are on the grounds, too. Yurts, which sleep three to six people, are like canvas-covered cabins. They are insulated, have bunk beds with mattresses, a locking door, inside lighting and heating, and a small table with chairs - so it's not quite camping, but still in the great outdoors. There are also a few one and two-bedroom cabins, with kitchenettes and bathrooms, that boast a front-row lake view.

Hours: Most activities are open year round. Day use hours for the general park are 6am - sunset, so it's open until 8pm or 8:30pm in the summer. The Nature Center is open Wed. - Sat., 10am - 4pm; Sun., 10am - 2pm; closed Mon. and Tues. Eagle Cruises are offered November - February, Fri. and Sat. at 10am and 2pm; Sun. at 10am. Wildlife Cruises are offered March - October, Fri. at 3pm; Sat. at 10am and 3pm; Sun. at 10am. The swimming pools are open mid- June - end of August, daily, noon - 2:30pm and 3pm - 5:30pm; daily Labor Day weekend; and end of August - September, Sat. only - same hours.

Price: Day use entrance is $10 per automobile; $3 for dogs. The Nature Center is free, after paying the park entrance fee. Camping starts at $25 (tent - off season) - $50 (with full hook-ups - in season,). There is also a $8 camping fee. Yurts are $75 (sleeps 3 to 5) off season - $120 (sleeps 5 to 6) peak season. Cabins are $125 (weekday - off season) - $175 (weekend - in season). There is also a $20 reservation fee for yurts and cabins. The swimming pools are $3 per person for each two+ hour session. Cruises are $15 for adults; $10 for ages 5 - 12; children 4 and under are not allowed; $5 for school groups. Boat rentals are $10 an hour for single kayak and $12 for a double; $12 an hour for a paddle boat; $35 for a two-hour rental for a four-passenger motorboat; and $90 for two hours on patio deck boat that accommodates up to 10 passengers.

Ages: All

CARPINTERIA BLUFFS NATURE PRESERVE AND TRAIL

(805) 684-5405 / www.carpinteria.ca.us
at the south end of Bailard Avenue, Carpinteria

This bluffs' nature preserve is 53 acres of open space with stunning front views of the ocean, coastline, and Channel Islands, and Santa Ynez mountains behind.

The trail runs from about 4th Street, at CARPINTERIA STATE BEACH (pg. 598), to just south of Bailard Avenue for a total of about five miles, round trip. Much of the trail is hard-packed dirt, while some parts are sandier and some parts are unimproved, so you might have to look for the path. It follows the coastline (and parallels, then crosses, the railroad tracks) mostly along the top of the bluffs, with an ocean view at almost every step. There is some beach access along the way via stairs. You'll also pass by the HARBOR SEAL PRESERVE (pg. 647) so look down to see the seals, as well as whales (as they migrate seasonally), dolphins, and more.

At the eastern end of the preserve is Viola Fields park with athletic fields for baseball/softball and soccer, plus kite flying (and a restroom!).
Hours: Open daily, sunrise to sunset.
 Price: Free
  Ages: 5 years and up.

CARPINTERIA CREEK PARK

(805) 684-5405 / www.carpinteria.ca.us
5775 Carpinteria Avenue, Carpinteria

This small (one-acre) park not only has a creek running adjacent to it (hence the name), but unique play structures of two climbing boulders. One is a large, sphere-shaped rock with deliberate cracks and footholds and the other is a taller, thinner rock (more real-looking) with more finger and foot holds - both are easy to climb up and jump down on to a cushy landing. Five picnic tables, grassy space bordered by lovely plants, including some large trees, interpretive signs, and a short paved pathway that runs throughout complete this fun stop off. It is also adjacent to a bike path. There are no bbq or restrooms.
Hours: Open daily, sunrise - sunset.
 Price: Free
  Ages: 4 - 10 years

CARPINTERIA SALT MARSH NATURE PARK

(805) 684-5405 / www.sblandtrust.org; www.carpinteria.com/points_of_interest
Sandyland Road and Ash Avenue, Carpinteria

Appearances can be deceiving. This 230-acre salt marsh preserve is not just a boring, swampy wasteland, as it might appear at first glance, but a thriving, ecological community for a variety of plant and animal species, all bordered by houses, streets, ocean, and train tracks. That said, kids will not find it a thrill a minute, but it is intriguing and educational. Over half of the marsh is a preserve, open only for research, while the other half comprises the nature "park", with several acres open to the public for ready access to walk and view.

You can enjoy the several overlooks and stroll the graveled and boardwalk-style trails that meander along the marsh amid lots of plants, reading its twenty interpretive signs on your own, or, one of the best ways to really experience it - join a docent-led tour offered on Saturdays at 10am, May through November. Look for the birds that consider the reserve home - herons, egrets, brown pelicans, osprey, and numerous other shore birds. Many birds also stop here during the annual migrations. Numerous plants, fish (including leopard sharks which feed at the mouth of the estuary in the summer), and other sea creatures also reside here. Remember, that CARPINTERIA STATE BEACH (pg. 598) is just a few steps away!
Hours: Open daily, sunrise - sunset.
 Price: Free
  Ages: 7 years and up.

CHASE PALM PARK

(805) 564-5418 / www.santabarbaraca.gov
323 E. Cabrillo Boulevard at Garden Street, Santa Barbara

This imaginative park runs parallel to the main street of Cabrillo Boulevard, across the street from EAST BEACH (pg. 599) and SANTA BARBARA HARBOR / STEARNS WHARF (pg. 635). The east end of the park holds the treasure of a shipwreck playground complete with sand; big cement octopus tentacles; large climbing structures; small bridges; slides; tubes to crawl through; and a few rocks to climb on. One area also has kid-size, adobe-style walls and doors to play hide and seek, and a tepee-like building. Just beyond the playground is a grassy area with gently rolling hills and a stage for outdoor concerts and events. Check out the family concerts given in the summer. A snack bar here sells hot dogs, churros, popsicles, and other necessary food items in the summer.

Stroll along the cement and hard-packed dirt pathway as it winds the length of the park, over bridges and through pretty garden landscape, around a scenic pond with a few ducks, along with cement picnic tables and wooden benches scattered throughout to reach the west end of the park where there is a fountain and some park benches.

Hours: Open daily, sunrise - sunset.
Price: Free. There is some free street parking, or park at the beach lot for $2 an hour; $12 max.
Ages: 9 months to 14 years.

CHUMASH PAINTED CAVE

(805) 733-3713 or (805) 968-1033 / www.parks.ca.gov
Painted Cave Road, Santa Barbara

Almost exactly two miles up a very narrow, sometimes one-lane, winding, woodland-laced road with hairpin turns, is your destination - the Painted Cave. (Be on the lookout for the brown sign that says "park" on the left.) Climb up a few boulders to peer through gratings into the cave. Its walls are covered with still-vivid paintings drawn by Chumash Indians hundreds of years ago. Yes, it's a rather precarious drive for just a few moments of sight-seeing, but to actually view such paintings can be exciting.

A trail, if one can call it that, leads up the boulder-covered hill. Be sure-footed to indulge in this short hike. We also found adventure on the opposite side of the road. A rock-lined dry creek bed (I assume the creek is seasonal!) and the surrounding woods provided my boys with a good deal of entertainment (and made the drive more justifiable).

Hours: Open daily, sunrise - sunset.
Price: Free
Ages: 8 years and up.

COAL OIL POINT RESERVE

$$$

(805) 893-5092 / coaloilpoint.ucnrs.org
Slough Road, adjacent to the UCSB campus, Isla Vista

This 158-acre reserve is a rich combination of undisturbed coastal dunes and estuarine habitats. The tidal lagoon area is flooded seasonally and then dries out in the summer to form salt flats and small hypersaline ponds and channels. Thousand of migratory birds, including (and most importantly), the endangered Snowy Plover, rest and nest here. A three+-mile, looping trail goes around the perimeter of the reserve, with eighteen interpretative placards along the way. One trail, the Pond Trail, shortcuts through it. The adjacent university offers the only way to see this place, via a guided tour.

Note that just around the "corner," on West Campus Beach by the Del Playa entrance, is one of best spots for year-round tidepooling. Peak under small boulders to observe the teeming marine life. Have no *reserve*ations about coming here for an educational and fun day!

Hours: Tours are given the 1st Sat. at 10am - with advanced reservations, only.
Price: $10 per person. Free parking is on the street outside the campus, or pay $3 for on-campus parking.
Ages: 6 years and up.

ELINGS PARK

(805) 569-5611 - park; (805) 698-5442 - tennis courts / www.elingspark.org
1298 Las Positas Rd, Santa Barbara

Elings Park has two distinct components to it. North Park is games-oriented recreational fun with a BMX course, three softball/baseball fields and two soccer fields, and adjacent Las Positas Tennis Courts, plus a playground, several picnic areas, a pavilion and park office. There are nine miles of multi-use trails. South Park has a hiking only (no bikes) dirt trail that traverses the hillside around plants up to a beautiful viewpoint of the ocean and beyond. The plateau is a paragliding and hand gliding training hill. It's fun to sit on the bench up here and just watch. If you want to do more than just watch, contact the park office to find out what companies are using the hill and take to the skies yourself. Or, continue taking the windy trail back down the other side of the hill for more of a workout and more beautiful scenery.

Other fun things to do here include radio-controlled car racing - races take place the 2nd and 4th Saturdays every month at 9:30am. Come participate, or watch. The track is open during park hours; $5 for the day. Become a member of Santa Barbara Radio Control Modelers (SBRCM) to be allowed to fly your RC plane here. Contact www.sbrcm.org

for more info.

Hours: Open daily, sunrise - sunset.
Price: Free. Weekday parking is free; weekends are $5. Tennis is $8 a day.
Ages: 3 years and up.

FIGUEROA MOUNTAIN

(805) 925-9538 - U.S. Forest Service; (805) 968-6640 - Los Padres National Forest Headquarters; (805) 688-6144 - Solvang Visitors Bureau / www.fs.usda.gov

Figueroa Mountain Road/Happy Canyon Road, Solvang

This over twenty miles of winding road goes through some of the most gorgeous scenery in all of Santa Barbara County. We drove a good portion of it and stopped at numerous spots along the way, sometimes at marked trails, and sometimes just where the countryside beckoned us. This mountain area, with canyons, waterfalls, chaparral, trees, and more, has over fifteen hiking trails and numerous unmarked "trails". The scenery changes drastically depending on the season. In the spring, the slopes are ablaze with wild flowers, including California poppies, shooting stars, and blue lupines. Indian summers bring fewer people and unmatched beauty. Be forewarned - the road is oftentimes closed during the rainy season. Snow can sometimes fall during the winter months. Contact the forest service for maps and more information. Fishing is available year-round at Davy Brown Creek, below the Davy Brown campground, and in Manzana Creek from March to mid-May, when it's stocked with trout. Check out Figueroa Campground, which has about thirty sites and is the only one with piped in water, or one of the other campgrounds to spend more time in this beautiful area.

Hours: Trails are open daily, sunrise - sunset. The picnic sites are open until 10pm.
Price: Most parking areas require the $5 Adventure Pass to be posted on your windshield.
Ages: 4 years and up.

FLETCHER PARK

(805) 925-0951 / www.cityofsantamaria.org

2200 S. College Drive, Santa Maria

This is a lovely, three-acre corner park with some fun features. An enclosed, portable-looking skatepark sports a variety of ramps, plus rails, a hubba ledge, a half pipe, boxes and plenty of skate room. Next to this is a half basketball court and then a favorite thing - climbing rocks. These three large, fake boulders are mostly flat on the top and of varying sizes, shapes and configurations. They have finger grips, cracks, and foot holds crafted into them and suggestions for how to climb them most effectively and how to switch up a route. Take the bridge across the drainage ditch to a small playground that has a tire swing, monkey bars, slides, and climbing elements surrounded by some grassy space, a small hill, and a covered picnic area with a bbq. An asphalt pathway goes between the houses and back along the ditch for a ways. Across the street is a sunken field for soccer games.

Hours: Open daily, sunrise - sunset.
Price: Free
Ages: All

HANS CHRISTIAN ANDERSEN PARK

(805) 688-PLAY (7529) / www.cityofsolvang.com

633 Chalk Hill Road, Solvang

Drive through the castle-like turrets (with cool wooden doors) into a delightful, back-to-nature park which has something for everyone. We especially enjoyed the numerous, huge, gnarled oak trees for shade and to climb on, and the seasonal creek. One picnic area has picnic tables and small barbecue pits. Another picnic area has huge charcoal pits, a nice grass area, horseshoe pits (bring your own horseshoes), and a bridge over the creek. The 1.3-mile round-trip dirt trail is great for hikers and horseback riders.

An enclosed, really nice-sized, cement skate park is towards the front of the park. It has several bowls and ramps, rails, steps, a pyramid and other street features. There are two playgrounds; one is tiny and the other, larger one has several slides, swings, a rock climbing wall, other climbing apparatus, and an activity board. Toward the back of the park are four tennis courts and more climbing trees. After a hard day of shopping in Solvang, give your family a storybook ending by coming to play at the park.

Hours: Open daily, 8am - sunset.
Price: Free
Ages: All

JIM MAY PARK

(805) 925-0951 / www.cityofsantamaria.org
809 Stanford Drive, Santa Maria

The outstanding feature of this park is its medium-size lake, surrounded by homes. A short pier/observation deck allows you to walk out a bit and see the wildlife. I saw a lot of coots. (And I don't mean old coots; I mean birds.) A paved, bike path encircles the lake while another path branches off, paralleling the riverbed. A small playground has some grassy areas with trees behind it. Get more physical by using the exercise stations staggered along the street.

Hours: Open daily, sunrise - sunset.
Price: Free
Ages: 2 - 15 years.

KID'S WORLD / ALAMEDA PARK

(805) 564-5418 / www.santabarbaraca.gov
1400 Santa Barbara Street, Santa Barbara

Partially designed by kids, and totally designed for them, this part of the park is a favorite - a truly awesome Kid's World. A large, enclosed, multi-level, wooden play fort, with cupolas on top and sawdust on the floor, is the main feature and is packed with imaginative "extras." It has stairways, slides, tube bridges, maze-like crawl spaces (made for kid-size bodies!), a zip line, climbing apparatus, a rope bridge, speaking tubes, and more. In the center of the fort are benches made so that parents can chat with each other while keeping an eye on the kids. A toddler area has swings and a large tic-tac-toe board.

The fort is under a sprawling shade tree, with big roots above ground. Plenty of picnic tables are right outside the fort perimeter, as are a sizable cement beached whale and shark, and more swings.

The rest of the park is pretty and restful, composed of lots of grassy areas and more shade trees, plus a few cement pathways. Look up ALICE KECK PARK MEMORIAL GARDENS (pg. 605), as it is just across the street.

Hours: Open daily, sunrise - 10pm.
Price: Free
Ages: 1 to 12 years.

LAKE LOS CARNEROS PARK

(805) 961-7500 / www.cityofgoleta.org
304 N. Los Carneros Road at Calle Real, Goleta

This large (140 acre) park/nature reserve, just beyond the STOW HOUSE / RANCHO LA PATERA (pg. 634) and SOUTH COAST RAILROAD MUSEUM (pg. 633), is pretty much in its natural state. Depending on the season, you'll find the park to be a green oasis of plants, mostly shrubbery, surrounding a lake, or very dry grass fields with a smaller lake. The ducks and a myriad of birds seem to be plentiful either way. The hard-packed dirt hiking trails branch off in different directions, with the one cutting almost through the center of the park and around the lake being a short, easy walk for most ages. The zig-zagging wooden bridge add a special element to the park. Look up STOW GROVE PARK (pg. 620), a neighboring park just north of Los Carneros.

Hours: Open daily, 8am - sunset.
Price: Free
Ages: All

LA PURISIMA MISSION STATE HISTORIC PARK

(805) 733-3713 / www.lapurisimamission.org
2295 Purisima Road, Lompoc

Situated on just a portion of the almost 2,000 acres of undeveloped parkland, this eleventh mission in the California chain was first founded in 1787. It is one of the most authentically-restored missions as the adobe bricks, structures, mission furniture, and decor have been replicated using tools, materials, and construction methods similar to the originals. Even the types of plants in the garden and representative livestock in the corrals harken back to that era.

You're invited to peer into and/or walk through the numerous buildings sprawled over this section of rural land, and to read the informational signs. We began our self-guided tour with the visitors' center. Just beyond this building is a shady picnic grove with California black walnut trees, coastal live oaks, a seasonal creek, and picnic tables. There old building near here once served as an infirmary and still contains rows of beds. Tip: Make sure to look up under the outside rafters at the birds and their mud nests.

The Tule village has three roomy huts made from tule reed. The blacksmith shop displays anvils, tools, and bellows, along with living quarters that has a bed and kitchen. A beehive oven plus kitchen, gourds, a granary, grinding mill stone, storeroom, and pottery shop are some of the components of the next series of rooms. The adjacent long building has a wine cellar; bedrooms; a large living and dining area; guest bedrooms (notice the pre-box-spring ropes across the bed frames); simply furnished padres' quarters; a tanning room (not used for humans to suntan, but to cure animal hides) with several hides; a leather shop; wooden horses with saddles; and a nave with vestments behind glass. Further rooms and items of interest include the mission bell; a Mexican ox yoke; bricks to touch; a large seventeenth-century, hand-written choir book made of sheepskin parchment; a weaving room with looms and spinning wheels; a candle room with strings of hanging candles waiting to be dipped; and military sleeping quarters where weapons hang on the walls, over the heads of beds.

Walk through the long main church with old paintings, outside to the cemetery and on to the huge tallow vats on the "back" side of the mission. The central courtyard is composed of beautiful gardens, a fountain, the lavanderia cistern (used for washing clothes and for bathing), and a corral. Long-horn cattle, horses, four-horn sheep, turkeys, geese, and burros dwell here.

Walking along the dusty paths between buildings gives present-time visitors a real sense of the past, as do the Mission Life Days which are held March through September, one Saturday of the month from 11am to 2pm. These special days feature costumed docents who recreate padres, soldiers, Indians, and other residents from the mission's heyday. Demonstrations can include wool spinning, brick making, candlemaking, and blacksmithing.

One hour guided tours for individuals are offered daily at 1pm (except during Living History Days or special events). Age-appropriate guided tours for groups of school-age children and for adults are offered throughout the year, for a minimum of ten people. Ask about the special evening candlelight tours and other events such as Village Days, Purisima's People Day, El Pastor, Mountain Men, Founding Day, and Sheep Shearing Day. The latter is a one-day event in April where you can see big, fluffy sheep sheared down to look like little naked things, plus learn how wool was processed and used at the mission.

Another pleasure of La Purisima is the miles and miles of hiking, biking, and equestrian trails that crisscross throughout the back country. The terrain varies from rolling hills to canyons to a pond. Trails range from the short climb of the Trail to the Landmark Cross, which does have a cross at the end of the path; to the 2.7 miles of Roadrunner Road, which is a service road forming a loop near the mission; to the miles of trails extending into the heart of the park's chaparral. Be on the lookout for all sorts of animals, especially the numerous birds that use this route for their migration. Pack your own water and/or bring a picnic lunch to enjoy on the mission grounds.

Hours: Open daily, 9am - 5pm. The buildings close at 4:30pm. The visitor center is open September - June, Tues. - Sun. and holiday Mon., 10am - 4pm. It is open July and August, Mon. 11am - 3pm; Tues. - Sun., 10am- 4pm. Everything is closed New Year's Day, Thanksgiving, and Christmas.

Price: Free to the mission. Parking is $6 per vehicle; $5 for seniors.

Ages: 5 years and up.

LOMPOC AQUATIC CENTER / COLLEGE PARK (skate park)

(805) 875-8100 or (805) 736-1261- park; (805) 875-2700 - aquatic center / www.cityoflompoc.com !/$$

207 W. College Avenue, Lompoc

This small park's central focus is a 10,000 square-foot skate park. It has ramps and bowls and all the "extras" that make a skate park fun and challenging. Skaters - wear protective safety gear. The surrounding park has shade trees, an open grassy area, a good-sized playground, and picnic tables and BBQs.

The park is next to a state-of-the-art, indoors, aquatic center with glass and aluminum framing and retractable roof panels (i.e. skylights) so it feels like the outdoors. The center has a competition, a therapeutic, and a lap/recreation pool, plus two long and winding water slides and a colorful aquatic play structure. The structure, which has zero depth entry, has enclosed mini slides, steps, water-squirting elements, and space to splash around. There is also a picnic area outside.

Hours: The park is open daily, sunrise - sunset. The aquatics center is open daily for lap swim. For recreational swim (and this includes the water play area), it is open most of the year, Sat. - Sun., 1pm - 3pm. It's open in the summer, usually daily, 1pm - 3pm, plus Tues. and Thurs. from 7pm - 9pm. The pool is closed New Years Eve, Thanksgiving and Christmas week.

Price: The park is free. The aquatics center is $4.50 for adults; $4 for seniors and ages 13 - 17; $3.50 for ages 2 - 12.

Ages: 7 years and up.

LOOKOUT COUNTY PARK

(805) 568-2461 or (805) 568-2465 / www.countyofsb.org

2297 Finney Road, Summerland

If you're on the lookout for some fun, this bluff-top park offers an incredible panoramic view of the ocean and shoreline. Kids are most interested in the small playground on rubber-type flooring with its slides, swings, toddler swings, a mini (mini!) zip-line, short "rock" climbing wall, sand pit, and adjacent volleyball court. There are also a few picnic tables, barbecue pits, horseshoe pit, a strip of grass, shade trees, and an asphalt pathway leading down to the long stretch of beach below. The beach is popular for both swimming and bodysurfing.

Hours: Open daily, 8am - sunset

Price: Free

Ages: All

LOPEZ LAKE RECREATION AREA and MUSTANG WATERPARK

(805) 489-1006 - marina and store; (805) 781-5930 or (805) 788-2381 - recreation area/camping; (805) 489-8898 - Mustang Waterpark / www.slocountyparks.com; www.mustangwaterpark.com; www.lopezlakemarina.com; www.vistalagoadventurepark.com

6800 Lopez Drive, Arroyo Grande

Well off the beaten path and snuggled into the surrounding mountains, the 4,600-acre, beautiful, year-round, get-away Lopez Lake is worth the drive from nearby Santa Barbara County. Fishing is a popular activity with rainbow trout, bass, crappie (not crappy, necessarily), and catfish available for catching in their seasons. Fish from the twenty-two miles of lake shoreline or from a boat. The marina boasts a boat launch, tackle shop, restaurant, and convenience store. Kayak rentals are $15 for a single for two hours, $25 for a double. Canoes are $30 for two hours. Stand Up Paddle boards are $15 for two hours. Pedal boats are $30 for two hours. Three-person wave runners are $90 for an hour, plus a gas charge. Motorized fishing boats are $75 for two hours. Ten-passenger, double-decker patio boats are $115 for two hours. There are also pontoon boats, ski boats, cabin boats and more available, too. Two-hour nature boat cruises of the lake are offered one weekend day a month at 9am for $6 for adults; $3 for ages 17 and under, plus the $10 park entrance fee. Explore the lakefront and surrounding property via mountain bike ($15 an hour) or pedal-powered kart ($17 an hour for kids' kart, $25 for 8 years and up). Hike on the several short, easy trails, or on the few more moderate ones, and be on the lookout for wildlife including deer, wild turkeys, and lots of birds. Or, just enjoy the grassy areas, the vast amount of mature oak trees, and the scattered picnic tables.

Summertime fun includes swimming at the Vista Lago swim area, complete with a beach. For the slightly more adventuresome, the adjacent small Mustang Waterpark offers two, long (600 feet), curvy, water slides that wind through the hillsides, ending in a splash pool. An inner tube ride zips you down one side of a thirty-eight-foot half pipe, back up the other side and back down - backwards. Younger kids, ages 9 and under, are not left out of the water fun as there are two wading pools for them (called pony pools) with mini slides and waterfall trees (that look more like giant mushrooms) embedded in perimeter boulders. A snack bar and lockers are also on the premises - no outside food is allowed in.

For s'more fun, stay at any of the over 350 campsites, from primitive camping to full hook-ups. Most of the sites have a picnic table, a grassy spot, and a huge oak tree at least nearby. Hot shower facilities are at several campgrounds. Look at specific sites online. To avoid some of the noise and for a campsite with a view of the lake, try Conejo or Buck campgrounds.

Hours: The marina is open most of the year, Mon. - Thurs., 8am - 5:30pm; Fri. 8am - 6:30pm; Sat., 7:30am - 6:30pm; Sun., 7:30am - 5:30pm. The recreation area is open daily, 6am - 8pm. The lake is open daily, 6am - dusk. Boat rentals are available daily, 7:30am - 5pm; open later in the summer. Mustang Waterpark is usually open late March - Labor Day daily, 10:30am - 5pm.

Price: Parking at Lopez Lake is $10. Camping is $23 (primitive, off peak) - $40 (full hook-up, peak), plus a $9 reservation fee. $3.50 per pet. Admission for Mustang Waterpark is $21 for 48" and taller; $18 for 47" and under; $13 for seniors; $15 for 42" - 47" (may ride all slides and go double with adult); $12 for 41" and under (restricted to kiddie slides only). Admission after 3pm is $4 off.

Ages: All

LOS ALAMOS COUNTY PARK and UNION HOTEL

(805) 934-6211 / www.countyofsb.org/parks

500 Drum Canyon Road, Los Alamos

Snug up against the hills of Drum Canyon, this lovely fifty-one-acre park is a refreshing place to visit and seemingly far removed from city life. Three group picnic areas encourage families to gather together for a day, or at least a meal. Each "site" has plenty of picnic tables and a huge barbecue grill - big enough to roast a pig!

Plentiful old oak trees spread their mighty (and shady) branches, beckoning kids to climb on them. A large grass area offers run around space. A seasonal creek runs through parts of the park. Horseshoe pits (bring your own shoes), a playground with slides and swings, a ball field, two sand volleyball courts, and hills to hike up and around make this an ideal park as there is something for everyone.

Note: Since you're out this way, and even passed it on the way in, stop off at the historic, wooden 1880 Union Hotel on 362 Bell St. It was rebuilt in the early 1900's and is truly great for photo ops - both outside and inside. Decorated with a feel of that era, there are richly wallpapered rooms, lamps, and wood accents in the upstairs hotel rooms and the downstairs rooms of the gorgeous lobby and the lounge. The Saloon Bar has ornate wood paneling on the walls and ceilings, plus rustic decor of stuffed animal heads. Grab a meal in the Saloon from a limited menu of quesadillas ($12); veggie spring rolls ($9); chicken and jalapeno poppers ($9); bbq sliders on a pretzel bun ($12); burgers ($13); tri tip sandwich ($15); and mac and cheese ($9). Call (805) 344-2744 for more info. There are also several antique shops on Bell St.

Hours: The park is open daily, 8am - sunset. Eat at the Union Hotel Mon., Wed. - Thurs., 4pm - 11pm; Fri. - Sun., 11am - 11pm. Closed. Tues.

Price: Free

Ages: All

LOTUSLAND

(805) 969-9990 / www.lotusland.org

695 Ashley Road, Montecito

$$$$$

Plant it and they will come. This thirty-seven-acre estate boasts a botanical garden of dreams. The main pathway branches off into various themed sections, each one focused on a particular grouping or type of plant in a breathtakingly-beautiful setting. A two-hour walking tour takes visitors through it all.

Begin at the visitor's center, which has oddly bent cactus in the patio courtyard, as well as a small mosaic tile fountain, tile benches, and a garden shop. Enter the Australian Garden, where the plants are native to Australia. The intriguing and serene Japanese Garden features a pond with lily pads and koi that is surrounded by native trees and plants, and a wisteria arbor. The Epiphyllum Garden pathway leads visitors past shady oak trees and eucalyptus tree trunks that are decorated with blooming orchid cacti and other plants. A rock-lined streambed meanders throughout this area. The Cycad (i.e., cone bearing) Garden offers a small pond with lily pads and a little waterfall, all enhanced by encircling palm plants. Feeling blue? The plants in the Blue Garden have silver and blue-gray foliage. The Water Garden was the original swimming pool, but the only thing floating in here now are the numerous Indian lotus plants. Side ponds hold other species of lotus and water lilies.

Cacti, bromeliads, succulents, and aloes all have their own area to call home. The aloe area also has a kidney-shaped pool with a cascading fountain made of giant clam shells. The parterre (i.e., formal planting beds) is divided into two sections by hedges: One side has a rose garden and star-shaped fountain, while the other has an intricate pebble mosaic and fanciful Neptune fountain. The Fern Garden flourishes with giant ferns hanging in baskets from trees, as well as with tree ferns and other species. The garden is bordered by another pool, a sandy "beach" with giant clam shells, and a stone wall lined with succulents. The colorful Butterfly Garden attracts garden-friendly insects, including butterflies. Look for Monarchs, or butterfly wannabes (i.e., caterpillars).

The orchard grows citrus, such as oranges, lemons and limes, as well as deciduous trees - plums, peaches, apples, persimmons, and more. Rows of olive trees, also produced here, end abruptly at a wall fountain with a figure of a mythological horse/sea monster. Last, but not least, is the Topiary Garden which has a twenty-five-foot (in diameter) working clock as its centerpiece. I think it's a bit hard to tell the time this way. The garden also features something particularly fun for kids - a zoo of topiary plants growing in shapes of a camel, gorilla, giraffe, seal, and other animals. Advanced reservation are required for this exotic plant tour as it is located in a residential neighborhood and the maximum number for a group is ten.

Hours: Open mid-February - mid-November, Wed. - Sat. for tours at 10am and 1:30pm. Ask about Family Tours, which is the only time children 9 years may visit.

Price: $48 for adults; $24 ages 3 - 17; children 2 and under are free.

Ages: 10 years and up, except for Family Tours.

MANNING PARK

(805) 969-0201 or (805) 568-2461 / www.countyofsb.org

449 San Ysidro Road, Montecito

There are two different facets to this park. To the west side of San Ysidro Road is a multi-level park that still feels like the estate it once was. This lush little park, with portions that could be classified as botanic gardens, has a green stretch of grass that is dotted with pine and other trees, lots of birds, a few scattered picnic tables and barbecue pits, and a really nice-looking youth center building. Just up the stairs and ramp is a small playground and a few covered picnic sites. There is a tennis court on the south side of this park. No admission is charged.

On the east side of the street is a more typical park, which is accessible by walking across the street, or driving to the other parking lot via Santa Rosa Lane. This medium-size park has a ball field that doubles as a field of grass, plus a volleyball court, a playground, large barbecue pits, and a creek that runs along one side. This park is subject to group reservations.

Hours: Open daily, 8am - sunset.
Price: Free
Ages: All

MINAMI PARK

(805) 925-0951 / www.cityofsantamaria.org
600 West Enos, Santa Maria

This sprawling park has everyone-appeal. There are wide, wide, wide open grass areas and trees interspersed throughout; hard-packed dirt pathways; two sand volleyball courts; softball fields; several lighted tennis courts; bocce ball; a basketball court; and a nice playground. The multi-level playground features long and twisty slides, bridges, short rock climbing walls, metal apparatus to play on and climb, and swings, all in a wood chip base. The community center has a multi-purpose room. Just across the street is a long sunken field for soccer, or other sports.

Hours: Open daily sunrise - sunset.
Price: Free
Ages: All

MORETON BAY FIG TREE

(805) 564-5418 / www.santabarbaraca.gov
Chapala and Montecito streets, Santa Barbara

This is not an end destination, but it is an interesting, natural wonder to stop off, see and take a photo. This fig tree, originally a seedling brought over from Australia in 1876, now has a top that spans 160 feet - it's absolutely huge!!! Its roots cover half a city block. The coolest fact for kids? It's listed in the Guinness Book of World Records. Note that there is a vintage train car near it as the Amtrak station is adjacent.

Hours: Open daily, sunrise to sunset.
Price: Free
Ages: All

NOJOQUI FALLS

(805) 568-2461 / www.countyofsb.org/parks
3200 Alisal Road, Solvang

Driving the tree-lined road leading to Nojoqui Falls is like a drive in the country. The first part of the park has group picnic areas with both large and small barbecue pits, a small playground, a sand volleyball court, a large grassy area, and lots of trees.

One reason for this beautiful park's popularity is the ten-minute, or so, hike to the limestone cliff waterfall. Located toward the back of the park, walk the dirt-packed, stroller-friendly trail that meanders along a seasonal creek, past boulders, and over bridges to the seasonal 100-foot waterfall. (In the summer and fall, it can become a tricklefall.) The surrounding scenery is admirable in any season.

Hours: Open daily, 8am - sunset.
Price: Free
Ages: All

OAK PARK

(805) 564-5418 / www.santabarbaraca.gov; www.santabarbaraparks.com
300 W. Alamar Street, Santa Barbara

Bordered by a street and a creek (or rocky creek bed during the dry season) this lovely park has numerous old, sprawling oak trees - great for climbing and great for picnicking under. Picnic tables are scattered throughout, with one large picnic area that has a fire pit covered with grates big enough to roast a pig. One of the play areas has a large sandbox and a tire swing, plus a few slides, and critters on big springs for kids to ride and rock back and forth on - all in a wood-chip base. The other playground is for slightly older kids with a swing set, taller slides, monkey bars and rings, and bridges that connect various climbing apparatus, all in a sand base. A very shallow (eighteen-inch) wading pool is open May through September. Other amenities include two tennis courts and horseshoe pits.

Hours: Open daily, sunrise - one-half hour after sunset.
Price: Free
Ages: All

PREISKER PARK

(805) 925-0951 / www.cityofsantamaria.org
330 Hidden Pines Way, Santa Maria

Ahhhhh! This large circular park - one of my favorites - is located at the northern end of the city and has a plethora of mature pine and oak trees (good for climbing!) that offer shade and a peaceful ambiance. There is also plenty of open, grassy areas to run around, plus gently rolling green hills, a baseball diamond, and two good-sized playgrounds. The playgrounds have a sand base, are dotted with big rocks, and host a few rock climbing walls, slides and swings, and a few other pieces of play equipment. A main attraction is the small wood and cement ship (a little replica of the Santa Maria) for young mateys to climb aboard. Located in a small pond (with a gangplank entrance), it's "armed" with cannon turrets. The pond has a fountain in the middle of it and is home to ducks who quack for handouts. A rock-lined stream with a short waterfall runs through a portion of the park and flows into the pond. Picnic tables are plentiful. This park also has an eighteen-hole disc golf course over mostly flat and lightly-wooded terrain, plus horseshoes, and a decent, paved perimeter walk.

A park within a park is found at North Preisker Ranch Park, just down the street at the corner of Hidden Pines and Railroad Avenue. The park features a large, multi-level children's play area. Besides the main, tall structure with slides, a rock climbing wall, monkey bars, and climbing apparatus, it also has several small railroad cars for your children with an attitoot toot! This area also has a grass area, picnic tables, tennis courts, and basketball courts that are shared with the Junior High School that the public can use when school is not in session. Enjoy a day in these delightful parks.

Hours: Open daily, sunrise - sunset.
Price: Free
Ages: All

RANCHO GUADALUPE-NIPOMO DUNES PRESERVE / OSO FLACO LAKE NATURAL AREA / OCEANO DUNES STATE VEHICULAR RECREATION AREA / DUNES CENTER

Dunes Center - (805) 343-2455; Dunes ranger station - (805) 473-7223 or 7220 or (805) 773-7170; camping reservations at Oceano -(800) 444-7275 or (805) 473-7223 / www.dunescenter.org; www.ohv.parks.ca.gov
The southern entrance is West Main Street/Hwy. 166 in Guadalupe; the central entrance is Oso Flaco Lake Road in Nipomo; and the northern one is Pier Avenue in Oceano. The visitors center museum is located at 1065 Guadalupe Street/Highway 1 in Guadalupe.

Maps of the preserve, an events calendar, and helpful docents make the Dunes Center (i.e. visitors' center and museum) a good starting point for your trip to the dunes. The Center also has interactive displays for kids (and adults) such as a sand pit filled with hidden treasures; skulls and other plaster bones to touch; microscopes and slides; a puppet stage and animal puppets; and award-winning computer programs written specifically to educate and fascinate visitors to the dunes. You can choose from such video topics as birds of prey, amphibians, geology, and the making of the 1923 Cecil B. DeMille movie, *The Ten Commandments*, which was filmed here. The Center has information about the movie set, which still lays buried in the area, intact, under layers of sand. There are also a few taxidermied animals, photographs, a small art gallery displaying local art regarding the Dune, and a small gift shop. Ask about the educational programs offered here and group walks.

There are three entrances for three very different experiences to the eighteen miles, and acres and acres and acres of sand dunes. In **Rancho Guadalupe**, the Southern-most entrance, drive past a working sand mine, through marshlands where cattle are grazing, until you almost reach the shoreline of Guadalupe Beach. Spend time exploring the rolling sandy hills, strolling along the beach, and frolicking in the water.

At **Oso Flaco**, park the car in the lot, and walk along the hard-packed dirt path to a long wooden bridge and boardwalk that cross over a portion of one of the fresh-water lakes in the preserve. The pathway extends all the way to the beach (at some points the trail is almost obliterated by sand), making it a total trek of about a mile-and-a-half. Other paths branch off into the dunes. The diversity of plant and animal life here is amazing. The dunes are constantly being resculpted as the wind and water shift the sands to new depths and new heights (up to 500 feet!) We hiked to the beach, but the boys really enjoyed exploring the more dramatic dunes. We took a trail that cut to the right, before the beach, and turned right again at the fence, going "off road" to reach our play area. The kids cavorted, ran, jumped, rolled, slid (with plastic sleds even), and crawled up and down the dunes. I took pictures. They were happy and tired. My pictures were great. When all is said and *dune*, we had a great day.

At the northern, **Oceano** entrance, park right near the beach, or take your four-wheel drive directly onto it! (Mini vans can only go so far.) You can drive quite a few miles on the beach, right up to the waves or dunes. Let the kids go wild! (Within reason, of course.) There are three-and-a-half miles of beach and 1,500 acres of sand dunes in this area available for OHV use. For those without the necessary vehicle you've got a few options. Humvee tours are quite the thrill, zooming up and over the dunes like riding a roller coaster. Prices are $55 an hour per person. Contact Pacific Adventure Tours (805) 481-9330 / www.pacificadventuretours.com. Or, rent an all-terrain vehicle - this is one of our favorite choices. The vehicles rent for about $45 for two hours for the smallest bikes (geared for 9 year olds, or so) on up to $90 for a more powerful model. The following are a few numbers to get you started on this quest: BJ's at (888) 481-5411 / www.bjsatvrentals.com; Arnie's at (800) 213-1590 or (805) 474-6060 / www.pismoatvrentals.com; and Steve's at (805) 481-2597 / www.stevesatv.com.

Camping is also available at the Oceano Dunes and reservations are highly recommended. Swim, surf, and/or fish in the water. This is quite a popular place to be, especially at night. It does get foggy and cold here, even in August, so grab a jacket. Bring your own wood to start a fire directly on the sand. Just outside the Oceano entrance is Pier Avenue, a short street that offers a Nature Center and a fun store stop - the Salt Water Taffy Coffee and Candy House. Delectable candies of all kinds, plus freshly-dipped caramel apples, shaved ice, firewood, and a small gift shop make up the varied selection of items. While in Oceano, which is just north of Santa Barbara County, check out the Pismo State Beach Campground which is just down the street.

There are numerous, docent-led tours of the dunes and the lakes offered for specific groups and for the general public, including adults, school kids, scouts, and more. Learn about the eco system, history, geology, and preservation of the dunes; wildlife; habitats; and more. Note that dune access is severely limited from March to September because the California least tern and the western snowy plover (birds) nest in the sands. Large sections of the area are fenced off.

Hours: Rancho Guadalupe dunes are open daily, 7am - sunset (but access is limited March - September). Oso Flaco Lake area is open daily, dawn - dusk. Oceano is open daily, 6am - 11pm. Dune Center is open Wed. - Sun., 10am - 4pm.

Price: Dunes Center is $6 for adults; free for ages 12 and under. Rancho Guadalupe is free. Oso Flaco is $5 per vehicle. Oceano is $5 per vehicle for day use, or find the few spaces on the street if not venturing by car out to the dunes. Dune camping here is $10 a night.

Ages: All

RIVER PARK

(805) 875-8100 or (805) 736-1261 - park; (805) 875-8034 - camping; (805) 757-8047 - Kids Moto Park / www.cityoflompoc.com;www.kidsmotopark.com

Highway 246 and Sweeny Road, Lompoc

Shall we gather at the river? River Park, that is? Yes. This mostly natural, linear park runs parallel to the Santa Ynez River (hence the name) and is great for a family gathering. It boasts sand volleyball courts; horseshoe pits; picnic areas; a playground; a walking pathway; chunks of open, grassy play space; and the smallish, man-made Kiwanis Lake. Just right for fishing (and apparently a lot of ducks and other wildlife), the lake also adds a spot of beauty to the park. Adults need to have a fishing license. There are thirty-five campsites with full hook-ups for RVs and tent camping sites, too.

Just when you thought it couldn't get any more fun, it can. There is (on a long-term, temporary basis) a Kids Moto Fun Park. This OHV facility is here to promote interest in the future Lompoc Valley Motorsports Park. It has a ¼ mile OHV course for motorcycles and ATVs up to 50cc for kids up to 12 years old to ride, for free! (I wish I was younger, for a lot of reasons, but this is one.) Also in the immediate vicinity is a safety class training room, plus benches and a shade area for parents to watch. This Park is open by appointment only.

Hours: The park is open daily, sunrise - sunset. The Kids Moto Fun Park is available weekends and holidays, 10am - 4pm, by reservation only.

Price: Free. Tent camping is $15 a night. RV campsites are $30 a night.

Ages: All

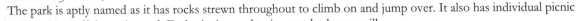

ROCKY NOOK COUNTY PARK

(805) 568-2461 / www.countyofsb.org

610 Mission Canyon Road, Santa Barbara

The park is aptly named as it has rocks strewn throughout to climb on and jump over. It also has individual picnic nooks, branching off the main road. Each picnic area has its own barbecue grill.

Oak, sycamore, eucalyptus, and pine trees form a shady "ceiling" and give the park a woodsy feel. The seasonal Mission Creek is almost more fun to explore in the summer when the water level is low as the numerous exposed rocks lining the sides and bottom practically beg kids to clamber on and around them. A small playground, a horseshoe pit, some short hiking trails, a few huge fallen logs, and two mosaic alligators near the entrance complete the park's offerings. Note: This park is near MISSION SANTA BARBARA (pg. 625), SANTA BARBARA MUSEUM OF NATURAL HISTORY (pg. 629), and SANTA BARBARA BOTANIC GARDEN (pg. 618).

Hours: Open daily, 8am - sunset.

Price: Free

Ages: 3 years and up.

ROTARY CENTENNIAL PARK

(805) 925-0951 / www.cityofsantamaria.org

2625 South College Drive, Santa Maria

This extensive park has a variety of components. At the northern end is attractive landscaping and a perimeter walking trail encircling an island of grass and a tight circle of trees. The borders also have a variety of ten, legitimate exercise stations. Further south is a great, tri-story play gym with slides, rock climbing walls, learning panels, ramps and bridges. Built-in play space under the equipment is always fun for younger ones. There is a similar, but shorter and smaller, play gym for tots that has speaking tubes and attached musical instruments to play. A basketball court, gazebo, a cluster of picnic tables, open grassy areas, some shade trees, and a massive field for soccer and other sports round out this park.

Hours: Open daily, sunrise - sunset.

Price: Free

Ages: All

SANTA BARBARA BOTANIC GARDEN

$$$

(805) 682-4726 / www.sbbg.org

1212 Mission Canyon Road, Santa Barbara

Picture walking on a dirt trails through a lovely, natural setting of chaparral and oak woodlands, oftentimes alongside the meandering Mission Creek, branching off in all directions, passing by a waterfall and an authentic Japanese Teahouse and Tea Garden, with an occasional bridge or even the creek to cross (using boulders). It feels like you're out in the woods, surrounded by canyons and hills - I could live here! The 5.5 miles of trails are mostly easy walking and stroller friendly, with a few quarter-mile hiking trails being the exception. Past Campbell Bridge is a small, but fun children's maze made of native brush - look for the gnome houses in there. You'll find benches and a few drinking fountains along the trails, plus a picnic area, so pack a lunch, or at least a snack.

Trees - pine, oak and even a redwood cluster - and shrubbery make up the majority of the 1,000 species of indigenous plants at this mid-size botanic garden. There are also a number of various plants sections - a small desert; a good-size meadow (look for turtles in the pond here); a manzanita section; and more, plus a wide variety of flowers adding brilliant color and beauty. Different seasons bring a variety of wildflowers and wildlife. The Discovery Garden, designed for younger gardeners, has a slab of redwood to inspect the rings, a small pond, a pollination garden, and other vegetation with either an interactive feature and/or information plaques.

A small nursery is on site if you're interested in purchasing plants. Ask about guided group and school tours. Across the street are a few more trails amidst the plants, so hike up one to see great views of Santa Barbara - the hills and beyond. Enjoy your time at the Garden which is so close to the city, but so far removed from city life.

Hours: Open March - October daily, 9am - 6pm; open November - February daily, 9am - 5pm. Closed Thanksgiving, Christmas Eve, and Christmas Day. Guided tours for individuals are offered Sat. at 11 and sometimes at 2pm; Sun. at 11am and 2pm; and Mon. at 2pm.

Price: $12 for adults; $10 for seniors; $8 for ages 13 - 17 and college students; $6 for ages 2- 12; children under 2 are free. See American Horticultural Society (pg. x) for info on reciprocal memberships.

Ages: All

SANTA YNEZ RECREATION AREA

(805) 967-3481 - USDA Forest Service / Los Padres National Forest; (805) 967-8766 - Rocky Mountain
Recreation - campgrounds / www.recreation.gov; www.fs.usda.gov/lpnf

Paradise Road, Santa Barbara

The Santa Ynez Recreation Area, part of the massive Los Padres National Forest, covers an extensive, accessible portion of Santa Barbara County's wilderness. The above phone numbers are references for the following: Contact the Forest Service for information on field trips, education programs, and publications that enable visitors to enjoy and protect the forest. Contact the Los Padres Forest Association for more information at (805) 640-9060. Rocky Mountain Recreation provides information on campgrounds and picnic areas, and they have a good map of the area trails. Note that trails are open for hikers, equestrians, and hardy mountain bikers. Stop by the Los Prietos Ranger Station on Paradise Road, within the Lower Santa Ynez Recreation Area, for maps and books that show designated roads, trails, recreation facilities, and more. The ranger station is open year round Monday through Friday from 8am to noon, then it reopens from 1pm to 4:30pm. It's closed weekends and holidays. It's open the same hours, plus Saturdays, during the summer.

Both the Lower Santa Ynez Recreation Area and the Upper S.Y.R.A. have beautiful scenery, plus trails, camping, and picnic areas. The lower area is easily accessible by car, if it hasn't rained. You do have to cross over a shallow part of the river a few times, which we did in the minivan. The upper is more remote with unpaved roads and more rustic campgrounds. Some lower S.Y.R.A. trail highlights include Aliso National Recreation Trail, which is just east of the Los Prietos Ranger Station. The trail head is at the east end of the Sage Hill campground. Pick up an interpretive brochure here (don't you just love adding to your kids' education?) and take the easy one-mile hike along the seasonal Aliso Creek. If your troops are energetic, and you've packed water, hike the entire, moderately graded, three-and-a-half-mile loop trail.

If you continue driving east on Paradise Road, past Sage Hill, and turn left on the road past the Lower Oso picnic area up to the Upper Oso campgrounds, you'll be near the trail head for the popular Santa Cruz National Recreation Trail. This delightful trail follows along Oso Creek, through a sandstone canyon, and past nature-made pools, which are usually fairly shallow. If the kids are tired (and hungry), Nineteen Oaks Trailcamp makes a good stopping point. (You have to provide the snacks.) Past this spot, the trail ascends up three-and-a-half miles to Little Pine Mountain, and another five miles to another trailcamp.

Another popular trail, Red Rock - Gibraltar, starts at the end of Paradise Road. This area has restrooms. The trail meanders alongside the Santa Ynez River. Going to the right, you'll go uphill, which is very steep at some points, past some tall rocks, encountering some wonderful vistas, with the midway point at Gibralter Dam and Reservoir. Take the same trail back or continue on a loop along a fairly unmaintained dirt trail, which goes briefly through marshland, back to the parking lot. The entire loop is seven miles long and moderately tough. Heading left from the trailhead at the parking lot, a short hike in, is a wading and swimming area in rock pools in the refreshingly cold Santa Ynez River. We hiked a few miles further back and found some very small lakes, surrounded by rocks and lush plant life, almost hidden, that were amazingly delightful - worth the hike.

Fish the stocked river for rainbow trout. A license is required for ages 17 and older. The four family campgrounds at the lower S.Y.R.A. have water, barbecues, fire pits, tables, and toilets. No sites offer full-service hook-ups.

Hours: Open daily, sunrise - sunset.

Price: $5 per automobile for a day-use pass (i.e., Adventure Pass) for stopping anywhere within the national forest. The camping fee is $30 a night.

Ages: 4 years and up.

SKATER'S POINT

(805) 564-5418 or (805) 564-5495 / www.santabarbaraca.gov

Cabrillo Boulevard at Garden Street, Santa Barbara

This is where the skate meets the sand. This popular, unsupervised, 14,600-foot concrete playground for skaters is just off the beach, next to Stearn's Wharf. Boarders and bladers work up a sweat on the ledges, rails, quarter-pipes, and bowls, and can then go take a swim in the ocean. A helmet and pads are required (for the skate park, not swimming in the ocean).

Hours: Open daily, 8am - sunset. Sat., 9am - 11am is for skater 12 years old and under only!

Price: Free. Parking at the beach lot is $2 an hour; $12 max. There is some free street parking.

Ages: 7 years and up.

STEVENS PARK

(805) 564-5418 / www.santabarbaraca.gov

258 Canon Drive, San Roque

This slightly off-the-beaten path park is a good find. The immediately visible part of the park has shade trees, a rock-lined creek, a playground, some picnic tables, and barbecues. Discover the more hidden part of the park by taking the dirt trail that leads under the road, through San Roque Canyon, and up the hillside to the Santa Ynez mountain range, where it branches off. Either part of the park you choose makes for a fun outing.

Hours: Open daily, 8am - sunset.
Price: Free
Ages: All

STOW GROVE PARK

(805) 961-7500 / www.cityofgoleta.org

580 N. La Patera Lane, Goleta

This delightful park, which is just up the road from LAKE LOS CARNEROS PARK (pg. 611), STOW HOUSE / RANCHO LA PATERA (pg. 634), and SOUTH COAST RAILROAD MUSEUM (pg. 633), has a redwood grove encircling its picnic area. Other amenities include barbecue pits, a ball field, two volleyball courts, playgrounds, horseshoe pits (bring your own equipment), and a grassy green lawn.

Hours: Open daily, 8am - sunset.
Price: Free
Ages: All

SUNNY FIELDS PARK

(805) 688-PLAY (7529) / www.cityofsolvang.com

900 Alamo Pintado Road, Solvang

Bring your sveinbarn (Norse for boy child) and girl child to this huge Viking wonderland of leike (i.e. play), that includes European and Western influences, too. The enclosed, multi-level wooden structures, painted in rich earth tones, form a village that urges imaginations to go wild.

Enter through a castle-like building to run on the wooden ramps that go everywhere; cross over bridges; play in a large Viking bateau (i.e. boat); go into a gingerbread-style house that is decorated on the inside, too; climb medieval towers; put on a show at the puppet theater (bring your own puppets); climb aboard a square, wooden wagon; dance in a Native American structure; enter the several kid-size playhouses; play under the mini buildings; scamper up a rock climbing wall; hang from the monkey bars; go high on the swings, including a tire swing; and enjoy the enclosed and open slides. There are plenty of benches for parents, and adjacent covered and uncovered picnic areas. If that's not enough, there is a baseball field and lots of open, grassy, run-around space, too. Your kids will come, see and conquer!

Hours: Open daily, sunrise - sunset.
Price: Free
Ages: 1 - 12 years old.

TOMOL INTERPRETATIVE PLAY AREA

(805) 684-5405 / www.carpinteria.ca.us

390 Linden Avenue, Carpinteria

A blue walkway, lined by a border wall crawling with life-like and life-size gecko statues, leads under and then onto a rainbow bridge, then into this nicely-landscaped, imaginative playground which is like a kids version of a replicated Chumash village. A central (fake) rock is designed to climb on and walk under. Large cement dolphin, seal and sea lion statues await riders, as does tomol, a Chumash word for plank boat. Several small huts - some with coverings, some without - are ready for inhabitants, or at least visitors. A few slides, several boulders (with pictographs) lining the small park perimeters, and a stone bench sitting area complete the village.

This play area is adjacent to the huge open field of Linden Field; a free beach area at the end of Linden Avenue; and CARPINTERIA STATE BEACH (pg. 598). It is also next door to the Palm to Linden trail, which is a block long, lush walkway (with lights and interpretive signage) that ultimately connects to CARPINTERIA BLUFFS NATURE PRESERVE AND TRAIL (pg. 608).

Hours: Open daily, sunrise - sunset
Price: Free
Ages: 1 - 10 years

TORO CANYON PARK

(805) 568-2461 / www.countyofsb.org/parks
Toro Canyon Park Road, Carpinteria

This beautiful, remote park sports numerous old oak trees along boulder-strewn hillsides. It also has picnic tables, barbecue pits, a horseshoe pit (bring your own equipment), and a dirt/sand volleyball court. Kids can play on man-made play equipment of the playground with swing and slides and/or on God-made play equipment of rocks and trees and a seasonal creek that meanders throughout the park. A short hiking trail leads visitors up a hillside to an overlook gazebo. Longer hiking and equestrian trails can also be accessed through the park.

Hours: Open daily, 8am - sunset.
Price: Free
Ages: All

WALLER PARK

(805) 934-6123 or (805) 934-6211 - park; (805) 925-4964 - pony rides / www.countyofsb.org
3107 Orcutt Road, Santa Maria

Waller Park, located at the south end of town, is 153 acres big and almost bursting with fun things to do. It's a very natural park, too. It has two small lakes with fountains in them (and a few rocks that my boys climbed on); several huge parcels of grassy lawns to run around on; shady picnic areas with a slew of picnic tables; basketball and volleyball courts; a disc golf course toward the main entrance; softball fields; barbecue grills; horseshoe pits; plenty of huge, shade trees; and bike trails that branch off throughout the park. The playgrounds are worth coming to the park in and of themselves because of their innovative equipment. One has fake boulders with hand and foot holds, and twisty slides. Another is really big and very colorful. It has several rock climbing walls, swings, pretend animals on big springs to ride, metal poles and spirals to climb about and hang from, tunnels and ramps. And yet another is equally large with some enclosed slides and other fun apparatus. Just go from playground to playground! There are two small, rock-lined lakes connected by a short waterfall. They are quite pretty with greenery and fountains, and a walkway around them. The upper one has an island in the middle with a plethora (and I mean that) of ducks, geese, and other fowl. There are also pony rides in a small walking ring in front of a cute Western facade that's open weekends and holidays, 11am to 4pm, weather permitting. We played, ran, ate, and played some more at the park, making a full day of it.

Woof-Pac Park, a fenced-off part of Waller Park, is a place for off-leash dogs to race around, sniff, and make new friends. This park is subdivided into enclosed sections for large dogs and a section for smaller dogs. If your dog needs to be cleaned, before or after park usage, use the pet spa - a coin-operated station that has doggie shampoo (more coins), warm-water rinse, and blow dry (more coins). I wonder if we could use this for kids, for a few more coins.

Adjacent to Waller Park is Hagerman Sports Complex with a great, new-style playground surrounded by several lighted ball fields with stadium seats, plus a cafe and inside/outside eating area.

Hours: Open daily, 8am - sunset. Pony rides are $5.
Price: Free
Ages: All

—MUSEUMS—

ART, DESIGN & ARCHITECTURE MUSEUM

(805) 893-2951 or (805) 593-5257 / www.museum.ucsb.edu
552 University Road, at University of California, Isla Vista

This picturesque campus by the sea has many special features, such as Storke Tower, which is a 175-foot tower with a sixty-one bell carillon that sounds twice per hour. The campus museum's focus is twofold - one is the fine arts; the other is architecture and design. Permanent works in the galleries include those from the 15th through 17th centuries, such as European Old Master Paintings and Renaissance metals and plaquettes; contemporary art, including some Polaroids and gelatin silver prints from Andy Warhol and a selection from local artists; historical photographs and daguerreotypes; writings; and a spotlight on the architectural renderings and design collection. The furniture, model homes, and decorative objects will probably appeal to kids more than the drawings. All of this, combined with rotating contemporary exhibits such as drawings and prints from Italian Masters; examples of Greek and Roman art; African sculpture; and Native California baskets, allow the museum to appeal to variety of artistic tastes. One object of the permanent collection is a Renaissance Cabinet (i.e. cabinet of curiosity) - a wall-to-wall cabinet concisely representing the world from the collector's perspective. It is filled with a mixture of items such as shells, stuffed animals, gemstones, musical instruments, and fossils. Remember to check out the outdoor sculpture garden. Look at the museum's calendar of events as some exhibits appeal more to kids than others.

Guided tours are offered for school groups that include curriculum and, for elementary-aged children, an in-class art lesson, as well.

Hours: Open Wed. - Sun., noon - 5pm (open Thurs. until 8pm). Closed Mon., Tues., school holidays, and major holidays.

Price: Free to the museum. Parking is about $3.

Ages: 7 years and up.

CARPINTERIA VALLEY MUSEUM OF HISTORY

(805) 684-3112 / www.carpinteriahistoricalmuseum.org

956 Maple Avenue, Carpinteria

In the middle of Carpinteria's downtown area is this surprisingly fine historical museum. One long room is separated into smaller rooms that depict segments of early life in this area. The rooms house steamer trunks and pictures of old Carpinteria; old dolls and toys; a living room with furniture, plus a melodeon, spindle, phonograph, and sweeper broom (i.e., an early-day vacuum cleaner); Chumash arrowheads, baskets, and several stone mortar and pestles; a bedroom set; saddles and chaps; and an adobe diorama.

A back room holds old machinery such as a collection of typewriters and cameras, plus a piano, and a butterfly collection. Another small section displays an apple press, washboard, water pump, and wall murals. Warning to the faint-hearted - if you stomp on the platform in this particular area, or clap your hands, the fake rat in the rattrap will twitch!

The museum also contains life-size cutouts of people dressed in period clothing throughout, as well as a stagecoach, an early Ford, and a small classroom with desks, books, slate boards, and a blackboard. A kitchen scenario holds implements such as a butter churn, dishes, and a stove. An adjacent workshop area has old tools and a walnut huller. Outside in the courtyard is an open grassy area, a few old pieces of old farm equipment, and a another stagecoach.

Walk around the museum on your own or ask about taking a guided tour. See the website calendar of events as the museum is host to numerous community events throughout the year, such as the Museum Marketplace (flea market with antiques, collectibles, household goods, clothing, jewelry, etc.) that takes place from 8am to 3pm the last Saturday of each month.

Hours: Open Tues. - Sat., 1pm - 4pm. Closed Sun., Mon., and major holidays.

Price: Free. Suggested donations of $2 for adults; $1 for seniors and children.

Ages: 6 years and up.

THE CARRIAGE AND WESTERN ART MUSEUM

(805) 962-2353 / www.carriagemuseum.org; www.santabarbaraca.gov

129 Castillo Street, Santa Barbara

Almost hidden in a corner of the Pershing Park Ball Field are treasures from California's early golden days contained in the wood and brick building called the Carriage and Western Art Museum. Over seventy horse-drawn conveyances manufactured from 1850 to 1911 have been lovingly restored and are finely displayed. Many of the carriages, buggies, and wagons are used in August for the OLD SPANISH DAYS FIESTA (pg. 729) during Santa Barbara's annual Fiesta Celebration. Some of our favorite vehicles include the Hearst carriage, a four-passenger pony runabout, the old fire wagons, surreys, and "typical" covered wagons.

The museum also displays spurs, bits, harnesses, whips, jackets, and over fifty ornately decorated saddles. Some of the more famous saddles include one that belonged to Clark Gable, another that was Will Rogers', and others owned by the Cisco kid and by Jimmy Stewart. The room in the back also has a small stage/restaurant/bar area with western facades and neon signs.

Looking at the carriages was interesting, but taking a tour was more fascinating as we learned from the docent some of the history associated with them and with the equestrian paraphernalia.

The adjacent Pershing Park has several areas of open grassy fields, shade trees, ball fields, and eight tennis courts. Call (805) 564-5573 for more details on the courts.

Hours: The museum is open Mon. - Fri., 9am - 3pm to walk through on your own. Closed on weekends, except the third Sun., 1pm - 4pm, when it's open for guided tours. Call to arrange for a group tour. The park tennis courts are available Mon. - Fri., 5pm - 9pm (they have lights!); Sat. - Sun., 8:30am - 9pm.

Price: Free

Ages: 4 years and up.

CASA DE LA GUERRA

(805) 965-0093 / www.sbthp.org

$

15 East De La Guerra Street, Santa Barbara

This historic adobe, originally built in the 1820's, is now a restored house museum. Once belonging to the commander of El Presidio, it features period rooms and special art. School tours are offered by reservation. The De la Guerra Plaza city park is in front of the Casa and plays host to many of the city festivals and events, such as Cinco de Mayo celebrations and a mercado (i.e., marketplace) during Old Spanish Days.

Hours: Open Tues. - Sun., noon - 4pm. Closed major holidays.

Price: $5 for adults; $4 for seniors; ages 16 and under are free. Note: Admission fee here includes admission to EL PRESIDIO DE SANTA BARBARA STATE HISTORIC PARK (pg. 623).

Ages: 6 years and up.

CASA DEL HERRERO

(805) 565-5653 / www.casadelherrero.com

$$$$$

1387 E. Valley Road, Montecito

Visit a bygone era when coming to this classy, Spanish-style house located in a residential neighborhood. It was completed in 1925 and shows heavy influences of Islamic and Moorish architecture. Colorful Mediterranean mosaic tiles are prevalent outside around the courtyard and inside the house, as well. The foyer boasts of tapestries, ornate panels on the ceiling and walls, and church pews for seats. The house is noted for its 13th- to 18th- century Spanish furniture. The living room contains red velvet furniture, pictures, and an early stereo. Walk through the smallish kitchen, bathrooms, formal dining room, enclosed porch with a garden view, and decorative bedrooms. The children's bedrooms have beds, trunks, gold mirrors, and clocks. Look at the sculptures, wood-carved doors and furniture, fireplaces with tiles, and other fine details throughout the two-story house.

The seven acres of cultivated gardens are meticulously groomed and designed in a Moorish fashion. Go through garden gates and an archway that looks like it leads to a secret garden. Take a walk past a rose garden, a little pond, a sundial, a camellia garden, an herb garden, a Spanish patio, and even orange orchards. The tour guide explains the layout of the gardens, the types of plants, and the entertaining that was once done here.

The owner was a blacksmith and his workshop is probably one of the most intriguing stops on the tour for kids. It is filled with his tools, plus workbenches, a casting furnace, forge, and anvils. My boys' fingers were itching to try out, or at least touch, the tools.

The ninety-minute tour includes forty-five minutes inside and forty-five minutes outside in the gardens. Note that the rooms are small and groups cannot be have more than twelve people. Note, too, that the parking lot only holds eight cars. Ask about Holiday Tours when the Casa is festooned for Christmas. Reservations are required for all tours.

Hours: Tours are offered Wed. and Sat. at 10am and 2pm, by reservation only. Groups of twelve or more may book reservations for Tues. - Sat. at 10am and 2pm.

Price: $25 per person. Holiday tours are $30. See American Horticultural Society (pg. x) for info on reciprocal memberships.

Ages: Children must be at least 10 years old.

EL PRESIDIO DE SANTA BARBARA STATE HISTORIC PARK

(805) 965-0093 / www.sbthp.org

$

123 East Canon Perdido Street, Santa Barbara

Originally built in 1792 to protect the mission, the reconstructed presidio (i.e., military fort) was the last Spanish military outpost built in North America. I appreciated the kid's info kit about the Presidio that the docent handed us upon arrival. Take a walk through the courtyards and the buildings and look into the sparsely furnished commander's, padre's, and lieutenant's quarters. The fort also features a decorated chapel and bell tower. Across the street is El Cuartel, the guard's house, which is the second-oldest building in California! For the oldest building, see MISSION SAN JUAN CAPISTRANO (pg. 309). Ask about the special events and educational programs offered here throughout the year.

Hours: Open daily, 10:30am - 4:30pm. Closed major holidays.

Price: $5 for adults; $4 for seniors; ages 16 and under are free. Note: Admission fee here includes admission to CASA DE LA GUERRA (pg. 623).

Ages: 6 years and up.

ELVERHOJ MUSEUM

(805) 686-1211 / www.elverhoj.org

1624 Elverhoy Way, Solvang

This quaint museum is tucked away amongst residential houses near the main shopping areas of Solvang. Built in 18th-century Danish-farmhouse style, the inside displays also depict this culture and time period.

The lobby holds a traveling desk and a sample of the red Danish national costume. The country kitchen is designed with typically simple lines and folk paintings. The Early Room contains clogs, shoes made of reeds, thatch (i.e., the plant used for roofs), dresses, a spinning wheel, and furniture. The parlor, or Best Room, features Danish costumes in a display case and furniture from an 1890's Danish farmhouse. Other rooms feature a children's canopy bed with a wonderful dollhouse, and clothing such as a colorful red postman's uniform and a naval officer's uniform. The other wing of the house contains a small art gallery.

Once a week docents demonstrate a traditional craft from the old country, such as lace making or paper cutting. Check the website as they have almost 40 special events in a year! Guided tours are available by request.

Hours: Open Wed. - Sun., 11am - 4pm. Closed Mon., Tues., and some holidays.

Price: Free; a donation of $5 for ages 13 and up is suggested.

Ages: 8 years and up.

FABING-MCKAY-SPANNE HISTORICAL HOUSE

(805) 735-4626 / www.lompochistory.org

207 North 'L' Street, Lompoc

This fully restored, two-story, wooden Victorian residence was originally built in 1875 and is furnished with items from that era. The front parlor was a music room of sorts and holds a melodeon, music box, two phonographs, and other musical instruments. Walk through the second parlor with a pump organ and fireplace; the dining room, with a table set for dinner; the kitchen; the pantry - check out the ice box; the bedroom; and the bathroom. Upstairs are more bedrooms filled with period furniture, including a washbasin and stand, and toys, dolls, and books in the children's room. Notice the wreath in the hallway - it's made out of human hair; perhaps an early form of knitting?

Adjacent to the home are three other buildings: The Carriage House houses several buggies and wagons lined up along the walls, and a 1908 Model 'S' Ford, plus saddles, tacks, spurs and more. The Blacksmith Shop has a forge, anvil and all the other necessary tools, plus burned cattle brands on the walls. The Museum Room showcases a 1920's kitchen with all of its implements; a laundry section with washing and drying wringers and other time-consuming machines; old-fashioned household items such as bottles, cans, and pans; artifacts from a shipwreck; and a Doctor's Office with shelves of medical tools (some look scary!), a bed, and mannequins.

Hours: Open Mon. (except legal holidays) and Thurs., 9am - 11am, and the fourth Sat., 10am - 1pm. Closed major holidays, Thanksgiving and the last 2 weeks of December.

Price: Free; donations appreciated.

Ages: 8 years and up.

FERNALD MANSION and TRUSSELL-WINCHESTER ADOBE

(805) 966-1601 / www.sbhistorical.org

414 W. Montecito Street, Santa Barbara

These small, historic homes played an important role in Santa Barbara's history and are worth a look-through and tour. The fourteen-room, Queen Anne-style house, called Fernald Mansion, was constructed in 1862 for Judge Fernald. It contains original furnishings from the nineteenth-century that are beautifully maintained and displayed. Although there is not a lot of maneuverability, the forty-five-minute tour will take you through the living room, kitchen, music room with its harp at the ready, and up the curved wooden staircase to the bedrooms and the bathrooms.

Next door is the adobe, built in 1854, which was constructed with timbers from a shipwreck. It contains items salvaged from a sea captain's ship and other furnishings. Note that the museum/homes are located in a residential district.

Hours: Tours are offered Sat. at 11am by appointment.

Price: $10 per person.

Ages: 10 years and up.

HANS CHRISTIAN ANDERSEN MUSEUM and BOOK LOFT

(805) 688-6010 - book store/museum; (805) 686-9770 - Solvang Coffee Company /
www.bookloftsolvang.com

1680 Mission Drive, Solvang

Fairytale favorites such as *The Steadfast Tin Soldier*, *The Ugly Duckling*, *Little Mermaid*, *Thumbelina*, *The Emperor's New Clothes*, and *The Princess and the Pea* were all penned by Hans Christian Andersen. This very small museum, located in the second story of Book Loft, is dedicated to the Danish-born author. His books (including first and early editions), manuscripts, letters, paper cuttings (which he did for friends), a bust of Andersen, and pictures of him and of his birthplace, are on display. One glass case is dedicated entirely to the Little Mermaid. You might not be in the museum long, but it is a fun, sentimental adventure. Guided group tours are available by appointment.

The rest of the book store is a book lover's treat! The Book Loft sells both new and used books, as well as classics and rare editions, and even games. The children's section is delightful. Make sure to take a look at the small, working model of the Gutenberg Press. Adding to the charm of the store is the attached Solvang Coffee Company where you can sip a cup of coffee and/or enjoy a pastry or sandwich while reading your new/old book.

Hours: The book store/museum is open Sun. - Mon., 9am - 6pm; Tues. - Thurs., 9am - 8pm; Fri. - Sat., 9am - 9pm.
The hours might be shorter in the winter.

Price: Free

Ages: 7 years and up.

KARPELES MANUSCRIPT LIBRARY MUSEUM

(805) 962-5322 / www.rain.org/~karpeles

21 West Anapamu, Santa Barbara

View actual pages of history at this museum which has millions of original documents in its archives, and several select ones on display. Each original document is enclosed in glass in a podium-like case, all artfully arranged throughout the museum. Each one also has a description of the contents, including the how, why, and when the document was written. Small busts of well-known people are also on display.

The exhibits rotate every three months. Each feature presentation focuses on a particular person, or topic, and incorporates about twenty-five documents. Past exhibits have included pages of Webster's dictionary; the final agreement from King Ferdinand and Queen Isabella regarding the New World and Columbus' voyage; scientific manuscripts of Galileo, Newton, and Einstein; and the surrender agreement of World War II. Most of the free pamphlets that correspond to and describe past exhibits also include an insert - a scaled down copy of an original manuscript. What a great teaching tool! One of the small permanent exhibits contains photocopied pages of sheet music from Beethoven, Handel, Mozart, Bach, and others, accompanied by that specific composer's bust. An encouraging observation for kids (and adults) is that those display manuscripts have cross outs, rewrites, or editing notes on them and that means the final, perfect-sounding draft doesn't come out perfect the first time around! Other permanent displays include ancient Egyptian plaques and carvings; models of ships from ancient Rome to the USS Constitution; an original Stone copy of the Declaration of Independence; a replica of the globe used by Christopher Columbus; the computer guidance system used on the first Apollo lander flight to the moon; and other space-related artifacts.

Ask about the Cultural Literacy Program for grades three up to college level, and other educational programs including on-site tours and off-site presentations. Note that there are fourteen other such Karpeles museums across the county.

Hours: Open Wed. - Sun., noon - 4pm. Closed Mon., Tues., New Years Day, Thanksgiving, and Christmas.

Price: Free

Ages: 8 years and up.

LA PURISIMA MISSION STATE HISTORIC PARK

See the entry for LA PURISIMA MISSION STATE HISTORIC PARK (pg. 611) for details.

$$

MISSION SANTA BARBARA

(805) 682-4713 / www.sbmission.org

2201 Laguna Street, Santa Barbara

$$$

Originally founded in 1786, this tenth mission, in the chain of twenty-one, is considered "Queen of the Missions" and has been occupied consistently by the Franciscan Order. The outside of the handsome mission has long been a favorite of photographers and painters, with its long front building and twin bell towers. Just outside, too, is a Moorish fountain, the basin of which was a lavanderia used by Indian women to wash clothing.

Take a self-guided tour through the buildings that are open, where one room leads easily into the next. Looking at glass-covered displays visitors see Chumash baskets and tools; a missionary's bedroom (with a tattered tall hat); religious portraits and sculptures; samples of weaving and candle making products; blacksmith's tools; and a kitchen with cookware and dishes. The chapel room contains an exhibit of ornate vestments and musical instruments, and offers a video about the history of the mission. Continue your tour outside through the garden courtyard and into the (still-active) mission church decorated with Mexican art. The door on the other side of the church leads to the cemetery, where early settlers and 4,000 Indians are buried. Juana Maria, the woman portrayed in the book, *Island of the Blue Dolphins*, is also buried here. Guided tours of the mission are available for adult groups and school kids.

Just across the street is Mission Park, with its expanse of green grass and a good-size garden with a plethora of roses. Come for a picnic or to just relax, although the latter can be hard with little ones running around.

Hours: Open daily, 9am - 4:30pm. It closes early on Good Friday and Christmas Eve. Closed Easter, Thanksgiving and Christmas.

Price: $9 for adults; $7 for seniors; $4 for ages 5 - 17; children 4 and under are free.

Ages: 7 years and up.

MOXI (The Wolf Museum of Exploration and Innovation)

(805) 770-5000 / www.moxi.org

125 State Street, Santa Barbara

$$$$

A visit here might seem like a day of play. And it is. But, it's also so much more than that! The well-lit and spacious MOXI has three floors of completely hands-on fun and learning experiences and experiments, dedicated to and cleverly integrated with themes that relate to science, technology, engineering, arts and math.

Enter under a kaleidoscope to the first floor where you can put your handprints, digitally, on a huge, suspended globe. Makerspace at the Innovation Workshop is where what you can imagine, you can invent, using 3-D printers and laser cutters, as well as popsicle sticks, glue and other high and low tech materials. It all sounds like fun at Sound Track where you can walk into and "strum" a giant guitar, and learn about sound waves; make your own sound effects in sync (or not) to a movie clip and play it back at the three small Foley Studios; produce futuristic (or just really different!) music at the Sound Machine using just your hands to direct the noise; and mix a variety of sounds and musical sounds with volume and other elements on the computer to create a sound masterpiece. The founding donors' name are incorporated with a massive, on-the-wall, pinball machine/game. (Look up at this station to see the kids on the glass portion of the roof laying down, looking at you!) There are really large, interlocking building sticks here so all ages can create and play.

The Fantastic Forces courtyard exhibits focus on gravity, magnetism, propulsion, and centripetal force. A humongous, clear, pneumatic tube system on the wall sends balls through the pipes, and then little parachutes fly out from the top, landing gently at your feet. Launch an air rocket, or two, here. Try your wings while conducting test flights and experimenting with wind at the Wind Column Workshop. See how attractive you are by playing with variously-shaped magnets.

Go full speed ahead on the second floor when you build your own race car and watch it zoom down a long, curved, downhill racetrack. Mix colors and designs as you control a large wheel that manipulates them on the wall until the colorful pattern is as you want it to be. Form another you on the large light wall that helps imprint and then shift your shape. Play with a jumbo, wall-sized Lite Brite. Watch a film in the interactive theater. Move a ball just using your brain power.

The roofless Sky Garden on the third floor takes water play to a whole new level - literally. The large water feature includes a giant Archimedes screw that kids can turn, plus pumps and cranks and wheels to make water move - you probably will get wet. Fret not because there are air drying tubes here! Become a conductor at the Weather Orchestra, a wind-, sun- and human-powered symphony station. Hear your heart beat played on a drum as you walk/run in place. Some may bravely walk, and almost all kids will get down on their hands and knees, on the glass grid Sky Deck to look down at the courtyard below them. Go inside the Lookout Tower and peer through five different observation scopes and lenses to see the city and beyond. Bonus - the Sky Garden offers an outstanding view of all of Santa Barbara - the city, ocean and the mountains!

Hours: Open daily, 10am - 5pm. Closed Thanksgiving and Christmas; closed at 1pm on Christmas Eve.

Price: $15 for ages 13 and up; $10 for ages 3 - 12; children 2 and under are free. Educators in Santa Barbara or Ventura Counties (grades K-12) receive free admission with valid ID from employer. See info on the Association of Science - Technology Centers (pg. xi) for reciprocal museum memberships.

Ages: 3 years and up.

NATURAL HISTORY MUSEUM OF SANTA MARIA

!

(805) 614-0806 / www.smnature.org
412 S. McClelland Street, Santa Maria

    This small museum houses quite a decent collection of natural history. Look for the eye-catching head cast of a Tyrannosaurus rex behind the reception desk. The first small room features a terrific, realistic seaside mural with stuffed shore birds, fake kelp, rocks and sea stars giving it a 3-D effect, while beach sounds are piped in. There is a fish quiz board here. A Monarch butterfly display and video is also here.

    The next room, and a side room, showcases more murals of the woodlands, with stuffed animals in the foreground of a roaring grizzly bear, as well as deer, bobcats, birds in flight, foxes, beavers, raccoon, coyote, beavers (and their habitat) and wild boar, plus "music" of animal sounds. There is also a "please touch" table with snake skin sheddings, bobcat fur, feathers, animals tracks, and rocks, plus displays of bird nests, eggs, and more. The bat exhibit has nocturnal rooms with a few stuffed barn owls, several bats (with bat sounds) and interactive bat quiz board.

    The backroom contains display cases of sea shells, crab shells, and sea stars; rocks; arrowheads; butterflies and other insects; a great whale jaw and teeth; a saber tooth cat skull; copies of baleen whale bone; mortar and pestle stones; and the Earth's timeline (with some pretty scary and strange-looking creatures) and a quiz board regarding it. A seven-minute video shows the geological history of the Santa Maria region.

    The side yard features life-size cut outs of sea mammals such as a Great White shark, orcas, and dolphins, all in a sand base, plus a table imprinted with sea life to do rubbings. The backyard also has a small grassy area and a few picnic tables. Ask about special family programs offered on select Saturdays, such as a visit with live animals and their handlers.

Hours: Open Wed. - Sat., 11am - 4pm; Sun., 1pm - 4pm. Closed Mon., Tues., and most major holidays. Tours are given by appointment.
Price: Free
Ages: 3 years and up.

OLD MISSION SANTA INES

$

(805) 688-4815 / www.missionsantaines.org
1760 Mission Drive, Solvang

    Named in honor of Saint Agnes (the Spanish spelling is Ines), there are only a few rooms of the original mission building, which was completed in 1807, to tour through. Learn the history of the nineteenth mission (out of twenty-one) and its artifacts by pressing the several push buttons that give a narration. The buttons are located throughout the building and the grounds.

    The first room is the Vestment Room, which contains numerous ornate vestments from several centuries. Paintings adorn the walls. Walk to the second room that has a wall map of the Spanish Colonial Empire, a 19th-century confessional booth, and old mission bells. An adjoining room displays cases of old nails, candlesticks, pottery, holy implements, branding irons, Bibles, firearms, and stone mortars and pestles. Next are the Madonna Room and the adjacent church, which still holds mass on a regular basis administered by the Franciscan order. The church contains many of the original paintings and wall decorations.

    The courtyard, laid out in the shape of a Celtic cross, contains a fountain and a large, lovely garden with grassy areas and a rose garden toward the back. The garden path leads to the mission's cemetery where 1,700 Indians are buried. Along a walkway on the side of the mission are the fourteen stations of the cross, each depicted by a wooden cross and picture of Christ. Note: This mission borders the quaint shopping district of Solvang, so you can combine a history lesson with a day of shopping!

Hours: Open daily 9am - 4:30pm. Closed New Year's Day, Easter, Thanksgiving, and Christmas.
Price: $5 for adults; children 11 years and under are free.
Ages: 6 years and up.

REAGAN RANCH CENTER

!

(805) 957-1980 / www.reaganranch.yaf.org
217 State Street, Santa Barbara

    It helps to like former President Ronald Reagan to appreciate visiting this small center. Santa Barbara, and specifically Rancho del Cielo, Reagan's home for twenty-five years, was known as the Western White House during his presidential years. Step into the lobby of this graceful, multi-storied building and you'll first see a big (5,000 pound) chunk of the Berlin wall, accompanied by a video explaining its importance.

    The adjoining, main room's centerpiece is an almost thirty-foot-long interactive "timeline" table with headsets and touch screens for visitors to learn more about Reagan's Ranch and countryside, plus his history and life as president and beyond. Along the walls are room-size vignettes that each showcase a portion of his life and presidency along with Reagan's belongings and artifacts - his saddle, cowboy hat, living room chair, the desk where he signed the tax cut, his farm tools, favorite books, and his blue Jeep with "Gipper" license plates. All of the exhibits are accompanied by photos, placards, and an audio and/or video explanation, too - very well done. You can also listen to and see some of his speeches, interviews, and more in the theater room and video kiosks. Other displays include letters written by Reagan, info on his Secret Service detail, and campaign memorabilia such as buttons, posters and commemoratives. The second story features a map of the ranch and a small chapel room, just like the one at his ranch. The third floor has more personal letters, art, and more. Tip: Kids can earn their "Junior Secret Service Clearance" by filling out info found throughout the museum and getting a stamp when it's completed.

Hours: Open Mon. - Thurs., 11am - 4pm. Closed on most federal holidays.
Price: Free
Ages: 7 years and up.

SANTA BARBARA HISTORICAL MUSEUM

(805) 966-1601 / www.sbhistorical.org

$$

136 East De La Guerra Street, Santa Barbara

This small, simple adobe museum complex offers a sampling of artifacts, photographs, furnishings, costumes, and fine art that represents Santa Barbara's rich multi-cultural history. One room features paintings of all twenty-one California missions. Walk through to the lovely courtyard that has a fountain and large, old pepper trees. The adjacent library contains rare literature, documents, and photographs.

Hours: Open Tues. - Sat., 10am - 5pm; Sun., noon - 5pm. Closed Mon. and holidays. Guided tours are offered Sat. and Sun. at 2pm.
Price: $7 for adults; $5 for seniors and students 18 and over; ages 17 and under are free.
Ages: 6 years and up.

SANTA BARBARA MARITIME MUSEUM

(805) 962-8404 / www.sbmm.org

$$$

113 Harbor Way, Santa Barbara

On the waterfront, surrounded by restaurants and gift shops, is the Maritime Museum, a tribute to this area's maritime past that's worth *sea*ing. Out front are statues of a massive harpoon gun and spear, and anchor. Once inside, ask for a treasure map to aid the kids in hunting for certain items in the museum's collection.

The Jimsuit - a one-person, incredibly heavy duty, atmospheric diving suit that looks like something from an old sci-fi movie - is in the entry to greet visitors. Some of the first floor exhibits are a Chumash plank canoe; an explorer's light-up display to aid in learning about early explorers and their routes (great as a supplement to California studies); and displays on otter and seal hunting, and whaling. Feel otter pelts, wool, and the hides of cattle. Lift up flaps to see and smell trade spices. Other exhibits include numerous model boats of various sizes; a fairly extensive diving helmet display from various decades; wall space dedicated to the fishing industry; displays of ranching artifacts; several ships' parts, such as a propeller and wheel; and the huge, restored, 150-year old Point Conception Lighthouse Fresnel lens, surrounded by information panels and photos that shed light on the details of its history.

The sportfishing chair is one of the most fun exhibits. Sit down, grab onto the stationary fishing pole, and, from the screen, choose the type of fish you are hoping to land. (Hint - read the instructions first.) The salmon, barracuda, marlin, tuna, or bass you choose shows like a movie clip on screen as the fishing pole in your hands starts really jerking around. Reeling in the big one, tension and all, feels very real!

The colorful kids area has a board with various types of knots to try (or tie); life jackets to try on; computers with nautical-themed programs; craft supplies to create; a puppet theater; a boat to into and fake kelp forest to "swim" through; and a video screen playing in a surfboard.

Look up - you'll see the massive, replicated hull of a schooner, as well as a seaplane and a few other planes in flight. Upstairs, contained within that schooner hull, is an eighty-six-seat theater which presents a continuous series of films regarding El Nino, octopuses, surf movies, documentaries on sharks, and sailing around Cape Horn, as well as movies such as *Shackleton's Antarctic Adventure*. Check the schedule for show times. There are more model boats up here - ranging from a royal barge from China to a Grecian fishing boat to an Inuit canoe. Check out the maritime cannons and cannon balls. Look through a working U.S. Navy periscope to see the ocean, beach, harbor, and houses just outside. An impressive Mark 46 torpedo (inert) is just outside the periscope station. A weather kiosk and radar display showing real-time image of the Santa Barbara Channel are also here. There are several surfboards here, and a visual and information display of surfing history, but you can't hang ten. At the Survival at Sea exhibit, watch the video of ships out in drastic storm conditions. Don't get steered in the wrong direction at the exhibit where you can virtually pilot a vessel.

The museum has a few other exhibits regarding art, surfing, pilot boats, commercial fisherman, coast guard, weather, and the environment. Ask about activities for kids, such as singing sea chanteys and learning how to tie knots, plus classes and tours for children and adults, live broadcasts, harbor tours, tall ships programs, outreach programs, and a lot more. Tip: Take the elevator up to the fourth floor of this building for an incredible view of the Santa Barbara Harbor and mountains! Also see SANTA BARBARA HARBOR / STEARNS WHARF (pg. 635) for more things to do in this immediate area.

Hours: Open Sun. - Tues. and Thurs. - Fri., 10am - 5pm; Sat., 9am - 3pm. Closed Wed., New Year's Day, the first Friday in August, Thanksgiving, and Christmas.

Price: $8 for adults; $5 for seniors, students, and ages 6 - 17; children 5 and under and active military are free. The third Thurs. of every month is free admission. Parking in beach lot is about $2 an hour; $12 max. There is some free street parking.

Ages: 3 years and up.

SANTA BARBARA MUSEUM OF ART   ☀

(805) 963-4364 / www.sbma.net $$$
1130 State Street, Santa Barbara

The colorful outside museum mural was painted by the world-renowned Mexican artist, David Alfaro Siqueiros. Degas, Matisse, Monet, Picasso, Dali, O'Keeffe, and Chagall all make appearances inside this museum of fine art, as do other masters. A diverse collection of American, 19th-century European, Latin American, and Asian artwork decorate its walls and halls. The museum also features modern art, photography exhibits, and ancient Greek, Roman, and Egyptian sculptures. Ask for a children's activity sheet upon entering the museum because the more that kids are involved with the art, in whatever capacity, the more they will remember. Downstairs is a small, Family Resource center, open for kids to discuss and learn more about current exhibits.

Take the time to stroll the galleries on your own, or join a free, guided gallery talk offered daily at noon and at 1pm. Age-appropriate guided tours for school kids and other groups are offered by reservation. Family days, studio art classes, workshops, holiday camps, and outreach programs are just a few of the museum's other features.

Hours: Open Tues. - Sun., 11am - 5pm (open until 8pm on Thurs.). Closed Mon., New Year's Day, 4th of July, Veteran's Day, Thanksgiving Day, and Christmas Day.

Price: $10 for adults; $6 for seniors, students, and ages 6 - 17; children 5 years and under, Santa Barbara students (with proof of residency), S.B. teachers, and active military and their families all with ID, are free. Admission is also free to everyone every Thurs., 5pm - 8pm, and there is special programming those nights.

Ages: 6 years and up.

SANTA BARBARA MUSEUM OF NATURAL HISTORY   ☾

(805) 682-4711 / www.sbnature.org $$$
2559 Puesta del Sol Road, Santa Barbara

Outside this good-sized, adobe-styled museum that's nestled into a woodland area is an impressive, seventy-three-foot skeleton of the largest animal ever known - the blue whale. Walk under it, into the rib cage. (Think of Jonah from the Old Testament.) Inside, the museum has sections devoted to geology, paleontology, minerals, native wildlife, marine life, and the culture of the Chumash Indians.

The Cartwright Hall features Santa Barbara biomes and contains small enclosures with live animals such as lizards, salamanders, tarantulas, various snakes (including rattlesnakes), and a few turtles. We liked the X-ray of the snake that swallowed light bulbs. Thousands of pinned butterflies, moths, bees, flies, grasshoppers, and other insects are on display at the insect and plant room. Inquisitive kids can lift panels to find answers to questions. See a termite colony, look at realistic-looking plants and flowers in diorama settings behind glass, and watch short films about ecological interactions.

The marine building has large dry aquariums showcasing fake fish suspended in air and a Japanese Giant Squid, plus coral, kelp, and other sea life in their "natural" habitats. Other stuffed sea creatures and models include sharks, batrays, octopus, lobsters, jellyfish, and sponges. There is also a real preserved giant squid in this room.

The paleontology/geology rooms hold skeletons of pygmy mammoths, bones of other mammoths and mastodons, a jawbone of a giant-toothed whale, and several fossils. The small Mineral and Gem Gallery showcases a collection of rocks, minerals, and gems. (Learn what the difference is between them.) See tourmaline, crystals, fluorescent specimens (whose characteristics glow under black light) and more. Briefly walk through the crystal mine that holds touchable minerals, including aquamarines and geodes. The Chumash Life displays include dioramas of Indian life, baskets, and tools. The Fleischmann Hall features wonderful changing exhibits such as Dinosaurs, the Next Generation.

The mammal hall showcases traditional dioramas of taxidermied animals in natural poses. The collection includes sea lions, tule elk, bats, a grizzly bear, opossum, mountain lion, raccoon, gray wolf, and several more creatures. The bird habitats room contains hundreds of stuffed birds in "flight", such as a California condor with its nine-foot wingspan, a barn owl with its babies, brown pelicans, orioles, cranes, a golden eagle, and several species of shore birds. This room also contains numerous eggs and nests, as well as habitat dioramas. An art gallery and library are also located in this section of the museum.

Kids (and adults) can arouse and satisfy their curiosity at the hands-on Curiosity Lab with its various stations. Use microscopes to look more closely at shells, invertebrates, plants and more. Draw a variety of specimens on display. Look at x-rays and skeletons. Slither into a pretend snake skin, and then touch actual snake skins. See a replica skeleton of an extinct elephant bird. Learn how birds fly by using wind. Make an animal track, then identify it. Go "camping" - read a story in a tent, find hidden animals and make a fake meal over "campfire".

Toward the back of the museum is the Space Lab where visitors can test their knowledge of stars, planets, and constellations by pushing buttons to match up the picture with the name of the celestial object. Watch NASA TV that features lift-off to landing coverage of space shuttle missions, as well as frequent live coverage on board the International Space Station. Touch a meteor. Check out the Magic Planet, a four-foot, "floating" globe that changes surface appearance according to if it's showing atmospheric, oceanographic, or geological changes.

The adjacent fifty-five-seat planetarium features forty-minute, or so, programs on the evening sky, as well as specialty programs for young children. These include the fifteen-minute *Twinkle Twinkle for Little Stars* show which changes every week, geared for ages 5 and under, and *Kid's Space Adventure*, a thirty-minute interactive show with time for q and a. Come at a scheduled show time or book a time for a group field trip. Observe the stars for real at the Museum's Palmer Observatory. Join the astronomy club, or just join them in star gazing, especially at the monthly star parties. These parties are for visitors to observe stars and planets through provided telescopes, as well as seeing a show in the planetarium.

The Museum Backyard is wonderful to explore! It is pretty, oak woodland with the Mission Creek running through it, plus some terrific activities to do. Pass through arches made of willow to climb on a pathway of boulders (designed for kids to climb on them!) that form a zig zag trail; build a fort (poles and materials supplied); gaze at a few redwoods; enjoy a presentation at the outdoor amphitheater; eat lunch, or a snack, at the picnic tables; relax and enjoy the beauty; and/or take a short hike on trails, one that actually leaves the museum property. Hundreds of butterflies and moths gracefully fly around in a butterfly house here that is open May through the beginning of September.

A variety of guided tours and programs are available for adult and for school groups. For instance, Nature Adventures, for ages 4 to 10 years old, incorporates lots of hands-on activities along with their classes, workshops, and camps. Traveling astronomy and Audubon Society programs and presentations are available to come to the facility of your choice. Other programs and special exhibitions at the museum often incorporate themed activities for the family. Note: The museum's satellite facility is the SEA CENTER (pg. 650), located on SANTA BARBARA HARBOR / STEARNS WHARF (pg. 635).

Hours: Open daily, 10am - 5pm. Closed New Year's Day, the last Sat. in June, Thanksgiving, and Christmas, with a 3pm closure on Christmas Eve. Planetarium shows are offered weekdays at 3pm; Sat. and Sun., 11am - 3pm, on the hour. The 3pm Sun. show is presented in Spanish. *Twinkle Twinkle for Little Stars* is Sat. - Sun. at 11am. *Kid's Space Adventure* is Tues. and Fri. at 3pm; Sat. - Sun. at 1pm. School planetarium shows are offered October - June, Tues. - Fri. at 10am and 11am, by reservation. Star parties are the second Sat., 7pm - 10pm.

Price: $12 for adults; $8 for seniors and ages 13 - 17; $7 for ages 2 - 12. Admission is free on the third Sun. (but not May - August), for the museum only. Planetarium admission is an additional $4 per person, with paid admission to the museum. Admission for just the star party is free. See info on the Association of Science - Technology Centers (pg. xi) for reciprocal museum memberships.

Ages: 3 years and up.

SANTA MARIA MUSEUM OF FLIGHT

(805) 922-8758 / www.smmof.org
3015 Airpark Drive, Santa Maria

Ready to take off to a place where the sky's the limit? This fine museum fills two hangars with small aircraft and flying memorabilia - one specializing in pre-WWII artifacts; the other from WWII to present day. Upon entering, attention is riveted on the bright red plane, a Hunt Special, featured in the movie *Rocketeer*. There is other *Rocketeer* memorabilia, too. Overhead is a replica of the Wright Brothers' glider, as well as a collection of radio control planes.

The hangar also contains dioramas of aviation history, a library of books and videos on aviation, model planes in display cases, a WWI gas mask, a skeleton plane that shows the inner workings of a radio control plane, and a gift shop.

Outside are miscellaneous parts of space rockets and a missile launcher, as well as a few small planes, such as the F4 Phantom Fighter, an A4 Skylark and an L5 Observation plane, which are grounded here. This is also a prime spot to watch small planes take off and land.

The metal, second hangar contains a few ejection seats (that look used); the Hughes H-1 Racer used in the movie, *Aviator*; a homebuilt, half-size, Lockheed P-38 Lightning; a small mock up of a space ship launch; one of the few Norden bombsights still around; inert missiles; an army truck; a British Gnat Trainer; and a working Link Trainer, which is a vintage instrument flight trainer/early simulator. The hangar also holds WWII displays, such as uniforms; airplane pieces, such as propellers and engines; lots of model airplanes and photos; and a display with mannequins featuring women pilots.

Hour-long, guided, age-appropriate tours of the museum are offered for school-age kids. The minimum number of students needed is fifteen; the maximum, twenty-five. Note that outside the second hanger is a sweet little picnic area/memorial park with tables and benches, trees and flowers, informational panels, and a timeline and a mural, all dedicated to women pilots from past to present.

Hours: Open Fri. - Sat., 10am - 4pm; Sun., noon - 4pm. Closed for special events, New Year's Day, and Christmas.
Price: $5 for adults; $4 for seniors; $3 for ages 12 - 17 and college students; $2 for ages 7 - 11; children 6 years and under are free, as are active military and their dependents.
Ages: 5 years and up.

SANTA MARIA VALLEY DISCOVERY MUSEUM

(805) 928-8414 / www.smvdiscoverymuseum.org
705 S. McClelland Street, Santa Maria

There is so much for kids to discover at the sizable, terrific, hands-on Discovery Museum, starting with an outside sand pit. Inside, the overarching theme is coastal. There are a multitude of other wonderful themed areas or "stations", each one having special activities for young ones to do, accompanied by great murals and props. Right by the entrance is a conglomeration of clear, interconnecting, floor-to-ceiling pneumatic tubes that balls and other items whoosh through to learn about movement and the power of air.

A beachy sand area, accompanied by buckets and shovels, is located next to a wooden dock that is part of a ship facade that you can walk up into and steer the big wheel. Kids can crawl under the ship, too (and be stowaways?). A real speed boat is parked next to this "ship" that sailors can board, put on life jackets and spin the captain's wheel to pretend pilot around. There are also glass displays that hold shells, sea stars and other treasures from the ocean. "Shop" at the fish market that sells buckets of the (plastic) catch of the day. A few tanks along a wall contain a variety of real fish, interspersed with information and activities, like a wide choice of magnetic words to make sentences all against a fish mural. I like the kelp hanging overhead to give that immersion feel.

An insect area features a friendly centipede to climb on, bugs to inspect via microscopes and a huge mural of a insect that shows its body parts. Discovery Reading Tree was my childhood dream - a tree trunk filled with a library of books and then climbing the (fake) treehouse to read. The good-sized play Moxie Cafe next door has tables and chairs and condiments, plus a cashier station, kitchen, food and menu - be the cook, server, or customer. Kids are encouraged to "Eat a Rainbow" in learning about nutrition and healthy eating here. Put a melody in your heart, or at least in your feet, and dance away the calories on the adjacent floor piano keyboard. At the fire and rescue area, with a mural of firefighters fighting a fire, kids can join in by dressing in fireman uniforms, including boots and helmets, and using the hose. Play a song, of sorts, by using a paddle to strike the pvc-style tubes that ring out different notes. Try your hand at an impromptu play at the tiny puppet theater. Plant a seedling to take home at the Planting Station.

The long STEAM tinkering maker lab bar supplies kids everything needed to create and do experiments and projects. I love the seemingly random big tree with fake birds and the real stuffed bear in the center of the museum. The cut-away whale in the center is hard to miss. Walk through its middle to take the short slide down its mouth and even watch a sea-related video towards its tail. Climb up and down and sideways at the eight-foot high and fairly long rock wall covered with hand and foot grips.

Things got a little sticky at the real tar pits, but here kids can don helmets and (re)discover fossils and bones in the mock excavation pit. Learn about water flow by going through a tunnel and looking at the 3-D wall mural of a neighborhood. Join the Money Club and learn about money by playing money games, dropping a coin in the top of board to make it go into the charity of your choice, and sitting at the bank teller's desk to be the financial advisor, or the customer.

At the barn and bunkhouse, look at all the brands on the walls; put on some cowboy boots and a hat; saddle up on real saddles; ride rocking horses; gather round a pretend campfire and/or cook at the back end of the wagon; practice your blacksmithing expertise with an anvil, hammer and horseshoe; and sit on a real John Deere tractor and shift gears. Space is the final frontier and kids can simulate a space launch using an actual Control computer console, or journey to Mars while seeing live feeds from Vandenberg on a projection screen at the Vandenberg Launch Experience. They can also become an astronaut and sit in a really cool mock-up of a space shuttle.

Another big nautical nook, for toddlers, has wonderful undersea murals, and sand and water-colored carpeting. It beckons bitty beachcombers to crawl through plushy "undersea" rocks and caves with portholes. There are also soft block toys to play with and enclosed play "pits", and some manipulatives.

And this list of things to see and do is not comprehensive! The Discovery Museum offers a variety of classes, workshops, and school or group tours, too.

Hours: Open Tues. - Sat., 10am - 5pm; Sun., noon - 4pm. Closed Mon. (except for field trips), and most major holidays.

Price: $6 per person; children under 2 are free.

Ages: 1 - 11 years.

SANTA MARIA VALLEY HISTORICAL SOCIETY MUSEUM

(805) 922-3130 / www.santamariahistory.com

616 S. Broadway Street, Santa Maria

For a relatively small museum, this one is packed with a lot of eclectic and wonderful old memorabilia! The first thing to see is a wall of brands, along with a few saddles, and a beautiful wooden organ, followed by a spring wagon and a statue of a cow. The main room is subdivided by representative rooms and mannequins dressed in period costumes. A vintage living room set is front and center. A side room contains portraits, mini trains, musical instruments and a cast of a saber-tooth cat - because somehow they all go together. jk. Towards the back is a wonderful mishmash of old cameras; fossils; fire fighting equipment - buckets, hoses, and cart - and uniforms; a kitchen, of sorts, with furniture and a cast iron stove; an old-fashioned switchboard along with a collection of various telephones; a nineteenth-century buggy; guns and swords; medical tools; a jail cell with a mannequin behind bars wearing an ankle ball and chain; a noose in a display case; and a mini schoolroom with a desk, books, and a copy of teacher's rules from 1872. Guided tours, offered by reservation, lend insight into the exhibits.

Hours: Open Tues. - Sat., 11am - 4pm. Closed Sun., Mon., and major holidays.

Price: Free - donations appreciated.

Ages: 6 years and up.

SANTA MARIA VALLEY RAILWAY HISTORICAL MUSEUM

(805) 863-6645 / www.smvrhm.org

708 S. Miller Street (this address is for the Souza Student Center, just south of the museum), Santa Maria

This is a quick, but fun stop off for railroad buffs. The three restored railcars here include a late 1800's engine used by the Betteravia Union Sugar Company, a 1930's box car, and a 1930's caboose - all of which are a treat to walk through. Inside the box car are several layouts with working model trains that travel past mini mountains, canyons, and cities - always fascinating to watch while learning about old Santa Maria. There is also some train paraphernalia on display and some for sale.

Hours: Open the 2nd and 4th Sat., noon - 4pm.

Price: Free

Ages: 3 years and up.

SANTA YNEZ VALLEY HISTORICAL SOCIETY MUSEUM / PARKS-JANEWAY CARRIAGE HOUSE

(805) 688-7889 / www.santaynezmuseum.org

3596 Sagunto Street, Santa Ynez

Go west, young man! On the main street of Santa Ynez, with its western-looking storefronts, dwells a vintage museum. Composed of a small complex of buildings, the museum offers all that the Old West time period held dear.

Outside is a reproduction of a Bodie Stage Line mud wagon. Inside, the lobby showcases a wonderful collections of spurs, bits, bridles, saddles, branding irons, chaps, barbed wire, riata (i.e., rope made of rawhide), and guns, as well as a stuffed golden eagle and a mounted boar's head. It also contains a nice display of Native American baskets, pottery, and stone mortars and pestles, plus samples of beadwork and shell bead money.

Meander back outside to the center courtyard where a fountain and a shady arbor with picnic tables invites visitors to sit and relax a spell. The next series of rooms form a U-shape around the courtyard. First stop is the Pioneer

Room, which is divided into three sections - a kitchen, bedroom, and parlor-living room - all furnished with items from the late nineteenth century. Walk through to see butter molds and churns, a cast iron stove, an 1847 sleigh bed, a crib, quilts, a treadle sewing machine, and an organ. The next room features changing displays of period clothing and accessories. We saw elegantly arranged, off-white wedding gowns, along with ornately beaded hand bags. The adjoining Valley Room's changing exhibits highlight the five small, nearby town's beginnings and early development. The exhibits include historical and cultural artifacts, and photos, as well as a narrow gauge train display, with models of the trains that ran through the area from 1887 to 1934, plus a depot, Mattie's Tavern, and more. Outside are farm implements and vehicles such as horse-drawn farm machinery, a 1907 Harvester pickup truck, and an early McCormick-Deering tractor. Forge ahead to look at the complete blacksmith shop also located back here.

Across the courtyard is the fascinating carriage house. Enter this large room and stroll down the streets of time as you admire the over thirty-five carriages parked here. Our favorites include the hunt wagons; a Goddard Buggy; a military supply wagon; the basket-style governesses' carts; surreys; stagecoaches; a still-functioning 1906 popcorn wagon; a hearse; a hitch wagon; a 1927 Model T school bus; and a fancifully-painted donkey cart from Sicily. O.K. - we like them all! There are also some saddles, bits, bridles, and other equestrian gear on display.

Guided tours that allow visitors to gain insight to the memorabilia and time period are available with advanced reservations. Check out the summer Wild West kids camps. Note that the Santa Ynez County Park is just down the street, with the entry off Edison and Numancia Sts. This park offers a few pieces of play equipment, a volleyball court, horseshoe pits, some trees, grassy areas, and picnic tables.

Hours: Open Wed. - Sun., 12pm - 4pm. Closed Mon., Tues., and major holidays.
Price: $5 for adults; children 12 and under are free.
Ages: 6 years and up.

SOLVANG MOTORCYCLE MUSEUM

(805) 686-9522 / www.motosolvang.com $$$
320 Alisal Road, Solvang

Over ninety vintage, rare, and classic motorcycles in excellent condition are lined up on the showroom floor, seemingly ready to roar to life. Each beautifully-restored vehicle has an accompanying description of its make and history. This eclectic private collection ranges from a 1902 Mitchell to a 1989 custom Harley - the emphasis is on racing motorcycles.

Some of the extra special bikes include an MV Agusta, Brough Superior, 1936 Nimbus sidecar, 1960 Jawa Factory Racer, 1949 Vincent Black Lightning - Supercharged, 1950 Vincent TT Grey Flash (one of four ever made), and 1946 Indian Chief - a classic with fringe on the seat. Note that the museum rotates the bikes on exhibit. The museum also has a replica of the first combustion automobile ever originally built by Karl Benz of Mercedes-Benz.

Hours: Open Sat. - Sun., 11am - 5pm, or by appointment during the week.
Price: $10 for adults; children 9 years and under are free when accompanied by an adult. Cash only.
Ages: 6 years and up.

SOUTH COAST RAILROAD MUSEUM

(805) 964-3540 / www.goletadepot.wordpress.com !/$
300 North Los Carneros Road, Goleta

Engineer some time for the kids to conduct their way to this satisfying railroad museum. Walk through an old caboose that shares this section of tracks with a handcar that is powered by passengers. In one of the small rooms at the 1901 depot building, watch a model train making tracks through mountains, over a cut-away bridge, and even past a mini circus. The depot waiting room features an old stove, trunks, and a motor car indicator - a signaling device that warned maintenance crews that a train was coming. You can also see a short slide show about the Goleta Depot project. Look into the ticket office which has several pieces of old equipment in place, and look into the freight office with its roll-top desk, candlestick phone, and scale. Check out the well-stocked gift shop. There is also a pleasant little park on the grounds with picnic tables and shade trees - a spot to rest your *toot*sies!

The highlight of a child's trip here is the nine-minute train ride, of course. The miniature train chugs its way around the depot grounds, past the picnic tables and scattered trees. Adults enjoy it just as much as the kids. Riders must be at least 34" tall for the train ride. Riders must be 48" for the handcar.

Many special events are held here throughout the year, including the Easter Bunny Express and Depot Day (in August). School and youth group tours include a free ride on the train. Ask for a copy of the self guided tour information sheet. Note that the railroad museum is located right next to STOW HOUSE / RANCHO LA PATERA (pg. 634) and is in LAKE LOS CARNEROS PARK (pg. 611).

Hours: Open Fri. - Sun., 1pm - 4pm. Mini trains run Fri., 2pm - 3:45pm; Sat. - Sun., 1pm - 3:45pm. Closed New Year's Day, Easter, Thanksgiving, and Christmas.
Price: Admission to the grounds is free. Train rides are $2.50 per person or $10 for 5 rides. Handcar rides are offered on the third Sat. of each month, or ask for a private ride on other days for a small fee.
Ages: 3 to 14 years.

STOW HOUSE / RANCHO LA PATERA

(805) 681-7216 / www.goletahistory.org
304 N. Los Carneros Road, Goleta

Woodsy surroundings and era-appropriate landscaped grounds make this Rancho and restored 1870's two-story Gothic Revival house, the Stow House, seem as though they have never met up with modern times. I love the porch that practically encircles the huge white house. (Notice the bench under the crossroad "street" signs made from horseshoes welded together.) Take the one-hour tour through the beautiful home to see all the rooms - the six or so upstairs and several more downstairs - that are filled with period furnishings, clothing and hats, toys, knickknacks, china, kitchen gadgets, and more. The dining room is elegantly set for a meal. The laundry room has wringers and washboards, and kids' clothes hanging around. The kitchen has a wonderful old stove, old tins, jars, and kitchen implements. The parlor contains a phonograph, old-fashioned phone, a desk, photos and more. The sewing room and the bedrooms upstairs, especially, while containing all the furniture and things that make a house a lived in home, also allow a closer look at the back-East-style of architecture and decor with alcoves and wallpapering. The docents, dressed in period costume, do an outstanding job of making history be engaging as they show and tell visitors how things work, give the back stories to many of the items, and point out objects that could be overlooked, like the wreath made out of hair, the "port-a-potty", the speaking tube, the unusual refrigerator, and much more.

The ranch grounds are extensive. The back farmyard contains old tractors, a variety of old-fashioned farm machinery, mining cars, and, most importantly, a three-person outhouse - bonding time. Other historic buildings on the ranch grounds are the carriage house with yes, carriages, although the horse stalls in this area contain farm equipment, a fire engine, and a tack display. A blacksmith shop is filled with tools of the trade. On certain days there are blacksmith demonstrations, and visitors can purchase newly-fashioned horseshoes (with their name engraved), wrought iron items, and more.

Inside the History Education Center building are exhibits, many of them hands-on, that cover local history from indigenous people to modern day, with a focus on ranching and agriculture. Things to do in here include sorting lemons; using carpentry tools; lifting panels to discover the answer to why some eggs are brown and some are white, for instance; writing/branding your name on the wall of brands; watching a slideshow of elementary-school kids from long ago; and lots more.

Call for information about the great educational programs for third graders, as well as other school, youth, and group tours that are offered during the week. Don't miss the small museum room off the visitors center. Note that this land is shared with the SOUTH COAST RAILROAD MUSEUM (pg. 633) and LAKE LOS CARNEROS PARK (pg. 611).
Hours: Open Sat. - Sun., 1pm - 4pm; tours given at 2pm and 3pm. Call for guided tour during the week. Closed Easter, Thanksgiving, and Christmas.
Price: $5 for adults; ages 12 and under are free.
Ages: 6 years and up.

SUSAN QUINLAN DOLL & TEDDY BEAR MUSEUM & LIBRARY

(805) 730-1707 / www.quinlanmuseum.com
122 West Canon Perdido Street, Santa Barbara

There is something about teddy bears and dolls that touch a young (and older) girl's heart and this charming museum has both in spades with over 2,500 dolls (!!) and over 500 teddy bears (!) on exhibit. Just past the five-foot stuffed warthog on roller skates is a small, lovely area near the window with tables and chairs in front of the playful and colorful wall murals of a teddy picnic and tea party - actually the bears are cavorting at local Santa Barbara spots. This is the party room.

One-of-a-kind dolls, ethnic dolls from all over the world, and dolls of every size (small to near life-size), plus rare bears are clearly and cleverly arranged here in huge glass display cases with each gallery having a different emphasis. The Historical Gallery traces California's history through a doll timeline starting with the Native American dolls. The Collector's Gallery includes the bear necessities - a tribute to the bear's namesake, Teddy Roosevelt, plus numerous bears in seasonal settings. Puppets and even fairytale characters are here, too. The museum's founder was a children's librarian and this love shows through especially in the Literary Gallery which shows dolls and bears representing literary characters, inspired by books from Winnie the Pooh to Harry Potter and everything in between. This is a child's favorite area. Boys aren't left out - there is a collection of space toys, robots, and figures from *Star Wars*, *Star Trek*, *Power Rangers*, and more. Another section contains dolls made of various materials - wood, wax, metal, cloth, and bisque. The children's sewing machines shows how models have changed over the years. Lastly is a Fairy Forest, with more fantasy dolls and teddy bears.

I love this unique place and was enthralled with the size of this collection, and the incredible variety and breadth of dolls here. One-hour (or more) tours are offered explaining the history of many of the dolls and a bit about their time periods. Browse the gift shop which offers a variety of dolls, teddy bears, books, toys, and collectibles. Tip: Visit the bathrooms while here as they are theme-decorated with dolls and bears, too.

Hours: Usually open Fri. - Mon., 11am - 5pm. Closed Tues. - Thurs.

Price: $7 for adults; $5.50 for seniors; $4 for ages 5 - 12; children 4 and under are free. Groups of 6 or more are $5 for adults; $2.50 for kids.

Ages: 3 years and up.

WATERSHED RESOURCE CENTER / EXPLORE ECOLOGY

(805) 884-0459 / www.artfromscrap.org; www.exploreecology.org

2981 Cliff Drive at Arroyo Burro / Hendry's Beach, Santa Barbara

Managed with the ART FROM SCRAP CREATIVE RESUSE STORE and EXPLORE ECOLOGY (pg. 598) environmental education program, this model of a green building serves as an education center with a focus on water quality issues. It plays hosts to several groups and programs that the entire family can participate in, such as creek water testing, beach clean ups, demonstrations, and even watching ecological movies. A variety of school field trips are offered that teach students about water pollution, solutions, the effect of plastic trash on the ocean and ocean life, watersheds, and more.

The center is open to the public the 2nd Sunday. Kids might not be here long, but the small center offers a great opportunity to become environmental aware through interactive games, maps, watershed models, a hands-on wet lab, and by the docents who want to educate youngsters (and us older folk).

Hours: Open to the public the 2nd Sun., 10am - 4pm; help clean up the beach this day, too, from noon - 2pm. Call for a schedule of programs.

Price: Free. Call for program information.

Ages: 5 years and up.

—PIERS AND SEAPORTS—

SANTA BARBARA HARBOR / STEARNS WHARF

(805) 564-5530 - harbor patrol; (805) 966-6676 - Santa Barbara Shellfish Co.; (805) 966-6110 - Los Banos pool; (805) 564-5523 - parking / www.stearnswharf.org; www.santabarbaraca.gov; www.shellfishcompany.com

State Street and Cabrillo Boulevard, Santa Barbara

This harbor is encompassed by long stretches of beach - from EAST BEACH (pg. 599) to WEST BEACH (pg. 601) to LEADBETTER BEACH (pg. 601) - with a lot of fun in the sun in between. Walk or drive onto the wharf's creaky wooden planks. Originally built in 1872, the wharf features the SEA CENTER (pg. 650); several restaurants - be sure to check out Santa Barbara Shellfish Co. at the end to see the tanks of live lobsters and shellfish (which make good food, too); and fun shops that sell shell-encrusted treasures, salt water taffy, and more. Fish from the pier, and during whale-watching seasons - late December through March for gray whales and in the summer for the blue whales - be on the lookout for the mighty marine mammals.

Adjacent to the wharf is the harbor where yachts, commercial fishing boats, and sailboats are moored. Pick up fresh crabs and lobsters from the fishing boats on Market Day, which is Saturdays from 6am - 11am. The harbor is also the place to book a cruise, rent kayaks, go out whale watching on a boat, and check out other nautical excursions. See the Transportation section for specific places to contact. More restaurants, shops, and the wonderful SANTA BARBARA MARITIME MUSEUM (pg. 628) are also located here. Make sure to visit the tiny visitor's center on the 4th floor of the maritime museum building because it has one of the most incredible views, for free, of all of Santa Barbara, and beyond, plus it carries resources and maps.

Walk, skate, or bike along the waterfront paved path which extends for three miles. See BIKE TRAIL: CABRILLO BEACHWAY (BIKEWAY) (pg. 642) for more information. This area is also home to a skate park [see SKATER'S POINT (pg. 619)]; art shows on the sidewalks every Sunday and on select Saturdays; a playground; and the

Los Banos swimming pool. This fifty-meter municipal pool has a diving board. It is located at 401 Shoreline Drive. In this vicinity is the Cabrillo Pavilion Boathouse with showers, lockers, beach wheelchair rentals, and volleyball rentals. Across the street from the beach is the fabulous CHASE PALM PARK (pg. 608).

Getting around from State Street to the wharf to the zoo is easy on the SANTA BARBARA WATERFRONT / DOWNTOWN SHUTTLE (pg. 645). It operates daily from 9am to 6pm and costs 50¢ per person one-way; 25¢ for seniors; children 45" and under are free. Also look under SANTA BARBARA TROLLEY COMPANY (pg. 644), as the wharf is one of the many stops along the trolley's route. If you can't decide if you want to tour the city by land or by sea - do both, by way of the amphibious "boat on wheels" of the LAND AND SEA TOURS (pg. 643).

Hours: Open daily. Los Banos Pools are open year-round for lap swim and only in the summer for recreational swim, usually Mon. - Fri., 7:30am - 9am and noon - 2pm; open weekends and some holidays, noon - 2pm.

Price: Recreation swim at Los Banos pool is $7 for non-resident adults, $6 for residents; $1 for ages 17 and under. There is limited street parking. On the east side of the beach, parking is about $2 an hour, $12 max with 1½ hours free with validation from the Maritime Museum, restaurant or store.

Ages: All

—POTPOURRI—

MARINE SCIENCE INSTITUTE

(805) 893-4093 / www.msi.ucsb.edu

!

Lagoon Road on the campus of University of California, Santa Barbara, Isla Vista

Educators, especially: Fantastic marine-based programs are offered via MSI - the REEF (Research Experience and Education Facility), which hosts thousands of school kids, educators, researchers and more every year. The Outreach Center for Teaching Ocean Science (OCTOS) building, perched on a bluff overlooking the ocean, contains two huge (2,000 gallon) fish tanks in the "wet laboratory"; overhead stuffed sharks and other sea life; an immersive theater; scenario-based activities utilizing a transect of the ocean floor (experience it to understand it); Nautilus Live - experiencing the ocean in realtime; touch tanks to touch and hold local sea life; and a "magic planet" (i.e. extra large globe) that allows viewers to see what is going on all over the world, as the surface of it changes according to global conditions based on data input.

Other programs offered include a mobile REEF program (where the aquariums and other equipment come to you), Family Science Night, after school activities, Marine Science 4 Scouts, and Floating Labs. The latter are 1.5 hour cruises that take place on the *Condor Express*, whale watching and sight *seaing*. Once anchored, students rotate through a series of stations exploring fields such as marine biology, navigation systems, earth science, oceanography, and more.

Hours: The REEF is open to the public on Sat., 11am - 2pm. Call regarding the group program you're interested in.

Price: Free on the public days. Call for program prices.

Ages: 5 years and up.

MURALS

(805) 736-4567 - chamber of commerce / www.lompoc.com; www.lompocmurals.com

!

throughout the city, Lompoc

Mural, mural on the wall, which is the fairest one of all? Lompoc, dubbed "City of Murals in the Valley of Flowers," combines the best of both of these elements, and more, in the over seventy murals gracing the buildings throughout the city. I thought I'd have to drag the kids to view the murals and consider it a quick art experience. While I did make them accompany me, they became enamored with the paintings - with the variety of scenes and collages, characters, time periods, locations, styles, colors, and even sizes. The murals depict flowers, portraits, rocket launches, an old-fashioned train depot, people, and much more.

For a self-guided "tour," pick up a free murals project brochure from the chamber of commerce (also available at www.lompocmurals.com), then drive around to admire and appreciate this free, unique outdoor art exhibit. Note: See the Calendar entry for details about the FLOWER FIELDS / FLOWER FESTIVAL (pg. 717) and combine these two attractions in one visit.

Hours: The murals can be seen during any daylight hours. The chamber of commerce is open Mon. - Fri., 8am - 5pm.

Price: Free

Ages: 4 years and up.

PAUL NELSON AQUATIC CENTER and COMMUNITY YOUTH CENTER

(805) 925-0951 / www.cityofsantamaria.org

516 McClelland Street, Santa Maria

Enjoy year-round swimming at this huge pool with a diving board and a short twisting water slide. An adjacent shallow wading pool features a little frog slide and a large mushroom-shaped shower that elicits giggles from young children. Parents can relax pool side in lounge chairs. The field beyond the fence has a grass area with basketball courts and a baseball field.

The indoor community youth center, geared for Jr. and Sr. high schoolers, has pool tables, air hockey, a few arcade games, basketball courts, exercise equipment, a computer lab, home movie theater with hundreds of DVDs, and even a cafe. Just outside, at the adjacent Simas Park, is an expanse of green lawn for baseball, other sports and running around, and a basketball court.

Hours: The wading pool opens in April and the rec pool in early June: Both are open through August, Mon., Wed., and Fri., 3pm - 4:30pm; Sat., 12:30pm - 3:30pm. Hours fluctuate so call first. The youth center is open daily - the mornings are for adults and kids, but kids, 7th - 12th graders, have it exclusively in the afternoons (after 2:30pm) until closing.

Price: Swimming is $2.75 for adults; $1.40 for ages 6 - 16; seniors and ages 5 and under are free. Ask about purchasing a pool pass. The community center is free.

Ages: 1 year and up.

SANTA BARBARA COUNTY COURTHOUSE

(805) 962-6464 / www.santabarbaracourthouse.org; www.sbcourthouse.org

1100 Anacapa Street, Santa Barbara

The verdict is in - this magnificent, historic courthouse is one of the city's most fascinating places to tour. The grandiose building, designed in Spanish-Moorish architecture, and its elegant surrounding gardens take up a city block.

Walk around and through the palace-like building on your own to admire the outside fountain, archways, graceful curved staircases inside, ornately carved doors, colorful mosaic tiles, unusual iron and glass hanging lanterns, paintings, and decorative floors, walls, and ceilings. Note that the Courthouse is still used for trials and houses civic offices.

The free, forty-five-minute guided tour is a terrific option as the guide explains the history of California, particularly Santa Barbara, and the history of the Courthouse, including the explanations of the various artistic styles used throughout, especially the Muslim influence. The tour begins in the beautiful mural room, so nicknamed because the walls are covered with murals depicting Chumash Indians, Cabrillo, California under Mexican rule, the building of the mission, and the beginning of the California/American era. Make sure to look at the fancy ceiling beams. Meetings are still held in here. Going into the law library with its painted stars on the ceiling, then down massive hallways, and learn the meaning of the Latin inscriptions over the outside pointed archways. The Hall of Records room is decorated in the original 1920's decor - wild! Other tour highlights (for us) included learning who Saint Barbara (the town's namesake) was; seeing, from across the courtyard, the jail and the solitary confinement quarters in a wing of the Courthouse; and looking at the stained glass window in the lobby. Note that parts of the tour incorporate walking in and out of the building, as well as up and down stairs. Some outside ramps and an inside elevator are available.

While here, take a ride eighty feet up in the elevator, walk up a few stairs, and out onto the balcony of the Courthouse clock tower for a wonderful, panoramic view of Santa Barbara. See the mountains, the ocean, and all the red-tiled roofs in the vicinity.

The meticulously-landscaped sunken garden in the center courtyard has an expansive lawn and bordering bushes, trees, and flowers. It's a peaceful haven for a picnic, and a relaxing place to ponder.

Hours: The Courthouse is open Mon. - Fri., 8am - 5pm; Sat. - Sun., 10am - 4:30pm. Closed all federal, court and major holidays. Tours are offered Mon. - Fri. at 10:30am and 2pm; Sat. - Sun., 2pm.

Price: Free

Ages: 8 years and up.

SOLVANG

(800) 468-6765 or (805) 688-6144 - visitor's center; (805) 688-0091 - Wheel Fun bike rentals / www.solvangusa.com; www.wheelfunrentals.com

Mission Drive, Alisal Road, Atterdag Road, and Copenhagen Drive form the perimeter of the core of the village, Solvang

Velkommen! The word Solvang is Danish for "sunny field." This sunny field is both an authentic Old World village and a tourist haven. Established in 1911, Solvang, which has become the Danish capitol of America, looks like a page out of one of Hans Christian Andersen's storybooks. Adults, and even kids, will notice and be enamored with the ethnic heritage and Scandinavian architecture including thatched roofs, colorful storefronts, window boxes filled with flowers, windmills, and decorative wood work. It truly is like being in a different country.

The over 300 eateries and shops include antique shops, smorgasbords, clothing stores, bakeries, souvenir shops, cafes, cobbler shops, and restaurants, all within walking distance of one another. Browse the stores to look for unique gifts and collectibles, such as cuckoo clocks, clogs, hand-crafted lace, glasswork, dolls, miniature ceramic windmills, a family coat of arms, and lots more. Snack on an aebleskiver - a Danish pancake ball concoction made with powdered sugar and served with raspberry jam. Just a few of our favorite stops include the Solvang Restaurant at 1672 Copenhagen Drive for great aebleskivers; Solvang Toyland at 1664 Copenhagen Drive for a selection of toys; Ingebrog's Danish Chocolate at 1679 Copenhagen for delectable chocolates and rich ice cream; Solvang Trolley Ice Cream Parlor at 16 18 Copenhagen Drive (because you can never have enough ice cream) with 20 flavors, including whiskey; and the Book Loft at 1680 Mission Drive for new, used, and rare books. The bookstore is also host to the HANS CHRISTIAN ANDERSEN MUSEUM and BOOK LOFT (pg. 625). The Farmer's Market is every Wednesday from 2:30pm tp 6pm.

Besides driving and walking around the village, other modes of transportation include renting a tandem, or two- to six-passenger surrey to pedal from Wheel Fun Rentals, 475 First Street (open daily, year round, 9am to 6pm, 7pm on the weekends), or taking a trolley ride. For the latter excursion, Belgian draft horses pull a replica 1915 Danish streetcar, or *honen* (Danish for "hen"), for about twenty-five minutes through the heart of downtown Solvang so visitors can see the town as well as hear about its history. The horse-drawn trolley rides of Solvang Trolley depart from the Visitor's Center on Copenhagen Drive most of the year Fridays through Mondays, 11:30am to 5pm (last ride leaves), and during the summer every day with extended hours (closed on Tuesdays) - weather permitting. Trolley rides are $14 for adults; $12 for seniors; $9 for ages 3 - 12; children 2 and under are free. Prices are sometimes higher in the summer or on holidays. Call (805) 794-8958 / www.solvangtrolley.com for more info and other carriage ride options.

Be on the lookout for the town's four windmills, the red and white Danish national flags, the half-scale model of Copenhagen's Little Mermaid (at the intersection of Mission and Alisal streets), and storks (not real ones) on roofs that are supposed to bring good luck. While in Solvang, you can also visit the ELVERHOJ MUSEUM (pg. 624), the SOLVANG MOTORCYCLE MUSEUM (pg. 633), PCPA THEATERFEST (pg. 640, 720) (during the summer only), and OLD MISSION SANTA INES (pg. 627). See the back of this book, under Index by City, for the numerous other nearby attractions besides just shopping and eating - although that works fine for our family! Also check the Calendar section for annual events. Mange tak. (Many thanks.)

Hours: The shops are usually open daily, 10am - 6pm. The visitor's center is open daily, 10am - 5pm.
Price: Free entrance and parking to Solvang. Bike rentals run from $15 an hour for road bikes to $50 an hour for six-passenger surreys.
Ages: All

—SHOWS AND THEATERS—

ARLINGTON THEATER AND CENTER FOR PERFORMING ARTS

(805) 963-4408 / www.thearlingtontheatre.com

$$$$$

1317 State Street, Santa Barbara

Enter via a Spanish courtyard, through a lobby decorated with ceiling murals of fiesta dancers and into the actual theater that was built to resemble a Spanish town, complete with elegant balconies and electronic "stars" twinkling overhead. The theater plays host to Broadway performances, such as *Cats*, plus Metropolitan Opera broadcasts, live headliner entertainers (i.e. Jerry Seinfeld), Michael Bolton, Cirque Wings, and so many more. In between live shows, the theater shows first-run, blockbuster movies.

Hours: Call for specific dates and times.
Price: Prices vary greatly depending on the show and date.
Ages: 8 years and up.

ENSEMBLE THEATER COMPANY

(805) 965-5400 / www.etcsb.org

$$$$

33 West Victoria Street, Santa Barbara

This resident theater troupe performs about four plays, or musicals, a year in the intimate, 300-seat theater. At least one of the plays is family-appropriate. School field trips are invited at the Student Matinee Series in particular, and school assemblies are offered.

Hours: Plays are usually performed Tues., 7pm; Wed. - Sat., 8pm; Sun. at 2pm and 7pm.

Price: Plays range from $35 (for preview performances) to $55 - $75 for regular performances, depending on the day, date, and time; $20 students and youth.

Ages: 7 years and up.

THE GRANADA

(805) 899-2222 - tickets; (805) 899-3000 or (805) 898-1417 - Concerts for Young People / www.granadasb.org

1214 State Street, Santa Barbara

A blend of old-time and contemporary grand theater, this sophisticated, restored theater is host and home to a wide variety of venues, including State Street Ballet, Broadway musicals, Opera Santa Barbara, Tony award winning musicals, Santa Barbara Choral Society, a family series, national and international touring groups, CAMA, Musical Academy of the West, headlining concerts, and special speaker series. The theater is also home to the Santa Barbara Symphony which performs a repertoire of traditional choral and pops selections throughout the year, including the Classics and Family Series. Educators, look online for information about the Mobile Music classroom series and for Concerts for Young People, where students can attend first-class performances in these stunning surroundings, accompanied by study guides. They sometimes have the opportunity to meet the performers, too. Check out the Music Mentors, where visiting artist present workshops, classes, and demonstrations.

Hours: Call for a schedule of performances.

Price: Prices vary according to show. Parking is about $3 an hour.

Ages: 4 years and up, depending on the production.

THE GREAT AMERICAN MELODRAMA & VAUDEVILLE

(805) 489-2499 / www.americanmelodrama.com

1863 Front Street, Oceano

For an evening of good, old-fashioned, light-hearted family entertainment, come boo, hiss, and cheer for the villains and heros (and heroines), respectively. (Participation is a must!) The music clues the audience in - if they can't figure out for themselves - as to when to do these actions. Each silly storyline is accompanied by lots of music and singing.

Upbeat piano music greets you as soon as you enter through the doors to the melodrama, getting you in the mood for a rollicking good time. Chairs are crowded around small round tables on the sawdust-covered floor. Other seating is available on benches around the raised perimeter of the room. The setting is intimate enough that the actors perform on stage without microphones. The show starts off with a sing along - the words are printed in the newspaper playbill. The hour-and-a-half feature presentation is just plain fun for all ages. Past productions have included *The Mark of Morro*, *Around the World in 80 Days*, *Less Miserable*, and *Scary Poppins*. After the melodrama, enjoy the half-hour vaudeville revue, with its song, dance, and comedy routine. Are your kids interested in performing on stage? Sign them up for summer Camp Melodrama where they can try out their acting chops.

During intermission, or before the main show, food and drinks are available from the servers, who are also the performers. The bill of fare includes hot dogs ($5.50); pulled pork sandwich ($7.50); nachos ($5.50); baked potato ($6 - $7); bowl of chili ($4.25); popcorn ($3.75); and assorted candy ($1.25). Kid's meals of a hot dog, chips, and soda served on a frisbee - $7.50. Tip: If you are interested in getting "real" dinner elsewhere before you arrive, check out ROCK AND ROLL DINER (pg. 603) which is just down the street. Note: I know that this theater isn't in Santa Barbara County, but it's so close to the border and the format was too unique and fun to pass up!

Hours: Show times are Wed., Thurs. and Fri. at 7pm; Sat., 3pm and 7pm; Sun., 6pm. Doors open a half hour before the show.

Price: $21 - $28 for adults, depending on the seat; $19 - $26 for seniors, students 13 - 17 year, and active military; $17 - $24 for ages 12 and under; children 2 and under are free if they are lap sitting, but it's best for kids at least 4 years old. Prices are slightly higher for the Holiday Extravaganza. A $2 handling fee is charged for all phone reservations. No performances on Easter, Thanksgiving, Christmas Eve and Christmas Day.

Ages: 5 years and up.

LOBERO THEATER

(888) 4LOBERO (456-2376) or (805) 963-0761- box office; (805) 679-6011 - tours and other info. / www.lobero.com

33 E. Canon Perdido Street, Santa Barbara

The Lobero is quite a busy theater, as well as the one of the oldest California theaters (originally built in 1873) in continuous operation. Attracting audiences from all age groups and cultural backgrounds, it hosts a wide variety of programming such as the Santa Barbara Grand Opera, Sings Like Hell concert series, and State Street Ballet, plus magic shows, concerts, dance programs, dramatic presentations, and other first-class performances. The theater also offers fifty-minute behind-the-scenes tours, by reservation only.

Hours: Call for performance schedules.

Price: Tickets prices vary depending on show title and date.

Ages: Depends on performance.

PCPA THEATERFEST

(805) 922-8313 - box office; (805) 928-7731 - bus. office / www.pcpa.org

2 locations: Santa Maria - 800 S. College Drive at the Marian and Severson Theaters at the Allan Hancock College (GPS users use 835 S. Bradley); Solvang - 420 2nd Street at the outdoor Festival Theater

Put a star next to this entry because the Pacific Conservatory of the Performing Arts (PCPA) knows how to make a theater experience a memorable one! Both theater locations have intimate settings, so the audience feels close to the on-stage action and professional actors. Many of the nine yearly plays and musicals are family friendly. Past shows have included *Hello Dolly!*, *Peter Pan*, *Little Women*, *Forever Plaid*, and *Shrek the Musical*.

We are especially enchanted by the 700-plus-seat Festival Theater in Solvang because the theater is outdoors. In the middle of this quaint Danish town, under a canopy of trees and starlight, as a cozy semi-circle of tiered seats surrounds the center stage, the magic of theater comes to life. Although the Solvang season runs mid-June through August, bring a blanket and/or jacket because the nights can get chilly. Note that last minute tickets are sometimes available.

The PCPA also has Outreach programs and tours that take age-appropriate shows to classrooms or other facilities. Program prices range from $12.50 - $15.

Hours: Call for show dates and times.

Price: Prices range, depending on date and show time. In Santa Maria - $30 - $46.50 for adults; $27.50 - $42.25 for seniors; $21 - $34 for students; $18.50 - $30.75 for ages 5 - 12 years. In Solvang - $39 - $57.50 for adults; $35.50 - $52.50 for seniors; $23.75 - $35.25 for students; $25.25 - $38.75 for children. Children 4 years and under are not admitted to shows. Thursday previews are sometimes less expensive.

Ages: 8 years and up.

SANTA MARIA CIVIC THEATER

(805) 922-4442 / www.smct.org

1660 North McClelland Street, Santa Maria

This 100-seat theater is host to nonprofessional actors who produce some good, area theater. Some of the shows are family friendly and some are even interactive; call first.

Hours: Call for specific shows and times.

Price: Call for specific show prices.

Ages: 5 years and up, depending on the performance.

STATE STREET BALLET

(805) 563-3262 - the ballet company; (805) 899-2222 - Granada box office; (805) 963-0761 - Lobero box office / www.statestreetballet.com; www.granadasb.org

1214 State Street at The Granada, Santa Barbara

This professional company tours nationally and also performs at "home", at The Granada, presenting both classic and contemporary ballets. The company occasionally performs at the Lobero Theatre - www.lobero.com. Make sure to catch at least one of four graceful and passionate shows performed each year. At Christmas time the holiday staple, *Nutcracker* is performed. Ask about the ballet's school and community outreach programs. For instance, students can be invited to performances during school hours when the troupe is in town, or the performers will come to schools for an on-site performance. The public is sometimes invited to open rehearsals.

Hours: Performances are usually given October - April, Fri., 7:30pm; Sat., 2pm, 7pm or 8pm; Sun., 2pm or 3pm.

Price: $40 - $60 for adults, depending on the date and the seats; $25 for students and ages 12 and under. Parking is $5.

Ages: 6 years and up.

—TOURS—

BRAILLE INSTITUTE (Santa Barbara County)

(805) 682-6222 / www.brailleinstitute.org

2031 De La Vina, Santa Barbara

A one-hour, or so, tour of the Braille Institute enables visitors to better understand how well the visually impaired can function in the world. The classrooms, library, art rooms, and computer labs are set up to enable the blind to gain life skills. Try the adaptive computer software which has zoom text and screen reader programs, or type something on the Braille embosser. Ask for permission to sit in on an orientation on how to use the white cane.

Hours: Call to schedule a tour for a group, or call as they will show individuals around, too. The Institute is open Mon. - Fri., 8:30am - 5pm.

Price: Free

Ages: 8 years old and up.

CALIFORNIA PIZZA KITCHEN (Santa Barbara County)

See the entry for CALIFORNIA PIZZA KITCHEN (Los Angeles County) (pg. 196) for more information.

GOLETA SANITARY DISTRICT

(805) 967-4519 / www.goletasanitary.org

One William Moffett Place, Goleta

Students can take a tour of this water resource recovery plant that complements school standards. (Other groups are welcome as well.) They learn about the water cycle by first listening to a talk on "following" a water stream (such as flushed toilet water) to see what happens to the water along its passage and at its destination. This is a very realistic and functional tour! Then, they visit the lab to analyze water samples and to learn to recognize chemical properties and components. Last, they walk through the treatment plant and huge water tanks to see the mechanics of how it all works. The minimum needed for a tour is ten students. Check out their fun and interactive open house given for the general public in the fall, in odd years, from 10am - 3pm, where hundreds of people come to explore, play and learn.

Hours: Tours are offered Tues. - Thurs. Call to make a reservation.

Price: Free

Ages: 4th graders and up.

SANTA BARBARA AVIATION EDUCATION CENTER

(805) 964-7622 or (805) 967-7111 /
www.santabarbaraca.gov/gov/depts/flysba/about/insidesba/visitorcenter.asp

45 Hartley Place, Goleta

Come learn about flying the friendly skies through a very-well presented tour at this airport and visitors center. The guided tour, which is the only way to see this facility, includes on-site classroom time and activities such as making and flying balsa wood airplanes. There are also a few hands-on aviation exhibits such as a small wooden plane to climb aboard, a flight simulator, and a radio-controlled aircraft that students fly in wind tunnels to get the feel for currents and navigation. One wind tunnel is similar to the one in the Smithsonian Air and Space Museum, but better aerodynamically.

The small exhibit hall also contains several model airplanes and lots of literature and videos (over 200 of them!) pertaining to flight. These are great resources for teachers. The local history of aviation and Santa Barbara's contribution to flight and space exploration is also spotlighted. The age-appropriate tours are usually about an hour long, depending on the age and attention span of the attendees. Tours are given for a minimum of ten students and a maximum of fifty. In-class presentations are available upon request, too. Note that once a year the center hosts a wonderful, GATE certified class on aviation for area 6th graders who excel in math and science. The visitors center is also the home base for the Santa Barbara Radio Modelers and for the YOUNG EAGLES PROGRAM (Santa Barbara County) (pg. 646).

Since the visitors center, which is wheelchair and stroller accessible, is adjacent to the airport, guests can also watch small planes land and take off. Note that the Santa Barbara airport is in the city of Santa Barbara on paper, but it's in the heart of Goleta. (I am taking no political stance on this one.)

Hours: Tours are available on Tues., Wed., and Thurs., 9am - 4pm, by appointment only. Call at least two weeks ahead of the time you'd like to visit.

Price: Free

Ages: Kindergarten and up.

SANTA MARIA TIMES

(805) 739-2143 or (805) 925-2691 / www.santamariatimes.com

3200 Skyway Drive, Santa Maria

Take a tour of this small-town newspaper to see how production is done. Walk through the newsroom seeing various departments to see and learn how a paper is put together. You'll also see old publications, dating from the 1800s, and see "cut and paste" via the computer. Depending on the time of your tour you can view the presses running, from a safe distance. See the papers coming off the conveyor and being set up on pallets. Your group needs to be a minimum of four and a maximum of fifteen.

Try to set up a tour, which lasts about forty-five minutes, in the afternoon when more of the staff are working. Morning tours will find a skeleton crew.

Hours: Tours are offered by appointment.

Price: Free

Ages: 6 years and up.

—TRANSPORTATION—

AMTRAK (Santa Barbara County)

(800) USA RAIL (872-7245) / www.amtrakcalifornia.com

Ride the rails! See AMTRAK (Los Angeles County) (pg. 208) for more information.

BIKE MAPS (Santa Barbara County)

See BIKE MAPS (Orange County) (pg. 328) for information. Also check the Santa Barbara Traffic Solution, (805) 963-SAVE (7283) or (805) 961-8900 / www.sbcag.org.

BIKE TRAIL: CABRILLO BEACHWAY (BIKEWAY)

bike.lacity.org; www.labikepaths.com

parallel to Cabrillo Boulevard, Santa Barbara

This mostly flat, three-mile, palm-lined path runs along the waterfront, from the LEADBETTER BEACH (pg. 601) parking lot to the ANDREE CLARK BIRD REFUGE (pg. 606) near the SANTA BARBARA ZOO (pg. 649). Note: The paved path gets very crowded on the weekends, especially during the summer.

Hours: Open daily, sunrise - sunset.

Price: Free

Ages: 4 years and up.

CLOUD CLIMBERS JEEP TOURS

(805) 646-3200 / www.ccjeeps.com

6/$

Departs from Santa Barbara and Solvang

A jeep ride is sometimes simply the best way to see a portion of the world, and I appreciate it when someone else, besides me, does the driving. (It's easier to sightsee!) The three-hour, narrated, Family Discovery Tour is designed with kids in mind. As the jeep climbs up and around the back country and the rugged mountains of Santa Ynez, the driver/tour guide shares the tales and history of the region, including its human and animal inhabitants, and facts about plant life. Kids (and adults) really understand and learn about nature, the Chumash Indians, and early settlers as they travel along portions of the original stagecoach road, and around rock formations and sandstone cliffs while looking and listening for clues during the Discovery Game. This tour also includes a short hike and a stop off at the painted cave, where you can peek in at a cave with Chumash drawings. All this, plus a panoramic view make for a memorable experience. There are several other tours available, too, including Horse-n-Around (which includes horseback riding) and "It's a Blast" which includes a stop at a private gun club.

The open-sided jeeps have canopies and seat five to seven people. Pack sunscreen and/or a hat, and bring a light jacket. Bottled water and blankets are provided.

Hours: Call to make a reservation for tours. The Discovery Tour departs at 9am and 1pm.

Price: The Discovery tour is $550 for up to 5 passengers. The three-hour Santa Ynez Mountain Tour is $89 per person, with a four person minimum.

Ages: Must be at least 6 years old.

CLOUD NINE GLIDER RIDES

(805) 602-6620 / www.cloud9gliderrides.com
900 Airport Road, Santa Ynez

Talk about quietly soaring above it all! A breath-taking sensation and scenery adds up to an unforgettable experience as you lift off and up in the one or two-seater glider plane with amazing wingspans. It's like sailing in the sky. It is *almost* as much fun to bring a blanket and some snacks to just watch the pilots and passengers. (Call first to see if anyone is flying, though.)

Hours: Call to book a flight.
Price: $185 for a 10 - 15-minute, 2,500 feet above sea level, Scenic Flight with a view of the Santa Ynez Valley and a little beyond; $279 per person for a 15 - 20-minute Mountain Adventure flight; $375 for 5,200 feet, 30-minute Mile High adventure to see the entire Central Coast and points inland.
Ages: 14 years and up to fly; all ages to watch.

CONDOR EXPRESS CRUISES

(888) 77WHALE (779-4253) or (805) 882-0088 / www.condorcruises.com; www.sealanding.net
301 W. Cabrillo Boulevard at Sea Landing, Santa Barbara

Board the *Condor Express,* a seventy-five-foot, double deck, full-service bar and galley, high-speed catamaran along the coast to look for gray whales from mid-February through mid-May. A naturalist explains what you see and why you are seeing it on the two-and-a-half hour excursions. Take a four-and-a-half-hour island trip to the Channel Islands the rest of the year to watch for blue whales and humpbacks, as well as numerous other marine mammals. You'll probably also get to check out the Painted Cave on Santa Cruz Island.

Hours: Coastal whale watching trips are daily, in season, at 9am, noon, and 3pm. Island cruises are offered daily, weather permitting, at 10am. Closed Thanksgiving, Christmas Eve and Christmas Day.
Price: Coastal whale watching excursions are $50 for adults; $30 for ages 5 - 12; children 4 and under are free. Island excursions are $99 for adults most of the year; $50 for ages 5 - 12; children 4 and under are free. Parking in beach lot is about $2 an hour; $12 max; $3 with validation.
Ages: 6 years and up for most cruises.

LAND AND SEA TOURS

(805) 683-7600 / www.out2seesb.com
10 East Cabrillo Boulevard, Santa Barbara

Land Shark! This oversized, forty-four passenger, odd-looking "bus", or boat with wheels, is amphibious, meaning it is capable of operating on both land and water. Your wonderful, ninety-minute, narrated tour starts off on land, traveling up and down the streets of Santa Barbara and the waterfront, seeing and assimilating information and anecdotes about the history, culture, and people of this town, both past and present. You'll pass by the Moreton Bay Fig tree, historic adobes, the Courthouse, and more landmarks, as well as travel along State Street.

The last half is spent in the water - it's a fun adventure just feeling the vehicle dip in! You'll navigate the harbor and hear how it was formed via dredging, learn about the commercial fishing industry, float past expensive yachts and Stearns Wharf, and cruise out to the seal lions. You might see some dolphins, too. Keep an eye out for the various sea birds, such as egrets, gulls, and pelicans.

Throughout your adventure, the captain keeps you well-informed on your surroundings in an entertaining manner. Visual aids are also incorporated, such as charts and sea urchins, making this an ideal excursion for both kids and adults. Bring a light jacket, regardless of the time of year.

Hours: Tours usually depart daily November - April at noon and 2pm; May - October at noon, 2pm and 4pm. Trips may be sold out in advance, so call first. (They don't take reservations.) Private bookings may call to schedule departure at other times. Closed New Year's Day, Thanksgiving and Christmas.
Price: $30 for adults; $15 for ages 10 and under; children under 2 are free. Parking at the beach is about $2 an hour; $12 max.
Ages: 5 years and up.

METROPOLITAN TRANSIT DISTRICT

(805) 963-3366 - transit center; (805) 683-3364 - bus. office / www.sbmtd.gov
1020 Chapala Street, Santa Barbara

Catch the inexpensive MTD service that runs from the waterfront to over ten highlights of Santa Barbara, including the Mission, the Botanic Garden, County Courthouse, and Museum of Art. The transit runs from Carpinteria to Goleta. The address given above is for the main station. Pick up a schedule here, on any MTD bus, or online.

Hours: Open daily. Call for hours and scheduled stops. No service on Thanksgiving or Christmas.
Price: One-way fare is $1.75; a day pass is $6. 3 children under 45" are free with a paying adult; other children, 5 - 17, are $1.75 each. .85¢ for seniors. Exact change is needed.
Ages: All

PADDLE SPORTS CENTER

(805) 617-3425 / www.islandpackers.com; www.paddlesportsca.com
117-B Harbor Way, Santa Barbara

$$$$

Rent kayaks at $15 for one hour for a single; $30 for a two-seater. Stand up paddle boards are $30 for one hour. Surfboards are $15 an hour; boogie boards are $10; wetsuits are $10. Locker rentals ($2 an hour) and showers are here, too. Kayaking and SUP lessons, plus classes and summer camps are also available.

Time for an adventure! Guided tours are the best way to become educated about the environment; soaking in knowledge while soaking in the sun. The History and Wildlife kayak excursion, for instance, is in the harbor - two hours for $55, gliding in and out of the pier pilings, along the shoreline, getting almost nose to snout with sea lions, and really learning about and *sea*ing the water and all that is in it, on it and near it. Or take a two-hour sunset tour for the same price. SUP tours are also available. Wear a hat, and bring sunscreen and a water bottle.

Hours: Generally open daily, 8am (open at 7am in the summer) - an hour before sunset. Closed in rainy weather. Excursions take place at various times and dates throughout the year - check the website for specific info.
Price: Prices are listed above. Parking is generally $2 an hour; $12 max.
Ages: Must be able to swim.

SANTA BARBARA SAILING CENTER / DOUBLE DOLPHIN CRUISE

(805) 962-2826 / www.sbsail.com
133 Harbor Way, Santa Barbara

$$$$

Almost anything water-oriented is offered here. Single kayaks rent for $12 an hour, $10 for college students 24 years old and under; double kayaks are $24, $20 for college students. Pedal boats are $30 for an hour. Stand-Up paddle boards are $25 an hour. For rowing champs, rent a rowing scull at $25 an hour. A 22' Capri sailing boat is $65 an hour. Two-and-a-half, narrated Whale Watching cruises are available seasonally, mid-February through mid-May for $50 for adults; $25 for college students; $30 for ages 12 and under. On this tour also be on the lookout for dolphins, sea lions, and seals. Or, take the one-hour Harbor Cruise out and around the harbor, especially near the buoys where the mammals tend to hang out, sunbathe and bark, and keep an eye out for other marine life. This tour is offered on certain dates throughout the year for $20 per person. Reservations are required.

Other cruises include a two-hour sunset cruise offered at select times year round for $40 for adults and kids; $30 for 12 and under; discounts given for college students Monday through Thursday. Kids and adults can also learn the ropes of sailing by taking a class, so why *knot*? The center also offers classes on kayaking, plus kids camps, and more. Call for a full schedule.

Hours: The Sailing Center is open daily, March - October, 9am - 6pm; November - February, 9am - 5pm. Whale watching cruises depart daily during the season at 10am and 1pm, although these hours can change.
Price: Some prices are given above. Parking in beach lot is $2 an hour; $12 max.
Ages: 6 years and up, depending on excursion.

SANTA BARBARA TROLLEY COMPANY

(805) 965-0353 / www.sbtrolley.com
23 E. Cabrillo, Santa Barbara

$$$$

Clang, clang, clang goes the trolley! Come aboard and see the highlights of Santa Barbara while hearing its history and hearing anecdotes about the town and some of its citizens. Take the ninety-minute narrated tour nonstop, or stop off at Stearns Wharf, the Mission, the Courthouse, downtown (to shop), and/or numerous other places, and reboard any time throughout the day at no extra cost. Remember, too, that for kids, this traditional trolley ride is part of the excursion fun.

Hours: Trolley tours operate daily, leaving once an hour from each of the 14 destinations, starting at 10am to about 3pm (last tour leaves from the visitor center). Note that the last 2 tours of the day may have no return trip to the pick-up location.

Price: $22 for adults; one child 12 and under is free with each paid adult; additional child day pass is $8. Infants are free if they are sitting on your lap. The second consecutive day is free. Ask about family deals or check online for discounts for area attractions with the purchase of a trolley ticket. Parking at the beach lot is about $2 an hour; $12 max.

Ages: 3 years and up.

SANTA BARBARA WATERFRONT / DOWNTOWN SHUTTLE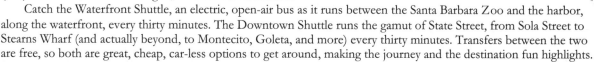

(805) 963-3366 / www.sbmtd.gov; www.santabarbara.com $

Catch the Waterfront Shuttle, an electric, open-air bus as it runs between the Santa Barbara Zoo and the harbor, along the waterfront, every thirty minutes. The Downtown Shuttle runs the gamut of State Street, from Sola Street to Stearns Wharf (and actually beyond, to Montecito, Goleta, and more) every thirty minutes. Transfers between the two are free, so both are great, cheap, car-less options to get around, making the journey and the destination fun highlights.

Hours: Shuttles run every 15 min. daily, 10am - 6pm. Shuttles also run the day before Memorial Day - day after Labor Day until 9pm on Fri. and Sat.

Price: 50¢ per person one-way; 25¢ for seniors; 3 children 45" and under are free with a paying adult; otherwise, ages 5 - 17 are 50¢ each. Exact change is needed.

Ages: All

SANTA BARBARA WATER TAXI / LIL TOOT

(805) 896-6900 or (805) 465-6676 / www.celebrationsantabarbara.com; www.sbwatertaxi.com $$

237 Stearns Wharf off W. Cabrillo Boulevard, and 113 Harbor Way, Santa Barbara

Board *Lil Toot,* which looks like a tug boat, for a fun, half-hour roundtrip, or fifteen minutes one-way excursion, in the harbor of Santa Barbara. You'll start (or end) at Stearns Wharf, go past the Sea Center, the pier, and restaurants along the waterfront, and out to the breakwater - what a fantastic view! You'll learn a little local history along the way of the area, the sea life, and the shore birds. You also cruise among the yachts (some worth millions of dollars) and sailboats at the marina. You can also start (or end) at the harbor near the Maritime Museum, at the end of Harbor Way. Get your cameras ready as kids get to play jr. captain and steer the boat (briefly) and sound the boat's steam whistle. Note that kid's birthday parties are $99 for a 45-minute cruise in the harbor and every child gets a chance to drive the boat.

Hours: Shuttles run every half hour during the summer daily, noon - sunset; open on weekends only in the winter, noon - 6pm.

Price: One-way fare is $5 for adults; $2 for ages 3 - 12; children 2 and under are free. Parking is free for 90 minutes with validation at either boarding point.

Ages: 2 years and up.

SANTA MARIA SPEEDWAY

(805) 992-2232 / www.racesantamariaspeedway.com $$$$

1900 Hutton Road, Santa Maria

Factory stocks, street stocks, sprint cars, minis, and more take to the track seasonally bringing excitement (and noise!) to spectators. The one-third-mile clay surface oval track has a three-foot-high concrete crash wall encircling it and a row of trees at the ridgeline, behind the bleachers, that provide a natural windbreak.

Hours: April - October on most Sat. nights - the gates open at 3pm; races start at 6pm. Check the website for Sunday Funday races, too.

Price: $16 - $25 for adults, depending on race and date; $6 for seniors and ages 6 - 12.

Ages: 5 years and up.

SEA LANDING

(805) 963-3564 or (888) 77WHALE (779-4253) - Sea Landing; (805) 570-2351 - Jet Boats / $$$$
www.sealanding.net; www.sbjetboats.com

301 W. Cabrillo Boulevard at Sea Landing, Santa Barbara

Sea Landing is the hub for renting kayaks and jet skis, as well as reserving boat tours for CONDOR EXPRESS CRUISES (pg. 643). Jet ski rentals, available only in the summer, are $135 per hour. (The rental comes with wet suits, etc.) An 18-foot jet boat that holds up to seven people is $285 for an hour; one that holds five people is $225 an hour. SUPs are $15 for an hour; $20 for two hours. Kayaks are a great price at $18 for singles and $30 for doubles - for up to three hours!

Hours: Open daily, 7:30am - 6pm. Rentals are available from 10am - 6pm (last rental) Thurs. - Sun. most of the year; open daily May - August. Closed some holidays.

Price: See above.

Ages: 6 years and up.

SUNSET KIDD SAILING

(805) 962-8222 / www.sunsetkidd.com

125 Harbor Way, Santa Barbara

$$$$$

Sailing cruises have a whole different feel than that of a more typical, large, noisy passenger cruise. Experience the sea waters on a two-hour morning or afternoon sail; two-and-a-half-hours on a whale watching cruise, available mid-February through mid-May; or ninety-minutes for a lovely sunset cruise.

Hours: Cruises set sail daily, mid-February - September at 10am, 2pm and 5:15pm. They set sail October - mid-February, Mon., Thurs. - Sun., at 10am, 2pm, and 5:15pm. Closed Tues., Wed., Thanksgiving, Christmas Eve and Christmas Day.

Price: $40 per person for most cruises. On the morning whale watching cruises, ages 4 - 10 are $25; ages 3 and under are free. Parking in beach lots varies by lot - one is about $2 an hour; $12 max.

Ages: 8 years and up.

WHEEL FUN RENTALS

(805) 966-2282 / www.wheelfunrentalssb.com

34 East Mason Street, Santa Barbara

$$$$

If you forgot to bring your own, you can still have some *wheel* along Santa Barbara's bike paths and harbor by renting transportation. Mountain bikes are $12.95 an hour; $10.96 for a cruiser; $8.95 for kids bike; $20.95 for tandems; and $29.95 for a single surrey; $39.95 for a double. They also rent roller blades, boogie boards, wheel chairs, and more. This company has multiple locations in Santa Barbara and throughout Southern California.

Hours: Open day after Labor Day - Memorial Day, daily, 8am - 6pm. Open Memorial Day - Labor Day, daily, 8am - 9pm.

Price: Prices are listed above.

Ages: 3 years and up.

YOUNG EAGLES PROGRAM (Santa Barbara County)

National number - (877) 806-8902; Santa Barbara - (805) 967-2943 - chapter #527; Santa Ynez - (805) 688-3169 - chapter #491 / www.youngeagles.org; www.sbaero.com - Santa Barbara; www.491.eeachapter.org - Santa Ynez

Santa Barbara - 45 Hartley Road; Santa Ynez - 900 Airport Road

See the entry for YOUNG EAGLES PROGRAM (Los Angeles County) (pg. 216) for details.

Hours: Santa Barbara - The program doesn't have set times as it is by reservation only, so call to schedule a time to be flying high! Santa Ynez - Offered usually once in the spring and once in the fall - call for exact dates and times.

Price: Free

Ages: 8 - 17 years.

—ZOOS AND ANIMALS—

CABRILLO HIGH SCHOOL AQUARIUM

(805) 742-2888 / www.cabrilloaquarium.org

4350 Constellation Road, Lompoc

This is an impressive aquarium, especially for a high school campus! The aquarium is composed of several large tanks, a few smaller ones, a theater, computers, murals, and static models fish. Murals, located in a city renowned for its murals, are depictions of Pacific Blue whales, of the local coastline, of the underwater kelp forest with local animals, and of the tropical rainforest. Aquatic-related photographs and artwork also decorate the room. Fish "swimming" overhead include a full-sized dolphin and a ten-foot model of a Great White Shark. Computers record every angle of the aquarium and are available to use for research.

One tank holds jellyfish. Actually, they're called moon jellies, and they look other-worldly. The warm water reef tank is visually exciting because the coral habitat holds brilliantly-colored fish such as clown fish, yellow tangs, damselfish, rainbow wrasse, and firefish. Two tanks hold sea horses; one for potbelly sea horses and another for tropical, lined sea horses. Crustaceans, such as spiny lobsters and crabs, are in another tank; one Pacific spiny lobster is fifteen pounds and eighty-years-old! The tropical marine life tank showcases puffer fish, angelfish, several wrasse, and brittle stars. Other containers hold bass, eels, perch, octopus, and sea anemones. An incubator is really a nursery for the main in-house food source - brine shrimp. A light shines through swell shark egg casings enabling visitors to see shark embryos. Marine life, such as sea cucumbers, sea stars, and sea urchins, are in a touch tank. The outside of the state-of-the-art, thirty-five-seat theater resembles a weathered lighthouse. Inside, various films are shown on the screen that can also be used as touch screen.

Community outreach programs, summer camps, and tours for schools and other groups are available by reservation.

Hours: Usually open once a month to the public, usually at nighttime at 6:30pm. Call for date and time, or to book a tour.
Price: Free
Ages: 3 years and up.

HARBOR SEAL PRESERVE

www.carpinteriacoast.com; www.carpinteria.com
at the end of Bailard Avenue, Carpinteria

Seal lovers enjoy a stop-off at this bluff-top observation point. Although the seals are here year long, the best viewing is December through May, during pupping season. (Although one never *really* knows when the seals will decide to visit.) For the half-mile trek, take the CARPINTERIA BLUFFS NATURE PRESERVE AND TRAIL (pg. 608) dirt trail south towards the beach, hang a right, follow the path south over the railroad tracks, and go right. (This is not a stroller/wheelchair friendly excursion.) The rookery is located at the south end of the pier - look for its sign and a bench. Note - it is illegal to walk on this section of beach from December through May, so, essentially, you just look down below at the seals, sunning themselves on the beach or splashing around in the water, and listen to their bellows. You can also take the trail and hike north, about two and a half miles round trip, to reach CARPINTERIA STATE BEACH (pg. 598).

Hours: Open daily, sunrise - sunset.
Price: Free
Ages: 5 years and up.

OSTRICH LAND USA

(805) 686-9696 / www.ostrichlandusa.com
610 E. Hwy. 246, Buellton

What are the differences between an ostrich and an emu? Stop by and see for yourself! Ostrichland has about fifty ostriches roaming around in a twenty-acre enclosure just off the highway. Pay your money and go behind the store on the walkway in front of the ranch to get a closer peek (not a closer peck). You can also purchase ostrich feed ($1) to bring them within breathing distance. Although you won't be here long (maybe 20 minutes), it's a good opportunity to see ostriches and the ten, or so, emus, which are in a separate enclosure, up close.

Ostriches, one of the world's largest birds, lay equally huge eggs: One ostrich egg is equivalent to about twenty-four chicken eggs. (We purchased one and invited the neighborhood over for a huge omelet.) The small produce stand/gift shop here, which is Ostrich Land's main business, offers fresh ostrich eggs, emu eggs (which are avocado green in color and available in the winter and spring), ostrich meat (which doesn't come from the ostriches on this ranch), feathers, and other ostrich products. A small selection of seasonal fruits and vegetables are also available here. A parting thought: If you are what you eat, consider that ostriches can run forty-five mph, they can live to 100 years old, and they breed three times a day.

Hours: Open most of the year daily, 9am - dusk.
Price: $5 for adults; $4 for seniors; $2 for ages 12 and under.
Ages: 3 years and up.

QUICKSILVER RANCH

(805) 686-4002
1555 Alamo Pintado Road, Solvang

Question: What's small and says "neigh"? Answer: Miniature horses. Quicksilver Ranch is a working breeding facility and home to over eighty miniature horses. (A horse must not exceed thirty-four inches to be registered as a miniature.) The small "so cute!" horses romp and graze in the twenty acres of lush, grassy enclosures. Even young visitors will enjoy strolling the grounds as they can get up close and personal with the animals because the pens are down-scaled. Oftentimes a handler brings out a horse to pet. Please keep in mind that this is not a petting zoo and don't bring food to feed the horses. If you want to see baby miniature horses (making them mini minis), twenty to thirty are usually born during the months of April, May, and June. You won't be here long, but it's a fun mini-excursion. Note: You'll drive past goats and full-size horses that live on adjacent ranches.

Hours: Open Mon. - Sat., 10am - 3pm. Closed Sun., Thanksgiving and Christmas.
Price: Free
Ages: 3 years and up.

RETURN TO FREEDOM WILD HORSE SANCTUARY ☼

(805) 737-9246 / www.returntofreedom.org $$$$$
4115 Jalama Road, Lompoc

Picture wild horses running with abandon through tall grasses, past oak trees, and over hills; their manes and tails flowing behind them. Welcome to Return to Freedom, where almost 400 wild mustangs, the last true vestiges of the American West, roam the grounds with their natural (and diverse) herds, or family groups, on this 310-acre ranch sanctuary. The sanctuary's goals are to preserve these majestic mustangs in their natural habitat and to educate visitors through direct encounters with them. Children and adults have the rare opportunity to observe the wild horses (and their colts) on their own turf, to gently and respectfully approach them, and to develop compassion as they learn the history (and hopefully the future) of the horses. Be prepared to do some walking over hilly terrain and to have romanticized images of cowboy roundups revamped.

Though most of the horses live in herds that free-range the hills, a few of the horses are in open-air paddocks. Some of these animals have come from abusive owners and need special care or supplements. One horse, however, has had a starring role. The beautiful stallion used as the model for Disney's animated movie *Spirit, Stallion of Cimarron* has been retired and now lives at the ranch. Other animals that consider the sanctuary home include burros and a few goats and chickens.

Most "tours" start in the barn area/learning center. Depending on the type of tour, visitors can watch a video about the sanctuary; see maps of where the horse herds are located; hear about the history of the horses, which are descendants of the Spanish conquistador's horses; learn about the government's role in the harsh treatment of mustangs; and learn horse behavior such as grooming, communication, social structure, head tosses, and how a lead horse acts.

The over three hour, introductory, Sanctuary Tour involves the above plus a walk into the hills to quietly observe the horses, examine herd behavior, and perhaps interact with them, if the horses invite it. Youth and Family Day at the Ranch is where kids can help out at the ranch by feeding them, cleaning up manure, grooming the tamer animals, and doing other ranch chores, plus interacting with the horses. Volunteering opportunities, for ages 8 and up, are available on Volunteer Work Days, the last Saturday of each month from 10am to 3pm. Volunteers do whatever needs to be done - weeding, carpentry, cleaning manure, painting, repairing fences, prepping for events, whatever! A short walk to see the herds is included at the end, plus volunteers are invited then to join the Sanctuary Tour that follows. Three-hour Photo Safaris, led by equine photographer, are a unique opportunity to photograph, and learn how to photograph, these beautiful animals. These are just some of the programs offered. If wild horses can't drag you here, hop in your mini van!

Hours: All tours are usually offered May - September: Sanctuary Tours are offered the last Sat. of each month from 3pm - 6pm (right after the volunteer day hours); Youth and Family Day is held the 3 summer months on the first Sat., 10am - 3pm; Photo Safaris are offered the second Sat. Check the online calendar or call for other tours, events, and information.
Price: Youth and Family Day is $45 per adult/child pair; $15 for each additional child, adult, friend, etc. The Sanctuary Tour is $50 for adults; $15 for ages 12 and under. Photo Safaris are $200. Call for other event prices.
Ages: 8 years and up, depending on the tour.

SANTA BARBARA POLO ☼

(805) 684-6683 or (805) 684-5819; (805) 684-3093 - clubhouse / www.sbpolo.com $$$
3300 Via Real, Carpinteria

Watching a polo game was an unexpectedly enthralling event. At the start, eight players, four per team, astride their thoroughbreds with long mallets in hand, loosely gathered around the mounted umpire who bowled in the ball. Whack! A player swung the mallet in an arch, connected with the ball and sent it down the field as the other players galloped in pursuit. Each horse and rider pair ran, pivoted, stopped, and maneuvered their way up and down the court with skill and finesse, racing each other, side by side. FYI - the beautifully manicured field is three football fields in length.

We learned a new word, "chukker," which is the seven minutes of playing time per period. There are six chukkers per game, with four minutes in-between each one. At the ten-minute half-time during the main match on Sunday, everyone is invited out onto the field for a Divot Stomp - stomping to help replace the divots (and to run around and socialize, plus a free glass of apple cider or champagne is included). Grandstand seats are not shaded at all, so bring sunscreen. Seats are first come, first served.

Bring your own food to have a tailgate party, or order food from the adjacent snack bar which offers burgers, salads, sandwiches, hot dogs, soda, and more. The clubhouse restaurant, also attached to the stands, is for members only. Note that the club offers polo classes for adults and youth, as well as summer camps.

Hours: Polo season runs May - mid-October. Tournament games are sometimes played on Fri. and Sat., but usually played on Sun. at 1pm, with the main match at 3pm; gates open at noon. Practice games are sometimes held on Wed., Thurs. or Sat.

Price: $10 per person Sunday tournament games; free for the practices.

Ages: 6 years and up.

SANTA BARBARA ZOO

(805) 962-6310 - recording; (805) 962-5339 - live person, Mon. - Fri. or (805) 963-5695 on weekends. / www.sbzoo.org

500 Niños Drive, Santa Barbara

This engaging, mid-size zoo lives up to the zoological gardens part of its description in that the over 500 animals in naturalistic settings dwell in and amongst a myriad of lush plants.

Brightly-colored macaws, although centralized in the parrot garden, are also found in several locations throughout the zoo. The flamingoes have their own lagoon area. Walk through the tropical aviary to view more beautiful birds. You can feed the red, purple, blue, and green lorikeets, or just go into their aviary and watch them land on your arm or head. Bring a camera!

The nocturnal hall contains a sloth and other nighttime animals. The aquarium and reptile complex houses some unique creatures, such as snake-necked turtles and a matamata turtle with its snorkel-like nose and lizard-like head and neck. A python, some bats, various types of frogs, Madagascar hissing cockroaches, stingrays, and arowana fish - with their fish heads and eel-like bodies - are also in here.

Look at the sea lions, with both above and below ground viewing. Feeding time is usually from 1pm to 2pm. The playful River Otters are also fun to watch, especially at feeding time, which happens four times a day. You can hear the gibbons screeching and hooting before actually reaching their enclosure. The Lowland Gorillas, meerkats, anteater, Asian elephants, coatimundi, alligators, monkeys, and even penguins are not only fascinating to observe, but easy to see as their habitats are relatively small. Watch the big cats (lions, snow leopards, Amur leopards, etc.) pace, play around, or indulge in their favorite activity - sleep. On weekdays, usually from 11:30am until 1:30pm, and until 2:30pm on weekends, you can hand-feed the giraffes from the Giraffe Deck for $8 for adults; $4 for kids. (Their tongues are long, black, and a little bit sticky!) A small playground has large, pretend, dinosaur eggs to play in, a rope spider web to climb, an anthill to act like a roly poly and roll down, and more. You can also pet and maybe feed llamas, goats, and sheep through the fence at the Barnyard. On the weekends, school breaks and holidays, climb a 26-foot rock wall for $6 to reach new heights. For an additional $6.50 for adults, $6 for ages 2 to 12 (children under 2 are free), hop on board a mini train (which is handicap accessible) for a ten-minute ride around the perimeter of the zoo. Picnic grounds are just around the corner and you are allowed to bring outside food inside.

Ask about the zoo's numerous age-appropriate workshops, geared for tiny tots up to junior zookeepers. Other interactive zoo happenings include camp outs, which means spending the night at the zoo and meeting some of the animals, especially nocturnal ones; breakfast with the animals, for members only; behind-the-scenes tours; Backstage Pass, a ninety-minute program for ages 5 and up to work alongside a zookeeper, see how they are cared for, and/or feed some of them - it's all up close and personal; discovery kits for classroom use; and Theater Gone Wild. This theater group puts on performances both at the zoo, like *How to Train Your Dinosaurs,* and at school or Scout facilities. Note that the ANDREE CLARK BIRD REFUGE (pg. 606) is just outside the zoo perimeter. Have a wild time at this great zoo!

Hours: Open daily, 10am - 5pm. Closed at 3:30pm on Thanksgiving, Christmas Eve., and Christmas, and sometimes for special events.

Price: $18 for adults; $13 for seniors; $10 for ages 2 - 12; children under 2 are free. Parking is $8 on weekdays; $11 on weekends and holidays.

Ages: All

SEA CENTER

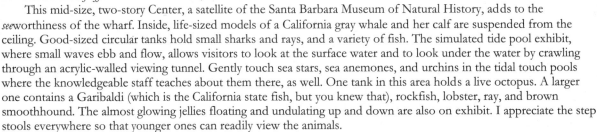

(805) 962-2526 or (805) 682-4711 / www.sbnature.org

211 Stearns Wharf off W. Cabrillo Boulevard, Santa Barbara

This mid-size, two-story Center, a satellite of the Santa Barbara Museum of Natural History, adds to the *see*worthiness of the wharf. Inside, life-sized models of a California gray whale and her calf are suspended from the ceiling. Good-sized circular tanks hold small sharks and rays, and a variety of fish. The simulated tide pool exhibit, where small waves ebb and flow, allows visitors to look at the surface water and to look under the water by crawling through an acrylic-walled viewing tunnel. Gently touch sea stars, sea anemones, and urchins in the tidal touch pools where the knowledgeable staff teaches about them there, as well. One tank in this area holds a live octopus. A larger one contains a Garibaldi (which is the California state fish, but you knew that), rockfish, lobster, ray, and brown smoothhound. The almost glowing jellies floating and undulating up and down are also on exhibit. I appreciate the step stools everywhere so that younger ones can readily view the animals.

The Bio Lab is set up like a working marine laboratory that allows tactile encounters of sea cucumbers and up close observation of swell sharks and other inhabitants. In the back room is a Wet Deck, which means you peer down through an opening in the floor to the water below. Using research equipment, you may help dredge, collect, and sift through samples of the water, sediments, and whatever else gets captured. You might be surprised at what tiny creatures you see. Make sure you open the lockers placed throughout the Center. As you do, you'll hear a recording about the person pictured on the front - what they do and why they became a marine biologist or oceanographer. You'll also see some of the tools of their trade and some personal belongings.

Upstairs you can test water, via a video magnifier, for salinity, pH balance, and temperature. A small theater continuously shows a short film on the sea life in the Santa Barbara channel. Can you sound like an angry orca? How about a romantic sea lion? Tucked in the nook of a wall is a computer kiosk, known as Whale Karaoke. Here you select a mammal, then an emotion, and push play for that recorded sound. Mimic and record your own take on the sound and watch as the computer matches the comparison graphically. One profound exhibit is a preserved pregnant female dolphin who washed on shore. A segment of her is cut away to expose her internal organs and her baby. While you're up here, don't forget to check out the view of the coastline and ocean.

Even if you live by the sea, you might not know a lot about it or its creatures. The Sea Center offers the opportunity to remedy that in a fairly intimate setting. School tours, birthday parties, and other groups and individuals are welcome. Look up SANTA BARBARA HARBOR / STEARNS WHARF (pg. 635) for details about the immediate area, and take a walk on the pier for a bite to eat and to shop while you are here.

Hours: Open daily, 10am - 5pm. Closed first Friday in August for Old Spanish Days Fiesta, as well as New Year's Day, Thanksgiving, Christmas Eve (at noon), and Christmas Day.

Price: $8.50 for adults; $7.50 for seniors and ages 13 - 17; $6 for ages 2 - 12; children under 2 are free. Parking is free for the first ninety minutes with validation. Otherwise, parking in beach lot is about $2.50 an hour; $12 max. There is some free street parking. Parking on the pier is about $2.50 an hour.

Ages: 3 years and up.

WHALE WATCHING

See the TRANSPORTATION section.

VENTURA COUNTY

Located between two major tourist markets, Los Angeles and Santa Barbara, Ventura County is a low-key, but worthy destination. As coastal fog along the shores of Oxnard and Ventura lift, the distant Channel Islands are unveiled. Take a cruise out to them. Walk along Main Street in Ventura for a cluster of attractions, as well as some terrific shopping. Inland and northward are the towns of Ojai, with its refined atmosphere, and Santa Paula, with its mid-West open-door policy, but better weather than that part of the U.S.

—AMUSEMENT PARKS—

CASITAS WATER ADVENTURE

(805) 649-2233 / www.lakecasitas.info
11311 Santa Ana Road, Ventura

This small, but refreshing water park is located inside LAKE CASITAS RECREATION AREA (pg. 666). The main component of the water park is a spacious, multi-level, colorful, water play area with six slides, chutes, climbing structures, wheels to turn to adjust the water spray, anchored squirt guns, and water spurting out of its pipes - all in only eighteen inches of water. Although designed for children 10 years and under, kids on the upper end of this spectrum will probably find this wading pool too tame. Several lifeguards patrol the pool.

Visitors can also cool off by taking an inner tube ride around on a slow moving "river" that winds through the nicely-landscaped water park. You'll go under bridges, and through waterfalls and jet sprays. Two other small, water play areas contain waterfalls, fountains, and umbrellas that pour water over their sides, deluging those underneath.

Relax on the adjacent grassy areas on the lounge chairs that surround this aquatic playground. A concession stand sells snacks, drinks, and ice cream, or there are picnic facilities just outside the water park. Locker rentals are available. Note: If your younger child is not quite potty trained, swim diapers are available to purchase here. Proper swimwear is required for all ages.

Hours: The lake and most amenities are open daily, sunrise - sunset. The water playground is open Memorial Day weekend - Labor Day, mostly Sun. - Thurs., 11am - 6pm; Fri. - Sat., 11am - 7pm. Check the calendar as there are some weekdays on either end that it's not open.

Price: Vehicle entrance to the lake is $10 per on weekdays, $20 on weekends and holidays. There is some free parking just outside the main entrance gate. The water playground is an additional $13 per person during the week; $14 on the weekend; children 1 year and under are free. 3 hours before closing, the price drops to $7.50

Ages: 1 - 10 years old.

—ARTS AND CRAFTS—

AS YOU WISH (Ventura County)

(805) 520-9500 / www.asyouwishpottery.com
1555 Simi Town Center Way, suite 675 at Simi Valley Town Center, Simi Valley

See AS YOU WISH (Los Angeles County) (pg. 8) for details.

Hours: Open Mon. - Thurs., 10am - 9m; Fri. - Sat., 10am - 10pm; Sun., 11am - 7pm.

Price: $7.50 studio fee, plus the cost of your item.

Ages: 4 years and up.

COLOR ME MINE (Ventura County)

Oxnard - (805) 981-8631; Thousand Oaks - (805) 370-3703 / www.oxnard.colormemine.com;
www.thousandoaks.colormemine.com
Oxnard - 2710 Portico Way at The Collection at Riverpark; Thousand Oaks - 3707 E. Thousand Oaks Blvd.

See the entry for COLOR ME MINE (Los Angeles County) (pg. 8) for details.

CREATE STUDIO

(818) 575-9566 / www.createstudiofun.com
31840 Village Center Road, Westlake Village

I walked into Create Studio and immediately exclaimed, "Yes!" The mid-size room exudes inspiration and space for creativity. Paint-splattered tables and benches are in the center while the walls (titled the Wall of Wow) are lined with bins and bins of art projects waiting to happen. They are filled with all sorts of recycled and craft items - buttons, hangers, yarn, bottles, glitter, pom poms, corks, paper punches, plastic thingamajigs (personal favorite), puzzle pieces, cardboard, ribbon, fabric, paint, broken pottery - you get the picture. Aprons, smocks, markers, glue, paint brushes and even easels for those who "just" want to paint are all supplied - all that's missing is you and your kids. Come in to design and craft an open-ended art something, or come to work on a school project. Create Studio actually gives back $1 of each student's studio fee to their school if they work on a school appointed project. This studio is like the art space you'd like to set up at home, but you don't have the wide variety of materials available and you want your house to stay clean. Crafters on the go can purchase an Eco Craft Kit consisting of over forty different, new and recycled items packaged in a gallon container for $20 plus tax, per can.

Hours: Open Tues. - Fri., 11am - 6p; Sat., noon - 5pm; Sun., noon - 4pm. Closed Mon. and certain holidays.

Price: $12 for ages 11 and up; $10 for ages 10 and under. The price includes two hours of studio time and all the materials available. Parents are welcome to assist their kids at no charge.

Ages: 3 years and up.

FIREFLY CERAMICS

(805) 650-1468 / www.fireflyceramics.com

$$$$

1580 Saratoga Avenue, suite C, Ventura

Choices, choices - what to paint? What colors? Free-hand design or use a stencil? What size brush to use? Give the finished product to someone or keep it? Painting your own ceramic piece is supposed to be a stress-free activity! Actually, creating a unique keepsake together with your child is time well spent. Choose from an array of items, decorative and practical, including dinnerware, animal banks, plant stakes, boxes, vases, figurines, and more. It will be glazed, fired, and ready to pick up in just a few days. Precut frames, plaques, clocks, and mirrors can also be purchased to fill in with glass or tile pieces also sold at Firefly. Inquire about summer camp art classes and year-round school fields trips.

Hours: Open Mon., Wed. - Sat., 10am - 7pm; Sun., noon - 6pm. Closed Tues. and holidays.

Price: The cost of the pieces, plus a studio fee of $7 for adults; $4 for ages 10 and under.

Ages: 4 years and up.

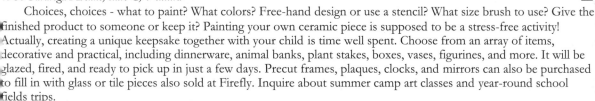

—BEACHES—

MCGRATH STATE BEACH

(805) 968-1033 / www.parks.ca.gov

$$

North Harbor Boulevard, Oxnard

There are three main reasons to visit McGrath State Beach: two miles of beach, campsites right by the beach, and bird watching. The two mile stretch of beach and coastline water, dotted with sand dunes, is great for surfing and fishing. Swimming is O.K. here, you just need to be cautious of riptides. Each of the over 170 campsites has a fire ring and picnic table. The most desirable sections (i.e. those closest to the beach) are sites 35 to 37, 41 to 44, and 102 to 107. If you are a bird watcher, this is an ideal spot as over 240 bird species have been recorded here. Grassy areas next to the beach are great for running around and tossing a ball. Picnic tables are here, too, so bring a picnic lunch or dinner.

Hours: Open daily, sunrise - sunset.

Price: $10 per vehicle for day use. Camping starts at $35 a night for tent camping.

Ages: All

OXNARD BEACH PARK / OXNARD - MANDALAY BEACH

(805) 385-7950 / www.visitoxnard.com; www.parks.ca.gov

$

1601 South Harbor Boulevard, Oxnard

This all-encompassing beach is where Southern Californians flock in the summer, and even throughout the year. The sizable grass area, ringed with palm trees, next to the parking lot, is perfect for running around and for picnicking. And the playground here is *masterfully* designed for kids to set sail on an adventurous playtime. There are two, huge pirate ships - metal outlines of ships that are filled in with ramps, bridges, lots of play cannons, chain ladders, several slides, speaking tubes, and plenty of play space under the ships, as well as on them. There are masts and "pirate only" signs, and the kids I observed were completely engaged in make believe. A few, good-sized fake boulders with rock climbing holdings in them; a sea serpent with his head and parts of his body out of the "water" to climb on; swings; animals on large springs to ride; a giant sea turtle; monkey bars; and more, plus a number of benches surrounding it, complete this park.

The pathway separating the lawn from the dunes and beach is ideal for biking, strolling, jogging, and blading. Just over the picturesque dunes (which are great backdrops for photos) is a broad and long stretch of sandy beach. Bring a volleyball to play on the sand courts, or tote a Frisbee, kite, boogie board, or bucket and shovel to enjoy your day of fun in the sun. Note that Rehab Point, adjacent to the park, provides wheelchair/stroller access through the dunes to the ocean.

Hours: Open daily, sunrise - sunset.

Price: Parking costs $1 an hour; $5 max. Cash only.

Ages: All

PORT HUENEME BEACH PARK - SURFSIDE SEAFOOD (cafe)

(805) 986-6542 or (805) 488-9533 - Surfside / www.ci.port-hueneme.ca.us; www.beachcalifornia.com
550 Surfside Drive, Port Hueneme

There is more to life in Port Hueneme than the Marines - there is marine life! A long fishing pier extends over the ocean. Kids like to race out to its end and play under it, during low tide, of course. This fifty-acre beach (therefore large and very wide) has several cement picnic tables with walls for wind breaks, a few swing sets and volleyball courts, sandy knolls, and a grassy area dotted with palm trees.

At the land end of the pier is an atypical snack bar - Surfside Seafood cafe. This hole-in-the-wall place, with only outside seating that is surrounded by plexiglass to keep the wind out, serves up great sea food. Try Surfside's eight-piece breaded shrimp with fries for $16.95; lobster tacos, $13.95; lobster tail, $39.95; bacon cheeseburger, $8.95; corn dog with fries, $8.95; grilled chicken salad, $12.95; and some of our favorites - clam chowder in a bread bowl for $13.95, and two-piece fish and chips for $11.95. All you can eat fish and chips is every Wed., 4pm to 8pm for $11.95 for adults and $9 for ages 12 and under. Come here for dinner and watch the sunset. This restaurant's tiny shop also sells tackle and bait, summer beach products, and ice cream - all the beach essentials.

There is a bike/pedestrian path that goes along the beach front and across the road, hooking up to a trail along the green belt of Bubbling Springs Creek. This cement pathway is a lovely ride through green grasses and next to waters that are home to various types of sea birds. At the end of the bike route is the small Evergreen Springs Park. Travel a shorter distance, about midway, to arrive at MORANDA PARK (pg. 668).

Hours: Open daily, sunrise - sunset. Surfside is open most of the year daily, 10am - 7pm. It's open in the summer, 9:30am - 9pm.

Price: Parking at the beach is $2 an hour, $8 max.

Ages: All

SAN BUENAVENTURA STATE BEACH / VENTURA PIER

(805) 968-1033 - park / www.parks.ca.gov
901 San Pedro Street, Ventura

The best entrance point to the beach, heading southward from the pier on Harbor, is on San Pedro Street. The beach is fairly wide and very long - about two miles! Next to the parking lot is a sizable grass area lined with palm trees, plenty of picnic tables, barbecue pits, and showers. Walk over the dunes to get to the sand where you can frolic in the water and play some volleyball on the sand courts.

At the northern end of the beach is one of California's oldest wooden piers. It was renovated in the 1990's though, so it's O.K. Ventura Pier offers a nice stroll and awesome view of Channel Islands and coastline, plus fishing, so bring your pole. (Tip: The view makes for iconic sunset photographs.) The base of the pier features interpretive display panels, a bait shop, snack bar, restrooms, and a nice seafood restaurant called Beach House Fish. Order chowder bread bowl, $9; coconut shrimp, $18; chicken gyro, ahi tacos, or pasta, $12 per; Caesar salad, $10; lobster, $25; and more, with lavender lemonade $5 to drink, ginger beer, $3, and more. The restaurant has both inside and patio seating. Call (805) 643-4783 / www.beachhousefish.com for more info.

A sandy beach stretches beneath the pier and surrounds it. Bikers and pedestrians make good use of the adjacent thirteen-mile Coastal Bikeway. Bike rentals are available on weekends during the summer and on holidays. Several seasonal events occur at the beach, so call to see what's scheduled. See BIKE TRAIL: COASTAL BIKEWAY (pg. 688) for more information about the bike path.

Hours: Open daily, 7am - sunset.

Price: There is some free street parking, or pay $10 for day use at the lot. Parking near the pier is $2 an hour; $10 max.

Ages: All

—EDIBLE ADVENTURES—

BENNETT'S HONEY FARM

(805) 521-1375 / www.bennetthoney.com
3176 Honey Lane, Fillmore

Here's the buzz: This honey farm is a fun (and educational) stop off if you are in the area, and if you like honey! The attraction is a small retail store/tasting room that sells games, toys, books, figurines, etc. that have to do with honey. I never knew there was this many honey-related items! It also sells products made from honey such as candles, soap, candy, raw honeycomb, sauces, and granola, as well as a wide array of flavors of very fresh honey. Visitors are encouraged to sample the honey, so try wildflower, orange, buckwheat, avocado, eucalyptus, and others. Yum! There is also a glass-encased beehive inside with the queen bee clearly marked. Outside are a few round picnic tables and benches under shade trees, with the ranch and mountains in the background, so *bee* seated and indulge your sweet tooth a little bit longer.

Hours: Open Mon. - Fri., 8am - 4:30pm; Sat. - Sun., 9am - 5pm. Closed on some holidays.
Price: Free; bring spending money.
Ages: 2 and up.

BUCA DI BEPPO (Ventura County)
(866) EAT BUCA (328-2822) for all locations; (805) 449-3688 - local / www.bucadibeppo.com
205 North Moorpark Road, Thousand Oaks
    See BUCA DI BEPPO (Los Angeles County) (pg. 16) for details.

BUSY BEE CAFE
(805) 643-4864 / www.busybeecafe.biz
478 E. Main Street, Ventura

    This 50's diner is indeed busy - busy with customers and busy in decor with red-and-white-checkered tiles on the walls, black-and-white-checkered tiles on the floor, and splotches of red on lamps, beams, vinyl booth seats, and more. The walls are covered with movie posters featuring stars from the 50's, neon signs, street signs, and pictures. Booths have personal jukeboxes that play two songs for 25¢, while music from the large jukebox plays over the loudspeakers.

    The cafe boasts an extensive menu for all meals. In the am, three eggs any style is $8.29; three pancakes, 5.95; strawberry waffles, $7.95; French toast, $7.55; and omelets start at $9.95. Lunch and dinner items include a cheeseburger, $9.95; tuna sandwich, $9.95; hot pastrami sandwich, $13.59; and hot dip sandwich, $11.59. Tempting desserts and fountain creations are apple dumplings, $6.49; bread pudding, $3.79; lime phosphate, $4.69; egg cream, $3.59; or a malt, $4.89. Kids' meals choices are pancakes; an egg and piece of bacon; a Belgian waffle; a peanut butter and jelly sandwich, with fruit; chicken strips; a burger; pizza; or junior hot dog with fries. These meals cost $5.69 each and come with a small drink. Note to all antique and thrift store shoppers - there are several shops along Main Street to appease your appetite!

Hours: Open daily, 7am - 10pm. Closed early on Thanksgiving and closed Christmas day.
Price: See menu prices above.
Ages: All

CHUCK E. CHEESE'S (Ventura County)
    See the entry for CHUCK E. CHEESE'S (Los Angeles County) (pg. 18) for details.

FARMER'S MARKETS (Ventura County)
    See the entry for FARMER'S MARKETS (Los Angeles County) (pg. 21) for details.

FILLMORE & WESTERN RAILWAY COMPANY
    See the entry for FILLMORE & WESTERN RAILWAY COMPANY (pg. 690), under TRANSPORTATION, for details.

ROCKET FIZZ SODA POPS AND CANDY SHOP (Ventura County)
Camarillo - (805) 987-SODA (7632); Simi Valley - (805) 526-SODA (7632); Thousand Oaks - (805) 494-SODA (7632); Ventura - (805) 641-1222 / www.rocketfizz.com
Camarillo - 2619 Ventura Blvd.; Simi Valley - 1555 Simi Town Center Way #420; Thousand Oaks - 593 North Moorpark Road, suite D; Ventura - 315 E Main St.

    See ROCKET FIZZ SODA POPS AND CANDY SHOP (Los Angeles County) (pg. 26) for details on this shop with an incredible array of unusual sodas, candy and more. The one in Camarillo is the flagship store. It has a small outside patio. Inside is a rocket ship fish tank filled with real, bright, candy-color fish. Push the button to hear the countdown for launch.

Price: Technically, free
Ages: 3 years and up.

UNDERWOOD FAMILY FARMS - Moorpark

(805) 529-3690 or (805) 523-2957 / www.underwoodfamilyfarms.com

3370 Sunset Valley Road, Moorpark

Underwood Family Farms is a huge (160-acre) working produce farm, as well as an animal farm. Let's talk food, first. There are two ways to enjoy the crops: 1) Stop by the on-site roadside market to purchase fresh produce (tasty, but boring), or 2) Let the kids pick their own fruits and vegetables. (Ya-hoo - we've got a winner!) There are rows and rows (and rows and rows) of seasonal crops including artichokes, strawberries, blackberries, peaches, squash, potatoes, lettuces, green beans, apricots, apples, onions, garlic, tomatoes, eggplant, peppers, pumpkins, melons, corn, and herbs. Signs here indicate the price per pound, and if the crop is ready to be picked. My boys were excited to eat strawberries they picked from the vines, carrots they pulled from the ground, beans they harvested from the stalks, and other good-for-you foods they won't normally eat, proving that kids really enjoy the fruits (and vegetables) of their labor.

Heavy-duty pull wagons and wheelbarrows are available to transport your prize pickings (or tired little ones) at no extra charge. A grassy picnic area, with tables, is located at the front of the farm, near the restroom facilities. Tips: Wear sunscreen and walking shoes; prepare to get a little muddy if you visit here after a rain; and bring a cooler to store your fresh produce.

The animal farm and play area is adjacent to the produce farm. This very pleasantly-landscaped area is a superb place to spend some time with your children, especially as there are lots of activities, plus several grassy patches and plenty of benches. Antique and modern farm equipment dotted around add to the atmosphere. Round up your darlings in the Kids Corral that has a small, two-story, mini fort with a slide, swings, and short rock-climbing wall, plus a shaded sand pit. Look up to see pygmy goats walking on skinny wooden ramps over your head - forty feet off the ground! A stationary, scale-size wooden train, with several cars, is great for kids to climb aboard and use their imaginations, as are a wooden fire truck and bus. Run through a short tunnel built under a hill. Climb up and steer a tractor, whoosh down a combine slide, and even jump up and on a wide and tall stack of hay bales (i.e. the hay pyramid). Enjoy funny and educational twenty-five-minute animal presentations on the weekends at 11:30am, 1:30pm and 3:30pm, featuring mostly barnyard animals. You may also wander around pens to see sheep, bunnies, jersey cows, donkeys, turkeys, alpacas, emus, ponies, and ducks. Check out the chicken coop with its freshly-laid eggs. All of the above is included with the price of admission. Entrance into the Petting Corral is 3 tickets. Other "extras", with per ticket admission price (ticket prices are listed below), include a moonbounce (3 tickets); hand-led pony rides around a small ring (5); a looping trike trail - the bike is supplied (3); tractor-drawn hayrides (3); a three-minute ride on a self-pedaled play tractor in an enclosed area (3); cow train ride - cow-shaped carts pulled by a tractor that go around a portion of the farm (4); gem mining at a sluice (8 tickets for a regular bag); and a mini-electric train ride (3). Experience the animal farm on your own, or take a guided tour. October and Easter time bring a slew of special activities such as a corn maze, ring a pumpkin, corn cannon, pig races, egg hunt, and more.

The farm offers a variety of guided field trips/tours of the fields for groups of twenty or more. The variety of ninety-minute to over four-hour Farm Tours include learning about a designated crop (or crops) of strawberries and/or vegetables, their care, growth cycle, and more; picking the crop(s) to take home; a tractor-drawn hayride; an animal presentation - learning about the characteristics and behaviors of animals; feeding and petting the animals; and more. All tours include a coloring book. There is plenty of time for a picnic lunch, too. What a great combination of fun and education! Crops do grow seasonally, so call or check the website to see what is currently ready to harvest. Ask about summer farm camps. Tip: See the Calendar entry FALL HARVEST FESTIVAL / PUMPKIN TOURS (pg. 736). Note: There is also an UNDERWOOD FAMILY FARMS in the nearby city of Somis. (See the next entry.)

Hours: The food and animal farm are open March - mid-November daily, 9am to 6pm; then weekends only through mid-December, weather permitting. Closed January, February, Thanksgiving and Christmas.

Price: The following price includes entrance to the animal farm, as well as entrance to the fields to pick your own crops: $3 per person Mon. - Fri., $6 per person, Sat. - Sun. and major holidays (which includes a tractor-drawn wagon ride to the fields and admission to the animal show); children under 2 are free. Season passes are available. Prices for crops are charged per pound and change per season/availability. Admission is $15 - $20 per person on Sat. - Sun. in October during the Fall Harvest Festival. Farm Tours start at $8 per student and go up to $14, depending on the tour. Ticket prices for extra activities are $1 = 1 ticket; $20 = 23 tickets, etc.

Ages: 18 months - 10 years for the animal farm; 4 years and up for food tours, and 3 years to pick crops.

UNDERWOOD FAMILY FARMS - Somis

(805) 386-4660 / www.underwoodfamilyfarms.com
5696 Los Angeles Avenue, Somis

!/$

If you're in the area, stop at this roadside stand which sells freshly-picked, seasonal produce. From the end of May to mid-June, you may pick your own blueberries daily, 9am to 4pm. Other seasonal picking includes strawberries, March - August; raspberries, May - November; and blackberries, June - December. The biggest draw for kids is the burros, jersey cows, rabbits, guinea pigs, alpacas (i.e., furry llamas that look like they're having a bad hair day), and most fascinating, the pygmy goats. The goats nimbly climb on very narrow wooden ramps that crisscross thirty feet above your head! An adjacent grassy area beckons picnickers. Kids can climb on the wooden vehicle stationed here and play in the sandbox. See the previous entry for UNDERWOOD FAMILY FARMS - Moorpark for a nearby, full-fledged, farm attraction.

Hours: Open April - October daily, 9am to 6pm. Open November - March daily, 9am to 5pm.
Price: Free
Ages: 2 - 12 years (although those overhead goats are quite a cool sight for all ages).

WAYPOINT CAFE

(805) 388-2535 / www.thewaypointcafe.com
325 Durley Avenue, Camarillo

$$$$

Just off the runway of the small Camarillo airport is a place with a great view, as well as great food. The cafe inside is decorated with lots of aviation photos, and a few pieces of airplane paraphernalia. The outside patio offers fresh air with mountains in the background, a stretch of lawn with a miniature runway and the sight of actual small planes (and helicopters) landing and taking off. Other "extras" include watching them grill the food on the outside BBQ (on certain days) and listening, live, to the air traffic control tower.

Breakfast offerings include omelettes, waffles, pancakes and more for $10.50 - $14 each. Lunch offerings include cheeseburgers, pepper jack turkey melt, smokehouse BBQ chicken salad, and more for $11.50 - $16 each. Indulge in an old-fashioned, made-right milkshake that has the outside of the glass dipped in chocolate! - about $7.50. Kid's meals are $7 - $8 per. Expect long waits at prime time, but enjoy some plane old-fashioned fun meal time, too. Note that this restaurant is just down the way from COMMEMORATIVE AIR FORCE MUSEUM (WWII Aviation Heritage Museum) (pg. 677).

Hours: Open Mon. - Fri., 7am - 3pm; Sat. - Sun., 7am - 4pm.
Price: Some prices are listed above.
Ages: 2 years and up.

—FAMILY PAY AND PLAY—

AMBUSH PAINTBALL & AIRSOFT PARK

(805) 259-3200 / www.ambushpaintballpark.com
8643 Shekell Road, Moorpark

$$$$

Both kid and adult friendly, the eight different fields/scenarios at this mid-size paintball and airsoft park give you enough variety and space to play ten-minute games of tag and hide and seek, or simply, capture the flag with markers. Not necessarily elaborate, yet a lot of fun with the various scenarios, battle your way around bunkers, across fields, through obstacles and in and out of buildings; deep dirt trenches (called WWI Field); huge wooden spools; over 350 hay bales (spread across a 25,000 square foot field); the junkyard (which resembles how our backyard looked at one time); and other objects, plus inflatables at the airball field. Bring lots of water - it gets hot out here! Pizza can be delivered or you can bring your own food. Players must wear paintball goggles with a full face mask; rentals are available here. Note that Splatmaster, a gentler game of paintball, is offered to groups of younger kids, in particular, to play.

Hours: Open Sat. - Sun., 9am - 4pm. Airsoft is only offered on Sun.
Price: $20 for full day of paintball or airsoft with your own equipment; $40 for all day admission plus rental equipment for both games.
Ages: 8 - 11 years for Splatmaster; 10 years and up for airsoft and paintball.

BEDFORD PINKARD SKATE PARK

(805) 385-8230 - skate park; (805) 385-7950/(805) 488-4324 - College Park / www.visitoxnard.com; www.socalskateparks.com

3250 South Rose Avenue, Oxnard

Skate 'til your hearts content at this 14,500 square-feet "skate-of-the-art" park with cement bowls, grinding blocks, rails, tombstones, pyramids, and quarter pipes. Helmets are required as is a parent-signed waiver for ages 17 and under. The skate part is in a section of College Park.

Other amenities at College Park include basketball courts, a tennis court, volleyball court, picnic area, exercise station, playground, concrete walkways throughout, and nifty dog park (with a dog washing station).

Hours: Both parks are open daily, noon - dusk. Closed on holidays and inclement weather.

Price: Free

Ages: 7 years and up.

BLAST CITY LASER TAG

(818)-233-8944 / www.blastcityla.com

618 Lindero Canyon Road, Oak Park

$$$

Laser Tag is a blast, especially here in this two-story, tech-inspired, blacklit arena that hosts up to 20 players at one time. Vests on, lasers in hand, doors open, fog's rolling, music's playing and GO! Run, point and zap, hide, and run some more. Ten minute+ games can be play in different chase game scenarios, such as Dracula, king of the hill, and capture the flag; as well as different game chapters for different levels; or as a free-for-all. Serious fun, and not just for kids!

In between games, play some games at the mini arcade such as Walking Dead, Space Invaders, a roller coaster simulator, motorcycle racing, air hockey and a few others. All that running works up an appetite, so enjoy the cafe servings of hamburger, chicken wings or chicken wrap, $10 per; buffalo cauliflower bites, $6; a variety of personal pizzas, average $12; kid's meals, $6; and more. Private party rooms are available here, too. Note that Laser Tag is adjacent to KID'S WORLD (pg. 659).

Hours: Open most of the year, Mon. - Thurs. for private events and field trips only; open to the public Fri., 3pm-10pm; Sat., 10am - 10pm; Sun., 10pm - 8pm. Open longer hours in the summer time and school holidays.

Price: $10 for the first game, $8 for the second.

Ages: 6 years and up.

BOULDERDASH INDOOR ROCK CLIMBING (Ventura County)

Thousand Oaks - (805) 557-1300; Ventura - (805) 557-1300 / www.boulderdashclimbing.com

Thousand Oaks - 880 Hampshire Road, Thousand Oaks; Ventura - 2879 Seaborg Ave.

$$$$

Do your kids have you climbing the walls? Then you'll feel right at home at Boulderdash! Both the novice and experienced climber have level-appropriate challenges at these 10,000 square-feet rock climbing centers. The beginner has walls that extend up to twenty-five feet, while the more advanced participant can climb walls as high as forty-five feet. The latter section also has a slab, aretes, roofs, and a rappel ledge. (Although these may be familiar terms for climbers, I needed to look up some of those words.) The dedicated bouldering areas are good-sized with a traverse of over 100 feet long. Routes change frequently, so there is always something new to try. Rock climbing is not only a fantastic, all-body workout, but almost any age level and any athletic ability can give it a go. Parents can (and dare I say, should?) participate too!

A locker area, soda and snacks area, and pro shop are also on the premises, as is a separate party room. A waiver for all ages (signed by parents for those 17 years and under) is mandatory. One of the most cost effective ways to have your child rock climb is for you, or another adult, to take a two-hour belay class, for $40 (minimum age is 13), so that you learn to belay and tie in your child. Or, make a reservation for him/her (only 5 climbers allowed per session) to come to a forty-five-minute Off the Deck class offered for ages 4 to 12 years old. You and your child can also sign up for Climb Time, which is open for all ages. Either class provides a belayer and all the necessary equipment. Have your child join the rock-climbing team, enroll in a camp or take a class. Safe, exhilarating, and confidence building - if kids are looking for a sport to grab hold of, have them grab the hand and toe holds of a rock climbing wall.

Hours: Open Mon. - Fri., 11am - 10pm; Sat., 10am - 8pm; Sun., 10am - 6pm. Off the Deck classes are Mon. - Fri., 3:30pm - 5pm. Climb Time sessions are Mon., Wed., Fri., 5pm - 5:45pm and 6pm - 6:45pm.

Price: Daily climb fees are $17 for adults, $15 for ages 24 and under. Rental gear - harness, shoes, and chalk - is $6, inclusive. Off the Deck is $25 per child. Climb Time is $20 per person.

Ages: 6 years and up.

CHUCK E. CHEESE'S (Ventura County)

See the entry for CHUCK E. CHEESE'S (Los Angeles County) (pg. 18) for details.

DOJOBOOM

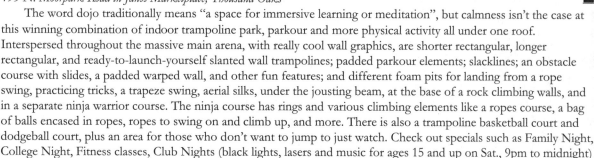

(805) 410-4690 / www.dojoboom.com
193 N. Moorpark Road in Janss Marketplace, Thousand Oaks

$$$

The word dojo traditionally means "a space for immersive learning or meditation", but calmness isn't the case at this winning combination of indoor trampoline park, parkour and more physical activity all under one roof. Interspersed throughout the massive main arena, with really cool wall graphics, are shorter rectangular, longer rectangular, and ready-to-launch-yourself slanted wall trampolines; padded parkour elements; slacklines; an obstacle course with slides, a padded warped wall, and other fun features; and different foam pits for landing from a rope swing, practicing tricks, a trapeze swing, aerial silks, under the jousting beam, at the base of a rock climbing walls, and in a separate ninja warrior course. The ninja course has rings and various climbing elements like a ropes course, a bag of balls encased in ropes, ropes to swing on and climb up, and more. There is also a trampoline basketball court and dodgeball court, plus an area for those who don't want to jump to just watch. Check out specials such as Family Night, College Night, Fitness classes, Club Nights (black lights, lasers and music for ages 15 and up on Sat., 9pm to midnight) and more.

Things to know: Jumpers need to purchase the grip socks here for $3 per. Pre-register for a jump time as they can get filled up. Jump times are every half hour. Come at least 30 minutes prior to your jump time as registration can take a bit. Observers - parents or others who want to just watch and not jump, are free. You receive a special wristband. Waivers must be signed for everyone.

Hours: Open for all ages Mon. - Sat., 10am - 9pm; Sun., 9am - 9pm. Kid Jump, open for ages 6 and under only, is Mon. - Sat., 9am - 10pm.

Price: Daily, one hour is $17 for ages 7 and up; $13 for ages 6 and under. Mon. - Fri., 1.5 hours is $22 for ages 7 and up; $17 for ages 6 and under; Sat. - Sun., $25 for 7 and up; $19 for 6 and under. Observers are free. On Kid Jump, one parent jumps for free with each paid child.

Ages: 3 years and up.

GOLF 'N STUFF (Ventura County)

(805) 644-7131 / www.golfnstuff.com
5555 Walker Drive, Ventura

$$$

If you and the kids are in the mood for a little golf 'n stuff, here's the place for you. There are two **miniature golf** courses with windmills, a tower, and other fanciful buildings (I love the castle!), to putt around on at $10 per round for adults; children under 3 years play for free with a paying adult. **Indy cars** ($8 for drivers) have a height requirement for drivers of 56", while **bumper cars** and **water bumper boats** ($8 ride) both have height requirements for drivers of 48". Passengers for the above attractions are $4. Play the action-packed game of **lazer tag** here for $7.50 per game. The center also features a big arcade with over 100 games, even some old-school ones, and a full-service snack bar.

Hours: Open September - mid-June, Mon. - Thurs., noon - 9pm (rides open at 3pm); Fri., noon - midnight (rides open at 3pm); Sat., 10am - midnight (rides and lazer tag open at 11am); Sun., 10am - 10pm (rides and lazer tag open at 11am). Lazer tag is only available on the weekends in the winter. Open mid-June - August, Sun. - Thurs., 10am - 10pm; Sat. - Sun., 10am - midnight (rides and lazer tag open at 11am). Golf and rides close about an hour before the park closes.

Price: Prices are listed above. Ask about package deals such as two hours of unlimited play on the weekends for $27.

Ages: 4 years and up.

KID'S WORLD

(818) 338-8888 / www.kidsworldla.com
618 Lindero Canyon Road, Oak Park

$$$

For a world of fun come to Kid's World, a spacious, colorful, indoor play place. There are two huge, connected, multi-level, mostly-padded, play structures with so many fun elements - a lot of tubes to crawl through (one looks like a shark); cargo netting; a variety of obstacles courses; slides (even three slides side-by-side and a few that are enclosed);

things to climb over and under; and lots more. The structure with foam ball blasters provokes lots of giggles, both for the ones shooting and those getting shot. A small, separate soft play area for toddlers has some short slides, foam blocks, and play mats. Younger-kid-friendly video, virtual reality and arcade games - Dizzy Chicken, air hockey, skee ball, driving cars, and more - are on the other side of the main room. Win tickets to spend at the prize redemption counter.

Kids (and adults) can run, dance, and jump on the virtual playground floor, which is real fun. Motion-activated games projecting sounds and graphics allows players to use their entire body. At Atomic Rush, interactive arcade gaming is at a new level as players must run and touch certain sequences of lights and buttons. The small basketball room (with stands that have adjustable rims) are great for all heights and ages. Inflatable bumper balls, for kids to get inside of and roll around (think hamster balls), are in a separate room. Ten to fifteen minutes sessions, when available, are an additional $5 per person.

Toward the back is a full-service cafe with cheeseburgers, pizza, a variety of salads, and turkey, tuna or veggie sandwiches for about $10 - $12 each. A choice of kids meals includes hot dogs, grilled cheese, chicken tenders, and more for about $6. Snack items and beverages are also available. There are plenty of table and chairs back here. Party rooms are located upstairs.

Everyone must wear socks in the play center. This place is wild, crazy, and sometimes loud, but always fun. I hope a visit here brightens your kid's world! See BLAST CITY LASER TAG (pg. 658) for an adjacent laser tag arena.

Hours: Open Tues. - Thurs., 10am - 8pm; Fri. - Sat., 10am - 9pm; Sun., 10am - 7pm. Closed Mon.

Price: $11.99 for 24 months - 15 years; $10.99 for a sibling on weekdays (except on holidays); $5.99 for ages 13 months - 23 months; children 12 months and under are free. Two adults are free with each paying child; $4 each additional adult.

Ages: 18 months - 12 years

LAZERTAG EXTREME

(805) 577-8400 / www.lazertagextreme.com

$$$

591 Country Club Drive in the Wood Ranch Shopping Center, Simi Valley

Two teams compete against each other armed with laser guns and wearing a lighted vest in this foggy, large (5,000 square feet), multi-level arena. Futuristically-themed, the grays and blacks of the walls, ramps, partitions, towers and markings are interspersed with some colorful neon lights. Accompanied by pulsating background music, this is a great place to play hide and seek. Zap your opponent with your laser gun to complete your goal of scoring the most points. Mission, not-so-impossible.

For another mission, should you choose to accept it, and more thrills, try Lazer Maze. In this room, the laser beams intersect and cross over each other so that the participant, should he/she be up to the challenge, must crawl, jump and walk over and under the beams and beat the clock - it's a timed laser obstacle course and your time could go by rather quickly if you break a beam.

There is a good selection of current video and arcade games in the lobby, as well as ticket and prize redemption, plus Starbooth where you can record a song onto a CD for $5. All the important food groups are here, too - a snack bar with hot dogs, chips, pizza, chicken strips, popcorn, and dippin' dots. Note that Lazertag Extreme and Archery Tag are mobile games, meaning that they can come to you for a party or special event.

Hours: Open Wed. - Thurs., 3pm - 9pm; Fri., 3pm - midnight; Sat., 11am - midnight; Sun., noon - 6pm. Closed Mon. and Tues., except for special events and some holidays.

Price: $10 for one mission. Lazer maze is $2 a mission.

Ages: 5 years and up.

MB2 RACEWAY (Ventura County)

(805) 214-9999 / www.mb2raceway.com

$$$$$

1475 Lawrence Drive, Thousand Oaks

See MB2 RACEWAY (Los Angeles County) (pg. 35) for details.

Hours: Open Mon. - Thurs., noon - 10pm; Fri. - Sat., 11am - midnight; Sun., 11am - 8pm.

Price: Licensed drivers are $23 for a fourteen-lap race; juniors are $20 for a nine-lap race.

Ages: At least 48" tall.

PUMP IT UP (Ventura County)

(805) 339-9669 / www.pumpitupparty.com

5120 Ralston Street, Ventura

See PUMP IT UP (San Diego County) (pg. 487) for details. This facility offers a variety of specialty Open Jumps including PreK only, Sunday Fun Day, and more.

Hours: Check the website calendar for details on Open Jump and other speciality jump times as the times vary even within a particular month.

Price: Open Jump is $11 per child; adults are free.

Ages: 2 years and up, depending on the Open Jump day/event.

SCOOTER'S JUNGLE (Ventura County)

(805) 203-9200 / www.scootersjungle.com

2250 Union Place, suite B, Simi Valley

See SCOOTER'S JUNGLE (Orange County) (pg. 266) for details.

Hours: Check the website calendar as the event times change every month.

Price: All Ages is $10 per child. Toddler Playtime is $9 per child. All playtimes include one adult; additional adults are an additional $4.

Ages: 2 years and up.

SKATELAB

(805) 578-0040; (805) 578-9928 / www.skatelab.com

4226 Valley Fair Street, Simi Valley

Yeowser! This hip, sprawling (20,000 square feet), indoor skate park has it all, and then some. It has a street section with two half-pipes - one is six feet high and the other is four feet high. It also has grinding boxes, a really large bowl, and much more. There is even a half pipe outside. Family-friendly Skatelab is both popular with kids and adults as parents can go upstairs to the overlook, sit down to watch the action, and enjoy a snack. This park is definitely geared for the intermediate to advanced skater, although there are sessions just for beginners. Bikes, roller blades and scooters are welcome at all times. All skaters and riders 17 years and under must have a waiver signed by their parent or legal guardian at the time of registration. A helmet, elbow, and knee pads are mandatory. Rentals are available.

The entrance hallway to Skatelab is lined with hundreds of skateboards. There is a small, free museum, upstairs, devoted to vintage skateboards and skateboard paraphernalia, showcasing the history of the sport. I never knew there was so many "extras" in skateboarding!

Hours: Sessions are Mon., 4pm - 7pm, 7pm - 10pm and 8:30pm - 10pm; Tues. - Fri., 3pm - 6pm and 4:30pm - 6pm, 7pm -10pm and 8:30pm - 10pm; Sat., 10am - 1pm for beginning skaters; 1pm - 4pm, 4pm - 7pm, and 7pm - 10pm; Sun., 10am - 1pm for beginning skaters; 1pm - 4pm and 4pm - 7pm.

Price: $17 for an all-day pass, or $10 each three-hour session; $6 each ninety-minute session Mon. - Thurs.; $8 each ninety-minutes Fri. - Sun. Check out the weekly specials where the price often drops to $5 per session.

Ages: 7 years and up.

SKY HIGH SPORTS (Ventura County)

(805) 484-6300 / cam.skyhighsports.com

166 Aviador Street, Camarillo

See SKY HIGH SPORTS (Los Angeles County) (pg. 40) for details about this fantastic, indoor trampoline place. This facility doesn't have Ninja Course. Note that SO CAL TACTICAL ADVENTURES (pg. 662) is also located in this complex.

Hours: Open most of the year, Mon. - Thurs., 3pm - 9pm; Fri., 3pm - 11pm; Sat., 11am - 11pm; Sun., 11am - 9pm. Usually open during school breaks and holidays, Sun. - Thurs., 11am - 9pm; Fri. - Sat., 11am -11pm.

Price: $15 for the first hour; $20 for ninety minutes; $25 for two hours. Children under 2 are free with paying adult.

Ages: 4 years and up.

SKY ZONE (Ventura County)

(805) 804-9555 / www.skyzone.com

2825 Johnson Dr., Ventura

See SKY ZONE (Los Angeles County) (pg. 40) for details.

Hours: Open Mon. - Thurs., 3pm - 8pm; Fri., 2pm - 10pm; Sat., 10am - 10pm; Sun., 10am - 8pm. Check out the calendar for all the Toddler Times, Family Fun Night, and other special programs. Open during the summer and holidays extended hours.

Price: $12 for 60 min., $15 for 90 min., etc.

Ages: 2 years and up.

SO CAL TACTICAL ADVENTURES

(805)384-0941 / www.socaltacticaladventures.com

166 N. Aviador, Camarillo

Sharing the same space with SKY HIGH SPORTS (Ventura County) (pg. 661) this 10,000 square foot indoor Reball arena has inflatable obstacles and objects all around to hide and shoot from behind, surrounded by wall murals of mountains and military equipment. FYI - Reball is paint-less paintball, so it's the same action-packed running around and strategy, using face masks for protection and paintball gear and guns for the reusable balls, but no messy paint. So Cal Tactical Adventures offers recreational, speedball and tactical play options.

Hours: Open Mon. - Thurs., 3pm - 9pm; Fri., 3pm - 11pm; Sat., 11am - 11pm; Sun., 11am - 9pm. Open longer on school breaks.

Price: A two-hour session is $45 and includes all gear - goggle mask, gun with hopper and air tank, vest, unlimited air and unlimited Reball. It's $35 for the session if you bring your own gear.

Ages: Minimum 10 years old.

THE CLUBHOUSE FUN ZONE

(805) 639-0414 / www.theclubhousefunzone.com

4535 McGrath Street, Ventura

Join the club and have fun at this smallish, indoor play place. The main, two-story play structure has a ball pit, tubes, slides, obstacle courses and padding all over. Other fun elements inside the Clubhouse are tyke-size vehicles, mini (mini) racers, a train table, a bounce, and a few toys and small playhouses. There are some comfy couches for adults and some tables and chairs, as well as a computer station and snack shop - you can bring your own food. Socks are required.

Hours: Open Mon. - Fri., 10am - 4pm. Closed Sat. and Sun. for private parties.

Price: $9 per child; $8 for siblings; adults are free.

Ages: 6 years and under

VENTURA AQUATICS CENTER

(805) 654-7511 / www.cityofventura.net/aquatics

901 S. Kimball Road in the Ventura Community Park, Ventura

It's hot. Question: Where do you go for refreshment? Answer: Go to the outdoor Ventura Aquatics Center. The Center has a competition pool, with three diving boards; a recreational pool for everyone; a small pool with two, twisty, twenty-five-foot slides - sliders must be 46" tall; and a separate, colorful water playground in shallow water for younger children. It features a short slide, steps, a little tunnel, pipes that burst with water (reminds me of home), a water umbrella, and buckets on tall poles that fill with water and tip over. Lifeguards are on duty.

In between the pools is a lovely patio area with round tables and chairs, surrounded by palm trees. There are also lounge chairs by the pools and the water play pool. Lockers are available to use free of charge; just bring your own lock. Children 9 and under must be accompanied by an adult. You are allowed to bring outside food in - yea! Ahh, now the day isn't unbearably hot.

Hours: Recreational swim and the water playground is open mid-May - mid-June, and September, Sat. - Sun., noon - 3pm; open mid-June - August, Mon., Wed., and Fri., noon - 4pm; Tues. and Thurs., 1pm - 4pm; Sat. - Sun., 11:30am - 4pm.

Price: $8 for ages 3 and up; $5 for seniors; children 2 and under are free and must have a swim diaper.

Ages: 1 ½ years and up.

—GREAT OUTDOORS—

CAMINO REAL PARK

(805) 652-4550 / www.cityofventura.net

Dean Drive and Validity Street, Ventura

This sporting park has several ball fields, eight tennis courts, a basketball court, sand volleyball courts, picnic tables, barbecue pits, and three playgrounds. Two of the playgrounds are good-sized with slides, swings, and other play equipment. A paved pathway runs throughout. Although it is right off the freeway, the perimeter of the park has groves of trees and a ravine, giving it *somewhat* of a country feel.

A main draw is the eucalyptus groves because they are roosting places for Monarch butterflies from mid-October - February. The monarchs look like dead leaves hanging from branches, but then they rustle, "come to life," and flutter about - this cycle is a very cool thing to observe.

Hours: Open daily, sunrise - sunset.
 Price: Free
 Ages: All

CHANNEL ISLANDS NATIONAL PARK ☼

(805) 658-5730 - National Park; (805) 642-7688 or (805) 642-1393 - Island Packers; (805) 987-1301 - Channel   6/$
Islands Aviation / www.nps.gov/chis; www.islandpackers.com; www.flycia.com;
www.recreation.gov/camping
The park headquarters is at 1901 Spinnaker Drive; Island Packers is at 1867 Spinnaker, Ventura

The Channel Islands comprise eight islands off the main coastline of Southern California, five of which make up Channel Islands National Park and marine sanctuary. Prepare your kids for a half or whole day excursion to an island by first obtaining information from the park service. The islands were originally the home of Chumash Indians. Then, hunters came and killed certain otter, seal, and sea lion species almost to extinction. Finally, ranchers settled here. Some parts of the islands are still privately owned. It's important to emphasize to your child that Channel Islands is a national preserve, so "take only memories, leave only footprints."

Climate on the islands is different from mainland climate, even during the summer. The harsher conditions have produced various terrains within the relatively small parcels of land, from sandy beaches to rocky hills. Cruise to the islands and explore nature at its best and wildest. Kids get especially excited about seeing the numerous seals and sea lions that are plentiful because they breed on many of the islands. Be on the lookout for blue sharks and dolphins, and note that whale watching is included with all cruises from the end of December through March. Once on an island, be on the lookout for some unusual birds and animals, like the island fox. Reservations are strongly recommended for all excursions. Bring jackets and your camera; wear sneakers; pack a water bottle; and have a terrific outing!

Here is a very brief overview of the islands (enough to whet your adventuring appetite), along with cruise prices from Island Packers. Note that campers must reserve boat transportation before booking a campsite - no walk-ons.

Anacapa - This is the closest island to Ventura, only twelve miles away. It is five miles long and one of the most popular islands to visit. On East Anacapa, climb up the 153 steps to a sweeping panoramic view. Enjoy a small visitor's center, and nearly two miles of hiking trails. There is no beach here, but swimming is allowed at the landing cove on calm summer days, as is scuba and skin diving, and snorkeling. Enjoy the kelp forest! On days of low tide, Frenchy's Cove, towards the western part of the island, is great for tidepooling. Picnicking is always welcomed. This trip, offered year round, takes about seven hours round trip, including approximately sixty minutes for the channel crossing then time on the island to explore. Adult fare is $59; seniors are $54; children 3 - 12 years are $41. Overnight camping trip fares to the island are $79 for adults; $74 for seniors; $57 for children.

Santa Cruz - At over ninety-six square miles, this is the largest island off California. Topography varies from sea caves (the Painted Cave here is one of the world's largest known sea caves at almost 100 feet wide!) and steep cliffs, to rolling hills and grasslands. Kayaking, swimming, and snorkeling (particularly in and through the wondrous sea cave and grottoes, and around the kelp) are some favorites pastimes here: Note that you must bring your own equipment, rent it before you head out, or sign up for a guided kayaking tour. Hiking is another favorite. If you land near Scorpion Ranch, the one-mile walk to Cavern Point is easy, but make the most of your trip and time here by going along the bluff on North Bluff Trail for incredible view points. Then go inland (look for the endemic island fox), into oak canyons and groves. Another landing point, Prisoner's Harbor, offers other trails and is more forested. Going to the island is offered year-round, though excursions to and through the sea cave are offered only spring to early fall. The round trip takes eight to nine hours, including about sixty minutes for the channel crossings, then time on the island for exploration. Adult fare is $59; seniors are $54; children 3 - 12 years are $41. Overnight camping trip fares to the island are $79 for adults; $74 for seniors; $57 for kids.

Santa Rosa - This island is fifteen miles long and, although eighty-five percent of it is grasslands, there are still canyons, volcanic formations, and fossil beds that vary the landscape. There is plenty to see and do for those who thrive on being in the midst of nature. Hikes, led by a ranger, are offered as well. Available April through November, the round trip takes about eleven hours, including the channel crossings of almost three hours each way and about four hours on the island. Adult fare is $82; seniors are $74; children 3 - 12 years are $65. Overnight camping trip fares to the island are $114 for adults; $104 for seniors; $90 for kids.

San Miguel - This eight-mile-long island has beaches and an incredible number of seals and sea lions. The most popular destination here is the Caliche Forest (i.e., mineral sand castings), which is a 3.5-mile hike from the beach. Be prepared for strong winds, plus rain and fog any time of year. The varying island terrain reflects the assault of weather upon San Miguel. Channel crossings take three-and-a-half to four hours. Weekend camping, offered June through October, and round-trip transportation costs are $147 for adults; $136 for seniors; $126 for children 3 - 12 years. Day trips, recommended for hardier kids, are offered September and October. They cost $105 for adults; $95 for seniors; $84 for kids.

Santa Barbara - This is the smallest island, only 640 acres, and is the farthest away from mainland Ventura. It has steep cliffs, a small "museum," and hiking trails. There are no shade trees on the island, so load up with sunscreen. You may stay for three days or longer on this remote island, but bring everything because there is nowhere to obtain any articles once you've arrived. Day-time round trips, offered April through October, take about eleven hours, including about four hours on the island. Adult day fare is $82; seniors are $74; children 3 - 12 years are $65. Overnight camping trip fares to the island are $114 for adults; $104 for seniors; $90 for kids.

Note that Island Packers does not rent kayaks or snorkeling equipment. For kayak rentals, contact CHANNEL ISLANDS KAYAK CENTER (pg. 689). They also offer guided kayak tours. There is an additional charge for bringing kayaks on board ($19 for a single; $28 for a double). See Island Packer's website for other companies that they work with who also give guided kayaking tours. Contact CONDOR EXPRESS CRUISES (pg. 643) for cruising to the islands from Santa Barbara.

If you prefer to fly, check out Channel Islands Aviation located at both the Camarillo Airport and at the Goleta airport. One of their options is, following a half-hour scenic flight over Anacapa and Santa Cruz Islands, to land on Santa Rosa Island and be here for about four-and-a-half hours. A ranger drives around the island where you'll see a century-old cattle ranch and other island highlights. You can hike around a bit, have a picnic lunch (which you supply), and explore more of the island before you fly back. Trips are sold on an exclusive charter basis meaning you will have the entire airplane to yourself, but it seats up to eight passengers so bring family and friends. Trips are available from $1,200 plus tax. Also check out CHANNEL ISLANDS NATIONAL PARK VISITOR CENTER (pg. 676) and VENTURA HARBOR VILLAGE (pg. 684) for other things to do while you're in this area.

Hours: Listed under each island.
Price: Listed under each island.
Ages: 6 years and up.

CONEJO COMMUNITY PARK / CONEJO VALLEY BOTANIC GARDEN

(805) 495-2163 - park; (805) 494-7630 - garden / www.crpd.org; www.conejogarden.org
350 Gainsborough Road and 1175 Hendrix, Thousand Oaks

This nature park is delightful in size and scope. There are acres and acres of green rolling hills, and a creek running throughout. The creek, by itself, is a major attraction. My boys loved looking for crawdads and, of course, stepping on the rocks, with the possible thrill of slipping and getting a bit wet. Almost a full day's adventure can be had by climbing the gnarled, old oak trees. There are cement pathways throughout the park, making much of it stroller accessible. The ambiance here is peaceful, unless you bring your kids, of course!

The upper field sports a baseball diamond; a basketball court is across the way. A covered picnic area with barbecue pits, a horseshoe pit, and shuffleboard court is also available here, as is a community center. The playgrounds in front of the community center building are great - they have slides, a rope climbing structure, and short climbing wall partially in sand, plus several fake rock formations to climb on, under and through, with connecting ropes to incorporate with imaginative play.

The adjoining botanic garden is thirty-three acres; only part of it is developed and open to walk through. One short path traverses through a variety of landscapes, looping around and covering most of the garden. Another nature trail goes up and around the hillside, following a creek through oak and willow trees before looping back around. Drought-tolerant plants, a meadow section, fruit trees, bird habitats, and a butterfly garden are all part of the landscape. A favorite area is the Kid's Adventure Garden. Children are encouraged to climb up into a tree trunk (or use the ramp) to the treehouse on top; crawl into the beehive (not a real one); walk through the small hydroponic greenhouse (i.e., a soil-less environment for plants); imagine at the zoo garden with animal statues (to play on and just look at) and topiaries; check out the pirates cave; look at the vegetable garden; and make garden-themed crafts. I don't know how much actual plant knowledge my kids gained from our time here, but I hope they are more rooted in appreciating the beautiful gift of nature.

Hours: The park is open October - March daily, 7am - 6pm; April - September daily, 7am - 8pm. The botanic garden is open daily, sunrise - sunset. The Kid's Adventure Garden is open Sun., 11am - 3pm. Both are closed on major holidays and during inclement weather.
Price: Free
Ages: All

CONEJO CREEK NORTH PARK

(805) 495-6471 - park; (805) 449-2660 - library / www.crpd.org

1379 E. Janss Road, Thousand Oaks

    Around the back of the library, near the freeway, is a long strip of land that is a delightful park. Trees block the view of the freeway, and some of its sound. A rock-lined creek runs through most of the park. My boys could spend hours playing just here, and getting a little wet. There are also two ponds (at each end of the park), sand volleyball courts, a ball field, picnic shelters, grassy areas, shade trees and natural play areas, an ornamental fountain, and quite a few bridges, one of which leads directly to the library and some join up with walkways. The playgrounds have great amenities - slides (some long and enclosed), bridges, speaking tubes, more rocks to climb on, swings, sand, digger tools, chain ladders, and even a wall featuring the competitive electronic games of Neos. A visit to the library and/or adjacent senior/teen community center can round out your trip.

Hours: Open daily, 7am - sunset. Call for library hours.

  Price: Free

   Ages: All

CORRIGANVILLE PARK

(805) 584-4400 / www.rsrpd.org; www.lamountains.com

7001 Smith Road, Simi Valley

    Almost 250 acres of rocky parkland was once the setting of thousands of movies and T.V. Westerns and shows. Now, the public can hike the trails past sandstone formations and caves, climb the boulders, and enjoy the rugged landscape. An easy, one-mile-round trip walk for kids is the Interpretation Trail, which is studded with oak trees alongside a small creek. Labels tell of the movies produced here. There are even a few remnants from old movie sets, mostly foundations, from *African Queen* and *Robin Hood*. Movie buffs will appreciate it! (Bring your own video camera, use your imagination, and roll 'em!) Picnic tables and huge shade trees make this a great place to enjoy your lunch. There are several other trails throughout the park, including some that parallel the old stagecoach route, one that leads to the wildlife corridor via the Santa Susana Pass Road and onto the mountains, and one that leads to Foothill Park via a quarter mile connector trail. Foothill Park has a half basketball court, bbq, a small playground, and an open, grassy field lined with large shade trees. See FAERY HUNT (Los Angeles County) (pg. 183) for information on a fun, interactive "production" for kids involving fairies and nature held here at certain times throughout the year. Across the driveway is a movie studio with facades (no public access).

Hours: The park is open daily, sunrise - sunset.

  Price: Free

   Ages: 3 years and up.

DENNISON PARK

(805) 654-3951 / www.ventura.org

7250 Ojai Santa Paula Rd., Ojai

    I recommend the very rural Dennison Park more for the camping than day use as the day use picnic area isn't very big. It contains some trees, a picnic table, a small playground and a horseshoe pit. However, the unspoiled views of the surrounding mountains, valleys, fields, and all of Ojai are quite stunning. And I recommend the campsites for older kids as, because of the view, the sites are high up and many, along the outer ring, are near the edges of hills. Having said all that, it is beautiful here. Most of the sites feel almost private with mature shade trees and shrubbery, and each has a stone or wooden picnic table and bbq pit. There is a park host onsite.

Hours: Open daily, 7:30am - sunset.

  Price: $2 per vehicle Mon. - Fri; $4, Sat. - Sun. Camping is $21 per night.

   Ages: 6 years and up.

GARDENS OF THE WORLD

(805) 557-1135 / www.gardensoftheworld.info

2001 Thousand Oaks Boulevard, Thousand Oaks

    Exit the busy streets through huge wrought iron gates and enter a peaceful and beautiful world of immaculate gardens. This four-and-a-half-acre park features distinctive samplings of gardens, in themed settings, of plants native to Japan, Italy, England, France, and America (specifically, California). The Japanese section evokes a sense of serenity with a koi pond, short brook and waterfall, small bamboo "forest," bridges, lush foliage, and authentic pagoda. The enclosed Mission Courtyard showcases each of the California missions on its walls, along with a fountain in the center. Outside, a life-sized statue of Father Serra beckons visitors. The centerpiece of the French garden is a tiered, horizontal fountain whose waters cascade over large steps into graduated pools. (No wading or splashing - however tempting!) Vibrantly-colored flowers and hedges complete this section. The English garden bursts with a variety of brilliant blooms and the adjacent rose garden, grouped by color, boasts over 400 bushes. Grape arbors, Cypress trees, and a fountain define the Italian garden.

A centrally-placed bandstand provides a stage for seasonal concerts. Sit and watch the show on the grassy knoll in front of the bandstand. Note that this area is the only place for kids (and adults) to run around in the gardens. This elegant park has strategically placed benches throughout, as well as several cement pathways that crisscross, making the gardens stroller and wheelchair friendly. Bring a lunch to enjoy at the picnic tables under the shade awning. Challenge the kids to a game of chess using the faux stone chess set, with pieces over a foot high, in front of the resource center.

Explore the park leisurely on your own, as all the plants are labeled, or take a forty-five-minute guided tour, offered to adults and to school children, with a maximum of about fifteen people. Learn about the rock formations at the Japanese garden; add new words, such as "deciduous", to your vocabulary; touch a lamb's ear (plant); and much more.

Hours: Open most of the year, Tues. - Sun., 9am - 5pm. Closed Mon., holidays, and during inclement weather.
Price: Free
Ages: 7 years and up

LAKE CASITAS RECREATION AREA

(805) 649-2233 - park; (805) 649-1122 - camping info; (805) 649-2043 - bait, boat rentals and Marina Cafe; (805) 304-6544 - Cycles 4 Rent / www.casitaswater.org; www.casitasboatrentals.com
11311 Santa Ana Road, Ventura

$$$

A day at Lake Casitas is pure pleasure. The main attractions at this beautiful huge lake have traditionally been fishing, biking, and camping. The lake is stocked seasonally with bass, rainbow trout, crappie, and catfish. A fishing license is needed for those 16 years and older. Night fishing from the shoreline until 11pm is offered on full moon weekends throughout the year. If you don't have any luck catching your own meal, catch breakfast or lunch at the lakeside Marina cafe, with its indoor/outdoor seating. The bait and tackle shop has boats for rent. A four-passenger aluminum motorboat is $50 an hour, $85 for the day; a ten-passenger pontoon boat is $105 an hour, $220 for the day; single kayaks are $15 an hour; double kayaks and canoes are $20. No waterskiing is allowed.

Play a round of disc golf at the eighteen-hole, lakeside course. See how well you aim as you attempt to fly your disc into each of the chain-link baskets before your opponent does. If you don't have a disc, purchase one here. They also carry course maps and scorecards. Park at Campsite M to play this challenging game. Younger kids will probably have more fun on the several playgrounds scattered around the recreation area.

Over 400 campsites range from basic tent camping to full RV hookups. Different spots offer different vistas. Each site has a picnic table and fire ring. There is a two-night minimum on weekends. There is a park store on site, too, in case you forget something. Beat the summer heat with the lake's CASITAS WATER ADVENTURE (pg. 652), a small, but refreshing water park.

Hours: The lake and most amenities, including the Cafe, are open daily, sunrise - sunset.
Price: Vehicle entrance to the lake is $10 on weekdays, $20 on weekends and holidays. There is some free parking just outside the main entrance gate. Walk in and bicycles are free. If you want to just come in and eat at the Cafe, your vehicle admission price will be credited to your Cafe food bill. Camping prices range from $30 - $66, depending on the site and time of year, plus a $9 non-refundable reservation fee.
Ages: 3 years and up.

LAKE PIRU RECREATION AREA

(805) 521-1500 / www.campone.com
4780 Piru Canyon Road, Piru

$$$

This beautiful mountain lake is huge at over four miles long and about one mile wide - no wonder there are two floating restrooms (aptly titled S.S. Reliefs) on it. Located at the foothills, Lake Piru offers year-round respite from "real" life. The marina, open daily except Christmas, offers boat rentals - quoted here for two hours - such as pontoons, $200; fourteen-foot fishing boats, $60; single kayak or SUP, $25. If you want to go waterskiing, you'll need to bring your own boat. No jet skis allowed. The lake is stocked with rainbow trout and bass, so reel 'em in. A California fishing license is needed for ages 16 and up. (Not available for purchase here.) Ask about the annual fishing derby held in the spring. Seasonally, the swim beach is open (using imported sand - so very chic!). Lifeguards are on duty in the summer on the weekends.

Day use picnic areas have covered eating areas, a grassy lawn, barbecue grills, a great children's playground and plenty of trees dotting the land. The general store, which carries bait and tackle, is open April through October. Over 250 tent and RV camping sites are intertwined with shade trees and great views of the lake. Note that Lake Piru is next to the Sespe Condor Sanctuary, so take a good look at the birds flying overhead. Since this is a natural environment, be on the lookout also for ospreys, geese, deer, skunks, squirrels, and an occasional bobcat.

Hours: Open daily, 7am - sunset.
Price: $10 per vehicle, October - March; $13, April - September. Camping for up to four people ranges from $20 (non-season, tent camping) - $44 (summer, full hook-up). Reservation fees are $8.
Ages: All

LIBBEY PARK

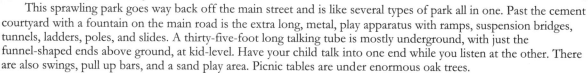

(805) 646-5581 / www.ojaicity.org; www.libbeybowl.org
Ojai Avenue & Signal Street, Ojai

This sprawling park goes way back off the main street and is like several types of park all in one. Past the cement courtyard with a fountain on the main road is the extra long, metal, play apparatus with ramps, suspension bridges, tunnels, ladders, poles, and slides. A thirty-five-foot long talking tube is mostly underground, with just the funnel-shaped ends above ground, at kid-level. Have your child talk into one end while you listen at the other. There are also swings, pull up bars, and a sand play area. Picnic tables are under enormous oak trees.

An abundant number of tennis courts are here - in the front area and then numerous more towards the back. Some have stadium seating as this is the home of an annual spring tournament that attracts the country's top-ranked collegiate players. Amateurs can play on a first come, first serve basis. The lower courts have lights for nighttime play. Cross under the sound arch with pipes that play a melody when activated by motion. The half-dome-shaped Libbey Bowl has graded seating for concerts in the springs and summer, or for your young stars to make their (pretend) debut. The Ojai Music Festival takes place here as does the annual storytelling festival in October, and many other musical forums and programs.

Further back, or entering from Montgomery Street, is the nature section of the park. Kids naturally gravitate to the seasonal creek that is surrounded by glorious old oak and sycamore trees. A natureish trail leads from here to the front and then crisscrosses through the park. For just a little while, perhaps, you'll feel refreshingly removed from civilization. The BIKE TRAIL: OJAI VALLEY TRAIL - VENTURA RIVER TRAIL (pg. 689) also begins (or ends) here. Tips: Top off your time with a visit to the ice cream store across Ojai Street. You can also catch a ride around town on the Ojai Trolley which runs daily from about 6:30am (7am on Sundays) to about 8:30pm. The cost per trip is $1.50 for ages 5 and up and 45" and taller; 75¢ for seniors and children 44" and under. Day trip prices are $4 and $2. Call (805) 646-5581 / www.ojaitrolley.com for more information.

Hours: The park is open daily, 6am - 11pm.
Price: Free
Ages: All

LOS PADRES NATIONAL FOREST: MATILIJA WILDERNESS AND SESPE WILDERNESS

$

(805) 640-9060 - Los Padres Forest / Wheeler Gorge Visitors Center; (805) 646-4348 - Ojai Ranger Station / www.lpforest.org; www.fs.usda.gov/lpnf
Highway 33 and beyond, Ojai

I'm already doing you a disservice, clumping thousands of acres of phenomenal hiking and camping terrain into one entry, but I wanted to make sure you at least had a starting point. I mention WHEELER GORGE VISITORS CENTER, NATURE TRAIL and CAMPGROUND (pg. 671) in a separate section simply because it is the most accessible trail (just eight miles outside of town) in the national forest. And it's a beaut! The next closest trail is Rose Valley, which has a waterfall and awesome scenery. The country further up and further in is even more spectacular and varied.

Call, check out the websites, or visit either the Wheeler Gorge Visitors Center, at 17017 Maricopa Hwy., or the Ojai Ranger Station, at 1190 E. Ojai Ave., for complete information on the trails, trail closures and territory in these wilderness areas.

Hours: The Visitors Center is open Sat. - Sun., 9am - 3pm. The Ranger Station is open most of the year, Mon. - Fri., 8am - 4:30pm.
Price: $5 per vehicle for an Adventure Pass.
Ages: 6 years and up.

MARINA PARK

(805) 652-4550 / www.cityofventura.net
at the end of Pierpont Boulevard, Ventura

This very cool park is part beach, part grass. The big expanse of open grass area (no shade trees) has a few picnic tables and precedes a pirate ship themed playground that has fake cannons, portholes, a slide and port and starboard rails. Other elements, all on rubberized flooring, include swings and toddler swings; a series of metal ladders to climb; a good-sized rock climbing wall with holes and holds; a tunnel to climb over and under; and other fun and creative apparatus.

At the adjacent beach part has a relatively large, cement and wooden replica Spanish galleon, masts and all, that is beached to play in and on. The ship has a zip line, or cable slide, that goes from the ship to a post about fifty feet away on the sand, so whoosh away. The beach also has a volleyball court and rock jetties with a paved pathway that goes out to a point. Sand dunes along the path, with the ocean and sailboats parading in and out of the marina, make it ideal for taking pictures, or just for meditating. A small cove (with waves) for swimming, and a surfing area are here, too. Note that VENTURA HARBOR VILLAGE (pg. 684) is just around the corner.

Hours: Open daily, sunrise - sunset.
Price: Free
Ages: All

MORANDA PARK

(805) 986 - 6500 or (805) 986-6542 / www.ci.port-hueneme.ca.us
200 Moranda Parkway, Port Hueneme

This hilly green park is spread out and diverse with eight tennis courts, two softball fields, a basketball court, and a good and good-sized playground. A paved path goes around and through the park, making it a great place to stroll, jog, or bike. It also connects about midway with the green belt of Bubbling Springs Creek, a lovely bike/pedestrian path that goes along from the beach front inland along a creek that is home to various types of sea birds. Stop at Moranda Park to play, or have a picnic while exploring Oxnard and Ventura.

Hours: Open daily, dawn - dusk. Tennis courts are open daily, 6am - 10pm.
Price: Free. Tennis is free, too.
Ages: All

OAKBROOK REGIONAL PARK

(805) 495-6471; (805) 449-2505 / www.conejo-openspace.org; www.crpd.org
3290 Lang Ranch Parkway, Thousand Oaks

See CHUMASH INDIAN MUSEUM (pg. 676) for details on this lovely, wooded regional park with a Chumash Indian Museum on the property.

Hours: Open daily, 7am - sunset.
Price: Free
Ages: 2 years and up.

OJAI SKATE PARK

(805) 646-5581 / www.ojaiskatepark.com; www.ojaicity.org
414 E. Ojai Avenue, Ojai

This good-sized, enclosed, unsupervised cement skate park has several bowls, with a central one that has a small mound in the middle, plus rails, steps, benches and platforms. Practice ollies, board slides, 50-50 grinds, method air, and more at this popular skate park. A helmet and pads are required.

Hours: Open daily, dawn to 10pm.
Price: Free
Ages: 7 years and up.

POINT MUGU STATE PARK

(310) 457-8143; (805) 488-1827 - park; (800) 444-7275 - camping reservations / www.parks.ca.gov;
www.lamountains.com; www.beachcalifornia.com
9000 W. Pacific Coast Highway at Sycamore Cove and Sycamore Canyon, Malibu

This westernmost park in the Santa Monica Mountain Recreation Area consists of miles of beach, plus inland hiking and biking trails; more than seventy miles in all. A passageway under the highway allows visitors access to both parts of the park. The beach is a popular spot for swimming, seasonal whale watching (end of December through March), and viewing flocks of Monarch butterflies (November through January). The inland, mountainside trails vary in length, difficulty, and scenery. Some trail heads are found at the campground.

The La Jolla Valley Loop Trail is about seven miles round trip. It is a relatively easy walk (about ¾ of a mile) to a little waterfall and pond before the trail enters valley grasslands and gets more strenuous. You can follow the Loop trail to reconnect to the canyon, or continue to Mugu Peak Trail and the 1,266-foot summit, which is an additional three miles. Other trails offer high-walled canyons, oak trees groves, fields of wild flowers (in the spring), and more. Note that Backbone Trail, a trail that extends nearly seventy miles across and through the Santa Monica Mountains, has a trailhead here. For more information on Backbone, call the Santa Monica Mountains National Recreation Area at (805) 370-2301 or (310) 589-3200 / www.smmc.ca.gov. The rugged ten-mile hike of Boney Mountains State Wilderness Loop, which includes craggy pinnacles, are also part of the Point Mugu system.

Camping is available in Sycamore Canyon, which is part of this park system. Most of the closely-spaced, fifty-eight sites are nestled in the mountainside, where the hiking trails are. These spaces are nice looking and have large shade trees. Adjacent to the campground is the Sycamore Nature Center, with exhibits housed in a 1928 mission-style bungalow. Very primitive beach camping is available a little over one mile north at the Thornhill Broome exit.

Hours: Open daily, 8am - 10pm. The nature center is open Sat. and Sun., 10am - 3pm.

Price: $8 - $12 per vehicle for day use during the week, depending on location; $20 on weekends and holidays. There is limited street parking available. Camping at Big Sycamore Canyon, which has showers and running water, starts at $45 a night. Camping at Thornhill Broome starts at $35 a night. A $8 camping reservation fee is charged. Admission is free to the nature center with paid vehicle fee.

Ages: All

RANCHO SIERRA VISTA / SATWIWA NATIVE AMERICAN CULTURE CENTER

(805) 370-2300; (805) 370-2301 / www.nps.gov/samo; www.lamountains.com
4121 Potrero Road, Newbury Park

Since the cultural center is not visible from the parking area, you need to walk about a quarter of a mile on a tree-lined gravel road to reach it. A small garden, a large reconstructed Chumash ap (i.e., round house dwelling made of willow and tule) to walk through, and the center's building containing informational display panels and a few Native American artifacts, are just the beginning. On Sundays the culture center plays host to traditionally-dressed Native Americans who tell stories, or talk about aspects of their ancestor's life and culture; share tribal songs; demonstrate crafts; and/or lead workshops. Ask or check the website regarding special presentations, and guided, educational hikes.

The trailhead for the two-mile Satwiwa loop trail is just outside the center. This trail traverses amongst oak and sycamore trees, and around the chaparral-covered hillsides that are particularly lovely after the winter rains, and while the spring wildflowers are in bloom. This fairly easy hike is good for almost all ages. Tip: Bring your own water. Go just another mile, round trip, off the loop trail to connect to Boney Mountain trail, which crosses a stream several times to reach a seasonal waterfall. Several other trails intersperse throughout, as this area extends into POINT MUGU STATE PARK (see the above entry). You can even hike to the beach, which is about eight miles each way. A shorter option, and more bike/stroller friendly, is the paved pathway that runs about three miles, one way.

Hours: The park is open daily, dawn - dusk. The Culture Center is open Sat. - Sun., 9am - 5pm; closed on major holidays.

Price: Free

Ages: 8 years and up.

RANCHO TAPO COMMUNITY PARK

(805) 584-4400 / www.rsrpd.org
3700 Avenida Simi, Simi Valley

Massive and wonderful, this park's amenities include four full basketball courts, side-by-side; a baseball diamond; tennis courts; pickleball courts; bocce ball courts (bring your own equipment); a nice-size fitness area with legitimate work out machines and equipment; a .5 walking path frequented by joggers and moms pushing strollers; lots of picnic tables and mature shade trees; shuffleboard courts; a good-sized pond with fountains and lots of ducks, surrounded by a veteran's memorial plaza; and a playground and water spray area. The playground, bordered by rocks, has slides, tunnels, swings, bridges, and metal climbing apparatus. The large, circular water spray area has fountain spurting up from the ground and a rainbow of spheres to run through that squirt water every which way.

Hours: The park is open daily, sunrise - sunset. The water spray area is open Memorial Day - Labor Day, daily, 11am - 2:30pm and 3:30pm - 7pm. (Closed in between for maintenance.)
  Price: Free
  Ages: All

SANTA SUSANA PARK / SANTA SUSANA DEPOT AND MUSEUM

(805) 584-4400 - park; (805) 581-3462 - depot/museum / www.rsrpd.org; www.santasusanna\depot.org
6503 Katherine Road (South of the Railroad bridge), Simi Valley

This great back-to-nature park is right next door to a train depot and museum. The large park is studded with huge, old shade trees. Some run-around grassy areas, picnic tables, a basketball court, baseball diamond, and volleyball court are here, plus a good-sized and fun playground that is reminiscent of a fort with bridges and slides, but what makes this park a stand out are the large boulders and rock mounds for kids to climb on and play. There is also a tunnel that connects this park to the an untamed area and more rocks on the other side. Trains are always zooming by the park, too, so train lovers get an eye-full.

The quaint railroad depot, authentically restored to how it looked in 1903, is just next door to the park. The old waiting room is now a museum filled with numerous railroad paraphernalia, as well as an extensive HO scale model railroad layout. The model trains run through a rural and city representation of Simi Valley as it was in the 1950's - kids and adults are enthralled. The tracks just outside the depot are still quite busy, used by both Amtrak and Metrolink.

Hours: The park is open daily, sunrise - sunset. The depot and museum are open Sat. - Sun. for tours and for the model train to run, 1pm - 4pm.
  Price: $1 for ages 9 and up.
  Ages: All

SHELF ROAD TRAIL / PRATT TRAIL

(805) 654-3951 / www.ventura.org
Shelf Road, near Signal St., Ojai

Shelf Road is a .6 mile old dirt fire road located at the foothills of the mountains that used to be open to cars. Now, it's a trail that leads hikers up and across a portion of the hills, past orange and avocado groves, for a great view of the valley below and mountains on the horizon. The road does tend to get steep at times, but it is wide and well-maintained, so it seems easier, somehow! If you are here around sunset, stop and drink in the "pink moment" that Ojai is famous for. (When the sun is just about to set, the sky blazes pink - really.)

The other trail accessible from this point is Pratt Trail, a more strenuous hike. This "true" hiking trail is almost five miles long, and narrow, with many ups and downs. Certain sections cross over the creek. There are numerous routes branching off from Pratt, so take your pick. It ends at Nordhoff Ridge. Note that the lower end of the trail cuts through private property.

Hours: Open daily, 7am - sunset.
  Price: Free
  Ages: 5 years and up.

SOULE PARK

(805) 654-3951 / www.ventura.org
1301 Soule Park Drive, Ojai

Located next to Soule Park Golf Course, this elongated, 223-acre park offers a not-too-far-away get away. Snuggled up against the mountains, so the view is amazing, the park consists of long and fairly wide expanses of grassy areas; lots of mature trees and picnic tables sprinkled throughout; three paddle-tennis courts; a dog park; and a throwback playground. The playground has a metal rocket ship with a slide to launch imaginations; a metal frame of a flying saucer disc to climb up, into and around; a metal frame of a submarine (and yes, its yellow; peeling paint, but yellow); toddler swings; horseshoe pits; and a baseball field towards the entrance.

Hours: Open daily 7:30am - sunset.
  Price: $2 per vehicle weekday; $4 on the weekends or holidays.
  Ages: 2 years and up.

STECKEL PARK

(805) 654-3951 / www.ventura.org
8080 Mistletoe Road, Santa Paula

This rural park offers an enticing hiatus from city life. The day-use picnic area is along the street, and along the banks of the Santa Paula Creek, which teems with bubbling waters, creek life, and boulders. Bring a fishing pole and see what you catch! Or, just go splashing in it during the summer months. Picnic tables and run-around space are tucked amongst big, shady, oak and walnut woodlands. Entertainment for kids, besides the gorgeous scenery, includes a small playground, a volleyball court, a horseshoe pit, and a field. A small aviary, just past the park office, has several cages holding peacocks, lovebirds, parrots, and other birds that you can peek into the cages and look at.

The adjacent tent campsites, to the west of Santa Paula Creek, each have trees, some shrubbery, and a barbecue pit. Although the campground is just off the highway, the noise is minimal and the surroundings make up for it.

Hours: Open daily, 7:30am - sunset.

Price: $2 per vehicle Mon. - Fri; $4, Sat. - Sun. Camping is $23 - $37 per night, depending on the season and if hook ups are needed.

Ages: All

WHEELER GORGE VISITORS CENTER, NATURE TRAIL and CAMPGROUND ☀

(805) 640-9060 - Los Padres Forest / Wheeler Gorge Visitors Center; (805) 646-4348 - Ojai Ranger Station; $$
(805) 640-1977 - Wheeler Gorge Campground; (877) 444-6777 - camping reservations /
www.fs.usda.gov/lpnf; www.lpforest.org; www.reserveamerica.com
17017 Maricopa Highway/ State 33, Ojai

"♬ Country roads, take me home to the place I belong ♪ . . . ." Just driving the mountain roads lined with oak, sycamore, and cottonwood trees, while listening to the sounds of birds trilling, and breathing in the crisp clean air, feels good. Getting out and walking around feels even better! Make your first stop the Los Padres Forest Wheeler Gorge Visitors Center, located about eight miles out of Ojai on the right-hand side. It is the hub station for going into the Los Padres Forest. Free hiking maps and advice are available here, as are special, interpretative, and educational weekend programs. Some favorites include the Herpetological Society presenting live lizards and snakes, and the Open House. Enjoy the displays of taxidermied local wildlife, such as a bear, coyote, and raccoon, plus some from the prehistoric past, such as a T-rex skull, inside and a picnic area outside. Just south of this immediate area, you may pull off onto the side of the road and hike around, and/or splash in the Matilija Creek, without having to pay $5 for an Adventure Pass for your vehicle.

Directly across the street from the Visitors Center is Wheeler Gorge Campground, run by Ojai Rangers. Its backcountry sites delight naturalists. Each of the sixty-eight sites (five of which are handicapped accessible) has a fire ring, barbecue pit, and picnic table, but no potable water. Two-night stays are required on the weekend. At the north end of the campground is the trailhead, with limited parking, for the Wheeler Gorge Nature Trail. This narrow, half-mile, looping trail runs along and crosses over Matilija Creek, into the hillsides and up for a breathtaking view. The creek has boulders that line it and are strewn across it at points. Be on the lookout for poison oak. Plant life on the trail changes from cool, shady riparian vegetation to drier chaparral plants. With ten trails that range in length and difficulty, toddlers to hardy hikers will find at least one that suits them.

Hours: The Visitors Center is open Sat. - Sun., 9am - 3pm. Day use for the campground area is open 8am - 6pm. The trail is open daily, sunrise - sunset. The campground is open year round.

Price: Free to the trail. Day use vehicle fee is $10. Tent camping is about $25 a night; RV camping, $50. The camping reservation fee is $10.

Ages: 5 years and up.

WILDWOOD REGIONAL PARK ☀

(805) 495-2163 or (805) 495-6471 / www.crpd.org; www.cosf.org   !/$
928 W. Avenue de los Arboles, Thousand Oaks

Take a walk on the wild side at Wildwood Regional Park. The narrow, dirt trails and service roads are great for real hiking. There are two major trail heads that lead to an extensive trail system for hikers, bikers, and equestrians. Come prepared by bringing water bottles, sunscreen, and backpacks with food, for designated picnic areas. Although hiking downhill is easy, plan twice as much time for the hike back up.

Some highlights along the somewhat shorter trails, which are still an almost all-day event, include the Nature Center, Little Falls, and Paradise Falls, which is a forty-foot waterfall that you'll hear before you actually reach it. A hardy 3.2 mile looping hike from the parking lot is down the wooden stairs and over the bridge of Moonridge Trail, into the canyon, past a tepee, to Paradise Falls, then onto Indian Creek Trail (take the side trip to the cave) and along the creek, through the chaparral and woodlands - be on the lookout for wildlife, such as mule deers and lizards - and finally, back up some stairs to the car.

Hike here during the spring months and you'll see an abundance of wildflowers. I encourage you to get a trail map, as different routes have different highlights that you'll want to explore and/or check the second website above for specific trail info. The park offers wonderful, fun, and educational programs like Saturday Night S'Mores, Full Moon Hikes, and Outdoor Experiential Workshops. Enjoy nature, almost in your backyard!

Hours: Open daily, 7am - dusk.
Price: Free. Some of the programs cost $6 - $8.
Ages: 4 years and up. Kids will tire easily.

—MALLS—

THE LAKES KIDS CLUB

(805) 637-8938 or (818) 637-8923 / www.shoplakes.com
2200 E. Thousand Oaks Boulevard, Thousand Oaks

The Lakes - this beautifully-landscaped, upscale, outdoor shopping center (dare I call it a mall?) with two lakes (hence the name), a fountain, and plaza, offers a free kid's club once a week. The productions are first class, featuring name entertainers for your youngsters. Come see marionettes, storytelling, dancing, and singing, and sometimes balloon animals and face painting. Then, grab a bite to eat here. The Lakes also hosts seasonal events and activities, including, ice skating during the winter months. See HOLIDAY ICE RINK (pg. 748) in the Calendar section for details.

Hours: The Club meets March - October, every Wed., 11am - noon.
Price: Free
Ages: 2 - 10 years.

PACIFIC VIEW

(805) 312-9650 or (805) 642-5530 / www.shoppacificview.com; www.mallkidsclub.com
3301 East Main Street, Ventura

This is a mall that might not have it all, but it's close. The Kids Club, powered by National Geographic Kids, incorporates free fun and a time of learning, activities, and games for kids that focus on discovery through play. Music, dance, art, crafts, puppetry, comedy, character performances and more are offered, plus free National Geographic publications, demos and prizes.

Other mall offerings, besides shopping and eateries, include BUILD-A-BEAR WORKSHOP (Ventura County) (pg. 685); VC Arts Collective, a Kids Saturday Morning Art class, that teaches real art techniques at $20 per class - contact (805) 676-1540 for more info; a DISNEY STORE (Ventura County) (pg. 685); and Le Funland, located next to Target. Funland is a fairly small place for children, 50" and shorter, to run around and play. It has four mini slides, that end into a little ball pit; foam blocks; play dolphins on a very slow moving merry-go-round; and a few other toys to play on and with. The cost is $10 for kids during the week ($12 on weekends); $8 for siblings during the week ($10 on weekends). Adults are free. Call (805) 535-4387 for more info.

Hours: The Kids Club is the third Sat. from 3pm - 4pm, usually in Center Court. The mall is open Mon. - Sat., 10am - 9pm; Sun., 11am - 7pm.
Price: Free for the Kids Club. Other activities cost.
Ages: 1 - 10 for the Kids Club.

THE OAKS

(805) 395-2300 / www.shoptheoaksmall.com
350 West Hillcrest Dr., Thousand Oaks

Most importantly for kids here is the Kids Zone, hosted by JCPenney. This Zone offers monthly events to participate in and/or seasonal projects for kids to do, create and take home, such as the Marvel Super Hero event, decorating a Mother's Day flower and sprucing up a Father's Day tie. Coupons and prizes are also given out, too.

The mall also has BUILD-A-BEAR WORKSHOP (Ventura County) (pg. 685); DISNEY STORE (Ventura County) (pg. 685); a mom mixer and craft and storytime on the third Friday from 10am to 11am; Star Kids toy store; a children's soft play area near the food court; and a Farmer's Market. The market is open every Thursday (but closed between Thanksgiving and New Year's Day) from 1:30pm - 6pm with over 50 food vendors for artisan bakery goods, fresh fish, and more.

Hours: Kids Zone events are on selected Sat., 11am - noon. The mall is open Mon. - Sat., 10am - 9pm; Sun., 11am - 7pm.
Price: Free
Ages: 1 - 10 for the Kids Club.

—MUSEUMS—

AGRICULTURE MUSEUM

(805) 525-3100 - museum; (805) 653-0323 - ag tours / www.venturamuseum.org
926 Railroad Avenue, Santa Paula

Hoping to plant a seed of interest, the story of agriculture in Ventura is vividly depicted throughout this barn-like museum. A gift shop and Ford Model A farm truck are the first things you see when you enter. Proceed into the spacious main room, with wooden floors, to see old farm machinery such as the first gasoline tractor and several other vintage tractors; a spring wagon; a Holt Caterpillar; a John Deere tractor; and the massive John Deere thresher, circa 1940 - all with explanatory placards. Old farm equipment and tools line the walls, as do old-time photographs, old signs, crates, branding irons, and even saddles, including one that you can sit on. One of the several interactive displays asks questions that you open the panels (via a sprinkler head knob) to find out the answers. Another is a 120-year old warehouse scale originally used to weigh lima beans that you can use, and another is a tractor to sit on. A blacksmith display is in the corner.

The next room is more geared for kids with a fake horse and 1890's real buggy to sit in and pose; a dress up area with old farm clothes; short, wooden trees laden with bean bag oranges, lemons and avocados to pick; lift up panels; an electronic match-the-crop game; a beautiful bee and flower mural with a real (encased) bee hive and bee info; a play cafe; and lots more. Out back are themed garden beds, as well as a planting area for students to participate in. The ninety-minute guided school tours, for K through 8th graders, reap a harvest of knowledge and fun as they include all that the museum has to offer, plus planting a seed to take home, participating in a five sense taste testing and perhaps a related craft. Note that free family fun days are the first Sunday of every month with free craft activities, too.

To learn even more about the agriculture-related businesses throughout Ventura County, check out the one-hour+ Ag Industry Tours offered on select dates May through August where you go on-site. Tours include Alpacas and Beyond, fleece producers; the lavender farm; Ojai Olive Oil Company; and Limoneira, a major citrus (and avocado) producer. Tours are $10 per person. If you are looking for something fun to do on the first Friday of the month, April through October, the Museum hosts music night with live music, food trucks, and more, all starting at dusk.

Don't have a cow when you go into the restrooms, though there is a statue of one right outside the door, along with an old cream separator and packing crate signs. The front of the museum has hitching posts for horses, plus benches, a little garden area, and interpretative signs. The museum is located across the railroad tracks from the historic depot, which is now a visitors center. Check out the CALIFORNIA OIL MUSEUM (pg. 674) and SANTA PAULA ART MUSEUM (pg. 681) that are right around the corner. Take a tour of the nine murals around town that show the history of Santa Paula and its inhabitants. See www.santapaulamurals.org for more info. Note that the FILLMORE & WESTERN RAILWAY COMPANY (pg. 690) has a regularly-scheduled stop here.

Hours: Open Wed. - Sun., 10am - 4pm. Closed major holidays.
Price: $5 for adults; $3 for seniors; $1 for ages 6 - 17; children 5 and under are free. Guided school tours are $5 per student; self-guided school tours are $1 per person. Admission is free on the first Sun. of every month.
Ages: 3 years and up.

AVIATION MUSEUM OF SANTA PAULA

(805) 525-1109 / www.aviationmuseumofsantapaula.org
830 E. Santa Maria Street, Santa Paula

Take your child to new heights at this aviation museum, adjacent to the Santa Paula Airport. Watch small planes land and take off. The museum consists of a chain of hangars, each one featuring different exhibits. Inside the first hangar, displays pertain to the history of the Santa Paula airport. See the short video here, too. Other hangars showcase restored vintage, military, classic, and experimental aircraft, plus items from the hangar owner's personal collection. More unusual exhibits (at least unusual for an aviation museum) are vintage and unusual radios, jukeboxes, antique and classic cars, vintage racing cars, paintings, photos, collectibles, and more. You can walk the grounds to the hangars or take a shuttle. The museum's goals are to expand to include other hangars, and to incorporate more historical aircraft, especially from the various war eras. School and other group tours are offered during the week. Call to make a reservation.

Enjoy the numerous classic airplanes that come in for a landing on the first Sunday, coinciding with the museum being open. There are often other "specials" on these days, such as a classic car show, and the gift shop is open. What a great way to spend time with the whole family! See SANTA PAULA AIRPORT - CP AVIATION (pg. 692) if you're interested in taking an airplane rides and YOUNG EAGLES PROGRAM (Ventura County) (pg. 692) for a free program for the kids.

Hours: Open the first Sun. of every month, 9am - 2pm, unless it's raining.
Price: Free
Ages: 4 years and up.

CALIFORNIA OIL MUSEUM
(805) 933-0076 / www.caoilmuseum.org
1001 E. Main Street, Santa Paula

The California Oil Museum is housed in the original headquarters of the Union Oil Company. The interior and exterior of the 1890 building has meticulously been restored to its original luster. Outside is a small, enclosed mini park for visitors with a bit of grass, benches and shade trees.

Enter the museum which walls are covered with great pictures and murals regarding the history and technology of the oil industry; of black gold. Quite a few of the exhibits are interactive, such as the Lubricity Exhibit. Kids can turn the gears and see how much easier the figures on bicycles can pedal when the gears are oiled. They can push a button and watch a model rig "drill" for oil through the layers of the earth. With a touch of a button, the Centrifuge Exhibit spins to separate water, and other substances from crude oil. A few touch screens here impart interesting information about how the oil industry affects so many aspects of our lives. See lighter and darker vials of oil depending on how heavy it is; a display of early uses of petroleum; and the transporting, pumping and marketing gasoline via models, tubes and a collection of vintage gas pumps. It's all visually well done and interesting.

Since geology is vital to finding oil, several terrific geological displays are in the museum. Some of the fossils on display include shells, dinosaur bones, and shark teeth. Rotating exhibits of science, transportation, history, and art are also presented here throughout the year.

The back room has rotating displays and is used as a classroom for school groups. One exhibit featured small planes - a Kitfox Model 1 and a Flying Flea, and other aviation-themed displays. Another was prehistoric California with a life-size saber-toothed cat with fur, plus numerous skeletons and bones and fossils from that time period.

The upstairs, which can only be seen by a half-hour guided tour, is interesting to older kids. It contains restored 1890s offices, a 1930s-era bedroom, a kitchen, and fireplaces with ornate tiles around them. A walk-in safe here looks like a secret, hidden room.

Walk through the main building to a side gallery room that features rotating displays. I saw an homage to our servicemen and women with mannequins dressed in military uniforms from WWII, plus canteens, medals, photographs, newspaper clippings, and a video.

Walk outside to reach the Rig Room. Besides the row of more antique gas pumps, the room is taken up by an immense, full-size drilling rig and a huge cable rig in action. The engine turns the sand wheel that turns the band wheel that moves the wooden walking beam and the huge drill bits. I hope you feel like we did when we visited the museum - like we struck oil! Several one- to two-hour guided tours (at only $4 per person) are available for adult and school guests.

Just a block down the street, at Ventura Street, is Veteran's Park, which has a gated, cement skate park; play equipment; picnic tables; and a large patch of grass. Check out the AGRICULTURE MUSEUM (pg. 673) and SANTA PAULA ART MUSEUM (pg. 681) that are right around the corner. Take a tour of the nine murals around town that show the history of Santa Paula and its inhabitants. See www.santapaulamurals.org for more info. Note that the FILLMORE & WESTERN RAILWAY COMPANY (pg. 690) has a regularly-scheduled stop here.

Hours: Open Wed. - Sun., 10am - 4pm. Tours of the upstairs are offered by appointment only on weekends. Closed major holidays.
Price: $4 for adults; $3 for seniors; $1 for ages 6 - 17; children 5 and under are free.
Ages: 4 years and up.

CAMARILLO RANCH MUSEUM
(805) 389-8182 / www.camarilloranch.org
201 Camarillo Ranch Road, Camarillo

This three-story, fifteen-room house is one of the most lovely restored Victorian homes I've had the pleasure of touring. The distinguished architecture - the archways, twelve-foot-high ceilings, octagon-shaped rooms, beautiful wood staircase, wrap around porch, and other special features, enhance the elegant furniture and colorful wallpaper and borders. On the forty-five-minute tour, the guide explained the past owners' history and all about the house, but truthfully, I mostly enjoyed just looking at all the rooms.

Adjacent to the house is the original mule barn and stables (one of which now houses a gift shop), as well as a huge Moreton Bay Fig tree, and attractively-landscaped grounds. Picnic tables are here, too. School and other group tours are available. The Ranch Museum is now surrounded by a business park, which seems out of place (or time).

Hours: The Ranch grounds are open daily, 9am - 5pm. The house is open for tours Sat. - Mon., 11am - 3pm. Closed on holidays. Group tours may be arranged at other times. School tours are offered Tues. and Wed., 9am - 11:30am.

Price: Public and group tours are $5 per person for ages 12 and over. School tours, geared for third graders, are free.

Ages: 8 years and up.

CARNEGIE ART MUSEUM

(805) 385-8158 / www.carnegieam.org

$

424 S. 'C' Street, Oxnard

Come see the permanent and rotating exhibits of paintings, photographs, and sculptures at this museum. Have your children draw a picture of their outing! I mention this small, beautiful fine arts museum mainly because of the kid-friendly workshops offered. (Tell your kids the building is done in neo-classical design, though they'll just think the columns look really neat.) I take my kids through art museums, explaining what I can and hoping that some understanding and appreciation for art will take root. However, I think the best way to reach and teach our kids is through guided tours and hands-on workshops.

In a group tour here, kids learn about a particular style, artist, or medium, depending on the current exhibit. Then, they create their own art projects in a workshop taught by a local artist. Reservations are needed. Ask about other classes offered, too.

Hours: Open Thurs. - Sat., 10am - 5pm; Sun., 1pm - 5pm. Closed during public holidays and during installation of new exhibits.

Price: $4 for adults; $2 for seniors; $3 for college students; $1 for age 6 - 18; children 5 and under are free. Call for tour and class prices.

Ages: 6 years and up.

CHANNEL ISLANDS MARITIME MUSEUM

(805) 984-6260 / www.cimmvc.org

$$

3900 Bluefin Circle, Oxnard

Explore the seas without leaving port! This unique nautical museum focuses on displaying maritime paintings and its outstanding (and massive) collection of model ships all beautifully arrayed and presented in a light and airy building with windows overlooking the picturesque marina. The striking paintings include works from Dutch masters from the 1700's and up. The intricate model ships of all sizes, mostly behind glass cases, are amazing - what attention to detail! Each of the ships is labeled with the specifics of what it is modeled after. Many of ships also feature tiny crewmen and equipment. There are so many models that intrigue, like the Prisoner of War ones made out of animal bones, the clipper ships, and the 1637 *Sovereign of the Seas* with its numerous minute cannons and all that rigging.

Upstairs are more models, including some larger ones and more special ones. There are also flags that the docents here gladly use to teach visitors what they are used for; a steering wheel from a wreck that can be turned; gages to be touched; a board with a variety of knots to try; ships in bottles; whale bones; and scrimshaw. Ask for a paper and pencil scavenger hunt for your kids as they look for objects in the museum and out the windows. Techies become the captain of a ship and navigate with the help of their crew via virtual reality, here, too.

The outside of the museum features an interactive mosaic fountain, plus round tables and chairs, so bring a snack to enjoy here, and soak in the view. Guided tours are offered upon request and the knowledge dispensed is well, indispensable.

Hours: Open to the public Mon., Thurs., Fri. and Sat., 10am - 4pm; Sun., noon - 4pm. Open for group tours Tues. and Wed., 10am - 4pm. Closed Sun., New Year's Day, Thanksgiving and Christmas.

Price: $7 for adults; $5 for seniors; $3 for ages 6 - 17; children 5 and under are free. Admission is free the third Thurs. of every month. School tours are $3 - $5 per student.

Ages: 4 years and up.

CHANNEL ISLANDS NATIONAL PARK VISITOR CENTER

(805) 658-5730 / www.nps.gov/chis
1901 Spinnaker Drive, Ventura

The Channel Islands Visitor Center is worthy of a trip in itself. You'll pass by beaches and stores (see VENTURA HARBOR VILLAGE (pg. 684)), but pacify the kids with a, "We'll stop there on the way out." (And then do so.) The Center is a good combination of museum, store, and resource center. The kids will head straight for the indoor tidepool (not a touch tank), which offers an up-close look at sea stars, anemones, lobsters, and other small, ocean creatures. Other eye-catching displays are the taxidermied animals, such as birds in flight, plus a topographical model of the islands, a life-size replica of an elephant seal, and a cast of a pygmy mammoth skeleton. My boys also enjoyed sifting sand in the mini-sand pit and grinding pretend meal with a Chumash Indian stone mortar and pestle. Have your kids participate in the Jr. Ranger program here. And go up the observation steps outside a few flights up to the top for a panoramic view.

The twenty-five-minute movie, *A Treasure In the Sea,* is shown throughout the day, and is a fun way to learn more about sea life. There are other films shown, as well. Tidepool talks are available on weekends and holidays. Note that rangers lead ninety-minute educational programs here, with a minimum of twelve students. They also come to local schools for presentations. Look under CHANNEL ISLANDS NATIONAL PARK (pg. 663) if you are interested in taking a trip to the islands.

Hours: Open daily, 8:30am - 5pm. Closed Thanksgiving and Christmas. The weekend and holiday ranger
presentations are at 11am and 3pm.
Price: Free
Ages: 2 years and up.

CHUMASH INDIAN MUSEUM

(805) 492-8076 - museum; (805) 449-2505 or (805) 495-6471 - park / www.chumashmuseum.org;
www.conejo-openspace.org
3290 Lang Ranch Parkway, Thousand Oaks

Long ago, the Chumash Indians occupied this area of land, which is now Ventura County, and other surrounding areas. An alcove off the main desk features a large selection of basketry from several Native American tribes, with a majority from the Chumash. There are also mounted deer, rams, and wild boar heads, plus a saddle and historical info and other artifacts from the Lang Ranch.

The small, one-room museum nicely and naturally displays artifacts representative of the Chumash way of life. The glass cases contain a collection stone mortar and pestles; stone, shell and bone tools and jewelry (from 9000 B.C. on); pictures of rock paintings and pigments; plants and herbal remedies; fragments of tomol, or canoe planks; and games using walnuts and other natural game pieces. Paintings and other artwork decorate the walls. There are several taxidermied animals such as a cougar, raccoon, eagle and fox. The centerpiece exhibit is the life-size diorama against the back wall. Five Chumash figures are wearing indigenous clothing and necklaces. They are on a sandy beach, obviously done fishing for the day. A recreated tomol is on the beach as are some baskets, shells, and a small (pretend) campfire. The table in front of the diorama holds some items not behind glass. A smaller, encased diorama showcases a young Chumash man in ceremonial paint and dance regalia wearing a deer bone pin, hawk feathers and deer hide.

Don't miss the gift shop, even if you don't come into the museum. It is like a mini-museum with Native American handcrafted articles such as deer antler stone knives, arrowhead necklaces, animal fur, rattles made from turtle shells, dolls, necklaces, beautifully painted stones, and more.

Walk outside .7 miles to see a replicated Chumash village with six different buildings (aps), other structures, and ceremonial grounds all under oak trees. (You don't have to pay the museum fee to see the village.) There are also benches out here for the school programs that take place. School or group tours, minimum twenty-five students, are about two-and-a-half hours long, very informative, and one of the most effective ways to really see and understand what the museum and grounds have to offer. Hear an explanation of the museum exhibits, listen to storytelling, play a few native games, make a craft to take home, and take a guided walk through the park and archaeological preserve, from a Chumash perspective. You'll learn about their way of life, hear how different plants and trees were used, and inspect the village. Guided nature walks, given on select weekends at 10am for the general public, are offered on select weekends. The cost is $10 for adults; $5 for ages 12 and under. It is only via a guided walk that you can see the centuries-old pictographs, or rock paintings, visible from the caves/overhangs as they are protect to preserve them. Note that the annual Chumash celebration is held at the museum and park in September.

The 436-acre Oakbrook Regional Park itself, adjacent to the museum and Lang Ranch Open Space, is beautiful, and can be visited without going into the museum. There are picnic tables, multitudes of mature shady oak trees, and miles of hiking trails, such as the moderate, 4+ mile Lang Ranch Loop.

Hours: The museum is open Sat., 10am - 4pm; the 1st and 3rd Sun., noon - 4pm. The park is open daily, 7am - dusk. School groups are welcome during the week for tours, 10am - 1pm.

Price: Entrance to the regional park is free. Admission to the museum is $5 for adults; $3 for seniors, students, and ages 5 - 12; children 4 and under are free. School tours are $8 per student, which includes a craft.

Ages: 7 years and up for the museum.

COMMEMORATIVE AIR FORCE MUSEUM (WWII Aviation Heritage Museum)

(805) 482-0064 / www.cafsocal.com

$$$

455 Aviation Drive at Camarillo Airport, Camarillo

Several World War II aircraft, and other items, are on display at this two-hangar museum. Most of the artifacts on exhibit date from WWII and include helmets, flags, airplane parts, canteens, maps, posters, swords, remote-controlled planes, uniforms, a teletype machine, and more. Some of the planes are in flyable condition; some are in the process of being restored; and some can be boarded . All of them make this museum-in-process a hit with visitors. Workers explain what they are doing to fix up planes, and it really is interesting to see the metal sheets, rivets, and huge tires that are being used. Volunteers are working on the aircraft on Tuesdays, Thursdays and Saturdays. Come see the permanent and visiting planes such as a YAK-9, a Curtiss C-46-F transport, a Grumman F8F-2 Bearcat fighter, a North American SNJ Navy trainer, a B-25 Mitchell bomber, P51D Mustang Man-O-War, a Japanese Zero (one of three flying ones in the world!), and several others. School or other group guided tours are given on request.

Kids can climb in a cargo airplane cockpit, buckle up, don the heavy WWII helmets, and turn the knobs on the console. They are also invited to put on a headset and practice Morse code; pick up an old field telephone and pretend to call someone; look through a B-29 gunsight; walk through a plane that looks as it did when the Air Force Chief of Staff used it; and look under a B-25 bomber to see where bombs were once lodged. The docents are affable, knowledgeable, and ready to impart aviation facts whenever asked. The museum is involved with air shows and several special events throughout the year. It also offers twenty-minute Warbird rides starting at $295.

Outside, children may climb on a cannon that was originally from a battleship, and look at a few jeeps located between hangars. As the museum is adjacent to the airport, you can spend some time watching small planes take off and land. If you get hungry for breakfast or lunch, jet on over to Waypoint cafe - see WAYPOINT CAFE (pg. 657). At the end of the air field is Freedom Park, which has a large, run-around field, a sports field, a small playground, horseshoe pits, lighted baseball fields, roller hockey rink, and a BMX track for practice and competitions. Contact (805) 482-1996 / www.pvrpd.org for more info on the park.

Hours: Open Tues. - Sat., 10am - 4pm. Tues., Thurs. and Sat. are work days, so planes are being worked on and even flown. Closed Sun., Mon., New Year's Day, Thanksgiving, and Christmas.

Price: $10 for adults; $5 for ages 10 - 18; $3 for ages 6 - 9; children 5 and under are free.

Ages: 4 years and up.

THE DUDLEY HOUSE

(805) 667-8042 or (805) 641-3563 / www.dudleyhouse.org

!

197 N. Ashwood Avenue, Ventura

This historic, gracious, two-and-a-half-story, Queen Anne-style mansion stands on the corner as a monument to days gone by. The grounds hold lemon trees and purple morning glories. Inside the house, which was originally completed in 1892, are furnishings that typify that era. Walk through the bedrooms, living room, dining room, the very old-fashioned kitchen, and other rooms, to get a feel for this time period. Music recorded in the early 1900's (and since copied onto CDs) plays while you take your guided tour. Guided tours for groups can make reservations to visit during the week.

The museum is host to numerous special events throughout the year, so please check the website or call for more information. For instance, it is decorated with patriotic bunting for 4th of July, and hosts a flea market. A craft boutique is held, along with the usual Open House, on the three weekends following Thanksgiving.

Hours: Open the first Sun. of every month, 1pm - 4pm. Open 4th of July, 1pm - 4pm. Closed December and holiday Sundays.

Price: Free - $5 donation appreciated.

Ages: 7 years and up.

FILLMORE HISTORICAL MUSEUM

(805) 524-0948 / www.fillmorehistoricalmuseum.com $

350 Main Street, Fillmore

Fillmore was founded in 1887 and this museum celebrates its origins in three unique buildings, all clustered around the FILLMORE & WESTERN RAILWAY COMPANY (pg. 690). The main museum is a two-story building, the Sespe Bunkhouse, with several small rooms packed with artifacts and history. There are lots of old photographs; clothing, especially dresses, plus hats, shoes, and accessories; furniture, such a roll top desk with an old telephone; farming and ranching tools; dolls, including a porcelain doll collection, and toys; a school desk; books; a Chumash room with baskets, rocks, and stone mortar and pestles; military war uniforms and medals; old cameras; a small weapons collection - guns and swords; musical instruments; an insect collection; items from packing house days with equipment used in harvesting citrus; and lots more. It's an interesting museum to explore and the docents explain many of the displays. I encourage you to take a guided tours to gain more inside info and especially to have students take a tour.

Inside the railroad depot building is a beautiful, wall-to-wall wooden freight room containing old trunks, a mural, a bell, and display cases holding farm tools, household items, lanterns, model railroad collection and more. The front room was an agent's office and still looks like one. The switchboard and old telephones, and the wood-burning stoves, are neat to look at.

The Hinckley House is beautiful and each of its rooms hold furniture and other household items that one would expect to see in the early 1900's. Walk through the front room, with its pump organ and chairs and living room furniture; to the dining room with the table all set; then, the kitchen with all of its old cooking implements, plus an oven and stove; into the bedroom (check out the baby carriage and antique sewing machine); then into Dr. Hinckley's dentist office. (He was the first dentist in Fillmore.) Enjoy relatively quiet exploration during the week. It gets busy on the weekends as that's when the railcars come and go.

Hours: Open Tues., Wed., and Fri., 9am- noon; Thurs., 1pm - 4pm; Sat., 10am - 3pm. Closed Sun., Mon. and holidays.

Price: $4 for adults; ages 17 and under are free.

Ages: 6 years and up.

MULLIN AUTOMOTIVE MUSEUM

(805) 385-5400 / www.mullinautomotivemuseum.com $$$$

1421 Emerson Avenue, Oxnard

Bonjour. With a nod to the layout and the feel of an elegant art museum, this classy and spacious museum, once owned by Otis Chandler, is home to more than 100 restored French cars exhibited in such a way as to make each one important while still allowing plenty of space to walk in between them and throughout. Also on display are French-stylized furniture, decorative art, and photography from the Art Deco Movement and era. Referred to as "streamlined, symmetrical, and striking", this movement (and museum) showcases cars such as the 1939 Delage D8-120, 1946 Delage D-6, 1938ish Delahaye T145 Coupe, 1937 Peugeot, 1928 Bugatti, and other extremely fine cars that a classic car enthusiast appreciates (and covets). Most of the cars are gleaming. A 1925 Bugatti was rescued from lake waters after being submerged for seventy years - it's a bit corroded. A few others are also in their somewhat original condition. Race cars are displayed on the second level. Should you see this museum? Oui.

Hours: Usually open the second and fourth Sat. (and occasionally other days, by reservation only), 10am - 3pm. Semi-private visits are offered on most Tues. at 10am and Thurs. at 11am. Closed Thanksgiving and Christmas.

Price: $15 for adults; $12 for seniors; $8 for ages 3 - 11; ages 2 and under and active military are free. There is a $2 per ticket processing fee, as well. Tickets must be purchased in advance. Semi-private visits are $40 per person.

Ages: 8 years and up.

MURPHY AUTO MUSEUM

(805) 487-4333 / www.murphyautomuseum.org   !/$$

2230 Statham Boulevard, Oxnard

Over ninety vintage automobiles, mostly on loan from collectors, are in rows, lined up in one, huge room on checkered flooring. There might be several Packards, ranging from 1937 to 1947, as well as a 1952 Chevrolet Suburban Woody, 1926 Ford Model T Roadster, 1970 Plymouth Barracuda, 1966 Chevrolet Corvette Stingray, and 1966 Litecloud Station Wagon Camper. A few vintage gas pumps are sprinkled about the room, and a HUGE scale model train layout (1,800 square feet!) chugs along, delighting onlookers. There are also rotating displays, such as vintage trailers, all about corvettes, and motorcycles, as well as special events held in the parking lot. Shoppers, check out the attached Atta Boy Vintage shop that has a little bit of everything from the recent (and further back) past. There is something to please everyone at Murphy's.

Hours: Open year round, Sat. - Sun., 10am - 4pm. It's also open on Fri., 10am - 4pm, April - December. Open by special arrangement for groups and tours on weekdays.

Price: Free; a suggested donation is $9 for adults; free for ages 12 and under and active military.

Ages: 8 years and up.

OJAI VALLEY MUSEUM

(805) 640-1390 / www.ojaivalleymuseum.org $$

130 W. Ojai Avenue, Ojai

This small museum, located inside an old chapel, has a mission - keeping historic Ojai alive by preserving the valley's cultural and natural heritage. Outside, the grounds are lovely with patches of grass and statues, including a sleeping bear, a huge condor (which is in front of the adjacent Ojai Visitor Center) and a Chumash garden in the back.

Inside, there are two rooms. One houses permanent displays of photos; glassware; Chumash tools, such as arrowheads and mortar and pestle; and a ranchero's or cowboy's equipment, like ropes and spurs. Kids especially like the deer hunter - a Chumash man wearing deer skin. A domed diorama of wildlife includes a wild cat, deer, bears, and a coyote. The second room nicely showcases temporary exhibits. A short video shows Rancho Casitas and its history. Guided tours for students and adults are offered. Call to schedule one.

Hours: Open Tues. - Sat., 10am - 4pm; Sun., noon - 4pm. Closed Mon. and most holidays.

Price: $5 for adults; $1 for ages 6 - 18; children 5 and under are free. Admission is free the first Fri. of every month.

Ages: 3 years and up.

OLIVAS ADOBE HISTORICAL PARK

(805) 658-4728 or (805) 644-4346 / www.cityofventura.net/olivasadobe   !/$$

4200 Olivas Park Drive, Ventura

The Olivas Adobe is a restored, two-story adobe home built in 1847 that once housed Senor Olivas, his wife, and their twenty-one children! It is representative of the rancho period in California's history and, as such, offers tour to the general public and school tours geared for fourth graders. These latter tours are great and very interactive, as students can participate in making bricks, rope a wooden steer, make tortillas, use stone and mortar pestle, and so much more. The residence has bedrooms, a living room, a large chapel room, and a kitchen to look into that are all furnished just as they were over 100 years ago.

The grounds are beautifully landscaped. The open courtyard, with its lovely bell gate entrance, contains a Spanish beehive oven and some farming equipment, plus it gives younger ones some running-around space. A small exhibit building, across from the rose garden, contains items that relate to this particular time period, such as saddles, pictures, and ranching equipment. While this is not an all-day visit, kids enjoy the opportunity to "see" the past. Ask about the many special programs hosted by the park, such as concerts, and candlelight tours at Christmastime.

Hours: The grounds are open daily, 8am - 4pm. The adobe is open for guided tours Sat. - Sun., 10am - 4pm, though tours are given 11am - 3pm. Closed Easter and major holidays that fall on weekends.

Price: Free for just the grounds. Docent guided tours of the house are $5 for adults; $3 for seniors and children 11 and under; or $10 for a family of 4.

Ages: 6 years and up.

PORT HUENEME LIGHTHOUSE

www.huenemelight.org $

120 W. Port Hueneme Road, Port Hueneme

"Let your light shine before men" (and before ships). (Matthew 5:16a) A Victorian-style lighthouse was originally built on this site in 1874. The forty-eight-foot cement tower you now see was constructed in 1941, and its light still stands guard over this section of sea. While not particularly picturesque, the lure of actually going inside a lighthouse beacons, I mean beckons, many people. A few pieces of old lighthouse gear are on display, and some old photographs of the tower line the walls. Walk up the three sets of stairs that wind around to reach the top, a domed chamber called the lantern room. The focal point is the old-fashioned lens - a beveled, brass-encased set of glass prisms. Up here, too, you can scan the horizon, just as lighthouse keepers of yesteryear. Visitors, often lighthouse afficionados, leave the place beaming.

Hours: Open the third Sat., 10am - 3pm (the last tour is at 2:30).
Price: Free. Parking in the promenade is $2 an hour.
Ages: 8 years and up.

RANCHO CAMULOS

(805) 521-1501 / www.ranchocamulos.org $$
5164 E. Telegraph Road, Piru

This forty-acre early rancho, a working citrus ranch, remains in its original countryside setting, so it's just how you picture it would have been in 1853, when it was first built. The lovely grounds include an arbor, rose garden, fish pond, and brick fountain that all complement the complex of over fifteen buildings. The buildings include the main adobe ranch house, a colonial-style adobe, a free-standing kitchen, olive press, a schoolroom, a barn, a chapel, and a brick winery - a treat to walk through and interesting to inspect. With all of this, the rancho is probably best known for being the setting of Helen Hunt Jackson's novel, *Ramona*.

Guided tours, for all ages, are offered. School kids are invited to do some hands-on activities, as well, and have lunch on the grounds. The Early California History tour shares details of the Tatavian Indians and the family that lived in the rancho during the Mexican/American period. Students tour the home and grounds and see demonstrations of adobe brick making, household chores, and cooking. The Old California Tour is similar, but the emphasis is on taking students back a little bit further in time, when the Spanish were exploring the region. This tour focuses on the Spanish influence and the historical context of the events.

Hours: Open to the public, Sun., 1pm - 4pm, with tours given on the hour. Open for school tours during the week. Closed during rainy weather.
Price: $5 for adults; $3 for ages 6 - 12; children 5 and under are free. School tours are $5 for students 13 - 17 years; $4 per student 12 years and under.
Ages: 6 years and up.

RONALD REAGAN PRESIDENTIAL LIBRARY AND MUSEUM

(805)-577-4000 or (800) 410-8354 / www.reaganlibrary.gov; www.reaganfoundation.org $$$$
40 Presidential Drive, Simi Valley

The massive, Spanish-style Ronald Reagan Library and Museum sits alone on a hilltop, surrounded by beautifully-landscaped grounds, a gracious courtyard, and gorgeous mountains. The fantastic museum is purposefully arranged to walk visitors through Reagan's road to the presidency. It starts with his growing up years, then his career as an actor, as governor, his terms as president, and his legacy. Videos, a plethora of photos and memorabilia all entertainingly arranged, and interactive exhibits guide visitors along the time line. Although your tour is self-guided, there are numerous docents posted in rooms ready and willing to answer your questions. Interspersed throughout the museum are mini theaters that show inauguration speeches; the tearing down of the Berlin wall; Reagan's meetings with international leaders; his time with Nancy Reagan; a remembrance of the Challenger crew; his assassination attempt; and more - all captivating footage.

Interactive features of the museum include sitting on a model horse, next to Reagan on a horse, so it looks like you're riding together; acting in a movie with the president (before he was the president) via a screen showing the movie and a camera pointed at you; going under and into a crawl section (kids like this) of a large recreation of the Berlin wall which has barbed wire on top and a blaring siren; playing six electronic, educational games on the game table that incorporate Reagan's economic politics; standing at a podium and delivering his inaugural address while people on the wall mural, including Nancy Reagan, cheer you on; and, via video screens built into what looks like an elegant dining room table, seeing more of what goes on in the White House. Use the dining table's screens to view guests that visited the Reagans; food that was served at State dinners; China dishes used on the table (you can even create your own pattern); and more. These are all great features and make the museum that much more interesting.

Other rooms and exhibits include the suit Reagan had cut off him after his assassination attempt (you can see the bullet hole); a full-size replica of the Oval Office decorated from when he was president in Reagan's style of warmth and Western, and a jar of jelly bellies; homemade, as well as ultra expensive gifts given to him; a room of Nancy Reagan's gowns and some of her jewelry; a hallway with videos, photos and more, called Peace Through Strength; video information on Reagan's summits; his saddles and other memorabilia from his ranch; and a room that has photos and signatures of most of the past U.S. presidents. A majority of the exhibits are accompanied by both written and audio commentary. If you want to know even more, rent an iPod for $7 (or download a free App beforehand to get a discount), that gives more in-depth information at various stations around the museum, plus you can use it to take photos that are emailed to you.

The Air Force One Pavilion is striking! Watch the video interviewing the President onboard Air Force One as the film details the logistical planning it takes to get a president airborne. The plane is massive! Facing a gigantic glass window that looks out over the mountains, it looks ready for take-off. Feeling presidential? Board this retired Air Force One plane used by seven past presidents, from Nixon to George W. Bush. Dubbed the "flying White House," you'll see the cockpit, communications center (where the "football" was kept), state rooms, Reagan's office, the lounge (this is my kind of airplane travel), and private rooms. Have a friend take a picture of you as you wave when you exit the plane. The pavilion also houses a Marine One helicopter, a bullet-proof limousine, a motorcade with police escort, a Cold War gallery with photos and videos of signing the treaty, and a copy of a pub Reagan frequented in Ireland.

Out back is a huge, decoratively spray-painted chunk of the actual Berlin wall. There are picnic tables out front, with a beautiful vista, so you could come here for just a picnic, but the museum is too good to miss. A full cafe is on the grounds with views that overlook the valley. Note that the gift shop sells great aids for teaching history. Outstanding school tours are offered. Check the website for the numerous special events held here throughout the year.

Hours: Open daily, 10am - 5pm. Closed New Year's Day, Thanksgiving, and Christmas.

Price: Tickets range in price, depending on what special exhibits are currently featured: $16 - $25 for adults; $13 - $22 for seniors; $9 - $18 for ages 11 - 17; $6 - $15 for ages 3 - 10; children 2 and under are free.

Ages: 5 years and up.

SAN BUENAVENTURA MISSION

(805) 643-4318 - mission; (805) 648-4496 - gift shop / www.sanbuenaventuramission.org $
211 E. Main Street, Ventura

Built in 1792, and ninth in the chain of California missions, San Buenaventura exudes old-world charm. Although the mission is readily seen from the street, a tour through the rooms and grounds offer a better picture of life during this historical time period. You'll see a small courtyard, artifacts from mission days in the several rooms, and even a small cemetery around the outside. Guided 4th grade school tours are offered during the school year - $35 for up to 35 students and one teacher. The tour includes information about the mission's past inhabitants and usually involves doing a mission-related craft. Teacher tip: If getting a docent doesn't work out they have a guide on line to download.

Hours: Open Sun. - Fri., 10am - 5pm; Sat., 9am - 5pm. Closed New Year's Day, Easter, Thanksgiving, and Christmas.

Price: $4 for adults; $3 for seniors; $1 for ages 17 and under.

Ages: 6 years and up.

SANTA PAULA ART MUSEUM

(805) 525-5554 / www.santapaulaartmuseum.org $
117 N. 10th Street, Santa Paula

Fine art finely displayed sums up this small art museum. The main gallery and two small, side rooms showcase local and national artists in this historic bank building. The safe is a tiny gallery. Towards the back is another room with rotating exhibits. A kid draw, literally, to the museum are the art trading cards where kids draw pictures of a standard size, as they are traded all over the world, and trade their drawing for someone else's. Guided tours, gallery talks, and other special events help make this museum an artistic destination. Check out the CALIFORNIA OIL MUSEUM (pg. 674) and AGRICULTURE MUSEUM (pg. 673) that are right around the corner. Take a tour of the nine murals around town that show the history of Santa Paula and its inhabitants. See www.santapaulamurals.org for more info.

Hours: Open Wed. - Sat., 10am - 4pm; Sun., noon - 4pm. Closed Mon., Tues., and most major holidays.

Price: $4 for adults; $3 for seniors; free for ages 17 and under. Admission is free on the first Sun. of every month.

Ages: 9 years and up.

SANTA SUSANA PARK / SANTA SUSANA DEPOT AND MUSEUM

See SANTA SUSANA PARK / SANTA SUSANA DEPOT AND MUSEUM (pg. 670), under GREAT OUTDOORS, for information.

STAGECOACH INN MUSEUM

(805) 498-9441 / www.stagecoachmuseum.org
51 N. Ventu Park Road, Newbury Park

$$

This beautiful 1870's hotel and stagecoach stop is both interesting and educational, and seen only by guided tour. The downstairs consists mainly of the parlor, dining room, and kitchen. The furniture, decor, and history are interesting to older kids, but younger kids get antsy. The Anderson Hall houses articles relating to the Chumash, with display cases of arrowheads, tools, weapons, baskets, drawings, and more. The Jungleland exhibit, when a lion and tiger farm was in the area many moons ago, is fun to look at with pictures and memorabilia from that time. (Makes me sad to have missed it.) Oooooo - a man named Pierre was supposedly shot here and his ghost still haunts the Inn. Now, the Inn becomes fascinating to kids!

A small "cowboy" bedroom has a saddle, bear skin rug, and other western paraphernalia. A child's room is filled with toys of yesteryear (no Xbox!), and contains a bed that Robert Todd Lincoln (Abe's son) slept in.

Outside the hotel, take a short wooded, nature trail that's dotted with old farming equipment and lots of steps. As it passes by and leads to other historic points of interest you'll see the Carriage House which contains stagecoaches, the old-looking Pioneer Newbury House, the Spanish Adobe House, and a replica of the first schoolhouse in the area. A beehive oven is also interesting, but explain to your kids that the oven is named for its design, not for cooking bees. Go down to see The Chumash Indian ap (i.e. home) and then down a flight of wooden steps into a mini forest. Several bang-up school tours ($4 per student) and other tours are available.

When the kids have seen all they want, head out to the small Stagecoach Park on a grassy hill just above the Inn. The playground fits the theme of the museum as there is a stagecoach-shaped play structure to climb in and on, with a slide and steps attached to it, as well as several black horses on big springs to ride back and forth on - all in a big sand-based play area. There are also a few swings, a basketball court, a picnic table under a shade tree, and a baseball field.

Hours: The Inn is open Wed. - Sun., 1pm - 4pm. The entire complex is open Sat. - Sun., 1pm - 4pm. Closed New Year's Day, Easter, Thanksgiving, and Christmas.

Price: $5 for adults; $4 for seniors and students; $2 for ages 5 - 12; children 4 and under are free.

Ages: 5 years and up.

STRATHEARN HISTORICAL PARK AND MUSEUM

(805) 526-6453 / www.simihistory.com
137 Strathearn Place, Simi Valley

$$

In a lovely, park-like setting, this six-acre, outdoor museum is a conglomeration of several historical buildings moved here from their original locations. Start your one-hour guided tour at the visitor's center, where you learn about the early days of Simi by watching a fifteen-minute video about the Valley's history. Some of the exhibits in the center include saddles, an old-fashioned switchboard, fossils, kitchen gadgets, early laundry equipment, and more.

Next, walk through one of the very first local colony houses. Though the inside decor is from the 1930's, the building itself still retains its original charm. An adobe house, built in the early 1700's, displays an owner's furnishings from the 1950's. The Strathearn House, which is a Victorian house built in 1893, has antique treasures throughout including furniture, clothing, and a pump organ. The library contains some fossils, as well as books. The small church is beautiful and quaint.

Read placards about the corrugated tin garage and the enclosed barn. In an open barn, and around the perimeter of the historic park, see all of the old (and rusted) farm equipment, including several types of wagons, tractors, and threshing tools, plus a few old automobiles. The restoration area is also housed here. Docent-led school tours for 3rd graders help make history come to life for kids. Look at the web calendar, too, for special events such as Civil War Days, Living History Days, and more.

Hours: The grounds are open Mon. - Fri., 9am - 3pm; Sat. - Sun., 1pm - 4pm. The inside buildings, which can only be seen on a tour, are open Wed. - Fri. at 1pm (sharp); Sat. - Sun., 1pm - 4pm, weather permitting. The last tour starts at about 2:30pm. Open for large groups, and for free, school tours during the week upon request (but make sure you get your request in by December for the next school year!).

Price: $3 per person.

Ages: 5 years and up.

U.S. NAVY SEABEE MUSEUM

(805) 982-5165 / www.history.navy.mil/museums/Seabee/seabee_museum.htm

3201 N. Ventura Road, Port Hueneme

This extensive, state-of-the-art museum is dedicated to documenting, preserving, and displaying material relating to the contributions of the Naval Construction Force, better known as the Seabees, and the U.S. Navy Civil Engineer Corps. While the mission statement is formal sounding, the museum is incredibly rich with fascinating exhibits in several distinctive areas. The Grand Hall is devoted to portraits of heroes, Seabees "firsts", and those killed in action, from World War II to the present. There is also a wall featuring all of the battalion plaques.

The theater continuously shows movies pertaining to the Seabees and the various wars. The larger adjacent gallery walks visitors through the history of Seabees, from its inception in WWII after the bombing of Pearl Harbor, and through all the wars since then. Each section is accompanied by mural-size photos, placards, medals, war posters, and gear - backpacks, field telephones, gas masks, and more - plus original artifacts significant to that time period or place, like a large bell from a camp park. In addition, there are numerous life-size models of men and women depicted in scenes of battle and peacetime, wearing authentic uniforms and costumes from around the world. Vehicles are also plentiful, particularly jeeps, tanks, and fully-outfitted Humvees, as are weapons - machine guns, rifles, and swords. Everything, in fact, that represents the many facets of a Seabee's life in action. The "We Build/We Fight" section, showcases just some of the accomplishments that Seabees have provided to America.

Another gallery features a 2/3 scale timber tower/guard tower in Afghanistan; a wooden two-hole burnout (latrine); personal items of maps, language guides, coins, books, etc.; a control station with a myriad of dials; a wooden bunkhouse with sandbags and camouflage netting; Antarctic tools; diving helmets; bullets; ship models; and artwork. And - we found Nemo! It actually stands for Naval Experimental Manned Observatory. This submersible is featured against an underseas mural complete with a sand floor and model divers.

"We Help, We Care" is a gallery focusing on the humanitarian efforts around the globe during wartime and in natural disasters. Interactive exhibits allow visitors to get a glimpse of what it's like, and the challenges that come with, managing a huge military construction project. It also allows youth a sense of what being an engineer is, and perhaps inspires them to consider careers in the CEC. Note: Bring a picnic lunch to enjoy outside in the museum's Memorial Garden.

Hours: Open Mon. - Sat., 10am - 5pm. Closed Sun. and all federal holidays.

Price: Free

Ages: 4 years and up.

WESTERN FOUNDATION OF VERTEBRATE ZOOLOGY

(805) 388-9944 / www.wfvz.org $$

439 Calle San Pablo, Camarillo

If you, or your kids, have ever wanted to be an oologist, this place is *egg*sactly what you're looking for. Oology, by the way, is the study of eggs, particularly bird eggs. The Foundation, started by one avid collector, has grown and now contains over 1 million eggs!, 53,000 bird skin specimens!, and 18,000 nests!!

Upon entering the one gigantic room (i.e., the research center/museum), the huge wall mural of sky, sea, and birds, and the incredible variety and number of mounted birds both in "flight" and in glass displays, make quite a visual impact. The birds are condors, owls, penguins, shore birds, mummified falcons, and many, many more. Several of the rows and rows of what look like big filing cabinets are filled with trays of study skins (odd terminology, I think, since they have feathers) of birds. Some of them are on a stick. Guests are invited to gently hold some of the skins/birds, such as brilliantly-colored tanagers, hummingbirds, toucans, and others, as they learn about the species - their design, their habitats, and their way of life.

The egg collection is astounding. They've all been single-hole drilled and drained. You'll see the very rare and enormous elephant bird egg (elephant birds became extinct in the 1600's), teeny tiny hummingbird eggs, fossilized dinosaur eggs, blue eggs, shiny green eggs, and more.

What a variety of nests! There are "typical" nests composed of sticks, as well as mud nests of swallows; intricate woven nests from weavers; shore bird's nests of sand kicked around; nests found in rope (the rope is here, too); and, again - so many more.

The Foundation's main objective is to manage this massive ornithological collection - one of the largest in the world, gathered from all parts of the globe - for research purposes. School, civic, and other groups of up to forty people may schedule a private tour. Teaching kits are available to educate the public. Who knows - a career desire might very well be hatched within your child! Bring a jacket as the room is usually kept cool.

Hours: One-hour public tours, for up to twenty-two people, are scheduled on the second Wed. from 3:30 - 4:30 and the last Fri., 3pm - 4pm. Call about a month in advance to reserve your spot. Call to book a group tour at other days and times for fourth graders through college age.

Price: $5 per person; ages 5 and under are free.

Ages: 4th grade and up.

—PIERS AND SEAPORTS—

VENTURA HARBOR VILLAGE

(805) 642-8538 or (877) 89-HARBOR (894-2726) / www.venturaharborvillage.com; www.venturaharbor.com   !/$
1583 Spinnaker Drive, Ventura

This harbor harbors a lot of fun. The picturesque "village" has thirty-five unusual gift shops, waterfront restaurants, and cafes. Come for lunch or, my personal favorite, dessert! The Parlor restaurant is small, but fun for kids with its 1920's theme, player piano, tin inlaid ceiling, old ice cream makers on display, and bar stools around the soda fountain. (Tip: Don't call the man behind the soda fountain a jerk.) The restaurant serves burgers, hot dogs, salads, and an array of shakes and malts. The Parlor also has outside seating, overlooking the harbor. I also like the fresh seafood restaurant with its tanks of live lobsters and some really big fish. Enjoy a stroll around, look at the boats, and check out all the colorful, ceramic tiled marine murals.

Take a ride on the indoor, thirty-six smallish horse (and other animals) carousel, at $3 a ride. (Parents can ride for free with kids ages 5 and under.) The compact adjacent arcade has mostly benign video games (yeah!), and a kiddie room with a few rides and little kid games. A birthday party room, redemption center, and snack bar with caramel apples, cotton candy, and homemade fudge, help make this place a child magnet. Call (805) 644-3234 for more information.

Free, outdoor concerts are given on most weekends, usually on Sundays, in the summer. A Fisherman's Market is held every Saturday from 8am to 11am in front of Andria's Restaurant. Come early for the catch of the day directly from fishermens' boats - you can even get your fish fileted. The harbor also sponsors numerous annual events, such as the Parade of Lights in December, the tallships in January/February, and Pirates Day Festival in June. (See the Calendar section under corresponding months for details.) Note that adults will probably enjoy the Ventura Harbor Comedy Club inside, depending on who's headlining.

While here, take a whale watching cruise, a cruise around the harbor or one out to the Channel Islands. Look up CHANNEL ISLANDS NATIONAL PARK (pg. 663) and ISLAND PACKERS (pg. 691) for more info. For other cruise information, and rentals of kayaks, pedal boats, and SUPs see VENTURA BOAT RENTALS (pg. 692). Enjoy sifting sand between your toes and/or swimming at the small Harbor Cove Beach, which is just across the street from the CHANNEL ISLANDS NATIONAL PARK VISITOR CENTER (pg. 676). Facilities include restrooms and a children's play area. The waters are protected by rock jetties, which adventuresome kids like to climb on. The rock jetties are not for the faint of heart, however, or for really young kids, as part of the "walkway" on the rocks is washed away. Bring your fishing poles if you have the time and patience. There are picnic areas and barbecues here. You may also play at the nearby MARINA PARK (pg. 668) which has a playground, a play cement ship, a walkway around a harbor, and more. Enjoy your day here with all there is to do and *sea*!

Tip: Hop aboard a old-fashioned trolley on the Downtown Ventura Harbor Trolley which tours visitors around from Ventura Harbor Village north to the Amtrak/Fairgrounds on Harbor Blvd., with several stops that riders can disembark at along the way. This free, fifty-five-minute loop ride is available year round, Wednesday through Sunday (and holiday Mondays), 11am - 11pm, with breaks from 2pm - 2:30pm and 7:35pm - 8:05pm. For more information, call (805) 827-4444 / www.downtownventura.org/downtown-harbor-trolley. I love free fun!

Hours: Most stores are open daily, 11am - 6pm. Many restaurants serve breakfast, lunch and dinner, so they are open earlier and later. The carousel and games are open Mon. - Thurs., 10am - 6pm; Fri. - Sat., 10am - 9pm; Sun., 10am - 7pm. Most places are open extended hours in the summertime.
Price: Technically free, but bring spending money.
Ages: All

—POTPOURRI—

BART'S BOOKS

(805) 646-3755 / www.bartsbooksojai.com

302 W. Matilija, Ojai

This is one of my happy places. Bart's Books is a large, unique, "outdoor" (i.e. no roof), used bookstore that is worth at least a browse-through, weather permitting. You and your reader-child will delight in this big, Bohemian-style store. It's like exploring an old, comfortable (albeit mostly roofless) house maze, except that most of the "rooms" are created by bookshelves. There are hundreds of books here on every subject, including a small, but packed, children's section and a roofed room of poetry and literature. Sit down on an assortment of benches and chairs, picnic tables, or in a recliner by a fireplace, and even under huge palm and other trees, to peruse your purchase.

Books that are on shelves on and facing the outside of the store are available for purchase any time of day or night. The trusting (or hopeful) store sign reads: "When closed please throw coins in slot in the door for the amount marked on the book. Thank you." The atmosphere here is worth the trip.

Hours: Open daily, 9:30am - sunset. Closed Thanksgiving and Christmas.
Price: Technically, free
Ages: All readers.

BUILD-A-BEAR WORKSHOP (Ventura County)

Thousand Oaks - (805) 449-8704; Ventura - (805) 626-3016 / www.buildabear.com

Thousand Oaks - 550 W. Hillcrest Dr. at The Oaks; Ventura - 3301-1 E Main St. at Pacific View Mall

See the entry for BUILD-A-BEAR WORKSHOP (Orange County) (pg. 315) for details.

Hours: Open Mon. - Sat., 10am - 9pm; Sun. at Thousand Oaks, 11am - 7pm, Ventura, noon - 6pm.

CHANNEL ISLANDS MARINE FLOATING LAB

(805) 382-4563 / www.floatinglab.com

4151 S. Victoria Avenue, Oxnard

This floating marine lab (i.e., boat) offers terrific in-harbor and out-of-harbor learning excursions. Students of all ages can book a "tour" here and receive hands-on teaching instruction. The tours incorporate going out of the harbor and dredging to gather whatever from the sea floor, anchoring and then participating in rotating learning stations on board the R/V Coral Sea. This enables students to gain knowledge about marine life, marine environments, and specifically, marine biology. What better way to involve and aid kids in understanding ocean life than for them to inspect it, as close up as under a microscope; to analyze it by investigating samples that they help to haul up from the ocean floor; to touch it by gently stroking live tidepool creatures such as sea stars and sea urchins, plus bat rays, octopus, and more; to explore it by actually being on the ocean; and to hear about it from naturalists.

The learning labs can be combined with whale watching when the Pacific gray whales migrate - January through April. Note that classes on board the boat are usually three-and-a-half hours long, but can be adjusted according to age and interest level. The maximum number of participants is forty. Bring a lunch to enjoy dockside.

Hours: Call to schedule a class, September - June, Mon. - Fri.
Price: Minimum fee of $650 for a three-plus-hour class. Ask about other classes and add-ons.
Ages: Kindergartners and up.

DISNEY STORE (Ventura County)

Thousand Oaks - (805) 379-2215; Ventura - (805) 477-9776 / www.stores.disneystore.com

Thousand Oaks - 350 West Hillcrest Dr. at The Oaks; Ventura - 3301 East Main Street at Pacific View

See DISNEY STORE (Orange County) (pg. 316) for details about this interactive, Disney store - it's a whole new world! See PACIFIC VIEW (pg. 672) and THE OAKS (pg. 672) to see what else these malls have to offer.

Hours: Open Mon. - Sat., 10am - 9pm; Sun., 11am - 7pm.
Price: Free
Ages: 1 - 10 years.

FRY'S ELECTRONICS (Ventura County)

(805) 751-1300 / www.frys.com
1901 E. Ventura Boulevard, Oxnard
    See the entry for FRY'S ELECTRONICS (Los Angeles County) (pg. 170) for details.

—SHOWS AND THEATERS—

FAERY HUNT (Ventura County)

    See FAERY HUNT (Los Angeles County) (pg. 183), under SHOWS AND THEATERS, for details.

$$$$

FAIRY TALES IN THE PARK

(661) 718-3968 / www.fairytalesinthepark.com
    Just like a band of gypsies, this volunteer, roving group of actors and actresses, collectively known as Gypsies in a Trunk, travel from place to place. Their purpose is to put on free, forty-five-minute performances for young children all around Ventura County to promote and inspire a love for live theater. They retell fairy tales and other tales, such as *Jack and the Beanstalk*, *The Hare and the Tortoise*, *Robin Hood*, and *The Wizard of Oz*. Live theater, geared for children, outdoors, for free = perfect! The cities and locations have included outdoor venues at Camarillo, Channel Islands Harbor, Simi Valley, Westlake Village, and Ventura. Bring a blanket or a low-back lawn chair, sunscreen, and some picnicky foods to enjoy.
Hours: Plays are performed May - September at various times throughout the day, depending on the location. Check their calendar website for specific info.
Price: Free; a hat is passed at the end - donations appreciated.
Ages: 3 - 9 years

OXNARD PERFORMING ARTS AND CONVENTION CENTER

(805) 385-8147 - theater; (805) 486-2424 - box office / www.oxnardperformingarts.com
800 Hobson Way at the Oxnard Performing Arts Center, Oxnard

$$$$

    Shows performed at this 1,654-seat theater for the general public include Broadway musicals; concerts; Shangri-La acrobats; and performances by the Ventura County Ballet Company, (805) 323-6620 / www.venturacountyballet.com and the New West Symphony, (805) 497-5800 / www.newwestsymphony.org. Specific kid-friendly acts have included *Sesame Street*, *Nutcracker*, *Anne Frank*, and *Wiggles Live*. School groups often rent the theater to see special performances put on by American Theater for Youth / www.omytheater.org, or other touring groups. Call for a schedule.
    Not quite a live performance, but still a special night out, the Dinner and Movie series incorporates dinner (menu choices might include pasta or chicken, soup, salad, dessert, and beverage) and watching a great movie such as *Les Miserable*, *Roman Holiday*, *Raiders of the Lost Ark*, etc. Some movie only dates, which are family friendly, are free such as showings of *Babe* and *Jungle Book*.
Hours: Call for show dates and times.
Price: Varies, depending on the show. The Dinner and Movie Series is $25 for adults; $22.50 for seniors and kids.
Ages: 3 years and up, depending on the show.

PERFORMANCES TO GROW ON

(805) 646-8907 / www.ptgo.org
various locations in Ventura County

$$$$

    What a refreshing take on theater, in the sense that these shows are geared for families and offer a variety of types of performance. Performances and past titles have included *Anne of Green Gables*; Kuniko Yamamoto, *Japanese Storytelling with Magic, Masks and Mime*; *Puss 'N Boots*, Oregon Shadow Theatre (done with shadow puppets); *Soul Street Dance Co.*; and *Fresh Roasted Concerts*. School groups are welcome to enjoy special performances on a field trip, such as the entertaining and educational *King Tut Theatreworks*, or via a school assemble. Teacher's workshops are also available.

Hours: Call for performance schedules and locations.
Price: $15 - $25 for adults; $10 - $14 for children, depending on the show and location.
Ages: 4 years and up, depending on the show.

THOUSAND OAKS CIVIC ARTS PLAZA / BANK OF AMERICA PERFORMING ARTS CENTER

(805) 449-ARTS (2787) / www.civicartsplaza.com; www.toaks.org
2100 E. Thousand Oaks Boulevard, Thousand Oaks

$$$$

This arts plaza, with beautiful fountains out front, is home to the Bank of America Performing Arts Center which consists of two theaters: the Scherr Forum Theatre, which seats 400 people, and the Kavli, which seats 1,800. Both theaters keep a packed calendar of events so there is something going on almost every night. Professional local and national touring production groups put on numerous, first-class shows and presentations including ballet; comedies; juggling; musicals; distinguished speakers (such as David McCullough); concerts; symphonies (a home to New West Symphony, (805) 497-5800 / www.newwestsymphony.org); dance (such as the Moscow dance theater); dramas; and more. A variety of family and children's concerts are offered. Past programs include Jim Gamble's Marionettes, *Do Jump! Acrobatic Theater, Freedom Train, The Music Man, Oregon Trail,* and *Sesame Street Live.* See PERFORMANCES TO GROW ON (pg. 686) for shows that are especially family friendly and inspiring. That company put on shows here as well as at other locations. Note that there are plenty of restaurants in the immediate area at the adjacent mall, The Lakes.

Hours: Call for show dates and times.
Price: Prices vary, depending on the show. Parking is $8 at the adjacent six level parking structure; cash only.
Ages: Varies, depending on the show.

VENTURA COUNTY BALLET COMPANY

(805) 323-6620 / www.venturacountyballet.com
800 Hobson Way at the Oxnard Performing Arts Center, Oxnard

$$$$

All ages grace the stage with performances that are visual treats. Experience shows such as *Jungle Book, Sleeping Beauty,* and, of course, *The Nutcracker.*

Hours: Call for performance times.
Price: Call for prices.
Ages: 5 years and up, depending on the show.

—TOURS—

CALIFORNIA PIZZA KITCHEN (Ventura County)

!

See the entry for CALIFORNIA PIZZA KITCHEN (Los Angeles County) (pg. 196) for more information.

NAVAL BASE VENTURA COUNTY

!

(805) 989-8095 or (805) 989-9234 / www.cnic.navy.mil/Ventura
Construction Battalion Center, Port Hueneme, and Naval Air Station, Point Mugu

Tours on either base allow citizens the rare opportunity of exploring a military base. Groups of at least ten people, maximum thirty-five, have the opportunity to talk with people who protect our country, find out where tax dollars go in supporting the military, and maybe learn about a future career. The tours at Port Hueneme are Fire Station, Public Works Engineering Services, and Military Working Dogs. Tours offered at Point Mugu are Air Traffic Control Tower & Radar Room, Airborne Carrier Command and Control Squadrons (E2s), Bird Watching/Ornithology Tours, Fire Station/Crash Crew, VR-55 Minutemen, Naval Satellite Operations Center, and a Windshield tour. Check the website for descriptions.

Tours are usually about an hour in length, so visitors may sign up for more than one tour in the day, as long as they are at the same location. Stipulations include that all participants must be U.S. citizens, groups must provide their own bus for transportation (no cars allowed), students must be at least 10 years old, and requests must be made at least three weeks prior to your desired date, online. Don't miss the boat on taking these tours!

Hours: Tours can be schedule once a month on Fri., to start at 9am and end at around noon.

Price: Free
Ages: Must be 10 years or older.

OJAI OLIVE OIL

(805) 646-5964 / www.ojaioliveoil.com
1811 Ladera Road, Ojai

Learn about olive oil (not Popeye) on this forty-five acre, 3,000 tree ranch. The informal tours, about thirty minutes long, begin when some people gather for one. Outside, under a grove of trees, the history of the ranch and the area is explained, as well as how the olives are organically grown and harvested. Olives are hand-picked from mid-October through mid-January and milled for twelve days only in November/December.

Next, come inside to the small room where the machinery is kept. The milling process is explained from the 'Hopper', that cleans off the olives, to the 'Denocciolatore', which removes the pits and pulverizes the fruit, to the mixing containers, where it's churned, and finally to the centrifuge, which separates the oil. The tour guide/owner explains what the difference is in fresh extra virgin olive oil and in the products that is often sold in stores. In the tiny tasting room guests are invited to sample varieties of olive oil, from mild to robust, and some that are flavored. Olive oil is available to purchase, as are cosmetic products made from it such as lip balm, soap and face cream.

Hours: Open for tours Wed., Sat., Sun., 10am - 4pm, on the hour. Open daily for tasting and shopping.
Price: Free
Ages: 8 years and up.

VENTURA COUNTY COURTHOUSE

(805) 390-4035 - tour; (805) 650-7599 - bar association/courthouse / www.vcba.org
800 S. Victoria Avenue, Ventura

Now students (and adult groups) can have their day in court! This two-and-a-half-hour tour is for groups of twenty to thirty-five people. The process of the Ventura County court system is explained while it is being experienced as participants sit in on and observe a civil and/or criminal case, seeing an actual trial in process. Touring through the courthouse, see and learn about the law library, the ceremonial courtroom, the traffic court, and the jury room. When available, judges, commissioners, attorneys, or other court personnel speak to the group, and answer questions. The tour also consists of seeing the administration building (where residents pay property taxes and obtain licenses), the sheriff's department, and the jail. Here visitors learn what happens when an inmate is incarcerated - from frisking, to showers, to where they eat and sleep.

A highlight of the tour is a grade-appropriate, mock trial of an actual court case. Participants read from scripts as they become members of the jury, lawyers, the bailiff, and even the judge (along with a robe and gavel). The tour ends with a video of the Sheriff's Detention Center. I think this is a fascinating tour, but I'll let you be the judge!

Hours: Tours are given November - April, Mon. and Tues. at 10:30am, by advanced reservations only.
Price: Free
Ages: 6th, 8th, and 12th graders, and adults.

—TRANSPORTATION—

AMTRAK (Ventura County)

(800) USA RAIL (872-7245) / www.amtrakcalifornia.com
Ride the rails! See AMTRAK (Los Angeles County) (pg. 208) for more information.

BIKE MAPS (Ventura County)

See BIKE MAPS (Orange County) (pg. 328) for information. Two other contacts include the Ventura County Transportation Commission at (805) 642-1591 / www.goventura.org and County of Ventura Transit Information at (800) 438-1112 - ask for a map. A great website for trails in Ventura is www.visitventuraca.com/blog/top-bike-trails-in-ventura.

BIKE TRAIL: COASTAL BIKEWAY

(805) 654-3951 - parks; (805) 648-4127 - ranger office; (805) 646-8126 - Chamber of Commerce; (805) 585-1850 - beach / www.bike.lacity.org; www.labikepaths.com

One end is on Harbor Boulevard at San Buenaventura State Beach - the other is past Emma Wood State Beach of Hwy. 101.

Thirteen miles of coastal bike trail makes for some beautiful scenery while enjoying a day of family and exercise. Stretching from the south at SAN BUENAVENTURA STATE BEACH / VENTURA PIER (pg. 654), northward to Emma Wood State Beach, the trail is popular, especially in the summer.

Surrey cycles, quad sports, choppers, slingshots, and bike rentals are available at Wheel Fun Rentals, www.wheelfunrentals.com. See the next entry for other places to rent bikes, and for another local bike path.

Hours: Open daily, sunrise - sunset.

Price: Free to ride. Parking is $10 at San Buenaventura Beach.

Ages: 4 years and up, depending on how long and far you want to ride.

BIKE TRAIL: OJAI VALLEY TRAIL - VENTURA RIVER TRAIL ☼

(805) 654-3951 - parks; (805) 646-8126 - Chamber of Commerce / www.ventura.org;   !/$
www.visitventuraca.com/blog/top-bike-trails-in-ventura
One end is on Ojai Avenue in Ojai - the other is at San Buenaventura State Beach in Ventura. Or, start in the middle at Foster County Park in Casitas Springs

This scenic, paved route is about sixteen miles long one way, officially ending (or beginning) on Main Street in Ventura. From the northern end point at Libbey Park, riding to Foster Park is about nine miles. The grade of the trail is a gentle slope from north to south, and therefore noticeably easier to pedal than vice versa. Although the trail follows along the major street of Ventura Avenue (Highway 33), oak and sycamore trees adorn it, making it pretty while shading good portions of it. Major sections are hidden from the main thoroughfare and give it a ride-in-the-country feel. The trail is frequented by bikers, skaters, strollers, equestrians, and joggers. The nine-mile trail from Foster Park to Main Street to the ocean includes a connection to the Coastal Bikeway. (See the previous entry.) That section is not all easy on the eyes, as it goes through industrial areas, but pathway artists have enlivened it somewhat with murals.

Forgot your wheels? Bicycle rentals are available at Bicycles of Ojai, (805) 646-7736 / www.bicyclesofojai.com, at 108 Canada Street, Ojai for $6 an hour. Note: No child-size bikes are available here. Ventura Bike Depot, (805) 652-1114 / www.venturabikedepot.com, near the base of Hwy. 33 at 239 W. Main Street in Ventura, offers rentals for kids and adults starting at $20 for adults for two hours; $15 for kids. Wheel Fun Rentalswww.wheelfunrentals.com, has several locations in Ventura and Oxnard.

Hours: The trail is open daily, dawn - dusk.

Price: Free at the Ojai end at Libbey Park; $2 parking at Foster Park during the week, $4 on the weekends.

Ages: 4 years and up, depending on how long and far you want to ride.

CHANNEL ISLANDS KAYAK CENTER ☼

(805) 984-5995 / www.cikayak.com $$$$
3600 S. Harbor Boulevard, suite 2-108 Channel Islands Harbor, Oxnard

Kayaking is a fun and relatively easy sport for most people to participate in. This company offers hourly, part-day, and full-day, sit-on-top kayak rentals and stand up paddle board rentals, as well as lessons and tours. If you want to get your feet wet, so to speak, take the two-and-a-half hour, guided History and Wildlife kayak tour, which begins with lessons, then heads out through the channel and around the coast. You'll see tall ships, and seals and other marine animals at almost eye level and enjoy the incredible scenery while learning the history of the area. You'll also be entertained by paddling by a replica of a small Mammoth and through an artificial sea cave, perhaps even finding "pirate" skulls - all in good fun.

The all-day, all-inclusive Channel Islands Kayak guided tour includes transportation out to Anacapa or Santa Cruz Channel Islands, where dolphins and seals are often encountered, as the guide paddles alongside you and shares some of the island's history. Another service that the center offers is kayak rentals to those booking their own passage out to the Channel Islands via Island Packers. See CHANNEL ISLANDS NATIONAL PARK (pg. 663) for details.

Hours: Open Mon. - Fri., noon - 5pm; Sat. - Sun., 10am - 5pm. Closed some holidays.

Price: Rentals in the harbor are $12.50 an hour for a single kayak; $20 for doubles. SUPs are $25 an hour. The History and Wildlife tour is $79.95 per person. The Caves Tour is $199.95 per person for a two-person tour. Kayaks rentals to take on your own excursion to the Channel Islands are $35 for a full day for a single; $55 for double.

Ages: 5 years and up.

CHANNEL ISLANDS SPORTFISHING

(805) 382-1612 or (805) 382-2900 / www.channelislandssportfishing.com $$$$$

4151 S. Victoria Avenue, Oxnard

Mature males and pregnant female Pacific gray whales are the first to migrate south to Mexico, and then head back north, toward home. Juvenile whales are the last to make the journey, toward the end of the season. Go out for three hours+ on one of several boats in the fleet with a naturalist and learn about the mammals while, hopefully, seeing some of them. The company also, obviously, offers sport fishing excursions.

Hours: The season runs the end of December - April. Departure times are usually Mon. - Fri., 9am; Sat. - Sun. and holidays at 9am and 1pm.

Price: $50 for adults; $40 for seniors (this doesn't apply on the weekends); $30 for ages 12 and under.

Ages: 6 years and up.

FILLMORE & WESTERN RAILWAY COMPANY

(805) 524-2546 / www.fwry.com $$$$$

364 Main Street, Central Park Depot, Fillmore

"More powerful than a locomotive"; *The Great Train Robbery*; and *The Little Engine That Could* - what does this potpourri of things bring to mind? A train ride, of course! Riding on a train is a real adventure for children. The countryside is scenic along this route, with citrus groves and beautiful landscapes. This railway line is also a favorite Hollywood location, so many of the trains you see and ride on have appeared in movies and television shows. Ride the rails in an open air railcar, a restored passenger coach (circa 1930); a 1929 parlour car; a restored, 1950's Streamlined diner; or a more modern car.

There are several types of weekend excursions offered. The "regular" ride, or Weekend Scenic Excursion, is on a Saturday and it's a three-and-a-half-hour round trip between Fillmore and Santa Paula, which includes a seventy-five-minute stopover in Santa Paula. During this time you are invited to tour whatever else is within walking distance, which is most of the town, such as the historic depot, the AGRICULTURE MUSEUM (pg. 673), CALIFORNIA OIL MUSEUM (pg. 674), or the SANTA PAULA ART MUSEUM (pg. 681). A second stopover is at Loose Caboose Garden Center, an eclectic mix of garden art, plants, a koi pond, farm animals, caged birds, fresh seasonal produce and a gift shop. Lunches are offered in the 1929 parlour car en route for an additional fee. (No outside food is allowed on the trains.) The Sunday Scenic Excursion travels to Piru and then to Bennetts Honey Farm. (See BENNETT'S HONEY FARM (pg. 654) for details.)

Many specialty train rides are available, too, including Easter, Father's Day, Pumpkinliner, Christmas Tree Trains, North Pole Express, and more. The Murder Express Lunch Train is a murder mystery comedy offered on select Saturdays and includes a four-hour ride, three-course lunch, and entertainment as you guess "who-done-it", plus a stop over at Loose Caboose. Ask about the hour-long School Trains, where students ride the rails to the Fillmore Fish Hatchery (and back), or non-stop enjoy the countryside as they learn about and see the workings of a train, vintage cars, and more. A snack bar and gift shop are on board. See the Calendar entry for details about the wonderful, annual FILLMORE STEAM RAILFEST (pg. 702).

The park-like area surrounding the train depot is nicely landscaped with stretches of green grass and a courtyard with a fountain. A few stationary train cars are actually stores that carry antiques and train-related merchandise. An ice cream shop is on the premises, too. Check out the FILLMORE HISTORICAL MUSEUM (pg. 678) near the depot, too. Walk around the block, or on the bike path, and you'll see numerous more train cars, in various states of repair.

Note: Several fresh produce stands dot Hwy. 26, just east of the train depot, which offer an awesome selection of in-season fruit and vegetables, with specialties of oranges and strawberries.

Hours: Weekend Scenic train rides depart most Sat., at noon (boarding at 11:30am), returning at 3pm; plus select Sun., at noon. Call or check the website for specialty rides.

Price: Round-trip fare for the Weekend Scenic rides are $26 for adults; $24 for seniors; $16 for ages 4 - 12; $12 for ages 3 and under. Murder Express lunch rides are $70 for adults; $40 for ages 7 - 12; Murder Express dinner, for ages 18 and up only, is $90. School Trains are $9 per person. Thomas trains are $21 - $25 per person. Call or check the website for prices for other specialty rides.

Ages: 3 years and up.

HOPPER BOAT RENTALS

(805) 382-1100 / www.hopperboatrentals.com $$$$

2741 S. Victoria Avenue, Oxnard

    Hop to it and rent an ocean kayak, paddle boat, seacycle (which is a water bike on pontoons), a motor or electric boat right on the Channel Islands Harbor. Reservations are recommended.

Hours: Open November - February, Mon. - Fri., noon - 5pm; Sat. - Sun., 10am - 5pm. Open March - October, daily, 10am - 5pm.

Price: All prices are per hour: Single kayaks are $12; doubles are $20. Paddle boats, for one to four passengers, are $20. Electric boats, for one to eight passengers, are $65; up to twelve passengers, $85. Stand Up Paddle boards are $24 an hour. Cash or check only.

Ages: 3 years and up.

ISLAND PACKERS

(805) 642-7688; (805) 642-1393 / www.islandpackers.com   6/$

Oxnard - 3600 South Harbor Boulevard at the Marine Emporium Landing; Ventura - 1691 Spinnaker Drive at Ventura Harbor

    This is a prime company to use when cruising out to the Channel Islands. See CHANNEL ISLANDS NATIONAL PARK (pg. 663) for complete details on the islands, the price, length of time, and departure times.

    View the magnificent Pacific gray whales on their way to Mexico where they breed and give birth before heading home to the Bering Sea. Three hour, or so, excursions begin December 26 and continue through early April. You may also join Island Packers late June through September for an all-day trek - seven to eight hours, with no island landing - out to the north shore of Santa Rosa Island to gaze at the enormous blue and humpback whales. The journey's climax is seeing the whales, but there is much aquatic life to enjoy along the way, as well. Island Packers also offers three-hour Wildlife Watching school group cruises April through December. From June through October set sail on a two-hour Saturday dinner cruise - what a lovely way to simultaneously enjoy both food and scenery.

Hours: Departure times for whale watching are usually Sat. - Sun. at 9:30am in the summer and sometimes at 1pm, too, in the winter. Check the website for all other departure times.

Price: Blue and humpback whale watching tours are $68 for adults; $62 for seniors; $55 for ages 3 - 12. Gray whale watching tours or Wildlife Watching tours are $37 for adults; $34 for seniors; $28 for children 3 - 12 years. See CHANNEL ISLANDS NATIONAL PARK (pg. 663) for prices for island cruises. Dinner cruises, usually 7pm - 9pm, are $58 for adults; $45 for children.

Ages: 6 years and up.

JIM HALL RACING CLUB

(805) 278-4111 / www.jimhallracingclub.com   6/$

2600 Challenger Place, Oxnard

    What child doesn't like racing around? Now he/she can learn how to do it in karts and enjoy the thrill of racing without the danger. This racing school offers parent/child learning days, for kids 10 to 14 who haven't driven before, and Day One Sprint Kart programs minimum 4 feet, 8" tall. Classes range from half-day instruction to a week, or more. Drivers learn safety (yea!), how to drive, braking techniques (this could be especially valuable in just a few years), and banking. Racers will even get timed - watch out, Robby Gordon! Ventura County beaches are just a short drive away from this school.

Hours: Call for class hours. Call two days in advance to reserve for a weekend time.

Price: Varies, depending on the length of class. The Day One Sprint Kart program, which is four hours of instruction and driving, starts at $249.

Ages: 10 years and up.

METROLINK (Ventura County)

(800) 371-LINK (5465) / www.metrolinktrains.com $$$

    See the entry for METROLINK (Orange County) (pg. 331) for details.

Ages: All

SANTA PAULA AIRPORT - CP AVIATION

(805) 525-2138 / www.cpaviation.com   6/$

830 E. Santa Maria Street, Santa Paula

    This small airport is kid-friendly; partly because of its size, and partly because it's always fun to watch planes land and take off. Instead of just watching, however, why not take the kids up for a spin, literally! At the instructor's discretion, if your child is at least 12 years old (and doesn't get motion sickness), he/she can take an exhilarating half-hour acrobatic intro ride with loops, rolls, and G's (better than a roller coaster!), for $165 per person. For those who enjoy a calmer, scenic ride, a Cessna 172, which can seat up to three passengers, is about $100 (total!) for a half-hour flight; $200 for an hour. Other aircraft are available for flights, too. Learn to Fly Instruction is $99 for a half hour. Lunch at the airport restaurant will complete your lofty adventure.

    If you're visiting on the first Sunday of the month, take a walk through the adjacent hangars that house the AVIATION MUSEUM OF SANTA PAULA (pg. 673). Check out the YOUNG EAGLES PROGRAM (Ventura County) (pg. 692).

Hours: The airport is open daily. Call for hours for a flight.

Price: Prices listed above.

Ages: 4 years and up for a look around the airport and a scenic flight.

VENTURA BOAT RENTALS

(805) 642-7753 / www.venturaboatrentals.com $$$

1575 Spinnaker Drive, Ventura

    Enjoy a forty-minute cruise out of the harbor, past the boats and homes along the coastline. Other options include kayak rentals - $15 an hour for a single, $20 for a double; paddle boats - $15 an hour for a two-passenger, $20 for a four-passenger; stand up paddle boards - $20 an hour; electric boats - $65 for a six-passenger Duffy with an awning, for an hour. (There are more options available for bigger boats, too.) Ninety-minute California Sleigh Rides (boat cruises) depart twice nightly in December and include seeing other boats and buildings with holiday lights, plus hot chocolate and cookies. See VENTURA HARBOR VILLAGE (pg. 684) for other things to do in this area.

Hours: Boat rentals are available Memorial Day - Labor Day, Mon. - Fri., 10am - 6pm; Sat. - Sun., and holidays, 10am - dusk; Labor Day - Memorial Day, Mon. - Fri., 11am - 5pm; Sat. - Sun., and holidays, 10am - 5pm. Cruises depart Memorial Day - Labor Day, Mon. - Fri., noon, 2pm and 4pm; Sat. - Sun. and select holidays, noon - dusk, every hour on the hour. From Labor Day - Memorial Day, cruises depart Sat. - Sun., and holidays at noon, 2pm and 4pm.

Price: Harbor cruises are $10 for adults; $8 for seniors; $6 for ages 2 - 12; $3 for children under 2. Sleigh Rides during the week are $25 for adults; $23 for seniors; $15 for ages 2 - 12; children under 2 are free. Weekend rides are $35 per person. Paying by credit card is more $ for most boat rentals. Other prices are listed above.

Ages: All

YOUNG EAGLES PROGRAM (Ventura County)

National number - (877) 806-8902 / www.eaa723.org; www.youngeagles.org

Camarillo - 501 Aviation Drive/Convair Street; Santa Paula - 830 E. Santa Maria Street

    See the entry for YOUNG EAGLES PROGRAM (Los Angeles County) (pg. 216) for details. Camarillo - Reservations are necessary - complete them online! Check out the COMMEMORATIVE AIR FORCE MUSEUM (WWII Aviation Heritage Museum) (pg. 677) at the airport. Santa Paula - Reservations are necessary - complete them online! Young Eagle flights coincide with the AVIATION MUSEUM OF SANTA PAULA (pg. 673) being open.

Hours: Camarillo - Offered the first Sat. of every month at 10am, 10:45am and 11:30am. Santa Paula - Offered the first Sun. of every month at 10am, 10:45am and 11:30am.

Price: Free

Ages: 8 - 17 years.

—ZOOS AND ANIMALS—

AMERICA'S TEACHING ZOO

(805) 378-1441 / zoo.moorparkcollege.edu $$$

7075 Campus Road at Moorpark Community College, Moorpark

Students attend this teaching zoo, that contains 200 exotic animals, to become zoo keepers, veterinarians, and animal trainers. My favorite aspect of this very small zoo is that the knowledgeable staff members throughout (i.e., students) answer any and all of your child's questions. My kids and I learned so much here! As this is a teaching zoo, and not just here for public enjoyment, many of the caged animals are in rows, making it difficult, or impossible, to see most of them. However, the animals that are readily viewed can be seen more up close than at a typical zoo. We saw llamas, American alligator, baboons, a miniature horse, macaws, potbellied pigs, New Guinea singing dogs, spider monkeys, ring-tailed lemurs, lions, foxes, barn owls, hawks, eagles, Galapagos Island tortoises, birds in an aviary, and many more. Siamang primates are very loud when they get agitated! There is also a small reptile house to go into.

Almost half-hour demonstrations, featuring three to five animals per show, such as primates, hoofed animals, birds, or reptiles, are given on a small outdoor stage. The student trainers give a lot of good information as they talk about the animal's habitats, nutrition, learned behavior, and training. Afterwards, sometimes, kids can touch the animals. One of the reptiles we saw and touched was a huge boa. We were amazed at its strength and its under-belly softness. Don't miss the 3:30pm feeding of the carnivores! Actually, get there a little early and see animals being fed that aren't on the scheduled program. Trainers feed the lions (go ahead - ask what they're eating) as they "show-off" the lions' learned behavior. Take a behind-the-scenes tour for an additional $7 per person to tour the tiny kitchen zoo and see how and what the animals eat, see more of the carnivores and their habitat, and more. Forty-minute school tours, starting at 10am or 10:30am, are given during the week and include animal presentations followed by a half-hour guided tour of the zoo. See the Calendar entry for information on the SPRING SPECTACULAR (pg. 705). Ask about the week-long, summer Junior Zoo Safari for kids who like to work with animals. Note: Picnic tables are here for your lunching pleasure on weekends. There is also a park across the street from the college on Campus Drive with a playground and grassy area.

Hours: The Zoo is open weekends, 11am - 5pm. Trainer talks are given throughout the day. Animal presentations are given at noon and 2pm, weather permitting. You can call to see what animals will be shown. Feeding of the carnivores is at 3:30pm.

Price: $8 for adults; $6 for seniors and ages 3 - 12; children 2 and are free. School tours start at $75 minimum or, over 25 students, $3 per person. All admission requires cash or check only. Parking during the week is $2.

Ages: All

CHIVAS GOAT MILK SKIN CARE AND GOAT FARM

(805) 727-3121 / www.chivasskincare.com
2220 Bardsdale Avenue, Fillmore

Nineteen French alpine goats are raised and hand-milked to create a line of goat milk soaps, lotions and other beauty products at this small, family-owned farm. Several special events, such as the Spring Fling in April, and open houses are held throughout the year for the public to explore the farm a little, including meeting and feeding the goats, pot-bellied pigs, horses, and tortoises; seeing the intimate soap workshop; and shopping!

There are other ways to explore the farm throughout the year. One is to sign up for a one-hour Farm & Soap Workshop, for $12 - $25 per person, depending on the workshop. It includes the above open house activities with more access and hands-on of the soap-making. Take a ninety-minute school group farm tour, for a minimum of $200. Topics and activities can include interacting with farm animals; learning how to raise goats; playing farm games; exploring edible plants and herbs in the learning garden; hands-on learning of biology via goat milking; and/or the chemistry of soap making by touring the soap workshop. Bring a picnic lunch to enjoy. Note that baby goats are usually born in the spring. Also, schedule a private tour for a minimum fee of $200. Topics include DIY Essential Oil Blending, How to Make Goat Cheese, and more. Check out the summer camps for kids, too (and I don't mean goat kids).

Hours: Check the website, call about special events or to schedule a farm tour.

Price: Free - $7 per person for special events, depending; minimum $200 for tours.

Ages: Kindergarten and up.

FILLMORE FISH HATCHERY

(805) 524-0962 / www.dfg.ca.gov
612 Hwy. 126, Fillmore

Stop off and take a quick look around the fish hatchery to see hundreds of thousands of rainbow trout; actually over one million are produced here annually. This hatchery supplies fish to lakes and streams throughout San Luis

Obispo, Santa Barbara, Los Angeles, and Ventura counties. The long, narrow, concrete tanks have compartments that are labeled with the various species names. Coin-operated fish food dispensers (10¢) are here and the fish always seem to be hungry. Watch them almost jump out of the water for the food! School field trips on the FILLMORE & WESTERN RAILWAY COMPANY come through the hatchery as part of their train ride. By the way, no fishing allowed.

Hours: Open daily, 7am - 3pm.
Price: Free
Ages: 2 years and up.

PAINTED PONY

(805) 525-9820 / www.ourpaintedponyfarm.com
15315 Ojai Road, W. of Steckel Park, Santa Paula

Way out here in the country, you won't get to paint a pony, but you will get to spend a few hours on the farm holding baby chicks, milking a goat, and feeding and petting the animals while learning a lot about farming and sustainable living. Just some of the animals include pigs, tortoises, horses, goats, chickens (over seventy-five hens), bunnies, ducks, and sheep - some of which are available for purchase. The farm owners offer a host of seasonal group tours, too, such as Day on the Farm for a minimum of twenty people. This tour includes exploring and learning about the farm, plus holding baby chicks, milking a goat, and seeing and feeding some of the animals. Come apple picking, seasonally; visit the pumpkin patch where about 2,000 pumpkins are growing in the field that you can snip right off the vine; attend week-long spring and summer camps where kids bottle feed baby goats, make cheese from goat's milk, learn about canning, do arts and crafts, and go swimming; and more.

Hours: Open mid-March - October, Mon. - Fri., by appointment only.
Price: A Day on the Farm Tour is $5 per person. Camps are $230 for ages 5 - 10; $210 for ages 11 and up. Call for other tour options.
Ages: 3 years and up.

UNDERWOOD FAMILY FARMS - Moorpark

See UNDERWOOD FAMILY FARMS - Moorpark (pg. 656), under EDIBLE ADVENTURES, for details about this adventure with animals for younger children.

WHALE WATCHING

See the TRANSPORTATION section.

CALENDAR
(a listing of annual events)

Many places listed in the main section of this book offer special events throughout the year. Below is a calendar listing of other annual stand outs. Please keep in mind that some events change dates and locations from year to year, so <u>call the attraction at least a month in advance</u>. The prices and information quoted here are as of June, 2018.

- JANUARY -

BEN FRANKLIN BIRTHDAY CELEBRATION, Carson. (310) 515-7166 / www.printmuseum.org, 315 Torrance Blvd. at the INTERNATIONAL PRINTING MUSEUM (pg. 123) Celebrate Benjamin Franklin's birthday with special tours of the Museum, hands-on demonstrations, Revolutionary friends (Washington, Jefferson, Adams and others), a family show at 11am (experience his inventions and life in colonial America), and a special program for the older crowd at 1pm (Ben's politics and details of his life). There is a symposium following the 1pm performance. Reservations recommended. Open Sat., 10am - 4pm. $12 for adults; $10 for srs and students.

CHILL AT THE QUEEN MARY, Long Beach. / www.queenmary.com. See December entry (pg. 745) for details.

COIN & COLLECTIBLES EXPO, Long Beach. (888) 743-9316 / www.longbeachexpo.com, 100 S. Pine Ave. at the Long Beach Convention Center. A penny for your thoughts! Over 400 vendors buy and sell rare coins, paper money, foreign currency, collectible postcards, autographs, historical documents, jewelry, and stamps. A free coin and stamp are usually given out to younger children at the Young Numismatists and Young Stampers table, respectively. There is a kids treasure hunt and wheel of prizes on Sat. This event is held late January (or early February), mid-June and early September. Open Thurs. - Fri., 10am - 7pm; Sat., 10am - 5pm. Admission is $8 for adults for all three days; $4 for srs. and ages 8 - 16; children 7 and under are free. Parking is $15 a day.

CORONADO BUTTERFLY RESERVE, Goleta. (805) 966-4520; (805) 961-7500 / www.sblandtrust.org/coronado-butterfly-preserve-2; www.trails.com. Parking at 7731 Hollister Ave. (Sperling Preserve at Ellwood Mesa Open Space), across the street from Ellwood Elementary School. Hundreds of Monarch butterflies come to this grove to rest as they migrate south. The public is welcome on this part-wooded and part-coastal land. Park and then walk the ½ mile dirt trail back into the reserve and the specific trees. Take only rugged strollers as ruts and parts are covered with wood chips and tree roots. The trail is well marked and you can take it all the way to the beach. The grove is peaceful - all the butterflies fluttering around and no noise. They look like dead leaves when their wings are folded, but like a stunning orange and black mosaic when they open them and fly. The butterflies arrive in mid-November and usually depart around the end of February, with peak season December and January. Open daily, dawn to dusk. Admission is free

DISTRICT FREEZE ICE RINK, Tustin. See December entry (pg. 755) for details.

ENCHANTED: FOREST OF LIGHT, La Canada Flintridge. See December entry (pg. 756) for details.

FESTIVAL OF HUMAN ABILITIES, Long Beach. (562) 590-3100 / www.aquariumofpacific.org, 100 Aquarium Way. Billed as "a celebration of the creative spirit of people with disabilities" the festival features dance, music, storytelling and interactive displays for children, and includes interactive classes for people of all ages and abilities. Featured presentations include wheelchair dance, live music, signing choirs, service dog demonstrations and more. The event is held at the AQUARIUM OF THE PACIFIC (pg. 217) and includes interactive classes for people of all ages and abilities. The aquarium is open 9am - 6pm; the festival is 10am - 4pm. Free with admission to the aquarium. Parking is $8 with validation.

FESTIVAL OF LIGHTS, Riverside. See November entry (pg. 746) for details.

HERITAGE PARK U-PIC ORANGES, La Verne. (909) 293-9005 / www.laverneheritage.org, 5001 Via De Mansion at Heritage Park. Every Saturday, January through February, pick your own oranges at one of the last working orange groves in the area. Now, you can really have fresh squeezed o.j.! The Weber House is also open for free tours with a suggested donation of $5. Built in the 1880's, it is one of the oldest remaining houses in La Verne. Open Sat., 9am - 3pm. $5 per bag.

HITS DESERT CIRCUIT, Thermal. (760) 399-9200 or (845) 246-8833 / www.hitsshows.com, 85-555 Airport Blvd. at the HITS Desert Horse Park. For eight weeks horse-lovers can get an eyeful as more than 3,000 horses and riders - the top hunters and jumpers in North America - compete in America's largest horse show with over 1.5 million dollars of total prize money. Professional and amateur riders, both adults and juniors, compete in the show ring. Ask about Kids' Day where crafts, free pony rides, slides, clowns, and other kid-oriented activities happen. The circuit begins January and ends mid-March. Open Wed. - Sun., 8am -4pm. Admission is free Wed. - Sat.; Sun., $5 for ages 12 and over; children 11 and under are free. Parking is free.

HOLIDAY ICE RINK, Los Angeles. See the November entry (pg. 748) for details.

HOLIDAY ICE RINK, Thousand Oaks. See November entry (pg. 748) for details.

HOLIDAY ON ICE, Irvine. See November entry (pg. 748) for details.

ICE AT SANTA MONICA, Santa Monica. See November entry (pg. 748) for details.

JUNGLE BELLS AT SAN DIEGO ZOO, San Diego. See December entry (pg. 758) for details. It's only open in January the first few days of the month.

LA KINGS HOLIDAY ICE, Long Beach; Los Angeles; Woodland Hills. See November entry (pg. 749) for details.

LA ZOO LIGHTS, Los Angeles. See December entry (pg. 749) for details.

LUNAR FEST RIVERSIDE, Riverside. (951) 453-3548 / www.lunarfestriverside.com, Downtown Riverside at Mission Inn Avenue and Lemon Street. Be transported to the Ancient Orient beginning with the Parade of Nations at 10am, followed by the Opening Ceremonies. The festivities continue with traditional Asian music, including Taiko drums, dance performances, martial arts, and many cultural displays. There is also a children's village, tea pavilions, food and the grand finale of fireworks. Open Sat., 10am - 9pm. Parking and admission is free.

LUNAR NEW YEAR FESTIVAL, Los Angeles. (213) 617-0396 / www.lachinesechamber.org; www.lagoldendragonparade.com, 600 - 900 blocks of Broadway St. in Chinatown. This over 100-year-old, two-day Chinese New Year celebration's main event is the elaborate (and televised) Golden Dragon Parade on Saturday with floats, bands, and dragon dancers in wonderful costumes. The Little King and Queen contest is adorable. Other goings-on include a street fair with arts and crafts, live music, and a car show. The New Year is celebrated on the first Saturday of the Lunar New Year - "Gung Hay Fat Choy" (i.e. Happy New Year.) Open Sat. noon - 8pm. The parade is 1pm - 4pm. Admission is free, although certain activities cost. Grandstand seating for the parade is $20 per seat for adults; $10 for ages 3 - 11.

MARTIN LUTHER KING JR. DAY. Celebrations take place all over the Southland. Long Beach hosts the Annual Dr. Martin Luther King, Jr. Peace and Unity Parade Celebration - (562) 570-6816. Los Angeles has the MLK Kingdom Day Parade - (310) 250-2891. San Diego hosts a parade, www.alpha-zsl.org. Also see the SAN DIEGO MULTICULTURAL FESTIVAL / MARTIN LUTHER KING, JR. PARADE (pg. 696).

MONARCH BUTTERFLIES, Ventura. See November entry (pg. 749) for details.

MUSEUMS FREE-FOR-ALL, www.socalmuseums.org. Check this website about free admission to twenty museums on the fourth Saturday in January. Regular parking fees apply. Consult individual museum websites for hours and additional information.

NATIONAL PARKS - FREE ENTRANCE DAYS, www.nps.gov/planyourvisit/fee-free-parks.htm. Entrance to your local National parks (and those across the country - 400 altogether!) is free on the following days: Martin Luther King Jr. Day (January); sometimes Presidents Day weekend (February); the first day of National Park Week (April); National Public Lands Day (September), and Veterans Day (November). Entrance is free, but other fees, such as camping, reservations, tours, etc. still apply.

PISMO BEACH MONARCH GROVE, Pismo Beach. (805) 773-7170 / www.monarchbutterfly.org; www.classiccalifornia.com, off Hwy 1/ S. Dolliver St., at the extreme southern end of the town of Pismo Beach; S. of North Beach State Campground. Every year, from November through February, over 25,000 monarchs come to roost and rest at this grove, the largest gathering in the state and, depending on the year, the largest in the U.S. Sometimes you see what looks like dead leaves as dense clusters of the butterflies hang, wings downward, from the branches. At other times the butterflies flutter around, resplendent in their orange and black markings. This site is staffed with knowledgeable docents, in season, daily, 10am - 4pm (except for holidays). A trailer is here, too, with more info and souvenirs. Talks and a guided walk through the grove are offered daily at 11am and 2pm, weather allowing. You won't be here long, but I think butterflies trees and a walk on the adjacent beach - an unbeatable combination. Check the website for coloring pages and other activities for kids. The grove is open daily, sunrise to sunrise. Free.

RADY'S CHILDREN ICE RINK, San Diego. See November entry (pg. 751) for details.

REINDEER ROMP, Los Angeles. See November entry (pg. 751) for details.

SAN DIEGO CHINESE NEW YEAR FAIR, San Diego. (619) 398-7025 or (619) 234-4447 / www.sdcny.org, 3rd and J sts., downtown San Diego. More than 25,000 people attend these two days of celebrating the Chinese culture. Enjoy demonstrations, such as karate and acrobatics; dances, such as fire dances, Chinese folk dances, the lion dance, and the dragon dance (the dragon is thirty-five feet long!); a craft area where kids make a Chinese lantern and form a lantern parade; and cooking demonstrations with wonderful food. Open Sat. - Sun., 9am - 5pm. Admission is free.

SAN DIEGO MULTICULTURAL FESTIVAL / MARTIN LUTHER KING, JR. PARADE, San Diego. (619) 235-2222, (858) 735-5921 / www.sdmulticultural.com, along Martin Luther King, Jr. Promenade - Fourth Ave. to

Market St. on Harbor Dr., adjacent to the outstanding New Children's Museum. Starting the day off with the Martin Luther King, Jr. Parade Saturday at 10am, the celebration continues throughout the day. A feast for the eyes and ears, this festival features stages of multicultural music and dance performances. Kids enjoy all of that, plus storytellers telling tales originating from different continents, hands-on activities, food booths, community information, vending booths with merchandise that span the globe, and more. Ask about Global Villages, an educational program integrating with kids in the classroom. The closest parking is at 6th & K, or take the trolley (See www.sdcommute.com for details). Open 10am - 5pm. The parade begins at 2pm. Admission is free.

SAN DIEGO NEW YEAR TET FESTIVAL, San Diego. (858) 215-4838 / www.sdtet.com, Mira Mesa Community Park, 8575 New Salem Street. Celebrated mainly in the Vietnamese community, the coming of spring is ushered in via a three-day festival. Along with a kid's contest, where they are judged on talent, manners, wearing traditional clothing, and more, the cultural village has ethnic performances (i.e. a variety of traditional and modern dancing and singing), calligraphy, workshops, chess competition, crafts, royal impersonators, and vendors, plus a beauty pageant and singing competition for the slightly older crowd. Fri., 5pm - 10pm; Sat. - Sun., 11am - 10pm. Admission is free.

SKATING BY THE SEA, Coronado. See November entry (pg. 751) for details.

SNOW DAY, Fullerton. (714) 738-6575 / www.cityoffullerton.com, 1700 N. Harbor Blvd. at the Brea Dam. Because it's hard to make snowmen, have a snowball fight and go sledding without snow, the city of Fullerton brings in tons of the white stuff for one day so all these activities can happen. There are three, side-by-side 75-foot sled runs (sleds provided), a blast zone, younger kid's play area, bounce houses, crafts and games, and food vendors. You must pre-register! Open Sat., 11am - 2pm. Early registration is $15 per person for Fullerton residents, $18 later on; non-residents are $18 early on, $21 later on.

TALL SHIPS TOUR, Dana Point, Long Beach, Newport Beach, Oceanside, Oxnard, Redondo Beach, San Diego, San Pedro, Ventura. (800) 200-LADY (5239) - ship tour / www.historicalseaport.org; www.channelislandsharbor.org. The stately, two-masted tall ship *Lady Washington,* a faithful, full-scale reproduction of the first American square rigged ship, and the *Hawaiian Chieftain,* a replica of a typical, nineteenth-century, European merchant trader, glide into port for about six days per port. They dock at various destinations each year starting in late December through January before heading back up north. Seaports include Redondo Beach (181 N. Harbor Dr.), San Pedro ([310] 833-6055; Berth 84 at the L.A. Maritime Institute); Long Beach (200 Aquarium Way at the Long Beach Harbor), Newport Beach (1931 West Coast Hwy. at Newport Sea Base), Dana Point (Ocean Institute), Oceanside ([760] 435-4000; 1540 Harbor Drive S. at Oceanside Harbor), San Diego (1561 Shelter Island Dr.), and back up to Oxnard (Channel Islands Harbor) and Ventura (1583 Spinnaker Dr.). Visitors experience the life of sailors first hand, as well as coastal explorers, traders, and missionaries of the 18th century via a one-hour guided dockside tour, or three-hour sailing adventures led by period-dressed crew members. The dockside tour is hands-on, teaching the life of a sailor and of the cultures along the coast. The three-hour, family-oriented adventure sail includes demonstrations of how to handle a tall ship, singing sea shanties, storytelling, and exploring the open seas. Three-hour battle reenactments place you in the history hot seat as the two ships try to out maneuver each other. The highlight is the firing of cannons. (It's not real ammunition - just lots of noise and smoke.) Another three-hour excursion is for students, called the Voyages of Discovery. This is geared for fourth and fifth graders, although older students enjoy it as well. All hands are on deck as students set and trim the sails, steer the ship, and use traditional navigational tools while learning mathematics, cartography, astronomy, and other sciences, as well as how to work together as a team. Note that teachers are sent a packet of suggested pre-trip activities and a bibliography. Programs run rain or shine, just like the sailors of old worked. Whatever option you choose, come sail the high seas of adventure. Check the schedule for particular times and dates of tours. Dockside tours vary with location, but are usually offered Tues. - Fri., 4pm - 5pm; Sat. - Sun., 10am - 1pm. The tours are free, but a $5 per person donation is requested. Dockside educational tours, for school groups, are $8 per participant, with a minimum of 15. Family adventure sails begin at 11am and cost $49 for adults; $42 for kids. Battle reenactments go to sea at 2pm and cost $79 for adults; $69 for srs., students, and active military; $42 for children 12 and under. Evening sails are $49 for adults; $42 for kids.

TEMECULA ON ICE, Temecula. See December entry (pg. 764) for details.

TET FESTIVAL, Costa Mesa. (714) 890-1418 / www.tetfestival.org, 88 Fair Drive at the Orange County Fair and Event Center. This three-day festival marks the beginning of spring and is the most widely-celebrated festival in Asian cultures, specifically the Vietnamese community. Arts and crafts, food booths, a fashion show, traditional dances, and other entertainment are just some of the fun "events". Open Fri., 4pm - 10pm; Sat., 11am - 10pm; Sun., 11am - 9pm. Admission is $6; children 2 and under are free. Carnival rides are an additional fee. Parking is $8 or take a free shuttle from Freedom Park in Westminster.

THE RINK IN DOWNTOWN BURBANK. Burbank. See December entry (pg. 764) for details.

TOURNAMENT OF ROSES PARADE, Pasadena. (626) 449-ROSE (7673) - recording; (626) 449-4100 - real person; (877) 793-9911 - holiday hot line / www.tournamentofroses.com; www.visitpasadena.com, Pasadena City Hall. This two-hour, world-famous parade of fancifully- and elegantly-decorated floral floats, plus bands and equestrian units, is held on New Year's Day (unless that's on a Sunday; then it's held on Mon., Jan. 2). Camp out overnight on the streets to guarantee a viewing spot - check the website for the rules and regulations; try your luck by arriving in the early morning hours on the actual day; or call Sharp Seating Company, (626) 795-4171 / www.sharpseating.com, for grandstand seating. Watching the parade along the sidewalk/curb is free. Prices for grandstand seats range from $55 - $100. Make reservations at least two months in advance; they are actually open Feb. of that year! The parade begins at 8am. Call or check the website for the parade route. Parking can cost $35 and upward, so plan ahead! Parking passes are available online.

TOURNAMENT OF ROSES POST PARADE VIEWING OF FLOATS, Pasadena. (626) 449-ROSE (7673) or (626) 449-4100 / www.tournamentofroses.com; www.visitpasadena.com. Jan. 1 - 835 South Raymond Avenue at the Rose Palace; Jan. 2 - 3 - along Sierra Madre and W. Washington blvds., near Sierra Madre Villa Ave. Over 50 of the famous floats can be viewed up close the afternoon after the parade and the following day. Arrive early in hopes of bypassing some of the hordes of people to let your kids walk around and "oooh" and "aaah" at the intricate workmanship. Bring your camera! It is a two-mile walk to view all the floats. Jan. 1, 1pm - 5pm; Jan. 2, 7am - 9am for mobility-impaired and srs. only, then 9am - 5pm (4pm is the last entrance) for the general public. Admission Jan. 1 is $15 (pre-sale only); Jan. 2, $15 per person; children 5 and under are free. Expect to pay at least $5 for parking, though there are some free shuttles. Pre purchase tickets at www.sharpseating.com or at the door until 3pm each day.

WHALE FIESTA, San Pedro. (310) 548-7562 / www.cabrillomarineaquarium.org, 3720 Stephen M. White Dr. Celebrate the migration of the Pacific gray whale and the beginning of whale watching season. Enjoy the games, arts and crafts, puppet shows, food and gift vendors, guest speakers, music, sand sculpture contest and duct tape whale sculpture contest. Sun., 10am - 3pm. Free.

WHALE WATCHING. See the Transportation section in the main section of the book for places to call to take a whale-watching cruise. The season goes from the end of December through March. Cruises are usually two and a half hours of looking for (and finding!) gray whales as they migrate to and from Baja. Also, be on the lookout for dolphins, pilot whales, and sea lions. Dress warmly.

WINTER WONDERFEST, Santa Ana, Sylmar. See December entry (pg. 698, 766) for details.

- FEBRUARY -

ANAHEIM INVITATIONAL PROFESSIONAL BULL RIDERS, Anaheim. (719) 242-2800 or (800) 745-3000 / www.pbrnow.com; www.hondacenter.com, 2695 E. Katella Ave. at the Honda Center. About forty-five of the world's top bull riders come to town to ride. This indoor rodeo event is enhanced by pyrotechnics, light shows, rock 'n roll music, fireworks, and more. The performances are Fri. at 7:45pm and Sat. at 6:45pm. Tickets range from $20 - $125. Parking is $20 - $25.

CALICO CIVIL WAR DAYS, Yermo. (800) TO CALICO (862-2542) or (760) 254-2122 / www.calicotown.com, 36600 Ghost Town Rd. at Calico Ghost Town. Over President's Day weekend the North meets the South in Civil War reenactments (at 11:45am and 2:15pm) complete with drills, cannon demonstrations, period fashion shows, music, living history displays, Confederate and Union camps, and two battles a day. Lincoln, Grant, and/or Lee might make an appearance, too. The Gettysburg Address is presented after each battle. Children's crafts and activities are held throughout the days. Other special events include a cotillion on Saturday night at 7:15pm, and Ghost Walks or nighttime tours through the town. Reservations are needed. Open 9am - 5pm. Admission, which includes entrance to the town and most of the activities, is $10 - $20 for adults; $6 for ages 4 - 13; children 3 and under are free. On-site camping (minimum 2 nights) is $30 a night; $65 a night for cabins for 4 people. Reservations for special events are made typically 3 months in advance. Camping and cabins include free admission to the town.

CAMELLIA FESTIVAL, Temple City. (626) 285-2171 / www.camilliafestival.org, corner of Las Tunas Dr. and Golden West Ave. at Temple City Park. The festival, held the last weekend in February and running for over 70 years, is complete with carnival rides and an art show on Sunday. The highlight, the festival parade, is held on Saturday. About ten, camellia-covered floats (which <u>must</u> be finished only with parts of camellias), are designed and made by youth groups. Prizes, including a Sweepstakes Trophy, are given out. Over twenty marching bands and drill teams, plus other organizations that promote the welfare of children such as Brownies and Cub Scouts, participate. Carnival rides are open Fri., 4pm - 10pm. The parade begins Sat. at 11am and the festivities, including the rides, go on until 11pm. The festival also runs Sun., 2pm - 8pm. Admission is free. Certain activities cost.

CHINESE NEW YEAR. Chinese New Year can be celebrated in January or February. See entries for this event in the January listings.

CIVIL WAR ENCAMPMENT, Simi Valley. (805) 526-6453 / www.simihistory.com, 137 Strathearn Place at Strathearn Historical Park & Museum. The historical park feels like an authentic background for the two day Civil War Encampment (a non-battle event). Union, Confederate and civilian re-enactors realistically show a soldiers' and families' way of life during encampments. As tents are pitched, and cooking, cleaning, firing muskets and life is lived throughout the weekend, guests are invited to visit and interact with the re-enactors. Throughout the days there are artillery, Cavalry, infantry, civilian and other demonstrations, plus skirmishes, President Lincoln giving the Gettysburg Address and more. See STRATHEARN HISTORICAL PARK AND MUSEUM (pg. 682) for more details on the park and museum buildings are open for touring. Open Sat., 10am - 4pm; Sun., 10am - 3pm. $6 for ages 12 and over; $3 for children 5 - 12; ages 4 and under are free.

CORONADO BUTTERFLY RESERVE, Goleta. See January entry (pg. 695) for details.

DICKENS FESTIVAL, Riverside. (800) 430-4140 or (951) 781-3168 / www.dickensfest.com, 9th / Main , in front of City Hall. You'll have a Dickens of a time at this two-day festival! The parade is at 11:45am on both Sat. and Sun. morning. Walk the streets of a re-created London Marketplace where the entertainment, costumes, and food (try shepherd's pie, or fish and chips) are served up Victorian style. The Queen makes an appearance and is available for a meet and greet. Vendors ply their goods - antique jewelry, pottery, toys, hats, and more. A mini faire for kids includes making period crafts, storytelling, learning to juggle, and a scavenger hunt. A free children's mini tea, for ages 4 and up, is served twice on the weekends. Real tea and a show is served at the Congregational Church at 3504 Mission Inn Ave. on Sat. at 11am, 1:30pm and 4pm; and Sun. at 11:30am and 2pm. Tea is $25 for adults; $15 for children 12 and under. Call (951) 684-2494 / www.fccriverside.com for more information and to make a reservation. Other activities and events included dramatic and musical presentations, a costume fashion show, educational workshops, and a Civil War camp - catch at least one drill demonstration. Have a night out on the town at the ball at Mr. Fessiwig's place where you can do the (Oliver) Twist. Dance classes are held at a local senior center for a month before the ball. Fri. is pub night - it is very bawdy and for adults only. A murder mystery dinner theater is also available to participate in. The festival is open Sat. and Sun., 9:45am - 5pm. Entrance to the Marketplace is free. Certain activities cost. The ball is Sat. night at 7:30pm and costs $45 to dance; $10 to come watch. The Victorian fashion show is Sat. at 1:30pm and costs $10. Evensong is Sat. night at 4pm at the church and costs $10 per person.

FIRST FLIGHT FIELD TRIP, Anaheim. (714) 704-2509 / www.ducksscore.com/firstflight.aspx, 2695 East Katella Ave. in the Honda Center. This free event, put on by the Anaheim Ducks, explores a different theme every year, such as the "Heart of Hockey" which explores the health and fitness of pro hockey players using math and science. Geared for 3rd thru 6th graders, there is a "playground" for hands-on activities and a "classroom" with workbooks and demonstrations. Players and coaches from the Ducks teach and participate in all the activities. Dress warmly. Open 8am - 12:30pm. Free to all schools.

HARLEM GLOBETROTTERS, Anaheim, Los Angeles, Ontario, San Diego. (800) 641-HOOP (4667) / www.harlemglobetrotters.com. Basketball is brought to new heights with incredible plays and performances by the renown Harlem Globetrotters. It is a whole entertainment and sports package 'cause they got game and then some! Audience participation is part of the deal where kids can learn the art of ball spinning and other fun tricks. The Harlem Globetrotters usually play at several locations during this month -Anaheim ([714] 740-2000, Honda Center); Los Angeles ([213] 480-3232, Staples Center); Ontario ([909] 244-5500, Citizens Business Bank Arena); and San Diego ([619] 224-4171, Valley View Casino Center). Call for show times. Tickets range from $16 - $130.

HERITAGE PARK U-PIC ORANGES, La Verne. See January entry (pg. 695) for details.

HITS DESERT CIRCUIT, Thermal. See January entry (pg. 695) for details.

KUUMBA FEST, San Diego. (619) 544-1000 / www.kuumbafest.com, 79 Horton Plaza at the Lyceum Theatre. Kuumba is Swahili for creativity. The San Diego Repertory Theatre celebrates Black History month with this creative, four-day fest. Enjoy an ethnic marketplace, educational workshops, a pageant of Egyptian and Zulu monarchs, a fashion show, arts and crafts, dance competitions, children's performances, and music that ranges from gospel to hip-hop. The festivities are Thurs. from 3pm - 5:45pm; Fri., 2pm - 7pm; Sat., 10am - 9pm; Sun., 1pm - 6pm. Tickets start at $20 and some activities cost extra.

LINCOLN SHRINE OPEN HOUSE, Redlands. (909) 798-7632 / www.lincolnshrine.org, 125 W. Vine St. at the Lincoln Memorial Shrine. An encampment with Civil War reenactors, including a surgeon's tent and demonstrations of surgical techniques of the time, are the focal point of this one-day celebration and memorial for President Lincoln. Music includes songs from that era. A gun salute is featured, as well. There is a Watchorn Dinner around this date, too, which includes an evening with a Civil War scholar as the featured speaker. Tickets for the dinner are $58, but reservations are often filled by mid-January. The Shrine also hosts other Civil War reenactments and events throughout the year. Open Sun., 11pm - 3pm. Admission is free.

MUSEUM MONTH, SAN DIEGO, (619) 276-0101 / www.sandiegomuseumcouncil.org; www.balboapark.org. February is Museum Month and more than 40 museums in San Diego County participate. Beginning Feb. 1, pick up a free Museum Month pass at any Macy's and bring it to the participating museums to receive half-off admission during this month. Contact the San Diego Museum Council for a listing of participants and more details.

NATIONAL PARKS - FREE ENTRANCE DAYS. See January entry (pg. 696) for details.

PISMO BEACH MONARCH GROVE, Pismo Beach. See January entry (pg. 696) for details.

PRESIDENT'S DAY, Simi Valley. (805) 522-2977 / www.reagan.utexas.edu; www.reaganfoundation.org, 40 Presidential Dr. at the Ronald Reagan Presidential Library and Museum. On President's Day Monday, Washington and Lincoln are only two of the presidents honored here. Roving president lookalikes could also include Reagan (of course), as well as Jefferson and Theodore Roosevelt, plus lookalike first ladies. Each year the specific activities change, but there are usually storytellers and few educational presentations, as well as food booths. Note that on Feb. 6, Reagan's birthday, the museum has a tribute with music from the Marine Corp, a twenty-one gun salute, and complementary piece of cake for visitors. The hours for President's Day are from 10am - 3pm. Admission is free for the outside activities. Admission to the museum is $25 for adults; $22 for srs.; $18 for ages 11 - 17; $15 for ages 3 - 10; ages 2 and under are free. Parking is free.

PRESIDENT'S DAY, Yorba Linda. (714) 993-5075 / www.nixonfoundation.org, 18001 Yorba Linda Blvd. at the Richard Nixon Presidential Library and Birthplace. Presidential tributes begin on Monday, President's Day. Actors portraying the Mt. Rushmore presidents will have a round table discussion and tell stories about their lives and times, and pose for pictures. The Air Force band plays at 11am and 2pm. Explore the museum to experience a different presidential era. The first 1,000 guests receive a free slice of cherry pie - no lie. Open Mon., 10am - 5pm. Admission on Sun. is $16 for adults; $12 for srs.; $10 for students; $6 for ages 5 - 11 years; children 4 and under are free.

RIVERSIDE COUNTY FAIR & NATIONAL DATE FESTIVAL, Indio. (800) 811-FAIR (3247) or (760) 863-8247 / www.datefest.org; www.indiochamber.org, 82-503 Hwy. 111 at the Riverside County Fairgrounds. This ten-day county fair usually begins the Friday before President's Day. There are lots of special exhibits and activities, many with particular kid-appeal. These include the gem and mineral show; carnival-type rides; a model railroad; livestock shows; a petting zoo (we saw the usual array of farm animals as well as llamas, a zebra, and a kangaroo); camel rides; pony rides; and virtual reality rides. The camel and ostrich races (both animals are ridden bareback and also with "chariots") are some of the festival highlights. These races take place a few times a day, and you just never know what is going to happen with two such stubborn species of animals. On President's Day Monday there is a colorful parade starring Queen Scheherazade, that starts at 9am. An hour-and-a-half musical pageant is put on nightly. The festival is open Tues. - Thurs., noon - 10pm; Fri. - Mon., 9am - 10pm. Rides are open until midnight Fri. - Mon. Admission is $11 for adults; $10 for srs.; $7 for ages 6 - 12; children 5 and under are free. Carnival wristbands range from $25 - $28. Parking on the fairgrounds is $10.

SCOTSFESITVAL & INTERNATIONAL HIGHLAND GAMES, Long Beach. (877) 404-3753 / www.queenmary.com, 1126 Queens Hwy, adjacent to and on the Queen Mary. Bring your bagpipes and wear a kilt (although you don't have to) for this two-day event. At least twelve Scottish clans are on hand to entertain visitors with a parade (usually at noon); battle reenactments (on-going, but check website for exact times); traditional and contemporary music; pipe band competitions; Highland games requiring brute strength (e.g. tossing the caber, hammer throw, etc.); dart throwing; sheepdog herding demonstrations; Highland dancing; storytelling; one-hour versions of a Shakespearian play; vendors with Scottish wares; a parade of British automobiles; food (haggis, anyone?); evening concerts; and much more. Activities just for kids include pint-size adaptations to the Highland games and races, being knighted, and more. Admission to the festival includes admission to the ship and 20% off most of the activities. Open Sat. - Sun., 9am - 6pm. Admission is $25 for adults; $12 for ages 4 - 11; children 3 and under are free. (Advanced tickets are less expensive.) Parking is $18. Tips: Parking is really tough! Get here early, or take the free shuttle from Long Beach and save on parking cost. Very limited free parking is available on Queensway Dr. and Harbor Plaza in front of the park. A few of the games, which you may watch for free, take place at the park on the grassy lawn.

TALL SHIPS TOUR, Dana Point, Long Beach, Newport Beach, Oceanside, Oxnard, Redondo Beach, San Diego, San Pedro, Ventura. See January entry (pg. 697) for details.

TANAKA FARMS - STRAWBERRIES, Irvine. (949) 653-2100 / www.tanakafarms.com, 5380¾ University Dr. The time is ripe for tours of strawberry fields and to U-Pic them. Tours are about one-hour long; include a tractor-drawn wagon ride around the thirty-acre farm and seeing the various fruits and vegetables; learning about farming methods, and the history of farming and the area; and picking picking a one-pound basket to take home. (You can pick more and pay for it.) Tours are offered Sat. - Sun., in season, every half hour from 9:30am - 2:30pm for the general public. No reservations needed. School or group tours are offered during the week and reservations are required. Tours are $18 per person; children 2 and under are free.

TET FESTIVALS. Tet or Vietnamese New Year is the same time as Chinese New Year and can be celebrated in January or February. See entries for this event in the January listings.

WHALE WATCHING. See January entry (pg. 698) for details.

- MARCH -

BLESSING OF THE ANIMALS, Los Angeles. (213) 485-8372 / www.elpueblo.lacity.org; www.olvera-street.com, 125 Paseo de la Plaza at El Pueblo de Los Angeles Historical Monument. This event is held on the Saturday before Easter. Children can dress up their pets - all domestic animals are welcome - and bring them to the Plaza Church to be blessed by priests. Some participating zoos bring in more exotic animals. All this is done to honor animals' contributions to the world. It gets wild with all different kinds of animals "held" in children's arms! Open noon - 5pm, with the procession and blessing at about 2pm. Admission is free.

BUBBLEFEST, Santa Ana. (714) 542-2823 / www.discoverycube.org, 2500 N. Main Street. Discovery Cube's Mega Bubblefest Laser Show floats into Orange County for another spring break. International bubble artist and scientist Deni Yang showcases the science of bubbles under a big top in a grand scale production that's like a Las Vegas show for little ones. Open daily, 10am - 5pm. The shows are 11am, 12:30pm, 2pm and 3:30pm. General admission is $17.95 for adults; $14.95 for srs.; $12.95 for ages 3-14; kids 2 and under are free. Parking is $5, cash only. Tickets to the show by Deni Yang are as additional $7 for non-members; $5 for members. Preferred seating is $15. Tickets must be purchased in advance.

BUNNY DAYS, Mission Viejo. (949) 460-2725 / www.cityofmissionviejo.org, 24932 Veteran's Way at Norman P. Murray Community and Senior Center. Geared for ages 11 years and under, join the Easter Bunny and friends the Saturday before Easter for egg hunts (divided into age groups for fairness), carnival game booths, family crafts, petting zoo and a visit by the Easter Bunny. Open Sat., 10am - 1pm. Admission is free. The egg hunt is $1. All other activities cost.

CALIFORNIA IRISH FESTIVAL, Perris. (707) 780-2437 / www.californiairishfest.com, 18700 Lake Perris Dr. at the Lake Perris Fairgrounds. Like finding gold at the end of a rainbow is the California Irish Festival. Bagpipes, bands, Celtic dancing, folk singers, vendors, kids activities, food (and lots of beer) and more! Experience the Emerald Isle in the Golden State. Note that the venue for this event can change. Sat., 11am - 11pm - with opening ceremonies/parade at 11am; Sun., 11am - 10pm. $7 for adults; ages 12 and under are free. Parking is $5.

CELEBRATION OF THE WHALES FESTIVAL, Oxnard. (805) 985-4852 / www.channelislandsharbor.org, at Channel Islands Harbor on Harbor Blvd. near Marine Emporium Landing. It's a whale of a sight! As the majestic ocean mammals migrate, look for them from the shore or take a cruise. This one-day festival includes kayak racing, tide-pool touch tanks, aquarium presentations, an inflatable fun zone, a rock climbing wall, model ship building demonstrations, a farmer's market, and other events and activities. Celebrate on Sun., 10am - 5pm. Admission is free.

EASTER EGG HUNTS. Many parks, schools, churches, and cities put on free Easter egg hunts and/or Easter craft activities the weekend, or Saturday, before Easter. Call the recreation department of your local park, local city hall, or chamber of commerce for more information. Some are small, simply put-together hunts, and others are large *egg*stravaganzas with carnival rides, inflatables bounces, races, and more.

EASTER EGGSTRAVAGANZA, Orange. (714) 997-3968 / www.irvineparkrailroad.com, 1 Irvine Park Road inside Irvine Regional Park. For three weeks, enjoy a hoppy Easter with photos with the Easter bunny and Easter egg hunts - $12 each; and/or train rides, hay ride, moon bounce, cookie decorating, and carnival games - $5 each, plus a free coloring page. Other attractions in this vicinity include paddle boat rentals, bike rentals, pony rides, and the Orange County Zoo. See IRVINE REGIONAL PARK (pg. 284) for more details about what this terrific park has to offer. Open Mon. - Fri., 10am - 5pm; Sat. - Sun., 9am - 6pm. General admission is free, but vehicle entrance is $3, Mon. - Fri.; $5 on weekends; $7 on holidays.

EASTER ON THE FARM, Moorpark. (805) 529-3690 / www.underwoodfamilyfarms.com, 3370 Sunset Valley Rd. at Underwood Family Farms. This two-week-long, yearly *egg*agement at Underwood Family Farms offers a whole farmful of family fun, including animal shows, tractor-drawn wagon rides, face painting, eggy games, balloons, mazes, egg hunts, a visit with the Easter Bunny, and so much more. See UNDERWOOD FAMILY FARMS - Moorpark (pg. 656) for more activities and information. Open daily, 9am - 6pm. Admission Mon. - Fri. is $6 for ages 2 and up; Sat. - Sun., $10 for ages 2 and up. Some activities may cost extra.

FESTIVAL OF SCIENCE & ENGINEERING, San Diego. (858) 455-0300 / www.lovestemsd.com. Each year in March, the San Diego Festival of Science & Engineering hosts an 8 day-long celebration of science and engineering throughout San Diego County. The goal is to inspire the next generation of innovators and researchers. The event kick off, Expo Day, is held at Petco Park with more than 130 organizations providing hands-on activities. During the week you can find tours, talks, shows, demonstrations and hands on experiments. Past events have included: slime and molecules; building with bones; squid dissection; making ice cream with liquid nitrogen; and a tour of the Taylor Guitar factory. Events occur at different times and different venues throughout the week so check the website. Expo Day runs from 10am to 5pm on the first Sat. Parking is $5 for Expo Day. Almost all of the events are free.

FESTIVAL OF THE KITE, Redondo Beach. (310) 372-0308 / www.redondopier.com, 100 Fisherman's Wharf. On the second Sunday of this month watch brilliantly-colored kites of all shapes and sizes fly high above the shoreline. Hosted by Sunshine Kite Company (a company that really knows and teaches all about kite flying and yo yos), which is located on the pier, there are contests, awards for all categories of kites, activities for kids, marital arts demonstrations, dance performances, live music, synchronized acrobatic flying teams, and a mass group kite ascension flight at the festival culmination. Open noon - 5pm. Parking is $1.50. Admission is free.

FESTIVAL OF WHALES, Dana Point. (949) 496-1045 / www.festivalofwhales.org, 34675 Golden Lantern at Dana Point Harbor and the Ocean Institute. It's no fluke - this massive, two-weekend festival celebrates the gray whales' migration. The whole family can enjoy a variety of events offered throughout Dana Point, such as a parade (on the first Sat. at 10am along Pacific Coast Highway); art shows; sand castle workshops; tidepool explorations; street fairs; farmer's market; kid's coloring contests; film festivals; music; lots of food options; evening campfire programs at the adjacent Doheny State Beach; sailing and rowing lessons; sailing regatta; nature walk through Dana Cove with park rangers; kids karnival; rubber ducky race; antique & classic boat show; and a plethora of whale-watching excursions. The Ocean Institute is open during the festival, as is the tallship Pilgrim for living history demonstrations (10am - 2:30pm), and the Doheny State Beach Interpretive Center - whew! Have a whale of a time! Check the websites for specific details. Prices and hours vary depending on the event.

FIESTA DE LAS GOLONDRINAS (Festival of the Swallows), San Juan Capistrano. (949) 493-1976 / www.swallowsparade.com; www.missionsjc.com, Ortega Hwy. at Mission San Juan Capistrano. This three-day festival, celebrating the return of the swallows from their annual migration to Argentina, takes place in different areas throughout San Juan Capistrano, including the mission. The swallows actually return to the mission every year on March 19th, so the festivities happen the weekend before or after this date (for over 60 years!). A festival highlight is the parade along downtown San Juan with marching bands, horse-drawn carriages, equestrian units, and colorful dancers. The children's pet parade is fun, too, where kids dress up their pets to compete for cutest, most obedient, best team costume, etc. There are also pageants, adobe brick making for kids, demonstrations and the Mercado Street Faire with music, food, family entertainment and a kids play zone. The festival runs 10am to 3pm, with the parade beginning at 11am. (Arrive early.) The mission is open at 8:30am on the 19th (as the birds usually arrive in the morning) and it closes at 5pm. The street fair runs 9am - 5pm, the festival. Admission at the mission is $12 for adults; $11 for srs., $8 for ages 4 - 11; children 3 and under are free. The street fair, in near-by Historic Town Center is free, but some activities cost money.

FILLMORE STEAM RAILFEST, Fillmore. (800) 524-2546 / www.fwry.com, 364 Main Street. The Visitors Center has a huge model train display, plus lots of paraphernalia and collectibles. Antique tractors and equipment, engine demonstrations, craft booths, live entertainment, gunfighters, and barbecue cooking are part of the fun. Check out the open-top speeder cars used to maintain railroad tracks. Miniature live steamer rides cost a minimal fee. Gunslingers come into town have a shootout, rob a bank, and make a getaway on a train. One hour rides are offered on an antique steam cars. Four hour rides on Sat. and three hour rides on Sun. are diesel excursions all the way to Santa Paula and back, including a stopover in town, are also offered. Note: The Santa Paula train ride has food services available. All aboard for the Railfest on Sat. - Sun., 9am - 5pm. Admission is free. Steam train rides, departing at 10am, noon, and 2pm, are $26 for adults; $16 for ages 4 - 12; $11 for ages 2 - 3; children under 2 are free. A sunset ride departs at 4:30pm and includes dinner - $60 for adults; $28 for ages 2 - 12. Diesel rides, departing at noon are $26 for adults; $24 for srs.; $16 for ages 4 - 12; $12 for ages 2 - 3. Lunch boxes are available for purchase. Ask about specialty train rides, too, such as a dinner train with cowboys and other Old West characters.

FLOWER FIELDS, Carlsbad. (760) 431-0352 / www.theflowerfields.com, 5704 Paseo del Norte, off Palomar Airport Rd. Mid-March through mid-May walk through fifty-three acres of rows of blooming ranunculus. The colors are amazing, and the trails lead to bluffs overlooking the shoreline. Call first to make sure the flowers are in full bloom. Adding to your enjoyment are on-site picnic tables; an antique wagon tractor ride ($5 for adults, $3 for kids ages 3-10); a sweet pea maze; poinsettia displays; and a visit to Santa's Playground, which has a few play houses and giant (fake) mushrooms originally from Santa's Village in Lake Arrowhead. Forty-minute guided, educational tours are also available that include a fifteen-minute tractor-drawn wagon ride. School groups are offered three tour options, including one with a one-hour classroom presentation and a guided tour of the Flower Fields for $12 per student.

Special events can include Easter sunrise service at the Flower Fields; arts and crafts; flower arranging; basket weaving; Legoland hands-on mosaic building; bubble making; science adventures; puppet shows; and more. There are so many blooming things to do here! Open daily, 9am - 6pm. Admission is $16 for adults; $14 for srs.; $8 for ages 3 - 10; children 2 and under are free. Auto Club members receive a discount.

FREE ICE CREAM CONE DAY, www.dairyqueen.com. Get your licks in this one day by receiving a free ice cream cone at participating Dairy Queens.

GRUNION RUNS, San Pedro. (831) 649-2870 - official number; (310) 548-7562 - Cabrillo Marine Aquarium / www.wildlife.ca.gov/fishing/ocean/grunion; www.cabrillomarineaquarium.org, up and down the coast. Call beaches, the CABRILLO MARINE AQUARIUM (pg. 219), the OCEAN INSTITUTE (pg. 311), or BIRCH AQUARIUM (pg. 585) for more details, dates, and times. Grunions are small, silvery fish that venture out of the waters from March to August to lay their eggs on sandy beaches. They are very particular about when they do this - after every full and new moon, and usually around midnight. You may catch them only on certain months and no nets or gloves are allowed; only bare hands. (Did I mention that the fish are slippery?) Eat what you catch, or let them go, and enjoy a unique night of grunion hunting. Cabrillo Aquarium charges $5 for adults; $1 for srs., students and children, which includes a slide presentation and instructions. The beaches are free.

HERITAGE PARK U-PIC ORANGES, La Verne. See January entry (pg. 695) for details.

HERMOSA BEACH ST. PATRICK'S DAY PARADE, Hermosa Beach. (858) 268-9111 / www.hbchamber.net/news_events/st_patricks.aspx, Down Pier Ave. from Valley Drive to 10th and Hermosa. The Hermosa Beach Saint Patrick's Day Parade steps off near the tennis courts on Valley Drive and heads down Pier Avenue. The accompanying festival features a Kiddy Carnival, a petting zoo, international foods, vendors, and Irish music and dancing. The parade begins at 11am. Admission is free.

HITS DESERT CIRCUIT, Thermal. See January entry (pg. 695) for details.

IRON HORSE - FAMILY STEAMPUNK CARNIVALE, Perris. (951) 943-3020 / www.oerm.org, 2201 South "A" St. at the Southern California Railway Museum. Steampunk - *a genre of science fiction that typically features steam-powered machinery rather than advanced technology*. What better place to celebrate steampunk than with the backdrop of a live steam powered locomotive. Come for the steampunk costume contest; craft workshops (i.e. make your own Victorian hat, $20 or a ray gun, $10); steam locomotive and vintage trolley rides; games; steampunk artisans; various displays; and food. There is also a Victorian Era Tea for $10 per person. Sat. and Sun., 9am to 5pm. Admission is $15 for adults, $10 ages 5 - 11, ages 4 and under are free.

ISLA VISTA JUGGLERS FESTIVAL, Isla Vista. / www.sbjuggle.org. Part of the festivities are at People's Park south of Embarcadero Hall and also the multi-activity center on Ocean Rd. at the University of California Santa Barbara in Robertson Gym, and at Harold Frank lecture hall. For over forty years the campus juggling club has hosted this three-day event over a weekend in Spring (usually Easter), so juggle your schedule to try to attend. See beginner and advanced jugglers toss and catch various props - hats, juggling pins, balls, cigar boxes, and more. Also in attendance are clowns on unicycles, magicians, and prop vendors. Sometimes workshops are offered. Open juggling and workshops at People's Park, Fri., 6pm - 11pm and Sun., 10am - 5pm. Open juggling and workshops are at the multi-activity center, Sat. 10am - 5:30pm. The show is at the Isla Vista Theatre at UCSB, Sat., 7:30pm - 10pm. The festival is free. The Sat. show is $15 for adults; $8 for srs., students, and kids. Parking is $5.

KITE PARTY, Huntington Beach. (714) 536-3630 / www.kiteparty.com, 200 Pacific Coast Highway at the north and south side of Huntington Beach pier. This two-day "party" is by invitation only to participate, but anyone can watch. About 100 local and international fliers are just-for-the-fun-of-it fliers and some compete in stunt flying (some even have music to accompany their movements), but all fill the sky with their colorful, fanciful flying "machines". The public can pay minimal $22 for a kite and some official flying time, although anyone can fly their own kite outside the roped-off area. Sat. - Sun., 9am - dusk. Free general admission. beach parking is about $1.50 an hour; $15 for the day.

LANTERN FESTIVAL, Los Angeles. (213) 485-8567 / www.camla.org/lantern-festival, 425 N. Los Angeles St. The annual Lantern Festival brings together free arts, culture, and educational activities in a re-created traditional village street fair at the Chinese American Museum. Open noon - 7pm. General admission is free. Parking is about $7.

LONG BEACH TOUCH-A-TRUCK, Long Beach. / www.justinrudd.com/truck.html, 1 Granada Ave. beachfront at Belmont Shore. Can you touch 100 vehicles in 5 ½ hours? Here's your opportunity to try and have a truckload of fun! About 100 large trucks, tractors, military, public safety, and construction vehicles are here to touch, look at, climb into, honk their horns, and take photos with. The vehicle list includes firetrucks, police vehicles, buses, semi-trucks, tractors, military vehicles, concrete mixer, aquarium on wheels, American Red Cross, refuse truck, moving van, golf cart, dump truck, jeep and so many more. If this weren't enough, there are also vendors, numerous food trucks (to eat from, not go inside and honk their horn), LEGO play corral and other fun activities. The Long Beach Firefighters

Association also grills over 1,000 free hot dogs! Ironically, parking can be tight so walk or ride a bike, or park on Second St. Sun., 9:30am - 1pm. There will be a VIP half hour from 9am - 9:30am only for children with disabilities and special needs. Free. Please bring a jar of peanut-butter and/or cans of tuna to be donated to local food banks. Pre-registration is highly recommended.

LOS ANGELES REGIONAL ROBOTICS COMPETITION, (603) 666-3906 / www.firstinspires.org; www.nationalroboticsweek.org. Working with FIRST (For Inspiration and Recognition of Science and Technology), each team of students - for all ages! - has been given the same kit of parts and a six-week time frame to build a robot and solve a common problem. They must strategize, design, build, program, test, and refine. The results are amazing contraptions! The fun part for spectators is watching the intense competition in a sports-like atmosphere as the robots "battle" it out, completing certain tasks, and vying for prizes. Good manners for the team members count here, according to the judges. Participants are certainly the winners with what they've learned, and so is the audience. Check out the Lego League, as well. Tournaments take place in the Los Angeles area - see www.la.fll.org/tournatments - and sometimes in the San Diego region, as well. The competition is on Fri. and Sat., 9am - 5pm, with matches in the morning and final rounds in the afternoon. Free admission. There is usually a charge for parking.

LOS ENCINOS EASTER EGG HUNT, Encino. (805) 529-3690 / www.historicparks.org, 16756 Moorpark St. Come for this *eggciting shellabration*, with an egg hunt (for toddlers to 10-year olds), black smith demonstration, tradition games and old-time music. Tours of the historic adobe home are given by performers in period costume. The hunts are 1:30pm for 2 and under; 2pm for ages 3 - 4; 2:30pm for ages 5 - 6; 3pm for ages 7 - 10. Remember to bring your own basket. Admission is free.

MCGRATH FAMILY FARMS, Camarillo. U-pic - (805) 983-0333; Tours - (805) 485-4210 / www.mcgrathfamilyfarm.com, 1020 West Ventura Blvd. This family farm sells produce and offers U-pic strawberries, vegetables and pumpkins in-season. Tours are also available throughout most of the year on weekends. Groups of 20 or more can schedule a tour during the week. Open in season, 11am - 4pm. Tour is $5 per person on weekends, $7 for scheduled tours. Fruits are paid for by the pound.

OCEAN BEACH KITE FESTIVAL, San Diego. (619) 531-1527 / www.oceanbeachkiwanis.org, Dusty Rhodes Park. One Sat. a month join in on a colorful, high-flying festival (going strong for over 70 years!) celebrating the joy of kiting. You are invited to build and decorate kites from 9am to 12:30pm. Judging commences across the street at the school from 1pm to 2pm and a parade is at 2pm. From then on, just fly 'em. There is also an on-going crafts fair, with music and food. Open 10am - 4pm. There is no charge for admission or for the materials used for kite making.

PAGEANT OF OUR LORD, Rolling Hills Estates. (310) 521-2520 / www.pageantofourlord.org, 2222 Palos Verdes Dr. N. at Rolling Hills Covenant. Similar to Pageant of the Masters, but on a smaller scale and Christian-based, major works of art come to "life" as people dress up in costume and full make-up to impersonate, albeit statue-like, the people in the original paintings. Music accompanies each presentation. This is an amazingly powerful medium in which to express art. The program is offered for two weeks before Easter at various times - in the mornings, afternoons, and evenings. Admission is $13 - $25 for adults (depending on seat location); $11 - $17 for ages 6 - 12; children 5 and under are not admitted.

POPPY RESERVE, Lancaster. (661) 946-6092 - state park; (661) 724-1180 - recorded info from the poppy reserve / www.parks.ca.gov, 15101 W. Lancaster Rd. Do you hear echos of the wicked witch's voice in *The Wizard of Oz* cackling, "poppies, poppies"? During the months of March and April our bright orange California state flower blooms in this almost 1,800 acre reserve, as do several other types of wildflowers. (You'll notice wonderful patches of flowers along the roadside, too.) Call first to see how rains have affected the bloom schedule. Hike the seven miles of hilly trails that run through the reserve, including a paved section for stroller/wheelchair access, or go the 2.5-mile round trip from the visitor center to Antelope Butte Vista Point. Don't forget your camera!! Although poppies only bloom seasonally, the reserve is open year round from sun-up to sundown. The Visitors' Center is just open seasonally - March through Mother's Day, Mon. - Fri., 10am - 4pm; Sat. - Sun., 9am - 5pm. The staff at the center provides orientation to the reserve and educational information. Parking is $10.

RIVERSIDE AIRPORT OPEN HOUSE AND AIR SHOW, Riverside. (951) 351-6113 / www.riversideca.gov/events/airshow, 6951 Flight Rd. at Arlington and Airport Drs. at the Riverside Airport. Skydivers, aerobatics, and numerous other performances are part of this annual air show. Other activities and events include model aircraft, vintage aircraft, plus military helicopters on display; Riverside Police K-9 demonstrations; rides for kids; and a car show with hot rods, cruisers, and custom cars. The pancake breakfast is at 7am and costs $6. The cafe is also open. The Open House is Sat., 9am - 4pm. Admission is free. Parking is $10 per car.

SAINT PATRICK'S DAY PARADE AND FESTIVAL, San Diego. (858) 268-9111 / www.stpatsparade.org, Sixth Ave. and Maple St. near Balboa Park. On a Saturday around St. Patty's day think of little green men, and I don't mean Martians. Leprechauns, Celtic music, Irish folk dancing, marching bands, clowns, equestrian units, step dancers, floats, kiddie rides, arts and crafts booths, and food are top of the order for this huge, one-day of shenanigans. The parade begins at Juniper St. and Sixth Ave. Park near Balboa Park and take a free shuttle. The two-and-a-half-hour parade begins at 10:30am. The festival is Sat., 9am - 6pm. Admission is free.

SPRING BUSKER FESTIVAL, San Diego. (619) 235-4014 / www.seaportvillage.com/busker, 849 West Harbor Drive at Seaport Village. This is a family-friendly celebration of street performers, including sword swallowers, jugglers, acrobats, comedians, musicians and more. The event takes place throughout the shopping center, Sat. and Sun., noon - 6pm. More events begin at 7pm for ages 18 and up. Admission is free. Parking is $5 an hour, with the first 2 hours "free" with any $10 purchase in Seaport Village.

SPRING SPECTACULAR, Moorpark. (805) 378-1441 / zoo.moorparkcollege.edu, 7075 Campus Rd. at Moorpark College. Join in on two weekends of animal fun held at AMERICA'S TEACHING ZOO (pg. 692). These weekends incorporate guest presentations and booths from various animal organizations; behind-the-scenes tours of animals not normally on exhibit; scripted shows with costumes; a kid's zone; up-close educational animal programs and demonstrations; games; and an opportunity to see all the exotic animals. This is a terrific event. Open Sat. - Sun., 10am - 5pm. Admission is $10 for adults; $7 for srs. and ages 3.-.12; Kids 2 and under are free. Some activities may cost extra.

STRAWBERRIES - CAL POLY POMONA, Pomona. See April entry (pg. 710) for details.

STRAWBERRY STANDS. Strawberry stands pop up everywhere in season, which starts in February and ends in October - depending on the weather and the year. In Oxnard, call the Oxnard Convention and Visitors Bureau at (800) 269-6273 or (805) 385-7545 / www.visitoxnard.com for a map and guide to local fruit stands. Call the city chamber of commerce that you are in, or near, for more information on established stands. Additionally, check the website www.pickyourown.org.

TANAKA FARMS, Irvine. See February entry (pg. 700) for details.

VENTURA ST. PATRICK'S DAY PARADE, Ventura. (805) 639-0303 / www.venturastpatricksdayparade.com, Main Street The 30th annual County Ventura St. Patrick's Day Parade keeps the spirit with bands, Irish dancers, fire trucks, antique vehicles, four legged pets, and anything else remotely green that can march down Main Street. The parade begins at 10am. Admission is free.

VISIT WITH MICHELANGELO AND LEONARDO DA VINCI, Glendale. (323) 340-4564 or (323) 340-4742 / www.forestlawn.com, 1712 S. Glendale Ave. at Forest Lawn Memorial Park in Glendale. A costumed Michelangelo and Da Vinci talk to an audience of up to 350 people for about a half hour about "their" lives, achievements, and who was the better artist - history comes alive! Take a self-guided tour around the premises to view "their" art. (Note: The art does contain some nudity.) See FOREST LAWN MEMORIAL PARK (pg. 170) for details about what else this park has to offer. Check website or call for times. Reservations are necessary. Admission is free.

VISTA CIVIL WAR REENACTMENT, Vista, (760) 941-1791 / www.agsem.com, 2040 N. Santa Fe Ave. at the Antique Gas and Steam Engine Museum. One of the largest reenactments in the area, meet the soldiers in their encampments and watch the men and horses in great battles with live cannon fire in this rural setting. A great location for this type of event and lots of reenactors in period dress give a real feel for this era. President Lincoln (not the real one) usually shows up, as well. Battles take place both days at noon and 3pm. Admission includes touring the museum. See ANTIQUE GAS & STEAM ENGINE MUSEUM, INC. (pg. 523) for details about the museum. Open Sat. - Sun., 10am - 4pm. Admission is $10 for adults; $9 for srs.; $7 for ages 6 - 12; children 5 and under are free. Parking is $5.

WHALE OF A DAY FESTIVAL, Rancho Palos Verdes. (310) 544-5260 / www.losserenos.org/woad.htm, 31501 Palos Verdes Dr. W. at Pt. Vincente Interpretative Center. Palos Verdes' annual festival celebrating the migration of the Pacific Gray Whale is held on the main grounds of the Point Vicente Interpretive Center and at the adjacent lighthouse. Activities for children include face painting, crafts, stories, games, and whale watching. Tours of the lighthouse are available for kids ages seven and older. The festival commences on the first Sat., 10am - 4pm. Admission is free. Parking is available at Rancho Palos Verdes City Hall located at 30940 Hawthorne Blvd. with free shuttles.

WHALE WATCHING. See January entry (pg. 698) for details.

WONDERCON, Anaheim. / www.comic-con.org, 800 W Katella Ave. ,Anaheim Convention Center. WonderCon is literally the sister show, albeit smaller sister, to Comic-Con, so see (pg. 723) for details. It also features comics, movies, TV, animation, the Masquerade, and more. It has been held in Anaheim and in Los Angeles. Fri., 11:30am - 7pm; Sat., 10am - 7pm, tho there are some additional programs later on, too; Sun., 10am - 5pm Fri. or Sat. admission is $35 for adults; $17 for srs., ages 13 - 17, and military. Sun. admission is $20 for adults; $10 for srs., ages 13 - 17, and military. Children 12 and under are free with a paying adult. Parking is $16.

- APRIL -

AMERICA'S FAMILY PET EXPO, Costa Mesa. (800) 999-7295 or (626) 447-2222 / www.petexpooc.com, 88 Fair Dr. at Orange County Fairgrounds. Bark, meow, oink, baaa, sssss, neigh - this three-day weekend is for animals lovers. Over 1,000 animals - dogs, cats, reptiles, goats, rabbits, pigs, fish, snakes, and more - are at the expo. See bird shows; cat shows; a petting zoo; Frisbee dogs; wiener dog races; pet products; search and rescue demonstrations; stage shows; animal competitions; and educational demonstrations. Check out the pet adoption services. (Animals are not for sale here.) Open Fri., 10am - 6pm; Sat., 10am - 7pm; Sun., 10am - 6pm. Admission per day is $15 for adults; $13 for srs.; $10 for ages 6 - 12; children 5 and under are free. Parking is $8.

AVOCADO FESTIVAL, Fallbrook. (760) 728-5845 / www.fallbrookchamberofcommerce.org, Main St. Guacamole by the pound. Race cars made from avocados. Thousands of people thronging the streets. A flower show. Avocado croquet. A pit-spitting contest at the Avocado Olympics. These are glimpses of what this one-day festival has in store. Besides arts and crafts, kids activities, and agriculture displays, other happenings include packing house tours of the Del Rey Avocado Company, a walk through the Gem and Mineral Society Museum, and a vintage aircraft show at Fallbrook Airpark. Don't be green with envy; just get green with avocados. The festival is on a Sun., 9am - 5pm. Free admission.

BANNING HERITAGE WEEK, Wilmington. (310) 548-7777 / www.banningmuseum.org, 401 East M St. at the Banning Residence Museum. For seven days, not including weekends, the museum becomes a living classroom for fourth grade school groups. Intermingle with Victorian-dressed women and men folk; learn dance steps from that era; practice tying sailor knots; pan for gold; do chores such as churning butter and washing clothes by hand; play hoops, and other 19th-century games; learn animal husbandry; create and art project; take a guided tour of the museum; and more. The program runs Mon. - Fri., 9:15am - 12:15pm. Tip: Bring a picnic lunch. Call way in advance for reservations. Admission is free. Suggested donations are $1 for students; $5 for teachers/adults.

BUBBLEFEST, Santa Ana. See March entry (pg. 701) for details.

CARLSBAD STRAWBERRY COMPANY, Carlsbad. (760) 603-9608 / www.carlsbadstrawberrycompany.com, 1205 Aviara Pkwy. Pick your own sweet fruit from these 80 acres of strawberry fields, April through July. Pre-picked strawberries are also available to purchase. Field trips for schools or other organizations are offered, April - June, too, for more information and a lesson on strawberries, and then to go strawberry picking. The fields are open daily, 9am - 5pm.

CHILDREN'S EARTH DAY, Culver City. (310) 842-8060 / www.childrensearthday.org, 10101 W. Jefferson Blvd. at the Star Eco Station. This "green" event is wild! Hosted by the STAR ECO STATION (pg. 229), come join the exotic animals here and the fun - games, environmentally-conscious crafts, live entertainment, green shopping, food, celebrity guests, and more. Open Sun., 10am - 4pm. The festival is free. Take a tour of the Eco Station for $5 per person.

CHUMASH DAY, Malibu. (310) 317-1364 / www.malibucity.org, 24250 Pacific Coast Highway. Malibu's annual pow-wow and gathering of the tribes brings native traditions to Malibu Bluffs Park. Open from 10am to 6pm. Admission is free.

CICLAVIA, Los Angeles. (213) 355-8500 / www.ciclavia.org. During the CicLAvia, bikes (and runners, skaters and walkers) take over the city's streets for a day, creating a family-friendly 15 mile path from downtown Los Angeles to the sea at Venice Beach. See website for map. You may start and end anywhere along the route. Path open from 9am to 4pm Free for anyone to ride.

DEL MAR NATIONAL HORSE SHOW, Del Mar. (858) 792-4288 / www.delmarnational.com, 2260 Jimmy Durante Blvd. at the Del Mar fairgrounds. Saddle up for three weeks of exciting horse competition and Olympic selection. Each weekend features a main equestrian category: Western, Dressage, or Hunter/Jumper. Watch the horses being put through their paces during the week. Note: Check the website for exciting horse shows throughout the year. See website for schedule. Shows begin at 8:30am; the Sat. night shows are at 7pm. Free except for Sat. nights - $21 for adults; $16 for srs and children. Parking is $14.

DISCOVER RECYCLING OPEN HOUSE, (800) 773-2489 / www.lacitysan.org. Throughout LA One family's garbage is another family's.... favorite annual event. It may sound crazy, but the six open houses at LA's watershed district yards are some of the most popular, kid-friendly happenings. There are trash trucks and equipment demonstrations (plus sitting in the trucks - a highlight!) in addition to facility tours, information booths, compost areas, plants to plant and bring home, recycling games, and refreshments (that aren't recycled). Open House are held on Saturdays, 9am - 2:30pm in either Sun Valley, Northridge, Los Angeles, or San Pedro from April through June.

EARTH FAIR, San Diego. (858) 272-7370 / www.earthdayweb.org, Park Blvd. at Balboa Park. Celebrate the preservation of the environment in this huge, one-day event. Over 300 booths and exhibits are featured focusing on alternatives to lighting, power, and energy via goods, services and causes, including wildlife, conservation, organic gardening, ecotourism, alternative energy vehicles, and so much more. The day also features storytelling, a kids' area, crafts, and live entertainment on five stages. Kids (and parents) who attend Earth Day will hopefully become more planet smart. Open 10am to 5pm, with a parade at 10:30am at the Spanish Village. Admission is free.

EASTER. Since Easter can take place in March or April, all of the Easter-related activities are under March.

EASTER EGGSTRAVAGANZA, Orange. See March entry (pg. 701) for details.

ESCONDIDO RENAISSANCE FAIRE, Escondido. (805) 665-0359 / www.therenlist.com; www.oldetymeproductions.com, 742 Clarence Ln. at Felicita Park. The age of chivalry is recreated in a natural setting. Come dressed up, if you want, to experience the glories of the reign of Queen Elizabeth with battle pageants (knights in armor and all), archery demonstrations, jugglers, music in the streets, games, activities, a kid's play area, and entertainment from days of yore, including, perhaps, Shakespeare's plays. Note: As with any enactment from this time period, there are some bawdy events. Open for two weekends, Sat. - Sun., 10am to 6pm. Admission is $19 for adults; $14 for srs.; $9 for ages 4 -10; children 3 and under are free. Parking is $3.

FLOWER FIELDS, Carlsbad. See March entry (pg. 702) for details.

FREE CONE DAY, www.benjerry.com. Life doesn't get any better than free ice cream! You get a scoop of any flavor of Ben & Jerry's ice cream for free on this one day. They call it Customer Appreciation Day, but we are the ones who say "thanks."

GILMAN RANCH WILD WEST &WESTERN ART FESTIVAL. Banning. (951) 922-9200; (951) 205-0494 / www.rivcoparks.org, 1901 West Wilson Str. at Gilman Historic Ranch and Wagon Museum. This event features Western reenactments, exhibits and hands-on activities. Visit a 1700 to1800's-era living history encampment and see clothing, tools, and equipment from this time period. The day also includes gold panning, seeing blacksmith demonstrations, pettings the animals at the petting zoo and more. Bring your gold dust (i.e. cash) to use at the trading posts. A tour through the ranch and museum is also available. Food and drink is available. See GILMAN HISTORIC RANCH AND WAGON MUSEUM (pg. 363) for more information on the museum. Opens Sat. - Sun., 10am - 4pm. Admission is $5 for adults; $3 for kids; $1 dogs. Cash only for everything.

IMAGINATION CELEBRATION, Orange County. (714) 556-5160 / www.sparkOC.com; www.artsoc.org. The Orange County Performing Arts Center is a main host for this forty-five day event that's held mid-April through May. At least fifty of Orange County's artistic and educational organizations bring performances, workshops, and exhibitions to over seventy family-friendly events. This festival of arts for families takes place at malls, museums, parks, libraries, schools, etc. Some of the activities include puppet making, family art days, folk tales, band and theater performances, and dancing. Call for a schedule of events. Many events are free in this county-wide celebration of imagination!

IMAGINOLOGY YOUTH EXPO, Costa Mesa. (714) 708-1500 / www.ocfair.com, 88 Fair Dr. at the Orange County Fairgrounds. This huge, three-day expo highlights the talents of Orange County kids from elementary through high school age. Their artistic endeavors are showcased in different buildings according to age groups and categories, such as fine arts, photography, woodworking, and ceramics. 4-H Club members also have wonderful exhibits. The Science Fair is a highlight which draws people from all over the United States who offer money and/or scholarships to students whose experimentally-based research designs are outstanding. The Expo is great for admiring other kids' works, and for sparking the creative genius in your child. Other concurrent events include a petting zoo, wild science presentations, a carnival with rides, and tours of the adjacent Centennial Farm. Educators should check out the Education Resource Center during the expo as it features exhibits and displays from over 100 organizations as well as classroom handouts, posters, and other free, educational tools. Open Fri., 9am - 3pm (this day can get crowded with school tours); Sat. - Sun., 10am - 5pm. Admission is free. Parking is free on Fri., $8 on Sat. and Sun.

KIDS FISHING DERBY, Fullerton. (714) 738-3338 / www.cityoffullerton.com, 3120 Lakeview Dr. at Laguna Lake Park. This 12 annual event is all about the kids, only for ages 3 - 15 years, and fishing - what a great combo! Kids can learn, first, the how-tos at the Dept. of Fish and Wildlife learning stations and then borrow fishing gear from them. Register early as the event will sell out. You kids are almost guaranteed to catch more than a fish story. Open Sat., 8am - 10am for the learning stations; 8:30am - 12:30pm to fish. Free.

KIDS KRAZY KRAFTS DAY, Carson. (310) 515-7166 / www.printmuseum.org, 315 W. Torrance Blvd. at the INTERNATIONAL PRINTING MUSEUM (pg. 123). For one day kids of all ages learn by hands-on "playing" to create printing crafts and arts such as origami, cartoon characters, calligraphy, paper (from mushy pulp to paper), silk screen printed t-shirts (bring a clean one of your own to do), cards (using antique printing presses), and so much more. The museum itself is fascinating to tour and these activities make it truly a special day. Krafts and museum touring is 10am - 4pm. $10 per person; ages 5 and under are free.

LAKESIDE RODEO & WESTERN DAYS, Lakeside. (619) 561-4331 or (619) 443-8561 - rodeo; (619) 561-1031 - parade info / www.lakesiderodeo.com, 12854 Mapleview and Hwy 67 at the Lakeside Rodeo grounds. Corral your young broncos and bring them to the two-and-a-half-hour rodeo show the last weekend in April. This fantastic three-day rodeo features the major events of bull riding, team roping, calf roping, buckin' horses, barrel racing, bareback riding, saddle broncs, and steer wrestling. A down-home town parade begins at 9:45am on Sat. at Woodside St. and ends at Main St. Rodeo shows are Fri., 7:30pm; Sat., 2pm and 7:30pm; Sun., 2pm. Gates open 90 minutes before the show. Tickets range between $15 - $20 for adults, depending on the day and seat; $10 for ages 12 and under. Parking is $3.

LOS ANGELES TIMES FESTIVAL OF BOOKS, Los Angeles. / www.latimes.com/extras/festivalofbooks, Exposition Blvd and S. Figueroa St., University of Southern California campus. This weekend festival is absolutely the place for book lovers of all ages. 150,000 people come to see the over 400 well-known authors, illustrators, and celebrity authors sign their books, do book readings, give seminars, entertain, and participate in panel discussions. Besides the six outdoor stages geared for adults (and several indoor venues), there are special programs on-going at the two children's stages. These include renown storytellers, musicians, singers, character appearances (such as Barney), and book readings by favorite kids' writers. Other activities include free craft-making, clown acts, contests and give-aways by Radio Disney, and much more. Hundreds of publishers, book stores, and other vendors have booths in which they sell their books and related products and services, usually at a discount. This is a "don't miss" event! Open Sat., 10am - 6pm; Sun., 10am - 5pm. Admission is $12 per vehicle. The events are free, but tickets are needed for all indoor panel and speaker sessions, so get them the week before the festival.

MCGRATH FAMILY FARMS, Camarillo. See March entry (pg. 704) for details.

MISSION FEDERAL ARTWALK, San Diego. (619) 615-1090 / www.artwalksandiego.org, along India St. and Kettner Blvd. in the Little Italy neighborhood, downtown San Diego. For 17 blocks in Little Italy (the largest outdoor arts festival in Southern California), hundreds of visual and performing arts exhibitors strut their stuff in a weekend-long celebration of the arts. (Many events happen throughout the month, too.) In cooperation with Museum of Contemporary Art, San Diego Area Dance Alliance, San Diego Performing Arts League, and others, you'll see paintings, dance, ballet, poetry, performance art on stage, photography, sculpture, opera, folkloric dance, divas, and more. Just a few specific activities for kids in the past have included writing poetry, a photo scavenger hunt, creating an origami animal, making a 3-D paper model, and molding a sculpture. Open Sat. - Sun., 11am - 6pm. General admission is free. Parking is $10.

NATIONAL PARKS - FREE ENTRANCE DAYS. See January entry (pg. 696) for details.

PASADENA MODEL RAILROAD CLUB'S SPRING OPEN HOUSE, Pasadena. (323) 222-1718 / www.pmrrc.org, 5458 Alhambra Ave. Over a period of one weekend (and a Tues.), make tracks to see the largest model railroad layout, which covers 5,000 square feet, as well as lots of other railroad paraphernalia - a delight for all ages. Open Sat., 1pm - 5pm and 7pm - 9pm; Sun., 1pm - 5pm; Tues., 7:30pm - 9pm. Admission is $5 for adults; $1 for ages 7 - 17; free for children 6 and under.

POPPY FESTIVAL, Lancaster. (661) 723-6077 / www.poppyfestival.com, 43063 N. 10th St W. at Sgt. Steve Owen Memorial Park. The poppy festival, located fifteen miles east of the POPPY RESERVE (pg. 704), is held for one weekend in April. The festival offers carnival rides; craft vendors; environmental displays; aerospace displays; farmer's market area; live entertainment; circus acts; animals (reptiles and insects, and bird performances), including Sea Lion Splash, with real sea lions; racing remote-controlled NASCAR models; Motocross stunts (on Sat.) called Thrashed Kids; mission's exhibit; dinosaur exhibit; safety zone with police and fire department personnel; and more. Open Sat. and Sun., 10am - 6pm. Admission is $10 for adults; $5 for srs. and ages 6 - 12; children 5 and under are free.

POPPY RESERVE, Lancaster. See March entry (pg. 704) for details.

PRINCESSES AT THE CASTLE, Redlands. (909) 792-2111 / www.kimberlycrest.org, 1325 Prospect Drive at the Kimberly Crest House and Gardens. Treat your little princess to an afternoon of royal activities, refreshments, and photos with other princesses, such as Snow White, Cinderella, Ariel, and even a few fairies, at the beautiful KIMBERLY CREST HOUSE AND GARDENS (pg. 425). Get dressed up and indulge in the crown-shaped cookies, pink-frosted cupcakes, pink lemonade, and popcorn, while getting your face painted, watching balloon animals take shape, doing a craft, and participating in a scavenger. A highlight is the procession and proclamation, when your little princess is announced and escorted as she walks down the outside mansion steps, and gives a princess wave to the adoring crowd. There is even a royal coach and coachmen. This event sells out, so get your tickets early. Sun., 10am - noon and 2pm - 4pm. The price is $70 for princess, age 3 - 10, and one adult. Additional adults are $20.

RAMONA OUTDOOR PLAY, Hemet. (800) 645-4465 / www.ramonabowl.com, 27400 Ramona Bowl Rd. All the world's a stage, or at least all this mountainside is a stage in Hemet. For three weekends a cast of almost 400 (including children and animals) perform on the mountainside to tell the romantic story of Ramona and her Indian hero, Alessandro. The tale, which also reflects our early California heritage, is incredibly well told and fascinating. For more than 85 years this epic play has been presented here. Come early for lunch, or to walk around the Mercado, a Spanish marketplace with folk music, dancers, and artisans. Bring a jacket. Gates open at 1:30pm; preshow activities begin at 1:30; and performances begin at 3.30pm and end at 6:30pm. Tickets range from $30 - $44 for adults; $28 - $44 for srs.; $18 - $44 for ages 12 and under - all depending on seat location. There is a $4 handling fee per ticket. Parking is $5

RENAISSANCE PLEASURE FAIRE, Irwindale. (626) 969-4750 / www.renfair.com, 15501 E. Arrow Highway at the Santa Fe Dam Recreation Area. Heare ye, heare ye, this annual faire, one of the largest in Southern California, runs for eight weekends in April through May (sometimes into June), bringing the Renaissance time period to life. Note: Wenches dress accordingly, and there is bawdiness. Eat, drink, and be merry as you cheer on knights; play challenging games from times of yore; be entertained by juggling, dancing, singing, and artisans demonstrations; watch jousting tournaments; see animal shows; participate in children's activities on the weekend; and enjoy the delicious food and fare. Dress up! Meet Queen Elizabeth and her court, plus Sir Francis Drake, William Shakespeare, and other well-known people of the time. Teachers, check out the school day special offered one Fri., from 9:30am - 3:30pm. On this day some of the same activities are offered as during the regular faire, although they are more educationally-oriented and the costumed participants are usually more modestly attired. School-day ticket prices are $14 each and must be purchased ahead of time. The faire is open to the public Sat. - Sun., 10am - 7pm. Admission is $29.95 for adults; $15 for ages 5 - 12; children 4 and under are free. Parking is $10. Purchase discount tickets online.

SAN DIEGO KIDS EXPO AND FAIR, Del Mar. (619) 269 - 9441 / www.sandiegokidsexpo.com, 2260 Jimmy Durante Blvd. at the Del Mar Fairgrounds. This huge event (150 companies participate!) is not only a rich resource of fun and educational products and services geared specifically for kids, but a fun place to bring the family. It includes activities for all of your kids, from toddlers to teens, such as workshops (i.e. arts, self defense and robotics); experiments via STEAM; activities (zip line, laser tag, bungee jump, a trackless train ride, giant inflatables, bowling, and more); a petting zoo with exotic animals; photo ops with kid's movie characters; and live music by children's music artists and local musicians. Sat. - Sun., 10am - 5pm. Sat., $10 for ages 13 and up; children 12 and under are free. (Prices are cheaper online.) Some activities cost extra. Parking is $14.

SANTA BARBARA KITE FESTIVAL, Santa Barbara. (805) 963-2964 or (805) 637-6202 / www.sbkitefest.net, 721 Cliff Dr. on the lawn next to Garvin Theater at Santa Barbara City College's West Campus. A rainbow array of kites take to the skies, although some nose dive, at this annual one-day festival. Kites of all sizes, shapes, and colors fly in various competitions such as sport flying, highest flying, kite fighting, most beautiful, and largest kite. Prizes are awarded. The tail chase event is especially fun for kids as they try to catch the tail of a kite as it alternately dips, dives, and soars. Kites are available for purchase or bring your own. Fly some fun on Sun., 11am - 5pm. Free admission.

SANTA CLARITA COWBOY FESTIVAL, Newhall. (661) 250-3735 / www.cowboyfestival.org, 22400 13th St. (13th and Railroad Ave.) Howdy-doo! Over 10,000 people attend this four-day event that acknowledges that cowboys are still heroes. Thursday is the SVC Film Tour from 12:30pm to 4:30pm. Friday offers various options at different venues around the area. One highlight is the Western Film Tour which visits several movie sites like Disney's Golden Oak Ranch, Vasquez Rocks, Iverson Ranch and Corriganville. The tour leaves at 12:30pm and returns at 5:30pm. Thursday's and Friday's tours visit different places. Each tour cost $60 and leaves from the shuttle area. There are other shows, lectures and demonstrations on these days, too. Past events have included a demonstration of prairie cooking (and eating), an open mic night for cowboy poets and musicians, a walking tour of Old Town Newhall and more. See website for specific events and prices. Cowboy Church is Sun. at 8am at First Presbyterian Church at 24317 Newhall Ave. Call (661) 268-8863 for more info. At the actual festival, held on Sat. and Sun., there are several specifically family-oriented programs offered, including Western farces, trick ropers, panning for gold, steer roping, street shows/performances, magic shows, and more. Come listen to some of the finest poetry, storytelling, and music that the West has to offer. Some of these performances cost extra and are held at the Canyon Theatre Guild at 24242 Main St. Shop for Western merchandise at the vendors' booths and peruse cowboy art. Tip: Dress up in western duds and don't forget to wear your Stetson. Yeehaw! Sat., 10am - 7pm; Sun., 10am - 6pm. Admission to the festival is free; some activities and shows cost.

SANTA MARIA VALLEY STRAWBERRY FESTIVAL, Santa Maria. (805) 925-8824 / www.santamariafairpark.com, 937 S. Thornburg at the Santa Maria Fairgrounds. Bring your little shortcakes to this three-day festival to enjoy carnival rides, a petting zoo, train rides, kid's crafts, face painting, and, most importantly, eating strawberries! Join in on pie eating contests, watch food preparation demonstrations with strawberries, and indulge in this sweet fruit presented in so many scrumptious ways. The festival is open Fri. - Sun., 11am - 10pm; the carnival is open until midnight. General admission is $10 for adults; $7 for srs. and ages 6 - 11; children 5 and under are free. Rides are extra. Check the website for discounts. Parking is $7.

SCANDINAVIAN FESTIVAL, Thousand Oaks. (805) 241-0391 or (805) 493-3151 / www.scandinavianfest.org, 60 W. Olsen Rd. at California Lutheran University. Valkommen! Enjoy a presentation/program of a 16th-century Swedish royal court at this two-day festival which includes a Viking encampment, folk dancing, a colorful parade with authentic costumes, arts and crafts booths, and a replica of Tivoli Gardens, although it's not quite as large as the one in Denmark. Kids will particularly enjoy the jugglers, puppet shows, magicians, clowns, and moon bounces. A smorgasbord is served here, too. The festival is open Sat. and Sun., 10am - 5pm Admission is $10 for adults; $5 ages 13 to 19; 12 and under are free. Certain activities cost extra.

SPRING ON THE FARM FIELD TRIPS, Pomona. (909) 869-6722; (909) 869-4906 / www.cpp.edu/~agriscapes/index.html; www.csupomona.edu/~farmstore, 4102 S. University Dr. on the campus of Cal Poly Pomona. Under the umbrella name of AGRIscapes, tour choices include the Children's Garden, where kids plant seeds, learn the how-tos of growing plants and about healthy food choices; a tractor-pulled wagon ride around the farm; learning about and then picking seasonal crops - fruits (mostly strawberries, as well as blackberries and sometimes boysenberries) and vegetables; and/or time spent petting, feeding and learning about the miniature horses, goats, sheep, rabbits, dairy calves, and small breed pigs in the Petting Farm. The fields are next to the Farm Store at Kellogg Ranch, which sells fresh fruits, vegetables, honey (fill your own bottle from the vat), plants, flowers, and even meats (beef, pork, and lamb) and other grocery products that have been raised on the campus by students. Bring a cooler to pack your goodies. Wed. - Fri., 9am - 4pm for group tours; Sat., 10am - 1pm for individuals to pick-your-own strawberries and more. Tours range from $4 - $12 per person, depending on the activity; $4 per person for pick your own.

SPRING SPECTACULAR, Moorpark. See March entry (pg. 705) for details.

STRAWBERRIES - CAL POLY POMONA, Pomona. See March entry (pg. 705) for details.

TANAKA FARMS, Irvine. See February entry (pg. 700) for details.

THE BLUE AND THE GRAY, A CIVIL WAR REENACTMENT, Moorpark. (805) 433-9188 - event; (805) 279-5253 - Rotary Club / www.moorparkrotary.com, 100 High St. at Hitch Ranch Cannons, horses, swords, smoking rifles, stagecoaches, drums, the calvary - this weekend event is one of the largest gatherings of its kind in Southern California, with over 500 reenactors. The fields are transformed into living Union and Confederate encampments. Three battles with ground charges are reenacted on Saturday - at noon, 3pm and 5:15pm; and two on Sunday - at noon and 2:30pm. Other happenings include Living History demonstrations such as cooking, soldier school for kids, medical demos, abolitionists rallies, infantry demos, presidential press conferences, music, Victorian ballroom dance classes, conversing with reenactors in character, general stores, and more. A food court serving breakfast, lunch, dinner, and snacks is also on the grounds. The grounds are open Sat., 10am - 6:15pm; Sun., 10am - 4pm. Admission is $22 for adults; $17 for ages 6 - 17; children 5 and under are free. Parking is $5.

TOUCH-A-TRUCK, Santa Monica. (323) 957-4280, 1550 Pacific Coast Highway, beach lot 1 North. Who drives the big trucks? And why? Find out this and more, especially when you get to go inside them, at this Touch-A-Truck event put on by the Jr. League of Los Angeles. Talk to local first responders as you explore their vehicles, and truckers, and more. There is also an area for arts and crafts, food, vendors, safety tables and tips, and other hands-on activities. Sat., 9am - 1pm. A quiet hour is held from 9am to 10am for those who might not respond well to the sounds of the trucks or flashing lights. $10 per person or $35 per family; kids 2 and under are free.

TOYOTA GRAND PRIX, Long Beach. (562) 981-2600; for tickets (888) 82SPEED (827-7333) / www.gplb.com, 3000 Pacific Ave. at Shoreline Dr. This three-day, top-of-the-line racing event includes practice and qualifying runs on Friday; celebrity racing and final qualifying runs on Saturday; and final Champ car racing on Sunday. There is also a children's FunZone with interactive games, a video arcade, kid's races and more. But first, on the Tues. before the Grand Prix, take part in Grand Prix View, where you can take a lap or two as you walk, bike or hang out on the 1.5 miles of the Toyota Grand Prix of Long Beach road track from 11:30am - 1pm. Just because you can. See you at the races! Gates are open Fri. and Sat. 7am - 9pm, Sun. 7am - 5:30pm. General admission (unreserved seating) for adults is $33 on Fri., $65 on Sat., $70 on Sun.; $57 for ages 12 and under on Sun. Reserved seating ranges from $78 - $90 for adults; $57 - $68 for ages 12 and under. There are three-day passes available. Parking is available at Shoreline Village for $15 a day.

TRAIN DAYS, Redlands. (909) 307-2669 and (909) 798-8608 / www.sbcounty.gov/museum, 2024 N. Orange Tree Lane. Come see model trains and trolleys, real train artifacts, visit with train experts and engineers and make train related crafts. Open Sat. and Sun., 9am - 5pm. Make crafts from noon - 4pm. $10 for adults; $8 for srs.; $7 for students; $5 for ages 5 - 12; children 4 and under are free.

VAN OMMERING DAIRY, Lakeside. (619) 390-2929 / www.omaspumpkinpatch.com, 14950 El Monte Road. K through 6th graders are invited to take an hour-long tour of this family-owned dairy. The tour starts in the commodities shed where seed is stored for the 600 cows that live on the premises. Guests then go through the showers (not literally!) where the cows are washed down before they're milked. From the milking barn, with all of its fascinating modern machinery, the tour visits the maternity pen. Kids are welcome to gently pet the newborns and the animals in the petting zoo. The hay ride, with wheelchair ramps, goes all around the farm. Information is dispensed throughout the tour about the workings of a dairy, cows' eating habits, where the milk goes after it's outside the cows, and more. Visitors leave with lots of knowledge about these milk/meat/leather-producing animals, a greater understanding of how farmers' work affects everyone, an ice cream cup, and a souvenir water bottle. Tours are offered in April and May, Tues., Wed. and Thurs. at 9:30am and 11am. Groups from 15 to 100 people are welcome. Reservations are required. Admission is $8 per person.

VICTORIAN FAIR, City of Industry. (626) 968-8492 / www.homesteadmuseum.org, 15415 East Don Julian Road at the Homestead Museum. Get a taste of what life was like for people living in the Southland during the 1840s, '50s, and '60s through music, dancing, crafts, historic house tours, genteel games, and demonstrations and classes (etiquette, calligraphy, quilt-making, and more)! Victorian dress is encouraged. Bring money for shopping. Also see THE HOMESTEAD MUSEUM (pg. 121). Sat. and Sun., 1pm to 5pm. Admission free.

- MAY -

AIRPORT DAY, Fullerton. (714) 738-6323 / www.ci.fullerton.ca.us, 4011 W. Commonwealth Avenue. Give your spirits a lift on Airport Day, which is celebrated every even year. Come and see how the airport really functions as you tour around it and see displays and demonstrations with the OC Fire Authority, Anaheim Police Department, CA Highway Patrol, Air Combat USA, public library, Fullerton Radio Club and others. Look to the skies for the airplane demonstrations, too. Open Sat., 10am - 4pm. Free.

BUG FAIR, Los Angeles. (213) 763-3499 / www.nhm.org, 900 Exposition Blvd. at the Natural History Museum of Los Angeles. This weekend fair really *bugs* me! Come and gawk at and even touch a wide variety of live insects, such as Madagascar hissing cockroaches, millipedes, and more. Over fifty vendors showcase every kind of insect product available including jewelry, t-shirts, toys, silkworms, live critters, a butterfly house, chocolate-covered crickets (poor Jimminy!), mounted insects, and lots more. The fair includes educational presentations and hands-on activities. Walk through the museum's Insect Zoo while here. See NATURAL HISTORY MUSEUM OF LOS ANGELES COUNTY (pg. 140) for a description of the museum. Creep, crawl, or fly here on Sat. - Sun., 9:30am - 5pm. Admission to the museum includes admission to the fair: $15 for adults; $12 for srs., college students, and ages 13 - 17; $7 for ages 3 - 12; children 2 and under are free. Parking is $12 (cash only).

CALIFORNIA STRAWBERRY FESTIVAL, Oxnard. (888) 288-9242 or (805) 385-4739 / www.strawberry-fest.org, 3250 S. Rose Ave. at College Park. This big, juicy festival, held on the third weekend of May, offers unique strawberry culinary delights, an arts and crafts show with over 300 artisans, and contests, including a strawberry shortcake eating contest. Kids enjoy Strawberryland, in particular, because it has a petting zoo, puppet shows, clowns, hands-on arts and crafts, and carnival rides. Have a *berry* good time here! Open Sat. and Sun., 10am - 6pm. Admission is $12 for adults; $8 for srs.; $5 for ages 5 - 12; children 4 and under are free. Certain activities cost extra. Parking at the festival is $10 or there is a free shuttle service.

CARLSBAD STRAWBERRY COMPANY, Carlsbad. See April entry (pg. 706) for details.

CARLSBAD VILLAGE FAIRE SPRING, Carlsbad. (760) 945-9288 / www.carlsbad.org, Carlsbad Village - Grand Ave. from Carlsbad Blvd. to Jefferson St. Held on the first Sunday in May and November, this is the one of the largest one-day fairs held in California. It has over 850 exhibitors, international food, some kiddie rides, and a variety of live entertainment. This type of fair is especially fun for shoppers of all ages as you never know what kind of unique items you might find and *have* to purchase. Complimentary shuttles run throughout the event. It runs from 8am - 5pm. Admission is free, but bring spending money!

CHERRY FESTIVAL / CHERRY PICKING, Beaumont, Cherry Valley. See June entry (pg. 716) and (pg. 717) for details.

CINCO DE MAYO CELEBRATION. The fifth of May, a national Mexican holiday honoring Mexican victory over the French army at Puebla, is celebrated throughout Southern California with several days of Mexican folk dancing, mariachi music, parades, puppet shows, face painting, storytelling, booths, piñatas, and fun! In Los Angeles, for instance, contact (213) 485-8435 / www.elpueblo.lacity.org, at El Pueblo de Los Angeles Historical Monument in downtown. This particular festival runs Sat. - Sun., 10am - 10pm. In Old Town San Diego, contact (619) 291-4903 / www.cincodemayooldtown.com. This celebration features a reenactment of the 1862 Battle of Puebla and Lucha Libre matches.

DISCOVER RECYCLING OPEN HOUSE. Throughout LA. See April entry (pg. 706) for details.

FIESTA MATSURI, Los Angeles. (213) 628-2725 / www.jaccc.org, 244 S. San Pedro in Little Tokyo. Fiesta Matsuri (literally means Festival Festival) is where Kodomo no Hi (children's day in Japanese) and Dia de los Niños (children's day in Spanish) meet. This multiethnic celebration is for families, and particularly children ages 4 to 12. They are invited to participate in a running race, as well as making arts and crafts. Other attractions can include magic shows, sports clinics, calligraphy demonstrations, origami-making, kite-making, dancing, displays of traditional costumes, live entertainment, and more. Kids can even see a samurai armor demonstration and children's mariachi. Open Sat., 11am - 4pm. Admission is free, although certain activities cost.

FLOWER FIELDS, Carlsbad. See March entry (pg. 702) for details.

FREE COMIC BOOK DAY, www.freecomicbookday.com. Sponsored by the Comic Book Industry, publishers such as Marvel, Dark Horse, DC, Image, and others prepare giveaway editions of their best titles for this one day. Some stores also host comic book creator appearances. Note that it is independent and specialty stores that participate. Check the website or call your local store for the date, which is typically the first Sat. in May.

FULLERTON RAILROAD DAYS, Fullerton. (714) 278-0648 / www.scrmf.org; www.fullertrainmuseum.org, 120 E. Santa Fe Ave at the Fullerton Train Station. Usually held the first weekend in May, kids and adults go loco over touring through a large steam locomotive, Amtrak passenger cars, and vintage private rail cars. More activities and events include model trains running about the huge and beautifully-landscaped garden layout; more operating train layouts inside a circus tent; children's activities; vendors selling train-related paraphernalia; and a food court. Open Sat. - Sun., 9am - 5pm. Admission is free.

I MADONNARI ART FESTIVAL, Santa Barbara. (800) 793-7666 / www.imadonnarifestival.com, at the corner of Los Olivos and Laguna sts. at Santa Barbara Mission. Since the 16th century, street painting, using chalk as a medium, has been an Italian tradition. Over 200 blank pavement squares in front of the mission will be filled in with colorful drawings by artists and aspiring artists of all ages over the three-day Memorial weekend. The professional works are indeed works of art. (Hope it doesn't rain!) The festival also includes live music and an Italian marketplace. Open Sat. - Sun., 10am - 6pm. Free admission. Young artists who want to paint a patch pay $12, which includes chalk.

IMAGINATION CELEBRATION, Orange County. See April entry (pg. 707) for details.

INTERNATIONAL FESTIVAL, Aliso Viejo. (949) 480-4081 / www.soka.edu, 1 University Dr. at Soka University. Enjoy a day with international flare by tantalizing your taste buds with food from around the world, cultural dances (the costumes are exciting and beautiful) and music (700 performers on four stages), plus games, activities, over 250 exhibitors, and a children's play area. Abierto, ouverte, aperto, offen, or open Sat., 10:30am - 5pm. Admission is free. Parking is $10.

INTERNATIONAL MUSEUM DAY, www.icom.museum. Here's a little known fact - May 18th is officially International Museum Day. Each year around that date a theme is selected and many museums offer free admission. Some participants may also sponsor a family day of art and craft activities, storytelling, or other entertainment. Call your local (or favorite) museum and see what they have to offer.

INTERNATIONAL SPEEDWAY, Costa Mesa. (949) 492-9933 / www.costamesaspeedway.net, 88 Fair Dr. at the Orange County Fairgrounds. The Speedway roars to life usually two Saturday nights a month from mid-May through mid-October. Note: Racing in July is limited due to the Orange County Fair. This spectator sport of motorcycle racing can include sidecars, go karts, Quads, a kids' class (ages 6 to 12), and more. After the two-hour show, which can get long for younger ones, take the kids into the pits to get racer's autographs, or, when the bikes cool down, to sit on a cycle or two. Wear jeans and t-shirt (and bring a sweatshirt) as dirt tracks aren't noted for cleanliness. Gates open at 6pm; qualifying races start at 7:30pm. Admission is cash only: $20 for adults; $15 for srs. and ages 13 - 17; $10 for ages 3 - 12; children 2 and under are free. Special events are $5 more per person. Parking is $8.

KORONEBURG RENAISSANCE FESTIVAL, Corona. (951) 496-2478 / www.renfestcorona.com, 14600 Baron Drive at Crossroads Riverview Park. Peasants, lords and ladies, merchants, artisans, craftsmen, nobles, knights, travelers, and everyone else is invited to join in the seven weekends of festivities. The fictitious setting is the Baron's estate, a European Village along the Rhine River via 1450 - 1600. Archery competitions, jousting, sheep shearing, weaving, goat milking and spinning demonstrations, great food, and crafts of old are just some of the fun to be had here. Open mid-May through mid-June, Sat., 10am - 7pm; Sun., 10am - 6pm, and on Memorial Day. Admission is $25 for adults; $15 for srs. and ages 6 - 12; children 5 and under are free. Discount coupons are online. Parking is $5.

LA CANADA FIESTA DAYS, La Canada. (818) 790-4289 / www.lacanadaflintridge.com, Community Center of La Canada Flintridge, 4469 Chevy Chase Dr. La Canada's Memorial Day weekend celebration includes a community breakfast, live music, a BBQ, a family film, and fireworks - followed by a grand parade down Foothill Boulevard. Memorial day weekend, check website or call for time and events. Most events, excluding meals, are free.

LAFD OPEN HOUSE, www.lafd.org. The second Sat. in May is "Fire Service Recognition Day" throughout Los Angeles and neighborhood fire stations open their doors to welcome the public. This is an ideal time to meet your local firefighters and thank them. Take a tour of the station and see the equipment and apparatus. Some of the stations have special displays and demonstrations, and some host a pancake breakfast. Check the website to see which ones. Sat., 10am - 4pm. Some stations are open instead on Sun., 10am - 4pm. Admission is free.

RANCHEROS VISTADORES RIDE FOR THE CURE, Santa Ynez. (805) 688-4815 / www.missionsantaines.org, 1760 Mission Dr. at Mission Santa Ines. About 750 riders come for two reasons: 1) to support breast cancer awareness and raise money for the cause and 2) to have their horses blessed by the padres at the mission. Saturday at 2:30pm is the gathering and blessing, then from 3pm to 4:30pm is a processional ride out. If you're in the area and a horse lover, it is a colorful procession to watch. Free to observe.

MANZINITA HIGH MOUNTAIN RENDEZVOUS, Campo. (760) 745-2927 / manzinitarendezvous.com, North Cote Ranch near Lake Moreno. Experience an authentic 1700's to 1840's Rocky Mountain fur traders' encampment in a rustic mountain setting. Demonstrations of primitive survival skills such as cooking, tool making, tomahawk throwing, and black powder target shooting are given over two weekends, but the real draw is being immersed in this time period. This event is geared for fellow buckskinners and traders, with the public welcome to visit and watch, but not participate. Primitive and modern camping is available on site. Open daily, 10am - 5pm. Admission is $5 for adults; ages 10 and under, school groups, military, and scouts in uniform are free.

MCGRATH FAMILY FARMS, Camarillo. See March entry (pg. 704) for details.

MOTA DAY, Pasadena. (213) 740-8687 / www.museumsofthearroyo.com. The six organizations that comprise MOTA - Museums of the Arroyo - open their doors for free one Sunday a year and include fun family activities. The museums include HERITAGE SQUARE MUSEUM (pg. 118) at 3800 Homer St., (Los Angeles); the Lummis Home and Garden at 200 E. Ave. 43; THE GAMBLE HOUSE (pg. 110) at 4 Westmoreland Pl.; LOS ANGELES POLICE MUSEUM (pg. 133) at 6045 York Blvd.; PASADENA MUSEUM OF HISTORY (pg. 144) at 470 W. Walnut St. and the Autry Historic Southwest Museum Mt. Washington Campus at 234 Museum Dr. There is a free shuttle service between the museums. The museums are open noon - 5pm.

NATIONAL PUBLIC GARDENS DAY, www.publicgardens.org. April showers bring May flowers. They also bring a day in May where admission to many botanical gardens and arboretums is free. This annual celebration is designed to raise the awareness of the importance of public gardens. Check the website for a garden near you (and those across the nation). Free.

PIRATE DAYS, San Diego. (619) 234-9153 / sdmaritime.org, 1492 N Harbor Dr. at the Maritime Museum of San Diego. Avast ye landlubbers - bring your booty to this two-day celebration that includes kids costume contests (so wear one, and get a $2 discount on tickets!), cannon firings, weapon demonstrations, sword fighting shows, live parrots, a mermaid grotto and a scavenger hunt for pirate treasures, plus museum admission. See MARITIME MUSEUM OF SAN DIEGO (pg. 536) for more info on this great museum! BOARDED is an interactive, live show on board the tall ship, *Californian*, lending it authenticity. You become part of the pirate crew, learn how to sword fight, bail water, swab the decks and other piratey skills on this one-hour cruise. Mutiny and mayhem ensue. Sat. - Sun., 10am - 4pm. $18 for adults; $8 for ages 3 - 12 years; children 2 and under are free. BOARDED show is an additional fee.

PLANES OF FAME AIR SHOW, Chino. (909) 597-3722 / www.planesoffame.net, 14998 Cal Aero Drive at the Air Museum Planes of Fame at Chino airport. In-air displays of classic and antique aircraft, trainer, liaison, fighter and bomber warbirds, flybys, and jet aircraft are at this weekend event. A crowd favorite is the aerobatic acts in the sky, such as wing walking. Several static (i.e. ground) displays include military aircraft, helicopters, and fighter jets, plus a WWII bomber to tour through. Antique cars and vintage race cars are also on display. Bring a picnic or purchase lunch from food vendors. Gates open at 8am; flying begins around 11am and the show ends about 4pm. Admission is $25 for adults; children 11 and under are free. Tickets include entrance to the museum.

RAMONA OUTDOOR PLAY, Hemet. See April entry (pg. 708) for details.

RAMONA RODEO, Ramona. (760) 803-2001 / www.ramonarodeo.com, 5th St. and Aqua Ln. at the Fred Grand Arena. Kick up your heels 'cause the rodeo comes to town the third weekend in May! With a down-home flavor, the rodeo includes all the favorite featured events, plus numerous vendors. Sunday is kids' day, with special activities such as "dummy" steer roping, rope tricks, and cowboy/cowgirl contests. Rodeo shows are Fri. and Sat., 8pm; and Sun., 4pm. Gates open 1.5 hours before the show. Fri. and Sun. admission is $15 for adults, $10 for ages 12 and under. Sat., $20 for adults, all ages; Sun $12 - $17. Reserved seating is more, but worth it since shows can sell out. Parking is $5.

RENAISSANCE PLEASURE FAIRE, Irwindale. See April entry (pg. 709) for details.

ROBOTICS BY THE SEA, San Pedro. (310) 548-7562 / www.cabrillomarineaquarium.org, 3720 Stephen M. White Dr. This yearly event showcases underwater remotely operated vehicles (ROVs). Also included are demonstrations by local high school robotics clubs, information about land and underwater ROVs, and opportunities to drive an underwater ROV through an obstacle course. Usually the third Sat. of the month, 11am - 3pm. Free.

ROCKET LAUNCH, Huntington Beach. (714) 913-5039 / www.oc.discoverycube.org, 5301 Bolsa Ave. at the

Boeing Company. This propelling Rocket Launch competition is one for the whole family to enjoy. Bring a 2-liter plastic soda bottle to design, decorate, build and launch here (or build it at home). The "extras" are provided - fins, parachutes, noses, etc., and even real engineers to help out. Bottles are launched, via water pressure, throughout the day and the ones with longest "hang time" win. There are three categories - K - 6th grade; 7th - 12th grade; and Adult. (Younger children can enter with a parent under Adult.) Prizes include watching an actual rocket launch and gift cards. Bring a lawn chair (and hat - there isn't any shade), compete, or just watch, and enjoy the food trucks that conveniently appear at lunch time. Have a blast! Open Sat., 9am - 2pm. Admission is free. Please register beforehand if you want to participate.

SAN BERNARDINO COUNTY FAIR, Victorville. (760) 951-2200 / www.sbcfair.com, 14800 7th St. For nine days the desert really heats up with excitement when the county fair comes to town. There are eighty-six acres of carnival rides, attractions, farm animals, clowns, family entertainment, and lots more fun. Open first Mon., Thurs. and Fri., 4pm - 11pm; Sat. - Sun. and last Mon., noon - 11pm. Closed Tues. - Wed. Admission is $8 for ages 6 an up; children 5 and under are free with a paying adult. Activities cost extra. Parking is $10.

SCOTTISH FEST AND HIGHLAND GATHERING / SCOTSFEST, Costa Mesa. (714) 708-1500 / www.scottishfest.com, 88 Fair Drive at the Orange County Fair and Event Center. Calling all lads and lassies to join in this Memorial weekend festival, which has been around for over 70 years! It showcases the best of the Scottish and Celtic heritage with caber tossing, hammer throws, shot put, sheepdog herding, good food, clan booths, parades, and a lot of tartan with over sixty clans represented. Bagpipes and Highland Fling dancers, country dancing, pipe and drum bands, and other fantastic music and dance entertain you and the kids throughout the day. A highlight of the Highlands are the Massed Bands, performing at noon on Sat. and 5pm on Sun. Open Sat. - Sun., 9am - 6pm. One-day admission is $15 for adults; $13 for srs. and students; $3 for ages 5 - 11; children 4 and under, military, first responders, police, fire and sheriffs are free. Pre-sale discount tickets are available online. Parking is $8.

SEAL DAY, San Pedro. (310) 548-5677 / www.marinemammalcare.org, 3601 S. Gaffey Street at Marine Mammal Care Center. This fund raiser event, hosted by the Marine Mammal Care Center, has tours of the facility, feedings of the animals, demonstrations, speakers, games, special gifts, food trucks, an Anime Pavilion and raffle prizes. Open Sun., 10am - 4pm. Free.

SPRING ON THE FARM FIELD TRIPS, Pomona. See April entry (pg. 710) for details.

STRAWBERRIES - CAL POLY POMONA, Pomona. See March entry (pg. 705) for details.

STRAWBERRY FESTIVAL, Garden Grove. (714) 638-0981 / www.strawberryfestival.org, between Euclid Ave. and Main St. at Village Green. This four-day event, always held Memorial Day weekend, features carnival rides; games; a parade (Saturday at 10am); arts and crafts booths; entertainment at the amphitheater; dance recitals; kids karaoke contest; a Berry Beautiful Baby Pageant; the annual redhead round-up; and strawberries. Open Fri., 1pm - 10pm; Sat. - Sun., 10am - 10pm; Mon., 10am - 9pm. General admission is free. Certain activities cost. All ride pass $30 Fri., $35 Sat. - Mon.

TANAKA FARMS, Irvine. See February entry (pg. 700) for details.

TEMECULA BERRY COMPANY, Temecula. (951) 225-5552 / www.temeculaberryco.com, 39700 Cantrell Rd. Blueberries are not just a highly-touted source for anti-oxidants, but they taste great and freeze well. U-pic berries from the ten-acre farm, or just purchase them. Free field trips can be scheduled for pre-schooler and elementary-aged kids. It does get really hot here during peak daylight hours, so wear a hat and bring sunscreen, and wear closed-toed shoes. Plan on coming in the morning or late afternoon to participate in the U-pic. If you come on a Friday, stay for movie night at the farm beginning at 8pm (u-pic stays open until 8 on Fridays). Bring your own chair and a blanket! During U-pic season open daily, 8am - 6pm. (Last entrance is 5:30.) About $6 per pint - cash only.

TEMECULA VALLEY BALLOON AND WINE FESTIVAL, Temecula. (951) 676-6713 / www.tvbwf.com, 37701 Warren Rd. at Lake Skinner Recreation Area. Rise and shine for this colorful, three-day festival. On the weekends the balloons are filled with hot air starting around 6am, an event fascinating to watch. Lift-off is around 6:30am, with numerous balloons filling the sky in a kaleidoscope of color. Many of the balloons come back down around 8:30am. Other, less lofty, activities include live entertainment, a food court, arts and craft, and a kid's fair with kiddie rides, a petting zoo, free tethered balloon rides (7:30am - 9:30am), and more. The Friday and Saturday night "glows" (i.e. inflated, lighted balloons that glow almost magically in the evening sky) occur after sunset (8pm). Open Fri., 3pm - 10pm; Sat., 6am - 10pm; Sun., 6am - 5pm. Admission for adults is $30 on Fri. and Sun.; $45 on Sat. Admission for ages 6 - 12 is $5; children 5 and under are free. Parking is $10. Certain activities cost extra. One-hour balloon rides are also available for $225 per person on Sat. or Sun., which includes admission to the festival. Riders must be 48" or taller. Advanced reservations for the rides are necessary, so contact (951) 699-9987 / www.agrapeescape.com.

TOPANGA BANJO AND FIDDLE CONTEST AND FOLK FESTIVAL, Agoura Hills. (818) 382-4819 or (805) 370-2301 / www.topangabanjofiddle.org, Paramount Ranch, 2903 Cornell Rd. We dare you to keep your toes from tapping when Paramount Ranch plays host to the annual old-time, blue grass, folk song, folk dancing, and crafts festival and contests. Note that the graphic design, dance, banjo and fiddle contests pay out good money! (If you win.) The 3rd Sunday in May, 9am to 6pm. Admission is $23 for adults; $18 for srs. and ages 10-17; under 10 is free.

TOUCH-A-TRUCK, Arcadia. (626) 657-0357 / www.truckadventures.org, 285 W. Huntington Dr. at Santa Anita Park This popular event invites kids and adults of all ages to touch and inspect 130 trucks and other vehicles from the outside in and the inside out. Clamber into them, honk the horn and "drive". Trucks, recreational vehicles, emergency vehicles, heavy machinery and more are here and raring to go. There is food, vendors and some other fun activities, as well. Sat., 9am - 2pm., with a sensory, no horns hour from 9am - 10am. $5 per person; $15 for a family; children 1 and under are free.

TURTLE AND TORTOISE SHOW, Long Beach. (562) 570-1745 / www.tortoise.org; www.longbeach.gov/park, 7550 E. Spring St. at the El Dorado Nature Center. Do you know the difference between a turtle or a tortoise? Find out this weekend as members of the California Turtle and Tortoise Society bring their favorites, from the smallest turtle to the large Galapagos Island tortoise. All questions are welcome! Sat., 10am - 3pm. Admission is free. Parking is $7.

VALLEY GREEK FESTIVAL, Northridge. (818) 886-4040 / www.valleygreekfestival.com, St. Nicholas Greek Orthodox Church, 9501 Balboa Boulevard. It's all Greek to them, and that inspires this annual cultural event replete with live music, dancing, epic amounts of food, cooking demonstrations, children's activities, a Greek market, and tour of the church. Memorial day weekend, noon to 9pm. Admission is $3 per person, cash only.

VILLAGE OF TALES OJAI STORYTELLING FESTIVAL, Ojai. (805) 646-8907 / www.ojaistoryfest.org, W. Ojai Ave. and Signal St. at Libbey Bowl. Once upon a time. . . . This wonderful time of storytelling, put on by Performances to Grow On, is intertwined with workshops for storytelling, poetry, and movement. Story swaps (with stories from all over the globe) include traditional folk tales, stories of suspense, adventure, and humor from renowned tellers of tales. Check out the student outreach programs for school groups, or groups of at least ten kids. See the schedule for details and to decide which events you want to attend. Note there is a Continental breakfast at 11am on Sunday. Thurs., 9am - 1pm and 6pm - 9:30pm; Fri. - Sat., 9am - 10pm; Sun., 9am - 1pm. Admission for specific events is $15 to $30 for adults per session; $12 - $27 for srs.; $9 to $25 for kids. A pre-ordered festival pass is $125 for adults; $115 for srs; $60 for ages 15 and under.

WHITTIER POLICE OPEN HOUSE, Whittier. (562) 567-9210 or (562) 567-9200 - police; (562) 567-9400 - health fair / www.cityofwhittier.org, 13200 Penn St. Every year the Whittier Police Department holds an Open House in conjunction with the City's health fair. (The fair is at the adjacent city building, 13230 Penn St.) This is a wonderful time of interacting with police personnel, touring the police station, and visiting booths displaying law enforcement, fire, and other emergency equipment. It could also include demonstrations from the K-9 unit, tactical team, fire department jaws of life, live music, food and entertainment. Don't cop out - come! Sat., 9am - 1pm. Free.

- JUNE -

ADVENTURE PLAYGROUND, Huntington Beach. (714) 842-7442 - playground; (714) 536-5486 / www.huntingtonbeachca.gov, 7111 Talbot at Huntington Beach Central Park. (Park at the Central Library.) Open mid-June through mid-August, young Huck Finns can use a raft (push poles are provided) in the shallow waters of a small, man-made lake. Kids, ages 5 - 12, will also love the slide (i.e. tarp-covered hill) which ends in a little mud pool; a rope bridge leading to a tire swing and mini zip line; sand box; and a work-in-progress kid-built "city" of shacks and clubhouses (only for ages 7 years and up). Lumber, hammers, and nails are provided. All guest must wear tennis shoes; no sandals or water shoes allowed. Notes: Day campers usually invade during the morning hours. A shower and changing area are available. Children 9 and under must be accompanied by an adult. This reminiscent of days-of-old playground is located in the huge Huntington Central Park (HUNTINGTON CENTRAL PARK / SHIPLEY NATURE CENTER (pg. 283)). Open Mon. - Sat., 10am - 4pm (play ends at 3:40pm). Closed Sun. and 4th of July. Admission is $4 per child; free for ages 16 and up.

AIRSHOW SAN DIEGO, El Cajon. (619) 259-5541 / www.ag1caf.org, 1905 North Marshall Ave. Hanger #6 at the Gillespie Field Airport. Several fly bys and aerial demonstrations, plus displays of more than seventy airplanes, including warbirds and vintage aircraft, decorate the air and airfield the first Friday through Sunday in May. Visitors may also tour through a grounded B-17, view antique cars and motorcycles, purchase memorabilia, and talk with aviation celebrities such as WWII Aces, original Flying Tigers, and Tuskegee Airmen. For an additional cost, you can fly in a vintage aircraft. Students are particularly welcome on Friday when kids are given educational tours regarding the aircraft. Visit the nearby museum, AIR GROUP ONE COMMEMORATIVE AIR FORCE WORLD WAR II

FLYING MUSEUM (pg. 523). The air show is open 8am - 5pm. Admission is $12 for adults; children 9 and under are free.

ANTIQUE ENGINE AND TRACTOR SHOW, Vista. (800) 587-2286 or (760) 941-1791 / www.agsem.com, 2040 N. Santa Fe Ave. at the Antique Gas & Steam Engine Museum. This show is held on two consecutive weekends in June, and again in October. Watch demonstrations of American crafts, farming, log sawing, and blacksmithing, plus see many of the restored tractors in a parade each day at 1pm; a very unusual-looking parade! This show has become a favorite of mine. Join in some of the activities such as hayrides and square dancing, and taste the good, home-cooked food available for purchase. See ANTIQUE GAS & STEAM ENGINE MUSEUM, INC. (pg. 523) for more information about this museum. Open Sat. - Sun., 9am - 4:30pm. Admission is $10 for adults; $9 for srs.; $7 for ages 6 - 12; children 5 and under are free. Parking is $5. Camping, with reservations, is $60 for the weekend and includes two admissions to the show.

A TICKET TO EXPLORE JPL, Pasadena. (818) 354-1234 / www.jpl.nasa.gov, 4800 Oak Grove Dr., Jet Propulsion Laboratory. What a blast! This unique opportunity to see Jet Propulsion Laboratories invites you to tour mission control; see displays of rover prototypes, including a life-size model of the Curiosity Mars rover; view multiple spacecraft; watch demonstrations from numerous space missions; see JPL's machine shop; and talk with scientists and engineers about the technologies being developed such as rovers and other robots for current and future space missions. There are so many great visuals just at the Visitor Center - exhibits about JPL missions to the planets and beyond, a full scale model of the Galileo spacecraft and a lunar sample brought back by the Apollo 16 astronauts. Travel through the solar system and beyond exploring what missions have discovered and taught about the planets, their moons, and the rest of the universe via several movies, even 3-D ones. Coming here could launch your child's career. See JET PROPULSION LABORATORIES (pg. 199) for more info on the facility and other tours here. Sat. - Sun., 8:30am - 4pm. You must preregister and will be given an assigned entry time. Free. Children 2 and under don't need a ticket.

BIG IRISH FAIR, Irvine. (949) 724-6247 / www.irishfairandmusicfest.org, 6950 Marine Way, at the Great Park Top o' the mornin' to ye. This weekend Irish fair, the largest one in the Western U.S., features top-name entertainment, such as Cillian's Bridge, Humble Hooligans, and the Fenians, on four different stages; wonderful Irish dancing; parades; traditional contests, such as fiddle playing and more dancing; sheep-herding demonstrations; a dog show featuring Irish breeds; bagpipe music; over 100 vendors of Irish wares; and Leprechaun Kingdom for kids. The Kingdom features storytelling, jugglers, pony rides, and carnival rides. Another favorite at the festival is a recreation of a medieval Irish village, Tara, where sword-yielding performers recount the village's legends and history. The athletic field hosts hurling (might not be what you're thinking) and Gaelic football. Look at the website to get a feel for just how big this festival is and how much there is to do here (and that's no blarney). The festival runs Sat. - Sun., 10am - 7pm. (Church is at 10am on Sunday.) Admission is $15 for adults (in advance, $20 at the gate); $13 for srs. and students ($16 at the gate); children 12 and under are free with a paid adult. Get tickets online at a discount. Parking is free.

BRIAN RANCH AIRPORT U-PICK ORCHARD, Llano. (661) 261-3216 / www.brianranch.com, 34810 Largo Vista Rd. off Pearblossom Hwy. You can fly into this ranch, as it does have a small airstrip, though most of us just drive. The 40-acre ranch, waaay down a lonely highway and a mile of dirt road, is a fruit mecca with 600 fruit trees. Depending on the season, pick cherries (June) - Bing, Lapins, and Sunburst; apricots (mid-June); nectarines (mid-July); peaches (mid-July) - Delight, Fairtime, Nectar, Springcrest, Suncrest and Paradise; apples (starting mid-July - September) - Braeburn, Golden Supreme, Red Fuji; and pears (starting in August) - Morettini, Bronze Beauty, Bartlett, and Rosi-Red. Ask about education and scout programs to do with aviation and also with produce. Open in season, Sat. - Sun., 8am - 2pm and by appointment. Fruits are paid for by the pound - most are $1.50lb, cherries are $4lb.

CARLSBAD STRAWBERRY COMPANY, Carlsbad. See April entry (pg. 706) for details.

CHERRY FESTIVAL / CHERRY PICKING. Beaumont, Cherry Valley. (951) 527-3197 / www.beaumontcherryfestival.org, 650 E. 9th St. at Stewart Park
I tell you no lie - June is a month ripe for cherry picking, but the season could start in mid-May and go as long as July, depending on the weather. Call first. The three-week, or so, season starts with a four-day festival in Beaumont that includes a parade, carnival-type rides, game booths, amateur and professional live musical entertainment, and lots of family fun. Thursday admission is $5 for adults; $3 for srs. and ages 6 - 13; ages 5 and under are free. Fri. - Sun. admission is $7 for adults; the rest are the same. One place and number to try is Riley's, (909) 797-7534 / www.rileysfarm.com, at 12261 S. Glen Oak in Yucaipa. (This ranch has raspberries, too, in August.) Look for roadside signs along Live Oak Avenida, Brookside, and Cherry Ave., announcing other U-Pics. Note: Dowling Orchard, (951) 845-1217, www.dowlingfruitorchard.webstarts.com is not a U-Pic, but it does offer just-picked cherries and a year-round produce market. Checkout the website www.pickyourown.org for a fairly comprehensive list of other

orchards. The festival hours are Thurs. - Fri., 5pm - midnight; Sat., noon - midnight; Sun., noon - 8pm. Call for U-Pic hours.

CHERRY PICKING, Leona Valley. (661) 266-7116 - Leona Valley Cherry Growers hotline / www.cherriesupic.com. The orchards here don't produce enough of the delicious crop for commercial sale, so the public wins by getting to harvest the cherries themselves! Put a bucket around your neck and start picking, although many orchards also sell pre-picked cherries. The weather-dependent, short season can start as early as May and can last through July. Different types of cherries, such as Bing, Rainier, Cashmere, Montmorency, Tartarians, etc., ripen at various times throughout the season. Call first! Villa del Sol, (661) 270-1356 / www.upickcherries.com, at Elizabeth Lake Road and Godde Hill Road has 25 acres with 3000 cherry trees. There is a $6 minimum per person, which isn't hard to do! Rolling Thunder, (661) 270-9688 / www.rtcherryranch.com, at 10254 Leona Ave., is open 8am to 4pm on weekdays. Tip: If you pick a lot of cherries, purchase a cherry pitter! Checkout the website www.pickyourown.org for a fairly comprehensive list of other orchards.

CHILDREN'S DAY, Santa Fe Springs. (562) 946-6476 / www.santafesprings.org, 12100 Mora Dr. at Heritage Park. This day of old-fashioned fun is when kids can churn butter; pan for gold; play turn-of-the-century games; and make crafts. Open Sun., noon - 4pm. Admission and activities are free.

COIN & COLLECTIBLES EXPO, Long Beach. See January entry (pg. 695) for details.

COLORADO LAGOON MODEL BOAT SHOP, Long Beach. (562) 570-3215 or (562) 570-6555 - boat shop in season; (562) 570-1888 - out of season info / www.longbeach.gov/park/recreation-programs/aquatics/colorado-lagoon, 5119 E. Colorado Ave. and Appian Way at Colorado Lagoon. Pre-packaged craft kits have their place in our instant-gratification society, but they have nothing on actually hand crafting a one-of-a-kind, wooden, 12"- to 40"-long sailboat that is balanced by a lead keel. Participants, who must be at least 7 years old, glue, sand, file, lacquer, and paint before the final rigging is done and they learn sailing lingo along the way. All materials, including hand tools, are provided. Boats take between five to seven days to complete, consecutively or in whatever increments you choose. Parents can drop kids off (or stay) anytime mid-June through the beginning of August, Mon. - Fri., 10am - 3pm. The small building "shop", staffed mostly by older kids, is a fenced in area just off the beach by the COLORADO LAGOON (pg. 11). Bring a picnic lunch and sunscreen. All participants can sail their finished products in the weekly regattas held on Fri. at 2pm. Help your kids chart their course to a great summer! Registration is $61 per child, plus material fees: Boats range from $25 for a 12", up to $50 for a 40".

CONCERTS. There are numerous venues all over Southern California that offer free, outdoor family concerts during the summer. Check with your local parks and recreations department, or chamber of commerce. For most of them, simply bring a blanket, some food, sit back, and enjoy the entertainment.

DISCOVER RECYCLING OPEN HOUSE. Throughout LA. See April entry (pg. 706) for details.

ELKS RODEO AND PARADE, Santa Maria. (805) 925-4125 / www.elksrec.com, 4040 US 101 Frontage Rd. at Elks Rodeo grounds. Experience the Old West with a roundup and a Professional Rodeo Cowboys Association event with calf roping, bull riding, saddle bronc riding, steer wrestling, and barrel racing events. Don't forget to try some of Santa Maria's famous BBQ tri-tip. The rodeo parade is held on Sat. at 9am and runs from Broadway Mill to Stowell. Tickets are $25 for adults; $17srs and ages 12 and under. Save on pre-sale tickets.

FIRE & SAFETY EXPO / FIREFIGHTER DEMOLITION DERBY, Del Mar. (858) 541-2277 / www.burninstitute.org, 2260 Jimmy Durante Boulevard, at Del Mar Fairgrounds. Did the title of this event spark your interest? Join firefighters in the largest fire expo held in Southern California. The event is held on a Saturday during the San Diego County Fair. For one-day see live demonstrations of auto extrications and bomb robots; a canine dog demonstration; and a Burn Run where 70+ engines (one from each of the area's stations) converge in a siren blaring, lights flashing parade at 1pm. A highlight is the challenge where firefighters from all over, dressed in full bunker gear and breathing apparatus, which can weight up to 50 pounds, compete in five real-life firefighting tasks. Rides on fire engines, a rock climbing wall, "live" firefighting demonstrations, helicopter fly-overs, a firefighter obstacle course, a kiddie carnival (with puppet shows, clowns, and such), and community service group booths add to this special event. One of the highlights is the Firefighter Demolition Derby, which gives local firefighters the chance to "smash for cash" and everyone else a chance to cheer them on. Open 10pm - 11pm. Admission to the county fair, which includes admission to the expo, is $19 for adults; $12 for srs. and ages 6 - 12; children 5 and under are free. Parking is $15. Free shuttle services from free off-site parking is available.

FLOWER FIELDS / FLOWER FESTIVAL, Lompoc. (805) 736-4567 - flower fields info ; (805) 735-8511 - festival / www.lompocvalleyfestivals.com. The flower fields are usually in peak bloom June through August, and sometimes September depending on the weather, so drive your car up and down the numerous roads, especially between Central and Ocean avenues traveling west, to get an eye full of color and nose full of fragrance. (The sweet peas are really aromatic.) Pick up a route map from the chamber of commerce at 111 South I St. Cut flowers and flowers grown for seed include larkspur, stock, marigolds, and many more. You'll also see vegetables and other produce. Stop and smell the flowers, but don't pick them. Make the most of your flower experience by also attending the five-day Flower Festival at Ryon Park the last full weekend in June. The parade, starting Saturday at 10am, goes along H and Ocean avenues. The creative floats must be constructed of flowers or natural materials. (Think of a much smaller scale Rose Parade.) The parade also features equestrians, bands, drill teams, and clowns. The festival consists of carnival rides, food booths, an arts and crafts show, and a huge flower show, as well as flower displays and demonstrations. One more thing - look up the entry on Lompoc MURALS (pg. 636) to incorporate seeing them into this *field* trip. The flower fields are open daily. The festival is open daily, but check for hours and specific exhibit times. Admission to the fields is free. Admission to the festival is $5 for ages 13 and up; children 12 and under are free. Rides cost extra. Minimal fee for parking at the festival.

GREEK FEST, San Diego. (619) 297-4165 / www.sdgreekfestival.com, 3655 Park Blvd. at St. Spyridon Church. Live (and lively) Greek music and dancing, home-made pastries and other Greek food, a tour of this Greek Orthodox church, booths, kids' carnival games, and more are offered at this three-day festival. Open Fri., 5pm - 10pm; Sat., 11am - 10pm; Sun., 11am - 9pm. Free Fri. - Sun., 11am - 1pm. After 1pm Sat. - Sun. it's $3 for ages 13 and up; ages 12 and under are free.

HEROES AIR SHOW, Lake View Terrace. (818) 631-8132 / www.heroes-airshow.com, 11480 Foothill Blvd. at Hansen Dam Recreation and Sports Complex. This one-day show is the premier air show exclusively for helicopters and flight teams, and their vehicles' role in law enforcement, fire service, and search and rescue. See aerial demonstrations of rope/rescue techniques; take a helicopter ride; look at the vintage fire engines, police cars, and emergency service vehicles that make up the "Rolling to the Rescue" exhibit; gather information at the Code 3 Career Fair; and enjoy the vendors and entertainment. Open Sat., 9am - 4pm. Free admission. Rides cost extra.

HO'OLAULE'A or NATIVE FOR NATURE, San Dimas. (909) 599-7512 / www.sandimascanyonnaturecenter.com, 1628 N. Sycamore Canyon Rd. at the San Dimas Canyon Community Regional Park. For one weekend, enjoy Hawaiian and Native American dances, music, and food, plus nature hikes, face painting, pottery, weaving, beading, games, crafts, and Indian fry bread and sweet corn. The proceeds from the activities provide food and medical care for the animals in the center's sanctuary. See SAN DIMAS CANYON COMMUNITY REGIONAL PARK (pg. 83) for more information on the park. Open Sat. - Sun., 10am - 6pm. Admission and parking is free. Certain activities cost.

HOPE FOR FIREFIGHTERS, Los Angeles. (310) 776-0933 / www.hopeforfirefighters.org, 333 South Hope St. and Fourth St. When a building is burning, we rush out as firefighters rush in. This celebration/fundraiser is one big way to show appreciation for firefighters, as over 25 stations are represented. Come see fire apparatus and demonstrations, and pet a real dalmatian fire dog. For a really hot time, create your own team to compete at the firefighter "Muster" games, in races that include a bucket brigade; firefighter suit-up, then using a lifenet to save a dummy falling from a building; and an old-fashioned hose pull. Watch out for the water hoses filled up by the fire hydrants! Note to teams: To become proficient in the games, there is a practice held a few weeks beforehand, which includes a picnic for all the teams and their families. This practice includes a tour of the Hollywood station, the Historical Society Museum next door, and getting to meet some of the firefighters. Team sponsorship is $1,000. There is also live music at the fundraiser, LAFD gift merchandise booths, raffle drawings, and a competition between stations for the "best of" in fire house meals. Open the first Thurs. in June, 11:30am - 2:30pm. Free admission. A fire house meal is $9; dessert and blended beverages, $3.

INDEPENDENCE DAY CELEBRATION, Torrance. (310) 515-7166 / www.printmuseum.org, 315 W. Torrance Blvd. at the INTERNATIONAL PRINTING MUSEUM (pg. 123). Learn a version of how our country got its independence by watching a play in the small theater, *The Confounding Brothers*, featuring Benjamin Franklin, John Adams, and Thomas Jefferson. Attendees also get to print their own keepsake copy of the Declaration of Independence on a colonial press, partake in special crafts, enjoy lunch (hot dogs and apple pie), and take a tour of one of my favorite museum. The Sat. around 4th of July, 10am - 4pm, with performances at 11am and 1pm. Admission is $15 per person, which includes lunch, or $50 for a family of four.

INTERNATIONAL SPEEDWAY, Costa Mesa. See May entry (pg. 712) for details.

INTERNATIONAL SUMMER ORGAN FESTIVAL, San Diego. (619) 702-8138 / www.specklesorgan.org, Balboa Park at the Spreckels Organ Pavilion. Every Monday night from mid-June through August enjoy the sounds of Scott Joplin, Charles Tournemire, Maurice Durufle, and others at the Organ Pavilion. Bring a picnic lunch (or at least dessert) to eat on the lawn and listen to the sounds of summer. Note that there are free outdoor concerts often given during the week, too, and one every Sunday at 2pm year round. Concerts start at 7:30pm. Admission is free.

INTERTRIBAL POW WOW, Oceanside. (760) 724-8505 / www.slrmissionindians.org, 4050 Mission Ave. at Mission San Luis Rey de Franca. Join a weekend of tribal dancing, arts and crafts, and American Indian games and food. Open Sat., 9am -11pm; Sun., 9am - 6pm. Admission is free.

JUNETEENTH CELEBRATION, Long Beach. (562) 570-6816 / www.longbeach.gov/park, 1950 Lemon Avenue, at Martin Luther King Jr. Park Community Center. This open-air event celebrates the abolition of slavery in the U.S. and promotes remembrance and awareness with speakers, historians, bands, dance troops and local entertainers. There are a gospel celebration and a reading of the Emancipation Proclamation. Food is available for purchase and there is a children's area with games, jumpers and arts and crafts. Attendees are encouraged to bring chairs and blankets. Fri., 5pm - 9pm. Free.

KINGSMEN SHAKESPEARE FESTIVAL, Thousand Oaks. (805) 493-3014 / www.kingsmenshakespeare.org, 60 Olsen Rd., California Lutheran University, Kingsmen Park. Two of Shakespeare's plays are featured, such as *Taming of the Shrew* or *Merchant of Venice*, during the six-weekend festival. There are also Elizabethan vendors, crafts, foods, and more. The festival usually runs Fri. - Sun., with pre-show entertainment and food vendors beginning at 5:30pm; performances starting at 8pm. Call for a schedule of pre- and post-performance activities. Bring a low back chair or blanket to sit on, and dress warmly. Admission is $25 for adults; $20 for srs.; $15 for students 18 and up; ages 17 and under are free. Lawn Boxes hold six people each and are available for reserve starting at $90.

KORONEBURG RENAISSANCE FESTIVAL, Corona. See May entry (pg. 712) for details.

LIVE OAK MUSIC FESTIVAL, Santa Barbara. (805) 781-3030 / www.liveoakfest.org, Live Oak Camp. Come for the music - folk, blues, jazz, bluegrass, gospel, classical and more - but stay for all the other things you kids will enjoy - crafts, juggling, climbing wall, stories, hikes and a talent show. Live Oak Camp is located about 15 miles from Santa Barbara and is in the beautiful Santa Ynez Valley. The festival is held on Father's Day weekend. Tickets are $55 for adults on Fri. $65 for Sat. or Sun;; $20 for ages 4 - 12 each day. Parking is $15, but 3 or more in a car is only $5. Runs Fri., 2pm - midnight; Sat., 8am - midnight; Sun., 8am - 8:30pm.

MARIACHI USA FESTIVAL, Hollywood. (800) MARIACHI (627-4224) or (323) 848-7717 / www.mariachiusa.com; www.hollywoodbowl.org, 2301 N. Highland Ave. at the Hollywood Bowl. This one-day event celebrates family, culture, and tradition. Bring a picnic dinner (note that there are food vendors on site as well) and enjoy Mariachi music, Ballet Folkloric, and a fireworks finale. The four-and-a-half hour performance is given Sat. at 6pm; festivities begin at 1pm. Tip: Purchase tickets early as the concert is usually sold out. Admission is $43 - $257, depending on seating. Parking is $22 - $60. You can also take the Park & Ride shuttle from various parts of the city for $7 round trip if pre-purchased or $12 at the lot. See the Hollywood Bowl website for more info.

MCGRATH FAMILY FARMS, Camarillo. See March entry (pg. 704) for details.

MOONLIGHT STAGE PRODUCTIONS, Vista. (760) 724-2110 or (760) 643-5297 / www.moonlightstage.com, 1200 Vale Terrace at Brengle Terrace Park at the Moonlight Amphitheater. Four Broadway musicals are performed at this outside amphitheater each summer, often including one youth theater production. Past performances include *Beauty and the Beast, Peter Pan, Sister Act* and *Monte Python's Spamalot*. Come see a show under the stars (and moon) and bring a picnic to enjoy on the lawn or purchase dinner at the on-site cafe. Productions run mid-June through September, Wed. - Sun. at 8pm. Call for specific dates and times. The gates open at 6:30pm for picnicking. Tickets cost between $10 - $55, depending on age of guest and the seating from general lawn to reserved lawn to reserved seats.

MORRELL NUT & BERRY FARM, Solvang. (805) 688-8969, 1980 Alamo Pintado Road. Fresh, off-the-vine raspberries, olallieberries and blackberries are yours for the picking at this U-Pic farm. Walnuts available mid October through December. Berry season runs June through August; call first. Come pick Thurs. - Sat., 10am - 5pm (closed Sun. - Wed.).

MOVIE NIGHT / OUTDOOR FAMILY FILMS. Many parks offer free, nighttime, out-door family entertainment, G or PG movies. Bring a blanket, picnic dinner, and enjoy a show together! Call your local park for information.

MOVIES. Movie theaters in the summer often offer incredible bargain rates for G and PG films. UltraStar Movies in Mission Valley at Hazard Center, San Diego, offers Kids Summer Series where a different film shown every week, Mon. - Fri. at 9:30am from the end of June - September for only $1 per person, per movie. Contact www.UltraStarMovies.com for more info. Regal Cinemas, www.regmovies.com, located all over the Southland, offers Summer Movies Express where movie admission is $1 for each of the 2 different movies each week for nine weeks during the summer, shown at 10am on Tues. and Wed. Your local AMC Theaters offers Movie Summer Camp on Wed. at 10am - $4 includes movie, popcorn, drink and fruit snack. Check www.amctheatres.com for more info. The Krikorian Kids' Series, at Krikorian Theatres, offers $1 admission for family movies every Tues., mid-June - mid-August, with 2 showings per day (of the same movies) at 10am and 12:30pm. See www.kptmovies.com for more info. Harkins Theatres has Harkins Summer Movie Fun program for kids, www.harkinstheatres.com; 10 movies for $5 (a season pass), or $2 per movie, per person. Movies show at 9:45am. Cinemark Summer Movie Clubhouse charges $1 per show if purchased at the box office, or purchase all of the movies in advance for only $5 total for the 10 shows running June - August. Visit at www.cinemark.com/summer-movie-clubhouse for more details.

OLD SANTA YNEZ DAY, Santa Ynez. (805) 688-3448 / www.syvelks.com; www.visitsyv.com, 3558 Sagunto St. The Old West comes to life in modern day as this frontier town celebrates its birth on the second Sat. every June. Take part and enjoy the classic parade (11am), entertainment, kids games, arts and crafts, vendors, antiques, get thrown in jail, and delicious food. Top off your evening with Spaghetti Western Night at 5pm at the adjacent Santa Ynez Historical Museum. Open 9am - 6:30pm. Free

PASADENA CHALK FESTIVAL, Pasadena. (626) 795-8891 / www.pasadenachalkfestival.com, 280 East Colorado Boulevard. Chalk it all up to having a good time! Over 600 artists draw marvelous, if temporary, masterpieces out of chalk on the sidewalks of Pasadena at this two-day festival in June or July. A children's chalk area is also set up. Live music and food complete the ambiance. Pull up a piece of sidewalk, Sat. - Sun., 10m - 7pm. Admission is free to watch.

PCPA THEATERFEST, Solvang. (805) 922-8313 - box office; (805) 686-1789 - information / www.pcpa.org, 420 2nd St., at the outdoor Festival Theater. In the middle of the quaint town of Solvang, this 750-seat outdoor theater shows plays from mid-June through September. Come watch one of the four musicals, usually family-friendly, offered during the season (or all four!) under the canopy of trees and starlight. Make sure you bring a jacket as summer night air can be unexpectedly chilly. The Theaterfest is a favorite activity for our family for the show and ambiance. See PCPA THEATERFEST (pg. 640, 720) for more details. Shows are usually given Tues. - Sun., 8pm, but check website for a performance schedule. Prices range, depending on show time, from $41 - $57.50 for adults; $37.25 - $52 for srs.; $29.50 - $41.25 for students and ages 13 - 18; $26.50 - $36.75 for ages 5 - 12 years; children 4 and under are not permitted. Thursday previews are less expensive.

PEARSON PARK AMPHITHEATER, Anaheim. (714) 765-5274 or (714) 765-5191 or / www.anaheim.net, Lemon and Sycamore sts. The terrific programs put on through the "Summer Nights Under the Stars" series run from mid-June to mid-August and are geared for kids 4 years old through 6th graders. The shows run approximately ninety minutes. Past programs have included Make-a-Circus, magic shows, puppet shows, a wild west show, ballet and jazz troupes, the mad scientist, and audience participation shows with songs or storytellers. Check the website for specific show information. A concession stand is on site. The amphitheater also host some free, family-friendly outdoor movies and concerts throughout the summer. The every Fri. programs start at 6:30pm (seating starts at 6pm); check the website for movies and concerts. Tickets for the programs are $3 for adults; children 8 and under are free.

REDLANDS BOWL SUMMER MUSIC FESTIVAL, Redlands. (909) 793-7316 / www.redlandsbowl.org, 25 Grant St. Two nights a week, from late June through August, the bowl offers something absolutely incredible - professional and top-notch symphony music, jazz, and opera as well as musicals, ballet, and dance ensembles - FOR FREE. Many of these are great programs for the family! A freewill offering is taken at intermission. Seating is first come, first served. Bring a picnic dinner to enjoy before the performance. Note: Don't park in the underground parking since the gates are usually locked at 9pm. Programs are offered Tues. and Fri. evening at 8pm and are free. Free, forty-five minute music appreciation workshops are given for elementary-aged kids on Tues. at 3pm (at the Redlands Community Center) and Sat. at 10am (at the Mission Gables Bowl House).

RENAISSANCE PLEASURE FAIRE, Irwindale. See April entry (pg. 709) for details.

SAN DIEGO COUNTY FAIR, Del Mar. (858) 793-5555 - recording; (858) 755-1161 - fairgrounds / www.sdfair.com, 2260 Jimmy Durante Blvd. at the Del Mar Fairgrounds. This major, three-week event features everything wonderful in a county fair - carnival rides; flower and garden shows; gem and minerals exhibits; farm animals; livestock judging; food; craft booths; and a festive atmosphere. Call for a schedule of events. Usually open Mon. - Fri. 10am - 11pm.; Sat., 9am - 11pm; and Sun., 9am - 10pm. Kids Zone opens 1 hour later than fair hours. The fair is closed Mon. and Tues. in June. Admission is $19 for adults; $12 for srs. and ages 6 - 12 years; children 5 and under are free. Certain activities cost extra. Check the website for discount ticket information. Parking is $15. Free shuttle services from free off-site parking is available.

SAN DIEGO SCOTTISH HIGHLAND GAMES AND GATHERING OF CLANS, Vista. (760)726-3691 or (619) 425-3454 / www.sdhighlandgames.org, 1200 Vale Terrace Dr. at Brengle Terrace Park. For almost thirty years, fifty or so clans have come to participate and enjoy first class entertainment at this gathering. The last weekend in June is the one for Scottish merrymaking, which includes highland dancing, Celtic harping, bagpipe competitions, sheepdog herding trials, athletic competitions (such as caber tossing), a drumming competition, and lots of good food. Open Sat. - Sun., 9am - 5pm. Admission is $15 for adults per day; $10 for srs.; $5 for ages 6 - 16; children 5 and under are free. Parking is $4 at Brengle Terrace, or park at Vista High School and take a free shuttle.

SAWDUST FESTIVAL, Laguna Beach. (949) 494-3030 / www.sawdustartfestival.org, 935 Laguna Canyon Rd. This three-acre, outdoor arts and crafts festival, with over 200 artisans, goes from the end of June through August (almost simultaneous with the FESTIVAL OF ARTS (pg. 723, 728). On-going demonstrations include ceramics, throwing pots (so to speak), etching, glass blowing, and more. The Children's Art booth allows kids to create art projects - for free! Family-oriented daytime entertainment includes storytelling and juggling. Nighttime entertainment includes listening and dancing to bands. Restaurants and other food services are on site. Tram service is free. The festival is open daily, 10am - 10pm. Daily admission is $9 for adults; $7 for srs.; $4 for ages 6 - 12; children 5 and under are free. Parking is $10 Mon. - Fri.; $10 - $20, Fri. after 5pm and all day Sat. - Sun.

SHAKESPEARE BY THE SEA, (310) 217-7596 / www.shakespearebythesea.org. Outdoors, under the stars, free - this is how Shakespeare is meant to be enjoyed. From mid-June - mid-August (totaling 10 weeks) usually two plays a season are presented at 20+ venues (usually parks) throughout L.A. and Orange counties on various nights. Bring a beach chair or blanket (one to sit on and one get warm under) and enjoy the celebrated wordsmith's plays. Most plays start at 7pm but check the website. Free, but donations are appreciated.

SPECIAL OLYMPICS SOUTHERN CALIFORNIA GAMES, Los Angeles. (562) 502-1100 / www.sosc.org, 1250 Bellflower Blvd. at California State University of Long Beach. "Let me win, but if I cannot win, let me be brave in the attempt." That is the Special Olympics motto. Come to cheer on hundreds of mentally challenged children and adults as they compete in Olympic-type sports of aquatics, basketball, golf, gymnastics, flag football and more. These are gratifying events to witness. Help run the events if you can volunteer some time. The public also enjoys live entertainment, community exhibits, games, and sports clinics. Games run Sat., 9:30am - 5pm; Sun., 9am - 3pm, followed by the closing ceremony. Free admission.

SUMMER CONCERTS, Pasadena. (626) 683-3230 / www.levittpavilionpasadena.org, 85 E. Holly St. at Memorial Park at the Levitt Pavilion for the Performing Arts. This park and bandshell are host to over 30 free(!), evening "concerts" (and shows) during the summer months. Weekly themes encompass Children's nights on Thurs., which have included the Bob Baker Marionettes, Rhythm Child, Circus Skills, West African dancers, Russian folk music, Parachute Express, and others. Sat. is Musica Latina; and Sun., Jazz and Big Band. Bring your blanket and picnic basket and enjoy the sweet sounds of summer. The concerts are Thurs., Sat. and Sun. at 7pm.

SUMMER SOLSTICE PARADE AND FESTIVAL, Santa Barbara. (805) 965-3396 / www.solsticeparade.com, State and Cota sts. to Micheltorenia St. For a really hot time, celebrate the summer solstice with a wacky, goofy, creative, colorful parade. Over 1,000 participants (who pay a fee to participate) dress up in elaborate costumes, incorporating choreographed dancing, giant puppets, people-powered floats, and general silliness. Parade participants can attend workshops in May and June to create their ensembles and get help from artists in residence. Parade watchers grab curb space or set up lawn chairs along the street early. The festival, at Alameda Park, has musical entertainment, drummers, food and refreshment, arts and crafts, storytellers, short theater productions, air bounces, face painting, vendors, and an up-close view of the floats. The parade is at noon on the first Sat. after the summer solstice. The festival is Fri., 4pm - 9pm, Sat., noon - 8pm, Sun., noon - 6pm. Only participants pay an entry fee; admission is free for festival attendees.

SUNSET LUAU ON MISSION BAY, San Diego. (800) 422-8386 or (858) 488-1081 / www.catamaranresort.com, 3999 Mission Blvd. at the Catamaran Resort. You can easily be persuaded that Mission Bay is just like the Hawaiian islands as you enjoy a traditional Hawaiian buffet dinner and beachside show at sunset. After a lei greeting, feast your taste buds on spicy bay shrimp salad; tropical fruit with coconut and grilled pineapple; chicken salad with macadamia nuts; Kalua roast pig; roast salmon with ginger lime cream sauce; guava chicken; ginger stir-fry; rice; Hawaiian sweet rolls; and desserts of pineapple upside down cake, coconut cream cake, passion fruit creme brulee and haupia; and more. The Pride of Polynesia dancers perform traditional dances - which are so beautiful and graceful to watch - including the hula - and one of our favorites, the fire knife performance. Aloha! Enjoy the dinner and show mid-June through August every Fri., 6pm - 9pm; with additional shows on Tues., mid-July through August. The schedule is as follows: 6pm - 6:45pm, a lei greeting and musical entertainment; 6:45pm - 8pm, a buffet with background music; 8pm - 9pm, the show. Admission is $72 for adults; $32 for ages 5 - 12; children 4 and under are free. Hotel guests get a discount.

TANAKA FARMS, Irvine. See February entry (pg. 700) for details.

TEMECULA BERRY COMPANY, Temecula. See May entry (pg. 714) for details.

TEMECULA STREET PAINTING/ARTS FESTIVAL, Temecula. (951) 694-6412 / www.temeculaevents.org, Main Street & Town Square in Old Town Temecula. Painting the streets is different than painting the town, especially when it's done with chalk. Come see great works of art on the asphalt created by professionals, and come to see work that simply appeals to proud parents as the festival is open to all participants. Reserve a space or come to look. Entertainment is on-going. Open Fri., 5pm - 8pm; Sat., 10am - 6pm; Sun., 10am - 4pm. Free for artists and the public.

TOUCH A TRUCK, Costa Mesa. (714) 557-0420 / www.truckadventures.org; ocmarketplace.com, 88 Fair Dr. at the Orange County Market Place, OC Fair & Event Center. Come play on a tractor. And a dirt bike. And "operate" a fork lift. And emergency response vehicles, construction trucks, vintage cars, cranes, Fed Ex., school buses, fire trucks, Humvees, ambulances (lie down on a stretcher!), police cars and so many more at this huge event. Rows and rows of vehicles await guests to board and honk their horns. Other adventures here include talking to the vehicle drivers, especially first responders, live entertainment, food, arts and crafts and more. You'll have tons of fun here! Sat., 9am - 2pm. Horn and siren free hours are from 9am - 11am. $15 per person; children 1 and under are free. Parking is $8.

TOUCH A TRUCK, Redlands. / www.redlandstouchatruck.com, 1200 E Colton Ave. at Ted Runner Stadium. My youngest son used to run after the trash truck. At this most fun event for kids, the trucks come to them. At this event, put on by the rotary club of Redlands, dozens of vehicles - emergency vehicles, transport vehicles, tow trucks, public health and safety trucks, busses (even a helicopter) - are accessible for visitors to climb into the cabs, honk the horns, examine the equipment, flash the lights, and talk to the men and women who work in and with the vehicles about how they use their vehicles to do their jobs. There is also a free "Kids' Zone" with crafts, games, and educational and safety exhibits, and, of course, food trucks! Keep on truckin'. Sat., 9am- 2pm. Note that the first 90-min. are No Noise Ninety Minutes" so very young children and other persons who might have an adverse reaction to sudden, loud noises may participate undisturbed. $5 for ages 4 and up. There are some complementary tickets distributed via schools. Families with active duty military (up to 6 people) and children 3 and under are free.

TOUCH-A-TRUCK, Thousand Oaks. / www.crpd.org, 2525 N. Moorpark Rd. at the Thousand Oaks Community Center. Some people kick the tires when they buy a car. At this event you can do that, too, but even better, you can climb into the driver's seat, honk the horns, and "drive" all kinds of trucks and other vehicles such as a garbage truck, an Army truck, stretch limousine, tractor, excavator, dump truck, school bus, fire engine, ambulance, monster truck, bulldozer, police cruiser, SWAT vehicle, K-9 and Search & Rescue vehicles, motorcycles, and more. And if that's not enough, which I think it is, there are arts and crafts, a kids' construction zone, jolly jumps, a motorized train ride, a water balloon drop from a cherry picker, beach balls unloaded from a dump truck, and sometimes a helicopter landing. Come early to park to park at the Thousand Oaks high school parking lot. Sat., 10am - 2pm. Free.

WILL GEER THEATRICUM BOTANICUM, Topanga. (310) 455-3723 / www.theatricum.com, 1419 N. Topanga Blvd. This outdoor theater produces several kinds of summertime "edutainment." Family Fundays are offered in two formats: 1) Creative PlayGround - an interactive, In-the-Round, 45-minute theatre production for ages 1- 9 years old with titles like Aesop's Fables and the Velveteen Rabbit. These tickets are $9 for ages 2 and up. Performances start at 11am and are usually on Sun., June - October. 2) Kids Koncerts - tickets are $10 and performances run July through Sept. on select Sun. These are programs for young kids featuring name entertainment, such as the Parachute Express and Dan Crow. Older audiences enjoy plays such as *The Merry Wives of Windsor* and *St. Joan*. See WILL GEER THEATRICUM BOTANICUM (pg. 195). Show times vary. More mature productions are $15 - $39.50 for adults; $10 for ages 5 - 15. Parking is $7.

- JULY -

ADVENTURE PLAYGROUND, Huntington Beach. See June entry (pg. 715) for details.
BIG WORLD FUN FAMILY SERIES AT THE FORD, Hollywood. (323) 461-3673 / www.fordtheatres.org, 2580 Cahuenga Blvd. E. at the John Anson Ford Amphitheater. This outdoor amphitheater presents wonderful, one-hour family performances, geared for ages 4 - 11, on Saturdays in July and August. Check the schedule for a complete listing, as family-friendly shows are also given sometimes during the week. Enjoy an intimate setting with shows that feature top-name entertainment in magic, puppetry, storytelling, music, dance, or plays designed with the whole family in mind. Pre-show activities can include live animal presentations and/or craft activities. Stay after the show to have a picnic lunch that you may either bring or purchase at several options on site. Pizza, gourmet sandwiches, Cobb salad, nachos, and more are available. Educators note that the website offers curriculum supplement for the show series. Shows on Sat. start at 10am. Pre-show activities starting at 9am. Call for a schedule of other show times and dates. Reservations are recommended. Seats cost $5 for adults; children 12 and under are free. Ask about Family Day admission. Parking on site cost $5. Free shuttle services from 1718 Cherokee in Hollywood are available, tho parking in Hollywood is $14.

BRIAN RANCH AIRPORT U-PICK ORCHARD, Llano. See June entry (pg. 716) for details.
CALIFORNIA WATERMELON FESTIVAL, Lakeview Terrace. (818) 295-0334 / www.watermelonfest.org, 11480 Foothill Blvd. at the Hansen Dam Soccer complex. Would it surprise you to know there are a lot of watermelon

activities here? How about greased watermelon relay races, watermelon-eating and seed-spitting contests and melon-carving demos. But there is also live entertainment, food, carnival rides and games, vendor booths, kids' activities, pony rides and, of course, free watermelon samples. Sat. - Sun., 10am - 10pm. $10 for adults; $6 for ages 3 - 12; Free for children 2 and under. Parking is $7.

CAMP-A-PALOOZA, Temple City. (626) 579-0461 / www.ci.temple-city.ca.us, 10144 Bogue St. at Live Oak Park. Introduce your kids to the wonderful world of camping, close at home. You bring the tent, sleeping bags and your family, and the rest is done for you. Besides camping, there could be arts and crafts, live entertainment, bounces, a movie, a scavenger hunt, rock climbing wall, and more. Each year has a different, family-friendly theme. Dinner - sometimes it's In-N-Out, snacks and a continental breakfast are provided. Make new friends and have an in*tent*s experience! Camp setup begins Fri. at 2:30pm; activities begin at 4pm. $75 per family for up to four people; $10 per additional family member.

CARLSBAD STRAWBERRY COMPANY, Carlsbad. See April entry (pg. 706) for details.

COLORADO LAGOON MODEL BOAT SHOP, Long Beach. See June entry (pg. 717) for details.

COMIC-CON, San Diego. (619) 414-1020 / www.comic-con.org, 111 W. Harbor Dr. at the San Diego Convention Center. Simply *Marvel*ous! In*DC*ribable! This four-day, massive comic book convention with over 700 events features people and genres of comics, graphic novels, original art, toys, movie memorabilia, games, trading cards, clothing, comic book characters, creators (get autographs), screenings, film stars, props, shows, and lots more. If a sci-fi, fantasy, and or super hero movie has made it big during the year, or any year, there is paraphernalia and models from that movie. A majority of attendees dress up in costume as their favorite characters - great for people watching and photo ops. The Masquerade, when costumed participants dress up as their favorite comic book characters and compete on Saturday night, is a big event as well, but is geared for older guests. Please note that there are certain elements of adult entertainment at the convention. The edgy components that can make this genre exciting, can also lend itself to scantily clad female models, violent images, etc. Open Wed. night for preview (6pm - 9pm) then Thurs. - Sat., 9:30am - 7pm with other programs available after 7pm); Sun., 9:30am - 5pm. These are the hours for the general showroom. Check the website for film showings and other events. Admission Wed. is $45 for adults, $23 for srs., ages 13 - 17 and active military; Thurs. - Sat., $63 for adults, $31 for srs., et al; Sun., $42 for adults, $21 for srs., et al. Kids 12 and under are free every day with a paid adult ticket. Tickets are only available online and have been known to sell out months in advance. To purchase tickets you must first become a Comic-Con member, which is free.

CONCERTS. See June entry (pg. 717) for details.

FESTIVAL OF ARTS, Laguna Beach. (949) 494-1145 / www.foapom.com, 650 Laguna Canyon Rd. at Irvine Bowl Park. This event runs from July through August, drawing thousands of visitors. More than 140 artisans and craftsmen display their work here - jewelry, wood crafts, paintings, and more - and at the nearby SAWDUST FESTIVAL (pg. 721). Kids are particularly drawn to the ongoing demonstrations, such as print making, water color, and Japanese pottery making. Young, aspiring artists should visit the Art Workshops and Activities where some activities are free and some workshop/classes charge fees to create paintings, paper hat making, printing, mixed media, and more. The Jr. Art Gallery is juried art work of over 300 school children from Orange County. Kids love looking at other kids' work. Bands play continuously. Check the website for a schedule of special events. The festival is open Mon. - Fri., noon - 11:30pm; Sat. - Sun., 10am - 11:30pm. General admission is $10 Mon. - Fri. for adults, $7 for srs. and students 13 and up; $15 Sat. - Sun. for adults, $11 for srs. and kids. Ages 6 - 12 are $5 every day; children 5 and under and Laguna Beach residents are free. Certain activities cost extra. $29 = unlimited admission to Laguna Art-A-Fair, Festival of Arts, and Sawdust Art Festival. Parking is $10 - $15 for the day; or a three-hour-max metered parking is available on the streets, or take a free shuttle from city parking lots on PCH and Laguna Canyon Rd.

FIREWORKS and 4th OF JULY SHOWS. Call the recreation departments at your local parks, or call city hall for information. Note: The Hollywood Bowl, (323) 850-2000 / www.hollywoodbowl.org, features a fireworks spectacular, along with outstanding lively music. Channel Islands Harbor in Oxnard, (805) 985-4852 / www.channelislandsharbor.org, has a whole day of fun planned for the family called Fireworks by the Sea. Pony rides, arts, crafts, rock climbing wall, inflatables, water taxi rides, music, parade, and fireworks are just a few of the events.

FLOWER FIELDS / FLOWER FESTIVAL, Lompoc. See June entry (pg. 717) for details.

FREE FISHING DAY, www.wildlife.ca.gov/Licensing/Fishing/Free-Fishing-Days. One Saturday in July and September there is usually a free fishing day, meaning that no license is required. Call a park or your favorite fishing hole to see if they are participating in this "reel" deal.

FRENCH FESTIVAL, Santa Barbara. (805)-963-8198 / www.frenchfestival.com, 300 W. Alamar at Oak Park. Ooh la! Join French compatriots across the sea in celebrating Bastille Day (the French Revolution) - or come for the fun of it. Enjoy crepes, decadent pastries, French bread, quiche and escargot (don't tell the kids their more common name) at sidewalk cafes with Parisian ambiance. Continuous, free entertainment on three stages include the Cancan, Moroccan belly dancers, grand opera, Cajun and classical groups, folk dancing, jazz, and cabaret music. Look for artists wearing berets while painting at their easels, as well as mimes, jugglers, accordion players, puppet shows, and storytellers strolling the fair grounds. Kids will also enjoy the large replica of the Eiffel Tower, the classic car show, the poodle parade on Sunday evening, and the wading pool at the park. C'est magnifique! Open Sat. - Sun., 11am - 7pm. Free admission and parking.

GREEK FESTIVAL, Santa Barbara. (805) 7683-4491 / www.santabarbaragreekfestival.org, 300 W. Alamar at Oak Park. Come to my big fat Greek festival - well, it's not mine, but it is one of the largest Greek festivals around. Saint Barbara Greek Orthodox Church hosts this party. Baklava, shish-kabob, stuffed grape leaves, gyros, music, authentic Grecian dances, folk dance lessons and demonstrations, and lots of entertainment await festival goers. Open Sat. - Sun. 11am - 7pm. Admission and parking are free.

HOLY SPIRIT FESTIVAL, Artesia. (562) 865-4693 / www.artesiades.org, 11903 Ashworth Ave. at the D.E.S. Plaza. Held for eight days in July, Sunday to Monday, this four-day event celebrates several elements of the Portuguese culture. On Sunday, a grand religious procession is followed by marching bands, food booths (including a free lunch or dinner for every visitor), Mass, and entertainment. Monday night is the three-hour culmination of the festival with bloodless bullfights put on by professional matadors. (Velcro patches are worn by the bull to hold the Velcro tipped spears, but the danger to the matadors still remains.) The festival hours are Fri., 7pm - midnight (which includes the crowning of the festival queen, and then it's mostly a dance); Sat., 5pm - midnight (includes Mass, concert, and dancing); Sun., 11am - midnight; Mon., 6pm - 9pm. Admission is free, except on Mon., when admission is $25 for adults; children 8 and under are free.

INSECT AND LADYBUG FESTIVAL, Encinitas. (760) 436-3036 / www.sdbgarden.org, 230 Quail Gardens Dr. at San Diego Botanic Gardens. How about a bug cookie? Or, maybe bug jewelry? This weekend fair also offers live insects and snakes on display, plus crafts, story time, nature walks at the gardens, as well as everything else that could bug guests. Other live animals, such as snakes, rabbits, owls, and sometimes an anteater or porcupine, come for show and tell, too. See SAN DIEGO BOTANIC GARDEN (pg. 513). Open Sat. - Sun., 9am - 5pm. Admission allows you to walk around the gardens, as well - $14 for adults; $10 for srs. and students; children 12 and under and active military are free. Discount coupons are available online. Parking is $2.

INTERNATIONAL SPEEDWAY, Costa Mesa. See May entry (pg. 712) for details.

KINGSMEN SHAKESPEARE FESTIVAL, Thousand Oaks. See June entry ((pg. 719) for details.

LOTUS FESTIVAL, Los Angeles. (231) 485-5027 or (213) 485-1310 / www.laparks.org, Park Ave. and Glendale Blvd. at Echo Park. A blend of Asian and Pacific Island cultures celebrate the symbolism of the lotus flower, which represents divine creative power and purity. All of this at an old-LA. neighborhood park! The park contains a lake filled with an abundance of these flowers in bloom. What a beautiful sight! The lotus stay in bloom until late summer. The two-day festival also usually incorporates music, traditional food, martial arts exhibitions, Polynesian dancing, origami demonstrations, fireworks, dragon-boat races, ceremonial tea at the Teahouse and children's arts and crafts. One-hour pedal boat and swan boats (pedal boats that look like swans) rentals are available at the boathouse via Wheel Fun Rentals. Swan boats are $11 for each adult per hour; $6 for each child. Pedal boats that hold up to four people are $25 an hour. The festival is open Sat. - Sun., noon - 9pm Admission is free, although some activities cost.

MCGRATH FAMILY FARMS, Camarillo. See March entry (pg. 704) for details.

MOONLIGHT STAGE PRODUCTIONS, Vista. See June entry (pg. 719) for details.

MORRELL NUT & BERRY FARM, Solvang. See June entry (pg. 719) for details.

MOVIE NIGHT / OUTDOOR FAMILY FILMS. See June entry (pg. 719) for details.

MOVIES. See June entry (pg. 719) for details.

MUD MANIA, Long Beach. (562) 206-2040 / www.rancholoscerritos.org, 4600 Virginia Rd. at Rancho Los Cerritos. Get down and dirty at this one-day event. Stomp around in an adobe mud pit, make real adobe bricks, participate in mod relay races, sculpt a clay pot, join in on archeological adventures, and help whitewash the adobe oven. Tip: Bring change of clothing and towels - shoes are required. Refreshments and live musical entertainment round out the day. Open Sun., 12:30pm - 4:30pm. Admission is $7 for adults; $5 for ages 12 and under.

NATIONAL DAY OF THE AMERICAN COWBOY, Norco. (951)270-5632 / www.norco.ca.us, 3737 Crestview at George Ingalls Equestrian Event Center. Tenderfoots and real cowboys enjoy celebrating America's Western heritage with chuck wagon races, pony rides (of course), a petting zoo, cowchip throwing contest, chariot races, Mane Attraction equestrian drill team performances, vendors (if you forgot your cowboy duds you can buy them here!) and Kids Corral with crafts, panning for "gold", stick horse races, kids boot scrambles and a jr. bull riders rodeo. They will have mutton bustin and bull riding during the main event of the rodeo. Also enjoy the obstacle course, speed barrels, bandit shoot-out and at 5pm the grand entrance of the presentation of flags from all 50 states presented by riders on horseback. Sat. - gates open at 3pm and the main event begins at 5pm. Admission is free. Parking is $5.

OLD FORT MACARTHUR DAYS, San Pedro. (310) 548-2631 / www.ftmac.org, 3601 S. Gaffey St. at Angels Gate Park and Fort MacArthur Museum. Multi-period military encampments, set up chronologically, and reenactments, representing time periods from ancient days to modern times, are here on the weekend following the 4th of July weekend. The first event is the Parade of Troops. Observers can mingle with the soldiers and ask questions about their lives, including Roman legionnaires who are in full regalia re-creating a garrison camp circa A.D. 130 - 160. Reenactments of historic military skirmishes can include the Indian wars, the Calvary, both World Wars, and/or the Korean War. There are also marching drills, rifle-loading drills, and firing demonstrations. (It gets loud!) On Sunday, some cannons are shot, too. (More loudness!) Military vehicles are also on the grounds. Bring a sack lunch or purchase food from the vendors. See FORT MACARTHUR MUSEUM - ANGEL'S GATE PARK (pg. 109) for more details. Open Sat. - Sun., 10am - 4pm, with skirmishes throughout the day. Admission per day is $15. This includes entrance to the museum, as well.

ORANGE COUNTY FAIR, Costa Mesa. (714) 708-1500 / www.ocfair.com, 88 Fair Dr. at the Orange County Fairgrounds. This huge, twenty-one-day event is great fun for the whole family. There are lots of carnival rides and games; rodeos (that last a few hours); acrobats; headliner concerts; speedway racing; farm animals, featured in shows and races, and to pet; craft booths; exhibits; demonstrations, such as the firefighters combat challenge; and, of course great food. Each day brings new attractions and events. There is so much to see and do that one day might just not be enough! Call or check the website for information on discount days offered during the fair and for the calendar of special events. Open Wed. - Fri., noon - midnight; Sat. - Sun., 11am - midnight; closed Mon. and Tues. Admission Wed. - Fri., $12 for adults; $7 for srs. and ages 6 - 12; children 5 and under are free; Sat. - Sun., $14 for adults; other prices are the same. Multi-day passes are available. Discount tickets are available online before the fair opens. Parking is $10 - cash only. Most shows cost extra.

PAGEANT OF THE MASTERS, Laguna Beach. (800) 487-3378 - box office; (949) 494-1145 / www.foapom.com, 650 Laguna Canyon Rd. at Irvine Bowl Park. For over 85 years this masterful event runs from July through August, drawing thousands of visitors. The fantastic Pageant of the Masters is comprised of an enormous cast (over 250 participants) in full makeup and costume who pose and re-create live "pictures" of well-known art works, both classic and contemporary, with a different theme each year. Note that some of the live art works contain nudity (i.e. real, semi-naked bodies). Each ninety-second picture is accompanied by a narration and full orchestral music. Tip: Bring binoculars to see the art/people closer up. Note that it is right down the street, and held at the same time, as the FESTIVAL OF ARTS (FESTIVAL OF ARTS (pg. 723, 728)). This one-and-a-half-hour production is staged nightly at 8:30pm. Tickets range between $15 - $272 per person, depending on date and seating location, plus a $6 per ticket service fee.

PCPA THEATERFEST, Solvang. See June entry (pg. 640, 720) for details.

PEACH PICKING. Sweet, succulent, and juicy - only freshly-picked peaches taste like this. Usually ripe mid-July through early October, contact the following orchards for peaches: •M&M Peach Ranch, (661) 724-1398 @ 48745 Three Points Road, Lake Hughes. Peaches and cherries can be picked, usually, Fri. - Sun., 9am - 5pm (other days by appointment). •Youngblood Farm, (661) 944-5823 at 7624 East Avenue U in Littlerock. This farm offers fourteen varieties of peaches and two of apples. It is open July through the beginning of November, Sat. - Sun., 8am - 2pm. Call as they may be open other hours. • BRIAN RANCH AIRPORT U-PICK ORCHARD (pg. 716). Also check www.pickyourown.org for more orchards.

PEARSON PARK AMPHITHEATER, Anaheim. See June entry (pg. 720) for details.

PIRATE DAY, Ventura. (805) 642-8538 / www.venturaharborvillage.com, 1500 Spinnaker Dr. at Ventura Harbor Village. This two-day annual festival features pirate reenactors, strolling musicians, a treasure hunt ($3), knot tying and a pirate costume contest. Arrrrr you going to the festival? Of course you arrrrr! Sat., 11 - 4; Sun. 11am - 4pm. Free, but bring spending money.

RAMONA COUNTRY FAIR, Ramona. (760) 789-1311 / www.ramonachamber.com, Aqua Ln. and 5th St. Now this is a good, old-fashioned county fair aided by a rural setting. State fair contests are held with ribbons and prizes in canning, baked goods, science projects, photography, arts and crafts, animal showings, and more. Carnival rides, live entertainment (including a Wild West show), pie and watermelon eating contest, martial arts demonstrations, vendors, food, and crafts are all part of a *fairly* good day! Note that it is hot here, so bring water and sunscreen. Open Thurs., 5pm - 10pm; Fri., 5pm - 11pm; Sat. 11am - 11pm; Sun. 11am - 10pm. General admission is free. Ride wristbands are $20. (Pre-sale prices are cheaper.)

RASPBERRY PICKING, Oak Glen and Moorpark. The tastiest fruits are ones that have just been harvested. Raspberries are usually ripe from mid-July to mid-October. Here is a website - www.oakglen.net. - and a few places to call in the Oak Glen area: Los Rios Rancho - (909) 797-1005 / www.losriosrancho.com; Riley's Apple Farm and Log Cabin - (909) 797-4061 / www.rileysapplefarm.com; Los Rios Rancho / Riley's Frontier - (909) 790-2364 / www.rileysfrontier.com; Riley's Farm -(909) 797-7534 / www.rileysfarm.com; and Snow Line Orchard - (909) 256-0405 / www.snowlineorchard.com. In Ventura County in Moorpark, call Underwood Family Farms at (805) 529-3690 / www.underwoodfamilyfarms.com. The above entries are also listed in the main section of the book. A great website for finding fruit picking locations all over Southern California is www.pickyourown.org.

REDLANDS BOWL, Redlands. See June entry (pg. 720) for details.

REDLANDS THEATRE FESTIVAL, Redlands. (909) 792-0562 / www.rtfseason.com, corner of Highland and Cajon in Prospect Park. This outdoor festival has been running for more than 30 years. Each season, that goes the second week of July to the third week of August, features five plays in repertory. Past shows have been *Nunsense, Twelfth Night, Forever Plaid* and *Man of La Mancha*. The intimate theater sits outside in Prospect Park, and although the festival is in the middle of summer, the evening show times make for more comfortable viewing. The parking is a little way from the theatre which is up a hill, but there is a free tram available for those who want to ride. Guests are encouraged to come early and enjoy a picnic dinner on the grass surrounding the theatre. Note: while most shows are family appropriate, check out any show that you aren't familiar with before bringing kids. Shows start at 8:30pm. Complementary tram service begins at 6:30pm. Admission is $21 for all seats.

SANTA BARBARA COUNTY FAIR, Santa Maria. (805) 925-8824 / www.santamariafairpark.com, 937 S. Thornburg at the Santa Maria Fairpark. Have some family fun at this five-day county fair with the petting zoo; agricultural and livestock exhibits; train rides; top-name entertainment; carnival rides; a Fair Queen Pageant; dancing; booths; Destruction Derby; a rodeo; and much much more. The fair hours are daily, noon - 10pm; the carnival is open until midnight. Admission is $12 for adults; $8 ages 6 - 11; children 5 and under are free. Pre-sale tickets and season passes are available at a discount. Carnival wristbands area $35. Admission to the Destruction Derby is $12 for general seating. Parking is $7 before 6pm; $10 after 6pm.

SANTA BARBARA NATIONAL HORSE SHOW, Santa Barbara. (805) 687-0766 or (626) 390-8918 / www.earlwarren.com, Calle Real and Las Positas Rd. at the Earl Warren Showgrounds. *Neigh* doubt about it - this is one of the nation's most highly-regarded horse shows. It takes place on two consecutive, four-day weekends in July. Classes and events include champion hunters and jumpers; American saddle bred; Hackney ponies harnessed to their show buggies; walking horses that strut their stuff; and a Western Horse show. Check the website for a schedule of events. Admission is free.

SAWDUST FESTIVAL, Laguna Beach. See June entry (pg. 721) for details.

SHAKESPEARE BY THE SEA. See June entry (pg. 721) for details.

SOUTH BAY GREEK FESTIVAL, Redondo Beach. (310) 540-2434 / www.sbgreekfestival.com, 722 Knob Hill at St. Katherine's. Held the first weekend of the month, this thirty-five-year old annual ethnic and religious festival recreates the atmosphere of a Greek fishing village with costumed participants, live Greek music and dancing, fresh-baked pastries, cultural arts and crafts, and food booths. A small kiddie area is on the premises, too. Tours of the church offering insights into Greek Orthodox traditions and Byzantine iconography are also given. I don't know - it's all Greek to me! Open Fri., 5pm - 10pm; Sat., noon - 10pm; Sun., noon - 9pm. Admission is $2 for adults; $1 for srs.; children 11 and under are free. Check on the website for coupons. Free parking.

STARLIGHT BOWL SUMMER CONCERT SERIES. Burbank. (818) 328-5300 / www.starlightbowl.com, 1249 Lockheed View Dr. Warm summer nights, music wafting through the air, surrounded by family and friends - this is the scene for summer concerts at the bowl. The concerts run the range of musical interests, so check the schedule to see who's playing. Bring a picnic, or purchase food from the indoor cafe or outdoor food court. The season starts with a 4th of July concert (and fireworks - this show is more) and continues through mid-August. Concerts are given on Sat. and Sun. from 6:30pm - 8:30pm. Parking opens at 4:30pm; gates at 5:30pm. Admission is $15 for adults; $10 for srs. and ages 3 - 12. Parking is $8 - cash only.

SUNSET LUAU ON MISSION BAY, San Diego. See June entry (pg. 475) for details.

TANAKA FARMS WATERMELON TOURS, Irvine. (949) 653-2100 / www.tanakafarms.com, 5380¾ University Dr. This thirty-acre farm grows all sorts of wonderful crops and offers a variety of tours. This tour includes a guided wagon ride around the working farm, learning about nutrition, tasting select fruits and veggies, and finishing up in the watermelon patch to pick your own. The stand sells pre-picked fresh produce, or you can pick most of the seasonal crops yourself. No reservation needed for public weekend tours, which are every hour on the half hour from 9:30am to

2:30pm. You must call and reserve a time for weekday school and group tours. The farm and stand is open Mon. - Sun., 9am - 5pm. The tour is $18 per person; children 2 and under free.

TOUCH A TRUCKX, San Diego. (858) 621-3473 / www.touchatrucksd.com, 5975 Village Center Loop Rd. at Pacific Trails Middle School. For 10 years strong, Beat Nb Southern California organization has been raising funds to cure cancer for kids via Touch a TruckX, giving kids (and adults) the opportunity to toot their own horn; well, the horn of a bunch of different kinds of trucks and other vehicles. Climb in and pretend to start the engines of race cars; classic cars; construction trucks (concrete mixers, trash trucks, dump trucks); military vehicles (NAVY Seals boat, Humvees, Homeland security); emergency vehicles (fire engine, helicopter); transportation vehicles (stagecoach, UPS, big rig); and more. Of course there is some live entertainment, vendors, food and some other fun things to see and do. Sat., 11am - 3pm. $15 per person; children under 1 are free. Buy tickets in advance as they do sell out.

VANS U.S. OPEN OF SURFING, Huntington Beach. (424) 653-1900 / www.huntingtonbeachevents.com; www.vansusopenofsurfing.com, Huntington Beach Pier. For over a week, thousands (350,000 or so) flock to the beach as the crowd gets its fill of high competition, world class games. Come see the U.S. Open of Surfing (men's, women's, and jr's); pro beach volleyball; BMX; and skateboarding competitions, plus moto cross demonstrations, concert stages, beach-style fashion shows, and the village (with over 70 vending booths). Wear sunblock. Check the website for a complete schedule of events, which are free to spectators.

VENTURA COUNTY FAIR, Ventura. (805) 648-3376 / www.venturacountyfair.org, 10 W. Harbor Blvd. at Seaside Park. This major event, sometimes held in August, is a week and a half long. The fair offers lots of carnival rides, plus rodeos; pig races; a petting zoo; pony rides; livestock and equestrian events; on-going, first-class entertainment and concerts; and several buildings that have arts and crafts for sale, flower shows, fine arts, gems and minerals, and vendor demonstrations. Whew! The fair is open Mon. - Sun., 11am - 11pm. Carnival opens at noon and closes between 11pm and midnight. A fireworks show is on the weekends nights. Admission is $12 for adults; $9 for srs. and ages 6 - 12; children 5 and under are free. Rides and certain activities cost extra. Check the website for discount days and coupons. Parking is $10.

VISTA CIVIL WAR REENACTMENT, Vista. See March entry (pg. 705) for details.

WILL GEER THEATRICUM BOTANICUM, Topanga. See June entry (pg. 722) for details.

YOUTH OUTDOOR SAFARI DAY, Corona. (951) 735-7981 / www.youthsafariday.com, 14995 River Rd. at Mike Raahauge's Shooting Complex. For practice before going on a real safari, to infuse kids with a love for the outdoors, and to introduce or sharpen their skills in recreational shooting, come to Safari Day. Participants can try archery, BB guns, paintball games, and laser shots; go kayaking; make game calls; paint duck decoys; walk through the Sensory Safari Van; and watch shooting exhibitions. (The last few years members of the Olympic Shooting Team have participated.) If that's not enough, kids can fish, chat with mountain men and cowboys in an encampment-type setting, see hawks and falcons up close, pet animals at the petting zoo and enjoy being outside. The events begin Sat. at 8am sharp. (Preregistration is highly recommended - check the website for forms). The day ends at 3pm. $14 per person for pre-purchased tickets; $20 at the gate; children under 2 are free.

- AUGUST -

ADVENTURE PLAYGROUND, Huntington Beach. See June entry (pg. 715) for details.

ANTELOPE VALLEY FAIR AND ALFALFA FESTIVAL, Lancaster. (661) 948-6060 / www.avfair.com, 2551 W. Ave. H at the fair grounds. This ten day affair has all the good stuff - carnival rides ($35 for unlimited rides); lots of livestock events; a parade with decorated cars and trucks and marching bands; demonstrations from a variety of vendors, plus booths, and great food; and entertainment, including monster truck demonstrations, headlining concerts, and more. County fairs are a once-a-year treat. Open daily, 4pm - midnight. General admission is $11 for adults; $8 for srs. and ages 6 - 11; active military and dependents are free as are children 5 and under are with a paid adult. Check the website for discount tickets. Parking is $10, cash only.

APPLE PICKING - JULIAN, Julian. There are a few U-Pic apple orchards left in the Julian area that are open in season. Here are four: **Volcan Valley Apple Farm**, 1284 Julian Orchards Dr., (760) 302-4574. The largest orchard in Julian with 7,000 trees of seven varieties, including the Gravenstein, Red Delicious and Granny Smith. There are picnic tables here, too. Open Thurs. - Mon., 9am - 5pm. **Apple Starr Orchard,** 1020 Julian Orchards Dr., (760) 305-2169 / www.apple-starr.com. Certified organic apple and pear orchard that's open Sat. - Sun., 10am - 5pm. Open for groups of 15 or more Mon., 9am - noon; Fri., 1pm - 5pm. **Apples and Art,** 1052 Julian Orchards Dr., (760) 310-6368 / www.applesandartorchards.com. It is open only for groups of 20 or more, yet that includes not just picking the apples, but learning about them and even making fresh cider. Great for students, scouts, adults - any group. **Peacefield**

Orchard, 3803 Wynola Rd., (855) 936-2775 /peacefieldorchard.org. No pesticides or chemicals are used. Open on weekends, unless you have a group of 10 or more, then with a $50 minimum, you can take a tour, too that dispenses info on how to grow apples and history of the area. People can purchase pre-picked pecks at less per peck than personally picking them (say that five times fast), but then you lose out on the joy of actually picking the apples. The season is short, but tasty - it begins towards the end of August and most of the crop is gone by the end of October.

ARTWALK NTC @ LIBERTY STATION, San Diego. (619) 615-1090 / www.artwalksandiego.org, 2751 Dewey Road in Ingram Plaza. This fine art festival brings 200 visual artists/vendors from a variety of mediums, plus live music featuring. In addition, KidsWalk offers other nearby art destinations for kids to try their hand at various, free interactive "ARTivities" set to inspire their inner artist to bloom. See MISSION FEDERAL ARTWALK (pg. 708) for a similar, but much larger, event in April. Sat., 10am - 6pm; Sun., 10am - 5pm. Free Admission

BARONA POWWOW, Lakeside. (619) 443-6612 / www.baron.nsn.gov, 1095 Barona Road, Barona Baseball Field on the Barona Indian Reservation. This three-day event, held on Labor Day weekend, showcases more than 300 Native Americans from across the country competing in traditional Tribal dancing. In addition to beautiful regalia and dancing, spectators will also be able to enjoy the Hand Drum and other special contests, singing and music, Gourd Dancing, authentic Native American cuisine and exquisite handcrafted arts and jewelry. Fri., 6pm - 11pm; Sat.-Sun., 1pm - 11pm; Fri.-Sun., Grand Entry - 7pm. Free admission & camping on a first come, first served basis.

BIG BEAR AIR FAIR, Big Bear City. (909) 585-3219 / www.bigbearcityairport.com, 501 Valley Blvd. at the Big Bear Airport. This bi-annual event (every odd year) takes to the skies for one day. Skydivers make two jumps, at 9am and noon. Keep looking up as vintage aircraft come in for a landing. Back on the ground, there are vintage, static aircraft on display; possibly Blackhawk or Huey helicopters; a U.S. Forestry Service water drop; classic cars; flight simulators; and activities for kids like a bounce house, climbing wall, and inflatable slide. Barbecue food, vendors, and community and military booths complete this fair. Open Sat., 9am - 3pm. Free.

BIG BEAR RENAISSANCE FAIRE, Fawnskin. (909) 237-0448 / www.bbvrsinc.org, 39115 Rim of the World Dr. Where hail ye from? Perhaps 16th-century England, as the participants' dress indicates. Merry maids, gentlemen, wenches, knights, and good citizens roam the shire and encampment as the Queen presides over her court. Indeed, for only $10 per person you may join Queen Anne Bolynn who hosts special teas each day with various guests such as the Fairy Queen, Queens' of the Gypsy's, Pirate's, Scots, Wilds and others. The faire is comprised of four stages of shows; archery tournaments; knights jousting (at 1pm and 4pm daily); sword fighting; gypsies belly dancing; Shakespeare's plays presented in shortened versions; birds of prey (from Moonridge Animal Zoo); jugglers; and wandering minstrels. A children's area is set up like a midsummer fairy forest with special activities. Vendors sell pewter steins, potions, Renaissance clothing, swords, and more. Note that bawdy songsters abound. Open first three weekends in August, Sat. - Sun., 10am - 6pm. Admission during the week is $25 per day for adults; $18 for srs., students, and ages 6 - 13. Sat. - Sun., $46 for adults; $34 for srs, et al. Children 5 and under are free. Parking is $5

BIG WORLD FUN FAMILY SERIES AT THE FORD, Hollywood. See July entry (pg. 722) for details.

BRIAN RANCH AIRPORT U-PICK ORCHARD, Llano. See June entry (pg. 716) for details.

CAMARILLO AIR AND CAR SHOW, Camarillo. (805) 419-3530; (805) 389-1070 - helicopter ride info; (480) 217-1635 - airplane ride info / www.wingsovercamarillo.com, 555 Airport Way at Camarillo Airport. Fly bys in the morning and demonstration flights, usually in the afternoon, are highlights of this air show. Another high-flying adventure is taking a morning flight, yourself, in a AH-1 Bell Cobra (for $350 per person) or in a helicopter ($50 for adults; $40 for ages 12 and under). Other exhibits and activities include WWII warbirds; vintage aircraft; antique farm equipment; over eighty home-built airplanes; experimental aircraft; classic and custom cars; motorcycles; WWII re-enactment camp; food vendors; and a kids area with a bounce, a maze, and more. Don't miss touring the COMMEMORATIVE AIR FORCE MUSEUM (WWII Aviation Heritage Museum) (pg. 677) which is on the airfield. Bring a chair and umbrella. Open Sat. - Sun., gates open at 9am and close at 4:30pm. The air show starts at noon, but vintage plane fly bys start around 9am. The parade of cars is at 11:30am. The Sat. concert is 5pm - 7pm. Admission is $20 for adults; $10 for ages 6 - 12; children 5 and under are free.

COLORADO LAGOON MODEL BOAT SHOP, Long Beach. See June entry (pg. 717) for details.

CONCERTS. See June entry (pg. 717) for details.

FESTIVAL OF ARTS, Laguna Beach. See July entry (pg. 723, 728) for details.

FLOWER FIELDS / FLOWER FESTIVAL, Lompoc. See June entry (pg. 717) for details.

INTERNATIONAL CLOWN WEEK, San Diego. (619) 282-9668 / www.sandiegoallstarclowns.weebly.com; www.internationalclownweek.org. Don't stop clowning around! The San Diego All Star Clowns performs the first week of August in several locations throughout San Diego County. The public is invited to some of these funny functions. Call or check the website for place and time.

INTERNATIONAL SPEEDWAY, Costa Mesa. See May entry (pg. 712) for details.

LA HABRA CORN FESTIVAL, La Habra. (562) 889-2805; (562) 905-9792 / www.lahabracornfestival.com, 201 N. Cypress St. Not to sound corny, but I when I heard about this festival I was all ears. Saturday starts off with a parade at 9:30am, complete with bands, equestrian groups, floats, and even a few celebrities. This is followed by a carnival with rides, games, music, craft booths, and food, especially buttery corn on the cob. Shucks, I think you ought to come to this country fair. Open the first weekend in August, Fri., 5:30pm - 11pm; Sat., 11am - 11pm; Sun., noon - 8pm. Admission is free, but rides and some activities cost money.

MANHATTAN BEACH OPEN, Manhattan Beach. (949) 679-3599 / avp.com/event/avp-manhattan-beach-open, just south of the Manhattan Beach Pier. Called the "Wimbledon of Beach Volleyball", this tournament features top players from all over the world with qualifiers, semi-finals and finals being the main draws. Thurs. - Sat., 8am - 6pm; Sun., 8am - 5pm. Admission is free.

MOONLIGHT STAGE PRODUCTIONS, Vista. See June entry (pg. 719) for details.

MORRELL NUT & BERRY FARM, Solvang. See June entry (pg. 719) for details.

MOVIE NIGHT / OUTDOOR FAMILY FILMS. See June entry (pg. 719) for details.

MOVIES. See June entry (pg. 719) for details.

NATIONAL PARKS - FREE ENTRANCE DAYS. See January entry (pg. 696) for details.

NISEI WEEK JAPANESE FESTIVAL, Los Angeles. (213) 687-7193 / www.niseiweek.org, 244 S. San Pedro St. in Room 303. In Little Tokyo. This two weekend festival, the biggest Japanese festival of the year, takes place at several locations throughout Little Tokyo. A sampling of events and exhibits include martial arts demonstrations, traditional Japanese dancing, games, arts and crafts, Sumo wrestling, hoops tournament, fashion show, Taiko drumming (on huge drums), tofu tasting, calligraphy, bonsai arrangements, and a grand parade with floats held on first Sun. of the event at 4pm. Most of the activities and programs occur on the weekends, Sat. - Sun., 11am - 7pm. Check the website for a schedule of events. Admission is free, although some activities cost.

NORCO MOUNTED POSSE PRCA RODEO, Norco. (951) 371-1204 / www.norcoposse.com, 3737 Crestview Ave. at George Ingall's Equestrian Event Center. This PRCA (Professional Rodeo Cowboys Association) event not only offers bull riding, barrel racing, bareback and bronco riding, team roping, and steer wrestling but also has cowboy dances, music, vendors, and food. On Sun. there is free Cowboy church in the stands at 10am. Fri. and Sat., gates open at 5pm, rodeo at 7:30; Sun., gates open at 3pm, Challenged Children's Rodeo at 3:30pm; professional rodeo at 5:30pm. Fri., $18 for ages 9 and up; children 8 and under free; Sat., $23 per person, children 3 and under free; Sun., $12 per person, $10 for srs. Parking is $8.

OLD SPANISH DAYS FIESTA, Santa Barbara. (805) 962-8101 / www.oldspanishdays-fiesta.org, multiple locations throughout Santa Barbara. This major five-day Santa Barbara party is kicked off Wednesday night with "Little Fiesta" at Mission Santa Barbara where a program of early Californian, Spanish and Mexican song and dance features dancers, clicking castanets, and more. Bring lawn chairs. A highlight of the Fiesta is the Friday parade. Participants include the queen and her court; mounted color guards; marching bands; colorfully-costumed equestrian riders; numerous antique carriages and wagons; Native American groups; Spanish Colonial reenactors; costumed dancers; and historical figures on elaborate floats decorated with fresh flowers. The parade begins at the corner of Cabrillo Blvd. and Castillo St. at noon. Grab a spot for free or get a reserved seat at $18 per person. On Saturday, at 10am, the Children's Parade has niñas and niños in fiesta attire parade down State Street in home-constructed wagons and carts that are pushed and pulled by dogs, parents, and siblings. Open-air market places (in De La Guerra Plaza in downtown Santa Barbara and other locations) feature music, dancing, and authentic Mexican and Spanish food. The carnival, located at Mackenzie Park, is open 11am to 11pm daily with rides, midway games, and attractions. Other fair features include a weekend craft fair (Sat., 10am - 6pm; Sun., 10am - 5pm) and a tribute to Vaqueros (i.e. California's cowboys) at the Earl Warren Showgrounds (Sun., 2pm) via afternoon and nighttime rodeos (Thurs. - Sat. at 7:30pm) with bull and bronc riding, barrel racing, team penning, steer wrestling and stock horse classes. Watch cowkids do some mutton bustin', and wild cow milking, too. Call (805) 688-5093 / www.sbfiestarodeo.com for more information regarding the rodeo events which run Thurs. - Sun. There is admission charged to some of the performances, but there are many free events as well. Rodeos are $25 - $35 for adults; $10 - $15 for ages 11 and under. Nightlife at the sunken gardens of the County Court House showcases a free variety shows of mariachis, flamenco dancers, Mexican folklorico dancers in colorful regional costumes, and other Latin-flavored music. Bring blankets for lawn seating. Again, many of the events are free.

PAGEANT OF THE MASTERS, Laguna Beach. See July entry (pg. 725, 729) for details.

PCPA THEATERFEST, Solvang. See June entry (pg. 640, 720) for details.

PEACH PICKING. See July entry (pg. 725) for details.

PEAR PICKING, Oak Glen. More flavorful than store bought, Asian and Bartlett pears are usually ready for picking the beginning of August to October. Check out: • (pg. 716), Sat. - Sun., 8am - 2pm. •Rileys Farm, (909) 790-TIME (8463) or (909) 797-7534 / www.rileysfarm.com, at 12261 S. Oak Glen Blvd. in Oak Glen is open Mon. - Fri., 10am - 4pm.; Sat., 9am - 4pm. U-Pick is Sat., 10am - 4pm. Check out Rileys Farm in the main section of the book, too. •Apple Starr Orchard, 760) 305-2169 /www.apple-starr.com at 1020 Julian Orchard Dr. in Julian. It's open Sat. - Sun., 10am - 5pm for pear picking with varieties of Bartletts, Comice, Anjous, and Bosc; and apple varieties of Jonagold, Granny, Fuji, Gala, Red Delicious.

PEARSON PARK AMPHITHEATER, Anaheim. See June entry (pg. 720) for details.

RANCHO MISSION VIEJO PRCA RODEO, San Juan Capistrano. / www.rmvrodeo.com, 30753 La Pata Ave. at Oaks Blenheim Rancho Mission Viejo Riding Park. Ride 'em cowboy - the rodeo's back in town! See bareback riding, saddle bronc riding, bull riding, tie-down roping, team roping, steer wrestling, rodeo clowns, and more at this two-day, large purse (i.e. lots of prize money!) rodeo. There is also a vendor area with shopping, games (like a mechanical bull and rock climbing), and food. Gates open Sat. at 1pm, the rodeo begins at 4pm, and a concert starts at 6pm. Gates open Sun. at 11:30am and the rodeo begins at 1:30pm. Admission is $30 for adults; $10 for ages 4 - 12; children 3 and under are free. Parking is $10 - cash only.

RASPBERRY PICKING. See July entry (pg. 726) for details.

SAN CLEMENTE FIESTA MUSIC FESTIVAL, San Clemente. (949) 492-1131 / www.scchamber.com, 100 & 200 block of Avenida Del Mar This fiesta, held for over 60+ years!!, has everything - food and games booths, stages of live entertainment, contests, a salsa challenge, arts and craft exhibits, a business exposition, children's activities and a classic car & motorcycle show. Second Sun., 9am - 7pm. Free admission and parking.

SAWDUST FESTIVAL, Laguna Beach. See June entry (pg. 721) for details.

SHAKESPEARE BY THE SEA. See June entry (pg. 721) for details.

STARLIGHT BOWL SUMMER CONCERT SERIES, Burbank. See July entry (pg. 726) for details.

SUNSET LUAU ON MISSION BAY, San Diego. See June entry (pg. 475) for details.

TEHACHAPI MOUNTAIN FESTIVAL, Tehachapi. (661) 822-4180 / www.tehachapimountainfestival.com; www.tehachapiprorodeo.com; www.thunderonthemountain.net. Traditionally held the third weekend of August, this event, running for 53+ years, takes place throughout Tehachapi. It includes a pancake breakfast, PRCA rodeo, an arts and crafts show, parade, a carnival, 5K & 10K runs, Thunder on the Mountain Car and Truck Show ($40), food, live entertainment and more. Call or see the website for times, places, events and prices. Fri., 6pm - 11pm (the rodeo starts at 7pm); Sat., 6:30am - 11pm (the parade is at 10am; the rodeo starts at 6pm); Sun., 9am - 9pm. General admission is free. Rodeo admission is $17 for adults (at the gate); $15 for srs and ages 5 - 13; children 4 and under are free.

TIKI BEACH FESTIVAL, Belmont Shore. (562) 477-6820 / www.alfredosbeachclub.com, 5101 E Ocean Blvd. Like taking a tropical vacation, come experience hundreds of Polynesian dancers, musicians, and fire knife dancers perform on stage while you sample ono' (delicious) Hawaiian food, shop the island marketplace (over 100 vendors), check out a tiki museum, enjoy the kids zone, peruse the arts and crafts, and watch outrigger canoe races and tiki carving. Sat., 9am - 9pm; Sun., 10am - 6pm (with a Sunday 10am church of hula praise and worship). Free admission.

VENTURA COUNTY FAIR, Ventura. See July entry (pg. 727) for details.

WILL GEER THEATRICUM BOTANICUM, Topanga. See June entry (pg. 722) for details.

WORLD BODYSURFING CHAMPIONSHIP, Oceanside. (310) 924-5111 / www.worldbodysurfing.org, 1540 Harbor Drive S. at Oceanside Harbor, near the pier. This two-day event has been happening for over four decades! More than 350 participants, including several from foreign countries, equipped with swim fins are judged on length of ride, style, and tricks such as barrel rolls and somersaults. Contestants must be at least 12 years old to enter. Held Sat., 6:30am - 1pm; the semi-finals and finals are held on Sun., 6:30am - 3pm. Admission to watch is free; $75 to participate.

- SEPTEMBER -

APPLE PICKING - JULIAN, Julian. See August entry (pg. 727) for details.

APPLE PICKING - OAK GLEN, Oak Glen. See the main entry for OAK GLEN / APPLE PICKING (pg. 403). The season runs from mid-September through mid-November.

BANANA FESTIVAL, Port Hueneme. (805) 535-4060 / www.bananaportfest.com, 105 E Port Hueneme Rd. at the Port of Hueneme This festival might a*peel* to you. You will find something here for everyone with live bands, arts and crafts, port tours (boat tours around the Naval Base and/or land tours in a motorcoach - both leave every half hour), educational displays, great food, and, of course, bananas! The kids area features bounce houses, games, a climbing wall and animals. Open Sat., 10am - 5pm. Free admission and parking.

BANNING STAGECOACH DAYS, Banning. / www.stagecoachdays.org, 2107. Victory Street at Dysart Park. Commemorating the city as one of the major stops on the transcontinental stagecoach route, this four-day festival pulls out all the stops and features a carnival, a parade on Sat. at 10am, dances, Old West-themed gun fights and costume competition, living history encampment, crafts, food, and PRCA rodeos (Thurs. and Sun. at 5pm; Fri. and Sat. at 7pm) and a junior rodeo (Sun. at 9am, following cowboy church at 8am). Always weekend after Labor Day, open Thurs., 5pm - 10pm, Fri., 4pm - midnight; Sat., noon - midnight; Sun., 9am - 8pm. General admission is $5; one child 4 and under is free with a paying adult. Rodeos, which include general admission: Thurs. and Sun., $10; Fri. and Sat. $15. Parking is $5.

BATES NUT FARM PUMPKIN PATCH, Valley Center. The Pumpkin Patch opens the end of September. See October entry (pg. 735) for details.

BRIAN RANCH AIRPORT U-PICK ORCHARD, Llano. See June entry (pg. 716) for details.

CABRILLO FESTIVAL, Point Loma. (619) 557-5450 / www.cabrillofestival.org, Ballast Point, Naval Base Point Loma, south end of Rosecrans Street. Journey back in time to commemorate the life and times of Juan Cabrillo, one of the first explorers of California. Partake in a living history encampment as authentically-dressed Spanish soldiers and sailors from the 16th century give history talks and just live their 16th century lives. You can also enjoy colorful folkloric dancing and music; cultural demonstrations; watching a narrated reenactment of Cabrillo's landing at 1pm; observing weaving and knife-making; and sampling food from Mexico, Portugal, Spain, and Native America. See CABRILLO NATIONAL MONUMENT (pg. 495) for more details on the park and museum. Open Sat., 11am - 4pm. Free.

CALICO DAYS, Yermo. (800) TO-CALICO (862-2542) / www.calicotown.com, 36600 Ghost Town Rd. at Calico Ghost Town. During a weekend in September or October, relive Calico's glory days and enjoy music, old prospectors burro run, miner's triathlon, gunfight shows, and more in this 50+ years old festival/celebration. Walk around this living history town itself and enjoy its many attractions. See CALICO GHOST TOWN (pg. 433) for more details. Sat. - Sun., 9am - 5pm. Admission is $10 for adults; $5 for ages 6- 15 years; children 5 and under are free. On-site camping (minimum 2 nights) is $30 - $40 a night (camping for this weekend books up months in advance); $65 a night for cabins.

CALIFORNIA LEMON FESTIVAL IN GOLETA, Goleta. (805) 967-2500 / www.lemonfestival.com, 7050 Phelps Road at Girsch Park. When life gives you lemons, make lemonade, or lemon chicken, lemon meringue pie, lemon cotton candy, and many other puckery creations. Besides citrus-flavored food, enjoy pony rides; moon bounces; mini golf; police and fire safety and action demonstrations; arts and crafts; a classic car and motorcycle show; vending booths; and bands - country, folk, bluegrass, and pop. Open Sat., 10am - 6pm; Sun., 10am - 5pm. Admission is free.

CHALK ART FESTIVAL ON THE PIER, Redondo Beach. (310) 318-0631 / www.redondopier.com, 100 Fisherman's Wharf. Come make your own chalk drawing or just look at everyone else's. The event is free to enter and offers prizes in many categories including professional, family and various age groups. Chalk Art Festival, 12pm-4pm. No fee to register for the chalk drawing contest.

CIVIL WAR DAYS, Huntington Beach. (714) 842-4481 / www.hbhistory.org/civilwar, 7111 Talbert Ave. and Golden West Ave. in Huntington Beach Central Park. Live through the Civil War time period, if only for one weekend. Heralded as one of the best reenactments, come visit with soldiers from the North and South who are authentically dressed in uniform and stay in character throughout the duration. Watch mock battles and wander through the encampments, see historical weapons demonstrations and listen to President Lincoln's Gettysburg Address given honestly, a few times throughout the days. Open 10am - 4pm. Battles (which get really loud) are Sat. at 1:30pm and 4pm; Sun. at 11am and 2pm. Living history demonstrations follow each battle. A twilight concert is at 5:30pm on Sat. Church service is Sun. at 9am. Admission is free.

COIN & COLLECTIBLES EXPO, Long Beach. See January entry (pg. 695) for details.

DANISH DAYS, Solvang. (805) 688-6144 or (800) 468-6765 / www.solvangdanishdays.org; www.solvangusa.com, downtown Solvang Velkommen! Danish Days are good not just for eating Danish (the food, not the people), although you must try the aebleskivers, but to celebrate this colorful heritage with old world customs and pageantry. Expect and enjoy lots of folk dancing demonstrations by costumed participants; music; food; a Kids Korner at Solvang Park with games and shows; craft demonstrations, such as woodcarving, paper cutting, clog painting, and making Christmas ornaments; Viking living history festival and sometimes reenactments; readings from Hans Christian Andersen tales; and everything else Danish that can be packed into this three-day festival. The Sat. parade at 2:30 has decorated floats, equestrian units, traditional dancers and more; and the Sun. children's parade at 2pm features mostly kids parading in costume. Two other note-worthy events that occur at this time are the wonderful PCPA outdoor theater presentations and a (free) visit to the Elverhoj Museum. Look in the SOLVANG (pg. 637) for more things to do while here. Open the third weekend in September, Fri. 4pm - 9pm; Sat., 8:30am - 11pm; Sun., 8:30am - 4:30pm. Free admission to most activities.

E HULA MAU, Long Beach. (619) 991-Mamo (6266); (562) 436-3661 / www.ehulamau.org, 300 E. Ocean Blvd. at the Terrace Theater of the Long Beach Convention Center. Come and treat yourself to an authentically Hawaiian experience that includes hula and chant competitions and other traditional dances and performances; food of the islands; and Polynesian arts & crafts vending booths. The hula is poetry in motion and the competition is both soothing and fun to watch. Ninety-minute cultural workshops, $25 per, are for both traditional and contemporary arts. They include the learning the hula, learning to play the Ukelele, lei-making (out of yarn), learning the Hawaiian vocabulary, and more. Pre-sign up for workshops. The festival and competitions are held the four days of Labor Day weekend, Fri. noon - midnight; Sat., 8am - midnight; Sun., 8am - midnight; Mon., 8am - 11:30. Admission is $25 per day. Parking is $15.

ENGLISH MOTORS AT FAIRBROOK, Fallbrook. (760) 728-0101 / www.englishmotorsatfairbrook.org, 4949 South Mission Rd. at Fairbrook Farms. A unique gathering of fine English motor cars and motor bikes, nestled in the Fallbrook hills at Fairbrook Farms, a beautiful twenty-five acre horse ranch. Along with the 250 cars and motorcycles, there are also food and automotive-related booths. Purchase food or bring your own picnic. Sun., 10am - 3pm. Admission and parking are free.

FALL HARVEST FESTIVAL / PUMPKIN TOURS, Moorpark. (805) 529-3690, 3370 Sunset Valley Rd. at Underwood Family Farms. See October (pg. 736) for details.

FESTIVAL OF CHILDREN, Costa Mesa. (877) 492-KIDS (5437) / www.festivalofchildren.org, 333 Bristol St. at South Coast Plaza. This month-long immersion in arts, culture, and philanthropy involves more than 75 Southern California organizations and local charities. One focal point, is the South Coast Plaza, which has activities and entertainment every weekend during the festival. The events, which mostly occur on the weekends from noon - 4pm, could include musical and dance performances (Irish, ballet, folk, etc.); art displays; guest appearances by celebrities; exotic animal presentations; health information; cultural presentations; storytelling; circus acts; arts and crafts for kids to make; costumed character appearances; and marionette shows - a bonanza of free activity!

FREE FISHING DAY, www.wildlife.ca.gov/Licensing/Fishing/Free-Fishing-Days. One Saturday in July and September there is usually a free fishing day, meaning that no license is required. Call a park or your favorite fishing hole to see if they are participating in this *reel* deal.

GRACEFEST, Palmdale. (661) 942-4111 / www.gracefestav.com, 2723 Rancho Vista Blvd. at the Palmdale Amphitheater. Gracefest presents headline Christian music artists, Christian merchants/vendors and worldwide compassion ministries. The kid's area provides supervised fun, games and activities for the kids. The Prayer Tent offers many exciting speakers and ministries presenting their programs and messages. Note: This is an outdoor event so bring your own blankets, lawn chairs, coolers, and sunscreen. Fri., 4pm - 8pm - worship night; Sat., 1pm -10pm. Admission is free on Fri.; Sat. $30 for adults; $15 ages 11 - 17; $5 ages 6 - 10; ages 5 and under are free. Parking is free.

GREEK FESTIVAL, Cardiff-by-the-Sea. (760) 942-0920 / www.cardiffgreekfestival.com, 3459 Manchester Ave. Park at the adjoining Mira Costa College. Live Greek music and dancing, Greek cuisine, like dolmathes (i.e. stuffed grape leaves), tiropites (cheese pita), Greek caviar dip and baklava, games, a bazaar, a live auction, and craft booths are a few of the goings-on at this weekend festival. Church tours of Saints Constantine and Helen Greek Orthodox Church are given as requested. The festival is Sat., 10am - 10pm; Sun., 11am - 9pm. Admission is $3 for adults; free for children 11 and under. Free parking.

INTERNATIONAL SPEEDWAY, Costa Mesa. See May entry (pg. 712) for details.

IRVINE GLOBAL VILLAGE FESTIVAL, Irvine. (949) 724-6606 / www.cityofirvine.org, 6950 Marine Way at the Orange County Great Park. Go global right here at home where over 100 performances are given on five stages - cultural music, colorful dances, martial arts, and so much more. These are some of the highlights of the Festival! The Festival also features a world of authentic food - try something different, with over seventy restaurants participating, this is a highlight. No, wait - so are the world religious displays; international marketplace; crafts; and Kid's Village. The Village features large inflatables, games, sports, and lots of activities for your worldly child. The festival is Sat., 10am - 6pm. Admission is free.

IRVINE PARK RAILROAD'S PUMPKIN PATCH, Orange. See October entry (pg. 739) for details.

JULIAN GRAPE STOMP FESTA, Julian. (760) 765-1857 / www.visitjulian.com, 1150 Julian Orchards at the Menghini Winery. For one juicy Saturday enjoy a bunch of fun and stomp around in a ton (literally) of grapes - and yes, this means you. Your feet are first sterilized in a vat of vodka and then you can squish the grapes between your toes. (This wine is not sold commercially!) Other activities include listening to Italian bands, dancing, playing Bocce ball (an

Italian lawn game), participating in arts and crafts, and sampling wine (this last part is not for children, obviously). Open 11am - 6pm. Admission is $15 for adults; $5 for ages 6 - 20; bambinos 5 and under are gratis (free).

LIVE OAK CANYON PUMPKIN PATCH, Yucaipa. See October entry (pg. 740) for details.

LOBSTER FESTIVAL, San Pedro / www.lobsterfest.com, check the website for location info "Here lobster, lobster." A Lobster Call is one of the activities at the three-day festival. (Do they really come?) Come to this annual *shellabration* and enjoy great Maine lobsters, plus street performers, which are always entertaining to watch, lots of musical performances, a kid's area with some games and crafts, touring the USS IOWA, and seeing the tall ships add to the fun. Maine lobster meals are 1.25 oz. of lobster, plus lobster rolls, lobster mac and cheese, lobster quesadillas, etc. Other food choices are available, too. Open Fri. - Sun. Check the website for current pictures.

LONG BEACH GREEK FESTIVAL BY THE SEA, Long Beach. (562) 494-8929 / www.lbgreekfest.org, 5761 E. Colorado St. at the Assumption of the Blessed Virgin Mary Greek Orthodox Church. Everything Greek - Greek dance groups; free Greek dance lessons; authentic Greek food and Greek pastries, Greek cooking lessons, snacks, full meals and beverages (food and dancing - Greek staples!); vendor booths; childrens area; carnival rides; and more. Opa! Labor Day Weekend Sat. - Mon., noon - 9pm. Admission $5, Children 12 and under are free.

LOS ANGELES COUNTY FAIR, Pomona. (909) 623-3111 / www.lacountyfair.com, 1101 W. McKinley Ave. at Fairplex. Billed as the world's largest county fair, this four-week event is wonderful (and exhausting). It has lots (and lots) of carnival rides and games, workshops, pig racing, goat and cow milking demonstrations, country contests, headliner concerts, livestock shows, petting zoo, horse-racing, flower and garden shows, music, dancing, booths, fun food (fried Twinkies, anyone?), and several long buildings filled with exhibits and truly unique items and products for sale. Come early and plan to spend the whole day - there is a lot to see and do (and buy!). Teachers - ask about the wonderful free Fairkids field trips!! The fair is open 3 hours earlier than usual for all age student field trippers who learn while doing activities related to agriculture, art, science, literature, California heritage, and life on a real farm. This is offered Wed. - Fri., only, with advanced registration. Supplemental curriculum focuses on particular aspects of the fair, such as animals or history, and allow students to enjoy a free day at the fair (no carnival rides, though!). Call (909) 865-4267 or (909) 865-4075 for more information. Fair hours are Wed., noon - 10pm; Thurs., noon - 11pm; Fri., noon - midnight; Sat., 10am - midnight; Sun., 10am - 10pm. Closed Mon. and Tues., but open Labor Day Mon., 10am - 10pm. Regular admission Wed. - Fri. is $14 for adults; $10 for srs; $8 for ages 6 - 12; children 5 and under are free. Admission Sat., Sun. and Labor Day is $20 for adults; $15 srs.; $12 for ages 6 - 12. Call or check the website for discounts. Certain activities cost extra. Parking is $15.

MOONLIGHT STAGE PRODUCTIONS, Vista. See June entry (pg. 719) for details.

MUSEUM DAY LIVE, www.smithsonianmag.com. On one Saturday in September, *Smithsonian Magazine* sponsors Museum Day. Go to the website and download a ticket good for free admission for two, to several museums in Southern California.

NATIONAL PARKS - FREE ENTRANCE DAYS. See January entry (pg. 696) for details.

OKTOBERFEST, Big Bear. See October entry (pg. 741) for details.

ORANGE COUNTY CHILDREN'S BOOK FESTIVAL, Costa Mesa. (714) 838-4528 - festival info / www.kidsbookfestival.com, 2701 Fairview Dr. at Orange Coast College. This one-day festival is designed to encourage kids to experience the wonder of books. 125 authors and 25 illustrators do book readings and signings. Stage presentations include a little bit of everything - interactive storytelling; musical entertainment; model trains; Radio Disney deejays and contests; cultural dances; magicians; clown acts; exotic animal presentations that can include boas, birds of prey, wild cats, and camels; and more. Additional kids' activities can include a science and technology area, puppet shows, face paintings, inflatable jumps, and mini train rides. Literary-based vendors and food booths abound. Don't just read about this festival - come! Open Sun., 9:30am - 4pm. Admission is free.

ORANGE INTERNATIONAL STREET FAIR, Orange. (714) 633-4816 / www.orangestreetfair.org, 112 E Chapman Ave., Chapman Ave. and Glassell Street at Old Towne Orange Plaza. This massively popular, multi-street fair boasts over nine stages of international entertainment, including a children's stage, international foods, crafts, folk dancing and music. The Street Fair has also become known for the variety of food reflecting cuisine from around the world and unique vendors items. Labor Day weekend - Fri., 5pm-10pm; Sat. - Sun., 10am - 10pm. Free admission. Prepare to park far(ish) away.

ORIGINAL LONG BEACH LOBSTER FESTIVAL, Long Beach. (562) 495-5959 / www.originallobsterfestival.com, 400 Shoreline Village Dr. at Rainbow Lagoon Park. One of *maine* attractions at this largest Lobster Festival outside of Maine, is the freshly flown, live Maine lobster. It also features live entertainment, a children's stage, inflatable bounces, a reptile exhibit, karaoke lounge, a giant food court, carnival games, arts and crafts booth, and more. Fri., 5pm -10pm; Sat. - Sun., noon - 10pm $15 for adults, 12 and under free, does not include food. Packages available that include a lobster feast. Discounts available on-line.

PACIFIC ISLANDER FESTIVAL, San Diego. (619) 699-8797 / www.pifasandiego.com, Ski Beach, Mission Bay. This event invites the thousands of Melanesian, Micronesian, and Polynesian residents of Southern California to celebrate their heritage. Each community sets up their own village where singing and chanting, cultural dances, storytelling, arts and crafts, foods, and even artifacts keep visitors entertained. Open Sat. - Sun., 8am - 4pm. Admission is free.

PASADENA GREEK FESTIVAL, Pasadena. (626) 449-6943 / www.pasadenagreekfest.org, 778 South Rosemead Blvd. This festival celebrates Greek culture with three days of socializing, dancing, and lightning-bolt throwing, plus a kid-zone and the awesome Greek food such as moussaka, spanakopita, lamb chops and gyros! 3rd weekend in Sept., Fri., 5pm-10pm; Sat. - Sun., noon - 10pm. $4 for adults; ages 12 and under free.

PCPA THEATERFEST, Solvang. See June entry (pg. 640, 720) for details.

PEACH PICKING. See July entry (pg. 725) for details.

PORTUGUESE BEND NATIONAL HORSE SHOW, Rolling Hills Estates. (310) 318-8258 or (310) 463-8892 / www.pcch.net, 25851 Hawthorne Blvd. at Ernie Howlett Park. For sixty years, this classy three-day show has featured numerous equestrian events in two sand rings. Past shows have also included, besides the main feature of horse competitions, a children's games area, crafts, demonstrations by the Long Beach Mounted Police, puppet shows (Sat. at noon and 1:30pm), pony rides, a moon bounce, food booths, petting zoo (Sat. and Sun.), Wildlife Safari with animals from around the world (Sun. only, 1pm - 2pm) and more. Feel free to bring a picnic lunch. Riding events begin at noon on Fri., and go from 7:30am - 5pm on Sat.; 7:30am - 3pm on Sun. Children's area open Fri., 10am - 4pm; Sat., 10pm - 3pm; Sun. 10am - 4pm. Pony rides are Sat. and Sun. 10:30am to 3pm. Admission free on Fri.; Sat. and Sun., it's $5 per person; children 12 and under are free. Ask about reserved seating prices. Parking and shuttle service to the site is free.

POWAY RODEO, Poway. (866) 776-7633 / www.powayrodeo.com, 14336 Tierra Bonita Rd. at the PVRA Arena. This "Brand Above the Rest" rodeo is yet another reason to come to Poway! The PRCA rodeos (i.e., Professional Rodeo Cowboys Association) are some of the best in the nation, with cowboys competing in several categories. Favorite events include kid's mutton bustin', rodeo clown acts, bareback riding, tie-down roping, bull riding, and Jr. barrel races will have your kids hootin' and hollerin' for more. Vendors and food are on-site. Rodeos are Fri and Sat. at 7:30pm, gates open at 5:30pm; Sat. at 1pm, gates open at 10am. The Pacific Coast Jr. Bull Riders event is at 10am on Sat. Admission is $19 - $25 for ages 13 and up, depending on seating; $12 - $17 for ages 6 - 12; children 5 and under are free with a paid adult. Parking ranges from $5 - $10, depending on where you park.

RASPBERRY PICKING. See July entry (pg. 726) for details.

RENDEZVOUS IN POWAY, Poway. (858) 668-4576; (858) 668-4579 - educational tours / www.poway.org/oldpowaypark, 14134 Midland Rd. in Old Poway Park. Be a part of history for a long weekend as you walk among the twenty-five, or so, interactive encampments and learn about and talk with mountain men, cowboys, buckaroos, and more from the 1820s to 1890s lifestyle. Mock gunfights, Civil War-era cannons, Gatling gun, train rides, crafts, an evening barn dance, train robberies, gold panning, folk dancing performances, and more await you. Two-hour educational tours and train rides are offered to school groups on the Thurs. and Fri. before the rendezvous for $4 per person. Look up OLD POWAY PARK (pg. 566) for more details on the park. Open Sat, 10am - 4pm; Sun., 10am - 2pm. Admission is free.

ROUTE 66 CRUISIN' REUNION, Ontario. (800) 867-8366 or (909) 891-1151 / www.route66cruisinreunion.com, Euclid Avenue. Let's go cruisin'! Car buffs from all over the country (as evidenced by the 200,000 attendees) come to get their kicks on Route 66 for this three-day rendezvous that encompasses 22 blocks of historic Euclid Avenue near Ontario Town Square, the library and city hall. Classics, muscle cars, hot rods, and trucks from 1900 to 1975 can be participating vehicles (usually more than 2,000 total!). The cars are cool to look at, plus there cars cruisin', live entertainment, a model car contest, vendors, wall to wall people at times and some kid's activities. The rendezvous is Fri., 5pm - 10pm; Sat., 9am - 9pm; Sun., 9am - 4pm. Admission is free.

TALL SHIPS FESTIVAL, Dana Point. (949) 496-2274 / www.ocean-institute.org, 24200 Dana Point Harbor Dr. at the Ocean Institute. This festival, held the weekend after Labor Day, is one of the largest gathering of tall ships on the West Coast. It begins as majestic tall ships sail into port. Go aboard to join in the Parade of Sail on Friday, 4pm - 7pm to work with the crew hauling up sail or watch how they handle the ship, and definitely watch the mock cannon battles. Other days, tour the ships and enjoy demonstrations and exhibits of the sailing arts, such as knot tying, scrimshaw, and wood carvings, plus cannon battles towards the evening. Pirate encampment activities include sea chantey concerts, storytelling, mock trials and weddings, and perhaps, walkin' the plank. All this, plus mermaid encounters (even breakfast with them with storytelling and crafts for $50 for ages 12 and up, $45 for ages 2 - 11, ages under 2 are free -

everyone must register in advance), music, crafts, and food make this festival worth *seeing*. Don't forget to explore the touch tank in the OCEAN INSTITUTE (pg. 311). Open Sat - Sun., 10am - 4pm. Fri. is the ship parade from 4pm - 7:30pm. General admission to the Festival - which includes tours of the *Brig Pilgrim,* the *Spirit of Dana Point*, and all visiting vessels; and access to shop and food vendors, pirate encampments, exhibitions, crafts, activities, and more - is $10 for adults; $7.50 for srs and ages 2 - 12. Sailing in the parade on Fri. is $50 for adults; $40 for ages 3 - 14. Cannon battle cruises on the weekends are $65 for adults; $55 for ages 3 - 14.

TANAKA FARMS PUMPKIN PATCH, Irvine. See October entry (pg. 745) for details.

VISTA VIKING FESTIVAL, Vista. (760) 726-6526 / www.vistachamber.com, 2006 East Vista Way at the Norway Hall. *Sven* the day indulging in all things Viking at this annual event. Test your strength with the Viking log toss, horn blowing, battle cries, and fish-flinging competitions. Add to this weapon and artisan demonstrations, Norwegian crafts, live entertainment, Viking encampments and villages, ethnic foods, and a KidZone and you *Thor* have the makings of a great day. Open Sat. - Sun., 10am - 7. Admission is $10 for adults; $3 ages 3 - 12, ages 2 and under are free. Parking is $5.

WESTERN DAYS, Temecula. (951) 694-6480 / temecula.ca.gov, 41970 Moreno Blvd. at Sam Hicks Monument Park in Old Town. Happy trails to you as you walk around this wonderful, old Western-style town any day of the week, but particularly this weekend. Goings on include a carnival, visiting the Temecula Valley Museum, face painting, vendor and craftsmen booths and watching gun fighters at a high noon shoot-out (this is at Hotel Temecula). Come dressed in your best western duds. Open Sat., 10am - 3pm. Admission is free.

WILL GEER THEATRICUM BOTANICUM, Topanga. See June entry (pg. 722) for details.

- OCTOBER -

AMY'S FARM PUMPKIN TOUR, Ontario. (844) 4AMYSFARM (426–9732) / www.amysfarm.com, 7698 Eucalyptus Avenue. Make a reservation to take a one-hour-plus tour of this working calf ranch with numerous animals, to learn how pumpkins grow, pick a pumpkin from the patch, pet the animals in the petting zoo, feed baby calves bottles of milk, and more. A shaded picnic area with plenty of open grassy space is available. There must be a minimum of ten paying people in a group. But you are welcome to drop by the pumpkin patch and walk around the farm any day it's open without a reservation! See the main entry of AMY'S FARM TOURS (pg. 441) for more details. Open October and November, Mon. - Fri. in the morning for tours, and on select Sat. at 10:30am. Call to book a date and time. The pumpkin tour is $8 per person, or $10 for adults not picking a pumpkin.

ANTIQUE ENGINE AND TRACTOR SHOW, Vista. See the entry in June, ANTIQUE ENGINE AND TRACTOR SHOW (pg. 716), for details.

APPLE PICKING - JULIAN, Julian. See August entry (pg. 727) for details.

APPLE PICKING - OAK GLEN, Oak Glen. See the main entry for OAK GLEN / APPLE PICKING (pg. 403). The season runs from mid-September through mid-November.

AVOCADO FESTIVAL, Carpinteria. (805) 684-0038 / www.avofest.com, 800 Linden Ave. Holy guacamole! This hugely popular festival has everything avocado, at least food-wise. Try avocado ice-cream, avocado Key lime tarts, roasted corn with avocado butter, or at least some guacamole from a huge vat. Over seventy acts provide entertainment on four stages. Arts and crafts booths as well as commercial booths and an expo tent offering educational information add to the weekend events. At the Children's Venue (ie. kids' block party), young ones enjoy face painting, a petting zoo, make-and-take crafts, miniature golf, a rock climbing wall, storytelling, and theater performances. At the "best-dressed" avocado contest, your entry could win for best hair, funniest, or scariest. Open Fri., 1pm - 10pm; Sat., 10am - 10pm; Sun., 10am - 6pm. Admission is free.

BANNING HERITAGE WEEK, Wilmington. See April entry (pg. 706) for details.

BATES NUT FARM PUMPKIN PATCH, Valley Center. (760) 749-3333; (800) 642-0348 / www.batesnutfarm.biz, 15954 Woods Valley Rd. Spend a delightful day in the country at this great farm [see the main entry (pg. 561)]. It has an eight-acre (pre-cut) pumpkin patch, along with (for $2.50 each) - a straw maze, tractor-drawn hayrides all around the farm, petting corral, and moon bounce; plus pony rides ($7.50), and more. Purchase lunch/dinner here from food trucks and other vendors (weekends only), or bring your own to enjoy at the large picnic area. Weekday educational programs are available for school groups. Special weekend events can include live entertainment, face painting, a rock climbing wall, costume contests, and more. Open daily during the month of October, Mon. - Fri., 9am - 5:30pm (tho open the last 3 Fri., 9am - 8pm); Sat. - Sun., 8:30am - 6pm. Admission is free; $5 for parking in October. Pumpkins are about $7 each.

BOCCALI'S RANCH PUMPKIN PATCH, Ojai. (805) 669-7077 / www.boccalis.com, 3277 Ojai Ave., behind the Boccali's restaurant. For over twenty years this ranch/garden has been an Ojai fixture. The pumpkin patch features home-grown pumpkins (pick them on or off the vine), gourds, and Indian corn in an authentic farm setting. Visitors can also enjoy tractor-drawn hay rides on the weekends (11am - 5pm, $2 per person), a free children's hay maze, and purchasing fruits, vegetables, and herbs from the produce stand at anytime. Haunted Hayrides, with scares and suspense and limited gore, are offered on Fri. and Sat. nights, 7pm to 9pm, for $10 per person. No-reservation Italian buffet dinners are offered on haunted hayride evenings for $15 for adults; $8 for ages 3 to 9 years; free for ages 2 and under with a paid adult. Note that Boccali's Pizza and Pasta restaurant is just next door, serving fresh and genuine Italian food. The pumpkin patch is open the month of October daily, 10am - 7pm. Open on Fri. and Sat. starting mid-October, until 9pm. Free general admission.

CALABASAS PUMPKIN FESTIVAL, Agoura. (818) 224-1600; (818) 222-5680 / www.calabasaspumpkinfestival.com; www.cityofcalabasas.com, 3701 Lost Hills Rd. at Juan Bautista de Anza Park. Join in contests of pumpkin pie eating, pumpkin seed spitting, pumpkin carving, and pumpkin bowling. Besides picking up a pumpkin, or two, in the pumpkin patch (and eating lots of pumpkin treats) there are - included in the price of admission - inflatables and giant slide, reptile and bug shows, a Saturday morning costume parade, kiddie carnival rides, craft vendors, live stage entertainment, and even a classic car show. Open Sat. and Sun., 10am - 5pm. Admission $5, children under 2 are free. Parking is free.

CALICO DAYS, Yermo. See September entry (pg. 731) for details.

CHILDREN'S FALL HARVEST FESTIVAL, Long Beach. (562) 431-3541 / www.rancholosalamitos.com, 6400 Bixby Hill Rd. at Rancho Los Alamitos. In back-at-the-farm surroundings, this geared-for-kids festival offers storytellers, demonstrations, pony rides, a costume parade (have the kids dress up) around the barnyard, crafts, games, and food. See RANCHO LOS ALAMITOS (pg. 148) for more information about this rancho. Open Sun., noon - 4pm. Free.

ENCINITAS OKTOBERFEST, Encinitas. (760) 753-6041 / www.encinitasoktoberfest.com, Mountain Vista Drive and El Camino Real. This festival includes music, Bavarian dancers, a street craft faire featuring over 200 vendors, a family food and refreshment tent, a family fun zone with children's games and family oriented activities. Sun., 10am -6pm; ceremonial parade noon. Admission and parking are free.

ESCONDIDO RENAISSANCE FAIRE, Escondido. See April entry (pg. 707) for details.

FALL FESTIVAL, Los Angeles. (323) 933-9211 / www.farmersmarketla.com, 3rd St. and Fairfax at Farmers Market. Enjoy this two-day, old-fashioned festival in the heart of historic L.A. See FARMERS MARKET (pg. 21) for info. Past activities and events (which could change every year) have included a petting zoo; pig racing; pumpkin patch; live country music; cooking, spinning, gardening, and pottery demonstrations; bobbing for apples; pie-eating contests; and more. The Market and its merchants are all decorated, too! Open Sat., 9am - 8pm; Sun., 10am - 7pm. Admission is free. Parking is free for the first 2 hours with merchant validation.

FALL HARVEST FESTIVAL / PUMPKIN TOURS, Moorpark. (805) 529-3690 or (805) 523-8552 / www.underwoodfamilyfarms.com, 3370 Sunset Valley Rd. at Underwood Family Farms. See UNDERWOOD FAMILY FARMS - Moorpark (pg. 656) for more details on this fantastic farm. Weekday admission includes access to corn mazes; pumpkin house and playhouses; chicken show; gourd tunnel; tractor-drawn hayride; hay bale spiders (more fun than it might sound); the combine slide, hay pyramid, fun hill, and play equipment; plus tractor displays, country store, and pumpkin patch. All of the above is available on the weekends, too, plus live entertainment (which could include stunt ropers, Jumbo Shrimp circus, country music and more); a 30-minute animal show; pig races; and country games and activities (that are an additional cost) such as pitch a pumpkin, duck races, corn cannon (a favorite), sling shot, cow train ride, make-a-scarecrow, horse-drawn wagon ride, and more. Farm fresh produce is available for purchase as well as gourds, squash, corn stalks, Indian corn, food, drinks, and much more. The farm has 16 acres of U-pic pumpkins, including the Atlantic Giants which can weight more than 500 pounds. Food vendors are here on the weekend serving hamburgers, Mexican food, kettle corn, roasted corn on the cob, and more. Educational Pumpkin Tours feature an educational presentation from the farmer; a tractor drawn wagon ride around the farm and pumpkin patch; picking sugarbaby pumpkins; visiting the Farm Animal Center; going through the corn maze; getting a coloring book; and use of the picnic area. The tours are $6 - $14 per person. (Teachers are free.) Open for the month of October daily, 9am - 6pm. Admission Mon. - Fri. is $6 for ages 2 and up; the first two Sat. - Sun., $15 for ages 2 and up; the latter Sat. - Sun., $20. Parking is free.

FERN STREET CIRCUS, San Diego. (619) 320-2055 / www.fernstreetcircus.com. This is not a three-ring circus; it's actually one ring. A mix of adults, teens, and children, professionals and students, make up this unusual circus that teaches circus and life skills to low income youth. The annual, free-of-charge Neighborhood Tour performs in several

Mid-City San Diego parks featuring professional circus and musical artists, live music, a bilingual presentation, and student performers. See the website for more info. Free.

FLEET WEEK, San Diego. (619) 858-1545 / www.fleetweeksandiego.org, 1000 N. Harbor Dr. at the Broadway Pier and Port Pavilion. This tribute to the military occurs all along the San Diego waterfront, especially around the USS Midway, offering displays in action. The Sea and Air parade, from noon - 2pm on Sat., showcases cruisers, amphibious ships, destroyers, frigates, submarines, and landing craft in addition to a demonstration of SEAL capabilities, Coast Guard Search and Rescue, a fly-over of contemporary Navy and World War II aircraft, and more. Parked at the entrance are current Navy jets and helicopters, special boats and hovercraft, vintage aircraft, tanks, guns, and other displays. A car show is also held on the grounds. Flyovers can take place throughout the weekend. Two other highlights are ship tours (the only time you get to do this!) and an interactive Innovation Zone for kids to create, experiment and experience. These FREE activities are offered Fri. - Sun., 10am - 4:30pm. Do these things! Check the website for details on specific events, times, places, and prices. Most events are free, such as the naval tours.

FORNERIS FARMS and HARVEST FESTIVAL, Mission Hills. (818) 730-7709 / www.fornerisfarms.com, 15200 Rinaldi Street, Mission Hills. For a month of amazing fun, come play in the corn fields. Walk through the four-acre cornstalk maze, trying to find your way out and seeking the CORNundrums (i.e. picture puns and riddles). Other activities include going through the Farm Frolic area (mini hay bale maze, bounce house and hay pyramid - $5); taking a narrated, tractor-pulled train ride ($4); picking a pumpkin at the patch; viewing the antique tractors and cars scattered around; and perusing the farm market with fresh produce and fall decorations. On weekends only enjoy pony rides ($6) and petting zoo ($5), too. Fresh produce is available at Forneris Farms from March through December. The farm activities are open the month of October, Mon. - Fri., 1pm - 5pm; Sat. - Sun., 9am - 5pm. The pumpkin patch is open daily 9am - 6pm. General admission is free to the farm and pumpkin patch. Attractions admission is $15 per person (ages 2 and under are free) and includes the corn maze, train ride, and Farm Frolic area. Cash only.

GEM-O-RAMA, Trona. (760) 372-5356 / www1.iwvisp.com/tronagemclub, 3½ hours north of L.A., near Ridgecrest. This two-day event, which occurs the second weekend in the month, is worth the trek! It's explanation deserves a full page, however space in this section is limited. A free gem and mineral show; a free, guided bus trip around the on-site minerals' plants; and touring a small museum and fire house are the clean activities. Messy highlights (and I mean messy and I mean highlights!) on Saturday morning include mineral collecting for two-and-a-half hours from gooey black mud for hanksite and borax crystals and, in the afternoon, collecting borax and halite from a blow hole. The Sunday highlight is trudging/wading knee to hip deep in the salt lake, which crunches like newly-fallen snow, to chip out halite crystals - small pieces or large chunks. (Note that mineral retailers come here to supply their stores.) Bring sacrificial clothes and shoes, water (to use to wash off), gloves, a heavy hammer, a crowbar (for prying out the specimens), and large boxes lined with trash bags to bring home your treasures. What a unique opportunity to collect saline minerals! Show opens 7:30am on both days and end at 5pm on Sat., 4pm on Sun. Sat. mud trip from 9am - 11:30am; Sat. blow hole from 2:30pm - 5pm; Sun. halite lake from 9am - 1:30pm. Registration is 1½ hour before each trip. Admission is $15 per vehicle on the Sat. mud trip; $15 for the Sat. blow hole; $20 for the Sun. halite lake - such a deal! Note that Pinnacles National Natural Landmark is down the road. Take the time to drive closer and walk around these other-worldly looking formations.

GREENSPOT FARMS, Mentone. (909) 794-7653 or (909) 583-1257 / www.greenspotfarms.com, 10133 Ward Way. I love visiting real farms! Choose and pick your pumpkin in the field and then enjoy a hay bale maze, corn maze, tractor-pull hay ride, face painting, petting zoo, and refreshments at this twenty-eight acre farm. The nighttime "haunted" hayride (called "Terror on the Farm") is a big draw for those who really like to be scared, open mid-October thru the end of October. Note that apples and berries are available here at certain times to U-Pic. School tours are available here, as well. Check out the honey house where you can look at live honey bees through a window (and purchase honey fresh from the hive). Open the month of October daily, 9am - 6pm. Free general admission. The hayride is $15 for adults; $12 for ages 12 and under; the haunted trail is $12 for adults; $10 for kids.

HALLOWEEN. Lots of "regular" attractions offer something special at Halloween. Zoos, for instance, offer Boo at the Zoo, where spooky, creepy, and crawly fun reign. Aquariums (Scarium of the Pacific instead of Aquarium of the Pacific in Long Beach), amusement parks (i.e. Knott's *Scary* Farm), museums (i.e. the *Queen Mary*), and even some botanic gardens go all out in decorating for Halloween and putting on special events. If you are looking for pumpkin patches and corn mazes check out the events listed in this October section and check the following website for a plethora of places - www.pumpkinpatchesandmore.org.

HALLOWEEN ALTERNATIVES. For alternatives to door-to-door trick or treating, check your local park, mall, or church as many of them offer carnival-type fun, a safer atmosphere, and still plenty of candy!

HARBOR AND SEAFOOD FESTIVAL, Santa Barbara. (805) 897-1962 or (805) 962-8404 / www.sbmm.org, 113 Harbor Way, Suite 190. You might have to *sea* it all, to believe it. Come talk with fishermen and purchase some fresh catches of the day, and other fresh seafood - a multitude of choices, plus food and retail vendors. There is also a touch tank, or two, of marine critters; free entrance into the wonderful SANTA BARBARA MARITIME MUSEUM (pg. 628); harbor patrol fire boat demonstrations; live music; free boat rides; and several dockside tours of various ships in port, such as a research vessel. Tall Ship Spirit of Dana Point, US Coast Guard Cutter Blackfin and more. Sometimes Tall Ships sails are available, too. Held on the second Sat., 10:30am - 5pm. Free. Dockside tours of the Tall Ship are $8 for adults; $5 for srs and ages 6 -17; children 5 and under are free. Parking is $2 an hour; $12 max.

HART OF THE WEST POW WOW AND NATIVE AMERICAN CRAFT FAIR, Newhall. (661) 298-3014 / www.friendsofhartpark.org; www.hartmuseum.org, 24151 San Fernando Rd. at the William S. Hart Park and Museum. This celebration of "California is a nation" encompasses many facets of the Old West. A Pow Wow, held at the large picnic area, begins 10am with the Grand Entry, followed by the Blessing, and ongoing dancing (with narration and interpretation) and drumming from several Indian nations. Native American regalia are for sale at booths. Sometime mountain men set up in encampments next to the Pow Wow, showing how people lived in the mid-1800's, by using period tools, campfire cooking, and display booths. There are also demonstrations for children and adults, Native American storytellers, and arts and crafts. Parking is tight. See WILLIAM S. HART MUSEUM AND PARK (pg. 158) for more information. The celebration hours are Sat., 10am - 7pm; Sun., 10am 6pm. Admission is free. You're welcome to bring a blanket and a picnic lunch.

HAUTE DOG HOWL'OWEEN PARADE, Long Beach. (562) 439-3316 / www.hautedogs.org, 5355 East Eliot St. at Marina Vista Park. More than 500 dogs put their best paw forward, decked out in their Halloween best for this ten block, pooch parade. Owners and dogs are often dressed alike as participants vie for best canine costume, best costume on a person, best group, best float (usually a decorated wagon), and more, with great prizes awarded. Yappy hour events have included a kid's costume contest, a bulldog kissing booth, dogs bobbing for hot dogs, a pet adoption fair, and more furry fun. Money raised goes towards a nonprofit organization. Haute Dogs is the Sunday before Halloween, opening at 11am; the parade is at 2:30pm. Free for spectators; $20 to participate.

HUCK FINN JUBILEE, Ontario. / www.huckfinn.com, 800 N. Archibald Ave. in Cucamonga-Guasti Regional Park. The huge, three-day jubilee is known for it's famous Blue Grass music festival, and there are lots of other things to do here. Cucamonga-Guasti Park offers two lakes for year-round trout and catfish fishing - a CA state fishing license is required. The long weekend is filled with a kid's parade, an art station, a Kid Zone, peddle boats, food and craft vendors, and a Splash Pad - a zero depth water park with with water-spraying nozzles in the shapes of flowers and mushrooms and more; poles and apparatus shooting out water. Put on a straw hat and join the throngs of people. Note: Camping is available here, too. Check the website for hours, tho traditionally they have been Fri. - Sat., 7am - 11pm; Sun., 7am - 8pm. Pre-sale admission is $45 for adults on Fri., $65 on Sta., $55 on Sun. Kids 6 - 15 are $15 on Fri., $25 on Sat., $20 on Sun. Children 5 and under are free. Camping starts at $75 for Fri. - Mon. morning for tents. Various attractions cost extra.

HURST RANCH HARVEST FESTIVAL, West Covina. (626) 549-0700 / www.hurstranch.com, 1227 South Orange Ave. Kids will have a great time making butter, pumping water, grinding coffee, picking pumpkins, and doing other farm chores (and yet you can't get them to pick up their socks). The festival affords opportunities to also find out about quilting, weaving, and more, take a house tour, explore the 4H farm petting zoo, pan for gold, and make a craft. They also have fairy gardens and visit an Indian encampment. Open the third Sat., 10am - 2pm Admission is $5 per person; children 2 and under free. Lunch is $6, or bring your own.

INDUSTRY HILLS CHARITY PRO RODEO, City of Industry. (626) 961-6892 / www.industrycharityevents.org, 16200 Temple Ave. at the Industry Hills Center. Everyone benefits from this rodeo - several charities receive needed funds, top performers compete in the rodeo for a large purse, and guests have a great time! Besides the main event of the rodeo with bareback riding, steer wrestling, team roping, saddle bronc riding, bull riding, and tie down roping, visitors enjoy petting zoo, crafts, pony rides, clowns, Western theme booths, a visit by Smokey the Bear, entertainment, food, and motocross. Come before the weekend shows begin to enjoy the pre-show fun. Note that a Community Kids Day precedes the event where local school kids come to watch the rodeo with their teachers as part of a lesson plan covering early western days. The rodeo commences Sat. at 6pm; Sun. at 2pm. Gates open 2 hours before show time. Admission is $20 for adults; $15 for srs.; $10 for ages 3 - 11. Parking is $7.

INSECT FAIR, Pomona. (909) 869-2215 or (909) 869-2200 / www.cpp.edu/~agriscapes/index.html; www.csupomona.edu, 4102 S. University Dr., at the AGRIscapes Visitor Center, on the campus of Cal Poly Pomona. This huge, two day Insect Fair will drive you buggy! You can see, learn about and even purchase some live millipedes, tarantulas, spiders, leaf bugs, scorpions, cockroaches, and so much more, as well as preserved insects, display cases, jewelry designed to look like insects, and more. See October entry (pg. 743) for this festival that is often held at the same time as this fair. Open Sat. - Sun., 9am - 5pm. $3 for adults; $2 for ages 2 - 12.

IRVINE PARK RAILROAD'S PUMPKIN PATCH, Orange. (714) 997-3968 / www.irvineparkrailroad.com, 1 Irvine Park Road inside Irvine Regional Park. *Orange* you looking for some fun this month? This pumpkin patch, located near the train station, offers more than just pumpkins. Take a twelve-minute ride through part of the park (1 ticket); a twenty-minute, tractor-drawn hayride (1 ticket); peddle a kid-size, John Deere tractor racer through an obstacle course (1 ticket); jump in a Halloween-themed bounce for fifteen minutes (1 ticket); pan for gold and keep a small bag of "gold" (2 tickets); enjoy carnival games (1 ticket); walk through a not-too-spooky haunted house (free); chart your course through a hay bale maze (free); climb a hay pyramid (free); get your face painted (2 tickets); and eat! Other attractions in this vicinity include paddle boat rentals, bike rentals, pony rides, and the Orange County Zoo. See IRVINE REGIONAL PARK (pg. 284) for more details about what this terrific park has to offer. Open Mon. - Fri., 10am - 5pm; Sat. - Sun., 10am - 6pm. Vehicle entry fees are $3, Mon. - Fri.; $5 on weekends; $7 on holidays. General admission to the pumpkin patch is free. Tickets are $5 per or $60 for 15.

JOHNSON BROTHERS PUMPKIN PATCH, Irvine. (949) 733-0650 /(714) 891-7456 / www.johnsonbros.net, 15500 Jeffrey Rd. These patches offer pumpkins (from giants to minis); bounce houses and obstacles (3-4 tickets); inflatable slide (3-4 tickets); barnyard animals (free); and a free kiddie play area with activity gyms, hay loft, straw ponies to sit on, and bouncing bags to play with. An unusual attraction, but theme-fitting, is an Indian Village replete with tipis, corn grinders to try, and free, do-it-yourself face painting. Johnson Brothers is also a good source for autumn items and decor, such as pre-made scarecrows, gourds, bundles of cornstalks, and more. Open daily in October, 9am - 9pm. Free general admission. Tickets are $1.50 each or 30 tickets for $40.

JULIAN FARM AND ORCHARD, Julian. (951) 313-0166 / www.julianminingcompany.com, 4444 Hwy. 78., across the street from Julian Mining Company. What do giants, minis, and princesses all have in common? They are all types of pumpkins. This terrific place offers an assortment of activities from picking on-the-vine pumpkins to taking a tractor-drawn hayride ($5); petting the animals at the petting zoo ($5); cider pressing ($5); hand-dipping candles; gold panning; the gem sluice; roping; marshmallow "wars" and much. See JULIAN MINING COMPANY (pg. 575) for all the wonderful activities that this place offers - it's like a farm from the 1800's, but more fun. Open in October, Sat., 10am - 5pm; Sun., noon - 5pm. General admission is free.

JULIAN TRIANGLE CLUB MELODRAMA, Julian. (760) 765-1857 / www.julianmelodrama.com, 2129 Main St. at Julian Town Hall. The last three weekends during the month of October you are invited to participate in a two-hour, old-time melodrama by booing the villain, cheering the hero, and sighing with the heroine. The shows feature local actors and incorporate a community sing-a-long (song lyrics are on the website). Shows are Fri. and Sat. at 7pm. Admission is $10 for adults; $5 for ages 4 - 12.

L.A. GREEK FESTIVAL, Los Angeles. (323) 737-2424 / www.lagreekfest.com, 1324 S. Normandie Ave. at Saint Sophia Greek Orthodox Cathedral. This fest features authentic Greek food (sample souvlaki, baklava, gyros, and more); music; traditional folk dances; theatrical performances; cooking demonstrations; Kid's Arcade; game booths; a marketplace; and tours of the cathedral. Open Fri., 5pm - 11pm; Sat., noon - 11pm; Sun., noon - 10pm. Admission is $5 per person. Discount coupons are online.

LAGUNA MOUNTAIN RENDEZVOUS, Santa Ysabel. / www.lagunamountainrendezvous.com, Mataguay Scout Reservation, 27955 Hwy 79. For over a week, experience an authentic 1700's - 1840's Rocky Mountain fur traders encampment in a rustic mountain setting. Demonstrations of primitive survival skills such as cooking, tool making, tomahawk throwing, and black powder target shooting are given, but really, it's just kind of living in this time period that's the attraction. Beginners and the public are welcome to learn the "how-tos" and to purchase items to become mountain men or women. Primitive and modern camping is available on site. Open daily, 8am - 6pm; Fri. until 8pm. Admission is $5 per person; scouts and scout leaders are free.

LANE FAMILY FARM PUMPKIN PATCH, Santa Barbara. (805) 964-3773 / www.lanefarmssb.com, 308 Walnut Ln. A long-standing tradition, family-owned Lane's has 2½ acres of U-pic pumpkins, plus a small (but worthy of going through) corn maze (open at 3pm weekdays); tractor-drawn hayride (offered weekends only); a petting zoo - not to go into - with pigs, goats, and donkeys; a talking scarecrow; a fresh-from-the-fields produce stand; and scattered tractors and antique farming equipment. Kids can learn about agriculture and farming by taking a field trip which fulfills California curriculum requirements, and it's fun! This is $5 per student Open the end of September through October, weekdays, 10am - 8pm; weekends, 9am - 8pm. Free, including hayride and corn maze.

LAVENDER HILL PUMPKINS, Fallbrook. (760) 715-8495 / www.lavenderhillpumpkins.com, 1509 E. Mission Rd. At this family-owned farm, it's all about pumpkins; just pumpkins. Thousands of them. And not just the traditional, roundish, orange ones, but tall ones, white ones, ones with "warts", pale orange ones, bright orange ones, colossus kinds, and minis. The variety, the names given to some of their pumpkins, and the opportunity to pick them from the field make this excursion a unique one. Open the end of September through October, Mon. - Fri., 2pm - 5pm; Sat - Sun., 10am - 5pm. Free.

LIVE OAK CANYON PUMPKIN PATCH, Yucaipa. (909) 795-TREE (8733) / www.thepumpkinfactory.com/liveoak, 32335 Live Oak Canyon Rd. This huge (at least in my city eyes) family-operated farm yields bushels of fun in the fall. A petting zoo is on the grounds, with goats, sheep, pigs, donkeys, ponies, chickens, and ducks. Watch the goats surefootedly "walk the plank" for food. Bring money to purchase feed. Some of the other fun includes tractor-drawn hayrides (free; on weekends only!); a giant hay "castle" created from hundreds of bales of hay spread out, as well as staggered on top of each other, to climb up and on (free!); several huge inflatables of bounces, obstacle courses and slides; mechanical kiddie rides; a bird aviary; a zip line; bungee jump; mini ATV; train rides; traditional scale model train rides; bobbles (walking inside a huge "bubble" on water); pony rides; archery; gold mining; games; and so much more. At Cowboy Corner, weekends only from 11am - 6pm, visitors are entertained with hold-ups, gun fights, skits and songs of the Old West. Weekends only, usually, also offers a variety of performances on stage - magic, comedy, dancing, music, storytelling and more. Two huge corn mazes have over 12,000 feet of pathways with games that, if done correctly, give players a combination to pass through "doors" of the mazes and receive a prize. The maze is 5 tickets Tues. - Thurs.; $6, Fri. - Sun. during the day and 8 at nighttime. Walk along the rows of the best pumpkin patch in Southern California (my opinion), which feature twenty-five acres of vine-cut pumpkins!! There are also huge piles of pre-picked pumpkins that range from giant pumpkins (make pies for everyone in the neighborhood), to sweet-tasting white pumpkins, Cinderellas, and mini pumpkins. Wagons are available to help tote your load. An on-site store sells decorative fall items such as Indian corn (in all colors), corn stalks, scarecrows, pumpkin carving supplies and kits, and numerous gourds, including the kind used by artists for making instruments, baskets, and other creative endeavors. Buy food from food trucks or bring a sack lunch and eat at the numerous picnic tables scattered under shade trees. One-hour tours, offered Tues. - Fri., 9am - 3pm, and adaptable to any age group and size, costs $8 per person and includes a tractor-drawn hayride past pumpkin, corn, and gourd fields; picking a pumpkin to take home; a visit to the petting zoo with the farm animals; coloring book; and learning all about pumpkins - from seed to full-grown pumpkin. Participants can pay for additional activities. Open mid-September, Tues. - Sun., 9am - 6pm. Open October Tues. - Sun., 9am - 9pm, and mid-Oct., Fri. - Sat., open until 10pm. Closed Mon., except Columbus Day. Amusements open at 3pm on weekdays. Check the website to see when specific activities are open. General admission is free Tues. - Thurs.; $5 on Fri. - Sun. for ages 3 and up; children 2 and under are free. Rides and some attractions and activities are extra.

LONDON BRASS RUBBING CENTER, Long Beach. (562) 436-4047 - church; (562) 439-9496 / www.stlukeslb.org/brass-rubbings.html, 525 E. 7th Street at St. Luke's Episcopal Church. Cheerio! Your child will thoroughly enjoy making a medieval brass rubbing, offered mid-October through mid-November. On black paper, use a wax rubbing crayon of gold, silver, or bronze to capture the intricate designs. The facsimiles of over 100 tombstones/reproduction-engraved plates of brass from England vary in size, and depict knights, Lords, ladies in fancy dress, griffins, Shakespeare, and others. Groups of at least ten people can incorporate a half-hour talk, given by a docent in period dress, to learn more about Medieval times and the stories behind some of the people and images in the engravings. A complete English tea can be added on to your time here, too, with advanced reservations and a group of at least ten people. The center is open to the public Sat., 11am - 3pm; weekdays by appointment (because of group scheduling). It is open to groups during this time, too, as well as Tues. - Sat., 9:30am - 3pm. There are 3 dates to sign up for, all at 1pm. The price to rub cost between $8 - $15, depending on the size of the brass plate. Groups of ten or more pay $8 per person. Teas are $26 for adults; $16 for ages 17 and under. This price includes a half-hour lesson/talk and a rubbing, too.

LOS ANGELES COUNTY FAIR, Pomona. See September entry (pg. 733) for details.

LOS ANGELES KOREAN FESTIVAL, Los Angeles. (213) 487-9696 / www.lakoreanfestival.org, 3250 San Marino St. at the Seoul International Park. This four-day festival includes a little bit of everything Korean: live cultural performances; playing traditional instrument; exhibitions; doing and watching traditional dances; music; crafts of making flowers and lanterns, paper folding, calligraphy and more; international foods; vendors; and kids' activities. Thurs., 2pm - 10pm; Fri. - Sat., 10am - 11pm; Sun., 10am - 10pm. Free admission.

LOS ANGELES PRINTERS FAIR, Torrance. (310) 515-7166 / www.printmuseum.org, 315 W. Torrance Blvd. at the INTERNATIONAL PRINTING MUSEUM (pg. 123). I hope this premier fair makes a good impression on you! Don't just read all about it, experience the world of printing through demonstrations and do-it-yourself - using the equipment - bookbinding, papermaking, letterpress printing, and more; plus 100 vendors from all over the country; crafts for kids; and exploring the museum with printing presses and other equipment dating from Gutenberg's time to today. Open Sat. - Sun., 10am - 4pm. Admission is $10 for adults; $5 for kids 11 and under. Cash only.

MCGRATH BROTHERS GREAT PACIFIC PUMPKINS, Ventura. (805) 644-1235 / www.greatpacificpumpkins.com, 5100 Olivas Park Dr. Looking for the Great Pumpkin? Open to the public and for school tours during the month of October, come walk the patch, take a tractor-drawn hayride ($2), find your way through the hay maze ($2), play a few games, and purchase product from the produce stand. Tours ($5 per person), which last about an hour, are offered for pre-K to elementary-aged school kids to learn about the life cycle of a pumpkin. Visitors are then invited to enjoy the other activities, and pick a pumpkin to take home. Open daily in October, 9am - 6pm. Admission is free.

MCGRATH FAMILY FARMS, Camarillo. See March entry (pg. 704) for details.

MCGRATH STREET PUMPKIN PATCH and GOURD FARM, Ventura. (805) 658-9972 / www.mcgrathstreetpumpkinpatch.com, 5156 McGrath St. During the month of October, walk the fields and choose a vine-cut pumpkin from the patch. Multi-colored Indian corn and gourds (the hard-shell kind used by artists and musicians), are for sale here year round. Tractor-drawn hayrides ($2) are given on the weekends. A few animals are on the site to look at and gently pet, plus face painting and pony rides. Groups of ten or more can take a field trip during the week to learn all about pumpkins, Native Americans, and more - $5 per student. Open daily, 9am - dusk. Admission is free.

MIRAMAR AIR SHOW, Miramar. (858) 577-1000 or (858) 577-1011; (858) 577-1016 or (888) 435-9746 for reserved seats / www.miramarairshow.com, Miramar Road at the Marine Corps Air Station. This three-day air show (one of the best!) features the Blue Angels, military, and civilian pilots performing thrilling aviation stunts and maneuvers, including wing walking. On the ground are over 100 displays of airplanes, helicopters, and military equipment, and some simulator rides, plus vendor booths and Consumer Fair exhibits. The Fun Zone includes a Ferris Wheel, climbing wall, obstacle course, mega slides, carousel, train ride, and bungee jump at various prices. No backpacks of any kind are allowed in. Note that a valid driver's license, current registration, and proof of insurance are necessary to get onto base. Gates open at 8am; a radio-controlled aircraft demonstration runs 8am - 9:30am, the show runs Fri. - Sun., 9am - 4pm. The Blue Angels usually fly at about 2pm. Parking, general admission, and blanket seating are free for all shows. Reserved seating ranges from $15 - $20 for adults; $10 - $12 for ages 3 - 9 for regular grandstand seats. VIP and other seats are available, too.

MOUNTAIN VALLEY RANCH PUMPKIN PATCH, Ramona. (760) 788-8703 / www.mountainvalleyranch.com, 842 Hwy. 78. You can almost make a day of this outing by visiting fields of pumpkins where you can pick your own, taking a hayride around the farm (weekends only), trying to find your way out of the large cornfield maze, looking at some of the old farm equipment, pony rides and enjoying the petting zoo with pigs, ponies, calves, birds and a corn cannon. Open daily, 9am - 6pm. Call for activity prices.

MR. BONES PUMPKIN PATCH, West Hollywood. (310) 276-9827 / www.mrbonespumpkinpatch.com, 702 North Doheny Drive. Pre-picked pumpkins of all sizes and shapes are available here, as well as farm-fresh goods, Halloween merchandise and decor, carving tools, gourds, and food. Activities for young ones include a pumpkin bounce (3 tickets); face painting (7 - 14 tickets); a straw maze ($3); hay bale tunnels; a petting zoo (5 tickets); and pony rides ($7). Mr. Bones is available for school groups and for birthday parties, too. Open mid-October through October 31, Mon. - Thurs., 9am - 8pm; Fri. - Sat., 9am - 9pm; Sun., 9am - 8pm. General admission is free Mon. - Thurs. all day and Fri., 9am - 4:59pm. Fri., 5pm - 9pm, admission is $10 for adults; $5 for children; ages 2 and under are free. Admission is Sat. - Sun., $15 per person; free for ages 2 and under.

NANCY'S RANCH, Santa Clarita. (661) 255-6943 / www.nancysranch.com, 25039 ½ W. Magic Mountain Pkwy. Fairytale, lumina, gold rush, and more types of pumpkins are available for the picking' from the vine. (Some of these suckers are really huge!) Straw, bales of hay, and cornstalks surround the pre-picked pumpkin patch adding to the ambiance of autumn. Squash and gourds are also available for purchase. Open the first Sat. in October through Halloween daily, 10am - 7pm.

NATIONAL FIRE PREVENTION WEEK. Call your local fire station to see if they are doing something special this week. Many offer tours of the fire engines and station houses, and sometimes kids can even dress up like firemen. The safety tips are lifesavers.

OAK GLEN - PUMPKIN PATCHES, Oak Glen. See the main entry for OAK GLEN / APPLE PICKING (pg. 403). Many of these orchards, including almost all the Riley's, have pumpkin patches, the kinds where visitors pick the pumpkins fresh from the field.

OKTOBERFEST, Big Bear. (909) 585-3000 / www.bigbearevents.com, 42900 Big Bear Blvd. at the Big Bear Lake Convention Center. This sehr gut (ie. very good!) event runs for seven weekends starting in September and has everything you would expect from an Oktoberfest - German Bands, dancing (polka and more), competitions (log-sawing, stein holding, and more), kids' contests, arts and crafts, vendors and of course German food (brats, pretzels, etc.) and beer. Little Oktoberfest fans will enjoy the Kinder Garten complete with bounce houses, face painting, airbrush tattoos and carnival games. Open Sat. noon - midnight; Sun. noon - 6pm. Entrance tickets in Sept. are $14.99 for adults on Sat., $8 on Sun.; srs., $10.99 on Sat., $6 on Sun.; ages 3- - 12 are $8 on Sat., free on Sun. Oct.

prices are $19.99 for adults on Sat., $9 on Sun.; srs., $14.99 on Sat., $6 on Sun.; ages 3 - 12 are $9.99 on Sat., free on Sun.

OMA'S PUMPKIN PATCH, Lakeside. (619) 390-2929 / www.omaspumpkinpatch.com, 14950 El Monte Road at Van Ommering Dairy. Admission to this pumpkin patch, located at a genuine dairy farm, includes a Jack pumpkin, a bottle of water, pumpkin education presentation, cottonseed mountain (to climb and dig through), hayrides around the farm and past all the cows, hay bale maze, milk bottle bowling, a petting zoo, playground equipment (with a sand pile and toys), and a shaded place to enjoy a picnic lunch (that you bring). Open the month of October, Tues. - Sat., 10am - 7pm. Reservations are required for groups of twenty or more. Admission is $10 for ages 1 - 13; $5 for ages 14 and up.

ORANGE COUNTY INTERNATIONAL AUTO SHOW, Anaheim. (717) 566-6100 - regional; (714) 765-8950 - local / www.motortrendautoshows.com, 800 W. Katella Ave. at the Anaheim Convention Center. This must be automotive afficionado's paradise! Hundreds of the latest concept cars, muscle cars, sporty imports, luxury, trucks, minivans, sport utility, celebrity rides, hybrids, tricked-out, classics, and exotics (i.e. Lamborghini, Ferrari, and Lotus) are on view for the public to look at, touch, and drool over. Here is where some of the hottest new cars make their debut. Live D.J.'s spin music, although they and some of the car models aren't always entirely clothed. Some of the things for kids include a kid's scavenger hunt, testing their driving at Camp Jeep on mini electric cars or directing a radio-controlled car at RIDEMAKERZ® RC Experience. Open Thurs., 4pm - 10pm; Fri., noon - 10pm; Sat., 9am - 10pm; Sun., 9am - 7pm. Admission is $12; $10 for srs.; free for ages 12 and under. Check online for discounts and an exact schedule. Parking is $16 per vehicle.

PACIFIC BEACHFEST, Pacific Beach. (858) 273-3303 / www.pacificbeachfest.org, between Garnet and Thomas Aves. on and near the boardwalk. This one-day event signifies the official end of summer in Southern California. Festival activities include a volleyball competition, sand castle building, dancing to live bands and a pro/am surf competition with surfers from around the world. Purchase food from twenty Pacific Beach restaurants here, such as Asian chicken salads, jambalaya, feta cheese ravioli, and chocolate mousse cake. Kids can be kept busy with face painting, clowns, cookie decorating, clay painting, a rock climbing wall and a Kids Action Alley with a large slide and dry-land surfboard (for practice). Nearby museums participate by having booths for children. A fire truck is also on hand to explore. Open 11am - 7pm. Admission is free. Some activities cost. Beach parking is limited.

PA'S PUMPKIN PATCH, Long Beach. (562) 596-7741 / www.paspumpkinpatch.com, 6701 E. Pacific Coast Highway. Besides the rows and rows of the orange vegetable/fruit, there is a snack bar, fall-related merchandise, petting zoo, train rides, pony rides around a ring, games, a huge tepee, giant inflatable bounces and slides, and some kiddie carnival rides like a carousel, roller coaster and swing ride. School and scout groups are welcome (as is the general public!). Open the month of October daily, usually 10am - 9pm. General admission is free but rides require tickets, which are $2.50 each. Most rides are 1 - 3 tickets.

PEACH PICKING. See July entry (pg. 725) for details.

PELTZER FARMS, Temecula. (951) 695-1115 / www.peltzerfarms.com, 39925 Calle Contento. This patch features a real farm experience with pumpkins, naturally, plus pony rides ($5); train rides ($4); gem mining ($5); a good-size petting zoo with pygmy goats, bunnies, sheep, baby chicks, and more ($2); and free activities of going through a one-acre cornfield maze, watching pig races, climbing the mound-o-hay, and viewing the John Deere Tractor display. Burgers, hot dogs, ice cream, and other food are available on weekends, or bring your own lunch and enjoy a picnic here. School tours, which take about an hour, are offered Mon. - Fri., 9am - 1pm and are $8 per student; teachers and supervising adults are $4. Participants will learn about working on a farm and growing crops. Also included is a booklet, pumpkin, and time in the corn maze and the petting farm. Open the end of September through October daily, 9am - 8pm. Most of the rides are available Mon. - Fri., 3pm - 8pm, plus regular weekend hours. Admission is free.

PIONEER DAYS, Twentynine Palms. (760) 367-3445 / www.visit29.org, Two Mile Road and Utah Trail at Luckie Park. The carnival starts on Thurs.; the parade is Sat. at 10am; and the other down home festivities continue through Sun. These include pumpkin patches, decorated bike parade, arm wrestling tournament, haunted house, pet parade, outhouse race, vending booths, live entertainment like a Wild West shoot out show, and competitions like skateboard and Lego building. Open Thurs. 6pm - 10pm; Fri., 6pm - 11pm; Sat., 10am - 11pm; Sun., noon - 8pm. General admission is free.

THE PUMPKIN EXPRESS, Campo. (619) 465-7776 / www.psrm.org, Sheridan Rd. off Hwy 94 at the PACIFIC SOUTHWEST RAILWAY MUSEUM (pg. 582). There are a lot of places with miniature train rides for kids, but why not go on a real train ride? Each weekend in October you can take a train ride from the PACIFIC SOUTHWEST RAILWAY MUSEUM (pg. 582) in Campo to the Great Pumpkin Patch. Afterward kids can tour the Haunted Train, and each child can pick out a pumpkin and decorate it. Trains depart, for the approx. one-hour ride, at 10am, 12:15pm and 2:30pm. The depot opens 2 hours before your trip, plan to arrive at least 45 minutes before departure. Call early to make a reservation. Fares are $18 for adults; $15 for srs.; $14 for ages 3 - 12; $5 for toddlers.

PUMPKIN CITY'S PUMPKIN FARM, Anaheim, Laguna Hills, Rancho Santa Margarita. Anaheim - (949) 880-5106; Laguna Hills - (949) 239 - 9009; Rancho Santa Margarita - (949) 589-2075 / www.pumpkincity.com, Anaheim - 2190 E. Lincoln Ave.; Laguna Hills - 24203 Avenida de la Carlota at Laguna Hills Mall; Rancho Santa Margarita - 30606 Santa Margarita Pkwy. This fenced-in "farm" takes over part of a parking lot for the month of October. The ground is covered with hay, while tractors, cornstalks and bales of hay all around enhance the autumn mood. There is a petting zoo to visit ($2.50), gem mining, pony rides ($7.50), a scale train, a few kiddie rides and carnival games (3 to 8 tickets with $1.25 per ticket at Laguna, $3.75 at Anaheim and Rancho Santa Margarita). Not all attractions are at all locations. Weekend entertainment is provided by costumed characters, country bands, and puppeteers. Group reservations are offered that include special rates on pumpkins and pony rides. And oh yes, there are thousands of pumpkins here of all shapes and sizes - mini pumpkins to ones that weigh up to 200 pounds! Open Mon. - Thurs., 11am - 8:30pm; Fri. - Sun., 10am - 10pm. General admission is free.

THE PUMPKIN FACTORY, Corona. / www.thepumpkinfactory.net, 1545 Circle City Dr. Several giant inflatables - thirty-foot slides, bounces, and obstacle courses; an ATV train ride (just like the olden days!); John Deere ride-on vehicles; a petting zoo and aviary; child-sized hay bale maze; pony rides ($10); other rides; and pumpkins already gathered from the field make this October outing a fun one. Open daily in October usually 4pm - 9pm weekdays; Sat., 10am - 10pm; Sun., 10am - 9pm. Rides are open after 4pm on the weekdays, and all day on weekends. General admission is free. Attractions cost 1 - 8 tickets, per. One ticket package is $20 for 22 tickets.

THE PUMPKIN FACTORY, Westminster. (805) 294-3654, 1025 Westminster Mall. See above entry for details. Not all activities are available at this location. Open Mon. - Thurs., 3pm - 9pm; Fri., noon - 10pm; Sat. , 10am - 10pm; Sun., 10am - 9pm.

PUMPKIN FESTIVAL, Pomona. (909) 869-2215 or (909) 869-2200 / www.cpp.edu/~agriscapes/index.html; www.csupomona.edu, 4102 S. University Dr. on the campus of Cal Poly Pomona. This two-day pumpkin festival is a very popular local event. Pick your own (pre-cut) pumpkin in the field ($5); pig out at a pancake breakfast ($5 per person); listen to live music; enter the Petting Farm; ride a horse; jump in a bounce house; participate in games; get your face painted; and munch on food. See October entry (pg. 738) for this fair that is often held at the same time as the pumpkin festival. Open Sat. - Sun., 10am - 5pm. Admission is $4 per person; some activities cost extra.

PUMPKIN LINER, Fillmore. (800) 773-8724 or (805) 524-2546 / www.fwry.com, 364 Main Street. Catch a vintage train to ride to a "private" pumpkin patch and then join in the festivities. There are games, haunted hay maze, jumps, a carousel, arts and crafts booths, food booths, and pumpkins. The train company also offers haunted hayride Family Dinner Train with delicious food, and a train ride that ends at the pumpkin patch. There ARE scary elements to this excursion. Open the month of October, Sat. - Sun., departing 10:30am and 2pm. The haunted hayrides is Sat. at 7pm. Pumpkin Liner rides are $22 for adults; $15 for ages 4 - 12; $10 for ages 2 - 3; children under 2 are free, as they occupy a lap, not a seat. Pumpkins are extra. Haunted hayrides are $62 for adults; $45 for ages 4 - 12; $30 for ages 3 and under. All reservations must be made online or by phone.

PUMPKIN PATCH EXPRESS, Perris. (951) 943-3020 / www.oerm.org, 2201 South A Street at the Southern California Railway Museum. Ride the rails to adventure! The train ride doesn't go far, but far enough for it be fun and a fun destination - a pumpkin patch. Guest choose and decorate their own pumpkin, go on a hay ride, visit the coloring station, and enjoy temporary tattoos, a bounce house, and trick or treating. Wear your Halloween costume! (Come as Thomas the Tank Engine!) And, of course, you can explore the museum, too, plus ride on the vintage trolley and streetcars, take a hay ride, go thru the small hay maze and enjoy some other activities and entertainment. Open select weekends, Sat. - Sun., 9am - 5pm. Tickets are $25 for adults; $15 for ages 2 - 11; children under 2 are free.

PUMPKIN PATCH FIELD TRIPS / YOU PICK PUMPKINS, Pomona. (909) 869-6722; (909) 869-4906 / www.cpp.edu/~agriscapes/index.html, 4102 S. University Dr. on the campus of Cal Poly Pomona. Under the umbrella name of AGRIscapes, pumpkin patch educational field trips are offered to learn about this fruit or vegetable?!, pick one (or two), meander through the corn maze, climb on the hay pyramid and pet the animals in the Petting Farm. There are over 80,000 pumpkins growing in the field - not on a patch of cement, as most pumpkin patches promote! Individuals are welcome at non-tour times to pretty much do the same. Tues. - Fri., 9am - noon for group tours; Tues. - Wed., noon - 6pm; Thurs. - Fri., noon - 8pm; Sat. - Sun., 10am - 8pm for individuals to pick-your-own. Tours are about $5 per person. Free general admission after the pumpkin festival - check the web calendar.

PUMPKIN STATION, Bonita, Escondido. Bonita - (858) 566-7466; Escondido (Rancho Bernardo Farm) - (858) 566-7466 / www.pumpkinstation.com, Bonita - 5437 Bonita Rd.; Escondido - 13421 Highland Valley Rd. Pre-picked pumpkins are fine, but there's nothing like getting them straight off the vine. These working farms offer pick-your-own pumpkin; a corn field maze to wander through; tractor-drawn hayrides; farm animals to gently touch (free); and plenty of space for picnicking. School tours, $10 per student (adults are free), include a pumpkin (up to $5 value), and all of the attractions, plus a coloring book and educational info about pumpkins. Bonita is open beginning of October -

mid-October, daily, 9am - 6pm; mid-October - end of October, daily, 9am - 8pm. Escondido is open in October, Mon. - Thurs., 9am - 5pm; Fri. - Sun., 9am - 6pm. General admission is free. Hayrides and corn maze are $2 each.

PUMPKIN STATION, Del Mar; El Cajon; Mission Valley; National City. Del Mar - (858) 566-7466; El Cajon - (858) 566-7466; Mission Valley - (858) 566-7466; National City - (858) 566-7466 / www.pumpkinstation.com, Del Mar - 15555 Jimmy Durante Blvd.; El Cajon - 415 Parkway Plaza at Westfield; Mission Valley - 1640½ Camino Del Rio N. at Westfield; National City - 3030 Plaza Bonita Rd. at Plaza Bonita Shopping Center. Halloween is not just about the pumpkins, although these stations (not farms, as the other Pumpkin Stations are) have plenty of them. Other important elements at these patches include train rides, kiddie rides, carousel, small Ferris wheel, a swing ride, game zone, petting zoo (with bunnies, llamas, goats, and chickens), photo ops, giant slide, and an inflatable bounce, jump, and play center. Note that not all locations have all the attractions. School tours, $10 per student (free for adults), include a pumpkin (up to a $5 limit), plus several of the attractions, coloring book, and a short educational presentation about pumpkins. Open from the end of September through October all the stations are open Fri. - Sun., 9am - 9pm. Other hours are - Del Mar: Sun. - Thurs., 9am - 7pm. El Cajon: Mon. - Thurs., 3pm - 9pm. Mission Valley: Mon. - Thurs., 11am - 9pm. National City: Mon. - Thurs., 1pm - 9pm. Free general admission. Attractions cost one ticket each. Tickets are $3.50 each, or 12 tickets for $36.

RASPBERRY PICKING. See July entry (pg. 726) for details.

RENDEZVOUS BACK TO ROUTE 66, San Bernardino. (909) 885-7515 / www.rendezvoustoroute66.com, Bordering "E" St., 5th St., Arrowhead and 2nd St. This classic car gathering is reminiscent of good old days, where people got together to socialize, admire each other's cars, eat and enjoy live entertainment. Over 950 cars are usually on display on the streets to walk around and oogle. Sat., 10am - 10pm. Free.

SANDCASTLE CONTEST, Newport Beach. (949) 729-4400 / www.newportbeach.com, near Iris St. and Ocean Blvd. at Corona Del Mar State Beach. Call about participating in this one-day sandy event, or just come to "sea" the most imaginative things created with sand. Both experts and novice builders compete. Sun., 10am - 3:30pm. It's free to watch. There is a fee to participate. Parking is $4/hr. or $15.

SAN DIEGO KIDS EXPO AND FAIR, Del Mar. See April entry (pg. 709) for details.

SAN DIEGO ZOO / SAN DIEGO ZOO SAFARI PARK, Escondido, San Diego. (619) 234-3153 or (619) 231-1515 / www.sandiegozoo.org. The Zoo is on Park Blvd. in Balboa Park, San Diego; the Safari Park is at 15500 San Pasqual Valley Road, Escondido. The world-famous Zoo and the Safari Park are both free for ages 11 and under, when accompanied by a paying adult, for the entire month of October. Now, that's wild! See the long write-ups for these wonderful places in the main section of the book.

SAN DIMAS WESTERN DAYS RODEO, San Dimas. (909) 394-RODEO (7633) or (909) 592-3818 / www.sandimasrodeo.com, San Dimas Canyon Rd. at Horsethief Canyon Park. Yee ha! This weekend PRCA rodeo, which raises money for Veterans, victims of domestic violence and more, features all a cowboys' (and cowgirls') favorite rodeo events. Come early for pre-rodeo activities, then enjoy the shows including bareback riding, saddle bronc riding, tie down roping, steer wrestling, clown, bull riding, barrel racing, and more. A rodeo clown and other half-time entertainment, plus food and vendors selling Western themed everything are also part of the happenings. On Sunday, the Cowboy Church starts at 9am, and the Challenged Buckaroos perform in their own rodeo at 1pm. Shuttles pick up at the Post Office starting at 11am, and run every 15 minutes. Gates open at 11am; pre-show activities on Sat. and Sun. begin at 1pm; the shows starts at 2pm and ends around 4:30pm. Admission is $18 for adults; $11 for ages 3 - 12. Discount tickets available via the website.

SEASONAL ADVENTURES, INC. (pumpkin patch), Eastvale; Hesperia; Lancaster; Murrieta; Rancho Cucamonga; San Marcos; Simi Valley; Thousand Oaks. (805) 532-2333 - corporate number / www.seasonaladventures.com. This franchise has 8 locations in Southern California, so look at the website for more info on your specific city. There are hundreds of pumpkins to choose from here, plus kiddie carnival rides, a bounce house, inflatable slide, and a petting zoo, making this a fun, Halloween stop-off. School field trips ($7 per student) and birthday parties are also welcome. Open the month of October Mon. - Fri., 11am - 9pm; Sat. - Sun., 9am - 9pm. General admission is free.

SOUTHERN CALIFORNIA FAIR, Perris. (951) 657-4221 / www.socalfair.com, 18700 Lake Perris Dr. at Lake Perris Fairgrounds. For nine days and nights, enjoy top-name entertainment; PRCA rodeos; livestock shows; monster trucks; demolition derby; petting zoo; extreme sports demonstrations; fishing demonstrations; carnival rides and games; and horticulture and fine art exhibits. Open Mon. - Thurs., 4pm - 11pm; Fri., noon - 11pm; Sat. - Sun., 11am - 11pm. Admission on weekdays is $10 for adults; $8 for srs.; $5 ages 5 - 12; children 4 and under are free. Rides and some activities cost extra. An unlimited ride wristband is $30. Parking is $8.

TANAKA FARMS PUMPKIN PATCH, Irvine. (949) 653-2100 / www.tanakafarms.com, 5380 ¾ University Dr. One unique feature of this pumpkin patch is that visitors can pick their pumpkins right off the vine. This thirty-acre working farm, in the heart of Irvine, also offers other autumn fun such as a good-size petting zoo ($3), wagon rides around the farm ($6), and a corn maze (free with admission), plus special weekend activities such as games ($2 - $6), a pumpkin cannon ($5 to launch one), some carnival rides, ATV rides, Bigger Digger, and lots of food choices. Tanaka also offers fresh U-pick vegetables (carrots, onions, green beans, and radishes) and fruit, depending on what's in season, and a produce stand. Fall items, such as decorative corn and gourds, corn stalks, and painted pumpkins, are also available for purchase. School and other groups, consisting of at least ten children, are welcome for tours and an educational adventure, daily. Individuals and groups can take the Fall Harvest Tour on weekends which includes a guided wagon ride around the farm, petting zoo, learning about produce, sampling veggies, and walking the corn maze. There is a holiday tour, too at Christmas time with seasonal offerings. Check out spring and summer months in this Calendar section to see other Tanaka food offerings. Notes: Active military receive free admission, wagon ride, and petting zoo admission. Open the end of September through October daily, 9am - 6pm. $3 admission per person; ages 2 and under are free.

TICKET TO THE TWENTIES, City of Industry. (626) 968-8492 / www.homesteadmuseum.org, 15415 East Don Julian Road at the Homestead Museum. Dress up (or not) and celebrate the Roaring Twenties as you enjoy music, dancing, crafts, historic house tours, games from the 20's, silent films with live musical accompaniment, demonstrations, 20's cars and vintage bicycles, and more! Also see THE HOMESTEAD MUSEUM (pg. 121). Sat. and Sun., 3pm - 7pm. Admission free, but bring spending money for food and shopping.

TRICK-OR-TREAT FESTIVAL, Costa Mesa. (949) 723-6616 or (714) 557-0420 / www.ocmarketplace.com, 88 Fair Drive at the Orange County Fair and Event Center. While this is one of the biggest (and best) swap meets in the area, with plenty of food choices, on the Sunday before Halloween, it is also a trick or treat festival with free face painting; daytime trick or treating for kids in costume; freaky puppet show (geared for kids); strolling entertainment; a pumpkin sculptor; blood drive; show; and a hearse (and ambulance) procession. Shop with the 1,000 vendors and be entertained. Open Sun., 8am - 4pm. Admission is $2 for adults; children 12 and under are free.

THE WICKERD FARM PUMPKIN PATCH, Menifee. (951) 672-3020 or (909) 286-8288 / www.wickerdfarm.com, 26852 Scott Rd. While this farm doesn't grow pumpkins it sells them in every shape and size. They are scattered throughout a portion of the farm, and amongst the trees, bales of hay and picnic area. Haunted hayrides are $10 for adults; $5 for kids. Educational field trips are offered as are hay rides upon request and a visit to the butterfly garden and small play area. Open the end of September - October 31st, Sun. - Thurs., 10am - 8pm, Fri. - Sat., 10am - 9pm. Admission is free.

WILL GEER THEATRICUM BOTANICUM, Topanga. See June entry (pg. 722) for details.

- NOVEMBER -

AMERICAN INDIAN ARTS MARKETPLACE, Los Angeles. (323) 667-2000 / www.theautry.org, 4700 Western Heritage Way at the Autry National Center in Griffith Park. More than 200 American Indian artists who represent more than 40 tribes offer sculpture, pottery, beadwork, basketry, photography, paintings, jewelry, textiles, carvings, mixed-media works, and more. Traditional dancers, storytellers, theater performances, children's activities, and films, plus a plethora of ethnic food and craft demonstration add up to a wonderful weekend marketplace. Explore the THE AUTRY MUSEUM (pg. 153) while you're here. Open Sat. - Sun., 10am - 5pm. Admission is $14 adults; $10 seniors and students; $6 children; ages 3 and under are free. This includes admission to the museum.

CARLSBAD VILLAGE FAIRE FALL, Carlsbad. See May entry for (pg. 711) for details.

CHILL AT THE QUEEN MARY, Long Beach. (562) 435-3511 or (877) 342-0752 / www.queenmary.com, 1126 Queens Highway at the Queen Mary. CHILL can feature some of the "coolest", and most expensive, experiences this season. There are a few staple elements, but every year is differently themed with different attractions. The constants are the many food snack shacks (serving hot chocolate, gingerbread cookies, corn dogs, and lots more); several small gift shops with Christmas merchandise; outdoor area decorated like Santa's village; live entertainment; visits with Santa; a few rides; an ice tube slide with side-by-side lanes; and an outdoor ice skating rink. Yet, even the rink changes as one year it was a traditional square rink, another it also had ice pathways that intersected and went around a huge Christmas tree, under a bridge and back to the main area. Some years have featured ice bumper cars ($5); riding ice bikes ($5); seeing a 4-D movie; a 300-foot zipline ($5); walking through an entire ice palace (a "palace" literally made of ice, with differently-themed rooms); and a very colorful, creative, lively and interactive set of rooms, hallways, and mazes with detailed lighting and some special effects - like a gigantic movie set - to go thru called *Alice in Winterland*. You can also walk through the Queen Mary on your own (i.e. not a guided tour). There are fireworks on some nights, too. Check the calender for days and times of operation as they fluctuate a lot, from 5pm - 10pm on Thurs. and Fri. nights to noon - 10pm on other days/nights. Basic admission gets you into the Queen Mary, the ice skating rink (with ice skates), the ice tube slide and on a giant rocking horse - $29.99 for adults; $19.99 for ages 4 - 11 years; children 3 and under are free. Other activities cost extra. Parking is $20 - or park elsewhere and take the free Passport shuttle.

CHRISTMAS ON THE FARM, Moorpark. (805) 529-3690; (805) 218-0282 / www.underwoodfamilyfarms.com, 3370 Sunset Valley Rd. at Underwood Family Farms. See UNDERWOOD FAMILY FARMS - Moorpark (pg. 656) for more details on this fantastic farm. Big Wave Dave's Christmas trees are sold here along with wreaths, mistletoe, and lots of Christmas decor. The trees and some farm activities are available daily, but admission to the animal center, vintage tractor-drawn wagon rides and rides with Santa (11am - 4pm); most of the farm, and farmer's market are available only on weekends. Note: Wagon rides are only offered on select weekends. Open the weekends after Thanksgiving - December 21, 9:30am - 7:30pm. Wagon rides are available 11am - 4pm. $6 covers the cost of a wagon ride and entry to the animal center.

CHRISTMAS RANCH TREE FARMS, Thousand Oaks. (805) 624-0031 / www.christmasranchtreefarms.com, 1586 Pederson Rd. Don't just go over the river and through the woods to grandmother's house, but stop in these woods and smell the fresh Christmas trees. For over 47 years going to Christmas Ranch Tree Farms has been a tradition for numerous families. On these fifteen acres, you can choose and cut your own Monterey Pine, Leyland Cypress, Aleppo Pine, and others kinds, via walking the farm or taking a vintage Jeep over a steep hill and to its other side - how fun! Also available here are pre-cut trees, wreaths, garland, and a picnic area. Open the Friday after Thanksgiving until December 24, Mon. - Fri., 2pm - 7pm; Sat. - Sun., 9am - 7pm. Admission is free.

CHRISTMAS TRAIN, Orange. See December entry (pg. 754) for details.

CORONADO BUTTERFLY RESERVE, Goleta. See January entry (pg. 695) for details.

DAY OUT WITH THOMAS, Perris. (951) 943-3020 / www.oerm.org, 2201 South A Street at the Southern California Railway Museum Inspired from the classic story, *Thomas the Tank Engine*, this popular event offers Thomas afficionados the opportunity to take a twenty-five minute ride on this friendly storybook engine. Thomas and Friends, Sir Topham Hatt, who is the Controller of the Railway on the Island of Sodor, and Percy the Small Engine will be here, too. (Percy might have to leave early in December, though.) Besides the train ride with Thomas, your day includes admission to the museum, train-themed entertainment, such as story telling and arts and crafts. 2 weekends, Sat. - Sun. (and a holiday Monday), 9am - 5pm (last ride at 4pm). Thomas rides leave every hour on the hour. Tickets are $25 per person, though there are some discounted dates and times, as low as $19; children under two are free. Advanced ticket purchases are recommended as sometimes this event sells out.

DISTRICT FREEZE ICE RINK, Tustin. See December entry (pg. 755) for details.

DOO-DAH PARADE, Pasadena. (626) 590-1134 / www.pasadenadoodahparade.info, It's time again for that off-the-wall, definitely-not-the-Rose Parade to march the streets of Pasadena. See the web side for a map of the route. Starts at 11am. The parade is free to watch.

ENCHANTED: FOREST OF LIGHT, La Canada Flintridge. See December entry (pg. 756) for details.

FAMILY CHRISTMAS TREE FARM, El Cajon. (619) 448-5331 / www.familychristmastreefarm.com; www.cachristmas.com, 300 Pepper Dr. Select your own Monterey pine from this ten-acre farm, or choose an already cut Noble, Douglas Fir or Grand Fir tree, or even a potted tree. A petting zoo, hayrides, and a small store with fresh winter greens, wreaths, cinnamon brooms and pinecones are also on the premises. School tours can be made by reservation. Open the day after Thanksgiving through December 22 daily, 9am - 8:30pm.

FESTIVAL OF BANDS, Arcadia. / www.worldofpagentry.com/events; www.arcadiamusic.org, Huntington Dr. and moving south on Baldwin Ave. for the parade; 180 Campus Dr. at Arcadia High School. Come out early on a Sat. morning to watch the procession of more than 40 marching bands down Baldwin Avenue. Immediately following the parade with the bands, drill teams, color guard, and drum majors, go as they assemble at Salter Stadium at Arcadia High School to face off in percussion performances and precision events that are rousing to watch and listen to. That night there is an evening field show at Citrus College at 1000 W. Foothill Blvd. in Glendora which showcases competing bands from all over Southern California. The parade begins at 8:40am. Gates open at 5pm. Performances are 6pm - 10pm. The parade is free. Admission for the evening performances are $12 for adults; ages 5 and under are free.

FESTIVAL OF LIGHTS, Riverside. (951) 826-2427 ; (951) 826-2370 / www.riversideca.gov/fol, 3900 Main St. at the Mission Inn Hotel and along Main St. Pedestrian Mall. The Festival of Lights Switch-On Ceremony (self explanatory) begins at 4:30pm, with live band and singing performances, a thank-you ceremony, and finally, the turning on of the 5 million twinkling lights and over 400 holiday decorations and animated figures surrounding the historic Mission Inn Hotel and pedestrian mall. What a fantastic sight! This night ends with fireworks and a visit from Santa Claus. Ranked as one of the top lighting festivals in the country, each evening following the Switch-On Ceremony is the Festival of Lights featuring the lights (and animated characters) lavishly decorating the outside of the huge Inn and surrounding buildings. Walk around to take in the festive ambiance; unique holiday vendors on the pedestrian strip; shopping; visits with Santa; horse-drawn carriage rides; trackless train rides ($5); a carousel ($5); skating rink ($15 + $3 for skate rentals) and Ferris wheel ($5). Sometimes strolling carolers, dance performances, and other entertainment are part of the festival fun, too. You are invited to enter the Inn's beautifully lit up inner courtyard, the tree, and the lobby, as well, but note that the line can be up to 90 minutes long to enter - get there early. There are a lot of special events going on at this place and time, even breakfast with Santa at the Inn and free children's Christmas movies - so check the website to make sure you don't miss anything! Also check out the Festival of Trees, the below entry, for another fun event. The Festival of Lights kicks off the Friday after Thanksgiving and continues until the beginning of January. The lights before Christmas are Mon. - Thurs., 5pm - 11pm; Fri., 3pm - 11pm; Sat., 3pm - 10pm. Note that the shops, rides and other activities run during the day, as well. The light hours after Christmas are Mon. - Sat., 3pm - midnight. The festival is closed Sun. and Christmas Day and closes early on Christmas Eve. General admission to the festival is free.

FESTIVAL OF TREES, Riverside. (951) 486-4213 or (951) 486-4238 / www.ruhealth.org, 3637 5th St. at the Riverside Convention Center. Fifty, elaborately-decorated trees, each with a unique theme, are the centerpiece of this three-day Festival of Trees. The trees are a fund raiser, sponsored and pre-purchased with proceeds going to the pediatric unit at Riverside County Regional Medical Center. For kids, the trees are simply magical. The rest of the convention center is equally transformed. There are also has visits with Santa; storytime with Santa (for a nominal fee as it includes cookie decorating); holiday vendors; craft-making; entertainment on stage by local youth; and stroll for seniors to take a tour of the trees and have free cocoa and a chocolate bar. Also see Festival of Lights, the above entry. The Festival of Trees is the Fri. after Thanksgiving, 10am - 9m; Sat., 10am - 8pm; Sun., 10am - 2pm. General admission is free. Parking at the Convention Center is $10.

FIRST FLIGHT FIELD TRIP. See February entry (pg. 699) for more info.

FROSTY'S VILLAGE AT LIVE OAK CANYON, Yucaipa. (909) 795-TREE (8733) / www.thepumpkinfactory.com/frostys-village, 32335 Live Oak Canyon Rd. Come join in the festivities celebrated here around Christmas time. Warm yourself by a large fire pit, and purchase a s'mores kit; visit with Santa Claus (on certain weekends); listen to carolers (usually on the weekends); look at real reindeer; and grab a bite at the refreshment stands. Other activities include the petting zoo, slide, moon bounces, a carousel and train ride - 3 tickets each; horse-drawn carriage - $5 per person on Sat. and Sun. starting at noon, available only the full week just before Christmas; pony rides - 6 tickets; plus a few other rides and attractions. Walk among a twenty-five acre forest of home-grown Monterey Pines, Sierra Redwoods, and Aleppo Pines. Choose your own Christmas tree here and have a worker cut it down, or purchase a fir tree shipped from Oregon. A tented gift shop sells fresh wreaths, garland, and other decorations and gift items. Note that outside food and coolers are allowed. Open late November - mid-December, Sun. - Thurs., 9am - 8pm; Fri. - Sat., 9am - 9pm. Rides and attractions are usually open on weekends only, 10am - 8pm. Admission is free. Some activities are free; ticket packages starting at 22 tickets for $20.

GREENSPOT FARMS, Mentone. (909) 794-7653 or (909) 583-1257 / www.greenspotfarms.com, 10133 Ward Wy. This farm is acres upon acres of Christmas trees and just being here generates a family feel, making this place a favorite holiday destination for over twenty years. Walk among the "forest" to pick your own tree - come and tag it early (even in October) and then come back in November or December to pick it up or cut it down, and to take it home the day you visit. This working ranch, filled with a variety of fruit trees, also has a petting zoo, small gift shop with wreaths and mistletoe, a refreshment stand, and picnic area, bounce house, and, depending on the day and season, tractor-drawn hayrides, and maybe a visit with Santa. Check out the honey house where you can look at live honey bees through a window (and purchase honey fresh from the hive). Open the Friday after Thanksgiving through December 23 daily, 9am - 6pm. Admission is free. The hayride is $10 for adults; $8 for children; free for ages 3 and under. Some activities cost extra.

HAGLE TREE FARM, Somis. (805) 630-4580 / www.hagletreefarm.com, 3442 Somis Road. Bring a little of the country home by choosing and cutting your own Christmas tree here. Most weekends include extras such as visits with Santa Claus, a hay hill to play on, pony rides, a petting zoo, hayrides, music, hot chocolate and trip-tip bbq sandwiches, plus a few picnic tables, and wreaths and garlands for sale to make your Christmas complete. Open the Friday after Thanksgiving through December 24 (open mid-December thru December 24 just to buy trees), Mon. - Fri., noon to 5pm; Sat. - Sun., 9am to 5pm. Weekend activities are Thanksgiving weekend and the first two weekends in December, Fri. - Sun., 10am - 4pm. General admission is free.

HOLIDAY BY THE BAY, San Diego. See December entry (pg. 747, 757) for details.

HOLIDAY FEST, Yermo. (800) TO-CALICO (862-2542) / www.calicotown.com, 36600 Ghost Town Rd. at Calico Ghost Town. On the Sat. after Thanksgiving enjoy a rootin' tootin' time at Calico. Live music, including carolers; visits with Santa; Native American dancers in full ceremonial dress performing; a holiday craft corner; animal shows; staged gun fights; tree lighting ceremony; and demonstrations of blacksmithing and rope-making give city slickers a feel for Christmas, Old West-style. Look up CALICO GHOST TOWN (pg. 433) for more details about the museum. Sat., 9am - 7pm. Admission is $8 for adults; $5 for ages 4 - 11 years; children 3 and under are free. On-site camping (minimum 2 nights) is $35 - $40 a night (camping for this weekend books up months in advance); $65 a night for cabins.

HOLIDAY ICE RINK, Thousand Oaks. (818) 637-8923 / www.conejovalleyguide.com, 2200 E. Thousand Oaks Blvd. at The Lakes. Baby, it's cold outside. Well, even if it isn't, you can still go ice skating outside. One of the two man-made lakes at this outdoor shopping complex is frozen over from Thanksgiving through January. The ambiance is lovely, so enjoy shopping and taking in a restaurant at the mall before or after your winter wonderland excursion. Classes are also available and you can rent out the rink for a birthday party or other event. Note: This rink is small and it can get crowded. The rink is open Mon. - Thurs., noon - 9pm; Fri., noon - 10pm; Sat., 10am - 11pm; Sun., 10am - 9pm. Open mid-December - Jan. 2 daily at 10am. Admission is $15 for the day, which includes skate rentals.

HOLIDAY ICE RINK, Los Angeles. (213) 847-4970 or (213) 624-4289 / www.laparks.org/pershingsquare; www.holidayicerinkdowntownla.com, 532 S. Olive near Hill St. and 5th and 6th sts. at Pershing Square. On a huge (7,200 square-foot) rink made of real ice and surrounded by L.A. skyscrapers, ice skate outside in sunny Southern California mid-November through mid-January. Special events such as live DJ's, professional skaters, and more are part of the seasonal offerings. The hours fluctuate but usually open mid-November - mid- December, and in January, Mon. - Thurs., 11:30am - 9:30pm; Fri., 11:30am - 11pm; Sat., 10am - 11pm; Sun., 10am - 9:30pm. Open mid-December - end of December daily, 10am - 11pm. Admission is $9, plus $4 for skate rental. Lockers are $3. Parking is $6.

HOLIDAY LIGHTS ON MAIN, El Cajon. (619) 334-3000 / downtownelcajon.com, 100 E. Main St. in downtown El Cajon. This one-day festival features a Santa's Village (and Santa!); carnival rides; an ice skating rink; live music/entertainment; scale model train rides; and food and craft vendors. The tree lighting is at 6pm. What a great day!! Open Sat., noon - 7pm. Free.

HOLIDAY ON ICE, Irvine. (949) 748-8280 or (949) 753-5180 / www.shopirvinespectrumcenter.com, 71 Fortune Dr. at Irvine Spectrum Center. One of the coolest places to be in Southern California in the winter is at the outdoor ice rink. The skating is fun to do and interesting to watch, plus you can always go eat or shop before or after. Look up IRVINE SPECTRUM CENTER (pg. 300) in the main section in the book, for details about the mall. Open day after Thanksgiving, November through New Year's Day, usually Mon. - Fri., 1pm - 11pm. Admission is per session, which are usually 2 to 2.5 hours long - $20 per person, which includes skate rental. $18 if you bring your own skates. Toddlers (size 8T to 13T) and srs. are $16. Lockers are .75¢

HOLLYWOOD CHRISTMAS PARADE, Hollywood. (310) 631-0691; (866) 727-2331 - grandstand tickets / www.thehollywoodchristmasparade.com, starting at Hollywood Blvd. and Orange; check to see this year's route. Starting at noon the Hollywood Christmas Parade offers information booths, games, and some live entertainment. All the stars come out at night - I mean the stars of Hollywood - for this celebrity-packed parade that is put on the Sunday after Thanksgiving. There are fantastic floats, live bands, drill units, cartoon characters, equestrian units, and of course, Santa Claus. The two-hour parade goes along a three-mile course through the streets of Hollywood. An all-star concert with multiple headliners is given at the end of this 85+ year tradition! A grandstand ticket is required to attend the concert. Pre-show concert is at 5pm. The parade starts at 6pm. The "big" concert follows the parade. Reserved grandstand seating is $65 - $85 per person. Standing room past Highland Blvd. is free, but it does get crowded and it's hard to see over people, so get here early. All-day parking in nearby lots runs from $5 - $15. Or, take the metro red line to the Hollywood/Highland exit or Hollywood/Vine.

HOW THE GRINCH STOLE CHRISTMAS, San Diego. (619) 234-5623 / www.oldglobe.org, Balboa Park at the Old Globe Theater. This seventy-five-minute, Dr. Seuss-inspired musical production stars a fuzzy green villain who learns how to have a heart in the magical, musical world of Who-ville. The show runs through most of November and December. Call for show times. Admission depends on the date and time. Prices range from $40 - $100.

ICE AT SANTA MONICA, Santa Monica. (310) 260 -1199 or (310) 393-8355 / www.downtownsm.com, 1324 5th St. (and Arizona Ave.). Chill out by iceskating so close to the ocean. This 8,000 foot ice rink operates daily from the beginning of November through mid-January so you can skate everyday (you'd be really good if you did that!). There is also a 20' by 20' enclosed Tot Spot rink for ages 6 and under. The rinks are available for birthday parties and lessons. Note that towards the beginning of November is the kick off of ICE with a one-day celebration of a kids craft station, dance music and a live performance by some of California's most elite skaters. The rest of Third Street Promenade (aka Downtown Santa Monica) is dramatically lit up, has decorated Christmas trees, and throughout the season (check the website for specifics) there are visits from Santa Claus, strolling carolers, and other entertainment keep visitors feeling merry. Look up THIRD STREET PROMENADE (pg. 95) for more details. Come on a Wed. or Sat. morning to also enjoy a Farmer's Market. General hours are Mon. - Thurs., 2pm - 10pm; Fri., 2pm - midnight; Sat., 10am - midnight;

Sun., 10am - 10pm. Call, or check the website calendar, as the hours fluctuate a lot. Admission and skate rental is $15 per person.

INDIO POWWOW, Indio. (760) 238-5770 or (800) 827-2946 / www.fantasyspringsresort.com, 84245 Indio Springs Dr. at Fantasy Springs Casino. Hosted by the Cabazon Band of Mission Indians, this three-day indoor Pow Wow brings together Native Americans and non-Indians in a celebration and competition of music with drum performances, bird singing, and dance contests for all ages, plus food and arts and crafts. Don't miss the "grand entrance" where all the Indians, in elaborate regalia, dance as they come in. The Pow Wow begins Fri., 5pm - midnight (grand entrance at 8pm); Sat., 11am - midnight (grand entrance at 1pm and 8pm); Sun., 11am - 6pm (grand entrance at noon). Admission is free.

LA KINGS HOLIDAY ICE, Long Beach; Los Angeles; Woodland Hills, (818) 296-5887 / www.nhl.com/kings; www.lakingsholidayice.com, Long Beach - 95 S Pine Ave. at The Pike; Los Angeles - 800 W Olympic Blvd. at Nokia Plaza at L.A. LIVE complex; Woodland Hills - 6100 Topanga Canyon Blvd. at Westfield Promenade Only in Southern California can you ice skate in a t-shirt and not only not get cold, but get a suntan! LA Kings run all three outside rinks, which are each about 7,000+ square feet of real ice. They offer recreational skating, skating exhibitions, field trips, birthday parties, and more. Nighttime skating, under the stars, is an almost magical treat. All of the rinks are located in places that have lots of restaurants and other activities to also do in the immediate area. Open mid-November - mid-December, Mon. - Fri., 5pm -8pm and 8:30pm - 10:30pm; Sat. - Sun., 4pm - 7pm. Open mid-December - mid-January daily, 4pm -7pm and 7:30pm - 10:30pm. Every session of skating, which includes skate rentals, is $17 for adults; $13 for srs, ages 6 and under.

LA ZOO LIGHTS, Los Angeles. (323) 644-4200 / www.lazoolights.org; ww.lazoo.org, 5300 Zoo Dr., Griffith Park at the Los Angeles Zoo. Truly magical, a winter wonderland of lights and music makes these nights at the zoo really special. A large portion of the zoo is decorated and open to walk around featuring animal-themed LEDs, laser lights, 3D projections, animated displays, glittering light tunnels to walk through, a disco-ball forest and a water show where fountains dance to music and lights. Other extras include visits with Santa (on certain dates); food for purchase; riding the carousel ($3); and seeing real reindeer. Note that all other animals, except those amphibians and reptiles in the L.A.I.R., are not on view on these nights. Note, too, that daytime zoo admission is not valid for this separate, nighttime event. Open mid-November - beginning of January, 6pm - 10pm nightly. Closed Christmas Eve and Christmas Day. Tickets are $21 for adults; $18 for srs.; $16 for ages 2 - 12. Tickets are sometimes cheaper on the front end of the event.

LOGAN'S CANDIES, Ontario. (909) 984-5410 / www.loganscandies.com, 125 W. "B" St. This small, family-owned retail candy store makes delicious candy canes (and other sweet treats). A limited number of thirty-minute demonstrations are offered to watch the fascinating process of the striped candy become a sweet reality. First you'll stand outside and hear a description of the procedure, some candy cane history and funny commentary, as you peer in through the storefront window. Flavoring is added and kneaded through a huge amber blob which is then stretched and pulled (think taffy pull) to form the white part of the cane. A smaller blob is dyed red. Next, you'll go inside the store to see the two colors twisted together and shaped into variously-sized candy canes. The samples of warm, fresh candy are delectable. Buy a ticket to bend your own candy cane in whatever shape you want. This is one of our favorite seasonal excursions! The store is open year round and other times throughout the year you can watch them (without a full demonstration and explanation, tho) make ribbon candy, and even candy canes for special events. Demonstrations, for a limited group size, are given the end of November through the third week in December at various times. Reservations are needed and make sure to reserve a spot early as these sometimes fill up in the summer! There are free and no-reservation-needed demos for families at several dates and times throughout the season, too - first come, first served. Note: Sometimes a few people can be added onto group tours - call first and find out. Group demonstrations are $6.50 per child, which includes a bag of candy; $1.85 for adults. The cost for anyone to bend their own candy cane is $1.85.

LONDON BRASS RUBBING CENTER, Long Beach. See October entry (pg. 740) for details.

MONARCH BUTTERFLIES, Ventura. (805) 652-4550 / www.cityofventura.ca.gov, Dean and Varsity Drs. at Camino Real Park. Hundreds of monarch butterflies arrive at the park during this month and hang on the trees at Dean Court. Go on a warm day when they reach out their orange and black wings toward the sun and flutter about. Free.

MOTHER GOOSE PARADE, El Cajon. (619) 333-0771 / www.mothergooseparade.org, The parade goes along Main St. between El Cajon and First sts. Note: The parade route can change so check the website first. This three-mile mother of parades has been going strong and gaining momentum since 1946. It features over 5,000 participants - marching bands, drill units, equestrian units, specialty units, clown acts, street performers, celebrities, military, dignitaries, vintage automobiles, fire trucks, Santa Claus, and the best part of all - lots of motorized floats depicting Mother Goose rhymes and fairy tales in a different theme each year. The parade takes place the Sun. before

Thanksgiving beginning at 1pm. The pre-parade show/concert begins at 11am in front of the grand stand only. Admission is free.

NATIONAL PARKS - FREE ENTRANCE DAYS. See January entry (pg. 696) for details.

NORTH POLE EXPRESS, Fillmore. (800) 773-8724 or (805) 524-2546 / www.fwry.com, 364 Main Street. Enjoy the train ride to the North Pole to pick up Santa Claus; you can even wear your jammies if you want to. (Actually, it's a much shorter ride to the North Pole than I thought - only an hour!) There are storytellers, caroling, cookies, and chocolate milk on board, too. Once you get to the destination of Santa's Village, you can ride the carousel and maybe some other kiddie rides, and purchase something fun at the gift shop. Bring your camera. Note that the train company also offers dinner with Santa rides, consisting of turkey or ham, mashed potatoes, and dessert for adults, and chicken fingers, potatoes, and fruit cup for kids. North Pole rides are offered mid-November through December 26, most weekends and some weekday evenings, usually departing at 6pm and 7:30pm. Note: The Dec. 26 train returns Santa to the North Pole. The train ride is $32 for adults; $22 for ages 2 - 12; children under 2 are free as they sit on your lap. Dinner with Santa is $62 for adults; $45 for ages 2 - 12.

NORTH POLE LIMITED, Campo. (619) 465-7776 / www.psrm.org, Sheridan Rd. off Hwy 94 at the PACIFIC SOUTHWEST RAILWAY MUSEUM (pg. 582). There are many ways to reach Santa instead of just waiting for a visit from him. From the end of November through mid-December on Fri. and Sat. evenings, take a train ride on railcars decked out for the holidays. While on board, you can make your list (and check it twice); enjoy hot chocolate and cookies (you are welcome to bring a picnic dinner on board); listen to a Christmas story read out loud; and sing carols. You stop at Santa's Workshop to pick up Santa and Mrs. Claus who visit with passengers on the train on the way back to the depot. Kids are given a jingle bell as a gift and as a reminder to ring in the Christmas season. Trains depart, for the approx. two-hour ride, at 5pm and 7pm on Fri. and Sat. The depot opens before your trip so plan to arrive at least 45 minutes before your departure to look around and check out the gift shop. Call early to make a reservation. Fares for coach class (in a restored 1920's commuter car) are $35 for adults; $25 for ages 3 - 12. Fares for first class (in a Union Pacific long-distance chair car or Santa Fe business car) includes bigger seats and complimentary soft drinks and candies for $50 for adults; $40 for ages 3 - 12. Prices on both railcars is $10 for ages 2 and under riding in an adult's lap.

PASADENA MODEL RAILROAD CLUB'S FALL OPEN HOUSE, Pasadena. See April entry (pg. 708) for details.

PELTZER PINES, Brea, Silverado. (714) 649-9291 / www.peltzerpines.com, Brea - 3400 Rose Dr.; Silverado - 7851 Blackstar Canyon Road. Walk among the pine trees on these farms and breath in their fresh pine fragrance - Christmas in the air! You choose the tree - either Monterey Pine or Leyland Cypress - and they will cut it down for you. Open mid-November - December 23, Mon. - Fri., 11:30am - 5pm; Sat. and Sun., 9am - 5pm.

PILGRIM PLACE FESTIVAL, Claremont. (909) 399-5500 / www.pilgrimplace.org, 625 Mayflower Rd. For over 70 years and counting, this timely festival takes place on the second Friday and Saturday in November. Thanksgiving is a time to be thankful (and to eat), but do your kids know how this holiday began? Find out by watching the educational highlight here - an hour-long, live reenactment of the pilgrim story, a retelling of the important story of our heritage, performed at the outdoor stage each day by the retired church professionals who live at this center. Bring a picnic lunch to enjoy at nearby parks. A favorite activity at the festival is called the Glue In. Tables full of recycled items are available for kids to glue onto a piece of cardboard to create a masterpiece (50¢). Other activities include riding the (motorized) Festival Ship (50¢); taking a mini-train ride (50¢); visiting the on-site cultural museum; shopping at the bazaar and craft fair; face painting; eating good food; and going to the Wampanoag Indian Village for story time and games. The festival runs from 10am - 4pm. Free admission, and free, but hard-to-come-by, parking. Free shuttles are available.

PINE TREE ACRES, Ramona. (760) 420-7289 / www.pinetreeacres.com, 620 Haverford Rd. Walk amongst the hundreds of Monterey Pines to choose the perfect one for your family. Cut it down and bring it home. Pine Tree Acres also has fresh pre-harvested trees, potted trees, ornaments and crafts for sale. Weekend fun includes ornament and cookie decorating, cider, a party jump, petting zoo ($5), pony rides and visits from Santa (on certain weekends, only). Make a day of this excursion! Open the Friday after Thanksgiving through mid-December weekdays, noon - 5pm; weekends, 9am - 5pm. Admission is free; some activities cost.

PISMO BEACH MONARCH GROVE, Pismo Beach. See January entry (pg. 696) for details.

PLANETARIUM SHOWS - CHRISTMAS SHOW / STAR OF BETHLEHEM. Look up planetariums in the main section of this book under Shows and Theaters, in your county. Starting mid-November through mid-December, some of them reset the nighttime skies back to the time of Jesus' birth. For instance, at Tessmann Planetarium in Santa Ana ([714] 564-6356 / www.sac.edu.), after an introduction to astronomy, the astronomer/narrator discusses how (and when) the miraculous phenomena called the Star of Bethlehem came about using the planetarium "skies", a slide show, and Bible passages. He includes the possible origins of a nova, comet, star, meteorite, or aligning planets. I won't give away the ending. The one-hour presentation is educational, as well as a wonderful blend of science and faith. See the main entry TESSMANN PLANETARIUM AT SANTA ANA COLLEGE (pg. 324) for more information about this planetarium. Also see George F. Beattie Planetarium in San Bernardino, which has three shows in December - GEORGE F. BEATTIE PLANETARIUM (pg. 436), www.valleycollege.edu/about-sbvc/facilities/planetarium; and Robert T. Dixon Planetarium at Riverside Community College, known as the RCC Planetarium, in Riverside - RIVERSIDE COMMUNITY COLLEGE PLANETARIUM (ROBERT T. DIXON PLANETARIUM) (pg. 371), www.rccshows.weebly.com. Tessmann's daytime shows start at 9:30am; nighttime shows at 7pm. Beattie's shows are 6:30pm. RCC shows are at 7pm. Tessman's tickets are $7 per person; but weekday shows before 4pm are $6. Beattie's tickets are $3 for adults; $2 for srs., students and alumni; $1 for ages 10 and under. RCC tickets are $5 for adults; $4 for students; $2.50 for children 12 and under. Reserve your space early as shows sell out.

RADY'S CHILDREN ICE RINK, San Diego. (858) 966-8477 / www.radyfoundation.org/icerink, 2875 Dewey Rd. at Liberty Station. Ice skating outside, surrounded by a shopping center, with a huge Christmas tree all lit up is *so* New York, but now it's also so Southern California! The temporary ice rink appears mid-November and welcomes skaters through the beginning of January. Wear gloves! You'll probably want to incorporate a visit to an adjacent restaurant, such as CORVETTE DINER (pg. 471). Open for two-hour sessions, every two hours, daily, 10am - 10pm. The rink is closed Thanksgiving and Christmas, and closes at 5pm on Christmas Eve and New Year's Eve. Admission for the two-hour sessions is $14 for adults; $12 for ages 11 and under; $10 for military. Prices include skate rentals.

RANCHO CHRISTMAS, Vista. (760) 724-4082 / www.sdparks.com, 2210 N. Santa Fe Ave. at Rancho Guajome Adobe. Celebrate Christmas in an atmosphere of yesteryear. The adobe, RANCHO GUAJOME ADOBE (pg. 547), is adorned with seasonal decor from the 1800s. Kids crafts, such as candlemaking, dipping candy apples, and making corn husk angels, plus tractor-drawn wagon rides, demonstrations by blacksmiths, shopping at vending booths, and other fun activities are all here - most of which are included in the admission price. On Saturday the events culminate in the lighting of the luminaries and a caroling program. Open the last Sat. of the month, 10am - 4pm. Admission is $5 for adults; $3 for ages 4 - 12; children 3 and under are free. Cash only.

RANCHO NOEL / POTRERO VALLEY CHRISTMAS TREE FARM, Potrero. (760) 583-5287 / www.ranchonoeltrees.com, 25655 Potrero Park Dr. For a true country excursion, fa la la your way through this twenty acre, no-other-frills, Christmas tree farm where you can "just" choose your own Monterey Pine to be cut and then take it home. Open the Friday after Thanksgiving through mid-December Tues. - Fri., 11am - 5pm; Sat. - Sun., 9am - 5pm. Closed Mon.

REINDEER ROMP, Los Angeles. (323) 644-4200 / www.lazoo.org, 5300 Zoo Dr., Griffith Park at the Los Angeles Zoo. Reindeer fly in to join their animal and human friends at the LOS ANGELES ZOO (pg. 222) during this season. Guests can visit with the reindeer (their antlers are fuzzy!) every day. On weekends, learn about them from the keepers; make paper reindeer antlers; enjoy a puppet show and ice-carving demonstrations; and take photos with Santa (extra fee). Of course you'll also walk around and see everything else at the zoo. Bring your herd! Also See November entry for (pg. 749) for another festive offering. The reindeer are here Thanksgiving through the beginning of January. Admission is regular zoo admission - $21 for adults; $18 for srs.; $16 for ages 2 - 12.

SANTA'S ELECTRIC LIGHT PARADE, Temecula. (951) 694-6480 / www.cityoftemecula.org, through Old Town on Jefferson Ave., between Rancho California and Del Rio Rd. A special Friday evening parade, in either November or early December, features over ninety entries with lights on cars and home-crafted floats, plus fire engines, marching bands, sheriff's posse, equestrian groups, and Santa. Stake out your spot early, bring a blanket and picnic dinner, enjoy the vendors, and dress warmly. The shows begins at 7pm. Admission is free.

SEASIDE HIGHLAND GAMES, Ventura. (818) 886-4968; (818) 645-6092 / www.seaside-games.com, 10 W Harbor Blvd. at the Ventura County Fairgrounds Welcome to the clan! Visit "Auld Scotia" - ancient Scotland - via fiddling and drumming competitions; clan tents; bagpipes; British cars; herding dogs; highland re-enactments; more bagpipes; vendors; dancing (with classes offered); food; lots of pipebands; harp gathering and playing; even more bagpipes; and lots of kilts. Scottish games and competitions include weight, stone ("shot put"), hammer tossing, and the original extreme sport - caber tossing. (Who thought of this sport?! And why?). Wee ones enjoy the Children's Glen with scaled down games for their age and size; a castle beanbag toss; learning bagpipes some dance steps; an archaeological dig for Scottish treasure; petting zoo; and more. Open Fri. at 5pm - 10pm for pre-show events; Sat. - Sun., 9am - 5pm. $20 for ages 13 and up; $17 for srs.; $5 for ages 6 -12; ages 5 and under are free. Some activities cost extra.

SKATING BY THE SEA, Coronado. (619) 522-8490 or (619) 435-6611 / www.hoteldel.com, 1500 Orange Ave. by the Hotel Del Coronado. Only in California can you ice skate on a rink ringed by palm trees, right next to the Pacific Ocean from Thanksgiving to the beginning of January! And by a world famous hotel! Open Nov. - mid-December,

Mon. - Fri., 4pm - 10pm; Sat., 10am - 10pm; Sun., 11am - 8pm. Open mid-December - Jan 2, Mon. - Fri., 10am - 10pm; Sat., 10am - 9pm; Sun., 11am - 8pm. Note that some sessions may be limited to 90 minutes if it's really crowded. Admission is $30 per person, which includes skate rentals.

SUGAR PLUM EXPRESS, Fillmore. (800) 773-8724 or (805) 524-2546 / www.fwry.com, 364 Main Street. Not the Sugar Plum fairy, but something maybe more fun for the family: Take a 3 hour vintage train adventure and have some holiday fun. Starting at Fillmore, take a forty-five minute train ride, with Santa on board. Stop at Holiday Village at Loose Caboose to walk through the Winter Wonderland ($3), play on holiday jumpers ($3), take a hayride ($3), see Santa's workshop, purchase gifts from craft and food vendors, and look at the Koi fish, goats and birds there. Choose a pre-cut tree (optional and additional cost) and enjoy the scenery on the ride back. Rides are offered the day after Thanksgiving through December 24 on weekends, leaving at 10:30am and 2pm. The train ride is $26 for adults; $24 for srs.; $16 for ages 4 - 12; $12 for ages 2 - 3; children under 2 are free. The tree costs extra. Netting is required and available.

TANAKA FARMS FALL HARVEST TOUR AND CHRISTMAS TREE LOT, Irvine. See October entry (pg. 745) for details.

VETERANS DAY CELEBRATION, Chiriaco Summit. (760) 227-3483 / www.generalpattonmuseum.com, 62 510 Chiriaco Summit at the General Patton Memorial Museum. Veterans are remembered and celebrated during this one-day event. Entertainment, which changes from year to year, can include a military band, military reenactments (in the tank yard), an "appearance" by General Patton giving a speech, an air salute fly-over by WWII aircraft, and definitely vendors, special exhibits, raffles, and a walk through the museum and tank yard. See GENERAL PATTON MEMORIAL MUSEUM (pg. 384) for more info on the museum. Open 9am - 5pm. The small parade starts at 11am. Admission is free.

WILDLIGHTS, Palm Desert. (760) 346-5694 / www.livingdesert.org, 47900 Portola Ave. at the Living Desert Wildlife and Botanical Park. Come have a wild night at the park! A special display, up for only six-weeks, features nearly a dozen, larger-than-life animal and other sculptures illuminated in hundreds of thousands of lights. This can include a gigantic teddy bear, a thirty-foot snowman, assorted desert critters, tunnel of lights, a golfing Santa, and much more. Live entertainment; keeper chats at various cages; camel rides; a trackless train ride; a visit with Santa; holiday-themed Wildlife Wonders Shows; wood-burning fireplaces; carousel rides ($4); crafts; and more, add to the holiday festivities. Wildlights is open on select Fri. and Sat. nights, Thanksgiving - Christmas Eve, 6pm - 9pm. Note that most of the animals are put to bed at nighttime so it's a people-only party. Admission is $10 for adults; $8 for military and ages 3 - 12.

WINTER FANTASY SAWDUST FESTIVAL, Laguna Beach. (949) 494-3030 / www.sawdustartfestival.org, 935 Laguna Canyon Rd. Three acres of shopping, craft and entertainment fun in a quaint outdoor festival with booths decorated to look like an old-fashioned Christmas. Synthetic snow is brought in daily in one area so you can teach your little angels how to make snow angels. Family entertainment includes jugglers, balloon artists, storytellers, and carolers. Children's art activities, like mask making or creating pottery, are different each day and range from free to $18. Over 175 artists have booths here, with on-going crafting demonstration. To complete the fantasy, visit Santa Claus in his house and/or sleigh. Get your holiday shopping done and keep the kids happy - all at the same time! Open five consecutive weekends (and sometimes a few Fridays) beginning the weekend before Thanksgiving (and Black Friday), 10am - 7pm. Admission is $9 for adults; $7 for srs.; $4 for ages 6 - 12; children 5 and under are free. All military and their family are free with ID. Parking fees vary depending on which lot you choose.

- DECEMBER -

A CHRISTMAS JOURNEY, Redondo Beach. (310) 372-4641 / www.journeyoffaith.com, 1935 Manhattan Beach Blvd. at Redondo Beach Performing Arts Center. Presented by Journey of Faith church, this 75-minute Christmas and holiday musical experience - singing, dancing, a video, message and more - is delightful new tradition. Fri., 7pm; Sat. and Sun., 4pm and 7pm. Tickets are available one hour before each show. Free

ARCTIC LIGHTS SNOW PLAYDAY, Moorpark. (805) 378-1441 / www.moorparkcollege.edu/teaching-zoo, 7075 Campus Rd. at Moorpark College. Literally tons of snow are brought in to AMERICA'S TEACHING ZOO (pg. 692) for both animals and kids to play in. The zoo is decorated with lots of light, plus there are winter-theme crafts and games and hot chocolate, too. Animal presentations are at noon and 2pm each day, plus you can walk around the zoo to see the animals, do a meet-and-greet and see the big cat feeding at 3:30pm. For an extra $7 per person guests can tour the back areas and interact with some of the animals. Open Sat. and Sun., 11am - 5pm. Admission is $8 for adults; $6 for ages 3 - 12; 2 and under are free. $7 extra for behind-the-scenes tour. Some activities may cost extra.

BALBOA PARK DECEMBER NIGHTS, San Diego. (619) 239-0512 / www.balboapark.org; www.sandiego.gov/december-nights, Park Blvd. and President's Way at Balboa Park. This festival marks the opening of the holiday season in San Diego as thousands of people (350,000) join the celebration. The almost overwhelming amount of activities and events include looking outside and inside all the buildings glowing spectacularly with Christmas lights and other decorations; tasting holiday fare from around the world; listening to strolling carolers; participating in kid's crafts and carnival-style games offered in the walkway and inside many museums; riding on 14 carnival rides (giant carousel, spinning rides, cliff hanger and more), plus coconut tree climbs, bungees, obstacle course, and ziplining; seeing and hearing musical and dance presentations (including ballet, hip hop, Polynesian, bagpipes, country, gospel, jazz, and lots more); sampling from food vendors galore; being mesmerized by a puppet show; enjoying free admission to the many museums here (including Reuben H. Fleet Science Center, San Diego Museum of Man, San Diego Air & Space and San Diego Natural History); watching the Santa Lucia procession; delighting in the Singing Christmas Story Tree at the organ pavilion; looking at the display of the Nativity scenes in the Organ Pavilion, and Santa and the reindeer; touring the Old Globe theater; applauding holiday favorites performed at the Casa Del Prado Theatre; shopping at the Spanish Village Art Centre where 250 artists display their works of art; and more!!! Usually open the first weekend in December, Fri., 3pm - 11pm; Sat., noon - 11pm. Participating museums are free from 5pm - 9pm these evenings (and some are also free during the day - check the website). Free parking and shuttle service is available at the downtown County Administration Building and City College. Admission is free.

BELMONT SHORE CHRISTMAS PARADE, Long Beach. (562) 434-3066 / www.belmontshore.org, 2nd St. between Bayshore and Livingston. This almost two-hour street parade is usually held on the first Saturday in December from 6pm - 9pm. It has over 100 entries, including bands, homemade floats, lots of locals, and Santa Claus. Admission is free.

THE BETHLEHEM EXPERIENCE, Westlake Village. (818) 889-1491 / www.gotobethlehem.com, 32111 Watergate Rd. at Westminster Presbyterian Church. Enter from Westgate Blvd. on Agoura Rd. At this event, which only happens on even years, a centurion greets you as you wait in line in your car - it's a true blend of ancient and modern. Drive slowly through and past vignettes of the streets of Bethlehem on the night that Jesus was born. Over a hundred costumed participants; sets - from marketplace to manger; props; and live animals (goats, sheep, chicken, a donkey, and a camel) make this pivotal time period come to life. Usually open the second weekend in December, Fri. and Sat., continuously from 5:30pm - 9:30pm. Free admission.

BETHLEHEM STORY, Spring Valley. (619) 461-7451 / www.fchapel.org, 9400 Campo Road at Faith Chapel Experience life as it was on the very first Christmas as re-enactors re-create this pivotal time. Cast members interact with you and engage you in conversation, in character, as you walk about the outdoor town of Bethlehem (i.e. the parking lot of the church) with its tradespeople - potters, blacksmiths, vendors, tanners, candle makers, yarn spinners, carpenters, brick layers, scribes, etc; townsfolk; guards; tax collectors; and even corralled animals - real sheep, chickens and goats. Use the free shekels given you at the entry to purchase samples of authentic food and make a craft. Enjoy the hustle and bustle of the town and the music; try your hand at making some of the wares; play some games; pet the animals; listen to the angels proclaim Jesus's birth; check into the inn to visit the stable where Mary and Joseph and baby Jesus are; and be a part of the story. Free hot chocolate and cider are available. Open for four nights, Thurs. - Sun., 6pm - 9pm. Free.

BETHLEHEM WALK, Escondido. (760) 745-5100 / firstunited.echurch.net, 341 S. Kalmia St. at the First United Methodist Church. Walk the streets of Bethlehem, or at least a re-creation of them, the second weekend in December. Visitors can walk through a marketplace to experience the everyday life of this ancient town as villagers sell merchandise at stores, work at their trades, and talk to each other (and you). You might get hassled by soldiers, and then go onto the inn to try to get accommodations. Being redirected to the stable, guests then see Mary, Joseph, and baby Jesus, and the live animals. Afterward, enjoy refreshments in the church's social hall. Reservations (ironically) are highly recommended and can be taken the Sun. after Thanksgiving. Open second weekend of December, Fri., 5:30pm - 9pm; Sat., 4pm - 8:30pm; Sun., 4pm - 8pm. Admission is free, but it is a ticketed/timed event to keep the "tour" numbers reasonable. Reservations are recommended.

BOAT RIDES WITH SANTA, Dana Point. (949) 496-5794 or (949) 923-2255 / www.danapointharbor.com; www.danawharf.com, 34675 Golden Lantern - east end of Dana Point Harbor at Dana Wharf Ho ho ho - and off we go! Instead of a sleigh, take a twenty-minute boat ride with Santa Claus and his helpers. He'll listen to your Christmas wishes and take some photos with you (and your kids). On this Sat. there is usually additional activities that night, like crafts, games, ceremonial lighting of the Ocean Institutes' tall ship, the Pilgrim and watching a classic holiday movie on board. Sat. and Sun., 10am - 2pm. $3 per person.

BREAKFAST WITH SANTA, Long Beach. (562) 431-3541 / www.rancholosalamitos.com, 6400 Bixby Hill Rd. at Rancho Los Alamitos. This is a fun adventure for the kids, geared for ages 12 and under. They get to eat a pancake breakfast (plus scrambled eggs, sausages, bacon, country potatoes, apple cider, hot chocolate with all the trimmings, and seasonal fresh fruits) with Santa while enjoying a live performance. There are also activities such as crafts, a petting coral, games, pony rides ($5), and decorating evergreens to take home. Sat., 9am - noon. Admission is $25 for adults; $18 for ages 3 - 14. This price includes entertainment and craft activities. Call early to reserve your ticket as the event sells out.

CANDLELIGHT WALK, Lake Forest. (949) 923-2230 / www.ocparks.com, 25151 Serrano Rd. at Heritage Hill Historical Park. For one magical weekend experience this historic park and four buildings by candlelight as over 1,000 luminaries light the pathways. Along the way, outside and inside, are strolling carolers, musicians, other genteel entertainment, visits with Santa, refreshments to purchase, and, inside the one-room schoolhouse, holiday storytelling. Tour the turn-of-the-century buildings that are festooned with old-fashioned decorations. Open Fri. - Sun., 5:30pm - 8:30pm. Admission is $5 per person; children 2 and under are free.

CAROLING CRUISE, Ventura. (805) 642-1393 / www.islandpackers.com, 1691 Spinnaker Dr. at Ventura Harbor. Sing your favorite Christmas carols (out loud!) while enjoying a one-hour tour of the harbor and Ventura Keys, looking at boats and houses lit up with holiday lights. Oh what fun it is to ride in a one-horse open boat! Bring a flashlight to read your caroling book. Dress warmly. Snacks and beverages are available to purchase. Cruises depart several nights throughout December at 6:30pm. Tickets are $16 for adults; $13 for srs.; $10 for ages 3 - 12.

CELEBRATING FAMILY & FRIENDS, Rancho Santa Margarita. (949) 216-9700 / www.cityofrsm.org, 22232 El Paseo at the Civic Plaza. Celebrate the new year with this alcohol-free party that features live stage musical entertainment; children's games and activities; inflatable slides and bounces; visual arts; street entertainers; interactive art booths; food booths; and more. Open December 31, 5pm - 9pm. Admission is free; some activities cost.

CHANUKAH AT THE HARBOR, Ventura. (805) 382-4770 / www.chabadofoxnard.com, 1583 Spinnaker Dr. at Ventura Harbor Village. This festival features latkes (yumm), snow (dress warmly!); a Judaica boutique; carnival rides (sometimes!), bounces, entertainment (comedy, music and more) and a Grand Menorah Lighting Ceremony (with a 20 foot menorah) at 4pm. Open 2:30pm to 4:30pm. Free admission.

CHILL AT THE QUEEN MARY, Long Beach. / www.queenmary.com. See November entry (pg. 745) for details.

CHRISTMAS IN THE PARK, Poway. (858) 668-4576 / www.poway.org, 13134 Midland Rd. in Old Poway Park. It is the most wonderful time of the year to spend an afternoon in this park. Live entertainment - caroling, music, dancing, comedy and other live holiday entertainment; a children's theater performance; craft boutique; horse-drawn hayrides; holiday ornament making; ginger bread house-making; a great model railroad display; petting zoo; and more activities for the family are offered on this second Sat. from 3:30pm - 8:30pm, for free. Pony rides and train rides are available for a minimal cost. The tree lighting ceremony at 5:15pm is followed by Santa's arrival via train. Refreshments (like hot chocolate and baked goods) and dinner food (like chili, corn dogs, and tamales) are available to purchase. Look up OLD POWAY PARK (pg. 566) for more details on the park. Free shuttles are available at Poway City Hall, 13325 Civic Center Drive, or the Poway Adult School, 13626 Twin Peaks Road.

CHRISTMAS ON THE FARM, Moorpark. See November entry (pg. 746) for details.

CHRISTMAS PARADE AND OPEN HOUSE, Coronado. (619) 435-7242 or (619) 435-9260 / www.coronadochamber.com; www.ecoronado.com, at First Street at the Ferry Landing Marketplace; the parade is along Orange Ave. On the first Friday in December the party starts as kids play in the snow, beginning at 2pm, then it really kicks into ho ho high gear when Santa arrives by ferry (the reindeer are taking a rest) at about 3:15. Make sure to see the 100,000 twinkling lights at Hotel Del Coronado, visit Santa's village, and skate at the outdoor ice rink right by the beach. See November entry (pg. 751) for details. Shop the fun boutique stores (5:30pm - 9pm). A parade commences down Orange Ave. at 6pm, complete with floats, bands, a fire truck (with Santa), cheerleaders, animals, and kids, to Rotary Park. (Prime viewing spots are between 8th St. and RH Dana Place.) The festivities conclude with a tree lighting ceremony at 7pm, followed by a holiday concert. The festival runs from 2pm - 8pm. Admission is free.

CHRISTMAS RANCH TREE FARMS, Thousand Oaks. (805) 501-0874. See November entry (pg. 746) for details about this farm.

CHRISTMAS TRAIN, Orange. (714) 997-3968 / www.irvineparkrailroad.com, 1 Irvine Park Rd. in Irvine Regional Park. Santa isn't always accessible by train, but he is at this park. While waiting for your turn to ride the scale model train to Santa's Village, which isn't quite as far as the North Pole, enjoy story time with Mrs. Claus (free) and/or, for $5 per activity - decorate a cookie, jump around in the bounce house, go ice "fishing", and play some carnival games. When you disembark, meet with Santa (bring your camera!), and purchase some goodies, like hot chocolate and popcorn, at the Elf House snack bar. On your ride back, you see colorful Christmas lights around the park and go through the glowing "Tunnel of Lights". Your experience is like getting an early Christmas present! Other attractions in this vicinity include paddle boat rentals, bike rentals, pony rides, and the Orange County Zoo. See IRVINE

REGIONAL PARK (pg. 284) for more details about what this terrific park has to offer. Open the last weekend in November - December 23, Mon. - Fri., 4pm - 8pm; Sat. - Sun., 10am - 8pm. Admission for the Christmas Train is $15 per person; ages 12 months and under are free. Parking at the Park is $3, Mon. - Fri.; $5 on weekends; $7 on holidays; free after 5pm.

CHRISTMAS TREE LANE AND WINTER ARTS AND CRAFTS FESTIVAL, Altadena. (626) 403-1123 / dev.christmastreelane.net, Santa Rosa Ave., between Woodbury Ave. and Altadena Dr. The festival is at the Altadena Public Library parking lot. On the second Saturday in December (usually!) the festivities begin with a holiday boutique and craft festival at 2pm, along with a snowplay area, free hot chocolate, and sometimes music by choirs and drum corps. Along with the arrival of Santa Claus, the lighting ceremony is at 6pm where the 150 majestic (huge!), 135-year old, classic Christmas trees (deodras/Himalayan cedars), that stretch along Santa Rosa Avenue for 3 long blocks, or so - almost a mile, are beautifully lit up. If you miss the ceremony, the lights are on nightly, dusk to midnight. Enjoy a short, but enchanting drive if you are in the area. Nightly thru Jan. 3, or so. Free.

CHRISTMAS TREES. If you're looking for Christmas tree farms where you can either choose and have it cut, or ones that offer pre-cut trees (besides store parking lots), and other Christmasy activities, check out www.pickyourownchristmastree.org and www.cachristmas.com. Hope your season is blessed.

CORONADO BUTTERFLY RESERVE, Goleta. See January entry (pg. 695) for details.

CRUISE OF LIGHTS, Huntington Beach. (714) 840-7542 / www.cruiseoflights.org, 16889 Algonquin St. by Huntington Harbor. The Philharmonic Society of Orange County sponsors this event (for over 56 years!), raising money to donate to the youth music programs in Orange County. For eight days (two long weekends) in the middle of December, forty-five-minute boat tours are given around the decorated homes of the Huntington Harbor area. These homes have entered a competition, so you will see the creme de la creme, like the Sweepstakes winner, the Most Beautiful, the Most Traditional, etc. You'll also hear interesting commentary. Some boats along the way are also decked out in their Christmas best. Other cruise options include a seventy-minute ride (more and closer as you go thru narrow channels), and a land and sea night of a boat tour, plus a stop to see some places closer up, followed by dinner at the Yacht Club. Tours are offered between 5:30pm and 8:30pm. Call for specific dates. 45-minute cruises are $19 or $21 for adults (depending on the night), $12 or $14 for ages 2 to 12; ages 1 and under are free. 70-minute cruises are $32 for adults; $25 for kids. Land and sea tickets are $75 for adults; $68 for kids.

DANA POINT HARBOR BOAT PARADE OF LIGHTS, Dana Point. (949) 496-5794 / www.danapointharbor.com; wwwdanawharf.com, 34624 Golden Lantern. This event has been going strong for over 43 years! Each year boats go all-out to compete for awards of Best Theme, Best Use of Lights, Best Animation, Most Colorful, Most Original, and more. The boats can be seen from anywhere in the harbor, or make a reservation at a restaurant for en*light*ening entertainment while you dine! Take a boat ride to participate in the parade with Dana Wharf Sportfishing for $29 for adults; $19 for kids. Some daytime activities on these parade nights include visits with Santa Claus, holiday crafts, performances by characters, and a twenty-minute harbor cruise with Santa. A treat within a treat - catch a free trolley ride to the boat parade, after paying $3 to park at Doheny State Beach. The trolley runs from 5:30pm - 10:30pm and drops off and picks up along Dana Point Harbor Dr. Family activities are from 4:30pm - 7:30pm. The two-weekend boat parade is Fri. and Sat. at 7:30pm. Watching is free.

DICKEN'S HOLIDAY CELEBRATION, Torrance. (310) 515-7166 / www.printmuseum.org, 315 W. Torrance Blvd. at the INTERNATIONAL PRINTING MUSEUM (pg. 123). You'll have the best of times, not the worst of times, at this event designed for the whole family. Characters from *The Christmas Carol*, *Great Expectations,* and *Tale of Two Cities*, as well as Dickens himself (not really himself, but a guy who plays him incredibly well), come to life as actors play the parts, retell his stories, and interact with the guests. (A highlight is a retelling of *A Christmas Carol* and using the audience as cast members.) Enjoy music for that time period, food (like Banger and gingerbread), printing holiday cards, and of course, all the wonderful printing presses at this awesome museum. Ask about a two-hour, more educational version of this program called *The Dickens Holiday Tour* for scheduled groups, available for two weeks in December. Open Sat. and Sun., 10am - 4pm. Admission, including lunch, is $25 per person, or $80 for a family of four.

DISNEY ON ICE, Anaheim; Long Beach; Los Angeles; Ontario. / www.disneyonice.com. Each year Disney on Ice produces a spectacular ice skating show starring beloved Disney characters from various movies performing stunts, wearing fantastic costumes, and telling stories all with various sets, lighting, music, and special effects. Let it go and come to the show! Performances are for a few days at each - the Honda Center in Anaheim, Long Beach Arena, Staples Center in Los Angeles, and at the Citizen's Bank Arena in Ontario. Matinees and evening shows. Tickets start at $25.

DISTRICT FREEZE ICE RINK, Tustin. (714) 259-9090 / thedistricttl.com, 2437 Park Ave. The District is a very hip place ("mall") to be anytime of year, particularly in the winter when the largest outdoor ice skating rink in Orange County is open here, in the parking lot. Enjoy the music, the special lights, and shopping and eating at the adjacent stores and restaurants. Open the end of November - mid-January, Mon. - Thurs., 1pm - 8:30pm; Fri., 1pm - 10:30pm;

Sat., 11am - 10:30pm; Sun., 11am - 8:30pm. Extended hours closer to the holidays; closed Thanksgiving and Christmas. For each 90-min. session, $19 per person (which includes skate rentals), $16 if you bring your own skates; $16 for toddlers (which includes skate rentals).

DOWNTOWN SANTA BARBARA HOLIDAY PARADE, Santa Barbara. (805) 962-2098 / www.downtownsb.org, State St., from Sola to Cota. Now this is a parade! High-stepping marching bands, floats all decked out for the holidays, performance groups, and of course, an appearance by Santa Claus make for a great parade down State Street which is festooned with lights and lots of decorations, and with more than 65,000 spectators! Usually held the first Fri. in December, 6:30pm - 8:30pm. Admission is free.

ENCHANTED: FOREST OF LIGHT, La Canada Flintridge. (818) 952-4390 or (818) 949-4200 / www.descansogardens.org, 1418 Descanso Drive. Descanso Gardens Enchanted is exactly the way I would describe this experience. A mile long walk through the beautiful gardens is made even more so as the trees and other plants, lake, and specific garden sections are beautifully and colorfully lit up, as is the pathway. There are some animated scenes along the way, larger scale lighted figures and even some interactive displays to control the lights and music. The end destination is the stunning Japanese Gardens. Stop by for hot cocoa, gingerbread decorating station and more at the illuminated Lakeside Lounge. Open the end of November - the beginning of January, nightly, 5pm - 10pm. Closed Thanksgiving and Christmas Day. Note that this is after the regular garden hours. $28 for adults; $24 for srs. ages 3 - 17; children 2 and under are free. Tickets are timed and must be purchased in advance.

ENCINITAS HOLIDAY PARADE, Encinitas. (760) 633-2760 or (760) 633-2600 / www.ci.encinitas.ca.us, from D St. on the Coast Highway 101 to J St. Parking shuttles are available. This is a huge small-town parade! Vying for awards in several categories, entrants include marching bands, floats of all kinds, equestrian units, drill teams, dancing groups and lots more trimmed with lots of lights and holiday decorations. It's like a moving party. Dress warm and come early for a viewing spot. Sat., a tree lighting ceremony is at 5pm; the parade goes from 5:30pm - 7:30pm. Free.

FALLBROOK CHRISTMAS PARADE, Fallbrook. / www.fallbrookchamberofcommerce.org. This one-day Christmas parade, held the first Sat. in December, includes over 100 groups of marching bands; decorated and lighted floats; highway patrol vehicles; dancers; fire engines; baton twirlers; Ramona mounted patrol; animals; Santa Claus; and more. The parade starts at 5pm on Main Street. Admission is free.

FAMILY CHRISTMAS TREE FARM, El Cajón. See November entry (pg. 746) for details.

FESTIVAL OF CAROLS, Los Angeles. (213) 972-7282 / www.lamc.org, 111 South Grand Ave. at Walt Disney Concert Hall. Falalala your way to and through this two-hour Festival of Carols featuring music and the beautifully singing of 115 singers of the Master Chorale. Traditional favorites plus some new arrangements and lots of spirit make this a joyous event for the whole family. Two Sat., at 2pm. Tickets range from $49 - $109.

FESTIVAL OF LIGHTS PARADE, Palm Springs. (760) 323-8276 / psfestivaloflights.com, on Palm Canyon Dr. between Ramon Rd. and Tamarisk Rd. The one-day holiday parade, held the first Sat. in December, includes over 100 entries including floats, big rigs, marching bands, equestrians, people, vehicles, and even animals festooned in white lights. The parade is 1.25 miles long and runs from 5:45pm - 8pm. Admission is free.

FESTIVAL OF LIGHTS, Riverside. See November entry (pg. 746) for details.

FIRST NIGHT, Fullerton. (714) 738-6545 / www.cityoffullerton.com, bordered by Lemon, Malden, Chapman, and Commonwealth sts. Downtown Fullerton on Harbor Blvd., Pomona Ave., and Wilshire Ave. Bring in the New Year all night long! This alcohol-free event could includes entertainment - music and dancing; a magic show; food booths; tethered hot air balloon ride (it goes fifty feet high!); free admission to the Fullerton Museum; and a Kids' Lane with giant bounces, obstacle course, jousting, bungee run, velcro wall, quad jumper, face painting and lots more. Fireworks light up your life at midnight! First Night fun happens between 7pm - midnight. Admission is free. Activities are $2 - $7 per.

FROSTY'S VILLAGE AT LIVE OAK CANYON, Yucaipa. See November entry (pg. 747) for details.

GREENSPOT FARMS, Mentone. See November entry (pg. 747) for details.

HAGLE TREE FARM, Somis. See November entry (pg. 747) for details.

HANUKKAH FAMILY FESTIVAL, Los Angeles. (310) 440-4500 or (310) 440-4636 / www.skirball.org, 2701 N. Sepulveda Blvd. at the Skirball Cultural Center. This is one of the bigger celebrations for the Festival of Lights in the area. It features storytelling, musical performances, a participatory retelling of the story of Hanukkah, playing traditional games, and making crafts such as paper lanterns, clay oil maps, and edible dreidels. Explore the museum, including Noah's Ark, too. See SKIRBALL CULTURAL CENTER (pg. 151) for more details on the museum. The one-day event takes place on a Sun., 11am- 4pm. Admission is $12 for adults; $9 for srs. and students; ages 2 - 12 are $7.

HANUKKAH HAPPENING, La Jolla. (858) 457-3030 / www.lfjcc.org, 4126 Executive Dr. at Lawrence Family Jewish Community Center. This family celebration includes carnival games, a climbing wall, inflatables, toddler dress up area, arts and crafts, food, shopping booths and more. Sun., 11am - 2pm. Admission is $7 for a family; ages under 2 are free. Activities are $1 per.

HOLIDAY AT THE RANCH, Goleta. (805) 681-7216 / goletahistory.org, 304 N. Los Carneros Rd. This weekend open house beckons visitors to not only see Santa and his "rein-goats", but also craft-making, hayrides, cookie decorating, story time, live music, and a guided tour through the historic house beautifully decked out in holiday style. Note that SOUTH COAST RAILROAD MUSEUM (pg. 633) is just next door, offering scale model train rides. See STOW HOUSE / RANCHO LA PATERA (pg. 634) for more details about the ranch. Open Sat. - Sun., 11am - 4pm. Admission is $5 for adults; $2 for ages 12 and under.

HOLIDAY BY THE BAY, San Diego. (619) 564-3333 / www.hiltonsandiegobayfront.com, 1 Park Boulevard at the Hilton San Diego Bayfront (sung to Jingle Bells, kind of) - "Oh what fun it is to skate, outside in California!" This ice rink, brightly decorated for Christmas, is attached to the Hilton, with all of its amenities. (The Hilton also offers holiday movies under the stars, breakfast with Santa and more for visitors staying there.) Open the end of November - mid-December, Mon. - Fri., 4pm - 10pm; Sat. - Sun., noon - 10pm. Open mid-December - Jan. 1, daily, noon - 10pm. Admission, per 90-minute session which includes skate rentals, is $20 for adults; $15 for ages 5 and under. Two-hour self-parking is validated next to Hilton San Diego Bayfront is $10 with minimum $30 spent at the ice rink.

HOLIDAY ICE RINK, Thousand Oaks. See November entry (pg. 748) for details.

HOLIDAY ICE RINK, Los Angeles. See the November entry (pg. 748) for details.

HOLIDAY IN THE PARK, Valencia. (661) 255-4111 / www.sixflags.com, 26101 Magic Mountain Parkway. This park is lit! With 1.5 million lights, Magic Mountain is transformed into a magical mountain. Walk around and soak in the ambiance as trees, walkways, rides and buildings are decorated with lights and animated scenes. Snowfall, tasty seasonal treats, music, larger than life toy soldiers, and live shows at Full Throttle stage that can include dancers, music and acrobatic and trapeze acts all add to the festival atmosphere. Various areas of Magic Mountain are themed such as DC UNIVERSE which becomes Rockin' Universe, featuring three dancing light shows synced with contemporary holiday music - so cool! At the Gleampunk District, a steampunk-inspired experience is now the setting of the sights and sounds of the industrial revolution, tho more fun, with a Steampunk Candy and Toy Factory and steampunk sleigh. Looney Tune characters makes their appearances. Take a ride on "Santa's Wild Sleigh Ride," an VR experience on The New Revolution. It's an immersive virtual world on a sleight with Santa and his reindeer to help battle a mischievous Elf who wants to ruin Christmas. And, of course, Santa and the Mrs. are in a classic Santa's village for photo ops and meet and greet. Know that your ticket includes an all day pass with all that Magic Mountain has to offer - it just really comes to life more at night with the lights and above special offerings! See SIX FLAGS MAGIC MOUNTAIN (pg. 4) for details. Open mid-November to mid-December, weekends only, 10:30am - 9pm; lights are on at 5pm. Open mid-December - December 31, daily, 10:30am - 9pm; lights are on at 5pm. $84.99 for adults; $59.99 for children 3 - 48"; children 2 and under are free. Parking is $25.

HOLIDAY IN THE VILLAGE / STARLIGHT PARADE, Chula Vista. (619) 422-1982 / thirdavenuevillage.com; www.starlightparade.com, 373 Park Way / near Third Ave. at Memorial Park. Get in the holiday spirit with some great stage entertainment, such as (from past years) Dance of the Sugar Plum Fairy, a Snow White Christmas with the Lyceum Theatre, Polar Express Conductor, music by the youth symphony, and more. Costumed characters abound, joining Santa for photo ops and holiday cheer. There are also vendors, arts and crafts, and some real snow, including a snow hill for sledding (at least on some years). Definitely stay for the parade, which goes down Third Ave., featuring floats, military and other marching bands, dancing, equestrians, and more merriment. Trophies are awarded in 12 categories! Munch on a snack such as popcorn, funnel cakes, cotton candy, roasted corn, and more. Sat., noon - 5pm; the parade starts at 6pm. Free.

HOLIDAY LIGHTS CRUISE, Newport Beach. (949) 673-1434 / www.christmasparadeboats.com. Take a seventy-five minute, "light"-hearted cruise any night in December around Newport Beach to see the beautifully decorated homes, yachts and other boats that are all dressed up for the holidays. Relaxing and lovely! Dress warmly. Cruises depart nightly at 5:30pm, 7pm and 8:30pm. $36 for adults; $32 for ages 3 - 12; $5 for ages 2 and under.

HOLIDAY ON ICE, Irvine. See November entry (pg. 748) for details.

HOLIDAY OPEN HOUSE AT RANCHO LOS ALAMITOS, Long Beach. (562) 431-3541 / www.rancholosalamitos.com, 6400 Bixby Hill Rd. at Rancho Los Alamitos. Ring in the holidays with tours of the festively decorated Ranch House, festooned in 1930's style. Enjoy the music and light refreshments, too. Reservations are required for parking. Open Wed. - Fri., 4pm - 8pm, with a final reservation at 7pm. Free.

HOLIDAY PARADE OF BOATS, San Pedro. (310) 549-8111 / www.laharborholidayafloat.org. For over 55 years owners go all out to decorate their boats - tall ships, tugboats, sailboats, harbor working craft, and leisure boats large and small - and compete for trophies for the best of in a wonderful parade, complete with celebrity grand marshals.

You can view this televised, ninety-minute parade along the San Pedro waterfront, Ports O' Call, Warehouse #1, Cabrillo and Holiday Harbor Marina. Dress warmly. The first Sat. in December at 6pm. Free.

HOLIDAY IN THE VILLAGE, La Mesa. (619) 784-MESA (6372) / www.lamesavillageassociation.org; www.lmvma.com, La Mesa Blvd. between Spring St. and Acacia Ave. One weekend in December the street section is closed to through traffic so this winter wonderland can boast twinkling lights, holiday foods, live music, strolling carolers, horse-drawn carriage rides, bonfires, and a children's carnival with snow, bounces, holiday crafts, rides, puppet shows, holiday movies shown on a big screen at 6pm, and a visit from Santa. Open Sat. - Sun., 10am - 10pm. General admission is free.

HOLIDAY TREE LIGHTING AND WINTER WONDERLAND FESTIVAL, Escondido. (800) 988-4253 / www.artcenter.org, 340 N Escondido Blvd. at California Center for the Arts. The Center wishes you a Merry Christmas with a real snow to play in; decorating Christmas cookies; seeing and photo ops with live reindeer(!), and Santa; entertainment - stilt walkers, hula dancers, carolers and more; face paintings; arts and crafts; vendors; and the "forest" of Christmas trees lit up at night. Sat., 3pm - 8pm. Free.

HOLLY TROLLEY HOLIDAY LIGHT TOUR, Oxnard. (805) 247-0197 / www.heritagesquareoxnard.com, 327 North 5th St. For three nights, the 50-minute tour on an open-top, double decker bus includes driving through Christmas Tree Lane in the Henry T. Oxnard Historic District (where rows of houses are decorated to the hilt); a stop at Heritage Square to see the gingerbread houses and Victorian homes; and the (pg. 752, 765) in Plaza Park. The price includes hot cocoa and some sweets along the way. Tues. - Thurs. the trolley departs at 6pm, 7pm and 8pm. $12 per person.

HOW THE GRINCH STOLE CHRISTMAS, San Diego. See November entry (pg. 748) for details.

ICE AT SANTA MONICA, Santa Monica. See November entry (pg. 748) for details.

INDIO INTERNATIONAL TAMALE FESTIVAL, Indio. (760) 832-8620 / www.tamalefestival.net, between Hwy 111 and Indio Blvd., filling the streets of Miles, Towne, Smurr & Requa. Hot tamales, mild tamales and everything in between are cooked and served fresh here at this massively attended festival. Besides just eating, there is a parade (at 10am on Saturday); kid's petting zoo; bike show; rock climbing wall; inflatable bounces; carnival rides and games; car show; contests; and traditional Mexican Folkloric dancing and singing, and other entertainment on two stages. Grab your amigos and come fiesta. Open the first weekend in December, Sat., 10am - 6pm; Sun., 10am - 5pm. Free.

JULEFEST, Solvang. (805) 688-6144 / www.solvangusa.com. This Julefest is really the name for the quaint town of Solvang following Yule traditions and dressing up for Christmas. The town looks like a small European village that twinkle with thousands of lights around and in the shops. Throughout the month, at certain times, there are crafts for kids, carolers, dances performed, carriage rides (for a fee), and lighting of the Christmas tree. One Saturday a parade begins at 11am, originating at 1760 Mission Dr. at Old Mission Santa Ines. Enjoy the 50+ entries costumed Danish dancers, musical performers, vintage vehicles, horses, carriages, and animals. A few other highlights include gawking at a gigantic gingerbread house (8' by 11' by 10') on display at Olsen's Danish Village Bakery at 1529 Mission Drive (you can decorate your own cookie here, too) and a Farmer's Markets on Wednesdays. Take a free, candlelight tour of the town at 5pm on Sat. nights in December. Take a Christmas lights tour of the homes all lit up at the Holidays Lights & Sounds Trolley Tour - $13. Look up (pg. 761) for details on another special attraction during this fest. General admission is free.

JUNGLE BELLS AT SAN DIEGO ZOO, San Diego. (619) 231-1515 / www.sandiegozoo.org, 2920 Zoo Dr. in Balboa Park. For a few weeks this month, see the zoo in a whole new light - lots of them! Holiday and animal-themed animated figures move, and light up the sky (and some enclosures) to celebrate the holiday season. Walk all around the zoo or take a thirty-minute ride on the Twinkle Light Trolley ($3 for adults, $2 for children) to see the trees marvelously all lit up, plus a fifty-two-foot lighted train, six-foot-tall toy soldiers, animated horse and buggy, a giant teddy bear, two "dancing" light experiences with musical accompaniment; and much more. Create holiday crafts; meet Santa; listen to storytellers; play reindeer (and other) games; enjoy the fifteen-minute animal encounters; watch a holiday-themed 4D movie ($6 for adults; $5 for children); take a miniature train ride; clap your hands to the live entertainment; and enjoy all that the zoo regularly has to offer. Open the beginning of December - Jan. 1, daily, 9am - 8pm. Closed at 5pm on Christmas Eve (so no real special Jungle Bell features) and closed Christmas Day. Admission to these attractions is included with the price of admission to the zoo - $54 for adults; $44 for ages 3 - 11; children 2 and under are free.

KING HARBOR YACHT CLUB CHRISTMAS BOAT PARADE, Redondo Beach. (310) 376-6926 / kingharbor.com/holiday-boat-parade, 181 N. Harbor Dr. at King Harbor and Redondo Beach Pier. *Watt* a spectacular sight! For 27+ years and going strong, lighted and fancifully decorated boats and paddle-craft parade from King

Harbor Marina to the Redondo Beach Pier competing for the trophy. Live commentary is provided just south of Polly's on the Pier. The parade is in mid-December, 5pm - 7pm. Admission is free.

L.A. COUNTY HOLIDAY CELEBRATION, Los Angeles. (213) 972-3099 / www.musiccenter.org, 135 N. Grand Ave. at the Dorothy Chandler Pavilion of the Music Center. Think of it as a gift offering: This free holiday extravaganza (even the parking is free) is three hours long and filled with dance and music performances of all nationalities and cultures. Ballet, barbershop quartets, gospel choirs, Chinese Classical Musical Ensemble, folk dance, and soooo much more. You do not have to stay for the entire three hours, but whatever you see and hear, you'll feel the richer for it. December 24, 3pm - 6pm. Doors open at 2:30pm and seating is first come, first served.

LA INTERNATIONAL CHILDREN'S FILM FESTIVAL, Los Angeles. (323) 857-6000 / www.lacama.org, 5905 Wilshire Blvd., at the Bing Theatre at the Los Angeles County Museum of Art. Can you watch 50 shows in one day? Probably not, but there are that many to choose from at this festival - so have it! Early shows are geared for toddlers. Kids get to act as reviewers, too - so a way for them to interact. Sat., 10:30am - 4pm. Street parking is free; otherwise $12 or so. Free.

LA JOLLA CHRISTMAS PARADE AND HOLIDAY FESTIVAL, La Jolla. (858) 922-4046 / www.ljparade.com, Parade route - Girard Ave. and Prospect St. Festival - 615 Prospect St. at the La Jolla Recreation Center. This holiday parade marches to the beat of a different drummer as various marching bands are accompanied by drill teams, costumed groups, scouts, floats, vintage automobiles, equestrian units and of course, Jolly St. Nick. Other festivities include a Kid Zone, entertainment, educational exhibits, photos with Santa and a tree lighting ceremony. The parade starts at 1:30pm on Sun.; other festivities run from 2:30pm - 5:30pm. Free.

LA KINGS HOLIDAY ICE, Long Beach; Los Angeles; Woodland Hills. See November entry (pg. 749) for details.

LAS POSADAS and OLD TOWN HOLIDAY IN THE PARK, San Diego. (619) 220-5422 or (619) 297-3100 / www.parks.ca.gov/oldtownsandiego; www.oldtownsandiegoguide.com, between San Diego Ave. and Twiggs St. in Old Town San Diego State Historic Park. The one-day Las Posadas event celebrates Christmas in an early California manner. Las Posadas retells the trek that Mary and Joseph made to Bethlehem, looking for lodging. Join in the candlelit procession weaving through the park, symbolically asking for lodging, and singing traditional Mexican and American carols. (Or just hum along.) The procession ends with a live nativity scene in front of Casa de Estudillo along with a choir performance. For most of the month of December, Old Town San Diego museums, historic homes, stores and restaurants are totally decorated in a way befitting the period and offer up some holiday entertainment. Look up OLD TOWN SAN DIEGO and STATE HISTORIC PARK (pg. 544) for more info on the park. Open Sun., 4:45pm - 6pm. Old Town is open 10am - 5pm, sometimes until 9pm.) Free.

LAS POSADAS, Los Angeles. / www.olvera-street.com, Olvera St. For nine consecutive nights, guests are invited to join in this Mexican tradition of singing and a candlelight procession led by actors portraying Mary and Joseph as the couple searches for shelter in Bethlehem. The Christmas pageant also includes a more modern celebration of breaking open a pinata. Then, enjoy Olvera Street and all that it has to offer with restaurants and shops. The festival is nightly, 5:30pm - 8:30pm. Admission is free.

LAS POSADAS, Santa Fe Springs. (562) 946-6476 / www.santafesprings.org, 12100 Mora Dr. at Heritage Park. In step with Mexican traditions, carols in both English and Spanish are sung along the candle lit processional route, as participants (who are encouraged to dress up according to the time period) follow "Mary" and "Joseph" as they seek to find shelter in Bethlehem. (Posada means lodging, shelter or inn.) Once it is found, the fiesta begins with folkloric dancers and mariachis, and refreshments to purchase. This one-day, Fri. evening procession begins at 6:30pm. Admission is free.

LA ZOO LIGHTS, Los Angeles. See December entry (pg. 749) for details.

LET IT SNOW HOLIDAY FESTIVAL, Rancho Palos Verdes. (310) 521-4460 / www.greenhillsmemorial.com, 27501 S Western Ave. at Green Hills Memorial Park. This festival is held on the beautiful grounds of this cemetery, at the church grounds. It has a little bit of everything - hayrides, caroling, photos with Santa, music, art and crafts for kids, tree lighting at 5:15pm, a lot of fun and a small hill of snow for sledding; just for the snow of it. Sun., 2:30pm - 5:30pm. Free.

LIGHTED STREETS. Is there a street or two in your neighborhood that the owners have gone all out to decorate every year? A great family tradition is to choose one special night during the Christmas season, go out to a restaurant, and walk or drive up and down the festive streets to enjoy the lights and displays. *Just a few* choice streets include: **Los Angeles County**: Candy Cane Lane in Woodland Hills - Most of the home-owners on this eight-block neighborhood of Winnetka St. - 5966 Lubao Ave. - bordered by Corbin Ave. and Victory Blvd go all out. Lights, animated scenes, inflatable snowmen, and more - and lots of traffic. Upper Hastings Ranch in Pasadena - This forty-four block area is bordered by Michillinda Ave., Sierra Madre Blvd. - 3725 E Sierra Madre Blvd. - and Riviera Dr. Numerous homes participate and each block decides on and decorates according to a certain theme. Call (626) 793-9911 (a holiday hotline) for other Pasadena light displays. Santa Fe Springs has an annual Christmas Home Decorating Contest - contact (562) 863-4896 or www.santafesprings.org for winners. Altadena's Christmas Tree Lane has earned a spot on the National Register of Historic Places - check out www.christmastreelane.net. **Orange County:** Eagle Hills in Brea has around 100 homes that decorate - enter on E. Birch and S. Starflower Sts. or E. Lambert Rd. and Sunflower St. - 2960-2970 Primrose Ave. Check out www.lakeforestchristmas.com for a map of houses and streets in south Orange County. **Riverside County:** Bainbridge Circle in Murrieta goes all out for the holidays; sometimes there is even a scavenger list on Facebook to get everyone more involved. **San Bernardino County:** Alta Loma has some great houses, especially Thoroughbred Street - exit 210 fwy N. on Carnelian. **San Diego County:** Check San Diego Family magazine for the best and specific map of Christmas lights sandiegofamily.com, such as 92128 Fairway Village in Carmel Mountain Ranch with other 80 homes decorated. **Santa Barbara County:** Old Town Santa Barbara Trolley of Lights Tour - for $26.50 for adults, $15 for children 12 & under, you can sit back and let the decorated trolley take you on a narrated, 90-minute tour of the best displays in Santa Barbara. **Ventura County:** Christmas Tree Lane Oxnard in Oxnard - Along F and G sts., between 5th and Palm, and the surrounding area of a 10-block loop - thousands of lights and decorations light up the night in this old and elegant area, 6pm - 10pm. There is even a porta potty available! Call (805) 385-7545 for more info. Weeknight Holly Trolley Tours see (pg. 758) and see (pg. 752, 765). Check (805) 385-7545 / www.oxnardhistoricdistrict.com or visitoxnard.com for more info.

LIGHTS ON TEMPLE CITY, Temple City. (626) 656-7321 / www.ci.temple-city.ca.us, 9701 Las Tunas Dr. at Temple City Park. No matter the weather, forty tons of snow will arrive at the park to help ring in the holidays in this community event. Besides the two play areas and snow run for children 12 and under, there are visits with Santa, crafts for kids, bounce houses, a merry-go-round, scale model train rides, snacks, musical entertainment by the high school, and a lighting of the 100' redwood tree. Festivities are Fri., 5pm - 9pm, with a mini-parade at 7pm. Admission is free.

LOGAN'S CANDIES, Ontario. See November entry (pg. 749) for details.

MARINA DEL REY HOLIDAY BOAT PARADE, Marina del Rey. (310) 670-7130 / www.mdrboatparade.org, Admiralty Way. On the second Sat. of December over eighty boats, decorated to the hilt with Christmas lights and decorations, circle around the marina's main channel. The parade is exciting with winners chosen for Best Theme, Best Humor, Best Music, Best Animation, etc. The best views are at 13650 Mindanao Way at Burton Chase Park (where the "live" action and music is played throughout), or 13755 Fiji Way at Fisherman's Village. But first, bring the kids for (pg. 763) for some snow play at the park. Fireworks start the evening off with a bang at 5:55pm. The parade is 5:55pm - 8pm. Free. Parking at the park is $8.

MENORAH LIGHTING AT FASHION ISLAND, Newport Beach. (949) 721-2000 / www.jewishnewport.com, 401 Newport Center Dr. at Fashion Island. Celebrate light over darkness with this Menorah Lighting Celebration. There are also special performances, dreidle-making and other crafts, doughnuts, balloon animal, face painting, treats and more. 5:30pm - 7:30pm.

MESSIAH SING-ALONG, Los Angeles. (213) 972-7282 / lamasterchorale.org, 111 South Grand Ave. at Walt Disney Concert Hall. Sing it out (but maybe practice first!) as you join in at this beautiful venue on one of the most acclaimed chorale presentations. There are numerous soloists, but you are part of the chorus in this 2.5 hour performance. Buy a score in the lobby for about $10, or bring your own. This is the grandest avenue of all this type of event, but call your local orchestra as several others offer this same opportunity. One night, at 7:30pm. Tickets are $39 - $99.

MONARCH BUTTERFLIES, Ventura. See November entry (pg. 749) for details.

MUSEUMS. Many of your favorite museums get all decked out for the holidays, particularly the historical homes. Many also offer holiday programs, with special family activities.

NAPLES ISLAND, Long Beach. / www.naplesca.com. Access Naples off 2nd Street on a number of streets, including Naples Plaza, Revenna, Tivoli and The Toledo. It is best to park and walk. This small "island" in Long Beach is always on our list of places to go at Christmas. The homes here are beautiful any time of the year, but from Thanksgiving until New Years, they take on a magical quality with the elaborate and wonderful decorations. This community is known as Naples because it is surrounded by canals, so you can start your walk anywhere along the water and end up back where you started from. The only thing not magical about this place is the parking. Although it is free, you will probably spend several minutes looking for a space. Just do what I do and sing Christmas carols loudly while you look - my kids always enjoy me doing this. See the next entry for information about the boat parade here. Evenings in December. Free.

NAPLES ISLAND HOLIDAY BOAT PARADE, Long Beach. (562) 570-5333 or (562) 436-3645 / www.naplesca.com, 5437 E. Ocean Blvd. at Los Alamitos Bay around the Naples Canals, and along 2nd St. by the Long

Beach Yacht Club. See the website for viewing opportunities. For over 70 years boat-owners have covered their boats with Christmas lights, and paraded past decorated homes along the Naples canals, competing in several different categories. Note that there are many restaurants along the waterfront to eat and see the parade. If you miss the boat (parade), just seeing the homes along here is a special treat, too (see above entry). Sat., 6pm - 8:30pm. Admission is free.

NATIVITY PAGEANT, Solvang. (800) 468-6765 or (805) 688-6144 / www.solvangusa.com, 420 Second St. at the outdoor Solvang Festival Theater. The narrated nativity pageant is performed in Solvang's outdoor theater (dress warmly) on a Saturday evening in December. The program features a choir, Christmas carols, renowned singers and musicians, and adult and children characters in full costumes, along with live animals, to tell the story of Christmas. It is held in conjunction with (pg. 758). The first show starts at 5pm; the second at 7pm. Free admission - first come, first served.

NEWPORT BEACH CHRISTMAS BOAT PARADE, Newport Beach. (949) 729-4400 / www.christmasboatparade.com, Newport Beach Harbor. The largest and oldest boat parade (over 110 years!), with more than 100 participants of yachts, boats, kayaks, and more, sets sail for five nights, Wed. - Sun., in mid-December. Holiday lights and music fill the air as some owners spend thousands of dollars decorating their floating vessels. The Ring of Lights contest goes on simultaneously, where bayside homes and businesses go all out in decorating to compete for prizes in various categories. (It's kind of 2-for-1 nights!) An ideal location for viewing the boat parade is Balboa Island, but you should arrive before 5:30pm, as parking is very limited. If you are going to have dinner in this area, be sure to make reservations and get reserved seating (and food!). Reserved lawn seating is available at Newport Sea Base, (949) 642-5031, located at 1931 W. Coast Highway for $10, in advance. Consider becoming a part of the cruise, and get a closer look at the beautiful boats and surrounding, decorated estates. Davey's Locker, (949) 673-1434, or Newport Landing, (949) 675-0551, offer three almost ninety-minute cruises a night (on their decorated boats) on parade nights, departing at 5:30pm, 7:15pm and 8:30pm for about $36 for adults; $32 for ages 3 - 12. Call for more details and to make reservations. The parade hours are about 6:30pm - 9pm, with fireworks at 6:15pm on Wed. and at 9pm on Sun.

NIGHTS OF 1,000 LIGHTS, (949) 673-2261 / www.slgardens.org. A colorful spot to spend a night with 1,000 lights, at least decorate smallish Sherman Library and Gardens for a Friday and Saturday night. Tunnel of lights to walk thru, visits with Santa, hot chocolate and live music. $10 for members; $15 for non-members. 6pm - 9pm.

NORTH PARK TOYLAND PARADE AND FESTIVAL, San Diego. (619) 269-2860 / www.toylandparade.com, University Ave., between Utah and Iowa sts., then North Park Way. For over 55 years this parade and festival has been like receiving an early Christmas present. The parade features vintage cars, enormous character balloons, marching bands, dance groups, beauty queens, city officials and Santa Claus riding a fire engine and ringing jingle bells. The festival has vendors, arts and crafts and fun activities for all ages. The parade is Sat., 11am - 1pm; the festival, 10am - 3pm. Free. Parking at North Park Parking Garage for $1.

NORTH POLE EXPRESS, Fillmore. See November entry (pg. 750) for details.

NORTH POLE LIMITED, Campo. See November entry (pg. 750) for details.

NUTCRACKER. Numerous venues all over Southern California present this classic ballet to the timeless music of Tchaikovsky. This is an enchanting way to expose your children to the beauty of ballet and classical music because of the costumed characters and gripping storyline. Look in the main section of the book under Shows and Theaters for ballet companies, and/or call your local theater.

OCEAN BEACH HOLIDAY PARADE, Ocean Beach. (619) 515-4400 / www.obtowncouncil.org, on Newport Ave. from Sunset Cliffs Blvd. to the beach. Sunny California boasts some "winter" fun with this Saturday evening parade, running 38+ years. Marching bands strut and play; roller derby players zoom past in colorful costumes; dance troupes bogey on by; decorated cars - classics and others, cruise down the street, as so motorcycles, floats and other vehicles; and Santa makes an appearance. Come early to shop at the craft fair that day, at the foot of Newport Ave. Craft fair, 11am - 1pm; parade, 5pm. Free.

OCEANSIDE HARBOR PARADE OF LIGHTS, Oceanside. (760) 722-5751 / www.ci.oceanside.ca.us; www.oceansideyc.net, 1540 Harbor Drive S. at Oceanside Harbor. For one bright evening, boats decked out in lights compete for awards and go on parade circling the inner harbor. It is one time when being judged is OK! For best viewing, come early and stand near the Harbor Police and fishing dock. Sat., 7pm - 9pm. Free.

AN OLD-FASHIONED CHRISTMAS MELODRAMA & ICE CREAM SOCIAL, Costa Mesa. (714) 432-5880 / www.orangecoastcollege.edu; www.occtickets.com, 2701 Fairview Rd. at Orange Coast College at the Drama Lab Theatre. Yea for the hero! Boo to the villain! Fa la la with the music! Yum for the ice cream! This annual Christmas Melodrama, that runs for several weekends, is great fun for the family to participate in, plus the audience enjoys ice cream with elves at intermission and singing classic Christmas carols. And whohoho do you think comes for a visit at the end of the show? Shows are Fri., 7pm; Sat. at 2:30pm and 7pm; Sun. at 2:30pm. Tickets are $7 in advance, $9 at the door ($5/$7 for students, seniors and children).

OXNARD CHRISTMAS PARADE / TAMALE FESTIVAL, Oxnard. (805) 247-0197 - parade; (805) 766-4906 - tamale / www.downtownoxnard.org; www.oxnardtamalefestival.com. Parade route is A, 5th and C Sts. The Tamale Festival is at Plaza Park - 5th & B sts. The hometown parade includes floats decorated to a new theme each year, plus marching bands, entertainment, equestrian units, and an awards ceremony. Gobble up authentic homemade tamales during the Tamale Festival, held in conjunction with the parade. Tamale-making demos, live mariachi music, arts and crafts, visits with Santa Claus, and more fun are to be had. The parade is Sat., 10am - noon. The Tamale Festival is 9am - 6:30pm. Admission is free.

PARADE OF 1,000 LIGHTS, Long Beach. (562) 435-2668; (562) 435-4093 / www.shorelineyachtclub.com, 429 Shoreline Village Dr.- the route is Shoreline Marina, Rainbow Harbor, and Queen Mary. Come enjoy the boats on parade (going on 36 years!) that are adorned with Christmas lights and decorations. Prizes are awarded in several categories. The best views are from Shoreline Village, particularly Parkers Lighthouse, although parking is at a premium, as well as the Queen Mary. The parade is on a Sat., 5:30 - 8pm. Admission is free.

PARADE OF LIGHTS, Mission Bay. (858) 488-0501 / www.mbyc.org. The best parade viewing of these more than 100 boats is along Crown Point, the east side of Vacation Island, or the west side of Fiesta Island. Sometimes fireworks, courtesy of SeaWorld, cap off the evening with a dazzling display of color. The boat parade usually begins at 6pm. Free.

PARADE OF LIGHTS BOAT CRUISE, Ventura. (805) 642-1393 / www.islandpackers.com, 1691 Spinnaker Dr. at Ventura Harbor. Depart for a cruise around the harbor, seeing the houses all decked out in their holiday finest. Then, watch the wonderful boat parade - (pg. 762) from your prime location and the fireworks show at 8pm before returning the to dock at about 8:30pm. Snacks and beverages can be purchased on board. Dress warmly!! Arrive early as parking can be tough on parade nights. Arrive earlier and enjoy the festivities of (pg. 766) in the harbor. Cruises depart Fri. at 6:15pm, 6:30pm and 6:40pm; on Sat. at 6:15pm and 6:30pm. Reservations are needed. $35 for adults; $32 for srs.; $25 for ages 3 - 12.

PARADE OF LIGHTS, Oxnard. (805) 985-4852 or (805) 247-0197 or (800) 269-6273 parade / www.channelislandsharbor.org, 3600 S. Harbor Blvd. at Channel Islands Harbor at Marine Emporium Landing. During this event*full* Saturday kids have tons of cold fun at the snowplay area, available from noon until it melts. Live music including carolers; rides and games, such as a rock climbing wall, inflatable fun zones, and water taxi rides; holiday arts and crafts boutique; arts and crafts for kids to do; and visits with Santa and Mrs. Claus are some of the other seasonal offerings. The parade (going on for 50+ years!) is officially kicked off at 7pm when Santa and his reindeers fly over head (via a helicopter - but don't tell the kids). Watch as numerous boats are decked out for the *hulladays* with lights and animated displays. The parade begins in front of Peninsula Park, heads to the main channel, and loops back around for a second run. Dress warmly (or drink some hot chocolate!). Sat., 10am - 8pm. General admission is free.

PARADE OF LIGHTS / SANTA'S VILLAGE, Santa Barbara. (805) 564-553 / www.santabarbaraca.gov, Cabrillo Street, at Harbor and along the beach near Stearns Wharf. At 3pm on this Sunday, Santa and his elves arrive at the pier escorted by the Harbor Patrol - come by and chat with them. (And arrive early as the first 400 receive a goody bag.) Carolers and special activities, like playing in the snow, in this one-day Santa's Village add to the enchantment. From 5:30pm - 7pm watch the over thirty decorated boats sail out of the harbor and parade up and down the shoreline, vying for prizes. The evening ends with a firework display at about 7pm. The best vantage point for the parade is along Stearns Wharf and the breakwater. Sun., 3pm - 7pm. Free.

PARADE OF LIGHTS, Ventura. (805) 642-8538 / www.venturaharborvillage.com, 1500 Spinnaker Dr. at Ventura Harbor Village. For over 40 years this two-night festive boat parade has been making the nights really light up. Pre-parade events include live music, visits with Santa, a fly-by with Santa (via helicopter), visiting reindeer, carousel rides, carnival rides, games, and indulging in shopping and eating. See (pg. 766) for more details on that festival. Located at 1575 Spinnaker Drive and dubbed California Sleigh Rides, Ventura Boat Rentals offers cruises most evenings at 5:45pm and 7:30pm during December to see the boat and shoreline home lights even more close up, traveling along the same route as the parade. Adults are $18; seniors are $16; and children are $12. Call (805) 642-7753 / www.venturaboatrentals.com for more details. Also See December entry (pg. 762) for other cruises during this parade. The evening festivities, after the wonderful parade, end with a fireworks display at 7:30 or 8pm. Fri. and Sat., 5pm (or earlier!) for pre-parade fun; 6:30pm for boat parade. General admission is free.

PELTZER PINES, Brea, Silverado. See November entry (pg. 750) for details.

PINE TREE ACRES, Ramona. See November entry (pg. 750) for details.

PISMO BEACH MONARCH GROVE, Pismo Beach. See January entry (pg. 696) for details.

PLANETARIUM SHOWS - CHRISTMAS SHOW / STAR OF BETHLEHEM. See November entry (pg. 750) for details.

PORT OF SAN DIEGO HOLIDAY BOWL PARADE, San Diego. (619) 283-5808 / www.holidaybowl.com, N. Harbor Dr. near Ash St. and W. Harbor. Although football is often the focal point of this one-day Holiday Bowl, the colorful parade, which is televised, is the real highlight for kids. Dubbed "America's Largest Balloon Parade" you'll see floats, a huge variety of gigantic character and other massive balloons, numerous marching bands, drill teams, and other entertainment that await sports fans of all ages. A lot, A LOT of people attend this so get here early and/or take a trolley (another fun treat). See www.sdmts.com for trolley info. Look at the event website for where to park and other tips. A few days after Christmas: The two-hour parade begins at 10am. Battle of the Bands, at the Broadway Pier, begins around 11:45am. Admission is free. Grandstand seating is $22 per person.

RADY'S CHILDREN ICE RINK, San Diego. See November entry (pg. 751) for details.

RANCHO NOEL POTRERO VALLEY CHRISTMAS TREE FARM, Potrero. See November entry (pg. 751) for details.

REINDEER ROMP, Los Angeles. See November entry (pg. 751) for details.

ROSE PARADE FLOAT DECORATING, Pasadena. (626) 449-4100 / www.tournamentofroses.com. Volunteers are always needed so call to ask where you can help decorate the Rose Parade floats. Children at least 13 years old and whose parents are Auto Club members can help decorate the AAA float. Check the listed website for other companies who need volunteers as well.

ROSE PARADE PRE FLOAT VIEWING, Irwindale, Pasadena. (626) 795-4171; (626) 449-4100 / www.tournamentofroses.com, Irwindale - 5400 Irwindale Ave.; Pasadena - Rosemont Pavilion at 700 Seco St. This is a wonderful opportunity to come "backstage" to see the world-famous floats as they are being made. Workers spend weeks meticulously decorating them using plants, seeds, tree bark, flowers, and single petals to turn them into works of art. Rosemont - open Dec. 28, 11am - 5pm; Dec. 29, 9am - 5pm; Dec. 30, 11am - 5pm; Dec. 31, 11am - 1pm. Irwindale - open Dec. 28 - Dec. 30, 11am - 5pm. Admission is $15 for ages 6 and up; ages 5 and under are free.

SAN DIEGO BAY PARADE OF LIGHTS, San Diego. (619) 224-2240 / www.sdparadeoflights.org, San Diego Bay. Over 80+ boats wonderfully decked out with lights and decorations participate in this parade (going on 46 years!) from Shelter Island, to Harbor Island, the Embarcadero, Seaport Village, the Pier at Cesar Chavez Park, and ending at the Ferry Landing in Coronado. The parade takes about an hour to pass by from any view point. Participants compete for prizes in the "best of" in several categories. There are even announcers along parts of the route. It runs on two consecutive Sun., 5pm - 9pm. Free viewing from the shoreline.

SAN PASQUAL BATTLE REENACTMENT, San Pasqual. (760) 737-2201 / www.parks.ca.gov, 15808 San Pasqual Valley Rd. at San Pasqual Battlefield State Historic Park. On a Sunday nearest to December 6, reenactors dress up as mountain men and other pivotal figures from the mid-1800's and they pitch tents; provide music, crafts (i.e. adobe brick making, candle making, etc.), and dance of the era; and best of all, they reenact the battle (one of the bloodiest fought in California during the Mexican War more than 150 years) ago - they even fire cannons! at 11:30am and 2:30pm. See the SAN PASQUAL BATTLEFIELD STATE HISTORIC PARK (pg. 515) for more details on the park. Open 11:30am - 3:30pm. Admission is free.

SANTA'S ELECTRIC LIGHT PARADE, Temecula. See November entry (pg. 751) for details.

SKATING BY THE SEA, Coronado. See November entry (pg. 751) for details.

SNOW DAYS AT KIDSPACE, Pasadena. (626) 449-9144 / www.kidspacemuseum.org, 480 N. Arroyo Blvd. at Kidspace Museum. Walking, or playing, in a winter wonderland of real snow in the courtyard of Kidspace Museum is cold, so bring mittens, boots and warm jackets. Prance around under falling snow (from the snow machine), decorate cookies (additional $3), make a winter craft, enjoy different live performances every day (dancing, puppets, circus acts, live animals, etc.) and explore all that the museum has to offer. See KIDSPACE CHILDREN'S MUSEUM (pg. 125) for details about this great children's museum. Dec. 26 - Dec. 30, 9:30am - 5pm. Price includes admission to the museum: $13 per person; infants under 1 are free.

SNOW WONDER, Marina del Rey. (310) 305-9545 / www.visitmarinadelrey.com, 13650 Mindanao Way at Burton Chace Park It's snow wonder people look forward to this one-day event! Lots of real snow is brought in for sledding, making snowmen and just playing. Other activities include arts and crafts, face painting, music, food trucks and more winter fun. Stay in the park to enjoy the (pg. 760) with fireworks at 5:55pm and the boat parade at 6pm. Open Sat., noon - 6pm. (Then the boat parade, so 8pm) Free. Parking is $8.

SPIRIT OF SAN PEDRO HOLIDAY PARADE, San Pedro. (310) 832-7272 / www.spholidayparade.com; www.sanpedrochamber.com. It starts at 13th and Pacific, head north to 6th St., east to Palos Verdes. 3 viewing areas: 11th and Pacific; 6th and Pacific; and 6th and Palos Verdes St. Get in the spirit of Christmas with this holiday parade put on the first Sunday of the month at 1pm. Enjoy local drill teams, decorated floats, bands, fire engines, police motorcycle brigades, equestrian groups and more. Sun., 1pm - 3pm.

SUGAR PLUM EXPRESS, Fillmore. See November entry (pg. 752) for details.

TANAKA FARMS FALL HARVEST TOUR AND CHRISTMAS TREE LOT, Irvine. See October entry (pg. 745) for details.

TEMECULA ON ICE, Temecula. (951) 694-6480 or (951) 297-9423 / www.temeculaca.gov, 41902 Main St., Old Town Temecula. Can you do a double axel or salchow? Me neither, but I enjoy outdoor skating so this rink is great. The grand opening features special skating exhibitions and the rest of the season is just fun. Open mid-December - beginning January, Sun. - Thurs., 10am - 9:30pm; Fri. - Sat., 10am - 11pm. Check on the holiday schedule. $10 per person for unlimited skating; $6 for skate rentals.

THE RINK IN DOWNTOWN BURBANK, Burbank. (818) 238-5180 / www.dtnbur.com, 150 North 3rd St. Ah, Burbank - so much history and so many celebrities, and now, so much ice! Join skaters from all over and then go shopping and/or eating at the nearby shops. There are also special events that go on at the rink throughout the season. Open mid-December - the beginning of January, Sun. - Thurs., 10am - 10pm; Fri. - Sat., 10am - 11:30pm - unlimited skating. Admission is $10 per person + $6 for skate rentals.

TIS THE SEASON, Costa Mesa. (714)-556-2787 / www.scfta.org, 600 Town Center Drive at Segerstrom Center for the Arts. Tis the season for joy, and singing, hence the Pacific Chorale, joined by the Pacific Symphony and Southern California Children's Chorus, present an evening of musical Christmas delights for the whole family. Usually a Sat. at 5pm and Sun. at 3pm. Tickets run between $29 - $140, depending on seating.

TOUCH A TRUCK, Simi Valley. (855) 478-7300 / www.svpf.org, 2929 Tapo Canyon Rd., in front of City Hall. Who doesn't want to touch a truck? Except maybe truck drivers cause they do it all the time. The Simi Valley Police Foundation presents its annual Touch A Truck toy drive where attendees can get up close and even inside all kinds of trucks and other vehicles including construction equipment trucks, police cars, firetrucks, SWAT vehicles, and more. There are also some vendors there, plus food trucks (yea!) and other activities to do. Open Sat., 10am - 3pm. Free. Please donate a new, unwrapped toy for the Salvation Army Toy Drive.

TOURNAMENT OF ROSES EVENTS, Pasadena. (877) 793-9911 - holiday hotline; (626) 449-4100 / www.tournamentofroses.com, 1001 Rose Bowl Dr. at the Rose Bowl. For three or four days before the big parade and football game, fans can participate in several activities and events that occur at various times at the bowl and off-site. See the **floats being decorated**, ROSE PARADE PRE FLOAT VIEWING (pg. 763). **Bandfest** is the opportunity to watch the practice of the award-winning marching bands from around the world that will be in the parade. It is held at 1570 E. Colorado Blvd. at Robinson Stadium at Pasadena City College. The three shows are usually Dec. 29 at 1:30pm; Dec. 30 at 9:30am and 2pm. The cost is $15 per person; free for ages 5 and under. **Equestfest** is held at 480 Riverside Drive in Burbank at the Los Angeles Equestrian Center usually on Dec. 29 from 10am - 3pm. Stroll through the stables, talk with riders, and most of all enjoy the show from noon - 2pm where riders and mounts perform drills as they practice for their turn in the parade. Trick roping and riding demonstrations, live entertainment, horse-drawn fire wagons, and food round out your day here. The cost is $15 per person; children 5 and under are free. Parking is $5. Tickets are available through Ticketmaster at (800) 745-3000 or www.ticketmaster.com. Exact events and times could change every year, so check the website to plan your outing.

TRAIN TO SANTA'S WORKSHOP, Perris. (951) 943-3020 / www.oerm.org, 2201 South "A" St. at the Southern California Railway Museum. For 2 long weekends before Christmas help build anticipation for the big day by taking your kids on a train ride to visit Santa at his (pseudo) North Pole workshop. The train is decked out and you'll sing Christmas songs, listen to storytelling and play some games. At the workshop there is a play area with Thomas the Tank Engine train tables (of course!), a kid-powered coaster ride, crafts, refreshments, and a lots of ho ho hoing. Enjoy all else that the Railway Museum has to offer - see SOUTHERN CALIFORNIA RAILWAY MUSEUM (pg. 373) for more details about this great museum. Train times are Fri., 5:30pm and 7pm; Sat. - Sun., 11am, 1pm, 3pm, 5:30pm and 7pm. Tickets are $20 for adults; $15 for ages 2 - 11; children under 2 are free.

TROLLEY TOUR OF LIGHTS, Long Beach. (562) 888-2870 / www.longbeachtrolley.com, 5236 E. 2nd St. You can drive around and look at the Christmas lights, and the driver misses out, or you can take the trolley and everyone enjoys the sights! This classic cable-car trolley goes around the waterfront and street of Long Beach, including the floating Christmas trees of Alamitos Bay, and beautifully decorated houses and boats of Naples Island. The tour is quick, a half an hour. It includes hot cocoa and a sugar cookie, an inexpensive souvenir Santa hat and candy cane, holiday music (you can sing along, or not) and some narration of the area. Most of the month of December, departing at 5:15pm, 6pm 6:45pm, 7:30pm, 8:15pm and 9pm. $30 for adults; $20 for ages 3 - 12; children 2 and under are free and must sit on a parent's lap.

TWAS THE LIGHTS BEFORE CHRISTMAS BUS TOURS, Temecula. (951) 694-6480 / www.temeculaca.gov, Meet at Old Town Parking Garage at 41000 Main St., Temecula Civic Center. Almost like a sleigh ride, but not: On select nights take a ninety-minute, open-air, double decker bus tour around Temecula's most decorated homes. Each evening includes refreshments, prize drawing and corny holiday jokes. Pre-registration is required. Dress warmly! Note: Bike riding families can join in on a free bike tour of homes on one night, too. See the website for details. Thurs. - Sun. in December, from 7pm - 8:30pm. $10 per person; under 2 not requiring a seat are free.

UNA NOCHE DE LAS POSADAS, Santa Barbara. (805) 965-0093 / www.sbthp.org, 123 East Canon Perdido St. at El Presidio de Santa Barbara State Historic Park. A reenactment of Joseph and Mary's search for shelter in Bethlehem is traditionally celebrated throughout Mexico and South America, as well as by early California inhabitants. After a short mass and singing of classic Christmas songs, join the procession, led by Joseph and Mary, and walk and sing from State Street, through the Paseo Nuevo mall, ending at Casa de la Guerra, where the young couple finds lodging. Everyone, then, enjoys more singing, hot chocolate, and a pinata (for the kids - just like in Bethlehem over 2,000 years ago!) Fri., starting at 7pm Admission is free.

UPTOWN CHRISTMAS PARADE, Whittier. (562) 696-2662 / www.whittieruptown.org. This one-day, uptown parade, for us downtown folks, too, features more than 120 entries including highschool bands, equestrian and marching units, dance troupes, vintage automobiles, floats, and Santa Claus. The route is down Greenleaf from Hadley to Mar Vista, ending at Whittier Community Center. Come early or stay after and do some shopping or eat at one of the local restaurants. Sat., 10am - noon. Admission is free.

VICTORIAN CHRISTMAS, Wilmington. (310) 548-7777 / www.banningmuseum.org, 401 E. M St. at the General Phineas Banning Residence Museum. Kick off the Yuletide season by immersing yourself in the 19th century on the first weekend in December at the BANNING MUSEUM (pg. 100). Docents greet you dressed in period costumes and show you around the beautifully-decorated house/museum. The lavish Victorian adornments are quite lovely and the costumed carolers, bell ringers, and musicians complete the ambiance. Take a horse-drawn trolley ride to and from the THE DRUM BARRACKS CIVIL WAR MUSEUM (pg. 107), which is just down the street, watch blacksmith demonstration, do a craft, shop with craft vendors and buy something to eat from food vendors. Open Sat. - Sun., 11am - 4pm. Admission is free.

VICTORIAN HOLIDAY HOME TOURS, Oxnard. (805) 247-0197 or (805) 483-7960 / www.heritagesquareoxnard.com, 715 S. "A" St. at Heritage Square. Take advantage of this rare opportunity to see the interiors of select Victorian homes as they are completely decked out for the holidays. Period Christmas music, living history performances, and an old-time ambiance add to the festive atmosphere. Guided tours by docents dressed from that era talk about the pioneers who originally owned the homes, and the architecture. You can also visit the near-by, free, gingerbread house display, at the Heritage Square Hall, 731 S. A Street, Tues. - Sat., 10am - 5pm and Sun., 1pm - 4pm. Tours take place through the month of December on Sat., 10am - 4pm; Sun., 1pm - 4pm. Reservations are suggested. Admission is $7 per person.

THE WICKERD FARM CHRISTMAS TREES, Menifee. (951) 672-3020 / www.wickerdfarm.com, 26852 Scott Rd. Help to cut your own tree at this five-acre farm - the fun is walking around all the trees (I actually really like this part!). Monetery pines are $10 a foot. There is a giant oak tree with a tire swing, picnic areas, and a small store selling fresh greens. Santa makes an appearance on certain weekends. Open the day after Thanksgiving until Christmas, Sun - Thurs., 10am - 8pm; Fri. - Sat. 10am - 9pm. Admission is free.

WILDLIGHTS, Palm Desert. See November entry (pg. 752) for details.

WINTER FANTASY MUSIC & LIGHT SHOW, Oxnard. (805) 385-2705 / www.downtownoxnard.org, corner of B and Fifth sts. at Plaza Park. This is an if-you-are-in-the-area thing to do: Put some sparkle in your life with this short light show at the Plaza Park Pagoda. Holiday music plays while 30,000 flashing colored lights and animated characters come to life amidst decorated trees. Indulge in dinner and/or a movie at the adjacent Centennial Plaza, or a holiday offering (see the rest of this December section for ideas). Every fifteen minutes in the month of December from 5pm - 10pm. Free.

WINTER FANTASY SAWDUST FESTIVAL, Laguna Beach. See November entry (pg. 752, 765) for details.

WINTERFEST, Garden Grove. (714) 741-5200 / www.ci.garden-grove.ca.us, 13630 Atlantis Way, at Atlantis Park. A lot of holiday fun is packed into the first Saturday of this month: Snow play and sledding (50 tons of snow!); pictures with Santa (in the evening); carnival games; inflatable bounces; train rides; entertainment; food for sale; and a crafts area where kids can make a variety of projects such as ornaments, wrapping paper, and Christmas cards. Open 2pm - 5pm. Admission is $10; children 2 and under are free. Tickets are limited only sold in advance at City Hall at 11222 Acacia Parkway.

WINTER FEST OC, Costa Mesa. (714) 855-1187 / www.winterfestoc.com, 88 Fair Dr. Santa Claus is coming to town and so is the huge Winter Fest, wintry fun with an outdoor ice rink; eight lane ice slide; snow play park for making snow angels and snowmen (and just to play in); a gigantic rocking horse; over 20 carnival rides; Alpine Village; model train exhibit; bounce houses; make and take crafts; petting zoo; toddler area; live entertainment, including mini shows starring favorite kid's characters, like Thomas and Friends and PJ Masks; inflatable light maze; strolling carolers; a carousel; nightly parade; snowboard simulator; fireworks (5:30 every night); lots and lots of Christmas sweet treats; nighttime concerts; a walk-thru Festival of Lights with thousands of sparkly lights and decorations; and more. Open mid-December to beginning of Jan., usually Mon. - Thurs., 2pm - 10pm; Fri., 2pm - 11pm; Sat. - Sun., noon - 11pm, or so. Holidays have different hours. Check for specific times. Basic admission is $17 for adults on line, $22 at the door; $12 for ages 3 -12 online, $17 at the door. Online opening hour, $10. Ice skating is $12 online; unlimited rides is $20, etc.

WINTER GATHERING POW WOW, Coachella. (866) 377-6829 / www.spotlight29.com, 46-200 Harrison Place at Spotlight29 Casino. This three-day, annual gathering of the Coachella Valley native peoples - from the U.S., Canada, and Mexico - is energetic, colorful, and memorable. Traditional dress, dances, and songs take the stage, with drum and dance cash-payout contests on-going, while Native American arts and crafts and food vie for your attention, too. Open Fri. - Sun., noon - evening. The Grand Entrance is Fri. at 7pm; Sat. at 1pm and 7pm; Sun. at 1pm. Free.

WINTER WONDERFEST, Santa Ana; Sylmar. (818) 890-1761 - Sylmar; (714) 542-2823 - Santa Ana / oc.discoverycube.org, 2500 North Main St., Santa Ana and 11800 Foothill Blvd., Sylmar. It's snow fun to come and play at the Discovery Cube and learn about the science of snow! Real snow is flurried in for sledding, tubing down a 75-foot ramp, and making snowmen. Build and race your own candy car in the annual Gingerbread Derby (then eat it!); smell, view and learn about the Science of Gingerbread during the stage show and exhibits; study weather at the learning station; watch a classic holiday movie; and have a blast exploring all the fantastic, hands-on exhibits at the here. A ticket for both Wonderfest and the museum are required. See DISCOVERY CUBE (Los Angeles County) (pg. 105) and DISCOVERY CUBE (Orange County) (pg. 304) for more details about these science museums. Open mid-December - early January, daily 10am - 5pm; closed Christmas Day. Wonderfest is $5 for adults; $7 for kids ages 3 - 14 for Wonderfest; plus general admission of $17.95 for adults; $14.95 for srs; $12.95 for ages 3 - 14.

WINTER WONDERLAND AND HOLIDAY MARKETPLACE, Ventura. (805) 642-8538 / www.venturaharborvillage.com, 1500 Spinnaker Dr. at Ventura Harbor Village. Celebrate the holiday season with this one-day event with snow flurries (faux snow), a visit with Santa and some of his reindeers (I can't tell which ones), strolling carolers, and other live entertainment, ice carving demonstrations, free crafts, and all the fun - carnival rides and games - that the Village has to offer. Stay for the evening boat parade and fireworks - see (pg. 762) for details!! Open Sat., 1pm - 5pm. General admission is free.

YOUNG AMERICANS HOLIDAY SHOW, La Mirada. (562) 944-9801 / lamiradatheatre.com, 14900 La Mirada Blvd. at the La Mirada Theatre. 250 Young Americans cast members come together for this absolutely marvelous holiday show. With 30 scene changes, more costume changes than you can count, fantastic numbers of singing and dancing, plus dancing Santas, Toyland, the Polar Express and Handel's Messiah represented, it's a dazzling feast for the eyes and ears. The show runs for a few weeks, Wed. - Fri. at 8pm; Sat., 2pm and 8pm; Sun., 2pm and 7pm. Tickets are $29 - $60.

IDEAS and RESOURCES

(General ideas of where else to go and what to do, plus where to find specific resource information.)

AIRPLANE or HELICOPTER RIDES. Look in the phone book; call small, local airports for flight information; and/or check the Transportation section in this book for specific flying venues.

ANIMALS

AA Laboratories, (714) 893-5675 / www.egglab.com - They sell fertilized eggs, such as a dozen chick eggs for $18 for a dozen. They also have fertile duck, quail and goose eggs, blown goose eggs for crafts and 50-pound bundles of sugar cane. Incubators rent for $10 a week - home births without the labor pains! Be forewarned, however, that very little instruction comes with your eggs and incubator. They have retail locations in Westminster and San Diego. Tips: Go to the library to research the process by checking out picture books of developing chicks and ducks. Or pick up an information sheet and feed at a pet store, such as Blacksmith's Corner in Bellflower (pg. 775). And yes, if you do not want to raise the birds, AA Labs will (usually) take them back and donate them to farms, zoos, etc.

Insect Lore, (800) LIVE BUG (548-3284) / www.insectlore.com - This website offers living science kits, giving families the opportunity to observe insects and other critters growing and transforming. Our favorite kits are the butterfly, caterpillar, ant, praying mantis, and ladybird beetles (i.e. ladybugs, to lay people). Each kit comes with instructions, information, and live insects. The website also offers other science experiments, books, and visual aids.

Wagon Train Feed & Pet in Orange, (714) 639-7932 / www.wagontrainoc.com - This small pet store sells chick and duck eggs, as well as incubators. See Wagon Train Feed & Pet (pg. 775) for more detail.

ARCHERY. Look under the Great Outdoors sections in each county for local parks that offer archery ranges. You can also check out USA Archery at www.usarchery.org or call (719) 866-4576. They will refer callers to local clubs and places to practice.

ARTS AND CRAFTS. Many places, including libraries and bookstores, offer free or minimal fee classes, or workshops, for kids. Also check out the ARTS AND CRAFTS sections of the book, as well as craft, handicraft stores and home repair stores below:

Home Depot, (800) 553-3199 / www.homedepot.com/workshops - Most offer free workshops between 9am and noon on the 1st Sat. of each month.

Lakeshore Learning Materials stores, (800) 428-4414 / www.lakeshorelearning.com - Most stores offer free crafts for kids every Sat. from 11am - 3pm for ages 3 - 9, or so. Some locations also have crafts on Sun., 11am - 3pm.

Michaels, (800) MICHAEL (642-4235) / www.michaels.com - Ask about their kids' programs including Camp Creativity and Kids Club®.

Piecemakers Country Store, (714) 641-3112 / www.piecemakers.com - Take a class in needlework, quilting, beading or other old-time country crafts. Also offers music and free demonstrations, such as soap making, bookbinding, and painting.

AUDIO CDS The following are some of our favorite, non just singing, audio recordings:

Adventures in Odyssey, (800) A-FAMILY (232-6459) / www.family.org - Focus on the Family puts out this series consisting of six, half-hour-long, Biblically-based, radio dramas. The stories are centered around a fictional soda shop/Bible room/imagination station/kid's hang-out called Whit's End, and the people that live in the small (made-up) town of Odyssey. Each episode involves kids, families, dilemmas, solutions, morals, wit, and wisdom. I can't recommend these adventures highly enough! TIP: visit www.whitsend.org and follow the links to listen to the current episode on your computer. Make sure that the digital audio works with your chosen player.

Audio Memory, (800)365-7464 / www.audiomemory.com - These CDs, DVDs and MP3 recordings teach different subjects, like geography, math, and history, through song. They say that you never forget what you sing. May that be true in this case.

Classical Kids Series, (888) 841-3456 / www.rainbowresource.com - They can be found in most larger retail record stores or ordered through Amazon or catalogs such as Rainbow Resource Center. Each hour-long recording in this wonderful series tells the story, told in play format, of a famous composer while the composer's music plays in the background. Titles include *Beethoven Lives Upstairs*, *Mozart's Magical Fantasy*, and *Tchaikovsky Discovers America*.

Focus on the Family Radio Theatre Drama, (800) A-FAMILY (232-6459) / www.family.org - Put out by Focus on the Family, as are the above-mentioned Adventures in Odyssey, this series presents fantastic dramatizations using a variety of voices, sound effects, and music. Titles include the *Chronicles of Narnia, Squanto, My Secret Garden, Ben Hur, A Christmas Carol*, and many more.

Well-Trained Mind, (800) 477-6234 / www.welltrainedmind.com; www.jimweiss.com - Well-Trained Mind sells many resources for parent and home educators, including recordings by the enthralling storyteller, Jim Weis. Kids (and adults) of all ages will enjoy the masterful recounting of history, from ancient to modern, and the retelling of (mostly) classic stories. Titles include *Ancient Times, The Story of the World, Abraham Lincoln and the Heart of America, Arabian Nights, Sherlock Holmes for Children, Three Musketeers, Greek Myths, Shakespeare for Children, Fairytale Favorites* and *Animal Tales*.

BASEBALL Call for a game schedule and ask about special days, such as fan appreciation day.

 Angels in Anaheim, www.angelsbaseball.com

 California Winter League, (760) 778-HITS (4487) / www.californiawinterleague.com

 Dodgers in Los Angeles, (866) DODGERS (363-4377) / www.dodgers.com

 Inland Empire 66ers in San Bernardino, (909) 888-9922 / www.ie66ers.com

 Inland Valley Bucs, (951) 830-3258 / www.inlandvalleybaseball.com

 Inland Valley Pirates, (951) 830-3258 / www.inlandvalleybaseball.com

 Lake Elsinore Storm, (951) 245-HITS (4487) / www.stormbaseball.com

 Lancaster JetHawks, (661) 726-5400 / www.jethawks.com

 Long Beach Legends, (714) 322-7306 / www.sunsetleaguebaseball.com

 Padres in San Diego, (877) 374-2784 / www.padres.com

 Palm Springs POWER, (760) 778-HITS (4487) / www.palmspringspowerbaseball.com

 Rancho Cucamonga Quakes, (909) 481-5000 / www.rcquakes.com

 Riverside Bulldogs, www.sccbaseball.com

 Signal Hill Oilers, www.sunsetleaguebaseball.com

 San Diego Force, (619) 723-0671 / www.leaguelineup.com/welcome.asp?url=sdforcebaseball

 Southern California Bombers, (951) 902-5863 / www.sccbaseball.com/rebels

 SOCAL Sparrows, (818) 912-3121 / www.sparrowsbaseballclub.org

 Solana Beach Redbirds, (619) 602 5669 / www.troskyredbirds.com

BASKETBALL

 Agua Caliente Clippers of Ontario, (909) 406-9090 / aguacaliente.gleague.nba.com

 Clippers in Los Angeles, www.clippers.com

 Lakers in Los Angeles, (310) 426-6000 / www.lakers.com

 Orange County Novastars, www.facebook.com/NovastarBasketball

 San Diego Guardians, www.thesdguardians.com

 San Diego Kings, (619) 302-3532 / www.sdkingsbasketball.com

 San Diego Surf, (858) 622-0111 / www.surfbasketball.com

 South Bay Lakers, (310) 343-3131 / southbay.gleague.nba.com

 Sparks in Los Angeles, (844) GO-SPARKS (467-7275) / www.wnba.com/sparks

 Highschool and college games can be fun, too. See www.usbasket.com for an exhaustive list of basketball teams from highschool, college, semi-pro and professional.

BATTING CAGES. "Hey batter batter." Cages are great for hitting practice, in season or out.

BILLIARDS. Many billiard parlors have a family-friendly atmosphere.

BOOKS. Numerous bookstores offer story times and/or craft times. Some of the bigger bookstores, such as Barnes & Noble, have a huge children's selection, as well as a children's reading area. Many smaller bookstores cater specifically to kids and are delightful to browse through. Look under the main section of the book, under Potpourri, to find some specific bookstore gems.

 Thrift stores and garage sales are a great resource for used books as are libraries, as they often host sales once or twice a year. Used bookstores are also a terrific bargain. Hot tip: There are several $1 bookstores, too, such as the Dollar Bookfair stores (www.dollarbookfair.com) in Buena Park, Hemet, Laguna Hills, and Moreno Valley, and the One Dollar Bookstore shops (www.theonedollarbookstore.com) in Orange, Lake Forest and Eagle Rock.

BOWLING. Many alleys offer bumper bowling for kids, where the gutters are covered so kids almost always knock down a pin or two. (This sounds like something right up my alley, also.) Cosmic Bowling, sometimes known as Rock 'n Roll Bowl, is great fun, too. Usually played at nighttime, ordinary lights are turned out and neon lights take over. The pins, balls, and lanes glow in the dark and rock music and/or videos play. All this while trying to bowl! Call your local bowling alley.

CAMPING. Campgrounds mentioned in this book are usually listed under the Great Outdoors section. Check your library or local bookstore for books written just about camping. A starting point are several books put out by Peterson (not me!) and the Guide to ACA-Accredited Camps in Southern California. You can make reservations for any California State Park at (800) 444-7275 or www.reservecalifornia.com.

CELEBRITIES. Find out when the next celebrity will be honored with a ceremony dedicating his/her star along this famous "Walk of Fame" in Hollywood, by checking www.hollywoodchamber.net or calling (323) 469-8311. Ceremonies occur almost monthly.

CIRCUS. You have to run away far to join or see the circus. Check newspapers and sports arenas, or try the following numbers to see when the circus is coming to town. Ask about specials or opening day events.

Carson & Barnes, (580) 743-7292 / www.carsonbarnescircus.com - Features three rings of continual action, with hundreds of animals, international performers, and lots of razzle-dazzle.

Circus Vargas, (877) GOTFUN1 (468-3861) / www.circusvargas.com - A real "Big Top" circus. Come early to be invited into the ring to see what it is like to be in a circus.

Cirque Du Solei, www.cirquedusoleil.com - Artsy and eccentric, much-acclaimed productions with frequent theme changes that focus on "impossible" body movements. Very unique! Note: No animals are used in this circus.

Community Circus Arts Corporation, (909) 798-9622 / docircus.org - The Great All American Youth Circus is classes that trains kids and then enables them to put on performances featuring genuine circus acts.

Fern Street Circus, (619) 320-2055 / www.fernstreetcircus.com - San Diego-based troupe with aerialists, clowns, and acrobats for whimsical entertainment; from a single clown to a full cast. The highlight of Fern Street's year is the annual Neighborhood Tour each October. Ask about programs that teach children circus skills in San Diego.

Great Y Circus in Redlands, (909) 798-9622 / www.ymcaeastvalley.org/programs/circus/ - Not only are small performances given through the year, your kids can actually take classes and learn circus skills. Founded in 1929 through the YMCA, this is oldest community circus in the world.

CONSTRUCTION SITES. If you're "toolin" around, these sites can give your youngster constructive ideas to build on.

CONVENTION CENTERS. For Kid's Stuff Expos, toy shows, circuses, and much more. Check the websites intermittently to see what's going on.

    Anaheim, (714) 765-8950 / www.anaheimconventioncenter.com

    Long Beach, (562) 436-3636 / www.longbeachcc.com

    Los Angeles, (213) 741-1151 / www.lacclink.com

    Ontario, (909) 930-1480 / www.ontariocc.com

    Palm Springs, (760) 325-6611 / www.palmspringscc.com

    Pasadena, (626) 795-9311 / www.pasadenacenter.com

    Riverside, (951) 222-4700 / www.riversidecvb.com

    San Diego, (619) 525-5000 / www.visitsandiego.com

COOKING. There are a lot of kid's cooking classes offered throughout the year through local parks and recreation departments. A few other suggestions are listed below:

Bristol Farms in Manhattan Beach, (310) 233-4752 / www.bristolfarms.com - Three-hour classes offer a variety of subjects for kids grade K-8.

San Diego Culinary Institute in La Mesa, (619) 644-2100 / www.sdci-inc.com - Adult and teen cooking classes are available.

Summer Art Academy Cooking Camp, (818) 386-2107 / www.summerartacademy.com - Campuses in La Canada and North Hollywood with classes for kids ages 7- 14.

Sur La Table, (800) 243-0852 / www.surlatable.com - Five-day classes are offered for ages 8 - 12 and 13-17.

COUPONS. Always check the website of the attraction you are visiting, for coupons. Hotel lobbies often have displays with brochures that contain coupons to local attractions. Also, call the visitors center of the city you are planning to visit as they often offer discount coupons.

CPR/FIRST AID CLASSES. Call your local Red Cross or hospital for class information. This is a great class for you, your kids (when they are old enough), and for babysitters to take.

DRIVE-IN MOVIES. Once a staple of family entertainment, there are not many drive-ins left. However, they can still be a fun outing. The shows are usually less expensive then a theater and many have double features. A great source for current information about drive-ins is www.drive-ins.com. Use it to find a drive-in theater near you or to reminisce about drive-ins that closed years ago:

Electric Dusk Drive-In, www.electricduskdrivein.com - Not a true drive-in, but has periodic showings using a large inflatable screen.

Hi-Way Drive-In in Santa Maria, (805) 937-3515 / www.playingtoday.com/hiway-drivein - 1 screen.

Mission Tiki Drive-In in Montclair, (909) 628-0511 / www.missiontiki.com - 4 screens.

Paramount Drive-In, (562) 630-7469 / www.paramountswap.com - 2 screens.

Rubidoux Drive-In in Riverside, (951) 683-4455 / www.rubidouxdrivein.com - 3 screens.

Santa Barbara Drive-In, (805) 964-9050 / www.westwinddriveins.com - 1 screen.

Santee Drive-In, (619) 448-7447 / www.santeedriveintheatre.com - 2 screens.

Skyline Drive-In in Barstow, (760) 256-3333 / www.facebook.com/Skylinedriveinbarstowca - 2 screens.

Smith's Ranch Drive-In in Twentynine Palms, (760) 367-7713 / www.29drive-in.com - 1 screen.

South Bay Drive-In in Imperial Beach, (619) 423-2727 / www.southbaydrivein.com - 3 screens.

Van Buren Cinema 3 Drive-In in Riverside, (951) 688-2360 / www.vanburendrivein.com - 3 screens.

Vineland Drive-In in Industry, (626) 961-9262 / www.vinelanddriveintheater.com - 4 screens.

EDUCATIONAL TOYS. There are numerous stores and catalogs that offer good quality, educational products. Goggle two other great resources - teacher supply stores (such as Lakeshore Learning) and children's bookstores. Many museum gift shops offer a terrific line of educational (and fun) supplies. The website, www.learningwrapups.com, has a store locator for their product that lists many educational stores in the Southland. Also, check out some of the following companies that offer catalogs and/or home workshops for their products:

EDUCATIONAL PRESENTATIONS. This section is written for all kinds of educators as most of these programs / presentations travel to schools or other off-site facilities. It is by no means complete, just *some* of the treasures we've discovered.

Amusement Parks. Look under the Amusement Parks section, as they are unexpected places to find educational classes. KNOTT'S BERRY FARM (pg. 238), in particular, has over fifteen specialized classes.

California Weekly Explorer, Inc. (714) 247-2250 / www.californiaweekly.com - This company sends knowledgeable staff members to your school for outstanding, interactive, and educational two-and-a-half-hour presentations. The three different presentations offered are called "walk throughs," as they walk students through particular time periods via costumes, role playing, skits, games, flags, props, music, hands-on quizzes, models, maps, and/or timelines, consistent with the California state framework and requires. Excellent! Programs are offered Mon. - Fri. and are limited to thirty-six students.

Discovery Toys, (800) 341-8697 / www.discoverytoys.net - A fantastic line of toys, books, games, and computer software.

Dorling Kindersley Books, (212) 213-4800 / www.dk.com - They offer outstanding books.

Jim Weiss - Storyteller Extraordinaire, (800) 477-6234 / www.jimweiss.com - Golden-voiced Jim Weiss is a nationally acclaimed storyteller. He's won over 100 prestigious awards for his over fifty recordings. Retelling (mostly) classic stories such as *Three Musketeers, Sherlock Holmes*, and *Fairytales in Song and Dance*.

As wonderful as he is to listen to on CD, he is even more enthralling in person. Jim does storytelling as well as workshops for both kids and adults. He explains the twists and turns good stories need, teaching how to choose a topic, map a plot, create and develop characters, use voice inflections masterfully, and more. He is the best!

Jurassic Parties, (714) 500-0593 / www.jurassicparties.com - They bring an assortment of animals, including snakes, lizards, tarantulas, and scorpions to you, or you come to them. Great for birthday parties (and getting over fears of these critters).

Kites for Kids, (714) 536-3630; (800) 431-3339 / www.kitesforkids.com - Presentation includes an educational demonstration and kite making for every participant. Cost is $495 for 1 - 250 students; per student pricing for groups over 250.

Mad Science, (800) 586-5231 - call to find your local mad scientist! / www.madscience.org - Bubbling potions, rocket launches, magnets, lasers, super bounce ball, cool chemical reactions, slime, and more hands-on learning fun. Programs include after-school enrichment classes, summer camps, school assemblies, and "edutainment" birthday parties.

Museums. Numerous museums, especially the art, science and children's museums, have "traveling programs," designed specifically to bring great, hands-on educational programs to your choice of locale. Contact, for example, CALIFORNIA SCIENCE CENTER (pg. 102), DISCOVERY CUBE (Los Angeles County) (pg. 105), DISCOVERY CUBE (Orange County) (pg. 304), INTERNATIONAL PRINTING MUSEUM (pg. 123), JURUPA MOUNTAINS DISCOVERY CENTER / EARTH SCIENCE MUSEUM (pg. 364), CHILDREN'S MUSEUM AT LA HABRA (pg. 303), RAYMOND M. ALF MUSEUM (pg. 149) and SANTA BARBARA MUSEUM OF NATURAL HISTORY (pg. 629) with it's Waves on Wheels program.

Shows and Theaters. This is another category that often has traveling shows - whether it's a play presented to children, or it's a theatrical workshop of some sort.

Usborne Books, (800) 475-4522 / www.edcpub.com - Top-notch, visually-exciting books.

Zoos and Animals. Many zoos have fantastic in-house programs as well as traveling presentations. Call the one nearest you for more information.

EQUESTRIAN SHOWS. English and Western riding, jumping, and prancing are all part of seeing a horse show. Call your local equestrian center for dates and times and/or check the Calendar section for special event shows.

ESCAPE ROOMS. A tremendous array and variety of themed escape rooms are available throughout So. Cal, and beyond. This game is essentially rooms that a team of people must figure out how to escape from using whatever clues, puzzles, and codes they discover, interpret and solve to lead them to the end goal, and doing so within the hour time limit.

ETHNIC NEIGHBORHOODS. Where can you take your family to experience another culture? Oftentimes, right in your own neighborhood, where people from other countries have settled and carved out a niche based on their homeland. Here are just a few options to check out, whether it's to try different foods or to shop for items not found in Target.

Armenian foods in Glendale. Located near Colorado St. and Glendale Ave, there are several Armenian cuisine restaurants, including several kabob places, pastries, lamb, quail, chicken, and more.

Chinatown in Los Angeles, www.chinatownla.com - Walk the streets to see a proliferation of red and gold colored buildings with pagoda-style roofs. See CHINATOWN (pg. 167) for more details on restaurant, shopping, etc.

Little Cambodia in Long Beach, www.littlecambodia.org - Long Beach is home to the largest population of Cambodians in the United States. Located on Anaheim St. between Atlantic Ave. and Junipero Ave., this area has Cambodian restaurants, groceries, gift shops, clothing stores and more.

Little Ethiopia in Los Angeles, www.littleethiopiabusinessassociation.com - Come visit this collection of Ethiopian shops and restaurants along Fairfax Ave. in the Carthay district, between Olympic and Pico Blvds.

Little India in Artesia, www.artesiaindia.us - Its aromatic restaurants, small grocery stores that carry an array of spices, and shops that prefer brightly-colored saris, among other items, beckon customers along Pioneer Boulevard, between Ashtoreth and South sts.

Little Italy in San Diego, www.littleitalysd.com - Located between Laurel and A sts., W. on of the 5 Fwy. Besides several Italian restaurants, the area offers many programs and festivals throughout the year.

Little Saigon in Westminster, www.littlesaigonnow.com - A mile-long stretch of Bolsa Ave. has bakeries, deli's, supermarkets, and dozens of excellent, inexpensive Vietnamese restaurants.

Little Tokyo in Los Angeles, www.visitlittletokyo.com - This area, near 1st and Central sts., has the JAPANESE AMERICAN NATIONAL MUSEUM (pg. 124), lots of shops and restaurants, and many yearly activities.

FAIRGROUNDS. Numerous events are held at the following locations throughout the year, such as gem shows, reptiles expos, fairs, cat shows, circuses, demolition derbies, Scottish games, horse shows, and lots more. Call or check websites for a schedule:

Los Angeles in Lancaster, (661) 948-6060 / www.avfair.com

Los Angeles in Pomona, (909) 623-3111 / www.fairplex.com

Orange in Costa Mesa, (714) 708-1500 or recorded info: (714) 708-FAIR (3247) / www.ocfair.com

Riverside in Indio, (800) 811-FAIR (3247) / www.datefest.org
Riverside in Lake Perris, (951) 657-4221 / www.socalfair.com
San Bernardino in Victorville, (760) 951-2200 / www.sbcfair.com
San Diego in Del Mar, (858) 755-1161 / www.sdfair.com
Santa Barbara in Santa Barbara, (805) 687-0766 / www.earlwarren.com
Santa Barbara in Santa Maria, (805) 925-8824 / www.santamariafairpark.com
Ventura in Ventura, (805) 648-3376 / www.venturacountyfair.org

FARMER'S MARKETS. See Edible Adventures in the main section of the book for details.

FISHING. Here's the hook - you have to look under the Great Outdoors section for places to go fish. You can also contact:

Department of Fish and Wildlife, (888) 773-8450 / www.wildlife.ca.gov - Free information on fishing, including maps to local lakes, fishing events, hatcheries, stocking guides, fishing clinics, regulations, and more. They also offer free fishing days during the year.

Fishing Network, www.fishingnetwork.net - This website is dedicated to providing information on fishing in Southern California.

Take Me Fishing, www.takemefishing.org - The website is designed to help families find places to fish and boat.

FOOTBALL

Chargers at StubHub Center in Carson, 877-CHARGERS (242-7437) / www.chargers.com - Currently play at StubHub Center until a new stadium is built in Inglewood.

Rams at Los Angeles Memorial Coliseum in Los Angeles, www.therams.com - Currently play at Los Angeles Memorial Coliseum until a new stadium is built in Inglewood.

Highschool and college games are exciting, too.

GEOCACHING, www.geocaching.com - This hobby/sport mixes high-tech and adventure. Participants hunt for hidden "treasure" by using a hand-held Global Positioning System (GPS) device. The only thing you need is the GPS and the coordinates of a geocache near you. A cache may be a hidden trinket, a log book to write your name in, an interesting place or view, or all three. It may be anywhere in the world, but use discretion when searching. Some park officials frown on hunters veering off established paths to search for the "cache" prize.

GYM CLASSES. There are multitudes of gyms and classes to choose from, including WE ROCK THE SPECTRUM KIDS GYM (Los Angeles County) (pg. 44) in the main section of the book. Here are just a very few others:

Creative Kids in Los Angeles, (310) 473-6090 / www.mycreativekids.com - Classes in gymnastics, music, art, fairytale theater, cooking, and more.

Gymboree, (415) 604-3092 / www.gymboreeclasses.com - Check website or your local phone book for listings. Classes are offered for parents and their children - newborns through 4 years old - that include easy exercise, songs, bubbles, and visits from Gymbo, the clown.

My Gym, www.mygym.com - Classes in tumbling, songs, games, and gymnastics are offered for the younger set. The franchises are everywhere in Southern California.

HOBBIES AND MODELS. Kids like to collect - anything! For example - bottle caps, dolls, miniatures (dollhouses), postcards, rocks, sports cards, and stamps. Other hobby ideas include model-making (i.e. cars, planes, rockets, and trains), creating jewelry, and sewing. Find local hobby shops to support your habit.

HOCKEY

Anaheim Ducks at Arrowhead Pond in Anaheim, (800) 559-2333 / www.nhl.com/ducks
Kings at Staples Center in Los Angeles, (800) 559-2333 / www.nhl.com/kings
San Diego Gulls at the Sports Arena in San Diego, (619) 359-4730 / www.sandiegogulls.com
Southern California Bombers in Lakewood, (562) 429-1805 / www.jrbombers.org
Valencia Flyers, (661) 775-8686 / www.valenciaflyers.net

HORSEBACK RIDING. Saddle up for a terrific family outing! Call your local equestrian center and note that there are some places mentioned in the main section of the book.

HOT AIR BALLOON RIDES. Up, up and away! Hot air balloon rides are recommended for ages 8 and up, as younger children might get scared of the flames shooting out (i.e. the "hot air"); they might get bored; safety; and they can't see very well over the basket. All ages, however, are enthralled by watching the balloon being inflated, either in the morning or at sunset! For a real colorful outing, look in the Calendar section for Hot Air Balloon Festivals. Most of the companies listed fly over Del Mar, Palm Springs, and/or Temecula. Flights are about an hour and some include a champagne breakfast. Prices are per person. These are just a few names and numbers to get you started:

California Dreamin' in Del Mar and Temecula, (951) 699-0601 / www.californiadreamin.com - Starting at $148 per person in Temecula; $298 per person in Del Mar. Check website for specials.

Fantasy Balloon Flights, (760) 568-0997 / www.fantasyballoonflight.com - Serving Palm Springs, Temecula and Ventura - $195 per person with discounts for groups, families, children, and seniors.

Sunrise Balloons in Temecula, (800) 548-9912 / www.sunriseballoons.com - $249 per person.

ICE SKATING. Go figure! Call, for instance, the arenas listed below:

The Rinks, www.therinks.com - The Rinks operates five ice rinks - Anaheim ICE (where the Anaheim Ducks practice!), Lakewood ICE, Westminster ICE, Yorba Linda ICE, and Poway ICE, plus three inline facilities -Corona Inline, Huntington Beach Inline and Irvine Inline. The Rinks offers public sessions, plus figure skating and hockey classes.

Toyota Sports Center, (310) 535-4400 / www.toyotasportscenter.com - This ice arena, where the Los Angeles Kings train, has public sessions, hockey, and figure skating.

IMAX THEATRES, www.imax.com - See it BIG! See it in your face! IMAX theaters really intensify your movie-going experience.

JUNKYARDS. One man's trash is another child's treasure. For kids who like to take things apart and make new creations, junkyards are inspiring places to investigate.

KITE FLYING. Go fly a kite! Really. Check the Calendar section for Kite Festivals.

LIBRARIES. Your local library has a lot to offer. Get a group together and ask for a tour. Besides book, video, and audio CD lending, many offer free storytelling on a regular basis and/or finger plays, puppet shows, magic shows, and crafts. Some libraries also encourage your bookworms by offering summer reading programs. A few times throughout the year libraries hold sales where book prices are practically a steal.

MAGAZINES. If you only receive one magazine, make it *Family Fun*. Contact them at www.parents.com/familyfun-magazine or (800) 289-4849. Put out by Disney, each edition is packed with do-able crafts, snacks, party ideas, games, activities, and family-friendly places to travel. Pick it up at the newsstand or get a subscription.

MALLS. Going to the mall can be a fun excursion with kids (honest!), especially if the mall has "extra" features, such as a merry-go-round or fountains, or, if it's spectacular in design, has unique shops and restaurants, etc. See the Malls section in the main part of the book for some of our top picks, that include free kid's clubs.

MONEY. Collect money from foreign countries without the expense of traveling there. Call (800) CURRENCY (287-7362) or check www.travelex.com to find the nearest Travelex location. You may exchange any sum of money for currency from an unlimited number of countries, for only one transaction fee. The fee is usually a $5 service fee or 1% of the U.S. amount, whichever amount is greater. You may also purchase money online.

MOVIE THEATERS. An obvious choice, but movies, and especially matinees, can be a relatively inexpensive and fun treat. Check the following theaters. Note that some also offer great bargains in the summertime for kids. See MOVIES (pg. 719), in the Calendar section, for details.

AMC THEATRES, www.amctheatres.com - $5 on Tues.

Cinemark, (800) 326-3264 / www.cinemark.com - $5 - $6 (depending on which theater) admission all day, usually on Tues.

Harkins Theatres, www.harkins.com - Besides comfy lounge-type seats, these theaters offer, for an additional fee, on-site Child PlayCenters where ages 3 - 8 years old can play games, read books, enjoy toys, and of course, watch movies, while parents are watching a movie in the adjacent theater. Summer movies for kids/families are $2 per person. Tuesday nights classic movies are $5. Anime, opera, ballet, documentaries, concerts and other special interest presentations are also shown on the big screen. Note that the Cerritos location offers Sensory Friendly Screenings one Sat. a month. **Cerritos** - (562) 865-4140; **Chino Hills** - (909) 627-8010; **Moreno Valley** - (951) 653-6161

Mommy Movie Monday, (714) 826-7469 / www.kptmovies.com - Stroller check-in, reduced sound levels, and dimmed lights (for baby visibility) make these Mon. 10am showings ideal for a new mom's or dad's outing. **Buena Park** - Krikorian Buena Park Metroplex 18 - $7.75

Monday Morning Mommy Movies, www.pacifictheatres.com - Babies are welcome and expected at special 11am showings. **Chatsworth** - (866) 722-9790; **Glendale** - (866) 722-9790; **Lakewood** - (866) 722-9790; **Los Angeles** - (866) 722-9790; **Northridge** - (866) 722-9790.

Picture Show, info - (714) 836-7469; office - (714) 953-8467 / www.pictureshowent.com - **Santa Ana** - Main Place Mall offers first and later run movies play at this theater, for $6.75 before 6pm, daily.

Regency Theatres, www.regencymovies.com - Some theaters offer discounted days, times and even food. Some also offer classic film screenings. Check website for times and prices at specific locations.

    Agoura Hills - Agoura Hills Stadium 8, (818) 707-9966. $6 on Wed. This location offers D-BOX, too - gentle motion forwards, backwards, side to side and up and down, in sync with on-screen action and sound - for an additional $8.

    Cathedral City - Cathedral City 10, (760) 324-7674. $1.50 on Sun.

    City of Commerce - Commerce 14, (323) 726-8022. $6.50 on Tues.

    Fontana - Fontana 8, (951) 341-5720. $6.50 on Sun.

    Lancaster - Blvd Cinemas, (661) 726-1537. $5.75 on Tues.

    Moreno Valley - Towngate 8, (951) 653-5500. $2.50 - $3.50 daily; $1.50 on Sun.; $11 after 6 on Wed. for 2 admissions, 2 popcorns, and 2 sodas.

    North Hollywood - Valley Plaza 6, (818) 760-8400. $2.50 - $3.50 daily; $1.75 on Sun. and Tues.

    Norwalk - Norwalk 8, (562) 804-5615. $2 - $3 daily; $1.50 on Tues.; $2 extra for 3-D movies.

    Pasadena - Academy Cinemas, (626) 229-9400. $2.50 - $3.50 daily; $10 after 6 on Wed. for 2 admissions, 2 popcorns and 2 sodas.

    Riverside - University Village 10, (951) 784-4342. $6 on Sun.

    San Bernardino - Sterling 6, (909) 864-1588. $6 on Sun. and matinees.

    San Juan Capistrano - (949) 661-3456. $6.50 on Tues.

    Santa Paula - Santa Paula 7, (805) 933-6707. $16 after 6 on Tues. for 2 admissions, 2 popcorns and 2 sodas.

    Van Nuys - Van Nuys Plant 16, (818) 779-0323. This location offers D-BOX, too for an additional $8.

    Ventura - Buenaventura 6, (805) 658-6544. $3.50 daily; $1 on Tues.; $10 after 6 on Wed. for 2 admissions, 2 popcorns and 2 sodas.

    Westminster - Westminster 10, (714) 893-4222. $6.50 on Sun.

Starlight Cinemas, www.starlightcinemas.com - Each theater offers huge discounts. Note that 3-D movies are $ extra. Check with the particular theater for the days they offer their special prices, plus senior discount days and more. Note that some locations offer an inexpensive Summer Series for kids/families.

    Anaheim - Starlight Cinema City Theatres, (714) 970-6700. $6 on Mon. and Tues., and before 6pm on Sun. $ before noon any day; $7 before 6pm. This location offers Cinema Classics, too.

    Corona - Starlight Dos Lagos 15, (877) 795-4410. $5 on Tues. and Thurs., and before 6pm on Sun. $5 before noon any day; $7 before 6pm. This location offers Cinema Classics, too.

    Costa Mesa - Starlight Triangle Square Cinemas, (949) 650-4300. $6 on Tues. and Wed. $6 before noon any day; $8 before 6pm.

    Garden Grove - Starlight 4 Star Cinemas, (714) 934-6377. $5 on Tues. and Thurs., and before 6pm on Sun. $ before noon any day; $7 before 6pm.

    Rancho Palos Verdes - Starlight Terrace Cinemas, (310) 831-1100. $6 on Tues. and Thurs. $6 before noon any day; $8 before 6pm.

    Whittier - Starlight Whittier Village Cinemas, (562) 907-3300. $6 on Tues. and Thurs. $6 before noon any day $8 before 6pm.

Studio Movie Grill, www.studiomoviegrill.com - Restaurant food fresh from the grill delivered to your seat while watching a movie! And $5 tickets on Tues.

    Downey - (562) 622-3999; **Monrovia** - (626) 305-7469; **Redlands** - (909) 793-6393

Tristone Cinemas, www.tristonecinemas.com -

    Brea - (714) 257-9377. $4.95 all day Tues., and Mon. - Fri. before noon

    Palm Desert - (760) 340-0033. $5.57 all day Tues.

    Rancho Cucamonga - (909) 483-8373. $5.95 Mon. - Fri. before noon

    Riverside - (951) 361-3163. $6.50 Mon. - Fri. before noon

    Simi Valley - (805) 526-4329. $4.95 all day Tues.

Temecula - (951) 296-9728. General admission is $4.75; matinees before 5pm are $3.95; Mon. - Fri. before noon is $3.50.

UltraStar Cinemas, (619) 685-2841 / www.ultrastarmovies.com - **San Diego** - Mission Valley at Hazard Center, offers Parent Movie Morning every Wed. at 10am and Baby's Night Out on some Wed. at 7pm. Bring your infants to see a current (and not children's) movie where crying and feedings are expected.

MUSEUMS. If you have a Bank of America card, you can get free admission on certain days to more than 100 museums worldwide through Bank of America's Museums on Us program. Check out the website museums.bankofamerica.com for dates and participating museums. Check the Bank of America Museums on Us (pg. xi) for more great tips.

PARKS. Almost every local park offers classes or sports programs for free, or at a minimal cost. Ask about kid's cooking classes, sidewalk chalk art day, and so much more. Check out #www.parks.ca.gov for information about parks throughout California.

PET STORES. This is a fun, mini-outing. Ask about tours. There are several larger chain stores, such as Petco and Petsmart, which are sufficient. However, while cuddly puppies and adorable rabbits are great, unusual and exotic animals can add a unique element to your outing. They can be found at some of the independent stores listed below. Look in your phone book for reptile, fish and bird stores, too. You can also find pet stores by looking up the pet product suppliers and finding local dealers.

Blacksmith's Corner in Bellflower, (562) 531-0386 / www.blacksmithscorner.com - Like visiting a mini farm, with its chickens, ducks, pheasants, etc.

Prehistoric Pets in Fountain Valley, (714) 500-0592 / www.prehistoricpets.com - Incredible! See exotic snakes (some twenty-feet long) and monitor lizards from all over the world, plus a small fish pond in the middle of the store, and more. See PREHISTORIC PETS / THE REPTILE ZOO (pg. 336) for more info.

Wagon Train Feed & Pet, (714) 639-7932 / www.wagontrainoc.com - When we visited this small pet store it had chicks, ducks, a lamb, a pot-bellied pig, turtles, and chinchillas. The stop here was worth a peek and pet. Note: They also sell fertilized chick eggs and incubators.

PHOTO ALBUMS. Tapped dry on how to put together a creative and memorable photo album? There is a plethora of photo book companies available to compile your digital photos in a slimline book. I use Blurb and found that they have some of the best prices.

PLAYGROUPS. Check local parks, newspapers, parenting "magazines" or onsite social media groups for information on getting involved with a playgroup near you. They are great ways to share the joys and trials of raising children. Other resources include:

MOMS, www.momsclub.org - An international, non-profit support group specifically for stay-at-home moms. Weekly meetings, kept at a low number of attendees, consist of talking and eating together, listening to a speaker, and going on various outings. All age children are welcome at all meetings and activities. MOMS groups are everywhere.

MOPS (Mothers Of Preschooler), (888) 910-6677 or (303) 733-5353 / www.mops.org - An international, Christian-based organization that has local meetings in almost every city. Moms usually meet at a church and talk, eat together, listen to a speaker, and make a craft while their preschoolers are being cared for by a Moppet helper. Great organization! Check online to find a MOPS near you.

Tot Lot. A playgroup designed for preschoolers (and their parents) to meet and play together at community parks on a regular basis during the week, building those all-important socialization skills. Registration fees go towards crafts, snacks, and even field trips. Call, for example, Lakewood Recreation and Community Services, (562) 866-9771 / www.lakewoodcity.org for information on Tot Lot at Bolivar, Del Valle, and Mayfair parks. Call your local parks and recreation department to see what programs they offer.

RESTAURANTS. See the Edible Adventures section in the main part of the book. Try eating at some unusual locations, such as at airports, on boats (try the *Queen Mary*), etc. Take your kids out for ethnic foods, too.

ROCKETRY. You can get you in touch with model rocketry classes (for ages 10 and older) and launch sites in Los Angeles and San Bernardino counties by checking the website home.earthlink.net/~mebowitz or calling (714) 529-1598.

RODEO. Southern California plays host to rodeos throughout the year. Several annual ones are listed in the Calendar section. Check these websites to find out the schedule of some of the touring events: Professional Bull Riders - www.pbr.com; Professional Rodeo Cowboy Association - www.prorodeo.com; Women's Professional Rodeo

Association - www.wpra.com; California Circuit Finals Rodeo - www.cafinalsrodeo.com; and Rodeoz Authority Guide - www.rodeoz.com.

ROLLER SKATING. Roll at rinks, on the sidewalks, around parks, and along beach fronts. (See Bike Paths, in the main section of the book for specific paved pathways.)

SOCCER

Los Angeles FC, (323) 648-6000 / www.lafc.com - Los Angeles Football Club plays at Banc of California Stadium in Exposition Park next to the LA Memorial Coliseum.

Los Angeles Galaxy, (877) - 3GALAXY (342-5299) or (310) 630-2200 / www.lagalaxy.com - Plays at the StubHub Center on the campus of Cal State University, Dominguez Hills.

Major League Soccer, www.mlssoccer.com - Men's professional soccer league info.

San Diego Soccers, (866) 799-GOAL (4625) / www.sdsockers.com - Home games are at Valley View Casino Center

SPORTING EVENTS. Check out high school and college events. These local games are a fun and inexpensive introduction to sports and fun for sports enthusiasts as well.

SPORTS ARENAS. Many special events are held at sports arenas including sporting events like the Harlem Globetrotters, rodeos, concerts, Walt Disney's World on Ice, circuses, etc.

Honda Center in Anaheim, (714) 704-2400 / www.hondacenter.com

L.A. Memorial Coliseum in Los Angeles, (213) 747-7111 / www.lacoliseum.com

SDCCU Stadium in San Diego, (619) 641-3100 / www.sandiego.gov/stadium

Staples Center in Los Angeles, (213) 742-7340 / www.staplescenter.com

StubHub Center in Carson, (310) 630-2000 / www.stubhubcenter.com

Valley View Casino Center in San Diego, (619) 224-4171 / www.valleyviewcasinocenter.com

SUN CLOTHING. The following companies make a full line of clothing specially designed to block out harmful rays from the sun:

SunGrubbies, (888) 970-1600 / www.sungrubbies.com

Sun Precautions / Solumbra, (800) 882-7860 / www.sunprecautions.com

Sun Protection Zone, (877) 266-7297 / www.sunprotectionzone.com

SWAP MEETS / FLEA MARKETS. Give your kids a dollar or two to call their own, as there are a lot of inexpensive toys or jewelry items for them to choose from at swap meets. Everyone goes home happy with their treasures! Here's a list of just a few good swap meets / flea markets.

Anaheim Marketplace (indoor) in Anaheim, (714) 999-0888 / www.anaheimindoormarketplace.com - Over 200 shops and 10 restaurants, plus 35 special events, including weekly happenings and live weekend entertainment, too. They also have adjacent soccer fields and arcade games. Open Wed. - Mon., 10am - 7pm (closed Tues.). Free admission.

Beaumont Outdoor Market in Beaumont, (323) 560-7469 / www.rgcshows.com - This smaller market, offering new, antique, and garage type merchandise, is held every Wed. Fri., Sat. and Sun. from 6am - 2pm. Admission is 50¢; children 11 and under are free. Parking is free.

College of the Desert Street Fair (outdoor) in Palm Desert, (760) 636-7957 / www.codaastreetfair.com - New and used items, antiques, a Farmer's market, arts and crafts courtyard, jewelry, and more make this more of a street fair than swap meet ambiance. Held Sat. - Sun., 7am - 2pm; summer hours are 7am - noon. Admission and parking are free.

Cypress College Swap Meet (outdoor), (714) 952-1847 / www.cypresscollegeswapmeet.com - Open Sat. and Sun, 8am - 4pm with over 500 vendors! Admission is free.

Foothill Swap Meet (outdoor) in Glendora, (626) 852-0030 / www.foothillswapmeet.com - Open Sun., 6:30am - 3pm.

Golden West College Swap Meet, (714) 895-0888 / www.gwc.info/swapmeet/ - New & used items, fresh produce, and flowers, antiques. Open Sat. & Sun. 8 a.m. to 3 p.m., rain or shine. Free admission and parking.

Kobey's Swap Meet (outdoor) at the sports arena parking lot in San Diego, (619) 226-0650 / www.kobeyswap.com - The equivalent of twelve football fields, this swap meet offers bargains on everything under the sun. Open Fri. - Sun., 7am - 3pm. Admission is $1 on Fri.; $2 on Sat. and Sun. Children 11 and under are free.

Long Beach Antique Market (outdoor) in Long Beach, (323) 655-5703 / www.longbeachantiquemarket.com - Held at Veterans Stadium on the 3rd Sun. from 6:30am - 2pm with over 800 sellers of cllectibles, home decor, vintage clothing, jewelry, antiques, and lots of just stuff. $7 per person; ages 11 and under are free.

Los Angeles City College Swap Meet (outdoor), (323) 913-3931 / www.laccswapmeet.com - Open Sat. and Sun, 9am - 3:30pm with over 200 vendors. Admission is $1 on Sun; children under 54" are free.

Orange County Market Place (outdoor) in Costa Mesa, (949) 723-6616 / www.ocmarketplace.com - One of the best and biggest with hundreds of vendors, plus food courts. Open weekends, 8am - 4pm. (Some weekends in July and August are closed due to the Orange County Fair.) Admission is $2 for adults; children 12 years and under are free.

Pasadena City College Flea Market (outdoor), (626) 585-7906 / www.pasadena.edu/fleamarket - A mishmash mixture of merchandise, including many antiques, from about 400 vendors - some great deals, some garage sale items. Open the first Sun. of every month, 8am - 3pm. Admission is free; $2 for parking.

Roadium (outdoor) in Torrance, (323) 532-5678 / www.roadium.com - 450 merchants sell new items, some collectibles, bargains, garage-sale stuff, and food daily, 7am - 4pm. Admission on Mon. and Fri. is $1 for the driver and 50¢ per person; Tues. and Thurs., 50¢ per person; Wed., $1.25 per person; Sat. and Sun., $2 per car and driver, plus $1 per additional passengers. Children 4 and under are always free.

Rosebowl Flea Mart (outdoor) in Pasadena, (323) 560-7469 / www.rgcshows.com - Known for antiques and collectibles, the more than 2,500 vendors offer everything you've ever seen and many things you've never heard of. Held the second Sun. of each month. Admission is $20 from 5am - 7am; $15 from 7am - 8am; $12 from 8am - 9am; $9 from 9am until it closes at 4:30pm. Ages 11 and under are free. Sellers begin leaving at 3pm. Parking is free.

San Bernardino Outdoor Market (outdoor) in San Bernardino, (323) 560-7469 / www.rgcshows.com - A large flea market, 300 vendors, is held at the National Orange Showgrounds. Open most Sun., 7am - 2pm. Admission is 75¢ per person, ages 11 and under free. Parking is free.

San Fernando Swap Meet (outdoor) in San Fernando, (818) 361-1431 / www.sanfernandoswapmeet.com - With a few hundred vendors, it's open Tues., Thurs. - Sun., 6am to 3pm.

Santa Clarita Swap Meet (outdoor) in Santa Clarita, (661) 259-3886 / www.saugusspeedway.com - Over 550 vendors, plus live entertainment, at this huge swap meet held every Sun., 7am - 3pm. The Tues. swap meet, open 7am - 1pm, is smaller with a focus on collectibles. Sat., open 7am - 1pm, has an emphasis on produce, household goods, tools, and garage sale items. Admission on Tues. and Sat. is free; Sun., $2 for adults; children 11 years and under are free.

Santa Fe Springs Swap Meet (indoor) in Santa Fe Springs, (562) 921-4359 / www.sfsswapmeet.com - Over 500 vendors have been meeting here for thirty years to sell new wares. The meet boasts live entertainment, a food court open daily, and a kiddie ride area open on the weekends. There are a prize drawing and half-price food on Wednesdays. Open Tues. - Thurs., 7am - 2:30pm; Fri., 5pm - 11pm; Sat., 7am - 4:30pm; and Sun., 7am - 5pm. Admission is free for adults Tue. - Thurs.; $2.50 Fri. night; $1 on Sat.; $1.50 on Sun. Children under 54" are always free.

Ventura Flea Market (outdoor) in Ventura, (323) 560-7469 / www.rgcshows.com - Antiques, second hand, and used goods for sale. The flea market is held six times a year at Seaside Park (i.e. Ventura County Fairgrounds). Call or check the website for dates. Starting at 6am admission is $10; starting at 9am it is $5 for adults, children 11 and under are free. Parking is free.

Vineland Swap Meet (outdoor) in City of Industry, (626) 369-7224 / www.vinelandswapmeet.com - At the Vineland Drive-in with over 600 vendors. Open daily, 7am - 3pm. Admission is 50¢ on Mon., Tues., Thurs. and Fri.; $1 on Wed. and Sat.; $1.50 on Sun. Children 52" and under are free. Parking is free. After the swap meet closes watch a movie at this drive-in theatre open every night.

SWIMMING and WADING POOLS. Community pools are open seasonally. Call your local park for information.

THEATER. Check out the Shows and Theaters sections in each county. Below are a few places to get you started. Local colleges are also great places see shows and plays.

California Theatre - San Bernardino, (909) 885-5152 / www.californiatheatre.net

The Music Center - Los Angeles, (213) 972-7211 / www.musiccenter.org

Performance Riverside, (951) 222-8100 / www.performanceriverside.org

San Diego County, (858) 381-5595 / www.sdartstix.com

Santa Barbara County, www.santabarbaraca.com
Segerstrom Center for the Arts - Orange County, (714) 556-2787 / www.scfta.org
THRIFT STORES. Teach your children the gift of thrift! Give them a few dollars to buy a "new" article of clothing, a toy, or a book. Sav-Mor Discount in Fullerton and Sav Mor Thrift in Santa Ana are super cheap. Savers is a great chain. Goodwill is more "expensive" yet good finds and supports a great cause. ReStore, habitatsb.org/restore, supports Habitat for Humanity and has great home building supplies and furnishing, at times.

TICKETS

Audiences Unlimited, (818) 260-0041 / www.tvtickets.com - Offers free tickets to watch the filming of almost all of the network television shows and many of their specials. The minimum age for kids ranges from 10 years old for some shows, to 18 years old for most shows. Check the website for a schedule.

LAStageTIX, (213) 614-0556 / www.lastagetix.com - Operated by the Theatre League Alliance of Southern California it allows day-of-show tickets (or even a few days before the show) to be purchased for 50% off the regular price. Check the website for a list of the shows and availability.

On-Camera Audiences, (818) 295-2700 / www.on-camera-audiences.com - Is responsible for filling studio audiences for a huge variety of television shows across the country. See the website for a complete list.

Times Arts Tix in San Diego next to Horton Plaza, (858) 381-5595 / www.sdartstix.com - Has half-price, day-of-performance, theater tickets available on a first-come, first-served, cash-only basis. Call for a listing of the day's shows.

TOURS. See Tours in the main section of the book. The following are general ideas of where you can go for group tours:

Animal Shelter	College/University	Florist	Nurseries (plant)
Airport	Dairy	Grocery Store	Pet Store
Bakery	Dentist	Hospital	Police Station
Bank	Factory	Hotel	Post Office
Chiropractor	Fire Station	Newspaper Office	Restaurant

TOYS. Look in this part of the book under Discovery Toys (pg. 770). One other listing, in particular, worth mentioning is Oriental Trading Company at www.orientaltrading.com. This catalog company offers bulk and individual novelty items, usually priced at the lower end of the scale (and more cheaply made).

VOLUNTEERING. Volunteering is a terrific way to spend time with your children while teaching them the real values of life - giving and serving. Check with local missions, churches, and temples as many have regular times when they go to help feed the homeless or serve in some capacity. Here are other volunteer agencies to get you started on your quest:

30-Minute Beach Cleanup in Long Beach, justinrudd.com/beachcleanup - Group meets on the third Sat. of each month at 10am. at S. Granada Ave. and Ocean Blvd.

Adopt-a-Park and Adopt-a-Beach in Orange County, www.ocgov.com - Organizes ongoing park and beach cleanups at more than 30 local sites for all age participants.

Big Sunday, (323) 549-9944 / www.bigsunday.org - Their mission is to build community through community service.

California Coastal Cleanup Day, (949) 476-1144 x311 / www.coastal.ca.gov - Every year, on the third Saturday in September, people join together at sites all over California to take part in the State's largest volunteer event to clean up California's coast. Go to the website and search for 'cleanup day'.

Children's Hunger Fund, (800) 708-7589 x3009 or (818) 899-5122 / www.chfus.org - Volunteers of all ages assemble care packages for disadvantaged children on Wed., Thurs. and Sat., 9am - 11am at 13931 Balboa Blvd. in Sylmar. You can even volunteer to do some things at home.

Corazón de Vida Foundation, (949) 476-1144 x311 / www.corazondevida.org - On selected Saturdays, volunteers visit one of 14 orphanages in Baja, Mexico to play, work on craft projects, read with the children, help with a building project or simply hold an infant who needs love. Children must be at 8 and those under 16 must be accompanied by an adult. A fee, per person, is required to cover the cost of the bus, food, and craft.

Father Joe's Villages, (619) 645-6411 / www.my.neighbor.org - Programs aimed at helping the homeless.Children as young as 10 years old can volunteer.

Florence Crittenton Services in Yorba Linda, (714) 680-9000 / www.crittentonsocal.org - Abused children living here benefit from volunteers in numerous ways: rocking a baby; fixing a bike; becoming a mentor; planning a party; and more.

Food Finders, (562) 283-1400 / www.foodfinders.org - Families can donate, sort and deliver canned goods, toys, and food year-round.

Habitat For Humanity, (800) 422-4828 / www.habitat.org - Habitat is a non-profit organization committed to providing low-income, owner-occupied housing by utilizing volunteer labor and donated materials. (Former President Jimmy Carter is one of the more prominent members.) Volunteers are needed to build homes and serve on committees such as finance, construction, and public relations. Kids must be at least 16 years old to work on construction sites, but younger children can help with off-site activities such as registration, making lunches, etc. Check website for local affiliates or call information.

Heal the Bay, headquartered in Santa Monica, (800) HEAL BAY (432-5229) or (310) 451-1500 / www.healthebay.org - There's nothing like a day at the beach, especially if you're there to help make it cleaner. Clean up pollution in the Santa Monica Bay, San Pedro Bay, Orange County, and adjacent coastal waters. This program works in conjunction with Adopt-A-Beach and Coastal Clean Up. Call (800) COAST-4U (262-7848) / www.coastal.ca.gov/publiced/pendx.html for the annual coastal clean up day and all the other ones in-between.

I Love a Clean San Diego, (619) 291-0103 / www.ilacsd.org - An educational and environmental group sponsoring beach clean-ups, storm drain stenciling, and graffiti removal.

Kids Korps USA, (858) 259-3602 / www.handsonsandiego.org - Young people, ages 5 - 18, can participate in a wealth of programs from preserving the environment to befriending those in need to helping animals and more. Every child who has a desire to do something to help can find an activity with Kids Korps.

Los Angeles Midnight Mission, (213) 624-9258 / www.midnightmission.org - Volunteer to help set up, decorate, and help serve meals on Thanksgiving or another holiday.

Los Angeles Regional Foodbank in Los Angeles, (323) 234-3030 / www.lafoodbank.org - Ages 14 and up can help maintain 300 garden plots in a low income area, as well as participate in a local food drive and food collection.

Make-A-Wish, (800) 722-9474 / www.wish.org

Move a Child Higher in La Canada / Flintridge, (626) 798-1222 / www.moveachildhigher.org - The Riding Club offers therapeutic horseback riding activities to children with disabilities. Volunteers, ages 14 and up, can exercise and groom the horses, and lead and walk alongside the riders.

One OC, (714) 953-5757 / www.oneoc.org - A clearinghouse for a wide variety of age-appropriate opportunities, including feeding the homeless, visiting the elderly, planting trees, cleaning up parks, and removing graffiti. The center even has a guidebook on family volunteer activities.

Project Chicken Soup, (310) 836-5402 / www.projectchickensoup.org - Work with the Los Angeles Jewish AIDS Services to prepare and deliver kosher meals to those living with AIDS. All ages are welcome, but children under 12 cannot work in the kitchen and one adult volunteer is needed for every two children under the age of 16.

Ripple Kids, (714) 602-2295 / www.ripplekids.com - Dedicated to inspiring kids to help their community. On the website, kids can find out about volunteering opportunities, share ideas and are encouraged to find solutions to issues.

Ronald McDonald House Charities, 630-623-7048 / www.rmhc.org - This house provides a home-away-from-home for up to 20 families who have children receiving treatment for cancer and other serious illnesses at local medical facilities. Opportunities include making or sponsoring a meal, general housekeeping, and clerical opportunities. Note: There are facilities throughout So. Cal. so check the website for information about the one nearest you.

Salvation Army, (562) 436-7000 / westernusa.salvationarmy.org - Volunteers are needed year round, but especially around Christmas time.

Samaritan's Purse, www.samaritanspurse.org - One way to help is to gather, pack and check the packages (i.e. shoeboxes) filled with gifts sent to children around the world. We volunteer at a packing facility in Orange County in November, but sign up way beforehand.

San Diego Coastkeeper, (619) 758-7743 / www.sdcoastkeeper.org - This organization provides a listing of more than 40 coastal and inland cleanup sites throughout San Diego.

Second Harvest Foodbank of Orange County, (949) 653-2900 / www.feedoc.org - Kindergartners and up are allowed to actually harvest and glean food from fields in Orange County. The food is delivered to local food banks. Kids as young as 14 years old can help at the Food Distribution Center, Tues. - Sat. I love all of this!!!

Soldiers' Angels, (626) 529-5114 / www.soldiersangels.org - Provides comfort to the men and women of the armed forces and their families.

Southwest Minority Economic Development Association, (714) 547-4073 / www.homelessshelterdirectory.org - Volunteers of all ages participate in serving food to the homeless.

Surfrider Foundation, (949) 492-8170 / www.surfrider.org - Help clean up local beaches, and more.

Tierra Del Sol Foundation, (818) 352-1419 / www.tierradelsol.org - Serves adults with developmental and often physical disabilities.

Trails4all, (310) 344-9229 / www.trails4all.org - Coordinates volunteers, who are at least 8 years old, to help with coastal cleanups, trail maintenance, and other activities that are group specific.

VolunteerMatch, (415) 241-6872 / www.volunteermatch.org - Website that matches volunteers with organizations that need them through the U.S.

Youth Service America, (202) 296-2992 / www.ysa.org - A national organization committed to youth changing the world with tons of resources, training and opportunites.

WILDFLOWER HOTLINES

Antelope Valley California Poppy Reserve, (661) 724-1180 or (661) 942-0662 / www.parks.ca.gov

Anza Borrego Desert State Park in Anza Borrego, (760) 767-4684 / www.parks.ca.gov

Joshua Tree National Park in Joshua Tree / Twentynine Palms, (760) 367-5500 / www.nps.gov

Mojave Desert Information Center, (760) 252-6100 / www.nps.gov

Theodore Payne Foundation for Wildflowers & Native Plants, (818) 768-3533 or (818) 768-1802 / www.theodorepayne.org

INDEX BY NAME

INDEX BY CITY